The Rights of the Child:
Law and Practice

DEDICATION

To Penny with Love and Admiration

The Rights of the Child:
Law and Practice

Alistair MacDonald QC
St Philips Chambers, Birmingham

Family Law

Published by Family Law
a publishing imprint of
Jordan Publishing Limited
21 St Thomas Street
Bristol BS1 6JS

British Library Cataloguing-in-Publication Data

A catalogue record for this book is available from the British Library.

ISBN 978 1 84661 210 7

Typeset by Letterpart Ltd, Reigate, Surrey

Printed in Great Britain by CPI Antony Rowe, Chippenham and Eastbourne

FOREWORD

It is no mean feat to write a textbook for domestic practitioners about the relevance of the international law on children's rights to their day to day work in this country. After all, most of the relevant international instruments, and in particular the United Nations Convention on the Rights of the Child, have not been directly incorporated or transformed into our domestic law. A child cannot sue if her rights under that Convention have been breached. She cannot even make a complaint to the United Nations Committee on the Rights of the Child. So why should a practitioner in the United Kingdom concern himself with that or any other unincorporated Convention? Has he not got enough to worry about?

These questions can be answered on many levels. But the most compelling for a practitioner is that without having somewhere to look up the latest learning on children's rights you may miss something important about a case. Take the recent decision of the Supreme Court in *ZH (Tanzania) v Secretary of State for the Home Department* [2011] UKSC 4. There is no power to remove, expel or deport British citizens from this country. Yet if a non-citizen parent is removed, she may have no choice but to agree to take her children with her, and if she does so her children will also have no choice. Their individual rights, interests and views might not be taken into account. Until recently, this was all taken for granted.

The Supreme Court held that the best interests of these children had to be a primary consideration in assessing whether removing a parent would be a disproportionate interference with the right of all the family members to respect for their private and family lives, contrary to article 8 of the European Convention on Human Rights. The European Court of Human Rights in Strasbourg has given more and more weight to the Convention on the Rights of the Child in recent years. Article 3 of the Convention requires that in all actions concerning children, whether undertaken by social welfare institutions, courts of law, administrative authorities or legislative bodies, the best interests of the child shall be a primary consideration. This does not mean that they trump all other considerations. But it does mean that they must be considered first and given great weight. Citizen children should not be deprived of their right to live, grow up and be educated in their own country, culture and language without very strong countervailing considerations. Nor should they have to suffer for their parents' misdeeds.

Article 3 has found its way into our domestic law in other ways. The United Kingdom Borders Agency, for example, now has an explicit duty, under s 55 of the Borders, Citizenship and Immigration Act 2009, to discharge its functions 'having regard to the need to safeguard and promote the welfare of children who are in the United Kingdom'.

So the message is: 'think children's rights' and it may transform the case. And where do you go to 'think children's rights'? Well this is a good place to start ...

Brenda Hale
Supreme Court of the United Kingdom

PREFACE

'Constans et perpetua voluntas, jus sum cuique tribuendi'[1]

Institutes of Justinian

A combination of the uncertain nature of the domestic legal foundation of children's rights, the historic reluctance of successive governments to promote children's rights and a feeling that rights based arguments for children are somehow rather abstract, has made lawyers dealing with cases involving children chary of basing their submissions before the courts squarely upon the rights of children. The seeming complexity and diversity of what is perceived as an exotic subject matter, coupled with attendant controversies that can still see even the basic proposition that children have enforceable rights trigger objection, appears to have militated against the rights of children being articulated fully in the context of a comprehensive practitioners' reference text on the subject. Rather than treating children's rights as a fascinating but esoteric and to some controversial by-way of the law relating to children, this book seeks to place children's rights at the heart of the day to day application of the law relating to children. This is a book that seeks to promote children's rights in practice.

The book is accordingly designed to provide a comprehensive and detailed exposition of the law and practice of children's rights. It is not intended to be a scholarly treatment of the subject, of which there are a number of admirable examples, most particularly Jane Fortin's peerless *Children's Rights and the Developing Law*[2] and Geraldine Van Bueren's classic *International Law on the Rights of the Child*,[3] to both of which books I am hugely indebted in the construction of this work. Rather, this book is a reference work aimed at providing an account of the current law for legal practitioners who deal daily with cases involving children in the courts, tribunals and administrative bodies of this jurisdiction. The book seeks also to encourage regard for children's rights in the wide range of judicial, quasi-judicial and administrative decision making processes involving children.

The central message of the book is that the UN Convention on the Rights of the Child can be relied on before the domestic courts, tribunals and decision making bodies of this jurisdiction notwithstanding that it has not yet been formally incorporated or transformed into domestic law. Chapter 3 provides a

---

[1]   'The constant and perpetual will to secure to everyone his own right.'
[2]   (2009) 3rd edn Cambridge.
[3]   (1998) Martinus Nijhoff.

detailed explanation of the law which supports this proposition and which requires the domestic courts to interpret domestic legislation, including the Human Rights Act 1998, and common law in line with the provisions of the CRC and requires domestic decision makers to have regard to the provisions of the CRC when exercising administrative discretion.

Following the introductory chapter *The Rights of the Child – Law and Practice* commences with a detailed description of the international, European and domestic legal frameworks touching and concerning children's rights (chapter 2) before proceeding to consider how children's rights can be most effectively applied and enforced in the jurisdiction of England and Wales given the complex international and regional source material enshrining those rights (chapter 3). The cardinal legal principles underpinning children's rights are then examined (chapter 4) followed by a detailed chapter by chapter examination of the law and practice concerning each of the cardinal rights enjoyed by children and covering the child's right to life, survival and development (chapter 5), the child's right to participate (chapter 6), the child's right to identity (chapter 7), the child's right to family life (chapter 8), the child's right to private life (chapter 9), the child's right to freedom of thought, conscience and religion (chapter 10), the child's right to freedom of expression (chapter 11), the child's right to freedom of association, peaceful assembly and movement (chapter 12), the child's right to education (chapter 13), the child's right to liberty and security of the person (chapter 14), the child's right to freedom from harmful treatment (chapter 15) and the child's right to fair and equal treatment before the law (chapter 16). The book concludes by considering some issues for the future implementation of children's rights within the domestic jurisdiction (chapter 17).

The structure of this book has been arranged by reference to what might be termed the 'traditional' first generation civil and political human rights. It does however incorporate all of the rights enshrined in the UN Convention on the Rights of the Child, which deals with both first generation civil and political rights and second generation economic, social and cultural rights, discussing some of those rights under the umbrella of others. Thus, for example, the child's right to an adequate standard of living under Art 27 of the CRC is discussed as an element of the child's right to life, survival and development. Within the book, international, regional and domestic statutes and case law are cited in the normal fashion by name, date and reference if appropriate. Additional source material which may be unfamiliar to some readers is also relied on. Treaties such as the Convention on the Rights of the Child and the Vienna Convention on the Law of Treaties are cited by their full name or appropriate acronym and reference number where appropriate. Declarations such as the Declaration on the Elimination of All Forms of Intolerance and Discrimination Based on Religion or Belief are likewise cited by the full name or appropriate acronym and reference number where appropriate. The General Comments of relevant human rights committees of the United Nations, including the Committee on the Rights of the Child are cited by committee, name and their United Nations documentation reference system number, for example: 'Committee on the Rights of the Child General Comment No 10 *Children's Rights in Juvenile Justice* CRC/C/GC/10'. References in the footnotes to particular countries followed by a UN documentation reference system citation are references to the concluding observations of the Committee on the Rights of the Child on the reports submitted to the Committee by that state, for example: 'United Kingdom of Great Britain and Northern Ireland (2002) CRC/C/15/Add.188 or United Kingdom of Great Britain and Northern Ireland (2008) CRC/C/GBR/CO/4'. Session reports of the relevant UN Committees are cited by reference to their committee, date and UN documentation reference system number, for example: 'Committee on the Rights of the Child *Report on the Fifth Session* (1994) CRC/C/24'.

I hope that I may proceed without seeking to prove the importance of my subject.[4] Of necessity however, in the opening chapter I attempt a very brief précis of the historical context of children's rights and provide a general introduction to the cardinal principles that underpin their application and which are addressed in detail in chapter 4. This brief introductory chapter is not required reading for those who seek practical solutions to common, and not so common, legal problems concerning the rights of the child. However, whilst I assert no expertise in history, philosophy or sociology for those who do wish a basic overview of the deep foundations on which those practical solutions are built, it is hoped that the perspective taken by a humble lawyer will be of interest.

The law is up to date as of February 2011 and any mistakes or omissions are entirely those of the author.

Alistair MacDonald
St Philips Chambers
Birmingham

February 2011

---

4   Jean-Jacques Rousseau *Le Contrat social* (1762), p.1.

ACKNOWLEDGMENTS

I am deeply indebted to a large number of people for their assistance and forebearance whilst this work has been completed. I owe a particular debt of gratitude to Baroness Hale of Richmond who kindly agreed to write the Foreword to the book. I am also immensely grateful to Greg Woodgate of Jordans who has never waivered in his enthusiasm for this project, has always been ready with detailed guidance and has granted my considerable number of requests for deadline extensions with good grace. I am greatly indebted to my former pupil, Lucie French for proof reading the first half of the book and for making detailed comments which helped refine the early text and assisted in eradicating what has been described by one friend as my anarchic use of the apostrophe. I am also grateful to our Chambers librarian, Caroline Covington for never failing to locate documents I requested, no matter how obscure and to my clerks Mark Mansell, Ian Charlton, Eloise Aldridge and Wayne Scott for granting with good humour my repeated requests for days out of court whenever the book was falling behind schedule. Thanks must also go to Liz Goldthorpe for her valuable comments on the work of the SEND tribunal in relation to the child's right to participate, to Christine Smart for providing me with the child rights materials produced by the Children and Family Court Advisory and Support Service and to District Judge Nicholas Crichton and the Family Justice Council Voice of the Child Sub-Committee for allowing me to present to the Committee the chapter on the child's right to participate during its construction. My sincere thanks are also due to Liz Walsh for agreeing to publish in Family Law a number of articles which I have written during the course of compiling this book as a prelude to its publication and to Piers Pressdee QC whose support and advice deriving from his own experiences as a legal author has been invaluable. I wish also to express my enduring gratitude to the late David Hershman QC who inspired me as his pupil to take the first steps on the path that eventually led to this book. My love and thanks go to my wife Penny for her support and for patiently putting up with 'the book' as a competitor for my attentions over the past two and a half years. Finally, my lasting gratitude and affection goes to my parents who were well ahead of their time in recognising their children's right to participate.

CONTENTS

TABLE OF CASES

References are to paragraph numbers.

TABLE OF STATUTES

References are to paragraph numbers.

TABLE OF STATUTORY INSTRUMENTS

References are to paragraph numbers.

TABLE OF EUROPEAN AND INTERNATIONAL MATERIAL

References are to paragraph numbers.

TABLE OF ABBREVIATIONS

ACA 2002	Adoption and Children Act 2002
Art 2 1P	First Protocol of the ECHR
Beijing Rules	UN Standard Minimum Rules for the Administration of Juvenile Justice
Brussels II Revised	Council Regulation (EC) No 2201/2003 of 27 November 2003 on Jurisdiction and the Recognition and Enforcement of Judgments in Matrimonial Matters and Matters of Parental Responsibility
CA 1989	Children Act 1989
Cafcass	Children and Family Court Advisory and Support Service
CAT	UN Convention against Torture and Other Cruel, Inhuman or Degrading Treatment or Punishment
CCCC	European Convention on Contact Concerning Children
CDE	Convention against Discrimination in Education
CEAFRD	UN Convention on the Elimination of All Forms of Racial Discrimination
CECR	Convention on the Exercise of Children's Rights
CEDAW	UN Convention on the Elimination of All Forms of Discrimination against Women
CPAPED	UN Convention for the Protection of All Persons from Enforced Disappearance
CPCSESA	European Convention on the Protection of Children against Sexual Exploitation and Sexual Abuse
CPRAMW	UN Convention on the Protection of the Rights of All Migrant Workers and Members of Their Families
CRC	UN Convention on the Rights of the Child
CRPD	UN Convention on the Rights of Persons with Disabilities
CRSR	UN Convention Relating to the Status of Refugees
ECHR	European Convention on Human Rights and Fundamental Freedoms
ESC	European Social Charter
FHDRA	First Hearing Dispute Resolution Appointment
FPR 2010	Family Procedure Rules 2010, SI 2010/2955
HFEA 1990	Human Fertilisation and Embryology Act 1990
HFEA 2008	Human Fertilisation and Embryology Act 2008
HRA 1998	Human Rights Act 1998
HRC	Human Rights Council

ICCPR	International Covenant on Civil and Political Rights
ICESCR	International Covenant on Economic, Social and Cultural Rights
ILO	International Labour Organisation
IRO	Independent Reviewing Officer
OHCR	Office of the High Commissioner for Human Rights
OPCAT	Optional Protocol to the UN Convention against Torture and Other Cruel, Inhuman or Degrading Treatment or Punishment
OPCEDAW	Optional Protocol to the Convention on the Elimination of All Forms of Discrimination against Women
OPCRPD	Optional Protocol on the Rights of Persons with Disabilities
Riyadh Guidelines	UN Guidelines on the Prevention of Juvenile Delinquency
UN	United Nations
UNESCO	United Nations Educational, Scientific and Cultural Organization
UNICEF	United Nations Children's Fund
UNHCR	United Nations High Commissioner for Refugees
VCLT	Vienna Convention on the Law of Treaties 1969

Chapter 1

INTRODUCTION

'Come away, O human child: To the waters and the wild with a fairy, hand in hand,
For the world's more full of weeping than you can understand'

William Butler Yeats

AIMS AND OBJECTIVES

1.1   Jane Fortin has observed that the judiciary not uncommonly analyse the rights that adults have but fail to articulate those of the children.[1] This may be seen as much the fault of lawyers as that of judges in that the former retain responsibility for alerting the latter to all of the applicable principles of law. Progress is however being made. Three years after this observation, in the 3rd edition of her book '*Children's Rights and the Developing Law*', Fortin was able to conclude that 'practitioners and the judiciary are now not only far more open to arguments based on children's rights, but also more willing to consider international instruments as an important source of guidance over standards to be reached by domestic law.'[2]

1.2   This book aims to contribute to that trend by providing a reference work which brings together the international, regional and domestic law relevant to the implementation of children's rights in the domestic jurisdiction. The power of the law to effect incremental change through the repeated and consistent application of cardinal principles is great. The objective of this work is to assist in facilitating the implementation of children's rights through the day to day practice of the law, as well as within the myriad instances of daily administrative decision making which touch and concern children. This work is accordingly designed to provide a comprehensive and detailed account of the law and practice of children's rights for judges, legal practitioners and officials who deal with cases involving children in the courts, tribunals and administrative bodies of this jurisdiction.[3] As noted in the Preface, the central message of the book is that the UN Convention on the Rights of the Child (hereafter the 'CRC') can be relied on before the domestic courts, tribunals and decision making bodies of this jurisdiction notwithstanding that it has not been formally incorporated into domestic law. Chapter 3 provides a detailed explanation of the law which supports this proposition and which requires the domestic courts to interpret domestic legislation

---

[1]   Fortin, J *Accommodating Children's Rights in a Post Human Rights Act Era* (2006) Modern Law Review 299, pp 302–303.

[2]   Fortin, J *Children's Rights and the Developing Law* (2009) 3rd edn, Cambridge, p ix.

[3]   Note also that in relation to legislation and policy making the House of Lords and House of Commons Joint Committee on Human Rights has recommended in relation to the UN Convention on the Rights of the Child that 'The Convention should function as a source of child-centred considerations to be used as yardsticks by all departments of Government when evaluating legislation and in policy-making, whether in respect of the progressive realisation of economic, social and cultural rights or in relation to guarantees of civil and political rights. We recommend, particularly in relation to policy-making, that Government demonstrate more conspicuously a recognition of its obligation to implement the rights under the Convention' (JCHR *The UN Convention on the Rights of the Child*, Tenth Report of Session 2002–2003 HL Paper 117/HC 81).

and common law in line with the provisions of the CRC and requires domestic decision makers to have regard to the provisions of the CRC when exercising administrative discretion.

1.3   Before turning to the law and practice of children's rights in detail, this chapter attempts a brief précis of the historical context of children's rights and provides a general introduction to the cardinal principles which underpin their application in order to give the reader a basic overview of the deep foundations on which the modern law and practice of children's rights is built. As Fortin suggests, whilst the body of intellectual thought on children's rights has not taken particular account of the needs of practitioners, it provides a far better basis for translating the concept of children's rights into practice than mere intuition or prejudice.[4]

CHILDREN'S RIGHTS – A BRIEF HISTORY

The Historical Context

1.4   Van Bueren contends that the history of the international law on the rights of the child is a curious tale.[5] It is also a tale whose very earliest foundations are hard to excavate from the historical record. Feldman suggests that:[6]

> 'the idea at the root of human rights thinking is that there are certain rights which are so fundamental to society's wellbeing and to peoples' chance of leading a fulfilling life that governments are obliged to respect them, and the international order has to protect them.'

If we seek to gain an accurate picture of the extent to which, over time, this idea has been accepted in relation to children we must also acknowledge the difficulty in establishing such a history. Because of the small number of historical texts concerning children, many of them fictional in character, the risk of gaining a seriously distorted impression of the historical ideas of childhood is great.[7] It must be remembered that the authors of much of the early historical material in respect of children constituted a tiny minority of the population and were, above all, male, clerical and close to the narrow circles of the aristocracy and the urban patriciate. The authors of literary works, whilst providing source material, are not necessarily providing a direct reflection of contemporary ideas of childhood.[8] By reason of these difficulties it is for many periods of history virtually impossible to get a contemporaneous historical account of what childhood was, either from the child or from those who cared for children directly.[9]

Early History

1.5   The early written histories which discuss children are characterised by children being considered as the raw material for successful adulthood in society rather than as individuals with interests separate from those of the adult population. In Plato's dialogues children, or at least those who would become guardians of the state or philosopher kings, are considered objects to be molded by education rather than persons

---

4   Fortin, J *Children's Rights and the Developing Law* (2009) 3rd edn, Cambridge, p 29.
5   Van Bueren, G *The International Law on the Rights of the Child* (1998) Martinus Nijhoff, p 25.
6   Feldman, D *Civil Liberties and Human Rights in England and Wales* (2002) Oxford, pp 34–35.
7   Heywood, C *A History of Childhood* (2001) Polity Press, p 6.
8   Heywood, C *A History of Childhood* (2001) Polity Press, p 6.
9   Heywood, C *A History of Childhood* (2001) Polity Press, p 7.

in their own right.[10] The Aristotlean concept of child was likewise that the child is 'important not for himself but for his potential'.[11] Within this context, there are very few first hand accounts of childhood and the place of children in the early historical record, which record contains only glimpses of the position of children in society. Gaius considered that 'children have no intellect' and were completely incapable under the law.[12] The Emperor Hadrian sought to address the practice by which a father had the right under Roman law to kill his children by subjecting it to some form of judicial control.[13] St Augustine[14] gives some details his childhood following his birth in November AD354 but this account is very much the exception and not the rule.[15] Under Justinian,[16] selling a child was permitted where the family was in extreme poverty. The child could however free him or herself by paying the buyer the price the buyer had paid to his or her father.[17] Heywood notes that in the Middle Ages, accepting the paucity of material, children and childhood remained characterised by their relative unimportance.[18] Again, whilst Abbot Guibert of Nogent gave some details of his childhood experiences following his birth in 1053 such accounts were the exception.[19] Within this context it is perhaps unsurprising that the principles enshrined in Magna Carta in 1215, which themselves have their roots in the coronation oaths of the Anglo-Saxon kings and the Charter of Henry I,[20] make no reference to children.

Seventeenth Century

1.6 Children start to appear more commonly in the historical record, and in the legal historical record in the seventeenth century. However, once again this history contains little that we would recognise as a foundation of a rights based approach to children and childhood. Whilst the Massachusetts Body of Liberties in 1641 enjoins parents not to choose their children's spouses or use unnatural severity against their children and gives children 'free liberty to complain to the authorities for redress', it also permits the death penalty for children over the age of 16 who disobey their parents. In France in 1666 Pierre de Bérulle felt compelled to observe that childhood 'is the most vile and abject state of human nature, after that of death'.[21] Within the domestic context, the only law from which vulnerable children could benefit was the Poor Law of 1601 which, for

---

10 Plato *Republic* 369a–376b and 503b–505d.
11 Aristotle *Politics*. Dante echoes the classical tradition in dividing a person's regular life span into a period of growth (*adolescenzia*, up to the age of 25), a period of maturity (*gioventute*, from 25 to 45, peaking at 35) and a final period of decline (*senettute*, from 45 to 70).
12 Berger, A *Encyclopaedic Dictionary of Roman Law* Vol 43, p 500. From the time of Justinian or perhaps slightly earlier *infantia* (childhood) meant children under the age of 7 years. An *infans* (a child who cannot express his ideas reasonably) was considered completely incapable under the law. The *infans* would then become an *impubes* (a person below the age of puberty) and at the age of 14 the child became a *pubes* which lasted until the age of 25 (Berger, A *Encyclopaedic Dictionary of Roman Law* Vol 43, p 500).
13 Hadrian transported to an island a father who had used a hunting trip as the opportunity to kill his son (Gibbon, E *The History of the Decline and Fall of the Roman Empire* (1993) Everyman Vol III, p 170 citing Marcian. Institut. 1. xiv in Pandect. 1. xiviii ix leg.5). Note that the *patria potestas* power of the head of the family gradually evolved from an unlimited judicial, economic and moral power to a power in the interests of the persons subject to it embracing moral duties such as protection, maintenance and assistance (Berger, A *Encyclopaedic Dictionary of Roman Law* Vol 43, p 621).
14 St Augustine AD354–430 *Confessions* Book I Chapters IV to XVIII.
15 Heywood, C *A History of Childhood* (2001) Polity Press, p 2.
16 AD 483 to AD 414 or 413.
17 Berger, A *Encyclopaedic Dictionary of Roman Law* Vol 43, p 621.
18 Heywood, C *A History of Childhood* (2001) Polity Press, p 2.
19 Guibert of Nogent AD1053–1125 *De vita sua sive monodiarum suarum libri tres* Book I Chapters III to VI.
20 Hearn, W *The Government of England: Its Structure and Development* (1867) Longmans Chapter 3, para 7.
21 Pierre de Bérulle *Opuscules de piété*, 69 (1666) Lyons.

children as well as adults, produced grave injustice.[22] By reason of the law entitling the poor to relief from one parish only, unmarried pregnant women would be driven from parish to parish to avoid the child being 'dropped' on a parish's doorstep. It was not unknown for pauper infants to be farmed out by parishes to 'minders' or 'masters' for a small premium. If the infant died, no one asked questions.[23] Whilst the English Bill of Rights in 1689 was partly directed to the protection of individual rights, children were not singled out within its protective framework. However, despite this bleak context, the concept of children as valued individuals was stirring. Towards the close of the seventeenth century John Locke began turning his thoughts to education.[24] Whilst to a certain extent maintaining the classical view of children as citizens in the making with empty minds to be filled with experience,[25] Locke nonetheless considered that the child's needs and interests should be recognised for what they are by observant parents and that the child should be reasoned with and not simply beaten or coerced into conformity with the rules of required behaviour.[26]

Eighteenth Century

1.7   Although admittedly directed at a relatively narrow aspect of children's lives, Locke's enlightenment thinking must be contrasted with the continuing reality of life for many children in the eighteenth century. The Poor Law attained its purest expression in the 'Work House', described by the legal reformer Jeremy Bentham as a 'mill to grind rogues honest and idle men industrious'.[27] The death rate in some work houses was 100%. Jonas Hanway[28] considered that an infant of 1 to 3 years might on average survive a month in a London work house.[29] Out of 2,339 children received into the London workhouses in the 5 years after 1750 only 168 were still alive in 1755.[30] For those at home, children from more impoverished backgrounds generally experienced parents as figures of direct power.[31] Attitudes towards parenting meant that children in more well to do situations could suffer a paucity of emotional care from parents, with wet nurses and nurse maids, and later governesses, tutors, singing teachers and dancing masters taking on the parental role.[32] Parents habitually inflicted upon their children what today would be seen as physical abuse. John Wesley's Mother, Susanna, proudly stated of her babies that 'when turned a year old (and some before) they were taught to fear the rod and cry softly'.[33] Historical accounts record that for being 'naughty' Fanny Kemble was imprisoned for a week in a tool shed. Charlotte Clarke was tied to a table leg for a similar misdemeanour.[34] In 1793 William Blake wrote 'Songs of Experience',[35]

---

22   The Poor Law of 1601 envisaged that the unemployed poor should be 'set to work' with children being 'apprenticed' and that necessary relief should be given to the impotent poor (Cretney, S *Family Law in the Twentieth Century – A History* (2003) Oxford, p 635). The Poor Law has been described as 'the historic base from which Parliament advanced to meet the needs of the orphan, the deserted and the abandoned child' (see *Leeds City Council v West Yorkshire Metropolitan Police* [1983] 1 AC 29 at 41 per Lord Scarman).

23   Porter, R *English Society in the 18th Century* (1990) Penguin, pp 130–133.

24   Locke, J *Some Thoughts Concerning Education* (1693).

25   Echoing Plato's *Theatetus* which likens the mind to a wax tablet (see Simons, M *Why Can't a Man Be More Like a Woman? (A Note on John Locke's Educational Thought)* (1990) Educational Theory 40.1, p 143).

26   Archard, D *Children – Rights and Childhood* (2004) Routledge, pp 1 and 12–15.

27   Porter, R *English Society in the 18th Century* (1990) Penguin, p 131.

28   Jonas Hanway (1712–1786) was an English traveller and philanthropist. Hanway is said to be the very first person in London to have carried an umbrella (Thomas, WJ and others *Notes and Queries: Umbrellas* (1851) George Bell, p 25).

29   Porter, R *English Society in the 18th Century* (1990) Penguin, p 131.

30   Porter, R *English Society in the 18th Century* (1990) Penguin, pp 131–132.

31   Porter, R *English Society in the 18th Century* (1990) Penguin, p 149

32   Porter, R *English Society in the 18th Century* (1990) Penguin, pp 27–28

33   Susanna Wesley, Letter to John Wesley July 24, 1732.

34   Porter, R *English Society in the 18th Century* (1990) Penguin, p 150. Children from foreign countries also

motivated primarily by the vision of child deprivation Blake saw before him in London and in particular a young child chained on occasion in the street across from his house. Within this context, it is difficult to disagree with DeMause that 'The history of childhood is a nightmare from which we have only recently begun to awaken'.[36]

1.8   Whilst by virtue of statute and common law the legal landscape of the eighteenth century offered redress to many plaintiffs, children above all failed to benefit from the protection of the law. There was practically no legislation in place to safeguard the young.[37] Indeed Rodham argues that eighteenth century English common law would have considered the term 'children's rights' as a non-sequitur.[38] Blackstone spoke of the duty owed by 'prized possessions' to their fathers.[39] However, as with the seventeenth century it would be a mistake to view the eighteenth century as one in which no progress at all was being made concerning children's position in society. Other passages from Blackstone present a slightly different picture of the child's relationship to his or her family and one expressed in terms of rights, albeit rights arising out of the parents' moral duty as opposed to any legal rights of the child sounding in law. In particular Blackstone considered in respect of parents that:[40]

> '... this moral duty is laid on them by their own proper act, in bringing them into the world: for they would be in the highest manner injurious to their issue if they only gave their children life, that they might afterwards see them perish. By begetting them, therefore, they have entered into a voluntary obligation to Endeavour, as far as this lies, that the life which they have bestowed shall be supported and preserved. And thus the children will have the perfect right of receiving maintenance from their parents.'

1.9   Further, in 1762 Jean Jacques Rousseau had published *Émile or on Education* which is widely credited with pioneering a modern view of childhood. Rousseau criticised those 'seeking the man in the child without thinking of what he is before being a man'[41] and insisted that 'childhood has its place in the order of human life. The man must be considered in the man, and the child in the child'.[42] Rousseau moves away from the concept of children as important not for themselves but for their potential and articulates the necessity of having a concept of childhood. In doing so, in the years leading up to the Declaration of the Rights of Man and the Citizen,[43] the United States

---

suffered harshly as a result of the established practices of the time. The following appeared in the London Advertiser in 1756: 'To be sold, a Negro boy aged about 14 years old, warranted free from any distemper and has had those fatal to that colour; has been used two years at all kinds of household work, and to wait at table; his price is £25, and would not be sold but the person he belongs to is leaving off business' (cited in Porter, R *English Society in the 18th Century* (1990) Penguin, p 136).

[35]   In 'The Chimney-Sweeper' Blake described the plight of children in 18th century London: 'A little black thing among the snow Crying 'weep weep' in notes of woe! Where are thy Father and Mother? Say! They are both gone to the church to pray. Because I am happy upon the hearth, And smiled among the winters snow, They clothed me in clothes of death, and Taught me to sing notes of woe. And because I am happy and dance and sing, They think they have done me no injury, And are gone to praise God and his Priest and King Who made up a heaven of our misery' (William Blake Songs of Experience (1990) Oxford University Press, p 30).

[36]   DeMause, L *The History of Childhood* (1974) The Psychohistory Press 1.

[37]   Porter, R *English Society in the 18th Century* (1990) Penguin, p 270.

[38]   Rodham, H *Children under the Law* (1973) Harvard Educational Review 43, pp 487–514, p 488.

[39]   Blackstone Commentaries on the Laws of England 1.12 (1775) 7th edn.

[40]   Blackstone Commentaries on the Laws of England 1.16 (1775) 7th edn.

[41]   Rousseau, JJ. *Émile or On Education* Trans. Bloom, A (1979) Basic Books, p 34.

[42]   Rousseau, JJ. *Émile or On Education* Trans. Bloom, A (1979) Basic Books, p 80.

[43]   The Declaration of the Rights of Man and the Citizen, in French 'Déclaration de droits de l'homme et du citoyen', is the key document of the French Revolution and defines individual and collective rights as being universal. Completed on 27 August 1789 it is a precursor document to the international human rights instruments although it fails to deal with women, children or slavery.

Constitution[44] and the US Bill of Rights[45] Rousseau lays the foundation for the much later development of seeing children as the individual subjects of the human rights which those instruments presaged.[46] Prior to that seminal development however, the child emerging from the trials of the eighteenth century came first to be idealised and seen as an object of protection.

Nineteenth Century

1.10   The Romantics of the nineteenth century idealised children as creatures blessed by God, and saw childhood as a source of inspiration that would last a lifetime.[47] Jean Paul Richter,[48] writing in 1814, considered that the world of the child encapsulated the future which, 'like Moses at the entrance to the Promised Land, we can only look upon without ever penetrating'.[49] Once again this high romantic rhetoric must be placed in the context of the reality of life for many children at this time.[50] The anecdotal evidence from the eighteenth century is, by necessity, very much rooted in an examination of the socio-economic situation of children at the time and in many respects amounts to an overall examination of the direct consequences of poverty. By the nineteenth century it is however possible to look at the abuse of children as a discreet issue based on forensic evidence, and in particular the lot of children who were subject to sexual abuse. Between 1830 and 1910 67% of cases involving sexual assault coming before Middlesex Assizes concerned children, at the Old Bailey the figure was 64% and in the north of England 46% at the North Yorkshire Assizes and 41% at the West Riding Quarter Sessions.[51] These figures should not however be taken as necessarily showing that sexual abuse was dealt with effectively through criminal prosecution. Data from the Thames Police Court between 1885 and 1910 and from the Hampstead Petty Sessions between 1870 and 1914 shows that most sexual abuse cases were either acquitted or trivialised and convicted as lesser offences.[52] Indeed, for much of the 1800's there existed an enormous discrepancy between the condemnation of sexual abuse and the very small incidences reaching trial. In 1886 the rate of prosecutions amounted to 4 cases per 100,000 of the population. Extrapolating the level of sexual abuse in the current population tends, accounting for the risks attendant on such extrapolation, to suggest a very large number of cases went unreported.[53] Incest, although stigmatised as the most serious form of abuse was still

---

44   The United States Constitution was adopted on 17 September 1787. It makes no mention of children.

45   The US Bill of Rights was introduced by James Madison to the First United States Congress with Thomas Jefferson as the primary proponent of the Bill. It came into effect on 15 December 1791. Once again it is silent as to children.

46   In his *Le Contrat Social* Rousseau wrote further that 'Even if each man could alienate himself, he could not alienate his children. For they are born men; they are born free; their liberty belongs to them; no one but they themselves has the right to dispose of it. Before they come to the years of discretion, their father may, in their name, make certain rules for their protection and welfare but he cannot give away their liberty irrevocably and unconditionally: for such gift would be contrary to the ends of nature, and an abuse of paternal right.' (Jean-Jacques Rousseau *Le Contrat Social* (1762) Penguin Books, p 8).

47   Heywood, C *A History of Childhood* (2001) Polity Press, p 3 citing Egle Becchi *Le XIXe siècle* in Egle Becchi and Dominique Julia (eds), *Histoire de l'enfance en Occident* (Editions de Seuil 1987), pp 147–217 (pp 151–53). Note that this view once again harks back to the classical view of the 'preparatory' nature of childhood.

48   John Paul Richter (1763–1825) was a German romantic writer.

49   Heywood, C *A History of Childhood* (2001) Polity Press, p 3.

50   Eloquently captured in Elizabeth Barrett Browning's poem 'The Cry of the Children' (see Forster, M *Elizabeth Barrett Browning – Selected Poems* (1988) Johns Hopkins University Press, p 179).

51   Jackson, L *Child Sexual Abuse in Victorian England* (2000) Routledge, pp 18–20.

52   Jackson, L *Child Sexual Abuse in Victorian England* (2000) Routledge, p 21.

53   Jackson, L *Child Sexual Abuse in Victorian England* (2000) Routledge, p 35.

the most underreported.[54] Child victims of incest were more likely to be sent to an institution than those sexually assaulted by strangers.[55]

1.11   As with the trials and tribulations visited upon children in previous centuries, the terrible suffering that many children endured in the nineteenth century, of which sexual abuse was but one aspect,[56] should not lead to the conclusion that slow incremental progress, highlighted in earlier centuries by the works of Locke and Rousseau, had stalled. Whilst John Stuart Mill[57] considered that the concept of liberty 'is meant to apply only to human beings in the maturity of their faculties' and that 'children, or ... young persons below the age which the law may fix as that of manhood or womanhood ... must be protected against their own actions as well as against external injury',[58] the public and the law at least began to accept the latter proposition. Indeed, a whole range of both formal and unofficial strategies for dealing with the problem of sexual abuse existed in working class neigbourhoods long before Parliament legislated in respect of such social evils and prior to the founding of bodies such as the NSPCC.[59]

1.12   In the nineteenth century reformers became highly active in the field of child welfare. Following in the spirit of Thomas Coram[60] in the eighteenth century, figures such as Mary Carpenter, who brought previously unavailable education opportunities to poor children and young offenders in Bristol and greatly influenced the development of education and a more enlightened juvenile justice regime,[61] Anthony Ashley-Cooper, Seventh Earl of Shaftsbury, who introduced legislation seeking to reduce child labour, sought to abolish the use of children as chimney sweeps and child prostitution and was president of the Ragged Schools Union,[62] Octavia Hill, who sought to develop social housing for the poor[63] and was a founder member of the Charity Organisation Society which pioneered a home visiting service[64] and Thomas Barnardo who founded and

---

[54]   Jackson, L *Child Sexual Abuse in Victorian England* (2000) Routledge, p 46.

[55]   Jackson, L *Child Sexual Abuse in Victorian England* (2000) Routledge, p 66.

[56]   Flegel argues that the literature of the 19th century, including Dickens, Charlotte Brontë, George Meredith and Wilkie Collins all contain depictions of childhood that focus less on physical discomfort than they do on emotional isolation or lack of love (Flegel, M *Conceptualising Cruelty to Children in Nineteenth Century England* (2009) Ashgate, pp 14–15.

[57]   John Stuart Mill (1806–1873) was an English philosopher famous for his conception of liberty as justifying the freedom of the individual over unlimited state control (see Mill, J S *On Liberty* (1859) ('On Liberty is a rational justification of the freedom of the individual in opposition to the claims of the state to impose unlimited control and is thus a defence of the rights of the individual against the state')).

[58]   Mill, J S *On Liberty* (1859).

[59]   See Jackson, L *Child Sexual Abuse in Victorian England* (2000) Routledge, p 31 and Flegel, M *Conceptualising Cruelty to Children in Nineteenth Century England* (2009) Ashgate, p 40.

[60]   Thomas Coram (1668–1751) established the London Foundling Hospital in Bloomsbury in 1739 to care for abandoned and orphaned children (see Wagner, J *Thomas Coram, Gent* (2004) Boydell Press, pp 136–152).

[61]   See Manton, J *Mary Carpenter and the Children of the Streets* (1976) Heinemann and Gehring, T and Bowers, F Mary Carpenter: *19th Century English Correctional Education Hero* (2003) Journal of Correctional Education September, 2. Mary Carpenters key works include Carpenter, M *Reformatory Schools: For the Children of the Perishing and Dangerous Classes and for Juvenile Offenders* (1851) Gilpin; Carpenter, M *Juvenile Delinquents, their Condition and Treatment* (1853) W. & F. G. Cash and Carpenter, M *Reformatories for Convicted Girls* (1860) Transactions of the National Association for the Promotion of Social Science, pp 338–346. Note however that the reformatory school system pioneered by Mary Carpenter was in principle entirely penal when given statutory recognition (see the Reformatory Schools Act 1866).

[62]   See Best, GFA. *Shaftesbury* (1964) B. T. Batsford. Note that the standards in Ragged Schools were often very low (see *Report of the Select Committee on the Education of Destitute Children* (1861) HC 460, BPP 1861 vii 395 cited in Cretney, S *Family Law in the Twentieth Century – A History* (2003) Oxford, p 629).

[63]   See Wohl, A *Octavia Hill and the Homes of the London Poor* (1971) The Journal of British Studies Vol 10, No 2, pp 105–31.

[64]   See Darley, G *Hill, Octavia (1838–1912)* (2004) Oxford Dictionary of National Biography, OUP.

directed homes for homeless and destitute children,[65] all worked, along with many other social reformers to relieve the situation of children trapped in grinding poverty and abuse.

1.13   Social reformers were also active in other jurisdictions in the nineteenth century. Mary Carpenter was inspired in part by Joseph Tuckerman, an advocate of social reform in Boston, Massachusetts.[66] In New York in 1873 Etta Angle Wheeler found Mary Ellen Wilson badly beaten and chained to a bedpost at the property of Mary Connolly and Thomas McCormack.[67] Finding reluctance on the part of the authorities to use child cruelty laws to intercede on Mary Ellen's behalf on the basis that 'the right of parents to chastise their own children was still sacred'[68] Wheeler sought the assistance of Henry Bergh, the President of the American Society for the Prevention of Cruelty to Animals. Bergh ensured that Mary Ellen McCormack was represented by counsel for the ASPCA before the court, which granted a *writ of de homine replagiando* under the US Habeas Corpus Act removing Mary Ellen from the custody of Connolly and McCormack. The case of Mary Ellen Wilson lead to the founding of the New York Society for the Prevention of Cruelty to Children on 15 December 1874, the first child protection organisation in the world.[69] The New York Society provided the organisational blueprint for similar organisations in England[70] and lead to a range of organisations being set up in the 1880s including the National Society for the Prevention of Cruelty to Children in 1884.[71] Indeed Behlmer notes that in England 'a bewildering array of charitable institutions were created to make life less harsh for the young'[72] pointing to the fact that the Charities Register and Digest for 1884 distinguished between those charities offering the child 'relief in affliction', 'relief in sickness', 'relief in distress (permanent)', 'relief in distress (temporary)', 'reformatory relief' and miscellaneous services such as emigration. The NSPCC came under Royal patronage in 1890.

1.14   In addition to social reformers and social reform organisations, the law began to play an active role in the protection of children in the latter half of the 19th Century. In the 1860's William Shaen began to identify child welfare as a specialist branch of legal practice in his capacity as solicitor to the Associate Institute for the Protection of Women and Children.[73] The Infant Life Preservation Acts of 1872 and 1897 were passed in a effort to combat the evils of 'baby-farming' by which desperate mothers lacking means of support handed over their infants to a 'baby-farming house' in which they

---

[65]   See Williams, A E *Barnado of Stepney* (1966) George Allen & Unwin. The work of Thomas Barnardo was not without controversy and that parents were not always content to have their children in Dr Barnado's care (see *R v Barnado* (1889) 23 QBD 305, *R v Barnado* [1891] 1 QB 194; *Barnado v McHugh* [1891] AC 388 and *Barnado v Ford* [1892] AC 326 and see Heywood, J *Children in Care* (1964) 2nd edn, p 63). These habeas corpus claims led to the passing of the Custody of Children Act 1891 (Cretney, S *Family Law in the Twentieth Century – A History* (2003) Oxford, p 632 n.29). See **1.14** below.

[66]   Manton, J *Mary Carpenter and the Children of the Streets* (1976) Heinemann, pp 49–52.

[67]   Radbill, S *A History of Child Abuse and Infanticide* in Helfer, R and Kempe, C (eds) *The Battered Child* (1968) University of Chicago Press, p 13.

[68]   Radbill, S *A History of Child Abuse and Infanticide* in Helfer, R and Kempe, C (eds) *The Battered Child* (1968) University of Chicago Press, p 13. Note that Mary Connolly and Thomas McCormack were not the parents of Mary Ellen but rather carers with whom Mary Ellen had been placed by the New York Department of Charities (see Watkins, S.A. *The Mary Ellen Myth: Correcting Child Welfare History* (1990) *Social Work* 35(6), pp 500–503).

[69]   Flegel, M *Conceptualising Cruelty to Children in Nineteenth Century England* (2009) Ashgate, p 18.

[70]   Behlmer, G *Child Abuse and Moral Reform in England 1870–1908* (1982) Stanford University Press, p 52.

[71]   Jackson, L *Child Sexual Abuse in Victorian England* (2000) Routledge, p 52.

[72]   Behlmer, G *Child Abuse and Moral Reform in England 1870–1908* (1982) Stanford University Press, p 57.

[73]   Jackson, L *Child Sexual Abuse in Victorian England* (2000) Routledge, p 61.

were often starved to death.[74] In 1889 the Prevention of Cruelty to, and Protection of, Children Act 1889 entered the statutes books and created the general offence of ill-treating, neglecting, abandoning or exposing a boy under 14 or a girl under 16 in a manner likely to cause the child unnecessary suffering or injury to health.[75] The Act also conferred extensive powers to investigate what had happened to the child at home and to commit the child to the care of a 'fit person'. In 1891 the Custody of Children Act was passed, which gave the court discretion to refuse to enforce a parents' right to custody where the parent had abandoned or deserted a child or otherwise acted in a manner such as to make it inappropriate to enforce the parental right.[76] In *The Queen's Reign for Children* in 1897 barrister William Clarke Hall wrote that prior to the 1889 Act 'there was no such offence known to English Law as the mere ill-treatment, no such offence as the mere neglect of a child. The Society resolved to create these offences'.[77] The Prevention of Cruelty to, and Protection of, Children Act 1889 was described by Benjamin Waugh as the 'great awakening of the nation to a true and full recognition of the rights of children'.[78]

1.15 Within the private family sphere English law continued to view children as the property of their father.[79] A father had the right to inflict moderate and reasonable corporal punishment on his children.[80] However, here also progress was very slowly being made. The courts began to show willingness to exercise a protective jurisdiction in cases where the actions of the father seriously compromised the welfare of child,[81] albeit

---

[74] Cretney, S *Family Law in the Twentieth Century – A History* (2003) Oxford, p 632. Due to lack of resources the legislation fell short of what was required of it to be effective (see Behlmer, G *Child Abuse and Moral Reform in England 1870–1908* (1982) Stanford University Press, p 282).

[75] Note that by s 14 of the Act the parents 'right' to administer punishment to the child was preserved.

[76] The Custody of Children Act 1889 followed a series of habeas corpus claims against Thomas Barnado (Cretney, S *Family Law in the Twentieth Century – A History* (2003) Oxford, p 632, n 29 and see *R v Barnado* (1889) 23 QBD 305, *R v Barnado* [1891] 1 QB 194; *Barnado v McHugh* [1891] AC 388 and *Barnado v Ford* [1892] AC 326). Amongst his detractors the Custody of Children Act 1891 was known as the 'Barnado Relief Act' (Nelson, C *Family Ties in Victorian England* (2007) Praeger, p 155).

[77] Clarke Hall, W *The Queen's Reign for Children* (1897) Fisher Unwin, pp 159–160. The Prevention of Cruelty to, and Protection of, Children Act 1889 is commonly known as the 'Children's Charter'.

[78] Waugh, B in Clarke Hall, W *The Queen's Reign for Children* (1897) Fisher Unwin Introduction, p vii. For an excellent account of how children came to be considered the worthy objects of unique legal protections at the end of the 19th century see Flegel, M *Conceptualising Cruelty to Children in Nineteenth Century England* (2009) Ashgate.

[79] Cross, G *Wards of Court* (1967) 83 LQR 200, 201. See *Wellesley v Duke of Beaufort* (1827) 2 Russ 22 (the 'filial affection and duty towards their father operate to the utmost), *Symington v Symingtom* (1875) LR 2 Sc & Div ('in the material and moral interest of boys to leave them in the care of their natural and legal guardian'), *Re Plomley* (1882) 47 LT (LS) 284 and *Re Agar-Ellis* (1883) 3 Ch D 317 ('when by birth the child is subject to a father, it is for the general interest of families, and for the general interest of children, and really for the interests of the particular infant, that the court should not, except in very extreme cases, interfere with the discretion of the father but leave to him the responsibility of exercising that power which nature has given him by birth of the child'). See also the limited inroads into this principle made by statute in the Custody of Children Act 1839, the Custody of Infants Act 1873, the Matrimonial Causes Act 1857, the Matrimonial Causes Act 1878 and the Guardianship of Infants Act 1886.

[80] *R v Hopley* (1860) 2 F&F 202 per Cockburn CJ ('by the law of England, a parent or a schoolmaster (who for this purpose represents the parent an has the parental authority delegated to him), may for the purpose of correcting what is evil in the child inflict moderate and reasonable corporal punishment, always, however, with this condition that it is moderate and reasonable. If it be administered for the gratification of passion or of rage, or if it be immoderate an excessive in its nature or degree, or if it be protracted beyond the child's powers of endurance, or with an instrument unfitted for the purpose and calculated to produce danger to life and limb; in all such cases the punishment is excessive, the violence is unlawful, and if evil consequences to life or limb ensue, then the person inflicting it is answerable to the law, and if death ensues it will be manslaughter'). See **10.23**, **13.67** and **15.22** below.

[81] See *R v Dobbyn* (1818) 4 Ad & El 644n, *ex P Bailey* (1838) 6 Dowl 311, *Shelley v Westboroke* (1817) Jac 226 and *Re Besant* (1879) 11 Ch D 508. See also the US case of *Commonwealth v Briggs* 33 Mass (16 Pick.) 203, 205 (1834).

with the aim of protecting the child's commitment to the dominant social values of the time rather than protecting his or her welfare *per se*. As Eekelar observes, at the end of the 19 Century the courts had articulated an interest which children might have which was distinct from that of their father although 'the earliest measures for dealing with child neglect were activated by concerns about social cohesion rather than the implementation of children's interests in their own right'.[82] However, towards the very end of the 1800s even the idea of the interest of the child being linked to the interests of society rather than the good of the child *per se* showed signs of changing. In 1886 the Guardianship of Infants Act s.5 gave the court jurisdiction to make orders for custody and access on the application of the child's mother 'having regard to the welfare of the infant'.[83] In *Re McGrath*[84] Lindley J held that 'The word welfare must be taken in its widest sense. The moral and religious welfare of the child must be considered as well as its physical wellbeing, nor can the ties of affection be disregarded'. In 1881 the Kansas Supreme Court held in *Chapsky v Wood*[85] that the courts paramount consideration was to be the child's welfare. The domestic jurisdiction followed suit in *F v F*[86] in which Farwell J said 'The court is considering the question of guardianship has regard before all things to the infant's welfare; it has regard, of course, to the rights of the father and the mother, but the essential requirements of the infant are paramount'.[87]

1.16   At the end of the 1800s children had thus moved over the preceding centuries from being little more than the blank canvass upon which the future adult was gradually drawn, with the extreme deprivations consequent upon that lack of individual social status or juridical personality, to attaining the rank of individuals worthy of protection based on their welfare widely interpreted. Given the history that had gone before, these developments in the later part of the nineteenth century represented significant progress for children although, as Freeman points out, the protective legislation in respect of children arising in the nineteenth century still defended practices such as corporal punishment.[88] This allowed Henry Bergh, one of the founders of the New York Society for the Prevention of Cruelty to Children to uphold 'a good wholesome flogging' as being appropriate for 'disobedient children'.[89] However, between 1900 and 1989, the position of children would evolve even further from being the object of protection to being subjects recognised as entitled to their own rights. This process of evolution would however once again be a long one.

---

[82]   Eekelar, J *The Emergence of Children's Rights* (1986) Oxford Journal of Legal Studies 6, pp 161–182, p 168. An example of this can be seen in the treatment of children who were the victims of intra-familial sexual abuse. Whilst there were valiant attempts to 'save' abused children, the act of sexual abuse was deemed to have corrupted the female child. Once 'fallen' the child's status was morally dubious. This created a desire to institutionalise girls who had been sexually abused due to fears about their moral status as 'corrupted children' as much as concerns of child protection. Child victims of incest were more likely to be sent to an institution than those sexually assaulted by strangers (see Jackson, L *Child Sexual Abuse in Victorian England* (2000) Routledge, pp 6 and 66–68). See also *Constantinidi v Constantinidi and Lance* [1905] P 254 per Stirling LJ stating that the function of the court is to 'to promote virtue and morality and to discourage vice and immorality'.

[83]   The Custody of Infants Act 1873 had used the formulation 'the benefit of the infant'.

[84]   [1893] 1 Ch 143.

[85]   (1881) 26 Kan 650 per Justice Brewer.

[86]   [1902] 1 Ch 688.

[87]   Munby notes that this is probably the first occasion on which it was said by a domestic court that the child's welfare is the court's paramount consideration (see Munby, J *Families old and new – the family and Art 8* (2005) CFLQ Vol 17 No 4, p 498.

[88]   The legislative provision made in respect of children in the 19th century was seen by many at the time as constituting an unacceptable interference with family responsibility (see Fox-Harding, L *Perspectives in Child Policy* (1997) Longman, p 35).

[89]   Freeman, M *Laws, Conventions and Rights* (1993) Children & Society 7:1, p 37–48, p 38.

The Codification of Children's Rights

1.17 Within national jurisdictions the child's juridical personality had gradually become visible to the law at the end of the nineteenth century and the word 'rights' had even been used to describe some of the domestic legislation that pertained to children.[90] By contrast, within the context of international law children remained largely invisible. However, as Tobin and Alston point out, 'The relative invisibility of children on the nineteenth century's international agenda was to begin to change dramatically in the first quarter of the twentieth century'.[91] Beginning in 1901 Alston and Tobin identify five different phases in the international effort to promote the concept of children's rights, three of which fall to be considered in detail in this introduction.[92]

1901–1947

1.18 In the aftermath of the Paris Commune in 1871 Jean Vallés had attempted to establish a league for the protection of children's rights and had begun to advocate children's rights.[93] Through the main character in his book, *L'Enfant*, Vallés states that 'I will defend the rights of the child just like others defend the rights of man'.[94] In the United States Kate Douglas Wiggin was advocating and articulating the specific content of children's rights.[95] In the opening years of the twentieth century Ellen Key continued these themes, articulating in *The Century of the Child* the child's right to a family united by love and harmony, the right to equality between marital and non-marital children, the child's right to be born of healthy and robust mothers, to be educated without punishment and to have their personalities respected.[96] In 1920 Janusz Korczak published *How to Love a Child* expressing the view that the child must be seen as a separate being with the inalienable right to grow into the person he or she was meant to be. His writings advocated the right of children to respect, to make mistakes, to protest an injustice, to die prematurely and the right to a peaceful non-racist world.[97]

1.19 Janusz Korczak formulated his ideas during the First World War.[98] Following that great conflagration a number of international developments further assisted the

---

[90] Waugh, B in Clarke Hall, W *The Queen's Reign for Children* (1897) Fisher Unwin Introduction, p vii, in which Waugh described the Prevention of Cruelty to, and Protection of, Children Act 1889 as the 'great awakening of the nation to a true and full recognition of the rights of children'. See even earlier Blackstone: 'By begetting them, therefore, they have entered into a voluntary obligation to Endeavour, as far as this lies, that the life which they have bestowed shall be supported and preserved. And thus the children will have the perfect right of receiving maintenance from their parents' (Blackstone Commentaries on the Laws of England 1.16 (1775) 7th edn). For the seminal account of the development of the domestic law in the twentieth century in relation to children see Cretney, S *Family Law in the Twentieth Century – A History* (2003) Oxford Part IV.

[91] Alston, P and Tobin, J *Laying the Foundations for Children's Rights* (2005) UNICEF, p 3.

[92] Alston, P and Tobin, J *Laying the Foundations for Children's Rights* (2005) UNICEF, p 3. The final two phases between 1989 and 2000 and between 2001 and the present day are covered within the body of the main text.

[93] See Freeman, M *Laws, Conventions and Rights* (1993) Children & Society 7:1, pp 37–48, p 38. Note that as early as 1852 Slogvolk had published an article entitled '*The Rights of Children*' (Hodgson, D *The Rise and Demise of Children's International Human Rights* (2009) Forum on Public Policy Part A).

[94] Jean Vallés *L'Enfant* (1879) Le Pere Lachease.

[95] Wiggin, K *Children's Rights* (1892) Houghton Mifflin. Wiggin championed the eradication of corporal discipline, observing 'that the rod of reason will have to replace the rod of birch' (Wiggin, K *Children's Rights* (1892) Houghton Mifflin, p 19).

[96] Key, E *The Century of the Child* (1909) GP Putnam & Sons Chapter 1.

[97] Wollins, M (ed) *Selected Works of Janusz Korczak* (1995) Warsaw and Freeman, M *Laws, Conventions and Rights* (1993) Children & Society 7:1, pp 37–48, p 38. Janusz Korczak died with the children of the Warsaw Ghetto in Treblinka he having refused to leave the children of his orphanage alone.

[98] Freeman, M *Laws, Conventions and Rights* (1993) Children & Society 7:1, pp 37–48, p 38.

cause of children's rights. Most importantly the Covenant setting up the League of Nations provided at Art 23 *inter alia* that the members of the League would endeavour to secure and maintain fair conditions of labour for men, women and children and entrust the League with general supervision over the execution of agreements with regard to the traffic in women and children. Pursuant to this aim the League of Nations set up a Child Welfare Committee. Ultimately, in its later guise as the Advisory Committee on Social Questions, the committee came to bring 50 countries to accept the 1924 Declaration on the Rights of the Child.[99] This step has been described by Alston and Tobin as 'by far the most important action taken by the League of Nations in relation to children'.[100] In addition to this seminal development, in the period following the First World War many of the international labour standards adopted by the International Labour Organisation in the first few years after its creation in 1919 focused directly on children and helped to develop the notion that, in the area of labour, children possessed certain rights as children.[101]

The Declaration of the Rights of the Child 1924

1.20   As the Axis economies came close to collapse at the end of the First World War Eglantyne Jebb, who was born in 1876 in Shropshire the daughter of a well to do family with a strong social conscience, was appalled at the suffering of the children in the Axis countries caused by the war and the allied blockade. As a result she set up the 'Fight the Famine Council' which on 15 April 1919 set up a fund to raise money for German and Austrian children entitled the 'Save the Children Fund'. Jebb and her sister Dorothy went on to set up the International Save the Children Union in Geneva in 1920. As the difficulties consequent upon the First World War receded the fund turned in 1921 to address the developing tragedy in Russia born out of the Bolshevik revolution. Upon the Russian relief effort also coming to a close Jebb's attention turned to the issue of children's rights.[102] It is said that on a cloudless summer Sunday in 1922 Jebb climbed to the summit of Mount Saléve overlooking Lake Geneva and in the silence drafted a short and clear document asserting the rights of children and the duty of the international community to prioritise those rights in planning.[103] This document, which Jebb presented to the Save the Children International Union in Geneva in 1923, would become the basis of the 1924 Declaration on the Rights of the Child.

1.21   The Declaration of the Rights of the Child was adopted by the League of Nations on 26 November 1924. The Declaration is also known as the Declaration of Geneva. It is a short document and reads as follows:

---

[99]   Walters, F. P. *A History of the League of Nations* (1952) Oxford University Press, pp 186–187.

[100]   Alston, P and Tobin, J *Laying the Foundations for Children's Rights* (2005) UNICEF, p 4.

[101]   Alston, P and Tobin, J *Laying the Foundations for Children's Rights* (2005) UNICEF, p 3. See in particular the Night Work of Young Persons (Industry) Convention, No 6 of 1919; the Minimum Age (Sea) Convention, No 7 of 1920; the Minimum Age (Agriculture) Convention, No 10 of 1921; the Medical Examination of Young Persons (Sea) Convention, No 16 of 1921 and the ILO Convention Fixing the Minimum for Admission of Children to Industrial Employment (1919). See also the International Agreement for the Suppression of the White Slave Trade (1904) and the Intentional Convention for the Suppression of Traffic in Women and Children (1921).

[102]   See Harrison, B *Jebb, Eglantyne (1876–1928)* Oxford Dictionary of National Biography (2004) Oxford University Press and Francesca Wilson *Rebel Daughter of a Country House* (1967) Allen & Unwin.

[103]   Personal letters of Eglantyne Jebb cited in Van Bueren, G *The International Law on the Rights of the Child* (1998) Martinus Nijhoff, p 8. See also Harrison, B *Jebb, Eglantyne (1876–1928)* Oxford Dictionary of National Biography (2004) Oxford University Press and Francesca Wilson *Rebel Daughter of a Country House* (1967) Allen & Unwin.

'Formulated by the Save the Children International Union, Geneva, 1923, and adopted by the Fifth Assembly of the League of Nations, 1924.

By the present declaration of the Rights of the Child, commonly known as the declaration of Geneva, men and women of all nations, recognising that mankind owes to the Child the best that it has to give, declare and accept it as their duty that beyond and above all considerations of race, nationality or creed:

(i) THE CHILD must be given the means requisite for its normal development, both materially and spiritually.

(ii) THE CHILD that is hungry must be fed; the child that is sick must be nursed; the child that is backward must be helped; the delinquent child must be reclaimed; and the orphan and waif must be sheltered and succoured.

(iii) THE CHILD must be the first to receive relief in times of distress.

(iv) THE CHILD must be put in a position to earn a livelihood, and must be protected against every form of exploitation.

(v) THE CHILD must be brought up in the consciousness that its talents must be devoted to the service of its fellow-men.'

1.22 The President of the League of Nations Fifth Assembly described the Declaration on the Rights of the Child 1924 as being 'the Children's Charter of the League [of Nations]'.[104] The 1924 Declaration continued to emphasise protection and welfare over autonomy in line with the thinking of the time.[105] More radical thinkers such as Janusz Korczak criticised the 1924 Declaration. In his book *The Child's Right to Respect* Korczak complained that 'The authors of the Declaration of Geneva have mistaken duties for rights. The tone of this Declaration is persuasion, not one of making demands. The Declaration is only an appeal for good will, a request for more understanding'.[106] However, whilst it is probably going to far to describe the 1924 Declaration as 'the formal establishment of an international movement for children's rights'[107] in that it regards children as being recipients of specific treatment rather than holders of specific rights,[108] as Van Bueren observes the Declaration helped to establish internationally the concept of the rights of the child, laying the foundations of for future international standard setting in the field of children's rights.[109] As Alston and Tobin point out, the Declaration provided the inspiration for much that was to follow during the second phase of international efforts on behalf of children during the twentieth century.[110] The Declaration reaffirmed by the League in 1934 and the Heads of States and Governments of the member states pledged to incorporate its provisions into their respective domestic legislations.[111]

---

[104]   Documentary Records of the Fifth Assembly 177.

[105]   Freeman, M (ed) *Children's Rights* (2004) Ashgate, p xii. Freeman considers that the principles of the Declaration, and above all the fifth principle that the child 'must be brought up in the consciousness that its talents must be devoted to the service of its fellow-men' reflected the aftermath of an imperialist war (see Freeman, M *Laws, Conventions and Rights* (1993) Children & Society 7:1, pp 37–48, p 39).

[106]   Veerman, P *The Rights of the Child and the Changing Image of Childhood* (1992) Martinus Nijhoff, p 96.

[107]   Black, M *The Children and the Nations: The Story of Unicef* (1986) Unicef, p 199.

[108]   Van Bueren, G *The International Law on the Rights of the Child* (1998) Martinus Nijhoff, p 7.

[109]   Van Bueren, G *The International Law on the Rights of the Child* (1998) Martinus Nijhoff, p 8.

[110]   Alston, P and Tobin, J *Laying the Foundations for Children's Rights* (2005) UNICEF, p 4.

[111]   *Report of the Secretary General* (1934) International Child Welfare Review 30 cited in Van Bueren, G *The International Law on the Rights of the Child* (1998) Martinus Nijhoff, p 9.

1948–1977

The United Nations Charter

1.23 Whilst during the Second World War work continued in extending the international legal protection for children, culminating in 1943 in the adoption by the Post-War World Inter-Allied Conference on Educational Fellowship of a 'Children's Charter for the Post-War World',[112] the period between the creation of the United Nations in 1945 and 1977 was one in which the emphasis was on building and consolidating the human rights regime as a whole without the differentiating children's rights.[113] The United Nations Charter, the constitutional document establishing the United Nations in 1945, contains no specific reference to children. Indeed, for a document at the pinnacle of the human rights system it has been said that the Charter has relatively little to say about human rights.[114] The limited rights set out in the Charter have been described as 'more programmic than operational'.[115] However, the Charter can be said to have given formal and authoritative expression to the human rights movement that began after the Second World War and the United Nations proved an important spur for the development of the human rights movement, providing a forum for many-sided debates about human rights.[116]

Universal Declaration of Human Rights 1948

1.24 Despite proposals to the contrary, the UN Charter stopped short of including a bill or rights.[117] This object was fulfilled by the Universal Declaration of Human Rights. Unlike the UN Charter, the Universal Declaration of Human Rights does mention children. Within the context of declaring the family to be the 'natural and fundamental group unit of society' and as such 'entitled to protection by society and the State',[118] Art 25(2) of the 1948 Declaration provides that 'motherhood and childhood are entitled to special care and assistance' and that '[a]ll children, whether born in or out of wedlock, shall enjoy the same social protection'.[119] Arguments continue over the status of the Universal Declaration of Human Rights in international law. Van Bueren considers that the Universal Declaration of Human Rights, in articulating the child's right to special care and assistance directly protects the rights of the child.[120] At the very least, the Universal Declaration remains in some sense the constitution of the entire human rights movement.[121] As Steiner notes, the Universal Declaration of Human Rights:[122]

---

[112] Van Bueren, G *The International Law on the Rights of the Child* (1998) Martinus Nijhoff, p 9. Van Bueren notes that in the same year the Pan-American Child Congress adopted the 'Declaration of Opportunity for Children.'

[113] Alston, P and Tobin, J *Laying the Foundations for Children's Rights* (2005) UNICEF, p 4. But see also **1.28** below concerning the Declaration on the Rights of the Child 1959.

[114] Steiner, H, Alston, P and Goodman, R *International Human Rights in Context – Law, Politics, Morals* (2007) Oxford, p 137.

[115] Steiner, H, Alston, P and Goodman, R *International Human Rights in Context – Law, Politics, Morals* (2007) Oxford, p 115.

[116] Steiner, H, Alston, P and Goodman, R *International Human Rights in Context – Law, Politics, Morals* (2007) Oxford, p 134.

[117] Steiner, H, Alston, P and Goodman, R *International Human Rights in Context – Law, Politics, Morals* (2007) Oxford, p 135.

[118] Article 16(3).

[119] Note that Art 26(3) maintains that 'parents have a prior right to choose the kind of education that shall be given to their children'.

[120] Van Bueren, G *The International Law on the Rights of the Child* (1998) Martinus Nijhoff, p 18.

[121] Steiner, H, Alston, P and Goodman, R *International Human Rights in Context – Law, Politics, Morals* (2007) Oxford, p 136.

[122] Steiner, H *Securing Human Rights: The First Half-Century of the Universal Declaration and Beyond* (1998)

'... has retained its place of honour in the human rights movement. No other document has so caught the historical moment, achieved the same moral and rhetorical force, or exerted as much influence on the movement as a whole ... [T]he Declaration expressed in lean, eloquent language the hopes and idealism of a world released from the grip of World War II. However self evident it may appear today, the Declaration bore a more radical message than many of its framers perhaps recognised. It proceeded to work its subversive path through many rooted doctrines of international law, forever changing the discourse of international relations on issues vital to human decency and peace'.

Declaration of the Rights of the Child 1948

1.25 In 1948 the International Union for Child Welfare (IUCW) adopted a revised version of the Declaration on the Rights of the Child. This revised Declaration expanded the focus of the 1924 Declaration and revived interest in children's rights.[123] The revised Declaration formed part of the IUCW's lobbying effort of the United Nations. It is however unclear precisely what the results of this effort were. Alston and Tobin point out that although it is widely reported that the UN General Assembly took action in respect of children's rights in 1948 and adopted a second Declaration on the Rights of the Child,[124] Alston and Tobin can find no record of this in the records of the UN General Assembly for 1948 and consider that the IUCW Declaration has been misattributed to the UN General Assembly.[125]

Geneva Conventions 1949

1.26 In the aftermath of the Second World War the first, second and third Geneva Conventions[126] were updated and a fourth Convention added, the Geneva Convention relative to the Protection of Civilian Persons in Time of War. For the first time, children were included as a category of protected persons, leading to a very significant extension of the protections afforded to children during times of war and armed conflict.[127]

European Convention on Human Rights and Fundamental Freedoms 1950

1.27 The Statute of the Council of Europe signed in 1949 established the Counsel of Europe with a Committee of Ministers and a Parliamentary Assembly. For obvious

---

Harvard Magazine September–October, p 45. Note that The Universal Declaration of Human Rights was predated by the American Declaration on the Rights and Duties of Man by less than a year. Adopted by the nations of the Americas at the Ninth International Conference of American States, the Declaration provides at Art VII that all children have the right to special protection, care and aid. To this end Art XXX provides that it is the duty of every person to aid, support, educate and protect his minor children. Article XXX further provides that 'it is the duty of children to honor their parents always and to aid, support and protect them when they need it.'

[123] Alston, P and Tobin, J *Laying the Foundations for Children's Rights* (2005) UNICEF, p 4.
[124] *Child rights in action: Path to the Convention on the Rights of the Child* (2002) UNICEF.
[125] Alston, P and Tobin, J *Laying the Foundations for Children's Rights* (2005) UNICEF, p 5.
[126] The first Geneva Convention, the Convention for the Amelioration of the Condition of the Wounded and Sick in Armed Forces in the Field was initially adopted on 22 August 1864 by twelve nations. The second Convention, the Geneva Convention for the Amelioration of the Condition of the Wounded and Sick in Armies at Sea was adopted on 6 July 1906 and the third Convention, the Geneva Convention relative to the Treatment of Prisoners of War on 27 July 1929. In 1977 the four Conventions were supplemented by two additional protocols namely, Protocol I relating to the Protection of Victims of International Armed Conflicts and Protocol II relating to the Protection of Victims of Non-International Armed Conflicts. A third protocol was adopted in 2005, Protocol III relating to the Adoption of an Additional Distinctive Emblem, to make provision for a non-religious symbol as an alternative to the Red Cross and the Red Crescent. For a detailed description of the operation of the Geneva Conventions so far as they pertain to children see **14.46 et seq** and **15.121 et seq** below. See also the UN Declaration on the Protection of Women and Children in Emergency and Armed Conflict (1974).
[127] Alston, P and Tobin, J *Laying the Foundations for Children's Rights* (2005) UNICEF, p 6.

reasons, the human tragedies and physical dilapidations of the Second World War generated a desire in the newly formed Council to establish and codify basic human rights applicable to all. The Chair of the Council's Legal and Administrative Division, Sir David Maxwell-Fyfe, First Earl of Kilmur[128] oversaw the drafting of the European Convention on Human Rights and Fundamental Freedoms (hereafter the 'ECHR'). The drafting was heavily influenced by the Universal Declaration of Human Rights 1948.[129] The ECHR was opened for signature in Rome on 4 November 1950. It entered into force on 3 September 1953. Whilst not enshrining any child specific rights, as will be seen within the main body of this work, the ECHR has been and continues to be a valuable instrument for children.[130]

Declaration on the Rights of the Child 1959

1.28 Whilst in 1950 the UN Economic and Social Council adopted a further draft Declaration on the Rights of the Child[131] it did not look at the matter seriously again until nearly a decade later in 1959. The draft produced in 1959 benefited from the input of 21 countries.[132] Following its submission to the UN General Assembly, the Assembly proceeded to cut down the Commission's draft, which was described as 'verbose and repetitious'.[133] On 20 November 1959 the UN General Assembly adopted a much reduced version of the Commission's draft but a much expanded version of the Declaration of the Rights of the Child 1924 with ten principles in place of the original five.[134] Following a declaration in the Preamble that 'mankind owes to the child the best it has to give' the ten principles of the Declaration read as follows:

'1. The child shall enjoy all the rights set forth in this Declaration. Every child, without any exception whatsoever, shall be entitled to these rights, without distinction or discrimination on account of race, colour, sex, language, religion, political or other opinion, national or social origin, property, birth or other status, whether of himself or of his family.

2. The child shall enjoy special protection, and shall be given opportunities and facilities, by law and by other means, to enable him to develop physically, mentally, morally, spiritually and socially in a healthy and normal manner and in conditions of freedom and dignity. In the enactment of laws for this purpose, the best interests of the child shall be the paramount consideration.[135]

3. The child shall be entitled from his birth to a name and a nationality.

4. The child shall enjoy the benefits of social security. He shall be entitled to grow and develop in health; to this end, special care and protection shall be provided both to him and to his mother, including adequate pre-natal and post-natal care. The child shall have the right to adequate nutrition, housing, recreation and medical services.

---

[128] Sir David Maxwell-Fyfe was a prosecutor at the Nuremburg Trials. He is also remembered when British Home Secretary for refusing to request clemency from the Queen in respect of the death sentence passed on Derek Bentley.

[129] See the Preamble to the ECHR, paras 1, 2 and 5.

[130] Van Bueren, G *The International Law on the Rights of the Child* (1998) Martinus Nijhoff, p 22.

[131] UN doc. E/CN.4/512.

[132] Van Bueren, G *The International Law on the Rights of the Child* (1998) Martinus Nijhoff, pp 9–10.

[133] British Diplomat Samuel Hoare quoted in *The UN Commission on Human Rights* in Luard, E (ed.) *The International Protection of Human Rights* (1967) Praeger, p 76.

[134] United Nations General Assembly *Resolution* 1386 session 14 Declaration of the Rights of the Child on 20 November 1959.

[135] As Freeman notes, the 1959 Declaration expresses the best interests principle in stronger terms than Art 3(1) of the UN Convention on the Rights of the Child adopted 30 years later (see Freeman, M (ed) *Children's Rights* (2004) Ashgate, p xiii).

5. The child who is physically, mentally or socially handicapped shall be given the special treatment, education and care required by his particular condition.

6. The child, for the full and harmonious development of his personality, needs love and understanding. He shall, wherever possible, grow up in the care and under the responsibility of his parents, and, in any case, in an atmosphere of affection and of moral and material security; a child of tender years shall not, save in exceptional circumstances, be separated from his mother. Society and the public authorities shall have the duty to extend particular care to children without a family and to those without adequate means of support. Payment of State and other assistance towards the maintenance of children of large families is desirable.

7. The child is entitled to receive education, which shall be free and compulsory, at least in the elementary stages. He shall be given an education which will promote his general culture and enable him, on a basis of equal opportunity, to develop his abilities, his individual judgment, and his sense of moral and social responsibility, and to become a useful member of society. The best interests of the child shall be the guiding principle of those responsible for his education and guidance; that responsibility lies in the first place with his parents. The child shall have full opportunity for play and recreation, which should be directed to the same purposes as education; society and the public authorities shall endeavour to promote the enjoyment of this right.

8. The child shall in all circumstances be among the first to receive protection and relief.

9. The child shall be protected against all forms of neglect, cruelty and exploitation. He shall not be the subject of traffic, in any form. The child shall not be admitted to employment before an appropriate minimum age; he shall in no case be caused or permitted to engage in any occupation or employment which would prejudice his health or education, or interfere with his physical, mental or moral development.

10. The child shall be protected from practices which may foster racial, religious and any other form of discrimination. He shall be brought up in a spirit of understanding, tolerance, friendship among peoples, peace and universal brotherhood, and in full consciousness that his energy and talents should be devoted to the service of his fellow men.'

1.29   Within the context of its time the 1959 Declaration has rightly been described as groundbreaking.[136] For the first time the child's emotional wellbeing was emphasised in an international declaration.[137] Further, and perhaps most importantly the 1959 Declaration maintained the emphasis on the individual child, continuing the major contribution of the 1924 Declaration.[138] In addition, Alston and Tobin cite the fact that the 1959 Declaration accorded relative priority to the child's entitlement to emergency assistance and its recognition of the key role of non-state actors.[139] The UN General Assembly has concluded that 'the principles of the Declaration have played a significant

---

[136]   Alston, P and Tobin, J *Laying the Foundations for Children's Rights* (2005) UNICEF, p 5.

[137]   See Principle 6 ('The child, for the full and harmonious development of his personality, needs love and understanding').

[138]   Alston, P and Tobin, J *Laying the Foundations for Children's Rights* (2005) UNICEF, pp 5. But see also Van Bueren who considers that there is a significant difference between the manner in which the 1924 Declaration treats children, namely as the object of international law, and the way the 1959 Declaration treats children, namely as the subject of international law and recognised as being able to 'enjoy the benefits of' specific rights and freedoms (see Van Bueren, G *The International Law on the Rights of the Child* (1998) Martinus Nijhoff, p 12).

[139]   Alston, P and Tobin, J Laying the Foundations for Children's Rights (2005) UNICEF, pp 5–6. See the Proclamation following the preamble ('The General Assembly Proclaims this Declaration of the Rights of the Child to the end that he may have a happy childhood and enjoy for his own good and for the good of society the rights and freedoms herein set forth, and calls upon parents, upon men and women as

part in the promotion of the rights of children in the entire world as well as in shaping various forms of international cooperation in this sphere'.[140] Van Bueren describes the Declaration on the Rights of the Child as the conceptual parent of the 1989 UN Convention on the Rights of the Child.[141]

1.30   The 1959 Declaration on the Rights of the Child is not without its weaknesses. As with the 1924 Declaration, and indeed with the UN Convention on the Rights of the Child, there are no provisions for the enforcement of the rights it enshrines. Most importantly, the 1959 Declaration continues the emphasis on welfare and protection, rather than autonomy or participation.[142] However, the historical context of the 1959 Declaration must be remembered. In particular, it is important to recall that the 1959 Declaration was drafted before the civil rights movement gained momentum in the United States[143] and accordingly before the child liberation movement of the late 1960s and early 1970s sparked the debate on the issue of children's autonomy that preceded the drafting of the UN Convention on the Rights of the Child. As Thorpe LJ has pointed out, in terms of social development and in terms of understanding child development, much time has passed since the drafting of the 1959 Declaration.[144]

1.31   Following the adoption of the 1959 Declaration on the Rights of the Child, Alston and Tobin contend that 'despite the significance of the rights approach reflected in the 1959 Declaration, most of the international agencies continued to maintain a welfarist approach to children and this effectively excluded any particular significance being attributed to the concept of children's rights'.[145] This may have had much to do with the fact that attitudes to the autonomous exercise by children of their rights at the time of the adoption of the 1959 Declaration were not universally positive. Freeman gives the example of the views of the French Delegate to the Commission on Human Rights in 1959 that 'the child was not in a position to exercise his or her own rights. Adults exercised them for the child ... A child had special legal status resulting from his inability to exercise his rights'.[146] The rights of children did continue to be articulated to a limited extent within international conventions between 1959 and 1978. In 1966 the United Nations International Covenant on Civil and Political Rights provided that every child shall have, without any discrimination as to race, colour, sex, language, religion, national or social origin, property or birth, the right to such measures of protection as are required by his status as a minor, on the part of his family, society and the State, that every child shall be registered immediately after birth and shall have a name and that every child has the right to acquire a nationality.[147] In the same year the United Nations Covenant on Economic, Social and Cultural Rights further enshrined the child's right to protection both generally and in relation to economic exploitation.[148] In 1973 the ILO Minimum Age Convention was adopted whereby each State party ratifying the Convention undertook to pursue a national policy designed to ensure the effective abolition of child labour and to raise progressively the minimum age for

---

individuals, and upon voluntary organisations, local authorities and national Governments to recognise these rights and strive for their observance by legislative and other measures progressively taken in accordance with the following principles ...').
[140]   1979 A/33/45.
[141]   Van Bueren, G *The International Law on the Rights of the Child* (1998) Martinus Nijhoff, p 14.
[142]   Alston, P and Tobin, J *Laying the Foundations for Children's Rights* (2005) UNICEF, p 5.
[143]   Freeman, M (ed) *Children's Rights* (2004) Ashgate p xiii.
[144]   *Re A (Children: 1959 UN Declaration)* [1998] 1 FLR 354 at 358.
[145]   Alston, P and Tobin, J *Laying the Foundations for Children's Rights* (2005) UNICEF, p 5.
[146]   Freeman, M *Laws, Conventions and Rights* (1993) Children & Society 7:1, pp 37–48, p 39.
[147]   Article 24.
[148]   Article 10.

admission to employment or work to a level consistent with the fullest physical and mental development of young persons. However, despite the adoption of the 1959 Declaration and some further limited codification of children's rights in the years which followed, in 1973 Hilary Rodham[149] still felt compelled to describe the term 'children's rights' as a slogan in search of a definition.[150]

1978–1989

The Child Liberationists

1.32 During the late 1960s and early 1970s the child liberation movement gained momentum in the United States, lead by John Holt[151] and Richard Farson.[152] Within the context of this movement, Freeman identifies Robert Ollendorff as probably the first to argue for the adolescent's right to self-determination.[153] Holt advocated that '[T]he rights, privileges, duties of adult citizens be made available to any young person, of whatever age, who wants to make use of them'.[154] Both Farson and Holt enumerated rights for children which each derived from the right to self-determination, including the right to exercise choice in living arrangements, the right to self-education, the right to sexual freedom including access to pornography, the right to economic power, the right to political power, the right to responsive design, the right to freedom from physical punishment and the right to justice.[155] The views of the child liberationists were extreme and indeed, seen with modern eyes, simply reckless.[156] The views expressed by Holt, Farson and others ultimately damaged the concept of children's rights in that they conveyed the misleading impression that children's rights are almost wholly concerned with giving children adult freedoms.[157] The radical nature of the views advance by the liberationists continue to ground the two arguments most commonly used to gainsay the concept of children's rights, namely children's rights are incompatible with the developmental characteristics of childhood and children's rights are antithetic to family life.[158] However, the arguments of the child liberationists did ultimately assist in identifying a key issue in the continuing development of children's rights, namely that of children's autonomy. In particular, as Freeman notes, through consideration of arguments advanced by the child liberationists it has come to be realised that the dichotomy between protecting children and protecting their right to autonomy is a false one.[159] Whilst the child liberationist considered autonomy should be manifested in emancipation from adult tyranny, what their radical views ultimately bequeathed was the acceptance of the idea that children are individual human beings capable of being autonomous rights holders within the context of established family and social settings.

---

[149] Later Hilary Clinton, wife of President William Jefferson Clinton and US Secretary of State in the administration of President Barack Obama.

[150] Rodham, H *Children under the Law* (1973) Harvard Educational Review 43, pp 487–514, p 487.

[151] Holt, J *Escape from Childhood: The Needs and Rights of Childhood* (1974) EP Dutton and Co.

[152] Farson, R *Birthrights* (1974) Collier MacMillan. See also Foster, H and Freed, D *A Bill of Rights for Children* (1972) 6 Family Law Quarterly 343.

[153] Freeman, M *Laws, Conventions and Rights* (1993) Children & Society 7:1, pp 37–48, p 40.

[154] Holt, J *Escape from Childhood: The Needs and Rights of Childhood* (1974) EP Dutton and Co.

[155] Farson, R *Birthrights* (1974) Collier MacMillan. Holt also included the right to travel, to drive and to use drugs (Holt, J *Escape from Childhood: The Needs and Rights of Childhood* (1974) EP Dutton and Co).

[156] The views of the child liberationists also attracted much criticism at the time they were espoused (see for example Hafen, B *Children's Liberation and the New Egalitarianism: Some Reservations about Abandoning Youth to their Rights* (1976) Brigham Young University Law Review 605 and Wald, M *Children's Rights: A Framework for Analysis* (1979) 12 University of California Davis law Review 255).

[157] Fortin, J *Children's Rights and the Developing Law* (2009) 3rd edn, Cambridge, p 4.

[158] Fortin, J *Children's Rights and the Developing Law* (2009) 3rd edn, Cambridge, p 5. Both these arguments are considered in detail below at **1.36 et seq**.

[159] Freeman, M *Laws, Conventions and Rights* (1993) Children & Society 7:1, pp 37–48, p 42.

The United Nations Convention on the Rights of the Child

1.33 Alston and Tobin contend that the period between 1978 and 1989 was, after a period of general quiescence, characaterised by the emergence of a strong children's rights consciousness at the international level.[160] In response to a request from the Executive Board of UNICEF the UN General Assembly declared 1979 the 'International Year of the Child'. Following the adoption of the 1959 Declaration on the Rights of the Child, a number of states, including Poland, said they would have preferred to adopt a Convention on the Rights of the Child.[161] As part of its contribution to the International Year of the Child, Poland submitted a draft for a Convention on the Rights of the Child to the United Nations Commission on Human Rights. This draft came to form the initial basis of the Working Group of the United National Human Rights Committee which was set up to produce a finalised Convention. The Working Group operated on the basis of concensus and this inevitably resulted in a central tension between the desire for agreement and the effort to create an effective legal document.[162] Through the Working Group the Convention developed well beyond its initial draft.[163] A final draft was completed in 1988 and adopted by the United Nations General Assembly in 1989. The United Nations Convention on the Rights of the Child is the most widely ratified human rights treaty in the world and was ratified by the UK on 16 December 1991.[164] Only the United States of America and Somalia have yet to ratify the Convention.[165] The United Kingdom ratified the CRC in 1991 and it came into force as a binding treaty in the United Kingdom in January 1992. The ratification by the United Kingdom of the CRC has been described as 'an event of outstanding importance'.[166]

1.34 Van Bueren contends the progress represented by the adoption of the CRC was prompted less by reflections on the moral rights of children and more by the real political belief that the promotion and protection of children's rights was less divisive than other issues on the diplomatic agenda at the time.[167] Notwithstanding this, Van Buren argues that the CRC accomplishes five goals, namely it creates new rights under international law for children, it enshrines those rights in a global treaty, it contains binding standards in areas where previously there were only non-binding recommendations, it imposes new obligations in relation to the provision for and protection of children and it adds an express prohibition on discrimination against

---

[160] Alston, P and Tobin, J *Laying the Foundations for Children's Rights* (2005) UNICEF, p 6. Note in 1978 the American Convention on Human Rights was adopted, which provides at Art 19 that 'Every minor child has the right to the measures of protection required by his condition as a minor on the part of his family, society, and the state.'

[161] Van Bueren, G *The International Law on the Rights of the Child* (1998) Martinus Nijhoff, p 11.

[162] Todres, J *Emerging Limitations on the Rights of the Child: The UN Convention on the Rights of the Child and its Early Case Law* (1998) Columbia Human Rights Law Review 30, pp 159–200, p 165. Freeman identifies five areas in which concensus was difficult to achieve, namely freedom of thought, conscience and religion, inter-country adoption, the rights of the unborn child, traditional practices and the duties of children (Freeman, M *Laws, Conventions and Rights* (1993) Children & Society 7:1 pp 37–48 pp 42–43). The difficulties that result from such compromises are highlighted in the main text as they become relevant.

[163] UN Doc E/CN.4/1349.

[164] Article 51 of the CRC permits reservations to be registered by States Parties at the time of ratification (although reservations incompatible with the object and purpose of the Convention are not permitted) and the UK adopted a number of reservations on ratifying the CRC. These are dealt with in detail in the main text where they become relevant.

[165] Both Somalia and the United States have signalled their intention to ratify by formally signing the CRC.

[166] Fortin, J *Children's Rights and the Developing Law* (2009) 3rd edn, Cambridge, p 31.

[167] Van Bueren, G *The International Law on the Rights of the Child* (1998) Martinus Nijhoff, p 25. The period covered by the negotiations over the Convention coincided with the final years of the Cold War.

children in the enjoyment of their rights.[168] Veerman describes the CRC as 'an important and easily understood advocacy tool, one that promotes children's welfare as an issue of justice rather than one of charity'.[169] Similarly, whilst noting the inevitable compromises which marked its creation, Fortin acknowledges the CRC as a remarkable document, which provides a comprehensive set of standards against which ratifying states may measure the extent to which they fulfil children's rights.[170]

1.35 Placed within its historical context, the most dramatic development in children's rights achieved by the CRC comprises the participation rights embodied in Art 12 of the Convention.[171] The rights enshrined in Art 12, which entitle the child to a say in the processes affecting his or her life,[172] above all others[173] illuminate how far children have come from the Aristotlean concept of the child as important not for himself or herself but for his or her potential and the 19th Century characterisation of the child as largely an object of intervention.[174] Standing at the end of a long history, the right to participate enshrined in Art 12 of the CRC recognises the child as a full human being, with integrity and personality, and with the ability to participate fully in society.[175] The child is recognised not as a possession of parents, or of the State, or simply an object of concern[176] but as a holder of rights in his or her own right.

CHILDREN AND CHILDREN'S RIGHTS

Children as Holders of Rights

1.36 Whilst, ultimately, agreement over a universally acceptable theory of rights for children may always prove elusive[177] the long debate about whether children have rights must surely now be settled in the affirmative.[178] The shear weight of international and regional treaty law and jurisprudence developed in the context of the foregoing history

---

[168] Van Bueren, G *The International Law on the Rights of the Child* (1998) Martinus Nijhoff, p 16.

[169] Veerman, P *The Rights of the Child and the Changing Image of Childhood* (1992) Martinus Nijhoff, p 184.

[170] Fortin, J *Children's Rights and the Developing Law* (2009) 3rd edn, Cambridge, p 45.

[171] Article 12 of the CRC provides that '1. States Parties shall assure to the child who is capable of forming his or her own views the right to express those views freely in all matters affecting the child, the views of the child being given due weight in accordance with the age and maturity of the child. 2. For this purpose, the child shall in particular be provided the opportunity to be heard in any judicial and administrative proceedings affecting the child, either directly, or through a representative or an appropriate body, in a manner consistent with the procedural rules of national law.' See chapter 6 below.

[172] Freeman, M *Laws, Conventions and Rights* (1993) Children & Society 7:1, pp 37–48, p 44.

[173] Veerman argues that the other innovative features of the CRC are that State agencies will be responsible for the physical, psychological and social reintegration of children where their rights have been violated (see Art 39), that placements in residential care and foster care will be subject to review (see Art 25) and that the right to identity is for the first time formulated in an international Convention (see Arts 7 and 8 and see Veerman, P *The Rights of the Child and the Changing Image of Childhood* (1992) Martinus Nijhoff, pp 184–185).

[174] Following the adoption of the CRC in 1989 the first regional treaty on the rights of the child was adopted in 1990 in the form of the African Charter on the Rights and Welfare of the Child. Within this context, it should be noted that the Inter-American Court of Human Rights considers that the American Convention and the Convention on the Rights of the Child are now part of a very comprehensive international *corpus juris* on rights of children (see I/A Court H.R, *Juridical Condition and Human Rights of the Child*. Advisory Opinion OC-17/02 of August 28, 2002 Series A No 17, paras 37, 53, and *Case of the Street Children (Villagrán Morales et al)*. Judgment of November 19, 1999 Series C No 63, para 194).

[175] Freeman, M *Laws, Conventions and Rights* (1993) Children & Society 7:1, pp 37–48, p 45.

[176] Committee on the Rights of the Child General Comment No 8 *The Right of the Child to Protection from Corporal Punishment and Other Cruel or Degrading Forms of Punishment* CRC/C/GC/8, p 12, para 47.

[177] Fortin, J *Children's Rights and the Developing Law* (2009) 3rd edn, Cambridge, pp 12–14.

[178] For a comprehensive summary of the history of the philosophical debate concerning children as rights holders see Fortin, J *Children's Rights and the Developing Law* (2009) 3rd edn, Cambridge, pp 12–14.

makes any argument to the contrary a largely academic exercise and certainly one of little practical relevance to children themselves. As a matter of practice at least, children have certain inherent, inalienable, universal and equal human rights. The common themes of concern in relation to children's rights, namely how to identify children's rights, how to balance one set of rights against another in the event of conflict between them and how to mediate between children's rights and those of adults[179] are issues that the courts now deal with on a day to day basis. It remains important however to consider children's rights in their proper context if their efficacy is to be maximised. It is rightly recognised that children's rights cannot be allowed to 'become a 'religion or belief' which is itself as intolerant of other forms of value systems which may stand in opposition to its own central tenets as any of those it seeks to address'.[180] The quickest way to undermine children's rights is to allow those rights to undermine the rights of others. Within this context, the Committee on the Rights of the Child emphasises that the human rights of the child cannot be realised independently from the human rights of their parents, or in isolation from society at large.[181]

1.37   As set out above, the early American child liberationists of the 1960s and early 1970s did the concept of children's rights a disservice in so far as they conveyed the misleading impression that children's rights are almost wholly concerned with giving children adult freedoms.[182] As noted, the radical nature of the views of the liberationists grounded the two arguments most commonly used to gainsay the concept of children's rights, namely children's rights are incompatible with the developmental characteristics of childhood and children's rights are antithetic to family life.[183] Whilst neither of these arguments is a satisfactory reason for denying the existence of children rights, both arguments require careful examination as they serve to highlight the two key interpretative tools in the effective application of children's rights, namely the principle of best interests and the principle of evolving capacity.[184]

Children's Rights and Childhood

1.38   The first primary objection used to gainsay children's rights is that such rights are incompatible with the developmental characteristics of childhood. Advancing children as 'holders' of rights is not intended to deny the child's entitlement to a childhood, not least because children have the right to be children and not adults,[185] nor to deny children protection in accordance with their plainly vulnerable position within society arising from the physical and mental differences between childhood and adulthood. Rather, children's rights provide a normative framework within which children can go about the business of childhood. Children's rights define the boundaries of a space in which the full and harmonious development of the child's personality, talents and mental and physical abilities can be achieved, and ensure relief in circumstances where that space is invaded by factors which threaten the achievement of that end.[186] If one

---

[179] Fortin, J *Children's Rights and the Developing Law* (2009) 3rd edn, Cambridge, p 3.

[180] Evans, M *Religious Liberty and International Law in Europe* (1997), p 257.

[181] Islamic Republic of Iran CRC/C/15/Add.123, paras 35 and 36.

[182] Fortin, J *Children's Rights and the Developing Law* (2009) 3rd edn, Cambridge, p 4. See for example Holt, J *Escape from Childhood: The Needs and Rights of Childhood* (1974) EP Dutton and Co and Farson, R *Birthrights* (1974) Collier MacMillan. For a summary of the history of the children's liberation movement see above at **1.32** and Freeman, M (ed) *Children's Rights* (2004) Ashgate, p xiii–xiv.

[183] Fortin, J *Children's Rights and the Developing Law* (2009) 3rd edn, Cambridge, p 5.

[184] For a detailed discussion of the principles of 'best interests' and 'evolving capacity' see chapter 4 below.

[185] Campbell, T *The Rights of the Minor* in Alston, P, Parker, S and Seymour, J (eds) *Children, Rights and the Law* (1992) Clarendon, p 20.

[186] See also Rodham, H *Children under the Law* (1973) Harvard Educational Review 43, pp 487–514, p 487

acknowledges the impact of the world upon children, both positive and negative, then a child deprived of his or her rights will grow up very differently from a child to whom such rights are granted.[187] As Waldron points out the structure of rights is not constitutive of social life, but is instead to be understood as a position of security in case other constitutive elements of a social relationship ever come apart.[188]

1.39 Attempts to satisfy children's rights require considerable care.[189] The key to ensuring that the normative framework of children's rights promotes rather than undermines children and childhood lies in recognising the 'essential conflict'[190] between the child's need for special care and assistance arising out of his or her status as a child and the child's need to develop his or her capacity for autonomy and self-determination. The effective implementation of the normative framework of children's rights requires a balance to be achieved between the need to identify with children the special treatment they require by reason of their incapacity and the need to ensure children are able to develop capacity and maturity as they grow to the point of being able to take full responsibility as free, rational agents for their own system of ends.[191] It is important to note that in this context protection and autonomy are two sides of the same equation. It is possible for the same child to need both care for one purpose and autonomy or self-determination for another.[192] The precise relationship between the two sides of this equation and the answer which that equation produces in respect of any given right will differ for each child depending on the age, understanding and development of the child in question and his or her particular needs and interests.

Children's Rights and Children's Best Interests

1.40 Given the child's need for special care and assistance arising out of his or her status as a child, the interpretation and application of the rights of the child must be achieved in accordance with the best interests of the individual child concerned determined by reference to the child's particular needs. The application of the best interests principle does not act to change the substantive nature of the right or rights in question but rather simply affects the method of implementation in respect of the individual child.[193] In this context it is important to note that the child's welfare and child's rights are not mutually exclusive but rather co-terminus. Talk of a discrete 'rights based approach' versus a discrete 'welfare based approach' is misleading and indeed a contradiction in terms.[194] The rights of children remain constant. However, they must

---

('The needs and interests of a powerless individual must be asserted as rights if they are to be considered and eventually accepted as enforceable claims against other persons or institutions').

[187] Freeman, M (ed) *Children's Rights* (2004) Ashgate, p xiii.

[188] Waldron, J *Liberal Rights: Collected Papers 1891–1991* (1993) Cambridge, p 374.

[189] Fortin, J *Children's Rights and the Developing Law* (2009) 3rd edn, Cambridge, p 29.

[190] Fortin, J *Children's Rights and the Developing Law* (2009) 3rd edn, Cambridge, p 17.

[191] Freeman, M *The Rights and Wrongs of Children* (1983) Frances Pinter, p 57.

[192] Minow, M *Rights for the Next Generation: A Feminist Approach to Children's Rights* (1986) Harvard Women's Law Journal 1, p 14.

[193] Van Bueren, G *Child Rights in Europe* (2007) Council of Europe Publishing, p 34.

[194] Fortin, J *Children's Rights and the Developing Law* (2009) 3rd edn, Cambridge, p 26 and Fortin, J *Accommodating Children's Rights in a Post Human Rights Act Era* (2006) Modern Law Review 299, p 311. This is particularly the case where the 'interests' theory of children's rights is employed (as opposed to the 'will' or 'choice' theory) which states that a child benefits from a right where his or her interests are protected in certain ways 'by the imposition of (legal or moral) normative constraints on the acts and activities of other people with respect to the object of one's interests' (MacCormick, N *Legal Right and Social Democracy: Essays in Legal and Political Philosophy* (1982) Clarendon Press, p 154).

be interpreted and given effect in accordance with children's best interests. As a normative standard the best interest principle is not with its difficulties and these are dealt with in chapter 4 below.[195]

Children's Rights and Children's Evolving Capacity

1.41   With regard to the child's need to develop his or her capacity for autonomy and self-determination, in achieving the proper implementation of children's rights it is important not to think of children as a homogenous group.[196] The child's capacity for autonomy in respect of different aspects of life emerges at different points in his or her development.[197] The key to resolving this complexity when giving effect to children's rights is the principle of 'evolving capacity'. This principle stems from the acknowledgement that childhood is not a single, fixed and universal experience between birth and majority but rather one in which, at different stages in their lives, children require different degrees of protection and participation.[198] Within this context, a rights based system of protection and participation founded solely on identifying who is a child and who is not would be objectionable since such a system would take no account of what the continually developing child is capable of doing to ensure protection and participation for themselves.[199] The extent to which a 3 year old is competent to express a fully informed view as to which nursery he or she should attend is manifestly different to the extent to which a 16 year old is competent to express a fully informed view as to which sixth form college best meets his or her interests. Both children have the right to participate in the given decision, however the manner in which that universal right to participate is given effect must plainly differ as between the older and the younger child if their differing best interests are to be effectively safeguarded in the application of the same fundamental right.[200] Thus the rights of children remain constant but again the manner in which they are given effect is dependent on the age, development and understanding of the given child.

Children's Rights and the Family

1.42   Lord Mackay recalled in 1989 that 'the integrity and independence of the family is the basic building block of a free and democratic society and the need to defend it should be clearly perceivable in the law'.[201] The second objection used to gainsay the concept of children's rights is the assertion that children's rights risk disrupting intimate family relationships and family life and are thus antithetical to this basic building block.

---

[195]   See the discussion at **4.128–4.133** below.

[196]   See Archard, D *Philosophical Perspectives on Childhood* in Fionda, J (ed) *Legal Concepts of Childhood* (2007) Hart Publishing, p 47 where he observes that 'While it is easy to represent an infant as evidently not an adult, lacking all but the most basic, and unimportant, characteristics of the mature human being, it correspondingly harder to do so for the late adolescent. What is true of a six-month-old baby by contrast with an adult is false of a sixteen year-old adolescent. To the extent that this is true it is problematic to deny to the adolescent that standing which is denied to all children by virtue of their not being adults.'

[197]   Campbell, T *The Rights of the Minor* in Alston, P, Parker, S and Seymour, J (eds) *Children, Rights and the Law* (1992) Clarendon, p 19.

[198]   Van Bueren, G *Child Rights in Europe* (2007) Council of Europe Publishing, p 38.

[199]   Verhellen, E *Convention on the Rights of the Child* (2000) Garant, p 26.

[200]   This principle is recognised as the concept of 'evolving capacity' in Art 5 of the CRC which provides that 'States Parties shall respect the responsibilities, rights and duties of parents or, where applicable, the members of the extended family or community as provided for by local custom, legal guardians or other persons legally responsible for the child, to provide, in a manner consistent with the evolving capacities of the child, appropriate direction and guidance in the exercise by the child of the rights recognised in the present Convention.'

[201]   (1989) 139 NLJ 505, at 508.

This fear appears to be based on the twin assumptions that the more rights children have the less rights adults have[202] and that children's rights are concerned solely with the autonomy of the child. Having regard to the depth and breadth of the CRC and the depth and breadth of the Universal Declaration of Human Rights, the International Covenant on Civil and Political Rights, the International Covenant on Economic, Social and Cultural Rights and the ECHR, both these assumptions are plainly false.[203] Indeed, the primacy of the family as the most basic unit in human society and its importance to children is reflected in the majority of the human rights instruments relevant to the rights of the child.[204] The ideological basis of the CRC is that children have rights which transcend those of the family of which they are a part.[205] The child is not a possession of parents, nor of the State, nor simply an object of concern[206] but is a holder of rights in his or her own right. However, the CRC also repeatedly stresses the importance of family life as the primary context for children's rights in no less than 11 articles in addition to the preamble.[207] The preamble to the CRC makes clear that:

'Convinced that the family, as the fundamental group of society and the natural environment for the growth and well-being of all its members and particularly children, should be afforded the necessary protection and assistance so that it can fully assume its responsibilities within the community. Recognising that the child, for the full and harmonious development of his or her personality, should grow up in a family environment, in an atmosphere of happiness, love and understanding.'

Article 5 of the CRC provides that:

'States Parties shall respect the responsibilities, rights and duties of parents or, where applicable, the members of the extended family or community as provided for by local custom, legal guardians or other persons legally responsible for the child, to provide, in a manner consistent with the evolving capacities of the child, appropriate direction and guidance in the exercise by the child of the rights recognised in the present Convention.'[208]

---

[202] Alderson, P *Young Children's Rights* (2008) Jessica Kingsley Publishers, p 85.

[203] Fortin, J *Children's Rights and the Developing Law* (2009) 3rd edn, Cambridge, p 7.

[204] The African Charter on the Rights and Welfare of the Child, Art 18 ('The family shall be the natural unit and basis of society ...'), the African Youth Charter, Art 8 ('The family, as the most basic social institution ...'), the African (Banjul) Charter on Human and Peoples Rights, Art 18 ('The family shall be the natural unit and basis of society' and 'the family which is the custodian of morals and traditional values recognised by the community.'), the Ibero-American Convention on the Rights of Youth, Art 7 ('Prominence of Family'), the American Convention on Human Rights, Art 17 and the Revised Arab Charter on Human Rights, Art 33 ('The family is the natural and fundamental group unit of society').

[205] Durant, J *The Abolition of Corporal Punishment in Canada: Parent's Versus Children's Rights* (1994) 2 International Journal of Children's Rights, pp 129–136.

[206] Committee on the Rights of the Child General Comment No 8 *The Right of the Child to Protection from Corporal Punishment and Other Cruel or Degrading Forms of Punishment* CRC/C/GC/8, p 12, para 47.

[207] Alderson, P *Young Children's Rights* (2008) Jessica Kingsley Publishers, p 84. See CRC, Arts 5, 7, 8, 9, 10, 11, 18, 20, 22, 24 and 27. See in particular CRC, Art 5 (States Parties shall respect the responsibilities, rights and duties of parents ...to provide ...appropriate direction and guidance in the exercise by the child of the rights recognised in the ...Convention), Art 7 (The child ...shall have the right ...as far as possible ...to know and be cared for by his or her parents) and Art18 (States Parties shall use their best efforts to ensure recognition of the principle that both parents have common responsibilities for the upbringing and development of the child. Parents or, as the case may be, legal guardians, have the primary responsibility for the upbringing and development of the child. The best interests of the child will be their basic concern).

[208] Article 5 of the CRC is not without difficulty. Fortin notes that its provisions appear to conflict with the provisions of the CRC which seek to promote the child's capacity for independence (Fortin, J *Children's Rights and the Developing Law* (2009) 3rd edn, Cambridge, p 43) and MacCormick observes that those obliged to fulfill the provisions of Art 5 are the very individuals who may have a personal interest in ensuring that the child does not exercise his or her rights (McGoldrick, D *The United Nations Convention on the Rights of the Child* (1992) 5 International Journal of Law and the Family 132, pp 138–139).

Article 7 of the CRC provides that:

> 'The child shall be registered immediately after birth and shall have the right from birth to a name, the right to acquire a nationality and, as far as possible, the right to know and be cared for by his or her parents.'

Article 18 of the CRC stipulates that:

> '1. States Parties shall use their best efforts to ensure recognition of the principle that both parents have common responsibilities for the upbringing and development of the child. Parents or, as the case may be, legal guardians, have the primary responsibility for the upbringing and development of the child. The best interests of the child will be their basic concern.
>
> 2. For the purpose of guaranteeing and promoting the rights set forth in the present Convention, States Parties shall render appropriate assistance to parents and legal guardians in the performance of their child-rearing responsibilities and shall ensure the development of institutions, facilities and services for the care of children.
>
> 3. States Parties shall take all appropriate measures to ensure that children of working parents have the right to benefit from child-care services and facilities for which they are eligible.'

1.43   Within this context it can be seen that just as children's rights provide a normative framework within which children can go about the business of childhood they also provide a normative framework within which parents can go about the business of bringing up their children. Children's rights define the boundaries of a space in which the parents may to promote the full and harmonious development of the child's personality, talents and mental and physical abilities. Those rights also act to ensure relief in circumstances where that space is occupied by parents or others who are unable or unwilling to achieve this aim. The fact that a child has rights is not evidence that parental love or competence is absent.[209] Family relationships can be based on both the existence of love and affection and the existence of rights and duties.[210] As Rousseau recognised in his *Le Contrat Social* in 1762:[211]

> 'Even if each man could alienate himself, he could not alienate his children. For they are born men; they are born free; their liberty belongs to them; no one but they themselves has the right to dispose of it. Before they come to the years of discretion, their father may, in their name, make certain rules for their protection and welfare but he cannot give away their liberty irrevocably and unconditionally: for such gift would be contrary to the ends of nature, and an abuse of paternal right.'

Once again, to paraphrase Waldron, children's rights are not constitutive of family life but instead may be understood as a position of security in case other constitutive elements of family life, including the role of the parent, ever come apart.[212]

---

[209]   Archard, D *Children: Rights and Childhood* (2004) Routledge, pp 120–121.

[210]   MacCormick notes in this context that he is 'at once glad and regretful to discover that it is possible for me to acknowledge that my children have rights, without being thereby committed to the outrageous permissiveness to which my natural indolence inclines in me' (MacCormick, N *Legal Right and Social Democracy: Essays in Legal and Political Philosophy* (1982) Clarendon Press, p 166).

[211]   Jean-Jacques Rousseau *Le Contrat social* (1762), p 2.

[212]   See Waldron, J *Liberal Rights: Collected Papers 1891–1991* (1993) Cambridge, p 374. See also Freeman, M (ed) *Children's Rights* (2004) Ashgate, p xxii ('The importance of relationship and needs should not lead us to belittle the importance of rights as a resource in structuring and constraining relationships').

CONCLUSION

1.44 Fortin rightly cautions against the dangers of 'rights talk'.[213] Claiming rights for children that are incapable of standing up to rigorous theoretical and legal analysis serves only to devalue those rights which can be legitimately established as being based on sound analytical foundations. As Wellman observes, an inflation of rights devalues their currency and the assertion of ungrounded rights discredits the ones that are genuine.[214] Children's rights are not designed to assist children to dictate the menu for Sunday lunch, justify the failure to undertake homework or to achieve a later bedtime on a school night. They emphatically do not seek the kind of unrestrained emancipation of children from parental care envisioned by the child liberationists in the 1960s and early 1970s nor do they seek to undermine childhood or family life more generally. Rather, children's rights provide a comprehensive and consistent normative framework within which all children can grow through childhood as subjects entitled to the benefit of universally accepted legal norms to the point of being able to take full responsibility as free, rational agents for their own system of ends.[215] We shall now turn to consider in detail the rights to which the child is entitled as a subject, beginning with a detailed examination of the international, regional and domestic legal instruments which enshrine those rights.

---

[213] Fortin, J *Children's Rights and the Developing Law* (2009) 3rd edn, Cambridge, p 9.
[214] Wellman, C *The Proliferation of Rights: Moral Progress or Empty Rhetoric?* (1999) Westview, pp 3, 176–81.
[215] Freeman, M *The Rights and Wrongs of Children* (1983) Frances Pinter, p 57.

Chapter 2

LEGAL FRAMEWORKS AND INSTITUTIONS

'Let us put our minds together and see what life we can make for our children'

Tatanja Iyotanka ('Sitting Bull')

INTRODUCTION

2.1   As discussed in chapter 1, the evolution of children's rights and their codification has bequeathed to us primarily international and European legal instruments upon which to rest the law and practice of children's rights within this jurisdiction.[1] The consideration of the domestic law and practice in relation to children's rights in England and Wales must therefore of necessity start with a detailed précis of the international and European legal frameworks and principles touching and concerning children's rights in addition to the domestic law and practice which reflects and promotes the principles articulated by those international and European instruments.

2.2   As Brownlie notes, it is impossible in a general work to provide a detailed picture of the multiform and numerous institutions involved in the protection of human rights.[2] To provide the context of this work this chapter examines in broad overview first the international legal frameworks and institutions concerned with children's rights, including the impact of customary international law on the application and enforcement of children's rights, before turning to consider the applicable regional legal frameworks and institutions, including the European Convention on Human Rights and Fundamental Freedoms 1950 and the European Court of Human Rights. The chapter concludes with a summary of the domestic legislation which reflects, albeit incompletely, some of the principles enshrined by those international and regional frameworks. The application and enforcement of those international and regional frameworks in the domestic arena is then dealt with in detail in chapter 3.

UNITED NATIONS LEGAL FRAMEWORK AND INSTITUTIONS

The United Nations Convention on the Rights of the Child

Overview

2.3   On 20 November 1989 the UN General Assembly unanimously adopted the text of the Convention on the Rights of the Child.[3] The CRC is the most widely ratified

---

[1]   See Fortin, J *Children's Rights and the Developing Law*, (2005) 2nd edn, Cambridge, p 31.

[2]   Brownlie, I *Principles of Public International Law* (2008) 7th edn, OUP, p 583.

[3]   United Nations General Assembly *Resolution* 25 Session 44 Convention on the Rights of the Child on 20 November 1989.

human rights treaty in the world and was ratified by the UK on 16 December 1991.[4] Only the United States of America and Somalia have not ratified the CRC.[5] As Fortin highlights, the failure of the United States to ratify the treaty is unfortunate and based on the misplaced view that the Convention interferes in the lives of individual families rather than, as it does, providing a framework for the implementation of key principles through domestic government policies and programmes and within the context of the developing capacity of the child.[6] Art 41 of the CRC provides that nothing in the Convention shall affect any provisions of the law of the States Parties or the international law in force for States Parties which are more conducive to the realisation of the rights of the child than the CRC itself.[7]

2.4   The CRC is organised into four parts. First, the Preamble sets out the key principles underpinning the CRC. Thereafter, Part I comprises Arts 1–41 which constitute the substantive articles defining the rights of the child and setting out the obligations on States Parties to the CRC by which those substantive rights are given effect. Part II, comprising Arts 42–45 codifies the procedures for monitoring the implementation of the CRC including the constitution of the UN Committee on the Rights of the Child. Finally, Part III, containing Arts 46–54, embodies the provisions providing for the entry into force of the CRC.[8]

2.5   In addition, two optional protocols[9] to the Convention on the Rights of the Child were adopted by the UN General Assembly in 2000, namely the Protocol to the Convention on the Rights of the Child on the Sale of Children, Child Prostitution and Child Pornography, which entered into force on 18 January 2002, and the Protocol to the Convention on the Rights of the Child on the Involvement of Children in Armed Conflict, which entered into force on 12 February 2002. The optional protocols expand the rights of children beyond those prescribed by the original terms of the CRC and must be interpreted in light of the CRC. The United Kingdom ratified the optional protocol on the sale of children, child prostitution and child pornography on 3 July 2003 and the optional protocol on armed conflict on 24 June 2003.[10]

2.6   The Convention and its optional protocols form part of a wider UN 'human rights framework' within which wider context the CRC must be read and understood.

---

4   Article 51 of the CRC permits reservations to be registered by States Parties at the time of ratification (although reservations incompatible with the object and purpose of the Convention are not permitted) and the UK adopted a number of reservations on ratifying the CRC. These are dealt with in detail in the text where they become relevant.

5   Both Somalia and the United States have signalled their intention to ratify by formally signing the CRC. Note however that even though the United States has not ratified the CRC the Convention has been cited by US Courts (see *Sadeghi v IRS* 40F.3d. 1139 (10th Cir. 1994) Kane J dissenting and *Batista v Batista* (Conn. Supp Ct) (1992) where the CRC was used as persuasive authority.

6   Fortin, J *Children's Rights and the Developing Law* (2005) 2nd edn, Cambridge, p 43. Guggenheim argues that the failure of the United States to ratify the CRC has very little to do with children's rights and is certainly not evidence of their repudiation by the USA (Guggenheim, M *What's Wrong with Children's Rights* (2005) Harvard, p 15.

7   The Committee on the Rights of the Child has stated that Art 41, '... invites States Parties to always apply the norms which are more conducive to the realisation of the rights of the child, contained in either applicable international law or national legislation.' (Committee on the Rights of the Child, Report on the Second Session September/October 1992, CRC/C/10, para 68). The optional protocols contain similar provisions.

8   Verhellen, E *Convention on the Rights of the Child* (2000) Apeldoorn, p 76.

9   In addition, United Nations bodies have formulated further conventions which provide additional protection for children, see for example the ILO Convention 182 on the Worst Forms of Child Labour (1999) which came into force on 19 November 2000.

10   See **2.28** below.

The UN 'human rights framework' comprises the Universal Declaration of Human Rights and the six core human rights treaties:

- The Convention on the Rights of the Child.

- The International Covenant on Civil and Political Rights.

- The International Covenant on Economic, Social and Cultural Rights.

- The Convention against Torture and other Cruel, Inhuman or Degrading Treatment or Punishment.

- The International Convention on the Elimination of All Forms of Racial Discrimination.

- The Convention on the Elimination of All Forms of Discrimination against Women.[11]

2.7 Within the context of recognising the inherent, inalienable, universal and equal nature of human rights guaranteed by this UN framework,[12] the preamble to the CRC, the rights which are encompassed within its 54 articles and its optional protocols, seek to balance a number of fundamental (and potentially competing)[13] principles central to the lives of children. Whilst not incorporated into English law, the CRC exerts an increasingly powerful influence on the developing domestic law of the United Kingdom.[14]

CRC, Preamble

2.8 The preamble to the CRC does not itself prescribe binding principles but rather provides a frame of reference by which the succeeding articles are to be interpreted.[15] The CRC takes as its premise that the state of 'childhood' requires special care and assistance,[16] citing the Declaration of the Rights of the Child as providing that 'the child, by reason of his physical and mental immaturity, needs special safeguards and care, including appropriate legal protection, before as well as after birth'.[17] Within this context the CRC defines the family as 'the fundamental group of society and the natural environment for the growth and wellbeing of all its members and particularly children'.[18] The preamble goes on to record that the family 'should be afforded the necessary protection and assistance so that it can fully assume its responsibilities within

---

[11] In addition to these instruments, the preamble to the CRC also references the UN Charter, the Declaration of the Rights of the Child of 1924, the Declaration of the Rights of the Child 1959, the Declaration on Social and Legal Principles relating to the Welfare and Protection of Children, the UN Standard Minimum Rules for the Administration of Juvenile Justice (the 'Beijing Rules') and the Declaration of the Protection of Women and Children in Emergency and Armed Conflict.

[12] See the preamble to the CRC, paras 1–9.

[13] See the analysis in Fortin, J *Children's Rights and the Developing Law* (2009) 3rd edn, Cambridge, pp 47–54.

[14] Fortin, J *Children's Rights and the Developing Law* (2009) 3rd edn, Cambridge, p 53 and see **3.32–3.46** below.

[15] See Art 31 of the Vienna Convention on the Law of Treaties 1969 and Verhellen, E *Convention on the Rights of the Child* (2000) Apeldoorn, p 77.

[16] Preamble to the CRC, para 4.

[17] Declaration of the Rights of the Child 1959, Preamble.

[18] Preamble to the CRC, para 5.

the community, [r]ecognising that the child, for the full and harmonious development of his or her personality, should grow up in a family environment, in an atmosphere of happiness, love and understanding'.[19]

2.9 The preamble to the CRC further provides that 'the child should be fully prepared to live an individual life in society, and brought up in the spirit of the ideals proclaimed in the Charter of the United Nations, and in particular in the spirit of peace, dignity, tolerance, freedom, equality and solidarity'.[20] It has been argued that this proposition is in conflict with that which comes before it in the preamble stipulating that childhood is a state requiring care and assistance.[21] However, the words 'fully prepared to live an individual life in society' in para 7 of the preamble appear to be a reference to the preparation constituted by a child's upbringing rather than a requirement of the state of childhood itself, and to this extent do not conflict with childhood as a state requiring care and assistance within the context of a family. The reference to the principle of equality contained in the preamble[22] however, may be said to import a potential conflict with the concept of the child as a dependent member of a family. To the extent that the preamble does specify conflicting ideals, it does no more than reflect and codify some of the difficulties inherent in the formulation of children's rights discussed in chapter 3.[23]

CRC, Part I

2.10 Leading on from the concluding principles articulated by the preamble, namely 'the importance of the traditions and cultural values of each people for the protection and harmonious development of the child' and 'the importance of international co-operation for improving the living conditions of children in every country, in particular the developing countries',[24] the 41 articles of Part I of the CRC prescribe the substantive rights conferred by the Convention. Pursuant to Art 1 of the CRC, these substantive rights apply to 'every human being below the age of 18 years unless under the law applicable to the child,[25] majority is attained earlier'.[26] The standards set by the CRC are described as both 'interdependent and indivisible'[27] on the basis that one right cannot be assured at the expense of another. When considering the proper interpretation of the articles contained in Part I, assistance can be derived from the

---

19 Preamble to the paras 5 and 6.
20 Preamble to the para 7.
21 See for example Fortin, J *Children's Rights and the Developing Law* (2005) 2nd edn, Cambridge, pp 36–37 and p 41.
22 By reference to the UN Charter.
23 Fortin, J *Children's Rights and the Developing Law* (2005) 2nd edn, Cambridge, p 36 and see Verhellen, E *Convention on the Rights of the Child* (2000) Apeldoorn, p 63.
24 Preamble to the CRC, para 11.
25 Namely the law of the relevant domestic jurisdiction applicable to the particular child.
26 Whilst Art 1 defines the upper age of those to whom the CRC applies, it does not define the point at which the application of the CRC commences and, in particular, does not make clear whether the CRC applies to an unborn child. However, paragraph 9 of the preamble to the CRC compels States Parties to bear in mind that 'the child, by reason of his physical and mental immaturity, needs special safeguards and care, including appropriate legal protection, before as well as after birth.' For a detailed discussion see **4.2–4.24** below. In any event, the United Kingdom, on ratifying the CRC declared that it would interpret the Convention as applying only following a live birth (see **4.7 et seq**).
27 Newell, P and Hodgkin, R *Implementation Handbook for the Convention on the Rights of the Child* (2008) 3rd edn, UNICEF, p xix.

'Concluding Observations' of the Committee on the Rights of the Child[28] as indicating the Committees view of the Conventions intentions[29] and the General Comments issued by the Committee on the Rights of the Child.[30]

2.11   The rights set out in Part I of the CRC, which cover the broad canvass of civil, political, economic, social and cultural aspects of childhood, overlap each other to a considerable extent. Attempts have been made to classify the rights contained in Part I of the CRC by way of groups of rights having similar ends.[31] The Committee on the Rights of the Child has formulated its own classification comprising the following divisions[32] (which, as with other systems of classification, to a certain extent overlap):

Guiding Principles	Article 1 (Definition of a Child)
	Article 2 (Non-Discrimination)
	Article 3 (Best interests of the Child)
	Article 6 (Right to Survival & Development)
	Article 12 (Respect for views of the Child)
Survival and Development Rights	Article 4 (Protection of Rights)
	Article 5 (Parental Guidance)
	Article 6 (Survival and Development)
	Article 7 (Name, Nationality and Care)
	Article 8 (Preservation of Identity)
	Article 9 (Separation from Parents)
	Article 10 (Family Reunification)
	Article 14 (Freedom of Though, Conscience and Religion)
	Article 18 (Parental Responsibilities and State Assistance)
	Article 20 (Children deprived of Family Environment)
	Article 22 (Refugee Children)
	Article 23 (Children with Disabilities)
	Article 24 (Health and Health Services)
	Article 25 (Review of Treatment in Care)
	Article 26 (Social Security)
	Article 27 (Adequate Standard of Living)
	Article 28 (Right to Education)

---

[28]   See **2.23** below.

[29]   See Fortin, J *Children's Rights and the Developing Law* (2005) 2nd edn, Cambridge, p 37. As Fortin points out, the research that has analysed these 'Concluding Observations' is likewise of valuable assistance in interpreting the articles in Part I, in particular, the *Implementation Handbook on for the Convention on the Rights of the Child* (Newell, P and Hodgkin, R (2008) 3rd edn, UNICEF).

[30]   See **2.23** below.

[31]   For example Le Blanc's classification defines 'membership rights', survival rights', protection rights' and 'empowerment rights' (Le Blanc, L *The Convention on the Rights of the Child: United Nations Law Making on Human Rights* (1995) University of Nebraska Press, Part Two). Hammarberg creates a classification that encompasses the four 'P's, namely 'participation rights', 'protection rights', 'prevention rights' and 'provision rights' (Harmmaberg, T *The UN Convention on the Rights of the Child and How to Make it Work* (1990) 12 Human Rights Quarterly 97). Verhellen argues that a subdivision of rights into different categories would be a breach of the spirit of the convention, which makes no distinction between the different rights and establishes no hierarchy (Verhellen, E *Convention on the Rights of the Child* (2000) Apeldoorn, p 77).

[32]   UNICEF Information Sheets.

	Article 29 (Goals of Education)
	Article 30 (Children of Minorities/Indigenous Groups)
	Article 31 (Leisure, Play and Culture)
	Article 42 (Knowledge of Rights)
Participation Rights	Article 4 (Protection of Rights)
	Article 12 (Respect for the views of the child)
	Article 13 (Freedom of Expression)
	Article 14 (Freedom of Thought, Conscience and Religion)
	Article 15 (Freedom of Association)
	Article 16 (Right to Privacy)
	Article 17 (Access to Information; Mass Media)
Protection Rights	Article 4 (Protection of Rights)
	Article 11 (Kidnapping)
	Article 19 (Protection from all forms of Violence)
	Article 20 (Children Deprived of Family Environment)
	Article 21 (Adoption)
	Article 22 (Refugee Children)
	Article 32 (Child Labour)
	Article 33 (Drug Abuse)
	Article 34 (Sexual Exploitation)
	Article 35 (Abduction, Sale and Trafficking)
	Article 36 (Other Forms of Exploitation)
	Article 37 (Detention and Punishment)
	Article 38 (War and Armed Conflicts)
	Article 39 (Rehabilitation of child victims)
	Article 40 (Juvenile Justice)
	Article 41 (Respect for National Standards)

Guiding Principles

2.12　　The articles of the CRC comprising the 'Guiding Principles' are those which are required for any and all the other rights under the CRC to be realised. Thus, the 'Guiding Principles' comprise the definition of a child,[33] the principle of non-discrimination,[34] the principle of best interests of the child,[35] the right to survival and development[36] and the right to participate.[37]

---

[33]　CRC, Art 1.
[34]　CRC, Art 2.
[35]　CRC, Art 3(1).
[36]　CRC, Art 6.
[37]　CRC, Art 12. See also the Vienna Programme of Action (UN Doc A/CONF 157/24 Part 1 1993). Each of these principles is covered in greater detail in chapters 4, 5 and 6.

(i) CRC, Art 1 – Definition of the Child

2.13 The CRC does not restrict a State's discretion to provide under its domestic law the point at which childhood begins.[38] On ratification the United Kingdom declared that it interprets the convention as applying only following a live birth to ensure that the CRC does not conflict with domestic abortion legislation.[39] As to the date on which childhood ends, Art 1 of the CRC provides that:[40]

> 'For the purposes of the present Convention, a child means every human being below the age of eighteen years unless under the law applicable to the child, majority is attained earlier.'

(ii) CRC, Art 2 – Non-Discrimination

2.14 Article 2(1) of the CRC seeks to ensure that children enjoy each and all of the rights conferred by the CRC regardless of the child's, or the child's parents' or legal guardian's race, colour, sex, language, religion, political or other opinion, national, ethnic or social origin, property, birth or other status. The protection given by this non-discrimination provision is further extended to particularly vulnerable groups by Art 22(1) in respect of refugee children, Art 23(1) concerning children with disabilities,[41] Art 30 concerning children of minority or indigenous groups[42] and within the context of the right to education pursuant to Art 29(1)(c).[43] Beyond prohibiting discrimination in the enjoyment of rights under the CRC, Art 2(2) compels States Parties to protect the child from discrimination or punishment by reason of the status, activities, expressed opinions, or beliefs of the child's parents, legal guardians or family members.[44] Whether the provisions of Art 2(2) provide a prohibition against discrimination which extends beyond the exercise of rights enshrined by the CRC is the subject of debate.[45] The non-discrimination provisions of Art 2(1) of the CRC do not appear to extend to a prohibition on discrimination against children *per se*, the prohibitions against discrimination contained in the CRC being referable always to the exercise of the rights of the child enshrined in the Convention, the special status of particular groups of children or the activities of the child's parents, legal guardians or family members.[46]

(iii) CRC, Art 3 – Best Interests

2.15 Under the Children Act 1989 whenever the court is determining any question in relation to the upbringing of a child or the administration of a child's property the

---

[38] Van Bueren, G *The International Law on the Rights of the Child* (1998) Martinus Nijhoff, p 34. See **4.4** below.

[39] UN Doc CRC/C/2/Rev.8, p 42 1991. As with The Holy See, other States have taken a different approach. For example Argentina and Guatemala have lodged reservations to the effect that Art 1 of the CRC should apply from the moment of conception.

[40] See **4.4** below.

[41] In respect of children with disabilities, reference should also be made to the UN Convention on the Rights of Persons with Disabilities (CRPD) and the UN Standard Rules on the Equalisation of Opportunities for persons with Disabilities.

[42] See the Committee on the Rights of the Child General Comment No 11 *Indigenous Children and their Rights under the Convention* CRC/C/GC/11.

[43] In respect of education, reference should also be made to the UN Convention against Discrimination in Education (CDE).

[44] Reference should also be made to the UN Declaration on the Elimination of All Forms of Intolerance and of Discrimination Based on Religion or Belief.

[45] See **4.87** below.

[46] Contrast Art 26 of the International Covenant on Civil and Political Rights which confers a comprehensive and freestanding guarantee of equality before the law as opposed to a 'parasitic' right providing only for freedom from discrimination referable to the enjoyment of rights (Pannick QC and others *Human Rights Law and Practice* (1999) Lexis Nexis 1st edn, p 320).

child's welfare is the court's paramount consideration.[47] Whilst the Declaration of the Rights of the Child 1959 provided that the best interests of the child were to be the paramount consideration in the enactment of laws for the purpose of securing the aims of the Declaration,[48] Art 3(1) of the CRC provides that the best interests of the child shall be 'a primary consideration'. Given the wide scope of the rights conferred by the CRC, it has been argued that this formulation allows the interests of the child to be balanced against the interests of other members of society in appropriate cases.[49] Art 3(1) is a guiding principle to the application of the CRC. Thus, each of the rights conferred by the CRC must be interpreted and applied having regard to the primary status of the best interests of the child. As Archard points out, the language of best interests in Art 3(1) is 'maximising' in its effect on the other rights.[50] The Committee on the Rights of the Child has made clear that in considering whether a particular right conferred by the CRC has been properly implemented, 'it needs to be demonstrated that children's interests have been explored and taken into account as a primary consideration'.[51]

Survival and Development Rights

2.16 The importance of the right to survival and development under Art 6 of the CRC, and the reason for it constituting a guiding principle is self evident. However, the right is not simply a right to survival and development *per se* but rather also incorporates rights to the resources, skills and contributions required to give practical effect to that right. States Parties have a positive obligation to take proactive steps to promote the child's survival and development.[52] In addition the recognition under Art 6(1) of the CRC that every child has the inherent right to life, under Art 6(2) States Parties, 'shall ensure to the maximum extent possible the survival and development of the child'. Likewise, in addition to States Parties respecting the right of the child to preserve his or her identity under Art 8(1) of the CRC, pursuant to Art 8(2), 'Where a child has been illegally deprived of some or all of the elements of his or her identity, States Parties shall provide appropriate assistance and protection, with a view to re-establishing speedily his or her identity'. By coupling substantive rights with a positive obligation to give effect to those rights, the CRC ensures that rights pertaining to a child's continued wellbeing and full development are both recognised and given effect in areas including identity, family life, health, education and intellectual development, standards of living, and leisure, play and culture.

2.17 As with any legal instrument imposing positive obligations on States Parties to promote the rights of children, the inclusion within the CRC of obligations giving practical effect to substantive rights exacts a necessary price in resources. Article 4 of the CRC acknowledges this by providing that, 'With regard to economic, social and cultural

---

[47] Children Act 1989, s 1(1).

[48] Declaration of the Rights of the Child 1959 Principle 2.

[49] See Fortin, J *Children's Rights and the Developing Law* (2005) 2nd edn, Cambridge, p 38. Fortin gives the example of the need to balance the interests of a young offender with rights under the CRC with the interests of society in being adequately protected from such offending. See also Newell, P and Hodgkin, R *Implementation Handbook for the Convention on the Rights of the Child* (2008) 3rd edn, UNICEF, pp 38–39.

[50] Archard, D *Rights and Childhood* (2004) Routledge, p 62.

[51] Newell, P and Hodgkin, R *Implementation Handbook for the Convention on the Rights of the Child* (2008) 3rd edn, UNICEF, p 38.

[52] The European Convention on Human Rights and Fundamental Freedoms has been interpreted to place similarly positive obligations on contracting States. See for example the positive duty on the State to promote respect for family life pursuant to Art 8 of the ECHR (*Marckx v Belgium* (1979) 2 EHRR 330, ECtHR).

rights,[53] States Parties shall undertake such measures to the maximum extent of their available resources'. Within our domestic jurisdiction, resource issues have long impacted upon the extent to which children's rights can be fully implemented and continue to do so.[54] The Committee on the Rights of the Child has repeatedly criticised the United Kingdom in this regard.[55] The nature of the obligations imposed by the CRC to ensure the practical effect of the substantive rights it enshrines are such that a lack of commitment by States Parties to adequate resourcing can fundamentally undermine those rights.

Participation Rights

2.18 Verhellen contends that the CRC establishes the first recognition of children's participatory rights by an international convention.[56] Classified by some as the 'empowerment rights'[57] the participation rights recognise that children should be able to participate fully and directly in the ordering of their own destiny in a manner commensurate with their age, development and understanding.[58] Having regard to the preamble to the CRC, which provides that, '... the child should be fully prepared to live an individual life in society, and brought up in the spirit of the ideals proclaimed in the Charter of the United Nations, and in particular in the spirit of peace, dignity, tolerance, freedom, equality and solidarity ...',[59] children must be assisted to develop that individual life in society. As Fortin points out, children in particular 'require the liberties essential to notions of adult autonomy if they are to develop their own capacity for autonomy and play an active part in society'.[60] Within the context of court proceedings, in *Re D (A Child)*[61] Baroness Hale observed that:

> 'There is a growing understanding of the importance of listening to the children involved in children's cases. It is the child, more than anyone else, who will have to live with what the Court decides. Those who do listen to children understand that they often have a point of view which is quite distinct from that of the person looking after them. They are quite capable of being moral actors in their own right. Just as the adults may have to do what the court decides whether they like it or not, so may the child. But that is no more reason for failing to hear what the child has to say than it is for refusing to hear the parents' views.'

2.19 Article 12(1) of the CRC provides that States Parties shall assure to the child who is capable of forming his or her own views the right to express those views freely in all matters affecting the child, the views of the child being given due weight in accordance with the age and maturity of the child. Many writers consider that Art 12 of the CRC is

---

53 The so called 'second generation rights'. These rights are distinct from 'first generation rights' such as the right to life, the prohibition on torture and cruel, inhuman or degrading treatment and the right to freedom of expression. See below **3.7 et seq**.

54 See for example MacDonald, A *The Caustic Dichotomy – Political Vision and Resourcing in the Care System* (2009) CFLQ, pp 41–44 examining the impact of under-resourcing on the functioning of the care system in England and Wales.

55 See Committee on the Rights of the Child, *Concluding Observations of the Committee of the Rights of the Child: United Kingdom of Great Britain and Northern Island* CRC/C/15/Add 34, para 9 and Committee on the Rights of the Child, *Concluding Observations of the Committee of the Rights of the Child: United Kingdom of Great Britain and Northern Island* CRC/C/15/Add 188, paras 10 and 11.

56 Verhellen, E *Convention on the Rights of the Child* (2000) Apeldoorn, p 78. The 'participation rights' are arguably the most controversial of children's rights: see Van Bueren, G *The International Law on the Rights of the Child* (1998) Martinus Nijhoff, pp 15–16.

57 Le Blanc, L *The Convention on the Rights of the Child: United Nations Law Making on Human Rights* (1995) University of Nebraska Press, Part Two.

58 MacDonald, A *The Child's Voice in Private Law – Loud Enough?* [2009] Fam Law 40.

59 See **2.8–2.9** above.

60 Fortin, J *Children's Rights and the Developing Law* (2005) 2nd edn, Cambridge, pp 40–41.

61 [2006] UKHL 51, [2007] 1 AC 619.

the pre-eminent article in the Convention, certainly within the context of the 'Participation Rights'.[62] Pursuant to Art 12(2), the right to express views and have them taken into account applies, not only to judicial proceedings but also to administrative proceedings affecting the child and is thus apt to be of wide application.[63] Other 'Participation Rights' ensure that children are free to formulate and express their own views, including their views on religion,[64] that they are able to associate and share those views with others[65] or to benefit from privacy[66] and that they have access to information on which to base their views and make informed choices.[67]

Protection Rights

2.20   The protection rights secured by the CRC aim to protect children from harm consequent on a wide variety of situations, including abduction, kidnapping and human trafficking, all forms of violence, sexual exploitation and abuse, child labour, removal from the family and war and armed conflict.[68] Once again, these substantive protective rights are expressed in terms of, or provide for, positive obligations upon States Parties. By way of example, Art 19(1) requires that 'States Parties shall take all appropriate legislative, administrative, social and educational measures to protect the child from all forms of physical or mental violence injury or abuse, neglect or negligent treatment, maltreatment or exploitation, including sexual abuse, while in the care of parent(s), legal guardian(s) or any other person who has the care of the child'. In addition to Art 38(1) requiring States Parties to respect the rules of international humanitarian law on armed conflicts relevant to children, Art 38(2)–(4) require States Parties to take positive steps to ensure the rights conferred by Art 38(1) have practical effect.

2.21   The CRC does not only provide for preventative protection in respect of those children who are at risk of harm but also seeks to ensure retrospective assistance for those children who have been victims of harm. Article 39 provides that:

> 'States Parties shall take all appropriate measures to promote physical and psychological recovery and social reintegration of a child victim of: any form of neglect, exploitation, or abuse; torture or any other form of cruel, inhuman or degrading treatment or punishment; or armed conflicts. Such recovery and reintegration shall take place in an environment which fosters the health, self-respect and dignity of the child.'

---

[62]   See for example Price Cohen C and Kilbourne S *Jurisprudence of the Committee on the Rights of the Child: A Guide for Research and Analysis* (1998) 19 Michigan Journal of International Law 633 at 648 and Newell, P and Hodgkin, R *Implementation Handbook for the Convention on the Rights of the Child* (2008) 3rd edn, UNICEF, p 149.

[63]   Encompassing for example in the domestic sphere, not only the court proceedings in a case in which a local authority is applying for a care order under the Children Act 1989, s 31(1) but also the statutory meetings by which the local authority determines the care plan for the child pursuant to s 31A of that Act.

[64]   CRC, Arts 13 and 14.

[65]   CRC, Art 15.

[66]   CRC, Art 16.

[67]   CRC, Art 17. On the basis that a child cannot develop views and critical thought without education (see Fortin, J *Children's Rights and the Developing Law* (2005) 2nd edn, Cambridge, p 41) there is a strong argument that the right to education under Arts 28 and 29 should also be included in the list of 'Participation Rights', as it is in Le Blanc's classification of 'Empowerment Rights' (see Le Blanc, L *The Convention on the Rights of the Child: United Nations Law Making on Human Rights* (1995) University of Nebraska Press).

[68]   See Preamble to the CRC, para 9 recalling the preamble to the Declaration of the Rights of the Child 1959 that 'the child, by reason of his physical and mental immaturity, needs special safeguards and care, including appropriate legal protection, before as well as after birth.' See also chapter 15 below.

CRC Part II

Publicity of the Principles and Provisions of the CRC

2.22   The rights conferred by the CRC can only be effective if those who are bound to implement those rights and those who would benefit from their implementation have knowledge of them. Article 42 of the CRC provides that States Parties undertake to make the principles and provisions of the CRC widely known, by appropriate and active means, to adults and children alike.[69] This places a substantive duty on States Parties.[70] Research has indicated that when children are educated as to their rights they become more respecting of the rights of all other children.[71] Within the United Kingdom, whilst the programme of study for citizenship at Key Stage 3 and Key Stage 4 of the National Curriculum provides that 'Pupils should be taught about the legal and human rights and responsibilities underpinning society'[72] both UNICEF UK and Save the Children have argued for a greater articulation of the principles and practice of the CRC within this aspect of the National Curriculum pursuant to the obligations under Art 42 of the CRC.[73] In 2008 UNICEF UK launched its 'Rights Respecting Schools Campaign' designed to provide a framework to help schools use the CRC as the basis for their ethos.[74]

The UN Committee on the Rights of the Child[75]

2.23   Article 43 of the CRC establishes a Committee on the Rights of the Child. The purpose of this Committee is expressed to be 'examining the progress made by States Parties in achieving the realisation of the obligations undertaken by the present Convention'.[76] The Committee consists of eighteen 'experts of high moral standing and recognised competence in the field covered by this convention' with consideration being given to geographical distribution and principle legal systems. Members are elected by secret ballot for a term of 4 years from among the nationals of States Parties.[77] Members of the Committee serve in their personal capacity and do not represent their State or any organisation.[78] The Committees Rules of Procedure permit the Committee to make 'General Comments' based on the articles and provisions of the Convention with a view to promoting its further implementation and assisting States Parties in fulfilling their reporting obligations, together with general recommendations based on information received during the reporting process or from other sources.[79] Whilst General Comments are not internationally binding they have been treated as an

---

[69]   See CRC/C/GC 5 '*General Measures of Implementation for the Convention on the Rights of the Child.*' Upon implementation, Spain for example ran a mass-media campaign to publicise the aims of the CRC.

[70]   Van Bueren, G *The International Law on the Rights of the Child* (1998) Martinus Nijhoff, p 395.

[71]   Howe, B & Covell, K *Empowering Children – Children's Rights Education as a Pathway to Citizenship* (2005) University of Toronto Press and Wringe, C *Issues in citizenship at national, local and global levels* (1999) Development Education Journal, 6, 4–6.

[72]   Citizenship, The National Curriculum for England, Key Stages 3 to 4 (1999).

[73]   Save the Children, *Memorandum Submitted by Save the Children to the Select Committee of Education and Skills* (March 2006) and UNICEF UK *Submission to the House of Commons Education and Skills Select Committee* (Undated).

[74]   UNICEF UK, *UNICEF UK Rights Respecting Schools in England* (2008).

[75]   For a detailed exposition on the work of the UN Committee on the Rights of the child see Van Bueren *The International Law on the Rights of the Child* (1998) Martinus Nijhoff, pp 388–399.

[76]   CRC, Art 43(1).

[77]   CRC, Arts 43(2), 43(3) and 43(6). An amendment to Art 43 increasing the number of members of the Committee from 10 to 18 came into force in November 2002.

[78]   Newell, P and Hodgkin, R *Implementation Handbook for the Convention on the Rights of the Child* (2008) 3rd edn, UNICEF, pp 639.

[79]   CRC/C/4/Rev.1 and see Newell, P and Hodgkin, R *Implementation Handbook for the Convention on the Rights of the Child* (2008) 3rd edn, UNICEF, pp 640–641.

authoritative interpretation of the CRC and by some scholars as having moral authority.[80] The Committee on the Rights of the Child is not however empowered to receive or determine complaints against States Parties from either individuals or other States Parties in respect of issues of implementation or breach of the CRC.[81] This is considered a major weakness of the CRC. However, it would appear increasingly likely that the Committee on the Rights of the Child will produce an Optional Protocol which establishes a complaints procedure under which children, as individuals or part of a group, can submit complaints directly to the Committee.[82]

Reports to the Committee

2.24 States Parties to the CRC are required by Art 4 to take all appropriate legislative, administrative and other measures for the implementation of the rights set forth in the CRC and, in relation to the implementation of social and economic rights, steps commensurate with the maximum extent of their available resources. The method by which such implementation is monitored is through States Parties reporting their efforts to this end to the Committee on the Rights of the Child, rather than by way of complaint or by way of enforcement through court proceedings.[83]

2.25 Article 44 of the CRC provides that 'States Parties undertake to submit to the Committee, through the Secretary-General of the United Nations, reports on the measures they have adopted which give effect to the rights recognised herein and on the progress made on the enjoyment of those rights'.[84] Reports must be submitted pursuant to this provision within 2 years of ratification[85] and thereafter every 5 years[86] and must include factors and difficulties, if any, affecting the degree of fulfillment by the State Party of its obligations under the CRC.[87] The information required to be contained in the reports is extensive and includes a requirement for detailed statistical measures.[88] The Committee can request further information if insufficient detail is provided by a State Party.[89]

---

[80] See for example Boerefijn, I *The Reporting Procedure under the Covenant of Civil and Political Rights* (1999) Intersentia-Hart, pp 294 and 300 and Nowak, M *UN Covenant on Civil and Political Rights – CCPR Commentary* (1993) Engel, p XXIV, para 21 and p 576.

[81] Contrast the position under the International Covenant on Civil and Political Rights. See **2.32** and **2.33** below.

[82] See the *Comments by the Committee on the Rights of the Child on the proposal for a draft optional protocol prepared by the Chairperson-Rapporteur of the Open-ended Working Group on an optional protocol to the Convention on the Rights of the Child to provide a communications procedure* (2010) A/HRC/WG.7/2/3.

[83] Van Bueren, G *The International Law on the Rights of the Child* (1998) Martinus Nijhoff, p 389. Van Bueren argues that 'The requirement that States Parties include in their reports any difficulties, which they may have in implementing the Convention's rights ought to help contribute to national debates on the prioritisation of such difficulties and the measures necessary to overcome them, as well as indicating a need for technical advice and assistance' and that 'By providing regular reports the State Party is theoretically regularly monitoring the extent of the implementation of each of the rights.' (Van Bueren *The International Law on the Rights of the Child* (1998) Martinus Nijhoff, pp 388–393).

[84] Article 44(1). See also Newell, P and Hodgkin, R *Implementation Handbook for the Convention on the Rights of the Child* (2008) 3rd edn, UNICEF, pp 643–653.

[85] See *General Guidelines Regarding the Form and Contents of Initial Reports to be Submitted by States Parties under Article 44 paragraph 1(a) of the Convention* (CRC/C/5, 15 October 1991).

[86] See *Revised Guidelines Regarding the Form and Contents of Periodic Reports to be Submitted by States Parties under Article 44 paragraph 1(b) of the Convention* (CRC/C/58, 20 November 1996, revised 3rd June 2005).

[87] CRC, Arts 44(1(b) and 44(2).

[88] See Van Bueren, G *The International Law on the Rights of the Child* (1998) Martinus Nijhoff, pp 390–391. See also the Committee on the Rights of the Child *Treaty-specific guidelines regarding the form and content of periodic reports to be submitted by States parties under article 44, paragraph 1 (b), of the Convention on the Rights of the Child* (2010) CRC/C/58/Rev.2.

[89] CRC, Art 44(4).

2.26 Following receipt of the report the Committee on the Rights of the Child will draw up 'Concluding Observations' which provide an evaluation in general terms of the report submitted by a State Party, including comments and recommendations to that State Party.[90] Again, whilst of lesser weight than the Committee's General Comments, the Committees 'Concluding Observations' have been treated as an authoritative interpretation of the CRC and by some scholars as having moral authority.[91] The Committee may request the Secretary-General of the UN to undertake studies on specific issues relating to the rights of the child.[92] The Committee submits an annual report to the Third Committee of the UN General Assembly, which hears from the Chair of the Committee on the Rights of the Child and adopts a Resolution on the rights of the child.[93]

The Optional Protocols

2.27 The two Optional Protocols to the Convention on the Rights of the Child adopted by the UN General Assembly in 2000, namely the Protocol to the Convention on the Rights of the Child on the Sale of Children, Child Prostitution and Child Pornography and the Protocol to the Convention on the Rights of the Child on the Involvement of Children in Armed Conflict, expand on the obligations created by the CRC in their respective topic areas. The Optional Protocols are not automatically binding on States Parties and each protocol contains its own ratification mechanism independent of Part III if of the CRC.[94]

Protocol on the Sale of Children, Child Prostitution and Child Pornography[95]

2.28 This Optional Protocol aims to extend the measures States should take in order to guarantee the protection of children from being sold and from involvement in prostitution and pornography.[96] To this end, Art 1 of the Protocol prohibits the sale of children, child prostitution and child pornography as defined by Art 2 of the Protocol. Articles 3–7 of the Protocol make provision for the criminal prosecution within the State Parties' jurisdictions[97] of certain acts defined in Art 3, including their definition as extraditable offences[98] and provision for the confiscation of goods, materials and assets.[99] Art 8 of Protocol places upon States Parties a positive obligation to protect the rights and interests of child victims of the practices prohibited by the Protocol at all stages of the criminal justice process. Article 9 imposes a positive obligation on States

---

90   UN Doc CRC/C/15 (1993).
91   See Boerefijn, I *The Human Rights Committees Concluding Observations* in Castermans-Holleman, M, Van Hoof, F and Smith, J *The Role of the Nation State in the 21st Century, Foreign Policy, Human Rights, International Organisations* (1998) Kluwer, pp 232 and 248 and Boerefijn, I *The Reporting Procedure under the Covenant of Civil and Political Rights* (1999) Intersentia-Hart, pp 303–304.
92   CRC, Art 45.
93   CRC, Art 44(5).
94   See the Optional Protocol to the CRC on the Involvement of Children in Armed Conflict, Art 9 and the Optional Protocol to the CRC on the Sale of Children, Child Prostitution and Child Pornography, Art 13.
95   In contrast to the Protocol on the Involvement of Children in Armed Conflict, the Optional Protocol on the Sale of Children etc. did not receive the active support of the Committee on the Rights of the Child, it being felt that the CRC sufficiently addressed the matters dealt with by that Protocol (Newell, P and Hodgkin, R *Implementation Handbook for the Convention on the Rights of the Child* (2008) 3rd edn, UNICEF, pp 643–669). See **15.56 et seq** below.
96   Optional Protocol to the CRC on the Sale of Children, Child Prostitution and Child Pornography, Preamble.
97   Optional Protocol to the CRC on the Sale of Children, Child Prostitution and Child Pornography, Art 4.
98   Optional Protocol to the CRC on the Sale of Children, Child Prostitution and Child Pornography, Arts 5 and 6.
99   Optional Protocol to the CRC on the Sale of Children, Child Prostitution and Child Pornography, Art 7.

Parties to take proactive steps to prevent the sale of children, child prostitution and child pornography and Art 10 obligates States Parties to cooperate with each other in the prevention, detection, investigation prosecution and punishment of such offences. The UK ratified this Protocol on 29 February 2009.

Protocol on the Involvement of Children in Armed Conflict[100]

2.29   The Protocol on the involvement of children in armed conflict has the effect of extending the protection provided by Arts 38(2) and 38(3) of the CRC.[101] Art 38(2) of the CRC provides that:

> 'States Parties shall take all feasible measures to ensure that persons who have not attained the age of fifteen years do not take a direct part in hostilities.'

Article 38(3) of the CRC provides that:

> 'States Parties shall refrain from recruiting any person who has not attained the age of fifteen years into their armed forces.'

Article 1 of the Optional Protocol provides that States Parties shall take all feasible measures to ensure that members of their armed forces who have not attained the age of *18* years do not take part in hostilities. Further, Art 2 of the Protocol stipulates that persons who have not attained the age of *18* years should not be compulsorily recruited into the armed forces. Finally, Art 3 of the Protocol requires State Parties to raise the age for the voluntary recruitment provided for in Art 38(3) of the CRC from 15 to 18 years of age.[102] Article 4 of the Protocol applies the foregoing provisions to armed groups distinct from the armed forces of the State.[103] Once again, the Protocol provides for, through Arts 6 and 7, a positive duty on States Parties to effectively implement these provisions. The UK ratified this Protocol on 24 June 2003.

The Wider UN Human Rights Framework

2.30   As already noted, the CRC and its optional protocols form part of a wider UN 'human rights framework' comprising the Universal Declaration of Human Rights and the six core human rights treaties: the Convention on the Rights of the Child, the International Covenant on Civil and Political Rights, the International Covenant on Economic, Social and Cultural Rights, the Convention against Torture and other Cruel, Inhuman or Degrading Treatment or Punishment, the International Convention on the

---

[100]   See also the provisions of the Geneva Convention IV Relative to the Protection of Civilian Persons in Time of War 1949 and associated protocols and the Paris Commitments and Principles to protect children from unlawful recruitment or use by armed forces or armed groups. See further **15.121** below.

[101]   Following concern that Art 38 of the CRC was not consistent with the level of protection offered to children by the rest of the Convention (see Newell, P and Hodgkin, R *Implementation Handbook for the Convention on the Rights of the Child* (2008) 3rd edn, UNICEF, p 660).

[102]   The UK made a declaration on signing the optional protocol on involvement in armed conflict that it would take all feasible measures to ensure that members of its armed forces who have not attained the age of 18 years do not take a direct part in hostilities but that Art 1 of the Optional Protocol would not exclude the deployment of soldiers under the age of 18 to take a direct part in hostilities where a) there is a genuine military need to deploy and b) by reason of the nature and urgency of the situation i) it is not practicable to withdraw such persons before deployment; or ii) to do so would undermine operational effectiveness, and thereby put at risk the successful completion of the mission and/or the safety of other personnel.

[103]   This article is designed to criminalise the use of child soldiers by militia, guerrilla and other military groups (Newell, P and Hodgkin, R *Implementation Handbook for the Convention on the Rights of the Child* (2008) 3rd edn, UNICEF, pp 663–664).

Elimination of All Forms of Racial Discrimination and the Convention on the Elimination of All Forms of Discrimination against Women. These instruments do not generally make a distinction between adults and children in respect of the specific rights which they enshrine.[104]

Universal Declaration on Human Rights

2.31 Within the context of the declaration that 'All human beings are born free and equal in dignity and rights',[105] the Universal Declaration of Human Rights provides that 'motherhood and childhood are entitled to special care and assistance. All children, whether born in or out of wedlock, shall enjoy the same social protection'.[106] It further states that the family is 'the natural and fundamental group unit of society and is entitled to protection by society and the state'.[107] The 30 articles of the Universal Declaration of Human Rights presage many the rights contained in the CRC.

International Covenant on Civil and Political Rights

2.32 The International Covenant on Civil and Political Rights (hereafter the 'ICCPR') was ratified by the United Kingdom on 20 May 1976. The rights enshrined by the ICCPR are divided into five categories, being protection of an individual's integrity, procedural fairness in law, protection from discrimination, individual freedom of belief, speech, association, press and assembly and the right to political participation.[108] Art 24 of the ICCPR provides that children have the right without discrimination to such measures of protection as required by his or her status as a minor on the part of his or her family, society and the State, the right to be registered after birth and to have a name and the right to acquire a nationality. In its General Comment No 17 *Article 24 (Rights of the Child)*[109] the UN Committee on Human Rights states that the rights pertaining to children in Art 24 of the Covenant are not the only rights that the Covenant recognises for children and that, as individuals, children benefit from all of the civil rights enunciated in the ICCPR. Article 2 of the ICCPR provides that each State Party undertakes to respect and ensure to all individuals within its territory and subject to its jurisdiction the rights conferred by that Convention without distinction of any kind, such as race, colour, sex, language, religion, political or other opinion, national or social origin, property, birth or other status.[110] By contrast to the CRC, the ICCPR provides for a mechanism by which the Human Rights Committee,[111] the body which overseas the ICCPR and receives reports from States Parties on its implementation, can receive and adjudicate upon complaints.[112] Private individuals can pursue a complaint claiming

---

[104] This creates difficulties where the wording of these instruments differs from the wording adopted by the CRC in respect of the same substantive right (See Balton, D *The Convention on the Rights of the Child – Prospects for International Enforcement* (1990) 12 Hum Rts Q 120, pp 123–125 and *G (Children) (Foreign Contact Order: Enforcment)* [2003] EWCA Civ 1607, [2004] 1 FCR 266 per Thorpe LJ).

[105] Universal Declaration of Human Rights, Art 1.

[106] Universal Declaration of Human Rights, Art 25(2).

[107] Universal Declaration of Human Rights, Art 16(3).

[108] International Covenant on Civil and Political Rights, Arts 1–27.

[109] HRI/GEN/Rev.8, para 2, p 183.

[110] ICCPR, Art 2.

[111] The Human Rights Committee has been called a 'judicial body of high standing' (see *Tavista v Minister of Immigration* [1994] 2 NZLR 257).

[112] See International Covenant on Civil and Political Rights Part IV. The procedure is of a largely conciliatory nature.

violation of the Convention pursuant to the first optional protocol to the ICCPR.[113]
The Second Optional Protocol to the ICCPR[114] seeks to abolish the death penalty,
providing in Art 1 that:

> 'No one within the jurisdiction of a State Party to the present protocol shall be executed' and
> that 'Each State Party shall take all necessary measures to abolish the death penalty within
> its jurisdiction.'

UN International Covenant on Economic, Social and Cultural Rights

2.33   The International Covenant on Economic, Social and Cultural Rights (hereafter
the 'ICESCR'), also ratified by the United Kingdom on 20 May 1976, enshrines the
right to work under just and favourable conditions, the right to social security, the right
to family life, the right to an adequate standard of living, the right to the highest
attainable standard of physical and mental health, the right to education and the right
to participation in a cultural life.[115] Art 2 of the ICESCR places a positive obligation on
States parties to implement and enforce these rights.[116] Art 10 of the Covenant provides
as follows in respect of children and their families:

> '1. The widest possible protection and assistance should be accorded to the family, which is
> the natural and fundamental group unit of society, particularly for its establishment and
> while it is responsible for the care and education of dependent children. Marriage must be
> entered into with the free consent of the intending spouses.
>
> 2. Special protection should be accorded to mothers during a reasonable period before and
> after childbirth. During such period working mothers should be accorded paid leave or leave
> with adequate social security benefits.
>
> 3. Special measures of protection and assistance should be taken on behalf of all children
> and young persons without any discrimination for reasons of parentage or other conditions.
> Children and young persons should be protected from economic and social exploitation.
> Their employment in work harmful to their morals or health or dangerous to life or likely to
> hamper their normal development should be punishable by law. States should also set age
> limits below which the paid employment of child labour should be prohibited and
> punishable by law.'

2.34   The ICESCR is monitored by the UN Committee on Economic, Cultural and
Social Rights, the system of enforcement being one of reporting by States Parties.[117] On
18 June 2008, the General Assembly adopted the Optional Protocol to the International
Covenant on Economic, Social and Cultural Rights.[118] The optional protocol was
opened for signature in 2009.[119] It provides for the UN Committee on Economic,

---

[113]   Adopted by General Assembly resolution 2200A (XXI) on 16 December 1966. Whilst recognising the
competence of the Human Rights Committee to hear complaints against the UK by other State Parties in
respect of alleged violations of the ICCPR, the United Kingdom has declined to ratify the first optional
protocol to the ICCPR.

[114]   Adopted by General Assembly Resolution 44/128 of 15 December 1989. It was ratified by the United
Kingdom on 10 December 1999.

[115]   International Covenant on Economic, Social and Cultural Rights, Arts 6–15.

[116]   Article 2 provides that 'Each State Party undertakes to take steps individually and through international
assistance and co-operation, especially economic and technical, to the maximum of its available resources,
with a view to achieving progressively the full realisation of the rights recognised in the present Covenant by
all appropriate means, including particularly, the adoption of legislative measures.'

[117]   ICESCR Part IV.

[118]   General Assembly resolution A/RES/63/117.

[119]   General Assembly resolution A/RES/63/117.

Cultural and Social Rights to receive communications from individuals and groups of individuals claiming to be victims of a violation of any of the rights set forth in the ICESC and from States Parties claiming that another State Party is not fulfilling its obligations under the ICESC. The optional protocol also prescribes an inquiry procedure to facilitate inquiries into grave or systematic violations by a State Party.[120] The UN emphasises the interdependence of the ICCPR and the ICESCR, recognising that the rights enshrined in each instrument are heavily interrelated and cannot be divorced from each other in practical application.[121]

UN Convention against Torture and Other Cruel, Inhuman or Degrading Treatment or Punishment

2.35 The UN Convention against Torture and Other Cruel, Inhuman or Degrading Treatment or Punishment (hereafter 'CAT') was ratified by the United Kingdom on 8 December 1988. Article 1(1) of CAT defines torture as:

'Any act by which severe pain or suffering, whether physical or mental, is intentionally inflicted on a person for such purposes as obtaining from him or a third person information or a confession, punishing him for an act he or a third person has committed or is suspected of having committed, or intimidating or coercing him or a third person, or for any reason based on discrimination of any kind, when such pain or suffering is inflicted by or at the instigation of or with the consent or acquiescence of a public official or other person acting in an official capacity. It does not include pain or suffering arising only from, inherent in or incidental to lawful sanctions.'

Part I of the CAT obliges State Parties to take measures to prevent torture and other acts of cruel, inhuman or degrading treatment or punishment. This positive duty includes ensuring that torture is a criminal offence, ensuring jurisdiction over acts of torture and ensuring that torture is an extraditable offence. The CAT specifically prohibits the deportation or repatriation of persons for whom there are substantial grounds to believe that they will be tortured in the destination State or the State to which that person may be subsequently removed. The CAT is enforced by the UN Committee against Torture through a system of reporting and a complaints mechanism provided for by Part II of the Convention. The Committee against Torture is empowered to investigate allegations of systematic torture.[122] As with the Covenant on Civil and Political Rights, the UK recognises the jurisdiction of the Committee against Torture to receive interstate complaints[123] but not its competence to hear complaints from individuals.[124] The CAT has an optional protocol (hereafter 'OPCAT'), ratified by the United Kingdom on 10 December 2003 which establishes 'a system of regular visits undertaken by independent international and national bodies to places where people are deprived of their liberty, in order to prevent torture and other cruel, inhuman or degrading treatment or punishment'.[125]

---

[120] General Assembly resolution A/RES/63/117 Arts 1 and 10.
[121] See Steiner, H Alston, P and Goodman, R *International Human Rights in Context – Law, Politics, Morals* (2007) 3rd edn, Oxford, pp 275–276 and 370–374.
[122] CAT, Art 20.
[123] CAT, Art 21.
[124] CAT, Art 22.
[125] OPCAT, Art 1.

UN Convention on the Elimination of All Forms of Racial Discrimination[126]

2.36 The UN Convention on the Elimination of All Forms of Racial Discrimination (hereafter 'CEAFRD') commits State Parties to condemning and eliminating racial discrimination and promoting understanding among all races.[127] Art 1 of CEAFRD defines racial discrimination as:

'any distinction, exclusion, restriction or preference based on race, colour, descent, or national or ethnic origin which has the purpose or effect of nullifying or impairing the recognition, enjoyment or exercise, on an equal footing, of human rights and fundamental freedoms in the political, economic, social, cultural or any other field of public life.'

Part I of the CEAFRD imposes positive obligations on States Parties to ensure that they do not discriminate on the grounds of race and to prohibit racial discrimination. For example, under Part I, States Parties are obliged to provide public education to promote understanding and tolerance.[128] Part II of CEAFRD establishes the Committee on the Elimination of Racial Discrimination which monitors the implementation of the CEAFRD by means of reporting provisions and the issuing of general recommendations. In addition, Part II provides for a complaints mechanism by which the Committee can hear complaints between States Parties and by individuals. Once again, the UK recognises the jurisdiction of the Committee in respect of the former but not in respect of the latter.

UN Convention on the Elimination of All Forms of Discrimination against Women

2.37 Ratified by the United Kingdom on 7 April 2006, the UN Convention on the Elimination of all forms of Discrimination against Women (hereafter 'CEDAW') requires States Parties to condemn discrimination against women in all its forms and to take positive steps to eliminate any such discrimination.[129] The CEDAW defines discrimination against women as:

'any distinction, exclusion or restriction made on the basis of sex which has the effect or purpose of impairing or nullifying the recognition, enjoyment or exercise by women, irrespective of their marital status, on a basis of equality of men and women, of human rights and fundamental freedoms in the political, economic, social, cultural, civil or any other field.'[130]

The obligations on States Parties under CEDAW include the obligation:[131]

'To ensure that family education includes a proper understanding of maternity as a social function and the recognition of the common responsibility of men and women in the upbringing and development of their children, it being understood that the interest of the children is the primordial consideration in all cases.'

---

[126] See also Arts 1–9 of the UN Declaration on Race and Racial Prejudice adopted by the UNESCO General Conference on 27 November 1978.
[127] CEAFRD, Art 2(1).
[128] CEAFRD, Art 7.
[129] CEDAW, Art 2.
[130] CEDAW, Art 1.
[131] CEDAW, Art 5(1).

Implementation of the CEDAW is monitored by the Committee on the Elimination of Discrimination against Women through a reporting procedure established under Part V of the CEDAW. The Optional Protocol to the Convention on the Elimination of all forms of Discrimination against Women (OPCEDAW) provides a complaints mechanism by which individuals and groups of individuals may submit complaints to the Committee and an inquiry procedure which supports the investigation of systematic abuses.[132] The optional protocol was ratified by the United Kingdom on 17 December 2004.[133]

Related UN Instruments and Institutions

2.38   In addition to the substantive human rights instruments comprising the UN human rights framework, there are a number of other UN instruments and institutions which touch and concern the rights of children. These, in conjunction with a series of UN standard rules and guidelines, must be considered when examining the legal framework which underpins children's rights. Eight UN Conventions additional to those comprising the UN human rights framework must be born on mind when considering the law and practice of children's rights.

Related UN Conventions

UN Convention Relating to the Status of Refugees

2.39   The UN Convention Relating to the Status of Refugees[134] (hereafter the 'CRSR'), taken together with its 1967 Protocol,[135] provides for the status and welfare of refugees. The CRSR as amended by the 1967 Protocol defines a refugee as:

> 'A person who owing to a well-founded fear of being persecuted for reasons of race, religion, nationality, membership of a particular social group or political opinion, is outside the country of his nationality and is unable or, owing to such fear, is unwilling to avail himself of the protection of that country; or who, not having a nationality and being outside the country of his former habitual residence as a result of such events, is unable or, owing to such fear, is unwilling to return to it.'[136]

The Office of the United Nationals High Commissioner for Refugees (UNHCR) is the UN agency with responsibility for the protection of refugees.

UN Convention on the Protection of the Rights of All Migrant Workers and Members of Their Families

2.40   The UN Convention on the Protection of the Rights of All Migrant Workers and Members of Their Families (hereafter 'CPRAMW') assures to migrant workers and

---

[132]   OPCEDAW, Arts 1, 2 and 8.

[133]   Two cases have been brought under this provision to date, both of which were declared inadmissible on the basis of failure to exhaust domestic remedies (see *Ms. Constance Ragan Salgado v United Kingdom of Great Britain and Northern Ireland* CEDAW, Communication 11/2006, UN Doc CEDAW/C/37/D/11/2003 (22 January 2007) and *N.S.F. v United Kingdom of Great Britain and Northern Ireland*, CEDAW, Communication 10/2005, UN Doc. CEDAW/C/38/D/10/2005 (12 June 2007).

[134]   Ratified by the United Kingdom on 11 March 1954 with a series of jurisdictional and territorial reservations relating to Isle of Man and the Channel Islands. See generally Goodwin-Gill, G *The Refugee in International Law* (2007) 3rd edn, OUP.

[135]   Which extended the original scope of the CRSR beyond the European refugees of the Second World War whom the convention was originally drafted to protect.

[136]   CRSR, Art 1.

their families fundamental human rights including the right to life, the right to protection under the law and the right to respect for family and private life.[137] The CPRAMW assures to children of migrant workers the right to a name, to registration of birth and to a nationality[138] and the basic right of access to education on the basis of equality of treatment with nationals of the State concerned.[139] The United Kingdom has yet to become a signatory to the CPRAMW.

UN Convention on the Rights of Persons with Disabilities

2.41 The UN Convention on the Rights of Persons with Disabilities (hereafter the 'CRPD') is intended, 'to promote, protect and ensure the full and equal enjoyment of all human rights and fundamental freedoms by all persons with disabilities, and to promote respect for their inherent dignity'.[140] The rights of persons with disabilities are defined within Arts 4–32 of the CRPD, together with the obligations on States Parties to give effect to those rights. In respect of children, the CRPD recognises that, 'children with disabilities should have full enjoyment of all human rights and fundamental freedoms on an equal basis with other children'.[141] To this end, Art 3 provides that a key principle of the CRPD is 'Respect for the evolving capacities of children with disabilities and respect for the right of children with disabilities to preserve their identities'. Article 7 of the CRPD provides that 'States Parties shall take all necessary measures to ensure the full enjoyment by children with disabilities of all human rights and fundamental freedoms on an equal basis with other children', and that 'In all actions concerning children with disabilities, the best interests of the child shall be a primary consideration'. Further, Art 7 stipulates that:

> 'States Parties shall ensure that children with disabilities have the right to express their views freely on all matters affecting them, their views being given due weight in accordance with their age and maturity, on an equal basis with other children, and to be provided with disability and age-appropriate assistance to realise that right.'

2.42 The CRPD is monitored by the Committee on the Rights of Persons with Disabilities by means of the reporting provisions conferred by the CRPD.[142] The Optional Protocol on the Rights of Persons with Disabilities (hereafter 'OPCRPD') allows States Parties to recognise the competence of the Committee to consider complaints from individuals and provides a mechanism for the consideration of grave or systematic violations.[143] It entered into force on 3 May 2008. The United Kingdom ratified the CRPD on 8 June 2009 and the Optional Protocol on 7 August 2010.[144]

---

[137] See CPRAMW, Part III.
[138] CPRAMW, Art 29.
[139] CPRAMW, Art 30.
[140] CRPD, Art 1. See also the Standard Rules on the Equalisation of Opportunities for persons with Disabilities (General Assembly resolution 48/96 of 20 December 1993) and **2.54** below.
[141] CRPD, preamble, para (r). The preamble to the convention also recognises at para (q) that 'women and girls with disabilities are often at greater risk, both within and outside the home of violence, injury or abuse, neglect or negligent treatment, maltreatment or exploitation.'
[142] CRPD, Arts 34 and 35.
[143] OPCRPD, Arts 1 and 6.
[144] The Government announced its intention to ratify the CRPD in its response to the Joint Committee on Human Rights Report *A Life Like Any Other? Human Rights and Adults with Learning Disabilities* Cm7378, pp 4–5.

ILO Minimum Age Convention

2.43   On 26 June 1973 the General Conference of the International Labour Organisation[145] adopted the Minimum Age Convention.[146] Art 1 of the Convention provides that:

> 'Each Member for which this Convention is in force undertakes to pursue a national policy designed to ensure the effective abolition of child labor and to raise progressively the minimum age for admission to employment or work to a level consistent with the fullest physical and mental development of young persons.'

The 1973 Convention specifies that the minimum age for admission into employment shall not be less that the age of completion of compulsory education and in any event not less than 15 years.[147]

ILO Worst Forms of Child Labour Convention

2.44   In 1999 the UN General Conference on International Labour Resolution on Worst Forms of Child Labour established the Worst Forms of Child Labour Convention.[148] States Parties ratifying the 1999 convention must take immediate and effective measures to secure the prohibition of the worst forms of child labour as a matter of urgency.[149] The Convention defines the worst forms of child labour as all forms of slavery and practices similar to slavery, the use, procuring or offering a child for prostitution, for the production of pornography or pornographic performances and work which is likely to harm the health, safety or morals of children.[150] The United Kingdom ratified the Convention on 22 March 2000.

Convention against Discrimination in Education

2.45   The Convention against Discrimination in Education (hereafter 'CDE') was adopted by the General Conference of the United Nations Educational, Scientific and Cultural Organisation (UNESCO)[151] on 14 December 1960. As its name suggests, the CDE seeks to eliminate discrimination within the educational systems of State Parties. Article 4 of the CDE requires that States Parties, 'formulate, develop and apply a national policy that will tend to promote equality of opportunity and of treatment in the matter of education. To this end, Art 4 obligates States Parties to make primary education free and compulsory, make secondary education available and accessible to all, make higher education equally accessible to all on the basis of individual capacity and assure compliance by all with the obligation to attend school prescribed by law[152] and '[t]o ensure that the standards of education are equivalent in all public educational

---

[145]   A specialised agency of the United Nations, the International Labour Organisation seeks to improve working and living conditions through the adoption of international labour conventions and recommendations.

[146]   1973 (No 138).

[147]   See Art 2(3). Countries with underdeveloped economies and educational systems are permitted to lower the age to 14 initially. Work which is likely to jeopardise the health, safety or morals of young people carries a minimum age of 18 (see Art 3(1)) or 16 where the health, safety and morals of the young person concerned are fully protected and the young person fully trained (see Art 3(3)).

[148]   The full title is 'Convention concerning the Prohibition and Immediate Action for the Elimination of the Worst Forms of Child Labour C.182 (1999).'

[149]   See Art 1.

[150]   See Art 3(a) to 3(b).

[151]   The stated role of UNESCO is to contribute to peace, security and development through education and intellectual co-operation, including ensuring children's right to education.

[152]   See Art 4(a).

institutions of the same level, and that the conditions relating to the quality of the education provided are also equivalent'.[153] The Optional Protocol to the CDE establishes a 'Conciliation and Good Offices Commission' to seek amicable settlement of disputes under the convention between States Parties. The United Kingdom accepted the CDE on 14 March 1962 but has not ratified it.

UN Convention for the Protection of All Persons from Enforced Disappearance

2.46 UN Convention for the Protection of All Persons from Enforced Disappearance (hereafter 'CPAPED') provides that no one shall be subjected to enforced disappearance,[154] defining enforced disappearance as the arrest, detention, abduction or any other form of deprivation of liberty by agents of the State or by persons or groups of persons acting with the authorisation, support or acquiescence of the State, followed by a refusal to acknowledge the deprivation of liberty or by concealment of the fate or whereabouts of the disappeared person, which place such a person outside the protection of the law.[155] State Parties are required to investigate acts of forced disappearance[156] and to ensure that it constitutes an offence under their criminal laws.[157] State Parties must also criminalise and seek to prevent the wrongful removal of children who are subjected to enforced disappearance, the falsification, concealment or destruction of documents attesting to the true identity of the children subjected to enforced disappearance and must search for and identify such children.[158] The Convention entered into force on 23 December 2010. The United Kingdom has not yet signed the Convention.

UN Convention against Transnational Organised Crime – Protocol to Prevent, Suppress and Punish Trafficking in Persons, Especially Women and Children

2.47 In addition to the foregoing UN conventions, the Protocol to Prevent, Suppress and Punish Trafficking in Persons, Especially Women and Children, supplementing the UN Convention against Transnational Organised Crime is also of relevance when considering children's rights.[159] The purpose of the Protocol, as defined by Art 2 is to prevent and combat trafficking in person, paying particular attention to women and children. Article 3(a) of the Protocol defines the crime of trafficking in human beings as:

> '"Trafficking in persons" shall mean the recruitment, transportation, transfer, harbouring or receipt of persons, by means of the threat or use of force or other forms of coercion, of abduction, of fraud, of deception, of the abuse of power or of a position of vulnerability or of the giving or receiving of payments or benefits to achieve the consent of a person having control over another person, for the purpose of exploitation.'

Exploitation includes, at a minimum, the exploitation of the prostitution of others or other forms of sexual exploitation, forced labour or services, slavery or practices similar

---

[153] See Art 4(b).
[154] CPAPED, Art 1(1).
[155] CPAPED, Art 2.
[156] CPAPED, Art 3.
[157] CPAPED, Art 4.
[158] CPAPED, Art 25.
[159] This protocol entered into force on 25 December 2003.

to slavery, servitude or the removal of organs.[160] The protocol requires that States Parties criminalise trafficking[161] and take proactive steps to assist and protect victims of trafficking.[162]

Related UN Declarations

2.48   The preamble to the CRC refers to the Geneva Declaration of the Rights of the Child of 1924 and the 1959 Declaration of the Rights of the Child, which are dealt with in chapter 1 above.[163] In addition, the preamble to the CRC references the Declaration of the Protection of Women and Children in Emergency and Armed Conflict and the Declaration on Social and Legal Principles relating to the Welfare and Protection of Children with Special Reference to Foster Placement and Adoption Nationally.[164]

Declaration of the Protection of Women and Children in Emergency and Armed Conflict

2.49   The Declaration of the Protection of Women and Children in Emergency and Armed Conflict was adopted by the General Assembly on 14 December 1974.[165] The Declaration seeks to provide protection for women and children from the dilapidations of armed conflict by prohibiting attacks on the civilian population, condemning the use of chemical and bacteriological weapons, restating the obligations under the Geneva Conventions and requiring States involved in armed conflicts to make all efforts to spare women and children 'from the ravages of war'.[166] In addition, the Declaration stipulates that: 'All forms of repression and cruel and inhuman treatment of women and children, including imprisonment, torture, shooting, mass arrests, collective punishment, destruction of dwellings and forcible eviction' committed by combatants shall be considered criminal and that 'women and children caught up in armed conflict shall not be deprived of shelter, food, medical aid or other inalienable rights'.[167]

Declaration on Social and Legal Principles Relating to the Welfare and Protection of Children with Special Reference to Foster Placement and Adoption Nationally

2.50   Adopted by an resolution of the General Assembly on 3 December 1986[168] the Declaration on Social and Legal Principles relating to the Welfare and Protection of Children with Special Reference to Foster Placement and Adoption Nationally provides by Art 1 of the Declaration that 'Every State should give high priority to family and child welfare' and Art 2 recognises that 'Child welfare depends on good family welfare'. Article 3 provides that 'The first priority for a child is to be cared for by his or her own parents'. In addition to these fundamental declarations of principle, the 1986 Declaration sets principles applicable to children who require alternative care by reason of their own parents being unavailable or inappropriate. Key amongst those principles are those provided by:

•   Article 5, which states that:

---

[160]   See Art 3(a).
[161]   See Art 5(1).
[162]   See Arts 6–8.
[163]   See **1.20–1.28**.
[164]   See also the UN Declaration on Race and Racial Prejudice adopted by the UNESCO General Conference on 27 November 1978.
[165]   General Assembly Resolution 3318 (XXIX).
[166]   See Arts 1–4.
[167]   See Arts 5 and 6.
[168]   General Assembly resolution 41/85.

'In all matters relating to the placement of a child outside the care of the child's own parents, the best interests of the child, particularly his or her need for affection and right to security and continuing care, should be the paramount consideration.'

- Article 8, which provides that:

    'The child should not, as a result of foster placement, adoption or any alternative regime, be deprived or his or her name, nationality or legal representative unless the child thereby acquires a new name, nationality or legal representative.'

- Article 9, which stipulates that:

    'The need of a foster or an adopted child to know about his or her background should be recognised by persons responsible for the child's care unless this is contrary to the child's best interests.'

The Declaration goes on to set out detailed principles in relation to foster care[169] and adoption.[170]

Declaration on the Elimination of All Forms of Intolerance and of Discrimination Based on Religion or Belief

2.51   In addition to the Declarations referenced in the pre-amble to the CRC, the Declaration on the Elimination of All Forms of Intolerance and of Discrimination Based on Religion or Belief[171] must also be considered in relation to the rights of children. Article 1 of the Declaration provides that:

'Everyone shall have the right to freedom of thought, conscience and religion. This right shall include freedom to have a religion or whatever belief of his choice, and freedom, either individually or in community with others and in public or private, to manifest his religion or belief in worship, observance, practice and teaching.'

Article 5(1) prescribes the right of parents or legal guardians of a child to:

'organise the life within the family in accordance with their religion or belief and bearing in mind the moral education in which they believe the child should be brought up.'

However, whilst Art 5(2) confers upon the child the right to access to education in the matter of religion or belief in accordance with the expressed wishes of his or her parents or guardian and Art 5(3) protects children from discrimination on the grounds of that religion or belief, under Art 5 only a child who is *not* under the care of his or her parents of guardian may have their expressed wishes in the matter of religion of belief taken into account.[172] This position is in potential conflict with Art 12 of the CRC in that it arguably restricts the right of children cared for by parents or guardians to express their views freely in matters of religion and belief.[173] This is examined further below.

---

[169]   See Arts 10–12.
[170]   See Arts 13–24.
[171]   Proclaimed by General Assembly Resolution 36/55 of 25 November 1981.
[172]   Article 5(4).
[173]   Article 8 of the Declaration states 'Nothing in the present Declaration shall be construed as restricting or derogating from any right defined in the Universal Declaration of Human Rights and the International Covenants on Human Rights' but this does not include the CRC.

Related UN Standard Minimum Rules

UN Standard Minimum Rules for the Administration of Juvenile Justice

2.52   The United Nations has promulgated extensive rules relating to juvenile justice. The UN Standard Minimum Rules for the Administration of Juvenile Justice (hereafter the 'Beijing Rules') governs the treatment of juvenile prisoners and offenders by the member nations.[174] Article 1(4) of the 'Beijing Rules' provides that:[175]

> 'Juvenile Justice shall be conceived as an integral part of the national development process of each country, within a comprehensive framework of social justice for all juveniles, thus, at the same time contributing to the protection of the young and the maintenance of a peaceful order in society.'

UN Rules for the Protection of Juveniles Deprived of their Liberty

2.53   The UN Rules for the Protection of Juveniles Deprived of their Liberty[176] are designed to establish minimum standards for the protection of juveniles deprived of their liberty consistent with human rights and fundamental freedoms and with a view to counteracting the detrimental effects on children and young people of detention and fostering integration in society.[177] The rules are intended to serve as standards of reference to professionals involved in the management of the juvenile justice system.[178]

UN Standard Rules on the Equalisation of Opportunities for Persons with Disabilities

2.54   Rules have also been promulgated in relation to issues of disability. The Standard Rules on the Equalisation of Opportunities for persons with Disabilities adopted by the United Nations General Assembly[179] aim to serve as a basis for policy making by States Parties by implying 'a strong moral and political commitment on behalf of States to take action' for the equalisation of opportunities for persons with disabilities'.[180] The purpose of the rules is expressed to be to ensure that children and adults with disabilities, as members of society can exercise the same rights and obligations as others.[181]

Related UN Guidelines

UN Guidelines on the Prevention of Juvenile Delinquency

2.55   The UN Guidelines on the Prevention of Juvenile Delinquency (hereafter the 'Riyadh Guidelines') recognise in Art 1(1) that 'The prevention of juvenile delinquency is an essential part of crime prevention in society'. The 'Riyadh Guidelines'[182] articulate

---

[174]   Adopted by the UN General Assembly on 29 November 1985 (Resolution 40/33).

[175]   See also the 'Guidelines for Action on Children in the Criminal Justice System' which aim to provide a framework for the implementation of those elements of the CRC concerned with children in the context of the administration of juvenile justice (Economic and Social Council resolution 1997/30 of 21 July 1997).

[176]   Adopted by the UN General Assembly on 14 December 1990 (Resolution 45/113). See also the UN Minimum Standards for Non-Custodial Measures (the 'Tokyo Rules') adopted on 14 December 1990 (Resolution 45/110).

[177]   See Art 3.

[178]   See Art 5.

[179]   A/RES/48/96

[180]   See UN Standard Rules on the Equalisation of Opportunities for Persons with Disabilities Introduction, para 14.

[181]   UN Standard Rules on the Equalisation of Opportunities for Persons with Disabilities Introduction, para 15.

[182]   Adopted by the UN General Assembly on 14 December 1990 (Resolution 45/112).

standards for the prevention of juvenile delinquency, including measures to protect vulnerable children and young people, with the emphasis placed on 'preventative policies facilitating the successful socialisation and integration of all children and young persons, in particular through the family, the community, peer groups, schools, vocational training, the world of work, and voluntary organisations'.[183]

Paris Commitments to Protect Children from Unlawful Recruitment or Use by Armed Forces or Armed Groups

2.56 The United Nations Children's Fund (UNICEF)[184] 'Paris Commitments to protect children from unlawful recruitment or use by armed forces or armed groups'[185] promotes its commitment to this end by prescribing a number of measures designed to prevent unlawful recruitment of children and to mitigate the impact of such recruitment where it has taken place. A second instrument, the UNICEF 'Paris Principles: Principles and Guidelines on Children Associated with Armed Forces or Armed Groups to which the signatories to the Paris Commitments dedicated themselves',[186] provides highly detailed guidance on protecting children from recruitment by, and on providing assistance to those children involved in, armed groups and military forces.

Office of the High Commissioner for Human Rights

2.57 The Office of the High Commissioner for Human Rights (hereafter the 'OHCR') is a department of the United Nations Secretariat with a mandate to protect and promote the enjoyment and full realisation, by all people, of all rights established in the Charter of the United Nations and in international human rights laws and treaties. This mandate includes obligations pertaining to the prevention of human rights violations, securing respect for human rights and the promotion of international cooperation in defence of human rights.[187] The OHCR will provide, on request, technical assistance to Governments in relation to human rights issues.[188]

The Human Rights Council

2.58 The Human Rights Council (hereafter the 'HRC'), created in April 2006, exists to promote universal respect for all human rights and fundamental freedoms. It is a subsidiary organ of the UN General Assembly and replaces the UN Commission on Human Rights.[189]

---

[183] See Art 10.
[184] Created by the UN General Assembly on 11 December 1946 to make provision for emergency food and healthcare to children in the countries devastated by the Second World War it became a permanent institution of the UN in 1953.
[185] UNICEF (February 2007).
[186] UNICEF (February 2007).
[187] See Merrill *Human Rights in the World* (1996) 4th edn, pp 112–114. Professor Merrill's considers that the central role of the Human Rights Commissioner is to provide leadership in the human rights field.
[188] Newell, P and Hodgkin, R *Implementation Handbook for the Convention on the Rights of the Child* (2008) 3rd edn, UNICEF, p 681.
[189] Newell, P and Hodgkin, R *Implementation Handbook for the Convention on the Rights of the Child* (2008) 3rd edn, UNICEF, p 681.

ADDITIONAL INTERNATIONAL LEGAL FRAMEWORKS AND INSTITUTIONS

The Geneva Conventions

2.59   There are four Geneva Conventions[190] and three protocols to those conventions. Geneva Convention IV Relative to the Protection of Civilian Persons in Time of War 1949, published at the end of a conference held in Geneva from April 21 to August 12 1949 and in force from 21 October 1950, is the most relevant to children with seventeen of the one hundred and fifty-nine articles relating to children.[191] Convention IV affords both general protection to children as civilians but also special protection for children living in both unoccupied and occupied territory.[192] Two additional Protocols were added to the Geneva Conventions in 1977,[193] which had the effect of providing greater protection for children caught up in hostilities.[194] The scope of the armed conflicts covered by the Conventions is widened to include conflicts where 'peoples are fighting against colonial domination and alien occupation and against racist regimes in the exercise or their right to self determination'[195] and 'Armed Conflicts which take place in the territory of a High Contracting Party between its armed forces and dissident armed forces or other organised armed groups which, under responsible command, exercise such control over a part of its territory as to enable them to carry out sustained and concerted military operations and to implement [Protocol II]'.[196] These two Additional Protocols also, for the first time, give some protection to children specifically against *participation* in armed conflicts.[197] A third Protocol was added in 2005 which provides for the addition of the non-religious and politically neutral emblem of the 'red crystal' to the Red Cross and Red Crescent emblems. The content and application of the Geneva Conventions as they relate to children are dealt with in detail in chapter 15.

The Hague Conventions

2.60   The first Hague Conventions were international treaties negotiated and agreed at the First and Second Peace Conferences in the Hague in 1899 and 1907 and dealt with the laws of war and with war crimes.[198] The Hague Conference on Private International Law is now an intergovernmental body whose aim is to 'to work for the progressive unification of the rules of private international law'.[199] In furtherance of this goal, multilateral treaties (the 'Hague Conventions') are negotiated, drafted and ratified by

---

[190]   Comprising Convention I for the Amelioration of the Condition of the Wounded and Sick in Armed Forces in the Field, Convention II for the Amelioration of the Condition of Wounded, Sick and Shipwrecked members of the Armed Forces, Convention III Relative to the Treatment of Prisoners of War and Convention IV Relative to the Protection of Civilian Persons in Time of War.

[191]   See Arts 14, 17, 23, 24, 25, 26, 38, 49, 50, 51, 68, 76, 81, 82, 89, 94 and 132.

[192]   See Art 2 and Van Bueren, G *The International Law on the Rights of the Child* (1998) Martinus Nijhoff, p 330. At a time when the United Kingdom is involved in at least one major armed conflict, these provisions are of more than academic interest, governing as they do how UK forces treat children in the conflict zones.

[193]   The United Kingdom ratified Protocol I and Protocol II on 28 January 1998. The UK registered reservations in respect of Protocol I.

[194]   See Plattner, D *The Protection of Children in International Humanitarian Law*, International Review of the Red Cross, No 240, May–June 1984, pp 140–152 and Singer, S *The Protection of Children during Armed Conflict Situations*, International Review of the Red Cross, No 252, May–June 1986, p 133.

[195]   Protocol I, Art 1(4). The articles in Protocol I relevant to children are Arts 8, 70, 74, 75(5), 77 and 78.

[196]   Protocol II, Art 1(1). The articles in Protocol II relevant to children are Arts 4(3) and 6(4).

[197]   Protocol I, Art 77(2) and Protocol II, Art 4. See also the Protocol to the CRC on the Protection of Children from Involvement in Armed Conflict and the Paris Commitments and Principles to protect children from unlawful recruitment or use by armed forces or armed groups.

[198]   See the Hague Convention of 1899 and the Hague Convention of 1907.

[199]   Statute of the Hague Conference on International Private Law 1955, Article 1

member states. The Conference currently has 69 members, including the United Kingdom.[200] In large part, the Hague Conventions do not themselves confer rights upon children but rather seek to facilitate and reinforce the existing rights of both children and adults.[201] The following Hague Conventions deal with the international protection of children:[202]

- Convention on the Law Applicable to Maintenance Obligations towards Children 1956.

- Convention concerning the Recognition and Enforcement of Decisions Relating to Maintenance Obligations Towards Children 1958.

- Convention concerning the Powers of Authorities and the Law Applicable in Respect of the Protection of Infants 1961.

- Convention on Jurisdiction, Applicable Law and Recognition of Decrees relating to Adoptions 1965.

- Convention on the Law Applicable to Maintenance Obligations 1973.

- Convention on the Recognition and Enforcement of Decisions Relating to Maintenance Obligations 1973.

- Convention on the Civil Aspects of International Child Abduction 1980.[203]

- Convention on Protection of Children and Co-operation in Respect of Intercountry Adoption 1993.

- Convention on the Jurisdiction, Applicable Law, Recognition, Enforcement and Co-operation in respect of Parental Responsibility and Measures for the Protection of Children 1996.

- Convention on the International Recovery of Child Support and Other Forms of Maintenance 2007.

---

[200] See the information provided at www.hcch.net.

[201] The European Court of Human Rights has treated the Hague Convention on the Civil Aspects of International Child Abduction as being a fundamental facet of Article 8 of the ECHR (see *Ignaccolo-Zenide v Romania* [2000] ECHR 31679/96, *Sylvester v Austria* [2003] 2 FLR 210 and Van Bueren, G *Child Rights in Europe* (2007) Council of Europe Publishing, pp 28–30).

[202] These are dealt with in detail in the text where they become relevant.

[203] This Convention is given force of law in England and Wales by the Child Abduction and Custody Act 1985. In considering the Convention on the Civil Aspects of International Child Abduction it is important to understand its relationship with the Council Regulation (EC) No 2201/2003 of 27 November 2003 on Jurisdiction and the Recognition and Enforcement of Judgments in Matrimonial Matters and Matters of Parental Responsibility for Children of both Spouses ('Brussells II Revised') (see Lowe, N, Everall, M and Nicholls, M *International Movement of Children* (2004) Family Law, paras 18.26–18.27 and **8.244** below). See also *Re L (A Minor) (Abduction: Jurisdiction)* [2002] EWHC 1864 (Fam), [2002] 1 WLR 3208, sub nom *Re L (Abduction: Child's Objection to Return)* [2002] 2 FLR 1042. See further Art 11(1) of the CRC, **8.94** below and the European Convention on Recognition and Enforcement of Decisions Concerning the Custody of Children 1980 at **2.99** below.

CUSTOMARY INTERNATIONAL LAW AND *JUS COGENS*

2.61 Brownlie concludes that the 'vast majority of States and authoritative writers would now recognise that the fundamental principles of human rights form part of customary or general international law, although they would not necessarily agree on the identity of fundamental principles'.[204] Within this context, Van Bueren[205] raises the question of whether, given the unprecedented rate at which the CRC has been ratified or acceded to, the rights of children enshrined by the CRC can now be said to be part of customary international law, albeit perhaps instant customary international law.[206] In examining the extent to which elements of the CRC can be said also to constitute rules of customary international law, and thus a further legal framework within which to advance the rights of children, Van Bueren further queries whether some of the rights articulated by CRC can be said to be encompassed by the principle of *jus cogens*.[207]

Customary International Law[208]

2.62 Customary law is said to arise when 'states acquire the habit of adopting, with respect to a given situation and whenever that situation recurs, a given attitude to which legal significance is attributed'.[209] As the name suggests, customary international law is international law that is derived from such international custom and is one of the sources of international law prescribed by the Statute of the International Court of Justice 1946.[210] Customary law is derived from 'common, consistent and concordant' international practice'[211] coupled with the acceptance of that practice as obligatory.[212] As such, to prove a customary rule of law there must be demonstrated a general practice which conforms to the rule and which is accepted in law.[213] Once established, a norm of international customary law binds all states with the exception only of those states that have persistently rejected the practice prior to its becoming law. While a certain practice does not require universal acceptance to become a norm of customary international law, a norm which has been accepted by the majority of States has no binding effect upon a

---

204 Brownlie, I *Principles of Public International Law* (2008) 7th edn, OUP, p 562. In this context, see *Legal Consequences of the Construction of a Wall in the Occupied Palestinian Territory* ICJ Reports (2004), 136, p 171, para 86.

205 See Van Bueren *The International Law on the Rights of the Child* (1998) Martinus Nijhoff, p 53.

206 The International Court of Justice has recognised that the fact that only a short period of time has passed is not necessarily a bar to the formation of a new rule of customary international law. See *North Sea Continental Shelf Cases (Federal Republic of Germany v Denmark; Federal Republic of Germany v Netherlands)* [1969] ICJ Reports 4.

207 *Jus Cogens* translates as 'compelling law'. See **2.68** below.

208 For a detailed account of customary international law see Brownlie, I *Principles of Public International Law* (2008) 7th edn, Oxford, pp 6–12.

209 Van Bueren *The International Law on the Rights of the Child* (1998) Martinus Nijhoff, p 54 citing Schwarzenberger, G *International Law*, (1957) Vol 1, Parry, C *The Sources and Evidence of International Law*, (1965) Manchester University Press and D'Amato, A *The Concept of Custom in International Law* (1971) Cornell University Press.

210 Article 38(1) provides that the recognised sources of international law are (a) international conventions, whether general or particular, establishing rules expressly recognised by the contesting states, (b) international custom, as evidence of a general practice accepted as law, (c) the general principles of law recognised by civilised nations and (d) judicial decisions and the teachings of the most highly qualified publicists of the various nations, as subsidiary means for the determination of rules of law.

211 See *Fisheries Jurisdiction Case (United Kingdom v Iceland) (Merits)* [1974] ICJ Reports 3, p 50.

212 Or *opinio juris sive necessitatis* (usually abbreviated as *opinio juris*) and which translates as 'an opinion of law or necessity' (or, abbreviated, as 'an opinion of law'). See *North Sea Continental Shelf Cases (Federal Republic of Germany v Denmark; Federal Republic of Germany v Netherlands)* [1969] ICJ Reports.

213 Virally, M *The Sources of International Law*, in Sorenson (ed.) *Manual of Public International Law* (1968) MacMillan, p 116.

State which has persistently rejected the practice upon which the norm is based.[214] It must be remembered that rules of customary international law are closely interrelated with international conventions. Convention articles may in some cases be declaratory of rules of customary international law or have the effect of amending those rules. Convention law is also capable of giving rise to rules of customary international law which may then bind States which are not party to the relevant convention.[215]

2.63 In relation to rules of customary international law in general, the strongest claims to that status can be made in respect of those rights to which attach no qualifiers attach,[216] namely those pertaining to slavery and institutions and practices similar to slavery or to the slave trade,[217] to torture[218] and to the right to life.[219] However, Van Bueren recognises a fundamental difficulty in arguing that these rights can assume the status of customary international law *exclusively* in relation to children as embodied by the CRC, namely, an apparent lack of agreement (ie a lack of a 'common, consistent and concordant practice') in respect of a definition of the child to which the purported customary rules could attach themselves.[220]

The Roach and Pinkerton Case

2.64 The difficulty identified by Van Bueren arose in the case of *Roach and Pinkerton*.[221] In that case, heard before the Inter-American Commission on Human Rights, two juvenile offenders, Terry Roach and Jay Pinkerton, were sentenced to death in the states of South Carolina and Texas respectively for crimes committed when they were seventeen. Whilst considering that there existed a rule of customary international law or a *jus cogens* norm prohibiting the execution of children, the Commission found there was uncertainty as to the applicable age of majority under international law and accordingly concluded that there did not exist at that time a norm of *jus cogens* or other customary international law prohibiting the execution of persons under the age of 18. However, the Commission did observe as follows:[222]

> 'The Commission is convinced by the U.S. Government's argument that there does not now exist a norm of customary international law establishing 18 to be the minimum age for imposition of the death penalty. Nonetheless, in light of the increasing numbers of States which are ratifying the American Convention on Human Rights and the United Nations Covenant on Civil and Political Rights, and modifying their domestic legislation in conformity with these instruments, the norm is emerging. As mentioned above, thirteen states and the U.S. capital have abolished the death penalty entirely and nine retentionist states have abolished it for offenders under the age of 18.'

---

[214] See *Anglo-Norwegian Fisheries Case*, ICJ Reports (1951), p 131.
[215] Steiner, J Alston, P and Goodman, R *International Human Rights in Context – Law, Politics, Morals* (2007) 3rd edn, Oxford, p 74.
[216] See American Law Institute, *Restatement of the Law, the Third, the Foreign Relations Law of the United States*, (1987), Vol 2, p 161, para 702.
[217] Which must encompass specific forms of sexual exploitation of children and specific forms of economic exploitation of children (see Van Bueren, G *Child Sexual Abuse and Exploitation: A Suggested Human Rights Approach*, 2 International Journal of Children's Rights 45 (1994)).
[218] CRC, Art 37.
[219] CRC, Art 6.
[220] Van Bueren *The International Law on the Rights of the Child* (1998) Martinus Nijhoff, p 57. See **4.1–4.24** for a discussion on the definition of the child.
[221] *Roach and Pinkerton v United States*, Case 9647, Res. 3/87, 22 September 1987, Annual Report of the IACHR 1986–87.
[222] *Roach and Pinkerton v United States*, Case 9647, Res. 3/87, 22 September 1987, Annual Report of the IACHR 1986–87, para 59.

The Michael Domingues Case

2.65 The case of *Roach and Pinkerton* was decided prior to the coming into force of the CRC[223] and the decision has now been revisited in the case of *Michael Domingues*, a 16 year old convicted of murder and sentenced to death in Nevada. When the case came before the Inter-American Commission of Human Rights the Commission, in a non-legally binding report, rejected the submission repeated by the United States that no rule of customary international law existed establishing 18 as the minimum age at which offenders could be sentenced to death. The Commission held that there was indeed a rule of customary international law not to impose capital punishment on individuals who committed their crimes when they had not yet reached 18 years of age.[224] In reaching this decision, the Commission paid express and particular regard to the adoption of the CRC, observing that:[225]

> 'The [CRC] subsequently entered into force on September 2, 1990, and as of September 2001 the Convention had 191 state parties with no explicit reservations taken to Article 37(a). The United States signed the Convention in February 1995, but has not yet ratified the Convention, joining Somalia as the only two states that are not parties to this treaty. In the Commission's view, the extent of ratification of this instrument alone constitutes compelling evidence of a broad consensus on the part of the international community repudiating the execution of offenders under 18 years of age.'

2.66 Having examined also the Convention on Civil and Political Rights, the American Convention on Human Rights and the Fourth Geneva Convention, the Commission concluded that:

> '... since 1987, and consistent with events prior to that date, there has been concordant and widespread development and ratification of treaties by which nearly all of the world states have recognised, without reservation, a norm prohibiting the execution of individuals who were under 18 years of age at the time of committing their offense.'

The Commission noted that this approach had been consistently supported by the UN bodies responsible for human rights and criminal justice and reflected in other instruments concerned with the age of majority.[226] Within this context the commission concluded that:[227]

> 'The overwhelming evidence of global state practice as set out above displays a consistency and generality amongst world states indicating that the world community considers the execution of offenders aged below 18 years at the time of their offence to be inconsistent

---

[223] Van Bueren *The International Law on the Rights of the Child* (1998) Martinus Nijhoff, p 57, noting also that the case was decided prior to adoption of the UN Rules on the Protection of Juveniles Deprived of their Liberty and the UNHCR Guidelines on Refugee Children.

[224] *The Michael Domingues Case: Report on the Inter-American Commission on Human Rights*, Report No 62/02, Merits, Case 12.285 (2002).

[225] *The Michael Domingues Case: Report on the Inter-American Commission on Human Rights*, Report No 62/02, Merits, Case 12.285 (2002), para 57.

[226] *The Michael Domingues Case: Report on the Inter-American Commission on Human Rights*, Report No 62/02, Merits, Case 12.285 (2002), paras 68, 71 and 80. Indeed, in August 2000 the United Nations Sub-Commission on the Promotion and Protection of Human Rights adopted Resolution 2000/17 on *The Death Penalty in Relation to Juvenile Offenders* in which the Sub-Commission recognised that the use of the death penalty against child offenders 'is contrary to customary international law'.

[227] *The Michael Domingues Case: Report on the Inter-American Commission on Human Rights*, Report No 62/02, Merits, Case 12.285 (2002), para 84.

with prevailing standards of decency. The Commission is therefore of the view that a norm of international customary law has emerged prohibiting the execution of offenders under the age of 18 years at the time of their crime.'

Children's Rights as Rules of Customary International Law

2.67   If the approach of the Inter-American Commission on Human Rights in the *Michael Domingues Case* is accepted, it opens the door to certain of the rights articulated by the CRC also being considered as rules of customary international law in respect of the child.[228] Given the weight attached by the Commission to the adoption by the majority of States of the CRC, and the introduction of other instruments pertinent to children's rights,[229] similar conclusions as to the existence of customary rules of international law might now be expected in relation to discrimination,[230] specific forms of sexual and economic exploitation of children, being practices akin to slavery, torture, cruel, inhuman and degrading treatment and punishment of children and the child's right to life interpreted on narrow grounds.[231] Whether this prediction will hold true for the wider body of children's rights, and in particular the economic, social and cultural rights enshrined in the CRC is open to debate, as the wider the rights in issue the less likely the requisite 'common, consistent and concordant practice' will be found to ground a rule of customary international law.

Jus Cogens

The Principle of Jus Cogens

2.68   In *The Michael Domingues Case* the Commission went beyond finding the existence of a rule customary international law and found further as follows in relation to the execution of persons under 18 years of age:[232]

> 'Moreover, the Commission is satisfied, based upon the information before it, that this rule has been recognised as being of a sufficiently indelible nature to now constitute a norm of *jus cogens*, a development anticipated by the Commission in its *Roach and Pinkerton* decision. As noted above, nearly every nation state has rejected the imposition of capital punishment to individuals under the age of 18. They have done so through ratification of the ICCPR, U.N. Convention on the Rights of the Child, and the American Convention on Human Rights, treaties in which this proscription is recognised as non-derogable, as well as through corresponding amendments to their domestic laws. The acceptance of this norm crosses political and ideological boundaries and efforts to detract from this standard have been vigorously condemned by members of the international community as impermissible under contemporary human rights standards ... On this basis, the Commission considers that the United States is bound by a norm of *jus cogens* not to impose capital punishment on individuals who committed their crimes when they had not yet reached 18 years of age. As a

---

[228]   As defined by Art 1 of the CRC.

[229]   For example, the Council of Europe Convention on the Protection of Children against Sexual Exploitation and Sexual Abuse.

[230]   See below **4.93**.

[231]   See Van Bueren *The International Law on the Rights of the Child* (1998) Martinus Nijhoff, pp 56–57.

[232]   *The Michael Domingues Case: Report on the Inter-American Commission on Human Rights*, Report No 62/02, Merits, Case 12.285 (2002), para 85. The US objected, inter alia, to the conclusion of the Commission in relation to *jus cogens* (see para 101). However, whilst not in response to the report of the Commission, the US subsequently banned the practice of executing juvenile offenders (see the decision of the US Supreme Court in *Roper v Simmons* 543 US 551 (2005)). See also *Gary Graham v United States* Report No 97/03, Case No 11 December 29 2003; *Napoleon Beazley v United States* Report No 101/103, Merits Case 12.412 December 29 2003 and *Douglas Christopher Thomas v United States* Report No 100/03 Case No 12.240 December 29 2003.

jus cogens norm, this proscription binds the community of States, including the United States. The norm cannot be validly derogated from, whether by treaty or by the objection of a state, persistent or otherwise.'

2.69 *Jus cogens* or 'compelling law',[233] is considered by some[234] to be a set of fundamental principles of customary international law from which no derogation is permitted, either by way of 'international treaties or local or special customs or even general customary rules with the same normative force'.[235] Whereas customary international law rests on the consent of nations, with a state that persistently objects to a norm of customary international law not being bound by that norm, norms of *jus cogens* derive their status from fundamental values held by the international community irrespective of protest, recognition or acquiescence.[236] In *Prosecutor v Anto Furundzija*[237] the Court stated in relation to torture as follows:

'Because of the importance of the values it protects, [the prohibition of torture] has evolved into a peremptory norm or jus cogens, that is, a norm that enjoys a higher rank in the international hierarchy than treaty law and even 'ordinary' customary rules. The most conspicuous consequence of this higher rank is that the principle at issue cannot be derogated from by states through international treaties or local or special customs or even general customary rules not endowed with the same normative force ...'

Jus Cogens and Treaty Law

2.70 Pursuant to Art 53 of the Vienna Convention on the Law of Treaties 'A treaty is void if, at the time of its conclusion, it conflicts with a peremptory norm of general international law'. Article 53 further stipulates that 'For the purposes of the present Convention, a peremptory norm of general international law is a norm accepted and recognised by the international community of States as a whole as a norm from which no derogation is permitted and which can be modified only by a subsequent norm of general international law having the same character'. The standard for determining a principle of *jus cogens* is more rigorous than that applied in establishing a rule of customary international law, requiring evidence of recognition of the indelibility of the norm by the international community as a whole. This can occur where there is acceptance and recognition by a large majority of states, even if over dissent by a small number of states.[238]

Jus Cogens and Children's Rights

2.71 It has been argued that there are areas in which *jus cogens* could be extended specifically to enforce the rights of children.[239] In addition to the normative status of a

---

[233] Also sometimes termed a 'peremptory norm'.

[234] It is not a universally accepted principle. See for example the criticism in Weil, P *Towards Relative Normativity in International Law*, American Journal of International Law 77 (1983), p 413.

[235] *Prosecutor v Furundzija, International Criminal Tribunal for the Former Yugoslavia*, 2002, 121 International Law Reports 213 (2002) in which the court held that the prohibition against torture is *jus cogens*. See also *The Barcelona Traction Case* (Second Phase) ICJ Reports (1970) 3, para 33.

[236] *Barcelona Traction Case* (Second Phase), ICJ Reports (1970) 3 at 32, per Judge Ammoun. See similarly *East Timor Case*, ICJ Reports (1995) 90 at 102.

[237] (1998) ILR 121, para 153.

[238] Report of the Proceedings of the Committee of the Whole, May 21, 1968, UN Doc. A/Conf.39/11 at 471–72.

[239] See Van Bueren, G *The International Law on the Rights of the Child* (1998) Martinus Nijhoff, pp 55–56. Indeed, it is of note that Van Bueren had argued for precisely the position arrived at in the *Michael Domingues Case* in respect of the death penalty for offenders below the age of 18 some 4 years prior to the decision.

prohibition on the execution of those under the age of 18, Van Buren contends that in circumstances where the prohibition slavery is accepted as *jus cogens*[240] then the prohibition specific forms of sexual and economic exploitation of children should, in addition to being rules of customary international law, be considered *jus cogens*.[241] As with customary international law, it is argued that this analysis is also supported by the *jus cogens* nature of torture.[242] Further, in circumstances where the right to life has been described by the Human Rights Committee as the 'supreme right from which no derogation is permitted even in times of public emergency which threatens the life of the nation'.[243] Van Bueren argues that the norm constituted by a prohibition on the death penalty for those under 18 is of broader application having regard to the stipulation in Art 6(1) of the CRC that States Parties should ensure to the maximum extent possible the survival and development of the child.[244] Finally, arguing for an extension of Brownlie's observation[245] that if protection against race discrimination is part of *jus cogens* then so to should be sex discrimination, Van Bueren contends that discrimination against children can likewise be considered *jus cogens* on the grounds of unjustifiable distinctions stemming from inherent differences, which distinctions are used to justify *jus cogens* classifications in relation to discrimination on the grounds of race and sex.[246]

2.72   Whilst clearly still in its infancy, the field of customary international law and *jus cogens* as it relates to the rights of children constitutes, at least in respect of those rights from which there is no or very limited scope for derogation, fertile ground for further development in the context of enforcing the rights of the child, or at least limiting the reservations which States are permitted to place on those rights, articulated within both the CRC and other treaties touching and concerning the rights of children.[247]

---

[240]   Sunga, L *Individual Responsibility in International Law for Serious Human Rights Violations* (1992) Martinus Nijhoff, p 92. See also the *Barcelona Traction Case* (Second Phase), ICJ Reports (1970) 3, para 33 where the Court stated that slavery is one of a group of rights of such importance that 'all States can be held to have a legal interest in their protection, they are obligations *erga omnes* ('in relation to everyone').'

[241]   Van Bueren, G *The International Law on the Rights of the Child* (1998) Martinus Nijhoff, p 56 and see Van Bueren, G *Child Sexual Abuse and Exploitation: A Suggested Human Rights Approach* (1994) International Journal of Human Rights 2, 45.

[242]   See *Filártiga v Peña-Irala* 630 F.2d 876 at 890 in which the United States Court of Appeals Second Circuit stated 'Among the rights universally proclaimed by all nations ... is the right to be free from physical torture.' See Van Bueren, G *The International Law on the Rights of the Child* (1998) Martinus Nijhoff, p 56.

[243]   Human Rights Committee General Comment 6 *Article 6(The Right to Life)* UN Doc HRI/GEN/1/Rev.8, p 166, para 1.

[244]   Van Bueren, G *The International Law on the Rights of the Child* (1998) Martinus Nijhoff, pp 556–57 pointing out that the issue may be not so much the normative status of the right to life but whether a narrow or broad interpretation of the right is adopted.

[245]   See Brownlie, I *Principles of Public International Law* (1990) Clarendon Press.

[246]   Van Bueren *The International Law on the Rights of the Child* (1998) Martinus Nijhoff, p 55 cautioning however against the over extension of this extrapolation on the basis that there is a difference between the normative status of discrimination against children and other rights in the CRC. See **4.71–4.119** for a detailed discussion of discrimination.

[247]   Van Bueren *The International Law on the Rights of the Child* (1998) Martinus Nijhoff, p 57.

EUROPEAN LEGAL FRAMEWORK AND INSTITUTIONS

The European Convention on Human Rights and Fundamental Freedoms 1950

Overview

2.73 Drafted by the Council of Europe[248] at the end of the Second World War, the formulation of the European Convention on Human Rights and Fundamental Freedoms 1950 (hereafter the 'ECHR') was overseen by the Chair of the Council's Legal and Administrative Division, Sir David Maxwell-Fyfe, First Earl of Kilmur.[249] The drafting of the ECHR was heavily influenced by the Universal Declaration of Human Rights 1948.[250] The ECHR was opened for signature in Rome on 4 November 1950. It entered into force on 3 September 1953. In *R (Pretty) v DPP (Secretary of State for the Home Department Intervening)*[251] Lord Steyn observed as follows:

> 'The human rights movement evolved to protect fundamental rights of individuals either universally or regionally. The theme of the Declaration of 1948 was universal. It involved a common conception of human rights capable of commanding wide acceptance throughout the world despite huge differences between countries in culture, in religion, and in political systems ... The aspirational text of the Universal Declaration was the point of departure and inspiration of the European Convention which opened for signature in 1950. It is to be noted, however, that the European Convention embodied in some respects a narrower view of human rights than the Universal Declaration. The framers of the European Convention required a shorter and uncontroversial text which would secure general acceptance among European nations. Thus the European Convention contains, unlike the Universal Declaration, no guarantees of economic, social and cultural rights. A further illustration relates to the guarantees of equality in the two texts. The guarantee in the Universal Declaration is free standing and comprehensive: see art 7. In the European Convention the provision is parasitic: it is linked with other Convention rights: art 14. The language of the European Convention is often open textured. In 1950 The Lord Chancellor observed 'Vague and indefinite terms have been used just because they were vague and indefinite, so that all parties, hoping and expecting that these terms will be construed according to their separate points of view, could be induced to sign them.'... The generality of the language permits adaptation of the European Convention to modern conditions. It is also, however, necessary to take into account that in the field of fundamental beliefs the European Court of Human Rights does not readily adopt a creative role contrary to a European consensus, or virtual consensus.

2.74 The ECHR can be divided into five sections. The preamble sets out the principles which underpin the provisions of the ECHR. Next, Art 1 sets out the obligation upon High Contracting Parties[252] to respect the rights and freedoms set out in Section I. Section I itself, comprising Arts 2–18 sets out the substantive rights and freedoms stipulated by the ECHR and includes the provisions relating to discrimination,[253]

---

[248] Established by the Statute of the Council of Europe in 1949 ((1949) CETS No 001). The statutory aim of the Council of Europe is to achieve greater unity among its members through common action agreements and debates (see Statute of the Council of Europe art 1(a)). Its key institutions are the Parliamentary Assembly, the Committee of Ministers and the European Court of Human Rights.

[249] Sir David Maxwell-Fyfe was a prosecutor at the Nuremburg Trials. He is also remembered when British Home Secretary for refusing to request clemency from the Queen in respect of the death sentence passed on Derek Bentley.

[250] See the Preamble to the ECHR, paras 1, 2 and 5.

[251] [2001] UKHL 61, [2002] 1 AC 800, para 56.

[252] Those States who are party to the ECHR.

[253] ECHR, Art 14.

derogation in times of emergency,[254] prohibition on abuse of rights[255] and the limitations on the use of restrictions on rights.[256] Section II of the ECHR deals with the establishment of the European Court of Human Rights and the structural, procedural and administrative arrangements for that court, which has jurisdiction to hear complaints regarding the breach of rights conferred by the ECHR.[257] Section III sets out the miscellaneous provisions of the ECHR including the provisions for safeguarding existing human rights,[258] territorial application[259] and reservations.[260] In addition, the Convention has 14 protocols. Those protocols confer rights additional to those safeguarded by the ECHR[261]

2.75 As with the CRC, the ECHR exists within a wider body of instruments touching on the rights of children. These instruments include the Revised European Social Charter,[262] the European Convention on Adoption,[263] the European Convention on the Exercise of Children's Rights,[264] the European Convention on Contact Concerning Children[265] and the Council of Europe Convention on the Protection of Children against Sexual Exploitation and Sexual Abuse.[266]

2.76 By contrast to the position in respect of the CRC, the enactment of the Human Rights Act 1998[267] has brought the canon of rights encompassed by the ECHR to the core of our domestic law[268] and allowed practitioners dealing with cases involving children in this jurisdiction to take full advantage of its provisions in those cases.[269] By s 1(2) of the Human Rights Act 1998, Arts 2–12 and Art 14, together with Arts 1–3 of the First Protocol and Arts 1 and 2 of the Second Protocol, as read with Arts 16–18 are given effect in domestic law. Pursuant to s 3(1) of the Act, domestic primary legislation

---

[254] ECHR, Art 15.

[255] ECHR, Art 17.

[256] ECHR, Art 18.

[257] Since November 1998 the European Court of Human Rights has been the only judicial body dealing with complaints under the ECHR, the judicial roles of the European Commission and the Committee of Ministers having been abolished in November 1998 by Protocol 11 to the ECHR. It should be noted that the past decisions of the Commission and of the Committee *may* remain relevant when interpreting the ECHR.

[258] ECHR, Art 53.

[259] ECHR, Art 56.

[260] ECHR, Art 57.

[261] As opposed to those protocols which affect institutional and procedural elements of the ECHR. See Protocol 11 and Protocol 14 (introducing new provisions for determining the admissibility of claims to the European Court of Human Rights).

[262] (1961) CETS No 035. Ratified by the United Kingdom on 11 July 1972. The European Social Charter was revised in 1996 (CETS No 163) and an Additional Protocol providing a complaints procedure added in 1995 (CETS No 158). The UK has not accepted the Additional Protocol.

[263] (1967) CETS No 058. Ratified by the United Kingdom on 21 December 1967 and entered into force on 26 April 1968.

[264] (1996) CETS No 160. Ratified by the United Kingdom on 21 December 2006 and entered into force on 1 April 2007.

[265] (2003) CETS No 192. Ratified by the United Kingdom on 21 December 2006 and entered into force on 1 April 2007.

[266] (2007) CETS No 201. Signed by the United Kingdom on 5 May 2008 but not yet ratified.

[267] 1998 c.42. The Act came into force on 2 October 2000. It has been described as a 'constitutional measure' (see *McCartan Turkington Breen v Times Newspapers* [2001] 2 AC 277 per Lord Steyn). The ECHR had already had a significant impact on the domestic law prior to its incorporation in 2000, see for example *Re M and H (Minors)* [1990] 1 AC 721 per Lord Brandon and *DPP v Jones* [1999] 2 WLR 62 at 634. For an account of the pre–1998 position see Duffy *English Law and the European Convention on Human Rights* (1980) 29 ICLQ 585.

[268] Swindells, H and others, *Family Law and the Human Rights Act 1998,* (1999) Family Law, p 3.

[269] The HRA 1998 omits Art 1 (obligation to respect human rights), Art 13 (right to an effective remedy), Arts 15–50 (operational provisions for the European Court) and the remaining protocols, including Art 5 of the Seventh Protocol (equality between spouses).

and subordinate legislation must be read and given effect in a way which is compatible with the rights of the ECHR. By s 6(1) it is unlawful for a public authority to act in a way which is incompatible with a Convention right. Those alleging a breach of Convention rights can, pursuant to s 7(1) of the Act, bring a freestanding claim for relief under the Act or rely on the Act in any existing legal proceedings, thereby allowing children to seek specific redress where public authorities have infringed their rights under the ECHR or have failed adequately to take steps to protect them from the actions of private individuals.

ECHR, Preamble

2.77 The preamble to the ECHR sets out, within the context of the rights declared by the Universal Declaration of Human Rights 1948, the intention of the Council of Europe to achieve 'greater unity between its members' through 'the maintenance and further realisation of human rights and fundamental freedoms'.[270] The preamble expresses the ECHR as constituting, 'the first steps for the collective enforcement of certain of the rights stated in the Universal Declaration'. Within this context, it has been observed that the aim of the ECHR was to guarantee first generation civil and political rights, guaranteeing fundamental liberties rather than promoting civil, economic, social and cultural rights, and that as such the aims of the ECHR are relatively limited.[271]

ECHR, Art 1

2.78 By contrast to the CRC, the genesis and formulation of the ECHR was not directed at protecting children as a group.[272] Art 1 of the ECHR states 'The High Contracting Parties shall secure to everyone within their jurisdiction the rights and freedoms defined in Section I of this Convention'. However, the wording of Art 1 clearly encompasses children, who, as human beings, are entitled to claim the protection it confers.[273] That this is the case is demonstrated by the large canon of jurisprudence from the European Court of Human Rights dealing with the ECHR as it impacts upon children.[274] The ECHR has resulted in the most extensive body of jurisprudence concerning children's rights of any of the regional human rights instruments.[275]

2.79 Notwithstanding that it is plain from the scope of Art 1 that the ECHR does apply to children, the fact that such application is not formally expressed highlights one potentially significant lacuna in the ECHR lying between Art 1 and the substantive rights contained in Arts 2–18, namely the absence of a welfare or 'best interests' provision. This contrasts with both the CRC[276] and domestic legislation.[277] Whilst the

---

[270] ECHR Preamble, paras 1–3.

[271] Fortin, J *Children's Rights and the Developing Law* (2005) 2nd edn, Cambridge, pp 50 and 54. Fortin notes that Art 2 of the First Protocol is the exception to this position, protecting the right to education but points out that the narrow focus of the ECHR is brought into sharp relief when compared with the extensive social, economic and cultural rights secured by the CRC in addition to basic civil and political freedoms.

[272] It has been said that the ECHR does not confer rights on children, rather it confers rights on everyone, including children (White, R Carr, P and Lowe, N *The Children Act in Practice* (2009) 4th edn, Lexis/Nexis, p 17, para 1.48).

[273] Fortin, J *Children's Rights and the Developing Law* (2009) 2nd edn, Cambridge, p 31. Further Art 5(1)(d) is expressed to apply specifically to minors and Art 6(1) provides special protection to juveniles in respect of cases heard in public. Finally, it is submitted that the words 'other status' in article 14 must encompass age as a characteristic in respect of which there should be no discrimination.

[274] Fortin, J *Children's Rights and the Developing Law* (2005) 2nd edn, Cambridge, p 53.

[275] Van Bueren, G *Child Rights in Europe* (2007) Council of Europe Publishing, pp 15–16.

[276] See CRC, Art 3(1).

[277] See Children Act 1989, s 1(1) and the Adoption and Children Act 2002, s 1(2).

absence of a best interests principle was the subject of significant misgivings prior to the implementation of the Human Rights Act 1998[278] jurisprudence from the European Court of Human Rights has significantly assuaged such concerns[279] although difficulties clearly remain.[280] The issue of welfare and best interests in the context of the ECHR and children's rights in general is dealt with in detail in chapter 4.[281]

ECHR, Section I

2.80 Section I of the ECHR comprises Arts 2–18 and sets out the substantive rights and freedoms stipulated by the Convention. The substantive rights secured by the ECHR are as follows:

- Article 2 – Right to life.[282]

- Article 3 – Prohibition of torture, inhuman or degrading treatment or punishment.[283]

- Article 4 – Prohibition of slavery and forced labour.[284]

- Article 5 – Right to liberty and security.[285]

- Article 6 – Right to a fair trial.[286]

- Article 7 – No punishment without law.[287]

- Article 8 – Right to respect for private and family life.[288]

- Article 9 – Right to freedom of thought, conscience and religion.[289]

- Article 10 – Right to freedom of Expression.[290]

- Article 11 – Right to freedom of assembly and association.[291]

- Article 12 – Right to marry.[292]

---

[278] See the analysis in Fortin, J *Children's Rights and the Developing Law* (2005) 2nd edn, Cambridge, pp 56–60.

[279] See for example the repeated references in the case law to *Johansen v Norway* (1996) 23 EHRR 33 and the cases of *K and T v Finland* [2000] 3 FCR 248, [2000] 2 FLR 79, *Yousef v The Netherlands* [2002] 3 FCR 477, [2003] 1 FLR, para 73 and *Kearns v France* Application No 35991/04 [2008] 2 FCR 19, [2008] 1 FLR 888, para 83. See also **4.135** below in respect of the impact of the CRC on this issue.

[280] See Van Bueren, G *Child Rights in Europe* (2007) Council of Europe Publishing, pp 30–37 and **4.142–4.150**.

[281] See **4.4.120** below.

[282] See chapter 5.

[283] See chapter 15.

[284] See chapter 15.

[285] See chapter 14.

[286] See chapter 16.

[287] See chapter 16.

[288] See chapter 8.

[289] See chapter 10.

[290] See chapter 11.

[291] See chapter 12.

[292] See chapter 8.

- Article 13 – Right to an effective remedy.[293]

- Article 14 – Prohibition of discrimination.[294]

2.81 Section I of the ECHR also contains provisions dictating the circumstances in which a High Contracting Party may derogate from the provisions of the Convention, Art 15 providing that:[295]

> 'In time of war or other public emergency threatening the life of the nation any High Contracting Party may take measures derogating from its obligations under this Convention to the extent strictly required by the exigencies of the situation, provided that such measures are not inconsistent with its other obligations under international law.'

Derogations in respect of Arts 2,[296] 3, 4(1) and 7 are prohibited.[297] Arts 8, 9, 10 and 11 are qualified rights which may be breached in the circumstances set out in the 'qualification' clause of each article. Article 16 allows High Contracting Parties to restrict the political activities of aliens notwithstanding the provision of Arts 10, 11 and 14.[298] Article 17 prohibits the abuse or limitation of the rights contained in the ECHR.[299] Finally, Art 18 limits the use of the restrictions which the ECHR places on its substantive rights to the purpose for which they have been prescribed.[300]

2.82 The relatively narrow nature of the rights guaranteed by Section I of the ECHR, the apparent deficit within the drafting of positive obligations aimed at promoting those rights and the fact that the ECHR was is not specifically expressed as applying to children, with the concomitant absence of a 'best interests' principle, could have limited its application in the field of children's rights. However a number of factors have helped deflect this potential difficulty.

Purposive Interpretation[301]

2.83 That a broad purposive approach to the interpretation of the ECHR should be adopted has been repeatedly emphasised[302] with a view to the interpretation of the provisions of the Convention in a manner which renders the provisions practical and effective.[303] Utilising perhaps the most famous description as to the manner in which the ECHR should be interpreted, in *Tyrer v UK*,[304] a case concerning corporal punishment, the European Court said, 'The Court must also recall that the Convention is a living instrument which, as the Commission rightly stressed, must be interpreted in the light of present-day conditions'. In achieving a purposive interpretation of the ECHR three principles play a crucial role, namely the doctrine of 'the margin of appreciation', the

---

[293] See chapter 16.
[294] See chapter 4.
[295] See *Lawless v Ireland* (1961) 1 EHRR 1; *Vogt v Germany* (1995) 21 EHRR 205; *Brogan and Others v UK* (1988) 11 EHRR 117 and *Brannigan and McBride v UK* (1993) 17 EHRR 557.
[296] Save in respect of deaths resulting from lawful acts of war.
[297] ECHR, Art 15(2).
[298] See *Piermont v France* (1995) Series A No 314, 20 EHRR 301.
[299] See for example *Campbell and Cosans v UK* (1982) Series A No 48, 4 EHRR 293.
[300] See *Quinn v France* (1995) 21 EHRR 529, para 57.
[301] See **3.62–3.64** for a detailed discussion.
[302] *Golder v UK* (1975) 1 EHRR 524
[303] *Loizidou v Turkey* (1995) 20 EHRR 99, para 72.
[304] (1978) 2 EHRR 1, para 31.

doctrine of necessity and the principle of 'proportionality'.[305] The doctrine of 'margin of appreciation' confers upon a High Contracting Party a measure of discretion when taking a decision involving an ECHR right subject to the ultimate supervision of the ECHR institutions,[306] the doctrine of 'necessity' requires that any interference with a right under the ECHR must correspond with a 'pressing social need'[307] and the principle of 'proportionality' requires a reasonable relationship between the restriction on a Convention right and the aim sought to be realised.[308] The purposive interpretation of the ECHR by the Convention institutions has resulted in many cases in the efficient protection of children interests even given the problems identified in the paragraph above.[309] To use the example given by Fortin, the combined use of Arts 2 (right to life), 3 (prohibition on torture or inhuman or degrading treatment) and 8 (right to respect for family life) has resulted in the ECHR imposing on High Contracting Parties an obligation to protect children from abusive treatment.[310] Within this context, Art 8 of the Convention, whilst not containing any express reference to procedural fairness, has been interpreted by the European Court as providing just such a guarantee in relation to procedures constituting an interference with family life.[311]

Positive Obligations[312]

2.84   Whilst the ECHR does not on its face place positive obligations on High Contracting Parties to take proactive steps to promote the rights of children protected by the Convention, the purposive approach to interpretation adopted by the courts has, using in particular using the terms of Art 1, resulted in a number of the articles being interpreted as conferring positive obligations of the type outlined in the previous paragraph.[313] For example, the High Contracting Parties must not only refrain from intentionally depriving a child of their life under Art 2(1) of the ECHR, they must take 'appropriate steps to safeguard the lives of those within its jurisdiction'.[314] Similarly, there is a positive duty under Art 3 to protect a child against inhuman and degrading treatment. Thus in *Z v United Kingdom* the European Court observed:[315]

---

[305]   For a summary of the role played by these principles in the interpretation of the ECHR see Brownlie, I *Principles of Public International Law* (2008) 7th edn, OUP, pp 575–579 and also **3.61 et seq** below.

[306]   Swindells, H and others, *Family Law and the Human Rights Act 1998,* (1999) Family Law, p 7 and see *Handyside v UK* (1976) 1 EHRR 737, para 48 and *Times Newspapers Ltd (Nos 1 and 2) v UK* (2009) *The Times,* 11 March 2009.

[307]   See *Silver and Others v United Kingdom* ECHR Judgment of 25 March 1983, Series A No 61, ILR 72, 334, p 369, para 97.

[308]   *Handyside v UK* (1976) 1 EHRR 737, para 49. In respect of some rights, for example those secured by Art 8, infringements are permitted provided the interference can be said to be proportionate (see Art 8(2)).

[309]   See Fortin, J *Children's Rights and the Developing Law* (2005) 2nd edn, Cambridge, pp 60–61.

[310]   Fortin, J *Children's Rights and the Developing Law* (2005) 2nd edn, Cambridge, pp 60–61 and see *Z v United Kingdom* (2001) 34 EHRR 97, [2001] 2 FLR 612, paras 73–75.

[311]   *McMichael v UK* (1995) 20 EHRR 205, [1995] 2 FCR 718; *W (and R, O, B and H) v UK* (1987) 10 EHRR 29; *Mantovanelli v France* Application No 21497/93 (1997) 24 EHRR 370 and *Scott v UK* [2000] 1 FLR 958, ECHR. The principle of procedural fairness under Art 8 has been applied by the domestic courts (see *R (P) v Secretary of State for the Home Department; R (Q) v Secretary of State for the Home Department* [2001] EWCA Civ 1151, [2001] 2 FLR 1122 and *CF v Secretary of State for the Home Department* [2004] EWHC 111 (Fam), [2004] 2 FLR 517).

[312]   See **3.64** for a detailed discussion.

[313]   See Kilkelly, U *The Child and the European Convention on Human Rights* (1999) Ashgate, pp 12–13.

[314]   *Osman v United Kingdom* (1998) 29 EHRR 245, [1999] 1 FLR 193, para 115. Observing that such an obligation must be interpreted in such a way which does not impose an impossible and disproportionate burden on authorities, the Court went on to observe at para 116 that 'not every claimed risk to life can entail for the authorities a Convention requirement to take operational measures to prevent that risk from materialising.'

[315]   *Z v United Kingdom* (2001) 34 EHRR 97, [2001] 2 FLR 612, paras 73–75.

'The obligation on State Contracting Parties under Art 1 of the Convention to secure to everyone within their jurisdiction the rights and freedoms defined in the Convention, taken together with Art 3, requires States to take measures designed to ensure that individuals within their jurisdiction are not subjected to torture or inhuman or degrading treatment, including such ill-treatment administered by private individuals ... These measures should provide effective protection, in particular, of children and other vulnerable persons and include reasonable steps to prevent ill-treatment of which the authorities had or ought to have had knowledge ...'

The existence of a positive obligation has played a significant part in the formulation of the jurisprudence on Art 8 of the ECHR in relation to issues concerning children[316] and in particular the provision of contact between children and their parents.[317] The European Court has held that a positive obligation under Art 8 will exist where there is a 'direct and immediate link between the measures sought by an applicant and the latter's private and/or family life'.[318] This formulation is apt to confer an extremely wide ranging obligation to take positive steps to ensure respect for the family and private life of children.

Horizontal as well as Vertical Effect

2.85   The use of the ECHR to protect the rights of children is further strengthened in that the obligations that have been read into the rights secured by the ECHR act not only to protect individuals from the actions of the State, but act also, through the agency of the State, to protect individuals from the actions of other individuals.[319] This doctrine of 'horizontal effect' has been articulated by the European Court in the context of Art 8 rights as including, in some circumstances, an obligation upon the State to protect a private individual's rights under the ECHR against infringement by another private individual.[320] Thus, even where a dispute over the residence of a child arises between private individuals, the State is under a positive obligation to take steps to ensure that the relevant ECHR rights are protected within the context of that dispute. The extension of the jurisdiction encompassed by the ECHR which has been achieved by the application of the doctrine of 'horizontal effect' has been rightly described as dramatic[321] and operates to further extend the protection afforded by the ECHR to the rights of children.

Influence of the Convention on the Rights of the Child[322]

2.86   The European Court of Human Rights considers that it is appropriate to interpret the ECHR as far as possible in harmony with the other rules of international

---

[316]   See *Marckx v Belgium* (1979) 2 EHRR 330.

[317]   See *Hockkanen v Finland* (1994) 19 EHRR 139; *Hansen v Turkey* [2004] 1 FLR 142; *Kosmopoulou v Greece* (ECHR Application No 60457/00), [2004] 1 FLR 800 and *Maire v Portugal* [2004] 2 FLR 653 but see also *Glaser v United Kingdom* [2001] 1 FLR 153.

[318]   *Botta v Italy* (1998) 26 EHRR 241. See also *A, B and C v Ireland* (2010) Application No 25579/05, paras 247–248.

[319]   See Mowbray, A *The Development of Positive Obligations under the European Convention on Human Rights by the European Court of Human Rights* (2004) Hart Publishing.

[320]   *Hokkanen v Finland* (1994) 19 EHRR 139, [1996] 1 FLR 289. See also *X and Y v The Netherlands* (1985) 8 EHRR 235, para 23. For detailed discussion on the principle of 'horizontal effect' see Wade, H *Human Rights and the Judiciary* [1998] EHRLR 520, Buxton, R *The Human Rights Act and Private Law* (2000) 116 LQR 48 and Hunt, M *The 'Horizontal Effect' of the Human Rights Act* [1998] Public Law 423.

[321]   See Fortin, J *Children's Rights and the Developing Law* (2005) 2nd edn, Cambridge, p 62 and *Fuentes Bobo v Spain* (2001) 31 EHRR 1115, para 38.

[322]   See generally Kilkelly, U *The Best of Both Worlds for Children's Rights? Interpreting the European Convention*

law.[323] Within this context, reference to the CRC has been made increasingly in the jurisprudence arising under the ECHR.[324] In the case of *Sahin v Germany; Sommerfield v Germany*[325] the European Court of Human Rights stated that, 'The human rights of children and the standards to which all governments must aspire in realising these rights for all children are set out in the United Nations Convention on the Rights of the Child 1989'. It has been observed that in *Sahin* the Court was, by referencing the CRC, establishing an aspirational goal only and not a jurisdictional expansion in that it remains impossible for a party to petition the Court on the basis of a breach of the CRC which did not also constitute a breach of the ECHR.[326] However, the effect of using the CRC as an aspirational goal provides the European Court of Human Rights and the domestic courts with an additional source of guidance and legitimacy when seeking to interpret the ECHR in a manner which is specifically protective of the rights of children notwithstanding it was not drafted specifically to fulfill that role.

ECHR, Section II

2.87 Section II of the ECHR establishes the European Court of Human Rights and sets out the administrative provisions for its operation.[327] Art 19 states that:

> 'To ensure the observance of the engagements undertaken by the High Contracting Parties in the Convention and the Protocols thereto, there shall be set up a European Court of Human Rights.'

Pursuant to Art 35(1) of the ECHR, the Court can only deal with the matter in question after all domestic remedies have been exhausted according to the recognised rules of international law and within a period of 6 months from the date the final decision was taken.[328]

2.88 Notwithstanding its willingness to pursue a purposive, flexible and horizontal as well as vertical interpretation of the ECHR rights, in respect of the rights of children the European Court has been criticised by a number of commentators for taking an overly paternalistic approach to the claims of children, characterised by a cautious approach to the notion that child have rights of their own and an innate reluctance to see children as individuals in their own right.[329] In considering this issue, Douglas and

---

on Human Rights in the Light of the UN Convention on the Rights of the Child (2001) Human Rights Quarterly 23(2): 308–326, criticised by Van Bueren in Van Bueren, G *Child Rights in Europe* (2007) Council of Europe Publishing, p 23. See also **3.78** below.

[323] See *Forgarty v United Kingdom* ECHR Judgement 21 November 2001 (Grand Chamber), paras 35–36 and Brownlie, I *Principles of Public International Law* (2008) 7th edn, OUP, p 578.

[324] See for example *Costello-Roberts v United Kingdom* [1994] 1 FCR 65, para 35, *A v United Kingdom (Human Rights: Punishment of Child)* [1998] 2 FLR 959, para 22 and *V v United Kingdom* (1999) 30 EHRR 121, paras 73, 76 and 97.

[325] [2003] 2 FLR 671, p 680, para 39. See also *Juppala v Finland* Application No 18620/03 [2009] 1 FLR 617, paras 23 and 41.

[326] Van Bueren, G *Child Rights in Europe* (2007) Council of Europe Publishing, pp 18–19.

[327] See **3.85-3.88** below for a detailed discussion of the jurisdiction of the European Court of Human Rights.

[328] This requirement does not need to be met where the breach complained of involves the administrative practice of the State complained against (see *Ireland v United Kingdom* ILR 58, 190, paras 156–159).

[329] See the analysis in Fortin, J *Children's Rights and the Developing Law* (2005) 2nd edn, Cambridge, pp 54–56 which considers the cases of *Nielsen v Denmark* (1988) 11 EHRR 175, *Valsamis v Greece* (1996) 24 EHRR 294 and *Koniarska v United Kingdom* 12 October 2000, Application No 33670/96, and also Van Bueren *The International Law on the Rights of the Child* (1998) Martinus Nijhoff, p 404.

Lowe have observed that the European Court has not yet truly taken on board 'the increasing international recognition of the child's developing autonomy rights'.[330]

ECHR, Section III

2.89   Section III of the ECHR contains provisions dealing with the safeguarding of existing human rights,[331] territorial application[332] and reservations.[333] Article 53, dealing with safeguarding existing human rights states that:

'Nothing in this Convention shall be construed as limiting or derogating from any of the human rights and fundamental freedoms which may be ensured under the laws of any High Contracting Party or under any other agreement to which it is a Party.'

ECHR Protocols

2.90   The Protocols to the ECHR which expand on the substantive rights in the main body of the Convention are as follows:[334]

- Protocol 1, Art 1 – Right to peaceful enjoyment of property.

- Protocol 1, Art 2 – Right not to be denied education and for parents to have children education in accordance with their views.

- Protocol 1, Art 3 – Right to regular, free and fair elections.

- Protocol 4 – Prohibition on imprisonment for breach of contact, right to free movement internally, right to leave and prohibition on expulsion.

- Protocol 6 – Restriction on the use of the death penalty.

- Protocol 7 – Right to fair procedure for lawfully resident foreigners facing expulsion.

- Protocol 12 – Application of Art 14 (prohibition on discrimination) to any legal right and the actions of public authorities.

- Protocol 13 – Abolition of the death penalty.

2.91   Protocol 12 has not been signed by the United Kingdom on the basis that it is said by the UK to be drafted in terms that are too wide and likely to result in a flood of new litigation to determine the exact boundaries of the provision.[335] The United Kingdom has stated that, instead, it is in favour of extending Art 14 of the ECHR so as

---

[330]   Douglas, G and Lowe, N *Annual Review of International Family Law* in Bainham, A (ed) *The International Survey of Family Law* (2002) Family Law.

[331]   ECHR, Art 53.

[332]   ECHR, Art 56.

[333]   ECHR, Art 57.

[334]   These are referred to in detail in the text where they become relevant.

[335]   Parliamentary question, 27 September 2001.

to provide a freestanding right against discrimination.[336] Only Arts 1–3 of the First Protocol and Arts 1 and 2 of the Sixth Protocol are applied to domestic law by s 1(2) of the Human Rights Act 1998.

The Human Rights Act 1998

2.92   As noted above, the Human Rights Act 1998 applies the ECHR to domestic law.[337] It constitutes a system which facilitates the enactment, interpretation and application of domestic legislation and decision making in a manner compatible with the ECHR.[338] By s 1(2) of the HRA 1998 Arts 2–12 and Art 14, together with Arts 1–3 of the First Protocol and Arts 1 and 2 of the Second Protocol, as read with Arts 16–18 are given effect in domestic law as Sch 1 to the 1998 Act. The domestic courts must, when determining a question which arises in connection with the ECHR, take account of the jurisprudence of the European Court of Human Rights, the opinions and decisions of the European Commission and decisions of the Committee of Ministers.[339] This jurisprudence is not binding in any strict sense of precedent and the domestic courts may go further than the European Court of Human Rights in their interpretation of the ECHR.[340]

2.93   Pursuant to s 3(1) of the 1998 Act, domestic primary legislation and subordinate legislation must be read and given effect in a way which is compatible with the rights of the ECHR. Pursuant to s 5 of the Act, where the court considers that a provision of the primary or subordinate domestic legislation is incompatible it can make a declaration of incompatibility.[341] Further, by s 6(1) it is unlawful for a public authority[342] to act in a way which is incompatible with a Convention right save where (a) as the result of one or more provisions of primary legislation, the authority could not have acted differently; or (b) in the case of one or more provisions of, or made under, primary legislation which cannot be read or given effect in a way which is compatible with the Convention rights, the authority was acting so as to give effect to or enforce those provisions. Those alleging a breach of Convention rights can, pursuant to s 7(1) of the Act, bring a

---

[336]   Written answer 37, Parliamentary Under Secretary of State, Home Officer (Lord Bassam of Brighton) 11 October 2001.

[337]   The Human Rights Act 1998 does not strictly 'incorporate' the ECHR into domestic law and the ECHR is not part of the substantive law. Rather, the 1998 Act creates domestic rights in the same terms as those expressed by the ECHR. Those rights are domestic and not international and their interpretation and enforcement is a matter for the domestic courts not the European Court of Human Rights (see *Re McKerr* [2004] UKHL12, [2004] 2 All ER 409, [2004] 1 WLR 807, para 63 per Lord Hoffman and see Hershman, D and McFarlane, A *Children Law and Practice* Jordan Publishing and Pannick QC and others *Human Rights Law and Practice* (1999) Lexis Nexis 3rd edn, p 29).

[338]   Swindells, H and others, *Family Law and the Human Rights Act 1998,* (1999) Family Law, p 3.

[339]   HRA 1998, s 2(1). The following principles should be born in mind when considering this provision: (a) older decisions are a less reliable guide as the Convention is a 'living instrument; (b) decisions of the European Court have greater weight than admissibility decisions of the Commission (whose judicial role is now defunct); (c) decisions generally turn on the facts, although some general principles may be discerned from them and (d) the 'margin of appreciation' varies according to the particular point in issue (Swindells, H and others, *Family Law and the Human Rights Act 1998,* (1999) Family Law, p 13, para 2.21).

[340]   See *Fitzpatrick v Sterling Housing Association Ltd* [2001] 1 AC 27, [1999] 3 WLR 113, [1999] 4 All ER 705, HL and *Ghaidan v Godin-Mendoza* [2004] UKHL 30, [2004] 2 AC 557, [2004] 2 FCR 481, [2004] 2 FLR 600.

[341]   Pursuant to s 5 the Crown is entitled to notice that the court is considering making a declaration of incompatibility pursuant to s 4 and to be joined as a party to proceedings.

[342]   By s 6(3) a public authority is 'a court or tribunal, and any person certain of whose functions are functions of a public nature.' This definition includes central and local Government, including Children's Services departments and adoption agencies. Both Houses of Parliament are excluded (note that the House of Lords Judicial Committee was not excluded). Pursuant to s 6(5) a person is not a public authority if the nature of the act in question is private.

freestanding claim for relief under the Act or rely on the Act in any existing legal proceedings.[343] Pursuant to s 8 the court may grant such relief of remedy, or make such order, within its powers as it considers appropriate.[344]

2.94 Under s 11 of the Human Rights Act 1998:

'A person's reliance on a Convention right does not restrict any other right or freedom conferred on him by or under any law having effect in any part of the United Kingdom.'

Additional European Instruments

2.95 Through additional instruments detailed below,[345] the Council of Europe[346] has aimed to harmonise the laws of the European member states with a view to promoting and safeguarding the welfare of children more effectively.[347] As Fortin points out, using the example of the ratification by the United Kingdom of the European Convention on the Legal Status of Children Born Out of Wedlock, many of the instruments promulgated by the Council of Europe have, in combination with the jurisprudence of the European Court of Human Rights, led to improvements in the domestic law.[348] In addition to the conventions advanced by the Council of Europe, the Parliamentary Assembly[349] and the Committee of Ministers[350] have made a number of Resolutions and Recommendations[351] touching on the rights of children.[352]

---

[343] Pursuant to s 9(1), alleged breaches by the court must be addressed by way of appeal or judicial review.

[344] Sections 8(2) and 8(3) limit the power of the court to award damages.

[345] In addition to the instruments listed in the text, reference will also be made where they become relevant to the European Convention on Social and Medical Assistance (1953) CETS No 014, the European Convention for the Prevention of Torture, Inhuman or Degrading Treatment (1987) CETS No 126, the Framework Convention for the Protection of National Minorities (1995) CETS No 157, the European Convention on the Exercise of the Dignity of the Human Being with regard to the Application of Biology and Medicine (1997) CETS No 164, the Convention on Cybercrime (ETS No 185: 2001/2004) and the Council of Europe Convention on Action against Trafficking in Human Beings (CETS No 197: 2005/2008).

[346] The Council of Europe pursues the aim of strengthening the legal protection of children and promoting common legal standards in family law through its Committee of Experts on Family Law.

[347] See Fortin's analysis in Fortin, J *Children's Rights and the Developing Law* (2005) 2nd edn, Cambridge, pp 63–65.

[348] Fortin, J *Children's Rights and the Developing Law* (2005) 2nd edn, Cambridge, p 64. The UK's ratification of the Convention on the Legal Status of Children Born Out of Wedlock, in combination with the decision in *Marckx v Belgium* (1979) 2 EHRR 330 resulted in the Law Commission recommending widespread reform to the law relating to children born out of wedlock (see Law Commission (1982), paras 4.11–4.12) and culminated in the Law Reform Act 1987 (see **4.65 et seq** below).

[349] The Parliamentary Assembly of the Council of Europe is one of the two statutory organs of the Council of Europe, the other being the Committee of Ministers. It represents the political forces in each Member State. It should not be confused with the European Parliament, which is an institution of the European Union.

[350] The Committee of Ministers is the decision making body of the Council of Europe and comprises the Foreign Ministers of each Member State.

[351] For example, in relation to the Parliamentary Assembly: 1065 (1987) (on the traffic in children and other forms of child exploitation), 1071 (1988) (on providing institutional care for infants and children), 1286 (1996) (on a European strategy for children), 1307 (2002) (sexual exploitation of children: zero tolerance) and 1778 (2007) (child victims). In relation to Committee of Ministers see for example No R(84)4 (parental responsibilities), No R(85)4 (violence in the family), No R(87)20 (social reactions to juvenile delinquency), No R(98)8 (children's participation in family and social life) and No R (06)12 (empowering children in the new information and communications environment). These instruments are dealt with in more detail in the text where they become relevant.

[352] See the Statute of the Council of Europe, Art 15(b) and Art 29 of the European Social Charter. Recommendations have persuasive influence only.

Revised European Social Charter

2.96   The European Social Charter (ESC) was ratified by the UK in 1962 and entered into force in 1965.[353] The ESC was amended in 1988[354] and in 1991[355] and a revised version produced in 1996.[356] It is overseen by the European Committee of Social Rights. An Additional Protocol providing a complaints procedure added in 1995 which is administered by the Committee of Independent Experts.[357] The ESC deals with economic, social and cultural rights, the so called 'second generation' human rights and has been described as 'the economic and social counterpart of the ECHR'.[358] Part I of the ESC enshrines the principle that, 'Children and young persons have the right to appropriate social, legal and economic protection'.[359] Part I further states that, 'The family as a fundamental unit of society has the right to appropriate social, legal and economic protection to ensure its full development'.[360] A number of the substantive articles of the ESC refer directly to the rights of children.[361]

Revised European Convention on the Adoption of Children

2.97   The European Convention on Adoption seeks to ensure conformity of the adoption laws of its Contracting Parties with the principles set out in the convention so as to establish good adoption practice. A revised Convention was adopted by the Committee of Ministers on 7 May 2008 and opened for signature on 27 November 2008.[362] Article 2 of the revised Convention provides that:

> 'Each State Party shall adopt such legislative or other measures as may be necessary to ensure the conformity of its law with the provisions of this Convention.'

Article 4 stipulates that no competent authority[363] shall grant an adoption unless it is satisfied that the adoption will be in the best interests of the child. Importantly, Art 5 of the Convention provides for the consent of the child to adoption where the child is considered by law to have sufficient understanding.[364] Article 6 of the Convention thereafter stipulates that:

> 'If the child's consent is not necessary according to Art 5, paragraphs 1 and 3, he or she shall, as far as possible, be consulted and his or her views and wishes shall be taken into

---

[353]   (1961) CETS No 035. The UK has not accepted Arts 2(1), 4(3), 7(1), 7(4), (7) and (8), 8(2), (3) and (4) and 12(2), (3) and (4). The UK has also accepted none of the provisions of the 1998 Additional Protocol (see CET List of declarations made in respect to Treaty No 035).

[354]   Additional Protocol of 1988 (1988) CETS No 128.

[355]   Additional Protocol of 1991 (1991) CETS No 142.

[356]   Revised European Social Charter of 1996 (1996) CETS No 163. The United Kingdom has signed but not ratified the Revised European Social Charter.

[357]   Additional Protocol of 1995 (1995) CETS No 158. This mechanism has been used to protect children through the lodging of complaints concerning children's rights, see for example *Autisme-Europe v France* Complaint No 13/2002.

[358]   Pannick QC and others, *Human Rights Law and Practice* (1999) Lexis Nexis 1st edn, p 341.

[359]   ESC Part I, para 17.

[360]   ESC Part I, para 16.

[361]   See, for example, Art 7 (Right to protection of children and young persons) and Art 17 (Right of mothers and children to social and economic protection). See also Cullen, H A. *Is the European Social Charter a charter for children?* Irish Jurist 40, 2005, pp 62–85.

[362]   (2008) CETS No 202. The UK has signed the Convention but not yet ratified it.

[363]   Defined in Art 3 as a 'court or administrative authority.'

[364]   See Art 5(1)(b). Pursuant to that provision a child *shall* be considered as having sufficient understanding on attaining an age which shall be prescribed by law, which age shall not be greater than 14 years.

account having regard to his or her degree of maturity. Such consultation may be dispensed with if it would be manifestly contrary to the child's best interests.'

European Convention on the Legal Status of Children Born Out of Wedlock

2.98 The European Convention on the Legal Status of Children born out of Wedlock[365] was opened for signature on 15 October 1975 and entered into force on 11 August 1978.[366] The object of the Convention is stated as being 'to improve the legal status of children born out of wedlock by reducing the differences between their legal status and that of children born in wedlock which are to the legal or social disadvantage of the former'.[367] The Convention deals with maternal[368] and paternal[369] affiliation, parental obligations to children born out of wedlock,[370] parental authority,[371] parental contact rights,[372] children's rights of succession[373] and children's legitimacy.[374]

European Convention on Recognition and Enforcement of Decisions concerning Custody of Children and on Restoration of Custody of Children[375]

2.99 The European Convention on Recognition and Enforcement of Decisions concerning Custody of Children and on Restoration of Custody of Children[376] entered into force on 1 September 1983 and was ratified by the UK on 21 April 1986.[377] It is given effect to in English law by s 12(2) of and Sch 2 to the Child Abduction and Custody Act 1985. The Convention is designed to make, 'arrangements to ensure that decisions concerning the custody of a child can be more widely recognised and enforced'.[378] The Convention requires each State to set up a central authority to carry out the functions of the Convention.[379] Part II of the Convention deals with the recognition and enforcement of decisions and restoration of custody of children and Part III with the associated procedure. It should be noted that Brussels II, Council Regulation (EC) No 1347/2000 of 29 May 2000 on Jurisdiction and the Recognition and Enforcement of Judgments in Matrimonial Matters and Matters of Parental Responsibility for Children of both Spouses will take precedence over the European Convention on Recognition and Enforcement of Decisions concerning Custody of Children and on Restoration of Custody of Children where a custody or access decision has been made in matrimonial (but not freestanding) proceedings in another member

---

[365] (1975) CETS No 085.
[366] The UK ratified the Convention on 24 February 1981. For the reservations entered by the UK upon ratifying the Convention see the CET List of declarations made in respect to Treaty No 085.
[367] Preamble, para 2.
[368] Article 2.
[369] Articles 3–5.
[370] Article 6.
[371] Article 7.
[372] Article 8
[373] Article 9.
[374] Article 10.
[375] Note that Arts 11(2) and 11(3) of the Convention on Recognition and Enforcement of Decisions concerning Custody of Children etc. do not apply in relations between States Parties who are also party to the European Convention on Contact Concerning Children.
[376] (1980) CETS No 105.
[377] The UK entered a significant number of reservations upon ratifying the convention. See CET List of Declarations made with respect to Treaty No 105.
[378] (1980) CETS No 105.
[379] Part I.

state and enforcement is sought. Step children applications must be made under the European Convention on Recognition and Enforcement of Decisions concerning Custody of Children and on Restoration of Custody of Children.[380]

European Convention on the Exercise of Children's Rights

2.100 The Convention on the Exercise of Children's Rights[381] (hereafter the 'CECR') does not deal with substantive rights but rather makes provision for procedural rights to promote the implementation of the essential rights of children pursuant to the demands of Art 4 of the CRC.[382] The Explanatory Report for the CECR states that 'The present Convention facilitates the exercise of the substantive rights of children by strengthening and creating procedural rights which can be exercised by children themselves or through other persons or bodies'.[383] Art 1(2) of the CECR further refines its purpose, stating 'The object of the present Convention is, in the best interests of children, to promote their rights, to grant them procedural rights and to facilitate the exercise of these rights by ensuring that children are, themselves or through other persons or bodies, informed and allowed to participate in proceedings affecting them before a judicial authority'. Under Art 1(3) proceedings 'before a judicial authority' are defined as 'family proceedings'. Chapter II of the CECR sets out the procedural measures to promote the exercise of children's rights. These include the 'right to be informed and to express his or her views',[384] the 'right to apply for the appointment of a special representative',[385] and the 'duty to act speedily'.[386] Chapter III of the CECR establishes a Standing Committee to review problems arising under the CECR and to consider any relevant questions of interpretation and implementation.[387] The CECR entered into force on 1 July 2000 but has not yet been signed or ratified by the United Kingdom.

European Convention on Contact Concerning Children[388]

2.101 By contrast to the CECR, the European Convention on Contact Concerning Children[389] (hereafter the 'CCCC') does purport to enshrine substantive rights. The Explanatory report on the CCCC describes its objects as being, 'to determine general principles to be applied to contact orders; to fix appropriate safeguards and guarantees to ensure the proper exercise of contact and the immediate return of children at the end of the period of contact, and to establish co-operation between central authorities, judicial authorities and bodies which are concerned by a contact order'.[390] These aims, which on the face of it appear entirely procedural in nature, are embodied in Art 1 of

---

[380] For a detailed exposition of the jurisdiction and functioning of this Convention see Lowe, N, Everall, M, QC, and Nicholls, M *International Movement of Children: Law, Practice and Procedure* (2004) Jordan Publishing, Chapter 19.

[381] (1996) CETS No 160.

[382] CECR Explanatory Report. Verhellen argues that the Convention on the Exercise of Children's Rights by its language in fact signifies a weakening of the CRC within the European Union (see Verhellen, E *Convention on the Rights of the Child* (2000) Apeldoorn, p 136). See also Fortin's analysis in Fortin, J *Children's Rights and the Developing Law* (2005) 2nd edn, Cambridge, pp 199–202.

[383] CECR Explanatory Report, para 7.

[384] CECR, Art 3.

[385] CECR, Art 4.

[386] CECR, Art 7.

[387] CECR, Art 16.

[388] The Convention on Contact Concerning Children does not prejudice the application of the Hague Conventions of 5 October 1961 or 19 October 1996 or the European Convention on the Recognition of Decisions concerning Custody of children etc (subject to Art 19 of the CCCC).

[389] (2003) CETS No 192.

[390] CCCC Explanatory Report, para 16.

the CCCC. Article 2 defines what is meant by 'contact' within the context of the CCCC. Chapter II of the CCCC (comprising Arts 3–10) sets out the general principles to be applied to contact orders. Chapter III of the CCCC sets out measures to promote and improve transfrontier contact, including the appointment by each State Party of a central authority to deal with cases of transfrontier contact.[391]

2.102 However, the CCCC arguably goes further than simply conferring procedural rights related to contact. In prescribing the general principles applied to contact orders, Chapter II of the CCCC includes at Art 4 the stipulation that, 'A child and his or her parents shall have the right to obtain and maintain regular contact with each other'.[392] The CCCC thus prescribes regular contact as a substantive right of the child. When read with Art 3, which provides that, 'States Parties shall adopt such legislative and other measures as may be necessary to ensure that the principles contained in this chapter are applied by judicial authorities when making, amending, suspending or revoking contact orders', the effect of the CCCC is to seek to ensure that States Parties take measures, including legislative measures, to guarantee to children a right of regular contact with parents and others. Further, Art 6 of the CCCC confers on the child a substantive right to be informed, consulted and to express his or her views on the issue of contact. The CCCC entered into force on 1 September 2005 but has not yet been signed or ratified by the United Kingdom.

Convention on the Protection of Children against Sexual Exploitation and Sexual Abuse

2.103 The European Convention on the Protection of Children against Sexual Exploitation and Sexual Abuse[393] (hereafter the 'CPCSESA') was signed by the United Kingdom on 5 May 2008 but has not yet been ratified. According to the Explanatory Report on the convention, its two main aims are to prevent and combat sexual exploitation and sexual abuse and to protect the rights of child victims.[394] Chapter II of the convention prescribes preventative measures and Art 4 of the CPCSESA requires that 'Each Party shall take the necessary legislative or other measures to prevent all forms of sexual exploitation and sexual abuse of children and to protect children'. Chapter III of the CPCSESA makes provision for 'the co-ordination on a national or local level between the different agencies in charge of the protection from, the prevention of and the fight against sexual exploitation and sexual abuse of children'[395] and Chapter IV provides for the protection of child victims. Chapters VI and VII requires States Parties to take the necessary legislative measures to criminalise sexual abuse, child prostitution, child pornography and associated offences.

---

[391] CCC, Art 11.
[392] CCCC, Art 4(1). Article 5 extends this right to include contact with 'the child and persons other than his or her parents having family ties with the child.' The substantive right to contact conferred by the CCCC thus extends to members of the child's extended family.
[393] (2007) CETS No 201. Signed by the United Kingdom on 5 May 2008 but not yet ratified.
[394] CPCSESA Explanatory Report, para 37. The preamble to the convention makes specific reference to Art 34 of the CRC and the Optional Protocol on the sale of children, child prostitution and child pornography, the Protocol to Prevent, Suppress and Punish Trafficking in Persons, Especially Women and Children, supplementing the United Nations Convention against Transnational Organised Crime, as well as the International Labour Organisation Convention concerning the Prohibition and Immediate Action for the Elimination of the Worst Forms of Child Labour.
[395] CPCSESA, Art 10.

The European Union

2.104 The Treaty on the European Union requires the EU to 'respect fundamental rights, as guaranteed by the European Convention for the Protection of Human Rights and Fundamental Freedoms signed in Rome on 4 November 1950 and as they result from the constitutional traditions common to the Member States, as general principles of Community law'.[396] Further, the European Charter of Fundamental Rights of the European Union stipulates that 'Children shall have the right to such protection and care as is necessary for their well-being. They may express their views freely. Such views shall be taken into consideration on matters which concern them in accordance with their age and maturity', that 'In all actions relating to children, whether taken by public authorities or private institutions, the child's best interests must be a primary consideration' and that 'Every child shall have the right to maintain on a regular basis a personal relationship and direct contact with both his or her parents, unless that is contrary to his or her interests'.[397] In accordance with Art 52(3) of the European Charter of Fundamental Human Rights the meaning and scope of the rights under the Charter is the same as that under the corresponding articles of the ECHR and its related protocols.[398] The EU bodies and institutions and Member States need have regard to the Charter only when implementing EU law.[399]

OTHER REGIONAL INSTRUMENTS AND INSTITUTIONS

2.105 In the same way that the ECHR 'regionalised' the Universal Declaration of Human Rights 1948, the principles enshrined in that instrument have likewise been regionalised in other areas of the world.[400] Whilst not binding on the domestic courts, they assist in further illuminating the law and practice of children's rights and are thus of some interest when considering developing law and practice in this jurisdiction.[401] Reference will be made in the text where appropriate to:[402]

- The American Convention on Human Rights (also known as the 'Pact of San José').[403]

---

[396]   Treaty of the European Union, Art 6(2).

[397]   European Charter of Fundamental Rights of the European Union, Art 24.

[398]   Article 52(3) of the Charter provides that 'Insofar as this Charter contains rights which correspond to rights guaranteed by the Convention for the Protection of Human Rights and Fundamental Freedoms, the meaning and scope of those rights shall be the same as those laid down by the said Convention. This provision shall not prevent Union law providing more extensive protection.'

[399]   European Charter of Fundamental Rights of the European Union, Art 51.

[400]   Verhellen, E *Convention on the Rights of the Child* (2000) Apeldoorn, p 127.

[401]   However, regard should also be had to the observations of Silber J in *R (on the application of Axon) v Secretary of State for Health and another* [2006] EWHC 37 (Admin), [2006] QB 539, [2006] 1 FCR 175 that 'Another very important consideration is that the domestic courts in Human Rights Act cases have often warned against the dangers of incorporating jurisprudence from other jurisdictions which arises under Charters of Rights, which are very different to the Convention. The United States Constitution, which sets out absolute rights, leaves the courts to imply limitations on them while art 8 of Convention is a good example of a totally different approach (see also McCombe J in *R (on the application of British American Tobacco) v Secretary of State for Health* [2004] EWHC 2493 (Admin), [2004] All ER (D) 91)).

[402]   These international instruments are dealt with in detail in the main text where they become relevant. It has been observed that there is dearth of regional human rights systems in Asia. See Van Bueren, G *Child Rights in Europe* (2007) Council of Europe Publishing, pp 379–380 and Lutz et al *Prospects for the Development of Intergovernmental Human Rights Bodies in Asia and the Pacific in New Directions* (1989) Human Rights.

[403]   In *Villagrán Morales et al v Guatemala* the Inter-American Court of Human Rights Court expressed the opinion that the American Convention on Human Rights and the Convention on the Rights of the Child are part of an international *corpus juris* for protection of the rights of children, that accordingly there is a substantive connection between the two treaties and that they should be applied together in cases pertaining

- The Ibero-American Convention on Young People's Rights.

- The African (Banjul) Charter on Human and Peoples' Rights.

- The African Charter on the Rights and Welfare of the Child.

- The African Youth Charter.

- The League of Arab States Revised Arab Charter on Human Rights.[404]

DOMESTIC LEGAL FRAMEWORK AND INSTITUTIONS

2.106 In examining the legal provisions which underpin the law and practice of children's rights there is an understandable need to concentrate on the international and European instruments which explicitly codify those rights.[405] However, in considering the full ambit of instruments and institutions relevant to the law and practice of children's rights, the domestic legislation and jurisprudence which give effect, albeit sometimes incompletely, to those rights also falls to be considered.[406] These are considered in summary form here and in greater detail where appropriate in the text below.

Domestic Legal Instruments

2.107 The key statutes which may impact upon children within the domestic jurisdiction[407] deal with subjects as diverse as their welfare and protection (the Child Abduction Act 1984, the Child Abduction and Custody Act 1985, the Children Act 1989, the Human Fertilisation and Embryology Act 1990, the Family Law Act 1996, the Care Standards Act 2000, the Children and Adoption Act 2002, the Children Act 2004 and the Children and Adoption Act 2006), their economic wellbeing (the Child Support Act 1991), their education (the Education Acts and the School Standards and Framework Act 1998), their identity, nationality and legal status (the Births and Deaths Registration Act 1953, the Family Law Reform Act 1969, the Legitimacy Act 1976, the British Nationality Act 1981 and the Family Law Reform Act 1987), their equality (the Equality Act 2006 and the Equality Act 2010) and any involvement they may have in the criminal justice system (the Criminal Justice Acts and the Youth Justice and Criminal Evidence Act 1999). This summary is by no means exhaustive in its scope.

---

to children and adolescents (see I/A Court H.R, *The 'Street Children' Case (Villagrán Morales et al.).* Judgment of November 19, 1999 Series C No 63, para 194).

[404] Article 2(3) of the Revised Arab Charter has caused considerable controversy (Art 2(3) states 'All forms of racism, Zionism and foreign occupation and domination constitute an impediment to human dignity and a major barrier to the exercise of the fundamental rights of peoples; all such practices must be condemned and efforts must be deployed for their elimination'). See Rishmawi, M *The Revised Arab Charter on Human Rights: A Step Forward?* Human Rights Law Review 2005 5(2), pp 361–376.

[405] Archard describes the CRC as the 'unavoidable starting point for any discussion of the legal rights of children' Archard, D *Rights and Childhood* (2004) Routledge, p 58.

[406] See generally Roche, J *The Children Act 1989 and children's rights – A critical reassessment* in Franklin, B (ed) *The New Handbook of Children's Rights* (2002) Routledge. The domestic provisions summarised in this section are discussed in detail within the text when they arise.

[407] It is vital to remember that not all 'children within the jurisdiction' have the same legal status under domestic law and hence may not have the same entitlements under the domestic legislative provisions, which in turn may impact on how fully their rights are or can be realised solely under that legislation.

2.108 Even before the impact of the Human Rights Act 1998 is considered within the foregoing domestic legislative context, that domestic legislation can be seen, in places, to reflect some of the substantive rights recognised and codified in the cardinal human rights instruments. By way of example, s 1(1) of the Children Act 1989 ensures that the child's best interests are the court's paramount consideration in all decisions affecting the child's upbringing.[408] The Adoption and Children Act 2002, s 1(2) extends this principle, stipulating that, 'The paramount consideration of the court or adoption agency must be the child's welfare, throughout his life'. To this extent, it has been persuasively argued that the best interests principle in s 1(1) of the Children Act 1989 has, when the welfare checklist provided by s 1(3) is considered along side it, advanced considerably the welfare rights of children.[409] Section 1(3)(a) of the Children Act 1989, echoed in s 1(4)(a) of the Adoption and Children Act 2002,[410] reflects in part the cardinal elements of the child's right to participation codified in Art 12 of the CRC, domestic jurisprudence further illuminating and amplifying that partial reflection by way of Lord Scarman's famous judgment in *Gillick v West Norfolk and Wisbech AHA* in which he held:[411]

> 'The underlying principle of the law ... is that parental right yields to the child's right to make his own decision when he reaches a sufficient understanding and intelligence to be capable of making his own mind up on the matter in question.'

2.109 Further examples of domestic provisions under the Children Act 1989 and associated regulations which it has been argued reflect or facilitate the rights of children include the 'right' to refuse to submit to a medical examination pursuant to s 44(7) of the Children Act 1989 and the 'right' to instruct legal representation under r 16.6 of the Family Procedure Rules 2010.[412] Other statutes encompass to a limited extent further rights. The Birth and Deaths Registration Act 1953, s 1(1) provides that, 'the birth of every child born in England or Wales shall be registered by the registrar of births and deaths for the sub-district in which the child was born by entering in a register kept for that sub-district such particulars concerning the birth as may be prescribed', reflecting elements of Art 7(1) of the CRC. The Education and Inspections Act 2006 (amending the Education Act 1996) prescribes a 'right' to education for children, reflecting elements of Art 28 of the CRC.[413]

2.110 In addition to embodying some of the rights found in international and regional human rights instruments relating to children, the domestic law also incorporates at least two of the principles of interpretation familiar under those instruments. First, as noted above, the principle of best interests as enshrined in s 1(1) of the Children

---

[408] The Children Act 1989 cannot be said to encompass comprehensively children's civil, political, economic, social or cultural rights (see Van Bueren *The United Nations Convention on the Rights of the Child – The Necessity of Incorporation into United Kingdom Law* [1992] Fam Law 373).

[409] Roche, J *The Children Act 1989 and children's rights – A critical reassessment* in Franklin, B (ed) *The New Handbook of Children's Rights* (2002) Routledge, p 62.

[410] Schedule 1, Art 13 of the Child Abduction and Custody Act 1985 also makes provision in respect of the wishes and feelings of the child, providing 'The judicial or administrative authority may also refuse to order the return of the child if it finds that the child objects to being returned and has attained an age and degree of maturity at which it is appropriate to take account of its views.'

[411] [1985] 2 WLR 830 at 855. See Archard, D *Rights and Childhood* (2004) Routledge, p 64.

[412] See Roche, J *The Children Act 1989 and children's rights – A critical reassessment* in Franklin, B (ed) *The New Handbook of Children's Rights* (2002) Routledge, pp 64–65. Roche recognises that both in respect of the 'right' to refuse medical examination (see *South Glamorgan CC v W and B* [1993] 1 FLR 574) and the 'right' to instruct legal representation (see *Re H (Residence Order: Child's Application for Leave)* [2000] 1 FLR 780 these 'rights' have, historically, been significantly circumscribed by the jurisprudence associated with them.

[413] Education and Inspections Act 2006, s 1 inserting s 13A into the Education Act 1996.

Act 1989. The Children Act 1989 also embodies the concept of 'proportionality in s 1(5) in providing that a court shall not make an order under the 1989 Act unless to do so is better for the child than making no order at all.[414]

2.111 The Human Rights Act 1998 now requires these and other domestic provisions relating to children to be interpreted so as to give effect to the provisions of the ECHR enshrined within the 1998 Act (which provisions themselves must be interpreted in light of the rights of children enshrined in the CRC)[415] and permits freestanding remedies for the breach of cardinal rights.[416] This has further refined the extent to which domestic legislation and jurisprudence protects and promotes children's rights. Fortin argues that the application to domestic law of the rights embodied in the ECHR will gradually oblige the courts to re-cast many aspects of the domestic law in a human rights mold.[417]

Domestic Institutions

Office of the Children's Commissioner – '11 Million'

2.112 Section 1(1) of the Children Act 2004 states that 'There is to be an office of Children's Commissioner'. The general function of the Children's Commissioner is defined in s 2(1) of the 2004 Act as encouraging persons exercising functions or engaged in activities affecting children to take account of their views and interests, advising the Secretary of State on the views and interests of children, considering or researching the operation of complaints procedures so far as they relate to children and any other matter relating to the interests of children and publishing a report on any matter considered or researched by him or her under this section.

2.113 In particular, pursuant to s 2(3), the Children's Commissioner must be concerned with the physical and mental health and emotional wellbeing of children, their protection from harm and neglect, their education, training and recreation, the contribution made by them to society and their social and economic wellbeing. The Children's Commissioner has a statutory right of entry in to any premises other than a private dwelling for the purposes of interviewing any child and, if the child consents, to conduct that interview in private.[418] The Children's Commissioner may also request disclosure of information for the purpose of carrying out his statutory function.[419] The Officer of the Children's Commissioner for England has recently been renamed '11 Million' after children and young people were asked their views, '11 Million' being the approximate number of children in the United Kingdom. There is a Children's Commissioner in each of England, Wales, Scotland and Northern Island. The Commissioners have submitted a report to the UN Committee on the Rights of the Child on the implementation of the CRC in the United Kingdom.[420]

2.114 The United Kingdom Children's Commissioners have varying mandates and degrees of autonomy and independence. The Children's Commissioners in Wales and

---

[414] See in particular *Re K (Supervision Orders)* [1999] 2 FLR 303 per Wall J.

[415] See **3.43** below for a detailed discussion of the impact of this principle.

[416] See above **2.92**.

[417] Fortin, J *Children's Rights and the Developing Law* (2005) 2nd edn, Cambridge, p 53. A good example of this ongoing process is the evolution of the law relating to restraining publicity in respect of cases concerning children (see in particular *Re Roddy (A Child) (Identification: Restriction on Publication)* [2003] EWHC 2927 (Fam), [2004] 2 FLR 949 per Munby J).

[418] Children Act 2004, s 2(8).

[419] Children Act 2004, s 2(9).

[420] *UK Children's Commissioners' Report to the UN Committee on the Rights of the Child* (June 2008).

Northern Island have authority to deal with individual cases, whilst the Commissioners in England and Scotland do not. The English Commissioner's rights of entry are more extensive than those of the Commissioner in Scotland. The Commissioner in England may be directed by the Government to undertake an enquiry but it is the Government's decision as to whether it is subsequently published. The English Commissioner may initiate his own inquiry but must consult with the Government before doing so.[421] The funding for the English Commissioner is granted on such conditions the Government considers appropriate.[422] Perhaps of most concern for children residing in England, whilst the mandates of the Commissioners for Wales, Northern Ireland and Scotland are rights-based and use the CRC as their framework, the English Commissioner is required instead to use five aspects of child well-being that correspond to the five outcomes[423] for children in the Government's 'Every Child Matters' agenda as the basis for his work.[424] This generalisation of specific children's rights into vague goals arguably makes it more difficult for the English Children's Commissioner to promote for children and young people the implementation of their rights as articulated and enshrined in the CRC.[425]

Commission for Equality and Human Rights

2.115 Section 1 of the Equality Act 2006 establishes a corporate body known as the Commission for Equality and Human Rights.[426] Section 3 provides that the role of the Commission extends to encouraging and supporting the development of a society in which people's ability to achieve their potential is not limited by prejudice or discrimination, there is respect for and protection of each individual's human rights, there is respect for the dignity and worth of each individual, each individual has an equal opportunity to participate in society, and there is mutual respect between groups based on understanding and valuing of diversity and on shared respect for equality and human rights. Having regard to the terms of s 10 of the 2006 Act, children fall within the groups provided for by s 3. Pursuant to s 8 of the Act, the Commission must promote equality and diversity and, pursuant to s 9, must also promote human rights by promoting an understanding of their importance, encouraging good practice in relation to human rights, promoting awareness, understanding and protection of human rights and by encouraging authorities to comply with the ECHR pursuant to s 6 of the Human Rights Act 1998. By the provisions of s 30(1) of the Act, the Commission can initiate or intervene in legal proceedings, whether for judicial review or otherwise, where it appears to the Commission that the proceedings are relevant to a matter in connection with which the Commission has a function.

---

[421] *UK Children's Commissioners' Report to the UN Committee on the Rights of the Child* (June 2008), p 8.

[422] Children Act 2004, Sch 1(7).

[423] These are physical and mental health and emotional well-being; protection from harm and neglect; education, training and recreation; the contribution made by children to society; and social and economic well-being.

[424] *UK Children's Commissioners' Report to the UN Committee on the Rights of the Child* (June 2008), p 8. See *Every Child Matters* Cm 5860 (2003).

[425] The UK Committee for UNICEF has published a leaflet entitled '*Every Child Matters – The five Outcomes and the UN Convention on the Rights of the Child*' which map the five outcomes stipulated by 'Every Child Matters' against the articles of the CRC. A recent independent review of the office, role and functions of the Children's Commissioner in England described the record of the Children's Commissioner as disappointing by reason of its limited remit (see Dunford, J *Review of the Office of the Children's Commissioner (England)* (2010) Department of Education Cm 7981, p 6).

[426] Previously known as the 'Commission for Racial Equality', the Equality and Human Rights Commission, which was founded on 1 October 2007, has taken over the responsibilities of the Commission for Racial Equality, the Equal Opportunities Commission and the Disability Rights Commission. The organisation is in fact known as the Equality and Human Rights Commission.

CONCLUSION

2.116 It can be seen that there is now a large and ever growing canon of international law on children rights, including rules of customary international law and *jus cogens* norms.[427] Within this cannon, the CRC is the instrument of outstanding importance.[428] The ECHR is also of fundamental significance when examining the nature, extent of children's rights and in particular when seeking to give them domestic effect. Whilst the deep roots of children's rights have a domestic pedigree, the current domestic legislative and jurisprudential framework is insufficient to protect fully the rights of children within this jurisdiction without reference to those international and European instruments. By reason of its limitations as a *children's* rights instrument,[429] this is the position even with the significant step forward in the field of human rights represented by the application to domestic law of the ECHR through the agency of the Human Rights Act 1998. Given not only the pre-eminence of international and European instruments in the field of children's rights, but the clear need to rely on those instruments to supplement domestic legislation and jurisprudence in order to fully realise the rights of children and young people in this jurisdiction, we must now turn to examine how those instruments and the principles embodied within them can be most effectively applied and enforced in our domestic jurisdiction.

---

[427] Within this context, the warning of Thorpe LJ in *G (Children) (Foreign Contact Order: Enforcment)* [2003] EWCA Civ 1607, [2004] 1 FCR 266, where he observed in relation to the Convention on Contact Concerning Children that 'There are, therefore, a number of authorities with different responsibilities to promote conventions in similar areas. Although undoubtedly all the authorities strive to cooperate rather than to compete, the end result may be a proliferation of instruments which by their complexity promote confusion amongst judges and practitioners as much as good outcomes for children and families' should be noted. See also Balton, D *The Convention on the Rights of the Child – Prospects for International Enforcement* (1990) 12 Hum Rts Q 120, pp 123–125.

[428] Fortin, J *Children's Rights and the Developing Law* (2005) 2nd edn, Cambridge, p 31.

[429] See **2.78** above.

Chapter 3

DOMESTIC APPLICATION AND ENFORCEMENT

'States are not moral agents, people are, and can impose moral
standards on powerful institutions'

Noam Chomsky

INTRODUCTION

3.1   It is widely accepted that children are entitled to certain fundamental rights
carrying the force of international law. The many and various legal instruments
described in chapter 2 are evidence of this. However, there remains a distinction in
practice between children's *entitlement* to specific rights and the procedural capacity for
children to enforce those rights.[1] To be of real value to children, the rights articulated by
international and regional legal instruments must, in concert with domestic legal
provisions and procedure, be capable both of effective practical application and of
effective enforcement, so as to maintain the integrity of those rights and to achieve
proper redress on those occasions when they are violated. As Fortin observes, this leap
from the theoretical to the practical presents considerable difficulties when it is
considered that the domestic legal system is a system that has yet to develop a
comprehensive rights based-framework for children.[2] This problem is further amplified
by the fact that its solution within the domestic jurisdiction relies, in part, on the
domestic application and enforcement of complex international legal frameworks which
have not been incorporated formally into domestic law.

3.2   In examining the law and practice of children's rights in this jurisdiction it is vital
to have a clear understanding of how, and to what extent, the rights codified in the
primarily international and regional instruments set out in chapter 2 can be relied upon
and enforced effectively within our domestic legal system. The central message of this
book is that the CRC can be relied on before the domestic courts, tribunals and decision
making bodies of this jurisdiction notwithstanding that it has not been formally
incorporated into domestic law. This Chapter provides a detailed explanation of the law
which underpins this proposition and which requires the domestic courts to interpret
domestic legislation and common law in line with the provisions of the CRC and
requires domestic decision makers to have regard to the provisions of the CRC when
exercising administrative discretion. The chapter begins by looking at the domestic
status of those binding international legal frameworks embodying children's rights,
including the CRC, which have been ratified by the UK but which have not been
incorporated into domestic law. This is followed by an examination of the status in
domestic law of non-binding international legal instruments before turning to consider
the status of the UN reporting procedures, General Comments, rules and guidelines.

---

[1]   See Van Bueren *The International Law on the Rights of the Child* (1998) Martinus Nijhoff, p 378.

[2]   Fortin, J *Children's Rights and the Developing Law* (2005) 2nd edn, Cambridge, p 27.

The status and role of customary international law and _jus cogens_ rules in domestic law is then examined before consideration is given to the application and enforcement in domestic law of the principles enshrined in the ECHR. A summary in tabular form of the domestic status of each of the international and regional legal instruments touching and concerning children's rights is provided at the end of the chapter.[3] Before commencing this examination however, it is important first to consider some key systemic issues which impact on the application and enforcement of children's rights within the domestic jurisdiction.

KEY SYSTEMIC ISSUES

Systemic issues – accessibility of enforcement procedures

Accessibility – international legal frameworks

3.3   In respect of international human rights instruments, it is only when States _agree_ to grant standing for the prosecution of specific complaints concerning the breach of rights that individuals can initiate action on their own behalf.[4] This is normally achieved either by means of the State legislating for such procedures within laws that incorporate international instruments into the domestic legal framework or by States recognising the jurisdiction of international bodies to determine individual complaints by their citizens through enforcement procedures embodied within the international instruments themselves.

3.4   The fact that the CRC, the cardinal legal instrument codifying children's rights, is not incorporated by statute into our domestic law[5] means that the enforcement of the rights it describes cannot be achieved by direct petition to the domestic courts in the way possible in respect of the rights codified in the ECHR.[6] This difficulty is compounded by the fact that the CRC does not incorporate its own provisions for enforcement by individuals to stand as an alternative mechanism to enforcement in the domestic courts.[7] There is thus no method of direct petition by which individual children within this jurisdiction can seek to enforce the rights stipulated by the CRC.[8]

3.5   Similar difficulties arise in relation to the other international instruments touching and concerning the rights of children which do provide mechanisms for petition by the individual. In large part these instruments are likewise not incorporated

---

3   See **3.94**.

4   Van Bueren _The International Law on the Rights of the Child_ (1998) Martinus Nijhoff, p 378.

5   The prospects for incorporation of the CRC into domestic law may be considered more hopeful within the context of discussion of the introduction of a Bill of Rights (see in particular the _Tenth Report of the Parliamentary Joint Committee on Human Rights_ HL Paper 117/HC81, paras 22 and 145). See also chapter 17.

6   The concept of taking all appropriate legislative measures to implement the CRC pursuant to Art 4 of the CRC does not extend to implying that a State Party _must_ incorporate the CRC into domestic law (see Jackson, J _Status of Treaties in Domestic Legal Systems: A Policy Analysis_ (1992) American Journal of International Law, Vol 86, p 310).

7   The proposal by Amnesty International that the CRC should incorporate a system for individual petitions was rejected (see Van Bueren _The International Law on the Rights of the Child_ (1998) Martinus Nijhoff, p 411 and Kilkelly, U _The UN Committee on the Rights of the Child – an evaluation in light of recent UK experience_ (1996) 8 Child and Family Law Quarterly 105, p 117). See Fortin, J _Children's Rights and the Developing Law_ (2009) 3rd edn, Cambridge, pp 52–53 for the arguments in favour of a system of individual petition for the CRC.

8   By contrast, the African Charter on the Rights and Welfare of the Child incorporates a right of individual petition for all children.

into domestic law[9] and the United Kingdom has been consistent in its reluctance to recognise and ratify the provisions of those international instruments[10] which do permit complaints by individuals to the international institutions responsible for administering them.[11] Compliance reporting by States Parties, the provision of General Comments, technical advice and assistance to States Parties on implementation issues, investigations by impartial experts into alleged violations and inter-state complaints procedures may be helpful in ensuring that progress is made towards the implementation and application of children's rights at a macroscopic level. However, they are of far less value in ensuring the consistent domestic application and enforcement of children's rights in individual cases on a day to day basis.[12] As Van Bueren concludes:[13]

> 'The difficult in international law is not in identifying the duty holders, but in identifying effective procedures whereby individuals or groups of individuals can bring actions against governments.'

Accessibility – European Legal Frameworks

3.6 The position in relation to the enforcement of European instruments is rendered less problematic by a European legal framework in which the United Kingdom is heavily invested and plays a central role in shaping. Most importantly, within this context any issues of accessibility of enforcement procedures have been largely solved by the ECHR being given effect in domestic law through the agency of the Human Rights Act 1998. That Act of Parliament provides comprehensive provisions for the enforcement of the rights articulated by the ECHR in the domestic courts. However, the domestic picture of applying and enforcing those rights on behalf of children remains complicated by the fact that the ECHR is not an instrument which is specifically referable to the rights of children, and therefore must be the subject of significant additional interpretation by the domestic courts in order to illuminate properly those rights.[14]

Systemic Issues – Distinction between Civil and Political and Economic, Social and Cultural Rights

3.7 Overarching these issues of accessibility is the potential difficulty created by the distinction that is often drawn between so called first generation civil and political rights and second generation economic, social and cultural rights.[15] There is a strong argument

---

[9] The exception is the Hague Convention on the Civil Aspects of International Child Abduction 1980 which is incorporated into domestic law by the Child Abduction and Custody Act 1985.

[10] See the International Covenant on Civil and Political Rights, Part IV, the Convention against Torture and Other Cruel, Inhuman or Degrading Treatment or Punishment, Art 22, the UN Convention on the Elimination of all forms of Racial Discrimination, Part II, the Optional Protocol to the Convention on the Elimination of all forms of Discrimination against Women and the Optional Protocol on the Rights of Persons with Disabilities.

[11] Although the efficacy of an international system for individual petitions is arguably weakened by the fact that an individual petition rarely *prevents* the breach of a right, only provides a remedy subsequent to breach and can be subject to severe delays (see Van Bueren *The International Law on the Rights of the Child* (1998) Martinus Nijhoff, pp 378–379).

[12] Van Bueren *The International Law on the Rights of the Child* (1998) Martinus Nijhoff, pp 378–379. See also Balton, D *The Convention on the Rights of the Child – Prospects for International Enforcement* (1990) 12 Hum Rts. Q 120 at pp 126–129.

[13] Van Bueren *The International Law on the Rights of the Child* (1998) Martinus Nijhoff, p 297.

[14] See **2.78** above.

[15] See Verhellen, E *Convention on the Rights of the Child* (2000) Garant, p 85. There are those who now argue for 'third generation' human rights including the right to an adequate standard of living (sometimes expressed as the 'right to food'), the right to a decent environment, the right to development and the right to

that this distinction is both artificial and unhelpful and detracts from the fundamental principle of the indivisible nature of human rights.[16] However, it is also a distinction that must be examined and analysed when determining the extent to which, irrespective of the legal means by which it is achieved, the rights conferred on children are directly enforceable by individual children in the domestic legal sphere and the scope of their practical application otherwise. The basis for the argument that there exist qualitative distinctions between civil and political and economic, social and cultural rights is primarily linguistic in nature and most of the distinctions argued for stem from these linguistic distinctions.

Obligatory versus Declaratory Language

3.8   The impact of linguistic distinctions on the enforcement of children's rights can be seen most readily by comparing the wording adopted within the Covenant on Civil and Political Rights as against Covenant on Social, Economic and Cultural Rights to articulate the obligations of State Parties.[17] The former adopts language which enjoins States Parties to 'respect and to ensure ... the rights recognised in the present Covenant',[18] whilst the latter calls on States Parties to 'take steps, individually and through international assistance and co-operation ... to the maximum of its available resources, with a view to achieving progressively the full realisation of the rights'.[19] Whilst the former wording is clearly obligatory, the latter may best be described as declaratory in nature.

3.9   The CRC combines both obligatory and declaratory language. For example, Art 2(1) of the CRC provides that 'States Parties shall respect and ensure the rights set forth in the present Convention to each child within their jurisdiction without discrimination of any kind'.[20] By contrast, Art 27(1) stipulates that 'States Parties recognise the right of every child to a standard of living adequate for the child's physical, mental, spiritual, moral and social development'. Sometimes obligatory and declaratory statements are encompassed within the same article. For example, the initial paragraphs of Art 28(1) provide as follows:

> 'States Parties recognise the right of the child to education, and with a view to achieving this right progressively and on the basis of equal opportunity, they shall, in particular:
>
> (a) Make primary education compulsory and available free to all.'

These variations in the way the rights of the child are articulated form the foundation of two further issues that impact on the application and enforcement of the rights of children, namely the issue of justiciability and the impact of economic considerations.

---

peace. At least some of these rights are encompassed by the CRC and are dealt with in the text where they become relevant. For a critique of 'third generation' human rights see Brownlie, I *Principles of Public International Law* (2008) 7th edn, OUP, pp 567–568.

[16]   See the analysis in Van Bueren *The International Law on the Rights of the Child* (1998) Martinus Nijhoff, pp 381–383. The corollary of this position is that economic, social and cultural rights are arguably the superior rights in that the so called 'first generation' rights are ineffective without them (see Steiner, H Alston, P and Goodman, R *International Human Rights in Context – Law, Politics, Morals* (2007) 3rd edn, Oxford, p 263).

[17]   Verhellen, E *Convention on the Rights of the Child* (2000) Garant, p 85.

[18]   CCPR, Art 2(1).

[19]   CSECR, Art 2(1).

[20]   Van Bueren notes 'The term 'respect' implies a duty of good faith on the part of the State Party to refrain from actions which would breach the Convention' (Van Bueren *The International Law on the Rights of the Child* (1998) Martinus Nijhoff, p 391).

Justiciability

3.10   The difference in wording between obligatory articles and declaratory articles effects the extent to which a particular right may be *capable* of judicial enforcement even where a procedure for enforcement is accessible. To be enforceable, the precise nature and extent of a legal obligation in question must be capable of being ascertained with certainty. The more declaratory the article, the less certain will be its legal scope. An absence of certainty over the legal scope of a right will militate against its consistent enforcement by the courts and increases the risk of arbitrary decisions. Within this context, it is civil and political rights rather than economic, social or cultural rights which tend to be perceived as more readily enforceable in law.[21] This raises interesting questions in relation to the rule of law, namely whether the rule of law might be said to attach with greater tenacity to procedural equality than to economic and social equality.[22] In this regard, the CRC, with its mixture of obligatory and declaratory articles, presents a challenge to lawyers and the courts striving for legal consistency.

3.11   In this context, one of the key issues in respect of many of the rights enshrined in the CRC and other international instruments is therefore whether certain of those rights meet the 'benchmark of justiciability'.[23] The UN Committee on Economic, Social and Cultural Rights contends that the absence of a judicial remedy for the violation of economic, social or cultural rights is not warranted either by the nature of the rights or by the provisions of the ICESCR.[24] However, citing Wellman's view that the moral and legal reality of social and welfare rights is questionable,[25] Fortin observes that 'one might argue that some of the economic, social and cultural rights contained in the CRC are not rights at all but merely claims based on ideals regarding children's needs in a perfect world'.[26] Whilst this conclusion should not undermine the value of 'aspirational drafting' nor prevent those concerned with implementing the social, economic and cultural provisions of the CRC for children from aspiring to achieve those goals, it must be recognised that the *legal* enforcement of some of these provisions in respect of individual children is likely to be very difficult to achieve.[27] Indeed, the courts have demonstrated a reluctance to intervene in areas touching on social or economic policy.[28]

---

[21]   Van Bueren *The International Law on the Rights of the Child* (1998) Martinus Nijhoff, p 391. But see the decision of the Constitutional Court of South Africa in *Treatment Action Campaign v Minister of Health* 2002 (5) SA 721, para 106. See also Steiner, H, Alston, P, Goodman, R *International Human Rights in Context Law Politics and Morals* (2007) Oxford, p 313 in relation to the justiciability of second generation rights under the Covenant of Economic, Social and Cultural Rights.

[22]   Van Bueren *The International Law on the Rights of the Child* (1998) Martinus Nijhoff, p 383.

[23]   Steiner, H Alston, P and Goodman, R *International Human Rights in Context – Law, Politics, Morals* (2007) 3rd edn, Oxford, p 313.

[24]   Committee on Economic, Social and Cultural Rights General Comment No 9 *The Domestic Application of the Covenant* HRI/GEN/1/Rev.8 p 57, para 10. See also Vierdag, E *The Legal Nature of Rights Granted by the International Covenant on Economic, Social and Cultural Rights* (1978) 9 Neths. Ybk. Int. L. 69.

[25]   Wellman, C *The Proliferation of Rights: Moral Progress or Empty Rhetoric?* (1999) Westview Press, pp 20–29.

[26]   Fortin, J *Children's Rights and the Developing Law* (2009) 3rd edn, Cambridge, p 18.

[27]   See for example Case Comment *Education: placement of Roma children in special schools* European Human Rights Law Review (2006) 340 at 343 and the dissenting opinion of Judge Borrego in *DH and Others v Czech Republic* [2008] ELR 17, 23 BHRC 526, para 5.

[28]   See for example *Carson v United Kingdom* Application No 42184/05 [2008] All ER (D) 18 (Nov) in which the European Court of Human Rights noted that because of their direct knowledge of their society and its needs, the national authorities were in principle better placed than the international judge to appreciate what was in the public interest on social or economic grounds, and the court would generally respect the legislature's policy choice unless it was manifestly without reasonable foundation. See also *Fretté v France* (2002) 38 EHRR 438, [2003] 2 FLR 9; *F v Switzerland* (1987) 10 EHRR 411 especially at para 33; *Botta v*

Economic considerations

3.12 With the context of the distinction between obligatory and declaratory language it is common for civil and political rights to be expressed as prohibitions and for economic, social and cultural rights to expressed as duties, although this is far from being a hard and fast rule.[29] Within this context, civil and political rights which are expressed as requirements to refrain from taking certain specified actions may be seen as more economic to implement in contrast to economic, social and cultural rights which, by virtue of the duties they incorporate, often involve State expenditure.[30] This can make legislating for the enforcement of civil and political rights more attractive to Governments than for those rights of an economic, social and cultural nature. In any event, a lack of 'available resources' may militate against the consistent practical implementation of economic, social and cultural rights, preventing such rights becoming universal normative standards.[31]

3.13 Central to the implementation of rights qualified by reference to available resources is the concept of 'progressive realisation'. In its General Comment No 3 the Committee on Economic, Social and Cultural Rights explains that:

> 'The concept of progressive realisation constitutes a recognition of the fact that full realisation of all economic, social and cultural rights will generally not be able to be achieved in a short period of time. In this sense the obligation differs significantly from that contained in article 2 of the International Covenant on Civil and Political Rights which embodies an immediate obligation to respect and ensure all of the relevant rights. Nevertheless, the fact that realisation over time, or in other words progressively, is foreseen under the Covenant should not be misinterpreted as depriving the obligation of all meaningful content. It is on the one hand a necessary flexibility device, reflecting the realities of the real world and the difficulties involved for any country in ensuring full realisation of economic, social and cultural rights. On the other hand, the phrase must be read in the light of the overall objective, indeed the raison d'être, of the Covenant which is to establish clear obligations for States parties in respect of the full realisation of the rights in question. It thus imposes an obligation to move as expeditiously and effectively as possible towards that goal. Moreover, any deliberately retrogressive measures in that regard would require the most careful consideration and would need to be fully justified by reference to the totality of the rights provided for in the Covenant and in the context of the full use of the maximum available resources.'[32]

3.14 Courts have recognised the problems created by the enforcement of economic and social rights by individuals. In the seminal decision of the Constitutional Court of South Africa in the case of *Soobramoney v Minister of Health (Kwa-Zulu Natal)*[33] Chaskalson P observed:

    Italy (1998) 26 EHRR 241, para 35; and *Mata Estevez v Spain* Application No 56501/00 ((unreported)) 10 May 2001. For an opposing view see *Re P and others (adoption: unmarried couple)* [2008] UKHL 38, [2008] 2 FCR 366, para 48 per Lord Hope of Craighead.

[29]   The right to life has been expressed as a positive obligation by the European Court of Human Rights (see *Osman v United Kingdom* (1998) 29 EHRR 245, [1999] 1 FLR 193, para 115). The Court has also emphasised the positive duties in relation to the prohibition on torture and other cruel, inhuman and degrading treatment or punishment (see *Z v United Kingdom* (2001) 34 EHRR 97, [2001] 2 FLR 612, paras 73–75) and the right to respect for family life and privacy (see *Marckx v Belgium* (1979) 2 EHRR 330).

[30]   For this reason, the words 'to the maximum of its available resources' are often included in the body of those articles dealing with economic, social and cultural rights.

[31]   See Steiner, H Alston, P and Goodman, R *International Human Rights in Context – Law, Politics, Morals* (2007) 3rd edn, Oxford, pp 294–313.

[32]   Committee on Economic, Social and Cultural Rights General Comment No 3 *The Nature of States Parties' Obligations* HRI/GEN/1/Rev.8 p 17, para 9.

[33]   (1998) CCT 32/97 (1999) 50 BMLR 224.

'There are also those who need access to housing, food and water, employment opportunities and social security ... The state has to manage its limited resources in order to address all these claims. There will be times when this requires it to adopt a holistic approach to the larger needs of society rather than to focus on the specific needs of particular individuals within society.'

However, in *Treatment Action Campaign v Minister of Health*,[34] a case concerning the right to have access to public health care services and the right to children to be afforded special protection, the Court held that:

'Where a breach of any right has taken place, including a socio-economic right, a court is under a duty to ensure that effective relief is granted. The nature of the right infringed and the nature of the infringement will provide guidance as to the appropriate relief in a particular case.'

3.15 The economic conditions precedent attached to some rights have been the subject of much criticism.[35] At the 2002 United Nations General Assembly special session on children the Assembly observed that the market should not operate to the detriment of children and that children should be insulated from the effect of short term and long term financial crises. Within this context States resolved to:[36]

'Mobilise new and substantial additional resources for social development, both at national and international level, to reduce disparities within and among countries, and ensure the effective and efficient use of existing resources. Further, ensure to the greatest possible extent, that social expenditures that benefit children are protected and prioritised during both short-term and long-term economic and financial crises.'

3.16 The practical relevance of the foregoing debate on the distinction between civil and political and economic, social and cultural rights is the tension between aspiration and achievement which it highlights. The declarative value of legislation should not be under estimated. There is value in expressing in international instruments the aspirational rights that children *should* be entitled to.[37] However, it must also be recognised that there is a real risk that this approach also provides a mechanism by which States can articulate general and formulaic policies in relation to children's rights whilst failing to promote the application and enforcement of specific rights for individual children facing day to day difficulties. This is demonstrated aptly within the domestic jurisdiction by the decision of the Government to base its central policy in

---

[34] 2002 (5) SA 721.
[35] See Steiner, H, Alston, P, Goodman, R *International Human Rights in Context Law Politics and Morals* (2007) Oxford, p 275 and Van Bueren *The International Law on the Rights of the Child* (1998) Martinus Nijhoff, p 295.
[36] United Nations, Report of the Ad Hoc Committee of the Whole of the twenty-seventh special session of the General Assembly, 2002, A/S-27/19/Rev.1, para 52.
[37] Fienberg, J *Rights, Justice and the Bounds of Liberty* (1980) Princeton University Press, p 153 and O'Neill, O *Children's Rights and the Law* (1992) Clarendon Press, pp 37–40.

respect of children[38] on five general aspirations[39] rather than the specific and comprehensive rights articulated by the CRC.[40]

Systemic Issues – Overlapping and Conflicting Principles

3.17 The legal position of children in society is governed by a wide range of domestic laws and a large body of domestic jurisprudence which the courts are bound to apply. This body of law is not always consistent with the demands of the international canon of laws on children's rights. It is only natural that the domestic courts (and the lawyers that populate them) have a far greater knowledge base in respect of the relevant domestic legal provisions and jurisprudence as compared to the relevant international instruments and jurisprudence, further militating against the consistent application of the latter in day to day practice. Further, caution should in any event be exercised before applying domestic interpretations of cardinal principles to similar principles enshrined in international and regional legal instruments.[41]

3.18 A related difficulty is that the large number of international and European instruments enshrining children's rights do not always articulate given rights in precisely the same language or with precisely the same emphasis. This can lead to difficulties of interpretation and application for the domestic courts. By way of example, Balton points out that whilst Art 6 of the Universal Declaration of Human Rights proclaims that 'everyone has the right to recognition everywhere as a person before the law', as does the Covenant on Civil and Political Rights,[42] the CRC has no comparable provision. Whilst the saving clause in Art 41 of the CRC[43] mitigates the impact of this apparent omission, it raises the question of the extent to which the drafters of the CRC originally intended children to have this cardinal right.[44] In another example, Art 14 of the CRC, whilst requiring States Parties to 'respect the right of the child to freedom of though, conscience and religion', omits many of the additional elements of this right articulated in the Universal Declaration of Human Rights,[45] the Covenant on Civil and Political Rights[46] and the Declaration of All Forms of Intolerance and of Discrimination Based on Religion or Belief.[47] Balton notes that, as these latter instruments make no distinction between children and adults regarding the rights they encompass, the failure of the CRC to adopt comparable language again calls into

---

[38]   See *Every Child Matters* Cm 5860 (2003).

[39]   These are: (1) physical and mental health and emotional well-being; (2) protection from harm and neglect; (3) education, training and recreation; (4) the contribution made by children to society; and (5) social and economic well-being. The fact that these aspirations are primarily are expressed in the language of second generation rights further emphasises how attractive such rights are to Governments who have one eye to the Treasury when considering the implementation of children's rights.

[40]   The UK Committee for UNICEF has published a leaflet entitled '*Every Child Matters – The five Outcomes and the UN Convention on the Rights of the Child*' which map the five outcomes stipulated by 'Every Child Matters' against the articles of the CRC.

[41]   Alston, P *The Best Interests Principle: Towards a Reconciliation of Culture and Human Rights* in Freeman, M (ed) *Children's Rights* Vol 2 (2003) Ashgate Dartmouth, p 199.

[42]   ICCPR, Art 16.

[43]   Article 41 of the CRC reads 'Nothing in this Convention shall affect any provisions that are more conducive to the realisation of the rights of the child and that may be contained in (a) the law of the State Party; or (b) international law in force in that State.'

[44]   Balton, J *The Convention on the Rights of the Child – Prospects for Enforcement* (1990) 12 Hum Rts. Q. 120, p 123.

[45]   Universal Declaration of Human Rights, Art 18.

[46]   ICCPR, Art 18.

[47]   Article 1.

question the extent to which children specifically enjoy each of those rights.[48] The need to reconcile international and European instruments with each other and with the principles of domestic law further complicates the task of applying and enforcing those international and European instruments within the domestic context when seeking to give domestic effect to the rights of children.

3.19   There are therefore a number of significant and potentially difficult systemic issues centered on accessibility and enforcement, linguistic distinctions and overlapping principles that impact upon the application and enforcement of the rights of children within the domestic jurisdiction. These difficulties must be kept well in mind when considering the most appropriate way to apply and enforce in the domestic law arena the international and regional instruments touching and concerning children's rights. Within this context, we now turn to look at that process of domestic application and enforcement. In doing so it is useful to recall Verhellen's view that in relation to the CRC, 'Much depends on the willingness and creativity of the lawyers and [Courts] in making the Convention enforceable by individuals'.[49] This observation is applicable to many if not all of the international instruments which embody the rights of children.

DOMESTIC LAW AND INTERNATIONAL LEGAL FRAMEWORKS

Nomenclature

3.20   The Vienna Convention on the Law of Treaties 1969 (hereafter the 'VCLT')[50] entered into force on 27 January 1980 and stipulates the rules for treaties concluded between States.[51] It was signed by the United Kingdom on 20 April 1970 and was ratified by the UK on 25 June 1971. Article 1(a) of the VCLT states that:

'"treaty" means an international agreement concluded between States in written form and governed by international law, whether embodied in a single instrument or in two or more related instruments and whatever its particular designation.'

Article 2 of the VCLT provides that:

'The provisions of paragraph 1 regarding the use of terms in the present Convention are without prejudice to the use of those terms or to the meanings which may be given to them in the internal law of any State.'

3.21   There is no universally accepted nomenclature for binding and non-binding international agreements and the term 'treaty' is often used interchangeably with the other generic terms.[52] When describing formal, multilateral, multiparty binding international agreements dealing with children's rights, the generic term 'convention' is

---

[48]   Balton, J *The Convention on the Rights of the Child – Prospects for Enforcement* (1990) 12 Hum Rts. Q. 120, p 124.

[49]   Verhellen, E *Convention on the Rights of the Child* (2000) Garant, p 86.

[50]   United Nations *Treaty Series* Vol 1155, p 331. See also the 1986 *Vienna Convention on the Law of Treaties between States and International Organisations or between International Organisations* ('1986 Vienna Convention') which has not yet entered into force but adds rules for treaties with international organisations as parties.

[51]   Article 1. Pursuant to Art 4 the Convention is not retroactive in its effect.

[52]   In particular, 'covenant', 'convention', 'protocol' and 'international agreement'. The title 'Charter' is generally reserved for particularly significant legally binding international agreements (for example, the UN

that most often used. Whilst the terms are synonymous, in the following paragraphs the term 'convention' rather than the term 'treaty' is used save where the context requires otherwise.

The Domestic Status of Binding International Conventions

Relevant General Principles of International Law

Treaty Law

3.22   Article 11 of the VCLT dictates the means by which a State can express its consent to be bound by a convention as being those of 'signature, exchange of instruments constituting a treaty, ratification, acceptance, approval or accession, or by any other means if so agreed'.[53] The act of signing shows agreement with the text, but a State is not bound until the convention has been ratified and has entered into force.[54] A State is not obliged to ratify any convention which it has signed but, having signed the convention, the State is under a duty, in the period prior to its ratification and entry into force, to refrain from acts which defeat the object and purpose of a convention.[55] Once it has ratified[56] the convention the State is bound by that convention once it enters into force.[57]

Pacta Sunt Servanda

3.23   The central principle of what has historically been known as 'treaty law' is '*pacta sunt servanda*' or 'pacts must be respected'.[58] Art 26 of the VCLT stipulates that, 'Every treaty in force is binding upon the parties to it and must be performed by them in good faith'.[59] The classical method of enforcement of a State's obligations under a convention is by reference to this duty of performance of convention obligations imposed on States Parties.[60] Pleading insufficiency of domestic law is not, in international law, an acceptable excuse for failure to implement the provisions of a convention[61] nor can a State rely on the provisions of its domestic law as authority for failing to perform[62] or

---

Charter). The title 'Declaration' tends to be used to describe instruments that are not legally binding but can, in certain instances, denote a legally binding international agreement.

[53]   Articles 12–17 of the VCLT provide the detailed provisions for each means by which a State may consent to be bound by a treaty.

[54]   Foreign & Commonwealth Office, Treaty Section, *Treaties and MOUs – Guidance on Practice and Procedures* (April 2000) 2nd edn, revised May 2004, p 6.

[55]   Article 18 VCLT.

[56]   Foreign & Commonwealth Office, Treaty Section, *Treaties and MOUs – Guidance on Practice and Procedures* (April 2000) 2nd edn, revised May 2004, p 6. By tradition, States which have participated in drafting the treaty agree to be bound by it through ratification and the remaining States agree to be bound by means of accession (see Van Bueren *The International Law on the Rights of the Child* (1998) Martinus Nijhoff, p 380).

[57]   Article 24(1) of the VCLT provides that 'A treaty enters into force in such manner and upon such date as it may provide or as the negotiating States may agree' and Art 24(2) provides that 'Failing any such provision or agreement, a treaty enters into force as soon as consent to be bound by the treaty has been established from all negotiating States.'

[58]   Preamble to the Vienna Convention on the Law of Treaties 1969, United Nations *Treaty Series* Vol 1155, p 331.

[59]   To this end, it should be noted that Art 4 of the CRC states that, 'States Parties shall undertake all appropriate legislative, administrative, and other measures for the implementation of the rights recognised in the present Convention. With regard to economic, social and cultural rights, States Parties shall undertake such measures to the maximum extent of their available resources and, where needed, within the framework of international co-operation.'

[60]   Brownlie, I *Principles of Public International Law* (2008) 7th edn, OUP, p 562.

[61]   Foreign & Commonwealth Office, Treaty Section, *Treaties and MOUs – Guidance on Practice and Procedures* (April 2000) 2nd edn, revised May 2004, p 6 and VCLT, Art 27.

[62]   VCLT, Art 27.

for violating[63] the provisions of an international convention by which it is bound.[64] An individual may plead that the convention obligations of the State are relevant to the interests of that individual and must thus be recognised by the domestic court.[65]

Reservations

3.24 A State party to a convention may modify or exclude the obligations placed on it by a convention through the adoption of 'reservations'[66] in relation to elements of the convention.[67] Art 19 of the VCLT permits the formulations of reservations by a State unless they are prohibited or excluded by the terms of the convention or incompatible with the object and purpose of the convention in question. Article 21 of the VCLT describes the legal effect of reservations as modifying the provisions of the convention to which the reservation relates to the extent of that reservation. Thus a reservation has the effect of altering for the reserving State its relations with the other parties to the convention in respect of the provision to which the reservation applies. The reservation does not modify the relevant provision in respect of the relations between the other parties *inter se*.[68]

Domestic Standing

3.25 The precise domestic legal implications of becoming a party to the convention will vary from State to State dependent on the constitutional provisions governing that State. There is however a general duty to ensure that domestic law conforms to international law.[69] In the United Kingdom the Ministerial Code requires that Government Ministers to 'comply with the law including international law and treaty obligations'.[70] Generally, States will adopt either a transformational approach, where the convention provisions are used as the basis for enacting national legislative rules to reflect the convention obligations, or an incorporative approach, where the convention itself becomes part of domestic law.[71] Either way, the means of implementation of a convention's provisions are a matter of domestic jurisdiction.[72] Thus, convention rights become domestic principles rather than operating as extraneous principles under the relevant convention.[73] For example, the proper citation of the articles of the ECHR is by reference to Sch 1 of the Human Rights Act 1998 (the domestic legislation implementing the treaty) rather than by reference to the ECHR itself (the treaty). However, where the principles stipulated by the convention are not formally adopted by

---

63 See *Texaco v Libya* 53 ILR 389 (1977).
64 See the *Alabama Claims Arbitration* (1872), Moore, *Arbitrations*, p 653.
65 Brownlie, I *Principles of Public International Law* (2008) 7th edn, OUP, p 35 and see below **3.28 et seq**.
66 Article 2 of the Vienna Convention on the Law of Treaties defines 'reservation' as follows: "reservation' means a unilateral statement, however phrased or named, made by a State, when signing, ratifying, accepting, approving or acceding to a treaty, whereby it purports to exclude or to modify the legal effect of certain provisions of the treaty in their application to that State.'
67 Verhellen notes that 'Making reservations is an extremely bad thing, because the standards in the Convention [on the Rights of the Child] are only minimum standards ... and any reservations fundamentally undermine the universal nature of these standards.' (see Verhellen, E *Convention on the Rights of the Child* (2000) Garant, p 83).
68 Article 21(1)(a) and (b) and Art 21(2).
69 Brownlie, I *Principles of Public International Law* (2008) 7th edn, OUP, p 19 citing Fitzmaurice, 92 Hague *Recueil* (1957 II), 89; Oppenheim, i 82–6; Guggenheim, i 31–3 and *Exchange of Greek and Turkish Populations* (1925) PCIJ Ser B No 10 p 20. A breach of this duty will only arise where the State fails to observe its obligation on a *specific* occasion (McNair, *Law of Treaties* (1961) OUP, p 100).
70 Ministerial Code (2010), para 1.2.
71 Van Bueren *The International Law on the Rights of the Child* (1998) Martinus Nijhoff, p 380.
72 Brownlie, I *Principles of Public International Law* (2008) 7th edn, OUP, p 562.
73 Jennings, R *General Course on Principles of International Law* Recueil des cours, Vol 121 (1967–II), 502 cited in Brownlie, I *Principles of Public International Law* (2008) 7th edn, OUP, p 562.

domestic law through incorporation or transformation, as is the case with the CRC and other conventions touching and concerning the rights of the child, the State will none the less remain subject to a duty to perform the obligations under that convention in good faith.[74] The rules of customary international law continue to govern questions not regulated by the VCLT.[75]

Relevant General Principles of Domestic Law

Power to make Conventions

3.26   In the United Kingdom power to make conventions is a prerogative power vested in the Crown and there is no constitutional requirement for Parliament to approve a convention.[76] Since 1924 however, in accordance with the 'Ponsonby Rule',[77] all conventions subject to ratification have been laid before Parliament in the form of a Command Paper for 21 sitting days before the convention is ratified. Conventions laid after 1997 have been accompanied by an Explanatory Memoranda which brings to the attention of Parliament the main features of the convention with which it is laid.[78] The purpose of the Explanatory Memoranda is to ensure that Parliament has taken note of, and had the opportunity to consider, the nature of the international commitments the Government is proposing to enter into. Parliament is therefore on notice of the terms of the convention prior to ratification, acceptance or approval (which have the same legal effect as ratification). The giving of notice under the 'Ponsonby Rule' is important when considering the central principle employed to apply the principles of the CRC to the interpretation of domestic legislation, namely that Parliament would not maintain or pass legislation capable of being exercised in a manner inconsistent with the treaty obligations of this country.[79] The 'Ponsonby Rule' has also been applied to amendments to multilateral conventions which are themselves subject to ratification and amendments which require legislation.[80] Since January 1998 it has been the consistent practice of the Foreign and Commonwealth Officer to apply the 'Ponsonby Rule' to conventions which are not subject to formal ratification (or acceptance or approval) but simply to the mutual notification of the completion of constitutional and other procedures by each Party.[81]

Domestic Application of Binding Conventions Incorporated into Domestic Law

3.27   Conventions affecting private rights and liabilities or that require the modification of common law or statute for their enforcement will only become incorporated into English law if an enabling Act of Parliament is passed.[82] Where such

---

[74]   VCLT, Art 26. See below at **3.28**.
[75]   VCLT, Preamble, para 8. See below at **3.55**.
[76]   Select Committee on Constitution Fifteenth Report *Waging War: Parliament's role and responsibility* (Session 2005–2006) Volume I, HL Paper 236–I, para 6.
[77]   Named after Arthur Ponsonby, Under Secretary of State for Foreign Affairs in Ramsay MacDonald's first Labour Government.
[78]   H.C. Deb. (1996) 287, WA 94302; H.L. Deb. (1996) 576, WA 101. Examples of Explanatory Memoranda can be found on the FCO website at www.fco.gov.uk/treaty.
[79]   See **3.28–3.31** below.
[80]   Sixth Report to the Joint Committee on Statutory Instruments (Session 1981–82) [Cmnd. 8600]. The practice does not apply to treaties that enter into force by signature.
[81]   VCLT, Art 24(1). See also FCO *The Ponsonby Rule* (2001) at http://www.fco.gov.uk/resources/en/pdf/pdf4/fco_pdf_ponsonbyrule (accessed on 17 May 2009).
[82]   Brownlie, I *Principles of Public International Law* (2008) 7th edn, OUP, p 45 and see *J H Rayner (Mincing Lane) Ltd v Department of Trade and Industry* [1990] 2 AC 418 at 500C per Lord Oliver of Aylmerton.

enabling domestic legislation is passed to give effect to a convention, that legislation will be interpreted according to a presumption that Parliament intended to fulfil its international obligations.[83]

Domestic Application of Binding Conventions not Incorporated into Domestic Law

(i) Unincorporated Binding Conventions and Interpretation of Domestic Legislation

3.28 From the date a binding convention enters into force for the United Kingdom, it places upon the UK binding international obligations vis-à-vis the other party or parties.[84] Even where a binding international convention is not the subject of an enabling Act of Parliament, such as the CRC, the courts will, where domestic legislation is ambiguous, seek to interpret that legislation consistently with that binding convention.[85] In *A v Secretary of State for the Home Department (No 2)*[86] Lord Bingham noted:[87]

> 'The appellants' submission has a further, more international, dimension. They accept, as they must, that a treaty, even if ratified by the United Kingdom, has no binding force in the domestic law of this country unless it is given effect by statute or expresses principles of customary international law. But they rely on the well-established principle that the words of a United Kingdom statute, passed after the date of a treaty and dealing with the same subject matter, are to be construed, if they are reasonably capable of bearing such a meaning, as intended to carry out the treaty obligation and not to be inconsistent with it.'

It must be remembered however that it is also a cardinal principle of the common law that an international convention cannot *override* the intentions of Parliament as expressed in domestic legislation.[88] Thus, for example, whilst the interpretation of domestic legislation must take account of Parliament's international obligations under the CRC, those obligations will not take precedence over the requirements of domestic legislation.[89]

3.29 Within this context, as Brownlee notes, 'since 1974 the English Courts have with variable consistency been prepared to take the provisions of international conventions on human rights into account in the course of interpreting and applying statutes'.[90] By way of example, prior to the coming into force of the Human Rights Act 1998 the domestic courts none the less sought to give effect to the ECHR. In 1974 Lord Reid referred in the case of *Waddington v Miah*[91] to a presumption that, in enacting

---

83 Brownlie, I *Principles of Public International Law* (2008) 7th edn, OUP, p 45 and see *Salomon v Commissioners for Customs and Excise* [1967] 2 QB 116 at 141 per Lord Denning MR and 143 per Diplock LJ. A subsequent Act of Parliament will prevail over the provisions of a prior treaty in case of inconsistency between the Act and the treaty (*IRC v Collco Dealings Ltd* [1962] AC 1 and *Woodend Rubber Company v Commissioner for Inland Revenue* [1971] AC 321).

84 Foreign & Commonwealth Office, Treaty Section, *Treaties and MOUs – Guidance on Practice and Procedures* (April 2000) 2nd edn, revised May 2004, p 6.

85 *R v Secretary of State for the Home Department ex p Brind* [1991] 1 AC 696 at 747H–748A and see *Equal Opportunities Commission for Hong Kong v Director of Education* [2001] HKCFI 880, paras 89–91 and 109–110 per Hartman J applying the principle to the Convention for the Elimination of All Forms of Discrimination Against Women.

86 [2005] UKHL 71, [2006] 2 AC 221, para 27.

87 See also *Garland v British Rail Engineering Ltd* [1982] 2 All ER 402 at 415, [1983] 2 AC 751 at 771.

88 *R v Lyons* [2002] UKHL 44, [2003] 1 AC 976, para 17 per Lord Bingham. But see *Re McKerr* [2004] UKHL 12, [2004] 2 All ER, [2004] 1 WLR 807, paras 48–50 in which Lord Steyn suggested that '[a] critical re-examination of this branch of the law may become necessary in the future.'

89 See **3.32–3.40** below.

90 Brownlie, I *Principles of Public International Law* (2008) 7th edn, OUP, p 46.

91 [1974] 1 WLR 683 at 694.

legislation, Parliament would not intentionally breach the provisions of the ECHR. One year later, Lord Wilberforce, giving judgment in *Blathwayt v Lord Cawley*[92] held that the ECHR was a legitimate source of enabling courts to decide issues of public policy. In *Ahmad v I.L.E.A*[93] Lord Scarman stated in relation to the ECHR that 'The Convention is not part of English Law but, as I have often said, we will always have regard to it. We will do our best to see that our decisions are in conformity with it'.[94] Thus the short title of the Human Rights Act 1998 states that it is 'an Act to give *further* effect to the rights and freedoms guaranteed under the European Convention on Human Rights'.[95]

(ii)   Unincorporated Binding Conventions and Interpretation of the Common Law

3.30   Likewise, where the common law is uncertain, unclear or incomplete the courts will exercise judicial discretion in a manner consistent with binding international conventions. In *A v Secretary of State for the Home Department (No 2)*[96] Lord Bingham said, 'If, and to the extent that, development of the common law is called for, such development should ordinarily be in harmony with the United Kingdom's international obligations and not antithetical to them'.[97]

(iii)   Unincorporated Binding Conventions and Relationship with Administrative Discretion

3.31   Whilst public authorities exercising discretionary administrative powers are not under a strict legal duty to comply with unincorporated binding international conventions[98] the courts will have regard to the human rights context in determining whether the public authority has acted reasonably and with regard to all relevant considerations.[99] Accordingly, absent a clear legislative or executive statement to the contrary, the courts recognise a legitimate expectation that ministers and civil servants will comply with convention obligations.[100] In *Ahmed and Patel v Secretary of State for the Home Department*[101] Lord Woolf MR held that where a state has ratified an international convention, there is a legitimate expectation that the state will take account of those international obligations in domestic decision-making where a discretion exists. Thus, in *European Roma Rights Centre v Immigration Officer at Prague Airport (United Nations High Comr intervening)*[102] the House of Lords, in deciding that the Home Secretary had acted unlawfully, relied on unincorporated conventions, namely the International Covenant on Civil and Political Rights and the International Convention on the Elimination of All Forms of Racial Discrimination. This approach reflects the

---

[92]   [1976] AC 397 at 426.
[93]   [1978] 1 QB 36.
[94]   But see also *R v Secretary of State ex p Brind* [1991] 1 AC 696 per Lord Bridge; *Derbyshire County Council v Times Newspapers Ltd* [1993] AC 534.
[95]   Emphasis added.
[96]   [2005] UKHL 71, [2006] 2 AC 221, para 27.
[97]   Within this context it is of note that the Foreign and Commonwealth Guidance on conventions states that 'it is always the intention to perform all HMG's commitments, whether legally binding or not.' See Foreign & Commonwealth Office, Treaty Section, *Treaties and MOUs – Guidance on Practice and Procedures* (April 2000) 2nd edn, revised May 2004, p 2.
[98]   *R v Secretary of State ex p Brind* [1991] 1 AC 696 at 748A–748F per Lord Bridge.
[99]   Pannick QC and others, *Human Rights Law and Practice* (1999) Lexis Nexis 3rd edn, pp 28–29.
[100] Pannick QC and others, *Human Rights Law and Practice* (1999) Lexis Nexis 3rd edn, p 11.
[101] [1999] Imm AR 22 Lord Woolf MR approving the judgment of the High Court of Australia in *Minister for Immigration and Ethnic Affairs v Teoh* (1995) 183 CLR 273.
[102] [2004] UKHL 55, [2005] 2 AC 1.

stricter objective justification required in the exercise of public powers within the domestic jurisdiction where human rights are concerned.[103] In *R v Ministry of Defence, ex p Smith*[104] the court held that:

> 'The more substantial the interference with human rights, the more the court will require by way of justification before it is satisfied that the decision is 'reasonable' in the sense that it was with the range of responses of a reasonable decision maker.'

It should be noted that the role of the court in human rights adjudication concerning administrative action is quite different from the role of the court in an ordinary judicial review of administrative action.[105] In considering whether an authority has acted incompatibly with human rights, the court must focus on the decision itself, not the decision making process.[106]

Domestic Status of the CRC

3.32   The foregoing general principles of international treaty law and domestic law are significant in that they demonstrate that both domestic courts and administrative bodies making decisions concerning children, and the courts which review those decisions, must pay express regard to the provisions of the CRC in reaching their conclusions. There is now an extensive line of House of Lords and Supreme Court authority supporting this proposition.

Direct Reliance on the CRC in Domestic Law

(i)   Statutory Interpretation

3.33   The principle that even where a binding international convention is not the subject of an enabling Act of Parliament the courts will seek to interpret the legislation consistently with that unincorporated binding convention has been applied by the House of Lords and Supreme Court to the CRC.[107] In the case of *R v Secretary of State for the Home Department, ex p Venables and Thompson*[108] Lord Browne-Wilkinson held in respect of the CRC that:

---

[103]   Pannick QC and others, *Human Rights Law and Practice* (1999) Lexis Nexis 3rd edn, p 10.
[104]   [1996] QB 517 at 554E–554G per Sir Thomas Bingham MR.
[105]   *Miss Behavin' Ltd v Belfast City Council* [2007] UKHL 19, [2007] 3 All ER 1007, [2007] 1 WLR 1420, para 31 per Baroness Hale. See also *R (Daly) v Secretary of State for the Home Department* [2001] UKHL 26, [2001] 2 AC 532, para 28 per Lord Steyn and *E v Chief Constable of the Royal Ulster Constabulary* [2008] UKHL 66, [2008] 3 WLR 1208, [2009] 1 All ER 467, para 13 per Lord Carswell.
[106]   See *R (Begum) v Headteacher and Governors of Denbigh High School* [2006] UKHL 15, [2007] 1 AC 100, para 68 per Lord Hoffman.
[107]   Whilst in both *Re P (Children Act: Diplomatic Immunity)* [1998] 1 FLR 624 at 628 and *R v Central Criminal Court ex p S* [1999] 1 FLR 480 at 487 it was held that the courts are not able to rely on the CRC to assist in interpreting the provisions of domestic legislation it is suggested that both these authorities are wrong. They appear to be based on a misapplication of the dicta of Lord Diplock in the case of *British Airways v Laker Airways* [1985] AC 58 in which he held that 'The interpretation of treaties to which the United Kingdom is a party but the terms of which have not either expressly or by reference been incorporated in English domestic law by legislation is not a matter that falls within the interpretative jurisdiction of an English court of law' (see also *R (Corner House Research) v Director of Serious Fraud Office* [2008] UKHL 60, [2008] 4 All ER 927, [2008] 3 WLR 568, paras 43–45 per Lord Bingham). In both *Re P* and *R v Central Criminal Court ex p S* the courts appear to have incorrectly taken Lord Diplock's prohibition on the interpretation of the terms of unincorporated international conventions by domestic courts to be a prohibition also on the use of such conventions as an aid to the interpretation of domestic provisions subject to the principles set out in **3.28** above. See also Section III of the Vienna Convention on the Law of Treaties.
[108]   [1997] 3 WLR 23 at 49F and H.

'The convention has not been incorporated into English law. But it is legitimate in considering the nature of detention during Her Majesty's pleasure (as to which your Lordships are not in agreement) to assume that Parliament has not maintained on the statute book a power capable of being exercised in a manner inconsistent with the treaty obligations of this country. Article 3.1 requires that in the exercise of administrative, as well as court, powers the best interests of the child are a 'primary consideration'. Article 40.1 shows that the child offender is to be treated in a manner which takes into account 'the desirability of promoting the child's reintegration and the child's assuming a constructive role in society. The Secretary of State contends that he is entitled to fix a tariff which will endure throughout the childhood of the offender and that neither in fixing that tariff nor in considering any revision of it will he have any regard to the welfare of the child. Such a policy would infringe the treaty obligations of this country.'

3.34   In the *Venables and Thompson* case the House of Lords, examining the legality of a Government policy concerning children, was prepared both to take into account of the relevant obligations imposed on the Government by the CRC and to tackle the fact that the policy in question was inconsistent with those obligations. The House of Lords took a similar approach in *R (R) v Durham Constabulary*,[109] Baroness Hale observing in relation to the CRC that:

'The Beijing Rules are not binding on member states, but the same principle is reflected in the United Nations Convention on the Rights of the Child 1989 (New York, 20 November 1989; TS 44 (1998); Cm 1976) (UNCRC)), which has been ratified by all but two of the member states of the United Nations. This is not only binding in international law; it is reflected in the interpretation and application by the European Court of Human Rights (the European Court) of the rights guaranteed by the European Convention for the Protection of Human Rights and Fundamental Freedoms 1950 (as set out in Sch 1 to the Human Rights Act 1998): see, for example, *V v UK* (2000) 30 EHRR 121; to that extent at least, therefore, it must be taken into account in the interpretation and application of those rights in our national law.'

3.35   In the same year in *R (Williamson) v Secretary of State for Education*,[110] a case concerning the practice of corporal punishment in Christian independent schools pursuant to the Education Act 1996, s 548(1), Baroness Hale again held that:

'Above all, the state is entitled to give children the protection they are given by an international instrument to which the United Kingdom is a party, the United Nations Convention on the Rights of the Child 1989 (New York, 20 November 1989; TS 44 (1998); Cm 1976) (UN convention).'

3.36   Baroness Hale consolidated this line of reasoning in *Smith v Secretary of State for Work and Pensions*,[111] observing, in a case concerning the child support regulations, that the European Court of Human Rights looks to other international human rights instruments when interpreting the ECHR, and held that:

'Even if an international treaty has not been incorporated into domestic law, our domestic legislation has to be construed as far as possible so as to comply with the international obligations which we have undertaken. When two interpretations of [the Child Support (Maintenance Assessments and Special Cases) Regulations 1992] are possible, the

---

[109]   [2005] UKHL 21, [2005] 2 All ER 369, [2005] 1 WLR 1184.
[110]   [2005] UKHL 15, [2005] 2 AC 246, pp 84–86, [2005] 2 All ER 1.
[111]   [2006] UKHL 35, [2006] 1 WLR 2024, [2006] 3 All ER 907 at [78].

interpretation chosen should be that which better complies with the commitment to the welfare of children which this country has made in ratifying the United Nations Convention on the Rights of the Child.'

3.37 The Supreme Court continues to adopt this approach to the CRC. In *Re D (A Child) (Abduction: Custody Rights)*[112] the Court noted that the principle, enshrined in Art 11(2) of the Brussels II Revised Regulation, that a child is given the opportunity to be heard during proceedings unless it is inappropriate having regard to his or her age or maturity is 'of universal application and consistent with our international obligations under Art 12 of the United Nations Convention on the Rights of the Child'. In *Re B (Children) (Sexual Abuse: Standard of Proof)*[113] Baroness Hale again referred to the Convention in recognising the special protection afforded to the family in a democratic society.[114] In *R (on the application of E) v Office of the Schools Adjudicator*[115] Lord Mance made specific reference to Art 3 of the CRC, noting that 'under Art 3 of the United Nations Convention on the Rights of the Child 1989 it is the best interests of the child which the United Kingdom is obliged to treat as a primary consideration'. Most recently in *ZH v (Tanzania) (FC) v Secretary of State for the Home Department*,[116] the Supreme Court expressly relied on the terms of Art 3(1) of the CRC when considering the question of what weight should be given to the best interests of children who are affected by the decision to remove or deport one or both of their parents from the United Kingdom. Baroness Hale holding that:

> 'For our purposes the most relevant national and international obligation of the United Kingdom is contained in article 3(1) of the UNCRC: "In all actions concerning children, whether undertaken by public or private social welfare institutions, courts of law, administrative authorities or legislative bodies, the best interests of the child shall be a primary consideration." This is a binding obligation in international law, and the spirit, if not the precise language, has also been translated into our national law. Section 11 of the Children Act 2004 places a duty upon a wide range of public bodies to carry out their functions having regard to the need to safeguard and promote the welfare of children. The immigration authorities were at first excused from this duty, because the United Kingdom had entered a general reservation to the UNCRC concerning immigration matters. But that reservation was lifted in 2008 and, as a result, section 55 of the Borders, Citizenship and Immigration Act 2009 now provides that, in relation among other things to immigration, asylum or nationality, the Secretary of State must make arrangements for ensuring that those functions "are discharged having regard to the need to safeguard and promote the welfare of children who are in the United Kingdom" ... Further, it is clear from the recent jurisprudence that the Strasbourg Court will expect national authorities to apply article 3(1) of UNCRC and treat the best interests of a child as "a primary consideration".'

3.38 In interpreting domestic legislation, the House of Lords and the Supreme Court have thus been prepared not only to take account of the relevant provisions of the CRC in interpreting domestic legislation but also to require an interpretation of the domestic law which is consistent with those provisions. Arguably, this approach goes beyond one of interpreting *ambiguous* legislation consistently with binding international

---

[112] [2006] UKHL 51, [2007] 1 AC 619, para 58.

[113] [2008] UKHL 35, [2009] AC 11, para 20.

[114] See also *Re M and another (children) (abduction)* [2007] UKHL 55, [2008] 1 All ER 1157, para 46 per Baroness Hale and *AL (Serbia) v Secretary of State for the Home Department; R (on the application of Rudi) v Secretary of State for the Home Department* [2008] UKHL 42, [2008] 4 All ER 1127 per Baroness Hale.

[115] [2009] UKSC 15, [2010] 1 All ER 319.

[116] [2011] UKSC 4.

conventions to one of interpreting *all* legislation in such a manner.[117] The approach taken to the CRC by the House of Lords and latterly the Supreme Court has been adopted by the lower domestic courts.[118]

(ii)   Application of Common Law

3.39   Whilst the cases comprising the foregoing line of authority arose primarily from disputes concerning legislative interpretation, the House of Lords has also demonstrated willingness to resolves issues arising at common law by reference to the CRC, for example, in respect of issues of private nuisance[119] and in respect of the duty of confidentiality owed by a medical professional to a competent young person.[120]

(iii)   Application of Administrative Discretion

3.40   Applying the general propositions set out above, the domestic application of the CRC also extends to the exercise of administrative discretion.[121] In *D v Home Office*[122] Brooke LJ, examining the concept of *ultra vires* as applied to the actions of officials, held that:[123]

> 'If a court judges that in making his decision to detain, an immigration officer failed to take into account matters of material significance (viz he has overlooked relevant features of internal policy or paid no regard to the fact that the prospective detainee is a child protected by art 37(b) of the United Nations Convention on the Rights of the Child), then he will have

---

[117]   In *R v Secretary of State for the Home Department, ex p Simms* [2000] 2 AC 115 at 130 Lord Steyn said 'But one cannot lose sight that there is at stake a fundamental or basic right, namely the right of a prisoner to seek through oral interviews to persuade a journalist to investigate the safety of the prisoner's conviction and to publicise his findings in an effort to gain access to justice for the prisoner. In these circumstances even in the absence of an ambiguity there comes into play a presumption of general application operating as a constitutional principle as Sir Rupert Cross explained in successive editions of his classic work: Statutory Interpretation (3rd edn, 1995), pp 165–166. This is called 'the principle of legality': 8(2) Halsbury's Laws (4th edn reissue) (1996), para 6' and Lord Hoffman observed at 131–132 that 'the principle of legality means that Parliament must squarely confront what it is doing and accept the political cost. Fundamental rights cannot be overridden by general or ambiguous words. This is because there is too great a risk that the full implications of their unqualified meaning may have passed unnoticed in the democratic process. In the absence of express language or necessary implication to the contrary, the courts therefore presume that even the most general words were intended to be subject to the basic rights of the individual.'

[118]   See for example *R v Accrington Youth Court ex p. Flood* [1998] 1 WLR 156; *Payne v Payne* [2001] EWCA Civ 166, [2001] Fam 473 at 487 (citing the United Nations Declaration on the Rights of the Child 1959); *R (P) v Secretary of State for the Home Department* [2001] EWCA Civ 1151, [2001] 1 WLR 2002 at 2028, para 85; *R (on the application of the Howard League for Penal Reform) v Secretary of State for the Home Department* [2002] EWHC 2497 (Admin), [2002] All ER (D) 465 (Nov), paras 51–52; *R (Kenny) v Leeds Magistrates Court* [2004] 1 All ER 1333, para 41; *Haringey London Borough Council v C, E and Another Intervening* [2006] EWHC 1620 (Fam), [2007] 1 FLR 1035, para 15 and *Webster and others v Governors of the Ridgeway Foundation School* [2009] EWHC 1140 (QB), [2009] All ER (D) 196 (May).

[119]   *Hunter and Others v Canary Wharf Ltd; Hunter and Others v London Docklands Corporation* [1997] AC 655, [1997] 2 All ER 426, [1997] 2 FLR 342, para 120 and 121 where the House of Lords made reference to Art 16 of the CRC. See also *Cheall v Association of Professional, Executive, Clerical and Computer Staff* [1983] 2 AC 180, HL.

[120]   *R (on the application of Axon) v Secretary of State for Health* [2006] EWHC 37 (Admin), [2006] 1 FCR 175 per Silber J at para 64 ('It is appropriate to bear in mind that the Convention attaches great value to the rights of children as I will explain in [144] to [146] below. Furthermore the ratification by the United Kingdom of the United Nations Convention on the Rights of the Child (UNC) in November 1989 was significant as showing a desire to give children greater rights. The Convention and the UNC show why the duty of confidence owed by a medical professional to a competent young person is a high one and which therefore should not be overridden except for a very powerful reason').

[121]   See **3.28** above.

[122]   [2005] EWCA Civ 38, [2006] 1 All ER 183, para 111.

[123]   See also *R (on the Application of MXL and others v Secretary of State for the Home Department* [2010] EWHC 2397 (Admin) at **3.44** below.

strayed outside his wide-ranging powers. As a result he will have had "no power" to authorise the detention in question. This is what the doctrine of ultra vires is all about ... The critical questions we have to answer are whether the provisions of Sch 2 to the 1971 Act place the claimants in some special category in which they are afforded a weaker recognition of their right to liberty, and whether English law, now viewed through the prism of the ECHR, affords an immunity to immigration officers in any way comparable to that afforded to courts of law. If the answers to these questions are that the detentions were unlawful by English law, there will be no defence to the claim for damages for false imprisonment. If, on the other hand, there is no illegality under English law, then we have to determine whether the detention of this family with their two young children was disproportionate in the light not only of Home Office internal policy but also of art 37(b) of the United Nations Convention on the Rights of the Child.'

3.41   The line of authority commencing with *R v Secretary of State for the Home Department, ex p Venables and Thompson*, taken with the principles set out at **3.32–3.46** above, demonstrates clearly that domestic legislation and common law principles should be construed and applied, and administrative decisions concerning children should be taken, in a manner which does not infringe, and which promotes, the rights of children as enshrined in the CRC, notwithstanding that the CRC has not been incorporated into domestic law.[124]

3.42   The proposition that domestic legislation and common law principles should be construed and applied in a manner which does not infringe, and which promotes, the rights of children as enshrined in the CRC now draws added support from the fact that the CRC has begun to be explicitly cited in secondary legislation and statutory guidance. The Children's Commissioner for Wales Appointment Regulations 2001[125] require the Children's Commissioner for Wales to 'have regard' to the CRC in the discharge of his duties. This is the first reference to the CRC in United Kingdom legislation. It has been followed by reference to the CRC in the Immigration (European Economic Area) Regulations 2006.[126] In relation to the formulation of domestic policy and legislation law , in its Tenth Report the Parliamentary Joint Committee on Human Rights stated in respect of the CRC that:[127]

'The Convention should function as the source of a set of child centred considerations to be used as yardsticks by all departments of Government when evaluating legislation and in policy making, whether in respect of the progressive realisation of economic, social and cultural rights or in relation to the guarantees of civil and political rights. We recommend particularly in relation to policy making, that Government demonstrate more conspicuously a recognition of its obligation to implement the rights under the Convention.'

---

[124]   See *Re C (children)(abduction: separate representation of children)* [2008] EWHC 517 (Fam), [2009] 1 FCR 194 in which Ryder J, considering the House of Lords jurisprudence in respect of the joinder of children in Hague Convention proceedings, observed 'It has to be acknowledged that the formulation of the principles to be applied as described by the House of Lords is intended to and does enable these courts to comply with our international obligations. In particular, the direct applicability of Art 11(2) of BIIR, arts 6 and 8 of the European Convention for the Protection of Human Rights and Fundamental Freedoms 1950 (as set out in Part I of Sch 1 to the Human Rights Act 1998) and art 12 of the United Nations Convention on the Rights of the Child (New York, 20 November 1989; TS 44 (1998); Cm 1976).'

[125]   SI 2001/3121.

[126]   SI 2006/1003, r 21(4) ('(4) A relevant decision [ie a decision taken on the grounds of public policy, public security or public health] may not be taken except on imperative grounds of public security in respect of an EEA national who—(a) has resided in the United Kingdom for a continuous period of at least ten years prior to the relevant decision; or (b) is under the age of 18, unless the relevant decision is necessary in his best interests, as provided for in the Convention on the Rights of the Child adopted by the General Assembly of the United Nations on 20 November 1989').

[127]   *Tenth Report of the Parliamentary Joint Committee on Human Rights* HL Paper 117/HC81, para 25.

Gradual movement in this direction is now being seen. On 1 April 2010 the Children's Trust Board (Children and Young People's Plan) (England) Regulations 2010[128] came into force. Regulation 5(1) states that 'When preparing, reviewing or revising a plan, the Board must have regard to the importance of acting, so far as possible, in a way which is compatible with the United Nations Convention on the Rights of the Child'. Reference to the CRC is now also contained in statutory guidance to the UK Border Agency on making arrangements to safeguard and promote the welfare of children issued under s 55 of the Borders, Citizenship and Immigration Act 2009.[129]

The CRC and the ECHR

3.43   The European Court of Human Rights has held that, as an aspect of the issue proportionality, it is appropriate to interpret the ECHR as far as possible in harmony with the other rules of international law, including the CRC.[130] In *Al Adsani v United Kingdom*[131] the European Court of Human Rights said:

> 'The Court must next assess whether the restriction was proportionate to the aim pursued. It recalls that the convention has to be interpreted in the light of the rules set out in the Vienna Convention of 23 May 1969 on the Law of Treaties, and that art 31(3)(c) of that treaty indicates that account is to be taken of "any relevant rules of international law applicable in the relations between the parties". The convention, including art 6, cannot be interpreted in a vacuum. The court must be mindful of the convention's special character as a human rights treaty, and it must also take the relevant rules of international law into account. The convention should so far as possible be interpreted in harmony with other rules of international law of which it forms part, including those relating to the grant of state immunity.'[132]

3.44   As Baroness Hale noted in *R (R) v Durham Constabulary*[133] and *Smith v Secretary of State for Work and Pensions*,[134] the proposition that domestic legislation should be interpreted in a manner which does not infringe, and which promotes, the rights of children as enshrined in binding international conventions, including the CRC,

---

[128]   SI 2010/591.

[129]   See para 2.7 ('In accordance with the UN Convention on the Rights of the Child the best interests of the child will be a primary consideration (although not necessarily the only consideration) when making decisions affecting children'). See *R (on the Application of TS) v Secretary of State for the Home Department* [2010] EWHC 2614 (Admin), [2010] All ER (D) 275 (Oct), para 32 ('It seems to me that the effect of the 2009 guidance is clear. In discharging immigration and/or asylum functions concerning children the best interests of the child will be a primary consideration; it will not be the only consideration but the use of the word primary means that it will always be at least an important consideration. Further, the specific aspects of the UN Convention set out above (Articles 20 and 24) will obviously be important components when the best interests of the child are being considered').

[130]   See *Fogarty v United Kingdom* ECHR Judgement 21 November 2001 (Grand Chamber), paras 35–36; *Sahin v Germany; Sommerfield v Germany* [2003] 2 FLR 671, p 680, para 39; *Pini v Bertani; Manera and Atripaldi v Romania* Application Nos 78028/01 and 78030/01 [2005] 2 FLR 596, para 139; *Mubilanzila Mayeka and Kaniki Mitunga v Belgium* Application No 13178/03 [2007] 1 FLR 1726, para 83; *S and another v The United Kingdom* Application Nos 30562/04 and 30566/04 [2008] All ER (D) 56 (Dec), para 124; *Juppala v Finland* Application No 18620/03 [2009] 1 FLR 617, paras 23 and 41. See also Brownlie, I *Principles of Public International Law* (2008) 7th edn, OUP, p 578 and de Mello QC, R (ed) *Human Rights Act 1998 – A Practical Guide* (2000) Jordan Publishing, p 8.

[131]   (2001) 12 BHRC 88 at 103.

[132]   See also *Neulinger and Shuruk v Switzerland* (2010) Application No 41615/07, para 131 ('The Convention cannot be interpreted in a vacuum but must be interpreted in harmony with the general principles of international law. Account should be taken, as indicated in Article 31(3)(c) of the Vienna Convention on the Law of Treaties of 1969, of 'any relevant rules of international law applicable in the relations between the parties', and in particular the rules concerning the international protection of human rights').

[133]   [2005] UKHL 21, [2005] 2 All ER 369, [2005] 1 WLR 1184.

[134]   [2006] UKHL 35, [2006] 1 WLR 2024, [2006] 3 All ER 907 at [78].

is reinforced within the domestic jurisdiction by the fact that the ECHR itself, in accordance with which domestic law must be interpreted, should be interpreted as far as possible in harmony with the other rules of international law, including the CRC.[135] Thus, in *Dyer (Procurator Fiscal, Linlithgow) v Watson; JK v HM Advocate*[136] the Privy Council held that Art 6 of the ECHR must, when dealing with children, be interpreted in light of the provisions of the CRC. In *R (on the Application of MXL and others v Secretary of State for the Home Department*[137] Blake J held that:

> 'Once Article 8 is engaged, the exercise of judgment in a case falling within its ambit must comply with the principles identified by Strasbourg. In a case where the interests of children are affected this means that other principles of international law binding on contracting states should be complied with. In the case of children those principles are reflected in Article 3(1) of the UN Convention on the Rights of the Child 1989 to which the UK is now a party without any derogation in respect of immigration decision making ... By this route, the principle that the interests of the child are a primary consideration should be applied by public officials (including immigration judges) when making immigration decisions that have an impact on the welfare of children.'

3.45   Through the agency of the Human Rights Act 1998, the jurisprudential space for the European Court of Human Rights to import a more dynamic interpretation of the ECHR in line with the particular entitlements of children under the CRC[138] is also a space within which the domestic courts can apply the entitlements of children under the CRC in their search for compatibility with the ECHR. This allows the CRC to exert further influence over the application and enforcement of children's rights in the domestic courts. Van Bueren argues that 'the use of the UN Convention on the Rights of the Child, when well argued and utilising all the tools of international law, can significantly improve the protection of children's civil rights within the Council of Europe'.[139] As members of the Council of Europe, this observation applies with equal force to the children of the United Kingdom.

3.46   Accordingly, within the domestic jurisdiction the CRC is given persuasive effect both directly, through the line of House of Lords authority culminating in *Smith v Secretary of State for Work and Pensions* and *ZH v (Tanzania) (FC) v Secretary of State for the Home Department*,[140] and indirectly, through its influence on the proper interpretation of the rights enshrined by the ECHR as they relate to children.[141] It

---

[135]   See also *ZH v (Tanzania) (FC) v Secretary of State for the Home Department* [2011] UKSC 4 per Baroness Hale ('Further, it is clear from the recent jurisprudence that the Strasbourg Court will expect national authorities to apply article 3(1) of UNCRC and treat the best interests of a child as "a primary consideration"').

[136]   [2002] UKPC D1, [2004] 1 AC 379, [2002] 4 All ER 1.

[137]   [2010] EWHC 2397 (Admin). See also the decision of Blake J in *R (on the application of Pounder) v HM Coroner for the North and South Districts of Darlington* [2009] EWHC 76 (Admin), [2009] 3 All ER 150 examining the power to use force to maintain good order and discipline in respect of young persons held in secure training centres ('Moreover, it should have been clear to all properly self-directing public authorities that the limits on the use of force on children in custody was driven by the core principles set out in the United Nations Convention on the Rights of the Child, to which effect was designed to be given in United Kingdom law by the Children Act 1989, and which informs any detailed elaboration of human rights relating to children set out in the 1998 Act. Deliberate infliction of pain and force on children as young as 14 could only be justified by very compelling reasons such as those contemplated by the STC rules, rather than generally to support staff orders. The authors of the Smallridge and Williamson report to the ministers were very much mistaken if they believed that the requirements of the United Nations Convention on the Rights of the Child were irrelevant to the limits of restraint that could be used in the United Kingdom').

[138]   Van Bueren, G *Child Rights in Europe* (2007) Council of Europe Publishing, p 19.

[139]   Van Bueren, G *Child Rights in Europe* (2007) Council of Europe Publishing, p 23.

[140]   [2011] UKSC 4.

[141]   See above at **3.43**.

would also appear that public authorities must also have regard to the provisions of the CRC, at least to the extent of determining their obligations under the ECHR.[142]

Domestic Status of other Unincorporated Binding Conventions

3.47 The principles articulated above will apply not only to the CRC but also to the other binding international conventions which touch and concern children's rights, including the Covenant on Civil and Political Rights and the Covenant on Economic, Social and Cultural Rights.

Domestic Status of Non-binding International Agreements[143]

Relevant General Principles of International Law

3.48 A number of non-binding multilateral international agreements are relevant to consideration of the rights of children and to the domestic application and enforcement of them. These include the Universal Declaration of Human Rights 1948, the Declaration of the Protection of Women and Children in Emergency and Armed Conflict and the Declaration on Social and Legal Principles relating to the Welfare and Protection of Children with Special Reference to Foster Placement and Adoption Nationally. These declarations do not constitute binding legal instruments, however, the normative impact of a declaration does not necessarily depend upon its formal legal status.[144] A number of cases demonstrate that tribunals can and will invoke non-binding multilateral agreements and the same can thus influence the operation of the domestic law.[145] The European Court of Human Rights has employed the Universal Declaration of Human Rights as an aid to the interpretation of the ECHR[146] leading Brownlie to observe in relation to the Universal Declaration that 'the indirect legal effect of the Declaration is not to be underestimated ... [t]he Declaration is a good example of an informal prescription given legal significance by the actions of authoritative decision makers'.[147]

Non-binding International Agreements and the Domestic Law

3.49 The domestic courts appear prepared to treat non-binding multilateral international agreements as persuasive authority in the interpretation of the nature and extent of children's rights. For example, in *Payne v Payne*,[148] Thorpe LJ made reference to the United Nations Declaration on the Rights of the Child 1959. In *R (on the application of Baiai and Another) v Secretary of State for the Home Department (Nos 1 and 2); R (on the application of Bigoku and Another) v Secretary of State for the Home Department; R (on the application of Tilki) v Secretary of State for the Home*

---

[142] See *R (on the application of Pounder) v HM Coroner for the North and South Districts of Darlington* [2009] EWHC 76 (Admin), [2009] 3 All ER 150, para 51.

[143] The title 'Declaration' tends to be used to describe instruments that are not legally binding but can, in certain instances, denote a legally binding international agreement. See the discussion as to nomenclature at **3.20–3.21** above.

[144] Brownlie, I *Principles of Public International Law* (2008) 7th edn, OUP, p 559.

[145] See in relation to the Universal Declaration of Human Rights 1948 the *Basic Right to Marry Case* (1971) ILR 72, 295 at 298; *Police v Labat*, ILR 70, 191 at 203; *M v United Nations and Belgium*, ILR 69, 139 at 142–143 and *Beth El Mission v Minister of Social Welfare*, ILR 47, 205.

[146] *Golder case* ILR 57, 201 at 216–217. See also *Fogarty v United Kingdom* (2002) 34 EHRR 302 paras. 35–36.

[147] Brownlie, I *Principles of Public International Law* (2008) 7th edn, OUP, pp 559–560.

[148] [2001] EWCA Civ 166, [2001] Fam 473 at 487.

Department[149] the House of Lords, considering an issue arising under domestic legislation impacting on the right to marry, had regard to the provisions of Art 16 of the Universal Declaration of Human Rights.[150] Likewise, the courts have also made reference to the Declaration on Social and Legal Principles relating to the Welfare and Protection of Children with Special Reference to Foster Placement and Adoption Nationally in domestic cases concerning adoption.[151]

Domestic Status of UN Reporting Procedures, General Comments, Rules and Guidelines

Status of Reporting Procedures

3.50 As outlined in chapter 2, the method of monitoring implementation by States Parties of the CRC pursuant to the obligations contained in Art 4 is by means of States Parties reporting their efforts to this end to the Committee on the Rights of the Child.[152] Other international instruments also incorporate reporting provisions.[153] As already noted, whilst these systems for monitoring compliance may ensure that progress is made towards the implementation and application of children's rights on the macroscopic level within a given jurisdiction,[154] they are of far less value in ensuring the consistent domestic application and enforcement of children's rights in specific cases on a day to day basis.

3.51 However, the outcome of the reporting process, namely the concluding observations on the reports of States Parties compiled by the Committee on the Rights of the Child, can have some influence as persuasive authority in the application of the provisions of the CRC by the courts in individual cases. Baroness Hale in *R (Williamson) v Secretary of State for Education*[155] noted the views of the Committee on the Rights of the Child in respect of corporal punishment as set out in the Committees observations of the United Kingdom's first and second reports on its compliance with the CRC.[156] Her Ladyship characterised those observations as the 'authoritative international view of what the UN convention requires' and posed the question:

> 'How can it not be a legitimate and proportionate limitation on the practice of parents' religious beliefs to heed such a recommendation from the bodies charged with monitoring our compliance with the obligations which we have undertaken to respect the dignity of the individual and the rights of children?'

---

149 [2008] UKHL 53, [2008] 3 All ER 1094.
150 See also *Derbyshire and others v St Helens Metropolitan Borough Council* [2007] UKHL 16, 3 All ER 81, para 1 per Lord Bingham.
151 *R (Charlton Thomson and others) v Secretary of State for Education and Skills* [2005] EHC 1378 (Admin), [2006] 1 FLR 175 per Munby J at para 6. See also *Singh v Entry Clearance Officer New Delhi* [2004] EWCA Civ 1075, [2004] 3 FCR 72 and *R v Secretary of State for Health ex p Luff* [1992] 1 FLR 59.
152 See **2.24–2.26** above.
153 For example Part II of the UN Convention on the Elimination of all forms of Racial Discrimination and Part V of the UN Convention on the Elimination of all forms of Discrimination against Women.
154 For a critique of the reporting mechanism see Fortin, J *Children's Rights and the Developing Law* (2009) 3rd edn, Cambridge, pp 47–50.
155 [2005] UKHL 15, [2005] 2 AC 246, 84–86, [2005] 2 All ER 1.
156 As set out in the Committee's observations of the United Kingdom's first and second reports as to its compliance with the CRC: Committee on the Rights of the Child *Concluding Observations of the Committee on the Rights of the Child: United Kingdom* (1995) CRC/C/15/Add.34 and Committee on the Rights of the Child *Concluding Observations: United Kingdom of Great Britain and Northern Ireland*, (2002) CRC/C/15/Add.188.

Status of General Comments

3.52   The 'General Comments' made by the Committee on the Rights of the Child with a view to promoting the further implementation of the Convention[157] and assisting States Parties with their reporting obligations have also on occasion been given persuasive weight by the Court in cases concerning children. In *R (on the application of C) v Secretary of State for Justice*[158] Lord Justice Buxton, in a case concerning the restraint of children detained in Secure Training Centres, stated as follows:

> 'The [House of Lords and House of Commons Joint Committee on Human Rights] pointed out to the Secretary of State that General Comment 8 of the UN Committee states that deliberate infliction of pain is not permitted as a form of control of juveniles. The Secretary of State denied that he sanctions the use of "violence" against children but, as the JCHR pointed out, that is exactly what PCC, at least in the form of distraction techniques, does provide for. Further, the Secretary of State appeared to suggest to the JCHR that he was bound only by the Convention, and not by the view of the UN Committee. The JCHR, at para 30, stated that it was very disappointed by the Secretary of State's apparent lack of respect for the views of the UN Committee. So am I.[159] And in view of the observations of Baroness Hale of Richmond that must raise serious doubts as to the degree of understanding with which the Secretary of State approaches his obligations under art 3.'

The General Comments made by the Committee on the Rights of the Child have also been cited in other cases in which issues of interpretation concerning children's rights have arisen.[160] The General Comments thus provide a further source of persuasive guidance when considering children's rights in the domestic context.

Status of Standard Rules and Guidelines

3.53   The UN standard minimum rules include the Standard Minimum Rules on the Administration of Juvenile Justice (the 'Beijing Rules'),[161] the UN Rules for the Protection of Juveniles Deprived of their Liberty,[162] and the Standard Rules on the Equalisation of Opportunities for persons with Disabilities.[163] The UN Guidelines

---

[157]   See Newell, P and Hodgkin, R *Implementation Handbook for the Convention on the Rights of the Child* (2008) 3rd edn, UNICEF, pp 640–641.

[158]   [2008] EWCA Civ 882.

[159]   In the Government's response to the report of the House of Lords and House of Commons Joint Committee on Human Rights 11th Report on the Use of Restraint in Secure Training Centres Ministers David Hanson and Beverly Hughes had responded to criticism of the Governments apparent lack of respect for the Committee on the Rights of the Child's interpretation of international law in its general comments as follows 'The UN Committee is not a judicial body and its comments are not, and should not be seen as binding on signatory states' (*Government's Response to the Committees 11th Report* (2008) HL Paper 154/HC 979, p 6).

[160]   See *R v (on the application of A) v Secretary of State for the Home Department* [2008] EWHC 2844 (Admin), [2008] All ER (D) 196 (Nov); *AL (Serbia) v Secretary of State for the Home Department; R (on the application of Rudi) v Secretary of State for the Home Department* [2008] UKHL 42, [2008] 4 All ER 1127, para 32 ('If anything, children who arrived here without a family required more protection than those who arrived with the support of their families. International law recognises that children who are separated from their families need special protection. The United Nations Convention on the Rights of the Child (New York, 20 November 1989; TS 44 (1998); Cm 1976) (UNCRC), Art 2(2) prohibits discrimination on the basis of, among other things, the birth or other status of the child or his family; the UN Committee on the Rights of the Child has emphasised that this prohibits any discrimination on the basis of the status of the child being unaccompanied or separated (General Comment No 6, 2005); UNCRC, Art 22 requires appropriate protection and humanitarian assistance in the enjoyment of applicable rights for all asylum-seeking children, whether or not accompanied').

[161]   See **2.52** above.

[162]   See **2.53** above.

[163]   See **2.54** above.

include the Guidelines on the Prevention of Juvenile Delinquency (the 'Riyadh Guidelines'), the United Nations Children's Fund (UNICEF) 'Paris Commitments to protect children from unlawful recruitment or use by armed forces or armed groups'[164] and the 'Paris Principles: Principles and Guidelines on Children Associated with Armed Forces or Armed Groups'.[165] In *R (R) v Durham Constabulary*[166] Baroness Hale referred to both the 'Beijing Rules and the 'Riyadh Guidelines' in addition to the CRC in considering the lawfulness of warnings given to children under the provisions of the Crime and Disorder Act 1998, ss 65 and 66.

3.54   As to the weight to be attached to the Standard Rules and the Guidelines, in the case of *T v United Kingdom*[167] the European Court of Human Rights did not draw a distinction between the status of a binding treaty in international law (in that case the CRC) and the status of the 'Beijing Rules' when citing those instruments as persuasive guidance on the issues of the age of criminal responsibility and sentences of life imprisonment for children.[168]

DOMESTIC STATUS OF CUSTOMARY INTERNATIONAL LAW AND *JUS COGENS*

General Principles

3.55   The extent to which the rules of customary international law and *jus cogens* norms are enforceable within domestic jurisdictions will depend on whether those jurisdictions adopt a doctrine of incorporation or a doctrine of transformation in relation to the rules of customary international law.[169] The former approach considers rules of customary international law to be part of domestic law save in so far as they are inconsistent with domestic statute or jurisprudence.[170] The latter considers rules of customary international law to be part of domestic law only in so far as those rules have been clearly incorporated by legislation, jurisprudence or established usage.[171] Brownlie comments that the authorities, taken as whole, support the doctrine of incorporation as the preferable approach.[172]

Status of Customary International Law and *Jus Cogens* in Domestic Law

3.56   The domestic courts apply the 'doctrine of incorporation' and the rules of customary international law will be considered as part of domestic law and will be

---

[164]   See **2.55** above.
[165]   See **2.56** above.
[166]   [2005] UKHL 21, [2005] 2 All ER 369, [2005] 1 WLR 1184, para 26.
[167]   Application No 24724/94 (1999), paras 71–75 and 96.
[168]   See Van Bueren, G *Child Rights in Europe* (2000) Council of Europe Publishing, p 22.
[169]   For a full discussion of the competing merits of these two approaches see Brownlie, I Principles of Public International Law (2008) 7th edn, OUP, pp 41–44.
[170]   See for example *Trendex Trading Corporation v Central Bank of Nigeria* [1977] 2 WLR 356, p 365.
[171]   See for example *Regina v Keyn* (1876) 2 Ex D 63, 202,203 and *Chung Chi Cheung v The King* [1939] AC 160 per Lord Atkin, pp 167–168.
[172]   Brownlie, I Principles of Public International Law (2008) 7th edn, OUP, p 44. Although Brownlie also notes at p 48 that 'Legal systems rarely adhere to any very pure form of incorporation'.

enforced as domestic law save insofar as they are inconsistent with domestic legislation or jurisprudence.[173] In *Trendex Trading Corporation v Central Bank of Nigeria* Lord Denning MR concluded:[174]

> 'Seeing that the rules of international law have changed – and do change – and that the courts have given effect to the changes without any Act of Parliament, it follows to my mind inexorably that the rules of international law, as existing from time to time, do form part of our English law.'

Accordingly, where reference is made to a rule of customary international law, a court will be required to satisfy itself of the existence of the rule in international law on the basis of all available evidence, to consider the effect of that rule in the domestic context and to satisfy itself that the application of the rule does not conflict with domestic legislation or jurisprudence.[175] Once the court has determined that there are no bars in domestic law to applying the rules of international law or the provisions of a treaty, those rules are accepted as rules of law and are not required to be established as formal proof.[176] As with the CRC, the domestic impact of customary international law on the rights of children is reinforced by the fact that the ECHR, in accordance with which domestic law must be interpreted, should itself be interpreted as far as possible in harmony with the other rules of international law.[177]

DOMESTIC LAW AND EUROPEAN LEGAL FRAMEWORKS

Status of the European Convention on Human and Fundamental Freedoms 1950

Status in Domestic Law – The Human Rights Act 1998

3.57 The United Kingdom ratified the ECHR in March 1951. The principles of the ECHR are given effect in domestic Law through the Human Rights Act 1998 (hereafter the HRA 1998).[178] The HRA 1998 came into force on 2 October 2000.[179] The Act requires the domestic law, and the actions of public authorities pursuant to that law, to demonstrate compatibility with the principles enshrined in the ECHR[180] as set out in Sch 1 of the Act. It should be noted that Sch 1 of the 1998 Act omits Art 1 of the

---

173 Brownlie, I Principles of Public International Law (2008) 7th edn, OUP, p 41 citing Seidl-Hohenveldern, 12 ICLQ (1963), pp 90–94 and Fawcett, J *The British Commonwealth in International Law* (1963) Steven & Sons, pp 16–74.

174 [1977] 2 WLR 356, p 365. But see also *Regina v Keyn* (1876) 2 Ex D. 63, 202,203 and *Chung Chi Cheung v The King* [1939] AC 160 per Lord Atkin, pp 167–168.

175 Brownlie, I Principles of Public International Law (2008) 7th edn, OUP, p 42.

176 Brownlie, I Principles of Public International Law (2008) 7th edn, OUP, p 40.

177 See *Fogarty v United Kingdom* (2002) 34 EHRR 302, paras 35–36; *Loizidou v Turkey* (1996) 23 EHRR 513, para 43 and Brownlie, I Principles of Public International Law (2008) 7th edn, OUP, p 578.

178 HRA 1998, s 1.

179 Human Rights Act 1998 (Commencement No 2) Order 2000, SI 2000/1851. Once again, it is important to note that the HRA 1998 does not incorporate the ECHR into domestic law. Rather, as noted in *R (Al-Jedda) v Secretary of State for Defence* [2007] UKHL 58, [2008] 1 AC 332, rights under the HRA 1998 'are distinct obligations in the domestic legal systems of the United Kingdom. The Act does not incorporate into our domestic law the international law obligations under the Convention as such.' See also *Re McKerr* [2004] UKHL 12, [2004] 2 All ER, [2004] 1 WLR 807, para 25 per Lord Nicholls. It is important also to remember that the ECHR and the jurisprudence that arise from it are separate and distinct from the law of the European Community and the jurisprudence of the European Court of Justice.

180 HRA 1998, s 1(2).

ECHR (obligation to respect human rights), Art 13 (right to an effective remedy),[181] Arts 15–50 (operational provisions for the European Court) and the remaining protocols, including Art 5 of the Seventh Protocol (equality between spouses). It has been held that, in respect of the domestic application of the ECHR, Arts 6, 8 and 14 apply only to those within the domestic jurisdiction.[182]

Compatibility – Legislation

3.58   Section 3(1) of the HRA 1998 provides that:

> 'So far as it is possible to do so, primary legislation and subordinate legislation must be read and given effect in a way which is compatible with Convention rights.'

Accordingly, the domestic court must look for the interpretation of domestic primary and subordinate legislation that best gives effect to the rights enshrined within the ECHR.[183] The court is only relieved of this statutory duty where it is *impossible* to find such an interpretation.[184] Finding an interpretation which is compatible with the ECHR extends to reading words into a statutory provision or removing individual words from a statutory provision in order to achieve compatibility.[185] The duty to interpret domestic law in a manner compatible with the ECHR has retrospective effect in relation to primary and secondary legislation already enacted at the date on which the HRA 1998 came into force[186] and further means that prior case law interpreting those domestic provisions may have to be revisited in light of that duty; even where to do so would be contrary to the domestic law of precedent.[187] Thus, in so far as the provisions of the ECHR given effect in domestic law confer rights on children, domestic primary legislation and subordinate legislation must be read and given effect in a way which is compatible with those rights.

3.59   In *Re W and B (children) (care plan), Re W (children) (care plan)* Hale LJ observed that 'the 1998 Act was carefully designed to promote the search for compatibility, rather than incompatibility'.[188] However, where the High Court, Court of Appeal, Supreme Court or the Judicial Committee of the Privy Council is satisfied that

---

[181]   Although the domestic courts should have regard to the terms of Art 13 and its associated case law when applying the HRA 1998 (see *R (Al-Skeini) v Secretary of State for Defence* [2007] UKHL 26, [2008] 1 AC 153.

[182]   *Re J (Child Returned Abroad: Human Rights)* [2004] 2 FLR 85, para 34.

[183]   The wording of s 3(1) is sufficiently wide to encompass everyone concerned with interpreting legislation (see *Ghaidan v Godin-Mendoza* [2004] UKHL 30, [2004] 2 AC 557, para 106).

[184]   *Rights Brought Home: The Human Rights Bill* (1997) (Cm 3782), para 2.7. In *Re S (Care Order: Implementation of Care Plan)* [2002] UKHL 10, [2002] 2 AC 291 Lord Nicholls observed at paras 37–40 that s 3 is 'a powerful tool whose use is obligatory. It is not an optional cannon of construction. Nor is its use dependent on the existence of ambiguity. Further, the section applies retrospectively.' However, Lord Nicholls also stated at para 33 in *Ghaidan v Godin-Mendoza* [2004] UKHL 30, [2004] 2 AC 557 that s 3 does not permit the court to 'adopt a meaning inconsistent with a fundamental feature of the legislation.'

[185]   See *Pickstone v Freemans PLC* [1989] 1 AC 66 *O'Brien v Sim-Chem Ltd* [1980] ICR 573 at 580F, which deal with this practice in the context of European Union law, and *McMonagle v Westminster City Council* [1990] 2 AC 716, HL per Lord Bridge at 726E. But see also *De Freitas v Permanent Secretary for the Ministry of Agriculture, Fisheries, Lands and Housing* [1998] 3 WLR 675.

[186]   HRA 1998, s 3(2) and see *Re S (Care Order: Implementation of Care Plan)* [2002] UKHL 10, [2002] 2 AC 291 per Lord Nicholls, paras 37–40.

[187]   However, this does not entitle the court to legislate in place of Parliament (see *Re S (Minors) (Care Order: Implementation of Care Plan), Re W (Minors) (Care Order: Adequacy of Care Plan)* [2002] UKHL 10, [2002] 2 AC 291, [2002] 2 WLR 720, [2002] 2 All ER 192, para 39 per Lord Nicholls). For a comprehensive summary of the principles of interpretation relevant to s 3(1) of the HRA 1998 see de Mello QC, R (ed) *Human Rights Act 1998 – A Practical Guide* (2000) Jordan Publishing, pp 22–26.

[188]   [2001] EWCA Civ 757, para 50, [2001] 2 FCR 450, [2001] 2 FLR 582.

it is not possible to read and give effect to primary or subordinate legislation in a way which is compatible with the ECHR it may make a 'declaration of incompatibility'.[189] Such a declaration neither binds the parties to the proceedings nor changes the law.[190] Instead, s 10 of, and Sch 2 to, the HRA 1998 provide a 'fast track' mechanism by which remedial action can be taken to amend legislation declared incompatible with the ECHR. The Government may intervene in any proceedings in which a declaration of incompatibility is sought.[191]

Compatibility – Public Authorities

3.60   The duty to act in manner compatible with the ECHR extends to the conduct of public authorities. It is unlawful for such authorities to act[192] in a manner incompatible[193] with a Convention right.[194] The duty to act encompasses 'a failure to act'.[195] This duty is qualified in that a public authority may act in a manner incompatible with the ECHR if (a) it is unable to act differently by reason of primary legislation[196] or (b) the relevant primary or subordinate legislation cannot be read or given effect to in a manner compatible with the Convention.[197] A 'public authority' is not definitively defined by the Act[198] but is described as including a court or tribunal and any person certain of whose functions are functions of a public nature[199] save where if the nature of the act done by the person is private.[200] The definition of 'public authority' in the Act is not thus exhaustive and accordingly there is scope for argument as to what or who constitutes a public authority for the purpose of the legislation.[201]

---

[189]   Ibid. s 4(2). See *Wilson v First County Trust Ltd (No 2)* [2003] UKHL 40, [2004] 2 AC 816, [2003] 3 WLR 568, [2003] 4 All ER 97. Whether the incompatibility has to be established by reference to a Convention right under the ECHR binding on the UK in international law or by reference to a right given effect by the HRA 1998 and interpreted by the domestic courts is unclear (see *R v Animal Defenders International) v Secretary of State for Culture, Media and Sport* [2008] UKHL 15, [2008] 1 AC 1312, [2008] 2 WLR 781.

[190]   HRA 1998, s 4(6) although the court may strike down incompatible secondary legislation save where the terms of the primary legislation make that impossible.

[191]   Ibid. s 5(1). See also *Poplar Housing and Regeneration Community Association Ltd v Donoghue* [2001] EWCA Civ 595, [2002] QB 48, paras 15–20 per Lord Woolf CJ and CPR 1998 r 19.4A and associated *Practice Direction*).

[192]   It will generally be necessary to examine the compatibility of the act rather than the legislation under which the act is done (see *Miss Behavin' Ltd v Belfast City Council* [2007] UKHL 19, [2007] 3 All ER 1007, [2007] 1 WLR 1420, paras 84–87 per Lord Neuberger).

[193]   The word 'incompatible' bears its ordinary meaning of 'inconsistent' (see *A-G's Reference (No s of 2001)* [2003] UKHL 68, [2004] 2 AC 72, para 7 per Lord Bingham).

[194]   HRA 1998, s 6(1).

[195]   HRA 1998, s 6(6). See *Re S (Minors) (Care Order: Implementation of Care Plan), Re W (Minors) (Care Order: Adequacy of Care Plan)* [2002] UKHL 10, [2002] 2 AC 291, [2002] 2 WLR 720, [2002] 2 All ER 192, para 45 per Lord Nicholls.

[196]   HRA 1998, s 6(2)(a). See *R (Hooper) v Secretary of State for Work and Pensions* [2005] UKHL 29, [2006] All ER 487, [2005] 1 WLR 1681, para 71 per Lord Hope.

[197]   HRA 1998, s 6(2)(b).

[198]   See *Aston Cantlow and Wilmcote with Billesly Parochial Church Council v Wallbank* [2003] UKHL 37, [2004] 1 AC 546, para 6 per Lord Nicholls. In the White Paper *Rights Brought Home* (Cm 3782, 1997), para 2.2 the term 'public authority' was expressed to include 'central government (including executive agencies); local government; the police; immigration officers; prisons; courts and tribunals themselves; and, to the extent that they are exercising public functions, companies responsible for areas of activity which were previously within the public sector, such as privatised utilities, (in respect of the latter see *YL v Birmingham City Council* [2007] UKHL 27, [2008] 1 AC 95 and the comment in Pannick QC and others, *Human Rights Law and Practice* (1999) Lexis Nexis 3rd edn, pp 63–64).

[199]   HRA 1998, s 6(3). This does not include Parliament or a person exercising functions in connection with proceedings in Parliament (s 6(3)) but did include the House of Lords when acting in its judicial capacity (s 6(4)). Where the act complained of is a judicial act, redress can only be sought by way of an appeal or judicial review (s 9(1)).

[200]   HRA 1998, s 6(5).

[201]   See *R (on the Application of Johnson) v London Borough of Havering and Others;* [2006] EWHC 1714

Within the context of the law relating to children, 'public body' will include, for example, a local authority discharging its child protection duties and an immigration authority dealing with unaccompanied asylum seeking children. Thus in so far as the ECHR confers rights on children, it is unlawful for a public authority to act in a manner that is incompatible with those rights or to fail to act in a manner compatible with them. Section 6 of the HRA 1998 must be interpreted as applying to a UK public authority acting within its jurisdiction under Art 1 of the ECHR outside the UK as well as inside the UK.[202]

Principles of Domestic Application

3.61   In ensuring that legislation is read and given effect in a way which is compatible with the rights of children protected by the ECHR and that public authorities act in a manner compatible with those rights, there are a number of principles of interpretation specific[203] to the HRA 1998 which the domestic courts are bound to observe. Further, the ECHR is an international treaty and therefore it is also subject to the general principles of interpretation set out in the Vienna Convention on the Law of Treaties Arts 31–33.[204]

Purposive Interpretation

3.62   'Convention rights are to be seen as an expression of fundamental principles rather than as a set of mere rules'.[205] As noted in outline in chapter 2, that a broad purposive approach to the interpretation of the ECHR should be adopted has been repeatedly emphasised[206] with a view to the interpretation of the provisions of the Convention in a manner which renders the provisions practical and effective[207] rather than theoretical and illusory.[208] This principle applies equally to the interpretation of the HRA 1998. In approaching the interpretation of the HRA 1998 in this way, regard must be had to its object and purpose, and in particular that it is 'an instrument designed to promote the ideals and values of a democratic society'.[209] Chief Justice Dickson, examining the Canadian Charter of Rights and Freedoms in *R v Oakes*[210] articulated the cardinal elements of a democratic society:

> '... the values and principles essential to a free and democratic society ... embody, to name but a few, respect for the inherent dignity of the human person, commitment to social justice

---

(Admin), [2006] All ER (D) 133 (July) and *R (on the Application of Johnson) v London Borough of Havering and Others; YL v Birmingham City Council and Others* [2007] EWCA Civ 26, [2007] All ER (D) 271 (Jan) and *YL v Birmingham City Council and Others* [2007] UKHL 27, [2007] All ER (D) 207 (Jun).

[202]   *R (Al-Skieni) v Secretary of State for Defence* [2007] UKHL 26, [2008] 1 AC 153, paras 54–59 per Lord Roger.

[203]   See *Ministry of Home Affairs v Fisher* [1980] AC 319, PC at 328G–328H and 329C–329F per Lord Wilberforce who observed that the ECHR is '*sui generis*, calling for principles of interpretation of its own, suitable to its character ... without necessary acceptance of all the presumptions that are relevant to legislation of private law.'

[204]   See **3.22–3.25** above. Note also that Art 60 of the ECHR provides that 'Nothing in this Convention shall be construed as limiting or derogating from any of the human rights and fundamental freedoms which may be ensured under the laws of any High Contracting Party or under any other agreement to which it is a Party.'

[205]   *Wislon v First Country Trust Ltd* [2003] UKHL 40, [2004] 1 AC 816, para 181 per Lord Rodger.

[206]   *Golder v UK* (1975) 1 EHRR 524.

[207]   *Loizidou v Turkey* (1995) 20 EHRR 99, para 72.

[208]   *Airey v Ireland* (1979) 2 EHRR 305, para 24.

[209]   *Kjeldsen, Busk, Madsen and Pedesen v Denmark* (1976) 1 EHRR 711, para 53.

[210]   (1986) 26 DLR (4th) 200 at 255.

and equality, accommodation of a wide variety of beliefs, respect for cultural and group identity, and faith in social and political institutions, which enhance the participation of individuals and groups within society.'

In the case of *Klass v Germany*[211] the European Court of Human Rights, considering the ideals and values of a democratic society added the rule of law to those cardinal elements of democracy outlined by Chief Justice Dickson:[212]

> 'One of the fundamental principles of society is the rule of law, which is expressly referred to in the preamble to the Convention. The rule of law implies, inter alia, that an interference by the executive authorities should be subject of effective control which should normally be assured by the judiciary, at least in the last resort, judicial control offering the best guarantees of independence, impartiality and proper procedure.'

3.63   As the European Court pointed out in *Tyrer v UK*[213] the ECHR is a 'living instrument'. Thus to achieve a purposive interpretation of the ECHR that interpretation must itself be evolutionary in nature, with its interpretation evolving in the light of present-day conditions. Again, the same principle applies to the HRA 1998. Purposive interpretation therefore 'require[s] the courts to adopt a non-rigid and generous approach' in which the court 'looks at the substance and reality of what was involved and should not be over-concerned with what are no more than technicalities'.[214] Courts should approach issues with 'realism and good sense, and kept in proportion'.[215] In particular, the provisions of the HRA 1998 'call for a generous interpretation, avoiding what has been called "the austerity of tabulated legalism", suitable to give individuals the full measure of the fundamental rights and freedoms referred to'.[216] Thus the rights to which the HRA 1998 gives effect should be interpreted 'autonomously, purposively and giving primacy to substance'.[217] However, it is also important to note that the principle of purposive interpretation is not without boundaries. In *Johntson v Ireland* the European Court of Human Rights held in a case concerning the existence or otherwise of a 'right to divorce', stated that it would not 'by means of an evolutive interpretation, derive ... a right that was not included therein at the outset' noting that 'This is particularly so ... where the omission was deliberate'.[218]

3.64   In respect of the rights of children one of the most important outcomes of the purposive and evolutionary interpretation of the ECHR and the HRA 1998 is the recognition of the positive obligations inherent in the rights enshrined in the Convention and necessary to give full effect to those rights. When considering whether a right

---

[211]   (1978) 2 EHRR 214, para 55.

[212]   See also *United States, Appellants v Cinque and others, Africans, captured in the Schooner Amistad* 40 US (15 Pet) 518 (1841) in which John Quincy Adams famously submitted 'When I say I derive consolation from the consideration that I stand before a court of justice, I am obliged to take this ground, because, as I shall show, another Department of the Government of the United States has taken, with reference to this case, the ground of utter injustice, and these individuals for whom I appear, stand before this court, awaiting their fate from its decision, under the array of the whole Executive power of this nation against them.'

[213]   (1978) 2 EHRR 1, para 31.

[214]   *Huntley v A-G for Jamaica* [1995] 2 AC 1 per Lord Woolf at 12G–12H.

[215]   *A-G for Hong Kong v Lee Kwong-kut* [1993] AC 951, PC per Lord Woolf at 975B–975C.

[216]   *Minister for Home Affairs v Fisher* [1980] AC 319 PC at 328 G–328H per Lord Wilberforce.

[217]   *R (Uttley) v Secretary of State for the Home Department* [2004] UKHL 38, [2004] 4 All ER 1, [2004] 1 WLR 2278, para 64 per Lord Carswell. But see also *Matadeen v Pointu* [1999] 1 AC 98, PC at 108E–108F per Lord Hoffman.

[218]   (1986) 9 EHRR 203, ECtHR at 219, para 53. See also *Pretty v United Kingdom* (2002) 35 EHRR 1, para 39; *N v Secretary of State for the Home Department* [2005] UKHL 31, [2005] 2 AC 296, para 21 per Lord Hope and *R (Gentle) v Prime Minister* [2008] UKHL 20, [2008] 3 All ER 1, para 9 per Lord Bingham.

conferred by the HRA 1998 has been breached, it is important to remember that such a breach can arise not only by reason of an action but also by reason of a failure to take necessary action.

Balancing Rights

3.65   Whilst the ECHR does not confer primacy on any particular right or group of rights, practical realities mean that courts and public authorities considering its application or enforcement are often required to navigate between competing rights and to carefully balance the same in reaching a determination. The courts must, in carrying out this balancing exercise have regard not only to the rights of individuals but also to the rights of communities.[219] At the same time, the courts must acknowledge that 'democracy does not simply mean that the views of a majority always prevail' and that the balance of rights must ensure 'the fair and proper treatment of minorities and avoid the abuse of a dominant position'.[220] Art 10 of the ECHR concerning freedom of expression is the only right which expressly 'carries with it duties and responsibilities'. However, Lord Hope noted in *R (McCann) v Manchester Crown Court*[221] that responsibility 'is a theme which runs right through the Convention. Respect for the rights of others is the price that we must pay for the rights and freedoms that it guarantees'.

3.66   The starting point in balancing rights is the recognition that some rights under the ECHR are absolute and some are qualified.[222] The absolute rights comprise Arts 2 (right to life), 3 (prohibition on torture), 4(1) (prohibition on slavery) and 7 (prohibition on punishment without law). The qualified rights are those comprising Arts 8 (right to respect for family life and privacy), 9 (freedom of thought, conscience and religion), 10 (freedom of expression) and 11 (freedom of assembly). An absolute right may not be breached under any circumstances or otherwise restricted to accommodate a qualified right.[223] A qualified right may be breached in circumstances provided for in the qualifying provisions of that right.[224]

3.67   In respect of two of the rights enshrined in the ECHR, the HRA 1998 prescribes specific matters which the court *must* place in the balance when considering whether to grant relief which may affect those rights. In respect of the right to freedom of expression,[225] the court must have regard to 'the particular importance of the

---

[219]   *Brown v Stott (Procurator Fiscal, Dunfermline)* [2003] 1 AC 681 PC at 707 per Lord Steyn.

[220]   *Chassagnou v France* (1999) 29 EHRR 615, ECtHR, para 112.

[221]   [2002] UKHL 39, [2003] 1 AC 787, para 41. See also Art 29(1) of the Universal Declaration of Human Rights.

[222]   There is also a third group of rights which are best described as 'prescribed rights' which have affect only in carefully prescribed circumstances, these being Art 4(2) (forced labour), Art 5 (liberty and security of the person) and Art 6 (fair trial).

[223]   *Chahal v UK* (1997) 23 EHRR 413. However, the requirement to strike a fair balance may also be of relevance in respect of absolute rights in respect of the positive obligations often implied into those rights. See *In re Officer L* [2007] UKHL 36, [2007] NI 277, [2007] 4 All ER 965, [2007] 1 WLR 2135, para 21 per Lord Carswell and *E v Chief Constable of the Royal Ulster Constabulary* [2008] UKHL 66, [2008] 3 WLR 1208, [2009] 1 All ER 467, para 45 per Lord Carswell.

[224]   For example, the right to respect for private and family life under Art 8 may be breached in circumstances where that breach is 'in accordance with the law and is necessary in a democratic society in the interests of national security, public safety or the economic wellbeing of the country, for the prevention of disorder or crime, for the protection of health or morals, or the protection of the rights and freedoms of others.' See below at **8.177**.

[225]   ECHR, Art 10. In *Handyside v UK* 1 EHRR (1976) 737 the European Court of Human Rights said, 'Freedom of expression constitutes one of the essential foundations of a (democratic) society, one of the basic conditions for its progress and for the development of every man.' See **11.91** below.

Convention right to freedom of expression'.[226] In respect of the right to freedom of thought, conscience and religion,[227] the HRA 1998 requires the court to have regard to the importance of this right.[228]

3.68 The act of balancing rights under the ECHR is particularly relevant to cases concerning the rights of children by reason of the potential conflict between the domestic principle of the paramountcy of the child's interests[229] and the fact that the ECHR does not provide that the rights of children under the ECHR are paramount as against the rights of others. In *Yousef v The Netherlands*[230] the European Court of Human Rights appeared to settle this issue when it held:

> '... that in judicial decisions where the rights under Article 8 of parents and those of the child are at stake, the child's rights must be the paramount consideration. If any balancing of interests is necessary, the interests of the child must prevail ...'

From the domestic perspective, Thorpe LJ observed in *Payne v Payne*[231] that:

> '... whilst the advent of the 1998 Act requires revision of the judicial approach to conclusion, as a safeguard to an inadequate perception and application for a father's rights under Articles 6 and 8, it requires no re-evaluation of the judge's primary task to evaluate and uphold the welfare of the child as the paramount consideration, despite its inevitable conflict with adult rights.'

In *Re L (A Child) (Contact: Domestic Violence), Re V (A Child), Re M (A Child), Re H (Children)*[232] Butler-Sloss P likewise expressed no difficulty with the proposition that the principle that the child's interests remained paramount was compatible with Art 8(2) of the ECHR. However, significant doubts remain as to whether the confidence expressed in the foregoing authorities has a solid foundation. These doubts will be examined in detail in chapter 4 when dealing with the subject of the child's best interests in the context of children's rights.[233]

Proportionality

3.69 The doctrine of proportionality requires that any limitation imposed on a right conferred by the ECHR be 'proportionate to the legitimate aim pursued' by that limitation.[234] Accordingly, there must be 'a reasonable relationship between the means employed and the legitimate objective pursued by the contested limitation',[235] a concept expressed by the House of Lords as requiring that 'the means used to impair the right or freedom are no more than is necessary to accomplish the objective'.[236] Whilst the application of the principle of proportionality and the domestic principle of *Wednesbury* reasonableness may in some cases produce the same result, the role of the

---

[226] HRA 1998, s 12(4).
[227] ECHR, Art 9. See chapter 10 below.
[228] HRA 1998, s 13(1).
[229] CA 1989, s 1(1). The issue of the 'paramountcy principle' is dealt with in detail at **4.145** and **4.169** below.
[230] (2002) 36 EHRR 20, [2002] 3 FCR 577, [2003] 1 FLR 210, para 73. See also the decision of the European Commission in *Hendricks v Netherlands* (1982) 5 EHRR 223 and *Johansen v Norway* (1996) 23 EHRR 33.
[231] [2001] EWCA Civ 166, para 57, [2001] 1 FCR 425, [2001] 1 FLR 1052.
[232] [2001] Fam 260, [2000] 4 All ER 609.
[233] See **4.145** and **4.169** below.
[234] *Handyside v United Kingdom* (1976) 1 EHRR 737 at 374, ECT HR, para 49. See also *Ashingdane v UK* (1985) 7 EHRR 528 and *James v UK* (1986) 8 EHRR 123.
[235] *Fayed v United Kingdom* (1994) 18 EHRR 393 at 432, ECtHR, para 71.
[236] *R v Secretary of State for the Home Department ex p Daly* [2001] UKHL 26, [2001] 2 WLR 1622, [2001] UKHRR 887 per Lord Steyn.

court in applying the principle of proportionality is quite different from the role of the court in an ordinary judicial review of administrative action.[237] By contrast to judicial review, in considering proportionality, the court must focus on the decision itself, not the decision making process.[238]

3.70 In the case of *Samaroo v Secretary of State for the Home Department*[239] the Court of Appeal held that in determining whether a particular limiting course of action satisfies the principle of proportionality, two separate questions must be asked. First, can the objective of the step be achieved by a means which are less interfering of an individual's rights? Second, assuming that the step taken to achieve the legitimate aim is necessary in the sense that it is the least interfering of the Convention rights that can be devised to achieve that aim, does taking that step have an excessive or disproportionate effect upon the interests of the affected persons?[240] In *Fogarty v United Kingdom*[241] the Grand Chamber held that consideration of the principle of proportionality cannot take place in a vacuum but rather it is appropriate to interpret the ECHR as far as possible in harmony with other rules of international law of which it forms part. This will include the CRC.[242]

3.71 The principle of proportionality has particular significance when considering those rights in respect of which the ECHR expressly permits restrictions which are 'in accordance with the law' or 'prescribed by law'[243] and 'necessary in a democratic society', proportionality being a crucial element of 'necessity'.[244] These are the so-called qualified rights.[245]

'In Accordance with the Law' or 'Prescribed by Law'

3.72 In considering whether a particular restriction to a qualified right can be said to be in accordance with the law or prescribed by law, the restriction must not only have some basis in domestic law[246] but that law itself must be compatible with the rule of law in order that there can be 'a measure of legal protection in domestic law against arbitrary interference by public authorities with the rights safeguarded' by the ECHR.[247] This requires that the law in question is (a) adequately accessible and (b) formulated with sufficient precision to enable the citizen to regulate his conduct in accordance with the law such that he can foresee, to a degree that is reasonable in the circumstances, the

---

[237] *Miss Behavin' Ltd v Belfast City Council* [2007] UKHL 19, [2007] 3 All ER 1007, [2007] 1 WLR 1420, para 31 per Baroness Hale. See also *R (Daly) v Secretary of State for the Home Department* [2001] UKHL 26, [2001] 2 AC 532, para 28 per Lord Steyn and *E v Chief Constable of the Royal Ulster Constabulary* [2008] UKHL 66, [2008] 3 WLR 1208, [2009] 1 All ER 467, para 13 per Lord Carswell.

[238] See *R (Begum) v Headteacher and Governors of Denbigh High School* [2006] UKHL 15, [2007] 1 AC 100, para 68 per Lord Hoffman.

[239] [2001] EWCA Civ 1139, [2001] UKHRR 1150.

[240] Hershman & McFarlane, *Children Law and Practice* Jordan Publishing, para K[671]–[673] citing *Samaroo v Secretary of State for the Home Department* [2001] EWCA Civ 1139, para 25, [2001] UKHRR 1150.

[241] (2002) 34 EHRR 302.

[242] See **3.43** above.

[243] No distinction is made between these two formulations (*Silver v United Kingdom* (1983) 5 EHRR 347, para 85).

[244] Swindells, H and others *Family Law and the Human Rights Act 1998* (1999) Jordan Publishing, p 7.

[245] See **3.6** above.

[246] *Silver v United Kingdom* (1983) 5 EHRR 347, para 85 and *Sunday Times v United Kingdom* (1984) 7 EHRR 245, para 47.

[247] *Malone v United Kingdom* (1984) 7 EHRR 14, para 67.

consequences which a given action may entail.[248] Thus, where the law provides for the exercise of discretion, there must be an indication of its scope.[249]

'Necessary in a Democratic Society'

3.73 The European Court of Human Rights has held that the word 'necessary' in the context of a qualified right 'is not synonymous with "indispensable", neither has it the flexibility of such expressions as 'admissible', 'ordinary', 'useful', 'reasonable' or 'desirable' and that it implies the existence of a 'pressing social need'.[250] The same court in *Chassagnou v France*[251] observed that in assessing the necessity of a given restriction:

> '... a number of principles must be observed. The term 'necessary' does not have the flexibility of such expressions as 'useful' or 'desirable'. In addition, pluralism, tolerance and broadmindedness are hallmarks of a 'democratic society'. Although individual interests must on occasion be subordinated to those of a group, democracy does not simply mean that the views of the majority must always prevail: a balance must be achieved which ensures a fair and proper treatment of minorities and avoids any abuse of a dominant position. Lastly, any restriction imposed on a Convention right must be proportionate to the legitimate aim pursued.'

As noted, proportionality is a crucial element of necessity and a particular restriction on a qualified Convention right will not be considered necessary where a more proportionate restriction can be arrived at. Thus, in *Sunday Times v United Kingdom*[252] the European Court of Human Rights held that, in considering whether a particular restriction is necessary, the court must determine:

> 'whether the interference complained of corresponded to a pressing social need, whether it was proportionate to the legitimate aim pursued [and] whether the reasons given by the national authorities to justify it are relevant and sufficient ...'

The existence and extent of procedural safeguards may be relevant to whether the test of necessity is satisfied.[253] The degree of 'necessity' required to justify a restriction on a right will vary with the gravity of the restriction proposed.[254] The question of necessity may be evaluated by reference to the interests of, or the impact upon, the class of relevant persons even where the legislative aim applies harshly to the individual facts of the complainant's case.[255]

---

[248] *Sunday Times v United Kingdom* (1979) 2 EHRR 245, para 49. See also *Silver v United Kingdom* (1983) 5 EHRR 374, *Malone v United Kingdom* (1984) 7 EHRR 14 and *James v United Kingdom* (1986) 8 EHRR 123.

[249] *Sunday Times v United Kingdom* (1979) 2 EHRR 245, para 49. See also *Silver v United Kingdom* (1983) 5 EHRR 374, *Malone v United Kingdom* (1984) 7 EHRR 14 and *James v United Kingdom* (1986) 8 EHRR 123. Although the formulation of a law can scarcely be expected to cover every eventuality (see *Olsson v Sweden (No 1)* (1989) 11 EHRR 259).

[250] *Sunday Times v United Kingdom* (1979) 2 EHRR 245, para 59.

[251] (2000) 29 EHRR 615.

[252] (1979) 2 EHRR 245

[253] See *Chapman v United Kingdom* (2001) 33 EHRR 399, paras 92 and 110 and *Jokela v Finland* (2003) 37 EHRR 581, para 45.

[254] See *Johansen v Norway* (1997) 23 EHRR 33 (permanent removal of child from family can only be justified in 'exceptional circumstances') and *Smith and Grady v United Kingdom* (2000) 29 EHRR 493 (restrictions that concern 'the most intimate part of an individual's private life' require 'particularly serious reasons' for the restriction). See also *Ciliz v The Netherlands* [2000] 2 FLR 469.

[255] See *Pretty v United Kingdom* (2002) 35 EHRR 1, para 74.

Serving a Legitimate Purpose

3.74   Article 18 of the ECHR provides that:[256]

> 'The restrictions permitted under this Convention to the said rights and freedoms shall not be applied for any purpose other than those for which they have been prescribed.'

A restriction to a qualified right may be said to be applied for a 'legitimate purpose' pursuant to Art 18 where such a restriction is necessary in a democratic society (a) in the interests of national security, public safety or the economic wellbeing of the country, (b) for the prevention of disorder or crime, (c) for the protection of health or morals or (d) for the protection of the rights and freedoms of others.[257] It should be noted that not all those matters listed as constituting a 'legitimate purpose' appear in each of Arts 8–11. Article 10 also includes the protection of the reputation or rights of others, the prevention of disclosure of information received in confidence and maintaining the authority of the judiciary as matters constituting 'legitimate purpose'.

Margin of Appreciation

3.75   The doctrine of 'margin of appreciation' confers upon a State party to the Convention a measure of discretion when taking a decision involving ECHR rights, subject to the ultimate supervision of the Convention institutions.[258] The basis for this doctrine is the intention that 'the machinery of protection established by the Convention is subsidiary to the national systems of safeguarding human rights'.[259] The European Court of Human Rights recognises that 'By reason of their direct and continuous contact with the vital forces of their countries, the national authorities are in principal better placed than the international court to evaluate local needs and conditions'.[260] The European Court of Human Rights is however empowered to give the final ruling on whether a restriction is reconcilable with the right in question and 'the domestic margin of appreciation thus goes hand in hand with a European supervision'.[261] When considering the 'margin of appreciation', the approach of the European Court of Human Rights to the application of the doctrine will vary according to context. Relevant factors will include the nature of the Convention right in issue, its importance for the individual and the nature of the activities concerned'.[262]

3.76   It is important to remember that the doctrine of 'margin of appreciation' has no application where a *domestic* court is considering Convention rights under the Sch 1 of the HRA 1998. The role of the domestic courts is to determine the compatibility or otherwise of domestic legislation and administrative action with the ECHR. This is different to the supervisory role of the European Court of Human Rights.[263] The domestic court may however employ a similar concept to the doctrine of 'margin of appreciation', often labeled the 'discretionary area of judgment', whereby the court affords to an inferior decision making body its own margin of appreciation in that

---

[256]   Articles 8–11 each prescribe the legitimate purposes for which a restriction to a right may be applied.
[257]   Articles 8–11.
[258]   Swindells, H and others, *Family Law and the Human Rights Act 1998,* (1999) Family Law, p 7 and see *Handyside v United Kingdom* (1976) 1 EHRR 737, para 48 and *Times Newspapers Ltd (Nos 1 and 2) v UK* (2009) *The Times,* 11 March 2009.
[259]   *Handyside v United Kingdom* (1976) 1 EHRR 737, para 49.
[260]   *Buckley v United Kingdom* (1996) 23 EHRR 101, para 75.
[261]   *Handyside v United Kingdom* (1976) 1 EHRR 737, para 49.
[262]   *Buckley v United Kingdom* (1996) 23 EHRR 101, para 74 and see *Johansen v Norway* 23 (1997) EHRR 33, para 64.
[263]   Hershman, D and McFarlane, A *Children Law and Practice* Jordan Publishing, para K, [586]–[588].

body's decisions, the extent of that 'discretionary area of judgment' varying with the circumstances of the particular case.[264] The Court must still however comply with its responsibility to give its own judgment in accordance with the provisions of the ECHR.[265]

Principle of Non-discrimination

3.77 Any restriction imposed on a right conferred by the ECHR must not be discriminatory. Article 14 of the ECHR provides that 'The enjoyment of the rights and freedoms set forth in this Convention shall be secured without discrimination on any ground such as sex, race, colour, language, religion, political or other opinion, national or social origin, association with a national minority, property, birth or other status'. There will be discrimination where a distinction is made which 'has no objective or reasonable justification' and the prohibition against discrimination will be breached where it is established that there is 'no reasonable relationship of proportionality between the means employed and the aim sought to be pursued'.[266] The prohibition on discrimination is covered in detail in chapter 4.

Overlap with CRC – Convergence and Children's Rights

3.78 As already outlined above, as a matter of general principle, the European Court of Human Rights has held that, as an aspect of the issue proportionality, it is appropriate to interpret the ECHR as far as possible in harmony with the other rules of international law.[267] Within this context, reference to the CRC has increasingly been made in the jurisprudence arising under the ECHR.[268] As already noted in chapter 2, in the case of *Sahin v Germany; Sommerfield v Germany*[269] the European Court of Human Rights stated that 'The human rights of children and the standards to which all governments must aspire in realising these rights for all children are set out in the United Nations Convention on the Rights of the Child 1989'. In *Pini v Bertani; Manera and Atripaldi v Romania*[270] the European Court of Human Rights held that:[271]

> 'With regard in particular to the obligations imposed by Art 8 of the Convention on the Contracting States in the field of adoption, and to the effects of adoption on the relationship

---

[264] Pannick QC and others, *Human Rights Law and Practice* (1999) Lexis Nexis 1st edn, pp 73–76 (approved in *R v DPP, ex p Kebilene* [2000] 2 AC 326, HL at 380E–381E per Lord Hope) and see *Libman v AG of Quebec* (1998) 3 BHRC 269 at 289, para 59; *R v Ministry of Defence ex p Smith* [1996] QB 517 at 554E–554F per Sir Thomas Bingham MR; *A-G of Hong Kong v Lee Kwong-kut* [1993] AC 951 at 975C–975D per Lord Woolf; *A v Secretary of State for the Home Department* [2004] UKHL 56, [2005] 2 AC 68, para 29 per Lord Bingham and *R (Gillan) v Metropolitan Police Commissioner* [2006] UKHL 12, [2006] 2 AC 307, para 17 per Lord Bingham. For a detailed summary of the factors to be taken into account when considering what discretionary area of judgment to accord see Pannick QC and others, *Human Rights Law and Practice* (1999) Lexis Nexis 3rd edn, pp 125–129.

[265] Pannick QC and others, *Human Rights Law and Practice* (1999) Lexis Nexis 1st edn, p 76 and see *R (ProLife Alliance) v BBC* [2003] UKHL 23, [2004] 1 AC 185.

[266] *Belgian Linguistic Case (No 2)* 1 EHRR 252, para 10.

[267] See *Fogarty v United Kingdom* (2002) 34 EHRR 302, paras 35–36; *Al Adsani v United Kingdom* (2001) 34 EHRR 273, para 55 and Brownlie, I Principles of Public International Law (2008) 7th edn, OUP, p 578.

[268] See for example *Costello-Roberts v United Kingdom* [1994] 1 FCR 65, para 35, *A v United Kingdom (Human Rights: Punishment of Child)* [1998] 2 FLR 959, para 22 and *V v United Kingdom* (1999) 30 EHRR 121, paras 73, 76 and 97.

[269] [2003] 2 FLR 671, p 680, para 39. See also *Juppala v Finland* [2009] 1 FLR 617, paras 23 and 41.

[270] Application Nos 78028/01 and 78030/01 [2005] 2 FLR 596, para 139.

[271] See also *X, Y and Z v United Kingdom* [1997] 3 FCR 341 in which the concurring opinion of Judge Pettiti criticises the Court for not referring to, and considering the direct effect of, the CRC in a case involving an alleged breach of Art 8 of the ECHR (see the comment on this case in Van Bueren, G *Child Rights in Europe* (2007) Council of Europe Publishing, p 21–22).

between adopters and those being adopted, they must be interpreted in the light of the Hague Convention on Protection of Children and Co-operation in respect of Intercountry Adoption 1993, the United Nations Convention on the Rights of the Child 1989 and the European Convention on the Adoption of Children 1967.'

This approach of using the CRC to assist in the interpretation of the ECHR in cases involving children was further demonstrated in the case of *S and another v The United Kingdom*[272] where the European Court of Human Rights, having noted the terms of Art 40 of the CRC stated that it had drawn on its provisions in emphasising the special position of children in the criminal justice system and the need for the protection of their privacy at criminal trials.

3.79　As Van Bueren has noted:[273]

'as the European Convention is a living instrument and many of its rights are framed in identical terms to the Convention on the Rights of the Child, this creates jurisprudential space for the European Court of Human Rights to import a more dynamic interpretation, in line with the particular entitlements of children.'

By way of example, in *Mubilanzila Mayeka and Kaniki Mitunga v Belgium*[274] the European Court of Human Rights considered that the fact there were measures the Belgian Government could have taken that would have been more conducive to the primary interest of the child as guaranteed by Art 3 of the CRC was relevant to the Court's conclusion that there had been a violation of Art 8 of the ECHR. This case is particularly interesting because the European Court appears to come close to importing from the CRC the 'welfare' or 'best interests' principle that is conspicuously absent from the ECHR.[275]

Domestic Proceedings for Breach

Jurisdiction[276]

3.80　Where a public authority has acted in a manner incompatible with the rights of a child under the ECHR, s 7(1) of the HRA 1998 provides for two methods of redress for the victim[277] of that unlawful act. First, a freestanding application for relief may be made under the HRA 1998 to the appropriate court or tribunal.[278] The domestic courts do not expect freestanding proceedings under the HRA 1998 to be launched until all other remedial routes have been explored.[279] Where such applications relate to the rights of children they should be heard in the Family Division, if possible by a judge with experience of sitting in the Administrative Court.[280] Second, where proceedings are already ongoing the child affected may rely on the Convention right or rights concerned

---

272　[2008] All ER (D) 56 (Dec), para 124. A case concerning the retention of a fingerprint and DNA samples following acquittal of criminal charges. See also *Keegan v Ireland* [1994] 3 FCR 165, para 50 for an earlier example.

273　Van Bueren, G *Child Rights in Europe* (2007) Council of Europe Publishing, p 19.

274　[2007] 1 FLR 1726, para 83.

275　See above at **4.142 et seq**. See also *C v Finland* [2006] 2 FLR 597, para 52 and *R (on the application of E) v Office of the Schools Adjudicator (Governing Body of JFS and others)* [2009] UKSC 15, para 90.

276　See *Practice Direction: Human Rights Act* 1998 (24 July 2000) [2000] 2 FLR 429.

277　See **3.81** below.

278　HRA 1998, s 7(1)(a) and see CPR 1998, Part 8.

279　*Re S (Minors) (Care Order: Implementation of Care Plan); Re W (Minors) (Care Order: Adequacy of Care Plan)* [2002] UKHL 10, [2002] 2 AC 291, [2002] 1 FLR 815, para 62.

280　*C v Bury Metropolitan Borough Council* [2002] EWHC 1438 (Fam), [2002] 2 FLR 868, para 55.

within those proceedings.[281] Where the act complained of is a judicial act however, redress can only be sought by way of an appeal or judicial review.[282] If the court or tribunal finds that the act (or proposed act) complained of is (or would be) unlawful it may grant such relief or remedy or make such order within its powers as it considers appropriate.[283] The burden is on the complainant to show that there has been a breach of their rights under the ECHR and, where the right is a qualified right, it is for the respondent to show that the breach falls within any of the qualifications specific to that right.

3.81   Pursuant to s 7(1) of the HRA 1998 relief is only available where a child is or would be the 'victim' of the unlawful act complained of. Pursuant to s 7(7) of the HRA 1998 a child will be a 'victim' of the unlawful act complained of where that child would be a victim for the purposes of Art 34 of the ECHR if proceedings were brought in the European Court of Human Rights, namely that he or she is directly affected by the act or omission complained of. This includes children at *risk* of being affected by the act or omission.[284]

Procedure – Freestanding Claim

3.82   A claim under s 7(1)(a) of the HRA 1998 in respect of a judicial act may only be brought in the High Court and must be commenced in the administrative court as an application for judicial review[285] or by way of appeal.[286] Any other claim under s 7(1)(a) may be brought in any court[287] save where a claim of incompatibility is being made.[288] Such a claim should be commenced by issuing proceedings under the CPR 1998, Part 8 procedure using Form N208. The limitation period for freestanding proceedings is within one year beginning with the date on which the act complained of took place, or such longer period as the court or tribunal considers equitable having regard to all the circumstances.[289] There must be no other available remedy. The Claim Form must state the following: that Part 8 applies, the question which the Claimant wants the Court to decide or the remedy sought and the legal basis for the same.[290] Where the claim includes a claim for damages arising out of a judicial act, notice must be given to the

---

281   HRA 1998, s 7(1)(b). It is not necessary to transfer proceedings in which such a claim is relied on to the High Court unless transfer is merited in any event (see *Re L (Care Proceedings: Human Rights Claims)* [2003] EWHC 665 (Fam), [2003] 2 FLR 160, para 33. See also *Re V (A Child) (Care Proceedings: Human Rights Claims)* [2004] EWCA Civ 54, [2004] 1 FLR 944.

282   HRA 1998, s 9(1). See CPR 1998, r 7.11.

283   HRA 1998, s 8(1). Damages, a claim for which must be pleaded in accordance with CPR 1998, r 19.4A(3)), may only be awarded where (a) the court otherwise has power to award damages and (b) taking into account all the circumstances of the case, the court is satisfied that the award is necessary to afford just satisfaction to the person in whose favour it is made (ss 8(2) and 8(3)).

284   *Campbell and Cosans v UK* (1982) 4 EHRR 293; *Norris v Ireland* (1991) 13 EHRR 186; *Sutherland v UK* [1998] EHRLR 117 and *Open Door Counselling and Dublin Well Women v Ireland* (1993) 15 EHRR 244. For a detailed discussion of the principles applicable to establishing whether a person is a 'victim' under the Act see Pannick QC and others, *Human Rights Law and Practice* (1999) Lexis Nexis 3rd edn, pp 68–71.

285   See CPR 1998, Part 54 and *Practice Direction 54A* (the 'Judicial Review Practice Direction') for the correct procedure.

286   CPR 1998, r 7.11(1) and HRA 1998, s 9(1).

287   CPR 1998, r 7.11(2). It is not necessary to transfer proceedings in which such a claim is relied on in relation to children to the High Court unless transfer is merited in any event (see *Re L (Care Proceedings: Human Rights Claims)* [2003] EWHC 665 (Fam), [2003] 2 FLR 160, para 33. See also *Re V (A Child) (Care Proceedings: Human Rights Claims)* [2004] EWCA Civ 54, [2004] 1 FLR 944).

288   HRA 1998, s 4(5) and see **3.58–3.60** above.

289   HRA 1998, s 7(5) and subject to any rule imposing a stricter time limit in relation to the procedure in question.

290   CPR 1998, r 8.2.

Crown through the Lord Chancellor.[291] Likewise, where a claim for incompatibility is made, notice must be given to the Crown and the Crown or a Minister will be joined as a party.[292] Where the matter concerns a child, the case should be referred to Cafcass Legal.[293] The court will give directions for the filing of acknowledgment of service, the filing and serving of evidence and a date for hearing.[294] The issue of whether oral evidence is to be heard should be settled at the directions hearing.[295]

Procedure – Claim in Existing Proceedings

3.83   A claim made in existing family proceedings will be governed by r 29.5 of the Family Procedure Rules 2010. The claims should be made by the appropriate originating document[296] and specify: (a) that relief or remedy is sought under the HRA 1998; (b) the precise details of the convention right claimed to have been infringed and details of the alleged infringement; (c) the relief sought; (d) whether any declaration of incompatibility is claimed.[297] Where a claim for incompatibility is made, notice must be given to the Crown and the Crown or a Minister will be joined as a party.[298] Where the claim includes a claim arising out of a judicial act, including a claim for damages,[299] notice must be given to the Crown through the Lord Chancellor.[300] Where the claim is a made in existing proceedings, only where a claim of incompatibility is made does the matter need to be heard in the High Court.[301] It should be noted that any other claim under the HRA 1998 within in existing proceedings is not ordinarily a ground for transferring the matter to the High Court.[302]

Status of European Jurisprudence

3.84   The domestic courts must, when determining a question which arises in connection with the ECHR, take account of the jurisprudence of the European Court of Human Rights, the opinions and decisions of the European Commission and decisions of the Committee of Ministers.[303] Whilst this jurisprudence is not binding in any strict sense of precedent,[304] in the absence of special circumstances, the court should follow any clear and constant jurisprudence of the European Court of Human Rights.[305] The following principles should be born in mind when considering such

---

[291]   CPR 1998, r 19.4A; Family Procedure Rules 2010, r.29.5(5)(b).
[292]   HRA 1998, s 5; CPR 1998, r 19.4A, Annex to PD 66 (non-family proceedings) and PD 19, para 6.1 (family proceedings). Family Procedure Rules 2010, r 29.5(3).
[293]   See *Cafcass Practice Note* [2004] 1 FLR 1190.
[294]   CPR 1998, r 8.9.
[295]   *C v Bury Metropolitan Borough Council* [2002] EWHC 1438 (Fam), [2002] 2 FLR 868.
[296]   Previously defined by the Family Proceedings Rules 1991, r 10.26(1) as 'a petition, application, originating application, originating summons or other originating process.' The Family Proceedings Rules 1991 have now been replaced by the Family Procedure Rules 2010 which do not define the nature of the originating document.
[297]   Family Procedure Rules 2010, r 29.5(2). Where a party seeks to amend their originating documents to include these matters it must, unless the court orders otherwise, do so not less than 28 days before the hearing (r 10.26(3)).
[298]   Family Procedure Rules 2010, r 29.5(3) and CPR PD 19, para 6.1 (Family Proceedings).
[299]   CPR 1998, r 19.4A.
[300]   Family Procedure Rules 2010, r 29.5(5)(b).
[301]   HRA 1998, s 4(5). See also Family Procedure Rules 2010, r 2.5(2)
[302]   *Re V (Care Proceedings: Human Rights)* [2004] EWCA Civ 54, [2004] 1 WLR 1433, [2004] 1 All ER 997 and *Westminster City Council v RA, B and S* [2005] EWHC 970 (Fam), [2005] 2 FLR 1309.
[303]   HRA 1998, s 2(1).
[304]   See *Fitzpatrick v Sterling Housing Association Ltd* [2001] 1 AC 27, [1999] 3 WLR 113, [1999] 4 All ER 705, HL and *Ghaidan v Godin-Mendoza* [2004] UKHL 30, [2004] 2 AC 557, [2004] 2 FCR 481, [2004] 2 FLR 600.
[305]   See *R (Alconbury Developments Ltd) v Secretary of State for the Environment, Transport and the Regions*

jurisprudence: (a) older decisions are a less reliable guide as the Convention is a 'living instrument; (b) decisions of the European Court have greater weight than admissibility decisions of the Commission (whose judicial role is now defunct); (c) decisions generally turn on the facts, although some general principles may be discerned from them and (d) the 'margin of appreciation' will vary according to the particular point in issue.[306]

Proceedings for Breach in the European Court of Human Rights[307]

3.85   Where a child has exhausted all the domestic remedies available to address a complaint concerning a breach by the State of their rights under the ECHR, they may make an application to the European Court of Human Rights. This application must be in the proper application form obtained from the Registrar of the Court[308] and filed within 6 months of the date of the final decision made within the domestic jurisdiction.[309] The proceedings are conducted in writing and oral hearings are exceptional. The proceedings of the European Court of Human Rights are governed by the European Court of Human Rights Rules of Court, revised in December 2008.[310]

3.86   The first task of the Court is to consider whether the complaint is admissible.[311] Any plea of 'inadmissibility' by the Contracting State must be raised in its written or oral observations.[312] Where the complaint appears inadmissible on its face, it will be referred to a 'Committee' of three judges[313] which will determine whether to strike it out or to admit it to the Court sitting as a 'Chamber' of seven judges[314] for consideration.[315] The Chamber may itself strike out the complaint as inadmissible notwithstanding the complaint has been referred to the Chamber by the Committee.[316] Where the complaint appears admissible on its face, one or more Judge Rapporteurs will be appointed to consider the issue of admissibility[317] and will determine whether the application should be referred to a Committee (for the Committee to determine whether to strike out the complaint or admit it to the Court sitting as a Chamber for consideration) or admitted direct to the Court sitting as a Chamber for consideration.[318] Again, the Chamber may itself strike out the complaint as inadmissible notwithstanding the complaint has been referred to the Chamber by the Judge Rapporteur(s).[319]

3.87   In respect of cases referred to it, the Chamber may examine the issues of admissibility and merits at the same time.[320] Once the decision has been declared

---

[2001] UKHL 23, [2003] 2 AC 295, para 26 per Lord Slynn (cited with approval by Lord Bingham in *R (Ullah) v Special Adjudicator* [2004] UKHL 26, [2004] 2 AC 323, para 20) and *R (Anderson) v Secretary of State for the Home Department* [2002] UKHL 46, [2003] 1 AC 837, para 18 per Lord Bingham.

306   Swindells, H and others, *Family Law and the Human Rights Act 1998,* (1999) Family Law, p 13, para 2.21. For a comprehensive discussion of this topic see Pannick QC and others, *Human Rights Law and Practice* (1999) Lexis Nexis 3rd edn, pp 38–41.

307   For a detailed description of the practice and procedure of the European Court of Human Rights see Leach, P *Taking a Case to the European Court of Human Rights* (2005) 2nd edn, Blackstone Press.

308   ECHR, Art 35(1). ECtHR Rules of Court r 47.

309   ECHR, Art 35(1).

310   In force from 1 January 2009.

311   ECHR, Arts 35(2)–4).

312   ECtHR Rules of Court, r 55.

313   ECtHR Rules of Court, r 27.

314   ECtHR Rules of Court, r 26(1).

315   ECtHR Rules of Court, rr 49(1) and 54.

316   ECtHR Rules of Court, r 54(1).

317   ECtHR Rules of Court, rr 49(2) and 49(3).

318   ECtHR Rules of Court, rr 49(3) and 54.

319   ECtHR Rules of Court, r 54(1).

320   ECHR, Art 29(3) and ECt HR Rules of Court, r 54A.

admissible, the Court will first encourage the parties to reach settlement on the point in issue.[321] If no settlement is achieved, the Court sitting as a 'Chamber' will finally consider and determine the complaint.[322] The Chamber may invite the parties to submit further evidence and written observations.[323] The Chamber may decide, either at the request of the parties or of its own motion, to hold an oral hearing.[324]

3.88   In exceptional cases, within 3 months of the judgment of the Chamber any party may request that the case be referred to the Grand Chamber.[325] This request will be accepted if 'the case raises a serious question affecting the interpretation of the Convention or the protocols thereto, or a serious issue of general importance'.[326] The judgment of the Grand Chamber is final.[327] The High Contracting Parties undertake to abide by the final judgment of the Court in any case to which they are parties.[328]

Status of other Council of Europe Conventions not Incorporated into Domestic Law

3.89   The other Council of Europe conventions[329] which touch and concern children's rights are treaties and are therefore subject to the general rules of interpretation set out in the Vienna Convention on the Law of Treaties Arts 31–33.[330] Having regard to the principles articulated by the line of House of Lords authority considered at **3.32–3.46** above, it is likely that the domestic courts will, in cases concerning the rights of children, consider themselves bound to construe domestic law as far as possible so as to comply with the obligations under the other Council of Europe conventions which the United Kingdom has ratified.[331] Once again, support for this approach is gained from the fact that the European Court of Human Rights attributes weight to other Council of Europe conventions when interpreting the ECHR, in accordance with which domestic law must be interpreted. For example, in the case of *Sidabras v Lithuania*[332] the European Court of Human Rights, in considering the ambit of 'private life' under Art 8 of the ECHR, observed:

> '... having regard in particular to the notions currently prevailing in democratic states the court considers that a far reaching ban on taking up private sector employment does affect "private life". It attaches particular weight in this respect to the text of Article 1(2) of the European Social Charter and the interpretation given by the European Committee of Social Rights and to the text adopted by the ILO it further reiterates that there is no water tight division separating the sphere of social and economic rights from the field covered by the convention ...'

---

[321]   ECHR, Arts 38 and 39 and ECt HR Rules of Court, r 62.
[322]   ECtHR Rules of Court, r 56.
[323]   ECtHR Rules of Court, r 59(1).
[324]   ECtHR Rules of Court, r 59(3). Hearings are governed by Chapter VI of the Rules of Court.
[325]   ECt HR Rules of Court, r 50. The Grand Chamber comprises all seventeen Judges of the European Court of Human Rights. Proceedings before the Grand Chamber are governed by Chapter VII of the Rules of Court.
[326]   ECHR, Art 43.
[327]   ECHR, Art 44.
[328]   ECHR, Art 46.
[329]   See **2.95–2.103** for a detailed summary of these conventions.
[330]   See **3.22** above.
[331]   See *G (Children) (Foreign Contact Order: Enforcement)* [2003] EWCA Civ 1607, [2004] 1 FCR 266.
[332]   (2006) 42 EHRR 104. See also *Wilson and Others v United Kingdom* [2002] All ER (D) 35 (Jul) (European Social Charter) and *Inze v Austria* Application No 8695/79 (1987) 10 EHRR 394.

Within this context, the domestic courts have likewise used other Council of Europe Conventions to assist with interpretation when applying the ECHR in a domestic context.[333] There is no reason to suppose that a different approach will be taken in cases concerning the rights of children.

Status of Council of Europe Resolutions and Recommendations in Domestic Law

3.90	The Committee of Ministers of the Council of Europe may make recommendations to member States[334] and the Parliamentary Assembly of the Council of Europe may make recommendations and resolutions directed to member states.[335] A number of these recommendations and resolutions are relevant to the rights of children.[336] The recommendations and resolutions constitute non-binding legal texts. They are however intended to serve as guidelines for policy development in the member States of the Council. In addition, domestic courts will refer to resolutions and recommendations from the Council of Europe as an aid to interpretation of domestic legislation[337] and of the provisions of the ECHR.[338]

Domestic Status of European Union Law

3.91	The law of the European Community is superior to domestic law.[339] There is a duty on national courts to secure the full effectiveness of Community law, even where it is necessary to create a national remedy where none had previously existed.[340] The Supreme Court is thus under a duty to give a purposive construction to domestic legislation so as to accord with EU law.[341] This can be done by implying words necessary to achieve a result[342] or by using the power to discard individual words where necessary.[343]

---

[333]	See *Tekle v Secretary of State for the Home Department* [2008] EWHC 3064 (Admin), [2009] 2 All ER 193, para 35.
[334]	Statute of the Council of Europe, Art 15.b.
[335]	Statute of the Council of Europe, Art 30.
[336]	See for example in relation to the Parliamentary Assembly: 1065 (1987) (on the traffic in children and other forms of child exploitation), 1071 (1988) (on providing institutional care for infants and children), 1286 (1996) (on a European strategy for children), 1307 (2002) (sexual exploitation of children: zero tolerance) and 1778 (2007) (child victims). In relation to Committee of Ministers see for example No R(84)4 (parental responsibilities), No R(85)4 (violence in the family), No R(87)20 (social reactions to juvenile delinquency), No R(98)8 (children's participation in family and social life) and No R (06)12 (empowering children in the new information and communications environment).
[337]	See *R (on the application of Pretty) v Director of Public Prosecutions* [2001] UKHL 61, [2002] 1 All ER 1, para 28; *European Roma Rights Centre and others v Immigration Officer at Prague Airport and another (United Nations High Commissioner for Refugees intervening)* [2004] UKHL 55, [2005] 1 All ER 527 and *R (on the application of D) v Camberwell Green Youth Court; R (on the application of the Director of Public Prosecutions) v Camberwell Youth Court* [2005] UKHL4, [2005] 1 ALL ER 999, para 19.
[338]	See *Mosley v News Group Newspapers Ltd* [2008] EWHC 1777 (QB), para 126 , *OBG Ltd and another v Allan and others; Douglas and another v Hello! Ltd and others (No 3); Mainstream Properties Ltd v Young and others* [2007] UKHL 21, [2007] 4 All ER 545, para 281.
[339]	Case 6/64, *Falminio Costa v ENEL* [1964] ECR 585, 593 and see, *Factortame Ltd v Secretary of State for Transport* (No 2) [1991] 1 AC 603.
[340]	*Factortame I* C-213/89 [1990] ECR I-2433.
[341]	*Pickstone v Freemans PLC* [1989] 1 AC 66 and *Lister v Forth Dry Dock Co Ltd* [1990] 1 AC 546 at 554G–554H and 559D–559F.
[342]	*Pickstone v Freemans PLC* [1989] 1 AC 66.
[343]	*O'Brien v Sim-Chem Ltd* [1980] ICR 573 at 580F.

3.92   The European Charter of Fundamental Rights of the European Union stipulates that 'Children shall have the right to such protection and care as is necessary for their well-being. They may express their views freely. Such views shall be taken into consideration on matters which concern them in accordance with their age and maturity', that 'In all actions relating to children, whether taken by public authorities or private institutions, the child's best interests must be a primary consideration' and that 'Every child shall have the right to maintain on a regular basis a personal relationship and direct contact with both his or her parents, unless that is contrary to his or her interests'.[344] In accordance with Art 52(3) of the European Charter of Fundamental Human Rights the meaning and scope of the rights under the Charter is the same as that under the corresponding articles of the ECHR and its related protocols.[345] Where a case concerning children involves European Union law, the domestic courts will take account of the ECHR as its principles constitute general principles of European Union law.[346] The EU bodies and institutions and Member States need have regard to the Charter only when implementing EU law.[347] The Treaty on the European Union requires the EU to 'respect fundamental rights, as guaranteed by the European Convention for the Protection of Human Rights and Fundamental Freedoms signed in Rome on 4 November 1950 and as they result from the constitutional traditions common to the Member States, as general principles of Community law'.[348]

DOMESTIC LAW AND OTHER REGIONAL FRAMEWORKS

3.93   The regional frameworks beyond Europe have been considered on occasion by the domestic courts where they have become relevant on the particular facts of the case. In *Northumberland County Council v Z, Y and X*[349] the court had regard to the African Union Charter on the Rights and Welfare of the Child in a case involving a Kenyan child brought into the UK illegally. Likewise, the European Court of Human Rights has made reference to the African (Banjul) Charter on Human and Peoples' Rights when considering the proper interpretation of Art 2 of the ECHR.[350] Finally, the rights enshrined in the regional human rights instruments may give rise to and reinforce customary rules of international law, which rules will be applied in the matter set out above.[351]

---

[344] European Charter of Fundamental Rights of the European Union, Art 24.

[345] Article 52(3) of the Charter provides that 'Insofar as this Charter contains rights which correspond to rights guaranteed by the Convention for the Protection of Human Rights and Fundamental Freedoms, the meaning and scope of those rights shall be the same as those laid down by the said Convention. This provision shall not prevent Union law providing more extensive protection.'

[346] European Charter of Fundamental Rights of the European Union, Art 6(3) and see Cases 46/87, 227/88: *Hoechst AG v EC Commission* [1989] ECR 2859 at 2923, para 13.

[347] European Charter of Fundamental Rights of the European Union, Art 51.

[348] Treaty of the European Union, Art 6(2).

[349] [2009] EWHC 498 (Fam), para 57 per Munby J. See also *R (Mullen) v Secretary of State for the Home Department* [2004] UKHL 18, [2005] 1 AC 1, [2004] 3 All ER 65.

[350] *Vo v France* Application No 53924/00 [2004] 2 FCR 577, para 63.

[351] See Balton, D *The Convention on the Rights of the Child – Prospects for International Enforcement* (1990) 12 Hum Rts Q 120, pp 122–123.

DOMESTIC APPLICATION AND ENFORCEMENT – SUMMARY

3.94   The overall position in domestic law concerning the application and enforcement within this jurisdiction of international and European legal frameworks touching and concerning the rights of children can be summarised as follows:[352]

Legal Framework	Relevant Legal Instruments	Application & Enforcement
Binding Conventions 'incorporated' into domestic law (3.57–3.88 above).	• European Convention on Human Rights and Fundamental Freedoms	Must be applied and enforced in accordance with the domestic statutory regime 'incorporating' the Convention principles into domestic law.
Binding Conventions not 'incorporated' into domestic law (3.32–3.46 above).	• Convention on the Rights of the Child • Covenant on Civil and Political Rights • Covenant on Economic, Social and Cultural Rights • Convention against Torture and Other Cruel, Inhuman or Degrading Treatment • Convention on Elimination of all forms of Racial Discrimination • Convention on Elimination of all forms of Discrimination against Women • Convention Relating to the Status of Refugees • Convention on the Protection of the Rights of All Migrant Workers and Members of Their Families • Convention on the Rights of Persons with Disabilities • Worst Forms of Child Labour Convention • Convention against Discrimination in Education • European Social Charter • European Convention on Adoption of Children • European Convention on the Legal Status of Children born out of Wedlock • The Geneva Conventions	Domestic legislation (including Sch 1 of the HRA 1998) should be read, interpreted and applied in a manner which accords with the obligations prescribed by the relevant binding Convention.
	• European Convention on the Exercise of Children's Rights • European Convention on Contact Concerning Children • Council of Europe Convention on the Protection of Children against Sexual Exploitation and Sexual Abuse	Domestic legislation (including Schedule 1 of the HRA 1998) should be interpreted and applied in accordance with the obligations prescribed by the relevant binding Convention.
Non-Binding International Agreements / Conventions not incorporated into domestic law (3.48–3.49 above).	• Universal Declaration of Human Rights • Declaration of the Protection of Women and Children in Emergency and Armed Conflict • Declaration on Social and Legal Principles relating to the Welfare and Protection of Children with Special Reference to Foster Placement and Adoption Nationally • Declaration on the Elimination of All Forms of Intolerance and of Discrimination Based on Religion or Belief	Should be taken into account as persuasive authority when interpreting and applying domestic legislation, including Schedule 1 of the HRA 1998.

---

[352]   Only the key instruments touching and concerning children's rights are included in this table.

Legal Framework	Relevant Legal Instruments	Application & Enforcement
Customary International Law and *Jus Cogens* (**3.55–3.56** above).	• Rules of customary international law and *jus cogen* rules pertaining to the rights of children.	Must be considered as a part of domestic law and enforced as such unless inconsistent with domestic legislation.
UN Standard Rules and Guidelines (**3.50–3.54** above).	• Standard Minimum Rules for the Administration of Juvenile Justice (the 'Beijing Rules') • Standard Rules on the Equalisation of Opportunities for persons with Disabilities • Guidelines on the Prevention of Juvenile Delinquency (the 'Riyadh Guidelines') • Paris Commitments to protect children from unlawful recruitment or use by armed forces or armed groups • Paris Principles: Principles and Guidelines on Children Associated with Armed Forces or Armed Groups to which the signatories to the Paris Commitments dedicated themselves	Should *at least* be considered persuasive authority when interpreting and applying domestic legislation, including Sch 1 of the HRA 1998. Arguably, the position is more prescriptive and domestic legislation should be interpreted and applied as a matter of course in accordance with the Standard Rules and Guidance.[353]
UN General Comments (**3.50–3.54** above).	• General Comments made by the Committee on the Rights of the Child with a view to promoting the further implementation of the Convention and assisting States Parties with their reporting obligations	Should be taken into account as persuasive authority when interpreting and applying domestic legislation.
Reports from Monitoring Bodies (**3.50–3.54** above).	• Concluding observations compiled by the Committee on the Rights of the Child on implementation of the CRC by the United Kingdom.	Should be taken into account as persuasive authority when interpreting and applying domestic legislation.
Council of Europe Resolutions and Recommendations (**3.90** above).	• Resolutions and Recommendations of the Committee of Ministers and the Parliamentary Assembly.	Should be taken into account as guidance when interpreting and applying domestic legislation.

CONCLUSION

3.95   The Human Rights Act 1998 provides a domestic framework for the enforcement of a number of cardinal rights of children, providing a clear procedure for those rights to be argued for in the domestic courts. The fact that the ECHR must be interpreted in light of the CRC, and the clear line authority from the House of the Lords and latterly the Supreme Court that requires domestic legislation to be interpreted and applied in a manner consistent with the United Kingdom's obligations under the CRC, provides a canvass onto which elements of the CRC can be projected in domestic proceedings. Whilst this projection is not without its difficulties, it should be increasingly possible for children to rely on elements of the CRC in support of arguments before the domestic courts, in particular those grounded in applications made under the HRA 1998. The steadily increasing content of customary international law and the willingness of the courts to have regard to the provisions of non-binding international agreements and standard rules and guidelines further strengthen the position of children seeking to argue for their rights before the domestic courts.

---

[353]   *T v United Kingdom* Application No 24724/94 (1999), paras 71–75 and para 96 and see **3.53–3.54** above.

3.96   In 1992 Van Bueren observed that:[354]

> 'International human rights law treaties are capable of being utilised on three levels: as an educational instrument; as evidence of the need for national law reform and as a tool for advocates. The [CRC] can effectively be used for the first two purposes but at present there are overwhelming obstacles facing UK lawyers seeking to plead articles of the [CRC] in UK courts and before regional and international human rights fora.'

Whilst obstacles still remain, and whilst there remains a need 'to go one step further and respond by developing mechanisms which children trust and which they are able to utilise effectively',[355] based on domestic legislation and jurisprudence there are now a wider range of tools at the disposal of the advocate seeking to give effect to the CRC, and to children rights in general, within the domestic jurisdiction. The precise utility of those tools has yet to be determined and will only be determined through advocates being prepared to use them in argument. As Verhellen notes, 'Much depends on the willingness and creativity of lawyers'.[356] We now turn to look at the fundamental principles that should underpin those arguments.

---

[354]   Van Bueren *The United Nations Convention on the Rights of the Child – The Necessity of Incorporation into United Kingdom Law* [1992] Fam Law 373.

[355]   Van Buren *The International Law on the Rights of the Child* (1998) Martinus Nijhoff, p 380. In short, the Government must urgently table legislation to incorporate the CRC into domestic law.

[356]   Verhellen, E *Convention on the Rights of the Child* (2000) Garant, p 86.

Chapter 4

GUIDING PRINCIPLES

'Nature throws us all into the world equal and alike ...'

John Adams

INTRODUCTION

4.1   There are a number of overarching principles that are of cardinal importance to interpreting, applying and enforcing the rights of children. Those principles comprise the definition of a child, the principle of non-discrimination and the principle of the child's best interests. The Committee on the Rights of the Child considers these principles to be, together with the right to survival and development and the right to participate, 'Guiding Principles' by which all of the other rights within the CRC are realised.[1] This chapter examines the definition of a child, including the principle of evolving capacity, the principle of non-discrimination and the concept of best interests. The right to survival and development is then dealt with in chapter 5 and the right to participate in chapter 6. Each of these principles must be held at the forefront of the mind when seeking to give effect to each of the rights of the child.

THE CHILD

4.2   Beyond the strict confines of a legal classification arrived at to ensure certainty in the application of the law, the definition of a child is a subject fraught with the difficulties. However, for the purposes of examining the law and practice of children's rights it is a legal classification to ensure certainty in the application of the law that is required.[2] As such, in seeking a definition of a child, there are two key questions. Namely, when in law does childhood begin and when in law does childhood end.[3] Beyond those two key questions, and in order to articulate fully the definition of a child in law and illuminate fully its consequences for the application and enforcement children's rights, the evolving capacity inherent in childhood[4] and the differential legal status accorded to children in society also require detailed examination.[5]

---

[1]   See *General Guidelines regarding the form and content of initial reports to be submitted by States parties under article 44* CRC/C/5, para 1(a).

[2]   The Committee on the Rights of the Child continues to encourage States who have not yet done so to harmonise their definition of 'child' with that provided by Art 1 of the CRC, namely 'every human being below the age of eighteen years unless under the law applicable to the child, majority is attained earlier (see Newell, P and Hodgkin, R *Implementation Handbook for the Convention on the Rights of the Child* (2008) 3rd edn, UNICEF, p 4). The Committee has stated that the definition of the child should be gender neutral, explicit and be enforced by law (see CRC/C/15/Add.157, para 27 and CRC/C/15/Add.219, para 23).

[3]   Van Bueren, G *The International Law on the Rights of the Child* (1998) Martinus Nijhoff, p 33.

[4]   As acknowledged in Art 5 and 14 of the CRC.

[5]   See Newell, P and Hodgkin, R *Implementation Handbook for the Convention on the Rights of the Child* (2008) 3rd edn, UNICEF, p 1 and UN General Comment No 7 (CRC/C/GC/7/Rev.1, para 3).

When in Law Does Childhood Begin?

4.3   Whilst most legal frameworks define the point at which, in law, childhood comes to an end, few expressly define its commencement in strict terms.[6] In the absence of a strict legal definition of the commencement of childhood, the question of when in law childhood begins is largely one of interpretation, the aim being to establish precisely the point when the law acknowledges the existence of, and offers protection to, the child. The question of when childhood begins for the purpose of the application and enforcement of children's rights as a whole has become largely conflated with the specific question of whether the unborn child has or should have a right to life.[7] These two issues must however be treated separately as one is a question of general application impacting on all rights and one is a question of specific application impacting on one right. The latter will be examined in detail in chapter 5.[8]

When in Law Does Childhood Begin – CRC

4.4   The preamble to the CRC quotes the Declaration of the Rights of the Child, stating that: 'as indicated in the Declaration of the Rights of the Child, 'the child, by reason of his physical and mental immaturity, needs special safeguards and care, including appropriate legal protection, *before as well as after birth*'' (emphasis added). In circumstances where the starting point of childhood is left open by Art 1 of the CRC, the preamble would tend to suggest that childhood commences before birth for the purposes of the Convention. However, the drafting group responsible for the insertion of this paragraph in the preamble[9] insisted that the *travaux preparatoires* to the Convention record that:[10]

> 'In adopting this preambular paragraph, the Working Group does not intend to prejudice the interpretation of article 1 or any provision of the Convention by States Parties'.

The effect of this statement is such that the preamble to the CRC does not have any binding legal implications for determining the starting point of childhood.[11] As Van Bueren observes, the CRC therefore does not restrict a State's discretion to provide under its domestic law the point when childhood begins.[12] From the domestic perspective, on ratification the UK declared that it interprets the convention as applying only following a live birth to ensure that the CRC does not conflict with domestic abortion legislation.[13]

---

[6]   See for example *Roe v Wade* 410 U.S. 113 (1973) where the US Supreme Court was not willing to define the point at which life began.

[7]   This is due in large part to the fact that the cases in which the concept of the commencement of childhood has been examined have been cases in which the overarching issue has been whether the unborn child has a right to life as opposed to other rights under international law.

[8]   See **5.5**.

[9]   The Federal Republic of Germany, Ireland, Italy, The Netherlands, Poland, Sweden and the United States.

[10]   E/CN.4/1989/48, pp 8–15. Taking an alternative perspective, The Holy See lodged a declaration stating 'The Holy See remains confident that the ninth preambular paragraph will serve as the perspective through which the rest of the Convention will be interpreted, in conformity with article 31 of the Vienna Convention on the Law of Treaties of 23 May 1969' (CRC/C/2/Rev.8, p 24).

[11]   Van Bueren, G *The International Law on the Rights of the Child* (1998) Martinus Nijhoff, p 34.

[12]   Van Bueren, G *The International Law on the Rights of the Child* (1998) Martinus Nijhoff, p 34.

[13]   CRC/C/2/Rev.8, p 42 1991. As with The Holy See, other States have taken a different approach. For example Argentina and Guatemala lodged declarations to the effect that art 1 of the CRC should apply from the moment of conception.

When in Law Does Childhood Begin – ECHR

4.5   In *Paton v UK*[14] the European Commission on Human Rights rejected the proposition that an unborn child had an absolute right to life under Art 2 of the ECHR and hence, by implication, that childhood commenced prior to birth.[15] It is of note that the Commission, in interpreting the word 'everyone' as being of post-natal application only, was not prepared to entirely exclude the possibility of Art 2 being of pre-natal application in 'rare cases'.[16] However, the European Court of Human Rights revisited the issue in *Vo v France*[17] and determined that the question of when the right to life commenced fell within the margin of appreciation and that, accordingly, it was neither desirable nor possible to answer the question of whether an unborn child was a person for the purposes of Art 2 of the ECHR.[18] In *A, B and C v Ireland*[19] the European Court of Human Rights, holding that Art 8 cannot be interpreted as conferring a right of abortion, stated that 'The woman's right to respect for her private life must be weighed against other competing rights and freedoms invoked including those of the unborn child'. However, in a later passage Court used the phrase 'the rights *claimed* on behalf of the foetus and those of the Mother'[20] and expressly declined to decide whether the term 'others' in Art 8(2) extends to the unborn child.[21] Thus, as with the CRC, the position under the ECHR appears to be that its provisions do not restrict a State's discretion to provide for the point when childhood begins under its domestic law. The European Court of Human Rights has held that an embryo created by IVF and existing outside the womb is not a person for the purposes of Art 2 of the ECHR.[22]

When in Law Does Childhood Begin – Other Regional Conventions

4.6   The same approach of permitting States to determine the issue of when childhood begins has been taken in relation under other regional legal frameworks

---

14   (1980) 3 EHRR 408, paras 18–20.
15   The Commission did however note in *Paton v UK* that an unborn child is attributed with certain rights which become enforceable upon birth. See below at **5.33**.
16   (1980) 3 EHRR 408, para 7. See also *Brüggeman and Scheuten v Federal Republic of Germany* (1978) Application No 6959/75 (unreported) (which expressly left open the issue of whether an unborn child is covered by Art 2 of the ECHR), *H v Norway* Application (1992) Application No 17004/90 (unreported) (where the Commission did 'not exclude that in certain circumstances' a foetus would be protected under Art 2 of the ECHR) and *Open Door Counseling and Dublin Well Women v Ireland* (1992) 15 EHRR 244 (where the European Court of Human Rights acknowledged the possibility that Art 2 of the ECHR might in certain circumstances offer protection to an unborn child).
17   [2004] 2 FCR 577.
18   For an alternative view see Recommendation 874(1979) of the Parliamentary Assembly on a European Charter on the Rights of the Child which contended for 'the right of every child to life from the moment of conception.'
19   (2010) Application No 25579/05, para 214.
20   (2010) Application No 25579/05, para 237 emphasis added. The full passage reads 'Of central importance is the finding in the above-cited Vo case, referred to above, that the question of when the right to life begins came within the States' margin of appreciation because there was no European consensus on the scientific and legal definition of the beginning of life, so that it was impossible to answer the question whether the unborn was a person to be protected for the purposes of Article 2. Since the rights claimed on behalf of the foetus and those of the mother are inextricably interconnected, the margin of appreciation accorded to a State's protection of the unborn necessarily translates into a margin of appreciation for that State as to how it balances the conflicting rights of the mother. It follows that, even if it appears from the national laws referred to that most Contracting Parties may in their legislation have resolved those conflicting rights and interests in favour of greater legal access to abortion, this consensus cannot be a decisive factor in the Court's examination of whether the impugned prohibition on abortion in Ireland for health and well-being reasons struck a fair balance between the conflicting rights and interests, notwithstanding an evolutive interpretation of the Convention.'
21   (2010) Application No 25579/05, para 228.
22   *Evans v United Kingdom* (2007) 43 EHRR 21.

touching and concerning children's rights. In the *Baby Boy* case[23] the Inter-American Commission on Human Rights held by a majority judgment that Art 1 of the American Declaration of the Rights and Duties of Man permitted each State Party to determine in accordance with its domestic law both the point at which life, and hence childhood begins and the point at which State Parties consider it is necessary to provide protection. Article 2 of the African Charter on Human Rights and Welfare of the Child is also silent on the point at which childhood begins and presumably a similar conclusion as that reached in the *Baby Boy* case could be expected under this provision.[24] Amongst regional human rights conventions, the American Declaration of Human Rights is the exception in that Art 4(1) of that convention provides that life is protected in general from the moment of conception.[25]

When in Law Does Childhood Begin – Domestic Law

4.7   The Family Law Reform Act 1969 provides that a person attains full age on attaining the age of 18.[26] The Children Act 1989, s 105(1) defines a child as 'a person under the age of eighteen'.[27] The word 'person' means 'live person' and adopting the normal principles of statutory construction this definition would appear to exclude the unborn child.[28] Within this context, the domestic case law demonstrates the reluctance on the part of the legislature[29] and the courts to consider childhood as commencing at any point prior to the live birth of the child and his or her consequent separate existence from the Mother, subject to some very limited 'exceptions'.

Domestic Law – Separate Existence from the Mother

4.8   In *Paton v British Pregnancy Advisory Service Trustees*[30] Sir George Baker P held that the unborn child has no rights of its own 'at least until it is born and has a separate existence from its mother.[31] This proposition permeates the whole civil law of this country'.[32] An embryo created by IVF and existing outside the womb will fall within the definition of 'unborn'.[33]

---

[23]   Inter-American Commission on Human Rights Res.No23/81 Case 2141 (USA).

[24]   Van Bueren, G *The International Law on the Rights of the Child* (1998) Martinus Nijhoff, p 35.

[25]   In light of the foregoing treaty law and case law and applying the principles set out in chapter 3, it would not appear possible at present to derive support for definitions of childhood which encompass the unborn child from the rules of customary international law or treaty provisions concerning the right to life (Van Bueren, G *The International Law on the Rights of the Child* (1998) Martinus Nijhoff, p 35).

[26]   FLRA 1969, s 1(1). In *law* the Sovereign is never a child (see *Duchy of Lancaster Case* (1561) 1 Plowd 212; Co Litt 43a, 43b; 1 Roll Abr Enfants A; 1 Bl Com (14th edn) 247–248). A child may be declared of 'full age' before he or she attains the age of eighteen by an Act of Parliament (see 4 Co Inst 36).

[27]   Subject to the provisions of the Children Act 1989, Sch 1, para 16 which extends the definition of 'child' to a person who has attained the age of 18 when an application is made for financial relief under paras 2 or 6 of Sch 1 of the 1989 Act.

[28]   See *Elliot v Joicey* [1935] AC 209 and *R v Newham London Borough Council, ex p Dada* [1996] QB 507, [1995] 2 All ER 552.

[29]   See for example the Human Fertilisation and Embryology Act 1990, s 1.

[30]   [1979] QB 276, [1978] 2 All ER 987. See also *Patton v UK* (1980) 3 EHRR 408.

[31]   See also *Re F (in utero)* [1988] Fam 122.

[32]   See also *Kelly v Kelly* [1997] 2 FLR 828 per Lord Justice Clerk of Cullen in the Scottish Court of Session: 'Whether it is an actionable wrong to the unborn foetus for an abortion to be terminated depends essentially on whether Scots law confers on the foetus a right to continue to exist in the mother's womb. Our conclusion is that Scots law recognises no such right on the foetus.'; *Borowski v A-G for Canada* (1987) 39 DLR (4th) 731 per Gerwing JA in the Saskatchewan Court of Appeal, concluding that there were no cases in Anglo-Canadian law giving the foetus a status *qua* foetus; *Medhurst v Medhurst* (1984) 9 DLR (4th) 252 per Reid J in the Ontario High Court of Justice: 'It is only persons recognised by law who are the subject of legal

4.9   Thus no offence is committed if the termination of a pregnancy is carried out in accordance with the provisions of the Abortion Act 1967[34] and a father has no rights over an unborn foetus.[35] In respect of medical treatment, the unborn child is not considered a separate person from the mother and its need for medical treatment does not prevail over the rights of the mother.[36] There is no jurisdiction to make an unborn baby a ward of court.[37] It is not possible for an unborn child to be abducted in breach of the provision of the Hague Convention on the Civil Aspects of International Child Abduction 1980 by the movement of a pregnant mother from one State to another.[38] An unborn child is not a person for the purposes of s 75 of the Housing Act 1985.[39] A foetus has no right of action until it is subsequently born alive and therefore while it is unborn it cannot be a party to an action.[40]

4.10   In *Bury Metropolitan Borough Council v D; Re D (unborn baby) (birth plan: future harm)*[41] Munby J held that for the purposes of granting *anticipatory* declaratory relief under the inherent jurisdiction for the purposes of protecting the child upon birth, it made no difference that the child whose future welfare was in issue had not yet been born. In this case, Munby J granted anticipatory declaratory relief to a local authority for the purposes of safeguarding the child from a risk of harm arising from the Mother's mental health. Having heard evidence from a consultant clinical psychologist that to inform the mother of the local authority's plan of removal of the child at birth would lead to a distinct possibility that the mother may, immediately after birth, harm both herself and the child, Munby J declared it lawful for the local authority not to involve the mother in the birth planning process notwithstanding the imperatives of Art 8 of the ECHR. Whilst it can be argued that the anticipatory relief sought and granted in the *Bury* case had the effect of protecting the unborn child (insofar as it may have prevented the Mother taking any precipitous action against herself and/or the child whilst the child was still in the womb), the relief granted was clearly to prevent harm to the child immediately subsequent to the birth. As such, this is not a case which creates any inroad

---

rights and duties ... the law does not regard an unborn child as an independent legal entity prior to birth' and *Roe v Wade* (1973) 410 US 113 US Supreme Court: 'In short, the unborn have never been recognised in the law as persons in the whole sense.'

[33]   See *Evans v United Kingdom* (2007) 43 EHRR 21.

[34]   Abortion Act 1967, s 1(1). But see below at **4.12 et seq**.

[35]   See *Paton v British Pregnancy Advisory Service Trustees* [1979] QB 276, [1978] 2 All ER 987 and *Re F* [1988] Fam 122, [1988] 2 All ER 193.

[36]   *St Georges Healthcare Trust v S; R v Collins and others, ex p S* [1998] 3 All ER 673, [1998] 2 FLR 728. See also *Re MB (An Adult: Medical Treatment)* [1997] 2 FLR 426 at 444 per Balcombe J ('The foetus up to the moment of birth does not have any separate interests.'); *Re S (Medical Treatment: Consent: Late Termination)* [2002] 1 FLR 445 (where the position of the unborn child was not considered in terms of its rights or welfare in the decision to order treatment to protect the mother); *The Queen on the Application of Smeaton on Behalf of the Society for the Protection of Unborn Children v Secretary of State for Health (Schering Health Care Ltd and Family Planning Association as Interested Parties)* [2002] EWHC 610 (Admin); *R (on the application of Smeaton) v Secretary of State for Health (No 2)* [2002] EWHC 886 (Admin), [2002] 2 FLR 146 (where it was held that there was nothing in the Offences Against the Person Act 1861 to demonstrate a parliamentary intention to protect 'life' from the point of conception) and *Evans v Amicus Healthcare Ltd; Hadley v Midland Fertility Services Ltd* [2003] EWHC 2161 (Fam), [2004] 1 FLR 67 at 112 per Wall J ('If a foetus has no right to life under Art 2, it is difficult to see how an embryo can have such a right'). But see *Re S (Adult: Refusal of Medical Treatment)* [1993] Fam 123, [1993] 1 FLR 26 (the health authority could lawfully perform an emergency Caesarean section operation on the patient and give her the necessary consequential treatment on the grounds that it was in her and the unborn child's vital interests, despite the patient's refusal to give her consent).

[37]   *Re F (In Utero)* [1988] Fam 122, [1988] 2 All ER 193 CA at 325G.

[38]   *Re F (Abduction: Unborn Child)* [2006] EWHC 2199 (Fam), [2007] 1 FLR 627.

[39]   *R v Newham London Borough Council ex p Dada* [1995] 1 FLR 842.

[40]   *C v S* [1987] 1 All ER 1230 per Heilbron J, pp 1234–1235.

[41]   [2009] EWHC 446 (Fam), [2009] 2 FCR 93.

into the domestic principles that childhood does not commence until birth and that the unborn child has no rights of its own. Rather, it is best seen as an example of the species of cases based on the principle of *en ventre sa mere*.

Domestic Law – En Ventre Sa Mere

4.11   In a limited number of situations the unborn child may be said to have 'conditional rights', the protection conferred by those rights being subject to the child surviving following birth, ie conditional upon childhood commencing. In such cases a child who is *en ventre sa mere* is accepted to be a child provided they are born alive.[42] In *Occleston v Fullalove*[43] a child who was *en ventre sa mere* at the date of the will which was the subject of that litigation was permitted to share with his sister under the will, having been born alive. In *Burton v Islington Health Authority, De Martell v Merton and Sutton Health Authority*[44] it was held that a child can sue following its birth for injuries suffered prior to his birth. In *Attorney-General's Reference (No 3 of 1994)*[45] the court determined that injuries to a child in utero which wholly or mainly result in the child's death following birth could constitute murder. As all these cases are conditional on childhood commencing at birth they really take the position as to the commencement of childhood established in *Paton* no further.[46]

Domestic Law – Protection Afforded by the Criminal Law

4.12   The criminal law arguably however does take the position slightly further.[47] The offence of child destruction contrary to s 1(1) of the Infant Life (Preservation) Act 1929 confers conditional protection on an unborn child by providing that:[48]

> '... any person who, with intent to destroy the life of a child capable of being born alive, by any willful act causes a child to die before it has an existence independent of its mother shall be guilty of ... child destruction ...'

In this context, a child is accepted to be a child conditional upon that child being *capable* of being born alive.[49] However, attempts to extrapolate from this a definition for the commencement of childhood that precedes birth have not been successful.[50] Rather, the Courts have made a distinction between the recognition in law of the sanctity of the

---

42   'An infant *in ventre sa mere*, or in the mother's womb, is supposed in law to be born for many purposes' (Sir William Blackstone, 'Commentaries on the Laws of England,' Vol I, p 126 (1765)).

43   (1873–1874) L R 9 Ch App 147.

44   [1993] QB 204. See also *Watt v Rama* [1972] VR 353.

45   [1996] 2 WLR 412, [1996] 2 FLR 1. In some jurisdictions, case brought under the principle of *en ventre sa mere* have begun to breach the legal boundary represented by the child's birth. In *Amadio v Levin*, 509 Pa. 199 (1985) the Supreme Court of Pennsylvania held that 'it makes no difference in liability under the wrongful death and survival statutes whether the child dies of the injuries just prior to or just after birth.' In *Farley v Sartin Trucking*, 195 W.Va. 671, the Supreme Court of Appeals of West Virginia did away with a requirement that a tortiously killed foetus be viable outside the womb at the time the tort was committed.

46   In the Scottish case of *Kelly v Kelly* [1997] 2 FLR 828 the Lord Justice Clerk of Cullen described these situations as 'the well known fiction by which ... a child in utero is deemed to have already been born.'

47   See *Royal College of Nursing of the United Kingdom v Department of Health and Social Security* [1981] 1 All ER 545 at 554 per Lord Denning MR.

48   The description of the 1929 Act which follows the title reads 'An Act to amend the law with regard to the destruction of children at or before birth'. The Act provides a defence at s 1(1) of acting in good faith for the sole purpose of preserving the life of the Mother.

49   A pregnancy which has lasted for a period of 28 weeks or more is prima facie proof that the child was capable of being born alive (s 1(2)).

50   See *C v S* [1987] 1 All ER 1230.

lives of children capable being born alive and the existence of childhood giving rise to enforceable rights prior to birth. In *Rance and Another v Mid-Downs Health Authority and Another*[51] Brook J said:

> 'I have no difficulty in detecting in the 1929 Act a policy decision by Parliament that the sanctity of the lives of children capable of being born alive is to be respected by the law (see *McKay v Essex Area Health Authority* [1982] 2 All ER 771 at 780, [1982] QB 1166 at 1180 per Stephenson LJ), even if a foetus, before being born alive, has no directly enforceable rights itself (see *Paton v Trustees of BPAS* [1978] 2 All ER 987, [1979] QB 276 and *Re F (in utero)* [1988] 2 All ER 193, [1988] Fam 122). I also have no difficulty in concluding that in 1967 Parliament did not intend to change that policy when it made major changes in the law relating to abortions.'

The offence of procuring or attempting to procure a miscarriage under ss 58 and 59 of the Offences Against the Person Act 1861 also provides protection to the unborn child. The protection conferred by the 1861 Act is, by contrast to the Infant Life (Preservation) Act 1929, conditional on nothing more than conception.[52] However, such protection is also likely to be considered by the courts at present to be based on the recognition of the sanctity of the life of a foetus capable of being born alive rather than the foetus being considered a 'child' having an enforceable right to life.[53]

4.13 Having regard to the foregoing authorities, if the commencement of childhood in law is defined for present purposes as the point at which the law acknowledges the existence of, and offers protection to, the child then the commencement of childhood in domestic law remains delimited by birth, subject to a limited number of highly circumscribed 'exceptions', themselves largely conditional on the commencement of childhood occurring, or being capable of occurring, at birth.

When in Law Does Childhood End?

4.14 Globally, there are a number of common factors applied to determine the end of childhood, namely the attainment of a certain age, the ability to perform specific acts or the capacity to perform certain functions.[54] These factors however have not resulted in a universally accepted definition of the end of childhood. Even using the strict criteria of childhood ceasing when the law stops recognising and protecting a person as a child and starts recognising and protecting them as an adult, the issue of when in law childhood comes to an end remains complicated. This is largely because: (a) unlike adulthood childhood is sub-divided, with different minimum ages applying in relation to certain actions and activities;[55] and (b) the differential speed of development of each individual child renders an upper age limit on childhood arbitrary.[56] Within this context however, a number of general principles concerning the end of childhood can be identified. First, there has to be 'some congruity among the legal limits' and a rational relationship

---

[51] [1991] 1 All ER 801. See also *McKay and another v Essex Area Health Authority and Another* [1982] 2 All ER 771 at 780 per Lord Justice Stephenson.

[52] The victim of the offence of administering drugs or using instruments to procure abortion is defined as 'Every woman, being with child ...' (s 58).

[53] See *Rance and Another v Mid-Downs Health Authority and Another* [1991] 1 All ER 801.

[54] Van Bueren, G *The International Law on the Rights of the Child* (1998) Martinus Nijhoff, p 36.

[55] See for example the discussion by the European Court of Human Rights on the age of criminal responsibility in *T v United Kingdom* [2000] 2 All ER 1024, [2000] Crim LR 187. See also Newell, P and Hodgkin, R *Implementation Handbook for the Convention on the Rights of the Child* (2008) 3rd edn, UNICEF, pp 4–12.

[56] Van Bueren, G *Child Rights in Europe* (2007) Council of Europe Publishing, p 57.

between a particular minimum age and the purpose which it is supposed to serve.[57] Second, the minimum age set by States should not be 'unreasonably low'.[58]

When in Law Does Childhood End – CRC

4.15 Article 1 of the CRC provides that:

> 'For the purposes of the present Convention, a child means every human being below the age of eighteen years unless under the law applicable to the child, majority is attained earlier.'

The words 'unless under the law applicable to the child, majority is attained earlier' allow States Parties which set an age lower than 18 as the end of childhood to retain that lower age.[59] It should be noted that the word 'majority' in Art 1 is not qualified by the word 'age', recognising that childhood in international law can come to an end by criteria other than age, for example 'emancipation' in those jurisdictions that subscribe to that principle.[60]

4.16 A domestic definition of majority does not exonerate a State party from honouring rights conferred on children by UN conventions under which majority is attained at 18. In respect of the CRC, the Committee on the Rights of the Child has stated that 'adolescents up to the age of 18 years old are holders of all the rights enshrined in the Convention; they are entitled to special protective measures, and, according to their evolving capacities, they can progressively exercise their rights'.[61] The UN Human Rights Committee has commented in relation to the provisions of Covenant on Civil and Political Rights concerning children[62] that a State party to the Covenant cannot 'absolve itself from its obligations under the Covenant regarding persons under the age of 18, even though they have reached the age of majority under domestic law'.[63]

4.17 Notwithstanding the general definition of 'child' provided by the CRC, Art 1 the Committee on the Rights of the Child recognises that States parties set minimum ages in relation to certain areas of law touching and concerning children, such as consent to medical treatment, compulsory education, employment, sexual consent, marriage, voluntary enlistment and conscription and criminal responsibility. Each of these issues are covered in detail below where they become relevant. However, in general terms, the Committee on the Rights of the Child expects minimum ages that are *protective* to be set as high as possible and that minimum ages that relate to a child gaining *autonomy* demand a more flexible system that is sensitive to the needs of the individual child.[64] In setting minimum ages, States parties to the CRC must have regard to the entire

---

[57]   Pappas, A *Law and the Status of the Child* (1981) 13 Colum, HR Rev. No 1 quoted in Van Bueren, G *The International Law on the Rights of the Child* (1998) Martinus Nijhoff, p 36.

[58]   See UN General Comment No 17, UN Doc. HRI/GEN/Rev.2 at 24.

[59]   See the preamble to the CRC which states 'Taking due account of the importance of the traditions and cultural values of each people for the protection and harmonious development of the child'.

[60]   Van Bueren, G *The International Law on the Rights of the Child* (1998) Martinus Nijhoff, pp 36–37.

[61]   General Comment No 4 *Adolescent health and Development in the context of the Convention on the Rights of the Child* HRI/GEN/1/Rev.8 p 376.

[62]   See Art 24.

[63]   See Human Rights Committee General Comment No 17 *Article 24 (Rights of the Child)* HRI/GEN/1/Rev.8 p 184, para 4. Note that also the Human Rights Committee General Comment No 21 *Article 10 (Humane Treatment of Persons Deprived of their Liberty)* HRI/GEN/ 1/Rev.8 p 194, para 13 'all persons under the age of 18 should be treated as juveniles, at least in matters relating to criminal justice.'

[64]   Newell, P and Hodgkin, R *Implementation Handbook for the Convention on the Rights of the Child* (2008) 3rd edn, UNICEF, p 5.

Convention and in particular to the general principles covered in this chapter. As such, in setting minimum ages, there must be no discrimination, the child's best interests must be primary and the child's maximum survival and development must be ensured.[65]

When in Law Does Childhood End – Other International Conventions

4.18 The Hague Convention on Civil Aspects of International Child Abduction 1980 and the European Convention on the Enforcement of Decisions Concerning the Custody of Children and on Restoration of Custody of Children 1980 define a child as being under 16.[66] Article 1 of the International Labour Organisation Minimum Age Convention[67] provides that the minimum age for admission into employment shall not be less that the age of completion of compulsory education and in any event not less than 15 years.[68]

When in Law Does Childhood End – ECHR

4.19 ECHR makes limited reference to children but does not provide a definition of 'child'. Children are referred to only in those articles where the definition is unlikely to be the point in issue.[69] Given that the ECHR has so few rights which are expressed to apply specifically to children, the European Court has not yet had cause to consider when childhood ends.[70] Recent Council of Europe Treaties concerning children define childhood in terms of persons under the age of 18,[71] the age of 18 being the age of full legal capacity in all member States in the Council of Europe.[72]

When in Law Does Childhood End – Domestic Law

Domestic Definitions

4.20 As already noted, the Children Act 1989, s 105(1) defines a child as 'a person under the age of eighteen'. The Family Law Reform Act 1969, s 1(1) provides that 'a person shall attain full age on attaining the age of eighteen'.[73] Within this domestic law, childhood thus ends upon the child attaining the age of 18 years.[74]

---

[65] Newell, P and Hodgkin, R *Implementation Handbook for the Convention on the Rights of the Child* (2008) 3rd edn, UNICEF, p 5.

[66] Hague Convention on Civil Aspects of International Child Abduction, Art 4; European Convention on the Enforcement of Decisions Concerning the Custody of Children and on Restoration of Custody of Children, Art 1(a).

[67] 1973 (No 138).

[68] See Art 2(3). Countries with underdeveloped economies and educational systems are permitted to lower the age to 14 initially. Work which is likely to jeopardise the health, safety or morals of young people carries a minimum age of 18 (see Art 3(1)) or 16 where the health, safety and morals of the young person concerned are fully protected and the young person fully trained (see Art 3(3)). See further **15.85–15.86** below.

[69] Van Bueren, G *Child Rights in Europe* (2007) Council of Europe Publishing, p 51. Article 5(1)(d) of the ECHR concerning detention of minors is expressed to apply specifically to minors and Art 6(1) provides special protection to juveniles in respect of cases heard in public.

[70] Van Bueren, G *Child Rights in Europe* (2007) Council of Europe Publishing, p 51.

[71] European Convention on the Exercise of Children's Rights, Art 1(1); European Convention on Contact Concerning Children, Art 2(c). See also the Council of Europe Resolution CM(72)29.

[72] Commentary on the European Convention on the Exercise of Children's Rights (ETS No 160).

[73] See also the Family Proceedings Rules 1991, r 9.1(1) and the Civil Procedure Rules 1998, r 21.1(2) which provide that ''child' means person under 18.'

[74] As to the procedure to be adopted where there is a dispute as to whether a person is under the age of 18 see *R (B) v Merton LBC* [2003] 2 FLR 888; *Re (A) v London Borough of Croydon* [2008] EWHC 2921 (Admin), [2009] 2 FLR 173, *A v Croydon London Borough Council; Secretary of State for the Home Department Interested Party; WK v Secretary of State for the Home Department etc* [2009] EWHC 939 (Admin), [2009]

Minimum Age Limits

4.21 Within the context of this definition, the Children Act 1989 and other legislation also sets out minimum age limits in respect of specific areas of law and policy which touch and concern children during their childhood.[75] By way of example,[76] under the Children Act 1989 itself no care order may be made in respect of a child over the age of 17 or 16 where the child is married.[77] The Sexual Offences Act 2003 states that the age of consent for sex is age 16. The Education Act 1996, s 8(2) provides that a child begins to be of compulsory school age when he or she attains the age or 5 and at present ceases to be of compulsory school age on attaining the age of 16.[78] The Crime and Disorder Act 1998, s 34 provides that the age of criminal responsibility in England and Wales is 10 years old.[79] The domestic legislation providing for minimum ages has been described as 'muddled'.[80]

4.22 The setting of minimum ages in relation to specific areas of law and policy concerning children does not act to limit a child's rights as a child under other domestic provisions or under international law. Thus whilst a range of legal provisions provide for minimum ages in certain areas of a child's life, *Working Together to Safeguard Children*[81] states that in relation to child protection legislation:[82]

> 'The fact that a child has become sixteen years of age is living independently or is in Further Education, or is a member of the armed forces, or is in hospital, or in prison or a young offenders institution does not change their status or their entitlement to services or protection under the Children Act 1989.'

Domestic legislation concerning minimum age limits must be read so as to give effect to the rights of children under the ECHR and to their rights under the CRC.[83]

4.23 Domestic legislation also straddles the boundary between the end of childhood and the commencement of adulthood. For example, under the 1989 Act, a local authority is able to provide accommodation for a person between the ages of 16 and 21

Fam Law 659 and *R (A) v Croydon London Borough Council; R (M) v Lambeth Borough Council* [2009] UKSC 8, [2010] 1 FLR 959. See also Children's Rights Alliance for England, *State of Children's Rights in England* (2008), pp 35–36.

[75] This approach is not without significant disadvantages. In *Gillick v West Norfolk and Wisbech Area Health Authority* [1986] AC 112 Lord Scarman said 'If the law should impose on the process of "growing up" fixed limits where nature knows only a continuous process, the price would be artificiality and a lack of realism an area where the law must be sensitive to human development and social change.'

[76] Minimum age limits set by domestic legislation are dealt with in detail in the text where they become relevant.

[77] CA 1989, s 31(3).

[78] See also the Education (Start of Compulsory School Age) Order 1998, the Education Act 1996, s 7 and the Education and Skills Act 2008. Pursuant to the Education and Skills Act 2008, s 2 education or training by way of a contract of apprenticeship will become compulsory up to the age of 17 from 2013 and compulsory up to the age of 18 from 2015.

[79] The 2002 report from the UN Committee on the Rights of the Child (CRC/C/Add.188 2002) criticised this low age limit and recommended that the UK Government 'considerably raise the minimum age of criminal responsibility'. See also the Committee's criticism of Australia in CRC/C/15/Add.79, para 11.

[80] Children's Rights Alliance for England, *State of Children's Rights in England* (2008) p 6

[81] (2010) Department of Education and Skills, para 1.19. See also *Safeguarding children: working together under the Children Act 2004* (2007) Welsh Assembly Government.

[82] In *R (G) v London Borough of Southwark* [2009] UKHL 26, [2009] 3 All ER 189, [2009] 2 FCR 459, [2009] 2 FLR 380 Baroness Hale noted, in the context of s 20 of the Children Act 1989, that 'even a child on the verge of adulthood is considered and treated by Parliament as a vulnerable person to whom the state (through the relevant authority) owes a duty which is much wider than the mere provision of accommodation.'

[83] See **3.32–3.46** above. See also Art 17 of the ECHR.

if it would safeguard and promote their welfare.[84] Where children have been in care, amendments to the Children Act 1989 made by the Children (Leaving Care) Act 2000 require local authorities to keep in touch with certain care leavers until the age of 21, providing assistance with education, employment and training.[85] These provisions do not act to extend the domestic definition of a 'child' beyond the age of 18 but rather provide a degree of legal and social continuity as children transition from children with rights to adults with rights. Notwithstanding these provisions, children between the ages of 16 and 18 children can exist in a legal 'Twilight Zone' between childhood and adulthood.[86] Children under the age of 18 are unable to vote,[87] stand for Parliament[88] or local Government,[89] be a school governor, acquire a legal estate in land[90] or be a tenant for life or exercise the powers of a tenant for life of settled land,[91] serve on a jury,[92] enter into an enforceable contract[93] or make a will[94] and are subject to significant restrictions on their financial independence. Excepting contracts for the supply of necessaries and contracts of service, children cannot enter into legally binding contracts.[95] However, at 16 children can consent to surgical, medical or dental treatment,[96] leave school,[97] marry with the consent of their parents, enlist in the armed forces with the consent of their parents[98] and have lawful sexual intercourse.[99] Children over 17 can drive[100] and act as a pilot in command of an aircraft under a private pilots licence.[101]

---

[84]   CA 1989, s 20(5).
[85]   CA 1989, ss 23C, 24 and 24A–24D.
[86]   Bainham, A *Children, Parents and the State* (1988) Sweet & Maxwell, p 63.
[87]   Representation of the People Act 1983, s 1(1).
[88]   Electoral Administration Act 2006, s 17. However a child can be a sheriff (*Young v Fowler* (1640) Cro Car 555; *Claridge and Evelyn* (1821) 5 B & Ald 81 at 86 Abott CJ) or a goaler (2 Co Inst 382; Com Dig Officer (B 3); *Wittingham's Case* (1603) 8 Co Rep 42b at 44b per Coke CJ; *Young v Fowler* (1640) Cro Car 555; *Claridge and Evelyn* (1821) 5 B & Ald 81 at 86 Abott CJ) and may hold any office for which he or she may appoint a deputy (*Young v Stoell* (1632) Cro Car 279; *Young v Fowler* (1640) Cro Car 555; *Claridge and Evelyn* (1821) 5 B & Ald 81 at 86 Abott CJ) or which is ministerial and does not involve the exercise of discretion (Bac. Abr Infancy and Age (E); Com Dig Officer (B 3); *Crosbie v Huxley* (1833) Alc & N 431 at 440 per Bush CJ).
[89]   Local Government Act 1972, s 79.
[90]   Law of Property Act 1925, s 1(6).
[91]   Settled Land Act 1925, ss 19–20. Although a child may be lord of a manor and perform the functions of the office (*Swayne's Case* (1608) 8 Co Rep 63a at 63b per Coke J).
[92]   Juries Act 1974, s 1(a) as substituted by the Criminal Justice Act 2003, s 321 Sch 33, paras 1 and 2.
[93]   Minors Contracts Act 1987. However, a child may be liable for income tax (*R v Newmarket Income Tax Comrs, ex p Huxley* [1916] 1 KB 788, CA) and may be made bankrupt if the petition is based on an enforceable debt (*Re Debtor (No 564 of 1949), ex p Customs and Excise Comrs v Debtor* [1950] Ch 282, [1950] 1 All ER 308, CA; *Re A and M* [1926] Ch 274; *Re Davenport, ex p The Bankrupt v Eric Street Properties Limited* [1963] 2 All ER 850, [1963] 1 WLR 817, CA).
[94]   Wills Act 1837, s 7 (as amended by the Statute Law Revision (No 2) Act 1888 and the Family Law Reform Act 1969, s 3(1)(a)). However, a child who is a soldier or a sailor at sea may validly dispose of property by will (Wills Act 1837, s 11 and the Wills (Soldiers and Sailors) Act 1918, ss 1 and 2 as amended by the Family Law Reform Act 1969, s 3(1)(b)).
[95]   *Proform Sports Management Limited v Proactive Sports Management Limited and anor* [2006] EWHC 2812 (Ch), [2007] 1 All ER 542.
[96]   Family Law Reform Act 1969, s 8(1). See **6.98** below.
[97]   Pursuant to the Education and Skills Act 2008, s 2 education or training by way of a contract of apprenticeship will become compulsory up to the age of 17 from 2013 and compulsory up to the age of 18 from 2015.
[98]   Army Act 1955, s 2(3)(a).
[99]   Sexual Offences (Amendment) Act 2000.
[100] Road Traffic Act 1988, s 101(1).
[101] Air Navigation Order 2005, SI 2005/1970, Sch 8. A child aged 16 and over may act as a pilot in command of a glider (Air Navigation Order 2005, SI 2005/1970, art 37).

Deceased Children

4.24 The definition of a 'child' in domestic law does not encompass a deceased child. As noted above, the word 'person' in s 105(1) of the Children Act 1989 is interpreted as meaning a 'live person'.[102] Adopting the normal principles of statutory construction this definition would appear also to exclude a deceased child. Whilst the domestic courts have been prepared to determine disputes arising in respect of the burial of deceased children, such cases have been decided on the basis of the rights of surviving adults rather than on the basis that the deceased child is a person with whom the court is concerned.[103]

Evolving Capacity[104]

4.25 Whilst the foregoing discussion defines the point in law at which childhood commences and the point at which it ends, defining a child for the purposes of applying and enforcing children's rights is more complicated than simply identifying who is a child and who is not. At the heart of this complexity is what is termed the 'evolving capacity' of the child. This principle stems from the acknowledgement that childhood is not a single, fixed and universal experience between birth and majority but rather one in which, at different stages in their lives, children require different degrees of protection, provision, prevention and participation.[105] Within this context, a rights based system of protection, provision, prevention and participation based solely on identifying who is a child and who is not would be objectionable since such a system would take no account of what the continually developing child is capable of doing to protect, provide, prevent and participate for themselves.[106]

Evolving Capacity and the CRC

CRC, Art 5

4.26 The CRC introduces the concept of 'evolving capacity' in Art 5, which provides that:[107]

> 'States Parties shall respect the responsibilities, rights and duties of parents or, where applicable, the members of the extended family or community as provided for by local custom, legal guardians or other persons legally responsible for the child, to provide, *in a manner consistent with the evolving capacities of the child*, appropriate direction and guidance in the exercise by the child of the rights recognised in the present Convention.'

---

[102] See *Elliot v Joicey* [1935] AC 209 and *R v Newham London Borough Council, ex p Dada* [1996] QB 507, [1995] 2 All ER 552.

[103] See *Fessi v Whitmore* [1999] 1 FLR 767 per Boggis QC; *Borrows v HM Coroner for Preston (McManus Interested Party)* [2008] EWHC 1387 (QBD), [2008] 2 FLR 1225 and *Hartshorne v Gardner* [2008] EWHC 83 (Ch), [2008] 2 FLR 1681 and *Scotchings v Birch* [2008] EWHC 844 (Ch), [2008] All ER (D) 265 (Mar).

[104] For a highly detailed discussion of this topic in the context of the CRC see Lansdown, G *The Evolving Capacities of the Child* (2005) UNICEF/Save the Children.

[105] Van Bueren, G *Child Rights in Europe* (2007) Council of Europe Publishing, p 38.

[106] Verhellen, E *Convention on the Rights of the Child* (2000) Garant, p 26.

[107] Emphasis added. Article 14(2) of the CRC also refers to the evolving capacities of the child in the context of the right to freedom of though, conscience and religion, providing that 'States Parties shall respect the rights and duties of the parents and, when applicable, legal guardians, to provide direction to the child in the exercise of his or her right in a manner consistent with the evolving capacities of the child' (see **10.35 et seq** below). Article 12 of the CRC provides that the views of children should be given 'due weight in accordance with the age and maturity of the child' (see **6.11 et seq** below).

4.27 Article 5 of the CRC regulates the relationship between children, parents and the State by articulating a protective framework aimed at preventing exploitation, harm or abuse whilst at the same time extending increasing levels of autonomy and self-determination to the child as he or she develops.[108] For example, in its General Comment No 4 *Adolescent Health an Development in the Context of the Rights of the Child* the Committee on the Rights of the Child makes clear that:

> 'Before parents give their consent [in respect of health services], adolescents need to have a chance to express their views freely and their views should be given due weight, in accordance with article 12 of the Convention. However, if the adolescent is of sufficient maturity, informed consent shall be obtained from the adolescent her/himself, while informing the parents if that is in the "best interest of the child" (art. 3).'[109]

'Evolving Capacity'

4.28 The principle of 'evolving capacity' refers to the process of maturation and learning whereby children progressively acquire knowledge, competencies and understanding, including acquiring understanding about their rights and about how they can best be realised.[110] It establishes that as children acquire enhanced competencies, there is a reduced need for direction and a greater capacity to take responsibility for decisions affecting their lives.[111] The concept of 'evolving capacity' accepts that it is reasonable that children are informed and guided and gradually take over more responsibility in matters concerning them.[112] Art 5, together with Art 18 recognising parents' common responsibilities, emphasises that the child is the active subject of rights and recognises the cardinal importance of the exercise by the *child* of those rights.[113] Art 5 is about the child's path to maturity, which must come from increasing exercise of autonomy.[114]

4.29 To this end, the concept of 'evolving capacity' focuses on capacity rather than age as the determinant in the exercise of human rights.[115] The UN Committee on the Rights of the Child has stated:[116]

> 'Article 5 contains the principle that parents (and others) have the responsibility to continually adjust the levels of support and guidance they offer to a child. These adjustments take account of a child's interests and wishes as well as the child's capacities for autonomous decision-making and comprehension of his or her best interests. While a young child generally requires more guidance than an older child, it is important to take account of

---

[108] Lansdown, G *The Evolving Capacities of the Child* (2005) UNICEF/Save the Children, p 4. See also Art 3 of the UN Convention on the Rights of Persons with Disabilities which provides that a cardinal principle of that Convention is 'Respect for the evolving capacities of children with disabilities and respect for the right of children with disabilities to preserve their identities.'

[109] HRI/GEN/1/Rev.8 p 383.

[110] Committee on the Rights of the Child General Comment No 7 *Implementing Child Rights in Early Childhood* HRI/GEN/1/Rev.8 p 439, para 17.

[111] Lansdown, G *The Evolving Capacities of the Child* (2005) UNICEF/Save the Children, p 3 citing Van Bueren, G *The International Law on the Rights of the Child* (1998) Martinus Nijhoff.

[112] Flekkøy, M and Kaufmann, N *The Participation Rights of the Child* (1997) Jessica Kingsley, p 47.

[113] Newell, P and Hodgkin, R *Implementation Handbook for the Convention on the Rights of the Child* (2008) 3rd edn, UNICEF, p 75.

[114] Newell, P and Hodgkin, R *Implementation Handbook for the Convention on the Rights of the Child* (2008) 3rd edn, UNICEF, p 80. For a particularly difficult example of the issues arising from the concept of 'evolving capacity' see the comments of the Human Rights Committee concerning the applicability of Dutch laws on euthanasia to children aged 12 years old and over (CCPR/CO/72/NET and **5.13–5.14** below).

[115] Lansdown, G *The Evolving Capacities of the Child* (2005) UNICEF/Save the Children, p viii.

[116] Committee on the Rights of the Child General Comment No 7 *Implementing Child Rights in Early Childhood* HRI/GEN/1/Rev.8 p 439, para 17.

individual variations in the capacities of children of the same age and of their ways of reacting to situations. Evolving capacities should be seen as a positive and enabling process, not an excuse for authoritarian practices that restrict children's autonomy and self-expression and which have traditionally been justified by pointing to children's relative immaturity and their need for socialisation. Parents (and others) should be encouraged to offer 'direction and guidance' in a child-centered way, through dialogue and example, in ways that enhance young children's capacities to exercise their rights, including their right to participation (art. 12) and their right to freedom of thought, conscience and religion (art. 14).'

4.30   The concept of 'evolving capacity' should be considered by reference to the individual child. Lansdown observes that a parent's aspirations for their children, the expectations and demands placed on them, the cultural, economic and social environments in which children grow up, as well as their own unique life experiences, all impact on the ranges and level of capacities that children acquire and exercise.[117] The process of development is dynamic, influenced by a wide range of factors, including attachment,[118] cognitive development,[119] resilience[120] and, not least, the nature of the dispute in which a child may be involved.[121] It must be recognised that there is enormous variation between children in the process of evolving capacity, arising from these genetic and environmental influences.[122] Further, the adult tendency to underestimate the extent to which the capacity of the child has evolved must be held in mind when considering a child's capacity.[123] Likewise, it must be acknowledged that there may not necessarily be an exponential link between increasing knowledge, experience and cognitive capacity and an evolving capacity to make rational 'mature' decisions.[124]

Implementation Not Existence

4.31   The issue of evolving capacity does not, within the context of the practical application of children's rights, determine the *existence* of a child's rights only the

---

[117]   Within this context, McGoldrick points out that Art 5 is potentially problematic as those obliged to give effect to it may have a vested interest in ensuring that the child does not exercise his or her rights (see McGoldrick, D *The United Nations Convention on the Rights of the Child* (1991) 5 International Journal of Law and the Family 132, pp 138–139).

[118]   Bowlby, *Attachment and Loss, Volume 1 Attachment* (Hogarth Press 1969), Howe, Brandon, Hinings and Schofield, *Attachment Theory: Child Maltreatment ant and Family Support* (Macmiillan 1999).

[119]   Piaget and Inhelder, *The Psychology of the Child* (Routledge, Keegan and Paul, 1969).

[120]   Fonagy, Steele, Steele, Higgit and Target, *Theory and Practice of Resilience* (1994) Journal of Child Psychology and Psychiatry.

[121]   Fortin, J *Children's Rights and the Developing Law* (2005) 2nd edn, Cambridge, pp 254 and 257–267. See also Lansdown, G *The Evolving Capacities of the Child* (2005) UNICEF/Save the Children, p 13.

[122]   Jones, D *Communicating with Vulnerable Children* (2003) Gaskell, p 9. See also Archard, D *Children – Rights and Childhood* (2004) Routledge, p 96 and Fortin, J *Children's Rights and the Developing Law* (2005) 2nd edn, Cambridge, pp 72–74 and pp 253–254.

[123]   Lansdown, G *The Evolving Capacities of the Child* (2005) UNICEF/Save the Children, p ix. For example, there is evidence that pre-school children can take account of the views of other children, solve problems involving relative sizes, work with categories, appreciate possible causal action, construe objects symbolically and recognise discrete objects as persisting over time (Donaldson, M *Children's Minds* (1978) Fontana cited in Archard, D *Children – Rights and Childhood* (2004) Routledge, p 94).

[124]   See *R (on the application of Begum) v Headteacher and Governors of Denbigh High School* [2006] UKHL 15, [2006] 2 WLR 719 per Baroness Hale at para 93 ('Important physical, cognitive and psychological developments take place during adolescence. Adolescence begins with the onset of puberty; from puberty to adulthood, the 'capacity to acquire and utilise knowledge reaches its peak efficiency'; and the capacity for formal operational thought is the forerunner to developing the capacity to make autonomous moral judgments. Obviously, these developments happen at different times and at different rates for different people. But it is not at all surprising to find adolescents making different moral judgments from those of their parents. It is part of growing up. The fact that they are not yet fully adult may help to justify interference with the choices they have made. It cannot be assumed, as it can with adults, that these choices are the product of a fully developed individual autonomy').

method of their implementation. In law, an infant has no lesser rights than a teenager, notwithstanding their differential capacities. Their respective capacities simply influence the manner in which their equal rights are given *effect*. The issue of evolving capacity thus determines the question of how rights are realised not the question of whether such rights exist.[125] In *The Evolving Capacities of the Child* Lansdown concludes:[126]

> 'The concept of evolving capacities is central to the balance embodied in the Convention between recognising children as active agents in their own lives, entitled to be listened to, respected and granted increasing autonomy in the exercise of rights, while also being entitled to protection in accordance with their relative immaturity and youth. This concept provides the basis for an appropriate respect for children's agency without exposing them prematurely to the full responsibilities normally associated with adulthood. It is important to recognise that it is not respect for rights, as such, which is influenced by the evolving capacities of children: All the rights in the Convention on the Rights of the Child extend to all children irrespective of capacity. What is at issue is where responsibility for the exercise of the rights lies.'

Evolving Capacity and the ECHR

Neilsen v Denmark

4.32 The concept of 'evolving capacity' and its effect on the interrelationship between the rights of the child and the rights of parents and carers is also plainly relevant to the application and enforcement of children's rights under the ECHR. The European Court has historically taken an overtly paternalistic approach to 'evolving capacity' favouring the authority of parents. In *Nielsen v Denmark*[127] a 12 year old boy was placed at his mother's request in the psychiatric ward of a State hospital for a period of 5 1/2 months notwithstanding that he had no identifiable mental illness. The European Court held that this did not infringe the child's rights under Art 5 of the ECHR, the right to liberty and security of the person, as the parental decision to place the child in a psychiatric ward was for a 'proper purpose'. The basis of the decision appears to be a desire on the part of the court to ensure that Art 5 did not undermine Art 8, which the Court considered protected the right of parents to decide how children spent their time, holding that:[128]

> 'Family life in this sense, and especially the rights of parents to exercise parental authority over their children, having due regard to their corresponding responsibilities, is recognised and protected by the Convention, in particular by Article 8.'

4.33 As Fortin points out, there are significant difficulties with the decision in *Neilsen v Denmark*.[129] The Strasbourg judiciary were far from united on the issue, the European Commission on Human Rights having favoured the child's case and a significant number of the judges in the European Court of Human Rights giving dissenting judgements.[130] In any event, Fortin argues persuasively that it is difficult to accept that lengthy restrictions placed on a nervous boy of 12 who was not mentally ill could be said

---

[125] See Flekkøy, M and Kaufmann, N *The Participation Rights of the Child* (1997) Jessica Kingsley, p 47.
[126] (2005) UNICEF/Save the Children, p viii.
[127] (1988) 11 EHRR 175.
[128] (1988) 11 EHRR 175, para 61.
[129] Fortin, J *Children's Rights and the Developing Law* (2009) 3rd edn, Cambridge, p 101. See also *Re K (Secure Accommodation: Right to Liberty)* [2001] 1 FLR 526, paras 28 and 99 per Butler Sloss P and Judge LJ. See further **14.66** below.
[130] (1988) 11 EHRR 175, para 72. See **14.66** below.

to be a parental decision with a 'proper purpose'. By reason of these deficiencies, Fortin suggested in 2005 that a robust reassessment of *Nielsen v Denmark* was long overdue.[131]

4.34 In 2006, in *R (on the application of Axon) v Secretary of State for Health and another*,[132] in which the case of *Neilsen v Denmark* was cited in argument, Silber J held that:

> 'Turning to *Nielsen v Denmark* (1988) 11 EHRR 175, Mr Sales contends correctly in my view that it does not go further than establishing a limited parental right, but it is a right first only in relation to where the child must reside and other restrictions on the child's liberty, such as admission to hospital. The judgment referred to family life as incorporating 'a broad range of parental rights and responsibilities in regard to the care and custody of minor children' (para 61). It is significant that the complaint in that case (unlike the application in the present case) was not made under art 8 but under art 5(1) and so it is only an authority on the application of art 5(1) of the Convention.'

Having expressly considered *Neilsen v Denmark*, Silber J further observed, in respect of the question of whether Art 8 of the ECHR creates a 'right to parental authority over a child' that:

> 'In order to decide whether parents have what Mr Havers describes as 'the right of parental authority over a child' having regard to their having parental duties, the age and maturity of the young person is of critical importance. Lord Lester QC and Mr David Pannick QC state convincingly and correctly in my view that 'as a child matures, the burden of showing ongoing family life by reference to substantive links or factors grows' (*Human Rights Law and Practice* (Butterworths, 2nd Edn, 2004), para 4.8.48). This conclusion presupposes correctly that any right to family life on the part of a parent dwindles as their child gets older and is able to understand the consequence of different choices and then to make decisions relating to them ... The parental right to family life does not continue after that time and so parents do not have Art 8 rights to be notified of any advice of a medical professional after the young person is able to look after himself or herself and make his or her own decisions.'

This decision would appear to begin, within the context of domestic law, to decouple the link relied on in *Neilsen v Denmark* between Art 8 of the ECHR and parental authority at the point where a child reaches a level of development whereby he or she is able to understand the consequence of different choices and then to make decisions relating to them. This brings domestic jurisprudence in respect of the rights enshrined in the ECHR closer to the approach taken by the CRC and by the domestic courts to the concept of 'evolving capacity'.

'Evolving Capacity' in Domestic Law

Terminology – Capacity or Competence?

4.35 Within the context of the domestic definition of a child as 'a person under the age of eighteen' the balance between recognising children as active agents entitled to autonomy in the exercise of rights and recognising their need for protection in accordance with their relative immaturity has historically been discussed in terms of a child's 'competence' rather than his or her 'capacity', with the presumption being that the child 'lacks competence'.[133] By contrast, under the Mental Capacity Act 2005, the

---

[131]　See Fortin, J *Children's Rights and the Developing Law* (2005) 2nd edn, Cambridge, p 86. See **14.66** below.

[132]　[2006] EWHC 37 (Admin), [2006] 1 FCR 175.

[133]　*Gillick v West Norfolk and Wisbech Area Health Authority* [1986] AC 112.

extent to which the exercise of rights by persons over the age of 16 who suffer from an impairment of, or disturbance in the functioning of, the mind or brain can be the subject of interference is determined on the basis of 'capacity',[134] the presumption being that a person 'has capacity'.[135] The relevant terminology in this area and the burden of the applicable presumption thus differs as between children and incapacitated adults and as between the majority of children and those children aged between 16 and 18 who labour under mental incapacity.[136]

4.36 Within the international context, the concept of 'evolving capacity' is central to the application and enforcement of children's rights. Given the central role of international principles in the domestic application and enforcement of children's rights there is merit in the use of consistent terminology as between the international and domestic arenas. Further, it may be argued that 'capacity' is in any event a more appropriate term than 'competence' in that the term 'incompetent', in modern usage, carries a more pejorative meaning than the term 'incapacity'. Accordingly, save where the context requires, the term 'capacity' is used in place of the term 'competence' when discussing the domestic position.[137] The key question for examination here is how does the domestic law deal with the issue of a child's evolving capacity in the applying and enforcing the rights of that child?

Gillick v West Norfolk and Wisbech Area Health Authority[138]

4.37 In the case of *Gillick v West Norfolk and Wisbech Area Health Authority* Lord Scarman held that:[139]

'Parental rights clearly do exist, and they do not wholly disappear until the age of majority ... But the common law has never treated such rights as sovereign or beyond review and control. Nor has our law ever treated the child as other than a person with capacities and rights recognised by law. The principle of the law ... is that parental rights are derived from parental duty and exist only so long as they are needed for the protection of the person and property of the child ... parental rights yield to the child's right to make his own decisions when he reaches a sufficient understanding and intelligence to be capable of making up his own mind on the matter requiring decision.'

4.38 In explaining what he meant by the term 'sufficient understanding' Lord Scarman stated as follows:[140]

---

[134] Mental Capacity Act 2005, s 2(1). Section 2(1) provides that a person lacks capacity in relation to a matter if at the material time he is unable to make a decision for himself in relation to the matter because of a permanent or temporary impairment of, or a disturbance in the functioning of, the mind or brain.

[135] Many have argued that children should likewise be presumed to have capacity (see in particular Rodham, H *Children under the Law* Harvard Educational Review, 9, 22 1974).

[136] Under the Mental Capacity Act 2005 the Court of Protection may exercise its powers in relation to a persons property and affairs (other than by the execution of a will) even though he or she has not reached the age of 16 provided that he or she will still lack capacity to make decisions in respect of that matter when he reaches the age of 18 (see Mental Capacity Act 2005, s 18(3)).

[137] It should however be noted that imprecise terms such as 'capacity' have been criticised as being essentially meaningless without further refinement by reference to the body of research on children's developmental processes (see Fortin, J *Children's Rights and the Developing Law* (2005) 2nd edn, Cambridge, p 74 and **4.35** above).

[138] [1986] AC 112. See also Committee on the Rights of the Child General Comment No 4 *Adolescent Health and Development in the Context of the Convention on the Rights of the Child* HRI/GEN/1/Rev.8, paras 28, 33, 32, 39 and 41.

[139] See *Blackstone's Commentaries,* (1830) 17th edn, vol 1, p 452, where he states 'The power of parents over their children is derived from ... their duty' as cited in the judgment of Lord Fraser.

[140] [1985] 3 All ER 402 at 424, [1986] 1 AC 112 at 189. See also Committee on the Rights of the Child General Comment No 4 *Adolescent Health and Development in the Context of the Convention on the Rights of the*

'... when applying these conclusions to contraceptive advice and treatment it has to be borne in mind that there is *much* to be understood by a girl under the age of 16 if she is to have legal capacity to consent to such treatment. It is not enough that she should understand the nature of the advice which is being given; she must also have a sufficient maturity to *understand what is involved.* There are *moral and family questions*, especially her relationship with her parents; long term problems associated with the emotional impact of pregnancy and its termination; and there are risks to health of sexual intercourse at her age, risks which contraception may diminish but cannot eliminate. It follows that a doctor will have to satisfy himself that she is able to appraise these factors before he can safely proceed upon the basis that she has at law capacity to consent to contraceptive treatment.'

4.39 These principles have become known through usage as '*Gillick* competence' and reflect domestic recognition of the principle of the evolving capacity of the child.[141] Lord Scarman's judgment recognises, in the same way as Art 5 of the CRC, that as between children, parents and the State, the application and enforcement of children's rights moves from being an exercise of parental responsibility (or State intervention) to an exercise in participation and, finally, to an exercise of self-determination. The principle encompassed in *Gillick* applies in all areas of decision making by a child or young person.[142]

4.40 In Lord Scarman's formulation, parental rights exist only so long as they are necessary for the protection, welfare and promotion of the rights of the child. Once the child has developed the capacity to exercise those rights independently, the right of the parents to exercise their parental responsibility recedes.[143] In this regard '*Gillick* competence' is a developmental process centred on the evolving capacity of the child.[144] The child retains the same rights throughout this developmental process but becomes increasingly autonomous in the application and enforcement of those rights as his or her capacity evolves.

Evolving Capacity – A Continuing Parental Veto?

4.41 Lord Scarman's formulation of 'evolving capacity', that 'parental rights yield to the child's right to make his own decisions when he reaches a sufficient understanding and intelligence to be capable of making up his own mind on the matter requiring decision', has been the subject of further consideration by the Court of Appeal within the context of a child's ability to consent or refuse medical treatment.[145]

4.42 In *Re R (A Minor)(Wardship: Medical Treatment)*[146] Lord Donaldson MR held that the parents may override by parental veto a '*Gillick* competent' child's refusal to consent to medical treatment, although they may not veto a '*Gillick* competent' child's consent to treatment, drawing a distinction between the right of determination and the

---

Child HRI/GEN/1/Rev.8, para 32 and *C v Wren* 35 DLR (1986) (4th) 419 in which the Alberta Court of Appeal held that a child's disagreement with her parents did not imply that she had insufficient understanding to give informed consent to an abortion.

[141] The case has been described as 'a landmark in children's rights' (see Hale, B and others, *Family, Law & Society* (2009) Oxford, p 367).

[142] See *Re Roddy (A Child) (Identification: Restriction on Publication)* [2003] EWHC 2997 (Fam), [2004] 2 FLR 949.

[143] Lansdown, G *Children's Childhoods Observed and Experienced* in Mayall, B (ed) (1994) Falmer Press, pp 42–43.

[144] *Re R (A Minor) (Wardship: Medical Treatment)* [1992] Fam 11, [1991] 4 All ER, [1992] 1 FLR 190.

[145] See **6.43–6.46** for a detailed discussion of the child's right to participate in decisions concerning his or her own medical treatment.

[146] [1992] Fam 11 at 23, [1991] 4 All ER 177 at 185.

right of consent.[147] In *Re W (A Minor)(Medical Treatment: Court's Jurisdiction)*[148] on an appeal from a decision of Thorpe J, Lord Donaldson MR doubted that Lord Scarman's statement of principle in *Gillick* meant more than that the *exclusive* right of the parents to *consent* to treatment terminated.[149] Within this context, Lord Donaldson held that a child of any age who is '*Gillick* competent' in the context of particular medical treatment has a right to consent to that treatment, which consent cannot be overridden by those with parental responsibility, but reiterated that no child of whatever age has power by refusing consent to treatment to override a consent to treatment by someone who has parental responsibility for him or her. Pursuant to *Re W* therefore parents arguably retain the right to override a child's decision even if that child is '*Gillick* competent' at lease in respect of decisions which parents consider are adverse to the child's welfare.[150]

4.43 The interpretation of *Gillick* by the Court of Appeal in *Re R* and *Re W* appears to leave open two possible approaches by the courts to the wider role of 'evolving capacity' in domestic law when it comes to the role of continuing parental responsibility. First (per Lord Scarman's general statement of principle in *Gillick*) the decision of a child with sufficient understanding and intelligence to be capable of making up his own mind on the matter requiring decision is determinative of the issue being decided where the child expresses a preference. Second (per Lord Donaldson's interpretation of *Gillick*), that the decision of a child with sufficient understanding and intelligence to be capable of making up his own mind on the matter requiring decision is determinative of the issue being decided where the child expresses a preference, *save* where the child seeks to act against, or refuses to act in, what are considered by adults to be his or her own interests, in which case a parental veto remains until the child reaches majority notwithstanding the child's capacity. In examining these two positions, there are a number of difficulties with the more paternalistic view taken by the Court of Appeal.

4.44 First, the decisions of the Court of Appeal appear to ignore the fact that Lord Scarman plainly intended to go further than Lord Donaldson's formulation. Lord Scarman makes no distinction between a decision to consent to treatment and a decision to refuse consent to treatment and thus leaves open no possibility of a parental veto based on such a distinction once a child reaches a sufficient understanding and intelligence to be capable of making up his own mind on the matter requiring decision, be that decision consent or refusal to consent.[151]

4.45 Second, in any event there appears to be no logical distinction between consent and refusal of consent, Masson describing Lord Donaldson's attempt to create such a distinction on which a continuing parental veto is based as 'not convincing'.[152] As has

---

[147] Hershman, D and McFarlane, A *Children Law and Practice* Jordan Publishing, para A[55].

[148] [1993] Fam 64 at 75–76 and 87, [1992] 3 WLR 748,[1992] 4 All ER 627 at 633 and 642–643 *sub nom Re W (A Minor)(Consent to Medical Treatment)* [1993] 1 FLR 1.

[149] This analysis tends to ignore the fact that Lord Scarman's statement of principle was not limited to decisions concerning treatment but rather was expressed in relation to decisions in general, Lord Scarman holding that 'parental rights yield to the child's right to make his own decisions when he reaches a sufficient understanding and intelligence to be capable of making up his own mind *on the matter requiring decision*' (emphasis added). See **4.37** above.

[150] See also *Re P (Minors)(Wardship: Care and Control)* [1992] 2 FCR 681 per Butler-Sloss LJ and see s 8(1) of the Family Law Reform Act 1969.

[151] Balcombe LJ acknowledged *Re W* that 'I accept that the words "or not" in this passage suggest that Lord Scarman considered that the right to refuse treatment was co-existent with the right to consent to treatment.'

[152] Masson, J *Adolescent Crisis and Parental Power* (1991) Family Law 528–531. In particular, the distinction

been pointed out by many commentators, 'meaningful consent implies the possibility of saying "no" and having this refusal accepted'.[153] Fennell argues that:[154]

> 'What is not acceptable is the automatic assumption that refusal is irrational and can be overridden whether or not the patient is competent. This is the very assumption that underlies Lord Donaldson's guidance – that children under 16 are never competent even if they are *Gillick* competent, to refuse treatment as long as someone else with a concurrent power of consent agrees to it.'

4.46   Finally, Lord Scarman expressed the principle of 'evolving capacity' as being of general application to a 'matter requiring decision'.[155] The Court of Appeal cases which propose the existence of a continuing parental veto examine only a relatively narrow aspect of the issue of capacity. Further they concerned cases in which the children's refusal of medical treatment was rooted in their particular and difficult personal circumstances, which circumstances call into question whether the children in question had in fact reached, or were capable of reaching, a sufficient understanding and intelligence to be able to make up their own minds on the matters requiring decision.[156] Given their relatively narrow subject matter, and the question of whether these are cases which in fact deal with children with sufficient capacity, the *Re R* and *Re W* decisions give an incomplete picture of how a child's evolving capacity should be treated in the wider context of parental responsibility. Both cases were decided prior to the coming into force of the Human Rights Act 1998.[157]

4.47   The decisions in *Re R* and *Re W* have been heavily criticised as confusing the approach taken in *Gillick* to the extent that it is now difficult to give children very clear advice over their legal right to reach decisions for themselves.[158] Within the context of the difficulties with the Court of Appeal decisions in *Re R* and *Re W* it would appear that the domestic courts now prefer to apply the principles in *Gillick* without the gloss placed on that decision by the Court of Appeal in respect of the existence of a continuing parental veto. In *Re Roddy (A Child) (Identification: Restriction on Publication)*[159] Munby J, having considered the judgment of the Court of Appeal in *Re W* said:

> 'In my judgment (and I wish to emphasise this) it is the responsibility – it is the duty – of the court not merely to recognise but, as Nolan LJ said, to *defend* what, if I may respectfully say so, he correctly described as the *right* of the child who has sufficient understanding to make an informed decision, to make his or her own choice. This is not mere pragmatism, although as Nolan LJ pointed out, any other approach is likely to be both futile and

---

appears to rely on the questionable assumption that a decision to consent to treatment is likely to be correct and a decision to refuse treatment is likely to be incorrect.

[153]   Roberts, M *R v M: Refusal of Medical Treatment* (1999) Child Right 159, pp 14–15. See also Douglas, G *The Retreat from Gillick* (1992) 55 Modern Law Review 569.

[154]   Fennell, P *Informal Compulsion: the psychiatric treatment of juveniles under common law* (1992) Journal of Social Welfare and Family Law, 4: pp 311–313.

[155]   The judgment of Lord Fraser likewise suggests that the principles enunciated in *Gillick* were intended to be of general application to conflicts arising between parent and child, Lord Fraser observing 'It is, in my view, contrary to the ordinary experience of mankind, at least in Western Europe in the present century, to say that a child or a young person remains in fact under the complete control of his parents until he attains the definite age of majority, now 18 in the United Kingdom, and that on attaining that age he suddenly acquires independence.'

[156]   See **4.37** below.

[157]   See Fortin, J *Children's Rights and the Developing Law* (2005) 2nd edn, Cambridge, pp 130–131.

[158]   Ibid, p 71.

[159]   [2003] EWHC 2997 (Fam), [2004] 2 FLR 949.

counter-productive. It is also, as he said, a matter of principle. For, as Balcombe LJ recognised, the court must recognise the child's integrity as a human being.'

In *R (on the application of Axon) v Secretary of State for Health and another*[160] Silber J held in relation to Gillick that:

'the reasoning of the majority was that the parental right to determine whether a young person will have medical treatment terminates if and when the young person achieves a sufficient understanding and intelligence to understand fully what is proposed.'

and that:

'there is nothing in the speeches of the majority in *Gillick*, which suggests that parental authority has any place in decision-making for a young person, who in the words of Lord Scarman, which I have quoted in the last paragraph "achieves a sufficient understanding and intelligence to enable him or her to fully understand what is proposed".'

Evolving Capacity – A Continuing Judicial Veto?

4.48 The UN Committee on the Rights of the Child has emphasised that 'adolescents up to the age of 18 years old are holders of all the rights enshrined in the Convention; they are entitled to special protection measures and, according to their evolving capacities, they can progressively exercise their rights'.[161] Lord Donaldson's decisions in *Re R* and *Re W* are perhaps best seen as cases in which the application of the principle in *Gillick* created particular problems at the junction between a child's entitlement to special protection and a child's entitlement to exercise their rights, at which junction a balance must be struck between allowing young people as much freedom as they have the capacity for, whilst restraining them from making choices which restrict there own future development.[162] In *Re R* and *Re W* these particular difficulties centered on children with arguably sufficient capacity seeking to act against their own best interests. Such cases beg the question of whether children with sufficient capacity should be permitted to take a decision even though its consequences will be clearly detrimental to their welfare.[163] If they are not to be so permitted, the question becomes who, in the absence of a continuing parental veto, will countermand the child's decision?

4.49 In *Re R* the Court of Appeal held that in exercising its wardship jurisdiction the High Court had power to consent to medical treatment of a minor ward who was competent to consent to treatment but who had refused consent or was not asked and, conversely, the wardship court had an overriding power, which natural parents did not have, to refuse consent or forbid treatment even if the ward consented, if the consent or refusal of consent by the court was deemed to be in the child's best interests. In *Re W* the Court of Appeal held that the court, exercising its unlimited inherent jurisdiction over minors and whether the child was a ward of court or not, could, in the child's best interests objectively considered, override the decision of a '*Gillick* competent' child, Balcombe LJ stating that 'It is also clear that Lord Scarman was only considering the

---

[160] [2006] EWHC 37 (Admin), [2006] QB 539, [2006] 1 FCR 175, paras 56 and 95.

[161] Committee on the Rights of the Child General Comment No 4 *Adolescent Health and Development in the Context of the Convention on the Rights of the Child* HRI/GEN/1/Rev.8, para 1 and see Newell, P and Hodgkin, R Implementation Handbook for the Convention on the Rights of the Child (2008) 3rd edn, UNICEF, p 3.

[162] Fortin, J *Children's Rights and the Developing Law* (2005) 2nd edn, Cambridge, p 78.

[163] Cases will also arise where the decision of the child may conflict with the best interests of other children (see *R (on the application of Begum) v Headteacher and Governors of Denbigh High School* [2006] UKHL 15, [2006] 2 WLR 719 per Baroness Hale).

position of the child vis-à-vis its parents: he was not considering the position of the child vis-à-vis the court, whose powers, as I have already said, are wider than the parents'. The courts have historically demonstrated a willingness to exercise this judicial veto where the consequences of a child's decision are considered to be detrimental to that child's welfare.[164] It should also be noted that a court may also override the decision of a parent to consent or refuse to consent on behalf of a child.[165]

4.50   Unlike the basis for the 'parental veto' formulated in *Re R* and *Re W*, it is argued that there is a sound theoretical justification for the court overriding the decisions of children with sufficient capacity in circumstances where the consequences of those decisions will be manifestly to the detriment of child's future wellbeing.[166] In *Re W* Nolan LJ noted that it is the court's duty to ensure so far as it can that children survive to reach the age of majority. This proposition is reinforced by CRC which requires by Art 6(1) that 'States Parties shall ensure to the maximum extent possible the survival and development of the child'. Within this context, even if developmentally ready to make the decision in question, if that decision interferes with and restricts that child's ability for future choices that decision should be overborne.[167] Further, it is arguable that children have the right to be protected from such choices.[168]

4.51   Some notes of caution however must be sounded in respect of the continuing existence of a judicial veto to override decisions made by children with sufficient capacity to make the decision in question. Many of the decisions in respect of the courts jurisdiction to veto decisions made by children with sufficient capacity were decided prior to the implementation of the Human Rights Act 1998. Within the context of this legislation, there is a growing recognition that children 'are quite capable of being moral actors in their own right'.[169] An adult who has capacity to refuse medical treatment but is nonetheless treated is the victim of both a criminal and a tortuous act.[170] It is at least questionable whether some of the decisions concerning medical treatment of children would have been decided in the same way having regard to the provisions of the 1998 Act.[171]

4.52   The further difficulty with the judicial veto of decisions made by children with capacity is that this approach assesses capacity by reference to outcome. As Fortin

---

[164]   See for example *Re P (Minors) (Wardship: Care and Control)* [1992] 2 FCR 681 per Butler-Sloss LJ (the court is not restricted by the wishes and feelings of the child and should disregard those wishes and feelings where they diverge from the child's welfare); *Re W (Wardship: Publicity)* [1995] 2 FLR 466 (the court is required to consider whether children were sufficiently mature to be able to speak directly to, and be interviewed by, representatives of the press or broadcasting media); *Re C (Detention: Medical Treatment)* [1997] 2 FLR 180 per Wall J (the court had jurisdiction to direct that a child be detained as an in-patient at a clinic treating anorexia nervosa with the use of reasonable force if necessary); *Re M (Medical Treatment: Consent)* [1999] 2 FLR 1097 per Johnson J (court vetoed the decision of a 15 year old girl not to have a heart transplant on the basis she did not want someone else's heart) and *Re P (Medical Treatment: Best Interests)* [2003] EWHC 2327 (Fam), [2004] 2 FLR 1117 per Johnson J (whilst the views of a young man of 17 with established convictions demanded respect and whilst treatment imposed against the will of the patient was to be avoided wherever possible, a young Jehovah's witness should be administered blood and blood treatments against his will, there being no other form of treatment available).

[165]   See **5.55 et seq** below for a detailed discussion of this topic in the domestic context.

[166]   Fortin, J *Children's Rights and the Developing Law* (2005) 2nd edn, Cambridge, p 84.

[167]   Fortin, J *Children's Rights and the Developing Law* (2005) 2nd edn, Cambridge, p 76 citing MacCormick, N *Legal Right and Social Democracy: Essays in Legal and Political Philosophy* (1982) Clarendon Press, p 160.

[168]   Fortin, J *Children's Rights and the Developing Law* (2005) 2nd edn, Cambridge, p 84.

[169]   *Re D (A Child)* [2006] UKHL 51, [2007] 1 AC 619, [2007] 1 All ER 783, [2007] 1 FCR 1, [2007] 1 FLR 961.

[170]   See *Re JT (Adult: Refusal of Medical Treatment)* [1998] 1 FLR 48 and *Re C (Refusal of Medical Treatment)* [1994] 1 FLR 31.

[171]   Fortin, J *Children's Rights and the Developing Law* (2005) 2nd edn, Cambridge, pp 130–131.

points out, this carries with an implicit danger in that it involves imposing overtly adult criteria of rationality on young people, whilst ignoring their own individual beliefs and characters, which might provide perfectly sound reasons for their decisions, but according to their own system of values'.[172]

4.53 Finally, care must be taken to determine whether cases in which a judicial veto is being considered are cases that do in fact concern children with sufficient capacity and thus may be properly considered as authorities for the proposition that a child having sufficient capacity to make the decision which is the subject of dispute can be overborne by the court. In *Re W* Lord Donaldson held, in relation to a child with anorexia nervosa who did not wish to be treated that:[173]

> 'Where the wishes of the minor are themselves something which the doctors reasonably need to treated in the minors own best interests, those wishes clearly have a much reduced significance.'

It is possible to see how such a situation could not be characterised as one in which the child has reached a sufficient understanding and intelligence to be capable of making up his own mind on the matter requiring decision.

Evolving Capacity and Domestic Statutory Provisions

4.54 Within the domestic statutory regime there are a range of examples of the principle of 'evolving capacity' having been incorporated into the legislative regime in respect of children. The role of 'evolving capacity' in the domestic law as it touches and concerns children's rights, and the existence or otherwise or continuing parental or judicial vetoes, must also be considered in the context of these statutory provisions.

(i)   Family Law Reform Act 1969

4.55 Section 8(1) of the Family Law Reform Act 1969 gives explicit legal force to the effective consent of a child over the age of 16 to surgical, medical or dental treatment.

(ii)   Child Abduction and Custody Act 1985

4.56 Pursuant to Sch 1 Art 13 of the Child Abduction and Custody Act 1985 the judicial or administrative authority may also refuse to order the return of the child if it finds that the child objects to being returned and has 'attained an age and degree of maturity at which it is appropriate to take account of [his or her] views'.[174]

(iii)   Children Act 1989

4.57 During the Committee Stage of the Children Act 1989 the Lord Chancellor stated that the then Bill did nothing to change the underlying principle of *Gillick*.[175] To this end, the 1989 Act incorporates the principle that parental rights must be exercised in line with the evolving capacities of the child, the child's participation in a given decision

---

[172] Fortin, J *Children's Rights and the Developing Law* (2005) 2nd edn, Cambridge, p 83.

[173] See also *R v Waltham Forest London Borough ex p G* [1989] 2 FLR 138 in which Ewbank J questioned obiter whether *Gillick* had relevance in determining whether a child had sufficient capacity to give informed consent to a psychiatric assessment.

[174] See also the test in the Hague Convention on Protection of Children and Co-operation in Respect of Intercountry Adoption Art 4(d) 'having regard to the age and degree of maturity of the child'.

[175] *Hansard* HL, vol 502, col 1351.

being dependent on his or her 'age and understanding'.[176] The Act however stops short, save in certain narrowly specified situations,[177] of giving the child a right to act entirely independently of his or her parents upon reaching a sufficient understanding and intelligence to be capable of making up his own mind on the matter requiring decision.[178]

4.58 Elsewhere in the domestic statutory regime the language used to evoke the concept of 'evolving capacity' in domestic law is not qualified by the phrase 'age and understanding'.[179] The concept of 'evolving capacity' is also imported into domestic primary and secondary legislation concerning children by the use of the words 'sufficient understanding'.[180] For example, the concept of 'sufficient understanding' is central to the question of whether a child is considered to have the capacity to instruct a solicitor without an adult agent acting on his or her behalf in that instruction. As such, much of the domestic case law on 'evolving capacity' has centred on the issue of whether a child demonstrates 'understanding'. This topic is dealt with in detail in chapter 6.

Legal Status of the Child

4.59 The Universal Declaration of Human Rights provides that 'All are equal before the law and are entitled without any discrimination to equal protection of the law'.[181] Under the Universal Declaration, States Parties are thus under a duty to ensure that children are equal before the law. The granting to the child of sufficient *procedural* capacity and rights to protect this equality and the rights underpinning it, in which the concept of 'evolving capacity' is so central, is only the second step towards ensuring the child's equality before the law. This second step is dealt with in chapter 16 below. The first step is the recognition of the child's legal personality.[182] The Universal Declaration of Human Rights and the International Covenant on Civil and Political Rights provides that everyone shall have the right to recognition everywhere as a person before the law.[183] Within the context of children's rights, issues of legal personality have to date been articulated primarily in the context of a historical distinction between the legal status of those children born within and those children born outside marriage.[184] For ease of reference, these two groups of children will be referred to as marital and non-marital children.

---

[176] See for example s 1(3)(a) of the Children Act 1989. Coppock, V in *The New Handbook of Children's Rights* Franklin, B (ed) (2002) Routledge, p 150.

[177] See **6.112** below.

[178] Clarke, Hall & Morrison on Children, Lexis/Nexis, para 1[10].

[179] There are number of examples within the statutory regime where the consideration of the child's wishes and feelings is not qualified by the phrase 'age and understanding' or 'sufficient understanding'. See the Armed Forces Act 1991, s 22A, reg 16 of the Children (Secure Accommodation) Regulations 1991, SI 1991/1505, the Emergency Protection Order (Transfer of Responsibilities) Regulations 1991, r 5 and the Children (Leaving Care) (England) Regulations 2001, r 11(c)(i). See also s 25B of the Children Act 1989.

[180] Section 46(3)(c) of the Children Act 1989 (Police Protection) uses the phrase 'capable of understanding' in relation to the decision whether to inform the child of the steps taken and to be taken by the police under that section.

[181] Article 7.

[182] Van Bueren, G *The International Law on the Rights of the Child* (1998) Martinus Nijhoff, p 45.

[183] Universal Declaration of Human Rights, Art 6 and ICCPR, Art 16.

[184] There are however other potential distinctions in the legal status of children which require consideration, for example as between children who are aliens and children who are nationals (see UN Committee on the Rights of the Child General Comment No 6 *Treatment of Separated and Unaccompanied Children Outside their Country of Origin* HRI/GEN/1/Rev.8, para 18).

Legal Status of the Child – CRC

4.60 Article 25(2) of the Universal Declaration of Human Rights provides that 'All children, whether born in or out of wedlock, shall enjoy the same social protection'.[185] Although it contains in Art 2(1) a prohibition against discrimination, the CRC does not itself embody the concept of equality of children before the law. It would have been plainly preferable for the CRC to acknowledge explicitly that the recognition of the child's legal personality is a pre-condition of the child's recognition as a rights holder.[186] However, the comments of the UN Committee on the Rights of the Child make clear that differentiation between the legal status of individual children or groups of children, whether through an improper distinction being drawn between the status of marital and non-marital children or otherwise constitutes a breach of Art 2(1) of the CRC.[187] The *Study of Discrimination against Persons Born out of Wedlock* completed by the UN Sub-Commission on Prevention of Discrimination and Protection of Minorities also recognised the discriminatory nature of the differential legal position of marital and non-marital children.[188]

Legal Status of the Child – ECHR

4.61 Jurisprudence arising out of the ECHR makes it clear that differentiating between the legal status of children or groups of children can be a violation of the Art 8 right to respect for family life when read with Art 14 prohibiting discrimination on the grounds of 'birth or other status'.[189] In *Marckx v Belgium*[190] the European Court of Human Rights arrived at this conclusion by reason of the lack of any objective and reasonable justification for the differential treatment in Belgium of marital and non-marital children, stating that:

> 'When the State determines in its legal system the regime applicable to certain family ties such as between an unmarried mother and her child it must act in a manner calculated to allow those concerned to lead a normal family life.'

---

[185] Van Bueren observes that the ambit of this provision is limited as 'social protection' does not necessarily encompass legal protection, including the recognition of paternity, maternity and inheritance rights (Van Bueren, G *The International Law on the Rights of the Child* (1998) Martinus Nijhoff, pp 41–42). The equivalent provision in the American Convention on Human Rights is worded far more tightly, Art 17(5) providing that 'The law shall recognise the equal rights for children born out of wedlock and those born in wedlock.'

[186] See Van Bueren, G *The International Law on the Rights of the Child* (1998) Martinus Nijhoff, p 40.

[187] See for example the Committee's Report on Bulgaria CRC/C/15/Add.66 and Todorova, V *Family Law in Bulgaria: Legal Norms and Social Norms* (2000) International Journal of Family, Law and Policy, 14 148 at 162.

[188] E/CN.4/Sub.2/265/Rev.2.

[189] Article 17 of the revised European Social Charter also requires that there be no discrimination between children born without marriage and outside marriage. See for example the European Committee on Social Rights Conclusions XIII-2 (France, Malta) and Conclusions XVII-2 (Malta).

[190] (1979) 2 EHRR 330. See also *Brauer v Germany* (2009) Application No 3545/04, para 40 ('The Court reiterates in this connection that the Convention is a living instrument which must be interpreted in the light of present-day conditions. Today the member States of the Council of Europe attach great importance to the question of equality between children born in and children born out of wedlock as regards their civil rights. This is shown by the 1975 European Convention on the Legal Status of Children born out of Wedlock, which is currently in force in respect of twenty-one member States and has not been ratified by Germany. Very weighty reasons would accordingly have to be advanced before a difference of treatment on the ground of birth out of wedlock could be regarded as compatible with the Convention'). See further Lithuania: LTU-1995-2-005 01-06-1995/e 4/95 Restoration of the rights of ownership (g) *Valstybes Zinios* (Official Gazette) 47–1154, 7 June 2009 in which the Lithuanian Constitutional Court held that there are equal rights between adopted children, children who are fostered and marital children.

4.62   On 11 August 1978 the European Convention on the Legal Status of Children born out of Wedlock[191] entered into force.[192] The object of the Convention is 'to improve the legal status of children born out of wedlock by reducing the differences between their legal status and that of children born in wedlock which are to the legal or social disadvantage of the former'.[193] Art 2 provides that 'Maternal affiliation of every child born out of wedlock shall be based solely on the fact of the birth of the child' and Art 3 that 'Paternal affiliation of every child born out of wedlock may be evidenced or established by voluntary recognition or by judicial decision'. Specific provision is made in respect of issues of recognition of paternity,[194] maintenance for the child,[195] attribution of parental authority,[196] rights of access,[197] rights of succession,[198] and the effect of subsequent parental marriage.[199]

4.63   In cases decided subsequent to the coming into force of the Convention on the Legal Status of Children born out of Wedlock the European Court reiterated its position that differentiating between the legal status of children or groups of children can be a breach of the provisions of the ECHR when those provisions are read with Art 14. For example, in *Inze v Austria*[200] the applicant claimed a breach of Art 14 and Art 1 of the First Protocol, concerning peaceful enjoyment of possessions, on the basis that Austrian law denied him, as a child born out of wedlock, inheriting his mother's farm when she died intestate. The Court held that Austria could not satisfy the Court that such a difference in treatment had an objective and reasonable justification. Rather, the Court observed that Austrian had in fact had ratified the 1975 European Convention on the Legal Status of Children Born out of Wedlock and were also taking steps to modify the regional legislation on the point at issue. The Court found a breach of Art 14 and of Art 1 of the First Protocol.

Legal Status of the Child – Other Regional Instruments

4.64   Article 17(5) of the American Convention on Human Rights provides that 'The law shall recognise the equal rights for children born out of wedlock and those born in wedlock'. Article 18(3) of the African Charter on the Rights and Welfare of the Child provides that 'No child shall be deprived of maintenance by reference to the parents' marital status'.

Legal Status of the Child – Domestic Law

The Family Law Reform Acts

4.65   Reforms introduced by the Family Law Reform Act 1969 and the Family Law Reform Act 1987 have removed the majority of the distinctions that existed in domestic

---

[191]   (1975) CETS No 085.
[192]   The UK ratified the Convention on 24 February 1981. For the reservations entered by the UK upon ratifying the Convention see the CET List of declarations made in respect to Treaty No 085.
[193]   CLSCW Preamble, para 2. The preamble further notes that 'that in a great number of member States efforts have been, or are being, made to improve the legal status of children born out of wedlock by reducing the differences between their legal status and that of children born in wedlock which are to the legal or social disadvantage of the former'.
[194]   Article 5.
[195]   Article 6.
[196]   Article 7.
[197]   Article 8.
[198]   Article 9.
[199]   Article 10.
[200]   (1987) 10 EHRR 394. See also *Johnston v Ireland* (1986) 9 EHRR 203.

law between the legal status of children born inside marriage and the legal status those born outside marriage.[201] The Family Law Reform Act 1987 was designed to give effect to the recommendations of the Law Commission concerning non-marital children.[202] Section 1(1) of the Act provides as follows:

> 'In this Act and enactments passed and instruments made after the coming into force of this section,[203] references (however expressed) to any relationship between two persons shall, unless the contrary intention appears, be construed without regard to whether or not the father and mother of either of them, or the father and mother of any person through whom the relationship is deduced, have or had been married to each other at any time.'

4.66 The effect of s 1 is to remove the terms 'legitimate' and 'illegitimate' from the domestic legal lexicon.[204] The Act does not however abolish entirely the concepts of legitimacy and illegitimacy in domestic law in that these concepts remain relevant to the question of whether the father has parental responsibility for his child. Further, the Act includes within the category of marital children a number of children who the Act classifies using the concept of legitimacy, being those children legitimated at common law, certain children of void marriages, legitimated children, certain children who have a parent by virtue of s 42 or 43 of the Human Fertilisation and Embryology Act 2008, adopted children and those children 'otherwise treated in law as legitimate'.[205]

4.67 The concept of a child not being 'legitimate' in law should be an anathema to a legal system that purports to protect the rights of children.[206] The reforms introduced by the Family Law Reform Act 1987 result in the effective abolition of almost all of the distinctions drawn historically between the legal status of a marital child and the legal status of a non-marital child, including issues of succession on intestacy and dispositions of property.[207] However, the retention of the language of 'legitimacy' and 'illegitimacy' to determine the issue of parental responsibility and to categorise certain groups of children is unfortunate,[208] as is the fact that, by reason of the prospective nature of the Act, there will be a lengthy transitional period in which these classifications will remain relevant.[209]

Remaining Legal Distinctions

4.68 Within this context there remain three significant distinctions drawn in domestic law between the legal personality of marital children and that of non marital children. First, whilst upon separation and divorce the arrangements for marital children are the subject to scrutiny by the court,[210] non-marital children have no such protection on the

---

[201] Hale, B Pearl, D, Cooke, E and Monk, D *The Family, Law and Society* (2009) Oxford, p 447.
[202] See Law Com Nos 118 and 157 on Illegitimacy.
[203] The section came into force on 4 April 1988 (see Family Law Reform Act 1987 (Commencement No 1) Order 1988.
[204] See also the COE (70)15E Resolution *Social Protection of Unmarried Mothers and their Children* (1970) which resolves to avoid the use of terminology which discriminates against children.
[205] Family Law Reform Act 1987, s 1(3).
[206] See the Concluding Observations of the Committee on the Rights of the Child in respect of Libya in CRC/C/15/Add. 84, para 12.
[207] FLRA 1987 ss 18 and 19. See also the National Immigration and Asylum Act 2002 and the British Nationality (Proof of Paternity) Regulations 2006 which allow children born outside the UK to secure British Citizenship through an unmarried father.
[208] See Bainham, A *Is Legitimacy Legitimate?* [2009] Fam Law 673.
[209] Butterworths Family Law Service Lexis/Nexis, para 3A [472]. But see s 30 of the Act which permits the Lord Chancellor to promulgate secondary legislation to remove the terms 'legitimate' and 'illegitimate' from earlier legislation.
[210] FPR 1991, rr 2.2(2), 2.6(5).

separation of co-habiting parents. Second, it remains the position that non-marital children cannot inherit a dignity or a title of honour.[211] Finally, as Fortin points out, recent legislative reforms in respect of parental responsibility for unmarried fathers[212] has arguably resulted in the creation of three groups of children who enjoy subtly different legal relationships with their parents.[213]

4.69 The first of these three groups identified by Fortin are marital children, in respect of whom both parents have parental responsibility which cannot be terminated by court order.[214] The second group comprises non-marital children whose fathers are identified on their birth certificates, in respect of whom both parents have parental responsibility but in respect of whom the father's parental responsibility can be terminated by order of the court.[215] The third group is comprised of non marital children whose fathers are not identified on their birth certificates, in respect of whom only their mother has parental responsibility.[216] This latter group will be left with no parent with parental responsibility in the event of their mother dying, exposing them to, for example, acrimonious disputes as to whether their father should be permitted to care for them.[217]

4.70 Whilst European jurisprudence mitigates the position of non-marital children whose father's do not hold parental responsibility for them by placing a positive obligation on the state to enable children to be integrated within his or her marital or non-marital family from birth,[218] the European court has rejected arguments that the provisions of the Children Act 1989 that prevent fathers being recognised as such as a matter of course breach the provisions of the ECHR.[219] This position appears to persist even after the death of the mother.[220] Notwithstanding this position, it is difficult to see how the creation of a sub-group of children whose legal personality encompasses, without a choice on their part, no legal relationship with their fathers cannot but offend against the principles of non-discrimination which underpin children's rights.[221]

---

[211] Legitimacy Act 1976, Sch 1, para 4(2). During the drafting of the CRC the United Kingdom was not able to agree to an article on non-discrimination which incorporated a provision concerning marital and non-marital children on the basis that such an article may affect established lines of succession to the throne, a position which apparently caused much amusement to the Polish Chair and other delegates (Van Bueren, G *The International Law on the Rights of the Child* (1998) Martinus Nijhoff, p 43).

[212] Children Act 1989, s 4(1)(a) as amended by the Adoption and Children Act 2002, s 11 by which parental responsibility is automatically conferred on an unmarried father whose name appears on the child's birth certificate.

[213] Fortin, J *Children's Rights and the Developing Law* (2009) 3rd edn, Cambridge, pp 482–487.

[214] CA 1989, s 2(1).

[215] CA 1989, s 4(3).

[216] Fortin also proposes a fourth group of children, comprising those children born before the reforms whose unmarried father's are entered on their birth certificates but under the old law do not have parental responsibility.

[217] See for example *Re S (Custody: Habitual Residence)* [1998] 1 FLR 122.

[218] *Marckx v Belgium* (1979) 2 EHHR 330, para 31.

[219] *B v United Kingdom* [2000] 1 FLR 1. The justification for this position was held to be the fact that a relationship between children and their unmarried fathers 'varies from ignorance and indifference to a close stable relationship indistinguishable from the conventional family based unit'. See also *Re W (Minors) (Abduction: Father's Rights)* [1999] Fam 1 and *Paulik v Slovakia* Application No 106/05 [2006] 3 FCR 333, para 58.

[220] See *Yousef v Netherlands* [2002] 3 FCR 577, [2003] 1 FLR 210.

[221] See Lowe, N *The Meaning and Allocation of Parental Responsibility* (1997b) International Journal of Law, Policy and the Family, p 192 and Eekelaar, J *Rethinking Parental Responsibility* [2001] Fam Law 426.

PROTECTION FROM DISCRIMINATION

The Principle of Equality

4.71   An examination of the legal status and personality of the child highlights the central importance of the principle of equality to the application and enforcement of children's rights. As Van Bueren observes, 'the moral imperative lying behind much of international human rights law is to treat all humanity as of equal worth'.[222] Giving a dissenting judgement in the International Court of Justice in the *South West Africa Cases (Second Phase)*[223] Judge Tanaka, addressed the concept of equality as follows:

'In what way is each individual allotted his sphere of freedom by the principle of equality? What is the content of this principle? The principle is that what is equal is to be treated equally and what is different is to be treated differently, namely proportionately to the factual difference. This is what was indicated by Aristotle as *justitia commutativa* and *justicia distributive*. The most fundamental point in the equality principle is that all human beings as persons have an equal value in themselves, that they are the aim itself and not the means for others ... It underlies all modern, democratic and humanitarian law systems as a principle of natural law. This idea however does not exclude the different treatment of persons from the consideration of the differences of factual circumstances such as sex, age, language, religion, economic condition, education, etc. To treat different matters equally in a mechanical way would be as unjust to as to treat equal matters differently ... We can say accordingly that the principle of equality before the law does not mean the absolute equality, namely equal treatment of men without regard to individual, concrete circumstances, but it means the relative equality, namely the principle to treat equally what are equal and unequally what are unequal ... To treat unequal matters differently according to their inequality is not only permitted but required. The issue is whether the difference exists. Accordingly, not every different treatment can be justified by the existence of differences, but only such as corresponds to the differences themselves, namely that which is called for by the idea of justice – "the principle to treat equal equally and unequal according to its inequality, constitutes an essential content of the idea of justice (Goetz Hueck, *Der Grundsatz der Gleichmässigen Behandlung in Privatrecht, 1958, p 106) [Translation]* ... The question arises: what is equal and what is different ... All human beings, notwithstanding the differences in their appearance and other minor points, are equal in their dignity as persons. Accordingly, from the point of view of human rights and fundamental freedoms, they must be treated equally ... The principle of equality does not mean absolute equality, but recognises relative equality, namely different treatment proportionate to concrete individual circumstances ... Different treatment must not be give arbitrarily; it requires reasonableness, or must be in conformity with justice.'

4.72   Lord Hoffman, defining discrimination in *R (on the application of Carson) v Secretary of State for Work and Pensions*; *R (on the application of Reynolds) v Secretary of State for Work and Pensions* held:[224]

'Discrimination means a failure to treat like cases alike. There is obviously no discrimination when the cases are relevantly different. Indeed, it may be a breach of art 14 not to recognise the difference: see *Thlimmenos v Greece* (2000) 9 BHRC 12. There is discrimination only if the cases are not sufficiently different to justify the difference in treatment.'

---

[222]   Van Bueren, G *The International Law on the Rights of the Child* (1998) Martinus Nijhoff, p 38.
[223]   ICJ Reports 1966 305–306 and 313–314.
[224]   [2005] UKHL 37, [2005] 4 All ER 545, para 14.

When the case reached the European Court of Human Rights as *Carson v United Kingdom*, the Court reflected the approach taken by the House of Lords, holding that:[225]

> 'The Court has established in its case-law that only differences in treatment based on an identifiable characteristic, or "status", are capable of amounting to discrimination within the meaning of Article 14. Moreover, in order for an issue to arise under Article 14 there must be a difference in the treatment of persons in analogous, or relevantly similar, situations . . .Discrimination means a failure to treat like cases alike; there is no discrimination when the cases are relevantly different.'

4.73 In the application and enforcement of children's rights, it is accordingly necessary to be able to distinguish between discrimination on the one hand and reasonable measures of differentiation on the other.[226] Discrimination against children, as with discrimination against adults, challenges the principle of equality and fundamentally undermines children's rights. Such discrimination occurs not only when there is discrimination against children by adults, but also as between different groups of children.[227] Children may be themselves the source of discrimination against other children.[228] In addition to discrimination arising out of differential treatment concerning their fundamental rights, children may also be victims of economic and social discrimination. For example discrimination can result from a child's location, with children living in rural areas or on the margins of urban life experiencing discrimination in respect of economic and social rights.[229]

The CRC and Equality

The CRC and Equality – The Wider Context

4.74 The vast majority of international human rights instruments stress the primacy of equality between individuals, including those conventions comprising the UN human rights framework, namely the Universal Declaration of Human Rights and the six core human rights treaties.[230] None of the human rights conventions include a minimum age requirement for the protection from discrimination in the exercise of human rights.[231] The protection against discrimination with which the CRC underpins the rights of children must be considered within this much wider body of treaty law concerning discrimination, much of which is relevant to the application and enforcement of children's rights.

---

225 [2008] All ER (D) 18 (Nov), paras 73 and 77.
226 Brownlie, I *Principles of Public International Law* (2008) 7th edn, OUP, p 573.
227 Van Bueren *Child Rights in Europe* (2007) Council of Europe Publishing, p 40.
228 Besson, S *The Non-discrimination Principle in the Convention on the Rights of the Child* (2005) International Journal of Children's Rights, pp 433–461
229 See for example Boyden, J and Holden, P *Children of the Cities* (1991) Zed Books. The courts however demonstrate a marked reluctance to grant relief in respect of economic and social discrimination (see for example Case Comment *Education: placement of Roma children in special schools* European Human Rights Law Review (2006) 340 at 343 and the dissenting opinion of Judge Borrego in *DH and Others v Czech Republic* [2008] ELR 17, 23 BHRC 526, para 5). See also **3.7–3.16** above.
230 The Convention on the Rights of the Child, the International Covenant on Civil and Political Rights, the International Covenant on Economic, Social and Cultural Rights, the Convention against Torture and other Cruel, Inhuman or Degrading Treatment or Punishment, the International Convention on the Elimination of All Forms of Racial Discrimination and the Convention on the Elimination of All Forms of Discrimination against Women.
231 Children's Rights Alliance for England, *Making the Case: Why Children Should be Protected from Age Discrimination and How it Can be Done – Proposals for the Equality Bill* (2009), p 3.

Universal Declaration of Human Rights[232]

4.75   Having declared in Art 1 that 'All human beings are born free and equal in dignity and rights', Art 2 of the Universal Declaration of Human Rights provides that:[233]

> 'Everyone is entitled to all the rights and freedoms set forth in this Declaration, without distinction of any kind, such as race, colour, sex, language, religion, political or other opinion, national or social origin, property, birth or other status. Furthermore, no distinction shall be made on the basis of the political, jurisdictional or international status of the country or territory to which a person belongs, whether it be independent, trust, non-self-governing or under any other limitation of sovereignty.'

International Covenant on Civil and Political Rights[234]

4.76   Article 26 of International Covenant on Civil and Political Rights casts the primacy of equality in terms of equality before the law, prohibiting discrimination in the following terms:

> 'All persons are equal before the law and are entitled without any discrimination to the equal protection of the law. In this respect, the law shall prohibit any discrimination and guarantee to all persons equal and effective protection against discrimination on any ground such as race, colour, sex, language, religion, political or other opinion, national or social origin, property, birth or other status.'[235]

Article 24 of the Covenant applies the principle of non-discrimination to the right of children to specific protection arising out of their status as minors, stipulating that:

> 'Every child shall have, without any discrimination as to race, colour, sex, language, religion, national or social origin, property or birth, the right to such measures of protection as are required by his status as a minor, on the part of his family, society and the State.'

4.77   The United Nations Human Rights Committee, commenting upon the meaning of the term 'discrimination' in the Covenant on Civil and Political Rights has proposed the following definition:[236]

> '... the Committee believes that the term 'discrimination' as used in the Covenant should be understood to imply any distinction, exclusion, restriction or preference which is based on any ground such as race, colour, sex, language, religion, political or other opinion, national or social origin, property, birth or other status, and which has the purpose or effect of nullifying or impairing the recognition, enjoyment or exercise by all persons, on an equal footing, of all rights and freedoms.'

With specific reference to Art 24 of the Covenant, the Human Rights Committee has observed that:

---

[232]   See **2.31** above.
[233]   For the other Conventions prohibiting discrimination see **4.93** under 'The Position in International Law'.
[234]   See **2.32** above.
[235]   The UN International Covenant on Economic, Social and Cultural Rights provides at Art 2(2) that 'The States Parties to the present Covenant undertake to guarantee that the rights enunciated in the present Covenant will be exercised without discrimination of any kind as to race, colour, sex, language, religion, political or other opinion, national or social origin, property, birth or other status.'
[236]   General Observations No 18 of 10 November 1989 CCPR/C/21/Rev.1/Add.1. It has been observed that this comment is of relevance to the CRC (see Newell, P and Hodgkin, R *Implementation Handbook for the Convention on the Rights of the Child* (2008) 3rd edn, UNICEF, p 17).

'The Covenant requires that children should be protected against discrimination on any grounds such as race, colour, sex, language, religion, national or social origin, property or birth. In this connection, the Committee notes that, whereas non-discrimination in the enjoyment of the rights provided for in the Covenant also stems, in the case of children, from article 2, and their equality before the law from article 26, the non-discrimination clause contained in article 24 relates specifically to the measures of protection referred to in that provision. Reports by States Parties should indicate how legislation and practice ensure that measures of protection are aimed at removing discrimination in every field, including inheritance, particularly as between nationals and children who are aliens, or as between legitimate children and children born out of wedlock.'[237]

The International Convention on the Elimination of All Forms of Racial Discrimination[238]

4.78 The International Convention on the Elimination of All Forms of Racial Discrimination and the Convention on the Elimination of All Forms of Discrimination against Women have as there cardinal aim the elimination of specific forms of discrimination. Articles 1 and 2 of the International Convention on the Elimination of All Forms of Racial Discrimination provide that:[239]

'1. In this Convention the term "racial discrimination" shall mean any distinction, exclusion, restriction or preference based on race, colour, descent, or national or ethnic origin which has the purpose or effect of nullifying or impairing the recognition, enjoyment or exercise, on an equal footing, of human rights and fundamental freedoms in the political, economic, social, cultural or any other field of public life.

2. States Parties condemn racial discrimination and undertake to pursue by all appropriate means and without delay a policy of eliminating racial discrimination in all its forms and promoting understanding among all races, and, to this end: (a) Each State Party undertakes to engage in no act or practice of racial discrimination against persons, groups of persons or institutions and to ensure that all public authorities and public institutions, national and local, shall act in conformity with this obligation ...'

In its General Recommendation No 14 on the definition of discrimination, the Committee on the Elimination of Racial Discrimination stated:

'A distinction is contrary to the Convention if it has either the purpose or the effect of impairing particular rights and freedoms. This is confirmed by the obligation placed upon States parties by article 2, paragraph 1 (c), to nullify any law or practice which has the effect of creating or perpetuating racial discrimination ... In seeking to determine whether an action has an effect contrary to the Convention, [the Committee] will look to see whether that action has an unjustifiable disparate impact upon a group distinguished by race, colour, descent, or national or ethnic origin.'[240]

---

[237] See Human Rights Committee General Comment No 17 *Article 24 (Rights of the Child)* HRI/GEN/1/Rev.8, para 5.

[238] See **2.36** above. See also Lerner, N *The United Nations Convention on the Elimination of All Forms of Racial Discrimination* (1980) 2nd edn, Sijthoff & Noordhoff.

[239] See also Arts 1–9 of the UN Declaration on Race and Racial Prejudice adopted by the UNESCO General Conference on 27 November 1978.

[240] Committee on the Elimination of Racial Discrimination General Recommendation No 14 on Article 1 Paragraph 1 of the Convention HRI/GEN/1/Rev.8 p 247, para 1.

International Convention on the Elimination of All Forms of Discrimination against Women[241]

4.79   Articles 1 and 2 of the International Convention on the Elimination of All Forms of Discrimination against Women stipulate that:

'1. For the purposes of the present Convention, the term "discrimination against women" shall mean any distinction, exclusion or restriction made on the basis of sex which has the effect or purpose of impairing or nullifying the recognition, enjoyment or exercise by women, irrespective of their marital status, on a basis of equality of men and women, of human rights and fundamental freedoms in the political, economic, social, cultural, civil or any other field.

2. States Parties condemn discrimination against women in all its forms, agree to pursue by all appropriate means and without delay a policy of eliminating discrimination against women . . .'[242]

4.80   The obligations on States Parties under CEDAW include the obligation under Art 5(1) of the Convention:

'To ensure that family education includes a proper understanding of maternity as a social function and the recognition of the common responsibility of men and women in the upbringing and development of their children, it being understood that the interest of the children is the primordial consideration in all cases.'

4.81   Beyond conventions comprising the UN Human Rights Framework, the Convention on the Rights of Persons with Disabilities, the Convention against Discrimination in Education and the Declaration on the Elimination of all Forms of Intolerance and Discrimination based on Religion or Belief each deal with the principle of non-discrimination within the context of their specific subject matter.[243]

Convention on the Rights of Persons with Disabilities[244]

4.82   Article 4 of the UN Convention on the Rights of Persons with Disabilities provides that:

---

[241]   See **2.37** above.

[242]   The United Kingdom has entered a series of detailed reservations in relation to this Convention (see http://www.un.org/womenwatch/daw/cedaw/reservations-country.htm).

[243]   See also Art 3 of the Convention Relating to the Status of Refugees ('The Contracting States shall apply the provisions of this Convention to refugees without discrimination as to race, religion or country of origin.'), Art 1 of the Convention on the Protection of the Rights of All Migrant Workers and their Families ('The present Convention is applicable, except as otherwise provided hereafter, to all migrant workers and members of their families without distinction of any kind such as sex, race, colour, language, religion or conviction, political or other opinion, national, ethnic or social origin, nationality, age, economic position, property, marital status, birth or other status') and Art 24 of the Declaration on Social and Legal Principles relating to the Welfare and Protection of Children with Special Reference to Foster Placement and Adoption Nationally ('Where the nationality of the child differs from that of the prospective adoptive parents, all due weight shall be given to both the law of the State of which the child is a national and the law of the State of which the prospective adoptive parents are nationals. In this connection due regard shall be given to the child's cultural and religious background and interests').

[244]   See **2.41** above.

'States Parties undertake to ensure and promote the full realisation of all human rights and fundamental freedoms for all persons with disabilities without discrimination of any kind on the basis of disability.'[245]

Article 3 provides that a key principle of the CRPD is 'Respect for the evolving capacities of children with disabilities and respect for the right of children with disabilities to preserve their identities'. Article 7 of the CRPD provides that 'States Parties shall take all necessary measures to ensure the full enjoyment by children with disabilities of all human rights and fundamental freedoms on an equal basis with other children', and that 'In all actions concerning children with disabilities, the best interests of the child shall be a primary consideration'. Further, Art 7 stipulates that 'States Parties shall ensure that children with disabilities have the right to express their views freely on all matters affecting them, their views being given due weight in accordance with their age and maturity, on an equal basis with other children, and to be provided with disability and age-appropriate assistance to realise that right'.

Convention against Discrimination in Education[246]

4.83 Articles 1–3 of the Convention against Discrimination in Education stipulate that:

'1. For the purposes of this Convention, the term ' discrimination ' includes any distinction, exclusion, limitation or preference which, being based on race, colour, sex, language, religion, political or other opinion, national or social origin, economic condition or birth, has the purpose or effect of nullifying or impairing equality of treatment in education and in particular:[247]

(a) Of depriving any person or group of persons of access to education of any type or at any level;
(b) Of limiting any person or group of persons to education of an inferior standard;
(c) Subject to the provisions of Article 2 of this Convention, of establishing or maintaining separate educational systems or institutions for persons or groups of persons; or
(d) Of inflicting on any person or group of persons conditions which are incompatible with the dignity of man.

Declaration on the Elimination of all forms of Intolerance and Discrimination based on Religion or Belief[248]

4.84 Article 2 of the Declaration on the Elimination of all forms of Intolerance and Discrimination based on Religion or Belief stipulates that:

'1. No one shall be subject to discrimination by any State, institution, group of persons, or person on the grounds of religion or other belief.

---

[245] See also Art 5(2) ('States Parties shall prohibit all discrimination on the basis of disability and guarantee to persons with disabilities equal and effective legal protection against discrimination on all grounds').
[246] See **2.45** above.
[247] Article 2 permits establishment or maintenance of separate educational systems or institutions for pupils of the two sexes, establishment or maintenance, for religious or linguistic reasons, of separate educational systems or institutions offering an education which is in keeping with the wishes of the pupil's parents or legal guardians and establishment or maintenance of private educational institutions, if the object of the institutions is not to secure the exclusion of any group but to provide educational facilities in addition to those provided by the public authorities provided certain minimum criteria are met. See **10.30** below.
[248] See **2.51** above.

2. For the purposes of the present Declaration, the expression 'intolerance and discrimination based on religion or belief' means any distinction, exclusion, restriction or preference based on religion or belief and having as its purpose or as its effect nullification or impairment of the recognition, enjoyment or exercise of human rights and fundamental freedoms on an equal basis.'

The CRC and Equality – CRC, Art 2

4.85 Within the foregoing context, the preamble to the CRC begins, in reference to the Charter of the United Nations, by recognising 'the inherent dignity and the equal and inalienable rights of the all members of the human family'. The preamble to the CRC goes on to recongise 'that the United Nations has, in the Universal Declaration of Human Rights and in the International Covenants on Human Rights, proclaimed and agreed that everyone is entitled to all the rights and freedoms set forth therein, without distinction of any kind, such as race, colour, sex, language, religion, political or other opinion, national or social origin, property, birth or other status'. Non-discrimination has been identified by the Committee on the Rights of the Child as a general principle of fundamental importance for implementation of the whole of the CRC.[249]

4.86 Articulating the principle of non-discrimination within the body of the CRC, Art 2 of the CRC provides that:

'1. States Parties shall respect and ensure the rights set forth in the present Convention to each child within their jurisdiction without discrimination of any kind, irrespective of the child's or his or her parent's or legal guardian's race, colour, sex, language, religion, political or other opinion, national, ethnic or social origin, property, disability, birth or other status.

2. States Parties shall take all appropriate measures to ensure that the child is protected against all forms of discrimination or punishment on the basis of the status, activities, expressed opinions, or beliefs of the child's parents, legal guardians, or family members.'

Ambit of CRC, Art 2

(i)   CRC, Art 2 – Broad Scope of Article

4.87 Article 2(1) prohibits only discrimination in respect of the rights embodied within the CRC as between adults and children and as between different groups of children. Article 2(2) has a wider application in that the discrimination prohibited extends beyond the rights enshrined in the CRC to encompass the status, activities, expressed opinions, or beliefs of the child's parents, legal guardians, or family members.[250] It may even be broad enough, if coupled with a positive duty on States Parties, to deal with economic and social discrimination against children.[251] The principal of non-discrimination under Art 2 applies equally to private institutions and individuals as well as the State.[252] The words 'to each child within their jurisdiction' in

---

[249]   Newell, P and Hodgkin, R *Implementation Handbook for the Convention on the Rights of the Child* (2008) 3rd edn, UNICEF, p 17.

[250]   The potential implications of Art 2(2) have been described as 'very wide' (Newell, P and Hodgkin, R *Implementation Handbook for the Convention on the Rights of the Child* (2008) 3rd edn, UNICEF, p 30).

[251]   Newell, P and Hodgkin, R *Implementation Handbook for the Convention on the Rights of the Child* (2008) 3rd edn, UNICEF, p 41.

[252]   Newell, P and Hodgkin, R *Implementation Handbook for the Convention on the Rights of the Child* (2008) 3rd edn, UNICEF, p 22 and see Zimbabwe CRC/C/15/Add.55, para 12.

Art 2(1) make clear that the non-discrimination principle in Art 2 applies to all children in the jurisdiction, including visitors, children of migrant workers, refugees and children in the jurisdiction illegally.[253]

(ii)   CRC, Art 2 – Positive Obligations

4.88   Van Bueren considers that, by applying to Art 2(1) of the CRC the Human Rights Committee General Comment criteria in relation to the International Covenant on Civil and Political Rights Art 24[254] it is possible to imply that States Parties are not only under a duty to prevent discrimination but are also obliged to take positive steps to ensure children enjoy rights which enable them to be recognised as equally valuable members of society.[255] Newell and Hodgkin describe an 'active' obligation on States Parties to prevent discrimination.[256] Alston notes that the use of the phrase 'to ensure' in Art 2(1) implies an affirmative obligation on the part of the State to take measures necessary to enable children to enjoy and exercise their rights without discrimination.[257]

(iii)   CRC, Art 2 – Positive Discrimination

4.89   Relying on a further General Comment made by the Human Rights Committee,[258] it has been suggested that the non-discrimination principle does not bar positive discrimination, sometimes called 'affirmative action', in order to diminish or eliminate conditions which cause discrimination against children.[259] However, care must be taken with this proposition, and in particular that affirmative action does not itself lead to discrimination.[260] In *Equal Opportunities Commission v Director of Education*[261] Hartman J, sitting in the High Court of the Hong Kong Special Administrative Region, held that a scheme designed to ensure 'gender balance' in secondary schools by a process of scaling entrance exams to the advantage of male pupils constituted direct sex discrimination. Hartman J observed that whilst it was argued that the purpose of the scaling of exam results was to achieve equality of treatment for boys and girls, it did not take account of the underlying principle that fundamental rights, such as the right to equal treatment free of sex discrimination, attach to the individual child and not groups of children.[262]

---

[253]   Newell, P and Hodgkin, R *Implementation Handbook for the Convention on the Rights of the Child* (2008) 3rd edn, UNICEF, p 17 and see Committee on the Rights of the Child General Comment No 6 *Treatment of Unaccompanied and Separated Children Outside their Country of Origin* HRI/GEN/1/Rev 8, p 413, para 18.

[254]   See **4.76** above.

[255]   Van Bueren, G *The International Law on the Rights of the Child* (1998) Martinus Nijhoff, p 40. This would reflect the position under the ECHR (see **4.98** below).

[256]   Newell, P and Hodgkin, R *Implementation Handbook for the Convention on the Rights of the Child* (2008) 3rd edn, UNICEF, p 21.

[257]   Alston, P *The legal framework of the Convention on the Rights of the Child* (1992) Bulletin of Human Rights 91/2 p 5. See also Bolivia CRC/C/15/Add.1, para 14.

[258]   General Comment 18 *Non-Discrimination* HRI/GEN/1/Rev 8, p 187, para 10 ('The Committee also wishes to point out that the principle of equality sometimes requires States parties to take affirmative action in order to diminish or eliminate conditions which cause or help to perpetuate discrimination prohibited by the Covenant').

[259]   Newell, P and Hodgkin, R *Implementation Handbook for the Convention on the Rights of the Child* (2008) 3rd edn, UNICEF, p 17. This includes ensuring in so far as possible that implementation of Art 2 is not made dependent on budgetary constraints (Newell, P and Hodgkin, R *Implementation Handbook for the Convention on the Rights of the Child* (2008) 3rd edn, UNICEF, p 23). See also Art 1(4) on the International Covenant on the Elimination of All Forms of Racial Discrimination (temporary special measures permitted for the sole purpose of securing adequate advancement of certain racial or ethnic groups).

[260]   See *DH v Czech Republic* [2008] ELR 17, 23 BHRC 526, para 175.

[261]   [2001] 2 HKLRD 690.

[262]   For a discussion of positive discrimination in the context of the ECHR, in the context of EC law and in the context of domestic legislation see below at **4.98**, **4.112** and **4.119** respectively.

CRC, Art 2 and the Definition of 'Discrimination'

4.90 Article 2 does not contain a definition of the term 'discrimination' and to date the Committee on the Rights of the Child has not published a General Comment on Art 2. The grounds for discrimination set out in Art 2 are similar to those contained in the International Covenant on Civil and Political Rights, with the addition of 'ethnic origin' and 'disability'.[263] The Committee on the Rights of the Child has also identified numerous grounds for discrimination not specified in Art 2 in its examination of States parties' reports.[264] It is accordingly likely that any definition of discrimination in the context of Art 2 of the CRC would encompass a similar definition of discrimination to that provided by the Human Rights Committee[265] but incorporating also references to particular issues of discrimination experienced by children.[266] Whilst stopping short of a definition of 'discrimination', the Committee on the Rights of the Child has taken broadly this approach to Art 2 of the CRC in relation to young children, stating in its General Comment No 7 *Implementing Child Rights in Early Childhood* that:

> 'Article 2 means that young children in general must not be discriminated against on any grounds, for example where laws fail to offer equal protection against violence for all children, including young children. Young children are especially at risk of discrimination because they are relatively powerless and depend on others for the realisation of their rights ... Article 2 also means that particular groups of young children must not be discriminated against. Discrimination may take the form of reduced levels of nutrition; inadequate care and attention; restricted opportunities for play, learning and education; or inhibition of free expression of feelings and views. Discrimination may also be expressed through harsh treatment and unreasonable expectations, which may be exploitative or abusive ...'[267]

4.91 The general principal, reiterated by the Human Rights Committee,[268] that enjoyment of rights and freedoms on an equal footing does not mean identical treatment in every instance and that not every differentiation in treatment will constitute discrimination, will apply equally to children.[269] In particular, the application of the principle that equal situations are treated equally and unequal situations differently will be important having regard to the fact that childhood is not a single, fixed and universal experience between birth and majority.[270]

---

[263] The prohibition against discrimination on the grounds of disability is the first instance of such a prohibition in binding international law (Van Bueren, G *The International Law on the Rights of the Child* (1998) Martinus Nijhoff, p 40. See now also the Convention on the Rights of Persons with Disabilities at **4.82** above and Newell, P and Hodgkin, R *Implementation Handbook for the Convention on the Rights of the Child* (2008) 3rd edn, UNICEF, p 24.

[264] Newell, P and Hodgkin, R *Implementation Handbook for the Convention on the Rights of the Child* (2008) 3rd edn, UNICEF, p 24 and see United Kingdom – Isle of Man CRC/C/15 Add.134, paras 22 and 23 and United Kingdom – Overseas Territories CRC/C/15/Add.135, paras 25 and 26.

[265] General Observations No 18 of 10 November 1989 CCPR/C/21/Rev.1/Add.1.

[266] See the analysis in Newell, P and Hodgkin, R *Implementation Handbook for the Convention on the Rights of the Child* (2008) 3rd edn, UNICEF, pp 18–20.

[267] Committee on the Rights of the Child General Comment No 7 *Implementing Child Rights in Early Childhood* HRI?GEN/1/Rev.8 p 436, para 11. See also General Comment No 3 *HIV / Aids and the Rights of the Child* HRI/GEN/1/Rev.8 p 365, paras 5–7, General Comment No 4 *Adolescent Health and Development in the Context of the Rights of the Child* HRI/GEN/1/Rev.8 p 377, para 2 and General Comment No 9 *The Rights of Children with Disabilities* CRC/C/GC/9, paras 8–10.

[268] 1989 CCPR/C/21/Rev.1/Add.1

[269] Newell, P and Hodgkin, R *Implementation Handbook for the Convention on the Rights of the Child* (2008) 3rd edn, UNICEF, p 20.

[270] Newell, P and Hodgkin, R *Implementation Handbook for the Convention on the Rights of the Child* (2008) 3rd edn, UNICEF, p 26. See **4.107** below.

The CRC and Equality – Additional Articles Dealing with Discrimination

4.92   In addition to the provisions of Art 2 of the CRC, certain articles of the CRC deal with children who are particularly prone to discrimination by reason of their particular situation, for example Art 22 dealing with refugee children. Further, the principle of non-discrimination is also expressly enshrined within additional articles in the CRC. Article 21(c) of the CRC provides that in relation to adoption States Parties shall:

> 'Ensure that the child concerned by inter-country adoption enjoys safeguards and standards equivalent to those existing in the case of national adoption.'

Article 23(1) of the CRC provides that:

> '... a mentally or physically disabled child should enjoy a full and decent life, in conditions which ensure dignity, promote self-reliance and facilitate the child's active participation in the community.'

Article 28 of the CRC stipulates that:

> 'States Parties recognise the right of the child to education, and with a view to achieving this right progressively and on the basis of equal opportunity ...'

Article 29(1)(d) of the CRC provides that the education of a child shall be directed to:

> 'The preparation of the child for responsible life in a free society, in the spirit of understanding, peace, tolerance, equality of sexes, and friendship among all peoples, ethnic, national and religious groups and persons of indigenous origin.'

Article 31of the CRC requires that States Parties:

> '... shall encourage the provision of appropriate and equal opportunities for cultural, artistic, recreational and leisure activity.'

Article 40(2)(b)(iv) provides that States Parties shall ensure that every alleged as or accused of having infringed the penal law shall be guaranteed to:

> 'obtain the participation and examination of witnesses on his or her behalf under conditions of equality ... .'

International Law and Equality

4.93   International law has focused on addressing discrimination where embedded in legislation rather than discrimination arising out of policy.[271] However, international tribunals have recognised the need to consider the issue of equality on a broad front, the Permanent Court of International Justice observing that 'There must be equality in fact ... as well as ostensible legal equality ...'.[272] Within this context, there is considerable support for the view that there is established in international law a legal

---

[271]   Van Bueren, G *The International Law on the Rights of the Child* (1998) Martinus Nijhoff, p 39.
[272]   P.C.I.J. 1923 Ser. B, No 6, 24.

principle of non-discrimination which applies to matters of race and sex.[273] Positive discrimination is permissible in certain circumstances under international law.[274]

The ECHR and Equality

ECHR, Art 14

4.94 Article 14 of the European Convention on Human Rights prohibits discrimination by reference to the substantive rights and freedoms which are embodied in the Convention itself, stating:

> 'The enjoyment of the rights and freedoms set forth in this Convention shall be secured without discrimination on any ground such as sex, race,[275] colour, language, religion, political or other opinion, national or social origin, association with a national minority, property, birth or other status.'

ECHR, Art 14 – Ambit

4.95 Article 14 of the ECHR has been described as 'a parasitic prohibition of discrimination in relation only to the substantive rights and freedoms set out elsewhere in the Convention'.[276] The wording of Art 14 makes it clear that the article guarantees equality without discrimination by reference solely to the rights conferred by the ECHR.[277] This position should not be taken as limiting in any way the importance of the principle of non-discrimination articulated in Art 14, as Baroness Hale made clear in *Ghaidan v Mendoza:*[278]

> 'The State's duty under Art 14, to secure that those rights and freedoms are enjoyed without discrimination based on such suspect grounds, is fundamental to the scheme of the European Convention as a whole. It would be a poor human rights instrument indeed if it obliged the State to respect the homes or private lives of one group of people but not the homes or private lives of another. Such a guarantee of equal treatment is also essential to democracy. Democracy is founded on the principle that each individual has equal value. Treating some as automatically having less value than others not only causes pain and distress to that person but also violates his or her dignity as a human being. The essence of the European Convention, as has often been said, is respect for human dignity and human freedom: see *Pretty v United Kingdom* (2002) 35 EHRR 1, [2002] 2 FLR 45, at para 65. Secondly, such treatment is damaging to society as a whole. Wrongly to assume that some people have talent and others do not is a huge waste of human resources. It also damages social cohesion, creating not only an under-class, but an under-class with a rational

---

[273] Brownlie, I *Principles of Public International Law* (2008) 7th edn, Oxford, p 573 and see *South West Africa Cases (Ethiopia v South Africa) (Liberia v South Africa) (second phase)* ICJ Rep 6, 293 and *European Roma Rights Centre v Immigration Officer at Prague Airport (United Nations High Commissioner for Refugees intervening)* [2004] UKHL 55, [2005] 2 AC 1, [2005] 1 All ER 527, [2005] 2 WLR 1.

[274] See *Stalla Costa v Uruguay* (1985) No 198.

[275] Discrimination on the grounds of a persons *perceived* race is still a form of racial discrimination for the purposes of the ECHR (see *Timishev v Russia* (2007) 44 EHRR 37, para 56).

[276] Lord Lester QC, Lord Pannick QC and Herberg, J *Human Rights Law and Practice* (2009) 3rd edn, LexisNexis, p 587.

[277] But see *Wilson v United Kingdom* (2002) 35 EHRR 20, [2002] IRLR 568, 13 BHRC 39, [2002] All ER (D) 35 (Jul) where the European Court of Human Rights was prepared to consider the International Labour Organisation Conventions and the European Social Charter when considering whether there had been breaches of the ECHR.

[278] [2004] UKHL 30, [2004] 2 AC 557, paras 131–132. See also *A v Secretary of State for the Home Department* [2002] EWCA Civ 1502, [2004] QB 335, para 8 per Lord Woolf; *Belgian Linguistic Case (No 2)* (1968) 1 EHRR 252, para 9; *National Union of Belgian Police v Belgium* (1975) 1 EHRR 578, para 44 and *Marckx v Belgium* (1979) 2 EHRR, para 32.

grievance. Thirdly, it is the reverse of the rational behaviour we now expect of government and the state. Power must not be exercised arbitrarily. If distinctions are to be drawn, particularly upon a group basis, it is an important discipline to look for a rational basis for those distinctions. Finally, it is a purpose of all human rights instruments to secure the protection of the essential rights of members of minority groups, even when they are unpopular with the majority. Democracy values everyone equally even if the majority does not.

4.96   As Art 14 of the ECHR is not a freestanding right, a complaint in relation to an infringement of that article must be linked to one of the other articles of the Convention or its Protocols.[279] However, this does necessarily presuppose a violation of one of the substantive rights of the Convention. An action which itself satisfies the demands of the relevant article of the ECHR may nonetheless breach Art 14 by reason of that action being discriminatory.[280] Thus it is 'necessary but it is also sufficient for the facts of the case to fall 'within the ambit' of one or more of the Convention Articles'.[281] The European Court of Human Rights has adopted a flexible approach to the issue of whether the treatment complained of falls within the ambit of a Convention right.[282] The House of Lords has held that it is necessary to demonstrate that the discrimination complained of relates to a 'personal interest close to the core' of a Convention right.[283] How close to the core of the Convention right it is necessary for a child to be to come within the ambit of Art 14 will depend on which substantive right is in issue.[284] Where the applicant alleges the breach of a substantive right and of Art 14, the general approach of the court is to consider the alleged breach of Art 14 only if the breach of the substantive right is not made out.[285]

ECHR, Art 14 – Principles of Application

4.97   In *DH v Czech Republic*,[286] a case concerning the question of whether the decision to place Roma children in special schools, taken by the head teacher on the basis of the results of tests to measure the child's intellectual capacity carried out by an educational psychologist and requiring the consent of the parents to the placement, was discriminatory, the Grand Chamber of the European Court of Justice revisited and restated the fundamental principles underpinning Art 14:

(a)   Discrimination means treating differently, without objective and reasonable justification, persons in relevantly similar situations.[287]

---

[279]   See *Beldjoudi v France* (1992) 14 EHRR 801. Note that Art 14 extends to both the elements of the substantive right that the State is required to guarantee *and* aspects of the right the State chooses to guarantee (*Belgian Linguistic Case (No 2)* (1968) 1 EHRR 252, para 9). See for example *EB v France* (2008) 47 EHRR 21 (Grand Chamber), para 49.

[280]   *Belgian Linguistic Case (No 2)* (1968) 1 EHRR 252, para 9; *Airey v Ireland* (1979) 2 EHRR 305, para 30; *Marckx v Belgium* (1979) 2 EHRR 330, para 32.

[281]   *Burden and another v United Kingdom* Application No 13378/05, [2008] All ER (D) 391 (Apr), [2008] 2 FLR 787, para 58. See also *Belgian Linguistics Case (No 2)* (1968) 1 EHRR 252 277; *Rasmussen v Denmark* (1985) 7 EHRR 371, para 35; *Schmidt v Germany* [1994] ECHR 13580/88, para 22; *Van Raalte v Netherlands* (1997) 24 EHRR 503, para 33 and *Stec v United Kingdom* (2006) 20 BHRC 348.

[282]   See *Petrovic v Austria* (1998) 33 EHRR 14.

[283]   *R (Clift & Hidawi) v Secretary of State for the Home Department* [2006] UKHL 54, [2007] 1 AC 484, para 13 per Lord Bingham.

[284]   *M v Secretary of State for Work and Pensions* [2006] UKHL 11, [2006] 2 AC 91, paras 60–61 per Lord Walker.

[285]   See *Airey v Ireland* (1979) 2 EHRR 305, para 30.

[286]   (2008) 47 EHRR 3. See also *Oršuš and Others v Croatia* (2010) Application No 15766/03.

[287]   *DH and others v The Czech Republic* (2008) 47 EHRR 3, para 175.

(b)   A difference in treatment can be established from the co-existence of sufficiently strong, clear and concordant inferences or of similar unrebutted presumptions of fact.[288]

(c)   Article 14 does not prohibit the differential treatment of groups in order to correct 'factual inequalities' between them. In certain circumstances a failure to attempt to correct such inequality can itself amount to a breach of Art 14.[289]

(d)   A general policy or measure that has disproportionately prejudicial effects on a particular group may be considered discriminatory notwithstanding that it is not specifically aimed at that group.[290]

(e)   Once the applicant has shown a difference in treatment, it is for the respondent State to show that the difference in treatment was justified ie the burden of proof shifts.[291]

(f)   The level of persuasion necessary for reaching a particular conclusion and the distribution of the burden or proof are intrinsically linked to the specificity of the facts, the nature of the allegation made and the Convention right at stake.[292]

Accordingly, in order to successfully establish discrimination in contravention of Art 14 a child must demonstrate (i) that the facts fall within the ambit of one or more of the ECHR rights, (ii) that he or she has been treated differently on a prohibited ground (iii) to others in an analogous position and (iv) the difference in treatment cannot be objectively and reasonably justified having regard to the doctrine of proportionality and the margin of appreciation.[293]

ECHR, Art 14 – Positive Obligations

4.98   Article 14 places an obligation on member states, beyond the obligation to avoid discrimination, to secure equal treatment in the enjoyment of the rights enshrined in the Convention.[294] Further, the positive obligations created by some of the other Convention articles themselves create an indirect positive obligation that must be applied in a non-discriminatory fashion.[295]

---

[288]   *DH and others v The Czech Republic* (2008) 47 EHRR 3, para 178.
[289]   *DH and others v The Czech Republic* (2008) 47 EHRR 3, para 175.
[290]   *DH and others v The Czech Republic* (2008) 47 EHRR 3, para 175.
[291]   *DH and others v The Czech Republic* (2008) 47 EHRR 3, para 177.
[292]   *DH and others v The Czech Republic* (2008) 47 EHRR 3, para 178.
[293]   Swindells, H and others *Family Law and the Human Rights Act 1998* (1999) Jordan Publishing, p 234, Lord Lester QC, Lord Pannick QC and Herberg, J *Human Rights Law and Practice* (2009) 3rd edn, LexisNexis, p 594 and *A and others v Secretary of State for the Home Department* [2004] UKHL 56, [2005] 3 All ER 169 per Lord Bingham of Cornhill.
[294]   *Belgian Linguistic Case (No 2)* (1968) 1 EHRR 252 at 278. See also *Ghadian v Mendoza* [2002] EWCA Civ 1533, [2003] Ch 380, para 5 per Buxton LJ (not considered by the House of Lords).
[295]   Lord Lester QC, Lord Pannick QC and Herberg, J *Human Rights Law and Practice* (2009) 3rd edn, p 611. See for example *Nachova v Bulgaria* (2006) 42 EHRR 43, para 161; *Bekos and Koutropoulos v Greece* (2006) 43 EHRR 2, para 70; *Angelova and Iliev v Bulgaria* (2008) 47 EHRR, paras 115 and 117 and *Cobzaru v Romania* (2008) 47 EHRR 10.

ECHR Protocol No 12 Art 1

4.99　ECHR Protocol No 12 Article 1 further stipulates the following general prohibition of discrimination by reference to *any* right set forth by law,[296] stating:

> '1. The enjoyment of any right set forth by law shall be secured without discrimination on any ground such as sex, race, colour, language, religion, political or other opinion, national or social origin, association with a national minority, property, birth or other status.
>
> 2. No one shall be discriminated against by any public authority on any ground such as those mentioned in paragraph 1.'[297]

ECHR Protocol No 12, Art 1 – Ambit

4.100　The words 'any right set forth by law' in Protocol No 12 Art 1 confer upon that article a much wider scope that Art 14 of the ECHR. As such, in addition to providing a broader foundation for the principle of non-discrimination within the ECHR, Art 1 of Protocol No 12 illuminates further the limited scope of Art 14 of the Convention. In *R (Carson and Reynolds) v Secretary of State for Work and Pensions*[298] Laws LJ observed that:

> '... art 14 must surely stand in contrast to art 1 of the new Twelfth Protocol, which has been opened for signature but which the United Kingdom has not ratified. It clearly occupies much greater territory than art 14 ... Paragraph 1 of this provision remains adjectival, as is art 14, but now it is adjectival to '*any* right set forth by law', including, presumably, any provision of municipal law. If that is right, it represents a very much bigger anti-discrimination provision than that apparently contained in art 14. And para 2 creates a true free-standing right, applicable in relation to any action by a public authority. Now, I do not of course suggest that the Strasbourg cases have gone so far as to hold that art 14 as it presently stands possesses the reach of either paragraph of art 1 of the Twelfth Protocol. But the contrast between the two sets of provisions is a focused reminder of what must have been the intended limitations of art 14.

4.101　Van Bueren notes that both Art 14 and Protocol No 12 Art 1 offer much potential to children as the grounds of discrimination are open ended. The words 'such as' and the words 'other status' in Art 14 indicate that the list of prohibited grounds is not exhaustive. The term 'other status' includes discrimination on the basis of age.[299] Fortin notes that Art 14 has particular relevance to all children in that it protects individuals from discriminatory treatment on any ground, including age and further notes that the value of Art 14, provided it can be linked to with another convention right, is the prohibition of all discriminatory treatment unless it can be argued that children, because

---

[296]　The United Kingdom has not yet signed or ratified Protocol No 12 and has indicated it will not do so (617 HL Official Report (5th Series) written answers Col WA37 (11 October 2000).

[297]　See also ECHR, Protocol No 7, Art 5 which provides that 'Spouses shall enjoy equality of rights and responsibilities of a private law character between them, and in their relations with their children, as to marriage, during marriage and in the event of its dissolution. This Article shall not prevent States from taking such measures as are necessary in the interests of the children.'

[298]　[2003] EWCA 797, [2003] 3 All ER 577, para 39. See also *Secretary of State for Work and Pensions v M* [2006] UKHL 11, [2006] 2 AC 91, para 82 per Lord Walker.

[299]　*Sutherland v United Kingdom* [1998] 24 EHRR CD 22 (judgment striking out the application following the United Kingdom bringing into force the Sexual Offences (Amendment) Act 2000 by which the age of consent for homosexual acts between consenting males was equalised with the age of consent for heterosexual acts). See also Children's Rights Alliance for England, *Making the Case: Why Children Should be Protected from Age Discrimination and How it Can be Done – Proposals for the Equality Bill* (2009).

of their minority, require special measures of protection.[300] The principles of application common to both Art 14 and Protocol 12 Art 1 are now considered.

Different Treatment on a Prohibited Ground

Definition of 'Discrimination'

4.102 Both Art 14 and Art 1 of Protocol No 12 enshrine the same non-exhaustive[301] list of prohibited grounds for different treatment or 'discrimination'.[302] The European Court of Human Rights has demonstrated a preference not to limit or define restrictively the grounds on which discrimination is prohibited under Art 14.[303] Instead, the court considers whether the ground relied on is a personal characteristic ('status') by which persons or groups of persons are distinguishable from each other.[304] The domestic courts have reflected this generous interpretation of Art 14,[305] emphasising that to for a difference in treatment to fall within Art 14 it must be based on 'status'.[306] Discrimination can itself also amount to degrading treatment for the purposes of Art 3 of the ECHR.[307]

Indirect Discrimination

4.103 Article 14 also prohibits indirect discrimination. In *DH and Others v Czech Republic*[308] the Grand Chamber[309] held that there had been a violation of Art 14 and of Art 2 of Protocol No 1 on the basis that the Roma origin of the children was the reason for their assignment to special schools. The judgment was based on the view of the Grand Chamber that number of Roma children in special schools was sufficient to give rise to a strong presumption of indirect discrimination. The following key principles emerged from the Grand Chamber on the issue of indirect discrimination under Art 14:

(a)   The existence of a general rule, policy or measure that appears to apply to everyone equally but in fact has the effect of placing a particular group or individual at a disadvantage by creating a disproportionately adverse impact on

---

[300]   Fortin, J *Children's Rights and the Developing Law* (2005) 2nd edn, Cambridge, p 61.

[301]   See *James v UK* (1986) 8 EHRR 123, para 74, [1986] RVR 139. But see also *AL (Serbia) v Secretary of State for the Home Department; R (Rudi) v Secretary of State for the Home Department* [2008] UKHL 43, [2008] 1 WLR 1434 where Baroness Hale observed at para 26 in relation to Art 14 that 'The list of prohibited grounds is long and open-ended, but it must be there for a purpose and cannot therefore be endless.'

[302]   For a comprehensive analysis of the differences between Art 14 and Protocol No 12 see Wintemute, R *Within the Ambit – How Big is the 'Gap' in Article 14 European Convention on Human Rights?* [2004] European Human Rights Law Review 366 and Wintemute, R *Filling the Article 14 Gap: Government Ratification and Judicial Control of Protocol 12, ECHR Part 2* [2004] European Human Rights Law Review 34, 484.

[303]   Lord Lester QC, Lord Pannick QC and Herberg, J *Human Rights Law and Practice* (2009) 3rd edn, LexisNexis, p 604.

[304]   *Kjeldsen, Busk Madsen and Pedersen v Denmark* (1971) 1 EHRR 711, para 56.

[305]   *R (Clift & Hidawi) v Secretary of State for the Home Department* [2006] UKHL 54, [2007] 1 AC 484, para 48 and *R (RJM(FC)) v Secretary of State for Work and Pensions* [2008] UKHL 63, [2008] 3 WLR 1023, para 42.

[306]   *R (Carson and Reynolds) v Secretary of State for Work and Pensions* [2005] UKHL 37, [2006] 1 AC 173, para 50 per Lord Walker ('Discrimination must always be on some ground. Completely blind, motiveless malevolence may be anti-social and abhorrent but it cannot amount to discrimination, because it is indeed indiscriminate.')

[307]   *Cyprus v Turkey* (2001) 11 BHRC 45, [2001] ECHR 25781/94, paras 302–311.

[308]   [2006] ELR 121, [2006] ECHR 57325/00.

[309]   (2008) 47 EHRR 3, [2008] ELR 17, 23 BHRC 526.

that group can amount to a difference in treatment amounting to indirect discrimination, not withstanding a lack of discriminatory intent.[310]

(b)   Less onerous rules of evidence should apply in cases concerning allegations of indirect discrimination in order to guarantee the effective protection of rights.[311] Statistics appearing reliable and significant upon critical examination can constitute the prima facie evidence required to demonstrate indirect discrimination, but are not a requirement in order to do so.[312]

(c)   Where an applicant establishes a rebuttable presumption that the effect of the general rule, policy or measure is discriminatory in its effect, the burden of proof is reversed and it becomes incumbent on the respondent to demonstrate that the difference in treatment is not discriminatory.[313]

Applying these principles, the Grand Chamber found that their was a danger that the testing employed by the authorities in the *DH and Others v Czech Republic* case, which was conceived for the majority population and the results of which were not analysed in light of the particularities and special characteristics of Roma children, was biased. Thus the tests could not serve as justification for the impugned difference in treatment. Overall, the Chamber was not satisfied that the difference in treatment of the Roma children was objectively and reasonably justified and that there existed a reasonable relationship of proportionality between the means used and the aim pursued.[314] The domestic courts have been less fulsome in their endorsement of Art 14 as a basis for claims of indirect discrimination.[315]

Positive Discrimination

4.104 Positive discrimination will not violate Art 14 of the ECHR if such difference in treatment can be said to have an objective and reasonable justification.[316] Art 14 does not prohibit a member State from treating groups differently in order to correct 'factual inequalities' between them; indeed in certain circumstances a failure to attempt to correct inequality through different treatment may in itself give rise to a breach of the Article.[317] The existence of a positive obligation on States to ensure all can enjoy their ECHR rights without discrimination may itself create circumstances in which the State is obliged to take measures which can be characterised as positive discrimination.[318]

---

[310]   (2008) 47 EHRR 3, para 184.
[311]   (2008) 47 EHRR 3, para 186.
[312]   (2008) 47 EHRR 3, para 188.
[313]   (2008) 47 EHRR 3, para 189.
[314]   See also *McShane v UK* (2002) 35 EHRR 23; *Hoogendijk v Netherlands* (2005) 40 EHRR SE 22; *Zarb Adami v Malta* (2007) 44 EHRR 3 and *Griggs v Duke Power Co*, 401 U.S. 424 (1971) in which the US Supreme Court observed that discrimination (as prohibited by the Civil Rights Act of 1964) comprises not only overtly discriminatory practice but also practices which are 'fair in form, but discriminatory in operation.'
[315]   See *Esfandiari v Secretary of State for Work and Pensions* [2006] EWCA Civ 282, *The Times* 29 May 2006 (considered in *R (Primrose) v Secretary of State for Justice* [2008] EWHC 1625 (Admin), [2008] All ER (D) 156 (Jul)), *Gallagher (Valuation Officer) v Church of Jesus Christ of the Latter Day Saints* [2008] UKHL 56, [2008] 1 WLR 1852 and the analysis in Lord Lester QC, Lord Pannick QC and Herberg, J *Human Rights Law and Practice* (2009) 3rd edn, LexisNexis, p 608, para 4.14.26.
[316]   *Belgian Linguistic Case (No 2)* (1968) 1 EHRR 252, para 10. See for example *Lindsay v United Kingdom* (1987) 9 EHRR 555, para 1(a). See also the judgment of Powell J in *Regents of University of California v Bakke* 438 US 265 (1978).
[317]   *Belgian Linguistic Case (No 2)* (1968) 1 EHRR 252, para 10 and *DH v Czech Republic* (2008) 42 EHRR 3, para 175.
[318]   Lord Lester QC, Lord Pannick QC and Herberg, J *Human Rights Law and Practice* (2009) 3rd edn, p 611.

Analogous Situation

4.105 The Explanatory Report to Protocol No 12 of the Con-vention for the Protection of Human Rights and Fundamental Freedoms (ECHR), adopted by the Committee of Ministers of the Council of Europe on 26 June 2000, states:

> 'While the equality principle does not appear explicitly in the text of either Article 14 of the Convention or Article 1 of this Protocol, it should be noted that the non-discrimination and equality principles are closely intertwined. For example, the principle of equality requires that equal situations are treated equally and unequal situations differently.'

4.106 Article 14 has been interpreted, in line with the general principle of treating equal situations equally, as safeguarding against discriminatory differences of treatment. individuals who are 'placed in analogous situations'.[319] Different treatment is thus only relevant for the purposes of Art 14 where the applicant can also demonstrate that his situation is analogous to, or 'relevantly similar'[320] to that of those in the group he has identified as enjoying more favourable treatment by comparison. There is discrimination only if the cases being compared are not sufficiently different to justify the difference in treatment falling within the grounds of Art 14.[321] In relation to the question of 'analogous situation', the European Court of Human Rights does not necessarily seek direct comparators but rather has often subsumed the issue of analogous situation with the issue of justification by asking itself whether differences in otherwise similar situations justify different treatment.[322] This approach has been reflected by the domestic courts. In *R (on the application of Carson) v Secretary of State for Work and Pensions*[323] Lord Nicholls of Birkenhead said:

> 'the essential, question for the court is whether the alleged discrimination, that is, the difference in treatment of which complaint is made, can withstand scrutiny. Sometimes the answer to this question will be plain. There may be such an obvious, relevant difference between the claimant and those with whom he seeks to compare himself that their situations cannot be regarded as analogous. Sometimes, where the position is not so clear, a different approach is called for. Then the court's scrutiny may best be directed at considering whether the differentiation has a legitimate aim and whether the means chosen to achieve the aim is appropriate and not disproportionate in its adverse impact.'

---

[319] *Rasmussen v Denmark* (1985) 7 EHRR 371, para 35. Examples of family relationships which have been adjudged not to be analogous include comparisons between a married couple and an unmarried couple (see *Lindsay v United Kingdom* Application No 11089/84 (Dec), 11 November 1986 49 DR 181), a natural father and a natural mother (see *MB v United Kingdom* (6 April 1994) 77–A DR 108 and *Rasmussen v Denmark* (1984) 7 EHRR 371), a natural father and a married father concerning the rights of children (see *McMichael v United Kingdom* [1995] 2 FCR 718, (1995) 20 EHRR 205) and a stable lesbian relationship with family life (see *S v United Kingdom* Application No 11716/85, (1986) 47 DR 274). See also *Paulik v Slovakia* Application No 10699/05 [2006] 3 FCR 333 and *Ismailova v Russia* Application No 37614/02 [2008] 2 FCR 72.

[320] *Marckx v Belgium* (1979) 2 EHRR 330, para 32, *Van der Mussele v Belgium* (1983) 6 EHRR 163, para 46 and *Sunday Times v United Kingdom (No 2)* (1992) 14 EHRR 229, para 58. See also *Stubbing v United Kingdom* (1996) 23 EHRR 213, paras 66–73.

[321] *R (Carson and Reynolds) v Secretary of State for Work and Pensions* [2005] UKHL, [2006] 1 AC 173, para 14. Some differences will not preclude a finding that a person is in an analogous or relevantly similar situation.

[322] Lord Lester QC, Lord Pannick QC and Herberg, J *Human Rights Law and Practice* (2009) 3rd edn, p 613. See *Burden v UK* (2008) 47 EHRR 38, paras 60–66 (no 'analogous situation' between co-habiting adult siblings and married couples and couples in a civil partnership) and *Andrejeva v Latvia* (2009) Application No 55707/00 (unreported) ('analogous situation' between a non-Lativian citizen in an 'objectively similar situation' to Latvian citizens).

[323] [2005] UKHL 37, [2005] 4 All ER 545, para 3, [2006] 1 AC 173.

4.107 Having regard to the foregoing principles, whether a child is being discriminated against will depend in part on whether an analogy may be validly drawn between the situation of that child and the situation of the adult or child said to be enjoying more favourable treatment by comparison; in short, whether it can be said that the former and the latter are in a 'relevantly similar' or analogous situation. In this regard, the observations of Baroness Hale in *AL (Serbia) v Secretary of State for the Home Department; R (Rudi)v Secretary of State for the Home Department*[324] are pertinent in respect of any attempt to rely solely on the child's status as a child to demonstrate that the situations in issue are not analogous:

> 'There are, also, as Lord Walker recognised in *Carson*'s case, dangers in regarding differences between two people, which are inherent in a prohibited ground and cannot or should not be changed, as meaning that the situations are not analogous. For example, it would be no answer to a claim of sex discrimination to say that a man and a woman are not in an analogous situation because one can get pregnant and the other cannot. This is something that neither can be expected to change. If it is wrong to discriminate between them as individuals, it is wrong to focus on the personal characteristics which are inherent in their protected status to argue that their situations are not analogous ... I say all this because so much argument has been devoted in this case, and in too many others, to identifying the precise characteristics of the persons with whom these two young men should be compared. This is an arid exercise. They complain that they, who arrived here as children without their families and are still without their families, have been treated differently from other people who arrived here as children with their families and are still with their families. That is obviously correct. It matters little whether this is described as being 'parentless and childless' (as the appellants would have it) or as 'not being part of a family unit' (as the Secretary of State would now have it). It is common ground that their condition, however described, falls within the residuary category of 'other status' for the purposes of art 14.'

Reasonable and Objective Justification

4.108 Article 14 of the ECHR affords protection against different treatment of persons in similar situations which is without an objective and reasonable justification.[325] In the *Belgian Linguistic Cases*[326] the European Court of Human Rights identified the following test:

> '... the principle of equality of treatment is violated if the distinction has not objective and reasonable justification. The existence of such justification must be assessed in relation to the aim and effects of the measure under consideration regard being had to the principles, which normally prevail in democratic societies. A difference in treatment in the exercise of a right laid down in the Convention must not only pursue a legitimate aim; Article 14 is likewise violated when it is clearly established that there is no reasonable relationship of proportionality between the means employed and the aim sought to be reaslised.'[327]

In relation to this test, the European Court of Human Rights has emphasised the need to recall that the Convention is a living instrument, to be interpreted in the light of

---

[324] [2008] UKHL 43, [2008] 1 WLR 1434, para 27.
[325] *Belgian Linguistic Case (No 2)* (1968) 1 EHRR 252, para 10. See also *Fredin v Sweden* (1991) 13 EHRR 784, para 60. See also *McMichael v United Kingdom* [1995] 2 FCR 718, 20 EHRR 205.
[326] (1967) 1 EHRR 241 and (1968) 1 EHRR 252. See also *Darby v Sweden* (1991) 13 EHRR 774, para 31, *Hoffman v Austria* (1993) 17 EHRR 293, para 33 and *Saucedo Gomez v Spain* Application 37784/97 EComHR.
[327] (1968) 1 EHRR 252, para 34. See for example, *Ünal Tekeli v Turkey* [2005] 1 FCR 663, para 68 (the objective of reflecting family unity through a joint family name could not provide a justification for the gender-based difference in treatment complained of).

present-day conditions.[328] The burden of proving objective and reasonable justification is on the State. Within this context, some categories of discrimination require greater justification than others.

4.109 Contracting States enjoy a margin of appreciation in assessing whether and to what extent differences in otherwise similar situations justify a different treatment in law.[329] Whilst the margin of appreciation is narrow in relation to differential treatment based on gender, a much wider margin will be allowed in relation to general measures of economic of social strategy[330] and in relation to different treatment based on what a person has done or experienced as opposed to who he or she is.[331] Discrimination in the form of differences in treatment based on public interest considerations leaves a wide margin in this regard.[332]

European Union Law and Equality

European Union Law – Principle of Equality

4.110 The European Court of Justice has repeatedly held that the principle of equality is 'one of the fundamental principles of Community Law'.[333] The principle prohibiting discrimination and requiring equality of treatment is enshrined in Art 13(1) of the Treaty Establishing the European Community[334] which provides:

> 'Without prejudice to the other provisions of this Treaty and within the limits of the powers conferred by it upon the Community, the Council, acting unanimously on a proposal from the Commission and after consulting the European Parliament, may take appropriate action to combat discrimination based on sex, racial or ethnic origin, religion or belief, disability, age or sexual orientation.'

Article 21(1) of the European Charter of Fundamental Rights provides that any discrimination based on any ground such as sex, race, colour, ethnic or social origin, genetic features, language, religion or belief, political or any other opinion, membership of a national minority, property, birth, disability, age or sexual orientation shall be prohibited and Art 22 requests the European Union to respect cultural, religious and linguistic diversity. Article 23 requires that the equality of men and women must be ensured in the areas of employment, work and pay.

---

[328] *Mizzi v Malta* Application No 26111/02 [2006] 1 FCR 256, [2006] 1 FLR 1048, para 132.

[329] *Rasmussen v Denmark* (1984) 7 EHRR 371, para 40.

[330] *Runkee and another v United Kingdom* [2007] 2 FCR 178, para 35.

[331] *R (RJM(FC)) v Secretary of State for Work and Pension* [2008] UKHL 63, [2008] 3 WLR 1023, para 5 per Lord Walker.

[332] *Karlheinz Schmidt v Germany* (1994) 18 EHRR 513, [1994] ECHR 13580/88 in which the European Court of Human Rights held that although contracting states enjoyed a certain margin of appreciation in assessing what justified a difference in treatment, very weighty reasons had to be put forward before a difference of treatment based exclusively on the ground of sex could be regarded as compatible with the Convention. See also *Adami v Malta* (2006) 20 BHRC 703, [2006] ECHR 17209/02. See also Van Bueren, G *Child Rights in Europe* (2007) Council of Europe Publishing, p 41.

[333] See Case C-152/81: *Ferrario v Commission* [1983] ECR 2357 at 2367; Case C-215/85: *Bundesanstalt für Landwirschaftliche Marktordnung v Raiffeisen Hauptgenossenschaft* [1987] ECR 1279, para 23 and Case C-85/97: *Société Financière D'investissements SPRL (SFI) v Belgian State* [1998] ECR I-7447, para 30. For the application of the non-discrimination principles of the ECHR to EC law see Case C-117/01 *KB v National Health Service Pensions Agency* [2004] ICR 781 and *A v Chief Constable of the West Yorkshire Police* [2004] UKHL 21, [2005] 1 AC 51, para 13. For the application of the non-discrimination principles of EC law to the ECHR see *DH v Czech Republic* (2008) 47 EHRR 3, para 187.

[334] Article 13(1) Consolidated Version of the Treaty Establishing the European Community as amended by Art 2(7) of the Treaty of Amsterdam.

4.111 The European Commission has presented a proposal for an EC Directive on implementing the principle of equal treatment between persons irrespective or religion or belief, disability, age or sexual orientation.[335] In particular, in relation to the concept of discrimination the proposed directive provides as follows at Art 2:

> '1. For the purposes of this Directive, the principle of equal treatment shall mean that there shall be no direct or indirect discrimination based on any grounds referred to in article 1 [*religion or belief, disability, age, or sexual orientation*].
>
> 2. For the purposes of paragraph 1:
>
> (a) direct discrimination shall be taken to occur where one person is treated less favourably than another is, has been or would be treated in a comparable situation on any of the grounds referred to in Article 1;
>
> (b) indirect discrimination shall be taken to occur where an apparently neutral provision, criterion or practice would put persons of a particular religion or belief, a particular disability, a particular age or a particular sexual orientation at a particular disadvantage compared with other persons, unless that provision, criterion or practice is objectively justified by a legitimate aim and the means of achieving that aim are appropriate and necessary.'

European Union Law – Positive Discrimination

4.112 The proposed directive further makes it clear that positive discrimination is permitted, providing at Art 5 as follows:[336]

> 'With a view to ensuring full equality in practice, the principle of equal treatment shall not prevent any Member State from maintaining or adopting specific measures to prevent or compensate for disadvantages linked to religion or belief, disability, age, or sexual orientation.'

European Union Law – Discrimination on the Grounds of Age

4.113 The principle prohibiting discrimination or requiring equality of treatment enshrined in Art 13(1) of the Treaty Establishing the European Community expressly encompasses discrimination based on age.[337] The United Kingdom Government has sought to suggest that the prohibition of discrimination based on age does not extend to children.[338] Art 2(6) of the proposed EC Directive on implementing the principle of equal treatment between persons irrespective or religion or belief, disability, age or sexual orientation[339] permits, as do existing EC directives,[340] differences of treatment based on age:[341]

---

335 2008/0140 (CNS). See also EC Directives 2000/43/EC, 2000/78/EC and 2004/113/EC which deal with discrimination based on race or ethnic origin in employment, occupation and vocational training, as well as in non-employment areas such as social protection, health care, education and access to goods and services, discrimination based on sex in the same fields, with the exception of education and media and advertising, and discrimination based on age, religion and belief, sexual orientation and disability in respect of employment, occupation and vocational training.

336 See Case C-476/99 *Lommers v Minister Van Landbouw, Natuurbeheer en Visserij* [2002] ECR I-2891 and Case C-407/98 *Abrahamsson and Anderson v Fogelqvist* [2000] ECR I-5539.

337 Article 13(1) Consolidated Version of the Treaty Establishing the European Union as amended by Art 2(7) of the Treaty of Amsterdam.

338 See Select Committee on European Scrutiny Session 2007–2008, Thirteenth Report and **4.117** below.

339 2008/0140 (CNS). See also EC Directives 2000/43/EC, 2000/78/EC and 2004/113/EC which deal with discrimination based on race or ethnic origin in employment, occupation and vocational training, as well as in non-employment areas such as social protection, health care, education and access to goods and services,

'Notwithstanding paragraph 2, Member States may provide that differences of treatment on grounds of age shall not constitute discrimination, if, within the context of national law, they are justified by a legitimate aim, and if the means of achieving that aim are appropriate and necessary. In particular, this Directive shall not preclude the fixing of a specific age for access to social benefits, education and certain goods or services.'

There is nothing to suggest that, subject to this exception, the prohibition on discrimination on the grounds of age enshrined in Art 13(1) of the Treaty Establishing the European Community does not apply to children.

European Union Law – Discrimination and Marital and Family Status

4.114 The text of the proposed EC Directive on implementing the principle of equal treatment between persons irrespective or religion or belief, disability, age or sexual orientation does make it clear that matters related to marital and family status, which include adoption and reproductive rights, are outside the scope of the proposed directive.[342] The Explanatory Memorandum to the proposed directive states that:[343]

'The diversity of European societies is one of Europe's strengths, and is to be respected in line with the principle of subsidiarity. Issues such as the organisation and content of education, recognition of marital or family status, adoption, reproductive rights and other similar questions are best decided at national level. The Directive does not therefore require any Member State to amend its present laws and practices in relation to these issues. Nor does it affect national rules governing the activities of churches and other religious organisations or their relationship with the state. So, for example, it will remain for Member States alone to take decisions on questions such as whether to allow selective admission to schools, or prohibit or allow the wearing or display of religious symbols in schools, whether to recognise same-sex marriages, and the nature of any relationship between organised religion and the state.'

Domestic Law and Equality

Domestic Law and Equality – Statutory Provisions

4.115 There is no general statutory provision prohibiting discrimination against children in domestic law. However, domestic statute law contains extensive non-discrimination provisions which are applicable to children.[344] The Equal Pay Act 1970 is expressed to apply to 'persons of whatever age'.[345] The provisions of the Sex Discrimination Act 1975 apply to females and males of 'any age'.[346] Sections 17(1) and 18(1) of the Race Relations Act 1976 prohibit discrimination by educational

---

discrimination based on sex in the same fields, with the exception of education and media and advertising, and discrimination based on age, religion and belief, sexual orientation and disability in respect of employment, occupation and vocational training.

[340] 2008/0140 (CNS). See also EC Directives 2000/43/EC, 2000/78/EC and 2004/113/EC.

[341] See also Art 2(7) of the proposed directive which provides that 'in the provision of financial services Member States may permit proportionate differences in treatment where, for the product in question, the use of age or disability is a key factor in the assessment of risk based on relevant and accurate actuarial or statistical data.'

[342] 2008/0140 (CNS), p 8.

[343] 2008/0140 (CNS), p 6.

[344] See for example the Equal Pay Act 1970, the Sex Discrimination Act 1975, the Race Relations Act 1976, the Disability Discrimination Act 1995 and the Equality Act 2006. See also the Public Order Act 1986, s 18 and the Criminal Justice and Public Order Act 1994, s 154.

[345] Equal Pay Act 1970, s 11(2). See also s 11(2A).

[346] Sex Discrimination Act 1975, s 5(2).

establishments against pupils on the grounds of race.[347] Overall, the provisions of the Race Relations Act 1976 are expressed to apply to any person.[348] The Disability Discrimination Act 1995 applies to disabled persons without distinction between child and adult.[349] In dealing with discrimination on the grounds of religion or belief the Equality Act 2006, s 45 likewise does not distinguish between children and adults. Note that where discrimination is alleged to have taken place after 1 October 2010 the applicable statute will now be the Equality Act 2010 which repeals each of the Equal Pay Act 1970, the Sex Discrimination Act 1975, the Race Relations Act 1976 and the Disability Discrimination Act 1995.

4.116 Whilst not expressly prohibiting discrimination against children, the Children Act 1989 and the Adoption and Children Act 2002, together with their associated secondary legislation, contain provisions designed to ensure that those elements of the child's identity likely to promote welfare and prevent discrimination if given proper consideration are given proper consideration.[350] The Childcare Act 2006, s 1(1)(b) requires local authorities to reduce inequalities between young children in their area in relation to their physical and mental health and emotional well-being, protection from harm and neglect, education, training and recreation, the contribution made by them to society and their social and economic well-being.

4.117 The Equality Act 2010 prohibits discrimination on the basis of protection characteristics.[351] A failure to meet the requirement of the provisions of the proposed Act will not confer a cause of action in private law.[352] Rather, proceedings for contravention of the provisions are by way of proceedings pursuant to Part 9 of the Act or by way of judicial review.[353] Part VI of the Act prohibits discrimination within the context of education.[354] However, the Act explicitly excludes children from legal protection under the Act from unfair discrimination on the grounds age. Regrettably, the Government stated early on its intention to exclude children from the protection conferred by the provisions of the proposed Act in this regard, the responsible Minister stating that:[355]

> 'The provisions will not cover people under 18. It is right to treat children and young people differently, for example through age limits on alcohol consumption, and there is little evidence of harmful age discrimination against young people.'

Both the principle of 'evolving capacity' and the assertion that there is little domestic evidence of harmful age discrimination against children[356] are doubtful arguments for

---

347 Pursuant to s 17A of the Sex Discrimination Act 1975 'pupil' includes, in England and Wales, any person who receives education at a school or institution to which s 17 applies.

348 Race Relations Act 1976, s 1(1).

349 Disability Discrimination Act 1995, s 1(2).

350 See for example CA 1989, s 22(5)(c) and the ACA 2002, s 1(5). In respect of the latter provision see also *Re N (a minor) (adoption)* [1990] FCR 241; *Re P (a minor)* [1990] 1 FLR 96; *Re JK (adoption: transracial placement)* [1990] FCR 87; *R v Lancashire County Council* [1992] 1 FCR 283; LAC(98)20 'Adoption—Achieving the Right Balance', para 14 and *Re S; Newcastle City Council v Z* [2007] 1 FLR 861.

351 Equality Act 2010, ss 13–19. Pursuant to ss 4–12 of the Act the protected characteristics are age, disability, gender reassignment, marriage and civil partnership, race, religion or belief, sex and sexual orientation.

352 Equality Act 2010, s 3.

353 Equality Act 2010, ss 113–141.

354 Equality Act 2010, ss 84–99.

355 Harriet Harman, Minister for Women and Equality, 26 June 2008 Hansard Column 504.

356 See Willow, C, Franklin, A and Shaw, C *Meeting the obligations of the Convention on the Rights of the Child in England. Children and young people's messages to Government* (2007) DCSF and *Making the Case – Why*

not extending the protection afforded by the Act to children and have been criticised.[357] The exclusion of children from protection under the Act also appears to create a potential conflict with s 1(1)(b) of the Childcare Act 2006 which places a duty on local authorities to reduce inequalities between young children in their area in relation to their physical and mental health and emotional wellbeing, protection from harm and neglect, education, training and recreation, the contribution made by them to society and their social and economic well-being.

Domestic Law and Equality – Common Law

4.118 Within the domestic jurisdiction, equality of treatment is also a common law principle. In *A v Secretary of State for the Home Department*[358] Lord Woolf CJ said:

> 'The right not to be discriminated against is one of the most significant requirements of the protection provided by the rule of law. It is now enshrined in art 14 of the convention, but long before the 1998 Act came into force the common law recognised the importance of not discriminating. The importance of not discriminating explains why every judge on taking office makes a vow to 'do right to all manner of people ... without fear or favour affection or ill will.'

Domestic Law and Equality – Positive Discrimination

4.119 Positive discrimination is considered permissible in the context of the domestic law on discrimination. Each of the Employment Equality (Religion or Belief) Regulations 2003,[359] the Employment Equality (Sexual Orientation) Regulations 2003[360] and the Employment Equality (Age) Regulations 2006[361] allow for 'positive action' in specified situations.[362] The courts have also interpreted statutory non-discrimination provisions so as to permit positive discrimination.[363]

BEST INTERESTS

4.120 The principle that, in decisions concerning them, children's best interests or welfare should be the 'paramount' or a 'primary consideration' would appear at first glance an uncontroversial proposition.[364] However, having regard to the pre-eminent status accorded to this proposition as a 'guiding principle' for the application and enforcement of children's rights, detailed consideration of the precise nature and impact

---

Children should be Protected from Age Discrimination and How it Can be Done (2009) CRAE both of which tend to challenge the Government's assertion of a lack of evidence of age discrimination against children.

[357] Children's Rights Alliance for England, *Making the Case: Why Children Should be Protected from Age Discrimination and How it Can be Done* (2009) CRAE.

[358] [2002] EWCA Civ 1502, [2004] QB 335, para 7, [2003] 1 All ER 816, para 7. See also the judgment of Lord Bingham in this case in the House of Lords at [2004] UKHL 56, [2005] 2 AC 68, para 46 citing *Railway Express Agency Inc v New York* (1949) 336 US 106 at 112–113 per Jackson J; *Matadeen v Pointu* [1999] 1 AC 98 at 109 per Lord Hoffman (but see *R (Association of British Civilian Internees Far East Region) v Secretary of State for Defence* [2003] EWCA Cov 473, [2003] QB 1397, para 85) and *Arthur JS Hall and Co v Simons* [2002] 1 AC 615 at 688 per Lord Hoffman.

[359] SI 2003/1660.

[360] SI 2003/1661.

[361] SI 2006/1031.

[362] The Act also makes provision for positive discrimination in specified circumstances (see the Equality Act 2010, s 158 (this section is not yet in force)).

[363] See for example *Kent County Council v Mingo* [2000] IRLR 90. See also *Archibald v Fife Council* [2004] UKHL 32, [2004] IRLR 651.

[364] The principle has a long history. See for example *Chapsky v Wood* (1881) 26 Kan. 650 in which the court

of the best interests principle is required. In particular, it is important to acknowledge that whilst central to the consideration of children's rights, the 'best interests' or 'welfare' principle sometimes cited as an almost sacred mantra is not without its critics, nor is their universal agreement as to its correct application.

General Principles

General Principles – 'Best Interests' and 'Welfare'

4.121 The language of the CRC and other relevant international instruments in this area is that of the 'best interests' of the child. Within the domestic jurisdiction, the Children Act 1989 uses the term 'welfare' rather than 'best interests'.[365] In applying this statutory welfare principle however, the domestic courts ask as a matter of course 'what is in the child's best interests?' It is important to note that the terms 'best interests' and 'welfare' are used interchangeably by courts and commentators. Save where the context demands otherwise, the term 'best interests' is used below.

4.122 The principle of the child's best interests has been described as 'a fundamental legal principle of interpretation developed from the compassionate self-imposed limitation on adult power'.[366] Eekelar observes that the 'best interests' principle 'requires a decision made with respect to a child to be justified from the point of view of a judgment about the child's interests. Put another way: it would be inconsistent with the welfare principle to make a decision that is *overtly* justified by reference to the way the outcome benefited some *other* interest or interests'.[367] The question asked by the 'best interests' principle is not what the essential justice of a case requires but rather what the best interests of the child requires.[368] It has been said that '[d]eciding what is best for a child poses a question no less ultimate than the purposes and values of life itself.'[369] The principle of best interests does not act to change the substantive nature of the child's right or rights in question but rather it simply affects its method of application in respect of the individual child.[370]

4.123 The term 'welfare' in the context under discussion has been defined by Hardie Boys J in the New Zealand case of *Walker v Walker v Harrison*[371] as follows:

> '"Welfare" is an all encompassing word. It includes material welfare, both in the sense of adequacy of resources to provide a pleasant home and a comfortable standard of living and in the sense of adequacy of care to ensure that good health and due personal pride are maintained. However, while material considerations have their place they are secondary matters. More important are the stability and the security, the loving and understanding care

---

stated that its paramount consideration in determining custody of the child was her welfare. Within the domestic jurisdiction see *Re McGrath (Infants)* [1883] 1 Ch 143; *F v F* [1902] 1 Ch 688 and *Ward v Laverty and Another* [1925] AC 101.

[365] CA 1989, s 1(1).

[366] Van Beuren, G *Child Rights in Europe* (2007) Council of Europe Publishing, p 30.

[367] Eekelaar, J *Beyond the Welfare Principle* (2002) 14 Child and Family Law Quarterly 237. See also *Re A (Medical Treatment: Male Sterilisation)* [2000] 1 FCR 193 at 200, [2000] 1 FLR 549 at 555 per Butler-Sloss P ('best interests encompasses medical, emotional and other welfare issues').

[368] *S(BD) v S(DJ) (Infants: Care and Consent)* [1977] 1 All ER 656 at 660A and *Re K (Minors) (Wardship: Care and Control)* [1977] 1 All ER 647 at 649.

[369] Mnookin, R *Child Custody and Adjudication: Judicial Functions in the Face of Indeterminacy* (1975) 39 Law and Contemporary Problems 226, p 260.

[370] Van Beuren, G *Child Rights in Europe* (2007) Council of Europe Publishing, p 34.

[371] [1981] NZ Recent Law 257.

and guidance, the warm and compassionate relationships, that are essential for the full development of the child's own character, personality and talents.'

General Principles – 'Paramount' and 'Primary'

4.124 A key difficulty in the consistent application of the 'best interests' principle within the context of children's rights is the differing articulation within the key legal instruments enshrining those rights of the weight to be accorded to that principle.

4.125 In the CRC children's interests are held to be 'a primary consideration' by Art 3(1), the 'basic concern' in relation to a parent's responsibility under Art 18(1) and 'the paramount consideration' in Art 21 in respect of adoption.[372] Under Art 5(b) of the Convention on the Elimination of All Forms of Discrimination Against Women the interests of children in relation to family education must be 'the primordial consideration' and 'paramount' in all matters relating to marriage pursuant to Art 16(1)(d).[373] Art 5 of Declaration on Social and Legal Principles relating to the Welfare and Protection of Children with Special Reference to Foster Placement and Adoption Nationally provides that the child's best interests shall be 'the paramount consideration' in all matters relating to the placement of a child outside the care of the child's own parents. Whilst the welfare principle does not appear in either the Covenant on Civil and Political Rights or the Covenant on Economic, Social and Cultural Rights, the Human Rights Committee has stated that the child's interests are 'paramount' in cases involving parental separation and divorce.[374] The Executive Committee of the UN High Commissioner for Refugees has 'stressed that all action taken on behalf of refugee children must be guided by the principle of the best interests of the child as well as by the principle of family unity'.[375] In domestic law, children's interests are, within the context of certain legal proceedings, to be 'the paramount consideration'.[376] Within the ECHR there is no overarching expression of the 'best interests' principle or of the weight to be attached to such a principle.[377]

4.126 The word 'paramount' is defined in the Concise Oxford English Dictionary as '1. supreme; requiring first consideration; pre-eminent. 2. in supreme authority'.[378] The word 'primary' is defined as '1a. of the first importance; chief. b. fundamental, basic'.[379] In considering the weight to be attached to a child's best interests, it is also important to note the differential use of the definite article 'the' and the indefinite article 'a' in combination with the words paramount and primary. The meaning of the terms 'the paramount consideration' and 'a primary consideration' will be considered in detail below by reference to the specific legal instruments in which the terms are appear.

---

[372] The best interests of the child are also referred to without reference to the weight to be attached to them in Arts 9(1), 9(3), 20, 37(c) and 40(2)(b)(iii) of the CRC.

[373] CA 1989, s 1(1) and ACA 2002, s 1(2). The African Charter on the Rights and Welfare of the Child Art 4 stipulates that the child's best interests shall be 'the primary consideration'.

[374] Human Rights Committee General Comments No s 17 *Article 17 (Right to Privacy)* and 18 *Non-Discrimination* HRI/GEN/Rev.8, pp 185 and 189. See also Communication No 201/1985 Views of 27 July 1988 Appendix I in Report of Human Rights Committee A/43/40 (1988) Annex VII, para 1 (in which the Human Rights Committee noted 'the undoubted right and duty of a domestic court to decide 'in the best interests of the child'').

[375] Conclusion 47 (XXXVIII) (1987) on 'Refugee Children', para (d) in *Conclusions on the International Protection of Refugees Adopted by the Executive Committee of the UNHCR* (1991) UNHCR, p 105.

[376] CA 1989, s 1(1) and ACA 2002, s 1(2).

[377] Article 6(1) refers to the 'interests of juveniles' and Art 5 of Protocol No 7 refers to the 'interests of children'.

[378] *The Concise Oxford English Dictionary* (1990) 8th edn, Oxford, p 863.

[379] *The Concise Oxford English Dictionary* (1990) 8th edn, Oxford, p 946.

Overall however, it can be seen that the varied manner in which the best interests principle is articulated makes its consistent application across international, regional and domestic contexts problematic.

General Principles – Best Interests and Other Guiding Principles

4.127 When considering a child's best interests, the child's participation must be facilitated, allowing a child to express his or her wishes and feelings and taking account of those wishes and feelings. Thus the assessment of best interests ought to include the child's assessment of his or her own best interests.[380] For example, within the context of the CRC the need to consider the child's best interests should not unduly dilute the aims of Art 12 of the CRC, for example by imposing an age restriction on its application.[381]

General Principles – Criticism of the 'Best Interests' Principle

4.128 Whilst the 'best interests' principle represents settled law in international, regional and domestic legal jurisdictions which *must* be applied, the principle is not without criticism. Within this context, it is useful to consider briefly the censure that has been applied to the principle to ensure that proper thought and rigourous analysis is applied to its application.

Indeterminate Nature

4.129 One of the fundamental principles of the rule of law is certainty. Whilst a certain level of flexibility in the application of rights is dictated by the need to do justice in individual cases and by the unreasonable burden that would be created in defining exhaustively all factors to be taken into account by decision makers, the loudest criticism of the 'best interests' principle remains that of its indeterminate nature and the uncertainty that this introduces.[382] This uncertainty arises in part from the broad discretion the principle permits to the decision maker, risking arbitrariness and a lack of consistency and uniformity in decisions flowing from the application of 'raw judicial intuition'.[383] This difficulty is perpetuated and amplified within and across jurisdictions by the fact that the elements of a child's 'best interests' are multifarious and in reality incapable of exhaustive definition.[384] This means that the question 'what is in a child's best interests' is not one which can be settled by means of appeal only to facts but is also a question with a significant moral element, influenced by disagreements within society.[385] For this reason the 'best interests' principle is extremely vulnerable to the decision makers individual beliefs and values.[386]

---

[380] Van Bueren, G *The International Law on the Rights of the Child* (1998) Martinus Nijhoff, p 122.

[381] See Marshall, K *Children's Rights in the Balance: The Participation – Protection Debate* (1997), p 110.

[382] See Mnookin, R *Child Custody and Adjudication: Judicial Functions in the Face of Indeterminacy* (1975) 39 Law and Contempary Problems 226; Fineman, M *Dominant Discourse, Professional Language and Legal Change in Child Custody* (1988) 101 Harvard Law Review 707; Parker, S *The Best Interests of the Child – Principles and Problems* (1994) 8 International Journal of Law and Family 26; Reece, H *The Paramountcy Principle: Concensus or Construct?* (1996) Current Legal Problems 267; Herring, J *The Welfare Principle and Parents' Rights* in Bainham, A, Day Sclater, S and Richards, M (eds) *What is a Parent? A Socio-Legal Analysis* (1999) Hart Publishing and Eekelaar, J *Beyond the Welfare Principle* (2002) 14 Child and Family Law Quarterly 237.

[383] Wexler, J *Rethinking the Modification of Child Custody Decrees* (1984) 94 Yale L.J. 757 at 784.

[384] See *Ex parte Devine* (1981) 398 So. 2d 686 Ala.

[385] Archard, D *Rights and Childhood* (2004) Routledge, p 62. See also Mnookin, R (ed). *In the Interests of Children* (1985) 18 and Elster, J *Solomonic Judgment: Against the Best Interests of the Child* (1978) 54 University of Chicago Law Review 1–45.

[386] Guggenheim, M *What's Wrong with Children's Rights* (2005) Harvard, p 40.

4.130 This situation demonstrates one of the central paradoxes of the law of children's rights. On one side, the norms comprising children's rights must be sufficiently clear, comprehensive and inflexible to provide the international community with some certain basis on which it might seek to restrain actions which circumvent or undermine minimum standards. On the other side, any universal principles aimed at addressing a wide range of situations concerning the relationship between the child, adults and the state must be characterised by a significant degree of flexibility and adaptability in order to do justice in as many cases as possible.[387] The difficulties created by the indeterminate nature of the 'best interests' principle, whilst perhaps different in nature, are arguably no more detrimental in impact, to the difficulties created by the application of inflexible rules to human problems, the latter having the added disadvantage of tending towards the treatment of children as a homogenous group rather than as individuals. Whilst some commentators argue that substantive rules are preferable to the 'best interests' concept,[388] there is a pressing need with regard to children (and adults) to take into account the myriad of situations created by the confluence of the applicable law and the child's family situation, developmental stage, views and needs if the decision maker is to do justice to the position of the child as an individual. Within this context, the European Court of Human Rights has upheld a degree of indeterminacy, stating in *Sunday Times v UK (No 2)* that:[389]

> '[W]hile certainty is highly desirable, it may bring in its train excessive rigidity and the law must be able to keep pace with changing circumstances. Accordingly, many laws are couched in terms which, to a greater or lesser extent, are vague and whose interpretation and application are questions of practice.'

Undermining of a Rights Based Approach

4.131 These difficulties take on particular significance within a legal system that is aiming to promote and enforce children's rights. The indeterminate nature of the 'best interests' principle can militate against a rights based approach to child law.[390] The concept of 'welfare' is distinct from the concepts of 'rights'. The former is an interpretative principle in the context of the rights of children, the latter is an objective legal entitlement. Within the context of the difficulties outlined above, the 'best interests' principle, if not deployed carefully, risks substituting an objective legal entitlement with a subjective value judgment.[391] Rather than supporting the rights of children, its effect is potentially to undermine them by allowing decision makers to 'dress up' adult concerns which militate against the objective rights of the child as factors purportedly promoting the welfare of the child.[392] It has been argued that it is this unwillingness to place value on the child's autonomy as a rights holder by

---

[387] Alston, P *The Best Interests Principle: Towards a Reconciliation of Culture and Human Rights* in Freeman, M (edn) *Children's Rights* Vol 2 (2003) Ashgate Dartmouth, p 200.

[388] Guggenheim argues that 'in the final analysis, almost *any* clearly defined rule is vastly superior to the open-ended best interests standard' (Guggenheim, M *What's Wrong with Children's Rights* (2005) Harvard, p 173).

[389] (1979) Series A No 30, 2 EHRR 245, para 49.

[390] Fortin, J *Children's Rights and the Developing Law* (2005) 2nd edn, Cambridge, p 63.

[391] This issue is at the root of the mistaken idea that there is a distinction between a 'rights based approach' and a 'welfare based approach' to issues concerning children when in fact the correct approach is the consisten application of the rights of the child having regard to the child's welfare as a primary consideration. See 1 above.

[392] Fortin, J *Children's Rights and the Developing Law* (2005) 2nd edn, Cambridge, p 248. Guggenheim out that 'There is always a great danger that the calls for children's best interests are stalking horse real arguments.' (Guggenheim, M *What's Wrong with Children's Rights* (2005) Harvard, p 90).

concentrating exclusively or primarily on the child's best interests has hindered the international protection of the rights of children.[393]

4.132 A further difficulty that arises from the 'best interests' principle in addition to its impact on the application of the rights of children is the question of its impact on the rights of others, particularly where that principle is the paramount consideration. Eekelaar contends that 'It certainly appears that the welfare principle, in its orthodox form, can hardly be reconciled with due recognition of the rights of others'.[394] Certainly it is difficult to see at first glance how, on the domestic formulation of best interests as paramount,[395] the rights of others can even be relevant where they conflict with the best interests of the child.[396]

4.133 These difficulties are of particular significance when it comes to navigating the disparate approach taken to 'best interests' by the international, regional and domestic legal instruments which incorporate and apply that standard, to which disparate approaches consideration is now given.

The CRC and Best Interests

CRC, Art 3(1)

4.134 Article 3(1) of the CRC articulates the concept of 'best interests' within the context of children's rights as follows:[397]

> 'In all actions concerning children, whether undertaken by public or private social welfare institutions, courts of law, administrative authorities or legislative bodies, the best interests of the child shall be a primary consideration.'

CRC, Art 3(1) – 'Best Interests'

4.135 Article 3(1) does not enshrine a right but is rather a principle of interpretation in respect of each of the rights enshrined within the CRC.[398] The rational for implementing children's rights subject to the best interests principal is that, as recognised in the CRC Preamble, children require, by reason of their status as children, special care and assistance. According to the principal of evolving capacity enshrined in Art 5, this need for special care and assistance will vary in intensity depending on the age,

---

[393] See Van Bueren, G *The International Law on the Rights of the Child* (1998) Martinus Nijhoff, pp 15–16. In particular, it has been pointed out by Eekelaar that 'the very ease of the welfare test encourages a laziness and unwillingness to pay proper attention to all the interests that are at stake in these decisions and, possibly, also a tendency to abdicate responsibility for decision making to welfare professionals' (Eekelaar, J *Beyond the Welfare Principle* (2002) 14 Child and Family Law Quarterly 237, p 248).

[394] Eekelaar, J *Beyond the Welfare Principle* (2002) 14 Child and Family Law Quarterly 237.

[395] See *J v C* [1970] AC 668, 711.

[396] See **4.169–4.175** below.

The domestic courts have on occasion relied on Art 3(1) of the CRC through the agency of Art 8 of the ~~R~~ (see *R (on the Application of MXL and others v Secretary of State for the Home Department* [2010] ~~~7~~ (Admin) per Blake J: 'Once Article 8 is engaged, the exercise of judgment in a case falling ~~~~ust comply with the principles identified by Strasbourg. In a case where the interests of ~~~is means that other principles of international law binding on contracting states ~~~~the case of children those principles are reflected in Article 3(1) of the UN ~~~he Child 1989 to which the UK is now a party without any derogation in ~~~on making ... By this route, the principle that the interests of the child are a ~~~ld be applied by public officials (including immigration judges) when making ~~~ have an impact on the welfare of children.' ~~~hildhood (2004) Routledge, p 64.

understanding and development of the child and his or her circumstances. Thus, if the application of the child's rights under the CRC is not in some circumstances to risk harming the child, thereby defeating the object of the right, the interpretation and application of those rights must be achieved in accordance with the best interests of the individual child concerned.

4.136 The term 'best interests' was not defined or the subject of further discussion by the Working Group drafting the CRC.[399] No General Comment has been issued by the Committee on the Rights of the Child providing such a definition.[400] There is likewise, no guidance within Art 3(1) of the CRC as to the factors which can be taken into account when determining a child's best interests nor in respect of matters which may be legitimately capable of overriding those best interests. In this context, it has been observed that the question of *how* best interests are to be determined remains the principle dilemma under Art 3(1).[401] However, given the need to consider the CRC as a whole it is clear that each of the other guiding principles, namely non-discrimination, maximum survival and development and respect for the views of the child, must be relevant to determining the question of the child's best interests.[402] Further, any interpretation of a child's best interests must be consistent with the spirit of the entire CRC.[403] The interpretation of best interests under Art 3(1) should not be carried out in an overly 'culturally relativist' way[404] and States cannot use their own interpretation of 'best interests' to deny children their rights under the CRC.[405]

CRC, Art 3(1) – 'A Primary Consideration'

4.137 Under Art 3(1) the child's interests are *a* primary consideration not *the* primary consideration. As such, under Art 3(1) of the CRC the best interests of the child will not always be the single, overriding factor to be considered as between the child and other

---

[399] See Alston, P *The Best Interests Principle: Towards a Reconciliation of Culture and Human Rights* in Freeman, M (edn) *Children's Rights* Vol 2 (2003) Ashgate Dartmouth, pp 192–193.

[400] In some of its concluding observations on States' Reports the Committee on the Rights of the Child has suggested that it is for individual States to analyse and objectively implement Art 3(1). See for example Canada CRC/C/15/Add.215, para 25 and Czech Republic CRC/C/15/Add.201, para 32. This reflects the requirement of the implementation checklist for Art 3 which asks 'Where legislation requires the determination of the best interests of a child in particular circumstances, have criteria been adopted for the purpose which are compatible with the principles of the Convention, including giving due weight to the expressed views of the child?' (See Newell, P and Hodgkin, R *Implementation Handbook for the Convention on the Rights of the Child* (2008) 3rd edn, UNICEF, p 44.)

[401] Newell, P and Hodgkin, R *Implementation Handbook for the Convention on the Rights of the Child* (2008) 3rd edn, UNICEF, p 193.

[402] Newell, P and Hodgkin, R *Implementation Handbook for the Convention on the Rights of the Child* (2008) 3rd edn, UNICEF, p 37.

[403] Newell, P and Hodgkin, R *Implementation Handbook for the Convention on the Rights of the Child* (2008) 3rd edn, UNICEF, p 38.

[404] For a detailed discussion of the interrelationship between best interests and culture see Alston, P *The Best Interests Principle: Towards a Reconciliation of Culture and Human Rights* in Freeman, M (edn) *Children's Rights* Vol 2 (2003) Ashgate Dartmouth, p 183. See also Malawi CRC/C/15/Add. 174, para 26, Pakistan CRC/C/15/Add.217, para 33 and Zambia CRC/C/15/Add. 206, para 25 in which the Committee on the Rights of the Child stated that that all necessary measures should be taken to ensure that local customary law does not impede the implementation of the principle of best interests.

[405] Newell, P and Hodgkin, R *Implementation Handbook for the Convention on the Rights of the Child* (2008) 3rd edn, UNICEF, p 38. See for example the Committee on the Rights of the Child General Comment No 8 CRC/C/GC/8, para 26 in which the Committee observed that the best interests principle in article 3(1) cannot be used to justify practices, including corporal punishment and other forms of cruel or degrading punishment, which conflict with the child's human dignity and right to physical integrity.

children or the child and other adults who may have competing interests.[406] The wording used in Art 3 arose from concerns that there may be other interests that compete with those of the child and must be balanced against them, such as the public interest and the interests of justice.[407] The formulation adopted by Art 3(1) also allows the child's best interests to be more readily acceptable as a factor to be taken into account in decisions and proceedings in which children are not the subject but which nonetheless impact upon them.[408] Thus 'a primary consideration' means that the best interests of the child should be a primary but not the only consideration under CRC, Art 3(1).[409]

4.138   The Committee on the Rights of the Child has made clear that it will not permit the primary nature of the child's interests under Art 3(1) to be downplayed. Article 3(1) has been said to underpin all of the other guiding principles, namely, non-discrimination, the right to life and the right to participate.[410] As Archard points out, the language of best interests in Art 3(1) is 'maximising' in its effect on the other rights enshrined in the Convention.[411] All children's rights must be interpreted in accordance with their best interests.[412] Finally, use of the word 'consideration' demonstrates that the child's best interests must be the actively considered, such consideration being genuine as opposed to token or merely formal and ensuring all aspects of the child's interest are given thought.[413]

CRC, Art 3(1) – 'All Actions'

4.139   The words 'all actions' in Art 3(1) will encompass both action and inaction[414] and require active measures throughout Government, parliament and the judiciary to apply the best interests principle to decisions and actions affecting children both directly and indirectly and as individuals as well as a constituency.[415] The use of term 'all actions' represents a significant extension of the 'best interests' principle beyond the judicial application traditionally contemplated in the domestic jurisdiction. In addition to the judiciary, the article is plainly wide enough to encompass the actions of all

---

[406]   Newell, P and Hodgkin, R *Implementation Handbook for the Convention on the Rights of the Child* (2008) 3rd edn, UNICEF, p 38.

[407]   Barsh, R *The Convention on the Rights of the Child: a Reassessment of the Final Text* (1989), pp 143–144. See also E/CN.4/L.1575, pp 3–7 and Detrick, S (ed) *The United Nations Convention on the Rights of the Child – A Guide to the Travaux Préparatoires* (1992) Martinus Nijhoff, pp 132–133.

[408]   See Van Bueren, G *The International Law on the Rights of the Child* (1998) Martinus Nijhoff, p 62 n.100.

[409]   Van Bueren, G *The International Law on the Rights of the Child* (1998) Martinus Nijhoff, p 76.

[410]   Fortin, J *Children's Rights and the Developing Law* (2005) 2nd edn, Cambridge, p 37.

[411]   Archard, D *Rights and Childhood* (2004) Routledge, p 62.

[412]   Fortin, J *Children's Rights and the Developing Law* (2005) 2nd edn, Cambridge, p 38.

[413]   Alston, P *The Best Interests Principle: Towards a Reconciliation of Culture and Human Rights* in Freeman, M (edn) *Children's Rights* Vol 2 (2003) Ashgate Dartmouth, p 195.

[414]   See Van Bueren, G *The International Law on the Rights of the Child* (1998) Martinus Nijhoff, p 46. For further observations on the interpretation of the term "all actions" in Art 3(1) of the CRC see also the Australian cases of *Minister of State for Immigration and Ethnic Affairs v Teoh* (1995) 128 ALR 353; *Re Anais Moala Kailomani* (1996) IRT Ref No. N94.01675; *Yad Ram v Deparment for Immigration and Ethnic Affairs* (1996) No.Q95/646 and the New Zealand cases of *Schier v Removal Review Authority* [1998] NZAR 203; *Patel v Minister of Immigration* [1997] 1 LZLR 257; *Puli'uvea v Removal Review Authority* [1996] 3 NZLR 538; *Elika v Ministry of Immigration* [1996] 1 NZLR 741; *Walsh v Department of Social Security* (1996) No.5795. The term 'all actions' in Art 3(1) of the CRC does not cover the repossession of a parent's car used to drive the child to after school lessons (*Issaac John MacKay Shields v Official Receive in Bankrupcy and Official Trustee in Bankruptcy* (1995) Fed. Ct NSW No. 441/96).

[415]   Committee on the Rights of the Child General Comment No 5 CRC/GC/2003/5, para 12 and General Comment No 7 CRC/C/GC/7/Rev.1, para 13. See also Burundi CRC/C/15/Add.193 and Canada CRC/C/15/Add. 215.

agencies of the State in addition to private institutions concerned with social welfare.[416] As to its application to private bodies not concerned with social welfare, the position is less clear although the wording of Art 3(1) is inclusive rather than exclusive as to its application and commentators have suggested that it is wide enough to encompass private bodies in general.[417] Further, the word 'official' was deleted from the article during the drafting process[418] which may further suggest the article is intended to be of broader application in respect of private organisations and institutions.

4.140 Article 3(1) of the CRC does not appear to extend to encompass actions by private individuals. Article 18(1) of the CRC does appear, on first reading, to require parents and legal guardians have the best interests of the child as their 'basic concern'.[419] The full text of the article reads:

> 'States Parties shall use their best efforts to ensure recognition of the principle that both parents have common responsibilities for the upbringing and development of the child. Parents or, as the case may be, legal guardians, have the primary responsibility for the upbringing and development of the child. The best interests of the child will be their basic concern.'

This requirement appears out of place in a Convention which is binding only on States which have ratified it.[420] However, Art 18(1) does not extend the application of the 'best interests' principle to private individuals. It is in fact intended to address those States which are legislating in respect of parental responsibility which, when drafting legislation on parents' rights, must ensure that legislation on parental responsibility reflects the well established legal responsibility of parents to act in the best interests of their children.[421]

Additional Articles

4.141 The position as to best interests under the CRC is complicated by the fact that in relation to other articles which mention the child's best interests, namely Arts 9(1), 9(3), 18(1), 20, 37(c) and 40(2)(b)(iii), there is no guidance as to the weight to be attached to those best interests. Further, in Art 21(1) of the CRC the child's best interests are defined as paramount in nature in the context of adoption.[422] Whilst in addition to Art 3(1) only Art 21(1) expressly articulates the weight to be attached to the child's best interests, the fact that Arts 9(1), 9(3), 18(1), 20, 37(c) and 40(2)(b)(iii) refer to best interests has been taken as extending the primary nature of the child's best interests to

---

[416] In this context, the absence of the best interests principle from Part III of the Children Act 1989 should be noted. See **4.164** below.

[417] Newell, P and Hodgkin, R *Implementation Handbook for the Convention on the Rights of the Child* (2008) 3rd edn, UNICEF, pp 36 and Alston, P *The Best Interests Principle: Towards a Reconciliation of Culture and Human Rights* in Freeman, M (edn) *Children's Rights* Vol 2 (2003) Ashgate Dartmouth, p 197.

[418] UN Doc E/CN.4/L 1575. See Detrick, S (ed) *The United Nations Convention on the Rights of the Child – A Guide to the Travaux Préparatoires* (1992) Martinus Nijhoff, p 134.

[419] See **4.141** below.

[420] See E/CN.4/1989/48, pp 50–52 and Detrick, S (ed) *The United Nations Convention on the Rights of the Child – A Guide to the Travaux Préparatoires* (1992) Martinus Nijhoff, p 270.

[421] Newell, P and Hodgkin, R *Implementation Handbook for the Convention on the Rights of the Child* (2008) 3rd edn, UNICEF, p 232. See also **4.141** below.

[422] Newell, P and Hodgkin, R *Implementation Handbook for the Convention on the Rights of the Child* (2008) 3rd edn, UNICEF, pp 39. There are also instances of the Committee on the Rights of the Child characterising Art 3(1) as a 'paramount' as opposed to a 'primary' consideration in its Concluding Observations (see Romania CRC/C/15/Add. 199, para 29).

each of these articles.[423] As such, it would appear that no other interests, whether economic, political or otherwise should take precedence or be considered equal to the child in matters covered by these articles.[424]

The ECHR and Best Interests

4.142   The 'best interests' principle is found in the domestic legal systems of all Council of Europe member states.[425] The ECHR does not however contain any explicit 'best interests' formula. Within the context of the formulae adopted by the CRC and the domestic legal provisions, this begs the question of whether a 'best interests' test applies in the application of the rights enshrined in the ECHR to children, and if so which one.[426]

The ECHR and Best Interests – Balancing Rights

4.143   When viewed in the context of the ECHR, cases involving children often involve a tension between the rights of the child, most commonly under Art 8, and the rights of the parent under the same article. The response of the European Court of Human Rights to this tension has been to treat such cases not as classic cases of interference in an individual's rights but as 'positive obligation' cases, in which there is an obligation on the State to strike a 'fair balance' between competing interests, when determining whether interference in Art 8 rights is justified for the purposes of Art 8(2).[427] This 'fair balance' approach to cases where the rights of parents and children under Art 8 conflict was described in *Kearns v France*[428] in which the European Court of Human Rights, following an established line of authority, observed:

> 'The court reiterates that although the object of Art 8 is essentially that of protecting the individual against arbitrary interference by the public authorities, it does not merely compel the state to abstain from such interference: in addition to this primarily negative undertaking, there may be positive obligations inherent in effective respect for family life. These obligations may involve the adoption of measures designed to secure respect for private life even in the sphere of the relations of individuals between themselves. The boundaries between the state's positive and negative obligations under Art 8 do not lend themselves to precise definition. The applicable principles are nonetheless similar. In particular, in both instances regard must be had to the fair balance which has to be struck between the competing interests; and in both contexts the state enjoys a certain margin of appreciation (see *Keegan v Ireland* (1994) 18 EHRR 342, at para 49; *Odièvre*, cited above, at para 40; and *Evans v United Kingdom* (Application No 6339/05) [2007] 1 FLR 1990 (ECHR Grand Chamber), at para [75]). The Contracting States will usually enjoy a wide margin of appreciation if the public authorities are required to strike a balance between competing

---

423   Newell, P and Hodgkin, R *Implementation Handbook for the Convention on the Rights of the Child* (2008) 3rd edn, UNICEF, p 39.
424   Newell, P and Hodgkin, R *Implementation Handbook for the Convention on the Rights of the Child* (2008) 3rd edn, UNICEF, p 295. Those matters being separation from parents (Art 9), parents' joint responsibilities assisted by the state (Art 18), children deprived or their family environment (Art 20), deprivation of liberty (Art 37(c)) and right to a fair trial (Art 40(2)(b)(iii)).
425   Van Beuren, G *Child Rights in Europe* (2007) Council of Europe Publishing, p 33.
426   Article 24(2) of the European Union Charter of Fundamental Rights provides that 'In all actions relating to children, whether taken by public authorities or private institutions, the child's best interests must be a primary consideration.'
427   See Lord Lester QC, Lord Pannick QC and Herberg, J *Human Rights Law and Practice* (2009) 3rd edn, LexisNexis, pp 425–428 and see *Gaskin v United Kingdom* (1989) 12 EHRR 36, para 42.
428   [2008] 1 FLR 888, para 74. It should be noted that the 'fair balance' approach has also been deployed in cases where Art 8 rights conflict with other ECHR rights (see *Von Hanover v Germany* (2005) 40 EHRR 1, para 57 and *White v Sweden* (2008) 46 EHRR 3).

private and public interests or Convention rights. This applies all the more where there is no consensus within the member states of the Council of Europe as to the relative importance of the interest at stake or as to the best means of protecting it (see *Evans*, cited above, at paras [77]–[81]).'[429]

4.144 Within this context, historically the European Court of Human Rights has made it clear that whilst the ECHR does not contain a 'best interests' provision, the 'best interests' principle could be accommodated within the terms of the Convention and more particularly within the terms of Art 8 as an element of the 'fair balance' of the rights and interests of different parties where they conflicted.[430] In this regard, the European Court has made repeated reference to its decision in *Johansen v Norway*[431] in which it held:

> '... a fair balance has to be struck between the interests of the child in remaining in public care and those of the parent in being reunited with the child. In carrying out this balancing exercise, the Court will attach particular importance to the best interests of the child, which, depending on their nature and seriousness, may override those of the parent. In particular ... the parent cannot be entitled under article 8 of the Convention to have such measures taken as would harm the child's health and development.'

Having regard to the approach in *Johansen*, the question arises as to whether the European Court of Human Rights has yet moved from treating the child's best interests as an element of the 'fair balance' to one of treating the child's best interests as paramount, and therefore determinative, in cases where there is a conflict of rights and interests. This question has significant implications for the extent to which the domestic welfare principle enshrined in s 1(1) of the Children Act 1989 can be said to be compatible with the ECHR.[432]

The ECHR and Best Interests – Paramountcy

4.145 Whilst the European Court has been relatively consistent in articulating the need for a balancing exercise which incorporates preferentially the best interests of the child, unfortunately it has been inconsistent in the language that it has used to articulate the proper weight to be attached to the child's best interests within that balancing exercise.[433]

---

[429] The cases cited in this passage further demonstrate that in cases in which there is tension between the same Art 8 rights, the European Court of Human Rights is inclined to use a 'fair balance' analysis to determine whether interference is justified under Art 8(2) of the ECHR. See also *Dickson v United Kingdom* (2008) 46 EHRR 927, paras 72–85 for a case in which the 'fair balance' analysis was used where the Art 8 rights of the parties conflicted with the public interests contended for by the State.

[430] Fortin, J *Children's Rights and the Developing Law* (2005) 2nd edn, Cambridge, p 59.

[431] (1996) 23 EHRR 33.

[432] See **4.169-4.175** below.

[433] See *Hendricks v Netherlands* (1982) 5 EHRR 223 ('where as in the present case there is a serious conflict between the interests of the child and one of its parents which can only be resolved to the disadvantage of one of them, the interests of the child, under article 8(2) prevail'); *Olsson v Sweden (No 2)* (1992) 17 EHRR 134 ('the interests as well as the rights and freedoms of all concerned, must be taken into account, notably the children's interests and their rights under the Convention'); *Hoffman v Austria* (1993) 17 EHRR 293 ('the predominant consideration ... must be the best interest of the children, including the protection of their health and morals'); *Hokkanen v Finland* (1994) 19 EHRR, para 58 (the court should consider 'the rights and freedoms or all concerned ... and more particularly the best interests of the child and his or her rights under Article 8 of the Convention'); *X, Y and Z v United Kingdom* (1997) 24 EHRR 143, para 47 ('the community as a whole has an interest in maintaining a coherent system of family law which places the best

4.146 At its highest, in *Yousef v The Netherlands*[434] the European Court of Human Rights held in 2002 in relation to the weight to be attached to the child's best interests that:

> 'The court reiterates that in judicial decisions where the rights under Article 8 of parents and those of the child are at stake, the child's rights must be the paramount consideration. If any balancing of interests is necessary, the interests of the child must prevail.'

4.147 This passage has been seized upon as authority for the proposition that the European Court of Human Rights has finally endorsed paramount nature of children's best interests in cases engaging Art 8 of the ECHR.[435] However, it has also been argued persuasively that the European Court of Human Rights did not intend in this passage to signal a radical departure from the balancing exercise approach adopted in *Johansen* nor to suggest that the child's best interests will always override all other interests protected under the ECHR. In particular Choudry points out that the use of the word 'reiterates' demonstrates no new principle was being enunciated by the Court in *Yousef*, which cited only cases endorsing the balancing test in *Johansen* in support of its judgment.[436] More importantly, Choudry further notes that since *Yousef* the European Court of Human Rights has not relied on the judgment in *Yousef*, instead repeatedly returning to the test in *Johansen* and in particular to the formulation:[437]

---

interests of the child at the forefront'); *Bronda v Italy* (2001) 33 EHRR 81 (best interests of the child are of 'fundamental importance') and *P, C and S v United Kingdom* [2002] 3 FCR 1 (the child's best interests are described as an 'overriding requirement').

[434] (2002) 36 EHRR 20, [2002] 3 FCR 577, [2003] 1 FLR 210, para 73. See also *Hoppe v Germany* [2003] 1 FCR 176, para 51.

[435] See *CF v Sec State for Home Department* [2004] EWHC 111 (Fam), [2004] 1 FCR 577, [2004] 2 FLR 517 at 103 per Munby J and *Re S (Contact: Promoting Relationship with Absent Parent)* [2004] EWCA Civ 18, [2004] 1 FLR 1279, para 15 per Butler Sloss.

[436] See Choudry, S *The Adoption and Children Act 2002 – The Welfare Principle and the Human Rights Act 1998 – A Missed Opportunity?* (2003) 15 Child and Family Law Quarterly 119.

[437] See *Frette v France* [2003] 2 FLR 9, para 42 ('where a family tie is established between a parent and a child, 'particular importance must be attached to the best interests of the child, which, depending on their nature and seriousness, may override those of the parent'); *Haase v Germany* [2004] 2 FLR 39, para 93 ('a fair balance has to be struck between the interests of the child remaining in care and those of the parent in being reunited with the child. In carrying out this balancing exercise, the court will attach particular importance to the best interests of the child which, depending on their nature and seriousness, may override those of the parent'); *Pini and Bertani; Manera and Atripaldi v Romania* [2005] 2 FLR 596, para 155 ('The court has consistently held that particular importance must be attached to the best interests of the child in ascertaining whether the national authorities have taken all the necessary steps that can reasonably be demanded to facilitate the reunion of the child and his or her parents. In particular, it has held in such matters that the child's interests may, depending on their nature and seriousness, override those of the parent'); *Süss v Germany* [2006] 1 FLR 522, para 88 ('Article 8 requires that a fair balance must be struck between the interests of the child and those of the parent and, in striking such a balance, particular importance must be attached to the best interests of the child which, depending on their nature and seriousness, may override those of the parent'); *Hunt v Ukraine* [2006] 3 FCR 756, para 54 ('The court further recalls that a fair balance must be struck between the interests of the child and those of the parent … and that in doing so particular importance must be attached to the best interests of the child which, depending on their nature and seriousness, may override those of the parent'); *C v Finland* [2006] 2 FLR 597 ('Article 8 requires the domestic authorities to strike a fair balance between the interests of the child and those of the parents and that, in the balancing process, particular importance should be attached to the best interests of the child which, depending on their nature and seriousness, may override those of the parents.'); *HK v Finland* [2007] 1 FLR 633, para 109 ('a fair balance has to be struck between the interests of the child remaining in care and those of the parent in being reunited with the child. In carrying out this balancing exercise, the court will attach particular importance to the best interests of the child which, depending on their nature and seriousness, may override those of the parent') and *Dolhamre v Sweden* (2010) Application No 67/04, para 111 ('a fair balance has to be struck between the interests of the child remaining in care and those of the parent in being reunited with the child. In carrying out this balancing exercise, the Court will attach particular importance to the best interests of the child which, depending on their nature and seriousness, may override those of the parent').

'a fair balance must be struck between the interests of the child and those of the parent and, in striking such a balance, particular importance must be attached to the best interests of the child which, depending on their nature and seriousness, may override those of the parent.'

4.148 This approach, repeatedly endorsed by the European Court subsequent to the judgment in *Yousef*, is certainly more compatible with the rights based approach to be expected from that Court and also with the 'primary consideration' approach under Art 3(1) of the CRC, in accordance with which the ECHR should be interpreted.[438] In this context it is of note that in *Mubilanzila Mayeka and Kaniki Mitunga v Belgium*[439] the European Court of Human Rights reached its decision there had been a violation of Art 8 of the ECHR by reference to the 'higher' interests of the child as guaranteed by Art 3 of the CRC.

4.149 Having regard to the wealth of authority endorsing the approach in *Johansen* subsequent to the case of *Yousef* it would appear that the Court in *Yousef* was simply seeking, in somewhat unhelpful language, to re-iterate the primary status of the child's best interests in the 'fair balance' approach endorsed in *Johansen*.[440] Reading *Yousef* in its proper context it would appear that the European Court of Human Rights has still 'declined to forego the notion of 'a fair balance of the interests of all concerned' in favour of attaching paramountcy to the best interests of the child'[441] although it continues to recognise the privileged place of the child's interests in that balancing exercise. In *Neulinger and Shuruk v Switzerland*[442] whilst noting that 'there is currently a broad consensus, including in international law, in support of the idea that in all decisions concerning children, their best interests must be paramount' the European Court again reiterated, in the context of determining whether in applying the Hague Convention the domestic courts had secured the guarantees of the ECHR, that:

> 'In this area the decisive issue is whether a fair balance between the competing interests at stake, those of the child, of the two parents, and of public order, has been struck, within the margin of appreciation afforded to States in such matters, bearing in mind, however, that the child's best interests must be the primary consideration, as is indeed apparent from the Preamble to the Hague Convention, which provides that "the interests of children are of paramount importance in matters relating to their custody". The child's best interests may, depending on their nature and seriousness, override those of the parents. The parents' interests, especially in having regular contact with their child, nevertheless remain a factor when balancing the various interests at stake.'

4.150 The current, apparently settled view of the European Court of Human Rights that the child's best interests occupy a primary position within a test which balances all relevant rights rather than being of paramount importance has significant consequences for the domestic authorities which have held that the paramount nature of the child's best interests in domestic is compatible with the ECHR.[443] In this context, it should be noted that Art 24(2) of the European Charter on the Fundamental provides that 'In all

---

[438] See *Üner v The Netherlands* [2006] EHRR 873, para 8.

[439] [2007] 1 FLR 1726, para 83.

[440] If this is correct then in so far as *Yousef* has been used to further support the domestic contention that there is no material difference in the analysis of best interests under Art 8 and s 1(1) of the Children Act 1989, such usage is mistaken. See **4.169-4.175** below. *Yousef* is still cited before the domestic courts (see for example *R (on the application of Suppiah and others) v Secretary of State for the Home Department* [2011] EWHC 2 (Admin), [2011] All ER (D) 31 (Jan).

[441] Swindells, H *Crossing the Rubicon – Family Law Post the Human Rights Act 1998* in Cretney, S (ed) *Family Law – Essays for the New Millennium* (2000) Family Law, p 64.

[442] (2010) Application No 41615/07, para 134.

[443] See **4.169 et seq** below.

actions relating to children, whether taken by public authorities or private institutions, the child's best interests must be a primary consideration'.[444]

Domestic Law and Best Interests

Children Act 1989, s 1(1)

4.151 Children Act 1989, s 1(1) enshrines the best interests principle in statute in respect of cases in which a court is determining any question in relation to the upbringing of a child or the administration of the child's property or income from it. In such circumstances, the statute stipulates that 'the child's welfare shall be the court's paramount consideration'. The application of the principle in the situations prescribed by the Act is mandatory.[445] Under the Children Act 1989 the primary welfare focus is on the child's upbringing as a child rather than on the long term consequences for a child as an adult.[446] It has been persuasively argued that s 1 of the Children Act, and in particular the endorsement of the paramountcy principle and the provision of the welfare checklist, has advanced the rights of children within the domestic jurisdiction.[447]

Adoption and Children Act 2002, s 1(2) and s 52(1)(b)

4.152 Section 1(2) of the Adoption and Children Act 2002 requires a court or adoption agency to have as its paramount consideration the child's welfare, throughout his life. The fact that welfare is referable to the child 'throughout his life' demonstrates the fundamental difference between adoption orders, wherein family ties are permanently extinguished for the remainder of the child's life, and orders under the Children Act 1989, wherein parental responsibility is regulated for minority of the child. Section 52(1)(b) of the 2002 Act permits a court to dispense with a parents' consent to placement for adoption or adoption where the court is satisfied that the welfare of the child requires it.

'Welfare'

4.153 Neither the Children Act 1989 nor the Adoption and Children Act 2002 define 'welfare'. The Children Act 1989 and the Adoption and Children Act 2002 however do seek to address the problem of the indeterminate nature of the 'welfare' principle by providing some guidance as to those factors relevant to determining the best interests of the child in the welfare checklists at s 1(3) of the 1989 Act and s 1(4) of the 2002 Act respectively.[448]

---

[444] See also *R (on the application of E) v Office of the Schools Adjudicator* [2009] UKSC 15, [2010] 1 All ER 319, para 90 per Lord Mance ('under Art 3 of the United Nations Convention on the Rights of the Child 1989 it is the best interests of the child which the United Kingdom is obliged to treat as a primary consideration').

[445] *Re A (Children) (Conjoined Twins: Surgical Separation)* [2001] Fam] 147, [2000] 4 All ER 961, [2000] 3 FCR 577, sub nom *Re A (Conjoined Twins: Medical Treatment)* [2001] 1 FLR 1 per Ward LJ.

[446] *Re A (Leave to Remove: Cultural and Religious Considerations)* [2006] EWHC 421 (Fam), [2006] 2 FLR 572. Contrast s 1(2)(a) of the Adoption and Children Act 2002 at **4.152**.

[447] Roche, J *The Children Act 1989 and Children's Rights – A Critical Reassessment* in Franklin, B (edn) *The New Handbook of Children's Rights* (2002) Routledge, p 63.

[448] See the Law Commission, *Report on Guardianship and Custody* Law Co. No 172 (1988) London HMSO, para 3.18 for a concise summary of the perceived advantages which lead to the adoption of the checklist in CA 1989, s 1(3).

4.154 Under the Children Act 1989 the 'welfare checklist' must be considered by the court when dealing with contested applications under s 8 of the Act, all applications for special guardianship orders, and all applications for care and supervision orders.[449] An officer of Cafcass must have regard to the checklist when carrying out his or her duties in respect of the child.[450] The factors which the court is required to take into account, which are not exhaustive,[451] are prescribed by s 1(3) of the Act as follows:

(a) The ascertainable wishes and feelings of the child concerned (considered in light of his age and understanding).

(b) His physical, educational and emotional needs.

(c) The likely effect on him of any change in circumstances.[452]

(d) His age, sex, background and any characteristics of his which the court considers relevant.[453]

(e) Any harm which he has suffered or is at risk of suffering.[454]

(f) How capable each of his parents, and any other person in relation to whom the court considers the question to be relevant, is of meeting his needs.

(g) The range of powers available to the court under the Act in the proceedings in question.

4.155 Under the Adoption and Children Act 2002 the welfare checklist set out in s 1(4) of the Act must be considered by the court and the adoption agency whenever it is coming to a decision relating to the adoption of a child.[455] Section 1(4) of the 2002 Act contains the following, non-exhaustive list, of factors:

(a) The child's ascertainable wishes and feelings regarding the decision (considered in the light of the child's age and understanding),

(b) The child's particular needs,

---

[449] CA 1989, s 1(4). See also *Payne v Payne* [2001] EWCA Civ 166, para 30, [2001] 1 FCR 425, [2001] 1 FLR 1052 per Thorpe LJ and *Re G (Children) (Residence: Same Sex Partner)* [2006] UKHL 43, [2006] 1 WLR 2305, [2006] 4 All ER 241, [2006] 3 FCR 1, [2006] 2 FLR 629, para [40] per Baroness Hale on the merits of judges referring explicitly to the checklist when giving judgment in any event.

[450] Family Procedure Rules 2010, rr 16.33(1) and 16.38(3).

[451] See for example *Re R (A Minor) (Residence Order: Finance)* [1995] 3 FCR 334, [1995] 2 FLR 612.

[452] See *S v W* (1981) 11 Fam Law 81 at 82 in which Ormrod LJ highlighted that the argument that the status quo should only be altered if good reasons are adduced 'depends for its strength wholly and entirely on whether the status quo is satisfactory or not. The more satisfactory the status quo, the stronger the argument for not interfering. The less satisfactory the status quo, the less one requires before deciding to change.'

[453] This will include the child's religious upbringing (see chapter 10 below), racial origin, cultural and linguistic background and heritage (see chapter 7 below).

[454] See chapter 15. Section 105(1) of the CA 1989 provides that the word 'harm' has the meaning prescribed by s 31(9) of the CA 1989 which states '"harm" means ill treatment or the impairment of health or development including, for example, the impairment suffered from seeing or hearing the ill-treatment of another.'

[455] ACA 2002 s 1(1).

(c)   The likely effect on the child (throughout his life) of having ceased to be a member of the original family and become an adopted person,

(d)   The child's age, sex, background and any of the child's characteristics which the court or agency considers relevant,

(e)   Any harm (within the meaning of the Children Act 1989 (c 41)) which the child has suffered or is at risk of suffering,

(f)   The relationship which the child has with relatives, and with any other person in relation to whom the court or agency considers the relationship to be relevant, including:

(i)   the likelihood of any such relationship continuing and the value to the child of its doing so,
(ii)   the ability and willingness of any of the child's relatives, or of any such person, to provide the child with a secure environment in which the child can develop, and otherwise to meet the child's needs,
(iii)   the wishes and feelings of any of the child's relatives, or of any such person, regarding the child.

'Paramount Consideration'

4.156   The classic formulation of 'paramount' in domestic law, provided with reference to the words 'first and paramount consideration' in the now repealed Guardianship of Minors Act 1971, was given by Lord MacDermott in *J v C*:[456]

'Reading these words in their ordinary significance, and relating them to the various classes of proceedings which the section has already mentioned, it seems to me that they must mean more than that the child's welfare is to be treated as the top item in a list of items relevant to the matter in question. I think they connote a process whereby, when all the relevant facts, relationships, claims and wishes of parents, risks, choices and other circumstances are taken into account and weighed, the course to be followed will be that which is most in the interests of the child's welfare as that term has now to be understood. That is the first consideration because it is of first importance and the paramount consideration because it rules on or determines the course to be followed.'

4.157   During the passage of the Children Act through Parliament Lord McKay stated that the child's welfare must be placed 'before and above any other consideration in deciding whether to make an order'.[457] Within this context, the approach of Lord MacDermott in *J v C* was endorsed again in 2006 by Baroness Hale in *Re G (Children) (Residence: Same Sex Partner)*[458] in which she said:

'The statutory position is plain: the welfare of the child is the paramount consideration. As Lord McDermott explained in *J v C* [1970] AC 668, 711, this means that it rules upon or determines the course to be followed. There is no question of a parental right.'

---

[456]   [1970] AC 668.
[457]   Lord McKay, LC, *Hansard* HL Vol 502, col 1167.
[458]   [2006] UKHL 43, [2006] 1 WLR 2305.

Under s 1(1) of the Children Act 1989 and s 1(2) of the Adoption and Children Act 2002 ultimately, the answer to one question will be determinative, namely 'what is best for the welfare of the child?'.[459]

Scope of Domestic Application

Judicial Application

(i) Children Act 1989

4.158 The application of the welfare principle in domestic law is much narrower than under Art 3(1) of the CRC. As stated, under the Children Act 1989 the court must consider the welfare principle when dealing with cases in which a court is determining any question in relation to the upbringing[460] of a child or the administration of the child's property or income from it.[461] The principle is not restricted to proceedings under the 1989 Act[462] and will include cases brought between parents and cases brought between parents and other individuals.[463] The application of the welfare principle is thus narrowly construed within the domestic jurisdiction.[464] Cases in which the court is considering proceedings that only *indirectly* concern a child's upbringing will fall outside the scope of s 1(1) of the 1989 Act.[465] The court will nonetheless retain a protective

---

[459] Swindells, H, Neaves, A, Kushner, M, Skilbeck, R *Family Law and the Human Rights Act 1998* (1999) Jordan Publishing, p 90.

[460] CA 1989, s 105(1) provides that '"upbringing", in relation to any child, includes the care of the child but not his maintenance.'

[461] CA 1989, s 1(1).

[462] The welfare principle will apply in wardship proceedings (see *J v C* [1970 AC 668, [1969] 1 All ER 788), non-European or Hague Convention child abduction cases (*Re J (A Child) (Custody Rights: Jurisdiction)* [2005] UKHL 40, [2006] 1 AC 80, [2005] 3 WLR 14, [2005] 3 All ER 291, [2005] 2 FCR 381, [2005] 2 FLR 802) and to cases under the inherent jurisdiction of the High Court (see *Re W (A Minor) (Medical Treatment: Court's Jurisdiction)* [1993] Fam 64, [1992] 4 All ER 627; *Re T (A Minor) (Wardship: Medical Treatment)* [1997] 1 All ER 906, [1997] 1 WLR 242 and *Re A (Children) (Conjoined Twins: Surgical Separation)* [2001] Fam 147, [2000] 4 All ER 961, [2000] 3 FCR 577, sub nom *Re A (Conjoined Twins: Medical Treatment)* [2001] 1 FLR 1.

[463] *Re G (Children) (Residence: Same Sex Partner)* [2006] UKHL 43, [2006] 1 WLR 2305, [2006] 3 FCR 1, [2006] 2 FLR 629 per Baroness Hale, para 30.

[464] In addition to applications under s 4 of the 1989 Act (parental responsibility order), s 8 (private law order), s 13 (change of surname), s 16 (family assistance order), s 31 (care or supervision order), s 34 (contact to a child in care), s 36 (education supervision order), s 37 (direction to investigate a child's circumstances), s 43 (child assessment orders) and s 51 (recovery order) this will include cases concerning a child's religious upbringing (*Re J (Child's Religious Upbringing and Circumcision)* [2000] 1 FCR 307, CA), applications to discharge a care order (*Re T and E (Proceedings: Conflicting Interests)* [1995] 1 FLR 581), applications to withdraw proceedings (*Southwark Borough Council v B* [1993] 2 FLR 559), applications for the stay of an order (*Re M (Application for Stay of Order)* [1996] 3 FCR 185). The court should have the welfare principle in mind when deciding whether to grant an order pursuant to s 91(14) preventing further applications without the leave or the court (*B v B (Residence: Contact: Restricting Applications)* [1997] 1 FLR 139, p 146 and *Re P (A Minor) (Residence Order: Child's Welfare* Fam 15, p 37, [199] 2 FCR 289 at 310, sub nom *Re P (A Child) (Residence Order: Restriction Order)* [1999] 2 FLR 573 at 592 per Butler-Sloss LJ. But see also *Re R (Residence: Restricting Contact Applications)* [1998] 1 FLR 749 per Wilson J). The welfare principle will apply prospectively when the court is considering whether or not to make contact activity directions pursuant to s 11A(9) of the CA 1989.

[465] This will include applications for financial maintenance in so far as they are still permitted (*K v H (Child Maintenance* [1993] 2 FLR 61, p 64 per Sir Stephen Brown P; *J v C (Child: Financial Provision)* [1998] 3 FCR 79, [1999] 1 FLR 152), the question of whether to administer blood tests to establish paternity (*S v S, W v Official Solicitor* [1972] AC 24, [1970] 3 All ER 107, HL (considered in *Re S (A Child) (Identification: Restriction on Publication)* [2003] EWCA Civ 963, para 20, [2003] 2 FCR 577, [2003] 2 FLR 1253 per Hale LJ) and *Re H (A Minor) (Blood Tests: Parental Rights)* [1997] Fam 89, [1996] 4 All ER 28 sub nom *Re H (Paternity: Blood Test)* [1996] 2 FLR 65 but note that s 21(3)(b) of the Family Law Reform Act 1969 as amended refers to the child's best interests), an application within divorce proceedings to exclude a spouse from the matrimonial home (*Richards v Richards* [1984] AC 174, [1983] 2 All ER 807 HL), application to

jurisdiction to prevent the child suffering harm, although in exercising that jurisdiction the child's welfare is not the only, nor necessarily the most important consideration.[466] The application of the welfare principle is also excluded by statute in certain circumstances even where the child's upbringing is otherwise directly in issue.[467] Such statutory exclusion may also be implied.[468] The welfare principal will also be excluded by a successful claim for diplomatic immunity.[469]

4.159 Where the welfare of more than one child is involved in proceedings under the 1989 Act to which the welfare principle applies, not all of whom are the subject of the application, the welfare principle will only apply to the child who is the subject of the application.[470] Where two or more children are the subject of the application the welfare

---

restrain publication of material containing salacious details concerning a deceased parent (*Re X (A Minor) (Wardship: Jurisdiction)* [1975] Fam 47, [1975] 1 All ER 697. See also *Re S (A Child) (Identification: Restrictions on Publication)* [2004] UKHL 47, [2005] 1 AC 593, [2004] 3 WLR 1129, [2004] 4 All ER 683, [2004 3 FCR 407, [2005] 1 FLR 591), applications for permission to use evidence previously admitted in wardship proceedings in subsequent criminal proceedings (*Re S (Minors) (Wardship: Police Investigation)* [1987] 3 All ER 1076), applications by adults for leave to apply for an order under CA 1989, s 8 (*Re A (Minors) (Residence Orders: Leave to Apply)* [1992] Fam 182, [1992] 3 All ER 872), applications by children seeking leave to apply for s 8 orders (*Re SC (A Minor) (Leave to Seek a Residence Order)* [1994] 1 FLR 96 per Booth J; *Re C (Residence: Child's Application for Leave)* [1995] 1 FLR 927 per Stuart-White J and *Re S (Contact Application By Sibling)* [1998] 2 FLR 897 per Charles J but see *Re C (A Minor) (Leave to Seek Section 8 Orders)* [1994] 1 FLR 26 per Johnson J), determining whether an unmarried father should be served with care proceedings (*Re X (Care: Notice of Proceedings)* [1996] 1 FLR 186 per Stuart-White J), determining whether a parent should be committed to prison for breaching an order concerning a child (*A v N (Committal: Refusal of Contact)* [1997] 1 FLR 533 but see also *M v M (Breaches of Orders: Committal)* [2005] EWCA Civ 1722, [2006] 1 FLR 1154 and *Re V (Children)* [2008] EWCA Civ 635 where the child interests were held to remain a material consideration in committal applications), application by one party for another to cease to be a party to proceedings (*Re W (Discharge of Party to Proceedings)* [1997] 1 FLR 128 per Hogg J), determining whether to give leave to apply for the revocation of a placement order (*M v Warwickshire County Council* [2007] EWCA Civ 1084, [2008] 1 WLR 991, [2008] 1 FLR 1093), determining costs in family proceedings (*Q v Q (Costs: Summary Assessment)* [2002] 2 FLR 668 per Wilson J), determining whether to issue a witness summons against a child (*Re P (Witness Summons)* [1997] 2 FLR 447 per Wilson J. See also *R v Highbury Magistrates Court, ex p Deering* [1997] 1 FLR 683), applications for interim assessment pursuant to CA 1989, s 38(6) *Re M (Residential Assessment Directions)* [1998] 2 FLR 371 per Holman J and *Re P (Children Act 1989, ss22 and 26: Local Authority Compliance)* [2000] 2 FLR 910 per Charles J) and determination of a dispute concerning the disposal of a deceased adult child's remains (*Buchannan v Milton* [1999] 2 FLR 844 at 857 per Hale J deceased adult child's welfare not paramount). See *The Chief Constable of Greater Manchester v KI and KW (Children)* [2007] EWHC 1837 (Fam), [2008] 2 FCR 172, [2008] 1 FLR 504 in respect of leave to interview children involved in court proceedings for the purpose of preparing an adult's defence in criminal proceedings. See also *M v M (Stay of Proceedings: Return of Children)* [2005] EWHC 1159 (Fam), [2006] 1 FLR 138 per Wilson J; *Re V (Forum Conveniens)* [2004] EWHC 2663 (Fam) [2005] 1 FLR 718, per Munby J; *Re S (Residence Order: Forum Conveniens)* [1995] 1 FLR 314 at 325 per Thorpe J and *Hallam v Hallam* [1992] 2 FCR 197, sub nom *H v H (Minors) (Forum Conveniens) (Nos 1 and 2)* [1993] 1 FLR 958 per Waite J in respect of the determination of forum conveniens.

466 *S v S, W v Official Solicitor* [1972] AC 24, [1970] 3 All ER 107 HL and *Richards v Richards* [1984] AC 174, [1983] 2 All ER 807 HL.

467 See the Human Fertilisation and Embryology Act 1990, s 30, the Matrimonial Causes Act 1973, s 25(1) and the Children Act 1989, s 105(1).

468 See *Richards v Richards* [1984] AC 174 at 202 D per Lord Hailsham; *Re M (A Minor) (Secure Accommodation Order)* [1995] Fam 108, [1995] 3 All ER 407 (but see *Re C (Detention: Medical Treatment)* [1997] 2 FLR 180 per Wall J) and *Re A (Minors) (Residence Orders: Leave to Apply)* [1992] Fam 182, [1992] 3 All ER 872.

469 *Re P (Children Act: Diplomatic Immunity)* [1998] 2 FCR 480, [1998] 1 FLR 624.

470 *Birmingham City Council v H (A Minor) (No 2)* [1994] 2 AC 212, [1994] 1 All ER 12, [1994] 1 FCR 896, [1994] 1 FLR 224, HL; *F v Leeds City Council* [1994] 2 FCR 428, [1994] 2 FLR 60, CA; *Re F (A Minor) (Contact: Child in Care)* [1994] 2 FCR 1354, [1995] 1 FLR 510. See also Douglas *In Whose Best Interests?* (1994) 101 LQR 379 and Bainham, *The Nuances of Welfare* [1995] CLJ 512 (both arguing that each child's interests should be balanced against that of the others). See also Lowe, G and Douglas, G *Bromley's Family Law* (2007) 10th edn, p 466.

and the paramount interests of each child produce results which are incompatible with each other, the court must determine the case having treated each child separately, having considered the welfare of each child as paramount and finally having carried out a balancing exercise as between the children to arrive at the least detrimental solution.[471]

(ii) Adoption and Children Act 2002

4.160 The Adoption and Children Act 2002 for the first time extends the 'best interests' principle beyond the court room to encompass some species of administrative discretion by requiring adoption agencies to have as their paramount consideration the welfare of the child throughout his life when coming to any decision relating to the adoption of a child.[472]

Domestic Best Interests and Article 3(1) of the CRC

Domestic Application of the Best Interests Principle

4.161 Beyond the limited extension provided by s 1(1) of the Children Act 1989 and the Adoption and Children Act 2002, the best interests principle has historically not been applicable outside the judicial proceedings specified by the Acts incorporating that principle. By contrast to Art 3(1) of the CRC it has had no application to the 'public or private social welfare institutions ... administrative authorities or legislative bodies'.[473] This limitation has included the exercise of administrative discretion by local authorities under Part III of the Children Act 1989 in respect of the provision of services for children and families.[474] The highest the welfare principle may be put in relation to Part III is that the welfare of the child will remain 'an important consideration'.[475] There are no provisions applying the principle to the day to day activities and actions of parents. The overall result of this position is that, outside the narrow confines of those situations specified by the Children Act 1989 and Adoption and Children Act 2002 there has been no legal requirement in domestic law to consider the best interests of the child, whether as the paramount or a primary consideration, within the context of other actions and decisions which impact directly and indirectly on children.

Committee on the Rights of the Child

4.162 The UN Committee on the Rights of the Child has repeatedly criticised the United Kingdom for an insufficiency of measures to ensure the proper implementation of the 'best interests' principle enshrined in Art 3(1) of the CRC. In 1995, the Committee noted that 'the principle of best interests appears not to be reflected in legislation in such areas as health, education and social security which have a bearing on the respect for the rights of the child'.[476] In 2008 the Committee again noted that 'that the principle of the best interests of the child is still not reflected as a primary

---

[471] *Re D (Minors) (Appeal)* [1995] 1 FCR 301, CA and *Re A (Conjoined Twins: Surgical Separation)* [2000] 4 All ER 961, [2000] 3 FCR 577, [2001] 1 FLR 1. See also *Re T and E (Children's Proceedings: Conflicting Interests)* [1995] 3 FCR 260 at 267, [1995] 1 FLR 581 at 587 per Wall J.

[472] ACA 2002 s 1(1) and 1(2).

[473] For example, the principle is of no application to prison authorities (see *R (P) v Secretary of State for the Home Department, R (Q) v Secretary of State for the Home Department* [2001] EWCA Civ 1151, [2001] 1 WLR 2002, sub nom *R (P) and (Q) and QB v Secretary of State for the Home Department* [2001] 2 FLR 1122, para 89 per Lord Philips MR.

[474] *Re M (A Minor)(Secure Accommodation Order)* [1995] Fam 108, [1995] 3 All ER 407, [1995] 1 FLR 418. Indeed, s 22(6) of the CA 1989 the need to protect members of the public from serious harm overrides the duty to safeguard and promote the interests of individual child.

[475] *Re P (Children Act 1989, ss22 and 26: Local Authority Compliance)* [2000] 2 FLR 910, p 923 per Charles J.

[476] 1995 CRC/C/15/Add.34, para 11.

consideration in all legislative and policy matters affecting children, especially in the area of juvenile justice, immigration and freedom of movement and peaceful assembly'.[477]

Areas of Concern

4.163 Given the highly circumscribed application of the 'best interests' principle in domestic law the observations of the Committee are not surprising. There are four key areas in which the domestic law appears to contravene the UK's binding obligations[478] under Art 3(1) of the CRC to ensure that 'in all actions concerning children, whether undertaken by public or private social welfare institutions, courts of law, administrative authorities or legislative bodies, the best interests of the child shall be a primary consideration'.

(i)   Services for Children and Families

4.164 As noted, whilst an important consideration,[479] there is no obligation on local authorities under Part III of the Children Act 1989 to have as their paramount or primary consideration the best interests of the child when providing services to children and families. Note however that s 11 of the Children Act 2004 places a duty on local authorities and a wide range of other bodies to discharge their functions having regard to the need to safeguard and promote the welfare of children.[480]

(ii)   Certain Proceedings under Children Act 1989

4.165 There are a significant number of applications under the Children Act 1989 and which, whilst directly or indirectly concerning children, do not require the court to have as its paramount or primary consideration the best interests of the child.[481]

(iii)   Procedural Applications Concerning Children

4.166 There are a range of procedural applications which, whilst often directly concerning the interests of children, do not require the court to hold those interests as a paramount or primary consideration. For example, in considering the disclosure of documents about the child filed in proceedings under the Children Act 1989, the welfare of the child is not the paramount or a primary consideration but rather a major or very important factor.[482] Likewise, in considering whether the media should be excluded from attendance during family proceedings in respect of which the child is the subject, the welfare of the child is not a paramount or a primary consideration of the Court.[483]

---

[477]   2008 CRC/C/GBR/CO/4, para 26.

[478]   See **3.32–3.46**.

[479]   *Re P (Children Act 1989, ss 22 and 26: Local Authority Compliance)* [2000] 2 FLR 910, p 923 per Charles J.

[480]   The bodies include children's services authorities, district councils, Strategic Health Authorities, Special health Authorities, Primary Care Trusts, NHS Trusts, NHS Foundation Trusts, Police Authorities, the British Transport Police Authority, local probation boards, youth offending teams, prison governors and any person providing services under s 144 of the Learning and Skills Act 2000.

[481]   See **fn 470** above.

[482]   See *Re D (Minors) (Wardship: Disclosure)* [1994] 1 FLR 346 at 351A; *Re Manda* [1993] Fam 183 at 195E, sub nom *Re Manda (Wardship: Disclosure of Evidence)* [1993] 1 FLR 205, 215 and *Re C (A Minor) (Care Proceedings: Disclosure)* [1997] Fam 76, 85D, sub nom *Re EC (Disclosure of Material)* [1996] 2 FLR 725 at 733.

[483]   Family Procedure Rules 2010, r 27.11(3)(a)(i).

(iv) Other Legislation Touching and Concerning Children

4.167 In addition to certain proceedings under and related to the Children Act 1989, there are a number of domestic statutes concerning children which do not provide for children's best interests to be the paramount or a primary consideration. Examples include s 175 of the Education Act 2002 which requires local education authorities and school governing bodies to discharge their functions with a view to safeguarding and promoting the welfare of children who are pupils at the school, s 11 of the Children Act 2004 which requires public authorities working with children to have regard to the need to safeguard and promote the welfare of children and which excludes immigration agencies from even this requirement, s 1 of the Childcare Act 2006 which requires local authorities to improve the well being of young children under eight in their area, s 44 of the Children and Young Persons Act 1933 which requires courts dealing with child defendants to have regard to the welfare of the child and s 3(5) of the Immigration Act 1971 which permits the deportation of non-citizen family members of those deported under s 3(5) including children. Note however that s 55 of the Borders, Citizenship and Immigration Act 2009 now provides that the Secretary of State must make arrangements for ensuring that the functions under the Act 'are discharged having regard to the need to safeguard and promote the welfare of children who are in the United Kingdom'.

CRC, Art 3(1) in Domestic Law

4.168 The binding obligations of the United Kingdom under the CRC allow a cogent argument to be made that, in the situations outlined above, the courts and administrative bodies acting in respect of children under the foregoing statutory provisions and common law principles *must* interpret those provisions and principles in such a way as to ensure that the child best interests are a primary consideration.[484] In this respect, the courts are ahead of administrative bodies in recognising that weight should be attached to children's interests even where stature or common law does not prescribe the use of the domestic welfare principle.[485] Most recently, the Supreme Court reiterated this position by explicit reference to and application of Art 3(1) of the CRC in relation to the Immigration Act 1971. In *ZH v (Tanzania) (FC) v Secretary of State for the Home Department*,[486] Baroness Hale held in relation to the question of what weight should be given to the best interests of children who are affected by the decision to remove or deport one or both of their parents from the United Kingdom that:

> 'For our purposes the most relevant national and international obligation of the United Kingdom is contained in article 3(1) of the UNCRC: "In all actions concerning children, whether undertaken by public or private social welfare institutions, courts of law, administrative authorities or legislative bodies, the best interests of the child shall be a primary consideration." This is a binding obligation in international law, and the spirit, if not the precise language, has also been translated into our national law. Section 11 of the Children Act 2004 places a duty upon a wide range of public bodies to carry out their functions having regard to the need to safeguard and promote the welfare of children. The

---

[484] See **3.32–3.46** above.

[485] See for example *M v M (Breaches of Orders: Committal)* [2005] EWCA Civ 1722, [2006] 1 FLR 1154 and *Re V (Children)* [2008] EWCA Civ 635 in respect of committal applications and *Re C (A Minor) (Care Proceedings: Disclosure)* [1997] Fam 76, 85D, sub nom *Re EC (Disclosure of Material)* [1996] 2 FLR 725 at 733 in respect of disclosure issues. See also *R (on the application of E) v Office of the Schools Adjudicator* [2009] UKSC 15, [2010] 1 All ER 319, para 90 per Lord Mance ('under art 3 of the United Nations Convention on the Rights of the Child 1989 it is the best interests of the child which the United Kingdom is obliged to treat as a primary consideration').

[486] [2011] UKSC 4.

immigration authorities were at first excused from this duty, because the United Kingdom had entered a general reservation to the UNCRC concerning immigration matters. But that reservation was lifted in 2008 and, as a result, section 55 of the Borders, Citizenship and Immigration Act 2009 now provides that, in relation among other things to immigration, asylum or nationality, the Secretary of State must make arrangements for ensuring that those functions "are discharged having regard to the need to safeguard and promote the welfare of children who are in the United Kingdom"... Further, it is clear from the recent jurisprudence that the Strasbourg Court will expect national authorities to apply article 3(1) of UNCRC and treat the best interests of a child as "a primary consideration". Of course, despite the looseness with which these terms are sometimes used, "a primary consideration" is not the same as "the primary consideration", still less as "the paramount consideration"... In making the proportionality assessment under article 8, the best interests of the child must be a primary consideration. This means that they must be considered first. They can, of course, be outweighed by the cumulative effect of other considerations.'

Domestic Best Interests and Art 8 of the ECHR

The Defence of 'Paramountcy'

4.169 The question of the extent to which the domestic welfare principle enshrined in s 1(1) of the Children Act 1989 is compatible with the provisions of the ECHR, and in particular Art 8(2), has been a vexed one. Following the implementation of the Human Rights Act 1998, the domestic courts have pursued a defence of the 'paramountcy principle' based on the premise that there is no material difference in the analytical exercise under Art 8(2) of the ECHR and that under s 1(1) of the Children Act 1989. To this end, in *Dawson v Wearmouth*[487] Lord Hobhouse of Woodborough stated:

> '[t]here is nothing in the [European Convention for the Protection of Human Rights and Fundamental Freedoms] which requires the courts of this country to act otherwise than in accordance with the interests of the child'

Thorpe LJ observed in respect of this issue in *Payne v Payne*:[488]

> 'whilst the advent of the 1998 Act requires revision of the judicial approach to conclusion, as a safeguard to an inadequate perception and application for a father's rights under Articles 6 and 8, it requires no re-evaluation of the judge's primary task to evaluate and uphold the welfare of the child as the paramount consideration, despite its inevitable conflict with adult rights.'

4.170 In *Re L (A Child) (Contact: Domestic Violence), Re V (A Child), Re M (A Child), Re H (Children)*[489] Butler-Sloss P likewise expressed no difficulty with the proposition that the child's interests remained paramount was compatible with Art 8(2) of the ECHR. In the same year, the House of Lords again visited this issue in *Re B (Adoption by One Natural Parent)*.[490] Lord Nicholls of Birkenhead held as follows in respect of the ECHR concepts of 'pressing social need' and 'proportionality':

> 'Inherent in both these Convention concepts is a balancing exercise, weighing the advantages and the disadvantages. But this balancing exercise, required by Art 8, does not differ in

---

[487]   [1999] 2 AC 308 at 329, [1999] 2 All ER 353 at 366, [1999] 1 FCR at 640, [1999] 1 FLR 1167 at 1181. See also *Re KD (A Minor) (Ward: Termination of Access)* [1988] AC 806.

[488]   [2001] EWCA Civ 166, para 57, [2001] 1 FCR 425, [2001] 1 FLR 1052.

[489]   [2001] Fam 260, [2000] 4 All ER 609.

[490]   [2001] UKHL 70, [2002] 1 FLR 196. *See also Re S (Minors) (Care Order: Implementation of Care Plan); Re W (Minors) (Care Order: Adequacy of Care Plan)* [2002] 1 FLR 815, para 109.

substance from the like-balancing exercise undertaken by a court when deciding whether, in the conventional phraseology of English law, adoption would be in the best interests of the child. The like considerations fall to be taken into account. Although the phraseology is different, the criteria to be applied in deciding whether an adoption order is justified under Art 8(2) lead to the same result as the conventional tests applied by English law. Thus, unless the court misdirected itself in some material respect when balancing the competing factors, its conclusion that an adoption order is in the best interests of the child, even though this would exclude the mother from the child's life, identifies the pressing social need for adoption (the need to safeguard and promote the child's welfare) and represents the court's considered view on proportionality. That is the effect of the judge's decision in the present case. Article 8(2) does not call for more.'

This approach was reflected by Wall J in dealing with the welfare checklist under s 1(3) of the Children Act 1989 in the private law case of *Re H (Contact Order) (No 2)*[491] in which he held:

'... it seems to me that a proper application of the checklist in s 1(3) of the Children Act 1989 is equivalent to the balancing exercise required in the application of Art 8, which is then a useful cross-check to ensure that the order proposed is in accordance with the law, necessary for the protection of the rights and freedoms of others and proportionate.'

4.171 As noted above, the domestic courts have relied on the decision in *Yousef v The Netherlands*[492] as confirmation of the domestic approach to date in respect of the compatibility of s 1(1) of the Children Act 1989 and Art 8 of the ECHR. In *CF v Secretary of State for the Home Department*[493] Munby J held:

'To this I would only add, as I pointed out during the course of argument, that the court has now made clear that, as between parent and child, the child's interests are paramount. As the court said in *Yousef v The Netherlands* (2003) 36 EHRR 20, [2003] 1 FLR 210 at para 73: 'The court reiterates that in judicial decisions where the rights under Art 8 of parents and those of a child are at stake, the child's rights must be the paramount consideration. If any balancing of interests is necessary, the interests of the child must prevail.''

In *Re S (Contact: Promoting Relationship with Absent Parent)*[494] Butler-Sloss P placed similar reliance on *Yousef*:

The principle of the paramountcy of the welfare of the child is, nonetheless, recognised in the jurisprudence of the European Court of Human Rights. In *Yousef v Netherlands* [2002] ECHR 33711/96, at para 73, the European Court stated 'The Court reiterates that in judicial decisions where the rights under art 8 of parents and those of a child are at stake, the child's rights must be the "paramount" consideration. If any balancing of interests is necessary, the interests of the child must prevail (see *Elsholz v Germany* [2001] ECHR 25735/94 at para 52 and *TP and KM v UK* [2001] ECHR 28945/95 at para 72).'

'Paramountcy' and ECHR, Art 8(2)

4.172 The defence by the domestic courts of the 'paramountcy' principle in the context of Art 8 of the ECHR[495] demands detailed scrutiny. The need for such scrutiny arises in

---

[491] [2002] 1 FLR 22, para 59.
[492] (2002) 36 EHRR 20, [2002] 3 FCR 577, [2003] 1 FLR 210, para 73. See also *Hoppe v Germany* [2003] 1 FCR 176, para 51.
[493] [2004] EWHC 111 (Fam), [2004] 1 FCR 577, [2004] 2 FLR 517 at 103.
[494] [2004] EWCA Civ 18, [2004] 1 FLR 1279, para 15.
[495] Described by Fortin as the 'status quo ante bellum' (Fortin, J *Children's Rights and the Developing Law* (2005) 2nd edn, Cambridge, p 250).

part because, for the reasons discussed earlier in this chapter,[496] the case of *Yousef* may well not be able stand the weight which the domestic courts have sought to place on it as a European bulwark for the domestic welfare principle. Indeed, the House of Lords now appears tentatively to have recognised that *Yousef* is not authority for the inevitable paramountcy of children's interests over all other considerations under Art 8(2) of the ECHR, at least in cases concerning adoption. In *Down Lisburn Health and Social Services Trust v H*[497] Baroness Hale stated:

> 'The UK is unusual amongst members of the Council of Europe in permitting the total severance of family ties without parental consent. (Professor Triseliotis thought that only Portugal and perhaps one other European country allowed this.) It is, of course, the most draconian interference with family life possible. That is not to say that it can never be justified in the interests of the child. The European Court has said that where the interests of the child and the interests of the adults conflict, the interests of the child must prevail: for example *Yousef v The Netherlands* (2003) 36 EHRR 20, [2003] 1 FLR 210, at para [73]. But it can be expected that the European Court would scrutinise the relevance and sufficiency of the reasons given for such a drastic interference with the same intensity with which it has scrutinised severance decisions in other care cases: see, in particular, *P, C and S v United Kingdom* (2002) 35 EHRR 31, [2002] 2 FLR 631, para [118].'

However, the need to scrutinise the validity of the domestic courts' conclusion that the paramountcy principle is compatible with Art 8(2) of the ECHR goes beyond the difficulties discussed above[498] in relying on *Yousef* as support for that defence, extending to the requirements of Art 8(2) itself.

4.173 When carrying out the analysis required by Art 8 ECHR a child's best interests cannot automatically justify interference with the Art 8(1) rights of the parents or others because Art 8(2) mandates that such interference be justified according to its terms before that interference is permissible. In the circumstances, the child's best interests can only come into the equation at the Art 8(2) stage. At that stage, in a case where there are competing Art 8 rights, it would appear settled ECHR law that the court should adopt a 'fair balance' approach in addressing the issue of justification under Art 8(2).[499] If at this point, in line with *Re G (Children) (Residence: Same Sex Partner)*,[500] the child's best interests are taken to be paramount with 'no question of a parental right', then the concept of a 'fair balance' at the Art 8(2) stage in cases involving children necessarily becomes redundant, as do the other processes carefully followed by the European Court of Human Rights in considering the requirements of Art 8(2).[501]

4.174 On this analysis it is difficult to see how the 'paramount' nature of the child's welfare under domestic law can be compatible with the proper application of Art 8 of the ECHR, at least in cases where the Art 8 rights of children and parents compete.[502] As Harris-Short argues:[503]

---

[496] See **4.145** above.
[497] [2006] UKHL 36, [2007] 1 FLR 121.
[498] See **4.145**.
[499] See **4.145–4.150** above. See also Fortin, J *Children's Rights and the Developing Law* (2005) 2nd edn, Cambridge, p 249.
[500] [2006] UKHL 43, [2006] 1 WLR 2305.
[501] Fortin, J *Children's Rights and the Developing Law* (2005) 2nd edn, Cambridge, p 250.
[502] A proposition which the Court of Appeal in *Re B (Adoption: Natural Parent)* clearly appreciated (see *Re B (Adoption by One Natural Parent to Exclusion of Other)* [2001] 1 FLR 589).
[503] Harris-Short, S *Re B (Adoption: Natural Parent) – Putting the Child at the Heart of Adoption?* [2002] CFLQ 325 at 336–337. Eekelaar similarly observes in relation to *Re B (A Child) (Adoption by One Natural Parent)* that 'Article 8 makes the subservience of adults' rights to the child's best interests *conditional on*

'To suggest that the child's welfare will automatically justify any interference with Convention rights protected under Article 8(1), is to fail to appreciate the demands of the Article 8(2) requirement that any interference with Convention rights must be "necessary in a democratic society". Convention case-law has established that "necessary" does not mean "indispensable", but it does impose a stricter standard than the interference with Convention rights merely being useful, reasonable or desirable. In other words, just because it can be shown that, with a view to protecting the welfare of the child, the interference with Article 8(1) rights is "desirable", does not mean it will be justified under Article 8(2). Something more is required. That "something more" is encapsulated in the concept of 'proportionality'. In *James v United Kingdom* the principle of proportionality is held to impose a requirement that a 'reasonable relationship' exist "between the means employed and the aim sought to be realised". In other Convention case-law, it is described as requiring a 'fair balance' between the "demands of the general interest of the community and the requirements of the protection of the individual's fundamental human rights". To suggest that in every case, the child's welfare will always justify the interference with an individual's Article 8 rights – no matter how substantial the interference and how weak the concerns relating to the child's welfare – is simply to ignore these requirements.'

4.175 Many recognised from the inception of the Human Rights Act 1998 that the approach to the welfare principle under the ECHR was different to that adopted by the domestic courts. In particular, it was recognised that the European approach remained 'wedded to the notion of 'balancing of all interests''[504] and that this difference in approach was fundamental.[505] The difference was also recognised by the Court of Appeal prior to the coming into force of the Human Rights Act 1998.[506] The assertion by the domestic courts to the effect that this position has altered such that there is now compatibility between the domestic paramountcy principle and the ECHR, whilst currently the prevailing view, is by no means watertight.

CONCLUSION

4.176 The foregoing discussion of the overarching principles stipulated by the Committee on the Rights of the Child as being of cardinal importance to the existence and efficacy of children's rights highlights a number of areas of tension between the international and regional articulation of these principles and their articulation in the domestic law. Two areas in particular demonstrate this tension, namely 'evolving capacity' and 'best interests'. In respect of 'evolving capacity' the approach to children's participation in matters concerning their own welfare taken in *Gillick v West Norfolk and Wisbech Area Health Authority*[507] was rightly described as a domestic 'landmark in

---

proportionality, necessity in a democratic society, etc. These factors are designed to protect the adults' rights. If Lord Nicholls of Birkenhead is to be read as saying that a decision that an outcome is in the child's best interests in and of itself determines the issue of proportionality, etc, this removes the contingency and the protection it gives' (Eekelaar, J *Beyond the Welfare Principle* (2002) 14 Child and Family Law Quarterly 237). Fortin argues that the decision in *Re B (A Child) (Adoption by One Natural Parent)* demonstrates that the domestic courts are keen to show that article 8(2) hardly needs serious consideration (Fortin, J *Children's Rights and the Developing Law* (2005) 2nd edn, Cambridge, p 250). See also Choudry, S and Fenwick, H *Taking the Rights of Parents and Children Seriously: Confronting the Welfare Principle under the Human Rights Act* (2005) Oxford Journal of Legal Studies 453.

[504] See for example Swindells, H *Crossing the Rubicon – Family Law Post the Human Rights Act 1998* in Cretney, S (ed) *Family Law – Essays for the New Millennium* (2000) Family Law, p 62.

[505] Swindells, H, Neaves, A, Kushner, M, Skilbeck, R *Family Law and the Human Rights Act 1998* (1999) Jordan Publishing, pp 54 and 91.

[506] *R v Secretary of State for the Home Department, ex p Gangadeen and Khan* [1998] 1 FLR 762 at 773–774 per Hurst LJ.

[507] [1986] AC 112. See also CRC/GC/2003/4, paras 28, 33, 32, 39 and 41.

children's rights'.[508] Lord Scarman's careful formulation mirrored the rights based approach to participation articulated in Arts 5 and 12 of the CRC. Unfortunately, the subsequent approach by the Court of Appeal to *Gillick* in *Re R (A Minor)(Wardship: Medical Treatment)*[509] and *Re W (A Minor)(Medical Treatment: Court's Jurisdiction)*[510] cannot be the subject of the same approbation. Whilst the courts have started along the road back towards the unvarnished application of Lord Scarman's judgment,[511] with rights based principles such as that enunciated in *Gillick* seemingly so hard to accept, it might be a long time before rights based ideas such as a presumption that children are capable of exercising rights and responsibilities unless proven otherwise become palatable.[512]

4.177 Whilst the inestimable value of the concept of the child's 'best interests' is arguably beyond dispute, the tension between the 'paramount' position of best interests in the domestic jurisdiction and the 'best interests' formulations of the international and regional human rights instruments and jurisprudence constitute more than theoretical difficulties. The prevailing and quite possibly mistaken domestic view that the 'paramountcy' principle is compatible with the rights based approach of Art 8(2) of the ECHR has potentially detrimental consequences for both children and their parents. By subsuming the child's rights within arguments relating to his or her welfare and then conflating welfare with the technical requirements of Art 8(2) the domestic courts have arguably failed to articulate properly the concept of children being independent actors with Art 8 rights of their own. Conversely, the view that the domestic paramountcy principle is compatible with Art 8(2) has arguably led the domestic courts to ignore legitimate arguments concerning the infringement of parents' rights. Overall, holding that the 'paramountcy' principle satisfies the requirements of Art 8(2) does much more than simply reduce the weight of rights on the opposite side of the scale, rather it risks rendering completely irrelevant the qualitatively different cardinal legal rights of others. This is more likely to result in the courts oscillating between a dubious preference for adults' rights and their virtual submergence under the welfare principle than it is in a fair application of children's rights in the context of the rights of others.[513]

4.178 Within this context, the rights based approach of conferring on the child's best interests the status of 'primary consideration' to be balanced against the interests of adults is arguably far more conducive to the advancement of children's rights than the approach of treating those best interests as 'paramount'. In arguing for the fair and consistent application and enforcement of the rights of children, there is some difficulty in relying on a principle that appears to act to simply negate the rights of others where a

---

508   Hale, B and others, *Family, Law & Society* (2009) Oxford, p 367.
509   [1992] Fam 11 at 23, [1991] 4 All ER 177 at 185.
510   [1993] Fam 64 at 75–76 and 87, [1992] 3 WLR 748,[1992] 4 All ER 627 at 633 and 642–643 *sub nom Re W (A Minor)(Consent to Medical Treatment)* [1993] 1 FLR 1.
511   See *Re Roddy (A Child)(Identification: Restriction on Publication)* [2003] EWHC 2997 (Fam), [2004] 2 FLR 949 and *R (on the application of Axon) v Secretary of State for Health and another* [2006] EWHC 37 (Admin), [2006] QB 539, [2006] 1 FCR 175, paras 56 and 95.
512   See Rodham, H *Children under the Law* Harvard Educational Review, 9, 22 1974. As Van Buren comments, a presumption of capacity rather than incapacity for children shifts the burden of proof onto those denying a child's capacity to exercise rights. Adopting such a reform would also align the position of children with that of adults (see the Mental Capacity Act 2005, s 1(2)).
513   Eekelaar, J *Beyond the Welfare Principle* (2002) 14 Child and Family Law Quarterly 237. Eekelaar points out that the strict adherence by the European Court of Human Rights to the wording of Art 8(2) itself risks placing the child's best interests too low in the hierarchy of interests (see Eekelaar, J *Beyond the Welfare Principle* (2002) 14 Child and Family Law Quarterly 237 p 241 and *Elsholz v Germany* [2000] 2 FLR 486 and *Sahin v Germany; Sommerfield v Germany; Hoffman v Germany* [2002] 1 FLR 119 at 136 and 151).

conflict of rights arises.[514] Within this context, an argument can be made that the 'best interests' formulation adopted by the Art 3(1) of the CRC is far more conducive to the effective promotion, application and enforcement of children's rights than the 'paramount' formulation currently utilised in the domestic jurisdiction, the former permitting a balancing of the rights and interests of all parties, according special weight to the best interests of the child within the context of that balancing exercise.[515] The counter-intuitive corollary of this position is of course the disappearance of the exclusivity of children's rights.[516] In this context, and in light of the defence of the 'paramountcy' principle within the context of the demands of the ECHR, again it may be some time before the foregoing arguments are seen as palatable in the domestic forum.

---

[514] Even more so where, as Eekelaar points out 'there are many contexts in which the principle does not apply' (Eekelaar, J *Beyond the Welfare Principle* (2002) 14 Child and Family Law Quarterly 237).

[515] *Clarke Hall & Morrison on Children*, Lexis/Nexis, para [82.2].

[516] Fortin, J *Children's Rights and the Developing Law* (2005) 2nd edn, Cambridge, p 58.

Chapter 5

THE CHILD'S RIGHT TO LIFE, SURVIVAL AND DEVELOPMENT

'The care of human life and happiness and not their destruction, is the only object of good government'

Thomas Jefferson

INTRODUCTION

5.1   The most basic human right is the right to life.[1] It has been described by the Human Rights Committee as 'the supreme right'[2] and in the Manual of Human Rights Reporting as of 'paramount importance'.[3] The European Court of Human Rights has described the right to life as 'fundamental'[4] as has the Inter-American Commission on Human Rights.[5] Whilst a freestanding right of the child under Art 6(1) of the CRC, the right to life is considered by the Committee on the Rights of the Child to be a guiding principle of cardinal importance to the existence and efficacy of all other rights of the child.[6]

5.2   The ECHR also enshrines the right to life in Art 2, which article provides that:

'Everyone's right to life shall be protected by law. No one shall be deprived of his life intentionally save in the execution of a sentence of a court following his conviction of a crime for which this penalty is provided by law.'

The right to life is reflected in Art 3 of the Universal Declaration of Human Rights which provides that 'Everyone has the right to life, liberty and security of person'. The Covenant on Civil and Political Rights provides at Art 6 that 'Every human being has the inherent right to life'. Article 10 of the Convention of the Rights of Persons with Disabilities requires that 'States Parties reaffirm that every human being has the inherent right to life and shall take all necessary measures to ensure its effective enjoyment by persons with disabilities on an equal basis with others'.[7]

---

[1]   Human Rights Committee, General Comment No 14 *Article 6 (The Right to Life)* HRI/GEN/1/Rev.8, para 1 p 178.

[2]   Human Rights Committee, General Comment No 6 *Article 6 (The Right to Life)* HRI/GEN/1/Rev.8, para 1 p 166.

[3]   *Manual on Human Rights Reporting* (1997) HR/PUB/91/1 (Rev 1), p 193.

[4]   See *McCann v United Kingdom* (1995) 21 EHRR 97, para 147.

[5]   (1986–1987) IA Comm HR Annual Report, p 271.

[6]   Newell, P and Hodgkin, R *Implementation Handbook for the Convention on the Rights of the Child* (2008) 3rd edn, UNICEF, p 83 although it should also be noted that each of the rights within the CRC has been described as 'interdependent and indivisible' (Newell, P and Hodgkin, R *Implementation Handbook for the Convention on the Rights of the Child* (2008) 3rd edn, UNICEF, p xix).

[7]   See also the Standard Rules on the Equalisation of Opportunities for Persons with Disabilities, rr 2.3, 15.1 and 15.2.

5.3 As noted in chapter 4, discussion of the child's right to life has tended to coalesce around the issue of the extent to which that right should extend to the protection of the unborn child.[8] This however, should not be allowed to obscure the importance of the right to life of all children, including those who are at risk of suicide, infanticide, subject to the death penalty, involved in armed conflict or at risk of other life threatening violence such as 'honour' murders, as well as those children whose survival is prejudiced by exploitation or poor social and economic conditions.[9]

5.4 Beyond the fundamental right to life, the UN human rights framework, including the CRC, recognises that the right to life is of little practical value unless accompanied by rights securing the continuation and development of life and a life of right quality. In its General Comment No 3 the Committee on the Rights of the Child has observed that:[10]

> 'Children have the right not to have their lives arbitrarily taken, as well as to benefit from economic and social policies that will allow them to survive into adulthood and develop in the broadest sense of the word.'

As such, the child's right to life is complimented and further facilitated by the right to survival and development in Art 6(2) of the CRC, adding a further dimension to the right to life not limited to a physical perspective and promoting life that is compatible with the dignity of the child.[11] In this regard, the Covenant on Economic, Social and Cultural Rights is of particular relevance to the child's right to survival and development. This chapter deals first with the child's right to life under the CRC, the ECHR and in domestic law before moving on to consider the complimentary rights to survival and to development under these various legal regimes.

THE CHILD'S RIGHT TO LIFE

The Ambit of the Child's Right to Life – the Unborn Child

5.5 The answer to the question of whether in *law* an unborn child has a particular right is solely a product of the applicable legal criteria for the commencement of childhood within the jurisdiction in which that question arises.[12] Whilst often an emotive issue by reason of its relevance to issues of abortion and family planning, this is the appropriate *legal* analysis of the ambit of the child's right to life. The applicability of this analysis is reinforced in relation to the right to life by the fact that neither the CRC nor the ECHR seeks to restrict a State's discretion to provide under its domestic law the point at which childhood begins[13] although the European Court of Human Rights has

---

8   See **4.3**.

9   See for example the view of the Platform for Action of the Fourth World Conference on Women held in Beijing in 1995 that 'More than 15 million girls aged 15 to 19 give birth each year. Motherhood at a very young age entails complications during pregnancy and delivery and a risk of maternal death that is much greater than average. The children of young mothers have higher levels of morbidity and mortality ...' (Platform for Action A/CONF.177/20/Rev.1, para 268).

10   Committee on the Rights of the Child General Comment No 3 *HIV/AIDS and the Rights of the Child* HRI/GEN/1/Rev 8, p 366, para 9.

11   *Manual on Human Rights Reporting* (1997) HR/PUB/91/1 (Rev 1), p 425.

12   See **4.2**.

13   Van Bueren, G *The International Law on the Rights of the Child* (1998) Martinus Nijhoff, p 34. See also UN Doc E/CN.4/1989/48, pp 8–15 in which the Working Group drafting the CRC made clear that the words 'before as well as after birth' the preamble to the CRC were not intended to 'prejudice the interpretation of Art 1 or any provision of the Convention by States Parties.'

declined to exclude the possibility of the right to life being engaged for the unborn child.[14] As such, the broad position is that in law the right to life will extend to the unborn child in those jurisdictions which recognise the unborn child as having a legal personality. In those jurisdictions which do not recognise the unborn child as having a legal personality, including our domestic jurisdiction, the right to life will not be applicable to, or enforceable on behalf of the unborn child.[15] The point at which childhood commences in law for the purposes of the application and enforcement of children's rights within the domestic jurisdiction is dealt with in detail in chapter 4.[16]

The Child's Right to Life under the CRC

CRC, Art 6(1) – The Right to Life

5.6   Article 6(1) of the Convention on the Rights of the Child articulates the child's right to life by providing that 'States Parties recognise that every child has the inherent right to life'. The right to life applies to all children without exception. The Committee on the Rights of the Child has stated that the right to life warrants special consideration with regard to children with disabilities.[17] In its General Comment No 6 the Committee on the Rights of the Child observed as follows in respect of children who are unaccompanied or separated:[18]

> 'Separated and unaccompanied children are vulnerable to various risks that affect their life, survival and development such as trafficking for purposes of sexual or other exploitation or involvement in criminal activities which could result in harm to the child, or in extreme cases, death. Accordingly, article 6 necessitates vigilance by States Parties in this regard ...'

CRC, Art 6(1) – 'Inherent Right to Life'

5.7   The UN Human Rights Committee has commented that the term 'inherent right to life' should not be interpreted narrowly, stating:[19]

> 'The expression 'inherent right to life' cannot be properly understood in a restrictive manner, and the protection of this right requires that States adopt positive measures. In this connection the Committee considers that it would be desirable for States Parties to take all possible measures to reduce infant mortality and to increase life expectancy, especially adopting measures to eliminate malnutrition and epidemics.'

The *Manual of Human Rights Reporting* states that measures taken by States in respect of the right to life can be:[20]

> '... thus designed to protect life, by increasing life expectancy, diminishing infant and child mortality, combating diseases and rehabilitating health, providing adequate nutritious foods

---

[14]   See **4.5** above and **5.33** below.

[15]   The Committee on the Rights of the Child has made clear that in light of this position, reservations to the CRC to preserve national abortion and family laws are unnecessary, the Committee considering that it is for individual States to find a path through the conflicting rights and interests involved in abortion and family planning (see Newell, P and Hodgkin, R *Implementation Handbook for the Convention on the Rights of the Child* (2008) 3rd edn, UNICEF, p 83).

[16]   See **4.3–4.13** above.

[17]   Committee on the Rights of the Child General Comment No 9 *The Rights of Children with Disabilities* CRC/C/GC/9, para 31.

[18]   Committee on the Rights of the Child, General Comment No 6 *Treatment of Unaccompanied and Separated Children outside their Country of Origin* CRC/GC/2005/6 p 9, para 23.

[19]   Human Rights Committee, General Comment No 6, 1982, HRI/GEN/1/Rev.8, para 5, p 167.

[20]   *Manual on Human Rights Reporting* (1997) HR/PUB/91/1 (Rev 1), p 424.

and clean drinking water. And they may further aim at preventing deprivation of life, namely by prohibiting and preventing death penalty, extra legal, arbitrary or summary executions or any situation of enforced disappearance. States Parties should therefore refrain from any action that may intentionally take life away, as well as steps to safeguard life.'

In its General Comment No 6 the Committee on the Rights of the Child stated that:[21]

'The obligation of the State Party under article 6 includes protection from violence and exploitation, to the maximum extent possible, which would jeopardise a child's right to life, survival and development.'

5.8 The right enshrined by Art 6(1) of the CRC thus includes a positive obligation. Whilst others have argued for a very narrow interpretation of Art 6(1) of the CRC[22] a broader interpretation of the Art 6(1) right to life is consistent with the fundamental nature of the right and the link made by the CRC between the concept of 'inherent right to life' in Art 6(1) and the concept of 'maximum survival and development' in Art 6(2).[23] The positive obligation conferred by Art 6(1) is further illuminated by many other articles of the CRC. By way of example, Art 19 deals with protection from all forms of violence, Art 37 deals with protection from torture and cruel, inhuman or degrading treatment and Art 38 confers protection on children caught up in armed conflict.

CRC, Art 6(1) – Application

CRC, Art 6(1) – Right to Life and Human Embryology and Fertilisation

5.9 The Platform for Action adopted at the Fourth World Conference on Women noted that practices such as prenatal sex selection and infanticide in respect of female children are 'often compounded by the increasing use of technologies to determine foetal sex, resulting in the abortion of female feotuses'.[24] The issue of prenatal sex selection is, by reason of continuing technological advances, of potentially increasing relevance to children within the domestic jurisdiction but has yet to be tackled comprehensively within the context of the Art 6(1) right to life under the CRC.[25]

CRC, Art 6(1) – Right to Life and Abortion[26]

5.10 The Committee on the Rights of the Child, whilst making clear that the CRC does not seek to restrict a State's discretion to provide under its domestic law the point

---

21 Committee on the Rights of the Child, General Comment No 6 *Treatment of Unaccompanied and Separated Children outside their Country of Origin* CRC/GC/2005/6 p 9, para 23. Contrast the approach of the United States Supreme Court in *DeShaney v Winnebago Social Services Department* (1989) 489 US 189 at 195–6 in which the Court held that the due process clause in the US Constitution forbids the state to deprive individuals or life or liberty without the due process of law but cannot be extended to impose 'an affirmative obligation on the State to ensure that those interests do not come to harm through any other means.'

22 See for example Dinstein, Y *The Right to Life, Physical Integrity and Liberty* in Henkin, L (ed) *The International Bill of Rights; the Covenant on Civil and Political Rights* (1981), p 116 who argues that Art 6(1) would only be breached by the practice of infanticide.

23 Van Bueren, G *The International Law on the Rights of the Child* (1998) Martinus Nijhoff, p 303.

24 Fourth World Conference on Women in Beijing, China, September 1995, Platform for Action, A/CONF.177/20/Rev.1, paras 259,277(c) and 283(d). See also *Women 2000: gender equality, development and peace for the twenty-first century* Resolution S-23/3 annex.

25 See also the Universal Declaration on the Human Genome and Human Rights UNESCO 11 November 1997.

26 On ratification the UK declared that it interprets Art 6(1) the convention as applying only following a live birth to ensure that the right does not conflict with domestic abortion legislation.

at which childhood begins,[27] has made adverse comment on high rates of abortion, the use of abortion as a method of family planning, clandestine abortions and on selective abortions by gender.[28] The Committee's concern has been expressed largely from the perspective of protecting the best interests of young mothers and child victims of rape and incest where abortion is illegal even in cases of rape and incest.[29]

5.11 However, the Committee on the Rights of the Child has also commented negatively within the context of the right to life under Art 6(1) of the CRC on the issue of selective abortion following pre-natal gender selection.[30] The position taken by the Committee in this respect represents a potential conflict with its view that it is for individual States to determine the point at which childhood begins and thus the extent to which the unborn child benefits from the right to life.[31] That latter stance is likely to come under increasing pressure with the continuing advance of medical technology relating to the unborn child, especially in circumstances where that technology leads to ethically questionable policies or specific social practices involving abortion.[32]

CRC, Art 6(1) – Right to Life and Withholding Medical Treatment

5.12 Within the domestic jurisdiction the issues arising out of the complex relationship between the right to life of the child and decisions to relating to the medical treatment of terminally ill or severely disabled children and very premature babies have been extensively argued within the context of the ECHR and domestic law.[33] However, the Committee on the Rights of the Child has not yet tackled such issues comprehensively within the context of the right to life under Art 6(1) of the CRC.[34]

CRC, Art 6(1) – Right to Life and Euthanasia

5.13 The Committee on the Rights of the Child has examined the issue of euthanasia in relation to children in its Concluding Observations on the second report from the Netherlands[35] and that State's law concerning euthanasia, which law is applicable to children over the age of 12.[36] The Committee expressed concern about information it had received concerning the termination of the lives of newborn babies with severe abnormalities and commented that the legislation should be evaluated to ensure that children, including newborn infants with severe abnormalities, enjoy special protection and that they are in compliance with Art 6(1). The Committee further enjoined the

---

[27] Van Bueren, G *The International Law on the Rights of the Child* (1998) Martinus Nijhoff, p 34. See also UN Doc E/CN.4/1989/48, pp 8–15 and **4.4** above.

[28] Newell, P and Hodgkin, R *Implementation Handbook for the Convention on the Rights of the Child* (2008) 3rd edn, UNICEF, p 85.

[29] See Palau CRC/15/Add. 149, paras 46 and 47. This concern has been reflected by the Committee on the Elimination of Discrimination against Women (see Committee on the Elimination of Discrimination against Women General Recommendation No 24 *Article 12 of the Convention (Women and Health)* HRI/GEN/1/Rev 8, p 336, para 31(c)).

[30] See India CRC/C/15/Add.228, paras 33 and 34, China CRC/C/15/Add.56, paras 15 and 16 and China CRC/C/CHN/2, paras 28 and 29.

[31] See **4.4** above. A solution to such a potential conflict is the prohibition of selective abortions by reference to the rights of the mother where the selective abortion is the result of a State policy or practice or exploitative practices by third parties.

[32] Newell, P and Hodgkin, R *Implementation Handbook for the Convention on the Rights of the Child* (2008) 3rd edn, UNICEF, p 87.

[33] See **5.35** and **5.55 et seq** below.

[34] Newell, P and Hodgkin, R *Implementation Handbook for the Convention on the Rights of the Child* (2008) 3rd edn, UNICEF, p 85.

[35] Netherlands and Aruba CRC/C/15/Add.227.

[36] The Termination of Life on Request and Assisted Suicide (Review Procedures) Act 2001.

Netherlands to ensure that the mental and psychological status of the child and parents or guardians requesting termination are taken into consideration.[37]

5.14 The comments of the Committee on the Rights of the Child were made within the context of recommendations made in respect of the same Dutch legislation by the UN Human Rights Committee.[38] That Committee stated:[39]

> 'The Committee is seriously concerned that the new law is also applicable to minors who have reached the age of 12 years. The Committee notes that the law provides for the consent of parents or guardians of juveniles up to 16 years of age, while for those between 16 and 18 the parents' or guardians' consent may be replaced by the will of the minor, provided the minor can appropriately assess his or her interests in the matter. The Committee considers it difficult to reconcile a reasoned decision to terminate life with the evolving and maturing capacities of minors. In view of the irreversibility of euthanasia and assisted suicide, the Committee wishes to underline its conviction that minors are in particular need of protection.'

CRC, Art 6(1) – Right to Life and Life Threatening Traditional Practices

5.15 'Honour' killings[40] of children self evidently violate the right to life under Art 6(1) of the CRC. The Committee on the Rights of the Child has expressed concern about the violation of the right to life constituted by 'honour' killings.[41] In its General Comment No 4 the Committee on the Rights of the Child commented as follows in relation to harmful traditional practices, including 'honour' killings:[42]

> 'In light of articles 3, 6, 12, 19, and 24(3) of the Convention, States Parties should take all effective measures to eliminate all acts and activities which threaten the right to life of adolescents, including honour killings. The Committee strongly urges States Parties to develop and implement awareness raising campaigns, education programmes and legislation aimed at changing prevailing attitudes, and address gender roles and stereotypes that contribute to harmful traditional practices. Further, States Parties should facilitate the establishment of multidisciplinary information and advice centres regarding the harmful aspects of some traditional practices, including early marriage and female genital mutilation.'

---

37   Netherlands and Aruba CRC/C/15/Add.227, paras 33 and 34.
38   CCPR/CO/72/NET.
39   Ibid, para 5(c). The Committee stated that it was 'gravely concerned that new-born handicapped infants have had their lives ended by medical personnel.'
40   A term rightly described by Wall LJ in *AM v A Local Authority and Another, Re B-M Children (Care Orders: Risk)* [2009] 2 FCR 505 sub nom *Re B-M (Care Orders)* [2009] 2 FLR 20 as a 'wholly inappropriate oxymoron' in respect of which 'the time has surely come to re-think the phrase ... to describe what is, in reality, sordid criminal behaviour.'
41   See Turkey CRC/C/15/Add.152, para 31.
42   General Comment No 4 *Adolescent Health and Development in the context of the Convention on the Rights of the Child* HRI/GEN/1/Rev 8, p 381, para 20. See also Pakistan CRC/C/15/Add.217, paras 34 and 35, Lebanon CRC/C15/Add. 169, paras 28 and 29 and Lebanon CRC/C/LBN/CO/3, paras 32 and 33. See also the summary records of the meetings of the Committee: CRC Summary Record of the 701st Meeting: Turkey, 29 May 2001, CRC/C/SR.701, para 51; CRC Summary Record of the 702nd Meeting: Turkey, 11 Feb. 2002, CRC/C/SR.702, para 5; Concluding Observations: Jordan, 2 June 2000, UN doc. CRC/C/15/Add.125, para 35 and the CRC Summary Record of the 752nd Meeting: Lebanon, 17 Sept. 2002, UN doc. CRC/C/SR.752, para 3. See further Art 21 of the African Charter on the Rights and Welfare of the Child and Art 25 of the African Youth Charter.

5.16 On 24 October 2002 the UN General Assembly passed Resolution 57/179 entitled *Working Towards the Elimination of Crimes against Women Committed in the Name of Honour*.[43] In its preamble, the Resolution makes clear that:[44]

> '... crimes against women committed in the name of honour are a human rights issue and that States have an obligation to exercise due diligence to prevent, investigate and punish the perpetrators of such crimes and to provide protection to the victims, and that not doing so violates and impairs or nullifies the enjoyment of their human rights and fundamental freedoms ...'

The Resolution stresses the need to treat all forms of violence against women and girls, including that committed in the name of honour, as a criminal offence punishable by law.[45] Within this context, the resolution sets out a series of legislative, administrative and programmatic measures which States should adopt to ensure the elimination of 'honour' based crimes.[46]

CRC, Art 6(1) – Right to Life and the Death Penalty

5.17 Article 37(a) of the CRC prohibits capital punishment 'for offences committed by persons below eighteen years of age' which prohibition is reinforced by the fact that Art 6(1) permits of no derogations whatsoever.[47] The Committee on the Rights of the Child General Comment No 10 has made clear the proper interpretation to be placed on Art 37(a) of the CRC, stating:[48]

> 'Article 37(a) of CRC reaffirms the internationally accepted standard (see for example article 6(5) of ICCPR) that the death penalty cannot be imposed for a crime committed by a person who at that time was under 18 years of age. Although the text is clear, there are States parties that assume that the rule only prohibits the execution of persons below the age of 18 years. However, under this rule the explicit and decisive criterion is the age at the time of the commission of the offence. It means that a death penalty may not be imposed for a crime committed by a person under 18 regardless of his/her age at the time of the trial or sentencing or of the execution of the sanction.'

The Committee on the Rights of the Child emphasises the need for the prohibition on the execution of persons under the age of 18 to be confirmed in legislation.[49]

CRC, Art 6(1) – Procedural Requirements

5.18 The Committee on the Rights of the Child has recognised that for the Art 6(1) right to life to have practical effect, the deaths of children must be the subject of adequate investigation and reporting in order to encourage reporting, to reduce the possibility of the cause of death being misrepresented and to inform preventative

---

[43] A/Res/57/179. See also the report of the Special Rapporteur to the Fifty-eighth Session of the UN Commission on Human Rights (2002) E/CN.4/2002/83.

[44] A/Res/57/179, p 1.

[45] A/Res/57/179, p 2.

[46] A/Res/57/179, pp 3–4.

[47] See also Art 6 of the Covenant on Civil and Political Rights which states 'Sentence of death shall not be imposed for crimes committed by persons below eighteen years of age and shall not be carried out on pregnant women.' The Second Optional Protocol to the Covenant on Civil and Political Rights seeks the abolition of the death penalty by prohibiting execution of anyone within the jurisdiction of a State Party.

[48] Committee on the Rights of the Child General Comment No 10 *Children's Rights in Juvenile Justice* CRC/C/GC/10 p 21, para 75. See also The Michael Domingues Case: Report on the Inter-American Commission on Human Rights, Report No 62/02, Merits, Case 12.285 (2002), para 84.

[49] See Burkina Faso (CRC/C/15/Add.193, para 60 and Saudia Arabia (CRC/C/SAU/CO/, paras 32 and 33).

strategies.[50] Art 9(4) of the CRC confers on the parents of a child killed as the result of any action initiated by a State party the right, on request, to be provided with the essential information concerning the whereabouts of the child. Rule 57 of the UN Rules for the Protection of Juveniles Deprived of their Liberty provides that:

> 'Upon the death of a juvenile during the period of deprivation of liberty, the nearest relative should have the right to inspect the death certificate, see the body and determine the method of disposal of the body. Upon the death of a juvenile in detention, there should be an independent inquiry into the causes of death, the report of which should be made accessible to the nearest relative. This inquiry should also be made when the death of a juvenile occurs within six months from the date of his or her release from the detention facility and there is reason to believe that the death is related to the period of detention.'[51]

CRC, Art 6(1) – Derogations

5.19   The CRC contains no derogation provisions, suggesting each of the cardinal rights it enshrines are non-derogable. Article 6(1), by contrast to Art 2 of the ECHR, contains no exceptions to accommodate for example, the death penalty or armed conflict. In respect of the death penalty, the Art 6(1) CRC right to life is reinforced in respect of children by Art 37(a) which prohibits capital punishment 'for offences committed by persons below 18 years of age'. Further support for the non-derogable nature Art 6(1) as it relates to the death penalty is found in Art 6(5) of the International Covenant on Civil and Political Rights which provides that 'Sentence of death shall not be imposed for crimes committed by persons below 18 years of age and shall not be carried out on pregnant women'.[52] In respect of armed conflict, the Art 6(1) right to life is reinforced by Art 38 of the CRC which requires special measures of protection for children affected by armed conflict.

The Child's Right to Life under other International Instruments

Geneva Conventions and Additional Protocols

5.20   Pursuant to the Geneva Convention Relative to the Protection of Civilian Persons in Time of War (Geneva Convention IV)[53] Art 68 the death penalty may not be pronounced against a person who is a protected person under the Convention where that person is under 18 year of age at the time of the offence. Pursuant to Art 77(5) of the Protocol Additional to the Geneva Conventions of 12 August 1949, and relating to the Protection of Victims of International Armed Conflicts[54] the death penalty for an offence related to armed conflict shall not be executed on persons who had not attained the age of 18 years at the time the offence was committed. In relation to non-international armed conflicts, pursuant to Art 6(4) of the Protocol Additional to the Geneva Conventions of 12 August 1949, and Relating to the Protection of Victims of Non-International Armed Conflicts[55] the death penalty shall not be pronounced on persons who were under the age of 18 years at the time of the offence and shall not be carried out on pregnant women or mothers of young children.

---

[50]   Newell, P and Hodgkin, R *Implementation Handbook for the Convention on the Rights of the Child* (2008) 3rd edn, UNICEF, p 92.
[51]   A/RES/45/113.
[52]   The Second Optional Protocol to the Covenant on Civil and Political Rights aims by Art 1 of that Protocol to abolish the death penalty.
[53]   See **15.121** below.
[54]   See **15.123** below.
[55]   See **15.123** below.

The Child's Right to Life under Customary International Law

5.21 It has been suggested that the right to life is a rule of customary international law.[56] Indeed, the right is considered by some to be a norm of *jus cogens*.[57] In its report on Chile, the UN Human Rights Committee stated that 'The international community ... considers the right to life in the context of *jus cogens* in international human rights law ...'.[58] Van Bueren, recognising that the normative status of the right to life of still leaves the problem of whether a wide or narrow interpretation of the right is adopted, argues that the right to life as a customary rule of international law is wide enough to encompass the right to survival and development.[59] The precise ambit of the right to life as a rule of customary international law, or even a *jus cogens* norm, is not yet definitively established. However, it is at least clear that there is a rule of customary international law, and likely a *jus cogens* norm which prohibits the use of the death penalty against children.[60]

Children and the Death Penalty in Customary International Law

5.22 In August 2000, the United Nations Sub-Commission on the Promotion and Protection of Human Rights adopted Resolution 2000/17 on *The Death Penalty in Relation to Juvenile Offenders* in which the Sub-Commission recognised that the use of the death penalty against child offenders 'is contrary to customary international law'.[61] As noted in chapter 4, in the *Michael Domingues Case*[62] the Inter-American Commission on Human Rights concluded in relation to the practice in the US State of Nevada of executing children under 18 that:[63]

> 'The overwhelming evidence of global state practice as set out above displays a consistency and generality amongst world states indicating that the world community considers the execution of offenders aged below 18 years at the time of their offence to be inconsistent with prevailing standards of decency. The Commission is therefore of the view that a norm of international customary law has emerged prohibiting the execution of offenders under the age of 18 years at the time of their crime. Moreover, the Commission is satisfied, based upon the information before it, that this rule has been recognised as being of a sufficiently indelible nature to now constitute a norm of *jus cogens*, a development anticipated by the Commission in its Roach and Pinkerton decision. As noted above, nearly every nation state has rejected the imposition of capital punishment to individuals under the age of 18. They have done so through ratification of the ICCPR, U.N. Convention on the Rights of the Child, and the American Convention on Human Rights, treaties in which this proscription is recognised as non-derogable, as well as through corresponding amendments to their domestic laws. The acceptance of this norm crosses political and ideological boundaries and efforts to detract from this standard have been vigorously condemned by members of the

---

56 Dinstein *The Right to Life, Physical Integrity and Liberty* in Henkin (ed) *The International Bill of Rights: The Covenant on Civil and Political Rights* 115. See also **2.71** above.

57 See Nowak, M *UN Covenant on Civil and Political Rights CCPR Commentary* (Khel/Strasbourg/ Arlington) p 105; Ramcharan, B *The Concept and the Dimensions of the Right to Life* in Ramcharan, B (ed) *The Right to Life in International Law* (1985), pp 1–32, p 15. See also **4.71** above.

58 *Human Rights in Chile* UN ECOSOC Comm'n Human Rights E/CN.4/1983/9.

59 Van Bueren, G *The International Law on the Rights of the Child* (1998) Martinus Nijhoff, p 56.

60 See **2.61-2.72** and **5.22** for a detailed discussion.

61 Preamble to Resolution 2000/17 on *The Death Penalty in Relation to Juvenile Offenders.*

62 The Michael Domingues Case: Report on the Inter-American Commission on Human Rights, Report No 62/02, Merits, Case 12.285 (2002).

63 The Michael Domingues Case: Report on the Inter-American Commission on Human Rights, Report No 62/02, Merits, Case 12.285 (2002), para 85. The US objected, inter alia, to the conclusion of the Commission's conclusions in relation to *jus cogens* (see para 101). However, whilst not in response to the report of the Commission, the US subsequently banned the practice of executing juvenile offenders (see the decision of the US Supreme Court in *Roper v Simmons* 543 US 551 (2005)).

international community as impermissible under contemporary human rights standards ... On this basis, the Commission considers that the United States is bound by a norm of *jus cogens* not to impose capital punishment on individuals who committed their crimes when they had not yet reached 18 years of age. As a *jus cogens* norm, this proscription binds the community of States, including the United States. The norm cannot be validly derogated from, whether by treaty or by the objection of a state, persistent or otherwise.'

The Child's Right to Life under the ECHR

ECHR, Art 2 – Right to Life

5.23   Article 2 of the ECHR articulates the right to life, subject to a number of qualifications set out in the body of the article:

'1. Everyone's right to life shall be protected by law. No one shall be deprived of his life intentionally save in the execution of a sentence of a court following his conviction of a crime for which this penalty is provided by law.

2. Deprivation of life shall not be regarded as inflicted in contravention of this article when it results from the use of force which is no more than absolutely necessary:

(a)   in defence of any person from unlawful violence;
(b)   in order to effect a lawful arrest or to prevent escape of a person lawfully detained;
(c)   in action lawfully taken for the purpose of quelling a riot or insurrection.'

5.24   In characterising the right to life under Art 2, the European Court of Human Rights has held that the right to life, together with the Art 3 concerning the prohibition of torture and inhuman or degrading punishment or treatment, is a 'fundamental' right which 'enshrines one of the basic values of the democratic societies making up the Council of Europe.[64]

ECHR, Art 2 – Ambit

5.25   The circumstances in which deprivation of life may be justified must therefore be strictly construed.[65] Art 2 must, in line with the rest of the ECHR, be interpreted so as to give the right to life practical effect.[66] In line with the principles outlined in chapter 3, in respect of children Art 2 of the ECHR must also be interpreted as far as possible in accordance with the provisions of Art 6(1) of the CRC and the provisions of the CRC generally.[67]

---

[64]   See *McCann v United Kingdom* (1995) 21 EHRR 97, para 147 ('It must also be borne in mind that, as a provision which not only safeguards the right to life but sets out the circumstances when the deprivation of life may be justified, Article 2 ranks as one of the most fundamental provisions in the Convention – indeed one which, in peacetime, admits of no derogation under Article 15. Together with Article 3 of the Convention, it also enshrines one of the basic values of the democratic societies making up the Council of Europe. As such, its provisions must be strictly construed'; *Andronicou and Constantinou v Cyprus* (1997) 25 EHRR 491, para 171 and *Cakici v Turkey* (1999) 31 EHRR 133, para 134.
[65]   *Mikayil Mammadov v Azerbaijan* (2010) Application No 4762/05.
[66]   *McCann v United Kingdom* (1995) 21 EHRR 97, para 146 ('The Court's approach to the interpretation of Article 2 must be guided by the fact that the object and purpose of the Convention as an instrument for the protection of individual human beings requires that its provisions be interpreted and applied so as to make its safeguards practical and effective') and *Loizidou v Turkey* (1995) 20 EHRR 99, para 72.
[67]   See **3.43–3.46** above.

5.26 Article 2(1) constitutes a negative obligation to refrain from the unlawful taking of life.[68] This duty under Art 2 extends beyond deaths caused intentionally.[69] As with Art 6(1) of the CRC, the protection conferred by Art 2(1) also places a positive obligation on States to safeguard life.[70] States Parties must not only refrain from intentionally depriving a child of his or her life under Art 2(1) of the ECHR, they must take 'appropriate steps to safeguard the lives of those within its jurisdiction'.[71] A positive obligation will arise where it has been established that the authorities knew or ought to have known at the time of the existence of a real and immediate risk to the life of an identified individual from the criminal acts of a third party and that they failed to take measures within the scope of their powers which, judged reasonably, might have been expected to avoid that risk.[72]

5.27 Such 'appropriate steps' include the implementation of effective criminal laws to deter the commission of offences against the person, backed up by law-enforcement machinery for the prevention, suppression and punishment of breaches of such provisions, including investigative and operational procedures and criminal sanctions.[73] The positive duty also extends in appropriate circumstances to a positive obligation on the authorities to take preventive operational measures to protect an individual from another individual or, in particular circumstances, from himself.[74] There is also a positive obligation to protect persons in custody[75] and account for their treatment.[76] In respect of deaths in police custody, it is incumbent on the state to provide a plausible explanation of the events leading up to the death, absent which the authorities must be held responsible under Art 2.[77] The positive obligation to protect persons in custody and account for their treatment includes an obligation to ensure measures are taken for the effective prevention of suicide in custody.[78] This obligation in relation to the prevention

---

[68]   *LCB v United Kingdom* (1998) 27 EHRR 212, para 36.

[69]   *Stewart v United Kingdom* (1984) 39 DR 162 170, para 15.

[70]   *McCann v United Kingdom* (1995) 21 EHRR 97, para 184 and *W v United Kingdom* 32 DR 190 (1983) at 200.

[71]   *Osman v United Kingdom* (1998) 29 EHRR 245, [1999] 1 FLR 193, para 115. Observing that such an obligation must be interpreted in such a way which does not impose an impossible and disproportionate burden on authorities, the Court went on to observe at para 116 that 'not every claimed risk to life can entail for the authorities a Convention requirement to take operational measures to prevent that risk from materialising.' See also *Savage v South Essex Partnership NHS Foundation Trust* [2008] UKHL 74, [2009] 1 AC 681, [2009] 2 WLR 115, [2009] 1 All ER 1053 and *W v UK* (1983) 32 DR 190 at 200.

[72]   *Tomašić v Croatia* (2009) Application No 56598/06. See also *Rantsev v Cyprus and Russia* (2010) Application No 25965/04, para 232 in which the Court held that where the State has allegedly acted or failed to act in a manner which has caused the death of a person, for the State to be liable for a violation of Art 2 based on that act or omission by the State there must be established a real and immediate risk to life arising out of the act or omission which is foreseeable to the State.

[73]   *Kilic v Turkey* (2001) 33 EHRR 1357, para 62 and *Mahmut Kaya v Turkey* (unreported) 28 March 2000, para 85 citing *Osman v United Kingdom* (1998) 29 EHRR 245, para 115. As in *Osman*, the European Court of Human Rights recognises that this duty should not impose an impossible and disproportionate burden on authorities. See also *Rantsev v Cyprus and Russia* (2010) Application No 25965/04, para 218 ('In the first place, this obligation requires the State to secure the right to life by putting in place effective criminal law provisions to deter the commission of offences against the person backed up by law enforcement machinery for the prevention, suppression and punishment of breaches of such provisions. However, it also implies, in appropriate circumstances, a positive obligation on the authorities to take preventive operational measures to protect an individual whose life is at risk from the criminal acts of another individual').

[74]   *Mikayil Mammadov v Azerbaijan* (2010) Application No 4762/05.

[75]   *Salman v Turkey* (2002) 34 EHRR 425 and *Edwards v United Kingdom* (2002) 35 EHRR 487, para 56. This includes offering protection from the risk presented by cell mates and other prisoners (see *Edwards v United Kingdom* (2002) 35 EHRR 487).

[76]   *Ognyanova v Bulgaria* (2007) 44 EHRR 7. This will include children held in so called 'administrative custody' such as those awaiting deportation (see *Slimani v France* (2004) 43 EHRR 1068).

[77]   *Salman v Turkey* (2002) 34 EHRR 425, para 99 citing in support *Selmouni v France* (1999) 29 EHRR 403, para 87 (concerning Art 3). See also *Jordan v United Kingdom* (2003) 37 EHRR 52.

[78]   *Savage v South Essex Partnership NHS Foundation Trust* [2008] UKHL 74, [2009] 1 AC 681, [2009] 2 WLR

of suicide and self harm extends to military conscripts.[79] The positive obligation under Art 2 of the ECHR will also extend to compelling hospitals, both public and private, to adopt measures for the protection of their patients' lives.[80] However, this cannot be an unqualified obligation and nor have the courts been prepared to treat it as such. For example, even where a child's life expectancy is in issue, the domestic courts have held that they cannot interfere with a health authorities decisions concerning the allocation of a limited budget.[81] The question of whether the positive obligation under Art 2(1) could give rise to a duty to rescue a person in a life threatening situation, subject to the availability of resources and the extent to which the threat to the life of the rescuer was disproportionate, was left open in the case of *Hughes v United Kingdom*.[82]

5.28   The positive obligation to take steps to safeguard life must be discharged not only on the basis of what information the authorities have available but also on the information they ought reasonably to have available.[83] In *Osman v United Kingdom*, the European Court of Human Rights held that:[84]

> '... it is sufficient for an applicant to show that the authorities did not do all that could be reasonably expected of them to avoid a real and immediate risk to life of which they have or ought to have knowledge.'

5.29   There is thus a two stage test to determine whether the State has fulfilled its positive obligations under Art 2. Namely, (a) what was or should have been the extent of the State's knowledge and (b) were the steps taken by the State reasonable in light of that knowledge?[85] Thus, in *Kontrová v Slovakia*[86] a wife, who had been subjected to severe domestic abuse by her husband in respect of which the police had failed to bring criminal charges or investigate despite the situation being repeatedly reported, established a violation of Art 2 after the husband shot their two children dead and then

---

115, [2009] 1 All ER 1053, para 9). This obligation will extend to protecting detained patients from self-harm and suicide whilst at the same time balancing the need for personal dignity and autonomy (see *Savage v South Essex Partnership NHS Foundation Trust* (ibid); *Keenan v United Kingdom* (2001) 33 EHRR 913, para 92 and *R (JL) v Secretary of State for the Home Department* [2008] UKHL 68, [2009] 1 AC 588, [3 WLR 1325, para 39, [2009] 2 All ER 521).

79   See *Kilinc v Turkey* (2005) Application 48083/99 (unreported) and *Ataman v Turkey* (2006) Application 46252/99 (unreported) cited by Baroness Hale in *Savage v South Essex Partnership NHS Foundation Trust* [2008] UKHL 74, [2009] 1 AC 681, [2009] 2 WLR 115, [2009] 1 All ER 1053, para 61.

80   *Calvelli v Italy* (2002) Application 32967/96 2002 (unreported), para 49; *Dodov v Bulgaria* (2008) Application 59548/00 (unreported), para 80 and *Vo v France* (2005) 40 EHRR 259, para 89 ('The positive obligations require States to make regulations compelling hospitals, whether private or public, to adopt appropriate measures for the protection of patients' lives. They also require an effective independent judicial system to be set up so that the cause of death of patients in the care of the medical profession, whether in the public or the private sector, can be determined and those responsible made accountable'). Something more than simply a failure on the part of the hospital to meet the standard of care of the patient required by the duty of care will be needed to breach this positive obligation (see *Savage v South Essex Partnership NHS Foundation Trust* [2008] UKHL 74, [2009] 1 AC 681, [2009] 2 WLR 115, [2009] 1 All ER 1053, para 9).

81   *R v Cambridgeshire District Health Authority, ex p B* [1995] 2 All ER 129, [1995] 1 WLR 898. See also *Association X v United Kingdom* (1978) 14 DR 31 at 32; *Taylor Family and Others v United Kingdom* (1994) 79-A DR 127 and the decision of the Constitutional Court of South Africa in *Soobramoney v Minister of Health* (1997) 4 BHRC 308.

82   (1986) 48 DR 258.

83   *Van Colle v Chief Constable of Hertfordshire Police; Smith v Chief Constable of Sussex Police* [2008] UKHL 50, [2009] 1 AC 225, [2008] 3 All ER 977, para 32 per Lord Bingham.

84   (1998) 29 EHRR 245, para 116.

85   The threshold for meeting this test is a high one. See *Osman v United Kingdom* (1998) 29 EHRR 245; *Mastromatteo v Italy* (2002) Application 37703/97 (unreported), *Kontrová v Slovakia* (2007) Application 7510/04 (unreported) and *Keenan v United Kingdom* (2001) 33 EHRR 913, para 89 for examples of the application of the test.

86   (2007) Application No 7510/04 (unreported).

killed himself. The violation was found on the basis that the State had failed to intervene to safeguard the lives of the children. However, in *Keenan v United Kingdom*[87] the authorities were found to have responded reasonably to the known risk of suicide in the case of a mentally ill young man who hanged himself whilst detained in a young offender's institution as, whilst the risk had been real and therefore known, it was not immediate.[88]

Victims

5.30   As with all breaches of the ECHR complaints may be made only by someone who is a 'victim' of the act complained of. Pursuant to s 7(7) of the HRA 1998 a child will be a 'victim' of the unlawful act complained of where that child would be a victim for the purposes of Art 34 of the ECHR if proceedings were brought in the European Court of Human Rights. In respect of the right to life, the direct victim of the act complained off is often dead.[89] A child may make a complaint concerning the murder of a close relation.[90] Potential relatives may also make a complaint provided they can demonstrate they are 'closely affected', for example as in *Paton v United Kingdom*[91] in which the potential father of the unborn child was able to satisfy the European Commission on this basis he was a 'victim' of the termination of his wife's pregnancy. Brothers and sisters may make complaints under Art 2 concerning the death of their siblings.[92]

ECHR, Art 2(1) – Application

ECHR, Art 2(1) – Right to Life and Human Embryology and Fertilisation

5.31   The extent to which the Art 2 right to life has been considered within the context of issues raised by the subject of human embryology and fertilisation has been limited by the broad margin of appreciation conferred on States in respect of the point at which life begins.[93] That margin of appreciation has been further emphasised in relation to

---

[87]   (2001) 33 EHRR 913.

[88]   In the case of an attempted suicide, the positive obligation inherent in Art 2 requires an enhanced inquiry into the circumstances of the attempt (see *R (JL) v Secretary of State for the Home Department* [2008] UKHL 68, [2009] 1 AC 588, [2009] 3 WLR 1325, para 39, [2009] 2 All ER 521 and *SP v Secretary of State for Justice* [2009] EWHC 13 (Admin), [2009] All ER (D) 119 (Jan) concerning the serious self-harm of a young women detained in a young offenders institution.

[89]   It is not an absolute requirement for death to have occurred to establish a breach of Art 2 and a threat or an attempt may be sufficient to establish a breach (see *Makaratzis v Greece* (2004) 41 EHRR 1092 and *Venables v News Group Newspapers Ltd* [2001] Fam 430).

[90]   *Yasa v Turkey* (1998) 28 EHRR 408, para 66.

[91]   (1980) 3 EHRR 408.

[92]   See *Cakici v Turkey* (1999) 31 EHRR 133 and *Kilic v Turkey* (2001) 33 EHRR 1357. But see *Savage v South Essex Partnership NHS Foundation Trust* [2008] UKHL 74, [2009] 1 AC 681, [2009] 2 WLR 115, [2009] 1 All ER 1053, paras 2–5 in which Lord Scott observed 'I can well understand how a member of a deceased's family may be regarded as a 'victim' for the purposes of the art 2(1) investigative obligation. An important, and perhaps the main, purpose of the investigative obligation is to enable the family of the deceased to understand why and how the deceased died and who, if anyone, was responsible for the death. It would follow that a close family member, such as a daughter of the deceased, could properly be regarded as a 'victim' of a failure by the State to discharge its investigative obligation. But I am quite unable to understand how a close family member can claim to be a 'victim' in relation to an act, in breach of the art 2(1) negative obligation, or in relation to an omission, in breach of the art 2(1) positive obligation, that had led to the death.'

[93]   *Evans v United Kingdom* (2007) 43 EHRR 21, [2007] 1 FLR 1990, paras 54–56 ('In its judgment of 7 March 2006, the Chamber recalled that in *Vo v France*, the Grand Chamber had held that, in the absence of any European consensus on the scientific and legal definition of the beginning of life, the issue of when the right to life begins comes within the margin of appreciation which the Court generally considers that States should enjoy in this sphere. Under English law, as was made clear by the domestic courts in the present

issues of human embryology and fertilisation by reason of the fact that there is no international consensus with regard to such issues and because those issues give rise to sensitive moral and ethical issues against a background of fast moving medical and scientific developments.[94] In considering the Art 2 right to life in the context of in vitro fertilisation treatment in the case of *Evans v United Kingdom*[95] the Court held that the embryos created by the in vitro process do not have a right to life under Art 2 of the ECHR.

5.32 In 1997 the Council of Europe agreed the Convention for the Protection of Human Rights and Dignity of the Human Being with regard to the application of Biology and Medicine, the Convention on Human Rights and Biomedicine for short.[96] The United Kingdom is not yet a signatory to the 1997 Convention on Human Rights and Biomedicine.[97] However, Art 14 of the Convention states in relation to pre-natal gender selection that:

> 'The use of techniques of medically assisted procreation shall not be allowed for the purpose of choosing a future child's sex, except where serious hereditary sex-related disease is to be avoided.'

Article 18 of the Convention states:

> 'Where the law allows research on embryos in vitro, it shall ensure adequate protection of the embryo. The creation of human embryos for research purposes is prohibited.'

The Convention contains a number of additional protocols. The 1998 Additional Protocol to the Convention for the Protection of Human Rights and Dignity of the Human Being with regard to the Application of Biology and Medicine, on the Prohibition of Cloning Human Beings prohibits:[98]

> 'Any intervention seeking to create a human being genetically identical to another human being, whether living or dead.'

---

applicant's case, an embryo does not have independent rights or interests and cannot claim – or have claimed on its behalf – a right to life under Article 2. There had not, accordingly, been a violation of that provision. The Grand Chamber notes that the applicant has not pursued her complaint under Article 2 in her written or oral submissions to it. However, since cases referred to the Grand Chamber embrace all aspects of the application previously examined by the Chamber, it is necessary to consider the issue under Article 2. The Grand Chamber, for the reasons given by the Chamber, finds that the embryos created by the applicant and J do not have a right to life within the meaning of Article 2, and that there has not, therefore, been a violation of that provision.')

94 Ibid, paras 81 and 82.
95 (2007) 43 EHRR 21, [2007] 1 FLR 1990.
96 ETS No 164.
97 Article 3 of the EU Charter of Fundamental Rights also contains provisions in respect of medicine and biology ensuring free and informed consent according to the procedures laid down by law, the prohibition of eugenic practices, in particular those aiming at the selection of persons, the prohibition on making the human body and its parts as such a source of financial gain and the prohibition of the reproductive cloning of human beings. See also Directive 2004/23/EC of the European Parliament and of the Council on setting standards of quality and safety for the donation, procurement, testing, processing, preservation, storage and distribution of human tissues and cells.
98 Article 1.

ECHR, Art 2(1) – Right to Life and Abortion

5.33   As detailed in chapter 4 above[99] the Grand Chamber has determined that it is neither desirable nor possible to answer the question of whether an unborn child is a person for the purposes of Art 2 of the ECHR.[100] As also pointed out however, in rejecting the proposition that an unborn child had an absolute right to life under Art 2 the European Commission in *Paton v UK* [101] left open the question of whether its decision that there had been no breach was on the basis that the word 'everyone' did not include the feotus or that, whilst included, the rights of the feotus were not absolute or subject to limitation. Within this context, the Commission declined to entirely exclude the possibility of Art 2 being of pre-natal application in 'rare cases'.[102] In *A, B and C v Ireland*[103] the European Court of Human Rights, holding that Art 8 cannot be interpreted as conferring a right of abortion, stated that 'The woman's right to respect for her private life must be weighed against other competing rights and freedoms invoked including those of the unborn child'.[104] Accordingly, whilst the European Court of Human Rights has declined to hold that Art 2 is engaged in respect of the unborn child, the possibility that it may so hold in a future case cannot be excluded.

5.34   Thus, notwithstanding Art 2 of the ECHR, a member State is permitted to have in place domestic laws which permit abortion in order to protect the physical and mental health of the mother[105] and to protect the mother from social hardship.[106] Within this

---

[99]   See **4.5**.

[100]   *Vo v France* (2005) 40 EHRR 259, para 82 ('As is apparent from the above recapitulation of the case-law, the interpretation of Article 2 in this connection has been informed by a clear desire to strike a balance, and the Convention institutions' position in relation to the legal, medical, philosophical, ethical or religious dimensions of defining the human being has taken into account the various approaches to the matter at national level. This has been reflected in the consideration given to the diversity of views on the point at which life begins, of legal cultures and of national standards of protection, and the State has been left with considerable discretion in the matter, as the opinion of the European Group on Ethics in Science and New Technologies at the European Commission appositely puts it: 'the ... Community authorities have to address these ethical questions taking into account the moral and philosophical differences, reflected by the extreme diversity of legal rules applicable to human embryo research ... It is not only legally difficult to seek harmonisation of national laws at Community level, but because of lack of consensus, it would be inappropriate to impose one exclusive moral code'. It follows that the issue of when the right to life begins comes within the margin of appreciation which the Court generally considers that States should enjoy in this sphere, notwithstanding an evolutive interpretation of the Convention, a 'living instrument which must be interpreted in the light of present-day conditions'. The reasons for that conclusion are, firstly, that the issue of such protection has not been resolved within the majority of the Contracting States themselves, in France in particular, where it is the subject of debate and, secondly, that there is no European consensus on the scientific and legal definition of the beginning of life.')

[101]   (1980) 3 EHRR 408, paras 18–20.

[102]   (1980) 3 EHRR 408, para 7. See also *Brüggeman and Scheuten v Federal Republic of Germany* (1978) Application No 6959/75 (unreported) (which expressly left open the issue of whether an unborn child is covered by Art 2 of the ECHR), *H v Norway* (1992) Application No 17004/90 Unpublished (where the Commission did 'not exclude that in certain circumstances' a foetus would be protected under Art 2 of the ECHR); *Open Door Counseling and Dublin Well Women v Ireland* (1992) 15 EHRR 244 (where the European Court of Human Rights acknowledged the possibility that Art 2 of the ECHR might in certain circumstances offer protection to an unborn child); *Poku v United Kingdom* (1996) 22 EHRR CD 94 (in which the Commission found the Art 2 claim inadmissible on grounds other than the issue of whether the unborn child had Art 2 rights) and *Boso v Italy* (2002) Application No 50490/99 (unreported) in which the Court recognised the feotus could have Art 2 rights in certain circumstances but that the State had not exceeded its margin of appreciation in the circumstances of this case.

[103]   (2010) Application No 25579/05, para 214.

[104]   Note however at para 237 the Court used the phrase 'the rights *claimed* on behalf of the foetus and those of the Mother' (emphasis added). Further, the Court expressly declined to decide whether the term 'others' in Art 8(2) extends to the unborn child.

[105]   *X v United Kingdom* (1980) 19 DR 244.

[106]   *H v Norway* (1992) 73 DR 155.

context, the State is still likely to be held to have a general duty to give guidance on the lawful procurement of abortion facilities.[107] Further, the choice to become a parent or not will be protected as an aspect of the right to respect for private life under Art 8 of the ECHR.[108] Note however that Art 8 cannot be interpreted as meaning that pregnancy and its termination pertain uniquely to a woman's private life as, whenever a woman is pregnant, her private life becomes closely connected with the developing foetus.[109]

ECHR, Art 2(1) – Right to Life and Withdrawing Medical Treatment

5.35   As noted, pursuant to the obligations created by Art 2, member States are obliged to compel both public and private hospitals to protect the lives of their patients.[110] Once again, the issues arising out of the complex relationship between the right to life of the child and decisions to relating to the medical treatment of terminally ill or severely disabled children and very premature babies have not been extensively argued before the European Court of Human Rights. However, the domestic courts have considered the impact of Art 2 in such situations.[111] These cases are dealt with in detail below.

ECHR, Art 2(1) – Right to Life and Euthanasia

5.36   In *R v (Pretty) v DPP (Secretary of State for the Home Department Intervening)*[112] Lord Steyn observed as follows:

> 'The fact is that among the 41 member states, – North, South, East and West – there are deep cultural and religious differences in regard to euthanasia and assisted suicide. The legalisation of euthanasia and assisted suicide as adopted in the Netherlands would be unacceptable to predominantly Roman Catholic countries in Europe. The idea that the European Convention *requires* states to render lawful euthanasia and assisted suicide (as opposed to allowing democratically elected legislatures to adopt measures to that effect) must therefore be approached with scepticism. That does not involve support for the proposition that one must go back to the original intent of the European Convention. On the contrary, approaching the European Convention as a living instrument, the fact is that an interpretation *requiring* states to legalise euthanasia and assisted suicide would not only be enormously controversial but profoundly unacceptable to the peoples of many member states.'

5.37   It was argued in the House of Lords in *Pretty* that the wording of Art 2 did not confer protection on life itself but rather the right to life and that, accordingly, Art 2 protects (a) the individuals right to choose whether or not to live and (b) the individuals

---

[107]   See *Tysiac v Poland* (2007) 22 BHRC 155; *Open Door Counselling and Dublin Well Women Clinic Limited v Ireland* (1992) 15 EHRR 244, para 68 and *Family Planning Association of Northern Ireland v Minister of Health* [2004] NICA 39, paras 38–44 per Nicholson LJ.

[108]   *Evans v United Kingdom* (2008) 46 EHRR 728, para 71 and *Dickson v United Kingdom* (2008) 46 EHRR 41. In *A, B and C v Ireland* (2010) Application No 25579/05, para 212 the Court reiterated 'The Court recalls that the notion of 'private life' within the meaning of Article 8 of the Convention is a broad concept which encompasses, inter alia, the right to personal autonomy and personal development. It concerns subjects such as gender identification, sexual orientation and sexual life, a person's physical and psychological integrity as well as decisions both to have and not to have a child or to become genetic parents.'

[109]   *A, B and C v Ireland* (2010) Application No 25579/05, para 213.

[110]   *Vo v France* (2005) 40 EHRR 259.

[111]   *A National Health Service Trust v D* [2000] 2 FLR 677; *NHS Trust A v M, NHS Trust B v H* [2001] Fam 347 sub nom *An NHS Trust v M, An NHS Trust v H* [2001] 2 FLR 367 and see *NHS Trust A v H* [2001] 2 FLR 501 and *NHS Trust v D and D* [2006] 1 FLR 638. See also *D v United Kingdom* (1997) 24 EHRR 423.

[112]   [2001] UKHL 61, [2002] 1 AC 800, para 56, [2001] 3 WLR 1598, [2002] 2 Cr App Rep 1, [2002] 1 FCR 1, [2002] 1 FLR 268, [2002] Fam Law 170, 11 BHRC 589, 63 BMLR 1, [2001] NLJR 1819, (2001) *The Times*, 5 December, [2002] 3 LRC 163, [2001] All ER (D) 417 (Nov).

right to self determination in relation to life and death. The House of Lords rejected this argument, holding that the protection of life is the *sole* object of Art 2.[113] When the case of *Pretty* reached the European Court of Human Rights the court affirmed the House of Lord's position, holding that:[114]

> 'Article 2 cannot, without a distortion of language, be interpreted as conferring on an individual the diametrically opposed right, namely the right to die; nor can it create a right to self determination in the sense of conferring on an individual the entitlement to choose death rather than life.'

5.38 This is however very different from saying that Art 2 renders euthanasia unlawful. As noted by the House of Lords in *Pretty*:[115]

> 'The logic of the European Convention does not justify the conclusion that the House must rule that a state is obliged to legalise assisted suicide. It does not require the state to repeal a provision such as s 2(1) of the 1961 Act. On the other hand, it is open to a democratic legislature to introduce such a measure. Our Parliament, if so minded, may therefore repeal s 2(1) and put in its place a regulated system for assisted suicide (presumably doctor assisted) with appropriate safeguards.'

5.39 The application of Art 2 to the issue of euthanasia has not yet been the subject of domestic judicial consideration in relation to children. It is to be anticipated that if such a case did arise it would the subject of intense legal and moral debate. The experience in Holland of the application to children of the Termination of Life on Request and Assisted Suicide (Review Procedures) Act 2001, and the response of the UN Committee on the Rights of the Child to it, highlights some of the key areas which would require detailed consideration in any such debate.[116]

ECHR, Art 2(1) – Right to Life and Life Threatening Traditional Practices

5.40 As in respect of Art 6(1) of the CRC, the killing of a child for reasons of so called 'honour' is also self evidently a breach of Art 2(1) of the ECHR. Further, under the principles described above, the State will have a positive obligation to prevent such 'honour' killings.[117] In 2002, the Council of Europe's Committee of Ministers adopted a recommendation on the protection of women from violence which includes 'honour'

---

[113] *R v (Pretty) v DPP (Secretary of State for the Home Department Intervening)* [2001] UKHL 61, [2002] 1 AC 800, para 86 per Lord Hope.

[114] *Pretty v United Kingdom* (2002) 35 EHRR 1, para 39 ('The consistent emphasis in all the cases before the Court has been the obligation of the State to protect life. The Court is not persuaded that 'the right to life' guaranteed in Article 2 can be interpreted as involving a negative aspect. While, for example in the context of Article 11 of the Convention, the freedom of association has been found to involve not only a right to join an association but a corresponding right not to be forced to join an association, the Court observes that the notion of a freedom implies some measure of choice as to its exercise. Article 2 of the Convention is phrased in different terms. It is unconcerned with issues to do with the quality of living or what a person chooses to do with his or her life. To the extent that these aspects are recognised as so fundamental to the human condition that they require protection from State interference, they may be reflected in the rights guaranteed by other Articles of the Convention, or in other international human rights instruments. Article 2 cannot, without a distortion of language, be interpreted as conferring the diametrically opposite right, namely a right to die; nor can it create a right to self-determination in the sense of conferring on an individual the entitlement to choose death rather than life').

[115] See for example the Termination of Life on Request and Assisted Suicide (Review Procedures) Act 2001 in the Netherlands considered at **5.13** above. See also *R (on the application of Purdy) v Director of Public Prosecutions* [2009] UKHL 45, [2009] 3 WLR 403.

[116] See **5.13–5.14** above.

[117] See **5.15–5.16** above.

killings in the definition of violence against women.[118] In *Crimes of Honour – Outline Report*[119] the Parliamentary Assembly recommended that member states of the Council of Europe take legal, preventive and protective measures in relation to 'honour' killings. In the case of *Opuz v Turkey*[120] the European Court of Human Rights found a violation of Art 2 of the ECHR in respect of the applicant's mother who was killed by the applicant's ex-husband on the grounds his honour had been at stake as she had taken the applicant and children away from him and had led the applicant into an immoral way of life.[121]

ECHR, Art 2(1) – Right to Life and the Death Penalty

5.41 Article 2(1) of the ECHR expressly permits the continued use of the death penalty in specified circumstances. Whilst there is no express prohibition in Art 2 prohibiting the use of the death penalty against children, the need to interpret Art 2 of the ECHR as far as possible in accordance with the international law, including the provisions of the CRC, would likely permit Art 2 to play a central part in successfully challenging any proposed execution of a child.[122] Further, the Sixth Protocol to the ECHR, which permits no derogation or reservation, was ratified by the United Kingdom on 27 January 1999[123] and prohibits the use of such penalty in peacetime.[124] The United Kingdom has also now ratified the Thirteenth Protocol to the ECHR which prohibits, again without derogation or reservation, the death penalty in every circumstance including wartime.[125]

5.42 Within the context of the UK having abolished the death penalty, these provisions are likely to be most relevant in cases where it is proposed to deport a child who is subject to a sentence of death to a State which still has not fulfilled its obligations under Art 37(a) of the CRC concerning the prohibition on the execution of children. In such a situation, the ratification by the UK of the Thirteenth Protocol is likely to prevent deportation where it can be shown that there is an actual risk of the death

---

[118] Recommendation (2002) 5 of the Committee of Ministers to member States on the protection of women against violence, para 1 defining violence against women as 'any act of gender-based violence, which results in, or is likely to result in, physical, sexual or psychological harm or suffering to women, including threats of such acts, coercion, or arbitrary deprivation of liberty, whether occurring in public or private life.' Such acts include 'violence occurring within the family or domestic unit, inter alia, ... crimes committed in the name of honour ...'.

[119] AS/Ega(2002)7rev2, 4 June 2002.

[120] (2009) Application No 33401/02 (unreported).

[121] The court also found a violation of Art 14 of the ECHR on the grounds that the general and discriminatory judicial passivity in Turkey, including the mitigation of sentences on the grounds of custom, tradition or honour, created a climate that was conducive to domestic violence which affected mainly women.

[122] See **3.43–3.46** above.

[123] Note also that the substantive rights enshrined in the Sixth Protocol are 'Convention Rights' for the purposes of the HRA 1998.

[124] The United Kingdom has also ratified the Second Protocol of the International Covenant on Civil and Political Rights which seeks the complete abolition of the death penalty. The United Kingdom ratified the Second Protocol on 10 December 1999.

[125] The United Kingdom ratified the Thirteenth Protocol on 3 May 2002.

penalty being imposed.[126] Where a child may be at risk of extra-judicial killing if deported, such a situation is more likely to be dealt with under Art 3 of the ECHR rather than Art 2.[127]

ECHR, Art 2(1) – Procedural Safeguards

5.43 Implicit in Art 2 of the ECHR are a number of procedural safeguards necessary to give effect to the right to life, the absence of which safeguards may constitute a breach of that right. As Baroness Hale noted in the case of *Savage v South Essex Partnership NHS Foundation Trust*[128] 'There is not much point in prohibiting police and prison officers ... from taking life if there is no independent investigation of how a person in their charge came by her death'.

5.44 Thus, where the State may be responsible for the death of a child there is a positive duty on the State to investigate that death.[129] The authorities must act of their own motion once the matter has come to their attention. They cannot leave it to the initiative of the next-of-kin either to lodge a formal complaint or to take responsibility for the conduct of any investigative procedures.[130] Art 2 of the ECHR, when read with Art 1, imposes on the State a duty to undertake an effective official investigation where the death of an individual is the result of force.[131] An effective official investigation will comprise four key elements:[132]

---

[126] Lord Lester QC, Lord Pannick QC and Herberg, J *Human Rights Law and Practice* (2009) 3rd edn, LexisNexis, p 166. See *Ocalan v Turkey* (2005) 41 EHRR 985; *Aylor v France* (1994) 100 ILR 665 and the decision of the Netherlands Supreme Court in *Short v Netherlands* (1990) Rechtspraak van de Week 358 reprinted in (1990) 29 ILM 1378. See also the position taken by the Human Rights Committee in *Kindler v Canada* (Communication No 470/1991) (1994) 1 IHRR 98 and *NG v Canada* (Communication No 469/1991)(1992) 1 IHRR 161.

[127] See *Aspichi Dehwari v Netherlands* (2000) Application No 37014/97 (unreported) and *Abdurrahim Incedursum v Netherlands* (1999) Application No 33124/96 (unreported). But see also *MAR v United Kingdom* (1996) 23 EHRR CD 120 and *Bahddar v Netherlands* (1998) 26 EHRR 278.

[128] [2008] UKHL 74, [2009] 1 AC 681, [2009] 2 WLR 115, [2009] 1 All ER 1053.

[129] See *Savage v South Essex Partnership NHS Foundation Trust* [2008] UKHL 74, [2009] 2 WLR 115.

[130] *Rantsev v Cyprus and Russia* (2010) Application No 25965/04, para 232.

[131] *McCann v United Kingdom* (1995) 21 EHRR 97, para 161 ('The Court confines itself to noting, like the Commission, that a general legal prohibition of arbitrary killing by the agents of the State would be ineffective, in practice, if there existed no procedure for reviewing the lawfulness of the use of lethal force by State authorities. The obligation to protect the right to life under this provision, read in conjunction with the State's general duty under Article 1 of the Convention to 'secure to everyone within their jurisdiction the rights and freedoms defined in [the] Convention', requires by implication that there should be some form of effective official investigation when individuals have been killed as a result of the use of force by, inter alios, agents of the State. See also *Jordan v United Kingdom* (2003) 37 EHRR 52 and *McKerr v United Kingdom* (2002) 34 EHRR 553. See also *Tyamuskhanovy v Russia* (2010) Application No 11528/07, para 88 ('The Court reiterates that, in the light of the importance of the protection afforded by Article 2, it must subject deprivations of life to the most careful scrutiny, taking into consideration not only the actions of State agents but also all the surrounding circumstances. Detained persons are in a vulnerable position and the obligation on the authorities to account for the treatment of a detained individual is particularly stringent where that individual dies or disappears thereafter. Where the events in issue lie wholly or in large part within the exclusive knowledge of the authorities, as in the case of persons under their control in detention, strong presumptions of fact will arise in respect of injuries and death occurring during that detention. Indeed, the burden of proof may be regarded as resting on the authorities to provide a satisfactory and convincing explanation').

[132] *Jordan v United Kingdom* (2003) 37 EHRR 52. See also *R (JL) v Secretary of State for the Home Department* [2008] UKHL 68, [2009] 1 AC 588, 3 WLR 1325 in which Lord Philips adopted these criteria as those required in respect of the 'enhanced investigation' required in respect of suicides and near suicides of prisoners and detainees.

(a)　The persons carrying out the investigation must be independent of those implicated in the events being investigated. It is for the State to initiate the investigation and not the next of kin.[133]

(b)　The investigation must be capable of leading to a determination of whether the use of force was or was not justified and to the identification and punishment of those responsible. There is a duty to take all reasonable steps to unmask any racist motive and to establish whether or not ethnic prejudice could have played a role in the death.[134]

(c)　The investigation must be prompt and expeditious.

(d)　There must be a sufficient element of public scrutiny in the investigation to secure accountability in practice as well as in theory.[135]

(e)　The investigation must involve the next of kin in the investigative process to the extent necessary to protect their legitimate interests, including a requirement that they be granted 'victim' status.[136]

In the case of an attempted suicide, the positive obligation inherent in Art 2 requires an enhanced inquiry into the circumstances of the attempt. This enquiry must comply with the criteria identified above.[137]

ECHR, Art 2(1) – Derogations

5.45　Article 2 contains the circumstances in which the deprivation of life may be justified, namely (a) in the execution of a sentence of a court following conviction for a crime for which the death penalty is prescribed by law[138] and (b) the use of force which is no more than is absolutely necessary (i) in the defence of any person from unlawful violence,[139] (ii) in order to effect a lawful arrest or to prevent the escape of a person lawfully detained[140] and (iii) in action lawfully taken for the purpose of quelling a riot or insurrection.[141] These circumstances are construed strictly having regard to the fundamental nature of the right to life and the fact that Art 2 permits of no derogation from the right to life during peacetime.[142] As noted above, the need to interpret Art 2 of

---

[133]　*Menson v United Kingdom* (2003) 37 EHRR CE 220.

[134]　*Nachova v Bulgaria* [2005] ECHR 43577/98, para 160 citing *Menson v United Kingdom* (2003) 37 EHRR CE 220.

[135]　Note that if the infringement of the right to life or to personal integrity is not caused intentionally, the positive obligation imposed by Art 2 to set up an effective judicial system does not necessarily require the provision of a criminal-law remedy in every case (see for example *Oyal v Turkey* (2010) Application No 4864/05).

[136]　For this latter requirement see *Luluyev v Russia* (unreported) 9 November 2006, para 71.

[137]　See *R (JL) v Secretary of State for the Home Department* [2008] UKHL 68, [2009] 1 AC 588, 3 WLR 1325, para 39, [2009] 2 All ER 521 and *SP v Secretary of State for Justice* [2009] EWHC 13, [2009] All ER (D) 119 Jan concerning the serious self-harm of a young women detained in a young offenders institution.

[138]　Article 2(1).

[139]　Article 2(2)(a).

[140]　Article 2(2)(b).

[141]　Article 2(2)(c).

[142]　See *Soering v United Kingdom* (1989) 11 EHRR 439, para 89 and *McCann v United Kingdom* (1995) 21 EHRR 97, para 146.

the ECHR as far as possible in accordance with the international law, including the CRC, would likely allow Art 2 to play a central part in successfully challenging any proposed execution of a child.[143]

5.46   It is important to note that the circumstances set out in Art 2(2) are referable to the use of force which may result in death as an unintended outcome, not to the intentional taking of a person's life.[144] The use of the word 'absolutely' in Art 2(2) requires a more compelling test of necessity than that required by the term 'necessary in a democratic society'.[145] An honest belief at the time that the use of force is absolutely necessary may justify the use of force even if that belief turns out subsequently to be a mistaken one.[146]

The Child's Right to Life in European Union Law

5.47   The Charter of Fundamental Rights of the European Union[147] Art 2(1) states that 'Everyone has the right to life'. Article 2(2) prohibits the death penalty without reservation, stating that 'No one shall be condemned to the death penalty, or executed'. Article 3(2) of the Charter prohibits eugenic practices, in particular those aimed at the selection of persons, prohibits the making of the human body and its parts a source of financial gain and prohibits the reproductive cloning of human beings. In accordance with Art 52(3) of the European Charter,[148] the meaning and scope of the rights under Art 2 is the same as that under the corresponding Art 2 of the ECHR. As such, the exceptions that are permitted by Art 2(2) of the ECHR will be permitted in respect of the rights under Art 2 of the Charter.

The Child's Right to Life in other Regional Instruments

5.48   The African Charter on Human and People's Rights stipulates at Art 4 that:

> 'Human beings are inviolable. Every human being shall be entitled to respect for his life and the integrity of his person. No one may be arbitrarily deprived of this right.'

---

[143] See **3.43–3.46** above.

[144] *McCann v United Kingdom* (1995) 21 EHRR 97, para 148 ('The Court considers that the exceptions delineated in paragraph 2 indicate that this provision extends to, but is not concerned exclusively with, intentional killing. As the Commission has pointed out, the text of Article 2, read as a whole, demonstrates that paragraph 2 does not primarily define instances where it is permitted intentionally to kill an individual, but describes the situations where it is permitted to 'use force' which may result, as an unintended outcome, in the deprivation of life. The use of force, however, must be no more than 'absolutely necessary' for the achievement of one of the purposes set out in sub-paragraphs (a), (b) or (c. See also *Jordan v United Kingdom* (2003) 37 EHRR 52, para 104.)

[145] *McCann v United Kingdom* (1995) 21 EHRR 97, para 149 and *Andronicou and Constantinou v Cyprus* (1997) 25 EHRR 491, para 171.

[146] *McCann v United Kingdom* (1995) 21 EHRR 97, para 200. See also the UN Basic Principles on the Use of Force and Firearms by Law Enforcement Officials (Adopted by the Eighth United Nations Congress on the Prevention of Crime and the Treatment of Offenders, Havana, Cuba, 27 August to 7 September 1990) which states 'intentional lethal use of firearms may only be made when strictly unavoidable in order to protect life.'

[147] 2000/C364/01.

[148] Article 52(3) of the Charter provides that 'Insofar as this Charter contains rights which correspond to rights guaranteed by the Convention for the Protection of Human Rights and Fundamental Freedoms, the meaning and scope of those rights shall be the same as those laid down by the said Convention. This provision shall not prevent Union law providing more extensive protection.'

The African Charter of the Rights and Welfare of the Child[149] provides that the 'Death sentence shall not be pronounced for crimes committed by children'. Article 4 of the American Convention on Human Rights states that 'Every person has the right to have his life respected. This right shall be protected by law and, in general, from the moment of conception. No one shall be arbitrarily deprived of his life'. Article 4(2) circumscribes the use of the death penalty and specifically provides that 'Capital punishment shall not be imposed upon persons who, at the time the crime was committed, were under 18 years of age or over 70 years of age; nor shall it be applied to pregnant women'.[150] The Inter-American Court of Human Rights has concluded:[151]

> 'That respect for life, regarding children, encompasses not only prohibitions, including that of arbitrarily depriving a person of this right, as set forth in Article 4 of the American Convention on Human Rights, but also the obligation to adopt the measures required for children's existence to develop under decent conditions.'

The revised Arab Charter on Human Rights provides at Art 5 that 'Every human being has the inherent right to life. This right shall be protected by law. No one shall be arbitrarily deprived of his life.' Article 7 of the Arab Charter stipulates that 'Sentence of death shall not be imposed on persons under 18 years of age, unless otherwise stipulated in the laws in force at the time of the commission of the crime'.

The Child's Right to Life in Domestic Law

Domestic Ambit of the Child's Right to Life

5.49   The domestic courts consider the right to life as 'the most fundamental of all human rights'.[152] When the right to life is engaged, the options available to a reasonable decision maker are curtailed.[153] In respect of children, whilst there is a strong presumption that all steps capable of preserving a child's life should be taken save in exceptional circumstances, the domestic principle remains that the paramount consideration at all times is the child's best interests.[154]

5.50   Within the domestic jurisdiction the right to life enshrined in Art 2 of the ECHR is given effect by Sch 1 of the Human Rights Act 1998. It is not retrospective in its effect and applies only to deaths which occurred following the coming into force of the Human Rights Act 1998 on the 2 October 2000.[155] Pursuant to the principles outlined in chapter 3, in cases and administrative decisions concerning children domestic legislation (including the application of the Human Rights Act 1998) and common law should be

---

[149] OAU Doc.CAB/LEG/24.9/49 art 5(3). A child is defined in Art 2 as 'every human being below the age of 18 years.'

[150] Article 1 of the Protocol to the American Convention on Human Rights to Abolish the Death Penalty states 'The States Parties to this Protocol shall not apply the death penalty in their territory to any person subject to their jurisdiction.' See also Art 9 of the Ibero-American Convention on Young People's Rights.

[151] Inter-American Court of Human Rights Advisory Opinion of 28 August 2002 OC-17/2002.

[152] *Bugdaycay v Secretary of State for the Home Department* [1987] AC 514 at 531E per Lord Bridge. See also *R v Lord Saville of Newdigate ex p A* [1999] 4 All ER 860, [2000] 1 WLR 1855.

[153] *R v Lord Saville of Newdigate ex p A* [1999] 4 All ER 860, [2000] 1 WLR 1855, paras 34–37 citing *R v Ministry of Defence, ex p Smith* [1996] QB 517.

[154] See *A National Health Service Trust v D* [2000] 2 FLR 677, [2000] 2 FCR 577. Note Kennedy's view that the application of the 'best interests principle' to issues concerning the right to life risks turning complex and moral questions into simple questions of fact (see Kennedy, I *Treat Me Right: Essays in Medical Law and Ethics* (1988) Clarendon Press, pp 395–396).

[155] *R (Hurst) v HM Coroner for Northern District London* [2007] UKHL 13, [2007] 2 AC 189.

interpreted as far as possible in accordance with the child's right to life enshrined in Art 6(1) of the CRC and the spirit of that Convention generally.[156]

Domestic Application of the Child's Right to Life

Domestic Application of the Right to Life – Human Embryology and Fertilisation

5.51   As discussed in detail in chapter 4,[157] in domestic law a foetus has no rights of its own 'at least until it is born and has a separate existence from its mother'.[158] By reason of the margin of appreciation enjoyed by member States in respect of Art 2 of the ECHR this domestic principle does not offend against the Art 2 right to life.[159] As the CRC does not seek to restrict a State's discretion to provide under its domestic law the point at which childhood begins, the domestic principle likewise does not offend against Art 6(1) of the CRC. By extension, the domestic courts have not been prepared to consider an embryo as having a right to life, Wall J noting in *Evans v Amicus Healthcare Ltd; Hadley v Midland Fertility Services Ltd* that:[160]

> 'If a foetus has no right to life under Art 2, it is difficult to see how an embryo can have such a right.'

5.52   The handling and use of human embryos is regulated within the domestic jurisdiction by the Human Fertilisation and Embryology Act 1990 and the Human Fertilisation and Embryology Act 2008.[161] The Human Fertilisation and Embryology Authority is the independent regulator which oversees the use of gametes and embryos in fertility treatment and research.[162] The area of human fertilisation and embryology is likely to raise further questions concerning the right to life as medical science advances. Many of the issues raised will be social as well as legal. Within this context, and in relation to other controversial areas touching on the right to life, regard should be had to the observations of Lord Brown-Wilkinson in *NHS Trust v Bland*[163] concerning the proper boundary between the judiciary and the legislature:

> 'Where cases raise wholly new moral and social issues, in my judgment it is not legitimate for the judges to seek to develop new, all-embracing principles of law in a way which reflects the individual judges' moral stance when society as a whole is substantially divided on the relevant moral issues. Moreover, it is not legitimate for a judge in reaching a view as to what is for the benefit of the one individual whose life is in issue to take into account the wider practical issues as to allocation of limited financial resources or the impact on third parties of altering the time at which death occurs. For these reasons, it seems to me imperative that the moral, social and legal issues raised by this case should be considered by Parliament. The judges' function in this area of the law should be to apply the principles which society, through the democratic process, adopts, not to impose their standards on society. If Parliament fails to act, then judge-made law will of necessity through a gradual and uncertain process provide a legal answer to each new question as it arises. But in my judgment that is not the best way to proceed.'

---

[156]   See **3.43–3.46** above.
[157]   See **4.3–4.13**.
[158]   *Paton v British Pregnancy Advisory Service Trustees* [1979] QB 276, [1978] 2 All ER 987.
[159]   *Patton v UK* (1980) 3 EHRR 408.
[160]   [2003] EWHC 2161 (Fam), [2004] 1 FLR 67 at 112.
[161]   In force from 1 October 2009.
[162]   There is currently a proposal to abolish the Human Fertilisation and Embryology Authority and to subsume its responsibilities within the Department of Health.
[163]   [1993] AC 789, [1993] 1 All ER 858 at 879, [1993] 1 FLR 1026, [1994] 1 FCR 485.

Domestic Application of the Right to Life – Abortion

5.53   The right to life does not act to prohibit abortion in the domestic jurisdiction as under the current law the unborn child does not benefit from that right.[164] Again, by reason of the margin of appreciation afforded to the State, the domestic position does not at present contravene either Art 6(1) of the CRC nor Art 2 of the ECHR.[165] However, within the context of the provisions of the Abortion Act 1967, the Government is probably subject to a general duty to give guidance on the lawful procurement of abortion facilities.[166]

5.54   The Infant Life (Preservation) Act 1929, s 1(1) provides protection for the life of the unborn child capable of being born alive by providing '... any person who, with intent to destroy the life of a child capable of being born alive, by any willful act causes a child to die before it has an existence independent of its mother shall be guilty of ... child destruction ...'.[167] The offence of procuring or attempting to procure a miscarriage under ss 58 and 59 of the Offences Against the Person Act 1861 also provides some protection to the unborn child. However, the domestic criminal laws protecting unborn children appear to be based on the concept of the 'sanctity of life' itself rather than any specific right, to life or otherwise, referable to the unborn child. In *Rance and Another v Mid-Downs Health Authority and Another*[168] Brook J said:

> 'I have no difficulty in detecting in the 1929 Act a policy decision by Parliament that the sanctity of the lives of children capable of being born alive is to be respected by the law (see *McKay v Essex Area Health Authority* [1982] 2 All ER 771 at 780, [1982] QB 1166 at 1180 per Stephenson LJ), even if a foetus, before being born alive, has no directly enforceable rights itself (see *Paton v Trustees of BPAS* [1978] 2 All ER 987, [1979] QB 276 and *Re F (in utero)* [1988] 2 All ER 193, [1988] Fam 122). I also have no difficulty in concluding that in 1967 Parliament did not intend to change that policy when it made major changes in the law relating to abortions.'

The concept of the 'sanctity of life' has also been used to justify the conclusion that it would be contrary to public policy to permit 'wrongful life' actions based on some species of right to die conferred upon the foetus.[169]

---

[164]   *Paton v British Pregnancy Advisory Service Trustees* [1979] QB 276, [1978] 2 All ER 987. See the Abortion Act 1967, s 1(1).

[165]   Although note that socially or ethically questionable practices associated with abortion such as selective abortion based on pre-natal sex selection have drawn adverse comments from the Committee on the Rights of the Child. See **5.10** above.

[166]   See *Tysiac v Poland* (2007) 22 BHRC 155; *Open Door Counselling and Dublin Well Women Clinic Limited v Ireland* (1992) 15 EHRR 244, para 68 and *Family Planning Association of Northern Ireland v Minister of Health* [2004] NICA 39, paras 38–44 per Nicholson LJ.

[167]   The description of the 1929 Act which follows the title reads 'An Act to amend the law with regard to the destruction of children at or before birth'. The Act provides a defence at s 1(1) of acting in good faith for the sole purpose of preserving the life of the Mother.

[168]   [1991] 1 All ER 801. See also *McKay and another v Essex Area Health Authority and Another* [1982] 2 All ER 771 at 780 per Lord Justice Stephenson.

[169]   *McKay v Essex Area Health Authority* [1982] 2 All ER 771 and Fortin, J *Is the 'Wrongful Life' Action really Dead?* (1987) JSWL 306.

Domestic Application of the Right to Life – Medical Treatment

(i)   Medical Treatment – General Principles

5.55   Medical staff seeking to treat a child with a life threatening illness or disability will normally need consent to do so if they are to avoid a prosecution for assault.[170] Generally, anyone with parental responsibility for the child, including a local authority[171] may give valid consent for the child to undergo surgical, medical or dental treatment, subject to:

(a)   The provisions of s 8(1) of the Family Law Reform Act 1969 which provides that the consent of a child who has attained the age of 16 years to treatment[172] which, in the absence of consent would constitute a trespass to the person of the child, is effective consent and excludes the need to obtain consent from parent or guardian.

(b)   The child being assessed as '*Gillick* competent' in relation to the treatment decision in question.[173]

(c)   A declaration by the High Court.

5.56   Within this context, the parents of a child owe the child a duty to give (or withhold) consent to medical treatment in the best interests of the child and without regard to their own interests.[174] Pursuant to s 1 of the Children and Young Persons Act 1933 a person over the age of 16 who has responsibility for a child under the age of 16 has a duty to obtain essential medical assistance for that child.

5.57   Where a child has the capacity to give consent on the grounds that they are adjudged to be '*Gillick* competent', the Children Act 1989 Guidance and Regulations Volume 3 Family Placements provide as follows in relation to the issue of consent to medical treatment:[175]

> 'Children who are judged able to give consent cannot be medically examined or treated without their consent. The responsible authority should draw the child's attention to his [or her] rights to give or refuse consent to examination or treatment if he [or she] is 16 or over or if he [or she] is under 16 and the doctor considers him [or her] of sufficient understanding to understand the consequences of consent or refusal.'

---

[170]   *Re R (A Minor) (Wardship: Medical Treatment)* [1992] Fam 11 at 22, [1991] 4 All ER 177 at 184 per Lord Donaldson.

[171]   It must be remembered that the parental responsibility conferred upon a local authority by s 44 of the Children Act 1989 (emergency protection order), s 38 (interim care order) and s 31 (care order) is shared with those who also hold parental responsibility for the child and is subject to the limitations provided in ss 44(5)(b) and s 33(3)(b)(i). Where a local authority is uncertain as to its parental authority, it is sensible for a local authority to invite the medical team to apply to the High Court for a declaration in respect of medical treatment (see *Re B (Medical Treatment)* [2008] EWHC 1996 (Fam), [2009] 1 FLR 1264).

[172]   The Act uses the phrase 'surgical, medical or dental treatment' which it defines in s 8(2) as including 'any procedure undertaken for the purpose of diagnosis' and 'any procedure (including in particular the administration of an anaesthetic) which is ancillary to any treatment as it applies to that treatment'.

[173]   See **4.41 et seq** concerning the validity of the judgment in *Re R (A Minor) (Wardship: Medical Treatment)* [1992] Fam 11 at 23, [1991] 4 All ER 177 at 185 holding that whilst a '*Gillick* competent' child's consent to medical treatment cannot be overridden by his or her parents, a '*Gillick* competent' child's refusal of medical treatment can be.

[174]   See Lord Donaldson in *Re J (A Minor) Wardship: Medical Treatment)* [1990] 3 All ER 930 at 934.

[175]   Para 2.32.

5.58   In cases of medical emergency, where the common law doctrine of necessity will apply if the well-being of the child will suffer serious harm or death by reason of the delay caused in obtaining consent, doctors may treat a child without the consent of those with parental responsibility.[176] The circumstances of medical emergencies are many and diverse. However, in principle the doctrine of necessity will also presumably apply where the child is aged 16 or over but by reason of the nature of the medical emergency it is not possible to obtain the child's consent pursuant to s 8(1) of the Family Law Reform Act 1969. It is also likely to apply where doctors consider the child '*Gillick* competent' in respect of his or her treatment but a medical emergency arises during the course of that treatment as a consequence of which it is not possible to obtain the consent of the child to take the steps necessary to address that emergency.[177]

5.59   Advances in medical technique have extended the threshold for survival to increasingly premature and gravely ill or disabled children.[178] However, 'life has a natural end and the existence of such techniques presents doctors, patients and their families with dilemmas'.[179] A child may have a strong and settled view concerning the treatment proposed for them, based on belief or simply a wish not to undergo the further pain and suffering consequent upon the proposed treatment.[180] The question of whether a child should have medical treatment for a life threatening or disabling condition is not for some parents simply a question of the hope engendered by medical technology or a simple disagreement with a doctor's medical opinion. Religious faith, a firm humanistic belief that they are acting with compassion or a determination to support a child's clearly expressed wishes can all lead a parent to object to life saving treatment for their child. All these positions may be sincere and honestly held. Finally, whilst treatment may be available for a terminally ill child, administrative decision makers may deny such treatment on the grounds of a cost benefit analysis.

---

[176]   See HOC63/1968, MOHCF/19/1B and *Re F (Mental Patient: Sterilisation)* [1990] 2 AC 1 at 52 sub nom *F v West Berkshire Health Authority (Mental Health Act Comr intervening)* [1989] 2 All ER 545 at 548 per Lord Bridge.

[177]   See *Re F (Mental Patient: Sterilisation)* [1990] 2 AC 1 at 52 sub nom *F v West Berkshire Health Authority (Mental Health Act Comr intervening)* [1989] 2 All ER 545 at 548 per Lord Bridge ('It seems to me to be axiomatic that treatment which is necessary to preserve the life, health or well-being of the patient may lawfully be given without consent. But, if a rigid criterion of necessity were to be applied to determine what is and what is not lawful in the treatment of the unconscious and the incompetent, many of those unfortunate enough to be deprived of the capacity to make or communicate rational decisions by accident, illness or unsoundness of mind might be deprived of treatment which it would be entirely beneficial for them to receive').

[178]   It has been suggested that the consequence of medical technology reaching a point where all neonates, however seriously disabled, could be kept a live would be the need to clarify legally the attributes a neonate must posses in order to claim a right life (Fortin, J *Babies and the Challenges of Medical Technology* in s Cretney (ed) *Family Law Essays for the new Millennium* (2000) Family Law 173).

[179]   *Withholding and Withdrawing Life Prolonging Treatments: Good Practice in Decision Making* (2008) General Medical Council, p 1. See *Portsmouth NHS Trust v Wyatt and Wyatt, Southampton NHS Trust Intervening* [2004] EWHC 2247 (Fam), [2005] 1 FLR 21 per Hedley J ('This case evokes some of the fundamental principles that undergird our humanity. They are not to be found in Acts of Parliament or decisions of the courts but in the deep recesses of the common psyche of humanity whether they be attributed to humanity being created in the image of God or whether it be simply a self defining ethic of a generally acknowledged humanism).'

[180]   See for example *Re M (Medical Treatment: Consent)* [1999] 2 FLR 1097 (a 15 year old girl refused to consent to a heart transplant on the grounds that she did not want someone else's heart or a life of taking medication) and *Re P (Medical Treatment: Best Interests)* [2003] EWHC 1696 (Fam), [2004] 2 FLR 1117 (a 16 year old boy who objected to the administration of blood or blood products by reason of his being a staunch and committed Jehovah's Witness). Note that in this context the child's right to participate under Art 12 of the CRC will be of particular relevance.

5.60   These issues have resulted in some cases in the common law principles articulated above becoming strained in their application, with such cases often requiring the courts intervention.[181] The Mental Capacity Act 2005 will, in respect of person over the age of 16, place most issues concerning disputed medical treatment in the Court of Protection.[182] For children under 16 the inherent jurisdiction of the High Court will remain the primary arena for issues of lawfulness of proposed medical treatment.[183] The court cannot make advance declarations in respect of medical treatment in anticipation of a disagreement over whether to give or withhold treatment.[184]

(ii)   Medical Treatment – Rights versus Welfare

5.61   In dealing with the issues arising from the treatment of children with life threatening illnesses or disabilities, the domestic courts have tended to conflate the concept of welfare and the child's right to life rather than treating the former as a principle of interpretation to be applied to the latter.[185] In 1995, prior to the coming into force of the Human Rights Act 1998, Laws J in *R v Cambridge District Health Authority, ex parte B* cited the right to life under the ECHR in a case concerning the funding of treatment for a child suffering from acute myeloid leukaemia. Laws J took the view, later rejected by the Court of Appeal, that the right to life was so fundamental as to be a part of common law and held that funding difficulties constituted insufficient justification for breaching the right.[186] Ten years later, in *Portsmouth NHS Trust v Wyatt*

---

[181]   *Re C (A Baby)* [1996] 2 FLR 43 per Stephen Brown P ('… the courts are ready to assist with the taking of responsibility in cases of grave anxiety …'). In respect of parental views, permission of the High Court is required where parents are in dispute over issues which are 'irrevocable steps in the child's life' (see *Re J (Specific Issue Order: Muslim Upbringing and Circumcision)* [1999] 2 FLR 678 confirmed by the Court of Appeal at [2000] 1 FCR 307, [2000] 1 FLR 571). The High Court retains jurisdiction where parents are united in their opposition to a course of action (see *Re B (A Minor) (Wardship: Medical Treatment)* (1982) 3 FLR 117).

[182]   *A Primary Care Trust and P v AH and A and a Local Authority* [2008] EWHC 1403 (Fam). See the Court of Protection Rules 2007, SI 2007/1744 for the practice and procedure in the Court of Protection and the Court of Protection Practice (2010) Jordan Publishing.

[183]   In some cases applications concerning the withholding or withdrawing of medical treatment have been made under s 8 of the Children Act 1989 (see for example *Re R (A Minor) (Blood Transfusion)* [1993] 2 FLR 757 and *Re HG (Specific Issue Order: Sterilisation)* [1993] 1 FLR 587). However, where the application concerns life-threatening decisions or issues of public policy an application under the inherent jurisdiction is more appropriate (*Clarke, Hall & Morrison on Children* LexisNexis, para 1[899]). See also *Practice Note (Official Solicitor: Declaratory Proceedings: Medical and Welfare Decisions for Adults Who Lack Capacity)* [2006] 2 FLR 373).

[184]   *R v Portsmouth Hospitals NHS Trust, ex p Glass* [1999] 3 FCR 145. But see *Re P (Medical Treatment: Best Interests)* [2003] EWHC 1696 (Fam), [2004] 2 FLR 1117 in which Johnson J made an order permitting a hospital to administer blood or blood products to a child objecting on the grounds of being a staunch and committed Jehovah's witness even though there was no reason to believe it was inevitable that there would be further need for blood or blood products to be administered.

[185]   *Re A (Conjoined Twins: Surgical Separation)* [2001] Fam 147, [2000] 4 All ER 961, [2000] 3 FCR 577, [2001] 1 FLR 1. The right to life is not the only right potentially engaged in cases of this nature, see *Airedale NHS Trust v Bland* [1993] AC 789, [1993] 1 FLR 1026 at 826 per Lord Hoffman ('… the sanctity of life is only one of a cluster of ethical principles which we apply to decisions about how we should live. Another is respect for the individual human being and in particular for his right to choose how he should live his own life. We call this individual autonomy or the right of self determination. And another principle, closely connected, is respect for the dignity of the individual human being: our belief that quite irrespective of what the person concerned may think about it, it is wrong for someone to be humiliated or treated without respect for his value as a person. The fact that the dignity of an individual is an intrinsic value is shown by the fact that we feel embarrassed and think it wrong when someone behaves in a way which we think demeaning to himself, which does not show sufficient respect for himself as a person … what is not always realised … is that they are not always compatible with each other').

[186]   [1995] 1 FLR 1055 at 1061. Reversed on appeal in *R v Cambridge Health Authority, ex p B* sub nom *R v Cambridge District Health Authority, ex p B* [1995] 2 All ER 129, [1995] 1 WLR 898, [1995] 2 FCR 485, [1995] 1 FLR 1055.

and Wyatt, Southampton NHS Trust Intervening[187] Hedley J stated, in a case concerning
a gravely ill and disabled baby named Charlotte, that:

> 'In the course of argument the European Convention for the Protection of Human Rights
> and Fundamental Freedoms 1950 (the European Convention) was referred to but no
> separate submissions were developed even though key rights are undoubtedly engaged. That
> was because although English domestic law has undoubtedly been significantly affected by
> the concept of European Convention rights, it is recognised that in this case at least the
> Convention now adds nothing to domestic law.'

In *NHS Trust v A*[188] Holman J, in a case concerning parents' objections to a bone
marrow transplant for their terminally ill child on the grounds of compassion and faith,
stated:

> 'Clearly, several articles of the Convention are engaged by a case such as this. However, the
> Convention and the passing of the Human Rights Act 1998 does not alter or add to
> established principles of English domestic law in this field, and no separate consideration of,
> or reference to, the Convention is required.'

Butler-Sloss LJ reached similar conclusions in relation to the child's rights under the
CRC in a case concerning the question of whether a baby should be tested for HIV
contrary to the wishes of her HIV positive mother.[189]

5.62   The domestic courts thus at present appear to conflate the child's right to life
with the child's best interests, treating them as interchangeable.[190] In *NHS Trust A v M;
NHS Trust B v H*[191] Butler-Sloss P held that the positive obligations under Art 2 of the
ECHR only oblige medical teams to keep a terminally ill patient alive if, according to
responsible medical opinion, this would be in the child's best interests. Indeed, the
domestic courts have held that where the treatment or lack of treatment is covered by a
declaration that that course of action is in the child's best interests, there can be no
infringement of the ECHR, Art 2 right to life.[192]

---

[187]   [2004] EWHC 2247 (Fam), [2005] 1 FLR 21, para 25.
[188]   [2007] EWHC 1696 (Fam), [2008] 1 FLR 70, para 44.
[189]   *Re C (HIV Test)* [1999] 2 FLR 1004, para 1021.
[190]   Interestingly, the courts have however expressly recognised that the best interests test should not be conflated
        with the patients wishes and feelings, suggesting that the child's right to participate survives as a discrete
        right to be considered discretely as part of the decision making process (See *R (on the application of Burke)
        v General Medical Council* [2005] EWCA Civ 1003, [2006] QB 273, [2005] 3 FCR 169).
[191]   [2001] Fam 348, para 37 sub nom *An NHS Trust v M, An NHS Trust v H* [2001] 2 FLR 367. See also *NHS
        Trust A v H* [2001] 2 FLR 501.
[192]   *A National Health Service Trust v D* [2000] 2 FLR 677. Further, such a best interests declaration would
        comply with the right to die with dignity under Art 3 of the ECHR (see *A National Health Service Trust v D*
        [2000] 2 FLR 677 and *D v United Kingdom* (1997) 24 EHRR 423).

(iii)   Withholding or Withdrawing Treatment from Gravely Ill or Disabled Children[193]

5.63   Thus, in domestic law, the child's best interests will be determinative the outcome of an application to determine whether life saving treatment should be withheld or withdrawn.[194] In applying the welfare test, the court must navigate the following 'intellectual milestones':[195]

(a)   the judge must decide what is in the best interests of the child;[196]

(b)   in doing so the child's welfare is the court's paramount consideration;

(c)   the judge must look at the case from the assumed point of view of the patient;

(d)   there is strong presumption in favour of a course of action which will prolong life, but that presumption is not irrebutable;[197]

(e)   The term best interests encompasses medical, emotional and all other welfare issues;[198]

(f)   The court must conduct a balancing exercise in which all relevant factors are weighed (and a helpful way of doing this is to draw up a balance sheet).[199]

---

[193] There is no distinction for the purpose of the applicable legal principles between withdrawing and withholding life support (see *An NHS Trust v MB* [2006] EWHC 507 (Fam), [2006] 2 FLR 319). See also *Withholding or Withdrawing Life Saving Treatment in Children: A Framework for Practice* (1997) Royal College of Paediatrics and Child Health.

[194] *Re A (Conjoined Twins: Surgical Separation)* [2001] Fam 147, [2000] 4 All ER 961, [2000] 3 FCR 577, [2001] 1 FLR 1. For criticism of this decision see Fortin, J *Children's Rights and the Developing Law* (2005) 2nd edn, Cambridge, p 318. See also See *Airedale National Health Service Trust v Bland* [1993] AC 789 HL.

[195] *Wyatt v Portsmouth NHS Trust* [2005] EWCA Civ 1182, [2006] 1 FLR 554.

[196] The concept of intolerability in the sense of 'intolerable to the child' should not be seen as gloss on, much less a supplementary test to, best interests (*Wyatt v Portsmouth NHS Trust* [2005] EWCA Civ 1182, [2006] 1 FLR 554). In assessing best interests, the court must balance the advantages of giving or not giving potential treatments in order to determine the child's best interests with regard to future treatment (see *Re K (Medical Treatment: Declaration)* [2006] EWHC 1007 (Fam), [2006] 2 FLR 883).

[197] See *Re J (A Minor) (Wardship: Medical Treatment)*, [1991] Fam 33, [1991] 1 FLR 366 at 46 in which Lord Donaldson said 'There is without doubt a very strong presumption in favour of a course of action which will prolong life, but ... it is not irrebuttable ... Account has to be taken of the pain and suffering and quality of life which the child will experience if life is prolonged. Account has also to be taken of the pain and suffering involved in the proposed treatment ... We know that the instinct and desire for survival is very strong. We all believe in and assert the sanctity of human life ... Even very severely handicapped people find a quality of life rewarding which to the unhandicapped may seem manifestly intolerable. People have an amazing adaptability. But in the end there will be cases in which the answer must be that it is not in the interests of the child to subject it to treatment which will cause it increased suffering and produce no commensurate benefit, giving the fullest possible weight to the child's, and mankind's desire to survive.' See also *A National Health Service Trust v D* [2000] 2 FLR 677, [2000] 2 FCR 577.

[198] See also *Re A (Male Sterilisation)* [2000] 1 FLR 549; *Re S (Sterilisation: Patient's Best Interests)* [2000] 2 FLR 389; *Portsmouth NHS Trust v Wyatt* [2004] EWHC 2247 (Fam), [2005] 1 FLR 21; *Re L (Medical Treatment: Benefit)* [2004] EWHC 2713 (Fam), [2005] 1 FLR 491 and *An NHS Trust v A* [2007] EWHC 1696 (Fam), [2008] 1 FLR 70 in which Holman J noted 'Best interests are used in the widest sense and include every kind of consideration capable of impacting on the decision. These include, non-exhaustively, medical, emotional, sensory (pleasure, pain and suffering) and instinctive (the human instinct to survive) considerations.'

[199] See *An NHS Trust v A* [2007] EWHC 1696 (Fam), [2008] 1 FLR 70 in which Holman J noted 'It is impossible to weigh such considerations mathematically, but the court must do the best it can to balance all the conflicting considerations in a particular case and see where the final balance of the best interests lies.'

5.64   Under domestic law, a child's life does not have to be extended by any means regardless of the circumstances.[200] A child does not need to be dying before the medical team can contemplate withholding treatment.[201] Within this context, the domestic courts have demonstrated considerable reluctance to override the bona fide clinical judgment of treating doctors. In *Re J (A Minor) (Wardship: Medical Treatment)*[202] Lord Donaldson said:[203]

'The fundamental issue in this appeal is whether the court in the exercise of its inherent power to protect the interests of minors should ever require a medical practitioner or health authority acting by a medical practitioner to adopt a course of treatment which in the bona fide clinical judgment of the practitioner concerned is contraindicated as not being in the best interests of the patient. I have to say that I cannot at present conceive of any circumstances in which this would be other than an abuse of power as directly or indirectly requiring the practitioner to act contrary to the fundamental duty which he owes to his patient.'

5.65   However, in *Re K (Medical Treatment: Declaration)*[204] Sir Mark Potter P, considering whether artificial feeding should be withdrawn from a child born prematurely with an inherited and severe neuromuscular disorder, held:

'This is a comparatively unusual case to come before the court in the sense that the declaration sought is non-contentious, all parties concerned being in agreement with the views of the medical professionals involved that life-prolonging treatment should cease. Indeed, I was told in the course of argument that, had the necessity for parental consent simply rested with the father and mother in this case, the matter would not have come to court, the medical professionals being satisfied that their ethical and legal obligations would not be breached by the action now proposed. However, the case is now before the court for decision, and the court is not tied to or bound by the clinical assessment of what is in K's interests. The court must reach its own conclusion on the basis of a broad spectrum of considerations after careful consideration of the evidence before it ...'

(iv)   Religious and Ethical Objections to Medical Treatment

5.66   The issue of whether medical treatment should be withheld or withdrawn from a gravely ill or disabled child may arise out of the religious or ethical beliefs of the child or the adults caring for that child. Where the beliefs advanced in opposition are those of the parents, their decision may act to deprive the child of developing to a point where he or she can decide for him or herself whether to place weight on those beliefs or not. In the case of *Prince v Massachusetts*,[205] Supreme Court Justice Holmes held that:

---

[200]   *C (A Minor) (Wardship: Medical Treatment)* [1990] Fam 26 (medical staff not obliged to administer antibiotics or use intravenous feeding in the event of C acquiring an infection or becoming unable to feed orally. Rather medical staff could care for her in a way that preserved her dignity and allowed her to die peacefully). See also *Re Ward of Court (Withholding Medical Treatment) (No 2)* [1995] ILRM 401 (Irish Sup Ct.).

[201]   *Re J (A Minor)* [1990] 3 All ER 930.

[202]   [1993] Fam 15, [1992] 4 All ER 614 at 622. Cited on this point in *Re C (Medical Treatment)* [1998] 1 FLR 384.

[203]   See also the Wyatt judgment of Hedley J *Wyatt (A Child) (Medical Treatment: Continuation of Order)* [2005] EWHC 2293 (Fam), [2005] All ER 1325 which reinforces this approach.

[204]   [2006] EWHC 1007 (Fam), [2006] 2 FLR 883.

[205]   321 US 158 (1944), US Supreme Court.

'The family itself is not beyond regulation in the public interest, as against a claim of religious liberty. And neither the rights of religion nor the rights of parenthood are beyond limitation ... The right to practice religion freely does not include the right to expose the community or the child to communicable disease or the latter to ill-health or death ... Parents may be free to become martyrs themselves. But it does not follow they are free, in identical circumstances, to make martyrs of their children before they have reached the age of full and legal discretion when they can make that choice for themselves.'

Where the religious beliefs are those of the child, issues of evolving capacity and the right to participation will be particularly important. In all cases, not only the right to life is likely to be engaged, but also potentially the right to respect for private and family life, the right to freedom of thought, conscience and religion[206] and the right to freedom from discrimination.[207]

5.67 It is well established that the domestic courts have jurisdiction to override the religious belief of parents in ordering treatment be given to a child. The line of cases in relation to parents' religious beliefs is replete with examples of those beliefs being held subordinate to the paramount interests of the child.[208] In *NHS Trust v A*[209] Holman J authorised an invasive but life saving bone marrow transplant for a six month old girl over the objections of her parents who refused consent on the grounds that the treatment would cause pain and distress and that God would heal the child without treatment. Holman J held that:

'The views and opinions of both the doctors and the parents must be carefully considered. Where, as in this case, the parents spend a great deal of time with their child, their views may have particular value because they know the patient and how he reacts so well; although the court needs to be mindful that the views of any parents may, very understandably, be coloured by their own emotion or sentiment. It is important to stress that the reference is to the views and opinions of the parents. Their own wishes, however understandable in human terms, are wholly irrelevant to consideration of the objective best interests of the child save to the extent in any given case that they may illuminate the quality and value to the child of the child–parent relationship.'

5.68 *NHS Trust v A* goes a long way to address the difficulties created by the earlier decision of *Re T (A Minor)(Wardship: Medical Treatment)*[210] in which the Court of Appeal appeared to render the parents' perception of best interests as the decisive factor in cases of this nature. In *Re T*, following a failed liver transplant, the mother in question had refused consent to a second liver transplant for a child on the ground that the child should not have to go through the pain and distress of further invasive surgery. Overturning the first instance decision to override the mother's refusal to consent, the Court of Appeal held that, whilst the operation had a good chance of success, whilst if successful it would lead to many years of normal life and whilst the welfare of the child was paramount, the mother's refusal of consent was reasonable. The basis for the court's decision appears to have been that the first instance judge had failed to assess the relevance or the weight of the mother's concern as to the benefits to her child of the surgery and post-operative treatment, the dangers of failure both long term as well as short term, the possibility of the need for further transplants, the likely length of life

---

[206] See chapter 10 below.
[207] See **4.71 et seq** above.
[208] See *Re R (A Minor) (Medical Treatment)* [1993] 2 FLR 757; *Re O (A Minor) (Medical Treatment)* [1993] 2 FLR 149; *Re S (A Minor) (Medical Treatment)* [1993] 1 FLR 376 and *Re C (Medical Treatment)* [1998] 1 FLR 384.
[209] [2007] EWHC 1696 (Fam), [2008] 1 FLR 70.
[210] [1997] 1 All ER 906.

and the effect on her child of all those concerns, together with the strong reservations expressed by one of the consultants about coercing the mother into playing a crucial part in the aftermath of the operation and thereafter. Whilst expressly stated to be a decision 'on the most unusual facts of the case' *Re T* has been the subject of considerable criticism.[211] *Re T* does appear to be a decision that holds that the death of the child is better than post operative pain, risk of future complications and a consequent burden of care on the parent. It is difficult to see where the child's right to life figures in this analysis or to disagree with Fortin's observation that 'If the treatment available holds a good prognosis for the child's future health, then the presumption should be in favour of the courts ensuring the child's survival and not the parents' peace of mind'.[212]

5.69   Where it is the child who expresses strong religious objections to lifesaving treatment the courts have also tended to override those wishes and directed that treatment be given.[213] Once again, these decisions are expressed in terms of welfare rather than in terms of the child's right to life. These cases are covered in detail in chapter 6.[214]

(v)   Funding Medical Treatment and the Right to Life

5.70   Even where a child's life expectancy is in issue, the domestic courts have held that they cannot interfere with health authorities' decisions concerning the allocation of a limited treatment budget on the basis of the child's right to life. The decision of Laws J in *R v Cambridge District Health Authority, ex parte B*[215] that the right to life of a child suffering from acute myeloid leukaemia was so fundamental that funding difficulties constituted insufficient justification for breaching the right was immediately overturned by the Court of Appeal.[216] The judgment of the Court of Appeal makes no reference to the right to life under Art 2 of the ECHR or otherwise, Bingham MR stating:

> 'I have no doubt that in a perfect world any treatment which a patient, or a patient's family, sought would be provided if doctors were willing to give it, no matter how much it cost, particularly when a life was potentially at stake. It would however, in my view, be shutting one's eyes to the real world if the court were to proceed on the basis that we do live in such a world. It is common knowledge that health authorities of all kinds are constantly pressed to make ends meet. They cannot pay their nurses as much as they would like; they cannot provide all the treatments they would like; they cannot purchase all the extremely expensive medical equipment they would like; they cannot carry out all the research they would like; they cannot build all the hospitals and specialist units they would like. Difficult and agonising judgments have to be made as to how a limited budget is best allocated to the maximum advantage of the maximum number of patients. That is not a judgment which the court can make.'

---

[211]   See for example Michalowski, S *Is it in the best interests of the child to have a life saving liver transplantation?: Re T (Wardship: Medical Treatment)* (1997) 9 Child and Family Law Quarterly 179; Fox, M and McHale, J *In Whose Best Interests* (1997) 60 Modern Law Review 700 and Bainham, A *Do Babies Have Rights?* (1997) Cambridge Law Journal 48.

[212]   Fortin, J *Children's Rights and the Developing Law* (2005) 2nd edn, Cambridge, p 326.

[213]   *Re L (Medical Treatment: Gillick Competence)* [1998] 2 FLR 810; *Re M (Medical Treatment: Consent)* [1999] 2 FLR 1097 and *Re P (Medical Treatment: Best Interests)* [2003] EWHC 1696 (Fam), [2004] 2 FLR 1117.

[214]   See below **6.97–6.105** on the child's right to participate.

[215]   [1995] 1 FLR 1055.

[216]   *R v Cambridge Health Authority, ex p B* sub nom *R v Cambridge District Health Authority, ex p B* [1995] 2 All ER 129, [1995] 1 WLR 898, [1995] 2 FCR 485, [1995] 1 FLR 1055.

5.71   Support for this approach is to be found in *Osman v United Kingdom*[217] where the European Court of Human Rights held that the right to life must be interpreted in such a way so as not to impose an impossible and disproportionate burden on authorities. Thus the positive obligation under Art 2 of the ECHR extends to compelling hospitals, both public and private, to adopt measures for the protection of their patients' lives[218] but this cannot be an unqualified obligation in light of the foregoing principles. Where a decision is taken not to fund treatment for a child, provided that the State can show that 'it has acted reasonably in the allocation of resources, acting in good faith to strike a rational balance between competing needs'[219] the domestic courts are unlikely to find a breach of the right to life unless the decision making process is itself flawed.[220]

(vi)   Domestic Impact of the Right to Life on Life Saving Treatment

5.72   Within the context of the domestic courts adopting an approach centering on the concept of best interests rather than on the child's right to life in respect of children with life-threatening illness or disability, Fortin argues that the positive obligation to protect the right to life under Art 2 of the ECHR, combined with domestic case law, should provoke a reassessment of the principles of common law which have governed the treatment of seriously ill and dying children.[221] In particular, Fortin contends that a rights based approach to life-saving treatment reminds the adults involved that child patients have an independent status of their own and represents a powerful way of challenging existing orthodoxies, including the reluctance to override the clinical judgment of treating doctors.[222] These conclusions are given further force by the positive obligations implicit in Art 6(1) of the CRC.[223]

Domestic Application of the Right to Life – Euthanasia

5.73   As a result of the decision of the House of Lords in *R (on the application of Purdy) v DPP*[224] the Director of Public Prosecutions has issued guidance on the application of the Suicide Act 1961 describing the factors that will be taken into account by the State when deciding whether to prosecute a person under s 2(1) of the 1961 Act.[225] Section 2(1) of the Act provides that 'A person who aids, abets, counsels or procures the suicide of another, or an attempt by another to commit suicide, shall be

---

[217]   (1998) 29 EHRR 245, [1999] 1 FLR 193, para 115.
[218]   *Calvelli v Italy* (2002) Application No 32967/96 (unreported), para 49; *Dodov v Bulgaria* (2008) Application No 59548/00 (unreported), para 80 and *Vo v France* (2005) 40 EHRR 259, para 89. Something more than the simply a failure on the part of the hospital to meet the standard of care of the patient required by the duty of care will be needed to breach this positive obligation (see *Savage v South Essex Partnership NHS Foundation Trust* [2008] UKHL 74, [2009] 1 AC 681, [2009] 2 WLR 115, [2009] 1 All ER 1053, para 9).
[219]   See Havers, P and Neenan, C *Impact of the European Convention on Human Rights on medical law* Postgrad Med J. 2002 October; 78 (924): 573–574.
[220]   See for example North West Lancashire Health Authority v A, D and G (2000) 1 WLR 977. See also the decision of the South African Constitutional Court in *Soobramoney v Minister of Health, KwaZulu Natal* (1997) 4 BHRC; James and Longley *Judicial Review and Tragic Choices* [1995] PL 367; O' Sullivan *The Allocation of Scarce Resources and the Right to Life under the ECHR* [1998] PL 389 and Freeman, M *Death, Dying and the Human Rights Act 1998* (1999) 52 CLP 218.
[221]   Fortin, J *Children's Rights and the Developing Law* (2005) 2nd edn, Cambridge, pp 368–371.
[222]   Fortin, J *Children's Rights and the Developing Law* (2005) 2nd edn, Cambridge, pp 368–371.
[223]   See **5.8** above.
[224]   [2009] UKHL 45, [2009] 3 WLR 403. See also the first instance decision in the case: *R (Purdy) v DPP* [2008] EWHC 2565 (Admin) (2008). 152 Sol Jo (No 43) 31, [2008] All ER (D) 284 (Oct) and the decision of the Court of Appeal: *R (on the application of Purdy) v Direction of Public Prosecutions, Society for the Protection of Unborn Children intervening)* [2009] EWCA Civ 92, [2009] 1 Cr App Rep 455, [2009] All ER (D) 197 (Feb).
[225]   *Policy for Prosecutors in respect of Cases of Encouraging or Assisting Suicide* (2010) The Director of Public Prosecutions.

liable on conviction on indictment to imprisonment for a term not exceeding fourteen years'. The Suicide Act 1961 is applicable when a substantial part of the aiding, abetting, procuring or counseling of the suicide occurs in England or Wales. The suicide itself can be committed in any country.[226] In respect of children, the DPP's guidance stipulates that one of the public interest factors in favour of a prosecution will be the fact that the victim was under the age of 18 years.[227]

Domestic Application of the Right to Life – Life Threatening Traditional Practices

5.74 In *AM v A Local Authority and Another*[228] Wall LJ commented as follows in relation to the practice of so-called 'honour' killing:

> 'The message from this case, which must be sent out load and clear, is that this court applies a tolerant and human rights based rule of law: one which, under the Act of 1989 regards parents as equals and the welfare of the child as paramount ... That is the law of England, and that is the law which applies in this case. Arson, domestic violence and potential revenge likely to result in abduction or death are criminal acts which will be treated as such.'

One of the events which may precede the 'honour' killing of a child is that child being forced into marriage. The Forced Marriage Act 2007 permits the civil courts to make an order protecting a person from being forced into marriage or from any attempt to be forced into marriage or protecting a person who has been forced into marriage.[229] Orders made under these provisions can contain such prohibitions, restrictions, requirements or other terms as are required to prevent a person being forced into marriage or to protect a person who has been forced into marriage.[230] The terms of the order may relate to conduct outside England and Wales.[231] The Forced Marriage Act 2007 does not prevent the use of other remedies to protect a child from being the victim of an 'honour' murder including the inherent jurisdiction of the High Court, the criminal law, civil remedies under the Protection from Harassment Act 1997, the other provisions of the Family Law Act 1996, any protection or assistance available under the Children Act 1989, any civil claim in tort or the laws of marriage.[232]

Domestic Application of the Right to Life – Procedural Safeguards

5.75 As noted, the Committee on the Rights of the Child has recognised that for the Art 6(1) right to life enshrined in the CRC to have practical effect, the deaths of children must be the subject of adequate investigation in order to encourage reporting, to reduce the possibility of the cause of death being misrepresented and to inform preventative strategies.[233] Implicit in Art 2 of the ECHR are a number of procedural safeguards

---

[226] Thus, the current practice by those wishing to commit suicide of travelling to the Dignitas clinic in Switzerland, which offers 'assisted suicide', is potentially caught by s 2(1) of the Act.

[227] See also the Assisted Dying for the Terminally Ill Bill, 681 HL Official Report (5th series) col 1184 which would apply only to a person who has reached the age of majority and who meets the qualifying conditions set out in the Bill. The Bill was defeated on its second reading in the House of Lords.

[228] [2009] 2 FCR 505 sub nom *Re B-M (Care Orders)* [2009] 2 FLR 20.

[229] Family Law Act 1996, s 63A(1) as amended by the Forced Marriage (Civil Protection) Act 2007.

[230] Family Law Act 1996, s 63B(1).

[231] Family Law Act 1996, s 63B(2).

[232] Family Law Act 1996, s 63R. See also *Multi-agency Practice Guidelines: Handling Cases of Forced Marriage*, FCO Forced Marriage Unit (2009).

[233] Newell, P and Hodgkin, R *Implementation Handbook for the Convention on the Rights of the Child* (2008) 3rd edn, UNICEF, p 92.

necessary to give effect to the right to life, the absence of which safeguards may constitute a breach of that right.[234] Within the domestic jurisdiction these procedural safeguards centre on the investigation and reporting of sudden child deaths through the Coroner.[235] This system has been held to be the 'default' method of satisfying the procedural requirements of Art 2[236] although the domestic courts have also recognised the system is inadequate to satisfy such requirements.[237]

Procedural Safeguards – Deaths in Hospital

5.76 Where a child dies as the result of negligence in an NHS hospital there must be in place a system that permits of a practical and effective investigation of the facts surrounding the death and for the determination of any civil liability on the part of the authorities.[238]

Procedural Safeguards – Deaths in Custody

5.77 Where a child dies in custody, for example due to restraint techniques in secure training centers,[239] there must be an investigation which meets the procedural requirements implicit in Art 2 of the ECHR.[240] In *R (D) v Secretary of State for the Home Department (Inquest Intervening)*[241] the Court of Appeal held that the requirement to investigate deaths in custody also extends to the investigation of 'near deaths'. In the case of an attempted suicide, the positive procedural obligations inherent in Art 2 require an enhanced inquiry into the circumstances of the attempt which cannot be satisfied by an internal investigation of the facts and which must meet the minimum requirements set out in *Jordan v United Kingdom*.[242] In *SP v Secretary of State for Justice*,[243] a case concerning the serious self-harm of a young women detained in a young offenders institution, the court held that the Art 2 requirement that any investigation be independent means that 'current hierarchical or institutional connection by rank or responsibility ... will undoubtedly disqualify the investigator ...' and that past hierarchical or institutional connection between the investigator and someone implicated in the events under investigation could cause an objective lack of practical independence. It is not however a breach of the United Kingdom's obligations under Art 2 not to hold a public enquiry into the sentencing and incarcerating of young offenders. In *R (Scholes) v Secretary of State for the Home Department*[244] it was held that no breach of Art 2 had occurred where the Home Secretary refused to hold a public enquiry into the suicide of a 16 year old boy at a young offender institution.[245]

---

[234] The absence of, or failure to comply with, procedural safeguards under Art 2 may also constitute a breach of Art 13 of the ECHR (right to an effective remedy).

[235] See the Coroners and Justice Act 2009, s 1(2).

[236] *Death Certification in England, Wales and Northern Ireland: The Report of the Fundamental Review* (2003) Cm 5831, paras 58–75.

[237] *R (Davies) v HM Deputy Coroner for Birmingham* [2003] All ER (D) 40 (Dec, [2003] EWCA Civ 1739. See also *Jordan v United Kingdom* (2003) 37 EHRR 52 and *R (Wright) v Home Office* [2001] EWHC (Admin) 520, HRLR 1, [2001] UKHRR 1399.

[238] *R (Takoushis) v HM Coroner for Inner North London* [2005] EWCA Civ 1440, [2006] 1 WLR 461.

[239] See JCHR *The Use of Restraint in Secure Training Centers* HL Paper 65, HC Paper 378 (2007–2008). See also Children's Rights Alliance for England, *State of Children's Rights in England* (2008) p 11.

[240] See the Coroners and Justice Act 2009, s 1(2)(c) and *R (Davies) v HM Deputy Coroner for Birmingham* [2003] All ER (D) 40 (Dec), [2003] EWCA Civ 1739.

[241] [2006] EWCA Civ 134, [2006] 3 All ER 946.

[242] (2003) 37 EHRR 52. See *R (JL) v Secretary of State for the Home Department* [2008] UKHL 68, [2009] 1 AC 588, [2009] 3 WLR 1325, para 39, [2009] 2 All ER 521.

[243] [2009] EWHC 13 (Admin), [2009] All ER (D) 119 (Jan).

[244] [2006] EWCA Civ 1343, [2006] HRLR 44.

[245] In October 2008 the Council of Europe Commissioner for Human Rights observed that 'Remarkably, there is no obligation in [UK] domestic law to hold a public inquiry into a child's unexpected death in custody,

Procedural Safeguards – Serious Case Reviews

5.78   Where a child dies, including by way of suicide, and abuse or neglect is known to be or suspected to be a factor in the child's death a Serious Case Review will be undertaken as provided for in Chapter 8 of *Working Together to Safeguard Children*.[246] The function of a Serious Case Review is to establish whether lessons can be learned concerning the manner in which local professionals and agencies safeguard children, identify clearly the nature and extent of those lessons, how they can be acted upon and what change is expected and to improve inter-agency working to better safeguard and promote the welfare of children.[247] It is not the function of a Serious Case Review to determine how the child died or who is culpable. Those are issues for the Coroner and the criminal court and for an independent public enquiry where one is held.[248] Serious Case Reviews thus do not meet the procedural requirements of Art 2 of the ECHR.[249] The UN Committee on the Rights of the Child has urged the Government to introduce a system of statutory child death inquiries.[250]

THE CHILD'S RIGHT TO SURVIVAL AND DEVELOPMENT

Ambit of the Right to Survival and Development

5.79   The UN Manual on Human Rights Reporting[251] states in relation to the right to life under Art 6(1) of the CRC that:[252]

> 'States' action should promote life which is compatible with the human dignity of the child. Or, to use the language of the Convention, that fully ensures the right to an adequate standard of living, including the right to housing, nutrition, to the highest attainable standard of health, to information and education in the basic use of preventive healthcare measures, to develop respect for the natural environment.'

Further, the Manual makes clear:[253]

> 'Adding a new dimension to life, it clearly stresses the need to enhance children's health, to ensure preventive healthcare measures, including immunisation, the provision of adequate information or knowledge on nutrition, hygiene and environmental sanitation. But it is in no way limited to a physical perspective, rather further emphasising the need to ensure a full and harmonious development of the child, including at the spiritual, moral and social levels,

---

     although this is implicit in the case-law of the European Court of Human Rights on article 2 of the ECHR' (Comm DH (2008) 27, Strasbourg, 17 October 2008. See now the Coroners and Justice Act 2009, s 1(2)(c).

[246] (2010) DCSF. A Serious Case Review will also be held where a child sustains a potentially life-threatening injury or serious and permanent impairment of health and development through abuse or neglect, is subjected to particularly serious sexual abuse, where a parent has been murdered and a homicide review is being initiated, a child has been killed by a parent suffering from mental illness or the case gives rise to concern about inter-agency working to protect a child from harm (Local Safeguarding Children Board Regulations 2006, SI 2009/90, r 5(2)(b)(ii)).

[247] Working Together (2010) DCSF, para 8.5.

[248] Working Together (2010) DCSF, para 8.6. For public enquiries see for example The Victoria Climbié Inquiry Report (2003) Cm 5730 and Lord Laming, *The Protection of Children in England: A Progress Report* (2009) HC 330.

[249] For criticism of this position see Children's Rights Alliance for England, *State of Children's Rights in England* (2008), p 19.

[250] Committee on the Rights of the Child *Concluding Observations in respect of United Kingdom of Great Britain and Northern Ireland* CRC/C/15/Add.188, para 38.

[251] HR/PUB/91/1/(Rev.1).

[252] *Manual on Human Rights Reporting* (1997) HR/PUB/91/1 (Rev 1), p 425.

[253] *Manual on Human Rights Reporting* (1997) HR/PUB/91/1 (Rev.1), pp 425–426.

where education will play a key role. The promotion of survival and development therefore means to gain another and deeper challenge of self-betterment of the child, ensuring the capacity of developing talents and abilities to their fullest potential, preparing the child for responsible life in a free society and ensuring him or her the essential feeling of be longing to a world made of solidarity where there is no place for indifference or passivity.'

5.80 Commenting on the obligation of parents to provide maintenance for their children, Blackstone observed that parents 'would be in the highest manner injurious to their issue, if they only gave their children life, that they might afterwards see them perish'.[254] The UN human rights framework recognises that the right to life, although fundamental, is of little practical value unless accompanied by rights securing the continuation and development of life and a life of right quality.[255] Survival is the pre-condition to all other rights.[256] As already noted, in its General Comment No 3 the Committee on the Rights of the Child has observed that:[257]

> 'Children have the right not to have their lives arbitrarily taken, as well as to benefit from economic and social policies that will all them to survive into adulthood and develop in the broadest sense of the word.'

The right to life, survival and development is thus constituted by and encompasses both first and second generation rights. Within this context, Art 6(2) of the CRC reflects the provisions of both the Universal Declaration of Human Rights and the Covenant on Economic, Social and Cultural Rights, in particular Art 12 of that Covenant.[258] Within this context, the family is recognised by the preamble to the CRC as being central to the development of the child and as the 'natural environment for the growth and well-being of all its members and particularly children', acknowledging that the child 'for the full and harmonious development of his or her own personality, should grow up in a family environment, in an atmosphere of happiness, love and understanding'.[259] The concept of the evolving capacity of the child, enshrined in Art 5 of the CRC is a further cardinal concept in child development.[260] The UN Committee on the Rights of the Child considers specifically the development of young children in its General Comment No 7 *Implementing Child Rights in Early Childhood* [261] and the development of adolescents in its General Comment No 4 *Adolescent Health and Development in the Context of the Convention on the Rights of the Child.*[262]

---

[254] Blackstone, *Commentaries on the Laws of England*, Book 1, chapter XVI.

[255] See also the decision of the Supreme Court of India in *Olga Tellis v Bombay Municipal Corporation* AIR (1986) Supreme Court 18 in which Chandrachud C observed 'That which alone makes it possible to live, leave aside what makes life liveable, must be deemed to be an integral component of the right to life.' Ensalaco argues that the connection between development and the rights of the child is so strong that it is possible to conceive of the rights of the child as the right of the child to develop (Ensalaco, M *The Right of the Child to Development* in Ensalaco, M and Majka, L (eds) *Children's Human Rights: Progress and Challenges for Children Worldwide* (2005) Rowman & Littlefield, p 22).

[256] Van Bueren *The International Law on the Rights of the Child* (1998) Martinus Nijhoff, p 293.

[257] Committee on the Rights of the Child General Comment No 3 *HIV/AIDS and the Rights of the Child* HRI/GEN/1/Rev 8, p 366, para 9.

[258] See UN Declaration on the Right to Development 1986.

[259] This reflects the contents of Art 25 of the Universal of Declaration of Human Rights which states that 'Motherhood and childhood are entitled to special care and assistance. All children, whether born in or out of wedlock, shall enjoy the same social protection.'

[260] See **4.26-4.31** above.

[261] Committee on the Rights of the Child General Comment No 7 *Implementing Child Rights in Early Childhood* HRI/GEN/1/Rev 8, p 432.

[262] Committee on the Rights of the Child General Comment No 4 *Adolescent Health and Development in the Context of the Convention on the Rights of the Child* HRI/GEN/1/Rev 8, p 376.

The Right to Survival and Development and Resources

5.81   The right to survival and development under Art 6(2) of the CRC is not qualified by reference to available resources. However, a number of other rights which support the child's survival and development, both within the CRC and the Covenant on Economic, Social and Cultural Rights are qualified by reference to available resources.[263] Having regard to the fact that right to survival and development encompasses both first and second generation rights, the concept of the 'progressive realisation' of economic and social rights is of central importance to the enforcement of rights concerning the survival and development of the child.[264]

The Right to Survival and Development

Right to Survival and Development under the CRC

CRC, Art 6(2)

5.82   CRC, Art 6(2) provides as follows in respect to the child's right to survival and development:

> 'States Parties shall ensure to the maximum extent possible the survival and development of the child.'

CRC, Art 6(2) – Ambit

5.83   As Fortin observes, the State has an interest in the health and well-being of its next generation; their poor development will affect the whole of society.[265] Art 6(2) of the CRC provides that 'States Parties shall ensure to the maximum extent possible the survival and development of the child'. This prescription is crucial to the implementation of the entire CRC, prefacing as it does references to development in a range of articles under the Convention and acting as a guiding principle for their implementation. The Committee on the Rights of the Child expects implementation of all other articles of the CRC to be carried out with a view to achieving the maximum survival and development of the child.[266]

5.84   Responsibility for giving effect to the child's right to survival is placed primarily on the State, whereas the responsibility for giving effect to right of development is less clearly delineated by the CRC.[267] Art 6(2) places the responsibility for giving effect to the child's right to development on the State. However, in Art 27(1), concerning the child's right to an adequate standard of living, the parents of the child are compelled to take primary responsibility within their ability and financial capacity, with the State performing a secondary role of assisting parents in implementing the child's rights.[268]

---

[263]   For example, Art 27(3) of the CRC provides that assistance to parents and other responsible for the child to implement the right to an adequate standard of living shall be provided 'in accordance with national conditions and within their means.' Within the ICESCR Art 2(1) provides that 'Each State Party to the present Covenant undertakes to take steps, individually and through international assistance and co-operation, especially economic and technical, to the maximum of its available resources, with a view to achieving progressively the full realisation of the rights recognised in the present Covenant by all appropriate means, including particularly the adoption of legislative measures.'

[264]   See **3.13** above.

[265]   Fortin, J *Children's Rights and the Developing Law* (2009) 3rd edn, Cambridge, p 334.

[266]   Newell, P and Hodgkin, R *Implementation Handbook for the Convention on the Rights of the Child* (2008) 3rd edn, UNICEF, p 93.

[267]   Van Bueren *The International Law on the Rights of the Child* (1998) Martinus Nijhoff, p 317.

[268]   See Art 18 of the CRC and the Committee on the Rights of the Child General Comment No 7 *Implementing*

(i)   CRC, Art 6(2) – 'Maximum Extent Possible'

5.85   The words 'to the maximum extent possible' in Art 6(2), make clear that the child's right to survival and the child's right to development are dynamic concepts, encompassing the necessary positive steps which a State should take in order to promote the survival and development of children.[269]

(ii)   CRC, Art 6(2) 'Development'

5.86   The right to development has been described as 'an inalienable human right by virtue of which every human person and all peoples are entitled to participate in, contribute to, and enjoy economic, social, cultural and political development, in which all human rights and fundamental freedoms can be fully realised'.[270] Further, the right to development 'implies the full realisation of the right of peoples to self-determination, which includes, subject to the relevant provisions of both International Covenants on Human Rights, the exercise of their inalienable right to full sovereignty over all their natural wealth and resources'.[271] The individual is the central subject of development and should be the active participant and beneficiary of the right to development.[272] States have the right and the duty to formulate appropriate national development policies that aim at the constant improvement of the well-being of the entire population and of all individuals, on the basis of their active, free and meaningful participation in development and in the fair distribution of the benefits resulting therefrom.[273]

5.87   The concept of development as applied to children is not simply about preparing the child for adulthood but requires the provision of optimal conditions in the child's life at all times during childhood. The Committee on the Rights of the Child has stated that child development should be seen as a holistic concept.[274] The right of development also refers to a level health and development of the individual child which enables the child to benefit from the exercise of all the other rights of the child.[275]

Child Rights in Early Childhood HRI/GEN/1/Rev.8, para 20 where the Committee observes that 'realising children's rights is in large measure dependent on the well-being and resources available to those with responsibility for their care.'

[269]   Van Bueren *The International Law on the Rights of the Child* (1998) Martinus Nijhoff, p 293.

[270]   UN Declaration of the Right of Development (Resol. 41/128) art 1(1). See also the 1924 Declaration of the Rights of the Child, para 1 ('the child must be given the means requisite for normal material and spiritual development') and the 1959 Declaration on the Rights of the Child Principle 2 ('The child … shall be given opportunities and facilities, by law and by other means, to enable him to develop physically, mentally, morally, spiritually and socially in a healthy and normal manner in conditions of freedom and dignity'). The right to development is also well recognised in the literature on international law. See Schachter, O *The Evolving International Law of Development* (1976) 15 Columbia Journ. Trans. Law, pp 1–16; Dupuy, R (ed) *The Right to Development at the International Level* (1980) Hague Academy of International Law; Synder and Slinn (eds) *International Law of Development: Comparative Perspectives* (1987) Abingdon; De Waart, Peters, Dentres (eds) *International Law and Development* (1988) Martinus Nijhoff.

[271]   UN Declaration of the Right of Development (Resol 41/128), Art 1(2). The pre-amble to the CRC further refers to the 'harmonious development' of the child's personality.'

[272]   UN Declaration of the Right of Development (Resol 41/128), Art 2(1).

[273]   UN Declaration of the Right of Development (Resol 41/128), Art 2(3).

[274]   Newell, P and Hodgkin, R *Implementation Handbook for the Convention on the Rights of the Child* (2008) 3rd edn, UNICEF, p 93.

[275]   Van Bueren *The International Law on the Rights of the Child* (1998) Martinus Nijhoff, p 293. See also Committee on the Rights of the Child General Comment No 7 *Implementing Child Rights in Early Childhood* HRI/GEN/1/Rev.8, para 10.

(iii)   The Right to Survival and Development and Children with Disabilities

5.88   Particular groups of children will require specific measures to enable them to benefit from their right to survival and development. Children with disabilities have an equal right to development to the maximum extent possible. Article 23(3) of the CRC provides as follows:

> 'Recognising the special needs of a disabled child, assistance extended in accordance with paragraph 2 of the present article shall be provided free of charge, whenever possible, taking into account the financial resources of the parents or others caring for the child, and shall be designed to ensure that the disabled child has effective access to and receives education, training, health care services, rehabilitation services, preparation for employment and recreation opportunities in a manner conducive to the child's achieving the fullest possible social integration and individual development, including his or her cultural and spiritual development.'

(iv)   The Right to Survival and Development and Refugee Children

5.89   Having regard to the principle of non-discrimination enshrined in Art 2 of the CRC, refugee children have an equal right to survival and development. Pursuant to Art 22(1) of the CRC:

> 'States Parties shall take appropriate measures to ensure that a child who is seeking refugee status or who is considered a refugee in accordance with applicable international or domestic law and procedures shall, whether unaccompanied or accompanied by his or her parents or by any other person, receive appropriate protection and humanitarian assistance in the enjoyment of applicable rights set forth in the present Convention and in other international human rights or humanitarian instruments to which the said States are Parties.'

Right to Survival and Development under the ECHR

5.90   The ECHR does not contain any specific right to survival and development. The European Court of Human Rights has held that it is not the Court's task to substitute its views for the views of local authorities on the best way to deal with social and economic problems.[276] However, a number of the first generation rights enshrined in the ECHR are relevant when seeking to ensure the child's survival and development. The Art 2 right to life imports a positive obligations relating to the provision of adequate health care to child patients in hospitals and those detained in custody.[277] The Art 3 prohibition on inhuman or degrading treatment may also be engaged where a particularly prejudicial lack of health care, poor standard of living or withdrawal of welfare can be said to constitute treatment, particularly in relation to vulnerable groups.

5.91   A number of articles of revised European Social Charter are particularly relevant to the child's right to survival and development. Indeed, the European Social Charter has been described as 'the economic and social counterpart of the ECHR'.[278] Art 11 of the Charter secures the right to protection of health, Art 12 the right to social security, Art 13 the right to social and medical assistance and Art 14 the right to benefit from social welfare services. Article 7 of the Charter specifically articulates the right of children and young persons to protection and Art 17 the right of children and young persons to social, legal and economic protection. Article 30 deals with the right to

---

[276]   *Öneryildiz v Turkey* (2005) 41 EHRR 20, paras 99–102.
[277]   See **5.26** above.
[278]   Pannick QC and others, *Human Rights Law and Practice* (1999) Lexis Nexis 1st edn, p 341. Note that the United Kingdom has not yet ratified the revised European Social Charter.

protection against poverty and social exclusion and Art 31 with the right to housing. The rights enshrined in these articles secure for children maternal health protection, health protection,[279] welfare and social security, housing,[280] family life,[281] and education.

Right to Survival and Development under Other Regional Instruments

5.92 Article 5(2) of the African Charter on the Rights and Welfare of the Child provides that 'States Parties to the present Charter shall ensure, to the maximum extent possible, the survival, protection and development of the child'.[282] Art 34(1) of the Ibero-American Convention on Young People's Rights stipulates that 'Youth have the right to social, economic, political and cultural development and to be considered priority subjects of the initiatives taken with that aim'.[283] Art 33(b) of the revised Arab Charter on Human Rights provides that the State and society shall 'provide adolescents and young persons the most ample opportunities for physical and mental development' and states at Art 33(c) that:

> 'The States parties shall take all necessary legislative, administrative and judicial measures to guarantee the protection, survival, development and well-being of the child in an atmosphere of freedom and dignity.'

Article 37 of the Arab Charter provides that:

> 'The right to development is a fundamental human right and all States are required to establish the development policies and the measures necessary to guarantee this right. They have a duty to implement the values of solidarity and cooperation among them and at the international level with a view to eradicating poverty and achieving economic, social, cultural and political development. Pursuant to this right, every citizen has the right to participate in the realisation of development and to enjoy the benefits and fruits thereof.'

Right to Survival and Development in Domestic Law

5.93 Within the domestic context, the central governmental policy underpinning childhood survival and development is entitled 'Every Child Matters'.[284] The stated aim of the policy is to maximise developmental opportunities for children and minimise risk to them, seeking to ensure that children can achieve certain defined developmental and social outcomes.[285] These outcomes achieve statutory articulation in the Children Act 2004 as physical and mental health and emotional wellbeing; protection from harm and neglect; education, training and recreation; contribution to society and social and economic wellbeing.[286] The Child Poverty Act 2010 aims to create legally binding

---

[279] Health care must be available to all children without discrimination, including children of illegal or undocumented migrants. See *International Federation of Human Rights Leagues (FIDH) v France*, Collective complaint No 14/2002.

[280] See *European Roma Rights Center (ERRC) v Greece*, Collective complaint No 15/2003.

[281] The revised ESC makes no distinction between the various models of family except for ensuring that greater protection exists for certain more vulnerable types such as single parent families.

[282] See also Art 10 of the African Youth Charter which provides that 'Every young person shall have the right to social, economic, political and cultural development with due regard to their freedom and identity and in equal enjoyment of the common heritage of mankind.'

[283] See also Art 26 of the American Convention on Human Rights and Art 16 of the Additional Protocol to the American Convention on Human Rights in the Area of Economic, Social and Cultural Rights (The 'Protocol of San Salvador').

[284] HM Government, *Every Child Matters: Change for Children* (2004) DfES.

[285] Ibid, p 9.

[286] Children Act 2004, s 10(2).

Ministerial obligations in relation to the eradication of child poverty.[287] It remains to be seen how enforceable such obligations will be in practice. Domestic legislation and case law also deals with issues concerning the provision of housing, health and social welfare for children and young people. These aspects are dealt with in detail below.[288]

Key Elements of the Child's Right to Survival and Development

Rights Supportive of Survival and Development

5.94 The right to survival and development contains a number of key elements which are articulated in provisions beyond Art 6(2) of the CRC. In particular, the right of the child to the highest attainable standard of health under Art 24 of the CRC, the right to enjoy nutritious food, clean drinking water and an adequate standard of living under Art 27 of the CRC, the right to adequate welfare provision under Art 26 and the right to play under Art 31 of the CRC underpin the State's duty to ensure to the maximum extent possible the survival and development of the child.[289] Likewise, the ECHR contains a number of rights supportive of the survival and development of the child.

5.95 In this chapter particular attention is paid to the child's standard of health, the child's standard of living and welfare provision and the child's right to play, together with the health and development of particularly vulnerable groups of children, namely refugee children, children with disabilities, children in the care of the State and child victims. It is however important to remember that both the CRC and the ECHR must be read and given effect as a whole. As such, the health and development of a child will be benefited by many if not all of the provisions of the CRC and many in the ECHR. As Newell and Hodgkin observe, 'The concept of 'development' is not just about the preparation of the child for adulthood. It is about providing optimal conditions for childhood, for the child's life now'.[290] In this regard, many articles of the CRC represent elements key to ensuring the child's right to survival and development, including Arts 20, 23, 24, 25, 27, 28, 29 and 31. Beyond those articles which explicitly refer to development, those articles dealing with protection from violence and exploitation, including Art 19 and Arts 32–39 of the CRC, are also maximising in their effect on the child's right to survival and development.[291]

Rights Supportive of Survival and Development – The Right to Highest Attainable Standard of Health

5.96 General Comment 14 of the Committee on Economic, Social and Cultural Rights states that 'Health is a fundamental human right indispensable for the exercise of other human rights'.[292] Equally, the realisation of the right to health is dependent on

---

[287] Child Poverty Bill 2008–2009, art 1(1).

[288] See below **5.131-5.136** and **5.170–5.178**.

[289] Van Bueren *The International Law on the Rights of the Child* (1998) Martinus Nijhoff, p 293.

[290] Newell, P and Hodgkin, R *Implementation Handbook for the Convention on the Rights of the Child* (2008) 3rd edn, UNICEF, p 93.

[291] Newell, P and Hodgkin, R *Implementation Handbook for the Convention on the Rights of the Child* (2008) 3rd edn, UNICEF, p 83.

[292] Committee on Economic, Social and Cultural Rights General Comment No 14 *The Right to the Highest Attainable Standard of Health (Art 12)* HRI/GEN/1/Rev 8, p 86.

rights to food, housing, work, education, human dignity, life, non-discrimination, equality, the prohibition against torture, privacy, access to information and the freedoms of association, assembly and movement.[293]

5.97 Article 1 of the Declaration of Alma-Ata 1978 states that health 'is a state of complete physical, mental and social wellbeing, and not merely the absence of disease or infirmity'.[294] In its General Comment No 14 the Committee on Economic, Social and Cultural Rights noted that:[295]

> 'the right to health embraces a wide range of socio-economic factors that promote conditions in which people can lead a healthy life, and extends to the underlying determinants of health, such as food and nutrition, housing, access to safe and potable water and adequate sanitation, safe and healthy working conditions, and a healthy environment ... The right to health is not to be understood as a right to be *healthy*. The right to health contains both freedoms and entitlements. The freedoms include the right to control one's health and body, including sexual and reproductive freedom, and the right to be free from interference, such as the right to be free from torture, non-consensual medical treatment and experimentation. By contrast, the entitlements include the right to a system of health protection which provides equality of opportunity for people to enjoy the highest attainable level of health.'

5.98 Whilst this book concentrates on legal and procedural practice, it must be appreciated that any examination of the right to health, and indeed the other rights encompassing the right to survival and development, 'must concern itself with the social, political, economic and cultural factors that determine and shape it'.[296] In particular, with regard to the right to health it is important to recognise that good health cannot be assured by the State nor can the State protect against every possible cause of ill-health taking into account genetic factors, individual susceptibility to ill health and the adoption of unhealthy or risky lifestyles.[297]

Right to Highest Attainable Standard of Health under the CRC

(i) CRC, Art 24

5.99 The aim of the Declaration of Alma-Ata that all peoples should attain a level of health that permits them to lead socially and economically productive lives[298] has, for all children, been codified into a legally binding right to the highest attainable standard of

---

[293] Committee on Economic, Social and Cultural Rights General Comment No 14 *The Right to the Highest Attainable Standard of Health (Art 12)* HRI/GEN/1/Rev 8, p 87.

[294] This formulation was used in preamble to the Constitution of the World Health Organisation as adopted by the International Health Conference, New York, 19–22 June, 1946. It was signed on 22 July 1947 by the representatives of 61 States (Official Records of the World Health Organisation, No 2, p 100) and entered into force on 7 April 1948. See also World Health Organisation *Basic Documents* (2006) 45th edn, Supplement WHO. It was adopted by UNICEF and WHO as the Declaration of Alma-Ata at the International Conference on Primary Healthcare on 12 September 1978.

[295] Committee on Economic, Social and Cultural Rights General Comment No 14 *The Right to the Highest Attainable Standard of Health (Art 12)* HRI/GEN/1/Rev.8, paras 4 and 8. See also Committee on Economic, Social and Cultural Rights General Comment No 14 *The Right to the Highest Attainable Standard of Health (Art 12)*HRI/GEN/1/1Rev.8, paras 43–45 which provide in summary the core obligations of the right to health.

[296] Eze, O *The Right to Health as a Human Right* in *Colloque Hague* 27–29 (1978) Hague Academy of International Law, 76 cited in Van Bueren *The International Law on the Rights of the Child* (1998) Martinus Nijhoff, p 294.

[297] Committee on Economic, Social and Cultural Rights General Comment No 14 *The Right to the Highest Attainable Standard of Health (Art 12)* HRI/GEN/1/Rev.8, para 9.

[298] Declaration of Alma-Ata (1978) principle V.

health by Art 24 of the CRC.[299] Art 24 of the CRC articulates in detail the child's right to health, providing in respect of each child that:

'1. States Parties recognise the right of the child to the enjoyment of the highest attainable standard of health and to facilities for the treatment of illness and rehabilitation of health. States Parties shall strive to ensure that no child is deprived of his or her right of access to such health care services.

2. States Parties shall pursue full implementation of this right and, in particular, shall take appropriate measures:

(a) To diminish infant and child mortality;
(b) To ensure the provision of necessary medical assistance and health care to all children with emphasis on the development of primary health care;
(c) To combat disease and malnutrition, including within the framework of primary health care, through, inter alia, the application of readily available technology and through the provision of adequate nutritious foods and clean drinking-water, taking into consideration the dangers and risks of environmental pollution;
(d) To ensure appropriate pre-natal and post-natal health care for mothers;
(e) To ensure that all segments of society, in particular parents and children, are informed, have access to education and are supported in the use of basic knowledge of child health and nutrition, the advantages of breastfeeding, hygiene and environmental sanitation and the prevention of accidents;
(f) To develop preventive health care, guidance for parents and family planning education and services.

3. States Parties shall take all effective and appropriate measures with a view to abolishing traditional practices prejudicial to the health of children.

4. States Parties undertake to promote and encourage international co-operation with a view to achieving progressively the full realisation of the right recognised in the present article. In this regard, particular account shall be taken of the needs of developing countries.'

5.100 Article 12(1) of the Covenant on Economic, Social and Cultural Rights also articulates the right to the highest attainable standard of health, stating:

'The States Parties to the present Covenant recognise the right of everyone to the enjoyment of the highest attainable standard of physical and mental health.'

This is a narrower approach to the right to health than that contained in Art 24(1) of the CRC, concentrating on prevention, treatment and control of disease and access to medical services in the event of sickness.[300]

---

[299] Van Bueren *The International Law on the Rights of the Child* (1998) Martinus Nijhoff, p 297. The principles of the CRC concerning the health of children were developed from provisions contained in the Universal Declaration of Human Rights, the Covenant on Civil and Political Rights, the Covenant on Economic, Social and Cultural Rights and from definitions and principles formulated by UNICEF and the World Health Organisation (WHO) (see Newell, P and Hodgkin, R *Implementation Handbook for the Convention on the Rights of the Child* (2008) 3rd edn, UNICEF, p 344). The World Declaration on the Survival, Protection and Development of Children 1990 provides for both general and specific commitments to child health related to the standards set by the CRC. The UN Millennium Declaration (UN General Assembly Resolution 55/2) builds on the 1990 World Declaration in prescribing basic goals for child development, which were in turn reaffirmed in 2005 (see General Assembly Sixteenth Session, October 2005 A/RES/60/1).
[300] Van Bueren *The International Law on the Rights of the Child* (1998) Martinus Nijhoff, p 298 and Newell, P and Hodgkin, R *Implementation Handbook for the Convention on the Rights of the Child* (2008) 3rd edn, UNICEF, p 345.

(ii) CRC, Art 24 – 'the highest attainable standard of health'

5.101 The 'highest attainable standard of health' for the purposes of Art 24 of the CRC is referable to both what is attainable for each individual child and according to the progressive realisation of the State's resources.[301] In order to achieve this aim, States Parties must 'promote and encourage international co-operation with a view to achieving progressively the full realisation of the right' pursuant to Art 24(4). The approach to achieving the highest attainable standard of health under Art 24 is a broad one, encompassing environmental pollution[302] and sanitation, the prevention of accidents[303] and the eradication of harmful traditional practices.[304] There is specific provision not only for treatment but also for rehabilitation following illness.[305] The right is clearly drafted so as to place a positive obligation on the State.[306] The need to achieve the highest attainable standard of health for the child is further emphasised by the fact that the rights articulate by Art 24 must be fully implemented pursuant to Art 4 of the CRC. The Committee on Economic, Social and Cultural Rights makes it clear that the right to the highest attainable standard of health comprises the essential elements of availability, accessibility, acceptability and quality.[307]

(ii) CRC, Art 24 and Non-Discrimination

5.102 Article 24(1), in concert with the principle of non-discrimination in Art 2 of the CRC requires the State to eradicate any differentials in the standard of health and availability of facilities as between different children.[308] Art 2 of the CRC prohibits any discrimination in access to health care and the underlying determinants of health, as well as in respect of means and entitlements for their procurement on the grounds of race, colour, sex, language, religion, political or other opinion, national or social origin, property, birth, physical or mental disability, health status (including HIV/AIDS), sexual orientation and civil, political, social or other status which has the intention or effect of nullifying or impairing the equal enjoyment or exercise of the right to health.[309] Art 23 of the CRC requires recognition of 'the right of the disabled child to special care' and stipulates that the assistance provided:[310]

> 'shall be designed to ensure that the disabled child has effective access to and receives ... health care services, rehabilitation services ...in a manner conducive to the child's achieving the fullest possible social integration and individual development, including his or her cultural and spiritual development.'

---

[301] Van Bueren *The International Law on the Rights of the Child* (1998) Martinus Nijhoff, p 300.

[302] Article 24(2)(c).

[303] Article 24 (2)(e).

[304] Article 24(3).

[305] Article 24(1).

[306] Van Bueren *The International Law on the Rights of the Child* (1998) Martinus Nijhoff, p 299. Van Bueren notes however that the drafting is not perfect, for example the use of the words 'illness or rehabilitation' in Art 24 (1) appear to exclude facilities for girls under 18 who are pregnant.

[307] Committee on Economic, Social and Cultural Rights General Comment No 14 *The Right to the Highest Attainable Standard of Health (Art 12)* HRI/GEN/1/Rev.8, para 12.

[308] Committee on Economic, Social and Cultural Rights General Comment No 14 *The Right to the Highest Attainable Standard of Health (Art 12)* HRI/GEN/1/Rev.8, para 12.

[309] Newell, P and Hodgkin, R *Implementation Handbook for the Convention on the Rights of the Child* (2008) 3rd edn, UNICEF, p 353.

[310] See also Committee on the Rights of the Child General Comment No 9 *The Rights of Children with Disabilities* CRC/C/GC/9, paras 44 and 45.

5.103 Further, Art 25 of the Convention on the Rights of Persons with Disabilities[311] provides that:[312]

> 'States Parties recognise that persons with disabilities have the right to the enjoyment of the highest attainable standard of health without discrimination on the basis of disability. States Parties shall take all appropriate measures to ensure access for persons with disabilities to health services that are gender-sensitive, including health-related rehabilitation. In particular, States Parties shall:
>
> (a)   Provide persons with disabilities with the same range, quality and standard of free or affordable health care and programmes as provided to other persons, including in the area of sexual and reproductive health and population-based public health programmes;
> (b)   Provide those health services needed by persons with disabilities specifically because of their disabilities, including early identification and intervention as appropriate, and services designed to minimise and prevent further disabilities, including among children and older persons;
> (c)   Provide these health services as close as possible to people's own communities, including in rural areas;
> (d)   Require health professionals to provide care of the same quality to persons with disabilities as to others, including on the basis of free and informed consent by, inter alia, raising awareness of the human rights, dignity, autonomy and needs of persons with disabilities through training and the promulgation of ethical standards for public and private health care;
> (e) Prohibit discrimination against persons with disabilities in the provision of health insurance, and life insurance where such insurance is permitted by national law, which shall be provided in a fair and reasonable manner;
> (f)   Prevent discriminatory denial of health care or health services or food and fluids on the basis of disability.'

(iii)   CRC, Art 24 and Emphasis on Primary Healthcare

5.104 Article 24 places great emphasis on primary health care for children. This allows the article to have a greater impact on a larger number of children by concentrating on maximum community participation.[313] As a *minimum*, primary healthcare for children should include:[314]

> '... essential health care based on practical, scientifically sound and socially acceptable methods and technology made universally accessible to individuals and families in the community through their full participation and at a cost that the community and country can afford to maintain at every stage of their development in the spirit of self reliance and self-determination ... [to include] at least education concerning prevailing health problems and the methods of preventing and controlling them; promotion of food supply and proper nutrition; an adequate supply of safe water and basic sanitation; maternal and child health care, including family planning; immunisation against the major infectious diseases; prevention and control of locally endemic diseases; appropriate treatment of common diseases and injuries; and provision of essential drugs.'

(iv)   CRC, Art 24 and Specific Aspects of Child Health

5.105 Within the context of its emphasis on primary care Art 24(2) of the CRC places duties on States Parties in respect of specific elements of child health, namely infant and

---

[311] Ratified by the United Kingdom on 8 June 2009.
[312] See also CRC, Art 23(4).
[313] Ibid, p 301. See Declaration of Alma-Ata (1978), para VI.
[314] Declaration of Alma-Ata (1978) principle VI and VII.

child mortality, pre-natal and post-natal care, medical assistance and healthcare, combating disease and malnutrition, health education and preventative healthcare. Article 24(3) further requires the abolition of traditional practices prejudicial to the health of children. This is a non-exhaustive list of measures.[315] These obligations in respect of the health of children cannot be abandoned or derogated from in time of emergency, including an economic emergency, having regard to the non-derogable nature of the right to life under Art 6 of the CRC and under the Covenant on Civil and Political Rights Art 4.

CRC, Art 24(2)(a) – Infant Mortality

5.106 Article 24(2)(a) of the CRC requires that State parties 'diminish infant and child mortality'.[316] It is important to note that this provision relates to infant *and* child mortality and is thus concerned with reducing mortality throughout childhood up to the age of 18.[317] Other rights under the CRC will be relevant to the diminishing infant and child mortality, including appropriate support for parenting under Art 18 and the protection of children from violence, exploitation and abuse pursuant to Art 19 and Arts 32–38. Where a State Party has a high infant mortality rate it is arguably under a duty to create programmes designed to remedy this issue.[318] Within this context, the Human Rights Committee has observed:[319]

> 'The expression 'inherent right to life' cannot properly be understood in a restrictive manner, and the protection of this right requires that States adopt positive measures. In this connection, the Committee considers that it would be desirable for States parties to take all possible measures to reduce infant mortality and to increase life expectancy, especially in adopting measures to eliminate malnutrition and epidemics.'

The Committee on Economic, Social and Cultural Rights has further stated that reduction in infant mortality requires:[320]

> 'The provision for the reduction of the stillbirth rate and of infant mortality and for the health development of the child ... may be understood as requiring measures to improve child and maternal health, sexual and reproductive health services, including access to family planning, pre- and post-natal care, emergency obstetric services and access to information, as well as the resources necessary to act on that information.'

CRC, Art 24(2)(d) – Pre and Post Natal Care

5.107 Article 24(2)(d) of the CRC requires States parties ensure appropriate pre- and post-natal health care for mothers. Whilst infant mortality can be reduced by the

---

[315] Newell, P and Hodgkin, R *Implementation Handbook for the Convention on the Rights of the Child* (2008) 3rd edn, UNICEF, p 344 and 355. See also Committee on the Rights of the Child General Comment No 7 *Implementing Child Rights in Early Childhood* HRI/GEN/1/Rev 8, p 443, para 27.

[316] See also Art 12(2)(a) of the Covenant on Economic, Social and Cultural Rights which provides that 'The steps taken by States Parties to the present Covenant to achieve the full realisation of this right shall include those necessary for (a) the provision for the reduction of the stillbirth-rate and of infant mortality and for the health development of the child.'

[317] Newell, P and Hodgkin, R *Implementation Handbook for the Convention on the Rights of the Child* (2008) 3rd edn, UNICEF, p 356.

[318] Cooke, R (1986) 18 Columbia Human Rights Law Review 1, p 16. There are clear issues with enforcing such a duty given the difficulty of proving that an individual child failed to survive by reason of a breach of Art 24(2)(a) as opposed to some unrelated cause. In the circumstances, it is likely that enforcement will be achieved by reference to the overall infant mortality rate.

[319] Human Rights Committee General Comment No 6 *Article 6 (The Right to Life)* HRI/GEN/1/Rev.8, para 5.

[320] Committee on Economic, Social and Cultural Rights General Comment No 14 *The Right to the highest Attainable Standard of Health* HRI/GEN/1/Rev.8, para 14.

provision of pre and post-natal maternal health care, the right to such care is also the right of children already born whose health and welfare is dependent on the health of their mother.[321] Art 10(2) of the Covenant on Economic, Social and Cultural Rights provides that:

> 'Special protection should be accorded to mothers during a reasonable period before and after childbirth. During such period working mothers should be accorded paid leave or leave with adequate social security benefits.'

CRC, Art 24(2)(b) – Provision of Medical Assistance and Health Care

5.108 Article 24(2)(b) of the CRC requires State parties to ensure the provision of necessary medical assistance and health care to all children with emphasis on the development of primary health care, the emphasis being on provision for *all* children. Under Art 15(1)(b) of the Covenant on Economic, Social and Cultural Rights children enjoy the right to benefit from scientific progress and its implementation and thus to benefits from advances in medical assistance and health care which increase their chance of survival and development.[322] The steps taken by States parties to realise the right under Art 12(1) of the ICESCR include 'The creation of conditions which would assure to all medical service and medical attention in the event of sickness'.[323] The Committee on Economic, Social and Cultural Rights has commented that:[324]

> 'A further important aspect is the improvement and furtherance of participation of the population in the provision of preventive and curative health services, such as the organisation of the health sector, the insurance system and, in particular, participation in political decisions relating to the right to health taken at both the community and national levels.'

CRC, Art 24(2)(c) – Disease and Malnutrition

5.109 Pursuant to Art 24(2)(c) of the CRC, States parties must combat disease and malnutrition, including within the framework of primary health care, through amongst other measures the application of readily available technology and through the provision of adequate nutritious foods and clean drinking-water, taking into consideration the dangers and risks of environmental pollution. The steps taken by States parties to realise the right under Art 12(1) of the ICESCR must include 'The prevention, treatment and control of epidemic, endemic, occupational and other diseases'[325] The Committee on Economic, Social and Cultural Rights has commented that:[326]

> 'The prevention, treatment and control of epidemic, endemic, occupational and other diseases ... requires the establishment of prevention and education programmes for behaviour-related health concerns such as sexually transmitted diseases, in particular HIV/AIDS, and those adversely affecting sexual and reproductive health, and the promotion of social determinants of good health, such as environmental safety, education, economic development and gender equity. The right to treatment includes the creation of a system of urgent medical care in cases of accidents, epidemics and similar health hazards, and the

---

[321] Van Bueren *The International Law on the Rights of the Child* (1998) Martinus Nijhoff, p 305.
[322] Ibid, p 303.
[323] ICESCR Art 12(2)(d).
[324] Committee on Economic, Social and Cultural Rights General Comment No 14 *The Right to the highest Attainable Standard of Health* General Comment No 14 HRI/GEN/1/Rev.8, para 17.
[325] ICESCR Art 12(2)(c).
[326] Committee on Economic, Social and Cultural Rights General Comment No 14 *The Right to the Highest Attainable Standard of Health* General Comment No 14 HRI/GEN/1/Rev.8, para 16.

provision of disaster relief and humanitarian assistance in emergency situations. The control of diseases refers to States' individual and joint efforts to, inter alia, make available relevant technologies, using and improving epidemiological surveillance and data collection on a disaggregated basis, the implementation or enhancement of immunisation programmes and other strategies of infectious disease control.'

The prohibition on the arbitrary deprivation of life in the Covenant on Civil and Political Rights implies that cost effective health programmes aimed at preventing life-threatening diseases should neither be ended nor underfunded.[327]

CRC, Art 24(2)(c) – Combating Disease

5.110 In respect of the child's rights under Art 24(2)(c) of the CRC, in addition to providing specific guidance to how CRC can ensure the issue of HIV/AIDS is addressed in relation to children, the Committee on the Rights of the Child General Comment No 3 provides a wider demonstration of how the CRC can promote the treatment of disease.[328] In particular, the Committee has commented:[329]

'HIV/AIDS impacts so heavily on the lives of all children that it affects all their rights – civil, political, economic, social and cultural. The rights in the general principles of the Convention – the right to non-discrimination, (art. 2), the rights of the child to have her/his interest to be a primary consideration (art. 3), the right to life, survival and development (art. 6) and the rights to have her/his views respected (art. 12) – should therefore be the guiding themes in the consideration of HIV/AIDS at all levels of prevention, treatment, care and support. Adequate measures to address HIV/AIDS can be provided to children and adolescents only if their rights are fully respected. The most relevant rights in this regard are – in addition to the four above-referred general principles – the following: the right to access information and material aimed at the promotion of their social, spiritual and moral well-being, physical and mental health (art. 17), their right to preventive health care, sex education and family planning education and services (art. 24(f)), their right to an appropriate standard of living (art. 27) their rights to privacy (art. 6), the right not to be separated from parents (art. 9), the right to be protected from violence (art. 19), the rights to special protection and assistance by the State (art. 20), the rights of children with disabilities (art. 23), the right to health (art. 24), the right to social security, including social insurance (art. 26), the right to education and leisure (arts. 28 and 31), the right to be protected from economic and sexual exploitation and abuse, from illicit use of narcotic drugs (arts. 32, 33, 34 and 36), the right to be protected from abduction, sale and trafficking as well as torture or other cruel inhuman or degrading treatment or punishment (arts. 35 and 37) and the right to physical and psychological recovery and social reintegration (art. 39).'

5.111 Children should not serve as test subjects in medical research into disease until an intervention under investigation has been thoroughly tested on adults.[330] The child's right to participate and right to privacy are of particular relevance. The Committee on the Rights of the Child has commented that:[331]

'In line with the child's evolving capacities, consent of the child should be sought and consent may be sought from parents or guardians if necessary, but in all cases consent must

---

[327] Van Bueren *The International Law on the Rights of the Child* (1998) Martinus Nijhoff, p 303.

[328] Committee on the Rights of the Child General Comment No 3 *HIV/AIDS and the Rights of the Child* HRI/GEN/1/Rev 8, p 363.

[329] Paras 3 and 4. See also Children living in a world with AIDS (CRC/C/80).

[330] Committee on the Rights of the Child General Comment No 3 *HIV/AIDS and the Rights of the Child* HRI/GEN/1/Rev.8, para 26.

[331] Committee on the Rights of the Child General Comment No 3 *HIV/AIDS and the Rights of the Child* HRI/GEN/1/Rev.8, para 26.

be based on full disclosure of the risks and benefits of research to the child. States parties are further reminded to ensure that the privacy rights of children, in line with their obligation under article 16 of the Convention, are not inadvertently violated through the research process and that personal information about children which is accessed through research is, under no circumstances, used for purposes other than that for which consent was given. States parties must make every effort to ensure that children, and according to their evolving capacities their parents and/or their guardians, participate in decisions on research priorities and that a supportive environment is created for children that participate in such research.'

CRC, Art 24(2)(c) – Food and Clean Drinking Water

5.112 The reference to the provision of adequate nutritious foods in Art 24(2)(c) of the CRC does not create a new right to food for children but rather refines and focuses an existing right to food under the Covenant on Economic, Social and Cultural Rights.[332] Art 11(2) of the ICESCR states that:[333]

> 'The States Parties to the present Covenant recognise the fundamental right of everyone to be free from hunger, shall take, individually and through international cooperation, the measures, including specific programmes, which are needed (a) To improve methods of production, conservation and distribution of food by making full use of technical and scientific knowledge, by disseminating knowledge of the principles of nutrition and by developing or reforming agrarian systems in such a way as to achieve the most efficient development and utilisation of natural resources; (b) Taking into account the problems of both food-importing and food-exporting countries, to ensure an equitable distribution of world food supplies in relation to need.'

5.113 The right to adequate food has been interpreted as being broader than simply the right to freedom from hunger. It includes the right to acquire food in a manner compatible with human dignity and the right to reliability and sustainability in accessing food.[334] The Committee on Economic, Social and Cultural Rights has commented that the right to adequate food comprises physical and economic access at all times to adequate food or means for its procurement and therefore that the right should not be interpreted in a narrow or restrictive sense which equates it with a minimum package of calories, proteins and other specific nutrients.[335] Art 11(2) of the ICESCR does not mention nutritional value as a component of adequate food, although this must surely be implied, nor does it mention water.

5.114 Article 24(2)(c) of the CRC corrects in respect of children these omissions by requiring the '*provision of adequate nutritious foods and clean drinking-water*' as an element of the child's right to the highest attainable standard of health. Article 24(2)(e) makes specific reference to 'the advantages of breastfeeding'.[336] Breast milk has been highlighted by UNICEF and WHO as a key element of primary health care and as a basis for healthy growth and development.[337] Art 27(3) of the CRC cites nutrition as one

---

[332] Van Bueren *The International Law on the Rights of the Child* (1998) Martinus Nijhoff, p 315.

[333] See also UN Resolution 3348 (XXIX) of 17 December 1874 and Alston and Tomasevski (eds) *The Right to Food* (1984); Eide, Goonatilake, Gussor, Omawale (eds) *Food as a Human Right* (1984); Brownlie, I *The Human Right to Food* (1987) Commonwealth Secretariat.

[334] UN Doc E/CN.4/1989/SR.20.

[335] Committee on Economic, Social and Cultural Rights General Comment No 12 *The Right to Adequate Food (Art 11)* HRI/GEN/1/Rev.8, para 1 and see also paras 6 and 8.

[336] See **5.117** below.

[337] *Report on the WHO Collaborative Study on Breast Feeding* (1981) World Health Organisation, Geneva. See also the *International Code of Marketing of Breast Milk Substitutes* (1981) Resolution WHA 34.22, the Global Strategy for Infant and Young Child Feeding (WHA55/2002/REC/1, Annex 2 and the Innocenti Declaration on Infant and Young Child Feeding 2005.

of the areas in which support should be provided to parents and carers to implement the child's right to an adequate standard of living.[338] Pursuant to Art 24(2)(c) of the CRC consideration must also be given to the issues of childhood anorexia and bulimia as threats to childhood health.[339] In respect the right to clean drinking water, the Committee on Economic, Social and Cultural Rights has commented that:[340]

> 'The human right to water entitles everyone to sufficient, safe, acceptable, physically accessible and affordable water for personal and domestic uses … The adequacy of water should not be interpreted narrowly, by mere reference to volumetric quantities and technologies. Water should be treated as a social and cultural good, and not primarily as an economic good. The manner of the realisation of the right to water must also be sustainable, ensuring that the right can be realised for present and future generations.'

5.115 Whilst, as already highlighted, the enforcement of economic and social rights can be problematic, the Committee on Economic, Social and Cultural Rights has commented that 'Any person or group who is a victim of a violation of the right to adequate food should have access to effective judicial or other appropriate remedies at both national and international levels'.[341] The Supreme Court of India provides some examples of the enforcement of the right to food. In *Peoples Union for Civil Liberties v Union of India & Ors*[342] the court observed that:

> 'The anxiety of the Court is to see that the poor and the destitute and the weaker sections of society do not suffer from hunger and starvation. The prevention of the same is one of the prime responsibilities of the Government – whether Central or the State. Mere schemes without any implementation are of no use. What is important is that the food must reach the hungry.'

In recognising the right to food, the Supreme Court of India in *Peoples Union for Civil Liberties v Union of India & Ors* directed that all destitute people be identified and included in food based schemes, which the Court directed the Government to fully implement, together with further directions to better implement food security.[343] The Indian Supreme Court has also intervened to protect the right to water.[344] The African Commission on Human and Peoples' Rights has found a breach of the right to health under Art 16 of the African Charter on Human and Peoples' Rights based on a lack of safe drinking water, electricity and medicines.[345] Whilst these decisions go some way to establishing the justiciability of the right to food and water they also demonstrate that the right to food and water are most readily justiciable by reference to a groups rather than individuals. Significant problems might be expected in attempting to enforce such rights on behalf of individual children pursuant to Art 24(2)(c) of the CRC.[346]

---

[338] See also Art 25 of the Universal Declaration of Human Rights and Art 10(b) of the Declaration on Social Progress and Development 1969.

[339] Newell, P and Hodgkin, R *Implementation Handbook for the Convention on the Rights of the Child* (2008) 3rd edn, UNICEF, p 357 and Norway, CRC/C/15/Add.126, paras 36 and 37.

[340] Committee on Economic, Social and Cultural Rights General Comment No 15 *The Right to Water* HRI/GEN/1/Rev.8, paras 10–11.

[341] Committee on Economic, Social and Cultural Rights General Comment No 12 *The Right to Adequate Food (Art 11)* HRI/GEN/1/Rev.8, para 32.

[342] Writ Petition (Civil) 196 of 2001. See also *S Jaganath v Union of India* (1997) 2 SCC 87 and *Samatha v State of Andhra Pradesh* (1997) 8SCC 191, AIR 1997 SC 3297.

[343] The Committee on the Rights of the Child has also on occasion recommended national nutritional policies for children (see Bangladesh CRC/C/15/Add.74, para 41).

[344] *State of Karnataka v Appa Balu Ingale* (1995) Supp (4) SCC 469, AIR 1993 1126 (SC).

[345] *Union Interafricaine de Droits de l'Homme v Zaire* Communication 100/93, Ninth Activity Report 1995–1996, Annex VIII.

[346] But see Art 14(2)(c) of the African Charter on the Rights and Welfare of the Child which guarantees to the

CRC, Art 24(2)(c) – Impact of Environmental Pollution and Sanitation

5.116 In 1990 the UN General Assembly observed that environmental protection is indivisible from the achievement of full enjoyment of rights by all.[347] Art 24(2)(c) of the CRC highlights the dangers and risks of environmental pollution to the provision of adequate nutritious foods and clean drinking water for children.[348] The steps taken by States parties to realise the right under Art 12(1) of the ICESCR to the highest attainable standard of health include 'The improvement of all aspects of environmental and industrial hygiene'[349] The Committee on Economic, Social and Cultural Rights has commented that the improvement of all aspects of environmental and industrial hygiene includes 'the prevention and reduction of the population's exposure to harmful substances such as radiation and harmful chemicals or other detrimental environmental conditions that directly or indirectly impact upon human health'.[350]

CRC, Art 24(2)(e) – Education and Support in relation to Health

5.117 Article 24(2)(e) of the CRC requires State parties ensure that all segments of society, in particular parents and children, are informed, have access to education and are supported in the use of basic knowledge of child health and nutrition, the advantages of breastfeeding, hygiene and environmental sanitation and the prevention of accidents.[351] There is a self evident link between education and primary and preventative health care.[352] Whilst certain elements of Art 24(2)(e) necessarily require a significant exercise of parental duty, such as accident prevention, there remains an obligation on the State. In relation to the prevention of accidents for example, the State can influence transport and environmental issues and make provision for advice and financial support in the event of accidents.[353] Domestic law governing education may provide a means of enforcing the rights enshrined in Art 24(2)(e).[354] Art 17 of the CRC enshrining the right of the child to access to information promoting his or her physical

---

child the right to 'adequate nutrition and safe drinking water' in respect of which right the African Committee of Experts on the Rights and Welfare of the Child will have jurisdiction to receive individual communications under Art 44.

[347] *The Need to Ensure a Health Environment for the Well-being of Individuals* UN Resolution 45/94 (1990). For an erudite and comprehensive discussion of whether there is a general right to an environment of quality see Glazebrook, S *Human Rights and the Environment* (2009) 40 Victoria University of Wellington Law Review, p 293.

[348] See for example Philippines CRC/C/15/Add.259, paras 60–61 and Ecuador CRC/C/15/Add.93, para 24 and CRC/C/15/Add.262, para 54. Note also that Article 24(2)(e) points up the need to educate children and parents in respect of, and support the use of their basic knowledge of, environmental sanitation.

[349] ICESCR Art 12(2)(b).

[350] General Comment No 14 *The Right to the Highest Attainable Standard of Health* HRI/GEN/1/Rev.8, para 15. See also Principle 1 of the Stockholm Declaration of 1972 which states: 'Man has the fundamental right to freedom, equality and adequate conditions of life, in an environment of a quality that permits a life of dignity and well-being'. See further the General Assembly resolution 45/94 on the need to ensure a healthy environment for the well-being of individuals, Principle 1 of the Rio Declaration and regional human rights instruments such as Art 10 of the San Salvador Protocol to the American Convention on Human Rights.

[351] See also Art 28 (right to education) and Art 18 (requiring States to render assistance to the parents in the performance of their child-rearing duties).

[352] *World Health Organisation Global Strategy for Health for All by the Year 2000: 'Health for All' No 3* (1981) p 21. See also the Declaration of Alma-Ata and the Tehran Proclamation on Human Rights 1968, the UN Declaration on Social Progress and Development 1969 and the Plan of Action of the World Population Conference 1974.

[353] Newell, P and Hodgkin, R *Implementation Handbook for the Convention on the Rights of the Child* (2008) 3rd edn, UNICEF, p 361.

[354] See below **5.117**.

and mental health will also be of relevance to health education. In its General Comment on adolescent health and development, the Committee on the Rights of the Child observed:[355]

> 'Adolescents have the right to access adequate information essential for their health and development and for their ability to participate meaningfully in society. It is the obligation of States parties to ensure that all adolescent girls and boys, both in and out of school, are provided with, and not denied, accurate and appropriate information on how to protect their health and development and practice healthy behaviours. This should include information on the use and abuse, of tobacco, alcohol and other substances, safe and respectful social and sexual behaviours, diet and physical activity.'

CRC, Art 24(2)(f) – Preventative Health Care

5.118 Article 24(2)(f) requires the development by States Parties of preventive health care, guidance for parents and family planning education and services. Preventative health care measures will include immunisation. Family planning has proved to be a controversial topic in many jurisdictions.[356] The Committee on the Rights of the Child General Comments on HIV / AIDS[357] and on Adolescent Health and Development in the Context of the Convention[358] emphasise the need for uncensored information on sexuality and access to appropriate services. The UN General Assembly has adopted a resolution in relation to the reproductive and sexual health needs of children which provides for 'Governments, the private sector, non-governmental organisations and other actors of civil society' to:[359]

> 'Design and implement programmes with the full involvement of adolescents, as appropriate, to provide them with education, information and appropriate, specific, user-friendly and accessible services, without discrimination, to address effectively their reproductive and sexual health needs, taking into account their right to privacy, confidentiality, respect and informed consent, and the responsibilities, rights and duties of parents and legal guardians to provide in a manner consistent with the evolving capacities of the child appropriate direction and guidance in the exercise by the child of the rights recognised in the Convention on the Rights of the Child.'

CRC, Art 24(3) – Abolition of harmful traditional practices

5.119 Article 24(3) enjoins States Parties to take all effective and appropriate measures with a view to abolishing traditional practices which are prejudicial to the health of children.[360] The need to take 'all effective and appropriate measures' implies a balance between eradicating harmful traditional practices and the avoidance of discrimination

---

[355] Committee on the Rights of the Child General Comment No 4 *Adolescent Health an Development in the Context of the Convention on the Rights of the Child* HRI/GEN/1/Rev 8, p 382, para 22.

[356] See for example the reservation of the Holy See to Art 24(2)(f) which provides that it 'interprets the phrase 'family planning education and services' in Art 24(2) to mean only those methods of family planning which it considers morally acceptable, that is natural methods of family planning.'

[357] Committee on the Rights of the Child General Comment No 3 *HIV/AIS and the Rights of the Child* HRI/GEN/1/Rev 8, p 363.

[358] Committee on the Rights of the Child General Comment No 4 *Adolescent Health an Development in the Context of the Convention on the Rights of the Child* HRI/GEN/1/Rev 8, p 376. See also the Report of the International Conference on Population Development 1994 proposing as a principle that 'Reproductive healthcare should provide the widest range of services without any form of coercion' (A/CONF.171/13/ Principle 8).

[359] A/RES/S-23/3, para 79(f).

[360] The protection conferred by Art 24(3) is arguably weakened by the inclusion of the words 'with a view to' although such language is consistent with the principle of progressive realisation of economic and social rights.

and arbitrary measures. The phrase 'traditional practices prejudicial to the health of children' in Art 24(3) avoids specificity. However, practices in respect of children that should be reviewed in light of the principles under Art 24(3) extend to include all forms of genital mutilation, including female circumcision and male circumcision, traditional birth practices, binding, scarring, burning, branding, coin rubbing, tattooing, piercing, initiation ceremonies involving harmful practices, deliberate discriminatory treatment including the preferential feeding of male infants, witchcraft, violent forms of discipline and disciplinary techniques prejudicial to health.[361]

5.120 Article 24(3) was drafted due to particular concerns regarding female circumcision.[362] Female circumcision comes within this article rather those prohibiting torture, inhuman or degrading treatment by reason of the difficulty in demonstrating that such conduct constitutes the intentional infliction of pain for a specific purpose. Female circumcision is not classified as torture by the Inter-African Committee on Traditional Practices Affecting Women and Children. The African Charter on the Rights and Welfare of the Child likewise does not conceptualise female circumcision as torture but rather by Art 21 places a duty on States to eliminate harmful 'social and cultural practices' prejudicial to 'health or life' of the child and which are 'affecting the welfare, dignity, normal growth and development of the child'.[363] The aim underpinning this position is to eradicate the practice of female circumcision without decrying the intentions of the society or culture that practices it as a cultural or social activity.[364] However, Van Bueren argues convincingly that some female circumcision must come within the prohibition on torture, inhuman or degrading treatment where such action is against the will of the child.[365] Within this context, the Conseil d'Etat has accepted as a matter of principle that a girl who flees a country to avoid female circumcision will be entitled to refugee status based on a well founded fear of being persecuted by reason of her membership of a particular social group.[366] Male children forced into circumcision may also be accorded such status.[367]

Right to Highest Attainable Standard of Health under the ECHR

(i)   ECHR – Standards of Health and Art 2 ECHR

5.121 The ECHR does not articulate a right to the highest attainable standard of health. Pursuant to Art 2(1) of the ECHR States Parties must take 'appropriate steps to safeguard the lives of those within its jurisdiction'.[368] This positive duty has been primarily articulated within the context of life being deprived by criminal actions,

---

[361]   Newell, P and Hodgkin, R *Implementation Handbook for the Convention on the Rights of the Child* (2008) 3rd edn, UNICEF, p 344 and 373. See also UN Doc E/CN.4/Sub.2/1989/42 and the *Report of the Working Group on Traditional Practices Affecting the Health of Women and Children* (1986) UN Doc E/CN.4/1986/42 and United Nations General Assembly Resolution A/RES/56/128 19 December 2001. In relation to female circumcision see also Committee on the Elimination of Discrimination against Women General Recommendation No 14 *Female Circumcision* HRI/GEN/1/Rev 8, p 298. In relation to preferential treatment of male children see also the Committee on the Rights of the Child Report of the Eighth Session January 1995 CRC/C/38 p 49 and the Committee on the Elimination of Discrimination Against Women General Recommendation No 24 *Article 12 of the Convention (Women and Health)* HRI/GEN/1/Rev.8, pp 331 et seq.

[362]   Newell, P and Hodgkin, R *Implementation Handbook for the Convention on the Rights of the Child* (2008) 3rd edn, UNICEF, pp 344 and 371–372.

[363]   See OAU Doc.CAB/LEG/153/Rev 1.

[364]   Van Bueren *The International Law on the Rights of the Child* (1998) Martinus Nijhoff, p 309.

[365]   Van Bueren *The International Law on the Rights of the Child* (1998) Martinus Nijhoff, p 309.

[366]   See *Mademoiselle X* (1992) Public Law 196.

[367]   *BVerwG Bundesverwaltungsgericht* (1992) Federal Administrative Court 107 DVBI 828, p 829.

[368]   See *Osman v United Kingdom* (1998) 29 EHRR 245, [1999] 1 FLR 193, para 115.

although the duty has been held to extend to the need to take operational measures to prevent a person taking their own life.[369] Lord Rogers observed in *Savage v South Essex Partnership NHS Foundation Trust* that 'fundamentally, Art 2 requires a state to have in place a structure of laws which help to protect life'.[370] However, whether, subject to the need not to impose impossible or disproportionate burdens on the resources of the State,[371] this positive duty extends to encompass the need to ensure an adequate standard of health for children remains debatable.

5.122 It has been suggested that it is 'highly unlikely' that there is a general right to a particular standard of *healthcare* under Art 2 of the ECHR.[372] In *LCB v UK*[373] a women diagnosed with Leukemia contended that, by reason of the positive obligation on the State to protect her life under Art 2, the State had been under an obligation to warn her parents of the risks associated with her father's exposure to radiation during the British nuclear tests on Christmas Island in 1957 and 1958 and to monitor her own health during her lifetime. The Court held that:[374]

> 'the state could only have been required *of its own motion* to take these steps [ie provide advice to her parents and monitor her health] in relation to the applicant if it had appeared likely at that time that any such exposure of her father to radiation might have engendered a real risk to her health ... given the information available to the state at the relevant time concerning the likelihood of the applicant's father having been exposed to dangerous levels of radiation and of this having created a risk to her health, it could have been expected to act *of its own motion* to notify her parents of these matters or to take any other special action in relation to her.'

5.123 Thus, the positive duty under Art 2 of the ECHR to safeguard life is only likely to compel authorities to act to ensure the highest attainable standard of health through the provision of healthcare for a child where those authorities are on notice of a real risk to an individual child's health.[375] Summarising the effect of the decision in *LCB v UK* Lord Rogers observed in *Savage v South Essex Partnership NHS Foundation Trust* that:[376]

> 'The court proceeded on the basis that art 2 imposed on the United Kingdom authorities a general obligation to take appropriate steps to protect the lives of those within their jurisdiction. But the applicant was asserting that they had been obliged, of their own motion, to do something specific in respect of her, viz to warn her parents and monitor her health. The problem was that she was just one of millions of people within the jurisdiction of the United Kingdom. Resources are finite. The authorities could not have been expected to monitor the health of each and every individual. How to choose? The court held that the authorities would have been under this special obligation, of their own motion to advise the applicant's parents and to monitor her health, if it had appeared likely that any exposure of

---

[369] See also *Savage v South Essex Partnership NHS Foundation Trust* [2008] UKHL 74, [2009] 1 AC 681, [2009] 2 WLR 115, [2009] 1 All ER 1053.

[370] [2009] 1 All ER 1053, para 19.

[371] In *Osman v United Kingdom* (1998) 29 EHRR 245 the Court observed, para 116 that 'not every claimed risk to life can entail for the authorities a Convention requirement to take operational measures to prevent that risk from materialising.'

[372] Lord Pannick QC and others, *Human Rights, Law and Practice* (2009) 3rd edn, LexisNexis, p 150. See also *Buckley v United Kingdom* (1996) 23 EHRR 101, para 75 and *Hatton v United Kingdom* (2003) 27 EHRR 611, paras 97–103 in relation to the effect of the margin of appreciation.

[373] (1998) 4 BHRC 447, (1998) 27 EHRR 212.

[374] (1998) 4 BHRC 447, (1998) 27 EHRR 212, paras 38 and 41.

[375] But see *Wockel v Germany* (1997) 25 EHRR CD 156 and *Barratt v United Kingdom* (1997) 23 EHRR CD 185.

[376] [2009] 1 All ER 1053, para 22.

her father to radiation might have engendered 'a real risk' to her health. The trigger for the obligation would have been the authorities' awareness of the 'real risk'. On the facts, the court held that the obligation had not been triggered in respect of the applicant. In view of the trust's argument in the present case, it is worth noticing, however, that the decision in *LCB* suggests that, if triggered, the duty would have applied to the medical authorities, just as much as to any other public authorities.'

### (ii)	ECHR – Standards of Health and Environmental Hazards

5.124	In extreme cases it is arguable that the protection provided to children under Art 2 of the ECHR extends to the protection of a child's health from life-threatening environmental hazards.[377] The test is whether the state has done all that could reasonably be required of it to prevent a life from being avoidably put at risk.[378] In *Guerra and Others v Italy*[379] the Court found a violation of Art 8 of the ECHR where the authorities failed to provide local people with information about the risks to their health from a chemical factory. In 2004 the Fourth Ministerial Conference on Environment and Health for the European Region of the WHO agreed the Children's Environment and Health Action Plan for Europe.[380] This plan of action includes placing emphasis on policies, programmes and plans to improve the state of the physical environment, in particular through the integration of children's needs into housing, transport, infrastructure and planning, and actions to prevent and reduce exposures to environmental health hazards.[381]

### (iii)	ECHR – Health Education

5.125	Consideration of a child's right to education in respect of health issues under the ECHR has centred on arguments concerning the provision of sex education. Article 2 of the First Protocol to the ECHR enshrines the right to education.[382] In *Kjeldsen, Busk Madsen and Pedersen v Denmark*[383] the European Court of Human Rights held that States Parties may introduce sex education overriding parental objection provided that the lessons are presented in a balanced and objective manner, such education being intended to impart knowledge objectively and in the public interest. The Court

---

[377]	Lord Pannick QC and others, *Human Rights, Law and Practice* (2009) 3rd edn, LexisNexis, p 182 and see *Charan Lal Sahu v Union of India* [1990] LRC (Const) 638 (Ind Sup Ct) and *Indian Council for Enviro-Legal Action v Union of India* [1996] 2 LRC 226 (Ind Sup Ct).

[378]	*LCB v UK* (1998) 4 BHRC 447, (1998) 27 EHRR 212.

[379]	(1998) 26 ECHR 357. See also *López Ostra v Spain* [1994] ECHR 46.

[380]	EUR/04/5046267/7 25 June 2004.

[381]	EUR/04/5046267/7 25 June 2004, p 3. The specific goals agreed as part of the action plan were (a) to reduce the morbidity and mortality arising from gastrointestinal disorders and other health effects by ensuring that adequate measures are taken to improve access to safe and affordable water and adequate sanitation for all children, (b) to substantially reduce health consequences from accidents and injuries and pursue a decrease in morbidity from lack of adequate physical activity, by promoting safe, secure and supportive human settlements for all children, (c) to prevent and reduce respiratory disease due to outdoor and indoor air pollution, thereby contributing to a reduction in the frequency of asthmatic attacks, in order to ensure that children can live in an environment with clean air and (d) to reduce the risk of disease and disability arising from exposure to hazardous chemicals (such as heavy metals), physical agents (such as excessive noise) and biological agents and to hazardous working environments during pregnancy, childhood and adolescence.

[382]	See **13.106 et seq** below.

[383]	(1976) 1 EHRR 711. See also *Campbell and Cosnans v United Kingdom* (1981) 4 EHRR 293 and *Hartikainen v Finland* (40/1975), Doc A/36/40, p 147 (where the Human Rights Committee held that compulsory classes for children on religion and ethics violated Art 18(4) of the ICCPR).

emphasised that this does not affect 'the right of parents to enlighten and advise their children ... or to guide their children on a path in line with the parents' own religious or philosophical convictions'.[384]

(iv) The European Social Charter

5.126 The revised European Social Charter does impose a right to protection of health, Art 11 providing that States parties undertake, either directly or in co-operation with public or private organisations, to take appropriate measures to (a) remove as far as possible the causes of ill-health, (b) to provide advisory and educational facilities for the promotion of health and the encouragement of individual responsibility in matters of health and (c) to prevent as far as possible epidemic, endemic and other diseases, as well as accidents. Further, Art 13 of the Charter enshrines a right to medical assistance in circumstances where a person is 'without adequate resources and who is unable to secure such resources either by his own efforts or from other sources'. Article 13 requires that its provisions be extended to the nationals of other parties in accordance with European Convention on Social and Medical Assistance 1953.

Highest Attainable Standard of Health under European Union Law

5.127 Article 35 of the European Charter of Fundamental Rights provides that everyone has the right to access to preventative health care and the right to benefit from medical treatment under the conditions established by national laws and practices. Article 35 further provides that a high level of human health protection shall be ensured in the definition and implementation of all European Union policies and activities. Article 37 of the Charter provides that a high level of environmental protection and improvement to the quality of the environment must be integrated into the policies of the European Union and ensured in accordance with the principle of sustainable development.

Highest Attainable Standard of Health under Other Regional Instruments

5.128 Article 14(1) of the African Charter on the Rights and Welfare of the Child stipulates that 'Every child shall have the right to enjoy the best attainable state of physical, mental and spiritual health ...'. Art 14(2) of the Charter lists the particular healthcare aims supportive of this right, which reflect broadly those listed in Art 24(2) of the CRC. Article 16 of the African Charter on Human and Peoples' Rights provides that every individual shall have the right to enjoy the best attainable state of physical and mental health and that States parties to the present Charter shall take the necessary measures to protect the health of their people and to ensure that they receive medical attention when they are sick. As noted above, The African Commission on Human and Peoples' Rights has found a breach of the right to health based on a failure by the State to provide basic services such as safe drinking water, electricity and medicines.[385] Additionally, breaches have been found in relation to depriving medical assistance to detainees suffering from ill health.[386]

---

[384]   (1976) 1 EHRR 711, para 54. See also *Campbell and Cosnans v United Kingdom* (1981) 4 EHRR 293. See **10.87–10.94** below.

[385]   *Union Interafricaine de Droits de l'Homme v Zaire* Communication 100/93, Ninth Activity Report 1995–1996, Annex VIII.

[386]   *Media Rights Agenda and Constitutional Rights Project v Nigeria* Communications 105/93, 128/94 and 152/96.

5.129 Article 25 of the Ibero-American Convention on Young People's Rights stipulates that 'The States Parties recognise the right of youth to a comprehensive, high-quality health'. Pursuant to Art 25(2), the right includes free primary health care, preventive education, nutrition, specialised health care and care of youth health, promotion of sexual and reproductive health, research on young age health problems, information and prevention of alcoholism, nicotine poisoning and the improper use of drugs. Article 23(1) of the Ibero-American Convention provides that States Parties must recognise that the right to education also includes the right to sexual education. Article 10 of the Additional Protocol to the American Convention on Human Rights in the Area of Economic, Social and Cultural Rights stipulates that everyone shall have the right to health, understood to mean the enjoyment of the highest level of physical, mental and social well-being. To secure this right, Art 10 emphasises primary healthcare, the extension of health care to all individuals, immunisation against principle infectious diseases, prevention of endemic, occupational and other disease, health education and the health needs of high risk groups and the poor.[387] The Additional Protocol also enshrines the right to a healthy environment[388] and the right to food.[389]

5.130 The Revised Arab Charter on Human Rights provides at Art 39(1) in relation to the right to the highest attainable standard of health that: 'The State Parties shall recognise the right of everyone to the enjoyment of the highest attainable standard of physical and mental health and the right of every citizen to enjoy free and non-discriminatory access to health services and health care centres'. The steps to be taken to ensure this right pursuant to Art 39(2) include the prevention and cure of disease, health education, the deprecation of traditional practices harmful to health, the provision of basic nutrition and clean water, the eradication of environmental pollution and unsanitary conditions and the eradication of tobacco, drugs and psychotropic substances.

Highest Attainable Standard of Health under Domestic Law

(i)   Domestic Law – Healthcare and Medical Treatment

5.131 The National Service Framework for Children, Young People and Maternity Services is a national programme designed to improve children's health.[390] The Framework sets national standards for children's health and social care.[391] The Framework is designed to play a key role in achieving the outcomes set out in Every Child Matters. The Framework introduces national standards for children's health, including specific standards for children and young people who are ill,[392] children in

---

[387]   Article 10(2)(a)–(f).
[388]   Article 11 ('Everyone shall have the right to live in a healthy environment and to have access to basic public services').
[389]   Article 12 ('Everyone has the right to adequate nutrition which guarantees the possibility of enjoying the highest level of physical, emotional and intellectual development. In order to promote the exercise of this right and eradicate malnutrition, the States Parties undertake to improve methods of production, supply and distribution of food, and to this end, agree to promote greater international cooperation in support of the relevant national policies').
[390]   *National Service Framework for Children, Young People and Maternity Services – Executive Summary* (2004) Department of Health. See also *Healthy Lives, Brighter Futures: the Strategy for Children and Young People's Health* (2009) Department for Children, Schools and Families and Department of Health.
[391]   *Healthy Lives, Brighter Futures: the Strategy for Children and Young People's Health* (2009) Department for Children, Schools and Families and Department of Health, pp 6–7. See also *National Service Framework for Children, Young People and Maternity Services – Core Standards* (2004) Department of Health.
[392]   *National Service Framework for Children, Young People and Maternity Services – Children and Young People who are Ill* (2004) Department of Health.

hospital,[393] disabled children and young people and those with complex health needs,[394] the mental health and psychological well-being of children and young people,[395] and medicines for children and young people.[396] The policy also covers maternity care before or during pregnancy, throughout birth and for the first 3 months of parenthood.[397] The Framework emphasises the importance of primary care and identifies key issues in the delivery of primary health care to children.[398] Notwithstanding the National Service Framework, significant issues remain for children in within the jurisdiction in securing their right to highest attainable standard of health.[399]

5.132 Even where a child's life expectancy is in issue, the domestic courts have held that they cannot interfere with a health authorities decisions concerning the allocation of a limited treatment budget on the basis of the child's right to life.[400] It is likely that the same answer would be returned in respect of any attempt to challenge the deployment of resources on the basis of a breach of the child's right to the highest attainable standard of health.

(ii) Domestic Law – Immunisation

5.133 The immunisation of children within the domestic jurisdiction is not compulsory. However, pursuant to the Health Protection (Vaccination) Regulations 2009,[401] which came into force on 1 April 2009, the Secretary of State is required to ensure that the recommendations of the Joint Committee on Vaccination and Immunisation[402] are implemented so far as is reasonably practicable where that recommendation meets certain conditions.[403]

(iii) Domestic Law – Environmental Health

5.134 Domestic law provides a comprehensive body of legislation, policy, regulation and guidance in relation to issues of environmental health which impact on children a

---

[393] *Getting the Right Start: National Service Framework for Children, Young People and Maternity Services – Standard for Hospital Services* (2003) Department of Health.

[394] *National Service Framework for Children, Young People and Maternity Services – Disabled Children and Young People and those with Complex Health Needs* (2004) Department of Health.

[395] *National Service Framework for Children, Young People and Maternity Services – The Mental Health and Psychological Well-being of Children and Young People* (2004) Department of Health.

[396] *National Service Framework for Children, Young People and Maternity Services – Medicines for Children and Young People* (2004) Department of Health.

[397] *National Service Framework for Children, Young People and Maternity Services – Maternity Services* (2004) Department of Health.

[398] *National Service Framework for Children, Young People and Maternity Services – Key Issues for Primary Care* (2004) Department of Health.

[399] See Children's Rights Alliance for England, *State of Children's Rights in England* (2008), pp 25–27. This includes difficulties that may not immediately be associated with the United Kingdom including cases of under-nutrition (see House of Commons Written Answer, 6 October 2008, Hansard Column 441W).

[400] *R v Cambridge Health Authority, ex p B* sub nom *R v Cambridge District Health Authority, ex p B* [1995] 2 All ER 129, [1995] 1 WLR 898, [1995] 2 FCR 485, [1995] 1 FLR 1055.

[401] SI 2009/38.

[402] The Joint Committee on Vaccination and Immunisation was set up in 1963 and provides Ministers with evidence based advice on matters relating to communicable diseases, preventable and potentially preventable through vaccination and immunisation.

[403] Reg 2(3). The conditions are that the recommendation (a) relates to a new provision for vaccination under a national vaccination programme or changes to existing provision under such a programme, (b) is made by the Joint Committee, (c) is in response to a question referred to the Joint Committee by the Secretary of State, (d) is based on an assessment which demonstrates cost effectiveness and (e) is not related to a vaccination in respect of travel or occupational health. See also the NHS Constitution (2009) Department of Health, p 6.

detailed account of which is beyond the scope of this work.[404] In response to the Children's Environment and Health Action Plan for Europe[405] the Government has published a Children's Environment and Health Strategy for the UK.[406] This strategy seeks to 'make recommendations on the measures necessary to improve children's and young peoples' health by improving their environment, and to encourage a coherent cross-government approach to these issues'.[407]

(iv) Domestic Law – Health Education

5.135 Health, sex and relationship education in the United Kingdom is not currently part of the statutory curriculum. Where sex and relationship education is given, the local education authority, governing body and head teacher must take such steps as are practicable to secure that it is given in such a manner as to encourage pupils to have due regard to moral considerations and the value of family life.[408] There must be a written policy in respect of such education.[409] Parents may remove their children from sex and relationship education classes save where it is taught as part of a science lesson.[410] On 23 October 2008 the Government announced its intention to include 'Personal, Social, Health and Economic' education (PHSE) as part of the statutory curriculum. Following report from Sir Alasdair Macdonald[411] the Government announced on 28 April 2009 that PHSE would become a compulsory part of the primary and secondary school curriculum from September 2011. PHSE covers nutrition and physical activity; drugs, alcohol and tobacco; sex and relationships; emotional health and wellbeing; safety; careers; work-related learning; and personal finance.[412]

(v) Domestic Law – Vulnerable Children

5.136 The domestic legislation concerning children places specific duties on local authorities relevant to the standard of health and development of children. Specifically, s 17 of the Children Act 1989 requires a local authority to provide services for children in need. In the context of the right to the highest attainable standard of health, a child will be considered 'in need' where he or she is unlikely to achieve or maintain, or to have the opportunity of achieving and maintaining, a reasonable standard of health or development without the provision for them of services by the local authority under Part III of the Children Act 1989, or his or her health or development is likely to be significantly impaired, or further impaired, without the provision of such services, or he or she is disabled.[413]

---

[404] The provisions include the Environmental Protection Act 1990, the Environment Act 1995, the Waste Minimisation Act 1998, the Water Act 2003, the Clean Neighbourhoods and Environment Act 2005, the Noise Act 2006, the Climate Change Act 2008, the Air Quality (England) Regulations 2000, the Air Quality Limit Values Regulations 2001, SI 2001/2315, the Air Quality Limit Values Regulations 2003, SI 2003/2121, the Air Quality Standards Regulations 2007, SI 2007/64, the Genetically Modified (Contained Use) Regulations 2000 and the Genetically Modified (Deliberate Release) Regulations 2002.

[405] EUR/04/5046267/7 25 June 2004. See **5.124** above.

[406] (2009) Health Protection Agency.

[407] (2009) Health Protection Agency, p 5.

[408] Education Act 1996, s 403(1).

[409] Education Act 1996, s 404.

[410] Education Act 1996, s 405(1). This parental veto has been the subject of criticism (see Children's Rights Alliance for England, *State of Children's Rights in England* (2008), p 27.

[411] Macdonald, A *Independent Review of the proposal to make Personal, Social, Health and Economic (PHSE) education statutory* (2009) Department of Children, Schools and Families.

[412] Macdonald, A *Independent Review of the proposal to make Personal, Social, Health and Economic (PHSE) education statutory* (2009) Department of Children, Schools and Families, p 7.

[413] Children Act 1989, s 17(10).

Rights Supportive of Survival and Development – Right to an Adequate Standard of Living

5.137 Article 25 of the Universal Declaration of Human Rights provides as follows in relation to standard of living:

> 'Everyone has the right to a standard of living adequate for the health and well-being of himself and of his family, including food, clothing, housing and medical care and necessary social services ...'

An adequate standard of living is crucial in the realisation of the child's right to survival and development, living conditions affecting as they do the child's physical, mental, spiritual, moral and social development. The pre-amble to the CRC specifically recognises 'the importance of international cooperation for improving the living conditions of children in every country'. The child's right to an adequate standard of living will touch upon housing, living conditions, environmental health, clothing, food and water, health provision, financial provision and education. In this respect there is a considerable overlap between the right to an adequate standard of living and the right to the highest attainable standard of health.

Right to Adequate Standard of Living under the CRC

(i)   CRC, Art 27

5.138 Article 27 of the CRC articulates the child's right to an adequate standard of living in the following terms:

> '1. States Parties recognise the right of every child to a standard of living adequate for the child's physical, mental, spiritual, moral and social development.
>
> 2. The parent(s) or others responsible for the child have the primary responsibility to secure, within their abilities and financial capacities, the conditions of living necessary for the child's development.
>
> 3. States Parties, in accordance with national conditions and within their means, shall take appropriate measures to assist parents and others responsible for the child to implement this right and shall in case of need provide material assistance and support programmes, particularly with regard to nutrition, clothing and housing.
>
> 4. States Parties shall take all appropriate measures to secure the recovery of maintenance for the child from the parents or other persons having financial responsibility for the child, both within the State Party and from abroad. In particular, where the person having financial responsibility for the child lives in a State different from that of the child, States Parties shall promote the accession to international agreements or the conclusion of such agreements, as well as the making of other appropriate arrangements.'

5.139 The International Covenant on Economic, Social and Cultural Rights also enshrines the right to an adequate standard of living in Art 11, which article states:

> '1. The States Parties to the present Covenant recognise the right of everyone to an adequate standard of living for himself and his family, including adequate food, clothing and housing, and to the continuous improvement of living conditions. The States Parties will take appropriate steps to ensure the realisation of this right, recognising to this effect the essential importance of international co-operation based on free consent.'

5.140 The Art 27 right to an adequate standard of living under the CRC imposes on States parties a positive obligation to give effect to the right.[414] The Committee on the Rights of the Child has commented, by reference to the rights of young children, that:[415]

> 'All possible means should be employed, including 'material assistance and support programmes' for children and families (art. 27.3), in order to assure to young children a basic standard of living consistent with rights.'

Further, Art 4 of the CRC requires that State Parties implement Art 27 'to the maximum extent of their available resources and, where needed, within the framework of international co-operation'. Within this context, the Art 27 right to an adequate standard of living reiterates the 'progressive nature' of its implementation by the word 'recognise' in Art 27(1), the words 'in accordance with national conditions and within their means, shall take appropriate measures' in Art 27(3) and the words 'all appropriate measures' in Art 27(4). Hodgkin and Newell doubt however that the qualification in Art 27(4) dilutes the overarching principle contained in Art 4 to meet the economic rights of children 'to the maximum extent ... of available resources'.[416]

(ii) CRC, Art 27(1) – 'Adequate standard of living'

5.141 The standard of living for a child required by Art 27(1) of the CRC is that required to ensure a child's physical, mental, spiritual, moral and social development. The concept of an adequate standard of living encompasses a child's global development and is not simply limited to the child's health. As such, the CRC sees the child's right to an adequate standard of living as extending beyond the basic elements fundamental to the child's survival.[417] Above all, it recognises that a child's development cannot be divorced from and is intrinsically linked to his or her standard of living.[418]

5.142 Whilst the term 'adequate' is subjective, having regard to the requirement in Art 6(2) to ensure 'to the maximum extent possible' the survival and development of the child and the requirement in Art 24(1) to ensure 'the highest attainable standard of health', an 'adequate' standard of living equates to the minimum standard required to promote the child's maximum development and achieve for him or her the highest attainable standard of health.[419] Characteristically for the CRC, the term 'adequate' also makes clear that the standard sought is not perfection but rather that which is realistically achievable. As has been observed, 'The UNCRC is about children's rights to basic necessities and to an 'adequate standard of living', but not to luxuries and passing fads'.[420]

---

[414] CRC, Art 27(3).
[415] Committee on the Rights of the Child General Comment No 7 *Implementing Child Rights in Early Childhood* HRI/GEN/1/Rev 8, p 443, para 26.
[416] Newell, P and Hodgkin, R *Implementation Handbook for the Convention on the Rights of the Child* (2008) 3rd edn, UNICEF, p 395.
[417] Van Bueren *The International Law on the Rights of the Child* (1998) Martinus Nijhoff, p 317.
[418] Newell, P and Hodgkin, R *Implementation Handbook for the Convention on the Rights of the Child* (2008) 3rd edn, UNICEF, p 394.
[419] Candappa, M *Human Rights and Refugee Children in the UK* in Franklin, B (ed) *The New Handbook of Children's Rights* (2002) Routlege, p 226.
[420] Alderson, P *Young Children's Rights – Exploring Beliefs, Principles and Practice* (2008) 2nd edn, JKP, p 37.

(iii) CRC, Art 27(2) – Responsibility of Parents

5.143 Article 27(2) of the CRC requires that the parent(s) or others responsible for the child have the primary responsibility to secure, within their abilities and financial capacities, the conditions of living necessary for the child's development.[421] Art 27(2) links the child's right to development with the parents' responsibility to secure that development.[422] Art 27(2) stipulates that parents or others responsible for the child shall have 'primary' to secure living conditions necessary for the child's development, recognising the continuing duty of the State towards the child as articulated in Art 27(4).

5.144 The provisions of Art 27(2) are expressly qualified by reference to action by the parents or other responsible for the child 'within their abilities and financial capacities', emphasising the need for States parties to assist parents who lack ability or financial capacity to ensure conditions of living necessary for the child's development. Within the context of the obligation on parents, with the support of the State, to secure an adequate standard of living for the child pursuant to Art 27(2), the State retains an overarching obligation under Art 6(2) to ensure to the maximum extent possible the survival and development of the child.

(iii) CRC, Art 27(4) – Enforcement of Child Maintenance Responsibilities

5.145 Financial provision for children is vital to assuring an adequate standard of living. This includes children whose parents, or those with responsibility for them, live apart by reason of relationship breakdown or economic circumstance. Article 27(4) of the CRC requires that:

> 'States Parties shall take all appropriate measures to secure the recovery of maintenance for the child from the parents or other persons having financial responsibility for the child, both within the State Party and from abroad. In particular, where the person having financial responsibility for the child lives in a State different from that of the child, States Parties shall promote the accession to international agreements or the conclusion of such agreements, as well as the making of other appropriate arrangements.'

States parties should seek ensure the dissemination of widespread knowledge of laws relating to maintenance[423] and to avoid delays within systems designed to secure the recovery of maintenance for the child.[424] To ensure the recovery of maintenance, the Committee on the Rights of the Child has suggested the establishment of a central fund to ensure payment of overdue child maintenance coupled with enforcement procedures which ensure the automatic deduction of maintenance from the income of defaulting parties.[425] It should be noted that the 'common responsibility' principle in Art 18(1) of

---

[421] Fortin observes that the provisions of Art 27 'are conservative and reflect the way childcare is currently organised throughout most of world. It accepts that children are brought up in family units and that governments should leave them to a degree of privacy, expecting parents to provide for children out of their own resources.' (Fortin, J *Children's Rights and the Developing Law* (2009) 3rd edn, Cambridge, p 334).

[422] See also CRC, Art 5 (States Parties shall respect the responsibilities, rights and duties of parents ... to provide ... appropriate direction and guidance in the exercise by the child of the rights recognised in the ... Convention), Art 7 (The child ... shall have the right ... as far as possible ... to know and be cared for by his or her parents) and Art 18 (States Parties shall use their best efforts to ensure recognition of the principle that both parents have common responsibilities for the upbringing and development of the child. Parents or, as the case may be, legal guardians, have the primary responsibility for the upbringing and development of the child. The best interests of the child will be their basic concern). See also CRC, Art 3(2).

[423] See Côte d'Ivoire CRC/C/15/Add.155, para 33 and Zambia CRC/C/15/Add.206, paras 40 and 41.

[424] See Ukraine CRC/C/15/Add.191, para 42.

[425] See Republic of Korea CRC/C/15/Add. 197, para 47.

the CRC, stipulating that both parents have a common responsibility for the upbringing and development of their child, requires the term 'maintenance' to be read broadly, encompassing much more than simply financial assistance and requiring both parents to play an active part in their child's upbringing.[426]

5.146 Article 27(4) requires States Parties to take appropriate measures to recover maintenance from parents and persons responsible for the child who are abroad.[427] The provisions applicable within the domestic jurisdiction are dealt with below.[428]

5.147 In respect of Art 27(4) care needs to be taken to maintain focus on the Art 3 best interests of the child in order ensure that the issue of maintenance is not used to the detriment of the child, for example by a parent seeking to exert financial pressure to secure contact unwanted by the child or by parents seeking to obtain financial advantage by retaining residence of the child.[429]

(iv)   CRC, Art 27(3) – Responsibility of States Parties

5.148 It has been observed that, since children do not choose their parents and may not be able to influence their household circumstances, as innocent victims, they should not be allowed to suffer serious deprivations arising from the conduct or situation of their carers.[430] Art 27(3) recognises that there will be circumstances where parents or others with responsibility for the child are unable to meet their responsibilities pursuant to Art 27(2) and will require State assistance to do so to ensure the integrity of the child's rights under Art 27(1). Thus Art 27(3) provides that:

> 'States Parties, in accordance with national conditions and within their means, shall take appropriate measures to assist parents and others responsible for the child to implement this right and shall in case of need provide material assistance and support programmes, particularly with regard to nutrition, clothing and housing.'

5.149 The effect of Art 27(3) is such that where parents are unable to ensure conditions of living necessary for the child's development the State is under an obligation to assist within its means.[431] The primary State responsibility under Art 27(3) is to secure the living conditions of children as a group rather than to assist individual children. The emphasis on assisting parents and others responsible for the child helps reinforce the principle that parents or, as the case may be, legal guardians, have the primary responsibility for the upbringing and development of the child such that family life is not unduly encroached upon.[432] Art 27(3) is a 'safety net' provision rather than one

---

[426]   Newell, P and Hodgkin, R *Implementation Handbook for the Convention on the Rights of the Child* (2008) 3rd edn, UNICEF, p 235.

[427]   See also E/CN.4/1988/28, p 17.

[428]   See below **5.175–5.177**.

[429]   Newell, P and Hodgkin, R *Implementation Handbook for the Convention on the Rights of the Child* (2008) 3rd edn, UNICEF, p 401. For this reason domestic courts deal with issues of contact and residence separately from issues of maintenance and ancillary relief.

[430]   Adam, S and Brewer, M *Supporting Families: The Financial Costs and Benefits of Children Since 1975* (2004) Policy Press, pp 4–5; Hirsch, D *What Will it Take to End Child Poverty? Firing on All Cylinders* (2006) Joseph Rowntree Trust, p 15.

[431]   The 'means' qualification was introduced into the text of the CRC by the United Kingdom delegate (see E/CN.4/1985/64, pp 8–10).

[432]   See Newell, P and Hodgkin, R *Implementation Handbook for the Convention on the Rights of the Child* (2008) 3rd edn, UNICEF, p 397 and Art 18 of the CRC.

designed to take children into the care of the State.[433] However, the obligation to provide material assistance is also one that requires more than doing the bare minimum, as the assistance must be sufficient to foster the child's physical, mental, spiritual, moral and social development.[434]

5.150 In addition to the provisions of Art 27, Art 23(1) of the CRC is relevant to achieving an adequate standard of living for disabled children. Article 23(1) provides that:

'States Parties recognise that a mentally or physically disabled child should enjoy a full and decent life, in conditions which ensure dignity, promote self-reliance and facilitate the child's active participation in the community.'

5.151 The UN Convention on the Rights of Persons with Disabilities is also relevant to securing the right of children with disabilities to an adequate standard of living. In particular, Art 28 of the Convention stipulates that:

'1. States Parties recognise the right of persons with disabilities to an adequate standard of living for themselves and their families, including adequate food, clothing and housing, and to the continuous improvement of living conditions, and shall take appropriate steps to safeguard and promote the realisation of this right without discrimination on the basis of disability.

2. States Parties recognise the right of persons with disabilities to social protection and to the enjoyment of that right without discrimination on the basis of disability, and shall take appropriate steps to safeguard and promote the realisation of this right, including measures:

(a) To ensure equal access by persons with disabilities to clean water services, and to ensure access to appropriate and affordable services, devices and other assistance for disability-related needs;
(b) To ensure access by persons with disabilities, in particular women and girls with disabilities and older persons with disabilities, to social protection programmes and poverty reduction programmes;
(c) To ensure access by persons with disabilities and their families living in situations of poverty to assistance from the State with disability-related expenses, including adequate training, counseling, financial assistance and respite care;
(d) To ensure access by persons with disabilities to public housing programmes;
(e) To ensure equal access by persons with disabilities to retirement benefits and programmes.'

5.152 The Committee on Economic, Social and Cultural Rights, in its General Comment No 5 on persons with disabilities states that, in relation to the right to an adequate standard of living under Art 11(1) of the ICESCR:[435]

'In addition to the need to ensure that persons with disabilities have access to adequate food, accessible housing and other basic material needs, it is also necessary to ensure that 'support services, including assistive devices' are available 'for persons with disabilities, to assist them

---

[433] Walsh, B *The United Nations Convention on the Rights of the Child* (1991) 5 International Journal of Law and the Family 170, p 173.

[434] Kimbrough, R *Entitlement to 'Adequacy': Application of Article 27 to US Law* in Andrews, A.B. and Kaufman, N.H. (eds) *Implementing the UN Convention on the Rights of the Child: A Standard of Living Adequate for Development* (1999) Praeger, p 169–170.

[435] Committee on the Economic, Social and Cultural Rights General Comment No 5 *Persons with Disabilities* HRI/GEN/1/Rev 8, p 32, para 33.

to increase their level of independence in their daily living and to exercise their rights'.[436] The right to adequate clothing also assumes a special significance in the context of persons with disabilities who have particular clothing needs, so as to enable them to function fully and effectively in society. Wherever possible, appropriate personal assistance should also be provided in this connection. Such assistance should be undertaken in a manner and spirit which fully respect the human rights of the person(s) concerned. Similarly, as already noted by the Committee in paragraph 8 of General Comment No 4 (Sixth session, 1991), the right to adequate housing includes the right to accessible housing for persons with disabilities.'

5.153 Taken together with Art 22(1) of the CRC, Art 27 of the CRC should likewise ensure that the basic needs of refugee children are provided for such as to secure for them an adequate standard of living.[437]

5.154 In meeting the obligations under Art 27(3) to take appropriate measures to assist parents and others responsible for the child to secure for the child an adequate standard of living, States Parties must, in addition to recovery of maintenance pursuant to Art 27(4), pay particular regard to nutrition, clothing and housing.[438] The use of the word 'particularly' in Art 27(3) indicates that the list of particular factors which should be the subject of State support is not however limited to nutrition, clothing and housing.

CRC, Art 27(3) – Nutrition

5.155 The requirement to ensure provision of adequate nutritious food under Art 24(2)(c) has been dealt with above.[439] The principles articulated there will be relevant to the Art 27(3) requirement concerning nutrition. By the use of the word 'nutrition' on its own Art 27(3) places emphasis on the nutritional aspect of food rather than its provision *per se*. It recognises by reference to the nutritional value of food that children will fail to make any significant progress on the key indicators of an adequate standard of living, namely their physical, mental, spiritual, moral and social development, if they are malnourished.[440]

CRC, Art 27(3) – Clothing

5.156 The material assistance provided by States Parties pursuant to Art 27(3) should encompass the provision of suitable clothing.[441]

---

[436] Standard Rules on the Equalisation of Opportunities for Persons with Disabilities, r 4.

[437] Candappa, M *Human Rights and Refugee Children in the UK* in Franklin, B (ed) *The New Handbook of Children's Rights* (2002) Routlege, p 226. See also United Nations High Commissioner for Refugees *Refugee Children: Guidelines on Protection and Care* (1994) Geneva: UNHCR and the UN Convention Relating to the Status of Refugees Art 21 ('As regards housing, the Contracting States, in so far as the matter is regulated by laws or regulations or is subject to the control of public authorities, shall accord to refugees lawfully staying in their territory treatment as favourable as possible and, in any event, not less favourable than that accorded to aliens generally in the same circumstances'), Art 23 ('The Contracting States shall accord to refugees lawfully staying in their territory the same treatment with respect to public relief and assistance as is accorded to their nationals') and Art 24(1)(b) relating to social security.

[438] The rights dealt with in Art 24(2) in respect of clean drinking water, health, education, good hygiene and sanitation, breastfeeding and preventative action in relation to environmental pollution, child accidents and harmful traditional practices are also each relevant to ensuring an adequate standard of living. In addition, Arts 29 and 31 of the CRC are relevant to as are articles which contribute to the social, moral, mental and spiritual development of the child (see Arts 12, 17, 5, 7, 8, 9, 18, 20, 21, 29 and 30 of the CRC).

[439] See **5.112–5.115** above.

[440] Newell, P and Hodgkin, R *Implementation Handbook for the Convention on the Rights of the Child* (2008) 3rd edn, UNICEF, p 398.

[441] See for example the recommendation of the Committee on the Rights of the Child that street children in Bosnia-Herzegovina be provided with clothing, in addition to nutrition, housing, health-care and education opportunities (Bosnia-Herzegovina CRC/C/15/Add.260, para 66).

CRC, Art 27(3) – Housing

5.157 In 2002 the UN General Assembly special session on children concluded in respect of housing that:[442]

> 'Adequate housing fosters family integration, contributes to social equity and strengthens the feeling of belonging, security and human solidarity, which are essential for the well-being of children. Accordingly, we will attach a high priority to overcoming the housing shortage and other infrastructure needs, particularly for children in marginalised peri-urban and remote rural areas.'

5.158 In addition to the housing provision contained in Art 27(3) of the CRC, Art 11 of the Covenant on Economic, Social and Cultural Rights provides that 'States Parties to the present Covenant recognise the right of everyone to an adequate standard of living for himself and his family, including adequate ... housing, and to the continuous improvement of living conditions'. The Committee on Economic, Social and Cultural Rights has formulated a General Comment on the right to adequate housing pursuant to Art 11(1) of the ICESCR.[443] The Committee makes clear that Art 11(1) right to adequate housing 'individuals, as well as families, are entitled to adequate housing regardless of age, economic status, group or other affiliation or status and other such factors'.[444] The Committee further makes clear that:[445]

> '... the right to housing should not be interpreted in a narrow or restrictive sense which equates it with, for example, the shelter provided by merely having a roof over one's head or views shelter exclusively as a commodity. Rather it should be seen as the right to live somewhere in security, peace and dignity.'

Legal security of tenure, availability of services, materials, facilities and infrastructure, affordability, habitability, accessibility, location and cultural adequacy are all emphasised as key elements of the right to adequate housing.[446] Pursuant to the right to adequate housing under Art 11 of the ICESCR 'States parties must give due priority to those social groups living in unfavourable conditions by giving them particular consideration'.[447]

5.159 The General Comment of the Committee on Economic, Social and Cultural Rights on the right to adequate housing has been endorsed by the Committee on the Rights of the Child in its statement to the Second UN Conference on Human Settlements, Habitat II held in Istanbul, in which the Committee observed that:[448]

---

[442] United Nations, Report of the Ad Hoc Committee of the Whole of the twenty-seventh special session of the General Assembly, 2002, A/S-27/19/Rev.1, para 27.

[443] Committee on Economic, Social and Cultural Rights General Comment No 4 *The Right to Adequate Housing (Art 11(1) of the Covenant)* HRI/GEN/1/Rev 8, p 19.

[444] Committee on Economic, Social and Cultural Rights General Comment No 4 *The Right to Adequate Housing (Art 11(1) of the Covenant)* HRI/GEN/1/Rev 8, p 19, para 6.

[445] Committee on Economic, Social and Cultural Rights General Comment No 4 *The Right to Adequate Housing (Art 11(1) of the Covenant)* HRI/GEN/1/Rev 8, p 19, para 7.

[446] Committee on Economic, Social and Cultural Rights General Comment No 4 *The Right to Adequate Housing (Art 11(1) of the Covenant)* HRI/GEN/1/Rev 8, p 19, para 8. See also CESCR General Comment No 7 1997, HRI/GEN/1/Rev 8, p 46, para 10 which emphasises that enforced evictions have a disproportionate effect on children.

[447] Committee on Economic, Social and Cultural Rights General Comment No 4 *The Right to Adequate Housing (Art 11(1) of the Covenant)* HRI/GEN/1/Rev 8, p 19, para 11.

[448] Committee on the Rights of the Child, Report on the eleventh session, January 1996, CRC/C/50, pp 77 and 79.

'The Committee believes that ... the right to housing should not be interpreted in a narrow or restrictive sense, but has to be interpreted as a right to live somewhere in security, peace and dignity ... It is important to emphasise that the rights to housing of children are interrelated to and interdependent with nearly every other right contained in the Convention. This underlines the comprehensive and holistic thrust of the Convention, as well as of its process of implementation and monitoring.'

5.160 The right not to be subjected to arbitrary or unlawful interference with a person's privacy, family, home or correspondence constitutes a very important dimension in defining the right to adequate housing.[449] Art 16(1) of the CRC provides that no child shall be subjected to arbitrary or unlawful interference with his or her privacy, family, home or correspondence.[450] This protection will include the prohibition of interference with the amenities provided by the home.[451]

5.161 Although housing is singled out in Art 27, children's needs and views are vital in respect of the whole built environment and crucial in relation to areas used primarily by children, including schools, play areas, residential institutions, clinics and hospitals.[452] The Children's Rights and Habitat Declaration,[453] prepared and delivered at the UNICEF and UNCHS/Habitat meeting in New York in February 1996, identifies the following needs of children in respect of the built environment:[454]

'The child's need for a secure, safe, healthy environment begins in the prenatal period. A healthy home includes a safe and sufficient water supply, safe and accessible sanitation and waste management; also protection from traffic and other hazards, freedom from exposure to pollution, radiation and disease, and from excessive noise and overcrowding.[455] The home environment should facilitate care giving, and should meet children's basic physical, social and psychological needs. Children of both sexes should be provided with equal opportunities and challenges for play and learning in the home and its immediate surroundings. Particular attention should be given to the home-based needs of disabled and other vulnerable children. A supportive environment for children includes healthy, crime-free and peaceful communities. It is essential that conditions promote social justice, gender equality and participation in community life. Childhood and adolescence must be recognised as unique stages in human cultural development, requiring the respect and understanding of the community and society. Street children and others in difficult circumstances must be included. Health care, education and child-care services of high quality must be available and accessible within the community. It is essential that children have safe, secure and protected environments within the community where they can play, participate and learn about their social and natural world. Adolescents, too, need places where they can be together, experience autonomy and feel a sense of belonging. Children have a special interest in the creation of sustainable human settlements that will support long and fulfilling lives for themselves and future generations. They require opportunities to participate and contribute to a sustainable urban future.'

5.162 The Constitutional Court of South Africa provides an example of the right to adequate housing being enforced, albeit in the context of the South African

---

[449] Committee on the Rights of the Child, Report on the eleventh session, January 1996, CRC/C/50, para 9.
[450] See **8.69 et seq** below.
[451] See *Hunter and Others v Canary Wharf Ltd; Hunter and Others v London Docklands Corporation* [1997] AC 655, [1997] 2 All ER 426, [1997] 2 FLR 342, para 120.
[452] Newell, P and Hodgkin, R *Implementation Handbook for the Convention on the Rights of the Child* (2008) 3rd edn, UNICEF, p 400.
[453] *Children's Rights and Habitat: Working Towards Child Friendly Cities* (1997) UNICEF Appendix 1, p 27.
[454] *Children's Rights and Habitat: Working Towards Child Friendly Cities* (1997) UNICEF Appendix 1, pp 27–28.
[455] See **5.116** and **5.157 et seq** above.

Constitution. The case of *Government of South Africa v Grootboom*,[456] concerned s 26(1) of the South African Constitution which provides that everyone has the right to adequate housing and that the State must, within its available resources, achieve the progressive realisation of that right. On the basis of this constitutionally enshrined right to adequate housing, the Constitutional Court ordered the South African Government to implement, within its available resources, a comprehensive and co-coordinated housing programme to include reasonable measures to provide relief to people who have no access to land, no roof over their heads, and who are living in intolerable situations or crisis situations.

Right to Adequate Standard of Living under the ECHR

(i)   ECHR, Art 8(1) – Home and Environment

5.163   As with the right to the highest attainable standard of health, the ECHR does not enshrine a specific right to an adequate standard of living.[457] Art 8 of the ECHR however provides that everyone has the right to respect for his home. The term 'home' denotes a physically defined area in which private and family life develops[458] and is the place where a person 'lives and to which he returns and which forms the centre of his existence'.[459] No legal interest in property is required to constitute a physically defined area as a home[460] and such an interest will not necessarily equate with a home for the purposes of Art 8.[461] Overall:[462]

> '"Home" is an autonomous concept which does not depend on classification under domestic law. Whether or not a particular habitation constitutes a 'home' which attracts the protection under Art 8(1) will depend on the factual circumstances, namely, the existence of sufficient and continuing links. The factor of 'unlawfulness' is relevant rather to considerations under paragraph 2 of that provision of 'in accordance with the law' and to the balancing exercise undertaken between the interests of the community and those of the individual in assessing the necessity of any interference.'

5.164   Article 8 does not guarantee the right to a home[463] and the scope of the positive obligation to house the homeless is limited[464] to cases where the State is responsible for the destruction of the applicant's home,[465] where the applicant is suffering from a severe disease[466] or is labouring under a severe disability.[467] Homeless children are not guaranteed housing provision simply by virtue of the provisions of Art 8 of the ECHR.[468] However, the ECHR is likely to provide protection from certain

---

[456]   2000 (11) BCLE 1169.

[457]   Neither does the revised European Charter on Fundamental Rights.

[458]   *Giacomelli v Italy* (2007) 45 EHRR 38, para 76. It cannot however be extended to mean 'homeland' (*Loizidou v Turkey* (1996) 23 EHRR 513, para 66.

[459]   *Uratemp Ventures Ltd v Collins* [2001] UKHL 43, [2002] 1 AC 301, para 31.

[460]   *McCann v United Kingdom* (2008) 47 EHRR 40, paras 46–47 and *Buckley v United Kingdom* (1997) 23 EHRR 101, para 54.

[461]   *London Borough of Harrow v Qazi* [2003] UKHL 43, [2004] 1 AC 983.

[462]   *Buckley v United Kingdom* (1997) 23 EHRR 101, para 63. The State will be given a certain margin of appreciation when conducting the necessary balance (*Hatton v United Kingdom* (2003) 27 EHRR 611).

[463]   *X v Federal Republic of Germany* (1956) No 159/56 1 YB 202; *Chapman v United Kingdom* (2001) 33 EHRR 399, para 99; *Marzari v Italy* (1999) 28 EHRR CD 175 p 179; *O'Rourke v United Kingdom* (2001) Application No 39022/97 (unreported); *London Borough of Harrow v Qazi* [2003] UKHL 43, [2004] 1 AC 983 and *Kay v Lambeth London Borough Council* [2006] UKHL 10, [2006] 2 AC 465, para 90.

[464]   *O'Rourke v United Kingdom* (2001) Application No 39022/97 (unreported).

[465]   *Moldovan v Romania (No 2)* (2007) 44 EHRR 16.

[466]   *Marzari v Italy* (1999) 28 EHRR CD 175.

[467]   *R (Bernard) v Enfield London Borough Council* [2002] EWHC 2282 (Admin), [2003] LGR 423.

[468]   *R (W) v Lambeth London Borough Council* [2002] EWCA Civ 613, [2002] 2 All ER 901.

environmental hazards which may affect a child's standard of living.[469] There is no right to housing in pleasant circumstances or with pleasant amenities but interference in home life by environmental hazards can be challenged under Art 8 of the ECHR.[470] This is not a freestanding right to environmental protection[471] but protection under Art 8 that may exist in circumstances where the environment has a substantial[472] harmful effect on a person's private or family life.[473]

5.165 In *López Ostra v Spain*[474] the European Court of Human Rights held that environmental pollution may affect an individual's private and family life to the extent that it breaches Art 8 without needing to affect their health. The Court held that in determining of whether a violation had occurred the appropriate test was to strike a fair balance between economic interests and the applicant's effective enjoyment of his or her right to respect for private and family life. Thus Art 8 may protect against noise pollution,[475] emissions[476] and pollution.[477] The State must regulate private industry effectively and ensure that decision making in this regard takes account of the interests of the individual.[478] The Children's Environment and Health Action Plan for Europe[479] will also be of relevance to the child's standard of living. It may also be possible to rely on Art 8 where the accommodation itself is unsatisfactory based on the State's positive duties under Art 8.[480] Where a person has no choice but to reside in a property as their home it may be possible to claim under Art 3 in relation to features of the accommodation affecting standard of living, although at present this argument has been confined to claims relating to detention facilities.[481] Damages may be awarded for breach of Art 8 in relation to environmental interference.[482]

5.166 Adequacy of housing implies security of tenure. Respect for the home pursuant to Art 8 of the ECHR includes protection for occupation of and access to the home.[483] The housing protection afforded by Art 8 goes beyond possession or property rights.[484]

---

[469] *Guerra and Others v Italy* (1998) 26 ECHR 357. But see also *Kyrtatos v Greece* (2005) 40 EHRR 16, para 52. See **5.124** above.

[470] *Arrondelle v United Kingdom* (1982) 26 DR 5; *Rayner v United Kingdom* (1986) 47 DR 5; *López Ostra v Spain* (1995) 20 EHRR 277; *Taşkin v Turkey* (2006) 42 EHRR 50, para 115 and *Giacomelli v Italy* (2007) 45 EHRR 38, para 76. See also *Hunter and Others v Canary Wharf Ltd; Hunter and Others v London Docklands Corporation* [1997] AC 655, [1997] 2 All ER 426, [1997] 2 FLR 342, para 121.

[471] *Fadeyeva v Russia* (2007) 45 EHRR 10 and *Kyrtatos v Greece* (2005) 40 EHRR 16.

[472] See *Lough v First Secretary of State* [2004] EWCA Civ 905, [2004] 1 WLR 2557, para 43.

[473] *Kyrtatos v Greece* (2005) 40 EHRR 16, para 52.

[474] (1995) 20 EHRR 277.

[475] *Hatton v United Kingdom* (2003) 27 EHRR 611; *Baggs v United Kingdom* (1987) 9 EHRR CD; *Powell and Rayner v United Kingdom* (1990) 12 EHRR 355; *Dennis v Ministry of Defence* [2003] EWHC 793 (QB), [2003] NLJR 634, para 60.

[476] *Guerra and Others v Italy* (1998) 26 ECHR 357 and *López Ostra v Spain* (1995) 20 EHRR 277.

[477] *Fadeyeva v Russia* (2007) 45 EHRR 10 and *Taşkin v Turkey* (2006) 42 EHRR 50.

[478] *Hatton v United Kingdom* (2003) 37 EHRR 28.

[479] EUR/04/5046267/7 25 June 2004. See **5.124** above.

[480] See *Lismane v Hammersmith and Fulham LBC* (1998) *The Times* 27 July, CA. Munby has observed that a child's Art 8 rights may be engaged if he or she is being brought up in surroundings that isolate him or her socially or confine or stullify him or her emotionally (see Munby, J *Making Sure the Child is Heard* [2004] Fam Law 338, p 341).

[481] *B v United Kingdom* (1981) 32 DR 5. See also *The Greek Case* 12 YB1 (1969) Com Rep and *Guzzardi v Italy* (1980) 3 EHRR 333.

[482] *Moreno Gómez v Spain* (2005) 41 HER 40, para 67 and see *Andrews v Reading Borough Council* [2005] EWHC 256 (QB); *Dennis v Ministry of Defence* [2003] EWHC 793 (QB), [2003] NLJR 634 and *R (Bernard) v Enfield London Borough Council* [2002] EWHC 2282 (Admin), [2003] LGR 423.

[483] See *Wiggins v United Kingdom* (1978) 13 DR 40 and *Cyprus v Turkey* (1976) 4 EHRR 482. Any interference would have to be justified in accordance with the exceptions provided in Art 8(2) of the ECHR.

[484] Harris, D, O'Boyle, M and Warbrick, C *Law of the European Convention on Human Rights* (1995), OUP,

This latter point is important in relation to children as, in domestic law, a legal estate in land cannot be held by a child,[485] nor can a child be tenant for life or exercise the powers of a tenant for life of settled land.[486] Parents and those with responsibility for children may also obtain further protection from Art 1 of the First Protocol to the ECHR which stipulates that:[487]

> 'Every natural or legal person is entitled to the peaceful enjoyment of his possessions. No one shall be deprived of his possessions except in the public interest and subject to the conditions provided for by law and by the general principles of international law.'

(ii)   The European Social Charter

5.167   The revised European Social Charter provides by Art 16 that States Parties must guarantee an adequate standard of living for children and families. Within this context, Art 16 covers the availability and construction of suitable family housing, including social housing.[488] Art 31 of the revised European Social Charter provides detailed guarantees in respect of housing.

Right to Adequate Standard of Living under Other Regional Instruments

5.168   Article 30 of the Ibero-American Convention on Young People's Rights enshrines a right to decent housing of good quality. Article 31 of the Convention stipulates that young persons have the right to live in a healthy and balanced environment. The latter article recongises 'the importance of protecting and using properly the natural resources in order to satisfy the current needs without endangering the requirements of future generations'.

5.169   Article 20(2) of the African Charter on the Rights and Welfare of the Child provides that:

> 'States Parties to the present Charter shall in accordance with their means and national conditions the all appropriate measures ... to assist parents and other persons responsible for the child and in case of need provide material assistance and support programmes particularly with regard to nutrition, health, education, clothing and housing ...'

Article 24 of the African Charter on Human and Peoples Rights provides that 'All peoples shall have the right to a general satisfactory environment favourable to their development'. Article 38 of the revised Arab Charter on Human Rights states that:

> 'Every person has the right to an adequate standard of living for himself and his family, which ensures their well-being and a decent life, including food, clothing, housing, services and the right to a healthy environment.'

---

p 319 cited with approval in *Hunter and Others v Canary Wharf Ltd; Hunter and Others v London Docklands Corporation* [1997] AC 655, [1997] 2 All ER 426, [1997] 2 FLR 342, para 121,(1995) 20 EHRR 277.

[485]   Law of Property Act 1925, s 1(6). Where a person purports to convey a legal estate in land to a child the conveyance operates to as a declaration that the land is held in trust for the child (Trusts of Land and Appointment of Trustees Act 1996, s 2, Sch 1, para 1(1)).

[486]   Settled Land Act 1925, ss 19 and 20.

[487]   An interest in land falls within the definition of a 'possession' for the purpose of Art 1(1) of the First Protocol (de Mello, R (ed) *Human Rights Act 1998 – A Practical Guide* (2000) Jordan Publishing, p 237). Article 1 of the First Protocol contains the following rider 'The preceding provisions shall not, however, in any way impair the right of a State to enforce such laws as it deems necessary to control the use of property in accordance with the general interest or to secure the payment of taxes or other contributions or penalties.'

[488]   See *European Roma Rights Center (ERRC) v Greece*, Collective complaint No 15/2003. See also CoE Recommendation 869 on payment by the state on advances on child maintenance (1979).

Right to Adequate Standard of Living under Domestic Law

(i)   Domestic Law – Parental Responsibility and Adequate Standard of Living

5.170   At common law, parents or others with responsibility for the child have primary responsibility for ensuring a child's adequate standard of living as an element of their responsibility for the child. This duty extends to protecting the child from physical harm and providing him or her with the necessities of life and arises in respect of any person who is looking after the child.[489] Statutorily, the scope of parental responsibility defined as 'all the rights, duties, powers, responsibilities and authority which by law a parent of a child has in relation to the child and his property'.[490] This definition is clearly broad enough to encompass a duty on parents to ensure an adequate standard of living for the child. There is a statutory duty on any person who has responsibility for a child not to willfully assault, ill treat, neglect, abandon or expose that child, or cause that child to be so treated, in a manner liable to cause him or her unnecessary suffering or injury on pain of criminal liability.[491] In this context, criminal neglect means failing to provide the child with adequate food, clothing, medical aid or lodging.[492]

5.171   In domestic law the provision of financial maintenance for children is treated as separate from the issue of parental responsibility. Parents have statutory responsibility in domestic law for maintaining their own children financially.[493] Further, the maintenance obligation owed to children by their parents is considered to be a function of the parents' private relationship with each other rather than a right of the child.[494]

(ii)   Domestic Law – State Obligations and Standard of Living

5.172   The central Government policy relevant to ensuring children in this jurisdiction have an adequate standard of living is Every Child Matters'.[495] Every Child Matters sets out five key outcomes which should be achieved for all children. As noted above, these outcomes achieve statutory articulation in the Children Act 2004 as physical and mental health and emotional wellbeing; protection from harm and neglect; education, training and recreation; contribution to society and social and economic wellbeing.[496] The Childcare Act 2006 requires each English local authority to improve the wellbeing of young children in their area and reduce inequalities between young children in their areas of physical and mental health and emotional wellbeing; protection from harm and neglect; education, training and recreation; contribution to society and social and

---

[489]   *R v Gibbins and Proctor* (1918) 13 Cr App R 134. There is also a common law duty on schools to take reasonable care to protect pupils from bullying or other mistreatment by other pupils at school (*Faulkner v London Borough of Enfield and Lea Valley School* [2003] ELR 426).

[490]   Children Act 1989, s 3(1). The term 'parental responsibility' is designed to reflect that the true nature of parental rights is that of limited powers to carry out parental duties (*The Children Act 1989 Guidance and Regulations Volume 2 Family Support, Day Care and Educational Provision for Young Children*, Annex A, para 1.3).

[491]   Children and Young Persons Act 1933, s 1. Persons who have responsibility for children under 12 have an additional duty to prevent them from being exposed to the risk of burning (CYPA 1933, s 11).

[492]   CYPA 1933, s 1(1).

[493]   Child Support Act 1991, s 1(1). The detailed provisions of the Child Support legislation are beyond the scope of this book. For a comprehensive summary of the provisions see *Child Support Handbook 2010–2011* (2010) 18th edn, Child Poverty Action Group.

[494]   *R (on the application of Kehoe) v Secretary of State for Work and Pensions* [2005] UKHL 48, [2005] 4 All ER 905, paras 50–69. But see also below at **5.173 et seq**.

[495]   HM Government, *Every Child Matters: Change for Children* (2004) DfES. For a critique of the current performance of the UK in relation to the standard of living for children see Children's Rights Alliance for England, *State of Children's Rights in England* (2008) pp 27–29.

[496]   Children Act 2004, s 10(2).

economic wellbeing.[497] The Child Poverty Act 2010 aims to create legally binding Ministerial obligations in relation to the eradication of child poverty.[498] The Warm Homes and Energy Conservation Act 2000 sets legally binding targets for the eradication of fuel poverty.[499]

5.173 The Minister in charge the passage of the Child Poverty Bill through Parliament stated that it was the Government's intention that judicial review would lie against a Government which failed to show how it was seeking to abolish child poverty.[500] To date however, attempts to judicially review legally binding targets relevant to standards of living have not been successful.[501] At first instance in *R (Friends of the Earth and another) v Secretary of State for Energy and Climate Change*[502] McCombe J (in a passage endorsed by the Court of Appeal)[503] said in relation to the UK Fuel Poverty Strategy required by the Warm Homes an Energy Conservation Act 2000 that:

> 'There must be room for difference of opinion as to how one can best go about the implementation of such policy. When one looks at s 2(5) of the Act again it is clear that the defendants are only obliged to take such steps as 'in [their] opinion' are necessary in order to implement the strategy. Absent a challenge to rationality of particular decisions, taken in compliance with the Act, it is not open to this court to adjudicate upon the merits of the opinions so formed.'

5.174 The domestic legislation concerning children places specific duties on local authorities relevant to the standard of living of vulnerable children. Part III of the Children Act 1989 sets out the general and specific duties imposed on local authorities in respect of the services which they must or may provide for children and their families. In providing these services, the local authority has a duty to consider whether any local education authority, local housing authority, health authority or other local authority can help in the provision of services and, if they can, to seek that help.[504] Specifically, under s 17 of the Children Act 1989 a local authority may provide accommodation for a child in need and his family.[505] The local authority may provide money to assist with accommodation under s 17. Pursuant to Sch 2 of the Children Act 1989, local authorities must make provision for advice, guidance and counseling for children in need, the provision of occupational, social, cultural and recreational activities, home help, travel assistance and holiday assistance, for children in need.[506] Every local authority must provide such family centres as they consider appropriate in relation to

---

[497] Children Act 2006, ss 1(1) and 1(2).

[498] Child Poverty Act 2010, s 1(1). See also *The Child Poverty Review* (2004) HM Treasury and *Ending Child Poverty: Everybody's Business* (2008) HM Treasury, Department of Work and Pensions and Department for Children, Schools and Families. The last Labour Government also launched the Children's Fund in 2000 to assist Local Authorities in tackling disadvantage amongst children and young people. In 2007 the 10-year Children's Plan was launched to address standards of living for children in the United Kingdom accompanied by the launch of the Child Poverty Unit.

[499] Warm Homes and Energy Conservation Act 2000, s 2(2).

[500] *The Guardian*, 11 June 2009.

[501] See *R (Friends of the Earth and another) v Secretary of State for Energy and Climate Change* [2008] EWHC 2518 (Admin), [2009] PTSR 529 and *R (Friends of the Earth and another) v Secretary of State for Energy and Climate Change* [2009] EWCA Civ 810, [2009] WLR (D) 276 CA in relation to fuel poverty.

[502] [2008] EWHC 2518 (Admin), [2009] PTSR 529.

[503] [2009] EWCA Civ 810, [2009] WLR (D) 276, [2009] All ER (D) 331 (Jul), (2009) *The Times*, 13 October.

[504] CA 1989, s 27. The Children Act 2004 and the Children Act 2004 (Children's Services) Regulations 2005, SI 2005/1972 creates a framework whereby the provision by local government, national government and non-governmental organisations of 'children's services' is carried out co-operatively having regard to the need to safeguard and promote the welfare of children.

[505] CA 1989, s 17(6) as amended by the Adoption and Children Act 2002, s 116.

[506] CA 1989, Sch 2, para 8(a)–8(e).

children within their area, whether those children are in need or not. A 'family centre' is a centre at which a child, his parents, a person with parental responsibility for him or any other person looking after him may attend for: (a) occupational, cultural, social or recreational activities; or (b) advice, guidance or counseling.[507] Further, the Act imposes on local authorities a duty to provide services for children with disabilities so as to minimise the effect of their disabilities and give such children the opportunity to lead lives which are as normal as possible.[508] A local authority may provide care or supervised activities for any child attending school, outside school hours or during holidays whether that child is in need or not and may assist those caring for children in day care.[509] A local authority may provide, either inside or outside its area, such recreational facilities as it sees fit for all children with or without charge.[510] A local authority may also establish, maintain and manage for all children camps, holiday classes, playing fields and play centres.[511] Finally, a local authority has a general discretion to make provision for the economic or social well-being of its area under s 2 of the Local Government Act 2000.[512]

(iii)   Domestic Law – Child Maintenance

5.175   The foregoing domestic legal provisions demonstrate that domestic law has yet to properly articulate provision of an adequate standard of living for children in terms of the rights of the child as opposed to the duties of adults. This situation has found particular expression in relation to child maintenance. Expressing apparent frustration in her dissenting judgment in *R (on the application of Kehoe) v Secretary of State for Work and Pensions* Baroness Hale of Richmond observed:[513]

> '... this is another case which has been presented to us largely as a case about adults' rights when in reality it is a case about children's rights. It concerns the obligation to maintain ones children and the corresponding right of those children to obtain the benefit of that obligation.'

In *R (on the application of Kehoe) v Secretary of State for Work and Pensions* Baroness Hale went on to construct a dissenting judgment which placed the rights of the child at its centre, concluding that:[514]

> 'That being the case, it is clear to me that children have a civil right to be maintained by their parents which is such as to engage Article 6 of the European Convention on Human Rights. Their rights are not limited to the rights given to the parent with care under the Child Support Act. The provisions of that Act are simply a means of quantifying and enforcing part of their rights ... The children's civil right to the benefit of the parental obligation to maintain them survives the Child Support Act. The extent of that obligation is defined by the Act together with the remaining private law powers. But the Act operates, not only as a limit to the extent of the obligation but also as a limit to its enforcement. This is throughout

---

[507]   CA 1989, Sch 2, para 9.
[508]   CA 1989, Sch 2, para 6.
[509]   CA 1989, s 18(6).
[510]   Local Government (Miscellaneous Provisions) Act 1976, s 19(1).
[511]   Education Act 1996, s 508.
[512]   *R (J) v London Borough of Enfield* [2002] EWHC 432 (Admin), [2002] 2 FLR 1.
[513]   [2005] UKHL 48, [2005] 4 All ER 905, para 49.
[514]   *R (on the application of Kehoe) v Secretary of State for Work and Pensions* [2005] UKHL 48, [2005] 4 All ER 905, paras 71–73. In considering whether the scheme under the Child Support Act 1991 was compatible with the child's rights under art 6 of the ECHR, Baroness Hale concluded that 'it would be difficult to hold that the scheme as a whole is incompatible with the children's rights to a speedy determination and enforcement of their claims'. Presumably, the child's rights under art 12 of the CRC would also be engaged although this was not explored by the House of Lords.

a private civil right. Even in a benefit case the money paid by the non-resident parent is the children's money. All the Act does is take away the carer's right to enforce payment. That places the enforcement provisions on the procedural side of the line.'

5.176 Whilst Fortin argues that this view that children have an independent civil right under existing law to be maintained by their non-resident parent is difficult to substantiate, Art 27 of the CRC would appear in fact to support this conclusion.[515] It is correct that the Child Support Act 1991 articulates the legal position as a duty on the part of the parent to pay rather than a right of the child to be maintained.[516] Further, doubt has been expressed as to whether the common law duty to maintain children, upon which Baroness Hale in part bases her conclusions, survives.[517] Reliance has also been placed on decisions which have held that payments made in respect of child maintenance constitute the income of the parent and not of the child.[518] Whilst case law in relation to maintenance has suggested that a mother acts only 'in a representative capacity' when applying for maintenance for the benefit of the child,[519] that the child's needs should be seen as separate from the mother[520] and that the child may be separately represented,[521] none of these principles equate to a right to maintenance on the part of the child.[522]

5.177 The provisions of Art 27 of the CRC are however plainly supportive of the right of children to be maintained, which right is relevant to the application of the Child Support Act 1991. Article 27(4) makes clear that maintenance is 'for the child'. Further, taken together with Art 27(1) parental maintenance is clearly seen as an essential element of ensuring the child's right to an adequate standard of living. Taken together, the provisions of Art 27 of the CRC provide strong support for the argument that maintenance as a right of the child as well as an obligation of the parent; articulated by Blackstone as children's 'perfect *right* of receiving maintenance from their parents'.[523]

---

[515] Fortin, J *Children's Rights and the Developing Law* (2005) 2nd edn, Cambridge, p 350. See also Wikeley, N *Duty But Not a Right: Child Support After R (Kehoe) v Secretary of State for Work and Pensions* (2006) 18 Child and Family Law Quarterly 287.

[516] Child Support Act 1991, s 1. By contrast, it is broadly accepted in the United States that 'the right to support lies exclusively with the child, and that a parent holds the child support payments in trust for the child's benefit' (see *Bussert v Bussert* 677 NE 2d 68, at 71 (Indiana Court of Appeals, 1997). See also *Warsco v Hambright* 762 NE 2d 98 (Indiana Supreme Court, 2002). In New Zealand it is 'the right of the children to be maintained by their parents' (Child Support Act 1991 (NZ), s 4(a)). See also the Family Law (Scotland) Act 1985.

[517] See Wikeley, N *Duty But Not a Right: Child Support After R (Kehoe) v Secretary of State for Work and Pensions* (2006) 18 Child and Family Law Quarterly 287 citing *Re C (A Minor) (Contribution Notice)* [1994] 1 FLR 111, at 116 and *R (on the application of Kehoe) v Secretary of State for Work and Pensions* [2004] EWCA Civ 225, [2004] 1 FLR 1132,, para [10]. See also J.C. Hall, *Sources of Family Law* (Cambridge University Press, 1966), p 271.

[518] See Wikeley, N *Duty But Not a Right: Child Support After R (Kehoe) v Secretary of State for Work and Pensions* (2006) 18 Child and Family Law Quarterly 287 citing *Stevens (Inspector of Taxes) v Tirard* [1940] 1 KB 204 and *Supplementary Benefits Commission v Jull; Y v Supplementary Benefits Commission* [1981] AC 1025. Wikeley however points out that 'both decisions unquestionably reflect the values of their age and pre-date the development of the contemporary jurisprudence of children's rights.'

[519] *M-T v T* [2006] EWHC 2494 (Fam), [2007] 2 FLR 925 per Charles J, para 18.

[520] *Re S (Unmarried Parents: Financial Provision)* [2006] EWCA Civ 479, [2006] 2 FLR 950 per Thorpe J, para 15.

[521] *Re S (Unmarried Parents: Financial Provision)* [2006] EWCA Civ 479, [2006] 2 FLR 950 per Thorpe J, para 17.

[522] Fortin, J *Children's Rights and the Developing Law* (2009) 3rd edn, Cambridge, p 357.

[523] Blackstone's Commentaries, Book 1, Chapter XVI. This 'right' arguably continues even after a parent's death, the Inheritance (Provision for Family and Dependents) Act 1975 permitting a child of married or unmarried parents to claim a share in the deceased parents' estate on grounds that the will did not make

Curiously, no reference is made in *R (on the application of Kehoe) v Secretary of State for Work and Pensions* to Art 27 of the United Nations Convention on the Rights of the Child.

(iii)   Domestic Law – Housing[524]

5.178 The issue of housing provision for children provides a further example of an unsuccessful attempt at a rights based approach by the domestic courts to issues touching and concerning the child's standard of living, being again one which arises out of a dissenting judgment.[525] In *Hunter and Others v Canary Wharf Ltd; Hunter and Others v London Docklands Corporation*[526] the House of Lords considered whether a plaintiff without an exclusive right of occupation was entitled to sue in private nuisance. Whilst the majority of the House answered this question in the negative, in a dissenting opinion, Lord Cooke of Thorndon considered the position of children living at home and held:

> 'The status of children living at home is different and perhaps more problematical but, on consideration, I am persuaded by the majority of the Court of Appeal in *Khorasandjian v Bush* [1993] Q.B. 727 and the weight of North American jurisprudence to the view that they, too, should be entitled to relief for substantial and unlawful interference with the amenities of their home. Internationally the distinct interests of children are increasingly recognised. The United Nations Convention on the Rights of the Child, ratified by the United Kingdom in 1991 and the most widely ratified human rights treaty in history, acknowledges children as fully-fledged beneficiaries of human rights. Article 16 declares inter alia that no child shall be subjected to unlawful interference with his or her home and that the child has the right to the protection of law against such interference. International standards such as this may be taken into account in shaping the common law. The point just mentioned can be taken further. Article 16 of the Convention on the Rights of the Child adopts some of the language of Article 12 of the Universal Declaration of Human Rights and Article 8 of the European Convention for the Protection of Human Rights and Fundamental Freedoms (1953) (Cmd. 8969). These provisions are aimed, in part, at protecting the home and are construed to give protection against nuisances: see *Arrondelle v United Kingdom,* Application No 7889/77 (1982) 26 D.R.5 F. Sett. (aircraft noise) and *Lopez Ostra v Spain* (1994) 20 E.H.R.R. 277 (fumes and smells from a waste treatment plant). The protection is regarded as going beyond possession or property rights: see *Harris, O'Boyle and Warbrick, Law of the European Convention on Human Rights* (1995), p 319. Again I think that this is a legitimate consideration in support of treating residence as an acceptable basis of standing at common law in the present class of case.'

Rights Supportive of Survival and Development – Right to Social Security

5.179 The Universal Declaration of Human Rights Art 25 stipulates that:

---

reasonable provision for the him or her (see the Inheritance (Provision for Family and Dependents) Act 1975, s 3. See also *Sivyer v Sivyer* [1967] 1 WLR 1482 and *Re Collins (decd)* [1990] Fam 56 for the Courts' approach).

[524] For a comprehensive guide to housing law as it relates to homeless children see Luba, J and Davies, E *Housing Allocation and Homelessness: Law and Practice* (2010) 2nd edn, Jordan Publishing. See also Department for Communities and Local Government and Department for Children Schools and Families *Joint Working between Housing and Children's Services* (2008) DCLG publications chapter 3 and paras 3.4 and 3.3.

[525] For criticism by the UN Committee on the Rights of the Child in respect of housing issues in the domestic jurisdiction see *Concluding observations of the Committee on the Rights of the Child: United Kingdom of Great Britain and Northern Ireland* (1995), para 15 and *Concluding observations of the Committee on the Rights of the Child: United Kingdom of Great Britain and Northern Ireland* (2002), para 46(b).

[526] [1997] AC 655, [1997] 2 All ER 426, [1997] 2 FLR 342.

'Everyone has the right to ... security in the event of unemployment, sickness, disability, widowhood, old age or other lack of livelihood in circumstances beyond his control.'

Crucial to the survival and development of some children is adequate welfare provision from the State. The UN Committee on the Rights of the Child General Comment No 7 *Implementing Child Rights in Early Childhood* makes clear, in the context of young children, that implementing children's right to benefit from social security, including social insurance, is an important element of any strategy to ensure an adequate standard of living.[527]

Right to Benefit from Social Security under the CRC

(i) CRC, Art 26

5.180 With regard to adequate welfare provision for children, Art 26 of the CRC provides as follows:

'1. States Parties shall recognise for every child the right to benefit from social security, including social insurance, and shall take the necessary measures to achieve the full realisation of this right in accordance with their national law.

2. The benefits should, where appropriate, be granted, taking into account the resources and the circumstances of the child and persons having responsibility for the maintenance of the child, as well as any other consideration relevant to an application for benefits made by or on behalf of the child.'

(ii) CRC, Art 26 – 'Benefit'

5.181 It is important to note that the child's right under the CRC is to 'benefit' from social security rather than having an independent right to such welfare provision. Children do however have a right to social security, including social insurance, under Art 9 of the Covenant on Social, Economic and Cultural Rights, which states 'The States Parties to the present Covenant recognise the right of everyone to social security, including social insurance'. Article 26 of the CRC implies that States must take active steps to ensure there is full uptake of social security entitlements where appropriate by or on behalf of children[528] In particular, States must ensure that children receive their welfare entitlement without discrimination, social stigma, the loss of any other right or prejudice to their privacy.[529] The words 'taking into account the resources and the circumstances of the child and persons having responsibility for the maintenance of the child, as well as any other consideration relevant to an application for benefits' make clear that both the financial and caring responsibilities of adults should be considered when considering whether social security benefits should be granted.

5.182 All children up to the age of 18 are entitled to benefit from this right and national provision which limits the payment of social security to children by reference to a lower age limit will contravene the provisions of Art 26 of the CRC.[530] The words 'by

---

[527] Committee on the Rights of the Child General Comment No 7 *Implementing Child Rights in Early Childhood* HRI/GEN/1/Rev 8, p 443, para 26. See also UN General Assembly Twenty-fourth Special Session (A/RES/S-24/2, 15 December 2000) and UN General Assembly Resolution A/RES/55/2, para 19, p 5).

[528] Newell, P and Hodgkin, R *Implementation Handbook for the Convention on the Rights of the Child* (2008) 3rd edn, UNICEF, p 388.

[529] Newell, P and Hodgkin, R *Implementation Handbook for the Convention on the Rights of the Child* (2008) 3rd edn, UNICEF, p 388.

[530] See for example Iceland CRC/C/15/Add.203, para 20 and Georgia CRC/C?15/Add.222, para 52.

or on behalf of the child' in Art 26(2) demonstrate that children must be directly eligible, and entitled to applyfor welfare provision where necessary.[531]

(iii)   CRC, Art 26 – 'Social security, including social insurance'

5.183 The minimum standards of 'social security' are provided by the International Labour Organisation Social Security (Minimum Standards) Convention (No 102)[532] which provides for a minimum of medical care; sickness benefit; unemployment benefit; old-age benefit; employment injury benefit; family benefit; maternity benefit; invalidity benefit; and survivors' benefit. The Art 26 requirement that children 'benefit' from these branches of social security will mean that Art 26 will still apply in situations where the benefit in question is not payable to the child but rather the adult caring for them.

(iv)   CRC, Art 26 – 'Resources'

5.184 Whilst the benefits guaranteed by Art 26 of the CRC are contingent on the 'resources and the circumstances of the child and persons having responsibility for the maintenance of the child, as well as any other consideration relevant to an application for benefits', Art 26 must be read in light of the proviso provided by Art 4 of the CRC. Article 4 provides that 'With regard to economic, social and cultural rights, States Parties shall undertake such measures to the maximum extent of their available resources and, where needed, within the framework of international cooperation'. Means testing is generally considered desirable to ensure limited resources can be targeted at those children most in need of welfare provision.[533] Hodgkin and Newell go as far as to argue that Art 26 of the CRC requires that States 'anticipate the possibility of cyclical recessions or financial crises and lay contingency plans for the protecting their most important asset: children'.[534]

5.185 In considering the deployment of resources for welfare provision, it should be noted that the obligation under Art 26 to ensure that every child benefits from social security is referable to a national legal standard not an international one. The words 'In accordance with national law' in Art 26 mean that the standard against which the adequacy of social security is measured for the purposes of Art 26 is that of the State and not more widely against some minimum international standard.

Right to Benefit from Social Security under the ECHR

(i)   ECHR, Art 3

5.186 The ECHR does not contain a freestanding right to benefit from social security. However, Art 3 of the ECHR, prohibiting torture or inhuman or degrading treatment or punishment, may be relevant in the context of welfare provision. If it results in the requisite degree of suffering or injury, the *withdrawal* of welfare provision from a person who is unable to meet their essential living needs by reason of destitution and inability

---

[531]   Newell, P and Hodgkin, R *Implementation Handbook for the Convention on the Rights of the Child* (2008) 3rd edn, UNICEF, p 389.

[532]   ILO C102. This Convention was ratified by the United Kingdom on 27 April 1954.

[533]   Newell, P and Hodgkin, R *Implementation Handbook for the Convention on the Rights of the Child* (2008) 3rd edn, UNICEF, p 389. Hodgkin and Newell note however that some degree of financial support for all children, regardless of circumstances, should not be considered unreasonable or unviable.

[534]   Newell, P and Hodgkin, R *Implementation Handbook for the Convention on the Rights of the Child* (2008) 3rd edn, UNICEF, p 388.

to work can amount to a breach of Art 3.[535] Whether a failure to *provide* welfare provision would lead to a similar outcome is not yet clear.[536]

(ii) European Social Charter

5.187 Article 16 of the revised European Social Charter[537] requires States Parties to guarantee an adequate standard of living for families. A key element of this guarantee is the provision by the State of a family or child benefit scheme. Benefits may be subject to means testing[538] but must constitute an adequate income supplement for a significant number of families.[539] The obligations under Art 16 are more extensive than those under Art 12 of the European Social Charter, which guarantees access to social security.

Right to Benefit from Social Security under European Union Law

5.188 Article 34(1) of the European Charter of Fundamental Rights provides that the European Union recognises and respects the entitlement to social security benefits and social services providing protection in cases such as maternity, illness, industrial accidents, dependency or old age, and in the case of loss of employment, in accordance with the rules laid down by Community law and national laws and practices. Article 34(2) extends the protection afforded by Art 34(1) to all those residing and moving legally within the European Union. Recognising that not all those within the European Union are 'residing and moving' legally therein, Art 34(3) provides that, in order to combat social exclusion and poverty, the European Union recognises the right to social housing and assistance so as to ensure a decent existence for all those who lack sufficient resources, in accordance with the rules laid down by European Union law and national laws and practices.

Right to Benefit from Social Security under Other Regional Instruments

5.189 Article 28(1) of the Ibero-American Convention on Young People's Rights provides that youth have the right to social protection in situations of illness, accident in the workplace, disability, widowhood or orphanage and any other situation meaning a lack or decrease of means of subsistence or capacity to work. States Parties are required to take positive measures to implement this right.[540] Article 14(3) of the African Youth Charter recognises the right of every young person to benefit from social security, including social insurance. Article 36 of the revised Arab Charter on Human Rights guarantees to every citizen the right to social security, including social insurance.

Right to Benefit from Social Security under Domestic Law

5.190 The foundations of the current welfare system in the United Kingdom were laid down in the Beveridge Report of 1942. The classic formulation of welfare provision in this jurisdiction is one which provides for a guarantee of minimum standards, social protection in the event of insecurity and the provision of services at the best possible

---

535 See *R (Limbuela) v Secretary of State for the Home Department* [2005] UKHL 66, [2006] 1 AC 396; *R (Husain) v Asylum Support Adjudicator* [2001] EWHC (Admin) 852, [2001] All ER (D) 107 (Oct). See also *R (Chavda) v London Borough of Harrow* [2007] EWHC (Admin) 3064.
536 *R (Q) v Secretary of State for the Home Department* [2003] EWCA Civ 364, [2004] QB 36.
537 The United Kingdom has not yet ratified the revised European Social Charter.
538 See Slovakia Conclusions XVI-2, Romania Conclusions 2002, Bulgaria Conclusions 2004.
539 Other forms of economic protection, such as birth grants, additional payments to large families and tax relief in respect of the children are also relevant to the implementation of Art 16 (see *Children's Rights under the European Social Charter*, Council of Europe).
540 Article 28(2).

level.[541] However, the system of welfare support has been described as being in reality 'a confusing patchwork of contributory, non-contributory and means tested benefits'.[542]

5.191 A detailed description of the welfare system in the domestic jurisdiction as it relates to children is beyond the scope of this book.[543] From the perspective of the rights articulated above with regard to social security, including social insurance, it is only in the context of disability living allowance that children have an entitlement to benefit in their own right.[544] Beyond this, children under 16 have no independent right to social security. The social security provisions for 16 and 17 years olds are of labyrinthine complexity and have been recognised by the Government as 'incomprehensible to all but the most expert'.[545] The system has been specifically criticised by the UN Committee on the Rights of the Child[546] and also by domestic agencies, including the Government itself.[547] The Government is now moving to compulsory education or training for all 16–18 year olds,[548] making education or training by way of a contract of apprenticeship to 17 compulsory from 2013 and to 18 from 2015.[549] Within the context of children benefiting from welfare provision made available to their parents and others caring for them, concerns have been expressed on the impact on children of Government policies designed to restrict benefits in order to encourage parents to return to work.[550]

Rights Supportive of Survival and Development – The Right to Play[551]

5.192 Article 24 of the Universal Declaration of Human Rights states that 'Everyone has the right to rest and leisure, including reasonable limitation of working hours and

---

[541]   Briggs, A *The Welfare State in Historical Perspective* (1961) European Journal of Sociology, pp 221–258.

[542]   Lister, R *Income Maintenance for Families in Britain* in Rapoport, R.N, Fogarty, M and Rapoport, R *Families in Britain* (1982) Routledge and Kegan Paul, p 432.

[543]   For a comprehensive examination of the subject see *Welfare Benefits and Tax Credits Handbook 2010/2011* (2010) 18th edn, Child Poverty Action Group.

[544]   N. Wikeley, 'Children and Social Security', in J. Fionda (ed), *Legal Concepts of Childhood* (Hart Publishing, 2001), chapter 13, p 226.

[545]   See HM Treasury, Department for Work and Pensions and Department for Education and Skills *Supporting Young People to Achieve: Towards a New Deal for Skill* (2004) HMSO, para 3.1 (see Income Support (General) Regulations 1987, SI 1987/1967 as amended.

[546]   See Committee on the Rights of the Child *Concluding Observations of the Committee on the Rights of the Child: United Kingdom of Great Britain and Northern Ireland* (1995) CRC/C/15/Add.34, para 15 and Committee on the Rights of the Child *Concluding Observations of the Committee on the Rights of the Child: United Kingdom of Great Britain and Northern Ireland* (2002) CRC/C/15/Add.188, para 46(c).

[547]   See Social Exclusion Unit *Bridging the Gap: New Opportunities for 16–18 Year Olds not in Education, Employment or Training* (1999) Cm 4405 Cabinet Office, paras 5.20–5.24; HM Treasury, Department for Work and Pensions and Department for Education and Skills *Supporting Young People to Achieve: Towards a New Deal for Skill* (2004) HMSO; HM Treasury, Department for Work and Pensions and Department for Education and Skills *Supporting Young People to Achieve: The Government's Response to the Consultation* (2005) HMSO; Centre for Economic Inclusion *A UK Youth Allowance? Inclusion Policy Paper No 4* (2005) and Children's Rights Alliance for England, *State of Children's Rights in England* (2008), p 28.

[548]   See DfES *Raising Expectations: Staying in Education and Training Post-16* (2007) Cm 7065, para 5.28 and the Education and Skills Act 2008.

[549]   This provision has also been criticised as overlooking the fact that young people who require State support at the age of 16 and 17 have left home and often have fare more and complex personal problems than their peers nationally (Fortin, J *Children's Rights and the Developing Law* (2005) 2nd edn, Cambridge, p 126 citing Pleace, N, Fitzpatrick, S, Johnsen, S, Quiglars, D and Sanderson, D *Statutory Homelessness in England: The Experience of Families and 16–17 Year Olds* (2008) Department of Communities and Local Government, para 12.116).

[550]   Fortin, J *Children's Rights and the Developing Law* (2009) 3rd edn, Cambridge, p 340. See DWP *Working for Children* (2007) p 27 and DWP *Ready for Work: Full Employment in Our Generation* (2007) Cm 7290, p 37.

[551]   'You are worried about seeing him spend his early years in doing nothing. What! Is it nothing to be happy? Nothing to skip, play, and run around all day long? Never in his life will he be so busy again.' Jean-Jacques Rousseau *Emile* (1762).

periodic holidays'. Principle 7 of the Declaration of the Rights of the Child 1959 provides that 'The child shall have full opportunity for play and recreation, which should be directed to the same purposes as education'. In considering the development of the child, the importance of the child's right to play cannot be underestimated.[552] Play is an essential part of childhood development including the development of social and personal skills such as negotiation, sharing and self-control. Play is the fundamental means by which children learn about themselves, their family members, their local communities and the world around them.[553] The right to play is a means of promoting the creativity and spirit of curiosity of children and ensuring a needed space for them to rest and enjoy the happiness of being children.[554] One of the defining aspects of play is that it is not compulsory.[555]

The Child's Right to Play under the CRC

5.193 Article 31 of the CRC provides as follows in respect of the child's right to rest and leisure and to engage in play and recreational activities:

'1. States Parties recognise the right of the child to rest and leisure, to engage in play and recreational activities appropriate to the age of the child and to participate freely in cultural life and the arts.

2. States Parties shall respect and promote the right of the child to participate fully in cultural and artistic life and shall encourage the provision of appropriate and equal opportunities for cultural, artistic, recreational and leisure activity.'

5.194 The CRC is the first legally binding international human rights instrument to expressly recognise the right of the child to engage in play and recreational activities.[556] Art 31 of the CRC should be read in the context of the other rights of the child enshrined in the Convention and in particular should be considered in relation to Art 28 (the right to education), Art 29 (object of education) Art 32 (child labour) and Art 39 (recovery and reintegration of child victims).[557] States parties have a positive obligation arising out of Art 31 of the CRC to promote children's play.[558] In its General Comment No 7 *Implementing Child Rights in Early Childhood* the Committee on the Rights of the Child observed that:[559]

---

[552] The *travaux préparatoires* of the CRC demonstrate clearly that the intended aim of the rights enshrined Art 31 of the CRC is to promote and protect the child's development within the context of the child's community as well as the child's school and family (Detrick, S *A Commentary on the United Nations Convention on the Rights of the Child* (1999) Martinus Nijhoff, p 279 and E/CN.4/L.1575, p 547). See also Burghardt, G *The comparative reach of play and the brain: perspective, evidence and implications* (2010) American Journal of Play, Vol 2, No 3, pp 338–356 and Samuel, M *A critical enquiry into the influences of children's play and stories in the early years and how they contribute to the development of communication language and literacy* (2010) Early Childhood Practice, Vol 11, No 1–2, pp 59–79.

[553] Clements, R and Fiorentino, L (eds) *The Child's Right to Play: A Global Approach* (2004) Praeger, p xv.

[554] UN Manual on Human Rights Reporting HR/PUB/91/1/ (Rev.1) p 469.

[555] Newell, P and Hodgkin, R *Implementation Handbook for the Convention on the Rights of the Child* (2008) 3rd edn, UNICEF, pp 469 and 472.

[556] Detrick, S *A Commentary on the United Nations Convention on the Rights of the Child* (1999) Martinus Nijhoff, p 279 and E/CN.4/L.1575, p 551.

[557] Newell, P and Hodgkin, R *Implementation Handbook for the Convention on the Rights of the Child* (2008) 3rd edn, UNICEF, p 470.

[558] See Guinea Bissau CRC/C/15/Add.177, paras 46 and 47, Rwanda CRC/C/15/Add.234, para 59, Albania CRC/C/15/Add.249, paras 62 and 63 and Mexico CRC/C/MEX/CO/3, paras 58 and 59.

[559] Committee on the Rights of the Child General Comment No 7 *Implementing Child Rights in Early Childhood* HRI/GEN/1/Rev 8, p 446, para 34.

'The Committee notes that insufficient attention has been given by States parties and others to the implementation of the provisions of article 31 of the Convention, which guarantees 'the right of the child to rest and leisure, to engage in play and recreational activities appropriate to the age of the child and to participate freely in cultural life and the arts'. Play is one of the most distinctive features of early childhood. Through play, children both enjoy and challenge their current capacities, whether they are playing alone or with others. The value of creative play and exploratory learning is widely recognised in early childhood education. Yet realising the right to rest, leisure and play is often hindered by a shortage of opportunities for young children to meet, play and interact in child-centred, secure, supportive, stimulating and stress-free environments. Children's right-to-play space is especially at risk in many urban environments, where the design and density of housing, commercial centres and transport systems combine with noise, pollution and all manner of dangers to create a hazardous environment for young children. Children's right to play can also be frustrated by excessive domestic chores (especially affecting girls) or by competitive schooling. Accordingly, the Committee appeals to States parties, non-governmental organisations and private actors to identify and remove potential obstacles to the enjoyment of these rights by the youngest children, including as part of poverty reduction strategies. Planning for towns, and leisure and play facilities should take account of children's right to express their views (art. 12), through appropriate consultations. In all these respects, States parties are encouraged to pay greater attention and allocate adequate resources (human and financial) to the implementation of the right to rest, leisure and play.'

5.195 The provision of opportunities for rest, leisure, recreational activities and play should be achieved in accordance with the principles of non-discrimination set out in Art 2 of the CRC[560] and the principles set out in Art 23 of the CRC concerning children with disabilities.[561] In its General Comment No 9 *The Rights of Children with Disabilities* the Committee on the Rights of the Child notes that:[562]

'Play has been recognised as the best source of learning various skills, including social skills. The attainment of full inclusion of children with disabilities in the society is realised when children are given the opportunity, places, and time to play with each other (children with disabilities and no disabilities). Training for recreation, leisure and play should be included for school-aged children with disabilities ... Children with disabilities should be provided with equal opportunities to participate in various cultural and arts activities as well as sports. These activities must be viewed as both medium of expression and medium of realising self-satisfying, quality of life ... Competitive and non-competitive sports activities must be designed to include children with disabilities in an inclusive form whenever possible. That is to say, a child with a disability who is able to compete with children with no disability should be encouraged and supported to do so. But sports are an area where, because of the physical demands of the sport, children with disabilities will often need to have exclusive games and activities where they can compete fairly and safely. It must be emphasised though that when such exclusive events take place, the media must play its role responsibly by giving the same attention as it does to sports for children with no disabilities.'

---

[560] See also the UN Rules for the Protection of Juveniles Deprived of their Liberty rr 18(c) and 47, the Guidelines for the Alternative Care of Children A/RES/64/142 paras 37, 86 and the Committee on the Rights of the Child General Comment No 6 *Treatment of Unaccompanied and Separated Children Outside their Country of Origin* HRI/GEN/1/Rev 8, p 424, para 63.

[561] See also the Convention on the Rights of Persons with Disabilities, Art 30.

[562] General Comment No 9 *The Rights of Children with Disabilities* CRC/C/GC/9, paras 44–46. See also the Standard Rules on the Equalisation of Opportunities for Persons with Disabilities, rr 4(7) and 11 (A/RES/48/96).

(i) CRC, Art 31(1) – Rest, Leisure, Recreational Activities and Play

5.196 Hodgkin and Newell suggest that 'rest' includes the basic necessities of physical or mental relaxation and sleep,[563] that 'leisure' is a wider term implying the time and freedom to do as one pleases, 'recreational activities' embrace the whole range of activities undertaken by choice for pleasure and that 'play' includes children's activities which are not controlled by adults and which do not necessarily conform to any rules.[564] Note that, in contrast to Principle 7 of the Declaration on the Rights of the Child 1959, Art 31 does not prescribe the purpose of rest, leisure, recreational activities and play. There should be reasonable limitations on school and working hours in order to ensure that the rights under Art 31 are effective rights.[565]

(ii) CRC, Art 31(1) – 'Appropriate to the Age of the Child'

5.197 The UN Manual on Human Rights Reporting makes clear that activities under Art 31 of the CRC should be appropriate to the child's age which requires them not to be excessive, entail any inappropriate risk or in any way be harmful to the development, health of education of the child. Activities under Art 31 should further avoid any form of exploitation of the child in activities which may seem, prima facie, to be designed to promote the child's wellbeing.[566]

(iii) CRC, Art 31(2) – Cultural and Artistic Life

5.198 Article 31(2) of the CRC provides as follows in respect of the child's right to participate in cultural and artistic life:

---

[563] See also the ILO Night Work of Young Persons (Non-Industrial Occupations) Convention 1946 No 79, Art 2 ('1. Children under fourteen years of age who are admissible for full-time or part-time employment and children over fourteen years of age who are still subject to full-time compulsory school attendance shall not be employed nor work at night during a period of at least fourteen consecutive hours, including the interval between eight o'clock in the evening and eight o'clock in the morning. 2. Provided that national laws or regulations may, where local conditions so require, substitute another interval of twelve hours of which the beginning shall not be fixed later than eight thirty o'clock in the evening nor the termination earlier than six o'clock in the morning') and Art 3 ('1. Children over fourteen years of age who are no longer subject to full-time compulsory school attendance and young persons under eighteen years of age shall not be employed nor work at night during a period of at least twelve consecutive hours, including the interval between ten o'clock in the evening and six o'clock in the morning. 2. Provided that, where there are exceptional circumstances affecting a particular branch of activity or a particular area, the competent authority may, after consultation with the employers' and workers' organisations concerned, decide that in the case of children and young persons employed in that branch of activity or area, the interval between eleven o'clock in the evening and six o'clock in the morning may be substituted for that between ten o'clock in the evening and six o'clock in the morning'). See also the ILO Night Work of Young Persons (Industry) Convention (Revised) 1948 (No 90), Art 2 ('1. For the purpose of this Convention the term *night* signifies a period of at least twelve consecutive hours. 2. In the case of young persons under sixteen years of age, this period shall include the interval between ten o'clock in the evening and six o'clock in the morning. 3. In the case of young persons who have attained the age of sixteen years but are under the age of eighteen years, this period shall include an interval prescribed by the competent authority of at least seven consecutive hours falling between ten o'clock in the evening and seven o'clock in the morning; the competent authority may prescribe different intervals for different areas, industries, undertakings or branches of industries or undertakings, but shall consult the employers' and workers' organisations concerned before prescribing an interval beginning after eleven o'clock in the evening').

[564] Newell, P and Hodgkin, R *Implementation Handbook for the Convention on the Rights of the Child* (2008) 3rd edn, UNICEF, p 469. Note that 'play' may nonetheless be facilitated and overseen by adults.

[565] See Newell, P and Hodgkin, R *Implementation Handbook for the Convention on the Rights of the Child* (2008) 3rd edn, UNICEF, p 469 and see E/CN.4/1983/ 62 Annex II and Detrick, S (ed) *The United Convention on the Rights of the Child: A Guide to the Travaux Préparatoires* (1992) p 415.

[566] UN Manual on Human Rights Reporting HR/PUB/91/1/ (Rev.1) p 469. See also Art 24 of the Universal Declaration of Human Rights.

'2. States Parties shall respect and promote the right of the child to participate fully in cultural and artistic life and shall encourage the provision of appropriate and equal opportunities for cultural, artistic, recreational and leisure activity.'

5.199 Article 27 of the Universal Declaration of Human Rights provides that 'Everyone has the right to freely participate in the cultural life of the community, enjoy the arts and to share in scientific advancement and its benefits. Article 15(1)(a) of the ICESCR requires States parties to recognise the right of every one to take part in cultural life. The word 'culture' in Art 31 of the CRC should be interpreted in its artistic sense rather than denoting traditions and customs,[567] although the latter may include the former where artistic traditions and customs are concerned. The right of the child to participate fully in cultural and artistic life includes both the right to join with adults in their cultural and artistic pursuits and the right to child-centred culture and arts.[568] The right to participate fully in cultural and artistic life is closely linked to the child's right to participate under Art 12 of the CRC and the child's right to freedom of expression under Art 13 of the CRC.[569]

The Child's Right to Play under other International Instruments

(i)   The Geneva Convention relative to the Protection of Civilian Persons in Time of War

5.200 The Geneva Convention relative to the Protection of Civilian Persons in Time of War 1950 (Geneva Convention IV) provides at Art 94 that in relation to children interned the detaining power shall encourage recreational pursuits, sports and games among internees whilst leaving them free to take part or not and reserve special playgrounds for children and young people. Further, pursuant to Art 142 of Convention IV, detaining powers must assist with the organisation of leisure time within places of internment.[570]

The Child's Right to Play under other Regional Instruments

(i)   Ibero-American Convention on the Rights of Youth

5.201 Article 32 of the Ibero-American Convention on the Rights of Youth provides as follows in respect of the right to play:

'1. Youth have right to recreation and leisure, to travel and know other national, regional or international communities as a mechanism to promote cultural, educational, experience and leisure exchange in order to manage to know one another and the respect towards cultural diversity and solidarity.

2. The States Parties undertake to implement policies and programmes which promote the exercise of these rights and to adopt measures which enable the free movement of youth about their countries.'

---

[567] Newell, P and Hodgkin, R *Implementation Handbook for the Convention on the Rights of the Child* (2008) 3rd edn, UNICEF, p 469.

[568] Newell, P and Hodgkin, R *Implementation Handbook for the Convention on the Rights of the Child* (2008) 3rd edn, UNICEF, p 473.

[569] Article 15 (right to freedom of association), Art 17 (access to the media) and Art 30 (right to enjoy culture) may also be engaged together with Art 31(2).

[570] See also Art 108.

(ii)   African Charter on the Rights and Welfare of the Child

5.202   Article 12 of the African Charter on the Right and Welfare of the Child stipulates as follows in respect of the right to play:[571]

> '1. States Parties recognise the right of the child to rest and leisure, to engage in play and recreational activities appropriate to the age of the child and to participate freely in cultural life and the arts.
>
> 2. States Parties shall respect and promote the right of the child to fully participate in cultural and artistic life and shall encourage the provision of appropriate and equal opportunities for cultural, artistic, recreational and leisure activity.'

(iii)   African Youth Charter

5.203   The African Youth Charter provides as follows at Art 22 in respect of the right to play:[572]

> '1. Young people shall have the right to rest and leisure and to engage in play and recreational activities that are part of a health lifestyle as well as to participate freely in sport, physical education drama, the arts, music and other forms of cultural life. In this regard, States Parties shall:
>
> (a)   Make provision for equal access for young men and young women to sport, physical education, cultural, artistic, recreational and leisure activities;
> (b)   Put in place adequate infrastructure and services in rural and urban areas for youth to participate in sport, physical education, cultural, artistic, recreational and leisure activities.'

(iv)   Revised Arab Charter on Human Rights

5.204   Article 42 of the Revised Arab Charter on Human Rights states as follows in relation to the right to participation in cultural and artistic activities:

> '1. Every person has the right to take part in cultural life and to enjoy the benefits of scientific progress and its application.
>
> 2. The States parties undertake to respect the freedom of scientific research and creative activity and to ensure the protection of moral and material interests resulting form scientific, literary and artistic production.
>
> 3. The state parties shall work together and enhance cooperation among them at all levels, with the full participation of intellectuals and inventors and their organisations, in order to develop and implement recreational, cultural, artistic and scientific programmes.'

---

[571]   See also Art 13(2) ('States Parties to the present Charter shall ensure, subject to available resources, to a disabled child and to those responsible for his care, of assistance for which application is made and which is appropriate to the child's condition and in particular shall ensure that the disabled child has effective access to training, preparation for employment and recreation opportunities in a manner conducive to the child achieving the fullest possible social integration, individual development and his cultural and moral development').

[572]   See also Art 13(4)(m) and Art 24(1) ('States Parties recognise the right of mentally and physically challenged youth to special care and shall ensure that they have equal and effective access to education, training, health care services, employment, sport, physical education and cultural and recreational activities').

Child's Right to Play under Domestic Law

5.205 Pursuant to the Education Act 1996, s 507B requires local education authorities in England to, so far as is reasonably practicable, secure for persons aged 13 to 19 sufficient educational leisure-time activities for the improvement of their well being[573] and sufficient facilities for such activities and sufficient recreational leisure-time activities for the improvement of their well-being[574] and sufficient facilities for such activities. Note also the Children and Families (Wales) Measure 2010 Chapter 2 which provides that a local authority must assess the sufficiency of play opportunities in its area for children in accordance with regulations and secure sufficient play opportunities in its area for children, so far as reasonably practicable, having regard to its assessment.[575] For the purposes of the measure play is defined as including any recreational activity.[576]

5.206 Under the Children Act 1989, Sch 2, para 9 every local authority must provide such family centres as they consider appropriate in relation to children within their area whether those children are in need or not. A 'family centre' is a centre at which a child, his parents, a person with parental responsibility for him or any other person looking after him may attend for occupational, cultural, social or recreational activities or advice, guidance or counseling. The Children Act 1989 Guidance and Regulations, Vol 2, *Family Support, Day Care and Educational Provision for Young Children* provides for three types of family centre, namely therapeutic, community and self-help.[577]

5.207 Further, a local authority may provide, either inside or outside its area, such recreational facilities as it sees fit for all children with or without charge.[578] A local authority may also establish, maintain and manage for all children camps, holiday classes, playing fields and play centres.[579]

CONCLUSION

5.208 Debates on the nature and extent of the child's right to life are increasingly driven by more than the ethical and religious debate on abortion. As medical technology advances, the issues raised by the child's right to life will become more complex and pose an increasing number of ethical dilemmas and conflicts.[580] In particular, there is an increasing tension between the broad reach of developing technology and the reluctance of the international and regional human rights organisations to take a prescriptive line on whether the right to life should be extended prior to birth. Within the context of advances in medical science, there may now be an increasing number of the 'rare cases'

---

[573] 'Sufficient educational leisure-time activities' must include sufficient educational leisure-time activities which are for the improvement of children's personal and social development (s.507B(3)).

[574] 'Wellbeing' is defined for the purposes of s 407B as relating to physical and mental health and emotional wellbeing, protection from harm and neglect, education, training and recreation, the contribution made by the child to society and social and economic wellbeing (see Children Act 2004).

[575] Children and Families (Wales) Measure 2010, s 11(1) and (3). In assessing and making provision the local authority must take into account the needs of children with disabilities and the needs of children of different ages (see s 11(5)).

[576] Children and Families (Wales) Measure 2010 s 11(6).

[577] (1991) Department of Health, para 3.20.

[578] Local Government (Miscellaneous Provisions) Act 1976, s 19(1).

[579] Education Act 1996, s 508(2).

[580] Newell, P and Hodgkin, R *Implementation Handbook for the Convention on the Rights of the Child* (2008) 3rd edn, UNICEF, p 87.

contemplated by the European Commission in *Paton v UK*[581] in which the human rights bodies will have to consider definitively the applicability of the right to life to the unborn child rather than deferring the question to States Parties. What is clear is that if emerging medical issues are going to be dealt with effectively and consistently on a legal, as opposed to a moral or religious, platform, a clearer lead will have to be given by the human rights institutions and the courts on this issue.

5.209 A further disadvantage of the focus on abortion as the touchstone in the debate on the child's right to life is that it tends to obscure the breadth and depth of that right and the rights closely associated with it. The right to life is of little value unless the child's right to survival and development is also prioritised. If the child's right to life is to be properly and consistently implemented and enforced there is a need urgently to promote the understanding that the right to life is itself underpinned by the right to survival and development, which in turn encompasses the child's right to the highest attainable standard of health, to an adequate standard of living, to social security and to play.

5.210 Within the context of the right to life, survival and development the issue of resources is an ever present hurdle to proper implementation and enforcement. An acute focus on breadth and depth of the child's right to life, survival and development is vital if the means are to be secured to give effect to those rights. In its 1995 *Concluding observations of the Committee on the Rights of the Child: United Kingdom of Great Britain and Northern Ireland*[582] the UN Committee on the Rights of the Child expressed concern over the adequacy of measures taken by the United Kingdom to ensure the implementation of economic, social and cultural rights to the maximum extent of available resources.[583] The Committee expressed particular concern regarding poverty.[584] The Committee recommended that, with regard to matters relating to the health, welfare and standard of living of children in the United Kingdom, additional measures be taken to address, as a matter of priority, problems affecting the health status of children of different socio-economic groups and of children belonging to ethnic minorities and to the problems of homelessness affecting children and their families. In its 2002 Report,[585] the Committee reiterated its concerns regarding child poverty. Unless adequate means can be secured from a responsible and sympathetic Government, the right of children in the United Kingdom to life, survival and development will not be adequately honoured.

---

[581] (1980) 3 EHRR 408, paras 18–20.

[582] *Concluding observations of the Committee on the Rights of the Child: United Kingdom of Great Britain and Northern Ireland* CRC/C/15/Add.34.

[583] *Concluding observations of the Committee on the Rights of the Child: United Kingdom of Great Britain and Northern Ireland* CRC/C/15/Add.34, para 9.

[584] *Concluding observations of the Committee on the Rights of the Child: United Kingdom of Great Britain and Northern Ireland* CRC/C/15/Add.34, para 15.

[585] *Concluding observations of the Committee on the Rights of the Child: United Kingdom of Great Britain and Northern Ireland* CRC/C/15/Add.188.

Chapter 6

THE CHILD'S RIGHT TO PARTICIPATE

Participate / pɑː'tɪsɪ,peɪt / v.intr. *1.* (foll. by *in*) take a part or share (in).

Concise Oxford Dictionary

INTRODUCTION

6.1   With the right to survival and development, the child's right to participate is the second substantive right also constituting a 'Guiding Principles' under which all of the other rights enshrined in the CRC are given effect.[1] Arguably, the right to participate is the right that articulates with the greatest clarity the child's status as an equal member of the human family able to hold and exercise rights.[2] As Van Bueren observes:[3]

'If the hallmark of a democratic society is a plurality of expressed opinions and contributions by those living within it then the participation of children ought to be valued.'

The right to participate emphasises that children not only have discrete views on the affairs of society which affect them but that they also can have 'superior knowledge' in many areas, which knowledge is deserving of respect.[4] The right to participate is a right relevant to children of all ages.[5] In short, the right to participate emphasises the child's status as an individual with fundamental rights and views and feelings of their own.[6] Against the fundamental nature of the child's right to participate, Van Bueren however cautions that this right is often regarded in a far more circumspect manner than the 'traditional' first generation rights.[7]

---

[1]   See *General Guidelines regarding the form and content of initial reports to be submitted by States Parties under article 44* UN Doc. CRC/C/5, 1991, para 1(a) and para 6.1 above.

[2]   For the contrary view see Guggenheim, M *What's Wrong with Children's Rights* (2005) Harvard University Press, pp 94–95 and pp 159–167.

[3]   Van Bueren, G *The International Law on the Rights of the Child* (1998) Martinus Nijhoff, p 131. As Alderson and Goodwin observe, if children are to be respected as rational moral actors in their own right 'their experiences must be seen as profound sources of knowledge' (Alderson, P and Goodwin, M *Contradictions Within Concepts of Children's Competence* (1993) International Journal of Children's Rights 303, p 309).

[4]   Flekkoy, M *A Voice for Children – Speaking Out as their Ombudsmen* (1991) Jessica Kingsley, p 225. At the 1976 US Democratic Convention no one paid any attention when 12 year old Gilbert Giles, a child reporter for the Children's Express charity in New York, got into the lift with a group of Jimmy Carter's senior aids. Giles scooped the world's press on Carter's choice of Walter Mondale as his Vice-Presidential running mate (Williams, S *Children's Express – A Voice for Young People in an Adult World* in Franklin, B (ed) *The New Handbook of Children's Rights* (2002) Routledge, p 255 ('Children's Express' is now 'Headliners'. See www.headliners.org)).

[5]   Thoburn, J *Involving Children in Planning and Review Services, Hearing the Children*, Family Law 2004, p 121.

[6]   Newell, P and Hodgkin, R *Implementation Handbook for the Convention on the Rights of the Child* (2008) 3rd edn, UNICEF, p 149. Within this context, Newell and Hodgkin note that the Committee on the Rights of the Child has rejected what it termed the 'charity mentality and paternalistic approaches towards children's issues.'

[7]   Van Bueren, G *The International Law on the Rights of the Child* (1998) Martinus Nijhoff, p 131.

6.2   The child's right to participate is closely allied to the child's right to freedom of expression,[8] the child's right to freedom of thought, conscience and religion[9] and the child's right to freedom of association.[10] Art 12 of the CRC should be read with Arts 13 and 17 of the CRC which guarantee to children the right to freedom of expression and the right to information respectively, both being key elements of effective participation.[11] However, it should also be remembered in relation to the right to participate under Art 12 and the right to freedom of expression under Art 13 that:[12]

> '... while both articles are strongly linked, they do elaborate different rights. Freedom of expression relates to the right to hold and express opinions, and to seek and receive information through any media. It asserts the right of the child not to be restricted by the State party in the opinions she or he holds or expresses. As such, the obligation it imposes on States parties is to refrain from interference in the expression of those views, or in access to information, while protecting the right of access to means of communication and public dialogue. Article 12, however, relates to the right of expression of views specifically about matters which affect the child, and the right to be involved in actions and decisions that impact on her or his life. Article 12 imposes an obligation on States parties to introduce the legal framework and mechanisms necessary to facilitate active involvement of the child in all actions affecting the child and in decision-making, and to fulfill the obligation to give due weight to those views once expressed.'

6.3   It is a requirement of natural justice that a person be able to participate in matters that impact upon them. The opportunity for children to participate fully and directly in the formulation of their own destiny in a manner commensurate with their age, development and understanding is thus a cardinal right. This chapter considers both the nature and extent of the child's right to participate under the CRC, international law, the key regional human rights instruments and finally under domestic law. In addition to examining the nature and ambit of the right to participate under each of those legal frameworks, the chapter considers in detail within each of those jurisdictional contexts the practical application of the child's right to participate in the areas of family life, medicine and healthcare, judicial and administrative proceedings, education and wider society.

---

8   CRC, Art 13.
9   CRC, Art 14. See Sachs J in *Christian Education South Africa v Minister of Education* (2000) 9 BHRC 53, Const Ct of South Africa commenting on the desirability of hearing the views of children in a case concerning freedom of religion: 'We have not had the assistance of a *curator ad litem* to represent the interests of the children. It was accepted in the High Court that it was not necessary to appoint such a curator because the state would represent the interests of the child. This was unfortunate. The children concerned were from a highly conscientised community and many would have been in their late teens and capable of articulate expression. Although both the state and the parents were in a position to speak on their behalf, neither was able to speak in their name. A curator could have made sensitive enquiries so as to enable their voice or voices to be heard. Their actual experiences and opinions would not necessarily have been decisive, but they would have enriched the dialogue, and the factual and experiential foundations for the balancing exercise in this difficult matter would have been more secure.' See also the judgment of Langa CJ in *Kwazulu-Natal v Pillay* [2007] ZACC 21 (Const Ct South Africa) 'It is always desirable, and may sometimes be vital, to hear from the person whose religion or culture is at issue. That is often no less true when the belief in question is that of a child. Legal matters involving children often exclude the children and the matter is left to adults to argue and decide on their behalf.'
10   CRC, Art 15.
11   Children must be made aware of their right to participate if that right is to have meaning (Newell, P and Hodgkin, R *Implementation Handbook for the Convention on the Rights of the Child* (2008) 3rd edn, UNICEF, p 152). States parties have to ensure that the child receives all necessary information and advice to make a decision in favour of her or his best interests (Committee on the Rights of the Child General Comment No 12 *The Right of the Child to Be Heard* CRC/C/GC/12, para 16).
12   Committee on the Rights of the Child General Comment No 12 *The Right of the Child to Be Heard* (CRC/C/GC/12, para 81).

GENERAL PRINCIPLES

'Participation'

6.4 Article 12 of the CRC and, in the domestic context, s 1(3)(a) of the Children Act 1989 Act articulate the concept of the child's participation in terms of the opportunity to be heard.[13] These provisions facilitate the child's participation through the expression by the child of his or her views, wishes and feelings coupled with an allied duty to give due weight to those expressed views. Whilst the ECHR does not enshrine a right to participate, Arts 6 and 8 of the ECHR ensure the involvement of the child in narrower terms by requiring the adequate and independent representation of the child's interests within certain judicial and administrative processes.[14] At the heart of each approach is the concept of participation.

6.5 In its General Comment No 12 the UN Committee on the Rights of the Child observes in relation to processes through which the views expressed by children add relevant perspectives and experience that:

> 'These processes are usually called participation. The exercise of the child's or children's right to be heard is a crucial element of such processes. The concept of participation emphasises that including children should not only be a momentary act, but the starting point for an intense exchange between children and adults on the development of policies, programmes and measures in all relevant contexts of children's lives.'[15]

The UN Committee thus makes clear that if participation is to be an effective and meaningful right for children, it needs to be understood as a process, not as an individual one-off event.[16] Finally, crucial to the concept of participation is the allied duty to take account of the child's contribution in a manner and to an extent commensurate with their age, development and understanding.[17]

PARTICIPATION NOT SELF-DETERMINATION

6.6 The child's right to participate should not be confused with a right to 'self-determination'.[18] Art 12 does not confer complete autonomy on children as the article does not stipulate that a child's views, whilst expressed as of right, must be acceded to.[19] As such, Art 12 confers on children a right to participate in the decision

---

[13] See below **6.11** and **6.95**.

[14] See below **6.72**.

[15] Committee on the Rights of the Child General Comment No 12 (2009) *The Right of the Child to Be Heard* CRC/C/GC/12, para 13.

[16] Committee on the Rights of the Child General Comment No 12 (2009) *The Right of the Child to Be Heard* CRC/C/GC/12, para 133. For example, Hart describes a path to full child participation comprising manipulation; decoration; tokenism, assigned but informed participation, consulted and informed participation; adult initiated shared decisions with children; child initiated and directed and child initiated shared decisions with adults (Hart, R *Children's Participation – From Tokenship to Citizenship* (1992) UNICEF Innocenti Essays No 4, p 8).

[17] See **6.9** and **6.10** below.

[18] Whilst the term 'right to self determination' is used here to denote personal self-determination, in a legal context the term is more generally used to refer to the right of cohesive natural groups ('peoples') to choose for themselves a form of political organisation and their relation to other groups (Brownlie, I *Principles of Public International Law* (2008) Oxford, p 580).

[19] Fortin, J *Children's Rights and the Developing Law* (2009) 3rd edn, Cambridge, p 236.

being made, not a right to dictate the decisions that will be made.[20] The right of all children, regardless of age or understanding, to self determination in respect of the political, social, cultural, economic and legal order under which the child lives would not be compatible with Art 5 of the CRC, which requires States Parties to respect the responsibilities, rights of parents and legal guardians to provide, in a manner consistent with the evolving capacities of the child, appropriate direction and guidance in the exercise by the child of the rights recognised in the CRC.[21]

Participation and Best Interests

6.7 Within the domestic context, it has long been considered that there is a tension between the child's right to be heard in judicial proceedings concerning children, as enshrined in s 1(3)(a) of the Children Act 1989 and the principle that the child's best interest must be the court's paramount consideration.[22] Accordingly, where following the views of even the older child is antithetic to that child's welfare, the domestic courts will overrule those views.[23] In contrast, the UN Committee on the Rights of the Child sees no tension between the right to participate and the best interests of the child, observing:[24]

> 'There is no tension between articles 3 and 12, only a complementary role of the two general principles: one establishes the objective of achieving the best interests of the child and the other provides the methodology for reaching the goal of hearing either the child or the children. In fact, there can be no correct application of article 3 if the components of article 12 are not respected. Likewise, article 3 reinforces the functionality of article 12, facilitating the essential role of children in all decisions affecting their lives.'

6.8 This analysis is based on the argument that the twin propositions that a child's best interests cannot properly be determined without the participation of the child and that in ensuring the participation of the child the child's best interests must be respected are propositions which are complimentary rather than competitive. It remains the case however that the first proposition embodies within it a potential tension between the right to participate and the child's best interests, by reference to which that right must be given effect, in that facilitating the role of children in all decisions affecting their lives may, depending on the nature of the decision to be taken and the views of the child on that decision, be antithetic to the child's best interests. For example, in *Re W (A Minor)(Medical Treatment: Court's Jurisdiction)* Lord Donaldson observed in relation to a 16 year old child suffering from anorexia nervosa who was unwilling to receive treatment that:

> 'Where the wishes of the minor are themselves something which the doctors reasonably consider need to be treated in the minors own interests, those wishes clearly have a much reduced significance.'

Thus, it is only realistic to acknowledge that in circumstances where the child's right to participate must be exercised in a manner which ensures the child's right to protection

---

[20] But see **6.96** below comparing the position under CRC, Art 12 and *Gillick v West Norfolk and Wisbeach Health* Authority [1986] AC 122.

[21] Van Bueren, G *The International Law on the Rights of the Child* (1998) Martinus Nijhoff, p 138. For a detailed discussion of 'evolving capacity' see **4.25** et seq.

[22] See for example Schofield, *The Voice of the Child in Public Law Proceedings: A Developmental Model, Hearing the Children*, Family Law 2004, p 34.

[23] See for example *Re L (Medical Treatment: Gillick Competence)* [1998] 2 FLR 810.

[24] [1993] Fam 64.

from harm[25] compromises may sometimes be necessary when interpreting the child's right to participate through the interpretive prism of the child's best interests.

Participation and the Developmental Context

6.9   The child's right to participate, both under the CRC and in domestic legislation is closely linked to the concept of 'evolving capacity'.[26] This link is articulated in Art 12 of the CRC by the requirement that the views of the child be given due weight 'in accordance with the age and maturity of the child'.[27] Within the domestic jurisdiction, the link is made in s 1(3)(a) of the Children Act 1989 by the requirement that the child's wishes and feelings be considered 'in light of his age and understanding'.

6.10   Article 12 of the CRC, when read with Arts 5 and 13, is specifically designed to move the focus from the question of which decisions children are not competent to make to the question of how children can participate and which elements of decisions they are able to make.[28] This latter question demands that consideration be given to the developmental context in which it is asked. In particular, regard must be had to the chronological and developmental range covered by 'childhood' and the fact that chronological age and developmental age will not necessarily coincide. Thus, for a child of a given age, the implementation of his or her right to participate must be considered within the context of a number of key aspects of developmental psychology[29] and theories of attachment,[30] cognitive development[31] and resilience[32] as well as the child's chronological age. The UN Committee on the Rights of the Child observes that:[33]

> 'Children's levels of understanding are not uniformly linked to their biological age. Research has shown that information, experience, environment, social and cultural expectations, and levels of support all contribute to the development of a child's capacities to form a view. For this reason, the views of the child have to be assessed on a case-by-case examination.'

When it comes to the right to participate children cannot be 'treated as a homogenous group in relation to whether and how they wish to participate in decision making'.[34] It should also be remembered that the child's right to participate should not lead to the assumption that the child will always have a settled view on a given topic and may be, and remain, undecided in respect of the same. States Parties must ensure effective access to justice for children with disabilities on an equal basis to others, including measures to facilitate their effective role both as direct and indirect participants.[35]

---

[25]   Committee on the Rights of the Child General Comment No 12 (2009) *The Right of the Child to Be Heard* CRC/C/GC/12, para 21.

[26]   See **4.25** above.

[27]   CRC, Art 12(1).

[28]   Van Bueren, G *The International Law on the Rights of the Child* (1998) Martinus Nijhoff, p 137.

[29]   For an excellent summary of the current research evidence on child and adolescent developmental capacity for decision making see Fortin, J *Children's Rights and the Developing Law* (2009) 3rd edn, Cambridge, pp 82–86.

[30]   See Bowlby, *Attachment and Loss, Volume 1 Attachment* (1969) Hogarth Press 1969, Howe, Brandon, Hinings and Schofield, *Attachment Theory: Child Maltreatment and Family Support* (1999) Macmillan.

[31]   See Piaget and Inhelder, *The Psychology of the Child* (1969) Routledge, Keegan and Paul.

[32]   See Fonagy, Steele, Steele, Higgit and Target, *Theory and Practice of Resilience*, (1994) Journal of Child Psychology and Psychiatry.

[33]   Committee on the Rights of the Child General Comment No 12 *The Right of the Child to Be Heard* CRC/C/GC/12, para 29.

[34]   Day-Scalter, S and Piper, C *Social Exclusion and the Welfare of the Child* (2001) Journal of Law and Society 409, p 427.

[35]   UN Convention on the Rights of Persons with Disabilities, Art 13.

THE CHILD'S RIGHT TO PARTICIPATE

The Child's Right to Participate under the CRC

Right to Participate – Art 12 CRC

6.11 Article 12 of the CRC explicitly enshrines the child's right to participate in the following terms:

> '1. States Parties shall assure to the child who is capable of forming his or her own views the right to express those views freely in all matters affecting the child, the views of the child being given due weight in accordance with the age and maturity of the child.
>
> 2. For this purpose, the child shall in particular be provided the opportunity to be heard in any judicial and administrative proceedings affecting the child, either directly, or through a representative or an appropriate body, in a manner consistent with the procedural rules of national law.'

6.12 The UN Committee on the Rights of the Child has published a General Comment on Art 12, giving detailed guidance as to its application and interrelationship with the other articles of the CRC. General Comment No 12, *The Right of the Child to Be Heard* was adopted at the Fifty-first session of the Committee on 1 July 2009.[36]

Article 12 CRC – Ambit

6.13 The Committee on the Rights of the Child has emphasised that Art 12 is a general principle of fundamental importance to all aspects of the implementation of the CRC and to the interpretation of each of its other articles.[37] Its significance is that it not only requires that the child should be assured the right to express his or her views freely, but also that they should be heard and that their views shall be given 'due weight'.[38] It highlights the role of the child as an active participant in the promotion, protection and monitoring of his or her own rights.[39] The Committee has stressed that:[40]

> 'To speak, to participate, to have their views taken into account: these three phases describe the sequence of the enjoyment of the right to participate from a functional point of view. The new and deeper meaning of this right is that it should establish a new social contract. One by which children are fully recognised as rights-holders who are not only entitled to receive protection but also have the right to participate in all matters affecting them, a right which can be considered as the symbol for their recognition as rights holders. This implies, in the long term, changes in political, social, institutional and cultural structures.'

6.14 Article 12 of the CRC thus affirms that children should not be seen as passive members of society but as active participants with rights to express their own views on

---

[36] CRC/C/GC/12 (2009). See also Committee on the Rights of the Child, Report on the forty-third session, September 2006, Day of General Discussion, Recommendations, Preamble (this document was the pre-cursor to the Committee's General Comment No 12).

[37] Newell, P and Hodgkin, R *Implementation Handbook for the Convention on the Rights of the Child* (2008) 3rd edn, UNICEF, p 149. Committee on the Rights of the Child General Comment No 12 *The Right of the Child to Be Heard* CRC/C/GC/12, para 2.

[38] Newell, P and Hodgkin, R *Implementation Handbook for the Convention on the Rights of the Child* (2008) 3rd edn, UNICEF, p 150.

[39] Committee on the Rights of the Child General Comment No 5 *General Measures of Implementation of the Convention on the Rights of the Child* HRI/GEN/1/Rev, p 387.

[40] Committee on the Rights of the Child, Report on the forty-third session, September 2006, Day of General Discussion, Recommendations, Preamble.

all matters affecting them.[41] This requires the implementation of Art 12 to be more than paying lip-service to the principles enshrined in the CRC. The Committee on the Rights of the Child further observes that:[42]

> '... appearing to "listen" to children is relatively unchallenging; giving due weight to their views requires real change. Listening to children should not be seen as an end in itself, but rather as a means by which States make their interactions with children and their actions on behalf of children ever more sensitive to the implementation of children's rights ... article 12 requires consistent and ongoing arrangements. Involvement of and consultation with children must also avoid being tokenistic and aim to ascertain representative views.'

6.15   The corollary to these principles is that the child 'has the right not to exercise the right to participate. Expressing views is a choice for the child, not an obligation'.[43] Further, the right is that of the child to express his or her own views, not a right to express the views of others.[44]

6.16   The implementation of the rights under Art 12 should not be dependent on the availability of resources. The qualification contained in Art 4 of the Convention in respect of economic, social and cultural rights that States Parties shall undertake implementation 'to the maximum extent of their available resources' does not apply to civil and political rights, including those enshrined in Art 12.[45]

Article 12(1) CRC – Interpretation

(i)   'Shall assure to'

6.17   The term 'shall assure' is a legal term of special strength, which leaves no leeway for State parties' discretion. States parties are under a strict obligation to undertake appropriate measures to fully implement the right to participate for all children.[46] The UN Committee provides guidance on the steps required for implementation of the right to participate, proceeding from the proper preparation of the child through the assessment of the child's capacity, the hearing of the child, the feedback to be given to the child and concluding with arrangements for complaints, remedies and redress.[47] A key element to assuring the child's right to participate is the provision of proper training for all professionals working with children.[48] Overall, all processes in which a child or children are heard and participate must be transparent and informative, voluntary, respectful, relevant, child friendly, inclusive, supported by training, safe and sensitive to risk and accountable.[49] In its General Comment No 2 *The Role of Independent National*

---

[41]   Fortin, J *Children's Rights and the Developing Law* (2009) 3rd edn, Cambridge, p 235.

[42]   Committee on the Rights of the Child General Comment No 5 *General Measures of Implementation of the Convention on the Rights of the Child* HRI/GEN/1/Rev. p 391.

[43]   Committee on the Rights of the Child General Comment No 12 (2009) *The Right of the Child to Be Heard* (CRC/C/GC/12, para 16).

[44]   Committee on the Rights of the Child General Comment No 12 (2009) *The Right of the Child to Be Heard* (CRC/C/GC/12, para 22).

[45]   Newell, P and Hodgkin, R *Implementation Handbook for the Convention on the Rights of the Child* (2008) 3rd edn, UNICEF, p 160.

[46]   Committee on the Rights of the Child General Comment No 12 (2009) *The Right of the Child to Be Heard* (CRC/C/GC/12, para 19).

[47]   Committee on the Rights of the Child General Comment No 12 (2009) *The Right of the Child to Be Heard* CRC/C/GC/12, para 40.

[48]   Committee on the Rights of the Child General Comment No 12 (2009) *The Right of the Child to Be Heard* CRC/C/GC/12, para 49.

[49]   Committee on the Rights of the Child General Comment No 12 (2009) *The Right of the Child to Be Heard* (CRC/C/GC/12, para 134).

Human Rights Institutions in the Promotion and Protection of the Rights of the Child[50] the Committee on the Rights of the Child makes clear that such institutions:[51]

> '... have a key role to play in promoting respect for the views of children in all matters affecting them, as articulated in article 12 of the Convention, by Government and throughout society. This general principle should be applied to the establishment, organisation and activities of national human rights institutions. Institutions must ensure that they have direct contact with children and that children are appropriately involved and consulted. Children's councils, for example, could be created as advisory bodies for NHRIs to facilitate the participation of children in matters of concern to them.'

(ii) 'A child Who is Capable of Forming His or Her Own Views'

6.18 The right to participate enshrined in Art 12(1) applies to those children who are capable of *forming* their own views, not just children who are capable of expressing their own views. The right thus applies to pre-verbal children and children unable to express their views by reason of disability, in respect of whom Art 12(1) must be implemented without discrimination pursuant to Art 2 of the CRC.[52] The UN Committee has made clear that:[53]

> 'The Committee wishes to emphasise that article 12 applies both to younger and to older children. As holders of rights, even the youngest children are entitled to express their views, which should be 'given due weight in accordance with the age and maturity of the child' (art. 12.1). Young children are acutely sensitive to their surroundings and very rapidly acquire understanding of the people, places and routines in their lives, along with awareness of their own unique identity. They make choices and communicate their feelings, ideas and wishes in numerous ways, long before they are able to communicate through the conventions of spoken or written language.'

6.19 Within this context, the phrase 'capable of forming his or her own views' should not be seen as a limitation, but rather as an obligation for States parties to assess the capacity of the child to form an autonomous opinion to the greatest extent possible.[54] This requires that States parties begin with the presumption that a child has the capacity to form her or his own views and recognise that she or he has the right to express them; it is not up to the child to first prove her or his capacity.[55] As such, the imposition of specific age barriers in relation to Art 12 rights is of questionable legitimacy under the CRC as all children have the rights under that article.[56]

---

[50] Committee on the Rights of the Child General Comment No 2 *The Role of Independent National Human Rights Institutions in the Promotion and Protection of the Rights of the Child* HRI/GEN/1/Rev 8, p 356.

[51] Committee on the Rights of the Child General Comment No 2 *The Role of Independent National Human Rights Institutions in the Promotion and Protection of the Rights of the Child* HRI/GEN/1/Rev 8, p 359.

[52] Committee on the Rights of the Child General Comment No 12 (2009) *The Right of the Child to Be Heard* (CRC/C/GC/12, para 21) and see Newell, P and Hodgkin, R *Implementation Handbook for the Convention on the Rights of the Child* (2008) 3rd edn, UNICEF, pp 159–160. Disabled children and young people in England and Wales currently have no legal right to augmentative and alternative communication equipment essential for the enjoyment of their Art 12 rights (see Children's Rights Alliance, *State of Children's Rights in England* (2008), p 12).

[53] Committee on the Rights of the Child General Comment No 7 *Implementing Child Rights in Early Childhood* HRI/GEN/1/Rev 8, p 432.

[54] Committee on the Rights of the Child General Comment No 12 (2009) *The Right of the Child to Be Heard* (CRC/C/GC/12, para 20).

[55] Committee on the Rights of the Child General Comment No 12 (2009) *The Right of the Child to Be Heard* (CRC/C/GC/12, para 20).

[56] Newell, P and Hodgkin, R *Implementation Handbook for the Convention on the Rights of the Child* (2008) 3rd edn, UNICEF, p 130. General Comment No 12 (2009) *The Right of the Child to Be Heard* (CRC/C/GC/12, para 21).

6.20 Whilst capacity to form views on a particular issue requires understanding of that issue as a necessary pre-condition, the Committee on the Rights of the Child considers that a child needs only a 'sufficient understanding' (as opposed to a comprehensive understanding) to be considered capable of forming his or her own views on the matter in question pursuant to Art 12 of the CRC.[57]

(iii) 'The Right to Express Those Views Freely'

6.21 The use of the word 'freely' in Art 12(1) requires that the child should be able to express his or her own views without pressure, manipulation or undue influence.[58] This will include ensuring that the child's social situation is considered, an environment is provided in which the child feels respected and secure in expressing his or her opinions and the child is not interviewed more often than necessary.[59] For example, there is no area of traditional parental or adult authority comprising an environment in which the views of the child have no place.[60]

6.22 As noted above, the child's freedom to express a view does not equate to an obligation to express a view. The child should be able to choose whether or not he or she wants to exercise his or her right to be heard.[61] The child should not suffer any pressure, constraint or influence that might prevent the expression of a view or require such an expression.[62] Within this context, a key element of the child being able to decide whether to express a view and to express any view freely is ensuring that:[63]

> '... the child be informed about the matters, options and possible decisions to be taken and their consequences by those who are responsible for hearing the child, and by the child's parents or guardian. The child must also be informed about the conditions under which she or he will be asked to express her or his views. This right to information is essential, because it is the precondition of the child's clarified decisions.'

6.23 Article 12 of the CRC does not confer an unqualified right to express views directly. Article 12(2) provides simply that the child's views shall be communicated 'either directly, or through a representative or an appropriate body, in a manner consistent with the procedural rules of national law'. This position flows from the fact that Art 12 must be read having regard to the child's best interests pursuant to Art 3 of the CRC, those best interests requiring for some children specific measures to enable the child's direct participation or in some cases militating against the child's direct participation. There is no requirement that any representative or appropriate body who expresses the child's views on his or her behalf must be designated to act for the child.[64] However, the rules of fairness and natural justice are likely to demand that any

---

[57] Committee on the Rights of the Child General Comment No 12 (2009) *The Right of the Child to Be Heard* (CRC/C/GC/12, para 21). The concept of 'evolving capacity' enshrined in Art 5 of the CRC (see **4.25** above) will be highly relevant to whether given children can be said to be 'capable of forming their own views'.

[58] Newell, P and Hodgkin, R *Implementation Handbook for the Convention on the Rights of the Child* (2008) 3rd edn, UNICEF, p 154.

[59] Committee on the Rights of the Child General Comment No 12 (2009) *The Right of the Child to Be Heard* (CRC/C/GC/12, paras 22–24).

[60] Newell, P and Hodgkin, R *Implementation Handbook for the Convention on the Rights of the Child* (2008) 3rd edn, UNICEF, p 154.

[61] Newell, P and Hodgkin, R *Implementation Handbook for the Convention on the Rights of the Child* (2008) 3rd edn, UNICEF, p 154.

[62] Manual on Human Rights Reporting (1997) HR/PUB/91/1 (Rev 1), p 426.

[63] Committee on the Rights of the Child General Comment No 12 (2009) *The Right of the Child to Be Heard* (CRC/C/GC/12, paras 25).

[64] Fortin, J *Children's Rights and the Developing Law* (2009) 3rd edn, Cambridge, p 236.

representative charged with 'freely' expressing the child's views be able to demonstrate that there is no conflict of interest, including a parent and official bodies.[65]

(iv)   'In All Matters Affecting the Child'

6.24   Article 12(1) places a duty on States Parties to involve children in, and take account of their views in all matters which affect them, including those not specifically covered by the CRC.[66] In its General Comment No 5 *General Measures of Implementation of the Convention on the Rights of the Child* the UN Committee on the Rights of the Child notes:[67]

> 'The emphasis on 'matters that affect them' in article 12(1) implies the ascertainment of the views of particular groups of children on particular issues – for example children who have experience of the juvenile justice system on proposals for law reform in that area, or adopted children and children in adoptive families on adoption law and policy.'

6.25   The ambit of the term 'all matters' is further clarified in the Committee on the Rights of the Child General Comment No 12 which stipulates that 'the child must be heard if the matter under discussion affects the child'.[68] The inclusion of the words 'all matters' introduces a level of 'horizontality'[69] to the application of the Art 12 right to participate, ensuring that the duty of the State to ensure the participation of the child extends beyond the relationship between the State and the individual child to matters concerning the child's private sphere. The use of the phrase 'all matters affecting the child' thus means that there is no longer an area of decision making concerning children in which adults have exclusive input into the decision to be made. Rather, parental and family decision making in respect of the child, as well as decisions taken by the State, are subject to the views of the child with those views to be given due weight in accordance with the child's age and maturity.[70] Once again, the requirement to consider the child's views in all matters affecting them should not mean that the child is pressured into becoming the decision-maker or pressured into expressing their views where they choose not to.[71]

(v)   'Due Weight in Accordance with the Age and Maturity of the Child'

6.26   The inclusion of 'age and maturity' as a condition precedent to the weight to be attached to the child's expressed views seeks to ensure that States Parties do not have an unfettered discretion as to whether and when to listen to the views of the child.[72] Simply

---

[65]   Committee on the Rights of the Child General Comment No 12 (2009) *The Right of the Child to Be Heard* (CRC/C/GC/12, paras 36–37). See also the President's Direction 5 April 2004 *Representation of Children in Family Proceedings Pursuant to Family Proceedings Rules 1991, Rule 9.5* [2004] 1 FLR 1188 which provides that one of the factors which should guide the decision to appoint separate representation for the child is the extent to which the child has a standpoint or interests which are inconsistent with or incapable of being represented by any of the adult parties (note that separate representation in family proceedings is now governed by the Family Procedure Rules 2010, r 16). See also Art 4(1) of the European Convention on the Exercise of Children's Rights and the Committee on the Rights of the Child General Comment No 12 (2009) *The Right of the Child to Be Heard* CRC/C/GC/12, paras 36–37.

[66]   Manual on Human Rights Reporting (1997) HR/PUB/91/1 (Rev 1), pp 426–427.

[67]   Committee on the Rights of the Child General Comment No 5 *General Measures of Implementation of the Convention on the Rights of the Child* HRI/GEN/1/Rev. p 391.

[68]   Committee on the Rights of the Child General Comment No 12 (2009) *The Right of the Child to Be Heard* (CRC/C/GC/12, paras 26).

[69]   See **2.85** above.

[70]   See **6.42** below.

[71]   Van Bueren, G *The International Law on the Rights of the Child* (1998) Martinus Nijhoff, p 137.

[72]   Van Bueren, G *The International Law on the Rights of the Child* (1998) Martinus Nijhoff, p 136.

listening to the views expressed by the child is not sufficient. The views of the child must be considered seriously where the child is capable of forming those views.[73] Both the 'age' and 'maturity' criteria are of equal value as children vary developmentally within defined age ranges.[74] They are closely linked with the concept of evolving capacity.[75] The UN Committee observes that 'maturity':[76]

'... refers to the ability to understand and assess the implications of a particular matter, and must therefore be considered when determining the individual capacity of a child. Maturity is difficult to define; in the context of article 12, it is the capacity of a child to express her or his views on issues in a reasonable and independent manner. The impact of the matter on the child must also be taken into consideration. The greater the impact of the outcome on the life of the child, the more relevant the appropriate assessment of the maturity of that child.'

6.27   Thus, in considering the concept of age and maturity it is important to remember that a child's level of understanding is not uniformly linked to his or her biological age. For this reason, the views of the child have to be assessed on a case-by-case examination'.[77] For example, age alone should not be an impediment for the child to access complaints mechanisms within the justice system and administrative proceedings.[78] Further, the Committee on the Rights of the Child draws a distinction between the right to be heard of an individual child and the right to heard as applied to a group of children.[79] The reason for this is articulated by General Comment No 12 as follows:[80]

'The conditions of age and maturity can be assessed when an individual child is heard and also when a group of children chooses to express its views. The task of assessing a child's age and maturity is facilitated when the group in question is a component of an enduring structure, such as a family, a class of schoolchildren or the residents of a particular neighbourhood, but is made more difficult when children express themselves collectively. Even when confronting difficulties in assessing age and maturity, States parties should consider children as a group to be heard, and the Committee strongly recommends that States parties exert all efforts to listen to or seek the views of those children speaking collectively.'

Article 12(2) CRC – Interpretation

6.28   Article 12(2) of the CRC provides specifically as follows in respect of the child's right to be heard in judicial and administrative proceedings:[81]

---

[73]   Committee on the Rights of the Child General Comment No 12 (2009) *The Right of the Child to Be Heard* (CRC/C/GC/12, para 28).

[74]   Van Bueren, G *The International Law on the Rights of the Child* (1998) Martinus Nijhoff, p 136. See above **6.9**.

[75]   See **4.25** above.

[76]   Committee on the Rights of the Child General Comment No 12 (2009) *The Right of the Child to Be Heard* (CRC/C/GC/12, para 30).

[77]   Committee on the Rights of the Child General Comment No 12 (2009) *The Right of the Child to Be Heard* (CRC/C/GC/12, para 29).

[78]   CRC/GC/2005/6.

[79]   Committee on the Rights of the Child General Comment No 12 (2009) *The Right of the Child to Be Heard* (CRC/C/GC/12, para 9).

[80]   Committee on the Rights of the Child General Comment No 12 (2009) *The Right of the Child to Be Heard* (CRC/C/GC/12, para 10).

[81]   Article 12(2) was originally included in the CRC as the second paragraph of Art 3 (best interests) before being moved to Art 12 (E/CN.4/1989/48, pp 42–45).

'For this purpose, the child shall in particular be provided the opportunity to be heard in any judicial and administrative proceedings affecting the child, either directly, or through a representative or an appropriate body, in a manner consistent with the procedural rules of national law.'

(i) 'For This Purpose'

6.29   The opening words of Art 12(2) 'for this purpose' require Art 12(2) to be read with Art 12(1), ensuring that a child who is capable of forming his or her own views not only has the right to be heard within judicial and administrative proceedings, but also the right to have those views given due weight in accordance with the age and maturity of the child.[82]

(ii) 'Judicial and Administrative Proceedings'

6.30   The requirement that 'the child shall in particular be provided the opportunity to be heard in any judicial and administrative proceedings' emphasises the importance of the application of the child's right to participate within the context of judicial and administrative proceeding affecting the child's life and future. The UN Committee has stipulated that:[83]

'... all children involved in judicial and administrative proceedings must be informed in a child friendly manner about their right to be heard, modalities of doing so and other aspects of the proceedings.'

6.31   Article 12(2) covers all judicial and administrative proceedings affecting the child. In respect of judicial proceedings, it has been suggested that the term includes criminal prosecutions of parents, the outcome of which can affect children dramatically.[84] The rights under Art 12(2) apply equally to religious courts such as sharia courts.[85] The UN Committee has reminded States Parties that:[86]

'... the right of the child to be heard in judicial and administrative proceedings applies to all relevant settings without limitation, including children separated from their parents, custody and adoption cases, children in conflict with the law, children victims of physical violence, sexual abuse or other violent crimes, asylum seeking and refugee children and children who have been the victims of armed conflict and in emergencies.'

6.32   The term 'administrative proceedings' is a wide term in its application.[87] The term covers a very broad range of formal decision making processes, including those in respect of health, education, planning[88] and the environment.[89] For example, in

---

82   Van Bueren, G *The International Law on the Rights of the Child* (1998) Martinus Nijhoff, p 139.

83   Committee on the Rights of the Child, Report on the forty-third session, September 2006, Day of General Discussion, Recommendations, para 40.

84   Newell, P and Hodgkin, R *Implementation Handbook for the Convention on the Rights of the Child* (2008) 3rd edn, UNICEF, p 156. Theoretically, this assertion could be taken further to encompass all court proceedings concerning parents and carers the outcome of which would impact adversely on the child, including proceedings for child maintenance and civil actions affecting the families' income or home.

85   Lebanon CRC/C/LBN/CO/3, paras 35–36.

86   Committee on the Rights of the Child, Report on the forty-third session, September 2006, Day of General Discussion, Recommendations, para 239. General Comment No 12 (2009) *The Right of the Child to Be Heard* (CRC/C/GC/12, paras 32).

87   Van Bueren, G *The International Law on the Rights of the Child* (1998) Martinus Nijhoff, p 137. See also Fawcett, J *The Application of the European Convention on Human Rights* (1987).

88   See Committee on the Rights of the Child General Comment No 5 *General Measures of Implementation of the Convention on the Rights of the Child* HRI/GEN/1/Rev, p 446.

determining the administrative measures to be adopted with respect to unaccompanied asylum seeking children the child's wishes should be ascertained and taken into account, it further being imperative that such children are provided with all relevant information concerning, for example, their entitlements, services available including means of communication, the asylum process, family tracing and the situation in their country of origin.[90] Further examples are administrative mechanisms to address discipline issues in schools, for example suspensions and expulsions, refusals to grant school certificates and performance-related issues, disciplinary measures and refusals to grant privileges in juvenile detention centres and applications for driver's licences.[91] The term 'administrative proceedings' will also encompass alternative dispute mechanisms such as mediation and arbitration[92] and complaints procedures.[93]

(iii) 'Either Directly or Through a Representative or Appropriate Body'

6.33   As already noted, Art 12 of the CRC does not confer a right to express views directly.[94] Art 12(2) provides simply that the child's views shall be communicated 'either directly, or through a representative or an appropriate body, in a manner consistent with the procedural rules of national law'. Further, Art 12(2) does not specify when the child should be heard directly and when through a representative in judicial and administrative proceedings.[95] However, the Committee on the Rights of the Child recommends that wherever possible the child must be given the opportunity to be heard directly in the proceedings.[96] As to representatives, the Committee observes as follows:[97]

> 'The representative can be the parent(s), a lawyer, or another person (inter alia, a social worker). However, it must be stressed that in many cases (civil, penal or administrative), there are risks of a conflict of interest between the child and their most obvious representative (parent(s)). If the hearing of the child is undertaken through a representative, it is of utmost importance that the child's views are transmitted correctly to the decision maker by the representative. The method chosen should be determined by the child (or by the appropriate authority as necessary) according to her or his particular situation. Representatives must have sufficient knowledge and understanding of the various aspects of the decision-making process and experience in working with children. The representative must be aware that she or he represents exclusively the interests of the child and not the interests of other persons (parent(s)), institutions or bodies (eg residential home, administration or society). Codes of conduct should be developed for representatives who are appointed to represent the child's views.'

6.34   Hodgkin and Newell observe that given the general right under Art 12(1) of the CRC for children to 'express those views freely in all matters affecting the child' it should be assumed that wherever children wish to speak directly to adjudicators that

---

89   Newell, P and Hodgkin, R *Implementation Handbook for the Convention on the Rights of the Child* (2008) 3rd edn, UNICEF, p 149.

90   HRI/GEN/1/Rev 8, p 415.

91   Committee on the Rights of the Child General Comment No 12 (2009) *The Right of the Child to Be Heard* CRC/C/GC/12, para 67.

92   Committee on the Rights of the Child General Comment No 12 (2009) *The Right of the Child to Be Heard* CRC/C/GC/12, para 32.

93   Newell, P and Hodgkin, R *Implementation Handbook for the Convention on the Rights of the Child* (2008) 3rd edn, UNICEF, p 158 and see UN Committee on the Rights of the Child General Comment No 9 *The Rights of Children with Disabilities* (CRC/C/GC/9, paras 42–43).

94   See **6.23** above.

95   CRC, Art 12(2).

96   Committee on the Rights of the Child General Comment No 12 (2009) *The Right of the Child to Be Heard* (CRC/C/GC/12, para 35).

97   Committee on the Rights of the Child General Comment No 12 (2009) *The Right of the Child to Be Heard* (CRC/C/GC/12, paras 36–37).

this should be arranged.[98] Some caution is however required in respect of this view given that Art 12 must be read in light of the child's best interests under Art 3 of the CRC. As such, there will be cases where notwithstanding the child has indicated a wish to speak directly to the tribunal, this will not be in the child's best interests.[99] In this regard, reference should be made to the UN Economic and Social Council Resolution *Guidelines on Justice Involving Child Victims and Witnesses of Crime*[100] which defines 'child sensitive' in the context of the child's right to participate as an approach that 'balances the child's right to protection and that takes into account the child's individual needs and views'.[101]

6.35 Within this context, Hodgkin and Newell do concede that where the child is not able to represent their own views adequately or requires representation in adversarial proceedings appropriate arrangements for the child to participate through a representative should be made.[102] However, they consider that the appointment of such a representative is not the same as providing children with the 'opportunity to be heard' pursuant to Art 12(2) or 'an opportunity to... make their views known' pursuant to CRC, Art 9(2), the risk being that the child's views may conflict with the adult portrayal of such views.[103]

6.36 Judicial and administrative proceedings involving children should ensure child-friendly information, advice, advocacy, and access to independent complaints procedures and to the courts with necessary legal and other assistance.[104]

(iv) 'In a Manner Consistent with the Procedural Rules of National Law'

6.37 The reference to 'the procedural rules of national law' in Art 12(2) permits States Parties to enact procedural rules formulating the manner of the child's participation but *not* circumscribing the right to participate.[105]

Article 12 CRC – Other Relevant CRC Articles

(i) CRC, Art 9(2)

6.38 The CRC incorporates a number of articles which apply the right to participate to specific situations concerning children. Pursuant to Art 9(2) of the CRC in proceedings concerning the separation of children from their parents 'all interested parties shall be given an opportunity to participate in the proceedings and make their views known'. The child is clearly an interested party for the purpose of Art 9(2).[106] Art 9(2) of the CRC should be read in conjunction with Art 12 and as such, the views

---

98 Newell, P and Hodgkin, R *Implementation Handbook for the Convention on the Rights of the Child* (2008) 3rd edn, UNICEF, p 129.

99 See above **6.7**.

100 UNODC/UNICEF 2005/20 of 22 July 2005.

101 UNODC/UNICEF 2005/20 of 22 July 2005, para 9(d).

102 Newell, P and Hodgkin, R *Implementation Handbook for the Convention on the Rights of the Child* (2008) 3rd edn, UNICEF, p 129.

103 Newell, P and Hodgkin, R *Implementation Handbook for the Convention on the Rights of the Child* (2008) 3rd edn, UNICEF, p 129.

104 Committee on the Rights of the Child General Comment No 5 *General Measures of Implementation for the Convention on the Rights of the Child* (CRC/GC/2003/5, para 24).

105 Van Bueren, G *The International Law on the Rights of the Child* (1998) Martinus Nijhoff, p 139.

106 Newell, P and Hodgkin, R *Implementation Handbook for the Convention on the Rights of the Child* (2008) 3rd edn, UNICEF, p 129.

expressed by the child concerning separation from his or her parents must be considered by the judicial authority dealing with the proceedings in accordance with the child's age and maturity.[107]

(ii) CRC, Art 21(a)

6.39 Article 21(a) of the CRC requires that the 'informed consent of the persons concerned' be obtained in respect of adoption.[108] The child's views are not mentioned in the terms of Art 21(a) but proper consideration of the child's views in relation to adoption is implied as well as required under Art 12 of the CRC.[109] Given this, in relation to children who are capable of giving consent, Art 21(a) of the CRC is likely to require that such consent be obtained.

(iii) CRC, Art 37(d)

6.40 Pursuant to Art 37(d) of the CRC every child deprived or his or her liberty has the right to challenge the legality of that deprivation before the court implies the right to initiate court action in addition to being heard.[110]

(iv) CRC, Art 40

6.41 Article 40 of the CRC requires that children who are alleged as having, or accused of, or recognised as having infringed the penal law have the right to an active role in the proceedings (though he or she must not be compelled to give testimony or to confess guilt).[111]

Article 12 CRC – Application

(i) CRC, Art 12 – Family Life

6.42 States Parties should encourage, through legislation and policy, parents, guardians and child minders to listen to children and give due weight to their views in matters that concern them.[112] Parents should also be advised to support children in realising the right to express their views freely and to have children's views duly taken into account at all levels of society.[113] Parents should support children in order to promote the realisation of the child's participation in society'[114] Again a distinction

---

[107] Article 9(1) and see Newell, P and Hodgkin, R *Implementation Handbook for the Convention on the Rights of the Child* (2008) 3rd edn, UNICEF, p 128.

[108] See below **8.151**.

[109] Newell, P and Hodgkin, R *Implementation Handbook for the Convention on the Rights of the Child* (2008) 3rd edn, UNICEF, p 296. See also Mexico CRC/C/15/Add.13 and Germany CRC/C/15/Add.43, para 29).

[110] Newell, P and Hodgkin, R *Implementation Handbook for the Convention on the Rights of the Child* (2008) 3rd edn, UNICEF, p 150. See below at **14.40**.

[111] Newell, P and Hodgkin, R *Implementation Handbook for the Convention on the Rights of the Child* (2008) 3rd edn, UNICEF p 150. See below **16.26**.

[112] The UN Committee points out that 'A family where children can freely express views and be taken seriously from the earliest ages provides an important model, and is a preparation for the child to exercise the right to be heard in the wider society' and that 'Such an approach to parenting serves to promote individual development, enhance family relations and support children's socialisation and plays a preventive role against all forms of violence in the home and family' (Committee on the Rights of the Child General Comment No 12 (2009) *The Right of the Child to Be Heard* (CRC/C/GC/12, para 90).

[113] Committee on the Rights of the Child General Comment No 12 (2009) *The Right of the Child to Be Heard* (CRC/C/GC/12, para 92).

[114] Committee on the Rights of the Child Committee on the Rights of the Child, Report on the forty-third session, September 2006, Day of General Discussion, Recommendations, para 18.

must be drawn between participation and self determination. Having regard to the concept of 'evolving capacity' pursuant to Art 5 of the CRC, the UN Committee makes clear that:[115]

> 'The more the child himself or herself knows, has experienced and understands, the more the parent, legal guardian or other persons legally responsible for the child have to transform direction and guidance into reminders and advice and later to an exchange on an equal footing. This transformation will not take place at a fixed point in a child's development, but will steadily increase as the child is encouraged to contribute her or his views.'

(ii) CRC, Art 12 – Medicine and Healthcare

6.43 Children's right to participate pursuant to Art 12 of the CRC requires that they participate both in individual healthcare decisions concerning them and more widely in the development of healthcare policy and services.[116] For example, the rights enshrined in Art 12 should be a guiding theme in consideration of HIV/AIDS at all levels of prevention, treatment, care and support.[117]

6.44 In relation to participation in individual healthcare decisions Art 12 requires the provision of information concerning proposed treatments, their effects and their outcomes and access to confidential counseling without parental consent irrespective of the child's age where this is needed for the child's safety or wellbeing.[118] The CRC provides no support for the imposition of a minimum age below which a child cannot seek independent medical counseling, which independent counseling is particularly important where the views and/or interests of the child are distinct from those of parents or carers.[119] Children as well as parents must be informed of, have access to and be supported in the use of basic knowledge concerning child health and nutrition, the advantages of breastfeeding, hygiene and environmental sanitation and the prevention of accidents.[120]

6.45 Pursuant to Art 12, a child is entitled to participate in decision-making processes concerning his or her individual health care needs in a manner consistent with his or her evolving capacity. The UN Committee recommends that where a younger child can demonstrate capacity to express an informed view on his or her medical treatment, that view is given due weight.[121] In respect of older children, the Committee on the Rights of the Child stipulates in its General Comment No 4 *Adolescent Health an Development in the Context of the Rights of the Child* that:[122]

---

[115] Committee on the Rights of the Child General Comment No 12 (2009) *The Right of the Child to Be Heard* (CRC/C/GC/12, para 84).

[116] Committee on the Rights of the Child General Comment No 12 (2009) *The Right of the Child to Be Heard* (CRC/C/GC/12, para 98).

[117] Committee on the Rights of the Child General Comment No 3 *HIV/AIDS and the Rights of the Child* HRI/GEN/Rev.8 p 364. See also p 366.

[118] Committee on the Rights of the Child General Comment No 12 (2009) *The Right of the Child to Be Heard* (CRC/C/GC/12, paras 100–101). The right to counselling is distinct from the right to consent and should not be the subject to any age limit.

[119] Newell, P and Hodgkin, R *Implementation Handbook for the Convention on the Rights of the Child* (2008) 3rd edn, UNICEF, p 6.

[120] CRC, Art 24(2)(e).

[121] Committee on the Rights of the Child General Comment No 12 (2009) *The Right of the Child to Be Heard* (CRC/C/GC/12, para 102).

[122] Committee on the Rights of the Child General Comment No 4 *Adolescent Health an Development in the Context of the Rights of the Child* HRI/GEN/1/Rev 8, p 377.

'The right to express views freely and have them duly taken into account (art. 12) is also fundamental in realising adolescents' right to health and development. States parties need to ensure that adolescents are given a genuine chance to express their views freely on all matters affecting them, especially within the family, in school, and in their communities. In order for adolescents to be able safely and properly to exercise this right, public authorities, parents and other adults working with or for children need to create an environment based on trust, information-sharing, the capacity to listen and sound guidance that is conducive for adolescents' participating equally including in decision-making processes.'

6.46 Within this context, it must be remembered that older children of sufficient maturity will attain capacity to make informed decisions and give informed consent to their own medical treatment.[123] In its General Comment No 4 the Committee on the Rights of the Child recognises that:[124]

'Before parents give their consent, adolescents need to have a chance to express their views freely and their views should be given due weight, in accordance with article 12 of the Convention. However, if the adolescent is of sufficient maturity, informed consent shall be obtained from the adolescent her/himself, while informing the parents if that is in the 'best interest of the child' (art. 3).'

In its General Comment 14 *The Right to the Highest Attainable Standard of Health* the UN Committee on Economic, Social and Cultural Rights states that:[125]

'States parties should provide a safe and supportive environment for adolescents, that ensures the opportunity to participate in decisions affecting their health, to build life skills, to acquire appropriate information, to receive counseling and to negotiate the health-behaviour choices they make. The realisation of the right to health of adolescents is dependent on the development of youth-friendly health care, which respects confidentiality and privacy and includes appropriate sexual and reproductive health services.'

(iii) CRC, Art 12 – Judicial and Administrative Proceedings

6.47 As noted above, the right to participate in judicial and administrative proceedings is extremely wide in its ambit.[126] The right to participate in judicial and administrative proceedings will apply to *all* children within the jurisdiction, including those children who are within the jurisdiction illegally. In its General Comment No 6

---

[123] The UN Committee welcomes the introduction in some countries of a fixed age at which the right to consent transfers to the child, and encourages States parties to give consideration to the introduction of such legislation (Committee on the Rights of the Child General Comment No 12 (2009) *The Right of the Child to Be Heard* (CRC/C/GC/12, para 102). Within the domestic context see the Family Law Act 1969, s 8(1).

[124] Committee on the Rights of the Child General Comment No 4 *Adolescent Health an Development in the Context of the Rights of the Child* HRI/GEN/1/Rev 8, p 383. Paragraph 29 of General Comment No 4 makes clear that 'With regard to privacy and confidentiality, and the related issue of informed consent to treatment, States parties should (a) enact laws or regulations to ensure that confidential advice concerning treatment is provided to adolescents so that they can give their informed consent. Such laws or regulations should stipulate an age for this process, or refer to the evolving capacity of the child; and (b) provide training for health personnel on the rights of adolescents to privacy and confidentiality, to be informed about planned treatment and to give their informed consent to treatment.'

[125] Committee on Economic, Social and Cultural Rights General Comment 14 *The Right to the Highest Attainable Standard of Health* HRI/GEN/1/Rev 8, p 92, para 23. In relation to practices prejudicial to the health of children and the child's right to participate Hodgkin & Newell observe that 'presumably, mature children should have the same rights, if any, as adults have under the law in each society to consent to practices that involve a degree of violence but are not significantly prejudicial to health' (Newell, P and Hodgkin, R *Implementation Handbook for the Convention on the Rights of the Child* (2008) 3rd edn, UNICEF, p 371).

[126] See above **6.13**.

Treatment of Unaccompanied Children and Separated Children Outside Their Country of Origin[127] the Committee on the Rights of the Child emphasises that:[128]

'In guardianship, care and accommodation arrangements, and legal representation, children's views should also be taken into account. Such information must be provided in a manner that is appropriate to the maturity and level of understanding of each child. As participation is dependent on reliable communication, where necessary, interpreters should be made available at all stages of the procedure.'

6.48 All children involved in judicial and administrative proceedings must be informed in a child friendly manner about their right to be heard, the methods by which they can be heard and other necessary aspects of the judicial or administrative proceedings. Judges and other decision makers should explicitly state and explain the outcome of the proceedings, especially if the views of the child could not be accommodated within the decision reached.

Proceedings for Divorce and Separation

6.49 The UN Committee on the Rights of the Child stipulates that all legislation on separation and divorce must include the right of the child to be heard by decision makers and in mediation processes.[129]

Proceedings for Contact and Residence

6.50 Article 12 of the CRC requires that children participate in proceedings in respect of them concerning contact and residence through the free expression of their views and the giving of weight to those views in accordance with the age and maturity of the child. In proceedings where the parents are living separately and a decision must be made as to the child's place of residence, Art 9(2) of the CRC requires that the child be given the opportunity to participate in the proceedings and make his or her views known.[130]

Care Proceedings

6.51 Within the context of judicial or administrative proceedings concerning the protection of children from abuse or neglect, the child's right to participate remains a central factor prior to, during and following such proceedings. As such, both before and during measures designed to protect children from all forms of violence and abuse, and in the planning, implementation and monitoring of those measures, respect for the views of the child is vital.[131]

6.52 Any decision making process which may result in the removal of the child from his or her family by reason of child being a victim of abuse or neglect within the home must take into account the views of the child as being central to determining that child's

---

[127] Committee on the Rights of the Child General Comment No 6 *Treatment of Unaccompanied Children and Separated Children Outside Their Country of Origin* HRI/GEN/1/Rev 8, p 407.

[128] Committee on the Rights of the Child General Comment No 6 *Treatment of Unaccompanied Children and Separated Children Outside Their Country of Origin* HRI/GEN/1/Rev 8, p 415.

[129] Committee on the Rights of the Child General Comment No 12 (2009) *The Right of the Child to Be Heard* (CRC/C/GC/12, para 52).

[130] See **8.78** below.

[131] Newell, P and Hodgkin, R *Implementation Handbook for the Convention on the Rights of the Child* (2008) 3rd edn, UNICEF, p 165.

best interests.[132] The child's views must also be obtained in relation to placement in foster care or homes, development of care plans and their review, and contact with parents and family.[133]

6.53 Pursuant to Art 9(2) of the CRC, the child must be given an opportunity to participate in proceedings which may result in the separation of the child from his or her parents by reason of abuse or neglect and to make his or her views known in those proceedings. Proceedings in which the separation of the child from his or her parents is necessary by reason of abuse or neglect highlight the particular importance of the relationship between Art 12 and the child's best interests under Art 3 of the CRC.[134] Children should be provided with space to freely express their views and to have those views given due weight in all aspects of prevention, reporting and monitoring violence against them.[135] Within this context, the UN Committee has emphasised the need for:[136]

'... rules and proceedings for child victims of physical violence, sexual abuse or other violent crimes ensuring that repetition of testimonies be avoided by the use of video-taped interviews to reduce retraumatisation, that protective measures, health and psychosocial services be made available and that unnecessary contact with the perpetrator be avoided. The identity of the victim should be maintained confidential and, when required, the public and the media should be excluded from the courtroom during the proceedings.'

6.54 Rule 3(2) of the UN Standard Minimum Rules for the Administration of Juvenile Justice (the 'Beijing Rules') extends the scope of those rules to cover care and welfare proceedings. Rule 5 of the UN Standard Minimum Rules for the Administration of Juvenile Justice promotes the welfare of the child within proceedings and applies the principle of proportionality to proceedings, requiring the personal circumstances of the child to be taken into account when considering the proper conduct of those proceedings. Rule 14(2) stipulates that 'proceedings shall be conducted in an atmosphere of understanding which shall allow the juvenile to participate therein and to express herself or himself freely'. Finally, rule 15 provides for the child to be represented by a legal adviser and to apply for free legal aid where there is provision for such aid. Each of these rules is relevant to ensuring the proper participation of the child in care and welfare proceedings.

---

[132] Committee on the Rights of the Child General Comment No 12 (2009) *The Right of the Child to Be Heard* (CRC/C/GC/12, para 53).
[133] Committee on the Rights of the Child General Comment No 12 (2009) *The Right of the Child to Be Heard* (CRC/C/GC/12, para 54).
[134] See **6.7** above.
[135] Report of the independent expert for the United Nations Study on Violence against Children (A/61/299).
[136] Committee on the Rights of the Child, Report on the forty-third session, September 2006, Day of General Discussion, Recommendations, para 48. See also CRC, Art 39 below at **15.108 et seq.**

6.55   Following a child being taken into care, the UN Committee on the Rights of the Child has stipulated that:[137]

> 'Mechanisms must be introduced to ensure that children in all forms of alternative care, including in institutions, are able to express their views and that those views be given due weight in matters of their placement, the regulations of care in foster families or homes and their daily lives.'

Article 25 of the CRC requires that children placed[138] by the State in care, protection or for the treatment of their psychological or mental health must be the subject of periodic review, in which review the child will have the right to participate fully by virtue of Art 12. All institutions in which children are placed must establish easy access to individuals or organisations to which they can report in confidence and safety.[139]

Proceedings for Adoption

6.56   It is of crucial importance that the child's voice is heard in relation to decisions as to adoption. As noted above, the requirement of Art 21(a) of the CRC that 'the persons concerned have given their informed consent' should be considered in context of the right of the child to express his or her views and have them considered in accordance with the age of maturity of the child.[140] The child's views should be obtained not only in relation to the substantive issue of whether or not to make an adoption order placing the child outside the birth family but also in relation to adoption by step-parents.[141] Obtaining the child's views necessarily involves informing the child as to the meaning and effect of adoption.[142] The child's views must be the subject of proper investigation and reporting by independent and properly qualified professionals within the context of an adoption application. The Committee on the Rights of the Child has recommended a requirement that children of a certain age be required to consent to their adoption.[143]

Criminal Proceedings

6.57   Criminal Proceedings – Child in Conflict with the Criminal Law – The right of a child accused of, or recognised as having, infringed the criminal law to express his or her views and to have them given due weight in all judicial and administrative proceedings affecting them pursuant to Art 12 of the CRC must also be observed throughout the

---

[137]   Committee on the Rights of the Child General Comment No 12 (2009) *The Right of the Child to Be Heard* (CRC/C/GC/12, para 97).

[138]   Placements for the purpose of Art 25 of the CRC include foster and adoptive families, children's homes and institutions, immigration and refugee centres, hospitals, health units and wards, therapeutic centres, boarding schools, detention centres, prisons and residential schools (Newell, P and Hodgkin, R *Implementation Handbook for the Convention on the Rights of the Child* (2008) 3rd edn, UNICEF, p 380).

[139]   Committee on the Rights of the Child General Comment No 12 (2009) *The Right of the Child to Be Heard* (CRC/C/GC/12, para 121).

[140]   Newell, P and Hodgkin, R *Implementation Handbook for the Convention on the Rights of the Child* (2008) 3rd edn, UNICEF, pp 296–297. See also Committee on the Rights of the Child, Report on the forty-third session, September 2006, Day of General Discussion, Recommendations, para 44.

[141]   Committee on the Rights of the Child General Comment No 12 (2009) *The Right of the Child to Be Heard* (CRC/C/GC/12, para 55).

[142]   Committee on the Rights of the Child General Comment No 12 (2009) *The Right of the Child to Be Heard* (CRC/C/GC/12, para 56).

[143]   See New Zealand CRC/C/15/Add.216, para 34.

juvenile justice process.[144] In its General Comment No 10 *Children's Rights in Juvenile Justice*, the Committee on the Rights of the Child observes that:[145]

> '... the child, in order to effectively participate in the proceedings, must be informed not only about the charges, but also about the juvenile justice process as such and about the possible measures. The child should be given the opportunity to express his/her views concerning the (alternative) measures that may be imposed, and the specific wishes or preferences he/she may have in this regard should be given due weight. Alleging that the child is criminally responsible implies that he/she should be competent and able to effectively participate in the decisions regarding the most appropriate response to allegations of his/her infringement of the penal law. It may go without saying that the judges involved are responsible for and make the decisions. But to treat the child as a passive object does not recognise his/her rights or contribute to an effective response to his/her behaviour. This also applies to the implementation of the measure imposed. of the child in this implementation will in most cases contribute to a positive result ...'

6.58 In order to ensure that the views of the children in conflict with the law are duly taken into account, the following must be provided as a *minimum* in order to ensure their participation in criminal proceedings in accordance with Arts 12 and 40 of the CRC:

(a) Adequate legal or other appropriate assistance;[146]

(b) Free access to an interpreter if the child cannot speak or understand the language used;[147]

(c) Respect for his or her privacy during all stages of the proceedings;[148]

(d) Recognition that the child has a right to participate freely and cannot be compelled to give testimony.[149]

Rule 14(2) of the UN Standard Minimum Rules for the Administration of Juvenile Justice requires that the juvenile justice process must be conducted 'in an atmosphere of understanding, which shall allow the juvenile to participate therein and to express herself or himself freely'.[150] It is particularly important to note in the context of

---

[144] Newell, P and Hodgkin, R *Implementation Handbook for the Convention on the Rights of the Child* (2008) 3rd edn, UNICEF, p 604 and see General Comment No 10 *Children's Rights in Juvenile Justice* (CRC/C/GC/10, para 4).

[145] Committee on the Rights of the Child, General Comment No 10 *Children's Rights in Juvenile Justice* CRC/C/GC/10, para 23.

[146] CRC, Art 40(2)(b)(iii).

[147] CRC, Art 40(2)(b)(vii). Article 14(3)(f) of the Covenant on Civil and Political Rights guarantees the same right. This right also encompasses special measures to prevent discrimination against children with disabilities who are in conflict with the law (Committee on the Rights of the Child General Comment No 9 *The Rights of Children with Disabilities* (2006) CRC/C/GC/9, paras 73 and 74).

[148] CRC, Art 40(2)(b)(vii). Within this context, the UN Committee on the Rights of the Child has stated that: 'The court and other hearings of a child in conflict with the law should be conducted behind closed doors. Exceptions to this rule should be very limited, clearly outlined in national legislation and guided by the best interests of the child' (Committee on the Rights of the Child General Comment No 12 (2009) *The Right of the Child to Be Heard* (CRC/C/GC/12, para 61).

[149] CRC, Art 40(2)(b)(iv).

[150] In this regard, rules 8(1) and 8(2) of the UN Standard Minimum Rules on the Administration of Juvenile Justice expand on the provisions of CRC, Art 40(2)(b)(vii) by providing that 'The juvenile's right to privacy shall be respected at all stages in order to avoid harm being caused to her or him by undue publicity or by the process of labelling. In principle, no information that may lead to the identification of a juvenile offender

criminal proceedings that the child's right to be heard is a choice for the child, not an obligation and accordingly does not conflict with the right to remain silent conferred by article 40(2)(b)(iv) of the CRC and r 7 of the UN Standard Minimum Rules on the Administration of Juvenile Justice.[151]

6.59   Once again the provision of information is a crucial aspect of the effective implementation of the child's right to participate. As such, Art 40 of the CRC stipulates that the child has the right to be informed promptly and directly of the charges against him or her in language he or she understands.[152]

6.60   Where a child is deprived of his or her liberty as the result of the juvenile justice process, the UN Committee has emphasised the need for the provision of complaints procedures for children whose liberty is restricted in accordance with the principles enshrined in Art 12 of the CRC.[153] The Committee has observed:[154]

'Every child should have the right to make requests or complaints, without censorship as to the substance, to the central administration, the judicial authority or other proper independent authority and to be informed of the response without delay; children need to know about and have easy access to these mechanisms'.

6.61   Criminal Proceedings – Child Victims and Witnesses in Criminal Proceedings[155] – The UN Economic and Social Council Resolution *Guidelines on Justice Involving Child Victims and Witnesses of Crime*[156] requires that the child victim or witness of crime shall be given the opportunity to exercise fully his or her right to freely express his or her view.[157] The right of the child victim or witness to be heard is linked to the right to be informed and to have available health, psychological and social services to support and rehabilitate victims and witnesses of crime.[158]

Immigration Proceedings

6.62   Article 10(1) of the CRC requires that applications by a child or his or her parents to enter or leave a State Party for the purposes of family reunification should be dealt with in a positive, humane and expeditious manner. Article 22(1) of the CRC stipulates that States Parties shall take appropriate measures to ensure that a child who is seeking refugee status or who is considered a refugee to provide protection and humanitarian assistance in the enjoyment of the rights enshrined in the CRC. Within this context, the principles of Art 12 of the CRC should be applied in respect of all

shall be published.' The United Kingdom has been criticised for failing to ensure the privacy of children involved in criminal proceedings (United Kingdom CRC/C/15/Add.188, paras 60(d) and 62(d)).

[151]   Committee on the Rights of the Child General Comment No 12 (2009) *The Right of the Child to Be Heard* (CRC/C/GC/12, para 58).

[152]   Article 40(2)(b)(ii) CRC and see Committee on the Rights of the Child General Comment No 12 (2009) *The Right of the Child to Be Heard* (CRC/C/GC/12, para 59).

[153]   Newell, P and Hodgkin, R *Implementation Handbook for the Convention on the Rights of the Child* (2008) 3rd edn, UNICEF, p 566.

[154]   Committee on the Rights of the Child General Comment No 10 *Children's Rights in Juvenile Justice* CRC/C/GC/10, para 28c.

[155]   'Child victim or witness' means a person under the age of 18 who is a victim of or witness to a crime, regardless of his or her role in the offence or in the prosecution of the alleged offender or groups of offenders (UNODC/UNICEF 2005/20 of 22 July 2005).

[156]   UNODC/UNICEF 2005/20 of 22 July 2005.

[157]   See also the Committee on the Rights of the Child, Report on the forty-third session, September 2006, Day of General Discussion, Recommendations, para 48. See also CRC, Art 39.

[158]   Committee on the Rights of the Child General Comment No 12 (2009) *The Right of the Child to Be Heard* (CRC/C/GC/12, para 64) and see Art 39 CRC.

immigration procedures including asylum applications.[159] The UN Committee on the Rights of the Child has stated as follows concerning children's participation involved in the immigration and asylum process:[160]

> 'Pursuant to article 12 of the Convention, in determining the measures to be adopted with regard to unaccompanied or separated children, the child's views and wishes should be elicited and taken into account (art. 12(1)). To allow for a well-informed expression of such views and wishes, it is imperative that such children are provided with all relevant information concerning, for example, their entitlements, services available including means of communication, the asylum process, family tracing and the situation in their country of origin (arts. 13, 17 and 22(2)). In guardianship, care and accommodation arrangements, and legal representation, children's views should also be taken into account. Such information must be provided in a manner that is appropriate to the maturity and level of understanding of each child. As participation is dependent on reliable communication, where necessary, interpreters should be made available at all stages of the procedure.'

6.63 In order to facilitate the participation of children within immigration and asylum proceedings, the Committee on the Rights of the Child provides the following further guidance:[161]

> '... children have to be provided with all relevant information, in their own language, on their entitlements, the services available, including means of communication, and the immigration and asylum process, in order to make their voice heard and to be given due weight in the proceedings. A guardian or adviser should be appointed, free of charge. Asylum-seeking children may also need effective family tracing and relevant information about the situation in their country of origin to determine their best interests. Particular assistance may be needed for children formerly involved in armed conflict to allow them to pronounce their needs. Furthermore, attention is needed to ensure that stateless children are included in decision-making processes within the territories where they reside. The Committee requests that special attention be given to the right of the child to be heard in immigration, asylum and refugee procedures by taking measures to ensure that the rules and practices, including the provision of interpreters, are in full compliance with the requirements elaborated by the Committee on the Rights of the Child in its General Comment No 6 on the Treatment of Unaccompanied and Separated Children Outside Their Country of Origin (2005), in particular paragraph 25.

(iv)   CRC, Art 12 – Education

6.64 Both Arts 12(1) and 12(2) will be relevant to the child's education, the former to everyday school life and the latter to more formal processes such as disciplinary procedures, exclusion and the allocation of school places. The Committee on the Rights of the Child General Comment No 1 *The Aims of Education* provides that:

> '... the participation of children in school life, the creation of school communities and student councils, peer education and peer counseling, and the involvement of children in school disciplinary proceedings should be promoted as part of the process of learning and experiencing the realisation of rights.'[162]

---

[159]   Newell, P and Hodgkin, R *Implementation Handbook for the Convention on the Rights of the Child* (2008) 3rd edn, UNICEF, p 169. See also *Refugee children – Guidelines on Protection and Care,* (1994) Office of the United Nations High Commissioner for Refugees (UNHCR).

[160]   Committee on the Rights of the Child General Comment No 6 *The Treatment of Unaccompanied and Separated Children outside their Country of Origin* HRI/GEN/1/Rev 8, p 415, para 25.

[161]   Committee on the Rights of the Child General Comment No 12 (2009) *The Right of the Child to Be Heard* (CRC/C/GC/12, para 124).

[162]   Committee on the Rights of the Child General Comment No 1 *The Aims of Education* HRI/GEN/1 /Rev.8 p 350, para 8.

In relation to the participation of children in the *development* of the educative process, the Committee has further observed that an approach should be adopted which 'encourages the active consultation of children in the development and evaluation of school curricula, including in the development of methodology, as greater participation is conducive to increasing the involvement of children in the learning process'.[163] Thus, for example, education must be provided in a way that respects the inherent dignity of the child and enables the child to express his or her views freely in accordance with Art 12 and to participate in school life.[164]

(v)   CRC, Art 12 – Wider Participation in Society

6.65   Article 25 of the Covenant on Civil and Political Rights does not prevent a State party from defining citizens who have the right to vote as persons above a certain age. The UN Committee on the Rights of the Child has not yet explored the relevance of Art 12 to voting age.[165] However, the Committee has noted that 'Given that few States as yet have reduced the voting age below 18, there is all the more reason to ensure respect for the views of unenfranchised children in Government and parliament'.[166] Paragraph 3 of the UN Guidelines for the Prevention of Juvenile Delinquency (the 'Riyadh Guidelines') stipulates that young people should have an active role and partnership within society and should not be considered mere objects of socialisation or control. The Committee on the Rights of the Child has highlighted the central role of the child's participation in the process of ensuring an active role for children, stating that:[167]

> 'The Committee urges States parties to move from an events based approach of the right to participation to systematic inclusion in policy matters in order to ensure that children can express their views and effectively participate in all matters affecting them. The Committee calls on States parties to comply with their obligation to ensure that child participation is taken into account in resource allocation and that mechanisms to facilitate the participation of children be institutionalised as a tool for implementation.'

6.66   To this end the Committee on the Rights of the Child recommends that States parties take into account children's participation in the community at different levels.[168] This should include the establishment of a standing body to represent children's views in the political process[169] on policy issues including, for example, budget allocations in the areas of education, health, working conditions for young people and violence prevention,[170] the location of playgrounds and the prevention of accidents.[171] Children

---

163   Committee on the Rights of the Child, Report on the forty-third session, September 2006, Day of General Discussion, Recommendations, para 22. See also General Comment No 12 (2009) *The Right of the Child to Be Heard* (CRC/C/GC/12, paras 105–114).

164   Committee on the Rights of the Child General Comment No 1 *The Aims of Education* HRI/GEN/1/Rev 8, p 351.

165   Newell, P and Hodgkin, R *Implementation Handbook for the Convention on the Rights of the Child* (2008) 3rd edn, UNICEF, p 164. See also the Human Rights Committee General Comment No 25 (1996) HRI/GEN/1/Rev.8, para 4, p 208.

166   Committee on the Rights of the Child General Comment No 5 *General Measures of Implementation for the Convention on the Rights of the Child* CRC/GC/2003/5, para 12.

167   Committee on the Rights of the Child, Report on the forty-third session, September 2006, Day of General Discussion, Recommendations, para 25.

168   Committee on the Rights of the Child, Report on the forty-third session, September 2006, Day of General Discussion, Recommendations, para 38.

169   China CRC/C/CHN/CO/2, para 41.

170   Committee on the Rights of the Child, Report on the forty-third session, September 2006, Day of General Discussion, Recommendations, para 31.

171   Manual on Human Rights Reporting (1997) HR/PUB/91/1 (Rev 1), p 427.

should participate in particular at a local and national level in the implementation of 'their' UN Convention.[172] This requires training on the rights of the child to all public officials who influence government policy and implement programmes which involve children's issues in order to promote awareness of the rights of the child and the obligation of taking these views into account.[173] In this context, the Committee on the Rights of the Child has observed that:[174]

> 'It is important that Governments develop a direct relationship with children, not simply one mediated through non-governmental organisations (NGOs) or human rights institutions. In the early years of the Convention, NGOs had played a notable role in pioneering participatory approaches with children, but it is in the interests of both Governments and children to have appropriate direct contact.'

The Committee also encourages parents to support children in order to promote the realisation of child participation at different levels in society.[175]

The Child's Right to Participate under Other International Instruments

Convention on the Civil Aspects of International Child Abduction 1980[176]

6.67 The Convention on the Civil Aspects of International Child Abduction is designed to protect children from the harmful effects of cross-border abductions and wrongful retentions by providing a primarily summary procedure designed to bring about the prompt return of such children to the State of their habitual residence.[177] Art 13 of the Hague Convention on the Civil Aspects of International Child Abduction provides that the judicial or administrative authority may refuse to order the return of an abducted child if it finds that the child objects to being returned and has attained an age[178] and degree of maturity[179] at which it is appropriate to take account of his or her views.[180]

---

[172] Committee on the Rights of the Child General Comment No 5 *General Measures of Implementation for the Convention on the Rights of the Child* CRC/GC/2003/5, para 57.

[173] Committee on the Rights of the Child, Report on the forty-third session, September 2006, Day of General Discussion, Recommendations, paras 29–30.

[174] Committee on the Rights of the Child General Comment No 5 *General Measures of Implementation of the Convention on the Rights of the Child* HRI/GEN/1/Rev, p 391.

[175] Committee on the Rights of the Child, Report on the forty-third session, September 2006, Day of General Discussion, Recommendations, para 18.

[176] This Convention is give force of law in England and Wales by the Child Abduction and Custody Act 1985. In considering the Convention on the Civil Aspects of International Child Abduction it is important to understand its relationship with the Council Regulation (EC) No 2201/2003 of 27 November 2003 on Jurisdiction and the Recognition and Enforcement of Judgments in Matrimonial Matters and Matters of Parental Responsibility for Children of both Spouses ('Brussels II Revised') (see Lowe, N, Everall, M and Nicholls, M *International Movement of Children* (2004) Family Law, paras 18.26–18.27 and **8.244** below and *Re L (A Minor) (Abduction: Jurisdiction)* [2002] EWHC 1864 (Fam), [2002] 1 WLR 3208, sub nom *Re L (Abduction: Child's Objection to Return)* [2002] 2 FLR 1042. See also Art 11(1) of the CRC at **8.94** below and the European Convention on Recognition and Enforcement of Decisions Concerning the Custody of Children 1980.

[177] Article 1 Convention on the Civil Aspects of International Child Abduction 1980. For an excellent summary of the domestic practice and procedure in cases under the Hague Convention see Ryder, E and Goldrein, I (eds) *Child Case Management Practice* (2009) Family Law Ch 9.

[178] Practice varies within and between jurisdictions as to the age at which the child's objections should be taken into account. In *Re R (Child Abduction: Acquiescence)* [1995] 1 FLR 716 Balcombe LJ was prepared to take into account the views of children as young as six. In *Re J and K (Abduction: Objections of Child)* [2004] EWHC 1985 (Fam) the Court took account of the views of a 9 year old child. In the Scottish case of *AQ v JQ* (unreported) Court of Session 12 December 2001 the Court expressed the view that even an immature

6.68   There is an inherent tension between the summary nature of the procedure under the Hague Convention designed to mitigate speedily the adverse effect of abduction and the time that is required to conduct the welfare investigation necessary to ascertain and relate the views of the child who objects to being returned.[181] However, within the European context, Art 11(2) of Council Regulation (EC) No 2201/2003 of 27 November 2003 on Jurisdiction and the Recognition and Enforcement of Judgments in Matrimonial Matters and Matters of Parental Responsibility for Children of both Spouses ('Brussels II Revised') makes clear that:

> '... when applying Articles 12 and 13 of the Hague Convention, it shall be ensured that the child is given an opportunity to be heard during the proceedings unless this appears inappropriate have regard to his or her age or degree of maturity.'[182]

6.69   Within the domestic jurisdiction, the Supreme Court has held that the principles set out in Art 11(2) of Council Regulation (EC) No 2201/2003 of 27 November 2003 on Jurisdiction and the Recognition and Enforcement of Judgments in Matrimonial Matters and Matters of Parental Responsibility for Children of both Spouses ('Brussels II Revised') should be applied in all Hague Convention cases.[183] The domestic approach to the child's participation in child abduction proceedings is dealt with below.[184]

6.70   The requirement to provide the child with an opportunity to be heard when applying articles 12 and 13 of the Hague Convention, unless this appears inappropriate have regard to his or her age or degree of maturity, aligns the Hague Convention more closely with the principles enshrined in Art 12 of the CRC in that the child is treated less

---

child of 10 would normally be capable of forming a view. In the Australian case of *Temple* [1993] FLC 92–365 however, the Court held that a child of 10 is not old enough to weigh up all the circumstances.

[179]   Again, practice in relation to assessing maturity varies within and between jurisdictions. In *Re S (A Minor) (Abduction: Custody Rights)* [1993] Fam 242 the Court considered a 9 year old to be mature as she had the 'mental age' of 12. In *Re G (A Minor) (Abduction)* [1989] 2 FLR 475 a nine year old was held to be insufficiently mature because 'his worldly understanding at the age of 9 was not sufficiently broad to comprehend all the complex factors of the case.' In *A v A (Child Abduction)* [1993] 2 FLR 225 maturity was equated with an ability to provide valid reasons (but see the preferable broader approach at first instance in *PW v ALI* (unreported) Outer House of Court of Session 25 February 2003 per the Lord Ordinary (overturned on appeal in *W v W* [2004] SC 63)). In *Re T (Abduction: Child's Objections to Return)* [2000] 2 FLR 192 Wall LJ held 'I would not wish to venture and definition of maturity. Clearly the child has to know what has happened to her and to understand that there is a range of choice. A child may be mature enough for it to be appropriate for her views to be taken into account even though she may not have gained that level of maturity that she is fully emancipated from parental dependence and can claim autonomy of decision making.' In the Hong Kong case of *S v S* [1998] 2 HKC 316 a six year old child was held insufficiently mature because he was not precocious or mature beyond his age. In the US case of *McManus v McManus* 354 F. Supp. 2d (62) (2005) ambivalence was considered to be a sign of maturity, indicating an ability to weigh both sides of the argument. In the New Zealand case of *Clarke v Carson* [1995] NZFLR 926 the Court held that 'The position at which it is right to take into account the views of children seems to me in the normal course to be the time when they are able to reason. That is a position supported by the Convention on the Rights of the Child.' See also *Cameron v Cameron* [1996] SLT 306 and the minority opinion in the US case of *England v England* 234 F.3d 268 (5th Cir. 2000).

[180]   See generally Caldwell, J *Child Welfare Defences in Child Abduction Cases – Some Recent Developments* [2001] CFLQ 121 at 130–133.

[181]   See Schuz, R *Protection versus Autonomy: The Child Abduction Experience* in Ronen, Ya'ir and Charles W. Greenbaum (ed.), *The Case for the Child: Towards a New Agenda*, Antwerp: Intersentia, 269–308 and Schuz, R *The Hague Child Abduction Convention and Children's Rights* (2002) Transnational Law and Contemporary Problems Vol 12 No 2, 393, pp 435–447.

[182]   Note that Preamble 19 to the Regulations states 'The hearing of the child plays an important role in the application of this Regulation, although this Instrument is not intended to modify national procedures applicable.' See *S v B (Abduction: Human Rights)* [2005] EWHC 733 (Fam), [2005] 2 FLR 878, para 65.

[183]   *Re D (A Child)(Abduction Rights and Custody)* [2006] UKHL 51, [2007] 1 AC 619.

[184]   See **6.159**.

as an object of return and more as a person in his or her own right.[185] However, Art 13 of the Hague Convention is not, even when read with Art 11(2) of Brussels II Revised, wholly compliant with Art 12 of the CRC in that it only requires the views of the child to be taken into account where the child objects to being returned.[186] In this context, Fisher J pointed up in the New Zealand case of *S v S* that:[187]

> 'It is difficult to see why more weight would be given to a mature child's wishes to remain than the same child's wishes to return. Either a mature child's wishes are to be respected in Hague Convention applications or they are not.'

Hague Convention on Protection of Children and Cooperation in Respect of Intercountry Adoption

6.71   Article 4(d) of the Hague Convention on Protection of Children and Cooperation in Respect of Intercountry Adoption requires that an adoption shall only take place if the competent authorities of the State of origin of the child have, in addition to the other requirements of Art 4 of the Convention,[188] ensured having regard to the age and degree of maturity of the child that the child has been counseled and duly informed of the effects of the adoption and of his or her consent to the adoption where such consent is required, that consideration has been given to the child's wishes and opinions, that the child's consent to adoption, where such consent is required, has been given freely, in the required legal form, and expressed or evidenced in writing, and that such consent has not been induced by payment or compensation of any kind.

The Child's Right to Participate under the ECHR

Overall Position under the ECHR

6.72   The right to a fair trial under Art 6 of the European Convention on Human Rights encompasses a right to be heard fairly, in public and within a reasonable time in determination of civil rights and obligations or of any criminal charge.[189] Art 10 of the ECHR enshrines the right to freedom of expression, including the freedom to hold

---

[185]   See *Hollins v Crozier* [2000] NZ FLR 775. It is important to note that Art 12 of the CRC requires that children be able to express their views freely. As such, Clarkson J observed in the New Zealand case of *Winters v Cowen* [2002] NZFLR 927 that 'The tension between the Hague Convention and Art 12 of the United Nations Convention on the Rights to the Child is demonstrated in this case. The Convention directs the return of the child unless their expressed objection is accepted and acted upon by the Court. The real question to be answered is whether it is honouring the children's rights to be heard if one allows them to operate merely as mouthpieces of adults. To do so would, in fact, derogate from their rights to be heard and considered independently.'

[186]   Lowe, N, Everall, M and Nicholls, M *International Movement of Children* (2004) Family Law, paras 17.155–17.156 and See Schuz, R *Protection versus Autonomy: The Child Abduction Experience* in Ronen, Ya'ir and Charles W. Greenbaum (ed.), *The Case for the Child: Towards a New Agenda*, Antwerp: Intersentia, 269–308. See also *Winters v Cowen* [2002] NZFLR 927 per Clarkson J.

[187]   [1999] 3 NZLR 513 at 521.

[188]   Those requirements being that (a) the child is adoptable, (b) that intercountry adoption is in the child's best interests, (c) that those from whom consent to adoption is required have been counselled as may be necessary and duly informed of the effects of their consent, (d) any necessary consents have been given freely in the required legal form and expressed or evidenced in writing, (e) the necessary consents have not been induced by payment or compensation and have not been withdrawn and (f) the consent of the mother, where required, has been given only after the birth of the child.

[189]   ECHR, Art 6(1).

opinions and to receive and impart information and ideas without interference.[190] The ECHR does not however enshrine on its face a general right to participate in respect of children or adults.

6.73 Notwithstanding this position, there is a long tradition in Strasbourg jurisprudence which weighs the views of the children heavily in the balance in cases concerning family breakdown and dysfunction.[191] Further, Art 6 of the ECHR can support arguments concerning the child's participation in administrative procedures concerning children and their families.[192] In addition, Art 8 of the ECHR encompasses procedural safeguards[193] against inappropriate interference with the substantive rights protected by Art 8 and as such can provide further support for the child's right to participate.[194] Finally, as set out in detail in chapter 3, the ECHR must be read so as to give effect to the child's right to participate enshrined Art 12 of the CRC.[195]

6.74 There do however remain obstacles to the use of the ECHR to underpin the child's right to participate. As Fortin points out, in respect of the manner in which the child's views are conveyed, whilst Art 6 may ground an argument by a child that they are entitled to be present in Court to convey their views or to be represented in Court, there is no European case law under Art 6 supporting that proposition.[196] Whilst the European Court of Human Rights has recognised the need to hear the child within the context of disputes between adults, this has not extended to recognition of a right to be present in Court. In *Sahin v Germany*[197] the European Court of Human Rights held that:

> '... the German courts' failure to hear the child reveals an insufficient involvement of the applicant in the access proceedings. It is essential that the competent courts give careful consideration to what lies in the best interests of the child after having direct contact with the child.

However, when the Grand Chamber considered the case in *Sahin v Germany*[198] it rejected the conclusion that it was essential that courts should only consider what is in the best interests of a child after having direct contact with the child, the Grand Chamber holding that:

> 'It would be going too far to say that domestic courts are always required to hear a child in court on the issue of access to a parent not having custody, but this issue depends on the specific circumstances of each case having due regard to the age and maturity of the child concerned.

---

[190] ECHR, Art 13(1).
[191] Van Bueren, G *Child Rights in Europe* (2007) Council of Europe Publishing, p 82. See also *X v Austria* (Yearbook of the European Convention on Human Rights, 3, p 198), *X v Netherlands* 6 EHRR 133 and *Pini and Bertani; Manera and Atripaldi v Romania* [2005] 2 FLR 596, para 164.
[192] See *Re L (Care: Assessment Fair Trial)* [2002] EWHC 1379 (Fam), [2002] 2 FLR 730; *Mantovanelli v France* Application No 21497/93 (1997) 24 EHRR 370.
[193] See *R (P) v Secretary of State for the Home Department; R (Q) v Secretary of State for the Home Department* [2001] EWCA Civ 1151; [2001] 2 FLR 1122.
[194] *CF v Secretary of State for the Home Department* [2004] EWHC 111 (Fam), [2004] 2 FLR 517 and see *P, C and S v United Kingdom* [2002] 2 FLR 631.
[195] See **3.43–3.46** above.
[196] Fortin, J *Children's Rights and the Developing Law* (2009) 3rd edn, Cambridge, p 238.
[197] [2002] 1 FLR 119.
[198] [2003] 2 FLR 671, para 73.

ECHR, Art 6 and the Right to Participate

6.75 Article 6 of the ECHR provides as follows in relation to the right to a fair trial in determination of a child's civil rights and obligations or of any criminal charge against him or her:

> '1. In the determination of his civil rights and obligations or of any criminal charge against him, everyone is entitled to a fair and public hearing within a reasonable time by an independent and impartial tribunal established by law. Judgment shall be pronounced publicly but the press and public may be excluded from all or part of the trial in the interests of morals, public order or national security in a democratic society, where the interests of juveniles or the protection of the private life of the parties so require, or to the extent strictly necessary in the opinion of the court in special circumstances where publicity would prejudice the interests of justice.
>
> 2. Everyone charged with a criminal offence shall be presumed innocent until proved guilty according to law.
>
> 3. Everyone charged with a criminal offence has the following minimum rights:
>
> (a) to be informed promptly, in a language which he understands and in detail, of the nature and cause of the accusation against him;
> (b) to have adequate time and facilities for the preparation of his defence;
> (c) to defend himself in person or through legal assistance of his own choosing or, if he has not sufficient means to pay for legal assistance, to be given it free when the interests of justice so require;
> (d) to examine or have examined witnesses against him and to obtain the attendance and examination of witnesses on his behalf under the same conditions as witnesses against him;
> (e) to have the free assistance of an interpreter.'

6.76 Whilst consideration of Art 6 has largely been confined to issues concerning criminal proceedings,[199] it is supportive in a number of ways of the child's right to participate in all legal proceedings affecting him or her. For example, the Court of Appeal has held that despite secure accommodation proceedings not qualifying as criminal proceedings for the purposes of Art 6 of the ECHR, the rights accorded by Art 6(3) should be accorded to children who are the subject of such proceedings as a matter of procedural fairness under English common law.[200] Art 6 requires the appearance of the fair administration of justice which in turn demands that a party in must be able to participate effectively by being able to put forward the matters in support of his or her claims.[201] Art 6 embodies the right of access to the court for the determination of civil rights and obligations.[202] This in turn *may* require that a party to the proceedings be provided with the assistance of legal representation where such assistance is indispensable for effective access to the court, either because legal

---

[199] *V and T v United Kingdom* (1999) 30 EHRR 121, paras 85–91. See below **16.72**.
[200] *Re C (Secure Accommodation Order: Representation)* [2001] EWCA Civ 458, [2001] 2 FLR 169. This decision has been criticised on the basis that whilst the Court of Appeal found that the rights under Art 6(3) were engaged it failed properly to analyse and apply those rights to the case in question (see Fortin, J *Children's Rights and the Developing Law* (2009) 3rd edn, Cambridge, p 279. See also Masson, J *Re K (A Child) (Secure Accommodation Order: Right to Liberty) and Re C (Secure Accommodation Order: Representation) – Securing Human Rights for Children and Young People in Secure Accommodation* (2002) 14 Child and Family Law Quarterly 77).
[201] *P, C and S v United Kingdom* [2002] 2 FLR 631.
[202] *Golder v UK* (1979–80) 1 EHRR 524, para 36.

representation is compulsory or the proceedings are complex or of a certain type.[203] Whilst there is no specific requirement within the ECHR for the provision of civil legal aid,[204] the right of effective access to a court encompassed by Art 6 may require its provision.[205] The right of access is not absolute and may be subject to limitations provided those limitations pursue a legitimate aim, are proportionate and are not such as to affect the very essence of the right.[206] The guarantee of a 'public hearing' in Art 6 includes the right to an oral hearing in both civil and criminal cases.[207]

6.77   The fair trial guaranteed by Art 6 is not confined to the 'purely judicial' part of proceedings concerning children and, as with Art 12 of the CRC, also encompasses 'administrative' proceedings concerning children.[208] As such, Art 6 may also provide support for the child's right to participate within the context of administrative proceedings and decision making processes. For example, Art 6 requires that a child should be entitled to participate effectively in the process by which the Local Authority identifies, assesses and approves prospective adopters for that child.[209] Art 6 requires that a person be given reasonable notice of administrative decisions which affect him or her in order that there is adequate opportunity to challenge those decisions in court.[210] The full requirements of Art 6 of the ECHR as they relate to children are dealt with in detail in chapter 16 below.

ECHR, Art 8 and the Right to Participate

6.78   Article 8 of the ECHR provides as follows in relation to the child's right to respect for his or her private and family life:

'1. Everyone has the right to respect for his private and family life, his home and his correspondence.

2. There shall be no interference by a public authority with the exercise of this right except such as is in accordance with the law and is necessary in a democratic society in the interests

---

[203]   *Airey v Ireland* (1979–80) 2 EHRR 305, paras 26–28. Factors identified as relevant in the *Airey* case in determining whether a party is able to present his or her case properly and satisfactorily without the assistance of a lawyer include the complexity of the procedure, the necessity to address complicated points of law or to establish facts, involving expert evidence and the examination of witnesses, and the fact that the subject-matter of the marital dispute entails an emotional involvement that was scarcely compatible with the degree of objectivity required by advocacy in court. See **16.86** below.

[204]   Article 6(3)(c) of the ECHR requires the provision of legal aid in criminal cases where the defendant does not has not sufficient means to pay for legal assistance the interests of justice so require. See *Benham v United Kingdom* (1996) 22 EHRR 293 for the scope of Art 6(3)(c).

[205]   *Airey v Ireland* (1979–80) 1 EHRR 305. See also *Aerts v Belgium* (2000) 29 EHRR 50; *Faulkner v United Kingdom* (2000) Times 11 January and *MLB v SLJ* 516 US 102 (1997) 3 BHRC 47, US Sup Ct. But see also *McVicar v United Kingdom* (2002) 35 EHRR 22; *R (Jarrett) v Legal Services Commission* [2001] EWHC Admin 389, [2002] ACD 160 and *Pine v Law Society* [2001] EWCA Civ 1574, [2002] UKHRR 81.

[206]   See *Ashingdane v United Kingdom* (1985) 7 EHRR 528. See also *Re S (Minors)(Care Order: Implementation of Care Plan)* [2002] UKHL 10, [2002] 2 AC 291.

[207]   See *Fredin v Sweden (No 2)* A 283-A (1994), *Fischer v Austrian* (1995) 20 EHRR 349 and see *Göç v Turkey* Judgment of 11 July 2002 ECtHR (Grand Chamber), para 47. Note that the lack of an oral hearing at the appellate stage is permissible where the first instance decision has arisen from an oral hearing (*Miller v Sweden* (2006) 42 EHRR 1155).

[208]   See *Re L (Care: Assessment Fair Trial)* [2002] EWHC 1379 (Fam), [2002] 2 FLR 730; *Mantovanelli v France* Application No 21497/93 (1997) 24 EHRR 370.

[209]   *Re L (Care: Assessment Fair Trial)* [2002] EWHC 1379 (Fam), [2002] 2 FLR 730; *Mantovanelli v France* Application No 21497/93 (1997) 24 EHRR 370.

[210]   *De La Pradelle v France* (1992) A 253-B, para 34.

of national security, public safety or the economic well-being of the country, for the prevention of disorder or crime, for the protection of health or morals, or for the protection of the rights and freedoms of others.'

6.79 Whilst not expressly enshrining any right to participate, Art 8 has been held to bestow procedural protection within processes which may interfere with the substantive rights conferred by Art 8.[211] These procedural safeguards apply as much to children as they do to adults.[212] As Mr Justice Munby observed in *CF v Secretary of State for the Home Department*.[213]

'Children are not the largely passive objects of more or less paternalistic parental or judicial ... decision making. A child is as much entitled to the protection of the European Convention – and specifically of Art 8 – as anyone else. So, in the present case, [the child] is as much entitled as her mother, and in her own right, to the procedural guarantees afforded by Art 8 and recognised by the court in *W v United Kingdom* (1988) 10 EHRR 29, and in *McMichael v United Kingdom* (1995) 20 EHRR 205.'

6.80 The procedural protections afforded by Art 8 are highly relevant to the participation of the child in judicial and administrative proceedings as those procedural safeguards include the need to ensure that the child's point of view is adequately and independently represented in any decision process, however young the child may be.[214] In public law care proceedings concerning children this means that, in the same way natural parents must be properly involved in the decision making process and full account taken of their wishes and views,[215] so must this be the case in respect of children who are the subject of, and party to such proceedings.[216] This principle applies equally to administrative proceedings concerning children.[217] In relation to private law proceedings, Fortin observes that, since the outcome of parental disputes will affect their family lives, children might argue that there own procedural rights under Art 8 would be infringed if they are not provided with any change to influence the outcome directly.[218] Fortin also notes these arguments have not yet found full acceptance on the part of the European Court of Human Rights.[219] However, the domestic Courts have

---

[211] *W v United Kingdom* (1988) 10 EHRR 29; *McMichael v United Kingdom* (1995) 20 EHRR 205; *Buchberger v Austria* (unreported) 20 December 2001; *Venema v Netherlands* (unreported) 17 December 2002; *R (P) v Secretary of State for the Home Department; R (Q) v Secretary of State for the Home Department* [2001] EWCA Civ 1151, [2001] 2 FLR 1122. See also Munby, J *Making Sure the Child is Heard: Part 2 – Representation* (2004) Family Law, p 428.

[212] *Dolhamre v Sweden* (2010) Application No 67/04, para 116 ('Here the Court further wishes to point out that, whilst Article 8 contains no explicit procedural requirements, the decision-making process involved in measures of interference must be fair and the parents and, as appropriate, the children must have been involved in the process, seen as a whole, to a degree sufficient to provide them with the requisite protection of their interests. In this respect, it is essential that the parents be placed in a position where they may obtain access to information which is relied on by the authorities in order to be able to put forward in a fair or adequate manner those matters militating in favour of his or her ability to provide the child with proper care and protection').

[213] [2004] EWHC 111 (Fam), [2004] 2 FLR 517.

[214] *CF v Secretary of State for the Home Department* [2004] EWHC 111 (Fam), [2004] 2 FLR 517.

[215] *W v United Kingdom* (1987) 10 EHRR 29 and see *Re M (Care: Challenging Decisions by Local Authority)* [2001] 2 FLR 1300, *Re L (Care: Assessment: Fair Trial)* [2002] EWHC 1379 (Fam), [2002] 2 FLR 730, and *Re G (Care: Challenge to Local Authority's Decision)* [2003] EWHC 551 (Fam), [2003] 2 FLR 42.

[216] *CF v Secretary of State for the Home Department* [2004] EWHC 111 (Fam), [2004] 2 FLR 517. See also *Dolhamre v Sweden* (2010) Application No 67/04, para 116 at **fn 212** above.

[217] *McMichael v United Kingdom* (1995) 20 EHRR 205, para 91 and see *CF v Secretary of State for the Home Department* [2004] EWHC 111 (Fam), [2004] 2 FLR 517.

[218] Fortin, J *Children's Rights and the Developing Law* (2009) 3rd edn, Cambridge, pp 238–239.

[219] Fortin, J *Children's Rights and the Developing Law* (2009) 3rd edn, Cambridge, p 239 citing *Sahin v Germany* [2003] 2 FLR 671 (Grand Chamber), para 73.

been more amenable to them. As Thorpe LJ noted in *Mabon v Mabon*[220] when examining the participation of children in private law proceedings pursuant to r 9.2A of the Family Proceedings Rules 1991:

> 'In my judgment, the rule is sufficiently widely framed to meet our obligations to comply with both Art 12 of the UN Convention and Art 8 of the European Convention, providing that judges correctly focus on the sufficiency of the child's understanding and, in measuring that sufficiency, reflect the extent to which, in the twenty first century, there is a keener appreciation of the autonomy of the child and the child's consequential right to participate in decision making processes that fundamentally affect his family life.'

6.81   In determining whether the procedural protection afforded under Art 8 may be invoked to correct a failure to ensure participation, the European Court of Human Rights has articulated in relation to adults principles that must apply equally to children:[221]

> '[W]hat has to be determined is whether, having regard to the particular circumstances of the case and notably the serious nature of the decisions to be taken, the parents have been involved in the decision-making process, seen as a whole, to a degree sufficient to provide them with the requisite protection of their interests. If they have not, there will have been a failure to respect their family life and the interference resulting from the decision will not be capable of being regarded as 'necessary' within the meaning of Art 8.'

And:[222]

> 'The Court does however consider that it is essential that a parent be placed in a position where he or she may obtain access to information which is relied on by the authorities in taking measures of protective care. A parent may claim an interest in being informed of the nature and extent of the allegations of abuse made by his or her child. This is relevant not only to the parent's ability to put forward those matters militating in favour of his or her capability in providing the child with proper care and protection but also to enable the parent to understand and come to terms with traumatic events effecting the family as a whole.'

And:[223]

> 'It is essential that a parent be placed in a position where he or she may obtain access to information which is relied on by the authorities in taking measures of protective care or in taking decisions relevant to the care and custody of a child. Otherwise the parent will be unable to participate effectively in the decision-making process or put forward in a fair or adequate manner those matters militating in favour of his or her ability to provide the child with proper care and protection.'

---

[220]   [2005] EWCA Civ 634, [2005] 2 FLR 1011.
[221]   *W v United Kingdom* (1988) 10 EHRR 29, paras 62 and 64.
[222]   *TP and KM v United Kingdom* [2001] 2 FLR 549. *TP and KM v United Kingdom* however makes clear that the procedural safeguards are not absolute (see para 80).
[223]   *P, C and S v United Kingdom* [2002] 2 FLR 631, para 137.

Other European Conventions and the Right to Participate

The European Convention on the Adoption of Children (Revised)

6.82 Article 9(2)(f) of the original European Convention on Adoption requires that the competent authority[224] shall not grant an adoption until appropriate enquires have been made concerning the adopter, the child and the family, which enquires shall include the views of the child with respect to the proposed adoption. The revised European Convention on Adoption[225] provides at Art 6 that:[226]

> 'If the child's consent is not necessary according to Art 5, paragraphs 1 and 3, he or she shall, as far as possible, be consulted and his or her views and wishes shall be taken into account having regard to his or her degree of maturity. Such consultation may be dispensed with if it would be manifestly contrary to the child's best interests.'

European Convention on Recognition and Enforcement of Decisions concerning Custody of Children and on Restoration of Custody of Children

6.83 Article 15(1)(a) of the European Convention on Recognition and Enforcement of Decisions concerning Custody of Children and on Restoration of Custody of Children[227] provides that, following an improper removal, before reaching a decision on whether the effects of the original decision relating to custody is manifestly no longer in accordance with the welfare of the child the views of the child shall be ascertained unless this is impracticable having regard to the child's age and understanding.[228]

The European Convention on the Exercise of Children's Rights

6.84 The European Convention on the Exercise of Children's Rights, though not ratified by the United Kingdom, makes further provision concerning the participation of children in proceedings affecting them before a judicial authority.[229] Art 1(3) makes clear that for the purposes of the Convention, 'proceedings' before a judicial authority affecting children are family proceedings, in particular those involving the exercise of parental responsibilities such as residence and contact to children.[230]

6.85 Article 3 of the CECR provides that a child considered to have sufficient understanding for the purposes of internal law is entitled in proceedings before a judicial authority affecting him or her to receive all relevant information, to be consulted and express his or her views and to be informed of the possible consequences of compliance with these views and the possible consequences of any decision. The judicial authority must give effect to these rights by ensuring the child has received all relevant information, by consulting the child, if necessary privately, unless manifestly contrary to the child's best interests, by allowing the child to express his or her views and by giving

---

[224] Defined as a 'court or administrative authority'.
[225] (2008) CETS No 202. The UK has signed the Convention but not yet ratified it. The revised Convention is not yet in force and will not be until three States have ratified it.
[226] See also *European Convention on the Adoption of Children (Revised) Explanatory Report*.
[227] (1980) CETS No 105. The Convention was ratified by the UK on 21 April 1986. The UK entered a significant number of reservations upon ratifying the convention. See CET List of Declarations made with respect to Treaty No 105.
[228] Whilst there is no express requirement thereafter to take account of the child's views it is submitted that this must be implied.
[229] CECR, Art 1.
[230] Article 2(a) defines 'judicial authority' as 'a court or an administrative authority having equivalent powers'. In the circumstances, the ambit of the CECR may not extend to administrative decision making processes.

due weight to those views.[231] Pursuant to Art 4(1) of the Convention, a child has the right 'to apply, in person or through other persons or bodies, for a special representative in proceedings before a judicial authority affecting the child where internal law precludes the holders of parental responsibilities from representing the child as a result of a conflict of interest with the latter'. The term 'special representative' is defined by the Convention as 'a person, such as a lawyer, or a body appointed to act before a judicial authority on behalf of a child'.[232] Art 14 provides that where legal aid is available under national law, that aid shall be available in relation to the provision of a special representative.

6.86   It is important to note that the rights enshrined in Arts 3 and 4 of the CECR concerning the participation of children are qualified by the fact that they extend only to a child who is 'considered by internal law as having sufficient understanding'. Further, Art 5 of the Convention provides that States Parties shall only *consider* granting children the important procedural rights to apply to be assisted by an appropriate person to express their views, to apply themselves for the appointment of a special representative, to appoint their own representative and the right to exercise some or all of the rights of parties to proceedings. In addition, only those children who are subject to internal law 'which precludes the holders of parental responsibilities from representing the child as a result of a conflict of interest with the latter' have the right to apply for a special representative. A child whose internal law does not prevent parents from representing him or her is thus in a significantly disadvantaged position under the Convention where a conflict exists but is not recognised.[233] Finally, Sawyer observes that the special representative is given a worrying leeway in interpreting his or her duties by the phrase 'manifestly contrary to the best interests of the child' in Art 10(1) of the Convention.[234] These numerous difficulties arguably limit the efficacy of the CECR, moving the position of children backwards from that achieved under the CRC.[235]

The European Convention on Contact Concerning Children

6.87   Pursuant to Art 6 of the European Convention on Contact Concerning Children[236] a child of 'sufficient understanding' has the right, 'unless it would be manifestly contrary to his or her best interests' to receive all relevant information, to be consulted, to express his or her views and to have due weight given to those views and to his or her ascertainable wishes and feelings on the issue of contact.[237] It should be noted that these provisions also apply to the making or modifying of agreements between

---

[231]   CECR, Art 6(b) and 6(c).
[232]   CECR, Art 2(c). The role of the special representative is defined in article 10 as being to provide all relevant information to the child, provide explanations to the child concerning the possible consequences of compliance with his or her views and the possible consequences of any action by the special representative, and to determine the views of the child and present those views to the judicial authority. These duties are to be carried out unless to do so would be manifestly contrary to the best interests of the child (Art 10(1)).
[233]   Fortin, J *Children's Rights and the Developing Law* (2009) 3rd edn, Cambridge, p 237.
[234]   Sawyer, C *One Step Forward and Two Steps Back – the European Convention on the Exercise of Children's Rights* (1999), p 155.
[235]   Sawyer, C *One Step Forward and Two Steps Back – the European Convention on the Exercise of Children's Rights* (1999), p 156 and Fortin, J *Children's Rights and the Developing Law* (2009) 3rd edn, Cambridge, pp 237–238.
[236]   (2003) CETS No 192. The CCCC entered into force on 1 September 2005 but has not yet been signed or ratified by the United Kingdom. The Convention on Contact Concerning Children does not prejudice the application of the Hague Conventions of 5 October 1961 or 19 October 1996 or the European Convention on the Recognition of Decisions concerning Custody of children etc (subject to Art 19 of the CCCC).
[237]   CCCC, Art 6(1) and (2). Paragraph 56 of the Explanatory Report for the CCCC states in relation to Art 6(2) that 'this second paragraph of Article 6 does not grant the child an absolute right to consent or to veto a planned decision concerning contact, because it is not always in the best interests of the child to grant him

parents and other persons having family ties with the child in respect of contact.[238] The provisions in the CCCC concerning the views of the child are based on the European Convention on the Exercise of Children's Rights. Accordingly, they are open to the some of the same criticisms outlined above in relation to the CECR.[239] In particular, it is difficult to see how the statement contained in the explanatory report to the CCCC to the effect that States are free to set minimum age limits for the purposes of determining whether a child is of 'sufficient understanding' can possible be compliant with the requirements of Art 12 of the CRC.[240]

The Child's Right to Participate under European Law

6.88   The European Charter of Fundamental Rights of the European Union Art 24(1) stipulates that children may express their views freely and that such views shall be taken into consideration on matters which concern them in accordance with their age and maturity.

The Child's Right to Participate under other Regional Instruments

American Convention on Human Rights

6.89   The Art 8 right to a fair trial in the ACHR stipulates that every person has the right to a hearing in the substantiation of any accusation of a criminal nature made against him or for the determination of his rights and obligations of a civil, labor, fiscal, or any other nature. The Inter-American Court of Human Rights has observed in the context of children's rights that the right to a fair trial, which includes the right to a hearing, applies not only to judicial proceedings but also to any other proceedings conducted by the State.[241] The aim, having regard to the child's specific conditions and his or her best interests, must be to seek as much access as possible by the child to examination of his or her own case.[242] In its Advisory Opinion of 28 August 2002 the Court opined that:[243]

> 'Evidently, there is great diversity in terms of physical and intellectual development, of experience and of the information known by those who are included in that group. The decision-making ability of a 3-year-old child is not the same as that of a 16-year-old adolescent. For this reason, the degree of participation of a child in the proceedings must be reasonably adjusted, so as to attain effective protection of his or her best interests, which are the ultimate objective of International Human Rights Law in this regard ... those responsible for application of the law, whether in the administrative or judiciary sphere, must take into account the specific conditions of the minor and his or her best interests to decide on the child's participation, as appropriate, in establishing his or her rights. This consideration will seek as much access as possible by the minor to examination of his or her own case.'

6.90   Article 23(1) of the ACHR confers a right to participate in Government on every 'citizen' which includes the right to take part in the conduct of public affairs, either

---

or her such a right. It is for the judicial authority to make the final decision taking into account the wishes and feelings of the child as well as all other circumstances.'
[238]   CCCC Art 8(1). Such agreements should preferably in writing.
[239]   See **6.86** above.
[240]   Paragraph 53 of the Explanatory Report states that 'States are naturally free to make the age of children one of those criteria' which defines whether a child is of 'sufficient understanding".
[241]   Advisory Opinion of 28 August 2002 OC-17/2002, para 117.
[242]   Advisory Opinion OC-17/2002, para 102.
[243]   Advisory Opinion of 28 August 2002 OC-17/2002, paras 101–102.

directly of through freely chosen representatives, the right to vote and the right to access to the public service of his or her country. These rights may be regulated by reference to age.[244]

Ibero-American Convention on Young People's Rights

6.91   In respect of family proceedings concerning children, Art 19(2) of the Ibero-American Convention on Young Peoples Rights provides that 'Minor young people have the right to a hearing in case of divorce or separation of their parents for the effects of attribution of the own guardianship, as well as, to make their will determining in the case of adoption'. In considering the wider right to participation of young people,[245] Art 21 of the Convention emphasises participation in the political process by young people:

'1. Youth have the right to participation in politics.

2. The States Parties undertake to boost and strengthen social processes which generate forms and guaranties which make the participation of youth from all sectors of society effective in organisations which encourage their inclusion.

3. The States Parties shall promote measures which, in conformity with the inner law of each country, promote and encourage that youth exercise their right to register in political associations, to elect and be elected.

4. The States Parties undertake to promote that governmental and legislative institutions promote the participation of youth in the formulation of policies and laws concerning youth, drawing up the corresponding mechanisms to make effective the analysis and discussion of youth initiatives through their organisations and associations.'

African (Banjul) Charter on Human and Peoples' Rights

6.92   Article 7 of the African (Banjul) Charter on Human and Peoples' Rights stipulates that every individual shall have the right to have his cause heard. Article 9(1) enshrines the right to receive information. By Art 13 of the Convention every citizen shall have the right to participate freely in the government of his country, either directly or through freely chosen representatives in accordance with the provisions of the law.

African Charter on the Rights and Welfare of the Child

6.93   Article 4(1) of the African Charter on the Rights and Welfare of the Child stipulates that:

'In all judicial or administrative proceedings affecting a child who is capable of communicating his/her own views, an opportunity shall be provided for the views of the child to be heard either directly or through an impartial representative as a party to the proceedings, and those views shall be taken into consideration by the relevant authority in accordance with the provisions of appropriate law.'

---

[244]   Article 23(2).
[245]   Defined by Art 1 of the Convention as 'all people, nationals or residents in any Ibero-American country, aged between 15 and 24 years.'

African Youth Charter

6.94 The African Youth Charter defines 'youth' and 'young people' as referring to persons between 15 and 35 years of age. Within this context, Art 11 of the Charter enshrines the right to participate in all spheres of society[246] emphasising active youth participation within society at all levels.[247]

The Child's Right to Participate in Domestic Law

Domestic Ambit of the Child's Right to Participate

6.95 The Children (Scotland) Act 1995, s 6(1) requires any parent, when reaching a 'major decision' involving his child's upbringing, to 'have regard as far as is practicable to the views (if he wishes to express them) of the child concerned' taking into account the child's age and maturity, a child of 12 being considered to be of sufficient age and understanding to form a view.[248] Domestic statute law, whilst incorporating a requirement that in proceedings which determine any question with respect to the upbringing of the child or the administration of his property the court must have regard to the child's ascertainable wishes and feelings considered in light of his or her understanding,[249] does not require parents to take account of their children's wishes and feelings.

6.96 Domestic case law however clearly recognises that parental control yields increasingly to the child's right to participate and then to make his or her own decisions when the child reaches a sufficient understanding and intelligence to be capable of making up his or her own mind on a matter requiring decision.[250] A child of sufficient understanding and intelligence to be capable of making up his or her own mind is now commonly described as 'Gillick competent' following the seminal decision of the House of Lords in *Gillick v West Norfolk and Wisbeach Health Authority*. Fortin observes that *Gillick* in fact goes considerably further when articulating the child's right to participate than does Art 12 of the CRC. She notes that whilst Art 12 requires participation in decision making to an extent dependent on his age and maturity without a concomitant requirement to comply with the child's stated wishes, *Gillick* requires that children's wishes should be *complied* with where a child passes the test of sufficient understanding and intelligence.[251] If applied according to the principles set out in *Gillick* the child's right to participate in domestic law has the potential to run ahead of the international position achieved under the CRC.

---

[246] Article 11(1).

[247] Article 11(2). Article 11(2) enshrines the right to participate *inter alia* in parliament and other decision making bodies, in decision-making at local, national, regional, and continental levels of governance and in delegations to ordinary sessions and other relevant meetings to broaden channels of communication and enhance the discussion of youth related issues.'

[248] The Scottish jurisdiction is not without criticism in its implementation of children's rights (see for example Tisdall, E *The Children (Scotland) Act 1995: Developing Policy and Law for Scotland's Children* (1997) The Stationery Office, p 122).

[249] Children Act 1989, s 1(3)(a).

[250] *Gillick v West Norfolk and Wisbeach Health Authority* [1986] AC 122 per Lord Scarman. See **4.25** above in respect of evolving capacity.

[251] Fortin, J *Children's Rights and the Developing Law* (2009) 3rd edn, Cambridge, p 94.

Domestic Application of the Child's Right to Participate

Domestic Application of the Child's Right to Participate – Medicine and Healthcare

6.97   The general domestic principles governing the medical treatment of children have been dealt with in chapter 5 when dealing with the child's right to life.[252] The child's right to participate is relevant to decisions concerning a child's medical treatment in that, as the patient, the child may well have a clear view as to that treatment. Within domestic law, the issue of the child's participation in medical decisions can be dealt with under three separate categories.

(i)   Family Law Reform Act 1969

6.98   Pursuant to the Family Law Reform Act 1969, s 8(1) the consent of a child who has attained the age of 16 years to treatment[253] which, in the absence of consent would constitute a trespass to the person of the child, is effective consent, excluding the need to obtain consent from parent or guardian.

(ii)   'Gillick Competent' Children under 16

6.99   Where a child under 16 is deemed *Gillick* competent, he or she may give valid consent to medical treatment. In *Re R (A Minor) (Wardship: Medical Treatment)*[254] Lord Donaldson MR held that the parents may override by parental veto a '*Gillick* competent' child's refusal to consent to medical treatment, although they may not veto a '*Gillick* competent' child's consent to treatment, drawing a distinction between the right of determination and the right of consent. In *Re W (A Minor) (Medical Treatment: Court's Jurisdiction)*[255] on an appeal from a decision of Thorpe J, Lord Donaldson MR doubted that Lord Scarman's statement of principle in *Gillick* meant more than that the *exclusive* right of the parents to *consent* to treatment terminated.[256] Pursuant to *Re W* and *Re R* it has accordingly been argued that parents retain the right to override a child's decision to refuse medical treatment by means of parental veto of that decision even if that child is '*Gillick* competent' subject only to the ultimate jurisdiction of the court.[257]

6.100   The decision in *Re R (A Minor) (Wardship: Medical Treatment)* and *Re W (A Minor) (Medical Treatment: Court's Jurisdiction)* have been the subject of sustained criticism.[258] It is suggested that the approach to be preferred in relation to the participation of children who are *Gillick* competent in decisions concerning their own medical treatment is that outlined by Silber J in *R (on the application of Axon) v Secretary of State for Health and another*[259] in which he held in respect of *Gillick* that:

---

[252]   See above at **5.55–5.73**.
[253]   The Act uses the phrase 'surgical, medical or dental treatment' which it defines in s 8(2) as including 'any procedure undertaken for the purpose of diagnosis' and 'any procedure (including in particular the administration of an anaesthetic) which is ancillary to any treatment as it applies to that treatment'.
[254]   [1992] Fam 11 at 23, [1991] 4 All ER 177 at 185.
[255]   [1993] Fam 64 at 75–76 and 87, [1992] 3 WLR 748, [1992] 4 All ER 627 at 633 and 642–643 *sub nom Re W (A Minor) (Consent to Medical Treatment)* [1993] 1 FLR 1.
[256]   Lord Donaldson's analysis tends to ignore the fact that Lord Scarman's statement of principle in *Gillick* was not limited to decisions concerning treatment but rather was expressed in relation to decisions in general, Lord Scarman holding that 'parental rights yield to the child's right to make his own decisions when he reaches a sufficient understanding and intelligence to be capable of making up his own mind *on the matter requiring decision*' (emphasis added). See **6.100** below.
[257]   See also *Re P (Minors) (Wardship: Care and Control)* [1992] 2 FCR 681 per Butler-Sloss LJ.
[258]   See the detailed treatment of this topic at **4.41–4.47** above.
[259]   [2006] EWHC 37 (Admin), [2006] QB 539, [2006] 1 FCR 175, paras 56 and 95.

'... the reasoning of the majority was that the parental right to determine whether a young person will have medical treatment terminates if and when the young person achieves a sufficient understanding and intelligence to understand fully what is proposed' and that 'there is nothing in the speeches of the majority in *Gillick*, which suggests that parental authority has any place in decision-making for a young person, who in the words of Lord Scarman, which I have quoted in the last paragraph 'achieves a sufficient understanding and intelligence to enable him or her to fully understand what is proposed.'

6.101 The courts do retain jurisdiction to override the decision of a *Gillick* competent child in respect of his or her own medical treatment. In *Re W (A Minor) (Medical Treatment: Court's Jurisdiction)*[260] the Court of Appeal held that the court, exercising its unlimited inherent jurisdiction over minors, and whether the child was a ward of court or not, could in the child's best interests objectively considered override the decision of a '*Gillick* competent' child, Balcombe LJ stating that:[261]

'It is also clear that Lord Scarman was only considering the position of the child vis-à-vis its parents: he was not considering the position of the child vis-à-vis the court, whose powers, as I have already said, are wider than the parents.'

(iii) Children Under 16 who are Not 'Gillick' Competent

6.102 For children under the age of 16 who are not *Gillick* competent, the applicable test in determining whether a child should be subjected to medical treatment to which he or she objects is one of what is in his or her best interests.[262] In the normal course of events, the child's best interests will be determined by those having parental responsibility for the child, having regard to and giving due weight to the child's wishes and feelings having regard to their age and understanding. Where however the courts are required to determine the issue in applying the best interests test the court must navigate the following 'intellectual milestones':[263]

(a)   the judge must decide what is in the best interests of the child;[264]

(b)   in doing so the child's welfare is the court's paramount consideration;

(c)   the judge must look at it from the assumed point of view of the patient;

(d)   there is strong presumption in favour of a course of action which will prolong life, but that presumption is not irrebuttable;

(e)   The term best interests encompasses medical, emotional and all other welfare issues;[265]

---

[260]   [1993] Fam 64 at 75–76 and 87, [1992] 3 WLR 748, [1992] 4 All ER 627 at 633 and 642–643 *sub nom Re W (A Minor) (Consent to Medical Treatment)* [1993] 1 FLR 1.

[261]   See **4.50–4.53** for a discussion of the rational for this position.

[262]   *Re A (Conjoined Twins: Surgical Separation)* [2001] Fam 147, [2000] 4 All ER 961, [2000] 3 FCR 577, [2001] 1 FLR 1. For criticism of this decision see Fortin, J *Children's Rights and the Developing Law* (2005) 2nd edn, Cambridge, p 318. See also See *Airedale National Health Service Trust v Bland* [1993] AC 789 HL.

[263]   *Wyatt v Portsmouth NHS Trust* [2005] EWCA Civ 1182, [2006] 1 FLR 554.

[264]   The concept of intolerability in the sense of 'intolerable to the child' should not be seen as gloss on, much less a supplementary test to, best interests (*Wyatt v Portsmouth NHS Trust* [2005] EWCA Civ 1182, [2006] 1 FLR 554). In assessing best interests, the court must balance the advantages of giving or not giving potential treatments in order to determine the child's best interests with regard to future treatment (see *Re K (Medical Treatment: Declaration)* [2006] EWHC 1007 (Fam), [2006] 2 FLR 883).

[265]   See also *Re A (Male Sterilisation)* [2000] 1 FLR 549; *Re S (Sterilisation: Patient's Best Interests)* [2000]

(f)   The court must conduct a balancing exercise in which all relevant factors are weighed. A helpful way of doing this is to draw up a balance sheet.[266]

6.103 Accordingly, the child's wishes and feelings considered in light his or her age and understanding will be one factor to be taken into account in determining whether the treatment is or is not in the child's best interests.[267] The domestic courts have emphasised the importance of the child's wishes and feelings within the context of decisions concerning his or her medical treatment. In *Re W (A Minor) (Medical Treatment: Court's Discretion)*,[268] sub nom *Re W (A Minor) (Consent to Medical Treatment)*[269] Balcombe LJ observed that the court's discretion:

> 'is not to be exercised in a moral vacuum. Undoubtedly the philosophy ... is that, as children approach the age of majority, they are increasingly able to take their own decisions concerning their medical treatment. In logic there can be no difference between an ability to consent to treatment and an ability to refuse treatment ... Accordingly, the older the child concerned the greater the weight the court should give to its wishes, certainly in the field of medical treatment. In a sense this is merely one aspect of the application of the test that the welfare of the child is the paramount consideration. It will normally be in the best interests of a child of sufficient age and understanding to make an informed decision that the court should respect its integrity as a human being and not lightly override its decision on such a personal matter as medical treatment, all the more so if that treatment is invasive ... Nevertheless, if the court's powers are to be meaningful, there must come a point at which the court, while not disregarding the child's wishes, can override them in the child's own best interests, objectively considered. Clearly such a point will have come if the child is seeking to refuse treatment in circumstances which will in all probability lead to the death of the child or to severe permanent injury.'

6.104 Where the child expresses strong religious objections to lifesaving treatment the courts have also tended to override those wishes and directed that treatment be given.[270] In *Re L (Medical Treatment: Gillick Competence)*[271] Sir Stephen Brown P, in a case in which a 14 year old girl refused treatment for a life threatening condition on religious grounds, relied on the views of a consultant child psychiatrist (who did not speak to the child) drawing a distinction between the sincerely and strongly held religious belief of the child formed in the context of her sheltered family life and associated religious

---

        2 FLR 389; *Portsmouth NHS Trust v Wyatt* [2004] EWHC 2247 (Fam), [2005] 1 FLR 21; *Re L (Medical Treatment: Benefit)* [2004] EWHC 2713 (Fam), [2005] 1 FLR 491 and *An NHS Trust v A* [2007] EWHC 1696 (Fam), [2008] 1 FLR 70 in which Holman J noted 'Best interests are used in the widest sense and include every kind of consideration capable of impacting on the decision. These include, non-exhaustively, medical, emotional, sensory (pleasure, pain and suffering) and instinctive (the human instinct to survive) considerations.'

[266] See *An NHS Trust v A* [2007] EWHC 1696 (Fam), [2008] 1 FLR 70 in which Holman J noted 'It is impossible to weigh such considerations mathematically, but the court must do the best it can to balance all the conflicting considerations in a particular case and see where the final balance of the best interests lies.

[267] *Wyatt v Portsmouth NHS Trust* [2005] EWCA Civ 1182, [2006] 1 FLR 554. See also *R (on the application of Burke) v General Medical Council* [2005] EWCA Civ 1003, [2006] QB 273, [2005] 3 FCR 169) in which the House of Lords recognised that that the wishes of a patient might conflict with his best interests. See also (1993) 12 BMLR 64 at 111, 136 per Lord Goff of Chievely and Lord Mustill respectively: 'It seems to us that it is best to confine the use of the phrase 'best interests' to an objective test, which is of most use when considering the duty owed to a patient who is not competent and is easiest to apply when confined to a situation where the relevant interests are medical.'

[268] [1993] Fam 64.

[269] [1993] 1 FLR 1.

[270] *Re L (Medical Treatment: Gillick Competence)* [1998] 2 FLR 810; *Re M (Medical Treatment: Consent)* [1999] 2 FLR 1097 and *Re P (Medical Treatment: Best Interests)* [2003] EWHC 1696 (Fam), [2004] 2 FLR 1117.

[271] [1998] 2 FLR 810.

experience and the constructive formulation of an opinion which occurs with adult experience. Within this context, the President held that the girl's best interests dictated treatment against her will, observing:[272]

> 'It is, therefore, a limited experience of life which she has – inevitably so – but that is in no sense a criticism of her or of her upbringing. It is indeed refreshing to hear of children being brought up with the sensible disciplines of a well-conducted family. But it does necessarily limit her understanding of matters which are as grave as her own present situation. It may be that because of her belief she is willing to say, and to mean it, "I am willing to accept death rather than to have a blood transfusion", but it is quite clear in this case that she has not been able to be given all the details which it would be right and appropriate to have in mind when making such a decision.'

6.105 In *Re M (Medical Treatment: Consent)*[273] a 15 year old girl refused to consent to a heart transplant on the grounds that she did not want someone else's heart or a life of taking medication. Johnson J accepted the view of the Official Solicitor that M was an intelligent 15 year old girl whose wishes should carry considerable weight but found that M felt overwhelmed by her circumstances and the decision she was being asked to make. The Court authorised the transplant on the basis that it was in her best interests.

Domestic Application of the Child's Right to Participate – Judicial and Administrative Proceedings

(i) Family Proceedings

Family Proceedings General Principles – Children Act 1989, s 1(3)(a)

6.106 Pursuant to1(3)(a) of the Children Act 1989 the court is required to have regard in particular to the ascertainable wishes and feelings of the child concerned, considered in light of his age and understanding, in any proceedings which:

(a)   determine any question with respect to the upbringing of the child;[274]

(b)   determine any question with respect to the administration of the child's property or the application of the income arising from it;[275] and

(c)   the court is considering whether:

    (i)   to make, vary or discharge a s 8 order, and the making, variation or discharge of the order is opposed by any party to the proceedings;[276] or

    (ii)   to make, vary or discharge a special guardianship order or an order under Part IV of the Act.[277]

---

[272]   See also *Re P (Medical Treatment: Best Interests)* [2003] EWHC 1696 (Fam), [2004] 2 FLR 1117 (concerning a 16 year old boy who objected to the administration of blood or blood products by reason of his being a staunch and committed Jehovah's Witness).

[273]   [1999] 2 FLR 1097.

[274]   CA 1989, s 1(1)(a). The upbringing of the child includes his or her care but not maintenance (CA 1989, s 105).

[275]   CA 1989, s 1(1)(b).

[276]   CA 1989 ,s 1(4)(a). Such proceedings are generally termed 'private law' proceedings.

[277]   CA 1989, s 1(4)(b). Proceedings under Part IV of the Children Act 1989 are generally termed 'public law proceedings.'

'Regard to Ascertainable Wishes and Feelings'

6.107 The position of the child's ascertainable wishes and feelings at the head of the 'welfare checklist' contained in s 1(3) of the Children Act 1989 demonstrates that the child's perspective should carry greater weight.[278] In having regard to the ascertainable wishes and feelings of the child, the court must properly take account and weigh those wishes and feelings.[279] However, in accordance with the principle of participation not self-determination, whilst regard must be paid to the child's wishes and feelings, they will not inevitably be determinative.[280] Where the other factors relevant to the child's best interests are evenly balanced the child's ascertainable wishes and feelings may be determinative of the issue.[281]

'Age and Understanding'

6.108 The need to have regard to the ascertainable wishes and feelings of the child must be considered in light of the child's age and understanding. Both concepts are important and the element of 'understanding' should not overlooked.[282] In considering the 'age and understanding' of the child in question it is important to have regard to enormous variation between children in the process of evolving capacity and that chronological age alone is unlikely to be a valid determinative factor.[283] Further, as Fortin notes, a child's age and competence to form views cannot be assessed *in vacuo* since the context of the dispute and the risk involved in ignoring or acceding to the child's wishes will always impinge on the decision making process.[284] In the appendix to *Contact and Domestic Violence – the Experts' Court Report*[285] produced with the assistance of John Eekelaar, Sturge and Glaser highlight the difficulties which may interfere with the consideration of the child's wishes and feelings:

(a)   Distinguishing between wishes and deeper feelings.

(b)   Statements influenced by a specific context.

(c)   Separating out the incidental or transitory.

(d)   Pressure from disputing adults.

(e)   Risk of being burdened with guilt.

(f)   Risk of receiving hostility from others.

---

[278]   *Re P (Minors)(Wardship)* [1992] 2 FCR 681.

[279]   The Law Commission considered that 'the increasing recognition given both in practice and in law to the child's status as a human being in his own right' should be incorporated as an integral part of the courts' decision making process in respect of children (Law Commission *Review of Child Law, Guardianship and Custody* (1988) Law Comm No 172 HMSO, para 3.24).

[280]   *Re P (Minors)(Wardship)* [1992] 2 FCR 681. See also *C v Finland* Application No 18249/02 [2006] 2 FCR 195.

[281]   *Re W (Minors)(Residence Order)* [1992] 2 FCR 461 and *Re H (Care Order: Contact)* [2008] EWCA Civ 1245, [2009] 2 FLR 55.

[282]   *Re H (Care Order: Contact)* [2008] EWCA Civ 1245, [2009] 2 FLR 55 per Ward LJ.

[283]   Jones, D *Communicating with Vulnerable Children* (2003) Gaskell, p 9. See also Archard, D *Children – Rights and Childhood* (2004) Routledge, p 96 and Fortin, J *Children's Rights and the Developing Law* (2009) 3rd edn, Cambridge, pp 298–303. See also **6.9** above.

[284]   Fortin, J *Children's Rights and the Developing Law* (2009) 3rd edn, Cambridge, pp 298–303.

[285]   Sturge, C and Glaser, D [2000] Fam Law 615 and see *Re L (A Child) (Contact: Domestic Violence)* [2000] 4 All ER 609.

(g)   Decision affected by information quality and provider bias.

(h)   Articulation affected by age and how the child may think wishes will be received.

(i)   Whether the child has promised someone what to say or what not to say.

(j)   Whether the child has support.

(k)   Where and how the child is asked.

(l)   Where it is difficult to explain alternatives to the child.

6.109   As noted, whatever the child's 'age and understanding' the Children Act 1989, s 1(3)(a) was not drafted so as to make the wishes and feelings of the child determinative of the issue in question.[286] The concept of *Gillick* competence has not to date exerted influence on the application of s 1(3)(a) of the Children Act 1989. Whilst, applying *Gillick*, a child who is of sufficient understanding and intelligence to be capable of making up his own mind on the matter requiring decision might be thought to hold the trump card under s 1(3)(a) the Children Act 1989, the Act in fact requires a balance to be achieved between:[287]

> 'the need to recognise the child as an independent person and to ensure that his views are fully taken into account and the risk of casting on him the burden of resolving problems caused by his parents or requiring him to choose between them.'

6.110   However, whilst this balance remains central to the question of the child's participation in family proceedings, the case law in respect of 'age and understanding' for the purposes of s 1(3)(a) has increasingly recognised the significance of the views of children when determining the extent to which those wishes and feelings should be considered.[288] In *Re Roddy (A Child) (Identification: Restriction on Publication)*[289]

---

[286]   See *Re P (Minors) (Wardship: Care and Control)* [1992] 2 FCR 681 at 687 per Butler-Sloss LJ. See also *M v M (Minor: Custody Appeal)* [1987] 1 WLR 404 at 411 per May LJ.

[287]   *Introduction to the Children Act 1989* (1991) HMSO, para 1.25.

[288]   See for example *Re S (Minors) (Access: Religious Upbringing)* [1992] 2 FLR 313 (nobody should dictate to children of 13 and 11 years old; children are people entitled to be treated with respect); *Re P (A Minor) (Education)* [1992] 1 FLR 316 (the strong wish of a 14 year old boy to attend a particular school and to live with his Father should be listened to and proper regard paid to it. The Court observed that older children have an appreciation of their position that is worthy of respect by adults and by the courts); *M v M (Removal from Jurisdiction)* [1993] 1 FCR 5 (two intelligent and articulate children aged 10 and 11 should have considerable weight attached to their wishes and feelings on issues relevant to the application of their Mother to move to Israel); *Re B (Abduction; Children's Objections)* [1998] 1 FLR 667 (two boys aged 7 and 12 were sufficiently mature for the court to consider their objection to being returned to Ireland with their Father); *Re S (Change of Surname)* [1999] 1 FLR 672 (a 15 year old child who wanted her name changed to that of her Mother's family was *Gillick* competent and accordingly her wishes should be given careful consideration) and *Re KR (Abduction: Forcible Removal by Parents)* [1999] 2 FLR 542 (although the English court was sensitive to the strong concept of family, that sensitivity would usually have to give way to the integrity of the individual child or young person concerned. Within this context the voice of a 17 year old girl would be heard, and her opposition to an arranged or enforced marriage would prevail). But see also *Re C (A Minor) (Care: Child's Wishes)* [1993] 1 FLR 832, [1993] Fam Law 400 (wishes of 13 year old girl in local authority care to return to live with her divorced, 64 year old, ill father were overruled on the basis that she was too young to carry burden of decisions about her own future and to have to bear the weight of responsibility for a father who lacked authority and played on her feelings).

[289]   [2003] EWHC 2927 (Fam), [2004] 2 FLR 949.

Munby J referred to the Court of Appeals decision in *Re W (A Minor) (Medical Treatment: Court's Jurisdiction)*[290] and observed:

> 'In my judgment (and I wish to emphasise this) it is the responsibility – it is the duty – of the Court not merely to recognise but, as Nolan LJ said, to defend what, if I may respectfully say so, he correctly described as the right of the child who has sufficient age and understanding to make an informed decision, to make his or her own choice. This is not mere pragmatism, though as Nolan LJ pointed out, any other approach is likely to be both futile and counter productive. It is also, as he said, a matter of principle. For, as Balcombe J recognised, the Court must recognise the child's integrity as a human being.'

In *Mabon v Mabon*[291] the Court of appeal acknowledged the increasing recognition of the autonomy and consequential rights of children having regard in particular to Art 12 of the CRC, Lord Justice Thorpe observing:

> 'The applicants were at the date of judgment aged respectively 17, 15, and 13. What remained was a disposal hearing. As Mr Everall eloquently put it, without separate representation how were they to know what their parents were contending for: were there cross-applications for residence, what were the contact applications? It was simply unthinkable to exclude young men from knowledge of and participation in legal proceedings that affected them so fundamentally ... Unless we in this jurisdiction are to fall out of step with similar societies as they safeguard Art 12 rights, we must, in the case of articulate teenagers, accept that the right to freedom of expression and participation outweighs the paternalistic judgment of welfare ... In testing the sufficiency of a child's understanding, I would not say that welfare has no place. If direct participation would pose an obvious risk of harm to the child, arising out of the nature of the continuing proceedings and, if the child is incapable of comprehending that risk, then the judge is entitled to find that sufficient understanding has not been demonstrated. But judges have to be equally alive to the risk of emotional harm that might arise from denying the child knowledge of and participation in the continuing proceedings.'

In the same case, Wall LJ observed that there was a need for the young person:

> '... to emerge from the proceedings (whatever the result) with the knowledge that their position had been independently represented and their perspective fully advanced to the judge.'

In *Re D (A Child)*[292] Baroness Hale observed in relation to this issue that:

> 'There is a growing understanding of the importance of listening to the children involved in children's cases. It is the child, more than anyone else, who will have to live with what the Court decides. Those who do listen to children understand that they often have a point of view which is quite distinct from that of the person looking after them. They are quite capable of being moral actors in their own right. Just as the adults may have to do what the court decides whether they like it or not, so may the child. But that is no more reason for failing to hear what the child has to say than it is for refusing to hear the parents' views.'[293]

---

[290] [1993] Fam 64.
[291] [2005] EWCA Civ 634, [2005] 2 FLR 1011.
[292] [2006] UKHL 51.
[293] See also *R (Axon) v Secretary of State for Health and the Family Planning Association* [2006] EWHC 37 (Admin), [2006] 2 FLR 206, para 79 per Silber J ('... the right of young people to make decisions about their own lives by themselves at the expense of the views of their parents has now become an increasingly important and accepted feature of family life').

6.111 The increasing recognition of the autonomy and consequential rights of children is likely to sustain and expand this line of authority to encompass more and younger children.[294] Sturge and Glaser maintain that in relation to the wishes and feelings of the child:[295]

> '... the older the child the more seriously they should be viewed and the more insulting and discrediting to the child to have them ignored. As a rough rule we would see these as needing to be taken account of at any age; above 10 we see these as carrying considerable weight with 6–10 as an intermediate stage and at under 6 as often indisguishable in many ways from the wishes and feelings of the main carer (assuming normal development).'

6.112 The Children Act 1989 itself recognises the significance of increasing age by providing that no order pursuant to s 8 of the Act should be made in respect of a child over the age of 16 unless the circumstances are exceptional[296] and no care or supervision order may be made in respect of a child who has reached the age of 17 (or 16 where married).[297] When read with the principle embodied in *Gillick*, the effect of s 1(3)(a) may ultimately be held to be that where a child has reached a sufficient understanding and intelligence to be capable of making up her own mind on the matter concerning their upbringing, his or her wishes and feelings will be determinative of the issue in question.

'Making, Varying or Discharging a s 8 Order which is Opposed'

6.113 Pursuant to s 1(4)(a) of the Children Act 1989, in private law proceedings between parents or carers the court is only *required* to have regard to the ascertainable wishes and feelings of the child where the order being sought in the proceedings by one party is opposed by the other. This contrasts with the position under s 1(4)(b) in respect of public law proceedings and applications for special guardianship orders in which the court's duty to consider the ascertainable wishes and feelings of the child is absolute.[298] This creates a potentially stark differential between two groups of children as to the extent to which their wishes and feelings will be considered by the Court.

6.114 The primary difficulty with the position created by s 1(4)(a) of the Children Act 1989 is that it qualifies a child's cardinal rights by reference the nature of the dispute between adults. A child whose parents are in dispute will have a greater opportunity to participate in the process designed to order their future than a child whose parents may be agreed on the correct way forward, even though those respective positions may have equally far reaching ramifications for both children. Whilst there is some logic in this position in that parents who are in agreement may be considered more likely to meet their child's needs than parents in dispute, this conclusion does not invariably follow. Most importantly, the child's right to participate under Art 12 of the CRC, in accordance with which the Children Act 1989 must be interpreted, is not qualified by reference to the nature or degrees of dispute but rather is available equally to all children.

---

[294] See *Mabon v Mabon* [2005] EWCA Civ 634, [2005] 2 FLR 1011 and *Re D (A Child)* [2006] UKHL 51, [2007] 1 AC 619, [2007] 1 All ER 783, [2007] 1 FCR 1, [2007] 1 FLR 961.

[295] Sturge, C and Glaser, D *Contact and Domestic Violence – the Experts' Court Report* [2000] Fam Law 615, p 624.

[296] CA 1989, ss 9(6) and 9(7).

[297] CA 1989, s 31(3).

[298] See Law Commission Report (1988), paras 3.23 and 3.24.

'Making, Varying or Discharging Orders under Part IV'

6.115 By contrast to s 1(4)(a), pursuant to s 1(4)(b) of the Children Act 1989 the duty of the court to have regard to the ascertainable wishes and feelings of the child considered in light of his or her understanding is an absolute one and is not qualified by reference to whether or not the proceedings are contested.

Family Proceedings General Principles – The Adoption and Children Act 2002

6.116 The Adoption and Children Act 2002, s 1(4) requires the adoption agency to have regard to the child's wishes and feelings 'considered in light of the child's age and understanding'.[299] The observations in the paragraphs above apply also to the phrase 'age and understanding' in s 1(4)(a) of the Adoption and Children Act 2002.[300] Section 1(4)(a) has not been subject to extensive judicial consideration but earlier case law on the adoption legislation suggests that the concept of 'age and understanding' will have an impact similar to that seen in respect of s 1(3)(a) of the Children Act 1989. In *Re D (Minors)(Adoption by Step-Parent)*[301] the Court of Appeal held that where the child understands the broad implications of adoption, the court will require clear reasons to justify proceedings against his expressed wishes and feelings.[302] As the trend in adoption is increasingly towards older children, the concept of evolving capacity embodied in s 1(4)(a) of the Act by the words 'age and understanding' is likely to become of increasing significance.

Family Proceedings General Principles – Further Statutory Provisions

6.117 Domestic family primary and secondary legislation incorporates a wide range of additional provisions which facilitate the participation of children prior to, during and subsequent to family proceedings in the domestic courts. The following table summarises these provisions:

Statutory Provision	Terms
Children Act 1989, ss 4(3)(b), 4(4), 4ZA(7) and 4A(4)	A child who has 'sufficient understanding'[303] may apply to bring to an end a parental responsibility order made pursuant to s 4 of the Act.
Children Act 1989, s 6(7)(b)	A child may apply to bring the appointment of a testamentary guardian to an end.

[299] The 'age and understanding' formulation is also used in secondary legislation. See for example the Emergency Protection Order (Transfer of Responsibilities) Regulations 1991, r 3, the Fostering Services Regulations 2002, r 11(b)(i), the Children (Private Arrangements for Fostering) Regulations 2005, Sch 2, para 1(b), the Special Guardianship Regulations 2005, r 3(a) and the Adoptions with a Foreign Element Regulations 2005, r 28(6).

[300] One of the recommendations of the 1992 Adoption Review not incorporated into the 2002 Act was that no order adoption order should be permitted in relation to a child aged 12 or over save in circumstances where that child had agreed to it or the court dispensed with the child's consent (see Department of Health and Welsh Office, *Review of Adoption Law: Report to Ministers of an Interdepartmental working group*: a consultation document, October 1992).

[301] (1981) 2 FLR 102.

[302] But contrast this formulation with Lord Scarman's far stricter definition of 'sufficient understanding' in *Gillick* at [1985] 3 All ER 402 at 424, [1986] 1 AC 112 at 189. See also *Re O (Transracial Adoption: Contact)* [1995] 2 FLR 597 at 611E–611F per Thorpe LJ.

[303] See **6.154** below for a discussion of the meaning of the phrase 'sufficient understanding'. Section 46(3)(c) of the Children Act 1989 (concerning police protection powers) uses the phrase 'capable of understanding' in relation to the decision whether to inform the child of the steps taken and to be taken by the police under that section.

Statutory Provision	Terms
Children Act 1989, s 10(8)	A child who has 'sufficient understanding' to make the proposed application may apply for an order pursuant to s 8 of the 1989 Act.[304]
Children Act 1989, s 11J(7)	A child of 'sufficient understanding' may apply pursuant to s 11J(7) to enforce a contact order made under s 8 of the Act or for compensation for financial loss arising out of the breach of that order pursuant to s 11O(7).
Children Act 1989, s 14D(4)	A child who has 'sufficient understanding' may make an application to vary or discharge a special guardianship order.
Children Act 1989, s 17(4A)	Before determining what if any services to provide for a particular child pursuant to s 17 a local authority shall, so far as is reasonably practicable and consistent with the child's welfare, ascertain the child's wishes and feelings regarding the provision of those services and give due consideration to them having regard to his or her age and understanding.
Children Act 1989, s 20(6)	Before determining whether to provide accommodation pursuant to s 20 a local authority shall, so far as is reasonably practicable and consistent with the child's welfare, ascertain the child's wishes and feelings regarding the provision of accommodation and give due consideration to them having regard to his or her age and understanding.
Children Act 1989, ss 22(4)(a) and 22(5)(a)	Before making any decision in respect of a child it is looking after a local authority shall, so far as is reasonably practicable ascertain the child's wishes and feelings regarding the matter to be decided and give due consideration to them having regard to his or her age and understanding.
Children Act 1989, s 26(7)(b)(ii)	In considering a complaint under s 26 of the Act, the local authority must notify the child of its findings if the child is of 'sufficient understanding'.
Children Act 1989, s 34(3)(b)	A child may apply for leave to apply for a contact order to a child in care.[305]
Children Act 1989, s 34(4)	The child may apply for an order authorising the Local Authority to refuse to allow contact between the child and any person specified in s 34(1) or named in the order.
Children Act 1989, s 34(9)	The child may apply to vary or discharge an order made pursuant to s 34.
Children Act 1989, s 38(6)	A child of 'sufficient understanding' may refuse to submit to an examination or other assessment directed pursuant to s 38(6) of the Children Act 1989.[306]

---

[304] Applications for leave by children should be made in the High Court (see *Practice Direction of 22 February 1993*). For the situation where a child makes an application for leave to make an application in respect of another child pursuant to s 10(9) of the 1989 Act see *Re S (Contact: Application by Sibling)* [1998] 2 FLR 897 at 905.

[305] The correct approach to a leave application under s 34(3)(b) of the Children Act 1989 is set out in *Re M (Care: Contact: Grandmother's Application for Leave)* [1995] 2 FLR 86 in which it was held that whilst the criteria in s 10(9) of the Children Act 1989 do not strictly apply to an application under s 34(3)(b) the Court should still bear those criteria in mind in reaching its decision.

[306] See *The Children Act 1989 Guidance and Regulations Vol 4 – Residential Care* (1991) HMSO, paras 2.30–2.32.

Statutory Provision	Terms
Children Act 1989, ss 39(1) and 39(2)	The child may apply to discharge a care order or to vary or discharge a supervision order.
Children Act 1989, s 43(8)	A child of 'sufficient understanding' may refuse to submit to a medical or psychiatric examination or other assessment directed pursuant to a child assessment order.
Children Act 1989, s 44(7)	A child of 'sufficient understanding' may refuse to submit to a medical or psychiatric examination or other assessment directed upon the granting of an emergency protection order.
Children Act 1989, s 46(3)(c)	As soon as reasonably practicable after taking a child into police protection the constable concerned shall inform the child, if he or she appears capable of understanding, of the steps taken in respect of him or her and the reasons for those steps and of such further steps that may be taken.
Children Act 1989, s 46(3)(d)	As soon as reasonably practicable after taking a child into police protection the constable concerned shall take such steps as are reasonable practicable to discover the wishes and feelings of the child.
Children Act 1989, s 47(5A)	For the purposes of making determination whether to take any action to safeguard or promote the child's welfare the local authority shall so far as is reasonably practicable ascertain the child's wishes and feelings regarding the action to be taken and give due consideration to them having regard to his or her age and understanding.
Children Act 1989, ss 64(2) and 64(3)	Before making a decision in respect of a child who is accommodated in a private children's home the person carrying on the home shall, so far as is reasonably practicable, ascertain the wishes and feelings of the child and in making such a decision give due consideration to the child's wishes and feelings having regard to his or her age or understanding.
Children Act 1989, Sch 2, para 17	Where a child is of 'sufficient understanding' to make an informed decision and the child objects to the appointment of an independent visitor, the local authority must abide by the child's view
Children Act 1989, Sch 3, para 4(4)(a)	A requirement for the child to submit to a medical or psychiatric examination or other assessment directed may not be included in a supervision order unless the court is satisfied that, where the child is of sufficient understanding to make an informed decision, he or she consents to its inclusion.
Emergency Protection Order (Transfer of Responsibilities) Regulations 1991, SI 1991/1414, reg 3	Where an applicant who has secured an emergency protection order in respect of a child who is not the local authority in whose area the child is ordinarily resident that local authority must consider the ascertainable wishes and feelings of the child considered in light of his or her age and understanding before forming an opinion that it should assume the responsibilities under the order.
Contact with Children Regulations 1991, SI 1991/891, reg 3(a)	Where an agreement to vary a care contact order made under s 34 of the Act is reached between a local authority and the person named in order and the child is of 'sufficient understanding', the variation may only take place subject to the child's agreement.
Contact with Children Regulations 1991, SI 1991/891, reg 2.	Where a local authority decides to refuse contact with a child pursuant to s 34(6) of the 1989 Act, it must notify the child if he or she is of 'sufficient understanding'.

Statutory Provision	Terms
Review of Children's Cases Regulations 1991, SI 1991/895, reg 6(2)	Before conducting any review of the child case the responsible authority shall, unless it is not reasonably practicable to do so, seek and take into account the views of the child and shall so far as is reasonably practicable involve the child in the review, including his or her attendance.
Fostering Services Regulations 2002, reg 11(b)(i)	Before making any decision affecting a child placed or to be placed with foster parents due consideration must be given to the child's wishes and feelings in light of his or her age and understanding.
Children (Private Arrangements for Fostering) Regulations 2005, Sch 2 para 1(b)	Where a local authority receives notification that a child is to be fostered privately the local authority must establish within 7 working days the wishes and feelings of the child about the proposed arrangement.
Adoption Agencies Regulations 1983, SI 1983/1964, reg 12(2)(j)(ii)	An adoption agency shall, where the prospective adopter has accepted the adoption agency's proposals, arrange a medical exam for the child unless the child is of sufficient understanding and he refuses to submit to the examination.
Adoptions with a Foreign Element Regulations 2005, SI 2005/392, reg 28(6)	Before coming to a decision concerning the breakdown of an adoptive placement the local authority must have regard to the wishes and feelings of the child having regard to his or her age and understanding and, where appropriate, obtain his or her consent to measures to be taken under the regulations.
Family Law Act 1996, ss 43(1) and 43(2)	A child under 16 may apply for an occupation order or a non-molestation order if they are of 'sufficient understanding'.[307]
School Standards and Framework Act 1998, s 110(5)	Where a governing body consider that a registered pupil has a 'sufficient understanding' of a home-school agreement, they may invite the pupil to sign the parental declaration as an indication that he acknowledges and accepts the school's expectations of its pupils.[308]
Armed Forces Act 1991, ss 18(4) and 20(4)	A child to whom a service family assessment order or a protection order relates may, if of sufficient understanding to make an informed decision, refuse to submit to a medical or psychiatric examination or other assessment.

Children and Family Court Advisory and Support Service (Cafcass)

6.118 Subject to exceptions in relation to hearsay[309] the rules of evidence apply in the High Court (with the exception of wardship), the county court and the magistrates' court.[310] The wishes and feelings of the child must be communicated to the court by means of admissible evidence, including hearsay evidence.[311]

---

[307] Applications need no longer be made in the High Court but should be made in the county court where the application can be dealt with by any judge (see Allocation and Transfer of Proceedings Order 2008, SI 2008/2836).

[308] See also s 28C(7) of the Disability Discrimination Act 1995 concerning 'confidentiality requests' in respect of disabled pupils.

[309] Children (Admissibility of Hearsay) Order 1993, SI 1993/621.

[310] Unless they are relaxed by agreement between the parties (see *Re H (A Minor), Re K (Minors) (Child Abuse: Evidence)* [1989] 2 FLR 313) or by order of the Lord Chancellor (See the CA 1989, s 96(3)).

[311] Children (Admissibility of Hearsay) Order 1993, SI 1993/621.

8.119 The Children and Family Court Advice and Support Service (Cafcass) was set up on 1 April 2001 as a non-departmental public body.[312] Its remit covers family proceedings in which the welfare of the child is or may be in question and is specified by the Criminal Justice and Courts Services Act 2002, s 12. Pursuant to the Criminal Justice and Court Services Act 2000, s 12(1) the functions of CAFCASS are defined as follows:

(a)   To safeguard and promote the welfare of children.

(b)   To give advice to any court about any application made to it in any such [family] proceedings.

(c)   To make provision for the children to be represented in such proceedings.

(d)   To provide information, advice and other support for the children and their families.

These functions are limited by statute to 'family proceedings'[313] but in the light of (d) and the support element suggested by its title, the activities of Cafcass may extend to associated activities outside the court.[314]

6.120 Cafcass incorporates into its work what it terms 'basic practice rights' based on the principles enshrined in Art 12 of the CRC.[315] These 'basic practice rights' are defined as the right to be seen and heard, the right of reply, the right to be fully informed, the right to be actively involved and the right not to be put under pressure.[316] These 'basic practice rights' are expressed to be in addition to the child's fundamental right to safety.[317]

6.121 Cafcass Legal Services and Special Casework (known as Cafcass Legal) has largely taken over the responsibilities of the Official Solicitor for representing children whose welfare is the subject of non-specified family proceedings. A Cafcass Practice Note[318] sets out guidance for the work of this body. The involvement of Cafcass Legal will generally only arise where it appears to the court that the child ought to have party status and be legally represented. The cases which may require representation from Cafcass Legal will generally arise where the child needs someone to orchestrate an investigation of the case on their behalf.[319] Further particular examples of Cafcass Legal representing subject children are where:

---

[312]   The operation of Cafcass in Wales is devolved to the National Assembly for Wales where the agency is known as Cafcass Cymru.

[313]   Criminal Justice and Court Services Act 2000, s 17.

[314]   The present reality however is that a paucity of resources makes this latter function all but inoperable.

[315]   See also the Cafcass National Standards which include the stated intention to put children first, ensure that each child has a voice that is heard and listened to, to start with the child and stay with the child throughout the life of the proceedings and to articulate and convince others about the needs, wishes and feelings of individual children in family court cases (Cafcass National Minimum Standards 2007).

[316]   *Children's Rights in Practice* (2007) Cafcass, pp 2–3.

[317]   See also the Cafcass Safeguarding Framework (2007), para 1.6 which seeks to ensure accountability throughout the service for the safeguarding and promoting of the welfare of children by ensuring the Service works to make certain that outcomes for children in the family court system both keep them safe and promote their welfare and ensuring that the individual child's voice is heard and is taken into account in making decisions about them.

[318]   Cafcass Practice Note [2001] 2 FCR 562.

[319]   *Re A (Contact: Separate Representation)* [2001] 1 FLR 715.

(a) there is a significant foreign element such as a challenge to the English court's jurisdiction or a need for enquiries to be conducted abroad;

(b) there is a need for expert medical or other evidence to be adduced on behalf of the child in circumstances where a joint instruction by the parties is impossible;

(c) a child wants to instruct a solicitor direct but has been refused leave to instruct a solicitor in accordance with the FPR 1991, r 9.2A;

(d) an application is made for leave to seek contact with an adopted child; and

(e) there are exceptionally difficult, unusual or sensitive issues (usually dealt with in the High Court) making it necessary for the child to be granted party status within the proceedings.

6.122 Cafcass Legal may be invited to act or instruct counsel to appear as *amicus curiae* in proceedings under the Act in which, in the opinion of the court, an issue of general public importance has arisen or is likely to arise. An officer of the Service may be authorised to conduct litigation in relation to any proceedings in any court and to exercise a right of audience in any proceedings before any court in the exercise of the functions of the Service.[320] Cafcass Legal may not represent a child in the family proceedings court. Cafcass Legal will liaise with the Office of the Official Solicitor to avoid duplication of representation.

6.123 The effectiveness of Cafcass is now significantly dilapidated by a lack of resources, management issues and a consequent inability to meet effectively fluctuations in workload. Due to extreme pressure on the resources of Cafcass, in 2009 the President of the Family Division issued what is termed 'interim' guidance concerning the use of Cafcass resources.[321] The intent of the Guidance is to 'create a framework for local arrangements as the best method of achieving necessary improvements to assist Cafcass to deliver their services to children, families and the courts and thus secure timely outcomes to promote the welfare of children who are the subject of family proceedings'. The guidance is stated to be temporary but its period of operation has already been extended.

Official Solicitor

6.124 The Official Solicitor will continue in appropriate cases to represent the interests of children whose welfare is not the subject of the proceedings where those children do not meet the criteria for acting without a litigation friend or children's guardian in non-specified proceedings[322] although the Official Solicitor will generally liaise with Cafcass to determine which body is best placed to represent the particular child. The Official Solicitor's Practice Note sets out the ambit of the cases involving children in which the Official Solicitor may become involved.[323] These include cases where:

---

[320] Criminal Justice and Courts Services Act 2000, s 15. The Government has undertaken that this power will only be used in limited circumstances, so that most children will continue to be represented by an independent Children Panel solicitor, but the rule is clearly capable of wider application. See also Hinchcliffe, M *Comment* September [2001] Fam Law.

[321] *Practice Guidance: Interim Guidance to Assist Cafcass* [2009] 2 FLR 1407.

[322] See **6.163** below. Note that under the old rules an officer of Cafcass or equivalent person acting in non-specified proceedings retained the title of 'Guardian ad Litem'. Under the Family Procedure Rules 2010 this has been changed and the relevant person will be known as a Children's Guardian.

[323] Practice Note: Official Solicitor: Appointment in Family Proceedings [2001] 2 FLR 155.

(a)   a child who is also the parent of a child, and who is a respondent to a Children Act or Adoption and Children Act application. If a child respondent is already represented by an officer of Cafcass in pending proceedings of which he or she is the subject, then the Official Solicitor will liaise with Cafcass to agree the most appropriate arrangements;

(b)   a child who wishes to make an application for a Children Act order naming another child (typically a contact order naming a sibling). The Official Solicitor will need to satisfy himself that the proposed proceedings would benefit the child applicant before proceeding;

(c)   a child witness to some disputed factual issue in a children case and who may require intervener status. In such circumstances the need for party status and legal representation should be weighed in the light of *Re H (Care Proceedings: Intervener)*;[324]

(d)   a child party to a petition for a declaration of status under Part III of the Family Law Act 1986;

(e)   a child intervener in divorce or ancillary relief proceedings[325] (FPR 1991, r 2.57 or 9.5);

(f)   a child applicant for, or respondent to, an application for an order under Part IV of the Family Law Act 1996. In the case of a child applicant, the Official Solicitor will need to satisfy himself that the proposed proceedings would benefit the child before pursuing them, with leave under the Family Law Act 1996, s 43 if required.

The Child's Participation prior to the Issue of Family Proceedings

6.125 The concept children's participation in the family justice process children traditionally contemplates children and young people involved in proceedings. However, Art 12 of the CRC requires that children should be able to express their views in 'all matters' affecting them and, in particular, in any judicial and administrative proceedings. The fair trial guaranteed to a child by Art 6 of the ECHR is not confined to the 'purely judicial' part of the proceedings but extends across the decision making process.[326] Within the context of domestic public law cases, court proceedings represent the end of a process in which the life of the child will have been the subject of examination, assessment and decision making for many months and sometimes years prior to the case reaching court. When examining the extent to which the child has the right to participate in proceedings specific regard must also be had to the extent of that right to participate *prior* to proceedings commencing.[327]

Pre-Proceedings Participation – Divorce and Separation

6.126 Parents who initiate divorce proceedings are required to complete a Statement of Arrangements for Children, which sets out the proposed arrangements for the children following the breakdown of the marriage.[328] There is however at present no domestic

---

[324]   [2000] 1 FLR 775.
[325]   See **6.130–6.137** below.
[326]   *Re L (Care: Assessment Fair Trial)*, [2002] EWHC 1379 (Fam), [2002] 2 FLR 730.
[327]   Children Act 1989, s 20(6)(a) and s 20(6)(b); Children Act 1989, s 22(4) and see *Re C (Care: Consultation with Parents not in the Child's Best Interests)* [2005] EWHC 3390 (Fam), [2006] 2 FLR 787.
[328]   Family Procedure Rules 2010, rr 7.8(2)(c) and 7.12(7) and Matrimonial Causes Act 1973, s 41(1). This

provision providing children with a legal right to participate in the compilation of the Statement of Arrangements or otherwise to be heard on the arrangements for them formulated as a consequence breakdown of their parents' marriage prior to the case coming before the Courts. The same position applies to the resolution of financial arrangements between the adult parties.

Pre-Proceedings Participation – Private Law Proceedings

6.127 Research shows children are frequently not given the opportunity to express their wishes and feelings for their future care or contact with a non-residential parent where those arrangements are not before the court.[329] Within the context of parental relationship breakdown which may precede private law proceedings, the child has no domestic legal right to be consulted about the arrangements being made for their future.[330] Again, this position can be contrasted to the position under the Children (Scotland) Act 1995, s 6(1) which makes such provision.[331] Pre-proceedings mediation of parental disputes is preferable to litigation. However, in respect of mediation prior to proceedings, Fortin cautions that whilst this may assist adults it does not consistently encompass the child in the process and agreements reached between parents at a time of stress and conflict may not serve the child's best interests.[332]

Pre-Proceedings Participation – Public Law Proceedings

6.128 The pre-proceedings stage of domestic public law children proceedings are governed by the revised *Children Act 1989 Guidance Volume One: Court Orders*[333] and the Public Law Outline.[334] The revised *Children Act 1989 Guidance Volume One: Court Orders* and the Public Law Outline are the product of the widely recognised need to encourage early effective intervention where children's welfare is threatened, with a view to achieving partial or full resolution before cases reach court and, where proceedings are necessary, to ensure their proper preparation and effective case management. Central to achieving these twin aims is the pre-proceedings process, which provides parents with notice of the Local Authority's concerns by way of a letter before proceedings[335] and the opportunity to discuss, with the benefit of legal advice, ways of dealing with those concerns without the need for the involvement of the courts.[336] This process involves the adult parties facing each other on equal terms, and in particular with equality of arms, for the purpose of ordering the arrangements for the child or identifying the issues the court will need to resolve if the court is to order those arrangements.

6.129 However, whilst the central aim of the pre-proceedings process incorporated within *Children Act 1989 Guidance Volume One: Court Orders* is to fix safe arrangements for the child, there is no provision for the separate participation or representation of the

---

document permits the court in due course to consider, pursuant to s 41 of the Matrimonial Causes Act 1973, whether it should, in light of the arrangements that have been or are proposed to be made, exercise any of its powers under the Children Act 1989 (see below **6.130**).

[329] See Butler, I, Scanlan, L, Robinson, M, Douglas, G and Murch, M *Divorcing Children: Children's Experience of Their Parents' Divorce* (2003) Jessica Kingsley Publishers and Smith, A, Taylor, N, and Tapp, P *Rethinking Children's Involvement in Decision-Making after Parental Separation* (2003) 10 Childhood 201.

[330] Fortin, J *Children's Rights and the Developing Law* (2009) 3rd edn, Cambridge, p 240.

[331] See **6.95** above.

[332] Fortin, J *Children's Rights and the Developing Law* (2009) 3rd edn, Cambridge, pp 243–245.

[333] Department of Children, Schools and Families (2007).

[334] Judiciary of England and Wales (2008).

[335] See *Children Act 1989 Guidance Volume One: Court Orders* Department of Children, Schools and Families (2007), para 3.25 and 3.29.

[336] See *Children Act 1989 Guidance Volume One: Court Orders* Department of Children, Schools and Families (2007), paras 3.26 and 3.31.

child's interests within this pre-proceedings process. The limited access to funding for legal advice available to parents upon the local authority issuing its letter before proceedings is not available to children. Section 41 of the Children Act 1989 does not provide a Children's Guardian until proceedings are actually issued.[337] Accordingly, during the period in which the local authority and the parents are working, with the benefit of legal advice, to avoid proceedings or to ensure the efficacy of proceedings, the interests of the children, many already living away from their families,[338] are entirely unrepresented save by the local authority and their parents, whose respective agendas may not always be coincident with the best interests of the child. The only element of the process concerning the involvement of the child requires that where any affected child is of a sufficient age and level of understanding, the *intention* to initiate care or supervision proceedings must also be explained to him or her.[339] Whilst there is a duty on local authorities to make arrangements for the provision of advocacy services for children in need, looked after children and children leaving care, this duty is limited to children and young people intending to make a complaint.[340] Thus, decisions with the potential to fundamentally affect the child for the remainder of his or her minority are taken without any provision for the participation of the child independent of both the parents and the State. Whilst there are statutory duties which require a local authority to ascertain the wishes and feelings of the child when carrying out a child protection investigation[341]and to represent those in the decision making process when working under Part III of the 1989 Act,[342] the current pre-proceedings process increases the risk of the child's position being settled by way of 'adult' arrangements which fail fully to take account of the child's interests and can, in extreme cases, lead to tragedy.[343]

The Child's Participation during Family Proceedings[344]

Participation during Family Proceedings – Divorce and Separation

6.130 The Matrimonial Causes Act 1973, s 41(1) requires the court to consider whether it should, in light of the arrangements that have been or are proposed to be made in respect of the children within divorce proceedings, exercise any of its powers under the Children Act 1989. The procedure to be adopted by the court is set out in Family Procedure Rules 2010, rr 7.8(2)(c) and 7.12(7) and is a solely paper exercise based on the Statement of Arrangement for the Children completed by each parent.[345] Even where those statements raise concern, the court has limited powers to act, s 41(2) of the

---

[337] Children Act 1989, s 41(1).

[338] Brophy J, Research Review: Child Care Proceedings under the Children Act 1989, DCA Research Series 5/06, 2006, p 12.

[339] *Children Act 1989 Guidance Volume One: Court Orders* Department of Children, Schools and Families (2007), para 3.28.

[340] See Advocacy Services and Representations Procedure (Children) (Amendment) Regulations 2004, SI 2004/719. It is self evident that a child not properly involved in the pre-proceedings process may not know that there is something to complain about.

[341] CA 1989, s 47(5A). See table at **6.117** above.

[342] CA 1989, s 17(4A). See table at **6.117** above.

[343] *Report of the Committee of Inquiry into the Care and Supervision Provided in Relation to Maria Colwell* (Committee of Inquiry into the Care and Supervision Provided in Relation to Maria Colwell London) Thomas Gilbert Field Fisher, London: HMSO (1974). See also MacDonald, A *Whatever Happened to the Pre-Proceedings Protocol* [2007] Fam Law 991 and MacDonald, A *The Voice of the Child – Still a Faint Cry* [2008] Fam law 648.

[344] Fortin observes that the fact that the domestic system for ensuring children are able to participate in proceedings concerning them is variable and arbitrary in its operation is largely due to the Government's reluctance to devote sufficient resources to that system (Fortin, J *Children's Rights and the Developing Law* (2009) 3rd edn, Cambridge, p 235).

[345] See **6.126** above.

Matrimonial Causes Act 1973 permitting the court only to direct that the decree of divorce or nullity is not to be made absolute, or the decree of judicial separation is not to be granted, until the court orders otherwise. The test for the exercise of these limited powers is the existence of '*exceptional circumstances*'.[346] There is no provision in s 41 providing for the participation of the child on the issue of whether the court should exercise any of its powers under the Children Act 1989 within the context of parental divorce or separation. The operation of s 41 has been the subject of some criticism.[347]

Participation during Family Proceedings – Financial Proceedings[348]

6.131 Proceedings under the Matrimonial Causes Act 1973 – Section 41 of the Matrimonial Causes Act 1973 deals with the issue of the extent to which a court seized of an application for a decree of divorce, nullity of marriage or of judicial separation between the parents can act to ensure the best interests of the children of the family are provided for under the Children Act 1989. However, the question also arises as to what extent a child is entitled to, and can participate in the determination of any financial proceedings which arise in connection with such applications, either under the Matrimonial Causes Act 1973, the Civil Partnership Act 2004 or the Children Act 1989, Sch 1, Article 12 of the CRC requires that children be heard in such proceedings.[349]

6.132 Pursuant to the Matrimonial Causes Act 1973, s 25(1) it is the duty of the court when deciding whether to exercise its powers to make financial provision orders, property adjustment orders, orders for the sale of property or pension sharing orders in respect of matrimonial assets to give first consideration[350] to the welfare whilst a minor of any child of the family who has not attained the age of eighteen. Section 25(1) does not however provide for the participation of the child in proceedings under the Act. Section 25(3), which governs the exercise of the courts power to make financial orders for the benefit of the child of the family does not stipulate the wishes and feelings of the child amongst the factors to be considered.[351] However, as Williams and Bain point out by way of example:[352]

---

[346] Matrimonial Causes Act 1973, s 41(2)(c).

[347] See Murch, M, Douglas, G, Scanlan, L, Perry, A, Lisles, C, Bader, K and Borkowski, M *Safeguarding Children's Welfare in Uncontentious Divorce: A Study of s 41 of the Matrimonial Causes Act 1973* (1999) Research Series No 7/99, Lord Chancellors Department.

[348] Children in England and Wales have no direct means of initiating proceedings for financial support against their parents (unlike children in Scotland (see Child Support Act 1991, s 7(1)). The determination of child support has now been largely removed from the jurisdiction of the court and is governed by the Child Maintenance and Enforcement Commission. As Fortin notes, incomprehensibly this third attempt to create a workable child support scheme contains no provision giving children a right to take the law into their own hands in relation to the child support paid for them (Fortin, J *Children's Rights and the Developing Law* (2009) 3rd edn, Cambridge, p 353). By the terms of the Child Support Act 1991, s 3(3) 'children' over the age of 18 may utilise Sch 1, para 2(1) of the Children Act 1989 and the Matrimonial Causes Act 1973, s 23(1) by reference to their educational or other special needs and only if their parents have already separated or have instituted matrimonial proceedings (see FPR 1991, r 2.54 and *Downing v Downing (Downing intervening)* [1976] Fam 288).

[349] Committee on the Rights of the Child General Comment No 12 (2009) *The Right of the Child to Be Heard* (CRC/C/GC/12, para 52). See **6.49** above.

[350] This does not mean the child's welfare is paramount but rather that the child's welfare is to be regarded as a consideration of the first importance to be borne in mind throughout consideration of all the circumstances, particularly those listed in s 25(2) (see *Suter v Suter and Jones* [1987] Fam 111, [1987] 2 All ER 336 CA). See also *N v N (Consent Orders: Variation)* [1994] 2 FCR 275, [1993] 2 FLR 868.

[351] The factors set out in s 25(3) being the financial needs of the child, the income, earning capacity (if any), property and other financial resources of the child, any physical or mental disability of the child, the manner in which the child was and in which the parties expected him or her to be educated and trained and the considerations set out in s 25(2)(a),(b), (c), and (e).

[352] Williams, D Blain, S *Voices in the Wilderness: Hearing Children in Financial Applications* [2008] Fam Law

'The sale of the family home may well involve not only the inevitable move to a new home, neighbours and environment, but also new schools, friends and distance from close family. If a move to a new home is stressful for the parents, how much more so must it be for the children? Yet the children's views are not canvassed, despite their welfare being the first consideration of the court under s 25(1) of the Matrimonial Causes Act 1973 (MCA 1973).'

6.133 The Family Procedure Rules 2010 provide for children to be separately represented in applications for financial remedies including those sought by parents within ancillary relief proceedings and applications pursuant to Sch 1 of the Children Act 1989.[353] Where an application for a financial remedy includes an application for an order for a variation of settlement, the court must, unless it is satisfied that the proposed variation does not adversely affect the rights or interests of any child concerned, direct that the child be separately represented on the application.[354] On any other application for a financial remedy the court may direct that the child be separately represented on the application.[355] Where the child is separately represented on an application for a financial remedy, the court may, if the person consents, appoint a person other than the Official Solicitor or the Official Solicitor to be the children's guardian.[356] The Family Procedure Rules 2010, r 9.10(1)(f) permit a child of the family to make an application for a financial remedy where the child has been given permission to apply. In such circumstances r 16.24(5) and (6) and rr 16.25–16.28 of the Family Procedure Rules 2010 will apply in respect of the representation of the child.[357] Finally, the Family Procedure Rules 2010, r 16.6 permits a child to bring proceedings without a litigation friend or children's guardian where the conditions of the rule are satisfied.[358]

6.134 At present, there appears to be only one domestic example of children being joined as parties to proceedings under the Matrimonial Causes Act 1973. In _Mubarak v Mubarak_[359] the children were joined as parties to proceedings brought to set aside a family trust pursuant to s 37 of the Matrimonial Causes Act 1973 and to vary the trust pursuant to s 24 of the Matrimonial Causes Act 1973, both applications being part of an attempt to recover a lump sum awarded in the ancillary relief proceedings. McFarlane J joined the children to the proceedings on the basis that they were beneficiaries of the trust in question whose interests may be adversely affected by orders

---

135 at 137. The authors point out that it would seem anomalous to canvass the child's views in relation to a change of residence under the Children Act 1989 but not in relation to a change of property pursuant to an order made under the Matrimonial Causes Act 1973 despite both decisions having a similar impact on issues such as continuity of schooling and peer relationships (see also _Re S (Unmarried Parents: Financial Provision)_ [2006] EWCA Civ 479, [2006] 2 FLR 950 per Thorpe LJ at para 15 (a case decided under Schedule 1 of the Children Act 1989)).

353   Family Procedure Rules 2010, r 9.11(1). See also Williams, D Blain, S _Voices in the Wilderness: Hearing Children in Financial Applications_ [2008] Fam Law 135 at 138. The Family Procedure Rules 2010, r 2.3 defines 'financial remedies' as meaning a financial order under Matrimonial Causes Act 1973 or the Civil Partnership Act 2004 or an order under those acts or under Sch 1 of the Children Act 1989, the Matrimonial and Family Proceedings Act 1984 and the Domestic Proceedings and Magistrates Court Act 1978. See also the Matrimonial and Family Proceedings Act 1984, s 32 and the Supreme Court Act 1981, s 61 and Sch 1.

354   Family Procedure Rules 2010, r 9.11(1).

355   Family Procedure Rules 2010, r 9.11(2).

356   Family Procedure Rules 2010, r 9.11(3). In such circumstances r 16.24(5) and (6) and rr 16.25–16.28 of the Family Procedure Rules 2010 will apply.

357   These provisions cover applications for financial orders under the Matrimonial Causes Act 1973 and the Civil Partnership Act 2004 and orders under those acts and under Sch 1 of the Children Act 1989, the Matrimonial and Family Proceedings Act 1984 and the Domestic Proceedings and Magistrates Court Act 1978. See also _Downing v Downing_ [1976] 3 WLR 335.

358   See Family Procedure Rules 2010, r 16.6(3).

359   [2007] EWHC 220 (Fam), [2007] 2 FLR 364.

made in respect of the trust. During the proceedings, the children's wishes and feelings were reported to the judge together with their litigation friend's assessment of their best interests.[360]

6.135 Applicants under the Children Act 1989, Sch 1 – Finally, applications for financial provision solely for children can be made pursuant to Section 15 and Sch 1 of the Children Act 1989 without prejudice to the provisions under the Matrimonial Causes Act 1973. In determining an application under Sch 1 the child's interests are not paramount and the court is not required to apply s 1(3)(a) concerning the wishes and feelings of the child.[361] Schedule 1 para 4(1) likewise does not require the court to consider the wishes and feelings of the child in reaching it decision. However, the argument for taking account of the views of the child might be considered especially pertinent in relation to applications under Sch 1 where any relief granted is for the benefit of the child.[362] In a small number of cases the domestic courts have recognised this and utilised the provisions outlined above to ensure the participation of the children.

6.136 In *Re S (Unmarried Parents: Financial Provision)*[363] Thorpe LJ promoted the idea of children being joined in financial proceedings between the parents which had become highly acrimonious in order to ensure that focus on the children's welfare was maintained. Thorpe LJ concluded:[364]

'The authorities show that it has not been the practice in these cases for children to be separately represented, but the present case is in my opinion a neat illustration of the advantages of ensuring separate representation for the child in some cases is brought under s 15 of the Children Act 1989. Here there was an intense and bitter battle between two adults; the mother striving to harm the father by extracting the maximum investment fund, the father striving to worst the mother by concealing the extent of his fortune. It is easy to see how, in such circumstances, the real crux of the case can be lost to view unless there is some advocate there to urge constantly the needs and interests of the child. For that, in the end, is what the award is largely designed to satisfy.'

A further example of the child being made a party to proceedings under Sch 1 is *Re A Minor* (unreported, 8 June 2006)[365] in which Baron J joined the child as a party to proceedings under Schedule 1 by reason of a plain conflict of interest between the child and the applicant parent. The court directed that the Guardian should take the lead in preparing the budgets required in order that the court could be satisfied that they were prepared on the basis of the child's best interests.

---

[360] See also Williams, D Blain, S *Voices in the Wilderness: Hearing Children in Financial Applications* [2008] Fam Law 135 at 141.

[361] Children Act 1989, s 105(1). However, in *J v C (Child: Financial Provision)* [1998] 3 FCR 79, [1999] 1 FLR 152 the court held that 'the child's welfare must be one of the relevant circumstances to be taken into account when assessing whether and how to order provision.' See also *Re P (A Child) (Financial Provision)* [2003] EWCA Civ 837, [2003] 2 WLR 865, [2003] 2 FCR 481, [2003] 2 FLR 865 in which Thorpe LJ stated that welfare is 'in the generality of cases, a constant influence on the discretionary outcome.'

[362] Williams, D Blain, S *Voices in the Wilderness: Hearing Children in Financial Applications* [2008] Fam Law 135.

[363] [2006] EWCA Civ 479, [2006] 2 FLR 950.

[364] Thorpe LJ later qualified this passage in a further judgement on appeal in this case, making clear that separate representation for the child in such proceedings would only be appropriate in 'exceptional circumstances' (see EWCA Civ 1310).

[365] Summarised in Williams, D Blain, S *Voices in the Wilderness: Hearing Children in Financial Applications* [2008] Fam Law 135 at 140.

6.137 Thus, as Williams and Blain conclude,[366] the current position in domestic law appears therefore to be that, in exceptional circumstances,[367] children may be made parties to financial proceedings where it can be demonstrated that:

(a)   Their rights or interests in property are or may be affected;

(b)   There is a conflict of interest between the child and the parent making or defending the application;

(c)   The positions of the adult parties are so hostile or polarised or are otherwise such that the interests of the child might be obscured.

Participation during Family Proceedings – Private Law Family Proceedings

6.138 Fortin usefully identifies five procedural 'rungs' in private law cases by reference to the degree of participation by children in private law proceedings concerning arrangements for their future upbringing by their parents or carers.[368] Charting an increasing level of children's involvement, these 'rungs' are:

(a)   The proceedings are resolved prior to any substantive court hearing through parental agreement reached via in court conciliation procedures under the Private Law Programme.[369]

(b)   The proceedings are resolved by litigation in which the parents convey to the Court the child's wishes and feelings and their respective assessment of what outcome is in the child's best interests.

(c)   The proceedings are resolved by litigation in which the Children and Family Reporter prepares a report on the child's wishes and feelings and best interests in respect of the issues arising within the proceedings pursuant to the Children Act 1989, s 7.

(d)   The proceedings are resolved by litigation in which the child is given party status and separate representation by way of a Children's Guardian pursuant to Family Procedure Rules 2010, rr 16.2(1) and 16.4(1)(c).

(e)   The proceedings are resolved by litigation in which the child acts on their own behalf within proceedings pursuant to the Family Procedure Rules 2010, r 16.6.

6.139   The Private Law Programme[370] – The Private Law Programme[371] was introduced on 9 November 2004 by the then President of the Family Division, Dame Elizabeth Butler-Sloss.[372] A revised version of the Private Law Programme was published on 1

---

[366]   Williams, D Blain, S *Voices in the Wilderness: Hearing Children in Financial Applications* [2008] Fam Law 135 at 141–142.

[367]   It is far from certain that the 'exceptional circumstances' test meets the imperatives of Art 12 of the CRC.

[368]   Fortin, J *Children's Rights and the Developing Law* (2009) 3rd edn, Cambridge, p 248.

[369]   See **6.139** below.

[370]   See *Parental Separation: Children's Needs and Parents' Responsibilities* (2005) Cm 6452.

[371]   President's Guidance 9 November 2004 '*The Private Law Programme*'.

[372]   For a detailed description of the content and operation of the original Private Law Programme see Pressdee QC, P, Vater, J, Judd QC, F, and Baker QC, J *Contact: The New Deal* (2006) Jordans, paras 5.3–5.51.

April 2010.[373] The expressed aim of the programme is to achieve the optimum outcome for children through the collaborative efforts of the court, Cafcass, Her Majesty's Courts Service, lawyers and parents.[374] At the heart of the Private Law Programme is the concept of in-court conciliation. The revised Private Law Programme provides a model scheme for in-court conciliation comprising the following key elements:

(a) Private law applications will be issued by the court on the day they are received and will be sent to Cafcass on the same day and no later than 24 hours after issue (48 hours in courts where applications are first considered on paper).

(b) Information sheets concerning a First Hearing Dispute Resolution Appointment (FHDRA) and the role of Cafcass will be sent to the parties with a Notice of Hearing.

(c) Prior to the application being listed for the FHDRA Cafcass will carry out safeguarding checks to include police and local authority checks.[375]

(d) Cafcass advises the court as to the existence of any particular risk or safety issues which require placing before the court at the FHDRA rather than being addressed through discussions between the parties and the Cafcass officer at court.

(e) The FDHRA is listed within 4 weeks and no later than 6 weeks from the date of the application before a judge with a Cafcass practitioner available to facilitate early dispute resolution if appropriate. Both parents are expected to attend with their representatives (if they have them).

6.140 The FHDRA must consider the involvement of the child[376] and the wishes and feelings of the child, including whether the child is aware of the proceedings, how the wishes and feelings of the child should be ascertained and how is the child to be involved in the proceedings if at all and whether this should be at or after the FHDRA.[377] The court and the parties are also required to give consideration to whether the child should be joined as a party to the proceedings and who should inform the child of the outcome of the case where appropriate. The revised programme makes it a requirement that the parties assist the court in promoting the welfare of the child by the application of the welfare principle contained in s 1(1) of the Children Act 1989.[378]

6.141 Whilst the expressed aim if the Private Law Programme is to achieve an optimum outcome for children thought collaborative working, reviews carried out in respect of the operation of the original private law programme highlighted the danger that children's views may become lost in the in court conciliation process.[379] Research

---

[373] Practice Direction *The Revised Private Law Programme* (2010).
[374] Early results suggest that the programme leads to resolution at first hearing of about 60% of applications (speech of Sir Mark Potter, President of the Family Division *Report on the Private Law Programme* 13 May 2008).
[375] See CA 1989, s 16A and **6.142** below.
[376] Practice Direction *The Revised Private Law Programme* (2010), para 2.2.
[377] Practice Direction *The Revised Private Law Programme* (2010), para 5.5.
[378] Practice Direction *The Revised Private Law Programme* (2010), para 2.2.
[379] HMICA *Domestic Violence, Safety and Family Proceedings: Thematic Review of the Handling of Domestic Violence Issues by the Children and Family Court Advisory and Support Service (CAFCASS) and the Administration of Family Courts in Her Majesty's Court Service* (2005), para 3.75 ('In law, children's needs are paramount. But where the emphasis is on agreement-seeking, there is a risk that their views become marginalised as their parents' dispute takes centre stage'). Once again, this difficulty is exacerbated by the

entitled *Making Contact Happen or Making Contact Work? The Process and Outcomes of In Court Conciliation*[380] has reinforced this concern, noting that the rapid processing of cases and the focus on settlement under the Private Law Programme risks children being either excluded from the process or becoming responsible for decisions. Within this context, it is of concern that under the revised Private Law Programme the child appears to remain far from the centre of the process designed to determine his or her future wellbeing. Indeed, under the revised Private Law Programme there remains an express prohibition on the Cafcass Officer speaking to the child prior to the FHDRA[381] and that there is no requirement to consider the views of the child prior to the conclusion of a consent order.[382] The research of Trinder *et al* recommends the establishment of a 'child programme' as part of a wider differentiated case management system incorporating in-court conciliation.[383] The authors point to the Australian 'Children in Focus' project which combines two meetings away from Court between children aged 5 and over and a specially trained child consultant who feeds back to the parents the child's own worldview beyond the issues concerning the adults in order to support the capacity of the parent to hear the child and focus on that child's needs on a long term rather than on a one-off basis.[384]

6.142 Domestic Violence – Children's wishes and feelings are equally important where a risk of domestic violence between parents or carers is indentified by the initial risk assessment carried out by Cafcass as part of the Private Law Programme.[385] There is a clear rational for ensuring that the child's wishes and feelings are ascertained in such cases. The experts' report directed by the Court of Appeal in the case of *Re L (A Child) (Contact: Domestic Violence)*[386] and entitled *Contact and Domestic Violence – the Experts' Court Report*[387] identified clearly the dangers of forcing children into continuing contact arrangements with violent parents and emphasised the need to take into account the views of children in accordance with their age and circumstances.[388] Where a child is adamant in his or her expressed view that he or she does not wish to see a parent or contemplate contact Sturge and Glaser make the following important observations:

(a)   The child must be listened to a taken seriously;

(b)   The age and understanding of the child are highly relevant;

---

terms of s 1(4)(a) of the Children Act 1989 which only requires the wishes and feelings of the child to be considered by the court where the making of a private law order is opposed (see **6.114** above).

[380]   Trinder, L, Connolly, J, Kellett, J, Notley, C and Swift, L (2006) Department of Constitutional Affairs.

[381]   Practice Direction *The Revised Private Law Programme* (2010), para 3.9(d). Indeed, if the child attempts to speak to the Cafcass Officer the Private Law Programme stipulates that that conversation must be postponed to the day of the FHDRA.

[382]   Practice Direction *The Revised Private Law Programme* (2010), para 5.3.

[383]   Trinder, L, Connolly, J, Kellett, J, Notley, C and Swift, L *Making Contact Happen or Making Contact Work? The Process and Outcomes of In Court Conciliation* (2006) Department of Constitutional Affairs.

[384]   See www.childreninfocus.org. See also HM Magistrates Court Service Inspectorate *Seeking Agreement: Children and Family Court Advisory and Support Service (CAFCASS)* (2003) Department of Constitutional Affairs, paras 4.46–4.47.

[385]   Neither s 16A nor the *Practice Direction of 3*rd *September 2007 (Children Act 1989: Risk Assessments under Section 16A)* [2007] 2 FLR 625 specifically address the wishes and feelings of the child in the context of risk assessment. However, the Cafcass Guidance requires the Cafcass practitioner to talk to children about their experience of domestic violence and to understand them from the child's own perspective (see Cafcass *Domestic Violence Policy and Standards* (2005) Chs. 5 and 6).

[386]   2000] 4 All ER 609.

[387]   Sturge, C and Glaser, D [2000] Fam Law 615.

[388]   Sturge, C and Glaser, D *Contact and Domestic Violence – the Experts' Court Report*, [2000] Fam Law 615, p 624.

(c)   The child either for developmental or emotional reasons, if in a positive relationship with the resident parent will inevitably be influenced by (i) that parent's views and (ii) their wish to maintain her or his sense of security and stability within that household;

(d)   Going against the child's wishes must involve indications that there are no prospects of the child changing his or her mind as the result of preparatory work and careful consideration being given to the effects on the child of making a decision that appears to disregard their feelings/wishes, it being damaging to a child to feel he or she is forced to do something against his or her will and against his or her judgment if the child cannot see the sense of it.[389]

6.143   When it comes to the court determining the appropriate outcome of private law cases in which the child may be at risk of harm, usually from domestic violence, the court will have regard to guidance from the Family Justice Council[390] and a detailed Practice Direction.[391] The latter states as follows in relation to the participation of the child:[392]

> 'Subject to the seriousness of the allegations made and the difficulty of the case, the court shall consider whether it is appropriate for the child who is the subject of the application to be made a party to the proceedings and be separately represented. If the case is proceeding in the magistrates' court and the court considers that it may be appropriate for the child to be made a party to the proceedings, it may transfer the case to the relevant county court for determination of that issue and following such transfer the county court shall give such directions for the further conduct of the case as it considers appropriate.'

6.144   Welfare Reports under the Children Act 1989, s 7 – Pursuant to the Children Act 1989, s 7 a court *may*, when considering any question with respect to a child under the Act, ask either Cafcass or a local authority to report to the court 'on such matters relating to the welfare of that child as are required to be dealt with in the report'.[393] The discretion to ask for a report arises in relation to any issue under the Children Act 1989, but since a children's guardian will almost invariably be appointed in public law proceedings,[394] these provisions relate primarily to private law proceedings. A report should be called for in any case involving allegations of domestic violence.[395] Children may not file an affidavit giving their own views to the Court.[396] As such a report pursuant to s 7 has been the primary means of communicating the child's wishes and feelings to the court in private law proceedings.

---

[389]   Sturge, C and Glaser, D *Contact and Domestic Violence – the Experts' Court Report*, [2000] Fam Law 615, p 621.

[390]   Craig, J (Chair) *'Everybody's Business' – How Applications for Contact Orders by Consent Should be Approached by the Court in Cases Involving Domestic Violence* (2007) Family Justice Council, pp 5–6. See also Craig, J *Everybody's Business – Applications for Contact Orders by Consent* (2008) 37 Family Law, p 26 and Wall, N *A Report to the President of the Family Division on the Publication by the Woman's Aid Federation of England entitled 'Twenty-nine child homicides: Lessons still to be learnt on domestic violence and child protection'* with particular reference to the five cases in which there was judicial involvement (2006), paras 8.21 and 8.27.

[391]   *Practice Direction: Residence and Contact Orders: Domestic Violence and Harm* [2009] All ER (D) 122 (Jan).

[392]   *Practice Direction: Residence and Contact Orders: Domestic Violence and Harm* [2009] All ER (D) 122 (Jan), para 17.

[393]   Children Act 1989, s 7.

[394]   See **6.163 et seq** below.

[395]   *Practice Direction: Residence and Contact Orders: Domestic Violence and Harm* [2009] All ER (D) 122 (Jan).

[396]   *Re M (Family Proceedings: Affidavits)* [1995] 2 FLR 100, p 103.

6.145 In preparing a report the children and family court reporter[397] should get to know the child in his or her home and observe the relationship between the child and any adults.[398] An independent and objective assessment of the family relationships involved cannot be made in an office and must be made in a natural environment.[399] In addition, the children and family court reporter is required:[400]

(a)   To notify the child of such of the contents of the report as appropriate having regard to the child's age and understanding or explain them to the child in a manner appropriate to his age and understanding.[401]

(b)   Attend any hearing at which his report is considered.

(c)   Advise the court if he considers that the joinder of a person as a party to the proceedings would be likely to safeguard the interests of the child.

(d)   Consider whether it is in the child's best interests to be made a party to the proceedings and, if so, to notify the court of his opinion and the reasons for it.

Where the Children and Family Court Reporter, having met the child, comes to the conclusion that he is not able to represent the views of the child to the court adequately, he or she should report the matter to the court at an early stage so that consideration can be given to the separate representation of the child.[402]

6.146 The procedure pursuant to the Children Act 1989, s 7 is not without its drawbacks when considered in light of the imperatives of Art 12 of the CRC. First, the process of writing the reports risks filtering the children's views through the prism of an adult perspective or worse the selective reporting of those views. In *Re W (Leave to Remove)*[403] Thorpe LJ criticised the Cafcass officer for not properly representing the views of the children within the context of the report writing process, observing that:[404]

---

[397]   'Children and family reporter' means an officer of the Service or a Welsh family proceedings officer who has been asked to prepare a welfare report under s 7(1)(a) of the Children Act 1989 or s 102(3)(b) of the Adoption and Children Act 2002.

[398]   *Re W (A Minor) (Custody)* (1983) 4 FLR 492 at 501B. Whilst it can be argued that the expectations set out in *Re W* are a counsel of perfection and are now not often achieved, if the relationship between child and non-residential parent is at the core of the proceedings it is doubtful the court can reach a satisfactory decision without sufficiently cogent evidence as to the quality of that relationship.

[399]   *Re P (A Minor) (Inadequate Welfare Report)* [1996] 2 FCR 285, sub nom *Re P (Welfare Officer: Duties)* [1996] Fam Law 664.

[400]   Family Procedure Rules 2010, r 16.33 and FPR Practice Direction 16A.

[401]   In *Re W (Leave to Remove)* [2008] EWCA Civ 538, [2008] 2 FLR 1170 Wilson LJ took the view that the children (who were aged 15, 13 and 11) should have been sent complete copies of the report and asked to provide written comments prior to its filing with the Court.

[402]   *L v L (Minors) (Separate Representation)* [1994] 1 FLR 156 and see below **6.147**.

[403]   [2008] EWCA Civ 538, [2008] 2 FLR 1170.

[404]   See also Buchanan, A, Hunt, J, Bretherton, H and Bream, V *Families in Conflict: Perspectives of Children and Parents on the Family Court Welfare Service* (2001) The Policy Press, Fortin, J *Accommodating Children's Rights in a Post HRA Era* (2006) 69 Modern Law Review 299, Douglas, G, Murch, M, Miles, C and Scanlan, L *Research into the Operation of Rule 9.5 of the Family Proceedings Rules 1991* (2006) Department of Constitutional Affairs and James, A, James, A, and McNamee, S *Turn Down the Volume – Not Hearing the Children in Family Proceedings* (2004) 16 Child and Family Law Quarterly 189 for further discussion on the risk of Cafcass Officers interpreting and relaying the views of children through the filter of an adult perspective. See also Schuz, R *The Hague Child Abduction Convention and the United Nations Convention on the Rights of the Child* in Lødrup, P and Modvar, E (eds) *Family Life and Human Rights* (2004) Gyldendal, p 727 noting a similar issue in child abduction proceedings.

'The children's wishes and feelings came to the judge only through the report of the Cafcass officer ... The three children are particularly intelligent and also mature and sophisticated for their different ages. Accordingly it is not surprising that they were keen to ensure that the Cafcass officer recorded their position in terms that they had approved ... However, the Cafcass officer then applied her own analysis to the statement which the children wished her to advance on their behalf. The end result of that analysis was her advice to the judge to exercise a degree of caution in evaluating the children's stated wishes and feelings... at the conclusion of the process J can only feel that her wishes and feelings were insufficiently considered by the judge because they were diminished by the very professional whom she trusted to advance them.'

Second, whilst under the Cafcass National Standards, the Cafcass Safeguarding Framework and the Children's Rights in Practice programme[405] Cafcass aspires to ensure the child is heard through evidence giving or a written analysis, in practice this approach does not provide the direct advocacy and forensic argument required to take representation in private law proceedings beyond a simple account of wishes and feelings and on to the level of participation prescribed by Art 12 of the UNCRC and Art 6 and 8 of the ECHR. In *Re C (Abduction: Separate Representation of Children)*[406] Ryder J stated:

'However expert any Cafcass officer may be in obtaining a child's views, much will depend on the way that that officer elicits those views ie what questions he asks and how he interprets the answers. That officer is not able to advocate a child's views within the proceedings and in particular to respond to the evidence and submissions as they unfold, giving the child's position where appropriate. The process of reporting does not allow a child to engage in the proceedings.'

Finally, the central role of Cafcass in in-court conciliation has necessarily, in the absence of a concomitant increase in resources, impacted on the availability of Cafcass to complete reports in cases that cannot be resolved through such conciliation. As Fortin points out, this negatively impacts on those very cases in which the child's wishes and feelings are most likely to be lost, namely the most intractable long running disputes.[407] These difficulties, coupled with the fact that the court retains a discretion as to whether to order a report, have lead some commentators to argue that the process adopted pursuant to s 7 of the 1989 Act is not fully compliant with Art 12 of CRC.[408]

6.147 Party Status under R 16.2 – In the context of the foregoing difficulties, within private law disputes between parents there has been concern at the ability of Child and Family Court Reporters to 'sufficiently see and hear' the child,[409] especially where there is a conflict of interest between parents and child, and as to the extent that children's right to participate is being given effect in private law proceedings.[410] Whilst there is no automatic right for the child to be represented in private family law proceedings,[411] increasingly the domestic courts are recognising the need for such representation.

---

[405] See **6.118** above.
[406] [2008] EWHC 517 (Fam), [2008] 2 FLR 6, para 44.
[407] Fortin, J *Children's Rights and the Developing Law* (2009) 3rd edn, Cambridge, p 254.
[408] See for example Pressdee QC, P, Vater, J, Judd QC, F, and Baker QC, J Contact – the New Deal, para 8.50.
[409] *Re A (A Child) (Contact: Separate Representation)* [2001] 1 FLR 715, CA.
[410] See for example *Mabon v Mabon* [2005] EWCA Civ 634, [2005] 2 FLR 1011 and *Re L (Family Proceedings Court) (Appeal: Jurisdiction)* [2003] EWHC 1682 (Fam), [2005] 1 FLR 210.
[411] Section 41(6A) of the Children Act 1989 (inserted by s 122 of the Adoption and Children Act 2002) is designed to address this discrepancy by rendering applications under s 8 'specified proceedings' for the purposes of s 41 of the Act, thereby opening the door to children being separately represented in those proceedings unless not necessary to safeguard the child's welfare. The regulations required to give effect to s 41(4A) have not yet been laid before Parliament.

6.148 Part 16 of the Family Procedure Rules 2010 provides for a child to be made a party in private law children proceedings, to be separately represented in those proceedings and for a children's guardian to be appointed for a child with authority to take part in proceedings on the child's behalf.[412] A child can only be made a party in private law proceedings where it appears to the court that it is in the best interests of the child to be made a party to those proceedings.[413] This test is expanded upon in *FPR Practice Direction 16A*.[414] The Court should give consideration to the need for separate representation in any case involving allegations of domestic violence.[415]

6.149 An order under r 16.2 involves joining the child as a party to private law proceedings.[416] Once the appointment is made, the child is treated procedurally as any other party. The court may thereafter make an order appointing as a children's guardian an officer of the service or a Welsh family proceedings officer or, if the persons consents, a person other than the Official Solicitor or the Official Solicitor.[417] Such an appointment may be made of the court's own motion or on the application of a person who wishes to be a children's guardian or any party to the proceedings.[418] The application must be supported by evidence and the court must be satisfied that the proposed guardian has no interests adverse to the child, can fairly and competently conduct proceedings on behalf of the child and, save where the children's guardian is an officer of the service, a Welsh family proceedings officer or the Official Solicitor, undertakes to pay any costs which the child may be ordered to pay in relation to the proceedings.[419] The Children's Guardian appointed will have the powers and the duties set out in FPR Practice Direction 16A and must exercise the powers in accordance with that Practice Direction.[420] Cafcass have also issued a Practice Note dated June 2006 dealing with the practical aspects of involving Cafcass Officers in private law as Children's Guardians.[421]

6.150 Where the court makes an appointment under r 16.2 consideration should first be given to appointing an officer of Cafcass or Welsh Family Proceedings Officer as Children's Guardian. Where a Cafcass officer is appointed as a children's guardian under r 16.2 the duties under the Family Procedure Rules 2010, r 16.20 apply.[422] Whilst a child of sufficient understanding may participate in proceedings without a children's guardian,[423] there may be advantages to the child having a children's guardian in a case where there is severe acrimony between his parents within private law proceedings. Where a 'proper person' is appointed in place of an officer of Cafcass, that proper

---

[412] Family Procedure Rules 2010, rr 16.2, 16.4, 16.22 to 16.28 and 16.29 . See also *W v W (Abduction: Joinder as Party)* [2009] EWHC 3288 (Fam), [2010] 1 FLR 1342 per Baker J.
[413] Family Procedure Rules 2010, r 16.2(1).
[414] The Family Procedure Rules 2010 are accompanied by a series of new Practice Directions.
[415] *Practice Direction: Residence and Contact Orders: Domestic Violence and Harm* [2009] All ER (D) 122 (Jan), para 16.
[416] *L v L (Minors)(Separate Representation)* [1994] 1 FLR 156, p 159.
[417] Family Procedure Rules 2010, r 16.24(1).
[418] Family Procedure Rules 2010, r 16.24(2).
[419] Family Procedure Rules 2010, r 16.24(5).
[420] Family Procedure Rules 2010, r 16.27(1).
[421] [2006] 2 FLR 143.
[422] Family Procedure Rules 2010, r 16.27(2). Rule 16.20(1) provides that the children's guardian is to act on behalf of the child upon the hearing or any application in proceedings with the duty of safeguarding the interests of the child. Rule 16.20(2) requires that the children's guardian must give provide the court with such other assistance as it may require and r 16.20(3) requires the children's guardian, when carrying out duties in relation to specified proceedings, other than placement proceedings, must have regard to the principle set out in s 1(2) and the matters set out in s 1(3)(a) to (f) of the 1989 Act as if for the word "court" in that section there were substituted the words "children's guardian.
[423] Family Procedure Rules 2010, r 16.6(3).

person may be a solicitor who is already a solicitor for the child, although this is undesirable,[424] or a charitable organisation such as the National Youth Advocacy Service (NYAS).[425] The use of the NYAS has been endorsed by the Court of Appeal.[426] A protocol has been agreed between Cafcass and NYAS with respect to children made parties in private law proceedings.[427]

6.151 Children Bringing and Responding to Private Law Proceedings – Children Act 1989, s 10 – With leave pursuant to s 10 of the Children Act 1989 a child may apply for leave to apply for private law orders pursuant to s 8 of the Act.[428] According to Charles J in *Re S (Contact: Application by Sibling)*[429] where the applicant child is the subject of the family proceedings, his or her application for leave falls to be considered under s 10(8) and where the applicant is not the subject of the proceedings the application falls to be considered under s 10(9). This difference is significant in that pursuant to s 10(8) leave for the subject child is conditional solely upon the child being of 'sufficient understanding' whereas leave for the non-subject child pursuant to s 10(9) is not expressed to be conditional on 'sufficient understanding'.[430]

6.152 Where a child applies for permission to apply for an order under s 8 of the Children Act 1989, the welfare of the child is not paramount.[431] Even where a child can demonstrate 'sufficient understanding' applications by a child to involve themselves in private law proceedings should be approached cautiously.[432] Historically, the courts have not limited their considerations to whether 'sufficient understanding' is demonstrated when determining the position of the child. In *Re SC (A Minor) (Leave to Seek Residence Order)*[433] the Court determined that in addition to considering the issue of sufficiency of the child's understanding, in an application by a child under s 10(8) of the Children Act 1989 for permission to apply for a s 8 order, the court had also to consider the prospects of success of that application.[434] In *Re H (Residence Order: Child's Application for Leave)*[435] the court refused the child's application under s 10(8) of the 1989 Act notwithstanding that the court was satisfied the child had 'sufficient understanding' on the basis that there was no issue between the wishes of the child and his father as against the position of the mother and accordingly the father could

---

[424] *Re K (Replacement of Guardian ad Litem)* [2001] 1 FLR 663.
[425] *Re A (Contact: Separate Representation)* [2001] 1 FLR 715.
[426] *H (National Youth Advocacy Service)* [2006] EWCA Civ 896 and *Re B (A Child)* [2006] EWCA Civ 716.
[427] Protocol of December 2005 between the National Youth Advocacy Service and the Children and Family Court Advisory and Support Service [2006] Fam Law 243.
[428] Applications for leave by children should be heard in the High Court.
[429] [1998] 2 FLR 897.
[430] Charles J however considered that the question of whether the child is able to demonstrate 'sufficient understanding' can be considered alongside the other factors set out in s 10(9) (those factors being the nature of the proposed application, the applicant's connection with the child, any risk that the application will disrupt the subject child's life to the extent that he or she would be harmed by it and, where the child is looked after by the Local Authority, the authority's plans for the child's future and the wishes and feelings of the child's parents) as that list of factors is not exhaustive (*Re S (Contact: Application by Sibling)* [1998] 2 FLR 897).
[431] *Warwickshire CC v M* [2007] EWCA Civ 1084, [2008] 1 FLR 1093. See also see *Re SC (A Minor) (Leave to Seek a Residence Order)* [1994] 1 FLR 96; *Re C (Residence: Child's Application for Leave)* [1995] 1 FLR 927 and *Re H (Residence Order: Child's Application for Leave)* [2000] 1 FLR 780). Whether this is the position in respect of applications under s 4 of the Children Act 1989 has not yet been considered.
[432] *Re C (Residence Order: Child's Application for Leave)* [1995] 1 FLR 927.
[433] [1994] 1 FLR 96.
[434] See also *Warwickshire CC v M* [2007] EWCA Civ 1084, [2008] 1 FLR 1093 in which Wilson LJ considered that the family courts could usefully borrow the test set out in CPR 1998 Part 52.3(6) for prospect of success, namely is there 'a real prospect of success?' See also *Re M (Care: Contact: Grandmother's Application for Leave)* [1995] 2 FLR 86.
[435] [2000] 1 FLR 780.

advance his son's case. It is arguable that *Re H (Residence Order: Child's Application for Leave)* would not be decided in the same way today having regard to the growing acknowledgement of the autonomy and consequential rights of children.[436]

6.153   Children Bringing and Responding to Private Law Proceedings – FPR 2010, R 16.6
– In all family law proceedings under the Children Act 1989 the child is considered to be a 'person under a disability' for the purpose of legal proceedings.[437] Within this context, every child who begins and prosecutes or defends family proceedings must act by a litigation friend or children's guardian respectively unless (a) he or she obtains the leave of the court to proceed without one or other by demonstrating 'sufficient understanding'[438] or (b) he or she has instructed a solicitor who considers that he or she is able, 'having regard to his understanding', to given instructions in relation to the proceedings and the solicitor has accepted instructions from the child to act for the child in the proceedings and, if the proceedings have begun, is already so acting.[439]

6.154   Whether or not a child is able to give instructions to a solicitor is ultimately a matter for the court.[440] The courts have given extensive consideration to the meaning of the phrase 'sufficient understanding' within the context of a child's capacity to instruct a solicitor without an adult intermediary. In *Re S (A Minor) (Representation)*[441] Sir Thomas Bingham MR, accepting that the test of '*Gillick* competence' is the appropriate test of sufficiency of a child's understanding for the purposes of the Children Act 1989, held that:[442]

> 'Different children have differing levels of understanding at the same age. And understanding is not an absolute. It has to be assessed relatively to the issues in the proceedings. Where any sound judgment on these issues calls for insight and imagination which only maturity and experience can bring, both the court and the solicitor will be slow to conclude that the child's understanding is sufficient.'

In *Re H (A Minor) (Guardian ad Litem: Requirement)*[443] Booth J considered the specific context in which a child's understanding is measured in respect of family proceedings:

> 'Participating as a party, in my judgment, means much more than instructing a solicitor as to his own views. The child enters the arena among other adult parties. He may give evidence and he may be cross-examined. He will hear other parties, including in this case his parents, give evidence and be cross-examined. He must be able to give instructions on many different matters as the case goes through its stages and to make decisions as the need arises. Thus a child is exposed and not protected in these procedures ... The child also will be bound to abide by the rules which govern other parties, including rules as to confidentiality.'

---

[436]   *Mabon v Mabon* [2005] EWCA Civ 634, [2005] 2 FLR 1011. See below **6.155**.
[437]   Family Procedure Rules 2010, r 2.3.
[438]   Family Procedure Rules 2010, rr 16.6(3)(a) and 16.6(6). Pursuant to the Family Procedure Rules 2010, r 16.6(4) an application under r 16.6(3)(a) may be made by the child without notice.
[439]   Family Procedure Rules 2010, r 16.6(3)(b).
[440]   *Re T (A Minor: Child Representation)* [1994] Fam 49, [1993] FLR sub nom *Re CT (A Minor) (Wardship: Representation)* [1993] 2 FLR 278. Note that this is not the case where the issue is whether the child wishes to give instructions which conflict with those of the Children's Guardian in public law proceedings and the question is whether he or she able, having regard to his understanding, to give instructions on his own behalf pursuant to FPR 1991 r 4.12(1)(a), that question being a matter for the solicitor instructed on behalf of the child. See below **6.170**.
[441]   [1993] 2 WLR 810, [1993] 2 FLR 437.
[442]   See also *Re H (A Minor) (Role of Official Solicitor)* [1993] 2 FLR 552; *Re M (Minors)* [1994] 1 FLR 749 and *Re N (Contact: Minor Seeking Leave to Defend and Removal of Guardian)* [2003] 1 FLR 652.
[443]   [1994] 4 All ER 762.

In *Re N (Contact: Minor Seeking Leave to Defend and Removal of the Guardian)*[444] Coleridge J formulated the necessary question concerning the child's understanding as being 'not whether he is capable of articulating instructions but whether he is of sufficient understanding to participate as a party in the proceedings'.

6.155 Since *Re S* in 1993 the jurisprudence in respect of the child's participation in family proceedings has moved on significantly. In *Mabon v Mabon*[445] Thorpe LJ considered the older authorities and placed the principle of 'sufficient understanding' within the context of the growing appreciation of the autonomy and consequential rights of children. Within this context, considering the phrase 'sufficient understanding' in what was then FPR 1991 r 9.2A(6) and is now r 16.6(6) of the Family Procedure Rules 2010, Thorpe LJ stated in respect of a child's capacity that:

> 'The guidance given by this court in *Re S (A Minor) (Independent Representation)* [1993] Fam 263, [1993] 2 FLR 437 on the construction of r 9.2A is now 12 years old. Much has happened in that time. Although the UK had ratified the UN Convention some 15 months earlier, it did not have much impact initially and it is hardly surprising that it was not mentioned by this court on 26 February 1993. Although the tandem model has many strengths and virtues, at its heart lies the conflict between advancing the welfare of the child and upholding the child's freedom of expression and participation. Unless we in this jurisdiction are to fall out of step with similar societies as they safeguard Art 12 rights, we must, in the case of articulate teenagers, accept that the right to freedom of expression and participation outweighs the paternalistic judgment of welfare. In testing the sufficiency of a child's understanding, I would not say that welfare has no place. If direct participation would pose an obvious risk of harm to the child, arising out of the nature of the continuing proceedings and, if the child is incapable of comprehending that risk, then the judge is entitled to find that sufficient understanding has not been demonstrated. But judges have to be equally alive to the risk of emotional harm that might arise from denying the child knowledge of and participation in the continuing proceedings ... In conclusion, this case provides a timely opportunity to recognise the growing acknowledgement of the autonomy and consequential rights of children, both nationally and internationally. The FPR are sufficiently robustly drawn to accommodate that shift. In individual cases, trial judges must equally acknowledge the shift when they make a proportionate judgment of the sufficiency of the child's understanding.'

6.156 If a child is suffering emotional disturbance, his or her ability to instruct a solicitor depends on whether the level of disturbance is such as to remove the level of understanding required for giving rational instructions. If such a question arises it is a matter for expert opinion.[446] Where such a child is able to instruct a solicitor, that solicitor should be careful to take full instructions notwithstanding the child's emotional disturbance.[447]

6.157 A child may still act by a litigation friend or children's guardian even if he or she meets the criteria for acting without them.[448] Where the court considers that the child does not have the capacity to give instructions, including where a solicitor's assessment of a child's capacity to instruct him is unsustainable, the court can appoint a litigation

---

[444] [2003] 1 FLR 652.
[445] [2005] EWCA Civ 634, [2005] 2 FLR 1011.
[446] *Re L (Children) (Care Proceedings: Cohabiting Solicitors)* [2000] 3 FCR 71 and *Re H (A Minor) (Care Proceedings: Child's Wishes)* [1993] 1 FLR 440 in which Thorpe LJ concluded that a child suffering from a psychiatric disorder 'must have sufficient rationality within the understanding to instruct a solicitor'.
[447] *Re T and A* [2000] 1 FLR 859.
[448] Family Procedure Rules 2010, r 16.6(1). See also Family Procedure Rules 2010, r 16.6(7).

friend or children's guardian.[449] This will be achieved by reference to Cafcass Legal where the child's welfare is the subject of the application. Where the child's welfare is not the subject of the application (for example, an application by a child for contact to a sibling) the appointment will be facilitated through the Official Solicitor.[450]

6.158 It is important to note that the issue of whether or not a child should have leave to bring and prosecute or defend proceedings without a litigation friend or children's guardian is separate from the issue of whether a child should have leave to bring the proceedings themselves. For example, where a child seeks leave to apply for a s 8 order pursuant to s 10(8) of the Children Act 1989 and seeks to act without a litigation friend pursuant to the Family Procedure Rules 2010, r 16.6, that child will need to satisfy the court both that he meets the requirements for acting without a litigation friend or children's guardian[451] *and* the requirements for the granting of leave to make the application.[452]

Participation During Family Proceedings – Child Abduction Proceedings

6.159 In *Re G (Children)*[453] Thorpe LJ observed that 'There is, in this branch of international family law, a growing perception that the judge at trial should hear the voice of the child: that is implicit from the Convention itself but made explicit by the United Nations Convention on the Rights of the Child 1989'. The Child Abduction and Custody Act 1985 incorporates into domestic law the Hague Convention on the Civil Aspects of International Child Abduction and the European Convention on the Recognition and Enforcement of Decisions concerning Custody of Children and on the Restoration of Custody of Children. Schedule 1 of the Act sets out the Hague Convention, including Art 13 which provides that the judicial or administrative authority may refuse to order the return of an abducted child if it finds that the child objects to being returned and has attained an age and degree of maturity at which it is appropriate to take account of his or her views.[454] The provisions of Art 13 of the Hague Convention and of Council Regulation (EC) No 2201/2003 of 27 November 2003 on Jurisdiction and the Recognition and Enforcement of Judgments in Matrimonial Matters and Matters of Parental Responsibility for Children of both Spouses ('Brussels II Revised') relevant to the participation of the child in child abduction proceedings are considered in detail above.[455] As noted, Art 11(2) of Brussels II Revised provides that:

> '... when applying Articles 12 and 13 of the Hague Convention, it shall be ensured that the child is given an opportunity to be heard during the proceedings unless this appears inappropriate have regard to his or her age or degree of maturity.'

---

[449]   Family Procedure Rules 2010, r 16.6(8) and see *Re T* [1994] Fam 49, [1993] 2 FCR 445, sub nom *Re CT (A Minor) (Wardship Representation)* [1993] 2 FLR 278, CA.

[450]   *CAFCASS Practice Note* [2001] 2 FCR 562 and *Practice Note: Official Solicitor: Appointment in Family Proceedings* [2001] 2 FLR 155.

[451]   Family Procedure Rules 2010, rr 16.6(3) and 16.6(6).

[452]   CA 1989, s 10(8), (9); *Re N (Contact: Minor Seeking Leave to Defend and Removal of Guardian)* [2003] 1 FLR 652.

[453]   [2010] EWCA Civ 1232, para 15.

[454]   See *Re T (Abduction: Child's Objection to Return)* [2000] 2 FLR 192 per Ward LJ at 203–204 for the three stage test to be applied, namely (a) why does the child object to returning, (b) whether the child is of sufficient age and understanding to have his or her views taken into account and (c) whether the Court should exercise its discretion and depart from the usual presumption imposed by the Convention. See also *W v W (Abduction: Joinder as Party)* [2009] EWHC 3288 (Fam), [2010] 1 FLR 1342 per Baker J.

[455]   See **6.67–6.70**.

6.160 In reading Art 13 of the Hague Convention with Art 11(2) of Brussels II Revised, the domestic courts have recently moved from a historic reluctance to involve children directly in child abduction proceedings[456] to a greater willingness to permit the child's participation in such proceedings. Whilst this progression was gradual in nature,[457] in *Re M and anor (Children) (Abduction)*[458] Baroness Hale made clear that the child's views should be heard in both European Convention and Hague Convention cases and separate representation should be a matter of routine for applications under Art 12 of the Hague Convention. Her Ladyship stipulated that the test for separate representation is one of 'whether separate representation of the child will add enough to the court's understanding of the issues that arise under the convention to justify the intrusion, expense and the delay which may result' observing that 'I have no difficulty in predicting that in the general run of cases it will not'.[459] Baroness Hale stressed that the aims of Art 12 of the CRC should be given greater emphasis in child objection cases under Art 13 of the Hague Convention and that the 'exceptional circumstances' test for allowing a child's objection to prevail[460] was to be disapproved, thereby rejecting the gloss on the Art 13 requirements and returning it closer to the spirit of Art 12 of the CRC.[461]

Participation During Family Proceedings – Public Law Family Proceedings

6.161 Establishing a child's wishes and feelings in the context of proceedings concerning significant harm suffered by the child can be extremely problematic, as can be achieving a proper balance between the need to give weight to those wishes and feelings and the need to afford effective protection of the child. In particular, within the context of public law proceedings, the nature of the harm visited on the child can result in a conflict arising between the child's expressed wishes and the need to safeguard the child's welfare, requiring a careful approach to child's wishes and feelings.[462] In *Re F (Mental Health Act: Guardianship)*[463] Thorpe LJ observed that 'The deficiencies of the home are more apparent to other adults than to the young who have known no other'. In *Re C (A Minor) (Care: Child's Wishes)*[464] Waite J, considering the position of a 13 year old girl who was deeply attached to and felt a strong sense of responsibility for her inadequate father who was unable to protect her from harm, observed:

---

[456] See for example *Re S (Abduction: Children: Separate Representation)* [1997] 1 FLR 486 at 493 per Wall J ('exceptional circumstances which on the facts make it inappropriate for the child's wishes and feelings to be represented either by one of the existing parties to the proceedings or by the court welfare officer'), *Re J (Abduction: Child's Objections to Return)* [2004] EWCA Civ 428, [2004] 2 FLR 64, para 63 per Wall LJ ('highly unusual for a child to be represented in Hague Convention proceedings') and *Re H (Abduction)* [2006] EWCA Civ 1247, [2007] 1 FLR 242, para 16 per Thorpe J ('the test for the grant of party status should, if it is to be revised in any direction, be in future more rather than less stringently applied').

[457] See *S v B (Abduction: Human Rights)* [2005] EWHC 733 (Fam), [2005] 2 FLR 878 and *Re D (A Child) (Abduction: Rights of Custody)* [2006] UKHL 51, [2007] 1 All ER 783.

[458] [2007] UKHL 55, [2008] 1 All ER 1157.

[459] This test was not subsequently followed by the Court of Appeal in *Re F (Abduction: Removal Outside the Jurisdiction)* [2008] EWCA Civ 842, [2008] 2 FLR 1649, para 12 per Thorpe LJ but was followed in *Re C (Abduction: Separate Representation of Children)* [2008] EWHC 517 (Fam), [2008] 2 FLR 6, para 31 per Ryder J.

[460] See for example *Re M (Abduction: Child's Objections)* [2007] EWCA Civ 260, [2007] 2 FLR 72 and *JPC v SLW and SMW (Abduction)* [2007] EWHC 1349 (Fam), [2007] 2 FLR 900.

[461] See General Comment No 6 *Treatment of Unaccompanied Children and Separated Children Outside Their Country of Origin* HRI/GEN/1/Rev 8, pp 427–429.

[462] Schofield, G *Making Sense of the Ascertainable Wishes and Feelings of Insecurely Attached Children* (1998) 10 Child and Family Law Quarterly 363, p 365.

[463] [2000] 1 FLR 192, p 198 per Thorpe LJ.

[464] [1993] 1 FLR 832.

'Certainly the issue is not an easy one. Whichever way the decision goes, C is bound to suffer and to be at a degree of risk. If she returns to live with her father she will get what she most wants, or believes she wants, but will be at risk through exposure to undesirable companions from whom he still seems unable to protect her. There are doubts, too, as to her prospects of thriving emotionally in his care. If she goes to yet another set of foster-parents, on the other hand, she will experience further dislocation in her routine, and will pine for her father ... The child is fixed and determined, it is true, in her own decision as to what she wants, and very protective of her father in the pathetic demands which he makes of her in his physical weakness and unhappiness. Nevertheless, I agree with comments that were made by her guardian ad litem, both in the original report and in evidence on this appeal. Those are to the effect that C is too young to carry the burden of decision about her own future, and too young to have to bear the weight of responsibility for a parent who lacks authority and plays on her feelings of protectiveness.'

6.162 Against these difficulties, the potentially draconian nature of orders made in public law proceedings emphasises the need to ensure children participate appropriately in the decisions being made.[465] It is important to remember that the child may be telling the truth when denying that abuse has taken place.[466] For these reasons, as Fortin notes, a child's age and competence to form views cannot be assessed *in vacuo* since the risk involved in ignoring or acceding to the child's wishes will always impinge on the decision making process.[467] Further it is important that the concepts of participation and protection are not seen as mutually exclusive but rather as interdependent concepts which require development in parallel.[468]

6.163 Participation during Public Law Proceedings – Children Act 1989, s 41 – Section 41(6) of the Children Act 1989 specifies certain proceedings in which the child is made a respondent[469] and the court is required to appoint an officer of Cafcass or a Welsh Family Proceedings Officer, known as a 'Children's Guardian', to represent the child, unless satisfied that it is not necessary to do so in order to safeguard the child's interests. The presumption in respect of the appointment of a Children's Guardian applies only to a child who is the subject of the proceedings. Where a child is a respondent to the proceedings by reason of being the parent of the child who is subject to the proceedings, the representation of that child will be governed by the rules covering the legal representation of children.[470]

6.164 The specified proceedings in which a Children's Guardian will be appointed under s 41 are as follows:

(a)   on an application for a care order or supervision order;

(b)   in which the court has given a direction under s 37(1) and has made, or is considering whether to make, an interim care order;[471]

---

[465]   See *R v Devon County Council, ex p O (Adoption)* [1997] 2 FLR 388, pp 396–397 per Scott-Baker J.
[466]   *Leeds City Council v YX and ZX (Assessment of Sexual Abuse)* [2008] EWHC 802 (Fam), [2008] 2 FLR 869, para 127 per Holman J.
[467]   Fortin, J *Children's Rights and the Developing Law* (2009) 3rd edn, Cambridge, p 313.
[468]   Barry, M *Minor Rights and Major Concerns – The Views of Young People in Care* in Franklin, B (ed) *The New Handbook of Children's Rights* (2002) Routledge, pp 251–252.
[469]   Family Procedure Rules 2010, r 12.27. The proceedings are known as 'specified proceedings'.
[470]   See above **6.147**.
[471]   The proceedings are no longer specified when the local authority decides not to make an application under the CA 1989, s 31.

(c)   on an application for the discharge of a care order or the variation or discharge of a supervision order;

(d)   on an application under s 39(4) to substitute a care order for a supervision order;

(e)   in which the court is considering whether to make a residence order with respect to a child who is the subject of a care order;

(f)   with respect to contact between a child who is the subject of a care order and any other person;

(g)   under Part V;

(h)   on an appeal against—

    (i)   the making of, or refusal to make, a care order, supervision order or any order under s 34 (contact to a child in care);
    (ii)   the making of, or refusal to make, a residence order with respect to a child who is the subject of a care order; or
    (iii)   the variation or discharge, or refusal of an application to vary or discharge, an order of a kind mentioned in sub-paragraph (i) or (ii);
    (iv)   the refusal of an application under s 39(4); or
    (v)   the making of, or refusal to make, an order under Part V;

(hh)   on an application for the making or revocation of a placement order (within the meaning of s 21 of the Adoption and Children Act 2002); or

(i)   which are specified for the time being, for the purposes of this section, by rules of court.

6.165 Education supervision orders do not come within the ambit of s 41(6)[472] and orders under Part II of the Children Act 1989 are not provided for. The rules[473] add the following proceedings to the specified proceedings category:

(a)   family proceedings under s 25 for a child to be kept in secure accommodation;

(b)   application under s 33(7) enabling a child to be known by a new surname or removed from the United Kingdom;

(c)   proceedings under Sch 2, para 19(1) to approve a child in care living abroad;

(d)   applications under Sch 3, para 6(3) for extension of a supervision order; and

(e)   appeals against the determination of proceedings of the kind set out in paragraphs (a) to (d) above.[474]

---

[472] *Essex County Council v B* [1993] 1 FLR 866.
[473] Family Procedure Rules 2010, r 12.27(1).
[474] Following an amendment by s 122 of the Adoption and Children Act 2002, s 41(6A) of the Children Act 1989 provides that proceedings which may be specified by rules of court include (for example) proceedings for the making, varying or discharging of a s 8 order. Whilst this amendment raises the prospect

6.166 Proceedings may cease to be specified proceedings, such as where a local authority, having conducted an investigation under s 37, decides not to make an application for a care or supervision order.[475] Where proceedings are no longer specified, the role of the Children's Guardian will cease, although it is possible to identify cases where the court has allowed the appointment to continue despite the fact that proceedings were no longer specified under the Act where, subject to consent and the availability of funding, it would be appropriate for the Guardian to continue.[476] It is no longer possible for the court to extend the appointment of the children's guardian following the making of a final supervision order, s 12(5)(b) of the Criminal Justice and Court Services Act 2000 having been repealed by the Adoption and Children Act 2002.[477] The court has no jurisdiction to direct a Children's Guardian to continue his or her involvement following the making of a final care order.[478] A desire on the part of the court to monitor a rehabilitation process under a care order is not a matter for the Children's Guardian.[479]

6.167 A Children's Guardian is appointed in accordance with rules of court which provide that the appointment shall be made as soon as practicable after the commencement of proceedings, unless an appointment has already been made or the court considers such an appointment is not necessary to safeguard the interests of the child.[480] The Public Law Outline[481] provides that a Children's Guardian shall be appointed by no later than the third day following issue of proceedings and that Cafcass should allocate the Children's Guardian within the same timescale[482] although there is no statutory duty on Cafcass to comply with this timescale, the duty on Cafcass being to comply 'as soon as reasonably practicable'.[483] Where it is not possible to appoint a Children's Guardian in time for the first appointment, the appointment by the court of a solicitor for the child pending the appointment of a children's guardian is governed by best practice guidance issued in 2003.[484] When appointing a Children's Guardian the court is required to consider appointing the person who has previously acted as the Children's Guardian to the same child.[485]

6.168 Where a Children's Guardian is not appointed at the commencement of proceedings because the court is satisfied that such an appointment is not necessary to safeguard the interests of the child, at any stage thereafter a party to the specified

---

that private law proceedings will become specified proceedings, the rules that will give effect to s 41(6A) are still awaited and no timescale has been given for their implementation.

[475] If the s 37 direction has been made in private law proceedings, the court may direct a s 7 report within those proceedings notwithstanding a s 37 report has been completed. See the CA 1989, s 7(1).

[476] *Re CE (A Minor) (Section 37 Direction)* [1995] 1 FLR 26. See also *Oxfordshire County Council v L and F* [1997] 1 FLR 235 where it was held desirable for the child to be represented after the termination of care proceedings on an application for disclosure of documents. An alternative approach would be for a direction under FPR 1991, r 9.5 to be sought and a public funding application made.

[477] Thus *Re SB and MB (Children)* [2001] 2 FLR 1334 is no longer good law.

[478] *Kent County Council v C* [1993] 1 FLR 308.

[479] See *Re S (Care Order: Implementation of Care Plan)* [2002] 2 WLR 720. The Adoption and Children Act 2002 amends the Children Act 1989 to provide for the power of referral of cases to a CAFCASS officer where a care plan has not been carried out. See **6.192** below.

[480] Family Procedure Rules 2010, r 16.3(1).

[481] See **6.128**.

[482] See also *Practice Guidance: Interim Guidance to Assist Cafcass* [2009] 2 FLR 1407.

[483] *R v Children and Family Court Advisory and Support Service* [2003] EWHC 235 (Fam), [2003] 1 FLR 953.

[484] Best Practice Guidance – Appointment of Solicitors for Children where it falls to the Court to do so in Specified Proceedings, November 2003.

[485] Family Procedure Rules 2010, r 16.3(4).

proceedings may apply without notice for such an appointment.[486] The court must grant such an application unless the court considers such an appointment is not necessary to safeguard the interests of the child.[487]

6.169 Any appointment of the Children's Guardian should be terminated by a judicial rather than an administrative act[488] and the court should give reasons for doing so.[489] It is possible for the court to terminate the appointment of a Children's Guardian who has acted manifestly contrary to the best interests of the children even if that guardian has acted in good faith and with due diligence.[490]

6.170 Participation during Public Law Proceedings – The Children's Guardian – The Children's Guardian is under a duty to safeguard the interests of the child in accordance with the rules.[491] In particular, the Children's Guardian should ensure that the party status of children is a reality.[492] Children's Guardians should always explore with the child whether they wish to attend court proceedings.[493] Where there is a conflict of interest between the children involved in the case, this will not necessarily prevent the Children's Guardian from safeguarding the interests of each of the children concerned.[494]

6.171 Within the context of the general duty to safeguard the interests of the child, the Children's Guardian is under a duty to:[495]

(a) Have regard to the principle that delay is likely to prejudice the welfare of the child and the matters set out at s 1(3)(a) to 1(3)(f) of the Act (the 'welfare checklist').

(b) Make such investigations as are necessary for him to carry out his duties and, in particular, to contact or seek to interview such persons as he thinks appropriate and to obtain such professional assistance as is available to him which he thinks it appropriate or which the court directs.

(c) Provide the court with such other assistance as it may require.

(d) Appoint a solicitor to represent the child if one has not already been appointed[496] or the Children's guardian is authorised for the purposes of the Criminal Justice and Court Services Act 2000, s 15.[497]

---

[486] Family Procedure Rules 2010, r 16.3(2).
[487] Family Procedure Rules 2010, r 16.3(1).
[488] See the Family Procedure Rules 2010, r 16.19(1) and *Re M (Terminating Appointment of Guardian Ad Litem)* [1999] 2 FLR 717.
[489] Family Procedure Rules 2010, r 16.19(2).
[490] *Re A (Conjoined Twins: Medical Treatment) (No 2)* [2001] 1 FLR 267.
[491] CA 1989, s 41(2)(b).
[492] Masson, J and Winn-Oakley, M *Out of Hearing: Representing Children in Care Proceedings* (1999) John Wiley & Sons, p 117.
[493] Family Justice Council Voice of the Child Sub-Group *Enhancing the Participation of Children and Young People in Family Proceedings: Starting the Debate* (2008) Fam Law 431, p 434.
[494] *Re T and E (Proceedings: Conflicting Interests)* [1995] 1 FLR 581 but see *Re P (Representation)* [1996] 1 FLR 486.
[495] Family Procedure Rules 2010, r 16.20 and FPR Practice Direction 16A. Interestingly, the children's guardian is not required by the rules to have regard to s 1(3)(h), the range of orders available to the court but is required to advise the court respect of the options open to it (see Family Procedure Rules 2010, r 16.20(3)).
[496] FPR Practice Direction 16A, para 6.2(a).
[497] To conduct litigation and exercise rights of audience in any proceedings before any court.

(e)   Give such advice to the child as is appropriate having regard to his understanding.[498]

(f)   Subject to the child meeting the criteria for instructing the solicitor direct[499] to instruct the solicitor representing the child on all matter relevant to the interests of the child, including the possibilities for appeal, arising in the course of proceedings.[500]

(g)   Inform the court where it appears that the child wishes to instruct a solicitor direct and the children's guardian or the court considers the child is capable of conducting proceedings on his own behalf and thereafter to continue his duties and such other duties as the court may direct and take such part in the proceedings as the court directs (with the benefit of legal representation if given leave by the court).[501]

(h)   Attend, unless excused, all directions appointments and hearings of proceedings and shall advise on the following matters:

   (i)   whether the child is of sufficient understanding for any purpose including the child's refusal to submit to a medical or psychiatric examination or other assessment that the court has power to require, direct or order;
   (ii)   the wishes of the child in respect of any matter relevant to the proceedings, including his attendance at court;
   (iii) the appropriate forum for the proceedings;
   (iv)   the appropriate timing of the proceedings or any part of them;
   (v)   the options available to it in respect of the child and the suitability of each such option including what order should be made in determining the application;
   (vi)   any other matter on which the court seeks his advice or about which he considers that the court should be informed.[502]

(i)   Where practicable, notify any person whose joinder as a party to the proceedings would be likely, in the opinion of the children's guardian, to safeguard the interests of the child, of that person's right to apply to be joined and to notify the court accordingly.[503]

(j)   File a written report advising on the interests of the child in accordance with the timetable set by the court.[504] This report may contain hearsay or other technically inadmissible evidence which the court may take account of subject to the usual

---

[498]   FPR Practice Direction 16A, para 6.2(b).
[499]   FPR Practice Direction 16A, para 6.2(c).
[500]   FPR Practice Direction 16 A, para 6.2(c).
[501]   Family Procedure Rules 2010, r 16.21(1) and FPR Practice Direction 16A, para 6.3.
[502]   FPR Practice Direction 16A, paras 6.5 and 6.6.
[503]   FPR Practice Direction 16A, para 6.8(b).
[504]   FPR Practice Direction 16A, para 6.8(a). The requirements of this provision are now supplemented by the provisions of the Pubic Law Outline, which requires the Children's guardian to prepare an 'Analysis and Recommendations' before the First Appointment, the Case Management Conference, the Issues Resolution Hearing and the Final Hearing.

caveats in respect of such evidence.[505] The court should not take a course of action contrary to the recommendations of the children's guardian without giving reasons for doing so.[506]

(k)   Inspect appropriate records[507] and bring to the attention of the court, such records and documents which may, in his opinion, assist in the proper determination of the proceedings.

(l)   Ensure that, if he considers it appropriate, that the child is notified of the decision of the court in a manner appropriate to the child's age and understanding.[508] A children's guardian should not promise a child to withhold information from the court,[509] but may apply to the court for directions that information should not be revealed to another party.[510]

6.172 A Children's Guardian appointed for the purpose of specified proceedings has a right at all reasonable times to examine and take copies of any records of, or held by, a local authority or other authorised persons compiled in connection with the making or proposed making by any person of any application under the Act with respect to the child he represents and any other records of, or held by, an authority in relation to the child and compiled in connection with any function of the social services committee under the Local Authority Social Services Act 1970.[511] The provision is wide enough to include case conference minutes. It includes files compiled with a view to adoption[512] and a report prepared under Part 8 of Working Together for an Area Child Protection Committee.[513] The provision is limited to the local authority or any authorised person. The Arrangements for Placement of Children (General) Regulations 1991 make additional provision so that each voluntary organisation,[514] where it is not acting as an authorised person, and every person carrying on a registered children's home, shall provide a guardian with access to the case records and registers and information from, and copies of, such records or registers held in whatever form (such as by means of computer). The Children's Guardian has no right to inspect records of the Crown Prosecution Service, but disclosure can be ordered if documents are of real importance to a care case.[515]

6.173 Where copies of records are taken by the Children's Guardian they are admissible as evidence in proceedings, regardless of any enactment or rule of law which would otherwise prevent the record in question being admissible in evidence.[516] There is no issue of public interest immunity to be taken by the local authority when considering the right of the children's guardian to inspect and copy documents that fall within the ambit of s 42 of the Act although the children's guardian should be cautious about what is then disclosed to other parties.[517]

---

[505]   CA 1989, s 41(11).
[506]   *Re D (Grant of Care Order: Refusal of Freeing Order)* [2001] 1 FLR 862.
[507]   CA 1989, s 42; FPR Practice Direction 16A, para 6.10.
[508]   FPR Practice Direction 16A, para 6.11
[509]   *Re D (minors)* [1995] 4 All ER 385, [1995] 2 FLR 687, HL.
[510]   *Re C (Disclosure)* [1996] 1 FLR 797.
[511]   Children Act 1989, s 42.
[512]   *Re T (A Minor) (Guardian Ad Litem: Case Record)* [1994] 1 FLR 632, CA.
[513]   *Re R (Care Proceedings: Disclosure)* [2000] 2 FLR 751.
[514]   Arrangements of Placement of Children (General) Regulations 1991, SI 1991/890, r 11.
[515]   *Nottinghamshire County Council v H* [1995] 1 FLR 115.
[516]   Children Act 1989, s 42(2), (3).
[517]   *Re J (Care Proceedings: Disclosure)* [2003] EWHC 976 (Fam), [2003] 2 FLR 522.

6.174 Participation in Public Law Proceedings – Legal Representation for the Child – A Children's Guardian appointed pursuant to s 41 of the Children Act 1989[518] must themselves appoint a solicitor to represent the child[519] and shall instruct the solicitor on all matters relevant to the interests of the child in the course of proceedings.[520] Notwithstanding the duty to instruct a solicitor, the Legal Services Commission may decide that the merits of a case do not warrant legal representation and refuse public funding.[521]

6.175 As for the Children's Guardian, the duties of a solicitor appointed to represent the child in specified proceedings are specific and they must:[522]

(a) act in accordance with instructions received from the children's guardian;

(b) conduct the proceedings in accordance with instructions received from the child, if the solicitor considers, having taken into account the views of the children's guardian and any direction of the court, that the child wishes to give instructions which conflict with those of the children's guardian and that he is able, having regard to his understanding, to give such instructions on his own behalf;

(c) act in accordance with instructions received from the child, if no children's guardian has been appointed for the child and the child has sufficient understanding to instruct a solicitor and wishes to do so;

(d) in default of any instructions, act in furtherance of the best interests of the child;[523]

(e) inform the court and other parties how the child was to be represented and what views he was expressing;[524] and

(f) not advance a local authority care plan when representing one child and at the same time represent a child, capable of giving instructions, who is opposed to the care plan.[525]

6.176 Thus the test for the child having direct access his or her own legal representation in public law proceedings varies depending on the circumstances:

(a) Where is a solicitor is appointed by the Children's Guardian he must represent the child in accordance with instructions received from the children's guardian save

---

518 Known as 'specified proceedings'. See CA 1989, s 41(6) for the list of 'specified proceedings'.

519 FPR Practice Direction 16A, para 6.2. This has become known as the 'tandem model' of representation.

520 FPR Practice Direction 16A, para 6.2(c). See also the Guidance on the Working Relationship between Children Panel solicitors and Guardians (Law Society / CAFCASS February 2004).

521 While the LSC may seek to avoid public funding, they should take account of the mandatory requirement placed on the guardian to appoint a solicitor: *R v Legal Aid Board, ex p W* [2000] 3 FCR 352, [2000] 2 FLR 821 and Focus 32, September 2000.

522 Family Procedure Rules 2010, r 16.29 and see The Law Society's Guide to Good Practice for Solicitors Acting for Children (6th edn, 2002) Law Society and the Law Society Guidance on Representation of Children in Public Law Proceedings (October 2006) Law Society.

523 The solicitor for the child is not *functus officio* at the conclusion of proceedings and has a duty to consider the question of appeal and to serve notice of appeal if appropriate (*R v Plymouth Juvenile Court, ex p F* [1987] 1 FLR 169).

524 *Re M (minors) (care proceedings: child's wishes)* [1994] 1 FCR 866, [1994] 1 FLR 749.

525 *Re P (Minors) (Representation)* (1995) *The Times*, 30 November.

where the child wishes to give instructions which conflict with the children's guardian and is able, having regard to his 'understanding',[526] to give such instructions on his own behalf, in which case the child's instructions prevail.[527]

(b)   Where the children's guardian is an officer of Cafcass authorised to conduct litigation, he is not required to instruct a solicitor if he intends to have conduct of the proceedings on behalf of the child, unless the child wishes to instruct a solicitor direct and the children's guardian or the court considers that he is of 'sufficient understanding' to do so.[528] The test of whether a child may instruct his or her own solicitor is thus slightly different where it appears to the *Children's Guardian* that the child is as a matter of fact instructing his solicitor direct, or intends to. In such circumstances, the Children's Guardian shall inform the court of the position where the Guardian is of the view that the child is 'capable of conducting the proceedings on his own behalf'.[529] He then carries on with his duties, save for instructing the solicitor, but may, with leave, have legal representation.[530]

(c)   A court may appoint a solicitor for the child if there is no children's guardian or if the child has 'sufficient understanding' to instruct a solicitor and wishes to do so or if it appears to the court that it is in the child's interests for him to be represented by a solicitor.[531]

(d)   There is no requirement that the child be of 'sufficient understanding' before he may apply for the termination of the solicitor's appointment.[532] A solicitor whose firm had acted previously in unrelated matters for a party in family proceedings was not required to stand down unless there was a real risk of disclosure of confidential information.[533] Where solicitors representing different parties in the same proceedings have a close personal relationship, one of them should stand down.[534] Where the child or the Children's Guardian wishes an appointment of a solicitor to be terminated, he may apply to the court for an order for its termination. The solicitor and the child or children's guardian shall be given an opportunity to make representations.[535]

6.177 As above, in relation to each test care must be taken in assessing the child's understanding to have regard to developmental, medical and environmental factors which may affect the child's level of understanding. This is particularly important in care proceedings where the nature of the issues overall may impact on this particular issue specifically.[536] The Children's Guardian should be alert to the possibility of conflicts arising between what he considers to be in the best interests of the child and the child's wishes. Guidance as to the proper course of action in circumstances where there

---

[526] Family Procedure Rules 2010, r 16.29(1) and (2). Note that the rules omit the word 'sufficient' as a qualification to the word 'understanding'.

[527] Family Procedure Rules 2010, r 16.29(2).

[528] FPR Practice Direction 16A, para 6.3.

[529] Family Procedure Rules 2010, r 16.21(1).

[530] Family Procedure Rules 2010, r 16.21(2).

[531] CA 1989, s 41(3), (4). See also Best Practice Guidance Note – Appointment of Solicitors for Children where it falls to the Court to do so in Specified Proceedings, November 2003 and Winter, D *The Dilemmas of a Panel Solicitor who has no Children's Guardian* [2001] Fam Law 904.

[532] Family Procedure Rules 2010, r 16.29(7).

[533] *Re T and A* [2000] 1 FLR 859.

[534] *Re L (Children) (Care Proceedings: Cohabiting Solicitors)* [2000] 3 FCR 71.

[535] Family Procedure Rules 2010, r 16.29(7).

[536] *Re H (A Minor) (Care Proceedings: Child's Wishes)* [1993] 1 FLR 440 per Thorpe J, p 449.

is a divergence between the views of the Children's Guardian and the views of the child is provided in *Re M (Minors) (Care Proceedings: Child's Wishes).*[537]

Participation During Family Proceedings – Adoption and Children Act 2002

6.178 Proceedings for a Placement Order – Proceedings under the Adoption and Children Act 2002, s 21 are 'specified' for the purposes of the Children Act 1989, s 41 and accordingly a Children's Guardian will be appointed for the child in placement proceedings under the 2002 Act unless it is unnecessary to do so to safeguard the interests of the child.[538] As with proceedings under the Children Act 1989, the Children's Guardian must appoint a solicitor for the child.[539] No placement order may be made without the personal attendance of the child at court unless the court permits non-attendance.[540]

6.179 Proceedings for an Adoption Order – Where a child is made party to an adoption application in respect of him or her pursuant to the Family Procedure Rules 2010, r 14.3, the court must appoint a Children's Guardian unless it is not necessary to do so to safeguard the child's interests.[541] The Children's Guardian must appoint a solicitor for the child.[542] No adoption order may be made without the personal attendance of the child at court unless the court permits non-attendance.[543]

6.180 Party Status for Non-subject Children – A child may be joined in adoption proceedings concerning their sibling where, for example, they object to the plan for adoption or to the plan for post permanency contact.[544]

Participation During Family Proceedings – Attendance of Child at Court

6.181 Children tend to argue that, as the proceedings are determining their futures, they should be permitted to see the process which seeks to achieve that end.[545] However, even where a child is a party to specified proceedings or a party to private law proceedings the child does not have an absolute right in domestic law to attend the hearing.[546] The rules provide that hearings in family proceedings shall take place in the absence of the child if the court considers it in the interests of the child, having regard to the matters to be discussed or the evidence likely to be given, and whether the child is represented by a Children's Guardian or solicitor. The child, if of sufficient understanding, must be given an opportunity to make representations as to his or her

---

[537] [1994] 1 FLR 749. See also *Re K and H* [2006] EWCA Civ 1898, [2007] 1 FLR 2043 on the current approach to be taken in cases where the child seeks to instruct the solicitor direct.
[538] CA 1989, s 41(6)(hh) and Family Procedure Rules 2010, r 16.3(1)(b)(ii).
[539] FPR Practice Direction 16A, para 6.2. See **6.171** above.
[540] Family Procedure Rules 2010, r 14.16(6) and (7).
[541] Family Procedure Rules 2010, r 16.3(1).
[542] FPR Practice Direction 16A, para 6.2. See **6.171** above.
[543] Family Procedure Rule 2010, r 14.16(6) and (7).
[544] Family Procedure Rules 2010, r 14.3(2).
[545] See Masson, J and Winn-Oakley, M *Out of Hearing: Representing Children in Care Proceedings* (1999) p 115, Rueger, M *Children's Experience of the Guardian ad Litem Service and Public Law Proceedings* in Rueger, M (ed) *Hearing the Voice of the Child: Representation of Children's Interests in Public Law Proceedings* (2001) Russell House Publishing, pp 40–41 and Timms, J and Thoburn, J *Your Short* (2003) NSPCC, p 7.
[546] There is a constitutional right of access to the courts at common law (see *Raymond v Honey* [1983] 1 AC 1; *R v Secretary of State for the Home Department ex p Anderson* [1984] QB 778; *R v Secretary of State for the Home Department ex p Leech (No 2)* [1994] QB 198 and *R v Lord Chancellor, ex p Whitam* [1998] QB 575.

attendance.[547] As matters currently stand, except by direction of the Court children should not attend any Children Act 1989 hearings.[548]

6.182 The courts are generally reluctant to permit children to attend court during public law care proceedings.[549] However, attendance at court may, provided steps are taken to ensure the welfare of the child is not prejudiced, ensure a better understanding of his or her situation,[550] permit the court a better understanding of the case[551] by enabling immediate dialogue between the child and the Children's Guardian on points in issue, facilitate a better outcome by assuring to the child a sense of participating in the determination of their own futures and assist to maintain the child as the focus of the professionals and the court.[552]

6.183 To date it has likewise not been the general practice in family proceedings for children to give direct oral evidence as to their wishes and feelings in private law proceedings on the basis that, in a dispute between parents, it is unfair for the child to be dragged into the arena.[553]

Participation During Family Proceedings – Oral Evidence from Child

6.184 By reason of the admissibility of hearsay evidence in Children Act proceedings[554] and the use of video interviewing techniques, courts have tended to take the view that it is unnecessary to call children as witnesses of fact. Historically, the child's expressed wish to give evidence has not necessarily altered this approach.[555] However, it is suggested that in certain cases there is no reason in principle why special measures should not be put in place to protect children who are required to give evidence in the same way that such measures are deployed in criminal proceedings.[556] Until recently, the correct starting point was that it is unusual for children to give evidence in care proceedings and particular justification would be required for that course of action.[557] However, the Supreme Court has now disapproved that approach, Baroness Hale holding in *Re W*[558] that:

> 'When the court is considering whether a particular child should be called as a witness, the court will have to weigh two considerations: the advantages that that will bring to the determination of the truth and the damage it may do to the welfare of this or any other child. A fair trial is a trial which is fair in the light of the issues which have to be decided. Mr Geekie accepts that the welfare of the child is also a relevant consideration, albeit not the

---

[547] Family Procedure Rules 2010, rr 12.14(3) and (4). See also Family Procedure Rules 12.12(2)(d).

[548] See The Children Act Advisory Committee, Handbook of Best Practice in Children Act Cases (1997) CAAC, para 58.

[549] See for example *Re C (A Minor)(Care: Child's Wishes)* [1993] 1 FLR 832. Compare the position in respect of Secure Accommodation Orders under s 25 of the Children Act 1989, in respect of which the Courts have jealously guarded the procedural requirement for the children to attend court (see for example *Re AS (Secure Accommodation Order)* [1999] 1 FLR 103, *Re C (Secure Accommodation Order: Representation)* [2001] EWCA Civ 458, [2001] 2 FLR 169 and *Re K (A Child)(Secure Accommodation Order: Right to Liberty)* [2001] 1 FLR 526).

[550] HMICA *Safeguarding Children in Family Proceedings* (2005), para 3.4.

[551] Fortin, J *Children's Rights and the Developing Law* (2009) 3rd edn, Cambridge, p 276. See also *Re K (A Child)(Secure Accommodation Order: Right to Liberty)* [2001] 1 FLR 526 per Butler-Sloss P at para 44.

[552] Fortin, J *Children's Rights and the Developing Law* (2009) 3rd edn, Cambridge, pp 276–277.

[553] *Re M (Family Proceedings: Affidavits)* [1995] 2 FLR 100.

[554] Children (Admissibility of Hearsay Evidence) Order 1993, SI 1993/621.

[555] *Re O (Care Proceedings: Evidence)* [2003] EWHC 2011 (Fam), [2004] 1 FLR 161.

[556] Youth Justice and Criminal Evidence Act 1999, Part II.

[557] See *R v Torbay Council* [2007] 1 FLR 203.

[558] *Re W* [2010] UKSC 12, [2010] 2 All ER 418, [2010] 1 FLR 1485.

paramount consideration in this respect. He is right to do so, because the object of the proceedings is to promote the welfare of this and other children. The hearing cannot be fair to them unless their interests are given great weight… The essential test is whether justice can be done to all the parties without further questioning of the child.'[559]

6.185 It is likely that the following factors will need to be borne in mind when conducting the balancing exercise:[560]

(a)   The nature of the issues to be decided and whether it is possible to decide the case without needing to make findings on particular allegations.

(b)   The quality of the evidence already before the court and whether it is possible to determine the findings in issue whether or not the child is cross-examined.

(c)   The quality of the 'Achieving Best Evidence' Interview.[561]

(d)   The nature of the challenge to be made against the child's evidence.[562]

(e)   The age and maturity of the child and the length of time since the events in question.

(f)   The support or lack of it available to the child from family members of others.

(g)   The child's own wishes and feelings about giving evidence.[563]

(h)   The views of the children's guardian and, where appropriate, those with parental responsibility for the child.

(i)   The risk of further delay in the proceedings.

(j)   Whether there are parallel criminal proceedings are taking place.

(k)   The general evidence of the harm which giving evidence may do to children.[564]

(l)   Any features particular to the child and to the case.

---

[559] Baroness Hale observed in relation to this test that 'Our prediction is that, if the court is called upon to do it, the consequence of the balancing exercise will usually be that the additional benefits to the court's task in calling the child do not outweigh the additional harm that it will do to the child' (*Re W* [2010] UKSC 12, [2010] 2 All ER 418, [2010] 1 FLR 1485, para 30).

[560] *Re W* [2010] UKSC 12, [2010] 2 All ER 418, [2010] 1 FLR 1485.

[561] See *Achieving Best Evidence in Criminal Proceedings: Guidance for Vulnerable and Intimidated Witnesses Including Children* (2000) Home Office Chapter 2.

[562] *Re W* [2010] UKSC 12, [2010] 2 All ER 418, [2010] 1 FLR 1485. Baroness Hale stated that 'The court is unlikely to be helped by generalised accusations of lying, or by a fishing expedition in which the child is taken slowly through the story yet again in the hope that something will turn up, or by a cross-examination which is designed to intimidate the child and pave the way for accusations of inconsistency in a future criminal trial. On the other hand, focused questions which put forward a different explanation for certain events may help the court to do justice between the parties.'

[563] The Supreme Court stated that an unwilling child should rarely, if ever, be obliged to give evidence (*Re W* [2010] UKSC 12, [2010] 2 All ER 418, [2010] 1 FLR 1485, para 26).

[564] Baroness Hale held that 'That risk of harm is an ever-present feature to which, on the present evidence, the court must give great weight. The risk, and therefore the weight, may vary from case to case, but the court must always take it into account and does not need expert evidence in order to do so' (*Re W* [2010] UKSC 12, [2010] 2 All ER 418, [2010] 1 FLR 1485, para 26).

(m) The steps that can be taken to improve the quality of the child's evidence whilst at the same time decreasing the risk of harm to the child.[565]

6.186 The court may properly refuse to receive oral evidence from a child notwithstanding that he or she is sufficiently competent to be an independent party to those proceedings.[566] In respect of private law proceedings, Baroness Hale concluded as follows in *Re W* in relation to the child giving evidence in such proceedings:[567]

> 'In principle, the approach in private family proceedings between parents should be the same as the approach in care proceedings. However, there are specific risks to which the court must be alive. Allegations of abuse are not being made by a neutral and expert local authority which has nothing to gain by making them, but by a parent who is seeking to gain an advantage in the battle against the other parent. This does not mean that they are false but it does increase the risk of misinterpretation, exaggeration or downright fabrication. On the other hand, the child will not routinely have the protection and support of a Cafcass guardian. There are also many more litigants in person in private proceedings. So if the court does reach the conclusion that justice cannot be done unless the child gives evidence, it will have to take very careful precautions to ensure that the child is not harmed by this.'

6.187 Where a child is called to give evidence, the court must determine whether the child is competent to give evidence, either sworn or unsworn. At common law a child may give sworn evidence provided the court is satisfied after enquiry that the child is competent to give sworn evidence applying the test: 'the child has a sufficient appreciation of the solemnity of the occasion, and the added: responsibility to tell the truth which is involved in taking the oath, over and above the duty to tell the truth which is an ordinary duty of social conduct.[568] If in the court's opinion the child does not understand the nature of an oath, a child's evidence may still be heard by the Court if he understands that it is his duty to speak the truth and is of 'sufficient understanding' to justify his evidence being heard.[569]

6.188 If the court determines that the child is competent to give evidence, the child will be a compellable witness.[570] Any court has an inherent jurisdiction not to require the attendance of witnesses where it would be oppressive to do so.[571] A specific issue order may be used to prevent a parent calling his or her child to give evidence.[572] In deciding whether to issue a witness summons the child's welfare is of great relevance although not

---

[565] The Court considered that 'The important thing is that the questions which challenge the child's account are fairly put to the child so that she can answer them, not that counsel should be able to question her directly (*Re W* [2010] UKSC 12, [2010] 2 All ER 418, [2010] 1 FLR 1485).

[566] *Re O (Care Proceedings: Evidence)* [2003] EWHC 2011 (Fam); [2004] 1 FLR 161.

[567] *Re W* [2010] UKSC 12, [2010] 2 All ER 418, [2010] 1 FLR 1485.

[568] *R v Hayes* [1977] 1 WLR 234; [1977] 2 All ER 288) see also *R v N* (1992) 95 Cr App R 256 (CA Criminal Division). Pursuant to the Oaths Act 1978, s 5 a child who understands the nature of an oath but objects to being sworn may affirm. A child's evidence in criminal proceedings is always given unsworn irrespective of the child's understanding and that testimony must be received unless the child is incapable of giving intelligible testimony (see Criminal Justice Act 1988, s 33A; *DPP v M* [1997] 2 All ER 749, [1997] 2 FLR 804; DPP v G [1997] 2 All ER 755, *sub nom G v DPP* [1997] 2 FLR 810).

[569] CA 1989, s 96(2(b). See also FPC(CA)R 1991, r 16(2) and FPR 1991, r 4.16(2). See also *R v Z* [1990] 2 All ER 971. Where the child is considered to have the capacity to give evidence the child will be a compellable witness but the court retains an inherent jurisdiction not to require the attendance of the witness at court if it would be oppressive (see *R v B County Council ex p P* [1991] 2 All ER 654, [1991] 1 FLR 470). See also the position in respect of criminal proceedings below at **6.199**.

[570] *R v B County Council, ex p P* [1991] 2 All ER 654, [1991] 1 FLR 470.

[571] *R v B County Council, ex p P* [1991] 2 All ER 654, [1991] 1 FLR 470.

[572] [1992] Fam Law 278.

paramount.[573] In principle, the older the child, the more arguable is the application for a witness summons.[574] Children's Guardians should think carefully about arrangements for children to be present and be prepared to explain them to the court.[575] If a child is likely to be unruly the court could refuse to allow him or her to attend.[576]

Participation During Family Proceedings – Seeing the Judge

6.189 The question of whether the judge in family proceedings should see the child to ascertain his or her wishes and feelings remains a controversial one within the domestic jurisdiction.[577] In particular, issues concerning a fair trial for other parties arise in relation to matters communicated by the child to the judge.[578] Whilst the practice does occur in the county court and High Court,[579] in proceedings taking place in the family proceedings court, historically it was held that the magistrates have no right to see the child privately.[580] Under the current case law the circumstances in which magistrates should see a child in private are 'rare and exceptional' where a children's guardian or Cafcass Officer is involved in the case.[581]

6.190 In *Re W (Leave to Remove)*[582] Thorpe LJ opined that the difficulties that had arisen in the case concerning the manner in which the Cafcass intermediary had advanced the children's wishes and feelings might have been avoided had the judge had a meeting with the children. However, in the same appeal both Wilson LJ and Charles J deprecated the idea of the children seeing the judge, Wilson LJ holding that:

> 'Whether judges should meet children (and, even if so, whether they should do so for the purpose of collecting their wishes and feelings) is a difficult and controversial subject which, as Thorpe LJ points out, is currently under examination at a high level, no doubt in particular by reference to the experiences of jurisdictions in which such meetings are more common. It may be that, presumably under the guidance of a set of fully debated and carefully drawn principles and perhaps following a degree of judicial training, the practice of the family courts in England and Wales will come to encompass such meetings (at any rate

---

573   *Re P (Witness Summons)* [1997] 2 FLR 447.
574   *Re P (Witness Summons)* [1997] 2 FLR 447.
575   *Re C (A Minor) (Care: Child's Wishes)* [1993] 1 FLR 832.
576   *Re W (A Minor) (Secure Accommodation Order: Attendance at Court)* [1994] 2 FLR 1092.
577   See Fortin, J *Children's Rights and the Developing Law* (2009) 3rd edn, Cambridge, p 264. The issue is has been examined by a Family Justice Council subcommittee on the 'The Voice of the Child'. The former President of the Family Division has mooted the question of whether judges should in fact review the historic reluctance to allow children to speak to them (see [2006] Fam Law 150 and 170) and has encouraged judges to see children in appropriate cases (see Inaugural Resolution Annual Lecture *Does the Family Justice System serve the needs of Children?* (2008) and *JPC v SLW and SMW (Abduction)* [2007] EWHC 1349 (Fam), [2007] 2 FLR 900, para 47). Guidance has now been issued (see *Guidelines for Judges Meeting Children who are subject to Family Proceedings* Family Justice Council April 2010 and **6.191** below).
578   *B v B (Minors) (Interviews and Listing Arrangements)* [1994] 2 FLR 489 at 495.
579   See *Re D (A Child) (Abduction: Rights of Custody)* [2006] UKHL 51, [2007] 1 All ER 783 per Baroness Hale at para 60.
580   *Re W (A Minor)* (1980) Fam Law 120.
581   *Re M (Minor) (Justices Discretion)* [1993] 2 FLR 706.
582   [2008] EWCA Civ 538, [2008] 2 FLR 1170. See also Buchanan, A, Hunt, J, Bretherton, H and Bream, V *Families in Conflict: Perspectives of Children and Parents on the Family Court Welfare Service* (2001) The Policy Press, Fortin, J *Accommodating Children's Rights in a Post HRA Era* (2006) 69 Modern Law Review 299, Douglas, G, Murch, M, Miles, C and Scanlan, L *Research into the Operation of Rule 9.5 of the Family Proceedings Rules 1991* (2006) Department of Constitutional Affairs and James, A, James, A, and McNamee, S *Turn Down the Volume – Not Hearing the Children in Family Proceedings* (2004) 16 Child and Family Law Quarterly 189 for further discussion on the risk of FCA's interpreting and relaying the views of children through the filter of an adult perspective. See also Schuz, R *The Hague Child Abduction Convention and the United Nations Convention on the Rights of the Child* in Lødrup, P and Modvar, E (eds) *Family Life and Human Rights* (2004) Gyldendal, p 727 noting a similar issue in child abduction proceedings.

for some purposes) more frequently. Presently, however, the discretion of our judges to meet children privately is largely untrammelled by authority; and all that is clear is that such is currently the exception rather than the norm. I would be concerned that a parenthetical expression of opinion, in a case in which the judge was not pressed to see the children and was not criticised by counsel in this appeal for having failed to do so, might, because of the respect in which my Lord's opinions are held, pre-emptively alter that neutral state of affairs.'

6.191 As matters stand, the decision whether or not to see the child in private remains a matter for the discretion of the judge.[583] Guidance has now been issued by the Family Justice Council to assist the Court in making the decision whether to see a child.[584] The guidance provides as follows:

(a) The judge is entitled to expect the lawyer for the child and/or the Cafcass officer:

  (i) to advise whether the child wishes to meet the Judge;
  (ii) if so, to explain from the child's perspective, the purpose of the meeting;
  (iii) to advise whether it accords with the welfare interests of the child for such a meeting take place; and
  (iv) to identify the purpose of the proposed meeting as perceived by the child's professional representative/s.

(b) The other parties shall be entitled to make representations as to any proposed meeting with the Judge before the Judge decides whether or not it shall take place.[585]

(c) In deciding whether or not a meeting shall take place and, if so, in what circumstances, the child's chronological age is relevant but not determinative. Some children of seven or even younger have a clear understanding of their circumstances and very clear views which they may wish to express.[586]

(d) If the child wishes to meet the judge but the judge decides that a meeting would be inappropriate, the judge should consider providing a brief explanation in writing for the child.

(e) If a judge decides to meet a child, it is a matter for the discretion of the judge, having considered representations from the parties –

  (i) the purpose and proposed content of the meeting;
  (ii) at what stage during the proceedings, or after they have concluded, the meeting should take place;[587]
  (iii) where the meeting will take place;[588]
  (iv) who will bring the child to the meeting;
  (v) who will prepare the child for the meeting (this should usually be the Cafcass officer);

---

[583] *Re C (Section 8 order: Court Welfare Officer)* [1995] 1 FLR 617 and *Re CB (Access: Court Welfare Report)* [1995] 1 FLR 622.
[584] *Guidelines for Judges Meeting Children who are subject to Family Proceedings* Family Justice Council April 2010.
[585] *B v B (Minors) (Interviews and Listing Arrangements)* [1994] 2 FLR 489.
[586] *B v B (Minors) (Interviews and Listing Arrangements)* [1994] 2 FLR 489.
[587] *B v B (Minors) (Interviews and Listing Arrangements)* [1994] 2 FLR 489.
[588] *Re R (A Minor) (Residence: Religion)* [1993] 2 FLR 163.

(vi)   who shall attend during the meeting – although a Judge should never see a child alone;[589]

(vii) by whom a minute of the meeting shall be taken, how that minute is to be approved by the Judge, and how it is to be communicated to the other parties.

It cannot be stressed too often that the child's meeting with the judge is not for the purpose of gathering evidence. That is the responsibility of the Cafcass officer. The purpose is to enable the child to gain some understanding of what is going on, and to be reassured that the judge has understood him/her.[590]

(f)   If the meeting takes place prior to the conclusion of the proceedings –

(i)   The judge should explain to the child at an early stage that a judge cannot hold secrets. What is said by the child will, other than in exceptional circumstances, be communicated to his/her parents and other parties.[591]

(ii)   The judge should also explain that decisions in the case are the responsibility of the judge, who will have to weigh a number of factors, and that the outcome is never the responsibility of the child.

(iii) The judge should discuss with the child how his or her decisions will be communicated to the child.

(iv)   The parties or their representatives shall have the opportunity to respond to the content of the meeting, whether by way of oral evidence or submissions.[592]

Participation Post-Proceedings

Participation Post-Proceedings – Public Law

6.192 In public law proceedings, and subject to judicial review, the court's jurisdiction to dictate to the local authority the manner in which it implements its care plan ceases upon the making of a final care or supervision order. The court should determine major issues such as the transfer of parental rights and duties where there is or may be a dispute between parents and local authorities. Thereafter, the management of the case should be the responsibility of the local authority'.[593] Whilst judicial attempts have been made to breach this well defined boundary between judicial and administrative authority, the embargo on judicial intervention in the management of the care plan by the family courts remains.[594] Accordingly, subsequent to the granting of a care order, the following options remain open to the child to participate in the decisions made pursuant to that order and its associated care plan:

(a)   Participation in the statutory review procedures governing children who are the subject of care orders pursuant to s 26 and s 24D of the Children Act 1989.

---

[589]   *L v L (Access: Contempt)* [1991] 1 FCR 547.

[590]   *Re W (Leave to Remove)* [2008] EWCA Civ 538, [2008] 2 FLR 1170, para 61.

[591]   *H v H (Child: Judicial Interview)* [1974] 1 WLR 595; *Elder v Elder* [1986] 1 FLR 610.

[592]   *H v H (Child: Judicial Interview)* [1974] 1 WLR 595; *Elder v Elder* [1986] 1 FLR 610.

[593]   Review of Child Care Law (1985), para 2.20.

[594]   *Re S (Minors) (Care Order: Implementation of Care Plan)*; *Re W (Minors) (Care Order: Adequacy of Care Plan)* [2002] UKHL 10, [2002] 2 WLR 720, [2002] 1 FLR 815.

(b)   Participation in the complaints procedure provided by the Children Act 1989, s 26 and the Children Act 1989 Representations Procedure (England) Regulations 2006.

(c)   An action pursuant to the Human Rights Act 1998 alleging breach of one or more of the child's substantive rights under the ECHR arising out of the implementation or non-implementation of the care plan;[595]

(d)   An action for judicial review challenging one or more of the decisions made pursuant to the implementation of the care plan.[596]

6.193 Review Procedure under the Children Act 1989 – Review is one of the key components within the core process of working with children and families under the domestic public law framework.[597] Primary and secondary legislation provides for a comprehensive review process in respect of children who are 'looked after'[598] under care orders.[599] This process includes the duty to appoint an Independent Reviewing Officer (IRO)[600] who will participate in the review process,[601] monitor the performance of the local authority's functions in respect of the review and refer the case to Cafcass if the IRO considers it appropriate to do so.[602] Cafcass may then take further family proceedings, proceedings under the Human Rights Act 1998 or proceedings for judicial review.[603]

6.194 Where the child wishes to take his or her own proceedings the IRO must assist the child to obtain legal advice or establish whether an appropriate adult is able and

---

[595]   See **3.82** and *Re S (Minors) (Care Order: Implementation of Care Plan)*; *Re W (Minors) (Care Order: Adequacy of Care Plan)* [2002] UKHL 10, [2002] 2 WLR 720, [2002] 1 FLR 815 in which the House of Lords held that 'if a local authority fails to discharge its parental responsibilities properly, and in consequence the rights of the parents under Article 8 are violated, the parents may, as a longstop, bring proceedings against the authority under s 7 … I say 'as a longstop', because other remedies, both of an administrative nature and by way of court proceedings, may also be available in the particular case … Sometimes court proceedings by way of judicial review of a decision of a local authority may be the appropriate way to proceed. In a suitable case an application for discharge of the care order is available. One would not expect proceedings to be launched under s 7 until any other appropriate remedial routes have first been explored.' These principles will apply equally to children.

[596]   See for example *R (on the application of CD) v Isle of Anglesey County Council* [2004] EWHC 1635 (Admin), [2005] 1 FLR 59. Note however that whilst care proceedings subsist, judicial review is not an appropriate method by which to challenge the care plan (see *Re C (Adoption: Religious Observance)* [2002] 1 FLR 1119). A full account of the judicial review procedure is beyond the scope of this work. Reference should be made to Fordham QC, M *Judicial Review Handbook* (2008) 5th edn, Hart Publishing.

[597]   Clarke, Hall and Morrison *Children* LexisNexis, para 1660.3.

[598]   See CA 1989, s 22(1).

[599]   See CA 1989, s 26(1), Review of Children's Cases Regulations 1991, SI 1991/895, the Arrangements for Placement of Children (General) Regulations 1991, SI 1991/890 and the Review of Children's Cases (Amendment) (England) Regulations 2004, SI 2004/1419 (note that from July 2007 the regulations apply to England only. Cases in Wales are governed by the Placement of Children (Wales) Regulations 2007, SI 2007/310 (W 27) and the Review of Children's Cases (Wales) Regulations 2007, SI 2007/307 (W 26)). See also CAFCASS Practice Note, Cases Referred by Independent Reviewing Officers, (November 2004) which explains the functions and duties of the CAFCASS Officer where a case is referred by an IRO.

[600]   'Independent' is a misnomer in this context as the IRO is inevitably an employee of the local authority, although there are limited restrictions on which employees may act in the role of IRO (see Review of Children's Cases Regulations 1991, r 2A(4)).

[601]   See *Independent Reviewing Officers Guidance – Adoption and Children Act 2002* (2004) Dept. for Children, Schools and Families.

[602]   CA 1989, s 26(2A). Note that these provisions have been little used as they relay primarily on the willingness of the IRO referring the matter back to Cafcass.

[603]   See *Re S (Minors) (Care Order: Implementation of Care Plan)*; *Re W (Minors) (Care Order: Adequacy of Care Plan)* [2002] UKHL 10, [2002] 2 WLR 720, [2002] 1 FLR 815.

willing to provide such assistance or to bring proceedings on the child's behalf.[604] Where the child is not in a position to take proceedings and no adult is able or willing to do so, the IRO should, where there is a risk that the child's human rights will be breached, refer the case to Cafcass.[605] Cafcass may then take proceedings on the child's behalf.

6.195 Within the review process, the local authority is under a duty to seek and take into account the views of the child, including the child's views in relation to the particular matters to be considered during the course of the review.[606] This duty goes further than simply asking the child what he or she thinks as the local authority is also under an allied duty to involve the child in the review as so far as is reasonably practicable, including, where the authority considers it appropriate, attending the meeting.[607] In deciding whether attendance is appropriate, it is suggested that the local authority would have to have regard to the requirements of Art 12 of the CRC. The child must be notified of the result of the review and the decisions taken in consequence of it.[608] The duties of the local authority under the Review of Children's Cases Regulations 1991 are reinforced by the wider duties of the local authority to looked after children to ensure that their wishes and feelings are ascertained[609] and given due consideration in accordance with their age and understanding.[610]

6.196 Complaints Procedure under the Children Act 1989, s 26 – Local authorities, voluntary authorities providing accommodation for children and children's homes[611] are required to establish a procedure for considering representations made to them by any child in need or child looked after by it,[612] including any complaint, in respect of the discharge of the local authorities duties under Part III[613] of the CA 1989 and Parts IV and V in relation to functions specified by the appropriate national authority in the regulations.[614] Further, every local authority shall establish a procedure for representations, including complaints, in respect of children who are being given advice and assistance in respect of leaving care.[615] Failure to establish a procedure can be remedied by the default powers of the Secretary of State under CA 1989, s 84.[616] Where there is no dispute as to fact or law, the complaints procedures under s 26 and s 24D of the Children Act 1989 are likely to be a more appropriate remedy than judicial review.[617]

---

[604] Review of Children's Cases Regulations 1991, r 2A(7).

[605] *Independent Reviewing Officers Guidance – Adoption and Children Act 2002* (2004) Dept. for Children, Schools and Families, para 5.4. Cafcass should take the decision whether to issue proceedings within 14 days of the referral from the IRO.

[606] Review of Children's Cases Regulations 1991, r 7(1).

[607] Review of Children's Cases Regulations 1991, r 7(2).

[608] Review of Children's Cases Regulations 1991, r 7(3).

[609] CA 1989, s 22(4).

[610] CA 1989, s 22(5).

[611] See also Children's Homes Regulations 2001, SI 2001/3967, r 24.

[612] CA 1989, s 26(3) with the Children Act 1989 Representations Procedure (England) Regulations 2006, SI 2006/1738, r 21. In England, but not in Wales, the procedure established should extend to the discharge of adoption support services and special guardianship services (see CA 1989, s 26(3B) and r 4). For a detailed description of the complaints procedure see Hershman & McFarlane *Children Law and Practice* Jordan Publishing, para G862 et seq.

[613] See *R v East Sussex CC ex p W* [1998] 2 FLR 1082.

[614] The functions are specified in the Children Act 1989 Representations Procedure (England) Regulations 2006, SI 2006/1738, r 3.

[615] CA 1989, s 24D. See the Children Act 1989 Representations Procedure (England) Regulations 2006, SI 2006/1738.

[616] See *R v London Borough of Barnet ex p S* [1994] 1 FLR 592 at 598 per Auld J.

[617] *R v Birmingham City Council ex p A* [1997] 2 FLR 841.

6.197 A child may complain under the foregoing provisions where the child is being looked after, including a child who believes he or she should be accommodated but is being refused accommodation,[618] or is in need. The responsible authority should always check with the child, subject to their understanding, that a complaint submitted on their behalf reflects their views and that they wish the person submitting it to act on their behalf.[619] In England, but not in Wales, complaints must be made within one year after the grounds for the complaint arose,[620] subject to the local authority's discretion to consider representations made outside this time limit where it would not have been reasonable to expect the complainant to complain within one year and it is still possible to consider the complaint effectively and fairly.[621]

6.198 Pursuant to the Children Act 1989, s 26A(1) the local authority is under a duty to make provision for assistance, including assistance by way of representation, for children making or intending to make complaints under the foregoing provisions.[622] These arrangements must be publicised.[623] Advocacy services must be commissioned in accordance with the National Standards for the Provision of Children's Advocacy Services 2002.

(ii) Criminal Proceedings

Child in Conflict with the Criminal Law

6.199 The age of criminal responsibility in England and Wales is 10 and therefore it is not uncommon for children to before the criminal courts as defendants.[624] There is no distinction between children and adults in terms of the procedure for arrest. Where the child is under the age of 17 and does not seek the services of a solicitor, the child cannot be interviewed without an appropriate adult being present.

6.200 Unlike a child witness, the defendant who is a child must be present in court and is not eligible for any special measures directions under the Youth Justice and Criminal Evidence Act 1999.[625] Following the criticism of the domestic approach to the trial of children in *T v UK*[626] and *V v UK*[627] a Practice Direction entitled *Trial of Young Persons in the Crown Court*[628] was issued by the Lord Chief Justice. Paragraph 3 of the Practice Direction provides that:

> 'Some young defendants accused of committing serious crimes may be very young and very immature when standing trial and in the Crown Court. The purpose of such trial is to determine guilt (if that is in issue) and decide the appropriate sentence if the young defendant pleads guilty or is convicted. The trial process should not itself expose the young defendant to avoidable intimidation, humiliation or distress. All possible steps should be taken to assist the young defendant to understand and participate in the proceedings. The

---

[618] *Royal Borough of Kingston-Upon-Thames ex p T* [1994] 1 FLR 798 at 812 per Ward J.
[619] *Children Act 1989 Guidance and Regulations Vol 3, para* 10.7.
[620] Children Act 1989 Representations Procedure (England) Regulations 2006, r 9(1).
[621] Children Act 1989 Representations Procedure (England) Regulations 2006, r 9(2).
[622] See also Advocacy Services and Representations Procedure (Children)(Amendment) Regulations 2004 SI 2004/719.
[623] CA 1989, s 26A(5).
[624] See chapter 16 for a full discussion on the age of criminal responsibility.
[625] See **6.203** below.
[626] [2000] Crim LR 187.
[627] (1999) 30 EHRR 121.
[628] February 2000.

ordinary trial process should so far as necessary be adapted to meet those ends. Regard should be had to the welfare of the young defendant as required by section 44 of the Children and Young Persons Act 1933.'

6.201   Paragraphs 9 to 16 of the Practice Direction seek to ensure child can effectively participate in the trial process. The measures stipulated by the Practice Direction include the provision of a court room in which all the participants are on the same or almost the same level, where the child can, if he or she wishes, be free to sit with members of his family or others in a like relationship and which permits easy, informal communication with his legal representatives. Further, the Practice Direction provides that the court should explain the course of proceedings to a young defendant in terms he or she can understand. The trial should be conducted according to a timetable which takes full account of a young defendant's inability to concentrate for long periods and robes and wigs should not be worn unless the young defendant asks that they should or the court for good reason orders that they should. Any person responsible for the security of a young defendant who is in custody should not be in uniform. There should be no recognisable Police presence in the court room unless there is a good reason. Finally, facilities for reporting the trial, subject to any direction given under s 39 of the 1933 Act or s 45 of the 1999 Act, must be provided but the court may restrict the number of those attending in the court room. The Practice Direction also stipulates that any other exercise of the courts discretion should be exercised in accordance with the principles in paragraph 3 of the Practice Direction.

Child Witnesses and Victims

6.202   In 1989, the *Report of the Advisory Group on Video Evidence*[629] noted evidence in relation to criminal proceedings to that suggested that 'most children are disturbed to a greater or lesser extent by giving evidence in court' and that giving evidence was for children a 'harmful, oppressive and often traumatic experience'.[630] Within this context, the report recommended that both the evidence-in-chief and cross-examination of child witnesses should be video-recorded and the recording stand as their evidence at the trial. These recommendations were give effect in respect of examination in chief, but not cross examination, by the Criminal Justice Act 1991. In 1992 a *Memorandum of Good Practice on Video Recorded Interviews with Child Witnesses for Criminal Proceedings*[631] was published. This was replaced in 2002 by *Achieving Best Evidence in Criminal Proceedings: Guidance for Vulnerable or Intimidated Witnesses, including Children*[632] and again in 2007 by *Achieving Best Evidence in Criminal Proceedings: Guidance on Interviewing Victims and Witnesses, and Using Special Measures*.[633] This latter guidance stipulates best practice for conducting interviews with children and sets national standards for the preparation of young witnesses prior to the criminal trial.

6.203   Children under 17 years of age[634] acting as witnesses in criminal proceedings[635] can take advantage of the provisions of Part II of the Youth Justice and Criminal

---

[629]   (1989) Home Office ('The Pigot Report').

[630]   Ibid, para 2.10. The Review Group attached 'particular importance to the psychiatric opinion we received which suggests that not only do abused children who testify in court exhibit more signs of disturbed behaviour than those who do not, but that the effects of a court appearance are most severe and prolonged in those who have suffered the worst abuse and those without family support.'

[631]   (1992) HMSO.

[632]   (2002) Home Office Communication Directorate.

[633]   (2007) Home Office.

[634]   Youth Justice and Criminal Evidence Act 1999. Young people aged between 17 and 18 may be able to take advantage of the provisions of s 17 of the Act which allow special measures to be used where the quality of

Evidence Act 1999.[636] A number of special measures to assist children to give evidence in criminal cases are available,[637] including screens,[638] live television links,[639] using video-recordings as evidence-in-chief,[640] and cross-examination and re-examination,[641] the exclusion of specified persons from the court room during the giving of evidence,[642] providing aids to communication,[643] examining the witness through an approved intermediary[644] and the removal by advocates of their wigs and/or gowns.[645] Pursuant to s 35 of the Youth Justice and Criminal Evidence Act 1999 no person charged with an offence to which s 35 applies[646] may cross-examine in person a child[647] in connection with that offence or in connection with any other offence of whatever nature with which that person is charged in the proceedings. These provisions have been held by the House of Lords to be compliant with the requirements of Art 6 of the ECHR. In *R v Camberwell Green Youth Court ex p D (a minor)(by his mother and litigation friend)*[648] Baroness Hale held in relation to the special measures implemented to protect child witnesses pursuant to the Youth Justice and Criminal Evidence Act 1999, s 21(5) that:

> 'All the evidence is produced at the trial in the presence of the accused, some of it in pre-recorded form and some of it by contemporaneous television transmission. The accused can see and hear it all. The accused has every opportunity to challenge and question the witnesses against him at the trial itself. The only thing missing is a face to face confrontation, but the appellants accept that the Convention does not guarantee a right to face to face confrontation. This case is completely different from the case of anonymous witnesses. Even then the Strasbourg Court has accepted that exceptions may be made, provided that

---

evidence given by the witness is likely to be diminished by reason of fear or distress on the part of the witness in connection with testifying in the proceedings.

[635] Note that under s 36 of the Children and Young Persons Act 1933, as amended by s 73(1) of the Access to Justice Act 1999, no child other than an infant is permitted to be present in court except when required as a witness.

[636] See also *Achieving Best Evidence in Criminal Proceedings: Guidance on Interviewing Victims and Witnesses, and Using Special Measures* (2007) Home Office.

[637] Recent research has shown that, although special measures have made the experience better for children giving evidence in the criminal courts, many still find it difficult and stressful (see Plotnikoff, J and Woolfson, R *Measuring up? Evaluating implementation of Government commitments to young witnesses in criminal proceedings* (2009) Nuffield Foundation and NSPCC).

[638] Youth Justice and Criminal Evidence Act 1999, s 23.

[639] Youth Justice and Criminal Evidence Act 1999, s 24.

[640] Youth Justice and Criminal Evidence Act 1999, s 27.

[641] Youth Justice and Criminal Evidence Act 1999, s 28.

[642] Youth Justice and Criminal Evidence Act 1999, s 25.

[643] Youth Justice and Criminal Evidence Act 1999, s 30.

[644] Youth Justice and Criminal Evidence Act 1999, ss 29. See also the Criminal Justice Act 2003, ss 114–118 which now allow for hearsay evidence to be given in criminal trials in a much wider set of circumstances than previously.

[645] Youth Justice and Criminal Evidence Act 1999, s 26. See ss 31–33 for the status of evidence given under special measures. See also the Criminal Evidence (Witness Anonymity) Act 2008.

[646] Section 35 applies to offences under the Sexual Offences Act 1956, the Indecency with Children Act 1960, the Sexual Offences Act 1967, s 54 of the Criminal Law Act 1977, the Protection of Children Act 1978, offences of kidnapping, false imprisonment or offences under ss 1 or 2 of the Child Abduction Act 1984, any offence under s 1 of the Children and Young Persons Act 1933 and any offence which involves an assault on, or injury or threat of injury to any person. See ss 38–39 for the provisions concerning assistance to the accused in respect of cross-examination.

[647] Pursuant to s 35(4) of the Act, 'child' means a person under the age of 17 where the offence is one under the Sexual Offences Act 1956, the Indecency with Children Act 1960, the Sexual Offences Act 1967, s 54 of the Criminal Law Act 1977 or the Protection of Children Act 1978 and a person under the age of 14 where the offence is one of kidnapping, false imprisonment or offences under ss 1 or 2 of the Child Abduction Act 1984, any offence under s 1 of the Children and Young Persons Act 1933 and any offence which involves an assault on, or injury or threat of injury to any person.

[648] [2005] UKHL 4, [2005] 1 WLR 393, para 49.

sufficient steps are taken to counter-balance the handicaps under which the defence laboured and a conviction is not based solely or decisively on anonymous statements.'

6.204 The 1999 Act permits witnesses of any age to give unsworn evidence in criminal proceedings unless it appears to the court that they are unable to understand the questions put or to give intelligible answers. Pursuant to s 53 of the Youth Justice and Criminal Evidence Act 1999 at every stage in criminal proceedings all person are, whatever their age, competent to give evidence unless they are not able to understand question put to them and give answers which can be understood. In *R v Barker*[649] the Court of Appeal considered a case in which a child aged four had given evidence in chief by video recording and had been cross examined via video link. The Court of Appeal held that in applying the provisions of s 53 if the Act:[650]

'The question in each case is whether the individual witness, or, as in this case, the individual child, is competent to give evidence in the particular trial. The question is entirely witness or child specific. There are no presumptions or preconceptions. The witness need not understand the special importance that the truth should be told in court, and the witness need not understand every single question or give a readily understood answer to every question. Many competent adult witnesses would fail such a competency test. Dealing with it broadly and fairly, provided the witness can understand the questions put to him and can also provide understandable answers, he or she is competent. If the witness cannot understand the questions or his answers to questions which he understands cannot themselves be understood he is not. The questions come, of course, from both sides. If the child is called as a witness by the prosecution he or she must have the ability to understand the questions put to him by the defence as well as the prosecution and to provide answers to them which are understandable... In particular, although the chronological age of the child will inevitably help to inform the judicial decision about competency, in the end the decision is a decision about the individual child and his or her competence to give evidence in the particular trial ...'

The Court of Appeal further observed that:

'We emphasise that in our collective experience the age of a witness is not determinative on his or her ability to give truthful and accurate evidence. Like adults some children will provide truthful and accurate testimony, and some will not. However children are not miniature adults, but children, and to be treated and judged for what they are, not what they will, in years ahead, grow to be. Therefore, although due allowance must be made in the trial process for the fact that they are children with, for example, a shorter attention span than most adults, none of the characteristics of childhood, and none of the special measures which apply to the evidence of children carry with them the implicit stigma that children should be deemed in advance to be somehow less reliable than adults. The purpose of the trial process is to identify the evidence which is reliable and that which is not, whether it comes from an adult or a child. If competent, as defined by the statutory criteria, in the context of credibility in the forensic process, the child witness starts off on the basis of equality with every other witness. In trial by jury, his or her credibility is to be assessed by the jury, taking into account every specific personal characteristic which may bear on the issue of credibility, along with the rest of the available evidence.'

---

[649] [2010] EWCA Crim 4, [2010] All ER (D) 126 (Jan). See also *R v MacPherson* [2006] 1 CAR 30: *R v Powell* [2006] 1 CAR 31: *R v M* [2008] EWCA Crim 2751 and *R v Malicki* [2009] EWCA Crim 365.

[650] The competency test may be re-analysed at the end of the child's evidence (see *R v Barker* [2010] EWCA Crim 4, [2010] All ER (D) 126 (Jan), para 43).

(iii) Civil Proceedings

6.205 Within the context of civil litigation, CPR 1998, r 21.2(2) requires that a child must have a litigation friend to conduct civil proceedings on his behalf unless the court permits the child to conduct proceedings without a litigation friend pursuant to CPR, r 21.2(3).[651] Part 21 does not provide a test of 'sufficient understanding' but in *Masterman-Lister v Brutton & Co and Jewell & anor*[652] Chadwick LJ held that:

> '[T]he test to be applied ... is whether the party to legal proceedings is capable of understanding, with the assistance of such proper explanation from legal advisers and experts in other disciplines as the case may require, the issues on which his consent or decision is likely to be necessary in the course of those proceedings. If he has capacity to understand that which he needs to understand in order to pursue or defend a claim, I can see no reason why the law – whether substantive or procedural – should require the interposition of a next friend or guardian ad litem (or, as such a person is now described in the CPR, a litigation friend).'

(iv) Immigration Proceedings

Pre-Proceedings

6.206 Pursuant to r 349 of the Immigration Rules an unaccompanied child may claim asylum in their own right.[653] In assessing the claim account should be taken of the applicant's maturity and more weight should be given to objective indications of risk than to the child's state of mind and understanding of his situation. An asylum application made on behalf of a child should not be refused solely because the child is too young to understand his situation or to have formed a well founded fear of persecution. Close attention should be given to the welfare of the child at all times.[654] Any child over the age of 12 who has claimed asylum in his own right must be interviewed about the substance of his claim unless the child is unfit or unable to be interviewed. When an interview takes place it must be conducted in the presence of a parent, guardian, representative or another adult independent of the Secretary of State who has responsibility for the child. The interviewer must have specialist training in the interviewing of children and pay particular regard to the possibility that a child will feel inhibited or alarmed. The child must be allowed to express himself in his own way and at his own speed. If the child appears tired or distressed, the interview must be stopped.[655] As soon as possible after an unaccompanied child makes an application for asylum he or she must be provided with a representative to represent and/or assist the child with respect to the examination of the application, to inform the child about the meaning and possible consequences of the interview and, where appropriate, how to prepare himself for the interview. The representative has the right to be present at the interview and ask questions and make comments in the interview, within the framework set by the interviewer.[656]

---

[651] For an example of children taking part in civil proceedings see *Scotching v Birch* [2008] EWHC 844 (Ch), [2008] All ER (D) 265 (Mar) in which the children sought to argue that they had a right to participate in the arrangements for the funeral of their deceased sibling under Art 12 of the CRC and Art 8 of the ECHR.

[652] [2003] 3 All ER 162.

[653] Where the claim is made by an unaccompanied child it must still be made at the earliest opportunity (Immigration Rules, r 349).

[654] Immigration Rules, r 351.

[655] Immigration Rules, r 352.

[656] Immigration Rules, r 352ZA.

Proceedings before the First Tier Tribunal (Asylum and Immigration)

6.207 The Asylum and Immigration Tribunal *Guidance Note No 8 Unaccompanied Children* remains relevant to First Tier Tribunal (Asylum and Immigration) hearings. The Guidance provides that cases involving unaccompanied children should always be placed first on the list.[657] The child should be legal represented and where the child does not have legal representation, the case should be adjourned in order that the same can be obtained.[658] Where the age of the child is in dispute the appellant should be treated as a child for the purposes of the proceedings.[659] The child should have an appropriate adult with them at all hearings and every effort should be made to ensure that the child has an interpreter who speaks their primary language.[660] A statement should be taken from the child in accordance with the Statement *of Good Practice*.[661] An order should normally be made to exclude members of the public from the hearing in accordance with r 50(3)(b) of the Immigration and Asylum Appeals (Procedure) Rules 2003.[662] Whether the child gives evidence at the hearing should be assessed taking into account their age, maturity, their capacity to give evidence, any relevant expert evidence on the child's condition, and relevant cultural differences.[663] The assessment of the extent to which a child's fear of persecution is well founded 'may call for a liberal application of the benefit of the doubt'.[664]

Domestic Application of the Child's Right to Participate – Education

6.208 The Crick committee recommended that school administrations should consult with pupils over elements of school administration and life and, wherever possible, give pupils responsibility and experience in running parts of their school.[665] There is now a duty to invite and consider pupils' views over the conduct of the school pursuant to s 29B of the Education Act 2002 having regard to their age and understanding.[666] Likewise, pursuant to s 176(1) it is the duty of the local education authority, in the exercise of any of their school functions, and of the governing body of a maintained school in relation to the exercise of any function relating to the conduct of the school to have regard to any guidance given from time to time by the Secretary of State in relation to consultation with pupils in connection with the taking of decisions affecting them.[667] In this regard it is important to remember that children with special educational needs must be considered as people in their own right rather than simply accepting as

---

[657] Asylum and Immigration Tribunal *Guidance Note No 8 Unaccompanied Children*, para 2.2.

[658] Asylum and Immigration Tribunal *Guidance Note No 8 Unaccompanied Children*, para 3.1.

[659] Asylum and Immigration Tribunal *Guidance Note No 8 Unaccompanied Children*, para 3.4.

[660] Asylum and Immigration Tribunal *Guidance Note No 8 Unaccompanied Children*, paras 3.7 and 3.9.

[661] (2000) 2nd edn, Separated Children in Europe Programme.

[662] Para 3.17.

[663] Para 4.6. See also *Practice Direction First Tier and Upper Tribunal – Child, Vulnerable Adult and Sensitive Witnesses* (2008) Tribunals Judiciary.

[664] See *Jatikay* (12658) 15 November 1995 (IAT).

[665] Crick, B *Education for Citizenship and Teaching Democracy in Schools* (1998) Advisory Group on Citizenship, Qualifications and Curriculum Authority, p 36. Unfortunately, the minimum age for becoming a school governor is 18 (Education (No 2) Act 1986). Whilst a child may become an associate member of the Committee of Governors, associate members have no voting rights.

[666] As inserted by the Education and Skills Act 2008, s 157. For the likely content of regulations implementing this measure see the School Councils (Wales) Regulations 2005, SI 2005/3200.

[667] The Committee on the Rights of the Child expects systematic consultation over *any* matter regarding school administration (see Committee on the Rights of the Child *Concluding Observations of the Committee on the Rights of the Child: United Kingdom of Great Britain and Northern Ireland* (2002) CRC/C/15/Add.188, paras 29 and 30 and see Committee on the Rights of the Child *Concluding Observations of the Committee on the Rights of the Child: United Kingdom of Great Britain and Northern Ireland* (2008) CRC/C/GBR/CO/4, paras 32, 66(a) and 67(g).

definitive adult views on how they should be educated.[668] Head teaches must consult pupils prior to drawing up a behaviour policy pursuant to the Education and Inspections Act 2006, s 88(3)(c) and (d).

6.209 However, it remains the case that parents rather than children have the legal right to decide which school the child will attend with no legal provision for children with sufficient understanding to challenge parental choice. Children have no right to complain about the standard of their education and may only be associate members of governing bodies.[669]

Proceedings before the First Tier Tribunal (SEND)

6.208 As matters stand at present, children are not expected to play any formal part in SEND proceedings. Children do not have party status before the tribunal and are not entitled to representation.[670] Children cannot initiate appeals to the tribunal. As Fortin notes, this situation assumes that the interests of children with special educational needs and the interests of their parents are always co-terminus.[671] The current regulations which apply to SEND do not contain any provision for ascertaining the child's wishes and feelings and brining the same before the tribunal. The tribunal does receive a 'Child's statement',[672] the Local Authority must ascertain the views of the child as to the matter which is appealed, those views must be stated to the tribunal[673] and the child may attend the hearing.[674] It is difficult however to see these provisions at present as compliant with the requirements of Art 12(2) of the CRC, not least because the views of the child are ascertained by an authority whose interests may not, by the very fact that the matter is before SEND, be co-terminus with those of the child. Whilst it may be argued that parents are able to represent their child's position before the Tribunal, once again this relies on the questionable assumption that the interests of the child and those of the parents are always co-terminus.

Domestic Application of the Child's Right to Participate – Wider Participation in Society

6.211 Children under 16 must be in full time education.[675] Children between 16 and 18 will shortly be required to remain in formal education or accredited training.[676] Children

---

668 Fortin, J *Children's Rights and the Developing Law* (2009) 3rd edn, Cambridge, p 457 citing the example of *R V (Care or Supervision Order)* [1996] 1 FLR 776. See also the SEN Code of Practice, paras 3.1–3.2.

669 Children's Rights Alliance, *State of Children's Rights in England* (2008), p 12.

670 *S v Special Educational Needs Tribunal and the City of Westminster* [1996] ELR 228 and *London Borough of Wandsworth v Mrs K and Special Needs and Disability Tribunal* [2003] EWHC 1424 (Admin), [2003] ELR 554. This position has been critcised by the Committee on the Rights of the Child Committee on the Rights of the Child by reference to Art 12 of the CRC (see Concluding Observations of the Committee on the Rights of the Child: United Kingdom of Great Britain and Northern Ireland (1995) CRC/C/15/Add. 34, para 14 and Committee on the Rights of the Child Concluding Observations of the Committee on the Rights of the Child: United Kingdom of Great Britain and Northan Ireland (2008) CRC/C/GBR/CO/4, para 66(a) and 67(h)). It is however unlikely that it can be addressed by reference to Art 6 of the ECHR (see *Simpson v United Kingdom* (1989) 64 DR 188).

671 Fortin, J *Children's Rights and the Developing Law* (2009) 3rd edn, Cambridge, p 458.

672 Practice Direction: Health, Education and Social Care Chamber Special Educational Needs or Disability in Schools Cases, para 2(b).

673 The Tribunal Procedure (First-tier Tribunal) (Health Education and Social Care Chamber) Rules 2008, SI 2008/2699 (L 16), r 21(2)(e). Where the local authority has not ascertained the child's views it must explain why.

674 The Tribunal Procedure (First-tier Tribunal) (Health Education and Social Care Chamber) Rules 2008, SI 2008/2699 (L 16), r 24 and see Harris, N *Special Educational Needs and Access to Justice* (1997) Jordans, pp 146–151.

675 The rules governing extent to which children may work when under 16 are confusing and ineffective. (See the

under the age of 18 are unable to vote,[677] stand for Parliament[678] or local Government,[679] be a school governor, acquire a legal estate in land[680] or be a tenant for life or exercise the powers of a tenant for life of settled land,[681] serve on a jury,[682] enter into an enforceable contract[683] or make a will[684] and are subject to significant restrictions on their financial independence. They can claim only limited welfare benefits and, excepting contracts for the supply of necessaries and contracts of service, cannot enter into legally binding contracts.[685] As Fortin points out 'Freedom from the restrictions of family life is often a bleak experience for those who have no correlative rights to financial help or accommodation'.[686]

6.212 However, confusingly, at 16 children can consent to surgical, medical or dental treatment,[687] leave school,[688] marry with the consent of their parents, enlist in the armed forces with the consent of their parents[689] and have lawful sexual intercourse.[690] Children over 17 can drive[691] and act as a pilot in command of an aircraft under a private pilots licence.[692] Under the current law, children over 16 may leave school and

---

Children and Young Persons Act 1933, s 18 (as amended) which governs the hours and type of work that may be undertaken by children aged 13 to 15). These provisions must be considered in light of EC regulation and in particular European Council Directive on the Protection of Young People at Work (94/33/EC) (See also Children (Protection at Work) Regulations 1998, SI 1998/276, the Children (Protection at Work) Regulations 2000, SI 2000/1333 and the Children (Protection at Work)(No 2) Regulations 2000, SI 2000/2548.

676   Education and Skills Act 2008, s 2.
677   Representation of the People Act 1983, s 1(1). In 2004 the Electoral Commission rejected widespread calls to lower the voting age to 16 (see *Age of Electoral Majority: Report and Recommendations* (2004) The Electoral Commission).
678   Electoral Administration Act 2006, s 17. However a child can be a sheriff (*Young v Fowler* (1640) Cro Car 555; *Claridge and Evelyn* (1821) 5 B & Ald 81 at 86 Abbott CJ) or a goaler (2 Co Inst 382; Com Dig Officer (B 3); *Wittingham's Case* (1603) 8 Co Rep 42b at 44b per Coke CJ; *Young v Fowler* (1640) Cro Car 555; *Claridge and Evelyn* (1821) 5 B & Ald 81 at 86 Abbott CJ) and may hold any office for which he or she may appoint a deputy (*Young v Stoell* (1632) Cro Car 279; *Young v Fowler* (1640) Cro Car 555; *Claridge and Evelyn* (1821) 5 B & Ald 81 at 86 Abbott CJ) or which is ministerial and does not involve discretion (Bac. Abr Infancy and Age (E); Com Dig Officer (B 3); *Crosbie v Huxley* (1833) Alc & N 431 at 440 per Bush CJ).
679   Local Government Act 1972, s 79.
680   Law of Property Act 1925, s 1(6).
681   Settled Land Act 1925, ss 19–20. Although a child may be lord of a manor and perform the functions of the office (*Swayne's Case* (1608) 8 Co Rep 63a at 63b per Coke J).
682   Juries Act 1974, s 1(a) as substituted by the Criminal Justice Act 2003, s 321 Sch 33, paras 1 and 2.
683   Minors Contracts Act 1987. However, a child may be liable for income tax (*R v Newmarket Income Tax Comrs, ex p Huxley* [1916] 1 KB 788 CA) and may be made bankrupt if the petition is based on an enforceable debt (*Re Debtor (No 564 of 1949), ex p Customs and Excise Comrs v Debtor* [1950] Ch 282, [1950] 1 All ER 308 CA; *Re A and M* {1926] Ch 274; *Re Davenport, ex p The Bankrupt v Eric Street Properties Limited* [1963] 2 All ER 850, [1963] 1 WLR 817, CA).
684   Wills Act 1837, s 7 (as amended by the Statute Law Revision (No 2) Act 1888 and the Family Law Reform Act 1969, s 3(1)(a)). However, a child who is a soldier or a sailor at sea may validly dispose of property by will (Wills Act 1837, s 11 and the Wills (Soldiers and Sailors) Act 1918, ss 1 and 2 as amended by the Family Law Reform Act 1969, s 3(1)(b)).
685   *Proform Sports Management Limited v Proactive Sports Management Limited and anor.* [2006] EWHC 2812 (Ch), [2007] 1 All ER 542.
686   Fortin, J *Children's Rights and the Developing Law* (2009) 3rd edn, Cambridge, p 123.
687   Family Law Reform Act 1969, s 8(1).
688   Pursuant to the Education and Skills Act 2008, s 2 education or training by way of a contract of apprenticeship will become compulsory up to the age of 17 from 2013 and compulsory up to the age of 18 from 2015.
689   Army Act 1955, s 2(3)(a).
690   Sexual Offences (Amendment) Act 2000.
691   Road Traffic Act 1988, s 101(1).
692   Air Navigation Order 2005, SI 2005/1970, Sch 8. A child aged 16 and over may act as a pilot in command of a glider (Air Navigation Order 2005, SI 2005/1970, art 37).

begin full time work although their entitlement to the statutory minimum wage is limited to an 'introductory' rate lower than the 'development' rate paid to 18 to 21 year olds.

6.213 The question of whether the child can leave home to participate fully in society without parental restriction has not been definitively decided. The European case of *Nielsen v Denmark*[693] would suggest not but obiter comments in *Re K (Secure Accommodation Order: Right to Liberty)*[694] suggests a more liberal approach may be taken under domestic law. Both Butler-Sloss LJ[695] and Judge LJ[696] suggested obiter that the parent cannot restrict the liberty of a child for more than a few days.[697] Fortin suggests that if the Courts were to follow these obiter comments parents would find it difficult to justify preventing a child from leaving home[698] In *Re K* Butler-Sloss LJ considered that the Court's response should depend on whether the parents actions were 'within ordinary acceptable parental restrictions on the movement of a child'.

6.214 The law is in a state of confusion as to whether the courts can force the return of a child who has elected to leave home.[699] Section 2 of the Child Abduction and Custody Act 1985 is very wide in scope and can potentially result in a person who provides advice and assistance to a child under 16 who is running away from home[700] although the defence of reasonable excuse is likely to be available in respect of a '*Gillick*' competent child.[701] Department of Health Guidance provides that children who run away are likely to be children in need for the purposes of s 17 of the Children Act 1989 and as such are entitled to services from the Local Authority.[702] New guidance accordingly requires a full needs assessment and welfare interview.[703] Where a child seeks to live with another adult the Court may formalise the position with a residence order pursuant to s 8 of the Children Act 1989.[704] With leave under s 10(8) the child him or herself may apply for such relief.[705]

---

[693] (1988) 11 EHRR 175.

[694] [2001] 1 FLR 526.

[695] At para 29.

[696] At para 101.

[697] But see the views of Lord Justice Thorpe at para 61 where he considers that the deprivation of liberty as a necessary consequence of the exercise of parental responsibility for the protection and promotion of the child's welfare will not amount to a breach of Art 5 of the ECHR.

[698] Fortin, J *Children's Rights and the Developing Law* (2009) 3rd edn, Cambridge, p 117.

[699] Formerly, applications were made for writs of habeas corpus by parents attempting to secure the return of children who had elected to leave home. The Courts would refuse to issue such writs once the children in question had reached the 'age of discretion' which age was 14 for boys and 16 for girls (see *R v Howes* (1860) 3 E&E 332 and *Krishnan v London Borough of Sutton* [1970] Ch 181. See also *Regina v D* [1984] FLR 847 in relation to the role of the child's consent in cases of kidnap).

[700] See *R v Leather* [1993] 2 FLR 770. Where the child is over the age of 16 the criminal sanctions on neglect and harbouring cease.

[701] Fortin, J *Children's Rights and the Developing Law* (2009) 3rd edn, Cambridge, p 119.

[702] *Children Missing from Care and from Home: A Guide to Good Practice* (2002) Department of Health.

[703] *Young Runaways Action Plan* (2008) Department for Children, Schools and Families.

[704] Such an order will provide protection from the provisions of the Child Abduction Act 1984 and the Sexual Offences Act 1956 and also provide a degree legal certainty for the arrangement (see *B v B (A Minor) (Residence Order)* [1992] 2 FLR 327).

[705] The interests of the child are not paramount in such an application (see *Re SC (A Minor) (Leave to Seek a Residence Order)* [1994] 1 FLR 96; *Re C (Residence: Child's Application for Leave)* [1995] 1 FLR 927 and *Re H (Residence Order: Child's Application for Leave)* [2000] 1 FLR 780). Applications for leave by children should be heard in the High Court.

CONCLUSION

6.215 Article 12 of the CRC and Arts 6 and 8 of the ECHR provide a compelling foundation for the participation of the child in domestic legal, administrative and social contexts. However, the degree to which domestic systems measure up to the demands of these international and regional legal provisions is variable. Whilst Fortin has described the system for the representation of children in domestic public law proceedings as 'an impressive one which fully complies with the requirements of international instruments such as the CRC, the continuing validity of this description is increasingly threatened.[706] With Cafcass increasingly unable to match the performance of the systems of child representation that went before it, consistent domestic compliance with Art 12 of the CRC in public law proceedings is becoming ever more difficult.

6.216 Elsewhere the picture also leaves no room for complacency. There remains a stubborn domestic dichotomy between the position of children in private law and their position in public law proceedings, the case of *Re W (Leave to Remove)*[707] demonstrating how the private law system can fail children in giving effect to their right to participate. Moreover, by virtue of the provisions of s 1(4)(a) and s 1(4)(b) of the 1989 Act there remains a stark differential within private law proceedings in terms of participation by the child as between children whose parents contest their arrangements and parents who do not. For the latter group of children, in court conciliation is still not consistently ensuring that the child's right to participate is given effect in a manner commensurate with the child's age and understanding. Even when they are involved, there is a suggestion it is to break an adult impasses rather than truly to secure the views of the child and their genuine participation in the process and that the process may place too greater weight on children's shoulders.[708] In a wider context, the provision for children to participate in wider society and in decisions taken by Government which affect them are still in their fledgling stages. Participation in policy making tends to be facilitated by voluntary organisations and NGOs rather than by the Government directly engaging with children.[709] In both the legal sphere and more widely in society, we have a long way to go before it can be said that the imperatives of Art 12 of the CRC are met in the United Kingdom.

---

[706] Fortin, J *Children's Rights and the Developing Law* (2009) 3rd edn, Cambridge, p 273. Fortin however notes that the increasing concentration by Cafcass on private law cases, the implementation of the Public Law Outline and resource issues all threaten the systems current compliance with international human rights instruments.

[707] [2008] EWCA Civ 538, [2008] 2 FLR 1170. See also Buchanan, A, Hunt, J, Bretherton, H and Bream, V *Families in Conflict: Perspectives of Children and Parents on the Family Court Welfare Service* (2001) The Policy Press, Fortin, J *Accommodating Children's Rights in a Post HRA Era* (2006) 69 Modern Law Review 299, Douglas, G, Murch, M, Miles, C and Scanlan, L *Research into the Operation of Rule 9.5 of the Family Proceedings Rules 1991* (2006) Department of Constitutional Affairs and James, A, James, A, and McNamee, S *Turn Down the Volume – Not Hearing the Children in Family Proceedings* (2004) 16 Child and Family Law Quarterly 189 for further discussion on the risk of FCA's interpreting and relaying the views of children through the filter of an adult perspective.

[708] Trinder, L, Connolly, J, Kellett, J, Notley, C and Swift, L *Making Contact Happen or Making Contact Work? The Process and Outcomes of In Court Conciliation* (2006) Department of Constitutional Affairs, pp 97–98.

[709] See for example Williams, S *Children's Express – A Voice for Young People in an Adult World* in Franklin, B (ed) *The New Handbook of Children's Rights* (2002) Routledge, p 254.

Chapter 7

THE CHILD'S RIGHT TO IDENTITY

'Why does the wind blow upon me so wild?
Is it because I am nobody's child?'

Phila Henrietta Case fl. 1864

INTRODUCTION

7.1   Identity is the condition of being a specified, identifiable person both as a unique separate individual and as a recognised member of a group.[1] Identity also has an important cultural content and is essential for relationships between each individual and the rest of society, for his or her understanding of the outside world, and his or her place in it.[2] As Van Bueren eloquently points out, identity is what makes a person visible to society.[3] Given their often less than visible position in society, and the disadvantages and risks consequent on that lack of visibility, the right to identity is a particularly important right for children. It is also a right which prior to the CRC did not exist for children under international law.[4]

7.2   Articles 7 and 8 of the CRC make clear that the child's right to identity itself encompasses a number of further rights. Article 7 of the CRC states that:

> 'The child shall be registered immediately after birth and shall have the right from birth to a name, the right to acquire a nationality and as far as possible, the right to know and be cared for by his or her parents.'

Article 8 of the CRC provides that 'States Parties undertake to respect the right of the child to preserve his or her identity, including his or her nationality, name and family relations'.[5] The rights to name, registration and nationality articulated in Arts 7 and 8 are also enshrined in other international human rights instruments. In particular, Arts 24(2) and (3) of the International Covenant on Civil and Political Rights provide that every child shall be registered immediately after birth and shall have a name and that every child has the right to acquire a nationality. Within the context of the ECHR, the right to understand and determine one's identity is a fundamental element of the

---

[1]   Jenkins, R *Social Identity* (2004) Routledge.

[2]   Dissenting judgment of Judge Cançado Trindade in *Serrano-Cruz Sisters v El Salvador* IACHR 1 March 2005 Series C No 120.

[3]   Van Bueren, G *The International Law on the Rights of the Child* (1998) Martinus Nijhoff, p 117.

[4]   Van Bueren, G *The International Law on the Rights of the Child* (1998) Martinus Nijhoff, p 16. See also the Convention on the Prevention and Punishment of the Crime of Genocide 1948, Art 11(e).

[5]   Article 8 of the CRC was introduced by Argentina at a time when the country was attempting to locate children who disappeared under the military junta in the 1970s and 1980s (E/CN.4/1986/39, pp 8–10). As Van Bueren points out however, when read with the other articles of the CRC, Art 8 may have implications beyond the concerns of the principle drafters (see Van Bueren, G *The International Law on the Rights of the Child* (1998) Martinus Nijhoff, p 127). See also the UN Declaration on the Protection of All Persons from Enforced Disappearance (A/RES/47/133) and the International Convention for the Protection of All Persons from Enforced Disappearance Art 25.

right to respect for private life under Art 8 of the ECHR and is closely linked to family life.[6] The European Court of Human Rights recognises names as constituting 'central elements of self-identification and self-definition'.[7]

7.3   Under the provisions of the CRC and the ECHR, the child's right to identity is thus formulated by specific reference to name, nationality and family. However, whilst not specifically articulated by the CRC or the ECHR, it is important to remember that, in addition to name, nationality and family relations, a child's identity will also comprise his or her personal history since birth, his or her race, culture, religion[8] and language and the child's physical appearance, abilities, gender identity and sexual orientation.[9] The right to identity can thus also be inferred from other substantive rights including the right to freedom of thought, conscience and religion and the right to freedom of expression.[10] Each of these elements of the child's individuality fall to be preserved by the child's right to identity.

7.4   The broad composition of a child's identity, and in particular the function of family relationships as an element of that identity, renders the conceptualisation and preservation of the child's identity an increasingly complex task. In particular, developments in the science of donor conception and the practice of adoption have significantly complicated questions concerning the child's right to know and be cared for by his or her parents; whilst at the same time developments in DNA testing have made it infinitely easier for the child to identity accurately who his or her biological parents are. In this context, and having regard to the child's right to know and be cared for by his or her parents, arguments over the child's right to knowledge of his or her origins as a fundamental element of identity can now become easily conflated with arguments over whether the child should have a social relationship with his or her biological father.[11]

7.5   This chapter considers in detail the key principles underpinning the child's right to identity, including the right to a name, to a nationality and the right to know and be cared for by parents, and the key issues to which that right gives rise. The right to identity is considered within the context of both the framework provided by international and regional human rights instruments and under domestic law.[12]

---

6   Lord Lester QC, Lord Pannick QC and Herberg, J *Human Rights Law and Practice* (2009) 3rd edn, LexisNexis, p 375.

7   *Daroczy v Hungary* Application 44378/05 (unreported) 1 July 2008, para 32. This principle will also encompass titles (see *Ardgowan (Baron) v Lord Lyon King of Arms* [2008] CSOH 36).

8   See Scolnicov, A *The Child's Right to Religious Freedom and the Formation of Identity* (2007) 15 International Journal of Children's Rights 251 and below at chapter 10.

9   Newell, P and Hodgkin, R *Implementation Handbook for the Convention on the Rights of the Child* (2008) 3rd edn, UNICEF, p 115.

10   See the dissenting judgment of Judge Cançado Trindade in *Serrano-Cruz Sisters v El Salvador* IACHR 1 March 2005 Series C No 120, para 22.

11   Wallbank, J *The Role of Rights and Utility in Instituting a Child's Right to Know Her Genetic History* (2004) 13 Social and Legal Studies, p 253.

12   In this chapter, the concept of the right to be cared for parents is examined from the perspective of the child's right to identity. In chapter 8, the right is further examined in the context of the child's right to family life. In respect of the latter, it should be remembered that cases involving disputes as to contact and residence will necessarily involve some consideration of the child's right to identity when considering the proper outcome in such cases.

GENERAL PRINCIPLES

General Principles – Right to Identity from Birth

7.6   For children, the right to identity is not something which evolves or is earned over time. Identity, for the purposes of the child's human rights, is a fully developed concept from birth.[13] Whilst the child's development and evolving capacity may result in the growth of traits which come to form part of the individual child's identity, the child's right to identity exists independently from the concepts of child development and evolving capacity. Article 7(1) of the CRC makes clear that its provisions as concerning the child's right to identity apply immediately upon the birth of the child.[14]

General Principles – Right to Registration

7.7   Registration of birth constitutes 'a decisively important step to further ensure that children are recognised as persons'.[15] The right to registration is fundamental to the efficacy of the child's right to identity and to each of the child's other human rights. Registration constitutes the State's first official acknowledgment of the child's existence and represents the child's individual importance to the State and his or her identity under the law.[16]

7.8   Civil registration records of birth supply legal proof of identity and civil status, including name, age, parentage, place of birth and nationality. These records thus underpin rights dependent on age, citizenship or ancestry. For example, registration records will help to ensure the child's right to life, survival and development by facilitating public health activities such as post-natal care of mother and infant, infant and child immunisation, and infant feeding programmes.[17] Registration also has a protective function in that it reduces the danger of abduction, sale or trafficking of children, facilitating identification following abduction or abandonment, and of treatment incompatible with the child's other rights.[18] It further provides the protection of proof in respect of minimum age limits.[19] On a wider front, registration is also a key component of planning for children on a local and national basis both in terms of the formulation of policy and the distribution of resources.[20] A failure to register a child can impact negatively on a child's sense of personal identity and children may be denied entitlements to basic health, education and social welfare.[21]

---

[13] Alderson, P *Young Children's Rights* (2008) Jessica Kingsley Publishers, p 82.

[14] See the Declaration of the Rights of the Child 1959 Principle 3: 'The child shall be entitled from his birth to a name and a nationality.' See also Committee on the Rights of the Child General Comment No 7 *Implementing Child Rights in Early Childhood,* para 6(e) (HRI/GEN/1/Rev 8, p 434, 'Young children's earliest years are the foundation for their physical and mental health, emotional security, cultural and personal identity, and developing competencies.'

[15] *Manual on Human Rights Reporting* HR/PUB/91/1/ (Rev 1), p 431.

[16] Newell, P and Hodgkin, R *Implementation Handbook for the Convention on the Rights of the Child* (2008) 3rd edn, UNICEF, p 98.

[17] *Handbook on Civil Registration and Vital Statistics Systems* (1998) ST/ESA/STAT/SER.F /70, paras 7–8.

[18] Human Rights Committee General Comment No 17 *Article 24 (Rights of the Child)* HRI/GEN/1/Rev.87, p 185.

[19] Newell, P and Hodgkin, R *Implementation Handbook for the Convention on the Rights of the Child* (2008) 3rd edn, UNICEF, pp 98–99.

[20] Newell, P and Hodgkin, R *Implementation Handbook for the Convention on the Rights of the Child* (2008) 3rd edn, UNICEF, p 98.

[21] Committee on the Rights of the Child General Comment No 7 *Implementing Child Rights in Early Childhood* HRI/GEN/1/Rev 8, para 25.

General Principles – Right to a Name

7.9　A child's name is the first point of reference both for the child and society as a means of identifying the child and the family to whom the child is related.[22] In particular, the child's name provides a method by which the child is linked quickly and accurately to his or her birth parents.[23] The child's name also constitutes a crucial link to the child's cultural background and heritage[24] and thus is an essential element of the child's knowledge of his or her origins. The right to have a name is especially important for a child born out of wedlock.[25] The child's right to a name, together with the right to registration and to nationality, is linked closely to the child's right to the protection required by his or status as a minor and to the recognition of the child's legal personality.[26] The child's right to a name, and to registration and nationality, are particularly important for child refugees and unaccompanied asylum seeking children.[27]

General Principles – Right to Nationality

7.10　The Universal Declaration of Human Rights, Art 15(1) provides that everyone has the right to a nationality. Principle 3 of the Declaration of the Rights of the Child 1959 provides that a child is entitled to acquire a nationality from birth.[28] The child should at all times have a nationality and should not be deprived of it unless the child thereby acquires a new one.[29] The rights of children to nationality tend not to be strong in domestic legal systems although the Supreme Court has recognised that, in the context of immigration cases, nationality will be of particular importance in assessing the child's best interests.[30] The link between identity and nationality is therefore an important one not only by reason of nationality constituting an element of the child's identity but also in its own right.[31]

7.11　As a matter of international law, questions of nationality fall within the domestic jurisdiction of each state.[32] However, this does not prevent the principles of international law from impacting on issues of nationality.[33] The principles of granting

---

[22]　Van Bueren, G *The International Law on the Rights of the Child* (1998) Martinus Nijhoff, p 117.

[23]　Fortin, J *Children's Rights and the Developing Law* (2009) 3rd edn, Cambridge, p 470.

[24]　Fortin, J *Children's Rights and the Developing Law* (2009) 3rd edn, Cambridge, p 489.

[25]　Human Rights Committee General Comment No 17 *Article 24 (Rights of the Child)* HRI/GEN/1/Rev 8, p 185. See also Seychelles CRC/C/15/Add.189, paras 30 and 31.

[26]　Human Rights Committee General Comment No 17 *Article 24 (Rights of the Child)* HRI/GEN/1/Rev 8, p 185. See Art 24 of the Covenant on Civil and Political Rights, which expressly links the child's right to name, registration and nationality with the concept of the protection required by the child by reason of his or her status as a minor.

[27]　Van Bueren, G *The International Law on the Rights of the Child* (1998) Martinus Nijhoff, p 366.

[28]　Article 24(3) of the Covenant on Civil and Political Rights provides that every child has the right to acquire a nationality but, interestingly, does not stipulate that the right is a right from birth.

[29]　Declaration on Social and Legal Principles relating to the Protection and Welfare of Children with Special Reference to Foster Placement and Adoption Nationally and Internationally (A/RES/41/85).

[30]　*ZH (Tanzania) v Secretary of State for the Home Department* [2011] UKSC 4.

[31]　Newell, P and Hodgkin, R *Implementation Handbook for the Convention on the Rights of the Child* (2008) 3rd edn, UNICEF, p 114. Bhaba notes that 'In short, the fact of belonging to a country fundamentally affects the manner of exercise of a child's family and private life, during childhood and well beyond' (Bhaba, J *The Mere Fortuity of Birth? – Children, Mothers, Borders and the Meaning of Citizenship* in Benhabib, S and Resnik, J (eds) *Migrations and Mobilities: Citizenship, Borders and Gender* (2009) New York University Press, p 193).

[32]　See Hudson, M *Yrbk. ILC* (1952), ii 3 at 7 and the *Tunis and Morocco Nationality Decrees* PCIJ, Ser. B. No 4 (1923) 24. See also Hague Convention on Certain Questions Relating to the Conflict of Nationality Laws 1930, Art 1 and Art 14.

[33]　*Nottebohm* ICJ Reports (1955) 4.

nationality are universal[34] and there is no separate body of principles or jurisprudence applying only to children. Nationality may be acquired by *jus soli* (law of ground) as a result of being born in the territory of the State or by *jus sanguinis* (law of blood) as a result of the nationality of one or both parents or any other criteria applied by the State party.[35] The principle of *jus soli* may extend to children born on ships and aircraft registered under the flag of a nation.[36] Children born to persons having diplomatic immunity will not be nationals by birth of the state to which the diplomatic agent concerned is accredited notwithstanding the application of the principle of *jus soli*.[37] Aliens on the territory of a state produce a complex of legal relations consequent on their status as non-nationals.[38] Under the Hague Convention on Certain Questions Relating to the Conflict of Nationality Laws 1930 an abandoned child[39] will, unless the contrary is proved, be presumed to have been born in the territory of the State in which the child was found.[40]

7.12 Practices whereby a child automatically takes nationality from his or her father or can only inherit nationality from a married father are potentially discriminatory.[41] The Convention on the Elimination of All Forms of Discrimination against Women provides that 'States Parties shall grant women equal rights with men with respect to the nationality of children'.[42]

General Principles – Right to Know and Be Cared for by Family

7.13 The identity of a child is constituted not just by his or her personal characteristics but also by the context into which the child was born and continues to survive and develop. Indeed, the former will depend in large part on the latter. In order to preserve the identity of a child the child must have full knowledge of *each* of the components of their identity.[43] Whilst the child's right to know and be cared for by his or her parents is commonly articulated by reference to the child's right to family life,[44] the child's knowledge of and care by his or her parents and wider family is, in the context under discussion, also integral to the child's right to identity. Knowledge of and membership of family allows the child awareness and understanding of his or her ancestors, family history and cultural and religious heritage, allowing a child to gain continuity with the past and a complete and consistent biography.[45] Accordingly, in

---

[34] Jennings, R and Watts, A (eds) *Oppenheim's International Law* (1955) Vol 1, p 642.

[35] At the conclusion of the first reading of the CRC the principle of *jus soli* had was expressly preferred as the means of acquiring nationality which should apply. However, ultimately the Convention is silent on the point and leaves it to the States Parties discretion as to which mechanism is adopted (Van Bueren, G *The International Law on the Rights of the Child* (1998) Martinus Nijhoff, p 367). Both principles may be said to be sanctioned by customary law (see Van Panhuys, H *The Role of Nationality* (1959), pp 160–161).

[36] Brownlie, I *Principles of Public International Law* (2008) 7th edn, Oxford, p 390. See also Art 3 of the UN Convention on the Reduction of Statelessness 1961.

[37] Brownlie, I *Principles of Public International Law* (2008) 7th edn, Oxford, p 389. See also the Hague Convention on Certain Questions Relating to the Conflict of Nationality Laws 1930 Art 12, the UN Legis. Series *Laws Concerning Nationality* (1954), Supl. Vol 1959 and Art II of the Optional Protocol concerning Acquisition of Nationality 1961 500 UNTS 223.

[38] Brownlie, I *Principles of Public International Law* (2008) 7th edn, Oxford, p 384.

[39] The Convention uses the term 'foundling'.

[40] Hague Convention on Certain Questions Relating to the Conflict of Nationality Laws 1930, Art 14.

[41] Newell, P and Hodgkin, R *Implementation Handbook for the Convention on the Rights of the Child* (2008) 3rd edn, UNICEF, p 105.

[42] Article 9(2).

[43] Van Bueren, G *The International Law on the Rights of the Child* (1998) Martinus Nijhoff, p 122.

[44] See chapter 8 generally.

[45] Haimes, E *'Now I Know Who I Really Am': Identity Change and Redefinitions of the Self in Adoption* in Honess, T and Yardley, K (eds) *Self and Identity* (1987) Routledge, Keegan and Paul, p 363.

articulating the child's right to identity Arts 7 and 8 of the CRC make explicit reference to the child's right to have knowledge of and, where possible, to be cared for by his or her family.

7.14   Within this context, the child's biological origins are a particularly important element of the right to know and be cared for by his or her parents, those origins being a significant determinant of the child's identity.[46] Knowledge of parentage permits a child a clear view of his or her biological and genetic origins and hence his or her biological identity. The need to determine biological identity may be driven not only by a child's emotional imperative to establish parentage but also by the desire to know whether his or her genetic heritage presents a future risk to health.[47] It is important to note that a right to knowledge of biological origins only has meaning for children if parents are under a concurrent duty to reveal the truth of those origins.[48] The child also has a right not to know his or her biological origins.[49]

THE CHILD'S RIGHT TO IDENTITY

The Child's Right to Identity under the CRC

The Right to Identity under the CRC – CRC, Art 7

7.15   Article 7 of the CRC enshrines the child's right to registration, name, nationality and, as far as possible, to knowledge of and a relationship with his or her parents in the following terms:

> '1. The child shall be registered immediately after birth and shall have the right from birth to a name, the right to acquire a nationality and as far as possible, the right to know and be cared for by his or her parents.
>
> 2. States Parties shall ensure the implementation of these rights in accordance with their national law and their obligations under the relevant international instruments in this field, in particular where the child would otherwise be stateless.'

7.16   Article 7 of the CRC should be read in conjunction with Art 3 (best interests),[50] Art 8 (preservation of identity), Art 9 (separation from parents), Art 10 (family reunification), Art 20 (continuity in upbringing of children deprived from their family environment) and Art 29 (the aims of education).[51] Whilst Art 7 sets out the four

---

[46]   Freeman, T and Richards, M *DNA Testing and Kinship: Paternity, Genealogy and the search for the 'Truth' of our Genetic Origins* in Ebtehaj, F, Lindley, B and Richards, M (eds) *Kinship Matters* (2006) Hart Publishing. See also *Re G (Children) (Residence: Same Sex Partner)* [2006] UKHL 43, [2006] 4 All ER 241.

[47]   See *Re H (Adoption: Disclosure of Information)* [1995] 1 FLR 236.

[48]   Probert, R *Families, Assisted Reproduction and the Law* (2004) 16 Child and Family Law Quarterly 273 p 287.

[49]   Fortin, J *Children's Rights and the Developing Law* (2009) 3rd edn, Cambridge, p 481. Fortin argues persuasively that it cannot be right to *force* a child to identify his or her biological parents.

[50]   See General Comment No 6 *Treatment of Unaccompanied and Separated Children Outside their Country of Origin*, para 20 (HRI/GEN/1/Rev.8) which makes clear that 'A determination of what is in the best interests of the child requires a clear and comprehensive assessment of the child's identity, including her or his nationality, upbringing, ethnic, cultural and linguistic background, particular vulnerabilities and protection needs.'

[51]   See in particular Art 29(1)(c) which seeks to ensure an enhanced sense of identity and affiliation (Committee on the Rights of the Child General Comment No 1 *The Aims of Education*, para 1 (HRI/GEN/1/Rev 8, p 349).

cardinal elements of the child's identity, namely registration, name, nationality and knowledge of and relationship with family, as noted above, these elements of identity are not exhaustive.[52]

CRC, Art 7 – Right to a Registration

(i) Right from Birth

7.17 By reason of the central importance of registration to the efficacy of the remainder of the child's rights,[53] Art 7(1) requires that registration take place *immediately* after the birth of the child.[54] The word 'immediately' in Art 7(1) should be interpreted as meaning as soon as possible[55] and implies a defined period of days rather than months.[56]

(ii) Information to be Registered

7.18 Hodgkin and Newell suggest that, having regard to the to right to a name, nationality and the right to know and be cared for by parents articulated by Art 7(1), the minimum information contained on the registration document should comprise the child's name at birth, the child's sex, the child's date of birth, the location of the child's birth, the parents' names and addresses and the parents' nationality status.[57] Details of the parents are particularly important given the child's right under Art 7(1) to know and be cared for by his or her parents and the importance of that right to the child's identity. Particular care should be taken to ensure the accuracy of the data recorded on the registration documents.[58] Art 16(2) of the CRC will require registration records to be kept in such a way as to protect against arbitrary or unlawful interference in the child's privacy.[59]

(iii) Enforcement

7.19 The concept of universal registration inherent in Art 7(1) of the CRC requires that States Parties make registration a compulsory duty both of parents and of the relevant administrative authorities.[60] Birth registration should be ensured by States Parties in relation to every child under their jurisdiction, including non-nationals, asylum seekers, refugee and stateless children.[61] However, where a child is not registered, that lack of registration should not result in discrimination against the child in terms of access to health care, protection, education and other social services.[62]

---

[52] See **7.3** above. See also UN Manual of Human Rights Reporting (HR/PUB/91/1 (Rev 1)), p 491. In *R (on the Application of NA) v London Borough of Croydon* [2009] EWHC 2357 (Admin) the court found that, having regard to Art 7 and Art 8 of the CRC age is an important aspect of identity.

[53] See **7.7** above. See also General Comment No 7 *Implementing Child Rights in Early Childhood*, para 25 (HRI/GEN/1/Rev. 8, para 443).

[54] The right is also enshrined in Art 24(2) of the Covenant on Civil and Political Rights.

[55] *Manual on Human Rights Reporting* HR/PUB/91/1/ (Rev.1) p 431.

[56] Newell, P and Hodgkin, R *Implementation Handbook for the Convention on the Rights of the Child* (2008) 3rd edn, UNICEF, p 100.

[57] Newell, P and Hodgkin, R *Implementation Handbook for the Convention on the Rights of the Child* (2008) 3rd edn, UNICEF, p 101.

[58] See Azerbaijan CRC/C/AZE/CO/2, paras 31 and 32.

[59] See the *Handbook on Civil Registration and Vital Statistics Systems* (1998) ST/ESA/STAT/SER.F /70.

[60] Newell, P and Hodgkin, R *Implementation Handbook for the Convention on the Rights of the Child* (2008) 3rd edn, UNICEF, p 100. See Art 7(2). The Committee on the Rights of the Child has however concluded that the imposition of civil or criminal sanctions for failure to register is counter-productive (see Albania CRC/C/1/Add.249, para 34 and Guinea Bissau CRC/C/15/Add.177, para 33).

[61] *Manual on Human Rights Reporting* HR/PUB/91/1/ (Rev.1) p 431. See Art 7(2).

[62] General Comment No 7 *Implementing Child Rights in Early Childhood* HRI/GEN/1/Rev.8, para 25.

CRC, Art 7 – Right to a Name

(i)   Right from Birth

7.20   The requirement under Art 7(1) is to provide a name 'from birth'.[63] This means that delays, for example to await baptism, should be avoided and the child should be given his or her name immediately following birth.

(ii)   Specifying and Giving Names

7.21   The CRC does not specify the type of name the child should have, for example that the child should take his or her parents surname. Domestic law should however allow for mechanisms to prevent the registration of a name which might make the child the subject of ridicule or discrimination.[64] Any national law that seeks to prescribe the names given to children should not conflict with the principle of non-discrimination under Art 2 of the CRC nor with the child's right to peacefully enjoy cultural practices under Art 30.[65]

7.22   The naming of a child from birth is unavoidably a matter for adult caregivers, thus the child does not have the right to a name of their choice,[66] although children should have the opportunity to change their name at a later date in accordance with the principles of Art 5 and Art 12 of the CRC.[67] Unlawful changes to the child's name should be avoided. The child should not be deprived of their name unless the child thereby acquires a new name.[68]

CRC, Art 7 – Right to Nationality[69]

(i)   Right from Birth

7.23   As with the right to registration and the right to a name, the right to nationality is a right from birth.[70]

(ii)   Right to Nationality – Ambit

7.24   The right 'to acquire nationality' under Art 7 of the CRC implies a right to all the benefits which derive from nationality.[71] Further, it is implicit in the right that the child is entitled to acquire the nationality of a country in which they have lived for a

---

[63]   See also the Declaration of the Rights of the Child 1959 Principle 3.

[64]   Newell, P and Hodgkin, R *Implementation Handbook for the Convention on the Rights of the Child* (2008) 3rd edn, UNICEF, p 103 and see Malawi CRC/C/15/Add.174, paras 31–32.

[65]   Newell, P and Hodgkin, R *Implementation Handbook for the Convention on the Rights of the Child* (2008) 3rd edn, UNICEF, p 102.

[66]   Van Bueren, G *The International Law on the Rights of the Child* (1998) Martinus Nijhoff, p 117.

[67]   Newell, P and Hodgkin, R *Implementation Handbook for the Convention on the Rights of the Child* (2008) 3rd edn, UNICEF, p 103.

[68]   Declaration on Social and Legal Principles relating to the Protection and Welfare of Children with Special Reference to Foster Placement and Adoption Nationally and Internationally (A/RES/41/85).

[69]   In September 2008 the United Kingdom removed its general reservation relating to immigration and citizenship which it entered upon ratifying the CRC in 1991.

[70]   See Declaration of the Rights of the Child 1959 Principle 3: 'The child shall be entitled from his birth to a name and a nationality' and Van Bueren, G *The International Law on the Rights of the Child* (1998) Martinus-Nijhoff, p 367 who concludes that the best interests of the child dictates that the right to nationality arises at birth. See also Art 24(3) of the Covenant on Civil and Political Rights.

[71]   Newell, P and Hodgkin, R *Implementation Handbook for the Convention on the Rights of the Child* (2008) 3rd edn, UNICEF, p 103.

specified period.[72] Where a child's nationality can be acquired through residence as well as through parentage, provisions in national law which prevent a child from acquiring nationality notwithstanding a significant period of residence will not be compliant with the CRC.[73] Legislation which prevents a child from inheriting his or her nationality from their parents may not be compatible with the CRC. There should be no discrimination with regard to the acquisition of nationality as between children born in wedlock and children born out of wedlock or in respect of stateless parents or based on the nationality status of one or both of the parents.[74] The Convention on the Elimination of All Forms of Discrimination against Women Art 9(2) says 'States parties shall grant to women equal rights with men with respect to the nationality of their children'.

7.25 The Human Rights Committee has observed that the right to a nationality does not necessarily make it an obligation for States to give their nationality to every child born in their territory. Commenting on Art 24(3) of the Covenant on Civil and Political Rights, which provides that every child has the right to acquire a nationality, the Human Rights Committee has observed that:[75]

> 'Special attention should also be paid, in the context of the protection to be granted to children, to the right of every child to acquire a nationality, as provided for in article 24, paragraph 3. While the purpose of this provision is to prevent a child from being afforded less protection by society and the State because he is stateless, it does not necessarily make it an obligation for States to give their nationality to every child born in their territory. However, States are required to adopt every appropriate measure, both internally and in cooperation with other States, to ensure that every child has a nationality when he is born. In this connection, no discrimination with regard to the acquisition of nationality should be admissible under internal law as between legitimate children and children born out of wedlock or of stateless parents or based on the nationality status of one or both of the parents.'

7.26 Under Art 24 of the Covenant on Civil and Political Rights, what is required therefore is for States to adopt every appropriate measure, both internally and in cooperation with other states, to ensure that every child has a nationality when he is born.[76] It is unclear whether these limitations imposed on Art 24(3) of the ICCPR by the Human Rights Committee will apply to Art 7 of the CRC.

(iii) Convention on Reduction of Statelessness 1961

7.27 The right to acquire a nationality prevents children from being afforded less protection by society and the State because he or she is stateless. The Convention on Reduction of Statelessness[77] makes provision for the acquisition of nationality by

---

[72]   Newell, P and Hodgkin, R *Implementation Handbook for the Convention on the Rights of the Child* (2008) 3rd edn, UNICEF, p 105.

[73]   Newell, P and Hodgkin, R *Implementation Handbook for the Convention on the Rights of the Child* (2008) 3rd edn, UNICEF, p 114.

[74]   Human Rights Committee General Comment No 17 *Article 24 (Rights of the Child)* HRI/GEN/1/Rev 8, p 185.

[75]   Human Rights Committee General Comment No 17 *Article 24 (Rights of the Child)* HRI/GEN/1/Rev 8, p 185 and *Manual on Human Rights Reporting* HR/PUB/91/1/ (Rev.1) p 432.

[76]   Human Rights Committee General Comment No 17 *Article 24 (Rights of the Child)* HRI/GEN/1/Rev.8, p 185.

[77]   1961 Treaty Series Vol 989, p 175. It was ratified by the United Kingdom on 29 March 1966. See also the Convention Relating to the Status of Stateless Persons (1954). The 1961 Convention has been described as 'grossly inadequate' (Van Bueren, G *The International Law on the Rights of the Child* (1998) Martinus Nijhoff, p 368).

children in order to prevent statelessness. Article 1 of the Convention provides that a Contracting State shall grant its nationality to a person born in its territory who would otherwise be stateless.

(iv) Enforcement

7.28 Article 7(2) of the CRC stipulates that States Parties shall ensure the implementation of these rights in accordance with their national law and their obligations under the relevant international instruments in this field, in particular where the child would otherwise be stateless.

CRC, Art 7 – Right to Know and be Cared for by Parents

7.29 Paragraph 16 of the Committee on the Rights of the Child's General Comment No 7, *Implementing Child Rights in Early Childhood*[78] makes clear the role of parents in the formulation of the child's developing identity from a very young age:

> 'The responsibility vested in parents and other primary caregivers is linked to the requirement that they act in children's best interests. Article 5 states that parents' role is to offer appropriate direction and guidance in 'the exercise by the child of the rights in the ... Convention'. This applies equally to younger as to older children. Babies and infants are entirely dependent on others, but they are not passive recipients of care, direction and guidance. They are active social agents, who seek protection, nurturance and understanding from parents or other caregivers, which they require for their survival, growth and well-being. Newborn babies are able to recognise their parents (or other caregivers) very soon after birth, and they engage actively in non-verbal communication. Under normal circumstances, young children form strong mutual attachments with their parents or primary caregivers. These relationships offer children physical and emotional security, as well as consistent care and attention. Through these relationships children construct a personal identity and acquire culturally valued skills, knowledge and behaviours. In these ways, parents (and other caregivers) are normally the major conduit through which young children are able to realise their rights.'

(i) Right Applies from Birth

7.30 As with the rights to registration, name and nationality, the child's right to know and be cared for by his or her parents is a right that applies from birth.[79] The qualification to this right, namely that it is a right which applies 'as far as possible' having regard to the child's best interests, will likewise fall to be considered from birth.[80] The rights enshrined in Art 7(1) are the child's rights and not the parents'. This accords with the principle that the right to be cared for is the child's right to be cared for by the parent not the parent's right to care for the child.

(ii) Right to Know and be Cared for by Parents – Ambit

Relationship to Right to Identity

7.31 The words 'the right to know and be cared for by his or her parents' in Art 7(1) uphold the general principle that, in ordinary circumstances, it is in the child's best

---

[78] Committee on the Rights of the Child's General Comment No 7, *Implementing Child Rights in Early Childhood* HRI/GEN/1/Rev, p 439.

[79] Van Bueren, G *The International Law on the Rights of the Child* (1998) Martinus Nijhoff, p 367.

[80] See **7.35** below.

interests to be cared for by his or her parents.[81] However, whilst echoing the child's wider right to family life,[82] the child's right to know and be cared for by his or parents is articulated in Art 7(1) as an essential element of establishing and maintaining the child's identity. Whilst Art 7 does not expressly enshrine a right of the child to knowledge of origins it has been interpreted to confer precisely such a right.[83] Art 8 of the CRC expresses the right in even wider terms, the words 'family relations' demonstrating that, in addition to knowledge of and care by the child's parents, the child's relationships with his or her family as a whole are integral to the child's right to identity. Articles 7(1) and 8 recognise that the child's parents and wider family are formative and continuing elements of the child's identity and seek to ensure that the child has a complete and continuing knowledge of those cardinal elements of his or her individuality.

Meaning of 'Parent'

7.32 Social developments and progress in the science of donor conception have resulted in the term 'parent' attracting an increasingly wide definition. The term 'parent' can characterise a range of parental roles ranging from the child's natural parent, through 'psychological parents',[84] being those who have cared for the child for significant periods, adoptive parents and genetic parents, who donate eggs or sperm for the purposes of assisted births. It has been suggested that for the purposes of Art 7(1) of the CRC, the term 'parents' must include genetic parents, whose medical history may be of crucial importance to the child, birth parents and 'psychological' parents.[85] Upon ratifying the CRC, the United Kingdom entered a Declaration to the effect that:[86]

> 'The United Kingdom interprets the references in the Convention to 'parents' to mean only those persons who, as a matter of national law, are treated as parents. This includes cases where the law regards a child as having only one parent, for example where a child has been adopted by one person only and in certain cases where a child is conceived other than as a result of sexual intercourse by the woman who gives birth to it and she is treated as the only parent.'

7.33 As noted above, Art 8 of the CRC makes clear that, in addition to knowledge of and care by the child's parents, the child's relationships with his or her family as a whole are integral to the child's right to identity. The Committee on the Rights of the Child has recognised that:[87]

---

[81] Newell, P and Hodgkin, R *Implementation Handbook for the Convention on the Rights of the Child* (2008) 3rd edn, UNICEF, p 109.
[82] See chapter 8.
[83] Great Britain and Northern Ireland CRC/C/15/Add 188. Note that Van Bueren, highlighting the difference between children knowing the identity of their biological parents and knowing their parents, suggests that Arts 8 and 13 of the CRC apply to the former and that Art 7 only applies to the latter (see Van Bueren, G *The International Law on the Rights of the Child* (1998) Martinus Nijhoff, p 125).
[84] See Goldstein, J, Freud, A and Solnit, A *Beyond the Best Interests of the Child* (1973) Free Press, p 19.
[85] Newell, P and Hodgkin, R *Implementation Handbook for the Convention on the Rights of the Child* (2008) 3rd edn, UNICEF, p 106.
[86] See also the reservations entered by the Czech Republic (CRC/C/2/Rev.8, p 20) and Luxembourg (CRC/C/2/Rev.8, p 28).
[87] General Comment No 7 *Implementing Child Rights in Early Childhood* (2005) CRC/C/GC/7/Rev.1, para 15. See also CRC/C/GC/7/Rev.1, para 19, the Human Rights Committee General Comment No 17 *Article 24 (Rights of the Child)* (1989) HRI/GEN/Rev.8, para 6, p 184 and the Human Rights Committee General Comment No 19 *Article 23 (The Family)* HRI/GEN/1/Rev 8, p 188, para 2.

'... "family" ... refers to a variety of arrangements that can provide for young children's care, nurturance an development, including the nuclear family, the extended family, and other traditional and community-based arrangements, provided these are consistent with children's rights and best interests.'

Each of these definitions of family will be relevant to the child's right to identity as articulated by Art 7(1) and Art 8 depending on the particular make up of the child's family.

Meaning of 'Cared For'

7.34   The term 'cared for' in Art 7(1) of the CRC implies a more active involvement on the part of a non-resident parent than simply paying child maintenance.[88] The right to be cared for by parents is also a key element of the child's right to respect for family life and is dealt with in further detail in chapter 8 below.[89]

Meaning of 'As Far As Possible'

7.35   Both the right to know and the right to be cared for in Art 7(1) of the CRC are qualified by the words 'as far as possible'. This qualification recognises the fact that it might not be possible to identify or locate the child's parents and that, even if identified it may not be in the child's best interests to be cared for by his or her parents having regard to the best interests imperative contained in Art 3 of the CRC.[90]

7.36   The words 'as far as possible' in Art 7(1) constitute a stricter and less subjective test than the concept of best interests in Art 3.[91] Although Art 7 must be interpreted in accordance with Art 3, the words 'as far as possible' suggest that, whilst each case will fall to be determined on its own facts, the circumstances in which it will be in a child's best interests not to know and be cared for by his or her parents will be relatively narrow and strictly construed.[92] Further, having regard to the child's evolving capacity and his or her right to participate under Art 12, at an appropriate point the child must be given an opportunity to reconsider the position with a view to re-establishing a situation whereby her or she knows and is cared for by his or her parents and to participate fully in any process which considers this option. As Hodgkin and Newell point out, the best interests of a 6 year old child on the issue of whether they are provided with distressing information as to their origins may be very different from the best interests of a 16 year old in the same circumstances.[93]

7.37   Adopting this strict construction, the situations contemplated by the phrase 'as far as possible' in the context of the right to identity will likely include (i) circumstances where the parents cannot be identified, (ii) circumstances where one parent refuses to

---

[88]   Newell, P and Hodgkin, R *Implementation Handbook for the Convention on the Rights of the Child* (2008) 3rd edn, UNICEF, p 108.

[89]   See **8.73–8.77**.

[90]   Newell, P and Hodgkin, R *Implementation Handbook for the Convention on the Rights of the Child* (2008) 3rd edn, UNICEF, p 97.

[91]   Newell, P and Hodgkin, R *Implementation Handbook for the Convention on the Rights of the Child* (2008) 3rd edn, UNICEF, p 107.

[92]   Newell, P and Hodgkin, R *Implementation Handbook for the Convention on the Rights of the Child* (2008) 3rd edn, UNICEF, p 107. Hodgkin and Newell argue that it is clear that the child's right to know their parentage could only be refused on the grounds of best interests in the most extreme and unambiguous circumstances.

[93]   Newell, P and Hodgkin, R *Implementation Handbook for the Convention on the Rights of the Child* (2008) 3rd edn, UNICEF, p 107.

identify the other, for example in cases of incest, rape or risk of being ostracised[94] by family and (iii) circumstances where the State deems that parent(s) should not be identified, for example annonymising the identity of egg/sperm donors.[95] These examples must be considered in light of the requirements of Art 9 of the CRC which provides that a child shall not be separated from his or her parents against their will except when such separation is necessary for the best interests of the child.

(iii)   Right to Know and be cared for by Parents – Application

Paternity Testing

7.38   The child's right as far as possible to know and be cared for by his or her parents pursuant to Art 7(1) of the CRC would tend to support the establishment of the child's paternity by means of scientific testing unless contra-indicated by the child's best interests.[96] Where a father seeks to establish the child's true parentage, Art 7(1) and Art 3 of the CRC will require the merits of establishing paternity to be determined on the basis of the child's right to know his or her father, taking into account his or her best interests, rather than the father's right to establish whether the child is his.[97]

Adoption

7.39   In order to preserve the identity of a child the child must have full knowledge of each of the components of his or her identity.[98] This will include his or her birth parents. In order for the child to exercise his or her right to know and be cared for by his or her birth parents pursuant to Art 7(1), a child must have access to information identifying those parents. Van Bueren contends that the only point in issue should be whether or not the child is sufficiently mature to be able to benefit from access to such records.[99]

7.40   In respect of children who are adopted, access to birth records and associated information may be proscribed by law.[100] The adopted child's right under Art 7(1) as far as possible to know and be cared for by his or her parents will encompass the child's birth parents as well as his or her adoptive parents.[101] Provisions to discover the identity of parents may not comply with Art 8 of the CRC if they do not extend to cover other

---

[94]   See also the Hague Convention on Protection of Children and Cooperation in Respect of Intercountry Adoption 1993, Art 30. Where a decision is taken not to disclose the details of a parent in order to protect the mother from being ostracised by her wider family, the State must nonetheless make provision for the release of such information to the child by way either of the mother's consent or at a time when the mother will not suffer any harm (Newell, P and Hodgkin, R *Implementation Handbook for the Convention on the Rights of the Child* (2008) 3rd edn, UNICEF, p 108).

[95]   Newell, P and Hodgkin, R *Implementation Handbook for the Convention on the Rights of the Child* (2008) 3rd edn, UNICEF, p 107. See **7.42** below.

[96]   Hodgkin and Newell argue that it is clear that the child's right to know their parentage could only be refused on the grounds of best interests in the most extreme and unambiguous circumstances (Newell, P and Hodgkin, R *Implementation Handbook for the Convention on the Rights of the Child* (2008) 3rd edn, UNICEF, p 107).

[97]   But see **7.68** below as to the position under the ECHR.

[98]   Van Bueren, G *The International Law on the Rights of the Child* (1998) Martinus Nijhoff, p 122. See also the dissenting judgment of Judge Cançado Trindade in *Serrano-Cruz Sisters v El Salvador* IACHR 1 March 2005 Series C No 120 'The right to identity presumes the right to know personal and family information, and to have access to this, to satisfy an existential need and safeguard individual rights.'

[99]   Van Bueren, G *The International Law on the Rights of the Child* (1998) Martinus Nijhoff, p 125.

[100]   See **7.116** below for the position in domestic law.

[101]   It is unclear whether Art 8(1) confers a similar right on an adopted child to the preservation of 'family relations' with his or her birth family as an aspect of preserving his or her identity as most adoptions will not be considered to amount to 'unlawful interference' under Art 8(1) or 'illegal deprivation' under Art 8(2).

members of the child's biological family.[102] The position can be complicated by the birth parents' competing right to confidentiality, particularly in circumstances where the birth parent may be at risk of extreme forms of social condemnation such as ostracism, injury or death.[103] However, in contrast to the position under Art 8 of the ECHR, application of the child's right to know and be cared for by his or her parents under Art 7(1) of the CRC does not require that that right be balanced against any right of the birth parents to privacy.[104]

7.41 The Declaration on Social and Legal Principles relating to the Protection and Welfare of Children with Special Reference to Foster Placement and Adoption Nationally and Internationally, which is non-binding instrument,[105] provides at Art 9 that 'The need for a foster or an adopted child to know about his or her background should be recognised by persons responsible for the child's care unless this is contrary to the child's best interests'.[106] Within this context, the following principles arise from the operation of the child's right as far as possible to know and be cared for by his or her parents under Art 7(1) in relation to adopted children:

(a) Domestic legislation should ensure that information about birth parents is preserved to be made available to the child.[107]

(b) Domestic adoption law should guarantee the right of the child to know his or her origins and to have access to information about the background and vital medical history of both the child and biological parents.[108]

(c) Domestic adoption law should establish appropriate legal procedures for this purpose, including the provision of professional support measures.[109]

(d) Where a decision is taken not to disclose the details of a parent in order to protect the mother from being ostracised or harmed, the State must nonetheless make provision for the release of such information to the child by way either of the mother's consent or at a time when the mother will not suffer any harm.[110]

---

[102] Newell, P and Hodgkin, R *Implementation Handbook for the Convention on the Rights of the Child* (2008) 3rd edn, UNICEF, p 114.

[103] Newell, P and Hodgkin, R *Implementation Handbook for the Convention on the Rights of the Child* (2008) 3rd edn, UNICEF, p 108. See the Hague Convention on Protection of Children and Cooperation in respect of Intercountry Adoption (1993), Art 30.

[104] See Besson, S *Enforcing the Child's Right to Know Her Origins: Contrasting Approaches under the Convention on the Rights of the Child and the European Convention on Human Rights* (2007) 21 International Journal of Law, Policy and the Family, pp 137 – 159

[105] A/RES/41/85.

[106] See also Art 8 of the Declaration on Social and Legal Principles relating to the Protection and Welfare of Children with Special Reference to Foster Placement and Adoption Nationally and Internationally which provides that 'The child should at all times have a name, a nationality and a legal representative. The child should not, as a result of foster placement, adoption or any alternative regime, be deprived of his or her name, nationality or legal representative unless the child thereby acquires a new name, nationality or legal representative.'

[107] Newell, P and Hodgkin, R *Implementation Handbook for the Convention on the Rights of the Child* (2008) 3rd edn, UNICEF, p 107.

[108] See Armenia CRC/C/15/Add.225, para 38.

[109] See Russian Federation CRC/C/RUS/CO/3, paras 40 and 41.

[110] Newell, P and Hodgkin, R *Implementation Handbook for the Convention on the Rights of the Child* (2008) 3rd edn, UNICEF, p 108.

(e)   The CRC places no obligation on adopted children to trace their birth parents. Children should not be obliged to be told the details of their birth parents and/or to contact their birth parents.[111]

Human Fertilisation and Embryology

7.42   Whilst some similarities arise in the context of the child's right to identity as between adopted children and children conceived by way of donor conception,[112] the essential distinction is that whereas adoption provides children with parents, donor conception provides parents with children.[113] In considering the right to identity in the context of donor conception, the applicable principles must be framed so as to protect the rights and wellbeing of the child rather than to meet the needs of childless couples.[114]

7.43   The justification for a child obtaining knowledge of his or her genetic parentage most often cited is the child's need to discover future genetic medical conditions with a view to taking preventative measures or planning future treatment.[115] Whilst it is possible to implement genetic screening processes to reduce the risk of the transmission of genetic conditions during the process of donor conception these processes themselves may have scientific, genetic and ethical drawbacks. In the circumstances, it will be important for a child to know his or her genetic parents (or at least their medical history) for the purposes of predicting and addressing future illness. Within this context, it is difficult to anticipate a situation in which the right to knowledge of parents under Art 7(1) would not be strictly construed to enable the child to ascertain his or her genetic parentage.[116] Certainly the argument that without the maintenance of complete annonymisation donors will be deterred seems weak when compared with the deleterious consequences of a child growing up unaware of a serious but treatable genetic condition and prioritises the needs of childless couples over the health and welfare of the child.[117] The Committee on the Rights of the Child has criticised legal systems which withhold information on origins from children born by means of donor conception.[118]

7.44   A potentially more complex issue is the question of whether a child born by means of donor conception should have the right not only to have knowledge of but also to have a relationship with his or her genetic parents pursuant to Art 7(1) of the CRC. Those persons who donate eggs or sperm for use by couples who are finding it difficult to conceive naturally do not normally intend to have a relationship with the child born as a result and may have an expectation of confidentiality in respect of their identity at the time of making their donation. Donors who cannot benefit from such confidentiality may be reluctant to participate in donor programmes, whether by fear of incurring later maintenance obligations or otherwise. Within the context of Art 7(1),

---

[111]   Newell, P and Hodgkin, R *Implementation Handbook for the Convention on the Rights of the Child* (2008) 3rd edn, UNICEF, p 107.

[112]   See Fortin, J *Children's Rights and the Developing Law* (2009) 3rd edn, Cambridge, p 469.

[113]   Van Bueren, G *The International Law on the Rights of the Child* (1998) Martinus Nijhoff, p 126.

[114]   Newell, P and Hodgkin, R *Implementation Handbook for the Convention on the Rights of the Child* (2008) 3rd edn, UNICEF, p 108.

[115]   But see Van Bueren, G *The International Law on the Rights of the Child* (1998) Martinus Nijhoff, pp 125–126 on the disadvantages of requiring children unaware of the identity of their biological parents to provide a reason for knowing what is another's child's right.

[116]   See Switzerland CRC/C/15/Add. 182, paras 28 and 29.

[117]   Newell, P and Hodgkin, R *Implementation Handbook for the Convention on the Rights of the Child* (2008) 3rd edn, UNICEF, p 108.

[118]   United Kingdom CRC/C/15/Add 188.

Newell and Hodgkin argue that it is possible to balance the imperatives of Art 7(1) and the disadvantages of breaching the confidentiality of the donor process through legislation which protects the donor from maintenance suits and other parental obligations. The precise boundaries of such arrangements however remain unclear and potential problems abound.[119]

Identity of Children of Minorities or Indigenous Peoples – Art 30, CRC

7.45   A child's culture, religion and language constitute cardinal elements of his or her identity. Article 30 of the CRC stipulates that in those States in which ethnic, religious or linguistic minorities or persons of indigenous origin exist, a child belonging to such a minority or who is indigenous shall not be denied the right, in community with other members of his or her group, to enjoy his or her own culture, to profess and practice his or her own religion, or to use his or her own language. Article 30 of the CRC seeks to ensure that children belonging to minorities can develop and understanding of, and sustain their cultural identity,[120] including significant aspects such as language and values.[121]

The Right to Preservation of Identity under the CRC – Art 8, CRC

7.46   Article 8 of the CRC enshrines the child's right to *preserve* his or her identity once established, including his or her nationality, name and family relations in the following terms:

> '1. States Parties undertake to respect the right of the child to preserve his or her identity, including nationality, name and family relations as recognised by law without unlawful interference.
>
> 2. Where a child is illegally deprived of some or all of the elements of his or her identity, States Parties shall provide appropriate assistance and protection, with a view to re-establishing speedily his or her identity.'

CRC, Art 8(1) – Ambit

7.47   The aim of Art 8 of the CRC is to ensure the widest possible respect for the protection of the child's identity as established by right under Art 7(1).[122] Whilst expressly mentioning those elements of the child's identity in respect of which specific provision is made in Art 7(1), the CRC does not define 'identity' and the list of the elements of the child's identity in Art 8(1) is not exhaustive, as indicated by the use of the word 'including'.[123] In the circumstances, in addition to nationality, name and family relations, Art 8 will also operate to ensure the preservation of other elements of the child's identity, including personal history since birth, race, culture, religion and language and the child's physical appearance, abilities, gender identity and sexual orientation. In this regard, Art 8 will also be engaged where there is a breach of Art 30 in relation to children of minorities or indigenous peoples.

---

[119]   See **7.125 et seq** below.
[120]   See Human Rights Committee General Comment No 23: *Article 27 (Rights of Minorities)*, para 6.2 (HRI/GEN/1/Rev 8, p 199).
[121]   Report of the ad hoc Committee of the Whole of the twenty-seventh special session of the General Assembly (2002) A/S-27/19/Rev.1, p 17). See also General Recommendation XXIII on the Rights of Indigenous Peoples, paras 3 and 4 (HRI/GEN/1/Rev.8).
[122]   *Manual on Human Rights Reporting* HR/PUB/91/1/ (Rev 1), p 433.
[123]   Van Bueren, G *The International Law on the Rights of the Child* (1998) Martinus Nijhoff, p 119.

CRC, Art 8(1) – Interpretation

(i) 'Undertake to Respect'

7.48 Pursuant to Art 8(1) States Parties 'undertake to respect' the child's right to identity. As pointed out by Van Bueren, this is a relatively weak formulation, arising out of confusion over the precise content of the right.[124] From the perspective of the enforcement of the child's right to preservation of identity the use of declaratory as opposed to obligatory language in Art 8 is extremely unhelpful.[125] Art 8(2) provides some guidance as to what will constitute 'respect' by the State of the child's right to preservation of his or her identity, stipulating that where the child is deprived illegally of elements of his or her identity the State shall 'provide appropriate assistance and protection' with a view to remedying such deprivation.

(ii) 'Preserve'

7.49 The use of word 'preserve' in Art 8 implies both non-interference with, and the proactive maintenance of a child's identity.[126] The latter may be achieved by ensuring registration of the child's birth and name and the keeping of details which the child can not be expected initially to remember when an infant.[127] This will include keeping records in relation to adoption and fertility treatment. The positive nature of the obligation to preserve the child's identity is further emphasised by the obligation on the State pursuant to Art 8(2) to 'provide appropriate assistance and protection' where the child's identity is threatened.

(iii) 'Family Relations Recognised by Law'

7.50 The precise legal meaning of the phrase 'family relations recognised by law' as used in Art 8(1) is unclear. The use of the qualifier 'recognised by law' is particularly unfortunate because the child's right to identity extends well beyond the child's legal relationships with family members.[128] The term 'family relations' clearly demonstrates that the family element of a child's identity is taken for the purposes of Art 8(1) to extend beyond merely knowing the identity of his or her parents to the need for a relationship with those parents *and* with their extended family, including siblings, grandparents and other relatives.[129]

(iv) 'Without Unlawful Interference'

7.51 Notwithstanding the advisory nature of the language used in Art 8(1), Hodgkin and Newell suggest that the use of the term 'without unlawful interference' suggests that the child's right to preservation of identity can be the subject of illegal interference.[130] Precisely what will constitute unlawful interference in the right or illegal deprivation of it remains unclear and is a matter for further development within the jurisprudence.[131]

---

[124] Van Bueren, G *The International Law on the Rights of the Child* (1998) Martinus Nijhoff, p 119.

[125] See **3.8** and **3.10** above.

[126] Newell, P and Hodgkin, R *Implementation Handbook for the Convention on the Rights of the Child* (2008) 3rd edn, UNICEF, p 115.

[127] See also Protocol I to the Geneva Conventions and **7.58** below.

[128] Newell, P and Hodgkin, R *Implementation Handbook for the Convention on the Rights of the Child* (2008) 3rd edn, UNICEF, p 114. Hodgkin and Newell describe the drafting process by which the term 'family relations as recognised by law' was arrived at as being 'less than logical.'

[129] See E/CN.4/1986/39, pp 8–10 and Detrick, p 294.

[130] Newell, P and Hodgkin, R *Implementation Handbook for the Convention on the Rights of the Child* (2008) 3rd edn, UNICEF, p 116.

[131] Van Bueren, G *The International Law on the Rights of the Child* (1998) Martinus Nijhoff, p 117.

As nationality is an element of identity, removal of a child's nationality may constitute an unlawful assault on their identity.[132] The term further suggests that there will be circumstances in which it is lawful for the State to interfere with the preservation of the child's identity having regard to the best interests of the child pursuant to Art 3 of the CRC.

CRC, Art 8(2) – Enforcement Provisions

7.52   Article 8(2) of the CRC stipulates the response expected of the State where there is interference in the child's right to preservation of his or her identity in the following terms:

> '2. Where a child is illegally deprived of some or all of the elements of his or her identity, States Parties shall provide appropriate assistance and protection, with a view to re-establishing speedily his or her identity.'

Other articles relevant to enforcement in relation to breach of the child's right to have his or her identity preserved will be Art 2 (non-discrimination), Art 7 (right to name, nationality and to be cared for by parents), Art 16 (protection from arbitrary interference in privacy and family home) and Art 30 (right to enjoy culture, religion and language) and Art 20 (children deprived of their family should where possible have continuity of upbringing particularly with regard to their ethnic, cultural and linguistic background).[133]

Article 8(2) CRC – Interpretation

(i) 'Illegally Deprived'

7.53   The term 'illegally' in Art 8(2) of the CRC will apply both when the deprivation is illegal under domestic law and when the deprivation of identity is contrary to international law.[134]

(ii) 'Appropriate Assistance'

7.54   'Appropriate assistance' in re-establishing the child's identity should comprise legislative measures, including civil and penal sanctions.[135] Hodgkin and Newell suggest that 'appropriate assistance' might include genetic profiling to establish parentage, actively tracing relatives, the use of media to advertise missing children and to reunite families, ratifying the Hague Convention on the Civil Aspects of International Child Abduction and the Hague Convention on Protection of Children and Cooperation in respect of Intercountry Adoption, officially recording any changes in the child's name, nationality or parental rights, enabling children to have access to official files maintained in respect of them, encouraging children in state care to practice their

---

[132] Newell, P and Hodgkin, R *Implementation Handbook for the Convention on the Rights of the Child* (2008) 3rd edn, UNICEF, p 114.
[133] See also Principles 16 and 20 of the UN High Commissioner for Children's Rights *Guiding Principles on Internal Displacement* (E/CN.4/1998/53/Add.2) and Art (4) CRC and the International Convention for the Protection of All Persons from Enforced Disappearance Art 25.
[134] Van Bueren, G *The International Law on the Rights of the Child* (1998) Martinus Nijhoff, p 119.
[135] *Manual on Human Rights Reporting* HR/PUB/91/1/ (Rev 1), pp 432–433.

religion, culture and language of origin and applying the best interests principle in issues relating to asylum and deportation procedures.[136] Such assistance must be offered without delay.[137]

(iii) 'Protection'

7.55 'Protection' for the purposes of Art 8(2) will include making sure the child is safe whilst his or her identity is re-established and making sure the child understands his or her situation.[138] Protection may also encompass protection of data relating to identity.[139]

(iv) 'Speedily Re-establishing'

7.56 Within the context of the child's continuing development, failure to 'speedily' remedy the deprivation of the child's identity pursuant to Art 8(2) may mean that the child assumes the identity of the family or culture in which they temporarily reside, making any re-establishment of their original identity a second deprivation and unacceptable having regard to the child's best interests under Art 3 of the CRC.[140]

The Child's Right to Identity under other International Instruments

Hague Convention on the Protection of Children and Co-operation in Respect of Inter-Country Adoption 1993

7.57 Article 30 of the Hague Convention on the Protection of Children and Co-operation in respect of Inter-Country Adoption 1993 provides as follows:

'(1) The competent authorities of a Contracting State shall ensure that information held by them concerning the child's origin, in particular information concerning the identity of his or her parents, as well as the medical history, is preserved.

(2) They shall ensure that the child or his or her representative has access to such information, under appropriate guidance, in so far as is permitted by the law of that State.'

As Van Bueren points out, access to records concerning the child's identity is only permitted by Art 30 to the extent allowed by the law of the State in which the records are held. As such, Art 30 is of limited assistance for individual children seeking access to records pertinent to the establishment and maintenance of their identity.[141] Art 16(2) of the Convention is a further limiting factor in that it entitles the State of origin to withhold the identity of the birth parents from the State receiving the adopted child. This latter provision clearly conflicts with the provisions of Art 7(1) and Art 8(1) of the CRC.

---

[136] Newell, P and Hodgkin, R *Implementation Handbook for the Convention on the Rights of the Child* (2008) 3rd edn, UNICEF, p 117.

[137] Van Bueren, G *The International Law on the Rights of the Child* (1998) Martinus Nijhoff, p 119.

[138] Newell, P and Hodgkin, R *Implementation Handbook for the Convention on the Rights of the Child* (2008) 3rd edn, UNICEF, p 117.

[139] See CRC, Art 16(2) and **9.17** below.

[140] Newell, P and Hodgkin, R *Implementation Handbook for the Convention on the Rights of the Child* (2008) 3rd edn, UNICEF, p 117.

[141] Van Bueren, G *The International Law on the Rights of the Child* (1998) Martinus Nijhoff, p 122.

The Geneva Conventions

7.58 Article 78(3) of Protocol I of the Geneva Conventions seeks to ensure the preservation of the identity of children displaced during time of war by providing as follows in relation to such children:

'3. With a view to facilitating the return to their families and country of children evacuated pursuant to this Article, the authorities of the Party arranging for the evacuation and, as appropriate, the authorities of the receiving country shall establish for each child a card with photographs, which they shall send to the Central Tracing Agency of the International Committee of the Red Cross. Each card shall bear, wherever possible, and whenever it involves no risk of harm to the child, the following information:

(a) Surname(s) of the child;
(b) The child's first name(s);
(c) The child's sex;
(d) The place and date of birth (or, if that date is not known, the approximate age);
(e) The father's full name;
(f) The mother's full name and her maiden name;
(g) The child's next of kin;
(h) The child's nationality;
(i) The child's native language, and any other language he speaks;
(j) The address of the child's family;
(k) Any identification number for the child;
(l) The child's state of health;
(m) The child's blood group;
(n) Any distinguishing features;
(o) The date on which and the place where the child was found;
(p) The date on which and the place from which the child left the country;
(q) The child's religion, if any;
(r) The child's present address in the receiving country;
(s) Should the child die before his return, the date, place and circumstances of death and place of interment.'

The Child's Right to Identity under the ECHR

Article 8 – General Principles

7.59 The ECHR does not contain a provision which expressly enshrines a right to identity. However, the right to respect for private life has been interpreted by the European Court of Human Rights as incorporating the concept of identity.[142] The Court has held that everyone should be able to establish details of his or her identity as a human being.[143] Art 8 of the ECHR thus supports the child's right to identity as an element of the child's private life, encompassing both the cardinal elements of name, nationality and family relations, as well as wider aspects of the child's physical and social identity.[144] The right under Art 8 of the ECHR to establish personal identity is a very strong one requiring particularly rigorous scrutiny when the right is said to be outweighed by countervailing considerations.[145] It is a breach of Art 8 to allow a legal

---

[142] *Gaskin v United Kingdom* (1989) 12 EHRR 36. Note that where a particularly important facet of an individual's existence or identity is at stake, the margin allowed to the State will normally be restricted (see *A, B and C v Ireland* (2010) Application No 25579/05, para 232).

[143] *Johnston v Ireland* (1987) 9 EHRR 203, para 55.

[144] *Niemietz v Germany* (1992) 16 EHRR 97, para 29 ('Respect for private life must also comprise to a certain degree the right to establish and develop relationships with other human beings').

[145] *Jäggi v Switzerland* (2008) 47 EHRR 702, paras 37–38 ('The Court considers that the right to an identity,

presumption as to parentage to prevail over biological and social reality without regard to both established facts and the wishes of those concerned.[146]

7.60 Pannick *et al* identify both negative and positive dimensions of Art 8 as it relates to the right to identity.[147] The negative dimension of Art 8 mandates a prohibition on State interference with the right of an individual to live and exist under an identity of their choice.[148] The positive aspect of Art 8 grounds a duty on the State to recognise a person's identity[149] and, where elements of a person's identity are unclear or not established, to provide information and assistance to enable a person to establish clearly those elements.[150]

7.61 Within the context of the positive obligations under Art 8 in relation to the child's right to identity, difficult issues may arise as the result of a number of different rights competing for primacy.[151] Such tensions will be resolved by seeking to establish a 'fair balance' between the competing rights and/or by the use of appropriate procedural safeguards.[152] In *Hiedecker-Tiemann v Germany*[153] the Court observed as follows in relation to the positive and negative dimensions of the rights under Art 8 in relation to names:

> 'The boundaries between the State's positive and negative obligations under Art 8 do not lend themselves to precise definition. The Court has held that not all regulation of names will necessarily constitute interference. While it is true that an obligation to change one's name would be regarded as an interference, the refusal to allow an individual to adopt a new name cannot necessarily be considered an interference. The applicable principles are nonetheless similar. In particular, in both contexts regard must be had to the fair balance which has to be struck between the competing interests; and in both contexts the State enjoys a certain margin of appreciation.

Article 8 – Application

Article 8 – Right to Registration

7.62 There is no express duty under the ECHR to register the child but failure to do so may amount to an unlawful interference in the child's right to respect for family life

---

which includes the right to know one's parentage, is an integral part of the notion of private life. In such cases, particularly rigorous scrutiny is called for when weighing up the competing interests. The Court considers that persons seeking to establish the identity of their ascendants have a vital interest, protected by the Convention, in receiving the information necessary to uncover the truth about an important aspect of their personal identity. At the same time, it must be borne in mind that the protection of third persons may preclude their being compelled to make themselves available for medical testing of any kind, including DNA testing') and *Mikulic v Croatia* [2002] 1 FCR 720.

146 *Znamenskaya v Russia* [2005] 2 FCR 406.
147 Lord Lester QC, Lord Pannick QC and Herberg, J *Human Rights Law and Practice* (2009) 3rd edn, LexisNexis, p 375.
148 See for example *Burghartz v Switzerland* (1994) 18 EHRR 101, *B v France* (1993) 16 EHRR 1 and *Daroczy v Hungary* (2008) Application No 44378/05 (unreported).
149 See for example *R (Blood & Tarbuck) v Department of Health* (unreported) 30 April 2003 and *S & Marper v United Kingdom* Application 30562/04 (unreported) 2008.
150 See *Gaskin v United Kingdom* (1989) 12 EHRR 36.
151 Lord Lester QC, Lord Pannick QC and Herberg, J *Human Rights Law and Practice* (2009) 3rd edn, LexisNexis, p 430 citing *Gaskin v United Kingdom* (1989) 12 EHRR 36, paras 43–46.
152 See **3.65** above. This approach contrasts with that under the CRC which concentrates on the primacy of the child's best interests (see Besson, S *Enforcing the Child's Right to Know Her Origins: Contrasting Approaches under the Convention on the Rights of the Child and the European Convention on Human Rights* (2007) 21 International Journal of Law, Policy and the Family, pp 137–159).
153 (2008) 47 EHRR SE9.

pursuant to Art 8 of the ECHR.[154] Art 8 further mandates that registration should take place without additional procedural requirements regardless of the marital or non-marital status of the child.[155]

Article 8 – Right to a Name

7.63   The European Court of Human Rights recognises names as constituting 'central elements of self identification and self-definition'.[156] Whilst Art 8 does not explicitly refer to names as an element of private life, the right to determine personal identity falls within the concept of private life for the purposes of Art 8 and that right will include consideration of names as a means of personal identification, a link to family and a means of establishing and developing relationships with others. As such, the issue of a child's name will fall within the ambit of Art 8 of the ECHR.[157] The rights under Art 8 in respect of a child's name, and the associated affect on private life under Art 8, will arise from the moment of birth.[158]

7.64   By reason of the age at which a child is usually named, Art 8 will be engaged in relation to the names parents choose to give to children.[159] The European Court of Human Rights has afforded a wide margin of appreciation in respect of the naming of children[160] although the margin of appreciation should not be misinterpreted as being an unlimited or unfettered discretion.[161] Unless the name chosen is ridiculous, whimsical or likely to prejudice the child, it will be an unjustified interference with the rights under Art 8 for the State to forbid a chosen name.[162] Controls on surnames may be justified in the public interest, in order to ensure accurate population registration or to safeguard means of personal identification but they must not be overly inflexible in their application[163] nor can they be discriminatory in their operation.[164] In *Stjerna v Finland*[165] the Court observed that:

> 'Despite the increased use of personal identity numbers in Finland and in other Contracting States, names retain a crucial role in the identification of people. Whilst recognising that there may exist genuine reasons prompting an individual to wish to change his or her name, the Court accepts that legal restrictions on such a possibility may be justified in the public

---

[154]   *Kalderas' Gypsies v Federal Republic of Germany and Netherlands* Application No 7823 DR 11, 221 in which it was held that the failure to deliver a birth certificate amounted to a breach of the right to family life under Art 8.

[155]   *Marckx v Belgium* (1979) 2 EHRR 330.

[156]   *Daroczy v Hungary* (2008) Application 44378/05 (unreported), para 32 ('The Court underlines that, while it is true that States enjoy a wide margin of appreciation concerning the regulation of names, they cannot disregard its importance in the lives of private individuals: names are central elements of self-identification and self-definition. Imposing a restriction on one's right to bear or change a name without justified and relevant reasons is not compatible with the purpose of Article 8 of the Convention, which is to protect individuals' self-determination and personal development'). This principle will also encompass titles (see *Ardgowan (Baron) v Lord Lyon King of Arms* [2008] CSOH 36).

[157]   *Johannson v Finland* (2008) 42 EHRR 369.

[158]   *Znamenskaya v Russia* (2007) 44 EHRR 293.

[159]   See for example *Salonen v Finland* (1997) Application 27868/95 (unreported); *Guillot v France* (1996) V No 19 1593, paras 21–22; *GMB and KM v Switzerland* (2001) Application 36797/97 (unreported) and *Bijeveld v Netherlands* (2000) Application 42973/98 (unreported).

[160]   *Stjerna v Finland* (1997) 24 EHRR 195.

[161]   *Hiedecker-Tiemann v Germany* (2008) 47 EHRR SE9.

[162]   *Johannson v Finland* (2008) 42 EHRR 369.

[163]   *Stjerna v Finland* (1997) 24 EHRR 195; *Daroczy v Hungary* (2008) Application 44378/05 (unreported). But see also *Hiedecker-Tiemann v Germany* (2008) 47 EHRR SE9.

[164]   *Unal Tekeli v Turkey* (2006) 42 EHRR 1185 and *Burghartz v Switzerland* (1994) 18 EHRR 101.

[165]   (1994) 24 EHRR 195, para 39.

interest; for example in order to ensure accurate population registration or to safeguard the means of personal identification and of linking the bearers of a given name to a family.'

7.65 Whilst it is recognised by the European Court of Human Rights that names constitute not only a means of personal identification but also a link to family, the Court has held that changing the child's surname from the mother's to that of the mother's new husband was not a breach of the father's Art 8 rights as the mother's surname did not amount to an outward sign of the bond between the father and the child.[166] In *Hiedecker-Tiemann v Germany*,[167] a case concerning compound surnames, the Court held that a refusal by the German authorities to register the compound surname did not constitute a lack of respect for the applicants' private and family life under Art 8(1) of the Convention.[168] In relation to forenames, in *Guillot v France*[169] the Court recognised that, since they constitute a means of identifying persons within their families and community, forenames, like surnames do concern private and family life and accordingly come within the ambit of Art 8.

Article 8 – Right to a Nationality

7.66 The Convention does not enshrine a right to nationality.[170] Whilst Art 14 will prohibit discrimination on the grounds of nationality, that article can only be relied on in conjunction with other articles of the Convention, as it prohibits discrimination only in relation to the enjoyment of those rights. Thus, even though the denial of a right to nationality might amount to discrimination against a child, no freestanding remedy is available under Art 14.[171]

Article 8 – Right to know and be cared for by Parents

7.67 The need for the child to know and have a relationship with his or her parents as an essential component of the child's identity engages the rights under Art 8 of the ECHR.[172] Pursuant to Art 8, the State must act in a manner calculated to enable the tie between child and family to be developed, from the moment of birth or as soon as practicable thereafter and legal safeguards must be established to render that possible.[173] In balancing competing rights, the Court will give significant weight to the child's right under Art 8 to know his or her origins and true identity. In conducting a balancing exercise between the competing Art 8 rights of the child and the adults in *Re T (Paternity: Ordering Blood Tests)*[174] Bodey J held that:

'I am entirely satisfied that in evaluating and balancing the various rights of the adult parties and of T under Art 8, the weightiest emerges clearly as being that of T, namely that he

---

[166] *Petersen v Germany* (2001) Application 39793/98 (unreported). See also *Rogl v Germany* 85A DR 153 (1996) where interference with Art 8 was established by reason of the German courts refusing to accept objections on the part of the father to his daughter's surname being changed to that of the stepfather but it was held that the interference was justified under Art 8(2) by the need for the child to integrate into her 'new' family.

[167] (2008) 47 EHRR SE9.

[168] See also *Fornaciarini, Gianettoni and Fornaciarini v Switzerland* (1996) Application No 22940/93 (unreported).

[169] (1996) V No 19 1593.

[170] But see European Convention on Adoption, Art 11 in relation to adopted children.

[171] *Beldjoudi v France* (1992) 14 EHRR 801, paras 76–78. Query however whether a child's nationality might be argued to constitute an element of the child's right to a private life on the basis that it is an integral part of the child's identity.

[172] *Mikulic v Croatia* [2002] 1 FCR 720 and see *Rassmussen v Denmark* (1984) 7 EHRR 371.

[173] *Marckx v Belgium* (1979) 2 EHRR 330, *Johnston v Ireland* (1987) 9 EHRR 203 and *Keegan v Ireland* 18 EHRR 342.

[174] [2001] 2 FLR 1190.

should have the possibility of knowing, perhaps with certainty, his true roots and identity. I find any such interference as would occur to the right to respect for the family/private life of the mother and her husband, to be proportionate to the legitimate aim of providing T with the possibility of certainty as to his real paternity, a knowledge which would accompany him throughout his life.'[175]

Identity and Paternity Testing

7.68 Pursuant to Art 8 the child has the right to discover his or her genetic history and paternity through paternity testing, paternity being considered an aspect of the child's private life.[176] Indeed, the European Court of Human Rights has held that the right to knowledge of parentage is an integral part of the notion of private life.[177] In *Phinikaridou v Cyprus*[178] the European Court of Human Rights observed that:

'... birth, and in particular the circumstances in which a child is born, forms part of a child's, and subsequently the adult's, private life guaranteed by Article 8 of the Convention. Respect for private life requires that everyone should be able to establish details of their identity as individual human beings and that an individual's entitlement to such information is of importance because of its formative implications for his or her personality. This includes obtaining information necessary to discover the truth concerning important aspects of one's personal identity, such as the identity of one's parents.'

The corollary of this position is that the parent of the child has an equivalent right under Art 8 to know whether the child is (or is not) his or hers.[179]

7.69 Whilst the case law demonstrates that Art 8 enshrines the right to knowledge of paternity, as noted above a balance must be struck between child's right to knowledge of his or her origins as an integral element of identity and the right of the father not to be forced to undergo scientific testing as to paternity.[180] In achieving the proper balance,

---

[175] The correct balance to be struck will depend on the facts of each case and in many cases the balance may be a complicated one open to more than one conclusion (compare for example the first instance and appellate decisions in *Re H and A (Paternity: Blood Tests)* [2002] EWCA Civ 383, [2002] 1 FLR 1145). See also Besson, S *Enforcing the Child's Right to Know Her Origins: Contrasting Approaches under the Convention on the Rights of the Child and the European Convention on Human Rights* (2007) 21 International Journal of Law, Policy and the Family, p 138.

[176] *Mikulic v Croatia* [2002] 1 FCR 720 and *Rassmussen v Denmark* (1984) 7 EHRR 371. It should be noted that a person's right to establish their parentage does not disappear with age (see *Jäggi v Switzerland* (2006) Application No 58757/00 (unreported)).

[177] *Jäggi v Switzerland* (2006) Application No 58757/00 (unreported), para 37. Compare this decision with the decision of the majority in *Odièvre v France* [2003] 1 FCR 621 which has been the subject of much criticism (see Steiner, E *Odièvre v France – Desperately Seeking Mother – Anonymous Births in the European Court of Human Rights* (2003) and Besson, S *Enforcing the Child's Right to Know Her Origins: Contrasting Approaches under the Convention on the Rights of the Child and the European Convention on Human Rights* (2007) 21 International Journal of Law, Policy and the Family, pp 150–152). See also *Re L (Family Proceedings Court) (Appeal: Jurisdiction)* [2003] EWHC 1682 (Fam), [2005] 1 FLR 210, para 23 per Munby J.

[178] (2008) Application No 23890/02, para 45.

[179] *Rozanski v Poland* Application No 55339/00 [2006] 2 FCR 178; *Schoffman v Russia* (2007) 44 EHRR 741 and *Znamenskaya v Russia* (2007) 44 EHRR 293. The parents' right to seek information concerning their children is not unlimited (see *R (Addinell) v Sheffield City Council* [2001] ACD 331).

[180] Fortin, J *Children's Rights and the Developing Law* (2009) 3rd edn, Cambridge, p 472. See *Jevremović v Serbia* [2007] ECHR 612, paras 106–111.

the Courts will give significant weight to the child's right under Art 8 to know his or her true origins and identity[181] but will also weigh in the balance a range of other factors. In *Phinikaridou v Cyprus*[182] the Court held:

> 'On the one hand, people have a right to know their origins, that right being derived from a wide interpretation of the scope of the notion of private life. Persons in the applicant's situation have a vital interest, protected by the Convention, in receiving the information necessary to uncover the truth about an important aspect of their personal identity and eliminate any uncertainty in this respect. On the other hand, as stated above, a presumed father's interest in being protected from stale claims concerning facts that go back many years cannot be denied. Finally, in addition to that conflict of interest, other interests may come into play, such as those of third parties, essentially the presumed father's family. While performing the 'balancing of interests test' in the examination of cases concerning limitations on the institution of paternity claims, the Court has taken a number of factors into consideration. For instance, the particular point in time when an applicant becomes aware of the biological reality is pertinent, that is, the Court will examine whether the circumstances substantiating a particular paternity claim are met before or after the expiry of the applicable time-limit, concerning disavowal of paternity claims; both cited above). Furthermore, the Court looks into whether or not an alternative means of redress exists in the event the proceedings in question are time-barred. This would include for example the availability of effective domestic remedies to obtain the reopening of the time-limit or exceptions to the application of a time-limit in situations where a person becomes aware of the biological reality after the time-limit has expired. The yardstick against which the above factors are measured is whether a legal presumption has been allowed to prevail over biological and social reality and if so whether, in the circumstances, this is compatible, having regard to the margin of appreciation left to the State, with the obligation to secure effective 'respect' for private and family life, taking into account the established facts and the wishes of those concerned.'[183]

Identity and Adoption

Jurisprudence

7.70 When it considered the case of *Gaskin v United Kingdom*,[184] a case concerning access to records pertaining to the applicant's time in care, the European Commission observed in relation to Art 8 that:

> '... respect for private life requires that everyone should be able to establish details of their identity as individual human beings and that in principle they should not be obstructed by the authorities from obtaining such very basic information without specific justification.'

7.71 When *Gaskin v United Kingdom* came before the European Court of Human Rights[185] the Court held that:

---

[181] *Re T (Paternity: Ordering Blood Tests)* [2001] 2 FLR 1190. Again, this approach contrasts with that under the CRC which concentrates on the primacy of the child's best interests (see Besson, S *Enforcing the Child's Right to Know Her Origins: Contrasting Approaches under the Convention on the Rights of the Child and the European Convention on Human Rights* (2007) 21 International Journal of Law, Policy and the Family, pp 137–159).

[182] (2008) Application No 23890/02, paras 53–55.

[183] See also *Lambeth London Borough Council v S, C, V and J (By His Guardian)* [2006] EWHC 326 (Fam), [2007] 1 FLR 152 per Ryder J ('Having regard to the more modern practice of balancing parallel rights, the court would expect that balance to be weighed in favour of a child having the certainty of parentage as against the inevitable interference with the Art 8 Convention rights of a parent').

[184] Application No 10454/83.

[185] [1990] 1 FLR 167.

'In the Court's opinion persons in the situation of the applicant have a vital interest, protected by the Convention, in receiving the information necessary to know and to understand their childhood and early development. On the other hand, it must be borne in mind that confidentiality of public records is of importance for receiving objective and reliable information, and that such confidentiality can also be necessary for the protection of third persons. Under the latter aspect, a system like the British one, which makes access to records dependent on the consent of the contributor, can in principle be considered to be compatible with the obligations under art 8, taking into account the State's margin of appreciation. The Court considers, however, that under such a system the interests of the individual seeking access to records relating to his private and family life must be secured when a contributor to the records either is not available or improperly refuses consent. Such a system is only in conformity with the principle of proportionality if it provides that an independent authority finally decides whether access has to be granted in cases where a contributor fails to answer or withholds consent. No such procedure was available to the applicant in the present case. Accordingly, the procedures followed failed to secure respect for Mr Gaskin's private and family life as required by art 8 of the Convention. There has, therefore, been a breach of that provision.'[186]

7.72   Van Bueren suggests that it is arguable that the principles applied in *Gaskin v United Kingdom* are equally applicable to requests made for adoption records.[187] Caution however must be exercised in relying on *Gaskin* in this regard. The European Court of Human Rights has expressed the view that '[t]he issue of access to information about one's origins and the identity of one's natural parents is not of the same nature as that of access to a case record concerning a child in care or to evidence of alleged paternity'.[188] Further, whilst the *Gaskin* case established that Art 8(1) could be used to support arguments for access to information, the Court made clear that its findings were 'reached without expressing any opinion on whether general rights of access to personal data and information may be derived from Art 8(1) ...'.[189] In addition, following its decision in *Leander v Sweden*,[190] the Court held that, whilst the right to freedom to receive information pursuant to Art 10 of the ECHR prohibits a Government from restricting a person from receiving information that others wish or may be willing to impart to him, the right to freedom of information under Art 10 did not confer on the individual a right of access to a register containing information on his personal position, nor did it embody an obligation on the Government to impart such information to the individual. Finally, the use of Art 8 to craft a right to access to information necessarily gives rise to difficult questions as to the balance to be struck between the child's right to information concerning his or her identity and the right to privacy of his or her parents and others. The courts have struggled to achieve a proper balance in this regard.[191]

---

[186]   See also *MG v United Kingdom* (2002) 36 EHRR 22, [2002] 3 FCR 289.
[187]   Van Bueren, G *The International Law on the Rights of the Child* (1998) Martinus Nijhoff, p 124. Article 8 will encompass adoptive parent/child relationships (see *X v Belgium and Netherlands* (1975) D&R 75).
[188]   *Odièvre v France* (2004) 38 EHRR, [2003] 1 FCR 621, para 43.
[189]   But see *Martin v UK* (1996) 84 D & R 169 in which the Commission, in declaring the case inadmissible, held that 'the records to which the applicant requests access, though not relating to his childhood, contain information of a personal nature relating to personally significant incidents in his life and, accordingly, considers that access to such records falls within Art 8 of the Convention' and *Re X (disclosure of information)* [2001] 2 FLR 440 at 451, para 34 per Munby J.
[190]   (1987) 9 EHRR 433.
[191]   See *Odièvre v France* (2004) 38 EHRR, [2003] 1 FCR 621 and Steiner, E Odièvre v France – Desperately Seeking Mother – Anonymous Births in the European Court of Human Rights (2003) and Besson, S Enforcing the Child's Right to Know Her Origins: Contrasting Approaches under the Convention on the Rights of the Child and the European Convention on Human Rights (2007) 21 International Journal of Law, Policy and the Family, pp 150–152.

7.73 In the circumstances, the utility of *Gaskin v United Kingdom* and Art 8 in achieving access to adoption records pertinent to the child's identity remains to be definitively established.[192] However, as Van Bueren further points out, if failure at the stage of registering a child can amount to a breach of Art 8 of the ECHR with regard to the child's identity[193] then should not being deprived records at the stage the child is seeking to establish his or her identity also, adopting a teleological approach, amount to a breach of Art 8.[194]

Council of Europe Recommendations

7.74 In 1981, the Committee of Ministers adopted Recommendation No R(81)19 on the Access to Information Held by Public Authorities, which stipulated that:[195]

> 'I. Everyone within the jurisdiction of a member state shall have the right to obtain, on request, information held by the public authorities other than legislative bodies and judicial authorities ...'

Whilst application of Art I is subject to 'limitations and restrictions as are necessary in a democratic society for the protection of legitimate public interests (such as national security, public safety, public order, the economic well-being of the country, the prevention of crime, or for preventing the disclosure of information received in confidence), and for the protection of privacy and other legitimate private interests' the Recommendation specifically provides that due regard be given to the 'specific interest of an individual in information held by the public authorities which concerns him personally'.[196]

7.75 In 2002 the Council of Europe adopted COE Recommendation (2002)2 on Access to Official Documents reiterated that 'Member states should guarantee the right of everyone to have access, on request, to official documents held by public authorities. This principle should apply without discrimination on any ground, including that of national origin'.[197] The limitations on access provide by the 2002 Recommendation are more extensive in nature than stipulated by the 1981 Recommendation on Access to Information and the Recommendation no longer specifically provides for due regard be given to the specific interest of an individual in information held by the public authorities which concerns him personally. However, the 2002 Recommendation is in turn narrower in scope, applying to 'Official Documents' rather than to information more generally.

---

[192] No support is provided by the European Convention on Adoption, which does not provide the child with a right to know the identity of his or her birth parents.

[193] See *Kalderas' Gypsies v Federal Republic of Germany and Netherlands* Application No 7823 DR 11, 221 and *Marckx v Belgium* (1979) 2 EHRR 330.

[194] Van Bueren, G *The International Law on the Rights of the Child* (1998) Martinus Nijhoff, p 125.

[195] See also COE Rec 854 (1979) on Access by the Public to Government Records and Freedom of Information and the Convention for the Protection of Individuals with regard to Automatic Processing of Personal Data (Council of Europe ETS No 108).

[196] Recommendation No R(81)19 on the Access to Information Held by Public Authorities Art V.

[197] Article III.

Identity and Human Fertilisation and Embryology

7.76 In *R (Rose) v Secretary of State for Health*[198] Scott Baker J, in considering whether claimants born as the result of donor insemination were entitled to rely on Art 8 of the ECHR in seeking information about the donors, concluded that:[199]

> 'Respect for private and family life has been interpreted by the European Court to incorporate the concept of personal identity. Everyone should be able to establish details of his identity as a human being. That, to my mind, plainly includes the right to obtain information about a biological parent who will inevitably have contributed to the identity of his child. There is in my judgment no great leap in construing art 8 in this way. It seems to me to fall naturally into line with the existing jurisprudence of the European Court.'

7.77 In *R (Rose) v Secretary of State for Health* it was argued by the Government that the claimants could not take advantage of Art 8 in seeking information regarding donors as they could not establish 'family life' for the purposes of Art 8. In support of this argument, the Government relied on *M v Netherlands,*[200] in which the Commission considered that the situation in which a person donates sperm only to enable a woman to become pregnant through artificial insemination does not of itself give the donor a right to respect for family life with the child.[201] However, in *R (Rose) v Secretary of State for Health* Scott Baker J drew a distinction between 'family life' and 'private life' under Art 8, relying on the observations of the European Court of Human Rights in *Mikulic v Croatia*[202] to conclude that the claimant's did come within the ambit of Art 8 of the ECHR:

> 'For my part I do not consider the issue in the present case to be essentially a question of whether the relationships of the claimants and the donors fall within the ordinary concept of family life. This, to my mind, is really an identity case and involves the claimants' rights to know about their origins. The emphasis therefore is much more on 'private life' than 'family life ... what the claimants are trying to obtain is information about their biological fathers, something that goes to the very heart of their identity.'

7.78 As to what information the child conceived by means of donor conception might be entitled to seek by reliance on his or her rights under Art 8, Scott Baker J made the following observations in *R (Rose) v Secretary of State for Health*:

> 'In my judgment, at the stage of considering whether art 8 is engaged at all, it is artificial to distinguish between identifying and non-identifying information. If art 8 is engaged it is

---

[198]   [2002] EWHC 1593 (Admin), [2002] 3 FCR 731 sub nom *Rose v Secretary of State for Health and Human Fertilisation and Embryology Authority* [2002] 2 FLR 962.

[199]   See also *Leeds Teaching Hospitals NHS Trust v A and Others* [2003] EWHC 259 (QB), [2003] 1 FCR 599, para 47.

[200]   (1993) 74 D & R 120.

[201]   See also *G v The Netherlands* (1993) 16 EHRR CD 38 and *MB v United Kingdom* (1994) 77 A–DR 108.

[202]   [2002] 1 FCR 720. In this case the Court held that 'The present case differs from the paternity cases cited above in so far as no family tie has been established between the applicant and her alleged father. The court reiterates, however, that art 8, for its part, protects not only 'family' but also 'private' life. Private life, in the court's view, includes a person's physical and psychological integrity and can sometimes embrace aspects of an individual's physical and social identity. Respect for 'private life' must also comprise to a certain degree the right to establish relationships with other human beings (see, mutatis mutandis, *Niemietz v Germany* (1992) 16 EHRR 97, para 29). There appears, furthermore, to be no reason of principle why the notion of 'private life' should be taken to exclude the determination of the legal relationship between a child born out of wedlock and her natural father. The court has held that respect for private life requires that everyone should be able to establish details of their identity as individual human beings and that an individual's entitlement to such information is of importance because of its formative implications for his or her personality (see *Gaskin v UK* (1989) 12 EHRR 36, para 39).'

engaged to facilitate the establishment by the claimants of their personal identity. It is of course ... claimants' personal identity that is crucial and not that of the donor. Information about the donors is only relevant in so far as it helps the claimants to build up pictures about themselves. There will come a point where information about the donor is too remote to assist in this purpose ... The distinction between identifying and non-identifying information is not relevant at the engagement stage of art 8, but it is likely to become very relevant when one comes to the important balancing exercise of the other considerations in art 8(2).'

Wider Identity

7.79 As with CRC, the concept of identity under the ECHR is wider in its ambit than simply the cardinal aspects of name, nationality and knowledge of and relationship with family. Article 8 of the ECHR has also been held to protect a person's right to decide on their personal identity as an element of his or her private life in relation to mode of dress and personal appearance.[203]

The Child's Right to Identity under European Law

Right to a Name

7.80 Whilst, under European Union law, the rules governing a child's surname are matters falling within the competence of Member States of the Union, States are required to comply with Community Law when exercising that competence. Accordingly, the provisions of Art 17 of the EC Treaty relating to citizenship and Art 12 of the EC Treaty relating to non-discrimination will be relevant when applying domestic naming rules.[204]

The Child's Right to Identity under other Regional Instruments

Right to a Name

Right to a Name – American Convention on Human Rights

7.81 Article 18 of the American Convention on Human Rights provides as follows in relation to the right to a name:[205]

> 'Every person has the right to a given name and to the surnames of his parents or that of one of them. The law shall regulate the manner in which this right shall be ensured for all, by the use of assumed names if necessary.'

---

[203] *McFeeley v United Kingdom* (1980) 20 DR 44; *Sutter v Switzerland* (1979) 16 DR 166; *Kara v United Kingdom* (1998) 27 EHRR CD 272 and *R (E) v Ashworth Hospital Authority* [2001] EWHC (Admin) 1089, (2002) *The Times* 17 January.

[204] See Case C-148/02: *Garcia Avello v Belgium* [2003] ECR I-11613, [2004] All ER (EC) 740 in which it was held that Arts 12 and 17 had to be interpreted as precluding, in circumstances of the case, the administrative authority of a member state from refusing to grant an application for a change of surname made on behalf of children resident in that state and having dual nationality of that state and of another member state where the purpose of that application was to enable those children to bear the surname to which they were entitled according to the law and tradition of the other member state.'

[205] Other articles of the American Convention on Human Rights will also be relevant to the right to identity, including Art 3 (right to recognition as a person before the law), Art 5(1) (right to have physical, mental and moral integrity protected) and Art 11 (right to have honour respected and dignity recognised). See the dissenting judgment of Judge Cançado Trindade in *Serrano-Cruz Sisters v El Salvador* IACHR 1 March 2005 Series C No 120, para 22.

7.82 In *Yean and Bosico v Dominican Republic*[206] the Inter-American Court on Human Rights held with regard to the right to a name that that right 'constitutes a basic and essential element of the identity of each individual, without which he cannot be recognised by society or registered before the State'. The Court held that states have the duty not only to protect this right, but also to offer persons the necessary measures to facilitate the registration of the person immediately after birth. The Inter-American Court on Human Rights has recognised the right to a name as part of the wider right of the child to identity. In the case of *The Serrano Cruz Sisters v El Salvador*[207] the Inter-American Court on Human Rights, whilst concluding that it did not have jurisdiction to determine the complaint made pursuant to Art 18 of the ACHR observed that:

> 'As the International Jurists Commission had indicated, the right to identity, particularly in the case of children and of forced disappearance, is a complex legal issue that acquired relevance with the adoption of the Convention on the Rights of the Child. This right has been recognised by case law and by legal writings as both an autonomous right and as the expression of other rights or as a constituent element of these. The right to identity is intimately associated with the right to the recognition of legal personality, the right to a name, a nationality, and a family and to have family relationships. The total or partial suppression or modification of the right of the child to preserve his identity and its intrinsic elements entails State responsibility.'

Right to a Name – Ibero-American Convention on Young People's Rights

7.83 The Ibero-American Convention on Young People's Rights contains no express right to a name but Art 14 enshrines a wide ranging right to individual and personal identity, providing that:[208]

> '1. All young people have the right to: have a nationality, not be deprived of it and acquire another one voluntarily, and to an individual identity, consisting in the building of the own personality attending to specificities and characteristics of sex, nationality, ethnic origin, filiation, sexual orientation, religious belief and culture.
>
> 2. The States Parties shall promote respect for the identity of youth and shall guarantee their free expression ensuring the eradication of situations which discriminate them in any of the aspects concerning their identity.'

Right to a Name – African Charter on the Rights and Welfare of the Child

7.84 Article 6 of the African Charter on the Rights and Welfare of the Child provides that every child shall have the right from his birth to a name and every child shall be registered immediately after birth.

Right to Nationality

Right to Nationality – American Convention on Human Rights

7.85 Article 20 of the American Convention on Human Rights provides a right to nationality, stipulating as follows:

---

[206] *Case of the Girls Yean and Bosico* IACHR Judgement 8 September 2005 Series C No 130.
[207] *Serrano-Cruz Sisters v El Salvador* IACHR Judgement 1 March 2005 Series C No 120.
[208] Article 15 of the Convention further provides that all young people have a right to their own image and to the prevention of the exploitation of their image.

'1. Every person has the right to a nationality.

2. Every person has the right to the nationality of the state in whose territory he was born if he does not have the right to any other nationality.

3. No one shall be arbitrarily deprived of his nationality or of the right to change it.'

7.86 In *Yean and Bosico v Dominican Republic*,[209] a case concerning two children deprived of their right to nationality by refusal of the authorities to issue birth certificates despite the fact that they were born in the territory of a state which recognises the right to nationality by reason of *jus soli*, the Inter-American Court of Human Rights held that the condition of statelessness in which the two girls lived affected the free development of their personalities, since it impeded access to their rights, such as the right to education, health, and housing, among others, and the special protection to which they are entitled. In his partially dissenting judgement, Judge Cançado Trindade further observed that:[210]

'In this case of the *Yean and Bosico children*, the Court understood that the violation of the right to nationality and the rights of the child also resulted in the violation of the rights to juridical personality, to a name and to equal protection under the American Convention.'

Right to Nationality – African Charter on the Rights and Welfare of the Child

7.87 Article 6(3) and 6(4) of the African Charter on the Rights and Welfare of the Child provides as follows in respect of the child's right to nationality:

'3. Every child has the right to acquire a nationality.

4. States Parties to the present Charter shall undertake to ensure that their Constitutional legislation recognise the principles according to which a child shall acquire the nationality of the State in the territory of which he has been born if, at the time of the child's birth, he is not granted nationality by any other State in accordance with its laws.'

Right to Nationality – Revised Arab Charter on Human Rights

7.88 At Art 29(1) the Revised Arab Charter on Human Rights stipulates that everyone has the right to nationality and that no-one shall be arbitrarily deprived of his nationality. Under Art 29(2) the Charter stipulates that:

'States parties shall take such measures as they deem appropriate, in accordance with their domestic laws on nationality, to allow a child to acquire the mother's nationality, having due regard, in all cases, to the best interests of the child.'

Pursuant to Art 29(3) a person must not be prevented from acquiring another nationality having due regard to the domestic legal procedures of his or her country.

Right to be Cared for by Parents

7.89 The regional human rights instruments, including the ECHR, do not expressly articulate the right of the child to know and be cared for by his or her family as an

---

[209] *Case of the Girls Yean and Bosico* IACHR Judgement 8 September 2005 Series C No 130.
[210] Dissenting judgement of Judge Cançado Trindade in the *Case of the Girls Yean and Bosico* IACHR Judgement 8 September 2005 Series C No 130, para 14.

intrinsic element of the child's right to identity. As discussed above, the right to respect for privacy under Art 8 of the ECHR has however been clearly interpreted by the European Court of Human Rights as encompassing the child's right to know and be cared for by his or her parents as a cardinal element of identity.[211]

7.90 The Inter-American Commission on Human Rights has recognised that the right to identity under Art 11 of the American Convention on Human Rights 'encompass a range of factors pertaining to the dignity of the individual, including, for example, the ability to pursue the development of one's personality and aspirations, determine one's identity, and define one's personal relationships'.[212] In his dissenting judgement in *Yakye Axa Indigenous Community v Paraquay*[213] Judge Abreu Burelli observed that the right to privacy under Art 11 of the American Convention on Human Rights:

> '... includes the right of the members of ethnic and cultural groups not to suffer arbitrary or abusive interference with their private, family and community life, which involves protection of their culture and respect for the integrity of the values, practices and institutions of these peoples.'

7.91 Whilst the African Charter on the Rights and Welfare of the Child at Art 10 and the African Youth Charter at Art 7 each enshrine the right to privacy, and the Ibero-American Convention on Young People's Rights provides for a right to family intimacy at Art 15(1), it is unclear the extent to which these rights will be interpreted as encompassing right of the child to know and be cared for by his or her family as an intrinsic element of the child's right to identity under each of these regional instruments.[214] Art 23(2) of the African Charter on the Rights and Welfare of the Child stipulates that States Parties shall undertake to cooperate with existing international organisations which protect and assist refugees in their efforts to protect and assist such a child and to trace the parents or other close relatives or an unaccompanied refugee child in order to obtain information necessary for reunification with the family.

The Child's Right to Identity under Domestic Law

Domestic Law – Right to Registration

7.92 Pursuant to ss 1 and 2 of the Births and Deaths Registration Act 1953[215] the birth of every child born in England or Wales must be registered by the registrar of births and deaths for the sub-district in which the child was born within 42 days of the birth of the child. Both parents where married have the power and the duty to register the child's names.[216] An unmarried father cannot, even if he has parental responsibility,

---

[211] See **7.29 et seq** above.

[212] Inter-American Commission on Human Rights Report No 92/00. Note in this context that Art 17(5) of the American Convention on Human Rights requires the law to recognise equal rights for children born out of wedlock and those born in wedlock.

[213] *Yakye Axa Indigenous Community v Paraguay* Judgement 17 June 2005 IACHR Case 12.313, Report No 2/02.

[214] But see Advisory Opinion of the Inter-American Court of Human Rights *Legal Status and Human Rights of the Child* OC-17/2002 of August 28 2002, paras 71–72.

[215] As amended by the Registration of Births and Deaths (Amendment) Regulations 1994.

[216] Births and Deaths Registration Act 1953, s 2(1) and see *Re W, Re A, Re B (Change of Name)* [1999] 2 FLR 930. Note that were the child has a parent by virtue of s 42 or 43 of the Human Fertilisation and Embryology Act 2008 references to the father of the child in s 2(1) of the 1953 Act are to be read as references to the women who is a parent by virtue of that section (Births and Deaths Registration Act 1953, s 2(2)).

register the name, having no power or duty to do so.[217] The basis on which an unmarried father can seek to be entered onto the registers are limited to registration at the joint request of the mother and the father, at the request of either upon the production of a statutory declaration of paternity,[218] where there is a parental responsibility agreement in placed under s 4 of the Children Act 1989 or where the court has made an order pursuant to s 4 of the Children Act 1989 or Sch 1 of the Children Act 1989. An unmarried father cannot therefore intervene in the registration process and prevent the mother from choosing and registering a name.[219] Where the child is abandoned, it is the duty of the person who has charge of the child to apply to the Registrar General for the child's birth to be registered.[220] Once registered the registered name stands indefinitely and the register cannot be altered, only the name changed.[221] The inclusion of a man's name on the register is prima facie evidence of paternity.[222]

Domestic Law – Right to a Name

7.93   Domestic law more than adequately meets the imperatives of the child's right to a name.[223] Where parents act jointly they have an absolute right to name and rename their child.[224] Domestic law gives no indication of whose surname should be given to the child[225] but simply provides for registration of a name at a given time.[226] Lord Jauncey of Tullichettle's view in *Dawson v Wearmouth*[227] that it should be the father's surname that is given has been roundly criticised.[228]

Change of Name

Jurisdiction

7.94   The domestic courts are often asked to determine disputes between parents concerning the wish of one or other parent to change the name of the child. The jurisdiction of the court to settle such disputes has been questioned in light of the Children Act 1989, s 2(7), which provides that where more than one person has parental responsibility for a child each of them may act alone and without the other in meeting that responsibility. Within this context, Fortin contends that the court's power to

---

[217]   Births and Deaths Registration Act 1953, s 2A(1). See s 2B for the unmarried mother's duty to provide information relating to the father.
[218]   Registration of Births and Deaths Regulations 1987, Sch 2, as amended by the Registration of Births and Deaths (Amendment) (England and Wales) Regulations 2009.
[219]   *Dawson v Wearmouth* [1999] 2 All ER 353.
[220]   Births and Deaths Registration Act 1953, s 3A.
[221]   See *Re H (Child's Name: First Name)* [2002] EWCA Civ 190, [2002] Fam Law 340, [2002] 1 FLR 973 per Thorpe LJ. See also *Rees v United Kingdom* (1987) 9 EHRR 56, sub nom *The Rees Case* [1987] 2 FLR 111; *Cossey v United Kingdom* (1990) 13 EHRR 622, [1991] 2 FLR 492; *X, Y and Z v UK* (1997) 24 EHRR 143, [1997] 2 FLR 892, and *Sheffield and Horsham v United Kingdom* (1998) 27 EHRR 163, [1998] 2 FLR 928 and *I v United Kingdom* [2002] 2 FLR 518 and *Goodwin v United Kingdom* [2002] 2 FLR 487.
[222]   Births and Deaths Registration Act 1953, s 34(2); *Brierley v Brierley and Williams* [1918] P 257; *Re G (Parentage: Blood Sample)* [1997] 2 FCR 325, [1997] 1 FLR 360.
[223]   Fortin, J *Children's Rights and the Developing Law* (2009) 3rd edn, Cambridge, p 489.
[224]   Children Act 1989, s 13. This includes adoptive parents (see Adoption and Children Act 2002, s 77 and Sch 1).
[225]   See the Registration of Births and Deaths Regulations 1987, SI 1987/2088, r 9(3) which provides that the surname to be entered into the register 'shall be the surname by which at the date of the registration of birth it is intended that the child shall be known.'
[226]   Births and Deaths Registration Act 1953, s 2.
[227]   [1999] 2 All ER 353 at 361.
[228]   See Eekelar *Family Law and Personal Life* (2006) Oxford, p 63 and Hale LJ in *Re R (Surname: Using Both Parents')* [2001] EWCA Civ 1344, [2001] 2 FLR 1358, para 13.

determine disputes over name comes from a series of self referencing decisions.[229] However, Holman J in *Re PC (Change of Surname)*[230] rejected jurisdictional arguments based on s 2(7) in light of pre-Children Act authority which he concluded established the principle that a parent could not change the child's surname without his spouse's consent. In respect of unmarried parents, Holman J held that the parent with parental responsibility 'has the right and power lawfully to cause a change of surname without any other permission or consent', although he considered the consent of a child aged over 16 may be required. Perhaps the strongest practical justification for Holman J's view is that, in the absence of a requirement to refer the matter to the Court where there is a dispute, parents could simply engage in an endless round of name changing, damaging the child's welfare in the process. Change of surname applications must be made in accordance with the *Practice Direction (Child: Change of Surname)*.[231] There is no requirement to execute a formal deed of surname, but it may be useful for some purposes.[232] A deed poll is merely evidence of the maker's intention to change their name.[233]

Effect of Other Orders

7.95   Where a residence order is in force pursuant to the Children Act 1989, s 8, that order prohibits the holder from changing change the child's surname without the consent in writing of all those with parental responsibility or with permission of the Court.[234] As such there is no statutory requirement for the child to consent to a change of name but he or she may apply for a prohibited steps order to prevent the change if he or she objects.[235] Where no residence order is in force, an application to change the surname may be made by way of an application for a specific issue order. Upon granting a special guardianship order the court may cause the child to be known by a new surname.[236] Such an order should not be made where it will interfere with the child's identity.[237]

7.96   The granting of a care order does not entitle a local authority to cause a child to be known by a new name without the consent in writing of all those with parental responsibility for the child or with permission of the Court.[238] The local authority may apply for permission ex parte only in exceptional circumstances.[239] In determining whether to grant the application the court should consider the wishes, feelings and objectives of the applicant, take advice from the children's guardian and consider the motives and objectives of the respondent.[240] It is important to note that the factors for change of name under s 33(7) of the Children Act 1989 are different from those under s 13(1)(a) and therefore the authorities on private law and public law change of name

---

229 Fortin, J *Children's Rights and the Developing Law* (2009) 3rd edn, Cambridge, p 491.
230 [1997] 2 FLR 730, pp 736–739. See also *Y v Y (Child: Surname)* [1973] Fam 147 at 152G.
231 [1995] 1 All ER 832, [1995] 1 WLR 365.
232 See Enrolment of Deeds (Change of Name) Regulations 1994, SI 1994/604.
233 *D v B (otherwise D) (Child: Surname)* [1979] 1 All ER 92.
234 CA 1989, s 13(1)(a). Note the comment of Wilson J in *Re B (Change of Surname)* [1996] 1 FLR 791 at 795 that s 3(1)(a) can only act as an inhibition to the resident parent not to cause the child to be *known* by a different surname.
235 Clarke, Hall & Morrison (LexisNexis), para 1[717].
236 CA 1989, s 14B(2)(a).
237 *Re L (A Child)(Special Guardianship Order and Ancillary Orders)* (2007) EWCA Civ 196, [2007] All ER (D) 208 Mar sub nom *Re E (A Child)(Special Guardianship Order)* (2007) Times 11 April.
238 CA 1989, s 33(7).
239 *Re J (A Minor) (Change of Surname)* [1993] 1 FCR 74, [1993] 1 FLR 699 and also *Re M, P, T, K and B (Care: Change of Name)* [2000] 2 FLR 645.
240 *Re S (Change of Surname)* [1999] 1 FLR 672 and *Re M, P, T, K and B (Care: Change of Name)* [2000] 2 FLR 645.

cases are not interchangeable.[241] Foster parents cannot change a child's surname or forename.[242] The child may apply to change his or her own name.[243]

Best Interests

7.97   The change of a child's surname is an important matter not to be undertaken lightly.[244] The domestic test to be applied in determining whether the child's name should be changed is that of the child's best interests.[245] A change of surname should not be ordered unless there was some evidence that this would lead to an improvement from the point of view of the child's welfare.[246] The factors that require weighing in the balance when determining best interests in this area have included whether the court considers that the name is an important link to the non-resident father and thus to the child's identity,[247] how important the name is to links with cultural identity[248] and how detrimental to the child's welfare is having a surname which causes the child distress or is not used on a day to day basis.[249] Whether or not the parents are married may also be considered a relevant factor by the courts.[250] A change to the child's surname may also be held to be in the child's best interests where it will avoid further disruption to the life of the child.[251] Finally, the objection of the other parent may be an important factor.[252] The most advantageous solution to the dispute may be to use of both surnames on separation.[253]

7.98   Different principles apply as between surnames and given (first) names. In *Re H (Child's Name: First Name)*[254] Thorpe LJ observed in relation to given (first) names that:[255]

> '... none of the authorities that guide the court in determining disputes as to the surname by which a child should be known seems to be of any application to a dispute of this sort. The surname by which a child is registered and known is of particular significance insofar as it denotes the family to which the child belongs. Given names have a much less concrete character. It is commonplace for a child to receive statutory registration with one or more given names and, subsequently, to receive different given names, maybe at baptism or, maybe, by custom and adoption. During the course of family life, as a child develops personality and individuality, parents or other members of the family, may be attracted to some

---

[241]   *Re S (Change of Surname)* [1999] 1 FLR 672 and *Re M, P, T, K and B (Care: Change of Name)* [2000] 2 FLR 645.

[242]   *Re D L and LA (Care: Change of Surname)* [2003] 1 FLR 339.

[243]   In the context of care proceedings see *Re S (A Minor) (Change of Name)*[1999] 1 FCR 304, [1999] 1 FLR 672.

[244]   *Re F (Child Surname)* [1994] 1 FCR 110.

[245]   *Dawson v Wearmouth* [1999] 2 All ER 353 and *Re W, Re A, Re B (Change of Name)* [1999] 2 FLR 930.

[246]   *Dawson v Wearmouth* [1999] 2 All ER 353.

[247]   *W v A (Child: Surname)* [1981] Fam 14 and *Re C (C Child)(Change of Surname)* [1999] 1 FCR 318.

[248]   *Re S (Change of Names: Cultural Factors)* [2001] 2 FLR 1005 and *Re A (A Child)(Change of Name)* [2003] EWCA Civ 56, [2003] 1 FCR 493, [2003] 2 FLR 1 in which it was held that independent expert evidence as to the culture and practice of the parties, as well as the general cultural context, are relevant to the court's decision whether to change a name.

[249]   *D v B (otherwise D) (Child: Surname)* [1979] 1 All ER 92 and *Y v Y (Child's Surname)* [1999] 2 FLR 5.

[250]   *Re W, Re A, Re B (Change of Name)* [1999] 2 FLR 930.

[251]   *Re F (Contact)* [2007] EWHC 2543 (Fam), [2007] All ER (D) 52 (Nov) sub nom *Re F (Children) (Contact: Change of Name)* [2007] 3 FCR 832.

[252]   See *Re T (otherwise H)(An Infant)* [1963] Ch 238 at 242 followed in *Re B (Change of Surname)* [1996] 1 FLR 791. See also see *G v A (Children: Surname)* [1995] 2 FCR 223.

[253]   See *Re R (Surname: Using both Parents)* [2001] EWCA Civ 1344, [2001] 2 FLR 1358.

[254]   [2002] EWCA Civ 190, [2002] Fam law 340, [2002] 1 FLR 973.

[255]   A foster parent may not change the child's first name (see *Re D L and LA (Care: Change of Surname)* [2003] 1 FLR 339.

nickname or some alternative given name which will then adhere, possibly for the rest of the child's life, or possibly only until the child's individuality and maturity allow it to make a choice for itself as to the name by which he or she wishes to be known.'

The Child's Right to Participate

7.99 In considering a change of name, the court will take into account the views of children having regard to their age and understanding. In *Re B (Minors) (Change of Surname)*[256] Wilson J held that whilst the checklist of factors under s 1(3) of the Children Act 1989, which includes the requirement to have regard to the ascertainable wishes and feelings of the child considered in light of his or her understanding, was not a mandatory consideration in applications under s 13 of the Act, it provided a most useful aide memoir of the factors to be taken into account. In *Re M, P, T, K and B (Care: Change of Name)*[257] the court held that it should be particularly loathe to refuse applications which are consistent with the wishes of mature children, even though those wishes are neither paramount nor determinative on an application to for a change of name. Where a child is 'Gillick' competent an application to change his or her surname requires special consideration.[258] In *Re PC (Change of Surname)*[259] Holman J recognised that consent of older children, and in particular children over the age of 16, to change of surname may be a requirement. In determining an application to change his or her name by a 'Gillick' competent child in care under s 33(7) of the Children Act 1989 the court should give very careful consideration to the wishes, feelings, needs and objectives of the child.[260]

Domestic Law – Right to Nationality

7.100 The domestic rules as to nationality are extremely complex and are regularly amended.[261] Accordingly, a full account is beyond the scope of this work. The following is a broad summary of the position under domestic law and readers should refer to a specialist text on the subject for the detailed and up to date position.

Automatic Acquisition in the United Kingdom

7.101 Under the British Nationality Act 1981, s 1(1) a child born in the United Kingdom[262] after 1 January 1983 will be a British Citizen at birth if, at the time of the birth either parent[263] is a British citizen, either parent is settled[264] in the United

---

[256] [1996] 2 FCR 304, [1996] 1 FLR 791.
[257] [2000] 2 FLR 645.
[258] *Re S (Change of Surname)* [1999] 1 FLR 672 and *Re M, P, T, K and B (Care: Change of Name)* [2000] 2 FLR 645.
[259] [1997] 2 FLR 730.
[260] *Re S (Change of Surname)* [1999] 1 FLR 672.
[261] See in particular the British Nationality Act 1981, the British Nationality (General) Regulations 2003, the British Nationality (General) (Amendment) Regulations 2003, the British Nationality (General) (Amendment) Regulations 2004 and the British Nationality (General) (Amendment No 2) Regulations 2004.
[262] 'United Kingdom' means Great Britain (England, Wales, and Scotland), Northern Ireland, the Channel Islands and the Isle of Man taken together. United Kingdom territorial waters do not form part of the United Kingdom for nationality purposes (British Nationality Act 1981, s 50(1)).
[263] Where the child is born before 1 July 2006 'parent' means the mother of a marital or non-marital child or the father of a marital child. Where the child was born after 1 July 2006 and was conceived before 5 April 2009, 'parent' means the mother who gave birth to the child and the mother's husband at the time of the child's birth or any person who is treated as the father for the purposes of the Human Fertilisation and Embryology Act 1990, s 28 or a person who is proven to be the father by production of a birth certificate issued within 12 months of the date of the child's birth or such other evidence as may satisfy the Secretary of State. In relation to a child conceived on or after 6 April 2009 'parent' means the mother who gave birth to the child and the mother's husband at the time of the child's birth or any person who is treated as the father for the

Kingdom or, if born after 13 January 2010, his or her father or mother is a member of the armed forces.[265] The UN Committee on the Rights of the Child has criticised the fact that a child cannot take British citizenship if his or her father is not married to his or her mother.[266] For the purposes of nationality, entry on the birth certificate of the father's name within one year of the child's birth is accepted as proof of paternity.[267]

7.102 Under s 1(2) of the 1981 Act a new-born infant found abandoned in the United Kingdom on or after 1 January 1983 can be regarded for the purposes of s 1(1) as having been born in the United Kingdom after 1 January 1983 and born to a parent who at the time of the birth was a British citizen or settled in the United Kingdom unless either condition can be disproved.

Automatic Acquisition in the Qualifying Territories

7.103 Under s 1(1) of the 1981 Act, as amended by the British Overseas Territories Act 2002, a person born in a qualifying territory[268] on or after 21 May 2002 is a British citizen at birth if, at the time of the birth either parent is a British citizen; or either parent is settled in the United Kingdom; or either parent is settled in that qualifying territory; or from 13 January 2010, either parent is a member of the armed forces.[269] Under s 1(2) of the 1981 Act, as amended by the British Overseas Territories Act 2002, a new-born infant found abandoned in a qualifying territory on or after 21 May 2002 can be regarded, for the purposes of s 1(1), as having been born in that territory on or after 21 May 2002 and born to a parent who, at the time of the birth, was either a British citizen or settled in the United Kingdom or settled in that territory unless either condition can be disproved.

Acquisition outside United Kingdom and Qualifying Territories

7.104 Pursuant to s 2(1)(a) of the 1981 Act, a person born outside the United Kingdom on or after 1 January 1983 and before 21 May 2002 is a British citizen at birth if, at the time of the birth, either parent is a British citizen 'otherwise than by descent'.[270]

---

purposes of the Human Fertilisation and Embryology Act 2008, s 35 or 36, a person who is treated as the parent of the child for the purposes of the Human Fertilisation and Embryology Act 2008, s 42, or 43 or a person who is proven to be the father by production of a birth certificate issued within 12 months of the date of the child's or such other evidence as may satisfy the Secretary of State (British Nationality Act 1981, ss 50(9), 50(9A) and 50(9B) and see British Nationality (Proof of Paternity) Regulations 2006, SI 2006/1496, r 2).

[264] For a discussion of the definition of 'settled' see UK Border Agency *Nationality Instructions Volume 1: The British Nationality Act 1981* Chapter 6, Annex A, para 33).

[265] Defined as a member of the regular forces within the meaning of the Armed Forces Act 2006, or a member of the reserve forces within the meaning of the 2006 Act subject to service law by virtue of s 367(2)(a)–(c) of that Act.

[266] CRC/C/15/Add.188, para 23. See British Nationality Act 1981, s 50(9A).

[267] British Nationality (Proof of Paternity) Regulations 2006, SI 2006/1496, r 2.

[268] 'Qualifying territory' means a British overseas territory other than the Sovereign Base Areas of Akrotiri and Dhekelia (British Nationality Act 1981, s 50(1)).

[269] See the Borders, Citizenship and Immigration Act 2009, s 42(1), (2).

[270] A British citizen otherwise than by way of descent will generally be persons who are British citizens by birth, adoption (including adoption under the Hague Convention on or after 1 June 2003), registration or naturalisation or by reason of being British overseas territories citizens by birth, adoption, registration or naturalisation immediately before 21 May 2002 (there are however a number of exceptions and reference should be made to the UK Border Agency *Nationality Instructions Volume 1: The British Nationality Act 1981* Chapter 20. British citizens by descent are defined in s 14(1) of the British Nationality Act 1981. British citizens by descent cannot transmit their citizenship to children born abroad except in certain narrowly defined circumstances. British citizens otherwise than by descent automatically transmit their citizenship to children born abroad.

Further, under s 2(1)(b) and (c), a person born outside the United Kingdom or after 1 January 1983 and before 21 May 2002 is a British citizen at birth if, at the time of the birth: either parent is a British citizen and that parent is serving outside the United Kingdom in the Crown Service under the Government of the United Kingdom or in service of any description designated under s 2(3)[271] or in service under a Community institution[272] and was recruited in the United Kingdom for that service or, in the case of a Community institution, in a county which at the time was a member of the Communities.[273]

7.105 For children born outside the UK or qualifying territories after 21 May 2002 under s 2(1)(a), a person born outside the United Kingdom and the qualifying territories on or after 21 May 2002 is a British citizen at birth if, at the time of the birth, either parent is a British citizen 'otherwise than by descent'. Further, under s 2(1)(b) and (c), a person born outside the United Kingdom on or after 21 May 2002 is a British citizen at birth if, at the time of the birth: either parent is a British citizen and that parent is serving outside the United Kingdom in Crown Service[274] under the Government of the United Kingdom or in service of any description designated under s 2(3) or in service under a Community institution and was recruited in the United Kingdom for that service or, in the case of a Community institution, in a county which at the time was a member of the Communities. A child who is a British citizen under s 2(1) of the Act is a British citizen by descent if a British citizen by virtue of s 2(1)(a) only and a British citizen otherwise than by descent in all other circumstances.

Automatic Acquisition by Adopted Children

7.106 In respect of adopted children who are not already British citizens at the time of their adoption, under s 1(5) of the British Nationality Act a child becomes a British citizen at the date of the adoption order if either the adoption is authorised by order of a court in the United Kingdom on or after 1 January 1983, or the adoption is authorised by order of a court in a qualifying territory on or after 21 May 2002 and the adopter or, in the case of a joint adoption order, one of the adopters is a British citizen on the date of the adoption order, or it is a Convention adopted under the 1983 Hague Convention on Intercountry Adoptions, and the adopter or in the case of a joint adoption, one of the adopters is a British citizen at the date of the Convention adopter and the adopter or, in the case of a joint adoption, both of the adopters is habitually resident in the United Kingdom or in a territory designated for this purpose under s 50(14) of the 1981 Act[275] on the date of the Convention adoption.[276] Under s 1(6) of the 1981 Act, British citizenship acquired by virtue of s 1(5) is not lost if the adoption or parental order

---

[271] Section 2(3), as amended by the 2002 Act, explains that the Home Secretary may make an order by statutory instrument designating any service which he thinks is closely associated with the activities outside the United Kingdom and the qualifying territories of Her Majesty's government in the United Kingdom or in a qualifying territory.

[272] 'Community institution' is defined by the Interpretation Act 1978 as an institution of the European Community which is classified as such by Part 5 of the EC Treaty ('Institutions of the Community'), namely the European Parliament, the Council of Ministers, the European Commission, the European Court of Justice, the Court of Auditors, the Economic and Social Committee, the Committee of the Regions and the European Investment Bank.

[273] 'Community' and 'Communities' is not defined in the British Nationality Act 1981 but 'Community' is read to mean the European Community and 'Communities' is read to mean the European Economic Community, the European Coal and Steel Community and the European Atomic Energy Community (UK Border Agency *Nationality Instructions Volume 1: The British Nationality Act 1981* Chapter 6, Annex A, para 6).

[274] 'Crown service' means the service of the Crown, whether within Her Majesty's dominions or elsewhere (British Nationality Act 1981, s 50(1)).

[275] No territories have been designated at this time.

[276] British Nationality Act 1981, s 5A.

ceases to have effect at a later date, for example on annulment. Where, however, the order is merely set aside by a higher court on appeal by the Home Secretary, s 1(6) has no effect and the child will thereupon cease to be a British citizen. From 6 April 2010 a child who is the subject of a parental order made in a United Kingdom court, following a surrogacy arrangement, becomes a British citizen under s 1(5) from the date of the order, if either of the persons making the order is a British citizen.

Automatic Acquisition by Persons otherwise Stateless

7.107 In respect of persons born in the United Kingdom or in a British overseas territory[277] who would otherwise be stateless, in order to meet the United Kingdom's obligations under the United Nations Convention on the Reduction of Statelessness s 50(7) and Sch 2 to the British Nationality Act 1981 make provision for the acquisition of the citizenships and status created by the Act by certain persons who are or would otherwise be stateless, including those born on ships and aircraft.

Acquisition by Registration[278]

7.108 Pursuant to s 3(1) of the British Nationality Act 1981 a child may be registered as a British citizen at the discretion of the Secretary of State where the application is made whilst the child is a minor, the Secretary of State is satisfied that, where the child is aged 10 or over as at the date of application, the child is of good character and the Secretary of State thinks it fit to register the child. A child born outside the United Kingdom and qualifying territories may also be entitled to registration under s 3(2) by reason of descent, under s 3(5) otherwise than by descent and under s 4D by reason of being born to members of the Armed Forces, provided certain criteria are fulfilled. Minors, who are British overseas territories citizens, British Nationals (Overseas), British Overseas citizens, British subjects under the 1981 Act or British protected persons are entitled to registration as British citizens under s 4(2) or s 4B of the British Nationality Act 1981 or at the Secretary of State's discretion under s 4(5) or s 4A upon the meeting of specific criteria. Pursuant to Sch 2 a stateless child may acquire British citizenship by registration provided certain criteria are met.

---

[277] 'British overseas territory' means a territory mentioned in Sch 6 to the British Nationality Act 1981 (British Nationality Act 1981, s 50(1)).

[278] Children may be eligible for registration under more than one provision. By the operation of s 14(1) of the 1981 Act, registration under one provision may give British citizenship by descent and, under another, British citizenship otherwise than by descent. In such cases, the UK Border Agency should, whenever possible, choose the one which gives British citizenship 'otherwise than by descent' (UK Border Agency *Nationality Instructions Volume 1: The British Nationality Act 1981* Chapter 20, para 20.1.9).

Domestic Law – Right to Know and be Cared for by Parents

Relationship to the Right to Identity

7.109 The domestic courts have recognised the child's right to knowledge of his or her origins unless his or her welfare demands otherwise.[279] In *Re H (Paternity: Blood Test)*[280] Ward LJ held in relation to paternity testing in respect of a 14 year old boy that:[281]

> 'In my judgment every child has a right to know the truth unless his welfare clearly justifies the cover-up. The right to know is acknowledged in the UN Convention on the Rights of the Child 1989 (Cm 1976) which has been ratified by the UK and in particular Art 7 which provides 'that a child has, as far as possible, the right to know and be cared for by his or her parents' ... If the child has the right to know, then the sooner it is told the better. The issue of biological parentage should be divorced from psychological parentage. Acknowledging Mr B's parental responsibility should not dent Mr H's social responsibility for a child whom he is so admirably prepared to care for and love irrespective of whether or not he is the father.'

7.110 The child's right to know and be cared for by his or her parents as an element of his or her right to identity manifests itself in domestic law in a broadly similar manner to that discussed above. Namely, cases in which the child's paternity is in doubt,[282] cases in which the child has been adopted and cases in which the child has been conceived by way of donor conception.[283]

Paternity Testing

Legal Framework

7.111 In *Re H and A (Paternity: Blood Tests)*[284] Thorpe LJ emphasised the need for the paternity of a child to be established by scientific methodology and not by the use of legal presumptions or inferences, observing that:

---

[279]   *A v L (Contact)* [1998] 1 FLR 361 at 366 per Holman J. The courts will also place weight on the need to preserve links with the child's culture and heritage as elements of the his or her identity (see *Re M (Child's Upbringing)* [1996] 2 FCR 473, [1996] 2 FLR 441 and *Re M (Section 94 Appeals)* [1995] 1 FLR 456) subject to the paramount nature of the child's welfare (*Re P (A Child) (Residence Order: Restriction Order)* [1993] 3 All ER 734, sub nom *Re P (A Child: Residence Order: Child's Welfare)* [1999] 2 FCR 289, sub nom *Re P (Section 91(14) Guidelines) (Residence and Religious Heritage)* [1999] 2 FLR 573).

[280]   [1996] 2 FLR 65.

[281]   Questions of paternity should be divorced from questions of contact and parental responsibility (see *Re G (Parentage Blood Sample)* [1997] 1 FLR 360 at 366 per Ward LJ (contact with stepfather may still be beneficial) and *Re T (Paternity: Ordering Blood Tests)* [2001] 2 FLR 1190 at 1196 (contact and parental responsibility do not automatically follow establishment of paternity)).

[282]   The maternity of the child will generally be obvious although cases have arisen in relation to the question of maternity (see *Morrison v Jenkins* (1949) 80 CLR 626 and *The Ampthill Peerage Case* [1977] AC 547 per Lord Simon at 577). In addition, failed surrogacy arrangements in which the child has been retained and not informed of his or her biological maternity or other situations where a person seeks to pass of a child as their own ('a supposititious child') could also give rise to issues of the child's maternal identity (see *Slingsby v AG* (1916) 33 TLR 120 and see *Bromley's Family Law* (10th edn, (2007) Ch 7) and the Weekly Reporter v 41 (1893), pp 433 and 750).

[283]   As above, in this chapter the child's right to know and be cared for by his or her parents is considered from the perspective of the child's right to identity. In chapter 8 the right to know and be cared for by parents is considered within the context of the child's right to family life, encompassing issues of contact and residence. Again, in respect of the latter, it should be remembered that cases involving disputes as to contact and residence will necessarily involve some consideration of the child's right to identity when considering the proper outcome in such cases.

[284]   [2002] 1 FLR 1145, para 30.

'Twenty years on I question the relevance of the presumption or the justification for its application. In the nineteenth century, when science had nothing to offer and illegitimacy was a social stigma as well as a depriver of rights, the presumption was a necessary tool, the use of which required no justification. That common law presumption, only rebuttable by proof beyond reasonable doubt was modified by s 26 of the Family Law Reform Act 1969 by enabling the presumption to be rebutted on the balance of probabilities. But as science has hastened on and as more and more children are born out of marriage it seems to me that the paternity of any child is to be established by science and not by legal presumption or inference.'

7.112 The Family Law Reform Act 1969, s 20(1) provides the statutory framework for the use of scientific tests to determine parentage and the taking of bodily samples[285] to facilitate such testing.[286] The High Court and county court may direct that a person from whom the court directs a sample should be taken should also be joined as a party to the proceedings.[287] Testing cannot be directed under the inherent jurisdiction.[288] Testing may only be carried out by a body which has been accredited for the purposes of the Act.[289] The choice of the accredited body to carry out the test is with the person applying for the test on the basis that the applicant pays for the testing, has most to gain or lose from the result and knows how much he or she can afford.[290] Where the child may be HIV positive, special provisions apply in respect of testing.[291] The test is used to determine whether a party to the application is excluded from being the father (or mother) of the child whose parentage is in issue.[292] It is arguable that an applicant mother may make successive applications to determine paternity against different putative fathers.[293]

Consent

7.113 Taking samples from children should only be carried out by order of the court.[294] Consent of the child's carer is not required where such testing would be in the child's

---

[285] Defined as a sample of bodily fluid or bodily tissue taken for the purpose of scientific tests (see Family Law Reform Act 1969, s 25 as amended by the Family Law Reform Act 1987, s 23(3)).

[286] The standard direction for scientific testing pursuant to s 20(1) of the Family Law Reform Act 1969 should be drafted as follows:' It is directed pursuant to s 20(1) of the Family Law Reform Act 1969 as amended: (a) that scientific tests (including DNA tests) be used to ascertain whether such tests show that [Mr A] is or is not excluded from being the father of [child B] born on [...]; and (b) that for that purpose bodily samples be taken on or before [...] from the following persons: [Mr A], [Mrs X, mother of child B] and [child B]; and (c) that the person appearing to the court to have care and control of [child B], who is under the age of 16 is [...]; and (d) that such tests be carried out by [Mr/Mrs CD of ...]'(this formulation is taken from Ryder, E and Goldrien, I (eds) *Child Case Management Practice* (2009) Jordan Publishing, p 545. See also *Re F (children) (DNA evidence)* [2007] EWHC 3235 (Fam), [2008] 1 FLR 348, paras 19 32 which provides detailed guidance on the proper procedures for scientific testing).

[287] RSC Ord 112, r 4; CCR Ord 47, r 5(3).

[288] *Re O, Re J (children) (blood tests: constraint)* [2000] Fam 139, [2000] 2 All ER 29.

[289] Family Law Reform Act 1969, s 20(1A) as substituted by the Child Support, Pensions and Social Security Act 2000, s 82. See also the Blood Tests (Evidence of Paternity) Regulations 1971, SI 1971/1861, reg 8A(1) and (2) as substituted by the Blood Tests (Evidence of Paternity) (Amendment) Regulations 2008, SI 2008/596, reg 11.

[290] See HOC 91/1989, para 5.

[291] *President's Direction: HIV testing of children* [2003] 1 FLR 1299 replacing the procedure set out in *Re X (a minor)* [1994] 2 FCR 1110, sub nom *Re HIV Tests* [1994] 2 FLR 116.

[292] The term 'excluded' in this context means excluded subject to the occurrence of genetic mutation (see the Family Law Reform Act 1969, s 26 and *F v F* [1968] 1 All ER 242 at 246 per Rees J).

[293] See *Re GW (A Minor) (Blood Tests)* [1994] 2 FCR 908, sub nom *Re A (a minor) (paternity: refusal of blood test)* [1994] 2 FLR 463, CA and *Hager v Osborne* [1992] Fam 94, [1992] 2 All ER 494, sub nom *H v O* [1992] 1 FCR 125, [1992] 1 FLR 282.

[294] *Re F (children) (DNA evidence)* [2007] EWHC 3235 (Fam), [2008] 1 FLR 348, para 32.

best interests.295 A child who has attained the age of 16 can consent to being tested, which consent is effective as if he or she had attained the age of majority.296 Where a child over the age of 16 refuses consent, the omission from s 21 of the worlds '*which, in the absence of consent, would constitute a trespass*', contained s 8 of the Family Law Reform Act 1969, would tend to suggest that, in contrast to a refusal of consent to medical treatment,297 there is no scope for argument that the child's consent can be overridden by someone with parental responsibility for him or her.298 Whether the court may override a refusal of consent by a child over 16 is uncertain. The court may override the refusal of a child aged 16 or over to undergo medical treatment.299 If this approach were applied to scientific testing then the court would have power to override the child's refusal of consent,300 although criticisms similar to those made against this approach in the context of medical treatment would apply.301 A bodily sample may not be taken from an adult without his or her consent.302 Where an child over the age of 16 lacks capacity for the purposes of the Mental Capacity Act 2005 consent may be given by the court under the Family Law Act 1969, s 20 or by a donee with an enduring or lasting power or attorney or a deputy appointed, or any other person authorised by the Court of Protection with power to give consent to the taking of a bodily sample.303

Exercise of the Court's Discretion

7.114 In determining whether to direct bodily samples pursuant to the Family Law Reform Act 1969 the Court will direct testing if it is satisfied that to do so would be in the child's best interests having regard also to the competing interests of adults who will be affected by the making or not making of the direction.304 The authorities have emphasised that in most cases it will be in the child's best interest for his or her parentage to be definitively established by means of scientific testing and that cases where testing will be refused will be rare.305 Indeed, there must be cogent reasons for denying the child knowledge of his or her parentage in light of the imperative contained in Art 7 of the CRC.306

---

295 Family Law Reform Act 1969, s 21(3)(b) as amended following *Re O and J* [2000] 1 FLR 418 per Wall LJ at 434. See also *Re L (an infant)* [1968] P 119, [1968] 1 All ER 20.

296 Family Law Reform Act 1969, s 21(2). Where the parentage of the child is in issue (as opposed to whether the child is the parent) it is unnecessary to make the child a party (*Re E (A Minor) (Child Support: Blood Test)* [1995] 1 FCR 245, [1994] 2 FLR 548).

297 See **4.41** above.

298 See Butterworth's Family Law Service (LexisNexis), para D[387].

299 See **4.48** above.

300 See *Re R (A Minor) (Blood Tests; Constraint)* [1998] Fam 66, [1998] 1 FCR 41, sub nom *Re R (blood test: child: inherent jurisdiction)* [1998] 1 FLR 745.

301 See **4.48** above. See also *S v S, W v Official Solicitor* [1972] AC 24 at 45, [1970] 3 All ER 107 at per Lord Reid at 113: 'I would, therefore, hold that the court ought to permit a blood test of a young child to be taken unless satisfied that that would be against the child's interests. I say a young child because as soon as a child is able to understand these matters it would generally be unwise to subject it to this operation against its will'.

302 Family Law Reform Act 1969, s 21(1). See also *S v S, W v Official Solicitor* [1972] AC 24, [1970] 3 All ER 107 and *W v W (No 4)* [1964] P 67, [1963] 2 All ER 841.

303 Family Law Reform Act 1969, s 21(4) as amended by the Mental Capacity Act 2005, s 67(1), Sch 6, para 15.

304 *S v S, W v Official Solicitor* [1972] AC 24, [1970] 3 All ER 107 and *Re F (A Minor) (Blood Tests: Parental Rights)* [1993] Fam 314, [1993] 3 All ER 596.

305 *Re T (A Child) (DNA Tests: Paternity)* [2001] 3 FCR 577, [2001] 2 FLR 1190 and *Re H and A (Children)* [2002] EWCA Civ 383, [2002] 2 FCR 469 sub nom *Re H and A (Paternity: Blood Tests)* [2002] 1 FLR 1145. For examples where testing has been refused see *S v McC, W v Official Solicitor* [1972] AC 24 at 48, [1970] 3 All ER 107 at 115 (application a 'fishing' exercise designed to call into question the parentage of the child for some ulterior motive), *Re F (A Minor) (Blood Tests: Parental Rights)* [1993] Fam 314, sub nom *Re F (a minor: paternity test)* [1993] 3 All ER 596 and *K v M (paternity: contact)* [1996] 3 FCR 517, [1996] 1 FLR 312 (outcome of blood testing would make no difference to the outcome of the proceedings) and *CB (A Minor) (Blood Test)* [1994] 2 FCR 925, [1994] 2 FLR 762 (if the applicant were found to be the father there

7.115 There is no method of enforcing a direction for scientific tests in the face of default by the child's carer.[307] In *Re O and J*[308] Wall J suggested that in the circumstances, given the knowledge of paternity is both in a child's best interests and his or her right, the provisions of the Family Law Act 1969 may not be compliant with the ECHR and are out of line with Art 7 of the CRC. Pursuant to s 23(1) of the Family Law Reform Act 1969 a court may draw such inferences as appear proper if any fails to take any step required of him or her for the purpose of giving effect to a direction for scientific testing.[309] Only very clear and cogent reasons, which it is just and reasonable maintain, will justify a refusal to be tested.[310] Courts do have jurisdiction to compel a mother to inform the child of his or her true paternity once the results of the testing are known[311] even to the extent where a court will direct another person to inform the child.[312] The issues of whether a parent should be compelled to inform the child of the outcome of the scientific testing will be decided on the basis of the child's best interests.[313]

Adoption Records

7.116 Domestic legislation now makes extensive provision for adopted children to ascertain information relevant to their origins and identity.[314]

Adopted Children Register

7.117 The Adoption and Children Act 2002, Sch 1 provides for the registration of adoptions in an Adopted Children Register in the General Register Office.[315] This register is not open to the public for search or inspection.[316] However, there must also be maintained an index to the register which any person may search. Any person may obtain a certified copy of an entry in the Adopted Children Register for a person over aged 18 or over[317] or, subject to the provision of particulars prescribed in the Regulations, to a certified entry for a child.[318]

---

was a real risk that the child would be 'be projected into an emotional maelstrom in which the court, even in the exercise of its coercive powers, would be hard pushed to protect her.'

[306] *Re H and A (Children)* [2002] EWCA Civ 383, [2002] 2 FCR 469 sub nom *Re H and A (Paternity: Blood Tests)* [2002] 1 FLR 1145.

[307] *Re O and J* [2000] 1 FLR 418.

[308] [2000] 1 FLR 418.

[309] For example see *Re G (Parentage: Blood Sample)* [1997] 2 FCR 325, [1997] 1 FLR 360. An adverse inference may be drawn even where there is a presumption of legitimacy operating *F v Child Support Agency* [1999] 2 FCR 385, [1999] 2 FLR 244.

[310] *Re GW (A Minor) (Blood Tests)* [1994] 2 FCR 908, sub nom *Re A (A Minor) (Paternity: Refusal of Blood Test)* [1994] 2 FLR 463 and *Re G (Parentage: Blood Sample)* [1997] 2 FCR 325 at 332, [1997] 1 FLR 360 at 367.

[311] *Re F (Paternity: Jurisdiction)* [2007] EWCA Civ 873, [2008] 1 FLR 225, paras 8 and 14 per Thorpe LJ.

[312] *Re R (A Minor)(Contact)* [1993] 2 FLR 762 at 768.

[313] *Re K (Specific Issue Order)* [1999] 2 FLR 280 and *Re L (A Child)(Contact: Paternity)* [2008] EWCA Civ 1388, [2009] 1 FLR 1152 and *J v C* [2006] EWHC 2837 (Fam), [2007] 1 FCR 365, sub nom *Re J (paternity: welfare of child)* [2007] 1 FLR 1064.

[314] As to the right of a natural parent to obtain information about his or her adopted child see *Re L (Adoption: Disclosure of Information)* [1998] Fam 19, sub nom *D v Registrar General* [1996] 2 FCR 248, [1997] 1 FLR 715.

[315] Adoption and Children Act 2002, Sch 1, para 1. This will include adoptions made in England and Wales, adoptions in Scotland, Northern Ireland, the Isle of Man and the Channel Islands where the Registrar General is notified of such adoptions and foreign adoptions (being adoptions which are either Convention Adoptions or 'overseas adoptions') if the child lives in England (see Adoption and Children Act 2002, Sch 1, paras 1–3). See also the Adopted Children and Adoption Contact Registers Regulations 2005, SI2005/924.

[316] Adoption and Children Act 2002, ss 77(1) and 77(2).

[317] Adoption and Children Act 2002, ss 78(1) and 78(2).

[318] See the Adopted Children and Adoption Contact Registers Regulations 2005, SI 2005/924, reg 10.

Obtaining Details of Birth

7.118 Further, pursuant to the Adoption and Children Act 2002, s 79, the Registrar General must make traceable the connection between entries in the Adopted Children Register and any corresponding entries in the register of live births and other records where a person is marked as adopted. Information kept for the purpose of making traceable the relevant connections is not open to public inspection.[319] An adopted person may however obtain information kept for the purpose of making traceable entries in the register of live births and any other information which would enable him or her to obtain a certified copy of the record of his or her birth and thus his or her birth parent(s) by:

(a)   An application being made in the prescribed manner[320] by the appropriate adoption agency in respect of the adopted person where the applicant was adopted after 30 December 2005;[321]

(b)   An application being made in the prescribed manner by an adopted person who has attained the age of 18 years where the applicant was adopted before 30 December 2005;[322]

(c)   Order of the court against the Registrar General in exceptional circumstances where the applicant was adopted before 30 December 2005.[323]

Finally, an application may be made in the prescribed manner by an adopted person who is under the age of 18 and intends to be married or form a civil partnership, whereupon the Registrar General must inform that applicant whether or not it appears from the information contained in the register or live births or other records that the applicant and the intended spouse or civil partner may be within the prohibited degrees of relationship for the purposes of the Marriage Act 1949 or the Civil Partnership Act 2004.[324]

7.119 The Registrar General can refuse to allow access to birth records on the grounds of public policy.[325] Under its inherent jurisdiction, the High Court may attach a condition to an adoption order to the effect that the Registrar General should not reveal details of the adoption recorded in the Adopted Children's Register without the leave of the High Court.[326]

7.120 In relation to adoptions made after 30 December 2005 an adopted person who has attained the age of 18 also has the right, upon request, to receive information from the relevant adoption agency, or local authority in a non-agency case, that will enable

---

[319] Adoption and Children Act 2002, s 79(2).

[320] See the Adopted Children and Adoption Contact Regulations 2005, SI 2005/924, r 11.

[321] Adoption and Children Act 2002, s 79(5).

[322] Adoption and Children Act 2002, Sch 2, para 1. Before giving information to the applicant pursuant to Sch 2, para 1 the Registrar General must inform the applicant that counselling services are available which must be provided to the applicant if requested (Sch 2, paras 2 and 3). Where the person was adopted before 12 November 1975 it is obligatory for the applicant to first attend an interview with a counsellor (Sch 2, para 4).

[323] Adoption and Children Act 2002, s 79(4).

[324] Adoption and Children Act 2002, s 79(7).

[325] *R v Registrar General ex p Smith* [1990] 2 FLR 79.

[326] *Re X (A Minor) (Adoption: Details: Disclosure)* [1994] 2 FLR 450 and *Re W (Adoption Details: Disclosure)* [1998] 2 FLR 625. See also *President's Direction of 17 December 1998.*

him or her to obtain a certified copy of his or her birth record.[327] This disclosure can extend to copies of the prescribed information given to the adopters pursuant to the Adoption Agencies Regulations 2005 and copy documents from the court file.[328] In exceptional circumstances an application may be made to the High Court to prevent disclosure under these provisions.[329] The statutory right to disclosure from the adoption agency does not apply in relation to adoptions made before 30 December 2005.

Regulations – Disclosure in relation to Adoptions made before 30 December 2005

7.121 Disclosure of information in respect of adoptions which occurred before 30 December 2005 will be governed by the Adoption Information and Intermediary Services (Pre-Commencement Adoptions) Regulations 2005[330] and the Adoption Information and Intermediary Services (Pre-Commencement Adoptions) (Wales) Regulations 2005.[331]

Regulations – Disclosure in relation to Adoptions made after 30 December 2005

7.122 Disclosure of information in respect of adoptions which occurred after 30 December 2005 will be governed by the Adoption and Children Act 2002, ss 54–65 and the Disclosure of Adoption Information (Post-Commencement Adoptions) Regulations 2005,[332] and the Access to Information (Post Commencement Adoptions) (Wales) Regulations 2005.[333]

7.123 In relation to information held by adoption agencies Regulation 15(2)(a) of the Adoption Agencies Regulations 1983 historically conferred upon adoption agencies a wide discretion to disclose to adopted persons information held on the adoption file. Subject to the foregoing pre and post-commencement provisions, it is likely that the correct approach to deciding whether to exercise the discretion to disclose information from an adoption file is to balance, in respect of each piece of information the benefits of disclosure on the one hand and the disadvantages of disclosure on the other. In carrying out this exercise, it has been held that the right to access such information under the provisions of the ECHR are not greater than those which existed under the Adoption Agencies Regulations. Further, it would appear that there are limits on the amount of information a child or adult who has been adopted be entitled to receive from the adoption agency concerning his or her adoptive parents where the information requested predates the date on which he or she was adopted.[334]

The Adoption Contact Register

7.124 Pursuant to s 80 of the Adoption and Children Act 2002, the Registrar General is also obliged to hold an Adoption Contact Register.[335] Part I of the Register contains the details of adopted persons who have given the prescribed notice expressing their wishes as to making contact (or not making contact) with their relatives and have provided sufficient information to the Registrar to obtain a certified copy of the record

---

[327] Adoption and Children Act 2002, s 60.
[328] Adoption and Children Act 2002, s 60(4).
[329] Adoption and Children Act 2002, s 60(2)(a).
[330] SI 2005/890.
[331] SI 2005/2701.
[332] SI 2005/888.
[333] SI 2005/2689.
[334] *Gunn-Russo v Nugent Care Society* [2001] EWHC Admin 566, [2002] 1 FLR 1.
[335] See also the Adopted Children and Adoption Contact Registers Regulations 2005, SI 2005/924.

of their birth.[336] Part II of the Register will contain the details of any relative of an adopted person by blood, half-blood, marriage or civil partnership[337] who wishes to express a view about contact and has the information necessary to obtain a certified copy of the adopted person's birth record.[338] The Adoption Contact Register operates simply by ensuring that information concerning any relative who has requested contact which appears in Part II is transmitted to the adopted person whose details appear in Part I.[339]

Human Fertilisation and Embryology

7.125 The issues which arise in respect of an adopted child's right to know and be cared for by his or her parents can be seen reflected in the position of children conceived by way of donor conception, although care must be taken with the analogy.[340] The domestic courts have emphasised the importance of children so conceived in knowing the identity of their biological parents.[341] Within the context of the advent of donor conception, in considering the issue of the child's right to know and be cared for by his or her parents as a cardinal element of the child's right to identity, it is important to consider who under domestic law is considered to be the legal parent of the child as well as the methods by which a child may obtain information about his or her biological parents.

(ii) Parents[342]

The Mother

7.126 Pursuant to s 27(1) of the Human Fertilisation and Embryology Act 1990 ('HFEA 1990') a woman who is carrying or has carried a child as a result of the placing in her[343] of an embryo or of sperm and eggs, and no other woman, is to be treated as the mother of the child, save where the child is subsequently adopted[344] or a parental order[345] is subsequently made. Section 27 applies only to children carried as the result of the placing of embryos or of sperm or eggs or of their artificial insemination on or after 1 August 1991.[346] After 5 April 2009 the same position pertains under the Human Fertilisation and Embryology Act 2008 ('HFEA 2008').[347]

---

[336]   Adoption and Children Act 2002, s 80(2) and (3).

[337]   Adoption and Children Act 2002, s 81(2).

[338]   Adoption and Children Act 2002, s 80(5).

[339]   Adopted Children and Adoption Contact Registers Regulations 2005, r 8.

[340]   See Turkmenday, I, Dingwall, R and Murphy, T *The Removal of Donor Anonymity in the UK: The Silencing of Claims by Would-Be Parents* (2008) 21 International Journal of Law, Policy and the Family, p 289–290.

[341]   See *Leeds Teaching Hospitals NHS Trust v A and Others* [2003] EWHC 259 (QB), [2003] 1 FCR 599; *R (Rose) v Secretary of State for Health* [2002] EWHC 1593 (Admin), [2002] 3 FCR 731 sub nom *Rose v Secretary of State for Health and Human Fertilisation and Embryology Authority* [2002] 2 FLR 962. See also *Re G (Children) (Residence: Same Sex Partner)* [2006] UKHL 43, [2006] 4 All ER 241.

[342]   The fact that a parent changes their gender does not affect the status of that person as the father or mother of the child in question (see the Gender Recognition Act 2004, s 12). Note that upon ratifying the CRC the United Kingdom entered the following declaration: 'The United Kingdom interprets the references in the Convention to 'parents' to mean only those persons who, as a matter of national law, are treated as parents. This includes cases where the law regards a child as having only one parent, for example where a child has been adopted by one person only and in certain cases where a child is conceived other than as a result of sexual intercourse by the woman who gives birth to it and she is treated as the only parent.'

[343]   Section 27 applies regardless of where the implantation took place (HFEA 1990, s 27(3)).

[344]   HFEA 1990, s 28(2).

[345]   HFEA 1990, s 27 as applied by the Parental Orders (Human Fertilisation and Embryology) Regulations 1994, SI 1994/2767, Sch 3.

[346]   Prior to this date, the position will be governed by common law.

[347]   HFEA 2008, s 33.

7.127 Under the Surrogacy Arrangements Act 1985 an arrangement whereby one woman carries a child for another with the intention that the child will be handed over at birth is not enforceable by or against any of the persons making that arrangement.[348] The surrogate mother will remain the legal mother of the child unless and until that child is subsequently adopted or a parental order is made under the HFEA 1990 s 30. Disputes as to who should care for the child should be determined by the application of the best interests principle.[349]

Genetic Fathers

7.128 The genetic father is regarded as the legal father at common law[350] unless the statutory exceptions under the HFEA 1990 or the HFEA 2008 apply or there has been an adoption order or a parental order under the HFEA 1990 s 30.

Exceptions under the HFEA 1990

7.129 Pursuant to the HFEA 1990 s 28(6) the genetic father of the child will not be the legal father of the child where he is a donor whose sperm is used for 'licensed treatment'[351] and whose consent to use his sperm has been obtained in accordance with the requirements of the Act.[352] Pursuant to s 28(6) of the HFEA 1990 a man whose sperm is used after his death is not the legal father unless:[353]

(a) he was married to the mother before death; or

(b) not married to the mother but with whom they had been provided with treatment services before his death; and

(c) he consented in writing and did not withdraw his consent to that use; and

(d) the mother elected in writing within 42 days[354] of the child's birth to enable the father's particulars to be entered on the birth register;[355] and

(e) no other person is to be treated as the father.

Exceptions under the HFEA 2008

7.130 Pursuant to the HFEA 2008 s 41 the genetic father will not be regarded as the legal father of the child if he is a licensed sperm donor or his sperm was used after his death without his prior written consent.[356]

---

348 Surrogacy Arrangements Act 1985, s 1A as amended by the HFEA 1990, s 36(1).

349 *Re P (Residence: Appeal)* [2007] EWCA Civ 1053, [2008] 1 FLR 198 upholding *Re P (Surrogacy: Residence)* 1 FLR 177.

350 See *Re B (Parentage)* [1996] 2 FLR 15 and *Re M (Child Support Act: Parentage)* [1997] 2 FLR 90.

351 HFEA 1990, Sch 2.

352 HFEA 1990, Sch 3.

353 Human Fertilisation and Embryology (Deceased Fathers) Act 2003. Note that this Act has retrospective effect. Under the Act the same position will exist in relation to an embryo that was created before the father's death but implanted after his death (see HFEA 1990, s 28(5A) and 5B) as amended).

354 This period can be extended for compelling reasons on application to the Registrar General (HFEA 1990, s 28(5F) and (5G).

355 HFEA 1990, s 28(5I) and see Registration of Birth and Deaths (Amendment) Regulations 2003, SI 2003/3048.

356 However, pursuant to s 39 of the HFEA 2008 where the father consents in writing and does not withdraw that consent to the use of his sperm after his death and to being treated as the father for the purpose of being registered as the child's father, he will be treated as the father for this purpose upon the mother electing

Non-genetic Fathers

7.131 A non-genetic father may be treated as the legal father of the child notwithstanding that he did not provide the genetic material by which the child was conceived. Donor conception does not constitute adultery.[357]

Child born between 4 April 1988 and 1 August 1991

7.132 Pursuant to the Family Law Reform Act 1987, s 27(1) a man will be treated as the father of a child born by artificial insemination where he is married to the inseminated woman unless he can prove that he did not consent to the insemination. This provision does not apply where the parties to the 'marriage' are both female.[358]

Child born after 1 August 1991 under the HFEA 1990

7.133 A man will be treated as the legal father of the child carried by a woman as the result of the placing in her of an embryo or sperm and eggs or her artificial insemination after 1 August 1991 notwithstanding that his sperm did not result in the conception of that child provided he is married to the women, unless he can prove that he did not consent to his wife's treatment.[359] It should be noted that the common law presumption of legitimacy based on marriage continues to apply and takes priority over the husband's consent.[360] Under this provision, read with s 27 of the HFEA 1990, a child born to a married surrogate mother will have as his or her legal parents the surrogate mother and her husband.[361] Where an embryo is created before a man's death with the sperm of another man he will be treated as the father of the father if he consented and did not withdraw his consent to the embryo being placed in his widow and to being treated as the father of the child subsequently born for the purposes of the birth register provided the mother elected within 42 days of the child's birth to enable the man's details to be entered into the birth register and no other person is treated as the father.[362]

7.134 Where the man is not married to the women he may also be treated as the legal father of the child carried by a woman as the result of the placing in her of an embryo or sperm and eggs or her artificial insemination after 1 August 1991 notwithstanding that his sperm did not result in the conception of that child where the placing in her of an embryo or sperm and eggs or her artificial insemination was in the course of licensed treatment services[363] provided for them together.[364] The man treated as the father in these circumstances will not automatically acquire parental responsibility for the child.[365]

---

in writing no later than 42 days after the birth of the child for the man to be so treated (under this section no distinction is made between spouses and other relationships).

[357] *MacLennan v MacLennan* (1958) S C 105.

[358] *J v C (Void Marriage: Status of Children)* [2006] EWCA Civ 551, [2006] 2 FLR 1098 in which the applicant was a women whom the mother had 'married' in the mistaken belief that the applicant was a man. The court held that the applicant could not be treated as the father of the children born by artificial insemination by donor.

[359] HFEA 1990 s 28(2). See *Re CH (Contact: Parentage)* [1996] 1 FLR 569.

[360] HFEA 1990 s 28(5)(a).

[361] *Re X (Children) (Parental Order: Surrogacy)* [2008] EWHC 3030 (Fam), [2009] 2 WLR 1294, [2009] FCR 321, [2009] All ER (D) 183 (Apr) sub nom *Re X and Y (Foreign Surrogacy)* [2009] 1 FLR 733.

[362] HFEA 1990 s 28(5C).

[363] For the purposes of the HFEA 1990, s 28(3) 'treatment services' means medical, surgical or obstetric services provided to the public or a section of the public for the purpose of assisting women to carry children (HFEA 1990, s 2). It does not include the concept of counselling (see *Re B (Parentage)* [1996] 2 FLR 15 at 21).

7.135 Finally, where, in the course of licensed treatment provided to the man and women together, an embryo is created with the sperm of a second man, the first man will be treated as the legal father of the child provided he consented and did not withdraw his consent to the embryo being placed in the woman and to being treated as the father of the child subsequently born for the purposes of the birth register provided the mother elected within 42 days of the child's birth to enable the man's details to be entered into the birth register and no other person is treated as the father.[366]

Child born after 5 April 2009 under the HFEA 2008

7.136 A man will be treated as the legal father of the child carried by a woman as the result of the placing in her of an embryo or sperm and eggs or her artificial insemination after 5 April 2009 notwithstanding that his sperm did not result in the conception of that child provided he is married to the women, unless he can prove that he did not consent to his wife's treatment.[367] Again, under this provision, read with s 33 of the HFEA 2008, a child born to a married surrogate mother will have as his or her legal parents the surrogate mother and her husband.[368] Where an embryo is created before a man's death with the sperm of another man the former will be treated as the father if he consented and did not withdraw his consent to the embryo being placed in his widow and to being treated as the father of the child subsequently born for the purposes of the birth register provided the mother elected within 42 days of the child's birth to enable the man's details to be entered into the birth register and no other person is treated as the father.[369]

7.137 Where the man is not married to the women he may also be treated as the legal father of the child carried by a woman as the result of the placing in her of an embryo or sperm and eggs or her artificial insemination after 5 April 2009 notwithstanding that his sperm did not result in the conception of that child where the placing of an embryo or sperm and eggs or the artificial insemination was in the course of licensed treatment

---

[364] HFEA 1990, s 28(3). The meaning of the term 'treatment together' has been the subject of much judicial consideration. It would appear that the approach of Bracewell J in *Re B (Parentage)* [1996] 2 FLR 15 to consider whether the man and women could be said to have embarked on a joint enterprise the object of which was for the woman to conceive is the approach to be preferred (see *R v Human Fertilisation and Embryology Authority ex p Blood* [1999] Fam 151, [1997] 2 All ER 687 and *Evans v Amicus Healthcare Ltd* [2004] EWCA 727, [2005] Fam 1, [2004] 2 FCR 530, [2004] 2 FLR 766). Where circumstances change, for example the man and the woman separate, during the course of treatment the man will not be treated as the father of the child (see *Re D (A Child)* [2005] UKHL 33, sub nom *Re R (IVF: Paternity of Child)* [2005] 2 FLR 843. The man's consent will be vitiated if the hospital uses the wrong sperm (*Leeds Teaching Hospital NHS Trust v A* [2003] EWHC 259 (QB), [2003] 1 FCR 599, [2003] 1 FLR 1091. A clear withdrawal of consent will terminate treatment together (*Evans v Amicus Healthcare Ltd* [2004] EWCA 727, [2005] Fam 1, [2004] 2 FCR 530, [2004] 2 FLR 766). See also *Re Q (Parental Orders)* [1996] 1 FLR 369 and *U v W (A-G Intervening)* [1998] Fam 29, [1998] 1 FCR 526, [1997] 2 FLR 282 and see also Lowe, N and Douglas, G *Bromley's Family Law* (2007) p 306–320. The concept of 'treatment together' has now been replaced under the HFEA 2008 with the concept of 'agreed fatherhood conditions' (see **7.135** below).

[365] *Re R (Contact: Human Fertilisation and Embryology Act 1990)* [2001] 1 FLR 247.

[366] HFEA 1990, s 28(5D).

[367] HFEA 2008, s 35.

[368] *Re X (Children) (Parental Order: Surrogacy)* [2008] EWHC 3030 (Fam), [2009] 2 WLR 1294, [2009] FCR 321, [2009] All ER (D) 183 (Apr) sub nom *Re X and Y (Foreign Surrogacy)* [2009] 1 FLR 733.

[369] HFEA 2008, s 40(1).

services, the 'agreed fatherhood conditions'[370] are met by the man at the time of the placing of an embryo or sperm and eggs or the artificial insemination and the man remained alive at the time of treatment.[371]

7.138 Finally, where, in the course of licensed treatment provided to the man and women together, an embryo is created with the sperm of a second man, the first man will be treated as the legal father of the child provided he consented and did not withdraw his consent to the embryo being placed in the woman and to being treated as the father of the child subsequently born for the purposes of the birth register provided the mother elected within 42 days of the child's birth to enable the man's details to be entered into the birth register and no other person is treated as the father.[372]

Same Sex Female Couples

7.139 Where a female civil partner gives birth to a child conceived by donor insemination she will be the mother of the child and her civil partner will be the other parent, unless her partner did not consent to the mother's treatment.[373] Where a same sex female couple are not civil partners the mother's female partner will be treated as the other parent provided that the placing of an embryo or sperm and eggs or the artificial insemination took place as the result of licensed treatment, the 'agreed female parenthood conditions' have been satisfied and the other woman remains alive at the time of treatment.[374]

Parental Orders[375]

7.140 A parental order pursuant to the HFEA 1990 s 30 provides that a child shall be treated in law as the child to the parties to a marriage in circumstances where the child has been carried by a woman other than the wife as a result of the placing in that woman of an embryo or sperm and eggs or her artificial fertilisation following the use of gametes of one or both of the parties to the marriage. The application may be made only by the husband or wife, at least one of whom must be over 18 and domiciled in the United Kingdom, Channel Islands or Isle of Man.[376] Both the woman who carried the child and the father[377] must agree unconditionally to the making of a parental order.[378] The applicants must satisfy the court that no money or other benefit save expenses reasonably incurred has been paid in connection with the making of the order, the giving of agreement, the handing over the child or the making of any arrangements with

---

[370]   These require that the couple each give notice agreeing to the man being treated as the father pursuant to the HFEA 2008, s 37. The 'agreed fatherhood conditions' replace the concept of 'treatment together' under the HFEA 1990.

[371]   HFEA 2008, s 36.

[372]   HFEA 2008, s 40(2).

[373]   HFEA 2008, s 42.

[374]   HFEA 2008, ss 43 and 44.

[375]   Upon regulations being promulgated under s 55 of the HFEA 2008 parental orders will be available under s 54 of the HFEA 2008 in respect of husbands, wives, civil partners and two persons who are living in an enduring family relationship and who are not within prohibited degrees of relationship. The regulations are still awaited.

[376]   HFEA 1990, s 30(2), s 30(3)(a) and s 30(4).

[377]   This will include a man who is the father for the purposes of the HFEA 1990, s 28(2) and (3). These sections have effect outside the jurisdiction of England and Wales (see *Re X (Children) (Parental Order: Surrogacy)* [2008] EWHC 3030 (Fam), [2009] 2 WLR 1294, [2009] FCR 321, [2009] All ER (D) 183 (Apr) sub nom *Re X and Y (Foreign Surrogacy)* [2009] 1 FLR 733).

[378]   HFEA 1990, s 30(5). See the Adoption Act 1976, s 61 as applied by the Parental Orders (Human Fertilisation and Embryology) Regulations 1994, SI 1994/2767.

a view to the making of the parental order.[379] In considering whether to grant the order the court must give first consideration to the need to safeguard and promote the welfare of the child throughout his or her childhood.[380] Proceedings for a parental order are 'family proceedings' for the purpose of the Children Act 1989 and accordingly the court has jurisdiction to make orders pursuant to ss 8 and 37 of the Children Act 1989.[381] Once made, the parental order will confer parental responsibility upon the applicants to the exclusion of all others, extinguishing the parental responsibility of any person who held it prior to the making of the order.[382] Once a parental order has been made the child will be treated in law as if he or she had been born as the child of the marriage of the husband and wife[383] and as if he or she were not the child of any other person.[384]

(iii)   Obtaining Information about Biological Parents

The Warnock Report

7.141 In the *Report of the Committee of Enquiry into Human Fertilisation and Embryology*[385] ('the Warnock report') the Committee concluded in relation to children conceived by donor insemination that:[386]

> 'We recommend that on reaching the age of eighteen the child should have access to the basic information about the donor's ethnic origin and genetic health and that legislation be enacted to provide the right to access this. This legislation should not be retrospective.'

As to the provision of more detailed information to those children who were conceived by donor conception the Committee concluded:[387]

> 'We are agreed that there is a need to maintain the absolute anonymity of the donor ... Anonymity would give legal protection to the donor but it would also have the effect of minimising the invasion of the third party into the family. Without anonymity, men would, it is argued, be less likely to become donors in view of the risk that they might subsequently be identified and forced to accept parental responsibility for an AID child, by payment of maintenance or otherwise. Clearly in view of our recommendation (4.17) that the AID child should for all purposes be treated as the legitimate child of the couple who have benefited from successful treatment, the donor should have no responsibilities towards the child. We therefore recommend a change in the law so that the semen donor will have no parental rights or duties in relation to the child. We recognise that one consequence of this provision would be that AID children, even if informed about the circumstances of their conception would never be entitled to know the identity of their genetic fathers.'

---

[379]   HFEA 1990, s 30(7). Payments may be authorised and authorisation may be given retrospectively (see *Re X (Children) (Parental Order: Surrogacy)* [2008] EWHC 3030 (Fam), [2009] 2 WLR 1294, [2009] FCR 321, [2009] All ER (D) 183 (Apr) sub nom *Re X and Y (Foreign Surrogacy)* [2009] 1 FLR 733).

[380]   Adoption Act 1976, s 6(1) as applied by the Parental Orders (Human Fertilisation and Embryology) Regulations 1994, SI 1994/2767. Where an application is pending no parent or guardian can remove the child from the applicant's home against the applicant's will without the leave of the court (Adoption Act 1976, s 27(1)).

[381]   HFEA 1990 s 30(8).

[382]   Parental Orders (Human Fertilisation and Embryology) Regulations 1994, SI 1994/2767.

[383]   Adoption Act 1976, s 39(1) as applied by the Parental Orders (Human Fertilisation and Embryology) Regulations 1994, SI 1994/2767.

[384]   Adoption Act 1976, s 39(2) as applied by the Parental Orders (Human Fertilisation and Embryology) Regulations 1994, SI 1994/2767.

[385]   Warnock, M *Report of the Committee of Enquiry into Human Fertilisation and Embryology* (1984) Cmnd 9314.

[386]   Warnock, M *Report of the Committee of Enquiry into Human Fertilisation and Embryology* (1984) Cmnd 9314, para 4.21.

[387]   Warnock, M *Report of the Committee of Enquiry into Human Fertilisation and Embryology* (1984) Cmnd 9314, para 4.22.

The Committee further recommended that the 'fiction' created by donor insemination should be formalised by means of the register of births:[388]

> 'Where the mother is married and the father consents to AID (4.17) we recommend that the law should be changed so as to permit the husband to be registered as the father. We are fully aware that this can be criticised as legislating for a fiction since the husband of a woman who has conceived by AID will not be the genetic father of the child and the register of births has always been envisaged as a true genetic record. Nevertheless it would in our view be consistent with the husband's assuming all parental rights and duties with regard to the child. However, we are of the view that consideration should be given as a matter of urgency to making it possible for the parents in registering the birth to add 'by donation' after the man's name.'[389]

7.142 In relation to children conceived by means of egg donation by a female donor, the Warnock report concluded that:[390]

> '... so far as possible similar principles should apply in relation to the anonymity of the donor, screening, donor profiles, the child's right to know the facts of the donation and access for the couples to information about the donor's ethnic origin and genetic health and, similarly, access for the child to this information on reaching the age of majority ... The principles of good practice we have already considered ... should apply, including the anonymity of the donor [and] openness with the child about his genetic origins ...'

The report further recommended that in relation to children born as the result of egg donation by a female donor that:[391]

> 'legislation should provide that when a child is born to a woman following donation of another's egg the woman giving birth should, for all purposes, be regarded in law as the mother of that child, and the egg donor should have no rights or obligations in respect of the child.'

The Rose Case

7.143 In *R (Rose) v Secretary of State for Health*[392] Scott Baker J, in considering whether claimants born as the result of donor insemination were entitled to rely on Art 8 of the ECHR in seeking non-identifying information about the anonymous donors and a contact register or, where possible, identifying information in respect of the anonymous donors, concluded that:

> 'Respect for private and family life has been interpreted by the European Court to incorporate the concept of personal identity (see *Gaskin v UK*). Everyone should be able to establish details of his identity as a human being. That, to my mind, plainly includes the right to obtain information about a biological parent who will inevitably have contributed to

---

[388] Warnock's position has changed and she now argues that 'all such deception is an evil' (Warnock, M *Making Babies: Is there a Right to Have Children?* (2006) Oxford, OUP 66). See also Eekelaar, J *Family Law and Personal Life* (2006) Oxford, OUP, pp 75–76.

[389] Para 4.25.

[390] Para 6.6.

[391] Para 6.8.

[392] [2002] EWHC 1593 (Admin), [2002] 3 FCR 731 sub nom *Rose v Secretary of State for Health and Human Fertilisation and Embryology Authority* [2002] 2 FLR 962. This case required the court to consider only if Art 8 was engaged and not whether, if the claimant's arguments were accepted on this point, they would justify the making of a declaration of incompatibility.

the identity of his child. There is in my judgment no great leap in construing art 8 in this way. It seems to me to fall naturally into line with the existing jurisprudence of the European Court.'[393]

Disclosure of Donor Information Regulations 2004

7.144 The case of *R (Rose) v Secretary of State for Health*[394] presaged the Human Fertilisation and Embryology Authority (Disclosure of Donor Information) Regulations 2004.[395] Pursuant to reg 2(2) the Human Embryology and Fertilisation Authority ('the Authority') is required to given a person born as the result of donor conception who gives notice to the Authority information provided by the donor as to:

(a)   the sex, height, weight, ethnic group, eye colour, hair colour, skin colour, year of birth, country of birth and marital status of the donor,

(b)   whether the donor was adopted;

(c)   the ethnic group or groups of the donor's parents;

(d)   the screening tests carried out on the donor and information on his personal and family medical history;

(e)   where the donor has a child, the sex of that child and where the donor has children, the number of those children and the sex of each of them;

(f)   the donor's religion, occupation, interests and skills and why the donor provided sperm, eggs or embryos;

(g)   matters contained in any description of himself as a person which the donor has provided; and

(h)   any additional matter which the donor has provided with the intention that it be made available to an applicant;

and where person born by means of donor conception is over the age of 18 the following further information shall be provided under reg 2(3):

(i)   the surname and each forename of the donor and, if different, the surname and each forename of the donor used for the registration of his birth;

(j)   the date of birth of the donor and the town or district in which he was born;

(k)   the appearance of the donor;

(l)   the last known postal address of the donor.

---

[393]   See also *Leeds Teaching Hospitals NHS Trust v A and Others* [2003] EWHC 259 (QB), [2003] 1 FCR 599, para 47.

[394]   [2002] EWHC 1593 (Admin), [2002] 3 FCR 731 sub nom *Rose v Secretary of State for Health and Human Fertilisation and Embryology Authority* [2002] 2 FLR 962. This case required the court to consider only if Art 8 was engaged and not whether, if the claimant's arguments were accepted on this point, they would justify the making of a declaration of incompatibility.

[395]   SI 2004/1511.

Information will not be disclosed under reg 2(2) if it may identify the donor by itself or in combination with any other information which is, or likely to come into the possession of the person born as a result of the donor's donation.[396] The person born as the result of donor conception may request not to receive certain information.[397] These regulations continue to have effect notwithstanding the amendment of the HFEA 1990 s 31 by the HFEA 2008 s 24.[398]

HFEA 1990 as amended

Disclosure on Request

7.145 Pursuant to HFEA 1990 s 31 as amended by s 24 of the HFEA 2008 a person who has attained the age of 16 and has been given suitable opportunity to receive counseling can request that the Authority give notice stating whether or not the information contained in the Register maintained by the Authority[399] shows that some person other person would or might have been his or her parent but for the operation of to ss 27–29 of the HFEA 1990.[400] The Authority must comply with the request if the information contained in the register shows that the applicant was, or may have been, born in consequence of treatment services.[401] If the Register does indicate this then the Authority must provide the person with information pursuant to the regulations[402] and in respect of whether a person specified in the request or any other person might be related.[403] Where the applicant for the information is under the age of 18, he or she cannot require the Authority to give the applicant any information which identifies the donor.[404] Further, a minor may request information concerning the person they wish to marry, enter into a civil partnership or, in respect of children aged 16 or older,[405] with whom they are in, or propose to enter into, an intimate physical relationship.[406]

Disclosure by Court Order

7.146 Pursuant to the HFEA 1990 s 34(1) where in any proceedings before a court the question whether a person is or is not the parent of a child by virtue of ss 27–29 of the Act of 1990 falls to be determined, the court may, where it is satisfied that the interests of justice require taking into account any representations by any individual who may be affected by the disclosure proposed, the welfare of any child and of any other person under 18 who may be affected by disclosure, on the application of any party to the proceedings make an order requiring the Authority to disclose whether or not any

---

[396] SI 2004/1511, reg 2(3).
[397] SI 2004/1511, reg 2(4).
[398] See the Human Fertilisation and Embryology (Consequential Amendments and Transitional and Saving Provisions) Order 2009, SI 2009/1892, art 4, Sch 4, para 13.
[399] As required by the HFEA 1990 s 31 as amended by the HFEA 2008 s 24.
[400] See **7.141–7.144** above.
[401] HFEA 1990 s 31ZA(3)(a).
[402] HFEA 1990 s 31ZA(2)(a). Until further regulations are promulgated the applicable regulations are presumably the Human Fertilisation and Embryology Authority (Disclosure of Donor Information) Regulations 2004 SI 2004/1511 discussed at **7.144** above (see Human Fertilisation and Embryology (Consequential Amendments and Transitional and Saving Provisions) Order 2009, SI 2009/1892, art 4, Sch 4, para 13).
[403] HFEA 1990 s 31ZA(2)(b).
[404] HFEA 1990 s 31ZA(4).
[405] HFEA 1990 s 31ZB(4).
[406] HFEA 1990 s 31ZB(2).

information relevant to that question is contained in the Register and, if it is, to disclose so much of it as is specified in the order.[407] The application may be heard in private.[408]

Parental Orders

7.147 Each parental order must be registered on the Parental Order Register maintained by the Registrar General.[409] Upon request, the Registrar General shall cause a search to be made of the register on the behalf of an applicant or permit that person to search for himself and to issue any person with a certified copy of the register.[410] A person who is the subject of a parental order and has reached the age of 18 may be supplied with information to enable him or her to obtain a certified copy of his or her record of birth upon being advised of the counseling services available.[411]

CONCLUSION

7.148 The child's right to identity is central to the efficacy of his or her other rights. Fortin concludes that it may be said that domestic law fulfils the imperatives of the CRC and ECHR in terms of the child's right to identity very well given mechanisms for adopted children and, to a lesser extent, children born by donor conception to discover their biological origins.[412] However, problems do remain in giving proper effect to the child's right to identity within the domestic context.

7.149 Parents of children born by means of donor conception may still withhold information concerning their child's origins, that effort being assisted by the provisions of the domestic legislation governing reproductive technologies.[413] In so far as parents withhold such information for fear of alienating their children, such fear may be misplaced. Research tends to show that the danger of disrupting the bond with the psychological parent arising from identifying the genetic parent is relatively low.[414] However, save where the position is too stark to avoid intervention, the Courts will not act to correct the fiction.[415] There also remains a group of children who fall entirely outside any regulatory regime in respect of obtaining knowledge of their origins. Jackson points out that infidelity may present a statistically far greater threat to the child's right to know his or her genetic origins than assisted conception, pointing out that an estimated 10% of the population is not biologically related to their presumed father.[416]

---

[407] See also disclosure of information in proceedings under the Congenital Disabilities (Civil Liability) Act 1976.

[408] HFEA 1990, s 34(3) and s 34(4).

[409] Adoption Act 1976, s 50 as applied by the Parental Orders (Human Fertilisation and Embryology) Regulations 1994, SI 1994/2767. See also the Forms of Entry for Parental Orders Regulations 1994, SI 1994/2981.

[410] Adoption Act 1976, s 50(3) as applied by the Parental Orders (Human Fertilisation and Embryology) Regulations 1994 SI 1994/2767.

[411] Adoption Act 1976, s 51 as applied by the Parental Orders (Human Fertilisation and Embryology) Regulations 1994 SI 1994/2767.

[412] Fortin, J *Children's Rights and the Developing Law* (2009) 3rd edn, Cambridge, p 472. But see *State of Children's Rights in England* (2008) Children's Rights Alliance for England, p 14.

[413] Fortin, J *Children's Rights and the Developing Law* (2009) 3rd edn, Cambridge, p 466 and see **7.141–7.144** above.

[414] See Sheldon, S *Fragmenting Fatherhood: The Regulation of Reproductive Technologies* (2005) 68 Modern Law Review 523, pp 550–551 and (by reference to adoption) Howe, D and Feast, J *Adoption, Search and Reunion: The Long Term Experience of Adopted Adults* (2000) The Children's Society, p 127.

[415] See *Leeds Teaching Hospital NHS Trust v A* [2003] EWHC 259, [2003] 1 FLR 1091.

[416] Jackson, E *Regulating Reproduction* (2001) Hart Publishing.

7.150 The need for rigorous maintenance of the child's right to identity is perhaps best demonstrated by the identity of children as a group being regularly subverted by unjustified press generalisations in the press of children as 'feral youths', 'hoodies' and 'yobs' and a prevalence of television programmes purporting to give 'parenting advice' in respect of 'problem children'.[417] Art 16(1) of the CRC stipulates that the child shall not be the subject to unlawful attacks on his or her honour or reputation. In its report on the 1996 Day of General Discussion on the child and the media, the Committee on the Rights of the Child noted that:

> 'In their reporting the media give an 'image' of the child; they reflect and influence perceptions about who children are and how they behave. This image could create and convey respect for young people; however, it could also spread prejudices and stereotypes which may have a negative influence on public opinion and politicians. Nuanced and well informed reporting is to the benefit of the rights of the child.'[418]

This situation makes it clear that to be effective in underpinning the efficacy of the child's rights overall, the right to identity must be effectively applied well beyond the fields of paternity, adoption and donor conception.

---

[417] See *State of Children's Rights in England* (2008) Children's Rights Alliance for England, p 18 and *The Voices behind the Hood: Young People's Views on Anti-Social Behaviour, the Media and Older People* (2006) British Youth Council and YouthNet. See also the Serious Organised Crime and Police Act 2005, s 141 allowing children who breach their Anti-Social Behaviour Order to be 'named and shamed'.

[418] *Report of the 11th Session* (1996) CRC/C/50 Annex IX, pp 80 and 81. See also Nicaragua CRC/C/15/Add.36, paras 17 and 34.

Chapter 8

THE CHILD'S RIGHT TO RESPECT FOR FAMILY LIFE

'Family life etches itself into memory and personality.
It's difficult to imagine anything more nourishing to the soul'

Thomas Moore

INTRODUCTION

8.1   Universal Declaration of Human Rights proclaims that the family is 'the natural and fundamental group unit of society'.[1] The primacy of the family as the most basic unit in human society, and its importance to children, is reflected in many of the human rights instruments relevant to the rights of the child.[2] The UN Convention on the Rights of the Child describes the family as 'the fundamental group of society and the natural environment for the growth and well-being of all its members and particularly children'.[3] The CRC further declares that 'the child, for the full and harmonious development of his or personality, should grow up in a family environment, in an atmosphere of happiness, love and understanding'.[4] The UN Guidelines for the Prevention of Juvenile Delinquency (the 'Riyadh Guidelines') state that 'the family is the central unit responsible for the primary socialisation of children'.[5] For the vast majority of children the family provides the overarching context within which the rights of the child fall to be considered and given effect.[6] The rights of the child, whilst sovereign, are usually best protected and promoted within the context of the child's family life with his or her parents.

---

[1]   Universal Declaration of Human Rights Art 16(3). This formulation is also used in Art 10(1) of the Covenant on Economic, Social and Cultural Rights and Art 23(1) of the Covenant on Civil and Political Rights.

[2]   The African Charter on the Rights and Welfare of the Child, Art 18 ('The family shall be the natural unit and basis of society ...'), the African Youth Charter, Art 8 ('The family, as the most basic social institution ...'), the African (Banjul) Charter on Human and Peoples Rights, Art 18 ('The family shall be the natural unit and basis of society' and 'the family which is the custodian of morals and traditional values recognised by the community.'), the Ibero-American Convention on the Rights of Youth, Art 7 ('Prominence of Family'), the American Convention on Human Rights, Art 17 and the Revised Arab Charter on Human Rights, Art 33 ('The family is the natural and fundamental group unit of society').

[3]   CRC Preamble.

[4]   CRC Preamble. See also para 11 of CRC General Comment No 4 *Adolescent health and development in the context of the Convention on the Rights of the Child* HRI/GEN/1/Rev. 8 p 378 ('The Committee stresses the importance of the family environment, including the members of the extended family and community or other persons legally responsible for the child or adolescent (arts. 5 and 18)').

[5]   UN Guidelines for the Prevention of Juvenile Delinquency Section IV, para 10(A)(12). See also the Paris Principles, para 6.31 ('The family and community generally provide the most effective protection for children').

[6]   E/CN.4/1982/L.14.

8.2   The concept of 'family' must necessarily embrace the relationship between the parents and child[7] and between the child and members of the extended family. The object of family life is to ensure for the members of that family the normal development of family and social relationships.[8] The family is thus the societal unit by which children become socialised and bring the characteristics which result from that socialisation into their adult lives.[9] In its General Comment No 7 *Implementing Child Rights in Early Childhood* the Committee on the Rights of the Child notes that:[10]

> 'Young children's experiences of growth and development vary according to their individual nature, as well as their gender, living conditions, family organisation, care arrangements and education systems ... Young children's experiences of growth and development are powerfully shaped by cultural beliefs about their needs and proper treatment, and about their active role in family and community.'

In the domestic context, the House of Lords recognised in *Huang v Secretary of State for the Home Department*[11] that:

> 'Human beings are social animals. They depend on others. Their family, or extended family, is the group on which many people most heavily depend, socially, emotionally and often financially. There comes a point at which, for some, prolonged and unavoidable separation from this group seriously inhibits their ability to live full and fulfilling lives.'

8.3   In this context, international and regional human rights instruments emphasise the importance of the widest possible protection and assistance for the family. This protection and assistance often requires a careful balance to be struck between what is regarded as the proper autonomy of the family, the individual rights of its members and the role of the State as the main source of provision of such protection and assistance. This can result in considerable friction at the boundary between the rights of different members of the family, including those of the child, and the responsibilities and duties of the State owed to children, parents and other family members. This chapter commences with a consideration of the definition of family within the context of children's rights and the difficult balance required to be struck as between the positions of the child, the family and the State. After next examining the general requirement to provide protection and assistance to the family this chapter then considers each of the cardinal aspects of the child's right to family life under international, regional and domestic[12] provisions, including the right not to be separated from parents, the right to continuing contact with parents and family and the right to alternative care.

GENERAL PRINCIPLES

General Principles – The Definition of 'Family'

8.4   Given the recognition of the family as the fundamental group unit of society and the natural environment for the growth and well-being of its members and particularly

---

[7]   *Wim Hendricks v The Netherlands* (1985) No 201/1985 (decision of the UN Human Rights Committee).
[8]   *Marckx v Belgium* (1979) 2 EHRR 330 and *Olsson v Sweden* (1988) 11 EHRR 259.
[9]   See UN Guidelines for the Prevention of Juvenile Delinquency, Section IV, para 10.
[10]   Committee on the Rights of the Child General Comment No 7 *Implementing Child Rights in Early Childhood* HRI/GEN/1/Rev. 8 p 435, para 6(f)–6(g).
[11]   [2007] UKHL 11, [2007] 2 AC 167, para 18.
[12]   The right to family life under domestic law is now most commonly articulated by reference to Art 8 of the European Convention on Human Rights.

children, the manner in which the family is defined is crucial when considering the nature, extent and implementation of the rights of the child.[13] There is no treaty definition of the word 'family' *per se*.[14] Rather international law incorporates three overlapping concepts concerning the family, namely those of 'family', 'family life' and 'family environment'.[15] The concepts of 'family life' and 'family environment' add a qualitative element to the concept of 'family'.[16] For this reason, the concepts of 'family life' and 'family environment' are perhaps the most helpful when considering the rights of the child. Overall, the approach in international law is to see the family as a community of individuals possessing specific rights.[17]

Definition of 'Family' under the UN Human Rights Framework

CRC, Art 5

8.5   Article 5 of the CRC incorporates the following description of 'family' for the purposes of the Convention:[18]

> 'States Parties shall respect the responsibilities, rights and duties of parents or, where applicable, the members of the extended family or community as provided for by local custom, legal guardians or other persons legally responsible for the child, to provide, in a manner consistent with the evolving capacities of the child, appropriate direction and guidance in the exercise by the child of the rights recognised in the present Convention.'

8.6   Article 5 of the CRC has been described as providing a 'flexible' description of family[19] and should focus the attention of States Parties not only on the child's relationship with his or her parents but also towards the potential of the extended family and the community. The Committee on the Rights of the Child has articulated this approach in its General Comment No 7 *Implementing Child Rights in Early Childhood*, providing as follows:[20]

> 'Under normal circumstances, a young child's parents play a crucial role in the achievement of their rights, along with other members of family, extended family or community, including legal guardians, as appropriate. This is fully recognised within the Convention (especially article 5), along with the obligation on States parties to provide assistance, including quality childcare services (especially article 18). The preamble to the Convention refers to the family as 'the fundamental group of society and the natural environment for the growth and well-being of all its members and particularly children'. The Committee recognises that 'family' here refers to a variety of arrangements that can provide for young children's care, nurturance and development, including the nuclear family, the extended

---

[13]   Van Bueren, G *The International Law on the Rights of the Child* (1998) Martinus Nijhoff, p 67.

[14]   Hale et al point out that, within the context of our multi-ethnic and culturally diverse society the definition of 'family' is in any event far from static (see Hale, B, Pearl, D, Cooke, E and Monk, D *The Family, Law and Society* (2009) 6th edn, Oxford University Press, p 1). See also CRC General Comment No 7 *Implementing Child Rights in Early Childhood* HRI/GEN/1/Rev. 8 p 440, para 19 and the Human Rights Committee General Comment No 19 *Article 23 (The Family)* HRI/GEN/1/Rev 8, p 188, para 2.

[15]   See **8.1** above.

[16]   Van Bueren, G *Child Rights in Europe* (2007) Council of Europe Publishing, p 118.

[17]   Van Bueren, G *The International Law on the Rights of the Child* (1998) Martinus Nijhoff, p 72.

[18]   Van Bueren points out that this wider focus on kinship and community is not consistently reflected in the rest of the CRC, the Convention referring in the majority of its articles to 'the parents, legal guardians and other persons legally responsible' as in Arts 14 and 18 (Van Bueren, G *The International Law on the Rights of the Child* (1998) Martinus Nijhoff, p 71).

[19]   Newell, P and Hodgkin, R *Implementation Handbook for the Convention on the Rights of the Child* (2008) 3rd edn, UNICEF, p 75.

[20]   Committee on the Rights of the Child General Comment No 7 *Implementing Child Rights in Early Childhood* HRI/GEN/1/Rev. 8 p 440, para 15

family, and other traditional and modern community-based arrangements, provided these are consistent with children's rights and best interests.'

8.7   The description of the family incorporated into Art 5 of the CRC takes account of the divergent concepts of family which may exist in different States.[21] Van Bueren points out that this need to accommodate a range of different family and community structures and values creates a tension with the need to enshrine and apply universal agreed minimum standards on the rights of the child.[22] An example is polygamous families. The Committee on the Rights of the Child has recommended that polygamous or bi-linear families be investigated for any negative impact on children.[23] General Recommendation No 21 of the Committee on the Elimination of Discrimination against Women proposes a prohibition on bigamy and polygamy and the protection of the rights of children.[24] In interpreting the other provisions of the CRC and the provisions of the other UN human rights instruments as they relate to the definition of family, such provisions must also be read in conjunction with CRC, Art 5.[25]

Covenant on Civil and Political Rights, Art 17 and 23

8.8   The interpretation of the concepts of 'family', 'family life' and 'family environment' is assisted by considering the use of these terms in other UN human rights instruments. The UN Human Rights Committee has made clear that the concept of 'family' must be understood in the wide sense.[26] In its General Comment No 16 *Article 17 (Right to Privacy)* the UN Human Rights Committee made clear in relation to Art 17 of the Covenant on Civil and Political Rights that:[27]

> 'Regarding the term "family", the objectives of the Covenant require that for purposes of article 17 this term be given a broad interpretation to include all those comprising the family as understood in the society of the State party concerned.'

8.9   Article 23 of the Covenant on Civil and Political Rights states 'The family is the natural and fundamental group unit of society and is entitled to protection by society and the State'. In recognising that the concept of family may differ from State to State, in the case of *Shirin Aumeeruddy-Cziffra and Nineteen other Mauritian Women v Mauritius*[28] the UN Human Rights Committee observed in respect of Art 23(1) of the ICCPR that:

> 'The Committee is of the opinion that the legal protection or measures a society or a State can afford to the family may vary from country to country and depend on different social, economic, political and cultural conditions and traditions.'

---

[21]   Van Bueren, G *The International Law on the Rights of the Child* (1998) Martinus Nijhoff, p 70.

[22]   Van Bueren, G *The International Law on the Rights of the Child* (1998) Martinus Nijhoff, p 67.

[23]   See Yemen CRC/C/15/Add.267, para 48.

[24]   (1994) HRI/GEN/1/Rev.8, para 39, p 315.

[25]   See Art 31 Vienna Convention on the Law of Treaties.

[26]   Human Rights Committee General Comment No 4 *The Right to Adequate Housing (Art 11(1) of the Covenant)* HRI/GEN/1/Rev 8, p 20, para 6. See also *Manual on Human Rights Reporting* HR/PUB/91/1/ (Rev.1) p 117.

[27]   Human Rights Committee General Comment No 16 *Article 17 (Right to Privacy)*, para 5. HRI/GEN/1/Rev. 8 p 182. See also General Comment No 5 *Persons with Disabilities* (1994) HRI/GEN/1/Rev.8, para 30.p 31 ('In this and other contexts, the term 'family' should be interpreted broadly and in accordance with appropriate local usage').

[28]   Communication No 35/1978, U.N. Doc. CCPR/C/OP/2 at 226 (1990).

In *Hendriks v Netherlands*[29] the UN Human Rights Committee made clear that the concept of the family survives separation and divorce for the purposes of Art 23(1) of the ICCPR:

> 'The words 'the family' in article 23 paragraph 1 do not refer solely to the family as it exists during the marriage. The idea of the family must necessarily embrace the relations between parents and child. Although divorce legally ends a marriage, it cannot dissolve the bond uniting father – or mother – and child; this bond does not depend on the continuation of the parents' marriage.'

8.10 Whilst seeking to maintain a flexible description of 'family' capable of evolving with social, economic, political and cultural developments, the UN Human Rights Committee has made it clear that the there are limits on the concept of 'family', imposed by the need to ensure that the concept of 'family' does not result in discrimination.[30] In this regard, the Committee has observed that:

> 'Where the Covenant requires a substantial protection as in article 23, it follows from those provisions that such protection must be equal, that is to say not discriminatory, for example on the basis of sex.'

Definition of 'Family Life' under Art 8, ECHR

Article 8 'Family Life' – A Question of Fact

8.11 Under Art 8 of the European Convention on Human Rights 'family life' is an autonomous concept and has been described as being *de facto* family life rather than *de jure* family life.[31] As such, the existence or non-existence under Art 8 of 'family life' for children will be a question of fact depending on the real existence in practice of close personal ties between those children and others.[32] As noted by the House of Lords in relation to the concept of family life for the purposes of Art 8 of the ECHR:[33]

> 'Families differ widely, in their composition and in the mutual relations which exist between the members, and marked changes are likely to occur over time within the same family. Thus there is no pre-determined model of family or family life to which art 8 must be applied. The article requires respect to be shown for the right to such family life as is or may be enjoyed by the particular Applicant or Applicants before the court, always bearing in mind (since any family must have at least two members, and may have many more) the participation of other members who share in the life of that family. In this context, as in most Convention contexts, the facts of the particular case are crucial.'

---

[29] (1985) No 201/1985.
[30] Van Bueren, G *The International Law on the Rights of the Child* (1998) Martinus Nijhoff, p 69.
[31] *Marckx v Belgium* (1979) 2 EHRR 330. See also *X v Switzerland* Application No 8924/80 DR 24.
[32] *K v United Kingdom* (1986) 50 DR 199. Note that in *Şerife Yiğit v Turkey* (2010) Application No 3976/05, para 95 the European Court of Human Rights made clear that the concept of family life under the ECHR 'does not include only social, moral or cultural relations, for example in the sphere of children's education; it also comprises interests of a material kind, as is shown by, amongst other things, the obligations in respect of maintenance and the position occupied in the domestic legal systems of the majority of the Contracting States by the institution of the reserved portion of an estate.'
[33] *EM (Lebanon) v Secretary of State for the Home Department ALF intervening* [2008] UKHL 64, [2009] 1 All ER 539, para 37 per Lord Bingham.

Article 8 'Family Life' – Children and Parents

8.12   In most circumstances family life will exist for the purposes of Art 8 between a child and his or her biological parents.[34] Family life for a child born within marriage will exist from birth by the very fact of that birth.[35] Family life may arise whether or not that child is a marital or non-marital child.[36] This will include a non-marital child of an informal union between his or her parents.[37] The European Court of Human Rights observed in *Sommerfeld v Germany*[38] that:

> 'The Court recalls that the notion of family under this provision is not confined to marriage-based relationships and may encompass other *de facto* 'family' ties where the parties are living together out of wedlock. A child born out of such a relationship is *ipso jure* part of that 'family' unit from the moment and by the very fact of his birth. Thus there exists between the child and his parents a bond amounting to family life.'

Family life under Art 8 between an unmarried mother and her child is established by fact of birth itself.[39] Family life will exist between an unmarried father and his child[40] provided a sufficient nexus is maintained between child and his or her father.[41] In assessing the latter, it is the social reality that will be important.[42] A father who has never had any contact with his child will have no right to respect for family life with that child.[43] However, whilst family life presupposes the existence of family, potential family life may come within the ambit of Art 8.[44] Thus the potential relationship between a child born out of wedlock and his or her father may amount to 'family life' for the purposes of Art 8 of the ECHR.[45]

8.13   Co-habitation is not a necessary pre-condition of the existence of family life between parents and children.[46] Thus, divorce and separation will not bring family life between the child and the absent parent to an end, even if the divorce leads to a significant period of loss of contact.[47] The breakdown of a settled relationship will

---

[34]   *Sommerfeld v Germany* (2003) 36 EHRR.
[35]   *Ahmut v Netherlands* (1997) 24 EHRR 62. See also *Berrehab v Netherlands* (1988) 11 HERR 322 and *Gül v Switzerland* (1996) 22 EHRR 93 and *Johnston v Ireland* (1986) 9 EHRR 203.
[36]   See *Berrehab v Netherlands* (1988) 11 HERR 322, para 21). See also *Gül v Switzerland* (1996) 22 EHRR 93 and *Söderbeck v Sweden* (1998) 29 EHRR 95 and *Brauer v Germany* (2009) Application No 3545/04, para 40 ('The Court reiterates in this connection that the Convention is a living instrument which must be interpreted in the light of present-day conditions. Today the member States of the Council of Europe attach great importance to the question of equality between children born in and children born out of wedlock as regards their civil rights. This is shown by the 1975 European Convention on the Legal Status of Children born out of Wedlock, which is currently in force in respect of twenty-one member States and has not been ratified by Germany. Very weighty reasons would accordingly have to be advanced before a difference of treatment on the ground of birth out of wedlock could be regarded as compatible with the Convention').
[37]   *Johnston v Ireland* (1986) 9 EHRR 203.
[38]   (2003) 36 EHRR, para 32.
[39]   *Marckx v Belgium* (1979) 2 EHRR 330.
[40]   *Kroon v Netherlands* (1994) 19 EHRR 263.
[41]   *X v United Kingdom* (1980) 19 DR244, p 253–254; *MB v United Kingdom* (1994) 77–A DR 108; *Nylund v Finland* (1999) Application No 27110/95 (unreported) and *Lebbink v Netherlands* [2004] 2 FLR 463. In *Keegan v Ireland* (1994) 18 EHRR 342 the European Court of Human Rights was satisfied that family life existed between the unmarried father and child even though they had met only once.
[42]   *X, Y and Z v United Kingdom* [1997] 2 FLR 892.
[43]   *Lebbink v Netherlands* [2004] 2 FLR 463.
[44]   *Marckx v Belgium* (1979) 2 EHRR 330 and *Abdulaziz, Cabales and Balkandali* (1985) 7 EHRR 471.
[45]   *Nylund v Finland* (1999) Application No 27110/95 (unreported).
[46]   *Berrehab v Netherlands* (1988) 11 HERR 322 and *Boughanemi v France* (1996) 22 EHRR 227.
[47]   *Berrehab v Netherlands* (1988) 11 HERR 322 and *Gül v Switzerland* (1996) 22 EHRR 93. See also *Chepelev v Russia* (2008) 47 EHRR 37.

likewise not lead to the end of family life between child and parent.[48] The placing of the child in public care will not bring family life to an end for the purposes of Art 8.[49] Even periods of considerable separation between parent and child may not be sufficient to prevent a conclusion that family life exists.[50] Indeed, the Art 8 rights of the child may be engaged even after the death of a parent where the child's identity is in issue.[51] A right of succession between children and parents is so closely related to family life that it comes within the sphere of Art 8 of the ECHR.[52] The evolving capacity of the child may be relevant to the existence of family life, as the older the child the less dependent on adults that child becomes.[53]

Article 8 'Family Life' – Children and Extended Family

8.14 In respect of siblings, the existence of family life between a child and his or her siblings is consonant with the use of the word 'everyone' in Art 8 of the ECHR including family life as between half siblings.[54] A child's family life under the ECHR will, subject to the existence in practice of close personal ties, encompass near relatives, including grandparents[55] and uncles and aunts.[56] It would appear that more distant relatives will also be able to bring themselves within Art 8 of the ECHR.[57] However, again this proposition must always be tested against the 'existence in practice of close personal ties'.

Article 8 'Family Life' – Foster Care and Adoption

8.15 It has been argued that normally there will be, as a matter of fact, family life between foster carers and the children they care for.[58] The relationship between an adopted child and adoptive parents will be of the same nature as those relationships which fall within the ambit of Art 8 of the ECHR.[59] In *Pini and Others v Romania*[60] the

---

[48] *Keegan v Ireland* (1994) 18 EHRR 342.

[49] *Andersson v Sweden* (1992) 14 EHRR 615.

[50] *Moustaquim v Belgium* (1991) 13 EHRR 802. But see also *MB v United Kingdom* (1994) 77–A DR 108.

[51] *Mikulic v Croatia* [2002] 1 FCR 720, paras 64–66. But see also *Hass v Netherlands* (2004) Application No 36983/97 (unreported). Note that the dead do not have Art 8 rights (see *The Estate of Kresten Filtenborg Mortensen v Denmark* (2006) Application No 1338/03 (unreported)).

[52] *Brauer v Germany* (2009) Application No 3545/04, para 30.

[53] *Mokrani v France* (2003) 40 EHRR 123, para 33

[54] *Marckx v Belgium* (1979) 2 EHRR 330, para 31 ('The Court concurs entirely with the Commission's established case-law on a crucial point, namely that Article 8 makes no distinction between the 'legitimate' and the 'illegitimate' family. Such a distinction would not be consonant with the word 'everyone', and this is confirmed by Article 14 with its prohibition, in the enjoyment of the rights and freedoms enshrined in the Convention, of discrimination grounded on 'birth'. In addition, the Court notes that the Committee of Ministers of the Council of Europe regards the single woman and her child as one form of family no less than others'); *Keegan v Ireland* (1994) 18 EHRR 342, para 44 and *Kroon v Netherlands* (1994) 19 EHRR 263, para 30. See also *Moustaquim v Belgium* (1991) 13 EHRR 802 and *Burden v United Kingdom* [2008] 2 FLR 787.

[55] *Price v United Kingdom* (1988) 55 DR 1988; *GHB v United Kingdom* Application 42455/98 (unreported) 4 May 2000 and *Bronda v Italy* Application No 22430/93 (unreported) 1998. See also Douglas, G and Ferguson, N *The Role of Grandparents in Divorced Families* (2003) International Journal of Law, Policy and the Family 17, p 41.

[56] *Boyle v United Kingdom* (1994) 19 EHRR 179 in which the uncle in question lived close to the child and acted as a father figure to his nephew. Contrast the case of *R (Banks) v Governor of Wakefield Prison* [2001] EWHC 917 (Admin), [2002] 1 FCR 445.

[57] *Wandsworth London Borough Council v Michalak* [2002] EWCA Civ 271, [2002] 4 All ER 1136.

[58] See the dissenting opinion of Schermers J in *Eriksson v Sweden* (1989) 12 EHRR 183 and Recommendation No R (87)6 of the Committee of Ministers in Respect of Foster Families. See also *Gaskin v United Kingdom* (1989) 12 EHRR 36; *X v Switzerland* (1978) 13 DR 248; *Rieme v Sweden* (1993) 16 EHRR 155 and *R (R) v Manchester City Council* [2002] 1 FLR 43.

[59] *X v France* Application No 9993/82, *X v Belgium and the Netherlands* Application No 6482/74 and *Kurochkin v Ukraine* (2010) Application No 42276/08, para 37 ('The Court recalls that the relations between an

Court held that a relationship between the adopter and the adopted child amounted to family life even in the absence of any concrete direct contact between the adults and the child. On the basis that periods of considerable separation between a parent and child may not be sufficient to prevent a conclusion that family life exists[61] it is likely that, having established the existence of family life for the purposes of Art 8 prior to adoption, the adopted child and his or her natural parents will retain their respective Art 8 rights consequent upon their prior 'family life' even following the child's adoption.

Article 8 'Family Life' – Donor Conception

8.16   The donation of sperm does not, by virtue of the biologic link alone, establish for the donor a right to family life under Art 8 of the ECHR with any subsequent child.[62] In *G v Netherlands*[63] the court held that the donor of sperm did not have family life with the child subsequently born even where he had been involved in caring for the child for 7 months.[64] The European Court of Human Rights has also held that family life does not exist between a non-biological parent and a child born to a lesbian relationship by means of artificial insemination.[65] This decision was distinguished in *X, Y and Z v United Kingdom*[66] in which family life was held to exist for the purposes of Art 8 between a woman, her female to male transsexual partner and the child the woman had conceived by donor insemination from an anonymous donor.

Article 8 'Family Life' – Other Relationships

8.17   Engagements to marry with evidence of intention or the establishing of relations may give rise to family life.[67] Marriages not in accordance with national law will not prevent the existence of family life.[68] Polygamous relationships may give rise to family life for the purposes of Art 8 of the ECHR.[69] To date the European Court of Human Rights has declined to recognise the existence of family life between homosexual partners.[70] The domestic courts have declined to follow the European Court of Human Rights in this regard.[71]

---

adoptive parent and an adopted child are as a rule of the same nature as the family relations protected by Article 8 of the Convention and such a relationship, arising from a lawful and genuine adoption, may be deemed sufficient to attract such respect as may be due for family life under Article 8 of the Convention').

60   [2005] 2 FLR 596.

61   *Moustaquim v Belgium* (1991) 13 EHRR 802. But see also *MB v United Kingdom* (1994) 77–A DR 108.

62   *M v Netherlands* (1993) 74 DR 120. See also *Re R (A Child) (IVF Child: Paternity Rights)* [2003] EWCA Civ 182, [2003] Fam 129 (no family life between a man and a child to whom the mother had given birth through IVF after separation even though the mother planned to raise the child with the father and acknowledged he would be the legal father of any child resulting from IVF treatment).

63   (1993) 16 EHRR CD 38.

64   Whether this decision can be reconciled with the factual test of 'the real existence in practice of close personal ties' is highly questionable.

65   *Kerkhoven v Netherlands* (1992) Application No15666/89 (unreported).

66   (1997) 24 EHRR 143.

67   *Wakefield v United Kingdom* (1990) 66 DR 251 although engagement does not of itself create family life.

68   *Abdulaziz, Cabales and Balkandali* (1985) 7 EHRR 471. In relation to 'sham' marriages see *Benes v Austria* (1992) 72 DR 271.

69   See *Alam and Khan v United Kingdom* (1967) 10 YB 478 and *A and A v Netherlands* (1992) 72 DR 118 but see also **8.7** above.

70   *S v United Kingdom* (1986) DR 47 274. See also *Grant v South-West Trains Ltd* [1998] ICR 449 for the position of homosexual relationships under European Union Law.

71   See *Fitzpatrick v Sterling Housing Association Ltd* [2001] 1 AC 27 and *Mendoza v Ghaidan* [2002] EWCA Civ 1533, [2003] Ch 380.

Relationships stopping short of 'Family Life'

8.18   Close relationships of the child which fall short of 'family life' for the purposes of Art 8 of the ECHR will nonetheless generally fall within the scope of 'private life' for the purposes of Art 8.[72] The child's right to respect for private life is dealt with in chapter 9.

Definition of 'Family' under Other Regional Instruments

8.19   Article 18 of the African Charter on the Rights and Welfare of the Child provides that the family shall be the natural unit and basis of society.[73] Art 8 of the African Youth Charter defines the family as the most basic social institution. Article 18 of the African (Banjul) Charter on Human and Peoples Rights similarly defines the family as the natural unit and basis of society and identifies it as 'the custodian of morals and traditional values recognised by the community'.[74] Art 33 of the Revised Arab Charter on Human Rights provides that the family is the natural and fundamental group unit of society.

8.20   The Ibero-American Convention on the Rights of Youth does not seek to define the family but enjoins States Parties to recognise the importance of the family and the duties and responsibilities parents or their legal substitutes to guide children in the exercise of the rights conferred by the Convention.[75] Art 19 of the Convention articulates the family as that which promotes relations of mutual affection, respect and responsibility. Article 17 of the American Convention on Human Rights stipulates that the family is the natural and fundamental group unit of society and is entitled to protection by society and the state.[76] Art 17 recognises the central role of the family and family-life in the individual's existence and society in general.[77] According to the Inter-American Court of Human Rights the term 'next of kin' must be understood in a broad sense that encompasses all persons linked by close kinship.[78]

---

[72]   *Znamenskaya v Russia* (2007) 44 EHRR 293. See chapter 9 below.
[73]   See also Art 20 of the African Charter on the Rights and Welfare of the Child.
[74]   It has often been observed that in many African cultural contexts the concept of 'parent' is wider than the man and woman who are biological parents and that the idea of 'family' assumes an extended group of kin (see for example Ankut, P *The African Charter on the Rights and Welfare of the Child – Linking Principles with Practice* (2008) Open Society Initiative for West Africa, p 6). But see also Van Bueren, G *The International Law on the Rights of the Child* (1998) Martinus Nijhoff, p 69. Van Bueren observes that it is simplistic and erroneous to conclude simply that Europe and North America have nuclear families and Asia, Africa and South America have extended families.
[75]   Article 7.
[76]   See also Advisory Opinion OC-17/2002 of August 28 2002 requested by the Inter-American Commission on Human Rights, paras 67–70.
[77]   *Ms. X v Argentina* (1996) Case 10.506, Report No 38/96.
[78]   See *Cfr. Trujillo Oroza Case. Reparations* (Art 63(1) American Convention on Human Rights). February 27, 2002 Judgement. Series C No 92, para 57; *Bámaca Velásquez Case. Reparations* (Art 63(1) American Convention on Human Rights). February 22, 2002 Judgment. Series C No 91, para 34; and *Villagrán Morales et al. Case. Reparations (Art 63(1) American Convention on Human Rights)*. May 26, 2001 Judgment. Series C No 77, para 68.

Definition of Family in Domestic Law

8.21   In domestic law, the technical concept of 'family' and 'family life' has undergone a swift and arguably radical development.[79] Lord Asquith in *Gammans v Ekins*[80] commented that:

> 'If ... the relationship involves sexual relations, it seems to me anomalous that a person can acquire a "status of irremoveability" by having lived in sin, even if the liaison has been protracted in time and conclusive in character. To say that two people masquerading, as these two were, as husband and wife – there being no children to complicate the picture – that they were members of the same family, seems to me an abuse of the English language.'

8.22   Nearly 30 years later Lord Diplock in *Carga Properties (formerly known as Joram Development) v Sherratt*[81] citing Russell LJ in *Ross v Collins*[82] held that:

> '[Family] still requires, it seems to me, at least a broadly recognizable de facto familial nexus. This may be capable of being found and recognised as such by the ordinary man – where the link would be strictly familial had there been a marriage or where the link is through adoption of a minor, de jure or de facto, or where the link is 'step' or where the link is 'in-law' or by marriage.'

8.23   By 2001 in *Fitzpatrick v Sterling Housing Association Limited*[83] Lord Slynn of Hadley held that 'the word [family] is to be applied flexibly, and does not cover only legally binding relationships'. Within the context of the Rent Act 1977 Lord Slynn noted that the hallmarks of a family relationship were:[84]

> '... essentially that there should be a degree of mutual inter-dependence, of the sharing of lives, of caring and love, of commitment and support. In respect of legal relationships these are presumed, though evidently these are not always present, as the family law and criminal courts know only too well. In de facto relationships these are capable, if proved, of creating membership of the tenant's family.'

8.24   Section 17(10) of the Children Act 1989 also demonstrates the wide interpretation of the concept of family, defining the word 'family' in relation to children in need[85] as including any person who has parental responsibility for that child and any other person with whom the child has been living.

---

[79]   Demonstrating that the family does not 'stand outside and above economic restructuring, market forces and financial, legal, technological and political change' (Silva, E and Smart, C *The New Practices and Policies of Family Life* (1999) Sage Publications, p 2–4).

[80]   [1950] 2 KB 328, [1950] 2 All ER 140.

[81]   [1979] 1 WLR 928, [1979] 2 All ER 1084.

[82]   [1964] 1 WLR 425.

[83]   [2001] 1 AC 27, [1999] 3 WLR 1113. Contrast this case to the earlier decision of *Harrogate Borough Council v Simpson* [1986] 2 FLR 91. See also *Mendoza v Ghaidan* [2002] EWCA Civ 1533, [2003] Ch 380.

[84]   See also *M v Secretary of State for Work and Pensions* [2006] UKHL 11, [2006] 2 AC 91 in which Lord Bingham referred to 'the love, trust, confidence, mutual dependence and unconstrained social intercourse which are the essence of family life'.

[85]   A child is defined as being 'in need' if he or she is unlikely to achieve or maintain, or to have the opportunity of achieving and maintaining, a reasonable standard of health or development without the provision for him or her of services by the local authority under Part III of the Children Act 1989, or his health or development is likely to be significantly impaired, or further impaired, without the provision of such services, or he or she is disabled (CA 1989, s 17(10)).

General Principles – Balancing Child, Family and State

Balancing Rights

8.25 As noted above, the approach in international law is to see the family as a community of individuals possessing specific rights.[86] Defining the family as a community of individuals possessing specific rights will often give rise to the need to balance the rights of those individuals, both as between each other and as against the State. This balancing exercise will be influenced by the changing views and attitudes of society. Within this context issues arise as to the appropriate location of the boundary between the rights of the child and those of the parents and between rights of the child and the parents and the duties and responsibility of the State.[87]

Balancing Rights – Parents and Child

Parents and Child – CRC

8.26 The CRC and the international human rights instruments that underpin it emphasise the importance of the child growing up in the care and under the responsibility of his or her parents.[88] Art 5 of the CRC expressly requires that:

> 'States Parties shall respect the responsibilities, rights and duties of parents or, where applicable, the members of the extended family or community as provided for by local custom, legal guardians or other persons legally responsible for the child, to provide, in a manner consistent with the evolving capacities of the child, appropriate direction and guidance in the exercise by the child of the rights recognised in the present Convention.'[89]

The Declaration of Social and Legal Principles Relating to the Protection and Welfare of Children with Special Reference to Foster Care Placement and Adoption Nationally and Internationally[90] also reaffirms at Art 3 that the first priority for the child is to be cared for by his or her own parents.

8.27 Article 18 of the CRC concerning the balance of responsibilities as between the parents of the child and the State provides that:

> 'States Parties shall use their best efforts to ensure recognition of the principle that both parents have common responsibilities for the upbringing and development of the child.

---

86   Van Bueren, G *The International Law on the Rights of the Child* (1998) Martinus Nijhoff, p 72.

87   *Prince v Massachusetts* (1944) 321 US 158 p 165 per Justice Rutledge 'It is the interest of youth itself, and of the whole community, that children be both safeguarded from abuses and given opportunities for growth into free and independent well developed men and citizens.' Note that the CRC in large measure leaves to States Parties the balance to be struck between competing rights under the CRC (Newell, P and Hodgkin, R *Implementation Handbook for the Convention on the Rights of the Child* (2008) 3rd edn, UNICEF, p 2).

88   Declaration of the Rights of the Child, Principle 6.

89   See also CRC, Art 3(2) which requires acknowledgement of the rights and duties of parents, legal guardians and others legally responsible for the child when State Parties seek to ensure protection and care for the child, Art 18(1) which enshrines the principle that both parents have common responsibilities for the upbringing and development of the child, Art 27(2) of the CRC by which parents have a responsibility to secure within their abilities and financial capacities, the conditions of living necessary for the child's development and Art 29(1)(c) of the CRC which states that the child's education shall be directed to, inter alia, the development of respect for the child's parents.

90   A/RES/41/85 3rd December 1986.

Parents or, as the case may be, legal guardians, have the primary responsibility for the upbringing and development[91] of the child. The best interests of the child will be their basic concern.'[92]

8.28 Article 5 and Art 18(1) of the CRC constitute statements in support of the primacy of parental responsibility over the responsibility of the State. It is important to note that these statements are made as against the State and *not* as against the child. The concept of parental responsibility under Art 18 must be considered in the context of the overall requirements of all parts of the CRC. Accordingly, the legal relationship of parents to their child derives from their responsibility to act in their child's best interests rather than from an unimpeachable right over them.[93] Arts 5 and 18 of the CRC do not articulate parental dominion over the child. Rather they describe a level of adult responsibility circumscribed in its application by the rights of the child as enshrined in the CRC. The parents' position in respect of their child is thus better described as one of responsibility than one of right. The Committee on the Rights of the Child has observed that:[94]

'Article 18 of the Convention reaffirms that parents or legal guardians have the primary responsibility for promoting children's development and well-being, with the child's best interests as their basic concern (arts. 18.1 and 27.2). States parties should respect the primacy of parents, mothers and fathers. This includes the obligation not to separate children from their parents, unless it is in the child's best interests (art. 9) … The Committee urges States parties to take all necessary steps to ensure that parents are able to take primary responsibility for their children; to support parents in fulfilling their responsibilities, including by reducing harmful deprivations, disruptions and distortions in children's care; and to take action where young children's well-being may be at risk.'

8.29 The child's evolving capacity and right to participate will impact on the manner in which the exercise of parental responsibility is balanced by the rights of the child. The parental responsibility articulated in Art 18 must be viewed through the prism of evolving capacity as articulated in Art 5 and the child's right to participate pursuant to Art 12. In the US case of *Polovchak v Meese*[95] the court, in granting a 12 year old boy asylum in the USA against the wishes of his parents who considered he should return to the USSR, considered that he was 'near the lower end of an age range in which a minor may be mature enough to assert individual rights that equal or override those of his parents' which rights become 'more compelling with age'. In its General Comment No 12 *Right to be Heard* the Committee on the Rights of the Child noted that:[96]

---

[91] The use of the word 'development' suggests assessment of parental performance by reference to Art 18 is relatively objective in nature (see Newell, P and Hodgkin, R *Implementation Handbook for the Convention on the Rights of the Child* (2008) 3rd edn, UNICEF, p 232). In relation to 'development' see also Arts 6, 27 and 29.

[92] Despite the imperative nature of this element of Art 18(1) it is recognised that the State cannot 'make' parents have their child's best interests as their basic concern. Rather Art 18(1) of the CRC is directed at States who write the legislation which prescribes the exercise of parental responsibility of parents to ensure that legislation is drafted in terms of best interests rather than parental rights (see Newell, P and Hodgkin, R *Implementation Handbook for the Convention on the Rights of the Child* (2008) 3rd edn, UNICEF, p 232).

[93] Newell, P and Hodgkin, R *Implementation Handbook for the Convention on the Rights of the Child* (2008) 3rd edn, UNICEF, p 76.

[94] Committee on the Rights of the Child General Comment No 7 *Implementing Child Rights in Early Childhood* (2005) CRC/C/GC/7/Rev.1, para 18. Note that this does not mean, of course, that parents have no rights of their own simply that those adult rights do not include a right of dominion over the child.

[95] (1985) 774 F.2.d 731.

[96] Committee on the Rights of the Child General Comment No 12 *Right to be Heard* CRC/C/GC/12 p 18–19. See also Committee on the Rights of the Child General Comment No 4 *Adolescent health and development in the context of the Convention on the Rights of the Child* (HRI/GEN/1/Rev 8, p 377).

'Article 5 of the Convention states that States parties shall respect the responsibilities, rights and duties of parents, legal guardians, or members of the extended family or community as provided for by local custom, to give direction and guidance to the child in her or his exercise of the rights recognised in the Convention. Consequently, the child has a right to direction and guidance, which have to compensate for the lack of knowledge, experience and understanding of the child and are restricted by his or her evolving capacities, as stated in this article. The more the child himself or herself knows, has experienced and understands, the more the parent, legal guardian or other persons legally responsible for the child have to transform direction and guidance into reminders and advice and later to an exchange on an equal footing. This transformation will not take place at a fixed point in a child's development, but will steadily increase as the child is encouraged to contribute her or his views ... A family where children can freely express views and be taken seriously from the earliest ages provides an important model, and is a preparation for the child to exercise the right to be heard in the wider society. Such an approach to parenting serves to promote individual development, enhance family relations and support children's socialisation and plays a preventive role against all forms of violence in the home and family ... The Convention recognises the rights and responsibilities of parents, or other legal guardians, to provide appropriate direction and guidance to their children, but underlines that this is to enable the child to exercise his or her rights and requires that direction and guidance are undertaken in a manner consistent with the evolving capacities of the child ... States parties should encourage, through legislation and policy, parents, guardians and child-minders to listen to children and give due weight to their views in matters that concern them. Parents should also be advised to support children in realising the right to express their views freely and to have children's views duly taken into account at all levels of society.'

Parents and Child – EHCR

8.30   The mutual enjoyment by parent and child of each other's company constitutes a fundamental element of family life for the purposes of Art 8 of the ECHR.[97] In respect of the relationship between parental responsibility and children's rights, the starting point under the ECHR is that 'the upbringing of children remains essentially a parental duty encapsulated within the concept of family life'.[98] The European Court of Human Rights has made clear however that in respect of issues arising in respect of family life, a fair balance must be struck between the rights of the child and those of the parents.[99] In the balancing process, particular importance should be attached to the best interests of the child which, depending on their nature and seriousness, may override those of the parents. In particular, a parent cannot be entitled under Art 8 of the Convention to have such measures taken as would harm the child's health and development.[100] The balance between parental rights and the rights of the child under Art 8 can be difficult to achieve and is often highly fact specific. In *X and Y v Netherlands*[101] a 14 year old child's claim that her rights under Art 8 had been breached by actions taken by the State to return her home against her will was rejected. A decision of opposite effect was reached in *X v Denmark*[102] where the Commission rejected the parents argument that their Art 8 rights had been breached where the State had refused to take action to force a 14 year old child

---

[97]   *Olsson v Sweden (No 1)* (1988) 11 EHRR 259.

[98]   *Seven Individuals v Sweden* Application No 8811/79 (1982) 29 D&R 104, p 113.

[99]   *Hansen v Turkey* [2004] 1 FLR 142, para 106; *Ignaccolo-Zenide v Romania* (2001) 31 EHRR 7, para 106; *C v Finland* [2006] 2 FLR 597; *Sahin v Germany* [2003] 2 FLR 671 (Grand Chamber).

[100]   *Scozzari and Giunta v Italy* (2002) 35 EHRR 12, sub nom *S and G v Italy* [2000] 2 FLR 771; *P, C and S v United Kingdom* (2002) 35 EHRR 31, [2002] 2 FLR 631; *Görgülü v Germany* [2004] 1 FLR 894.

[101]   (1974) 2 DR 118. A case involving a 14 year old who ran away from home with her boyfriend and went into hiding before giving herself up to the Police who had returned her home.

[102]   (1977–78) 7–9 DR 81. A case involving a 14 year old who ran away from home to a 'children's community' before moving to stay with a friend cared for by the friend's mother. The State had provided financial assistance to the child when she refused to return home and had refused to use force to return her on the grounds that this approach had failed in the past.

to return home against her will. It has been argued that the ECHR is ill equipped to establish the appropriate balance between the exercise of parental responsibility and the rights of the child,[103] this difficulty being most acutely demonstrated by decisions such as *Nielsen v Denmark*.[104]

Parents and Child – Domestic Law

8.31   The Law Commission, in its report entitled *Review of Child Law: Guardianship*[105] recognised the principle that parents' rights in so far as they concern their children are only derived from their duties as parents and exist only to secure the welfare of their children.[106] Integral to the ethos of the subsequent Children Act 1989 is that family life should be independent and free from unjustified interference by the State. This ethos is crystallised within the Act by the central concept of parental *responsibility* rather than parental rights, whereby parental responsibility comprises 'all the rights, duties, powers, responsibilities and authority which by law a parent has in relation to a child and his property'[107] are ordinarily discharged by the parent(s) of a child as part of 'the every day reality of being a parent'.[108] This central concept is further reinforced by the presumption that no court order modifying or restricting the exercise of parental responsibility should be made unless it will promote the child's welfare (the so called 'no order' principle').[109] Where a dispute arises as to the exercise of parental responsibility, and the dispute is brought before the court, it will be determined having regard to the child's best interests as the paramount consideration,[110] assessed by reference to the child's wishes and feelings considered in light of his or her age and understanding,[111] the child's physical, emotional and educational needs, the likely effect on him or her of any change in circumstances, any harm which he or she has suffered or is at risk of suffering, the capability of parents or carers to meet his or her needs, the range of powers available to the court,[112] the principle that delay is ordinarily inimical to the child[113] and the principle that the court should make no order unless to do so is better for the child than making no order at all.[114]

Balancing Rights – The Family and the State

8.32   It follows from the principles set out above that the historical view of the family as an entity in which the parents had unimpeachable authority over the child is unsustainable. Parental responsibility, whilst given prominence in both international and

---

[103]   Fortin, J *Children's Rights and the Developing Law* (2009) 3rd edn, Cambridge, p 68 and see Fortin, J *Children's Rights and the Impact of Two International Conventions: the UNCRC and the ECHR* in Thorpe, M and Cowton, C (eds) *Delight and Dole: The Children Act 10 Years On* (2002) Jordan Publishing, p 22. See also *Valsamis v Greece* (1996) 24 EHRR 294 (no separate examination of the child's claim).

[104]   (1988) 11 EHRR 175. For a full discussion of this case see **14.66**.

[105]   Law Commission (1988), para 2.4.

[106]   See also *F v Wirral Metropolitan Borough Council* [1991] Fam 69, [1991] 2 FLR 114.

[107]   CA 1989, s 3(1). The Act does not set out a basic list of parental responsibilities in contrast to s 1(1) of the Children (Scotland) Act 1995, which lists those responsibilities as being, in so far as is practicable and in the interests of the child (a) to safeguard and promote the child's health, development and welfare; (b) to provide, in a manner appropriate to the stage of development of the child (i) direction and (ii) guidance to the child; (c) if the child is not living with the parent, to maintain personal relations and direct contact with the child on a regular basis; and (d) to act as the child's legal representative.

[108]   Guardianship and Custody (Law Comm 1988 No 172), para 2.4.

[109]   CA 1989, s 1(5).

[110]   CA 1989, s 1(1) and see **4.151** above.

[111]   CA 1989, ss 1(1) and s 1(3)(a).

[112]   CA 1989, s 1(3)(b) to s 1(3)(g).

[113]   CA 1989, s 1(2).

[114]   CA 1989, s 1(5).

regional human rights instruments, is not unrestricted and can be regulated by the State where the exercise of that parental responsibility falls short of the expected norms in a given society. This immediately creates a tension between the exercise of parental responsibility and the exercise of State responsibility. In taking State action to regulate the exercise of parental responsibility a proper balance must be achieved between the rights of the child and the family and the exercise of State power.[115] As Baroness Hale observed in *Re B (Care Proceedings: Standard of Proof)*:[116]

> 'Taking a child away from her family is a momentous step, not only for her, but for her whole family, and for the local authority which does so. In a totalitarian society, uniformity and conformity are valued. Hence the totalitarian state tries to separate the child from her family and mould her to its own design. Families in all their subversive variety are the breeding ground of diversity and individuality. In a free and democratic society we value diversity and individuality. Hence the family is given special protection in all the modern human rights instruments including the European Convention for the Protection of Human Rights and Fundamental Freedoms 1950, Art 8, (the Convention), the International Covenant on Civil and Political Rights 1966, Art 23, and throughout the United Nations Convention on the Rights of the Child 1989. As McReynolds J famously said in *Pierce v Society of Sisters* 268 US 510 (1925), at 535, "The child is not the mere creature of the State".'[117]

The Family and the State – CRC

8.33   The preamble to the CRC recognises that the child, by reason of his or her physical and mental immaturity needs special safeguards and care, including appropriate legal protection. Where the State provides such special safeguards and care it must do so respecting the responsibilities, rights and duties of parents to provide care for the child in a manner consistent with child's evolving capacity.[118] However, where parents cannot manage or choose not to manage their responsibilities to the child, the State must step in to secure the child's rights and needs.[119] Art 19(1) of the CRC compels the State to intervene in the care of parent(s) or legal guardian(s) or any other person who has care of the child in specific circumstances in which the child's welfare may be threatened:

> 'States Parties shall take all appropriate legislative, administrative, social and educational measures to protect the child from all forms of physical or mental violence, injury or abuse, neglect or negligent treatment, maltreatment or exploitation, including sexual abuse, while in the care of parent(s), legal guardian(s) or any other person who has the care of the child.'

8.34   Even where the State intervenes in the exercise of the parental responsibility, States Parties to the CRC must ensure that such protection and care as is necessary for the child's well-being is given taking into account the rights and duties of parents and

---

[115]   See again the decision of the US Supreme Court in *Prince v Massachusetts* (1944) 321 US 158 p 165 in which Justice Rutledge characterised the balance to be struck between parental responsibility and State power as follows: 'Against these sacred private interests, basic in a democracy, stand the interests of society to protect the welfare of children'. *Prince v Massachusetts* represented considerable progress from the 1646 Massachusetts Stubborn Child Statute which permitted stubborn or rebellious sons over the age of 15 to be put to death upon the complaint of their parents.

[116]   [2008] UKHL 35, [2008] 2 FLR 141, [2009] AC 11.

[117]   The full passage cited by Baroness Hale in *Pierce v Society of Sisters* 268 US 510 (1925) reads 'The fundamental theory of liberty upon which all governments in this Union repose excludes any general power of the state to standardise its children by forcing them to accept instruction from public teachers only. The child is not the mere creature of the state; those who nurture him and direct his destiny have the right, coupled with the high duty, to recognise and prepare him for additional obligations.'

[118]   CRC, Art 5.

[119]   Newell, P and Hodgkin, R *Implementation Handbook for the Convention on the Rights of the Child* (2008) 3rd edn, UNICEF, p 231.

others legally responsible for him or her.[120] State intervention, as distinct from State assistance under CRC, Art 18(2) should be a measure of last resort and steps should be taken to address risks to the child *in situ* before a decision is taken by the State to remove the child.

The Family and the State under the ECHR

8.35   Respect for family life under Art 8 of the ECHR implies the existence in law of safeguards that render possible from the moment of birth the child's integration in his or her family.[121] Within this context, only the most pressing grounds can be sufficient to permit State interference with family life, even where the material conditions of the family are poor.[122] The European Court of Human Rights has consistently reiterated this principle in respect of State intervention in family life. For example, there must be extraordinarily compelling reasons before a baby can be physically removed by the State from his or her mother against her will immediately after birth.[123] As regards the extreme step of the State severing all parental links with a child, the court has taken the view that such a measure would cut a child from its roots and could only be justified in exceptional circumstances or by the overriding requirement of the child's best interests.[124] Following State intervention in the family, a stricter scrutiny is called for in respect of any further limitations by the authorities on family life and in respect of legal safeguards designed to secure the effective protection of the right of parents and children to respect for their family life.[125] State interference in family life should normally be regarded as a temporary measure to be discontinued as soon as circumstances permit.[126]

8.36   In assessing whether State intervention in the family constitutes a breach of Art 8 of the ECHR the court will bear in mind that the national authorities have the benefit of direct contact with all the persons concerned, often at the very stage when measures are being envisaged or immediately after their implementation[127] The margin of appreciation given to States will however vary in the light of the nature of the issues and the seriousness of the interests at stake.[128] Whilst Art 8 contains no explicit procedural requirements such requirements are implicit. The decision-making process leading to State interference in family life must be fair and such as to afford due respect for the interests safeguarded by Art 8.[129] It is essential that the parents and the child be placed in a position where they may obtain access to information which is relied on by the State

---

[120]   CRC, Art 3(2).

[121]   *Johnston v Ireland* (1986) 9 EHRR 203.

[122]   *X and Y v Federal Republic of Germany* (1978) Application No 8059/77 (unreported).

[123]   *K and T v Finland* (2000) 31 EHRR 484, [2000] 2 FLR 79, para 168 ('... the taking of a new-born baby into public care at the moment of its birth is an extremely harsh measure. There must be extraordinarily compelling reasons before a baby can be physically removed from the care of its mother, against her will, immediately after birth as a consequence of a procedure in which neither she nor her partner has been involved. The shock and distress felt by even a perfectly healthy mother are easy to imagine'). See **8.195** below.

[124]   *Johansen v Norway* (1997) 23 EHRR 33 and *Gnahoré v France* (2002) 34 EHRR 38. Note that this approach may not apply in all contexts, depending on the nature of the parent-child relationship (see *Söderbäck v Sweden* (2000) 29 EHRR 95, [1999] 1 FLR 250 where the severance of links between a child and father, who had never had care and custody of the child, was found to fall within the margin of appreciation of the courts which had made the assessment of the child's best interests).

[125]   See *Elsholz v Germany* (2002) 34 EHRR 58, [2000] 2 FLR 486.

[126]   *Johansen v Norway* (1997) 23 EHRR 33 and *EP v Italy* (1999) Application No 31127/96 (unreported).

[127]   *Johansen v Norway* (1997) 23 EHRR 33 and *K and T v Finland* (2000) 31 EHRR 484, [2000] 2 FLR 79.

[128]   *K and T v Finland* (2000) 31 EHRR 484, [2000] 2 FLR 79 and *P, C and S v United Kingdom* (2002) 35 EHRR 31, [2002] 2 FLR 631.

[129]   *McMichael v United Kingdom* (1995) 20 EHRR 205 and see *R (P) v Secretary of State for the Home*

in taking measures of intervention and can participate effectively in the decision-making process.[130] Measures of State intervention require exceptional diligence be exercised in avoiding delay.[131] Effective respect for family life requires that future relations between parent and child should not be determined by the mere effluxion of time.[132]

The Family and the State in Domestic Law[133]

8.37 The central position in the Children Act 1989 of the concept of parental responsibility and the principle that the court should make no order unless to do so is better for the child than making no order at all[134] places emphasis on the exercise of parental responsibility by parents without interference on the part of the State unless the best interests of the child demand such interference. The Children Act 1989 prescribes strict conditions that must be satisfied before the State may interfere with the exercise of parental responsibility and even then it may only do so if such interference can be said to be in the child's best interests.[135] The child's best interests must be assessed holding the child's best interests as paramount and having regard to the child's wishes and feelings considered in light of his or her age and understanding.[136] Account must also be taken of the child's physical, emotional and educational needs, the likely effect on him or her of any change in circumstances, any harm which he or she has suffered or is at risk of suffering, the capability of parents or carers to meet his or her needs, the range of powers available to the court[137] and the principle that delay is ordinarily inimical to the child.[138] The domestic courts will apply with rigor the jurisprudence in respect of Art 8 of the ECHR that seeks to draw the appropriate boundary between the family and the State, both in judicial proceedings concerning children and more widely.[139]

General Principles – Protection and Assistance for Families

8.38 As the family is for the majority of children the principle arena for securing the rights of the child, a primary method of protecting the child from breaches of his or her rights is the protection of and assistance for the family when it is in need.[140] A duty to

---

130   *Department; R (Q) v Secretary of State for the Home Department* [2001] EWCA Civ 1151; [2001] 2 FLR 1122 and *CF v Secretary of State for the Home Department* [2004] EWHC 111 (Fam), [2004] 2 FLR 517).

130   *McMichael v United Kingdom* (1995) 20 EHRR 205; *TP and KM v United Kingdom* [2001] 2 FLR 549 and *Buchberger v Austria* (2001) Application No 32899/96 (unreported).

131   See **16.42** below.

132   *W v United Kingdom* (1987) 10 EHRR 29.

133   The Earl of Chatham famously said 'The poorest man in his cottage may bid defiance to all the forces of the Crown. It may be frail, its roof may shake, the wind may blow through it, the storm may enter, the rain may enter, but the King of England cannot enter, all his forces dare not cross the threshold of the ruined tenement' (Henry Lord Brougham, *Statesmen in the Time of George III* First Series (1845), p 52).

134   CA1989, s 1(5).

135   CA 1989, ss 1 and 31(2) (the court may make a care order or a supervision order only where (i) it is satisfied that the child concerned is suffering or is likely to suffer significant harm and that harm, or the likelihood of harm, is attributable to the care given to the child, or likely to be given to him or her were an order not made, not being what it would be reasonable to expect a parent to give him and (ii) such an order would be in the child's best interests). Criteria are also prescribed by law for investigation by the State into the child's welfare (CA 1989, s 7(1), s 37(1) and s 47(1)), the provision of State support (CA 1989, Part III) and the emergency protection of children by the State (Children Act 1989, ss 38(2), 44 and 46).

136   CA 1989, s 1(1) and (3)(a).

137   CA 1989, s 1(3)(b)–(3)(g).

138   CA 1989, s 1(2).

139   See **8.37** above and see for example *Re B (Care: Interference with Family Life)* [2003] EWCA Civ 786, [2003] 2 FLR 813 per Thorpe LJ and *R (P) v Secretary of State for the Home Department; R (Q) v Secretary of State for the Home Department* [2001] EWCA Civ 1151; [2001] 2 FLR 1122.

140   Van Bueren, G *The International Law on the Rights of the Child* (1998) Martinus Nijhoff, p 86.

protect and assist the family is explicitly enshrined in many of the international human rights instruments relevant to children's rights.[141] These human rights instruments mandate the protection of and assistance for the family in economic, social and legal terms.[142] The provision of protection and assistance for families is the responsibility of the family, society and the State. In its General Comment No 17 *Article 24 (Rights of the Child)* the UN Human Rights Committee observes that:[143]

'Responsibility for guaranteeing children the necessary protection lies with the family, society and the State. Although the Covenant does not indicate how such responsibility is to be apportioned, it is primarily incumbent on the family, which is interpreted broadly to include all persons composing it in the society of the State party concerned, and particularly on the parents, to create conditions to promote the harmonious development of the child's personality and his enjoyment of the rights recognised in the Covenant. However, since it is quite common for the father and mother to be gainfully employed outside the home, reports by States parties should indicate how society, social institutions and the State are discharging their responsibility to assist the family in ensuring the protection of the child. Moreover, in cases where the parents and the family seriously fail in their duties, ill-treat or neglect the child, the State should intervene to restrict parental authority and the child may be separated from his family when circumstances so require. If the marriage is dissolved, steps should be taken, keeping in view the paramount interest of the children, to give them necessary protection and, so far as is possible, to guarantee personal relations with both parents.'

8.39 Implicit in the State's duty to provide protection and assistance for the family is the requirement that such protection and assistance be advanced *before* a situation arises which may result in the separation of the child from the family, recognising that the need for protection may, where the best interests of the child demand, require the removal of the child from his or her family in order to safeguard his or her welfare.

Protection and Assistance for the Family under the CRC

CRC, Arts 18(2) and 18(3)

8.40 Article 18(2) and (3) of the CRC stipulate State support for parents in meeting their parental responsibilities, providing:

'2. For the purpose of guaranteeing and promoting the rights set forth in the present Convention, States Parties shall render appropriate assistance to parents and legal guardians

---

[141] See CRC Preamble ('Convinced that the family, as the fundamental group of society and the natural environment for the growth and well-being of all its members and particularly children, should be afforded the necessary protection and assistance so that it can fully assume its responsibilities within the community'); the Covenant on Economic, Social and Cultural Rights, Art 10 ('The widest possible protection and assistance should be accorded to the family, which is the natural and fundamental group unit of society, particularly for its establishment and while it is responsible for the care and education of dependent children') and the African Charter on the Rights and Welfare of the Child, Art 20(2)(a) ('States Parties to the present Charter shall in accordance with their means and national conditions the all appropriate measures ... to assist parents and other persons responsible for the child ...'). See also para 17(d) of the General Recommendation XXXI on the Prevention of Racial Discrimination in the Administration and Functioning of the Criminal Justice System (HRI/GEN/1/Rev. 8 p 283) which provides that the family must be protected against reprisals where a victim of crime is involved in judicial proceedings. See also the Paris Principles and Guidelines on Children Associated with Armed Forces or Armed Groups (2007), paras 6.35.2, 7.36, 7.45 and 7.58.1.

[142] None of these instruments however permit families to petition as a group in respect of alleged breaches (see Van Bueren, G *The International Law on the Rights of the Child* (1998) Martinus Nijhoff, p 78).

[143] Human Rights Committee General Comment No 17 *Article 24 (Rights of the Child)*, para 6. HRI/GEN/1/ Rev 8, p 183.

in the performance of their child-rearing responsibilities and shall ensure the development of institutions, facilities and services for the care of children.

3. States Parties shall take all appropriate measures to ensure that children of working parents have the right to benefit from child-care services and facilities for which they are eligible.'

8.41   Article 18(2) and (3) must be read with the other articles of the CRC which provide for forms of support and assistance for the child and/or family.[144] CRC, Art 3(2) enshrines a general duty enjoining States Parties to undertake to ensure to the child such protection and care as is necessary for his or her well-being, taking into account the rights and duties of his or her parents, legal guardians, or other individuals legally responsible for him or her. Article 19(1) requires that States Parties shall take all appropriate legislative, administrative, social and educational measures to protect the child from all forms of physical or mental violence, injury or abuse, neglect or negligent treatment, maltreatment or exploitation, including sexual abuse, while in the care of parent(s), legal guardian(s) or any other person who has the care of the child. Pursuant to Art 23 of the CRC, in respect of disabled children, States Parties must encourage and ensure the extension, subject to available resources, to the eligible child and those responsible for his or her care, of assistance for which application is made and which is appropriate to the child's condition and to the circumstances of the parents or others caring for the child. Article 27(3) requires that State Parties, in accordance with national conditions and within their means, take appropriate measures to assist parents and others responsible for the child to implement the child's right to an adequate standard of living with particular reference to nutrition, clothing and housing.[145]

8.42   Where parents are unable to fulfill their responsibilities to their children, culpability is irrelevant to the provision of State assistance.[146] State assistance should be anticipatory and directed at families at risk of breaking down. The need for the 'development' of institutions, facilities and services implies a wider duty on the part of the State than mere provision, encompassing monitoring, evaluation and improvement on an ongoing basis. The services provided should cover all children and not just the very young.[147] The measures adopted by the State to assist families should be practical and include financial benefits, day care, home help, housing provision as well as professional and psychological support. The Committee on the Rights of the Child recommends in its General Comment No 7 *Implementing Child Rights in Early Childhood* the following non-exhaustive measures:

'Assistance to parents will include provision of parenting education, parent counselling and other quality services for mothers, fathers, siblings, grandparents and others who from time to time may be responsible for promoting the child's best interests ... Assistance also includes offering support to parents and other family members in ways that encourage positive and sensitive relationships with young children and enhance understanding of children's rights and best interests ... In providing appropriate assistance to parents in the performance of their child-rearing responsibilities (art. 18.2), States parties should take all appropriate measures to enhance parents' understanding of their role in their children's early education, encourage child-rearing practices which are child-centred, encourage respect for

---

[144]   Newell, P and Hodgkin, R *Implementation Handbook for the Convention on the Rights of the Child* (2008) 3rd edn, UNICEF, p 231.

[145]   See **5.155-5.162**.

[146]   Newell, P and Hodgkin, R *Implementation Handbook for the Convention on the Rights of the Child* (2008) 3rd edn, UNICEF, p 237.

[147]   See Committee on the Rights of the Child General Comment No 4 *Adolescent Health and Development in the Context of the Convention on the Rights of the Child* (2003) CRC/GC/2003/4, para 16.

the child's dignity and provide opportunities for developing understanding, self-esteem and self-confidence ... In planning for early childhood, States parties should at all times aim to provide programmes that complement the parents' role and are developed as far as possible in partnership with parents, including through active cooperation between parents, professionals and others in developing 'the child's personality, talents and mental and physical abilities to their fullest potential.'[148]

8.43   In providing that States Parties shall take all appropriate measures[149] to ensure that children of working parents have the right to benefit from child-care services and facilities for which they are eligible, the emphasis of Art 18(3) is the provision of day care services for children.[150] The Committee on the Rights of the Child recommends:[151]

> '[T]hat States parties support early childhood development programmes, including home- and community-based preschool programmes, in which the empowerment and education of parents (and other caregivers) are main features. States parties have a key role to play in providing a legislative framework for the provision of quality, adequately resourced services, and for ensuring that standards are tailored to the circumstances of particular groups and individuals and to the developmental priorities of particular age groups, from infancy through to transition into school. They are encouraged to construct high-quality, developmentally appropriate and culturally relevant programmes and to achieve this by working with local communities rather by imposing a standardised approach to early childhood care and education'.

Paternity and maternity leave and benefits are central to meeting the imperatives of Art 18(3). The International Labour Organisation Recommendation *Supplementing the Maternity Protection Convention*[152] expressly supports the principles of Art 18 of the CRC and makes recommendations in respect of maternity leave, benefits, employment protection and non-discrimination, health protection and breast feeding. Article 7(a) of the Covenant on Economic, Social and Cultural Rights requires State Parties to 'reduce the constraints faced by men and women in reconciling professional and family responsibilities by promoting adequate policies for childcare and care of dependent family members'.[153]

---

[148]   General Comment No 7 *Implementing Child Rights in Early Childhood* CRC/C/GC/7/Rev.1, para 20(c) and (d) and 29(a) and (b). See also General Comment No 4 *Adolescent health and development in the context of the Convention on the Rights of the Child* HRI/GEN/1/Rev. 8 p 385, para 35(a) which provides that States Parties must fulfill the obligation to 'To create a safe and supportive environment for adolescents, including within their family ...'.

[149]   The term 'appropriate assistance' may be taken to mean assistance at a level which enables the family to assume its responsibilities fully within the community (see the Declaration of Social Progress and Development 1969, A/RES/24/2542, Art 4 which provides that 'The family as a basic unit of society and the natural environment for the growth and well-being of all its members, particularly children and youth, should be assisted and protected so that it may fully assume its responsibilities within the community. Parents have the exclusive right to determine freely and responsibly the number and spacing of their children.' Art 18(1) of the African Charter on Human and People's Rights enjoins States Parties to take care of the 'physical and moral health' of the family (see **8.231** below)).

[150]   Newell, P and Hodgkin, R *Implementation Handbook for the Convention on the Rights of the Child* (2008) 3rd edn, UNICEF, p 239.

[151]   Committee on the Rights of the Child General Comment No 7 *Implementing Rights in Early Childhood* (2005) CRC/C/GC/7/Rev.1, para 31. See also United Nationals International Conference on Population and Development (A/CONF.171/13 p 32) and World Summit for Children *Declaration and Plan of Action* Appendix II E(i).

[152]   2000 (No 191). See also the Maternity Protection Convention Revised 1952 (C103).

[153]   Committee on Economic, Social and Cultural Rights General Comment No 16 *The Equal Right of Men and Women to Enjoyment of All Economic, Social and Cultural Rights, para* 24 HRI/GEN/1/Rev 8, p 127.

Covenant on Civil and Political Rights, Art 23

8.44   Further assistance as to the ambit of Arts 18(2) and 18(3) of the CRC can be derived from examining the similar provisions in the Covenant on Civil and Political Rights and the Covenant on Economic, Social and Cultural Rights. In considering the ambit of Art 23 of the ICCPR, which provides that the family is the natural and fundamental group unit of society and is entitled to protection by society and the State, the UN Human Rights Committee in *Shirin Aumeeruddy-Cziffra and Nineteen other Mauritian Women v Mauritius*[154] the Human Rights Committee held that:

> 'The Committee is of the opinion that the legal protection or measures a society or a State can afford to the family may vary from country to country and depend on different social, economic, political and cultural conditions and traditions.'

Covenant on Economic, Social and Cultural Rights, Art 10

8.45   Article 10(1) of the ICESCR provides as follows in respect of the provision of protection and assistance to the family:

> 'The States Parties to the present Covenant recognise that:
>
> 1. The widest possible protection and assistance should be accorded to the family, which is the natural and fundamental group unit of society, particularly for its establishment and while it is responsible for the care and education of dependent children. Marriage must be entered into with the free consent of the intending spouses.
>
> 2. Special protection should be accorded to mothers during a reasonable period before and after childbirth.[155] During such period working mothers should be accorded paid leave or leave with adequate social security benefits.'

8.46   Article 10 of the ICESCR requires that State Parties recognise that the widest possible protection and assistance should be afforded to the family.[156] In respect of persons with disabilities this means that 'everything possible should be done to enable such persons, when they so wish, to live with their families'.[157] The term 'dependent children' should not be interpreted narrowly and equated only with infancy as a child may be financially and emotionally dependent until his or her majority.[158]

Protection and Assistance for Families under the ECHR

8.47   Whilst the Art 8 right to respect for family life will imply a duty of protection and assistance for the family within specific contexts, the European Convention of Human Rights does not enshrine a general right of protection and assistance for the family. However, the Committee of Independent Experts established under the European Social Charter noted in 1995 that 'family welfare cannot henceforth be left to

---

[154]   Communication No 35/1978, U.N. Doc. CCPR/C/OP/2 at 226 (1990).

[155]   See also ICESCR Art 12(2)(a).

[156]   Committee on Economic, Social and Cultural Rights General Comment No 16 *The Equal Right of Men and Women to Enjoyment of All Economic, Social and Cultural Rights*, para 27 (HRI/GEN/1/Rev 8, p 127).

[157]   Committee on Economic, Social and Cultural Rights General Comment No 5 *Persons with Disabilities, para* 30 HRI/GEN/1/Rev 8, p 31.

[158]   Van Bueren, G *The International Law on the Rights of the Child* (1998) Martinus Nijhoff, p 77. See also the Declaration of Social Progress and Development 1969 Art 4 A/RES/24/2542.

individual effort'.[159] Art 16 of the revised European Social Charter provides the main provisions in the Charter for the protection of the family:

> 'With a view to ensuring the necessary conditions for the full development of the family, which is a fundamental unit of society, the Parties undertake to promote the economic, legal and social protection of family life by such means as social and family benefits, fiscal arrangements, provision of family housing, benefits for the newly married and other appropriate means.'[160]

Article 7 of the Charter (The right of children and young persons to protection) and Art 17 (The right of children and young persons to social, legal and economic protection) will also apply in some respects to the protecting of young persons in the family circle'.[161] The Committee of Ministers Resolution (77) 33 on Placement of Children[162] stipulates that the need for alternative care for children should be avoided a far as possible through preventative measures of support for families in accordance with their special problems and needs.[163]

Protection and Assistance for Families under European Union Law

8.48   European Charter on Fundamental Rights, Art 33 provides as follows in respect of the protection and assistance of the family:

> '1. The family shall enjoy legal, economic and social protection.[164]

> 2. To reconcile family and professional life, everyone shall have the right to protection from dismissal for a reason connected with maternity and the right to paid maternity leave and to parental leave following the birth or adoption of a child.'[165]

Protection and Assistance for Families under other Regional Instruments

African Charter of Human and People's Rights

8.49   Article 18(1) of the African Charter of Human and People's Rights provides as follows in respect of the duty to provide protection and assistance for the family unit:

---

159 European Social Charter Committee of Independent Experts *Conclusions XIII-2* (1995) Council of Europe, p 41.
160 See also Recommendation (96)5 of the Committee of Ministers of 19 June 1996 on reconciling work and family life. Note that the United Kingdom has yet to ratify the revised European Social Charter.
161 European Social Charter Committee of Independent Experts *Conclusions XIII-2* (1995) Council of Europe, p 40.
162 Adopted on 3 November 1977.
163 Committee of Ministers Resolution (77) 33 on Placement of Children, para 1.1.
164 Article 33(1) is based on Art 16 of the European Social Charter. The second paragraph draws on Council Directive 92/85/EEC on the introduction of measures to encourage improvements in the safety and health at work of pregnant workers and workers who have recently given birth or are breast feeding and Directive 96/34/EC on the framework agreement on parental leave concluded by UNICE, CEEP and the ETUC. See also Council Recommendation 92/241/EEC, of 31 March 1992 on child care; Council Directive 96/34/EEC, of 3 June 1996 on the framework agreement on parental leave concluded by UNICE, CEEP and the ETUC and Council Directive 97/81/EC, of 15 December 1997 concerning the Framework Agreement on part-time work concluded by UNICE, CEEP and the ETUC.
165 Article 33(1) is based on Art 8 of the Revised European Social Charter and draws on Article 27 (right of workers with family responsibilities to equal opportunities and equal treatment) of the revised Social Charter.

'1. The family shall be the natural unit and basis of society. It shall enjoy the protection and support of the State for its establishment and development.

2. States Parties to the present Charter shall take appropriate steps to ensure equality of rights and responsibilities of spouses with regard to children during marriage and in the even of its dissolution. In case of the dissolution, provision shall be made for the necessary protection of the child.

3. No child shall be deprived of maintenance by reference to the parents' marital status.'

African Youth Charter

8.50 Article 8(1) of the African Youth Charter also provides that 'The family, as the most basic social institution, shall enjoy the full protection and support of States Parties for its establishment and development noting that the structure and form of families varies in different social and cultural contexts'.

Ibero-American Convention on the Rights of Youth

8.51 The Ibero-American Convention on the Rights of Youth likewise stipulates a duty to protect and assist families. Article 19(3) of the Convention provides that:

'3. The States Parties undertake to create and enable the educational, economic, social and cultural conditions which promote the values of the family, cohesion and strength of family life and healthy development of youth in it, through public policies and its corresponding financing.'

Article 20(2) of the Convention stipulates that:

'2. The States Parties shall promote all legal measures which guarantee the compatibility of work and family life and the responsible exercise of paternity and maternity and allow their continuous personal, educational, formation and vocational development.'

American Convention on Human Rights

8.52 Article 17 of the American Convention on Human Rights provides that 'The family is the natural and fundamental group unit of society and is entitled to protection by society and the state'.

Revised Arab Charter on Human Rights

8.53 Article 33 of the Revised Arab Charter on Human Rights also enshrines the principle that the family is the basic unit of society, whose protection it shall enjoy and a duty on the State to 'ensure the protection of the family, the strengthening of family ties, the protection of its members and the prohibition of all forms of violence or abuse in the relations among its members, and particularly against women and children' and to 'ensure the necessary protection and care for mothers, children, older persons and persons with special needs and shall provide adolescents and young persons with the best opportunities for physical and mental development'.

Protection and Assistance for Families in Domestic Law

Children Act 1989, Part III

8.54 Part III of the Children Act 1989 sets out the general and specific duties imposed on local authorities in respect of the services which they must or may provide for children and their families. In providing these services, the local authority has a duty to consider whether any local education authority, local housing authority, health authority or other local authority can help in the provision of services and, if they can, to seek that help.[166] The scheme set out under Part III imposes:

(a) A general duty in respect of the welfare of children in need (including children with a disability) coupled with specific duties and powers aimed at facilitating the general duty of the local authority to provide a range and level of services to children in need.[167]

(b) Duties and powers in respect of children under five (whether they are in need or not).[168]

(c) Duties and powers in respect of other children (whether or not they are under five and whether or not they are in need).[169]

(d) Duties and powers in relation to the accommodation of children including children who are 'looked after' by the local authority.[170]

(e) Duties and powers in respect of children leaving care and formerly looked after by the Local Authority.[171]

Each of the duties prescribed under Part III is intended to enable local authorities to work with a family in a manner which seeks to promote the independent exercise of parental responsibility.

8.55 Specifically, the work of local authorities under Part III should be directed at avoiding the need for proceedings under Part IV of the 1989 Act.[172] Working in partnership with those holding parental responsibility and members of the wider family is the guiding principle in the effective discharge of the local authority's duties under

---

[166] CA 1989, s 27. It should be noted that the Children Act 2004 and the Children Act 2004 (Children's Services) Regulations 2005, SI 2005/1972, now creates a framework whereby the provision by local government, national government and non-governmental organisations of 'children's services' is carried out co-operatively having regard to the need to safeguard and promote the welfare of children.

[167] CA 1989, s 17 and Sch 2. The specific duties to children in need include a duty to identify children in need (*R (Howard League for Penal Reform) v Secretary of State for the Home Department* [2002] EWHC 2497 (Admin), [2003] 1 FLR 484; *R (D) v Secretary of State for the Home Department* [2003] EWHC 155, [2003] 1 FLR 979), a duty to prevent abuse and neglect (CA 1989, Sch 2, para 4(1)), a duty to provide accommodation to a third party where it appears that a child is suffering or is likely to suffer ill-treatment at the hands of that person living at the same premises (CA 1989, Sch 2, para 5), a duty to promote the upbringing of children by their families by providing advice, guidance and counselling, occupational, social, cultural and recreational activities, home help, travel assistance and holiday provision (CA 1989, Sch 2, para 8), a duty to take steps to enable the child to live or have contact with his or her family home (CA 1989, Sch 2, para 10) and a duty to provide day care (CA 1989, s 18(1)).

[168] CA 1989, s 18(2). See also Education Act 1996, s 17.

[169] CA 1989, Sch 2, para 9.

[170] CA 1989, s 20(1).

[171] CA 1989, Sch 2, para 19A as inserted by the Children Leaving Care Act 2000, s 1.

[172] CA 1989, Sch 2, para 7(a)(i).

Part III of the Act.[173] This requires local authorities to maximise the involvement of families at all stages of the planning and decision-making process such that the decision-making process in respect of those families is characterised by transparency and fairness.[174] This means that issues affecting a family's ability to participate in the decision-making process, for example a learning disability, should not be allowed to frustrate the principle of working in partnership[175] and that families should be provided with correct and complete information to facilitate that partnership.[176] It should be remembered however, that partnership cannot be permitted to compromise the duty to safeguard and promote the child's welfare. Authorities are required to facilitate the provision of Part III services by others, in particular voluntary organisations, and may make such arrangements as they see fit for others to provide such services (for example, day care or fostering services).[177] Further, a local authority may request the help of another authority, including an education authority, a housing authority, or a health authority or special health authority, Primary Care Trust or National Health Service Trust, to carry out duties under Part III. An authority so requested shall comply with the request if it is compatible with its own statutory or other duties and obligations and does not unduly prejudice the discharge of any of its functions.[178] A housing authority is not obliged to provide accommodation, but it does have a duty to ascertain whether it could provide a solution to the problems of homeless families so as to prevent children suffering from lack of accommodation.[179]

State Benefits

8.56   The domestic system of welfare support, including that for children and families, has been described as being 'a confusing patchwork of contributory, non-contributory and means test benefits'.[180] The domestic system of state benefits for children and families is complex and changes on a regular basis. It is thus beyond the scope of this work. For a comprehensive examination of the subject see the *Welfare Benefits and Tax Credits Handbook 2010/11*.[181]

General Principles – Family Life and Non-Discrimination

8.57   The child's right to family life should be implemented having regard to the principle of non-discrimination. This principle will extend to both the make up of the child's family and the child's relationships with that family. In its General Comment No 28 *Article 3 (The Equality Rights Between Men and Women)*[182] the UN Human Rights Committee observes that:

---

[173]   The concept of partnership was introduced in the Guidance to the Act. See the Children Act 1989 Guidance and Regulations, Vol 2, Family Support, Day Care and Educational Provision for Young Children (1991) Department of Health, para 2.1 and Care of Children: Principles and Practice in Regulations and Guidance (1989) HMSO.

[174]   *Re L (Care: Assessment: Fair Trial)* [2002] EWHC 1379 (Fam), [2002] 2 FLR 730.

[175]   *Re G (Care: Challenge to Local Authority's Decision)* [2003] EWHC 551 (Fam), [2003] 2 FLR 42.

[176]   *Sahin v Germany* [2002] 1 FLR 119, [2002] Fam Law 94.

[177]   Section 17(5). See also the Children Act 1989 Guidance and Regulations, Vol 2, Family Support, Day Care and Educational Provision for Young Children (1991) Department of Health, para 2.11.

[178]   CA 1989, s 27.

[179]   *R v Northavon District Council, ex p Smith* [1994] 2 AC 402, HL.

[180]   Lister, R *Income Maintenance for Families in Britain* in Rapoport, R N, Fogarty, M and Rapoport, R *Families in Britain* (1982) Routledge and Kegan Paul, p 432.

[181]   (2010) 18th edn, Child Poverty Action Group.

[182]   Human Rights Committee General Comment No 28 *Article 3 (The Equality Rights Between Men and Women)* HRI/GEN/1/Rev. 8 p 223, para 27.

'In giving effect to recognition of the family in the context of article 23, it is important to accept the concept of the various forms of family, including unmarried couples and their children and single parents and their children, and to ensure the equal treatment of women in these contexts (see general comment No 19, paragraph 2). Single-parent families frequently consist of a single woman caring for one or more children, and States parties should describe what measures of support are in place to enable her to discharge her parental functions on the basis of equality with a man in a similar position.'

Self evidently, the expectation that female children will undertake excessive family responsibility will constitute discrimination and will deprive the child of opportunities to participate in early childhood and primary education.[183]

Family Life and Non-Discrimination – CRC

CRC, Art 18(1)

8.58 The importance of the application of the principle of non-discrimination enshrined in Art 2 of the CRC to the provisions of the CRC which articulate the elements of the child's right to family life is highlighted by the fact that the stipulation in Art 6 of the Declaration on the Rights of the Child 1959 that 'a child of tender years shall not, save in exceptional circumstances, be separated from his mother' does not appear in the CRC. Article 18(1) of the CRC provides that:[184]

'States Parties shall use their best efforts to ensure recognition of the principle that both parents have common responsibilities for the upbringing and development of the child.'

The provisions of Art 18(1) of the CRC reflect Art 5 of the Convention on the Elimination of All Forms of Discrimination Against Women which requires States Parties to recognise:[185]

'... the common responsibility of men and women in the upbringing and development of their children, it being understood that the interest of children is the primordial consideration in all cases.'

8.59 The wider provisions of the CRC must be read in light of the requirements of Art 18(1) that both parents have common responsibility for the upbringing and development of the child. For example, in relation to the duty on the State to take all appropriate measures to secure the recovery of maintenance for the child from the parents or other persons having financial responsibility for the child under Art 27(4) the 'common responsibility' principle in Art 18(1) requires the term 'maintenance' to be

---

[183] See Committee on the Rights of the Child General Comment No 7 *Implementing Child Rights in Early Childhood,* para 11(b)(i) HRI/GEN/1/Rev 8, p 436.

[184] See also General Recommendation No 21 *Equality in Marriage and Family Relations* HRI/GEN/1/Rev 8, p 308 in general and para 18 ('women should share equal rights and responsibilities with men for the care and raising of dependent children or family members') and Art 23(4) of the Covenant on Civil and Political Rights ('States Parties to the present Covenant shall take appropriate steps to ensure equally of rights and responsibilities of spouses as to marriage, during marriage and at its dissolution').

[185] See also Art 16 of the Convention on the Elimination of All Forms of Discrimination Against Women which requires that 'States Parties ... shall ensure, on the basis of equality of men and women ... The same rights and responsibilities as parents, irrespective of marital status, in matters relating to their children; in all cases the interests of the children shall be paramount.'

read broadly, encompassing much more than simply financial assistance and requiring both parents play an active part in their child's upbringing.[186]

8.60 Whilst the provisions of Art 18(1) appear to concentrate on the position of the parent rather than that of the child, the principles of equality they enshrine are drafted in terms of parental responsibilities rather than parental rights and are thus designed to ensure the promotion of the child's rights within the family. The provisions of Art 18(1) of the CRC must be read in light of the best interests principle in Art 3(1) of the CRC. Thus, for example, the Art 18(1) requirement of 'common responsibility' will be particularly significant when dealing with the consequences of parental separation. Any provisions which fail to incorporate recognition of the equality of parents in terms of ongoing participation in the upbringing of their child following separation may breach the child's right not to be separated from his parents and the child's right to maintain contact with his parents. As such, whilst recognising the strong bond between mothers and very young children, translating this recognition into a law or an inflexible presumption requiring all young children reside with their mothers on separation would contravene Art 18(1).[187] Equally, Art 18(1) cannot not be used to support an inflexible presumption that the child's time should be divided equally between each parent following separation as such a presumption would fail to account properly for the primary nature of the child's best interests under Art 3(1).

CRC, Art 2(2)

8.61 Article 2(2) of the CRC ensures that the rights of the child are not infringed by acts of discrimination which result not from the status or activities of the child but from the status, activities, expressed opinion or beliefs of his or her parents, legal guardians or family members which may bring those adults into conflict with the State, Art 2(2) providing that:

> '2. States Parties shall take all appropriate measures to ensure that the child is protected against all forms of discrimination or punishment on the basis of the status, activities, expressed opinions, or beliefs of the child's parents, legal guardians, or family members.'

Family Life and Non-Discrimination – ECHR

8.62 The ECHR, by reason of it not being an instrument drafted with children's rights in mind, articulates principles of equality in relation to family life from a primarily adult perspective. Article 5 of Protocol 7 of the ECHR provides as follows in relation to the position as between spouses:

> 'Spouses shall enjoy equality of rights and responsibilities of a private law character between them, and in their relations with their children, as to marriage, during marriage and in the event of its dissolution. This Article shall not prevent States from taking such measures as are necessary in the interests of the children.'

8.63 It is a breach of Art 8 of the ECHR read with Art 14 to treat an unmarried father less favourably than a married father in respect of contact to his children.[188] The principle of non-discrimination extends to ensuring that a parent is not treated

---

[186] Newell, P and Hodgkin, R *Implementation Handbook for the Convention on the Rights of the Child* (2008) 3rd edn, UNICEF, p 235.

[187] Newell, P and Hodgkin, R *Implementation Handbook for the Convention on the Rights of the Child* (2008) 3rd edn, UNICEF, p 236 and see Niger CRC/C/15/Add.179, para 38 and Pakistan CRC/C/15/Add, para 44.

[188] *Sommerfield v Germany* (2003) 36 EHRR 565, paras 51 and 55 and (2003) 38 EHRR 756, paras 93–94

differently in respect of contact with his or her children based on their sexual orientation[189] or religious convictions.[190] Likewise, it is a breach of Art 8 read with Art 14 to prevent the adoption of a child by an unmarried couple[191] or on the basis of a person's sexual orientation.[192] However, not all circumstances affecting the family will fall within the ambit of Art 8 and hence be amenable to a claim alleging discrimination under Art 8 read with Art 14.[193]

8.64   The existence of family life for a child who is part of a family as compared to a child who has lost his or her parents may justify a difference in treatment as between those children which will not breach the terms of Art 8 when read with Art 14 of the ECHR. In *AL (Serbia) v Secretary of State for the Home Department*,[194] whilst acknowledging that Art 2(2) of the CRC prohibits discrimination on the basis of, among other things, the birth or other status of the child or his family and that the UN Committee on the Rights of the Child has emphasised that this prohibits any discrimination on the basis of the status of the child being unaccompanied or separated,[195] the Court held that a one off exercise to grant asylum claimants indefinite leave to remain in the UK was not discriminatory even though it applied only to families with children who were living in a family unit and not to unaccompanied asylum seeking children. It should be noted however that whilst the claimants had arrived as unaccompanied children they had petitioned the court as adults. Baroness Hale acknowledged that the conclusion of the court may have been different if the alleged discrimination had occurred whilst the claimants were still children:

> 'I am quite prepared to accept that, in certain circumstances, a difference in treatment between children who did or did not have parents to look after them, unless designed to correct the factual inequalities between them, would require particularly careful scrutiny. To deny a benefit to a child whose parents were dead, had disappeared, or were incapable of looking after him, which was available to a child who had parents available to look after him, might be very hard indeed to justify. Not all asylum-seeking children fall into this category. Some do have parents who may be traced and their children reunited with them in due course. But we are assuming for the sake of argument that that is not the case here. Had this policy discriminated between the children while they were children it would have been particularly hard to justify.'

(Grand Chamber). See also *PM v United Kingdom* (2005) 18 BHRC 668 concerning the unequal tax treatment of maintenance payments made by an unmarried father compared to those made by a married father who had been separated or divorced.

189   *Salguiero Da Silva Mouta v Portugal* (1999) Application No 33290/96 (unreported).

190   *Hoffman v Austria* (1993) 17 EHRR 293. See also *Palau-Martinez v France* (2003) 41 EHRR 136, [2004] 2 FLR 810 and *Ismailova v Russia* [2008] 1 FLR 533.

191   *Re P (Adoption: Unmarried Couple)* [2008] UKHL 38, [2008] 2 FLR 1084.

192   *EB v France* [2008] 1 FLR 850.

193   *Secretary of State for Work and Pensions v M* [2006] UKHL11, [2006] 2 AC 91, [2006] 1 FCR 497. But see the dissenting judgement of Baroness Hale.

194   [2008] UKHL 42, [2008] 4 All ER 1127. See also *Stec v United Kingdom* (2006) 20 BHRC 348 in which the European Court of Human Rights held that 'A difference of treatment is, however, discriminatory if it has no objective and reasonable justification; in other words, if it does not pursue a legitimate aim or if there is not a reasonable relationship of proportionality between the means employed and the aim sought to be realised. The contracting state enjoys a margin of appreciation in assessing whether and to what extent differences in otherwise similar situations justify a different treatment ...' and **4.71** above.

195   UN Committee on the Rights of the Child General Comment No 6.

Family Life and Non-Discrimination – Other Regional Instruments

The American Convention on Human Rights

8.65   Article 17(4) of the American Convention on Human Rights provides as follows in respect of married life:[196]

'4. The States Parties shall take appropriate steps to ensure the equality of rights and the adequate balancing of responsibilities of the spouses as to marriage, during marriage, and in the event of its dissolution. In case of dissolution, provision shall be made for the necessary protection of any children solely on the basis of their own best interests.'

The African Charter on the Rights and Welfare of the Child

8.66   Article 18(2) of the African Charter on the Rights and Welfare of the Child stipulates that:

'2. States Parties to the present Charter shall take appropriate steps to ensure equality of rights and responsibilities of spouses with regard to children during marriage and in the even of its dissolution. In case of the dissolution, provision shall be made for the necessary protection of the child.'

Family Life and Non-Discrimination – Domestic Law

8.67   Within the domestic legal arena, issues of discrimination in the context of family life have centred on contact and residence disputes concerning the children of separated parents. There is no presumption in domestic law that the mother is to be considered the primary carer in preference for the father.[197] It is the proper application of the child's right to respect for family life interpreted in accordance with the best interests principle that ensures that the focus on the child is maintained and should ensure decisions are based on the child best interests rather than potentially discriminatory presumptions.[198] However, subject to the child's best interests, the domestic courts have historically recognised advantages in young children being cared for by their mother. In *Re K (Residence Order: Securing Contact)*[199] the court held that:

'Of course, all things being equal, it is likely that a child naturally would expect to live with the mother, particularly when that child is of tender years. That is always subject to the overriding factor that the child's welfare is the paramount consideration.'

In *Brixey v Lynas*[200] Lord Jauncey of Tullichettle held that:

'My Lords, to summarise, the advantage to a very young child of being with its mother is a consideration which must be taken into account in deciding where lie its best interests in custody proceedings in which the mother is involved. It is neither a presumption nor a principle but rather recognition of a widely held belief based on practical experience and the workings of nature. Its importance will vary according to the age of the child and to the

---

[196]   See also *María Eugenia Morales de Sierra v Guatemala* (2001) Case 11.6.25 No 4/01.

[197]   *Re S (A Minor) (Custody)* [1991] 2 FLR 388 (there is no starting-point that the mother should be preferred to the father and only displaced by a preponderance of evidence to the contrary); *Re A (a minor) (custody)* [1991] FCR 569 [1991] 2 FLR 394 and *Re A (a minor) (residence order)* [1998] 2 FCR 633, sub nom *Re A (children: 1959 UN declaration)* [1998] 1 FLR 354. See also **8.236** below for a discussion of the existence or otherwise of a 'natural parent presumption'.

[198]   *Re G (Children) (Residence: Same Sex Partner)* [2006] UKHL 43, [2006] 2 FLR 614, paras 30–31.

[199]   [1999] 1 FLR 583.

[200]   [1997] 1 FCR 220 at 226, [1996] 2 FLR 499 at 505.

other circumstances of each individual case such as whether the child has been living with or apart from the mother and whether she is or is not capable of providing proper care. Circumstances may be such that it has no importance at all. Furthermore it will always yield to other competing advantages which more effectively promote the welfare of the child. However, where a very young child has been with its mother since birth and there is no criticism of her ability to care for the child only the strongest competing advantages are likely to prevail.'[201]

THE CHILD'S RIGHT TO RESPECT FOR FAMILY LIFE

The Child's Right to Respect for Family Life under the CRC

8.68   There is no right to a family *per se* under the CRC. Rather, the CRC seeks to protect the existing family from arbitrary or unlawful interference,[202] to ensure that as far as possible the child knows and is cared for by his or her parents,[203] to ensure that the child is not separated from his or her parents save in certain narrowly defined circumstances,[204] to ensure that he or she maintains parental contact if separated[205] and to ensure that the child is provided with a proper alternative to family care where necessary.[206] Where that alternate care is adoption, the CRC ensures that the child's best interests are paramount in determining whether an adoption should proceed.[207]

CRC, Art 16 – Right to Respect for Family

CRC, Art 16

8.69   Article 16 of the CRC provides as follows in respect of the child's right to respect for family life:[208]

> '1. No child shall be subjected to arbitrary or unlawful interference with his or her privacy, family, home or correspondence, nor to unlawful attacks on his or her honour and reputation.
>
> 2. The child has the right to the protection of the law against such interference or attacks.'

This chapter deals with respect for family and home under Art 16 of the CRC. The child's right to respect for privacy, correspondence, honour and reputation are dealt with in chapter 9 below.

---

[201]   See also *A v A (custody appeal: role of appellate court)* [1988] FCR 205, [1988] 1 FLR 193, CA; *Re S (a minor) (custody)* [1991] FCR 155, [1991] 2 FLR 388 at 390 (likely that a young child, particularly a little girl, would be expected to be with her mother, but where there was a dispute it was a consideration rather than a presumption). See also *Re W (a minor) (interim custody)* [1990] FCR 540, [1990] 2 FLR 86 (assumption that an 8 month old child should be with mother); *Re W (residence order: baby)* [1992] 2 FCR 603, [1992] 2 FLR 332 (there is, however, a rebuttable presumption that a baby's best interests are best served by being with its with his or her mother; the mother wishing to breast feed).

[202]   CRC, Art 16.

[203]   CRC, Art 7.

[204]   CRC, Art 9(1).

[205]   CRC, Art 9(3).

[206]   CRC, Art 20.

[207]   CRC, Art 21. Contrast Art 21 with Art 3 in which the child's interests are a primary consideration.

[208]   Note that Art 12 of the Universal Declaration of Human Rights omits the word 'unlawful' in this context. Contrast the negative formulation adopted by CRC, Art 16 with the positive formulation of Art 8 of the ECHR.

CRC, Art 16 – Interpretation

(i) 'Family'

8.70 CRC, Art 16 uses the term 'family' in preference to the wider concept of 'family life' or 'family environment', both of which carry a qualitative element. Van Bueren notes that it is unfortunate that the narrower term 'family' was used in Art 16 of the CRC rather than the term 'family life' used in Art 8 of the ECHR.[209] However, having regard to the scope of the rights enshrined in the CRC relating to the child's life with his or her family and the need to read CRC, Art 16 with the terms of the CRC as a whole, including the 'flexible' description of 'family' enshrined in Art 5,[210] the proper application of the CRC will encompass the child's family life and environment as well as the bare constitution of that family. The protection provided by Art 16 against arbitrary or unlawful interference in the child's family will extend to the child's wider family and will include siblings and grandparents and others who are important to the child.[211] This mirrors the approach taken under Art 8(1) of the ECHR.

(ii) 'Arbitrary and Unlawful'

8.71 Both Art 16 of the CRC and Art 17 of the Covenant on Civil and Political Rights[212] establish a prohibition on arbitrary or unlawful interference with the child's family.[213] The term 'unlawful' as used in Art 17 of the ICCPR has been interpreted to imply that State interference with family and family life may only be justified on the basis of law, which laws themselves must conform to the ICCPR in that they should not be arbitrary in their operation. Thus, even where the interference in family life is lawful it should also be 'reasonable in the particular circumstances'.[214] Under Art 17 of the ICCPR arbitrary or unlawful interference in the family is prohibited in respect of both the actions of the State and the actions of natural or legal persons and there is a positive duty on the State to prevent arbitrary or unlawful interference.[215] Art 17 of the ICCPR also applies to aliens.[216]

8.72 The interpretation of the phrase 'unlawful' under Art 17 of the ICCPR will apply equally in relation to the rights concerning family life enshrined in CRC, Art 16.[217] Thus, pursuant to Art 16 of the CRC, any arrangements permitting interference with a child's family must be set out in law, must not be arbitrary, must be compatible with the other principles and provisions of the CRC and must be reasonable in the particular circumstances.[218]

---

[209] Van Bueren, G *The International Law on the Rights of the Child* (1998) Martinus Nijhoff, p 79–80.

[210] See **8.5** above.

[211] Newell, P and Hodgkin, R *Implementation Handbook for the Convention on the Rights of the Child* (2008) 3rd edn, UNICEF, p 210.

[212] Save for the insertion of the word 'child' the terms of Art 16 of the CRC and Art 17 of the ICCPR are identical. Article 4 of the ICCPR permits States Parties to derogate from their obligations under Art 17 when proclaiming a state of emergency. The CRC contains no derogation provisions.

[213] See ICCPR General Comment No 19 *Article 23 (The Family)*, para 1. (HRI/GEN/1/Rev 8, p 188).

[214] *Shirin Aumeeruddy-Cziffra and 19 other Mauritian women v Mauritius, Communication* No R.9/35 (2 May 1978), U.N. Doc. Supp. No 40 (A/36/40) at 134 (1981).

[215] *Shirin Aumeeruddy-Cziffra and 19 other Mauritian women v Mauritius, Communication* No R.9/35 (2 May 1978), U.N. Doc. Supp. No 40 (A/36/40) at 134 (1981).

[216] Human Rights Committee General Comment No 15 *The Position of Aliens under the Covenant, para* 7 (HRI/GEN/1/Rev 8, p 180).

[217] As noted above, save for the insertion of the word 'child' the terms of Art 16 of the CRC and Art 17 of the CCPR are identical.

[218] Newell, P and Hodgkin, R *Implementation Handbook for the Convention on the Rights of the Child* (2008) 3rd edn, UNICEF, p 210.

CRC, Art 7 – Right to Know and Be Cared for by Parents

CRC, Art 7

8.73 Article 7 of the CRC provides as follows in respect of the child's right to know and be cared for by his or her parents:

'1. The child shall be registered immediately after birth and shall have the right from birth to a name, the right to acquire a nationality and, as far as possible, the right to know and be cared for by his or her parents.

2. States Parties shall ensure the implementation of these rights in accordance with their national law and their obligations under the relevant international instruments in this field, in particular where the child would otherwise be stateless.'

The child's right to know his or her parents as an element of the child's identity is dealt with in chapter 7 above.[219] The following section considers the child's right to be cared for by his or her parents as an element of the child's family life and the rights which protect the same.

CRC, Art 7 – Ambit

8.74 The right to be cared for is the child's right to be cared for by the parent not the parent's right to care for the child.[220] The requirement of Art 7 that a child shall have the right from birth to be cared for by his or her parents must be read in concert with Art 5, Art 9 and Art 18 of the CRC. Article 7 of the CRC has been referred to by the domestic courts.[221]

CRC, Art 7 – Interpretation

(i) 'As Far as Possible'

8.75 The child's right to be cared for by his or her parents is qualified by the words 'as far as possible'. This qualification recognises the fact that, even if possible, it may not be in the child's interests to be cared for by his or her parents having regard to the best interests imperative stipulated by Art 3(1) of the CRC.[222] However, the words 'as far as possible' in Art 7(1) constitute a stricter and less subjective test than the concept of best interests in Art 3(1) of the CRC.[223] Although Art 7 must be interpreted in accordance with Art 3, the words 'as far as possible' suggest that, whilst each case will fall to be determined on its own facts, the circumstances in which it will be in a child's best interests not to be cared for by his or her parents will be relatively narrow and strictly construed.[224] Thus, within the context of the right to family life, only situations which present a risk of significant harm to the child are likely to justify a conclusion that it is

---

[219] See **7.29–7.44** above.
[220] The original formulation of 'to know and belong to his parents' in Art 7(1) was rejected at the drafting stage (see E/CN.4/1989/48, pp 18–22).
[221] *Re O (A Child) (Blood Tests: Constraint); Re J (A Child) (Blood Tests: Constraint)* [2000] 2 All ER 29; *Re H (A Minor) (Blood Tests: Parental Rights)* [1996] 4 All ER 28 and *Re F (A Minor) (Blood Tests: Parental Rights)* [1993] 3 All ER 596.
[222] Newell, P and Hodgkin, R *Implementation Handbook for the Convention on the Rights of the Child* (2008) 3rd edn, UNICEF, p 97.
[223] Newell, P and Hodgkin, R *Implementation Handbook for the Convention on the Rights of the Child* (2008) 3rd edn, UNICEF, p 107.
[224] Newell, P and Hodgkin, R *Implementation Handbook for the Convention on the Rights of the Child* (2008) 3rd edn, UNICEF, p 107.

not in the child's best interests to be cared for by his or her parents.[225] The onus will be on the State to prove the existence of such circumstances.[226] In circumstances where it is not in the child's best interests to be cared for by his or her parents it is nonetheless likely to be in the child's best interests to continue to know his or her parents. The circumstances where the child's *knowledge* of his or her parents is the subject of State limitation will be even narrower and more strictly construed than those which justify the removal of the child from his or her parents' care.[227] Having regard to the child's evolving capacity and his or her right to participate under Art 12 of the CRC, at an appropriate point the child who is not in the care of his or her parents must be given an opportunity to reconsider the position with a view to re-establishing care by his or her parents and to participate fully in any process which considers this option.

CRC, Art 7 – Application

8.76   Article 7(2) constitutes a positive duty on the State to ensure that a child can, as far as possible, know and be cared for by his or her parents. In addition to this general duty under Art 7(2) of the CRC, other instruments provide for specific action on the part of the State. The Covenant on Economic, Social and Cultural Rights requires States Parties to 'reduce the constraints faced by men and women in reconciling professional and family responsibilities by promoting adequate policies for childcare and care of dependent family members'.[228] Art 10(1) of the Covenant on Economic, Social and Cultural Rights. In respect of persons with disabilities 'everything possible should be done to enable such persons, when they so wish, to live with their families'.[229]

8.77   Where the child's parents have separated the child's right under Art 7 of the CRC to be cared for by his or her parents implies a more active involvement in the child's life by an absent parent than simply ensuring the financial security of the child through the payment of maintenance.[230] Where a child has elected not to be cared for by his or her parents by running away or otherwise leaving the family home, returning that child without listening to the views of the child and conducting an investigation and assessment of the circumstances which led the child to leave would be inconsistent with the child's rights under the CRC.[231]

---

[225]   See CRC, Art 9 and **8.78** et seq below.

[226]   Newell, P and Hodgkin, R *Implementation Handbook for the Convention on the Rights of the Child* (2008) 3rd edn, UNICEF, p 109.

[227]   Hodgkin and Newell argue that it is clear that the child's right to know their parentage could only be refused on the grounds of best interests in the most extreme and unambiguous circumstances (Newell, P and Hodgkin, R *Implementation Handbook for the Convention on the Rights of the Child* (2008) 3rd edn, UNICEF, p 107).

[228]   Committee on Economical, Social and Cultural Rights General Comment No 16 *The Equal Right of Men and Women to Enjoyment of All Economic, Social and Cultural Rights, para* 24 HRI/GEN/1/Rev 8, p 127.

[229]   Committee on Economic, Social and Cultural Rights General Comment No 5 *Persons with Disabilities, para* 30 HRI/GEN/1/Rev 8, p 31.

[230]   Newell, P and Hodgkin, R *Implementation Handbook for the Convention on the Rights of the Child* (2008) 3rd edn, UNICEF, p 108.

[231]   Newell, P and Hodgkin, R *Implementation Handbook for the Convention on the Rights of the Child* (2008) 3rd edn, UNICEF, p 109.

CRC, Art 9 – Right not to be Separated from Parents

CRC, Art 9

8.78 CRC, Art 9(1) provides as follows in respect of the child's right not to be separated from his or her parents and the right to participate in proceedings which may result in such separation:[232]

'1. States Parties shall ensure that a child shall not be separated from his or her parents against their will, except when competent authorities subject to judicial review determine, in accordance with applicable law and procedures, that such separation is necessary for the best interests of the child. Such determination may be necessary in a particular case such as one involving abuse or neglect of the child by the parents, or one where the parents are living separately and a decision must be made as to the child's place of residence.'

CRC, Art 9(1) – Ambit

(i) Right Not to be Separated from Parents

8.79 Article 9(1) enshrines the principle that children should not be separated from their parents unless their best interests demand such separation in circumstances such as the abuse or neglect of the child by the parents or where parental separation requires the child's place of residence to be with one or other parent. Whilst Art 9(1) is drafted so as to place an obligation on State Parties to ensure that the child is not separated from his or her parents, it is clear that Art 9(1) accords to the child the right not to be separated from his or her parents against his or her will.[233]

(ii) Right Applicable Regardless of Age

8.80 Article 9(1) reflects Principle 6 of the 1959 Declaration on the Rights of the Child. Principle 6 of the 1959 Declaration provides that a child shall wherever possible, grow up in the care and under the responsibility of his parents. The particular consequences of separating a young child from his or her parents have been recognised by the Committee on the Rights of the Child:[234]

'States parties should respect the primacy of parents, mothers and fathers. This includes the obligation not to separate children from their parents, unless it is in the child's best interests (art. 9). Young children are especially vulnerable to adverse consequences of separations because of their physical dependence on and emotional attachment to their parents/primary caregivers. They are also less able to comprehend the circumstances of any separation.'

However, in contrast to the Declaration of the Rights of the Child 1959, Art 9(1) makes no distinction based on the age of the child. The right not to be separated from his or her parents will apply to every child regardless of age save in circumstances specified in the Art 9(1).[235]

---

[232] These examples are not meant to be exhaustive (see E/1982/12/Add.1C, pp 49–55).

[233] Detrick, S *A Commentary on the United Nations Convention on the Rights of the Child* (1999) Martinus Nijhoff, p 171.

[234] Committee on the Rights of the Child General Comment No 7 *Implementing Child Rights in Early Childhood* (2005) CRC/C/GC/7/Rev.1, para 18.

[235] See **8.82** below.

(iii) Positive Obligations Inherent in Right Not to be Separated

8.81   The right not to be separated from his or her parents places upon States Parties a positive obligation to promote parental care with a view to preventing family separation. The UN Guidelines for the Alternative Care of Children[236] provide that States should actively address the root causes of child abandonment, child relinquishment and separation of the child from his/her family by ensuring, inter alia, the right to birth registration, and access to adequate housing and to basic health, education and social welfare services, as well as by promoting measures to combat poverty, discrimination, marginalisation, stigmatisation, violence, child maltreatment and sexual abuse, and substance abuse.[237] The obligation to keep the child with his or her family where possible will apply equally to children with disabilities.[238] In this respect, the UN Guidelines for the Alternative Care of Children enjoin States Parties to ensure that:[239]

> 'Organisations and authorities should make every effort to prevent the separation of children from their parents or primary caregivers, unless the best interests of the child so require, and ensure that their actions do not inadvertently encourage family separation by providing services and benefits to children alone rather than to families.'

Where separation has taken place, the State should take positive steps to promote reintegration of the child into the family unit, provided it is in the child's best interests to be reintegrated.[240]

(iv) Exceptions to the Right Not to be Separated from Parents

8.82   A child may only be separated from his or her parents contrary to the right enshrined in Art 9(1) where competent authorities have determined that such separation is necessary for the best interests of the child.[241] The determination by competent authorities that the child's best interests demand separation must be subject to judicial review in accordance with applicable law and procedures.[242] Whilst Art 9(1) provides examples of the circumstances in which it may be in the child's best interests to be separated from his or her parents, namely where there is abuse or neglect of the child by the parents,[243] or where the parents are living separately and a decision must be made as to the child's place of residence, these examples are not intended to be exhaustive.[244]

(v) Participation in Decisions Concerning Separation – Art 9(2)

8.83   Where competent authorities seek to effect the separation of a child from his or her parents pursuant to Art 9(1) of the CRC, Art 9(2) stipulates that:

---

[236]   UN Guidelines for the Alternative Care of Children (2010) A/RES/64/142.
[237]   UN Guidelines for the Alternative Care of Children (2010) A/RES/64/142, paras 32 and 34.
[238]   Newell, P and Hodgkin, R *Implementation Handbook for the Convention on the Rights of the Child* (2008) 3rd edn, UNICEF, p 286.
[239]   UN Guidelines for the Alternative Care of Children (2010) A/RES/64/142, paras 155–156.
[240]   UN Guidelines for the Alternative Care of Children (2010) A/RES/64/142, paras 49–52.
[241]   For best interests see Art 3(1) of the CRC and **4.120** above. The requirement that decisions be taken by 'competent authorities' implies that States Parties must establish public authorities especially designated as competent to make decisions regarding the separation of a child from his or her parents subject to the child's best interests (Detrick, S *A Commentary on the United Nations Convention on the Rights of the Child* (1999) Martinus Nijhoff, p 171).
[242]   Again, this implies that States Parties must have specific laws and procedures governing the separation of children from their parents (see Detrick, S *A Commentary on the United Nations Convention on the Rights of the Child* (1999) Martinus Nijhoff, p 171).
[243]   See also CRC, Art 19.
[244]   See E/1982/12/Add.1C, pp 49–55).

'2. In any proceedings pursuant to paragraph 1 of the present article, all interested parties shall be given an opportunity to participate in the proceedings and make their views known.'

8.84   The requirement in Art 9(2) that *all* interested parties must be given an opportunity to participate in proceedings by which competent authorities seek to effect the separation of the child from his or her parents and make their views known in those proceedings includes the child.[245] The child's right to participate in proceedings concerning a proposed separation from his or her parents is also guaranteed by Art 12 of the CRC.[246]

(vi)   Provision of Information upon Separation – Art 9(4)

8.85   Where the State initiates the separation of the family and specifically the separation of children from their parents Art 9(4) of the CRC provides that:

'4. Where such separation results from any action initiated by a State Party, such as the detention, imprisonment, exile, deportation or death (including death arising from any cause while the person is in the custody of the State) of one or both parents or of the child, that State Party shall, upon request, provide the parents, the child or, if appropriate, another member of the family with the essential information concerning the whereabouts of the absent member(s) of the family unless the provision of the information would be detrimental to the well-being of the child.[247] States Parties shall further ensure that the submission of such a request shall of itself entail no adverse consequences for the person(s) concerned.'

In relation to children who may be relinquished by their parents or abandoned by them, the UN Guidelines for the Alternative Care of Children[248] stipulate that:

'When a child is relinquished or abandoned, States should ensure that this may take place in conditions of confidentiality and safety for the child, respecting his/her right to access information on his/her origins where appropriate and possible under the law of the State.'

Article 9(1) CRC – Interpretation

(i)   'Against Their Will'

8.86   Van Bueren contends that, in light of the emphasis in the CRC on the evolving capacity and participation of the child, the use of the term 'against their will' in Art 9(1) must refer to both the parents *and* the child.[249] Hodgkin and Newell take the same view and consider that the grammar of Art 9(1) makes it plain that the term 'against their will' refers either to the parents will or the will of the parents and the child.[250]

(ii)   'Competent Authorities'

8.87   The qualifier 'competent' used in Art 9(1) in relation to authorities who can effect separation of children from their parents where the child's best interests demand

---

245   See CRC/C/58 p 17, para 69.
246   See **6.50–6.54** for detailed discussion of this provision within the context of the child's right to participate.
247   Circumstances where the provision of such information will be detrimental to the child are likely to be rare and exceptional (Newell, P and Hodgkin, R *Implementation Handbook for the Convention on the Rights of the Child* (2008) 3rd edn, UNICEF, p 131).
248   (2010) A/RES/64/142, para 42.
249   Van Bueren, G *The International Law on the Rights of the Child* (1998) Martinus Nijhoff, p 80.
250   Newell, P and Hodgkin, R *Implementation Handbook for the Convention on the Rights of the Child* (2008) 3rd edn, UNICEF, p 122. See *Re T (An Adoption)* [1996[1 NZLR 368 in which the court held that once an adoption order is made the word 'parent' in Art 9(1) of the CRC ceases to mean biological parent.

refers to the authorised position of the authority in question rather than the aptitude and ability of that authority, although the latter will also be crucial to the proper implementation of the child's rights under Art 9(1).[251]

(iii) 'Subject to Judicial Review'

8.88 The need for any decision making process whereby children are separated from their parents to be subject to judicial review also implies that such a process will adhere to the safeguards provided by the natural justice and the right to fair and equal treatment under the law.[252] The Courts dealing with hearings concerning the separation of children from their parents should be both specialised and properly funded.[253]

(iv) 'In Accordance with Applicable Law and Procedures'

8.89 The requirement that competent authorities take any decision to separate a child from his or her parents in accordance with applicable law and procedures implies that States Parties must have specific laws and procedures governing the separation of children from their parents.[254]

(v) 'Necessary for the Best Interests of the Child'[255]

8.90 The only ground for separating children from their parents contrary to the right of the child not to be so separated enshrined in Art 9(1) is where such separation is in the child's best interests. Poverty should never be a reason to justify separating a child from his or her family.[256] Art 23 of the Convention on the Rights of Persons with Disabilities further provides that 'In no case shall a child be separated from parents on the basis of a disability of either the child or one of both of the parents'.[257] The Committee on the Rights of the Child has expressed concern regarding accommodating children with their imprisoned parents.[258] To avoid separation of the child from his or her parent non-custodial sanctions for the parent should be used in preference[259] and where the placement of the child with their parent in prison is necessary in the best interests of the child clear guidelines should be formulated and implemented, including provision for ensuring that living conditions meet the imperatives of Art 27 of the CRC

---

[251] Newell, P and Hodgkin, R *Implementation Handbook for the Convention on the Rights of the Child* (2008) 3rd edn, UNICEF, p 127 and Slovenia CRC/C/15/Add.230, paras 30 and 31. The requirement that decisions be taken by 'competent authorities' implies that States Parties must establish public authorities especially designated as competent to make decisions regarding the separation of a child from his or her parents subject to the child's best interests (Detrick, S *A Commentary on the United Nations Convention on the Rights of the Child* (1999) Martinus Nijhoff, p 171).

[252] Dealt with in chapter 16 below.

[253] See Nicaragua CRC/C/15/Add.265, para 37.

[254] Detrick, S *A Commentary on the United Nations Convention on the Rights of the Child* (1999) Martinus Nijhoff, p 171.

[255] For a detailed discussion of best interests see **4.120–4.175**.

[256] Van Bueren, G *The International Law on the Rights of the Child* (1998) Martinus Nijhoff, p 70. See also Nepal CRC/C/15/Add.261, para 54, Azerbaijan CRC/C/AZE/CO/2, paras 37 and 38 and Hungary CRC/C/HUN/CO/2, para 30 and the UN Guidelines for the Alternative Care of Children (2010) A/RES/64/142, para 15 ('Financial and material poverty … should be seen as a signal for the need to provide appropriate support for the family').

[257] It is likely that this principle will be interpreted having regard to the child's best interests as a primary consideration.

[258] Nepal CRC/C/15/Add.261, paras 51 and 52.

[259] Newell, P and Hodgkin, R *Implementation Handbook for the Convention on the Rights of the Child* (2008) 3rd edn, UNICEF, p 124. See **14.21** below.

as adequate for the child's development.[260] The child should not be punished on the basis of the activities of his or her parents.[261]

Article 9(1) CRC – Application

(i)   General

8.91   Reflecting an oft expressed truism, Hodgkin and Newell observe that the '[r]emoval of children from their parents without justification is one of the gravest violations of rights the State can perpetrate against children'.[262] Set against this, circumstances will inevitably arise where the separation of the child from his or her parents is necessary in the child's best interests. Accordingly decisions to remove children from their parents will require a careful balance to be struck between the child's right to the love and society of his or her parents and the child's best interests as secured by CRC, Art 3(1). As set out above, within this context Art 9(1) contains a number of cardinal safeguards which combine to form the necessary foundation for the proper determination that balancing exercise, namely that:

(a)   a child may only be separated from his or her parents if that separation is in his or her best interests;

(b)   any decision to separate a child from his or parents must be made by competent authorities;

(c)   any decision to separate a child from his or her parents must be in accordance with the applicable law and procedures;

(d)   any decision to separate a child from his or her parents must be subject to judicial review;

(e)   any decision to separate a child from his or her parents must be taken only after all interested parties have had the opportunity to make their views known.

8.92   In applying the precepts of Art 9(1) in administrative and judicial decision making concerning the separation of children from their parents it is vital that those engaged in the decision making process do not lose sight of these cardinal principles. In addition, before considering the separation of the child from his or her parents, the duty to provide assistance and protection to the family requires that all reasonable steps be taken to prevent the need for such separation.[263] The need to avoid delay is also an implicit element of the application of Art 9(1).[264] Reading Art 3(1) of the CRC with Art 16 of the CRC concerning the child's right to privacy suggests a presumption that proceedings in respect of the separation of children governed by Art 9 should be held in private.[265]

---

[260]   See Mexico CRC/C/MEX/CO/3, para 40.

[261]   CRC, Art 2(2).

[262]   Newell, P and Hodgkin, R *Implementation Handbook for the Convention on the Rights of the Child* (2008) 3rd edn, UNICEF, p 127 and see also, p 129'the inclusion of care and welfare proceedings in the 'Beijing Rules' stresses the point that removing children from their parents is as serious a step as depriving them of their liberty, and merits a fair hearing under the rules of natural justice').

[263]   See **8.38–8.56** above.

[264]   See E/1982/12/Add.1 C, pp 49–55.

[265]   Newell, P and Hodgkin, R *Implementation Handbook for the Convention on the Rights of the Child* (2008)

(ii)   Private Law

Parental Separation and Divorce

8.93   When parents separate in many cases this will also involve the separation of a child from one or other of the parents in the sense that the child will no longer be residing with that parent. Where the State is called upon, by reason of parental disagreement, to determine the nature and extent of such separation, the principles enshrined in Art 9(1) will apply.[266] Whilst recognising the strong bond between mothers and very young children, translating this recognition into a law or an inflexible presumption requiring that on parental separation all young children reside with their mothers with contact to their fathers will contravene Art 18(1) of the CRC.[267] Equally, Art 18(1) cannot be used to support an inflexible presumption that the child's time should be divided equally between each parent following separation as such a presumption would fail to account properly for the primary nature of the child's best interests under Art 3(1). Having regard to the requirement in Art 9(2) that all interested parties shall be given an opportunity to participate in proceedings and make their views known, States Parties should make provision for disputes as to residence arising out of a dispute between parent and child as well as out of disputes between parents.[268]

Child Abduction – CRC, Art 11

8.94   CRC, Art 11 provides as follows in relation to the enforced separation of the child from one or both parents by reason of the illicit transfer and non-return of children abroad:[269]

'1. States Parties shall take measures to combat the illicit transfer and non-return of children abroad.

2. To this end, States Parties shall promote the conclusion of bilateral or multilateral agreements or accession to existing agreements.'

8.95   The terms 'illicit transfer' and 'non-return' are drafted in deliberately broad terms and encompass parental and non-parental abduction.[270] However, Art 11 is primarily concerned with parental abductions and retentions.[271] The *Manual on Human Rights Reporting* notes in this context that:

'... children may be abducted by one of the parents and are usually not permitted to return home, even when a previous judicial authority had already decided on the custody and place of residence of the child, as well as on the visiting rights of the parent with whom the child should no longer live. The situation often tends to permanently prevent the child from having

---

3rd edn, UNICEF, p 236. See also Art 14(1) of the International Convention on Civil and Political Rights, Art 3(2) of the UN Standard Minimum Rules of Juvenile Justice (the 'Beijing Rules') and **9.14** below.

[266]   Article 9(1) expressly provides for its application to circumstances where 'the parents are living separately and a decision must be made as to the child's place of residence.'

[267]   Newell, P and Hodgkin, R *Implementation Handbook for the Convention on the Rights of the Child* (2008) 3rd edn, UNICEF, p 236 and see Niger CRC/C/15/Add.179, para 38 and Pakistan CRC/C/15/Add, para 44.

[268]   Newell, P and Hodgkin, R *Implementation Handbook for the Convention on the Rights of the Child* (2008) 3rd edn, UNICEF, p 122.

[269]   See also CRC, Art 10 at **8.102** below.

[270]   Van Bueren, G *The International Law on the Rights of the Child* (1998) Martinus Nijhoff, p 90.

[271]   Newell, P and Hodgkin, R *Implementation Handbook for the Convention on the Rights of the Child* (2008) 3rd edn, UNICEF, p 143. For provisions covering the sale, trafficking and abduction of children see CRC, Art 35 and the Optional Protocol on the Sale of Children, Child Prostitution and Child Pornography at **15.57** below.

access to the parent with whom the child used to live or with whom the child had direct and regular contacts and personal relations (see Articles 9, para 3 and 10, para 2). It also shows how important it is to be guided by the best interests of the child and in ensuring, as a general rule, that both parents continue to assume their responsibilities for the upbringing and development of the child, even when separation or divorce has intervened.'

In UK the measures taken pursuant to Art 11(2) of the CRC are the ratification of the European and the Hague Conventions concerning abduction.[272]

(iii)   Public Law

Separation due to Neglect and Abuse

8.96   CRC, Art 9(1) expressly recognises that separation of a child from his or her parent 'may be necessary in a particular case such as one involving abuse or neglect of the child by the parents'.

8.97   Before considering separating a child from his or her family on the basis of reasonable grounds to believe that a child is at risk, States should apply proper criteria based on sound professional principles for assessing the child's and the family's situation, including the family's actual and potential capacity to care for the child, with subsequent decisions being made by suitably qualified and trained professionals, on behalf of or authorised by a competent authority, in full consultation with all concerned and bearing in mind the need to plan for the child's future.[273] The UN Guidelines for the Alternative Care of Children provide as follows in relation to the procedure to be adopted:[274]

> 'Decision-making on alternative care in the best interests of the child should take place through a judicial, administrative or other adequate and recognised procedure, with legal safeguards, including, where appropriate, legal representation on behalf of children in any legal proceedings. It should be based on rigorous assessment, planning and review, through established structures and mechanisms, and should be carried out on a case-by-case basis, by suitably qualified professionals in a multidisciplinary team, wherever possible. It should involve full consultation at all stages with the child, according to his/her evolving capacities, and with his/her parents or legal guardians. To this end, all concerned should be provided with the necessary information on which to base their opinion. States should make every effort to provide adequate resources and channels for the training and recognition of the professionals responsible for determining the best form of care so as to facilitate compliance with these provisions.'

8.98   CRC, Art 9(2) provides that in any proceedings pursuant to Art 9(1) all interested parties shall be given an opportunity to participate in the proceedings and make their views known. Whenever consideration is being given to separating a child from his or her parents because the child is or is thought to be a victim of abuse or neglect the views of the child must be taken into account when determining the best interests of the child.[275]

---

[272]   See below **8.168**.

[273]   UN Guidelines for the Alternative Care of Children (2010) A/RES/64/142, para 39.

[274]   (2010) A/RES/64/142, para 57. See also para 12(e) of Committee on the Rights of the Child General Comment No 4 *Adolescent health and development in the context of the Convention on the Rights of the Child* HRI/GEN/1/Rev 8, p 380.

[275]   Article 12 and Committee on the Rights of the Child General Comment No 12 *Right to be Heard*, para 53 CRC/C/GC/12, p 13.

8.99   Even though a child is taken into State care, the parents do not thereby lose their rights nor are they absolved of their responsibilities in respect of the child.[276] Ideally separation effected pursuant to Art 9(1) in cases of neglect or abuse should be temporary, it being recognised that:[277]

> 'Children's's rights to development are at serious risk when they are ... deprived of family care or when they suffer long-term disruptions to relationships or separations.'

Juvenile Offenders

8.100   Care orders removing parental responsibility should not be part of sentencing tariffs.[278] Rule 18(2) of the 'Beijing Rules' stipulates that 'No juvenile shall be removed from parental supervision, whether partly or entirely, unless the circumstances of her or his case make this necessary'. CRC, Art 37(b) provides that imprisonment (and consequent separation from parents) shall only be used as a measure of last resort.[279]

Immigration and Separation – CRC, Art 10

8.101   The UN General Recommendation XXX on Discrimination against Non-Citizens recommends that States must '[a]void expulsions of non-citizens, especially of long-term residents, that would result in disproportionate interference with the right to family life'.[280] The terms of Art 9(1) strongly suggest immigration law and procedures which result in the separation of children from their parents for reasons other than the children's best interests will contravene Art 9(1).

8.102   Article 10 of the CRC covers the processes by which family reunification may be achieved where the child has been separated from his or her parents by reason of the fact that the parents and the child reside in different States. In respect of the process required to remedy such separations Art 10 of the CRC provides as follows:

> '1. In accordance with the obligations of States Parties under article 9, paragraph 1, applications by a child or his or her parents to enter or leave a State Party for the purpose of family reunification shall be dealt with by the States Parties in a positive, humane and expeditious manner. States Parties shall further ensure that the submission of such a request shall entail no adverse consequences for the applicants and for the members of their family.
>
> 2. A child whose parents reside in different States shall have the right to maintain on a regular basis, save in exceptional circumstances, personal relations and direct contacts with both parents. Towards that end and in accordance with the obligation of States Parties under article 9, paragraph 1, States Parties shall respect the right of the child and his or her parents to leave any country, including their own,[281] and to enter their own country.[282] The right to

---

276   Luxembourg CRC/C/15/Add.250, paras 34 and 35.

277   Committee on the Rights of the Child General Comment No 7 *Implementing Child Rights in Early Childhood*, para 36(b) HRI/GEN/1/Rev 8, p 447. See also UN Guidelines for the Alternative Care of Children (2010) A/RES/64/142, para 2.

278   Newell, P and Hodgkin, R *Implementation Handbook for the Convention on the Rights of the Child* (2008) 3rd edn, UNICEF, p 125.

279   See **14.21** below.

280   HRI/GEN/1/Rev. 8 p 276, para 28. See also Committee on the Rights of the Child General Comment No 6 *Treatment of Unaccompanied and Separated Children Outside their Country of Origin* CRC/GC/2005/6, para 40 ('A child who has adult relatives arriving with him or her or already living in the country of asylum should be allowed to stay with them unless such action would be contrary to the best interests of the child. Given the particular vulnerabilities of the child, regular assessments should be conducted by social welfare personnel').

281   See Art 12(2) of the ICCPR ('Everyone shall be free to leave any country including his own').

leave any country shall be subject only to such restrictions as are prescribed by law and which are necessary to protect the national security, public order (ordre public)[283], public health or morals or the rights and freedoms of others and are consistent with the other rights recognised in the present Convention.'

8.103 Article 10 of the CRC should be read together with Art 9 of the CRC as Art 10 is expressly framed as being referable to the obligations contained in Art 9(1).[284] Following the adoption of Art 9, Art 10 was stated as 'not intended to affect the general right of States to establish and regulate their respective immigration laws in accordance with their international obligations.[285] However, the provisions of Art 10 will apply to children whose parents are under threat of deportation.[286]

8.104 Whilst Art 10(2) of the CRC recognises the right of children and parents to leave any country, including their own, and to enter their own country, Art 10 of the CRC does not expressly enshrine a 'right to family reunion' for parents and children residing in different countries and contains no express right to remain with a view to avoiding separation.[287] Art 10 of the CRC seeks only to ensure procedural protection in relation to applications to enter or leave the State by ensuring that such applications are dealt with in a positive, humane and expeditious manner and entail no adverse consequences for the applicants and for the members of their family.

Article 10, CRC Interpretation – 'Positive, humane and expeditious manner'

8.105 The word 'positive' was chosen to ensure that the state could apply Art 10 without compelling the State to invariably grant the application.[288] Its use emphasises the 'procedural' tenor of Art 10, the article creating no freestanding right to entry and exit for the purposes of family reunification with or for the child. The word 'humane' qualifies the word 'positive' and adds an additional dimension to the requirement that the State treat the application in a positive manner. It is implicit that the decision making procedure applied to the application must be 'humane' in execution.[289] In this regard there is a link between Art 10 and Art 37 of the CRC concerning the deprivation of liberty, which often accompanies the decision making process in relation to questions of immigration. The use of the word 'expeditious' reflects the need for State Parties to complete judicial or administrative processes in respect of children as soon as possible so as to avoid the need for decisions imposed solely by passage of time.

---

[282] See Art 12(4) of the ICCPR ('No one shall be arbitrarily deprived of the right to enter his own country').

[283] The French term 'ordre public' is said to be more precise than the English term 'public order' (see E/CN.4/1986/39, pp 5–8).

[284] Newell, P and Hodgkin, R *Implementation Handbook for the Convention on the Rights of the Child* (2008) 3rd edn, UNICEF, p 126.

[285] E/CN.4/1989/48, para 203. In relation to children separated from their parents due to immigration issues see also the decisions of the Human Rights Commission of Australia in its *Report on the Complaint of Mr and Mrs M. Yilmas* (1985) Volume 22 Issue 7 and *Report on the Complaint of Mr and Mrs Au Yeung* (1985) Volume 22 Issue 9.

[286] Newell, P and Hodgkin, R *Implementation Handbook for the Convention on the Rights of the Child* (2008) 3rd edn, UNICEF, p 137.

[287] Although Hodgkin and Newell argue that such a right to remain is implicit in Art 10 (Newell, P and Hodgkin, R *Implementation Handbook for the Convention on the Rights of the Child* (2008) 3rd edn, UNICEF, p 136).

[288] E/CN.4/1989/48, pp 37–40.

[289] Newell, P and Hodgkin, R *Implementation Handbook for the Convention on the Rights of the Child* (2008) 3rd edn, UNICEF, p 138.

Article 10, CRC Interpretation – 'No adverse consequences'

8.106 An application by a parent or a child for permission to enter or leave must not result in the persecution of or the discrimination against the applicant or his or her family. The 'adverse' consequences contemplated by Art 10 extend beyond 'malice' and encompass, for example, the adverse consequences of breaching the family's confidentiality in the course of investigations in a manner hazardous to them.[290]

Article 10, CRC Interpretation – 'Right to leave any country and enter their own country'

8.107 In applying the right to enter one's own country[291] to family reunification, the words 'own country' are likely to be interpreted more widely than denoting simply the concept of nationality and will embrace at the very least a child or parent who, by reason of his or her special ties to or claims in relation to a given country cannot be considered to be a mere alien.[292] The UN Human Rights Committee has observed that:[293]

> 'The right of a person to enter his or her own country recognises the special relationship of a person to that country. The right has various facets. It implies the right to remain in one's own country. It includes not only the right to return after having left one's own country; it may also entitle a person to come to the country for the first time if he or she was born outside the country (for example, if that country is the person's State of nationality). The right to return is of the utmost importance for refugees seeking voluntary repatriation. It also implies prohibition of enforced population transfers or mass expulsions to other countries.'

Article 10, CRC Interpretation – 'Restrictions prescribed by law and necessary'

8.108 The right to leave any country[294] as it is articulated by Art 10 of the CRC is not absolute. Rather, it is qualified by a number of exceptions, namely such restrictions as are prescribed by law and which are necessary to protect the national security, public order (ordre public), public health or morals or the rights and freedoms of others and are consistent with the other rights recognised in the CRC.[295] The use of the term 'subject only' in Art 10(2) suggests that the restrictions provided for in the article are exhaustive. The last words, 'and are consistent with the other rights recognised in the present Convention', in Art 10(2) are particularly important and indicate that any restrictions placed on the right of the child and parent to leave any country and enter their own must be measured not only against the law of the nation(s) in question but also against the CRC. It is important to note that, unlike the right to leave any country, the child and parents' right to enter their own country is not subject to any restriction or qualification.

---

[290] Newell, P and Hodgkin, R *Implementation Handbook for the Convention on the Rights of the Child* (2008) 3rd edn, UNICEF, p 316 and see CRC, Art 22(2).

[291] See Art 12(4) of the ICCPR ('No one shall be arbitrarily deprived of the right to enter his own country').

[292] Human Rights Committee General Comment No 27 *Freedom of Movement* (1999) HRI/GEN/1/Rev.8, para 20, p 217 and see Communication No 538/1993, *Stewart v Canada* U.N. Doc. CCPR/C/58/D/538/1993 (1996) in which the Human Rights Committee held in relation to the meaning of the phrase 'his own country' in Art 12(4) of the ICCPR that 'In short, while these individuals may not be nationals in the formal sense, neither are they aliens within the meaning of article 13. The language of article 12, paragraph 4, permits a broader interpretation, moreover, that might embrace other categories of long-term residents, particularly stateless persons arbitrarily deprived of the right to acquire the nationality of the country of such residence.'

[293] General Comment No 27 *Freedom of Movement* (1999) HRI/GEN/1/Rev 8, p 217, paras 19 and 20.

[294] See Art 12(2) of the ICCPR ('Everyone shall be free to leave any country including his own').

[295] CRC, Art 10(2).

8.109 Efforts at family reunification should include efforts to ensure that siblings can be maintained together.[296] Where children are separated from their parents by abandonment or conflict efforts must still be made to ensure their reunification with parents or family.[297]

Refugee Children – CRC, Art 22(2)

8.110 CRC, Art 22(2) provides as follows in respect of ensuring that refugee children separated from their parents and/or family can be reunited with them:

'2. ... States Parties shall provide, as they consider appropriate, co-operation in any efforts by the United Nations and other competent intergovernmental organisations or nongovernmental organisations co-operating with the United Nations to protect and assist such a child and to trace the parents or other members of the family of any refugee child in order to obtain information necessary for reunification with his or her family. In cases where no parents or other members of the family can be found, the child shall be accorded the same protection as any other child permanently or temporarily deprived of his or her family environment for any reason, as set forth in the present Convention.'

8.111 Article 22(2) should be read in conjunction with Art 9(1) and Art 10 of the CRC. Preserving or restoring the child's family unity is crucial in achieving sustainable outcomes for a refugee child.[298] The Committee on the Rights of the Child has emphasised that:

'In order to pay full respect to the obligation of States under article 9 of the Convention to ensure that a child shall not be separated from his or her parents against their will, all efforts should be made to return an unaccompanied or separated child to his or her parents except where further separation is necessary for the best interests of the child, taking full account of the right of the child to express his or her views (art. 12) (see also section IV (e), 'Right of the child to express his or her views freely'). While the considerations explicitly listed in article 9, paragraph 1, sentence 2, namely, cases involving abuse or neglect of the child by the parents, may prohibit reunification at any location, other best-interests considerations can provide an obstacle to reunification at specific locations only.'

8.112 In the context of unaccompanied and separated children outside their country of origin, reunification in their country of origin can raise particular issues.[299] The Committee on the Rights of the Child has observed that:[300]

'Family reunification in the country of origin is not in the best interests of the child and should therefore not be pursued where there is a 'reasonable risk' that such a return would lead to the violation of fundamental human rights of the child ... [T]he granting of refugee status constitutes a legally binding obstacle to return to the country of origin and, consequently, to family reunification therein. Where the circumstances in the country of origin contain lower level risks and there is concern, for example, of the child being affected by the indiscriminate effects of generalised violence, such risks must be given full attention and balanced against other rights-based considerations, including the consequences of

---

[296] Committee on the Rights of the Child General Comment No 6 Treatment of Unaccompanied and Separated Children Outside of their Country of Origin, para 40 (HRI/GEN/1/Rev. 8 p 419).

[297] Colombia CRC/C/15/Add.137, paras 40 and 42.

[298] Newell, P and Hodgkin, R *Implementation Handbook for the Convention on the Rights of the Child* (2008) 3rd edn, UNICEF, p 316.

[299] See generally Committee on the Rights of the Child General Comment No 6 *Treatment of Unaccompanied and Separated Children Outside of their Country of Origin* HRI/GEN/1/Rev. 8 p 407.

[300] Committee on the Rights of the Child General Comment No 6 *Treatment of Unaccompanied and Separated Children Outside their Country of Origin* (2005) CRC/GC/2005/6, paras 82 and 83.

further separation. In this context, it must be recalled that the survival of the child is of paramount importance and a precondition for the enjoyment of any other rights. Whenever family reunification in the country of origin is not possible, irrespective of whether this is due to legal obstacles to return or whether the best-interests-based balancing test has decided against return, the obligations under article 9 and 10 of the Convention come into effect and should govern the host country's decisions on family reunification therein.'

Children of Migrant Workers

8.113 In respect of migrant workers, Art 44 of the International Convention on the Protection of the Rights of All Migrant Workers and Members of their Families[301] provides as follows:

'1. States Parties, recognising that the family is the natural and fundamental group unit of society and is entitled to protection by society and the State, shall take appropriate measures to ensure the protection of the unity of the families of migrant workers.

2. States Parties shall take measures that they deem appropriate and that fall within their competence to facilitate the reunification of migrant workers with their spouses or persons who have with the migrant worker a relationship that, according to applicable law, produces effects equivalent to marriage, as well as with their minor dependent unmarried children.

3. States of employment, on humanitarian grounds, shall favourably consider granting equal treatment, as set forth in paragraph 2 of the present article, to other family members of migrant workers.'

CRC, Art 9(3) – Right to Maintain Contact with Parents

CRC, Art 9(3) – General Principle of Contact

8.114 CRC, Art 9(3) provides as follows in respect of the child's right to maintain contact with his or her parents:

'3. States Parties shall respect the right of the child who is separated from one or both parents to maintain personal relations and direct contact with both parents on a regular basis, except if it is contrary to the child's best interests.'

CRC, Art 9(3) – Ambit[302]

8.115 Article 9(3) of the CRC enshrines the child's right to maintain contact with his or her parents. Article 9(3) does not prescribe a right to contact with siblings and members of the extended family, although such contact is assured by the provisions of CRC, Art 16 in that denying a child contact with his or her siblings or extended family without justification will amount to an arbitrary and/or unlawful interference in his or her

---

[301] Adopted by General Assembly resolution 45/158 of 18 December 1990 but not yet ratified by the United Kingdom. Article 14 of the Convention provides that 'No migrant worker or member of his or her family shall be subjected to arbitrary or unlawful interference with his or her privacy, family, correspondence or other communications, or to unlawful attacks on his or her honour and reputation. Each migrant worker and member of his or her family shall have the right to the protection of the law against such interference or attacks.' Art 22(1) provides that 'Migrant workers and members of their families shall not be subject to measures of collective expulsion. Each case of expulsion shall be examined and decided individually.'

[302] Note that under Art 23(4) of the ICCPR children are entitled to have 'provision' made for them upon the dissolution of their parents' marriage. This provision will include the provision of contact with his or her parents (see the decision of the UN Human Rights Committee in *Wim Hendricks v The Netherlands* (1985) No 201/1985, D&R 5).

family.[303] When read with Arts 18 and 7 of the CRC, Art 9(3) implies that the law should presume that, unless it is proved to the contrary the continued involvement of both parents in the child's life is in his or her best interests.[304] Thus the child's best interests will generally require Art 9(3) to be interpreted as requiring that regular contact be maintained with both parents, although the courts may refuse to enforce the child's right to contact with both parents where such contact is likely to have adverse consequences for the child.[305] Contact should not be disrupted by the inability of parents or the child to travel significant distances or visit at set times.[306] Art 9(3) of the CRC has been referred to by the domestic courts in the context of contact proceedings.[307]

Contact Following Parental Separation

8.116 The child's right to maintain personal relations and continuing contact with his or her parents under CRC, Art 9(3) will be of particular significance for children whose parents have decided to terminate their own relationship. In *Hendriks v Netherlands*[308] the UN Human Rights Committee noted that, in the context of Art 23 of the ICCPR, the relationship between parent and child does not depend on the subsistence of the marriage between the parents:

> 'The words 'the family' in article 23 paragraph 1, do not refer solely to the family as it exists during the marriage. The idea of the family must necessarily embrace the relations between parents and child. Although divorce legally ends a marriage, it cannot dissolve the bond uniting father – or mother – and child; this bond does not depend on the continuation of the parents' marriage.'

In *Hendriks v Netherlands* the Human Rights Committee further held that it was necessary to provide for the child to have contact with both parents following separation save in 'exceptional circumstances'. Within that context, the Committee recognised that the child's best interests could result in a parent having no contact with the child.

Contact Following Removal from Parental Care

(i)   Contact Whilst in State Care

8.117 CRC, Art 9(3) will also operate to ensure contact between a child and his or her parents where that child is in the care of the State. The fact that a child's best interests requires his or her removal from parental care should not lead automatically to a conclusion that it is in the child's best interests not to have continuing contact with those parents. The best interest decisions as to separation and as to contact will rarely be co-terminus, it being important, in the context of State care being ideally a temporary measure,[309] to maintain the child's relationship with his or her parents.

---

[303] See **8.69** above. Note that it is definitively established that ECHR, Art 8 does extend to sibling contact (see **8.203** below).

[304] Newell, P and Hodgkin, R *Implementation Handbook for the Convention on the Rights of the Child* (2008) 3rd edn, UNICEF, p 237.

[305] Newell, P and Hodgkin, R *Implementation Handbook for the Convention on the Rights of the Child* (2008) 3rd edn, UNICEF, p 130.

[306] Newell, P and Hodgkin, R *Implementation Handbook for the Convention on the Rights of the Child* (2008) 3rd edn, UNICEF, p 123 and see Czech Republic CRC/C/15/Add. 201, para 44.

[307] *Re L (A Child) (Contact: Domestic Violence)* [2000] 4 All ER 609.

[308] (1985) No 201/1985, D&R 5.

[309] UN Guidelines for the Alternative Care of Children (2010) A/RES/64/142, para 2.

(ii)   Contact Following Adoption

8.118   The issue of whether a child should continue to have contact with his or her birth parents following adoption is a complex one. The Committee on the Rights of the Child has not yet specifically considered the extent to which CRC, Art 9(3) will act to compel the continuation of contact between an adopted child and his or her birth parents. In its General Comment No 7 *Implementing Child Rights in Early Childhood*[310] the Committee makes clear that in considering the option of adoption, States Parties must systematically bear in mind and respect *all* relevant rights of the child set out in the CRC.[311] It is to be anticipated that in considering the application of Art 9(3) in relation to adopted children a close analysis of the child's best interests will be required to determine whether such continuing contact would be beneficial in this particular context, having regard to the child's need for security, continuity of care and affection and the opportunity to form long-term attachments based on mutual trust and respect.[312]

Contact to Children in Custody

8.119   Children deprived of their liberty will be entitled pursuant to CRC, Art 9(3) to maintain personal relations and direct contact with both parents on a regular basis, except if it is contrary to his or her best interests. CRC, Art 37(c) expressly articulates this position, stating that the child deprived of his or her liberty 'shall have the right to maintain contact with his or her family through correspondence and visits, save in exceptional circumstances'.[313] The exceptional circumstances that may limit contact should be clearly described in the law and not be left to the discretion of the competent authorities.[314] In order to facilitate visits, the child should be placed in a facility that is as close as possible to the place of residence of his/her family.[315] The benefits of family ties being maintained by remaining at liberty prior to the trial must be weighed in the balance when considering pre-trial detention of children.[316] As to the meaning of the term 'regular basis' in CRC, Art 9(3) when applied in the context of contact to children deprived of their liberty, Rule 61 of the UN Rules for the Protection of Juveniles Deprived of their Liberty[317] provides that:

> 'Every juvenile should have the right to communicate in writing or by telephone at least twice a week with the person of his or her choice, unless legally restricted, and should be assisted as necessary in order effectively to enjoy this right. Every juvenile should have the right to receive correspondence.'

---

[310]   Committee on the Rights of the Child General Comment No 7 *Implementing Child Rights in Early Childhood* HRI/GEN/1/Rev 8, p 432.

[311]   Committee on the Rights of the Child General Comment No 7 *Implementing Child Rights in Early Childhood* HRI/GEN/1/Rev 8, p 448, para 36(b).

[312]   Committee on the Rights of the Child General Comment No 7 *Implementing Child Rights in Early Childhood* HRI/GEN/1/Rev 8, p 448, para 36(b).

[313]   See also CCPR Art 10(3) and CCPR General Comment No 19 *Article 23 (The Family)* (HRI/GEN/1/Rev 8, p 194, paras 12 and 13 and the UN Minimum Standard Rules for the Administration of Juvenile Justice (the 'Beijing Rules') 40/33 of 29 November 1985, r 1.1.

[314]   Committee on the Rights of the Child General Comment No 10 *Children's Rights in Juvenile Justice* CRC/C/GC/10 p 23, para 87.

[315]   Committee on the Rights of the Child General Comment No 10 *Children's Rights in Juvenile Justice* CRC/C/GC/10 p 23, para 87.

[316]   General recommendation XXXI on the Prevention of Racial Discrimination in the Administration and Functioning of the Criminal Justice System, para 26(c) (HRI/GEN/1/Rev. 8 p 285).

[317]   A/RES/45/113.

Immigration and Contact

8.120 The rights enshrined in CRC, Art 9(3) will apply to children whose parents reside in different States. CRC, Art 10(2) specifically legislates for these circumstances by providing that:[318]

> '2. A child whose parents reside in different States shall have the right to maintain on a regular basis, save in exceptional circumstances personal relations and direct contacts with both parents. Towards that end and in accordance with the obligation of States Parties under article 9, paragraph 1, States Parties shall respect the right of the child and his or her parents to leave any country, including their own, and to enter their own country. The right to leave any country shall be subject only to such restrictions as are prescribed by law and which are necessary to protect the national security, public order (ordre public), public health or morals or the rights and freedoms of others and are consistent with the other rights recognised in the present Convention.'

CRC, Art 20 – Right to Alternative Care

8.121 Where a child is unable to reside within his or her family environment, CRC, Art 20 provides as follows in relation to the provision for that child or alternative care:

> '1. A child temporarily or permanently deprived of his or her family environment, or in whose own best interests cannot be allowed to remain in that environment, shall be entitled to special protection and assistance provided by the State.[319]
>
> 2. States Parties shall in accordance with their national laws ensure alternative care for such a child.
>
> 3. Such care could include, inter alia, foster placement, kafalah of Islamic law,[320] adoption or if necessary placement in suitable institutions for the care of children. When considering solutions, due regard shall be paid to the desirability of continuity in a child's upbringing and to the child's ethnic, religious, cultural and linguistic background.'

CRC, Art 20 – General Principles

(i) Key Instruments

8.122 When considering the child's right to provision of alternative care, in addition to the provisions of CRC, Art 20 itself, a number of other international instruments fall for consideration. Principle 6 of the Declaration of the Rights of the Child[321] provides that where it is not possible to grow up in the care and under the responsibility of his or her parents, the child shall in any case grow up in an atmosphere of affection and or moral and material security. CRC, Art 20 must also be read with the Declaration of Social and Legal Principles Relating to the Protection and Welfare of Children with Special Reference to Foster Care Placement and Adoption Nationally and Internationally[322] Further the principles enshrined in CRC, Art 20 must also now be considered in light of

---

[318]   For the interpretation of the terminology used in Art 10(2), see **8.102–8.109** above.
[319]   See **8.38** above.
[320]   Defined in Art 116 of the Family Code of Algeria as 'the commitment to voluntarily take care of the maintenance, of the education and of the protection of a minor, in the same way as a father would do it for his son'. The need for kafalah arises out of the prohibition on adoption based on the interpretation of verses 4 and 5 of Sura Ahzab XXXIIII in the Koran.
[321]   G.A. Res. 1386 (XIV), 14 U.N. GAOR Supp. (No 16) at 19, U.N. Doc. A/4354.
[322]   A/RES/41/85 3rd December 1986.

the UN Guidelines for the Alternative Care of Children[323] which were adopted by the UN on 24 February 2010. These guidelines seek in particular:

(a) To support efforts to keep children in, or return them to, the care of their family or, failing this, to find another appropriate and permanent solution, including adoption and *kafala* of Islamic law;

(b) To ensure that, while such permanent solutions are being sought, or in cases where they are not possible or are not in the best interests of the child, the most suitable forms of alternative care are identified and provided, under conditions that promote the child's full and harmonious development;

(c) To assist and encourage Governments to better implement their responsibilities and obligations in these respects, bearing in mind the economic, social and cultural conditions prevailing in each State; and

(d) To guide policies, decisions and activities of all concerned with social protection and child welfare in both the public and the private sectors, including civil society.[324]

(ii) Definitions

8.123 The UN Guidelines for the Alternative Care of Children[325] provide a number of definitions pertinent to the child's right to alternative care. The concept of 'children without parental care' encompasses all children not in the overnight care of at least one of their parents, for whatever reason and under whatever circumstances.[326] Children without parental care who are outside their country of habitual residence or victims of emergency situations may be designated as 'unaccompanied' if they are not cared for by another relative or an adult who by law or custom is responsible for doing so, or 'separated' if they are separated from a previous legal or customary primary caregiver, but who may nevertheless be accompanied by another relative.[327]

8.124 In relation to alternative care for children, the UN Guidelines differentiate between (a) informal care, being any private arrangement provided in a family environment, whereby the child is looked after on an ongoing or indefinite basis by relatives or friends (informal kinship care) or by others in their individual capacity, at the initiative of the child, his/her parents or other person without this arrangement having been ordered by an administrative or judicial authority or a duly accredited body, and (b) formal care, being all care provided in a family environment which has been ordered by a competent administrative body or judicial authority, and all care provided in a residential environment, including in private facilities, whether or not as a result of administrative or judicial measures.[328] In terms of environment, alternative forms of care detailed in the UN Guidelines include:[329]

---

[323] (2010) A/RES/64/142. See also *Human Rights and Social Work: A Manual for Schools of Social Work and the Social Work Profession* (1994) Centre for Human Rights.

[324] UN Guidelines for the Alternative Care of Children (2010) A/RES/64/142, para 2.

[325] (2010) A/RES/64/142.

[326] (2010) A/RES/64/142, para 29(a).

[327] (2010) A/RES/64/142, paras 29(a)(i) and 29(a)(ii).

[328] (2010) A/RES/64/142, paras 29(b)(i) and 29(b)(ii).

[329] Note that the forms of alternative care contemplated by the UN Guidelines do not include (a) children deprived of their liberty by decision of a judicial or administrative authority and who situation is covered by the UN Standard Minimum Rules for the Administration of Juvenile Justice and the UN Rules for the

(a) Kinship care: family-based care within the child's extended family or with close friends of the family known to the child, whether formal or informal in nature;

(b) Foster care: situations where children are placed by a competent authority for the purpose of alternative care in the domestic environment of a family other than the children's own family that has been selected, qualified, approved and supervised for providing such care;

(c) Other forms of family-based or family-like care placements;

(d) Residential care: care provided in any non-family-based group setting, such as places of safety for emergency care, transit centres in emergency situations, and all other short- and long-term residential care facilities, including group homes;

(e) Supervised independent living arrangements for children.[330]

With respect to those responsible for alternative care the UN Guidelines contemplate both agencies that are public or private bodies, services that organise alternative care for children and facilities that provide residential care for children.

(iii) *Primacy of Family Care*

8.125 The preamble to the CRC stresses that 'the child, for the full and harmonious development of his or her personality, should grow up in a family environment, in an atmosphere of happiness, love and understanding'. The UN Guidelines for the Alternative Care of Children provide that:[331]

> 'The family being the fundamental group of society and the natural environment for the growth, well-being and protection of children, efforts should primarily be directed to enabling the child to remain in or return to the care of his/her parents, or when appropriate, other close family members. The State should ensure that families have access to forms of support in the care giving role.'

Likewise, Part A of Declaration of Social and Legal Principles Relating to the Protection and Welfare of Children with Special Reference to Foster Care Placement and Adoption Nationally and Internationally[332] emphasises that the primary aim should be care within the family if at all possible. Article 1 of the Declaration makes it clear

---

Protection of Juveniles Deprived of their Liberty, (b) care by adoptive parents from the moment the child concerned is effectively placed in their custody pursuant to a final adoption order, the child being considered from that moment to be 'in parental care' (the Guidelines will apply to adoptive placements prior to the final adoption order) and (c) informal arrangements whereby a child voluntarily stays with relatives or friends for recreational purposes and reasons not connected with parents inability or unwillingness to provide adequate care (UN Guidelines for the Alternative Care of Children (2010) A/RES/64/142, para 30).

330 UN Guidelines for the Alternative Care of Children (2010) A/RES/64/142, para 29(c). Competent authorities and others concerned are also encouraged to make use of the UN Guidelines at boarding schools, hospitals, centres for children with mental and physical disabilities or other special needs, camps, the workplace and other places which may be responsible for the care of children (UN Guidelines for the Alternative Care of Children (2010) A/RES/64/142, para 31).

331 A/RES/64/142, para II A 3. This will involve the need for positive action on the part of the State 'To support family care giving environments whose capacities are limited by factors such as disability, drug and alcohol misuse, discrimination against families with indigenous or minority backgrounds, and living in armed conflict regions or under foreign occupation' (A/RES/64/142, para 9 and see also paras 32–52).

332 A/RES/41/85 3rd December 1986.

that State should give a high priority to the child to be cared for by his or her parents and Art 3 goes further in stipulating that '[t]he first priority for a child is to be cared for by his or her own parents'.[333]

8.126 Even where alternative care is unavoidable, the CRC and the Committee on the Rights of the Child emphasise the importance of 'family like' solutions when considering alternative care for children.[334] In its General Comment No 7 *Implementing Child Rights in Early Childhood* the Committee makes clear that:[335]

> 'To the extent that alternative care is required, early placement in family-based or family-like care is more likely to produce positive outcomes for young children. States parties are encouraged to invest in and support forms of alternative care that can ensure security, continuity of care and affection, and the opportunity for young children to form long-term attachments based on mutual trust and respect, for example through fostering, adoption and support for members of extended families.'

(iv)   Best Interests

8.127 It is important to note that in respect of adoption in the context of the CRC 'the best interests of the child shall be the paramount consideration'[336] and not, as in respect of the other rights under the CRC, simply 'a primary consideration'.[337] Indeed, it is arguable that in *all* matters relating to the placement of the child outside the care of the child's own parents, the best interests of the child should be the paramount consideration.[338] In considering alternative care arrangement for children, States parties must 'systematically bear in mind' all relevant rights of the child and obligations of States parties set out in the CRC.[339]

(v)   Continuity and Avoidance of Delay

Continuity

8.128 Article 20(3) requires that in considering solutions to the need for alternative care, due regard shall be paid to the desirability of continuity in a child's upbringing.

---

[333] The Declaration makes clear that the placement of a child in foster care should not preclude the return of the child to the care of his or her family (Art 11). See also UN Guidelines for the Alternative Care of Children A/RES/64/142, para 3.

[334] *Manual on Human Rights Reporting* HR/PUB/91/1/ (Rev1), p 450.

[335] Committee on the Rights of the Child General Comment No 7 *Implementing Child Rights in Early Childhood* HRI/GEN/1/Rev 8, p 448, para 36(b). See also UN Guidelines for the Alternative Care of Children (2010) A/RES/64/142, para 22 which provides that 'In accordance with the predominant opinion of experts, alternative care for young children, especially those under the age of 3 years, should be provided in family-based settings. Exceptions to this principle may be warranted in order to prevent the separation of siblings and in cases where the placement is of an emergency nature or is for a predetermined and very limited duration, with planned family reintegration or other appropriate long-term care solution as its outcome.'

[336] CRC, Art 21. See **8.143** below.

[337] CRC, Art 3.

[338] Declaration of Social and Legal Principles Relating to the Protection and Welfare of Children with Special Reference to Foster Care Placement and Adoption Nationally and Internationally Art 5 (A/RES/41/85 3rd December 1986). See also UN Guidelines for the Alternative Care of Children, para 7 (A/RES/64/142) which requires that the best interests of the child in the context of the provision of alternative care shall be determined by reference to the course of action best suited to satisfying the child's needs and rights, taking into account the full and personal development of their rights in their family, social and cultural environment and their status as subjects of rights, both at the time of the determination and in the longer term.

[339] Committee on the Rights of the Child General Comment No 7 *Implementing Child Rights in Early Childhood*, para 36(b) (HRI/GEN/1/Rev. 8 p 448).

When considering alternative care for the child States parties to the CRC should prioritise alternative placements which are able to ensure security, continuity of care and affection, and the opportunity for young children to form long-term attachments based on mutual trust and respect.[340] The UN Guidelines for the Alternative Care of Children stipulate:[341]

> 'Frequent changes in care setting are detrimental to the child's development and ability to form attachments, and should be avoided. Short-term placements should aim at enabling an appropriate permanent solution to be arranged.'

8.129 The need for continuity in alternative care also implies, subject to the best interests of the child, continuity of contact with parents, family and the wider community.[342] This proposition is likely to create particular issues in relation to children placed for adoption.[343] Stability and continuity will also require, pursuant to CRC, Art 20(3) that when considering alternative care due regard be paid to the 'desirability of continuity and the child's ethnic, religious, cultural and linguistic background'.[344]

Avoidance of Delay

8.130 Where required in the child's best interests, alternative care should be secured without delay. The UN Guidelines for the Alternative Care of Children provide that, in relation to alternative care:[345]

> 'Permanency for the child should be secured without undue delay through reintegration in his/her nuclear or extended family or, if this is not possible, in an alternative stable family setting or, where paragraph 21 above applies, in stable and appropriate residential care.'

The UN Guidelines further stipulate:[346]

> 'Planning for care provision and permanency should be carried out from the earliest possible time, ideally before the child enters care, taking into account the immediate and longer-term advantages and disadvantages of each option considered, and should comprise short- and long-term propositions.'

(vi) Children's Participation in Decision Making

8.131 Decisions concerning alternative care, including decisions regarding placement in foster care or home, development of care plans and their review and visits with parents and family must be taken having regard to the views of the child in accordance with

---

[340] Committee on the Rights of the Child General Comment No 7 *Implementing Child Rights in Early Childhood*, para 36(b) (HRI/GEN/1/Rev. 8 p 448). See also Declaration of Social and Legal Principles Relating to the Protection and Welfare of Children with Special Reference to Foster Care Placement and Adoption Nationally and Internationally, Art 5 (A/RES/41/85 3rd December 1986).

[341] A/RES/64/142, para 60.

[342] Newell, P and Hodgkin, R *Implementation Handbook for the Convention on the Rights of the Child* (2008) 3rd edn, UNICEF, p 289.

[343] See **8.142** below. Newell and Hodgkin suggest this principle will apply even after a child is adopted (Newell, P and Hodgkin, R *Implementation Handbook for the Convention on the Rights of the Child* (2008) 3rd edn, UNICEF, p 289).

[344] Report on the Fortieth Session *Day of Discussion on Children Without Parental Care* (2005) CRC/C/153, para 673 and see **8.138** below.

[345] A/RES/64/142, para 60.

[346] A/RES/64/142, para 61.

Art 12 of the CRC.[347] The obligation to have regard to the views of the child applies equally to any judicial or administrative procedure by which decisions concerning the alternative placement of the child are made.[348] In respect of alternative placement, the child's best interests cannot be defined without consideration of the child's views, which should if possible be taken within the context of the child having been informed about the effects and consequences of the alternative placement, including the consequences of adoption if relevant.[349] The requirement to hear the child is no less important where an adoption is by a step-parent or foster carer.[350] The child's right to be heard continues to apply with equal force within any alternative placement:[351]

> 'Mechanisms must be introduced to ensure that children in all forms of alternative care, including in institutions, are able to express their views and that those views be given due weight in matters of their placement, the regulations of care in foster families or homes and their daily lives.'

(vii) Legal Responsibility

8.132 In ensuring an alternative placement which meets the best interests of the child and ensures the protection and promotion of the child's rights, it is vital that legal responsibility for the child within the context of the alternative placement is clearly defined. The UN Guidelines for the Alternative Care of Children[352] provide that:

> 'In situations where the child's parents are absent or are incapable of making day-to-day decisions in the best interests of the child, and the child's placement in alternative care has been ordered or authorised by a competent administrative body or judicial authority, a designated individual or competent entity should be vested with the legal right and responsibility to make such decisions in the place of parents, in full consultation with the child.'

Pursuant to the Guidelines, the role and specific responsibilities of the 'designated person' or 'competent entity' should include:

(a)   Ensuring that the rights of the child are protected and, in particular, that the child has appropriate care, accommodation, health-care provision, developmental opportunities, psychosocial support, education and language support;

(b)   Ensuring that the child has access to legal and other representation where necessary, consulting with the child so that the child's views are taken into account by decision-making authorities, and advising and keeping the child informed of his/her rights;

---

[347]   CRC, Art 12 and see Committee on the Rights of the Child General Comment No 12 *Right to be Heard*, para 54 (CRC/C/GC/12 p 13). See also UN Guidelines for the Alternative Care of Children, para 6 (A/RES/64/142).

[348]   UN Guidelines for the Alternative Care of Children, para 57 (A/RES/64/142).

[349]   Committee on the Rights of the Child General Comment No 12 *Right to be Heard*, para 56 (CRC/C/GC/12 p 13). It is also important within this context that the child's need to know about his or her background should be recognised by those responsible for the child's care (see Declaration of Social and Legal Principles Relating to the Protection and Welfare of Children with Special Reference to Foster Care Placement and Adoption Nationally and Internationally Art 9 (A/RES/41/85 3rd December 1986)).

[350]   Committee on the Rights of the Child General Comment No 12 *Right to be Heard*, para 55 (CRC/C/GC/12, p 13).

[351]   Committee on the Rights of the Child General Comment No 12 *Right to be Heard*, para 97 (CRC/C/GC/12, p 19).

[352]   A/RES/64/142, para 101.

(c)　　Contributing to the identification of a stable solution in the best interests of the child;

(d)　　Providing a link between the child and various organisations that may provide services to the child;

(e)　　Assisting the child in family tracing;

(f)　　Ensuring that, if repatriation or family reunification is carried out, it is done in the best interests of the child;

(g)　　Helping the child to keep in touch with his/her family, when appropriate.[353]

(viii)　Standards of State Care

8.133　In evaluating the adequacy of alternative care provided by the State, the State must be judged fit or unfit to care for a child on similar criteria to those applied to the family.[354] In addition to ensuring that the child's best interests are the primary consideration when the State is providing alternative care[355] the standards to be applied by the State in providing such alternative care to children will be measured in part against the provisions of Art 3(3) of the CRC which provides:

> '3. States Parties shall ensure that the institutions, services and facilities responsible for the care or protection of children shall conform to the standards established by competent authorities, particularly in the areas of safety, health, in the number and suitability of their staff, as well as competent supervision.'

This will require that legislation stipulates that all agencies and facilities be registered and authorised, which authorisation should be the subject of regular review by competent authorities on the basis of standard criteria covering the agency or facility's objectives, functioning, staff recruitment and qualifications, conditions of care, financial resources and management.[356]

(ix)　Alternative Care – Key Principles of Good Practice

8.134　The key principles of the primacy of family care, the consistent application of the best interests principle, the need for continuity and avoidance of delay and the need to secure the effective participation of the child are contained in Part B of the UN Guidelines for the Alternative Care of Children[357] which stipulate that in making decisions about alternative care decision makers should ensure that:

(a)　　Full account is taken of the desirability, in principle, of maintaining the child as close as possible to his/her habitual place of residence, in order to facilitate contact and potential reintegration with his/her family and to minimise disruption of his/her educational, cultural and social life;

---

[353]　A/RES/64/142, para 104.
[354]　Van Bueren, G *The International Law on the Rights of the Child* (1998) Martinus Nijhoff, p 87.
[355]　CRC, Art 3(1).
[356]　UN Guidelines for the Alternative Care of Children, para 105 (A/RES/64/142). See also paras 106–117 and 128–130 for the detailed requirements.
[357]　A/RES/64/142.

(b)   Due regard is given to the importance of ensuring children a stable home and of meeting their basic need for safe and continuous attachment to their caregivers;

(c)   Removal of a child from the care of the family is seen as a measure of last resort and should, whenever possible, be temporary and for the shortest possible duration;

(d)   Removal decisions are regularly reviewed and the child's return to parental care;

(e)   Attention is paid to promoting and safeguarding all other rights of special pertinence to the situation of children without parental care, including, but not limited to, access to education, health and other basic services, the right to identity, freedom of religion or belief, language and protection of property and inheritance rights;

(f)   Siblings with existing bonds are not separated by placements in alternative care unless there is a clear risk of abuse or other justification in the best interests of the child and that every effort is made to enable siblings to maintain contact with each other, unless this is against their wishes or interests;

(g)   The child is not without the support and protection of a legal guardian or other recognised responsible adult or competent public body at any time;

(h)   The use of residential care is limited to cases where such a setting is specifically appropriate, necessary and constructive for the individual child concerned and in his/her best interests.

CRC, Art 20 – Interpretation

(i)   'Temporarily or permanently deprived of his or her family environment'

8.135   The use of the words 'family environment' in Art 20(1) makes clear that the child's removal from his or her *parents* does not automatically mean the provision of alternative care outside the wider family. When a child's best interests demand removal from his or her immediate family environment, usually comprising his or her parents, the State should seek to give effect to the child's right to alternative care by placing the child with his or her wider family *before* considering alternative options for care.[358] As such, the wider family should be first in the hierarchy of options for alternative care:[359]

'When care by the child's own parents is unavailable or inappropriate, care by relatives of the child's parents, by another substitute – foster or adoptive – family or, if necessary, by an appropriate institution should be considered.'

---

[358]   CRC, Art 5 and see Committee on the Rights of the Child General Comment No 7 *Implementing Child Rights in Early Childhood* (2005) CRC/C/GC/7/Rev.1, para 15.

[359]   Declaration of Social and Legal Principles Relating to the Protection and Welfare of Children with Special Reference to Foster Care Placement and Adoption Nationally and Internationally A/RES/41/85 3 December 1986.

(ii) 'Entitled to Special Protection and Assistance'

8.136 The use of the word 'entitled' stresses the obligation owed by the State to children who are not able to be cared for by their own parents.[360] When read with the CRC as a whole, Art 20(1) of the CRC implies that children separated from their families and provided with alternate care are entitled to an additional level of protection and assistance to that ordinarily provided to the child under the CRC.[361] The provision of alternative care pursuant to Art 20(2) should be considered in this context.

(iii) 'Such Care Could Include ...'

8.137 The use of the phrase 'could include' clearly demonstrates that the list of options for alternative care contained in CRC, Art 20(3), namely foster placement, kafalah of Islamic law, adoption or, if necessary, placement in suitable institutions for the care of children, is not exhaustive.[362] The use of the term 'if necessary' before the option of institutional care and the fact that this is listed as the last solution to the need for alternative care demonstrates clearly that the use of institutional care is to be considered an option of last resort.[363] In particular, in relation to children with special needs, including disabilities, there should be an avoidance of unnecessary institutionalisation.[364]

(iv) 'Child's Ethnic, Religious, Cultural and Linguistic Background'

8.138 Child's ethnic, religious, cultural and linguistic background must be considered in accordance with Art 20(3) when determining whether and which option for alternative care is in the child's best interests. In the context of adoption, this principle will apply in both domestic and intercountry adoptions. It should be noted that a blanket policy to place children into alternative placements with the same ethnicity or religion is not required by Art 20(3) because of the words 'due regard' and by reason of the fact that such a placement may not meet the child best interests in other respects.

Article 20 CRC – Application

(i) Alternative Care – Extended Family

8.139 Whilst Art 20(3) does not specifically mention the child's wider family, the words 'family environment' in Art 20(1) make clear that the child's removal from his or her *parents* does not automatically require the provision of alternative care outside the wider family. Further, in circumstances where the parents are incapable or unwilling to care for the child the child's extended family should be the first choice for alternative care save in circumstances where the extended family are themselves unsuitable or notifying the extended family would place the child or the parent at risk.[365] Placements with extended

---

[360] Newell, P and Hodgkin, R *Implementation Handbook for the Convention on the Rights of the Child* (2008) 3rd edn, UNICEF, p 279.

[361] Van Bueren, G *The International Law on the Rights of the Child* (1998) Martinus Nijhoff, p 94.

[362] Van Bueren, G *The International Law on the Rights of the Child* (1998) Martinus Nijhoff, p 102.

[363] *Manual on Human Rights Reporting* HR/PUB/91/1/ (Rev.1) p 450 and see UN Guidelines for the Alternative Care of Children, para 23 (A/RES/64/142).

[364] UN Guidelines for the Alternative Care of Children, para 132 (A/RES/64/142).

[365] CRC, Art 5 and see Committee on the Rights of the Child General Comment No 7 *Implementing Child Rights in Early Childhood* (2005) CRC/C/GC/7/Rev.1, para 15. See also **8.125–8.136** above and Declaration of Social and Legal Principles Relating to the Protection and Welfare of Children with Special Reference to Foster Care Placement and Adoption Nationally and Internationally A/RES/41/85 3 December 1986.

family members must still be regulated to ensure the welfare of the child, the UN Guidelines for the Alternative Care of Children providing that:[366]

'Recognising that, in most countries, the majority of children without parental care are looked after informally by relatives or others, States should seek to devise appropriate means, consistent with the present Guidelines, to ensure their welfare and protection while in such informal care arrangements, with due respect for cultural, economic, gender and religious differences and practices that do not conflict with the rights and best interests of the child.'

(ii)   Alternative Care – Foster Care

8.140   In contrast to Art 21 of the CRC which further elaborates the rights of the child in relation to adoption, Art 20 CRC does not articulate further the principles governing the placement of a child in foster care. However, a number of other provisions assist in determining the principles which will be applicable.

8.141   Pursuant to the CRC, Art 25 a child placed in foster care has the right to a periodic review of the foster care placement and all circumstances relevant to that placement.[367] The oversight required of the State by CRC, Art 3(3) will also apply to foster carers.[368] Further, the Declaration of Social and Legal Principles Relating to the Protection and Welfare of Children with Special Reference to Foster Care Placement and Adoption Nationally and Internationally sets out the following principles in relation to foster care:[369]

(a)   Persons responsible for foster placement or adoption procedures should have professional or other appropriate training.

(b)   Foster placement of children should be regulated by law.

(c)   Foster family care, though temporary in nature, may continue, if necessary, until adulthood but should not preclude either prior return to the child's own parents or adoption.

(d)   In all matters of foster family care, the prospective foster parents and, as appropriate, the child and his or her own parents should be properly involved. A competent authority or agency should be responsible for supervision to ensure the welfare of the child.

(iii)   Alternative Care – Adoption

8.142   CRC, Art 20 does not promote adoption, but rather lists it as one of the options for alternative care where a child has to be separated from his or her family environment. It is however implicit from the place given to adoption in the list of options for alternative care provided by CRC, Art 20(3) that it is an option for

---

[366]   A/RES/64/142, para 18.
[367]   Newell, P and Hodgkin, R *Implementation Handbook for the Convention on the Rights of the Child* (2008) 3rd edn, UNICEF, p 380.
[368]   Newell, P and Hodgkin, R *Implementation Handbook for the Convention on the Rights of the Child* (2008) 3rd edn, UNICEF, p 282. See **8.125** above.
[369]   Declaration of Social and Legal Principles Relating to the Protection and Welfare of Children with Special Reference to Foster Care Placement and Adoption Nationally and Internationally Arts 6, 10, 11 and 12 (A/RES/41/85 3 December 1986). See also UN Guidelines for the Alternative Care of Children, paras 118–122 (A/RES/64/142).

alternative care that should only be considered once rehabilitation to the care of the family has been ruled out by means of due process.[370]

Adoption – CRC, Art 21

8.143 Whilst the principles enshrined in CRC, Art 20 will apply to adoption as a form of alternative care, CRC, Art 21 encompasses specific rights of the child in relation to adoption.[371] CRC, Art 20 must thus be considered together with the provision of CRC, Art 21 when considering the rights of the child in the context of alternative care provided by means of adoption. Article 21 of the CRC provides as follows:

> 'States Parties that recognise and/or permit the system of adoption[372] shall ensure that the best interests of the child shall be the paramount consideration and they shall:
>
> (a)   Ensure that the adoption of a child is authorised only by competent authorities who determine, in accordance with applicable law and procedures and on the basis of all pertinent and reliable information, that the adoption is permissible in view of the child's status concerning parents, relatives and legal guardians and that, if required, the persons concerned have given their informed consent to the adoption on the basis of such counselling as may be necessary;
>
> (b)   Recognise that inter-country adoption may be considered as an alternative means of child's care, if the child cannot be placed in a foster or an adoptive family or cannot in any suitable manner be cared for in the child's country of origin;
>
> (c)   Ensure that the child concerned by inter-country adoption enjoys safeguards and standards equivalent to those existing in the case of national adoption;
>
> (d)   Take all appropriate measures to ensure that, in inter-country adoption, the placement does not result in improper financial gain for those involved in it;
>
> (e)   Promote, where appropriate, the objectives of the present article by concluding bilateral or multilateral arrangements or agreements, and endeavour, within this framework, to ensure that the placement of the child in another country is carried out by competent authorities or organs.'

Adoption – General Principles

8.144 The Declaration of Social and Legal Principles Relating to the Protection and Welfare of Children with Special Reference to Foster Care Placement and Adoption Nationally and Internationally[373] sets out a series of general principles concerning adoption:

(a)   The primary aim of adoption is to provide the child who cannot be cared for by his or her own parents with a permanent family.

(b)   In considering possible adoptive placements, persons responsible for them should select the most appropriate environment for the child.

(c)   If a child cannot be placed in a foster or an adoptive family or cannot in any suitable manner be cared for in the country of origin, intercountry adoption may be considered as an alternative means of providing the child with a family.

---

[370]   See above **8.125**.

[371]   Article 21(c) of the CRC has been referred to by the domestic courts (see *Re R (Minor) (Inter-country Adoption; Practice Note* [1999] 4 All ER 1015).

[372]   Not all countries permit adoption. For example, Islamic law does not recognise the concept of adoption.

[373]   Articles 13, 14, 17 and 24 A/RES/41/85 3 December 1986.

(d)   Where the nationality of the child differs from that of the prospective adoptive parents, all due weight shall be given to both the law of the State of which the child is a national and the law of the State of which the prospective adoptive parents are nationals. In this connection due regard shall be given to the child's cultural and religious background and interests.

8.145 In accordance with the general principle outlined above delay in determining a decision as to adoption will be inimical to the child's best interest.[374] Sufficient time and adequate counselling should be given to the child's own parents, the prospective adoptive parents and, as appropriate, the child in order to reach a decision on the child's future as early as possible.[375]

Adoption and Best Interests

8.146 CRC, Art 21 requires that 'States Parties that recognise and/or permit the system of adoption shall ensure that the best interests of the child shall be the paramount consideration'. This provision contrasts with the requirements of Art 3 of the CRC in that, in relation to adoption, the best interests of the child must be the 'paramount' rather than 'a primary consideration' as required by Art 3. Accordingly, under CRC, Art 21, no other interests, be they economic, political, matters of national security or the interests of the adoptive parents will take precedence over the best interests of the child.[376] The 'child' whose best interests are referred to in Art 21 is the child being considered for adoption.

8.147 The best interests of the child who it is proposed is adopted must be considered and evaluated by reference to, amongst other factors the child's need for affection and right to security and continuing care.[377] The child's best interests in relation to adoption cannot be effectively determined and defined without consideration of the child's views in accordance with Art 12 of the CRC.[378]

Adoption Jurisdiction

8.148 In order to determine whether the adoption of a child is permissible States parties to the CRC must, in addition to being satisfied that adoption is in the child's best interests, ensure that three cardinal principles are adhered to within the adoption decision making process. Namely, that the adoption is in accordance with applicable law and procedure, is based on proper evidence and takes place following informed consent having been given.

Jurisdiction – In Accordance with Applicable Law and Procedure

8.149 In respect of the jurisdiction governing adoption of children, Art 21(a) of the CRC requires that the adoption of a child is authorised only by competent authorities in

---

[374] Switzerland CRC/C/15/Add.182, para 36 and Philippines CRC/C/15/Add.259, para 48.

[375] Declaration of Social and Legal Principles Relating to the Protection and Welfare of Children with Special Reference to Foster Care Placement and Adoption Nationally and Internationally, Art 15 (A/RES/41/85 3 December 1986.).

[376] Newell, P and Hodgkin, R *Implementation Handbook for the Convention on the Rights of the Child* (2008) 3rd edn, UNICEF, p 295.

[377] Declaration of Social and Legal Principles Relating to the Protection and Welfare of Children with Special Reference to Foster Care Placement and Adoption Nationally and Internationally, Art 5 (A/RES/41/85 3 December 1986).

[378] Committee on the Rights of the Child General Comment No 12 *Right to be Heard*, paras 55–56 CRC/C/GC/12, p 13.

accordance with applicable law and procedures. The term 'competent authorities' covers those judicial and administrative authorities charged with considering the best interests of the child, the suitability of the adoptive placement considered in light of the child's best interests and ensuring the relevant information has been considered and consents obtained.[379] The term competent relates to the legal status of the authority rather than the skill of the authority.

Jurisdiction – Based on Evidence

8.150 Article 21(a) further requires that the adoption of the child occurs only on the basis of 'all pertinent and reliable information'. The need for 'all pertinent and reliable information' means that an adoption must be conditional upon a proper investigation and assessment by qualified professionals independent of the authority considering the adoption application. Pertinent and reliable information will certainly include the views and wishes of the child[380] and the views and position of the parents. Such information is also likely to include as a minimum the anticipated impact on the child of an adoption, the availability and suitability of any prospective adopters and the arrangements for any ongoing contact between the child and his or her birth parents.

Jurisdiction – Based on Informed Consent

8.151 CRC, Art 21(a) further stipulates that, if required, the persons concerned with the adoption have given their informed consent to the adoption on the basis of such counselling as may be necessary. Care must be taken with the term 'if required' in Art 21(a). The term 'if required' in relation to the provision of consent does no more than recognise that there will be situations where, notwithstanding that consent is withheld by the persons concerned, adoption will nonetheless remain in the child best interests. Informed consent to adoption thus remains required in all circumstances save those where, in accordance with applicable law and procedure, a competent authority has determined that it is in the child's best interests for the need for consent to be dispensed with. Consent must be obtained from 'persons concerned' which term will encompass the parents, including an unmarried father, and, where of sufficient age and understanding, the child.[381] Those giving consent should be provided with such counselling as may be necessary to assist with the decision as to whether to consent or not.[382]

Adoption – Inter-Country Adoptions

General Principles

8.152 Article 21 CRC makes specific provision as to inter-country adoption, which provision recognises that inter-country adoption may be considered as an alternative means of securing the child's care if the child cannot be placed in a foster or an adoptive family or cannot in any suitable manner be cared for in the child's country of origin. It

---

[379] Newell, P and Hodgkin, R *Implementation Handbook for the Convention on the Rights of the Child* (2008) 3rd edn, UNICEF, p 295.
[380] See **8.131** above.
[381] CRC, Art 12. See also the Hague Convention on Protection of Children and Cooperation in respect of Intercountry Adoption, Art 4(d) which provides that the adoption can only proceed where the State of origin has 'ensured, having regard to the age and degree of maturity of the child, that he or she has been counselled and duly informed of the effects of the adoption and of his or her consent to the adopted, where such consent is required' and that 'consideration has been given to the child's wishes and opinions.'
[382] CRC, Art 21(a) and see Newell, P and Hodgkin, R *Implementation Handbook for the Convention on the Rights of the Child* (2008) 3rd edn, UNICEF, p 296.

seeks to ensure that the child involved in an inter-country adoption enjoys safeguards and standards equivalent to those existing in the case of national adoption and that the inter-country placement does not result in improper financial gain for those involved in it. Article 21(e) invites States Parties to promote, where appropriate, the objectives of Art 21 by concluding bilateral or multilateral arrangements or agreements, and endeavour, within the framework of Art 21, to ensure that the placement of the child in another country is carried out by competent authorities or organs.

8.153 The CRC implicitly incorporates the principle that intercountry adoption should be an option of last resort within the available options for adoption.[383] Art 21(b) of the CRC provides that States Parties shall recognise that inter-country adoption may be considered as an alternative means of child's care *if* the child cannot be placed in a foster or an adoptive family or cannot in any suitable manner be cared for in the child's country of origin.[384] Prolonged residential care is unlikely to constitute a 'suitable' placement in the child's country of origin for the purposes of Art 21(b).[385]

8.154 Pursuant to CRC, Art 21(c) a child involved in intercountry adoption must enjoy the same safeguards and standards to those applying to domestic adoptions.[386] The requirements of Art 21(c) implicitly recognise that each inter-country adoption must be measured against the standard of the child's best interests by competent authorities acting on information obtained by means of professional investigation and assessment. In particular, pursuant to CRC, Art 21(d), States Parties must ensure that an inter-country adoptive placement does not result in improper financial gain for those involved in it.[387]

8.155 States Parties must, where appropriate, ensure pursuant to CRC, Art 21(2) that the aims and objectives of Art 21 as it relates to inter-country adoption are promoted by the conclusion of bilateral or multilateral arrangements or agreements, thus endeavouring to ensure that inter-country adoptions are carried out by competent authorities.[388] The Declaration of Social and Legal Principles Relating to the Protection and Welfare of Children with Special Reference to Foster Care Placement and Adoption Nationally and Internationally[389] emphasises the provisions of CRC, Art 21(e) by providing at Art 18 that Governments should establish policy, legislation and effective supervision for the protection of children involved in intercountry adoption and that

---

[383] Van Bueren, G *The International Law on the Rights of the Child* (1998) Martinus Nijhoff, p 102. See also Art 20(3) CRC and Newell, P and Hodgkin, R *Implementation Handbook for the Convention on the Rights of the Child* (2008) 3rd edn, UNICEF, pp 297 and 298. See also the guidelines provided by the Supreme Court of India in *Lakshmi Kant Pandey v Union of India* (1984) 2 SCC 244, AIR 1984 SC 469.

[384] See also the Hague Convention on Protection of Children and Co-operation in respect of Inter-country Adoption Art 4(b) ('An adoption within the scope of the Convention shall take place only if the competent authorities of the State of origin ... have determined, after possibilities for placement of the which within the State of origin have been given due consideration, that an inter-country adoption is in the child's best interests').

[385] Newell, P and Hodgkin, R *Implementation Handbook for the Convention on the Rights of the Child* (2008) 3rd edn, UNICEF, pp 297 and 298.

[386] See also the Optional Protocol to the Convention on the Rights of the Child on the Sale of Children, Child Prostitution and Child Pornography, Arts 2, 3 and 5, which requires States Parties to take measures to criminalise the trafficking of children, including 'Improperly inducing consent, as an intermediary, for adoption of a child in violation of application internal legal instruments on adoption' (Art 3(1)(a)(ii)).

[387] See also Art 35 of the CRC, Arts 2, 3 and 5 of the Optional Protocol to the Convention on the Rights of the Child on the Sale of children, Child Prostitution and Child Pornography and Art 32 of the Hague Convention on Protection of Children and Co-operation in respect of Inter-country Adoption.

[388] The key multilateral agreement in this regard is the Hague Convention on Protection of Children and Co-operation in respect of Inter-country Adoption. See Art 1(a) of the Convention and **8.169** below.

[389] A/RES/41/85 3 December 1986.

inter-country adoption should, wherever possible, only be undertaken when such measures have been established in the States concerned.[390]

Inter-Country Adoption and Unaccompanied and Refugee Children

8.156 The guidance set out in General Comment No 6 *Treatment of Unaccompanied and Separated Children Outside their Country of Origin*[391] emphasises the care that must be taken by States Parties when considering the option of adoption in relation to unaccompanied and refugee children.[392] The UN Guidelines for the Alternative Care of Children make clear that:

> 'Placement with a view to adoption or *kafala* of Islamic law should not be considered a suitable initial option for an unaccompanied or separated child. States are encouraged to consider this option only after efforts to determine the location of his/her parents, extended family or habitual carers have been exhausted.'

8.157 Accordingly, when considering the adoption of unaccompanied and separated children States Parties must respect both the preconditions to adoption provided under Art 21 of the Convention and other relevant international instruments, including in particular the Hague Convention on Protection of Children and Co-operation in Respect of Inter-Country Adoption and the Recommendation Concerning the Application to Refugee Children and Other Internationally Displaced Children of the Hague Convention on Protection of Children and Co-Operation in Respect of Inter-country Adoption.[393] In considering the issue of adoption in relation to unaccompanied or refugee children, States Parties must recognises the particular circumstances of those children and ensure the application of the following principles:

(a) Adoption of unaccompanied or separated children should only be considered once it has been established that the child is in a position to be adopted. In practice, this means that efforts with regard to tracing and family reunification have failed, or that the parents have consented to the adoption. The consent of parents and the consent of other persons, institutions and authorities that are necessary for adoption must be free and informed. This presupposes that such consent has not been induced by payment or compensation of any kind and has not been withdrawn.

(b) Unaccompanied or separated children must not be adopted in haste at the height of an emergency.

(c) Any adoption must be determined as being in the child's best interests and carried out in keeping with applicable national, international and customary law.

(d) The views of the child should be sought and taken into account in all adoption procedures subject to his or her age and degree of maturity. This requirement implies that the child has been counselled and duly informed of the consequences

---

[390] See also Declaration of Social and Legal Principles Relating to the Protection and Welfare of Children with Special Reference to Foster Care Placement and Adoption Nationally and Internationally, Arts 19–23.

[391] Committee on the Rights of the Child General Comment No 6 *Treatment of Unaccompanied and Separated Children Outside their Country of Origin* CRC/GC/2005/6, para 91

[392] The UN Guidelines for the Alternative Care of Children, para 141 provides that 'Unaccompanied or separated children already abroad should, in principle, enjoy the same level of protection and care as national children in the country concerned' (A/RES/64/142).

[393] Hague Conference on Private International Law 1994.

of adoption and of his or her consent to adoption, where such consent is required. Such consent must have been given freely and not induced by payment or compensation of any kind.

(e)   Priority must be given to adoption by relatives in the child's country of residence. Where this is not an option, preference should be given to adoption within the community from which the child came or at least within his or her own culture, subject always to the best interests of the child.

(f)   Adoption should not be considered where there is reasonable hope of successful tracing and family reunification is in the child's best interests, if it is contrary to the expressed wishes of the child or the parents or unless a reasonable time has passed during which all feasible steps to trace the parents or other surviving family members has been carried out.[394] This period of time will vary with the circumstances of each case, in particular those relating to difficulties in conducting a proper tracing exercise.[395] However, the process of tracing must itself be completed within a reasonable period of time.

(g)   Adoption in a country of asylum should not be effected where there is the possibility of voluntary repatriation under conditions of safety and dignity in the near future.[396]

(iv)   Alternative Care – Residential Care

General Principles

8.158   The terms of CRC, Art 20 imply that the use of residential care is a last resort, to be used only 'if necessary'.[397] The Committee on the Rights of the Child has interpreted Art 20 to require that residential care should only be used where such care is professionally indicated and in the best interests of the child.[398] The UN Guidelines for the Alternative Care of Children state that 'The use of residential care should be limited to cases where such a setting is specifically appropriate, necessary and constructive for the individual child concerned and in his/her best interests'.[399] This principle applies equally to children with disabilities.[400] Residential care is likely to be particularly inappropriate for younger children.[401] Overall, States Parties should pursue a policy of the deinstitutionalisation of children, the UN Guidelines for the Alternative Care of Children making clear that:[402]

---

[394]   The UN Guidelines for the Alternative Care of Children, para 146 provides that 'As soon as an unaccompanied or separated child is taken into care, all reasonable efforts should be made to trace his/her family and re-establish family ties, when this is in the best interests of the child and would not endanger those involved.' (A/RES/64/142).

[395]   See **8.125** above in relation to the rights of the child in respect of family reunification.

[396]   Committee on the Rights of the Child General Comment No 6 *Treatment of Unaccompanied and Separated Children Outside their Country of Origin* CRC/GC/2005/6, para 91.

[397]   Newell, P and Hodgkin, R *Implementation Handbook for the Convention on the Rights of the Child* (2008) 3rd edn, UNICEF, p 282. See **8.121** above.

[398]   Lithuania CRC/C/LTU/CO/2, para 42.

[399]   A/RES/64/142, para 21.

[400]   Convention on the Rights of Persons with Disabilities 2006 Art 23. See also the Standard Rules on the Equalisation of Opportunities for Persons with Disabilities, r 9(1) and General Comment No 9 *The Rights of Children with Disabilities* CRC/C/GC/9, paras 47–49.

[401]   Committee on the Rights of the Child General Comment No 7 *Implementing Child Rights in Early Childhood* (2005) CRC/C/GC/7/ Rev 1, para 36.

[402]   A/RES/64/142, para 23.

'While recognising that residential care facilities and family-based care complement each other in meeting the needs of children, where large residential care facilities (institutions) remain, alternatives should be developed in the context of an overall deinstitutionalisation strategy, with precise goals and objectives, which will allow for their progressive elimination. To this end, States should establish care standards to ensure the quality and conditions that are conducive to the child's development, such as individualised and small-group care, and should evaluate existing facilities against these standards. Decisions regarding the establishment of, or permission to establish, new residential care facilities, whether public or private, should take full account of this deinstitutionalisation objective and strategy.'

Standards of Institutional Care[403]

8.159 In relation to the standards of care provided to children by residential institutions CRC, Art 3(3) requires that:

'3. States Parties shall ensure that the institutions, services and facilities responsible for the care or protection of children shall conform to the standards established by competent authorities, particularly in the areas of safety, health, in the number and suitability of their staff, as well as competent supervision.'

Article 3(3) is not an exhaustive list and will cover not only State care but will extend to alternative care provided by all those responsible for the care or protection of children. As such, the applicability of the provision will extend beyond public care to encompass foster placements and provision made by private and voluntary agencies.[404]

8.160 The words 'the standards established by competent authorities' in CRC, Art 3(3) are not defined by the CRC. However, the State must be judged fit or unfit to care for a child on similar criteria to those applied to the family.[405] The UN Guidelines for the Alternative Care of Children emphasise in particular that the residential setting should be as close as possible to a family or small group situation,[406] with the objective generally to provide temporary care and to contribute actively to the child's reintegration with his or her family or move into permanent alternative care by way of adoption.[407] In its General Comment No 7 *Implementing Child Rights in Early Childhood* the Committee on the Rights of the Child has emphasised that:[408]

'States parties must ensure that the institutions, services and facilities responsible for early childhood conform to quality standards, particularly in the areas of health and safety, and that staff possess the appropriate psychosocial qualities and are suitable, sufficiently numerous and well-trained. Provision of services appropriate to the circumstances, age and individuality of young children requires that all staff be trained to work with this age group. Work with young children should be socially valued and properly paid, in order to attract a highly qualified workforce, men as well as women. It is essential that they have sound, up-to-date theoretical and practical understanding about children's rights and development (see also paragraph 41); that they adopt appropriate child-centred care practices, curricula

---

[403] See **8.159** above in relation to the standards of State care.
[404] Newell, P and Hodgkin, R *Implementation Handbook for the Convention on the Rights of the Child* (2008) 3rd edn, UNICEF, p 42.
[405] Van Bueren, G *The International Law on the Rights of the Child* (1998) Martinus Nijhoff, p 87.
[406] A/RES/64/142, paras 123–127. See also Report on the Twenty-Fifth Session *Day of General Discussion on State Violence Against Children* (2000) CRC/C/100, 688.2 and 688.24.
[407] See also General Comment No 3 *HIV/AIDS and the Rights of the Child* (2003) CRC/GC/2003/3, para 35.
[408] Committee on the Rights of the Child General Comment No 7 *Implementing Child Rights in Early Childhood* CRC/C/GC/7/Rev.1, para 23.

and pedagogies; and that they have access to specialist professional resources and support, including a supervisory and monitoring system for public and private programmes, institutions and services.'

8.161 In addition to the requirements of CRC, Art 3(3), the precepts of Art 3(1) (best interests) and Art 12 (the right to participate) must also be rigorously adhered to when setting appropriate standards in residential care, as must the provisions of Art 13 (freedom of expression), Art 16 (the right to privacy) and Art 19 (protection from violence). Where residential care is provided to children with disabilities that care must meet the requirements of CRC, Art 23 and in particular make certain that the child with a disability enjoys a full and decent life in conditions which ensure dignity, promote self-reliance and facilitate the child's active participation in the community.[409] In relation to children who have infringed the penal law, when considering the institutionalisation of such children regard must be had to CRC, Art 40(4), which provides that:[410]

'A variety of dispositions, such as care, guidance and supervision orders; counseling; probation; foster care; education and vocational training programmes and other alternatives to institutional care shall be available to ensure that children are dealt with in a manner appropriate to their well-being and proportionate both to their circumstances and the offence.'

(v) Alternative Care – Proper Review

Proper Review – General Principles

8.162 In order to ensure the protection and promotion of the rights of children provided with alternative care, the proper review of such alternative placements is vital. Within this context, the UN Guidelines for the Alternative Care of Children provide that it is the role of the State, through its competent authorities, to ensure the supervision of the safety, well-being and development of any child placed in alternative care and the regular review of the appropriateness of the care arrangement.[411] In respect of the detailed requirements arising from this role, the Guidelines stipulate that:[412]

'States should ensure the right of any child who has been placed in temporary care to regular and thorough review – preferably at least every three months – of the appropriateness of his/her care and treatment, taking into account, notably, his/her personal development and any changing needs, developments in his/her family environment, and the adequacy and necessity of the current placement in these circumstances. The review should be carried out by duly qualified and authorised persons, and should fully involve the child and all relevant persons in the child's life.'

8.163 In requiring States Parties to ensure that the institutions, services and facilities responsible for the care or protection of children conform to the standards established by competent authorities, it is implicit in CRC, Art 3(3) that an adequate system of independent inspection and monitoring is required.[413] This implicit requirement will

---

[409] See also CRC, Art 39.
[410] See also CRC, Art 37(b) and the UN Standard Minimum Rules for the Administration of Juvenile Justice (the 'Beijing Rules'), r 17.
[411] A/RES/64/142, para 5
[412] A/RES/64/142, para 67.
[413] Newell, P and Hodgkin, R *Implementation Handbook for the Convention on the Rights of the Child* (2008) 3rd edn, UNICEF, p 41.

extend to institutions, services and facilities run by voluntary or private organisations that will be required to adhere to the precepts of Art 3(3) of the CRC.[414]

Proper Review – CRC, Art 25

8.164 Whereas CRC, Art 3(3) ensures the monitoring of institutions and staff caring for children, CRC, Art 25 ensures the review of each individual child[415] by providing that:

> 'States Parties recognise the right of a child who has been placed by the competent authorities for the purposes of care, protection or treatment of his or her physical or mental health, to a periodic review of the treatment provided to the child and all other circumstances relevant to his or her placement.'

8.165 The provisions of Art 25 of the CRC will cover placements in families, both foster and adoptive, and placements in residential care, both State and private.[416] By reason of the words 'for the purposes of care, protection or treatment of his or her physical or mental health' CRC, Art 25 will also cover placements in hospitals, health units, therapeutic centres, boarding schools and immigration and refugee detention centres. Article 25 will also apply to children deprived of their liberty.[417] The term 'all other circumstances relevant to his or her placement' will necessarily encompass the reasons for that placement and whether such reasons persist.[418] The provisions of Art 25 will apply to interim and temporary placements.[419] In respect of foster care placements, the Declaration of Social and Legal Principles Relating to the Protection and Welfare of Children with Special Reference to Foster Care Placement and Adoption Nationally and Internationally[420] requires that a competent[421] authority or agency should be responsible for supervision to ensure the welfare of the child.

8.166 In reviewing a child's alternative placement, the views of the child must be sought and taken into account in respect of the review in question.[422] It is also important that the review process for alternative care can respond to particular issues in respect of

---

[414] Newell, P and Hodgkin, R *Implementation Handbook for the Convention on the Rights of the Child* (2008) 3rd edn, UNICEF, p 42. See also Day of General Discussion on *The Private Sector as Service Provider and its Role in Implementing Child Rights* Report on Thirty-First Session September/October 2002 CRC/C/121 p 152 et seq and Committee on the Rights of the Child General Comment No 7 *Implementing Child Rights in Early Childhood* (2005) CRC/C/GC/7/Rev.1, para 32: 'Where non-State services play a major role, the Committee reminds State Parties that they have an obligation to monitor and regulate the quality of provision to ensure that children's rights are protected and their best interests served.'

[415] See the Report of the Fortieth Session *General Day of Discussion on Children Without Parental Care* (2005) CRC/C/153, paras 667 and 669 in which the Committee on the Rights of the Child emphasises the principle of 'individualisation' by which the position of the child should be considered on a case by case basis.

[416] Report of the Thirty-First Session *Day of General Discussion on the Private Sector as Service Provider and its Role in Implementing Child Rights* (2002) CRC/C/121, para 653. Private placements arranged by parents will not fall within the ambit of Art 25 (see E/CN.4/1986/39, pp 11–13 and Detrick, p 360 but see also Guinea CRC/C/15/Add.100, para 21 and Chad CRC/C/15/Add.107, para 22).

[417] Newell, P and Hodgkin, R *Implementation Handbook for the Convention on the Rights of the Child* (2008) 3rd edn, UNICEF, pp 379 and 380.

[418] Newell, P and Hodgkin, R *Implementation Handbook for the Convention on the Rights of the Child* (2008) 3rd edn, UNICEF, p 381.

[419] Costa Rica CRC/C/15/Add.266, paras 33 and 34.

[420] A/RES/41/85 3 December 1986.

[421] Once again, the term competent refers to legal authority rather than professional ability.

[422] CRC, Art 12 and see Report of the Fortieth Session *General Day of Discussion on Children Without Parental Care* (2005) CRC/C/153, paras 663 and 664.

individual placements outside the formal review period for that placement. The UN Guidelines for the Alternative Care of Children provide that:[423]

> 'Children in care should have access to a known, effective and impartial mechanism whereby they can notify complaints or concerns regarding their treatment or conditions of placement. Such mechanisms should include initial consultation, feedback, implementation and further consultation. Young people with previous care experience should be involved in this process, due weight being given to their opinions. This process should be conducted by competent persons trained to work with children and young people.'

The Child's Right to Family Life under other International Instruments

The Geneva Convention

8.167 Article 25 of the Geneva Convention IV[424] requires that all persons in the territory of a Party to an armed conflict or a territory occupied by it must be enabled to give and receive news of a personal nature to members of their families speedily and without undue delay. Where as the result of circumstances it becomes difficult to facilitate this obligation the Parties to the conflict must employ the services of a neutral intermediary to do so and decide in consultation with that agency on the best way to meet their obligations in this regard. Where Parties to the conflict deem it necessary to restrict family correspondence those restrictions must be confined to the compulsory use of standard forms containing 25 freely chosen words dispatched at a minimum of once per month.

The Hague Conventions

Child Abduction

8.168 The Hague Convention on the Civil Aspects of International Child Abduction[425] seeks to protect children from the harmful effects of their wrongful removal from, and ensure their prompt return to, family members caring for them as well as ensuring that contact between the child and those family members is maintained by the implementation of expeditious legal and administrative measures.[426] The emphasis of the Convention is on the return of the child in a timely fashion in order that the child's relationship with both parents can be determined by the court of the jurisdiction from which the child was removed. This procedure, together with the strict interpretation of the exceptions within the Convention[427] bolsters the child's right to family life.[428] Note that the European Court of Human Rights has made clear that it is competent to review the procedure of the domestic courts in relation to the Hague Convention by reference to Art 8 of the ECHR.[429]

---

[423] A/RES/64/142, para 99.
[424] See **15.130** below.
[425] As enacted by the United Kingdom in Sch 1 of the Child Abduction and Custody Act 1985.
[426] Preamble to the Convention. The Preamble is not specifically enacted by the United Kingdom but it has been referred to by the domestic courts (see *Re A (A Minor) (Abduction)* [1988] 1 FLR 365; *Re M (Abduction: Psychological Harm)* [1997] 2 FLR 690; *Re S (A Minor) (Custody: Habitual Residence)* [1998] AC 750 sub nom *Re S (Custody: Habitual Residence)* [1998] 1 FLR 122).
[427] See Arts 12 and 13.
[428] A detailed discussion of the operation of the Hague Convention on the Civil Aspects of International Child Abduction is beyond the scope of this work. For the authoritative treatise on the Hague Convention see Lowe N, Everall M, and Nicholls, M *International Movement of Children* (2004) Jordan Publishing.
[429] *Neulinger and Shuruk v Switzerland* (2010) Application No 41615/07, paras 132–133 and 138 ('In matters of international child abduction, the obligations that Article 8 imposes on the Contracting States must

Intercountry Adoption

8.169 The Hague Convention on Protection of Children and Cooperation in respect of Intercountry Adoption recalls in its pre-amble that each State should take, as a matter of priority, appropriate measures to enable the child to remain in the care of his or her family of origin.[430] Art 1 of the Convention makes clear that the aims of the Convention include the establishment of safeguards which ensure that intercountry adoptions take place only in the best interests of the child and with respect to the child's fundamental rights as recognised by international law, which rights will include the right to respect for family life. In order to pursue these aims, the Convention sets out strict criteria governing the intercountry adoption of children.[431]

The Child's Right to Family Life under the ECHR

Key Provisions

8.170 There are three articles of the ECHR and its associated Protocols which directly touch and concern the child's right to respect for family life. Article 8 of the ECHR enshrines the right to respect for private and family life, preventing any interference in family life which is not in accordance with the law, in pursuit of a legitimate aim and necessary in a democratic society. Article 12 of the ECHR incorporates the right to marry and found a family.[432] Finally, Art 5 of Protocol No 7 to the ECHR ensures equality between spouses for the benefit of children both during and upon dissolution of marriage.

ECHR, Art 8 – Ambit

8.171 Article 8 of the ECHR provides as follows in respect the right to respect for family life and the qualifications that may be placed on that right in certain defined circumstances:

---

therefore be interpreted taking into account, in particular, the Hague Convention on the Civil Aspects of International Child Abduction of 25 October 1980 ... However, the Court must also bear in mind the special character of the Convention as an instrument of European public order (ordre public) for the protection of individual human beings and its own mission, as set out in Article 19, 'to ensure the observance of the engagements undertaken by the High Contracting Parties' to the Convention. For that reason the Court is competent to review the procedure followed by domestic courts, in particular to ascertain whether the domestic courts, in applying and interpreting the provisions of the Hague Convention, have secured the guarantees of the Convention and especially those of Article 8 ... It follows from Article 8 that a child's return cannot be ordered automatically or mechanically when the Hague Convention is applicable. The child's best interests, from a personal development perspective, will depend on a variety of individual circumstances, in particular his age and level of maturity, the presence or absence of his parents and his environment and experiences (see the UNHCR Guidelines, paragraph 52 above). For that reason, those best interests must be assessed in each individual case. That task is primarily one for the domestic authorities, which often have the benefit of direct contact with the persons concerned. To that end they enjoy a certain margin of appreciation, which remains subject, however, to a European supervision whereby the Court reviews under the Convention the decisions that those authorities have taken in the exercise of that power').

[430] See also Recommendation Concerning the Application to Refugee Children and Other Internationally Displaced Children of the Hague Convention on Protection of Children and Co-Operation in Respect of Inter-country Adoption (Hague Conference on Private International Law 1994).

[431] Hague Convention on Protection of Children and Co-operation in Respect of Inter-country Adoption, Arts 4 and 5.

[432] Article 12 of the ECHR will apply in England and Wales to children over the age of 16 as, with the written consent of parents (and the local authority if a care order is in force) or the person with whom the child lives under a residence order, a child can marry upon reaching the age of 16 (Marriage Act 1949, s 3(1A)).

'1. Everyone has the right to respect for his private and family life, his home and his correspondence.

2. There shall be no interference by a public authority with the exercise of this right except such as is in accordance with the law and is necessary in a democratic society in the interests of national security, public safety or the economic well-being of the country, for the prevention of disorder or crime, for the protection of health or morals, or for the protection of the rights and freedoms of others.'

The scope of Art 8 is clearly very wide.[433] Lester and Pannick describe Art 8 as a broad range of loosely allied personal interests: physical or bodily integrity; personal identity and lifestyle, family life, the home and home environment and correspondence, embracing all forms of communication.[434] In the broadest terms, Art 8 seeks to ensure, in the words of Lord Hoffman, a person's 'own limited area of sovereignty in which he is free to act without state constraint, in which he is immune from the tyranny of the majority'.[435] This section concentrates on the ambit of Art 8 as it concerns the child's family life.

Article 8, ECHR – General Principles[436]

Article 8 General Principles – Purpose

8.172 The purpose of Art 8, in so far as it enshrines the right to respect for family life, is to protect the individual against arbitrary interferences with his or her family life.[437] The burden is on the applicant to establish to the requisite standard of proof that interference has occurred. Interference with the family life of the child will be considered arbitrary unless it can be said to fall within the justifications set out in Art 8(2) of the ECHR. In *Kroon v Netherlands*[438] the European Court of Human Rights emphasised that:

'The Court reiterates that the essential object of Article 8 is to protect the individual against arbitrary action by the public authorities. There may in addition be positive obligations inherent in effective 'respect' for family life. However, the boundaries between the State's positive and negative obligations under this provision do not lend themselves to precise definition. The applicable principles are nonetheless similar. In both contexts regard must be had to the fair balance that has to be struck between the competing interests of the individual and of the community as a whole; and in both contexts the states enjoys a certain margin of appreciation.'

---

433 Article 8 was described by Stanley Burton J in *R (Wright) v Secretary of State for Health* [2006] EWHC 2886 (Admin), [2007] 1 All ER 825 as 'the least defined and most unruly' of the rights enshrined in the ECHR (a view cited with approval by the House of Lords on appeal at [2009] UKHL 3, [2009] AC 739, para 30 per Baroness Hale).

434 Lord Lester QC, Lord Pannick QC and Herberg, J *Human Rights Law and Practice* (2009) 3rd edn, LexisNexis, p 359.

435 Lord Hoffman, *Separation of Powers: the Combar Lecture 2001* [2002] JR 137.

436 These principles will also be applicable when it comes to considering the right to respect for privacy under Art 8 at **9.23–9.54** below.

437 See **8.71** above in relation to the purpose of CRC, Art 16.

438 (1994) 19 EHRR 263.

Article 8 General Principles – 'Respect'

8.173 The requirements inherent in the term 'respect' as used in Art 8 of the ECHR will, given the positive obligations[439] that can arise under Art 8, be contextual in character. In *Goodwin v United Kingdom*[440] the Court made clear that:

> '... the notion of "respect" as understood in Art 8 is not clear cut, especially as far as the positive obligations inherent in that concept are concerned: having regard to the diversity of practices followed and the situations obtaining in the contracting states, the notion's requirements will vary considerably from case to case and the margin of appreciation to be accorded to the authorities may be wider than that applied in other areas under the Convention. In determining whether or not a positive obligation exists, regard must also be had to the fair balance that has to be struck between the general interests of the community and the interests of the individual, the search for which balance in inherent in the whole of the Convention.'[441]

Pursuant to Art 8, where family life is found to exist, the children of the family will be entitled to respect for their family life.

Article 8 General Principles – Positive Obligations[442]

8.174 In addition to the negative obligations imposed on the State by Art 8 the State may also have positive obligations to secure respect for family and private life where there is a direct and immediate link established between the measures sought by the applicant and the applicant's family life.[443] The case of *X & Y v The Netherlands*[444] demonstrates that Art 8:[445]

> '... does not merely compel the State to abstain from such interference: in addition to this primarily negative undertaking, there may be positive obligations inherent in an effective respect for private or family life ... These obligations may involve the adoption of measures designed to secure respect for private life even in the sphere of the relations of individuals between themselves.'

8.175 In relation to children, the positive duties inherent in Art 8 of the ECHR include a requirement to ensure a non-marital child's integration into his or her family,[446] a requirement to provide a person with access to records which constituted a substitute record of the memories and experience of, and the principle source of information for

---

[439] See **8.174** below.

[440] (2002) 35 EHRR 447, para 72.

[441] See also *A, B and C v Ireland* (2010) Application No 25579/05, paras 247–248 ('The notion of "respect" is not clear cut especially as far as positive obligations are concerned: having regard to the diversity of the practices followed and the situations obtaining in the Contracting States, the notion's requirements will vary considerably from case to case. Nonetheless, certain factors have been considered relevant for the assessment of the content of those positive obligations on States. Some factors concern the applicant: the importance of the interest at stake and whether "fundamental values" or "essential aspects" of private life are in issue; and the impact on an applicant of a discordance between the social reality and the law, the coherence of the administrative and legal practices within the domestic system being regarded as an important factor in the assessment carried out under Article 8. Some factors concern the position of the State: whether the alleged obligation is narrow and defined or broad and indeterminate').

[442] See also **2.84** above.

[443] *Botta v Italy* (1998) 26 EHRR 241, para 34 and see *Kroon v Netherlands* (1994) 19 EHRR 263.

[444] (1985) 8 EHRR 235.

[445] See also *Kroon v Netherlands* (1994) 19 EHRR 263, para 31 and *X, Y and Z v United Kingdom* (1997) 24 EHRR 143, [1997] 2 FLR 892, para 41. See also *A, B and C v Ireland* (2010) Application No 25579/05, paras 247–248.

[446] *Marckx v Belgium* (1979) 2 EHRR 330.

his or her formative childhood years,[447] a requirement to ensure protection for family from a violent parent,[448] a requirement to ensure a child is returned following abduction by one parent from another[449] and a requirement to ensure the return of the body of a dead child to the family as soon as possible after the post-mortem is carried out.[450] The positive obligations under Art 8 may further include a requirement that the State to provide resources to improve the circumstances of and the protection for vulnerable children.[451] However, Art 8 will not compel full financial support for the family from the State or financial support in a specified manner.[452] The state will enjoy a particularly wide margin of appreciation in deciding whether to implement a positive obligation arising under Art 8.[453]

8.176 The positive duties under Art 8 will also lead to 'horizontality' of effect.[454] The principle of horizontality requires that the rights enshrined in the ECHR operate not only to protect individuals from the actions of the State, but also to protect individuals through the agency of the State from the actions of other individuals.[455] This doctrine of 'horizontal effect' has been articulated by the European Court in the context of Art 8 as including, in some circumstances, an obligation upon the State to protect a private individual's rights under the ECHR against infringement by another private individual.[456] Thus, even where a dispute over the residence of a child arises between private individuals, the State is under a positive obligation to take steps to ensure that the relevant ECHR rights of the child and the parents are protected within the context of that dispute.[457] The concept of horizontality under Art 8 is particularly important where the rights of children and their parents may be in conflict.[458]

Article 8 General Principles – Justification

8.177 Article 8(2) of the ECHR makes clear that the right to respect for family life enshrined in Art 8 is qualified rather than absolute. Interference by a public authority in the right to respect for family life enshrined by Art 8 will not be considered arbitrary and will be justified in circumstances where such interference is:

---

[447] *Gaskin v United Kingdom* (1990) 12 EHRR 36 and see also *MG v United Kingdom* (2002) 36 EHRR 22.

[448] *Airey v Ireland* (1979) 2 EHRR 305.

[449] *Igesias Gil and AIU v Spain* (2005) 40 EHRR 3.

[450] *Pannullo and Forte v France* (2003) 36 EHRR 757, paras 38–40.

[451] See *X and Y v Netherlands* (1985) 8 EHRR 235, para 23; *Johnston v Ireland* (1986) 9 EHRR 203, para 55; *R (Bernard) v Enfield Borough Council* [2002] EWHC 2282 (Admin), [2003] LGR 423, [2003] HRLR 111 and *R v G* [2008] UKHL 37, [2009] 1 AC 92.

[452] *Petrovic v Austria* (2001) 33 EHRR 14 and see also *Chapman v United Kingdom* (2001) 33 EHRR 18.

[453] *Abdulaziz, Cabales and Balkandali v United Kingdom* (1985) 7 EHRR 471, para 67; *Buckley v United Kingdom* (1996) 23 EHRR 101 and *Handyside v United Kingdom* (1976) 1 EHRR 737.

[454] See **2.85** above.

[455] See Mowbray, A *The Development of Positive Obligations under the European Convention on Human Rights by the European Court of Human Rights* (2004) Hart Publishing.

[456] *Hokkanen v Finland* (1994) 19 EHRR 139, [1996] 1 FLR 289. See also *X and Y v The Netherlands* (1985) 8 EHRR 235, para 23. For detailed discussion on the principle of 'horizontal effect' see Wade, H *Human Rights and the Judiciary* [1998] EHRLR 520, Buxton, R *The Human Rights Act and Private Law* (2000) 116 LQR 48 and Hunt, M *The 'Horizontal Effect' of the Human Rights Act* [1998] Public Law 423.

[457] *Hokkanen v Finland* (1994) 19 EHRR 139, [1996] 1 FLR 289. See also *X and Y v The Netherlands* (1985) 8 EHRR 235.

[458] See for example *Evans v United Kingdom* (2008) 46 EHRR 728.

'in accordance with the law[459] and is necessary in a democratic society[460] in the interests of national security, public safety or the economic well-being of the country, for the prevention of disorder or crime, for the protection of health or morals, or for the protection of the rights and freedoms of others.'[461]

If an action is not in accordance with the law there is no need for the court to then go on to consider whether the action is justified by reference to the further requirements of Art 8(2) as such an action will *a fortiori* constitute an unjustified interference in the right to respect for family life. If the action in issue is in accordance with the law then the test for necessity must be applied, which test involves asking whether there is a 'pressing social need' for the interference alleged and whether the means of interference employed are proportionate to the legitimate aims pursued.[462] However, it should also be noted that, particularly in cases where a positive obligation under Art 8 is engaged, the concept of 'fair balance' must also be considered in determining whether a particular action can be justified by reference to Art 8.

Article 8 General Principles – 'Fair Balance'

8.178 In the case of purely negative State obligations, whether or not interference in the Art 8 rights is justified can in most cases be determined solely by reference to the requirements of Art 8(2).[463] However, by reason of the positive as well as negative obligations inherent in Art 8 and the difficulty in some cases in determining whether the relevant obligation is a positive or a negative one, the proper application of Art 8 in case of positive obligation is achieved on the basis of 'fair balance'.[464] In *Gaskin v United Kingdom* [465] the European Court of Human Rights stated that:

> 'In accordance with its established case-law, the Court, in determining whether or not such a positive obligation exists, will have regard to the 'fair balance that has to be struck between the general interest of the community and the interests of the individual ... In striking this balance the aims mentioned in the second paragraph of Article 8 (art. 8) may be of a certain relevance, although this provision refers in terms only to 'interferences' with the right protected by the first paragraph – in other words is concerned with the negative obligations flowing therefrom.'

---

[459] See for example *Olsson v Sweden (No 2)* (1992) 17 EHRR 134 (restrictions on contact to children in care without legal basis and accordingly not in accordance with the law).

[460] See for example *W v United Kingdom* (1987) 10 EHRR 29 (exclusion of parents from decisions in relation to removal of children and adoption not necessary to protect the rights of the child). The concept of 'necessity' encompasses the requirement that any interference pursues a 'legitimate aim'. See further **3.69** and **3.73** above.

[461] What Lord Bingham terms 'the community exceptions' to the right to respect for private and family life (see Bingham, T *The Rule of Law* (2010) Allen Lane, p 75).

[462] See **3.73** above.

[463] Note however that the European Court of Human Rights is increasingly importing the fair balance test into the determination of negative as well as positive obligations under Art 8 of the ECHR (See *A, B and C v Ireland* (2010) Application No 25579/05, para 247 ('The principles applicable to assessing a State's positive and negative obligations under the Convention are similar. Regard must be had to the fair balance that has to be struck between the competing interests of the individual and of the community as a whole, the aims in the second paragraph of Article 8 being of a certain relevance')).

[464] See for example *Odiévre v France* (2004) 38 EHRR 43, paras 40–49; *Mikulic v Croatia* [2002] 1 FCR 720, paras 57–59 and *Jevremovic v Serbia* [2007] 2 FCR 671, [2008] 1 FLR 550. See also *Cossey v United Kingdom* (1990) 13 EHRR 622, para 37 in which the Court emphasised that the search for a 'fair balance' is 'inherent in the whole convention.'

[465] (1989) 12 EHRR 36, para 42.

8.179 Thus, at least in respect of positive obligations,[466] the requirements of Art 8(2) are not exhaustive criteria for determining whether a particular action is justified and other factors will be relevant to establishing the requisite 'fair balance'. The 'fair balance' approach will be particularly relevant in cases in which Art 8 has a 'horizontal' effect as between private individuals whose Art 8 rights are in competition.[467] In *Evans v United Kingdom* the European Court of Human Rights reiterated this approach to the principle of 'fair balance':[468]

> 'Although the object of Article 8 is essentially that of protecting the individual against arbitrary interference by the public authorities, it does not merely compel the State to abstain from such interference: in addition to this primarily negative undertaking, there may be positive obligations inherent in an effective respect for private life. These obligations may involve the adoption of measures designed to secure respect for private life even in the sphere of the relations of individuals between themselves. The boundaries between the State's positive and negative obligations under Article 8 do not lend themselves to precise definition. The applicable principles are nonetheless similar. In particular, in both instances regard must be had to the fair balance which has to be struck between the competing interests; and in both contexts the State enjoys a certain margin of appreciation.'

Article 8 General Principles – Procedural Protection

8.180 Whilst Art 8 does not embody explicit procedural safeguards the European Court of Human Rights has made it clear that any decision making process concerning measures which would have the effect of interfering with rights under Art 8 must be fair and must themselves be conducted in a manner which ensures the efficacy of the rights protected by Art 8 of the ECHR.[469] Thus, even though not expressly articulated in the body of the article, Art 8 affords procedural safeguards against inappropriate interference with the substantive rights protected by the article.[470] These procedural safeguards relating to a child's Article 8 rights will include the need to ensure that the child's point of view is adequately and independently represented in any decision process, however young the child may be.[471] Delay should be avoided in decisions

---

[466] In *Paulik v Slovakia* (2008) 46 EHRR 41 the European Court of Human Rights went further and suggested that the need to find a 'fair balance' between the competing interests of the individual and the community as a whole will apply equally to cases of positive obligation and negative obligation under Art 8. See also *A, B and C v Ireland* (2010) Application No 25579/05, para 247 ('The principles applicable to assessing a State's positive and negative obligations under the Convention are similar. Regard must be had to the fair balance that has to be struck between the competing interests of the individual and of the community as a whole, the aims in the second paragraph of Article 8 being of a certain relevance').

[467] This approach will also be adopted where Art 8 rights conflict with other rights under the Convention (see for example *Von Hannover v Germany* (2005) 40 EHRR 1, para 57).

[468] (2008) 46 EHRR 728, para 75. Contrast this approach with that taken by the Court of Appeal in analysing the Art 8 rights of the parties, treating the case as one of negative interference (*Evans v Amicus Healthcare Ltd* [2004] EWCA 727, [2005] Fam 1). See also *Dickson v United Kingdom* (2008) 46 EHRR 41 and *Iosub Caras v Romania* (2008) 47 EHRR 35.

[469] See *TP and KM v United Kingdom* [2001] 2 FCR 289, para 72 and see also *Karadzic v Croatia* (2007) 44 EHRR 45; *Bajrami v Albania* (2008) 47 EHRR 22 and *Covezzi and Morselli v Italy* (1993) Application No 52763/99 (unreported).

[470] *R (P) v Secretary of State for the Home Department; R (Q) v Secretary of State for the Home Department* [2001] EWCA Civ 1151, [2001] 2 FLR 1122.

[471] *Dolhamre v Sweden* (2010) Application No 67/04, para 116 ('Here the Court further wishes to point out that, whilst Article 8 contains no explicit procedural requirements, the decision-making process involved in measures of interference must be fair and the parents and, as appropriate, the children must have been involved in the process, seen as a whole, to a degree sufficient to provide them with the requisite protection of their interests. In this respect, it is essential that the parents be placed in a position where they may obtain access to information which is relied on by the authorities in order to be able to put forward in a fair or

concerning the child's right to respect for family life.[472] Whether procedural delay amounts to a breach of Art 8 will depend on the circumstances of the case. There will be no breach where procedures are not particularly effective but are not negligent.[473]

ECHR, Art 8 – Application

Article 8 – Right to know and be cared for by Parents

8.181 The mutual enjoyment by parent and child of each other's company constitutes a fundamental element of family life.[474] The right to respect for family life under Art 8 of the ECHR implies the existence in law of safeguards that render possible from the moment of birth the child's integration in his or her family.[475] The right to know and be cared for by parents is generally described as the right of the child to be cared for by the parent rather than the right of the parent to care for the child.[476] In order for family life to be maintained as the child grows older, a continuing relationship between the parent and child is necessary.[477] The fact that a person is the natural parent of the child will not automatically justify a legal recognition of the relationship between parent and child.[478] The European Court of Human Rights has not expressly articulated a principle of primacy of family care although such a principle would seem arguably implicit in decisions concerning reunification of children separated from their parents after an extended period of time.[479]

Article 8 – Right not to be separated from Parents

Right not to be Separated – General Principles

8.182 In determining whether the separation of a child from his or her parents is justified for the purposes of Art 8 of the ECHR a fair balance must be struck between the interests of the child in being separated from his or her parents and the interests of the parents in being reunited with the child.[480] There will be situations where the child's

---

adequate manner those matters militating in favour of his or her ability to provide the child with proper care and protection'). See also *CF v Secretary of State for the Home Department* [2004] EWHC 111 (Fam), [2004] 2 FLR 517.

[472] *B v United Kingdom* (1987) 10 EHRR 87.

[473] *HN v Poland* (2007) 45 EHRR 46. See also *Siemianowski v Poland* (2007) 44 EHRR 24; *Iosub Caras v Romania* (2008) 47 EHRR 35 and *Nuutinen v Finland* (2002) 34 EHRR 358.

[474] *Johansen v Norway* (1996) 23 EHRR 33.

[475] *Johnston v Ireland* (1986) 9 EHRR 203.

[476] See **8.1** above. However, see the dissenting judgement of Martens J in *Gül v Switzerland* (1996) 22 EHRR 93 in which he argued that the parents' right to care for their children is a 'fundamental element of an elementary human right.' See also Eekelaar, J *The Wardship Jurisdiction, Children's Welfare and Parents' Rights* (1991) Law Quarterly Review, p 388.

[477] See *Berrehab v Netherlands* (1988) 11 EHRR 322 and *Singh v UK* (1967) 10 YB 478.

[478] *Yousef v Netherlands* (2003) 36 EHRR 345.

[479] See *Hokkanen v Finland* (1994) 19 EHRR 139 and *Görgülü v Germany* [2004] 1 FLR 894 (for criticism of the decision in *Görgülü v Germany* see Fortin, J *Children's Rights and the Developing Law* (2009) 3rd edn, Cambridge, pp 528–529). Note however that any principle of the primacy of family care under Art 8 must be subject to the child's best interests (see *Bronda v Italy* (2001) 33 EHRR 4 and see also *Söderbäck v Sweden* [1999] 1 FR 250; *Eski v Austria* [2007] 1 FLR 1650 and *Pini and Bertani; Manera and Atripaldi v Romania* [2005] 2 FLR 596.

[480] *Johansen v Norway* (1996) 23 EHRR 33, para 78. See also *Neulinger and Shuruk v Switzerland* (2010) Application No 41615/07, para 136 ('The child's interest comprises two limbs. On the one hand, it dictates that the child's ties with its family must be maintained, except in cases where the family has proved particularly unfit. It follows that family ties may only be severed in very exceptional circumstances and that everything must be done to preserve personal relations and, if and when appropriate, to 'rebuild' the family.

welfare demands that the child cannot be cared for by birth parents.[481] However, within this context, Art 8 imposes on every State the obligation to aim at reuniting a natural parent with his or her child as soon as circumstances permit following any removal.[482]

8.183 The separation of a child from his or her parents should not be permitted to come about as the result of circumstances caused by mere effluxion of time.[483] In particular, procedural delay must not be permitted to lead to a situation whereby permanent separation is achieved by a *de facto* determination of the case based on a *status quo* established by such delay.[484]

8.184 Any separation of a child from his or her parents must be based on legal certainties.[485] Art 8 requires that parents are sufficiently involved in the decision making processes which determine whether or not the child should be separated from them. This principle must, *a fortiori* apply to the child as well.[486] The European Court of Human Rights has stated that:[487]

> 'what has to be determined is whether, having regard to the particular circumstances of the case and notably the serious nature of the decisions to be taken, the parents have been involved in the decision-making process, seen as a whole, to a degree sufficient to provide them with the requisite protection of their interests. If they have not, there will have been a failure to respect their family life and the interference resulting from the decision will not be capable of being regarded as 'necessary' within the meaning of Article 8.'

When considering the parents rights under Art 8 in the context of being reunited with their children, the child's rights and the rights of any *de facto* carers will also fall to be considered in the balance.[488] In such cases failing to hear evidence to allow this balance to be undertaken will itself be a breach of Art 8 of the ECHR.[489]

Right not to be Separated – Private Law

Parental Separation and Divorce

8.185 Parental separation or divorce often results in the 'separation' of the child from one of his or her parents. Whilst both parents will retain a right to respect for their

---

On the other hand, it is clearly also in the child's interest to ensure its development in a sound environment, and a parent cannot be entitled under Article 8 to have such measures taken as would harm the child's health and development').

[481] *Hokkanen v Finland* (1994) 19 EHRR 139.

[482] *Görgülü v Germany* [2004] 1 FLR 894.

[483] *W v United Kingdom)* (1987) 10 EHRR 313.

[484] *Iosub Caras v Romania* (2008) 47 EHRR 35 and *Nuutinen v Finland* (2002) 34 EHRR 358.

[485] See *Olsson v Sweden (No 2)* (1992) 17 EHRR 134 and *Eriksson v Sweden* (1990) 12 EHRR 183.

[486] *Dolhamre v Sweden* (2010) Application No 67/04, para 116 ('Here the Court further wishes to point out that, whilst Article 8 contains no explicit procedural requirements, the decision-making process involved in measures of interference must be fair and the parents and, as appropriate, the children must have been involved in the process, seen as a whole, to a degree sufficient to provide them with the requisite protection of their interests. In this respect, it is essential that the parents be placed in a position where they may obtain access to information which is relied on by the authorities in order to be able to put forward in a fair or adequate manner those matters militating in favour of his or her ability to provide the child with proper care and protection').

[487] *W v United Kingdom)* (1987) 10 EHRR 313. This will include the disclosure of documents to the parents (see *McMichael v United Kingdom* (1995) 20 EHRR 205, [1995] 2 FCR 718). Note however that disclosure is not an absolute right and must be balanced against the need to protect the child (see *Hokkanen v Finland* (1994) 19 EHRR 139, [1995] 2 FCR 320, [1996] 1 FLR 289).

[488] See *Söderbäck v Sweden* [1999] 1 FLR 250 and *Eski v Austria* [2007] 1 FLR 1650.

[489] *Elsholz v Germany* [2000] 2 FLR 486 and *Jucius and Juciuvienė v Lithuania* [2009] 1 FLR 403.

family life with the child and the child a right to respect for his or her family life with his or her parents, neither parent can claim a 'right' to have residence of the child following parental separation or divorce.[490] The child's right to respect for family life under Art 8 of the ECHR will continue to apply following parental separation or divorce having regard to the child's best interests.

8.186 Where one parent applies to remove the child from the jurisdiction, thereby separating the child from the remaining parent, a prima facie interference with the right to respect for family life falls to be considered.[491] Having regard to the horizontal effect of Art 8 of the ECHR, Art 8(2) requires that the right to respect for family life of the child and the remaining parent must be balanced against the right of the emigrating parent to live his or her private life as they wish and his or her freedom to work where he or she reasonably chooses to do so.[492] Art 8 requires the court to ask itself whether the application is genuine, in the sense of not being motivated to exclude the other parent, and realistic, being founded on well researched and investigated proposals.[493]

Child Abduction

8.187 A failure to take adequate measures to enforce a return order made in respect of a child abducted by his or her parent will constitute a breach of Art 8 of the ECHR on the basis of the State's failure to meet its positive obligation to ensure effective respect for family life by taking measures to reunite child and parent.[494]

Immigration and Separation[495]

8.188 Decisions taken by States in the immigration sphere can in some cases amount to interference with the right to respect for private and family life secured by Art 8 of the ECHR, in particular where the persons concerned possess strong personal or family ties in the host country which are liable to be seriously affected by application of the measure in question.[496] However, where a child is separated from his or her parents by reason of immigration rules or policies, Art 8 of the ECHR does not confer upon the child a general right to acceptance for settlement in a country in which his or her parents are settled. In *Abdulaziz, Cabales and Balkandali v United Kingdom*[497] the court held:

> '[T]his is an area in which the Contracting Parties enjoy a wide margin of appreciation in determining the steps to be taken to ensure compliance with the Convention with due regard

---

[490] *X v Sweden* Application No 172/56 1 YB 211.

[491] *Payne v Payne* [2001] EWCA Civ 166, [2001] Fam 473, [2001] 1 FLR 1052.

[492] *Re A (Permission to Remove Child from Jurisdiction: Human Rights)* [2000] 2 FLR 225. See also Art 2 of Protocol 4 to the ECHR.

[493] Lowe N, Everall M, and Nicholls, M *International Movement of Children* (2004) Jordan Publishing, p 99.

[494] *Ignaccola-Zenide v Romania* (2001) 31 EHRR 7; *Sylvester v Austria* [2003] 2 FLR 210 and *Maire v Portugal* (2003) 43 EHRR 231, [2004] 2 FLR 653. See also See *Glaser v United Kingdom* [2001] 1 FLR 153.

[495] See also ECHR, Protocol 4, Art 2 ('1.Everyone lawfully within the territory of a State shall, within that territory, have the right to liberty of movement and freedom to choose his residence. 2. Everyone shall be free to leave any country, including his own. 3. No restrictions shall be placed on the exercise of these rights other than such as are in accordance with law and are necessary in a democratic society in the interests of national security or public safety, for the maintenance of ordre public, for the prevention of crime, for the protection of health or morals, or for the protection of the rights and freedoms of others. 4. The rights set forth in paragraph 1 may also be subject, in particular areas, to restrictions imposed in accordance with law and justified by the public interest in a democratic society'), Protocol 4, Art 3 ('1. No one shall be expelled, by means either of an individual or of a collective measure, from the territory of the State of which he is a national. 2. No one shall be deprived of the right to enter the territory of the state of which he is a national') and Protocol 4, Art 4 ('Collective expulsion of aliens is prohibited'). See also ECHR, Protocol 7, Art 1.

[496] *Kurić v Slovenia* (2010) Application No 26828/06, para 351.

[497] (1985) 7 EHRR 47, para 67.

to the needs and resources of the community and of individuals. In particular, in the area now under consideration, the extent of a State's obligation to admit to its territory relatives of settled immigrants will vary according to the particular circumstances of the persons involved. Moreover, the Court cannot ignore that the present case is concerned not only with family life but also with immigration and that, as a matter of well-established international law and subject to its treaty obligations, a State has the right to control the entry of non-nationals into its territory.'

8.189 Article 8 of the ECHR thus does not require the granting of residency to all family members in all circumstances, even where the applicant is a close family member. In this context it is of further note that Art 8 only protects the rights of established families.[498] Thus where a refusal of entry or an order for deportation would result in the separation of an established family, Art 8 will be engaged and may be breached by the refusal or deportation.[499] In determining whether a person's Art 8 rights have been breached by removal from the United Kingdom, the court must take into account the effect of his or her proposed removal upon all the members of his or her family unit.[500] In *Abdulaziz, Cabales and Balkandali v United Kingdom*[501] the European Court of Human Rights held that the State in which a person has settled is in principle obliged to respect their choice in bringing into the country relatives left behind. *Da Silva v Netherlands*[502] sets out the factors which the court should consider in determining whether Art 8 would be violated by enforcing separation or preventing re-unification between parents and children in established families:

'Factors to be taken into account in this context are the extent to which family life is effectively ruptured, the extent of the ties in the Contracting State, whether there are insurmountable obstacles to the family living in the country of origin of one or more of them and whether there are factors of immigration control (for example, a history of breaches of immigration law) or considerations of public order weighing in favour of exclusion (see *Solomon v the Netherlands* (dec.), No 44328/98, 5 September 2000). Another important consideration will also be whether family life was created at a time when the persons involved were aware that the immigration status of one of them was such that the persistence of that family life within the host State would from the outset be precarious. The Court has previously held that where this is the case it is likely only to be in the most exceptional circumstances that the removal of the non-national family member will constitute a violation of Article 8.'

In respect of measures concerning the expulsion of a child from a country in which he or she has settled, in *Neulinger and Shuruk v Switzerland*[503] the European Court of Human Rights observed that:[504]

---

[498] Provided that family life was established before the persons involved were aware that the immigration status of one of them was such that the persistence of that family life would be from the outset precarious (see *Mitchell v the United Kingdom* (1998) Application No 40447/98 (unreported) and *Ajayi and Others v the United Kingdom* (1999) Application No 27663/95 (unreported)).

[499] *Yildiz v Austria* (2003) 36 EHRR 553 and *Mayeka v Belgium* (2008) 46 EHRR 23.

[500] *Beoku-Betts v Secretary of State for the Home Depart*ment [2008] UKHL 39, [2009] 1 AC 115, [2008] 3 WLR 166.

[501] (1985) 7 EHRR 471.

[502] (2007) 44 EHRR 34.

[503] (2010) Application No 41615/07, para 146.

[504] See also *Maslov v Austria* (2008) Application No 1638/03. Note that regardless of the existence or otherwise of a family life, therefore, the Court considers that the expulsion of a settled migrant constitutes interference with his or her right to respect for private life. It will depend on the circumstances of the particular case whether it is appropriate for the Court to focus on the family life rather than the private life aspect (*Kurić v Slovenia* (2010) Application No 26828/06, para 353).

'... in order to assess the proportionality of an expulsion measure concerning a child who has settled in the host country, it is necessary to take into account the child's best interests and well-being, and in particular the seriousness of the difficulties which he or she is likely to encounter in the country of destination and the solidity of social, cultural and family ties both with the host country and with the country of destination. The seriousness of any difficulties which may be encountered in the destination country by the family members who would be accompanying the deportee must also be taken into account.'

8.190 The principles governing the application of Art 8 to the question of immigration and family life tend to be construed and applied strictly. The court is likely to require strong grounds for suggesting the legal or practical impossibility of return or substantial detrimental consequences upon such return before reliance can be placed on Art 8 of the ECHR in this context.[505] Where the justification contended for removal is the criminal conduct of a parent, the court has made clear in *Boultif v Switzerland*[506] that it will apply the following criteria:

'In assessing the relevant criteria in such a case, the Court will consider the nature and seriousness of the offence committed by the applicant;[507] the duration of the applicant's stay in the country from which he is going to be expelled; the time which has elapsed since the commission of the offence and the applicant's conduct during that period; the nationalities of the various persons concerned; the applicant's family situation, such as the length of the marriage; other factors revealing whether the couple lead a real and genuine family life; whether the spouse knew about the offence at the time when he or she entered into a family relationship; and whether there are children in the marriage and, if so, their age. Not least, the Court will also consider the seriousness of the difficulties which the spouse would be likely to encounter in the applicant's country of origin, although the mere fact that a person might face certain difficulties in accompanying her or his spouse cannot in itself preclude expulsion.'

8.191 The authorities suggest that overall the key criteria in these cases will be the extent to which the family life for which protection is claimed under Art 8 of the ECHR is already established, which in turn provides a measure of the extent to which refusal of entry or deportation would interfere with that family life.[508] Where family life is established to the requisite degree the question then becomes whether the decision in question can be said to be proportionate.[509]

Right not to be Separated – Public Law

Public Law – Removal into Public Care

8.192 The removal into public care of a child from his or her parents will constitute interference in the Art 8 right to respect for family life of the child and the parents.[510]

---

505 *Beldjoudi v France* (1992) 14 EHRR 801.
506 (2001) 33 EHRR 50. See also *Keles v Germany* (2007) 44 EHRR 12 and *Radavanovic v Austria* (2005) 41 EHRR 6.
507 Criminal offences must go beyond repeat petty crime and involve something more serious (see *Boujilfa v France* (2000) 30 EHRR 419; *Aoulmi v France* (2008) 46 EHRR 1; *Keles v Germany* (2007) 44 EHRR 12; *Maslov v Austria* (2008) 47 EHRR 20; *Lupsa v Romania* (2008) 46 EHRR 36 and *Al-Nashif v Bulgaria* (2003) 36 EHRR 37. See also *AS (Pakistan) v Secretary of State for the Home Department* [2008] EWCA Civ 1118, [2008] All ER (D) 128 (Oct).
508 *Berrehab v Netherlands* (1989) 11 EHRR 322; *Moustaquim v Belgium* (1991) 13 EHRR 802; *Beldjoudi v France* (1992) 14 EHRR 801; *Boughanemi v France* (1996) 22 EHRR 228; *Bouchelkia v France* (1997) 25 EHRR 686 and *Nasri v France* (1995) 21 EHRR 458.
509 *Beldjoudi v France* (1992) 14 EHRR 801. See also *Ciliz v Netherlands* [2000] 2 FLR 469.
510 Note that Art 8 does not require a common law duty of care by local authorities towards a parent of a child

The issue in most cases of proposed or actual removal is therefore one of whether such separation can be said to be justified by reference to the criteria set out in Art 8(2) and the principle of 'fair balance'.[511] In *Saviny v Ukraine*[512] the European Court of Human Rights summarised its approach to cases concerning the taking of children into public care:[513]

> 'The Court further reiterates that, notwithstanding a margin of appreciation enjoyed by the domestic authorities in deciding on placing a child into public care, severing family ties means cutting a child off from its roots, which can only be justified in very exceptional circumstances. A relevant decision must therefore be supported by sufficiently sound and weighty considerations in the interests of the child, and it is for the respondent State to establish that a careful assessment of the impact of the proposed care measure on the parents and the child has been made. In particular, where the decision is explained in terms of a need to protect the child from danger, the existence of such a danger should be actually established. In taking a decision on removal of a child, a variety of factors may be pertinent, such as whether by virtue of remaining in the care of its parents the child would suffer abuse or neglect, educational deficiencies and lack of emotional support, or whether the child's placement in public care is necessitated by the state of its physical or mental health. On the other hand, the mere fact that a child could be placed in a more beneficial environment for his or her upbringing does not on its own justify a compulsory measure of removal. Neither can this measure be justified by a mere reference to the parents' precarious situation, which can be addressed by less radical means than the splitting of the family, such as targeted financial assistance and social counselling. Further, in assessing the quality of a decision-making process leading to splitting up the family, the Court will see, in particular, whether the conclusions of the domestic authorities were based on sufficient evidentiary basis (including, as appropriate, statements by witnesses, reports by competent authorities, psychological and other expert assessments and medical notes) and whether the interested parties, in particular the parents, had sufficient opportunity to participate in the procedure in question. The Court will also have regard to whether, where appropriate, the children themselves were able to express their views. In any event, taking a child into care should normally be regarded as a temporary measure, to be discontinued as soon as circumstances permit. It cannot, therefore, be justified without prior consideration of the possible alternatives and should be viewed in the context of the State's positive obligation to make serious and sustained efforts to facilitate the reuniting of children with their natural parents and until then enable regular contact between them, including, where possible, by keeping the siblings together.'

8.193 Importance of Procedural Safeguards – It is vital that consideration of whether a child should be removed from his or her parents takes place within a framework of procedural measures sufficient to ensure that the rights of all family members, including

---

when exercising their child protection duties. (see *Lawrence v Pembrokeshire County Council* [2007] EWCA Civ 446, [2007] 1 WLR 2991; *JD v East Berkshire County Community Health NHS Trust* (2005) UKHL 23, [2005] 2 AC 373).

[511] Note that the application of Art 8 of the ECHR in domestic care proceedings is complicated by the bright line which exists between the jurisdiction of the court prior to the granting of a final care order and the responsibility of the local authority once a final care order has been made (see *A v Liverpool City Council* (1981) 2 FLR 222). Article 8 will apply to the actions of local authorities once a care order has been made but the role of the domestic courts in policing alleged breaches of Art 8 will operate subject to the 'cardinal principle' of the Children Act 1989, namely that once a care order has been made the local authority is responsible for the manner in which parental responsibility is exercised independent of the courts (see *Re S (Children: Care Order: Implementation of Care Plan)* [2002] UKHL 10, [2002] 2 AC 291. In practice, this means that any intercession by the courts following the granting of a final care order must be under the jurisdiction provided by the Human Rights Act 1998 or judicial review rather than under the Children Act 1989 (see **8.28** below).

[512] (2008) Application No 39948/06, paras 49–52.

[513] See also *AD and OD v United Kingdom* (2010) Application No 28680/06.

the children are adequately protected.[514] This will include sufficiently involving the members of the family, including the children in the process.[515] Both the parents and the child must be placed in a position where they may obtain access to information which is relied on by the authorities in taking measures of protective care or in taking decisions relevant to the care of the child.[516] The European Court of Human Rights has recognised that there will be cases where participation of the parents in the decision making process will not be possible or meaningful.[517]

8.194 Margin of Appreciation – The European Court of Human Rights will permit a wide margin of appreciation in respect of decisions concerning the removal of children on the basis that domestic authorities 'on the ground' are best placed to balance the rights of the child, considered in light of his or her best interests, and the rights of the parents.[518] In *Kutzner v Germany*[519] the Court observed that its role is not:

> 'to substitute itself for the domestic authorities in the exercise of their responsibilities for the regulation of the public care of children and the rights of parents whose children have been taken into care, but rather to review under the Convention the decisions that those authorities have taken in the exercise of their power of appreciation.'

Social workers and care workers will likewise be accorded a wider margin of appreciation in substantive decision making concerning the public care of children.[520]

8.195 Strict Test – The summary removal of a baby into public care following birth requires 'exceptional justification' and 'extraordinarily compelling reasons' under Art 8 of the ECHR.[521] The fact that the situation of removal is one of an emergency will not excuse the authorities from adhering to the precepts stipulated by Art 8 of the ECHR. As a general rule inappropriate recourse to emergency procedures which do not permit effective judicial scrutiny will undermine the procedural safeguards inherent in Art 8 of the ECHR.[522] In *K and T v Finland*[523] the European Court of Human Rights held that:

---

[514]   *W v United Kingdom* (1987) 10 EHRR 29.
[515]   See *Buchberger v Austria* (2001) Application No 32899/96 (unreported); *P, C and S v United Kingdom* (2002) EHRR 1075 and *Venema v Netherlands* (2002) Application No 35731/97 (unreported). See also *Dolhamre v Sweden* (2010) Application No 67/04, para 116 ('Here the Court further wishes to point out that, whilst Article 8 contains no explicit procedural requirements, the decision-making process involved in measures of interference must be fair and the parents and, as appropriate, the children must have been involved in the process, seen as a whole, to a degree sufficient to provide them with the requisite protection of their interests. In this respect, it is essential that the parents be placed in a position where they may obtain access to information which is relied on by the authorities in order to be able to put forward in a fair or adequate manner those matters militating in favour of his or her ability to provide the child with proper care and protection').
[516]   *McMichael v United Kingdom* (1995) 20 EHRR 205 and *TP and KM v United Kingdom* [2001] 2 FLR 549.
[517]   *B v United Kingdom* (1987) 10 EHRR 87.
[518]   See *X v Croatia* (2008) Application No 11223/04, para 47 ('The Court reiterates that it is an interference of a very serious order to split up a family. The Court recognises that, in reaching decisions in so sensitive an area, local authorities are faced with a task that is extremely difficult. To require them to follow on each occasion an inflexible procedure would only add to their problems. They must therefore be allowed a measure of discretion in this respect. On the other hand, predominant in any consideration of this aspect of the present case must be the fact that the decisions may well prove to be irreversible as in a case where a child has been taken away from his parents and freed for adoption. This is accordingly a domain in which there is an even greater call than usual for protection against arbitrary interferences').
[519]   [2003] 1 FCR 249.
[520]   Lord Pannick QC and others, *Human Rights Law and Practice* (2009) 3rd edn, LexisNexis, para 4.8.107 and *Andersson (M and R) v Sweden* (1992) 14 EHRR 615.
[521]   *K and T v Finland* [2001] 2 FCR 673, [2001] 2 FLR 707 and *P, C and S v United Kingdom* (2002) 35 EHRR 31, [2002] 2 FLR 631.
[522]   Van Bueren, G *Child Rights in Europe* (2007) Council of Europe Publishing, p 142.

'when such a drastic measure for the mother, depriving her absolutely of her new born child immediately on birth, was contemplated, it was incumbent on the competent national authorities to examine whether some less intrusive interference into family life, at such a critical point in the lives of the parents and child, was not possible.'

There will be cases where an emergency without notice summary application is justified but these are likely to be very rare.[524] The test as to the efficacy of such a procedure (as distinct from the strict test for removal) will be whether the step of not involving the parents in the planning of the proposed removal and not communicating that plan to the parents is justified by the overriding necessity of the best interests of the child or something which is essential to secure the child's safety.[525]

8.196 Beyond situations of emergency, the test for whether the removal of a child from the care of his or her parents is justified at any stage remains a strict one. Article 8 of the ECHR requires the Sate to demonstrate that in the particular circumstances of the case there exist reasons justifying the removal of the child as being necessary.[526] In, *P, C and S v United Kingdom*[527] the European Court of Human Rights held that:

'The margin of appreciation so to be accorded to the competent national authorities will vary in the light of the nature of the issues and the seriousness of the interests at stake. While the authorities enjoy a wide margin of appreciation in assessing the necessity of taking a child into care, in particular where an emergency situation arises, the Court must still be satisfied in the particular case that there existed circumstances justifying the removal of the child, and it is for the respondent State to establish that a careful assessment of the impact of the proposed care measure on the parents and the child, as well as of the possible alternatives to taking the child into public care, was carried out prior to implementation of such a measure.'

8.197 The fact that a child may be placed in a more beneficial environment than that provided by the parents is not a sufficient justification for separating a child from his or parents. In *Kutzner v Germany*[528] the European Court of Human Rights stipulated that:

'a child could be placed in a more beneficial environment but this is insufficient to justify a compulsory measure of removal from the care of the biological parents; there must exist other circumstances pointing to the 'necessity' for such an interference.'

8.198 Best Interests – In determining the extent to which there exist circumstances justifying the removal of the child into public care, consideration of the child's best interests will be central. In *Johansen v Norway*[529] the court made clear that:

'[A] fair balance has to be struck between the interests of the child in remaining in public care and those of the parent in being reunited with the child. In carrying out this balancing exercise, the Court will attach particular importance to the best interests of the child, which, depending on their nature and seriousness, may override those of the parent. In particular, as

---

[523] [2001] 2 FCR 673, [2001] 2 FLR 707
[524] *Venema v Netherlands* [2003] 1 FLR 552 and *Haase v Germany* [2004] 2 FLR 39.
[525] *Re D (Unborn Baby)* [2009] EWHC 446 (Fam), [2009] 2 FLR 313. Note that Art 12 of the CRC will require the involvement of the child in planning unless the same exceptions apply.
[526] *Kutzner v Germany*[2003] 1 FCR 249.
[527] (2002) 35 EHRR 31, [2002] 2 FLR 631.
[528] [2003] 1 FCR 249.
[529] (1996) 23 EHRR 33, para 78.

suggested by the Government, the parent cannot be entitled under Article 8 of the Convention (art. 8) to have such measures taken as would harm the child's health and development.'

8.199 Removal should be Temporary – Taking a child into public care should normally be regarded as a 'temporary measure' to be discontinued as soon as circumstances permit and any measure of implementation of temporary care should be consistent with the ultimate aim of reuniting the parent and the child.[530] In this regard a fair balance has to be struck between the interests of the child remaining in care and those of the parent in being reunited with the child. In carrying out this balancing exercise, the Court will attach particular importance to the best interests of the child which, depending on their nature and seriousness, may override those of the parent.[531] Implicit in the principle of 'temporary care' is a duty on the State to take proactive measures to rehabilitate the child to the care of his or her parents, although this duty is not an absolute one.[532] In *K and T v Finland*[533] the court held that:

> 'The positive duty to take measures to facilitate family reunification as soon as reasonably feasible will begin to weigh on the responsible authorities with progressively increasing force as from the commencement of the period of care, subject always to its being balanced against the duty to consider the best interests of the child.'

Whilst the removal of the child subsists, a stricter scrutiny is required in respect of any further steps which may interfere with the right of the child and parents to respect for family life, for example limitations in respect of contact between the child and his or her parents.[534] To justify permanent removal, the State must satisfy the court that exceptional circumstances exist and that the permanent removal is motivated by an overriding requirement pertaining to the child's best interests.[535]

Right not to be Separated – Child's Right to Choose Separation from Parents

8.200 Particularly difficult legal, social and policy issues arise where a child *chooses* to be separated from his or her parents. Historically, the European Commission has responded inconsistently to children who have decided themselves to leave home. In *X v Netherlands*[536] the Commission rejected a 14 year old girl's claim that her rights under Art 8 had been breached by actions taken by the State to return her home. A decision of opposite effect was reached in *X v Denmark*[537] where the Court rejected the parents argument that their Art 8 rights had been breached where the State had refused to take action to force a 14 year old child to return home against her will. Whilst in *Nielsen v Denmark*[538] the European Court of Human Rights acknowledged that parental decision making power is not unlimited, there is no more recent case law than that of *X v Netherlands*[539] and *X v Denmark*[540] to provide guidance on the extent to which a child

---

[530] *Olsson v Sweden* (1988) 10 EHRR 259 and *Johansen v Norway* (1996) 23 EHRR 33, para 78.

[531] *Dolhamre v Sweden* (2010) Application No, 67/04, para 111.

[532] *Olsson v Sweden (No 2)* (1992) 17 EHRR 134.

[533] (2001) 31 EHRR 18, [2001] 2 FLR 707.

[534] *Johansen v Norway* (1996) 23 EHRR 33, para 64 and *Kutzner v Germany* [2003] 1 FCR 249, para 67.

[535] *Johansen v Norway* (1996) 23 EHRR 33.

[536] (1974) 2 DR 118.

[537] (1977–78) 7–9 DR 81.

[538] (1988) 11 EHRR 175. Van Bueren notes that the application by the court of this principle to the facts in *Nielsen v Denmark* left a great deal to be desired (Van Bueren, G *The International Law on the Rights of the Child* (1998) Martinus Nijhoff, p 74). See further **14.66** below.

[539] (1974) 2 DR 118.

[540] (1977–78) 7–9 DR 81.

might rely on Art 8 or other provisions of the ECHR, in particular Art 5 and Art 2 of Protocol 4, in respect of supporting his or her unilateral decision to leave home.[541]

8.201 Van Bueren considers the position to be that a child is under an obligation to reside with his or her parents but the State is not under a corresponding obligation to overrule the child and return the child to the care of his or her parents, citing the approach in other jurisdictions[542] and in particular the US case of *Polovchack v Meese*.[543] In that case the Court of Appeals Seventh Circuit determined that a 12 year old Russian boy, who objected against the wish of his parents to returning to the Soviet Union with them, could be granted political asylum notwithstanding his parents claim that the grant of asylum violated substantive constitutional rights protecting their privacy and the integrity of their family, as well as their right to raise and control their son and to participate in his major life decisions. However, it should be noted that in *Polovchack v Meese* the court plainly based its decision not to overrule the child and return him to the care of his parents in large part on its conclusion that the child in question was 'near the lower end of an age range in which a minor may be mature enough to assert individual rights that equal or override those of his parents' which rights become 'more compelling with age'. In determining the extent to which the State is found to be under a positive obligation to overrule the child who has elected to leave home and return the child to the care of his or her parents it is likely that the principles of evolving capacity and best interests will play a central role.

Article 8 – Right to Maintain Contact

Right to Maintain Contact – General Principle

8.202 The mutual enjoyment by child and parent of each other's company constitutes a fundamental element of family life under Art 8 of the ECHR.[544] Contact between a child and his or her parents is a key means of promoting this element of the right to respect for family life.[545] The European Court of Human Rights has accepted the principle that contact between child and parent is a right of the child rather than a right of the parent.[546] Any interference with this right must be justified by reference to Art 8(2), balancing the interests of the child and the rights of the parent, particular importance being attached to the child's best interests.[547] As with the separation of the child from his or her parents' care, the maintenance of contact between a child and his or her parents is an area in which there is an even greater call than usual for protection against arbitrary interferences.[548]

---

[541] See also Art 12 of the Covenant on Civil and Political Rights.
[542] Van Bueren, G *The International Law on the Rights of the Child* (1998) Martinus Nijhoff, p 75.
[543] 774 F.2d 731 (7th Cir. 1985).
[544] *Hoppe v Germany* [2003] 1 FLR 384, para 44.
[545] The word 'contact' is defined in Art 2(a) of the European Convention on Contact Concerning Children (ETS No 192) as '(i) the child staying for a limited period of time with or meeting [his or her parents or a person having family ties with the child] with whom he or she is not usually living; (ii) any form of communication between the child and such person; (iii) the provision of information to such a person about the child or to the child about such a person.'
[546] *B v United Kingdom* (1987) 10 EHRR 87 and *Mustaquim v Belgium* (1991) 13 EHRR 802. See however the Art 4(1) of the European Convention on Contact Concerning Children (ETS No 192) which provides that 'A child and his or her parents shall have the right to obtain and maintain contact with each other.'
[547] *Hoppe v Germany* [2003] 1 FLR 384, para 44 and *Elsholz v Germany* [2000] 2 FLR 486, para 50.
[548] *W v United Kingdom* (1987) 10 EHRR 29.

Right to Maintain Contact following Parental Separation

Principle of Contact

8.203 In *Sommerfeld v Germany*[549] the court made clear that contact between a child and his or her parents should be promoted notwithstanding parental separation:

> '[T]he mutual enjoyment by parent and child of each other's company constitutes a fundamental element of family life, even if the relationship between the parents has broken down, and domestic measures hindering such enjoyment amount to an interference with the right protected by Article 8 of the Convention.'

Contact should take place between a child and his or her non-resident parent unless there are grounds which militate against such contact based on the best interests of the child.[550] The test of proportionality will be applied strictly to any interference with such contact in cases of parental separation.[551] Where contact between the child and the non-resident parent has not taken place for some time, preparation work prior to contact being reinstated should take place.[552] Where it is not in the best interests of the child to maintain unsupervised contact with one or both of his or her parents the possibility of supervised personal contact or other forms of contact with his or her parents must be considered.[553] Contact should extend to persons other than the parents having family ties with the child, including siblings, grandparents and other members of the extended family.[554]

Child's Wishes and Feelings

8.204 The child's wishes and feelings in respect of contact must be taken into account[555] and balanced against the right of parents to a family life with their children. Whilst the court recognises that measures against children obliging them to have contact with their non-resident parent are an option of last resort, the court does not rule out such measures in the event of non-compliance or unlawful behaviour on the part of the parent with whom the child lives.[556] In such circumstances States parties should provide a parent with reasonable assistance to persuade children to accede to contact if such contact can be said, on proper evidence, to e in the child's best interests.[557] However, such assistance must take into account the child's best interests, be sensitive to the child's needs and be non-punitive in respect of the child, with a fair balance being struck between the needs of the absent parent and the needs of the child.[558] The parents' rights

---

[549] (2003) 36 EHRR, para 32.
[550] *Hendriks v Netherlands* (1982) 29 DR 5. See also Art 4(2) of the European Convention on Contact Concerning Children (ETS No 192).
[551] *Scozzari v Giunta v Italy* [2000] 3 FCR 430.
[552] *Hansen v Turkey* [2004] 1 FLR 142 and *Ignaccolo-Zenide v Romania* (2001) 31 EHRR 7.
[553] Article 4(3) of the European Convention on Contact Concerning Children (ETS No 192).
[554] Article 5(1) of the European Convention on Contact Concerning Children (ETS No 192).
[555] *C v Finland* (2006) 46 EHRR 485, [2006] 2 FCR 195, [2006] 2 FLR 597. See also Art 6 of the European Convention on Contact Concerning Children (ETS No 192).
[556] *Hansen v Turkey* [2004] 1 FLR 142, para 106.
[557] *Ignaccolo-Zenide v Romania* (2001) 31 EHRR 7, para 106; *C v Finland* [2006] 2 FLR 597, para 58 and *Sahin v Germany* [2003] 2 FLR 671 (Grand Chamber).
[558] *Hansen v Turkey* [2004] 1 FLR 142 and *Ignaccolo-Zenide v Romania* (2001) 31 EHRR 7.

under Art 8 of the ECHR do not extend as far as forcing a child to have contact with his or her biological parent against his or her wishes.[559] In *C v Finland*[560] the court made clear that:

> 'It is generally accepted that courts must take into account the wishes of children in such proceedings. On a practical basis, there may also come a stage where it becomes pointless, if not counter-productive and harmful, to attempt to force a child to conform to a situation, which, for whatever reasons, he or she resists.'

8.205 Parents must be involved in the decision making process in relation to contact decisions in the context of private law cases.[561] This principle must apply equally to children.[562]

Enforcement of Contact

8.206 Decisions as to contact must be enforced effectively so as to ensure that contact ordered by the court or organised by the social care authorities takes place.[563] Failure to enforce contact orders made by the Court will engage the Art 8 right to maintain contact.[564] The relevant authorities must take all necessary steps to facilitate contact within the particular circumstances of the case.[565] In the case of *Ignaccolo-Zenide v Romania*[566] the court accepted that, whilst coercive measures are undesirable in general, there may be cases in which sanctions for failure to comply with orders will be justified where the parent with residence of the child acts unlawfully. However, the obligation to facilitate contact between a child and his or her non-resident parent is not an absolute one.[567] In *Nuutinen v Finland*[568] the Court held that:

> 'The obligation of the national authorities to take measures to facilitate meetings between a parent and his or her child is not absolute, especially where the two are still strangers to one another. Such access may not be possible immediately and may require preparatory measures being taken to this effect. The nature and extent of such preparation will depend on the circumstances of each case, but the understanding and cooperation of all concerned will always be an important ingredient. Whilst national authorities must do their utmost to facilitate such cooperation, any obligation to apply coercion in this area must be limited since the interests as well as the rights and freedoms of all concerned must be taken into account, and more particularly the best interests of the child and his or her rights under Article 8 of the Convention. Where contacts with the parent might appear to threaten those interests or interfere with those rights, it is for the national authorities to strike a fair balance between them. What is decisive is whether the national authorities have taken all necessary steps to facilitate access as can reasonably be demanded in the special circumstances of each case.'

---

[559] See the decision of the Supreme Court of the Netherlands in *Rechtspraak van de Week* (1996) First Division 8643, 10.

[560] (2006) 46 EHRR 485, [2006] 2 FCR 195, [2006] 2 FLR 597.

[561] *Elsholz v Germany* [2000] 3 FCR 385, [2000] 2 FLR 486.

[562] See *Scozzari v Giunta v Italy* [2000] 3 FCR 430, para 138.

[563] *Scozzari v Giunta v Italy* [2000] 3 FCR 430. See also Art 9 of the European Convention on Contact Concerning Children (ETS No 192).

[564] *Ignaccolo-Zenide v Romania* (2001) 31 EHRR 7.

[565] *Glaser v United Kingdom* [2002] 3 FCR 193 and *K and T v Finland* (2000) 31 EHRR 484.

[566] (2001) 31 EHRR 7.

[567] *Kaleta v Poland* [2009] 1 FLR 927.

[568] (2002) 34 EHRR 15, para 128.

Right to Maintain Contact following Removal into Care

8.207 Family relationships are not terminated by the taking of the child into public care.[569] The wide margin of appreciation afforded to domestic authorities in the decision to remove a child from the care of his or her parents does not extend to measures which thereafter further limit the right to respect for family life, for example by way of proscribing or terminating contact to a child in care.[570] Whilst the removal of the child subsists, a stricter scrutiny is required in respect of any further steps which may interfere with the right of the child and parents to respect for family life, for example limitations in respect of contact between the child and his or her parents.[571] The European Court of Human Rights has made clear that unnecessary restrictions on contact to children in care will constitute an unjustified breach of Art 8 of the ECHR.[572] In *Johansen v Norway*[573] the court stipulated that any deprivation of contact between parents and a child in care must be justified by particularly strong reasons.

Post Adoption Contact

8.208 Whilst it would appear that no case has yet been taken to the European Court of Human Rights in respect of post-adoption contact,[574] it has been argued that Art 8 of the ECHR grounds an argument that an adopted child has the right to maintain familial links with his or her natural parents post adoption, provided such contact is in the child's best interests.[575]

Contact to Children in Custody

8.209 It is an essential part of a prisoner's right to respect for family life that the prison authorities assist him or her in maintaining contact with his or her close family.[576] Applying the principles set out above, the child will likewise retain a right to have contact with a parent who is imprisoned and there will be a duty on the State to ensure measures are in place to facilitate such contact having regard to the child's best interests.[577]

Immigration and Contact

8.210 Immigration measures which prevent contact between a child and his or her parents may amount to an unjustifiable interference with the right to respect for family life under Art 8 of the ECHR.[578]

---

[569] *Eriksson v Sweden* (1990) 12 EHRR 183 and see *B v United Kingdom* (1987) 10 EHRR 87.
[570] Van Bueren, G *Child Rights in Europe* (2007) Council of Europe Publishing, pp 142–143.
[571] *Johansen v Norway* (1996) 23 EHRR 33, para 64 and *Kutzner v Germany*[2003] 1 FCR 249, para 67.
[572] *Andersson (M and R) v Sweden* (1992) 14 EHRR 615; *Hokkanen v Finland* (1994) 19 EHRR 139 and *Rieme v Sweden* (1993) 16 EHRR 155.
[573] (1996) 23 EHRR 33.
[574] The case of *Clark v United Kingdom* Application No 23387/94, which would have required the court to consider the issue of post-adoption contact in the context of the ECHR, was settled prior to hearing.
[575] See Harris-Short, S *Making and Breaking Family Life: Adoption, the State and Human Rights* (2008) Journal of Law and Society, pp 38–41. See also Hale, B and Fortin, J *Legal Issues in the Care and Treatment of Children with Mental Health Problems* in Rutter, M, Bishop, D, Pine, D, Scott, S, Stevenson, J, Taylor, E and Thapar, A (eds) *Rutter Child and Adolescent Psychiatry* (2008) Blackwell Publishing, p 102.
[576] *Ostrovar v Moldova* (2007) 44 EHRR 19. See also the decision of the Inter-American Commission on Human Rights in *X and Y v Argentina* Report No 38/96 Case 10.506.
[577] See *R (L) v Secretary of State for Health* [2001] 1 FCR 326, [2001] 1 FLR 406.
[578] *Berrehab v Netherlands* (1988) 11 EHRR 322.

Article 8 – Right to Alternative Care

8.211 The Committee of Ministers Resolution (77) 33 on Placement of Children[579] stipulates that the need for alternative care for children should be avoided a far as possible through preventative measures of support for families in accordance with their special problems and needs.[580] Where alternative care is necessary placement decisions should be made on the basis of advice given by a multidisciplinary team.[581] The child's alternative placement should facilitate the child's links to his or her family and promote working in partnership with parents.[582] This must include the use of a placement sufficiently proximate to the parents to allow the maintenance of the family relationships.[583] Siblings should be placed together where possible and in the best interests of each child.

(i) Alternative Care – Extended Family

8.212 The principle of proportionality is likely to demand that in considering options for alternative care the extended family are, subject to consideration of the child's best interests, to be considered as the first option for the care of the child in circumstances where the parents are unable or unwilling to care for the child.[584]

(ii) Alternative Care – Foster Care

8.213 The Council of Europe Recommendation on Foster Families R(87) 6 recommends that national legislation provide a system of supervision of foster parents in order to ensure that they provide 'the necessary moral and material conditions for the proper development of the child'. During the period of foster care the personal relationships of the child with his or her family should be maintained and information concerning the child's well-being must be made available to the family.[585] Art 8 of the ECHR, read with Art 14, will be violated where the State differentiates financially between those foster parents who foster children unrelated to them and those who foster children related to them.[586]

(iii) Alternative Care – Adoption

8.214 The European Court of Human Rights recognises that a point may come where the balance to be struck between the rights of the parents and those of the child dictates that adoption is appropriate.[587] Adoption means providing a child with a family not providing a family with a child.[588] Placement for adoption which severs all links between the child and his or her birth parents is an extreme step when measured against the requirements of the Art 8 of the ECHR and can only be justified by reference to Art 8(2) in exceptional circumstances or by the overriding requirement of the child's best interests.[589] The State has a broad discretion as to the content of the rules which regulate

---

[579] Adopted on 3 November 1977.
[580] Committee of Ministers Resolution (77) 33 on Placement of Children, para 1.1.
[581] Committee of Ministers Resolution (77) 33 on Placement of Children, para 1.4.
[582] Committee of Ministers Resolution (77) 33 on Placement of Children, para 2.11.
[583] *Olsson v Sweden (No 1)* (1988) 11 EHRR 259.
[584] See also Committee of Ministers Resolution (77) 33 on Placement of Children, para 1.3.
[585] Council of Europe Recommendation on Foster Families R(87) 6 Principle 2.
[586] *R (R) v Manchester City Council* [2002] 1 FLR 43.
[587] *Johansen v Norway* (1996) 23 EHRR 33, para 78 and 80 and *Scott v United Kingdom* [2000] 1 FLR 958 at 970.
[588] *Fretté v France* (2002) 38 EHRR 438, [2003] 2 FLR 9.
[589] *Johansen v Norway* (1996) 23 EHRR 33 and *Gnahoré v France* (2002) 34 EHRR 38. See also *Soderback v*

adoption.[590] However, the natural parents must be properly involved in the decision making process concerning adoption,[591] including an unmarried father, both in a situation where a *de facto* family exists between him and the mother[592] and otherwise.[593] Likewise, it is submitted that Art 8 and Art 6 of the ECHR require that the child must be properly involved in the decision making process concerning adoption.[594]

8.215 The European Convention on the Adoption of Children[595] stipulates that an adoption shall be valid only if it is granted by a judicial or administrative authority and on the basis that consent has been given or been overruled on exceptional grounds determined by law.[596] Pursuant to the Convention, a judicial or administrative authority shall not grant an adoption unless it is satisfied that the adoption will be in the interest of the child.[597]

(iv) Alternative Care – Residential Care

8.216 Residential care should be avoided for all children where possible, including children with disabilities.[598] The Committee of Ministers Recommendation to Member States on the Rights of Children Living in Residential Institutions[599] makes clear that children should only be placed in residential institutions to meet needs that have been established as imperative on the basis of a multidisciplinary assessment and then only in circumstances that ensure the protection and promotion of their fundamental rights. In providing guidelines on quality standards, the Recommendation to Member States on the Rights of Children Living in Residential Institutions stipulates that a placement should be selected which is as close as possible to the child's known environment and organised to allow parents to exercise their responsibilities and to maintain parent-child contact on a regular basis, preferably a small family style residential unit. Priority should be given to the physical and mental health of the child and his or her full, harmonious development and an individual care plan should be drawn up which is based on both the development of the child's capacities and abilities and respect for his or her autonomy, as well as on maintaining contacts with the outside world and preparation for living outside the institution in the future.

Sweden [1999] 1 FLR 250. In *X v Croatia* (2008) Application No 11223/04 the European Court of Human Rights described adoption as 'a very restrictive measure which results in complete disruption of the relation between a parent and a child …'.

590 *X and Y v United Kingdom* (1977) 12 DR 32 and *X v Netherlands* (1981) 24 DR 176. Such rules as are promulgated will however be subject to scrutiny against the principles enshrined in the ECHR.

591 *McMichael v United Kingdom* (1995) 20 EHRR 205. This obligation does not extend to informing relatives of the parents and child prior to the placement of the child for adoption (*Z County v R* [2001] 1 FLR 365).

592 *Re H (A Child)(Adoption: Disclosure)* [2001] 1 FCR 726, [2001] 1 FLR 646.

593 *Keegan v Ireland* (1994) 18 EHRR 342; *Re H (A Child)(Adoption: Disclosure)* [2001] 1 FCR 726, [2001] 1 FLR 646 and *Re R (Adoption: Father's Involvement)* [2001] 1 FLR 302.

594 *Re L (Care: Assessment Fair Trial)* [2002] EWHC 1379 (Fam), [2002] 2 FLR 730; *Mantovanelli v France* (1997) 24 EHRR 370.

595 ETS No 058.

596 European Convention on the Adoption of Children, Arts 4 and 5. The consent of the Mother is not valid if given within 6 weeks of the birth of the child (Art 5(4)).

597 European Convention on the Adoption of Children, Art 8(1). Note that the article uses the term 'interests' rather than 'best interests'.

598 Committee of Ministers Resolution (77) 33 on Placement of Children, para 1.6 and 2.2.

599 (2005)5.

ECHR, Art 12 – Right to Marry and Found a Family

ECHR, Art 12

8.217 Article 12 of the ECHR provides as follows in relation to the right to marry and found a family:

> 'Men and women of marriageable age have the right to marry and to found a family, according to the national laws governing the exercise of this right'.[600]

ECHR, Art 12 – Ambit

8.218 The right to marry has been described as a strong right and one which must be protected from interference by the promulgation of national laws.[601] It has also been characterised as being concerned mainly with the protection of marriage as the basis of the family.[602] The right not to marry is implicit in Art 12 of the ECHR[603] but Art 12 does not confer a right to divorce.[604] The right to found a family pursuant to Art 12 of the ECHR is a right only of those who have first married.[605] However, the ability to found a family is not a condition precedent of the right to marry.[606] The right to found a family under Art 12 will not provide the basis for claiming residence in respect of a child[607] or entitle an unmarried person to adopt a child.[608]

8.219 The words 'according to the national laws governing the exercise of this right' in Art 12 permit States parties to impose proportionate restrictions on marriage in

---

[600] Article 9 of the European Charter of Fundamental Rights states that 'The right to marry and the right to found a family shall be guaranteed in accordance with the national laws governing the exercise of these rights' Art 16(1) of the Universal Declaration of Human Rights which stipulates that 'Men and women of full age, without any limitation due to race, nationality or religion, have the right to marry and to found a family. They are entitled to equal rights as to marriage, during marriage and at its dissolution.' Art 16(2) provides that 'Marriage shall be entered into only with the free and full consent of the intending spouses.' Art 10 of the Covenant on Economic, Social and Cultural Rights implies the right of persons with disabilities to marry and have their own family (CESCR General Comment No 5 *Persons with Disabilities*, para 30 (HRI/GEN/1/Rev 8, p 31). See also Art 23(2) of the Covenant on Civil and Political Rights and Art 2 of the Supplementary Convention on the Abolition of the Slavery, the Slave Trade and Institutions and Practices Similar to Slavery 1956 which provides 'With a view to bringing to an end the institutions and practices [of marriage for payment, transfer of women for value received or inheritance of women on the death of a husband] the States Parties undertake to prescribe, where appropriate, suitable minimum ages of marriage, to encourage the use of facilities whereby the consent of both parties to a marriage may be freely expressed in the presence of a competent civil or religious authority, and to encourage the registration of marriages', UN General Assembly Resolution 843(IX) Status of Women in Private Law and Art 16(1) of the Convention on the Elimination of All Forms of Discrimination Against Women with General Recommendation No 21 *Equality in Marriage and Family Relations* (HRI/GEN/1/Rev. 8 p 308).

[601] *R (Baiai) v Secretary of State for the Home Department* [2008] UKHL 53, [2008] 3 WLR 549.

[602] *Rees v United Kingdom* (1986) 9 EHRR 56.

[603] *Pretty v DPP* [2001] UKHL 61, [2002] 1 AC 800 and see *Marckx v Belgium* (1979) 2 EHRR 330, para 67. Paragraph 4 of the Council of Europe Resolution 1468 entitled *Forced Marriages and Child Marriages* defines forced marriage as the union of two persons at least one of whom has not given their full and free consent to the marriage.

[604] *Johnston v Ireland* (1986) 9 EHRR 203.

[605] *Emonet v Switzerland* (2007) 49 EHRR 234. Laws and regulations governing alternative means of married couples founding a family, including adoption and artificial reproductive techniques will be covered by Art 12 but States parties will be accorded a wide margin of appreciation in respect of the content of national laws and regulations in this regard (see *X and Y v United Kingdom* (1977) 12 DR 32 (adoption) and *X, Y and Z v United Kingdom* (1997) 24 EHRR 143 and *Dickson v United Kingdom* (2007) 46 EHRR 927 (artificial insemination)).

[606] *Goodwin v United Kingdom* (2002) 35 EHRR 447. See also *Hamer v United Kingdom* (1979) 24 DR 5 and *Draper v United Kingdom* (1980) 24 DR 72.

[607] *B, R and J v Federal Republic of Germany* (1984) 36 DR 130.

[608] *X v Belgium and Netherlands* (1975) 7 DR 75 and *Emonet v Switzerland* (2007) 49 EHRR 234.

accordance with national laws, for example by imposing rules on capacity, consent, prohibited degrees of consanguinity[609] and the prevention of bigamy,[610] but such laws must not impair the very essence of the right to marry.[611] In *O'Donoghue v United Kingdom*[612] the European Court of Human Rights observed as follows:

> 'The Convention institutions have accepted that limitations on the right to marry laid down in the national laws may comprise formal rules concerning such matters as publicity and the solemnisation of marriage. They may also include substantive provisions based on generally recognised considerations of public interest, in particular concerning capacity, consent, prohibited degrees of affinity or the prevention of bigamy. In the context of immigration laws and for justified reasons, the States may be entitled to prevent marriages of convenience, entered solely for the purpose of securing an immigration advantage. However, the relevant laws – which must also meet the standards of accessibility and clarity required by the Convention – may not otherwise deprive a person or a category of persons of full legal capacity of the right to marry with the partners of their choice.'

ECHR, Art 12 – 'Marriageable Age'

8.220 The term 'marriageable age' in Art 12 of the ECHR is not further defined. The Council of Europe Resolution 1468 entitled Forced Marriages and Child Marriages notes that child marriage in itself infringes children's rights as children and that it is prejudicial to their physical and psychological welfare. Article 16(2) of the Convention on the Elimination of All Forms of Discrimination Against Women states that:

> 'The betrothal and the marriage of a child shall have no legal effect, and all necessary action, including legislation, shall be taken to specify a minimum age for marriage and to make the registration of marriages in an official registry compulsory.'

8.221 There is however little agreement as to what constitutes 'child marriage'. The Council of Europe Resolution defines 'child marriage' as the union of two persons at least one of whom is under 18 years of age and stresses the need to take the requisite legislative measures to prohibit child marriage by making 18 years the minimum marriageable age.[613] Art 21(2) of the African Charter on the Rights and Welfare of the Child provides that child marriage and the betrothal of girls and boys shall be prohibited and effective action, including legislation, shall be taken to specify the minimum age of marriage to be 18 years. The UN Convention on Consent to Marriage, Minimum Age for Marriage and Registration of Marriages[614] provides that States Parties shall take legislative action to specify a minimum age for marriage and that no marriage shall be legally entered into by any person under that age, except where a competent authority has 'for serious reasons' granted a dispensation as to age in the interest of the intending spouses. There was no agreement in relation to minimum age in relation to this Convention and accordingly, only a non-binding UN Resolution specifies the minimum age as not less than 15 years old.[615] The UN Human Rights

---

[609] See *B v United Kingdom* [2006] 1 FLR 35.
[610] *Hamer v United Kingdom* (1979) 24 DR 5, para 62.
[611] *Rees v United Kingdom* (1986) 9 EHRR 56 and *F v Switzerland* (1987) 10 EHRR 411.
[612] (2010) Application No 34848/07, para 83.
[613] Council of Europe Resolution 1468, paras 7 and 12.
[614] GA Res 1763 A (XVII) (1962).
[615] Recommendation on Consent to Marriage, Minimum Age for Marriage and Registration of Marriages (GA Res 2018 (XX) (1965)). See also Art 20 of the Ibero-American Convention on Rights of Youth which provides that 'Youth have the right to freely choose a partner, to common life and to the constitution of marriage ...'.

Committee has stated that 'marriageable age' should be such as to enable each of the intending spouses to give his or her free and full personal consent in a form and under conditions prescribed by law.[616]

8.222 In England and Wales a child under the age of 18 but over the age of 16, not being a widow or widower, may marry with the consent of each parent with parental responsibility, each guardian (if any), the person or persons with whom the child lives if a residence order was in force immediately before the child's sixteenth birthday or, where there is a care order in force, with the consent of the local authority as well as each parent with parental responsibility and each guardian.[617] Where the requisite consent has been refused by those required to give it, the Court may give consent.[618] Where the child is ward, the consent of the High Court must be obtained.[619]

The Child's Right to Family Life under European Union Law

European Charter of Fundamental Rights

8.223 Article 7 of the European Charter of Fundamental Rights provides as follows in respect of the right to family life:

> 'Everyone has the right to respect for his or her private and family[620] life, home and communications.'

The rights guaranteed by Art 7 correspond with those enshrined in Art 8 of the European Convention on Human Rights and, in accordance with Art 52(3) of the European Charter,[621] the meaning and scope of the rights under Art 7 is the same as that under the corresponding Art 8 of the ECHR. As such, the limitations that are permitted by Art 8(2) of the ECHR will be permitted in respect of the rights under Art 7 of the Charter.[622]

The Child's Right to Family Life under other Regional Instruments

American Convention on Human Rights

8.224 Article 17(1) of the American Convention on Human Rights states that the family is the natural and fundamental group unit in society and is entitled to protection by society and the State. Article 16 of the Protocol to the Convention, known as the Pact of San Salvador provides that:

> 'Every child, whatever his parentage, has the right to the protection that his status as a minor requires from his family, society and the State. Every child has the right to grow under the

---

[616] CCPR General Comment No 19 *Article 23 (The Family), para* 4 (HRI/GEN/1/Rev 8, p 188).

[617] Marriage Act 1949, ss 2 and 3(1A).

[618] Marriage Act 1949, s 3(1)(b).

[619] Marriage Act 1949, s 3(6).

[620] In respect of the meaning of 'family' in the context of European Union law see C249/96 *Grant v South West Trains* [1998] ICR 449, para 35.

[621] Article 52(3) of the Charter provides that 'Insofar as this Charter contains rights which correspond to rights guaranteed by the Convention for the Protection of Human Rights and Fundamental Freedoms, the meaning and scope of those rights shall be the same as those laid down by the said Convention. This provision shall not prevent Union law providing more extensive protection.'

[622] See **8.177–8.179** above.

protection and responsibility of his parents; save in exceptional, judicially recognised circumstances, a child of young age ought not to be separated from his mother.'

In *X and Y v Argentina*[623] the Inter-American Court of Human Rights held that the right to respect for family life is a right so basic that it is considered to be non-derogable even in extreme circumstances. Article 11(2) of the Convention provides that no one may be the object of arbitrary or abusive interference with his private life his family, his home or his correspondence, or unlawful attacks on his honour or reputation. Article 11(3) provides that everyone has the right to the protection of the law against such interference or attacks. Article 19 of the Convention enshrines the child's right to measures of protection from his or her family, society and the State.[624] Article 32(1) places responsibility on every person to his or her family, community and mankind. Finally, Art 17(2) of the American Convention on Human Rights stipulates that the right of men and women of marriageable age to marry and raise a family shall be recognised if they meet the conditions required by domestic laws.

8.225 In its Advisory Opinion on the Legal Status and Human Rights of the Child[625] the Inter-American Court of Human Rights stated that the child has the right to live with his or her family, which is responsible for satisfying his or her material, emotional, and psychological needs.[626] The Court made clear that the child must remain in his or her household, unless there are determining reasons, based on the child's best interests, to decide to separate him or her from the family and, even then, separation must be exceptional and, preferably, temporary.[627]

Ibero-American Convention on the Rights of Youth

8.226 Article 7 of the Ibero-American Convention on the Rights of Youth 'recognises the importance of the family and the duties and responsibilities of parents, or their legal substitutes, of guiding their young children, minors, in the exercise of the rights' recognised by the Convention. Article 19 provides that youth have the right to form an active part of a family and that States parties undertake to enable educational, economic, social and cultural conditions which promote the values of the family, cohesion and strength of family life. Article 20 enshrines the right of youth to marry and found a family.

African Charter on the Rights and Welfare of the Child

8.227 Article 18 of the African Charter on the Rights and Welfare of the Child stipulates the family shall be the natural unit and basis of society. Article 10 provides as follows in respect of the child's right to respect for family life:

'No child shall be subject to arbitrary or unlawful interference with his privacy, family home or correspondence, or to the attacks upon his honour or reputation, provided that parents or

---

623 Report No 38/96 Case 10.506 Argentina [1].
624 See *X and Y v Argentina* Report No 38/96 Case 10.506 Argentina [1] in which the Inter-American Court on Human Rights noted 'The state has a special duty to protect children and to ensure that, whenever state authorities take actions that may in any way affect a child, special care is taken to guarantee the child's rights and well being.'
625 OC-17/2002.
626 OC-17/2002, para 71.
627 OC-17/2002, para 77. See also the Inter-American Convention on the International Return of Children and the Inter-American Convention on Conflict of Laws concerning the Adoption of Minors.

legal guardians shall have the right to exercise reasonable supervision over the conduct of their children. The child has the right to the protection of the law against such interference or attacks.'

8.228 The African Charter provides specific provisions relating to the separation of the child from his or her parents. Article 19 provides as follows:

'1. Every child shall be entitled to the enjoyment of parental care and protection and shall, whenever possible, have the right to reside with his or her parents. No child shall be separated from his parents against his will, except when a judicial authority determines in accordance with the appropriate law, that such separation is in the best interest of the child.[628]

2. Every child who is separated from one or both parents shall have the right to maintain personal relations and direct contact with both parents on a regular basis.[629]

3. Where separation results from the action of a State Party, the State Party shall provide the child, or if appropriate, another member of the family with essential information concerning the whereabouts of the absent member or members of the family.[630] States Parties shall also ensure that the submission of such a request shall not entail any adverse consequences for the person or persons in whose respect it is made.

4. Where a child is apprehended by a State Party, his parents or guardians shall, as soon as possible, be notified of such apprehension by that State Party.'

8.229 By contrast to the ECHR and the CRC, the Art 31 of the African Charter enshrines responsibilities on the part of the child towards his or her family, society and the State. Pursuant to the Charter, the child has the *duty* to work for the cohesion of the family, to respect his or her parents, superiors and elders at all times and to assist them in case of need. In addition, wider responsibilities such as the duty to preserve and strengthen social and national solidarity and preserve and strengthen the independence and integrity of his or her country are also incorporated into Art 31. Whilst the concept of responsibility is important for children and both implicit and necessary in any system of rights, and accepting that Art 31 must be placed properly in its cultural context, it nevertheless must be questioned whether the language used in Art 31 can be said to be co-terminus with the protection and promotion of the rights of the child set out in the African Charter on the Rights and Welfare of the Child.[631]

---

[628] Article 24(b) of the African Charter stipulates that inter-country adoption shall be a measure of last resort where the child cannot be placed in a foster or adoptive family or cannot be cared for in a suitable manner in the child's country of origin.

[629] See also Art 17(3) which requires that during trial and any subsequent period of detention the essential aim shall be the reintegration of the child into his or her family and social rehabilitation. Article 25 requires that a child who is permanently or temporarily deprived of his family environment shall be entitled to special protection and assistance, including alternative family care.

[630] See also Art 23(2) which requires the State to cooperation in the tracing of parent or other close relatives in cases where the child is a refugee.

[631] See Van Bueren, G *The International Law on the Rights of the Child* (1998) Martinus Nijhoff, p 76. Van Bueren concludes that the responsibility to respect parents and their elders at all times is too unquestioning and general. Van Bueren also points out that it is difficult to envisage a situation arising whereby parents would initiate actions against their children before human rights tribunals based on their children's failure to support them in times of need (Van Bueren, G *The International Law on the Rights of the Child* (1998) Martinus Nijhoff, p 77).

The African Youth Charter

8.230 Article 8 of the African Youth Charter provides that the family, as the most basic social institution, shall enjoy the full protection and support of States Parties. As with the African Charter on the Rights and Welfare of the Child, the African Youth Charter stipulates at Art 26 the responsibilities which every young person shall have towards his or her family and society, the State and the international community.

The African Charter on Human and Peoples' Rights

8.231 Article 18 of the African Charter on Human and People's Rights states that the family shall be the natural unit and basis of society and shall be protection by the State which shall take care of its physical health and moral. Article 27 stipulates that every individual shall have duties towards his family and society, the State and other legally recognised communities and the international community and Art 29 provides that every individual shall have the duty to preserve the harmonious development of the family and to work for the cohesion and respect of the family, to respect his or her parents at all times and to maintain them in case of need.[632]

Revised Arab Charter on Human Rights

8.232 Article 33(1) of the revised Arab Charter on Human Rights recognises the family as the natural and fundamental group unit of society and provides enshrines a right to marry and found a family.[633] Art 21 provides that no one shall be subjected to arbitrary or unlawful interference with regard to his privacy, family, home or correspondence, nor unlawful attacks on his honour or his reputation and that everyone has the right to the protection of the law against such interference or attacks.

The Child's Right to Family Life under Domestic Law

Domestic Law – Right to Respect for Family Life

The Children Act 1989[634]

8.233 Integral to the ethos of domestic legislation concerning the family life of the child is that family life should be independent and free from unjustified interference by the State. This ethos is crystallised within the Children Act 1989 by the concept of parental responsibility, whereby 'all the rights, duties, powers, responsibilities and authority which by law a parent has in relation to a child and his property'[635] are ordinarily discharged by the parent(s) of a child as part of 'the every day reality of being a parent'.[636] This central concept of parental responsibility is further reinforced by the presumption that no court order modifying or restricting the exercise of that responsibility should be made unless it will promote the child's welfare (the so called 'no

---

[632] See **8.229** commenting on the similar provisions in the African Charter on the Rights and Welfare of the Child.

[633] Article 33 of the Arab Charter states specifically that the family is based on a marriage between a man and a woman.

[634] A full account of the operation of the Children Act 1989 in so far as it relates to family life is beyond the scope of this work. For a detailed account of practice and procedure under the Act see White, R, Carr, P, Lowe, N, and MacDonald, A *The Children Act in Practice* (2008) 4th edn, LexisNexis.

[635] Children Act 1989, s 3(1).

[636] *Guardianship and Custody* (Law Com 1988 No 172), para 2.4.

order' principle').[637] Fortin criticises the Children Act 1989 as appearing to operate on the underlying assumption that the interests of the child and the interests of the parents will be co-terminus.[638] Such an assumption must be guarded against and it should be noted that the concept of the 'exercise of parental responsibility' was designed to move away from the concept of parents having right's over their children. In this regard, the Law Commission, in its report entitled *Review of Child Law: Guardianship*[639] recognised the principle that parents' rights are only derived from their duties and that such 'rights' exist only to secure the welfare of their children.[640]

8.234 The Children Act 1989 prescribes strict conditions that must be satisfied before the State may interfere with the family. Before it may mediate the exercise of parental responsibility as between two parents the State must be able to show that such interference is in the child's best interests.[641] The child's best interests must be assessed by holding those interests as paramount and by having regard to the child's wishes and feelings considered in light of his or her age and understanding.[642] Account must also be taken of the child's physical, emotional and educational needs, the likely effect on him or her of any change in circumstances, any harm which he or she has suffered or is at risk of suffering, the capability of parents or carers to meet his or her needs, the range of powers available to the court[643] and the principle that delay is ordinarily inimical to the child.[644] Where the State seeks to take the child into care or undertake State supervision of family life, the Children Act 1989 imposes an additional preliminary hurdle of requiring actual or likely significant harm attributable to the parents or cares to be proved.[645] Even if satisfied of this, the court must still go on to determine whether taking the child into care or supervising his or her care is in the child's best interests holding those interests as paramount[646] Within the context of the respect that family life is accorded in domestic law, as Hedley J observed in *Re L (Care: Threshold Criteria)*:[647]

> 'It follows inexorably from that, that society must be willing to tolerate very diverse standards of parenting, including the eccentric, the barely adequate and the inconsistent. It follows too that children will inevitably have both very different experiences of parenting and very unequal consequences flowing from it. It means that some children will experienced disadvantage and harm, while others flourish in atmospheres of loving security and emotional stability. These are the consequences of our fallible humanity and it is not the provenance of the State to spare children all the consequences of defective parenting. In any event, it simply could not be done.'

---

[637] Children Act 1989, s 1(5).

[638] Fortin, J *Children's Rights and the Developing Law* (2009) 3rd edn, Cambridge, p 324. In particular, Fortin notes that, unlike the Children (Scotland) Act 1995, the Children Act 1989 does not set out a list of parental responsibilities.

[639] Law Commission (1988), para 2.4.

[640] See also *F v Wirral Metropolitan Borough Council* [1991] Fam 69, [1991] 2 FLR 114.

[641] CA 1989, s 1(1).

[642] CA 1989, ss 1(1) and s 1(3)(a).

[643] CA 1989, s 1(3)(b)–(g).

[644] CA 1989, s 1(2).

[645] CA 1989, s 31(2) (the court may make a care order or a supervision order only where (i) it is satisfied that the child concerned is suffering or is likely to suffer significant harm and that harm, or the likelihood of harm, is attributable to the care given to the child, or likely to be given to him or her were an order not made, not being what it would be reasonable to expect a parent to give him and (ii) such an order would be in the child's best interests). Criteria are also prescribed by law for investigation by the State into the child's welfare (CA 1989, s 7(1), s 37(1) and s 47(1)), the provision of State support (CA 1989 Part III) and the emergency protection of children (Children Act 1989, ss 38(2), 44 and 46). See also the Revised Children Act 1989 Guidance and Regulations, Vol 1, Court Orders (2008) Department of Health, para 3.6.

[646] See *Re B (Care Interference with Family Life)* [2003] EWCA Civ 786, [2003] 2 FLR 813.

[647] [2007] 1 FLR 2050.

Human Rights Instruments and the Domestic Right to Family Life

8.235 The domestic statutory foundation for an independent family life is now underpinned in domestic law by regional and international human rights instruments. The Human Rights Act 1998 gives effect in domestic law to the provisions of the European Convention on Human Rights and Fundamental Freedoms 1950 and in particular Art 8. Accordingly, the principles outlined above in respect of Art 8 must be considered cardinal principles in domestic law.[648] The domestic courts will apply with rigor the jurisprudence in respect of Art 8 of the ECHR that seeks to draw the appropriate boundary between the family and the State, both in judicial proceedings[649] concerning children and more widely.[650] The Courts must also have regard to the principles of the CRC and the other international human rights instruments ratified by the United Kingdom as being of persuasive effect.[651] In *Re B (Care Proceedings: Standard of Proof)*[652] Baroness Hale stated:

> 'In a totalitarian society, uniformity and conformity are valued. Hence the totalitarian state tries to separate the child from her family and mould her to its own design. Families in all their subversive variety are the breeding ground of diversity and individuality. In a free and democratic society we value diversity and individuality. Hence the family is given special protection in all the modern human rights instruments including the European Convention on Human Rights (Article 8), the International Covenant on Civil and Political Rights (Article 23) and throughout the United Nations Convention on the Rights of the Child. As McReynolds J famously said in *Pierce v Society of Sisters* (1925) 268 US 510, 535, 'The child is not the mere creature of the State'.

Domestic Law – Right to Know and be Cared for by Parents

Care by the Natural Parent[653]

8.236 The significance of the status of a natural parent when it comes to determining whether a child should be cared for by his or her parents has been the subject of extensive treatment by the domestic courts. In *J v C*[654] Lord McDermott cited with approval the words of Wilberforce J in *Re Adoption Application (No 2)*:[655]

> 'The tie ... between the child and his natural father (or any other relative) may properly be regarded in this connexion, not on the basis that the person concerned has a claim which he has a right to have satisfied, but, only if, and to the extent that, the conclusion can be drawn that the child will benefit from the recognition of this tie ... While there is now no rule of law that the rights and wishes of unimpeachable parents must prevail over other considerations,

---

[648] See *Re MA (Care Threshold)* [2010] 1 FLR 431 in which Ward LJ said 'At all times the spectre of Art 8 of the European Convention for the Protection of Human Rights and Fundamental Freedoms 1950 hangs over us all.'

[649] See **8.37** above and *Re B (Care: Interference with Family Life)* [2003] EWCA Civ 786, [2003] 2 FLR 813 per Thorpe LJ and *R (P) v Secretary of State for the Home Department; R (Q) v Secretary of State for the Home Department* [2001] EWCA Civ 1151; [2001] 2 FLR 1122.

[650] See *Ghaidan v Mendoza* [2004] UKHL 30, [2004] 2 AC 557 (Art 8 encompasses the right to respect for the home) and the dissenting judgment of Baroness Hale in *M v Secretary of State for Work and Pensions* [2006] UKHL 11, [2006] 2 AC 91 (Art 8 is engaged in relation to the domestic child support scheme).

[651] See **3.32-3.46** above.

[652] [2009] 1 AC 11.

[653] For the meaning of natural parent see *Re G (Children) (Residence: Same Sex Partners)* [2006] UKHL 43, [2006] 1 WLR 2305, [2006] 2 FLR 629, paras 32–37. For the concept of a 'psychological parent' see Goldstein, J, Freud, A and Solnit, A *Beyond the Best Interests of the Child* (1973) Free Press, p 19.

[654] [1970] AC 668.

[655] [1963] 2 All ER 1082 at 1085.

such rights and wishes, recognised as they are by nature and society, can be capable of ministering to the total welfare of the child in a special way, and must therefore preponderate in many cases.'[656]

8.237 In 1988 Lord Templeman took a narrower view in the case of *Re KD (A Minor) (Ward: Termination of Access)*[657] concluding, by reference to Art 8 of the ECHR that:

'The best person to bring up a child is the natural parent. It matters not whether the parent is wise or foolish, rich or poor, educated or illiterate, provided the child's moral and physical health are not endangered.'

Whilst this famous passage is often cited, it should be noted that Lord Oliver, in the leading judgment, nonetheless considered that the parent was to be given no special consideration in terms of his or her status as the natural parent, the decision to be made by the court being determined by the child's welfare:

'... the natural bond and relation between parent and child gives rise to universally recognised which ought not to be gratuitously interfered with and which, if interfered with at all, ought to be so only if the welfare of the child dictates it ... Parenthood, in most civilised societies, in generally conceived as conferring upon parents the exclusive privilege of ordering, within the family, the upbringing of children of tender age, with all that that entails. That is a privilege which, if interfered with without authority, would be protected by the courts, but it is a privilege circumscribed by many limitations imposed both by the general law and, where the circumstances demand, by the courts of by the authorities upon whom the legislature has imposed the duty of supervising the welfare of children and young persons. When the jurisdiction of the court is invoked for the protection of the child the parental privileges do not terminate. They do, however, become immediately subservient to the paramount consideration which the court has always in mind, that is to say, the welfare of the child.'

8.238 The Court of Appeal appeared to move closer to endowing the natural parent with a pre-eminent status in *Re K (Minor) (Ward: Care and Control)*[658] in holding that:

'The question was not: where would R get the better home? The question was: was it demonstrated that the welfare of the child positively demanded the displacement of the parental right? The word 'right' is not really accurate in so far as it might connote something in the nature of a property right (which it is not) but it will serve for the present purposes. The 'right', if there is one, is perhaps more that of the child.'[659]

However, in *Re H (A Minor) (Custody: Interim Care and Control)*[660] Lord Donaldson made clear that he was:

'slightly apprehensive that *Re K (A Minor) (Ward: Care and Control)* may be misconstrued ... it is not a case of parental right opposed to the interests of the child, with an assumption that prevails unless there are strong reasons in terms of the interests of the child ... all that *Re K* is saying, as I understand it, is that of course there is a strong

---

[656] [1970] AC 668 at 715.
[657] [1988] AC 806 per Lord Templeman at 812.
[658] [1990] 3 All ER 795 at 798.
[659] Fortin notes that it is unfortunate that what amounts to a natural parent presumption is concealed behind the language of child rights (Fortin, J *Children's Rights and the Developing Law* (2009) 3rd edn, Cambridge, p 524).
[660] [1991] 2 FLR 109 at 112–113.

supposition that, other things being equal, it is in the interests of the child that it shall remain with its natural parents. But that has to give way to particular needs in particular situations.'

8.239 The approach espoused by Lord Donaldson in *Re H* calls for no more than a proper application of the test that is now set out in s 1 of the Children Act 1989 by the court weighing up which option will be in the child's best interests taking into account 'particular needs in particular situations'. Whilst the courts have often allowed the 'presumption' in favour of natural parent articulated by Lord Templeman to obscure this approach,[661] the strict application of the best interests principle in the context of the child's right to family life under the CRC and ECHR, considered in light of the 'welfare checklist' in s 1(3) of the Children Act 1989 and the principle of proportionality under Art 8 of the ECHR is the proper way of ensuring the best course for the child is determined and accordingly of ensuring to the child the integrity of his or her rights. Unfortunately, as Fortin observes the courts have been reluctant to apply the interpretation in *Re H* when evaluating the relative merits of care by natural parents verses alternative care arrangements.[662] This despite it being well recognised that it is 'a history of social interaction, not kinship that breeds attachment'.[663]

8.240 However, the primacy of the child's best interests over parenthood *per se* received significant support from the House of Lords in *Re G (Children)(Residence: Same Sex Partners)*[664] and from the Supreme Court in *Re B (A Child)*.[665] In *Re G* Baroness Hale made clear that:

> 'The statutory position is plain: the welfare of the child is the paramount consideration. As Lord MacDermott explained, this means that it 'rules upon or determines the course to be followed'. There is no question of a parental right. As the Law Commission explained, 'the welfare test itself is well able to encompass any special contribution which natural parents can make to the emotional needs of their child' or, as Lord MacDermott put it, the claims and wishes of parents "can be capable of ministering to the total welfare of the child in a special way".'[666]

8.241 In *Re G* Lord Nicholls stated that the child's 'welfare is the court's paramount consideration. In reaching its decision the court should always have in mind that in the ordinary way the rearing of a child by his or biological parent can be expected to be in the child's best interests, both in the short term and also, and importantly, in the longer term. I decry any tendency to diminish the significance of this factor'. In *Re B (A Child)*,[667] considering the import of Lord Nicholls' statement, Lord Kerr made clear that:

> 'As we have observed, it appears to have been in reliance on the latter passage that the justices stated that a child should not be removed from the primary care of biological parents. A careful reading of what Lord Nicholls of Birkenhead actually said reveals, of course, that he

---

[661] See for example *Re W (A Minor)(Residence Order)* [1993] 2 FLR 625; *Re M (Child's Upbringing)* [1996] 2 FLR 441; *Re D (Care: Natural Parent Presumption)* [1999] 1 FLR 134.

[662] See Fortin, J *Children's Rights and the Developing Law* (2009) 3rd edn, Cambridge, pp 525–528 and her discussion of *Re W (A Minor) (Residence Order)* [1993] 2 FLR 625, *Re M (Child's Upbringing)* [1996] 2 FLR 441 and *Re D (Care: Natural Parent Presumption)* [1999] 1 FLR 134.

[663] Schaffer, H *Making Decisions About Children* (1998) Blackwell, p 62.

[664] [2006] UKHL 43, [2006] 1 WLR 2305, [2006] 2 FLR 629.

[665] [2009] UKSC 9, [2010] 1 FLR 551.

[666] Baroness Hale made clear that this does not mean that the fact of parentage is irrelevant but rather is an important and significant factor to be considered in the overall welfare judgement (see paras 32–38 and 44).

[667] [2009] UKSC 9, [2010] 1 FLR 551.

did not propound any general rule to that effect. It is important at the outset to recognise that Lord Nicholls' comment about the rearing of a child by a biological parent is set firmly in the context of the child's welfare. This he identified as "the courts paramount consideration". It must be the dominant and overriding factor that ultimately determines disputes about residence and contact and there can be no dilution of its importance by reference to extraneous matters ... all consideration of the importance of parenthood in private law disputes about residence must be firmly rooted in an examination of what is in the child's best interests. This is the paramount consideration. It is only as a contributor to the child's welfare that parenthood assumes any significance.'

Domestic Law – Right not to be Separated from Parents

Right not to be Separated – Domestic Private Law

(i) Parental Separation and Divorce

8.242 Residence orders pursuant to s 8 of the Children Act 1989 determine with whom a child is to live subject to consideration of the child's best interests and the matters set out in the welfare checklist in s 1(3) of the 1989 Act.[668] Changes in a child's residence following parental separation or divorce should interfere as little as possible in his or her relationship with both parents.[669]

8.243 In relation to the argument that the care of children should, as a matter of course, be shared equally between parents following parental separation, it has been readily acknowledged by the Government that 'Children are not a commodity to be apportioned equally after separation. The best arrangements for them will depend on a variety of issues particular to their circumstances: a one size fits all formula will not work'.[670] Good reasons must exist if a shared residence order is not to be made[671] but the order that is made must reflect the reality of the position on the ground.[672] A shared residence order may be made for the purpose of giving parental responsibility to the child's 'psychological' parent.[673]

(ii) Child Abduction

8.244 The domestic law provides a comprehensive statutory framework in the Child Abduction and Custody Act 1985, which incorporates into domestic law the Hague Convention on the Civil Aspects of International Child Abduction International Child Abduction[674] and the European Convention on the Recognition and Enforcement of Decisions Concerning Custody of Children and on the Restoration of Custody of Children, the latter having been largely superseded by Brussels II Revised. The operation

---

[668] Although note that, curiously, where the making of a residence order is not opposed by any party there is no requirement to consider the matters in the welfare checklist (Children Act 1989, s 1(4)(a)).

[669] Law Com No 172, para 4.16. This will include cases in which one parent proposes to remove the child from the jurisdiction for the purposes of relocating (see *Payne v Payne* [2001] EWCA Civ 166, [2001 Fam 473). The preponderance of research shows that the children who achieve the best outcomes following parental separation or divorce are those who are able to maintain and good relationship with both their parents (see Harold, G and Murch, M *Inter-Parental Conflict and Children's Adaptation to Separation and Divorce: Theory, Research and Implications for Family Law, Practice and Policy* [2005] CFLQ 185).

[670] *Parental Separation: Children's Needs and Parents' Responsibilities* (2004) Cm 6273 TSO, para 42.

[671] *Re P (Shared Residence)* [2005] EWCA Civ 1639, [2006] 2 FLR 347, para 22. Note that a decade earlier, the test was 'exceptional circumstances' (see *Re H (A Minor) (Shared Residence)* [1994] 1 FLR 717).

[672] *Re K (Shared Residence Order)* [2008] EWCA Civ 526, [2008] 2 FLR 380.

[673] *Re A (A Child: Joint Residence/Parental Responsibility)* [2008] EWCA 867 Civ, [2008] 2 FLR 1593.

[674] See **8.168** above.

of this legislation is beyond the scope of this work and reference should be made to the seminal work *International Movement of Children*[675] for detailed discussion of the practice and procedure.

Right not to be separated – Domestic Public Law

(i)   Public Law – Separation due to Child Protection Concerns

Public Law – Duty to Avoid Separation

8.245   As under the ECHR jurisprudence, the first priority of the domestic authorities should be to ensure that children are not separated from their families. This should be achieved by the provision of appropriate support and assistance to the family to address issues which may otherwise evolve to a point where the removal of the child is dictated by his or her best interests. Part III of the Children Act 1989 provides the statutory framework by which such assistance can be rendered to children and families[676] and the revised *Children Act 1989 Guidance and Regulations Volume1, Court Orders* seek to ensure that court proceedings in relation to State intervention in the family are avoided by working in partnership with families.[677] Key to the operation of this guidance is that the local authority should communicate to the parents at the earliest stage:

(a)   The nature and extent of the local authority's concerns.

(b)   The actions the family will need to take to address the concerns of the local authority.

(c)   The assistance, guidance and services that will be provided to the family to help them address the concerns of the local authority.

(d)   The timescale within which the concerns of the local authority need to be addressed.

(e)   The criteria for successfully addressing the concerns of the local authority.

(f)   The consequences of failing to address the concerns of the local authority.[678]

Where a child is of sufficient age and understanding, it is vital that the local authority speak to the child about its concerns and involves the child in the assessment process and its plans for the child.[679] Voluntary arrangements should always be fully explored ahead of any application for a care or supervision order, provided this does not jeopardise the safety of the child.[680]

---

[675]   Lowe N, Everall M, and Nicholls, M (2004) Jordan Publishing.

[676]   See **8.54** above.

[677]   There is a strong argument that these provisions are but a pale reflection of what is actually required to ensure that work carried out prior to court proceedings being issued operates effectively to reduce the number of children separated from their families (see MacDonald, A *Whatever Happened to the Pre-Proceedings Protocol?* [2007] Fam Law 991).

[678]   Revised Children Act 1989 Guidance and Regulations, Vol 1, Court Orders (2008) Department of Health, paras 3.3 and 3.24. See also para 7.39.

[679]   Children Act 1989 Guidance and Regulations, Vol 1, Court Orders (1991) Department of Health, para 3.24.

[680]   Children Act 1989 Guidance and Regulations, Vol 1, Court Orders (1991) Department of Health, para 3.7.

Public Law – Strict Test

8.246 In *Re B (Children)(Sexual Abuse: Standard of Proof)*[681] Baroness Hale reiterated that '[t]aking away a child from his or her family is a momentous step, not only for her, but for her whole family, and for the local authority which does so'. The test applied by the domestic courts to the issue of whether a child should be separated from his or her parents by removal from the family home is a rigorous one. The court must first be satisfied that the threshold for State intervention in family life is met in accordance with the applicable statutory criteria.[682] Thereafter, the court must satisfy itself that the plan of removal is in the child's best interests having regard to the paramount nature of those interests and the factors set out in the statutory welfare checklist.[683] In considering this question, removal should only be contemplated where the safety of the child demands immediate separation[684] such that removal is required by the overriding necessity of the interests of the child[685] and no other less radical form of order would achieve the essential end of promoting his or her welfare.[686] The domestic decision making process by which a decision is taken to remove a child from the care of his or her parents must incorporate procedural safeguards which ensure respect for the child and parents' family life under Art 8 of the ECHR and pay full regard to the child's rights under the CRC.[687]

Public Law – Duty to Rehabilitate

8.247 Where a child has been removed from the care of his or her parents the local authority remains under a duty to rehabilitate the child to the parents' care.[688] The domestic courts must have regard to the duty to rehabilitate and to the fact that a situation may redeemed with appropriate support and work with the family.[689] A Local Authority should work to support, and eventually reunite, a family unless the risks are so high that the children's welfare requires alternative family care.[690] A decision to permanently remove children from a parents care should not be made until such time as it is clear that rehabilitation within an acceptable time span is not possible.[691] This balance has been reinforced by statutory guidance:[692]

> 'Where a child is in the care of the local authority, the Children Act 1989 places a duty on them to make all reasonable efforts to rehabilitate the child with his or her family wherever possible unless it is clear that the child can no longer live with his family or that the authority has sufficient evidence to suggest that further attempts at rehabilitation are unlikely to succeed.'

---

[681] [2008] UKHL 35, [2008] 3 WLR 1, para 20.

[682] See CA 1989, s 38(2) and s 31(2). Note that a local authority cannot apply for a residence order nor use s 8 proceedings for the purpose of retaining control of a child (*Nottingham County Council v P* [1994] Fam 18, [1993] 3 All ER 815, CA).

[683] CA 1989, s 1(1) and s 1(3).

[684] *Re H (A Child)(Inter Care Order)* [2002] EWCA Civ 1932, [2003] 1 FCR 350, para 39

[685] *Re C and B (Care Order: Future Harm)* [2001] 1 FLR 611.

[686] *Re B (Care: Interference with Family Life)* [2003] EWCA Civ 786, [2003] 2 FLR 813, para 34.

[687] *Re C (Care Proceeding: Disclosure of the Local Authority's Decision Making Process)* [2002] EWHC 1379 (Fam), [2002] 2 FCR 673 and *CF v Secretary of State for the Home Department* [2004] EWHC 111 (Fam), [2004] 2 FLR 517.

[688] CA 1989, s 23(4) (which provides that unless to do so would not be reasonably practicable or consistent with the child's welfare, the authority must make arrangements to enable him to live with his parents or other person with parental responsibility or a relative, friend or other person connected with him).

[689] See *Re D (Grant of Care Order: Refusal of Freeing Order)* [2001] 1 FLR 862 and *Re G (A Child) (Interim Care Order: Residential Assessment)* [2005] UKHL 68, [2006] AC 576.

[690] *Re C and B (Care Order: Future Harm)* [2001] 1 FLR 611.

[691] *Re Y (A Minor)* [1985] FLR 294.

[692] LAC (98) 20 Appendix 4.

(ii)   Public Law – Permanent Separation by way of Adoption[693]

8.248   The domestic courts draw heavily on the Art 8 jurisprudence of the European Court of Human Rights in determining whether a child should be permanently separated from his or her parents by means of adoption. Thus, the domestic courts will endeavour to strike a fair balance between the various competing factors, including the child's relationship with his or her parents and the need for the child to have the security, stability and permanence of a family who can meet all or most of his or her needs.[694] The balancing exercise can be extremely complicated.[695] In *Re M (Adoption or Residence Order)*[696] Ward LJ held as follows:

> 'The legal nature and effect of an adoption order is ... [that] ... it changes status. The child is treated in law as if she had been born a child of the marriage of the applicants. She ceases in law to be a child of her mother and the sister of her siblings. The old family link is destroyed and new family ties are created. The psychological effect is that the child loses one identity and gains another. Adoption is inconsistent with being a member of both old and new family at the same time. Long-term fostering does enable the child to have the best of both worlds by feeling she belongs to both families though she must reside with and will anyway usually choose to live with only one – the one who gives her the daily love and care. The significant advantage of adoption is that it can promote much-needed security and stability, the younger the age of placement, the fuller the advantage. The disadvantage is that it is unlike any other decision made by adults during the child's minority because it is irrevocable. The child cannot at a later stage even in adulthood reverse the process. That is a salutary reminder of the seriousness of the decision. The advantage of the care/residence order is the converse – it can be adapted to meet changing needs, but therein lies its disadvantage – it does not provide absolute certainty and security. Section 91(14) of the Children Act 1989 minimises, if not eliminates, the uncertainty. In weighing up these considerations, the court must have an eye to the realities of the child's situation, bearing in mind the torture of adolescence through which the child must live, finding and then asserting the independence of growing adulthood. When times are bad – and it would be surprising if there were not such times – it will be the emotional attachment forged between the adopters and the child, not that piece of paper entitled 'adoption order', which will prevent a disaffected child searching for a grass which will always seem so much greener in the pastures occupied by the old family.'[697]

8.249   Within the domestic legislation, the framework for undertaking this balancing exercise is provided by s 1(4) of the Adoption and Children Act 2002 and s 1(4)(c) and 1(4)(f) of the 2002 Act compels the court to have regard to the effect on the child of the separation from his or her family.[698] Where a child is old enough to understand the broad implications of adoption, the court will require some fairly clear reason to justify proceeding against his or her expressed wishes and feelings.[699] In taking the decision whether to sanction adoption the court must hold the child's best interests as

---

[693]   For a comprehensive treatment of the domestic law on adoption see Swindells, H and Heaton, C *Adoption: The Modern Procedure* (2006) Jordan Publishing.

[694]   *Re B (Adoption: Natural Parent)* [2001] UKHL 70, [2002] 1 FLR 196, para 31.

[695]   See for example *SB v County Council* [2008] EWCA Civ 535, [2008] 2 FCR 185 and *Re O (Adoption: Withholding Agreement)* [1999] 1 FLR 451.

[696]   [1998] 1 FLR 570.

[697]   Complexities also arise when it is sought to adopt a child within the birth family (see *Re S (Adoption Order or Special Guardianship Order)* [2007] EWCA Civ 54, [2007] 1 FLR 819).

[698]   *Re C (A Child) v XYZ County Council* [2007] EWCA Civ 1206, [2008] 1 FLR 1294, para 18. Where the choice is between an adoption order in favour of a member of the birth family and an order under the Children Act 1989 both the welfare checklist under the Children Act 1989, s 1(3) and the checklist under the Adoption and Children Act 2002, s 1(4) will need to be considered (see *Re S (Adoption Order or Special Guardianship Order)* [2007] EWCA Civ 54, [2007] 1 FLR 819).

[699]   *Re D (Minors) (Adoption by Stepparent)* (1981) 2 FLR 102.

paramount[700] and permanent separation by means of adoption must be a proportionate response to the concerns which give rise to the proposal for such an adoption.[701] In *SB v County Council*[702] Wall LJ observed at para 124 that in applying the test of proportionality:

> 'In assessing what is proportionate, the court has, of course, always to bear in mind that adoption without parental consent is an extreme – indeed the most extreme – interference with family life. Cogent justification must there exist before parental consent is dispensed with.'

Right not to be Separated – Immigration and Separation

8.250 Section 55 of the Borders, Citizenship and Immigration Act 2009 requires that the United Kingdom Border Agency (UKBA) carry out its functions in a manner which takes into account the need to safeguard and promote the welfare of children in the United Kingdom. The United Kingdom has now removed its reservation to the CRC in respect of domestic immigration laws.[703] However, the immigration rules in respect of children remain extremely complicated.[704] The objective of those rules is to allow a child to join a parent or relative in the United Kingdom *only* where that child could not be adequately cared for by his parents or relatives in his own country.[705] In respect of unaccompanied children entering or found in the United Kingdom, each case must be treated on its merits in light of all available information and welfare considerations may take precedence over the immigration implications of allowing the child to remain in the United Kingdom.[706] In cases before the court which involve issues of immigration courts must be slow to trespass on the Secretary of State's powers in respect of immigration control[707] although breaches of the immigration legislation may be excused by the court where to do so would be in the child's best interests.[708] In considering the position of families subject to the immigration rules, the Secretary of State and the immigration appellate authorities must consider the child's best interests as a primary consideration.[709] This will involve asking whether it is reasonable to expect the child to live in another country.[710] Relevant to this will be the level of the child's integration in this country and the length of absence from the other country; where and with whom the child is to live and the arrangements for looking after the child in the other country; and the strength of the child's relationships with parents or other family members which will be severed if the child has to move away.[711] The Supreme Court has recognised that, in the context of immigration cases, nationality will be of particular importance in assessing the child's best interests.[712] In carrying out this exercise the Art 8 rights of all the family members who may be affected by the immigration decision and not just the

---

[700] Adoption and Children Act 2002, s 1(1).
[701] *Down Lisburn Health and Social Services Trust v H* [2006] UKHL 36, [2007] 1 FLR 121, para 34.
[702] [2008] EWCA Civ 535, [2008] 2 FCR 185.
[703] See United Kingdom CRC/C/15/Add.34, paras 7 and 29 and United Kingdom 2nd Report CRC/C/15/Add.188, para 6.
[704] See Immigration Rules rr 296–316F.
[705] Immigration Directorate's Instructions *Children* Ch 8 s 5A, para 1 November 2009.
[706] Immigration Directorate's Instructions *Children* Ch 8 s 5A, para 6.1 November 2009
[707] *Re M (A Minor)(Immigration: Residence Order)* [1993] 2 FLR 858.
[708] *ASB and KBS v MQS (Secretary of State for the Home Department Intervening)* [2009] EWHC 2491 (Fam), [2010] 1 FLR 748.
[709] *ZH (Tanzania) v Secretary of State for the Home Department* [2011] UKSC 4.
[710] *EB (Kosovo) v Secretary of State for the Home Department* [2008] UKHL 41, [2009] AC 1159.
[711] *ZH (Tanzania) v Secretary of State for the Home Department* [2011] UKSC 4.
[712] *ZH (Tanzania) v Secretary of State for the Home Department* [2011] UKSC 4.

claimant or the appellant in question. In *Beoku-Betts v Secretary of State for the Home Department*[713] Lord Brown held as follows in this regard:

'Together these members enjoy a single family life and whether or not the removal would interfere disproportionately with it has to be looked at by reference to the family unit as a whole and the impact of removal upon each member. If overall the removal would be disproportionate, all affected family members are to be regarded as victims.'

8.251 The UKBA operates a family reunion programme for persons who are recognised refugees or are benefiting from humanitarian protection in the United Kingdom with a view to reuniting them with their family members, including children.[714] However, only pre-existing families, defined as the spouse, civil partner or unmarried or same sex partner plus any children under 18 who formed part of the family unit at the time asylum was sought may apply to enter the United Kingdom under the family reunion programme.[715] Those falling outside these parameters may be permitted entry on compassionate grounds. In *Huang v Secretary of State for the Home Department, Kasmiri v Secretary of State for the Home Department*[716] the House of Lords observed that:

'Human beings are social animals. They depend on others. The family, or extended family, is the group on which many people most heavily depend, socially, emotionally and often financially. There comes a point at which, for some, prolonged and unavoidable separation from this group seriously inhibits their ability to live full and fulfilling lives. Matters such as age, health and vulnerability of the applicant, the closeness and previous history of the family, the applicant's dependence on the financial and emotional support of the family, the prevailing cultural tradition and conditions in the country of origin and many other factors may all be relevant.'

Domestic Law – Right to Maintain Contact

Contact following Parental Separation

(i)   Contact Right of Child not of Parent

8.252 In *M v M (Child: Access)*[717] Wrangham J made the following statement of principle in relation to the right to contact between a child and his or her parents:

'... the companionship of a parent is in any ordinary circumstances of such immense value to the child that there is a basic right in him to such companionship. I for my part would

---

713   [2008] UKHL 39, [2009] AC 115.
714   In respect of children see Immigration Rules (HC395) r 352D which sets out the requirements to be met by a person seeking leave to enter or remain in the United Kingdom in order to join or remain with the parent who has been granted asylum in the United Kingdom, those requirements being (i) is the child of a parent who has been granted asylum in the United Kingdom; and (ii) is under the age of 18, and (iii) is not leading an independent life, is unmarried and is not a civil partner, and has not formed an independent family unit; and (iv) was part of the family unit of the person granted asylum at the time that the person granted asylum left the country of his habitual residence in order to seek asylum; and (v) would not be excluded from protection by virtue of Art 1F of the United Nations Convention and Protocol relating to the Status of Refugees if he were to seek asylum in his own right; and (vi) if seeking leave to enter, holds a valid United Kingdom entry clearance for entry in this capacity.
715   See *ZN (Afghanistan)(FC) and others v Entry Clearance Officer (Karachi) and one other action* [2010] UKSC 21, [2010] All ER (D) 88 (May) in which the Supreme Court held that a parent need not be a 'current' refugee at the time an entry clearance application is made by any of their children who are under the age of 18 at the time of the application.
716   [2007] UKHL 11, [2007] 2 AC 167.
717   [1973] 2 All ER 81 at 85.

prefer to call it a basic right in the child rather than a basic right in the parent. That only means this, that no court should deprive a child of access to either parent unless it is wholly satisfied that it is in the interests of that child that access should cease, and that is a conclusion at which a court should be extremely slow to arrive.'[718]

These principles should also apply to sibling contact[719] and to contact with members of the child's wider extended family.[720]

(ii) No Presumption of Contact

8.253 There is no presumption of contact between a child and his or her parents in the Children Act 1989. The statute is careful to ensure that each case is dealt with by reference to the paramount nature of the child best interests assessed against a non-exhaustive list of factors to ensure that each order under the act is tailored to that child's particular needs.[721] The introduction of a 'presumption' into this process would militate against the welfare based analysis required by the Children Act 1989 and would undermine a rights based approach to issues of contact.[722] As Fortin pointedly observes, '[t]he assumption that the blood tie between parent and child has magical properties which, if enhanced by physical proximity, will inevitably produce a happy and long-term relationship certainly seems misguided'.[723] To ensure the rights of children are protected and promoted each case must be carefully considered on its own facts and determined on the basis of the applicable principles under the Children Act 1989, the ECHR and the CRC.[724] Notwithstanding this, the domestic courts have tended to commence their analysis upon the premise that contact to the non-resident parent is in the child's best interests. In *Re Bradford; Re O'Connell*[725] Wall LJ held:

---

[718] See also *Re S (Minors) (Access)* [1990] 2 FLR 166 at 170 ('access is the right of the child, not of the parent. The child has a right, even though his parents are separated and the child may be living with one and not with the other, to know his other parent'); *Re R (A Minor) (Contact)* [1993] 2 FLR 762 at 767 ('It is the right of a child to have a relationship with both parents wherever possible.') and *A v Y (Child's Surname)* [1999] 2 FLR 5 at 8 ('It is the child's right to have that relationship with her father, supported, encouraged and enlarged'). See also Holman J in *A v L (Contact)* [1998] 1 FLR 361 at 365 ('it is very important, if at all possible, for a child to grow up with some knowledge of and some contact at least with his natural father. This is a fundamental right of a child and it is ordinarily very much in the welfare of a child to grow up having some contact at least with both his parents').

[719] *Re S (Minors) (Access)* [1990] 2 FLR 166 at 170 ('access is the right of the child, not of the parent. The child has a right, even though his parents are separated and the child may be living with one and not with the other, to know his other parent. Even more so has a child the right to know his siblings, his brothers and sisters').

[720] *A v Y (Child's Surname)* [1999] 2 FLR 5 at 8 ('It is the child's right to have that relationship with her father, supported, encouraged and enlarged. It is also, in my judgment, the child's right to have a relationship with her paternal grandparents').

[721] CA 1989, s 1(1) and 1(3).

[722] Fortin, J *Children's Rights and the Developing Law* (2009) 3rd edn, Cambridge, pp 502–511.

[723] Fortin, J *Children's Rights and the Developing Law* (2009) 3rd edn, Cambridge, p 510.

[724] It is particularly important that courts do not simply 'rubber stamp' consent orders reached between parents on the assumption that such consent must mean the order is in the child's best interests (see Wall, N *A Report to the President of the Family Division on the Publication by the Woman's Aid Federation of England entitled 'Twenty-Nine Child Homicides: Lessons Still to be Learnt on Domestic Violence and Child Protection'* with particular Reference to the Five Cases in which there was Judicial Involvement (2006), paras 8.21 and 8.27 and *Practice Direction: Residence and Contact Orders: Domestic Violence and Harm* [2009] All ER (D) 122 (Jan)).

[725] [2006] EWCA Civ 1199, [2007] 1 FLR 530, para 70.

'The court starts from the premise that, generally speaking, the application of the welfare test in s 1 of the Children Act 1989 means: (1) that contact with a non-resident parent is in the bests interests of children; and (2) that it requires compelling evidence for such contact to be refused.'[726]

(iii) Contact and Domestic Abuse

8.254 The need to approach each contact application on its own facts on the basis of the applicable principles under the Children Act 1989 is particularly acute in cases where the parent seeking contact may present a risk of harm to the child. In the context of private law disputes, such risk of harm usually takes the form of domestic abuse. Fortin suggests children must have a right not to have contact of any kind with an extremely violent parent.[727] The caustic effect of domestic violence on children is certainly well recognised.[728] Within this context the domestic courts and legislature have developed a clear approach to cases of domestic violence.[729] Where the outcome of a contact application under s 8 of the Children Act 1989 may be affected by allegations of domestic violence the court must determine whether those allegations are proved. Where such violence is proved, it does not act of itself as a bar to contact but must be considered in the overall exercise of the court's discretion.[730]

(iv) Enforcement of Contact

8.255 The domestic courts take an increasingly strong line in enforcing the contact rights of children where one parent seeks, without objective justification, to frustrate the child's contact with the non-resident parent. In *Re O (Contact: Imposition of Conditions)*[731] the Master of the Rolls stated in clear terms that:

'The courts should not at all readily accept that the child's welfare will be injured by direct contact. Judging that question the court should take a medium-term and long-term view of the child's development and not accord excessive weight to what appear likely to be short-term or transient problems. Neither parent should be encouraged or permitted to think that the more intransigent, the more unreasonable, the more obdurate and the more unco-operative they are, the more likely they are to get their own way. Courts should remember that in these cases they are dealing with parents who are adults, who must be treated as rational adults, who must be assumed to have the welfare of the child at heart, and who have once been close enough to each other to have produced the child. It would be as well if parents also were to bear these points in mind.'

8.256 In *Re M (Contact: Committal Order)*[732] Ward LJ recognised that whilst the committal of a parent to prison is a potential remedy where a parent refuses to obey a contact order facilitating contact with the child's non-resident parent, it should be the

---

[726] Fortin points out that the research does not necessarily support to assertion that contact with the non-resident parent will generally be in the child's best interests (see Fortin, J *Children's Rights and the Developing Law* (2009) 3rd edn, Cambridge, pp 498–499 and 510).

[727] Fortin, J *Children's Rights and the Developing Law* (2009) 3rd edn, Cambridge p 507.

[728] See *Contact and Domestic Violence: The Experts' Court Report* [2000] Fam Law 615 and the broadened definition of harm in the Children Act 1989, s 31(10) as amended by the Adoption and Children Act 2002.

[729] See *Re L (A Child)(Contact: Domestic Violence) and other appeals* [2000] 4 All ER 609 and the Children Act 1989, s 16A and *Practice Direction of 3 September 2007 (Children Act 1989: Risk Assessments under Section 16A)* [2007] 2 FLR 625.

[730] *Re L (A Child)(Contact: Domestic Violence) and other appeals* [2000] 4 All ER 609. See also *K and S (Children)* [2005] EWCA Civ 1660, [2006] 1 FCR 316 per Thorpe LJ, para 27.

[731] [1995] 2 FLR 124 at 129–130.

[732] [1999] 1 FLR 810. See also *Re H (A Child)(Contact: Mother's Opposition)* [2001] 1 FCR 59 and *Re S (Un-cooperative Mother)* [2004] EWCA Civ 597, [2004] 2 FLR 710.

remedy of last resort.[733] Other options, including family therapy and changing the residence of the child[734] should be considered before an order for the committal of the parent is made. The court may, in exceptional circumstances, also consider utilising the provisions of s 37 of the children Act 1989 to order an investigation by the local authority as a prelude to the granting of an interim care order.[735] The court should not give up easily in seeking to ensure contact between a child and his or her non-resident parent, even in the face of strong opposition by the resident parent, always ensuring that an evaluation of whether the opposition of the opposing parent has an objective foundation and, where such a foundation exists, balance that against other relevant considerations.[736] By virtue of the Children and Adoption Act 2006, which arose out of a lack of realistic options for enforcement,[737] the courts now have a wider range of options to implement contact.[738]

Contact following Removal from Parents

(i) Contact following Removal into Public Care

8.257 Where a child is removed by the local authority and placed into care, the local authority has a continuing duty to ensure contact between the child and his or her parents and extended family. Where a child is being looked after by a local authority, whether subject to a care order or not, the authority shall, unless it is not reasonably practicable or consistent with his welfare, endeavour to promote contact between the child and his parents, others who have parental responsibility and relatives, friends and others.[739] Where the child is the subject of a care order, the local authority must allow the child reasonable contact with his or her parents.[740]

8.258 The word 'reasonable' implies contact which is agreed between the local authority and the parents or in the absence of an agreement, contact which is objectively reasonable.[741] The advantage of maintaining a link via contact where to do so is in the best interests of the child operates in respect of fathers just as much as it does for mothers.[742] The local authority cannot subordinate the welfare of the child by reducing or ending contact in order to make finding a permanent placement for that child easier.[743] The parents of the child, his or her guardian or a person in whose favour there was a residence order immediately before the making of the care order, may apply for an order for contact to a child in care.[744] The child may also apply for such an order.[745] In determining such an application the child's best interests are paramount and the court must consider the welfare checklist under s 1(3) of the Children Act 1989.

---

[733] See also *Re D (Intractable Contact Dispute: Publicity)* [2004] EWHC 727 (Fam), [2004] 1 FLR 1226 per Munby J, paras 56–57 and *Re S (Contact Dispute: Committal)* [2004] EWCA Civ 1790, [2005] 1 FLR 812.
[734] See *V v V (Contact: Implacable Hostility)* [2004] EWHC 1215 (Fam), [2004] 2 FLR 851 and *Re C (Residence Order)* [2007] EWCA Civ 866, [2008] 1 FLR 211.
[735] *Re M (Intractable Contact Dispute: Interim Care Order)* [2003] EWHC 1024 (Fam), [2003] 2 FLR 636 and *Re F (Family Proceedings: Section 37 Investigation)* [2005] EWHC 2935, [2006] 1 FLR 1122.
[736] *Re H (A Child)(Contact: Mother's Opposition)* [2001] 1 FCR 59.
[737] See *V v V (Contact: Implacable Hostility)* [2004] EWHC 1215 (Fam), [2004] 2 FLR 851.
[738] For a comprehensive treatment of contact in the domestic context see Pressdee, P, Vater, J, Judd, F and Baker, J *Contact: The New Deal* (2006) Jordan Publishing.
[739] CA 1989, sch 2, para 15.
[740] CA 1989, s 34(1).
[741] *Re P (Minors) (Contact With Children In Care)* [1993] 2 FLR 156.
[742] *Re G (Adoption: Contact)* [2003] 1 FLR 270.
[743] *Re H (Children)(Termination of Contact)* [2005] EWCA Civ 318, [2005] 2 FLR 408.
[744] CA 1989, s 34(3)(a). Other persons may apply with the permission of the court (CA 1989, s 34(3)).
[745] CA 1989, s 34(2).

8.259 The Children Act 1989 empowers a local authority to refuse contact between a child and his or her parents for no more than 7 days, provided it is satisfied that this is necessary to safeguard and promote the child's welfare.[746] Thereafter, any continued cessation of contact must be sanctioned by the court.[747] An order giving authority to refuse contact should only be made where matters are so exceptional and the risk so severe that contact must be stopped.[748] The court does not have power to make an order prohibiting a local authority from allowing contact between child and parent, only an order authorising the local authority to refuse contact.[749]

(ii) Post Adoption Contact

8.260 The Adoption and Children Act 2002, s 1(4)(f)(i) requires the court or adoption agency to have regard to the relationship the child has with relatives including the likelihood of any such relationship continuing and the value to the child of it doing so. Before making an adoption order the court must consider whether there should be arrangements for allowing any person contact with the child.[750] The domestic courts have recognised the importance of ongoing contact following the permanent placement of the child away from his or her birth family. In *Re E (A Minor) (Care Order: Contact)*[751] Simon-Brown LJ noted:

> 'In short, even when the s 31 criteria are satisfied, contact may well be of singular importance to the long-term welfare of the child: first, in giving the child the security of knowing that his parents love him and are interested in his welfare; secondly, by avoiding any damaging sense of loss to the child in seeing himself abandoned by his parents; thirdly, by enabling the child to commit himself to the substitute family with the seal of approval of the natural parents; and, fourthly, by giving the child the necessary sense of family and personal identity. Contact, if maintained, is capable of reinforcing and increasing the chances of success of a permanent placement, whether on a long-term fostering basis or by adoption.'[752]

Pursuant to s 26(5) of the Adoption and Children Act 1989 the court may hear an application under s 8 of the Children Act 1989 for a contact order when it determines an application for an adoption order. The courts thus have the power to make contact orders post adoption where such orders are in the interests of the child concerned.[753]

Domestic Law – Right to Alternative Care

8.261 A detailed account of the domestic law and guidance on alternative care in the form of extended family placements, foster care, adoption and residential care is extensive and a comprehensive treatment is beyond the scope of this work.[754] The

---

[746] CA 1989, s 34(6).
[747] CA 1989, s 34(4). Note that an order made under this section is not an order terminating contact but rather an order *authorising* the local authority to continue to refuse contact.
[748] *A v M and Walsall Metropolitan Borough Council* [1994] 1 FCR 606, [1993] 2 FLR 244.
[749] *Re W (Parental Contact: Prohibition)* [2000] 1 FLR 502.
[750] Adoption and Children Act 2002, s 46(6). The imposition on adopters of contact orders with which they are not in agreement is extremely unusual (see *Re R (Adoption: Contact)* [2006] 1 FLR 373).
[751] [1994] 1 FLR 146.
[752] See also *Re C (Minor) (Adoption Order: Conditions)* [1989] AC 1, *Re O (Transracial Adoption: Contact)* [1996] 1 FCR 540, *Re G (Adoption: Contact)* [2003] 1 FLR 270 per Ward LJ, *Down Lisburn Health and Social Services Trust v H* [2007] 1 FLR 121, para 44 per Lord Carswell and *SB v County Council* [2008] EWCA Civ 535, [2008] 2 FCR 185, paras 141–154.
[753] *SB v County Council* [2008] EWCA Civ 535, [2008] 2 FCR 185, para 154.
[754] For a complete account of the relevant law in this area see Hershman, D and McFarlane, A *Children Law and Practice* Jordan Publishing.

following areas of domestic law should be considered as the starting point when considering the right of the child to alternative care in the domestic context.

Extended Family

8.262 When local authorities assess the needs of a child for alternative placement, they must consider the possibility of placement with the extended family.[755] Before reaching a decision to take care proceedings, the local authority should have taken such steps as are possible to explore whether care for the child can be safely provided by a relative or friend, have assessed the suitability of possible arrangements and considered the most appropriate legal status of such arrangements.[756] When the court is considering the best outcome for the child, it must give weight to the right of the child to grow up within his own family unless to do so would not be in his best interests. Where the local authority seeks alternative care for the child it is for the local authority to demonstrate why a family placement is not in the child's best interests. If the court accedes to the case put forward by the local authority it must clearly articulate the risks presented by such a family placement.[757]

Foster Care

(i) Private Fostering

8.263 Private fostering arrangements[758] are subject to the *Replacement Children Act 1989 Guidance on Private Fostering*.[759] A local authority must ensure that the welfare of privately fostered children is being satisfactorily safeguarded and promoted by those with parental responsibility.[760] This of course depends on the local authority being aware that a child is privately fostered. A private foster carer must safeguard and promote the welfare of the child, protect the child from physical harm, comply with his or her duties under the Children Act 1989 and carry out certain duties in respect of the child's education.[761] A private foster parent has no right to retain the care of the child against the will of the person(s) with parental responsibility for the child, although whilst the child is in the care of the foster carer the foster carer may do what is reasonable in all the circumstances to safeguard and promote the welfare of the child, subject to the provisions of the Children Act 1989.[762] Even where the 'fostering' arrangement falls outside the definition of private fostering, those caring for the child will be subject to the duty to protect any child under 16 from unnecessary suffering or injury to health,[763] the common law duty to take reasonable care and not to act negligently in the care of the child and duties under the education legislation.

(ii) Local Authority Fostering

8.264 A child looked after by the local authority is a child who is either in the care of the local authority under a care order[764] or a child provided with continuous

---

[755] Revised Children Act 1989 Guidance and Regulations, Vol 1, Court Orders (2008) Department of Health, para 3.7.
[756] Revised Children Act 1989 Guidance and Regulations, Vol 1, Court Orders (2008) Department of Health, para 3.24.
[757] *Re G (Care Proceedings: Placement for Adoption)* [2005] EWCA Civ 896, [2006] 1 FLR 47.
[758] For the definition of 'private fostering' see Children Act 1989, s 66.
[759] DfES July 2005.
[760] CA 1989, s 67(1) and see the Children (Private Arrangements for Fostering) Regulations 2005, SI 2005/1533.
[761] Education Act 1996, s 576.
[762] CA 1989, s 3(5).
[763] Children and Young Persons Act 1933, s 1 as amended by CA 1989, Sch 13, paras 2–5.
[764] CA 1989, s 105(1).

accommodation[765] by the local authority for a period of more than 24 hours.[766] A local authority foster carer is a person who cares for a child looked after by the local authority unless that person is the parent of the child, a person who has parental responsibility or a person in whose favour there was a residence order in force immediately prior to the making of any current care order.[767] Local authority foster placements are subject to statutory guidance entitled *The Children Act 1989 Guidance and Regulations Volume 3* and *Volume 6*.[768] The local authority will be responsible for the child placed with a local authority foster carer.[769] The Care Quality Commission monitors the extent to which local authorities fulfil their regulatory requirements in relation to foster care.[770] A local authority foster carer must care for the child as if he or she were a member of the foster carers own family and promote his or her welfare and must not wilfully assault, ill-treat, neglect, abandon or expose the child in a manner likely to cause him or her unnecessary suffering or injury to health.[771] A foster carer does not have the right to change a foster child's name.[772] A local authority foster carer comes within the definition of 'parent' for the purposes of making an appeal to the Special Educational Needs and Disability Tribunal.[773]

Adoption[774]

8.265 The domestic statutory framework for adoption is provided by the Adoption and Children Act 2002 and associated secondary legislation. An overview of the legislation is provided by the *Adoption and Children Act 2002: President's Guidance* and the *Adoption Guidance*.[775] Whenever the court or an adoption agency is considering a decision relating to adoption of a child the paramount consideration must be the welfare of the child throughout his or her life[776] having regard to the matters set out in the 'adoption welfare checklist'.[777] The House of Lords has held that the balancing exercise under s 1 of the Adoption and Children Act 2002 does not differ in substance to the exercise which the court must undertake to ensure that the decision is compatible with Art 8 of the ECHR.[778] Section 1(5) of the Adoption and Children Act 2002 requires that, in placing a child for adoption, the adoption agency must give due consideration to the child's religious persuasion, racial origin and cultural and linguistic

---

[765] CA 1989, s 20.

[766] CA 1989, s 22(1). Fostering services may also be provided by independent fostering agencies (see Care Standards Act 2000, s 4(4)).

[767] CA 1989, s 23 and the Fostering Services Regulations 2005. A local authority foster placement with be subject to the Fostering Service Regulations 2002 and the Arrangements for Placement of Children (General) Regulations 1991 SI 1991/890. Note that where a child who is in the care of the local authority under a care order is placed at home with parents a person who has parental responsibility or a person in whose favour there was a residence order in force immediately prior to the making of any current care order that placement will be governed by the Placement of Children with Parents etc. Regulations 1991, SI 1991/893 and the Arrangements for Placement of Children (General) Regulations 1991, SI 1991/890.

[768] LAC (97)17.

[769] Fostering Service Regulations 2002, r 2(1) and the Arrangements for Placement of Children (General) Regulations 1991, r 1(2).

[770] Care Standards Act 2000.

[771] Children and Young Persons Act 1933, s 1 as amended by CA 1989, Sch 13, paras 2–5. See also CYPA 1933, s 11 with regard to the duty to protect the child from burning or scalding.

[772] *Re D, L, LA (Care: Change of Forename)* [2003] 1 FLR 339.

[773] *Fairpo v Humberside County Council* [1997] 1 FLR 339.

[774] For a comprehensive treatment of the domestic law on adoption see Swindells, H and Heaton, C *Adoption: The Modern Procedure* (2006) Jordan Publishing.

[775] DCSF (2005).

[776] See *Re D (A Minor) (Adoption Order: Validity)* [1991] Fam] 137, [1991] 2 FLR 66.

[777] Adoption and Children Act 2002, s 1(2) and s 1(4).

[778] *Re B (Adoption: Natural Parent)* [2001] UKHL 70, [2002] 1 FLR 196. See chapter 4 for the difficulties with this approach.

background.[779] Since 1 June 2003 the Hague Convention on Protection of Children and Co-operation with respect to Inter-country Adoption has had full effect in England and Wales.[780]

Residential Care

8.266 A child may be placed in alternative care in a 'community home' which homes are governed by the Children Act 1989 Part IV and provided by a local authority or voluntary organisation.[781] A child may be kept in secure accommodation in a community home pursuant to s 25 of the Children Act 1989 and the Children (Secure Accommodation) Regulations 1991[782] where the community home has been authorised for such use by the Secretary of State. A community home accommodating children must be registered as a children's home.[783] All children's homes must be registered in accordance with the Children's Homes Regulations 2001. Failure to register is a criminal offence.[784] In respect of children accommodated in children's homes the local authority has the duties set out in ss 22–24 of the Children Act 1989 and, in respect of children accommodated by a voluntary organisation, the duties set out in the Children Act 1989, s 62(1), (2) and (5). The management of children's homes is governed by the Children Act 1989, Part IV and the Children's Homes Regulations 2001.[785] The person carrying on the children's home will have specific duties towards the children accommodated under the Children Act 1989, s 64 and the Arrangements for Placement of Children (General) Regulations 1991.

Proper Review

8.267 Where a local authority is looking after a child by reason of their being accommodated by the local authority or the subject of a care order, the local authority must draw up an individual plan for the child being looked after and carry out regular reviews with the regulations and amended if necessary pursuant to s 26(1) of the Children Act 1989.[786] The planning in respect of the child should take place with the aim of safeguarding and promoting that child's welfare, preventing drift and focusing work with the family and child. The planning process should comprise the stages set out in the *Children Act 1989 Guidance and Regulations, Vol 4, Residential Care.*[787] The process of review should ensure that the child's welfare is being promoted and safeguarded in the most effective manner and should result in amendments to the individual plan if necessary. Any failure to implement a recommendation of the review process must be notified by the local authority to the Independent Reviewing Officer.[788]

---

[779] Generally, as to race and culture in this context see *Children Act 1989, Guidance and Regulations*, vol 3, paras 2.40 and 2.41.

[780] See the Adoptions with a Foreign Element Regulations 2005, SI 2005/392. See also the Adoption and Children Act 2002, ss 83–85.

[781] For the definition of 'voluntary organisation' see CA 1989, s 105(1). Where the home is provided by a voluntary organisation it may be designated a controlled community home under CA 1989, s 53(4) and Sch 4, para 3(1) (if the local authority is responsible for its management) or an assisted community home under CA 1989, s 53(5) (where the voluntary organisation is responsible for its management).

[782] SI 1991/1505. See **14.122** below.

[783] Care Standards Act 2000, s 1(2).

[784] Care Standards Act 2000, s 11.

[785] SI 2001/3967.

[786] Arrangements for Placement of Children (General) Regulations 1991 and the Review of Children's Cases Regulations 1991. Cases in Wales are governed by the Placement of Children (Wales) Regulations 2007 and the Review of Children's Cases (Wales) Regulations 2007. See also the Children (Private Arrangements for Fostering) Regulations 2005, r 8.

[787] (1991), paras 2.43–2.72.

[788] Review of Children's Cases Regulations 1991, r 8A.

8.268 Upon the making of a final care order, the court cedes jurisdiction to the local authority in relation to decisions concerning the child and may not thereafter interfere with those decisions unless a further application is made to the court. Particular difficulties arise where a local authority which is caring for a child under a care order seeks to change the care plan for the child in a manner not agreed by others holding parental responsibility for the child or in a manner antithetic to the child's interests. Traditionally, the remedy of the aggrieved parent was to apply to discharge the care order as a means of bringing to the attention of the court the disputed actions of the local authority. However, following the coming into force of the Human Rights Act 1998 in *Re S (Minors) (Care Order: Implementation of Care Plan)*; *Re W (Minors) (Care Order: Adequacy of Care Plan)*[789] the House of Lords held that:

> '... if a local authority fails to discharge its parental responsibilities properly, and in consequence the rights of the parents under Article 8 are violated, the parents may, as a longstop, bring proceedings against the authority under s 7 ... I say 'as a longstop', because other remedies, both of an administrative nature and by way of court proceedings, may also be available in the particular case ... Sometimes court proceedings by way of judicial review of a decision of a local authority may be the appropriate way to proceed. In a suitable case an application for discharge of the care order is available. One would not expect proceedings to be launched under s 7 until any other appropriate remedial routes have first been explored.'[790]

CONCLUSION

8.269 One of the oft cited objections to the concept of children's rights is that such rights risk the disruption of family life and the dilution of appropriate parental authority.[791] This view however is extremely difficult to square with a reading of the key human rights instruments which repeatedly emphasise the importance of family life and the need to balance the rights of children with those of parents. The CRC time and again stresses the importance of the family in the life of the child and the importance to the child of parental guidance.[792] The ECHR requires constant attention to the proper balance between the respective rights of the parents and the child.[793] The domestic courts have repeatedly sought to emphasise that the advantages of parental care and parental contact as the starting point in considering proposals for the child in the context of family breakdown and dysfunction. There can be little doubt that the substantive instruments which enshrine children's rights recognise the primacy of family life and that it must be protected.

8.270 Likewise, arguments that children's rights encourage the overreaching of State power are difficult to sustain in the real world. Gugenheim argues that keeping families free from State oversight will do more for children than encouraging litigation and judicial intervention,[794] citing Justice Brandeis famous ruling that:[795]

---

[789]   [2002] UKHL 10, [2002] 2 WLR 720, [2002] 1 FLR 815.
[790]   These principles will apply equally to children.
[791]   See for example Ross, L *Families and Health Care Decision Making* (1998) Oxford University Press. Alderson points out that the validity of this view depends on whether children's rights are viewed as 'zero-sum' (the more rights children have the fewer their parents can have) or 'win-win' (where everyone gains) (see Alderson, P *Young Children's Rights* (2008) Jessica Kingsley, p 85).
[792]   See Arts 3(2), 5, 7, 8, 9, 10, 11, 18, 20, 22, 24 and 27.
[793]   See **8.30** above.
[794]   Guggenheim, M *What's Wrong with Children's Rights* (2005) Harvard University Press, p 249.
[795]   *Olmstead v United States* (1928) 277 US 438.

'Experience should teach us to be most on our guard to protect liberty when the Government's purposes are beneficent. Men born to freedom are naturally alert to repel invasion of their liberty by evil minded rulers. The greatest dangers to liberty lurk in insidious encroachment by men of zeal, well meaning but without understanding.'

State intervention in family life must always remain an intervention of very last resort but Gugenhiem's generalisation regarding State intervention is at best naïve. The sad reality of the human condition is that some children suffer significant harm or are at risk of suffering significant harm by reason of family breakdown or dysfunction and the State is the appropriate, and indeed only, agency to address which has the will and the resources to address that issue. Within the context of this reality, and as Gugenheim himself recognises,[796] it is by the existence of and the proper application of children's rights that the necessary limits of State intervention can be properly prescribed to ensure the correct balance between personal freedom and State power is maintained, and maintained by reference to the needs of children as well as those of adults.

---

[796] Guggenheim, M *What's Wrong with Children's Rights* (2005) Harvard University Press, p 250.

Chapter 9

THE CHILD'S RIGHT TO A PRIVATE LIFE

'All significant truths are private truths'

T.S. Eliot

INTRODUCTION

9.1   Article 12 of the Universal Declaration of Human Rights stipulates that no one shall be subjected to arbitrary interference with his privacy. This right is reflected in Art 17 of the Covenant on Civil and Political Rights, Art 22 of the Convention on the Rights of Persons with Disabilities and Art 16 of the CRC. The right to privacy has not, historically, been much considered from the perspective of the child due to its apparent conflict with the concept of parental responsibility and the very nature of traditional family life.[1] Whilst the right to privacy can, at least in so far as it concerns personal privacy, give rise to complex issues in relation to children, this reluctance to consider the right to a private life from the perspective of the child is based on a restricted interpretation of the concept of privacy. Within the context of children's rights, the concept of privacy is in fact a wide one. It encompasses not only the narrow concept of personal freedom from intrusion or public attention but also, and importantly in relation to children, psychological and physical integrity, personal development and the development of social relationships and physical and social identity. As such, the child's right to a private life is crucial to the child's growth as a human being and must be considered a cardinal right of the child.

GENERAL PRINCIPLES

The Concept of Privacy

9.2   In their seminal article *The Right to Privacy*[2] Warren and Brandeis considered whether the law of the United States as it then stood could accommodate a right to privacy for the individual. They decided that:

'We must therefore conclude that the rights, so protected, whatever their exact nature, are not rights arising from contract or from special trust, but are rights as against the world; and, as above stated, the principle which has been applied to protect these rights is in reality not the principle of private property, unless that word be used in an extended and unusual sense. The principle which protects personal writings and any other productions of the intellect or of

---

[1]   Van Bueren, G *Child Rights in Europe* (2007) Council of Europe Publishing, p 63. For examples of such consideration see Michael, J *A Child's Right to Privacy or Open Justice* in Douglas, G and Sebba, L (eds) *Children's Rights and Traditional Values* (1998) Programme on International Rights of the Child, p 194 and MacDonald, A *Bringing Rights Home for Children: Transparency and the Child's Right to Respect for Private Life* [2010] Fam Law 190.

[2]   (1890) 4 Harv L Rev 193.

the emotions, is the right to privacy, and the law has no new principle to formulate when it extends this protection to the personal appearance, sayings, acts, and to personal relations, domestic or otherwise.'

9.3   In the South African case of *Bernstein v Bester*[3] Ackerman J described the concept of privacy as being graduated in its ambit:

'A very high level of protection is given to the individual's intimate personal sphere of life and the maintenance of its basic preconditions and there is a final untouchable sphere of human freedom that is beyond interference from any public authority. So much so that, in regard to this most intimate core of privacy, no justifiable limitation thereof can take place.[4] But this most intimate core is narrowly construed. This inviolable core is left behind once an individual enters into relationships with persons outside this closest intimate sphere; the individuals then acquire a social dimension and the right of privacy in this context becomes subject to limitation.'

9.4   The foregoing descriptions of privacy make clear that the concept of privacy extends well beyond the simple idea of personal freedom from intrusion or public attention.[5] In *R (Countryside Alliance) v A-G*[6] Lord Roger observed that 'the European Human Rights Commission long ago rejected any Anglo-Saxon notion that the right to respect for private life was to be equated with the right to privacy'. Summarising the position, Pannick and others conclude that 'the notion of privacy is a continuum, starting from an inviolable core of personal autonomy in a private context and radiating out (yet becoming more subject to qualification or justified interference) into personal and social relationships in the wider world'.[7]

---

[3]   (1996) (4) BCLR 449, (1996) (2) SA 751 (CC).

[4]   See chapter 10 below on the child's right to freedom of thought, conscience and religion.

[5]   In this context it is important to note that an act may not be considered private simply because it is not done in public. In *Australian Broadcasting Corp v Lenah Game Meats Pty Ltd* (2002) 185 ALR 1 Gleeson CJ explained the difficulty of distinguishing between public and private information or actions, observing that 'There is no bright line which can be drawn between what is private and what is not. Use of the term 'public' is often a convenient method of contrast, but there is a large area in between what is necessarily public and what is necessarily private. An activity is not private simply because it is not done in public. It does not suffice to make an act private that, because it occurs on private property, it has such measure of protection from the public gaze as the characteristics of the property, the nature of the activity, the locality, and the disposition of the property owner combine to afford. Certain kinds of information about a person, such as information relating to health, personal relationships, or finances, may be easy to identify as private; as may certain kinds of activity, which a reasonable person, applying contemporary standards of morals and behaviour, would understand to be meant to be unobserved. The requirement that disclosure or observation of information or conduct would be highly offensive to a reasonable person of ordinary sensibilities is in many circumstances a useful practical test of what is private.' Note that within the domestic jurisdiction the threshold test of privacy is one of 'reasonable expectation' rather than Gleeson CJ's 'highly offensive to a reasonable person' test (see *Campell v MGN Ltd* [2004] UKHL 22, [2004] 2 AC 457 per Baroness Hale, paras 135–137).

[6]   [2007] UKHL 52, [2008] 1 AC 719.

[7]   Lord Lester QC, Lord Pannick QC and Herberg, J *Human Rights Law and Practice* (2009) 3rd edn, LexisNexis, p 359.

THE CHILD'S RIGHT TO RESPECT FOR PRIVATE LIFE

The Child's Right to Respect for Private Life under the CRC

CRC, Article 16

9.5   Article 16 of the CRC provides as follows in respect of the child's right to a private life:

'1. No child shall be subjected to arbitrary or unlawful interference with his or her privacy, family, home or correspondence, nor to unlawful attacks on his or her honour and reputation.

2. The child has the right to the protection of the law against such interference or attacks.'

CRC, Art 16 – Ambit

9.6   Subject to the principles of best interests under Art 3 and evolving capacity under Art 5, the child's right to privacy under Art 16 of the CRC must be protected in all situations, including within the family, in alternative care and in the provision of all facilities and services.[8] For example, the concept of privacy will even extend to the design of institutions in which children reside.[9] The Committee on Economic, Social and Cultural Rights General Comment No 4 *The Right to Adequate Housing*[10] makes clear that 'adequate shelter' includes adequate privacy. The right to a private life is also vital in ensuring the efficacy of other rights of children, for example the provision of appropriate sexual and reproductive health services for young people as part of their right to survival and development.[11] The child's right to privacy will also encompass the child's beliefs. The *Manual on Human Rights Reporting*[12] states that:

'The respect ... for the right to privacy, as recognised in Article 16 of the Convention, implies that no child should be compelled to reveal his or her religion. This may assume a special importance as a means of preventing discrimination of children on the basis of their religion or of the religion of their parents, legal guardians or family members, as recognised by Article 2.'

---

[8]   Newell, P and Hodgkin, R *Implementation Handbook for the Convention on the Rights of the Child* (2008) 3rd edn, UNICEF, p 203.

[9]   See Art 3(3) of the CRC and Art 32 of the Rules for the Protection of Juveniles Deprived of their Liberty: 'The design of detention facilities for juveniles and the physical environment should be in keeping with the rehabilitative aim of residential treatment, with due regard to the need of the juvenile for privacy ...' See also UN Rules for the Protection of Juveniles deprived of their Liberty Rule 34 on private sanitary arrangements, Rule 35 on the possession of personal effects as a basic element of the right to privacy, Rule 60 the need for privacy for conversations with defence counsel and Rule 87(e) need for professionals to preserve the privacy of confidential matters learned as a result of their professional capacity. The UN Rules for the Protection of Juveniles deprived of their Liberty will be relevant to all residential placements (see Newell, P and Hodgkin, R *Implementation Handbook for the Convention on the Rights of the Child* (2008) 3rd edn, UNICEF, p 206).

[10]   Committee on Economic, Social and Cultural Rights General Comment No 4 *The Right to Adequate Housing* HRI/GEN/1/Rev 8, p 20.

[11]   Committee on Economic, Social and Cultural Rights General comment No 14: *The right to the highest attainable standard of health* HRI/GEN/1/Rev.8.

[12]   HR/PUB/91/1/ (Rev.1) p 436.

CRC, Art 16(1) – Interpretation

(i) 'Arbitrary'

9.7 In relation to Art 17 of the Covenant on Civil and Political Rights the expression 'arbitrary interference' is considered by the UN Human Rights Committee to extend to interference provided for under the law. The introduction of the concept of arbitrariness in Art 16 of the CRC is intended to guarantee that even interference in the child's right to privacy provided for by law should be in accordance with the provisions, aims and objectives of the CRC and should be, in any event, reasonable in the particular circumstances.[13] Thus interference in the child's right to privacy may be arbitrary even though it is lawful.

(ii) 'Unlawful'

9.8 In relation to Art 17 of the Covenant on Civil and Political Rights, the word 'unlawful' has been taken by the UN Human Rights Committee to mean that no interference can take place except in cases envisaged by the law, which law itself must comply with the provisions, aims and objectives of the Covenant.[14] It is likely that a similar interpretation would be applied to the use of the word 'unlawful' in Art 16 of the CRC by the Committee on the Rights of the Child.

(iii) 'Interference'

9.9 In interpreting the meaning of the word 'interference' in Art 17 of the Covenant on Civil and Political Rights the UN Human Rights Committee makes no distinction between interference by State authorities and interference from natural or legal persons.[15] The Human Rights Committee further makes the point that '[a]s all persons live in society, the protection of privacy is necessarily relative'.[16] These principles will apply equally to the application of the child's right to privacy under Art 16 of the CRC although in determining the level of protection to be afforded to the child's privacy, the child's status as a child and his or her consequent need for special protection and assistance[17] must be taken into account. In determining whether there has been 'interference' under Art 16 account must also be taken of Art 5 of the CRC which requires States Parties to respect the responsibility of parents and members of the extended family to provide appropriate direction and guidance in the exercise of the child's rights under the Convention.

Article 16(1) CRC – Application

(i) CRC, Art 16 – Privacy of Court Proceedings

Competing Rights

9.10 The child's right to privacy in relation to court hearings creates a friction between the child's right to a private life and the right to freedom of expression that ensures the administration of justice is transparent and accountable to all members of society. The right to freedom of expression has been described as the 'touchstone of all human rights'.[18] Accordingly, in protecting the child's right to a private life within the context of

---

[13]   Human Rights Committee General Comment No 17 *Right to Privacy* HRI/GEN/1/Rev. 8 p 181, para 4.
[14]   Human Rights Committee General Comment No 17 *Right to Privacy* HRI/GEN/1/Rev 8 p 181, para 3.
[15]   Human Rights Committee General Comment No 17 *Right to Privacy* HRI/GEN/1/1Rev.8 p 181.
[16]   Human Rights Committee General Comment No 17 *Right to Privacy* HRI/GEN/1/Rev. 8 p 181, para 7.
[17]   CRC Preamble.
[18]   UN General Assembly Resolution 59(1) of 14 December 1946.

court proceedings a careful balance has to be struck between the child's right to privacy and the freedom of expression necessary to ensure the transparency of, and public confidence in the administration of public justice.

Privacy in Criminal Proceedings

9.11   Article 40(2)(b)(vii) of the CRC requires that a child accused of having infringed the penal law should 'have his or her privacy full respected at all stages of the proceedings'. This will include ensuring that communications between a child and his or her legal advisers take place in conditions of confidentiality.[19] The Committee on the Rights of the Child has made clear that the provisions of Art 16 of the CRC in respect of the child's right to privacy will be applicable to all stages of the juvenile justice process. In its General Comment No 10 *Children's Rights in Juvenile Justice*:[20]

> 'The right of a child to have his/her privacy fully respected during all stages of the proceedings reflects the right to protection of privacy enshrined in article 16 of CRC. 'All stages of the proceedings' includes from the initial contact with law enforcement (eg a request for information and identification) up until the final decision by a competent authority, or release from supervision, custody or deprivation of liberty. In this particular context, it is meant to avoid harm caused by undue publicity or by the process of labelling. No information shall be published that may lead to the identification of a child offender because of its effect of stigmatisation, and possible impact on his/her ability to have access to education, work, housing or to be safe. It means that a public authority should be very reluctant with press releases related to offences allegedly committed by children and limit them to very exceptional cases. They must take measures to guarantee that children are not identifiable via these press releases. Journalists who violate the right to privacy of a child in conflict with the law should be sanctioned with disciplinary and when necessary (eg in case of recidivism) with penal law sanctions.'

9.12   In addition to the provisions of Art 40(2)(b)(vii) and Art 16 of the CRC, Rule 8.1 of the UN Standard Minimum Rules for the Administration of Juvenile Justice (the 'Beijing Rules') requires that:[21]

> 'The juveniles right to privacy shall be respected at all stages in order to avoid harm being caused to her or him by undue publicity or by the process of labeling ... In principle, no information that may lead to the identification of a juvenile offender shall be published.'

9.13   Exceptions to the principle that hearings in relation to children who are in conflict with law should be conducted in private should be very limited and clearly stated in the law.[22] Art 14(1) of the Covenant on Civil and Political Rights stipulates that:

---

[19]   Committee on the Rights of the Child General Comment No 10 *Children's Rights in Juvenile Justice* CRC/C/GC/10, para 50.

[20]   CRC/C/GC/10, para 64.

[21]   This will include records in respect of juvenile offenders ('Beijing Rules', r 21.1). Note that the Commentary to r 8 of the UN Standard Minimum Rules for the Administration of Juvenile Justice provides that 'Rule 8 stresses the importance of the protection of the juvenile's right to privacy. Young persons are particularly susceptible to stigmatisation. Criminological research into labeling processes has provided evidence of the detrimental effects (of different kinds) resulting from the permanent identification of young persons as 'delinquent' or 'criminal'. Rule 8 stresses the importance of protecting the juvenile from the adverse effects that may result from the publication in the mass media of information about the case (for example the names of young offenders, alleged or convicted). The interest of the individual should be protected and upheld, at least in principle.'

[22]   Committee on the Rights of the Child General Comment No 10 *Children's Rights in Juvenile Justice* CRC/C/GC/10, para 66.

'All persons shall be equal before the courts and tribunals. In the determination of any criminal charge against him, or of his rights and obligations in a suit at law, everyone shall be entitled to a fair and public hearing by a competent, independent and impartial tribunal established by law. The press and the public may be excluded from all or part of a trial for reasons of morals, public order (ordre public) or national security in a democratic society, or when the interest of the private lives of the parties so requires, or to the extent strictly necessary in the opinion of the court in special circumstances where publicity would prejudice the interests of justice; but any judgement rendered in a criminal case or in a suit at law shall be made public except where the interest of juvenile persons otherwise requires or the proceedings concern matrimonial disputes or the guardianship of children.'

The verdict and, if convicted, the sentence in respect of the child should be pronounced in public at a court session in such a way that the identity of the child is not revealed.[23]

Family Proceedings

9.14   Whilst there is no specific provision contained in the various international human rights instruments requiring family proceedings to be held in private, it is clearly established that those instruments support that proposition. Article 16 of the CRC when read with the best interests principle enshrined in Art 3 suggests that judicial proceedings under Art 9 of the CRC concerning the separation of children from their parents should be held in private.[24] The Committee on the Rights of the Child has stated that the principle articulated by Art 40(20(b)(vii) that the child has a right in criminal proceedings to 'have his or her privacy full respected at all stages of the proceedings' should also apply to family proceedings and where children are the victims of violence, which latter category must include family proceedings concerning the alleged abuse of the child.[25] As set out above,[26] Art 14(1) of the Covenant on Civil and Political Rights contains a specific exception in respect of the publication of any judgment in proceedings concerning 'matrimonial disputes or the guardianship of children'. Finally, Rule 3(2) of the UN Standard Minimum Rules for the Administration of Juvenile Justice (the 'Beijing Rules') extends the scope of those Standard Minimum Rules to encompass care and welfare proceedings in respect of children, providing that '[e]fforts shall be made to extend the principles embodied in the Rules to all juveniles who are dealt with in welfare and care proceedings'. The 'Beijing Rules' themselves call for such hearings to be conducted 'in an atmosphere of understanding'[27] and stress the need for privacy.[28]

9.15   It is also important to note that professionals and experts involved proceedings concerning children and their families will, in addition to any existing duty of patient or client confidentiality, be required by Art 16 of the CRC to protect the child's privacy. In its General Comment No 10 *Children's Rights in Juvenile Justice*[29] the Committee on the Rights of the Child stipulates that:

---

23   Committee on the Rights of the Child General Comment No 10 *Children's Rights in Juvenile Justice* CRC/C/GC/10, para 66.
24   Newell, P and Hodgkin, R *Implementation Handbook for the Convention on the Rights of the Child* (2008) 3rd edn, UNICEF, p 128.
25   Committee on the Rights of the Child *Report of the Eleventh Session* (1996) CRC/C/50/ Annex IX, p 80 and Newell, P and Hodgkin, R *Implementation Handbook for the Convention on the Rights of the Child* (2008) 3rd edn, UNICEF, p 203.
26   See **9.13**.
27   Rule 14.2.
28   Rule 8.
29   Committee on the Rights of the Child General Comment No 10 *Children's Rights in Juvenile Justice* CRC/C/GC/10, para 66.

'The right to privacy (art.16) requires all professionals involved in the implementation of the measures taken by the court or another competent authority to keep all information that may result in the identification of the child confidential in all their external contacts.'

(ii) CRC, Art 16 – Confidentiality of Advice and Counselling

9.16 The effective counselling of the child in respect of health matters requires privacy and confidentiality as does the opportunity to give informed consent.[30] In its General Comment No 4 *Adolescent Health and Development in the Context of the Convention on the Rights of the Child*[31] the Committee on the Rights of the Child notes that:

'In order to promote the health and development of adolescents, States parties are also encouraged to respect strictly their right to privacy and confidentiality, including with respect to advice and counselling on health matters (art. 16). Health-care providers have an obligation to keep confidential medical information concerning adolescents, bearing in mind the basic principles of the Convention. Such information may only be disclosed with the consent of the adolescent, or in the same situations applying to the violation of an adult's confidentiality. Adolescents deemed mature enough to receive counselling without the presence of a parent or other person are entitled to privacy and may request confidential services, including treatment.'[32]

(iii) CRC, Art 16 – Privacy of Information

9.17 Fried argues that the control over information relating to oneself is inherent in the right to privacy.[33] In its General Comment No 16 *Article 17 (Right to Privacy)*[34] the UN Human Rights Committee make clear that public authorities should only be able to call for such information relating to an individual's private life where the same is essential in the interests of society.[35] The Committee further observes that:[36]

'The gathering and holding of personal information on computers, data banks and other devices, whether by public authorities or private individuals or bodies, must be regulated by law. Effective measures have to be taken by States to ensure that information concerning a person's private life does not reach the hands of persons who are not authorised by law to receive, process and use it, and is never used for purposes incompatible with the Covenant. In order to have the most effective protection of his private life, every individual should have the right to ascertain in an intelligible form, whether, and if so, what personal data is stored in automatic data files, and for what purposes. Every individual should also be able to ascertain which public authorities or private individuals or bodies control or may control their files. If such files contain incorrect personal data or have been collected or processed contrary to the provisions of the law, every individual should have the right to request rectification or elimination.'

---

[30] See **5.118** above.

[31] Committee on the Rights of the Child General Comment No 4 *Adolescent Health and Development in the Context of the Convention on the Rights of the Child* CRC/GC/2003/4, para 7.

[32] The right to privacy will also be relevant to the implementation of Art 39 of the CRC by which State Parties must take all appropriate measures to promote physical and psychological recovery and social reintegration of a child victim.

[33] Fried, C *Privacy* Yale Law Journal (1968) 77, pp 475, 483.

[34] Human Rights Committee General Comment No 16 *Article 17 (Right to Privacy)* HRI/GEN/1/Rev. 8 p 181.

[35] Human Rights Committee General Comment No 16 *Article 17 (Right to Privacy)* HRI/GEN/1/Rev. 8 p 181, para 7.

[36] Human Rights Committee General Comment No 16 *Article 17 (Right to Privacy)* HRI/GEN/1/Rev. 8 p 181, para 10.

9.18 The protection conferred on the child in respect of his or her privacy under Art 16 of the CRC will likewise require that the child knows of the existence of the information stored about him or her, knows why such information is stored and by whom it is controlled, has access to such records and is able to challenge, if necessary, correct their content. The child should also know who else has access to the information and access by others must be limited.[37] In relation to children deprived of their liberty, Rule 19 of the UN Rules for the Protection of Juveniles Deprived of their Liberty provides that:[38]

> 'All reports, including legal records, medical records and records of disciplinary proceedings, and all other documents relating to the form, content and details of treatment, should be placed in a confidential individual file, which should be kept up to date, accessible only to authorised persons and classified in such a way as to be easily understood. Where possible, every juvenile should have the right to contest any fact or opinion contained in his or her file so as to permit rectification of inaccurate, unfounded or unfair statements. In order to exercise this right, there should be procedures that allow an appropriate third party to have access to and to consult the file on request. Upon release, the records of juveniles shall be sealed, and, at an appropriate time, expunged.'

(iv) CRC, Art 16 – Privacy of Correspondence

9.19 Pursuant to Art 16 of the CRC a child has the right not to have their correspondence, which will encompass both letters and more modern forms of communication such as telephone, e-mail, texting and instant messaging, interfered with arbitrarily or unlawfully. The contents of the Human Rights Committee General Comment No 16 *Right to Privacy*[39] in respect of Art 17 of the Covenant on Civil and Political Rights will apply equally in respect of children's correspondence subject to the best interests principle and the principle of evolving capacity enshrined in Art 5 of the CRC:

> 'Compliance with article 17 requires that the integrity and confidentiality of correspondence should be guaranteed de jure and de facto. Correspondence should be delivered to the addressee without interception and without being opened or otherwise read. Surveillance, whether electronic or otherwise, interceptions of telephonic, telegraphic and other forms of communication, wire-tapping and recording of conversations should be prohibited.'

9.20 Any arrangements permitting interference with a child's correspondence must be set out in law and must not be arbitrary, must be compatible with the other principles and provisions of the Convention and must be reasonable in the particular circumstances.[40] This will include correspondence for the purposes of Art 37(c) of the CRC which provides that 'Every child deprived of liberty ... shall have the right to maintain contact with his or her family through correspondence ... save in exceptional circumstances'.

---

[37] Newell, P and Hodgkin, R *Implementation Handbook for the Convention on the Rights of the Child* (2008) 3rd edn, UNICEF, p 209.

[38] See also the 'Beijing Rules', r 21(2) which provides that 'Records of juvenile offenders shall be kept strictly confidential and closed to third parties. Access to such records shall be limited to persons directly concerned with the disposition of the case at hand or other duly authorised persons.'

[39] Human Rights Committee General Comment No 16 *Right to Privacy* HRI/GEN/1/Rev. 8 p 181, para 8.

[40] Newell, P and Hodgkin, R *Implementation Handbook for the Convention on the Rights of the Child* (2008) 3rd edn, UNICEF, p 210.

(v) CRC, Art 16 – Protection of Honour and Reputation

9.21 Article 16(1) of the CRC stipulates that the child shall not be the subject to unlawful attacks on his or her honour or reputation. In its report on the 1996 Day of General Discussion on the child and the media, the Committee on the Rights of the Child noted that:[41]

> 'In their reporting the media give an 'image' of the child; they reflect and influence perceptions about who children are and how they behave. This image could create and convey respect for young people; however, it could also spread prejudices and stereotypes which may have a negative influence on public opinion and politicians. Nuanced and well informed reporting is to the benefit of the rights of the child.'

Article 16(2) CRC – Protection of the Law

9.22 Article 16(2) of the CRC provides that the child has the right to the protection of the law against interference with his or her privacy, family, home or correspondence or attacks on his or her honour and reputation.

The Child's Right to Respect for Private Life under the ECHR

ECHR, Art 8

9.23 Article 8 of the ECHR enshrines the right to respect for private life, home and correspondence as follows:

> '1 Everyone has the right to respect for his private and family life, his home and his correspondence.
>
> 2 There shall be no interference by a public authority with the exercise of this right except such as is in accordance with the law and is necessary in a democratic society in the interests of national security, public safety or the economic well-being of the country, for the prevention of disorder or crime, for the protection of health or morals, or for the protection of the rights and freedoms of others.'

Article 8, ECHR – General Principles

9.24 The general principles applicable to the operation of Art 8 of the ECHR are covered in detail in chapter 8 above in relation to the right to family life.[42] The general principles articulated in that chapter will also be applicable to the operation of Art 8 as it relates to the right to a private life and reference should be made thereto. In accordance with those general principles, the right to respect for private life under Art 8 will also ground positive obligations on the State to take steps to protect an individual child's right to respect for private life.

---

[41] *Report of the 11th Session* (1996) CRC/C/50 Annex IX, pp 80 and 81 and see Nicaragua CRC/C/15/Add.36, paras 17 and 34. See also Art 17 of the CRC which recognises the importance of the mass media in providing the child with access to information.

[42] See **8.172–8.180**.

Article 8(1), ECHR – Ambit

Ambit of Art 8 Right to Private Life

9.25 A child has his or her own right to respect for his or her private life under Art 8 of the ECHR, as distinct from his or her parents' right to respect for private life by reason of the child having a reasonable expectation of privacy in certain circumstances.[43]

9.26 The child's Art 8 right to a private life ranges far wider than the notion of personal privacy at common law and equity.[44] As already noted, in *R (Countryside Alliance) v A-G*[45] Lord Roger observed that 'the European Human Rights Commission long ago rejected any Anglo-Saxon notion that the right to respect for private life was to be equated with the right to privacy'. This means that, in so far as the private life of a child has a necessary boundary with activities undertaken in public, the child's Art 8 right to private life under Art 8 of the ECHR will extend to areas of communal activity. Within this context, in *Niemietz v Germany*[46] the European Court of Human Rights held that:

> 'The court does not consider it possible or necessary to attempt an exhaustive definition of the notion of 'private life'. However, it would be too restrictive to limit the notion to an 'inner circle' in which the individual may live his own personal life as he chooses and to exclude therefrom entirely the outside world not encompassed within that circle. Respect for private life must also comprise to a certain degree the right to establish and develop relationships with other human beings.'[47]

9.27 Within this context, the European Commission and the European Court of Human Rights has stressed that Art 8 protects a wide range of aspects of private life.[48] This will include both a person's personality and personal relationships.[49] In *Botta v Italy*[50] the European Court of Human Rights, holding that the State has a positive obligation to ensure respect for private life under Art 8, observed that:

---

[43] *Murray v Express Newspapers Plc* [2008] EWCA Civ 446, [2008] 2 FLR 599 per Sir Arthur Clarke MR, para 16 but see para 58 and Loughrey, J *Can You Keep a Secret? Children, Human Rights and the Law of Medical Confidentiality* (2008) 20 Child and Family Law Quarterly 312.

[44] Lord Pannick QC et al, *Human Rights Law and Practice* (LexisNexis, 3rd edn, 2009) and see **9.4** above. In *S and Marper v United Kingdom* (2008) Application Nos. 30562/04 and 30566/04 (unreported) the European Court of Human Rights said 'The Court recalls that the concept of 'private life' is a broad term not susceptible to exhaustive definition. It covers the physical and psychological integrity of a person. It can therefore embrace multiple aspects of the person's physical and social identity. Elements such as, for example, gender identification, name and sexual orientation and sexual life fall within the personal sphere protected by Art 8. Beyond a person's name, his or her private and family life may include other means of personal identification and of linking to a family. Information about the person's health is an important element of private life. The Court furthermore considers that an individual's ethnic identity must be regarded as another such element. Article 8 protects in addition a right to personal development, and the right to establish and develop relationships with other human beings and the outside world.'

[45] [2007] UKHL 52, [2008] 1 AC 719.

[46] (1993) 16 EHRR 97.

[47] In *Whaley and another v Lord Advocate* [2007] UKHL 53, [2008] SCLR 128 the House of Lords emphasised the words 'to a certain degree' in *Niemietz v Germany* when examining the extent to which the element of the right to a private life comprising the right to establish and develop personal relationships is protected by Art 8 of the ECHR.

[48] *Dudgeon v United Kingdom* (1981) 4 EHRR 149; *Sutherland v United Kingdom* (1997) 24 EHRR CD 22, para [56].

[49] Note however that just because a certain activity establishes relationships with others does not automatically mean that it will fall within the scope of private life for the purposes of Art 8 (see *Adams v Scottish Ministers* [2004] SC 665, paras 62–68).

[50] (1998) 26 EHRR 97.

'Private life, in the court's view, includes a person's physical and psychological integrity; the guarantee afforded by Art 8 of the Convention is primarily intended to ensure the development, without outside interference, of the personality of each individual in his relations with other human beings.'

9.28   The European Court has continued to develop this theme in relation to the ambit of the right to private life under Art 8 of the ECHR. In *Von Hanover v Germany*[51] the Court held that:

'[P]rivate life, in the Court's view, includes a person's physical and psychological integrity; the guarantee afforded by Art 8 of the Convention is primarily intended to ensure the development, without outside interference, of the personality of each individual in his relations with other human beings. There is therefore a zone of interaction of a person with others, even in a public context, which may fall within the scope of 'private life'... The Court has also indicated that, in certain circumstances, a person has a 'legitimate expectation' of protection and respect for his or her private life ... The Court reiterates the fundamental importance of protecting private life from the point of view of the development of every human being's personality. That protection – as stated above – extends beyond the private family circle and also includes a social dimension. The Court considers that anyone, even if they are known to the general public, must be able to enjoy a 'legitimate expectation' of protection of and respect for their private life.'

In *Pretty v United Kingdom*[52] the Court held:

'As the court has had previous occasion to remark, the concept of 'private life' is a broad term not susceptible to exhaustive definition. It covers the physical and psychological integrity of a person. It can sometimes embrace aspects of an individual's physical and social identity. Elements such as, for example, gender identification, name and sexual orientation and sexual life fall within the personal sphere protected by Art 8. Article 8 also protects a right to personal development, and the right to establish and develop relationships with other human beings and the outside world. Though no previous case has established as such any right to self-determination as being contained in Art 8 of the Convention, the court considers that the notion of personal autonomy is an important principle underlying the interpretation of its guarantees.'[53]

9.29   As to the limits of the extent to which the right to respect for private life operates within the communal sphere with which the child has contact or in which he or she operates in *R (Countryside Alliance) v A-G*[54] Baroness Hale stated that:

'Article 8, seems to me, reflects two separate but related fundamental values. One is the inviolability of the home and personal communications from official snooping, entry and interference without a very good reason. It protects a private space, whether in a building, or through the post, the telephone lines, the airwaves or the ether, within which people can both be themselves and communicate privately with one another. The other is the inviolability of a different kind of space, the personal and psychological space within which each individual develops his or her own sense of self and relationships with other people. This is fundamentally what families are for and why democracies value family life so highly. Families are subversive. They nurture individuality and difference. One of the first things a totalitarian regime tries to do is to distance the young from the individuality of their own families and indoctrinate them in the dominant view. Article 8 protects the private space,

---

51   (2005) 40 EHRR 1.
52   (2002) 35 EHRR 1, [2002] 2 FLR 45.
53   See also *X v Iceland* (1976) 5 DR 86; *McFeeley v United Kingdom* (1980) 20 DR 44; *Beljoudi v France* (1992) 14 EHRR 801 per Martin J.
54   [2007] UKHL 52, [2008] 1 AC 719.

both physical and psychological, within which individuals can develop and relate to others around them. But that falls some way short of protecting everything they might want to do even in that private space; and it certainly does not protect things that they can only do by leaving it and engaging in a very public gathering and activity.'

9.30　A child's reasonable expectation of privacy will be relevant, although not conclusive, in determining whether a particular activity of the child falls within the scope of 'private life' for the purposes of Art 8. In *Pay v United Kingdom*[55] the European Court of Human Rights held that:

'There is, therefore, a zone of interaction of a person with others, even in a public context, which may fall within the scope of 'private life'. There are a number of elements relevant to a consideration of whether a person private life is concerned in measures effected outside a person's home or private premises. Since there are occasions when people knowingly or intentionally involve themselves in activities which are or may be recorded or reported in a public manner, a person's reasonable expectation as to privacy may be a significant, although not necessarily conclusive, factor.'

Ambit of Child's Art 8 Right to Private Life

9.31　In respect of children therefore, the ambit of the right to a private life under Art 8 of the ECHR will operate to protect and promote the psychological and physical integrity of the child, their personal development, the development of their social relationships and/or their physical and social identity in addition to ensuring in certain circumstances personal freedom from intrusion or public attention in respect of their daily lives and correspondence.

Article 8, ECHR – Application

9.32　The categorisation of the elements of the right to a private life protected under Art 8 of the ECHR is an exercise capable of a number of solutions.[56] The categorisation adopted below is suggested as the most logical in relation to the child's right to respect for privacy having regard to the jurisprudence from the European Court of Human Rights summarised above.

Child's Private Life under Art 8 – Psychological and Physical Integrity

9.33　The child's right to a private life under Art 8 will encompass the child's psychological integrity, mental health and also his or her physical integrity.[57] In relation to psychological integrity or mental health, in *Bensaid v United Kingdom*[58] the Court observed that:

'Not every act or measure which adversely affects moral or physical integrity will interfere with the right to respect to private life guaranteed by Art 8. However, the court's case-law does not exclude that treatment which does not reach the severity of Art 3 treatment may

---

[55]　(2009) 48 EHRR 15.

[56]　See for example Moreham, N *The Right to Respect for Private Life in the European Convention on Human Rights: A Re-examination* (2008) EHRLR 44 who identifies the following elements of the right to privacy (a) freedom from interference with physical and psychological integrity, (b) freedom from unwanted access to and collection of information, (c) freedom from serious environmental pollution, (d) to develop personality and identity and (e) to live in the manner of one's choosing.

[57]　*YF v Turkey* (2004) 39 EHRR 34. See also *X and Y v Netherlands* (1985) 8 EHRR 235; *Costello-Roberts v United Kingdom* (1993) 19 EHRR 112 and *Stubbings v United Kingdom* (1996) 23 EHRR 213.

[58]　(2001) 33 EHRR 205.

nonetheless breach Art 8 in its private life aspect where there are sufficiently adverse effects on physical and moral integrity. Private life is a broad term not susceptible to exhaustive definition. The court has already held that elements such as gender identification, name and sexual orientation and sexual life are important elements of the personal sphere protected by Art 8. Mental health must also be regarded as a crucial part of private life associated with the aspect of moral integrity. Art 8 protects a right to identity and personal development, and the right to establish and develop relationships with other human beings and the outside world. The preservation of mental stability is in that context an indispensable precondition to effective enjoyment of the right to respect for private life.'

9.34 Physical integrity will include the child's right not to be subjected to corporal punishment falling outside the ambit of Art 3 of the ECHR[59] as the right to physical integrity will operate notwithstanding that the conduct in question may not attain the level of severity that would engage Art 3 of the ECHR.[60] Any interference in bodily integrity must be clearly prescribed by the law[61] and requires very careful contextual justification.[62] However, in cases where the Art 8 right to privacy is relied on in relation to compulsory medical treatment of patients lacking capacity, the State will be granted a wide margin of appreciation.[63] This wider margin of appreciation will also pertain in cases involving positive obligations under the Art 8 right to physical and psychological integrity.[64]

9.35 The right of the child to respect for physical and psychological integrity will, as a constituent of the right to respect for private life under Art 8, carry with it an element of positive duty which may involve the adoption of measures designed to secure respect for the child's physical and psychological integrity as an element of private life.[65] The concept of 'horizontality'[66] may give rise to such a positive duty even in the sphere of the relationships between the child and other private individuals.[67] These positive duties may extend to the provision of financial assistance[68] and information relevant to the protection and promotion of physical and psychological integrity.[69]

---

[59]   *Costello-Roberts v United Kingdom* (1993) 19 EHRR 112. See also *A v United Kingdom* (1998) 27 EHRR 611.

[60]   *Raninen v Finland* (1997) 25 EHRR 563.

[61]   *YF v Turkey* (2004) EHRR 715, para 43 ('any interference with a person's physical integrity must be prescribed by law and requires the consent of that person. Otherwise, a person in a vulnerable situation, such as a detainee, would be deprived of legal guarantees against arbitrary acts').

[62]   *Wainwright v United Kingdom* (2007) 44 EHRR 809, para 47 and *Herczegfalvy v Austria* (1992) 15 EHRR, para 82.

[63]   See *Matter v Slovakia* (2001) 31 EHRR 32, para 69. The court will require comprehensive evidence when deciding issues of competence and justification for treatment, including actual as opposed to hypothetical evidence of impact on mental health (*R (Wilkinson) v Broadmoor Special Hospital Authority* [2001] EWCA Civ 1545, [2002] 1 WLR 419 and *Bensaid v United Kingdom* (2001) 33 EHRR 205).

[64]   See *Osman v United Kingdom* (2000) EHRR 245. The margin of appreciation extends to the remedies available for breach (see *Stubbings v United Kingdom* (1996) 23 EHRR 213 'Article 8 does not necessarily require that States fulfill their positive obligation to secure respect for private life by the provision of unlimited civil remedies in circumstances where criminal law sanctions are in operation').

[65]   *Stubbings v United Kingdom* (1996) 23 EHRR 213 concerning a failure to institute adequate criminal and civil sanctions against child abuse (cited with approval in *Deep Vein Thrombosis and Air Travel Group Litigation* [2002] EWHC 2825 (QB), [2002] All ER 935, para 176). See also *X and Y v Netherlands* (1985) 8 EHRR 235, para 23 (applied in *R v G* [2008] UKHL 37, [2009] 1 AC 92); *August v United Kingdom* (2003) 36 EHRR CD 15, *Ivison v United Kingdom* (2002) 35 EHRR CD 20 and *R v G* [2008] UKHL 37, [2008] 1 WLR 1379, [2009] 1 AC 92, [2008] 3 All ER 1071, para 54.

[66]   See **2.85**.

[67]   *Osman v United Kingdom* (1998) 29 EHRR 245.

[68]   See *R (Bernard) v Enfield London Borough Council* [2002] EWHC 2282 (Admin), [2003] LGR 423, [2003] HRLR 111.

[69]   *McGinley and Egan v United Kingdom* (1998) 27 EHRR 1 and *Roche v United Kingdom* (2006) 42 EHRR 600.

9.36 The application of these principles to the lives of children is potentially very wide. All measures which interfere with the physical and psychological integrity of a child will constitute a *prima facie* breach of the child's right to respect for that private life, subject only to the existence of justification under Art 8(2). Thus, for example, where the presence of the media in court during proceedings concerning a child interferes with the psychological integrity of the child the presence of the media will constitute a breach of the child's right to a private life unless the exceptions set out in Art 8(2) apply.[70]

Child's Private Life under Art 8 – Personal Autonomy and Development

9.37 Article 8 of the ECHR guarantees the right of a person to shape who they are through personal choice as a constituent of the right to a private life. Thus a person can decide his or her sexual orientation, whether or not to drink alcohol,[71] decide whether or not to smoke,[72] decide whether or not to become a parent,[73] which family member to have appointed as a litigation friend,[74] and may even extend to choice of burial.[75]

9.38 Within the context of the best interests principle, the child's evolving capacity and the child's right to participate , the right to personal autonomy and development as an element of the right to private life raises difficult and potentially controversial issues in respect of children.[76] For example, the age of consent for sexual relations in the United Kingdom is 16 years old. Accordingly, for young people aged 16 and over choices concerning sexual relations, orientation and identity may lawfully fall to be made and will accordingly be treated as core aspects of the young person's private life.[77] At the same time, young people aged 16 to 18 may not wish to engage in sexual activity and as children will continue to benefit from the 'protective' rights that will apply to guard children and young people from inappropriate or unwanted sexual advances. In relation to younger children, as recognised by Baroness Hale in *R v G*,[78] whilst a child of 13 *may* be capable of fully understanding and freely agreeing to sexual activity, society enacts legislation to protect younger children and the moral ethos of society as a whole which renders such actions unlawful.[79] In the area of sexual relations, and other areas of self-determination, the extent to which a child may benefit from the right to shape who they are through personal choice as a constituent of the right to a private life will be dependent on the child being of an age and understanding to make an informed

---

[70]   MacDonald, A *Bringing Rights Home for Children: Transparency and the Child's Right to Respect for Private Life* [2010] Fam Law 190. Note that in such circumstances it would also be necessary to place in the balance the right to freedom of expression under Art 10 of the ECHR. See **9.54** below.

[71]   *Whitefield v General Medical Council* [2003] HRLR 243 but see also *R v Taylor* [2001] EWCA Crim 2263, [2002] 1 Cr App Rep 519.

[72]   *R (G) v Nottinghamshire Healthcare NHS Trust* [2008] EWHC 1096 (Admin), [2008] UKHRR 788, paras 98–109.

[73]   *Evans v United Kingdom* (2008) 46 EHRR 728 and *Dickson v United Kingdom* (2008) 46 EHRR 41. Note that it is still unclear whether or not Art 8 of the ECHR protects a person's wish to have an abortion.

[74]   *JT v United Kingdom* [2000] 1 FLR 909 and *R (M) v Secretary of State for Health* [2003] EWHC 1094 (Admin), [2003] 3 All ER 672.

[75]   See *Dödsbo v Sweden* (2007) 45 EHRR 581, para 23 ('The Court reiterates that the concepts of 'private and family life' are broad terms not susceptible to exhaustive definition. It notes the findings of the Commission that an applicant's wish to have his ashes spread over his own land fell within the sphere of private life. However, in that case, the Commission also found, given the personal choices involved, that not every regulation on burials constituted an interference with the exercise of this right') and see also *Estate of Kresten Filtenborg Mortensen v Denmark* (2006) Application No 1338/03 (unreported).

[76]   See for example *R v G* [2008] UKHL 37, [2008] 1 WLR 1379, [2009] 1 AC 92, [2008] 3 All ER 1071.

[77]   *X and Y v Netherlands* (1985) 8 EHRR 235, para 27.

[78]   [2008] UKHL 37, [2008] 1 WLR 1379, [2009] 1 AC 92, [2008] 3 All ER 1071.

[79]   *Dudgeon v United Kingdom* (1981) 4 EHRR 149.

decision within the context of the child's evolving capacity and best interests and upon the decision made being lawful according to legislative provisions designed to protect the child.

Child's Private Life under Art 8 – Personal Relationships

9.39 The right to form personal relationships with others is an aspect of the child's right to a private life under Art 8 of the ECHR. However, whether the formation of such relationships falls within Art 8 will be a question to be determined on a case by case basis. Just because a child undertakes an activity which establishes relationships with others does not automatically mean that the activity in question will fall within the scope of private life for the purposes of Art 8 of the EHCR.[80]

Child's Private Life under Art 8 – Personal Identity

9.40 The right to a personal identity as an element of the Art 8 right to respect for private life is dealt with in detail in chapter 7 above.[81] A child's reputation and honour will also form a constituent element of the child's right to a private life.[82] The positive obligations arising under Art 8 of the ECHR in respect of the right to a private life may require action be taken to correct an individual child's reputation after the same has been unjustly damaged.

Child's Right to Private Life under Art 8 – The Child's Image

9.41 In *Reklos and Davourlis v Greece*[83] the European Court of Human Rights considered a case in which a newborn infant had been photographed without his parents' permission by the official photographer for the clinic in which the baby had been born who had then retained the negatives. In relation to the concept of a person's image, the Court observed as follows:[84]

> '... a person's image constitutes one of the chief attributes of his or her personality, as it reveals the person's unique characteristics and distinguishes the person from his or her peers. The right to the protection of one's image is thus one of the essential components of personal development and presupposes the right to control the use of that image. Whilst in most cases the right to control such use involves the possibility for an individual to refuse publication of his or her image, it also covers the individual's right to object to the recording, conservation and reproduction of the image by another person. As a person's image is one of the characteristics attached to his or her personality, its effective protection presupposes, in principle and in circumstances such as those of the present case, obtaining the consent of the person concerned at the time the picture is taken and not simply if and when it is published. Otherwise an essential attribute of personality would be retained in the hands of a third party and the person concerned would have no control over any subsequent use of the image.'

---

80   *Adams v Scottish Ministers* [2004] SC 665, paras 62–68.

81   See **7.59–7.79**.

82   *Pfeifer v Austria* (2009) 48 EHRR 175, para 35 ('What is at issue in the present case is a publication affecting the applicant's reputation. It has already been accepted in the Convention organs' case-law that a person's right to protection of his or her reputation is encompassed by Article 8 as being part of the right to respect for private life ... The Court considers that a person's reputation, even if that person is criticised in the context of a public debate, forms part of his or her personal identity and psychological integrity and therefore also falls within the scope of his or her 'private life'. Article 8 therefore applies'). See also *W v Westminster City Council* [2004] EWHC 2866, [2005] 1 FCR 39, [2005] 1 FLR 816.

83   (2009) Application No 1234/05.

84   (2009) Application No 1234/05, para 40.

In finding a violation of Art 8 of the ECHR the court placed weight on the fact that the child had not knowingly or accidentally lain himself open to the possibility of having his photograph taken in the context of an activity that was likely to be recorded or reported in a public manner[85] nor had the parents at any time given their consent to the photographs being taken. The court further gave weight to the fact that the child was not a public or newsworthy figure and did not fall within a category which in certain circumstances may justify, on public-interest grounds, the recording of a person's image without his knowledge or consent.[86] However, holding that there is a positive duty on State parties under Art 8 of the ECHR to protect a person's picture against abuse by others even in the sphere of the relations of individuals between themselves, the key factor on which the court based its finding that there had been violation of Art 8 was the fact that the photographer kept the photographs without the applicants' consent and the baby's image was thus retained by another in an identifiable form with the possibility of subsequent use against the wishes of the person concerned and/or his parents.

Child's Private Life under Art 8 – Personal Privacy

Personal Privacy

9.42   Article 8(1) of the ECHR encompasses a general right to privacy, namely the opportunity to maintain a private life free of undue interference, comment, intrusion, recording or monitoring, in both private and, where appropriate, public spaces.[87] As with other elements of the Art 8 right to respect for private life, the general right to privacy guaranteed by Art 8 will give rise to a positive duty on the State to take steps to ensure the personal privacy protected by the Convention. The broad test of whether Art 8 will act to protect the private life of the child from intrusion by others is one of whether it can be said that the child has, in the circumstances of the case, a 'reasonable expectation' of privacy.[88] In *Campbell v Mirror Group Newspapers Ltd*[89] Lord Nicholls held that:

> 'Essentially the touchstone of private life is whether in respect of the disclosed facts the person in question had a reasonable expectation of privacy.'

9.43   In applying the 'reasonable expectation' test the court should consider (a) the location in which the activity in question took place or from which the information in issue was obtained,[90] (b) the identity of the aggrieved party, (c) the nature of the activity or information for which protection is sought, (d) how the information was gathered[91] and in particular whether it was obtained through a private or confidential relationship

---

[85]   *Murray v Express Newspapers plc* [2008] EWCA Civ 446, [2008] 3 WLR 1360, para 57 ('It seems to us that, subject to the facts of the particular case, the law should indeed protect children from intrusive media attention, at any rate to the extent of holding that a child has a reasonable expectation that he or she will not be targeted in order to obtain photographs in a public place for publication which the person who took or procured the taking of the photographs knew would be objected to on behalf of the child').

[86]   See *Krone Verlag GmbH & Co KG v Austria* (2003) 36 EHRR 1059.

[87]   Lord Lester QC, Lord Pannick QC and Herberg, J *Human Rights Law and Practice* (2009) 3rd edn, LexisNexis, p 386.

[88]   *Murray v Express Newspapers plc* [2008] EWCA Civ 446, [2008] 3 WLR 1360.

[89]   [2004] UKHL 22, [2004] 2 AC 457.

[90]   The fact that the activity in question takes place in a public space is a factor to be considered in the overall evaluation of whether there is a reasonable expectation of privacy and acts in public may be protected if there is (see *Peck v United Kingdom* (2003) 36 EHRR 719 and *Von Hanover v Germany* (2005) 40 EHRR 1 concerning the applicant's children).

[91]   The manner of observation in a public place will be relevant in this regard (see *PG and JH v United Kingdom* (2008) 34 EHRR 1272 and *Sciacca v Italy* (2006) 43 EHRR 400. See also *Rotaru v Romania* (2000) 8 BHRC 449 and *Amann v Switzerland* (2000) 30 EHRR 843).

or other covert means and (e) the intrusive effect of the gathering,[92] retention, use or publication of information and the nature of the alleged intrusion and its intrusive effect.[93] In cases involving children, the fact that the complainant is a child will be relevant to the application of the reasonable expectation test, the child having his or her own right to a private life as distinct from his or her parents and a reasonable expectation of privacy.[94] Note that this does not amount to a guarantee of privacy for the child. Once a reasonable expectation of privacy on the part of the child has been established the court must go on to consider the fair balance between the child's right to respect for private life under Art 8 and the media's right to freedom of expression under Art 10 of the ECHR.[95]

9.44   Subject to the satisfaction of the 'reasonable expectation' test, the child's privacy within a personal or private space will, subject to the provisions of Art 8(2) and balancing the right to freedom of expression under Art 10 of the ECHR, be protected by Art 8(1) as a reasonable expectation of privacy will arise in such spaces. Such spaces will include not only the home but the homes of friends,[96] telephone calls made in work premises,[97] private functions in potentially public places such as rented rooms in restaurants and bars,[98] prison cells[99] and custody suites.[100] The domestic courts consider that Art 8(1) will cover even prosaic conversations which take place in, and information concerning, such spaces.[101]

Personal Information and Personal Data

9.45   In *S & Marper v United Kingdom*[102] the European Court of Human Rights held that:

> 'The protection of personal data is of fundamental importance to a person's enjoyment of his or her right to respect for private and family life, as guaranteed by Article 8 of the Convention.'

In *S & Marper v United Kingdom* the Court held that the mere storing of data relating to the private life of an individual may amount to an interference within the meaning of Art 8. However, in determining whether in a particular case the personal information

---

[92]   For the proper approach to the relevance of the nature and effect of the intrusion compare the approach in *Campbell v Mirror Group Newspapers Ltd* [2004] UKHL 22, [2004] 2 AC 457, para 22 with the approach taken by the European Court of Human Rights in *PG and JH v United Kingdom* (2008) 34 EHRR 1272.

[93]   *Murray v Express Newspapers plc* [2008] EWCA Civ 446, [2008] 3 WLR 1360, para 36 ('As we see it, the question whether there is a reasonable expectation of privacy is a broad one, which takes account of all the circumstances of the case. They include the attributes of the claimant, the nature of the activity in which the claimant was engaged, the place at which it was happening, the nature and purpose of the intrusion, the absence of consent and whether it was known or could be inferred, the effect on the claimant and the circumstances in which and the purposes for which the information came into the hands of the publisher').

[94]   *Murray v Express Newspapers plc* [2008] EWCA Civ 446, [2008] 3 WLR 1360, para 57 ('It seems to us that, subject to the facts of the particular case, the law should indeed protect children from intrusive media attention, at any rate to the extent of holding that a child has a reasonable expectation that he or she will not be targeted in order to obtain photographs in a public place for publication which the person who took or procured the taking of the photographs knew would be objected to on behalf of the child').

[95]   *Murray v Express Newspapers plc* [2008] EWCA Civ 446, [2008] 3 WLR 1360, para 58.

[96]   *Armstrong v United Kingdom* (2003) 36 EHRR 30.

[97]   *Halford v United Kingdom* (1997) 24 EHRR 523.

[98]   *Douglas v Hello! Ltd* [2005] EWCA Civ 595, [2006] QB 125.

[99]   *PG and JH v United Kingdom* (2008) 34 EHRR 1272.

[100]   *Perry v United Kingdom* (2003) Application No 63737/00 (unreported).

[101]   *McKennitt v Ash* [2005] EWHC 3003 (QB), [2006] IP&T 605, [2006] EMLR 178 and [2006] EWCA Civ 1714, [2008] QB 73.

[102]   (2008) Application No 30562/04 (unreported).

retained by the authorities involves any of the aspects of private life for the purposes of Art 8(2) mentioned above, the Court will have due regard to the specific context in which the information at issue has been recorded and retained, the nature of the records, the way in which these records are used and processed and the results that may be obtained. In order to come within the ambit of Art 8(1) right to respect for privacy the personal information or data in issue must have the character of private information.[103] Whilst information concerning identity,[104] time in care,[105] medical history,[106] personal relationships[107] and private events may fall within the ambit of this requirement, the right to a private life under Art 8 will not act to protection information or data of an anodyne or trivial nature.

9.46   Data on individuals which is systematically stored, processed and disseminated by the State or by other individuals will also be encompassed by Art 8 of the ECHR.[108] This will include information held on child protection registers,[109] DNA,[110] information resulting from security checks,[111] information arising from surveillance[112] and information contained on the electoral register.[113] The individual has no automatic right to know what information is stored about him or her.[114]

---

[103]   Lord Lester QC, Lord Pannick QC and Herberg, J *Human Rights Law and Practice* (2009) 3rd edn, LexisNexis, p 392.

[104]   *Odievre v France* (2004) 38 EHRR 43 (note that this case has been heavily criticised in relation to the child's right to identity), *Venables and Thompson v News Group Newspapers Ltd* [2001] Fam 340, *X (a woman formerly known as Mary Bell) v O'Brien* [2003] EWHC 1101 (QB), [2003] 2 FCR 686; *Chief Constable of Greater Manchester v McNally* [2002] EWCA Civ 14, [2002] Cr App Rep 617 and *Ashworth Hospital Authority v MGN Ltd* [2001] 1 WLR 515 CA and HL at [2002] UKHL 29, [2002] 1 WLR 2033. Note that a parent has a right under Art 8 to know whether a child is (or is not) his or hers (see *Schoffman v Russia* (2007) 44 EHRR 741 and *Znamenskaya v Russia* (2007) 44 EHRR 293. See *R (Addinell) v Sheffield City Council* [2001] ACD 331 for limits on parent's right to information concerning their children.

[105]   *R (S) v Plymouth City Council* [2002] EWCA Civ 388, [2002] 1 WLR 2583.

[106]   See *Z v Finland* (1998) 25 EHRR 37, *MS v Sweden* (1997) 28 EHRR 313, *A Health Authority v X* [2002] 1 FLR 1045, *Ashworth Hospital Authority v MGN Ltd* [2001] 1 WLR 515 (Court of Appeal) and [2002] UKHL 29, [2002] 1 WLR 2033 (House of Lords), *Ackroyd v Mersey Care NHS Trust (No 1)* [2003] EWCA Civ 663, 73 BMLR 88, *Mersey Care NHS Trust v Ackroyd (No 2)* [2007] EWCA Civ 101, [2008] EMLR 1 and *Archer v Williams* [2003] EWHC 1670 (QB), [2003] EMLR 869.

[107]   See *A v B (a Company)* [2002] EWCA Civ 337, [2003] QB 195, para 11(xi); *X v Persons Unknown* [2006] EWHC 2783, [2007] EMLR 290; *CC v AB* [2006] EWHC 3083 (QB), [2008] 2 FCR 505 and *Brown of Madingley (Lord) v Associated Newspapers Ltd* [2007] EWCA Civ 295, [2007] EMLR 538.

[108]   See *S & Marper v United Kingdom* (2008) Application No 30562/04 (unreported) and Art 1 of the Convention for the Protection of Individuals with regard to Automatic Processing of Personal Data (Council of Europe ETS No 108). See also EC Directives 95/46/EC and 97/66/EC.

[109]   *R (Ellis) v Chief Constable of Essex Police* [2003] EWHC 1321 (Admin), [2003] 2 FLR 566, *J and P v West Sussex County Council* [2002] EWHC 1143 (Admin), [2002] 2 FLR 1192, *R v Local Police Authority in the Midlands, ex p LM* [2000] 1 FCR 736, [2000] 1 FLR 612 and *R v Chief Constable of North Wales Police, ex p Thorpe* [1999] QB 396.

[110]   *S & Marper v United Kingdom* Application 30562/04 (unreported) 4 December 2008 following the decision in *R (S & Marper) v Chief Constable of South Yorkshire* [2004] UKHL 39, [2004] 4 All ER 193, [2004] 1 WLR 2196.

[111]   *Hilton v United Kingdom* (1988) 57 DR 108.

[112]   *Klass v Germany* (1978) 2 EHRR 214; *Hewitt and Harman v United Kingdom* (1992) 14 EHRR 657; *Mersch v Luxembourg* (1985) 43 DR 34; *Leander v Sweden* (1987) 9 EHRR 433; *X v United Kingdom* (1982) 30 DR 239; *Murray v United Kingdom* (1994) 19 EHRR 193 and *Chare (née Jullien) v France* (1991) 71 DR 141.

[113]   *R (Robertson) v Wakefield Metropolitan District Council* [2001] EWHC Admin 915, [2002] QB 1052.

[114]   *Leander v Sweden* (1987) 9 EHRR 433. See also *Hewitt and Harman v United Kingdom* (1992) 14 EHRR 657); *Amann v Switzerland* (2000) 30 EHRR 843 and *Rotaru v Romania* (2000) 8 BHRC 449, para 43 ('... public information can fall within the scope of private life where it is systematically collected and stored in files held by the authorities. That is all the truer where such information concerns a person's distant past').

Child's Private Life under Art 8 – Correspondence

9.47 Article 8(1) of the ECHR specifically articulates a right to respect for correspondence. This right will be engaged in relation to the opening or censoring of correspondence,[115] the protection of correspondence after it has been received[116] and a refusal to send or deliver correspondence[117] or the dictation of the mode of correspondence.[118] The concept of 'correspondence' under Art 8(1) will include private telephone calls.[119] In *Andersson v Sweden*[120] the European Commission found that telephone conversations between a child and his or her parents for the purposes of contact constituted 'correspondence' for the purposes of Art 8(1) of the ECHR. Surveillance likely to record conversations or communications may also contravene Art 8(1) of the ECHR.[121]

Child's Private Life under Art 8 – Surveillance

9.48 In order for surveillance of an individual not to constitute an unjustified interference with the right to a private life under Art 8(1) of the ECHR there must be a legally certain basis for such surveillance. The more serious and intrusive the nature of the interference created by the surveillance the greater the requirement for legal certainty underpinning that surveillance.[122] This will require laws sufficiently clear to give citizens an adequate indication as to the circumstances in which authorities are empowered to resort to surveillance.[123] In *Copland v United Kingdom*[124] it was held that a statutory power to do anything necessary or expedient for the purposes of providing further education did not extend to justifying surveillance of students.

Child's Right to Private Life under Art 8 – Court Proceedings

(i)   ECHR, Art 6(1)

9.49 In *B v United Kingdom; P v United Kingdom*[125] the European Court of Human Rights, considering the right to a public hearing under Art 6(1) of the ECHR, held as follows in respect of the purpose of holding court hearings in public:

> 'The public character of proceedings protects litigants against the administration of justice in secret with no public scrutiny; it is also one of the means whereby confidence in the courts can be maintained. By rendering the administration of justice visible, publicity contributes to the achievement of the aim of Art 6(1), a fair hearing, the guarantee of which is one of the foundations of a democratic society.'[126]

---

[115] *Puzinas v Lithuania* (2002) Application No 44800/98 (unreported).
[116] *Warner v Verfides* [2008] EWHC 2609 (Ch), (2008) *The Times*, 6 November.
[117] *Faulkner v United Kingdom* (2002) 35 EHRR 686. See also *R (Nilson) v Governor of Whitmore Prison* [2002] EWHC 668 (Admin), [2002] All ER (D) 275 (Mar).
[118] *R (Hirst) v Secretary of State for the Home Department* [2002] EWHC 602 (Admin), [2002] 1 WLR 2929 (a case determined by reference to Art 10 ECHR).
[119] *Halford v United Kingdom* (1997) 24 EHRR 523, paras 53–58 and see *A v France* (1993) 17 EHRR 462.
[120] (1992) 14 EHRR 615.
[121] See *Khan v United Kingdom* (2001) 31 EHRR 1016; *PG and JH v United Kingdom* (2008) 46 EHRR 51; *Taylor-Sabori v United Kingdom* (2003) 36 EHRR 248 and *Allan v United Kingdom* (2003) 36 EHRR 143.
[122] *Kopp v Switzerland* (1999) 27 EHRR 91 and *Malone v United Kingdom* (1984) 7 EHRR 14 and *Hewitson v United Kingdom* (2003) 37 EHRR 31. See also *Liberty v United Kingdom* (2009) 48 EHRR 1, paras 62 and 63.
[123] *Kruslin v France* (1990) 12 EHRR 547 and *Weber v Saravia v Germany* (2008) 46 EHRR 5.
[124] (2007) Application No 62617/00 (unreported).
[125] [2001] 2 FCR 22, [2001] 2 FLR 261.
[126] See also *Sutter v Switzerland* (1984) 6 EHRR 272.

9.50   The European Court of Human Rights went on to point out in *B v United Kingdom; P v United Kingdom however* that Art 6(1) of the ECHR contains exceptions to the right to a public hearing in that it provides that:

> '... the press and public may be excluded from all or part of the trial ... where the interests of juveniles or the private life of the parties so require, or to the extent strictly necessary in the opinion of the court in special circumstances where publicity would prejudice the interests of justice.'

Within this context, in *B v United Kingdom; P v United Kingdom* the European Court of Human Rights considered that proceedings concerning disputes as to the residence of children following parental separation or divorce are prime examples of cases where the exclusion of the press and public may be justified in order to protect the privacy of the child and the parties and to avoid prejudicing the interests of justice, the court commenting that:

> 'To enable the deciding judge to gain as full and accurate a picture as possible of the advantages and disadvantages of the various residence and contact options open to the child, it is essential that the parents and other witnesses feel able to express themselves candidly on highly personal issues without fear of public curiosity or comment.'

To this end, the court did not consider that designating an entire class of cases as an exception to the general rule that proceedings should be heard in public contravened Art 6(1) of the ECHR provided that such measures were always subject to the control of the court.[127] The form of publicity given to any subsequent judgment in such proceedings must be assessed in light of the special features of the proceedings in question and by reference to the object and purpose of Art 6(1).[128] These principles will apply equally to proceedings concerning State intervention in the family in cases of alleged abuse of children and in criminal proceedings.[129]

(ii)   ECHR, Art 8

9.51   Article 8(1) of the ECHR may also require the exclusion of the press and public from all or part of proceedings concerning children having regard to the child's right to a private life under Art 8(1). Measures which interfere with the psychological and physical integrity, the personal development, the development of social relationships and the physical and social identity that comprise cardinal elements of a child's 'private life' will constitute a breach of the right to respect for that private life save where such interference is justified under Art 8(2) of the ECHR.[130] Where the admission of the press of public to proceedings concerning children has the effect of interfering with the child's psychological and physical integrity, personal development, development of social relationships and physical and social identity[131] such admission will constitute a breach of the child's right to respect for private life under Art 8(1) requiring justification under Art 8(2).[132]

---

[127]   But see the dissenting judgement of Judge Loucaides joined by Judge Tulkens.
[128]   *Sutter v Switzerland* (1984) 6 EHRR 272.
[129]   *Doorson v Netherlands* (1996) 22 EHRR 300, *Jasper v United Kingdom* (2000) 30 EHRR 441, *Z v Finland* (1998) 25 EHRR 371 and *T v United Kingdom* (2000) 30 EHRR 121.
[130]   See **9.26** above.
[131]   See Sturge, C *'Transparency in Family Proceedings'* [2006] Fam Law 409.
[132]   See MacDonald, A *Bringing Rights Home for Children: Transparency and the Child's Right to Respect for Private Life* [2010] Fam Law 190.

(iii)   ECHR, Art 10

9.52   Once again, as with the right to privacy under Art 16 of the CRC, there is a friction between the exceptions provided for in Art 6(1) of the ECHR, the child's right to respect for private life under Art 8(1) and the right to freedom of expression under Art 10 of the ECHR, the latter article seeking to ensure *inter alia* that the administration of justice is transparent and accountable to all members of society in the manner articulated by the European Court of Human Rights in *B v United Kingdom; P v United Kingdom*.[133] As such, in considering the extent to which the exclusion of the press and public from judicial proceedings concerning children is justified under the exceptions in Art 6(1) and/or Art 8 a balance must be struck between the requirements of those provisions and Art 10 of the ECHR.

9.53   In the domestic case of *Re S (Identification: Restrictions on Publication)*[134] the House of Lords stipulated the approach to be taken in cases where the dilemma posed is whether a child is entitled to have his right to respect for private life protected or whether the restriction of the right to freedom of expression which such protection involves cannot be justified. The balancing exercise to be carried out between Arts 8 and 10 when considering this dilemma was described by Lord Steyn as follows:

> 'First, neither article has as such precedence over the other. Secondly, where the values under the two articles are in conflict, an intense focus on the comparative importance of the specific rights being claimed in the individual case is necessary. Thirdly, the justifications for interfering with or restricting each right must be taken into account. Finally, the proportionality test must be applied to each. For convenience, I will call this the ultimate balancing test.'

9.54   In carrying out this balancing exercise, it should not be forgotten that children too have the right to freedom of expression under Art 10. The exercise of this right by children is particularly valuable when it comes to the need for a dialogue between vulnerable children and professionals, including the court, which communicative activity is in principle within the scope of Art 10 of the ECHR.[135] Measures which act to prevent or restrict the disclosure by children of matters detrimental to their welfare must accordingly be justified by reference to Art 10(2). In this regard, it is suggested that the curtailment by reason of the fear of publication of the child's freedom of expression within investigative and therapeutic scenarios can itself amount to a breach of the child's rights under Art 10.

The Child's Right to Respect for Private Life under European Union Law

9.55   Article 7 of the European Charter of Fundamental Rights provides as follows in respect of the right to family life:

> 'Everyone has the right to respect for his or her private and family life, home and communications.'

The right to privacy guaranteed by Art 7 of the European Charter of Fundamental Rights corresponds with that enshrined in Art 8 of the European Convention on

---

[133]   See **9.49** above.
[134]   [2004] UKHL 47, [2005] 1 FLR 591.
[135]   *Belfast City Council v Miss Behavin' Ltd* [2007] UKHL 19, [2007] 1 WLR 1420.

Human Rights and, in accordance with Art 52(3) of the European Charter,[136] the meaning and scope of the rights under Art 7 is the same as that under the corresponding Art 8 of the ECHR. As such, the limitations that are permitted by Art 8(2) of the ECHR in respect to the right to a private life will be permitted in respect of the rights under Art 7 of the Charter.[137]

The Child's Right to a Private Life under other Regional Instruments

American Convention on Human Rights

9.56   Article 11 of the American Convention on Human Rights provides as follows in respect of the right to privacy:

> '1. Everyone has the right to have his honor respected and his dignity recognised.
>
> 2. No one may be the object of arbitrary or abusive interference with his private life, his family, his home, or his correspondence, or of unlawful attacks on his honor or reputation.
>
> 3. Everyone has the right to the protection of the law against such interference or attacks.'

9.57   The right to privacy guaranteed by this provision covers, in addition to the protection against publicity, the physical and moral integrity of the person. The object of Art 11 is to protect the individual against arbitrary interference by public officials. It also requires the state to adopt all necessary legislation in order to ensure this provision's effectiveness. In *X and Y v Argentina*[138] the Inter-American Court of Human Rights held that the right to privacy guarantees that each individual has a sphere into which no one can intrude, a zone of activity which is wholly his or her own and that, in this sense, the various guarantees throughout the Convention which protect the sanctity of the person create zones of privacy. In his dissenting judgment in *Yakye Axa Indigenous Community v Paraguay*[139] Judge Burelli held that the Art 11 right to privacy protected the culture of, and ensures respect for the integrity of the values, practices and institutions of members of, ethnic and cultural groups.[140] Note that the implementation of Art 8(5) of the ACHR[141] must take into account the privacy of the child, without diminishing either the right of the parties to defence or the transparency of judicial actions and avoiding absolute secrecy of what occurs during the proceedings, especially with respect to the parties. When minors are involved in proceedings, publicity must be limited to benefit their dignity or privacy, and in situations where debate of the case may have negative consequences or lead to stigmatisation.[142]

---

[136]   Article 52(3) of the Charter provides that 'Insofar as this Charter contains rights which correspond to rights guaranteed by the Convention for the Protection of Human Rights and Fundamental Freedoms, the meaning and scope of those rights shall be the same as those laid down by the said Convention. This provision shall not prevent Union law providing more extensive protection.'

[137]   See **8.177** above.

[138]   Report No 38/96 Case 10.506 Argentina.

[139]   Case 12.313.

[140]   See also Report No 31/96 Case 10.526 Guatemala (1996).

[141]   Article 8(5) provides that 'Criminal proceedings shall be public, except insofar as may be necessary to protect the interests of justice.'

[142]   Inter-American Court of Human Rights *Advisory Opinion on the Legal Status and Human Rights of the Child* OC-17/2002, para 134.

African Charter on the Rights and Welfare of the Child

9.58 Article 10 if the African Charter on the Rights and Welfare of the Child stipulates that:

> 'No child shall be subject to arbitrary or unlawful interference with his privacy, family home or correspondence, or to the attacks upon his honour or reputation, provided that parents or legal guardians shall have the right to exercise reasonable supervision over the conduct of their children. The child has the right to the protection of the law against such interference or attacks.'

The African Youth Charter

9.59 Article 7 of the African Youth Charter provides that 'No young person shall be subject to the arbitrary or unlawful interference with his/her privacy, residence or correspondence, or to attacks upon his/her honour or reputation'.

Revised Arab Charter on Human Rights

9.60 Article 21 of the Revised Arab Charter on Human Rights provides that no-one shall be subjected to arbitrary or unlawful interference with regard to his privacy, family, home or correspondence, nor to unlawful attacks on his honour or his reputation and that everyone has the right to the protection of the law against such interference or attacks.

The Child's Right to a Private Life under Domestic Law

Article 8 and Respect for Privacy in Domestic Law

Confidentiality and the Right to Respect for Privacy

(i) The Domestic Principle of Confidentiality

9.61 The domestic principal that confidentiality is capable of protection by the courts has a long history. In *The Duke of Queensbury v Shebbeare*[143] the court restrained a printer from publishing confidential information and in *Thompson v Stanhope*[144] the court restrained the publication of family letters. In the famous case of *Prince Albert v Strange*[145] the court restrained the defendant from publishing a catalogue of private etchings made by Queen Victoria and Prince Albert. In *Saltman Engineering Co Ltd. v Campbell Engineering Co Ltd*[146] the Court of Appeal confirmed the existence of an equitable doctrine of confidence.

9.62 Within the context of the domestic law on confidentiality confidential information is broadly defined as information intended to be kept secret. The essential features of confidential information are its limited public availability[147] and its specific character, which must be capable of clear definition.[148] Further clarification on the

---

[143] (1758) 2 Eden 329.
[144] (1774) Amb 737.
[145] [1894] 1 Mac & G 25.
[146] (1948) 65 RPC 203, [1963] 3 All ER 413.
[147] *Robb v Green* [1895] 2 QB 1 at 18.
[148] *Prince Albert v Strange* [1894] 1 Mac & G 25.

meaning of 'confidential information' can be found in a number of domestic statutes.[149] Where information is confidential, the confidentiality belongs to the person about whom information is kept and not the keeper of the information.[150] Historically, in addition to the information being confidential in quality, the necessary ingredients for an action for breach of confidence were that the information was imparted so as to import an obligation of confidence and that the information was put to unauthorised use to the detriment of the party communicating it.[151] The duty of confidentiality was qualified where the confidential information has already entered the public domain, where the information was useless or trivial and where the public interest in the preservation of confidentiality was outweighed by the public interest in the disclosure of the confidential information in question.[152]

(ii)   Confidentiality and Art 8 ECHR

9.63   Obligations in confidence continue to be of importance in relation to confidential information held by public agencies and the right not to have confidential information published by such agencies save in specific and defined circumstances is well established[153] However, Art 8 of the ECHR has acted to modify the domestic law on confidentiality.[154] In *A v B (a company)*[155] the Court of Appeal recognised that in domestic cases involving issues of confidentiality, having regard to the ECHR and the Human Rights Act 1998, s 12 a balance must now be struck between the protection of the privacy of the claimant and the importance of the defendant's right to freedom of expression, to which freedom must be attached particular importance. In *A v B* the Court of Appeal considered that this balancing exercise could be carried out within an action for breach of confidence, the Court holding that if there is an intrusion within the context of a situation where a person can reasonably expect his or her privacy to be respected then that intrusion will be capable of giving rise to liability in an action for breach of confidence unless the intrusion can be justified.[156] Within this context, the Court of Appeal saw no need for this approach to lead to a new domestic right to privacy, Lord Woolf observing:

> '[Articles 8 and 10] have provided new parameters within which the court will decide, in an action for breach of confidence, whether a person is entitled to have his privacy protected by the court or whether the restriction of freedom of expression which such protection involves cannot be justified. The court's approach to the issues which the applications raise has been modified because under s 6 of the 1998 Act, the court, as a public authority, is required not to act 'in a way which is incompatible with a Convention right'. The court is able to achieve this by absorbing the rights which arts 8 and 10 protect into the long-established action for breach of confidence. This involves giving a new strength and breadth to the action so that it accommodates the requirements of those articles ... It is most unlikely that any purpose will be served by a judge seeking to decide whether there exists a new cause of action in tort which protects privacy. In the great majority of situations, if not all situations, where the protection of privacy is justified, relating to events after the 1998 Act came into force, an action for breach of confidence now will, where this is appropriate, provide the necessary

---

149   See for example the Health and Social Care Act 2001, s 60(9), the Local Government Act 1972, s 100A(3) and the Financial Services and Markets Act 2000, Part IV.
150   *Ashworth Hospital Authority v MGN* [2002] UKHL 29, para 63.
151   *Coco v A.N.Clark (Engineers) Ltd* (1969) R.P.C. 41.
152   *Attorney-General v Observer Ltd; A-G v Times Newspapers Ltd* [1990] 1 AC 109 (the 'Spycatcher' case).
153   See Halsbury's Laws, Vol 8(2), para 110 and *Helewell v Chief Constable of Derbyshire* [1995] 4 All ER 473 and *Marcel v Metropolitan Police Commissioner* [1992] Ch 225.
154   *Campbell v Mirror Group Newspapers Ltd* [2004] UKHL 22, [2004] 2 AC 457, paras 42–43. See also *A v B (a company)* [2002] EWCA Civ 337, [2003] QB 195, para 11.
155   [2002] EWCA Civ 337, [2003] QB 195.
156   See also *Venables v News Group Newspapers Ltd* [2001] 1 All ER 908.

protection. This means that at first instance it can be readily accepted that it is not necessary to tackle the vexed question of whether there is a separate cause of action based upon a new tort involving the infringement of privacy.'

9.64 This approach was endorsed and reinforced by the House of Lords in *Campbell v Mirror Group Newspapers Ltd*[157] in which case the House of Lords recognised that the effect of Art 8 and Art 10 of the ECHR was that the right to privacy which lies at the heart of an action for breach of confidence has to be balanced against the right to freedom of expression under Art 10 of the ECHR, which in turn must be balanced against the right to respect for private life under Art 8. In achieving this balance, the House of Lords made clear, within the context of the historical approach taken in actions for breach of confidence, that it is no longer a relationship 'importing an obligation of confidence' which will dictate the outcome of an action for breach of confidence[158] but rather an examination of nature of the information itself and the proper balance between the competing rights of the claimant and defendant.[159] The exercise of balancing the requirements of Art 8 and Art 10 of the ECHR must begin where the person publishing the information knows or ought to know that there is a 'reasonable expectation' that the information in question will be kept confidential. In balancing the rights under Arts 8 and 10 neither right takes precedence over the other.[160] As noted above, in *Re S (Identification: Restrictions on Publication)*[161] concerning the publication of information in respect of proceedings involving children the House of Lords stipulated the general approach to the required balancing exercise as between Arts 8 and 10 of the ECHR, Lord Steyn holding that:

'First, neither Art has as such precedence over the other. Secondly, where the values under the two Arts are in conflict, an intense focus on the comparative importance of the specific rights being claimed in the individual case is necessary. Thirdly, the justifications for interfering with or restricting each right must be taken into account. Finally, the proportionality test must be applied to each. For convenience, I will call this the ultimate balancing test.'

9.65 Thus issues of privacy concerning children in the domestic sphere are now primarily dealt with by reference to Art 8(1) of the ECHR within the framework of the domestic law on confidentiality.[162] Importantly, the domestic courts have clearly recognised that under Art 8(1) of the ECHR a child has his or her *own* right to respect for private life as distinct from that of his or her parents and a reasonable expectation of privacy.[163] Where parents seek to waive their child's right to privacy Thorpe LJ held in *Re G (Celebrities: Publicity)*[164] that 'there can be no doubt that the court has jurisdiction in personam to restrain any act by a parent that if unrestrained would or might adversely affect the welfare of the child the subject of the proceedings'.

---

[157] [2004] UKHL 22, [2004] 2 AC 457, Lord Nicholls of Birkenhead stating that 'The time has come to recognise that the values enshrined in arts 8 and 10 are now part of the cause of action for breach of confidence.

[158] In *Campbell v Mirror Group Newspapers Ltd* Lord Nicholls held that the essence of the tort of breach of confidence is, in the context of information concerning an individual's private life, better encapsulated as 'misuse of private information', which tort affords respect for one aspect of an individual's privacy.

[159] See also *A-G v Guardian Newspapers (No 2)* [1988] 3 All ER 545, 1 AC 109.

[160] See Resolution 1165 of 1998 of the Parliamentary Assembly of the Council of Europe, para 10.

[161] [2004] UKHL 47, [2005] 1 FLR 591.

[162] *Campbell v Mirror Group Newspapers Ltd* [2004] UKHL 22, [2004] 2 AC 457, paras 42–43. See also *A v B (a company)* [2002] EWCA Civ 337, [2003] QB 195, para 11.

[163] *Murray v Express Newspapers Plc* [2008] EWCA Civ 446, [2008] 2 FLR 599. See also *Ambrisiadou v Coward* [2010] EWHC 1794 (QB), [2010] 2 FLR 1775.

[164] [1999] 1 FLR 409 at 414–415.

9.66   The application of Art 8 of the ECHR by the domestic courts in cases concerning physical and psychological integrity, personal autonomy and development, identity and personal privacy of children are dealt with above at **9.32–9.54**. In the following section, further areas touching and concerning the privacy of children under the domestic law are considered.

Child's Right to Respect for Privacy in Domestic Law

Privacy of Information in Domestic Law

(i)   Medical Records

9.67   A doctor is under an obligation of confidence to his patient with regard to personal information acquired for the purpose of treatment and must not disclose it to others unless (a) the patient consents or (b) the doctor can justify the disclosure in the absence of consent. It follows that medical records are themselves confidential, with such confidentiality governed by the same two principles. The boundaries of medical confidentiality are therefore prescribed by the operation of consent and exceptional circumstances.[165] The importance of the confidentiality of medical records has been reiterated repeatedly by the Courts over an extended period of time.[166] In *Campbell v MGN Limited*[167] Baroness Hale observed that:

> 'It has always been accepted that information about a person's health and treatment for ill-health is both private and confidential. This stems not only from the confidentiality of the doctor-patient relationship but from the nature of the information itself.'

9.68   A person over the age of 16 is entitled to full medical confidentiality. In the case of patients below that age where a doctor is not satisfied that the patient has sufficient maturity and understanding to appreciate what is involved in a medical treatment or procedure, the doctor may inform the parents or the guardian. If the patient does have sufficient maturity and understanding then full confidence applies.[168] In *R (Axon) v Secretary of State for Health*[169] Silber J made clear that the ECHR and the CRC demonstrate clearly that the duty of confidence owed by the medical profession to a competent young person is a high one and one which therefore should not be overridden except for very powerful reasons.

---

165   Detailed guidance for doctors on the boundaries of medical confidentiality is provided by the General Medical Council's guide entitled *Confidentiality: Protecting and Providing Information* (2000). Further, guidance on the issue of confidentiality in exceptional situations is dealt with by situation specific guidance. For example, *Reporting Gun Shot Wounds Guidance for Doctors in Accident and Emergency Departments* (GMC, September, 2003) and the *Guide to Serious Communicable Diseases* (GMC, October 1997). Legislation concerning data protection also operates to safeguard and place boundaries on medical confidentiality. In particular, the Health and Social Care Act 2001, s 60, the Access to Medical Reports Act 1988, s 3(1), the Access to Health Records Act 1990, the Access to Health Records (Control of Access) Regulations 1993, SI 1993/746, the Data Protection Act 1998 and the Data Protection (Subject Access Modification) (Health) Order 2000, SI 2000/413 may be relevant to issues of confidentiality and disclosure that come before the Court. Guidance in relation to medical and health records held by social services is provided in Local Authority Circular (88) 17 (as continued in force by LASSL (92)9).
166   See for example *Wyatt v Wilson* [1820] (unreported).
167   [2004] 2 AC 457, para 145.
168   *Gillick v West Norfolk and Wisbech Area Health Authority and DHSS* [1986] AC 112.
169   [2006] 2 WLR 1130, para 64.

(ii) Records held by Social Services

9.69 All personal information concerning the child held on social services records must be treated as confidential. All social services staff have a duty to respect confidentiality during the course of carrying out their social work duties. As with medical records, a social worker is not permitted to breach confidentiality in relation to social work records unless (a) consent has been given or (b) in exceptional circumstances exist.[170] Disclosure without consent is permitted for the purposes of carrying out social work duties.[171] The Local Government (Access to Information) Act 1985 provides for greater access to information held by local authorities but most, if not all, matters referred to social services committees are excluded from its provisions by Sch 12A of the Local Government Act 1972 (as amended by the Local Government (Access to Information) Act 1985) and the law relating to the disclosure of information held by social services is contained in the Data Protection Act 1998.

(iii) Police Records

9.70 Information concerning children which comes into the possession of the police is treated as confidential and must not be divulged to other parties except in the proper course of police duty.[172] Within this context, limited reasonable disclosures are permitted to the extent that such disclosures are necessary in purpose and degree to carry out the public duties of the police.[173] Following a prosecution, the Police are not bound by any implied undertaking not to use the material obtained in the course of an investigation for any purpose other than criminal proceedings. The police will continue to owe a duty of confidence to the owner of the material although this may be overridden in the public interest.[174]

(iv) School Records

9.71 Teachers and other educational staff are bound by the general obligations of the professions as to confidentiality[175] and the law as to confidentiality in general.[176] In this regard, a teacher who learns of confidential information about the child or his family from the child or other sources has a duty to keep such information confidential except in so far as to do so would conflict with the child's best interests. Where a teacher has real grounds to suppose a child is the subject of abuse, he or she will not be in breach of any duty of confidentiality if he or she reports the concern to the authorities.[177] School records on pupils' academic achievements, others skills and abilities are confidential but may be used for the purpose of the pupil's welfare, for example, in assisting a child care officer in preparing a report for Court. A school pupil has subject access rights under the Data Protection Act 1998, subject to the Data Protection (Subject Access

---

[170] These principles are set out in Local Authority Circular (88)17 (as continued by LASSL (92)9)). This guidance is issued under the Local Authority Social Services Act 1970, s 7 and therefore has statutory force. See also the Local Government (Access to Information) Act 1985 (amending Sch 12A of the Local Government Act 1972).

[171] This will extend only to disclosure to social services department staff, other social carers, other departments to enable the Local Authority to discharge its statutory duties, management, students and children's guardians.

[172] Police (Conduct) Regulations 2004, Sch 1, para 7.

[173] *R v Chief Constable of the North Wales Police, ex p AB* [1999] QB 396 (a case concerning the public identification of convicted paedophiles).

[174] *Preston BC v McGrath* (2000) *The Times*, May 19.

[175] See *Brown v IRC* [1965] AC 244 at 265.

[176] *Duchess of Argyll v Duke of Argyll* [1967] Ch 302.

[177] Toulson, R & Phipps, C *Confidentiality* (2006) 2nd edn, Sweet and Maxwell. See also the Education (School Records) Regulations 1989.

Modification) (Education) Order 2000. In *Webster and others v Governors of the Ridgeway Foundation School*[178] the Court had regard to Art 3(1) of the CRC in determining whether to disclose school records containing identifying particulars of pupils for the purposes of an action in negligence arising out of an assault which had occurred within the school.

(v)   Information in Court Proceedings

9.72   That the domestic family courts deal with the private affairs of children and families at a time when they are arguably at their most vulnerable has been long appreciated, Lord Shaw of Dunfermline observing in 1913 in *Scott v Scott*[179] that such matters are:

> '... truly private affairs; the transactions are transactions truly *intra familiam* and it has long been recognised that an appeal for the protection of the court in the case of such persons does not involve the consequence of placing in the light of publicity their truly domestic affairs.'

It is axiomatic that a family's domestic affairs form part of the foundation upon which children develop physical and emotional integrity and formulate the character, personality and relationships by which they come to fulfill their potential as children and as adults and which in turn form cardinal elements of the child's private life under Art 8 of the ECHR as defined above.

9.73   The confidentiality of information within family proceedings is circumscribed by a wide range of statutes, secondary legislation and common law and this area has been the subject of recent major statutory reform.[180] Where the court holds the information in question, any issue of personal confidentiality having been dealt with in the appropriate manner prior to being filed with the court, any right of confidentiality at that stage is a right of confidentiality that belongs to the court imposed to protect the proper functioning of the court's role in protecting children.[181]

Privacy of Court Proceedings.

9.74   The Family Procedure Rules 2010 provide for the hearing of family proceedings to take place in private save where any rules or enactment provides for the attendance of representatives of the media and others during family proceedings and the communication of certain information.[182]

9.75   The Family Procedure Rules 2010, r 27.11 provide that in the family proceedings court, the county court and High Court duly accredited representatives of the news gathering and reporting organisations, and any other accredited person whom the court

---

[178]   [2009] EWHC 1140 (QB).

[179]   [1913] AC 417.

[180]   The most recent of which is the Children, Schools and Families Act 2010 Part II which is not yet in force. It has been argued that these provisions are not complaint with Art 8 of the ECHR (see MacDonald, A *Bringing Rights Home for Children – Transparency and the Child's Right to Respect for Private Life* [2010] Fam Law 190. See also Sturge, C *Transparency in Family Proceedings* [2006] Fam Law 409 and *Teenage Pregnancy* (1999) Social Exclusion Unit Cm 4342; *Get Real: Providing Dedicated Sexual Health Services for Young People* (2002) Save the Children and *Tracking Survey Wave 12 Evaluation of Teenage Pregnancy Strategy* (2004) BMRB International).

[181]   *Oxfordshire CC v L and F* [1997] 1 FLR 235.

[182]   Family Procedure Rules 2010, r 27.10(1) The word 'private' means proceedings at which the general public have no right to be present (see Family Procedure Rules 2010 r 27.10(1)).

permits,[183] are able to be present at hearings of all family proceedings,[184] as defined by the Matrimonial and Family Proceedings Act 1984, s 32, subject to the power of the court to exclude such accredited persons.[185] The provisions cover a wide range of proceedings, including public and private law proceedings under the Children Act 1989 and claims for ancillary relief under the Matrimonial Causes Act 1973. In the Family Proceedings Court, media representatives are admitted under s 69(2) of the Magistrates Courts Act 1980 with that attendance now regulated by r 27.11 of the Family Procedure Rules 2010, which in turn provides for the court to exclude accredited persons. The burden on demonstrating the media should be excluded is on the party seeking their exclusion.[186] The appellate courts will continue to sit in public as they have done to date. An appellate court has the power sit in private when hearing an appeal but very rarely does so.[187]

Publication of Information from court proceedings

9.76 The right of the media to attend hearings in family proceedings must be distinguished from the statutory restrictions on publication and disclosure of information relating to those proceedings, which continue to apply and are at present unaffected by the rules and associated guidance on the admission of media representatives to family proceedings.[188]

---

[183] Family Procedure Rules 2010, rr 27.11(2)(f) and 27.11(2)(g). The production identification issued by the UK Press Card Authority is sufficient evidence of the requisite accreditation (see r 27.11(7)) although the court retains the power under the general power to admit persons provided by r 27.11(2)(g) to admit unaccredited media representatives to be present. Note that these provisions do not expressly cover communication of information to accredited representatives of the media or the public at large nor to they permit the media to receive or peruse documents.

[184] Hearings conducted for the purpose of judicially assisted conciliation or negotiation, including Financial Dispute Resolution hearings and First Hearing Dispute Resolution hearings in private law children cases and Case Management Conferences and Issues Resolution Hearings in public law cases are excluded (Family Procedure Rules 2010, r 27.11(1)).

[185] The court may direct exclusion where it is satisfied that to do so in necessary in the interests of any child concerned in, or connected with, the proceedings, or that to do so is necessary for the safety or protection of a party, a witness in the proceedings, or a person connected with such a party or witness, or that to do so is necessary for the orderly conduct of the proceedings or because justice would otherwise be impeded or prejudiced (Family Procedure Rules 2010, r 27.11(3)). For the guidance see Practice Direction 20 April 2009, paras 5.1–5.2, Practice Direction (FPC) 20 April 2009, paras 5.1–5.2. and *Re X (Residence and Contact: Rights of Media Attendance: FPR r 10.28(4))* [2009] EWHC 1728 (Fam), [2009] 2 FLR 1467.

[186] *Spencer v Spencer* [2009] EWHC 1529 (Fam), [2009] Fam Law 790; *Re X (Residence and Contact: Rights of Media Attendance: FPR r 10.28(4))* [2009] EWHC 1728 (Fam), [2009] Fam Law 930.

[187] Domestic and Appellate Proceedings (Restriction of Publicity) Act 1968, s 1.

[188] See the Family Procedure Rules 2010, r 27.11. See also Practice Direction 20 April 2009, para 2.4 and Practice Direction (FPC) 20 April 2009, para 2.4. See also the President's Guidance of 22 April 2009, paras 7 and 8. Upon commencement, Part II of the Children, Schools and Families Act 2010 will apply to any relevant family proceedings at which the public are not (or in the case of proceedings which have already taken place, were not) entitled to be present. Pursuant to s 11(2) of the 2010 Act publication of information relating to the proceedings is a contempt of court committed by the publisher unless the publication of the information is (a) an authorised publication of the text, or a summary, of the whole or part of an order made or judgement given by the court in the proceedings; (b) an authorised news publication; (c)authorised by the rules of court. These provisions will apply to all tiers of court and replace the statutory restrictions on publication contained in s 12(1)(a) of the Administration of Justice Act 1960 in a case where the proceedings are adoption proceedings or parental order proceedings or a case where the publication of the text or summary contains identification information relating to an individual involved in the proceedings, to the extent that the publication of the text or summary is permitted by the court for the purposes of this section, s 97(2)–(9) of the Children Act 1989 and the Adoption and Children Act 2002, s 101(1) and s 101(2).

Children Act 1989, s 97(2)

9.77   Pursuant to the Children Act 1989, s 97(2) provides that no person shall publish to the public at large or any section of the public any material which is intended or likely to identify any child involved in proceedings under the Children Act 1989 or the Adoption and Children Act 2002 or the address or school of that child.[189] 'Publishing' includes radio and television broadcasts or to cause to be published, and 'material' includes any picture or representation.[190] It is a defence if the publisher can prove that he or she did not know and had no reason to suspect that the published material was intended, or likely, to identify the child.[191] The courts may lift the restriction imposed by s 97(2)[192] and are increasingly willing to do so.[193] In *Clayton v Clayton*[194] the Court of Appeal clarified that the provisions of s 97(2) provide confidentiality only during the currency of proceedings. Any further prohibition enduring beyond the end of proceedings must be based on the Administration of Justice Act 1960, s 12 where relevant[195] or a discretionary welfare based decision under the inherent jurisdiction of the High Court, itself balancing the child's rights protected by Arts 8 with the rights under Art 10 of the ECHR.[196]

Administration of Justice Act 1960, s 12

9.78   The Administration of Justice Act 1960, s 12(1) as amended[197] provides that the publication of information relating to proceedings before any Court sitting in private shall not of itself be a contempt of court except where the proceedings relate to the exercise of the inherent jurisdiction of the High Court with respect to minors, are brought under the Children Act 1989 or the Adoption and Children Act 2002 or otherwise relate wholly or mainly to the maintenance or upbringing of a minor. Section 12(1) does not prohibit publication of the names and addresses or photograph of the child nor of details about the order[198] and accordingly does not prohibit publications, including publishing pictures of the parents, that do not relate to the care

---

189   To do is an offence punishable on summary conviction by a fine not exceeding level 4 on the standard scale.
190   CA 1989, s 97(5). Note that CA 1989, s 97(8) expressly preserves the operation of the MCA 1980, s 71 under which only the grounds of the application, submissions on points of law and the court decision, including any observations made by the court in giving it, may be published or broadcast.
191   CA 1989, s 97(3).
192   CA 1989, s 97(4).
193   See in particular *Re Webster, Norfolk County Council v Webster and others* [2007] 1 FLR 1146 per Munby J (holding that the court had the power pursuant to s 97(4) to lift the restriction imposed by s 97(2) whenever Convention rights so required and that that power was not limited by express reference to the interests of the child); *Re LM (Reporting Restrictions: Coroner's Inquest)* [2008] 1 FLR 1360 (permission to report at an inquest into the death of the child's sister); *Re B; X County Council v B* [2008] 1 FLR 482 (permission to name the local authority); *Re B; X County Council v B (No 2)* [2008] 1 FLR 1460 (permission to the mother and two of the children to waive their anonymity if they chose to do so); *Re H (Care Plan)* [2008] 2 FLR 21 (permission to publish a summary of the judicial criticism of social workers and the local authority's response to local Family Court User Groups); *Medway Council v G and Others* [2008] 2 FLR 1687 (permission to newspaper to interview a stepfather about related criminal proceedings on the basis of an agreed statement of facts prepared by the parties and subject to the child not being identified). But see also *Re R (Identification: Restrictions on Publication)* [2008] 1 FLR 1252 (restraining parents from seeking to identify the prospective adopters and from contacting and publishing details of the children).
194   [2006] EWCA Civ 878.
195   See **9.78** below.
196   See **9.79** below. Note that the Children and Young Persons Act 1933, s 39(1) also provides that no newspaper report shall reveal the name, address or school or include any particular calculated to lead to the identification of the subject child or child witness in proceedings nor the publication of any picture of them.
197   By CA 1989, sch 13, para 14.
198   *Re L (a minor) (Wardship: Freedom of Publication)* [1988] 1 All ER 418, [1988] 1 FLR 255; *Re W (Wards) (Publication of Information)* [1989] 1 FLR 246.

or upbringing of the child.[199] What may be restricted under s 12(1) includes the contents of any reports made in connection with the hearing, proofs of witnesses and submissions made during proceedings[200] and the fact that witnesses in a contested residence case would be giving evidence that they thought the mother was unfit to look after the children.[201] The prohibition is not limited in time and remains even if proceedings are discharged.[202] The Court has the power to allow disclosure of material that is otherwise protected by s 12(1).[203] In *A v Ward*,[204] Munby J gave a comprehensive description of the limitations on the protection afforded by s 12 of the Administration of Justice Act 1960.

Inherent Jurisdiction

9.79 Beyond the statutory provisions concerning information in proceedings, the court retains a power to issue injunctions to restrain publication of information concerning proceedings in respect of children or the child who is the subject of those proceedings.[205] As set out in **9.53** above, in determining whether such an injunction should be granted the court will balance the Art 8 right of the child to respect for his or her private life with the Art 10 right to freedom of expression.[206] Once again, in *(Re S (Identification: Restrictions on Publication)*[207] the balancing exercise to be carried out between Arts 8 and 10 was described by Lord Steyn as follows:[208]

> 'First, neither Art has as such precedence over the other. Secondly, where the values under the two Arts are in conflict, an intense focus on the comparative importance of the specific rights being claimed in the individual case is necessary. Thirdly, the justifications for interfering with or restricting each right must be taken into account. Finally, the proportionality test must be applied to each. For convenience, I will call this the ultimate balancing test.'

---

[199] *R v Central Independent Television plc* [1994] Fam 192, [1994] 3 All ER 641, CA. But see also *Re West (minors)* [1995] 2 FCR 206, *Re G (Minors) (Celebrities: Publicity)* [1999] 3 FCR 181 and *Medway Council v BBC* [2001] Fam Law 883.

[200] *Official Solicitor v Newsgroup Newspapers* [1994] 2 FCR 552, [1994] 2 FLR 174 and *Re EC (Disclosure of Material)* [1996] 2 FLR 123 at 130. See also *Re B* [2004] EWHC 411 (Fam), [2004] 2 FLR 142.

[201] *X v Dempster [1999] 1 FLR 894*.

[202] *Re E (A Minor)(Child Abuse: Evidence)* [1991] 1 FLR 420.

[203] *Norfolk County Council v Webster and Others* [2006] EWHC 2733 (Fam), [2007] 1 FLR 1146.

[204] [2010] EWHC 16 (Fam), [2010] 1 FLR 1497.

[205] See for example *X County Council v A* [1985] 1 All ER 53, *sub nom Re X (A Minor) (Wardship: Injunction)* [1984] 1 WLR 1422; *Re C (A Minor) (Wardship: Medical Treatment) (No 2)* [1990] Fam 39, [1989] 2 All ER 791, CA; *Re M and N (Minors) (Publication of Information)* [1990] Fam 211, [1990] 1 All ER 205, CA and *Re H-S (Minors) (Protection of Identity)* [1994] 3 All ER 390, [1994] 1 WLR 1141, *sub nom Re H (Minors) (Injunction: Public Interest)* [1994] 1 FLR 519, CA; *A v M (Family Proceedings: Publicity)* [2000] 1 FCR 577, [2000] 1 FLR 562, FD. See also *British Broadcasting Co v Rochdale Metropolitan Borough Council & X Y* [2007] 1 FLR 101 in which the court permitted publication of the identity of social workers involved in the earlier social work investigation, the balancing of Art 10 and Art 8 rights resolving in favour of Art 10 and publication.

[206] Note that other rights held by the child may justify interference with the Art 10 right to freedom of expression. In *T v United Kingdom* [2000] 30 EHRR 121 the ECtHR held that a child's Art 6 right to a fair hearing had been breached by reason of the hearing taking place in public. The child's right to life under Art 2 and the child's right to freedom from inhuman or degrading treatment under Art 3 have likewise been held in to justify interference with the right to freedom of expression in certain circumstances (*Venables v News Group Newspapers* [2001] Fam 430, [2001] 1 FLR 791; *X (A Woman formerly known as Mary Bell) v O'Brien* [2003] EWHC 1101 (QB)).

[207] [2004] UKHL 47, [2005] 1 FLR 591.

[208] See also *Re W (Children) (Identification: Restriction on Publication)* [2007] 3 FCR 69, [2006] 1 FLR 1.

9.80   As discussed above, in achieving this balance the domestic courts must have particular regard to the importance of the right to freedom of expression.[209] Any curtailment of the right to freedom of expression must be convincingly established by a compelling countervailing consideration.[210] In carrying out this balancing exercise, it should not be forgotten that children too have the right to freedom of expression under Art 10. The exercise of this right by children is particularly valuable when it comes to the need for a dialogue between children and professionals, which communicative activity is in principle within the scope of Art 10.[211] Measures which act to prevent or restrict the disclosure by children of matters detrimental to their welfare must accordingly be justified by reference to Art 10(2). In this regard, it is suggested that the curtailment by reason of the fear of publication of the child's freedom of expression within investigative and therapeutic scenarios can itself amount to a breach of the child's rights under Art 10.

9.81   It has been suggested that the maintenance of public confidence in the judicial system must also be weighed as part of the requisite balancing exercise. In *A v Ward*[212] Munby J observed that:

> '... the law has to have regard to current realities and one of those realities, unhappily, is a decreasing confidence in some quarters in the family justice system – something which although it is often linked to strident complaints about so-called 'secret justice' is too much of the time based upon ignorance, misunderstanding, misrepresentation or worse. The maintenance of public confidence in the judicial system is central to the values which underlie both Article 6 and Article 10 and something which, in my judgment, has to be brought into account as a very weighty factor in any application of the balancing exercise. And where the lack of public confidence is caused even if only in part by misunderstanding or, on occasions, the peddling of falsehoods, then there is surely a resonance, even for the family justice system, in what Brandeis J said so many years ago. I have in mind, of course, not merely what he said in *Whitney v California* (1927) 274 US 357 at page 77:
>
> > 'If there be time to expose through discussion the falsehood and fallacies, to avert the evil by the processes of education, the remedy to be applied is more speech, not enforced silence.'
>
> I have in mind also his extra-judicial observation that, and I paraphrase, the remedy for such ills is not the enforced silence of judicially conferred anonymity but rather the disinfectant power of exposure to forensic sunlight.'

Privacy of Information in Domestic Law – Disclosure of Information

9.82   Issues will inevitably arise in respect of the disclosure of confidential or private information concerning children arising from proceedings or elsewhere. This issue usually arises either in the context of disclosure for the purposes of litigation or disclosure for the purposes of publication by the media as dealt with above. The following section deals primarily with disclosure of private or confidential information concerning children for the purposes of court proceedings.

---

[209]   Human Rights Act 1998, s 12(4).
[210]   *Re S (Identification: Restrictions on Publication)* [2004] UKHL 47, [2005] 1 FLR 591.
[211]   *Belfast City Council v Miss Behavin' Ltd* [2007] UKHL 19, [2007] 1 WLR 1420.
[212]   [2010] EWHC 16 (Fam), [2010] 1 FLR 1497.

(i) Domestic Duty of 'Full and Frank' Disclosure

9.83 It is a duty owed to the court both by the parties and by their legal representatives to give full and frank disclosure in all matters in respect of children.[213] A local authority which brings care proceedings has a duty to disclose all relevant information in its possession or power which might assist parents to rebut allegations made against them. In *R v Hampshire County Council, ex p K* [214] the court held that local authorities:

> 'had a high duty in law, not only on grounds of general fairness but also in the direct interests of a child whose welfare they served, to be open in the disclosure of all relevant material affecting that child in their possession or power (excluding documents protected on established grounds of public immunity) which might be of assistance to the natural parent or parents in rebutting charges against one or both of them of in any way ill-treating the child.'

9.84 This position is reinforced by the provisions of Art 6 of the ECHR which requires that each party must be afforded an equal opportunity to present his case, including his evidence, under conditions that do not place him at a substantial disadvantage. This includes the right to the disclosure of relevant documents.[215] The fair trial guaranteed by Art 6 is not confined to the 'purely judicial' part of the proceedings but extends prior to and subsequent to the proceedings themselves.[216] Article 8 also affords procedural safeguards against inappropriate interference with the substantive rights protected by Art 8 which safeguards arguably compel proper disclosure of documents relevant to the issue and/or proceedings in question.[217]

9.85 However, none of these provisions translate to an absolute and unqualified right of parties to see all documents, including those which are confidential, prior to or during proceedings. The right to a fair hearing pursuant to Art 6 of the European Convention on Human Rights is an unqualified right but the several ancillary rights under Art 6 are not themselves unqualified, including the right to disclosure of relevant evidence.[218] Further, the procedural rights under Art 8 are subject to the usual principles of legality, necessity and proportionality.[219] Finally, the interests of anyone whose Art 6, 8 and 10 rights are engaged in the issue of disclosure, whether as a witness, party or victim, must be considered and balanced when determining whether disclosure of confidential documents should be withheld or made.[220] Accordingly, whilst relevant to the balancing exercise the domestic court must carry out when determining whether to order or withhold disclosure, the rights guaranteed by the ECHR are not definitive in themselves on the issue of whether confidential documents should be disclosed.

---

[213] *Practice Direction: Case Management* [1995] 1 FLR 456. It is probable that the duty of the parties under the PLO to help the court further the overriding objective encompasses a duty of full and frank disclosure. See also *Re B, R and C (Children)* [2002] EWCA Civ 1825, [2003] Fam Law 305.

[214] [1990] 2 QB 71, [1990] 2 All ER 129, [1990] 1 FLR 330.

[215] *Feldbrugge v The Netherlands* (1986) 8 EHRR 425; *McGinley and Egan v UK* (1998) 27 EHRR 1.

[216] *Re L (Care: Assessment Fair Trial)* [2002] EWHC 1379 (Fam), [2002] 2 FLR 730; *Mantovanelli v France* (1997) 24 EHRR 370.

[217] See *R (P) v Secretary of State for the Home Department; R (Q) v Secretary of State for the Home Department* [2001] EWCA Civ 1151; [2001] 2 FLR 1122.

[218] *R v H* [2004] UKHL 3, [2004] 2 AC 134 ('... some derogation from the golden rule of full disclosure may be justified but such derogation must always be the minimum derogation necessary to protect the public interest in question and must never imperil the overall fairness of the trial').

[219] *R (on the application of TB) v Stafford Crown Court* [2006] EWHC 1645 (Admin), [2007] 1 All ER 102.

[220] *Re B (Disclosure to other Parties)* [2001] 2 FLR 1017, paras 64–66.

(ii) Confidentiality and Disclosure of Information

9.86 Where the information in issue is necessary for the fair disposal of the proceedings[221] confidentiality is not a valid reason for non-disclosure.[222] Further, it is important to note that in domestic law a child has no more right to confidentiality than anyone else coming before the court.[223]

(iii) Consent to Disclosure

9.87 The general rule applicable to confidential information is that such information should not be disclosed without the consent of the person who holds the confidentiality. To be valid, that consent must be both informed and freely given without pressure or undue influence being exerted having had access to and an opportunity to consider information relevant to the question of informed consent. Acquiescence where the person does not know what the request entails is not 'consent'. The seeking and giving of consent is usually a process, rather than a one-off event. Whether consent has been given should always be the subject of proper verification.[224] Proper adherence to these provisions is particularly important when dealing with confidential information concerning children who are capable of giving or withholding consent.

9.88 Traditionally, the child's right to waive confidentiality in domestic law has been a right to be exercised by the child's parents on its behalf.[225] However, in accordance with the rights enshrined in the CRC and the rights from which children benefit under the ECHR, the domestic courts increasingly recognise the autonomy of children mature enough to make informed decisions on their own behalf.[226] Again, where parents seek to waive their child's right to privacy Thorpe LJ held in *Re G (Celebrities: Publicity)*[227] that 'there can be no doubt that the court has jurisdiction in personam to restrain any act by a parent that if unrestrained would or might adversely affect the welfare of the child the subject of the proceedings'.

---

[221] *Re R (Care: Disclosure: nature of Proceedings)* [2002] 1 FLR 755 (FD).

[222] Note that third parties whose information is included in confidential records which are to be disclosed have an independent right separate from the subject to have their personal information kept confidential and must give their consent to disclosure. For example, this principle is enshrined in LAC (88)17 in relation to Social Work Records. In relation to medical records, the principle is enshrined in the Access to Health Records Act 1990, s 5(1)(a)(ii) which section stipulates a restriction on access to health records by those whom they relate and others where disclosure would identify a third party who provided the information.

[223] *B v B (Child Abuse: Evidence)* [1991] 2 FLR 591.

[224] See for example the guidance contained in *Reference Guide to Consent For Examination or Treatment*, Department of Health 2001, the Children Act 1989 Guidance and Regulations Volume 3, *Family Placements*, para 2.30 and The Children Act 1989 Guidance and Regulations Volume 4, *Residential Care*, para 1.92.

[225] See *Re Z (A Minor)(Identification: Restrictions on Publication)* [1997] Fam 1 at 25 per Ward LJ. Under the Data Protection Act 1998, under which a parent is entitled to disclosure of records relating to their child unless disclosure would be likely to cause serious harm an individual is entitled to have communicated to him in an intelligible form personal data of which that individual is the data subject: Data Protection Act 1998, s 7. The Information Commissioner takes the view that an individual can exercise parental responsibility in relation to his child in this regard. Data is exempt from disclosure if the supply of the information to the data subject would be likely to cause serious harm to his or any other person's physical or mental health or condition: Data Protection (Subject Access Modification) (Social Work) Order 2000, SI 2000/415. See also the Data Protection (Subject Access Modification) (Health) Order 2000, SI 2000/413 and the Data Protection (Subject Access Modification) (Education) Order 2000, SI 2000/414 for similar provisions.

[226] See *Torbay Borough Council v News Group Newspapers* [2003] EWHC 2927 (Fam), [2004] EMLR 8 at [45–60] and *Gillick v West Norfolk and Wisbech Health Authority* [1986] AC 112.

[227] [1999] 1 FLR 409 at 414–415.

(iv) Public Interest Immunity

9.89 Where the disclosure of otherwise relevant private or confidential material is not consented to or otherwise permitted or governed by primary or secondary legislation, the issue of whether such information should be disclosed will generally involve the application of the principles of public interest immunity.[228]

9.90 Information can be withheld from disclosure if the public interest requires it to be excluded. This is known as 'public interest immunity'.[229] The categories of public interest immunity are not closed[230] and public interest immunity is unlikely to attach to material simply because it belongs to a class of documents.[231] Each claim for public interest immunity must therefore be considered by reference to the individual documents themselves.[232] It would appear that the public interest immunity in respect of records concerning children is based on the duty owed to children that what they say in confidence will not be disclosed without good reason. However, ultimately the question of disclosure is a matter for the court. Accordingly, a child should not be given an undertaking that what they say will remain confidential.[233] If records appear to be protected by public interest immunity, the authority holding such records should draw their existence to the attention of the other parties, so that they can apply for them to be disclosed.[234] This is so even where the document in question is detrimental to the authority's case.[235]

9.91 In considering whether the information in question is protected from disclosure by public interest immunity, the Court must weigh up the balance between the public interest favouring confidentiality as against the public interest that justice should be done.[236] The public interest in confidentiality is strong enough to compete with, and sometimes prevail over, the public interest in a fair trial and disclosure of all material that passes the relevant threshold test. Even if relevant, evidence must be excluded if, as a matter of public policy, the public interests requires that it should be so excluded when set against the competing public interests requiring the full and frank disclosure of relevant facts. In the context of proceedings involving children, in *Re D (Minors) (Wardship: Disclosure)*[237] the Court highlighted the need when determining whether to exercise its discretion to order disclosure to balance the public interest of ensuring the frankness induced by confidentiality with the public interest of a fair trial (in that case a

---

[228] See also the Family Procedure Rules 2010, r 21.3(1).

[229] *D v NSPCC* [1978] AC 178.

[230] *D v NSPCC* [1978] AC 178.

[231] *R v Chief Constable of West Midlands Police, ex p Wiley; R v Chief Constable of Nottinghamshire Police, ex p Sunderland* [1995] 1 AC 274, [1994] 3 All ER 420. Note that in *Re R (Care: Disclosure: Nature of Proceedings)* [2002] 1 FLR 755 Charles J commented that any case on public interest immunity prior to *Wiley* in 1995 should be regarded with caution and carefully reconsidered.

[232] *R v Chief Constable of West Midlands Police, ex p Wiley; R v Chief Constable of Nottinghamshire Police, ex p Sunderland* [1995] 1 AC 274, [1994] 3 All ER 420.

[233] *Re G (Minors) (Welfare Report: Disclosure)* [1993] 2 FLR 293, CA.

[234] *Re C (Expert Evidence: Disclosure: Practice)* [1995] 1 FLR 204.

[235] *Re R (Care: Disclosure: Nature of Proceedings)* [2002] 1 FLR 755.

[236] See *Duncan v Cammell Laird & Co Ltd* [1942] AC 624 per Lord Simon at 641 and *Air Canada v Secretary of State for Trade (No 2)* [1983] 2 AC 394 at 436.

[237] [1994] 1 FLR 346. See also *Kent County Council v K* [1994] 1 WLR 912 sub nom *Re K and Others (Minors) (Disclosure)* [1994] 1 FLR 377; *Oxfordshire County Council v P* [1995] Fam 161, [1995] 1 FLR 552; *Re A (Criminal Proceedings: Disclosure)* [1996] 1 FLR 221, *Oxfordshire CC v L and F* [1997] 1 FLR 235), *Re C (A Minor) (Care Proceedings: Disclosure)* [1997] Fam 76 and *Re X (Disclosure of Information)* [2001] 2 FLR 440 where the court gave leave to disclose a judgement in care proceedings to children who were not the subject of the proceedings to enable those children to see that their evidence had been believed, to enable them to obtain therapeutic help and to enable them to obtain compensation.

criminal trial). In particular, the Court must include in the balance the competing factors of the need to protect the interests of the child in maintaining the confidentiality and privacy of the proceedings, the need to encourage candour by all involved in the proceedings by maintaining the confidentiality and privacy of proceedings, the public interest of free exchange of information between agencies and the public interest in protecting vulnerable members of the community. The balancing exercise will include consideration of whether disclosure is in accordance with the law and necessary for the purposes of Art 8 of the ECHR.[238]

9.92 There are limits to the reach of public interest immunity. In the case of *L v L*[239] Tugendhat J made clear that, whilst the rights of privacy and of confidentiality may be overridden by public interest in full disclosure before trial, if relevant rights of privilege would not be overridden where such documents were not relevant, neither would other rights be overridden. Whilst confidentiality is not a separate head of privilege it may be a very material consideration when privilege is claimed on public interest immunity grounds.[240]

(v) Disclosure and Harm

Disclosure to Prevent Harm

9.93 Where a child may suffer serious harm if disclosure does not take place the normal rule that disclosure may only take place by way of consent may be overridden. By way of example, statements made in conciliation should not to be disclosed into proceedings under the Children Act 1989 unless such a statement indicates that the maker has in the past, or was likely to in the future to cause serious harm to the wellbeing of the child.[241] In relation to medical records, disclosures may be made in the public interest without consent where disclosure is essential to protect the patient or third parties from risk of death or serious harm.[242]

Non-Disclosure to Prevent Harm

9.94 Records which are otherwise disclosable, either because consent is given or otherwise, may be withheld to prevent harm. The Access to Health Records Act 1990, s 5(1)(a)(i) prohibits access to health records by those whom they relate and others where disclosure would be likely to cause serious harm to mental or physical health. In relation to evidence filed in proceedings, in narrowly defined circumstances the court has the power to refuse to disclose information filed within proceedings to a person notwithstanding that the person is a party to those proceedings. In *Re D (Minors) (Adoption Reports: Confidentiality)*[243] Lord Mustill said there must be a strong presumption in favour of disclosure on the grounds of natural justice. He went on to set out the test for non-disclosure:

> '... the Court should first consider whether disclosure of the material would involve a real possibility of significant harm to the child. If it would, the court should next consider

[238] *R (on the application of TB) v Stafford Crown Court* [2006] EWHC 1645 (Admin), [2007] 1 All ER 102.

[239] [2007] EWHC 140 (QB), [2007] 2 FLR 171.

[240] *Alfred Crompton Amusement Machines Ltd v Customs and Excise Commissioners (No 2)* [1974] AC 405 at 433 per Lord Cross.

[241] *Re D (minors) (Conciliation: Disclosure of Information)* [1993] 1 FLR 932.

[242] *Confidentiality: Protecting and Providing Information* (2000), paras 14 and 36, *C (A Minor) (Evidence: Confidential Information)* [1991] 2 FLR 478 and *Re L Minors (Police Investigation: Privilege)* (1995) *The Times* 25 April. See also *W v Egdell* [1990] 1 Ch 359.

[243] [1996] AC 593.

whether the overall interests of the child would benefit from non-disclosure, weighing on the one hand the interest of the child in having material properly tested, and on the other both the magnitude of the risk that harm will occur and the gravity of the harm if it does occur. If the Court is satisfied that the interests of the child point towards non-disclosure, the next and final step is for the Court to weigh that consideration, and its strength in the circumstances of the case, against the interest of the parent or other party in having an opportunity to see and respond to the material. In the latter regard the court should take into account the importance of the material to the issues in the case. Non-disclosure should be the exception not the rule. The Court should be rigorous in the examination of the risk and gravity of the feared harm to the child and should order non-disclosure only when the case for doing so is compelling.'

This decision is still valid following the implementation of the Human Rights Act 1998 but there is now a need to consider in the balance the rights of *anyone* whose Art 6, 8 and 10 rights are engaged when determining whether disclosure should be refused to a party in a case.[244] Information from the child which has influenced the expert but which has not been disclosed should be disclosed save where exceptional circumstances exist such as a breach of the child's rights under Art 2 or Art 3 of the ECHR.[245]

Child's Personal Privacy in Domestic Law

9.95 In the case of *Murray v Express Newspapers Plc*[246] the Court of Appeal, considering a case in which a photographer had covertly taken a photograph of the child of a world famous author in a public place, which photograph was sold to a national media organisation and published in a magazine, held that:

'It seems to us that, subject to the facts of the particular case, the law should indeed protect children from intrusive media attention, at any rate to the extent of holding that a child has a reasonable expectation that he or she will not be targeted in order to obtain photographs in a public place for publication which the person who took or procured the taking of the photographs knew would be objected to on behalf of the child.'[247]

CONCLUSION

9.96 The child's right to respect for private life is plainly crucial for the development of the child's psychological and physical integrity, social relationships and physical and social identity. For children involved in legal proceedings concerning their family, for children involved in criminal proceedings and for children whose parents are in the public eye and the subject of interest by the more prurient elements of the press,[248] there is increasing pressure on that private life. Further concerns have been expressed as to the

---

[244] *Re B (Disclosure to other Parties)* [2001] 2 FLR 1017, paras 64–66.

[245] *A County Council v SB and others* [2010] EWHC 2528 (Fam), [2010] All ER (D) 182 (Oct).

[246] [2008] EWCA Civ 446, [2008] 2 FLR 599, [2008] 3 WLR 360.

[247] And presumably, where the child was of sufficient age and understanding, knew would be objected to by the child.

[248] In considering this issue it is salutary to reflect on a warning given by Warren and Brandeis as long ago as 1890 in relation to those elements of the press who do no more than peddle gossip: '[Gossip] belittles by inverting the relative importance of things, thus dwarfing the thoughts and aspirations of a people. When personal gossip attains the dignity of print, and crowds the space available for matters of real interest to the community, what wonder that the ignorant and thoughtless mistake its relative importance. Easy of comprehension, appealing to that weak side of human nature which is never wholly cast down by the misfortunes and frailties of our neighbours, no one can be surprised that it usurps the place of interest in brains capable of other things. Triviality destroys at once robustness of thought and delicacy of feeling. No enthusiasm can flourish, no generous impulse can survive under its blighting influence' ((1890) 4 Harvard Law Review, p 193).

erosion of the child's right to privacy consequent upon the use of CCTV and other electronic monitoring devices which are currently the subject of no statutory regulation.[249] Whilst it is plain that the 'naming and shaming' of children under anti-social behaviour orders risks alienating and stigmatising children and thereby entrenching their errant behaviour[250] the domestic courts have failed to take the opportunity to rule that the practice breaches the child's right to privacy under Art 8 of the ECHR.[251] As Hammarberg notes, it is difficult to comprehend why any civilised government would permit such a practice, let alone pro-actively pursue it.[252]

9.97 Whilst, domestically, there remains no overarching, all embracing cause of action for invasion of privacy[253] the ECHR has spurred the development of the protection of privacy under the law of confidentiality and is likely to continue to do so. The explicit acknowledgment by the domestic courts that these developments extend to protect children independent of the interests of adults is to be particularly welcomed.[254] In the face of grave concerns regarding the admission of the press into the domestic family courts and the increasingly sophistication of technology for monitoring the actions of children there is plainly an urgent need for this advance to be reinforced by those provisions of the CRC which also protect the child's right to a private life and in light of which the ECHR must be interpreted and applied. Only in this way can the law ensure that the necessary balance between the child's right to a private life and the cardinal right to freedom of expression is properly drawn so as to both protect and advance the interests and welfare of children.

---

[249]　CRAE *The State of Children's Rights in England* (2008), p 15.

[250]　Gil-Robles, A *Report by Mr Alvaro Gil-Robles Commissioner for Human Rights on his visit to the United Kingdom* (2005) CommDH 6 Council of Europe, para 119.

[251]　*R (Stanley, Marshall and Kelly) v Metropolitan Police Commissioner* [2004] EWHC 2229 (Admin), [2005] UKHRR 115.

[252]　Hammarberg, T *Memorandum by Thomas Hammarberg, Commissioner for Human Rights of the Council of Europe* (2008) CommDH Council of Europe, para 30.

[253]　*Wainwright v Home Office* [2003] UKHL 53, [2003] 4 All ER 969.

[254]　*Murray v Express Newspapers Plc* [2008] EWCA Civ 446, [2008] 2 FLR 599, [2008] 3 WLR 360.

Chapter 10

THE CHILD'S RIGHT TO FREEDOM OF THOUGHT, CONSCIENCE AND RELIGION

'Remember only that I was innocent
and, just like you, mortal on that day,
I, too, had had a face marked by rage, by pity and joy,
quite simply, a human face!'

Benjamin Fondane

INTRODUCTION

10.1 The right to freedom of thought, conscience and religion has been described as a far reaching and profound right encompassing freedom of thought on all matters, personal conviction and the commitment to religion or belief, whether manifested individually or in community with others.[1] It is a right which is derived from the inherent dignity of the human person[2] and underpins the very foundation of democracy.[3] In *R v Big M Drug Mart*[4] the Supreme Court of Canada recognised the right to freedom of religion as a cardinal aspect of society, which should 'accommodate a wide range of beliefs, diversity of tastes and pursuits, customs and codes of conduct'.

10.2 International law does not establish a minimum age above which a person enjoys freedom of thought, conscience and religion.[5] Art 1 of the Universal Declaration of Human Rights recognises that *all* human beings are endowed with reason and conscience. Within this context, the Universal Declaration of Human Rights upholds the freedom of thought, conscience and religion of *everyone*.[6] The European Convention on Human Rights likewise guarantees freedom of thought, conscience and religion to everyone.[7] Within this context Art 14 of the CRC provides that States Parties shall respect the right of the child to freedom or thought, conscience and religion. The domestic law recognises that religious beliefs and convictions are part of the humanity of every individual.[8] However, whilst accordingly the right to freedom of thought, conscience and religion is thus conferred upon children, the right has historically been

---

[1] Human Rights Committee General Comment No 22 1993 HRI/GEN/1/Rev 8, p 194, para 1.
[2] Partsch, K *Freedom of Conscience and Expression, and Political Freedoms* in Henking, L (ed) *The International Bill of Rights: The Covenant on Civil and Political Rights* (1981), p 209.
[3] *Multani v Commission Scolaire Marguerite-Bourgeoys* 2006 SCC 6 (CanLII). So fundamental is the right to freedom of thought, conscience and religion that it is not permissible for States to derogate from the right as enshrined in Art 18(1) of the Covenant on Civil and Political Rights (see ICCPR Art 4).
[4] [1985] 1 SCR 295.
[5] Van Bueren *The International Law on the Rights of the Child* (1998) Martinus Nijhoff, p 151.
[6] Universal Declaration of Human Rights Art 18.
[7] ECHR, Art 9(1).
[8] *R (Williamson) v Secretary of State for Education and Employment* [2005] UKHL 15, [2005] 2 AC 246.

the subject of little consideration in relation to the child,[9] and then primarily from the perspective of the parents' religion and beliefs rather than those of the child individually.[10]

10.3   The lack of specific consideration of the child's right to freedom of thought, conscience and religion arises in part from the fact that the traditional approach of international law has been to consider the relationship between State duties and parental rights in respect of a child's religious upbringing and not the child's own right to freedom of thought, conscience and religion.[11] This traditional approach is demonstrated in a number of the international human rights instruments. A particular example is the non-binding Declaration on the Elimination of All Forms of Intolerance and Discrimination Based on Religion or Belief.[12] This Declaration gives specific content to the general statements of the rights to freedom of religion or belief and freedom from discrimination based on religion of belief contained in the major human rights instruments, including Art 18 of the Covenant on Civil and Political Rights.[13] The Declaration is intended to be normative.[14] However the Declaration, whilst incorporating specific provisions in relation to the rights of the parents and children, views these rights only from the parents' perspective.[15]

10.4   In addition to the primarily adult perspective on the child's religious life contained in the majority of international human rights instruments, the interpretation and application of the child's right to freedom of thought, conscience and religion is further complicated by the fact that the relationship between children and religion is an emotive one and capable of generating great controversy. More State parties have made reservations concerning the child's right to freedom of thought, conscience and religion under Art 14 of the CRC than any other article of the Convention. Many of these

---

9   The first dedicated work on this area, Langlaude, S *The Right of the Child to Religious Freedom in International Law* (2007) Martinus Nijhoff was published in 2007.
10   Van Bueren, G *Child Rights in Europe* (2007) Council of Europe Publishing, p 77.
11   Van Bueren *The International Law on the Rights of the Child* (1998) Martinus Nijhoff, p 159.
12   General Assembly Resolution 36/55. See also Art 5 of the UN Convention against Discrimination in Education UNTS, vol 429, p 93.
13   Sullivan, D *Advancing the Freedom of Religion or Belief Through the UN Declaration on the Elimination of Religious Intolerance and Discrimination* (1988) 82 Am. J. Int. L. 487.
14   See Arts 4 and 7.
15   See Art 5 which considers the religious life of the child entirely from the perspective of the child's parents or legal guardian:
     '5(1) The parents or, as the case may be, the legal guardians of the child have the right to organise the life within the family in accordance with their religion or belief and bearing in mind the moral education in which they believe the child should be brought up.
     (2) Every child shall enjoy the right to have access to education in the matter of religion or belief in accordance with the wishes of his parents or, as the case may be, legal guardians, and shall not be compelled to receive teaching on religion or belief against the wishes of his parents or legal guardians, the best interests of the child being the guiding principle.
     (3) The child shall be protected from any form of discrimination on the ground of religion or belief. He shall be brought up in a spirit of understanding, tolerance, friendship among peoples, peace and universal brotherhood, respect for freedom of religion or belief of others, and in full consciousness that his energy and talents should be devoted to the service of his fellow men.
     (4) In the case of a child who is not under the care either of his parents or of legal guardians, due account shall be taken of their expressed wishes or of any other proof of their wishes in the matter of religion or belief, the best interests of the child being the guiding principle.
     (5) Practices of a religion or belief in which a child is brought up must not be injurious to his physical or mental health or to his full development, taking into account article 1, paragraph 3, of the present Declaration.'

reservations are maintained notwithstanding that they are incompatible with the object and purpose of the CRC having regard to the provisions of the Art 51 of the Convention.[16]

10.5   Notwithstanding this position, children do have a religious dimension which the law should not be able to ignore.[17] Further, children's rights are not detached or isolated values devoid of context, but exist within a broader ethical, moral, spiritual, cultural and social framework. Most children's rights, far from being externally imposed, are embedded within the values of local communities, which communities themselves have a cohesive religious dimension.[18] In particular, children are commonly socialised and nurtured into a religious faith in connection with their family and religious community.[19] Within this context, the child's right to freedom of thought, conscience and religion as enshrined in Art 14 of the CRC is extremely important both in its own right and to ensure the efficacy of the wider rights of the child. Issues of thought, conscience and religion which concern children range from the child's views on issues such a diet and pacifism and the wearing religious clothing and symbols, through the nature of the child's right to education to the relationship between children's rights and parental responsibilities when it comes to religious practices such as circumcision.

10.6   The right to freedom of thought, conscience and religion has been described as one of the most complex of human rights and its complexities increase when considered in the context of the rights of the child.[20] This chapter begins by examining the general principles which underpin the child's right to freedom of thought, conscience and religion before going on to consider the right, and its application, in the context of the key international and regional human rights instruments and finally, within the context of our domestic law.

---

[16]   See for example Algeria, Iraq, the Republic of the Maldives, the Kingdom of Morocco, and the Sultanate of Oman, each of which have entered reservations on the basis that granting a child the right to freedom of choice of religion would be contrary to the principles of Islam, and the reservation of the Holy See, which stipulates that it interprets the articles of the CRC in a way which 'safeguards the primary and inalienable rights of parents, in particular in so far as these rights concern ... religion.'

[17]   See Langlaude, S *The Right of the Child to Religious Freedom in International Law* (2007) Martinus Nijhoff, Chapters 1 and 2. Langlaude formulates the child's right to freedom of religion as being 'based on the interests of the child to be unhindered in their growth as an independent autonomous actor in the matrix of parents, religious community and society.' See also the decision of the US Supreme Court in *Board of Education v Barnette* 319 US 624.

[18]   CRC General Comment No 1 *The Aims of Education* HRI/GEN/Rev.8 p 350.

[19]   Langlaude, S *The Right of the Child to Religious Freedom in International Law* (2007) Martinus Nijhoff, p 34. See also *Christian Education South Africa v Minister of Education* (2000) 9 BHRC 53, Const Ct of South Africa, per Sachs J: 'Religious belief has the capacity to awake concepts of self-worth and human dignity which form the cornerstone of human rights.'

[20]   Langlaude, S *The Right of the Child to Religious Freedom in International Law* (2007) Martinus Nijhoff, p xxiv. See Sachs J's description of the difficulties in *Christian Education South Africa v Minister of Education* (2000) 9 BHRC 53, Const Ct of South Africa: '... religious and secular activities are, for purposes of balancing, frequently as difficult to disentangle from a conceptual point of view as they are to separate in day to day practice. While certain aspects may clearly be said to belong to the citizen's Caesar and others to the believer's God, there is a vast area of overlap and interpenetration between the two. It is in this area that balancing becomes doubly difficult, first because of the problems of weighing considerations of faith against those of reason, and secondly because of the problems of separating out what aspects of an activity are religious and protected by the Bill of Rights and what are secular and open to regulation in the ordinary way.'

GENERAL PRINCIPLES

'Thought, Conscience and Religion'

10.7 The international and regional human rights instruments do not contain definitions of 'thought', 'conscience' or 'religion'. Van Bueren notes that there are advantages to not adopting a definition of these concepts as it avoids unnecessarily excluding certain beliefs.[21] Used together, the terms 'thought, conscience and religion' have been described as encompassing:

> '[A]ll possible attitudes of the individual toward the world, toward society, and toward that which determines his fate and the destiny of the world, be it divinity, some superior being or just reason and rationalism or chance. 'Thought' includes political[22] and social thought; 'conscience' includes morality. 'Religion' or 'belief' is not limited to theistic belief but comprises equally nontheistic and even atheistic beliefs.'[23]

10.8 In so far as the courts have attempted a definition of religion, the primary components of a religion have been stipulated as being (a) the existence of a system of faith which addresses ultimate questions by reference to spiritual or supernatural existence or experience and (b) the external manifestations of such beliefs by adherents in religious practices which formalise and express spiritual or supernatural beliefs.[24] Such religious beliefs may be theistic, non-theistic beliefs, whether or not traditional or institutional in character, with the concept of religion and belief being broadly construed.[25]

---

21 Van Bueren *The International Law on the Rights of the Child* (1998) Martinus Nijhoff, p 165 n.41 and see Sullivan, D *Advancing the Freedom of Religion or Belief Through the UN Declaration on the Elimination of Religious Intolerance and Discrimination* (1988) 82 Am. J. Int. L. 487.

22 See *Roach v Canada (Minister of State for Multiculturalism and Citizenship)* [1994] 2 FC 406 (decision of the Canadian Federal Court) and *NHGH and RA v Turkey* (1992) 27 DR 200.

23 Partsch, K *Freedom of Conscience and Expression, and Political Freedoms* in Henking, L (ed) *The International Bill of Rights: The Covenant on Civil and Political Rights* (1981) p 209–245. See also the Nuremberg Principles, Principle IV 'The fact that a person acted pursuant to order of his Government or of a superior does not relieve him from responsibility under international law, provided a moral choice was in fact possible to him.'

24 See *Malnak v Yogi* (1979) 592 F 2d 197 (US Court of Appeals, Third Circuit) and *Church of New Faith v Comr For Pay-Roll Tax* (1982) 154 CLR 120 (High Court of Australia). Note also the observation of Sachs J in *Christian Education South Africa v Minister of Education* (2000) 9 BHRC 53, Const Ct of South Africa that 'Religion is not just a question of belief or doctrine. It is part of a way of life, of a people's temper and culture.'

25 Human Rights Committee General Comment No 22 *Article 18 (Freedom of Thought, Conscience and Religion* HRI/GEN/1/Rev 8, p 195, para 2. The Committee on the Rights of the Child has not published a General Comment on the right to freedom of thought, conscience and religion. The general principles set out in Human Rights Committee General Comment No 22 *Article 18 (Freedom of Thought, Conscience and Religion* HRI/GEN/1/Rev.8 concerning Art 18 of the ICCPR will be some relevance in interpreting Art 14 of the CRC, subject always to exercising the caution required when transposing the position of adults and children.

Freedom of Thought, Conscience and Religion

Scope of Freedom of Thought Conscience and Religion

10.9   The *freedom* of thought, conscience and religion means that the State does not prescribe religious orthodoxy or prohibit particular religions or beliefs.[26] In *Church of New Faith v Comr For Pay-Roll Tax*[27] the High Court of Australia held that:

> 'Freedom of religion, the paradigm freedom of conscience, is the essence of a free society. The chief function in the law of a definition of religion is to mark out an area within which a person subject to the law is free to believe and act in accordance with his belief without legal restraint …'[28]

In *R v Big M Drug Mart*[29] the Supreme Court of Canada considered the concept of freedom of religion and observed that:

> 'The essence of the concept of freedom of religion is the right to entertain such religious beliefs as a person chooses, the right to declare religious beliefs openly and without fear of hindrance or reprisal, and the right to manifest religious belief by worship and practice or by teaching and dissemination.'

The German Federal Constitutional Court has held that freedom of religion guarantees not only the freedom to believe or not to believe but also the right of a person to orientate their entire behaviour to the tenets of their faith and to act according to their convictions.[30] It should be noted that the ambit and approach to freedom of thought, conscience and religion in a given State will inevitably be influenced by the history and nature of the relationship between personal conscience, the practice of religion and the State in question.[31]

Absence of Coercion

10.10   The concept of 'freedom' necessarily implies an absence of coercion, pressure or constraint. In *R v Big M Drug Mart*[32] Dickson CJ held as follows in respect of the concept of freedom as it pertained to matters of religion:

> 'Freedom can primarily be characterised by the absence of coercion or constraint. If a person is compelled by the state or the will of another to a course of action or inaction which he would not otherwise have chosen, he is not acting of his own volition and he cannot be said to be truly free … Coercion includes not only such blatant forms of compulsion as direct commands to act or refrain from acting on pain of sanction, coercion includes indirect forms of control which determine or limit alternative courses of conduct available to others. Freedom in a broad sense embraces both the absence of coercion and constraint, and the right to manifest beliefs and practices. Freedom means that, subject to

---

[26]   Shelton, D and Kiss, A *A Draft Model Law on Freedom of Religion* in van der Vyver, J and Witte, J (eds) *Religious Human Rights in Global Perspective* (1996) p 572.

[27]   (1982) 154 CLR 120.

[28]   See also *Centrepoint Community Growth Trust v IRC* [1985] 1 NZLR 673 (endorsing the approach in *Church of New Faith v Comr For Pay-Roll Tax*). For the approach in the US see *Torcasco v Watkins* (1961) 367 US 488 (United States Supreme Court), in Canada see *Syndicat Northcrest v Amselem* (2004) 241 DLR (Supreme Court of Canada) and in India see *Hindu Religious Endowments, Madras (Comr) v Sri Lakshmiranda Thirtha Swamiar of Sri Shirur Mutt* [1954] SCR 105 (Supreme Court of India).

[29]   [1985] 1 SCR 295.

[30]   BVerfG 11 April 1972 2 BvR 75/71.

[31]   Van Bueren *The International Law on the Rights of the Child* (1998) Martinus Nijhoff, p 155.

[32]   [1985] 1 SCR 295.

such limitations as are necessary to protect public safety, order, health, or morals or the fundamental rights and freedoms of others, no one is to be forced to act in a way contrary to his beliefs or his conscience.'

Article 18(2) of the ICCPR expressly provides that 'No one shall be subject to coercion which would impair his freedom to have or to adopt a religion or belief of his choice'. Article 1(2) of the Declaration on the Elimination of All Forms of Intolerance and Discrimination Based on Religion or Belief provides that 'No one shall be subject to coercion which would impair his freedom to have a religion or belief of his choice'. Thus, for example, the freedom of girls to practice religion should not be constrained by rules requiring permission from third parties, or by interference from fathers, husbands, brothers or others.[33]

10.11 Article 14 of the CRC is considerably less detailed than Art 18 of the ICCPR and omits any express reference to the absence of coercion in respect of having or adopting a religion of the child's choice. However, the use of the term 'freedom' in Art 14 of the CRC clearly implies absence of coercion or pressure on the child. This issue is considered in depth below when examining Art 14 of the CRC in detail. The Standard Rules on the Equalisation of Opportunities for Persons with Disabilities r 12 provide that States should encourage, in consultation with religious authorities, measures to eliminate discrimination and make religious activities accessible to persons with disabilities, including encouraging the accessibility of religious literature to persons with sensory impairments.

Best Interests and Freedom of Thought, Conscience and Religion

10.12 Whilst the best interests of the child are paramount in domestic decisions concerning the religious upbringing of children[34] and are routinely considered to be so, in many other national jurisdictions, the best interests principle has been very little discussed in the context of the child's right to freedom of thought, conscience and religion in international law.[35] However, the child's right to freedom of thought, conscience and religion pursuant to Art 14 of the CRC must be interpreted in line with the best interests of the child in accordance with Art 3 of the Convention such that where the child's right to freedom of thought, conscience and religion is in potential conflict with his or her own best interests, those interests will be a primary consideration. The child's best interests will likewise be a primary consideration where the parents' religious beliefs are in potential conflict with the welfare of the child. In the Canadian case of *P v S*[36] L'Heureux-Dube J observed that:

> '[I]n ruling on a child's best interests, a court is not putting religion on trial nor its exercise by a parent for himself or herself, but is merely examining the way in which the exercise of a given religion by a parent throughout his or her right to access affects the child's best interests ... As the court has reiterated many times, freedom of religion, like any freedom, is

---

[33]   Committee on Economic, Social and Cultural Rights General Comment No 28 *Article 3 (The Equality of Rights between Men and Women)* HRI/GEN/Rev.8 page 222, para 21.

[34]   See *Re S (Minors)(Access: Religious Upbringing)* [1992] 2 FLR 313, *Re P (Section 91(14) Guidelines)(Residence and Religious Heritage)* [1999] 2 FLR 573, *Re J (Specific Issue Orders: Muslim Upbringing and Circumcision)* [1999] 2 FLR 678 and *Re J (Specific Issue Orders: Child's Religious Upbringing and Circumcision)* [2000] 1 FLR 571 CA.

[35]   Langlaude, S *The Right of the Child to Religious Freedom in International Law* (2007) Martinus Nijhoff, pp 111–112.

[36]   108 DLR (4th) 287 at 317.

not absolute.[37] It is inherently limited by the rights and freedoms of others. Whereas parents are free to choose and practise the religion of their choice, such activities can and must be restricted when they are against the child's best interests, without thereby infringing the parents' freedom of religion.'

Likewise, in the US Supreme Court case of *Prince v Massachusetts*[38] Rutledge J considered that parents' rights to manifest their religion are necessarily circumscribed by the interests of the child and held that:

'... neither rights of religion nor rights of parenthood are beyond limitation. Acting to guard the general interest in youth's well being, the state as *parens patriae* may restrict the parent's control by requiring school attendance, regulating or prohibiting the child's labor [sic] and in many other ways. Its authority is not nullified merely because the parent grounds his claim to control the child's course of conduct on religion or conscience. Thus, he cannot claim freedom from compulsory vaccination for the child more than for himself on religious grounds. The right to practice religion freely does not include liberty to expose the community or the child to communicable disease or the latter to ill health or death ... [T]he state has a wide range of power for limiting parental freedom and authority in things affecting the child's welfare; and that this includes, to some extent, matters of conscience and religious conviction ...'

Evolving Capacity and Freedom of Thought, Conscience and Religion

10.13 The concepts of thought, conscience and religion imply a capacity to understand, appreciate and engage rationally with competing ideas and beliefs and, ultimately, the capacity to exercise choice in respect of those ideas and beliefs. In the context of the right of the child to freedom of thought, conscience and religion it is self evident that these faculties are ones that develop and become more sophisticated as the child develops and matures during the course of childhood. The right of the child who is capable of forming his or her own views to express them freely pursuant to the child's right to participate under Art 12 of the CRC and the child's right to freedom of expression under Art 13 of the CRC will also encompass matters of thought, conscience and religion.[39] Accordingly, the concept of evolving capacity,[40] as enshrined in Arts 5,

---

[37]   This statement is not strictly accurate and would have been better articulated by stating that the freedom to *manifest* religion or belief is not absolute. See below **10.45**.

[38]   (1944) 321 US 158. See also *Christian Education South Africa v Minister of Education* (2000) 9 BHRC 53, Const Ct of South Africa per Sachs J: 'Courts throughout the world have shown special solicitude for protecting children from what they have regarded as the potentially injurious consequences of their parents' religious practices. It is now widely accepted that in every matter concerning the child, the child's best interests must be of paramount importance. This Court has recently reaffirmed the significance of this right which every child has. The principle is not excluded in cases where the religious rights of the parent are involved.'

[39]   Note that Art 5 of the Declaration on the Elimination of All Forms of Intolerance and Discrimination Based on Religion or Belief would appear to conflict with this principle. Article 5 provides that:
' '1. The parents or, as the case may be, the legal guardians of the child have the right to organise the life within the family in accordance with their religion or belief and bearing in mind the moral education in which they believe the child should be brought up.
2. Every child shall enjoy the right to have access to education in the matter of religion or belief in accordance with the wishes of his parents or, as the case may be, legal guardians, and shall not be compelled to receive teaching on religion or belief against the wishes of his parents or legal guardians, the best interests of the child being the guiding principle.
3. The child shall be protected from any form of discrimination on the ground of religion or belief. He shall be brought up in a spirit of understanding, tolerance, friendship among peoples, peace and universal brotherhood, respect for freedom of religion or belief of others, and in full consciousness that his energy and talents should be devoted to the service of his fellow men.
4. In the case of a child who is not under the care either of his parents or of legal guardians, due account shall be taken of their expressed wishes or of any other proof of their wishes in the matter of religion or

12 and 14(2) of the CRC[41] is of central importance to the implementation of the child's right to freedom of thought, conscience and religion.

10.14 As a child's capacity evolves over time the child's facility to understand, appreciate and engage rationally with competing ideas and beliefs will also evolve. In relation to matters of thought, conscience and religion, children will move along a continuum from relying on the direction and guidance provided by their parents to ultimately having their own ideas and making their own choices about matters of religion and conscience.[42] In *Prince v Massachusetts*[43] the US Supreme Court described the desirability of achieving a proper balance between the rights of the parents, the power of the State and the developing capacity of the child in respect of the right to freedom of thought, conscience and religion:

> 'On one side is the obviously earnest claim for freedom of conscience and religious practice. With it is allied the parent's claim to authority in her own household and in the rearing of her children. The parent's conflict with the state over control of the child and his training is serious enough when only secular matters are concerned. It becomes the more so when an element of religious conviction enters. Against these sacred private interests, basic in a democracy, stand the interests of society to protect the welfare of children, and the state's assertion of authority to that end, made here in a manner conceded valid if only secular things were involved. The last is no mere corporate concern of official authority. It is the interest of youth itself, and of the whole community, that children be both safeguarded from

---

belief, the best interests of the child being the guiding principle.

5. Practices of a religion or beliefs in which a child is brought up must not be injurious to his physical or mental health or to his full development, taking into account article 1, paragraph 3, of the present Declaration.'

The effect of this provision is that children who are 'not under the care either of his parents or of legal guardians' have greater right to participate than those who are. As it is a non-binding declaration the provisions of Art 12 of the CRC will take precedence over Art 5 of the Declaration on the Elimination of All Forms of Intolerance and Discrimination Based on Religion or Belief.

40   See **4.25** above.

41   Article 14(2) of the CRC requires State parties to respect the role of the parents of the child in providing direction to the child in matters concerning thought, conscience and religion 'in a manner consistent with the evolving capacities of the child' (see **10.35** below). Newell and Hodgkin characterise Art 14(2) as providing for 'qualified parental direction' in respect of matter of thought, conscience and religion (see Newell, P and Hodgkin, R *Implementation Handbook for the Convention on the Rights of the Child* (2008) 3rd edn, UNICEF, p 189).

42   See Sachs J in *Christian Education South Africa v Minister of Education* (2000) 9 BHRC 53, Const Ct of South Africa commenting on the desirability of hearing the views of children in a case concerning freedom of religion: 'We have not had the assistance of a *curator ad litem* to represent the interests of the children. It was accepted in the High Court that it was not necessary to appoint such a curator because the state would represent the interests of the child. This was unfortunate. The children concerned were from a highly conscientised community and many would have been in their late teens and capable of articulate expression. Although both the state and the parents were in a position to speak on their behalf, neither was able to speak in their name. A curator could have made sensitive enquiries so as to enable their voice or voices to be heard. Their actual experiences and opinions would not necessarily have been decisive, but they would have enriched the dialogue, and the factual and experiential foundations for the balancing exercise in this difficult matter would have been more secure.' See also the judgment of Langa CJ in *Kwazulu-Natal v Pillay* [2007] ZACC 21 (Const Ct South Africa) 'It is always desirable, and may sometimes be vital, to hear from the person whose religion or culture is at issue. That is often no less true when the belief in question is that of a child. Legal matters involving children often exclude the children and the matter is left to adults to argue and decide on their behalf.' In Switzerland a child above the age of 16 may choose his or her religion (Swiss Civil Code Art 277: 'Independent decisions as to their religious faith shall not be forbidden to children who have reached their sixteenth year') as can a child aged 15 or over in Finland (Act of Freedom of Religion). The Spanish Constitutional Court has recognised that children have the right not to share their parents' beliefs and not to be exposed to proselytising by the parents (*Pedro Carrasco Carrasco* Boletín Official del Estado 156 30 June 200 40–46).

43   (1944) 321 US 158. See also the decision of the US Supreme Court in *Wisconsin v Yoder* (1972) 406 US 205 and in particular the dissenting judgment of Justice Douglas.

abuses and given opportunities for growth into free and independent well developed men and citizens ... neither rights of religion nor rights of parenthood are beyond limitation.'

10.15 In *Christian Education South Africa v Minister of Education*[44] the Constitutional Court of South Africa, in considering a claim that the prohibition of corporal punishment contained in s 10 of the South African Schools Act 1996 violated Christian parents' right to freedom of thought, conscience and religion in that it prevented their 'divinely imposed responsibility for the corporal punishment of their children',[45] highlighted the complexity of the issues raised as between the child, the parents and the State within which context the child's evolving capacity must be considered:

'It is clear from the above that a multiplicity of intersecting constitutional values and interests are involved in the present matter – some overlapping, some competing. The parents have a general interest in living their lives in a community setting according to their religious beliefs, and a more specific interest in directing the education of their children. The child, who is at the centre of the enquiry, is probably a believer, and a member of a family and a participant in a religious community that seeks to enjoy such freedom. Yet the same child is also an individual person who may find himself 'at the other end of the stick', and as such be entitled to the protections of sections 10, 12 and 28. Then, the broad community has an interest in reducing violence wherever possible and protecting children from harm. The overlap and tension between the different clusters of rights reflect themselves in contradictory assessments of how the central constitutional value of dignity is implicated. On the one hand, the dignity of the parents may be negatively affected when the state tells them how to bring up and discipline their children and limits the manner in which they may express their religious beliefs. The child who has grown up in the particular faith may regard the punishment, although hurtful, as designed to strengthen his character. On the other hand, the child is being subjected to what an outsider might regard as the indignity of suffering a painful and humiliating hiding deliberately inflicted on him in an institutional setting. Indeed, it would be unusual if the child did not have ambivalent emotions. It is in this complex factual and psychological setting that the matter must be decided.'

Non-Discrimination and Freedom of Thought, Conscience and Religion

10.16 In the human rights instruments which prohibit discrimination, the prohibition of discrimination on the grounds of religion is rightly ubiquitous.[46] Art 2 of the non-binding Declaration on the Elimination of All Forms of Intolerance and Discrimination Based on Religion or Belief[47] provides that:

'1. No one shall be subject to discrimination by any State, institution, group of persons, or person on the grounds of religion or other belief.

2. For the purposes of the present Declaration, the expression 'intolerance and discrimination based on religion or belief' means any distinction, exclusion, restriction or preference based on religion or belief and having as its purpose or as its effect nullification or impairment of the recognition, enjoyment or exercise of human rights and fundamental freedoms on an equal basis.'[48]

---

[44] (2000) 9 BHRC 53, Const Ct of South Africa.
[45] The claimants relied on Proverbs 22:6, 22:15, 19:18 and 23:13–14 and Deuteronomy 6:4–7 to support their contention that Christian parents had a divinely imposed responsibility to use corporal punishment against their children.
[46] See amongst many examples Art 2(1) ICCPR, Art 2(2) ICESCR and Art 14 ECHR.
[47] General Assembly Resolution 36/55.
[48] See also Art 20(2) of the ICCPR which requires that 'Any advocacy of national, racial or religious hatred that constitutes incitement to discrimination, hostility or violence shall be prohibited by law.'

In addition to the definition provided by Art 2(2) of this Declaration, the use of the word 'intolerance' has been taken to describe the emotional, psychological, philosophical and religious attitudes which may prompt acts of discrimination or violations of religious freedoms, which may in turn also constitute violations of other fundamental rights as well as national laws.[49] Art 4 of the Declaration places a positive duty on States to prevent and eliminate discrimination on the grounds of religion or belief:

'1. All States shall take effective measures[50] to prevent and eliminate discrimination on the grounds of religion or belief in the recognition, exercise and enjoyment of human rights and fundamental freedoms in all fields of civil, economic, political, social and cultural life.

2. All States shall make all efforts to enact or rescind legislation where necessary to prohibit any such discrimination, and to take all appropriate measures to combat intolerance on the grounds of religion or other beliefs in this matter.'

10.17 In respect of children, Art 2(1) of the CRC requires States parties to respect and ensure the rights set forth in the CRC without discrimination of any kind irrespective of, *inter alia*, the child's religion. Further, Art 5(3) of the Declaration on the Elimination of All Forms of Intolerance and Discrimination Based on Religion or Belief provides that:

'3. The child shall be protected from any form of discrimination on the ground of religion or belief.[51] He shall be brought up in a spirit of understanding, tolerance, friendship among peoples, peace and universal brotherhood, respect for freedom of religion or belief of others, and in full consciousness that his energy and talents should be devoted to the service of his fellow men.'[52]

FREEDOM OF THOUGHT, CONSCIENCE AND RELIGION

The Child's Right to Freedom of Thought, Conscience and Religion under the CRC

CRC, Art 14 – Child's Right to Freedom of Thought, Conscience and Religion

10.18 Article 14 of the CRC provides as follows in respect of the child's right to freedom of though, conscience and religion:

'1. States Parties shall respect the right of the child to freedom of thought, conscience and religion.

---

[49] Sullivan, D *Advancing the Freedom of Religion or Belief Through the UN Declaration on the Elimination of Religious Intolerance and Discrimination* (1988) 82 Am. J. Int. L. 487.

[50] The concept of 'effective measures' will include education (Sullivan, D *Advancing the Freedom of Religion or Belief Through the UN Declaration on the Elimination of Religious Intolerance and Discrimination* (1988) 82 Am. J. Int. L. 487).

[51] See also the Committee on the Rights of the Child General Comment No 6 *Treatment of Unaccompanied and Separated Children outside their Country of Origin* HRI/GEN/Rev.8 p 408, para 31(iii) and Art 1A (2) of the 1951 Refugee Convention concerning the requirement to demonstrate a well founded fear of being persecuted on the grounds of race, religion, nationality, membership of a particular social group or political opinion.

[52] See also the UN Convention against Discrimination in Education, Art 5 (UNTS, vol. 429, p 93). The United Kingdom accepted the Convention against Discrimination in Education on 14 March 1962.

2. States Parties shall respect the rights and duties of the parents and, when applicable, legal guardians, to provide direction to the child in the exercise of his or her right in a manner consistent with the evolving capacities of the child.

3. Freedom to manifest one's religion or beliefs may be subject only to such limitations as are prescribed by law and are necessary to protect public safety, order, health or morals, or the fundamental rights and freedoms of others.'

The wording of Art 14 represents a hitherto unusual approach to the child's freedom of thought, conscience and religion in that it eschews the normal approach of international law, namely to consider State duties and parental rights in respect of matters of conscience and religion concerning children, primarily in the sphere of education, rather than, as enshrined in Art 14, the child's right to freedom of thought, conscience and religion as a freestanding concept.[53]

CRC, Art 14(1) – Ambit

10.19 Article 14(1) of the CRC stipulates that States Parties shall respect the right of the child to freedom of thought, conscience and religion.

(i) Freedom of thought

10.20 The concept of freedom of thought enshrined in Art 14 of the CRC is closely linked to the child's right to form and express views as enshrined in Art 12 of the CRC. Likewise, the practical implementation of the child's right to freedom of thought, conscience and religion is related to the freedom to seek, receive and impart information and ideas of all kinds under Art 13 of the CRC, the child's right to access to appropriate information under Art 17 of the CRC and to the education of the child under Arts 28 and 29 of the CRC. The child's right to privacy under Art 16 of the CRC will also be relevant in that the child's right to privacy implies that the child has a right to the privacy of his or her own thoughts.[54] It should be noted that the restrictions set out in Art 14(3) concerning the manifestation of religion and belief do not apply to the right to freedom of thought. The only check on the child's right to freedom of thought is the direction that may be provided to the child by his or her parents under Art 14(2). Accordingly, no child can be compelled to reveal his or her thoughts.[55]

(ii) Freedom of Conscience

10.21 Issues of conscience for children may manifest in a variety of contexts and in respect of a wide range of subjects, for example dietary issues such as vegetarianism, philosophies such as pacifism[56] and conscientious objection[57] concerning armed conflict and political beliefs centred on educational, social or environmental concerns to name

---

[53] Van Bueren *The International Law on the Rights of the Child* (1998) Martinus Nijhoff, p 159.
[54] Newell, P and Hodgkin, R *Implementation Handbook for the Convention on the Rights of the Child* (2008) 3rd edn, UNICEF, p 186.
[55] Human Rights Committee General Comment No 22 *Article 18 (Freedom of Thought, Conscience and Religion)* 1993 HRI/GEN/1/Rev 8, p 195, para 3.
[56] In his Nobel Lecture Seán McBride noted that 'To the rights enshrined in the Universal Declaration of Human Rights one more might, with relevance, be added. It is 'The Right to Refuse to Kill' (MacBride, S *The Imperatives of Survival* Nobel Lecture, December 12 1974).
[57] See the Report of the UN Secretary General E/CN.4/1997/99 and the Commission on Human Rights Resolution No 1998/77 *Conscientious Objection to Military Service* which recognises that persons already performing military service may develop conscientious objections. Conscientious objection may be defined as the refusal to perform armed service or any other direct or indirect participation in armed conflicts for reasons of conscience or profound conviction arising from religious, ethical, moral, humanitarian,

but a very few. In relation to conscientious objection, any right to the same is implied from the international human rights instruments as there is no express right to object to participating in armed conflict on the grounds of conscience.[58] Langlaude argues that, given the international effort to eradicate the recruitment of child soldiers, consideration of the issue of conscientious objection in respect of children constitutes an improper focus.[59] However, given persons already performing military service may develop conscientious objections[60] and in circumstances where many States, including the United Kingdom, permit voluntary entry into the armed forces prior to the age of 18, it seems unrealistic not to acknowledge this as a potential issue for children and young people.[61]

10.22 As with respect to the right to freedom of thought, the restrictions on the manifestation of religion and belief set out in Art 14(3) of the CRC do not apply to the right to freedom of conscience. The only check on the child's right to freedom of conscience is the direction which may be provided by his or her parents under Art 14(2).

(iii) Freedom of Religion

Freedom of Religion – Art 14(1) CRC

Ambit of the Child's Right to Freedom of Religion under Art 14(1) CRC

10.23 Article 14(1) of the CRC enshrines the right to freedom of religion for the child subject only to the provisions of Art 14(2) concerning parental direction and the very limited restrictions set out in Art 14(3) concerning the *manifestation* of religion and belief. The right to freedom of religion under Art 14 of the CRC will protect theistic, non-theistic and atheistic beliefs on the part of the child, whether or not traditional or institutional in character, as well as the child's right not to profess any religion or belief, with the terms religion and belief being broadly construed.[62] Read together, Art 14 and

---

philosophical or political motive (see UN Doc E/CN.4/1989/30 and Van Bueren *The International Law on the Rights of the Child* (1998) Martinus Nijhoff, p 152).

[58] Van Bueren *The International Law on the Rights of the Child* (1998) Martinus Nijhoff, p 152. But see Art 8(3) of the ICCPR ('No one shall be required to perform forced or compulsory labour ... For the purposes of this paragraph the term 'forced or compulsory labour' shall not include ... Any service of a military character and, in countries where conscientious objection is recognised, any national service required by law of conscientious objectors'), Art 4 of the ECHR ('No one shall be required to perform forced or compulsory labour ... For the purposes of this article the term 'forced or compulsory labour' shall not include any service of a military character or, in case of conscientious objectors in countries where they are recognised, service exacted instead of compulsory military service') and Art 6(3)(b) of the American Convention on Human Rights ('No one shall be required to perform forced or compulsory labour ... For the purposes of this article, the following do not constitute forced or compulsory labor ... military service and, in countries in which conscientious objectors are recognised, national service that the law may provide for in lieu of military service'). See also Recommendation 1518 (2001) Exercise of the Right of Conscientious Objection to Military Service in Council of Europe Member States which provides that 'The right of conscientious objection is a fundamental aspect of the right to freedom of thought, conscience and religion enshrined in the Universal Declaration of Human Rights and the European Convention on Human Rights.'

[59] Langlaude, S *The Right of the Child to Religious Freedom in International Law* (2007) Martinus Nijhoff, p 202 criticising the approach of Van Bueren in *The International Law on the Rights of the Child* (1998) Martinus Nijhoff, p 152.

[60] See Commission on Human Rights Resolution No 1998/77 *Conscientious Objection to Military Service*.

[61] See **10.59** below.

[62] Human Rights Committee General Comment No 22 *Article 18 (Freedom of Thought, Conscience and Religion)* HRI/GEN/1/Rev 8, p 195, para 2. The general principles set out in Human Rights Committee General Comment No 22 *Article 18 (Freedom of Thought, Conscience and Religion)* HRI/GEN/1/Rev.8 concerning Art 18 of the CCPR will be some relevance in interpreting Art 14 of the CRC, subject always to exercising the caution required when transposing the position of adults and children. By Art 4(2) of the ICCPR the right to freedom of religion cannot be derogated from even in times of public emergency.

Art 16 of the CRC (child's right to privacy) will operate to ensure that no child can be compelled to reveal his or her adherence to a particular religion or belief.

10.24 The child's right to freedom of religion comprises both negative and positive rights. The negative rights ensure the child is protected against unjustified intervention by the State in his or her religious freedom, which right will also protect the child's relationship with his or her parents as it concerns religion and belief and/or his or her religious community. The child's positive rights will compel the State to take steps to ensure that the child can exercise his or her right to freedom of religion by protecting the child from actions of third parties, including parents and organs of the State itself, which may interfere with the child's rights by providing access to procedural measures to facilitate the child's rights. Such measures will include procedures which facilitate the participation of the child in matters of religion and measures which ensure the efficacy of other substantive rights of the child which are relevant to the implementation of the child's right to freedom of religion.[63]

The Child's Freedom to Choose a Religion

10.25 The primary questions raised by the provisions of Art 14 of the CRC within the context of the child's right to freedom of religion are when can a child choose a religion for themselves and in what circumstances can children change or abandon a religion of their own volition.

10.26 Article 14 of the CRC omits the express right to choice of religion which is enshrined in the International Covenant on Civil and Political Rights.[64] Art 18(1) of the ICCPR elaborates on the bare elements of the right to freedom of religion, providing that:

> 'This right shall include freedom to have or to adopt a religion or belief of his choice,[65] and freedom, either individually or in community with others and in public or private, to manifest his religion or belief in worship, observance, practice and teaching.'[66]

Whilst this passage was originally contained in the draft of Art 14(1) of the CRC it was subsequently removed by reason of a failure between States to reach agreement on the appropriate terms.[67] This however does not necessarily militate against a conclusion that the right of children to choose a religion is implied by Art 14(1) of the CRC.

---

[63] Langlaude, S *The Right of the Child to Religious Freedom in International Law* (2007) Martinus Nijhoff, pp 56–61.

[64] See Van Bueren, G *The Right to be the Same, the Right to be Different* in Lindholm, T, Durham, C and Tahzib-Lie, B (eds) *Facilitating Freedom of Religion and Belief* (2004) 561 and Cohen, C *United Nations Convention on the Rights of the Child: Introductory Note* (1990) 44 Int'l Comm'n Jurists Rev 36.

[65] See **10.35** below concerning the role of parents in the child's having or adopting a religion or belief of his or her choice.

[66] See also the similar terms of Art 1(1) of the UN Declaration on the Elimination of All Forms of Intolerance and Discrimination Based on Religion or Belief (General Assembly Resolution 36/55) 'Everyone shall have the right to freedom of thought, conscience and religion. This right shall include the freedom to have a religion or whatever belief of his choice, and freedom, either individually or in community with others and in public or private, to manifest his religion or belief in worship, observance, practice and teaching.'

[67] The failure to reach agreement on the inclusion of this passage in Art 14(1) stemmed from the fact that in some religions children follow the religion of their parents as a matter of divine law (see Van Bueren *The International Law on the Rights of the Child* (1998) Martinus Nijhoff, p 157). Note that Sweden, the Netherlands and Belgium each issued an interpretive declaration to the effect that they had joined in the consensus on the final wording of Art 14 on the understanding that such wording encompassed the child's right to have or adopt a religion or belief of his or choice as soon as the child is capable of making such a choice having regard to his or her age and maturity. See also Art 41 of the CRC.

10.27 In its General Comment No 22 *Article 18 (Freedom of Thought, Conscience and Religion)* the Human Rights Committee makes clear that the freedom to 'have or adopt' a religion or belief in Art 18(1) necessarily entails the freedom to choose a religion or belief, including the right to replace one's current religion or belief with another or to adopt atheistic views, as well as the right to retain one's religion or belief.[68] Further, the Human Rights Committee has accepted in principle that under Art 18(1) of the ICCPR the child has a right to adopt a religion of his or her choice.[69] Within this context, the Human Rights Committee has suggested that the inability of a child of Muslim parents to change religion may conflict with Art 18 of the ICCPR.[70] Further, the Universal Declaration of Human Rights, which upholds the freedom of thought, conscience and religion of *everyone*[71] stipulates that the right to freedom of though, conscience and religion includes the freedom to change religion or belief[72] as does Art 9(1) of the ECHR and Art 12 of the American Convention on Human Rights. Article 12 of the CRC requires the views of the child to be taken into account in the choice of religion.[73] Within this context, the Committee on the Rights of the Child has recognised clearly that children have the right to select a religion of their choice, which choice must be made of their own free will.[74] The Committee has expressed the view that the child's right to choose a religion must rely on a rights-based approach as opposed to 'an approach based on concern for the welfare or protection of the child as a passive subject of the law'.[75]

10.28 Having regard to the foregoing matters, it is submitted that the 'freedom of religion' enshrined in Art 14(1) of the CRC must encompass the right of the child to choose a religion or belief subject to the provisions of Art 14(2) and the principle of evolving capacity.[76] In addition to the applicability of the principle of evolving capacity, this right of the child to choose his or her religion will be implemented having regard to the principles of best interests under Art 3 of the CRC. It must be acknowledged that the precise ambit of the child's right to choose a religion remains uncertain.[77] In particular, in respect of religions which consider that the child should not be permitted to choose any religion other than that practiced by his or her parents the traditional

---

[68] Human Rights Committee General Comment No 22 1993 HRI/GEN/1/Rev 8, p 195, para 5 and see Langlaude, S *The Right of the Child to Religious Freedom in International Law* (2007) Martinus Nijhoff, p 70. However, see also Evans, M *Religious Liberty and International Law in Europe* (1997) Cambridge University Press, p 202 (arguing that the text of Art 18 is open to the interpretation that it allows an individual to continue in a faith, to adopt a faith but not to abandon a faith already held) and Evans, M *Human Rights, Religious Liberty and the Universality Debate* in O'Dair, R and Lewis, A (eds) *Law and Religion* (2001) Oxford University Press 205–226, p 218. See also McBride, J *Autonomy of Will and Religious Freedom* in Flauss, J-F. (ed) *International Protection of Religious Freedom* (2002) Bruylant 93, p 103.

[69] UN Doc A/36/40/1981.

[70] UN Doc A/37/40 (1982), p 40, para 180.

[71] Universal Declaration of Human Rights, Art 18.

[72] Universal Declaration of Human Rights, Art 18. Note that Art 8 of the UN Declaration on the Elimination of All Forms of Intolerance and Discrimination Based on Religion or Belief (General Assembly Resolution 36/55) provides that 'Nothing in the present Declaration shall be construed as restricting or derogating from any right defined in the Universal Declaration of Human Rights and the International Covenants on Human Rights.'

[73] See Croatia CRC/C/SR.280 (1996), para 12.

[74] See Morroco CRC/C/SR.317 (1996), para 51 and Lithuania CRC/C/SR.1101 (2006), para 36. Note that the Committee has also made clear that a child of sufficient understanding may choose to be exempted from religious education (Lithuania CRC/C/SR.1101 (2006), para 36) and that a child who chooses to participate in religious education may give up such classes before the completion of the school year (see Croatia CRC/C/SR.280 (1996) at 12).

[75] See Monaco CRC/C/SR.717 (2001) at 62.

[76] See **10.35** below.

[77] Sullivan, D *Advancing the Freedom of Religion or Belief Through the UN Declaration on the Elimination of Religious Intolerance and Discrimination* (1988) 82 Am. J. Int. L. 487.

public/private distinction in international law is likely to be employed where divine law is relied on as taking precedence over the rights enshrined in Art 14(1) of the CRC.[78]

Child's Freedom to Change or Abandon Religions

10.29 A further question in relation to the right to freedom of religion under Art 14(1) of the CRC is whether that right encompasses a right of the child to *change* religions or to abandon religious belief.[79] Having regard to the principles outlined in the previous section, it is at least arguable that the rights enshrined in Art 14(1) of the CRC must include the right to reject a current belief or religion and choose to accept or not accept another,[80] or to adopt atheistic views in addition to the right to retain one's religion or belief.[81] However, as with the child's right to choose a religion, the ambit of the child's right to change or abandon religion altogether remain at present uncertain.[82]

Non-Discrimination and the Child's Right to Freedom of Religion under Art 14(1), CRC

10.30 Article 14 of the CRC must be read with Art 2 of the CRC, which provides not only that States parties must ensure the rights set forth in the CRC to each child without discrimination on, *inter alia*, the grounds of religion but also that 'States Parties shall take all appropriate measures to ensure that the child is protected against all forms of discrimination or punishment on the basis of the status, activities, expressed opinions, or beliefs of the child's parents, legal guardians, or family members'.[83] The child should accordingly not only be protected from discrimination on the grounds of his or her religion but should also not be subject to discrimination on the grounds of the religion or beliefs of his or her parents or legal guardian. The fact that a religion is a 'State' religion or is practiced by the majority of the population in the State should not result in the impairment of the child's right under Art 14(1) or any of the other rights enshrined in the CRC and should not cause the child to be discriminated against on the grounds that the child adheres to a different religion or does not have a religious belief.[84] The implementation of the child's rights under Art 14(1) must not be the cause of discrimination in relation to any other right under the CRC.

Freedom of Religion – Art 30, CRC

10.31 Article 30 of the CRC enshrines the right of a child who belongs to an ethnic, religious or linguistic minority or who is indigenous to profess and practice his or her own religion in the following terms:

> 'In those States in which ethnic, religious or linguistic minorities or persons of indigenous origin exist, a child belonging to such a minority or who is indigenous shall not be denied the right, in community with other members of his or her group, to enjoy his or her own culture, to profess and practise his or her own religion, or to use his or her own language.'

---

[78] Van Bueren *The International Law on the Rights of the Child* (1998) Martinus Nijhoff, p 158.

[79] This question is particularly relevant in respect of religions in which the abandonment of that religion or the adoption of another religion is contrary to the divine law of the original religion.

[80] Sullivan, D *Advancing the Freedom of Religion or Belief Through the UN Declaration on the Elimination of Religious Intolerance and Discrimination* (1988) 82 Am. J. Int. L. 487.

[81] Human Rights Committee General Comment No 22 1993 HRI/GEN/1/Rev 8, p 195, para 5.

[82] Sullivan, D *Advancing the Freedom of Religion or Belief Through the UN Declaration on the Elimination of Religious Intolerance and Discrimination* (1988) 82 Am. J. Int. L. 487.

[83] CRC, Art 2(2).

[84] Human Rights Committee General Comment No 22 *Article 18 (Freedom of Thought, Conscience and Religion)* 1993 HRI/GEN/1/Rev 8, p 196, para 9.

Fortin points out that the words 'in community with other members of his or her group' concentrates on the minority group as a cohesive whole rather than the individual child members of that group.[85] The wording of Art 30 of the CRC reflects that of Art 27 of the ICCPR which provides that 'In those States in which ethnic, religious or linguistic minorities exist, persons belonging to such minorities shall not be denied the right, in community with the other members of their group, to enjoy their own culture, to profess and practice their own religion, or to use their own language'. In its General Comment No 23 *Article 27 (Rights of Minorities)*[86] the Human Rights Committee makes clear that:

> 'The terms used in article 27 indicate that the persons designed to be protected are those who belong to a group and who share in common a culture, a religion and/or a language. Those terms also indicate that the individuals designed to be protected need not be citizens of the State party ... Although the rights protected under article 27 are individual rights, they depend in turn on the ability of the minority group to maintain its culture, language or religion. Accordingly, positive measures by States may also be necessary to protect the identity of a minority and the rights of its members to enjoy and develop their culture and language and to practice their religion, in community with the other members of the group.'[87]

10.32 In the context of minority groups, the child's individual right to freedom of thought, conscience and religion presents particular issues arising from the fact that the right must considered in the context of the collective right of the minority or indigenous group to maintain minority identity, requiring a balance to be struck between these two potentially competing entitlements.[88] The issue of the correct balance between the child's right to individual religious freedom and the rights of the minority community to renew itself spiritually from generation to generation and to preserve its identity often arises in the context of the child's education. Cullen argues that the proper emphasis should be on whether the education in question fulfils the child's individual potential rather than whether it protects minority characteristics.[89]

10.33 Albeit not a case considering the rights under the CRC, in *Wisconsin v Yoder*[90] the US Supreme Court considered a claim by the Amish community that compulsory education for children until the age of 16 was contrary to the practices of their religion, which required the removal of Amish children from school prior to the age of 16 and their continued vocational education within the Amish community.[91] The Amish communities advanced uncontroverted expert evidence on the effect compulsory high school attendance could have on the continued survival of Amish communities as they existed in the United States. The Supreme Court held that:

---

85   Fortin, J *Children's Rights and the Developing Law* (2009) 3rd edn, Cambridge, p 412.
86   HRI/GEN/1/Rev 8, p 197 at 198–199.
87   See also General Recommendation XXI on the Right to Self Determination (1996) HRI/GEN/1/Rev 8, p 253.
88   Cullen, H *Education Rights and Minority Rights* (1993) International Journal of Law and the Family 143, p 144.
89   Cullen, H *Education Rights and Minority Rights* (1993) International Journal of Law and the Family 143, p 144.
90   (1972) 406 US 205.
91   The primary objection by the Amish communities to compulsory education to the age of 16 was the marked variance between the object of high school and higher education and the Amish religious values and the Amish way of life. In this context, Chief Justice Burger noted that 'The high school tends to emphasise intellectual and scientific accomplishments, self-distinction, competitiveness, worldly success, and social life with other students. Amish society emphasizes informal learning-through-doing; a life of 'goodness,' rather than a life of intellect; wisdom, rather than technical knowledge; community welfare, rather than competition; and separation from, rather than integration with, contemporary worldly society.'

'The conclusion is inescapable that secondary schooling, by exposing Amish children to worldly influences in terms of attitudes, goals, and values contrary to beliefs, and by substantially interfering with the religious development of the Amish child and his integration into the way of life of the Amish faith community at the crucial adolescent stage of development, contravenes the basic religious tenets and practice of the Amish faith, both as to the parent and the child.'

10.34 Whilst the issues in *Wisconsin v Yoder* clearly engaged not only the religious rights of a minority but also the child's right to individual religious freedom, in reaching this conclusion, the majority of the Supreme Court did not consider it necessary to examine the rights of the Amish children who would be affected by their decision, the majority considering that, in circumstances where the children themselves did not seek to attend school beyond the period allowed for by the Amish religion, the dispute in issue was between the parents and the State.[92] However, in a dissenting judgment Justice Douglas rejected this approach, holding that the view of the majority did not sufficiently consider the position of the Amish children themselves in endorsing the exemption which affected them, stating that:

'The Court's analysis assumes that the only interests at stake in the case are those of the Amish parents on the one hand, and those of the State on the other. The difficulty with this approach is that, despite the Court's claim, the parents are seeking to vindicate not only their own free exercise claims, but also those of their high-school-age children ... no analysis of religious-liberty claims can take place in a vacuum. If the parents in this case are allowed a religious exemption, the inevitable effect is to impose the parents' notions of religious duty upon their children. Where the child is mature enough to express potentially conflicting desires, it would be an invasion of the child's rights to permit such an imposition without canvassing his views ... if an Amish child desires to attend high school, and is mature enough to have that desire respected, the State may well be able to override the parents' religiously motivated objections.'

CRC 14(2) – Ambit

(i) Parental Direction and Evolving Capacity under Art 14(2), CRC

10.35 The foregoing analysis of the child's right to freedom of thought, conscience and religion must be considered subject to the provisions of Art 14(2) of the CRC which requires State parties to respect the rights of parents to provide 'direction' to the child in matters of religion subject to the evolving capacity of the child. Article 14(2) of the CRC provides as follows in respect of the role of evolving capacity in the implementation of the child's right to freedom of thought, conscience and religion:

'2. States Parties shall respect the rights and duties of the parents and, when applicable, legal guardians, to provide direction to the child in the exercise of his or her right in a manner consistent with the evolving capacities[93] of the child.

---

[92]   Chief Justice Burger expressly noted that 'Our holding in no way determines the proper resolution of possible competing interests of parents, children, and the State in an appropriate state court proceeding in which the power of the State is asserted on the theory that Amish parents are preventing their minor children from attending high school despite their expressed desires to the contrary. Recognition of the claim of the State in such a proceeding would, of course, call into question traditional concepts of parental control over the religious up-bringing and education of their minor children recognised in this Court's past decisions. It is clear that such an intrusion by a State into family decisions in the area of religious training would give rise to grave questions of religious freedom comparable to those raised here.'

[93]   See **4.25** above.

10.36 The child's right to freedom of thought, conscience and religion pursuant to Art 14(1) as described above is accordingly subject to qualified parental direction.[94] The permissible nature and extent of that parental direction will be dependent on the age, development and understanding of the child. As the child's capacity evolves the child's capacity to understand, appreciate and engage rationally with competing ideas and beliefs also evolves. Article 14(2) maintains the CRC's emphasis on the child's right to freedom of thought, conscience and religion by expressly linking parental direction with the child's evolving capacity,[95] ensuring that a child who is of sufficient age and understanding can participate in decisions concerning, and eventually make up his or her own mind on matters of thought, conscience and religion. The provisions of Art 14(2) are reinforced by the terms of Art 5 of the CRC. The right of the child who can form views to express them freely pursuant to Art 12 of the CRC will also encompass matters of religion, as will the child's right to freedom of expression under Art 13 of the CRC.

10.37 The effect of these provisions when read together is that whilst parents provide direction to the child in relation to matters of religion and conscience, that direction must respect the child's right to express his or her views concerning religion and to participate in decisions concerning the same in a manner consistent with the evolving capacities of the child. As such parental intervention in matters of religion and conscience should not go beyond what is necessary to provide direction and guidance to the child.[96] Parental direction in relation to matters of thought, conscience and religion does not equate with their chosen religious and moral education.[97] It is the child who exercises the right to freedom of thought, conscience and religion.[98] In principle, the child's right to freedom of thought, conscience and religion is non-derogable.[99]

10.38 It has been suggested that Art 14(2) of the CRC will operate to place a duty on States parties to ensure that parents exercise their qualified right of direction in a manner consistent with the evolving capacities of the child.[100] States parties are certainly under a duty to recognise that parental power to provide direction to children in respect of matters of thought, conscience and religion is not unlimited and decreases as the child matures. In its General Comment No 7 *Implementing Child Rights in Early Childhood*[101] the Committee on the Rights of the Child stipulated that:

---

[94] Newell, P and Hodgkin, R *Implementation Handbook for the Convention on the Rights of the Child* (2008) 3rd edn, UNICEF, p 189.

[95] Newell, P and Hodgkin, R *Implementation Handbook for the Convention on the Rights of the Child* (2008) 3rd edn, UNICEF, p 185.

[96] Direction and guidance should be 'child-centred' and achieved through dialogue and example with the aim of enhancing the child's capacities to exercise his or her rights (see Committee on the Rights of the Child General Comment No 7 *Implementing Child Rights in Early Childhood* CRC/C/GC/7, para 17).

[97] See Republic of Korea CRC/C/SR.277 (1996) at 31.

[98] Newell, P and Hodgkin, R *Implementation Handbook for the Convention on the Rights of the Child* (2008) 3rd edn, UNICEF, p 188. See also Norway CRC/C/SR.150 (1994) at 42, The Holy See CRC/C/SR.256 (1995) at 10 and Turkey CRC/C/SR.701 (2001) at 25. Fortin asserts that the right to freedom of religion is unambiguously that of the child with parents only able to provide direction consistent with the child's developing competence and his or her right to participate and right to freedom of expression (Fortin, J *Children's Rights and the Developing Law* (2009) 3rd edn, Cambridge, p 44).

[99] See Bangladesh CRC/C/SR.380 (1997) at 19.

[100] Brems, E *Article 14: The Right to Freedom of Thought, Conscience and Religion* in Alen, J, Vande Lanotte, J, Verhellen, E, Anf, F, Berghmans, E and Verheyde, M (eds) *A Commentary on the United Nations Convention on the Rights of the Child* (2006) Martinus Nijhoff 1, p 29.

[101] Committee on the Rights of the Child General Comment No 7 *Implementing Child Rights in Early Childhood* HRI/GEN/Rev.8 p 440, para 17.

'Parents (and others) should be encouraged to offer 'direction and guidance' in a child-centred way, through dialogue and example, in ways that enhance young children's capacities to exercise their rights, including their right to participation (art. 12) and their right to freedom of thought, conscience and religion (art. 14).'

(ii) Parental Direction and Religious Education

10.39 The position of the child in relation to parental direction in respect of matters of conscience and religion generally is significantly stronger under Art 14(2) of the CRC than is the position of the child in relation to the international law governing parental direction as to the provision of religious education for children. Article 26(3) of the Universal Declaration of Human Rights stipulates that 'Parents have a prior right to choose the kind of education that shall be given to their children'. Article 18(4) of the International Covenant on Civil and Political Rights states that:

'4. The States Parties to the present Covenant undertake to have respect for the liberty of parents and, when applicable, legal guardians to ensure the religious and moral education of their children in conformity with their own convictions.'[102]

Article 13(3) of the International Covenant on Economic, Social and Cultural Rights provides as follows in relation to the provision of religious education for children:

'3. The States Parties to the present Covenant undertake to have respect for the liberty of parents and, when applicable, legal guardians to choose for their children schools, other than those established by the public authorities, which conform to such minimum educational standards as may be laid down or approved by the State and to ensure the religious and moral education of their children in conformity with their own convictions.'

Article 5(2) of the Declaration on the Elimination of All Forms of Intolerance and Discrimination Based on Religion or Belief provides that:

'2. Every child shall enjoy the right to have access to education in the matter of religion or belief in accordance with the wishes of his parents or, as the case may be, legal guardians, and shall not be compelled to receive teaching on religion or belief against the wishes of his parents or legal guardians, the best interests of the child being the guiding principle.'

10.40 In relation to the religious education of the child, the traditional approach in international law has been to place a clear duty on the State to educate the child in accordance with the religious convictions and beliefs of the parents. The Human Rights Committee has commented that the liberty of parents and guardians to ensure religious and moral education cannot be restricted.[103] This approach, and the foregoing provisions that articulate it, were drafted when the political indoctrination that preceded World War II was fresh in the memory. Within this context such provisions are designed to be enabling in nature by providing parents with a means to protect children against the use of education by the State to ideologically indoctrinate the child.[104] In considering these provisions it is important to remember that their context is the

---

[102]   In its General Comment No 22 *Article 18 (Freedom of Thought, Conscience and Religion)* HRI/GEN/1/Rev.8 at page 196, para 6 the Human Rights Committee suggests that Art 18(4) is primarily aimed at ensuring that freedom to teach a religion or belief enshrined in Art 18(1) of the ICCPR is exercised subject to the need to ensure provision for non-discriminatory exemptions or alternatives that would accommodate the wishes of parents and guardians.

[103]   Human Rights Committee General Comment No 22 *Article 18 (Freedom of Thought, Conscience and Religion)* HRI/GEN/1/Rev 8, p 196, para 8.

[104]   Van Bueren *The International Law on the Rights of the Child* (1998) Martinus Nijhoff, p 159.

protection of the rights of parents as against State. The provisions were not intended to result in interference with the child's rights, although to date this has often been their effect.

10.41 The requirement in Art 14(2) of the CRC for parents 'to provide direction to the child in the exercise of his or her right in a manner consistent with the evolving capacities of the child' implies a right on the part of the child to have his or her choice of religious or moral education respected by his or her parents and the State.[105] The right of children to be educated in accordance with their religious and philosophical convictions is thus advanced by Art 14(2) in respect of children who are sufficiently mature to have their wishes in relation to religious education taken into account.[106]

10.42 Thus, having regard to Art 18(4) of the ICCPR, Art 13(3) of the ICESCR and Art 5(2) of the Declaration on the Elimination of All Forms of Intolerance and Discrimination Based on Religion or Belief, the aim of ensuring that education is not used against parents by the State as a method of religious or political indoctrination of their children does not appear to properly allow for the correct balance between parental rights and the rights of the child in relation to the issue of religious education when the need to account for the child's evolving capacity, his or her right to participate and his or her right to freedom of expression is considered.[107] In particular, Art 18(4) of the ICCPR, Art 13(3) of the ICESCR and Art 5(2) of the Declaration on the Elimination of All Forms of Intolerance and Discrimination Based on Religion or Belief militate against the consideration by the courts of the rights of children as individuals in cases concerning religious education.[108] As Van Bueren rightly observes, whilst these provisions assume that the interests of the child and the parents will always coincide, merely because the wishes of the child and the parents frequently coincide does not necessarily imply that the child can never have an independent interest in matters of thought, conscience and religion or otherwise.[109]

10.43 In the context of these potential difficulties it is important to remember that Art 18(4) of the ICCPR and similar provisions are simply designed to ensure that the State does not interfere with parental discretion as to the religious and moral education of children.[110] The right of the child, both as against the parent and as against the State, to freedom of religion considered in light of his or her age and understanding exists *separately* and is a separate right to be considered under Art 14(1) of the CRC read with Arts 5, 28(1) and 12 of the CRC. Further, Art 18(4) does not compel States parties to

---

[105]   Van Bueren *The International Law on the Rights of the Child* (1998) Martinus Nijhoff, p 160 and see UN Doc. E/CN.4/1989/WG.1/WP.2. See also Art 5(1)(b) of the UN Convention against Discrimination in Education (UNTS, vol. 429, p 93).

[106]   Fortin however cautions that even the CRC contains compromises concerning the child's educational rights which could reduce the child's ability to break away from his or her parent's beliefs through the receipt of a liberal education, citing the potentially competing requirements of Art 29(1)(a) of the CRC, which stresses the need for education to develop the child's personality, talents and abilities to their fullest potential, and Art 29(1)(c) of the CRC which requires that the child's education should develop a respect for the child's parents and his or her own cultural identity, language and values (Fortin, J *Children's Rights and the Developing Law* (2009) 3rd edn, Cambridge, pp 411–412).

[107]   See Van Bueren *The International Law on the Rights of the Child* (1998) Martinus Nijhoff, p 151. This is in part a product of the time the provisions were drafted, being a period prior to the widespread development and acceptance of the concept of children as autonomous holders of rights.

[108]   See **10.53–10.58** below.

[109]   Van Bueren *The International Law on the Rights of the Child* (1998) Martinus Nijhoff, pp 242–243. See also the commentary on *Wisconsin v Yoder* (1972) 406 US 205 above at **10.43**.

[110]   Langlaude, S *The Right of the Child to Religious Freedom in International Law* (2007) Martinus Nijhoff, p 91.

provide education of the parents' choice but rather simply to respect the wishes of parents.[111] Thus, in cases where a parent seeks to persuade a court that the State is failing to ensure the religious and moral education of their children in conformity with the parents' own convictions it is vital that the court also consider, as a separate albeit related question, whether and to what extent the *child's* right to freedom of education is engaged in the decision the court is being asked to make. By taking such an approach all of the competing rights can be properly balanced and, where necessary, the child can obtain protection from education which is pursued in conformity with the parents' own convictions but which in the particular circumstances of the case conflicts with the child's own right to freedom of thought, conscience and religion.[112]

(iii) Parental Disagreement as to the Child's Religion

10.44 International law contains no guidance as to the position where parents cannot agree in relation to the religious upbringing of their children and it has been left to domestic legislatures to deal with these issues, necessarily resulting in such measures taking on the national character of religious debate.[113] However, where parents disagree as between themselves as to the direction to be given to a child in respect of religion under Art 14(2), the dispute should be decided having regard to the child's right to freedom of thought, conscience and religion under Art 14(1) of the CRC and taking into account the views of the child in light of his or her evolving capacity and his or her best interests as a primary consideration under Art 3(1) of the CRC.[114]

CRC 14(3) – Ambit

(i) Restriction on Manifestation of Religion or Beliefs

10.45 Unlike Art 18(1) of the ICCPR, Art 14(1) of the CRC does not contain an express right of the child to freedom to manifest his or religion or belief in worship, observance, practice and teaching.[115] However, Art 14(1) is the specific subject of the limitations prescribed by Art 14(3).[116] The limitations in Art 14(3) deal solely with the legitimate restrictions that may be placed on the freedom to manifest religion or beliefs.

> '3. Freedom to manifest one's religion or beliefs may be subject only to such limitations as are prescribed by law and are necessary to protect public safety, order, health or morals, or the fundamental rights and freedoms of others.'

Hence, the wording of Art 14(3) of the CRC would appear to suggest that Art 14(1) does, or was at least intended by the drafters of the Convention to, enshrine the child's right to freedom to manifest his or her religion or beliefs.

10.46 The limitations in Art 14(3) are restricted solely to the freedom to *manifest* religion or beliefs. Thus no limitation is permitted upon a child's inner thought or moral consciousness, or his or her attitude towards the universe or its creator, religious or

---

[111]   UN Doc A/C.3/SR 1024.

[112]   Fortin, J *Children's Rights and the Developing Law* (2009) 3rd edn, Cambridge, p 411.

[113]   For the approach in domestic law see **10.109–10.113** below.

[114]   Newell, P and Hodgkin, R *Implementation Handbook for the Convention on the Rights of the Child* (2008) 3rd edn, UNICEF, p 189.

[115]   Article 18(1) of the ICCPR stipulates the right to 'either individually or in community with others and in public or private, to manifest his religion or belief in worship, observance, practice and teaching.'

[116]   Detrick, *A Commentary on the Convention on the Rights of the Child*, pp 247 and 252.

otherwise (this being the child's *forum internum)*[117] but rather only on external manifestations of religion or belief and then only in narrowly defined circumstances.[118] In *Christian Education South Africa v Minister of Education*[119] Sachs J articulated the justification for tempering the unimpeded individual right to freedom of thought, conscience and religion with limitations on the manifestation of religion or beliefs within a society:

> 'The underlying problem in any open and democratic society based on human dignity, equality and freedom in which conscientious and religious freedom has to be regarded with appropriate seriousness, is how far such democracy can and must go in allowing members of religious communities to define for themselves which laws they will obey and which not. Such a society can cohere only if all its participants accept that certain basic norms and standards are binding. Accordingly, believers cannot claim an automatic right to be exempted by their beliefs from the laws of the land. At the same time, the state should, wherever reasonably possible, seek to avoid putting believers to extremely painful and intensely burdensome choices of either being true to their faith or else respectful of the law.'

'Manifest'

10.47 Article 14(3) of the CRC and Art 18(3) of the ICCPR are drafted in identical terms.[120] In the context of Art 18(3) of the ICCPR the ambit of the freedom to *manifest* religion, as distinct from the freedom to maintain a religion or belief the Human Rights Committee has stated as follows:[121]

> 'The freedom to manifest religion or belief may be exercised 'either individually or in community with others and in public or private'. The freedom to manifest religion or belief in worship, observance, practice and teaching encompasses a broad range of acts. The concept of worship extends to ritual and ceremonial acts giving direct expression to belief, as well as various practices integral to such acts, including the building of places of worship, the use of ritual formulae and objects, the display of symbols, and the observance of holidays and days of rest. The observance and practice of religion or belief may include not only ceremonial acts but also such customs as the observance of dietary regulations, the wearing of distinctive clothing or head coverings, participation in rituals associated with certain stages of life, and the use of a particular language customarily spoken by a group. In

---

[117] This principle was perhaps most famously articulated by Elizabeth I when she announced that 'I have no desire to make windows into men's souls.'

[118] UN Doc A/4625, para 48 reproduced in Bossuyt, M *Guide to the 'Travaux Préparatoires' of the International Covenant on Civil and Political Rights* (1987), pp 357–358 and see Human Rights Committee General Comment No 22 1993 HRI/GEN/1/Rev.8. The proper boundary between the *forum internum* and actions constituting manifestation of religion or beliefs is the matter of some debate (see for example Taylor who argues that the ambit of the *forum internum* has been unduly limited by the improper characterisation of certain matters as 'manifestations' (Taylor, P *Freedom of Religion: UN and European Human Rights Law and Practice* (2005) Cambridge University Press).

[119] (2000) 9 BHRC 53, Const Ct of South Africa.

[120] See also the Declaration on the Elimination of All Forms of Intolerance and Discrimination Based on Religion or Belief (General Assembly Resolution 36/55) Art 1(3) 'Freedom to manifest one's religion or belief may be subject only to such limitations as are prescribed by law and are necessary to protect public safety, order, health or morals or the fundamental rights and freedoms of others.'

[121] Human Rights Committee General Comment No 22 *Article 18 (Freedom of Thought, Conscience and Religion)* HRI/GEN/1/Rev 8, p 195, para 4. See also the decisions of the Human Rights Committee in *Boodoo v Trinidad and Tobago* (2002) Communication 721/1997 (the freedom to manifest religion or belief in worship, observance, practice and teaching encompasses a broad range of acts and that the concept of worship extends to ritual and ceremonial acts giving expression of belief, as well as various practices integral to such acts) and *Sister Immaculate Joseph and 80 Teaching Sisters of the Holy Cross of the Third Order of St Francis in Mensingen of Sri Lanka v Sri Lanka* (2005) 1249/2004 (the requirement of a religion to spread knowledge, to propagate their beliefs to others and to provide assistance to others will be part of an individuals manifestation of religion and belief).

addition, the practice and teaching of religion or belief includes acts integral to the conduct by religious groups of their basic affairs, such as the freedom to choose their religious leaders, priests and teachers, the freedom to establish seminaries or religious schools and the freedom to prepare and distribute religious texts or publications.'

'Religion or Beliefs'

10.48 Article 14(1) speaks of 'thought, conscience and religion' whilst Art 14(3) speaks of 'religion or beliefs. In its General Comment No 22 the Human Rights Committee makes clear that 'The terms 'belief' and 'religion' in Art 18(3) of the ICCPR are to be broadly construed'.[122]

Limitations on Manifesting Religion or Belief

10.49 Limitations can only be placed on the child's manifestation of religion or beliefs in accordance with the precepts of Art 14(3) of the CRC, namely the protection of public safety, order, health or morals, or the fundamental rights and freedoms of others.[123] In contrast to CRC, Art 10 (family reunification), Art 13 (freedom of expression) and Art 15 (freedom of association) Art 14(3) contains no 'national security' ground for limiting freedom of manifestation of religion or beliefs. The term 'morals' describes 'principles which are not always legally enforceable but which are accepted by a great majority of the citizens as general guidelines for their individual and collective behaviour'[124] The term 'the rights and freedoms of others' does not indicate which rights or freedoms of others may be protected at the expense of the freedoms in question but Henkin suggests that whilst the term might well authorise States to choose between rights enshrined in the CRC, it will not permit States to prefer other rights and interests which it might create by its own law for its own purposes.[125]

10.50 The Human Rights Committee has made clear that in seeking to establish the boundaries of permissible limitation under Art 18(3) of the ICCPR the starting point should be the need to guarantee the right to freedom to manifest religion or belief. Limitations must be established by law and must not be applied in a manner which would vitiate the overall right to freedom of thought, conscience and religion. Thus, by analogy, limitations which *prevent* a child from practicing or not practicing a religion are likely to constitute a breach of Art 14 and Art 12 of the CRC.[126] The limitations stipulated in Art 14(3) are to be strictly interpreted and may be applied only for the purposes for which they were prescribed and must be directly related and proportionate to the specific need on which they are predicated. Limitations may not be imposed for discriminatory purposes or applied in a discriminatory manner.[127]

10.51 In considering the scope of limitations imposed on the child's right to manifest religion or beliefs on the grounds of protecting morals pursuant to Art 14(3) of the CRC it should be remembered that as the concept of morals derives from many social,

---

[122] 1993 HRI/GEN/1/Rev 8, para 2.

[123] See China CRC/C/15/Add.56 (1996) at 17. Langlaude notes that the Committee on the Rights of the Child complies strictly with the wording of Art 14(3) and does not tolerate any exceptions (see Langlaude, S *The Right of the Child to Religious Freedom in International Law* (2007) Martinus Nijhoff, p 137).

[124] Kiss, A *Permissible Limitations on Rights* in Henkin, L (ed) *The International Bill of Rights: The Covenant on Civil and Political Rights* (1981), pp 290–310, p 304.

[125] Henkin, L *Introduction* in Henkin, L (ed) *The International Bill of Rights: The Covenant on Civil and Political Rights* (1981), pp 1–31, p 31.

[126] See Colombia CRC/C/SR.114 (1995) at 28.

[127] See Human Rights Committee General Comment No 22 *Article 18 (Freedom of Thought, Conscience and Religion)* HRI/GEN/1/Rev 8, p 196, paras 3 and 8.

philosophical and religious traditions, limitations on the freedom to manifest a religion or belief for the purpose of protecting morals must be based on principles not deriving exclusively from a single tradition.[128]

10.52 Article 5(5) of the Declaration on the Elimination of Religious Intolerance and of Discrimination based on Religion and Belief provides that practices of a religion or belief in which a child is brought up must not be injurious to his physical or mental health or to his full development. This provision represents one aspect of the wider protection provided with regard to health and morals by Art 14(3).[129]

CRC, Art 14 – Application

(i) Freedom of Thought, Conscience and Religion in Education

10.53 Outside the home, education may form a significant element of a child's religious life. As has been repeatedly emphasised, children do not lose their human rights by virtue of passing through the school gates.[130] The child's right to freedom of thought, conscience and religion under Art 14(1) of the CRC will continue to apply within the context of the child's education and in particular in the implentation of the child's right to the development of his or personality, talents and mental and physical abilities pursuant to Art 29(1)(a) of the CRC.

10.54 It should be noted that it is in the context of education that the potential friction between the child's right to freedom of thought conscience and religion under Art 14(1) of the CRC and the protection accorded to parents against indoctrination of their children by the State in Art 18(4) of the ICCPR, Art 13(3) of the ICESCR and Art 5(2) of the Declaration on the Elimination of All Forms of Intolerance and Discrimination Based on Religion or Belief is most readily seen.[131]

Religious Content of the Curriculum

10.55 CRC, Art 14(1) – Pursuant to the child's right to freedom of thought, conscience and religion a child may choose not to undergo religious education when sufficiently mature to make the choice.[132] Where a child is of sufficient capacity to choose not to participate or to participate in religious education he or she should not require the consent of his of her parents to do so.[133] Children must not be marginalised in education if they abstain from religious instruction.[134] Under Art 14(1) of the CRC children must be able to obtain a dispensation from compulsory religious education.[135]

---

[128] See Human Rights Committee General Comment No 22 *Article 18 (Freedom of Thought, Conscience and Religion)* HRI/GEN/1/Rev 8, p 196, para 8. Note that the concept of margin of appreciation will be important when considering the issue of 'morals' under the ECHR. In *A, B and C v Ireland* (2010) Application No 25579/05, para 222 the European Court of Human Rights stated that 'The Court recalls that it is not possible to find in the legal and social orders of the Contracting States a uniform European conception of morals including on the question of when life begins. By reason of their 'direct and continuous contact with the vital forces of their countries', State authorities are in principle in a better position than the international judge to give an opinion on the 'exact content of the requirements of morals' in their country, as well as on the necessity of a restriction intended to meet them.'

[129] See also CRC, Arts 6(2) and 24(3).

[130] Committee on the Rights of the Child, General Comment No 1 *The Aims of Education* CRC/GC/2001/1, para 8.

[131] See **10.3** above. See also CRC, Art 29(1)(c).

[132] See Cyprus CRC/C/SR.1173 (1996), para 29.

[133] See Poland CRC/C/15/Add.194 (2002), para 32.

[134] See Italy CRC/C/15/Ad.198, paras 29 and 30.

[135] See Ireland CRC/C/SR.1182 (2006), para 9.

If it is possible to choose an alternative subject to that of religious education the child's school must allow for such a choice in an adequate manner.[136] The Committee on the Rights of the Child has also made clear that a child who chooses to participate in religious education may give up such classes before the completion of the school year.[137] Faith schools should not privilege religious instruction to the detriment of professional and scientific instruction.[138] The religious education provided by schools should present the values of all religions rather than focusing on any one religion to encourage social integration for all believers.[139] As such, any compulsory curriculum must provide for the child's right to freedom of religion.[140]

10.56 ICCPR, Art 18(4) and ICESCR, Art 13(3) – In respect of parental views concerning the religious education of children, the Human Rights Committee has suggested that Art 18(4) of the ICCPR means that:[141]

> '... public education that includes instruction in a particular belief or religion is inconsistent with article 18(4) unless provision is made for non-discriminatory exemptions or alternatives that would accommodate the wishes of parents and guardians.'

The alternative educational provision may include the study of the history of religions and ethics provided such alternative instruction is given in a neutral and objective way and respects the convictions of parents and guardians.[142] It should be noted that Art 18(4) of the ICCPR does not compel States parties to provide education of the parents' choice but rather to respect the wishes of parents.[143]

Religious Symbols and Clothing at School

10.57 The Committee on the Rights of the Child has deprecated the prohibition on the wearing of headscarves in school by female pupils[144] and teachers[145] and the prohibition on displaying religious symbols.[146] In *Hudoyberganova v Uzbekistan*[147] the Human Rights Committee considered a claim by a university student that a prohibition on her wearing a headscarf ('hijab') violated her rights under Art 18 and 19 of the ICCPR. The Committee held that:

---

[136]   See Poland CRC/C/15/Add.194 (2002), para 32.
[137]   See Croatia CRC/C/SR.280 (1996) at 12.
[138]   See Gambia CRC/C/SR.739 (2002) at 83 and Benin CRC/C/SR.1183 (2005), para 56.
[139]   See Finland CRC/C/SR.284 (1996) at 28.
[140]   See Armenia CRC/C/15/Add.225, paras 31–32 and Costa Rica CRC/C/15/Add.266, paras 25–26.
[141]   Human Rights Committee General Comment No 22 *Article 18 (Freedom of Thought, Conscience and Religion)* HRI/GEN/1/Rev 8, p 196, para 6. See also Art 13(3) of the CESCR and General Comment No 13 *The Right to Education* HRI/GEN/1/Rev 8, p 71 of the Committee on Economic, Social and Cultural Rights.
[142]   *Hartikainen v Finland* R 9/40 HRC 36, 147 and *Leirvåg et al v Norway* (2003) Communication 1155/2003.
[143]   UN Doc A/C.3/SR 1024.
[144]   See Tunisia CRC/C/15/Add.181, paras 29 and 30.
[145]   See Germany CRC/C/15/Add.226, paras 30 and 31. See also the Human Rights Committee General Comment No 28 *Article 3 (The Equality of Rights Between Men and Women)* HRI/GEN/1/Rev 8, para 13 'The Committee stresses that [regulation of clothing] may involve a violation of a number of rights guaranteed by the Covenant, such as: article 26, on non-discrimination; article 7, if corporal punishment is imposed in order to enforce such a regulation; article 9, when failure to comply with the regulation is punished by arrest; article 12, if liberty of movement is subject to such a constraint; article 17, which guarantees all persons the right to privacy without arbitrary or unlawful interference; articles 18 and 19, when women are subjected to clothing requirements that are not in keeping with their religion or their right of self-expression; and, lastly, article 27, when the clothing requirements conflict with the culture to which the woman can lay a claim'.
[146]   See France CRC/C/15/Add.240, paras 25 and 26.
[147]   Communication 931/2000 (2005).

'... her right to freedom of thought, conscience and religion was violated as she was excluded from University because she refused to remove the headscarf that she wore in accordance with her beliefs. The Committee considers that the freedom to manifest one's religion encompasses the right to wear clothes or attire in public which is in conformity with the individual's faith or religion. Furthermore, it considers that to prevent a person from wearing religious clothing in public or private may constitute a violation of article 18, paragraph 2, which prohibits any coercion that would impair the individual's freedom to have or adopt a religion. As reflected in the Committee's General Comment No 22 (para.5), policies or practices that have the same intention or effect as direct coercion, such as those restricting access to education, are inconsistent with article 18, paragraph 2.... In the particular circumstances of the present case, and without either prejudging the right of a State party to limit expressions of religion and belief in the context of article 18 of the Covenant and duly taking into account the specifics of the context, or prejudging the right of academic institutions to adopt specific regulations relating to their own functioning, the Committee is led to conclude, in the absence of any justification provided by the State party, that there has been a violation of article 18, paragraph 2.'

10.58   In *Multani v Commission Scolaire Marguerite-Bourgeoys*[148] the Supreme Court of Canada considered a dispute concerning the carrying of metal kirpans[149] by a child of the Sikh religion at school. In holding that the school's decision to prohibit the child from wearing his kirpan at school and to permit him to wear a plastic or wooden version infringed his right to freedom of religion, the Supreme Court of Canada noted that the child genuinely believed he would not be complying with the requirement of his religion were he to wear a plastic or wooden version and that the interference with his religion was neither trivial nor insignificant. The Supreme Court further noted that:

'If some students consider it unfair that G may wear his kirpan to school while they are not allowed to have knives in their possession, it is incumbent on the schools to discharge their obligation to instill in their students [the religious tolerance] that is at the very foundation of our democracy. A total prohibition against wearing a kirpan at school undermines the value of this religious symbol and sends students the message that some religious practices do not merit the same protection as others. Accommodating G and allowing him to wear his kirpan under certain conditions demonstrates the importance that our society attaches to protecting freedom of religion and showing respect for its minorities.'

(ii) Freedom of Thought, Conscience and Religion and Armed Conflict

10.59   The Committee on Human Rights has observed that in relation to the concept of conscientious objection to military service that:[150]

'The Covenant does not explicitly refer to a right to conscientious objection, but the Committee believes that such a right can be derived from article 18, inasmuch as the obligation to use lethal force may seriously conflict with the freedom of conscience and the right to manifest one's religion or belief. When this right is recognised by law or practice, there shall be no differentiation among conscientious objectors on the basis of the nature of their particular beliefs; likewise, there shall be no discrimination against conscientious objectors because they have failed to perform military service.'

10.60   In relation to the recruitment of children into the armed forces of a State party Art 38(3) of the CRC provides that:[151]

---

[148]   2006 SCC 6 (CanLII).
[149]   The Sikh religion requires that the kirpan must be made of metal.
[150]   Human Rights Committee General Comment No 22 1993 HRI/GEN/1/Rev 8, p 198, para 11.
[151]   See **15.98** below for a detailed discussion of this provision.

'States Parties shall refrain from recruiting any person who has not attained the age of fifteen years into their armed forces. In recruiting among those persons who have attained the age of fifteen years but who have not attained the age of eighteen years, States Parties shall endeavour to give priority to those who are oldest.'

Conscientious objection[152] to military service will plainly be relevant to children where the State operates a national service system of conscription encompassing persons under the age of 18. However, given persons already performing military service may develop conscientious objections[153] and in circumstances where many States, including the United Kingdom, permit voluntary entry into the armed forces prior to the age of 18, conscientious objection may also be relevant to children where conscription is not an issue. The interpretation of Art 18 of the ICCPR by the Human Rights Committee with regard to the issue of conscientious objection would suggest that it is implicit in Art 14(1) of the CRC that the obligation to use lethal force will conflict with the child's freedom of conscience and the right to manifest his or her religion or belief where the child objects to military service. Further, military service against the child's expressions of conscience, and arguably in any event, will fail to adhere to the requirements of Art 29(1)(d) of the CRC which provides that the education of the child shall be directed to:

'The preparation of the child for responsible life in a free society, in the spirit of understanding, peace, tolerance, equality of sexes, and friendship among all peoples, ethnic, national and religious groups and persons of indigenous origin.'

(iii) Freedom of Religion for Children deprived of their Liberty

10.61 Where children are deprived of their liberty Art 14(1) of the CRC will continue to apply. Rule 48 of the UN Rules for the Protection of Juveniles Deprived of the Liberty provides as follows:

'Every juvenile should be allowed to satisfy the needs of his or her religious and spiritual life, in particular by attending the services or meetings provided in the detention facility or by conducting his or her own services and having possession of the necessary books or items of religious observance and instruction of his or her denomination. If a detention facility contains a sufficient number of juveniles of a given religion, one or more qualified representatives of that religion should be appointed or approved and allowed to hold regular services and to pay pastoral visits in private to juveniles at their request. Every juvenile should have the right to receive visits from a qualified representative of any religion of his or her choice, as well as the right not to participate in religious services and freely to decline religious education, counseling or indoctrination.'[154]

Van Bueren points out that it is ironic that a child must be deprived of his or liberty to take advantage of the most comprehensive international instrument concerning his or her religious freedom.[155]

---

[152] Conscientious objection may be defined as the refusal to perform armed service or any other direct or indirect participation in armed conflicts for reasons of conscience or profound conviction arising from religious, ethical, moral, humanitarian, philosophical or political motive (see UN Doc E/CN.4/1989/30 and Van Bueren *The International Law on the Rights of the Child* (1998) Martinus Nijhoff, p 152).

[153] See Commission on Human Rights Resolution No 1998/77 *Conscientious Objection to Military Service.*

[154] See also Human Rights Committee General Comment No 22 *Article 18 (Freedom of Thought, Conscience and Religion)* HRI/GEN/1/Rev 8, p 196, para 8.

[155] Van Bueren, G *Child Rights in Europe* (2007) Council of Europe Publishing, p 79.

The Child's Right to Freedom of Thought, Conscience and Religion under the ECHR

ECHR, Art 9 – Freedom of Thought, Conscience and Religion

10.62 Article 9 of the ECHR provides as follows in relation to the right to freedom of thought, conscience and religion:

'1. Everyone has the right to freedom of thought, conscience and religion; this right includes freedom to change his religion or belief and freedom, either alone or in community with others and in public or private, to manifest his religion or belief, in worship, teaching,[156] practice and observance.

2. Freedom to manifest one's religion or beliefs shall be subject only to such limitations as are prescribed by law and are necessary in a democratic society in the interests of public safety, for the protection of public order, health or morals, or for the protection of the rights and freedoms of others.'[157]

10.63 The principles enshrined in Art 9(1) of the ECHR have, together with the right to freedom of expression under ECHR, Art 10 and the right to freedom of assembly and association under ECHR, Art 11, been described as the foundations of democratic society.[158] In *Grzelak v Poland*[159] the European Court of Human Rights reiterated that:

'... freedom of thought, conscience and religion, as enshrined in Article 9, is one of the foundations of a 'democratic society' within the meaning of the Convention. It is, in its religious dimension, one of the most vital elements that go to make up the identity of believers and their conception of life, but it is also a precious asset for atheists, agnostics, sceptics and the unconcerned. The pluralism indissociable from a democratic society, which has been dearly won over the centuries, depends on it. That freedom entails, inter alia, freedom to hold or not to hold religious beliefs and to practise or not to practise a religion.'

10.64 In the context of the ECHR, most of the decisions which touch and concern the child's right to freedom of thought, conscience and religion have been decided by reference to the parental rights concerning the provision of education under Art 2 of the First Protocol to the ECHR rather than by specific reference to the child's right to freedom of thought, conscience and religion under Art 9(1) of the ECHR. Whilst Art 9(1) is expressed as applying to 'everyone', historically, the European Court of Human Rights has failed to account for the right of the child to freedom of thought, conscience and religion in cases brought under Art 9(1) concerning children, preferring an adult centred analysis of the issues even where children are the applicants.[160] However, in considering the historical case law, it is important to remember that the

---

[156] The term 'teaching' in Art 9(1) of the ECHR cannot be interpreted to entail an obligation on States parties to permit religious education in public schools of nurseries (see *Savex Crkava 'Riječ Života' v Croatia* (2010) Application No 7798/08, para 57).

[157] Note that Art 2 of the First Protocol of the ECHR also deals with matters of religion in the context of parental religious and philosophical convictions concerning the education of children (see **10.87–10.99** below).

[158] Lord Lester QC, Lord Pannick QC and Herberg, J *Human Rights Law and Practice* (2009) 3rd edn, LexisNexis, p 453.

[159] (2010) Application No 7710/02, para 85.

[160] Langlaude, S *The Right of the Child to Religious Freedom in International Law* (2007) Martinus Nijhoff, p 198.

court has at least started to recognise that parents and children can have separate rights and interests when it comes to the right to freedom of thought conscience and religion.[161]

ECHR, Art 9(1) – Ambit

(i) Thought, Conscience, Religion and Belief

10.65 In *Kokkinakis v Greece*[162] the European Court of Human Rights observed in relation to the right to freedom of thought, conscience and religion enshrined in Art 9(1) of the ECHR that:

> '[Art 9(1)] is, in its religious dimension, one of the most vital elements that go to make up the identity of believers and of their conception of life, but it is also a precious asset for atheists, agnostics, sceptics and the unconcerned.'

10.66 Article 9 of the ECHR primarily protects religious creeds and personal beliefs, for example pacifism,[163] together with acts which are linked with the same, including those acts which manifest such religion or belief as opposed to ideologies.[164] As such Art 9(1) will cover religious as well as non-religious beliefs based on thought and conscience.[165] The European Court of Human Rights has suggested that the word 'belief' in Art 9(1) denotes views which attain a certain level of cogency, seriousness, cohesion or importance and requires more than firmness.[166] It is unclear how suitable this definition is when considering the beliefs and convictions of children. Whilst a child's belief may be less cogent, coherent or solemn than a comparable belief of an adult it may nonetheless be similarly important and spiritual.[167]

10.67 In order to come within the ambit of Art 9(1), a non-religious belief must relate to an aspect of human life or behaviour of comparable importance to that normally found with religious belief.[168] It should be noted that the European Court of Human

---

[161] *Folgerø and others v Norway* (2004) Application No 15472/02 (unreported). Unfortunately the recognition of the separate position of the children in this case resulted in their application being declared inadmissible on the grounds that they had failed to exhaust domestic remedies.

[162] *Kokkinakis v Greece* (1993) 17 EHRR 397.

[163] *Arrowsmith v United Kingdom* (1978) 3 EHRR 218.

[164] See the decision of the European Commission in *Vereniging v Rechtswinkels Utrecht v Netherlands* (1986) 46 DR 200. However, a refusal by the State to grant a religious organisation legal personality can amount to a breach of Art 9 (see *Moscow Branch of the Salvation Army v Russia* (2007) 44 EHRR 46 and *Church of Scientology Moscow v Russia* (2008) 46 EHRR 16).

[165] *Arrowsmith v United Kingdom* (1980) 19 DR 5.

[166] *Campbell and Cosans v United Kingdom* (1982) 4 EHRR 293. This definition of 'belief' has been criticised as unsophisticated in failing to take into account that religious belief is not merely a set of intellectual propositions but may include moral, ethical, supernatural, communal or symbolic elements (see Evans, C *Freedom of Religion under the European Convention on Human Rights* (2001) Oxford University Press, pp 65–66). In *R (Williamson) v Secretary of State for Education and Employment* [2005] UKHL 15, [2005] 2 AC 286, citing Arden LJ in *R (Williamson) v Secretary of State for Education and Employment* [2002] EWCA Civ 1926, [2003] QB 1300, the House of Lords held that to fall within Art 9(1) a belief must be consistent with the ideals of a democratic society and must be compatible with human dignity, serious and important, cogent and coherent. These threshold conditions were considered met in *Christian Institutes Application for Judicial Review* [2007] NIQB 66 in relation to the orthodox Christian belief that the practice of homosexuality is sinful ('Whether the belief is to be accepted or rejected is not the issue. The belief is a long established part of the belief system of the world's major religions. This is not a belief that is unworthy of recognition. I am satisfied that Article 9 is engaged in the present case. The extent to which the manifestation of the belief may be limited is a different issue').

[167] Langlaude, S *The Right of the Child to Religious Freedom in International Law* (2007) Martinus Nijhoff, p 202.

[168] *Campbell & Cosans v United Kingdom* (1982) 4 EHRR 293 cited with approval in *R (Williamson) v Secretary*

Rights is reluctant to consider cases as falling within the ambit of Art 9(1) where those cases may also fall within the ambit of other articles of the Convention.[169] The freedom of thought and conscience will cover pacifism, on the basis that it is a 'philosophy'[170] and vegetarianism and veganism.[171] It is unclear whether Art 9 covers political beliefs.[172] As to religions, Art 9 has been held to protect Scientology,[173] the Krishna Consciousness movement,[174] and Jehovah's Witnesses.[175] However the question of whether Druidism falls within Art 9(1) has been left open.[176] The burden is on the applicant to demonstrate that he or she is an adherent to a particular religion and that the practice or belief in issue is an essential aspect of that religion.[177]

(ii) Legitimacy of Religion and Belief

10.68 The freedom of thought, conscience and religion enshrined in Art 9(1) of the ECHR places limits on the extent to which the State may assess the legitimacy of religious views or the legitimacy of the manner in which those views are expressed. In *Hasan and Chaush v Bulgaria*[178] the court observed that:

> '... but for very exceptional cases, the right to freedom of religion as guaranteed under the Convention excludes any discretion on the part of the State to determine whether religious beliefs or the means used to express such beliefs are legitimate.'

---

of State for Education and Employment [2005] UKHL 15, [2005] 2 AC 286. See also *Refah Partisi (Welfare Party) v Turkey (No 2)* (2003) 37 EHRR 1, para 93 ('... the principle of secularism is certainly one of the fundamental principles of the State which are in harmony with the rule of law and respect for human rights and democracy. An attitude which fails to respect that principle will not necessarily be accepted as being covered by the freedom to manifest one's religion and will not enjoy the protection of Article 9 of the Convention') and *Whaley v Lord Advocate* [2007] UKHL 53, (2008) SC (HL) 107, (2008) HRLR 11 ('The current jurisprudence does not support the proposition that a person's belief in his right to engage in an activity which he carries on for pleasure or recreation, however fervent or passionate, can be equated with beliefs of the kind that are protected by article 9. It would be surprising if it did so, as it would be hard in that event to set any limits to the range of beliefs that would be opened up for protection').

[169] See for example *Hoffman v Austria* (1993) 17 EHRR 293 (residence dispute between parents of different religious persuasions considered under Art 8), *Palau-Martinez v France* (2005) 41 EHRR 9 (residence dispute concerning allegations of breach of Arts 8 and 9 dealt with under Art 8), *Zengin v Turkey* (2008) 46 EHRR 44 (refusal to exempt children from religious and ethics lessons dealt with under Art 2 of the First Protocol) and *Khan v United Kingdom* (1986) 48 DR 253 (claim of right to marry at a lower age than permitted under domestic law due to religious rules dealt with under Art 12).

[170] *Arrowsmith v United Kingdom* (1980) 19 DR 5. It will not however guarantee the right to conscientious objection (see *Bayatyan v Armenia* (2010) Application No 23459/03). See also Council of Europe Resolution 337 (1967) on the right of conscientious objection and Recommendation 816 (1977) on the right of conscientious objection to military service. See further the Recommendation No R (87) 8 of the Committee of Ministers regarding conscientious objection to compulsory military service and the Recommendation 1518 (2001). Exercise of the right of conscientious objection to military service in Council of Europe member states which provides that 'The right of conscientious objection is a fundamental aspect of the right to freedom of thought, conscience and religion enshrined in the Universal Declaration of Human Rights and the European Convention on Human Rights.'

[171] *H v United Kingdom* (1993) 16 EHRR CD 44.

[172] See *NHGH and RA v Turkey* (1992) 27 DR 200. See also the decision of the Canadian Federal Court in *Roach v Canada (Minister of State for Multiculturalism and Citizenship)* [1994] 2 FC 406.

[173] *Sweden* (1979) 16 DR 68.

[174] *Ishkon v UK* 76–A DR 90.

[175] *Kokkinakis v Greece* (1993) 17 EHRR 397.

[176] *Chappell v UK* (1987) 53 DR 241.

[177] *Guzzardi v Italy* (1980) 3 EHRR 333.

[178] (2002) 34 EHRR 55, para 78.

Likewise, in the case of *Metropolitan Church of Bessarabia v Moldova*[179] the court held that 'in principle the right to freedom of religion for the purposes of the Convention excludes assessment by the State of the legitimacy of religious beliefs or the ways in which those beliefs are expressed'.

10.69 As such, in determining cases brought under Art 9(1) of the ECHR the European Court of Human Rights will often start from the assumption that the religion or belief in issue comes within the ambit of Art 9(1) of the ECHR.[180] Where the legitimacy of the belief in question is in issue before the court, the role of the courts under Art 9(1) is to conduct a limited enquiry into the genuineness of that professed belief.[181] Thus, only in extreme cases will a claim to religious or non-religious belief be disregarded entirely.[182]

10.70 However, this position is complicated when elements of the system of belief in question conflict with other principles protected by the Convention.[183] Whilst questioning of the legitimacy of Islam as a religion, in *Refah Partisi (The Welfare Party) v Turkey*[184] the European Court of Human Rights considered the 'political' manifestation of Islamic sharia law and observed that:

> '... the Court considers that sharia, which faithfully reflects the dogmas and divine rules laid down by religion, is stable and invariable. Principles such as pluralism in the political sphere or the constant evolution of public freedoms have no place in it. The Court notes that, when read together, the offending statements, which contain explicit references to the introduction of sharia, are difficult to reconcile with the fundamental principles of democracy, as conceived in the Convention taken as a whole. It is difficult to declare one's respect for democracy and human rights while at the same time supporting a regime based on sharia, which clearly diverges from Convention values, particularly with regard to its criminal law and criminal procedure, its rules on the legal status of women and the way it intervenes in all spheres of private and public life in accordance with religious precepts ... In the Court's view, a political party whose actions seem to be aimed at introducing sharia in a State party to the Convention can hardly be regarded as an association complying with the democratic ideal that underlies the whole of the Convention.'

Thus some beliefs will not be protected by Art 9(1) where they do not respect other rights enshrined in the ECHR. In *Refah Partisi (The Welfare Party) (No 2)*[185] the Grand Chamber, concurring with the Court, observed that:

> '... the principle of secularism is certainly one of the fundamental principles of the State which are in harmony with the rule of law and respect for human rights and democracy. An attitude which fails to respect that principle will not necessarily be accepted as being covered by the freedom to manifest one's religion and will not enjoy the protection of Article 9 of the Convention.'[186]

---

[179] (2002) 35 EHRR 306.

[180] See for example *Chappell v United Kingdom* (1987) 53 DR 241.

[181] *R (Williamson) v Secretary of State for Education and Employment* [2005] UKHL 15, [2005] 2 AC 286.

[182] *X v United Kingdom* (1977) 11 DR 55.

[183] See again *R (Williamson) v Secretary of State for Education and Employment* [2005] UKHL 15, [2005] 2 AC 286, citing Arden LJ in *R (Williamson) v Secretary of State for Education and Employment* [2002] EWCA Civ 1926, [2003] QB 1300, in which the House of Lords held that to fall within Art 9(1) a belief must be consistent with the ideals of a democratic society and must be compatible with human dignity.

[184] (2001) 31 EHRR 51.

[185] (2003) 37 EHRR 1, para 93

[186] See Boyle, K *Human Rights, Religion and Democracy: The Refah Party Case* (2004) 1 (1) Essex Human Rights Review 1, p 14 for criticism of this approach to secularism.

10.71 The views expressed in the *Refah* case arguably amount to the proposition that there should be no freedom of thought, conscience and religion for those who do not respect the freedom of thought, conscience and religion of others. This proposition is extremely problematic and has been rightly criticised.[187] The better approach is that of Lord Walker in *R v Secretary of State for Education and Employment and Others (Respondents) ex parte Williamson (Appellant) and others*[188] in which he stated shortly the preferable approach, namely that 'in matters of human rights the court should not show liberal tolerance only to tolerant liberals'.

(iii) Freedom to Change Religion

10.72 Article 9(1) expressly incorporates the freedom to change religion or belief. The freedom to change religion implies an absence of coercion. Thus, in considering changing religion, the individual should be able to make a considered and unrestrained choice in matters of religious belief and affiliation.[189] Any form of compulsion to express thoughts or convictions or treatment intended to change the process of thinking may infringe Art 9(1).[190] This principle will have particular relevance to children.[191] Within this context, Art 9(1) provides protection to the individual against indoctrination into religious belief by the State.[192] However, Art 9(1) does not excuse a person from having applied to them generally applicable laws where that person refuses to obey such laws by reason of conscience.[193]

10.73 The freedom to change religion does not prohibit acts of proselytisation in an attempt to convert a person from one belief to another. In *Kokkinakis v Greece*[194] the court held that:

> 'According to Article 9, freedom to manifest one's religion is not only exercisable in community with others, 'in public' and within the circle of those whose faith one shares, but can also be asserted 'alone' and 'in private'; furthermore, it includes in principle the right to try to convince one's neighbour, for example through 'teaching', failing which, moreover, 'freedom to change (one's) religion or belief', enshrined in Article 9, would be likely to remain a dead letter.'

---

[187] See Boyle, K *Human Rights, Religion and Democracy: The Refah Party Case* (2004) 1(1) Essex Human Rights Review 1 at 12–14 and Evans, M *Believing in Communities, European Style* in Ghanea, N (ed) *The Challenge of Religious Discrimination at the Dawn of the New Millennium* (2004) Martinus Nijhoff Publishers 133 at 153–154.

[188] [2005] UKHL 15 [2005] 2 AC 286.

[189] Stahnke, T *Proselytism and the Freedom to Change Religion in International Human Rights Law* [1999] BYU L. rev. 251 at 330.

[190] Van Dijk, P and Van Hoof, F *Theory and Practice of the European Convention on Human Rights* (1998) 3rd edn, Kluwer, p 752.

[191] See for example *Riera Blume v Spain* (2000) 30 EHRR 632.

[192] *Angelini v Sweden* (1986) 51 DR 41. See also **10.87** below in respect of the provisions of Art 2 of the First Protocol of the ECHR. Voluntary membership of an established State religion will not constitute a breach of Art 9(1) (see *Darby v Sweden* (1990) 13 EHRR 774).

[193] *Vergos v Greece* (2005) 41 EHRR 41 and see in the domestic context *R v Taylor (Paul)* [2001] EWCA Crim 2263, [2002] 1 Cr App Rep 37. The corollary of this position is that a failure to apply generally applicable laws to persons by reason of their religious conviction or belief may constitute discrimination under Art 14 read with Art 9(1) (see *Campbell v South Northamptonshire District Council and Another* [2004] EWCA Civ 409, [2004] 3 All ER 387).

[194] (1994) 17 EHRR 397.

The European Court of Human Rights accordingly held that the freedom to change religion will justify acts of proselytisation by 'bearing witness in words and deeds' provide that the acts in question could not be characterised as 'improper proselytism', this being defined as:[195]

> 'activities offering material or social advantages with a view to gaining new members for a Church or exerting improper pressure on people in distress or in need; it may even entail the use of violence or brainwashing; more generally, it is not compatible with respect for the freedom of thought, conscience and religion of others.'

The Spanish Constitutional Court has recognised that children have the right not to share their parents' beliefs and not to be exposed to proselytising by the parents.[196]

ECHR, Art 9(2) – Ambit

10.74 Article 9(2) of the ECHR provides as follows in respect of the right to freedom to manifest region or beliefs enshrined in Art 9(1) of the Convention:

> '2. Freedom to manifest one's religion or beliefs shall be subject only to such limitations as are prescribed by law and are necessary in a democratic society in the interests of public safety, for the protection of public order, health or morals, or for the protection of the rights and freedoms of others.'[197]

(i) Manifesting Religion and Belief

10.75 As with Art 14(3) of the CRC,[198] the limitations set out in Art 9(2) apply only to the right to *manifest* religion. The right to freedom of thought, conscience and religion *per se* is an absolute right which may not be the subject to any form of limitation or restriction.[199] The stipulated limitations on the freedom to manifest religion or belief recognises that in democratic societies, in which several religions coexist within one and the same population, it may be necessary to place restrictions on this freedom in order to reconcile the interests of the various groups and ensure that everyone's beliefs are respected.[200] In *R (Williamson) v Secretary of State for Education and Employment*[201] Lord Nicholls noted that:

> '[A]rt 9 of the convention safeguards freedom of religion. This freedom is not confined to freedom to hold a religious belief. It includes the right to express and practice one's beliefs. Without this, freedom of religion would be emasculated. Invariably religious faiths call for more than belief. To a greater or lesser extent adherents are required or encouraged to act in certain ways, most obviously and directly in forms of communal or personal worship, supplication and meditation. But under art 9 there is a difference between freedom to hold a belief and freedom to express or 'manifest' a belief. The former right, freedom of belief, is absolute. The latter right, freedom to manifest belief, is qualified. This is to be expected, because the way a belief is expressed in practice may impact on others. Familiar instances of conduct shaped by particular religious beliefs are the days or times when worship is

---

[195] *Kokkinakis v Greece* (1993) 17 EHRR 397.

[196] *Pedro Carrasco Carrasco* Boletín Official del Estado 156 30 June 200 40–46.

[197] See *Kokkinakis v Greece* (1993) 17 EHRR 397 'While religious freedom is primarily a matter of individual conscience, it also implies, inter alia, freedom to 'manifest [one's] religion.'

[198] See **10.45** above.

[199] See *Kokkinakis v Greece* (1993) 17 EHRR 397, para 33, *R (Williamson) v Secretary of State for Education and Employment* [2002] EWCA Civ 1926, [2003] QB 1300 and *R (Williamson) v Secretary of State for Education and Employment* [2005] UKHL 15, [2005] 2 AC 286.

[200] *Kokkinakis v Greece* (1993) 17 EHRR 397.

[201] [2005] UKHL 15, [2005] 2 AC 286.

prescribed or encouraged, the need to abstain from work on certain days, forms of dress, rituals connected with the preparation of food, the need for total abstinence from certain types of food or drink, and the need for abstinence from all or some types of food at certain times. In a more generalised and non-specific form the tenets of a religion may affect the entirety of a believer's way of life: for example, 'thou shalt love thy neighbour as thyself'. The manner in which children should be brought up is another subject on which religious teachings are not silent. So in a pluralist society a balance has to be held between freedom to practice one's own beliefs and the interests of others affected by those practices.'

10.76 In respect of the freedom to manifest belief under Art 9(2) a distinction is drawn between the manifestation of the religion or belief in question, which will be protected under Art 9 and other practices merely motivated by a religion of belief.[202] The act constituting manifestation must be intimately linked to the belief it is said to manifest.[203] The wearing of a headscarf by Muslim women has been held to be a manifestation of religious belief rather than being simply motivated by such a belief.[204] A prohibition on a Buddhist prisoner submitting a publication to a religious journal was held not to be a manifestation of his belief as opposed to being motivated by such belief as his religion did not require him to be able to make such submissions even though it motivated him to do so.[205] By contrast, in *Jakóbski v Poland*[206] the European Court of Human Rights found a breach of Art 9 in respect of the failure to make available a meat free diet to a Buddhist prisoner on the grounds that compliance with such a diet was motivated and inspired by his religion.

(ii) Limitations

10.77 Under Art 9(2) the manifestation of religion or beliefs by an individual may be interfered with provided such interference is prescribed by law and necessary in a democratic society in pursuit of a legitimate aim, namely public safety, the protection of public order, health or morals, or the protection of the rights and freedoms of others.[207] The application of Art 9(2) has evolved from the courts taking a restrictive interpretation of 'religion and belief' to now pursuing a more flexible approach to questions of justification under Art 9(2).[208] As such, whether a particular act constitutes interference in the rights enshrined in Art 9(1) will depend on all the circumstances of the case in question, including the extent to which in the circumstances an individual can reasonably be expected to be at liberty to manifest his or her beliefs in practice.[209]

202　*Arrowsmith v United Kingdom* (1980) 19 DR 5, *Kalac v Turkey* (1997) 27 EHRR 552 ('Art 9 lists a number of forms which manifestation of one's religion or belief may take, namely worship, teaching, practice and observance. Nevertheless, Art 9 does not protect every act motivated or inspired by a religion or belief'), *Metropolitan Church of Bessarabia v Moldova* (2002) 35 EHRR 306 and *Şahin v Turkey* (2007) 44 EHRR 5. See also *R (Williamson) v Secretary of State for Education and Employment* [2002] EWCA Civ 1926, [2003] QB 1300 and *R (Williamson) v Secretary of State for Education and Employment* [2005] UKHL 15, [2005] 2 AC 286.

203　*X v United Kingdom* (1983) 6 EHRR 558. See also *R (Playfoot) v Governing Body of Millais School* [2007] EWHC 1698 (Admin), [2007] LGR 851, [2007] 3 FCR 754 in which the court held that if a belief took the form of a perceived obligation to act in a specific way then in principle doing that act pursuant to that belief is itself a manifestation of that belief in practice as the act was intimately linked to the belief.

204　*Leyla Şahin* (2007) 44 EHRR 5.

205　*Khan v United Kingdom* (1986) 48 DR 253.

206　(2010) Application No 18429/06, para 45.

207　Note that, by contrast to the other qualified rights of the ECHR, there is no 'national security' justification for interfering with a persons Art 9 rights.

208　Lord Lester QC, Lord Pannick QC and Herberg, J *Human Rights Law and Practice* (2009) 3rd edn, LexisNexis, p 453. See *Şahin v Turkey* (2007) 44 EHRR 5, *R (Williamson) v Secretary of State for Education and Employment* [2005] UKHL 15, [2005] 2 AC 286 and *R (on the application of Shabina Begum) v Denbigh High School Governors* [2006] UKHL 15, [2006] 2 WLR 719, [2007] 1 AC 100.

209　*Kalac v Turkey* (1997) 27 EHRR 552 cited in *R (Williamson) v Secretary of State for Education and*

ECHR, Art 9 – Application

(i) ECHR, Art 9 – Freedom of Religion and the Child's Family Life

10.78 Whilst Art 9(1) has been considered in the context of family life, the child's right to freedom of thought, conscience and religion has been little considered, if at all. Instead, the European Court of Human Rights has taken a welfare based approach to the issue of the potential impact of a parents' religion on the child. The Spanish Constitutional Court has recognised that children have the right not to share their parents' beliefs and not to be exposed to proselytising by the parents.[210]

10.79 In *Hoffman v Austria*[211] the European Court of Human Rights considered a claim by a mother that she had been denied residence of her children on the basis of her religious convictions as a Jehovah's witness. The court found a breach under Art 8 of the ECHR and accordingly found it unnecessary to consider the claim under Art 9(1). The court made no reference to the rights of the children concerned under Art 9(1). In *Palau-Martinez v France*[212] on similar facts the court found a violation of Art 8 read with Art 14 of the ECHR. Again, the court made no reference to the rights of the children concerned.[213] Finally, in *Deschomets v France*[214] a mother who was a member of the Brethren movement contended that the decision to change the residence of the children to the father did not take account all of the circumstances of the case, including the wishes of the children who had been represented in the domestic proceedings, but rather relied solely on her religion. Whilst making reference to the fact that the children had, as evidenced by the welfare report, 'expressed their rejection of their mother's religious practice and way of life' the court dealt with this factor part of the welfare considerations rather than by reference to the children's rights under Art 9(1) of the ECHR. Indeed the Court expressly noted that the decisions in *Hoffman v Austria* and *Palau-Martinez v France*:

> '... were based on the children's best interests, taking into account their reactions to the lifestyles of both their parents, in conformity with the Court's case-law, which has been inspired in particular by Article 3 of the United Nations Convention on the Rights of the Child.'

(ii) ECHR, Art 9(1) – Religious Dress and Symbols and Education

Personal Religious Dress and Symbols

10.80 In *Karaduman v Turkey*[215] the applicant had been denied a certificate of graduation because she would not submit to being photographed without a head scarf. The court found no violation of Art 9(1) on the grounds that:

Employment [2005] UKHL 15, [2005] 2 AC 286, para 38. See also *Şahin v Turkey* (2007) 44 EHRR 5 ('... the freedom of religion, as guaranteed by Article 9, is not absolute, but subject to the limitations set out in Article 9(2). Moreover, it may, as regards the modality of a particular religious manifestation, be influenced by the situation of the person claiming that freedom') and *R (on the application of Shabina Begum) v Denbigh High School Governors* [2006] UKHL 15, [2006] 2 WLR 719.

210 *Pedro Carrasco Carrasco* Boletín Official del Estado 156 30 June 200 40–46.
211 (1993) 17 EHRR 293.
212 (2005) 41 EHRR 9.
213 See also *FL v France* (2005) Application No 61162/00 (unreported).
214 (2006) Application No 31956/02 (unreported).
215 (1993) 74 DR 93.

'... by choosing to pursue her higher education in a secular university a student submits to those university rule, which may make freedom of students to manifest their religion subject to such restrictions as to place and manner intended to ensure harmonious co-existence between students of different beliefs.'

10.81 In *Dahlab v Switzerland*[216] the court justified the ban on the wearing of a headscarf by a female teacher on the grounds that it might have a proselytising effect on the children she taught, given that it appeared to be a requirement imposed on women by a precept laid down in the Qur'an, which precept the court considered was difficult to square with gender equality. The court thus considered the ban justified on the basis of protection of the child's right to freedom of thought, conscience and religion:

'The Court accepts that it is very difficult to assess the impact that a powerful external symbol such as the wearing of a headscarf may have on the freedom of conscience and religion of very young children. The applicant's pupils were aged between four and eight, an age at which children wonder about many things and are also more easily influenced than older pupils. In those circumstances, it cannot be denied outright that the wearing of a headscarf might have some kind of proselytising effect, seeing that it appears to be imposed on women by a precept which is laid down in the Koran and which, as the Federal Court noted, is hard to square with the principle of gender equality. It therefore appears difficult to reconcile the wearing of an Islamic headscarf with the message of tolerance, respect for others and, above all, equality and non-discrimination that all teachers in a democratic society must convey to their pupils. Accordingly, weighing the right of a teacher to manifest her religion against the need to protect pupils by preserving religious harmony, the Court considers that, in the circumstances of the case and having regard, above all, to the tender age of the children for whom the applicant was responsible as a representative of the State, the Geneva authorities did not exceed their margin of appreciation and that the measure they took was therefore not unreasonable.'[217]

10.82 The fact that the court considered the position of the young children involved in *Dahlab v Switzerland* represents a rare departure from the normal approach of the European Court of Human Rights to situations which may violate the child's right to freedom of thought, conscience and religion. However, the decision in *Dahlab v Switzerland* is open to criticism.[218] In *Dahlab*, in addition to the decision amounting to a requirement that teachers choose between their faith and their profession, there does not appear to have been any forensic basis, for example in the form of evidence demonstrating the particularly proselytising effect of religious dress on young children, for the courts conclusion that the wearing of an Islamic headscarf by a teacher would have an adverse effect on the freedom of thought, conscience and religion of young children.[219] The rights of the child to freedom of thought, conscience and religion under Art 9(1) of the ECHR are plainly engaged in cases of this nature and should always be

---

[216] (2001) Application No 42393/98 (unreported).

[217] The approach in *Dahlab* was endorsed in *Şahin v Turkey* (2007) 44 ECHR 5 concerning a ban on wearing the Islamic headscarf in institutions of higher education ('... it is the principle of secularism, as elucidated by the Constitutional Court, which is the paramount consideration underlying the ban on the wearing of religious symbols in universities. In such a context, where the values of pluralism, respect for the rights of others and, in particular, equality before the law of men and women are being taught and applied in practice, it is understandable that the relevant authorities should wish to preserve the secular nature of the institution concerned and so consider it contrary to such values to allow religious attire, including, as in the present case, the Islamic headscarf, to be worn ... the Court finds that the interference in issue was justified in principle and proportionate to the aim pursued'). In that case the court noted that the place of the Islamic headscarf in State education had been the subject of debate across Europe for more than 20 years.

[218] See Gibson, N *Faith in the Courts: Religious Dress and Human Rights* [2007] CLJ 66(3) 657–697. The European Court of Human Rights nonetheless appears intent on following the line of authority (see *Dogru v France* (2008) Application No 27058/05 (unreported)).

[219] See the German Federal Constitutional Court case of *Ludin* ((BVerfG) *Ludin* 2 BvR 1436/02) where the

considered. They should not however be used simply as a makeweight argument in the absence of forensic evidence that the right has been violated.

Religious Symbols displayed in Schools

10.83 In *Lautsi v Italy*[220] the European Court of Human Rights considered a claim by a Mother that the display of a crucifix in the classrooms of school attended by her children aged 11 and 13, contrary to her wish to bring up her children in accordance with secular principles, breached her rights under Art 9(1) and Art 2 1P of the ECHR. In a judgment which once again did not consider the children's views or their rights under Art 9(1), the court held that freedom not to have a religious belief is not restricted to the absence of religious services or religious education but rather extends to practices and symbols expressing, in particular or in general, a belief, a religion or atheism and that freedom not to believe deserves special protection if it is the State which expresses a belief. Within this context, the court found a violation of Art 2 1P of the ECHR read with Art 9 on the grounds that the compulsory display of a symbol of a particular faith by the exercise of public authority in relation to specific situations subject to governmental supervision, particularly in classrooms, restricts the right of parents to educate their children in conformity with their convictions and the right of school children to believe or not believe, such restrictions being incompatible with the State's duty to respect neutrality in the exercise of public authority, particularly in the field of education.[221]

10.84 The approach to issues of religious clothing and symbols in the context of educational establishments adopted by the European Court of Human Rights should be contrasted with the approach taken by the Constitutional Court of South Africa in *Kwazulu-Natal v Pillay*[222] to the question of the place of religious and cultural expression by children in school:

> 'The traditional basis for invalidating laws that prohibit the exercise of an obligatory religious practice is that it confronts the adherents with a Hobson's choice between observance of their faith and adherence to the law. There is however more to the protection of religious and cultural practices than saving believers from hard choices. As stated above, religious and cultural practices are protected because they are central to human identity and hence to human dignity which is in turn central to equality ... The practice to which Sunali adheres is that once she inserts the nose stud, she must never remove it. Preventing her from wearing it for several hours of each school day would undermine the practice and therefore constitute a significant infringement of her religious and cultural identity. What is relevant is the symbolic effect of denying her the right to wear it for even a short period; it sends a message that Sunali, her religion and her culture are not welcome.'

(iii) ECHR, Art 9(1) – Religion and Content of the Curriculum

10.85 In *CJ, JJ and EJ v Poland*[223] the European Commission was required to consider the case of a child exempted from attending Catholic instruction. As part of the

---

court investigated the extent of the knowledge base in the area of child psychology concerning the effect of religious dress worn by teachers on the development of children and came to the conclusion that little was known.

[220] (2010) Application 30814/06.

[221] (2010) Application 30814/06, para 57. Note that this case has been referred to the Grand Chamber.

[222] [2007] ZACC 21 (Const Ct South Africa). At the beginning of his judgment in *Kwazulu-Natal v Pillay* Langa CJ noted that 'At the centre of the storm is a tiny gold nose stud.' For the domestic approach see below at **10.126** the domestic case of *R (on the application of Shabina Begum) v Denbigh High School Governors* [2006] UKHL 15, [2006] 2 WLR 719.

[223] (1996) D&R 46.

requirements of her exemption, she was compelled to wait in a corridor during the instruction and was subject to detailed questioning by those in authority. Eventually, the child acquiesced and commenced Catholic instruction. In finding that there had been no breach of Art 9(1) of the ECHR the Commission clearly failed to appreciate the link between the distress felt by the child and her decision to commence classes or its relevance, given that any form of compulsion to express thoughts or convictions or treatment intended to change the process of thinking may infringe Art 9(1).[224]

10.86 A more child centred approach was taken by the European Court of Human Rights in the case of *Grzelak v Poland*[225] in which a 7 year old boy alleged discrimination under Art 9 of the ECHR read with Art 14 arising out of the decision of his parents that he should not attend religious instruction at school. As a result of this decision and his non-attendance at religious classes the child received no mark for 'religion/ethics' on his school report, the relevant sections being simply scored through with a line. Despite requests, the school made no provision for alternative lessons to replace religious instruction. Reiterating that religious beliefs do not constitute information that can be used to distinguish an individual citizen in his or her relations with the State, they being not only a matter of individual conscience but also matters that may change over a person's lifetime, the European Court of Human Rights found a violation of Art 9(1) of the ECHR read with Art 14 on the basis that the absence of a mark on the child's report in respect of religious instruction did not constitute 'neutral information' on the fact that a child did or did not follow a course offered at the school. Rather, the Court held that the absence of a mark for 'religion/ethics' would be understood by any reasonable person as an indication that the child did not follow religious education classes, which were widely available, and that he was thus likely to be regarded as a person without religious beliefs; a finding which the Court considered took on particular significance in respect of a country like Poland where the great majority of the population owe allegiance to one particular religion. Further, in circumstances where the mark for religious instruction was taken into account in calculating the student's average score and in the absence of an available alternative course within the curriculum, the Court considered that children in the situation of the applicant would either find it more difficult to increase their average mark as they could not follow the desired optional subject or might feel pressurised against their conscience to attend a religion class in order to improve their average.

ECHR, Art 2 of the First Protocol

10.87 Article 2 of the First Protocol of the ECHR (hereafter 'Art 2 1P') provides as follows in respect of the right education:

> 'No person shall be denied the right to education. In the exercise of any functions which it assumes in relation to education and to teaching, the State shall respect the right of parents to ensure such education and teaching in conformity with their own religious and philosophical convictions.'

---

[224] Van Dijk, P and Van Hoof, F *Theory and Practice of the European Convention on Human Rights* (1998) 3rd edn, Kluwer, p 752. Contrast the decision in *CJ, JJ and EJ v Poland* (1996) D&R 46 with the decision in *Grzelak v Poland* (2010) Application No 7710/02 discussed at **10.86** below.

[225] (2010) Application No 7710/02.

ECHR, Art 2 of the First Protocol – Ambit

Parental Convictions and the Child's Rights under Art 9(1)

10.88 The first sentence of Art 2 1P primarily concerns the rights of children. The second sentence concerns the right of parents. It has been held that Art 2 1P is dominated by its first sentence, 'No person shall be denied the right to education'.[226] The aim of Art 2 1P has been described as 'safeguarding the possibility of pluralism in education which possibility is essential for the preservation of the 'democratic society' as conceived by the Convention' it being noted that, in view of the power of the modern State, it is above all through teaching that this aim must be realised.[227] The State is thus prohibited by Art 2 1P from educating children in a manner which does not respect parents' religious and philosophical convictions.[228] Parents have the right to establish private schools or to send their children to private schools that teach a curriculum which better accords with their religious beliefs.[229] Art 2 1P will apply to public and private education as well as the functions which States parties exercise in relation to education.[230]

10.89 The extent to which the words 'the State shall respect the rights of parents to ensure such education and teaching in conformity with their own religious and philosophical convictions' in Art 2 1P undermine the child's right to freedom of thought, conscience and religion under Art 9(1) of the ECHR has not been the subject of definitive consideration by the European Court of Human Rights. However, although the aim of Art 2 1P to protect parents from religious and racial persecution by the State attempting to indoctrinate their children through their schooling[231] is laudable, it seems clear that Art 2 1P does not on its own sufficiently provide for child's right to freedom of thought, conscience and religion to be taken into account where his or her convictions differ from those of their parents, having regard to the child's right to freedom of thought, conscience and religion under Art 9(1) of the ECHR and the child's freedom of expression under Art 10 of the ECHR.[232] Indeed, in his concurring Opinion in the case of *Kjeldsen, Busk and Madsen v Denmark* Judge Kellberg considered that Art 2 1P placed insufficient stress on the rights of the child, concluding that: 'It is hardly conceivable that the drafters would have intended to give parents something like dictatorial powers over the education of their children'.[233] In *Kjeldsen, Busk and Madsen v Denmark* the European Court of Human Rights made clear that:[234]

> '… the provisions of the Convention and Protocol must be read as a whole. Accordingly, the two sentences of Article 2 must be read not only in the light of each other but also, in particular, of Articles 8, 9 and 10 of the Convention, which proclaim the right of everyone, including parents *and children*, 'to respect for his private and family life', to 'freedom of thought, conscience and religion', and to 'freedom […] to receive and impart information and ideas'.

---

[226]   *Cohen v UK* (1996) 21 EHRR 104.

[227]   *Kjeldsen, Busk, Madsen & Pedersen v Denmark* 1 EHRR 711 and see *Çiftçi v Turkey* (2004) Application No 71860 (unreported). See also *Family H v UK* (1984) 37 DR 105; *Ford v UK* (1996) EHRLR 534; *PD and LD v UK* (1989) 62 DR 292 and *Simpson v UK* (1989) 64 DR 188.

[228]   *Kjeldsen, Busk and, Madsen v Denmark* 1 EHRR 711.

[229]   *Graeme v United Kingdom* (1990) 64 DR 158.

[230]   *Campbell and Cosans v United Kingdom* (1982) 4 EHRR, para 36–41.

[231]   Fortin, J *The Human Rights Act 1998 – Human Rights for Children Too* in Franklin, B (ed) *The New Handbook of Children's Rights* (2002) Routledge 119–135, p 132.

[232]   Van Bueren, G *Child Rights in Europe* (2007) Council of Europe Publishing, pp 151 and 162–163.

[233]   *Kjeldsen, Busk, Madsen & Pedersen v Denmark* Series A No 21, 50.

[234]   *Kjeldsen, Busk, Madsen & Pedersen v Denmark* 1 EHRR 711, para 52 emphasis added.

10.90 Thus, as with the friction between Art 14 of the CRC and Art 18(4) of the ICCPR,[235] in resolving the potential conflict between Art 9(1) of the ECHR and Art 2 1P it is important to remember that Art 2 1 P is designed to ensure that the State does not interfere with parental discretion as to the religious and moral education of children. The right of the child, both as against the parent and as against the State, to freedom of religion considered in light of his or her age and understanding exists *separately* is a separate right to be considered under Art 9(1) of the ECHR. Further, Art 2 1P does not create an absolute right for the parent to have a child educated in accordance with that parent's religious or philosophical convictions but only to have that right respected.[236] Thus, in cases where a parent seeks to persuade a court pursuant to Art 2 1P that the State is failing to ensure the religious and moral education of their children in conformity with the parents' own convictions it is vital that the court also consider, as a separate albeit related question, whether and to what extent the *child's* right to freedom of education under Art 9(1) is also engaged in the decision the court is being asked to make. Within this context it is vital that Art 9(1) of the ECHR is interpreted and applied in accordance with the provisions of the CRC.[237] Adopting such an approach will ensure that all of the competing rights can be properly balanced and, where necessary, the child can obtain protection from education pursued in conformity with the parents' own convictions but which conflicts with the child's own right to freedom of thought, conscience and religion.[238] It would be wrong for children who hold different philosophical convictions from their parents to abide by their decision concerning educational matters.[239] Note that the rights of parents under Art 2 1P are not removed by reason of the making of a care order.[240] However, it has been held that a parent whose child has been adopted no longer has the right to ensure the education of the child in accordance with his or her own religious and philosophical convictions.[241]

Parental Convictions and the Child's Right to Education

10.91 The European Court of Human Rights has clearly established that when there is a conflict between the parent's right to respect for their religious convictions and the child's right to education, the interests of the child will prevail.[242] The child's right to

---

[235] See **10.39–10.43** above.

[236] *Family H v UK* (1984) 37 DR 105.

[237] See *Fogarty v United Kingdom* ECHR Judgement 21 November 2001 (Grand Chamber), paras 35–36; *Sahin v Germany; Sommerfield v Germany* [2003] 2 FLR 671, p 680, para 39 ('The human rights of children and the standards to which all States must aspire in realising these rights for all children are set out in the United Nations Convention on the Rights of the Child'); *Pini and Bertani; Manera and Atripaldi v Romania* [2005] 2 FLR 596, para 139; *Mubilanzila Mayeka and Kaniki Mitunga v Belgium* Application No 13178/03 [2007] 1 FLR 1726, para 83; *S and another v The United Kingdom* (Application Nos 30562/04 and 30566/04) [2008] All ER (D) 56 (Dec), para 124; *Juppala v Finland* Application No 18620/03 [2009] 1 FLR 617, paras 23 and 41. See also Brownlie, I Principles of Public International Law (2008) 7th edn, OUP, p 578 and de Mello QC, R (ed) *Human Rights Act 1998 – A Practical Guide* (2000) Jordan Publishing, p 8. Van Bueren contends that reading the provisions of Art 5 of the UN Convention against Discrimination in Education, Arts 5 and Art 14(2) of the CRC and Art 10 of the ECHR (which is not limited by age) demonstrates that children are entitled to participate in decisions which help to ensure that their education is in conformity with the *child's* religious and philosophical convictions (Van Bueren, G *Child Rights in Europe* (2007) Council of Europe Publishing, pp 163–164).

[238] Fortin, J *Children's Rights and the Developing Law* (2009) 3rd edn, Cambridge, p 411.

[239] *Kjeldsen, Busk, Madsen & Pedersen v Denmark* Series A.No 21, 50. per Judge Kellberg.

[240] *Olsson v Sweden (No 1)* (1989) 11 EHRR 259.

[241] *X v United Kingdom* 11 DR 160 (1978).

[242] *Çiftçi v Turkey* (2004) Application No 71860 (unreported) and *Martins Casimiro and Cerveira Ferreira v Luxembourg* (1999) Application No 44888/98 (unreported). Note however that the latter case is another example of the European Court of Human Rights failing to consider the rights of the child to freedom of religion in addition in this case to the child's right to education. This contrasts sharply with the approach of the UN Committee on the Rights of the Child in a similar case (see Japan CRC/C/SR.465 (1998) at 6).

education under Art 2 1P is of primary importance and accordingly the 'philosophical convictions' relied on by parents under Art 2 1P must not, even if valid and validly held, conflict with the fundamental right of the child to education.[243] Further, Art 2 1P does not create an absolute right for the parent to have a child educated in accordance with that parent's religious or philosophical convictions but only to have that right respected.[244] In *Kjeldsen, Busk and Madsen v Denmark*[245] the European Court of Human Rights held in relation to Art 2 1P that:

> 'As is shown by its very structure, Article 2 constitutes a whole that is dominated by its first sentence. By binding themselves not to 'deny the right to education', the Contracting States guarantee to anyone within their jurisdiction 'a right of access to educational institutions existing at a given time' and 'the possibility of drawing', by 'official recognition of the studies which he has completed', 'profit from the education received.' The right set out in the second sentence of Article 2 is an adjunct of this fundamental right to education. It is in the discharge of a natural duty towards their children – parents being primarily responsible for the 'education and teaching' of their children – that parents may require the state to respect their religious and philosophical conviction. Their right thus corresponds to a responsibility closely linked to the enjoyment and the exercise of the right to education.'

10.92 The United Kingdom has entered a reservation on that part of Art 2 1P which provides:

> '... in view of certain provisions of the Education Acts in force in the United Kingdom, the principle affirmed in the second sentence of Article 2 is accepted by the United Kingdom only so far as it is compatible with the provision of efficient instruction and training, and the avoidance of unreasonable public expenditure.'[246]

In doing so, the UK Government has gone a little way to recognising the tension between Art 2 1P and the rights of the child, noting that the reservation recognises that in the provision of State-funded education a balance must be struck in some cases between the convictions of the parents and what is educationally sound and affordable.[247]

'Philosophical Convictions'

10.93 Considering the term 'philosophical convictions' in Art 2 1P of the ECHR in *Campbell and Cosans v United Kingdom*[248] the European Court of Human Rights held as follows:

---

[243]   *Campbell and Cosans v UK* 4 EHRR 293. In *Cohen v UK* (1996) 21 EHRR 104 a child argued before the European Court of Human Rights that Art 2 1P gave a right to free transportation to the school of his choice on the basis that the State could not respect his parents' right to ensure his education and teaching according to their convictions if State permitted him to go to the school of his parents choice but then fail to provide free transport for. The court held that: 'Article 2 of Protocol No 1 cannot be used to derive a right to free transport to the school of one's choice where an alternative is available which would involve free transport and which has not been shown to conflict with the parents' convictions.'

[244]   *Family H v UK* (1984) 37 DR 105.

[245]   1 EHRR 711.

[246]   This reservation is preserved by the Human Rights Act 1998, s 15 and reflects the wording of s 9 of the Education Act 1996 which provides that 'In exercising or performing all their respective powers and duties under the Education Acts, the Secretary of State and local education authorities shall have regard to the general principle that pupils are to be educated in accordance with the wishes of their parents, so far as that is compatible with the provision of efficient instruction and training and the avoidance of unreasonable public expenditure.' The reservation has been questioned by the European Court of Human Rights (see *Cohen v UK* (1996) 21 EHRR 104).

[247]   *Rights Brought Home* Cm 3782, para 4.6.

[248]   (1982) 4 EHRR 293, para 36 and see *Young, James and Webster v United Kingdom* (1981) 4 EHRR 38,

'In its ordinary meaning the word "convictions", taken on its own, is not synonymous with the words "opinions" and "ideas", such as are utilised in Article 10 of the Convention, which guarantees freedom of expression; it is more akin to the term "beliefs" (in the French text: "convictions") appearing in Article 9 – which guarantees freedom of thought, conscience and religion – and denotes views that attain a certain level of cogency, seriousness, cohesion and importance. As regards the adjective "philosophical", it is not capable of exhaustive definition and little assistance as to its precise significance is to be gleaned from the travaux préparatoires. The Commission pointed out that the word "philosophy" bears numerous meanings: it is used to allude to a fully-fledged system of thought or, rather loosely, to views on more or less trivial matters. The Courts agrees with the Commission that neither of these two extremes can be adopted for the purposes of interpreting Article 2: the former would too narrowly restrict the scope of a right that is guaranteed to all parents and the latter might result in the inclusion of matters of insufficient weight or substance. Having regard to the Convention as a whole, including Article 17, the expression 'philosophical convictions' in the present context denotes, in the Court's opinion, such convictions as are worthy of respect in a 'democratic society' and are not incompatible with human dignity; in addition, they must not conflict with the fundamental right of the child to education, the whole of Article 2 being dominated by its first sentence.'[249]

10.94 The 'philosophical conviction' in question must be genuinely held and the burden of proving that it is remains a heavy one.[250] In the dissenting judgments of Thór Vilhjálmsson and Jambrek in *Valsamis v Greece*[251] it was suggested that a parental objection based on philosophical convictions must be accepted unless 'obviously unfounded or unreasonable'. The word 'respect' in Art 2 1P means more than 'take account of' or 'acknowledge' but less than 'comply with' and implies a positive obligation on States parties concerning the means by which parents rights are respected.[252] The State is not required to provide special facilities to accommodate particular convictions.[253]

ECHR, Art 2 1P – Application

(i) Education

10.95 Pannick and others describe the position of students at educational establishments in respect of the right to freedom of thought, conscience and religion to be a nebulous one, with the authorities not providing a consistent line of decision making.[254] In the context of the ECHR, most of the decisions which touch and concern the child's right to freedom of thought, conscience and religion have been decided by reference to parental rights concerning education under Art 2 1P to the ECHR rather than by specific reference to the child's right to freedom of thought, conscience and religion under Art 9(1) of the ECHR. The record of the court in considering cases from the perspective of the right of the child to freedom of thought, conscience and religion is not an impressive one.

---

para 63 ('Although individual interests must on occasion be subordinated to those of a group, democracy does not simply mean that the views of a majority must always prevail: a balance must be achieved which ensures the fair and proper treatment of minorities and avoids any abuse of a dominant position').

[249]   For example, parental enthusiasm for linguistic preferences in education does not amount to a 'philosophical conviction' for the purposes of Art 2 1P (see *Belgian Linguistics Case (No 2)* (1968) 1 EHRR 252, para 5).

[250]   *Warwick v United Kingdom* (1989) 60 DR 5 at 18. Note that the objection should be raised initially with the national education authorities (see *B and D v United Kingdom* (1986) 49 DR 44).

[251]   (1996) 24 EHRR 294.

[252]   *Campbell and Cosans v United Kingdom* (1982) 4 EHRR 293, para 37.

[253]   *PD and LD v United Kingdom* (1989) 62 DR 292, *Simpson v United Kingdom* (1989) 64 DR 188 and *Graeme v United Kingdom* (1990) 64 DR 158.

[254]   Lord Lester QC, Lord Pannick QC and Herberg, J *Human Rights Law and Practice* (2009) 3rd edn, LexisNexis, p 469.

Participation in Religious Education and Activities

10.96 In *Valsamis v Greece*[255] the court was required to examine compulsory attendance at a school parade away from the school grounds and outside of school hours in order to mark the national day in Greece. A student who was a Jehovah's Witness refused to attend claiming the parade violated her and her parents' pacifist views. She was punished by the school. The majority of the court held that the parade did not advocate anything contrary to pacifism and didn't find a violation. Demonstrating the adult centred approach of the court, notwithstanding that the child was the person most affected by the impugned measures the court found that because the obligation to take part in the school parade was not such as to offend her *parents'* religious convictions the measure did not amount to an interference with the child's religious freedom. Having dismissed the parents' claim, the court felt it was not necessary to consider the child's perspective separately.

10.97 Likewise, in *Efstratiou v Greece*[256] the child's claim was considered as secondary to that of her parents rather than as a claim in its own right. Having found the parents religious convictions were not offended the majority found that the child's religious convictions were not offended either. By contrast, in their dissenting judgment Judges Thór Vilhjálmsson and Jambrek, finding violations of both Art 2 1P and Art 9(1) of the ECHR at least took time to examine the child's perspective in considering whether there had been a violation of Art 9(1):

> 'Sophia Efstratiou stated that the parade she did not participate in had a character and symbolism that were clearly contrary to her neutralist, pacifist, and thus religious, beliefs. We are of the opinion that the Court has to accept that and we find no basis for seeing Sophia's participation in this parade as necessary in a democratic society, even if this public event clearly was for most people an expression of national values and unity.'

Content of School Curriculum

10.98 In *Kjeldsen, Busk, Madsen & Pedersen v Denmark*[257] the European Court of Human Rights held as follows in respect of a claim that compulsory sex education was against the philosophical convictions of the parents as Christians and accordingly a breach of Art 2 P1:

> 'The second sentence of Article 2 is binding upon the Contracting States in the exercise of each and every function – it speaks of 'any functions' – that they undertake in the sphere of education and teaching, including that consisting of the organisation and financing of public education ... The second sentence of Article 2 aims in short at safeguarding the possibility of pluralism in education which possibility is essential for the preservation of the 'democratic society' as conceived by the Convention. In view of the power of the modern State, it is above all through State teaching that this aim must be realised ... Article 2, which applies to each of the State's functions in relation to education and to teaching, does not permit a distinction to be drawn between religious instruction and other subjects. It enjoins the State to respect parents' convictions, be they religious or philosophical, throughout the entire State education programme ...'

Having considered the meaning and ambit of the second sentence of Art 2 1P the court went on to consider the relationship of the second sentence with the first sentence of that Article:

---

[255] (1996) 24 EHRR 294.
[256] (1997) 24 EHRR 298.
[257] 1 EHRR 711.

'As is shown by its very structure, Article 2 constitutes a whole that is dominated by its first sentence. By binding themselves not to 'deny the right to education', the Contracting States guarantee to anyone within their jurisdiction 'a right of access to educational institutions existing at a given time' and 'the possibility of drawing', by 'official recognition of the studies which he has completed', 'profit from the education received'. The right set out in the second sentence of Article 2 is an adjunct of this fundamental right to education. It is in the discharge of a natural duty towards their children – parents being primarily responsible for the 'education and teaching' of their children – that parents may require the State to respect their religious and philosophical convictions. Their right thus corresponds to a responsibility closely linked to the enjoyment and the exercise of the right to education ... On the other hand, 'the provisions of the Convention and Protocol must be read as a whole'. Accordingly, the two sentences of Article 2 must be read not only in the light of each other but also, in particular, of Articles 8, 9 and 10 of the Convention which proclaim the right of everyone, including parents and children, 'to respect for his private and family life', to 'freedom of thought, conscience and religion', and to 'freedom ... to receive and impart information and ideas'.

After considering the interrelationship between the second sentence and the first sentence of Art 2 1P the court considered the impact of the Article on the setting and planning of the school curriculum:

'It follows in the first place ... that the setting and planning of the curriculum fall in principle within the competence of the Contracting States. This mainly involves questions of expediency on which it is not for the Court to rule and whose solution may legitimately vary according to the country and the era. In particular, the second sentence of Article 2 of the Protocol does not prevent States from imparting through teaching or education information or knowledge of a directly or indirectly religious or philosophical kind. It does not even permit parents to object to the integration of such teaching or education in the school curriculum, for otherwise all institutionalised teaching would run the risk of proving impracticable. In fact, it seems very difficult for many subjects taught at school not to have, to a greater or lesser extent, some philosophical complexion or implications. The same is true of religious affinities if one remembers the existence of religions forming a very broad dogmatic and moral entity which has or may have answers to every question of a philosophical, cosmological or moral nature. The second sentence of Article 2 implies on the other hand that the State, in fulfilling the functions assumed by it in regard to education and teaching, must take care that information or knowledge included in the curriculum is conveyed in an objective, critical and pluralistic manner. The State is forbidden to pursue an aim of indoctrination that might be considered as not respecting parents' religious and philosophical convictions. That is the limit that must not be exceeded. Such an interpretation is consistent at one and the same time with the first sentence of Article 2 of the Protocol, with Articles 8 to 10 of the Convention and with the general spirit of the Convention itself, an instrument designed to maintain and promote the ideals and values of a democratic society. Furthermore, the second sentence of Article 2 must be read together with the first which enshrines the right of everyone to education. It is on to this fundamental right that is grafted the right of parents to respect for their religious and philosophical convictions, and the first sentence does not distinguish, any more than the second, between State and private teaching.'

Finally, the court in *Kjeldsen, Busk, Madsen & Pedersen v Denmark*[258] considered within the context of Art 2 1P the issue of compulsory sex education in the context of the parents philosophical convictions in respect of the same:

'The instruction on the subject given in State schools is aimed less at instilling knowledge [children] do not have or cannot acquire by other means than at giving them such knowledge

---

[258]   1 EHRR 711.

more correctly, precisely, objectively and scientifically. The instruction, as provided for and organised by the contested legislation, is principally intended to give pupils better information ... Even when circumscribed in this way, such instruction clearly cannot exclude on the part of teachers certain assessments capable of encroaching on the religious or philosophical sphere; for what are involved are matters where appraisals of fact easily lead on to value-judgments. The minority of the Commission rightly emphasised this ... The public authorities wish to enable pupils, when the time comes, 'to take care of themselves and show consideration for others in that respect', 'not ... [to] land themselves or others in difficulties solely on account of lack of knowledge'... These considerations are indeed of a moral order, but they are very general in character and do not entail overstepping the bounds of what a democratic State may regard as the public interest. Examination of the legislation in dispute establishes in fact that it in no way amounts to an attempt at indoctrination aimed at advocating a specific kind of sexual behaviour. It does not make a point of exalting sex or inciting pupils to indulge precociously in practices that are dangerous for their stability, health or future or that many parents consider reprehensible. Further, it does not affect the right of parents to enlighten and advise their children, to exercise with regard to their children natural parental functions as educators, or to guide their children on a path in line with the parents' own religious or philosophical convictions. Certainly, abuses can occur as to the manner in which the provisions in force are applied by a given school or teacher and the competent authorities have a duty to take the utmost care to see to it that parents' religious and philosophical convictions are not disregarded at this level by carelessness, lack of judgment or misplaced proselytism ... The Court consequently reaches the conclusion that the disputed legislation in itself in no way offends the applicants' religious and philosophical convictions to the extent forbidden by the second sentence of Article 2 of the Protocol (P1–2), interpreted in the light of its first sentence and of the whole of the Convention.[259]

Discipline in Education

10.99 In *Campbell and Cosans v United Kingdom*[260] the European Court of Human Rights held that an objection to the use or threatened use of violence as a form of disciplinary measure against children amounted to a philosophical conviction in that it forms part of an individual's concept of human behaviour in society.[261] In finding that the child's year long suspension consequent on the parents refusal to agree that he be subject to the rules as to corporal punishment amounted to a violation of Art 2 1P the court held:

'Discipline is an integral, even indispensable, part of any educational system, with the result that the functions assumed by the State in Scotland must be taken to extend to question of discipline in general, even if not to its everyday maintenance ... The right to education

---

[259] In *Angelini v Sweden* (1986) 51 DR 41 at 48 the European Court of Human Rights considered a distinction drawn by Sweden between education *about* religion and education *in* religion. The Court held that religious instruction on a particular state religion is not a violation of Art 2 1P provided that exceptions are available. Exceptions which themselves provide information concerning religion only are not in breach of Art 9 or Art 2 1P. See also *Zengin v Turkey* (2008) 46 EHRR 44 'In the Court's view, [the fact primary school textbooks give greater priority to knowledge of Islam than they do to that of other religions] itself cannot be viewed as a departure from the principles of pluralism and objectivity which would amount to indoctrination having regard to the fact that, notwithstanding the State's secular nature, Islam is the majority religion practiced in Turkey.' Contrast the *Kejeldsen* case with the approach of the Human Rights Committee in *Hartikainen v Finland* (40/1975) Doc A/36/40, p 147 which held that compulsory classes on religion and ethics violated Art 18(4) of the ICCPR.

[260] (1982) 4 EHRR 293.

[261] Note that the *Campbell and Cosans* case establishes only that the child has the right to attend school where he or she will not be subject to corporal punishment which is against his or her parents' wishes. It is not authority for the general proposition that corporal punishment will breach Art 3 of the ECHR (Van Bueren, G *The International Law on the Rights of the Child* (1998) Martinus Nijhoff, p 250). For further discussion of this point see **13.123 et seq** below.

guaranteed by the first sentence of Article 2 by its very nature calls for regulation by the State, but such regulation must never injure the substance of the right nor conflict with other rights enshrined in the Convention or its Protocols ... The suspension of Jeffrey Cosans – which remained in force for nearly a whole school year – was motivated by his and his parents' refusal to accept that he receive or be liable to corporal chastisement. His return to school could have been secured only if his parents had acted contrary to their convictions, convictions which the United Kingdom is obliged to respect under the second sentence of Article 2. A condition of access to an educational establishment that conflicts in this way with another right enshrined in Protocol No 1 cannot be described as reasonable and in any event falls outside the State's power of regulation under Article 2. There has accordingly also been, as regards Jeffrey Cosans, breach of the first sentence of that Article.'[262]

The Child's Right to Freedom of Thought, Conscience and Religion under European Union Law

10.100 Article 10 of the Charter of Fundamental Rights of the European Union provides as follows in respect of the right to freedom of thought, conscience and religion:

'1. Everyone has the right to freedom of thought, conscience and religion. This right includes freedom to change religion or belief and freedom, either alone or in community with others and in public or in private, to manifest religion or belief, in worship, teaching, practice and observance.

2. The right to conscientious objection is recognised, in accordance with the national laws governing the exercise of this right.'

In accordance with Art 52(3) of the European Charter,[263] the meaning and scope of the rights under Art 10 is the same as that under the corresponding Art 9 of the ECHR and its related protocols. As such, the limitations that are permitted by Art 9(2) of the ECHR will be permitted in respect of the rights under Art 10 of the Charter.[264]

The Child's Right to Freedom of Thought, Conscience and Religion under other Regional Instruments

American Convention on Human Rights

10.101 Article 12 of the American Convention on Human Rights articulates the right to freedom of thought, conscience and religion as 'freedom of conscience and religion' as 'freedom of thought' is incorporated into the Art 13 right to freedom of 'thought and expression'. Article 12 of the Convention provides as follows:

---

[262] See below at **10.124** the domestic case of *R v Secretary of State for Education and Employment and Others (Respondents) ex part Williamson (Appellant) and others* [2005] UKHL 15, [2005] 2 AC 286 which also examined the issue of corporal punishment from the perspective of Art 9(1) in addition to Art 2 1P of the ECHR.

[263] Article 52(3) of the Charter provides that 'Insofar as this Charter contains rights which correspond to rights guaranteed by the Convention for the Protection of Human Rights and Fundamental Freedoms, the meaning and scope of those rights shall be the same as those laid down by the said Convention. This provision shall not prevent Union law providing more extensive protection.'

[264] See **10.77** above.

'1. Everyone has the right to freedom of conscience[265] and of religion. This right includes freedom to maintain or to change one's religion or beliefs, and freedom to profess or disseminate one's religion or beliefs, either individually or together with others, in public or in private.

2. No one shall be subject to restrictions that might impair his freedom to maintain or to change his religion or beliefs.

3. Freedom to manifest one's religion and beliefs may be subject only to the limitations prescribed by law that are necessary to protect public safety, order, health, or morals, or the rights or freedoms of others.

4. Parents or guardians, as the case may be, have the right to provide for the religious and moral education of their children or wards that is in accord with their own convictions.'[266]

Ibero-American Convention on the Rights of Youth

10.102 Article 17 of the Ibero-American Convention on the Rights of Youth provides as follows in respect of the right to freedom of thought, conscience and religion:

'1. Youth have the right to freedom of thought, conscience and religion, being any kind of persecution or thought repression prohibited.

2. The States Parties undertake to promote such measures as may be necessary to guarantee the exercise of this right.'

10.103 In addition to the provisions of Art 17 of the Convention, Art 12 of the Ibero-American Convention on the Rights of Youth enshrines a right to conscientious objection, providing:

'1. Youth have the right to make conscientious objection towards obligatory military service.

2. The States Parties undertake to promote the pertinent legal measures to guarantee the exercise of this right and advance in the progressive elimination of the obligatory military service.

3. The States Parties undertake to assure youth under 18 years of age that they shall not be called up or involved, in any way, in military hostilities.'

African Charter on the Rights and Welfare of the Child

10.104 Article 9 of the African Charter on the Rights and Welfare of the Child enshrines the right of the child to freedom of thought, conscience and religion:

'1. Every child shall have the right to freedom of thought conscience and religion.

---

[265] Article 12 will encompass a right to conscientious objection in those countries which recognise the right to conscientious objector status (see *Cristián Daniel Sahli Vera et al v Chile* Case 12.219 Report No 43/05).

[266] See also the case of *Jehovah's Witnesses v Argentina* (1978) Case 2137 in which the American Commission on Human Rights declared the expulsion of 300 school age children by reason of their religion a violation of Art III of the American Declaration of the Rights and Duties of Man.

2. Parents, and where applicable, legal guardians shall have a duty to provide guidance and direction in the exercise of these rights having regard to the evolving capacities, and best interests of the child.

3. States Parties shall respect the duty of parents and where applicable, legal guardians to provide guidance and direction in the enjoyment of these rights subject to the national laws and policies.'

10.105 It should be noted that Art 9(2) of the African Charter places a *duty* on parents and, where appropriate, legal guardians to provide guidance and direction to the child in the exercise of his or her right to freedom of thought, conscience and religion. This differs from the approach adopted by Art 14(2) of the CRC which maintains a right as well as a duty on the part of parents to give such direction. Article 9(3) of the African Charter requires that the State respect the parents' duty to provide guidance and direction on matters of thought, conscience and religion subject to national laws and policies.

The African Youth Charter

10.106 Article 6 of the African Youth Charter stipulates that 'Every young person shall have the right to freedom of thought, conscience and religion. Article 2(3) of the Charter requires that 'State Parties shall recognise the rights of Young people from ethnic, religious and linguistic marginalised groups or youth of indigenous origin, to enjoy their own culture, freely practice their own religion or to use their own language in community with other members of their group'.

The African Charter on Human and Peoples' Rights

10.107 The African Charter on Human and Peoples' Rights enshrines the right to freedom of thought, conscience and religion in Art 8 which provides that 'Freedom of conscience, the profession and free practice of religion shall be guaranteed. No one may, subject to law and order, be submitted to measures restricting the exercise of these freedoms'.

Revised Arab Charter on Human Rights

10.108 The revised Arab Charter on Human Rights refers expressly to the 'noble Islamic religion and other divinely revealed religions' in its preamble.[267] Art 30 of the revised Arab Charter provides that:

'1. Everyone has the right to freedom of thought, conscience and religion and no restrictions may be imposed on the exercise of such freedoms except as provided for by law.

2. The freedom to manifest one's religion or beliefs or to perform religious observances, either alone or in community with others, shall be subject only to such limitations as are

---

[267] Note that the terms of Art 3(3) of the revised Charter ('Men and women are equal in respect of human dignity, rights and obligations within the framework of the positive discrimination established in favour of women by the Islamic Shariah, other divine laws and by applicable laws and legal instruments. Accordingly, each State party pledges to take all the requisite measures to guarantee equal opportunities and effective equality between men and women in the enjoyment of all the rights set out in this Charter') suggests that the Charter will be interpreted in accordance with the Islamic Shariah and divine law.

prescribed by law and are necessary in a tolerant society that respects human rights and freedoms for the protection of public safety, public order, public health or morals or the fundamental rights and freedoms of others.

3. Parents or guardians have the freedom to provide for the religious and moral education of their children.'

The Child's Right to Freedom of Thought, Conscience and Religion under Domestic Law

Domestic Law – Children, Parents and Religion

Religion and the Role of Parents

10.109   Historically, the domestic common law required that, unless there were exceptional circumstances, a child had to be brought up in the religion of his or her father.[268] In the case of *Re Agar-Ellis*[269] the parents had agreed that their children would be brought up Roman Catholics. Following the parents' separation, the mother continued the children's Catholic instruction and the children refused to attend Anglican services with their father. In response, the father obtained an injunction against the mother preventing her acting against his wishes in respect of the children's religious upbringing and removed the children from her care. The Court of Appeal refused to interfere with the first instance decision of Malins V-C that a 'father is the head of his house, he must have the control of his family, he must say how and by whom they are to be educated and where they are to be educated'.

10.110   The domestic rule that children had to be brought up in the religion of their father was abolished by the Guardianship of Infants Act 1925, s 1 and the decision in *Re Agar-Ellis*[270] has been the subject of much condemnation.[271] However, the child's religious upbringing remains a function of parental responsibility[272] in the discharge of which the court will not readily interfere. In *Re T (Minors) (Custody: Upbringing)*[273] Lord Scarman made clear that 'it was not for the court to pass any judgment on the beliefs of parents where they are socially acceptable and consistent with a decent and respectable life'.[274] The continuing strength of the parental role in the child's religious upbringing is demonstrated by s 33(6)(a) of the Children Act 1989 which requires that:

'(6) While a care order is in force with respect to a child, the local authority designated in the order shall not –

---

[268]   *Hawksworth v Hawksworth* (1871) LR Ch App 539 and *Andrews v Salt* (1873) 8 Ch App 622.

[269]   (1878) 10 Ch D 49.

[270]   (1878) 10 Ch D 49.

[271]   See the summary of Lord Fraser in *Gillick v West Norfolk and Wisbech Area Health Authority and another* [1986] AC 112.

[272]   Children Act 1989, s 3(1) and see *Re J (Specific Issue Orders: Muslim Upbringing and Circumcision)* [1999] 2 FLR 678 per Wall J.

[273]   (1981) 2 FLR 239. See also *Re H (A Minor)(Custody: Religious Upbringing)* (1981) 2 FLR 253 ('mere indoctrination with the beliefs and tenets of this narrow faith is not of itself indicative of harm or that harm will occur to the child so indoctrinated, provided there is an understanding and level headed parent in charge of the child'). For the rare contrasting position see *Re B and G (Minors)(Custody)* [1985] FLR 493 (where a father and stepmother were denied residence of the children for whom they had been caring for 5 years on the basis that they were scientologists, held views that were found by the court to be 'immoral and obnoxious' and the father would not provide an undertaking to remove the children the 'evil forces of scientology') and *Hewison v Hewison* (1977) Fam Law 207.

[274]   Repeated by Purchas LJ in *Re R (A Minor)(Residence: Religion)* [1993] 2 FLR 163.

(a)   cause the child to be brought up in any religious persuasion other than that in which
        he would have been brought up if the order had not been made; or ...'[275]

Religion and Welfare

10.111   Whilst a person with parental responsibility may determine the child's religious
education, there is no duty in domestic law to give the child a religious upbringing.[276]
Where there is a dispute as between parents as to the religious upbringing of the child,
whilst serious heed will be paid by the Court to the religious wishes of a parent,[277] in the
event agreement cannot be reached the child's best interests will be paramount.[278] In
considering the matters under the welfare checklist in s 1(3) of the Children Act 1989 the
child's 'background' for the purposes of s 1(3)(d) may include the child's religion.[279] In
this context it should be noted that religion will not be an overriding consideration when
determining any matter in relation to the upbringing of a child.[280] However, when a
religion which provides a way of life and permeates every activity forms part of the
child's background, the child's religious and cultural heritage will be a very important
factor in the assessment of the child's welfare. Overall, religion will always remain one
factor amongst a range of factors to be weighed and taken into account.[281] In assessing
the impact of particular beliefs, tenets or doctrines on the welfare of the child it is not a
function of the court to determine the validity of those beliefs only their effect or
otherwise on the welfare of the child in question.[282]

Religion and the Child's Wishes

10.112   The child's wishes and feelings in relation to the issue of religion in dispute will
also fall to be considered in light of the child's age and understanding pursuant to
s 1(3)(a) of the Children Act 1989.[283] Indeed, the child's right to understand and
appreciate religion will be a factor in the welfare decision[284] and the court will be slow to
force any particular religion on a child in the event of a dispute.[285]

10.113   The domestic courts have recognised the right of a child of sufficient age and
understanding to participate in choosing a religion. In *Re S (Specific Issue Order:*

---

[275]   Although see also the evolution in the adoption legislation from the consideration of the parents wishes in
        respect of religious upbringing contained in s 7 of the Adoption Act 1976 ('An adoption agency shall in
        placing a child for adoption have regard (so far as is practicable) to any wishes of a child's parents and
        guardians as to the religious upbringing of the child') to the consideration of the child's religious persuasion
        in s 1(5) of the Adoption and Children Act 2002 ('In placing the child for adoption, the adoption agency
        must give due consideration to the child's religious persuasion, racial origin and cultural and linguistic
        background').
[276]   *Re J (Specific Issue Orders: Muslim Upbringing and Circumcision)* [1999] 2 FLR 678, FD and *Re J (Specific
        Issue Orders: Child's Religious Upbringing and Circumcision)* [2000] 1 FLR 571, CA.
[277]   *J v C* [1969] 1 All ER 788.
[278]   See *Re S (Minors) (Access: Religious Upbringing)* [1992] 2 FLR 313, *Re P (Section 91(14) Guidelines)
        (Residence and Religious Heritage)* [1999] 2 FLR 573, *Re J (Specific Issue Orders: Muslim Upbringing and
        Circumcision)* [1999] 2 FLR 678 and *Re J (Specific Issue Orders: Child's Religious Upbringing and
        Circumcision)* [2000] 1 FLR 571, CA. See also *Re E (An Infant)* [1963] 3 All ER 874 per Wiberforce J.
        ('Welfare is not limited to material welfare. The religious upbringing is an element of great importance).
[279]   See *Re M (Infants)* [1967] 3 All ER 1071 at 1074.
[280]   *Haleem v Haleem* (1975) Fam Law 184.
[281]   *Re P (A Child) (Residence Order: Child's Welfare)* [2000] Fam 15, [1999] 3 All ER 734.
[282]   *Re R (A Minor) (Residence: Religion)* [1993] 2 FLR 163.
[283]   *Re S (Specific Issue Order: Religion: Circumcision)* [2004] EWHC 1282 (Fam), [2005] 1 FLR 236,
        paras 76–78.
[284]   *Re P (Section 91(14) Guidelines)(Residence and Religious Heritage)* [1999] 2 FLR 573
[285]   *Re C (MA) (An Infant)* [1966] 1 ALL ER 838. The court made clear in this case that the fact that a child
        had been baptised in a particular faith does not mean that the court will order the child to be brought up in
        that faith.

Religion: Circumcision)[286] Baron J held that two children aged almost 10 and 8 ½ who were the subject of a dispute between their parents as to whether they should be raised as Hindus or Muslims were too old for the court to impose a religion upon them. The court held that the children of mixed religious background should be permitted to decided for themselves which, if any, religion they wished to follow. This extended to refusing to sanction the circumcision of the male child so as to allow him to make an informed decision when he reached an age where he had the capacity to do so having regard to the principles set out in *Gillick v West Norfolk and Wisbech Area Health Authority.*[287]

Domestic Law – Human Rights Act 1998

10.114 Before the Human Rights Act came into force the concept of religious freedom was recognised in domestic common law as an interest demanding strong countervailing interests to justify administrative action interfering with such freedom.[288] This approach finds continued expression in the Human Rights Act 1998.[289] Section 13 of the Act provides as follows in respect of the right to freedom of thought, conscience and religion:

> '1. If a court's determination of any question arising under this Act might affect the exercise by a religious organisation (itself or its members collectively) of the Convention right to freedom of thought, conscience and religion, it must have particular regard to the importance of that right.[290]
>
> 2. In this section 'court' includes tribunal.'

10.115 In respect of Church law, the Measures of the Church of England are classified under the Human Rights Act 1998 as primary legislation.[291] As such, Measures are to be interpreted in a manner compatible with the rights enshrined in the ECHR. The Church of England, as an established church in part of the United Kingdom is not a 'public authority' for the purposes of the Human Rights Act 1998.[292]

Domestic Law – Children and Religious Practices[293]

10.116 In *Re J (Specific Issue Orders: Muslim Upbringing and Circumcision)*[294] Wall J considered an application by a Muslim father for specific issue orders requiring the non-Muslim mother of the parents' 5 year old son to raise him as a Muslim and requiring her to have the child circumcised. Wall J refused both applications, holding in relation to the application for an order requiring the mother to raise the child as a Muslim that only in unusual circumstances would the court require that a child be

---

[286] [2004] EWHC 1282 (Fam), [2005] 1 FLR 236.

[287] [1986] AC 112.

[288] *R v Secretary of State for the Home Department, ex p Moon* [1996] COD 54, 8 Admin LR 477 and *Redmond-Bate DPP* (1999) 7 BHRC 375 (DC).

[289] See Cumper, P *The Protection of Religious Rights under Section 13 of the Human Rights Act 1998* [2000] Public Law 265.

[290] Note however that s 13 does not permit freedom of religion to override other rights enshrined in the ECHR (See *R (on the application of Ullah) v Special Adjudicator* [2002] EWHC 1584 (Admin) [2002] All ER (D) 235 (Jul)).

[291] Human Rights Act 1998, s 21.

[292] *Aston Cantlow Parochial Church Council v Wallbank* [2003] UKHL 37, [2004] 1 AC 546.

[293] See also **5.66** above for discussion on refusal of treatment on religious grounds.

[294] [1999] 2 FLR 678.

brought up in a religion which was not that of the parent with whom the child was residing. In respect of the application for an order requiring circumcision of the child, refusing the order and emphasising his decision turned on the facts of the case Wall J held:

> '... A case can be made for describing ritual male circumcision without any medical need for it as an assault on the bodily integrity of the child; indeed, that is the case which is made in much of the medical literature to which I was referred. However, although the origins of ritual circumcision are unknown, the fact remains that there have, historically, been a number of medical justifications put forward for male circumcision, and there are certain specific, albeit rare, medical conditions for which it is currently deemed necessary. Whilst the medical benefits of ritual male circumcision are now controversial, the fact remains that not only is it insisted upon by Muslims and Jews, but that male circumcision itself has, over the years, become an accepted practice amongst a significant number of parents in England. In my judgment, therefore, where two parents, jointly exercising parental responsibility for a male child, cause him to be ritually circumcised in accordance with the tenets of their religion, that exercise of parental responsibility is lawful ... where there is a disagreement between those who have parental responsibility for the child as to whether or not he should be circumcised, the issue is one within the court's jurisdiction under s 8 of the Children Act 1989; and ... the court must decide the question by the application of s 1 of the Children Act 1989 to the facts of the individual case ... I repeat that my decision in this case turns on its particular facts. I do not think it can be said that the court would not, in any circumstances, order a child to be circumcised.'[295]

On appeal in *Re J (Specific Issue Orders: Child's Religious Upbringing and Circumcision)*[296] the Court of Appeal upheld Wall J's decision.

10.117 The Female Genital Mutilation Act 2003, s 1(1) provides that a person is guilty of an offence if he excises, infibulates[297] or otherwise mutilates the whole or any part of a girl's labia majora, labia minora or clitoris'. The maximum term on conviction on indictment is 14 years imprisonment or a fine or both.[298] Section 2 of the Act makes it an offence to aid, abet, counsel or procure a girl to excise, infibulate or otherwise mutilate the whole or any part of a girl's labia majora, labia minora or clitoris and s 3 extends the offence of aiding and abetting to girls who are not United Kingdom nationals or permanent United Kingdom residents. By s 4(1) these provisions extend to any act done outside the United Kingdom by a United Kingdom National or permanent United Kingdom resident.

---

[295] Fortin questions whether the fact that a procedure comprises a popular or long accepted parental practice is sufficient legal justification for its use (Fortin, J *Children's Rights and the Developing Law* (2009) 3rd edn, Cambridge, p 394). Arguing that there is no compelling legal authority for the view that circumcision is lawful, Fox and Thomson place the concept of male circumcision in stark context by pointing out that 'Only limited consideration has been given to the seemingly obvious fact that circumcision is the excision of healthy tissue from a child unable to give his consent for no demonstrable medical benefit' (Fox, M and Thomson, M *A Covenant with the Status Quo? – Male Circumcision and the New BMA Guidance to Doctors* (2005) J Med Ethics 31: 463–469).

[296] [2000] 1 FLR 571, CA. Note that the court approved the proposition that circumcision fell into that small category of cases where, in the event of parental disagreement, the issue should be referred to the court notwithstanding s 2(7) of the Children Act 1989 (s 2(7) providing that 'Where more than one person has parental responsibility for a child, each of them may act alone and without the other (or others) in meeting that responsibility; but nothing in this part shall be taken to affect the operation of any enactment which requires the consent of more than one person in a matter affecting the child').

[297] The act of closing off or obstructing the genitals.

[298] Female Genital Mutilation Act 2003, s 5(a). Note that the maximum term on summary conviction is 6 months or a fine not exceeding the statutory maximum or both.

Domestic Law – Education and Religion

Religion and the Curriculum

(i) Religious Education

Statutory Framework

10.118 Domestic law obliges all maintained schools to promote the Christian religion through a daily act of collective worship, which act must be broadly Christian in character.[299] The provisions which make it illegal to discriminate against pupils on the grounds of their religion or belief do not apply to acts of collective worship or to the provision of religious education.[300] It is also a legal requirement for all maintained schools to make provision for religious education for all registered pupils in accordance with the School Standards and Framework Act Sch 19.[301] The Education Act 1996, s 375(3) provides that 'Every agreed syllabus shall reflect the fact that religious traditions in Great Britain are in the main Christian whilst taking account of the teaching and practices of the other principal religions represented in Great Britain'.[302]

Exemptions

10.119 A parent may withdraw their child from participation in collective religious worship and/or religious education.[303] Where a parent wishes a child to receive religious education of a kind not provided by their school, the child may be withdrawn from school for such periods as are reasonably necessary for the purposes of enabling him or her to receive such religious education.[304] Note that young persons in sixth form may request to be wholly or partly excused from attendance at religious worship.[305] As such, under the domestic education legislation, children under 16 may not elect to forego religious education without parental consent. Only children who have attained the age of 16 may, without parental intervention, elect not to attend acts of worship in school. As Fortin notes, the lack provision for the participation of children under the age of 16 in decisions concerning their education in respect of religious matters and their participation in the same does send the message that such views are not important.[306] Fortin further notes that, as with many of the international human rights instruments, it is regrettable that the principles of law applying to collective worship and religious education assume that the parents' right to freedom of thought, conscience and religion is necessarily co-terminus with that of their children.[307] The Committee on the Rights of

---

[299] School Standards and Framework Act 1998, s 70 and Sch 20, para 3(2). In areas where there are few pupils of the Christian religion the Standing Council on Religious Education may permit no form of collective worship or one which accords with the pupils' family backgrounds.

[300] Equality Act 2006, s 50(2)(a) and (b).

[301] Education Act 2002, s 80 and the School Standards and Framework Act 1998, s 69(1). Note that nursery and primary education is exempt from this requirement as are maintained special schools (Education Act 2002, s 80(2)).

[302] Education Act 1996, s 375(3).

[303] School Standards and Framework Act 1998, s 71(1). See also the Education Act 1996, s 9 'In exercising or performing all their respective powers and duties under the Education Acts, the Secretary of State and local education authorities shall have regard to the general principle that pupils are to be educated in accordance with the wishes of their parents, so far as that is compatible with the provision of efficient instruction and training and the avoidance of unreasonable public expenditure.'

[304] School Standards and Framework Act 1998, s 71(3).

[305] School Standards and Framework Act 1998, s 71(1B).

[306] Fortin, J *Children's Rights and the Developing Law* (2009) 3rd edn, Cambridge, p 427.

[307] Fortin, J *Children's Rights and the Developing Law* (2009) 3rd edn, Cambridge, p 427 and see Harris, N *Education, Law and Diversity* (2007) Hart Publishing, pp 434–437.

the Child has suggested that the availability in domestic law of exemptions for children under the age of 16 only at the behest of parents may not be compatible with Art 14 of the CRC.[308]

10.120   The domestic law empowers the State to intervene in independent faith schools irrespective of the religious or ethnic group those schools cater for.[309] The aim and ambit of the religious education provided by independent faith schools is prescribed by regulation.[310] Children who attend independent faith schools must, like every other child of compulsory school age, receive efficient full time education which is suitable to his or her age, ability and aptitude and to any special educational needs he or she may have. Within the context of independent faith schools, in *R v Secretary of State for Education and Science, ex p Talmud Torah Machzikei Haddass School Trust*[311] the court held that education is 'suitable' if it primarily equips a child for life within the community of which he or she is a member, rather than the way of life in the wider country as a whole, as long as it does not foreclose the child's options in later years to adopt some other form of life if he wishes to do so.

(ii) Sex Education:

10.121   Provision for Sex and Relationships Education (SRE) is made by the Learning and Skills Act 2000, s 148 amending the Education Act 1996, s 403. The latter section provides that the governing body and head teacher shall take such steps as are reasonably practicable to secure that where sex education is given to any registered pupils at a maintained school, it is given in such a manner as to encourage those pupils to have due regard to moral considerations and the value of family life.[312] Pursuant to the Education Act 1996, s 405 parents can withdraw their children from SRE classes except so far as such education is comprised in the National Curriculum.[313] It is difficult to see how this exemption can comply with Arts 10, 12 and 14 of the CRC. Within the context of domestic law the absence of any provision for participation in accordance with his or her understanding by the child in any request for exemption from sex education means that under domestic law a child who is *Gillick* competent may seek contraception without parental knowledge whilst at the same time being lawfully prevented by his or her parents from receiving sex education.[314]

---

[308]   See Norway CRC/C/SR.625 (2000) at 55.

[309]   See Education Act 2002, Part X and the Education and Skills Act 2008, Part IV.

[310]   Education (Independent School Standards) (England) Regulations 2003, SI 2003/1910. These regulations have been criticised as being relatively vague in meaning (see Bradney, A *The Inspection of Ultra-Orthodox Scholls: 'The Audit Society' and 'The Society of Scholars'* (2009) 21 Child and Family Law Quarterly 131).

[311]   (1985) *The Times* 12 April. Hamilton argues that education provided by a faith school should only be accepted as suitable if it fulfils the child's right to equality of opportunity protected by international human rights instruments, which education equipping a child only for life within the community of a religious group does not (Hamilton, C *Family, Law and Religion* (1995) Sweet & Maxwell, pp 259–263).

[312]   Education Act 1996, s 403(1). The Secretary of State is required by s 403(2) to issue guidance to secure that when sex education is given children learn 'the nature of marriage and its importance for family life and the upbringing of children; and they are protected from teaching and materials which are inappropriate having regard to the age and the religious and cultural background of the pupils concerned' (see Guidance from the Department for Education and Employment *Sex and Relationship Education Guidance* (2000) 0116/2000 DfEE).

[313]   This provision has been criticised by the Committee on the Rights of the Child *Concluding Observations of the Committee on the Rights of the Child: United Kingdom of Great Britain and Northern Ireland* (1995) CRC/C/15/Add 34, para 14.

[314]   See Fortin, J *Children's Rights and the Developing Law* (2009) 3rd edn, Cambridge, pp 226–227.

Religion and School Admissions

10.122   In *R (E) v Governing Body of JFS; R (E) v Office of the Schools Adjudicator*[315] the Court of Appeal noted that the exemption of faith schools from the prohibition on discrimination on grounds of religion and belief contained in the Equality Act 2006 means that where a faith school is undersubscribed it may not use religious criteria to allocate places but that once it is oversubscribed the school may lawfully restrict admissions to those children who, or whose parents, share the school's faith.[316] The Court of Appeal further noted that this does not permit the school to discriminate in its admissions policy on the grounds of race, the same being forbidden by the Race Relations Act 1976, or where the alleged discrimination occurred after 1 October 2010 by the Equality Act 2010. *In R (on the application of K) v London Borough of Newham*[317] Colins J held that in order for the State to comply with Art 2 1P of the ECHR there has to be some positive action on the part of the State in respect of admissions, which action should include the implementation of a mechanism for ensuring that the potential importance of a child's religious convictions is appreciated by the authorities considering admission applications.

Religion and School Discipline

(i) Statutory Framework

10.123   Section 47 of the Education Act 1986 made physical punishment in maintained schools illegal. The prohibition was extended to private schools in 1998. Section 131 of the School Standards and Framework Act 1998 amended s 548(1) of the Education Act 1996 to provide that corporal punishment given by a member of school staff to a child cannot be justified in any proceedings on the ground that it was given in pursuance of a right exercisable by the member of the staff by virtue of their position as such. Members of staff may use force in certain specified circumstances, namely to prevent a pupil from committing an offence, causing personal injury or damage to property or prejudicing the maintenance of good order and discipline at the school.[318]

(ii) School Discipline and Religion

10.124   In *R v Secretary of State for Education and Employment and Others (Respondents) ex part Williamson (Appellant) and others*[319] the House of Lords was required to consider the terms of the Education Act 1996, s 548(1). The claimants, who comprised head teachers, teachers and parents of children at four independent schools, challenged the statutory prohibition on corporal punishment in all schools as a breach of their right to freedom or religion. The basis of their claim was that the commitment to so called 'loving corporal correction'[320] in the upbringing of children was an essential element of their faith based on their interpretation biblical scripture. The claimants argued that religious liberty required that parents be able to delegate to schools the ability to train children according to these 'biblical' principles.[321]

---

[315]   [2009] EWCA Civ 626, [2009] 4 All ER 375. See also *A v Special Educational Needs and Disability Tribunal and London Borough of Barnett* [2003] EWHC 3368 (Admin), [2004] ELR 293 and *London Oratory School v Schools Adjudicator* [2004] EWHC 3014 (Admin), (2005) ELR 162.

[316]   See Equality Act 2006, s 50(1)(a).

[317]   [2002] EWHC 405 (Admin), [2002] ELR 390, pp 398–99.

[318]   Education and Inspections Act 2006, s 93.

[319]   [2005] UKHL 15, [2005] 2 AC 286.

[320]   The practice in question took the form, for boys, of a thin broad 'paddle' to the buttocks and, for girls, a strap on the hand, followed for both boys and girls by comfort from an adult and an encouragement to pray.

[321]   See Committee on the Rights of the Child General Comment No 8 *The Right of the Child to Protection from Corporal Punishment and other Cruel or Degrading forms of Punishment* (Arts 19; 28, para 2; and 37, inter

10.125   The House of Lords held that the Education Act 1996, s 548(1) prevented the delegation by parents to teachers of the parental right to administer reasonable physical chastisement. The House of Lords were clear that this position materially interfered with the right of the parents to manifest their Christian beliefs pursuant to Art 9(1) and Art 2 1P of the ECHR but that that the interference was justified under Art 9(2) as being prescribed by law, necessary in a democratic society to protect children and promote their wellbeing. Whilst this case was about the punishment of children by adults using physical means only Baroness Hale made any reference to the rights of the child as constituting a separate consideration in the case, observing that:

> 'This is, and has always been, a case about children, their rights and the rights of their parents and teachers. Yet there has been no-one here or in the courts below to speak on behalf of the children. No litigation friend has been appointed to consider the rights of the pupils involved separately from those of the adults. No non-governmental organisation, such as the Children's Rights Alliance, has intervened to argue a case on behalf of children as a whole. The battle has been fought on ground selected by the adults. This has clouded and over-complicated what should have been a simple issue ... The practice of corporal punishment involves what would otherwise be an assault upon another person. The essential question, therefore, has always been whether the legislation achieves a fair balance between the rights and freedoms of the parents and teachers and the rights, freedoms and interests, not only of their children, but also of any other children who might be affected by the persistence of corporal punishment in some schools. The mechanism for achieving that balance lies in article 9.2... The real question is whether any limits set by the state can be justified under article 9.2... There can be no doubt that the ban on corporal punishment in schools pursues the legitimate aim of protecting the rights and freedoms of children. It has long been held that these are not limited to their rights under the European Convention. The appellants were anxious to stress that the corporal punishment in which they believe would not breach the child's rights under either article 3 or article 8. But it can still be legitimate for the state to prohibit it for the sake of the child. A child has the same right as anyone else not to be assaulted; the defence of lawful chastisement is an exception to that right. It has long been held in the context of article 8 that the rights and freedoms of the child include his interests... Even if it could be shown that a particular act of corporal punishment was in the interests of the individual child, it is clear that a universal or blanket ban may be justified to protect a vulnerable class ... Above all, the state is entitled to give children the protection they are given by an international instrument to which the United Kingdom is a party, the United Nations Convention on the Rights of the Child (UNCRC). There was also a large body of professional educational and child care opinion in support of the ban ... With such an array of international and professional support, it is quite impossible to say that Parliament was not entitled to limit the practice of corporal punishment in all schools in order to protect the rights and freedoms of all children. Furthermore, the state has a positive obligation to protect children from inhuman or degrading punishment which violates their rights under article 3. But prohibiting only such punishment as would violate their rights under article 3 (or possibly article 8) would bring difficult problems of definition, demarcation and enforcement. It would not meet the authoritative international view of what the UNCRC requires. The appellants' solution is that they and other schools which share their views should be exempted from the ban. But this would raise exactly the same problems. How could it be justified in terms of the rights and protection of the child to allow some schools to inflict corporal punishment while prohibiting the rest from doing so? If a child has a right to be brought up without institutional violence, as he does, that right should

---

alia) CRC/C/GC/8, para 29 ('Some raise faith-based justifications for corporal punishment, suggesting that certain interpretations of religious texts not only justify its use, but provide a duty to use it. Freedom of religious belief is upheld for everyone in the International Covenant on Civil and Political Rights (art. 18), but practice of a religion or belief must be consistent with respect for others' human dignity and physical integrity. Freedom to practise one's religion or belief may be legitimately limited in order to protect the fundamental rights and freedoms of others').

be respected whether or not his parents and teachers believe otherwise. For very different reasons from those given by the Court of Appeal, therefore, I would dismiss this appeal.'

Whilst this analysis has been criticised as complicating what is essentially a claim between two competing views of the child's best interests,[322] Baroness Hale's approach explicitly recognises that in law it is not only the parents whose rights are engaged in determining the appropriate resolution between the position of the parents and the position of the State on a matter religious freedom which impact upon children.

Religion and School Uniform

(i) Religion and School Uniform – Claims under the Human Rights Act 1998

10.126 In *R (On the application of Shabina Begum) v Denbigh High School Governors*[323] the House of Lords considered a claim by a Muslim pupil that a prohibition on the wearing of a jilbab at school violated her right to freedom of religion under Art 9(1) of the ECHR.[324] The majority of the House of Lords (Lord Nicholls and Baroness Hale dissenting in part) held that there had been no violation of the child's rights under Art 9(1) as there was no prohibition on her attending a school where her religion did not require a jilbab or where she was allowed to wear one.[325] Lord Nicholls and Baroness Hale dissented from the conclusion of the majority that Shabina Begum's rights were not engaged, holding instead that the prohibition on wearing the jilbab interfered with her Art 9(1) rights but that such interference was justified under Art 9(2). Baroness Hale observed that:

'The reality is that the choice of secondary school is usually made by parents or guardians rather than by the child herself. The child is on the brink of, but has not yet reached, adolescence. She may have views but they are unlikely to be decisive. More importantly, she has not yet reached the critical stage in her development where this particular choice may matter to her. Important physical, cognitive and psychological developments take place during adolescence. Adolescence begins with the onset of puberty; from puberty to adulthood, the 'capacity to acquire and utilise knowledge reaches its peak efficiency'; and the capacity for formal operational thought is the forerunner to developing the capacity to make autonomous moral judgments. Obviously, these developments happen at different times and at different rates for different people. But it is not at all surprising to find adolescents making different moral judgments from those of their parents. It is part of growing up. The fact that they are not yet fully adult may help to justify interference with the choices they have made.

---

[322] Hill, M *Interpreting the European Convention on Human Rights in the United Kingdom Courts: The Impact on Religious Organisations* (2007) European Consortium for Church and State Research. Hill's view appears to ignore the existence in law of children's rights under the ECHR and the CRC.

[323] [2006] UKHL 15, [2006] 2 WLR 719. See also Brems, E *Above Children's Heads: The Headscarf Controversy in European Schools from the Perspective of Children's Rights* (2006) 14 International Journal of Children's Rights 119, pp 129–133; Hill, M *Interpreting the European Convention on Human Rights in the United Kingdom Courts: The Impact on Religious Organisations* (2007) and Hill, M and Sandberg, R *Is Nothing Sacred? Clashing Symbols in a Secular World* [2007] *Public Law* 488–506 and Hill, M *Interpreting the European Convention on Human Rights in the United Kingdom Courts: The Impact on Religious Organisations* (2007) Cardiff.

[324] The school dress code permitted the wearing of a shalwar kameze and the claimant had done so for 2 years. She later however came to believe that the shalwar kameze was not appropriate for a Muslim girl who had reached puberty, believing the jilbab more appropriately concealed the shape of her arms and legs. See also Department for Children, Schools and Families (DCSF) *DCSF Guidance to Schools on Uniform and Related Policies* (2007) DCSF.

[325] In reaching this decision, the majority placed heavy reliance on the European jurisprudence including *X v Denmark* (1976) 5 DR 157; *Kjeldsen, Busk Madsen and Pedersen v Denmark* (1976) 1 EHRR 711; *Karaduman v Turkey* (1993) 74 DR 93; *Konttinen v Finland* (1996) 87–A DR 68; *Valsamis v Greece* (1996) 24 EHRR 294; *Stedman v United Kingdom* (1997) 23 EHRR CD 168 and *Liturgical Association Cha'are Shalom Ve Tsedek v France* (2000) 9 BHRC 27.

It cannot be assumed, as it can with adults, that these choices are the product of a fully developed individual autonomy. But it may still count as an interference. I am therefore inclined to agree with my noble and learned friend, Lord Nicholls of Birkenhead, that there was an interference with Shabina Begum's right to manifest her religion.'

In holding however that the interference with Shabina Begum's right to manifest her religion under Art 9(1) of the ECHR was justified Baroness Hale went on to hold that:

'If a woman freely chooses to adopt a way of life for herself, it is not for others, including other women who have chosen differently, to criticise or prevent her ... The European Court of Human Rights has never accepted that interference with the right of freedom of expression is justified by the fact that the ideas expressed may offend someone. Likewise, the sight of a woman in full purdah may offend some people, and especially those western feminists who believe that it is a symbol of her oppression, but that could not be a good reason for prohibiting her from wearing it. But schools are different. Their task is to educate the young from all the many and diverse families and communities in this country in accordance with the national curriculum. Their task is to help all of their pupils achieve their full potential. This includes growing up to play whatever part they choose in the society in which they are living. The school's task is also to promote the ability of people of diverse races, religions and cultures to live together in harmony. Fostering a sense of community and cohesion within the school is an important part of that. A uniform dress code can play its role in smoothing over ethnic, religious and social divisions. But it does more than that. Like it or not, this is a society committed, in principle and in law, to equal freedom for men and women to choose how they will lead their lives within the law. Young girls from ethnic, cultural or religious minorities growing up here face particularly difficult choices: how far to adopt or to distance themselves from the dominant culture. A good school will enable and support them.'

10.127   The issue of school uniform in the context of religion has been considered in a number of cases since *R (On the application of Shabina Begum) v Denbigh High School Governors*[326] In *R (On the application of X) v Y High School*[327] Sibler J applied the reasoning of the majority in the *Begum* case and found that there had been no infringement of the Art 9(1) rights of a 12 year old Muslim girl prevented from wearing a niqab by her schools uniform policy on the grounds that there was a school nearby which achieved good results and permitted the wearing of the niqab. In *R (Playfoot) v Governing Body of Millais School*[328] the court rejected the claim of a 16 year old girl that a prohibition on her wearing a 'purity ring' violated her rights under Art 9(1). The court found that Art 9(1) was not engaged as the wearing of the ring was not intimately linked to her belief in chastity before marriage and therefore not a manifestation of her belief.

(ii) Religion and School Uniform – Claims under the Anti-Discrimination Legislation

10.128   In *Mandla v Lee and Ors*[329] the court held that the refusal to allow a Sikh boy to wear a turban amounted to unlawful discrimination under the Race Relations Act 1976, the rule banning the turban not being justifiable within the meaning of s 1(b)(ii) of the Act[330] merely because the school had a genuine belief that it would provide a better system of education if it were permitted to discriminate against those

---

[326]   [2006] UKHL 15, [2006] 2 WLR 719.
[327]   [2007] EWHC 298 (Admin), [2008] 1 All ER 249.
[328]   [2007] EWHC 1698 (Admin), [2007] LGR 851, [2007] 3 FCR 754.
[329]   [1983] 2 AC 548.
[330]   See now also s 1A of the Act.

children who wore turbans.[331] The Race Relations Act 1976 has been replaced by the Equality Act 2010 in respect of allegations of discrimination occurring after 1 October 2010.[332]

10.129   Under the Equality Act 2006, s 49(1)(c)(iv) where a person is a pupil at an educational establishment it is unlawful for the responsible body of that establishment to discriminate against a person by 'subjecting him to any other detriment'. This section may allow a claim for indirect religious discrimination under s 45(3) of the Equality Act 2006 in refusing to permit the wearing of a visible sign of the membership of a particular group or faith if the child can demonstrate that he or she is a member of a particular racial or religious group and that he or she has suffered 'detriment' in being prevented from wearing the clothing or item concerned. In *R (Watkins-Singh) v Governing Body of Aberdare Girls' High School*[333] Silber J considered the claim of a 14 year old Sikh girl who had been prohibited from wearing her Kara in school. The court held that schools decision to prohibit the wearing of a Kara amounted to indirect discrimination on the grounds that the child suffered detriment by being forbidden from wearing an item that she personally believed to be of exceptional importance to her religion. Silber J noted that the wearing of the clothing or item need not be a compulsory element of the faith or belief although the person must genuinely believe on reasonable grounds that wearing the clothing or item is a matter of exceptional importance to his or her racial identity or religious belief and that the wearing of the clothing or item is objectively of exceptional importance to his or her religion or race, even if not a compulsory requirement of the same. Note the Equality Act 2006 contains an exception based on reasonable justification by surrounding circumstances.[334] In the instant case the court held that the school's arguments as to reasonable justification for the ban did not stand up to scrutiny.

CONCLUSION

10.130   As Baroness Hale observed in *R (On the application of Shabina Begum) v Denbigh High School Governors*[335] 'it is not at all surprising to find adolescents making different moral judgments from those of their parents. It is part of growing up'. Such judgments form a key element of the child's developing understanding of the wider concept that mankind does not have a single way of life but rather a flourishing diversity of religions and philosophies which must be accommodated within the society that children join at birth and in which they increasingly participate as they grow up. The nurturing and development of this understanding through parental direction which progressively gives way to informed decision making protected by the child's freedom of thought, conscience and religion is a vital element in sustaining and renewing a democratic, vibrant and fair society; the 'rights of children to exercise their religion, and of parents to give them religious training and to encourage them in the practice of religious belief, as against preponderant sentiment and assertion of state power'[336] being

---

[331]   The school had argued that the wearing of a turban was a manifestation of the child's ethnic origins and would accentuate religious and social distinctions in the school which the school wished to minimise.

[332]   Equality Act 2010, s 211 and Sch 27. The Act defines religion as 'any religion and a reference to religion includes lack of religion' and defines belief as 'any religious or philosophical belief and a reference to belief includes lack of belief' (Equality Act 2010, s 10).

[333]   [2008] EWHC 1865 (Admin), [2008] ELR 561.

[334]   Equality Act 2006, s 45(3)(d).

[335]   [2006] UKHL 15, [2006] 2 WLR 719.

[336]   *Prince v Massachusetts* (1944) 321 US 158 (Supreme Court).

crucial to that end. In *Race and History*[337] Levi-Strauss observed that 'no section of humanity has succeeded in finding universally applicable formulas ... it is impossible to imagine mankind pursuing a single way of life for, in such a case mankind would be ossified'.

10.131 Historically, international instruments and regional and domestic case law demonstrate a reluctance to consider children as capable of thought, conscience and religious belief separate from that of their parents. Whilst this approach in part has its foundations both in the well-meaning desire to prevent the educational indoctrination of children and to preserve the cohesion of family and community, it is an approach which ultimately militates against the child's ability to develop independent thought and to explore the beliefs and views he or she may wish to adopt as he or she grows into adulthood. This in turn risks the child being unable to accommodate the beliefs and philosophies of others with whom he or she must co-exist in society. If this is to be avoided, the parental direction that is necessary in relation to young children not yet mature enough to make, or be expected to make, independent decisions concerning religion and matters of conscience needs ultimately to give way, as the child's capacity evolves, to the desire to ensure that children are encouraged to think for themselves and make for themselves decisions concerning religion and matters of conscience. This is a process which the State must facilitate where appropriate. In this regard, the courts must recognise that children have a right to freedom of thought, conscience and religion under Art 14(2) of the CRC and Art 9(1) of the ECHR *independent* of the rights held by their parents. Having regard to the child's best interests and his or her evolving capacity, these are rights of the child that the courts should be more ready to consider in their own right when examining matters of religion and conscience which impact on the upon the family.

---

[337]   (1952) UNESCO, p 12.

Chapter 11

THE CHILD'S RIGHT TO FREEDOM OF EXPRESSION

'Pretty much all the honest truth telling in the world is done by children'.

Oliver Wendell Holmes

INTRODUCTION

11.1   Whilst the inclusion of the right to freedom of expression in Art 13 of the UN Convention on the Rights of the Child makes clear that the use of the word 'everyone' in Art 19 of the Universal Declaration of Human Rights[1] and Art 19 and the UN Covenant on Civil and Political Rights[2] must include children,[3] Van Buren notes that the full application of the right to freedom of expression for children is still evolving.[4] Children's expression often takes place in a context where 'there is no dialectical confrontation between the concerned parties'[5] and children often lack structure to convey their opinions to official bodies.[6] However, the importance to children of the right to freedom of expression cannot be underestimated.

---

[1]   Article 19 of the Universal Declaration of Human Rights provides that 'Everyone has the right to freedom of opinion and expression; this right includes freedom to hold opinions without interference and to seek, receive and impart information and ideas through any media and regardless of frontiers.'

[2]   Article 19 of the ICCPR provides that '1. Everyone shall have the right to hold opinions without interference. 2. Everyone shall have the right to freedom of expression; this right shall include freedom to seek, receive and impart information and ideas of all kinds, regardless of frontiers, either orally, in writing or in print, in the form of art, or through any other media of his choice. 3. The exercise of the rights provided for in paragraph 2 of this article carries with it special duties and responsibilities. It may therefore be subject to certain restrictions, but these shall only be such as are provided by law and are necessary: (a) For respect of the rights or reputations of others; (b) For the protection of national security or of public order (ordre public), or of public health or morals.'

[3]   Newell, P and Hodgkin, R *Implementation Handbook for the Convention on the Rights of the Child* (2008) 3rd edn, UNICEF, p 177. Note however that the application of Art 19 of the Universal Declaration of Human Rights has rarely been discussed in relation to children (Van Bueren *The International Law on the Rights of the Child* (1998) Martinus Nijhoff, p 131). See also Human Rights Committee General Comment No 17 *The Rights of the Child (Art 24)* HRI/GEN/1/Rev 8, p 183, para 2 (as individuals, children benefit from the civil rights enunciated in the ICCPR).

[4]   Van Bueren, G *Child Rights in Europe* (2007) Council of Europe Publishing, pp 81–82 citing Smith, A *Interpreting and Supporting Cultural Rights – Contributions from Socio-Cultural Theory* (2002) International Journal of Children's Rights 10 p 73 and Walker, S *Consulting with Children and Young People* (2001) International Journal of Children's Rights 9, p 45.

[5]   UN Doc E/CN.4/Sub.2/1991/42.

[6]   Van Bueren *The International Law on the Rights of the Child* (1998) Martinus Nijhoff, p 131.

11.2   The right to freedom of expression has been referred to as 'the touchstone of all the freedoms to which the United Nations is consecrated'.[7] Within the European context the right to freedom of expression has been described as being:[8]

> '... based on the need of a democratic society to promote the individual self fulfillment of its members, the attainment of truth, participation in decision making and the striking of a balance between stability and change. The aim is to have an open and pluralistic society.'

11.3   Within the domestic context, the House of Lords in *R v Secretary of State for the Home Department ex p Simms* noted that in a democracy, the right to freedom of expression is a primary right without which the effective rule of law is not possible.[9] In *Simms* Lord Steyn stated that:

> 'Freedom of expression is, of course, intrinsically important: it is valued for its own sake. But it is well recognised that it is also instrumentally important. It serves a number of broad objectives. First, it promotes the self-fulfillment of individuals in society. Secondly, in the famous words of Holmes J (echoing John Stuart Mill), 'the best test of truth is the power of the thought to get itself accepted in the competition of the market': *Abrams v US* (1919) 250 US 616 at 630 per Holmes J (dissent). Thirdly, freedom of speech is the lifeblood of democracy. The free flow of information and ideas informs political debate. It is a safety valve: people are more ready to accept decisions that go against them if they can in principle seek to influence them. It acts as a brake on the abuse of power by public officials. It facilitates the exposure of errors in the governance and administration of justice of the country: see Stone, Seidman, Sunstein and Tushnett *Constitutional Law* (3rd Edn, 1996) pp 1078–1086. It is this last interest which is engaged in the present case. The prisoners argue that in their cases the criminal justice system has failed, and that they have been wrongly convicted. They seek with the assistance of journalists, who have the resources to do the necessary investigations, to make public the wrongs which they allegedly suffered.'

11.4   Within this context, the importance to children of the right to freedom of expression is plain both by reason of the value of the right itself and by reason of the interplay between the child's right to freedom of expression and the child's other substantive rights. In particular, the right to freedom of expression under Art 13 of the CRC and the right to participate under Art 12 of the CRC are allied rights.[10] As Verhellen points out '[t]he Convention clearly makes an inseparable link between the right to information, freedom of opinion, freedom of expression and participation' noting that these rights cannot exist independently of one and other.[11] Likewise, there is a close interplay between Art 13 and Art 14 of the CRC, concerning the freedom to express religious belief through clothing, symbols and proselytism, between Art 13 and Art 30 of the CRC, emphasising the linked cultural, religious and linguistic rights of children and between Art 13 and Art 31 of the CRC, the right of children to engage in play and recreation and in cultural life and the arts. Finally, it is also important to remember that there is also a close symbiosis between the right to freedom of expression

---

7   UN General Assembly Resolution 59(I) of 14 December 1946. Note that the right to freedom of expression is important in itself in addition to having a functional value (see Dworkin, R *Life's Dominion: An Argument about Abortion, Euthanasia and Individual Freedom* (1993) Vintage, pp 69–74).

8   *Handyside v United Kingdom* (1976) 1 EHRR 737. See also Brandies J in *Whitney v California* 274 US (1927) 375–376 ('the path to safety lies in the opportunity to discuss freely supposed grievances and remedies').

9   *R v Secretary of State for the Home Department ex, p Simms* [2000] AC 115.

10   See chapter 6 above and see Committee on the Rights of the Child General Comment No 12 *The Right of the Child to be Heard* CRC/C/GC/12, p 15, para 68.

11   Verhellen, E *Convention on the Rights of the Child* (2000) Garant, p 122.

and the right to information under Art 17 of the CRC. Article 13 specifically articulates the right to freedom to seek, receive and impart information as an essential element of the right to freedom of expression.

11.5   Given the close relationship between Arts 12, 13 and 14 of the CRC, many of the principles relevant to the child's right to freedom of expression have been covered in chapter 6 concerning the child's right to participate and chapter 10 concerning the child's right to freedom of thought, conscience and religion. This chapter deals with the additional principles relevant to the child's right to freedom of expression under the international human rights instruments, including the CRC, the regional instruments, including the ECHR and under domestic law.

GENERAL PRINCIPLES

Freedom of Expression

Opinion

11.6   The freedom of expression is the freedom to outwardly manifest an opinion. Both historically and conceptually, the right to freedom of expression begins with the liberty to believe differently.[12] In order to have freedom to express an opinion it is necessary to have the freedom to hold it. The holding of an opinion is a purely internal and personal ability encompassed by the *forum internum* of the child who is capable of forming his or her own views and is uncontrollable by the State.[13] Art 19(1) of the ICCPR provides that 'Everyone shall have the right to hold opinions without interference'. The right to hold opinions is absolute and cannot be the subject of restriction. Thus no limitation is permitted upon a person's inner thought or moral consciousness, or his or her attitude towards the universe or its creator, religious or otherwise.[14]

Expression

11.7   The UN Manual on Human Rights Reporting states that 'Freedom of expression has a broad scope that includes all aspects relating to the circulation of information in any form and through any media'.[15] In *Texas v Gregory Lee Johnson*[16] the US Supreme Court held as follows in relation to whether a particular act constituted expressive conduct:

> 'In deciding whether particular conduct possesses sufficient communicative elements ... we have asked whether '[a]n intent to convey a particularised message was present and [whether] the likelihood was great that the message would be understood by those who viewed it.'

---

12   Van Bueren *The International Law on the Rights of the Child* (1998) Martinus Nijhoff, p 136.
13   Van Bueren *The International Law on the Rights of the Child* (1998) Martinus Nijhoff, p 136.
14   This principle was perhaps most famously articulated by the statement of Elizabeth I that 'I have no desire to make windows into men's souls.' As such, the freedom of opinion is not susceptible to external forces with regard to the protection of the forum internum (see Thorgeirsdóttir, H *Article 13 – The Right to Freedom of Expression* in Alen, A, Vande Lanotte, J, Verhellen, E, Berghams, E and Verheyde, M (eds) *A Commentary on the Untited Nations Convention on the Rights of the Child* (2006) Martinus Nijhoff, p 8).
15   *Manual on Human Rights Reporting* HR/PUB/91/1/ (Rev.1) p 234.
16   491 US 397 (1989), US Sup Ct.

11.8   Silence may constitute 'expression' for the purposes of the right to freedom of expression[17] and expression will encompass not only ideas capable of relatively precise, detached explication, but otherwise inexpressible emotions as well.[18] Note however that according to the European Commission expression for the purposes of Art 10 of the ECHR does not extend to the physical expression of feelings of love.[19] The right to freedom of expression will encompass the right to vote. Article 25(b) of the ICCPR provides that elections 'shall be by universal and equal suffrage and shall be held by secret ballot, guaranteeing the free expression of the will of the electors'. In the Australian case of *Levy v Victoria*[20] Kirby J held:

> 'For the purpose of the Constitution, freedom of communication is not limited to verbal utterances. Signs, symbols, gestures and images are perceived by all and used by many to communicate information, ideas and opinions. Indeed, in an appropriate context any form of expressive conduct is capable of communicating a political or government message to those who witness it.'

11.9   It is well established that unpopular and offensive opinions will fall within the protection afforded by the right to freedom of expression. In Redmond-*Bate v DPP*[21] Sedley J stated that:

> 'Free speech includes not only the inoffensive but the irritating, the contentious, the eccentric, the heretical, the unwelcome and the provocative provided it does not tend to provoke violence. Freedom only to speak inoffensively is not worth having.'[22]

However, it should be noted that the prohibition of the dissemination of ideas based upon racial superiority or hatred is considered incompatible with the right to freedom of opinion and expression embodied in Art 19 of the ICCPR.[23]

Derogation

11.10   The right to freedom of expression is a right which may be the subject of derogation under the ICCPR.[24] However, derogation from the right to freedom of expression is only permissible as an exceptional measure[25] and must also aim to preserve

---

17   *Brown v Louisiana* 383 US 131 (1966), US Sup Ct.
18   *Cohen v California* 403 US 15 at 26 (1971), US Sup Ct.
19   *X v United Kingdom* (1977) 3 EHRR 63.
20   (1997) 189 CLR 579 at 638.
21   (1999) 163 JP 789.
22   See however the approach taken under the ECHR discussed at **11.54-11.55** below.
23   Committee on the Elimination of Racial Discrimination *General Recommendation XV on Article 4 of the Convention* HRI/GEN/1/Rev 8, p 248, para 4.
24   See CCPR Art 4 ('1. In time of public emergency which threatens the life of the nation and the existence of which is officially proclaimed, the States Parties to the present Covenant may take measures derogating from their obligations under the present Covenant to the extent strictly required by the exigencies of the situation, provided that such measures are not inconsistent with their other obligations under international law and do not involve discrimination solely on the ground of race, colour, sex, language, religion or social origin'), ECHR, Art 15 ('1. In time of war or other public emergency threatening the life of the nation any High Contracting Party may take measures derogating from its obligations under this Convention to the extent strictly required by the exigencies of the situation, provided that such measures are not inconsistent with its other obligations under international law) and Art 27 American Convention on Human Rights ('1. In time of war, public danger, or other emergency that threatens the independence or security of a State Party, it may take measures derogating from its obligations under the present Convention to the extent and for the period of time strictly required by the exigencies of the situation, provided that such measures are not inconsistent with its other obligations under international law and do not involve discrimination on the ground of race, color, sex, language, religion, or social origin').
25   UN Doc CCPR/C/21/Add 2.

the rule of law.[26] The CRC contains no provision for the derogation of rights and accordingly there is no basis for derogation from the child's the right to freedom of expression under the CRC.

RIGHT TO FREEDOM OF EXPRESSION

The Child's Right to Freedom of Expression under the CRC

CRC, Art 13

11.11 Article 13 of the CRC provides as follows in respect of the child's right to freedom of expression:[27]

> '1. The child shall have the right to freedom of expression; this right shall include freedom to seek, receive and impart information and ideas of all kinds, regardless of frontiers, either orally, in writing or in print, in the form of art, or through any other media of the child's choice.
>
> 2. The exercise of this right may be subject to certain restrictions, but these shall only be such as are provided by law and are necessary:
>
> (a)   For respect of the rights or reputations of others; or
> (b)   For the protection of national security or of public order (ordre public), or of public health or morals.'

CRC, Art 13(1) – Ambit

(i)   CRC, Art 13(1) 'Freedom of Expression'

CRC, Art 13(1) – Freedom of Expression and Freedom of Opinion

11.12 As noted above, the freedom to *hold* opinions is a condition precedent to the right to freedom of expression.[28] However, Art 13 of the CRC does not reflect Art 19 of the ICCPR and enshrine the right of the child to hold opinions, omitting as it does the words 'everyone shall have the right to hold opinions without interference'.[29] Freeman argues that because the child's right to freedom of expression under Art 13(1) is stated to 'include' the forms of expression listed in it the freedom to hold opinions is also encompassed in Art 13(1) of the CRC.[30] Whilst this analysis is problematic in that the freedom to hold opinions is a condition precedent to each of the forms of expression provided for in Art 13(1) rather than a form of expression itself, by reason of the fact that holding an opinion is a condition precedent to expressing that opinion the freedom to hold opinions must be implicit in Art 13(1).[31] In this regard, it has been argued that

---

[26]   UN Doc E/CN.4/Sub.2/1982/15.

[27]   Article 13 of the CRC falls under the rubric of civil and political rights and is both a substantive and procedural right (Thorgeirsdóttir, H *Article 13 – The Right to Freedom of Expression* in Alen, A, Vande Lanotte, J, Verhellen, E, Berghams, E and Verheyde, M (eds) *A Commentary on the Untited Nations Convention on the Rights of the Child* (2006) Martinus Nijhoff, p 4).

[28]   See **11.6** above.

[29]   Note that Art 13(1) also does not follow Art 19 in that Art 13(2) omits the words '[t]he exercise of the rights provided for in paragraph 2 of this article carries with it special duties and responsibilities' contained in Art 19(3). See **11.13** below.

[30]   Freeman, M *Children's Rights Ten Years After Ratification* in Franklin, B (ed) *The New Handbook of Children's Rights* (2002) Routledge 97–118, p 106.

[31]   It has been suggested that the absence of any explanation in the *travaux préparatoires* for the omission of the words 'the right to hold opinions without interference' suggests that the omission was an 'accident' rather

whilst its omission is not crucial, the holding of an opinion being a purely internal and personal ability uncontrollable by the State, its omission from the CRC is illogical because, both historically and conceptually, the right to freedom of expression begins with the liberty to believe differently.[32] It has however been pointed out that, despite its omission, the need to protect the delicate process of forming an opinion is evident from the Concluding Observations of the Committee on the Rights of the Child.[33]

CRC, Art 13(1) – Scope of Child's Right to Freedom of Expression

11.13 The child's right to freedom of expression under Art 13(1) of the CRC encompasses the right to hold and express opinions, and to seek and receive information through any media. It asserts the right of the child not to be restricted by the State party in the opinions she or he holds or expresses.[34] The obligation it imposes on States parties is to refrain from interference in the expression of those views, or in access to information, while protecting the right of access to means of communication and public dialogue.[35]

11.14 The child's right to freedom of expression under Art 13(1) will operate not only as between the child and the State but as between the child and his or her family.[36] Art 13(1) of the CRC should be read together with Art 12. Van Bueren notes that this arguably results in a right to freedom of expression for children which is wider than that encompassed in other international rights instruments.[37] Reading the two articles together confers on the child the right to freedom of expression 'in all matters affecting the child'. Article 13(1) will impose on the State a duty to take positive steps to facilitate the child's right to freedom of expression. For example, in the context of culture, the Human Rights Committee has observed in relation to children that:[38]

> 'In the cultural field, every possible measure should be taken to foster the development of their personality and to provide them with a level of education that will enable them to enjoy the rights recognised in the Covenant, particularly the right to freedom of opinion and expression.'

---

than 'deliberate' (see Thorgeirsdóttir, H *Article 13 – The Right to Freedom of Expression* in Alen, A, Vande Lanotte, J, Verhellen, E, Berghams, E and Verheyde, M (eds) *A Commentary on the Untited Nations Convention on the Rights of the Child* (2006) Martinus Nijhoff, p 22).

[32] Van Bueren *The International Law on the Rights of the Child* (1998) Martinus Nijhoff, p 136. See also Thorgeirsdóttir, H *Article 13 – The Right to Freedom of Expression* in Alen, A, Vande Lanotte, J, Verhellen, E, Berghams, E and Verheyde, M (eds) *A Commentary on the Untited Nations Convention on the Rights of the Child* (2006) Martinus Nijhoff, pp 10–14.

[33] Thorgeirsdóttir, H *Article 13 – The Right to Freedom of Expression* in Alen, A, Vande Lanotte, J, Verhellen, E, Berghams, E and Verheyde, M (eds) *A Commentary on the Untited Nations Convention on the Rights of the Child* (2006) Martinus Nijhoff, p 24.

[34] See Thorgeirsdóttir, H *Article 13 – The Right to Freedom of Expression* in Alen, A, Vande Lanotte, J, Verhellen, E, Berghams, E and Verheyde, M (eds) *A Commentary on the Untited Nations Convention on the Rights of the Child* (2006) Martinus Nijhoff, p 19 ('Freedom of expression, if properly protected, will enable the child to develop [his or her] mind and [his or her] self in society with others and grow into a citizen participating in public life as such and not merely as a mindless consumer').

[35] Committee on the Rights of the Child General Comment No 12 *The Right of the Child to be Heard* CRC/C/GC/12 p 17, para 81.

[36] Van Bueren *The International Law on the Rights of the Child* (1998) Martinus Nijhoff, p 147, n.36.

[37] Van Bueren *The International Law on the Rights of the Child* (1998) Martinus Nijhoff, p 137.

[38] Human Rights Committee General Comment No 17 *Article 24 (Rights of the Child)* HRI/GEN/1/Rev 8, p 184, para 3.

CRC, Art 13(1) – Expression, Best Interests and Evolving Capacity

11.15 Article 13 of the CRC contains no limitation based on the authorities, rights or responsibilities of parents or legal guardians.[39] That said, as with the other substantive rights enshrined in the CRC, the child's right to freedom of expression under Art 13(1) must be read with Art 3 of the CRC concerning the child's best interests and Art 5 concerning the child's evolving capacity. Within this context, in applying Art 13(1) of the CRC there is a need to consider appropriate ways of ensuring balance between parental guidance and the realisation of the right of the child to freedom of expression.[40] However, Art 13(1) of the CRC, read with Art 12 and 17 of the CRC makes plain that the child is the subject of the right to freedom of expression and, together with Art 5, that the child is entitled to exercise that right on his or her own behalf, in accordance with her or his evolving capacity.[41] The restrictions that can legitimately be placed on the child's right to freedom of expression are confined to the narrow limitations provided for in Art 13(2) of the CRC.[42]

11.16 Article 21 of the UN Convention on the Rights of Persons with Disabilities provides as follows in respect of the right to freedom of expression:

> 'States Parties shall take all appropriate measures to ensure that persons with disabilities can exercise the right to freedom of expression and opinion, including the freedom to seek, receive and impart information and ideas on an equal basis with others and through all forms of communication of their choice, as defined in article 2 of the present Convention, including by:

> (a)   Providing information intended for the general public to persons with disabilities in accessible formats and technologies appropriate to different kinds of disabilities in a timely manner and without additional cost;
> (b)   Accepting and facilitating the use of sign languages, Braille, augmentative and alternative communication, and all other accessible means, modes and formats of communication of their choice by persons with disabilities in official interactions;
> (c)   Urging private entities that provide services to the general public, including through the Internet, to provide information and services in accessible and usable formats for persons with disabilities;
> (d)   Encouraging the mass media, including providers of information through the Internet, to make their services accessible to persons with disabilities;
> (e)   Recognising and promoting the use of sign languages.[43]

11.17 In respect of the right of children with disabilities and children from minority, indigenous and migrant communities to freedom of expression the Committee on the Rights of the Child has stated that:[44]

> '... children with disabilities should be equipped with, and enabled to use, any mode of communication necessary to facilitate the expression of their views. Efforts must also be

---

[39]   See UN Docs E/CN.4/1986/39, p 17; E/CN.4/1987/25, pp 26 and 27; E/CN.4/1988/28, pp 9–13.
[40]   Committee on the Rights of the Child, Report on the Fifth Session (1994) CRC/C/24, Annex V, p 63.
[41]   Committee on the Rights of the Child General Comment No 12 *The Right of the Child to be Heard* CRC/C/GC/12 p 16, para 80.
[42]   See **11.39** below.
[43]   Note also that Art 7(1) of the Convention on the Rights of Persons with Disabilities provides that 'States Parties shall take all necessary measures to ensure the full enjoyment by children with disabilities of all human rights and fundamental freedoms on an equal basis with other children.'
[44]   Committee on the Rights of the Child General Comment No 12 *The Right of the Child to be Heard* CRC/C/GC/12, p 7.

made to recognise the right to expression of views for minority, indigenous and migrant children and other children who do not speak the majority language.'

CRC, Art 13(1) – Freedom of Expression and Freedom of Participation

11.18 In its General Comment No 12 *The Right of the Child to be Heard*[45] the Committee on the Rights of the Child makes clear the difference between the right to participate and the right to freedom of expression:

'The right to freedom of expression embodied in article 13 is often confused with article 12. However, while both articles are strongly linked, they do elaborate different rights. Freedom of expression relates to the right to hold and express opinions, and to seek and receive information through any media. It asserts the right of the child not to be restricted by the State party in the opinions she or he holds or expresses. As such, the obligation it imposes on States parties is to refrain from interference in the expression of those views, or in access to information, while protecting the right of access to means of communication and public dialogue. Article 12, however, relates to the right of expression of views specifically about matters which affect the child, and the right to be involved in actions and decisions that impact on her or his life. Article 12 imposes an obligation on States parties to introduce the legal framework and mechanisms necessary to facilitate active involvement of the child in all actions affecting the child and in decision-making, and to fulfill the obligation to give due weight to those views once expressed. Freedom of expression in article 13 requires no such engagement or response from States parties. However, creating an environment of respect for children to express their views, consistent with article 12, also contributes towards building children's capacities to exercise their right to freedom of expression.'

(ii)   *CRC, Art 13(1) – 'Freedom to Seek, Receive and Impart Information and Ideas'*

Freedom to Seek, and Receive Information – CRC, Art 13(1)

11.19 Access to information is an essential component of the right to freedom of expression, information being a necessary ingredient for the formation of opinion.[46] The child's right to freedom of expression under Art 13(1) of the CRC includes the freedom to seek, receive and impart information and ideas of all kinds. The concept of seeking information in Art 13(1) implies an active enquiry with an element of probing.[47] The right to receive information implies that children must be treated on an equal basis with regard to the enjoyment of any civil right.[48] The right to receive information under Art 13 of the CRC is a right which operates regardless of frontiers.[49]

11.20 The restrictions on the child's right to freedom of expression contained in Art 13(2) of the CRC will apply to the right to seek and receive information under Art 13(1). There will be categories of information which it is not in the child's best interests to receive on the grounds set out in Art 13(2). CRC jurisprudence clearly implies that States parties have positive obligations to protect the child from injurious

45   CRC/C/GC/12, p 17, para 81.
46   Thorgeirsdóttir, H *Article 13 – The Right to Freedom of Expression* in Alen, A, Vande Lanotte, J, Verhellen, E, Berghams, E and Verheyde, M (eds) *A Commentary on the Untited Nations Convention on the Rights of the Child* (2006) Martinus Nijhoff, p 25.
47   Van Bueren *The International Law on the Rights of the Child* (1998) Martinus Nijhoff, p 132.
48   Thorgeirsdóttir, H *Article 13 – The Right to Freedom of Expression* in Alen, A, Vande Lanotte, J, Verhellen, E, Berghams, E and Verheyde, M (eds) *A Commentary on the Untited Nations Convention on the Rights of the Child* (2006) Martinus Nijhoff, p 35.
49   Thorgeirsdóttir, H *Article 13 – The Right to Freedom of Expression* in Alen, A, Vande Lanotte, J, Verhellen, E, Berghams, E and Verheyde, M (eds) *A Commentary on the Untited Nations Convention on the Rights of the Child* (2006) Martinus Nijhoff, p 43. As such, the right to receive information as an element of the right freedom of expression will apply to methods of communication which span frontiers including the internet.

material when the child is exercising his or her right to seek information on the grounds that it is in the best interests of the child to take into account his or her vulnerability and need for protection within the process of seeking that information.[50] Van Buren argues that to help ensure the restrictions in Art 13(2) do not unduly limit the child's right to freedom of expression children ought to be entitled to exercise their right to freedom of expression and participation in determining whether it is in their best interests not to receive particular classes of information.[51]

Freedom to Seek, and Receive Information – CRC, Art 17

11.21 Article 13(1) is not the only part of the CRC which enshrines the child's right to access to information. Article 17 of the CRC provides as follows in respect of the role of the mass media and the child's right to access to information:

> 'States Parties recognise the important function performed by the mass media and shall ensure that the child has access to information and material from a diversity of national and international sources, especially those aimed at the promotion of his or her social, spiritual and moral well-being and physical and mental health. To this end, States Parties shall:
>
> (a)   Encourage the mass media to disseminate information and material of social and cultural benefit to the child and in accordance with the spirit of article 29;
>
> (b)   Encourage international co-operation in the production, exchange and dissemination of such information and material from a diversity of cultural, national and international sources;
>
> (c)   Encourage the production and dissemination of children's books;
>
> (d)   Encourage the mass media to have particular regard to the linguistic needs of the child who belongs to a minority group or who is indigenous;
>
> (e)   Encourage the development of appropriate guidelines for the protection of the child from information and material injurious to his or her well-being, bearing in mind the provisions of articles 13 and 18.'[52]

11.22 Article 17 of the CRC is particularly focused on the role of the mass media in relation to children's rights[53] but also includes a general obligation on State Parties to ensure that the child has access to information and material from diverse sources.[54] Art 17 of the CRC helps to ensure the child's participatory rights under Art 12 of the CRC and the child's right to freedom of expression under Art 13(1) of the CRC, which right includes the right to 'seek, receive and impart information and ideas of all kinds, regardless of frontiers, either orally, in writing or in print, in the form of art, or through any other media of the child's choice'. In addition, Art 17 is relevant to the child's right

---

[50]   Thorgeirsdóttir, H *Article 13 – The Right to Freedom of Expression* in Alen, A, Vande Lanotte, J, Verhellen, E, Berghams, E and Verheyde, M (eds) *A Commentary on the Untited Nations Convention on the Rights of the Child* (2006) Martinus Nijhoff, p 33.

[51]   Van Bueren *The International Law on the Rights of the Child* (1998) Martinus Nijhoff, p 135.

[52]   Note that the initial draft of Art 17 sought to protect the child 'against harmful influence that mass media, and in particular the radio, film, television, printed materials and exhibitions, on account of their contents, may exert on his mental and moral development' however, following a suggestion that the media did more good than harm, Art 17 was re-drafted in positive terms (see Detrick, S *A Commentary on the United Nations Convention on the Rights of the Child* (1999) Martinus Nijhoff, p 279 and E/CN.4/L.1575, pp 19–20).

[53]   See the recommendations arising out of the General Day of Discussion 1996 Committee on the Rights of the Child *Report on the Thirteenth Session* CRC/C/57, paras 242 et seq.

[54]   Newell, P and Hodgkin, R *Implementation Handbook for the Convention on the Rights of the Child* (2008) 3rd edn, UNICEF, p 217. See also r 62 of the United Nations Rules for the Protection of Juveniles Deprived of their Liberty: 'Juveniles should have the opportunity to keep themselves informed regularly of the news by reading newspapers, periodicals and other publications, through access to radio and television programmes and motion pictures ...' See further the UNESCO Declaration on Mass Media.

to survival and development under Art 6 of the CRC and the child's right to participate fully and freely in cultural and artistic life under Art 31 of the CRC.

CRC, Art 17 – 'Important Function Performed by the Mass Media'

11.23 The Committee on the Rights of the Child has commented as followed in respect of the importance of mass media to children:[55]

> '... the media is important for offering children the possibility of expressing themselves. One of the principles of the Convention is that the views of children be heard and given due respect (art. 12). This is also reflected in articles about freedom of expression, thought, conscience and religion (arts. 13–14). It is in the spirit of these provisions that children should not only be able to consume information material but also to participate themselves in the media. This requires that there exist media which communicate with children. The Committee on the Rights of the Child has noted that there have been experiments in several countries to develop child-oriented media; some daily newspapers have special pages for children and radio and television programmes also devote special segments for the young audience. Further efforts are, however, needed ... The Committee also reminds States parties that the media are an important means both of promoting awareness of the right of children to express their views, and of providing opportunities for the public expression of such views. It urges various forms of the media to dedicate further resources to the inclusion of children in the development of programmes and the creation of opportunities for children to develop and lead media initiatives on their rights.'

11.24 The media should respect and promote the participatory rights of children.[56] However, the Committee on the Rights of the Child has also commented on the potentially harmful influence of the media.[57] In this context, it is important that Art 17 is read in light of Art 3 to ensure that the child's best interests are the primary consideration when looking to the implementation of Art 17. Once again, CRC jurisprudence clearly implies that States parties have positive obligations to protect children from injurious material in exercising their right to seek information by reason of the fact that it is in the best interests of the child to take into account his or her vulnerability and need for protection within the process of seeking information.[58]

CRC, Art 17 – 'Promotion of social, spiritual and moral well-being and physical and mental health'

11.25 The promotion of the child's social, spiritual and moral well-being and physical and mental health is the overall aim of the five strategies set out in Art 17(a)–(e).[59] In

---

[55] Committee on the Rights of the Child, Report on the eleventh session, January 1996, CRC/C/50, Annex IX, pp 80–83. See also Committee on the Rights of the Child, General Comment No 7, 2005, CRC/C/GC/7/Rev.1, para 35: 'Early childhood is a specialist market for publishers and media producers, who should be encouraged to disseminate material that is appropriate to the capacities and interests of young children, socially and educationally beneficial to their well-being, and which reflects the national and regional diversities of children's circumstances, culture and language. Particular attention should be given to the need of minority groups for access to media that promote their recognition and social inclusion ...'

[56] Newell, P and Hodgkin, R *Implementation Handbook for the Convention on the Rights of the Child* (2008) 3rd edn, UNICEF, p 217.

[57] See **11.32** below.

[58] Thorgeirsdóttir, H *Article 13 – The Right to Freedom of Expression* in Alen, A, Vande Lanotte, J, Verhellen, E, Berghams, E and Verheyde, M (eds) *A Commentary on the Untited Nations Convention on the Rights of the Child* (2006) Martinus Nijhoff, p 33.

[59] Newell, P and Hodgkin, R *Implementation Handbook for the Convention on the Rights of the Child* (2008) 3rd edn, UNICEF, p 220.

relation to the role of the media in the positive socialisation of children the UN Guidelines for the Prevention of Juvenile Delinquency (the 'Riyadh Guidelines') provide as follows:

'40. The mass media should be encouraged to ensure that young persons have access to information and material from a diversity of national and international sources.

41. The mass media should be encouraged to portray the positive contribution of young persons to society.

42. The mass media should be encouraged to disseminate information on the existence of services, facilities and opportunities for young persons in society.

43. The mass media generally, and the television and film media in particular, should be encouraged to minimise the level of pornography, drugs and violence portrayed and to display violence and exploitation disfavourably, as well as to avoid demeaning and degrading presentations, especially of children, women and interpersonal relations, and to promote egalitarian principles and roles.

44. The mass media should be aware of its extensive social role and responsibility, as well as its influence, in communications relating to youthful drug and alcohol abuse. It should use its power for drug abuse prevention by relaying consistent messages through a balanced approach. Effective drug awareness campaigns at all levels should be promoted.'

CRC, Art 17(a) – 'Dissemination of information and material in accordance with Art 29'

11.26 Article 17(a) of the CRC requires that the function of the media in relation to children is in part dictated by the requirements of Art 29 of the CRC. Importantly, the activities of the media should not undermine the aims of Art 29 of the CRC.[60] Art 29 of the CRC provides as follows in relation to the aims of education:

'1. States Parties agree that the education of the child shall be directed to:

(a) The development of the child's personality, talents and mental and physical abilities to their fullest potential;

(b) The development of respect for human rights and fundamental freedoms, and for the principles enshrined in the Charter of the United Nations;

(c) The development of respect for the child's parents, his or her own cultural identity, language and values, for the national values of the country in which the child is living, the country from which he or she may originate, and for civilisations different from his or her own;

(d) The preparation of the child for responsible life in a free society, in the spirit of understanding, peace, tolerance, equality of sexes, and friendship among all peoples, ethnic, national and religious groups and persons of indigenous origin;

(e) The development of respect for the natural environment.'[61]

---

[60] Committee on the Rights of the Child General Comment No 1 *The Aims of Education* CRC/GC/2001/1, para 21.

[61] See also the UNESCO Declaration on Fundamental Principles concerning the Contribution of the Mass Media to Strengthening Peace and International Understanding, to the Promotion of Human Rights and to Countering Racialism, Apartheid and Incitement to War.

CRC, Art 17(b) – 'International Co-operation in the Production, Exchange and Dissemination of Information'

11.27 The requirement under Art 17(b) that State Parties 'Encourage international co-operation in the production, exchange and dissemination of such information and material from a diversity of cultural, national and international sources' emphasises the diversity of information that should be available to the child.[62]

CRC, Art 17(c) – 'Production and Dissemination of Children's Books'

11.28 Article 17(c) of the CRC requires that States parties encourage the production and dissemination of children's books.[63]

CRC, Art 17(d) – 'Regard for Linguistic Needs of Children of Minority and Indigenous Groups'

11.29 Article 17(d) of the CRC requires that State parties encourage the mass media to have particular regard to the linguistic needs of children who belong to a minority group or who are indigenous and should be read with Art 30 of the CRC and Art 29 (d) concerning children of religious and linguistic minorities and children of indigenous origin.

11.30 In relation to children with disabilities, the Committee on the Rights of the Child has made clear that in its General Comment No 9 *The Rights of Children with Disabilities* in relation to access to information and communications that:[64]

> 'Access to information and communications, including information and communications technologies and systems, enables children with disabilities to live independently and participate fully in all aspects of life. Children with disabilities and their caregivers should have access to information concerning their disabilities that educates them on the process of disability, including causes, management and prognosis. This knowledge is extremely valuable as it not only enables them to adjust to their disabilities, it also allows them to be involved and make informed decisions regarding their own care. Children with disabilities should also have the appropriate technology and other services and languages, e g Braille and sign language, that enables them to access all forms of media, including television, radio and printed material as well as new information and communication technologies and systems, such as the Internet.'

11.31 Article 8(2)(c) of the Convention on the Rights of Persons with Disabilities requires that State parties to the Convention adopt immediate, effective and appropriate measures 'Encouraging all organs of the media to portray persons with disabilities in a manner consistent with the purpose of the present Convention'. Rule 1(3) of the UN Standard Rules on the Equalisation of Opportunities for Persons with Disabilities requires that 'States should encourage the portrayal of persons with disabilities by the mass media in a positive way ...'[65]

---

[62] Newell, P and Hodgkin, R *Implementation Handbook for the Convention on the Rights of the Child* (2008) 3rd edn, UNICEF, p 223.

[63] For the history of this provision see Detrick, S *A Commentary on the United Nations Convention on the Rights of the Child* (1999) Martinus Nijhoff, p 287 and E/CN.4/1987/25, p 7).

[64] Committee on the Rights of the Child General Comment No 9 *The Rights of Children with Disabilities* CRC/C/GC/9, para 37. See also Art 23 CRC.

[65] See also r 9(3) of the UN Standard Rules on the Equalisation of Opportunities for Persons with Disabilities ('States should promote measures to change negative attitudes towards marriage, sexuality and parenthood of persons with disabilities, especially of girls and women with disabilities, which still prevail in society. The media should be encouraged to play an important role in removing such negative attitudes').

CRC, Art 17(e) – 'Appropriate Guidelines'

11.32 Pursuant to Art 17(e) of the CRC, States parties must encourage the development of appropriate guidelines for the protection of the child from information and material injurious to his or her well-being, bearing in mind the Art 13(1) right to freedom of expression and the principle enshrined in Art 18(1) of the CRC that parents or, as the case may be, legal guardians, have the primary responsibility for the upbringing and development of the child. Article 17(e) is designed to ensure that children are protected from the negative aspects of mass media, which negative aspects have been recognised by the Committee on the Rights of the Child:[66]

> '... Concern has also been expressed about the influence on children of negative aspects of the media, primarily programmes containing brutal violence and pornography. There is discussion in a number of countries about how to protect children from violence on television, in video films and in other modern media. Again, voluntary agreements have been attempted, with varied impact. This particular problem is raised in article 17 of the Convention which recommends that appropriate guidelines be developed 'for the protection of the child from information and material injurious to his or her well-being'.'

The Committee on the Rights of the Child has further noted the potentially negative impact of modern technology in this area:[67]

> 'Rapid increases in the variety and accessibility of modern technologies, including Internet-based media, are a particular cause for concern. Young children are especially at risk if they are exposed to inappropriate or offensive material. States parties are urged to regulate media production and delivery in ways that protect young children, as well as support parents/caregivers to fulfill their child-rearing responsibilities in this regard.'

11.33 In formulating 'appropriate guidelines' under Art 17(e) of the CRC States parties should bear in mind the children's right to freedom of expression under Art 13(1) of the CRC and that, pursuant to Art 18(1) of the CRC, the parents, and not the State, are responsible for the development of children by providing appropriate direction and guidance commensurate with the child's evolving capacity pursuant to Art 5 of the CRC. Thus, such guidelines as are formulated pursuant to Art 17(e) must not interfere with the child's right to access information or parental discretion within the ambit of Arts 5 and 18 of the CRC.[68]

Freedom to Seek, and Receive Information – CRC, Art 24(2)(e)

11.34 The child's right to access information is also incorporated in Art 24(2)(e) of the CRC which provides that, in ensuring the right of the child to the highest attainable standard of health, States parties shall take appropriate measures 'To ensure that all segments of society, in particular parents and children, are informed, have access to education and are supported in the use of basic knowledge of child health and nutrition,

---

[66] Committee on the Rights of the Child, Report on the eleventh session, January 1996, CRC/C/50, Annex IX, pp 80 and 81.

[67] Committee on the Rights of the Child, General Comment No 7 *Implementing Child Rights in Early Childhood* CRC/C/GC/7/Rev.1, para 35.

[68] Van Bueren *The International Law on the Rights of the Child* (1998) Martinus Nijhoff, p 134 and see Newell, P and Hodgkin, R *Implementation Handbook for the Convention on the Rights of the Child* (2008) 3rd edn, UNICEF, p 225.

the advantages of breastfeeding, hygiene and environmental sanitation and the prevention of accidents'.[69] The Committee on the Rights of the Child has observed that:[70]

> 'Adolescents have the right to access adequate information essential for their health and development and for their ability to participate meaningfully in society. It is the obligation of States Parties to ensure that all adolescent girls and boys, both in and out of school, are provided with, and not denied, accurate and appropriate information on how to protect their health and development and practice healthy behaviours. This should include information on the use and abuse, of tobacco, alcohol and other substances, safe and respectful social and sexual behaviours, diet and physical activity.'

Freedom to Seek, and Receive Information – CRC, Art 9(4)

11.35 Article 9(4) of the CRC enshrines the right of the child to Right to receive information concerning the whereabouts of family, stipulating that the State party shall upon request 'provide the parents, the child or, if appropriate, another member of the family with the essential information concerning the whereabouts of the absent member(s) of the family unless the provision of the information would be detrimental to the well-being of the child'.[71]

Freedom to Seek, and Receive Information – CRC, Art 42

11.36 The child's right to information encompasses the receiving of information concerning the CRC itself, in respect of which the media will play an important role.[72] Art 42 of the CRC provides as follows concerning the dissemination of knowledge regarding the CRC:

> 'States Parties undertake to make the principles and provisions of the Convention widely known, by appropriate and active means, to adults and children alike.'

(iii)   CRC, Art 13(1) – 'Regardless of Frontiers'

11.37 The term 'regardless of frontiers' was inserted into Art 19(2) of the ICCPR to make it clear that the right to freedom of expression was not to be limited within the confines of any political or territorial entity.[73] The wording of Art 19(2) is reflected in Art 13(1) of the CRC.[74]

(iv)   CRC, Art 13(1) – 'Choice'

11.38 Article 13(1) makes clear that children may choose the media by which they express themselves. Verhellen notes that Art 13(1), and in particular the words 'any

---

[69]   For detailed discussion of Art 24(2)(e) see **5.117** above.
[70]   Committee on the Rights of the Child, General Comment No 4 *Adolescent Health and Development in the Context of the Convention on the Rights of the Child* CRC/GC/2003/4, para 26. See also General Comment No 3 *HIV/AIDS and the Rights of the Child* CRC/GC/2003/3, para 17.
[71]   For a detailed discussion of Art 9(4) see **8.85** above.
[72]   Newell, P and Hodgkin, R *Implementation Handbook for the Convention on the Rights of the Child* (2008) 3rd edn, UNICEF, pp 217–218.
[73]   Detrick, S A *Commentary on the United Nations Convention on the Rights of the Child* (1999) Martinus Nijhoff, p 235.
[74]   See Thorgeirsdóttir, H *Article 13 – The Right to Freedom of Expression* in Alen, A, Vande Lanotte, J, Verhellen, E, Berghams, E and Verheyde, M (eds) *A Commentary on the Untited Nations Convention on the Rights of the Child* (2006) Martinus Nijhoff, p 43. As such, the right to receive information as an element of the right freedom of expression will apply to methods of communication which span frontiers including the internet.

other media of the child's choice' mean that whilst a number of known forms of media are specified in Art 13(1), the State must look for those media which come naturally to children and show respect for their choice.[75] This will include the right to choose non-verbal forms of communication appropriate to young children or children too traumatised to communicate verbally.[76] Read with Art 12 of the CRC, the child's choice of media pursuant to Art 13(1) will apply in respect of all matters affecting the child.

CRC, Art 13(2) – Ambit

11.39 The rights enshrined in Art 13(1) of the CRC are neither absolute nor non-derogable.[77] Art 13(2) of the CRC provides as follows in respect of the limitations that may be imposed on the child's right to freedom of expression under Art 13(1) of the CRC:

> '2. The exercise of this right may be subject to certain restrictions, but these shall only be such as are provided by law and are necessary:
>
> (a)   For respect of the rights or reputations of others; or
> (b)   For the protection of national security or of public order (ordre public), or of public health or morals.'

11.40 Note that Art 13(2) of the CRC does not follow Art 19 of the ICCPR in that Art 13(2) omits the words '[t]he exercise of the rights provided for in ... this article carries with it special duties and responsibilities' contained in Art 19(3). Van Bueren states that the implication of this omission is that the right of children to express their opinions does not necessarily mean having to accept full legal responsibility for the consequences, which responsibility children may not be able to deal with or comprehend.[78] The 'special duties and responsibilities' added by Art 19(3) in respect of the right to freedom of expression were included in the ICCPR in recognition of the powerful influence of the modern media exerted upon the minds of men and women and upon national and international affairs.[79] As such, the provisions of Art 19(3) of the ICCPR should operate with protective effect in respect of children in so far as they act to regulate the freedom of expression exercised by the media.

(i)   CRC, Art 13(2) – 'Provided by Law and are Necessary'

11.41 The only restrictions that may be placed on the child's right to freedom of expression under Art 13(1) of the CRC[80] are those narrow restrictions prescribed in Art 13(2), namely such restrictions as are provided by law[81] and are necessary for respect of the rights or reputations of others or for the protection of national security or of public order (ordre public), or of public health or morals. Thus the restriction must be prescribed by law *and* necessary to constitute a restriction permitted by Art 13(2). The

---

[75]   Verhellen, E *Convention on the Rights of the Child* (2000) Garant, p 123.

[76]   Van Bueren *The International Law on the Rights of the Child* (1998) Martinus Nijhoff, p 142.

[77]   Thorgeirsdóttir, H *Article 13 – The Right to Freedom of Expression* in Alen, A, Vande Lanotte, J, Verhellen, E, Berghams, E and Verheyde, M (eds) *A Commentary on the Untited Nations Convention on the Rights of the Child* (2006) Martinus Nijhoff, p 21.

[78]   Van Bueren *The International Law on the Rights of the Child* (1998) Martinus Nijhoff, p 143.

[79]   Detrick, S A Commentary on the United Nations Convention on the Rights of the Child (1999) Martinus Nijhoff, p 34.

[80]   The provisions of Art 13(2) of the CRC mirror the provisions of Art 19 of the ICCPR in this regard. Note that the terms of Art 13(2) are narrower than the restrictions on the right to freedom of expression enshrined in Art 10(2) of the ECHR. See **11.61** below.

[81]   Any restrictions must be set out in legislation (Newell, P and Hodgkin, R *Implementation Handbook for the Convention on the Rights of the Child* (2008) 3rd edn, UNICEF, p 180).

restrictions must be applied only for the purposes for which they are prescribed and must be directly related and proportionate to the specific needs on which they are predicated.[82] In accordance with the general rules of international law the limitations prescribed by Art 13(2) are exceptions and must be interpreted restrictively.[83] It has been suggested that to be necessary in a democratic society the restrictions must be essential.[84] The concept of the 'democratic society' implies political freedom and individual rights which reduce or moderate the authority of the State and the existence of appropriate supervisory institutions to monitor respect for human rights.[85] It is the interplay between the principle of freedom of expression and the limitations and restrictions permitted under Art 13(2) which determines the actual scope of the child's right under Art 13(1) of the CRC.[86]

(iii) CRC, Art 13(2) – Grounds for Restriction

11.42 The grounds upon which restriction of the child's right to freedom of expression may be permitted under Art 13(2) of the CRC are the respect of the rights or reputations of others, the protection of national security or of public order (ordre public) or the protection of public health or morals.

CRC, Art 13(2) – 'Respect of the rights or reputations of others'

11.43 The term 'the rights and reputations of others' does not indicate which rights of others may be protected at the expense of the freedoms in question but Henkin suggests that whilst the term might well authorise States to choose between rights enshrined in the CRC it will not permit States to prefer other rights and interests which it might create by its own law for its own purposes.[87]

CRC, Art 13(2) – For the protection of public health or morals.

11.44 The term 'public morals' describes 'principles which are not always legally enforceable but which are accepted by a great majority of the citizens as general guidelines for their individual and collective behaviour'.[88] In considering the scope of limitations imposed on the child's right to freedom of expression on the grounds of protecting morals it should be remembered that as the concept of morals derives from many social, philosophical and religious traditions, limitations on the freedom of expression for the purpose of protecting morals must be based on principles not deriving exclusively from a single tradition.[89]

---

[82]　Human Rights Committee General Comment No 10 1993 HRI/GEN/1/Rev 8, p 172, para 4.

[83]　Detrick, S A *Commentary on the United Nations Convention on the Rights of the Child* (1999) Martinus Nijhoff, p 37.

[84]　Kiss, A *Permissible Limitations on Rights* in Henkin, L (ed) *The International Bill of Rights: The Covenant on Civil and Political Rights* (1981) p 290, p 308.

[85]　Kiss, A *Permissible Limitations on Rights* in Henkin, L (ed) *The International Bill of Rights: The Covenant on Civil and Political Rights* (1981) p 290, p 304.

[86]　See The Human Rights Committee General Comment No 10 1983 HRI/GEN/1/Rev.8, para 3, p 171.

[87]　Henkin, L *Introduction* in Henkin, L (ed) *The International Bill of Rights: The Covenant on Civil and Political Rights* (1981), pp 1–31, p 31.

[88]　Kiss, A *Permissible Limitations on Rights* in Henkin, L (ed) *The International Bill of Rights: The Covenant on Civil and Political Rights* (1981), pp 290–310, p 304. See also *Reno v American Civil Liberties Union* 521 US 844 (1997), US Sup Ct; *Ashcroft v ACLU* 535 US 564 (2002), US Sup Ct; *Curtis v Minister of Safety* (1996) BHRC 541, Const Ct of South Africa; *De Reuck v DPP* [2004] 4 LRC 72, Const Ct of South Africa.

[89]　See Human Rights Committee General Comment No 22 *Art 18 (Freedom of Thought, Conscience and Religion)* HRI/GEN/1/Rev.8, p 196, para 8. Note that the concept of margin of appreciation will be important when considering the issue of 'morals' under the ECHR. In *A, B and C v Ireland* (2010) Application No 25579/05, para 222 the European Court of Human Rights stated that 'The Court recalls that it is not possible to find in the legal and social orders of the Contracting States a uniform European

CRC, Art 13 – Application

(i)   CRC, Art 13 – Freedom of Expression within the Family

11.45 As noted above Art 13 of the CRC contains no limitation based on the authorities, rights or responsibilities of parents or legal guardians.[90] Art 13 must however be interpreted with regard to the requirements of Art 5 of the CRC and there is a need to consider appropriate ways of ensuring balance between parental responsibility and the realisation of the child's right to freedom of expression.[91] Parents should support children in realising the right to express their views freely and to have their views duly taken into account at all levels of society.[92] The UN Committee points out that '[a] family where children can freely express views and be taken seriously from the earliest ages provides an important model, and is a preparation for the child to exercise the right to be heard in the wider society' and that '[s]uch an approach to parenting serves to promote individual development, enhance family relations and support children's socialisation and plays a preventive role against all forms of violence in the home and family'.[93] The child's right to freedom of expression should not be unduly curtailed on the internet subject to the need for the child to be protected from inappropriate material.[94]

(ii)   CRC, Art 13 – Freedom of Expression at School

11.46 The child's right to freedom of expression should not be unduly curtailed within school.[95] In the US Supreme Court case of *Tinker v Des Moines Community School District*[96] three teenagers were suspended from school for wearing black armbands in protest at the US Government's policy in Vietnam. Justice Fortas held that rights, including the right to free speech:

> '... applied in light of the special characteristics of the school environment, are available to teachers and students. It can hardly be argued that either students or teachers shed their constitutional rights to freedom of speech or expression at the schoolhouse gate ... There is here no evidence whatever of petitioners' interference, actual or nascent, with the schools' work or of collision with the rights of other students to be secure and to be let alone. Accordingly, this case does not concern speech or action that intrudes upon the work of the schools or the rights of other students ... in our system, undifferentiated fear or apprehension of disturbance is not enough to overcome the right to freedom of expression. Any departure from absolute regimentation may cause trouble. Any variation from the majority's opinion may inspire fear. Any word spoken, in class, in the lunchroom, or on the campus, that deviates from the views of another person may start an argument or cause a disturbance. But our Constitution says we must take this risk ... In order for the State in the person of school officials to justify prohibition of a particular expression of opinion, it must be able to show that its action was caused by something more than a mere desire to avoid the

---

conception of morals including on the question of when life begins. By reason of their 'direct and continuous contact with the vital forces of their countries', state authorities are in principle in a better position than the international judge to give an opinion on the 'exact content of the requirements of morals' in their country, as well as on the necessity of a restriction intended to meet them.'

90   See E/CN.4/1986/39, p 17; E/CN.4/1987/25, pp 26 and 27; E/CN.4/1988/28, pp 9–13.

91   Committee on the Rights of the Child, Report on the Fifth Session (1994) CRC/C/24, Annex V, p 63.

92   Committee on the Rights of the Child General Comment No 12 (2009) *The Right of the Child to Be Heard* (CRC/C/GC/12, para 92).

93   Committee on the Rights of the Child General Comment No 12 (2009) *The Right of the Child to Be Heard* (CRC/C/GC/12, para 90.

94   Republic of Korea CRC/C/Add.197, para 36.

95   See Committee of the Rights of the Child General Comment No 1 *The Aims of Education* CRC/GC/2001/1, para 8 and see Japan CRC/C/15/Add.231, paras 29 and 30.

96   (1969) 393 US 503.

discomfort and unpleasantness that always accompany an unpopular viewpoint. Certainly where there is no finding and no showing that engaging in the forbidden conduct would 'materially and substantially interfere with the requirements of appropriate discipline in the operation of the school,' the prohibition cannot be sustained ... In our system, state-operated schools may not be enclaves of totalitarianism. School officials do not possess absolute authority over their students. Students in school, as well as out of school, are 'persons' under our Constitution. They are possessed of fundamental rights which the State must respect, just as they themselves must respect their obligations to the State. In our system, students may not be regarded as closed-circuit recipients of only that which the State chooses to communicate. They may not be confined to the expression of those sentiments that are officially approved. In the absence of a specific showing of constitutionally valid reasons to regulate their speech, students are entitled to freedom of expression of their views. As Judge Gewin, speaking for the Fifth Circuit, said, school officials cannot suppress 'expressions of feelings with which they do not wish to contend'.'[97]

11.47 In the decision of the Human Rights Committee in *William Eduardo Delgado Páez v Colombia*[98] the Committee held that the right of freedom of expression and of opinion provided by Art 19(1) of the CCPR will usually cover the freedom of teachers to teach their subjects in accordance with their own views, without interference.

(iii)   CRC, Art 13 – Freedom of Expression through Voting

11.48 The child's right to freedom of expression under Art 13(1) does not extend to the formal expression of political ideas through the medium of suffrage where national laws do not permit voting by children. Article 25(b) of the ICCPR stipulates that every citizen shall have the right and the opportunity '[t]o vote and to be elected at genuine periodic elections which shall be by universal and equal suffrage and shall be held by secret ballot, guaranteeing the free expression of the will of the electors' and thus no lower age limit is put in place in international law. However, age restrictions on the right to vote are considered reasonable by the Human Rights Committee which states that '[t]he right to vote at elections and referendums must be established by law and may be subject only to reasonable restrictions, such as setting a minimum age limit for the right to vote'.[99]

(iv)   CRC, Art 13 – Freedom of Expression for Children Deprived of their Liberty

11.49 Aspects of freedom of expression not incompatible with the deprivation of liberty must be preserved in all forms of restriction of liberty.[100] The UN rules for the Protection of Juveniles Deprived of their Liberty provide that juveniles deprived of their liberty shall not for any reason related to their status be denied the civil, economic, political, social or cultural rights to which they are entitled under national or

---

[97]   In his opinion Justice Fortas made reference to the opinion of Justice Jackson in *West Virginia v Barnette* 319 U.S. 624 (1943) in which Justice Jackson observed: 'That they are educating the young for citizenship is reason for scrupulous protection of Constitutional freedoms of the individual, if we are not to strangle the free mind at its source and teach youth to discount important principles of our government as mere platitudes.' See also *Hazelwood School District v Cathy Kuhlmeier* 484 US 260 (teachers permitted to exercise editorial control over the style and content of speech in school provided their actions are 'reasonably related to pedagogical concerns') and *Bethel School District No 403 v Fraser* 478 US (1986) 549 (the right to free speech for school students is not automatically co-extensive with that of adults in other settings).

[98]   Human Rights Committee Communication No 195/1985.

[99]   Human Rights Committee General Comment No 25 *Article 25 (Participation in Public Affairs and the Right to Vote)* HRI/GEN/1/Rev 8, p 209, para 10. For discussion of the principles relating to voting by children see Archard, D *Children – Rights and Childhood* (2004) 2nd edn, Routlege, pp 98–105.

[100]   Newell, P and Hodgkin, R *Implementation Handbook for the Convention on the Rights of the Child* (2008) 3rd edn, UNICEF, p 180.

international law, and which are compatible with the deprivation of liberty. This will include the right to freedom of expression under Art 13(1) of the CRC.[101]

The Child's Right to Freedom of Expression under other International Instruments

11.50 For discussion of the other international instruments which touch and concern the child's right to freedom of expression see chapter 6 which deals with the child's right to participate under the Convention on the Civil Aspects of International Child Abduction 1980 and the Hague Convention on Protection of Children and Cooperation in Respect of Intercountry Adoption.[102]

The Child's Right to Freedom of Expression under the ECHR

ECHR, Art 10 – The Right to Freedom of Expression

11.51 Article 10 of the European Convention on Human Rights provides as follows in respect of the right to freedom of expression:

> '1. Everyone has the right to freedom of expression. This right shall include freedom to hold opinions and to receive and impart information and ideas without interference by public authority and regardless of frontiers. This article shall not prevent States from requiring the licensing of broadcasting, television or cinema enterprises.
>
> 2. The exercise of these freedoms, since it carries with it duties and responsibilities, may be subject to such formalities, conditions, restrictions or penalties as are prescribed by law and are necessary in a democratic society, in the interests of national security, territorial integrity or public safety, for the prevention of disorder or crime, for the protection of health or morals, for the protection of the reputation or rights of others, for preventing the disclosure of information received in confidence, or for maintaining the authority and impartiality of the judiciary.'

ECHR, Art 10(1) – Ambit[103]

(i) Article 10 and the Child's Right to Freedom of Expression'

11.52 Whilst Art 10 does not refer explicitly to children, they are clearly encompassed by the word 'everyone' in the first line. Article 10 of the ECHR should be interpreted having regard to the CRC and in particular to Art 12 and Art 13 of the CRC.[104] Art 10 of the ECHR does not contain the final part of the final sentence of Art 13 of the CRC namely, 'through any other media of the child's choice'. Van Bueren argues that in order to make the Art 10 right to freedom of expression appropriate for application to children these words must be read into the first sentence of Art 10.[105]

---

[101] UN rules for the Protection of Juveniles Deprived of their Liberty, r 13.

[102] See **6.67–6.71** above.

[103] The law on Art 10 of the ECHR is extremely extensive and a full account is beyond the scope of this work, which accordingly limits its consideration to Art 10 in so far as it effects children. For a detailed study of the law relating to Art 10 see Lord Lester QC, Lord Pannick QC and Herberg, J *Human Rights Law and Practice* (2009) 3rd edn, LexisNexis.

[104] See **3.43–3.46** above.

[105] Van Bueren, G *Child Rights in Europe* (2007) Council of Europe Publishing, p 83.

(ii)   Article 10 – 'Freedom of Expression'

11.53 Any form of communicative activity is in principle within the scope of Art 10 of
the ECHR.[106] The right to freedom of expression under Art 10 includes the negative
right of freedom not to speak. There is a positive duty on the State to take steps to
ensure that the right to freedom of expression is protected from interference by private
individuals as well as by the State.[107] Beyond content, freedom of expression will also
protect the manner in which the expression is made.[108] Expressions constituting value
judgments are also protected and any requirement in law to prove a value judgment will
constitute a breach of Art 10 of the ECHR.[109] In respect of value judgments, in *Lindon,
Otchakovsky-Laurens and July v France*[110] the court stated that:

> 'It reiterates in this connection that in order to assess the justification of an impugned
> statement, a distinction needs to be made between statements of fact and value judgments.
> While the existence of facts can be demonstrated, the truth of value judgments is not
> susceptible of proof. The requirement to prove the truth of a value judgment is impossible to
> fulfil and infringes freedom of opinion itself, which is a fundamental part of the right
> secured by Article 10. The classification of a statement as a fact or as a value judgment is a
> matter which in the first place falls within the margin of appreciation of the national
> authorities, in particular the domestic courts. However, even where a statement amounts to a
> value judgment, there must exist a sufficient factual basis to support it, failing which it will
> be excessive.'

11.54 Whether Art 10 will protect communicative activity which itself breaches the
values of the ECHR is debatable. In *Jersild v Denmark*[111] and *Lehideux and Isorni v
France*[112] the European Court of Human Rights made clear that the right to freedom of
expression under Art 10 does not extend to remarks which run directly against the
underlying values of the ECHR. However, within the domestic context, as noted above,
it is well established that unpopular and offensive opinions will fall within the protection
afforded by the right to freedom of expression.[113] This latter approach is reflected in
other common law jurisdictions. In the Canadian case of *R v Keegstra*[114] a
schoolteacher was charged with the offence of promoting hatred by making anti-Semitic
statements to students. The Canadian Supreme Court held that the content of the
communication was irrelevant to the protection afforded by the right to freedom of
expression, even if that content willfully promotes hatred against and identifiable group,
but that limits on the right to freedom of expression designed to prevent the willful
promotion of hatred are lawful. It is submitted that, given the importance of the right to
freedom of expression, the preferable approach under the ECHR is to consider offensive

---

[106]   *Belfast City Council v Miss Behavin' Ltd* [2007] UKHL 19, [2007] 1 WLR 1420.
[107]   *Özgür Gundem v Turkey* (2001) 31 EHRR 1082, para 43 ('The Court recalls the key importance of freedom
        of expression as one of the preconditions for a functioning democracy. Genuine, effective exercise of this
        freedom does not depend merely on the State's duty not to interfere, but may require positive measures of
        protection, even in the sphere of relations between individuals'). See also *Artze für das Leben v Austria*
        (1988) 13 EHRR 204.
[108]   *Jersild v Denmark* (1994) 19 EHRR 1 and *Da Silva v Portugal* (2002) 34 EHRR 56.
[109]   *Ferihumer v Austria* (2008) 47 EHRR 42, para 24 ('While the existence of facts can be demonstrated, the
        truth of value judgments is not susceptible of proof. The requirement to prove the truth of a value judgment
        is impossible to fulfill and infringes freedom of opinion itself, which is a fundamental part of the right
        secured by Article 10').
[110]   (2008) 46 EHRR 761.
[111]   (1994) 19 EHRR 1, para 35.
[112]   (1998) 30 EHRR, para 53 ('There is no doubt that, like any other remark directed against the Convention's
        underlying values the justification of a pro-Nazi policy could not be allowed to enjoy the protection afforded
        by Article 10').
[113]   *Redmond-Bate v DPP* (1999) 163 JP 789.
[114]   [1990] 3 SCR 697 Canadian Supreme Court.

material prima facie protected by the right to freedom of expression under Art 10(1) and then consider whether any restriction placed upon it is justified under Art 10(2). In the case of racist language or conduct, the justification for the imposition of comprehensive restrictions may be found easily.[115]

11.55 In relation to unpopular or offensive opinions it is in any event important to distinguish between expressions properly categorised as hate speech and expressions constituting a genuine critique on a matter of public interest.[116] Likewise, whilst forms of expression which seek to negate or revise 'clearly established historical facts' will not be protected by Art 10 having regard to the terms of Art 17 of the ECHR,[117] historical debate must be permitted given the demands of pluralism, tolerance and broadmindedness in a democratic society.[118]

11.56 Whilst Art 10 will thus cover most forms of communicative activity, the extent to which communicative activity is protected by Art 10 in a particular case will be evaluated by reference to the character of what is communicated when assessing the proportionality of any restriction and the margin of appreciation to be accorded to the State.[119]

(iii) Freedom to Receive and Impart Information without Interference

The Right to Receive Information

11.57 The right to receive information is a key aspect of Art 10. In *London Regional Transport v Mayor of London*[120] Sedley LJ observed that:

> 'Article 10 of the European Convention on Human Rights is not just about freedom of expression. It is also about the right to receive and impart information, a right which (to borrow Lord Steyn's metaphor in *R v Home Secretary, ex parte Simms* [2000] 2 AC 115, [1999] 3 All ER 400 at 126 of the former report) is the lifeblood of a democracy.'

11.58 In contrast to Art 13(1) of the CRC, Art 10 of the ECHR does not enshrine the right to *seek* information in addition to receiving and imparting information. Further, the right to receive information enshrined in Art 10 does not impart a positive obligation on the State to provide a person with information.[121] However, it should be noted that the European Convention on the Protection of Individuals with regard to

---

[115] See for example *Zdrahal v Wellington City Council* [1995] 1 NZLR 700.

[116] *Ergin v Turkey* (No 6) (2008) 47 EHRR 829, para 34.

[117] Article 17 of the ECHR states that 'Nothing in this Convention may be interpreted as implying for any State, group or person any right to engage in any activity or perform any act aimed at the destruction of any of the rights and freedoms set forth herein or at their limitation to a greater extent than is provided for in the Convention.'

[118] *Lehideux v France* (1998) 30 EHRR 665, para 47 ('The Court considers that it is not its task to settle this point, which is part of an ongoing debate among historians about the events in question and their interpretation. As such, it does not belong to the category of clearly established historical facts – such as the Holocaust – whose negation or revision would be removed from the protection of Article 10 by Article 17. In the present case, it does not appear that the applicants attempted to deny or revise what they themselves referred to in their publication as 'Nazi atrocities and persecutions' or 'German omnipotence and barbarism'. In describing Philippe Pétain's policy as 'supremely skilful', the authors of the text were rather supporting one of the conflicting theories in the debate about the role of the head of the Vichy government, the so-called 'double game' theory') and *Garaudy v France* (2003) Application No 65831/01 (unreported).

[119] *R v Secretary of State for the Home Department, ex p Simms* [2000] 2 AC 115.

[120] [2001] EWCA Civ 1491, [2003] EMLR 88, para 55. See also *Observer and Guardian v United Kingdom* (1991) 14 EHRR 153, para 59.

[121] See *Leaner v Sweden* (1987) 9 EHRR 433 and *Gaskin v United Kingdom* (1989) 12 EHRR 36.

Automatic Processing of Personal Data[122] does not prescribe a minimum age for access and accordingly permits children access to their electronic files. Further, in *Open Door and Dublin Well Women v Ireland*[123] a perpetual injunction restraining information services concerning abortion was held to breach Art 10 of the ECHR. Whilst this decision was predicated on the court being satisfied that the injunction in question interfered with the rights of counselors to impart information and the right of pregnant women to receive information the impugned injunction also affected those who sought information concerning abortion.

The Right to Impart Information

11.59 The role of the media in imparting information has been emphasised by the European Court of Human Rights. In *Observer and Guardian v United Kingdom*[124] the court held that:

> 'Freedom of expression constitutes one of the essential foundations of a democratic society; subject to paragraph 2 of Article 10, it is applicable not only to "information" or "ideas" that are favourably received or regarded as inoffensive or as a matter of indifference, but also to those that offend, shock or disturb. Freedom of expression, as enshrined in Article 10, is subject to a number of exceptions which, however, must be narrowly interpreted and the necessity for any restrictions must be convincingly established. These principles are of particular importance as far as the press is concerned. Whilst it must not overstep the bounds set, inter alia, in the "interests of national security" or for "maintaining the authority of the judiciary", it is nevertheless incumbent on it to impart information and ideas on matters of public interest.[125] Not only does the press have the task of imparting such information and ideas: the public also has a right to receive them. Were it otherwise, the press would be unable to play its vital role of 'public watchdog'.[126]

11.60 However, within this context, the European Court of Human Rights has increasingly developed a doctrine of 'responsible journalism' when evaluating alleged breaches of Art 10 of the ECHR in relation to journalistic activity. In *Lindon, Otchakovsky-Laurens and July v France*[127] the court stated:

---

[122] ETS No 108.

[123] (1992) 15 EHRR 244.

[124] (1991) 14 EHRR 153, para 59.

[125] Note that publications whose sole aim is to satisfy the curiosity of a certain public as to the details of the private life of a person, whatever their fame, should not be regarded as contributing to any debate of general interest to society (*Leempoel & SA Ed Cine Review v Belgium* (2006), para 68 and *Von Hannover v Germany* (2004) 16 BHRC 545, para 63).

[126] See also *Castells v Spain* (1992) 14 EHRR 445, para 43 ('Freedom of the press affords the public one of the best means of discovering and forming an opinion of the ideas and attitudes of their political leaders. In particular, it gives politicians the opportunity to reflect and comment on the preoccupations of public opinion; it thus enables everyone to participate in the free political debate which is at the very core of the concept of a democratic society'), *Lingens v Austria* (1986) 8 EHRR 407, *Bergens Tidende v Norway* (2001) 31 EHRR 16, para 52 ('Where, as in the present case, measures taken by the national authorities are capable of discouraging the press from disseminating information on matters of legitimate public concern, careful scrutiny of the proportionality of the measures on the part of the Court is called for') and *Samoma Uitgevers v Netherlands* (2010) Application No 38224/03, para 50 ('The right of journalists to protect their sources is part of the freedom to 'receive and impart information and ideas without interference by public authorities' protected by Article 10 of the Convention and serves as one of its important safeguards. It is a cornerstone of freedom of the press, without which sources may be deterred from assisting the press in informing the public on matters of public interest. As a result the vital public-watchdog role of the press may be undermined and the ability of the press to provide accurate and reliable information to the public may be adversely affected').

[127] (2008) 46 EHRR 761.

'The Court reiterates in this connection that protection of the right of journalists to impart information on issues of general interest requires that they should act in good faith and on an accurate factual basis and provide 'reliable and precise' information in accordance with the ethics of journalism. Under the terms of paragraph 2 of Article 10 of the Convention, freedom of expression carries with it 'duties and responsibilities', which also apply to the media even with respect to matters of serious public concern. Moreover, these 'duties and responsibilities' are liable to assume significance when there is a question of attacking the reputation of a named individual and infringing the 'rights of others'. Thus, special grounds are required before the media can be dispensed from their ordinary obligation to verify factual statements that are defamatory of private individuals. Whether such grounds exist depends in particular on the nature and degree of the defamation in question and the extent to which the media can reasonably regard their sources as reliable with respect to the allegations.'

In *Stoll v Switzerland*[128] the European Court of Human Rights reiterated this approach to journalistic activity:

'... the Court reiterates that, by reason of the "duties and responsibilities" inherent in the exercise of freedom of expression, the safeguard afforded by Article 10 to journalists in relation to reporting on issues of general interest is subject to the proviso that they are acting in good faith in order to provide accurate and reliable information in accordance with the ethics of journalism.'

Whilst this development of a doctrine of responsible journalism by the European Court of Human Rights has been criticised as a dangerous limitation on the role and duties of the press in a democratic society,[129] encouraging the practice of journalism in good faith in order to provide accurate and reliable information in accordance with the ethics of journalism is also a step that can act to reinforce the right to freedom of expression by increasing public confidence in the utility of that cardinal right.

ECHR, Art 10(2) – Ambit

(i) ECHR, Art 10(2) – 'Restrictions'

11.61 Article 10(2) of the ECHR provides as follows in respect of the limitations which may be placed on the right to freedom of expression:

'2. The exercise of these freedoms, since it carries with it duties and responsibilities, may be subject to such formalities, conditions, restrictions or penalties as are prescribed by law and are necessary in a democratic society, in the interests of national security, territorial integrity or public safety, for the prevention of disorder or crime, for the protection of health or morals, for the protection of the reputation or rights of others, for preventing the disclosure of information received in confidence, or for maintaining the authority and impartiality of the judiciary.'

11.62 The ambit of Art 10(2) of the ECHR was described by the House of Lords in *R v Shayler*[130] as follows:

'It is plain from the language of art 10(2), and the European Court has repeatedly held, that any national restriction on freedom of expression can be consistent with art 10(2) only if it is prescribed by law, is directed to one or more of the objectives specified in the article and is

---

[128] (2008) 47 EHRR 1270.

[129] See Lord Lester QC, Lord Pannick QC and Herberg, J *Human Rights Law and Practice* (2009) 3rd edn, LexisNexis, p 542.

[130] [2002] UKHL 11, [2003] 1 AC 247, para 23 per Lord Bingham.

shown by the state concerned to be necessary in a democratic society. "Necessary" has been strongly interpreted: it is not synonymous with "indispensable", neither has it the flexibility of such expressions as "admissible", "ordinary", "useful", "reasonable" or "desirable" (see *Handyside v UK* (1979) 1 EHRR 737 at 754 (para 48)). One must consider whether the interference complained of corresponded to a pressing social need, whether it was proportionate to the legitimate aim pursued and whether the reasons given by the national authority to justify it are relevant and sufficient under art 10(2).'

11.63 The restrictions under Art 10(2) must thus be narrowly interpreted and the necessity for any restriction must be convincingly established[131] on the basis of cogent evidence.[132] The burden of proving necessity is on the defendant. Restrictions may be constituted by prior restraint on expression[133] or post expression restraints which may have a 'chilling' effect on the future exercise of freedom of expression.[134] Rights held by the child under the ECHR have been held to justify the interference with the right to freedom of expression under Art 10. In *T v United Kingdom*[135] the European Court of Human Rights held that a child's Art 6 right to a fair hearing had been breached by reason of the hearing taking place in public. The child's right to life under Art 2 of the ECHR and the child's right to freedom from inhuman or degrading treatment under Art 3 have likewise been held in to justify interference with the right to freedom of expression in certain circumstances.[136]

(ii)   ECHR, Art 10(2) – 'Duties and Responsibilities'

11.64 Article 10(2) of the ECHR stipulates that the right to freedom and expression 'carries with it duties and responsibilities', which duties and responsibilities justify the limitations provided for in Art 10(2).[137] The precise scope of the term 'duties and responsibilities' will depend on the situation of the person exercising the rights under Art 10(1) and the means employed to do so.[138] The 'duties and responsibilities' are liable to assume significance when there is a question of infringing the 'rights of others'.[139] The term encompasses the duty to avoid expressions that are gratuitously offensive to others and which to not contribute to legitimate public debate.[140] In the context of a case concerning the issue of whether the seizure of a publication aimed at children was necessary to protect the health or morals of children, in *Handyside v UK*[141] the European Court of Human Rights observed:

> 'From another standpoint, whoever exercises his freedom of expression undertakes "duties and responsibilities" the scope of which depends on his situation and the technical means he uses. The Court cannot overlook such a person's "duties' and 'responsibilities" when it enquires, as in this case, whether "restrictions" or "penalties" were conducive to the 'protection of morals' which made them "necessary" in a "democratic society".'

---

[131]   *Thorgierson v Iceland* 14 EHRR 843, para 63.
[132]   *Kelly v BBC* [2001] Fam 59.
[133]   See *Wingrove v United Kingdom* (1996) 24 EHRR 1. Prior restraint requires special scrutiny.
[134]   See *Godlevsky v Russian* (2008), para 36 and *Lingens v Austria* (1986) 8 EHRR 407.
[135]   [2000] 30 EHRR 121.
[136]   *Venables v News Group Newspapers* [2001] Fam 430; *X (A Women formerly known as Mary Bell) v O'Brien* [2003] EWHC 1101 (QB), [2003] 2 FCR 686.
[137]   See also **11.61–11.63** above.
[138]   *Müller v Switzerland* (1988) 13 EHRR 212 and see *Otto Preminger Institut v Austria* (1994) 19 EHRR 34.
[139]   *Lindon, Otchakovsky-Laurens and July v France* (2008) 46 EHRR 761.
[140]   *Giniewski v France* (2007) 45 EHRR 589.
[141]   (1979) 1 EHRR 737.

(iii) ECHR, Art 10(2) – 'Formalities, Conditions, Restrictions or Penalties'

Prescribed by Law

11.65 Within the context of Art 10(2) of the ECHR, in *Lindon, Otchakovsky-Laurens and July v France*[142] the European Court of Human Rights articulated the requirements of the phrase 'prescribed by law', which includes both statute and common law, in Art 10(2) as follows:[143]

> 'The Court reiterates that a norm cannot be regarded as a "law" within the meaning of Article 10(2) unless it is formulated with sufficient precision to enable the citizen to regulate his conduct; he must be able – if need be with appropriate advice – to foresee, to a degree that is reasonable in the circumstances, the consequences which a given action may entail. Those consequences need not be foreseeable with absolute certainty. Whilst certainty is desirable, it may bring in its train excessive rigidity and the law must be able to keep pace with changing circumstances. Accordingly, many laws are inevitably couched in terms which, to a greater or lesser extent, are vague and whose interpretation and application are questions of practice. The Court further reiterates that the scope of the notion of foreseeability depends to a considerable degree on the content of the text in issue, the field it is designed to cover and the number and status of those to whom it is addressed. A law may still satisfy the requirement of foreseeability even if the person concerned has to take appropriate legal advice to assess, to a degree that is reasonable in the circumstances, the consequences which a given action may entail. This is particularly true in relation to persons carrying on a professional activity, who are used to having to proceed with a high degree of caution when pursuing their occupation. They can on this account be expected to take special care in assessing the risks that such activity entails.'

Necessary in a Democratic Society

11.66 The adjective 'necessary', within the meaning of Art 10(2) is not synonymous with 'indispensable', neither has it the flexibility of such expressions as 'admissible', 'ordinary', 'reasonable' or 'desirable'. Nevertheless, it is for the national authorities to make the initial assessment of the reality of the pressing social need implied by the notion of 'necessity' in this context.[144] In *Christian Democratic People's Party v Moldova (No 2)*[145] the European Court of Human Rights stated as follows in relation to the meaning of 'democratic society' in the ECHR:

> 'Referring to the hallmarks of a "democratic society", the Court has attached particular importance to pluralism, tolerance and broadmindedness. In that context, it has held that although individual interests must on occasion be subordinated to those of a group, democracy does not simply mean that the views of the majority must always prevail: a balance must be achieved which ensures the fair and proper treatment of minorities and avoids any abuse of a dominant position.'

11.67 The examples of restrictions necessary in a democratic society provided by Art 10(2) are national security, territorial integrity, public safety and the prevention of disorder and crime, protection of health or morals, protection of the reputation and

---

[142] (2008) 46 EHRR 761.
[143] See also *Sunday Times v United Kingdom* (1979) 2 EHRR 245, and *Gaweda v Poland* (2002) 12 BHRC 486, para 39 ('The Court observes that one of the requirements flowing from the expression 'prescribed by law' is the foreseeability of the measure concerned. A norm cannot be regarded as a 'law' unless it is formulated with sufficient precision to enable the citizen to regulate his conduct: he must be able – if need be with appropriate advice – to foresee, to a degree that is reasonable in the circumstances, the consequences which a given action may entail').
[144] *Handyside v UK* (1979) 1 EHRR 737.
[145] (No 2) (2010) Application 25196/04 (unreported).

rights of others, preventing disclosure of information received in confidence and maintaining the authority and impartiality of the judiciary. Whilst each of these may be relevant to children, the key exceptions under Art 10(2) of the ECHR most commonly touching and concerning children will be the protection of health or morals, the protection of the reputation and rights of others and preventing disclosure of information received in confidence.

Protection of Health or Morals

11.68 Because of the wide range of domestic standards concerning health and morals States parties enjoy a wide margin of appreciation when imposing restrictions on freedom of expression based on the need to protect health and morals. It is thus primarily for the State to assess the content of morals having regard to the importance of the Art 10(1) right to freedom of expression in a democracy, mediation between different groups in society, respect for legislation based on considered balancing of interests, recognition of 'holistic' policy areas which are not readily justiciable and respect for legislation representing the democratic will on moral and ethical questions.[146] In *Handyside v UK*,[147] a case concerning the protection of the health and morals of children, the European Court of Human Rights observed that:

> '... it is not possible to find in the domestic law of the various Contracting States a uniform European conception of morals. The view taken by their respective laws of the requirements of morals varies from time to time and from place to place, especially in our era which is characterised by a rapid and far-reaching evolution of opinions on the subject. By reason of their direct and continuous contact with the vital forces of their countries, State authorities are in principle in a better position than the international judge to give an opinion on the exact content of these requirements as well as on the "necessity" of a "restriction" or "penalty"' intended to meet them. The Court notes at this juncture that, whilst the adjective "necessary", within the meaning of Article 10 para 2, is not synonymous with "indispensable", neither has it the flexibility of such expressions as "admissible", "ordinary", "reasonable" or "desirable". Nevertheless, it is for the national authorities to make the initial assessment of the reality of the pressing social need implied by the notion of "necessity" in this context.'[148]

However, whilst a wide margin of appreciation is permitted in settling the content of morals in a national jurisdiction, where the means employed by the State in protecting such morals violates Art 10(1) of the ECHR, the protection employed must be demonstrably necessary in a democratic society for the purposes of Art 10(2).[149]

Protection of Health and Morals – Publications aimed at Children

11.69 In *Handyside v UK*,[150] the European Court of Human Rights recognised that States parties are permitted to restrict the right to freedom of expression in the interests of the child's health, morals and for the protection of their other rights. The case concerned restrictions imposed on the circulation of a publication entitled 'The Little

---

[146]   *R (on the application of Pro Life Alliance) v BBC* [2003] UKHL 23, [2004] 1 AC 185.
[147]   (1979) 1 EHRR 737.
[148]   See also *Muller v Switzerland* (1988) 13 EHRR 212 and *R (on the application of Pro Life Alliance) v BBC* [2003] UKHL 23, [2004] 1 AC 185 on the need for evidence as to the domestic concept of morals on a particular subject ('Public opinion in these matters is often diverse, sometimes unexpected and in constant flux. Generally accepted standards on these questions are not a matter of intuition on the part of elderly male judges').
[149]   *Open Door Counseling and Dublin Well Women v Ireland* (1992) 15 EHRR 244.
[150]   (1979) 1 EHRR 737.

Red Schoolbook' which dealt with issues relevant to children and young people.[151] The British publisher of the book, Mr Handyside, brought a claim for breach of Art 10(1) of the ECHR following the seizure of his stock of the books and his arrest and conviction for having in his possession obscene books contrary to the Obscene Publications Act 1959. On the basis of the margin of appreciation doctrine the European Court of Human Rights held that, having regard to the wide margin of appreciation is permitted in settling the content of morals in a national jurisdiction, the court could not find established a breach of Art 10(1) of the ECHR. Van Bueren notes that the fact that the book had been contributed to by children and had been read, without ill effects, by children in other States carried little weight with the court, which appeared to conceptualise the issues as the protection of the children's welfare rather than their rights.[152] It is of particular note that the child's right to receive information and ideas under Art 10(1) of the ECHR was not considered by the court in this case. Likewise, when the 'Little Red School Book' came to be considered again by the European Court of Human Rights in *X, Y and Z v United Kingdom*[153] apart from relying on the fact that the book had not been substantially altered in its content, no cogent reasoning was advanced by the court as to the justification for older children not being entitled to receive information on sex education or drugs.[154]

Protection of Health and Morals – Child Protection Reports

11.70 In *Juppala v Finland*[155] a maternal grandmother alleged violation of her right to freedom of expression under Art 10(1) of the ECHR after having been found guilty of 'defamation without better knowledge' for reporting bruising on her grandson, that her grandson's behaviour had been abnormal since he had visited his father and that her grandson had reported that the bruising had been caused by a punch from his father. The doctor to whom the grandmother reported these matters wrote in his report that the bruise noted on the boy's back was consistent with a punch, thereby supporting the boy's account, given also to the doctor, that he had been hit by his father. In finding a violation of the applicant's right to freedom of expression under Art 10(1) of the ECHR the court held that:

> 'This case calls into consideration two countervailing interests, each of high social importance: the need to safeguard children from abuse by their own parents, and the need to protect parents from unnecessary interference with their right to respect for their private and family life or the risk of unjustified arrest and prosecution. The first of these interests involves protection of children as the victims of crime. The Court has emphasised that children and other vulnerable individuals in particular are entitled to State protection, in the form of effective deterrence, against such serious breaches of personal integrity ...If the source of the abuse is the parent, the child is at risk from his primary and natural protector within the privacy of his home. Child abuse is indeed a hard form of criminal conduct to combat, because its existence is difficult to uncover. Babies and young children are unable to tell, older children are often too frightened. The question raised by this application is how to strike a proper balance when a parent is wrongly suspected of having abused his or her child,

---

[151] The court summarised the contents of the book as follows 'It contained an introduction headed 'All grown-ups are paper tigers', an 'Introduction to the British edition', and chapters on the following subjects: Education, Learning, Teachers, Pupils and The System. The chapter on Pupils contained a twenty-six page section concerning 'Sex' which included the following sub-sections: Masturbation, Orgasm, Intercourse and petting, Contraceptives, Wet dreams, Menstruation, Child-molesters or 'dirty old men', Pornography, Impotence, Homosexuality, Normal and abnormal, Find out more, Venereal diseases, Abortion, Legal and illegal abortion, Remember, Methods of abortion, Addresses for help and advice on sexual matters.'

[152] Van Bueren *The International Law on the Rights of the Child* (1998) Martinus Nijhoff, p 135.

[153] (1976) Application No 5528/72.

[154] See Van Bueren, G *Child Rights in Europe* (2007) Council of Europe Publishing, p 85.

[155] (2008) Application No 18620/03 (unreported).

while protecting children at risk of significant harm. In considering these questions, the starting point is to note that the applicant acted properly in considering whether the bruise on the boy's back had been deliberately inflicted. Having become suspicious, she consulted a medical doctor who rightly decided to communicate to the child welfare authorities the suspicion which he personally formed having examined and interviewed the boy. That is the essential next step in child protection. The seriousness of child abuse as a social problem requires that persons who act in good faith, in what they believe are the best interests of the child, should not be influenced by fear of being prosecuted or sued when deciding whether and when their doubts should be communicated to health care professionals or social services. There is a delicate and difficult line to tread between taking action too soon and not taking it soon enough. The duty to the child in making these decisions should not be clouded by a risk of exposure to claims by a distressed parent if the suspicion of abuse proves unfounded ... the threat of an *ex post facto* review in criminal proceedings of a concerned grandmother's statement made in good faith to the child's doctor accords ill with every adult's moral duty to defend a child's interests ... The possibility to voice a suspicion of child abuse, formed in good faith, in the context of an appropriate reporting procedure should be available to any individual without the potential 'chilling effect' of a criminal conviction or an obligation to pay compensation for harm suffered or costs incurred... It is therefore only in exceptional cases that restriction of the right to freedom of expression in this sphere can be accepted as necessary in a democratic society.'

Protection of Health and Morals – Content of Broadcast Media

11.71 In *Nederlandse Omroeppogramma Stichting v Netherlands*[156] the European Commission considered restrictions placed on commercial statements made in the context of television programmes aimed primarily at a young audience. Holding programmes aimed at children cannot be excluded from the scope of Art 10(1), the Commission held that the restrictions imposed constituted an interference with Art 10(1) but that the interference pursued the legitimate aim of protecting children from indirect advertising in television programmes and could reasonably be considered as necessary in a democratic society for the protection of the rights of others. In its Recommendation No (84)3 *On Principles on Television Advertising* the Committee of Ministers recommends that television advertising aimed at children should 'avoid anything likely to harm their interests and should respect their physical, mental and moral personality'.[157]

Protection of the Reputation and Rights of Others

11.72 Article 10(2) permits the right to reputation to be invoked as a counterveilling interest to the right to freedom of expression.[158] The limits of acceptable criticism of an individual will vary depending on the status of the individual in question.[159] The limit of acceptable criticism of private citizens is narrower than that for those in the public eye.[160] The reputation of children as a group is often a particularly pressing issue.[161] In general terms, an interference with free speech which seeks to protect a group of persons from defamation on account of their membership of a specific religious group falls within Art 10(2) and is consonant with the aim of the protections provided by Art 9 of the ECHR.[162] The duties and responsibilities that accompany the right to freedom of expression require the avoidance of expressions which are gratuitously offensive to

[156] (1991) Application No 16844/90 (unreported).
[157] Recommendation No (84)3 *On Principles on Television Advertising* Principle 5.
[158] *Pfeifer v Austria* (2009) 48 EHRR 175.
[159] *Lingens v Austria* (1986) 8 EHRR 407.
[160] *Lingens v Austria* (1986) 8 EHRR 407.
[161] See CRAE *State of Children's Rights in England* (2008), pp 15–18.
[162] Lord Lester QC, Lord Pannick QC and Herberg, J *Human Rights Law and Practice* (2009) 3rd edn, LexisNexis, p 531 and see *Klein v Slovakia* (2006) 21 BHRC 457.

others and which to not contribute to legitimate public debate.[163] However, Pannick and others caution that care must be taken in determining whether the rights of specific groups have been violated.[164] In *Wingrove v United Kingdom*[165] the court observed that:

> 'Moreover, as in the field of morals, and perhaps to an even greater degree, there is no uniform European conception of the requirements of 'the protection of the rights of others' in relation to attacks on their religious convictions. What is likely to cause substantial offence to persons of a particular religious persuasion will vary significantly from time to time and from place to place, especially in an era characterised by an ever growing array of faiths and denominations. By reason of their direct and continuous contact with the vital forces of their countries, State authorities are in principle in a better position than the international judge to give an opinion on the exact content of these requirements with regard to the rights of others as well as on the 'necessity' of a 'restriction' intended to protect from such material those whose deepest feelings and convictions would be seriously offended.'

Children as a group were considered in *B v United Kingdom; P v United Kingdom*[166] where by the privacy rights of children in residence proceedings and the need to avoid prejudicing the interests of justice justified limitations on public hearings and public pronouncement of judgments.

Preventing Disclosure of Information Received in Confidence

11.73 In *Stoll v Switzerland*[167] the European Court of Human Rights interpreted the phrase 'preventing the disclosure of information received in confidence' as follows:

> 'The Court accepts that clauses which allow interference with Convention rights must be interpreted restrictively. Nevertheless, in the light of paragraph 3 of Article 33 of the Vienna Convention, and in the absence of any indication to the contrary in the drafting history of Article 10, the Court considers it appropriate to adopt an interpretation of the phrase 'preventing the disclosure of information received in confidence' which encompasses confidential information disclosed either by a person subject to a duty of confidence or by a third party and, in particular, as in the present case, by a journalist.'

The protection of information revealed by children in confidence is particularly important in the context of the protection of the health and morals of children. For example, in light of the principle that any form of communicative activity is in principle within the scope of Art 10 of the ECHR[168] information disclosed in confidence by children to counselors and experts within family proceedings will fall to be protected under Art 10(1) of the ECHR.[169]

ECHR, Art 10 – Application

ECHR, Art 10 – Media and the Courts

11.75 The right to receive information under Art 10(1) of the ECHR will be engaged in the question of whether courts hearing cases concerning children should be open to the

---

[163] *Giniewski v France* (2007) 45 EHRR 589.
[164] Lord Lester QC, Lord Pannick QC and Herberg, J *Human Rights Law and Practice* (2009) 3rd edn, LexisNexis, p 531 and see *Klein v Slovakia* (2006) 21 BHRC 457.
[165] (1996) 24 EHRR 1.
[166] (2002) 11 BHRC 667, [2001] 2 FLR 261.
[167] (2008) 47 EHRR 1270, para 61.
[168] *Belfast City Council v Miss Behavin' Ltd* [2007] UKHL 19, [2007] 1 WLR 1420.
[169] MacDonald, A *Bringing Rights Home for Children: Transparency and the Child's Right to Respect for Private Life* [2010] Fam Law 190.

press and public given the centrality of open justice to a legal system based on the rule of law[170] and the press being one of the means by which politicians and the public can verify that the judiciary is discharging its responsibilities competently.[171]

11.75 The right to freedom of expression and the right receive information under Art 10(1) may be curtailed where the protection of vulnerable witnesses who might be otherwise unwilling to testify fully or at all.[172] The European Court of Human Rights recognised in *B v United Kingdom; P v United Kingdom*[173] that the purpose of hearing cases concerning children in private was to protect the private lives of children and to promote the administration of justice by encouraging the parties and witnesses to give full and frank evidence. The Court held that in such circumstances it may be necessary to limit the open and public nature of proceedings in order to protect the safety or privacy of witnesses or to promote the free exchange of information and opinion in the pursuit of justice.[174]

11.76 In examining the extent to which the restriction of publication by the media of information concerning family proceedings may be justified, it is important to bear in mind that Art 10(1) of the ECHR, guaranteeing freedom of expression, is held to be a 'touchstone of all human rights'.[175] As such, any curtailment of the right to freedom of expression by the exclusion of the media from the court must be convincingly established by a compelling countervailing consideration.[176] Usually, this consideration will be the child's right to respect for private life under Art 8 of the ECHR. In *Re S (A Child)(Identification: Restrictions on Publication)*[177] the House of Lords stipulated the approach to be taken in cases where the dilemma posed is whether a child is entitled to have his right to respect for private life protected or whether the right to freedom of expression should prevail. The balancing exercise to be carried out between Art 8(1) and Art 10(1) of the ECHR when considering this dilemma was described by Lord Steyn:

> 'First, neither Article has as such precedence over the other. Secondly, where the values under the two Articles are in conflict, an intense focus on the comparative importance of the specific rights being claimed in the individual case is necessary. Thirdly, the justifications for interfering with or restricting each right must be taken into account. Finally, the proportionality test must be applied to each. For convenience, I will call this the ultimate balancing test.'

11.77 In carrying out this balancing exercise, it should not be forgotten that as noted above children too have the right to freedom of expression under Art 10(1) of the ECHR. The exercise of this right by children is particularly valuable when it comes to

---

[170]   *Re Vancouver Sun* [2005] 2 LRC 248, Sup Ct of Canada.
[171]   *Prager and Oberschlick v Austria* (1995) 21 EHRR 1, para 34 ('The Court reiterates that the press plays a pre-eminent role in a State governed by the rule of law. Although it must not overstep certain bounds set, inter alia, for the protection of the reputation of others, it is nevertheless incumbent on it to impart – in a way consistent with its duties and responsibilities – information and ideas on political questions and on other matters of public interest'). Note that the European Court of Human Rights acknowledges the importance of the reputation of judges (see *Barford v Denmark* (1989) 13 EHRR 493, paras 61–64) and that protection from destructive attacks against the reputation of the judiciary may justify a limitation on the freedom of expression under the provisions of Art 10(2) for 'for maintaining the authority and impartiality of the judiciary' (see *Kobenter and Standard Verlags GMBH v Austria* (2006) Application No 60899/00 (unreported)).
[172]   See *R (Wagstaff) v Secretary of State for Health* [2001] 1 WLR 292 at 320F.
[173]   (2002) 11 BHRC 667, [2001] 2 FLR 261.
[174]   See **9.49** above.
[175]   UN General Assembly Resolution 59(1) of 14 December 1946.
[176]   *Re S (A Child)(Identification: Restrictions on Publication)* [2004] UKHL 47, [2005] 1 AC 593.
[177]   [2004] UKHL 47, [2005] 1 AC 593.

the need for a dialogue between vulnerable children and professionals, which communicative activity is in principle within the scope of Art 10(1).[178] Measures which act to prevent or restrict the disclosure by children of matters detrimental to their welfare or risk the disclosure of such information given in confidence must accordingly be justified by reference to Art 10(2). In this regard, it is suggested that the curtailment by reason of the fear of publication of the child's freedom of expression within the investigative and therapeutic scenarios that often precede or accompany proceedings concerning harm to children can itself amount to a breach of the child's rights under Art 10(1).

ECHR, Art 10 – Voting

11.78 The protection afforded by Art 10(1) of the ECHR is unlikely to be held to extend to conferring on the child a right to vote. In *W, X, Y, Z v Belgium*[179] the European Commission on Human Rights held that, in establishing a minimum age of 25 for those wishing to stand for election, the State of Belgium could not be considered to be imposing an unreasonable or arbitrary restriction nor interfering with the right to freedom of expression.

The Child's Right to Freedom of Expression under European Union Law

11.79 Article 11 of the European Charter of Fundamental Rights provides as follows in relation to the right to freedom of expression:

> '1. Everyone has the right to freedom of expression. This right shall include freedom to hold opinions and to receive and impart information and ideas without interference by public authority and regardless of frontiers.
>
> 2. The freedom and pluralism of the media shall be respected.'

In accordance with Art 52(3) of the European Charter,[180] the meaning and scope of the rights under Art 11 is the same as that under the corresponding Art 10 of the ECHR and its related protocols. As such, the limitations that are permitted by Art 10(2) of the ECHR will be permitted in respect of the rights under Art 10 of the Charter. The European Court of Justice has referred to Art 17 of the CRC in the context of considering the relationship between the mass media and the welfare of the child.[181]

11.80 Article 22 of the EC Broadcasting Directive of 3 October 1989 stipulates as follows in respect of television broadcasts which may affect the health or morals of children:[182]

---

[178] *Belfast City Council v Miss Behavin' Ltd* [2007] UKHL 19, [2007] 1 WLR 1420.

[179] 6745 6/74 DR2, 110.

[180] Article 52(3) of the Charter provides that 'Insofar as this Charter contains rights which correspond to rights guaranteed by the Convention for the Protection of Human Rights and Fundamental Freedoms, the meaning and scope of those rights shall be the same as those laid down by the said Convention. This provision shall not prevent Union law providing more extensive protection.'

[181] See *Dynamic Medien Vertriebs GmbH v Avides Media AG* (Case C-244/06) [2008] All ER (D) 198 (Feb).

[182] See also Recommendation 963 (1983) *On Cultural and Educational Means of Reducing Violence* which recommends that the Committee of Ministers invite member Governments to 'consider introducing legislation to ensure that media violence involving individuals is condemned alongside incitement to racial hatred or obscenity, to take the appropriate measures to ensure that broadcasting companies give particular attention to means of protecting sensitive people, especially children, from prolonged exposure to media violence and to make clear to the press and to the audio-visual media their special responsibility as regards

'Member States shall take appropriate measures to ensure that television broadcasts by broadcasters under their jurisdiction do not include programmes which might seriously impair the physical, mental or moral development of minors, in particular those that involve pornography or gratuitous violence. This provision shall extend to other programmes which are likely to impair the physical, mental or moral development of minors, except where it is ensured, by selecting the time of the broadcast or by any technical measure, that minors in the area of transmission will not normally hear or see such broadcasts.'

The Child's Right to Freedom of Expression under other Regional Instruments

American Convention on Human Rights

11.81 Article 13 of the American Convention on Human Rights[183] enshrines the right to freedom of thought and expression, providing as follows:

'1. Everyone has the right to freedom of thought and expression. This right includes freedom to seek, receive, and impart information and ideas of all kinds, regardless of frontiers, either orally, in writing, in print, in the form of art, or through any other medium of one's choice.

2. The exercise of the right provided for in the foregoing paragraph shall not be subject to prior censorship but shall be subject to subsequent imposition of liability, which shall be expressly established by law to the extent necessary to ensure:

a.   respect for the rights or reputations of others; or
b.   the protection of national security, public order, or public health or morals.

3. The right of expression may not be restricted by indirect methods or means, such as the abuse of government or private controls over newsprint, radio broadcasting frequencies, or equipment used in the dissemination of information, or by any other means tending to impede the communication and circulation of ideas and opinions.

4. Notwithstanding the provisions of paragraph 2 above, public entertainments may be subject by law to prior censorship for the sole purpose of regulating access to them for the moral protection of childhood and adolescence.

5. Any propaganda for war and any advocacy of national, racial, or religious hatred that constitute incitements to lawless violence or to any other similar action against any person or group of persons on any grounds including those of race, color, religion, language, or national origin shall be considered as offenses punishable by law.'[184]

11.82 The Inter-American Court of Human Rights has observed that the right to freedom of expression is:[185]

'... a cornerstone upon which the very existence of a democratic society rests. It is indispensable for the formation of public opinion. It is also a condition *sine qua non* for the

---

the dissemination of models of political violence, and therefore make proper understanding of the effects of the media a necessary part of the qualification of all personnel employed in the media field.'

[183] See also the Declaration of Principles on Freedom of Expression.

[184] See also Art 23(b) which provides that every citizen shall enjoy the right and opportunity to 'to vote and to be elected in genuine periodic elections, which shall be by universal and equal suffrage and by secret ballot that guarantees the free expression of the will of the voters.'

[185] *Ricardo Canese* Judgment of August 31, 2004 Series C No 111, para 82 and *Herrera Ulloa* Judgment of July 2, 2004 Series C No 107, para 70.

development of political parties, trade unions, scientific and cultural societies and, in general, those who wish to influence the public. It represents, in short, the means that enable the community, when exercising its options, to be sufficiently informed. Consequently, it can be said that a society that is not well informed is not a society that is truly free.'

The court has stated that the protection granted by the American Convention in respect of the right to freedom of thought and expression includes 'not only the right and freedom to express one's own thoughts, but also the right and freedom to *seek, receive and impart* information and ideas of all kinds.[186] The Inter-American Court of Human Rights has also held that freedom of expression extends to the free circulation of information, ideas, and the exhibition of works of art that may or may not be approved by state authorities.[187] The court has further stated that:[188]

'The right protected by Article 13 [of the American Convention] ... has a special scope and character, which are evidenced by the dual aspect of freedom of expression. It requires, on the one hand, that no one be arbitrarily limited or impeded in expressing his own thoughts. In that sense, it is a right that belongs to each individual. Its second aspect, on the other hand, implies a collective right to receive any information whatsoever and to have access to the thoughts expressed by others.'

11.83 In *Reyes v Chile* the Inter-American Court of Human Rights confirmed that the right to freedom of expression enshrined in Art 13(1) of the American Convention contained a positive obligation on the part of the State to provide access to the information it holds, stating:

'... the Court finds that, by expressly stipulating the right to 'seek' and 'receive' 'information,' Article 13 of the Convention protects the right of all individuals to request access to State-held information, with the exceptions permitted by the restrictions established in the Convention. Consequently, this article protects the right of the individual to receive such information and the positive obligation of the State to provide it, so that the individual may have access to such information or receive an answer that includes a justification when, for any reason permitted by the Convention, the State is allowed to restrict access to the information in a specific case. The information should be provided without the need to prove direct interest or personal involvement in order to obtain it, except in cases in which a legitimate restriction is applied. The delivery of information to an individual can, in turn, permit it to circulate in society, so that the latter can become acquainted with it, have access to it, and assess it. In this way, the right to freedom of thought and expression includes the protection of the right of access to State-held information, which also clearly includes the two dimensions, individual and social, of the right to freedom of thought and expression that must be guaranteed simultaneously by the State.'

11.84 Article 13 of the American Convention contains a virtually complete ban on prior censorship, which ban is not found in other international human rights instruments. The Inter-American Commission on Human Rights has observed that this indicates the high regard the drafters of the Convention had for the right to freedom of expression.[189] Note however that the Inter-American Court has stated that the blanket ban of censorship will not apply in relation to Art 13(4) of the American Convention

---

[186] *López Álvarez* Judgment of February 1, 2006 Series C No 141, para 163, *Ricardo Canese* Judgment of August 31, 2004 Series C No 111, paras 77–80 and *Herrera Ulloa* Judgment of July 2, 2004 Series C No 107, paras 108–111.

[187] *Alejandra Marcela Matus Acuña et al v Chile* (2005) Case 12.142 Report No 90/05.

[188] *Alejandra Marcela Matus Acuña et al v Chile* (2005) Case 12.142 Report No 90/05.

[189] IACHR, *Report on Terrorism and Human Rights*, OAS/Ser.L/V/II.116, Doc. 5, rev. 1, corr. October 22, 2002, paragraph 312.

which permits censorship for the sole purpose of regulating access to public entertainments for the moral protection of childhood and adolescence.[190]

Ibero-American Convention on the Rights of Youth

11.85 Article 14(2) of the Ibero-American Convention on the Rights of Youth provides as follows:

'The States Parties shall promote respect for the identity of youth and shall guarantee their free expression ensuring the eradication of situations which discriminate them in any of the aspects concerning their identity.'

Article 18(1) of the Convention stipulates the following in respect of the right to freedom of expression, assembly:

'Youth have the right to freedom of opinion, expression, assembly and information, to have youth forums at their disposal and create organisations and associations where their problems are analysed and may present proposals of political initiatives before public authorities in charge of attending youth matters, with no kind of interference of limitation.'[191]

African Charter on the Rights and Welfare of the Child

11.86 The African Charter on the Rights and Welfare of the Child enshrines the child's right to freedom of expression as follows in Art 7:

'Every child who is capable of communicating his or her own views shall be assured the rights to express his opinions freely in all matters and to disseminate his opinions subject to such restrictions as are prescribed by laws.'

The African Youth Charter

11.87 Article 4 of the African Youth Charter provides as follows in respect of the right to freedom of expression:

'1. Every young person shall be assured the right to express his or her ideas and opinions freely in all matters and to disseminate his or her ideas and opinions subject to the restrictions as are prescribed by laws.

2. Every young person shall have the freedom to seek, receive and disseminate information and ideas of all kinds, either orally, in writing, in print, in the form of art or through any media of the young person's choice subject to the restrictions as are prescribed by laws.'

---

[190] *Alejandra Marcela Matus Acuña et al v Chile* (2005) Case 12.142 Report No 90/05.
[191] See also Art 23(1) ('The States Parties recognise that the right to education also includes the right to sexual education as a source of personal, affective development and communicative expression, as well as to the information concerning reproduction and its consequences') and Art 24(1) ('Youth have the right to cultural life and free creation and artistic expression. The practice of these rights shall be connected to their comprehensive formation').

The African Charter on Human and Peoples' Rights

11.88 The African Charter on Human and People's Rights frames the right to freedom of expression as the right to receive information and to express and disseminate opinions in Art 9 of the Charter:

> '1. Every individual shall have the right to receive information.
>
> 2. Every individual shall have the right to express and disseminate his opinions within the law.'

Revised Arab Charter on Human Rights

11.89 The Revised Arab Charter on Human Rights provides at Art 32 as follows in respect of the right to freedom of expression:

> '1. The present Charter guarantees the right to information and to freedom of opinion and expression, as well as the right to seek, receive and impart information and ideas through any medium, regardless of geographical boundaries.
>
> 2. Such rights and freedoms shall be exercised in conformity with the fundamental values of society and shall be subject only to such limitations as are required to ensure respect for the rights or reputation of others or the protection of national security, public order and public health or morals.'[192]

The Child's Right to Freedom of Expression under Domestic Law

Domestic Law – Freedom of Expression

11.90 As with the right to respect for family life, domestic decisions engaging the child's right to freedom of expression will now fall to be determined under Art 10(1) of the ECHR as applied by the Human Rights Act 1998. For example, following the coming into force of the 1998 Act, the House of Lords held that the foundation of the jurisdiction to restrain publicity concerning children now derives from the ECHR.[193] It should be noted however that the Human Rights Act 1998 does no more than reinforce and give greater weight to the principles of freedom of expression that were already embodied in the domestic common law.[194] The key change engineered by the Human Rights Act 1998 is the use of principle of proportionality as the means of scrutinising restrictions of the right to freedom of expression. In *London Regional Transport v The Mayor of London*[195] Sedly LJ observed that in respect of balancing countervailing considerations against the right to freedom of expression:

> 'The difficulty ... is to know by what instrument this balance is to be struck. Is it to be, in Coke's phrase (4 Inst. 41), the golden and straight metwand of the law or the incertain and crooked cord of discretion? The contribution which Art 10 and the jurisprudence of the European Court of Human Rights can make towards an answer is, in my view, real. It lies in the methodical concept of proportionality. Proportionality is not a word found in the text of

---

[192] See also Art 24.

[193] *Re S (A Child) (Identification: Restrictions on Publication)* [2004] UKHL 47, [2005] 1 AC 593.

[194] See *A-G v Guardian Newspapers (No 2)* [1990] 1 AC 109 at 283; *Derbyshire County Council v Times Newspapers* [1993] AC 534; *Reynolds v Times Newspapers* [2001] 2 AC 127; *R v Shayler* [2002] UKHL 11, [2003] 1 AC 247 and *McCartan Turkington Breen v Times Newspapers Ltd* [2001] 2 AC 277.

[195] [2001] EWCA Civ 1491, [2003] EMLR 88.

the Convention: it is the tool – the metwand – which the Court has adopted (from 19th-century German jurisprudence) for deciding a variety of Convention issues including, for the purposes of the qualifications to arts 8 to 11, what is and is not necessary in a democratic society. It replaces an elastic concept with which political scientists are more at home than lawyers with a structured inquiry: does the measure meet a recognised and pressing social need? Does it negate the primary right or restrict it more than is necessary? Are the reasons given for it logical? These tests of what is acceptable by way of restriction of basic rights in a democratic society reappear, with variations of phrasing and emphasis, in the jurisprudence of (among others) the Privy Council, the Constitutional Court of South Africa, the Supreme Court of Zimbabwe and the Supreme Court of Canada in its Charter jurisdiction, the courts of the Republic of Ireland and the Court of Justice of the European Communities.'

The convention thus requires domestic law, in the words of Lord Nicholls in *Reynolds v Times Newspapers*[196] to consider whether a restriction on the right to freedom of expression is 'convincingly established by a compelling countervailing consideration'.

Domestic Law – Human Rights Act 1998, s 12

11.91 Section 12 of the Human Rights Act 1998 provides as follows in relation to the right to freedom of expression:

'(1) This section applies if a court is considering whether to grant any relief which, if granted, might affect the exercise of the Convention right to freedom of expression.

(2) If the person against whom the application for relief is made ('the respondent') is neither present nor represented, no such relief is to be granted unless the court is satisfied—

(a)   that the applicant has taken all practicable steps to notify the respondent; or
(b)   that there are compelling reasons why the respondent should not be notified.

(3) No such relief is to be granted so as to restrain publication before trial unless the court is satisfied that the applicant is likely[197] to establish that publication should not be allowed.

(4) The court must have particular regard to the importance of the Convention right to freedom of expression and, where the proceedings relate to material which the respondent claims, or which appears to the court, to be journalistic, literary or artistic material (or to conduct connected with such material), to—

(a)   the extent to which—
        (i)   the material has, or is about to, become available to the public; or

---

[196]   [2001] AC 127 at 200F–200G.
[197]   As to the meaning of 'likely' see *Cream Holdings Ltd v Bannerjee* [2004] UKHL 44, [2005] 1 AC 253, para 22. ('There can be no single, rigid standard governing all applications for interim restraint orders. Rather, on its proper construction the effect of s 12(3) is that the court is not to make an interim restraint order unless satisfied the applicant's prospects of success at the trial are sufficiently favourable to justify such an order being made in the particular circumstances of the case. As to what degree of likelihood makes the prospects of success "sufficiently favourable", the general approach should be that courts will be exceedingly slow to make interim restraint orders where the applicant has not satisfied the court he will probably ("more likely than not") succeed at the trial. In general, that should be the threshold an applicant must cross before the court embarks on exercising its discretion, duly taking into account the relevant jurisprudence on art 10 and any countervailing convention rights. But there will be cases where it is necessary for a court to depart from this general approach and a lesser degree of likelihood will suffice as a prerequisite. Circumstances where this may be so include those mentioned above: where the potential adverse consequences of disclosure are particularly grave, or where a short-lived injunction is needed to enable the court to hear and give proper consideration to an application for interim relief pending the trial or any relevant appeal.')

(ii)   it is, or would be, in the public interest for the material to be published;
  (b)   any relevant privacy code.

(5) In this section—

'court' includes a tribunal; and

'relief' includes any remedy or order (other than in criminal proceedings).'

11.92   The Human Rights Act 1998, s 12 requires the court to pay particular regard to the importance of the right to freedom of expression when considering the granting of relief which may affect that right. Section 12 of the 1998 Act emphasises the cardinal importance of the right to freedom of expression. It does not however act to give the right to freedom of expression a presumptive priority in domestic law. In *Douglas v Hello! Ltd*[198] Sedley LJ observed as follows in relation to s 12 of the Human Rights Act 1998:

'There is no need to look at the parliamentary genesis of this section in order to see that it, with s 13, is of a different kind from the rest of the Human Rights Act 1998. It descends from the general to the particular, singling out one Convention right and making procedural and substantive provision for litigation in which the right is directly or indirectly implicated. The Convention right in question is the right to freedom of expression (Art 10) ... Two initial points need to be made about s 12 of the Human Rights Act 1998. First, by s 12(4) it puts beyond question the direct applicability of at least one Article of the Convention as between one private party to litigation and another – in the jargon, its horizontal effect ... The other point, well made by Mr Tugendhat, is that it is 'the Convention right' to freedom of expression which both triggers the section (see s 12(1)) and to which particular regard is to be had. That Convention right, when one turns to it, is qualified in favour of the reputation and rights of others and the protection of information received in confidence. In other words, you cannot have particular regard to Art 10 without having equally particular regard at the very least to Art 8 ... The European Court of Human Rights has always recognised the high importance of free media of communication in a democracy, but its jurisprudence does not – and could not consistently with the Convention itself – give Art 10(1) the presumptive priority which is given, for example, to the First Amendment in the jurisprudence of the United States' courts. Everything will ultimately depend on the proper balance between privacy and publicity in the situation facing the court ... It will be necessary for the court, in applying the test set out in s 12(3), to bear in mind that by virtue of s 12(1) and (4) the qualifications set out in Art 10(2) are as relevant as the right set out in Art 10(1). This means that, for example, the reputations and rights of others – not only but not least their Convention rights – are as material as the defendant's right of free expression. So is the prohibition on the use of one party's Convention rights to injure the Convention rights of others ... The case being one which affects the Convention right of freedom of expression, s 12 of the Human Rights Act 1998 requires the court to have regard to Art 10 (as, in its absence, would s 6). This, however, cannot, consistently with s 3 and Art 17, give the Art 10(1) right of free expression a presumptive priority over other rights. What it does is require the court to consider Art 10(2) along with Art 10(1), and by doing so to bring into the frame the conflicting right to respect for privacy. This right, contained in Art 8 and reflected in English law, is in turn qualified in both contexts by the right of others to free expression. The outcome, which self-evidently has to be the same under both Articles, is determined principally by considerations of proportionality.'[199]

---

[198]   [2001] QB 967 per Sedley LJ, paras 132–137.
[199]   Note that in his 1996 Goodman Lecture Lord Hoffman made clear that his use in *R v Central Television plc* [1994] Fam 192, 203, sub nom *Mrs R v Central Independent Television plc* [1994] 2 FLR 151 at 162 of the phrase 'trump card' in relation to the right to freedom of expression meant only that '... in order to be put [in] the balance against freedom of speech, another interest must fall within some established exception that

Domestic Law – Restrictions on Freedom of Expression

11.93 Within the context of domestic law, the issue relating to children in respect of which the right to freedom of expression is most commonly engaged is that of applications to restrain publicity concerning them.

11.94 The domestic courts jealously guard the right to freedom of expression of the press.[200] In *R v Shayler*[201] Lord Bingham stated:

> 'Modern democratic government means government of the people by the people for the people. But there can be no government by the people if they are ignorant of the issues to be resolved, the arguments for and against different solutions and the facts underlying those arguments. The business of government is not an activity about which only those professionally engaged are entitled to receive information and express opinions. It is, or should be, a participatory process. But there can be no assurance that government is carried out for the people unless the facts are made known, the issues publicly ventilated. Sometimes, inevitably, those involved in the conduct of government, as in any other walk of life, are guilty of error, incompetence, misbehaviour, dereliction of duty, even dishonesty and malpractice. Those concerned may very strongly wish that the facts relating to such matters are not made public. Publicity may reflect discredit on them or their predecessors. It may embarrass the authorities. It may impede the process of administration. Experience however shows, in this country and elsewhere, that publicity is a powerful disinfectant. Where abuses are exposed, they can be remedied. Even where abuses have already been remedied, the public may be entitled to know that they occurred. The role of the press in exposing abuses and miscarriages of justice has been a potent and honourable one. But the press cannot expose that of which it is denied knowledge.'

11.95 As such, any curtailment of the right to freedom of expression by the exclusion of the media from the court must be convincingly established by a compelling countervailing consideration.[202] As noted above, in cases concerning children this consideration will usually be the child's right to respect for private life under Art 8 of the ECHR. Once again, in *Re S (A Child) (Identification: Restrictions on Publication)*[203] the House of Lords stipulated the approach to be taken in cases where the dilemma posed is whether a child is entitled to have his right to respect for private life protected or whether the restriction of the right to freedom of expression which such protection involves cannot be justified.[204] The balancing exercise to be carried out between Art 8 and Art 10 was formulated by Lord Steyn as follows:

> 'First, neither Article has as such precedence over the other. Secondly, where the values under the two Articles are in conflict, an intense focus on the comparative importance of the specific rights being claimed in the individual case is necessary. Thirdly, the justifications for interfering with or restricting each right must be taken into account. Finally, the proportionality test must be applied to each. For convenience, I will call this the ultimate balancing test.'

---

could be justified under Art 10 of the Convention.' In other words, if freedom of expression is to be impeded it must be on cogent grounds recognised by law (per Sedley J *Douglas v Hello! Ltd* [2001] QB 967, para 136).

[200]　See *McCartan Turkington Breen v Times Newspapers Ltd* [2001] 2 AC 277 at 290–291.
[201]　[2003] 1 AC 247, para 21.
[202]　*Re S (A Child) (Identification: Restrictions on Publication)* [2004] UKHL 47, [2005] 1 AC 593.
[203]　[2004] UKHL 47, [2005] 1 AC 593.
[204]　See also **9.49 et seq** above.

CONCLUSION

11.96 Verhellen contends that 'children should not longer be treated as passive consumers [of media] but as active participants.'[205] The myriad of new information and communications technology and electronic social networking applications facilitated by that technology allow children a broad range of new avenues by which to express themselves to ever wider sections of society. Within this context the media should respect and promote the participatory rights of children in order to facilitate to the maximum possible extent the child's right to freedom of expression.[206] However, as Verhellen also acknowledges, there is a tension between the child's participation through the right to freedom of expression and the child's need for protection in this area.[207] At the same time as opportunities for children to exercise their right to freedom of expression expands so does the risk presented to children by the exercise of the right of freedom of expression. The growth of modern and accessible media through which children can exercise their right to freedom of expression has developed alongside media which exploits children for the purposes of entertainment.[208] If the child's right to freedom of expression is to be of any value, it must be a right exercised by the child on the child's terms and rather than by adults acting as proxies with a view to selling cheap entertainment inconsistent with the wider rights of the child.

---

[205] Verhellen, E *Convention on the Rights of the Child* (2000) Garant, p 124.
[206] Newell, P and Hodgkin, R *Implementation Handbook for the Convention on the Rights of the Child* (2008) 3rd edn, UNICEF, p 217.
[207] Verhellen, E *Convention on the Rights of the Child* (2000) Garant, p 124.
[208] See CRAE *State of Children's Rights in England* (2008), p 18.

Chapter 12

THE CHILD'S RIGHT TO FREEDOM OF ASSOCIATION AND PEACEFUL ASSEMBLY

'[T]he aim of every political association is the preservation of the
natural and imprescriptible rights of man'

Marquis de Lafayete

INTRODUCTION

12.1   Article 20 of the Universal Declaration of Human Rights stipulates that 'Everyone has the right to freedom of peaceful assembly and association'. The International Covenant on Civil and Political Rights provides at Art 21 for the right to peaceful assembly and at Art 22 for the right to freedom of association.[1] The right is a fundamental right in a democratic society and, like the right to freedom of expression, is one of the foundations of such a society.[2] In the Canadian case of *Re Public Service Employee Relations Act*[3] Chief Justice Dickson described the right to freedom of association as follows:

> 'Freedom of association is the freedom to combine together for the pursuit of common purposes or the advancement of common causes ... a *sine qua non* of any free and democratic society, protecting individuals from the vulnerability of isolation and ensuring the potential of effective participation in society. In every area of human endeavour and throughout history individuals have formed associations for the pursuit of common interests and aspirations. Through association individuals are able to ensure that they have a voice in shaping the circumstances integral to their needs, rights and freedoms.'

12.2   In describing the importance of civil rights for children during the drafting of the CRC, including the right to freedom of association and peaceful assembly, the US delegation pointed out that the child as defined in Art 1 of the CRC included adolescents who have often acquired the skills required to participate fully and

---

[1]   See also Art 8 of the Covenant on Economic, Social and Cultural Rights which states *inter alia* that '1. The States Parties to the present Covenant undertake to ensure: (a) The right of everyone to form trade unions and join the trade union of his choice, subject only to the rules of the organisation concerned, for the promotion and protection of his economic and social interests. No restrictions may be placed on the exercise of this right other than those prescribed by law and which are necessary in a democratic society in the interests of national security or public order or for the protection of the rights and freedoms of others.'

[2]   *Rassemblement Jurasien Unité v Switzerland* 17 DR 93 (1979) and *Ziliberberg v Moldova* (2004) Application No 61821/00 (unreported). In *Committee for the Commonwealth of Canada v Canada* (1991) 77 DLR (4th) 385 (Sup Ct of Canada) the Court noted the interrelationship between the right to freedom of association and peaceful assembly and the right to freedom of expression, stating that '... freedom of expression cannot be exercised in a vacuum ... it necessarily implies the use of physical space in order to meet its underlying objectives. No one could agree that the exercise of freedom of expression can be limited solely to places owned by the person wishing to communicate: such an approach would certainly deny the very foundation of the freedom of expression'

[3]   [1987] 1 SCR. 313 (Sup Ct of Canada).

effectively in society.[4] Together with the child's right to participate and the child's right to freedom of expression, the child's right to freedom of association and peaceful assembly promotes the child as an active and participating member of society,[5] the latter right being central to the child's sense of freedom and involvement in society.[6] As a more vulnerable member of society the child's right to freedom of association and peaceful assembly increases the power of the individual child by conferring on him or her the right to participate in group activity,[7] thereby increasing the child's ability to effect change for him or herself as an individual and for children as a group. The child's right to freedom of association and peaceful assembly also directly reinforces the efficacy of the child's right to freedom of expression,[8] the right to freedom of thought, conscience and religion and the child's right to participate. Associations relevant to children will include student councils, youth parliaments and children's organisations nationally and in local communities.[9]

12.3   Hodgkin and Newell note that the implications of recognising the child's right to freedom of association and peaceful assembly have still not been widely explored.[10] This chapter examines international, regional and domestic provisions which confer on children the right to freedom of association and peaceful assembly and the limited consideration that has been given to those provisions by the international human rights bodies and the regional and domestic courts.

GENERAL PRINCIPLES

Association and Peaceful Assembly

12.4   Whilst the ICCPR separates the right to freedom of association and the right to freedom of peaceful assembly into two separate articles, Art 15 of the CRC combines those rights into one article. Both the right to freedom of association and the right to freedom of peaceful assembly enshrined in Art 15 of the CRC are designed to protect the right of children to come together and co-operate for some joint action or purpose, with both rights being closely connected to the formation of the common 'will' of the people in a democratic society.[11] In *NAACP v Patterson*[12] the US Supreme Court noted that effective advocacy of both public and private points of view, particularly

---

4   UN Doc E/CN.4/1987/25, para 112.
5   Newell, P and Hodgkin, R *Implementation Handbook for the Convention on the Rights of the Child* (2008) 3rd edn, UNICEF, p 197.
6   Van Bueren, G *Child Rights in Europe* (2007) Council of Europe Publishing, p 86. See also Morrow, V *Children's Rights to Public Space: Environment and Curfews* in Franklin, B (ed) *The New Handbook of Children's Rights* (2002) Routledge, p 168.
7   Van Bueren, G *The International Law on the Rights of the Child* (1998) Martinus Nijhoff, p 144. Van Bueren gives the example of the impact of Brazilian 'street children' marching together in 1991 to protest the murder of many among their number. See also the decision of the Inter-American Court of Human Rights in *The 'Street Children' Case (Villagrán Morales et al.)*. Judgment of November 19, 1999 Series C No 63.
8   See *NAACP v Patterson* 357 U.S. 449 (1958) and *Committee for the Commonwealth of Canada v Canada* (1991) 77 DLR (4th) 385 (Sup Ct of Canada).
9   See Committee on the Rights of the Child, Report on the forty-third session, September 2006, Day of General Discussion, Recommendations, para 33 and *Guidelines for Periodic Reports (Revised 2005)* (CRC/C/58/Rev.1, Annex, paras 6 and 7).
10   Newell, P and Hodgkin, R *Implementation Handbook for the Convention on the Rights of the Child* (2008) 3rd edn, UNICEF, p 198. See also Van Bueren, G *Child Rights in Europe* (2007) Council of Europe Publishing, p 86.
11   Detrick, S *A Commentary on the United Nations Convention on the Rights of the Child* (1999) Martinus Nijhoff, p 279 and E/CN.4/L.1575, p 259.
12   357 U.S. 449 (1958).

controversial ones, is undeniably enhanced by group association. However, there are also material differences between the right to freedom of association and the right to peaceful assembly. The freedom of association tends to protect formal organisations whereas the freedom of peaceful assembly is more applicable to ad hoc gatherings.[13] The difference between formal associations and ad hoc gatherings may justify different grounds upon which restrictions on the right to freedom of association and restrictions on the right to freedom of peaceful assembly are justified.[14]

Association

12.5   The International Covenant on Civil and Political Rights provides at Art 21 for the right to peaceful assembly and at Art 22 for the right to freedom of association.[15] In relation to the freedom of association, Art 22 of the ICCPR provides as follows:

> '1. Everyone shall have the right to freedom of association with others, including the right to form and join trade unions for the protection of his interests.[16]
>
> 2. No restrictions may be placed on the exercise of this right other than those which are prescribed by law and which are necessary in a democratic society in the interests of national security or public safety, public order (ordre public), the protection of public health or morals or the protection of the rights and freedoms of others. This article shall not prevent the imposition of lawful restrictions on members of the armed forces and of the police in their exercise of this right.
>
> 3. Nothing in this article shall authorise States Parties to the International Labour Organisation Convention of 1948 concerning Freedom of Association and Protection of the Right to Organise to take legislative measures which would prejudice, or to apply the law in such a manner as to prejudice, the guarantees provided for in that Convention.'

12.6   Of particular significance for children is the question of whether the right to freedom of association is limited to protecting political associations or extends to the protection of wider social and cultural associations, the latter being more relevant to children in their earlier years. The right to association under Art 22 of the ICCPR has been said to include the right to come together with one or more other persons for social, cultural, economic or political purposes and will include association with a group assembly, casual as well as formal associations and single and temporary as well as organised and continuing associations.[17] In the Privy Council decision of *Collymore v Attorney-General*[18] Lord Donovan agreed with the statement of Wooding CJ in the Trinidad and Tobago Court of Appeal decision in *Collymore v Attorney-General*[19] that:

---

[13] Detrick, S *A Commentary on the United Nations Convention on the Rights of the Child* (1999) Martinus Nijhoff, p 279 and E/CN.4/L.1575, p 259.

[14] Partsch, K *Freedom of Conscience and Expression, and Political Freedoms* in Henking, L (ed) *The International Bill of Rights: The Covenant on Civil and Political Rights* (1981) p 209, pp 230–231.

[15] See also Art 8 of the Covenant on Economic Social and Cultural Rights.

[16] Note Art 20(2) of the Universal Declaration of Human Rights states that 'No one may be compelled to belong to an association.'

[17] Partsch, K *Freedom of Conscience and Expression, and Political Freedoms* in Henking, L (ed) *The International Bill of Rights: The Covenant on Civil and Political Rights* (1981) p 209, p 235. But see also the decision of the European Court of Human Rights in *Anderson v United Kingdom* [1998] EHRR CD 172 at **12.29** below.

[18] [1970] AC 538. See also the decision of the US Supreme Court in *Healy v James* 408 U.S. 169 (1972) where the Court held that the need to protect the integral activities of an association as a necessary component of the right to freedom of association.

[19] (1967) 12 WIR 5. Note that Wooding CJ went on to hold state 'But the freedom to associate confers neither right nor licence for a course of conduct or for the commission of acts which in the view of Parliament are

'... freedom of association means no more than freedom to enter into consensual arrangements to promote the common-interest objects of the associating group. The objects may be any of many. They may be religious or social, political or philosophical, economic or professional, educational or cultural, sporting or charitable.'

Peaceful Assembly

12.7   Article 21 of the ICCPR states as follows in relation to the right to freedom of peaceful assembly:

'The right of peaceful assembly shall be recognised. No restrictions may be placed on the exercise of this right other than those imposed in conformity with the law and which are necessary in a democratic society in the interests of national security or public safety, public order (ordre public), the protection of public health or morals or the protection of the rights and freedoms of others.'

12.8   The word 'peaceful' in Art 21 refers exclusively to the conditions under which the assembly in question is held and not the object for which the assembly is called or the opinions which may be expressed at the assembly.[20] The right to freedom of peaceful assembly includes the right not to participate in peaceful assembly.[21]

Association and Peaceful Assembly, Best Interests and Evolving Capacity

12.9   The *travaux préparatoires* of the CRC indicate that it was anticipated that the child's freedom of association and peaceful assembly would be exercised commensurate with the child's age, maturity and development.[22] As with the other rights enshrined in the CRC, the Art 15 right to freedom of association and peaceful assembly must be read in light of Art 3 of the CRC (best interests) and Art 5 of the CRC (evolving capacity). However, Art 15(1) of the Convention cannot be taken as providing support for limitations on the child's freedom of association based on parental consent.[23]

12.10   Article 29(b)(i) of the Convention on the Rights of Persons with Disabilities requires that States parties shall guarantee to persons with disabilities the right to participate in non-governmental organisations and associations concerned with the public and political life of the country.[24] Art 23(1) of the CRC requires that States

---

inimical to the peace, order and good government of the country. What is or is not inimical to the peace, order and good government of the country is not for the courts to decide.'

[20]   Nowak, M *UN Covenant on Civil and Political Rights: CCPR Commentary* (1993), pp 373–375 and Partsch, K *Freedom of Conscience and Expression, and Political Freedoms* in Henking, L (ed) *The International Bill of Rights: The Covenant on Civil and Political Rights* (1981) p 209, p 231. Note that the right to assembly under Art 11 of the African Charter of Human and People's Rights omits the word 'peaceful'.

[21]   Partsch, K *Freedom of Conscience and Expression, and Political Freedoms* in Henking, L (ed) *The International Bill of Rights: The Covenant on Civil and Political Rights* (1981) p 209, p 231.

[22]   UN Doc E/CN.4/1988/28, para 48.

[23]   See Japan CRC/C/15/Add.231, paras 29 and 30.

[24]   See also Committee on Economic, Social and Cultural Rights General Comment No 5 Persons *with Disabilities* HRI/GEN/1/Rev 8, p 30, para 26 ('Trade union-related rights (Art 8) apply equally to workers with disabilities and regardless of whether they work in special work facilities or in the open labour market. In addition, Art 8, read in conjunction with other rights such as the right to freedom of association, serves to emphasise the importance of the right of persons with disabilities to form their own organisations. If these organisations are to be effective in 'the promotion and protection of [the] economic and social interests' (Art 8(1)(a)) of such persons, they should be consulted regularly by government bodies and others in relation to all matters affecting them; it may also be necessary that they be supported financially and otherwise so as to ensure their viability').

Parties recognise that a mentally or physically disabled child should enjoy a full and decent life, in conditions which ensure dignity, promote self-reliance and facilitate the child's active participation in the community. When read with Art 2 and Art 23 of the CRC, Art 15(1) requires children with disabilities to benefit equally from the right to freedom of association and freedom of peaceful assembly.

Derogation

12.11 The rights to freedom of association and freedom of peaceful assembly under the ICCPR are rights which may be the subject of derogation.[25] However, derogation from the right to freedom of association and freedom of peaceful assembly is only permissible as an exceptional measure[26] and must also aim to preserve the rule of law.[27] The CRC contains no provision for the derogation of rights and accordingly there is no basis for derogation from the child's the right to freedom of association and peaceful assembly under the CRC.

FREEDOM OF ASSOCIATION AND PEACEFUL ASSEMBLY

Child's Right to Freedom of Association and Peaceful Assembly under the CRC

CRC, Art 15

12.12 Article 15 of the CRC provides as follows in respect of the child's right to freedom of association and freedom of peaceful assembly:

> '1. States Parties recognise the rights of the child to freedom of association and to freedom of peaceful assembly.
>
> 2. No restrictions may be placed on the exercise of these rights other than those imposed in conformity with the law and which are necessary in a democratic society in the interests of national security or public safety, public order (ordre public), the protection of public health or morals or the protection of the rights and freedoms of others.'

CRC, Art 15(1) – Ambit

12.13 The right to freedom of association and peaceful assembly is granted by the Universal Declaration of Human Rights to 'everyone'. In requiring States parties to

---

[25] See ICCPR Art 4 ('1. In time of public emergency which threatens the life of the nation and the existence of which is officially proclaimed, the States Parties to the present Covenant may take measures derogating from their obligations under the present Covenant to the extent strictly required by the exigencies of the situation, provided that such measures are not inconsistent with their other obligations under international law and do not involve discrimination solely on the ground of race, colour, sex, language, religion or social origin'), ECHR, Art 15 ('1. In time of war or other public emergency threatening the life of the nation any High Contracting Party may take measures derogating from its obligations under this Convention to the extent strictly required by the exigencies of the situation, provided that such measures are not inconsistent with its other obligations under international law) and Art 27 American Convention on Human Rights ('1. In time of war, public danger, or other emergency that threatens the independence or security of a State Party, it may take measures derogating from its obligations under the present Convention to the extent and for the period of time strictly required by the exigencies of the situation, provided that such measures are not inconsistent with its other obligations under international law and do not involve discrimination on the ground of race, color, sex, language, religion, or social origin').

[26] UN Doc CCPR/C/21/Add 2.

[27] UN Doc E/CN.4/Sub.2/1982/15.

'recognise' the rights of the child to freedom of association and to freedom of peaceful assembly, Art 15(1) of the CRC ensures the recognition of an existing human right in relation to children rather than granting the right itself.[28] However, whilst the wording of Art 15 of the CRC does no more than reiterate the terms of other international human rights instruments, and the restrictions contained in Art 15(2) are identical to those in such instruments, Art 15(1) compels state parties to consider the right to freedom of association and peaceful assembly in respect of children.[29]

12.14 The child's right to freedom of association and peaceful assembly includes association with an individual as well as with a group so long as the individual does not threaten the child's other rights, including those concerned with the protection of the child.[30] Note that Art 15(1) of the CRC does not repeat the terms of Art 20(2) of the Universal Declaration of Human Rights, namely that 'No one may be compelled to belong to an association'. However Hodgkin and Newell argue that the freedom of association contained in Art 15(1) of the CRC implies the right to join *and* leave associations.[31] Likewise, Art 15 of the CRC does not explicitly enshrine the right of children to form and join trade unions for the protection of their interests as provided by for in Art 22(1) of the ICCPR. However, again Hodgkin and Newell argue that the right is implied in the child's right to freedom of association and that the limitations in Art 15(2) of the CRC would not justify preventing children from forming or joining unions.[32] Likewise, Van Bueren argues that the general international legal principles concerning the right to join a trade union apply equally to children above the legal minimum age for employment.[33] Within this context it should be noted that the right to form and join trade unions under Art 22(1) of the ICCPR and Art 8 of the ICESCR apply to 'everyone'.[34] Restrictions on children joining or establishing political organisations may breach Art 15(1) of the CRC.[35]

---

[28] See UN Doc A/2929 Chapter VI, para 140 in relation to the use of term 'shall be recognised' in Art 21 of the ICCPR and Partsch, K *Freedom of Conscience and Expression, and Political Freedoms* in Henking, L (ed) *The International Bill of Rights: The Covenant on Civil and Political Rights* (1981) p 209, pp 231–232.

[29] Van Bueren, G *The International Law on the Rights of the Child* (1998) Martinus Nijhoff, p 144. See also Rule 59 of the UN Rules for the Protection of Children Deprived of their Liberty which provides that 'Every means should be provided to ensure that juveniles have adequate communication with the outside world, which is an integral part of the right to fair and humane treatment and is essential to the preparation of juveniles for their return to society. Juveniles should be allowed to communicate with their families, friends and other persons or representatives of reputable outside organisations, to leave detention facilities for a visit to their home and family and to receive special permission to leave the detention facility for educational, vocational or other important reasons. Should the juvenile be serving a sentence, the time spent outside a detention facility should be counted as part of the period of sentence.'

[30] Newell, P and Hodgkin, R *Implementation Handbook for the Convention on the Rights of the Child* (2008) 3rd edn, UNICEF, p 198.

[31] Newell, P and Hodgkin, R *Implementation Handbook for the Convention on the Rights of the Child* (2008) 3rd edn, UNICEF, p 198 and see Detrick, S *A Commentary on the United Nations Convention on the Rights of the Child* (1999) Martinus Nijhoff, p 279 and E/CN.4/L.1575, p 261.

[32] Newell, P and Hodgkin, R *Implementation Handbook for the Convention on the Rights of the Child* (2008) 3rd edn, UNICEF, p 199 and see also Art 32 of the CRC ('States Parties recognise the right of the child to be protected from economic exploitation and from performing any work that is likely to be hazardous or to interfere with the child's education, or to be harmful to the child's health or physical, mental, spiritual, moral or social development').

[33] Van Bueren, G *The International Law on the Rights of the Child* (1998) Martinus Nijhoff, p 145. The ILO Minimum Age Convention 1973 Art 2(3) stipulates that the minimum age for admission to employment shall be 15 years. For detailed consideration of these provisions see chapter 15 below.

[34] The law on the right to freedom of association as it relates to trade unions and labour laws is extensive and is beyond the scope of this work. For an excellent summary in the context of human rights see Lord Lester QC, Lord Pannick QC and Herberg, J *Human Rights Law and Practice* (2009) 3rd edn, LexisNexis, 553 et seq.

[35] See Japan CRC/C/15/Add.231, paras 29 and 30 and Costa Rica CRC/C/15/Add.266, paras 23 and 24.

CRC, Art 15(2) – Ambit

12.15 The child's right to freedom of association and peaceful assembly may only be restricted in accordance with terms of Art 15(2) of the CRC which provides that:

> '2. No restrictions may be placed on the exercise of these rights other than those imposed in conformity with the law and which are necessary in a democratic society in the interests of national security or public safety, public order (ordre public), the protection of public health or morals or the protection of the rights and freedoms of others.'

12.16 The only restrictions that may be placed on the child's right to freedom of association and freedom of peaceful assembly are thus such restrictions as are in conformity with the law and are necessary in a democratic society in the interests of national security or public safety, public order (ordre public), the protection of public health or morals or the protection of the rights and freedoms of others. It is the interplay between the principle of freedom of association and peaceful assembly and the limitations and restrictions permitted under Art 15(2) which determines the actual scope of the child's right under Art 15(1) of the CRC.[36] In accordance with the general rules of international law the limitations prescribed by Art 15(2) on the child's right to freedom of association and peaceful assembly must be interpreted restrictively.[37] Such restrictions must be applied only for the purposes for which they are prescribed and must be directly related and proportionate to the specific needs on which they are predicated.[38]

(i)   Article 15(2) – Conformity with the Law

12.17 In requiring that restrictions to the right to freedom of association and freedom of peaceful assembly to be in 'conformity with the law' Art 15(2) of the CRC differs from the restrictions prescribed by Arts 10(2) and Art 14(3) of the CRC, which require restrictions to the child's right to leave any country and the child's right to freedom of thought conscience and religion respectively to be 'prescribed by law', and Art 13(2), which requires restrictions on the child's right to freedom of expression to be 'provided by law'.[39] The latter provisions suggest that the restrictions under each of Arts 10(2), 13(2) and 14(3) must be embodied in statute or common law.[40] By contrast, the term 'conformity with the law' in Art 15(2) of the CRC suggests that the restrictions must be lawful by reference to existing laws but that the restrictions themselves need not be embodied in the substantive law. The use of the phrase 'conformity with the law' in Art 15(2) of the CRC may indicate a wider discretion to administrative authorities in placing restrictions on the child's right to freedom of association and freedom of peaceful assembly provided the same are in accordance with the restrictions set out in Art 15(2).[41] In the circumstances, Art 15(2) of the CRC appears to provide less stringent protection from administrative interference with the child's right to freedom of association than Art 22 of the ICCPR which stipulates that the restrictions to be placed on the exercise of the right to freedom of expression must be 'prescribed by law'.

---

[36]   See The Human Rights Committee General Comment No 10 1983 HRI/GEN/1/Rev 8, p 171, para 3.

[37]   Detrick, S A Commentary on the United Nations Convention on the Rights of the Child (1999) Martinus Nijhoff, p 37.

[38]   Human Rights Committee General Comment No 10 *Article 19 (Freedom of Opinion)* HRI/GEN/1/Rev 8, p 172, para 4.

[39]   Note however that the term 'conformity with the law' is used in Art 37(b) of the CRC concerning the right to liberty. See below **14.17**.

[40]   Nowak, M *UN Covenant on Civil and Political Rights: CCPR Commentary* (1993) p 208 and, p 394.

[41]   Partsch, K *Freedom of Conscience and Expression, and Political Freedoms* in Henking, L (ed) *The International Bill of Rights: The Covenant on Civil and Political Rights* (1981) p 209, pp 232–233.

(ii)   Article 15(2) – 'Necessary in a Democratic Society'

12.18 It has been suggested that to be necessary in a democratic society the restrictions must be 'essential'.[42] The concept of the 'democratic society' for the purposes of Art 15(2) of the CRC implies political freedom and individual rights which reduce or moderate the authority of the State and the existence of appropriate supervisory institutions to monitor respect for human rights.[43]

(iii)   Article 15(2) – Grounds for Restriction

12.19 The grounds upon which restriction of the child's right to freedom of association and peaceful assembly may be permitted under Art 15(2) of the CRC are the interests of national security or public safety, public order (ordre public), the protection of public health or morals or the protection of the rights and freedoms of others.

Interests of National Security or Public Safety and Public Order

12.20 A curfew that restricts the child's right to freedom of association and peaceful assembly to specific hours is likely to breach the child's right under Art 15(1) of the CRC as not falling within the narrow national security, public safety and public order justifications provided by Art 15(2).[44] Note that the term public order cannot be assimilated into public safety although the two concepts are plainly linked.

Protection of Public Health or Morals

12.21 The term 'public morals' describes 'principles which are not always legally enforceable but which are accepted by a great majority of the citizens as general guidelines for their individual and collective behaviour.'[45] In considering the scope of limitations imposed on the child's right to freedom of association and peaceful assembly on the grounds of protecting morals it should be remembered that as the concept of morals derives from many social, philosophical and religious traditions, limitations on the freedom of association and peaceful assembly for the purpose of protecting morals must be based on principles not deriving exclusively from a single tradition.[46]

---

[42]   Kiss, A *Permissible Limitations on Rights* in Henking, L (ed) *The International Bill of Rights: The Covenant on Civil and Political Rights* (1981) p 290, p 308.

[43]   Kiss, A *Permissible Limitations on Rights* in Henking, L (ed) *The International Bill of Rights: The Covenant on Civil and Political Rights* (1981) p 290, p 304.

[44]   See Newell, P and Hodgkin, R *Implementation Handbook for the Convention on the Rights of the Child* (2008) 3rd edn, UNICEF, p 200 and Panama CRC/C/15/Add.233, paras 31 and 32.

[45]   Kiss, A *Permissible Limitations on Rights* in Henkin, L (ed) *The International Bill of Rights: The Covenant on Civil and Political Rights* (1981), pp 290–310, p 304. See also *Reno v American Civil Liberties Union* 521 US 844 (1997), US Sup Ct; *Ashcroft v ACLU* 535 US 564 (2002), US Sup Ct; *Curtis v Minister of Safety* (1996) BHRC 541, Const Ct of South Africa; *De Reuck v DPP* [2004] 4 LRC 72, Const Ct of South Africa.

[46]   See Human Rights Committee General Comment No 22 *Aricle 18 (Freedom of Thought, Conscience and Religion* HRI/GEN/1/Rev.8, p 196, para 8. Note that the concept of margin of appreciation will be important when considering the issue of 'morals' under the ECHR. Note that the concept of the margin of appreciation will be important in considering the issue of 'morals' under the ECHR. In *A, B and C v Ireland* (2010) Application No 25579/05, para 222 the European Court of Human Rights stated that 'The Court recalls that it is not possible to find in the legal and social orders of the Contracting States a uniform European conception of morals including on the question of when life begins. By reason of their 'direct and continuous contact with the vital forces of their countries', State authorities are in principle in a better position than the international judge to give an opinion on the 'exact content of the requirements of morals' in their country, as well as on the necessity of a restriction intended to meet them.'

Protection of the Rights and Freedoms of Others

12.22 The term 'the rights and reputations of others' does not indicate which rights of others may be protected at the expense of the freedoms of association and peaceful assembly in question but Henkin suggests that whilst the term might well authorise States to choose between the rights that are enshrined in the CRC, it will not permit States to prefer other rights and interests which it might create by its own law for its own purposes.[47]

Child's Right Freedom of Association and Peaceful Assembly under the ECHR

ECHR, Art 11 – Freedom of Association and Peaceful Assembly

12.23 Article 11 of the ECHR provides as follows in respect of the right to freedom of peaceful assembly and freedom of association:

> '1. Everyone has the right to freedom of peaceful assembly and to freedom of association with others, including the right to form and to join trade unions for the protection of his interests.
>
> 2. No restrictions shall be placed on the exercise of these rights other than such as are prescribed by law and are necessary in a democratic society in the interests of national security or public safety, for the prevention of disorder or crime, for the protection of health or morals or for the protection of the rights and freedoms of others. This article shall not prevent the imposition of lawful restrictions on the exercise of these rights by members of the armed forces, of the police or or of the administration of the State.'

12.24 The protection of personal opinions including political beliefs is one of the objectives of the right to freedom of peaceful assembly and to freedom of association under Art 11 of the ECHR.[48] As such, the European institutions have often subsumed the right to freedom of expression within the right to freedom of peaceful assembly and association under Art 11(1) of the ECHR.[49]

ECHR, Art 11(1) – Positive Obligations

12.25 Article 11(1) of the ECHR will encompass a positive duty on the State to ensure freedom of association and freedom of peaceful assembly, even as between individuals.[50] In *Plattform Arzte für das Leben v Austria*[51] the European Commission held that:

> 'Genuine, effective freedom of peaceful assembly cannot … be reduced to a mere duty on the part of the State not to interfere: a purely negative conception would not be compatible with the object and purpose of Article 11. Like Article 8, Article 11 sometimes requires positive measures to be taken, even in the sphere of relations between individuals, if need be.'

---

[47] Henkin, L *Introduction* in Henkin, L (ed) *The International Bill of Rights: The Covenant on Civil and Political Rights* (1981), pp 1–31, p 31.

[48] *Vogt v Germany* (1995) 21 EHRR 205 and *Refah Partisi v Turkey* (2002) 35 EHRR 56.

[49] See for example the decisions of the European Commission in *Rassemblement Jurrasien Unité v Switzerland* 17 DR 93 (1979) and *Plattform Arzte für das Leben v Austria* 44 DR 65 (1985).

[50] *Plattform Arzte für ds Leben v Austria* 44 DR 65 (1985).

[51] 44 DR 65 (1985).

ECHR, Art 11(1) – Ambit

(i)   ECHR, Art 11(1) – Right to Freedom of Peaceful Assembly

12.26 The right to freedom of peaceful assembly under Art 11(1) of the ECHR encompasses fixed meetings and assemblies as well as processions and marches[52] both in private and in public.[53] State authorities must show a certain degree of tolerance towards peaceful gatherings in order that the Art 11(1) right to freedom of peaceful assembly is not deprived of its substance.[54]

12.27 The word 'everyone' in Art 11(1) demonstrates that the freedom of peaceful assembly applies also to children. In *Christian Democratic People's Party v Moldova*[55] the European Court of Human Rights considered a claim that the prohibition of peaceful demonstrations by adults and children against the decision of the Moldovan government to make Russian language tuition compulsory for children breached Art 11(1) of the ECHR. One of the grounds relied on by the Moldovan Government in prohibiting the demonstration was the involvement of children in the same. In finding a violation of Art 11(1) the court stated:

> 'Where the presence of children is concerned, the Court notes that it has not been established by the domestic courts that they were there as a result of any action or policy on the part of the applicant party. Since the gatherings were held in a public place anyone, including children, could attend. Moreover, in the Court's view, it was rather a matter of personal choice for the parents to decide whether to allow their children to attend those gatherings and it would appear to be contrary to the parents' and children's freedom of assembly to prevent them from attending such events which, it must be recalled, were to protest against government policy on schooling. Accordingly, the Court is not satisfied that this reason was relevant and sufficient.'

12.28 As noted above, peaceful assembly for social and cultural purposes, as opposed to for political purposes, is also important for children and is clearly encompassed with Art 22 of the ICCPR[56] and Art 15(1) of the CRC.[57] However, in *Anderson v United Kingdom*[58] the European Court of Human Rights rejected as inadmissible a claim for breach of Art 11(1) by a group of nine young people who had been excluded from a shopping centre on the grounds of their alleged misconduct and disorderly behaviour, holding that:

> 'The right to freedom of assembly is one of the foundations of a democratic society and should not be interpreted restrictively. The right is applicable to private meetings and to meetings in public thoroughfares, marches and sit-ins. There is, however, no indication ... that freedom of assembly is intended to guarantee a right to pass and re-pass in public places, or to assemble for purely social purposes anywhere one wishes. Freedom of

---

52   *Christians Against Racism and Fascism v United Kingdom* 21 DR 148 (1980).
53   *Rassemblement Jurrasien Unité v Switzerland* 17 DR 93 (1979).
54   *Saya v Turkey* (2008) Application 4327/02 (unreported), para 46 ('In the Court's view, where demonstrators do not engage in acts of violence, it is important for the public authorities to show a certain degree of tolerance towards peaceful gatherings if the freedom of assembly guaranteed by Article 11 of the Convention is not to be deprived of all substance').
55   (2006) 45 EHRR 13.
56   Partsch, K *Freedom of Conscience and Expression, and Political Freedoms* in Henking, L (ed) *The International Bill of Rights: The Covenant on Civil and Political Rights* (1981) p 209, p 235. But see also the decision of the European Court of Human Rights in *Anderson v United Kingdom* [1998] EHRR CD 172 at **12.29** below.
57   Newell, P and Hodgkin, R *Implementation Handbook for the Convention on the Rights of the Child* (2008) 3rd edn, UNICEF, p 198.
58   [1998] EHRR CD 172.

association, too, has been described as a right for individuals to associate 'in order to attain various ends. Moreover, the Commission notes that Protocol No 4 to the Convention, Article 2 of which guarantees the right to liberty of movement within the territory of a State, has not been ratified by the United Kingdom. The Commission notes that the applicants had no history of using the Centre for any form of organised assembly or association. The Commission thus finds no indication in the present case that the exclusion of the applicants from the Centre interfered with their rights under Article 11 of the Convention.'

12.29   The interpretation of the scope of the right to freedom of peaceful assembly adopted in *Anderson v United Kingdom*[59] excluding a right to peaceful assembly by children for social purposes appears narrow when one considers that the ECHR protects the right of the child to establish and develop relationships with other human beings,[60] and the child's right to develop without outside interference his or her personality through relations with other human beings[61] as elements of the child's right to respect for private life under Art 8(1) of the ECHR. Van Bueren contends that it is arguable that the national courts are giving insufficient weight to the importance of the right to freedom of peaceful assembly for children *qua* children.[62] The same can be said of the decision of the European Court of Human Rights in *Anderson v United Kingdom*, especially when one considers that Art 11(1) of the ECHR must be interpreted in accordance with the provisions of Art 15(1) of the CRC and Art 22 of the ICCPR.[63]

(ii)   ECHR, Art 11(1) – Right to Freedom of Association

12.30   For the purpose of the ECHR the word 'association' encompasses the concept of a voluntary grouping of people for a common goal.[64] In *Association X v Sweden*[65] the European Commission stated that the right to freedom of association under Art 11(1) protects the 'general capacity for the citizens to join without interference by the state in association in order to attain various ends'. The European Court's definition of 'association' in Art 11(1) should take precedence over definitions advanced by the State when considering the application of Art 11(1) of the ECHR.[66] The definition of 'association' will include trade unions[67] and political parties. In *Christian Democratic People's Party v Moldova*[68] the European Court of Human Rights observed that:

> 'The Court reiterates that, notwithstanding its autonomous role and particular sphere of application, Article 11 must also be considered in the light of Article 10. The protection of opinions and the freedom to express them is one of the objectives of the freedoms of assembly and association as enshrined in Article 11. That applies all the more in relation to political parties in view of their essential role in ensuring pluralism and the proper functioning of democracy.'

---

[59]   [1998] EHRR CD 172.

[60]   *Niemietz v Germany* (1993) 16 EHRR 97 and see **9.25 et seq** above.

[61]   *Botta v Italy* (1998) 26 EHRR 97 and *Von Hanover v Germany* (2005) 40 EHRR 1. See **9.25 et seq** above.

[62]   Van Bueren, G *Child Rights in Europe* (2007) Council of Europe Publishing, p 88.

[63]   See **3.43–3.46** above.

[64]   *Young, James and Webster v United Kingdom* (1982) 3 EHRR 38.

[65]   9 DR 1 (1978).

[66]   *Chassagnou v France* (1999) 26 EHRR 615, para 100 ('If Contracting States were able, at their discretion, by classifying an association as 'public' or 'para-administrative', to remove it from the scope of Article 11, that would give them such latitude that it might lead to results incompatible with the object and purpose of the Convention, which is to protect rights that are not theoretical or illusory but practical and effective').

[67]   The law on the right to freedom of association as it relates to trade unions and labour laws is extensive and is beyond the scope of this work. For an excellent summary in the context of human rights see Lord Lester QC, Lord Pannick QC and Herberg, J *Human Rights Law and Practice* (2009) 3rd edn, LexisNexis, pp 553 et seq.

[68]   (2006) 45 EHRR 13 and see *United Communist Party of Turkey v Turkey* (1998) 26 EHRR 121. But see also *Refah Partisi v Turkey* (2002) 35 EHRR 56.

12.31 There is implied in Art 11(1) of the ECHR the negative right not to associate, in part by reason of the protection of personal opinions guaranteed by Arts 9 and 10 of the ECHR.[69] The cases of *Sørensen v Denmark* and *Rassmussen v Denmark*[70] do not exclude in principle of equality of protection for the positive and negative rights to freedom of association under Art 11(1). The requirement to join a professional association in order to practice a profession does not violate Art 11(1) of the ECHR.[71] There is no right for an individual to join an existing association and no obligation on an existing association to permit a person to remain a member of the association.[72]

12.32 As with the right to freedom of assembly, the right to freedom of association has been held not to concern the right of individuals simply to share the company of others.[73] Neither does the right to freedom of association encompass recreational activities with others. In *R (Countryside Alliance) v Attorney General*[74] Lord Hope of Craighead held that:

> 'The essence of the freedom of assembly that art 11 guarantees is that it is a fundamental right in a democracy and, like the right to freedom of expression, is one of the foundations of such a society. The situations to which it applies must relate to activities that are of that character, of which the right to form and join a trade union which art 11 refers to is an example. The purpose of the activity provides the key to its application. It covers meetings in private as well as in public, but it does not guarantee a right to assemble for purely social purposes. The right of assembly that the claimants seek to assert is really no more than a right to gather together for pleasure and recreation ... I agree with Lord Bingham that, where the activity which brings people together is prohibited, the effect is in reality to restrict their right to assemble. But the claimants' position is no different from that of any other people who wish to assemble with others in a public place for sporting or recreational purposes. It falls well short of the kind of assembly whose protection is fundamental to the proper functioning of a modern democracy and is, for that reason, guaranteed by art 11. No decision of the Strasbourg court has gone that far.'

ECHR, Art 11(2) – Ambit

(i) Restrictions

12.33 The right to freedom of peaceful assembly and peaceful association under Art 11(1) of the ECHR may only be restricted on the grounds set out in Art 11(2) which provides as follows:

> '2. No restrictions shall be placed on the exercise of these rights other than such as are prescribed by law and are necessary in a democratic society in the interests of national security or public safety, for the prevention of disorder or crime, for the protection of health or morals or for the protection of the rights and freedoms of others. This article shall not prevent the imposition of lawful restrictions on the exercise of these rights by members of the armed forces, of the police or of the administration of the State.'

---

69 *Sigurour A Sigurjonnson v Iceland* (1993) 16 EHRR 462, para 35 and *Sørensen v Denmark; Rassmussen v Denmark* (2008) 46 EHRR 29.
70 (2008) 46 EHRR 29, para 56.
71 *Le Compte, Van Leuven and De Meyere v Beligum* (1981) 4 EHRR 1; *A v Spain* 66 DR 1988 (1990) and see *Sigurour A Sigurjonnson v Iceland* (1993) 16 EHRR 462.
72 *Cheall v United Kingdom* 42 DR 178 (1985) at 185 and A*SLEF v United Kingdom* (2007) 45 EHRR 34. See also *Damyanti v Union* [1971] 3 SCR 840 (Sup Ct of India).
73 *McFeeley v United Kingdom* 20 DR 44 (1980). See also *Anderson v United Kingdom* [1998] EHRR CD 172 discussed at **12.29** above.
74 [2007] UKHL 52, [2008] 1 AC 719. See also *Whaley v Lord Advocate* [2007] UKHL 53, 2008 SC (HL) 107.

12.34 In *Christian Democratic People's Party v Moldova (No 2)*[75] the European Court of Human Rights commented on the task of determining whether a particular action meets the imperatives of Art 11 of the ECHR as follows:

> 'When carrying out its scrutiny under Article 11 the Court's task is not to substitute its own view for that of the relevant national authorities but rather to review under Article 11 the decisions they have delivered in the exercise of their discretion. This does not mean that it has to confine itself to ascertaining whether the respondent State exercised its discretion reasonably, carefully and in good faith; it must look at the interference complained of in the light of the case as a whole and determine whether it was 'proportionate to the legitimate aim pursued' and whether the reasons adduced by the national authorities to justify it are 'relevant and sufficient'. In so doing, the Court has to satisfy itself that the national authorities applied standards which were in conformity with the principles embodied in Article 11 and, moreover, that they based their decisions on an acceptable assessment of the relevant facts.'[76]

(ii)   Prescribed by Law

12.35 Where those seeking to assemble or associate are not able to foresee all the legal consequences which might ensue if they continue to assemble or associate such a lack of foreseeability may in itself be a sufficient basis for the conclusion that the impugned measures are not prescribed by law for the purposes of Art 11(2) of the ECHR.[77]

(iii)   Necessary in a Democratic Society

12.36 The adjective 'necessary' is not synonymous with 'indispensable', neither has it the flexibility of such expressions as 'admissible', 'ordinary', 'reasonable' or 'desirable'. Nevertheless, it is for the national authorities to make the initial assessment of the reality of the pressing social need implied by the notion of 'necessity'.[78] In considering 'necessity' it is important to remember that notwithstanding its autonomous role and particular sphere of application, Art 11 must also be considered in the light of Art 10 and that the protection of opinions and the freedom to express them is one of the objectives of the freedoms of assembly and association as enshrined in Art 11 of the ECHR.[79] The European Court of Human Rights has emphasised that the only type of necessity capable of justifying an interference with the rights enshrined in Arts 8, 9, 10 and 11 of the ECHR is one which originates from 'democratic society', that democracy appears to be the only political model contemplated by the ECHR and, accordingly, the only one compatible with it.[80] In *Christian Democratic People's Party v Moldova*

---

[75]   (No 2) (2010) Application 25196/04 (unreported) and see *United Communist Party of Turkey and Others v Turkey* (1998) 26 EHRR 121, para 47 ('When the Court carries out its scrutiny, its task is not to substitute its own view for that of the relevant national authorities but rather to review under Article 11 the decisions they delivered in the exercise of their discretion. This does not mean that it has to confine itself to ascertaining whether the respondent State exercised its discretion reasonably, carefully and in good faith; it must look at the interference complained of in the light of the case as a whole and determine whether it was 'proportionate to the legitimate aim pursued' and whether the reasons adduced by the national authorities to justify it are 'relevant and sufficient'. In so doing, the Court has to satisfy itself that the national authorities applied standards which were in conformity with the principles embodied in Article 11 and, moreover, that they based their decisions on an acceptable assessment of the relevant facts').

[76]   In *United Communist Party of Turkey and Others v Turkey* (1998) 26 EHRR 121 the European Court of Human Rights emphasised that in relation to political parties the exceptions set out in Art 11(2) of the ECHR will be construed strictly with only convincing and compelling reasons being capable of justifying restrictions on such parties.

[77]   *Christian Democratic People's Party v Moldova* (2006) 45 EHRR 13, para 53.

[78]   *Handyside v UK* (1979) 1 EHRR 737.

[79]   *United Communist Party of Turkey and Others v Turkey* (1998) 26 EHRR 121.

[80]   *United Communist Party of Turkey and Others v Turkey* (1998) 26 EHRR 121.

(No 2)[81] the European Court of Human Rights stated as follows in relation to the meaning of 'democratic society' in the ECHR:

'Referring to the hallmarks of a 'democratic society', the Court has attached particular importance to pluralism, tolerance and broadmindedness. In that context, it has held that although individual interests must on occasion be subordinated to those of a group, democracy does not simply mean that the views of the majority must always prevail: a balance must be achieved which ensures the fair and proper treatment of minorities and avoids any abuse of a dominant position.'

12.37 The examples of restrictions necessary in a democratic society given in Art 11(2) of the ECHR are the interests of national security or public safety, the prevention of disorder or crime, the protection of health or morals and the protection of the rights and freedoms of others. Whilst each of these may be relevant to children, the key exceptions under Art 11(2) of the ECHR most commonly touching and concerning children will be public safety, the prevention of disorder or crime, the protection of health or morals and the protection of the rights and freedoms of others.

12.38 Note that term 'morals' describes 'principles which are not always legally enforceable but which are accepted by a great majority of the citizens as general guidelines for their individual and collective behaviour.'[82] In considering the scope of limitations imposed on the child's right to freedom of peaceful assembly and association on the grounds of protecting morals it should be remembered that as the concept of morals derives from many social, philosophical and religious traditions, limitations on the freedom of expression for the purpose of protecting morals must be based on principles not deriving exclusively from a single tradition.[83] The term 'the rights and reputations of others' does not indicate which rights of others may be protected at the expense of the freedoms in question but Henkin suggests that whilst the term might well authorise States to choose between rights enshrined in the CRC it will not permit States to prefer other rights and interests which it might create by its own law for its own purposes.[84]

ECHR, Art 11(2) – Application

(i) **Restrictions on the Right to Freedom of Peaceful Assembly**

12.39 Once a foreseeable danger of disorder arising out of an assembly is identified the State has a wide margin of appreciation as to the measures it adopts to forestall that disorder.[85] However, absent evidence that the assembly is likely to lead to violence or serious public disorder, sweeping measures by the State aimed at preventing assembly and the expression of views are unlawful notwithstanding that those views may be shocking or unacceptable.[86] However, where such views are contrary to the text and spirit of the ECHR, Art 17 of the ECHR may prevent reliance on the Art 11(1) right to

---

[81] (No 2) (2010) Application 25196/04 (unreported).

[82] Kiss, A *Permissible Limitations on Rights* in Henkin, L (ed) *The International Bill of Rights: The Covenant on Civil and Political Rights* (1981), pp 290–310, p 304. See also *Reno v American Civil Liberties Union* 521 US 844 (1997) US Sup Ct; *Ashcroft v ACLU* 535 US 564 (2002) US Sup Ct; *Curtis v Minister of Safety* (1996) BHRC 541, Const Ct of South Africa; *De Reuck v DPP* [2004] 4 LRC 72, Const Ct of South Africa.

[83] See Human Rights Committee General Comment No 22 *Art 18 (Freedom of Thought, Conscience and Religion)* HRI/GEN/1/Rev.8, p 196, para 8.

[84] Henkin, L *Introduction* in Henkin, L (ed) *The International Bill of Rights: The Covenant on Civil and Political Rights* (1981), pp 1–31, p 31.

[85] *Rassamblement Jurrasien Unité v Switzerland* 17 DR 93 (1979) and see *Christians Against Racism and Fascism v United Kingdom* 21 DR 148 (1980) and *Ezelin v France* (1991) 14 EHRR 362.

[86] *Stankov v Bulgaria* (2001) Application No 29221/95 (unreported).

peaceful assembly in order to protect them.[87] Further, given the close link between Art 11(1) and Art 10(1) of the ECHR it is likely that the authorities on the prohibition of freedom of expression in respect of opinions which undermine the values of the ECHR will be also be relevant.[88] The court must have cogent evidence to support reasons for preventing peaceful assembly or association.[89] The prevention of an assembly at a time the issue that is the subject of the assembly is relevant can amount to an interference in the right to freedom of peaceful assembly.[90] However, the right to hold a spontaneous assembly will override the obligation to give prior notice[91] only in circumstances where an immediate response to an event is warranted in the form of peaceful assembly.[92]

(ii)   Restrictions on the Right to Freedom of Association

12.40 In *Vogt v Germany*[93] the European Court of Human Rights considered the dismissal of teacher whose capabilities and work were described as entirely satisfactory and who was held in high regard by her pupils and their parents and by her colleagues but who refused to dissociate himself from the German Communist Party. In finding a breach of Art 11(1) the court held that the dismissal was disproportionate to the legitimate aim pursued, namely protecting national security, preventing disorder and protecting the rights of others.

12.41 The risk of causing tension within society does not of itself justify an interference with the right to freedom of association.[94] However, Art 17 of the ECHR[95] may prevent the application of the Art 11(1) right to freedom of association where such an association would undermine the values of the ECHR itself. In *WP and others v Poland*[96] the Court held in relation to the prohibition by the State of the formation of a right wing association entitled 'The National and Patriotic Association of Polish Victims of Bolshevism and Zionism' that:

> '... the Court notes that the memorandum of association of the National and Patriotic Association of Polish Victims of Bolshevism and Zionism included in points 6, 12 and 15 statements alleging the persecution of Poles by the Jewish minority and the existence of inequality between them. The Court agrees with the Government that these ideas can be seen as reviving anti-Semitism. The applicants' racist attitudes also transpire from the anti-Semitic tenor of some of their submissions made before the Court. It is therefore satisfied that the evidence in the present case justifies the need to bring Article 17 into play. The applicants essentially seek to employ Article 11 as a basis under the Convention for a

---

[87]   See *WP and others v Poland* (2005) 40 EHRR SE1 and **12.41** below.
[88]   See **11.53–11.56** above.
[89]   *Makhmudov v Russia* (2008) 46 EHRR 37.
[90]   *Bączkowski v Poland* (2007) Application No 1543/06 (unreported).
[91]   *Bukta v Hungary* (2007) Application No 25691/04 (unreported).
[92]   *Molnár v Hungary* (2008) Application No 22592/02 (unreported).
[93]   (1995) 21 EHRR 205.
[94]   *Ouranio Toxo v Greece* (2007) 45 EHRR 277, para 37 ('... it is incumbent upon public authorities to guarantee the proper functioning of an association or political party, even when they annoy or give offence to persons opposed to the lawful ideas or claims that they are seeking to promote. Their members must be able to hold meetings without having to fear that they will be subjected to physical violence by their opponents. Such a fear would be liable to deter other associations or political parties from openly expressing their opinions on highly controversial issues affecting the community. In a democracy the right to counter-demonstrate cannot extend to inhibiting the exercise of the right of association').
[95]   Article 17 of the ECHR provides that 'Nothing in this Convention may be interpreted as implying for any State, group or person any right to engage in any activity or perform any act aimed at the destruction of any of the rights and freedoms set forth herein or at their limitation to a greater extent than is provided for in the Convention.'
[96]   (2005) 40 EHRR SE1.

right to engage in activities which are contrary to the text and spirit of the Convention and which right, if granted, would contribute to the destruction of the rights and freedoms set forth in the Convention. Consequently, the Court finds that, by reason of the provisions of Article 17 of the Convention, the applicants cannot rely on Article 11 of the Convention to challenge the prohibition of the formation of the National and Patriotic Association of Polish Victims of Bolshevism and Zionism.'

Child's Right to Freedom of Association and Peaceful Assembly under European Union Law

12.42 Article 12 of the European Charter of Fundamental Rights provides as follows in relation to the right to freedom of peaceful assembly and freedom of association:

'1. Everyone has the right to freedom of peaceful assembly and to freedom of association at all levels, in particular in political, trade union and civic matters, which implies the right of everyone to form and to join trade unions for the protection of his or her interests.

2. Political parties at Union level contribute to expressing the political will of the citizens of the Union.'

In accordance with Art 52(3) of the European Charter,[97] the meaning and scope of the rights under Art 12 is the same as that under the corresponding Art 11 of the ECHR and its related protocols. As such, the limitations that are permitted by Art 11(2) of the ECHR will be permitted in respect of the rights under Art 12 of the Charter.

Child's Right to Freedom of Association and Peaceful Assembly under other Regional Instruments

American Convention on Human Rights

ACHR Art 15 – Freedom of Peaceful Assembly

12.43 Article 15 of the American Convention on Human Rights stipulates as follows in respect of the right to freedom of peaceful assembly:

'The right of peaceful assembly, without arms, is recognised. No restrictions may be placed on the exercise of this right other than those imposed in conformity with the law and necessary in a democratic society in the interest of national security, public safety or public order, or to protect public health or morals or the rights or freedom of others.'[98]

12.44 The Inter-American Commission on Human Rights has held that the right of assembly ensures that persons are able to meet freely in private places with the consent of their owners, public places, and workplaces and the right to participate in the organisation and conduct of a meeting or demonstration and to take part in it.[99]

---

[97] Article 52(3) of the Charter provides that 'Insofar as this Charter contains rights which correspond to rights guaranteed by the Convention for the Protection of Human Rights and Fundamental Freedoms, the meaning and scope of those rights shall be the same as those laid down by the said Convention. This provision shall not prevent Union law providing more extensive protection.'

[98] See also Art XXI of the American Declaration of the Rights and Duties of Man ('Every person has the right to assemble peaceably with others in a formal public meeting or an informal gathering, in connection with matters of common interest of any nature').

[99] *Matia Nicolasa García v Mexico* (2007) Report No 53/07 and see IACHR, *Report on the Situation of Human Rights Defenders in the Americas,* OEA/Ser.L/V/II.124 Doc-5 rev. 1 March 7, 2006, para 53. See also the decision of the Inter-American Commission in *Oscar Elías Biscet et al v Cuba* (2006) Report No 67/06 as to

ACHR Art 16 – Freedom of Association

12.45 Article 16 of the American Convention on Human Rights provides as follows in relation to the right to freedom of association:

> '1. Everyone has the right to associate freely for ideological, religious, political, economic, labor, social, cultural, sports, or other purposes.
>
> 2. The exercise of this right shall be subject only to such restrictions established by law as may be necessary in a democratic society, in the interest of national security, public safety or public order, or to protect public health or morals or the rights and freedoms of others.
>
> 3. The provisions of this article do not bar the imposition of legal restrictions, including even deprivation of the exercise of the right of association, on members of the armed forces and the police.'[100]

12.46 The Inter-American Commission on Human Rights has held that freedom of association includes protection against arbitrary interference by the State when persons decide to associate with others.[101]

12.47 Note that the scope of the express terms of Art 16(1) of the American Convention on Human Rights are much broader than the interpretation applied by the European Court of Human Rights in determining the scope of the right to freedom of association under Art 11(1) of the ECHR.[102] In particular, the breadth of the provision in Art 16(1) for freedom of association for 'social, cultural and sports or other purposes' appears to allow greater weight to be accorded to the importance of the right to freedom of peaceful assembly and association for children *qua* children in appropriate cases.[103] As such, the provisions of Art 16(1) of the AMCHR may permit more broadly construed decisions concerning the scope of the child's right to freedom of peaceful assembly and association on the facts of such European cases as *Anderson v United Kingdom*.[104]

Ibero-American Convention on the Rights of Youth

12.48 Article 18 of the Ibero-American Convention on the Rights of Youth provides as follows in respect of the right to freedom of expression, assembly and association:

---

the ambit of the right of assembly under Art XXI of the American Declaration of the Rights and Duties of Man ('The right of assembly [in the American Declaration of the Rights and Duties of Man], for its part, is every person's right to assemble in groups, either publicly or privately, to discuss or defend his or her ideas').

[100] See also Art XXII of the American Declaration of the Rights and Duties of Man ('E very person has the right to associate with others to promote, exercise and protect his legitimate interests of a political, economic, religious, social, cultural, professional, labor union or other nature').

[101] *Matia Nicolasa García v Mexico* (2007) Report No 53/07 and see IACHR, *Report on the Situation of Human Rights Defenders in the Americas,* OEA/Ser.L/V/II.124 Doc-5 rev. 1 March 7, 2006, para 50; *Report on Terrorism and Human Rights* OEA/Ser.L/V/II.116 Doc. 5 rev. 1 corr. October 22, 2002, para 359. See also the decision of the Inter-American Commission in *Oscar Elias Biscet et al v Cuba* (2006) Report No 67/06 as to the ambit of the right of association under Art XXII of the American Declaration of the Rights and Duties of Man ('The right of association [in the American Declaration of the Rights and Duties of Man] gives the individual the right to associate with whomever he or she chooses, without having the exercise of one's other civil, political, economic and social rights in any way restricted as a consequence of that association. This includes the right to form associations, and the right to join existing associations. It encompasses all facets of life in modern society').

[102] See **12.29** above.

[103] Van Bueren, G *Child Rights in Europe* (2007) Council of Europe Publishing, p 88.

[104] [1998] EHRR CD 172.

'1. Youth have the right to freedom of opinion, expression, assembly and information, to have youth forums at their disposal and create organisations and associations where their problems are analysed and may present proposals of political initiatives before public authorities in charge of attending youth matters, with no kind of interference of limitation.[105]

2. The States Parties undertake to promote such measures as may be necessary to enable them to obtain the existing resources for the financing of their activities, projects and programmes, respecting the independence and autonomy of youth organisations and associations.'

12.49 Article 21 of the Ibero-American Convention on the Rights of Youth concerns the right to participate in politics and provides as follows:

'1. Youth have the right to participation in politics.

2. The States Parties undertake to boost and strengthen social processes which generate forms and guaranties which make the participation of youth from all sectors of society effective in organisations which encourage their inclusion.

3. The States Parties shall promote measures which, in conformity with the inner law of each country, promote and encourage that youth exercise their right to register in political associations, to elect and be elected.

4. The States Parties undertake to promote that governmental and legislative institutions promote the participation of youth in the formulation of policies and laws concerning youth, drawing up the corresponding mechanisms to make effective the analysis and discussion of youth initiatives through their organisations and associations.'[106]

African Charter on the Rights and Welfare of the Child

12.50 Article 8 of the African Charter on the Rights and Welfare of the Child provides as follows in relation to the child's right to freedom of association and freedom of peaceful assembly:

'Every child shall have the right to free association and freedom of peaceful assembly in conformity with the law.'

The African Youth Charter

12.51 The African Youth Charter Art 5 stipulates as follows in respect of the child's right to freedom of association and freedom of peaceful assembly:

'1. Every young person shall have the right to free association and freedom of peaceful assembly in conformity with the law.

2. Young people shall not be compelled to belong to an association.'

---

[105] The inclusion of the right to freedom of expression, freedom of assembly and freedom of association in the same article highlights the close inter-relationship between these rights.

[106] See also Art 35(2) ('The States Parties undertake to promote all legal measures, as well as any other one, aiming the promotion of organisation and consolidation of youth participation structures in the local, regional and national scope, as tools to promote the participation in associations, exchange, cooperation and representation before public authorities').

The African Charter on Human and Peoples' Rights

12.52 Article 10 of the African Charter on Human and Peoples' Rights provides as follows in respect of the right to freedom of association:

> '1. Every individual shall have the right to free association provided that he abides by the law.
>
> 2. Subject to the obligation of solidarity provided for in Art 29 no one may be compelled to join an association.'[107]

12.53 Article 11 of the African Charter on Human and Peoples' Rights provides as follows in respect of the right to freedom of assembly:[108]

> 'Every individual shall have the right to assemble freely with others. The exercise of this right shall be subject only to necessary restrictions provided for by law in particular those enacted in the interest of national security, the safety, health, ethics and rights and freedoms of others.'

Revised Arab Charter on Human Rights

12.54 Article 24 of the Revised Arab Charter on Human Rights provides as follows concerning freedom of association and freedom of peaceful assembly:

> 'Every citizen has the right:
>
> 1. To freely pursue a political activity.
>
> 2. To take part in the conduct of public affairs, directly or through freely chosen representatives.
>
> 3. To stand for election or choose his representatives in free and impartial elections, in conditions of equality among all citizens that guarantee the free expression of his will.
>
> 4. To the opportunity to gain access, on an equal footing with others, to public office in his country in accordance with the principle of equality of opportunity.
>
> 5. To freely form and join associations with others.
>
> 6. To freedom of association and peaceful assembly.
>
> 7. No restrictions may be placed on the exercise of these rights other than those which are prescribed by law and which are necessary in a democratic society in the interests of national security or public safety, public health or morals or the protection of the rights and freedoms of others.'

---

[107] Article 29 of the African Charter on Human and Peoples' Rights imposes duties on the individual to preserve and promote the development of the family and of the State including under Art 29(7) the duty to 'To preserve and strengthen positive African cultural values in his relations with other members of the society, in the spirit of tolerance, dialogue and consultation and, in general, to contribute to the promotion of the moral well being of society.'

[108] Note that Art 11 of the African Charter on Human and Peoples' Rights omits the words 'and peacefully' after the word 'freely'.

Child's Right to Freedom of Association and Peaceful Assembly under Domestic Law

Domestic Law – Freedom of Association and Peaceful Assembly

12.55 Whilst in Lord Hewart CJ observed in *Duncan v Jones*[109] that 'English law does not recognise any special right of public meeting for political or other purposes', Lord Denning famously held as follows in *Hubbard v Pitt*[110] in relation to the right of assembly in domestic law:

> 'Here we have to consider the right to demonstrate and the right to protest on matters of public concern. These are rights which it is in the public interest that individuals should possess; and, indeed, that they should exercise without impediment so long as no wrongful act is done. It is often the only means by which grievances can be brought to the knowledge of those in authority—at any rate with such impact as to gain a remedy. Our history is full of warnings against suppression of these rights. Most notable was the demonstration at St Peter's Fields, Manchester, in 1819 in support of universal suffrage. The magistrates sought to stop it. Hundreds were killed and injured. Afterwards the Court of Common Council of London affirmed 'the undoubted right of Englishmen to assemble together for the purpose of deliberating upon public grievances'. Such is the right of assembly. So also is the right to meet together, to go in procession, to demonstrate and to protest on matters of public concern. As long as all is done peaceably and in good order without threats or incitement to violence or obstruction to traffic, it is not prohibited. I stress the need for peace and good order. Only too often violence may break out: and then it should be firmly handled and severely punished. But, so long as good order is maintained, the right to demonstrate must be preserved.'[111]

Domestic Law – Human Rights Act 1998

12.56 The impact of the Human Rights Act 1998 on the domestic approach to freedom of assembly was considered by the House of Lords in *R (Laporte) v Chief Constable of Gloucestershire*[112] in which case Lord Bingham observed that:

> 'The approach of the English common law to freedom of expression and assembly was hesitant and negative, permitting that which was not prohibited. Thus although Dicey in *An Introduction to the Study of the Law of the Constitution* (10th Edn, 1959), in Pt II on the 'Rule of Law', included Chs VI and VII entitled 'The Right to Freedom of Discussion' and 'The Right of Public Meeting', he wrote of the first (at pp 239–240) that 'At no time has there in England been any proclamation of the right to liberty of thought or to freedom of speech' and of the second (at p 271) that 'it can hardly be said that our constitution knows of such a thing as any specific right of public meeting'. Lord Hewart CJ reflected the then current orthodoxy when he observed in *Duncan v Jones* [1936] 1 KB 218 at 222, [1935] All ER Rep 710 at 712, that 'English law does not recognise any special right of public meeting for political or other purposes'. The 1998 Act, giving domestic effect to arts 10 and 11 of the convention, represented what Sedley LJ in *Redmond-Bate v DPP* (1999) 7 BHRC 375 at 380, aptly called a 'constitutional shift'.'[113]

---

[109]   [1936] 1 KB 218 at 222, [1935] All ER Rep 710 at 712.
[110]   [1976] QB 142 at 178.
[111]   See also *DPP v Jones* [1999] 2 AC 240 per Lord Irvine of Lairg LC ('… the public highway is a public place which the public may enjoy for any reasonable purpose, provided the activity in question does not amount to a public or private nuisance and does not obstruct the highway by unreasonably impeding the primary right of the public to pass and repass; within these qualifications there is a public right of peaceful assembly on the highway') and *Cheall v Association of Professional, Executive, Clerical and Computer Staff* [1983] 2 AC 180, HL.
[112]   [2006] UKHL 55, [2007] 2 AC 105 at 126–127.
[113]   See also *Kay v Commissioner of Police for the Metropolis* [2008] UKHL 69, [2008] 1 WLR 2723 per

Domestic Law – Children and Freedom of Association and Peaceful Assembly

12.57 Developments in the domestic law designed to address alleged anti-social behaviour[114] by children and young people have lead the domestic courts to give limited consideration to the issue of the child's right to freedom of peaceful assembly and association in the domestic context. In *R v Dean Bonness and others*[115] the Court recognised that the application of legislation of this nature would engage Art 11(1) of the ECHR, noting that:

> 'Not only must the court before imposing an order prohibiting the offender from doing something consider that such an order is necessary to protect persons from further anti-social acts by him, the terms of the order must be *proportionate* in the sense that they must be commensurate with the risk to be guarded against. This is particularly important where an order may interfere with an ECHR right protected by the Human Rights Act 1998, e.g articles 8, 10 and 11.'[116]

12.58 However, notwithstanding this recognition the domestic courts have demonstrated very little sympathy for arguments that the powers under the anti-social behaviour legislation should be analysed by reference to the child's right to freedom of peaceful assembly or association under Art 11(1) of the ECHR. In *R (on the application of W) v Commissioner of Police for the Metropolis and Richmond Upon Thames Borough Council (Secretary of State for the Home Department, Interested Party)*[117] the claimant, who was under the age of 16, and lived in a area designated a dispersal area pursuant to the Anti-Social Behaviour Act 2003, s 30(6) sought judicial review of the authorisation by the first defendant police commissioner and the consent given by the second defendant local authority 'granting the police power to forcibly remove persons under 16 from the Richmond area during the curfew hours', which power was granted on the basis that there were reasonable grounds for believing that the presence or behaviour of a group of two or more persons in any public place has resulted or is likely to result in members of the public being intimidated, harassed, alarmed or distressed.[118]

12.59 Reversing the decision of Brookes LJ at first instance and holding that the 2003 Act permitted the police to use reasonable force to compel a child to return to his or her home[119] the Court of Appeal, despite the obvious issues of liberty, privacy, freedom of

---

Lord Carswell at para 55 ('The ability to balance the freedom of citizens to hold protests and processions with the amount of regulation necessary to preserve order and protect the rights of others is one of the distinguishing features of a developed democracy').

[114] See the Crime and Disorder Act 1998, s 1 and the Anti-Social Behaviour Act 2003, s 30. The Home Office in a 2002 publication entitled *'A Guide to Anti-Social Behaviour Orders and Acceptable Behaviour Contracts'* gave examples of the types of anti-social behaviour which the Home Office considered could be tackled by ASBOs. The list (which does not purport to be exhaustive) comprises: harassment of residents or passers-by, verbal abuse, criminal damage, vandalism, noise nuisance, writing graffiti, engaging in threatening behaviour in large groups, racial abuse, smoking or drinking alcohol while under age, substance misuse, joyriding, begging, prostitution, kerb-crawling, throwing missiles, assault and vehicle crime. See also *R (McCann and others) v Crown Court at Manchester* [2002] UKHL 39; [2003] 1 AC 787 Lord Steyn at para 16.

[115] [2005] EWCA Crim 2393, [2006] 1 Cr App R (S) 120.

[116] See also Walsh, C *Curfews: No More Hanging Around* (2002) 2 Youth Justice 70.

[117] [2005] EWHC 1586 (Admin), [2005] 3 All ER 749 (DC); [2006] EWCA Civ 458, [2006] 3 All ER 458 (CA).

[118] Anti-Social Behaviour Act 2003, s 30(3) (Note that Unless there are exceptional circumstances, a reasonable belief for the purposes of this subsection must normally depend, in part at least, on some behaviour of the group which indicates in some way or other harassment, intimidation, the cause of alarm or the cause of distress (*MB v DPP* [2006] EWHC 1888 (Admin), 171 JP 10)).

[119] The power of removal is not to be exercised arbitrarily, constables must have regard to circumstances such as the age of the child, the lateness of the hour, whether the child is vulnerable or distressed, the child's explanation for his or her conduct and continued presence in the area, and the nature of the actual or imminently anticipated anti-social behaviour (*R (on the application of W) v Commissioner of Police for the*

association and discrimination raised by the case, dismissed peremptorily any need to examine the Act from the perspective of the child's ECHR rights, holding:[120]

> '... s 30(6) of the 2003 Act does not have a curfew effect such as W apprehended. It also follows that, since the power was never used to remove W to his place of residence, there was no reasonable or sufficiently serious, real or immediate apprehension by him that the legislation, if it were operated in his case, would infringe any convention right to give him the standing of a victim to challenge the legislation on human rights grounds (see s 7 of the Human Rights Act 1998). The gathering together in the present appeal of sixty or so authorities to that and related ends was largely unnecessary.'

12.60 By contrast to the approach taken by the Court of Appeal in *R (on the application of W) v Commissioner of Police for the Metropolis and Richmond Upon Thames Borough Council (Secretary of State for the Home Department, Interested Party)*[121] commentators argue that the anti-social behaviour provisions are clearly in breach of the child's rights under Art 11(1) of the ECHR and should be analysed by reference to those rights.[122] In light of the decision of the Court of Appeal in *R (W)* that the Anti-Social Behaviour Act 2003, s 30(6) permitted the police to use reasonable force to compel a child to return to his or her home, and thus the issues of liberty, privacy, freedom of association and discrimination raised by the case, this argument has even greater force. The fact that anti-social behaviour proceedings are determined to be civil rather than criminal in nature and thus the fact that the normal protections afforded by a higher standard of proof, strict rules of evidence and the procedural guarantees under Art 6(2) and 6(3) of the ECHR are unavailable reinforces this point.[123] However, perhaps the strongest argument for an approach which analyses the provisions of the 2003 Act and similar legislation by reference to the rights of the child is the fact

---

    Metropolis and Richmond Upon Thames Borough Council (Secretary of State for the Home Department, Interested Party) [2006] EWCA Civ 458, [2006] 3 All ER 458.

[120] In *R (on the application of W) v Commissioner of Police for the Metropolis and Richmond Upon Thames Borough Council (Secretary of State for the Home Department, Interested Party)* [2005] EWHC 1586 (Admin), [2005] 3 All ER 749 Brooke LJ took a similar approach at first instance ('[21] As is now customary on these occasions we were treated by counsel to scholarly expositions of convention law (the European Convention for the Protection of Human Rights and Fundamental Freedoms 1950 (Rome, 4 November 1950, TS 71 (1953); Cmnd 8969)). It is often forgotten, however, that English common lawyers contributed to the drafting of the convention, and the resolution of points of statutory interpretation in cases like this can very often be achieved without any need to refer to Strasbourg law at all. After all, all of us have the right to walk the streets without interference from police constables or CSOs unless they possess common law or statutory powers to stop us') although, unlike the Court of Appeal, he did make an indirect reference to the CRC ('Part 4 of the 2003 Act is intended to give police officers enhanced powers to minimise anti-social behaviour in defined areas. If Parliament were to be taken to have regarded all children found in such areas between the relevant hours as potential sources of anti-social behaviour, a coercive power to remove them might be a natural corollary. However, to attribute such an intention to Parliament would be to assume that it ignored this country's international obligations to treat each child as an autonomous human being').

[121] [2005] EWHC 1586 (Admin), [2005] 3 All ER 749 (Divisional Court) and [2006] EWCA Civ 458, [2006] 3 All ER 458 (Court of Appeal).

[122] See Hollingsworth, K *R (W) v Commissioner of Police of the Metropolis and Another – Interpreting Child Curfews: A Question of Rights?* (2006) 18 Child and Family Law Quarterly 253 on the first instance decision in *R (on the application of W) v Commissioner of Police for the Metropolis and Richmond Upon Thames Borough Council (Secretary of State for the Home Department, Interested Party)* [2005] EWHC 1586 (Admin), [2005] 3 All ER 749 ('The case of *R (W)* provided the opportunity for the courts to make clear that children are 'persons' under the European Convention and, like adults, have rights worthy of protection. The outcome of the case is to be welcomed, but it would have been an even stronger decision if the reasoning had at least explicitly addressed the issue of the rights of children, and made clear that children's Convention rights can only be restricted in a justifiable and proportionate way').

[123] Hammarberg, T *Memorandum by Thomas Hammarberg, Commissioner for Human Rights of the Council of Europe* (2008) CommDH Council of Europe, para 29. Hammarberg comments that this situation leaves the potential recipient of an anti-social behaviour order especially vulnerable to human rights violations.

that the Court of Appeal has demonstrated itself more than willing to analyse the same piece of legislation by reference to the rights of adults under Art 11(1) of the ECHR.[124]

12.61 Fortin notes that it is surprising that not more challenges are mounted to the draconian terms[125] that may be attached to anti-social behaviour orders given the way in which many such terms restrict the family life of the young person involved and may well interfere with their Art 10 and 11 rights in a manner disproportionate to the need to protect the community or may not be 'necessary' as it is possible to prevent repeat behaviour by other means.[126] The legislation clearly creates forensic space for such arguments to be pursued on the basis of proportionality and necessity by reference to the child's rights under the CRC and ECHR, both in relation to the order itself and the terms of that order.[127]

CONCLUSION

12.62 With legislation on the statute books which permits police and local councils to designate a dispersal zone where a member of the public is alarmed, harassed or distressed by a group of two or more children and a blanket power to return home

---

[124] See *R (on the application of Singh and another) v Chief Constable of West Midlands Police* [2006] EWCA Civ 1118, [2007] 2 All ER 297.

[125] See for example *R (on the application of W) v Commissioner of Police for the Metropolis and Richmond Upon Thames Borough Council (Secretary of State for the Home Department, Interested Party)* [2005] EWHC 1586 (Admin), [2005] 3 All ER 749 and *Hills v Chief Constable of Essex Police* [2006] EWHC 2633 (Admin), (2007) 171 JP 14.

[126] Fortin, J *Children's Rights and the Developing Law* (2009) 3rd edn, Cambridge, pp 699–700. See also the approach taken by the Supreme Court of Washington in *City of Seattle v Ronny Gene Pullman* 82 Wash. 2d. 794 in which the court held that a curfew for children under the age 18 which did not make a distinction between conduct calculated to harm and conduct which was essentially innocent constituted the unreasonable exercise of police powers, such curfews in relation to children under the age of 18 being permitted only where they contain specific prohibitions needed to remedy a demonstrable social evil.

[127] See in particular the Crime and Disorder Act 1998, s 1(1)(b) and 1C(b) and see *R v W and anor* [2006] EWCA Crim 686, [2006] 3 All ER 562 at 41: '(1) Proceedings under s 1C of the CDA 1998 are civil in nature, so that hearsay evidence is admissible. But a court must be satisfied to a criminal standard that the Defendant has acted in the anti-social manner alleged. (2) The test of 'necessity' set out in s 1C(2)(b) requires the exercise of judgment or evaluation; it does not require proof beyond reasonable doubt that the order is 'necessary'. (3) The findings of fact giving rise to the making of the order must be recorded by the Court. We regard this as particularly important. (4) The terms of the order made must be precise and capable of being understood by the offender: (5) The conditions in the order must be enforceable in the sense that the conditions should allow a breach to be readily identified and capable of being proved. Therefore the conditions should not impose generic prohibitions, but should identify and prohibit the particular type of anti-social behaviour that gives rise to the necessity of an ASBO. (6) There is power under s 1C(5) of the CDA 1998 to suspend the starting point of an ASBO until an offender has been released from a custodial sentence. However, where custodial sentences in excess of a few months are passed and the offender is liable to be released on licence and is thus subject to recall, the circumstances in which there would be a demonstrable necessity to make a suspended ASBO, to take effect on release, will be limited. But there might be cases where geographical restraints could supplement licence conditions. (7) Because the test for making an ASBO and prohibiting an offender from doing something is one of necessity, each separate order prohibiting a person from doing a specified thing must be necessary to protect persons from anti-social behaviour by the offender. Therefore each order must be specifically fashioned to deal with the offender concerned. The court has to ask: 'is this order necessary to protect persons in any place in England and Wales from further anti-social acts by him'. (8) Not all conditions set out in an ASBO have to run for the full term of the ASBO itself. The test must always be is what is necessary to deal with the particular anti-social behaviour of the offender and what is proportionate in the circumstances: *ibid. Paragraphs 27, 29 and 37*. (9) The order is there to protect others from anti-social behaviour by the offender. Therefore the court should not impose an order which prohibits an offender from committing specified criminal offences if the sentence which could be passed following conviction (or a guilty plea) for the offence should be a sufficient deterrent. (10) It is unlawful to make an ASBO as if it were a further sentence or punishment. An ASBO must therefore not be used merely to increase the sentence of imprisonment that the offender is to receive.'

children under the age of 16 years old between the hours of 9.00pm and 6.00am, there are clearly pressing issues concerning the child's right to freedom of association and peaceful assembly in domestic law.[128] Not the least of these issues is the need to ensure that the domestic courts consider such legislation having regard to the rights of the child under international and regional human rights instruments which are binding on, or have persuasive effect in those courts as they are so clearly prepared to do in cases concerning adults. In addition to the reluctance of the courts to address these issues by reference to the rights of the child, the government appears likewise ambivalent to other threats to the child's right to peaceful assembly, such as the 'Mosquito' anti-social dispersal device, designed specifically to prevent children gathering in public places by regardless of their reasons for assembling.[129] Without greater willingness on the part of the Courts, and indeed lawyers, to address issues touching and concerning children's freedom of peaceful assembly and freedom of association by reference to their established rights the chorus of domestic, regional and international criticism concerning anti-social behaviour legislation and devices such as the 'Mosquito' is unlikely to subside in the near future.[130]

---

[128] See also s 103 of the Education and Inspections Act 2006 which places parents under a legal obligation to ensure that, following school exclusion, their child is not found in a public place during normal school hours without reasonable justification.

[129] CRAE *State of Child Rights in England* (2008), p 15. The 'Mosquito' is an electronic device which emits a high pitched noise designed to be uncomfortable to those under the age of 25 (the sound being largely undetectable to those over the age of 25). See Walsh, C *The Mosquito: A Repellent Response* (2008) 8 Youth Justice 122, pp 123 et seq.

[130] Anti-Social Behaviour legislation has been the subject of repeated criticism by the UK Children's Commissioners (see *UK Children's Commissioners' Report to the UN Committee on the Rights of the Child* (2008) 11 Million, p 33), domestic commentators (see Margo, J and Stevens, A *Make me a Criminal: Preventing Youth Crime* (2008) IPPR, pp 48–49), the European Commissioner for Human Rights (see Gil-Robles, A *Report by Mr Alvaro Gil-Robles, Commisioner for Human Rights on His Visit to the United Kingdom* (2005) CommDH 6 Council of Europe, paras 108–120 and 79–80 and Hammarberg, T *Memorandum by Thomas Hammarberg, Commissioner for Human Rights of the Council of Europe* (2008), paras 29–30) and by international human rights bodies (see Human Rights Committee *Concluding Observations of the Human Rights Committee: United Kingdom of Great Britain and Northern Ireland* (2008) CCPR/C/GBR/6, para 20 and the Committee on the Rights of the Child *Concluding Observations of the Committee on the Rights of the Child: United Kingdom of Great Britain and Northern Ireland* (2008) CRC/C/GBR/ CO/4, paras 34–35). See also the Committee on the Rights of the Child *Concluding Observations of the Committee on the Rights of the Child: United Kingdom of Great Britain and Northern Ireland* (2008) CRC/C/GBR/CO/4, paras 34–35 (criticism of the governments response to the 'Mosquito' device).

Chapter 13

THE CHILD'S RIGHT TO EDUCATION

'Wisdom and knowledge, as well as virtue, diffused generally among the body of the
people being necessary for the preservation of their rights and liberties'

A Constitution or Form of Government for the Commonwealth of Massachusetts
John Adams[1]

INTRODUCTION

13.1   Education is both a core human right of children and fundamental to the
development of society. Article 26 of the Universal Declaration of Human Rights states
that everyone has the right to education.[2] The provision of basic education and literacy
is among the most important contributions that can be made to the development of the
world's children.[3] Education is a key factor in reducing poverty and child labour,
protecting human rights, promoting democracy, peace and tolerance and driving social
and economic development.[4] The Committee on Economic, Social and Cultural Rights
has stated that 'Education is both a human right in itself and an indispensable means of
realising other human rights' and that 'a well-educated, enlightened and active mind,
able to wander freely and widely, is one of the joys and rewards of human existence'.[5] In
Unni Krishnan, J.P., v State of A.P. and Others[6] the Indian Supreme Court held that the
right to education is part of the fundamental right to personal liberty as without
education life cannot be lived with dignity:

---

[1]   In a further appreciation of the importance of education in the promotion and preservation of rights John
      Adams wrote 'I must study politics and war that my sons may have liberty to study mathematics and
      philosophy. My sons ought to study mathematics and philosophy, geography, natural history, naval
      architecture, navigation, commerce, and agriculture in order to give their children a right to study paintings,
      poetry, music, architecture, statuary, tapestry and porcelain' (MCullough, M *John Adams* (2001) Simon &
      Schuster, pp 236–237).
[2]   The full text of Art 26 of the Universal Declaration of Human Rights provides that '1. Everyone has the
      right to education. Education shall be free, at least in the elementary and fundamental stages. Elementary
      education shall be compulsory. Technical and professional education shall be made generally available and
      higher education shall be equally accessible to all on the basis of merit. 2. Education shall be directed to the
      full development of the human personality and to the strengthening of respect for human rights and
      fundamental freedoms. It shall promote understanding, tolerance and friendship among all nations, racial or
      religious groups, and shall further the activities of the United Nations for the maintenance of peace. 3.
      Parents have a prior right to choose the kind of education that shall be given to their children.'
[3]   World Summit for Children (1990), para 13.
[4]   See '*A World Fit for Children*', Report of the Ad Hoc Committee of the Whole of the twenty-seventh special
      session of the General Assembly, 2002, A/S-27/19/Rev.1, para 38. See also *Education in Sub-Saharan Africa*
      (1988) World Bank ('without education development will not occur') and the Plan of Action agreed at the
      World Education Forum at Dakar in 2000, para 6 as endorsed by the UN General Assembly's special session
      on childhood in 2002 '*A World Fit for Children*', Report of the Ad Hoc Committee of the Whole of the
      twenty-seventh special session of the General Assembly, 2002, A/S-27/19/Rev.1, paras 39 and 40 ('Education
      is a fundamental human right. It is the key to sustainable development and peace and stability within and
      among countries, and thus an indispensable means for effective participation in the societies and economies
      of the twenty-first century').
[5]   General Comment No 13 *The Right to Education* HRI/GEN/1/Rev 8, p 71, para 1.
[6]   [1993] 4 LRC 234.

'The right to education flows directly from right to life. The right to life … and the dignity of an individual cannot be assured unless it is accompanied by the right to education … Education is enlightenment. It is the one that lends dignity to a man … Without education, dignity of the individual cannot be assured.'

13.2   Within this context Fortin describes the child's right to education as one of the most important of children's moral and legal rights.[7] In her dissenting judgment in *Ali v Head Teacher and Governors of Lord Grey School*[8] Baroness Hale acknowledged that:

'Education plays an indispensable and fundamental role in a democratic society. Without it, children will not grow up to play their part in the adult world, to exercise their rights but also to meet their responsibilities. That is why children must not be denied their right to the education which the state provides for them.'

13.3   Education is not a static commodity to be considered in isolation from its greater context; it is an ongoing process and holds its own inherent value as a human right.[9] The preamble to the CRC provides that 'the child should be fully prepared to live an individual life in society, and brought up in the spirit of the ideals proclaimed in the Charter of the United Nations, and in particular in the spirit of peace, dignity, tolerance, freedom, equality and solidarity'. Within this context, this chapter begins by examining the nature and purpose of 'education'. The chapter then goes on to consider the extent and application of the child's right to education under the CRC and other international human rights instruments and the ECHR and other regional instruments. The chapter concludes with a summary of the position under domestic law from a rights based perspective.

GENERAL PRINCIPLES

General Principles – Definition of 'Education'

Broad Ambit of Definition

13.4   Within the context of the rights of the child the concept of 'education' is a much broader concept than simply schooling, teaching or instruction.[10] Education starts from birth and begins with adults listening and responding to children.[11] Art 1(a) of the Recommendation Concerning Education for International Understanding, Cooperation and Peace and Education relating to Human Rights and Fundamental Freedoms[12] stipulates that:

'The word 'education' implies the entire process of social life by means of which individuals and social groups learn to develop consciously within, and for the benefit of, the national

---

7   Fortin, J *Children's Rights and the Developing Law* (2009) 3rd edn, Cambridge, p 189.
8   [2006] UKHL 14, [2006] 2 All ER 457, para 81.
9   A Human Rights-based Approach to Education for All: A Framework for the Realisation of Children's Right to Education and Rights within Education', UNICEF/UNESCO (2007), p xii.
10   For example, see the definition proposed in Peiris *Missing the Wood for the Trees* in Fortuyn and de Langen (eds) *Towards the Realisation of Human Rights for Children* (1992) cited in Van Bueren, G *The International Law on the Rights of the Child* (1998) Martinus Nijhoff, p 256 (namely to be 'nurtured psychologically to fit with ease into the world of the future').
11   Alderson, P *Young Children's Rights* (2008) 2nd edn, JKP, p 39. See also Art 5 of the non-binding 1990 World Declaration on Education for All (the 'Jomtien Declaration') which states *inter alia* that: 'Learning begins at birth. This calls for early childhood care and initial education. These can be provided through arrangements involving families, communities, or institutional programmes, as appropriate.'
12   (1974) UNESCO Eighteenth Session.

and international communities, the whole of their personal capacities, attitudes, aptitudes and knowledge. This process is not limited to any specific activities.'[13]

13.5 In its General Comment No 1 *The Aims of Education* the Committee on the Rights of the Child articulated a similarly broad definition of 'education' as follows:[14]

'The education to which every child has a right is one designed to provide the child with life skills, to strengthen the child's capacity to enjoy the full range of human rights and to promote a culture which is infused by appropriate human rights values. The goal is to empower the child by developing his or her skills, learning and other capacities, human dignity, self-esteem and self-confidence. 'Education' in this context goes far beyond formal schooling to embrace the broad range of life experiences and learning processes which enable children, individually and collectively, to develop their personalities, talents and abilities and to live a full and satisfying life within society.'

13.6 Likewise, in examining the concept of 'education', the European Court of Human Rights has identified a difference between instruction and education. In *Campbell and Cosans v United Kingdom*[15] the Court distinguished instruction from education, holding that education comprised a much broader canvass, namely:

'... the whole process whereby in any society adults endeavour to transmit their beliefs, culture and other values to the young, where as teaching or instruction refers in particular to the transmission of knowledge and to intellectual development.'[16]

'Basic Education'

13.7 The Plan of Action agreed in 2000 at the World Education Forum at Dakar[17] arrived at a definition of 'basic education' as follows:

'Basic education allows personal development, intellectual autonomy, integration into professional life and participation in the development of the society in the context of democracy. In order to achieve these aims, basic education must lead to the acquisition of:

(a) key skills used as personal development tools and, later on, as a basis for lifelong learning;

(b) initial vocational guidance;

(c) the knowledge, values and abilities that are needed for individual development, and for the exercise of participatory and responsible citizenship in a democracy.'

---

[13] See also Art 1(1) of the non-binding 1990 World Declaration on Education for All (the 'Jomtien Declaration') which states that 'Every person – child, youth and adult – shall be able to benefit from educational opportunities designed to meet his basic learning needs. These needs comprise both essential learning tools (such as literacy, oral expression, numeracy, and problem solving) and the basic learning content (such as knowledge, skills, values, and attitudes) required by human beings to be able to survive, to develop their full capacities, to live and work in dignity, to improve the quality of their lives, to make informed decisions, and to continue learning'.

[14] Committee on the Rights of the Child General Comment No 1 *The Aims of Education* HRI/GEN/1/Rev 8, p 349, para 2.

[15] (1980) 3 EHRR 531.

[16] See also *Pierce v Society of Sisters* 268 US 510 (1925), US Sup Ct ('The fundamental theory of liberty upon which all governments in this Union repose excludes any general power of the State to standardise its children by forcing them to accept instruction from public teachers only. The child is not the mere creature of the State; those who nurture him and direct his destiny have the right, coupled with the high duty, to recognise and prepare him for additional obligations').

[17] Endorsed by the UN General Assembly's special session on childhood in 2002 '*A World Fit for Children*', Report of the Ad Hoc Committee of the Whole of the twenty-seventh special session of the General Assembly, 2002, A/S-27/19/Rev.1, paras 39 and 40.

General Principles – The Purpose and Objectives of Education

UN Human Rights Framework

13.8   Within the context of the broad definition given to 'education' the purpose and objectives of 'education' are defined in similarly broad terms. Article 26(2) of the Universal Declaration of Human Rights provides that:

> 'Education shall be directed to the full development of the human personality and to the strengthening of respect for human rights and fundamental freedoms. It shall promote understanding, tolerance and friendship among all nations, racial or religious groups, and shall further the activities of the United Nations for the maintenance of peace.'

13.9   The scope of the purpose and objectives of education was expanded in Art 13(1) of the International Covenant on Economic, Social and Cultural Rights by the addition of the twin objects of developing the sense of the dignity of human personality and enabling persons to participate effectively in a free society. Accordingly, Art 13(1) of the ICESCR provides as follows:

> 'The States Parties to the present Covenant recognise the right of everyone to education. They agree that education shall be directed to the full development of the human personality and the sense of its dignity, and shall strengthen the respect for human rights and fundamental freedoms. They further agree that education shall enable all persons to participate effectively in a free society, promote understanding, tolerance and friendship among all nations and all racial, ethnic or religious groups, and further the activities of the United Nations for the maintenance of peace.'

Purpose and Objectives of Education – CRC, Art 29(1)

CRC, Art 29(1)

13.10   Whereas Art 26(2) of the Universal Declaration of Human Rights and Art 13(1) of the ICESCR enshrine the object of education for everyone, Art 29 of the CRC represents a consensus of world opinion about the fundamental purposes of educating *children*.[18] Whilst Art 28 of the CRC deals with child's right to education in terms of provision, access and equality of opportunity,[19] Art 29 of the CRC deals with the aims of education, providing part of the broader ethical framework within which the child's right to education exists. Article 29 of the CRC provides as follows:

> '1. States Parties agree that the education of the child shall be directed to:
>
> (a)   The development of the child's personality, talents and mental and physical abilities to their fullest potential;
>
> (b)   The development of respect for human rights and fundamental freedoms, and for the principles enshrined in the Charter of the United Nations;
>
> (c)   The development of respect for the child's parents, his or her own cultural identity, language and values, for the national values of the country in which the child is living, the country from which he or she may originate, and for civilisations different from his or her own;

---

[18]   As indicated by the words 'States Parties agree' at the commencement of Art 29(1). Van Bueren notes that, by contrast to Art 26(2) of the Universal Declaration of Human Rights and Art 13(1) of the ICESCR Art 29 of the CRC has the advantage of seeking to evaluate the aims of education from the perspective of the child (Van Bueren, G *The International Law on the Rights of the Child* (1998) Martinus Nijhoff, p 254).

[19]   See below **13.38–13.76**.

(d)   The preparation of the child for responsible life in a free society, in the spirit of understanding, peace, tolerance, equality of sexes, and friendship among all peoples, ethnic, national and religious groups and persons of indigenous origin;

(e)   The development of respect for the natural environment.'

13.11 In its General Comment No 1 *The Aims of Education*[20] the Committee on the Rights of the Child notes in respect of Art 29 of the CRC that:

> 'The aims of education that it sets out, which have been agreed to by all States parties, promote, support and protect the core value of the Convention: the human dignity innate in every child and his or her equal and inalienable rights ... Article 29 (1) not only adds to the right to education recognised in article 28 a qualitative dimension which reflects the rights and inherent dignity of the child; it also insists upon the need for education to be child-centred, child-friendly and empowering, and it highlights the need for educational processes to be based upon the very principles it enunciates ... The goal is to empower the child by developing his or her skills, learning and other capacities, human dignity, self-esteem and self-confidence.'[21]

13.12 Van Bueren notes that international law does not provide any guidance as to the relative importance of each aim of education and as such the aims must be assumed to have equal weight, preventing States from selectively implementing such aims.[22] Overall, UNESCO emphasizes the goal of a human rights based approach to the purpose and objectives of education as one which seeks to assure to every child a quality education that respects and promotes her or his right to dignity and optimum development[23] in which children are recognised as active agents in their own learning and which is designed to promote and respect their rights and needs.[24] It is self-evident that education should be used to inform impartially and not to indoctrinate.[25]

13.13 Article 29(1) of the CRC must be read in the context of the other rights of the child enshrined in the CRC and in particular in light of the child's right to participate pursuant to Art 12 of the CRC. The child's participation is a tool to stimulate the full development of the personality and evolving capacities of the child consistent with the aims of Art 29 of the CRC.[26] In its General Comment No 12 *The Right of the Child to be Heard* the Committee on the Rights of the Child notes that:[27]

> 'In all educational environments, including educational programmes in the early years, the active role of children in a participatory learning environment should be promoted. Teaching and learning must take into account life conditions and prospects of the children. For this reason, education authorities have to include children's and their parents' views in the

---

[20]   Committee on the Rights of the Child General Comment No 1 *The Aims of Education* HRI/GEN/1/Rev 8, p 349, para 1 and 2.

[21]   See also Article 7 (2) Convention on the Worst Forms of Child Labour 1999 ILO Convention 182 ('Each Member shall, taking into account the importance of education in eliminating child labour, take effective and time-bound measures to: (c) ensure access to free basic education, and, wherever possible and appropriate, vocational training, for all children removed from the worst forms of child labour').

[22]   Van Bueren, G *The International Law on the Rights of the Child* (1998) Martinus Nijhoff, p 253.

[23]   *A Human Rights-based Approach to Education for All: A Framework for the Realization of Children's Right to Education and Rights within Education* UNICEF/UNESCO (2007), p 1.

[24]   *A Human Rights-based Approach to Education for All: A Framework for the Realization of Children's Right to Education and Rights within Education* UNICEF/UNESCO (2007), p 8.

[25]   See Van Bueren, G *The International Law on the Rights of the Child* (1998) Martinus Nijhoff, p 255.

[26]   Committee on the Rights of the Child General Comment No 12 (2009) *The Right of the Child to be Heard* CRC/C/GC/12 p 16, para 79.

[27]   Committee on the Rights of the Child General Comment No 12 (2009) *The Right of the Child to be Heard* CRC/C/GC/12, pp 21–22, paras 106–110.

planning of curricula and school programmes. Human rights education can shape the motivations and behaviours of children only when human rights are practised in the institutions in which the child learns, plays and lives together with other children and adults. In particular, the child's right to be heard is under critical scrutiny by children in these institutions, where children can observe, whether in fact due weight is given to their views as declared in the Convention. Children's participation is indispensable for the creation of a social climate in the classroom, which stimulates cooperation and mutual support needed for child centred interactive learning. Giving children's views weight is particularly important in the elimination of discrimination, prevention of bullying and disciplinary measures. The Committee welcomes the expansion of peer education and peer counseling. Steady participation of children in decision-making processes should be achieved through, inter alia, class councils, student councils and student representation on school boards and committees, where they can freely express their views on the development and implementation of school policies and codes of behaviour. These rights need to be enshrined in legislation, rather than relying on the goodwill of authorities, schools and head teachers to implement them.'

CRC, Art 29(1) – Ambit

(i) Article 29(1)(a) – Development of Personality, Talents and Mental & Physical Abilities

13.14 Article 29(1)(a) of the CRC records that States Parties agree that the education of the child shall be directed to the development of the child's personality, talents and mental and physical abilities to their fullest potential. In relation to Art 29(1)(a) the Committee on the Rights of the Child has stated that:[28]

'... the key goal of education is the development of the individual child's personality, talents and abilities, in recognition of the fact that every child has unique characteristics, interests, abilities, and learning needs. Thus, the curriculum must be of direct relevance to the child's social, cultural, environmental and economic context and to his or her present and future needs and take full account of the child's evolving capacities; teaching methods should be tailored to the different needs of different children. Education must also be aimed at ensuring that essential life skills are learnt by every child and that no child leaves school without being equipped to face the challenges that he or she can expect to be confronted with in life. Basic skills include not only literacy and numeracy but also life skills such as the ability to make well-balanced decisions; to resolve conflicts in a non-violent manner; and to develop a healthy lifestyle, good social relationships and responsibility, critical thinking, creative talents, and other abilities which give children the tools needed to pursue their options in life.'

13.15 The use of the word 'talents' in Art 29(1)(a) of the CRC indicates that the aims of education should extend beyond simply the child's academic ability to encompass vocational, sporting and artistic skills. Overall, the requirement to develop personality, talents and mental and physical abilities demonstrates the extremely wide ambit of the word 'education' as used in the CRC. Within this context, the Committee on the Rights of the Child stipulates that:[29]

'Education must also be aimed at ensuring that ... no child leaves school without being equipped to face the challenges that he or she can expect to be confronted with in life. Basic

---

[28]   Committee on the Rights of the Child, General Comment No 1 *The Aims of Education* CRC/GC/2001/1, p 351, para 9.

[29]   Committee on the Rights of Child General Comment No 4 *Adolescent Health and Development in the Context of the Rights of the Child* HRI/GEN/1/Rev 8, p 380, para 13. See also Art 21 of the Riyadh Guidelines on the Prevention of Juvenile Delinquency.

skills should include ... the ability to make well-balanced decisions; to resolve conflicts in a non-violent manner; and to develop a healthy lifestyle [and] good social relationships ...'

(ii) Article 29(1)(b) – Respect for Human Rights and the Charter of the United Nations.[30]

13.16 Article 29(1)(b) of the CRC records that States Parties agree that the education of the child shall be directed to the development of respect for human rights and fundamental freedoms, and for the principles enshrined in the Charter of the United Nations.[31] Art 29(1)(b) seeks to achieve more than simply educating children as to the content of human rights instruments including the CRC. Rather, it seeks to promote the development of *respect* for human rights.[32] In this context, human rights education is seen as a tool for social change and development.[33] As such, not only the curriculum but the administrative arrangements, behavioural codes and the teaching methods adopted in educational provision should therefore reflect the contents of the CRC.[34] In this regard, the Committee on the Rights of the Child has noted that:[35]

'[Art 29(1)(b)] attaches importance to the process by which the right to education is to be promoted. Thus, efforts to promote the enjoyment of other rights must not be undermined, and should be reinforced, by the values imparted in the educational process. This includes not only the content of the curriculum but also the educational processes, the pedagogical methods and the environment within which education takes place, whether it be the home, school, or elsewhere. Children do not lose their human rights by virtue of passing through the school gates. Thus, for example, education must be provided in a way that respects the inherent dignity of the child and enables the child to express his or her views freely in accordance with article 12(1) and to participate in school life. Education must also be provided in a way that respects the strict limits on discipline reflected in article 28(2) and promotes non-violence in school. The Committee has repeatedly made clear in its concluding observations that the use of corporal punishment does not respect the inherent dignity of the child nor the strict limits on school discipline. Compliance with the values recognised in article 29(1) clearly requires that schools be child-friendly in the fullest sense of the term and that they be consistent in all respects with the dignity of the child. The participation of children in school life, the creation of school communities and student councils, peer

---

[30] See Charter of the United Nations, June 26 1945.

[31] See also the UNESCO Convention against Discrimination in Education, Art 5(1)(a) ('Education shall be directed to the full development of the human personality and to the strengthening of respect for human rights and fundamental freedoms; it shall promote understanding, tolerance and friendship among all nations, racial or religious groups, and shall further the activities of the United Nations for the maintenance of peace').

[32] Newell, P and Hodgkin, R *Implementation Handbook for the Convention on the Rights of the Child* (2008) 3rd edn, UNICEF, p 442. See also the Committee on the Rights of the Child General Comment No 1 *The Aims of Education* CRC/GC/2001/1, p 353–354, para 19 ('The term 'human rights education' is too often used in a way which greatly oversimplifies its connotations. What is needed, in addition to formal human rights education, is the promotion of values and policies conducive to human rights not only within schools and universities but also within the broader community'). See also CRC, Art 42 ('States Parties undertake to make the principles and provisions of the Convention widely known, by appropriate and active means, to adults and children alike').

[33] Armenia CRC/C/15/Add. 225, para 53.

[34] Newell, P and Hodgkin, R *Implementation Handbook for the Convention on the Rights of the Child* (2008) 3rd edn, UNICEF, p 442.

[35] Committee on the Rights of the Child, General Comment No 1 *The Aims of Education* CRC/GC/2001/1, para 8. See also Committee on the Rights of the Child General Comment No 5 *General Measures of Implementation of the Convention on the Rights of the Child (Arts 4, 42 and 44(6)* HRI/GEN/1/Rev 8, p 402, para 68 ('Children need to acquire knowledge of their rights and the Committee places special emphasis on incorporating learning about the Convention and human rights in general into the school curriculum at all stages').

education and peer counseling, and the involvement of children in school disciplinary proceedings should be promoted as part of the process of learning and experiencing the realisation of rights.'

(iii) Article 29(1)(c) – Respect for Parents, Culture, National Values and Others

13.17 Article 29(1)(c) records that States Parties agree that the education of the child shall be directed to the development of respect for the child's parents, his or her own cultural identity, language and values, for the national values of the country in which the child is living, the country from which he or she may originate, and for civilisations different from his or her own.[36]

'Respect'

13.18 The use of word 'respect' in Art 29(1)(c) implies more than just tolerance and understanding and means acknowledging the equal worth of peoples of all cultures, without condescension.[37] Further, the wording of Art 29(1)(c) seeks to ensure that the value systems of the ratifying State party and of other States parties are equally respected.[38] The Committee on the Rights of the Child has noted that:[39]

'Discrimination is learned, observed, experienced, suffered and acquired through life. Therefore, education can play an essential role not only in combating discrimination, but also in preventing it. Education is a process that takes place within the family and the community as well as in schools. If education deliberately aims to prevent and combat racisms and intolerance instead of condoning them or contributing to their development, it will make the greatest possible contribution to improving respect for human rights.'

13.19 Adherence to the provisions of Art 29(1)(c) will be important in achieving the aims of Art 29(1)(d), namely the preparation of the child for responsible life in a free society, in the spirit of understanding, peace, tolerance, equality of sexes, and friendship among all peoples, ethnic, national and religious groups and persons of indigenous origin.[40]

(iv) Article 29(1)(d) – Preparation for a Responsible Life in Free Society

13.20 Article 29(1)(d) records that States Parties agree that the education of the child shall be directed to the preparation of the child for a responsible life in a free society, in the spirit of understanding, peace, tolerance, equality of sexes, and friendship among all peoples, ethnic, national and religious groups and persons of indigenous origin.[41] Art 29(1)(d) once again reflects the broader aim of education beyond the academic

---

[36] See also CRC, Art 30, Art 8 of the Convention on the Rights of Persons with Disabilities and the Committee on the Elimination of Racial Discrimination, General Recommendation XXIX, 2002, HRI/GEN/1/Rev.8, p 272.

[37] Newell, P and Hodgkin, R *Implementation Handbook for the Convention on the Rights of the Child* (2008) 3rd edn, UNICEF, p 445.

[38] Committee on the Rights of the Child, General Comment No 1 *The Aims of Education* CRC/GC/2001/1, para 4.

[39] Committee on the Rights of the Child, Report on the twenty-ninth session, January/February 2002, CRC/C/114, p 191. See also See Committee on the Rights of the Child, General Comment No 1, *The Aims of Education* CRC/GC/ 2001 /1, para 10.

[40] See **13.20** below.

[41] See also the UNESCO Convention against Discrimination in Education, Art 5(1)(a) ('Education shall be directed to the full development of the human personality and to the strengthening of respect for human rights and fundamental freedoms; it shall promote understanding, tolerance and friendship among all nations, racial or religious groups, and shall further the activities of the United Nations for the maintenance of peace').

tuition of children and mandates subjects such as citizenship, politics, health education, including sex education, social responsibility and participation and financial management.[42]

CRC, Art 33

13.21 In addition to Art 29(1)(d), the CRC also makes specific provision directed in part to the preparation of the child for responsible life in a free society in relation to drugs, health and nutrition and children leaving care. Article 33 of the CRC provides that 'States Parties shall take all appropriate measures, including legislative, administrative, social and educational measures, to protect children from the illicit use of narcotic drugs and psychotropic substances as defined in the relevant international treaties, and to prevent the use of children in the illicit production and trafficking of such substances'.

CRC, Art 24(2)(e)

13.22 Article 24(2)(e) of the CRC requires States parties 'To ensure that all segments of society, in particular parents and children, are informed, have access to education and are supported in the use of basic knowledge of child health and nutrition, the advantages of breastfeeding, hygiene and environmental sanitation and the prevention of accidents'.[43]

Children Leaving Care

13.23 The Guidelines for the Alternative Care of Children stipulate that 'Ongoing educational and vocational training opportunities should be imparted as part of life skills education to young people leaving care in order to help them to become financially independent and generate their own income'.[44]

(v) Article 29(1)(e) – Development of Respect for the Natural Environment

13.24 The CRC is the only international human rights instrument which deals with respect for the environment from an educational perspective. Article 29(1)(e) of the CRC

---

[42] See also UNESCO Recommendation concerning Education for International Understanding, Human Rights and Fundamental Freedoms, Art 4(g).

[43] See **5.117** above. See also Committee on the Rights of the Child, General Comment No 4 *Adolescent Health and Development in the Context of the Convention on the Rights of the Child* CRC/GC/2003/4, paras 26, 27 and 28 and Committee on the Rights of the Child, General Comment No 3 *HIV/AIDS and the Rights of the Child* CRC/GC/2003/3, para 16.

[44] A/RES/64/142 p 19, para 135. See also Committee on the Rights of the Child General Comment No 10 *Children's Rights in Juvenile Justice* CRC/C/GC/10 p 10, para 28 ('juvenile justice system should provide for ample opportunities to deal with children in conflict with the law by using social and/or educational measures, and to strictly limit the use of deprivation of liberty').

records that States Parties agree that the education of the child shall be directed to the development of respect for the natural environment.[45] The Committee on the Rights of the Child has stated that:[46]

> '... the development of respect for the natural environment, education must link issues of environmental and sustainable development with socio-economic, socio-cultural and demographic issues. Similarly, respect for the natural environment should be learnt by children at home, in school and within the community, encompass both national and international problems, and actively involve children in local, regional or global environmental projects.'

General Principles – Education and Non-Discrimination

Education and Non-Discrimination – Principles

Equality of Opportunity

13.25 In the seminal United States Supreme Court case of *Brown v Board of Education*[47] Chief Justice Warren held as follows in relation to the cardinal requirement of equality in education:

> 'Today education is perhaps the most important function of state and local governments. Compulsory school attendance laws and the great expenditures for education both demonstrate our recognition of the importance of education to our democratic society. It is required in the performance of our most basic public responsibilities, even service in the armed forces. It is the very foundation of good citizenship. Today it is a principal instrument in awakening the child to cultural values, in preparing him for later professional training, and in helping him to adjust normally to his environment. In these days, it is doubtful that any child may reasonably be expected to succeed in life if he is denied the opportunity of an education. Such an opportunity, where the state has undertaken to provide it, is a right which must be made available to all on equal terms.'

Convention against Discrimination in Education 1960

13.26 On 14 December 1960 UNESCO adopted the Convention against Discrimination in Education. Article 1 of the Convention provides as follows in respect of non-discrimination in education:

> '1. For the purposes of this Convention, the term 'discrimination' includes any distinction, exclusion, limitation or preference which, being based on race, colour, sex, language, religion, political or other opinion, national or social origin, economic condition or birth, has the purpose or effect of nullifying or impairing equality of treatment in education and in particular:

---

[45] See also the Rio Declaration on Environment and Development (1992) Principle 10 ('Environmental issues are best handled with the participation of all concerned citizens, at the relevant level. At the national level, each individual shall have appropriate access to information concerning the environment that is held by public authorities, including information on hazardous materials and activities in their communities, and the opportunity to participate in decision-making processes. States shall facilitate and encourage public awareness and participation by making information widely available.'), Principle 21 ('The creativity, ideals and courage of the youth of the world should be mobilised to forge a global partnership in order to achieve sustainable development and ensure a better future for all').

[46] Committee on the Rights of the Child, General Comment No, 1 *The Aims of Education* CRC/GC/2001/1, para 13.

[47] 347 US 483 (1954), US Sup Ct.

(a)   Of depriving any person or group of persons of access to education of any type or at any level;

(b)   Of limiting any person or group of persons to education of an inferior standard;

(c)   Subject to the provisions of Article 2 of this Convention,[48] of establishing or maintaining separate educational systems or institutions for persons or groups of persons; or

(d)   Of inflicting on any person or group of persons conditions which are incompatible with the dignity of man.

2. For the purposes of this Convention, the term 'education' refers to all types and levels of education, and includes access to education, the standard and quality of education, and the conditions under which it is given.'

CRC, Art 28(1)

13.27   Article 28(1) of the CRC requires that the child's right to education be recognised on the basis of equal opportunity.[49] Read with Art 2 of the CRC, Art 28(1) requires that the child's right to education be recogised without discrimination of any kind, irrespective of the child's or his or her parent's or legal guardian's race, colour, sex, language, religion, political or other opinion, national, ethnic or social origin, property, disability, birth or other status. Discrimination on the basis of any of the grounds listed in Art 2 of the CRC, whether it is overt or hidden, offends the human dignity of the child and is capable of undermining or even destroying the capacity of the child to benefit from educational opportunities.[50] The Committee on the Rights of the Child observes that:[51]

'Racism and related phenomena thrive where there is ignorance, unfounded fears of racial, ethnic, religious, cultural and linguistic or other forms of difference, the exploitation of prejudices, or the teaching or dissemination of distorted values. A reliable and enduring antidote to all of these failings is the provision of education which promotes an understanding and appreciation of the values reflected in article 29 (1), including respect for differences, and challenges all aspects of discrimination and prejudice.'

And:[52]

'Discrimination is learned, observed, experienced, suffered and acquired through life. Therefore, education can play an essential role not only in combating discrimination, but also in preventing it. Education is a process that takes place within the family and the community as well as in schools. If education deliberately aims to prevent and combat racisms and intolerance instead of condoning them or contributing to their development, it will make the greatest possible contribution to improving respect for human rights.'

Education and Non-Discrimination – Vulnerable Groups

13.28   The Committee on the Rights of the Child has identified a number of groups who are particularly prone to discrimination in relation to education, namely girls,

---

[48]   Article 2 of the Convention contains three narrow exceptions to Art 1 in respect of the provision of single sex education, separate religious or linguistic education and private education.

[49]   See Van Bueren, G *The International Law on the Rights of the Child* (1998) Martinus Nijhoff, p 245.

[50]   Committee on the Rights of the Child, General Comment No 1 *The Aims of Education* CRC/GC/2001/1, p 351, para 10.

[51]   Committee on the Rights of the Child, General Comment No 1 *The Aims of Education* CRC/GC/2001/1, p 352, para 11.

[52]   Committee on the Rights of the Child, Report on the twenty-ninth session, January/February 2002, CRC/C/114, p 191.

children from rural communities, children of minority or indigenous groups, children with disabilities, children with or affected by HIV/AIDS and children deprived of their liberty.[53] This is not an exhaustive list.[54] Each of these groups is discussed in detail below when considering the application of the child's right to education under Art 28(1) of the CRC.[55]

Education and Evolving Capacity

13.29 Article 26(3) of the Universal Declaration of Human Rights provides that 'Parents have a prior right to choose the kind of education that shall be given to their children'. Article 13(3) of the ICESCR states that:

> 'The States Parties to the present Covenant undertake to have respect for the liberty of parents and, when applicable, legal guardians to choose for their children schools, other than those established by the public authorities, which conform to such minimum educational standards as may be laid down or approved by the State and to ensure the religious and moral education of their children in conformity with their own convictions.'[56]

In a similar provision, Art 18(4) of the ICCPR stipulates that 'The States Parties to the present Covenant undertake to have respect for the liberty of parents and, when applicable, legal guardians to ensure the religious and moral education of their children in conformity with their own convictions'.[57]

13.30 Neither Art 28 or Art 29 of the CRC contains provisions enshrining the right of parents to choose educational establishments for their children and to ensure their religious and moral education in conformity with their own convictions.[58] Such provisions were rejected by the Working Party at the drafting stage on the basis that parents' overall rights and responsibilities are dealt with elsewhere in the CRC.[59] As such, the CRC does not, as is contended for by the Holy See in its reservation to Art 28(1),[60] recognise the 'primary and inalienable' rights of parents in education. Rather, by virtue of the CRC the parental rights set out in the Universal Declaration, the ICESCR and the ICCPR are made expressly subject to the child's best interests, evolving capacity and the right to participate, to the wider canon of the child's rights under the CRC and to the nature of parental responsibility as prescribed in Art 18 of the CRC.[61]

---

[53] See Newell, P and Hodgkin, R *Implementation Handbook for the Convention on the Rights of the Child* (2008) 3rd edn, UNICEF, pp 414–420 and see UN Doc E/1988/5.

[54] Van Bueren, G *The International Law on the Rights of the Child* (1998) Martinus Nijhoff, p 246.

[55] See **13.77–13.102**.

[56] See also Art 13(4) of the ICESCR ('No part of this article shall be construed so as to interfere with the liberty of individuals and bodies to establish and direct educational institutions, subject always to the observance of the principles set forth in paragraph I of this article and to the requirement that the education given in such institutions shall conform to such minimum standards as may be laid down by the State').

[57] See **10.56** above.

[58] See chapter 10 above for a detailed discussion of the child's right to freedom of thought, conscience and religion in the context of education.

[59] Detrick, S *A Commentary on the United Nations Convention on the Rights of the Child* (1999) Martinus Nijhoff, pp 384 and 394 and E/CN.4/1985/64, pp 11–15 and E/CN.4/1989/48, pp 79–84. See in particular CRC, Arts 5 and 18.

[60] CRC/C/Rev.8, p 23.

[61] Newell, P and Hodgkin, R *Implementation Handbook for the Convention on the Rights of the Child* (2008) 3rd edn, UNICEF, p 411. Note however that Art 29(2) does safeguard the rights of parents and others to establish schools outside the state system.

THE RIGHT TO EDUCATION

Universal Declaration of Human Rights

13.31 Article 26 of the Universal Declaration of Human Rights provides as follows in respect of the right to education:

> '1. Everyone has the right to education. Education shall be free, at least in the elementary and fundamental stages. Elementary education shall be compulsory. Technical and professional education shall be made generally available and higher education shall be equally accessible to all on the basis of merit.
>
> 2. Education shall be directed to the full development of the human personality and to the strengthening of respect for human rights and fundamental freedoms. It shall promote understanding, tolerance and friendship among all nations, racial or religious groups, and shall further the activities of the United Nations for the maintenance of peace.
>
> 3. Parents have a prior right to choose the kind of education that shall be given to their children.'

13.32 The right to education has been classed both as a social right and a cultural right.[62] Van Bueren notes that the right to education illustrates the artificiality of the traditional distinctions between economic, social and cultural rights on the one hand and civil and political rights on the other.[63] The Committee on Economic, Social and Cultural Rights General Comment No 11 *Plans for Action for Primary Education (Art 14)* observes as follows:[64]

> 'The right to education, recognised in articles 13 and 14 of the Covenant, as well as in a variety of other international treaties, such as the Convention on the Rights of the Child and the Convention on the Elimination of All Forms of Discrimination against Women, is of vital importance. It has been variously classified as an economic right, a social right and a cultural right. It is all of these. It is also, in many ways, a civil right and a political right, since it is central to the full and effective realisation of those rights as well. In this respect, the right to education epitomizes the indivisibility and interdependence of all human rights.'

International Covenant on Economic, Social and Cultural Rights[65]

13.33 The International Covenant on Economic, Social and Cultural Rights also enshrines the right to education, providing at Art 13:

> '1. The States Parties to the present Covenant recognise the right of everyone to education. They agree that education shall be directed to the full development of the human personality and the sense of its dignity, and shall strengthen the respect for human rights and fundamental freedoms. They further agree that education shall enable all persons to

---

[62] Verheyde, M *Article 28: The Right to Education* in Alen, A, Vande Lanotte, J, Verhellen, E, Berghams, E and Verheyde, M (eds) *A Commentary on the Untitled Nations Convention on the Rights of the Child* (2006) Martinus Nijhoff, p 1. See also Van Bueren, G *Deconstructing the Mythologies of International Human Rights Law* in Gearty and Tomkin (eds) *Understanding Human Rights* (1996) 596.

[63] Van Bueren, G *The International Law on the Rights of the Child* (1998) Martinus Nijhoff, p 233.

[64] Committee on Economic, Social and Cultural Rights General Comment No 11 *Plans for Action for Primary Education (Art 14)* HRI/GEN/1/Rev 8, p 61, para 2.

[65] Note that Art 18(4) of the ICCPR states "The States Parties to the present Covenant undertake to have respect for the liberty of parents and, when applicable, legal guardians to ensure the religious and moral education of their children in conformity with their own convictions.' This provision is discussed in detail at **10.56** above.

participate effectively in a free society, promote understanding, tolerance and friendship among all nations and all racial, ethnic or religious groups, and further the activities of the United Nations for the maintenance of peace.[66]

2. The States Parties to the present Covenant recognise that, with a view to achieving the full realisation of this right:[67]

(a)   Primary education shall be compulsory and available free to all;[68]
(b)   Secondary education in its different forms, including technical and vocational secondary education, shall be made generally available and accessible to all by every appropriate means, and in particular by the progressive introduction of free education;
(c)   Higher education shall be made equally accessible to all, on the basis of capacity, by every appropriate means, and in particular by the progressive introduction of free education;
(d)   Fundamental education shall be encouraged or intensified as far as possible for those persons who have not received or completed the whole period of their primary education;
(e)   The development of a system of schools at all levels shall be actively pursued, an adequate fellowship system shall be established, and the material conditions of teaching staff shall be continuously improved.

3. The States Parties to the present Covenant undertake to have respect for the liberty of parents and, when applicable, legal guardians to choose for their children schools, other than those established by the public authorities, which conform to such minimum educational standards as may be laid down or approved by the State and to ensure the religious and moral education of their children in conformity with their own convictions.[69]

4. No part of this article shall be construed so as to interfere with the liberty of individuals and bodies to establish and direct educational institutions,[70] subject always to the observance of the principles set forth in paragraph I of this article and to the requirement that the education given in such institutions shall conform to such minimum standards as may be laid down by the State.'[71]

13.34   The term 'fundamental education' in Art 13(2)(d) of the ICESCR is not used in the CRC. The term 'fundamental education' corresponds to the term 'basic education' as

---

[66]   States parties are required to ensure that curricula for all levels of the educational system are directed to the objectives identified in article 13 (1) (Committee on Economic, Social and Cultural Rights General Comment No 13 *The Right to Education (Art 13)* HRI/GEN/1/Rev.8, p 81, para 49).

[67]   In relation to Art 13(2) States have obligations to respect, protect and fulfill each of the 'essential features' (availability, accessibility, acceptability, adaptability) of the right to education (Committee on Economic, Social and Cultural Rights, General Comment No 13 *The Right to Education (Art 13)* HRI/GEN/1/Rev.8, p 81, para 50).

[68]   The obligations of States parties in relation to primary, secondary, higher and fundamental education are not identical. Given the wording of article 13 (2), States parties are obliged to prioritise the introduction of compulsory, free primary education (Committee on Economic, Social and Cultural Rights, General Comment No 13 *The Right to Education (Art 13)* HRI/GEN/1/Rev.8, p 81, para 51).

[69]   The provisions of Art 13(3) of the ICESCR is covered in chapter 10 above.

[70]   A State party has no obligation to fund institutions established in accordance with article 13(3) and (4). However, if a State elects to make a financial contribution to private educational institutions, it must do so without discrimination on any of the prohibited grounds (Committee on Economic, Social and Cultural Rights, General Comment No 13 *The Right to Education (Art 13)* HRI/GEN/1/Rev.8, p 81, para 54).

[71]   States parties are obliged to establish 'minimum educational standards' to which all educational institutions established in accordance with article 13 (3) and (4) are required to conform. They must also maintain a transparent and effective system to monitor such standards (Committee on Economic, Social and Cultural Rights, General Comment No 13 *The Right to Education (Art 13)* HRI/GEN/1/Rev.8, p 81, para 54).

set out in the *World Declaration on Education for All*.[72] By virtue of Art 13(2)(d) of the ICESCR individuals 'who have not received or completed the whole period of their primary education' have a right to fundamental education, or basic education as defined in the *World Declaration on Education For All*. However, the right to fundamental education is not confined to this group alone as everyone has the right to the satisfaction of their basic learning needs.[73]

Child's Right to Education under the CRC

Right to Education under the CRC – Structure

13.35 The first mention of the child's right to education in an international human rights instrument was contained in Principle 7 of the 1959 UN Declaration of the Rights of the Child which provided that:

> 'The child is entitled to receive education, which shall be free and compulsory, at least in the elementary stages. He shall be given an education which will promote his general culture and enable him, on a basis of equal opportunity, to develop his abilities, his individual judgement, and his sense of moral and social responsibility, and to become a useful member of society. The best interests of the child shall be the guiding principle of those responsible for his education and guidance; that responsibility lies in the first place with his parents.'

13.36 In its preamble, the CRC highlights the need for children to be fully prepared to live an individual life in society, and brought up in the spirit of the ideals proclaimed in the Charter of the United Nations, and in particular in the spirit of peace, dignity, tolerance, freedom, equality and solidarity. The child's right to education is crucial to achieving this aim. Article 28 of the CRC articulates the child's right to education. Article 29 of the CRC stipulates the purpose and objectives of that education. Article 24(2)(e) and Art 33 also articulate the child's right to education by reference to health care and narcotics respectively.

13.37 Articles 28 and 29 of the CRC should be read together and with Art 2 (non-discrimination), Art 3 (best interests), Art 4 (implementation of rights), Art 6 (right to life, survival and development) and Art 12 (right to participate) of the CRC.[74] Art 12 of the CRC will mandate the child's involvement in decisions concerning their education having regard to his or her age and maturity.[75] The Committee on the Rights of the Child has observed in this regard that:[76]

---

[72] Endorsed by the UN General Assembly's special session on childhood in 2002 '*A World Fit for Children*', Report of the Ad Hoc Committee of the Whole of the twenty-seventh special session of the General Assembly, 2002, A/S-27/19/Rev.1, paras 39 and 40.

[73] Committee on Economic, Social and Cultural Rights, General Comment No 13 *The Right to Education (Art 13)* HRI/GEN/1/Rev.8, p 76, para 23.

[74] See also Arts 19 (protection from maltreatment), Art 23(3), effective education for children with disabilities), Art 24(2)(e) (health education), Art 30 (rights of children belonging to minority or indigenous groups, Art 32 (concerning child labour), Art 33 (concerning narcotics) and Art 43 and 44(6) (concerning human rights education) (Verheyde, M *Article 28: The Right to Education* in Alen, A, Vande Lanotte, J, Verhellen, E, Berghams, E and Verheyde, M (eds) *A Commentary on the Untitled Nations Convention on the Rights of the Child* (2006) Martinus Nijhoff, p 2).

[75] Committee on the Rights of the Child General Comment No 12 (2009) *The Right of the Child to be Heard* CRC/C/GC/12, p 9, para 32.

[76] Committee on the Rights of the Child General Comment No 1 *The Aims of Education* HRI/GEN/1/Rev 8, p 351, para 8. See also Art 16 of the UNESCO Recommendation concerning Education for International Understanding, Human Rights and Fundamental Freedoms ('Student participation in the organisation of studies and of the educational establishment they are attending should itself be considered a factor in civic education and an important element in international education').

'The participation of children in school life, the creation of school communities and student councils, peer education and peer counseling, and the involvement of children in school disciplinary proceedings should be promoted as part of the process of learning and experiencing the realisation of rights.'

Right to Education under the CRC – CRC, Article 28

13.38 Article 28 of the CRC provides as follows in respect of the child's right to education:

'1. States Parties recognise the right of the child to education, and with a view to achieving this right progressively and on the basis of equal opportunity, they shall, in particular:

(a)   Make primary education compulsory and available free to all;

(b)   Encourage the development of different forms of secondary education, including general and vocational education, make them available and accessible to every child, and take appropriate measures such as the introduction of free education and offering financial assistance in case of need;

(c)   Make higher education accessible to all on the basis of capacity by every appropriate means;

(d)   Make educational and vocational information and guidance available and accessible to all children;

(e)   Take measures to encourage regular attendance at schools and the reduction of drop-out rates.

2. States Parties shall take all appropriate measures to ensure that school discipline is administered in a manner consistent with the child's human dignity and in conformity with the present Convention.

3. States Parties shall promote and encourage international cooperation in matters relating to education, in particular with a view to contributing to the elimination of ignorance and illiteracy throughout the world and facilitating access to scientific and technical knowledge and modern teaching methods. In this regard, particular account shall be taken of the needs of developing countries.

CRC, Art 28 – Ambit

(i)   CRC, Art 28 – The Child's Right to Education

13.39 In respect of the child's right to education the CRC does not create that right but rather requires the recognition of the pre-exiting right to education. Article 28(1) of the CRC accordingly provides as follows in respect of the child's right to education:

'States Parties recognise the right of the child to education, and with a view to achieving this right progressively and on the basis of equal opportunity ...'

'Education'

13.40 In accordance with the general principles outlined above, the definition of the word 'education' in the CRC is not limited to formal instruction delivered within schools but recognises informal education as well, for example education conducted over the Internet.[77] Hodgkin and Newell however suggest that the reference in Art 28(e) to 'attendance at schools' and in Art 29(2) to private 'educational institutions' implies that

---

77   Newell, P and Hodgkin, R *Implementation Handbook for the Convention on the Rights of the Child* (2008) 3rd edn, UNICEF, p 411.

education through attendance at school is the norm contemplated by the CRC.[78] This view is reinforced by the particular duties on states to take measures to encourage regular attendance and reduce dropout rates under Art 28(e).

'The Right of the Child to Education'

13.41 The key elements of the child's right to education are the right to access education, the right to quality education and the right to respect in the learning environment.[79] Note that there is no requirement on the part of a child that she or he demonstrate a responsible attitude in order to 'earn' an entitlement to education.[80]

The Right to Access to Education

13.42 The right to access education requires the provision of education throughout all stages of childhood, the provision of sufficient, accessible school places or learning opportunities and equality of opportunity.[81] The core minimum provision encompassed by the right to education under Art 28(1) is the provision of free, compulsory primary education and the provision of different forms of secondary education and vocational guidance.[82]

13.43 Article 29(2) of the CRC preserves the rights of individuals and groups to order their own education provision subject to the aims of Art 29(2) and the CRC as a whole being fulfilled, allowing for greater diversity and flexibility in the provision of education. Article 29(2) of the CRC provides as follows in respect of the liberty of individuals to establish and direct educational institutions:[83]

> '2. No part of the present article or article 28 shall be construed so as to interfere with the liberty of individuals and bodies to establish and direct educational institutions, subject always to the observance of the principle set forth in paragraph 1 of the present article and to the requirements that the education given in such institutions shall conform to such minimum standards as may be laid down by the State.'

13.44 Article 29(2) is qualified by the words 'subject always to the observance of the principle set forth in paragraph 1 of the present article and to the requirements that the education given in such institutions shall conform to such minimum standards as may be laid down by the State'.[84] Thus a private school which, for example, focuses exclusively on the religious education of children using doctrinal texts would fall foul of

---

[78] Newell, P and Hodgkin, R *Implementation Handbook for the Convention on the Rights of the Child* (2008) 3rd edn, UNICEF, pp 411–412. See also Szabo, I *Cultural Rights* (1974) Leiden.

[79] *A Human Rights-based Approach to Education for All: A Framework for the Realization of Children's Right to Education and Rights within Education* UNICEF/UNESCO (2007), p 28.

[80] *A Human Rights-based Approach to Education for All: A Framework for the Realization of Children's Right to Education and Rights within Education* UNICEF/UNESCO (2007), p 22.

[81] *A Human Rights-based Approach to Education for All: A Framework for the Realization of Children's Right to Education and Rights within Education* UNICEF/UNESCO (2007), pp 29–31.

[82] Newell, P and Hodgkin, R *Implementation Handbook for the Convention on the Rights of the Child* (2008) 3rd edn, UNICEF, p 408.

[83] See also Art 5(1)(b) of the UNESCO Convention against Discrimination in Education.

[84] There appears to be no *duty* on States parties to lay down minimum standards in education but see Art 3(3) of the CRC which provides that 'States Parties shall ensure that the institutions, services and facilities responsible for the care or protection of children shall conform with the standards established by competent authorities, particularly in the areas of safety, health, in the number and suitability of their staff, as well as competent supervision.'

this provision.[85] Given the principles of non-discrimination, equal opportunity and effective participation for all, the State has an obligation to ensure that the provisions of Art 29(2) of the CRC do not lead to extreme disparities of educational opportunity for some groups of children.[86]

The Right to Quality Education

13.45 The Committee on the Rights of the Child has emphasised that the right to education encompasses not only the content of education but also its quality.[87] A quality education is one that satisfies basic learning needs, and enriches the lives of pupils and their overall experience of living.[88] The right to quality education requires as a minimum cognitive development to be the primary objective, with the effectiveness of education measured against its success in achieving this objective, together with the promotion of creative and emotional development, the supporting of the objectives of peace, citizenship and security, the fostering of equality and the passing on of global and local cultural values.[89] Quality of education implies a broader definition of quality than simply good teaching and includes addressing the wellbeing of pupils, including health, and nutrition, the quality of the curricula including assessment and materials, the quality of the learning process, including teachers and technologies to enhance learning and the quality of the learning environment which should be child-centred, gender-sensitive, healthy and safe.[90] Quality must not suffer as access expands and improvements in quality should not benefit the economically well-off at the expense of the poor.[91] Education must encompass the basic skills of literacy and numeracy.[92]

The Right to Respect in the Learning Environment

13.46 The right to respect in the learning environment must be understood as incorporating respect for the child's identity, their right to express their views in all matters that concern them and their physical and personal integrity.[93]

---

[85] Newell, P and Hodgkin, R *Implementation Handbook for the Convention on the Rights of the Child* (2008) 3rd edn, UNICEF, p 451.

[86] See Committee on Economic, Social and Cultural Rights, General Comment No 13 *The Right to Education* HRI/GEN/1/Rev 8, p 77, para 30 commenting on the application of Art 13(3) of the ICESCR which provides that 'No part of this article shall be construed so as to interfere with the liberty of individuals and bodies to establish and direct educational institutions, subject always to the observance of the principles set forth in paragraph I of this article and to the requirement that the education given in such institutions shall conform to such minimum standards as may be laid down by the State.'

[87] See Armenia CRC/C/15/Add. 225, para 55.

[88] *A Human Rights-based Approach to Education for All: A Framework for the Realization of Children's Right to Education and Rights within Education* UNICEF/UNESCO (2007) p 17 and Art 29 CRC above. Plan of Action agreed in 2000 at the World Education Forum at Dakar, p 67 as endorsed by the UN General Assembly's special session on childhood in 2002 '*A World Fit for Children*', Report of the Ad Hoc Committee of the Whole of the twenty-seventh special session of the General Assembly, 2002, A/S-27/19/Rev.1, paras 39 and 40.

[89] *A Human Rights-based Approach to Education for All: A Framework for the Realization of Children's Right to Education and Rights within Education* UNICEF/UNESCO (2007) p 32 and Art 29 CRC above.

[90] Plan of Action agreed in 2000 at the World Education Forum at Dakar, p 67 as endorsed by the UN General Assembly's special session on childhood in 2002 '*A World Fit for Children*', Report of the Ad Hoc Committee of the Whole of the twenty-seventh special session of the General Assembly, 2002, A/S-27/19/Rev.1, paras 39 and 40.

[91] Plan of Action agreed in 2000 at the World Education Forum at Dakar, p 16.

[92] See Brazil CRC/C/15/Add. 241, para 58.

[93] *A Human Rights-based Approach to Education for All: A Framework for the Realization of Children's Right to Education and Rights within Education* UNICEF/UNESCO (2007), p 35.

'Progressively'

13.47 The words 'achieving this right progressively' recognise that the provision of education is expensive.[94] However, the word 'progressively' does not just refer to financial expenditure on education provision but also relates to the administration of education.[95] The Committee on Economic, Social and Cultural Rights defines the word 'progressively' in its General Comment No 3 *The Nature of the State Parties' Obligations*:[96]

> 'The concept of progressive realisation constitutes a recognition of the fact that full realisation of all economic, social and cultural rights will generally not be able to be achieved in a short period of time ... Nevertheless, the fact that realisation over time, or in other words progressively, is foreseen under the Covenant should not be misinterpreted as depriving the obligation of all meaningful content. It is on the one hand a necessary flexibility device, reflecting the realities of the real world and the difficulties involved for any country in ensuring full realisation of economic, social and cultural rights. On the other hand, the phrase must be read in the light of the overall objective, indeed the *raison d'être* of the Covenant which is to establish clear obligations for States Parties in respect of the full realisation of the rights in question. It thus imposes an obligation to move as expeditiously and effectively as possible towards that goal. Moreover, any deliberately retrogressive measures in that regard would require the most careful consideration and would need to be fully justified by reference to the totality of the rights provided for in the Covenant and in the context of the full use of the maximum available resources ... the Committee is of the view that a minimum core obligation to ensure the satisfaction of, at the very least, minimum essential levels of each of the rights is incumbent upon every State Party . . . If the Covenant were to be read in such a way as not to establish such a minimum core obligation, it would be largely deprived of its *raison d'être*. By the same token, it must be noted that any assessment as to whether a State has discharged its minimum core obligation must also take account of resource constraints applying within the country concerned. Article 2(1) obligates each State Party to take the necessary steps 'to the maximum of its available resources'. In order for a State Party to be able to attribute its failure to meet at least its minimum core obligations to a lack of available resources, it must demonstrate that every effort has been made to use all resources that are at its disposition in an effort to satisfy, as a matter of priority, those minimum obligations ... The Committee wishes to emphasize, however, that even where the available resources are demonstrably inadequate, the obligation remains for a State Party to strive to ensure the widest possible enjoyment of the relevant rights under the prevailing circumstances. Moreover, the obligations to monitor the extent of the realisation, or more especially of the non-realisation, of economic, social and cultural rights, and to devise strategies and programmes for their promotion, are not in any way eliminated as a result of resource constraints ...'[97]

---

[94] Newell, P and Hodgkin, R *Implementation Handbook for the Convention on the Rights of the Child* (2008) 3rd edn, UNICEF, p 407. See also Art 4 of the CRC which requires State parties to undertake measures to the maximum extent of their available resources in implementing economic, social and cultural rights.

[95] Newell, P and Hodgkin, R *Implementation Handbook for the Convention on the Rights of the Child* (2008) 3rd edn, UNICEF, p 413.

[96] Committee on Economic, Social and Cultural Rights, General Comment No 3 *The Nature of the State Parties' Obligations* HRI/GEN/1/Rev.8, para 11, pp 17 and 18 (with which the Committee on the Rights of the Child has concurred in its General Comment No 5 *General measures of implementation of the Convention on the Rights of the Child* CRC/GC/2003/5, para 8).

[97] See also Art 14 of the ICESCR which provides that: 'Each State Party to the present Covenant which, at the time of becoming a Party, has not been able to secure in its metropolitan territory or other territories under its jurisdiction compulsory primary education, free of charge, undertakes, within two years, to work out and adopt a detailed plan of action for the progressive implementation, within a reasonable number of years, to be fixed in the plan, of the principle of compulsory education free of charge for all.' See also the Committee on Economic, Social and Cultural Rights General Comment No 11 *Plans for Action for Primary Education (Art 14)* HRI/GEN/1/Rev 8, p 60 and Art 2(1) of the ICESCR.

(ii)   CRC, Art 28 – Provision of Primary Education

13.48   Article 28(1)(a) of the CRC provides in respect of primary education for children that State Parties shall in particular 'Make primary education compulsory and available free to all'.[98]

'Primary Education'

13.49   Primary education that is free, compulsory and of good quality is the cornerstone of an inclusive basic education.[99] The Art 5 of the UNESCO World Declaration on Education for All provides that:

> 'Primary education must be universal, ensure that the basic learning needs of all children are satisfied, and take into account the culture, needs, and opportunities of the community. Supplementary alternative programmes can help meet the basic learning needs of children with limited or no access to formal schooling, provided that they share the same standards of learning applied to schools, and are adequately supported.'

The obligations of States parties in relation to primary, secondary, higher and fundamental education are not identical. Given the wording of Art 28(1)(a) and Art 28(1)(b) of the CRC concerning the provision of secondary education, States parties are obliged to prioritise the introduction of compulsory, free primary education.[100]

Pre-Primary Education

13.50   Whilst State parties to the CRC are required to make primary education compulsory and available free to all there is no corresponding duty under international law for States to provide pre-primary or 'early years' education.[101] Art 28(1)(a) of the CRC does not mention pre-primary or 'early years' education. However, the Committee on the Rights of the Child has recognised the importance of this form of education:[102]

> 'The Committee interprets the right to education during early childhood as beginning at birth and closely linked to young children's right to maximum development (art. 6.2) ... States parties are reminded that children's right to education include all children, and that girls should be enabled to participate in education, without discrimination of any kind ...

---

[98]   See also Committee on Economic, Social and Cultural Rights General Comment No 11 *Plans for Action for Primary Education (Art 14)* HRI/GEN/1/Rev 8, p 60. Article 28(1)(a) of the CRC should be read in light of Art 2 and Art 14 of the ICESCR (Van Bueren, G *The International Law on the Rights of the Child* (1998) Martinus Nijhoff, p 235).

[99]   *A World Fit for Children'*, Report of the Ad Hoc Committee of the Whole of the twenty-seventh special session of the General Assembly, 2002, A/S-27/19/Rev.1, para 7. Note that primary education is not synonymous with basic education as defined in the Plan of Action agreed in 2000 at the World Education Forum at Dakar although there is close correspondence between the two (Committee on Economic, Social and Cultural Rights, General Comment No 13, 1999, HRI/GEN/1/Rev.8, para 9, p 73).

[100]   See Committee on Economic, Social and Cultural Rights, General Comment No 13 *The Right to Education* HRI/GEN/1/Rev.8, p 81, para 51 in relation to Art 13(2)(a) and 13(2)(b) of the ICESCR.

[101]   Van Bueren, G *The International Law on the Rights of the Child* (1998) Martinus Nijhoff, p 234.

[102]   Committee on the Rights of the Child, General Comment No 7 *Implementing child Rights in Early Childhood* CRC/C/GC/7/Rev.1, paras 28 and 30 and 33. The provision of pre-primary or early years education will be closely linked to the right to play under Art 31(1) of the CRC which provides that States Parties recognise the right of the child to rest and leisure, to engage in play and recreational activities appropriate to the age of the child and to participate freely in cultural life and the arts' (Committee on the Rights of the Child, General Comment No 7 *Implementing Child Rights in Early Childhood* CRC/C/GC/7/Rev.1, para 34). See also the International Charter of Physical Education and Sport Art 1 (UNESCO 21 November 1978) which provides in relation to the practice of physical education and sport that 'Special opportunities must be made available for young people, including children of pre-school age ...'.

The Committee calls on States parties to ensure that all young children receive education in the broadest sense (as outlined in paragraph 28 above), which acknowledges a key role for parents, wider family and community, as well as the contribution of organised programmes of early childhood education provided by the State, the community or civil society institutions ... Such education should be participatory and empowering to children, providing them with practical opportunities to exercise their rights and responsibilities in ways adapted to their interests, concerns and evolving capacities. Human rights education of young children should be anchored in everyday issues at home, in childcare centres, in early education programmes and other community settings with which young children can identify.'

The Committee on the Rights of the Child thus expects that pre-primary or 'early years' educational provision will be included in the State parties' general framework of education provision.[103]

'Compulsory'

13.51 Primary education must be compulsory. Note that it is the provision by the State of primary education and not school attendance that is compulsory under Art 28(1)(a) of the CRC. Thus the requirement can be fulfilled by primary education at home.[104] The element of compulsion serves to highlight the fact that neither parents, nor guardians, nor the State are entitled to treat as optional the decision as to whether the child should have access to primary education.[105] Whilst none of the international human rights instruments prescribe the duration or expected curriculum of primary education. The Committee on the Rights of the Child has indicated that compulsory primary education should comprise at least 6 years and that a minimum of 9 years primary and secondary education is expected.[106] Further, the terms of Art 29(1) of the CRC will apply to the provision of primary education.[107]

13.52 The international and regional human rights instruments make no provision for the accommodation of children's wishes in the matter of school attendance.[108] This suggests, along with the principle of compulsory primary education for children, that it is beyond argument that education, at least at a primary level, is in the child's best interests.[109] However, whilst international law provides for primary education to children to be compulsory it does not place a duty on the child to receive an education.[110]

'Free'

13.53 The word 'free' in Art 28(1)(a) of the CRC means that education at the primary stage should be secured for all children regardless of family means.[111] However, this does

---

[103] See India CRC/C/15/Add. 228, para 65.

[104] Newell, P and Hodgkin, R *Implementation Handbook for the Convention on the Rights of the Child* (2008) 3rd edn, UNICEF, p 422.

[105] Committee on Economic, Social and Cultural Rights General Comment No 11 *Plans for Action for Primary Education (Art 14)* HRI/GEN/1/Rev 8, p 61, para 6.

[106] Newell, P and Hodgkin, R *Implementation Handbook for the Convention on the Rights of the Child* (2008) 3rd edn, UNICEF, p 412.

[107] See **13.10** above.

[108] Fortin, J *Children's Rights and the Developing Law* (2009) 3rd edn, Cambridge, p 192. However, note that Art 28(1) of the CRC must be read in light of Art 12.

[109] Van Bueren, G *The International Law on the Rights of the Child* (1998) Martinus Nijhoff, p 237.

[110] Van Bueren, G *The International Law on the Rights of the Child* (1998) Martinus Nijhoff, p 237 although see Art XXXI of the American Declaration of the Rights and Duties of Man which provides that 'It is the duty of every person to acquire at least an elementary education.'

[111] Newell, P and Hodgkin, R *Implementation Handbook for the Convention on the Rights of the Child* (2008) 3rd edn, UNICEF, p 421. See also Art 26(1) of the Universal Declaration of Human Rights which provides

not require States to make all primary education free but rather to ensure that free primary education is available.[112] For example, free education provided through charitable institutions which meets the other requirements of the CRC will meet the objectives of Art 28(1)(a). All children who live in States which are party either to the ICESCR or the CRC are entitled to receive free primary education.[113] The Committee on Economic, Social and Cultural Rights has observed in relation to the requirement that primary education be free that:

> 'The nature of this requirement is unequivocal. The right is expressly formulated so as to ensure the availability of primary education without charge to the child, parents or guardians. Fees imposed by the Government, the local authorities or the school, and other direct costs, constitute disincentives to the enjoyment of the right and may jeopardise its realisation. They are also often highly regressive in effect.[114] Their elimination is a matter which must be addressed by the required plan of action. Indirect costs, such as compulsory levies on parents (sometimes portrayed as being voluntary, when in fact they are not), or the obligation to wear a relatively expensive school uniform,[115] can also fall into the same category.'[116]

(iii)   CRC, Art 28 – Provision of Secondary Education

13.54   Article 28(1)(b) of the CRC provides in respect of secondary education that State Parties shall in particular:

> 'Encourage the development of different forms of secondary education, including general and vocational education, make them available and accessible to every child, and take appropriate measures such as the introduction of free education and offering financial assistance in case of need.'

'Secondary Education'

13.55   The Committee on Economic, Social and Cultural Rights has stated in relation to the definition of 'secondary education' that:[117]

---

that 'Education shall be free, at least in the elementary and fundamental stages' and Art 13(2)(a) of the ICESCR 'Primary education shall be compulsory and available free to all.' The wording of the Universal Declaration of Human Rights Art 26(1) suggests that States should be moving in the direction of free education at secondary and higher levels as well (Van Bueren, G *The International Law on the Rights of the Child* (1998) Martinus Nijhoff, p 235. Note that the Soviet delegation proposed an amendment to the Declaration of the Rights of the Child which would have resulted in the extension of the principle of free education to secondary education (see UN Doc E/CN.4/L 539 Rev.1). See also Art XII of the American Declaration of the Rights and Duties of Man ('Every person has the right to receive, free, at least a primary education') and Principle 7 of the Declaration of the Rights of the Child 1959 ('The child is entitled to receive education, which shall be free and compulsory, at least in the elementary stages').

112   Newell, P and Hodgkin, R *Implementation Handbook for the Convention on the Rights of the Child* (2008) 3rd edn, UNICEF, p 421.

113   Van Bueren, G *The International Law on the Rights of the Child* (1998) Martinus Nijhoff, p 235.

114   See Colombia CRC/C/COL/CO/3, para 76, Republic of Congo CRC/C/COG/CO/1, para 68 and Nicaragua CRC/C/15/Add. 265, para 57.

115   See Myanmar CRC/C/15/Add. 237, para 62.

116   Committee on Economic, Social and Cultural Rights, General Comment No 11 *Plans of Action for Primary Education (Art 14)* HRI/GEN/1/Rev 8, p 62, para 7.

117   Committee on Economic, Social and Cultural Rights, General Comment No 13 *The Right to Education* HRI/GEN/1/Rev 8, p 74, para 12. The ILO Minimum Age Convention 1973 Art 2 would suggest that the minimum age for the end of secondary education is 15 years of age.

'While the content of secondary education will vary among States parties and over time, it includes completion of basic education and consolidation of the foundations for life-long learning and human development. It prepares students for vocational and higher educational opportunities.'

'Different Forms of Secondary Education'

13.56 The inclusion of vocational training in Art 28(1)(b) of the CRC recognises that secondary education must have relevance to the child's current and future life and must increase opportunity, emphasising the need for flexible curricula and delivery systems to respond to the needs of the child in his or her social setting.[118]

Available and Accessible

13.57 Article 28(1)(b) does not make secondary education compulsory in the manner Art 28(1)(a) does in respect of primary education. Nor does Art 28(1)(b) require the provision of secondary education to be dependent on the student's apparent capacity or ability as does Art 28(1)(c) in respect of the provision of higher education. The wording of Art 28(1)(b) reflects a pragmatic recognition that secondary education which is both compulsory and free is simply beyond the means of some State parties to the CRC[119] but should nonetheless be available to all regardless of capacity or ability.

13.58 The Committee on Economic, Social and Cultural Rights has interpreted the words 'available and accessible' in relation to secondary education:[120]

'The phrase "generally available" signifies, firstly, that secondary education is not dependent on a student's apparent capacity or ability and, secondly, that secondary education will be distributed throughout the State in such a way that it is available on the same basis to all. For the Committee's interpretation of "accessible", see paragraph 6 above. The phrase "every appropriate means" reinforces the point that States parties should adopt varied and innovative approaches to the delivery of secondary education in different social and cultural contexts.'

13.59 Hodgkin and Newell suggest that the words 'take appropriate measures such as the introduction of free education and offering financial assistance in case of need' in Art 28(1)(b) imply that means testing for secondary education would not contravene Art 28(1)(b) but caution that such an approach can militate against availability and accessibility to every child.[121] Van Bueren notes that whilst this interpretation is possible it should not be allowed to detract from the State's overriding duty under Art 28(1)(b) to make secondary education progressively available and accessible to every child.[122]

---

[118] Newell, P and Hodgkin, R *Implementation Handbook for the Convention on the Rights of the Child* (2008) 3rd edn, UNICEF, p 423 and see Committee on Economic, Social and Cultural Rights, General Comment No 13, 1999, HRI/GEN/1/Rev 8, p 74, para 12.

[119] Newell, P and Hodgkin, R *Implementation Handbook for the Convention on the Rights of the Child* (2008) 3rd edn, UNICEF, p 422.

[120] Committee on Economic, Social and Cultural Rights, General Comment No 13 *The Right to Education* HRI/GEN/1/Rev 8, p 74, para 13. Accessibility has three overlapping dimensions, namely non-discrimination, physical accessibility and economic accessibility (Committee on Economic, Social and Cultural Rights General Comment No 13 *The Right to Education* HRI/GEN/1/Rev 8, p 73, para 6).

[121] Newell, P and Hodgkin, R *Implementation Handbook for the Convention on the Rights of the Child* (2008) 3rd edn, UNICEF, p 422.

[122] Van Bueren, G *The International Law on the Rights of the Child* (1998) Martinus Nijhoff, p 236.

'General and Vocational Education'[123]

13.60 Both Art 28(1)(b) of the CRC and Art 13(2)(b) of the ICESCR incorporate vocational training as an integral element of secondary education, reflecting the particular importance of vocational education at that level.[124] However, note that the Committee on Economic, Social and Cultural Rights takes the view that vocational training should be an integral element of education at all levels.[125] Art 1(a) of the UNESCO Convention on Technical and Vocational Education defines vocational education as:[126]

> '... all forms and levels of the educational process involving, in addition to general knowledge, the study of technologies and related sciences and the acquisition of practical skills, know-how, attitudes and understanding relating to occupations in the various sectors of economic and social life.'

(iv) CRC, Art 28 – Provision of Higher Education

13.61 Many of those accessing high education will not be of an age to come within the definition of 'child' for the purposes of Art 1 of the CRC but the inclusion of higher education is logical given its place in the continuum of the child's education and the fact that there will be circumstances where children younger than 18 will qualify for higher education based on their capacity. Article 28(1)(c) of the CRC provides in respect of higher education that State Parties shall in particular 'Make higher education accessible to all on the basis of capacity by every appropriate means'.

13.62 Note that the terms of Art 28(1)(c) differ from the corresponding provision in the ICESCR in that there is no reference in the CRC to the progressive introduction of free higher education. Article 28(1)(c) did originally contain a reference to the progressive introduction of free higher education but this was removed at the behest of the United Kingdom during the second reading of the CRC.[127]

'Accessible'

13.63 Article 28(1)(c) uses the term 'accessible' rather than the term 'available and accessible'. In respect of the accessability of higher education the Committee on Economic, Social and Cultural Rights suggests that in practice higher education, like

---

123 See also the discussion of Art 28(1)(d) of the CRC in relation to educational and vocational information and guidance at **13.65** below.

124 See also Committee on Economic, Social and Cultural Rights General Comment No 18 *The Right to Work* HRI/GEN/1/Rev 8, p 152, para 15 ('The Committee reaffirms the need to protect children from economic exploitation, to enable them to pursue their full development and acquire technical and vocational education ...').

125 Committee on Economic, Social and Cultural Rights, General Comment No 13 *The Right to Education* HRI/GEN/1/Rev 8, p 74, para 15. See also Art 6(a)(i) of the Revised Recommendation Concerning Technical and Vocational Education (adopted by the General Conference of UNESCO in 1974) which stipulates that vocational and technical training should be integrated into all education streams above primary level and the ILO Convention No 142 *Human Resources and Development Convention* concerning Vocational Guidance Art 2 ('With the above ends in view, each Member shall establish and develop open, flexible and complementary systems of general, technical and vocational education, educational and vocational guidance and vocational training, whether these activities take place within the system of formal education or outside it').

126 See also Committee on Economic, Social and Cultural Rights General Comment No 13 *The Right to Education* HRI/GEN/1/Rev 8, p 75, para 16.

127 Van Bueren, G *The International Law on the Rights of the Child* (1998) Martinus Nijhoff, p 236.

secondary education, must be available 'in different forms' if it is to respond to the needs of students in different social and cultural settings.[128]

'On the basis of capacity'

13.64 The term 'on the basis of capacity' refers to the capacity of the student rather than the capacity of the State to make provision for higher education. In determining the capacity of the child for the purposes of admission to higher education care must be taken that capacity is measured in ways which do not discriminate against children from poorer backgrounds, for example by measuring more than just 'teachable' skills.[129] The 'capacity' of individuals should be assessed by reference to all their relevant expertise and experience.[130]

(v)   CRC, Art 28 – Information and Guidance

13.65 Article 28(1)(d) of the CRC provides that State Parties shall in particular 'Make educational and vocational information and guidance available and accessible to all children'.[131] Children can only develop their potential if a range of opportunities are available and they know how to obtain information on those opportunities.[132] Art 28(1)(d) requires States parties to make the information available to *and* accessible by children on the basis of equal opportunity in education under Art 28(1) of the CRC.[133]

(vi)   CRC, Art 28 – Attendance at School

13.66 Article 28(1)(e) of the CRC provides in relation to school attendance that State parties shall in particular 'Take measures to encourage regular attendance at schools and the reduction of drop-out rates'. Article 28(1)(e) of the CRC mandates State parties to take positive steps to ensure children remain in school. This will require, *inter alia*, measures which ensure a high quality of teaching, relevant and interesting curricula, including vocational education, the eradication of financial disincentives to remain in education, measures to combat teenage pregnancy, programmes to increase the participation of children in their schooling provision under Art 12 of the CRC, programmes for minority and indigenous cultures and languages and systems to establish the causes of lack of attendance and to generate policies to address them. The Committee on the Rights of the Child has, in relation to prevention of juvenile delinquency, emphasised the need for particular attention to be given to children who drop out of school or otherwise do not complete their education.[134]

---

[128] Committee on Economic, Social and Cultural Rights, General Comment No 13 *The Right to Education* HRI/GEN/1/Rev.8, p 75, para 18.

[129] Newell, P and Hodgkin, R *Implementation Handbook for the Convention on the Rights of the Child* (2008) 3rd edn, UNICEF, p 425.

[130] Committee on Economic, Social and Cultural Rights, General Comment No 13 *The Right to Education* HRI/GEN/1/Rev.8, p 76, para 19.

[131] See also the ILO Human Resources Development Convention No 142 Art 2.

[132] Newell, P and Hodgkin, R *Implementation Handbook for the Convention on the Rights of the Child* (2008) 3rd edn, UNICEF, p 426.

[133] Van Bueren, G *The International Law on the Rights of the Child* (1998) Martinus Nijhoff, p 239.

[134] Committee on the Rights of the Child General Comment No 10 *Children's Rights in Juvenile Justice* CRC/C/GC/10 p 7, para 18.

(vii)   CRC, Art 28 – Administration of School Discipline

13.67 Article 28(2) of the CRC stipulates in relation to discipline in schools[135] that State parties shall in particular:

> 'States Parties shall take all appropriate measures to ensure that school discipline is administered in a manner consistent with the child's human dignity and in conformity with the present Convention.'[136]

Consistent with Human Dignity and in Conformity with the CRC

13.68 The key principle articulated by Art 28(2) of the CRC is that school discipline should conform to a manner consistent with the child's human dignity and in conformity with CRC as a whole.[137] Further, teaching methods, including methods of discipline, should reflect the philosophy of the CRC as a whole.[138]

Prohibition on Corporal Punishment in Schools

13.69 Article 28(2) of the CRC makes no specific mention of corporal punishment and there is no reference to the issue in the *travaux préparatoires* for the CRC. However, as a living instrument the Committee on the Rights of the Child has made clear that within the context of the CRC generally[139] and of Art 28(2) in particular the practice of

---

[135] There is no distinction drawn between public and private schools for the purposes of Art 28(2) of the CRC (see United Kingdom CRC/C/15/ Add.34, para 16 and CRC/C/SR.206, para 5: 'The right not to receive corporal punishment was a fundamental right, and one could not therefore lay down a different regime according to whether the school was public or private, all the more so as that would give rise to the question of discrimination and the application of article 2 of the Convention to the education system, since whether a child was sent to a state or private school was generally linked to the family's standard of living').

[136] By reason of the words 'in conformity with the present Convention' in Art 28(2) of the CRC it should be read with Art 19(1) ('States Parties shall take all appropriate legislative, administrative, social and educational measures to protect the child from all forms of physical or mental violence, injury or abuse, neglect or negligent treatment, maltreatment or exploitation, including sexual abuse, while in the care of parent(s), legal guardian(s) or any other person who has the care of the child.'). The provisions of Art 19(1) will encompass the actions of teachers (Van Bueren, G *The International Law on the Rights of the Child* (1998) Martinus Nijhoff, p 249). See also Art 37 of the CRC ('no child shall be subjected to torture or other cruel, inhuman or degrading treatment or punishment' and the Human Rights Committee General Comment No 7 *(Prohibition of Torture or Cruel, Inhuman or Degrading Treatment or Punishment)* HRI/GEN/1/Rev 8, p 168, para 2 ('In the view of the Committee the prohibition [on torture or cruel, inhuman or degrading treatment or punishment] must extend to corporal punishment, including excessive chastisement as an educational or disciplinary measure').

[137] See also the preamble to the CRC.

[138] See CRC/C/15/Add. 46, para 12.

[139] Note that Art 3(3) of the CRC stipulates that 'States Parties shall ensure that the institutions, services and facilities responsible for the care or protection of children shall conform with the standards established by competent authorities, particularly in the areas of safety, health, in the number and suitability of their staff, as well as competent supervision.' Art 3(3) will require clear standards to be established in legislation prohibiting corporal punishment and any other inhuman or degrading treatment or punishment in institutions, clear policies for the prevent of any forms of violence by children against child in institutions and clear and well advertised procedures to enable children to seek confidential advice and to make representations and complaints about their treatment to an independent body, with access where necessary to independent advocates or representatives (see Newell, P and Hodgkin, R *Implementation Handbook for the Convention on the Rights of the Child* (2008) 3rd edn, UNICEF, p 264).

corporal punishment directly conflicts with the equal and inalienable right of children to respect for their human dignity and physical integrity.[140] The Committee on the Rights of the Child has commented that:[141]

> 'Children do not lose their human rights by virtue of passing through the school gates. Thus, for example, education must be provided in a way that respects the inherent dignity of the child ... Education must also be provided in a way that respects the strict limits on discipline reflected in article 28 (2) and promotes non-violence in school. The Committee has repeatedly made clear in its concluding observations that the use of corporal punishment does not respect the inherent dignity of the child nor the strict limits on school discipline. Compliance with the values recognised in article 29 (1) clearly requires that schools be child-friendly in the fullest sense of the term and that they be consistent in all respects with the dignity of the child. The participation of children in school life, the creation of school communities and student councils, peer education and peer counseling, and the involvement of children in school disciplinary proceedings should be promoted as part of the process of learning and experiencing the realisation of rights.'

13.70 The Committee on the Rights of the Child deprecates *all* forms of corporal punishment, however mild, as unacceptable forms of discipline in schools. This also encompasses the prevention of bullying as between students and by teachers of students.[142] The Committee on the Rights of the Child defines 'corporal' or 'physical' punishment as follows:[143]

> '... any punishment in which physical force is used and intended to cause some degree of pain or discomfort, however light. Most involves hitting ("smacking", "slapping", "spanking") children, with the hand or with an implement – a whip, stick, belt, shoe, wooden spoon, etc. But it can also involve, for example, kicking, shaking or throwing children, scratching, pinching, biting, pulling hair or boxing ears, forcing children to stay in uncomfortable positions, burning, scalding or forced ingestion (for example, washing children's mouths out with soap or forcing them to swallow hot spices). In the view of the Committee, corporal punishment is invariably degrading. In addition, there are other non-physical forms of punishment that are also cruel and degrading and thus incompatible with the Convention. These include, for example, punishment which belittles, humiliates, denigrates, scapegoats, threatens, scares or ridicules the child.'

---

[140] Committee on the Rights of the Child General Comment No 8 *The Right of the Child to Protection from Corporal Punishment and other Cruel or Degrading forms of Punishment (arts. 19; 28, para 2; and 37, inter alia)* CRC/C/GC/8, paras 20 and 21.

[141] Committee on the Rights of the Child, General Comment No 1 *The Aims of Education*, CRC/GC/2001/1, para 8.

[142] Newell, P and Hodgkin, R *Implementation Handbook for the Convention on the Rights of the Child* (2008) 3rd edn, UNICEF, p 431. The Committee on the Rights of the Child has made clear that a 'school which allows bullying or other violent and exclusionary practices to occur is not one which meets the requirements of article 29 (1)' (Committee on the Rights of the Child, General Comment No 1, 2001, CRC/GC/2001/1, p 353–354, para 19). See also Sweden CRC/C/15/Add.248, paras 35 and 36.

[143] Committee on the Rights of the Child General Comment No 8 *The Right of the Child to Protection from Corporal Punishment and other Cruel or Degrading forms of Punishment (arts. 19; 28, para 2; and 37, inter alia)* CRC/C/GC/8, para 11. See also Committee on Economic, Social and Cultural Rights, General Comment No 13 *The Right to Education* HRI/GEN/1/Rev.8, p 79, para 41 ('In the Committee's view, corporal punishment is inconsistent with the fundamental guiding principle of international human rights law enshrined in the Preambles to the Universal Declaration of Human Rights and both Covenants: the dignity of the individual. Other aspects of school discipline may also be inconsistent with human dignity, such as public humiliation. Nor should any form of discipline breach other rights under the Covenant, such as the right to food. A State party is required to take measures to ensure that discipline which is inconsistent with the Covenant does not occur in any public or private educational institution within its jurisdiction. The Committee welcomes initiatives taken by some States parties which actively encourage schools to introduce 'positive', non-violent approaches to school discipline').

13.71 It is important to note that the prohibition on violence and humiliation as forms of punishment should not be taken as rejecting the positive concept of discipline in respect of children. The Committee on the Rights of the Child recognises that 'The healthy development of children depends on parents and other adults for necessary guidance and direction, in line with children's evolving capacities, to assist their growth towards responsible life in society'.[144] In this regard, the Committee distinguishes between physical actions and interventions designed to protect children and the deliberate and punitive use of force to cause some degree of pain, discomfort or humiliation.[145] Note also that the Committee recognises that there are exceptional circumstances in which teachers and others may be confronted by dangerous behaviour which justifies the use of reasonable restraint to control it. Here too there is a clear distinction between the use of force motivated by the need to protect a child or others and the use of force to punish. In all the circumstances, the principle of the minimum necessary use of force for the shortest necessary period of time must always apply.[146] There can be no religious justification for corporal punishment in schools.[147]

13.72 The term 'appropriate measures' in Art 28(2) of the CRC will include measures to ensure the enforcement of legal prohibitions on corporal punishment[148] and equipping children with measures to protect themselves from corporal punishment.[149]

Exclusion from School – Due Process

13.73 Where a child is excluded from school the process of exclusion should conform to the rules of natural justice and with the child's right to participate under Art 12 of the CRC.[150] The Committee on the Rights of the Child has observed that:[151]

> 'In decisions about the transition to the next level of schools or choice of tracks or streams, the right of the child to be heard has to be assured as these decisions deeply affect the child's best interests. Such decisions must be subject to administrative or judicial review. Additionally, in disciplinary matters, the right of the child to be heard has to be fully respected. In particular, in the case of exclusion of a child from instruction or school, this decision must be subject to judicial review as it contradicts the child's right to education.'

13.74 In *Goss v Lopez*[152] the US Supreme Court held that due process requires, in connection with a suspension of 10 days or less, that that the student be given oral or written notice of the charges against him or her and, if he or she denies them, an

---

[144] See Committee on the Rights of the Child General Comment No 8 *The Right of the Child to Protection from Corporal Punishment and other Cruel or Degrading forms of Punishment (arts. 19; 28, para 2; and 37, inter alia)* CRC/C/GC/8, para 13.

[145] Committee on the Rights of the Child General Comment No 8 *The Right of the Child to Protection from Corporal Punishment and other Cruel or Degrading forms of Punishment (arts. 19; 28, para 2; and 37, inter alia)* CRC/C/GC/8, para 14.

[146] Committee on the Rights of the Child General Comment No 8 *The Right of the Child to Protection from Corporal Punishment and other Cruel or Degrading forms of Punishment (arts. 19; 28, para 2; and 37, inter alia)* CRC/C/GC/8, para 15.

[147] Committee on the Rights of the Child General Comment No 8 *The Right of the Child to Protection from Corporal Punishment and other Cruel or Degrading forms of Punishment (arts. 19; 28, para 2; and 37, inter alia)* CRC/C/GC/8, para 29.

[148] See Hungary CRC/C/HUN/CO/2, paras 54 and 55.

[149] See Malawi CRC/C/15/Add. 174, para 56.

[150] Newell, P and Hodgkin, R *Implementation Handbook for the Convention on the Rights of the Child* (2008) 3rd edn, UNICEF, p 430.

[151] Committee on the Rights of the Child General Comment No 12 (2009) *The Right of the Child to be Heard* CRC/C/GC/12 p 22, para 113.

[152] 419 US 565 (1975).

explanation of the evidence the authorities have and an opportunity to present his or her version. Justice White held, Justices Powell, Burger, Blackmun and Rehnquist dissenting, that:

> 'School authorities here suspended appellees from school for periods of up to 10 days based on charges of misconduct. If sustained and recorded, those charges could seriously damage the students' standing with their fellow pupils and their teachers as well as interfere with later opportunities for higher education and employment ... "education is perhaps the most important function of state and local governments" and the total exclusion from the educational process for more than a trivial period, and certainly if the suspension is for 10 days, is a serious event in the life of the suspended child ... At the very minimum, therefore, students facing suspension and the consequent interference with a protected property interest must be given some kind of notice and afforded some kind of hearing. "Parties whose rights are to be affected are entitled to be heard; and in order that they may enjoy that right they must first be notified."... Some modicum of discipline and order is essential if the educational function is to be performed. Events calling for discipline are frequent occurrences and sometimes require immediate, effective action. Suspension is considered not only to be a necessary tool to maintain order but a valuable educational device. The prospect of imposing elaborate hearing requirements in every suspension case is viewed with great concern, and many school authorities may well prefer the untrammeled power to act unilaterally, unhampered by rules about notice and hearing. But it would be a strange disciplinary system in an educational institution if no communication was sought by the disciplinarian with the student in an effort to inform him of his dereliction and to let him tell his side of the story in order to make sure that an injustice is not done.'[153]

Other Forms of Discipline

13.75 The words 'consistent with the child's human dignity and in conformity with the present Convention' also require that other forms of punishment that are inconsistent with the child's human dignity and rights under the Convention are prohibited under Art 28(2), including forms such as public humiliation, prevention of access to friends and family and denial of rest or leisure.[154]

(viii) CRC, Art 28 – International Cooperation in respect of Education

13.76 Article 28(3) of the CRC provides in relation to international cooperation on matters concerning education that State parties:

> 'States Parties shall promote and encourage international cooperation in matters relating to education, in particular with a view to contributing to the elimination of ignorance and illiteracy throughout the world and facilitating access to scientific and technical knowledge and modern teaching methods. In this regard, particular account shall be taken of the needs of developing countries.'

---

[153] Note that the Supreme Court held that there need be no delay between the time 'notice' is given and the time of the hearing and that, in the great majority of cases, the disciplinarian may informally discuss the alleged misconduct with the student, the student being given an opportunity to explain his version of the facts at this discussion after first being told what he or she is accused of doing and what the basis of the accusation is. Further, in respect of recurring situations in which prior notice and hearing cannot be insisted upon and in situations where students whose presence poses a continuing danger to persons or property or an ongoing threat of disrupting the academic process, the Supreme Court accepted that the student may be immediately removed from school and the necessary notice and rudimentary hearing should follow as soon as practicable thereafter. Finally, in relation to suspensions of more than 10 days in length or unusual situations leading to shorter suspensions, the Supreme Court accepted that these may require more formal procedures.

[154] Committee on Economic, Social and Cultural Rights, General Comment No 11 *Plans of action for primary education (art. 14)* HRI/GEN/1/Rev 8, p 79, para 41.

Right to Education under the CRC – Application

Education and Girls

13.77 In its Resolution entitled Further Actions and Initiatives to implement the Beijing Declaration and Platform for Action[155] the UN General Assembly observed that:

> 'In some countries, efforts to eradicate illiteracy and strengthen literacy among women and girls and to increase their access to all levels and types of education were constrained by the lack of resources and insufficient political will and commitment to improve educational infrastructure and undertake educational reforms; persisting gender discrimination and bias, including in teacher training; gender-based occupational stereotyping in schools, institutions of further education and communities; lack of childcare facilities; persistent use of gender stereotypes in educational materials; and insufficient attention paid to the link between women's enrolment in higher educational institutions and labour market dynamics. The remote location of some communities and, in some cases, inadequate salaries and benefits make attracting and retaining teaching professionals difficult and can result in lower quality education. Additionally, in a number of countries, economic, social and infrastructural barriers, as well as traditional discriminatory practices, have contributed to lower enrolment and retention rates for girls.'

13.78 Gender disparities in primary and secondary education should be eliminated.[156] Note however that equality of education between girls and boys requires more than mere parity in the number of girls and boys registered to attend school.[157] Further, a focus on eliminating discrimination in education in respect of girls should not result in a loss of focus on discriminatory practices which may affect boys. In its Resolution entitled *A World Fit for Children* the UN General Assembly recorded that 'All girls and boys must have access to and complete primary education that is free, compulsory and of good quality as a cornerstone of an inclusive basic education.[158] Teenage pregnancy can have a detrimental effect on adolescent girls' education, as can early marriage. In its General Comment No 4 *Adolescent Health and Development in the Context of the Rights of the Child* the Committee on the Rights of Child states that:[159]

> 'Adolescent girls should have access to information on the harm that early marriage and early pregnancy can cause ... The Committee urges States parties ... to develop policies that will allow adolescent mothers to continue their education.'

---

[155] See the Fourth World Conference on Women, Platform for Action, Beijing 1995 A/CONF.177/20/Rev. 1, paras 263 and 279.

[156] Report of the Ad Hoc Committee of the Whole of the 27th special session of the General Assembly, 2002, A/S-27/19/Rev.1, para 7(5). See also General Comment No 16 *The Equal Right of Men and Women to the Enjoyment of All Economic, Social and Cultural Rights* HRI/GEN/1/Rev 8, p 128, para 30.

[157] United Nations, Economic and Social Council, Commission on Human Rights, 62nd Session, *Girls' Right to Education*, Report submitted by the Special Rapporteur on the right to education E/CN.4/2006/45 p 10, para 61. See also the Convention on the Elimination of All Forms of Discrimination against Women Art 10 (GA Res 34/180 1979) which is also applicable to girls (Van Bueren, G *The International Law on the Rights of the Child* (1998) Martinus Nijhoff, p 246).

[158] See also the recommendations for addressing discrimination against girls in education in Fourth World Conference on Women, Platform for Action, Beijing, 1995 A/CONF.177/20/Rev.1, paras 276, 277, 279 and 280.

[159] Committee on the Rights of the Child General Comment No 4 *Adolescent Health and Development in the Context of the Rights of the Child* HRI/GEN/1/Rev 8, p 383, para 27.

Education and Rural children

13.79 Children in rural areas face more limitations on their educational opportunities than their urban counterparts.[160] Steps should be taken to ensure equality of educational opportunity as between rural and urban populations of children, including equality of opportunity in respect of vocational and technical training.[161]

Education and Children of Minority and Indigenous Groups

13.80 The maintenance of a separate identity by minority and indigenous groups depends in large part on their ability to maintain its continuity by educating their children to understand and respect their own customs, religion and culture.[162]

(i) Children of Minority Groups

13.81 In relation to educational provision for children from national minority populations, Art 5(1)(c) of the UNESCO Convention against Discrimination in Education stipulates that:

'It is essential to recognise the right of members of national minorities to carry on their own educational activities, including the maintenance of schools and, depending on the educational policy of each State, the use or the teaching of their own language, provided however:

(i)   That this right is not exercised in a manner which prevents the members of these minorities from understanding the culture and language of the community as a whole and from participating in its activities, or which prejudices national sovereignty;

(ii)   That the standard of education is not lower than the general standard laid down or approved by the competent authorities; and

(iii)   That attendance at such schools is optional.'

(ii) Children of Indigenous Groups

13.82 In respect of education for the children of indigenous communities, the Committee on the Rights of the Child has highlighted that:[163]

'The education of indigenous children contributes both to their individual and community development as well as to their participation in the wider society. Quality education enables indigenous children to exercise and enjoy economic, social and cultural rights for their personal benefit as well as for the benefit of their community. Furthermore, it strengthens children's ability to exercise their civil rights in order to influence political policy processes for improved protection of human rights. Thus, the implementation of the right to education of indigenous children is an essential means of achieving individual empowerment and self-determination of indigenous peoples.'

13.83 The preamble to the UN Declaration on the Rights of Indigenous Peoples[164] recognises the right of indigenous families and communities to retain shared

---

[160]   See UN *The Millennium Development Goals Report 2006 p* 7. See also Mozambique CRFC/C/83/ Add.1, para 35 and Marshall Islands CRC/C/15/Add.139.
[161]   See the Revised Recommendation Concerning Technical and Vocational Education (2001), para 40.
[162]   Fortin, J *Children's Rights and the Developing Law* (2009) 3rd edn, Cambridge, p 406.
[163]   Committee on the Rights of the Child General Comment No 11 *Indigenous Children and their Rights under the Convention* CRC/C/GC/11, para 57.
[164]   GA Res. 61/295 2007, p 3.

responsibility for the upbringing, training, education and well-being of their children, consistent with the rights of the child.[165] To this end, Art 14 of the Declaration provides that:

'1. Indigenous peoples have the right to establish and control their educational systems and institutions providing education in their own languages, in a manner appropriate to their cultural methods of teaching and learning.

2. Indigenous individuals, particularly children, have the right to all levels and forms of education of the State without discrimination.[166]

3. States shall, in conjunction with indigenous peoples,[167] take effective measures, in order for indigenous individuals, particularly children, including those living outside their communities, to have access, when possible, to an education in their own culture and provided in their own language.'[168]

13.84 In respect of indigenous children Art 30 of the CRC is also relevant to the provision of non-discriminatory educational provision, stipulating that:

'In those States in which ethnic, religious or linguistic minorities or persons of indigenous origin exist, a child belonging to such a minority or who is indigenous shall not be denied the right, in community with other members of his or her group, to enjoy his or her own culture, to profess and practise his or her own religion, or to use his or her own language.'[169]

---

[165] See also Committee on the Rights of the Child General Comment No 11 *Indigenous Children and their Rights under the Convention* CRC/C/GC/11, paras 56–63.

[166] See the Committee on the Rights of the Child General Comment No 11 *Indigenous Children and their Rights under the Convention* CRC/C/GC/11, para 58 ('In order to ensure that the aims of education are in line with the Convention, States parties are responsible for protecting children from all forms of discrimination as set out in article 2 of the Convention and for actively combating racism. This duty is particularly pertinent in relation to indigenous children. In order to effectively implement this obligation, States parties should ensure that the curricula, educational materials and history text books provide a fair, accurate and informative portrayal of the societies and cultures of indigenous peoples. Discriminatory practices, such as restrictions on the use cultural and traditional dress, should be avoided in the school setting').

[167] States parties must identify the existing barriers to education and the specific rights and needs of indigenous children with respect to school education and vocational training. This requires that special efforts be taken to maintain a dialogue with indigenous communities and parents regarding the importance and benefits of education (Committee on the Rights of the Child General Comment No 11 *Indigenous Children and their Rights under the Convention* CRC/C/GC/11, para 71).

[168] See also United Nations Declaration on the Rights of Indigenous Peoples (GA Res. 61/295 2007) Art 15 ('Indigenous peoples have the right to the dignity and diversity of their cultures, traditions, histories and aspirations which shall be appropriately reflected in education and public information'), Art 17 ('States shall in consultation and cooperation with indigenous peoples take specific measures to protect indigenous children from economic exploitation and from performing any work that is likely to be hazardous or to interfere with the child's education, or to be harmful to the child's health or physical, mental, spiritual, moral or social development, taking into account their special vulnerability and the importance of education for their empowerment') and Art 21 ('Indigenous peoples have the right, without discrimination, to the improvement of their economic and social conditions, including, inter alia, in the areas of education, employment, vocational training and retraining, housing, sanitation, health and social security'). See further the ILO Convention No 169 Concerning Indigenous and Tribal Peoples which highlights the rights of indigenous children in the area of education and Committee on the Rights of the Child General Comment No 11 *Indigenous Children and their Rights under the Convention* CRC/C/GC/11, paras 60–61.

[169] See also the United Nations Declaration on the Rights of Indigenous Peoples (GA Res. 61/295 2007), Art 44.

(iii)   Access to Education for Minority and Indigenous Groups

13.85 Minority and indigenous groups should have equality of access to educational provision.[170] Such equality of access will comprise access either to all levels and forms of education provided by the State or to forms of education in their own languages, in a manner appropriate to their cultural methods of teaching and learning to a standard which is not lower than the general standard laid down or approved by the competent authorities.[171] The World Conference against Racism, Racial Discrimination, Xenophobia and Related Intolerance Programme of Action[172] stipulates that States should ensure equal access to education for all, in law and in practice, refrain from any legal or other measures leading to imposed racial segregation in access to schooling and:

> 'Urges States to adopt, where applicable, appropriate measures to ensure that persons belonging to national or ethnic, religious and linguistic minorities have access to education without discrimination of any kind and, where possible, have an opportunity to learn their own language in order to protect them from any form of racism, racial discrimination, xenophobia and related intolerance that they may be subjected to.'[173]

(iv)   Standard of Education for Minority and Indigenous Groups

13.86 The standard of education for children of minority and indigenous groups should be equal to the general standard laid down and approved by competent national authorities.[174] Van Bueren notes that the quality of education provided in the minority language should be on the basis of reasonable equality with the major language although it need not be identical.[175] In *Jean Claude Mahe v Alberta*[176] the Supreme Court of Canada expressed the *obita* opinion that:

> '... the quality of education provided to the minority should in principle be on a basis of equality with the majority ... However, the specific form of educational system provided to the minority need not be identical to that provided to the majority. The different circumstances under which various schools find themselves, as well as the demands of a minority language education itself, make such a requirement impractical and undesirable.'

Article 13(3) of the ICESCR permits the imposition by the state of minimum standards on schools other than those established by the public authorities in order to balance the need to respect the religious and moral convictions of parents with the child's right to an education that prepares them fully for life.[177] Respect for the religious and moral liberty

---

[170] Committee on the Rights of the Child General Comment No 11 *Indigenous Children and their Rights under the Convention* CRC/C/GC/11, para 25.

[171] Article 5(1)(c) UNESCO Convention against Discrimination in Education and Art 14 United Nations Declaration on the Rights of Indigenous Peoples.

[172] (2001) A/CONF.189/12, paras 121 and 122.

[173] See for example the measures proposed to ensure the inclusion in national school systems of all children of Roma origin in Committee on the Elimination of Racial Discrimination General Recommendation XXVII (2000) HRI/GEN/1/Rev.8, pp 261 and 262, paras 17–26.

[174] See Art 5(c)(ii) UNESCO Convention against Discrimination in Education. Note that by reason of the fact that the attendance at schools arising out of the exercise of the right of members of national minorities to carry on their own educational activities, including the maintenance of schools is optional, the entitlements under Art 5 of the UNESCO are not unconditional (see Art 5(c)(iii)). See also Committee on the Elimination of Racial Discrimination General Recommendation XXIX (2002) HRI/GEN/1/Rev.8, p 272.

[175] Van Bueren, G *The International Law on the Rights of the Child* (1998) Martinus Nijhoff, p 259.

[176] [1980] 1 SCR 342 (Sup Ct Canada).

[177] See also *Wisconsin v Yoder* 406 US 205 (1972), US Sup Ct and *Prince v Massachusetts* 321 US 158 (1944), US Sup Ct.

of parents and guardians must not be allowed to lead to extreme disparities of educational opportunity between different groups in society.[178]

(v) Minority Languages and the Right to Education

13.87 In addition to providing a means of communication, language is also a means by which peoples may express and promote their cultural identities.[179] In *Jean Claude Mahe v Alberta*[180] the Dickson CJ discussed the importance of language and observed:

> 'My reference to cultures is significant: it is based on the fact that any broad guarantee of language rights, especially in the context of education, cannot be separated from a concern for the culture associated with the language. Language is more than a mere means of communication, it is part and parcel of the identity and culture of the people speaking it. It is the means by which individuals understand themselves and the world around them ... Language is not merely a means or medium of expression; it colors the content and meaning of expression ... Language is also the key to cultural development. Language and culture are not synonymous, but the vitality of the language is a necessary condition for the complete preservation of a culture.'

13.88 Within the context of education in A Human Rights-based Approach to Education for All: A Framework for the Realisation of Children's Right to Education and Rights within Education[181] UNESCO notes that:

> 'there is an implication that States should facilitate the use of a child's first language especially in the earliest years of education ... It encourages community mobilisation and social development, overcomes exclusion and marginalisation, and provides for a political voice. It also increases economic opportunity and mobility.'[182]

Note that the Convention on the Rights of Persons with Disabilities Art 24(3)(c) requires that States parties ensure that 'the education of persons, and in particular children, who are blind, deaf or deaf-blind, is delivered in the most appropriate languages and modes and means of communication for the individual'.[183]

Education and Unaccompanied and Separated Children

13.89 The right of the unaccompanied or separated child to education is the same as that enjoyed by national children.[184] The Committee on the Rights of the Child has stipulated the following particular requirements concerning educational provision for unaccompanied and asylum seeking children:[185]

---

[178] Committee on Economic, Social and Cultural Rights General Comment No 13 *The Right to Education (article 13)* E/C.12/1999/10, paras 28, 29, 30. See also *A Human Rights-based Approach to Education for All: A Framework for the Realization of Children's Right to Education and Rights within Education'*, UNICEF/UNESCO (2007), pp 78–79.

[179] See Van Bueren, G *The International Law on the Rights of the Child* (1998) Martinus Nijhoff, p 247 and *Ford v Attorney General of Quebec* (1988) SCR 712 at 748–749 (Sup Ct Canada), para 40.

[180] [1980] 1 SCR 342 (Sup Ct Canada).

[181] UNICEF/UNESCO (2007), p 78. See also *Access to German Minority Schools in Upper Silesia* PCIJ Ser. No 40 8 (1931). However, see also the discussion of the *Belgian Linguistic Case (No 2)* (1968) 1 EHRR 252 at **13.109** below.

[182] See Ireland CRC/C/IRL/CO/2, paras 60 and 61. See also the decision of the Human Rights Committee in *EP et al v Colombia* Communication 318/1988 CCPR/C/OP/3, p 87 and the decision of the UN Human Rights Committee in *Diergardt v Namibia* Communication No 760/1997 CCPR/C/69/D/760/1997.

[183] Discussed further at **13.92** below.

[184] Committee on the Rights of the Child General Comment No 6: *Treatment of Unaccompanied and Separated Children outside their Country of Origin* HRI/GEN/1/Rev 8, p 429, para 90.

[185] These principles will also be applicable to migrant children (Newell, P and Hodgkin, R *Implementation*

'States should ensure that access to education is maintained during all phases of the displacement cycle. Every unaccompanied and separated child, irrespective of status, shall have full access to education in the country that they have entered ... Such access should be granted without discrimination and, in particular, separated and unaccompanied girls shall have equal access to formal and informal education, including vocational training at all levels. Access to quality education should also be ensured for children with special needs, in particular children with disabilities ... The unaccompanied or separated child should be registered with appropriate school authorities as soon as possible and get assistance in maximising learning opportunities. All unaccompanied and separated children have the right to maintain their cultural identity and values, including the maintenance and development of their native language. All adolescents should be allowed to enroll in vocational/professional training or education, and early learning programmes should be made available to young children. States should ensure that unaccompanied or separated children are provided with school certificates or other documentation indicating their level of education, in particular in preparation of relocation, resettlement or return.'[186]

13.90 Where the unaccompanied or separated child is detained the Committee on the Rights of the Child requires that during their period in detention, children have the right to education which ought, ideally, to take place outside the detention premises in order to facilitate the continuance of their education upon release.[187]

Education and Children with Disabilities

13.91 All children, no matter what their disability, are entitled to education that maximizes their potential.[188] Denial of education to children with disabilities represents an invidious form of discrimination.[189]

(i) Children with Disabilities – Right to Education

13.92 Extensive provision in respect of education for persons with disabilities is made in the Convention on the Rights of Persons with Disabilities Art 24.[190] Art 24(1) of the Convention requires that:

'1. States Parties recognise the right of persons with disabilities to education. With a view to realising this right without discrimination and on the basis of equal opportunity, States Parties shall ensure an inclusive education system at all levels and lifelong learning directed to:

(a) The full development of human potential and sense of dignity and self-worth, and the strengthening of respect for human rights, fundamental freedoms and human diversity;

Handbook for the Convention on the Rights of the Child (2008) 3rd edn, UNICEF, p 417). See also Committee on the Rights of the Child General Comment No 12 (2009) *The Right of the Child to be Heard* CRC/C/GC/12, p 24, para 123: 'In the case of migration, the child has to be heard on his or her educational expectations ...'.

[186] Committee on the Rights of the Child General Comment No 6: *Treatment of Unaccompanied and Separated Children outside their Country of Origin* HRI/GEN/1/Rev 8, p 419, paras 41–43.

[187] Committee on the Rights of the Child General Comment No 6: *Treatment of Unaccompanied and Separated Children outside their Country of Origin* HRI/GEN/1/Rev 8, p 424, para 63.

[188] Newell, P and Hodgkin, R *Implementation Handbook for the Convention on the Rights of the Child* (2008) 3rd edn, UNICEF, p 418.

[189] Committee on Economic, Social and Cultural Rights General Comment No 5 *Persons with Disabilities* HRI/GEN/1/Rev 8, p 28, para 15.

[190] See also the UNESCO Revised Recommendation Concerning Technical and Vocational Education (2001), paras 7(g), 29 and 52 in respect of the provision of vocational and technical training for persons with disabilities.

(b)   The development by persons with disabilities of their personality, talents and creativity, as well as their mental and physical abilities, to their fullest potential;

(c)   Enabling persons with disabilities to participate effectively in a free society.'[191]

13.93 Article 23(3) of the CRC requires States parties ensure that the disabled child has effective access to and receives education in a manner conducive to the child's achieving the fullest possible social integration and individual development, including his or her cultural and spiritual development.[192] The Salamanca Statement and Framework for Action on Special Needs[193] noted that 'every child has unique characteristics, interests, abilities and learning needs ... those with special educational needs must have access to regular schools which should accommodate them within a child-centred pedagogy capable of meeting those needs'.[194]

(ii)   Children with Disabilities – Education and Inclusion

13.94 The concept of inclusion in education has been described as 'a dynamic approach of responding positively to pupil diversity and of seeing individual differences not as problems, but as opportunities to enrich learning'.[195] Art 23(3) of the CRC requires the education of children with disabilities in a manner which, *inter alia*, achieves the fullest possible social integration[196] of the child. Whilst Art 23 of the CRC does not specifically mandate inclusive education,[197] Art 23(2) argues against the formation of two separate systems of educational provision for children with disabilities

---

[191]   Note that Art 24(4) of the Convention states that 'In order to help ensure the realisation of this right, States Parties shall take appropriate measures to employ teachers, including teachers with disabilities, who are qualified in sign language and/or Braille, and to train professionals and staff who work at all levels of education. Such training shall incorporate disability awareness and the use of appropriate augmentative and alternative modes, means and formats of communication, educational techniques and materials to support persons with disabilities.'

[192]   Article 23(4) of the CRC further requires State parties to promote, in the spirit of international cooperation, the exchange of appropriate information in the field of, *inter alia*, educational and vocational services with the aim of enabling States Parties to improve their capabilities and skills and to widen their experience in these areas.

[193]   UNESCO World Conference on Special Needs Education: Access and Quality (1994) UNESCO ED-94/WS/18, para 2.

[194]   In the context of the Plan for Action, the term 'special educational needs' refers to all those children and youth whose needs arise from disabilities or learning difficulties (see para 3).

[195]   UNESCO Guidelines for Inclusion: Ensuring Access to Education for All (2005) UNESCO, p 12. Note that the concept of educational inclusion for children with disabilities is not one that is embraced universally as a positive principle (see Low, C *A Defence of Moderate Inclusion and an end of Ideology* in Cigman, R (ed) *Included or Excluded? The Challenge of Mainstream for some SEN Children* (2007) Routledge, Wing, L *Children With Autistic Spectrum Disorders* in Cigman, R (ed) *Included or Excluded? The Challenge of Mainstream for some SEN Children* (2007) Routledge and Jarvis, J *'Jigsawing it Together': Reflections on Deaf Pupils and Inclusion* in Cigman, R (ed) *Included or Excluded? The Challenge of Mainstream for some SEN Children* (2007) Routledge and Mencap *Don't Stick It, Stop It* (2007) Mencap. See further discussion at **13.115** below).

[196]   Note that in the context of inclusive education there is an important distinction between 'integration' and 'inclusion'. Policies of integration tend to seek to change the child in order to fit into the school. Inclusion, on the other hand, seeks to change the school environment in order to meet the needs of the disabled child. Inclusive education needs to be introduced as part of a strategy for promoting an inclusive society (UN General Discussion Day on Children with Disabilities UN Doc CRC/C/66 (1997), para 335).

[197]   Freeman, M *The Future of Children's Rights* (2000) 14 Children and Society 277, p 283.

and children without disabilities.[198] Arts 24(2) and 24(3) of the Convention on the Rights of Persons with Disabilities, which Convention will apply to children,[199] goes further in providing:

'2. In realising [the right of persons with disabilities to education], States Parties shall ensure that:

(a)   Persons with disabilities are not excluded from the general education system on the basis of disability, and that children with disabilities are not excluded from free and compulsory primary education, or from secondary education, on the basis of disability;

(b)   Persons with disabilities can access an inclusive, quality and free primary education and secondary education on an equal basis with others in the communities in which they live;

(c)   Reasonable accommodation of the individual's requirements is provided;

(d)   Persons with disabilities receive the support required, within the general education system, to facilitate their effective education;

(e)   Effective individualised support measures are provided in environments that maximise academic and social development, consistent with the goal of full inclusion.

3. States Parties shall enable persons with disabilities to learn life and social development skills to facilitate their full and equal participation in education and as members of the community. To this end, States Parties shall take appropriate measures, including:

(a)   Facilitating the learning of Braille, alternative script, augmentative and alternative modes, means and formats of communication and orientation and mobility skills, and facilitating peer support and mentoring;

(b)   Facilitating the learning of sign language and the promotion of the linguistic identity of the deaf community;

(c)   Ensuring that the education of persons, and in particular children, who are blind, deaf or deaf-blind, is delivered in the most appropriate languages and modes and means of communication for the individual, and in environments which maximise academic and social development.'[200]

13.95 Within this context, the Committee on the Rights of the Child stipulates that States parties should aim to provide appropriate and effective education for children with disabilities in mainstream schools alongside children without disabilities:[201]

'At its core, inclusive education is a set of values, principles, and practices that seeks meaningful, effective, and quality education for all students, that does justice to the diversity of learning conditions and requirements not only of children with disabilities, but for all students. This goal can be achieved by different organisational means which respect the diversity of children. Inclusion may range from full-time placement of all students with

---

[198] Van Bueren, G *The International Law on the Rights of the Child* (1998) Martinus Nijhoff, p 248. See also the UN General Discussion Day on Children with Disabilities UN Doc CRC/C/66 (1997), para 335 ('The inclusion of disabled children was a right, not a privilege').

[199] See Art 1(1) ('The purpose of the present Convention is to promote, protect and ensure the full and equal enjoyment of all human rights and fundamental freedoms by *all persons* [emphasis added] with disabilities, and to promote respect for their inherent dignity').

[200] See also the Standard Rules on the Equalisation of Opportunities for Persons with Disabilities Rule 6 annexed to General Assembly resolution 48/96 of 20 December 1993 ('States should recognise the principle of equal primary, secondary and tertiary educational opportunities for children, youth and adults with disabilities, in integrated settings'). See also Art 8 of the Convention on the Rights of Persons with Disabilities.

[201] Committee on the Rights of the Child General Comment No 9 *The Rights of Children with Disabilities* 2006, CRC/C/GC/9, para 67.

disabilities into one regular classroom or placement into the regular classroom with varying degree of inclusion including a certain portion of special education. It is important to understand that inclusion should not be understood nor practiced as simply integrating children with disabilities into the regular system regardless of their challenges and needs. Close cooperation among special educators and regular educators is essential. Schools' curricula must be re-evaluated and developed to meet the needs of children with and without disabilities. Modification in training programmes for teachers and other personnel involved in the educational system must be achieved in order to fully implement the philosophy of inclusive education.'

13.96 In relation to children with special educational needs the *Salamanca Statement and Framework for Action on Special Needs Education*[202] states that:

'... those with special educational needs must have access to regular schools which should accommodate them within a child-centred pedagogy capable of meeting those needs; regular schools with this inclusive orientation are the most effective means of combating discriminatory attitudes, creating welcoming communities, building an inclusive society and achieving education for all; moreover, they provide an effective education to the majority of children and improve the efficiency and ultimately the cost-effectiveness of the entire education system.'[203]

Education and Children with or affected by HIV/AIDS

13.97 In relation to children with or affected by HIV or AIDS the Committee on the Rights of the Child has commented as follows:[204]

'... the Committee wishes to remind States Parties of their obligation to ensure that primary education is available to all children, whether infected, orphaned or otherwise affected by HIV/AIDS. In many communities where HIV has spread widely, children from affected families, in particular girls, are facing serious difficulties staying in school and the number of teachers and other school employees lost to AIDS is limiting and threatening to destroy the ability of children to access education. States Parties must make adequate provision to ensure that children affected by HIV/AIDS can stay in school and ensure the qualified replacement of sick teachers so that children's regular attendance at schools is not affected, and that the right to education (art. 28) of all children living within these communities is fully protected.'

Education and Children Deprived of their Liberty

13.98 The requirements of the international and regional human rights instruments enshrine the right to education are not reduced by reason of the child being deprived of his or her liberty.[205]

---

[202] UNESCO World Conference on Special Needs Education: Access and Quality (1994) UNESCO ED-94/WS/18, paras 6–14.

[203] See also the UNESCO Review of the Present Situation in Special Education (1995) UNESCO ED-95/WS7.

[204] Committee on the Rights of the Child General Comment No 3 *HIV/AIDS and the rights of the child* 2003, CRC/GC//2003/3, para 15.

[205] Van Bueren, G *The International Law on the Rights of the Child* (1998) Martinus Nijhoff, p 248. See also the UN Rules for the Protection of Juveniles Deprived of their Liberty r 13 ('Juveniles deprived of their liberty shall not for any reason related to their status be denied the civil, economic, political, social or cultural rights to which they are entitled under national or international law, and which are compatible with the deprivation of liberty').

(i) Education and Prevention

13.99 Prior to considering the rights to education of children deprived of their liberty, it should be noted that the child's right to education is a cardinal element of measures aimed at preventing children from becoming involved in situations which may lead to the deprivation of their liberty. In respect of homeless children and adolescents State parties should develop strategies for the provision of appropriate education and opportunities for the development of livelihood skills.[206] Art 5(a) of the Riyadh Guidelines on the Prevention of Juvenile Delinquency requires delinquency prevention polices which involve *inter alia*:

> 'The provision of opportunities, in particular educational opportunities, to meet the varying needs of young persons and to serve as a supportive framework for safeguarding the personal development of all young persons, particularly those who are demonstrably endangered or at social risk and are in need of special care and protection.'[207]

The Committee on the Rights of the Child has fully endorsed the 'Riyadh Guidelines' and the principle of prevention through education:[208]

> 'The Committee fully supports the Riyadh Guidelines and agrees that emphasis should be placed on prevention policies that facilitate the successful socialisation and integration of all children, in particular through the family, the community, peer groups, schools, vocational training and the world of work, as well as through voluntary organisations. This means, inter alia that prevention programmes should focus on support for particularly vulnerable families, the involvement of schools in teaching basic values (including information about the rights and responsibilities of children and parents under the law), and extending special care and attention to young persons at risk. In this regard, particular attention should also be given to children who drop out of school or otherwise do not complete their education.'

(ii) Education of Children Deprived of their Liberty

13.100 The juvenile justice system should provide for opportunities to deal with children in conflict with the law by using social and/or educational measures, and to strictly limit the use of deprivation of liberty.[209] Where the deprivation of the child's liberty cannot be avoided, the UN Rules for the Protection of Juveniles Deprived or their Liberty set out the rules governing the provision and content of education.[210] Rule 38 provides:[211]

---

[206] Committee on the Rights of Child General Comment No 4 *Adolescent Health and Development in the Context of the Rights of the Child* HRI/GEN/1/Rev 8, p 384, para 32. See also Guidelines for the Alternative Care of Children A/RES/64/142 p 22, para 156.

[207] See also Art 24 ('Educational systems should extend particular care and attention to young persons who are at social risk. Specialised prevention programmes and educational materials, curricula, approaches and tools should be developed and fully utilised').

[208] Committee on the Rights of the Child General Comment No 10 *Children's Rights in Juvenile Justice* CRC/C/GC/10, p 7, para 18.

[209] Committee on the Rights of the Child General Comment No 10 *Children's Rights in Juvenile Justice* CRC/C/GC/10, p 10, para 28.

[210] UN Rules for the Protection of Juveniles Deprived or their Liberty, rr 38–43. See also Art 37(c) of the CRC.

[211] Rule 42 further provides that 'Every juvenile should have the right to receive vocational training in occupations likely to prepare him or her for future employment.' See also Committee on the Rights of the Child General Comment No 10 *Children's Rights in Juvenile Justice* CRC/C/GC/10, p 21, para 89 concerning children deprived of their liberty ('Every child of compulsory school age has the right to education suited to his/her needs and abilities, and designed to prepare him/her for return to society; in addition, every child should, when appropriate, receive vocational training in occupations likely to prepare him/her for future employment').

'Every juvenile of compulsory school age has the right to education suited to his or her needs and abilities and designed to prepare him or her for return to society. Such education should be provided outside the detention facility in community schools wherever possible and, in any case, by qualified teachers through programmes integrated with the education system of the country so that, after release, juveniles may continue their education without difficulty. Special attention should be given by the administration of the detention facilities to the education of juveniles of foreign origin or with particular cultural or ethnic needs. Juveniles who are illiterate or have cognitive or learning difficulties should have the right to special education.'

13.101 Article 29(1)(b) of the CRC requires that the education of children within the juvenile justice system shall be directed to the development of respect for human rights and freedoms.[212] A child deprived of his or her liberty should receive education aiming at his or her release, reintegration and ability to assume a constructive role in society.[213] Measures should be taken to provide former child offenders with appropriate support and assistance to reintegrate into society, including measures to prevent discrimination in respect of access to education.[214]

Education of Children in Care

13.102 Where a child is taken into alternative care, in order to minimise disruption of his or her educational life the child should be accommodated as close as possible to his or her habitual place of residence.[215] Whilst in alternative care children should have access to formal, non-formal and vocational education in accordance with their rights, to the maximum extent possible in educational facilities in the local community.[216] Ongoing educational and vocational training opportunities should be imparted as part of life skills education to young people leaving care in order to help them to become financially independent and generate their own income.[217] Where parents or guardians are unable to support young persons Government agencies should provide them with the opportunity of continuing in full-time education funded by the State and with opportunities for receiving work experience.[218]

Child's Right to Education under other International Instruments

The Geneva Conventions

13.103 Article 24 of the Geneva Convention relative to the Protection of Civilian Persons in Time of War 1950 provides as follows in respect of the education of children under the age of 15 who are orphaned or separated from their families as a result of war:

'The Parties to the conflict shall take the necessary measures to ensure that children under fifteen, who are orphaned or are separated from their families as a result of the war, are not left to their own resources, and that their maintenance, the exercise of their religion and their

---

[212] Committee on the Rights of the Child General Comment No 10 Children's *Rights in Juvenile Justice* CRC/C/GC/10, p 6, para 13.
[213] Committee on the Rights of the Child General Comment No 10 *Children's Rights in Juvenile Justice* CRC/C/GC/10, p 21, para 77.
[214] Committee on the Rights of the Child General Comment No 10 *Children's Rights in Juvenile Justice* CRC/C/GC/10, p 4, para 7.
[215] Guidelines for the Alternative Care of Children A/RES/64/142, p 4.
[216] Guidelines for the Alternative Care of Children A/RES/64/142, p 14, para 85.
[217] Guidelines for the Alternative Care of Children A/RES/64/142, p 19, para 135.
[218] Riyadh Guidelines on the Prevention of Juvenile Delinquency, Art 47.

education are facilitated in all circumstances. Their education shall, as far as possible, be entrusted to persons of a similar cultural tradition.'

13.104 In relation to occupying powers, Art 50 of the Geneva Convention relative to the Protection of Civilian Persons in Time of War stipulates as follows:

'The Occupying Power shall, with the cooperation of the national and local authorities, facilitate the proper working of all institutions devoted to the care and education of children. The Occupying Power shall take all necessary steps to facilitate the identification of children and the registration of their parentage. It may not, in any case, change their personal status, nor enlist them in formations or organisations subordinate to it. Should the local institutions be inadequate for the purpose, the Occupying Power shall make arrangements for the maintenance and education, if possible by persons of their own nationality, language and religion, of children who are orphaned or separated from their parents as a result of the war and who cannot be adequately cared for by a near relative or friend.'

13.105 In respect of persons interned during time of war, Art 94 of the Geneva Convention relative to the Protection of Civilian Persons in Time of War requires that:

'The Detaining Power shall encourage intellectual, educational and recreational pursuits, sports and games amongst internees, whilst leaving them free to take part in them or not. It shall take all practicable measures to ensure the exercise thereof, in particular by providing suitable premises. All possible facilities shall be granted to internees to continue their studies or to take up new subjects. The education of children and young people shall be ensured; they shall be allowed to attend schools either within the place of internment or outside. Internees shall be given opportunities for physical exercise, sports and outdoor games. For this purpose, sufficient open spaces shall be set aside in all places of internment. Special playgrounds shall be reserved for children and young people.'[219]

Child's Right to Education under the ECHR

ECHR, Art 2 of the First Protocol[220]

13.106 Article 2 of the First Protocol to the European Convention of Human Rights (hereafter 'Art 2 1P') provides as follows:

'No person shall be denied the right to education. In the exercise of any functions which it assumes in relation to education and to teaching, the State shall respect the right of parents to ensure such education and teaching in conformity with their own religious and philosophical convictions.'[221]

---

[219] See also Art 108 and 142. See also Arts 78(2) and 77(5) of Protocol I to the Geneva Conventions.

[220] Note that United Kingdom has entered a reservation on that part of Art 2 1P which reservation reads '… in view of certain provisions of the Education Acts in force in the United Kingdom, the principle affirmed in the second sentence of Art 2 is accepted by the United Kingdom only so far as it is compatible with the provision of efficient instruction and training, and the avoidance of unreasonable public expenditure.' This reservation is preserved by the Human Rights Act 1998, s 15 and reflects the wording of s 9 of the Education Act 1996 which provides that 'In exercising or performing all their respective powers and duties under the Education Acts, the Secretary of State and local education authorities shall have regard to the general principle that pupils are to be educated in accordance with the wishes of their parents, so far as that is compatible with the provision of efficient instruction and training and the avoidance of unreasonable public expenditure.' The reservation has been questioned by the European Court of Human Rights (see *Cohen v UK* (1996) 21 EHRR 104).

[221] Note that the provision in Art 2 1P requiring the State to respect the right of parents to ensure such education and teaching in conformity with their own religious and philosophical convictions is dealt with in chapter 10 above. See also Art 17 of the revised European Social Charter ('With a view to ensuring the

Article 2 1P of the ECHR should not be interpreted restrictively[222] and must be read and interpreted in light of the provisions of the CRC.[223] In *Oršuš and Others v Croatia*[224] the Grand Chamber described the right to education under Art 2 1P as follows:

> '... the right to education, as set out in the first sentence of Article 2 of Protocol No 1, guarantees everyone within the jurisdiction of the Contracting States 'a right of access to educational institutions existing at a given time', but such access constitutes only a part of the right to education. For that right 'to be effective, it is further necessary that, *inter alia*, the individual who is the beneficiary should have the possibility of drawing profit from the education received, that is to say, the right to obtain, in conformity with the rules in force in each State, and in one form or another, official recognition of the studies which he has completed.'

ECHR, Art 2 1P – The Scope of the Right to Education

Article 2 1P – 'Education'

13.107 The European Court of Human Rights draws a distinction between the broader concept of education and the narrower concept of teaching. In *Campbell and Cosans v United Kingdom*[225] the Court held that for the purposes of Art 2 1P of the ECHR, 'education' is the whole process whereby, in any society, adults endeavour to transmit their beliefs, culture and other values to the young, whereas teaching or instruction refers in particular to the transmission of knowledge and to intellectual development.

Article 2 1P – First Sentence

13.108 The first sentence of Art 2 1P, 'No person shall be denied the right to education' is the dominant sentence in the article. In *Kjeldsen, Busk and Madsen v Denmark*[226] the European Court of Human Rights held in relation to Art 2 1P that:

> 'As is shown by its very structure, Article 2 constitutes a whole that is dominated by its first sentence. By binding themselves not to 'deny the right to education', the Contracting States guarantee to anyone within their jurisdiction 'a right of access to educational institutions existing at a given time' and 'the possibility of drawing', by 'official recognition of the studies which he has completed', 'profit from the education received.' The right set out in the second sentence of Article 2 is an adjunct of this fundamental right to education. It is in the

---

effective exercise of the right of children and young persons to grow up in an environment which encourages the full development of their personality and of their physical and mental capacities, the Parties undertake, either directly or in co operation with public and private organisations, to take all appropriate and necessary measures designed: 1(a) to ensure that children and young persons, taking account of the rights and duties of their parents, have the care, the assistance, the education and the training they need, in particular by providing for the establishment or maintenance of institutions and services sufficient and adequate for this purpose; (b) to protect children and young persons against negligence, violence or exploitation; (c) to provide protection and special aid from the state for children and young persons temporarily or definitively deprived of their family's support; 2 to provide to children and young persons a free primary and secondary education as well as to encourage regular attendance at schools'). Article 17 covers all children under the age of 18 and does not provide any obligation to provide education to persons over the age of 18. The United Kingdom has not yet ratified the revised European Social Charter.

[222] *Timishev v Russia* (2008) 47 EHRR 13 ('In a democratic society, the right to education, which is indispensable to the furtherance of human rights, plays such a fundamental role that a restrictive interpretation of the first sentence of Article 2 of Protocol No 1 would not be consistent with the aim or purpose of that provision').

[223] See **3.43–3.46** above.

[224] (2010) Application No 15766/03, para 146.

[225] (1982) 4 EHRR 293, para 33.

[226] 1 EHRR 711.

discharge of a natural duty towards their children – parents being primarily responsible for the 'education and teaching' of their children – that parents may require the state to respect their religious and philosophical conviction. Their right thus corresponds to a responsibility closely linked to the enjoyment and the exercise of the right to education.'

Article 2 1P – Negative Formulation

13.109 Unlike all other international and regional human rights instruments which enshrine the right to education, Art 2 1P of the ECHR adopts a negative formulation of the right to education.[227] Pannick and others note that the negative formulation of the opening sentence of Art 2 1P indicates the qualified scope of the right to education under the ECHR.[228] In *Belgian Linguistic Case (No 2)*[229] the European Court of Human Rights held as follows in relation to the scope of the first sentence of Art 2 1P of the ECHR:

'3. By the terms of the first sentence of [Art 2 1P], 'no person shall be denied the right to education'. In spite of its negative formulation, this provision uses the term "right" and speaks of a "right to education". Likewise the preamble to the Protocol specifies that the object of the Protocol lies in the collective enforcement of "rights and freedoms". There is therefore no doubt that Article 2 does enshrine a right. It remains however to determine the content of this right and the scope of the obligation which is thereby placed upon States. The negative formulation indicates, as is confirmed by the preparatory work, that the Contracting Parties do not recognise such a right to education as would require them to establish at their own expense, or to subsidise, education of any particular type or at any particular level. However, it cannot be concluded from this that the State has no positive obligation to ensure respect for such a right as is protected by Article 2 of the Protocol. As a "right" does exist, it is secured, by virtue of Article 1 of the Convention, to everyone within the jurisdiction of a Contracting State. To determine the scope of the "right to education", within the meaning of the first sentence of Article 2 of the Protocol, the Court must bear in mind the aim of this provision. It notes in this context that all member States of the Council of Europe possessed, at the time of the opening of the Protocol to their signature, and still do possess, a general and official educational system. There neither was, nor is now, therefore, any question of requiring each State to establish such a system, but merely of guaranteeing to persons subject to the jurisdiction of the Contracting Parties the right, in principle, to avail themselves of the means of instruction existing at a given time. The Convention lays down no specific obligations concerning the extent of these means and the manner of their organisation or subsidisation. In particular, the first sentence of Article 2 does not specify the language in which education must be conducted in order that the right to education should be respected. It does not contain precise provisions similar to those which appear in Articles 5(2) and 6(3)(a) and (e). However, the right to education would be meaningless if it did not imply, in favour of its beneficiaries, the right to be educated in the national language or in one of the national languages, as the case may be.

4. The first sentence of Article 2 of the Protocol consequently guarantees, in the first place, a right of access to educational institutions existing at a given time, but such access constitutes only a part of the right to education. For the "right to education" to be effective, it is further necessary that, inter alia, the individual who is the beneficiary should have the possibility of drawing profit from the education received, that is to say, the right to obtain, in conformity with the rules in force in each State, and in one form or another, official recognition of the

---

[227] For the reasoning behind this formulation see the *travaux preparatoires* for the ECHR (Docs. CM/WP VI(51)7, 4 and AS/JA(3)13, 4.
[228] Lord Lester QC, Lord Pannick QC and Herberg, J *Human Rights Law and Practice* (2009) 3rd edn, LexisNexis, p 669.
[229] (1968) 1 EHRR 252.

studies which he has completed. The Court will deal with this matter in greater detail when it examines the last of the six specific questions listed in the submissions of those who appeared before it.

5. The right to education guaranteed by the first sentence of Article 2 of the Protocol by its very nature calls for regulation by the State, regulation which may vary in time and place according to the needs and resources of the community and of individuals. It goes without saying that such regulation must never injure the substance of the right to education nor conflict with other rights enshrined in the Convention. The Court considers that the general aim set for themselves by the Contracting Parties through the medium of the European Convention on Human Rights was to provide effective protection of fundamental human rights, and this, without doubt, not only because of the historical context in which the Convention was concluded, but also of the social and technical developments in our age which offer to States considerable possibilities for regulating the exercise of these rights. The Convention therefore implies a just balance between the protection of the general interest of the community and the respect due to fundamental human rights while attaching particular importance to the latter ...

7. The first sentence of Article 2 contains in itself no linguistic requirement. It guarantees the right of access to educational establishments existing at a given time and the right to obtain, in conformity with the rules in force in each State and in one form or another, the official recognition of studies which have been completed, this last right not being relevant to the point which is being dealt with here.'

13.110 Thus by reason of its negative formulation, whilst guaranteeing access to educational institutions and stipulating the right to an 'effective' education, the right to education under Art 2 1P does not imply a duty on States parties to provide free or subsidised education of a specific type or at a specific level nor does it dictate the means or manner of the provision of such education.[230] Further, it does not guarantee the specific standards or content of education[231] or a right to vocational training.[232] The fact that Art 2 1P leaves the structure, aims, content, standards and funding of education to State parties thus means that the scope of the right is largely defined by how States parties exercise their discretion in this regard.[233] The child's right to education under Art 2 1P is engaged only once the method of education has been established.[234] The *content* of the right to education under the ECHR may thus differ from child to child.[235] Within this context, the right to education under Art 2 1P of the ECHR has been described as a 'weak' right.[236] It should be noted that the negative formulation of Art 2 1P of the ECHR does not prevent positive obligations arising under it.[237] There is however at present no guidance as to precise ambit of the positive obligations under Art 2 1P. As to the factors relevant to determining the validity of limitations placed on the right to education by the State, in *Ali v United Kingdom*[238] the European Court of Human Rights held noted that:

---

[230] *Belgian Linguistic Case (No 2)* (1968) 1 EHRR 252.

[231] See *R (Holub) v Secretary of State for the Home Department* [2001] 1 WLR 1359.

[232] *R v Birmingham City Council ex p Youngson* [2001] LGR 218.

[233] Lord Lester QC, Lord Pannick QC and Herberg, J *Human Rights Law and Practice* (2009) 3rd edn, LexisNexis, p 669. See *Simpson v United Kingdom* 64 DR188 (1989).

[234] Van Buren, G *Child Rights in Europe* (2007).

[235] *A v Essex County Council* [2010] UKSC 33, [2010] 4 All ER 199, para 107 per Baroness Hale.

[236] See *Ali v Head Teacher and Governors of Lord Grey School* [2006] UKHL 14, [2006] 2 All ER 457 per Lord Bingham at para 24. See also *A v Essex County Council* [2008] EWCA Civ 364, para 10 and *R (O) v London Borough of Hackney* [2006] EWHC 3405 (Admin), [2007] ELR 405, para 35.

[237] *Belgian Linguistic Case (No 2)* (1968) 1 EHRR 252, para 3. See also *Gemeinsam Lernen* v Austria (1995) 20 EHRR CD 78 and *R (K) v London Borough of Newham* [2002] EWHC 405 (Admin), 2002) ELR 390.

[238] (2011) Application No 40385/06, paras 52–53.

'The Court recognises that in spite of its importance the right to education is not absolute, but may be subject to limitations. Provided that there is no injury to the substance of the right, these limitations are permitted by implication since the right of access 'by its very nature calls for regulation by the State ... Admittedly, the regulation of educational institutions may vary in time and in place, *inter alia*, according to the needs and resources of the community and the distinctive features of different levels of education. Consequently, the Contracting States enjoy a certain margin of appreciation in this sphere, although the final decision as to the observance of the Convention's requirements rests with the Court. In order to ensure that the restrictions that are imposed do not curtail the right in question to such an extent as to impair its very essence and deprive it of its effectiveness, the Court must satisfy itself that they are foreseeable for those concerned and pursue a legitimate aim. However, unlike the position with respect to Articles 8 to 11 of the Convention, it is not bound by an exhaustive list of "legitimate aims" under Article 2 of Protocol No 1. Furthermore, a limitation will only be compatible with Article 2 of Protocol No 1 if there is a reasonable relationship of proportionality between the means employed and the aim sought to be achieved.'

13.111   Having regard to the *Belgian Linguistic* judgment, the right to education under Art 2 1P of the ECHR can be divided into four separate rights, none of which are absolute.[239] Namely, a right of access to those educational establishments that exist at a given time, a right to an effective (but not the most effective possible) education, a right to official recognition of academic qualifications and a right not to be disadvantaged in the provision of education on any ground.

ECHR, Art 2 1P – Elements of the Right to Education

Right of Access to such Educational Establishments as Exist

(i)   Provision and Access

13.112   The first sentence of Art 2 1P guarantees a right of access to educational institutions existing at a given time. Note that such access constitutes only a part of the right to education.[240] There is no duty on States parties to establish at their expense or fund education of a particular type or at a particular level.[241] As such, there is no right to the provision of single sex or selective schools such as grammar schools under Art 2 1P of the ECHR.[242] Further, there is no obligation to recognise or continue to recognise any particular institution as an educational establishment.[243] The right to education under Art 2 1P of the ECHR does not include a right to access or to remain in any particular educational institution.[244] There is no right to be admitted to a particular

---

[239] See *Belgian Linguistic Case (No 2)* (1968) 1 EHRR 252. See also *Campbell and Cosans v United Kingdom* (1982) 4 EHRR 293; Lord Lester QC, Lord Pannick QC and Herberg, J *Human Rights Law and Practice* (2009) 3rd edn, LexisNexis, p 671 and Fortin, J *Children's Rights and the Developing Law* (2009) 3rd edn, Cambridge, p 191.

[240] *Belgian Linguistic Case (No 2)* (1968) 1 EHRR 252, para 4. See also *R (Douglas) v North Tyneside Metropolitan Borough Council* [2003] EWCA Civ 1847, [2004] 1 WLR 2363 in which Scott Baker LJ noted that there is no limit to any particular stage of education and that whilst education was in practice divided into primary, secondary and tertiary education, it is a continuing process and this division is, in one sense, artificial.

[241] *Belgian Linguistic Case (No 2)* (1968) 1 EHRR 252, para 5 and X v United Kingdom 14 DR 179 (1978).

[242] *W & DM and M & HI v United Kingdom* 37 DR 96 (1984).

[243] *Church of X v United Kingdom* 1 DR 41 (1974).

[244] *Simpson v United Kingdom* (1989) 64 DR 188) but see also *Ali v Head Teacher and Governors of Lord Grey School* [2006] UKHL 14, [2006] 2 All ER 457.

school where a number of proximate educational establishments exist.[245] States parties may refuse to provide assistance to independent schools provided this does not lead to discrimination.[246] Note however, that States parties may compel parents to send children to school or establish adequate education at home.[247] A foreign student has no right under Art 2 1P to pursue his or her education in a foreign country.[248]

(ii)   Admissions Policies and Entry Requirements

13.113   The right to access such educational establishments as exist will not be breached by statutory admissions policies[249] or entry requirements.[250] Within this context, there is a wide margin of appreciation concerning the establishment of school commencement and leaving ages.[251] The right to education is not restricted to persons under a particular age and will apply to both primary and secondary education. Article 2 1P of the ECHR permits State parties to restrict access to university courses to those who have attained the academic level required to benefit from the courses offered.[252] Denial of access to other educational institutions by reason of repeated disciplinary offences will not necessarily breach the right of access to education.[253]

(iii)   Access to Vocational Training and Higher Education

13.114   There is no right pursuant to Art 2 1P of the ECHR to the provision of vocational training[254] or to specialist advanced studies.[255] However, the European Court has determined that the right to higher education is a right of a civil nature.[256] Whilst there is no unfettered right under Art 2 1P of the ECHR to the provision of higher or tertiary education[257] there will be a right of access to such education were it exists.[258]

---

[245]   *Lee v United Kingdom* (2001) 33 EHRR 677, paras 122–125. See also *R v Vale of Glamorgan County Council ex p J* [2001] EWCA Civ 593, [2001] ELR 758 and *R (R) v Leeds City Council* [2005] EWHC 2495 (Admin), (2006) ELR 25.

[246]   *W and KL v Sweden* 45 DR 143 (1985) at 148–149.

[247]   *Family H v United Kingdom* 37 DR 105 (1984).

[248]   *Foreign Students v United Kingdom* 9 DR 185 (1977).

[249]   *R (Hounslow London Borough Council) v School Admission Appeal Panel* [2002] EWCA Civ 900, (2002) ELR 602.

[250]   *X v United Kingdom* 23 DR 228 (1980).

[251]   *X v United Kingdom* 2 DR 50 (1975) and *Foreign Students v United Kingdom* 9 DR 185 (1977).

[252]   *Patel v United Kingdom* (1982) 4 EHRR 256.

[253]   *Sulak v Turkey* 84-A DR 98 (1996) and *Yanasik v Turkey* 74 DR 14 (1993).

[254]   *X v United Kingdom* 2 DR 50 (1975). See however Arts 10(1) and 10(2) of the revised European Social Charter which provides that State parties undertake to provide or promote, as necessary, the technical and vocational training of all persons, including the handicapped, in consultation with employers' and workers' organisations, to grant facilities for access to higher technical and university education, based solely on individual aptitude and to provide or promote a system of apprenticeship and other systematic arrangements for training young boys and girls in their various employments. See also Art 7(6) of the Revised European Social Charter which provides that State parties undertake to provide that the time spent by young persons in vocational training during the normal working hours with the consent of the employer shall be treated as forming part of the working day. See further Art 15(1) of the Charter which provides that States parties undertake to take the necessary measures to provide persons with disabilities with guidance, education and vocational training in the framework of general schemes wherever possible or, where this is not possible, through specialised bodies, public or private. The United Kingdom has not yet ratified the revised European Social Charter.

[255]   *Sulak v Turkey* 84-A DR 98 (1996).

[256]   *Emine Araç v Turkey* (2008) Application No 9907/02.

[257]   *X v United Kingdom* 2 DR 50 (1975) and *Glazewska v Sweden* 45 DR 300 (1985).

[258]   *Sahin v Turkey* (2005) 41 EHRR 8, para 141 ('... it is clear that any institutions of higher education existing at a given time come within the scope of the first sentence of Article 2 of Protocol No 1, since the right of access to such institutions is an inherent part of the right set out in that provision. This is not an extensive

(iv)   Access for Children with Special Educational Needs

13.115   Children with special educational needs have no absolute right of parity of access with other pupils.[259] In *A v Essex County Council*[260] the Supreme Court held that Article 2 1P of the ECHR does not guarantee an absolute minimum standard of education and accordingly does not impose a positive obligation to provide effective education for children who had special educational needs.

13.116   The European Commission has acknowledged the view that whenever possible, children with special educational needs should be educated alongside children with no special educational needs.[261] However, the cases decided under the ECHR also recognise that inclusion cannot be applied as a blanket policy to all children. As such, a broad discretion is accorded to States parties in relation to the provision for children with special educational needs based on the States wide margin of appreciation accorded to States parties in the efficient use of educational resources.[262] In *Klerks v Netherlands*[263] the European Commission held that:

> 'The Commission observes that there is an increasing body of opinion which holds that, whenever possible, disabled children should be brought up with normal children of their own age. The Commission recognises, however, that this policy cannot apply to all handicapped children. It further recognises that there must be a wide measure of discretion left to the appropriate authorities as to how to make the best use possible of the resources available to them in the interests of disabled children generally. While these authorities must place weight on parental convictions, it cannot be said that the second sentence of Article 2 (P1–2) requires the placing of a child with a serious hearing impairment in a regular school (either with the expense of additional teaching staff which would be needed or to the detriment of the other pupils) rather than in an available place in a special school.'

Right to an Effective Form of Education

13.117   The right to education under Art 2 1P encompasses a right to an 'effective' form, but not the most effective possible form, of education.[264] Art 2 1P does not adopt the approach of the Universal Declaration of Human Rights Art 26(2) nor of Art 29 of the CRC by articulating the elements of effective education. However, the standard of education must reach a minimum standard.[265] An effective education for the purposes of Art 2 1P of the ECHR will also be a pluralist education.[266] Notwithstanding these

---

interpretation forcing new obligations on the Contracting States: it is based on the very terms of the first sentence of Article 2 of Protocol No 1 read in its context and having regard to the object and purpose of the Convention, a law-making treaty').

[259]   See *P and LD v United Kingdom* 62 DR 292 (1989) ('While these authorities must place weight on parental convictions, it cannot be said that the second sentence of Article 2 requires the placing of a child with severe development delay in a general school (with the expense of additional teaching staff which would be needed) rather than in an available place in a special school.') and Fortin, J *Children's Rights and the Developing Law* (2009) 3rd edn, Cambridge, p 433.

[260]   [2010] UKSC 33.

[261]   *P and LD v United Kingdom* 62 DR 292 (1989) and *Klerks v Netherlands* 82–A DR 129 (1995).

[262]   See *Ford v UK* (1996) EHRLR 534; *SP v United Kingdom* (1997) 23 EHRR CD 139 and *Graeme v United Kingdom* 64 DR 158 (1990).

[263]   82–A DR 129 (1995).

[264]   *Belgian Linguistic Case (No 2)* (1968) 1 EHRR 252.

[265]   *Belgian Linguistic Case (No 2)* (1968) 1 EHRR 252, para 5; *Ford v United Kingdom* [1996] EHRLR 534; *SP v United Kingdom* (1997) 23 EHRR CD 139 and *Cyprus v Turkey* (2001) 11 BHRC 45. See also *Ali v Head Teacher and Governors of Lord Grey School* [2006] UKHL 14, [2006] 2 All ER 457, paras 24, 57 and 61. See also Art 7(3) of the Revised European Social Charter which stipulates that persons who are still subject to compulsory education shall not be employed in such work as would deprive them of the full benefit of their education.

[266]   *Kjeldsen, Busk Madsen and Pedersen v Denmark* (1976) 1 EHRR 711, paras 52–54.

general principles, Kilkelly observes that 'As long as the child's needs have been assessed by a competent authority ... the court is unlikely to impose a contrary view unless it is established that the education received is clearly ineffective or discriminatory'.[267] The *content* of the right to an effective form of education may thus differ from child to child.[268]

Right to Official Recognition of Academic Qualifications

13.118   The State party is obligated under Art 2 1P to provide official recognition of any completed educational studies.[269]

Right Not to be Disadvantaged in the Provision of Education on Any Ground

13.119   Article 14 of the ECHR when read with Art 2 1P will act to prohibit discrimination in the provision of education on any ground. In *Belgian Linguistic Case (No 2)*[270] the European Court of Human Rights observed as follows:

> 'The right to education guaranteed by the first sentence of Article 2 of the Protocol by its very nature calls for regulation by the State, regulation which may vary in time and place according to the needs and resources of the community and of individuals. It goes without saying that such regulation must never injure the substance of the right to education nor conflict with other rights enshrined in the Convention. The Court considers that the general aim set for themselves by the Contracting Parties through the medium of the European Convention on Human Rights was to provide effective protection of fundamental human rights, and this, without doubt, not only because of the historical context in which the Convention was concluded, but also of the social and technical developments in our age which offer to States considerable possibilities for regulating the exercise of these rights. The Convention therefore implies a just balance between the protection of the general interest of the community and the respect due to fundamental human rights while attaching particular importance to the latter ...'

13.120   In *DH v Czech Republic*,[271] a case concerning the question of whether the decision to place Roma children in special schools, taken by the head teacher on the basis of the results of tests to measure the child's intellectual capacity carried out by an educational psychologist, and requiring the consent of the parents to the placement, was discriminatory, the Grand Chamber of the European Court of Justice revisited and restated the fundamental principles underpinning Art 14:

(a)   Discrimination means treating differently, without objective and reasonable justification, persons in relevantly similar situations.[272]

(b)   A difference in treatment can be established from the co-existence of sufficiently strong, clear and concordant inferences or of similar unrebutted presumptions of fact.[273]

---

[267]   Kilkelly, U *The Child and the European Court of Human Rights* (1999) Ashgate, p 68.
[268]   *A v Essex County Council* [2010] UKSC 33, [2010] 4 All ER 199, para 107 per Baroness Hale.
[269]   *Church of X v United Kingdom* 1 DR 41 (1974) and *Eren v Turkey* (2007) 44 EHRR 28. See also *EH v Greece* (2001) Application No 42079/98 (unreported).
[270]   (1968) 1 EHRR 252, para 5.
[271]   *DH and others v The Czech Republic* (2008) 47 EHRR 3.
[272]   *DH and others v The Czech Republic* (2008) 47 EHRR 3, para 175.
[273]   *DH and others v The Czech Republic* (2008) 47 EHRR 3, para 178.

(c)   Article 14 does not prohibit the differential treatment of groups in order to correct 'factual inequalities' between them. In certain circumstances a failure to attempt to correct such inequality can itself amount to a breach of article 14.[274]

(d)   A general policy or measure that has disproportionately prejudicial effects on a particular group may be considered discriminatory notwithstanding that it is not specifically aimed at that group.[275]

(e)   Once the applicant has shown a difference in treatment, it is for the respondent State to show that the difference in treatment was justified i e the burden of proof shifts.[276]

(f)   The level of persuasion necessary for reaching a particular conclusion and the distribution of the burden or proof are intrinsically linked to the specificity of the facts, the nature of the allegation made and the Convention right at stake.[277]

13.121   Accordingly, in order to successfully establish discrimination in contravention of Art 14 in respect of matters of education a child must demonstrate (i) that the facts fall within the ambit of Art 2 1P, (ii) that he or she has been treated differently on a prohibited ground (iii) to others in an analogous position and (iv) the difference in treatment cannot be objectively and reasonably justified having regard to the doctrine of proportionality and the margin of appreciation.[278]

13.122   In the case of *DH and others v The Czech Republic*[279] the Court held in relation to the impugned tests that the difference in treatment between Roma children and non-Roma children was not objectively and reasonably justified and that there did not exist a reasonable relationship of proportionality between the means used and the aim pursued. The nationwide practice of placing a disproportionate number of Roma children in schools for pupils with learning difficulties amounted to discrimination based on their ethnic origin. In *Sampanis and Others v Greece*[280] the Court found that the practice of denying Roma children enrolment in school and their subsequent placement in special classes located in an annex to the main building of a primary school, coupled with a number of racist incidents in the school instigated by the parents of non-Roma children, amounted to discrimination based on the applicants ' Roma origin. In *Oršuš v Croatia*[281] the Grand Chamber held that fact that the measure of placing children in separate classes on the basis of their insufficient command of the Croatian language was applied only in respect of Roma children clearly represented a difference in treatment and that such a difference in treatment had no objective or reasonable justification.[282] Refusal of a loan to fund education will not amount to

---

[274]   *DH and others v The Czech Republic* (2008) 47 EHRR 3, para 175.

[275]   *DH and others v The Czech Republic* (2008) 47 EHRR 3, para 175.

[276]   *DH and others v The Czech Republic* (2008) 47 EHRR 3, para 177.

[277]   *DH and others v The Czech Republic* (2008) 47 EHRR 3, para 178.

[278]   Swindells, H and others *Family Law and the Human Rights Act 1998* (1999) Jordan Publishing, p 234, Lord Lester QC, Lord Pannick QC and Herberg, J *Human Rights Law and Practice* (2009) 3rd edn, LexisNexis, p 594 and *A and others v Secretary of State for the Home Department* [2004] UKHL 56, [2005] 3 All ER 169 per Lord Bingham of Cornhill.

[279]   (2008) 47 EHRR 3.

[280]   (2008) Application No 32526/05 (unreported).

[281]   (2010) Application No 15766/03 (unreported).

[282]   Note that the Court held that the temporary placement of children in a separate class on the grounds that they lack an adequate command of the language is not, as such, automatically contrary to Article 14 of the

discrimination under Art 2 1P read with Art 14 of the ECHR[283] nor will a difference in treatment as between exceptionally gifted children and children with special educational needs.[284]

ECHR, Art 2 1P – Education and Discipline

ECHR, Art 2 1P and Discipline

13.123 Article 2 1P does not exclude recourse to disciplinary measures.[285] In *Sahin v Turkey*[286] the Grand Chamber held that:

> 'The right to education does not in principle exclude recourse to disciplinary measures, including suspension or expulsion from an educational institution in order to ensure compliance with its internal rules. The imposition of disciplinary penalties is an integral part of the process whereby a school seeks to achieve the object for which it was established, including the development and molding of the character and mental powers of its pupils.'

ECHR, Art 2 1P and Corporal Punishment

13.124 In *Campbell and Cosans v United Kingdom*[287] the European Court of Human Rights held that an objection to the use or threatened use of violence as a form of disciplinary measure against children within the educational system amounted to a philosophical conviction in that it forms part of an individual's concept of human behaviour in society. In finding that the child's year long suspension consequent on the parents refusal to agree that he be subject to the rules as to corporal punishment amounted to a violation of Art 2 1P the court held:

> 'Discipline is an integral, even indispensable, part of any educational system, with the result that the functions assumed by the State in Scotland must be taken to extend to question of discipline in general, even if not to its everyday maintenance ... The right to education guaranteed by the first sentence of Article 2 by its very nature calls for regulation by the State, but such regulation must never injure the substance of the right nor conflict with other rights enshrined in the Convention or its Protocols ... The suspension of Jeffrey Cosans – which remained in force for nearly a whole school year – was motivated by his and his parents' refusal to accept that he receive or be liable to corporal chastisement. His return to school could have been secured only if his parents had acted contrary to their convictions, convictions which the United Kingdom is obliged to respect under the second sentence of Article 2. A condition of access to an educational establishment that conflicts in this way with another right enshrined in Protocol No 1 cannot be described as reasonable and in any event falls outside the State's power of regulation under Article 2. There has accordingly also been, as regards Jeffrey Cosans, breach of the first sentence of that Article.'[288]

Convention. However, when such a measure disproportionately or even, as in the instant case, exclusively, affects members of a specific ethnic group, then appropriate safeguards have to be put in place (para 157). See also *Timishev v Russia* (2008) 47 EHRR 13.

[283] *R (Douglas) v North Tyneside Metropolitan Borough Council* [2003] EWCA Civ 1847, [2004] 1 WLR 2363.

[284] *S v Special Educational Needs and Disability Tribunal* [2005] EWHC 196 (Admin), [2005] ELR 443.

[285] *Ali v United Kingdom* (2011) Application No 40385/06, para 54 ('... the right to education does not in principle exclude recourse to disciplinary measures such as suspension or expulsion from an educational institution in order to ensure compliance with its internal rules. The imposition of disciplinary penalties is an integral part of the process whereby a school seeks to achieve the object for which it was established, including the development and moulding of the character and mental powers of its pupils').

[286] [2006] ELR 73, para 156.

[287] (1982) 4 EHRR 293.

[288] See below at **10.124** the domestic case of *R v Secretary of State for Education and Employment and others*

13.125 The case of *Campbell and Cosans v United Kingdom*[289] establishes only that the child has the right to attend school where he or she will not be subject to corporal punishment which is against his or her parents' wishes for the purposes of the second sentence of Art 2 1P. The case is not authority for the general proposition that corporal punishment will breach Art 3 of the ECHR.[290] However, in *Tyrer v United Kingdom*,[291] a case involving the birching of a teenage boy by a stranger in humiliating circumstances as a punishment for a criminal offence, the European Court of Human Rights appeared to suggest that all institutional corporal punishment will violate Art 3 of the ECHR. Within this context, in *Warwick v United Kingdom*[292] and *Y v United Kingdom*[293] the European Commission held that the corporal punishment of pupils by caning constituted degrading punishment for the purposes of Art 3 of the ECHR. In the latter case, the Commission observed that there was no good pedagogical reason for dealing with the child's bullying behaviour with punishment on the same level, namely bullying by use of superior strength to degrade another.[294] By contrast, in *Costello-Roberts v United Kingdom*[295] the European Court of Human Rights held that three blows inflicted on a child's clothed buttocks using a slipper did not engage the provisions of Art 3 of the ECHR, observing that:[296]

> 'Beyond the consequences to be expected from measures taken on a purely disciplinary plane, the applicant has adduced no evidence of any severe or long-lasting effects as a result of the treatment complained of. A punishment which does not occasion such effects may fall within the ambit of Article 3 (art. 3), provided that in the particular circumstances of the case it may be said to have reached the minimum threshold of severity required. While the Court has certain misgivings about the automatic nature of the punishment and the three-day wait before its imposition, it considers that minimum level of severity not to have been attained in this case. Accordingly, no violation of Article 3 (art. 3) has been established.'

13.126 The case law of the European Court of Human Rights does not therefore provide a consistent message deprecating the use of corporal punishment against children in educational contexts. However, it remains difficult to see how corporal punishment which would amount to an assault against an adult cannot amount to such an assault against a child.[297] Within this context, such forms of punishment are not only adverse to the child's best interests but are also discriminatory and thus antithetic to both the terms and the spirit of the ECHR.[298]

(Respondents) ex part Williamson (Appellant) and others [2005] UKHL 15, [2005] 2 AC 286 which also examined the issue of corporal punishment from the perspective of Art 9(1) in addition to Art 2 1P of the ECHR.

[289] (1982) 4 EHRR 293.

[290] Van Bueren, G *The International Law on the Rights of the Child* (1998) Martinus Nijhoff, p 250. For a detailed discussion of Art 3 see para 15 below.

[291] (1978) 2 EHRR 1.

[292] (1989) 60 DR 5.

[293] (1994) 17 EHRR 238.

[294] *Y v United Kingdom* (1994) 17 EHRR 238, para 44.

[295] (1993) 19 EHRR 112.

[296] Note that Van Bueren observes that the *Costello-Roberts* case was perhaps the weakest on its facts of a number of cases brought before the European Court of Human Rights, the remainder of which were the subject of friendly settlement (Van Bueren, G *The International Law on the Rights of the Child* (1998) Martinus Nijhoff, p 252).

[297] See European Committee of Social Rights General Observations Regarding Article 7, Paragraph 10, and Article 17 (2001) Conclusions XV-2, Vol 1, General Introduction, p 26 and *Eliminating Corporal Punishment: a Human Rights Imperative for Europe's Children* (2005) Council of Europe Publishing.

[298] See Van Bueren, G *The International Law on the Rights of the Child* (1998) Martinus Nijhoff, p 252. See also *Curtis Francis Doebbler v Sudan* Comm. No 236/2000 (2003), para 42 concerning a sentence of 'lashes' imposed on students of Ahlia University who held a picnic in Khartoum. The African Commission on

ECHR, Art 2 1P and Exclusion

13.127 In *Ali v United Kingdom*[299] the European Court of Human Rights held in respect of the factors relevant to determining the validity of excluding a child from school for the purposes of Art 2 1P of the ECHR that:

> 'In determining whether or not an exclusion resulted in a denial of the right to education, the Court will have to consider whether a fair balance was struck between the exclusion and the justification given for that measure. It will therefore have regard to factors such as the procedural safeguards in place to challenge the exclusion and to avoid arbitrariness; the duration of the exclusion; the extent of the co-operation shown by the pupil or his parents with respect to attempts to re-integrate him; the efforts of the school authorities to minimise the effects of exclusion and, in particular, the adequacy of alternative education provided by the school during the period of exclusion; and the extent to which the rights of any third parties were engaged.'

Child's Right to Education under European Union Law

13.128 Article 14 of the European Charter of Fundamental Rights provides as follows in respect of the right to education:

> '1. Everyone has the right to education and to have access to vocational and continuing training.
>
> 2. This right includes the possibility to receive free compulsory education.
>
> 3. The freedom to found educational establishments with due respect for democratic principles and the right of parents to ensure the education and teaching of their children in conformity with their religious, philosophical and pedagogical convictions shall be respected, in accordance with the national laws governing the exercise of such freedom and right.'[300]

13.129 In accordance with Art 52(3) of the European Charter,[301] the meaning and scope of the rights under Art 14 is the same as that under the corresponding Art 2 1P of the ECHR.

Child's Right to Education under other Regional Instruments

American Convention on Human Rights

13.130 The American Convention on Human Rights does not enshrine a right to education. However, the Protocol to the Convention, known as the Pact of San Salvador, provides at Art 13 as follows:

Human and Peoples' Rights held that 'There is no right for individuals, and particularly the Government of a country to apply physical violence to individuals for offences. Such a right would be tantamount to sanctioning State-sponsored torture under the Charter and contrary to the very nature of [the African Charter of Human and Peoples Rights].'

299 (2011) Application No 40385/06, para 58.

300 See also Art 32 ('Young people admitted to work must have working conditions appropriate to their age and be protected against economic exploitation and any work likely to harm their safety, health or physical, mental, moral or social development or to interfere with their education').

301 Article 52(3) of the Charter provides that 'Insofar as this Charter contains rights which correspond to rights guaranteed by the Convention for the Protection of Human Rights and Fundamental Freedoms, the meaning and scope of those rights shall be the same as those laid down by the said Convention. This provision shall not prevent Union law providing more extensive protection.'

'1. Everyone has the right to education.

2. The States Parties to this Protocol agree that education should be directed towards the full development of the human personality and human dignity and should strengthen respect for human rights, ideological pluralism, fundamental freedoms, justice and peace. They further agree that education ought to enable everyone to participate effectively in a democratic and pluralistic society and achieve a decent existence and should foster understanding, tolerance and friendship among all nations and all racial, ethnic or religious groups and promote activities for the maintenance of peace.

3. The States Parties to this Protocol recognise that in order to achieve the full exercise of the right to education:

a.   Primary education should be compulsory and accessible to all without cost;
b.   Secondary education in its different forms, including technical and vocational secondary education, should be made generally available and accessible to all by every appropriate means, and in particular, by the progressive introduction of free education;
c.   Higher education should be made equally accessible to all, on the basis of individual capacity, by every appropriate means, and in particular, by the progressive introduction of free education;
d.   Basic education should be encouraged or intensified as far as possible for those persons who have not received or completed the whole cycle of primary instruction;
e.   Programs of special education should be established for the handicapped, so as to provide special instruction and training to persons with physical disabilities or mental deficiencies.

4. In conformity with the domestic legislation of the States Parties, parents should have the right to select the type of education to be given to their children, provided that it conforms to the principles set forth above.

5. Nothing in this Protocol shall be interpreted as a restriction of the freedom of individuals and entities to establish and direct educational institutions in accordance with the domestic legislation of the States Parties.'[302]

Article 7(f) of the Pact of San Salvador provides that for children under the age of 16 the work day shall be subordinate to the provisions regarding compulsory education and that in no case shall work constitute an impediment to school attendance or limitation on benefiting from education received.

Ibero-American Convention on the Rights of Youth

13.131   Article 22 of the Ibero-American Convention on the Rights of Youth provides as follows in respect of the right to education:

'1. Youth have the right to education.

2. The States Parties recognise their obligation to guarantee a comprehensive, continuous, appropriate education of high quality.

3. The States Parties recognise that this right includes the freedom of choosing the educational centre and the active participation in its life.

---

[302]   See also Art 16 ('Every child has the right to free and compulsory education, at least in the elementary phase, and to continue his training at higher levels of the educational system').

4. The education shall promote the exercise of values, arts, science and technology in the transmission of teaching, interculturalism, respect of ethnic cultures and open access to new technologies and promote among the educated people the vocation for democracy, human rights, peace, solidarity, acceptance of diversity, tolerance and equal rights of men and women.

5. The States Parties recognise that education is a life-long learning process which includes elements from formal and non-formal education which contribute to the continuous and comprehensive development of youth.

6. The States Parties recognise that the right to education is opposite to any kind of discrimination and undertake to guarantee the universalisation of basic, compulsory and free education for all young people and, specifically, to enable and ensure the access and permanence in secondary education. The States Parties likewise undertake to stimulate the access to higher education, adopting the needed political and legislative measures to achieve so.

7. The States Parties undertake to promote the adoption of measures which enable the academic and scholar mobility of youth, and so agree to establish validation procedures which allow, when applicable, the equivalency of levels, academic degrees and professional qualifications of their respective national educational systems.'[303]

African Charter on the Rights and Welfare of the Child

13.132 Article 11 of the African Charter on the Rights and Welfare of the Child provides extensive provision in respect of the child's right to education:[304]

'1. Every child shall have the right to an education.

2. The education of the child shall be directed to:

(a)   the promotion and development of the child's personality, talents and mental and physical abilities to their fullest potential;

(b)   fostering respect for human rights and fundamental freedoms with particular reference to those set out in the provisions of various African instruments on human and peoples' rights and international human rights declarations and conventions;

(c)   the preservation and strengthening of positive African morals, traditional values and cultures;

(d)   the preparation of the child for responsible life in a free society, in the spirit of understanding tolerance, dialogue, mutual respect and friendship among all peoples ethnic, tribal and religious groups;

(e)   the preservation of national independence and territorial integrity;

---

[303]   See also Art 23 which states '1. The States Parties recognise that the right to education also includes the right to sexual education as a source of personal, affective development and communicative expression, as well as to the information concerning reproduction and its consequences. 2. Sexual education shall be taught at all educational levels and shall promote a responsible conduct in the exercise of sexuality, aiming the personal full acceptance and identity of youth, as well as the prevention of sexual diseases, HIV (AIDS), undesired pregnancy and sexual abuse or violence. 3. The States Parties recognise the important role and responsibility which corresponds to the family regarding sexual education of youth. 4. The States Parties shall adopt and implement sexual education policies, establishing plans and programmes which assure information and the full and responsible exercise of this right.'

[304]   See also Art 13 of the African Youth Charter. Note that Art 10(3)(d) of the African Youth Charter provides that 'State Parties shall ... Provide access to information and education and training for young people to learn their rights and responsibilities, to be schooled in democratic processes, citizenship, decision-making, governance and leadership such that they develop the technical skills and confidence to participate in these processes.'

(f)   the promotion and achievements of African Unity and Solidarity;

(g)   the development of respect for the environment and natural resources;

(h)   the promotion of the child's understanding of primary health care.

3. States Parties to the present Charter shall take all appropriate measures with a view to achieving the full realisation of this right and shall in particular:

(a)   provide free and compulsory basic education;

(b)   encourage the development of secondary education in its different forms and to progressively make it free and accessible to all;

(c)   make the higher education accessible to all on the basis of capacity and ability by every appropriate means;

(d)   take measures to encourage regular attendance at schools and the reduction of drop-out rates;

(e)   take special measures in respect of female, gifted and disadvantaged children, to ensure equal access to education for all sections of the community.[305]

4. States Parties to the present Charter shall respect the rights and duties of parents, and where applicable, of legal guardians to choose for their children's schools, other than those established by public authorities, which conform to such minimum standards may be approved by the State, to ensure the religious and moral education of the child in a manner with the evolving capacities of the child.

5. States Parties to the present Charter shall take all appropriate measures to ensure that a child who is subjected to schools or parental discipline shall be treated with humanity and with respect for the inherent dignity of the child and in conformity with the present Charter.

6. States Parties to the present Charter shall have all appropriate measures to ensure that children who become pregnant before completing their education shall have an opportunity to continue with their education on the basis of their individual ability.

7. No part of this Article shall be construed as to interfere with the liberty of individuals and bodies to establish and direct educational institutions subject to the observance of the principles set out in paragraph I of this Article and the requirement teal the education given in such institutions'

The African Charter on Human and Peoples' Rights

13.133   Article 17 of the African Charter on Human and People's Rights provides as follows in respect of the right to education:

'1. Every individual shall have the right to education.

2. Every individual may freely, take part in the cultural life of his community.

3. The promotion and protection of morals and traditional values recognised by the community shall be the duty of the State.'[306]

---

[305]   See Van Bueren, G *The International Law on the Rights of the Child* (1998) Martinus Nijhoff, p 247.

[306]   Note that Art 25 states that 'States parties to the present Charter shall have the duty to promote and ensure through teaching, education and publication, the respect of the rights and freedoms contained in the present Charter and to see to it that these freedoms and rights as well as corresponding obligations and duties are understood.'

Revised Arab Charter on Human Rights

13.134   Article 41 of the Revised Arab Charter on Human Rights enshrines the right to education in the following terms:

'1. The eradication of illiteracy is a binding obligation upon the State and everyone has the right to education.

2. The States parties shall guarantee their citizens free education at least throughout the primary and basic levels. All forms and levels of primary education shall be compulsory and accessible to all without discrimination of any kind.

3. The States parties shall take appropriate measures in all domains to ensure partnership between men and women with a view to achieving national development goals.

4. The States parties shall guarantee to provide education directed to the full development of the human person and to strengthening respect for human rights and fundamental freedoms.

5. The States parties shall endeavour to incorporate the principles of human rights and fundamental freedoms into formal and informal education curricula and educational and training programmes.

6. The States parties shall guarantee the establishment of the mechanisms necessary to provide ongoing education for every citizen and shall develop national plans for adult education.'[307]

Child's Right to Education under Domestic Law

Domestic Law – Context

13.135   Fortin argues that the huge body of English education legislation is oddly perverse in the way it largely ignores those who are the reason for its existence, citing the views of the UN Special Reporter Tomaševski that the provision of schooling in the United Kingdom is treated as a relationship between school and parents with children 'thus absent as actors in this process although it is aimed at their learning'.[308] By reason of the size of the 'huge body of English education legislation' only an overview of the domestic law by reference to the elements of the right to education enshrined in the international and regional human rights instruments can be encompassed within the scope of this work.[309]

---

[307] See also Art 34(3) ('The States parties recognise the right of the child to be protected from economic exploitation and from being forced to perform any work that is likely to be hazardous or to interfere with the child's education ...') and Art 40(4) ('The States parties shall provide full educational services suited to persons with disabilities, taking into account the importance of integrating these persons in the educational system and the importance of vocational training and apprenticeship and the creation of suitable job opportunities in the public or private sectors').

[308] Fortin, J *Children's Rights and the Developing Law* (2009) 3rd edn, Cambridge, p 189 and Tomaševski K. *Special Rapporteur on the Right to Education Addendum (England)* (1999) E/CN.4/20000/6/Add. 2, para 31.

[309] For a detailed account of domestic education law, reference should be made to McManus, J *Education and the Courts* (2004) Jordan Publishing.

Domestic Law – The Right to Education

The Right to Education

13.136 There is no express reference in domestic legislation to the child's *right* to education. However, the net effect of the relevant domestic statutory provisions concerning education is that all children have the right to free full time and appropriate education.[310]

The Domestic Definition of Education

13.137 Within the domestic context, the *Special Educational Needs Report of the Committee of Enquiry into the Education of Handicapped Children and Young People* [311] (known as 'the Warnock Report') concluded as follows in relation to the goals of education:

> 'We hold that education has certain long-term goals, that it has a general point or purpose, which can be definitely, though generally, stated. The goals are twofold, different from each other, but by no means incompatible. They are, first, to enlarge a child's knowledge, experience and imaginative understanding, and thus his awareness of moral values and capacity for enjoyment; and secondly, to enable him to enter the world after formal education is over as an active participant in society and a responsible contributor to it, capable of achieving as much independence as possible. The educational needs of every child are determined in relation to these goals. We are fully aware that for some children the first of these goals can be approached only by minute, though for them highly significant steps, while the second may never be achieved. But this does not entail that for these children the goals are different. The purpose of education for all children is the same; the goals are the same. But the help that individual children need in progressing towards them will be different. Whereas for some the road they have to travel towards the goals is smooth and easy, for others it is fraught with obstacles. For some the obstacles are so daunting that, even with the greatest possible help, they will not get very far. Nevertheless, for them too, progress will be possible, and their educational needs will be fulfilled, as they gradually overcome one obstacle after another on the way.'

Primary, Secondary and Further Education

13.138 From a structural perspective, the Education Act 1996 defines primary education as 'full-time or part-time education suitable to the requirements of children who have attained the age of two but are under compulsory school age, full-time education suitable to the requirements of junior pupils of compulsory school age who have not attained the age of 10 years and 6 months and full-time education suitable to the requirements of junior pupils who have attained the age of 10 years and 6 months and whom it is expedient to educate together with junior pupils.[312] The Act defines secondary education as full-time education suitable to the requirements of pupils of compulsory school age who are either senior pupils[313] or junior pupils who have attained the age of 10 years and 6 months and whom it is expedient to educate together with senior pupils of compulsory school age and full-time education suitable to the

---

[310] Fortin, J *Children's Rights and the Developing Law* (2009) 3rd edn, Cambridge, p 190. Pannick and others consider that the right to education is recognised by statute (see Lord Lester QC, Lord Pannick QC and Herberg, J *Human Rights Law and Practice* (2009) 3rd edn, LexisNexis, p 671).

[311] Warnock, H (Chairman) *Special Educational Needs Report of the Committee of Enquiry into the Education of Handicapped Children and Young People* (1978) Cmnd 7212, para 1.4.

[312] Education Act 1996, s 2(1). Pursuant to the Education Act 1996, s 3(2) ' junior pupil' means a child who has not attained the age of 12.

[313] Pursuant to s 3(2) of the Education Act 1996 ' senior pupil' means a person who has attained the age of 12 but not the age of 19.

requirements of pupils who are over compulsory school age but under the age of 19 which is provided at a school at which education of senior pupils takes place.[314] Further education is defined as full-time and part-time education suitable to the requirements of persons who are over compulsory school age including vocational, social, physical and recreational training and organised leisure-time occupation provided in connection with the provision of such education.[315]

Education and Pluralism

13.139   The domestic context of the right to education is in part provided by the multi-cultural nature of domestic society. The maintenance of a separate identity by minority groups within society depends in large part on their ability to maintain its continuity by educating their children to understand and respect their own customs, religion and culture.[316] The balance which domestic education seeks to achieve between respect for minority customs, religion and culture and the need for a cohesive and unified society is encompassed the concept of 'cultural pluralism within limits'.[317] This concept articulates the idea that a policy of pluralism must be limited by the need for a cohesive society founded on shared fundamental values.[318] Accordingly education should establish 'a sense of common citizenship, including a national identity that is secure enough to find a place for the plurality of nations, cultures, ethnic identities and religions found in the United Kingdom'.[319] Fortin however cautions that these broad principles provide no real answers as to how to define the fundamental values which provide the limits of 'cultural pluralism within limits'.[320]

13.140   In *R v Secretary of State for Education and Science, ex p Talmud Torah Machzikei Haddass School Trust*[321] the court held that education is 'suitable' if it primarily equips a child for life within the community of which he or she is a member, rather than the way of life in the wider country as a whole, as long as it does not foreclose the child's options in later years to adopt some other form of life if he wishes to do so.[322] In *R (E) v Governing Body of JFS; R (E) v Office of the Schools Adjudicator*[323] the Court of Appeal noted that the exemption of faith schools from the prohibition on discrimination on grounds of religion and belief contained in the Equality Act 2006 means that where a faith school is undersubscribed it may not use religious criteria to allocate places but that once it is oversubscribed, the school may

---

[314]   Education Act 1996, s 2(2). See also s 2(2A) and 2(B).

[315]   Education Act 1996, s 2(3). Note that 'organised leisure time occupation' means leisure-time occupation, in such organised cultural training and recreative activities as are suited to their requirements, for any persons over compulsory school age who are able and willing to profit by facilities provided for that purpose. See also s 2(5).

[316]   Fortin, J *Children's Rights and the Developing Law* (2009) 3rd edn, Cambridge, p 406.

[317]   Poulter, S *Ethnicity, Law and Human Rights: The English Experience* (1998) Oxford, p 21.

[318]   Swann, M *Education for All* (1985) Committee of Enquiry into the Education of Children from Ethnic Minority Groups Cmnd 9453, p 6.

[319]   Crick, B *Education for Citizenship and the Teaching of Democracy in Schools* (1998) Advisory Group on Citizenship, Qualifications and Curriculum Authority Cmnd, para 3.14.

[320]   Fortin, J *Children's Rights and the Developing Law* (2009) 3rd edn, Cambridge, p 407.

[321]   (1985) Times 12 April. See also *A v Special Educational Needs and Disability Tribunal and London Borough of Barnet* [2003] EWHC 3368 (Admin), [2004] ELR 293 and *R (on the application of K) v London Borough of Newham* [2002] EWHC 405 (Admin), [2002] ELR.

[322]   Hamilton argues that education provided by a faith school should only be accepted as suitable if it fulfils the child's right to equality of opportunity protected by international human rights instruments, which education equipping a child only for life within the community of a religious group does not (Hamilton, C *Family, Law and Religion* (1995) Sweet & Maxwell, pp 259–263).

[323]   [2009] EWCA Civ 626, [2009] 4 All ER 375. See also *A v Special Educational Needs and Disability Tribunal and London Borough of Barnett* [2003] EWHC 3368 (Admin), [2004] ELR 293 and London Oratory School v Schools Adjudicator [2004] EWHC 3014 (Admin), (2005) ELR 162.

lawfully restrict admissions to those children who, or whose parents, share the schools faith.324 The Court of Appeal further noted that this does not permit the school to discriminate in its admissions policy on the grounds of race, the same being forbidden by the Race Relations Act 1976.325 *In R (on the application of K) v London Borough of Newham*326 Colins J held that in order for the State to comply with Art 2 1P of the ECHR there has to be some positive action on the part of the State, which action should include the implementation of a mechanism for ensuring that the potential importance of a child's religious convictions is appreciated by the authorities considering admission applications.

Access to Education of a High Standard

13.141 The Education Act 1996 as amended327 provides that a local education authority shall contribute towards the spiritual, moral, mental and physical development of the community by securing that efficient primary education, and secondary education, and in the case of a local education authority in England, further education, are available to meet the needs of the population of their area.328 The Act stipulates that local education authorities shall secure sufficient329 schools providing primary and secondary education. The local education authority must also make arrangement for the provision of suitable education at school or otherwise330 than at school for those children of compulsory school age who by reason of illness, exclusion from school or otherwise are not able to receive education absent such arrangements being made.331

---

324   See Equality Act 2006, s 50(1)(a).
325   Note that in respect of allegations of discrimination on the grounds of race made after 1 October 2010 it is the Equality Act 2010 that will be the applicable statute.
326   [2002] EWHC 405 (Admin), [2002] ELR 390, pp 398–99.
327   By the Education Act 1997, the School Standards and Framework Act 1998, the Learning and Skills Act 2000, the Education Act 2002, the Education Act 2005, the Education and Inspections Act 2006 and the Apprenticeships, Skills, Children and Learning Act 2009. See also the Education Act 2002, ss 21(5)–(9) and s 29B.
328   Education Act 1996, s 13(1). Note that under s 15A(1ZA) A local education authority may secure the provision for their area of full-time or part-time education suitable to the requirements of persons over compulsory school age who have not attained the age of 19. In respect of persons who have attained the age of 19 s 15B provides that a local education authority may secure the provision for their area of full-time or part-time education suitable to the requirements of persons who have attained the age of 19 including training, to include vocational, social, physical and recreational training, and organised leisure time occupation (defined in s 2(6) as means leisure-time occupation, in such organised cultural training and recreative activities as are suited to their requirements, for any persons over compulsory school age who are able and willing to profit by facilities provided for that purpose) with particular regard to the needs of persons with learning difficulties.
329   The schools available for an area will not be regarded as sufficient unless they are sufficient in number, character and equipment to provide for all pupils the opportunity of appropriate education (s.14(2). 'Appropriate education' means education which offers such variety of instruction and training as may be desirable in view of the pupils' different ages, abilities and aptitudes and the different period for which they many be expected to remain in school including practical instruction and training appropriate to their needs (s.14(3)). Note that in *R v Inner London Education Authority ex p Ali* (1990) 2 Admin LR 822 Wolf LJ held that, in relation to the duty to provide sufficient primary schools that 'A local education authority which is faced with a situation where, without any fault on its part, it has not complied with the standard which the section sets for a limited period is not automatically in breach of the section. Here I refer to changing situations which could not be anticipated, not questions of resources or priorities.' See also *Meade v Harringay London Borough Council* [1979] 1 WLR 637.
330   Accordingly a parent may educate their child at home. Note however that this does not amount to a right to choose what he or she learns (see *Baker v Earl* [1960] Crim LR 363). See also the School Standards and Framework Act 1998, ss 110–111.
331   Education Act 1996, s 19(1). The question of what constitutes a 'suitable education' must be determined purely by reference to educational considerations, namely that the education must be 'efficient' and 'suitable to [the child's] age, ability and aptitude' and also suitable 'to any special educational needs he may have'. The

Cause every person to whom this subsection

13.142 Within this context, the Education Act 1996 provides that a local education authority in England must ensure that their relevant education functions and their relevant training functions are exercised by the authority with a view to promoting high standards, ensuring fair access to opportunity for education[332] and training and promoting the fulfillment of learning potential by every person to whom this subsection applies.[333] There is a statutory duty on parents to cause every child of compulsory school age to receive a full time education suitable to his or her age, ability or aptitude and to any special educational needs he or she may have, either by regular school attendance or otherwise.[334] The Secretary of State is under a duty to promote the education of the people of England and Wales.[335]

Special Educational Needs[336]

13.143 The *Special Educational Needs Report of the Committee of Enquiry into the Education of Handicapped Children and Young People[337]* (known as 'the Warnock Report') concluded in relation to the provision of education for children with special educational needs that:

> 'Though the general concept of education may remain constant, its interpretation will thus be widely different in the case of different children. There is in our society a vast range of differently disabled children, many of whom would not have survived infancy in other periods of history. In the case of the most profoundly disabled one is bound to face the questions: Why educate such children at all? Are they not ineducable? How can one justify such effort and such expense for so small a result? Such questions have to be faced, and must be answered. Our answer is that education, as we conceive it, is a good, and a specifically human good, to which all human beings are entitled. There exists, therefore, a clear obligation to educate the most severely disabled for no other reason than that they are human. No civilised society can be content just to look after these children; it must all the time seek ways of helping them, however slowly, towards the educational goals we have identified. To understand the ways in which help can be given is to begin to meet their educational needs. If we fail to do this, we are actually increasing and compounding their disadvantages. Moreover there are some children with disabilities who, through education along the common lines we advocate, may be able to lead a life very little poorer in quality than that of the non-handicapped child, whereas without this kind of education they might face a life of dependence or even institutionalisation. Education in such cases makes the difference between a proper and enjoyable life and something less than we believe life should be. From the point of view of the other members of the family, too, the process of drawing

---

availability or otherwise of resources is not relevant to the determination save where there is more that one way of providing 'suitable education'. In such circumstances the education authority is entitled to have regard to its resources in choosing between different ways of making such provision (*R v East Sussex County Council ex p Tandy* [1998] 2 All ER 769).

[332] The Education Act 1996, s 14(3A) requires that local education authorities exercise their functions with a view to securing diversity in the provision of schools and increasing opportunities for parental choice.

[333] Education Act 1996, s 13A(1). This section applies to persons under the age of 20 and persons over the age of 20 but under 25 who are subject to a learning difficulty assessment (s 13A(2)). Note however that local education authorities are not under an obligation to provide children with the best possible education or to provide a Utopian system (see *R v Surrey County Council Education Committee ex p H* (1984) 83 LGR 219 at 23).

[334] Education Act 1996, s 7.

[335] Education Act 1996, s 10.

[336] For a detailed discussion of the domestic law concerning the provision of education for children with special educational needs see Oliver, S and Clements, P *Special Educational Needs and the Law* (2007) 2nd edn, Jordan Publishing.

[337] Warnock, H (Chairman) *Special Educational Needs Report of the Committee of Enquiry into the Education of Handicapped Children and Young People* (1978) Cmnd 7212, para 1.4.

a severely handicapped child into the educational system may, through its very normality, help to maintain the effectiveness, stability and cohesion of the family unit.'[338]

13.144 In *A v Essex County Council*[339] the Supreme Court held that Art 2 1P of the ECHR does not guarantee an absolute minimum standard of education and accordingly does not impose a positive obligation to provide effective education for children who had special educational needs.[340] However, having regard to established elements of the right to education under Art 2 1P, namely a right of access to those educational establishments that exist at a given time, a right to an effective education and a right not to be disadvantaged in the provision of education on any ground, Black-Branch argues that the right to education requires the following from domestic authorities charged with the provision of education for children with special educational needs:[341]

'First, educators must make an accurate identification of the child's individual capacities and needs. Then, they must design a programme to meet these needs, one that is appropriate to the individual needs of the child in question. Thirdly, educators must insure the effective delivery of the programme of instruction, insuring a monitoring system to measure its success, introducing necessary modifications as the child progresses and as the set programme progresses. Parents need to participate in the process at all levels and in all respects of the decision-making.'

Domestic Law – Attendance

Compulsory Attendance

13.145 Domestic law imposes an absolute duty on parents to ensure that their children of compulsory school age attend full time education.[342] The Education Act 1996 makes provision for the prosecution of parents who fail to meet this duty, creating absolute offences to which there is no defence, a parent being liable to conviction whether or not he or she knew of the child's absences and irrespective of his or her attitude to attendance.[343] Fortin argues persuasively that truancy has become excessively criminalised to no useful end.[344]

---

[338] Warnock, H *Special Educational Needs, Report of the Committee of Enquiry into the Education of Handicapped Children and Young People* (1978) Cmnd 7212, paras 1.7 and 1.8. Notwithstanding these laudable principles, the picture of domestic provision for children with special educational needs is not a happy one. Blair reaches the bleak conclusion that it is 'a story not only of unfairness and indignation, but of tragic levels of neglect, disinterest and despair' (Blair, A *Local Government Ombudsmen Reports* (2008) 9 Education Law Journal 225, p 227). See also *A v Essex County Council* [2010] UKSC 33, para 104 per Baroness Hale.

[339] [2010] UKSC 33.

[340] The domestic courts have been willing to consider the provisions of the CRC where appropriate when considering domestic special educational needs legislation (see *Governing Body of X Endowed Primary School v Special Educational Needs and Disability Tribunal and others* [2009] EWHC 1842 (Admin), para 58)

[341] Black-Branch, J *Equality, Non-Discrimination and the Right to Special Education: from International Law to the Human Rights Act* [2000] EHLRR 297. To Black-Branch's requirements must be added the participation of the child in accordance with the principles enshrined in Art 12 of the CRC. See also see Fortin, J *Children's Rights and the Developing Law* (2009) 3rd edn, Cambridge, p 430 et seq. Local authorities have a duty of care to their pupils and must exercise reasonable care and skill in responding to their special educational needs (see *Phelps v Hillingdon London Borough Council, Anderton v Clwyd County Council, Jarvis v Hampshire County Council, Re G (A Minor)* [2000] 4 All ER 504 at 522, 531 and 538 and *Carty v Croydon London Borough Council* [2005] EWCA Civ 19, [2005] 2 All ER 517, para 51).

[342] Education Act 1996, s 7. See also Education Act 1996, s 463A.

[343] Education Act 1996, s 444. See *Crump v Gilmore* (1969) 113 Sol Jo 998 and see *Barnfather v Islington* LBC [2003] ELR 263; *Hampshire County Council v E* [2007] EWHC 2584 (Admin), [2008] ELR 260 and *R (P) v Liverpool City Magistrates* [2006] EWHC 887 (Admin), [2006] ELR 386.

[344] Fortin, J *Children's Rights and the Developing Law* (2009) 3rd edn, Cambridge, Cambridge, pp 193–194. See also CRAE *State of Children's Rights in England* (2008), p 9.

Domestic Law – Education and Discipline

Discipline by Teachers

13.146　Teachers have the legal power to discipline their pupils.[345] In administering discipline a teacher is required to show the same standard of care as that of a reasonably careful parent, taking into account the school context and the number of pupils.[346] Schools' governing bodies must draw up a written statement of discipline and good behaviour having consulted the head teacher, relevant school employees, parents and pupils.[347]

Prevention of Bullying

13.147　The written statement of discipline and good behaviour must encompass a policy on bullying.[348] Note that in relation to the issue of discipline and bullying, the schools duty to safeguard a pupil will extend beyond the school premises.[349] In addition to these provisions, there is also a common law duty on schools to take reasonable care to protect pupils from bullying or other mistreatment by other pupils at school.[350]

Corporal Punishment

13.148　Section 47 of the Education Act 1986 made physical punishment in maintained and schools illegal. The prohibition was extended to private schools in 1998. Section 131 of the School Standards and Framework Act 1998 amended s 548(1) of the Education Act 1996 to provide that corporal punishment given by a member of school staff to a child cannot be justified in any proceedings on the ground that it was given in pursuance of a right exercisable by the member of the staff by virtue of their position as such. Members of staff may use force in certain specified circumstances, namely to prevent a pupil from committing an offence, causing personal injury or damage to property or prejudicing the maintenance of good order and discipline at the school.[351]

13.149　In *R v Secretary of State for Education and Employment and Others (Respondents) ex part Williamson (Appellant) and others*[352] the House of Lords was required to consider the terms of the Education Act 1996, s 548(1). The claimants, who comprised head teachers, teachers and parents of children at four independent schools, challenged the statutory prohibition on corporal punishment in all schools as a breach of their right to freedom or religion. The basis of their claim was that the commitment

---

[345]　Education and Inspections Act 2006 Part 7 and see DfES guidance *School Discipline and Pupil Behaviour Polices: Guidance for Schools* (2007) DfES.

[346]　See *Van Oppen v Clerk to the Bedford Charity Trustees* [1989] 3 All ER 389 at 401 and *Gower v London Borough of Bromley* [1999] ELR 356 at 359.

[347]　Education and Inspections Act 2006, s 88.

[348]　Education and Inspections Act 2006, s 89(1)(a), (b) and (6). See also DfES guidance *School Discipline and Pupil Behaviour Polices: Guidance for Schools* 2007, para 3.1.2.

[349]　*Bradford-Smart v West Sussex County Council* [2002] EWCA Civ 07, [2002] ELR 139, paras 34–36 and see EIA 2006 s 89(5) ('The measures which the head teacher determines under subsection (1) [comprising measures of discipline] may, to such extent as is reasonable, include measures to be taken with a view to regulating the conduct of pupils at a time when they are not on the premises of the school and are not under the lawful control or charge of a member of the staff of the school').

[350]　*Faulkner v London Borough of Enfield and Lea Valley School* [2003] ELR 426.

[351]　Education and Inspections Act 2006, s 93 and see DfES guidance *School Discipline and Pupil Behaviour Polices: Guidance for Schools* 2007, para 17. See also Education Act 1996, s 550AA (power to search without consent where there is a reasonable suspicion that the pupil has a knife, blade or other offensive weapon in his or her possession).

[352]　[2005] UKHL 15, [2005] 2 AC 286.

to 'loving corporal correction'[353] in the upbringing of children was an essential element of their faith based on their interpretation biblical scripture. The claimants argued that religious liberty required that parents be able to delegate to schools the ability to train children according to these 'biblical' principles. The House of Lords held that the Education Act 1996, s 548(1) prevented the delegation by parents to teachers of the parental right to administer reasonable physical chastisement. The House of Lords were clear that this position materially interfered with the right of the parents to manifest their Christian beliefs pursuant to Art 9(1) and Art 2 1P of the ECHR but that that the interference was justified under Art 9(2) as being prescribed by law, necessary in a democratic society to protect children and promote their wellbeing. Whilst this case was about the punishment of children by adults using physical means only Baroness Hale made any reference to the rights of the child as constituting a separate consideration in the case, observing that:

'This is, and has always been, a case about children, their rights and the rights of their parents and teachers. Yet there has been no-one here or in the courts below to speak on behalf of the children. No litigation friend has been appointed to consider the rights of the pupils involved separately from those of the adults. No non-governmental organisation, such as the Children's Rights Alliance, has intervened to argue a case on behalf of children as a whole. The battle has been fought on ground selected by the adults. This has clouded and over-complicated what should have been a simple issue ... The practice of corporal punishment involves what would otherwise be an assault upon another person. The essential question, therefore, has always been whether the legislation achieves a fair balance between the rights and freedoms of the parents and teachers and the rights, freedoms and interests, not only of their children, but also of any other children who might be affected by the persistence of corporal punishment in some schools. The mechanism for achieving that balance lies in article 9.2 ... The real question is whether any limits set by the state can be justified under article 9.2 ... There can be no doubt that the ban on corporal punishment in schools pursues the legitimate aim of protecting the rights and freedoms of children. It has long been held that these are not limited to their rights under the European Convention. The appellants were anxious to stress that the corporal punishment in which they believe would not breach the child's rights under either article 3 or article 8. But it can still be legitimate for the state to prohibit it for the sake of the child. A child has the same right as anyone else not to be assaulted; the defence of lawful chastisement is an exception to that right. It has long been held in the context of article 8 that the rights and freedoms of the child include his interests ... Even if it could be shown that a particular act of corporal punishment was in the interests of the individual child, it is clear that a universal or blanket ban may be justified to protect a vulnerable class ... Above all, the state is entitled to give children the protection they are given by an international instrument to which the United Kingdom is a party, the United Nations Convention on the Rights of the Child (UNCRC). There was also a large body of professional educational and child care opinion in support of the ban ... With such an array of international and professional support, it is quite impossible to say that Parliament was not entitled to limit the practice of corporal punishment in all schools in order to protect the rights and freedoms of all children. Furthermore, the state has a positive obligation to protect children from inhuman or degrading punishment which violates their rights under article 3. But prohibiting only such punishment as would violate their rights under article 3 (or possibly article 8) would bring difficult problems of definition, demarcation and enforcement. It would not meet the authoritative international view of what the UNCRC requires. The appellants' solution is that they and other schools which share their views should be exempted from the ban. But this would raise exactly the same problems. How could it be justified in terms of the rights and protection of the child to allow some schools to inflict corporal punishment while prohibiting the rest from doing so? If a child has a right to be brought up without institutional violence, as he does, that right should

---

[353] The practice in question took the form, for boys, of a thin broad 'paddle' to the buttocks and, for girls, a strap on the hand, followed for both boys and girls by comfort from an adult and an encouragement to pray.

be respected whether or not his parents and teachers believe otherwise. For very different reasons from those given by the Court of Appeal, therefore, I would dismiss this appeal.'

Whilst this approach has been criticised as complicating what is essentially a claim between two competing views of the child's best interests,[354] Baroness Hale's approach explicitly recognises that in law it is not only the parents whose rights are engaged in determining the appropriate resolution between the position of the parents and the position of the State on a matter of religious and educational freedom which impact upon children.

Exclusion

13.150   An educational system is entitled to have rules and disciplinary procedures to enforce those rules. Discipline is an integral part of the educational process and that process may incorporate measures of exclusion.[355] However, the procedure for excluding a child from school must comply with the tenets of fairness and natural justice[356] and afford him or her with procedural protection.[357] The carefully regulated procedure for exclusion must be followed rigorously.[358] Whilst it has been held that Art 6(1) of the ECHR will not apply to hearings Independent Appeals Panel proceedings concerning exclusions,[359] it remains a fundamental principle that the pupil has a right to be heard.[360] Any decision to exclude must be based on basic facts established on the balance of probabilities.[361] Even then a pupil may only be excluded in response to serious breaches of the schools behaviour policy or if allowing the pupil to remain in school would seriously harm the education or welfare of the pupil or others in the school.[362] Account must be taken of the individual child's needs when considering their behaviour.[363] Even a much excluded pupil has a right to education in some form.[364]

---

[354]   Hill, M *Interpreting the European Convention on Human Rights in the United Kingdom Courts: The Impact on Religious Organisations* (2007). Hill's view appears to ignore the existence in law of children's rights under the ECHR and the CRC.

[355]   *Ali v Head Teacher and Governors of Lord Grey School* [2006] UKHL 14, [2006] 2 All ER 457, para 81.

[356]   *R v Headteacher and Independent Appeal Committee of Dunraven School, ex p B* [2000] ELR 156 and *R (S and B) v Independent Appeal Panel of Birmingham City Council* [2006] EWHC 2369 (Admin), [2007] ELR 57.

[357]   *Ali v Head Teacher and Governors of Lord Grey School* [2006] UKHL 14, [2006] 2 All ER 457, para 81.

[358]   See School Standards and Framework Act 1998, s 64, Education Act 2002, s 52, Education (Pupil Exclusions and Appeals) (Maintained School) (England) Regulations 2002, SI 2002/3178, Education (Pupil Exclusions) (Miscellaneous Amendment) (England) Regulations 2004, SI 2004/402, Education (Pupil Exclusions and Appeals) (Miscellaneous Amendments) (England) Regulations 2006, SI 2006/2189.

[359]   *Simpson v United Kingdom* (1989) 64 DR 188; *R (on the application of B) v Head Teacher of Alperton Community School* [2001] EWHC Admin 229, [2001] ELR 359, paras 46–49 and *S, T and P v London Borough of Brent* [2002] EWCA Civ 693, [2002] ELR 556, para 30.

[360]   *Improving Behaviour and Attendance: Guidance on Exclusion from Schools and Pupil Referral Units* (2008) DSCF, para 20 ('The pupil's participation in decisions related to their exclusion is not set out in primary legislation or regulations. Nevertheless the child or young person should be invited and encouraged to state their case at all stages of the exclusion process, where appropriate, taking account of their age and understanding'),102 ('An excluded pupil under the age of 18 should be allowed and encouraged to attend the hearing and to speak on his or her own behalf, if he or she wishes to do so, subject to their age and understanding') and 139. Note however that a child under 16 has no legal status in exclusion proceedings and no independent right of appeal. The position of children over the age of 16 is governed by the School Standards and Framework Act 1998, ss 86A, 86B and s 94 as amended by the Education and Skills Act 2008 (contrast right to appeal in Wales for children over the age of 11 since 2004 and in Scotland for children over the age of 12). The Government has consulted on changes that would allow children in England a right of appeal (see Consultation on Giving Children and Young People a Right to Appeal (2009) DCSF).

[361]   Department for Children, Schools and Families *Improving Behaviour and Attendance: Guidance on Exclusion from Schools and Pupil Referral Units* (2008) DSCF, para 16 (note however that the guidance currently cites an outdated authority in respect of the standard of proof, namely *Re H (Minors)(Sexual Abuse: Standard*

CONCLUSION

13.151 The right to education may be seen as the doorway through which children can access their other cardinal rights; the foundation stone of a rights based means of achieving their place in the world both as children and as adults. The foundational nature of the right to education highlights both its utility and the dangers created by its violation. With a variety of challenges remaining to the consistent and effective domestic implementation of the child's right to education, including discrimination in school admissions and access to education, limited student choice in decision making concerning education and continuing high levels of exclusions,[365] it is vital that practitioners remain vigilant in ensuring the rigorous application of the child's right to education. Only in this way can a firm foundation be assured for all children on which can be based a rewarding individual life in society underpinned by the cardinal rights to which they are entitled.

---

of Proof) [1996] 1 All ER 1, rather than the correct authority which is *Re B (Children)(Sexual Abuse: Standard of Proof)* [2008] UKHL 35, [2008] 4 All ER 1).

[362] *Improving Behaviour and Attendance: Guidance on Exclusion from Schools and Pupil Referral Units* (2008) DSCF, para 13. Note that exclusion should not be used in respect of minor incidents such as failure to do homework or bring dinner money, poor academic performance, lateness or truancy, pregnancy, breach of school uniform rules or rules on appearance, punishing pupils for the behaviour or their parents or protecting victims of bullying by excluding them from the school (see *Improving Behaviour and Attendance: Guidance on Exclusion from Schools and Pupil Referral Units* (2008) DSCF, para 26).

[363] *School Discipline and Pupil Behaviour Polices: Guidance for Schools* (2007) DfES, para 3.9. Teachers should take care to recognise that poor behaviour by SEN pupils may be attributable to their learning difficulties (Taylor, F *A Fair Hearing? Researching Young People's Involvement in the School Exclusion Process* (2005) Save the Children, pp 18–19 and see DfES guidance *School Discipline and Pupil Behaviour Polices: Guidance for Schools* 2007, para 63–67 and *R (T) v Independent Appeal Panel for Devon County Council, the Governing Body of X College [2007] EWHC 763 (Admin)* [2007] ELR 499). In respect of disabled pupils see *Lewisham London Borough Council v Malcolm* [2008] UKHL 43, [2008] 4 All ER 525.

[364] Fortin, J *Children's Rights and the Developing Law* (2009) 3rd edn, Cambridge, p 220. Reintergration plans must be drawn up in consultation with the local authority, pupil and parent within one month of permanent exclusion (see *Local Authority Responsibility to Provide Full Time Education and Reintegrate Permanently Excluded Pupils* (2007) DCSF, paras 23 and 24). Local authorities have the power to force admission of an excluded pupil's by a school (School Standards and Framework Act 1998, ss 96–97). Admission may not be refused on the bases of the child's poor record (Department of Children Schools and Families *School Admissions Code* (2009) DCSF, para 3.31. This guidance has statutory force pursuant to the School Standards and Framework Act s 84(3) as amended by the Education and Inspections Act 2006, s 40(4)).

[365] CRAE *State of Children's Rights in England* (2008), pp 8, 12, 30 and 31.

Chapter 14

THE CHILD'S RIGHT TO LIBERTY AND SECURITY OF THE PERSON

'He that would make his own liberty secure, must guard even his enemy from
oppression;
for if he violates this duty, he establishes a precedent that will reach to himself'

Thomas Paine

INTRODUCTION

14.1   The basis of a democratic state is liberty.[1] It is a fundamental principle of a
democratic society that the State must adhere to the rule of law when interfering with
the child's right to liberty and security of the person.[2] Art 3 of the Declaration of
Human Rights provides that everyone has the right to life, liberty and security of
person. Article 9(1) of the International Covenant on Civil and Political Rights provides
that everyone has the right to liberty and security of the person.[3] The Convention on the
Rights of Persons with Disabilities, Art 14(1)(a) provides that States Parties shall ensure
that persons with disabilities, on an equal basis with others, enjoy the right to liberty and
security of person. These formulations are reflected in Art 5(1) of the ECHR which
likewise stipulates that everyone has the right to liberty and security of the person.

14.2   The child's right to liberty and security of the person must be considered not
only within the context of the criminal justice system but also in respect of other areas
which may threaten the right such as mental health, educational supervision and asylum
and immigration.[4] This chapter deals with the child's right to liberty and security of the
person under the key international and regional human rights instruments before
considering the topic within the context of the domestic law.

---

[1]   Aristotle, *Politics*. In *R v Secretary of State for the Home Department ex p Cheblak* [1991] 1 WLR 890
Lord Donaldson said 'We have all been brought up to believe, and do believe, that the liberty of the citizen
under the law is the most fundamental of all freedoms.'

[2]   *Brogan v United Kingdom* (1988) 11 EHRR 117, para 58 ('it enshrines a fundamental human right, namely
the protection of the individual against arbitrary interferences by the State with his right to liberty. Judicial
control of interferences by the executive with the individual's right to liberty is an essential feature of the
guarantee ... which is intended to minimise the risk of arbitrariness. Judicial control is implied by the rule of
law, 'one of the fundamental principles of a democratic society').

[3]   Note for children living in States who are party to both the CRC and ICCPR it will be standards in Art 37
of the CRC rather than the standards in Art 9(3) of the ICCPR which will prevail (see Van Bueren, G *The
International Law on the Rights of the Child* (1998) Martinus Nijhoff, p 210).

[4]   Newell, P and Hodgkin, R *Implementation Handbook for the Convention on the Rights of the Child* (2008)
3rd edn, UNICEF, p 548.

GENERAL PRINCIPLES

General Principles – Liberty

14.3   In the context of the child's right to liberty and security of the person, the word 'liberty' is used in the sense of 'physical liberty'. The word liberty has a wide definition in this regard. Whilst the term 'deprivation of liberty' in respect of children applies to any form of detention, imprisonment or placement in a public or private custodial setting from which a child is not allowed to leave at will, by order of any judicial, administrative or other public authority,[5] its ambit extends beyond this definition. Thus deprivation of liberty is a broader concept than simply the act of arrest, detention or imprisonment.[6] The deprivation of liberty will not act to prevent the child from benefiting from all of his or her other rights under international law.[7]

General Principles – Security of the Person

14.4   The precise extent to which the concepts of 'liberty' and 'security of the person' are considered to be linked or co-terminus varies with the interpretation placed on the international and regional human rights instruments by their respective governing institutions. Thus in *Páez v Colombia*[8] the UN Human Rights Committee preferred an interpretation which considered liberty and the security of the person as separate concepts with security of the person denoting the physical security of all individuals, stating that:

> 'An interpretation of article 9(1) which would allow a State party to ignore threats to the personal security of non-detained persons within its jurisdiction would render totally ineffective the guarantees of the Covenant.'

By contrast, in examining the relationship between liberty and security of the person the European Court of Human Rights has emphasised that security of the person must be understood in the context of physical liberty rather than physical safety and that the word 'security' serves simply to emphasis that the requirement that a person's liberty may not be deprived in an arbitrary fashion.[9]

---

5   UN Rules for the Protection of Juveniles Deprived of their Liberty r 11(b) (A/Res/45/113).

6   Van Bueren, G *The International Law on the Rights of the Child* (1998) Martinus Nijhoff, p 206. Note that the term 'arrest, means apprehending a person for the alleged commission of an offence, 'detention' means any deprivation of liberty except as the result of a conviction for an offence and 'imprisonment' means deprivation of liberty arising out of a conviction (Body of Principles for the Protection of All Persons under any form of Detention or Imprisonment (GA Res 43/117 9 December 1988)).

7   Body of Principles for the Protection of All Persons under any form of Detention or Imprisonment Principle 2 (GA Res 43/117 9 December 1988).

8   UN Human Rights Committee Communication No 195/1985 (1990).

9   *East African Asians v United Kingdom* (1973) Application No 4626/70 ('The full text of Art 5 shows that the expression "liberty and security of the person" in para (1) must be read as a whole and that consequently, "security" should be understood in the context of 'liberty ... in the Commissions view, the protection of "security" is in this context concerned with arbitrary interference, by a public authority, with an individual's personal "liberty". Or, in other words, any decision taken with the sphere of Art 5 must, in order to safeguard the individuals right to "security of the person", conform to the procedural as well as the substantive requirements laid down by an already existing law ... protection against arbitrary arrest and detention was one of the principle considerations of the drafters of this treaty') and *Bozano v France* (1986) 9 EHRR 297, para 54 ('The main issue to be determined is whether the disputed detention was "lawful", including whether it was in accordance with "a procedure prescribed by law". The Convention here refers essentially to national law and establishes the need to apply its rules, but it also requires that any measure depriving the individual of his liberty must be compatible with the purpose of Art 5, namely to protect the individual from arbitrariness. What is at stake here is not only the "right to liberty" but also the "right to security of person"').

14.5 The interpretation of the ambit of the right to liberty and security of the person favoured by the Human Rights Committee in *Páez v Colombia*[10] highlights the close link between a person's right to liberty and security of the person and a person's right to protection from harmful treatment such as torture and cruel, inhuman or degrading treatment or punishment. For children, the close relationship between the right to liberty and the right to protection from harmful treatment is emphasised by the fact that the CRC enshrines the prohibition on the torture or other cruel, inhuman or degrading treatment or punishment of the child in the same article as the child's right to liberty.[11]

THE RIGHT TO LIBERTY AND SECURITY OF THE PERSON

The Child's Right to Liberty and Security of the Person under the CRC

CRC, Art 37

14.6 Article 37(a) of the CRC deals with the child's right to freedom from torture or other cruel, inhuman or degrading treatment or punishment, the prohibition on capital punishment in respect of children and the prohibition of life imprisonment without possibility of release in respect of children.[12] The child's right to freedom from torture or other cruel, inhuman or degrading treatment or punishment is dealt with in chapter 15 and the prohibition on capital punishment is dealt with in chapter 5. The prohibition on life imprisonment without possibility of release is dealt with below. The remainder of Art 37 of the CRC provides that States Parties shall ensure that in respect of the child's right to liberty:

'(b) No child[13] shall be deprived of his or her liberty unlawfully or arbitrarily. The arrest, detention or imprisonment of a child shall be in conformity with the law and shall be used only as a measure of last resort and for the shortest appropriate period of time;

(c) Every child deprived of liberty shall be treated with humanity and respect for the inherent dignity of the human person, and in a manner which takes into account the needs of persons of his or her age. In particular, every child deprived of liberty shall be separated from adults unless it is considered in the child's best interest not to do so and shall have the right to maintain contact with his or her family through correspondence and visits, save in exceptional circumstances;

(d) Every child deprived of his or her liberty shall have the right to prompt access to legal and other appropriate assistance, as well as the right to challenge the legality of the deprivation of his or her liberty before a court or other competent, independent and impartial authority, and to a prompt decision on any such action.'

---

[10] UN Human Rights Committee Communication No 195/1985 (1990).

[11] See CRC, Art 37(a) and Art 37(b). Note that Art 37(b) of the CRC does not use the term 'liberty and security of the person' but rather refers simply to 'liberty', suggesting that the under the CRC, as under the ICCPR, the concept of security of the person is more closely linked to physical security than the arbitrary deprivation of liberty.

[12] Article 37(a) of the CRC provides that 'No child shall be subjected to torture or other cruel, inhuman or degrading treatment or punishment. Neither capital punishment nor life imprisonment without possibility of release shall be imposed for offences committed by persons below eighteen years of age.'

[13] Note that in relation to the definition of 'child' in Art 37 of the CRC, Art 1 of the CRC will apply, namely 'a child means every human being below the age of eighteen years unless under the law applicable to the child, majority is attained earlier.' Note also the view of the Human Rights Committee that 'all persons under the age of 18 should be treated as juveniles, at least in matters relating to criminal justice' (Human Rights Committee General Comment No 21 *Article 10 (Humane Treatment of Persons Deprived of their Liberty* HRI/GEN/1/Rev 8, p 194, para 13).

CRC, Art 37 and Best Interests

14.7 Article 37 of the CRC must be read in the context of Art 3 and in all decisions taken in relation to decisions concerning the deprivation of the child's liberty under the provisions of Art 37 the child's best interests must be a primary consideration.[14] Thus, for example, the Committee on the Rights of the Children General Comment No 10 *Children's Rights in Juvenile Justice* notes that:

> 'The protection of the best interests of the child means, for instance, that the traditional objectives of criminal justice, such as repression/ retribution, must give way to rehabilitation and restorative justice objectives in dealing with child offenders.'

CRC, Art 37 – Related Provisions

(i) **Preventative Measures**

UN Guidelines on the Prevention of Juvenile Delinquency (the 'Riyadh Guidelines')

14.8 Article 37(b) of the CRC requires that the arrest, detention or imprisonment of a child shall be used only as a measure of last resort. Implicit in this requirement is the need to take steps to prevent children becoming involved in activities which may necessitate their arrest, detention or imprisonment. The UN Guidelines on the Prevention of Juvenile Delinquency (the 'Riyadh Guidelines') recognise in Art 1(1) that 'The prevention of juvenile delinquency is an essential part of crime prevention in society'. The 'Riyadh Guidelines' articulate standards for the prevention of juvenile delinquency, including measures to protect vulnerable children and young people, with the emphasis placed on:

> '... preventative policies facilitating the successful socialisation and integration of all children and young persons, in particular through the family, the community, peer groups, schools, vocational training, the world of work, and voluntary organisations.'[15]

14.9 The Committee on the Rights of the Child has endorsed the 'Riyadh Guidelines' in the context of the children who may come into conflict with the law:[16]

> 'The Committee fully supports the Riyadh Guidelines and agrees that emphasis should be placed on prevention policies that facilitate the successful socialisation and integration of all children, in particular through the family, the community, peer groups, schools, vocational training and the world of work, as well as through voluntary organisations. This means, inter alia that prevention programmes should focus on support for particularly vulnerable families, the involvement of schools in teaching basic values (including information about the rights and responsibilities of children and parents under the law), and extending special care and attention to young persons at risk. In this regard, particular attention should also be given to children who drop out of school or otherwise do not complete their education. The use of peer group support and a strong involvement of parents are recommended. The States parties should also develop community-based services and programmes that respond to the special needs, problems, concerns and interests of children, in particular of children repeatedly in conflict with the law, and that provide appropriate counseling and guidance to their families.'

---

[14] Committee on the Rights of the Children General Comment No 10 *Children's Rights in Juvenile Justice* CRC/C/GC/10 p 5, para 10.

[15] See Art 10.

[16] Committee on the Rights of the Children General Comment No 10 *Children's Rights in Juvenile Justice* CRC/C/GC/10 p 7, para 18.

(ii)   Alternatives to Deprivation of Liberty

CRC, Art 40(4)

14.10   Implicit in the requirement of Art 37(b) of the CRC that the arrest, detention or imprisonment of a child shall be used only as a measure of last resort is the need to identify and implement alternatives to depriving the child of his or her liberty.[17] Within the context of children who are at risk of being deprived of their liberty by reason of their coming into conflict with the law, Art 40(4) of the CRC provides that:

'A variety of dispositions, such as care, guidance and supervision orders; counselling; probation; foster care; education and vocational training programmes and other alternatives to institutional care shall be available to ensure that children are dealt with in a manner appropriate to their well-being and proportionate both to their circumstances and the offence.'[18]

(iii)   Proper Treatment of Children Deprived of their Liberty

CRC, Art 40(1)

14.11   CRC, Art 40(1) will be relevant in relation to children who have been deprived of their liberty by reason of their coming into conflict with the law.[19] Art 40(1) of the CRC provides as follows in this regard:

'States Parties recognise the right of every child alleged as, accused of, or recognised as having infringed the penal law to be treated in a manner consistent with the promotion of the child's sense of dignity and worth, which reinforces the child's respect for the human rights and fundamental freedoms of others and which takes into account the child's age and the desirability of promoting the child's reintegration and the child's assuming a constructive role in society.'[20]

UN Rules for the Protection of Juveniles Deprived of their Liberty

14.12   By reason of their broad scope Van Bueren points out that the UN Standard Minimum Rules for the Administration of Juvenile Justice (the 'Beijing Rules') rules were never intended to provide a thorough and systematic approach to the conditions of all forms of deprivation of liberty in respect of children.[21] Accordingly, in considering the conditions of children deprived of their liberty reference must also be made to the UN Rules for the Protection of Juveniles Deprived of their Liberty. The UN Rules for

---

[17]   See the Committee on the Rights of the Child General Comment No 9 *The Rights of Children with Disabilities* CRC/C/GC/9, paras 73 and 74.

[18]   Note also Art 40(3)(b) which provides that 'States Parties shall seek to promote the establishment of laws, procedures, authorities and institutions specifically applicable to children alleged as, accused of, or recognised as having infringed the penal law, and, in particular: ... (b) Whenever appropriate and desirable, measures for dealing with such children without resorting to judicial proceedings, providing that human rights and legal safeguards are fully respected.' See Committee on the Rights of the Children General Comment No 10 *Children's Rights in Juvenile Justice* CRC/C/GC/10, p 9, para 26.

[19]   Committee on the Rights of the Children General Comment No 10 *Children's Rights in Juvenile Justice* CRC/C/GC/10, p 7, para 13.

[20]   See **16.26** below for a detailed discussion of this provision. See also Art 14(4) of the ICCPR.

[21]   Van Bueren, G *The International Law on the Rights of the Child* (1998) Martinus Nijhoff, pp 206–207. Rule 1(4) of the 'Beijing Rules' provides that 'Juvenile Justice shall be conceived as an integral part of the national development process of each country, within a comprehensive framework of social justice for all juveniles, thus, at the same time contributing to the protection of the young and the maintenance of a peaceful order in society.' Rule 13(5) of the 'Beijing Rules' states that 'While in custody, juveniles shall receive care, protection and all necessary individual assistance-social, educational, vocational, psychological, medical and physical-that they may require in view of their age, sex and personality.'

the Protection of Juveniles Deprived of their Liberty[22] apply to any person under the age of 18 years of age[23] and are designed to establish minimum standards for the protection of children deprived of their liberty consistent with their human rights and fundamental freedoms with a view to counteracting the detrimental effects of detention and fostering integration in society.[24] The rules are intended to serve as standards of reference to professionals involved in the management of the juvenile justice system.[25] Van Bueren argues these rules should be used as a normative framework by the Committee on the Rights of the Child[26] and indeed the Committee on the Rights of the Child regards these provisions as providing relevant detailed standards for the implementation of Art 37 of the CRC.[27]

CRC, Art 37 – Ambit

(i) Wide Application of CRC, Art 37

14.13 The provisions of Art 37 of the CRC which relate to the deprivation of liberty are not limited in their application to children in conflict with the law but will also apply to restrictions of liberty on the grounds of welfare, mental health and in relation to asylum and immigration issues.[28] As such, the rights of a child deprived of his or her liberty enshrined in the CRC apply with respect to children in conflict with the law and to children placed in institutions for the purposes of care, protection or treatment, including mental health, educational, drug treatment, child protection or immigration institutions.[29]

(ii) CRC, Art 37(b)

14.14 Article 37(b) of the CRC provides as follows in respect of the child's right not to be deprived or his or her liberty:

> '(b) No child shall be deprived of his or her liberty unlawfully or arbitrarily. The arrest, detention or imprisonment of a child shall be in conformity with the law and shall be used only as a measure of last resort and for the shortest appropriate period of time.[30]

---

22 Adopted by the UN General Assembly on 14 December 1990 (Resolution 45/113). See also the UN Minimum Standards for Non-Custodial Measures (the 'Tokyo Rules') adopted on 14 December 1990 (Resolution 45/110).

23 See Art 11(a).

24 See Art 3.

25 See Art 5.

26 Van Bueren, G *The International Law on the Rights of the Child* (1998) Martinus Nijhoff, p 211.

27 Newell, P and Hodgkin, R Implementation Handbook for the Convention on the Rights of the Child (2008) 3rd edn, UNICEF, p 548. See also the 'Guidelines for Action on Children in the Criminal Justice System' which aim to provide a framework for the implementation of those elements of the CRC concerned with children in the context of the administration of juvenile justice (Economic and Social Council resolution 1997/30) and 'Guidelines on Justice in Matters involving Child Victims and Witnesses of Crime' (ESC Resolution 2005/20).

28 Newell, P and Hodgkin, R *Implementation Handbook for the Convention on the Rights of the Child* (2008) 3rd edn, UNICEF, pp 548 and 560.

29 Committee on the Rights of the Children General Comment No 10 *Children's Rights in Juvenile Justice* CRC/C/GC/10 p 5 n.1. See also the Human Rights Committee General Comment No 8 *The Right of the Child to Protection from Corporal Punishment and other Cruel or Degrading Forms of Punishment* HRI/GEN/1/Rev 8, p 169, para 1 and the Committee on the Rights of the Child General Comment No 11 *Indigenous Children and their Rights under the Convention* CRC/C/GC/11, paras 74–77.

30 The domestic courts have had regard to Art 37(b) of the CRC (see for example *R (on the Application of B) v Brent Youth Court* [2010] All ER (D) 76 (Jul) and *Re CK (A Minor)* [2009] NICA 17, [2010] NI 15).

Article 37(b) – 'Deprived or his or her Liberty'

14.15 The Committee on the Rights of the Child has adopted the definition of 'deprivation of liberty' provided by the UN Rules for the Protection of Juveniles Deprived of their Liberty r 11(b) namely:

> 'The deprivation of liberty means any form of detention or imprisonment or the placement of a person in another public or private setting from which this person is not permitted to leave at will, by order of any judicial, administrative or other public authority.'[31]

Article 37(b) – 'Unlawfully or Arbitrarily'

14.16 Article 37(b) sets out strict conditions for any arrest, detention or period of imprisonment which deprives the child of his or her liberty. For a deprivation of liberty consequent upon arrest, detention or imprisonment not to be unlawful and/or arbitrary it must fulfil the minimum conditions set out in Art 37(b) of being in conformity with the law, a measure of last resort and be for the shortest possible time. Note that there is no age based qualification in Art 37 of the CRC in respect of the deprivation of liberty although, self-evidently, the younger the child the more inappropriate will be the use of deprivation of liberty over family or 'family like' alternatives. Likewise, international law does not establish a minimum age below which States parties are prohibited from depriving a child of his or her liberty.[32] However, Art 40(3)(a) of the CRC provides that States Parties to the CRC shall in particular seek the 'establishment of a minimum age below which children shall be presumed not to have the capacity to infringe the penal law'. The appropriate age under Art 40(3)(a) should be set by reference to the UN Standard Minimum Rules for the Administration of Juvenile Justice (the 'Beijing Rules') r 4 of which provides that 'the beginning of that age shall not be fixed at too low an age level, bearing in mind the facts of emotional, mental and intellectual maturity'.[33] By implication, these provisions prevent children below a certain age from being deprived of their liberty by infringing the penal law.[34] However, given the wide ambit of Art 37, its failure to include an aged based qualification in respect of the deprivation of liberty will continue to effect children who may be deprived of their liberty other than by way of coming into conflict with the criminal law.

Article 37(b) – 'In Conformity with the Law'

14.17 In requiring that restrictions to the right to liberty be in 'conformity with the law' Art 37(b) of the CRC differs from the restrictions prescribed by Arts 10(2) and Art 14(3) of the CRC, which require restrictions to the child's right to leave any country and the child's right to freedom of thought conscience and religion respectively to be 'prescribed by law', and Art 13(2), which requires restrictions on the child's right to freedom of expression to be 'provided by law'.[35] The latter provisions suggest that the restrictions

---

[31] See also the Committee on the Rights of the Child Guidelines for Periodic Reports, paras 138–146 (CRC/C/58) and Newell, P and Hodgkin, R *Implementation Handbook for the Convention on the Rights of the Child* (2008) 3rd edn, UNICEF, p 557.

[32] Van Bueren, G *The International Law on the Rights of the Child* (1998) Martinus Nijhoff, p 208.

[33] See also Committee on the Rights of the Children General Comment No 10 *Children's Rights in Juvenile Justice* CRC/C/GC/10, paras 30–39.

[34] See also the UN Guidelines for the Alternative Care of Children A/RES/64/142, para 92 which provides that 'Measures aimed at protecting children in care should be in conformity with the law and should not involve unreasonable constraints on their liberty and conduct in comparison with children of similar age in their community.'

[35] Note however that the term 'conformity with the law' is used in Art 15(2) concerning the right to freedom of association and freedom of peaceful assembly.

under each of Arts 10(2), 13(2) and 14(3) must be embodied in statute or common law.[36] By contrast, the term 'conformity with the law' in Art 37(b) of the CRC suggests that the restrictions on the child's liberty must be lawful by reference to existing laws but that the restrictions themselves need not be embodied in the substantive law in order to comply with Art 37(b) of the CRC. Given the gravity of depriving a child of his or her liberty, it is unfortunate that Art 37(b) does not use the stronger formulation of 'prescribed by law'.

Deprivation of Liberty on the Grounds of Welfare

14.18 The Committee on the Rights of the Children deprecates the use of deprivation of liberty ostensibly to secure the child's welfare.[37] Deprivation of liberty on the grounds of welfare will not of itself justify that deprivation as lawful for the purposes of Art 37(b). Within this context the Committee has indicated that children with mental health problems should not be imprisoned.[38]

Deprivation of Liberty in respect of Asylum Seeking and Refugee Children

14.19 A child's status as an asylum seeker or refugee cannot of itself justify as lawful for the purposes of Art 37(b) a restriction on that child's liberty.[39] Further, uunaccompanied or separated children, including those who arrive irregularly in a country, should not, in principle, be deprived of their liberty solely for having breached any law governing access to and remaining within the territory.[40] Where children who are asylum seekers or refugees are deprived of their liberty that deprivation of liberty must be in accordance with the principles of international law if the deprivation of liberty is to be considered lawful.[41] Accordingly, any deprivation of liberty of a refugee or asylum seeking child must comply with the provisions of Art 37 of the CRC[42] and Art 31(1) of the Refugee Convention 1951 which provides as follows:

> '1. The Contracting States shall not impose penalties, on account of their illegal entry or presence, on refugees who, coming directly from a territory where their life or freedom was threatened in the sense of article 1, enter or are present in their territory without authorisation, provided they present themselves without delay to the authorities and show good cause for their illegal entry or presence.
>
> 2. The Contracting States shall not apply to the movements of such refugees restrictions other than those which are necessary and such restrictions shall only be applied until their status in the country is regularised or they obtain admission into another country. The Contracting States shall allow such refugees a reasonable period and all the necessary facilities to obtain admission into another country.'

[36] Nowak, M *UN Covenant on Civil and Political Rights: CCPR Commentary* (1993) p 208 and p 394.

[37] Newell, P and Hodgkin, R *Implementation Handbook for the Convention on the Rights of the Child* (2008) 3rd edn, UNICEF, p 562. See also the Committee on the Rights of the Child Report on the Tenth Session October/November 1995 CRC/C/46, para 228. Note that r 3.2 of the UN Standard Minimum Rules for the Administration of Juvenile Justice (the 'Beijing Rules') extends the ambit of those rules to welfare and care proceedings.

[38] See Nepal CRC/C/15/Add.57, para 38.

[39] Committee on the Rights of the Child General Comment No 6 *Treatment of Unaccompanied and Separated Children Outside their Country of Origin* CRC/GC/2005/6, paras 61–63.

[40] UN Guidelines for the Alternative Care of Children A/RES/64/142, para 43.

[41] Refugee Children – Guidelines on Protection and Care (1994) UNHCR, pp 86–88.

[42] See also the Human Rights Committee General Comment No 15 *The Position of Aliens under the Covenant* HRI/GEN/1/Rev 8, p 180, para 7 ('Aliens have the full right to liberty and security of the person. If lawfully deprived of their liberty, they shall be treated with humanity and with respect for the inherent dignity of their person. Aliens may not be imprisoned for failure to fulfill a contractual obligation. They have the right to liberty of movement and free choice of residence; they shall be free to leave the country').

14.20 The UNHCR Executive Conclusion *Detention of Refugees and Asylum Seekers*[43] provides that, if necessary, detention may be resorted to only on grounds prescribed by law to verify identity, to determine the elements on which the claim to refugee status or asylum is based, to deal with cases where refugees or asylum-seekers have destroyed their travel and/or identity documents or have used fraudulent documents in order to mislead the authorities of the State in which they intend to claim asylum or to protect national security or public order.[44]

Article 37(b) – 'Measure of Last Resort'

Scope of Application

14.21 The use of the term 'measure of last resort' in Art 37(b) emphasises that the deprivation of liberty of children should be viewed as an exceptional measure and will not be lawful unless it is so.[45] By the terms of Art 37(b) only the arrest, detention or imprisonment of a child has to meet the requirement of being a measure of last resort. Whilst on the face of it this suggests that notwithstanding the apparently wide application of Art 37 of the CRC[46] one of the cardinal principles of Art 37(b) does not apply to all forms of deprivation of liberty,[47] the wide definition of the word 'detention' means that all of the provisions of Art 37(b), including the 'measure of last resort' requirement, will apply within the context of mental health, secure accommodation and immigration.[48] The provisions of Art 37(b) will apply to refugee children.[49]

14.22 In addition to the provisions of Art 37(b) and the UN Standard Minimum Rules for the Administration of Juvenile Justice mandate a proportionate response concerning the deprivation of liberty in respect of children in conflict with the law. Rule 17 provides that:

> '17.1 The disposition of the competent authority shall be guided by the following principles:
>
> (a) The reaction taken shall always be in proportion not only to the circumstances and the gravity of the offence but also to the circumstances and the needs of the juvenile as well as to the needs of the society;
>
> (b) Restrictions on the personal liberty of the juvenile shall be imposed only after careful consideration and shall be limited to the possible minimum;[50]

---

43   No 44 (XXXVII) 1986 UNHCR.

44   See *Refugee Children: Guidelines on Protection and Care* (1995) UNHCR, p 86.

45   Newell, P and Hodgkin, R *Implementation Handbook for the Convention on the Rights of the Child* (2008) 3rd edn, UNICEF, p 556. See also the UN Rules for the Protection of Juveniles Deprived of their Liberty r 1 ('Imprisonment should be used as a last resort'), r 2 ('Deprivation of the liberty of a juvenile should be a disposition of last resort and for the minimum necessary period an should be limited to exceptional cases') and r 17 ('Detention before trial shall be avoided to the extent possible and limited to exceptional circumstances. Therefore, all efforts shall be made to apply alternative measures').

46   See **14.13** above.

47   Van Bueren, G *The International Law on the Rights of the Child* (1998) Martinus Nijhoff, p 209.

48   Note again that the term 'arrest, means apprehending a person for the alleged commission of an offence, 'detention' means any deprivation of liberty except as the result of a conviction for an offence and 'imprisonment' means deprivation of liberty arising out of a conviction (Body of Principles for the Protection of All Persons under any form of Detention or Imprisonment (GA Res 43/117 9 December 1988)).

49   See *Refugee Children: Guidelines on Protection and Care* (1995) UNHCR, pp 86–88.

50   Note that the Commentary provided with the 'Beijing Rules' states that 'Rule 17.1(b) implies that strictly punitive approaches are not appropriate. Whereas in adult cases, and possibly also in cases of severe offences by juveniles, just desert and retributive sanctions might be considered to have some merit, in juvenile cases such considerations should always be outweighed by the interest of safeguarding the well-being and the future of the young person ... rule 17.1(b) encourages the use of alternatives to institutionalisation to the

(c)   Deprivation of personal liberty shall not be imposed unless the juvenile is adjudicated of a serious act involving violence against another person or of persistence in committing other serious offences and unless there is no other appropriate response;[51]

(d)   The well-being of the juvenile shall be the guiding factor in the consideration of her or his case.'

Availability of Alternatives

14.23 The fact that deprivation of liberty in respect of the child must be a measure of last resort clearly implies a positive duty on State Parties to consider and make available alternatives to detention or imprisonment.[52] The UN Standard Minimum Rules for Non-custodial Measures (the 'Tokyo Rules') provide a framework of rules governing non-custodial measures and are applicable to children.[53] Rule 18 of the UN Standard Minimum Rules for the Administration of Juvenile Justice provides as follows in relation to the variety of 'disposition measures' which should be considered:

'18.1 A large variety of disposition measures shall be made available to the competent authority, allowing for flexibility so as to avoid institutionalisation to the greatest extent possible. Such measures, some of which may be combined, include:

(a)   Care, guidance and supervision orders;
(b)   Probation;
(c)   Community service orders;
(d)   Financial penalties, compensation and restitution;
(e)   Intermediate treatment and other treatment orders;
(f)   Orders to participate in group counseling and similar activities;
(g)   Orders concerning foster care, living communities or other educational settings;
(h)   Other relevant orders.

18.2 No juvenile shall be removed from parental supervision, whether partly or entirely, unless the circumstances of her or his case make this necessary.'[54]

Pre-Trial Detention

14.24 The use of deprivation of liberty as a measure of last resort pursuant to Art 37(b) of the CRC applies equally to detention pending trial.[55] The UN Rules for the Protection of Juveniles Deprived of their Liberty r 17 provides that detention before trial shall be avoided to the extent possible and limited to exceptional circumstances.[56] The UN Standard Minimum Rules for the Administration of Juvenile Justice require

---

maximum extent possible, bearing in mind the need to respond to the specific requirements of the young. Thus, full use should be made of the range of existing alternative sanctions and new alternative sanctions should be developed, bearing the public safety in mind. Probation should be granted to the greatest possible extent via suspended sentences, conditional sentences, board orders and other dispositions.'

[51]   See also the UN Secretary-General's *Study on Violence Against Children* (A/61/299, para 122(b)) which concludes that 'Detention should be reserved for child offenders who are assessed as posing a real danger to others, and significant resources should be invested in alternative arrangements, as well as community-based rehabilitation and reintegration programmes ...'.

[52]   Newell, P and Hodgkin, R *Implementation Handbook for the Convention on the Rights of the Child* (2008) 3rd edn, UNICEF, p 557. See also Canada CRC/C/15/Add.215, para 57(d) and Latvia CRC/C/LVA/CO/2, para 62(d).

[53]   See r 2(2).

[54]   Note that r 19.1 of the 'Beijing Rules 'provides that 'The placement of a juvenile in an institution shall always be a disposition of last resort and for the minimum necessary period.'

[55]   UN Standard Minimum Rules for the Administration of Juvenile Justice (the 'Beijing Rules'), r 13.1 ('Detention pending trial shall be used only as a measure of last resort and for the shortest possible period of time').

[56]   See also the 'Beijing Rules', r 13(1) ('Detention pending trial shall be used only as a measure of last resort

that, wherever possible, detention pending trial shall be replaced with alternative measures such as close supervision, intensive care or placement with a family or in an education setting or home.[57] Whilst in pre-trial detention children must receive care, protection and all necessary individual social, educational, vocational, psychological, medical and physical assistance that they require having regard to their age, sex and personality.[58] Juveniles who are detained pending trial are entitled to the guarantees enshrined in the UN Standard Minimum Rules for the Treatment of Prisoners.[59] The use of pre-trial detention as a form of punishment will violate the presumption of innocence.[60] Van Bueren argues that it is implicit in Art 40(4) of the CRC that States parties to the CRC are under a duty to develop alternate strategies to pre-trial detention by the use of social services to supervise the release of the child into some form of family environment.[61] Within this context, the Committee on the Rights of the Child stipulates that an effective package of alternatives to pre-trial detention should be available.[62] The law should clearly state the conditions that are required to determine whether to place or keep a child in pre-trial detention and the duration of pre-trial detention should be limited by law and be subject to regular review.[63] Refugee children should not be detained pending confirmation of their status save as a measure of last resort.[64]

Article 37(b) – 'Shortest Appropriate Period of Time'

14.25 The requirement to impose arrest, detention and imprisonment on a child for the 'shortest appropriate period of time'[65] pursuant to Art 37(b) of the CRC applies to both pre and post-trial deprivation of liberty.[66] The UN Standard Minimum Rules for the Administration of Juvenile Justice reinforce this stipulation.[67] The need to ensure that children are deprived of their liberty for the shortest appropriate period of time underpins the prohibition in Art 37(a) on life imprisonment without possibility of release. The duration of pre-trial detention should be limited in law and subject to

---

and for the shortest possible period of time') and r 13(2) ('Whenever possible, detention pending trial shall be replaced by alternative measures, such as close supervision, intensive care or placement with a family or in an educational setting or home').

[57] UN Standard Minimum Rules for the Administration of Juvenile Justice (the 'Beijing Rules'), r 13.2.

[58] UN Standard Minimum Rules for the Administration of Juvenile Justice (the 'Beijing Rules'), r 13.5.

[59] UN Standard Minimum Rules for the Administration of Juvenile Justice (the 'Beijing Rules'), r 13.3.

[60] Newell, P and Hodgkin, R *Implementation Handbook for the Convention on the Rights of the Child* (2008) 3rd edn, UNICEF, p 558 and Committee on the Rights of the Child General Comment No 10 CRC/C/GC/10 p 21, para 80.

[61] Van Bueren, G *The International Law on the Rights of the Child* (1998) Martinus Nijhoff, p 211. See the UN Standard Minimum Rules for the Administration of Juvenile Justice, r 13.2 ('Whenever possible, detention pending trial shall be replaced by alternative measures, such as close supervision, intensive care or placement with a family or in an educational setting or home') and see the UN Secretary-General's Study on Violence Against Children A/61/299, para 112(c).

[62] Committee on the Rights of the Child General Comment No 10 CRC/C/GC/10 p 21, para 80.

[63] Committee on the Rights of the Child General Comment No 10 CRC/C/GC/10 p 21, para 80.

[64] See *Refugee Children: Guidelines on Protection and Care* (1995) UNHCR, p 86.

[65] Note that the original wording proposed was the 'shortest possible period of time' but the need for compromise during the drafting of the CRC resulted in the adoption of the weaker formulation 'shortest appropriate period of time' (see UN Doc E/CN.4/1989/WG.1/L.4 cited in Van Bueren, G *The International Law on the Rights of the Child* (1998) Martinus Nijhoff, p 214). Note that the UN Rules for the Protection of Juveniles Deprived of their Liberty r 17 and the UN Standard Minimum Rules for the Administration of Juvenile Justice r 13.1 use the term 'shortest possible'.

[66] Contrast the provisions of Art 9(3) of the ICCPR. See also *Re CK (A Minor)* [2009] NICA 17, [2010] NI 15.

[67] See the 'Beijing Rules', r 19.1 ('The placement of a juvenile in an institution shall always be a disposition of last resort and for the minimum necessary period') and r 28.1 ('Conditional release from an institution shall be used by the appropriate authority to the greatest possible extent, and shall be granted at the earliest possible time').

regular review.[68] In relation to pre-trial detention, the UN Rules for the Protection of Juveniles Deprived of their Liberty and the UN Standard Minimum Rules for the Administration of Juvenile Justice both emphasise the need to ensure any deprivation of liberty lasts for the shortest possible period of time.[69]

(iii)   CRC, Art 37(c)

14.26   Article 37(c) of the CRC provides as follows in respect of the treatment of children who have been deprived of their liberty in accordance with the requirements of Art 37(b) of the Convention:

> 'Every child deprived of liberty shall be treated with humanity and respect for the inherent dignity of the human person, and in a manner which takes into account the needs of persons of his or her age. In particular, every child deprived of liberty shall be separated from adults unless it is considered in the child's best interest not to do so and shall have the right to maintain contact with his or her family through correspondence and visits, save in exceptional circumstances.'

CRC, Art 37(c) – Humanity, Respect, Dignity and Age Appropriate Treatment

14.27   Article 1 of the Universal Declaration of Human Rights provides that all human beings are born free and equal in dignity and rights. Within this context, Art 10(1) of the ICCPR provides that 'All persons deprived of their liberty shall be treated with humanity and with respect for the inherent dignity of the human person'. In its General Comment No 9 *Article 10 (Humane Treatment of Persons Deprived of their Liberty)* the Human Rights Committee has commented that:[70]

> 'Treating all persons deprived of their liberty with humanity and with respect for their dignity is a fundamental and universally applicable rule. Consequently, the application of this rule, as a minimum, cannot be dependent on the material resources available in the State party. This rule must be applied without distinction of any kind, such as race, colour, sex, language, religion, political or other opinion, national or social origin, property, birth or other status.'

14.28   With regard to children deprived of their liberty, the Committee on the Rights of the Child has stated that the requirement to treat children deprived of their liberty with humanity and respect of their inherent dignity as human beings:[71]

> '... reflects the fundamental human right enshrined in article 1 of Universal Declaration of Human Rights, which stipulates that all human beings are born free and equal in dignity and rights. This inherent right to dignity and worth, to which the preamble of CRC makes explicit reference, has to be respected and protected throughout the entire process of dealing with the child, from the first contact with law enforcement agencies and all the way to the implementation of all measures for dealing with the child.'

---

68   Newell, P and Hodgkin, R *Implementation Handbook for the Convention on the Rights of the Child* (2008) 3rd edn, UNICEF, p 558.

69   See the UN Rules for the Protection of Juveniles Deprived of their Liberty r 17 ('When preventive detention is nevertheless used, juvenile courts and investigative bodies shall give the highest priority to the most expeditious processing of such cases to ensure the shortest possible duration of detention') and UN Standard Minimum Rules for the Administration of Juvenile Justice r 13.1 ('Detention pending trial shall be used only as a measure of last resort and for the shortest possible period of time').

70   Human Rights Committee General Comment No 21 *Article 10 (Humane Treatment of Persons Deprived of their Liberty* HRI/GEN/1/Rev 8, p 193, para 4.

71   Committee on the Rights of the Child General Comment No 10 *Children's Rights in Juvenile Justice* CRC/C/GC/10 p 6, para 13.

14.29 Within this context, Art 37(c) of the CRC requires that children who are deprived of their liberty in accordance with the conditions laid down in Art 37(b) of the CRC should not lose their fundamental rights during the course of the deprivation of their liberty.[72] The UN Rules for the Protection of Juveniles deprived of their Liberty reinforces these principles, providing that 'Juveniles deprived of their liberty shall not for any reason related to their status be denied the civil, economic, political, social or cultural rights to which they are entitled under national or international law, and which are compatible with the deprivation of liberty'. The Human Rights Committee has expressed the view that the requirement to treat all persons deprived of their liberty with humanity and respect for the inherent dignity of the human person is non-derogable as a norm of general international law.[73]

14.30 The requirement to treat children with humanity and respect for their inherent dignity as human beings will apply to all institutions in which children are lawfully deprived of their liberty. Article 3(3) of the CRC[74] will also apply to such situations and requires that:

> 'States Parties shall ensure that the institutions, services and facilities responsible for the care or protection of children shall conform with the standards established by competent authorities, particularly in the areas of safety, health, in the number and suitability of their staff, as well as competent supervision.'

14.31 Further, in using the words 'in a manner which takes into account the needs of persons of his or her age' Art 37(c) applies the concept of the evolving capacity of the child as articulated by Art 5 of the CRC to the issue of the treatment of children deprived of their liberty. This latter principle must also be applied, observed and respected throughout the entire process of dealing with the child, from the first contact with law enforcement agencies all the way to the implementation of all measures for dealing with the child.[75]

14.32 The UN Standard Minimum Rules for the Administration of Juvenile Justice, r 13.5 provides that 'While in custody, juveniles shall receive care, protection and all necessary individual assistance-social, educational, vocational, psychological, medical and physical-that they may require in view of their age, sex and personality'. Pursuant to r 13.3 of the UN Standard Minimum Rules for the Administration of Juvenile Justice the UN Standard Minimum Rules will apply to juveniles detained pending trial. The UN Rules for the Protection of Children Deprived of their Liberty r 36 requires that to the extent possible children should have the right to use their own clothing, that detention facilities should ensure that each child has personal clothing suitable for the climate and adequate to ensure good health, and which should in no manner be degrading or humiliating and that children removed from or leaving a facility for any purpose should be allowed to wear their own clothing. Treatment with humanity will self evidently require an absence of corporal punishment in the context of the lawful

---

[72] Newell, P and Hodgkin, R *Implementation Handbook for the Convention on the Rights of the Child* (2008) 3rd edn, UNICEF, p 563.

[73] See Human Rights Committee General Comment No 29 *Article 4: Derogations during a State of Emergency* HRI/GEN/1/Rev 8, p 228, para 13(a).

[74] See also **8.159** above.

[75] Committee on the Rights of the Children General Comment No 10 *Children's Rights in Juvenile Justice* CRC/C/GC/10 p 6, para 13.

deprivation of the child's liberty.[76] The Committee on the Rights of the Child has summarised the minimum requirements for the treatment of children deprived of their liberty as follows:

'Children should be provided with a physical environment and accommodations which are in keeping with the rehabilitative aims of residential placement, and due regard must be given to their needs for privacy,[77] sensory stimuli, opportunities to associate with their peers, and to participate in sports, physical exercise, in arts, and leisure time activities;[78]

Every child of compulsory school age has the right to education suited to his/her needs and abilities, and designed to prepare him/her for return to society; in addition, every child should, when appropriate, receive vocational training in occupations likely to prepare him/her for future employment;

Every child has the right to be examined by a physician upon admission to the detention/correctional facility and shall receive adequate medical care throughout his/her stay in the facility, which should be provided, where possible, by health facilities and services of the community;[79]

The staff of the facility should promote and facilitate frequent contacts of the child with the wider community, including communications with his/her family, friends and other persons or representatives of reputable outside organisations, and the opportunity to visit his/her home and family;

Restraint or force can be used only when the child poses an imminent threat of injury to him or herself or others, and only when all other means of control have been exhausted;

The use of restraint or force, including physical, mechanical and medical restraints, should be under close and direct control of a medical and/or psychological professional. It must never be used as a means of punishment. Staff of the facility should receive training on the applicable standards and members of the staff who use restraint or force in violation of the rules and standards should be punished appropriately;

Any disciplinary measure must be consistent with upholding the inherent dignity of the juvenile and the fundamental objectives of institutional care; disciplinary measures in violation of article 37 of CRC must be strictly forbidden, including corporal punishment, placement in a dark cell, closed or solitary confinement, or any other punishment that may compromise the physical or mental health or well-being of the child concerned;

---

[76] See generally the Committee on the Rights of the Child General Comment No 8 *The Right of the Child to Protection from Corporal Punishment and Other Cruel or Degrading Forms of Punishment* CRC/C/GC/8.

[77] See also the UN Rules for the Protection of Children Deprived of their Liberty, r 35 ('The possession of personal effects is a basic element of the right to privacy and essential to the psychological well-being of the juvenile. The right of every juvenile to possess personal effects and to have adequate storage facilities for them should be fully recognised and respected').

[78] See also the UN Rules for the Protection of Children Deprived of their Liberty, r 86(f) ('All personnel should seek to minimise any differences between life inside and outside the detention facility which tend to lessen due respect for the dignity of juveniles as human beings').

[79] See also the UN Rules for the Protection of Children Deprived of their Liberty, r 27 ('As soon as possible after the moment of admission, each juvenile should be interviewed, and a psychological and social report identifying any factors relevant to the specific type and level of care and programme required by the juvenile should be prepared. This report, together with the report prepared by a medical officer who has examined the juvenile upon admission, should be forwarded to the director for purposes of determining the most appropriate placement for the juvenile within the facility and the specific type and level of care and programme required and to be pursued. When special rehabilitative treatment is required, and the length of stay in the facility permits, trained personnel of the facility should prepare a written, individualised treatment plan specifying treatment objectives and time-frame and the means, stages and delays with which the objectives should be approached').

Every child should have the right to make requests or complaints, without censorship as to the substance, to the central administration, the judicial authority or other proper independent authority, and to be informed of the response without delay; children need to know about and have easy access to these mechanisms;

Independent and qualified inspectors should be empowered to conduct inspections on a regular basis and to undertake unannounced inspections on their own initiative; they should place special emphasis on holding conversations with children in the facilities, in a confidential setting.'[80]

14.33 Training is a vital component in ensuring that the precepts of Art 37(c) are met by those responsible for the lawful deprivation of the child's liberty. As Van Bueren notes, 'training is the principle means of ensuring that the wide ambit of discretion, which is inevitably exercised by staff in institutions, is exercised in the best interests of the child within the framework of international legal standards'.[81] The design and administration of facilities in which children are lawfully deprived of their liberty will also contribute to meeting the requirements of Art 37(c) of the CRC.[82] The treatment of children deprived of their liberty with humanity and respect for the inherent dignity of the human person is a vital component of achieving the aims of Art 40(1) of the CRC in respect of the re-integration of children deprived of their liberty and their assumption of constructive roles in society.[83]

CRC, Art 37(c) – Separation from Adults

14.34 Article 37(c) of the CRC articulates two particular elements of the requirement that a child deprived of his or her liberty be treated with humanity and dignity in accordance with the needs of his or her age. Namely, that every child deprived of liberty shall be separated from adults unless it is considered in the child's best interest not to do so[84] and shall have the right to maintain contact with his or her family through correspondence and visits, save in exceptional circumstances.

Separation

14.35 The first of these particular requirements, that every child deprived of liberty shall be separated from adults unless it is considered in the child's best interest not to do so, will be applicable to all deprivations of liberty and not just to children who are

---

[80] Committee on the Rights of the Child General Comment No 10 *Children's Rights in Juvenile Justice* CRC/C/GC/10 p 23, para 89.

[81] Van Bueren, G *The International Law on the Rights of the Child* (1998) Martinus Nijhoff, p 217. See also the UN Rules for the Protection of Children Deprived of their Liberty r 85 ('The personnel should receive such training as will enable them to carry out their responsibilities effectively, in particular training in child psychology, child welfare and international standards and norms of human rights and the rights of the child, including the present Rules. The personnel should maintain and improve their knowledge and professional capacity by attending courses of in-service training, to be organised at suitable intervals throughout their career'). See also r 83.

[82] See the UN Rules for the Protection of Children Deprived of their Liberty rr 30 and 32.

[83] See also UN Rules for the Protection of Children Deprived of their Liberty r 79 ('All juveniles should benefit from arrangements designed to assist them in returning to society, family life, education or employment after release. Procedures, including early release, and special courses should be devised to this end').

[84] See also ICCPR Art 10(2)(b) ('Accused juvenile persons shall be separated from adults and brought as speedily as possible for adjudication') and Art 10(3) ('The penitentiary system shall comprise treatment of prisoners the essential aim of which shall be their reformation and social rehabilitation. Juvenile offenders shall be segregated from adults and be accorded treatment appropriate to their age and legal status'). See further the UN Standard Minimum Rules for Prisoners r 8(b). These latter provisions will apply to children (see Jordan CRC/C/15/Add.21, para 16, Paraguay CRC/C/15/Add.75, para 28 and Costa Rica CRC/C/15/Add. 266, para 56).

detained or imprisoned as the result of pending criminal charges or criminal conviction. The protection conferred by Art 37(c) is accordingly broader than the relevant provisions of the ICCPR.[85] The requirement that every child deprived of his or her liberty shall be separated from adults unless it is considered in the child's best interest not to do so implies the availability of either separate facilities or properly separated areas in the same facility. Note that the United Kingdom has entered a reservation in respect of the requirements of Art 10(2)(b) and Art 10(3) of the ICCPR.[86] The United Kingdom has not however entered a similar reservation in respect of Art 37(c) of the CRC. In the circumstances, it is unclear what practical effect if any the reservations entered in respect of the ICCPR can have in respect of children deprived of their liberty by the domestic authorities.

Best Interests

14.36 The Human Rights Committee has stipulated that the requirement under Art 10(2)(b) of the ICCPR that accused juvenile persons shall be separated from adults is an 'unconditional' requirement.[87] However, Art 37(c) of the CRC provides that the requirement to separate children deprived of their liberty from adults is expressly subject to the child's best interests. The best interests exception in Art 37(c) should however be interpreted narrowly and never for the convenience of the State parties.[88] Rule 29 of the UN Rules for the Protection of Juveniles Deprived of their Liberty provides examples of when it may be in the child's best interest not to be separated from adults, stating that:

> 'In all detention facilities juveniles should be separated from adults, unless they are members of the same family. Under controlled conditions, juveniles may be brought together with carefully selected adults as part of a special programme that has been shown to be beneficial for the juveniles concerned.'

Article 37(c) – Maintaining Contact

14.37 Maintaining Contact – Again, the requirement in Art 37(c) that the child shall have the right to maintain contact with his or her family through correspondence and visits, save in exceptional circumstances is a specific element of the right of the child deprived of his or her liberty to be treated with humanity and dignity in accordance with the needs of his or her age.[89] In order to facilitate contact visits between the child

---

[85]   See ICCPR Arts 10(2)(b) and 10(3).

[86]   The reservation reads 'Where at any time there is a lack of suitable prison facilities or where the mixing of adults and juveniles is deemed to be mutually beneficial, the Government of the United Kingdom reserve the right not to apply Arts 10(2)(b) and 10(3), so far as those provisions require juveniles who are detained to be accommodated separately from adults ...'.

[87]   Human Rights Committee General Comment No 9 *Article 10 (Humane Treatment of Persons Deprived of their Liberty)* HRI/GEN/1/Rev.8, para 2, pp 170–171.

[88]   Committee on the Rights of the Children General Comment No 10 *Children's Rights in Juvenile Justice* CRC/C/GC/10 p 22, para 85.

[89]   Note the importance of Art 9(4) of the CRC in this context ('4. Where such separation [of a child from his or her parents] results from any action initiated by a State Party, such as the detention, imprisonment, exile, deportation or death (including death arising from any cause while the person is in the custody of the State) of one or both parents or of the child, that State Party shall, upon request, provide the parents, the child or, if appropriate, another member of the family with the essential information concerning the whereabouts of the absent member(s) of the family unless the provision of the information would be detrimental to the well-being of the child. States Parties shall further ensure that the submission of such a request shall of itself entail no adverse consequences for the person(s) concerned').

deprived of his liberty and his or her family, the child should be placed in a facility that is as close as possible to the place of residence of his or her family.[90]

14.38 Exceptional Circumstances – The words 'save in exceptional circumstances' in Art 37(c) constitute an exception which should be exercised only in accordance with the child's best interests and not as a disciplinary measure or a measure designed to secure the cooperation of the child within the context of his or her detention.[91] The exceptional circumstances should be clearly described in law and not left to the discretion of competent authorities.[92]

14.39 Children of Detained or Imprisoned Mothers – The UN Standard Minimum Rules for the Treatment of Prisoners provide that in women's penal institutions there shall be special accommodation for all necessary pre-natal and post-natal care and treatment, that arrangements shall be made wherever practicable for children to be born in a hospital outside the institution and that if a child is born in prison, that fact shall not be mentioned in the birth certificate. Further, where nursing infants are allowed to remain in the institution with their mothers, provision shall be made for a nursery staffed by qualified persons, where the infants shall be placed when they are not in the care of their mothers.[93] In this context, the UN Guidelines for the Alternative Care of Children provide that:[94]

> 'When the child's sole or main carer may be the subject of deprivation of liberty as a result of preventive detention or sentencing decisions, non-custodial remand measures and sentences should be taken in appropriate cases wherever possible, the best interests of the child being given due consideration. States should take into account the best interests of the child when deciding whether to remove children born in prison and children living in prison with a parent. The removal of such children should be treated in the same way as other instances where separation is considered. Best efforts should be made to ensure that children remaining in custody with their parent benefit from adequate care and protection, while guaranteeing their own status as free individuals and access to activities in the community.'

(iv) CRC, Art 37(d)

14.40 Article 37(d) of the CRC provides as follows in respect of the child's right to challenge his or her deprivation of liberty:

> 'Every child deprived of his or her liberty shall have the right to prompt access to legal and other appropriate assistance, as well as the right to challenge the legality of the deprivation of his or her liberty before a court or other competent, independent and impartial authority, and to a prompt decision on any such action.'

---

[90] Committee on the Rights of the Children General Comment No 10 *Children's Rights in Juvenile Justice* CRC/C/GC/10 p 23, para 87.

[91] Van Bueren, G *The International Law on the Rights of the Child* (1998) Martinus Nijhoff, p 220.

[92] Committee on the Rights of the Children General Comment No 10 *Children's Rights in Juvenile Justice* CRC/C/GC/10 p 23, para 87.

[93] UN Standard Minimum Rules for the Treatment of Prisoners r 23. See also the Human Rights Committee General Comment No 28 *Article 3 (The Equality of Rights between Men and Women)* HRI/GEN/1/Rev 8, p 221, para 15 ('Pregnant women who are deprived of their liberty should receive humane treatment and respect for their inherent dignity at all times, and in particular during the birth and while caring for their newborn children').

[94] UN Guidelines for the Alternative Care of Children A/RES/64/142, para 48.

CRC, Art 37(d) – Prompt access to Legal and other Appropriate Assistance

14.41 Article 8 of the Universal Declaration of Human Rights provides that 'Everyone has the right to an effective remedy by the competent national tribunals for acts violating the fundamental rights granted him by the constitution or by law'. Within this context Art 9(4) of the ICCPR stipulates that 'Anyone who is deprived of his liberty by arrest or detention shall be entitled to take proceedings before a court, in order that that court may decide without delay on the lawfulness of his detention and order his release if the detention is not lawful'.[95] The Human Rights Committee has confirmed that the provisions of the ICCPR concerning challenges to deprivation of liberty extend to deprivations effected by administrative bodies as well as criminal courts.[96] Whilst not expressly stated in Art 37 of the CRC, the right of the child under Art 37(d) of the CRC to challenge the legality of any deprivation of liberty must imply a requirement that the child be informed promptly upon his or her arrest of the grounds for that arrest.[97] The provisions of Art 37(d) are examined in further detail in chapter 16.

CRC, Art 37(d) – Right to challenge the legality of the Deprivation

14.42 The Committee on the Rights of the Children in its General Comment No 10 *Children's Rights in Juvenile Justice* notes that in respect of the requirement under Art 37(d) of the CRC that the child have the right to challenge the legality of the deprivation of his or her liberty before a court or other competent, independent and impartial authority:[98]

> 'Every child arrested and deprived of his/her liberty should be brought before a competent authority to examine the legality of (the continuation of) this deprivation of liberty within 24 hours. The Committee also recommends that the States parties ensure by strict legal provisions that the legality of a pretrial detention is reviewed regularly, preferably every two weeks. In case a conditional release of the child, e g by applying alternative measures, is not possible, the child should be formally charged with the alleged offences and be brought before a court or other competent, independent and impartial authority or judicial body, not later than 30 days after his/her pretrial detention takes effect. The Committee, conscious of the practice of adjourning court hearings, often more than once, urges the States parties to introduce the legal provisions necessary to ensure that the court/juvenile judge or other competent body makes a final decision on the charges not later than six months after they have been presented.'

14.43 The right to challenge the legality of the deprivation of liberty includes not only the right to appeal, but also the right to access the court, or other competent, independent and impartial authority or judicial body in cases where the deprivation of liberty is an administrative decision.[99] Where the restriction of liberty is imposed by means of an administrative process it is vital that a proper complaints procedure is in place that meets the requirements of Art 37(d).

---

[95] See also the Body of Principles for the Protection of All Persons under Any Form of Detention or Imprisonment Principle 32 GA Res 43/173 1988 ('A detained person or his counsel shall be entitled at any time to take proceedings according to domestic law before a judicial or other authority to challenge the lawfulness of his detention in order to obtain his release without delay, if it is unlawful').

[96] Decision of the Human Rights Committee *Antti Vuolanne v Finland* (265/1987) A/44/40, Annex X.

[97] See Art 9(2) of the ICCPR ('Anyone who is arrested shall be informed, at the time of arrest, of the reasons for his arrest and shall be promptly informed of any charges against him').

[98] General Comment No 10 *Children's Rights in Juvenile Justice* CRC/C/GC/10, p 22, para 83.

[99] Committee on the Rights of the Children General Comment No 10 *Children's Rights in Juvenile Justice* CRC/C/GC/10, p 22, para 84.

14.44 All the procedures put in place to satisfy the requirement of Art 37(d) of the CRC must also satisfy the requirements of Art 12 of the Convention. In particular, the UN Rules for the Protection of Juveniles Deprived of their Liberty require that on admission to a facility depriving them of their liberty all juveniles shall be given a copy of the rules governing the detention facility and a written description of their rights and obligations in a language they can understand, together with the address of the authorities competent to receive complaints, as well as the address of public or private agencies and organisations which provide legal assistance. For those juveniles who are illiterate or who cannot understand the language in the written form, the information should be conveyed in a manner enabling full comprehension.[100] Every child should have the opportunity of making requests or complaints to the director of the detention facility and to his or her authorised representative and should have the right to make a request or complaint, without censorship as to substance, to the central administration, the judicial authority or other proper authorities through approved channels, and to be informed of the response without delay. Further, every child should have the right to request assistance from family members, legal counselors, humanitarian groups or others where possible, in order to make a complaint. Illiterate children should be provided with assistance should they need to use the services of public or private agencies and organisations which provide legal counsel or which are competent to receive complaints.[101]

CRC, Art 37(d) – Prompt Decision

14.45 The right to a 'prompt' decision under Art 37(d) of the CRC following a challenge to the legality of the deprivation of the child's liberty before a court or other competent, independent and impartial authority means that a decision must be rendered as soon as possible and within and not later than 2 weeks after the challenge is made.[102] The Committee on the Rights of the Child has pointed out that term 'prompt' is even stronger, and justifiably so given the seriousness of deprivation of liberty, than the term 'without delay' contained in Art 40(2)(b)(iii) of CRC,[103] which in turn is stronger than the term 'without undue delay' used in Art 14(3)(c) of ICCPR.[104]

---

[100] UN Rules for the Protection of Juveniles Deprived of their Liberty, r 24.

[101] UN Rules for the Protection of Juveniles Deprived of their Liberty, rr 75–78.

[102] Committee on the Rights of the Children General Comment No 10 *Children's Rights in Juvenile Justice* CRC/C/GC/10, p 22, para 84.

[103] Article 40(2)(b)(iii) provides that 'Every child alleged as or accused of having infringed the penal law has at least the following guarantees ... (iii) To have the matter determined without delay by a competent, independent and impartial authority or judicial body in a fair hearing according to law, in the presence of legal or other appropriate assistance and, unless it is considered not to be in the best interest of the child, in particular, taking into account his or her age or situation, his or her parents or legal guardians.'

[104] Committee on the Rights of the Children General Comment No 10 *Children's Rights in Juvenile Justice* CRC/C/GC/10, p 22, para 51. Article 14(3)(c) of the ICCPR provides that 'In the determination of any criminal charge against him, everyone shall be entitled to the following minimum guarantees ... (c) to be tried without undue delay.' See also the Human Rights Committee General Comment No 8 *Article 9 (Right to Liberty and Security of the Person)* HRI/GEN/1/Rev 8, p 169, paras 2 and 3 and r 10(2) of the 'Beijing Rules'.

The Child's Right to Liberty and Security of the Person under Other International Instruments

The Geneva Conventions

Child Prisoners of War

14.46 Pursuant to Art 4A of the Geneva Convention Relative to the Treatment of Prisoners of War 1949 ('Geneva Convention III'), the definition of a prisoner of war is not dependent on age. Thus, the protection provided to prisoners of war by Geneva Convention III will encompass all children even though the participation of children under the age of 15 in armed conflict is prohibited.[105] Note however that, in relation to members of militias and other volunteer corps, the requirement contained in Art 4A(2)(d) of Geneva Convention III that militias or volunteer corps conduct their operations 'in accordance with the laws and customs of war' will exclude from protection child members below the age of 15 years of age where this requirement is not met.[106] Children who participate in hostilities but do not fall within the definition of combatants remain subject to the domestic legislation of their national state and will, if they come within the category of persons protected by the Geneva Convention relative to the Protection of Civilian Persons in Time of War ('Geneva Convention IV'), be treated as civilian internees.[107] Note that in internal conflicts the status of the combatant is unrecognised in international law and therefore the status of 'prisoner of war' does not exist. However, child soldiers who are captured during internal conflicts will benefit from the protection afforded by Geneva Convention III as persons who have ceased to participate in hostilities.[108]

14.47 Pursuant to Art 5 the protection conferred on prisoners of war by Geneva Convention III applies from the time they fall into the power of the enemy until their final release and repatriation. Pursuant to Art 14 of Geneva Convention III all prisoners of war are entitled in all circumstances to respect for their persons and their honour. Note that there is no duty under Geneva Convention III to take into account the particular needs of child prisoners of war. However, the International Committee of the Red Cross will intervene to ensure the wellbeing of child prisoners of war.[109] Child prisoners of war will be subject to the same repatriation requirements of Art 117 of Geneva Convention III as adults, namely that repatriated persons may not be employed on active military service.

Arrest, Detention and Internment of Children in time of War

(i) Breach of Penal Laws of the Occupied Territory

14.48 During any occupation by an Occupying Power the penal laws of an occupied territory remain in force save in so far as they may be repealed by the Occupying Power in cases where such law constitutes a threat to the security of the Occupying Power or an obstacle to the application of the Geneva Convention.[110] Children in occupied territories may therefore be subject to the penal law of an occupied territory and may

---

[105] See **15.134** below.
[106] See **15.134** below.
[107] See Art 68 of Geneva Convention IV and **14.49** below.
[108] See Geneva Convention III Art 3(1). See also Art 4(3) of Protocol II to the Geneva Conventions.
[109] See *Report of the International Committee of the Red Cross on its Activities during the Second World War* September 1 1939 to 30 June 1947 Vol1 (1948), pp 297–300 and Dutli, M *Captured Child Combatants* (1990) International Review of the Red Cross 278.
[110] Geneva Convention IV, Art 64.

also be subject to penal consequences for committing acts prejudicial to the security of the Occupying Power.[111] Where children are detained under the penal law of an occupied territory during a time of occupation proper regard must be paid to the special treatment due to children.[112]

(ii) Internment

14.49 Under international law a party to an armed conflict may take measures against persons, including children, to ensure that party's security.[113] Such measures can include internment.[114] Pursuant to Art 42 of Geneva Convention IV internment may only be used if the security of the Detaining Power makes it absolutely necessary. Pursuant to Art 43 of the Geneva Convention IV a child who is interned is entitled to have his or her internment reconsidered as soon as possible by an appropriate court or administrative board designated by the Detaining Power and if the internment is maintained it must be periodically reviewed no less than twice per annum. Article 43 further provides that the names of any interred persons must be provided to the Protecting Power and details of any decisions made in respect of their internment.

14.50 Once interred, children are entitled under Geneva Convention IV to certain minimum conditions.[115] Internees must be accommodated and administered separately from prisoners of war and persons deprived of their liberty for any other reason.[116] If arrested, detained or interned for reasons related to the armed conflict, children shall be held in quarters separate from the quarters of adults, except where families are accommodated as family units.[117] Where they are interned with their families, children shall be lodged together with their families and wherever possible in the same premise separate from other internees and with facilities for leading a proper family life. Internees may request that their children who have been left at liberty without parental care shall be interned with them.[118] Children under the age of 15 years must be given additional food in proportion to their physiological needs.[119] The education of interned children and young people must be ensured by the Detaining Power and they must be allowed to attend schools either within the place of internment or outside it. Special playgrounds must be reserved for children and young people.[120] During the course of hostilities the combatants should in particular endeavour to conclude agreements for the release, repatriation and return to places of residence or a neutral country of children, pregnant women and mother's with infants and young children.[121]

---

[111] Geneva Convention IV, Arts 64–77.
[112] Geneva Convention IV, Art 76.
[113] Geneva Convention IV, Art 5.
[114] Geneva Convention IV, Art 41. 'Internment' is detention solely for the purposes of ensuring security rather than by reason of punishment.
[115] See Generally Geneva Convention, IV, Section IV.
[116] Geneva Convention IV, Art 84.
[117] Geneva Convention Protocol I, Art 77(4).
[118] Geneva Convention IV, Art 82. Note that internment camps must be clearly marked as such using the letters 'IC' clearly visible in daytime from the air (see Geneva Convention IV, Art 83).
[119] Geneva Convention IV, Art 89.
[120] Geneva Convention IV, Art 94.
[121] Geneva Convention IV, Art 132.

International Convention for the Protection of all Persons from Enforced Disappearance

14.51 Article 1 of the Declaration on the Protection of All Persons from Enforced Disappearance[122] provides that:

> 'Any act of enforced disappearance places the persons subjected thereto outside the protection of the law and inflicts severe suffering on them and their families. It constitutes a violation of the rules of international law guaranteeing, inter alia, the right to recognition as a person before the law, the right to liberty and security of the person and the right not to be subjected to torture and other cruel, inhuman or degrading treatment or punishment. It also violates or constitutes a grave threat to the right to life.'

14.52 Within this context, the International Convention for the Protection of all Persons from Enforced Disappearance[123] Art 1 provides that no one shall be subjected to enforced disappearance and that no exceptional circumstances whatsoever, whether a state of war or a threat of war, internal political instability or any other public emergency, may be invoked as a justification for enforced disappearance. Article 2 of the Convention defines enforced disappearance as:

> '... the arrest, detention, abduction or any other form of deprivation of liberty by agents of the State or by persons or groups of persons acting with the authorisation, support or acquiescence of the State, followed by a refusal to acknowledge the deprivation of liberty or by concealment of the fate or whereabouts of the disappeared person, which place such a person outside the protection of the law.'

14.53 Article 25 of the International Convention for the Protection of all Persons from Enforced Disappearance sets out the following provisions aimed at protecting children from enforced disappearance:

> '1. Each State Party shall take the necessary measures to prevent and punish under its criminal law:
>
> (a)   The wrongful removal of children who are subjected to enforced disappearance, children whose father, mother or legal guardian is subjected to enforced disappearance or children born during the captivity of a mother subjected to enforced disappearance;
> (b)   The falsification, concealment or destruction of documents attesting to the true identity of the children referred to in subparagraph (a) above.
>
> 2. Each State Party shall take the necessary measures to search for and identify the children referred to in paragraph 1 (*a*) of this article and to return them to their families of origin, in accordance with legal procedures and applicable international agreements.
>
> 3. States Parties shall assist one another in searching for, identifying and locating the children referred to in paragraph 1 (*a*) of this article.
>
> 4. Given the need to protect the best interests of the children referred to in paragraph 1 (*a*) of this article and their right to preserve, or to have reestablished, their identity, including their nationality, name and family relations as recognised by law, States Parties which recognise a system of adoption or other form of placement of children shall have legal procedures in

---

[122]   A/RES/47/133.
[123]   December 2006. Note that the United Kingdom is not yet a signatory to this Convention.

place to review the adoption or placement procedure, and, where appropriate, to annul any adoption or placement of children that originated in an enforced disappearance.

5. In all cases, and in particular in all matters relating to this article, the best interests of the child shall be a primary consideration, and a child who is capable of forming his or her own views shall have the right to express those views freely, the views of the child being given due weight in accordance with the age and maturity of the child.'[124]

The Child's Right to Liberty and Security of the Person under the ECHR

ECHR, Art 5

14.54 Article 5 of the ECHR provides as follows in respect of the right to liberty and security of the person and the lawful exceptions to the prohibition on deprivation of liberty:

'1. Everyone has the right to liberty and security of person. No one shall be deprived of his liberty save in the following cases and in accordance with a procedure prescribed by law:

a)   the lawful detention of a person after conviction by a competent court;

b)   the lawful arrest or detention of a person for non-compliance with the lawful order of a court or in order to secure the fulfilment of any obligation prescribed by law;

c)   the lawful arrest or detention of a person effected for the purpose of bringing him before the competent legal authority on reasonable suspicion of having committed an offence or when it is reasonably considered necessary to prevent his committing an offence or fleeing after having done so;

d)   the detention of a minor by lawful order for the purpose of educational supervision or his lawful detention for the purpose of bringing him before the competent legal authority;

e)   the lawful detention of persons for the prevention of the spreading of infectious diseases, of persons of unsound mind, alcoholics or drug addicts or vagrants;

f)   the lawful arrest or detention of a person to prevent his effecting an unauthorised entry into the country or of a person against whom action is being taken with a view to deportation or extradition.

2. Everyone who is arrested shall be informed promptly, in a language which he understands, of the reasons for his arrest and of any charge against him.

3. Everyone arrested or detained in accordance with the provisions of paragraph 1.c of this article shall be brought promptly before a judge or other officer authorised by law to exercise judicial power and shall be entitled to trial within a reasonable time or to release pending trial. Release may be conditioned by guarantees to appear for trial.

4. Everyone who is deprived of his liberty by arrest or detention shall be entitled to take proceedings by which the lawfulness of his detention shall be decided speedily by a court and his release ordered if the detention is not lawful.

5. Everyone who has been the victim of arrest or detention in contravention of the provisions of this article shall have an enforceable right to compensation.'

---

[124]   Note that Art 1 of the International Convention for the Protection of all Peoples from Enforced Disappearance provides that '1. No one shall be subjected to enforced disappearance. 2. No exceptional circumstances whatsoever, whether a state of war or a threat of war, internal political instability or any other public emergency, may be invoked as a justification for enforced disappearance.'

14.55 Note that the Council of Europe has expressly recognised the importance of having proper preventative strategies in place with a view to avoiding the deprivation of children's liberty.[125] Unlike the provisions of Art 37 of the CRC, States parties to the ECHR may derogate from Art 5 in times of war or other public emergency threatening the life of the nation.[126]

ECHR, Art 5 – 'Liberty and Security of Person'

14.56 The concept of liberty under Art 5(1) of the ECHR contemplates individual liberty in its classic sense, that is to say the physical liberty of the person.[127] Under Art 5(1) of the ECHR the relationship between liberty and security of the person emphasizes the fact that security of the person must be understood in the context of physical liberty rather than physical safety. Thus the word 'security' serves simply to emphasise that the requirement that a person's liberty may not be deprived in an arbitrary fashion.[128] Indeed, the definitive object and purpose of Art 5 has been held to be that of ensuring that no one should be disposed of his or her liberty in an arbitrary manner.[129] As such the 'security of the person' for the purposes of Art 5 of the ECHR will not be relevant, for example, in respect of applications relating to social security[130] or insecure personal circumstances.[131]

14.57 A deprivation of liberty will be considered arbitrary where it is not in keeping with the restrictions permissible under Art 5(1) or with the provisions of the ECHR generally.[132] There must be no element of arbitrariness in respect of the deprivation of

---

[125] See Council of Europe Committee of Ministers Recommendation No R(87)20 on Social Reactions to Juvenile Delinquency (1987).

[126] See ECHR, Art 15. Note that the derogation from Art 5 entered into by the United Kingdom after September 11 2001 under s 14 of the Human Rights Act 1998 was held to be disproportionate by the European Court of Human Rights and has since been withdrawn (see *A & Others v United Kingdom* (2009) Application No 3455/05).

[127] *Engel v Netherlands* (1976) 1 EHRR 647, para 58.

[128] *East African Asians v United Kingdom* (1973) Application No 4626/70 ('The full text of Art 5 shows that the expression 'liberty and security of the person' in para (1) must be read as a whole and that consequently, 'security' should be understood in the context of 'liberty' ... in the Commissions view, the protection of 'security' is in this context concerned with arbitrary interference, by a public authority, with an individual's personal 'liberty'. Or, in other words, any decision taken with the sphere of Art 5 must, in order to safeguard the individuals right to 'security of the person', conform to the procedural as well as the substantive requirements laid down by an already existing law ... protection against arbitrary arrest and detention was one of the principle considerations of the drafters of this treaty') and *Bozano v France* (1986) 9 EHRR, para 54 ('The main issue to be determined is whether the disputed detention was 'lawful', including whether it was in accordance with 'a procedure prescribed by law'. The Convention here refers essentially to national law and establishes the need to apply its rules, but it also requires that any measure depriving the individual of his liberty must be compatible with the purpose of Article 5, namely to protect the individual from arbitrariness. What is at stake here is not only the 'right to liberty' but also the 'right to security of person'').

[129] *Winterwerp v Netherlands* (1979) 2 EHRR 387, para 37; *Bozano v France* (1986) 9 EHRR 297, para 54 and *Engel v Netherlands* (1976) 1 EHRR 647, para 58 ('In proclaiming the 'right to liberty', paragraph 1 of Article 5 is contemplating individual liberty in its classic sense, that is to say the physical liberty of the person. Its aim is to ensure that no one should be dispossessed of this liberty in an arbitrary fashion. As pointed out by the Government and the Commission, it does not concern mere restrictions upon liberty of movement (Art 2 of Protocol No 4). This is clear both from the use of the terms 'deprived of his liberty', 'arrest' and 'detention', which appear also in paras 2–5, and from a comparison between Article 5 and the other normative provisions of the Convention and its Protocols').

[130] *X v Germany* (1972) 1 Digest 288.

[131] *Menteşe v Turkey* (2007) 44 EHRR 147, para 66 ('The applicants' insecure personal circumstances arising from the loss of their home do not fall within the notion of security of person as envisaged in Article 5(1) of the Convention') and *X v Ireland* 16 YB 388 (1973).

[132] *Winterwerp v Netherlands* (1979) 2 EHRR 387, paras 37–39 and see *Van Droogenbroeck v Belgium* (1982) 4 EHRR 443, para 48; *Weeks v United Kingdom* (1987) 10 EHRR 293, para 49; *Bozano v France* (1986) 9 EHRR 297, para 54 and *Ashingdane v United Kingdom* (1985) 7 EHRR 528, para 44.

liberty in question[133] and no detention that is arbitrary can ever be regarded as lawful.[134] The deprivation of liberty must also be proportionate to the attainment of its purpose.[135] Thus in *Bouamar v Belgium*[136] the detention of a child for the purposes of educational supervision was held to be arbitrary for the purposes of Art 5(1) of the ECHR on the grounds that the 'fruitless repetition' of interim custody measures prior to a regime of supervised education could not be regarded as furthering any educational aim.[137] Each period of custody thus had the effect of making such measures less and less lawful.

ECHR, Art 5 – 'Deprivation'

(i) Meaning of 'Deprivation'

14.58 In *Engel v Netherlands*[138] the European Court of Human Rights held in relation to the right to liberty enshrined in Art 5(1) of the ECHR that:

> 'In proclaiming the "right to liberty", paragraph 1 of Article 5 is contemplating individual liberty in its classic sense, that is to say the physical liberty of the person. Its aim is to ensure that no one should be dispossessed of this liberty in an arbitrary fashion. As pointed out by the Government and the Commission, it does not concern mere restrictions upon liberty of movement. This is clear both from the use of the terms "deprived of his liberty", "arrest" and "detention", which appear also in paragraphs 2 to 5, and from a comparison between Article 5 and the other normative provisions of the Convention and its Protocols.'

14.59 In the circumstances, for the purposes of Art 5(1) of the ECHR the 'deprivation' of liberty must be distinguished from 'restrictions' imposed upon liberty.[139] Further Art 5 of the ECHR is not concerned with the treatment and conditions consequent upon deprivation of liberty.[140] Art 5(1) of the ECHR is solely concerned with deprivation of liberty although the European Court does recognise the difficulty in distinguishing between loss of liberty and simple restrictions on movement.[141]

---

[133]   *Winterwerp v Netherlands* (1979) 2 EHRR 387, paras 37–39.

[134]   *Ashingdane v United Kingdom* (1985) 7 EHRR 528, para 44 ('it follows from the very aim of Article 5, para 1 that no detention that is arbitrary can ever be regarded as "lawful". The Court would further accept that there must be some relationship between the ground of permitted deprivation of liberty relied on and the place and conditions of detention').

[135]   *Winterwerp v Netherlands* (1979) 2 EHRR 387, paras 37–39 and *Van Droogenbroeck v Belgium* (1982) 4 EHRR 443.

[136]   (1988) 11 EHRR 1, para 53.

[137]   The European Court of Human Rights characterised the measures taken in *Bouamar* as constituting '[t]he detention of a young man in a remand prison in conditions of virtual isolation and without the assistance of staff with educational training ...'.

[138]   (1976) 1 EHRR 647, para 58. See also *Guzzardi v Italy* (1980) 3 EHRR 333, para 92; *Raimondo v Italy* (1994) 18 EHRR 237, para 39

[139]   Such restrictions are dealt with under Art 2 of the Fourth Protocol (Art 2 4P) to which the United Kingdom is not party. Article 2 4P stipulates that '1. Everyone lawfully within the territory of a State shall, within that territory, have the right to liberty of movement and freedom to choose his residence. 2. Everyone shall be free to leave any country, including his own. 3. No restrictions shall be placed on the exercise of these rights other than such as are in accordance with law and are necessary in a democratic society in the interests of national security or public safety, for the maintenance of ordre public, for the prevention of crime, for the protection of health or morals, or for the protection of the rights and freedoms of others. 4. The rights set forth in paragraph 1 may also be subject, in particular areas, to restrictions imposed in accordance with law and justified by the public interest in a democratic society.'

[140]   *Ashingdane v United Kingdom* (1985) 7 EHRR 528, para 52 ('the domestic remedy available under [Art5(4)] should enable review of the conditions which, according to [Art5(1)] are essential for the 'lawful detention' of a person ...') and see *D v Germany* 54 DR 116 (1987) at 121.

[141]   *Guzzardi v Italy* (1980) 3 EHRR 333, para 93 ('The difference between deprivation of and restriction upon liberty is nonetheless merely one of degree or intensity, and not one of nature or substance. Although the process of classification into one or other of these categories sometimes proves to be no easy task in that

(ii) Positive Obligations in respect of Deprivation of Liberty

14.60 As with a number of other articles under the ECHR, Art 5(1) imports positive obligations on States parties to protect the liberty of its citizens. In *Storck v Germany*[142] the European Court of Human Rights held in respect of Art 5(1) that:

> 'The Court has consistently held that the responsibility of a State is engaged if a violation of one of the rights and freedoms defined in the Convention is the result of non-observance by that State of its obligation under Article 1 to secure those rights and freedoms in its domestic law to everyone within its jurisdiction. Consequently, the Court has expressly found that Article 2 and Article 8 of the Convention require the State not only to refrain from an active infringement by its representatives of the rights in question, but also to take appropriate steps to provide protection against an interference with those rights either by State agents or by private parties. Having regard to this, the Court considers that Article 5(1), first sentence, of the Convention must equally be construed as laying down a positive obligation on the State to protect the liberty of its citizens. Any conclusion to the effect that this was not the case would not only be inconsistent with the Court's case-law, notably under Articles 2, 3 and 8 of the Convention, it would also leave a sizeable gap in the protection from arbitrary detention, which would be inconsistent with the importance of personal liberty in a democratic society. The State is therefore obliged to take measures providing effective protection of vulnerable persons, including reasonable steps to prevent a deprivation of liberty of which the authorities have or ought to have knowledge.'

14.61 The scope of this positive obligation under Art 5(1) of the ECHR will include the taking of effective measures to safeguard an individual's liberty and security of the person and to ensure procedural measures for the prompt investigation of claims that a person has been deprived of their liberty and not been seen since.[143]

(iii) Determining whether there has been 'Deprivation of Liberty'

14.62 In *Guzzardi v Italy*[144] the European Court of Human Rights stated that in respect of determining whether a person has been deprived of their liberty for the purposes of Art 5(1) of the ECHR that:

> 'In order to determine whether someone has been 'deprived of his liberty' within the meaning of Article 5, the starting point must be his concrete situation and account must be taken of a whole range of criteria such as the type, duration, effects and manner of implementation of the measure in question.'

---

some borderline cases are a matter of pure opinion, the Court cannot avoid making the selection upon which the applicability or inapplicability of Article 5 depends').

[142] (2006) 43 EHRR 6, para 102.

[143] *Çakici v Turkey* (1999) 31 EHRR 133, para 104 ('To minimise the risks of arbitrary detention, Article 5 provides a corpus of substantive rights intended to ensure that the act of deprivation of liberty is amenable to independent judicial scrutiny and secures the accountability of the authorities for that measure ... Given the responsibility of the authorities to account for individuals under their control, Article 5 requires them to take effective measures to safeguard against the risk of disappearance and to conduct a prompt and effective investigation into an arguable claim that a person has been taken into custody and has not been seen since'). See also *Cicek v Turkey* (2003) 37 EHRR 20, para 164 ('The Court stresses in this respect that the unacknowledged detention of an individual is a complete negation of these guarantees and a most grave violation of Article 5. Having assumed control over that individual, it is incumbent on the authorities to account for his or her whereabouts. For this reason, Article 5 must be seen as requiring the authorities to take effective measures to safeguard against the risk of disappearance and to conduct a prompt effective investigation into an arguable claim that a person has been taken into custody and has not been seen since') and *Imakayeva v Russia* (2008) 27 EHRR 4, para 171.

[144] (1980) 3 EHRR 333, para 92.

Intention and Deprivation of Liberty

14.63 Whether there has been a deprivation for the purposes of Art 5(1) is thus a relative question that will depend on a number of variable factors. The intention of the authorities in respect of the alleged deprivation will be a relevant factor. In *X v Germany*[145] the questioning of a 10 year old girl for two hours in a police station without formal arrest, detention or being held in a cell was held not to have breached the provisions of Art 5(1), the European Commission holding that:

> 'In the present case the children were only questioned and then made to wait in an unlocked room before being brought home. The purpose of their being taken to the police quarters was to question them and not to arrest and detain them. The Commission considers it to be regrettable that the children may not have been able to understand the police action and may have felt that they were deprived of their liberty. Nevertheless, in view of an objective appreciation of the information now before the Commission, it considers that in the circumstances of the case the action in question did not constitute a deprivation of liberty in the sense of Article 5(1) of the Convention.'

Consent to Deprivation of Liberty

14.64 Properly informed consent can prevent a deprivation breaching Art 5(1) but that consent may be withdrawn, after which point the deprivation may constitute a violation of Art 5 of the ECHR.[146] Further, consent to deprivation of liberty will never deny a person the protection of Art 5 of the ECHR. In *HL v United Kingdom*:[147]

> 'The Court reiterates that the right to liberty is too important in a democratic society for a person to lose the benefit of Convention protection for the single reason that he may have given himself up to be taken into detention especially when it is not disputed that that person is legally incapable of consenting to, or disagreeing with, the proposed action.'

14.65 The issue of consent to deprivation of liberty raises particular difficulties for children not only by way of the need to establish whether a child has the capacity to consent to the deprivation of his or her liberty[148] but also the extent to which the child's parents should be entitled to consent on his or her behalf.

14.66 The rightly criticised decision of *Nielsen v Denmark*[149] considered the latter issue of parental consent to deprivation of liberty and held, contrary to the view of the European Commission, that the admission of the child to a children's psychiatric ward at the behest of his mother against his will and at a time he was not suffering from any recognised mental illness did not engage Art 5 of the ECHR as the child's admission was decided by his mother in the exercise of her parental 'rights'.[150] Seven judges of the Court dissented from the majority opinion in *Nielsen v Denmark*. Judges Thór Vilhjálmsson, Pettiti, Russo, Speilman, De Meyer, Carriloor Salcedo and Valticos all considered that the specific conditions under which the child was admitted to the hospital, and placed against his will in the psychiatric ward, and the length and nature of the committal should be given weight in determining whether the applicant was

---

[145] 24 DR 158 (1981) at 161.
[146] *De Wilde, Ooms and Versyp v Belgium* (1971) 1 EHRR 373, para 65.
[147] (2005) 40 EHRR 761, para 90.
[148] See **4.25** above.
[149] (1988) 11 EHRR 75.
[150] The Commission recognised the seemingly obvious point missed by the majority of the Court that the case concerned 'detention in a psychiatric ward of a 12-year-old boy who was not mentally ill' (see *Nielsen v Denmark* DR 46 155 (1986)).

deprived of his liberty. Taking into account these factors they agreed with the European Commission that the fact that the committal lasted over a period of several months and involved the placing in a psychiatric ward of a twelve-year-old boy who was not mentally ill constituted a deprivation of the child's liberty for the purposes of Art 5 of the ECHR.[151]

14.67 Whilst the Court in *Nielsen v Denmark* noted that parental 'rights' are not absolute and safeguards against abuse are required, as Van Bueren points out, the decision of the European Court of Human Rights in *Nielsen v Denmark* leaves children who are deprived of their liberty with the consent of one or both of their parents but against their own wishes wholly unprotected.[152] It is suggested that, having regard to the decision of the European Commission, the force of the dissenting judgments in the European Court of Human Rights and the principles underpinning the application of Art 5 of the ECHR considered in the context of the Convention as a whole, that the decision of the court in *Nielsen v Denmark* cannot be considered safe and should not be relied upon.

Status of the Individual and Deprivation of Liberty

14.68 The status of the individual deprived of their liberty may be relevant to whether that deprivation engages Art 5(1) of the ECHR.[153] Thus the fact that the person deprived of their liberty is a child is likely to be a relevant factor when considering the application of Art 5(1).

Freedom to Leave and Deprivation of Liberty

14.69 Having the freedom to leave an area will only prevent a breach of Art 5(1) where that freedom to leave is an effective one.[154] Thus to establish a deprivation of liberty for the purposes of Art 5(1) it is not necessary to establish detention in a locked area.[155] What is required to demonstrate a deprivation of liberty is to show that a person's liberty, not just their freedom of movement, has been circumscribed both in fact and in law.[156]

---

[151]   In a separate dissenting judgment, Judges Pettiti and De Meyer made clear their view that 'The applicant's committal could not be based on any of the grounds which could have justified it under this paragraph (art. 5–1). It did not constitute the normal exercise of parental authority or the normal practice of psychiatry. In fact it represented an abuse of both.' In his own separate dissenting judgment Judge Pettiti observed that: 'The Nielsen case involved a minor who was already the victim of parental conflict and who could only have been very disturbed by living with the other children in the ward. Furthermore, even for adults, so-called 'voluntary' committal may be just as sensitive as 'compulsory' committal and must be subject to full supervision.'

[152]   Van Bueren, G *The International Law on the Rights of the Child* (1998) Martinus Nijhoff, p 213.

[153]   See *Engel v Netherlands* (1976) 1 EHRR 647, para 59 in which it was held that the engagement of Art 5(1) in the context of military discipline depended on whether the measures in issue 'clearly deviate' from normal conditions of military life of those detained.

[154]   See *Amuur v France* (1996) 22 EHRR 533, para 48 ('The mere fact that it is possible for asylum seekers to leave voluntarily the country where they wish to take refuge cannot exclude a restriction on liberty, the right to leave any country, including one's own, being guaranteed, moreover, by Protocol No 4 to the Convention. Furthermore, this possibility becomes theoretical if no other country offering protection comparable to the protection they expect to find in the country where they are seeking asylum is inclined or prepared to take them in') and *SM and MT v Austria* (1993) 74 DR 179.

[155]   See *Ashingdane v United Kingdom* (1985) 7 EHRR 528, para 42 and *HL v United Kingdom* (2005) 40 EHRR 761, paras 91–94.

[156]   *Ashingdane v United Kingdom* (1985) 7 EHRR 528, para 42.

Duration of Deprivation of Liberty

14.70 The period of time for which a person is detained or imprisoned is a relevant but not an overriding factor in determining whether that detention or imprisonment is lawful. Thus the duration of detention will not necessarily be a decisive indicator of whether there has been a deprivation for the purposes of Art 5(1) of the ECHR.[157]

ECHR, Art 5 – Permissible Grounds for Deprivation of Liberty

14.71 The list of permissible grounds for the deprivation of liberty contained in Art 5(1) of the ECHR is exhaustive.[158] The European Court of Human Rights has made clear that, in addition to being exhaustive, the exceptions contained in Art 5(1) call for a narrow interpretation.[159] The exceptions are not mutually exclusive.[160] Thus, deprivation of the liberty of children will be prima facie a breach of Art 5(1) unless they come within one of the stated exceptions.[161]

14.72 In *R v Governor of Brockhill Prison ex p Evans (No 2)*[162] the House of Lords considered the proper test for determining whether a deprivation of liberty falls within one of the permissible lawful grounds, holding that:

'The jurisprudence of the European Court of Human Rights indicates that there are various aspects to art 5(1) which must be satisfied in order to show that the detention is lawful for the purposes of that article. The first question is whether the detention is lawful under domestic law. Any detention which is unlawful in domestic law will automatically be unlawful under art 5(1).[163] It will thus give rise to an enforceable right to compensation under art 5(5), the provisions of which are not discretionary but mandatory. The second question is whether, assuming that the detention is lawful under domestic law, it nevertheless complies with the general requirements of the convention. These are based upon the principle that any restriction on human rights and fundamental freedoms must be prescribed by law (see arts 8 to 11 of the convention). They include the requirements that the domestic law must be sufficiently accessible to the individual and that it must be sufficiently precise to enable the individual to foresee the consequences of the restriction. The third question is whether, again assuming that the detention is lawful under domestic law, it is nevertheless open to criticism on the ground that it is arbitrary because, for example, it was resorted to in bad faith or was not proportionate.'[164]

---

[157] *X and Y v Sweden* 7 DR 123 (1976) and *X v Austria* 18 DR 154 (1979). See also *Boumar v Belgium* (1987) 11 EHRR 1.

[158] *Ireland v United Kingdom* (1978) 2 EHRR, para 194 and *Winterwerp v Netherlands* (1979) 2 EHRR 387, para 37.

[159] *Winterwerp v Netherlands* (1979) 2 EHRR 387, para 37 ('Article 5, para 1 obviously cannot be taken as permitting the detention of a person simply because his views or behaviour deviate from the norms prevailing in a particular society. To hold otherwise would not be reconcilable with the text of Article 5, para 1 which sets out an exhaustive list of exceptions calling for a narrow interpretation. Neither would it be in conformity with the object and purpose of Article 5, para 1, namely to ensure that no one should be dispossessed of his liberty in an arbitrary. Moreover, it would disregard the importance of the right to liberty in a democratic society').

[160] *McVeigh, O'Neill and Evans v United Kingdom* 25 DR 15 (1981) and *Koniarska v United Kingdom* (2000) Application No 33670/96.

[161] Swindells, H, Neaves, A, Kushner, M and Skilbeck, R *Family Law and the Human Rights Act 1998* (1999) Jordans, p 117.

[162] [2001] 2 AC 19 at 38B–38E.

[163] Note however that that lawfulness under domestic law will not always be a decisive element in determining whether there has been a breach of Art 5(1) (see *Kuudoyorov v Russia* (2007) 45 EHRR 144, para 124 and *Weeks v United Kingdom* (1987) 10 EHRR 293, para 42).

[164] See also *Bozano v France* (1986) 9 EHRR 297, para 58 and *Perks v United Kingdom* (2000) 30 EHRR 33, para 68.

14.73 The lawfulness of any detention is required to be demonstrated in respect of both the ordering and the execution of the measure depriving the individual of his or her liberty.[165] As such a detention must not only be lawful *per se* but must be carried out in accordance with a procedure prescribed by law[166] including directly applicable EC law[167] and international law.[168] The 'procedure prescribed by law' must be accessible and precise in its terms in order to avoid arbitrariness[169] and permit the individual to foresee to a degree reasonable in the circumstances the consequences which a given action may entail.[170]

(i)   ECHR, Art 5(1)(a) – Lawful Detention after Conviction

14.74 Article 5(1)(a) of the ECHR provides as follows concerning the lawful detention of persons after conviction:

> '1. Everyone has the right to liberty and security of person. No one shall be deprived of his liberty save in the following cases and in accordance with a procedure prescribed by law:
>
> a)   the lawful detention of a person after conviction by a competent court;'

14.75 For the purposes of Art 5(1)(a) the term 'conviction' means a finding of guilt in respect of an offence and the imposition of a penalty.[171] The word 'after' in Art 5(1)(a) is not simply temporal but denotes the need for a causal connection between the conviction and the deprivation of liberty.[172] The term 'competent court' for the purposes of Art 5(1) means a body which gives to the individuals concerned guarantees appropriate to the kind of deprivation of liberty in question, namely it must be

---

[165] *Ashingdane v United Kingdom* (1985) 7 EHRR 528, para 44.

[166] *Winterwerp v Netherlands* (1979) 2 EHRR 387, para 39; *Herczegfalvy v Austria* (1992) 15 EHRR 437, para 63 ('In order to comply with paragraph 1(e) (art 5–1-e), the detention in issue must first of all be 'lawful', including the observance of a procedure prescribed by law; in this respect the Convention refers back essentially to national law and lays down the obligation to conform to the substantive and procedural rules thereof. It requires in addition, however, that any deprivation of liberty should be consistent with the purpose of Article 5, namely to protect individuals from arbitrariness'); *Bozano v France* (1986) 9 EHRR 297, para 54 and *Weeks v United Kingdom* (1987) 10 EHRR 293, para 42. See also *E v Norway* (1990) 17 EHRR 30, para 49.

[167] *Caprino v United Kingdom* 12 DR 14 (1978).

[168] *Öcalam v Turkey* (2003) 37 EHRR 288.

[169] *Zamir v United Kingdom* 40 DR 42 (1983); *Sunday Times v United Kingdom* (1979) 2 EHRR 245, para 49 and *Amuur v France* (1992) 22 EHRR 533, para 50.

[170] *Steel v United Kingdom* (1998) 28 EHRR 603, para 54, *Laumont v France* (2003) 35 EHRR 625, para 45 and *Gusinsky v Russia* (2005) 41 EHRR 17, paras 63–64.

[171] *X v United Kingdom* (1981) 4 EHRR 188, para 39. See also *B v Austria* (1991) 13 EHRR 20, para 38 ('Having regard in particular to the French text, the word 'conviction', for the purposes of Article 5(1)(a), has to be understood as signifying both a finding of guilt, after it has been established in accordance with the law that there has been an offence, and the imposition of a penalty or other measure involving deprivation of liberty').

[172] *Weeks v United Kingdom* (1987) 10 EHRR 293, para 42 ('Furthermore, the word 'after' in sub-paragraph (a) does not simply mean that the detention must follow the 'conviction' in point of time: in addition, the 'detention' must result from, 'follow and depend upon' or occur 'by virtue of' the 'conviction'. In short, there must be a sufficient causal connection between the conviction and the deprivation of liberty at issue') and *B v Austria* (1991) 13 EHRR 20, para 38. See also *Waite v United Kingdom* (2003) 36 EHRR 54.

independent of both the executive and the parties and have the power to give a legally binding judgment concerning a persons release.[173] In the circumstances, the competent court does not need to be a court of law.[174]

(ii) ECHR, Art 5(1)(b) – Compliance with the Law

14.76 Article 5(1)(b) of the ECHR provides as follows in respect of the deprivation of liberty to secure compliance with the law:

'1. Everyone has the right to liberty and security of person. No one shall be deprived of his liberty save in the following cases and in accordance with a procedure prescribed by law:

b)   the lawful arrest or detention of a person for non-compliance with the lawful order of a court or in order to secure the fulfilment of any obligation prescribed by law;'

14.77 Article 5(1)(b) permits the deprivation of liberty following non-compliance with a civil order of the court such as an injunction.[175] The order must be made by a court of competent jurisdiction,[176] be capable of enforcement and denote clearly the nature of the conduct that is prohibited or the obligation that is required to be met.[177] Art 5(1)(b) is thus not concerned with punishing a person for the breach of a general obligation.[178] The words 'to secure the fulfilment of any obligation prescribed by law' in Art 5(1)(b) were defined in *Guzzardi v Italy*[179] as follows:

'As regards the words 'to secure the fulfilment of any obligation prescribed by law', they concern only those cases where the law permits the detention of a person to compel him to fulfil a 'specific and concrete' obligation which he has failed to satisfy.'

14.78 The fact that an order is *later* found to have been wrong in law will not necessarily retrospectively render the period of detention consequent upon the order unlawful for the purposes of Art 5(1) of the ECHR[180] Likewise the overturning of a

---

[173] *De Wilde, Ooms and Versyp v Belgium* (1971) 1 EHRR 373, para 76 ('… in order to constitute such a 'court' an authority must provide the fundamental guarantees of procedure applied in matters of deprivation of liberty. If the procedure of the competent authority does not provide them, the State could not be dispensed from making available to the person concerned a second authority which does provide all the guarantees of judicial procedure'). See also *X v United Kingdom* (1981) 4 EHRR 188 and *Weeks v United Kingdom* (1987) 10 EHRR 293.

[174] *Weeks v United Kingdom* (1987) 10 EHRR 293, para 61 ('The 'court' referred to in Article 5, para 4 does not necessarily have to be a court of law of the classic kind integrated within the standard judicial machinery of the country. The term 'court' serves to denote 'bodies which exhibit not only common fundamental features, of which the most important is independence of the executive and of the parties to the case …, but also the guarantees' – 'appropriate to the kind of deprivation of liberty in question' – 'of a judicial procedure', the forms of which may vary from one domain to. In addition, as the text of Article 5, para 4 makes clear, the body in question must not have merely advisory functions but must have the competence to 'decide' the 'lawfulness' of the detention and to order release if the detention is unlawful. There is thus nothing to preclude a specialised body such as the Parole Board being considered as a 'court' within the meaning of Article 5, para provided it fulfils the foregoing conditions').

[175] Note however Art 1 of the Fourth Protocol to the ECHR which provides that 'No one shall be deprived of his liberty merely on the ground of inability to fulfil a contractual obligation'. The United Kingdom is not a party to Art 1 of the Fourth Protocol.

[176] See **16.108 et seq** below.

[177] *Steel v United Kingdom* (1998) 28 EHRR 603 and *Hashman and Harrap v United Kingdom* (1999) 30 EHRR 241.

[178] *Guzzardi v Italy* (1980) 3 EHRR 333, para 101. See also *Johansen v Norway* 44 DR 155 (1985); *Ciulla v Italy* (1989) 13 EHRR 346, para 36; *McVeigh, O'Neill and Evans v United Kingdom* (1981) 5 EHRR 71 and *Vasileva v Denmark* (2005) 40 EHRR 27.

[179] (1980) 3 EHRR 333, para 101.

[180] *Douiyed v Netherlands* (2000) 30 EHRR 790, paras 44–45.

conviction on appeal will not render the sentence of imprisonment unlawful under Art 5(1) of the Convention.[181] However, where the court has no power to confer a sentence such a sentence will be unlawful even after the event.[182]

(iii)   ECHR, Art 5(1)(c) – Arrest on Reasonable Suspicion

14.79   Article 5(1)(c) of the ECHR provides as follows in respect of lawful detention following arrest on the basis of a reasonable suspicion:

> '1. Everyone has the right to liberty and security of person. No one shall be deprived of his liberty save in the following cases and in accordance with a procedure prescribed by law:
>
> c)   the lawful arrest or detention of a person effected for the purpose of bringing him before the competent legal authority on reasonable suspicion of having committed an offence or when it is reasonably considered necessary to prevent his committing an offence or fleeing after having done so;'

14.80   Article 5(1)(c) must be read in conjunction with Art 5(3) of the ECHR which provides that:

> 'Everyone arrested or detained in accordance with the provisions of paragraph 1.c of this article shall be brought promptly before a judge or other officer authorised by law to exercise judicial power and shall be entitled to trial within a reasonable time or to release pending trial. Release may be conditioned by guarantees to appear for trial.'

14.81   Article 5(1)(c) does not create a general power of detention.[183] The European Court of Human Rights has made clear that Art 5(1)(c) permits deprivation of liberty on the basis of reasonable suspicion only in connection with criminal proceedings[184] and only for the purpose of bringing a person before the competent legal authority.[185] A criminal offence will be one that is 'well in keeping with the idea of an offence'.[186] The term 'competent legal authority' was considered in *Schiesser v Switzerland*[187] where the court held that:

> '... the Government and the Commission note that throughout Article 5 use is made of expressions of two kinds, one precise – 'court' (para. 1 (a) and (b), para 4) and 'judge' (para. 3) – and the other rather vague – 'competent legal authority' (para. 1 (c)) and 'officer authorised by law to exercise judicial power' (para. 3). In their view, it is reasonable to deduce from this that the first kind of expression contemplates stricter requirements than the second kind. The Court shares this opinion but wishes to emphasise the limits of the distinction which it establishes. Since paragraph 1 (c) forms a whole with paragraph 3, 'competent legal authority' is a synonym, of abbreviated form, for 'judge or other officer authorised by law to

---

[181]   *Krzycki v Germany* 13 DR 57 (1978) at 61 and *Benham v United Kingdom* (1996) 22 EHRR 293, para 42 ('A period of detention will in principle be lawful if it is carried out pursuant to a court order. A subsequent finding that the court erred under domestic law in making the order will not necessarily retrospectively affect the validity of the intervening period of detention. For this reason, the Strasbourg organs have consistently refused to uphold applications from persons convicted of criminal offences who complain that their convictions or sentences were found by the appellate courts to have been based on errors of fact or law').

[182]   *Benham v United Kingdom* (1996) 22 EHRR 293, paras 42–46.

[183]   *Lawless v Ireland (No 3)* (1961) 1 EHRR 15, para 14.

[184]   *Ciulla v Italy* (1989) 13 EHRR 346, para 38; *De Jong, Baljet and Van Den Brink v Netherlands* (1984) 8 EHRR 20 and *Guzzardi v Italy* (1980) 3 EHRR 333, para 102.

[185]   *Jėčius v Lithuania* (2002) 35 EHRR 400, paras 50–51.

[186]   *Ireland v United Kingdom* (1978) 2 EHRR 25, para 196; *Brogan v United Kingdom* (1988) 11 EHRR 117, para 51 and *Steel v United Kingdom* (1998) 28 EHRR 603.

[187]   (1979) 2 EHRR 417, para 29.

exercise judicial power'... Before a body can properly be regarded as a 'court', it must, inter alia, be independent of the executive and of the parties, but this also holds good for the 'officer' mentioned in paragraph 3: while the 'judicial power' he is to exercise, unlike the duties set out in paragraph 4, may not take the form of adjudicating on legal disputes ('un caractère juridictionnel'), nonetheless judicial power is likewise inconceivable if the person empowered does not enjoy independence ... To sum up, the 'officer' is not identical with the 'judge' but must nevertheless have some of the latter's attributes, that is to say he must satisfy certain conditions each of which constitutes a guarantee for the person arrested. The first of such conditions is independence of the executive and of the parties. This does not mean that the 'officer' may not be to some extent subordinate to other judges or officers provided that they themselves enjoy similar independence. In addition, under Article 5 para 3, there is both a procedural and a substantive requirement. The procedural requirement places the 'officer' under the obligation of hearing himself the individual brought before him; the substantive requirement imposes on him the obligations of reviewing the circumstances militating for or against detention, of deciding, by reference to legal criteria, whether there are reasons to justify detention and of ordering release if there are no such.'

14.82 The 'reasonableness' of the suspicion on which an arrest must be based forms an essential part of the safeguard against arbitrary arrest and detention. Having a 'reasonable suspicion' presupposes the existence of facts or information which would satisfy an objective observer that the person concerned may have committed the offence.[188] What may be regarded as 'reasonable' will depend upon all the circumstances, including the nature of the suspected crime.[189] It is not however necessary to establish the offence has been committed nor that the person arrested has committed it before a deprivation of liberty may take place by means of an arrest on the basis of a reasonable suspicion.[190]

(iv)   ECHR, Art 5(1)(d) – Deprivation of the Liberty of Children

14.83 Article 5(1)(d) of the ECHR provides as follows in respect of the lawful deprivation of the liberty of children for the purposes of educational supervision:

> '1. Everyone has the right to liberty and security of person. No one shall be deprived of his liberty save in the following cases and in accordance with a procedure prescribed by law:
>
> d)   the detention of a minor by lawful order for the purpose of educational supervision or his lawful detention for the purpose of bringing him before the competent legal authority;'

14.84 Article 5(1)(d) provides a ground in respect of which only children can be detained.[191] Deprivation of liberty for the purposes of educational supervision is not recognised in the CRC or any other international human rights instrument. Whilst Art 5(1)(d) provides a specific example of the detention of children only, it is not meant to denote that educational supervision is the only purpose for which a child may be

---

[188]   *Fox, Campbell and Hartley v United Kingdom* (1990) 13 EHRR 157, para 32.

[189]   *Fox, Campbell and Hartley v United Kingdom* (1990) 13 EHRR 157, para 32 where the European Court of Human Rights held that terrorist crime falls into a special category.

[190]   *X v Austria* (1989) 11 EHRR 112; *Murray v United Kingdom* (1994) 19 EHRR 193, para 55 ('The object of questioning during detention under sub-paragraph (c) of Article 5, para 1 is to further the criminal investigation by way of confirming or dispelling the concrete suspicion grounding the arrest. Thus, facts which raise a suspicion need not be of the same level as those necessary to justify a conviction or even the bringing of a charge, which comes at the next stage of the process of criminal investigation').

[191]   Van Bueren, G *Child Rights in Europe* (2007) Council of Europe Publishing, p 95.

detained.[192] An order for educational supervision may be made by an administrative body provided sufficient safeguards pursuant to Art 5(4) of the ECHR are in place.

ECHR, Art 5(1)(d) – 'Educational Supervision'

14.85 The term 'educational supervision' is not to be equated rigidly with notions of classroom teaching.[193] In the context of a young person in local authority care it has been held that 'educational supervision' must embrace many aspects of the exercise by the local authority of parental rights for the benefit and protection of the person concerned. In *Koniarska v United Kingdom*[194] the European Court considered the domestic legislation concerning secure accommodation for children pursuant to s 25 of the Children Act 1989, which provision makes no mention of accommodation for the purposes of educational supervision. The European Court of Human Rights held that the child's complaint that she had been deprived of her liberty for no reason permitted by Art 5(1) of the ECHR was inadmissible as educational supervision for the purposes of Art 5(1)(d) must embrace many aspects of the exercise of parental rights for the benefit and protection of the person concerned. Van Bueren argues persuasively that in appearing to extend the ambit of Art 5(1)(d) to cover the deprivation of liberty for the purposes of local authority care *Koniarska v United Kingdom* stretches the concept 'educational supervision' beyond its natural meaning.[195]

ECHR, Art 5(1)(d) – Bringing before a Competent Legal Authority

14.86 Article 5(1)(d) also permits the detention of a minor for the purposes of bringing him or her before a competent legal authority.[196]

(v)   ECHR, Art 5(1)(e) – Medical and Social Reasons

14.87 Article 5(1)(e) of the ECHR provides as follows in respect of the deprivation of liberty for medical and social reasons:

> '1. Everyone has the right to liberty and security of person. No one shall be deprived of his liberty save in the following cases and in accordance with a procedure prescribed by law:
>
> e)   the lawful detention of persons for the prevention of the spreading of infectious diseases, of persons of unsound mind, alcoholics or drug addicts or vagrants;

14.88 In *Enhorn v Sweden*[197] the European Court of Human Rights articulated the justification for the provisions in Art 5(1)(e) of the ECHR as follows:

> '... Article 5(1)(e) of the Convention refers to several categories of individuals, namely persons spreading infectious diseases, persons of unsound mind, alcoholics, drug addicts and vagrants. There is a link between all those persons in that they may be deprived of their liberty either in order to be given medical treatment or because of considerations dictated by social policy, or on both medical and social grounds. It is therefore legitimate to conclude from this context that a predominant reason why the Convention allows the persons

---

[192]   *Mubilanzila Mayeka and Kaniki Mitunga v Belgium* (2008) 46 EHRR 449.
[193]   *DG v Ireland* (2002) 35 EHRR 1153, para 80 and *Re K (A Child)* [2001] Fam 377.
[194]   (2000) Application No 33670/96 (unreported). Contrast the outcome in the case of *Bouamar v Belgium* (1988) 11 EHRR 1.
[195]   Van Bueren, G *Child Rights in Europe* (2007) Council of Europe Publishing, p 99. See **14.122** below for the further discussion of this issue within the context of domestic law.
[196]   See *X v Switzerland* 18 DR 238 (1979).
[197]   (2005) 41 EHRR 633, para 43.

mentioned in paragraph 1 (e) of Article 5 to be deprived of their liberty is not only that they are a danger to public safety but also that their own interests may necessitate their detention.'

ECHR, Art 5(1)(e) – Infectious Diseases

14.89 The test for depriving persons of their liberty for the purpose of the prevention of the spreading of infectious diseases pursuant to Art 5(1)(e) of the ECHR is whether the spreading of the infectious disease is dangerous to public health or safety, and whether detention of the person infected is the last available measure in order to prevent the spreading of the disease, because less severe measures have been considered and found to be insufficient to safeguard the public interest. When these criteria are no longer fulfilled, the basis for the deprivation of liberty ceases to exist.[198]

ECHR, Art 5(1)(e) – Persons of Unsound Mind

14.90 In permitting the deprivation of liberty of persons of unsound mind Art 5(1)(e) of the ECHR does not permit the restriction of a person's liberty simply on the basis that their conduct differs from the norms which prevail within a particular society.[199] The criteria for depriving persons of unsound mind of their liberty are threefold, namely (i) the behaviour of the person is of a nature to justify an 'emergency' confinement,[200] (ii) other, less severe measures, have been considered and found to be insufficient to safeguard the individual or public interest which might require that the person concerned be detained such that the deprivation of liberty is necessary in the circumstances[201] and (iii) he has he or she has been reliably shown to be of 'unsound mind' by reason a mental disorder of a kind or degree warranting compulsory confinement established on the basis of objective medical expertise.[202] The validity of continued confinement depends upon these criteria continuing to be met.[203] There is a margin of appreciation allowed in the State's initial assessment of the person in question[204] and in respect of ongoing assessments.[205]

ECHR, Art 5(1)(e) – Vagrants[206] and Alcoholics

14.91 In *Guzzardi v Italy*[207] the European Court of Human Rights held as follows in relation to the justification for permitting the lawful deprivation of liberty of those persons considered to be vagrants:

'The reason why the Convention allows [persons of unsound mind, alcoholics or drug addicts or vagrants], all of whom are socially maladjusted, to be deprived of their liberty is not only that they have to be considered as occasionally dangerous for public safety but also that their own interests may necessitate their detention. One cannot therefore deduce from

---

[198] *Enhorn v Sweden* (2005) 41 EHRR 633, para 44.
[199] *Winterwerp v Netherlands* (1979) 2 EHRR 387, para 37.
[200] *Winterwerp v Netherlands* (1979) 2 EHRR 387, para 42 and see *HL v United Kingdom* (2005) 40 EHRR 761.
[201] *Varbanov v Bulgaria* (2000) Application No 31365/96, para 46.
[202] *Winterwerp v Netherlands* (1979) 2 EHRR 387, para 39 and see *Johnson v United Kingdom* (1997) 27 EHRR 296.
[203] *Winterwerp v Netherlands* (1979) 2 EHRR 387, para 39.
[204] *Winterwerp v Netherlands* (1979) 2 EHRR 387, para 40.
[205] *Johnson v United Kingdom* (1999) 27 EHRR 296.
[206] The term 'vagrant' has been defined as meaning 'persons who have no fixed abode, no means of subsistence and no regular trade or profession' (see *De Wilde, Ooms and Versyp v Belgium* (1971) 1 EHRR 373, para 68).
[207] (1980) 3 EHRR 333, para 98.

the fact that Article 5 authorises the detention of vagrants that the same or even stronger reasons apply to anyone who may be regarded as still more dangerous.'[208]

(vi)   ECHR, Art 5(1(f) – Immigration, Deportation and Extradition

14.92   Article 5(1)(f) of the ECHR stipulates the following in relation to deprivation of liberty associated with immigration, deportation and extradition issues:

> '1. Everyone has the right to liberty and security of person. No one shall be deprived of his liberty save in the following cases and in accordance with a procedure prescribed by law:
>
> f)   the lawful arrest or detention of a person to prevent his effecting an unauthorised entry into the country or of a person against whom action is being taken with a view to deportation or extradition.'

14.93   The word 'lawful' in Art 5(1)(f) of the ECHR means both lawful under domestic law and not arbitrary.[209] The deprivation of liberty need not be necessary to prevent the person from committing an offence or absconding in order to be lawful under Art 5(1)(f).[210] The deprivation of liberty, insofar as it is justified under Art 5(1)(f) of the ECHR will only remain justified whilst the deportation or extradition proceedings subsist, there being a requirement to prosecute those proceedings with due diligence.[211] However, care must be taken not to take decisions hastily without due regard to all the relevant issues and evidence.[212] Art 5(1)(f) of the ECHR must be read in the light of the international instruments discouraging the use of detention in respect of refugees and asylum seekers.[213] In particular, Art 5(1)(f) should be applied having regard to the principle that uunaccompanied or separated children, including those who arrive irregularly in a country, should not be deprived of their liberty solely for having breached any law governing access to and stay within the territory.[214]

ECHR, Art 5(2) – Ambit

14.94   ECHR, Art 5(2) provides as follows in respect of the right to be informed of the ground for detention:

> '2. Everyone who is arrested shall be informed promptly, in a language which he understands, of the reasons for his arrest and of any charge against him.'

14.95   The information concerning the reasons for arrest and any charge can be given orally or in writing provided they are in a language that the detained person will

---

[208]   See also *Witold Litwa v Poland* (2001) 33 EHRR 1267, para 60.

[209]   *De Jong, Baljet and Van Den Brink v Netherlands* (1984) 8 EHRR 20 and *Bozano v France* (1986) 9 EHRR 297, para 54 ('The main issue to be determined is whether the disputed detention was 'lawful', including whether it was in accordance with 'a procedure prescribed by law'. The Convention here refers essentially to national law and establishes the need to apply its rules, but it also requires that any measure depriving the individual of his liberty must be compatible with the purpose of Article 5, namely to protect the individual from arbitrariness. What is at stake here is not only the 'right to liberty' but also the 'right to security of person'').

[210]   *Bozano v France* (1986) 9 EHRR 297.

[211]   *Lynas v Switzerland* 6 DR 141 (1976) and *Chahal v United Kingdom* (1997) 23 EHRR 413, paras 113–117 ('any deprivation of liberty under Article 5, para 1(f) will be justified only for as long as deportation proceedings are in progress. If such proceedings are not prosecuted with due diligence, the detention will cease to be permissible under Article 5, para 1(f)').

[212]   *Chahal v United Kingdom* (1997) 23 EHRR 413, para 117.

[213]   See **14.19** above.

[214]   UN Guidelines for the Alternative Care of Children A/RES/64/142, para 43.

understand.[215] In *Van der Leer v Netherlands*[216] the European Court of Human Rights observed as follows in respect of the ambit of Art 5(2) of the ECHR:

> 'The Court is not unmindful of the criminal-law connotation of the words used in Article 5(2). However, it agrees with the Commission that they should be interpreted 'autonomously', in particular in accordance with the aim and purpose of Article 5, which are to protect everyone from arbitrary deprivations of liberty. Thus the 'arrest' referred to in paragraph 2 of Article 5 extends beyond the realm of criminal-law measures. Similarly, in using the words 'any charge' ('toute accusation') in this provision, the intention of the drafters was not to lay down a condition for its applicability, but to indicate an eventuality of which it takes account. The close link between paragraphs 2 and 4 of Article 5 supports this interpretation. Any person who is entitled to take proceedings to have the lawfulness of his detention decided speedily cannot make effective use of that right unless he is promptly and adequately informed of the reasons why he has been deprived of his liberty. Paragraph 4 does not make any distinction as between persons deprived of their liberty on the basis of whether they have been arrested or detained. There are therefore no grounds for excluding the latter from the scope of paragraph 2.'

14.96 The language used to indicate the reason for arrest and the nature of any charge will, depending on their age, development and understanding, be particularly important in relation to providing information to children. For all persons the language used should be simple and non-technical. In *Fox, Campbell and Hartley v United Kingdom*[217] the European Court of Human Rights observed that:

> 'Paragraph 2 of Article 5 contains the elementary safeguard that any person arrested should know why he is being deprived of his liberty. This provision is an integral part of the scheme of protection afforded by Article 5: by virtue of paragraph 2 any person arrested must be told, in simple, non-technical language that he can understand, the essential legal and factual grounds for his arrest, so as to be able, if he sees fit, to apply to a court to challenge its lawfulness in accordance with paragraph 4. Whilst this information must be conveyed 'promptly' (in French: 'dans le plus court délai'), it need not be related in its entirety by the arresting officer at the very moment of the arrest. Whether the content and promptness of the information conveyed were sufficient is to be assessed in each case according to its special features.'[218]

ECHR, Art 5(3) – Ambit

14.97 Article 5(3) of the ECHR seeks to ensure that once arrested and detained on the basis of a reasonable suspicion under Art 5(1)(c) that the person deprived of their liberty is dealt with expeditiously by providing that:

> '3. Everyone arrested or detained in accordance with the provisions of paragraph 1.c of this article shall be brought promptly before a judge or other officer authorised by law to exercise judicial power and shall be entitled to trial within a reasonable time or to release pending trial. Release may be conditioned by guarantees to appear for trial.'

---

[215] *Lamy v Belgium* (1989) 11 EHRR 529, para 31. There is no obligation under Art 5(2) of the ECHR to make the file concerning the arrest and charge available to the detained person (but see also *Lamy v Belgium* (1989) 11 EHRR 529, para 29). The requirement to inform a person promptly and in language they can understand will also apply to persons detained under the mental health legislation (see *Van der Leer v Netherlands* (1990) 12 EHRR 567, para 29).

[216] (1990) 12 EHRR 567, paras 27–29.

[217] (1990) 13 EHRR 157, para 40.

[218] See also *Ireland v United Kingdom* (1978) 2 EHRR 25, para 198. See further Art 6(3)(a) of the ECHR which is applicable following charge ('Everyone charged with a criminal offence has the following minimum rights: (a) to be informed promptly, in a language which he understands and in detail, of the nature and cause of the accusation against him') dealt with at **16.115** below.

(i)   ECHR, Art 5(3) – Objective

14.98   Article 5(3) of the ECHR applies only to criminal offences.[219] In *TW v Malta*[220] the European Court of Human Rights described the object of Art 5(3) as follows:

> 'As the Court has pointed out on many occasions, Article 5(3) of the Convention provides persons arrested or detained on suspicion of having committed a criminal offence with a guarantee against any arbitrary or unjustified deprivation of liberty. It is essentially the object of Article 5(3), which forms a whole with paragraph 1 (c), to require provisional release once detention ceases to be reasonable. The fact that an arrested person had access to a judicial authority is not sufficient to constitute compliance with the opening part of Article 5(3). This provision enjoins the judicial officer before whom the arrested person appears to review the circumstances militating for or against detention, to decide by reference to legal criteria whether there are reasons to justify detention, and to order release if there are no such reasons. In other words, Article 5(3) requires the judicial officer to consider the merits of the detention.'

(ii)   ECHR, Art 5(3) – 'Promptly'

14.99   Pursuant to Art 5(3) everyone arrested or detained in accordance with the Art 5(1)(c) must be brought promptly before a judge or other officer authorised by law. The French text of Art 5(3) the ECHR uses the word 'aussitôt' which denotes more urgency than the English word 'promptly'.[221] There is limited flexibility in the concept of 'promptness' and whilst promptness must be assessed according to the features of each case[222] those features must never be permitted to impair the essence of the right guaranteed by Art 5(3) of the ECHR.[223] In *TW v Malta*[224] the court observed that:

> 'To be in accordance with Article 5(3), judicial control must be prompt. Promptness has to be assessed in each case according to its special features. However, the scope of flexibility in interpreting and applying the notion of promptness is very limited. In addition to being prompt, the judicial control of the detention must be automatic. It cannot be made to depend on a previous application by the detained person. Such a requirement would not only change the nature of the safeguard provided for under Article 5(3), a safeguard distinct from that in Article 5(4), which guarantees the right to institute proceedings to have the lawfulness of detention reviewed by a court. It might even defeat the purpose of the safeguard under Article 5(3) which is to protect the individual from arbitrary detention by ensuring that the act of deprivation of liberty is subject to independent judicial scrutiny. Prompt judicial review of detention is also an important safeguard against ill-treatment of the individual

---

[219]   *De Wilde, Ooms and Versyp v Belgium* (1971) 1 EHRR 373, para 71 (Paragraph (1)(c) of Article 5, to which [Art 5(3)] refers, is solely concerned with 'the lawful arrest or detention of a person effected for the purpose of bringing him before the competent legal authority on reasonable suspicion of having committed an offence or when it is reasonably considered necessary to prevent his committing an offence or fleeing after having done so').

[220]   (2000) 29 EHRR 185, para 41.

[221]   *Brogan v United Kingdom* (1988) 11 EHRR 117, paras 58 and 59 ('The obligation expressed in English by the word 'promptly' and in French by the word 'aussitôt' is clearly distinguishable from the less strict requirement in the second part of paragraph 3 ('reasonable time'/'délai raisonnable') and even from that in paragraph 4 of Article 5 ('speedily'/'à bref délai'). The term 'promptly' also occurs in the English text of paragraph 2, where the French text uses the words 'dans le plus court délai'. As indicated in the *Ireland v the United Kingdom* judgment, 'promptly' in paragraph 3 may be understood as having a broader significance than 'aussitôt', which literally means immediately. Thus confronted with versions of a law-making treaty which are equally authentic but not exactly the same, the Court must interpret them in a way that reconciles them as far as possible and is most appropriate in order to realise the aim and achieve the object of the treaty').

[222]   *De Jong, Baljet and Van Den Brink v Netherlands* (1984) 8 EHRR 20, para 52.

[223]   *Koster v Netherlands* (1991) 14 EHRR 396, para 24.

[224]   (2000) 29 EHRR 185, para 41.

taken into. Furthermore, arrested persons who have been subjected to such treatment might be incapable of lodging an application asking the judge to review their detention. The same could hold true for other vulnerable categories of arrested persons, such as the mentally weak or those who do not speak the language of the judicial officer.'

(iii) ECHR, Art 5(3) – 'Judge or Other Officer Authorised by Law

14.100 The term 'judge or other officer authorised by law' in Art 5(3) of the ECHR has the same meaning as competent legal authority under Art 5(1)(c). As noted above, in *Schiesser v Switzerland*[225] the European Court of Human Rights held as follows:

'... the Government and the Commission note that throughout Article 5 use is made of expressions of two kinds, one precise – "court" (para. 1 (a) and (b), para 4) and 'judge' (para. 3) – and the other rather vague – 'competent legal authority' (para. 1 (c)) and 'officer authorised by law to exercise judicial power' (para. 3). In their view, it is reasonable to deduce from this that the first kind of expression contemplates stricter requirements than the second kind. The Court shares this opinion but wishes to emphasise the limits of the distinction which it establishes. Since paragraph 1 (c) forms a whole with paragraph 3, "competent legal authority" is a synonym, of abbreviated form, for "judge or other officer authorised by law to exercise judicial power" ... Before a body can properly be regarded as a "court", it must, inter alia, be independent of the executive and of the parties, but this also holds good for the "officer" mentioned in paragraph 3[226] while the 'judicial power' he is to exercise, unlike the duties set out in paragraph 4, may not take the form of adjudicating on legal disputes ("un caractère juridictionnel"), nonetheless judicial power is likewise inconceivable if the person empowered does not enjoy independence ... To sum up, the "officer" is not identical with the "judge" but must nevertheless have some of the latter's attributes, that is to say he must satisfy certain conditions each of which constitutes a guarantee for the person arrested. The first of such conditions is independence of the executive and of the parties. This does not mean that the "officer" may not be to some extent subordinate to other judges or officers provided that they themselves enjoy similar independence. In addition, under Article 5 para 3, there is both a procedural and a substantive requirement. The procedural requirement places the 'officer' under the obligation of hearing himself the individual brought before him; the substantive requirement imposes on him the obligations of reviewing the circumstances militating for or against detention, of deciding, by reference to legal criteria, whether there are reasons to justify detention and of ordering release if there are no such.'

The language of Art 5(3), read in the light of its object and purpose, makes evident that its inherent procedural requirement, namely the 'judge' or judicial 'officer' must actually hear the detained person before taking the appropriate decision.[227]

---

[225] (1979) 2 EHRR 417, para 29.

[226] See *Assenov v Bulgaria* (1998) 28 EHRR 652, para 146 ('The Court reiterates that judicial control of interferences by the executive with the individual's right to liberty is an essential feature of the guarantee embodied in Article 5(3). Before an 'officer' can be said to exercise 'judicial power' within the meaning of this provision, he or she must satisfy certain conditions providing a guarantee to the person detained against any arbitrary or unjustified deprivation of liberty. Thus, the 'officer' must be independent of the executive and the parties. In this respect, objective appearances at the time of the decision on detention are material: if it appears at that time that the 'officer' may later intervene in subsequent criminal proceedings on behalf of the prosecuting authority, his independence and impartiality may be open to doubt').

[227] *De Jong, Baljet and Van Den Brink v Netherlands* (1984) 8 EHRR 20, para 51; *Assenov v Bulgaria* (1998) 28 EHRR 652, para 146 ('The 'officer' must hear the individual brought before him in person and review, by reference to legal criteria, whether or not the detention is justified. If it is not so justified, the 'officer' must have the power to make a binding order for the detainee's release') and *TW v Malta* (2000) 29 EHRR 185, para 44. See also *McGoff v Sweden* 31 DR 72 (1982).

(iv)   ECHR, Art 5(3) – 'Trial within a Reasonable Time or to Release pending Trial'

14.101   The use of the word 'or' in the phrase 'trial within a reasonable time or to release pending trial' does not mean that a prompt trial is an alternative to release pending trial.[228] The criteria for continued detention are strict ones. In *Kudla v Poland*[229] the European Court of Human Rights observed that:

> 'The Court reiterates that the question of whether or not a period of detention is reasonable cannot be assessed in the abstract. Whether it is reasonable for an accused to remain in detention must be assessed in each case according to its special features. Continued detention can be justified in a given case only if there are specific indications of a genuine requirement of public interest which, notwithstanding the presumption of innocence, outweighs the rule of respect for individual liberty laid down in Article 5 of the Convention. It falls in the first place to the national judicial authorities to ensure that, in a given case, the pre-trial detention of an accused person does not exceed a reasonable time. To this end they must, paying due regard to the principle of the presumption of innocence, examine all the facts arguing for or against the existence of the above-mentioned requirement of public interest justifying a departure from the rule in Article 5 and must set them out in their decisions on the applications for release. It is essentially on the basis of the reasons given in these decisions and of the well-documented facts stated by the applicant in his appeals that the Court is called upon to decide whether or not there has been a violation of Article 5(3). The persistence of reasonable suspicion that the person arrested has committed an offence is a condition *sine qua non* for the lawfulness of the continued detention, but after a certain lapse of time it no longer suffices. The Court must then establish whether the other grounds given by the judicial authorities continued to justify the deprivation of liberty. Where such grounds were 'relevant' and 'sufficient', the Court must also be satisfied that the national authorities displayed 'special diligence' in the conduct of the proceedings.'

14.102   The need for trial within a reasonable time is particularly acute in relation to children. In *Assenov v Bulgaria*[230] the European Court of Human Rights held, in relation to a fourteen year old boy who had been held in pre-trial detention for approximately 2 years, that in respect of children it is more than usually important for the authorities to display special diligence in ensuring that the accused is brought to trial within a reasonable time.[231] The burden of demonstrating that the criteria for continued pre-trial detention are satisfied remains on the authorities.[232]

---

228   *Nuemeister v Austria* (1968) 1 EHRR 91.
229   (2002) 35 EHRR 11, paras 110–111. See also *Grisez v Belgium* (2003) 36 EHRR 854, para 49.
230   (1998) 28 EHRR 652.
231   (1998) 28 EHRR 652, para 147. The Court found that pre-trial detention lasting approximately 2 years had denied the applicant a 'trial within a reasonable time' in violation of Art 5(3) of the ECHR.
232   *Letellier v France* (1991) 14 EHRR 83, para 35 ('It falls in the first place to the national judicial authorities to ensure that, in a given case, the pre-trial detention of an accused person does not exceed a reasonable time. To this end they must examine all the facts arguing for or against the existence of a genuine requirement of public interest justifying, with due regard to the principle of the presumption of innocence, a departure from the rule of respect for individual liberty and set them out in their decisions on the applications for release'); *Ilijkov v Bulgaria* (2001) Application 33977/96 (unreported), paras 84–85 ('Shifting the burden of proof to the detained person in such matters is tantamount to overturning the rule of Article 5 of the Convention, a provision which makes detention an exceptional departure from the right to liberty and one that is only permissible in exhaustively enumerated and strictly defined cases') and *R (O) v Harrow Crown Court and another* [2006] UKHL 42, [2007] 1 AC 249, paras 27–28 ('The two key requirements imposed by art 5(3) are, first, that the prosecution must bear the overall burden of justifying a remand in custody—it must advance good and sufficient public interest reasons outweighing the presumption of innocence and the general presumption in favour of liberty; and, secondly, that the judge must be entitled to take account of all relevant considerations pointing for and against the grant of bail so as to exercise effective and meaningful judicial control over pre-trial detention').

(v)   ECHR, Art 5(3) – 'Release may be conditioned by Guarantees to Appear for Trial'

14.103   Where an application for bail pending trial is made that application may be refused only on relatively narrow grounds. Namely by reason of: (i) a risk that the accused will fail to appear for trial;[233] (ii) a risk that there will be interference with the course of justice;[234] (iii) the need to prevent further offences;[235] and (iv) the need to preserve of public order.[236]

ECHR, Art 5(4) – Ambit

14.104   Article 5(4) of the ECHR states as follows in respect of the right to challenge a deprivation of liberty by reason of arrest or detention:

> '4. Everyone who is deprived of his liberty by arrest or detention shall be entitled to take proceedings by which the lawfulness of his detention shall be decided speedily by a court and his release ordered if the detention is not lawful.'

14.105   Article 5(4) guarantees the right to a claim of *habeas corpus*[237] in order to challenge the legality of executive detention.[238] The claim of *habeas corpus* is the fundamental instrument for safeguarding individual freedom against arbitrary or unlawful state action.[239] The right to make an application of the type contemplated by Art 5(4) of the ECHR applies to all grounds of detention.[240] The burden of proving the lawfulness of the detention rests with the State.[241]

14.106   Art 5(4) expressly concerns deprivations of liberty by reason of arrest or detention rather than detention following conviction. However, whilst the general rule is

---

[233]   *Nuemeister v Austria* (1968) 1 EHRR 91.

[234]   *Wemhoff v Germany* (1968) 1 EHRR 55.

[235]   *Clooth v Belgium* (1991) 14 EHRR 717, para 40 ('The Court considers that the seriousness of a charge may lead the judicial authorities to place and leave a suspect in detention on remand in order to prevent any attempts to commit further offences. It is however necessary, among other conditions, that the danger be a plausible one and the measure appropriate, in the light of the circumstances of the case and in particular the past history and the personality of the person concerned').

[236]   *Letellier v France* (1991) 14 EHRR 83, para 51 ('The Court accepts that, by reason of their particular gravity and public reaction to them, certain offences may give rise to a social disturbance capable of justifying pre-trial detention, at least for a time. In exceptional circumstances this factor may therefore be taken into account for the purposes of the Convention ... However, this ground can be regarded as relevant and sufficient only provided that it is based on facts capable of showing that the accused's release would actually disturb public order. In addition detention will continue to be legitimate only if public order remains actually threatened; its continuation cannot be used to anticipate a custodial sentence').

[237]   Lat. 'that you have the body'. In *Bushell's Case* (1670) Vaughan 135, 136 Chief Justice Vaughan stated 'The writ of habeas corpus is now the most usual remedy by which a man is restored again to his liberty, if he have been against law deprived of it.'

[238]   *Musial v Poland* (1999) 31 EHRR 720, para 43 ('... in guaranteeing to persons arrested or detained a right to institute proceedings to challenge the lawfulness of their detention, also proclaims their right, following the institution of such proceedings, to a speedy judicial decision concerning the lawfulness of detention and ordering its termination if it proves unlawful') and *Brogan v United Kingdom* (1988) 1 EHRR 117, para 65 ('arrested or detained persons are entitled to a review bearing upon the procedural and substantive conditions which are essential for the 'lawfulness', in the sense of the Convention, of their deprivation of liberty').

[239]   *Harris v Nelson* 394 U.S. 286, 290–91 (1969) noting that the writ of habeas corpus must be 'administered with the initiative and flexibility essential to insure that miscarriages of justice within its reach are surfaced and corrected.' See also *R v Bournewood Community and Mental Health NHS Trust ex p L (Secretary of State for Health and others intervening)* [1998] 2 FCR 501 per Lord Nolan: 'the individuals right to liberty, and the remedy of habeas corpus, lie at the heart of our law.'

[240]   *De Wilde, Ooms and Versyp v Belgium* (1971) 1 EHRR 373, para 73.

[241]   *Zamir v United Kingdom* 40 DR 42 (1983); *E v Norway* (1990) 17 EHRR 30, para 50.

that detention in accordance with a determinate sentence imposed by a court is justified under Art 5(1)(a) without the need for further reviews of detention under Art 5(4),[242] preventative or indeterminate sentences will be subject to the provisions of Art 5(4) as the very nature of the deprivation of liberty under such sentences would appear to require a review of lawfulness to be available at regular intervals.[243] In *R (Giles) v Parole Board*[244] Lord Hope held that:

> 'Where the prisoner has been lawfully detained within the meaning of art 5(1)(a) following the imposition of a determinate sentence after his conviction by a competent court, the review which art 5(4) requires is incorporated in the original sentence passed by the sentencing court. Once the appeal process has been exhausted there is no right to have the lawfulness of the detention under that sentence reviewed by another court. The principle which underlies these propositions is that detention in accordance with a lawful sentence passed after conviction by a competent court cannot be described as arbitrary. The cases where the basic rule has been departed from are cases where decisions as to the length of the detention have passed from the court to the Executive and there is a risk that the factors which informed the original decision will change with the passage of time. In those cases the review which art 5(4) requires cannot be said to be incorporated in the original decision by the court. A further review in judicial proceedings is needed at reasonable intervals if the detention is not to be at risk of becoming arbitrary.'

ECHR, Art 5(4) – 'A Court'

14.107 The minimum requirements constituting 'a court' for the purposes of Art 5(4) are the same as for Art 5(1)(a), namely a body which gives to the individuals concerned guarantees appropriate to the kind of deprivation of liberty in question, namely it must be independent of both the executive and the parties and have the power to give a legally binding judgment concerning a persons release.[245] Within the process determining whether the deprivation of liberty is lawful there should be equality of arms.[246] The process by which the question of whether the deprivation of liberty is lawful should all incorporate special arrangements for vulnerable people and those who lack capacity.[247]

---

[242] Feldman, D *Civil Liberties and Human Rights in England and Wales* (2002) 2nd edn, Oxford, p 446.

[243] *Winterwerp v Netherlands* (1979) 2 EHRR 387, para 55 ('it would be contrary to the object and purpose of Article 5 (see paragraph 37 above) to interpret paragraph 4 thereof, read in its context, as making this category of confinement immune from subsequent review of lawfulness merely provided that the initial decision issued from a court. The very nature of the deprivation of liberty under consideration would appear to require a review of lawfulness to be available at reasonable intervals'). See also *Hussain v United Kingdom* (1996) 22 EHRR 1 and *T and V v United Kingdom* (2000) 30 EHRR 121.

[244] [2003] UKHL 42, [2004] 1 AC 1.

[245] *De Wilde, Ooms and Versyp v Belgium* (1971) 1 EHRR 373, para 76 ('... in order to constitute such a 'court' an authority must provide the fundamental guarantees of procedure applied in matters of deprivation of liberty. If the procedure of the competent authority does not provide them, the State could not be dispensed from making available to the person concerned a second authority which does provide all the guarantees of judicial procedure'). See also *Benjamin and Wilson v United Kingdom* (2003) 36 EHRR 1, para 34 ('the body in question must have not merely advisory functions but must have the competence to 'decide' the 'lawfulness' of the detention and to order release if the detention is unlawful') and *Megyeri v Germany* (1992) 15 EHRR 584, para 22 ('Article 5, para 4 requires that the procedure followed have a judicial character and give to the individual concerned guarantees appropriate to the kind of deprivation of liberty in question; in order to determine whether a proceeding provides adequate guarantees, regard must be had to the particular nature of the circumstances in which such proceeding takes place').

[246] *Toth v Austria* (1991) 14 EHRR 551, para 84. See also *Megyeri v Germany* (1992) 15 EHRR 584, para 22 and 27 ('The judicial proceedings referred to in Article 5, para 4 need not always be attended by the same guarantees as those required under Article 6, para 1 for civil or criminal litigation. None the less, it is essential that the person concerned should have access to a court and the opportunity to be heard either in person or, where necessary, through some form of representation').

[247] *Megyeri v Germany* (1992) 15 EHRR 584, paras 22 and 27.

ECHR, Art 5(4) – 'Decided Speedily'

14.108 Speedy determination for the purposes of Art 5(4) was considered in *E v Norway*[248] in which the court held that:

> '... the notion of 'promptly' (aussitôt) in the latter provision indicates greater urgency than that of 'speedily' (à bref délai) in Article 5(4). Even so, a period of approximately eight weeks from the filing of summons to judgment does appear, prima facie, difficult to reconcile with the notion of 'speedily'. However, in order to reach a firm conclusion, the special circumstances of the case have to be taken into account.'

The Child's Right to Liberty and Security of the Person under European Union Law

European Charter of Fundamental Rights Art 6

14.109 Article 6 of the European Charter of Fundamental Rights provides that 'Everyone has the right to liberty and security of person'. In accordance with Art 52(3) of the European Charter[249] the meaning and scope of the rights under Art 6 is the same as that under the corresponding Art 5 of the ECHR and its related protocols. As such, the exceptions that are permitted by Art 5(1) of the ECHR will be permitted in respect of the rights under Art 6 of the European Charter.

The Child's Right to Liberty and Security of the Person under other Regional Instruments

The American Convention on Human Rights

American Convention on Human Rights – Art 7

14.110 Article 7 of the American Convention on Human Rights provides as follows in respect of the right to personal liberty:

> '1. Every person has the right to personal liberty and security.

> 2. No one shall be deprived of his physical liberty except for the reasons and under the conditions established beforehand by the constitution of the State Party concerned or by a law established pursuant thereto.

> 3. No one shall be subject to arbitrary arrest[250] or imprisonment.

---

[248] (1990) 17 EHRR 30, para 64. See also *R (Spence) v Secretary of State for the Home Department* [2003] EWCA Civ 732, [2003] Prison LR 290.

[249] Article 52(3) of the Charter provides that 'Insofar as this Charter contains rights which correspond to rights guaranteed by the Convention for the Protection of Human Rights and Fundamental Freedoms, the meaning and scope of those rights shall be the same as those laid down by the said Convention. This provision shall not prevent Union law providing more extensive protection.'

[250] See *Jailton Neri Da Fonseca v Brazil* Case 11.634 Report No 33/04 (2004) concerning the death of a child arrested and murdered by military police in which it was held that 'An arrest is arbitrary and illegal when it does not occur in accordance with the causes and procedures established by law, when it is effected without observing the practices stipulated by law, and when it has been effected as a distortion of the authority to arrest, or in other words, when it is effected for purposes other than those stipulated and required by law. The Commission has also maintained that arrest for inappropriate purposes is, in and of itself, a punishment that constitutes a type of punishment without due process, or an extralegal punishment that violates the guarantee of a prior trial.'

4. Anyone who is detained shall be informed of the reasons for his detention and shall be promptly notified of the charge or charges against him.

5. Any person detained shall be brought promptly before a judge or other officer authorised by law to exercise judicial power and shall be entitled to trial within a reasonable time or to be released without prejudice to the continuation of the proceedings. His release may be subject to guarantees to assure his appearance for trial.

6. Anyone who is deprived of his liberty shall be entitled to recourse to a competent court, in order that the court may decide without delay on the lawfulness of his arrest or detention and order his release if the arrest or detention is unlawful. In States Parties whose laws provide that anyone who believes himself to be threatened with deprivation of his liberty is entitled to recourse to a competent court in order that it may decide on the lawfulness of such threat, this remedy may not be restricted or abolished. The interested party or another person in his behalf is entitled to seek these remedies.

7. No one shall be detained for debt. This principle shall not limit the orders of a competent judicial authority issued for non-fulfillment of duties of support.'

14.111   With respect to the right to liberty under Art 7 of the American Convention on Human Rights, the Inter-American Court of Human Rights indicated in *Bulacio v Argentina*[251] that in the case of children, detention must be exceptional and for the shortest possible time. Moreover, it held that in cases of the detention of children, the right to establish contact with next of kin takes on special importance to ensure that the child receives the necessary care. It also stressed the need for detention centers to have adequately trained staff to attend to and protect the children. The Inter-American Court of Human Rights has emphasised the state's position as guarantor in cases involving children and adolescents deprived of their liberty.[252] The detention of minors for noncriminal acts merely because they were in a situation of social abandonment, risk, orphanhood or vagrancy has been heavily deprecated by the Inter-American Commission on Human Rights.[253] Note that in respect of children detained in institutions, the Inter-American Court of Human Rights has stated that the children's substantive and procedural rights must be safeguarded and that:[254]

'Any action that affects them must be perfectly justified according to the law, it must be reasonable and relevant in substantive and formal terms, it must address the best interests of the child and abide by procedures and guarantees that at all times enable verification of its suitability and legitimacy.'

American Convention on Human Rights – Art 5

14.112   Article 5(1) of the American Convention on Human Rights stipulates that every person has the right to have his physical, mental and moral integrity respected. Article 5(2) requires that all persons deprived of their liberty shall be treated with respect for the inherent dignity of the human person. Within this context Art 5(4) of the Convention provides as follows in respect of children:

'Minors while subject to criminal proceedings shall be separated from adults and brought before specialised tribunals, as speedily as possible, so that they may be treated in accordance with their status as minors.'

---

[251]   I/A Court H R, *Case of Bulacio*. Judgment of September 18, 2003 Series C No 100, paras 126 ff.
[252]   I/A Court H R, *Case of the 'Juvenile Reeducation Institute'*. Judgment of September 2, 2004 Series C No 11.
[253]   See *Detained Minors v Honduras* Case No 11.491 IACHR, Report Nº 41/99 Case 11.491, para 109.
[254]   Advisory Opinion OC-17/2002, para 113.

14.113 In relation to the right to humane treatment under Art 5 of the American Convention on Human Rights the Inter American Court of Human Rights held in the case of *Bulacio v Argentina*[255] that in cases involving children deprived of their liberty it is particularly important that account be taken of children's special vulnerability, in accordance with the state's obligation to provide for a special guarantee of the rights of children. The Inter American Commission on Human Rights held in the case of *Detained Minors v Honduras*[256] that having regard to Art 19 of the American Convention on Human Rights:[257]

> 'In the view of the Commission, the duty of the state to keep minors in detention in separate establishments from those occupied by adults is based on Article 5(5), considered together with Article 19 of the Convention. It is obvious that the obligation emanating from Article 19, of according children special treatment, cannot be interpreted exclusively as the requirement to create a juvenile court and judges, but also, to ensure the 'protection required by his condition as a minor,' requires that the minor be held separately from adults, namely in specialised institutions.'

The Commission further held in the context of children that the State has a positive duty to protect the right to humane treatment, stating that:

> 'The obligation emanating from [the State's] position of guarantor implies that the agents of the state not only should refrain from carrying out acts that could be harmful to the life and physical safety of the detainee, but it should also endeavor by every means at its disposal to maintain the fundamental rights of the person in detention, and especially the right to life and humane treatment. The state has the specific obligation here to protect prisoners from attacks coming from third parties, including those from other inmates.'

The Ibero American Convention on the Rights of Youth

14.114 Article 16 of the Ibero-American Convention on the Rights of Youth provides as follows in respect of the right to liberty and security of the person:

> '1. The States Parties recognise youth, with the extension expressed in the International Covenant on Civil and Political Rights, the right to their liberty and its exercise, without being restricted or limited in the activities deriving from it and prohibiting any measure which may prejudice the liberty, integrity or physical or mental security of youth.
>
> 2. Consequent with the recognition and duty of protection of the right to liberty and security of youth, the States Parties guarantee that Youth shall not be arbitrarily arrested, detained, imprisoned or exiled.'

The African Charter on the Rights and Welfare on the Child

African Charter on the Rights and Welfare of the Child – Art 17

14.115 Article 17 of the African Charter on the Rights and Welfare of the Child provides as follows in respect of the right to liberty and security of the person:

---

[255] I/A Court H R, *Case of Bulacio*. Judgment of September 18, 2003 Series C No 100. See also Villagrán Morales et al v Guatemala (I/A Court H R, *The 'Street Children' Case (Villagrán Morales et al)*. Judgment of November 19, 1999 Series C No 63, para 194.

[256] Case No 11.491 IACHR, Report N° 41/99 Case 11.491, para 125.

[257] Article 19 provides that 'Every minor child has the right to the measures of protection required by his condition as a minor on the part of his family, society, and the state.'

'1. Every child accused or found guilty of having infringed penal law shall have the right to special treatment in a manner consistent with the child's sense of dignity and worth and which reinforces the child's respect for human rights and fundamental freedoms of others.

2. States Parties to the present Charter shall in particular:

(a)   ensure that no child who is detained or imprisoned or otherwise deprived of his/her liberty is subjected to torture, inhuman or degrading treatment or punishment;

(b)   ensure that children are separated from adults in their place of detention or Imprisonment ...'

African Charter on the Rights and Welfare of the Child – Art 30

14.116   Article 30 of the African Charter on the Rights and Welfare of the Child makes specific provision in respect of the children of imprisoned mothers by providing as follows:

'1. States Parties to the present Charter shall undertake to provide special treatment to expectant mothers and to mothers of infants and young children who have been accused or found guilty of infringing the penal law and shall in particular:

(a)   ensure that a non-custodial sentence will always be first considered when sentencing such mothers;

(b)   establish and promote measures alternative to institutional confinement for the treatment of such mothers;

(c)   establish special alternative institutions for holding such mothers;

(d)   ensure that a mother shall not be imprisoned with her child;

(e)   ensure that a death sentence shall not be imposed on such mothers;

(f)   the essential aim of the penitentiary system will be the reformation, the integration of the mother to the family and social rehabilitation.'

14.117   Article 30(1)(e) of the Charter should not be read as requiring that where a mother is sentenced to imprisonment the child should be separated from her and remain at liberty but rather as requiring that under no circumstances should a mother be sentenced to a period of imprisonment if it would mean that her child would have no alternative but to be placed in prison with her.[258]

The African Charter on Human and Peoples' Rights

14.118   Article 6 of the African Charter on Human and Peoples' Rights states as follows in respect of the right to liberty and security of the person:

'Every individual shall have the right to liberty and to the security of his person. No one may be deprived of his freedom except for reasons and conditions previously laid down by law. In particular, no one may be arbitrarily arrested or detained.'

Revised Arab Charter on Human Rights

14.119   The Revised Arab Charter on Human Rights Art 14 enshrines the right to liberty and security of the person in the following terms:

---

[258]   Van Bueren, G *The African Charter on the Rights and Welfare of the Child* (1991) International Human Rights Monitor 20.

'1. Everyone has the right to liberty and security of person. No one shall be subjected to arbitrary arrest, search or detention without a legal warrant.

2. No one shall be deprived of-his liberty except on such grounds and in such circumstances as are determined by law and in accordance with such procedure as is established thereby.

3. Anyone who is arrested shall be informed, at the time of arrest, in a language that he understands, of the reasons for his arrest and shall be promptly informed of any charges against him. He shall be entitled to contact his family members.

4. Anyone who is deprived of his liberty by arrest or detention shall have the right to request a medical examination and must be informed of that right.

5. Anyone arrested or detained on a criminal charge shall be brought promptly before a judge or other officer authorised by law to exercise judicial power and shall be entitled to trial within a reasonable time or to release. His release may be subject to guarantees to appear for trial. Pre-trial detention shall in no case be the general rule.

6. Anyone who is deprived of his liberty by arrest or detention shall be entitled to petition a competent court in order that it may decide without delay on the lawfulness of his arrest or detention and order his release if the arrest or detention is unlawful.

7. Anyone who has been the victim of arbitrary or unlawful arrest or detention shall be entitled to compensation.'

The Child's Right to Liberty and Security of the Person under Domestic Law

14.120   The domestic courts recognise that 'the individual's right to liberty, and the remedy of habeas corpus, lie at the heart of our law'.[259] Dicey considers that the right to liberty is one of the general principles of the Constitution.[260] Domestic laws touching and concerning the child's right to liberty must be read and applied in a manner compatible with Art 5 of the ECHR interpreted in light of the contents of Art 37 of the CRC.[261] Within this context many of the cardinal principles governing the deprivation of liberty in domestic law have been covered in the sections above.

14.121   The areas in which domestic law impacts most acutely on the child's right to liberty and security of the person are the areas of secure accommodation, school

---

[259]   *R v Bournewood Community and Mental Health NHS Trust ex p L (Secretary of State for Health and others intervening)* [1998] 2 FCR 501 per Lord Nolan. Note that there are limits to the proper application of habeas corpus within domestic law. See *Re S (Habeas Corpus); S v Harringey London Borough Council* [2003] EWHC 2734 (Admin) [2004] 1 FLR 590 per Munby J ('First, that the proper forum for litigating issues that arise whilst care proceedings are on foot (different considerations apply where the care proceedings have finally concluded) will almost always be the court where the care proceedings are being tried – the family proceedings court, the county court or the High Court, as the case may be. Such issues should ordinarily be dealt with in the family court which is dealing with the relevant care proceedings, and as part of the care proceedings, even if they involve Human Rights Act or other issues of the kind that might otherwise be litigated either in judicial review proceedings in the Administrative Court or by a free-standing application for relief under the Human Rights Act 1998 in the Administrative Court or elsewhere'). See also the US Supreme Court decision of *Lehman v Lycoming County Children's Services* 458 US 502 (1982) which held that State supervised foster care is not custody that is protected by habeas corpus.

[260]   Dicey, A V *An Introduction to the Study of the Law of the Constitution* (1885) 9th edn, MacMillan 1945, p 195.

[261]   See **3.43–3.46** above.

detention, youth and criminal justice, immigration and asylum and deprivation of liberty under the domestic mental health legislation.

Domestic Law – Secure Accommodation under the Children Act 1989[262]

The Decision in Re K (A Child)[263]

14.122 In *Re K (A Child)* Butler-Sloss P held that the detention of a child under the auspices of a secure accommodation order granted pursuant to s 25 of the Children Act 1989 was a deprivation of liberty within the meaning of Art 5 of the ECHR but that such deprivation of liberty came within the exception provided by Art 5(1)(d), namely detention for the purposes of educational supervision. The Court of Appeal was able to reach this conclusion by relying on the fact that, whilst s 25(1) of the Children Act 1989 does not mention educational supervision, under the Education Act 1996 education is compulsory to the age of 16 and, having regard to the decision in *Koniarska v United Kingdom*,[264] the meaning of 'educational supervision' should be given a broad interpretation. Pursuant to *Re K* proceedings for a secure accommodation order under s 25 of the 1989 Act will therefore engage Art 5 of the ECHR but will usually come within the exception under Art 5(1)(d).[265] However, the decision in *Re K* should be approached with caution.

14.123 Whilst relying on the fact that under the Education Act 1996 education is compulsory to the age of 16, the Court of Appeal did not consider s 562 of the Education Act 1996 which provides that no power or duty conferred or imposed by that Act 'shall be construed as relating to any person who is detained in pursuance of an order made by the court'.[266] Further, the decision of the Court of Appeal in *Re K* is based in part on the analysis in *Koniarska v United Kingdom*[267] of the scope of the term 'educational provision' in Art 5(1)(d) of the ECHR.[268] As set out above[269] the decision in *Koniarska v United Kingdom* that educational supervision for the purposes of Art 5(1)(d) must embrace many aspects of the exercise by the local authority of parental rights for the benefit and protection of the person concerned appears to extend the ambit of Art 5(1)(d) to cover the deprivation of liberty for the purposes of local authority care and in doing so stretches the concept 'educational supervision' well beyond its natural meaning.[270] Finally, the Court of Appeal's own analysis that a statutory duty to educate children renders all secure accommodation orders as made for

---

[262] For the detailed practice and procedure for secure accommodation orders see Hershman, D and McFarlane, A *Children Law and Practice* Jordan Publishing. See also Local Authority Circular (93)13 *Guidance of Permissible Forms of Control in Children's Residential Care*.

[263] [2001] Fam 377, [2001] 2 All ER 719, [2001] 1 FCR 249, [2001] 1 FLR 526.

[264] (2000) Application No 33670/96 (unreported). Contrast *Bouamar v Belgium* (1988) 11 EHRR 1.

[265] Pursuant to FPR 1991 r 10.26(22) on any application or appeal concerning a secure accommodation order under s 25 of the Children Act 1989 or the refusal to grant habeas corpus, if the court ordering the release of the person concludes that his or her Convention rights have been infringed by the making of the order to which the application or appeal relates, the judgment or order should so state, but if the court does not do so, that failure will not prevent another court deciding the matter.

[266] Note that this provision is itself expressly criticised by the Committee on the Rights of the Child as failing to impose a duty to provide education in respect of detained children (see Committee on the Rights of the Child *Concluding Observations: United Kingdom of Great Britain and Northern Ireland* CRC/C/GBR/CO/4, para 77(e)).

[267] (2000) Application No 33670/96 (unreported). Contrast *Bouamar v Belgium* (1988) 11 EHRR 1.

[268] Namely that 'educational supervision' must embrace many aspects of the exercise, by the local authority, of parental rights for the benefit and protection of the person concerned. In *Re K* Butler-Sloss P described the analysis in *Koniarska* as helpful.

[269] See **14.85**.

[270] Van Bueren, G *Child Rights in Europe* (2007) Council of Europe Publishing, p 99.

the purposes of educational supervision, in addition to being arguably incorrect, likewise appears to stretch the statutory language of s 25(1) of the Act to breaking point as the Act makes no mention of educational supervision.[271] Masson argues persuasively that in accepting that secure accommodation orders are compatible with Article 5(1)(d) when there is no legal duty to provide education within that context and no consideration of the educational regime for the detainee, the Court of Appeal interpreted the ECHR in a way that substantially limits the protection provided for young people detained on welfare grounds.[272]

14.124   In addition to these difficulties Fortin argues that *Re K* constitutes a surprising interpretation in that it seemingly ignores the central question of whether s 25 as drafted is sufficiently precise to have the quality of a law as required by the ECHR.[273] Fortin points out that, as drafted, s 25 of the Children Act 1989 fails to prevent the granting of an order which falls outside the bounds of the exception provided by Art 5(1)(d) since there is nothing in the wording of s 25 that requires every secure accommodation order to be made for the purposes of educational supervision.[274]

14.125   Accordingly, the decision in *Re K* to the effect that secure accommodation orders will not generally violate the provisions of Art 5(1) of the ECHR by reason of their coming within the exception provided by Art 5(1)(d) can by no means be considered a settled proposition.[275]

---

[271]   Section 25(1) of the Children Act 1989 defines secure accommodation as 'accommodation provided for the purpose of restricting liberty'. See also the definition by of 'educational supervision' given by Judge LJ in *Re K*, para 107 ('This goes far beyond school. It is not just about the restriction on liberty involved in requiring a reluctant child to remain at school for the school day. It arises in the context of the responsibilities of parents which extend well beyond ensuring the child's attendance at school. So it involves education in the broad sense, similar, I would respectfully suggest, to the general development of the child's physical, intellectual, emotional, social and behavioural abilities, all of which have to be encouraged by responsible parents, as part of his upbringing and education, and for this purpose, an appropriate level of supervision of the child to enhance his development, where necessary, by restricting his liberty is permitted.'

[272]   Masson, J *Securing human rights for children and young people in secure accommodation* [2002] CFLQ 77. Note that the detention on welfare grounds is not permitted under the CRC (see **14.18** above).

[273]   Fortin, J *Children's Rights and the Developing Law* (2009) 3rd edn, Cambridge, p 621.

[274]   See *Huvig v France* (1990) 12 EHRR 528 holding that the law must indicate with reasonable clarity the scope and manner of exercise of the relevant discretion conferred on public authorities, which public authorities will include the courts.

[275]   In a partly dissenting judgment Thorpe LJ concluded that secure accommodation was not a deprivation of liberty for the purposes of Art 5 since it was a necessary exercise of parental responsibility delegate by a parent to the local authority or acquired by the local authority under a care order and thus does not need justifying by reference to Art 5(1)(d). This analysis appears to ignore the fact that under the terms of s 25 of the Children Act 1989 it is plainly the court rather than the local authority that makes a secure accommodation order (Masson, J *Securing human rights for children and young people in secure accommodation* [2002] CFLQ 77.) In reaching his decision that secure accommodation is a necessary exercise of parental responsibility Thorpe LJ accepted the analysis of the European Court of Human Rights in the highly questionable decision in *Nielsen v Denmark* (1988) 11 EHRR 175, interpreting that decision as giving parents extensive powers to restrict their children's liberty. By contrast Butler-Sloss P made clear that 'If a parent exercised those powers by detaining a child in a similar restrictive fashion and was challenged to justify such detention, for my part, I doubt whether the general rights and responsibilities of a parent would cover such an exercise of parental authority.' Note however, that Butler-Sloss P also placed significant emphasis on the decision in *Nielsen v Denmark*. *Masson points out that* 'By accepting uncritically the approach in *Nielsen*, the Court of Appeal has not acknowledged the responsibilities parents have in making decisions for their children, the importance of balancing the rights of parents and children and the need to ensure that an objective consideration of children's welfare tips the balance' (Masson, J *Securing human rights for children and young people in secure accommodation* [2002] CFLQ 77).

Secure Accommodation and the Child's Right to Liberty and Security of the Person

14.126 In applying the provisions of s 25 of the Children Act 1989 the child's right to liberty and security of the person under Art 37(b) of the CRC[276] and Art 5 of the ECHR must be zealously protected even where the position of the local authority seeking to deprive the child of his or her liberty appears to be pragmatic and welfare focused. It is not permissible for pragmatic considerations to prevail over legal safeguards designed to protect the child's right to liberty and security of the person.[277]

14.127 Within this context it is vital that lawyers dealing with secure accommodation consider in each case Art 5 of the ECHR and Art 37(b) of the CRC.[278] The procedure by which the court deals with applications for secure accommodation orders must be rigorously fair having regard to the fact that making a secure accommodation order is a deprivation of the liberty of the child.[279] A child who is subject to proceedings for a secure accommodation order has the protection of the fair trial provisions in Art 6(1) of the Convention and while it has not been decided whether such proceedings should be categorised as civil or criminal in nature for the purpose of the Convention, such a child should be afforded the five specific minimum rights guaranteed under Art 6(3) to everyone charged with a criminal offence.[280]

Domestic Law – School Detention

14.128 The Education Act 1996 s 550B(1) provides as follows in relation to the imposition of school detention on a pupil:

> 'Where a pupil to whom this section applies is required on disciplinary grounds to spend a period of time in detention at his school after the end of any school session, his detention shall not be rendered unlawful by virtue of the absence of his parent's consent to it if the conditions set out in subsection (3) are satisfied.'

14.129 The requirements stipulated in s 550B(3) are that the head teacher of the school must have previously determined and made known within the school and to parents that the detention of pupils after the end of a school session is one the measures which may be taken with a view to regulating the conduct of pupils, the detention must be imposed by the head teacher or another teacher specifically authorised for the purpose, the detention must be reasonable in all the circumstances and the parents must be given at least 24 hours notice in writing that the detention is to take place. Section 550B(4) provides that in determining whether the imposition of a detention is reasonable in all the circumstances, particular account should be taken of whether the detention constitutes a proportionate punishment in the circumstances of the case and any special circumstances relevant to its imposition on the pupil which are known to the person

---

[276] Article 37(b) of the CRC does not appear to have been considered in the domestic decisions concerning secure accommodation. Note however that it would appear that the Revised Children Act 1989 Guidance and Regulations, Volume 1 Court Orders (2008) DCSF, paras 5.2–5.3 on secure accommodation conflicts with the provisions of Art 37(b) of the CRC in so far as it provides that secure accommodation 'should not be considered as a 'last resort' in the sense that all other options must have been tried without success.'

[277] *LM v Essex County Council* [1999] 1 FLR 988 per Holman J, pp 994–995. See also Revised Children Act 1989 Guidance and Regulations, Volume 1 Court Orders (2008) DCSF, para 5.2 ('Restricting the liberty of children is a serious step which should only be taken where the needs of the child cannot be met by a more suitable placement elsewhere').

[278] See *Good Practice in Child Care Cases* (2004) The Law Society, para 6.1.6.

[279] *Re AS (Secure Accommodation Order)* [1999] 1 FLR 103.

[280] *Re M (a child) (secure accommodation)* [2001] EWCA Civ 458, [2001] 1 FCR 692, sub nom *Re C (Secure Accommodation Order: Representation)* [2001] 2 FLR 169.

imposing it or of which he or she ought reasonably to be aware including in particular the pupils age, any special educational needs he or she may have, any religious requirements affecting him or her, whether suitable alternative travel arrangements can be made.[281]

Domestic Law – Youth and Criminal Justice

Domestic Provisions in Respect of Detention

14.130 The domestic provisions governing the detention of children within the criminal justice system are extensive and a comprehensive treatment is beyond the scope of this work.[282] It should be noted in particular that every court dealing with a child or young person brought before it, either as an offender or otherwise, must have regard to the welfare of that child or young person.[283] In addition to any other duty to which they are subject, it is also the duty of all persons carrying out functions in relation to the youth justice system to have regard to the welfare of the child or young person.[284] This principle will thus encompass the police, the Probation Service, social services, youth offending teams, the Crown Prosecution Service, defence lawyers, the Prison Service and the courts.[285] Local authorities are under a statutory duty to take reasonable steps designed to encourage children within their areas not to commit criminal offences and to reduce the need to bring criminal proceedings against such children.[286]

Domestic Penal Law and Children's Rights

14.131 Within the context of children's rights the domestic sentencing provisions concerning children have been the subject of criticism by the Committee on the Rights of the Child.[287] In particular the Committee has criticised the high numbers of children deprived of their liberty, suggesting that detention is not always applied as a measure of last resort, and that the number of children on remand is also high.[288] The Committee

---

[281] See also Children's Homes Regulations 2001 SI 2001/3937, reg 17 as amended and the Children's Homes (Wales) Regulations 2002, SI 2002/327, reg 17 as amended.

[282] For a comprehensive account of the youth justice system and domestic sentencing provision in respect of children see Clark Hall & Morrison on Children (Lexis Nexis) Division 7(5).

[283] Children and Young Persons Act 1933, s 44.

[284] Crime and Disorder Act 1998, s 37(2).

[285] *No More Excuses – A New Approach to Tackling Youth Crime in England and Wales* Cm 3809 (1997) Home Office, para 2.5.

[286] Children Act 1989, Sch 2, para 7. See also *R (Howard League for Penal Reform) v Secretary of State for the Home Department* [2002] EWHC 2497, [2003] 1 FLR 484, para 136 per Munby J ('... the law can, as it seems to me, be summarised in the following general propositions: (i) the 1989 Act does not confer or impose any functions, powers, duties, responsibilities or obligations on either the Prison Service (or any of its staff) or the Secretary of State for the Home Department; (ii) in that sense the Act does not apply as such either to the Prison Service or to YOIs; (iii) but the duties which a local authority would otherwise owe to a child either under s 17 or under s 47 of the Act do not cease to be owed merely because the child is currently detained in a YOI; (iv) in that sense the Act does apply to children in YOIs; (v) however, a local authority's functions, powers, duties and responsibilities under the Act, and specifically under ss 17 and 47 of the Act, take effect and operate subject to the necessary requirements of imprisonment'). See further Part III of the Crime and Disorder Act 1998 concerning the local provision of youth justice services including youth offending teams and the Youth Justice Board.

[287] See Committee on the Rights of the Child *Concluding Observations: United Kingdom of Great Britain and Northern Ireland* CRC/C/15/Add.188, para 59 and Committee on the Rights of the Child *Concluding Observations: United Kingdom of Great Britain and Northern Ireland* CRC/C/GBR/CO/4, paras 77 and 79.

[288] Committee on the Rights of the Child *Concluding Observations: United Kingdom of Great Britain and Northern Ireland* CRC/C/GBR/CO/4, para 77.

further criticises the application of domestic anti-social behaviour legislation and recommends the abolition of anti-social behaviour orders.[289]

14.132   In *R (Howard League for Penal Reform) v Secretary of State for the Home Department*[290] Munby J made clear that the CRC, the ECHR and the Charter of Fundamental Rights of the European Union are important sources of possible obligations both owed to and enforceable by children detained in young offender institutions. Munby J noted that in relation to the CRC that Art 3(1) and Art 37b are particularly relevant in the domestic context.[291] In this regard, Munby J held that:

'[65] In the first place, Arts 3 and 8 of the European Convention protect children in YOIs from those actions by members of the Prison Service which constitute inhuman or degrading treatment or punishment or which impact adversely and disproportionately on the child's physical or psychological integrity.

[66] Secondly, however, Arts 3 and 8 of the European Convention, read in the light of Arts 3 and 37 of the UN Convention and Art 24 of the European Charter, impose on the Prison Service positive obligations to take reasonable and appropriate measures designed to ensure that:

(i)   children in YOIs are treated, both by members of the Prison Service and by fellow inmates, with humanity, with respect for their inherent dignity and personal integrity as human beings, and not in such a way as to humiliate or debase them;

(ii)   children in YOIs are not subjected to torture or to inhuman or degrading treatment or punishment by fellow inmates or to other behaviour by fellow inmates which impacts adversely and disproportionately on their physical or psychological integrity.

[67] Such measures must strike a fair balance between the competing interests of the particular child and the general interests of the community as a whole (including the other inmates of the YOI) but always having regard:

(i)   first, to the principle that the best interests of the child are at all times a primary consideration;

(ii)   secondly, to the inherent vulnerability of children in a YOI; and

(iii)   thirdly, to the need for the State – the Prison Service – to take effective deterrent steps to prevent, and to provide children in YOIs with effective protection from, ill-treatment (whether at the hands of Prison Service staff or of other inmates) of which the Prison Service has or ought to have knowledge.

[68] In short, human rights law imposes on the Prison Service enforceable obligations, that is, obligations enforceable by or on behalf of children in YOIs:

(i)   to have regard to the 'welfare' principle encapsulated in the UN Convention and the European Charter; and
(ii) to take effective steps to protect children in YOIs from any ill-treatment, whether at the hands of Prison Service staff or of other inmates, of the type which engages either Arts 3 or 8 of the European Convention.

---

[289]   Committee on the Rights of the Child *Concluding Observations: United Kingdom of Great Britain and Northern Ireland* CRC/C/GBR/CO/4, para 79. The continuation of the anti-social legislation in its current form is now the subject of a Government Review.

[290]   [2002] EWHC 2497, [2003] 1 FLR 484.

[291]   Munby J concluded in relation to the CRC and the European Charter that 'both can, in my judgment, properly be consulted insofar as they proclaim, re-affirm or elucidate the content of those human rights that are generally recognised throughout the European family of nations, in particular the nature and scope of those fundamental rights that are guaranteed by the European Convention.' See **3.32–3.46** above.

[69] In this connection it is to be borne in mind that, quite apart from any other remedies which there may be arising out of the State's – the Prison Service's – failure to meet its human rights obligations, ss 7 and 8 of the Human Rights Act 1998 enable a victim to bring a free-standing action in the High Court. In the case of a claimant who is a child, such a claim is appropriately brought in the Family Division.'[292]

Domestic Law – Asylum Seeking and Unaccompanied Children

14.133 The detention of children with their families in United Kingdom Border Agency centres where their families have been judged by tribunal to have no right to remain in the United Kingdom has been the subject of much criticism.[293] This criticism has now been echoed by the domestic courts.[294] The Committee on the Rights of the child has made clear that a child's status as an asylum seeker or refugee cannot of itself justify as lawful a restriction on that child's liberty.[295] Further, uunaccompanied or separated children, including those who arrive irregularly in a country, should not, in principle, be deprived of their liberty solely for having breached any law governing access to and stay within the territory.[296]

14.134 The Committee on the Rights of the Child has criticised the United Kingdom for the detention of asylum seeking and refugee children as being incompatible with the principles and provisions of the CRC.[297] In particular, the Committee has deprecated the Asylum and Immigration (Treatment of Claimants etc.) Act 2004, s 2 which permits the prosecution of children over the age of 10 if they do not possess valid documentation upon entry into the United Kingdom.[298] In this context the United Kingdom has now removed its reservations to Art 37(c) and (d), Art 32 and Art 22 of CRC. Most importantly however, the domestic courts are now willing to expressly refer to the provisions of the CRC in the domestic context to determine whether there has been an unlawful deprivation of liberty. In *D v Home Office*[299] Brooke LJ, examining the concept of *ultra vires* as applied to detention of families by domestic immigration officials, held that:

'If a court judges that in making his decision to detain, an immigration officer failed to take into account matters of material significance (viz he has overlooked relevant features of internal policy or paid no regard to the fact that the prospective detainee is a child protected by art 37(b) of the United Nations Convention on the Rights of the Child), then he will have

---

[292] See also Prison Service Order No 4950 and the Youth Justice Board *Strategy for the Secure Estate of Children and Young People* (2005), p 9.

[293] See *The Arrest and Detention of Children Subject to Immigration Control* (2009) Children's Commissioner; the First Report of Session 2009–2010 of the House of Commons Home Affairs Committee *The Detention of Children in the Immigration System* (2009) HC73 and the *Children's Commissioner for England Follow Up Report to: The Arrest and Detention of Children Subject to Immigration Control* (2010).

[294] *R (on the application of Suppiah and others) v Secretary of State for the Home Department* [2011] EWHC 2 (Admin), [2011] All ER (D) 31 (Jan).

[295] Committee on the Rights of the Child General Comment No 6 *Treatment of Unaccompanied and Separated Children Outside their Country of Origin* CRC/GC/2005/6, paras 61–63.

[296] UN Guidelines for the Alternative Care of Children A/RES/64/142, para 43.

[297] Committee on the Rights of the Child Concluding Observations: United Kingdom of Great Britain and Northern Ireland CRC/C/15/Add.188, para 49 and Committee on the Rights of the Child Concluding Observations: United Kingdom of Great Britain and Northern Ireland CRC/C/GBR/CO/4, para 70. In December 2010 the Government announced that the detention of children in immigration detention centres would cease although children will remain at risk of being detained in 'pre-departure accommodation' for up to 72 hours prior to leaving the United Kingdom.

[298] Committee on the Rights of the Child *Concluding Observations: United Kingdom of Great Britain and Northern Ireland* CRC/C/GBR/CO/4, para 70. See *R (on the Application of HBH) v Secretary of State for the Home Department* [2009] EWHC 928 (Admin).

[299] [2005] EWCA Civ 38, [2006] 1 All ER 183, para 111.

strayed outside his wide-ranging powers. As a result he will have had 'no power' to authorise the detention in question. This is what the doctrine of ultra vires is all about ... The critical questions we have to answer are whether the provisions of Sch 2 to the 1971 Act place the claimants in some special category in which they are afforded a weaker recognition of their right to liberty, and whether English law, now viewed through the prism of the ECHR, affords an immunity to immigration officers in any way comparable to that afforded to courts of law. If the answers to these questions are that the detentions were unlawful by English law, there will be no defence to the claim for damages for false imprisonment. If, on the other hand, there is no illegality under English law, then we have to determine whether the detention of this family with their two young children was disproportionate in the light not only of Home Office internal policy but also of art 37(b) of the United Nations Convention on the Rights of the Child.'

Domestic Law – Deprivation of Liberty and Mental Health

14.135 The Mental Health Act ss 2 as amended by the Mental Health Act 2007 permits the detention of a patient[300] for assessment on the grounds that he or she is suffering from mental disorder of a nature or degree which warrants the detention of the patient in a hospital for assessment or for assessment followed by medical treatment for at least a limited period and he or she ought to be so detained in the interests of his own health or safety or with a view to the protection of other persons. Section 3 of the 1983 Act as amended provides for the detention of a patient for treatment on the grounds that he is suffering from a mental disorder of a nature or degree which makes it appropriate for him or her to receive medical treatment in a hospital, it is necessary for the health or safety of the patient or for the protection of other persons that he or she should receive such treatment and it cannot be provided unless he or she is detained under this section and appropriate medical treatment is available to him or her.[301] Mental disorder will not encompass unwise acts by children.[302]

14.136 The domestic mental health legislation is extensive and complex and again a comprehensive description is beyond the scope of this work.[303] Guidance relating to the application of the provisions of the Mental Health Act 1983 to children[304] and young people is provided by Chapter 36 of the *Code of Practice under the Mental Health Act 1983* published by the Department of Health.

Domestic Law – Deprivation of Liberty and the Family Home

14.137 The question of whether the child can leave home without parental restriction has not been definitively decided.[305] The European case of *Nielsen v Denmark*[306] would suggest not but obiter comments in *Re K (Secure Accommodation Order: Right to*

---

[300] The definition of a 'patient' under the Mental Health Act 1983, s 145 is 'a person suffering or appearing to be suffering from mental disorder' and thus will encompass children.

[301] See also *R (H) v London North and East Region Mental Health Review Tribunal* [2001] EWCA Civ 415, [2002] QB 1 and the Mental Health Act (Remedial) Order 2001, SI 2001/3712.

[302] *Re F (Mental Health Act: Guardianship)* [2000] 1 FLR 192.

[303] These provisions apply to the exclusion of the common law principle of necessity (see *R v Bournewood Community and Mental Health NHS Trust ex p L* [1998] 2 WLR 764). For a comprehensive account of the application of domestic mental health legislation to children see Clark Hall & Morrison on Children (Lexis Nexis) Division 1(14).

[304] The guidance defines 'children' as being under 16 years old and 'young people' as being those aged 16 or 17 years old (see para 36.1).

[305] Note that to engage Art 5 of the ECHR the deprivation of liberty must be imputable to the State (*Re A and C (Equality and Human Rights Commissioner Intervening)* [2010] EWHC 978 (Fam), [2010] 2 FLR 1363).

[306] (1988) 11 EHRR 175.

Liberty)[307] suggests a more liberal approach may be taken under domestic law. Both Butler-Sloss LJ[308] and Judge LJ[309] suggested obiter that the parent cannot restrict the liberty of a child for more than a few days.[310] Fortin suggests that if the Courts were to follow these obiter comments parents would find it difficult to justify preventing a child from leaving home.[311] In *Re K* Butler-Sloss LJ considered that the Court's response should depend on whether the parents actions were 'within ordinary acceptable parental restrictions on the movement of a child'. In this context, the best interests principle and the principle of evolving capacity would be crucial to determining whether this test was made out in any given case.[312]

14.138   The domestic law is in a state of confusion as to whether the courts can force the return of a child who has elected to leave home.[313] Section 2 of the Child Abduction Act 1984 is very wide in scope and can potentially result in a person who provides advice and assistance to a child under 16 who is running away from home[314] although the defence of reasonable excuse is likely to be available in respect of a *'Gillick'* competent child.[315] Department of Health Guidance provides that children who run away are likely to be children in need for the purposes of s 17 of the Children Act 1989 and as such are entitled to services from the Local Authority.[316] New guidance accordingly requires a full needs assessment and welfare interview.[317] Where a child seeks to live with another adult the court may formalise the position with a residence order pursuant to s 8 of the Children Act 1989.[318] With leave under s 10(8) of the Children Act 1989 the child him or herself may apply for such relief.[319]

CONCLUSION

14.139   The unlawful or arbitrary deprivation of a child's liberty constitutes a grave violation of his or her cardinal rights. The inherent gravity of any violation of the child's

---

[307]   [2001] 1 FLR 526.

[308]   At para 29.

[309]   At para 101.

[310]   But see the views of Lord Justice Thorpe, para 61 where he considers that the deprivation of liberty as a necessary consequence of the exercise of parental responsibility for the protection and promotion of the child's welfare will not amount to a breach of Art 5 of the ECHR. Note that Munby LJ considered in *Re A and C (Equality and Human Rights Commissioner Intervening)* [2010] EWHC 978 (Fam), [2010] 2 FLR 1363 that the care of children by their parents in the family home would not typically involve a deprivation of liberty.

[311]   Fortin, J *Children's Rights and the Developing Law* (2009) 3rd edn, Cambridge, p 117.

[312]   See *R v Howes* (1860) 3 E&E 332 and *Krishnan v London Borough of Sutton* [1970] Ch 181. See also *Regina v D* [1984] FLR 847 in relation to the role of the child's consent in cases of kidnap.

[313]   Formerly, applications were made for writs of habeas corpus by parents attempting to secure the return of children who had elected to leave home. The Courts would refuse to issue such writs once the children in question had reached the 'age of discretion' which age was 14 for boys and 16 for girls (see *R v Howes* (1860) 3 E&E 332 and *Krishnan v London Borough of Sutton* [1970] Ch 181. See also *Regina v D* [1984] FLR 847 in relation to the role of the child's consent in cases of kidnap).

[314]   See *R v Leather* [1993] 2 FLR 770. Where the child is over the age of 16 the criminal sanctions on neglect and harbouring cease.

[315]   Fortin, J *Children's Rights and the Developing Law* (2009) 3rd edn, Cambridge, p 119.

[316]   *Children Missing from Care and from Home: A Guide to Good Practice* (2002) Department of Health.

[317]   *Young Runaways Action Plan* (2008) Department for Children, Schools and Families.

[318]   Such an order will provide protection from the provisions of the Child Abduction Act 1984 and the Sexual Offences Act 1956 and also provide a degree legal certainty for the arrangement (see *B v B (A Minor) (Residence Order)* [1992] 2 FLR 327).

[319]   The interests of the child are not paramount in such an application (see *Re SC (A Minor) (Leave to Seek a Residence Order)* [1994] 1 FLR 96; *Re C (Residence: Child's Application for Leave)* [1995] 1 FLR 927 and *Re H (Residence Order: Child's Application for Leave)* [2000] 1 FLR 780). Applications for leave by children should be heard in the High Court.

right to liberty and security of the person makes it essential that the State adhere to the rule of law when seeking to deprive a child of his or her liberty.[320] If the child's right to liberty and security of the person is to be properly protected this principle must be applied not only within the context of the criminal justice system but also in respect of other areas which may threaten the right such as mental health, educational supervision, asylum and immigration.[321] The domestic courts are increasingly willing in individual cases to recognise the importance of not only the ECHR but also the CRC in ensuring that the child's right to liberty and security of the person is safeguarded effectively.[322] It is vital that lawyers take advantage of this judicial willingness and consider and seek to apply the provisions of these instruments in all circumstances in which a child may be deprived of his or her liberty.

14.140 On a macroscopic scale however the domestic picture is far from impressive with the United Kingdom being the subject of repeated criticism concerning what Fortin describes as 'the UK's predilection for locking up children'.[323] The United Kingdom has one of the highest rates of incarceration of children in Western Europe[324] The Committee on the Rights of the Child has repeatedly stressed that, in the context of its plain breach of Art 37 of the CRC in neither using detention as a last resort nor for the shortest period of time, the Government must seek preventative and rehabilitative solutions to problems that can lead to children being deprived of their liberty. It is plain that the Government must move away from punitive sanctions concerning criminal behaviour and immigration irregularities which inevitably violate the child's right to liberty and security of the person.[325]

14.141 In this regard there is an urgent need to appreciate that whilst the child may be responsible in the sense of having committed the offence in question he or she ought not to be liable only to a punitive response for the commission of the offence.[326] This proposition does not represent a contradiction if society is prepared to embrace a welfare driven response to offending by children rather than a response driven solely or primarily by the wish to satisfy a perceived public demand for punitive sanctions[327] and appreciate that any difference between a justice model and a welfare model of juvenile justice rests primarily in the manner the former is applied in order to achieve the latter. As Archard points out 'A juvenile court can, for instance, both impose a penalty on a child *and* make provision for the child's needs to be addressed'.[328]

---

[320] *Brogan v United Kingdom* (1988) 11 EHRR 117, para 58.

[321] Newell, P and Hodgkin, R *Implementation Handbook for the Convention on the Rights of the Child* (2008) 3rd edn, UNICEF, p 548.

[322] R (Howard League for Penal Reform) v Secretary of State for the Home Department [2002] EWHC 2497, [2003] 1 FLR 484.

[323] Fortin, J *Children's Rights and the Developing Law* (2009) 3rd edn, Cambridge, p 716.

[324] Gil-Robles, A *Report by Mr Alvar Gil-Robles, Commissioner for Human Rights on His Visit to the United Kingdom* (2005), paras 86 and 87 and Hammarberg, T *Memorandum by Thomas Harmmarberg, Commissioner for Human Rights of the Council of Europe* (2008), paras 28, 31 and 52.

[325] Committee on the Rights of the Child *Concluding Observations of the Committee on the Rights of the Child: United Kingdom of Great Britain and Northern Ireland* (2002) CRC/C/15/Add.188, paras 59 and 62 and Committee on the Rights of the Child *Concluding Observations of the Committee on the Rights of the Child: United Kingdom of Great Britain and Northern Ireland* (2008) CRC/C/GBR/CO/4, paras 77–78.

[326] Archard, D *Children – Rights and Childhood* (2004) 2nd edn, Routledge, p 133.

[327] What Muncie has described as 'the ever-desperate measures to placate tabloid and mid-market newspaper law-and-order campaigns' (Muncie, J *Children's Rights and Youth Justice* in Franklin, B (ed) *The New Handbook of Children's Rights* (2002) Routledge 81, p 94.

[328] Archard, D *Children – Rights and Childhood* (2004) 2nd edn, Routledge, p 133.

Chapter 15

THE CHILD'S RIGHT TO FREEDOM FROM HARMFUL TREATMENT

'Man hands on misery to man. It deepens like a coastal shelf'

Philip Larkin, This Be the Verse

INTRODUCTION

15.1   The right to freedom from harmful treatment is traditionally associated with and articulated by the prohibition on torture or cruel, inhuman or degrading treatment. However, in respect of children the right to freedom from harmful treatment, the child's basic right to physical and psychological integrity,[1] extends to his or her protection from physical and sexual abuse and exploitation, protection from economic harm, sale, trafficking and forced labour and protection from involvement in armed conflict. Within this context, in addition to the prohibition on torture and cruel, inhuman or degrading treatment or punishment, the CRC particularises in detail a number of further rights of the child pertaining to activities which threaten the child's physical and psychological integrity.[2] This reflects the reality that treatment which threatens a child's person is rarely due to the violation of a single right.[3]

15.2   This chapter collects together the cardinal rights protective of the child's physical and psychological integrity under the broad heading of the child's right to freedom from harmful treatment. The chapter examines each salient right in detail in addition to considering the child's right to rehabilitation where he or she has been the victim of harmful treatment.[4] The chapter then goes on to consider the prohibition on torture and inhuman or degrading treatment or punishment under other international instruments and the prohibitions on torture and slavery under customary international law before considering the relevant articles of the ECHR and other regional instruments. Finally, the child's right to freedom from harmful treatment is examined within the context of our domestic law.

---

[1]   See Lord Lester QC, Lord Pannick QC and Herberg, J *Human Rights Law and Practice* (2009) 3rd edn, LexisNexis, p 187. Note that the consequences of harmful treatment are not limited to interference with the child's physical integrity but may also cause psychological harm (see **15.7** below).
[2]   See CRC, Arts 19, 32, 34, 35, 36, 37 and 38.
[3]   Van Bueren, G *The International Law on the Rights of the Child* (1998) Martinus Nijhoff, p 262.
[4]   See CRC, Art 39.

GENERAL PRINCIPLES

The Child's Right to Protection

15.3   The Declaration on the Rights of the Child adopted by the League of Nations in 1924 stipulated that the child must be protected against every form of exploitation.[5] Having recognised in its preamble that 'the child, by reason of his physical and mental immaturity, needs special safeguards and care, including appropriate legal protection, before as well as after birth', the Declaration on the Rights of the Child 1959 Principle 9 elaborated on this broad principle by providing that:

> 'The child shall be protected against all forms of neglect, cruelty and exploitation. He shall not be the subject of traffic, in any form. The child shall not be admitted to employment before an appropriate minimum age; he shall in no case be caused or permitted to engage in any occupation or employment which would prejudice his health or education, or interfere with his physical, mental or moral development.'

15.4   Within this context, Art 24(1) of the Covenant on Civil and Political Rights (ICCPR) further articulated the broad right of the child to protection having regard to his or her status as a child from all those responsible for his or her care, Art 24(1) providing that:

> 'Every child shall have, without any discrimination as to race, colour, sex, language, religion, national or social origin, property or birth, the right to such measures of protection as are required by his status as a minor, on the part of his family, society and the State.'[6]

15.5   Article 10 of the Covenant on Economic, Civil and Political Rights (ICESCR) likewise articulates the child's right to protection in the context of his or her family as the fundamental group unit of society and in relation to the risk of economic and social exploitation, stating that:

> 'The States Parties to the present Covenant recognise that:
>
> 1. The widest possible protection and assistance should be accorded to the family, which is the natural and fundamental group unit of society, particularly for its establishment and while it is responsible for the care and education of dependent children. Marriage must be entered into with the free consent of the intending spouses.
>
> 2. Special protection should be accorded to mothers during a reasonable period before and after childbirth. During such period working mothers should be accorded paid leave or leave with adequate social security benefits.
>
> 3. Special measures of protection and assistance should be taken on behalf of all children and young persons without any discrimination for reasons of parentage or other conditions. Children and young persons should be protected from economic and social exploitation. Their employment in work harmful to their morals or health or dangerous to life or likely to hamper their normal development should be punishable by law. States should also set age limits below which the paid employment of child labour should be prohibited and punishable by law.'

---

5   Principle 4.
6   See also Art 23(1) of the ICCPR which provides that 'The family is the natural and fundamental group unit of society and is entitled to protection by society and the State.'

15.6 Before codifying specific rights protective of the child's physical and psychological integrity the preamble to the CRC reflects the principles articulated in the Declarations on the Rights of the Child, the ICCPR and the ICESCR and other international instruments in stating that:

'Bearing in mind that the need to extend particular care to the child has been stated in the Geneva Declaration of the Rights of the Child of 1924 and in the Declaration of the Rights of the Child adopted by the General Assembly on 20 November 1959 and recognised in the Universal Declaration of Human Rights, in the International Covenant on Civil and Political Rights (in particular in articles 23 and 24), in the International Covenant on Economic, Social and Cultural Rights (in particular in article 10) and in the statutes and relevant instruments of specialised agencies and international organisations concerned with the welfare of children, Bearing in mind that, as indicated in the Declaration of the Rights of the Child, 'the child, by reason of his physical and mental immaturity, needs special safeguards and care, including appropriate legal protection, before as well as after birth', Recalling the provisions of the Declaration on Social and Legal Principles relating to the Protection and Welfare of Children, with Special Reference to Foster Placement and Adoption Nationally and Internationally; the United Nations Standard Minimum Rules for the Administration of Juvenile Justice (The Beijing Rules); and the Declaration on the Protection of Women and Children in Emergency and Armed Conflict, Recognising that, in all countries in the world, there are children living in exceptionally difficult conditions, and that such children need special consideration, Taking due account of the importance of the traditions and cultural values of each people for the protection and harmonious development of the child ...'

Harmful Treatment

15.7 The chapter title 'freedom from harmful treatment' is used in preference to 'freedom from harm' to denote that what the relevant rights of the child seek to ensure is freedom from harm inflicted on the child's physical and/or psychological integrity by the actions or omissions of others.[7]

15.8 The nature of the treatment contemplated by the term 'harmful treatment' is indicated by the articles of the CRC and the other international and regional human rights instruments discussed below and ranges from torture, through abuse suffered within the family home to involvement in armed conflict. As to the extent of the harm required to constitute 'harmful treatment' it should be noted that the child's status as a child means that the degree of harm required to violate the rights which seek to ensure the child's freedom from harmful treatment may be less than the degree of harm required to violate the corresponding rights of adults. Van Bueren observes that whilst it is arguable that the level of treatment or punishment amounting to torture or inhuman treatment and punishment is the same for children and adults, a particular form conduct which does not amount to cruel or degrading treatment and punishment when inflicted upon adults may amount to cruel or degrading treatment and punishment when inflicted on a child.[8] Thus the ambit of the right to freedom from harmful treatment is potentially wider in respect of children than it is in respect of adults.

---

[7]   It would be absurd for example to argue that a child had the right to freedom from harm from earthquakes or other natural disasters *per se*, although the child is be entitled expect reasonable protective measures to be taken by others to mitigate the impact of such natural disasters pursuant to the child's right to life, survival and development (see chapter 5 above).

[8]   Van Bueren, G *The International Law on the Rights of the Child* (1998) Martinus Nijhoff, p 223. See also IACHR, Report N° 33/04, Jailton Neri Da Fonseca (Brazil), Case 11.634 of March 11, 2004, para 64.

Non-Derogable Nature of Right

15.9   The prohibition on torture and cruel, inhuman and degrading treatment or punishment under ICCPR Art 4(2) is non-derogable. Note further that Art 2(3) of the UN Convention against Torture provides that 'An order from a superior officer or a public authority may not be invoked as a justification of torture'.[9] The CRC contains no provisions permitting derogation in respect of any of the rights of the child enshrined in the Convention and accordingly derogation from the prohibition contained in Art 37(a) of the CRC in respect of torture and cruel, inhuman or degrading treatment or punishment is not permitted. It is also likely that any reservations seeking to reserve the right to torture or to treat in a cruel, inhuman or degrading a child way would fall foul of Art 51(2) of the CRC.[10] Within this context it is likely that the child's right to freedom from harmful treatment is likewise a non-derogable right[11] and reservations which seek to reserve the right to treat children in a manner harmful to them will contravene Art 51(2) of the CRC.

THE RIGHT TO FREEDOM FROM HARMFUL TREATMENT

The Child's Right to Freedom from Harmful Treatment under the CRC

15.10   The child's right to freedom from harmful treatment under the CRC is comprised of a number of elements incorporated into the CRC.[12] Namely, the right to protection from torture or other cruel, inhuman or degrading treatment or punishment,[13] the right to protection from all forms of physical or mental violence, injury or abuse, neglect or negligent treatment, maltreatment or exploitation while in the care of parent(s), legal guardian(s) or any other person who has the care of the child,[14] the right to protection from all forms of sexual exploitation and sexual abuse,[15] the right to protection from the illicit use of narcotic drugs and psychotropic substances,[16] the right to protection from

---

[9]   See Goodman, R *Human Rights Treaties, Invalid Reservations and State Consent* (2002) Vol 96:53 p 531. See also the Nuremberg Principles, Principle IV 'The fact that a person acted pursuant to order of his Government or of a superior does not relieve him from responsibility under international law, provided a moral choice was in fact possible to him.'

[10]   Article 51(2) of the CRC provides that 'A reservation incompatible with the object and purpose of the present Convention shall not be permitted.' See also Art 19(c) of the Vienna Convention on the Law of Treaties. See also *The Advisory Opinion of the International Court of Justice on Reservations to the Genocide Convention* (1961) 18, Goodman, R *Human Rights Treaties, Invalid Reservations and State Consent* (2002) Vol 96:53 p 531 and Ruda, J *Reservations to Treaties* 146 Recueil de Cours 101 (1975).

[11]   See the UN Committee Against Torture and Other Cruel, Inhuman or Degrading Treatment or Punishment General Comment No 2 *Implementation of Article 2 by State Parties* CAT/C/GC/2, para 3 'The obligations to prevent torture and other cruel, inhuman or degrading treatment or punishment (hereinafter 'ill-treatment') under article 16, paragraph 1, are indivisible, interdependent and interrelated. The obligation to prevent ill-treatment in practice overlaps with and is largely congruent with the obligation to prevent torture ... In practice, the definitional threshold between ill-treatment and torture is often not clear. Experience demonstrates that the conditions that give rise to ill-treatment frequently facilitate torture and therefore the measures required to prevent torture must be applied to prevent ill-treatment. Accordingly, the Committee has considered the prohibition of ill-treatment to be likewise non-derogable under the Convention and its prevention to be an effective and non-derogable measure.'

[12]   Note that whilst Art 32 of the CRC enshrines protection from exploitation in terms of a right, the remaining relevant articles do not articulate that protection in terms of a right but rather as an undertaking by or duty upon States Parties to take protective action (Arts 19, 33, 34, 36 and 38) or an absolute prohibition (Art 37(a)).

[13]   CRC, Art 37(a).

[14]   CRC, Art 19.

[15]   CRC, Art 34 and the Optional Protocol to the Convention on the Rights of the Child on the Sale of Children, Child Prostitution and Child Pornography.

[16]   CRC, Art 33.

abduction, sale and trafficking,[17] the right to protection from economic exploitation,[18] the right to protection from involvement in armed conflict[19] and the right to protection against all other forms of exploitation prejudicial to any aspects of the child's welfare.[20] In addition, Art 17 seeks to protect children from harmful information,[21] Art 24(3) seeks to protect children from traditional practices injurious to their health[22] and Art 28(3) of the CRC requires that school discipline be consistent with the child's human dignity and in conformity with the Convention.[23]

15.11 The CRC does not just seek to protect children from harmful treatment but also seeks to address the consequences of such treatment where it has taken place in violation of the rights enshrined in the Convention. Where a child has been the victim of any form of neglect, exploitation, or abuse; torture or any other form of cruel, inhuman or degrading treatment or punishment or armed conflicts the child has the right to physical and psychological recovery and social reintegration within an environment which fosters the health, self-respect and dignity of the child.[24]

The Child's Right to Freedom from Harmful Treatment under the CRC – CRC, Art 37 – Protection from Torture or other Cruel, Inhuman or Degrading Treatment or Punishment

CRC, Art 37(a)

(i) Prohibition on Torture or other Cruel, Inhuman or Degrading Treatment or Punishment

15.12 Article 37(a) enshrines an absolute prohibition on the torture or other cruel, inhuman or degrading treatment or punishment of the child.[25] In this regard Art 37(a) of the CRC provides that States Parties shall ensure that:

> '(a)   No child shall be subjected to torture or other cruel, inhuman or degrading treatment or punishment. Neither capital punishment nor life imprisonment without possibility of release shall be imposed for offences committed by persons below eighteen years of age.'

15.13 Article 37(a) of the CRC reflects the provisions of the Universal Declaration of Human Rights, Art 5 which provides that 'No one shall be subjected to torture or to cruel, inhuman or degrading treatment or punishment' and Art 7 of the ICCPR, which states that:[26]

> 'No one shall be subjected to torture or to cruel, inhuman or degrading treatment or punishment. In particular, no one shall be subjected without his free consent to medical or scientific experimentation.'

---

[17]   CRC, Art 11.
[18]   CRC, Art 32.
[19]   CRC, Art 38 and Optional Protocol to the Convention on the Rights of the Child on the Involvement of Children in Armed Conflict.
[20]   CRC, Art 36.
[21]   See **11.32** above.
[22]   See **5.15** above.
[23]   See **13.67** above.
[24]   CRC, Art 39.
[25]   The remainder of Art 37 of the CRC concerns the child's right to liberty and is dealt with in chapter 14 above.
[26]   See **15.15** below.

15.14 Within the context of these international instruments, the UN Convention against Torture and Other Cruel, Inhuman or Degrading Treatment or Punishment of 1984 stipulates at Art 2 that:

'1. Each State Party[27] shall take effective legislative, administrative, judicial or other measures[28] to prevent acts of torture in any territory under its jurisdiction.[29]

2. No exceptional circumstances whatsoever, whether a state of war or a threat of war, internal political in stability or any other public emergency, may be invoked as a justification of torture.

3. An order from a superior officer or a public authority may not be invoked as a justification of torture.'[30]

(ii) Medical and Scientific Experimentation

15.15 Article 37(a) of the CRC does not duplicate the provisions set out in Art 7 of the ICCPR relating to the prohibition of medical and scientific experimentation on human beings without valid consent. This prohibition is also contained in Art 15(1) of the Convention on the Rights of Persons with Disabilities which provides:[31]

---

[27] See UN Committee Against Torture and Other Cruel, Inhuman or Degrading Treatment or Punishment General Comment No 2 *Implementation of Article 2 by State Parties* CAT/C/GC/2, para 15 ('The Convention imposes obligations on States parties and not on individuals. States bear international responsibility for the acts and omissions of their officials and others, including agents, private contractors, and others acting in official capacity or acting on behalf of the State, in conjunction with the State, under its direction or control, or otherwise under colour of law.'

[28] Article 4 of the UN Convention against Torture and Other Cruel, Inhuman or Degrading Treatment or Punishment specifically requires state parties to ensure that all acts of torture are offences under its criminal law and punishable by appropriate penalties.

[29] In its UN Committee Against Torture and Other Cruel, Inhuman or Degrading Treatment or Punishment General Comment No 2 *Implementation of Article 2 by State Parties* CAT/C/GC/2, para 7 the Committee observes that 'The Committee also understands that the concept of 'any territory under its jurisdiction,' linked as it is with the principle of non-derogability, includes any territory or facilities and must be applied to protect any person, citizen or non-citizen without discrimination subject to the de jure or de facto control of a State party. The Committee emphasizes that the State's obligation to prevent torture also applies to all persons who act, de jure or de facto, in the name of, in conjunction with, or at the behest of the State party. It is a matter of urgency that each State party should closely monitor its officials and those acting on its behalf and should identify and report to the Committee any incidents of torture or ill-treatment as a consequence of anti terrorism measures, among others, and the measures taken to investigate, punish, and prevent further torture or ill-treatment in the future, with particular attention to the legal responsibility of both the direct perpetrators and officials in the chain of command, whether by acts of instigation, consent or acquiescence.' Pursuant to Art 3 of the UN Convention against Torture and Other Cruel, Inhuman or Degrading Treatment or Punishment 'No State Party shall expel, return ('refouler') or extradite a person to another State where there are substantial grounds for believing that he would be in danger of being subjected to torture.'

[30] See UN Committee Against Torture and Other Cruel, Inhuman or Degrading Treatment or Punishment General Comment No 2 *Implementation of Article 2 by State Parties* CAT/C/GC/2, para 26 ('The non derogability of the prohibition of torture is underscored by the long-standing principle embodied in article 2, paragraph 3, that an order of a superior or public authority can never be invoked as a justification of torture Thus, subordinates may not seek refuge in superior authority and should be held to account individually. At the same time, those exercising superior authority – including public officials – cannot avoid accountability or escape criminal responsibility for torture or ill-treatment committed by subordinates where they knew or should have known that such impermissible conduct was occurring, or was likely to occur, and they failed to take reasonable and necessary preventive measures').

[31] See also the Convention on the Rights of Persons with Disabilities, Art 17: 'Every person with disabilities has a right to respect for his or her physical and mental integrity on an equal basis with others.'

'No one shall be subjected to torture or to cruel, inhuman or degrading treatment or punishment. In particular, no one shall be subjected without his or her free consent to medical or scientific experimentation.'

However, it is clear that the general prohibition on the exploitation of children contained in Art 36 of the CRC would cover non-consensual medical or scientific experimentation on children as being forms of exploitation prejudicial to the welfare of children. Further, the Human Rights Committee has also made clear in its *General Comment No 20: Article 7 (Prohibition of Torture or Other Cruel, Inhuman or Degrading Treatment or Punishment*[32] in the context of Art 7 of the ICCPR that:

'... special protection in regard to such experiments is necessary in the case of persons not capable of giving valid consent, and in particular those under any form of detention or imprisonment. Such persons should not be subjected to any medical or scientific experimentation that may be detrimental to their health.'[33]

CRC, Art 37(a) – Ambit

(i) CRC, Art 37(a) – Absolute nature of Prohibition

15.16 The prohibition on subjecting children to torture or other cruel, inhuman or degrading treatment or punishment is absolute.[34] The UN Committee against Torture and Other Cruel, Inhuman or Degrading Treatment or Punishment General Comment No 2 *Implementation of Article 2 by State Parties*[35] makes clear that:[36]

'Article 2, paragraph 2 [of the UN Convention against Torture] provides that the prohibition against torture is absolute and nonderogable. It emphasises that *no exceptional circumstances whatsoever* may be invoked by a State Party to justify acts of torture in any territory under its jurisdiction. The Convention identifies as among such circumstances a state of war or threat thereof, internal political instability or any other public emergency. This includes any threat of terrorist acts or violent crime as well as armed conflict, international or non-international. The Committee is deeply concerned at and rejects absolutely any efforts by States to justify torture and ill-treatment as a means to protect public safety or avert emergencies in these and all other situations. Similarly, it rejects any religious or traditional justification that would violate this absolute prohibition. The Committee considers that amnesties or other impediments which preclude or indicate unwillingness to provide prompt and fair prosecution and punishment of perpetrators of torture or ill-treatment violate the principle of non-derogability.'

---

[32] Human Rights Committee General Comment No 20 *Article 7 (Prohibition of Torture or Other Cruel, Inhuman or Degrading Treatment or Punishment* HRI/GEN/1/Rev 8, p 190, para 7. See also the Committee on the Rights of the Child General Comment No 3 *HIV/AIDS and the Rights of the Child* CRC/GC/2003/3, para 29.

[33] The Human Rights Committee has adopted two General Comments on the issue of torture: Human Rights Committee General Comment No 7 *Prohibition of torture or cruel, inhuman or degrading treatment or punishment* HRI/GEN/1/Rev.8, pp 168–169 now replaced by Human Rights Committee General Comment No 20 *Prohibition of torture or cruel, inhuman or degrading treatment or punishment* HRI/GEN/1/Rev.8, pp 190–192.

[34] Newell, P and Hodgkin, R *Implementation Handbook for the Convention on the Rights of the Child* (2008) 3rd edn, UNICEF, p 548.

[35] UN Committee against Torture and Other Cruel, Inhuman or Degrading Treatment or Punishment General Comment No 2 *Implementation of Article 2 by State Parties* CAT/C/GC/2, para 5.

[36] Note that the Committee on the Rights of the Child has stipulated that any statement made as the result of torture or other cruel, inhuman or degrading treatment cannot be accepted as evidence (see General Comment No 10 *Children's Rights in Juvenile Justice* CRC/C/GC/10, para 56). See also Art 15 of the Convention against Torture and Other Cruel, Inhuman or Degrading Treatment or Punishment.

(ii)   CRC, Art 37(a) – 'Torture'

Relationship with Cruel, Inhuman or Degrading Treatment or Punishment

15.17 In considering the ambit of the prohibitions on torture or other cruel, inhuman or degrading treatment or punishment it should be noted that these forms of harmful treatment are considered to be indivisible, interdependent and interrelated. In its General Comment No 2 *Implementation of Article 2 by State Parties*[37] the UN Committee Against Torture and Other Cruel, Inhuman or Degrading Treatment or Punishment notes that:

> 'The obligations to prevent torture and other cruel, inhuman or degrading treatment or punishment (hereinafter 'ill-treatment') under article 16, paragraph 1, are indivisible, interdependent and interrelated. The obligation to prevent ill-treatment in practice overlaps with and is largely congruent with the obligation to prevent torture ... In practice, the definitional threshold between ill-treatment and torture is often not clear. Experience demonstrates that the conditions that give rise to ill-treatment frequently facilitate torture and therefore the measures required to prevent torture must be applied to prevent ill-treatment.'

15.18 Whilst the Human Rights Committee also posits that it may not be necessary to draw sharp distinctions between the prohibited forms of treatment,[38] Van Bueren argues that when it comes to children, such distinctions may serve some purpose.[39] As noted above, Van Bueren observes that whilst it is arguable that the level of treatment or punishment amounting to torture or inhuman treatment and punishment is the same for children and adults, a particular form of treatment or punishment that may not amount to cruel, or degrading treatment and punishment when inflicted upon adults may amount to cruel, or degrading treatment and punishment when inflicted on a child.[40] Thus in some cases the distinctions between the prohibited forms of treatment under Art 37(a) of the CRC may take on more significance for children than they would do for adults.

Definition of Torture

15.19 The UN Convention against Torture and Other Cruel, Inhuman or Degrading Treatment or Punishment Art 1(1) defines 'torture' as follows:

> 'For the purposes of this Convention, the term 'torture' means any act by which severe pain or suffering, whether physical or mental, is intentionally inflicted on a person for such purposes as obtaining from him or a third person information or a confession, punishing him for an act he or a third person has committed or is suspected of having committed, or intimidating or coercing him or a third person, or for any reason based on discrimination of any kind, when such pain or suffering is inflicted by or at the instigation of or with the consent or acquiescence of a public official or other person acting in an official capacity. It does not include pain or suffering arising only from, inherent in or incidental to lawful sanctions.'[41]

---

[37]   Committee Against Torture and Other Cruel, Inhuman or Degrading Treatment or Punishment General Comment No 2 *Implementation of Article 2 by State Parties* CAT/C/GC/2, para 3.

[38]   CCPR/C/21/Add 1.

[39]   Van Bueren, G *The International Law on the Rights of the Child* (1998) Martinus Nijhoff, p 224.

[40]   Van Bueren, G *The International Law on the Rights of the Child* (1998) Martinus Nijhoff, p 223.

[41]   Note that Art 1(2) of the Convention against Torture and Other Cruel, Inhuman or Degrading Treatment or Punishment makes clear that Art 1(1) '... is without prejudice to any international instrument or national legislation which does or may contain provisions of wider application.' See also *Quinteros v Uruguay* (1983) Human Rights Committee A/38/40.

(iii)   CRC, Art 37(a) – 'Other Cruel, Inhuman or Degrading Treatment or Punishment'

CRC, Art 37(a) – 'Cruel'

15.20   Whether conduct amounts to 'cruel' treatment for the purposes of Art 37(a) of the CRC will be a matter for assessment of the circumstances of each case.[42] Note that the addition of the word 'harsh' to the terms 'cruel, inhuman or degrading treatment, punishment, correction or discipline' in r 87(a) of the UN Rules on the Protection of Juveniles Deprived of their Liberty implies that, in relation to children, there is a prohibited form of treatment that is somewhat below the concept of cruelty.[43]

CRC, Art 37(a) – 'Inhuman or Degrading'

15.21   In *Antti Vuolanne v Finland*[44] the Human Rights Committee held as follows in relation to the question of what constitutes inhuman or degrading treatment:

> 'The Committee recalls that article 7 prohibits torture and cruel or other inhuman or degrading treatment. It observes that the assessment of what constitutes inhuman or degrading treatment falling within the meaning of article 7 depends on all the circumstances of the case, such as the duration and manner of the treatment, its physical or mental effects as well as the sex, age and state of health of the victim ... In this connection, the Committee expresses the view that for punishment to be degrading, the humiliation or debasement involved must exceed a particular level and must, in any event, entail other elements beyond the mere fact of deprivation of liberty.'[45]

CRC, Art 37(a) – Application

(i)   Corporal Punishment

Corporal Punishment at Home[46]

15.22   The Committee on the Rights of the Child considers that any form of corporal punishment of children, however light, is incompatible with the prohibition on torture or cruel, inhuman or degrading treatment or punishment contained in Art 37(a) of the CRC.[47] The Committee on the Rights of the Child General Comment No 8 *The Right of the Child to Protection from Corporal Punishment and Other Cruel or Degrading Forms of*

---

[42]   See *Pratt and Morgan v Jamaica* Human Rights Committee Communications Nos 210/1986 and 225/1987 (1989).

[43]   See Van Bueren, G *Standard Minimum Rules for Juveniles Deprived of their Liberty* in *Report of an International Seminar on Children in Prison* (1989) Amnesty International. Rule 87(a) provides that 'No member of the detention facility or institutional personnel may inflict, instigate or tolerate any act of torture or any form of harsh, cruel, inhuman or degrading treatment, punishment, correction or discipline under any pretext or circumstance whatsoever.'

[44]   Human Rights Committee Communication No 265/1987 (1989).

[45]   See also *The Greek Case* 12 Yearbook 186 (1969) decided under the ECHR defining degrading treatment as 'treatment or punishment of an individual may be said to be degrading if it grossly humiliates him before others or drives him to act against his will or conscience.'

[46]   The issue of corporal punishment in education as prohibited by the terms of CRC, Art 28(2) is dealt with at **10.99** and **13.67** above.

[47]   See also CRC, Art 19. The Committee on the Rights of the Child has consistently interpreted Art 19, read with the CRC as a whole, as requiring the prohibition of corporal punishment in all settings (Newell, P and Hodgkin, R *Implementation Handbook for the Convention on the Rights of the Child* (2008) 3rd edn, UNICEF, p 249). In this context the Committee on the Rights of the Child has commented that the words 'all forms of physical and mental violence' in Art 19(1) of the CRC leave no room for any level of legalised violence against children in the form of corporal punishment (Committee on the Rights of the Child General Comment No 8 *The Right of the Child to Protection from Corporal Punishment and Other Cruel or Degrading Forms of Punishment* CRC/C/GC/8 p 6, para 18).

Punishment[48] addresses the issue of corporal punishment of children and measures for eliminating it, in the family, schools and other settings. In its General Comment the Committee on the Rights of the Child recommends the prohibition of all corporal punishment, however light, in family settings.[49] Within this context, the term 'corporal punishment' is defined as:[50]

> 'The Committee defines "corporal" or "physical" punishment as any punishment in which physical force is used and intended to cause some degree of pain or discomfort, however light. Most involves hitting ("smacking", "slapping", "spanking") children, with the hand or with an implement – a whip, stick, belt, shoe, wooden spoon, etc. But it can also involve, for example, kicking, shaking or throwing children, scratching, pinching, biting, pulling hair or boxing ears, forcing children to stay in uncomfortable positions, burning, scalding or forced ingestion (for example, washing children's mouths out with soap or forcing them to swallow hot spices). In the view of the Committee, corporal punishment is invariably degrading. In addition, there are other non-physical forms of punishment that are also cruel and degrading and thus incompatible with the Convention. These include, for example, punishment which belittles, humiliates, denigrates, scapegoats, threatens, scares or ridicules the child.'

15.23 The best interests principle under Art 3 of the CRC cannot be used to justify 'reasonable' or 'moderate' corporal punishment at home, which punishment conflicts with the child's human dignity and right to physical integrity.[51] The Committee on the Rights of the Child has emphasised that corporal punishment should be prohibited 'however light'.[52] Neither does the term 'appropriate direction and guidance' in Art 5 of the CRC leave room for justification of corporal punishment within the family setting.[53] Provisions which permit the use of 'reasonable' or 'moderate' corporal punishment should be removed from national law and be replaced by criminal sanctions making it clear it is as unlawful to hit or 'smack' or 'spank' a child as it is to do so to an adult,[54] and that the criminal law on assault applies equally to such violence, regardless of whether it is termed 'discipline' or 'reasonable correction'.[55]

15.24 The prohibition of corporal punishment in the family setting should *not* be conflated with a prohibition in respect of discipline in the family environment. In its

---

[48] Committee on the Rights of the Child General Comment No 8 *The Right of the Child to Protection from Corporal Punishment and Other Cruel or Degrading Forms of Punishment* CRC/C/GC/8.

[49] Committee on the Rights of the Child General Comment No 8 *The Right of the Child to Protection from Corporal Punishment and Other Cruel or Degrading Forms of Punishment* CRC/C/GC/8 p 3, paras 5 and 8. Note that States Parties to the CRC are not able to invoke the provisions of domestic law to justify the violation of their human rights obligations in respect of the use of corporal punishment in the home and in other settings (see Report of the Special Rapporteur on Torture and other Cruel, Inhuman or Degrading Treatment or Punishment (2005) A/60/316, paras 18–28).

[50] Committee on the Rights of the Child General Comment No 8 *The Right of the Child to Protection from Corporal Punishment and Other Cruel or Degrading Forms of Punishment* CRC/C/GC/8 p 4, para 11.

[51] Committee on the Rights of the Child General Comment No 8 *The Right of the Child to Protection from Corporal Punishment and Other Cruel or Degrading Forms of Punishment* CRC/C/GC/8 p 7, para 26.

[52] See United Kingdom CRC/C/SR.205, para 72.

[53] Committee on the Rights of the Child General Comment No 8 *The Right of the Child to Protection from Corporal Punishment and Other Cruel or Degrading Forms of Punishment* CRC/C/GC/8, p 8, para 28.

[54] In commenting on the defence of 'lawful', 'reasonable' or 'moderate' chastisement in English common law and the 'right of correction' in French law the Committee on the Rights of the Child has observed that at one time in many States the same defence was also available to justify the chastisement of wives by their husbands and of slaves, servants and apprentices by their masters (Committee on the Rights of the Child General Comment No 8 *The Right of the Child to Protection from Corporal Punishment and Other Cruel or Degrading Forms of Punishment* CRC/C/GC/8, p 9, para 31).

[55] Committee on the Rights of the Child General Comment No 8 *The Right of the Child to Protection from Corporal Punishment and Other Cruel or Degrading Forms of Punishment* CRC/C/GC/8, p 9, paras 31 and 34.

General Comment No 8 *The Right of the Child to Protection from Corporal Punishment and Other Cruel or Degrading Forms of Punishment*[56] the Committee on the Rights of the Child observes that:

> 'In rejecting any justification of violence and humiliation as forms of punishment for children, the Committee is not in any sense rejecting the positive concept of discipline. The healthy development of children depends on parents and other adults for necessary guidance and direction, in line with children's evolving capacities, to assist their growth towards responsible life in society. The Committee recognises that parenting and caring for children, especially babies and young children, demand frequent physical actions and interventions to protect them. This is quite distinct from the deliberate and punitive use of force to cause some degree of pain, discomfort or humiliation. As adults, we know for ourselves the difference between a protective physical action and a punitive assault; it is no more difficult to make a distinction in relation to actions involving children. The law in all States, explicitly or implicitly, allows for the use of non-punitive and necessary force to protect people.'

Use of Corporal Punishment in Detention

15.25 The UN Standard Minimum Rules for the Administration of Juvenile Justice (the 'Beijing Rules') r 17(3) provides that 'Juveniles shall not be subject to corporal punishment'. Likewise, the UN Rules for the Protection of Children deprived of their Liberty r 67 provides that:

> 'All disciplinary measures constituting cruel, inhuman or degrading treatment shall be strictly prohibited, including corporal punishment, placement in a dark cell, closed or solitary confinement[57] or any other punishment that may compromise the physical or mental health of the juvenile concerned. The reduction of diet and the restriction or denial of contact with family members should be prohibited for any purpose. Labour should always be viewed as an educational tool and a means of promoting the self-respect of the juvenile in preparing him or her for return to the community and should not be imposed as a disciplinary sanction. No juvenile should be sanctioned more than once for the same disciplinary infraction. Collective sanctions should be prohibited.'[58]

---

[56] Committee on the Rights of the Child General Comment No 8 *The Right of the Child to Protection from Corporal Punishment and Other Cruel or Degrading Forms of Punishment* CRC/C/GC/8 p 5, paras 13 and 14.

[57] The use of solitary confinement will also raises issues linked to the child's right to liberty (Newell, P and Hodgkin, R *Implementation Handbook for the Convention on the Rights of the Child* (2008) 3rd edn, UNICEF, p 554 and see chapter 14 above). In its General Comment No 10 *Children's Rights in Juvenile Justice* CRC/C/GC/10 p 24 the Committee on the Rights of the Child records that 'disciplinary measures in violation of Art 37 of CRC must be strictly forbidden, including corporal punishment, placement in a dark cell, closed or solitary confinement, or any other punishment that may compromise the physical or mental health or well-being of the child concerned.'

[58] See also UN Rules for the Protection of Children deprived of their Liberty r 66 ('Any disciplinary measures and procedures should maintain the interest of safety and an ordered community life and should be consistent with the upholding of the inherent dignity of the juvenile and the fundamental objective of institutional care, namely, instilling a sense of justice, self-respect and respect for the basic rights of every person'). See also the Committee on the Rights of the Child General Comment No 8 *The Right of the Child to Protection from Corporal Punishment and Other Cruel or Degrading forms of Punishment* CRC/C/GC/8, para 39.

The Child's Right to Freedom from Harmful Treatment under the CRC – CRC, Art 19 – Protection from Harm Inflicted by Parents, Guardians and Carers

CRC, Art 19

15.26 Article 19 of the CRC stipulates as follows in respect of the child's right to protection from harm inflicted by parents, guardians or other carers:

> '1. States Parties shall take all appropriate legislative, administrative, social and educational measures to protect the child from all forms of physical or mental violence, injury or abuse, neglect or negligent treatment, maltreatment or exploitation, including sexual abuse, while in the care of parent(s), legal guardian(s) or any other person who has the care of the child.
>
> 2. Such protective measures should, as appropriate, include effective procedures for the establishment of social programmes to provide necessary support for the child and for those who have the care of the child, as well as for other forms of prevention and for identification, reporting, referral, investigation, treatment and follow-up of instances of child maltreatment described heretofore, and, as appropriate, for judicial involvement.'[59]

CRC, Art 19(1) – Ambit

15.27 Hodgkin and Newell observe that the child's rights under Art 19 of the CRC go beyond their protection from what is generically terms 'abuse' and beyond their right to protection from torture and cruel, inhuman or degrading treatment or punishment under Art 37 of the CRC, the protection under Art 19 being directed at the child's human right to equal respect for his or her dignity as well as his or her physical and psychological integrity.[60]

(i)   CRC, Art 19(1) – 'Physical violence, injury or abuse'

15.28 The meaning of physical violence, injury or abuse is largely self evident. It is defined in the context of children in the *World Report on Violence and Health*[61] as the intentional use of physical force or power, threatened or actual, against a child, by an individual or group, that either results in or has a high likelihood of resulting in actual or potential harm to the child's health, survival, development or dignity. In conceptualising violence as it affects children it is important to consult children and young people to ensure that physical violence and its effects is considered from the perspective of the potential victim of such treatment.[62] Physical violence is not rendered acceptable simply because it happens in the context of punishments administered at home or at school.[63] The Committee on the Rights of the Child has made clear that the words 'all forms of physical and mental violence' in Art 19(1) of the CRC leaves no room for any level of legalised violence against children in the form of corporal

---

[59] Note again that Art 24(1) of the Covenant on Civil and Political Rights thus recognises the family as a protective unit in addition the responsibility for protecting the family which is placed on society and upon the State '1. Every child shall have, without any discrimination as to race, colour, sex, language, religion, national or social origin, property or birth, the right to such measures of protection as are required by his status as a minor, on the part of his family, society and the State.'

[60] Newell, P and Hodgkin, R *Implementation Handbook for the Convention on the Rights of the Child* (2008) 3rd edn, UNICEF, p 249.

[61] Krug, E et al. (eds) *World Report on Violence and Health* (2002) World Health Organisation, p 5.

[62] Committee on the Rights of the Child Report on the Twenty-eighth Session (2001) CRC/C/111, paras 2 and 3.

[63] See **15.22** above concerning punishment at home and **10.99** and **13.67** above in relation to punishment at school.

punishment.[64] Note that protecting children from self harm, including suicide and attempted suicide comes within the ambit of Art 19 of the CRC as well as Art 6 of the CRC.[65] Art 19 of the CRC will also encompass abuse committed through the adoption of traditional practices[66] and by reason of the availability and dissemination of violent images and information.[67]

(ii)   CRC, Art 19(1) – 'Mental violence injury or abuse'

15.29   Mental violence, injury or abuse includes humiliation, harassment, verbal abuse, the effects of isolation and other practices that cause or may result in psychological harm, including the witnessing of violence or ill treatment of another person.[68]

(iii)   CRC, Art 19(1) – 'Neglect or Negligent Treatment'

15.30   Neglect may be deliberate or as the result of omission consequent on parental, family or community incapacity.[69] States Parties should take measures to prevent neglect of children having regard to their duties to ensure to the maximum extent possible the survival and development of the child,[70] to provide appropriate assistance to parents[71] and to ensure that the child benefits from health care,[72] social security,[73] an adequate standard of living[74] and education.[75] 'Negligent treatment' concerns accidental injury to children arising out of the negligence of parents, legal guardians or any other person who has care of the child.[76]

(iv)   CRC, Art 19(1) – 'Maltreatment or Exploitation, including Sexual Abuse'

Maltreatment or Exploitation

15.31   The term 'maltreatment or exploitation' in Art 19(1) of the CRC covers any other adverse treatment by parents, legal guardians or others with care of the child not necessarily encompassed by physical or mental violence, injury, abuse, neglect or negligent treatment.[77]

Sexual Abuse

15.32   The child's right to protection from sexual abuse is encompassed in both Art 19(1) and in Art 34 of the CRC.[78] In the context of Art 19(1) the term 'sexual abuse'

---

[64]   Committee on the Rights of the Child General Comment No 8 *The Right of the Child to Protection from Corporal Punishment and Other Cruel or Degrading Forms of Punishment* CRC/C/GC/8 p 6, para 18.

[65]   Newell, P and Hodgkin, R *Implementation Handbook for the Convention on the Rights of the Child* (2008) 3rd edn, UNICEF, p 265.

[66]   See **5.119** above in respect of CRC, Art 24(3).

[67]   See **11.32** concerning Art 17(e) of the CRC.

[68]   Newell, P and Hodgkin, R *Implementation Handbook for the Convention on the Rights of the Child* (2008) 3rd edn, UNICEF, p 256. Note that the term psychological harm is to be preferred to 'emotional harm'.

[69]   Newell, P and Hodgkin, R *Implementation Handbook for the Convention on the Rights of the Child* (2008) 3rd edn, UNICEF, p 257.

[70]   CRC, Art 6. See chapter 5 above.

[71]   CRC, Art 18.

[72]   CRC, Art 24. See **5.105** above.

[73]   CRC, Art 26. See **5.180** above.

[74]   CRC, Art 27. See chapter 5 above.

[75]   CRC, Art 28 and 29. See chapter 13 above.

[76]   See also CRC, Art 24(2)(e).

[77]   Newell, P and Hodgkin, R *Implementation Handbook for the Convention on the Rights of the Child* (2008) 3rd edn, UNICEF, p 257.

[78]   Article 34 of the CRC provides that 'States Parties undertake to protect the child from all forms of sexual exploitation and sexual abuse. For these purposes, States Parties shall in particular take all appropriate

contemplates familial and institutional sexual abuse having regard to the words 'care of parent(s), legal guardian(s) or any other person who has the care of the child' at the end of Art 19(1), with sexual exploitation by strangers and more widely being dealt with primarily under Art 34 and the Optional Protocol to the Convention on the Rights of the Child on the Sale of Children, Child Prostitution and Child Pornography.[79] However, the two articles and the Optional Protocol are closely linked and will overlap. Sexual abuse will include not only violent sexual assaults but other sexual activity, whether consensual or not, with children who are below the defined age of sexual consent.[80]

(v) CRC, Art 19(1) – 'In the care of Parent(s), Legal Guardian(s) or any other Person who has Care of the Child'

15.33 The term 'In the care of parent(s), legal guardian(s) or any other person who has care of the child' in Art 19(1) of the CRC will include foster care, day schools and all institutional settings.[81] The UN Guidelines for the Alternative Care of Children[82] provide that:

> 'Children must be treated with dignity and respect at all times and must benefit from effective protection from abuse, neglect and all forms of exploitation, whether on the part of care providers, peers or third parties, in whatever care setting they may find themselves.'[83]

CRC, Art 19(1) – Application

(i) Early Childhood

15.34 The Committee on the Rights of the Child notes in its General Comment No 7 *Implementing Child Rights in Early Childhood*[84] that:

> 'Young children are frequent victims of neglect, maltreatment and abuse, including physical and mental violence. Abuse very often happens within families, which can be especially destructive. Young children are least able to avoid or resist, least able to comprehend what is happening and least able to seek the protection of others. There is compelling evidence that trauma as a result of neglect and abuse has negative impacts on development, including, for the very youngest children, measurable effects on processes of brain maturation. Bearing in mind the prevalence of abuse and neglect in early childhood and the evidence that it has long-term repercussions, States parties should take all necessary measures to safeguard young children at risk and offer protection to victims of abuse, taking positive steps to support their recovery from trauma while avoiding stigmatisation for the violations they have suffered.'

---

national, bilateral and multilateral measures to prevent: (a) The inducement or coercion of a child to engage in any unlawful sexual activity; (b) The exploitative use of children in prostitution or other unlawful sexual practices; (c) The exploitative use of children in pornographic performances and materials.'

79 For detailed discussion of the provisions and application of Art 34 see **15.43–15.55** below.

80 Newell, P and Hodgkin, R *Implementation Handbook for the Convention on the Rights of the Child* (2008) 3rd edn, UNICEF, p 257.

81 Newell, P and Hodgkin, R *Implementation Handbook for the Convention on the Rights of the Child* (2008) 3rd edn, UNICEF, p 258.

82 A/RES/64/142, para 13.

83 See also Committee on the Rights of the Child General Comment No 3 *HIV/AIDS and the Rights of the Child* CRC/GC/2003/3, para 34 ('In keeping with the rights of the child according to article 19 of the Convention, States parties have the obligation to protect children from all forms of violence and abuse, whether at home, in school or other institutions, or in the community. Programmes must be specifically adapted to the environment in which children live, their ability to recognise and disclose abuses and their individual capacity and autonomy').

84 Committee on the Rights of the Child General Comment No 7 *Implementing Child Rights in Early Childhood* CRC/C/GC/7/Rev.1, para 36(a).

(ii) Children with Disabilities

15.35 Within the context of children with disabilities being more vulnerable to abuse in all settings, the Committee on the Rights of the Child General Comment No 9 *The Rights of Children with Disabilities*[85] urges States Parties to take all necessary measures for the prevention of abuse of and violence against children with disabilities including measures to:

(a) Train and educate parents or others caring for the child to understand the risks and detect the signs of abuse of the child;

(b) Ensure that parents are vigilant about choosing caregivers and facilities for their children and improve their ability to detect abuse;

(c) Provide and encourage support groups for parents, siblings and others taking care of the child to assist them in caring for their children and coping with their disabilities;

(d) Ensure that children and caregivers know that the child is entitled as a matter of right to be treated with dignity and respect and they have the right to complain to appropriate authorities if those rights are breached;

(e) Ensure that schools take all measures to combat school bullying and pay particular attention to children with disabilities providing them with the necessary protection while maintaining their inclusion into the mainstream education system;

(f) Ensure that institutions providing care for children with disabilities are staffed with specially trained personnel, subject to appropriate standards, regularly monitored and evaluated, and have accessible and sensitive complaint mechanisms;

(g) Establish an accessible, child-sensitive complaint mechanism and a functioning monitoring system based on the Paris Principles;

(h) Take all necessary legislative measures required to punish and remove perpetrators from the home ensuring that the child is not deprived of his or her family and continue to live in a safe and healthy environment;

(i) Ensure the treatment and re-integration of victims of abuse and violence with a special focus on their overall recovery programmes.'[86]

---

[85] CRC/C/GC/9, paras 43 and 44.

[86] See also Art 16(1) of the Convention on the Rights of Persons with Disabilities ('States Parties shall take all appropriate legislative, administrative, social, educational and other measures to protect persons with disabilities, both within and outside the home, from all forms of exploitation, violence and abuse, including their gender-based aspects.').

(iii)　Adolescence

15.36　The Committee on the Rights of the Child General Comment No 4 Adolescent Health and Development in the context of the Convention on the Rights of the Child[87]provides that:

> 'Under article 19 of the Convention, States parties must take all appropriate measures to prevent and eliminate: (a) institutional violence against adolescents, including through legislation and administrative measures in relation to public and private institutions for adolescents (schools, institutions for disabled adolescents, juvenile reformatories, etc.), and training and monitoring of personnel in charge of institutionalised children or who otherwise have contact with children through their work, including the police; and (b) interpersonal violence among adolescents, including by supporting adequate parenting and opportunities for social and educational development in early childhood, fostering non-violent cultural norms and values (as foreseen in article 29 of the Convention), strictly controlling firearms and restricting access to alcohol and drugs.'

CRC, Art 19(2) – Ambit

15.37　CRC, Art 19(2) provides as follows in respect of protective and preventative measures in respect of violence to children:

> '2. Such protective measures should, as appropriate, include effective procedures for the establishment of social programmes to provide necessary support for the child and for those who have the care of the child, as well as for other forms of prevention and for identification, reporting, referral, investigation, treatment and follow-up of instances of child maltreatment described heretofore, and, as appropriate, for judicial involvement.'

The use of the word 'include' in Art 19(2) of the CRC indicates that this list is non-exhaustive in terms of the protective and preventative measures which may taken by States parties to protect the child from physical or mental violence, injury or abuse, neglect or negligent treatment, maltreatment or exploitation of the child.

(i)　CRC, Art 19(2) – 'Social Programmes to Provide Necessary Support'

15.38　Social programmes for the protection from and prevention of violence to children will include educational and information campaigns, training for those working with children including specialist training in child protection.[88] Social Programmes should not only provide the necessary support but should contribute to requirements of Art 19(2) that violence against children be both identified and reported.

(ii)　CRC, Art 19(2) – 'Identification, reporting, referral, investigation, treatment and follow-up'

15.39　The identification of abuse is the precursor to protective measures being taken. Effective procedures for identification for the purposes of Art 19(2) will be those designed to ensure that the steps commonly taken by perpetrators to disguise the occurrence of physical or mental violence, injury or abuse, neglect or negligent treatment, maltreatment or exploitation are ineffective. The requirement for effective

---

[87]　Committee on the Rights of the Child General Comment No 4 *Adolescent Health and Development in the context of the Convention on the Rights of the Child* CRC/GC/2003/4, para 19.

[88]　Newell, P and Hodgkin, R *Implementation Handbook for the Convention on the Rights of the Child* (2008) 3rd edn, UNICEF, p 266. See also Committee on the Rights of the Child General Comment No 8 CRC/C/GC/8, paras 45 and 48 and the UN Guidelines for the Alternative Care of Children A/RES/64/142, paras 32–52.

procedures for the reporting of such abuse must include legal obligations to report violence against children.[89] The Committee on the Rights of the Child considers that reporting of abuse identified by professionals should be mandatory.[90] It should be noted that effective procedures for the reporting of physical or mental violence, injury or abuse, neglect or negligent treatment, maltreatment or exploitation should take account of the child's right to privacy under Art 16 of the CRC, the child's right to freedom of expression under Art 13 and the child's right to participate under Art 12 of the CRC. Such procedures should be well-publicised, confidential and accessible to all children, including those in care and juvenile justice institutions, who should be aware of the existence of mechanisms of complaint.[91] Hodgkin and Newell note that the requirement for referral in Art 19(2) implies the expectation of a specialised and trained response to violence inflicted on the child. Article 12 of the CRC will apply to any referral arrangements or processes.[92] The requirement to refer and the requirement to investigate must be read together as the latter must result from the former. Investigations in relation to violence against children must be 'child sensitive'.[93]

15.40 The requirement for treatment and follow up under Art 19(2) following abuse perpetrated against the child is supplemented by Art 25 and Art 39 of the CRC.[94] Read together, these Arts require a specialist and tailored approach to treatment and follow up in respect of violence which goes beyond the treatment of physical injuries and requires a holistic and multi-disciplinary approach to dealing with the aftermath of violence against a child.

(iii)   CRC, Art 19(2) – 'Judicial Involvement'

Criminal Sanctions

15.41 Violence towards children may, depending on its nature and severity, result in judicial involvement by way of the prosecution of the perpetrator of the violence. Such judicial involvement should occur having regard to the principles of the CRC and in particular with regard to Art 3 and Art 12 of the CRC. Violence within the family home and other care contexts may also be perpetrated by children. In such circumstances, such child perpetrators of abuse should also be treated by the courts, if they need to become involved, in accordance with the principles set out in the CRC.[95] In both scenarios judicial involvement should have proper regard to the fact that judicial proceedings themselves can be detrimental to the welfare of the child and the procedures adopted should be child sensitive.[96]

---

[89] See *Report of the independent expert for the United Nations study on violence against children* A/61/299, para 25.

[90] See Ghana CRC/C/GHA/CO/2, paras 44 and 45 and Belize CRC/C/15/Add.99, para 22.

[91] See *Report of the independent expert for the United Nations study on violence against children* A/61/299, para 104.

[92] Newell, P and Hodgkin, R *Implementation Handbook for the Convention on the Rights of the Child* (2008) 3rd edn, UNICEF, p 268.

[93] See Czech Republic CRC/C/15/Add.210, para 41.

[94] CRC, Art 25 provides that 'States Parties recognise the right of a child who has been placed by the competent authorities for the purposes of care, protection or treatment of his or her physical or mental health, to a periodic review of the treatment provided to the child and all other circumstances relevant to his or her placement.' CRC, Art 39 states that 'States Parties shall take all appropriate measures to promote physical and psychological recovery and social reintegration of a child victim of: any form of neglect, exploitation, or abuse; torture or any other form of cruel, inhuman or degrading treatment or punishment; or armed conflicts. Such recovery and reintegration shall take place in an environment which fosters the health, self-respect and dignity of the child.' See **15.108** below.

[95] See chapter 14 above and chapter 16 below generally.

[96] See Costa Rica CRC/C/15/Add.266, para 38. The ESC Guidelines on Justice in Matters involving Child

Protective Intervention by the State

15.42 Violence towards children by parents, legal guardians or other persons seized of the child's care may also trigger judicial involvement by way of State intervention in the child's family or care environment.[97] In addition to the provisions of Art 19 of the CRC regard must be had to Art 9(1) of the CRC in such circumstances.[98]

The Child's Right to Freedom from Harmful Treatment under the CRC – CRC, Art 34 – Protection from Sexual Exploitation and Abuse

CRC, Art 34

15.43 Article 34 of the CRC provides as follows in respect of the protection of children from sexual exploitation and abuse:

> 'States Parties undertake to protect the child from all forms of sexual exploitation and sexual abuse. For these purposes, States Parties shall in particular take all appropriate national, bilateral and multilateral measures to prevent:
>
> (a)   The inducement or coercion of a child to engage in any unlawful sexual activity;
> (b)   The exploitative use of children in prostitution or other unlawful sexual practices;
> (c)   The exploitative use of children in pornographic performances and materials.'

CRC, Art 34 – Related Provisions

15.44 The child's right to protection from sexual abuse is also encompassed Art 19(1) of the CRC.[99] In the context of Art 19(1) the term 'sexual abuse' contemplates familial and institutional sexual abuse.[100] Art 34 of the CRC contemplates the issue of sexual exploitation by strangers and more widely.[101] However, the two articles and the Optional Protocol are closely linked and will overlap as for example, some families do seek to

---

Victims and Witnesses of Crime, para 9(d) define 'child' sensitive' as an approach which 'balances the child's right to protection and that takes into account the child's individual needs and views'.

[97]   For the general principles applicable in this situation see **8.78–8.99** above.

[98]   Article 9(1) provides that 'States Parties shall ensure that a child shall not be separated from his or her parents against their will, except when competent authorities subject to judicial review determine, in accordance with applicable law and procedures, that such separation is necessary for the best interests of the child. Such determination may be necessary in a particular case such as one involving abuse or neglect of the child by the parents, or one where the parents are living separately and a decision must be made as to the child's place of residence.' See **8.78** above.

[99]   Article 19 of the CRC provides that '1. States Parties shall take all appropriate legislative, administrative, social and educational measures to protect the child from all forms of physical or mental violence, injury or abuse, neglect or negligent treatment, maltreatment or exploitation, including sexual abuse, while in the care of parent(s), legal guardian(s) or any other person who has the care of the child. 2. Such protective measures should, as appropriate, include effective procedures for the establishment of social programmes to provide necessary support for the child and for those who have the care of the child, as well as for other forms of prevention and for identification, reporting, referral, investigation, treatment and follow-up of instances of child maltreatment described heretofore, and, as appropriate, for judicial involvement.'

[100]   See **15.31** above.

[101]   Article 4 of the Universal Declaration of Human Rights ('No one shall be held in slavery or servitude; slavery and the slave trade shall be prohibited in all their forms') and the similar provisions of Art 8 of the ICCPR will also be relevant to preventing the sexual exploitation of children. See in particular Art 1(d) o the UN Supplementary Convention on the Abolition of Slavery, the Slave Trade and Institutions and Practices Similar to Slavery which provides that ('Each of the States Parties to this Convention shall take all practicable and necessary legislative and other measures to bring about progressively and as soon as possible the complete abolition or abandonment of the following institutions and practices, where they still exist and whether or not they are covered by the definition of slavery contained in article 1 of the Slavery Convention signed at Geneva on 25 September 1926: (d) Any institution or practice whereby a child or young person

engage their children in the exploitative activities dealt with by Art 34 of the CRC. Further, the sexual exploitation of children through child prostitution and child pornography may also engage Art 37(a) of the CRC on the grounds that they constitute degrading treatment.[102]

15.45 CRC, Art 34 is complimented by the Optional Protocol to the Convention on the Rights of the Child on the Sale of Children, Child Prostitution and Child Pornography[103] which further defines and enhances the protection afforded by Art 34 of the CRC. The Optional Protocol defines each of the terms contained in its title and places duties on States parties to criminalise and prosecute such conduct, during which prosecution children should be treated with humanity and with a view to their social rehabilitation. In contrast to the Protocol on the Involvement of Children in Armed Conflict, the Optional Protocol on the Sale of Children Child Prostitution and Child Pornography did not receive the active support of the Committee on the Rights of the Child, it being felt that the CRC sufficiently addressed the matters dealt with by the protocol.[104]

15.46 The Human Rights Committee has made it clear that Art 24 of the ICCPR encompasses a duty on States parties to prevent children from being exploited by means of prostitution or by any other means.[105] The Convention on the Elimination of All Forms of Discrimination against Women Art 6 provides that 'States Parties shall take all appropriate measures, including legislation, to suppress all forms of traffic in women and exploitation of prostitution of women'.[106] Article 2 of the ILO Forced Labour Convention 1930 (No 29)[107] and Art 3(b) of the ILO Worst Forms of Child Labour Convention 1999 (No 182)[108] also act to prohibit the sexual exploitation of children through prostitution, the production of pornography or pornographic performances. Article 16 of the UN Convention on the Rights of Persons with Disabilities requires State parties to take all appropriate legislative, administrative, social, educational and

---

under the age of 18 years, is delivered by either or both of his natural parents or by his guardian to another person, whether for reward or not, with a view to the exploitation of the child or young person or of his labour').

[102] Van Bueren, G *The International Law on the Rights of the Child* (1998) Martinus Nijhoff, p 279.

[103] The UK ratified the Optional Protocol on 29 February 2009.

[104] Newell, P and Hodgkin, R *Implementation Handbook for the Convention on the Rights of the Child* (2008) 3rd edn, UNICEF, pp 643–669. Article 11 of the Optional Protocol provides that 'Nothing in the present Protocol shall affect any provisions that are more conducive to the realisation of the rights of the child and that may be contained in (a) The law of a State Party; (b) International law in force for that State.'

[105] Human Rights Committee General Comment No 17 *Article 24 (Rights of the Child)* HRI/GEN/1/Rev 8, p 184, para 3. See also the UN Convention for the Suppression of the Traffic of Persons and of the Exploitation of the Prostitution of Others (GA Res 317(IV) 1949), Art 1 ('The Parties to the present Convention agree to punish any person who, to gratify the passions of another: (1) Procures, entices or leads away, for purposes of prostitution, another person, even with the consent of that person; (2) Exploits the prostitution of another person, even with the consent of that person') and Art 2 ('The Parties to the present Convention further agree to punish any person who: (1) Keeps or manages, or knowingly finances or takes part in the financing of a brothel; (2) Knowingly lets or rents a building or other place or any part thereof for the purpose of the prostitution of others'). See also discussion of the UN Convention against Transnational Organised Crime and the associated Protocol to Prevent, Suppress and Punish Trafficking in Persons, Especially Women and Children at **15.63** below.

[106] See also Committee on the Elimination of Discrimination against Women, General Recommendation No 19, 1991, HRI/GEN/1/ Rev.8, para 15.

[107] ILO Forced Labour Convention 1930 (No 29), Art 2 states that 'For the purposes of this Convention the term 'forced or compulsory labour' shall mean all work or service which is exacted from any person under the menace of any penalty and for which the said person has not offered himself voluntarily.'

[108] The ILO Worst Forms of Child Labour Convention 199 (No 182), Art 3(b) provides that 'For the purposes of this Convention, the term 'the worst forms of child labour' comprises: (b) the use, procuring or offering of a child for prostitution, for the production of pornography or for pornographic performances.'

other measures to protect persons with disabilities, both within and outside the home, from all forms of exploitation, violence and abuse, including their gender-based aspects.[109]

CRC, Art 34 – Ambit

(i)   CRC, Art 34 – 'Sexual Exploitation'

15.47   Neither the 1924 nor the 1959 Declarations on the Rights of the Child mention sexual exploitation explicitly. The 1997 Declaration and Agenda for Action of the World Congress against Commercial Sexual Exploitation of Children[110] defined commercial sexual exploitation of children as follows:

> '... commercial sexual exploitation of children ... comprises sexual abuse by the adult and remuneration in cash or kind to the child or to a third person or persons. The child is treated as a sexual object and as a commercial object. The commercial sexual exploitation of children constitutes a form of coercion and violence against children, and amounts to forced labour and a contemporary form of slavery.'

15.48   Van Bueren defines sexual exploitation as 'the use of children to meet the sexual needs of others at the expense of the children's emotional and physical needs' within a commercial context.[111] Article 34 of the CRC provides a list of specific aspects of sexual exploitation which States Parties to the CRC must prevent, namely the inducement or coercion of a child to engage in any unlawful sexual activity, the exploitative use of children in prostitution or other unlawful sexual practices and the exploitative use of children in pornographic performances and materials. Article 2 of the Optional Protocol to the Convention on the Rights of the Child on the Sale of Children, Child Prostitution and Child Pornography defines child prostitution as 'the use of a child in sexual activities for remuneration or any other form of consideration' and defines child pornography as 'any representation, by whatever means, of a child engaged in real or simulated explicit sexual activities or any representation of the sexual parts of a child for primarily sexual purposes'. Within the context of the definition of child prostitution, Art 3 of the Optional Protocol requires the criminalisation of the act of obtaining, procuring or providing a child for child prostitution.[112] Under Art 3 of the Optional Protocol, States Parties must ensure that the acts of producing, distributing, disseminating, importing, exporting, offering, selling or possessing child pornography are covered by the criminal and penal law.[113] The Optional Protocol further recognises that the sale of children may involve the offering, delivering or accepting, by whatever means, a child for the purposes of sexual exploitation.[114]

(ii)   CRC, Art 34 – 'Sexual Abuse'

15.49   There will obviously be an overlap between the terms 'sexual exploitation' and 'sexual abuse' in Art 34 of the CRC, with each term to an extent encompassing the

---

[109]   See also UN Standard Rules on the Equalisation of Opportunities for Persons with Disabilities, r 9(4) ('Persons with disabilities and their families need to be fully informed about taking precautions against sexual and other forms of abuse. Persons with disabilities are particularly vulnerable to abuse in the family, community or institutions and need to be educated on how to avoid the occurrence of abuse, recognise when abuse has occurred and report on such acts').

[110]   A/51/385, para 5.

[111]   Van Bueren, G *The International Law on the Rights of the Child* (1998) Martinus Nijhoff, p 275.

[112]   CRC, Art 3(1)(b).

[113]   CRC, Art 3(1)(c).

[114]   See Optional Protocol, Art 3(1)(a)(i)a.

other. Sexual abuse will include not only violent sexual assaults but other sexual activity, whether consensual or not, with children who are below the defined age of sexual consent.[115]

(iii)   CRC, Art 34 – 'All Appropriate National, Bilateral and Multilateral Measures'[116]

15.50 It is implicit in the use of the word 'appropriate' in Art 34 that the national, bilateral and multilateral measures adopted must be effective.[117] A key measure in preventing the activities prohibited by Art 34 of the CRC is the establishment of an appropriate age of consent to sexual activity. The Committee on the Rights of the Child is not prescriptive about the age of sexual consent but has stated that 12 years old is manifestly too low[118] and that 14 years old would give cause for concern.[119] Note that the protection afforded to children by Art 34 will extend to the age of 18 having regard to the definition of child in Art 1 of the CRC.[120] The required measures under Art 34 will also include the criminalisation of the use of child prostitutes and the possession of child pornography.[121]

15.51 The protection of children from sexual exploitation and abuse is closely linked with their protection from abduction, sale and trafficking[122] and with the protection of children within the context of armed conflict.[123] Refugee, unaccompanied and internally displaced children will be at high risk of sexual exploitation.[124] In relation to unaccompanied or separated children outside their country of origin, the Committee on the Rights of the Child has made clear that:[125]

---

[115] Newell, P and Hodgkin, R *Implementation Handbook for the Convention on the Rights of the Child* (2008) 3rd edn, UNICEF, p 257.

[116] See also CRC, Art 35 ('States Parties shall take all appropriate national, bilateral and multilateral measures to prevent the abduction of, the sale of or traffic in children for any purpose or in any form').

[117] For the measures contemplated see the Declaration from the First World Congress against Commercial Sexual Exploitation of Children Agenda for Action against Commercial Exploitation of Children (1996), paras 1–6.

[118] See Indonesia CRC/C/15/Add.233, para 81.

[119] See Iceland CRC/C/15/Add. 217, para 38.

[120] Newell, P and Hodgkin, R *Implementation Handbook for the Convention on the Rights of the Child* (2008) 3rd edn, UNICEF, p 523.

[121] See Finland CRC/C/15/Add. 53, para 19 and 29. See also the UN Convention for the Suppression of the Traffic in Persons and of the Exploitation of the Prostitution of Others 1949, Arts 1 and 2.

[122] CRC, Art 35. See **15.56** below.

[123] CRC, Art 38. See **15.91** below. See also *Impact of Armed Conflict on Children,* Report of the expert of the Secretary-General, Ms Graça Machel, 26 August 1996, A/51/306.

[124] See Sexual Violence against Refugees: Guidelines on Prevention and Response, UNHCR, 1995, preface and, para 1.2 and the Committee on the Rights of the Child General Comment No 6 *Treatment of Unaccompanied and Separated Children Outside their County of Origin* CRC/GC/2005/6, para 50. See also General Comment No 11 *Indigenous Children and their Rights under the Convention* CRC/C/GC/11, paras 72–73 ('Articles 34 and 35 of the [CRC] with consideration to the provisions of Art 20, call on States to ensure that children are protected against sexual exploitation and abuse as well as the abduction, sale or traffic of children for any purposes. The Committee is concerned that indigenous children whose communities are affected by poverty and urban migration are at a high risk of becoming victims of sexual exploitation and trafficking. Young girls, particularly those not registered at birth, are especially vulnerable. In order to improve the protection of all children, including indigenous, States parties are encouraged to ratify and implement the Optional Protocol on the sale of children, child prostitution and child pornography ... States should, in consultation with indigenous communities, including children, design preventive measures and allocate targeted financial and human resources for their implementation. States should base preventive measures on studies which include documentation of the patterns of violations and analysis of root causes').

[125] Committee on the Rights of the Child, General Comment No 6 *Treatment of Unaccompanied and Separated Children Outside their Country of Origin* CRC/GC/2005/6, paras 50 and 51.

'Articles 34 to 36 of the Convention must be read in conjunction with special protection and assistance obligations to be provided according to article 20 of the Convention, in order to ensure that unaccompanied and separated children are shielded from trafficking, and from sexual and other forms of exploitation, abuse and violence.'

15.52 The preamble to the Optional Protocol on the Sale of Children, Child Prostitution and Child Pornography notes the concern about the growing availability of child pornography on the internet and other evolving technologies. The use of information technology, and in particular the internet, constitutes a particular challenge to the implementation of effective national, bilateral and multilateral measures pursuant to CRC, Art 34 as well as underlining the need for a bilateral and multilateral approach. In his *World Report on Violence against Children*, Pinheiro notes that 'protecting children from the negative potential of technology is a serious challenge.' He identifies the need for an acute focus on prevention as an absolute imperative in addressing child safety within the context of information and communication technologies.[126] Thus, for the purposes of Art 34 'appropriate national, bilateral and multilateral measures' will include:[127]

'... cooperation between governments, intergovernmental organisations, the private sector and nongovernmental organisations to combat the criminal use of information technologies, including the Internet, for purposes of the sale of children, for child prostitution, child pornography, child sex tourism, paedophilia and other forms of violence and abuse against children and adolescents.'

(iv)   CRC, Art 34(a) – Inducement or Coercion of a Child to Engage in any Unlawful Sexual Activity

15.53 Article 34(a) of the CRC requires that States parties take all appropriate measures to prevent the inducement or coercion of a child to engage in any unlawful sexual activity. The prohibition on the inducement or coercion of a child to engage 'in any unlawful sexual activity' will encompass both sexual exploitation and sexual abuse.[128] Note that the use of the word 'unlawful' in Art 34(a) would appear to be otiose and unhelpful as the main body of Art 34 has the effect of prohibiting the use of children in *all* sexual practices which are exploitative, whether they are lawful or unlawful. Thus a sexual practice that is lawful but results in the exploitation of children will violate Art 34 of the CRC notwithstanding that the activity in question is legal. States Parties to the CRC are under a positive duty to take all appropriate measures to prevent both unlawful and exploitative sexual practices in respect of children.[129]

(v)   CRC, Art 34(b) – Exploitative use of Children in Prostitution or Other Unlawful Sexual Practices

15.54 Article 34(b) of the CRC requires States parties to take all appropriate measures to prevent the exploitative use of children in prostitution or other unlawful sexual practices. Prostitution can be defined as the 'enforced or voluntary hire or sale of sexuality by an individual to another individual for explicit material gain'.[130] Art 2 of the Optional Protocol to the Convention on the Rights of the Child on the Sale of

---

[126]   Pinheiro, P *World Report on Violence against Children*, United Nations, Geneva, 2006, pp 314 and 338.
[127]   Report of the Ad Hoc Committee of the Whole of the twenty-seventh special session of the General Assembly, 2002, A/S-27/19/Rev.1, paras 40–47.
[128]   Van Bueren, G *The International Law on the Rights of the Child* (1998) Martinus Nijhoff, p 276.
[129]   Van Bueren, G *The International Law on the Rights of the Child* (1998) Martinus Nijhoff, p 276.
[130]   Ennew, J *Children in Especially Difficult Circumstance: The Sexual Exploitation of Children; Prostitution and Pornography* (1985) Anti-Slavery Society.

Children, Child Prostitution and Child Pornography defines child prostitution as 'the use of a child in sexual activities for remuneration or any other form of consideration'. Within the context of the definition of child prostitution, Art 3 of the Optional Protocol requires the criminalisation of the act of obtaining, procuring or providing a child for child prostitution.[131] Once again, the use of the word 'other unlawful sexual practices' in Art 34(b) would appear to be otiose and unhelpful as the main body of Art 34 has the effect of prohibiting the use of children in *all* sexual practices which are exploitative, whether they are lawful or unlawful. Further, the term has the effect of also qualifying the word 'prostitution' in Art 34(b), implying that the use of children in lawful prostitution is not exploitative. This cannot have been what was intended.[132]

(vi) CRC, Art 34(c) – Exploitative use of Children in Pornographic Performances and Materials

15.55 Article 34(c) of the CRC requires States parties to take all appropriate measures to prevent the exploitative use of children in pornographic performances and materials. Article 2 of the Optional Protocol to the Convention on the Rights of the Child on the Sale of Children, Child Prostitution and Child Pornography defines child pornography as 'any representation, by whatever means, of a child engaged in real or simulated explicit sexual activities or any representation of the sexual parts of a child for primarily sexual purposes'. Under Art 3 of the Optional Protocol, States Parties must ensure that the acts of producing, distributing, disseminating, importing, exporting, offering, selling or possessing child pornography are covered by the criminal and penal law.[133] Again, the word 'exploitative' in Art 34(c) would appear otiose and unhelpful, implying as it does that provided the use of the child in pornographic performances or materials is not exploitative it does not come within the ambit of Art 34(c). Again, this cannot be what the drafters of the Convention intended.[134]

The Right to Freedom from Harmful Treatment under the CRC – CRC, Art 35 – Protection from Abduction, Sale and Trafficking

CRC, Art 35

15.56 Article 35 of the CRC provides as follows in respect of protecting children from abduction, sale and trafficking:

> 'States Parties shall take all appropriate national, bilateral and multilateral measures to prevent the abduction of, the sale of or traffic in children for any purpose or in any form.'[135]

CRC, Art 35 – Related Provisions

15.57 CRC, Art 35 is complimented by the Optional Protocol to the Convention on the Rights of the Child on the Sale of Children, Child Prostitution and Child

---

[131] CRC, Art 3(1)(b).
[132] See Van Bueren, G *The International Law on the Rights of the Child* (1998) Martinus Nijhoff, p 277.
[133] CRC, Art 3(1)(c).
[134] See Van Bueren, G *The International Law on the Rights of the Child* (1998) Martinus Nijhoff, p 277.
[135] See also CRC, Art 11 which concentrates on the transfer and non-return of children abroad, usually by relatives and not for profit. Article 11 provides: '1. States Parties shall take measures to combat the illicit transfer and non-return of children abroad. 2. To this end, States Parties shall promote the conclusion of bilateral or multilateral agreements or accession to existing agreements.' This provision is dealt with in detail at **8.94–8.95** above. The domestic courts have referred to Arts 11 and 35 of the CRC in the context of illegal adoptions (see *Northumberland County Council v Z and others* [2009] EWHC 498 (Fam), [2010] 1 FCR 494 and see also *Re S (Care: Jurisdiction)* [2008] EWHC 3013 (Fam), [2009] 2 FLR 550).

Pornography[136] which further defines and enhances the protection afforded by Art 35 of the CRC.[137] The Optional Protocol defines each of the terms contained in its title and places duties on States parties to criminalise and prosecute such conduct, during which prosecution children should be treated with humanity and with a view to their social rehabilitation.[138] Reference should also be made in the context of Art 35 of the CRC to the UN Convention for the Suppression of the Traffic of Persons and of the Exploitation of the Prostitution of Others[139] and the UN Convention against Transnational Organised Crime and its associated Protocol to Prevent, Suppress and Punish Trafficking in Persons, Especially Women and Children.

CRC, Art 35 – Ambit

15.58 In the context of the protections afforded by Art 21 of the CRC in respect of adoption for improper financial gain, Art 32 in respect of protection from exploitative or harmful work, Art 33 in respect of involvement in drug trafficking, Art 34 concerning sexual exploitation and Art 36 in respect of all other forms of exploitation, Art 35 has been described as a safety net to ensure that children are safe from being abducted or procured for these purposes or for any other purposes.[140] The words 'for any purpose or in any form' in Art 35 demonstrate that the protection from sale and trafficking of children contemplated by Art 35 is wider in scope than the protection afforded by Art 34 in relation specifically to forms of sexual exploitation.[141] Art 35 of the CRC was in particular designed to deal with the sale of children for adoption and reinforces the normative strength of Arts 19 and 20 of the UN Declaration of Social and Legal Principles Relating to Foster Placement and Adoption.[142] As such, Art 35 of the CRC must also be read with Hague Convention on International Cooperation and Protection of Children in Respect of Intercountry Adoption.[143]

15.59 The Optional Protocol to the Convention on the Rights of the Child on the Sale of Children, Child Prostitution and Child Pornography provides further provisions in respect of the sale of children which compliment the provisions of Art 35 of the CRC. Specifically, the provisions seek to ensure that any act or transaction whereby a child is transferred by any person or group of persons to another for remuneration or any other consideration should be made a criminal offence and be subject of penal sanction.[144]

---

[136] The UK ratified the Optional Protocol on 29 February 2009.

[137] See also the Supplementary Convention on the Abolition of Slavery, the Slave Trade and Practices Similar to Slavery 1956, Art 1(d) ('Each of the States Parties to this Convention shall take all practicable and necessary legislative and other measures to bring about progressively and as soon as possible the complete abolition or abandonment of the following institutions and practices, where they still exist and whether or not they are covered by the definition of slavery contained in article 1 of the Slavery Convention signed at Geneva on 25 September 1926: (d) Any institution or practice whereby a child or young person under the age of 18 years, is delivered by either or both of his natural parents or by his guardian to another person, whether for reward or not, with a view to the exploitation of the child or young person or of his labour').

[138] See also of the UN Guidelines for the Alternative Care of Children A/RES/64/142, para 93 ('All alternative care settings should provide adequate protection to children from abduction, trafficking, sale and all other forms of exploitation. Any consequent constraints on their liberty and conduct should be no more than are strictly necessary to ensure their effective protection from such acts').

[139] GA Res 317(IV).

[140] Newell, P and Hodgkin, R *Implementation Handbook for the Convention on the Rights of the Child* (2008) 3rd edn, UNICEF, p 531.

[141] See E/CN.4/1987/25, pp 15–24.

[142] Van Bueren, G *The International Law on the Rights of the Child* (1998) Martinus Nijhoff, p 281.

[143] See **15.138** below.

[144] Optional Protocol on the Sale of Children, Child Prostitution and Child Pornography, Art 3.

(i)   CRC, Art 35 – 'Abduction'

15.60   The word 'abduction' in Art 35 of the CRC is qualified by the words 'for any purpose'. Accordingly, the abduction of a child does not have to have a financial or commercial motive or involve remuneration to fall within the ambit of Art 35 of the CRC.[145]

(ii)   CRC, Art 35 – 'Sale'

15.61   The Optional Protocol to the Convention on the Rights of the Child on the Sale of Children, Child Prostitution and Child Pornography defines the sale of the children as any act or transaction whereby a child is transferred by any person or group of persons to another for remuneration or any other consideration.[146] Further guidance as to the meaning of 'sale' is given in Art 3 of the Optional Protocol. Article 3 provides that, as a minimum, State parties must, in the context of any act or transaction whereby a child is transferred by any person or group of persons to another for remuneration or any other consideration, criminalise the offering, delivering or accepting of a child for the purposes of the sexual exploitation of the child,[147] the transfer of organs of the child for profit[148] or the engagement of the child in forced labour[149] and the act of improperly inducing the consent, as an intermediary, for the adoption of a child.[150]

15.62   In relation to the issue of the trafficking of children's organs for profit, referenced should be made to the World Health Organisation's *Guiding Principles on Human Organ Transplantation*. Principle 4 provides that:

> 'No cells, tissues or organs should be removed from the body of a living minor for the purpose of transplantation other than narrow exceptions allowed under national law. Specific measures should be in place to protect the minor and, wherever possible the minor's assent should be obtained before donation. What is applicable to minors also applies to any legally incompetent person.'[151]

---

[145]   Newell, P and Hodgkin, R *Implementation Handbook for the Convention on the Rights of the Child* (2008) 3rd edn, UNICEF, p 533. See also see Art 3 of the Hague Convention on the Civil Aspects of International Child Abduction discussed at **15.138** below.

[146]   Optional Protocol on the Sale of Children, Child Prostitution and Child Pornography, Art 1(a).

[147]   CRC, Art 3(1)(a)(i)(a.). Note that Art 4 of the Optional Protocol deals with jurisdictional issues concerning the criminal actions stipulated in Arts 3, 5 and 6 deal with issues of extradition in respect of such offences. Article 7 requires the seizure of goods and proceeds and the closure of relevant premises relating to the commission of offences. Article 8 addresses the needs of child survivors of the offences described in the Optional Protocol. Article 9 imposes a positive obligation on States Parties to take proactive steps to prevent the sale of children, child prostitution and child pornography and Art 10 obligates States Parties to cooperate with each other in the prevention, detection, investigation prosecution and punishment of such offences.

[148]   CRC, Art 3(1)(a)(i)(b.). See also the Guiding Principles on Human Organ Transplantation (WHO) Principles 4 and 5 discussed at **15.62** below.

[149]   CRC, Art 3(1)(a)(i)(c.).

[150]   CRC, Art 3(1)(a)(ii). Note that Art 3(5) requires that 'States Parties shall take all appropriate legal and administrative measures to ensure that all persons involved in the adoption of a child act in conformity with applicable international legal instruments.'

[151]   See also Principle 5 ('Cells, tissues and organs should only be donated freely, without any monetary payment or other reward of monetary value. Purchasing, or offering to purchase, cells, tissues or organs for transplantation, or their sale by living persons or by the next of kin for deceased persons, should be banned. The prohibition on sale or purchase of cells, tissues and organs does not preclude reimbursing reasonable and verifiable expenses incurred by the donor, including loss of income, or paying the costs of recovering, processing, preserving and supplying human cells, tissues or organs for transplantation').

(ii)   CRC, Art 35 – 'Traffic'

15.63 Article 35 of the CRC prohibits trafficking both within one State or across borders.[152] Subject to Art 3(c), Art 3(a) of Protocol to the Prevent, Suppress and Punish Trafficking in Persons, Especially Women and Children, supplementing the UN Convention against Transnational Organised Crime defines 'trafficking in persons' as follows:

> '"Trafficking in persons" shall mean the recruitment, transportation, transfer, harbouring or receipt of persons, by means of the threat or use of force or other forms of coercion, of abduction, of fraud, of deception, of the abuse of power or of a position of vulnerability or of the giving or receiving of payments or benefits to achieve the consent of a person having control over another person, for the purposes of exploitation. Exploitation shall include, at a minimum, the exploitation of the prostitution of others or other forms of sexual exploitation, forced labour or services, slavery or practices similar to slavery, servitude or the removal of organs ... (c) The recruitment, transportation, transfer, harbouring or receipt of a child for the purpose of exploitation shall be considered 'trafficking in persons' even if this does not involve any of the means set forth in subparagraph (a) of this article.'[153]

15.64 It is important to note however that Art 3(c) of the Protocol to the Prevent, Suppress and Punish Trafficking in Persons, Especially Women and Children provides explicitly that the recruitment, transportation, transfer, harbouring or receipt of a child for the purpose of exploitation shall be considered 'trafficking in persons' even if this does not involve any of the means set forth in Art 3(a). Further, the consent of a victim of trafficking for the purposes of the intended forms of exploitation particularised in Art 3(a) of the Protocol to the Prevent, Suppress and Punish Trafficking in Persons, Especially Women and Children is irrelevant where any of the methods set out in Art 3(a) have been used.[154] In relation to the risk to unaccompanied and separated children of trafficking, the Committee on the Rights of the Child has stipulated that:

> 'Trafficking of such a child, or "re-trafficking" in cases where a child was already a victim of trafficking, is one of many dangers faced by unaccompanied or separated children. Trafficking in children is a threat to the fulfillment of their right to life, survival and development (art. 6). In accordance with article 35 of the Convention, States parties should take appropriate measures to prevent such trafficking. Necessary measures include identifying unaccompanied and separated children; regularly inquiring as to their whereabouts; and conducting information campaigns that are age-appropriate, gender-sensitive and in a language and medium that is understandable to the child. Adequate legislation should also be passed and effective mechanisms of enforcement be established with respect to labour regulations and border crossing.'[155]

(iv)   CRC, Art 35 – Treatment of Children who are Trafficked

15.65 No penalties should be imposed upon children who are the victims of trafficking even where they are in breach of immigration legislation. In particular, child victims of trafficking should neither be detained in police custody nor subjected to penalties for

---

[152]   Van Bueren, G *The International Law on the Rights of the Child* (1998) Martinus Nijhoff, p 281.

[153]   Note that pursuant to Art 6 of the Rome Statute of the International Criminal Court the forcible transferring of children of a national, ethnical, racial or religious group to another group with intent to destroy, in whole or in part, that national, ethnical, racial or religious group may constitute the crime of genocide.

[154]   Protocol to the Prevent, Suppress and Punish Trafficking in Persons, Especially Women and Children, Art 3(b).

[155]   Committee on the Rights of the Child General Comment No 6 *Treatment of Unaccompanied and Separated Children outside their Country of Origin* CRC/GC/2005/6, paras 52.

their involvement under compulsion in unlawful activities.[156] The Committee on the Rights of the Child has noted, in the context of unaccompanied and separated children, that:

> 'Risks are also great for a child who has already been a victim of trafficking, resulting in the status of being unaccompanied or separated. Such children should not be penalised and should receive assistance as victims of a serious human rights violation. Some trafficked children may be eligible for refugee status under the 1951 Convention, and States should ensure that separated and unaccompanied trafficked children who wish to seek asylum or in relation to whom there is otherwise indication that international protection needs exist, have access to asylum procedures. Children who are at risk of being re-trafficked should not be returned to their country of origin unless it is in their best interests and appropriate measures for their protection have been taken.[157] States should consider complementary forms of protection for trafficked children when return is not in their best interests.'[158]

15.66 The Protocol to the Prevent, Suppress and Punish Trafficking in Persons, Especially Women and Children stipulates that in appropriate cases and to the extent possible under its domestic law a State party shall protect the privacy and identity of victims of trafficking including making legal proceedings confidential,[159] as well as their physical safety.[160] Assistance must be given to victims of trafficking to provide them information concerning relevant court and administrative proceedings and to ensure that their views and concerns are presented in any criminal proceedings.[161] In providing assistance to child victims of trafficking, State parties must in particular of the special needs of children, including appropriate housing, education and care.[162] The domestic legal systems of State parties to the Protocol should contain measures to offer the victims of trafficking compensation for damage suffered.[163]

The Child's Right to Freedom from Harmful Treatment under the CRC – CRC, Art 33 – Protection from Harm by Narcotics

CRC, Art 33

15.67 Article 33 of the CRC provides as follows concerning the protection of children from harm caused by illicit narcotic drugs and psychotropic substances:

> 'States Parties shall take all appropriate measures, including legislative, administrative, social and educational measures, to protect children from the illicit use of narcotic drugs and psychotropic substances as defined in the relevant international treaties, and to prevent the use of children in the illicit production and trafficking of such substances.'

---

[156] UN Guidelines for the Alternative Care of Children A/RES/64/142, para 144.

[157] See also Protocol to the Prevent, Suppress and Punish Trafficking in Persons, Especially Women and Children, Art 8.

[158] Committee on the Rights of the Child General Comment No 6 *Treatment of Unaccompanied and Separated Children outside their Country of Origin* CRC/GC/2005/6, para 53.

[159] Protocol to the Prevent, Suppress and Punish Trafficking in Persons, Especially Women and Children, supplementing the UN Convention against Transnational Organised Crime, Art 6(1).

[160] Article 6(5).

[161] Article 6(2). Note that Art 12 of the CRC will apply in full to all children who are the victims of trafficking.

[162] Article 6(4). See also CRC, Art 22(1) ('States Parties shall take appropriate measures to ensure that a child who is seeking refugee status or who is considered a refugee in accordance with applicable international or domestic law and procedures shall, whether unaccompanied or accompanied by his or her parents or by any other person, receive appropriate protection and humanitarian assistance in the enjoyment of applicable rights set forth in the present Convention and in other international human rights or humanitarian instruments to which the said States are Parties').

[163] Article 6(6).

CRC, Art 33 – Ambit

(i) *'Illicit Narcotic Drugs and Psychotropic Substances'*

15.68 The illicit narcotic drugs and psychotropic substances covered by Art 33 are those defined as such by relevant international treaties. The key treaties defining illicit narcotic drugs and psychotropic substances are the Single Convention on Narcotic Drugs (1961) as amended by the 1972 Protocol and the Convention on Psychotropic Substances (1971). These Conventions categorise the following groups of illicit narcotics and psychotropic substances: (a) opiates, (b) products derived from the coca leaf, (c) cannabis products, (d) amphetamine type stimulants and (e) any other psychotropic or psychoactive drug capable of producing a state of dependence or the abuse of which could lead to public health problems warranting international control.

15.69 Note that whilst substances such as alcohol, tobacco and chemical solvents are often prohibited in respect of some or all children on the basis of minimum age requirements they are not the subject of the Single Convention on Narcotic Drugs (1961) as amended and accordingly do not come within the ambit of Art 33 of the CRC.[164] However, other articles of the CRC may be relevant in relation to these substances, such as the child's right to the highest attainable standard of health. The Committee on the Right of the Child notes that:[165]

> 'Adolescents have the right to access adequate information essential for their health and development and for their ability to participate meaningfully in society. It is the obligation of States parties to ensure that all adolescent girls and boys, both in and out of school, are provided with, and not denied, accurate and appropriate information on how to protect their health and development and practise healthy behaviours. This should include information on the use and abuse, of tobacco, alcohol and other substances, safe and respectful social and sexual behaviours, diet and physical activity.'

(ii) *'Use of Children in Illicit Production and Trafficking'*

15.70 The words 'the use of children in the illicit production and trafficking' refers to the use or employment of children in the illicit production and trafficking of illicit narcotic drugs and psychotropic substances. The ILO Worst Forms of Child Labour Convention (No 182) Art 3(c) provides that the term 'the worst forms of child labour' includes the use, procuring or offering of a child for illicit activities, in particular for the production and trafficking of drugs.

(iii) *'All Appropriate Measures'*

15.71 The use of the word 'including' after the term 'all appropriate measures' in Art 33 of the CRC indicates that legislative, administrative, social and educational measures are simply examples of the measures that States Parties should take to ensure the aims of Art 33 are met. Such measures should involve the use of mass media to assist in the prevention of substance abuse.[166] The measures taken under Art 33 are meant to be 'protective' rather than punitive. Custodial penalties on children for drug

---

[164] Newell, P and Hodgkin, R *Implementation Handbook for the Convention on the Rights of the Child* (2008) 3rd edn, UNICEF, p 503. But see Spain CRC/C/15/Add.185, para 38 (concerning alcohol and tobacco) and Finland CRC/C/15/add. 272, paras 38 and 39 (concerning the overuse of drugs to treat ADHD and ADD).

[165] Committee on the Right of the Child General Comment No 4 *Adolescent Health and Development in the Context of the Convention on the Rights of the Child* CRC/GC/2003/4, para 22. See also, paras 6, 19 and 21.

[166] See the UN Guidelines for the Prevention of Juvenile Delinquency (the 'Riyadh Guidelines'), para 44 ('The mass media should be aware of its extensive social role and responsibility, as well as its influence, in

use will not meet this imperative.[167] The obligation imposed on States parties to protect children under Art 33 will include taking measures to protect children from the effect of drug abuse by adults.[168] In its General Comment No 7 *Implementing Child Rights in Early Childhood*[169] the Committee on the Rights of the Child points out that:

'While very young children are only rarely likely to be substance abusers, they may require specialist health care if born to alcohol- or drug-addicted mothers, and protection where family members are abusers and they are at risk of exposure to drugs. They may also suffer adverse consequences of alcohol or drug abuse on family living standards and quality of care, as well as being at risk of early initiation into substance abuse.'

The Child's Right to Freedom from Harmful Treatment under the CRC – CRC, Art 32 – Protection from Economic Harm and Child Labour

CRC, Art 32

15.72 Article 32 of the CRC provides as follows in respect of the protection of children from economic exploitation and child labour:

'1. States Parties recognise the right of the child to be protected from economic exploitation and from performing any work that is likely to be hazardous or to interfere with the child's education, or to be harmful to the child's health or physical, mental, spiritual, moral or social development.

2. States Parties shall take legislative, administrative, social and educational measures to ensure the implementation of the present article. To this end, and having regard to the relevant provisions of other international instruments, States Parties shall in particular:

(a)   Provide for a minimum age or minimum ages for admission to employment;

(b)   Provide for appropriate regulation of the hours and conditions of employment;

(c)   Provide for appropriate penalties or other sanctions to ensure the effective enforcement of the present article.'

15.73 Article 32 of the CRC echoes the provisions of Arts 4 and 23 of the Universal Declaration of Human Rights[170] and Art 8 of the International Covenant on Civil and Political Rights.[171] Art 10(3) of the International Covenant on Economic, Social and Cultural Rights provides as follows:

communications relating to youthful drug and alcohol abuse. It should use its power for drug abuse prevention by relaying consistent messages through a balanced approach. Effective drug awareness campaigns at all levels should be promoted').

[167]   Newell, P and Hodgkin, R *Implementation Handbook for the Convention on the Rights of the Child* (2008) 3rd edn, UNICEF, p 508. See also UN Rules for the Protection of Juveniles Deprived of their Liberty, r 54 ('Juvenile detention facilities should adopt specialised drug abuse prevention and rehabilitation programmes administered by qualified personnel. These programmes should be adapted to the age, sex and other requirements of the juveniles concerned, and detoxification facilities and services staffed by trained personnel should be available to drug or alcohol dependent juveniles').

[168]   Newell, P and Hodgkin, R *Implementation Handbook for the Convention on the Rights of the Child* (2008) 3rd edn, UNICEF, p 506.

[169]   Committee on the Rights of the Child General Comment No 7 *Implementing Child Rights in Early Childhood* HRI/GEN/1/Rev 8, p 448, para 36(f).

[170]   Article 4 of the Universal Declaration of Human Rights provides that 'No one shall be held in slavery or servitude; slavery and the slave trade shall be prohibited in all their forms' and Art 23 provides that '1. Everyone has the right to work, to free choice of employment, to just and favourable conditions of work and to protection against unemployment. 2. Everyone, without any discrimination, has the right to equal pay for equal work. 3. Everyone who works has the right to just and favourable remuneration ensuring for himself

'Special measures of protection and assistance should be taken on behalf of all children and young persons without any discrimination for reasons of parentage or other conditions. Children and young persons should be protected from economic and social exploitation. Their employment in work harmful to their morals or health or dangerous to life or likely to hamper their normal development should be punishable by law. States should also set age limits below which the paid employment of child labour should be prohibited and punishable by law.'[172]

CRC, Art 32(1) – Ambit

15.74 The CRC is not designed to prohibit all work by children. Rather, the rights enshrined in Art 32 of the CRC are directed at preventing children from working in certain specified circumstances and to protecting children where they are doing work for which they are eligible.[173] Likewise, the international standards that compliment Art 32 of the CRC are designed to set parameters for distinguishing child labour that needs abolition on the one hand and acceptable work done by children, including such activities that allow children to acquire livelihood skills, identity and culture, on the other.[174]

15.75 As such, the generic term 'child labour'[175] does not encompass all work undertaken by children but rather that work which violates international standards.[176] Work which violates such international standards may affect children of any age and

---

and his family an existence worthy of human dignity, and supplemented, if necessary, by other means of social protection. 4. Everyone has the right to form and to join trade unions for the protection of his interests.'

[171] Article 8 of the ICCPR states that '1. No one shall be held in slavery; slavery and the slave-trade in all their forms shall be prohibited. 2. No one shall be held in servitude. 3. (a) No one shall be required to perform forced or compulsory labour; (b) Paragraph 3 (a) shall not be held to preclude, in countries where imprisonment with hard labour may be imposed as a punishment for a crime, the performance of hard labour in pursuance of a sentence to such punishment by a competent court; (c) For the purpose of this paragraph the term 'forced or compulsory labour' shall not include: (i) Any work or service, not referred to in subparagraph (b), normally required of a person who is under detention in consequence of a lawful order of a court, or of a person during conditional release from such detention; (ii) Any service of a military character and, in countries where conscientious objection is recognised, any national service required by law of conscientious objectors; (iii) Any service exacted in cases of emergency or calamity threatening the life or well-being of the community; (iv) Any work or service which forms part of normal civil obligations.'

[172] See Committee on Economic, Social and Cultural Rights General Comment No 13 HRI/GEN/1/Rev 8, p 82, para 55 ('States parties have an obligation to ensure that communities and families are not dependent on child labour'). See also the Committee on the Rights of the Child General Comment No 11 *Indigenous Children and their Rights under the Convention* CRC/C/GC/11, para 70 ('The Committee notes with grave concern that indigenous children are disproportionately affected by poverty and at particular risk of being used in child labour, especially its worst forms, such as slavery, bonded labour, child trafficking, including for domestic work, use in armed conflict, prostitution and hazardous work').

[173] Van Bueren, G *The International Law on the Rights of the Child* (1998) Martinus Nijhoff, p 263.

[174] General Comment No 11 *Indigenous Children and their Rights under the Convention* CRC/C/GC/11, para 69.

[175] See below at **15.80**.

[176] Newell, P and Hodgkin, R *Implementation Handbook for the Convention on the Rights of the Child* (2008) 3rd edn, UNICEF, p 480.

does not necessarily have to fall within the category of hazardous work or manual labour.[177] Within this context the Committee on the Rights of the Child has commented as follows:[178]

'During adolescence, an increasing number of young people are leaving school to start working to help support their families or for wages in the formal or informal sector. Participation in work activities in accordance with international standards, as long as it does not jeopardise the enjoyment of any of the other rights of adolescents, including health and education, may be beneficial for the development of the adolescent. The Committee urges States parties to take all necessary measures to abolish all forms of child labour, starting with the worst forms, to continuously review national regulations on minimum ages for employment with a view to making them compatible with international standards, and to regulate the working environment and conditions for adolescents who are working (in accordance with article 32 of the Convention, as well as ILO Conventions Nos. 138 and 182), so as to ensure that they are fully protected and have access to legal redress mechanisms.'

(i) CRC, Art 32 – 'Economic Exploitation'

'Exploitation'

15.76 The use of the term 'economic exploitation and from performing any work' in Art 32 of the CRC makes clear that the economic exploitation of children and work by children can be separate issues.[179] The Committee on the Rights of the Child in its *Report on the Fifth Session*[180] specifically identified as economically exploitative activities jeopardising the development of the child or contrary to human values and dignity; activities involving cruel, inhuman or degrading treatment, the sale of children or situations of servitude; activities that are dangerous or harmful to the child's harmonious physical, mental and spiritual development or are liable to jeopardise the future education and training of the child; activities involving discrimination, particularly with regard to vulnerable and marginalised social groups; all activities under the minimum ages referred to in Art 32(2) of the CRC and in particular those recommended by ILO and all activities using the child for legally punishable criminal acts, such as trafficking in drugs or prohibited goods. 'Exploitation' for the purposes of Art 32 of the CRC is not defined in terms of working hours or conditions and reference must be made to the ILO Minimum Age Convention (No 138) and ILO Recommendation 146 in this regard.[181] It has been held that working for less than the minimum wage prescribed by statute can constitute a form of forced service.[182]

---

[177] See Committee on the Rights of the Child General Comment No 7 *Implementing Child Rights in Early Childhood* HRI/GEN/1/Rev 8, para 36(e) ('young children may be initiated into domestic work or agricultural labour, or assist parents or siblings engaged in hazardous activities. Even very young babies may be vulnerable to economic exploitation, as when they are used or hired out for begging. Exploitation of young children in the entertainment industry, including television, film, advertising and other modern media, is also a cause for concern'). See also Committee on the Rights of the Child General Comment No 9 *The Rights of Children with Disabilities* CRC/C/GC/9, para 75.

[178] Child General Comment No 4 *Adolescent health and development in the context of the Convention on the Rights of the Child* CRC/GC/2003/4, paras 18. See also para 36(e).

[179] Van Bueren, G *The International Law on the Rights of the Child* (1998) Martinus Nijhoff, p 264.

[180] (1994) CRC/C/24, p 42.

[181] See **15.84** below for detailed discussion of these provisions.

[182] *People's Union for Democratic Rights v Union* (1982) 1 SCR 546 Supreme Court of India.

Relationship with Art 37(a) of the CRC

15.77 Where conditions of economic exploitation amount to cruel and degrading treatment for the purposes of Art 37(a) of the CRC the responsibility of State parties becomes one of immediate abolition irrespective of the extent of the developmental progress of the State in question.[183]

Slavery

15.78 Slavery is the most extreme form of the economic exploitation of children. The right not to be enslaved is one of the oldest internationally recognised human rights.[184] Slavery is defined by Art 1 of Slavery Convention 1926 as 'the status or condition of a person over whom any or all of the powers attaching to the right of ownership are exercised' and the slave trade as including 'all acts involved in the capture, acquisition or disposal of a person with intent to reduce him to slavery; all acts involved in the acquisition of a slave with a view to selling or exchanging him; all acts of disposal by sale or exchange of a slave acquired with a view to being sold or exchanged, and, in general, every act of trade or transport in slaves'. Slavery and the slave trade are outlawed by Art 4 Universal Declaration of Human Rights[185] and Art 8 of the ICCPR.[186] The prohibition on slavery and the slave trade is also a norm of *jus cogens*.[187] Enslavement committed as part of a widespread or systematic attack directed against any civilian population, with knowledge of the attack constitutes a crime against humanity for the purposes of Art 7 of the Rome Statute of the International Criminal Court.[188]

15.79 Pursuant to Art 1 of the Supplementary Convention on the Abolition of the Slavery, the Slave Trade and Institutions and Practices Similar to Slavery practices similar to slavery are also prohibited absolutely including debt bondage,[189] serfdom,[190] any institution or practice whereby a woman, without the right to refuse, is promised or given in marriage on payment of a consideration in money or in kind to her parents, guardian, family or any other person or group; or the husband of a woman, his family, or his clan, has the right to transfer her to another person for value received or otherwise; or a woman on the death of her husband is liable to be inherited by another

---

[183]   Van Bueren, G *The International Law on the Rights of the Child* (1998) Martinus Nijhoff, p 263.

[184]   Lord Lester QC, Lord Pannick QC and Herberg, J *Human Rights Law and Practice* (2009) 3rd edn, LexisNexis, p 217.

[185]   Article 4 provides that 'No one shall be held in slavery or servitude; slavery and the slave trade shall be prohibited in all their forms.'

[186]   Article 8 provides, inter alia, that '1. No one shall be held in slavery; slavery and the slave-trade in all their forms shall be prohibited. 2. No one shall be held in servitude.'

[187]   See the *Barcelona Traction Case* (Second Phase) ICJ Reports 3 at 32. See also Restatement of the Law, 3rd Restatement of the Foreign Relations Law of the United States 702(b).

[188]   Article 7 defines 'enslavement' as 'the exercise of any or all of the powers attaching to the right of ownership over a person and includes the exercise of such power in the course of trafficking in persons, in particular women and children.'

[189]   Being the status or condition arising from a pledge by a debtor of his personal services or of those of a person under his control as security for a debt, if the value of those services as reasonably assessed is not applied towards the liquidation of the debt or the length and nature of those services are not respectively limited and defined (Supplementary Convention on the Abolition of the Slavery, the Slave Trade an Institutions and Practices Similar to Slavery Art 1(a)). This may include 'family bondage' where children are required to work to help pay off a loan or other obligation incurred by the family (*Child Labour: Targeting the Intolerable* International Labour Conference, Eight-sixth Session (1998) ILO, p 13).

[190]   Being the condition or status of a tenant who is by law, custom or agreement bound to live and labour on land belonging to another person and to render some determinate service to such other person, whether for reward or not, and is not free to change his status (Supplementary Convention on the Abolition of the Slavery, the Slave Trade an Institutions and Practices Similar to Slavery, Art 1(b)).

person[191] and any institution or practice whereby a child or young person under the age of 18 years is delivered by either or both of his natural parents or by his guardian to another person, whether for reward or not, with a view to the exploitation of the child or young person or of his labour.[192] The ILO Convention (No 29) on Forced or Compulsory Labour Art 1 prohibits forced compulsory labour.[193]

(ii)   CRC, Art 32(1) – 'Work'

'Child Labour'

15.80   Article 32(1) of the CRC requires that the child be protected from 'work which is likely to be hazardous or to interfere with the child's education,[194] or to be harmful to the child's health or physical, mental, spiritual, moral or social development'. Whilst the word 'work' is used in Art 32(1) of the CRC, the other international instruments dealing this issue tend to use the term 'child labour' which term has attained common usage as a shorthand description of work likely to be hazardous or harmful to the child. As such, the definition of the term 'child labour' provides further assistance as to the forms of work in respect of which protection under Art 32(1) of the CRC will apply.

15.81   The term 'child labour' covers many diverse situations.[195] Fyfe divides child labour into five categories, namely domestic, non-domestic, non-monetary, bonded labour, wage labour and marginal economic activity.[196] In *A Future without Child Labour – Global Report under the Follow-up to the ILO Declaration on Fundamental Principles and Rights at Work*[197] child labour is defined as that which violates international standards as labour performed by a child who is under a minimum age specified in national legislation in line with international standards for that kind of work, labour that jeopardises the physical, mental and moral wellbeing of the child (known as hazardous work) and the unconditional worst forms of child labour[198]

---

[191]   Supplementary Convention on the Abolition of the Slavery, the Slave Trade an Institutions and Practices Similar to Slavery, Art 1(c).

[192]   Supplementary Convention on the Abolition of the Slavery, the Slave Trade an Institutions and Practices Similar to Slavery, Art 1(d).

[193]   Being all work or service which is exacted from any person under the menace of any penalty and for which the said person has not offered himself voluntarily (ILO Convention (No 29) on Forced or Compulsory Labour, Art 2(1)). See also ILO Convention (No 29) on Forced or Compulsory Labour, Art 2(2) for the exceptions to this definition.

[194]   In respect of interference with the child's education Art 32(1) should be read with Art 28 of the CRC and the Preamble to the Worst Forms of Child Labour Convention 1999 (No 182) ('Considering that the effective elimination of the worst forms of child labour requires immediate and comprehensive action, taking into account the importance of free basic education and the need to remove the children concerned from all such work and to provide for their rehabilitation and social integration while addressing the needs of their families').

[195]   Francis Blanchard, former Director General of the ILO observed that 'This what child labour is: *not* teenagers working a few hours a week for pocket money; *not* youngsters who help out at home; *not* children on farms who lend a helping hand; but children who, at an early age, lead the life of an adult, working long hours for a pittance in circumstances which can damage their health, and their physical and mental development, children who are often denied any opportunity of meaningful education an training, which might lead to a better future for them' (cited in Verhellen, E *Convention on the Rights of the Child* (2000) Garant, p 116).

[196]   Fyfe, A *Child Labour* (1989) Polity, p 73.

[197]   The Report of the Director General *A Future without Child Labour – Global Report under the Follow-up to the ILO Declaration on Fundamental Principles and Rights at Work* International Labour Conference, Ninetieth Session (2002) Report I(B) Executive Summary, p X.

[198]   Being those forms of child labour which in all cases represent extreme violations of children's rights (Newell, P and Hodgkin, R *Implementation Handbook for the Convention on the Rights of the Child* (2008) 3rd edn, UNICEF, p 481).

defined by international standards as slavery,[199] trafficking, debt bondage, forced recruitment for use in armed conflict, prostitution and pornography and illicit activities. In line with the absolute prohibition on corporal punishment the use of corporal punishment on children in the workplace is unlawful.[200]

Hazardous Work

15.82 Hazards to children engaged in work can relate to the nature of the work itself such as intrinsically hazardous processes, exposure to hazardous substances and agents or the exposure of the child to poor or dangerous working conditions.[201] Work that is not hazardous for adults may be hazardous for children by reason of their different anatomical, physiological and psychological characteristics, which may make them more susceptible to harm arising out of occupational hazards.[202]

CRC, Art 32(2) – Ambit

15.83 Article 32(2) of the CRC provides as follows in respect of the legislative, administrative, social and educational measures that must be taken by States parties to ensure the implementation of the prohibitions on economic exploitation and hazardous or harmful work enshrined in Art 32(1):

> 2. States Parties shall take legislative, administrative, social and educational measures to ensure the implementation of the present article. To this end, and having regard to the relevant provisions of other international instruments, States Parties shall in particular:
>
> (a)   Provide for a minimum age or minimum ages for admission to employment;
> (b)   Provide for appropriate regulation of the hours and conditions of employment;
> (c)   Provide for appropriate penalties or other sanctions to ensure the effective enforcement of the present article.'

(i)   CRC, Art 32(2) – 'Relevant Provisions of other International Instruments'

15.84 The term 'relevant provisions of other international instruments' in Art 32(2) will encompass the International Labour Organisation (ILO) Conventions and Recommendations and in particular the ILO Minimum Age Convention 1973 (No 138) read with ILO Recommendation (No 146) and the Worst Forms of Child Labour Convention 1999 (No 182) read with the Worst Forms of Child Labour Recommendation (No 190). The ILO Minimum Age Convention consolidates principles established in earlier instruments[203] and will apply to all sectors of economic activity in which children are

---

[199]   See also the Supplementary Convention on the Abolition of Slavery, the Slave Trade and Institutions and Practices Similar to Slavery 1956, Art 1(d) which provides the definition of slavery and practices similar to slavery in relation to children as 'Any institution or practice whereby a child or young person under the age of 18 is delivered by either or both of his natural parents or by his guardian to another person, whether for reward or not, with a view to the exploitation of the child or young person or of his labour.'

[200]   Committee on the Rights of the Child General Comment No 8 CRC/C/GC/8, paras 35 and 36. See also the *Report of the Independent Expert for the United Nations Study on Violence Against Children* General Assembly (2006) A/61/299, paras 64–68.

[201]   *Child Labour: Targeting the Intolerable* International Labour Conference, Eighty-sixth Session (1998) ILO, p 9.

[202]   *Child Labour: Targeting the Intolerable* International Labour Conference, Eighty-sixth Session (1998) ILO, p 9.

[203]   See also the Minimum Age (Industry) Convention 1919 (No 5) and the Minimum Age (Industry) Convention (Revised) 1937 (No 59), the Night Work of Young Persons (Industry) Convention 1919 (No 6) and the Night Work of Young Persons (Industry) Convention (Revised) 1948 (No 90), the Minimum Age (Sea) Convention 1920 (No 7) and the Minimum Age (Sea) Convention (Revised) 1936 (No 58), the Minimum Age (Agriculture) Convention 1921 (No 10), the Minimum Age (Trimmers and Stokers)

involved. Regard must also be had to the provisions of the ICESCR, the ICCPR, the Supplementary Convention on the Abolition of Slavery, the Slave Trade, and Institutions and Practices Similar to Slavery and to the Convention for the Suppression of the Traffic in Persons and of the Exploitation of the Prostitution of Others. Finally, both Optional Protocols to the CRC, in addressing the sale of children, child prostitution and child pornography[204] and the involvement of children in armed conflict[205] respectively both contain principles relevant to the protection of children from the worst forms of child labour.

(ii)   CRC, Art 32(2)(a) – 'Minimum Age or Minimum Ages'

15.85 Article 32(2)(a) of the CRC requires that a minimum age for admission to employment be set but does not define a minimum age. The minimum ages for the purposes of Art 32(2)(a) will thus be determined by reference to the ILO Minimum Age Convention 1973 (No 138) and the ILO Recommendation 146. The Minimum Age Convention Art 2(3) requires that the minimum age for admission to employment or work in any occupation shall not be less than the age of completion of compulsory schooling and, in any case, shall not be less than 15 years of age.[206] The provisions of Art 2(3) governing the minimum age for admission into employment must be read in the context of the general duty placed on States parties to the ILO Minimum Age Convention to raise progressively the minimum age for admission to employment or work to a level consistent with the fullest physical and mental development of young persons.[207] Note that the ILO Recommendation No 146 recommends that all States parties take as their objective the progressive raising to 16 years of the minimum age for admission to employment or work.[208] National laws and regulations may permit the employment or work of children aged 13 to 15 in 'light work' provided that such work is

---

Convention 1921 (No 15), the Forced Labour Convention 1930 (No 29), the Minimum Age (Non-Industrial Employment) Convention 1923 (No 33) and the Minimum Age (Non-Industrial Employment Convention (Revised) 1937 (No 60), the Medical Examination of Young Persons (Industry) Convention 1946 (No 77), the Medical Examination of Young Persons (Non-Industrial Occupations) Convention 1946 (No 78), the Nigh Work of Young Persons (Non-Industrial Occupations) Convention 1946 (No 79), the Minimum Age (Fisherman) Convention 1959 (No 112), the Minimum Age (Underground Work) Convention 1965 (No 132) and the Medical Examination of Young Persons (Underground Work) Convention 1965 (No 124).

[204] Optional Protocol to the Convention on the Rights of the Child on the Sale of Children, Child Prostitution and Child Pornography. See **15.57** above. See also the International Convention for the Suppression of the Traffic in Women and Children 1921 as amended by the Protocol, the Convention for the Suppression of the Traffic in Persons and of the Exploitation of the Prostitution of Others 1949 (GA Res 317(IV)) and the UN Convention Against Trans-national Organised Crime 2000 and its Protocol to Prevent, Suppress and Punish Trafficking in Persons, Especially Women and Children.

[205] Optional Protocol to the Convention on the Rights of the Child on the Involvement of Children in Armed Conflict. See **15.96** below.

[206] Note also the provisions of Art 2(4) which provides that 'Notwithstanding the provisions of paragraph 3 of this Article, a Member whose economy and educational facilities are insufficiently developed may, after consultation with the organisations of employers and workers concerned, where such exist, initially specify a minimum age of 14 years' and the exceptions provided in Art 6 ('This Convention does not apply to work done by children and young persons in schools for general, vocational or technical education or in other training institutions, or to work done by persons at least 14 years of age in undertakings, where such work is carried out in accordance with conditions prescribed by the competent authority, after consultation with the organisations of employers and workers concerned, where such exist, and is an integral part of (a) a course of education or training for which a school or training institution is primarily responsible; (b) a programme of training mainly or entirely in an undertaking, which programme has been approved by the competent authority; or (c) a programme of guidance or orientation designed to facilitate the choice of an occupation or of a line of training'). Exceptions may also be granted for such purposes as participation in artistic performances provided that such exceptions limit the number of hours during which and prescribe the conditions in which such employment or work is allowed (see ILO Minimum Age Convention (No 138) 1973, Art 8).

[207] ILO Minimum Age Convention (No 138) 1973, Art 1.

[208] ILO Recommendation No 146, Art 7(1).

not likely to be harmful to their health or development and will not prejudice their attendance at school, their participation in vocational orientation or training or their capacity to benefit from the instruction received.[209] Such work may also be done by children aged 15 who have not completed their compulsory education.[210] Van Bueren suggests that 'light work' comprises two categories, namely the assistance by the child in the family economy and the engagement of children in work outside schools hours to earn extra money or gain experience.[211]

15.86 In relation to any type of employment or work which by its nature or the circumstances in which it is carried out[212] is likely to jeopardise the health, safety or morals of children and young people the minimum age for admission to such employment is set by Art 3(1) of the ILO Minimum Age Convention at 18. Article 32(2) of the CRC imposes a positive duty on States parties to ensure that social pressures will not give rise to *de facto* situation in which children below the statutory minimum age will be vulnerable to economic exploitation or the need to work in a manner prohibited by the Convention.[213]

(iii)   CRC, Art 32(2)(b) – 'Regulation of Hours and Conditions'

Hours of Work

15.87 Where children are permitted to work, Art 32(2)(b) of the CRC requires that such work be subject to detailed regulation in respect of the hours worked and the conditions of work. In relation to the regulation of hours of work, international law does not define a minimum number of hours it is permissible for a child who meets the age requirements of international law to work. However, the ILO Recommendation No 146 does stipulate that special attention should be given to the strict limitation of the hours spent at work in a day and in a week, and the prohibition of overtime, so as to allow enough time for education and training, including the time needed for homework, enough time for rest during the day and for leisure activities, the granting, without possibility of exception save in genuine emergency, of a minimum consecutive period of 12 hours night rest, and of customary weekly rest days and the granting of an annual holiday with pay of at least 4 weeks and, in any case, not shorter than that granted to adults.[214] The emphasis on protecting the child's education in Art 32(1) of the CRC further implies that any working hours should not obstruct the child's school day or other educational provision. The ILO Conventions prohibit the involvement of children in night work in certain occupations.[215]

Conditions of Work

15.88 Article 12(1) of the ILO Recommendation No 146 provides that measures should be taken to ensure that the conditions in which children and young persons under the age of 18 years are employed or work reach and are maintained at a satisfactory

---

[209]   ILO Minimum Age Convention (No 138) 1973, Art 7(1).
[210]   ILO Minimum Age Convention (No 138) 1973, Art 7(2).
[211]   Van Bueren, G *The International Law on the Rights of the Child* (1998) Martinus Nijhoff, p 267.
[212]   See also ILO Recommendation No 146 Art 10(1) ('In determining the types of employment or work to which Article 3 of the Minimum Age Convention, 1973, applies, full account should be taken of relevant international labour standards, such as those concerning dangerous substances, agents or processes (including ionising radiations), the lifting of heavy weights and underground work').
[213]   Van Bueren, G *The International Law on the Rights of the Child* (1998) Martinus Nijhoff, p 269.
[214]   ILO Recommendation No 146, Art 13(1).
[215]   See the Night Work of Young Persons (Industry) Convention 1919 (No 6), Art 1 the Night Work of Young Persons (Industry) Convention (Revised) 1948 (No 90) and the Nigh Work of Young Persons (Non-Industrial Occupations) Convention 1946 (No 79).

standard with those conditions being supervised closely. Article 12(2) requires that measures should likewise be taken to safeguard and supervise the conditions in which children and young persons undergo vocational orientation and training within undertakings, training institutions and schools for vocational or technical education and to formulate standards for their protection and development. Further, the ILO provides three categories of Conventions concerning the conditions in which children work, namely (i) those which prohibit the involvement of children in certain occupations at night,[216] (ii) those which require the medical examination of children to establish fitness to work[217] and (iii) those which prohibit children from specific dangerous occupations.[218] It is essential that the prohibition of corporal punishment and other cruel or degrading forms of punishment be enforced in any situations in which children are working.[219]

15.89 The foregoing provisions will also apply to children deprived of their liberty.[220] In addition, the UN Rules for the Protection of Children Deprived of their Liberty provide further safeguards concerning work undertaken by children whilst detained. Rule 18(b) of the UN Rules for the Protection of Children Deprived of their Liberty requires that all juveniles should be provided, where possible, with opportunities to pursue work, with remuneration, and continue education or training, but should not be required to do so. Such work, education or training should not cause the continuation of the detention beyond the original sentence. Rule 45 provides that:

> 'Wherever possible, juveniles should be provided with the opportunity to perform remunerated labour, if possible within the local community, as a complement to the vocational training provided in order to enhance the possibility of finding suitable employment when they return to their communities. The type of work should be such as to provide appropriate training that will be of benefit to the juveniles following release. The organisation and methods of work offered in detention facilities should resemble as closely as possible those of similar work in the community, so as to prepare juveniles for the conditions of normal occupational life.'[221]

(iv)   CRC, Art 32(2)(c) – 'Appropriate Penalties and Sanctions'

15.90 Article 32(2)(c) does not define what appropriate penalties and sanctions must be implemented by States parties beyond providing that they must ensure the effective

---

[216] The Night Work of Young Persons (Industry) Convention 1919 (No 6), Art 1 the Night Work of Young Persons (Industry) Convention (Revised) 1948 (No 90) and the Night Work of Young Persons (Non-Industrial Occupations) Convention 1946 (No 79).

[217] The Medical Examination of Young Persons (Industry) Convention 1946 (No 77), the Medical Examination of Young Persons (Non-Industrial Occupations) Convention 1946 (No 78) and the Examination of Young Persons (Underground Work) Convention 1965 (No 124).

[218] The Minimum Age (Industry) Convention (Revised) 1937 (No 59), the Minimum Age (Sea) Convention (Revised) 1936 (No 58), the Forced Labour Convention 1930 (No 29), the Minimum Age (Non-Industrial Employment) Convention 1923 (No 33) and the Minimum Age (Non-Industrial Employment Convention (Revised) 1937 (No 60), the Minimum Age (Fisherman) Convention 1959 (No 112) and the Minimum Age (Underground Work) Convention 1965 (No 132).

[219] Committee on the Rights of the Child General Comment No 8 *The Right of the Child to Protection from Corporal Punishment and Other Cruel or Degrading Forms of Punishment* CRC/C/GC/8, p 9, para 36.

[220] UN Rules for the Protection of Children Deprived of their Liberty, r 44.

[221] See also UN Rules for the Protection of Children Deprived of their Liberty, r 46 ('Every juvenile who performs work should have the right to an equitable remuneration. The interests of the juveniles and of their vocational training should not be subordinated to the purpose of making a profit for the detention facility or a third party. Part of the earnings of a juvenile should normally be set aside to constitute a savings fund to be handed over to the juvenile on release. The juvenile should have the right to use the remainder of those earnings to purchase articles for his or her own use or to indemnify the victim injured by his or her offence or to send it to his or her family or other persons outside the detention facility').

enforcement of Art 32. The ILO Minimum Age Convention 1973 (No 138) Art 9 stipulates that all necessary measures, including the provision of appropriate penalties, shall be taken by the competent authority to ensure the effective enforcement of the provisions of the Convention and that national laws or regulations or the competent authority shall define the persons responsible for compliance with the provisions giving effect to the Convention. This will include stipulating the registers or other documents which shall be kept and made available by the employer, which registers or documents must contain the names and ages or dates of birth, duly certified wherever possible, of persons employed or working who are less than 18 years of age.[222] The ILO Worst Forms of Child Labour Convention (No 182) 1999 Art 7 requires State parties to take all necessary measures to ensure the effective implementation and enforcement of the provisions giving effect to the Convention including the taking of effective and time limited measures to prevent the engagement of children in the worst forms of child labour, to ensure the provision of the necessary and appropriate direct assistance for the removal of children from the worst forms of child labour and for their rehabilitation and social integration, to ensure access to free basic education and, wherever possible and appropriate, vocational training for all children removed from the worst forms of child labour, to identify and reach out to children at special risk and to take account of the special situation of girls.

The Child's Right to Freedom from Harmful Treatment under the CRC – CRC, Art 38 – Protection from Involvement in Armed Conflict

CRC, Art 38

15.91 Article 38 of the CRC[223] stipulates as follows in respect of the measures required of States Parties to protect children from involvement in armed conflict:

> '1. States Parties undertake to respect and to ensure respect for rules of international humanitarian law applicable to them in armed conflicts which are relevant to the child.
>
> 2. States Parties shall take all feasible measures to ensure that persons who have not attained the age of fifteen years do not take a direct part in hostilities.
>
> 3. States Parties shall refrain from recruiting any person who has not attained the age of fifteen years into their armed forces. In recruiting among those persons who have attained the age of fifteen years but who have not attained the age of eighteen years, States Parties shall endeavour to give priority to those who are oldest.
>
> 4. In accordance with their obligations under international humanitarian law to protect the civilian population in armed conflicts, States Parties shall take all feasible measures to ensure protection and care of children who are affected by an armed conflict.'

---

[222] See also ILO Recommendation No 146 Art 14 and *Child Labour: Targeting the Intolerable* International Labour Conference, Eighty-sixth Session (1998) ILO, pp 40–49.

[223] Note that the drafting and agreement of Art 38 of the CRC was considered by some to be the result of an entirely unsatisfactory process (see E/CN.4/1989/48, pp 110–116 and E/CN.4/1989/48, pp 50–58 and Detrick, S *The United Nations Convention on the Rights of the Child: A Guide to the Travaux Préparatoires* (1992) Martinus Nijhoff, pp 512 and 630. See also Van Bueren, G *The International Law on the Rights of the Child* (1998) Martinus Nijhoff, p 339).

CRC, Art 38(1) – Ambit

(i) 'Respect for International Humanitarian Law'

15.92 Armed conflict does not take place in a normative void but in accordance with rules of international humanitarian law.[224] The Committee on the Rights of the Child has defined 'rules of international humanitarian law' for the purposes of Art 38 of the CRC as including[225] the four Geneva Conventions and additional protocols thereto,[226] the Declaration on the Protection of Women and Children in Emergency and Armed Conflict,[227] the Declaration on the Rights of the Child and the CRC generally.[228] In addition, Art 38(1) of the CRC is supplemented by the Optional Protocol to the Convention on the Rights of the Child on the Involvement of Children in Armed Conflict which has the effect of amending Art 38 in relation to the minimum age for the involvement in armed conflict and for the recruitment into armed forces and armed groups.[229] Further, regard must be had to the United Nations Children's Fund (UNICEF) Paris Commitments to Protect Children from Unlawful Recruitment or use by Armed Forces or Armed Groups,[230] which prescribes a number of measures designed to prevent unlawful recruitment of children and to mitigate the impact of such recruitment where it has taken place, and the UNICEF Principles and Guidelines on Children Associated with Armed Forces or Armed Groups (the 'Paris Principles'),[231] which provide highly detailed guidance on protecting children from recruitment by, and on providing assistance to those children involved in, armed groups and military forces. Note that the Committee on the Rights of the Child has made clear that the principles of the CRC are not to be the subject of derogation during times of armed conflict.[232] Finally, the Rome Statute of the International Criminal Court 1998, the ILO Convention on the Worst Forms of Child Labour (No 182) Art 32, the Red Cross Resolution on Protection of Children in Armed Conflicts (1986), the Red Cross Resolution on Assistance to Children in Emergency Situations (1986) and Security Council Resolutions 1261 (1999), 1314 (2001), 1379 (2001), 1460 (2003), 1539 (2004) and 1612 (2006) will also be relevant.[233]

---

[224] HCJ 1730/96 *Sabih v The Commander of IDF Forces in the Judea and Samaria Area* 50(1) PD 353, 369 (Israeli Supreme Court).

[225] Committee on the Rights of the Child *Report of the Second Session: September/October 1992* CRC/C/10, para 65. Note that the International Committee of the Red Cross, the International Federation of Red Cross and Red Crescent Societies and the National Red Cross and Red Crescent Societies have adopted the following definition of international humanitarian law, namely the 'international rules, established by treaties or custom, which are specifically intended to solve humanitarian problems directly arising from international or non-international armed conflicts and which, for humanitarian reasons, limit the right of parties to a conflict to use the methods and means of warfare of their choice or protect persons and property that are, or may be, affected by conflict' (see Machal, G *Impact of Armed Conflict on Children* (1996) A/51/306, para 211 n.40).

[226] See **15.121–15.137** below.

[227] GA Resolution 3318 (XXIX).

[228] See for example Committee on the Rights of the Child General Comment No 1 CRC/GC/2001/1, para 16 on the role of education in conflict resolution and General Comment No 11 *Indigenous Children and their Rights under the Convention* CRC/C/GC/11, paras 64–68 on the effect of hostilities on indigenous children.

[229] See **15.96** below.

[230] UNICEF (February 2007).

[231] UNICEF (February 2007).

[232] Newell, P and Hodgkin, R *Implementation Handbook for the Convention on the Rights of the Child* (2008) 3rd edn, UNICEF, p 573.

[233] Regard must also be had to the 'traditional norms' of war adopted by belligerents as 'time honoured taboos' (see Report of the Special Representative to the Secretary General on Children and Armed Conflict to the Commission on Human Rights (2005) E/CN.4/2005.77, para 18).

CRC, Art 38(2) – Ambit

(i) Minimum Age for Participation in Hostilities

15.93 Article 38(2) of the CRC provides as follows in respect of the minimum age for the *participation* by children in hostilities:

> '2. States Parties shall take all feasible measures to ensure that persons who have not attained the age of fifteen years do not take a direct part in hostilities.'

Article 32(2) must be read with Art 1 of the Optional Protocol to the Convention on the Rights of the Child on the Involvement of Children in Armed Conflict which provides that 'States Parties shall take all feasible measures to ensure that members of their armed forces who have not attained the age of 18 years do not take a direct part in hostilities' and Art 4(1) which states that 'Armed groups that are distinct from the armed forces of a State should not, under any circumstances, recruit or use in hostilities persons under the age of 18 years'. Thus, pursuant to Art 38(2) no child under the age of 15 years may take direct part in hostilities.[234] Where a child over the age of 15 is a member of the armed forces or an armed group, that child should not take a direct part in hostilities where they have not attained the age of 18 pursuant to Art 1 of the Optional Protocol. It will be noted that these provisions leave a lacuna in respect of children who are aged between 15 and 18 and not a member of any armed forces or armed group. However, the Committee on the Rights of the Child has expressed the view that, given the definition of a child contained in Art 1 of the CRC and the best interests principle contained in Art 3(1), *no* child under the age of 18 should be allowed to be involved in hostilities, either directly or indirectly.[235]

15.94 There is a potential and difficult friction between the foregoing provisions and the child's right to participate under Art 12 of the CRC. The question arises as to the extent to which a child who is under the age of 15 or a soldier or a member of an armed group who is under the age of 18 and who is capable of forming his or her own views concerning participation in hostilities and expresses the wish to participate directly in an armed conflict should be entitled to do so. It is submitted that where this issue arises it must, as with all other matters which engage Art 12 of the CRC, be dealt with according to the principles which govern the operation of that article, including the provisions of Art 3 of the CRC concerning the child's best interests.[236]

CRC, Art 38(3) – Ambit

15.95 Article 38(3) of the CRC provides as follows concerning the minimum age for the *recruitment* of children into the armed forces of a state:

> '3. States Parties shall refrain from recruiting any person who has not attained the age of fifteen years into their armed forces. In recruiting among those persons who have attained the age of fifteen years but who have not attained the age of eighteen years, States Parties shall endeavour to give priority to those who are oldest.'

---

[234] See also Protocol I to the Geneva Conventions Art 77 ('The Parties to the conflict shall take all feasible measures in order that children who have not attained the age of fifteen years do not take a direct part in hostilities ...'). See **15.134** below.

[235] Committee on the Rights of the Child *General Discussion on Children in Armed Conflict* Report on the Second Session, September/October (1992) CRC/C/10, para 67 and see Newell, P and Hodgkin, R *Implementation Handbook for the Convention on the Rights of the Child* (2008) 3rd edn, UNICEF, pp 573 and 583.

[236] See chapter 6 for the detailed provisions concerning the application of Art 12 of the CRC.

15.96 Article 38(3) of the CRC must now be read in with Arts 2, 3 and 4 of the Optional Protocol to the Convention on the Rights of the Child on the Involvement of Children in Armed Conflict. Article 2 of the Optional Protocol to the Convention on the Rights of the Child on the Involvement of Children in Armed Conflict provide as follows in respect of the recruitment of children into the armed forces and armed groups:

'States Parties shall ensure that persons who have not attained the age of 18 years are not compulsorily recruited into their armed forces.'

Article 3 of the Optional Protocol to the Convention on the Rights of the Child on the Involvement of Children in Armed Conflict provides:

'1. States Parties shall raise the minimum age for the voluntary recruitment of persons into their national armed forces from that set out in article 38, paragraph 3, of the Convention on the Rights of the Child, taking account of the principles contained in that article and recognising that under the Convention persons under 18 are entitled to special protection.

2. Each State Party shall deposit a binding declaration upon ratification of or accession to this Protocol that sets forth the minimum age at which it will permit voluntary recruitment into its national armed forces and a description of the safeguards that it has adopted to ensure that such recruitment is not forced or coerced.

3. States Parties that permit voluntary recruitment into their national armed forces under the age of 18 shall maintain safeguards to ensure, as a minimum, that:

(a) Such recruitment is genuinely voluntary;
(b) Such recruitment is done with the informed consent of the persons parents or legal guardians;
(c) Such persons are fully informed of the duties involved in such military service;
(d) Such persons provide reliable proof of age prior to acceptance into national military service.

4. Each State Party may strengthen its declaration at any time by notification to that effect addressed to the Secretary-General of the United Nations, who shall inform all States Parties. Such notification shall take effect on the date on which it is received by the Secretary-General.

5. The requirement to raise the age in paragraph 1 of the present article does not apply to schools operated by or under the control of the armed forces of the States Parties, in keeping with articles 28 and 29 of the Convention on the Rights of the Child.'

Article 4 of the Optional Protocol to the Convention on the Rights of the Child on the Involvement of Children in Armed Conflict provides:

'1. Armed groups that are distinct from the armed forces of a State should not, under any circumstances, recruit or use in hostilities persons under the age of 18 years.

2. States Parties shall take all feasible measures to prevent such recruitment and use, including the adoption of legal measures necessary to prohibit and criminalise such practices.

3. The application of the present article under this Protocol shall not affect the legal status of any party to an armed conflict.'

(i)   CRC, Art 38(3) – 'Recruitment'

15.97 The term recruitment encompasses both voluntary and compulsory recruitment. Article 38(3) of the CRC does not make reference to 'conscription' in providing a minimum age for recruitment[237] however Arts 2 and 3 of the Optional Protocol do distinguish between voluntary recruitment and compulsory recruitment.[238] The distinction is important as, pursuant to the Optional Protocol, the compulsory recruitment of children under the age of 18 is prohibited[239] but is permitted in respect of voluntary recruitment subject to the safeguards set out in Art 3(3) of the Optional Protocol. Article 3(1) of the Optional Protocol requires States parties to raise the age of voluntary recruitment from that provided in Art 38(3) of the CRC, namely 15 years of age.[240] Note that the term 'recruitment' does not necessarily mean recruitment as front line soldiers.[241]

(ii)   CRC, Art 38(3) – Minimum Age for Recruitment

15.98 Read with the Optional Protocol to the Convention on the Rights of the Child on the Involvement of Children in Armed Conflict the minimum age for *compulsory* recruitment into the armed forces or armed groups under Art 38(3) of the CRC is 18 years of age. The minimum age for the *voluntary* recruitment under Art 38(3) of the CRC into the armed forces is 15 years of age although States parties to the Optional Protocol are under an obligation to raise this minimum age and, where they seek to recruit children under the age of 18, to ensure that such recruitment is genuinely voluntary, that it is done with the informed consent of the child's parents or legal guardians, that the child is fully informed of the duties involved in such military service and that the child provides reliable proof of age prior to acceptance into national military service.[242] Note that, pursuant to the use of the words 'under any

---

237 Happold argues that in English, the term 'recruitment' is broader than the word 'conscription', and thus covers both voluntary enlistment and conscription into the armed forces (Happold, M *Child Soldiers in International Law: The Legal Regulation of Children's Participation in Hostilities*, Netherlands International Law Review, Vol XLVII (2000), pp 37–38). This suggests that the prohibition on recruitment in Art 38(3) must also include turning away children who volunteer to be recruited notwithstanding that the article does not distinguish between compulsory and voluntary recruitment. In any event, Happold goes further to suggest that 'the object and purpose of the provision is ... to protect children from the effects of armed conflicts; it is concerned with their welfare. Given this, it becomes immaterial whether a child's recruitment is voluntary or coerced' (Happold, *Child Soldiers in International Law: The Legal Regulation of Children's Participation in Hostilities*, Netherlands International Law Review, Vol XLVII (2000), pp 37–38).

238 Within this context the *Paris Principles: Principles and Guidelines on Children Associated with Armed Forces or Armed Groups* (2007) UNICEF, para 2.4 defines 'recruitment' as 'compulsory, forced and voluntary conscription or enlistment of children into any kind of armed force or armed group.'

239 As it by ILO Convention on the Worst Forms of Child Labour (No 182) Art 3(a). Van Bueren notes that it was pointed out to the CRC Working Group that there are very few events in life more hazardous than having to face bullets from a semi-automatic rifle (see Van Bueren, G *The International Law on the Rights of the Child* (1998) Martinus Nijhoff, p 339).

240 Note that the Rome Statute of the International Criminal Court Art 8(2)(b)(xxvi) defines as a war crime 'Conscripting or enlisting children under the age of fifteen years into the national armed forces or using them to participate actively in hostilities' in respect of acts of conscripting and enlisting children under the age of 15 into the national armed forces or using them to participate actively in hostilities. Cottier observes in relation to children that '[E]ven though the Rome Conference adopted the language of 'using them to participate actively' instead of 'allowing them to take part', there is no need of any element of force in using them, and the simple acceptance of using their 'participation product' should be sufficient to subsume it under this prohibition' (Cottier, M *War Crimes – para 2(b)(xxvi)* in Triffterer, O (ed.) *Commentary on the Rome Statute of the International Criminal Court* (1999) p 261).

241 Newell, P and Hodgkin, R *Implementation Handbook for the Convention on the Rights of the Child* (2008) 3rd edn, UNICEF, p 583.

242 See also Protocol I to the Geneva Conventions Art 77 ('The Parties to the conflict shall take all feasible measures in order that children who have not attained the age of fifteen years do not take a direct part in hostilities and, in particular, they shall refrain from recruiting them into their armed forces. In recruiting

circumstances' in Art 4(1) of the Optional Protocol, the minimum age for voluntary recruitment into armed groups would appear to be 18 years of age. The reason for this distinction is unclear. It should be noted that in any event the Committee on the Rights of the Child has expressed the view that, given the definition of a child contained in Art 1 of the CRC and the best interests principle contained in Art 3(1), no child under the age of 18 should be recruited into the armed forces, either through conscription or voluntary enlistment.[243]

(iii)   CRC, Art 38 – Obligation to given Priority to Oldest Children when Recruiting

15.99   CRC, Art 38 requires that in recruiting among those persons who have attained the age of 15 years but who have not attained the age of 18 years, States Parties shall endeavour to give priority to those who are oldest.[244] Once again, it should be noted that the Committee on the Rights of the Child has expressed the view that no child under the age of 18 should be recruited into the armed forces, either through conscription or voluntary enlistment.[245]

CRC, Art 38(4) – Ambit

15.100   Article 38(4) of the CRC stipulates as follows in respect of the obligation on States parties to protect children affected by armed conflict:

> '4. In accordance with their obligations under international humanitarian law to protect the civilian population in armed conflicts,[246] States Parties shall take all feasible measures to ensure protection and care of children who are affected by an armed conflict.'

(i)   Obligation to Protect Children affected by Armed Conflict

'All Feasible Measures'

15.101   Article 38(4) of the CRC requires States parties to fulfil their obligations under international humanitarian law and in particular under the Geneva Convention IV Relative to the Protection of Civilian Persons in Time of War[247] by taking all feasible measures to ensure protection and care of children who are affected by an armed conflict. Van Bueren argues that the provisions of the CRC, Art 38(4) significantly lowers the standard of protection for children affected by armed conflict by reason of the fact that Art 38(4) uses the words 'take all feasible measures' rather than the words 'take all necessary measures'.[248] Van Bueren argues that whilst Art 38(4) requires State parties to have regard to existing duties under international humanitarian law, the

---

among those persons who have attained the age of fifteen years but who have not attained the age of eighteen years the Parties to the conflict shall endeavour to give priority to those who are oldest').

[243]   Committee on the Rights of the Child *General Discussion on Children in Armed Conflict* Report on the Second Session, September/October (1992) CRC/C/10, para 67 and see Newell, P and Hodgkin, R *Implementation Handbook for the Convention on the Rights of the Child* (2008) 3rd edn, UNICEF, pp 573 and 583.

[244]   See also Protocol I to the Geneva Conventions Art 77 ('... In recruiting among those persons who have attained the age of fifteen years but who have not attained the age of eighteen years the Parties to the conflict shall endeavour to give priority to those who are oldest').

[245]   Committee on the Rights of the Child *General Discussion on Children in Armed Conflict* Report on the Second Session, September/October (1992) CRC/C/10, para 67 and see Newell, P and Hodgkin, R *Implementation Handbook for the Convention on the Rights of the Child* (2008) 3rd edn, UNICEF, pp 573 and 583.

[246]   See **15.92** above.

[247]   See **15.121** below for a detailed discussion of the provisions of Geneva Convention IV Relative to the Protection of Civilian Persons in Time of War as they relate to children.

[248]   Van Bueren, G *The International Law on the Rights of the Child* (1998) Martinus Nijhoff, p 342.

wording of Art 38(4) obfuscates the position for children affected by armed conflict in a situation where clarity as to the duty on belligerent States is vital.[249] Later instruments adopt the stronger formulation of 'all necessary measures' in respect of the protection of civilians during situations of armed conflict, Art 11 of the Convention on the Rights of Persons with Disabilities providing that:

> 'States Parties shall take, in accordance with their obligations under international law, including international humanitarian law and international human rights law, all necessary measures to ensure the protection and safety of persons with disabilities in situations of risk, including situations of armed conflict, humanitarian emergencies and the occurrence of natural disasters.'[250]

15.102   It is arguably contrary to the non-discrimination provisions of international law for a child with a disability to be entitled to greater protection from the effects of armed conflict under Art 11 of the Convention on the Rights of Persons with Disabilities than a child without disability under Art 38(4) of the CRC. Further, having regard to the provisions of Art 41 of the CRC,[251] in those States where the Geneva Convention IV Relative to the Protection of Civilian Persons in Time of War has been ratified, the higher standards of protection afforded to children affected by armed conflict by that Convention[252] will apply in preference to the weaker provisions of Art 38(4) of the CRC.

15.103   In relation the protection to be provided under Art 38(4) of the CRC the Committee on the Rights of the Child has stated that:[253]

> 'Child soldiers should be considered primarily as victims of armed conflict. Former child soldiers, who often find themselves unaccompanied or separated at the cessation of the conflict or following defection, shall be given all the necessary support services to enable reintegration into normal life, including necessary psychosocial counseling. Such children shall be identified and demobilised on a priority basis during any identification and separation operation. Child soldiers, in particular, those who are unaccompanied or separated, should not normally be interned, but rather, benefit from special protection and assistance measures, in particular as regards their demobilisation and rehabilitation. Particular efforts must be made to provide support and facilitate the reintegration of girls who have been associated with the military, either as combatants or in any other capacity. If, under certain circumstances, exceptional internment of a child soldier over the age of 15 years is unavoidable and in compliance with international human rights and humanitarian law, for example, where she or he poses a serious security threat, the conditions of such internment should be in conformity with international standards, including article 37 of the Convention and those pertaining to juvenile justice, and should not preclude any tracing efforts and priority participation in rehabilitation programmes.'

---

[249]   Van Bueren, G *The International Law on the Rights of the Child* (1998) Martinus Nijhoff, p 342.

[250]   See also Committee on the Rights of the Child General Comment No 9 *The Rights of Children with Disabilities* CRC/C/GC/9, para 55 ('States parties are obliged to take all necessary measures to protect children from the detrimental effects of war and armed violence and to ensure that children affected by armed conflict have access to adequate health and social services, including psychosocial recovery and social reintegration') and the Standard Rules on the Equalisation of Opportunities for Persons with Disabilities r 22 ('The term 'prevention' means action aimed at preventing the occurrence of physical, intellectual, psychiatric or sensory impairments (primary prevention) or at preventing impairments from causing a permanent functional limitation or disability (secondary prevention). Prevention may include many different types of action, such as ... prevention of disability resulting from ... armed conflict').

[251]   Article 41 of the CRC provides that 'Nothing in the present Convention shall affect any provisions which are more conducive to the realisation of the rights of the child and which may be contained in: (a) The law of a State party; or (b) International law in force for that State.'

[252]   See **15.121** below.

[253]   General Comment No 6 CRC/GC/2005/6, para 56 and 57.

Unexploded Ordnance

15.104 Unexploded ordnance presents a particular hazard to children in areas of current or past armed conflict. Landmines in particular represent an acute danger by reason of the fact that States parties are often not privy to the plan of the sites where the landmines were planted and the cost of mine clearance is high.[254] The UN Convention on the Use, Stockpiling, Production and Transfer of Anti-personnel Mines and on their Destruction Art 1(1) requires that State Parties undertake never under any circumstances to use anti-personnel mines,[255] to develop, produce, otherwise acquire, stockpile, retain or transfer to anyone, directly or indirectly, anti-personnel mines or to assist, encourage or induce, in any way, anyone to engage in any activity prohibited to a State Party under the Convention. Article 1(2) requires state parties to destroy or ensure the destruction of all anti-personnel mines in accordance with the provisions of the Convention. The Committee on the Rights of the Child encourages State parties to ratify the Convention on the Use, Stockpiling, Production and Transfer of Anti-personnel Mines and on their Destruction and to take proactive action on all unexploded ordnance.[256]

Treatment of Children accused of War Crimes

15.105 Children should not be prosecuted for war crimes.[257] The Paris Principles make clear that children who are accused of crimes under international law allegedly committed while they were associated with armed forces or armed groups should be considered primarily as victims of offences against international law.[258] To this end the International Criminal Court has specifically excluded children under the age of 18 from its jurisdiction.[259]

The Child's Right to Freedom from Harmful Treatment under the CRC – CRC, Art 36 – Protection against All Other Forms of Exploitation

CRC, Art 36

15.106 CRC, Art 36 provides a catch all provision in relation to the exploitation of children as follows:

> 'States Parties shall protect the child against all other forms of exploitation prejudicial to any aspects of the child's welfare.'

---

[254] Committee on the Rights of the Child General Comment No 9 *The Rights of Children with Disabilities* CRC/C/GC/9, para 23.

[255] Article 2 of the Convention defines 'anti-personnel mines' as a munition designed to be placed under, on or near the ground or other surface area to be exploded by the presence, proximity or contact of a person and that will incapacitate, injure or kill one or more persons. Mines designed to be detonated by the presence, proximity or contact of a vehicle as opposed to a person, that are equipped with anti-handling devices (a device intended to protect a mine and which is part of, linked to, attached to or placed under the mine and which activates when an attempt is made to tamper with or otherwise intentionally disturb the mine), are not considered anti-personnel mines as a result of being so equipped.

[256] See the Committee on the Rights of the Child General Comment No 9 *The Rights of Children with Disabilities* CRC/C/GC/9, para 23. See also Cambodia CRC/C/15/Add.128 and Nicaragua CRC/C/OPAC/NIC/1, p 5.

[257] Newell, P and Hodgkin, R *Implementation Handbook for the Convention on the Rights of the Child* (2008) 3rd edn, UNICEF, p 584 and see Rawanda CRC/C/15/Add.234, paras 70 and 71.

[258] *Paris Principles: Principles and Guidelines on Children Associated with Armed Forces or Armed Groups* (2007) UNICEF, para 3.6.

[259] Rome Statute of the International Criminal Court, Art 26 ('The Court shall have no jurisdiction over any person who was under the age of 18 at the time of the alleged commission of a crime').

15.107 Article 36 is designed to ensure that the 'social exploitation' of children is recognised in addition to the more explicit forms of exploitation such as sexual and economic exploitation.[260] Forms of exploitation which may be covered by this article will include the use of children in criminal activities, the exploitation of gifted children, the exploitation of children in political activities, the exploitation of children in the media[261] and the use of children for medical or scientific experimentation.[262] In relation to scientific and medical experimentation, the Committee on the Rights of the Child General Comment No 3 *HIV/AIDS and the Rights of the Child* indicates the Committees approach to this issue:

> 'Consistent with article 24 of the Convention, States parties must ensure that HIV/AIDS research programmes include specific studies that contribute to effective prevention, care, treatment and impact reduction for children. States parties must, nonetheless, ensure that children do not serve as research subjects until an intervention has already been thoroughly tested on adults.[263] Rights and ethical concerns have arisen in relation to HIV/AIDS biomedical research, HIV/ADS operations, and social, cultural and behavioural research. Children have been subjected to unnecessary or inappropriately designed research with little or no voice to either refuse or consent to participation. In line with the child's evolving capacities, consent of the child should be sought and consent may be sought from parents or guardians if necessary, but in all cases consent must be based on full disclosure of the risks and benefits of research to the child. States parties are further reminded to ensure that the privacy rights of children, in line with their obligations under article 16 of the Convention, are not inadvertently violated through the research process and that personal information about children, which is accessed through research, is, under no circumstances, used for purposes other than that for which consent was given. States parties must make every effort to ensure that children and, according to their evolving capacities, their parents and/or their guardians participate in decisions on research priorities and that a supportive environment is created for children who participate in such research.'[264]

The Child's Right to Freedom from Harmful Treatment under the CRC – CRC, Art 39 – Rehabilitation of Child Victims

CRC, Art 39

15.108 Article 39 of the CRC provides as follows in respect of the treatment of child victims of neglect, exploitation or abuse,[265] torture or any other form of cruel, inhuman or degrading treatment or punishment[266] or armed conflict:[267]

---

[260] Newell, P and Hodgkin, R *Implementation Handbook for the Convention on the Rights of the Child* (2008) 3rd edn, UNICEF, p 543.

[261] See **11.32** above and See also the Committee on the Rights of the Child *Report on the 11th Session* CRC/C/50 p 80.

[262] See **15.15** above concerning Art 7 of the ICCPR. See also Human Rights Committee General Comment No 20 HRI/GEN/1/Rev 8, p 191, para 7 ('The Committee observes that special protection in regard to such experiments is necessary in the case of persons not capable of giving valid consent, and in particular those under any form of detention or imprisonment. Such persons should not be subjected to any medical or scientific experimentation that may be detrimental to their health'). See further the International Ethical Guidelines for Biomedical Research Involving Human Subjects (2002) Council for International Organisations of Medical Sciences and WHO Guideline 14.

[263] See also the International Ethical Guidelines for Biomedical Research Involving Human Subjects (2002) Council for International Organisations of Medical Sciences and WHO Guideline 13.

[264] CRC/GC/2003/3, para 29.

[265] See CRC, Arts 19, 32, 33, 34, 35 and 35.

[266] See CRC, Art 37.

[267] See CRC, Art 38.

'States Parties shall take all appropriate measures to promote physical and psychological recovery and social reintegration of a child victim of any form of neglect, exploitation, or abuse; torture or any other form of cruel, inhuman or degrading treatment or punishment; or armed conflicts. Such recovery and reintegration shall take place in an environment which fosters the health, self-respect and dignity of the child.'

CRC, Art 39 – Related Provisions

(i) Additional Provisions of the CRC

15.109 Article 39 of the CRC must be read in light of Art 2 of the CRC to ensure that the appropriate measures taken under Art 39 are available to all children without discrimination,[268] Art 3 of the CRC, to ensure that the best interests of the child are the primary consideration throughout the provision of such measures, Art 12 of the CRC, to ensure that the child's views are fully respected when seeking make provision for and to implement such measures and Art 6 of the CRC to ensure that the measures taken promote the maximum survival and development of the child.[269] In addition, reference should also be made to Art 19(1),[270] Art 20(1),[271] Art 25 and Art 40(1) of the CRC.[272] Note that Art 14(4) of the ICCPR provides that 'In the case of juvenile persons in conflict with the law the procedure shall be such as will take account of their age and the desirability of promoting their rehabilitation'.[273]

(ii) Optional Protocol to the Convention on the Rights of the Child on the Sale of Children, Child Prostitution and Child Pornography

15.110 The provisions of Art 39 of the CRC are supplemented by the Optional Protocol to the Convention on the Rights of the Child on the Sale of Children, Child Prostitution and Child Pornography Art 8 which mandates that appropriate support be provided to the child victim throughout any legal process resulting from his or her being the victim of sale, child prostitution or child pornography[274] and protecting, as appropriate, the privacy and identity of child victims and taking measures in accordance with national law to avoid the inappropriate dissemination of information that could lead to the identification of child victims.[275] The Optional Protocol requires that States Parties shall take all feasible measures with the aim of ensuring all appropriate assistance to victims of such offences, including their full social reintegration and their full physical and psychological recovery.[276] The Protocol places a duty on State parties

---

[268] See also Austria CRC/C/15/Add.98, para 21.

[269] Newell, P and Hodgkin, R *Implementation Handbook for the Convention on the Rights of the Child* (2008) 3rd edn, UNICEF, p 589. See also the ESC Guidelines on Justice in Matters Involving Child/Victims and Witnesses of Crime (Resolution 2005/20) and the UN Declaration of Basic Principles of Justice for Victims of Crime and the Abuse of Power, paras 14–17(GA Resolution 40/34 1985 Annex).

[270] See **15.26** above.

[271] See **8.121** above.

[272] See **16.26** above.

[273] The concept of 'rehabilitation' as set out in Art 14(4) of the ICCPR has been replaced by the concept of 'reintegration', the former concept being considered to hold unhelpful connotations of social control by the State and sole responsibility upon the individual, failing to reflect the multi-faceted causes of offending behaviour in children (Van Bueren, G *The International Law on the Rights of the Child* (1998) Martinus Nijhoff, p 173). The term reintegration is used in Art 39 of the CRC and Art 40(1) of the CRC and the 'Beijing Rules', r 80 Van Bueren submits that the term 'rehabilitation' in Art 14(4) of the ICCPR should be interpreted as 'the means by which the child can assume a constructive role in society' in order to avoid the creation of two different standards (Van Bueren, G *The International Law on the Rights of the Child* (1998) Martinus Nijhoff, p 173).

[274] Optional Protocol, Art 8(1)(d).

[275] Optional Protocol, Art 8(1)(e).

[276] Optional Protocol, Art 9(3).

to promote international cooperation to assist child victims in their physical and psychological recovery, social reintegration and repatriation.[277]

(iii)   *Optional Protocol to the Convention on the Rights of the Child on the Involvement of Children in Armed Conflict.*

15.111 The provisions of Art 39 of the CRC are further supplemented by the provisions of the Optional Protocol to the Convention on the Rights of the Child on the Involvement of Children in Armed Conflict. In particular, Art 6(3) of the Optional Protocol provides that:

> 'States Parties shall take all feasible measures to ensure that persons within their jurisdiction recruited or used in hostilities contrary to this Protocol are demobilised or otherwise released from service. States Parties shall, when necessary, accord to these persons all appropriate assistance for their physical and psychological recovery and their social reintegration.'[278]

(iv)   *Protocol to Prevent, Suppress and Punish Trafficking in Persons, Especially Women and Children supplementing the UN Convention against Transnational Organised Crime*

15.112 Article 6(3) and (4) of the Protocol to Prevent, Suppress and Punish Trafficking in Persons, Especially Women and Children provide as follows with regard to assistance to and protection of victims of trafficking in persons:

> '3. Each State Party shall consider implementing measures to provide for the physical, psychological and social recovery of victims of trafficking in persons, including, in appropriate cases, in cooperation with non-governmental organisations, other relevant organisations and other elements of civil society, and, in particular, the provision of:
>
> (a)   Appropriate housing;
> (b)   Counseling and information, in particular as regards their legal rights, in a language that the victims of trafficking in persons can understand;
> (c)   Medical, psychological and material assistance; and
> (d)   Employment, educational and training opportunities.
>
> 4. Each State Party shall take into account, in applying the provisions of this article, the age, gender and special needs of victims of trafficking in persons, in particular the special needs of children, including appropriate housing, education and care.'

(v)   *UN Convention on the Rights of Persons with Disabilities*

15.113 Article 16(4) of the Convention on the Rights of Persons with Disabilities provides as follows in respect of persons with disabilities who become victims in any form of exploitation, violence or abuse:

> '4. States Parties shall take all appropriate measures to promote the physical, cognitive and psychological recovery, rehabilitation and social reintegration of persons with disabilities who become victims of any form of exploitation, violence or abuse, including through the

---

[277]   Optional Protocol, Art 10(2).
[278]   See also Optional Protocol to the Convention on the Rights of the Child on the Involvement of Children in Armed Conflict, Art 7(1) ('States Parties shall cooperate in the implementation of the present Protocol, including in the prevention of any activity contrary to the Protocol and in the rehabilitation and social reintegration of persons who are victims of acts contrary to this Protocol, including through technical cooperation and financial assistance. Such assistance and cooperation will be undertaken in consultation with concerned States Parties and relevant international organisations').

provision of protection services. Such recovery and reintegration shall take place in an environment that fosters the health, welfare, self-respect, dignity and autonomy of the person and takes into account gender- and age-specific needs.'

(vi) UN Convention Against Torture and Other Cruel, Inhuman or Degrading Treatment or Punishment

15.114 Article 14(1) of the Convention Against Torture and Other Cruel, Inhuman or Degrading Treatment or Punishment requires that each State party shall ensure in its legal system that the victim of an act of torture obtains redress and has an enforceable right to fair and adequate compensation, including the means for as full a rehabilitation as possible.[279]

CRC, Art 39 – Ambit

(i) 'Child Victim'

15.115 The phrase 'child victim' has been interpreted widely by the Committee on the Rights of the Child and will extend beyond those children who have been the victim of neglect, exploitation or abuse, torture or any other form of cruel, inhuman or degrading treatment or punishment or armed conflict[280] to those children who are refugees,[281] children involved in child labour and forced labour,[282] children who are affected by family conflict,[283] children who have been sold and trafficked[284] and children involved in the juvenile justice system.[285] Art 39 will also be applicable to abuses which have occurred as the result of a child being deprived or his or her liberty and in respect of children who have suffered as the result of witnessing or knowing about their parents' torture.[286]

(ii) 'Appropriate Measures to Promote Psychological Recovery and Social Reintegration'

Appropriate Measures

15.116 Measures for psychological recovery and social reintegration which foster the health, self-respect and dignity of the child will include social, medical and psychological counseling, the prevention of the social stigmatisation of the child and his or her family, programmes to facilitate recovery and reintegration in the community and the promotion of alternative means of livelihood for child victims.[287] Within this context

---

[279] See also Art 15 of the International Convention for the Protection of All Persons from Enforced Disappearance ('States Parties shall cooperate with each other and shall afford one another the greatest measure of mutual assistance with a view to assisting victims of enforced disappearance, and in searching for, locating and releasing disappeared persons and, in the event of death, in exhuming and identifying them and returning their remains').

[280] See Committee on the Rights of the Child General Comment No 6 *Treatment of Unaccompanied and Separated Children Outside their Country of Origin* CRC/GC/2005/6, para 56.

[281] See CRC, Art 22. See also Committee on the Rights of the Child General Comment No 6 *Treatment of Unaccompanied and Separated Children outside their Country of Origin* CRC/GC/2005/6, para 47.

[282] See CRC, Art 32.

[283] See CRC, Art 9.

[284] See CRC, Art 35.

[285] See CRC, Arts 37 and 40. Newell, P and Hodgkin, R *Implementation Handbook for the Convention on the Rights of the Child* (2008) 3rd edn, UNICEF, p 590.

[286] Van Bueren, G *The International Law on the Rights of the Child* (1998) Martinus Nijhoff, p 225.

[287] Agenda for Action adopted by the First World Congress against Sexual Exploitation of Children (A/51/385, para 5. See also See *Gaurav Jain v Union of India* (1997) 8 SCC 114; AIR 1997 SC 3021 in which the Supreme Court of India held that the children of prostitutes have the right to equality of opportunity, dignity, care, protection and rehabilitation so as to be part of the mainstream of social life without any

it is important that children who are in need of protection by reason of their association with activities that are considered criminal are not treated as offenders but rather are dealt with under child protection mechanisms in order to promote psychological recovery and social reintegration.[288] The measures promoting psychological recovery and social reintegration should respect the child's right to privacy.[289]

The Role of the Juvenile Justice System

15.117 The juvenile justice system has a central role to play in the recovery and reintegration of child victims. As such States parties must ensure that the juvenile justice system promotes an effective system of physical and psychological recovery and social reintegration of the child, in an environment that fostered his or her health, self-respect and dignity.[290] Art 40(1) of the CRC requires that every child alleged as, accused of, or recognised as having infringed the penal law to be treated in a manner consistent with the promotion of the child's sense of dignity and worth, which reinforces the child's respect for the human rights and fundamental freedoms of others and which takes into account the child's age and the desirability of promoting the child's reintegration and the child's assuming a constructive role in society.[291] The Committee on the Rights of the Child has commented that:[292]

> 'This principle must be applied, observed and respected throughout the entire process of dealing with the child, from the first contact with law enforcement agencies all the way to the implementation of all measures for dealing with the child. It requires that all professionals involved in the administration of juvenile justice be knowledgeable about child development, the dynamic and continuing growth of children, what is appropriate to their well-being, and the pervasive forms of violence against children.'

The Committee on the Rights of the Child has made clear that a child sentenced to life imprisonment contrary to the prohibition contained in Art 37(a) of the CRC should receive education, treatment and care aiming at his or her social reintegration upon release.[293]

---

pre-stigma attached on them. The Court directed the constitution of a committee to formulate and implement a scheme for the rehabilitation of such children and child prostitutes.

[288] Committee on the Rights of the Child *Report on 25th Session* September/October 2000 CRC/C/100, para 688.9 and see also Brunei CRC/C/15/Add.219, para 53 and Bangladesh CRC/C/15/Add 221, para 49.

[289] Newell, P and Hodgkin, R *Implementation Handbook for the Convention on the Rights of the Child* (2008) 3rd edn, UNICEF, p 593.

[290] Committee on the Rights of the Child *Report on the 10th Session* October/November 1995 CRC/C/46, para 221. See also Committee on the Rights of the Child General Comment No 10 *Children's Rights in Juvenile Justice* CRC/C/GC/10, para 4.

[291] See also UN Rules for the Protection of Juveniles Deprived of their Liberty r 79 ('All juveniles should benefit from arrangements designed to assist them in returning to society, family life, education or employment after release. Procedures, including early release, and special courses should be devised to this end') and r 80 ('Competent authorities should provide or ensure services to assist juveniles in re-establishing themselves in society and to lessen prejudice against such juveniles. These services should ensure, to the extent possible, that the juvenile is provided with suitable residence, employment, clothing, and sufficient means to maintain himself or herself upon release in order to facilitate successful reintegration. The representatives of agencies providing such services should be consulted and should have access to juveniles while detained, with a view to assisting them in their return to the community'). See also r 28(2) of the 'Beijing Rules'.

[292] Committee on the Rights of the Child General Comment No 10 *Children's Rights in Juvenile Justice* CRC/C/GC/10, para 13. See also, paras 23, 29 and 40.

[293] Committee on the Rights of the Child General Comment No 10 *Children's Rights in Juvenile Justice* CRC/C/GC/10, para 77.

Recovery from the Effects of Armed Conflict

15.118   Article 6(3) of the Optional Protocol to the Convention on the Rights of the Child on the Involvement of Children in Armed Conflict provides that:[294]

> 'States Parties shall take all feasible measures to ensure that persons within their jurisdiction recruited or used in hostilities contrary to this Protocol are demobilised or otherwise released from service. States Parties shall, when necessary, accord to these persons all appropriate assistance for their physical and psychological recovery and their social reintegration.'

The Committee on the Rights of the Child General Comment No 6 Treatment of Unaccompanied and Separated Children Outside their Country of Origin states that:[295]

> 'Child soldiers should be considered primarily as victims of armed conflict. Former child soldiers, who often find themselves unaccompanied or separated at the cessation of the conflict or following defection, shall be given all the necessary support services to enable reintegration into normal life, including necessary psychosocial counseling. Such children shall be identified and demobilised on a priority basis during any identification and separation operation. Child soldiers, in particular, those who are unaccompanied or separated, should not normally be interned, but rather, benefit from special protection and assistance measures, in particular as regards their demobilisation and rehabilitation. Particular efforts must be made to provide support and facilitate the reintegration of girls who have been associated with the military, either as combatants or in any other capacity.'

Recovery from the Effects of Corporal Punishment

15.119   In its General Comment No 8 The Right of the Child to Protection from Corporal Punishment and Other Cruel or Degrading Forms of Punishment the Committee on the Rights of the Child stipulates that:

> 'Corporal punishment and other degrading forms of punishment may inflict serious damage to the physical, psychological and social development of children, requiring appropriate health and other care and treatment. This must take place in an environment that fosters the integral health, self-respect and dignity of the child, and be extended as appropriate to the child's family group. There should be an interdisciplinary approach to planning and providing care and treatment, with specialised training of the professionals involved. The child's views should be given due weight concerning all aspects of their treatment and in reviewing it.'[296]

Recovery from Economic Harm

15.120   In relation to recovery from economic harm the Committee on the Rights of the Child has made clear that the provisions of Art 39 of the CRC aimed at promoting the physical and psychological recovery and social reintegration of child victims in an

---

[294]   See also Optional Protocol to the Convention on the Rights of the Child on the Involvement of Children in Armed Conflict, Art 7(1) ('States Parties shall cooperate in the implementation of the present Protocol, including in the prevention of any activity contrary to the Protocol and in the rehabilitation and social reintegration of persons who are victims of acts contrary to this Protocol, including through technical cooperation and financial assistance. Such assistance and cooperation will be undertaken in consultation with concerned States Parties and relevant international organisations').

[295]   Committee on the Rights of the Child General Comment No 6 *Treatment of Unaccompanied and Separated Children Outside their Country of Origin* CRC/GC/2005/6, para 56. See also para 47.

[296]   Committee on the Rights of the Child General Comment No 8 *The Right of the Child to Protection from Corporal Punishment and Other Cruel or Degrading Forms of Punishment* CRC/C/GC/8, p 10, para 37.

environment which fosters the health, self-respect and dignity of the child will apply equally to child victims of any form of economic exploitation.[297] The Committee has observed in this regard that:[298]

> 'States parties must also take measures to ensure the rehabilitation of children who, as a result of economic exploitation, are exposed to serious physical and moral danger. It is essential to provide these children with the necessary social and medical assistance and to envisage social reintegration programmes for them in the light of article 39 of the Convention on the Rights of the Child.'

The Child's Right to Freedom from Harmful Treatment under Other International Instruments

The Geneva Conventions

15.121   The Geneva Conventions are self evidently important in protecting children from the harmful effects of armed conflict. There are four Geneva conventions[299] and three protocols to those conventions.[300] Geneva Convention IV Relative to the Protection of Civilian Persons in Time of War 1949, published at the end of a conference held in Geneva from April 21 to August 12 1949 and in force from 21 October 1950, is the most relevant to children with seventeen of the one hundred and fifty-nine articles relating to children.[301] Geneva Convention IV affords both general protection to children as civilians but also special protection for children living in unoccupied and occupied territory.[302] Two Additional Protocols were added to the Geneva Conventions in 1977,[303] which had the effect of providing greater protection for children caught up in hostilities.[304] The scope of the armed conflicts covered is widened to include conflicts where 'peoples are fighting against colonial domination and alien occupation and against racist regimes in the exercise or their right to self determination'[305] and conflicts which take place in the territory of a High Contracting

---

[297]   Committee on the Rights of the Child *Report on the 5th Session* January 1994 CRC/C/24, p 39. See also *Child Labour: Targeting the Intolerable* International Labour Conference Eighty-sixth Session (1998) ILO, p 54.

[298]   Committee on the Rights of the Child *Report on the 5th Session* January 1994 CRC/C/24, p 43.

[299]   Comprising Convention I for the Amelioration of the Condition of the Wounded and Sick in Armed Forces in the Field, Convention II for the Amelioration of the Condition of Wounded, Sick and Shipwrecked members of the Armed Forces, Convention III Relative to the Treatment of Prisoners of War and Convention IV Relative to the Protection of Civilian Persons in Time of War.

[300]   Comprising the Protocol Additional to the Geneva Conventions of 12 August 1949, and relating to the Protection of Victims of International Armed Conflicts (Protocol I) and the Protocol Additional to the Geneva Conventions of 12 August 1949, and Relating to the Protection of Victims of Non-International Armed Conflicts (Protocol II) which confer additional protection on civilian populations and the Protocol additional to the Geneva Conventions of 12 August 1949, and relating to the Adoption of an Additional Distinctive Emblem (Protocol III) which provides for the addition of the non-religious and politically neutral emblem of the 'Red Crystal' to the Red Cross and Red Crescent emblems.

[301]   See Arts 14, 17, 23, 24, 25, 26, 38, 49, 50, 51, 68, 76, 81, 82, 89, 94 and 132. See also **14.46–14.50** for the application to children of Geneva Convention III Relative to the Treatment of Prisoners of War.

[302]   See Art 2 and Van Bueren, G *The International Law on the Rights of the Child* (1998) Martinus Nijhoff, p 330. At a time when the United Kingdom is involved in at least one major armed conflict, these provisions and those of the Protocols are of more than academic interest, governing as they do how UK forces treat children in the conflict zones.

[303]   The United Kingdom ratified Protocol I and Protocol II on 28 January 1998. The UK registered reservations in respect of Protocol I.

[304]   See Plattner, D *The Protection of Children in International Humanitarian Law*, International Review of the Red Cross, No 240, May–June 1984, p 140–152 and Singer, S *The Protection of Children during Armed Conflict Situations*, International Review of the Red Cross, No 252, May–June 1986, p 133.

[305]   Protocol I, Art 1(4). The articles in Protocol I relevant to children are Arts 8, 70, 74, 75(5), 77 and 78.

Party between its armed forces and dissident armed forces or other organised armed groups.[306] These two Additional Protocols also, for the first time, give some protection to children specifically against *participation* in armed conflicts.[307] A third Protocol was added in 2005 which provides for the addition of the non-religious and politically neutral emblem of the 'red crystal' to the Red Cross and Red Crescent emblems.

Geneva Convention IV relative to the Protection of Civilian Persons in Time of War

(i)   Geneva Convention IV – Application

Geneva Convention IV

15.122   Article 1 of the Geneva Convention relative to the Protection of Civilian Persons in Time of War (Geneva Convention IV) provides that the High Contracting Parties to the Convention undertake to respect and to ensure respect for the Convention in all circumstances. Accordingly, the Geneva Convention will apply notwithstanding claims of 'just war' or 'jihad' or justifications of 'self defence'.[308] The Convention applies in all cases of declared war or of any other armed conflict which may arise between two or more of the High Contracting Parties, even if a state of war is not recognised by one of them and to all cases of partial or total occupation of a High Contracting Party even if the occupation meets with no armed resistance.[309] Note that even though one of the Powers to the conflict may not be a party to the Convention, the Power that is a party will remain bound by its obligations under the Convention. Individuals protected by the Convention, known as 'protected persons' are those who, at a given moment and in any manner whatsoever, find themselves in case of a conflict or occupation in the hands of a party to the conflict or Occupying power of which they are not nationals.[310] Note however that Part II of the Geneva Convention IV, concerning the general protection of populations covers the whole of the populations of the countries in conflict, without any adverse distinction based, in particular, on race, nationality, religion or political opinion, and is intended to alleviate the sufferings caused by war.[311]

Protocols I and II

15.123   Geneva Convention IV concerns armed conflicts having an international character. Whilst it makes some provision for armed conflicts not of an international character occurring in the territory of a High Contracting Party[312] it is Protocols I and II to the Geneva Conventions which provide the comprehensive protection in respect of other types of armed conflict. Protocol I applies to armed conflicts in which peoples are fighting against colonial domination and alien occupation and against racist regimes in

---

[306]   Protocol II, Art 1(1).

[307]   Ibid. Article 77(2) and Protocol II, Art 4. See also See also the Protocol to the CRC on the Protection of Children from Involvement in Armed Conflict and the Paris Commitments and Principles to protect children from unlawful recruitment or use by armed forces or armed groups.

[308]   Van Bueren, G *The International Law on the Rights of the Child* (1998) Martinus Nijhoff, p 330.

[309]   Geneva Convention IV, Art 2.

[310]   Geneva Convention IV, Art 4. Note that pursuant to Art 4 nationals of a State which is not bound by the Convention are not protected by it. Nationals of a neutral State who find themselves in the territory of a belligerent State, and nationals of a co-belligerent State, are not regarded as protected persons for the purposes of the Convention while the State of which they are nationals has normal diplomatic representation in the State in whose hands they are. Persons protected by the Geneva Conventions I, II and III shall not be considered as protected persons within the meaning of the Geneva Convention IV.

[311]   Geneva Convention IV, Art 13.

[312]   See Geneva Convention IV, Art 3.

the exercise of their right of self-determination.[313] Protocol II applies to all armed conflicts which are not covered by Art 1 of Protocol I and which take place in the territory of a High Contracting Party between its armed forces and dissident armed forces or other organised armed groups which, under responsible command, exercise such control over a part of its territory as to enable them to carry out sustained and concerted military operations and to implement the Protocol.[314] Protocol II concerns non-international armed conflicts and reflects long recognised[315] need to regulate conduct in internal conflicts such as civil wars. Note that in cases not covered by the Geneva Conventions and Protocols or any other international agreement civilians and combatants remain under the protection and authority of the principles of international law derived from established custom, from the principles of humanity and from the dictates of public conscience.[316]

Application to Children

15.124 In international humanitarian law children as a group are sub-divided into newborn babies, infants, those under 7 years of age, those children under 12 years of age, children under 15 and young people between the ages of 15 and 18. Under the Geneva Convention IV and Protocols I and II these distinctions govern a number of aspects of the protection afforded to children in times of armed conflict.[317] Geneva Convention IV does not set an upper age limit on the definition of child. Note that for the purposes of Protocol I the terms 'wounded' and 'sick' encompass newborn babies, expectant mothers and maternity cases.[318] Pursuant to Art 77(1) of Protocol I children must be the object of special respect and must be protected against any form of indecent assault and provided with the care and aid they require whether because of their age or for any other reason. In respect of non-international conflicts, Art 4(3) of Protocol II provides that children shall be provided with the care and aid they require.

(ii) Geneva Convention IV – Protection of Children from the effects of Armed Conflict

Safe Zones and Removal from Besieged Areas

15.125 During peacetime the High Contracting Parties and after the outbreak of hostilities the Parties to those hostilities may establish in their territory and in occupied areas hospital and safety zones and localities organised to protect children under 15, expectant mothers[319] and mothers of children under the age of 7 from the effects of war.[320] Agreements may be concluded between the Parties to the hostilities on the mutual recognition of these safe zones.[321] The Parties to the hostilities must endeavour to conclude local agreements for the removal of children from besieged or encircled areas and for the passage of ministers of all religions, medical personnel and medical equipment into such areas.[322]

---

[313] Protocol I, Art 1(4).
[314] Protocol II, Art 1(1).
[315] See for example De Vattel, E *Le Droit des Gens ou Principles du Droit Naturel* (1785) Edition Carnegie 1916.
[316] Protocol I, Art 1(2).
[317] See for example Geneva Convention IV Arts 14, 23, 24, 38(5) and 51 and Protocol I, Arts 76(2) and 77(3).
[318] Protocol I, Art 8(a).
[319] See Geneva Convention IV, Art 16 which requires that expectant mothers shall be the object of particular concern and respect.
[320] Geneva Convention IV, Art 14.
[321] Geneva Convention IV, Art 14.
[322] Geneva Convention IV, Art 17.

Provision of Essential Supplies

15.126 Article 23 of the Geneva Convention IV requires that each High Contracting Party shall allow the free passage as rapidly as possible of all consignments of medical and hospital stores and objects necessary for religious worship intended for the civilians of another High Contracting Party even if the latter is an adversary and, in particular, shall allow the free passage of all consignments of essential foodstuffs, clothing and tonics intended for children under the age of 15, expectant mothers and maternity cases. These provisions are subject to there being no serious reasons for fearing that the relevant consignments may be diverted from their destination, that control may not be effective or that a definite advantage may accrue to the military efforts or economy of the enemy consequent upon such consignments. Article 50 of the Geneva Convention IV requires that the Occupying Power shall not hinder the application of any preferential measures in regard to food, medical care and protection against the effects of war, which may have been adopted prior to the occupation in favour of children under fifteen years, expectant mothers, and mothers of children under 7 years. Where relief actions are undertaken in respect of civilian populations in a territory under the control of a party to the conflict other than occupied territory pursuant to Art 70 of Protocol I priority must be given to those persons, such as children, expectant mothers, maternity cases and nursing mothers, who, under the Geneva Convention IV or Protocol I are to be accorded privileged treatment or special protection.

Protection and Evacuation of Orphaned and Separated Children

15.127 Pursuant to Art 24 of the Geneva Convention IV the Parties to an armed conflict must take all necessary measures to ensure that children under the age of 15 who are orphaned or separated from their families as the result of war are not left to their own resources and that their maintenance, the exercise of their religion, and their education, which should be entrusted to persons of a similar cultural tradition, are facilitated. Further, the Parties to the conflict must facilitate the reception of orphaned and separated children in a neutral country for the duration of the conflict having regard to the foregoing duties. The Parties to the conflict must endeavour to arrange for any children under the age of 12 to be identified through the wearing of discs or by other means.[323] Note however that pursuant to Art 49 of Geneva Convention IV individual or mass forcible transfers, as well as deportations of protected persons from occupied territory to the territory of the Occupying Power or that of any other country are prohibited regardless of motive.[324]

---

[323] See also Protocol I, Art 78(3) ('With a view to facilitating the return to their families and country of children evacuated pursuant to this Article, the authorities of the Party arranging for the evacuation and, as appropriate, the authorities of the receiving country shall establish for each child a card with photographs, which they shall send to the Central Tracing Agency of the International Committee of the Red Cross. Each card shall bear, whenever possible, and whenever it involves no risk of harm to the child, the following information: (a) Surname(s) of the child; (b) The child's first name(s); (c) The child's sex; (d) The place and date of birth (or, if that date is not known, the approximate age); (e) The father's full name; (f) The mother's full name and her maiden name; (g) The child's next-of-kin; (h) The child's nationality; (i) The child's native language, and any other languages he speaks; (j) The address of the child's family; (k) Any identification number for the child; (l) The child's state of health; (m) The child's blood group; (n) Any distinguishing features; (o) The date on which and the place where the child was found; (p) The date on which and the place from which the child left the country; (q) The child's religion, if any; (r) The child's present address in the receiving country; (s) Should the child die before his return, the date, place and circumstances of death and place of interment'). See also Geneva Convention IV Art 50 ('A special section of the Bureau set up in accordance with Article 136 shall be responsible for taking all necessary steps to identify children whose identity is in doubt. Particulars of their parents or other near relatives should always be recorded if available').

[324] Note that this provision is subject to the exception that the Occupying Power may undertake a total or

15.128 Note that the provisions of Art 24 concerning facilitating the reception of orphaned and separated children in a neutral country for the duration of the conflict must be read with Art 78 of Protocol I concerning the evacuation of children and in particular the requirement of Art 78(1) that no Party to the conflict shall arrange for the evacuation of children, other than its own nationals, to a foreign country except for a temporary evacuation where compelling reasons of the health or medical treatment of the children or, except in occupied territory, their safety, so require. The list of reasons for evacuation in Art 78(1) is exhaustive and narrowly drawn. Van Bueren argues that evacuation of children should only be used where it is in the children's best interests.[325] In respect of orphaned or separated children whose parents or legal guardians are not available to give their consent to evacuation as required by Art 78(1) of Protocol I the written consent to such evacuation of the persons who by law or custom are primarily responsible for the care of the children is required.[326] Art 78(3) of Protocol I requires that whenever an evacuation occurs each child's education, including his religious and moral education shall be provided while he is away with the greatest possible continuity. In relation to non-international conflicts, Art 4(3)(e) of Protocol II will govern the temporary evacuation of children from the area in which hostilities are taking place.[327]

15.129 In applying Art 24 of the Geneva Convention IV regard should also be had to Art 74 of Protocol I which requires that The High Contracting Parties and the Parties to the conflict shall facilitate in every possible way the reunion of families dispersed as a result of armed conflicts and shall encourage in particular the work of the humanitarian organisations engaged in this task in accordance with the provisions of the Conventions and of the Protocol and in conformity with their respective security regulations.[328] Art 4(3)(b) of Protocol II makes similar provision in respect of non-international conflicts.[329]

Maintenance of Contact between Family Members

15.130 Article 25 of the Geneva Convention IV requires that all persons in the territory of a Party to the conflict or a territory occupied by it must be enabled to give and receive news of a personal nature to members of their families speedily and without undue delay. Where as the result of circumstances it becomes difficult to facilitate this obligation the Parties to the conflict must employ the services of a neutral intermediary to do so and decide in consultation with that agency on the best way to meet their obligations in this regard. Where Parties to the conflict deem it necessary to restrict

---

partial evacuation of a given area if the security of the population or imperative military reasons demand provided (a) such evacuations do not involve the displacement of protected persons outside the bounds of the occupied territory save where it is for material reasons impossible to avoid such placement, (b) such persons are transferred back to their homes as soon as hostilities in the area in question have ceased, (c) proper accommodation is provided to receive the protected persons, (d) that the evacuation takes place in satisfactory conditions of hygiene, health, safety and nutrition, (e) that members of the same family are not separated, (f) the Protecting Power is informed of such evacuations as soon as they take place, (g) the Occupying Power does not detain protected persons in an area particularly exposed to the dangers of war unless the security of the population of imperative military reasons demand it and (h) the Occupying Power does not deport or transfer parts of its own civilian population into the territory it occupies.

[325] Van Bueren, G *The International Law on the Rights of the Child* (1998) Martinus Nijhoff, p 343.

[326] Protocol I, Art 78(1). Note that in such circumstances the provisions of Art 12 of the CRC will also apply.

[327] Article 4(3)(e) of Protocol II provides that 'Measures shall be taken, if necessary, and whenever possible with the consent of their parents or persons who by law or custom are primarily responsible for their care, to remove children temporarily from the area in which hostilities are taking place to a safer area within the country and ensure that they are accompanied by persons responsible for their safety and well-being'.

[328] See also Geneva Convention IV, Art 26.

[329] Article 4(3)(b) provides that 'All appropriate steps shall be taken to facilitate the reunion of families temporarily separated.'

family correspondence those restrictions must be confined to the compulsory use of standard forms containing 25 freely chosen words dispatched at a minimum of once per month. Pursuant to Art 26 of the Convention, each Party to the conflict must facilitate enquiries made by family members who are dispersed as the result of war with the object of renewing contact with one another and meeting.

Equal Benefit from Preferential Treatment for Children who are Protected Persons

15.131 The position of children under 15 years of age, pregnant women and the mothers of children under the age of 7 years who are protected persons under the Geneva Convention IV must be regulated by the provisions concerning aliens during times of peace. However, such children, pregnant women and the mothers of children under the age of 7 years must also benefit by any preferential treatment to the same extent as the nationals of the State concerned.[330] Pursuant to Art 10(1) of Protocol I all newborn babies shall be respected and protected and must treated humanely and must receive, to the fullest extent practicable and with the least possible delay, the medical care and attention required by their condition. There must be no distinction among them founded on any grounds other than medical ones.

Duty to Maintain Institutions for the Care and Education of Children

15.132 Pursuant to Art 50 of Geneva Convention IV the Occupying Power must, in cooperation with national and local authorities, facilitate the proper working of all institutions devoted to the care and education of children. In relation to children who are orphaned or separated from their parents as a result of war and who cannot be adequately cared for by a near relative or friend the Occupying Power must make arrangements for their maintenance and education, if possible by persons of their own nationality, language and religion, should the local institutions be inadequate for this purpose. Within this context, the Occupying Power must not in any case change a child's personal status nor enlist a child in formations or organisation subordinate to the Occupying Power. The Occupying Power must not hinder the application of any preferential measures in regard to food, medical care and protection against the effects of war, which may have been adopted prior to the occupation in favour of children under 15 years, expectant mothers, and mothers of children under 7 years.[331] In relation to non-international conflicts, Art 4(3)(a) of Protocol II provides that children must receive an education, including religious and moral education, in keeping with the wishes of their parents, or in the absence of parents, of those responsible for their care.

No Recruitment or Compulsory Labour for Protected Persons

15.133 Pursuant to Art 51 of the Geneva Convention IV an Occupying Power may not compel protected persons to serve in its armed forces or auxiliary forces and no pressure or propaganda which aims at voluntary enlistment is permitted. Further, the Occupying Power may not compel any protected person under the age of 18 to work.

---

[330] Geneva Convention IV, Art 38(5).
[331] Geneva Convention IV, Art 50.

(iii)   Geneva Convention IV – Participation of Children in Armed Conflict

Prohibition on Children under 15 taking a Direct Part in Hostilities

15.134 Whilst dealing comprehensively with the protection of children in hostilities, none of the Geneva Conventions deal with the issue of recruitment of children into the armed forces. Protocols I and II however do now deal with this issue.

Protocol I

15.135 Article 77(2) of Protocol I provides as follows in respect of the participation of children in armed conflicts:

> 'The Parties to the conflict shall take all feasible measures in order that children who have not attained the age of fifteen years do not take a direct part in hostilities and, in particular, they shall refrain from recruiting them into their armed forces. In recruiting among those persons who have attained the age of fifteen years but who have not attained the age of eighteen years, the Parties to the conflict shall endeavour to give priority to those who are oldest.'

15.136 Kalshoven suggests that the words 'to take a direct part in hostilities' must be interpreted to mean that:[332]

> 'the person in question performs warlike acts which by their nature or purpose are designed to strike enemy combatants or materiel; acts, therefore, such as firing at enemy soldiers, throwing a Molotov-cocktail at an enemy tank ... and so on.'

Art 77(2) Protocol I thus arguably fails to prohibit other dangerous roles such as supplying the front lines or acting as a means of communication between units.

Protocol II

15.137 Article 4(3)(c) of Protocol II provides that:

> 'Children who have not attained the age of fifteen years shall neither be recruited in the armed forces or groups nor allowed to take part in hostilities.'

In contrast to Art 77(2) of Protocol I requiring 'all feasible measures' to be taken to ensure children under the age of 15 years do not take part in hostilities, Protocol II concerning internal conflicts prohibits *any* type of involvement for children under the age of 15 in non-international conflicts, resulting in a disparity of protection between the two Protocols. Note that Art 38(2) of the CRC adopts the weaker terminology used in Protocol I and prohibits only direct participation by children under the age of 15. Whilst Art 38(2) covers both international and internal conflicts, States parties who are party to both Protocol II of the Geneva Conventions and the CRC will be bound to apply the higher duties under Protocol II in relation to internal conflicts.[333]

---

[332] Kalshoven, F *Constraints on the Waging of War* (1987) ICRC, p 91.
[333] Van Bueren, G *The International Law on the Rights of the Child* (1998) Martinus Nijhoff, p 335 and see Art 41 of the CRC.

The Hague Conventions

Convention on Protection of Children and Co-operation in Respect of Intercountry Adoption

15.138 The aim of the Hague Convention on Protection of Children and Co-operation in Respect of Intercountry Adoption is to establish safeguards to ensure that intercountry adoptions take place in the best interests of the child with respect for his or her fundamental rights as recognised by international law and thereby to ensure the prevention of the abduction, sale or and traffic in children.[334] The Convention ensures that an adoption within the scope of the Convention will only take place if the competent authorities in the child's State of origin have established that the child is adoptable, have determined, after giving due consideration to the possibilities of placement within the State of origin, that adoption is in the child's best interests, have ensured that those whose consent to adoption is required have been counseled on the effect of adoption and that their consents have been freely given in the required form in writing, in respect of the Mother only after the child has been born, and have not been induced by payment or compensation or been withdrawn and have ensured that, having regard to the age and maturity of the child, that the child has been counseled on the effect of adoption, that his or her consent has been given freely in the required legal form in writing where required and not induced by payment or compensation and that consideration has been given to his or her wishes and opinions.[335]

The Hague Convention on the Civil Aspects of International Child Abduction

15.139 The Hague Convention on the Civil Aspects of International Child Abduction seeks to ensure that children who are wrongfully removed and retained in any Contracting State are returned promptly and that the rights of custody and access under the law of one Contracting State are effectively respected in other contracting States.[336]

The Child's Right to Freedom from Harmful Treatment under Customary International Law

Customary International Law – Torture

15.140 The prohibition on torture has become a norm of *jus cogens*[337] in international law.[338] Torture constitutes a crime against humanity under Art 7 of the Rome Statute of

---

[334] The Hague Convention on Protection of Children and Co-operation in Respect of Intercountry Adoption, Art 1.

[335] The Hague Convention on Protection of Children and Co-operation in Respect of Intercountry Adoption, Art 4. A detailed account of the operation of the Hague Convention on Protection of Children and Co-operation in Respect of Intercountry Adoption is beyond the scope of this work and reference should be made to Hershman, D and McFarlane A. *Children Law and Practice* Jordan Publishing.

[336] The Hague Convention on the Civil Aspects of International Child Abduction, Art 1. Again, a comprehensive account of the operation of the Hague Convention on the Civil Aspects of International Child Abduction is beyond the scope of this work and reference should be made to Lowe, N Everall, M and Nicholls, M *International Movement of Children* (2004) Jordan Publishing.

[337] See **2.61 et seq** above.

[338] See Brownlie, I *Principles of Public International Law* (2008) 7th edn, Oxford, p 528 and De Wet, E *The Prohibition of Torture as an International norm of Jus Cogens and its Implications for National and Customary Law* (2004) European Journal of International Law 15 p 97. See also *Prosecutor v Anto Furundzija* (1998) ILR 121, para 153 ('Because of the importance of the values it protects, [the prohibition of torture] has evolved into a peremptory norm or jus cogens, that is, a norm that enjoys a higher rank in the international hierarchy than treaty law and even 'ordinary' customary rules. The most conspicuous consequence of this higher rank is that the principle at issue cannot be derogated from by states through international treaties or

the International Criminal Court when committed as part of a widespread or systematic attack directed against any civilian population, with knowledge of the attack. Note also however that the status of torture as a norm of *jus cogens* means that the offence of torture exists independent of the existence of war or armed conflict (so called 'torture in time of peace') and of crimes against humanity.[339] Torture is accordingly a crime under general international law without requiring a particular pattern of activity[340] and has been described as an international crime in the highest sense.[341] In *Prosecutor v Anto Furundzija*[342] the International Criminal Tribunal for the Former Yugoslavia described the cardinal features of the prohibition against torture in international law, namely that (a) States are obliged not only to prohibit and punish torture, but also to forestall its occurrence and bound to put in place all those measures that may pre-empt the perpetration of torture, (b) that the prohibition on torture imposes on States obligations *erga omnes* or obligations owed towards all the other members of the international community each of which then has a correlative right and finally (c) that torture has acquired the status of *jus cogens* and is prohibited by a peremptory norm of international law. It is arguable that as a peremptory norm having the character of an obligation *erga omnes*[343] the prohibition on torture must be applied by States without regard to territorial limitation.[344] International law provides that offences that are *jus cogens* may be punished by any state because the offenders are 'common enemies of all mankind and all nations have an equal interest in their apprehension and prosecution'.[345] The *jus cogens* nature of the international crime of torture thus justifies States in taking universal jurisdiction over torture wherever it is committed.[346]

Customary International Law – Slavery and the Slave Trade

15.141   As noted above, the prohibition on slavery and the slave trade is also an international norm of *jus cogens*.[347] Enslavement committed as part of a widespread or

---

local or special customs or even general customary rules not endowed with the same normative force ... Clearly, the jus cogens nature of the prohibition against torture articulates the notion that the prohibition has now become one of the most fundamental standards of the international community. Furthermore, this prohibition is designed to produce a deterrent effect, in that it signals to all members of the international community and the individuals over whom they wield authority that the prohibition of torture is an absolute value from which nobody must deviate').

[339] See Judge Cassese Year Book ILC 1996 II (Part II), pp 42–43.

[340] *Prosecutor v Anto Furundzija* (1998) ILR 121 and *R v Bow Street Metropolitan Stipendiary Magistrate ex p Pinochet Ugarte* [1999] 1 AC 147 per Lord Brown-Wilkinson.

[341] *R v Bow Street Metropolitan Stipendiary Magistrate ex p Pinochet Ugarte* [1999] 1 AC 147 per Lord Brown-Wilkinson.

[342] (1998) ILR 121, paras 147–157.

[343] Lat. 'in relation to everyone'.

[344] Brownlie, I *Principles of Public International Law* (2008) 7th edn, Oxford, p 596.

[345] *R v Bow Street Metropolitan Stipendiary Magistrate ex p Pinochet Ugarte* [1999] 1 AC 147 per Lord Browne-Wilkinson citing *Demjanjuk v Petrovsky* (1985) 603 F Supp 1468, 776 F 2d 571.

[346] See *Jorgic v Germany* (2008) 47 EHRR 2007, para 68 in relation to genocide. But see also the UN Convention on Jurisdictional Immunities of States and Their Property Art 5 and *Democratic Republic of Congo v Belgium* ILM 41 (2002) 536 ('The Court accordingly concludes that the functions of a Minister of Foreign Affairs are such that, throughout the duration of his or her office, he or she when abroad enjoys full immunity from criminal jurisdiction and inviolability. That immunity and that inviolability protect the individual concerned against any act of authority of another State which would hinder him or her in the performance of his or her duties'). For the approach to the issue of immunity in domestic law see *Jones v Minister of the Interior of the Kingdom of Saudi Arabia* [2006] UKHL 26, [2007] 1 AC 270 and *R v Bow Street Metropolitan Stipendiary Magistrate ex p Pinochet Ugarte* [1999] 1 AC 147.

[347] See the *Barcelona Traction Case* (Second Phase) ICJ Reports 3 at 32. See also Restatement of the Law, 3rd Restatement of the Foreign Relations Law of the United States, 702(b).

systematic attack directed against any civilian population, with knowledge of the attack constitutes a crime against humanity for the purposes of Art 7 of the Rome Statute of the International Criminal Court.[348]

The Child's Right to Freedom from Harmful Treatment under the ECHR

ECHR, Art 3 – Torture, Inhuman or Degrading Treatment or Punishment

ECHR, Art 3

15.142 Article 3 of the ECHR has been described as 'arguably, one of the most influential of all Convention articles'.[349] In prohibiting torture and inhuman or degrading treatment or punishment it enshrines one of the fundamental values of the democratic societies making up the Council of Europe.[350] Art 3 of the ECHR provides as follows in respect of this prohibition:

'No one shall be subjected to torture or to inhuman or degrading treatment or punishment.'

(i) ECHR, Art 3 – Absolute Prohibition

15.143 The prohibition on torture and inhuman or degrading treatment or punishment under Art 3 of the ECHR is absolute. There are no exceptions permitted by the article of the type permitted, for example, by Art 8 of the ECHR.[351] This absolute prohibition, derived from the unqualified wording of Art 3, means that the State must not, either on its own behalf or through its agents,[352] subject its citizens and other persons within its territories, to torture or to inhuman or degrading treatment or punishment.[353] This will include responsibility for the actions of unofficial groups such

---

[348] Article 7 defines 'enslavement' as 'the exercise of any or all of the powers attaching to the right of ownership over a person and includes the exercise of such power in the course of trafficking in persons, in particular women and children.'

[349] Cooper, J *An Analysis of Article 3* (2003) Sweet & Maxwell, p ix.

[350] *Soering v United Kingdom* (1989) 11 EHRR 439.

[351] *Mayeka v Belgium* (2008) 46 EHRR 23 at 48 ('Article 3 makes no provision for exceptions. This absolute prohibition of torture and of inhuman or degrading treatment or punishment under the terms of the Convention shows that Article 3 enshrines one of the fundamental values of the democratic societies making up the Council of Europe'). See also *Chahal v United Kingdom* (1997) 23 EHRR 413 at 79–80 ('The Court is well aware of the immense difficulties faced by States in modern times in protecting their communities from terrorist violence. However, even in these circumstances, the Convention prohibits in absolute terms torture or inhuman or degrading treatment or punishment, irrespective of the victim's conduct') and *Aksoy v Turkey* (1997) 24 EHRR 533 at 62 ('Even in the most difficult of circumstances, such as the fight against organised terrorism and crime, the Convention prohibits in absolute terms torture or inhuman or degrading treatment or punishment. Unlike most of the substantive clauses of the Convention and of Protocols Nos. 1 and 4, Article 3 makes no provision for exceptions and no derogation from it is permissible under Article 15 even in the event of a public emergency threatening the life of the nation'). See also *Public Committee Against Torture v Israel* (1999) 7 BHRC 31.

[352] See *Ireland v United Kingdom* (1980) 2 EHRR 25, para 159 ('It is inconceivable that the higher authorities of a State should be, or at least should be entitled to be, unaware of the existence of such a practice [in breach of Art 3]. Furthermore, under the Convention those authorities are strictly liable for the conduct of their subordinates; they are under a duty to impose their will on subordinates and cannot shelter behind their inability to ensure that it is respected'). See also the UN Convention Against Torture and Other Cruel, Inhuman or Degrading Treatment or Punishment Art 1(1) ('... the term torture means any act ... inflicted by or at the instigation of or with the consent or acquiescence of a public official or other person acting in an official capacity').

[353] Lord Lester QC, Lord Pannick QC and Herberg, J *Human Rights Law and Practice* (2009) 3rd edn, LexisNexis, p 196.

as private schools where such actions are contrary to the principles enshrined in Art 3 of the ECHR.[354] Note that whilst a State will be potentially responsible for the acts of its agents carried out on foreign soil where it has effective control in that area[355] other principles of public international law may override the State's responsibilities under Art 3 of the ECHR.[356] No derogation from the rights enshrined in Art 3 of the ECHR is permitted in times of public emergency or war.[357]

(ii)   ECHR, Art 3 – Positive Obligation

Ambit of Positive Obligation

15.144   Under Art 3 of the ECHR States parties have a positive obligation to prevent torture or inhuman or degrading treatment. A purposive interpretation of Art 3 of the ECHR is required.[358] This positive obligation will include a duty to take proactive steps to prevent treatment that falls within the ambit of Art 3 of the ECHR, including that inflicted by private individuals.[359] In *Pretty v United Kingdom*[360] the European Court of Human Rights reiterated that:

> '... the Court has held that the obligation on the High Contracting Parties under Article 1 of the Convention to secure to everyone within their jurisdiction the rights and freedoms defined in the Convention, taken in conjunction with Article 3, requires States to take measures designed to ensure that individuals within their jurisdiction are not subjected to torture or inhuman and degrading treatment or punishment, including such treatment administered by private individuals. A positive obligation on the State to provide protection against inhuman or degrading treatment has been found to arise in a number of cases: see, for example, *A v the United Kingdom* where the child applicant had been caned by his stepfather, and *Z and Others v the United Kingdom*, where four child applicants were severely abused and neglected by their parents. Article 3 also imposes requirements on State authorities to protect the health of persons deprived of liberty.'[361]

Positive Obligation and Children

15.145   The European Court of Human Rights has noted that children and other vulnerable individuals, in particular, are entitled to State protection, in the form of

---

[354]   *Costello-Roberts v United Kingdom* (1993) 19 EHRR 112, paras 26–28 (... in the present case, which relates to the particular domain of school discipline, the treatment complained of although it was the act of a headmaster of an independent school, is none the less such as may engage the responsibility of the United Kingdom under the Convention if it proves to be incompatible with Article 3 or Article 8 or both').

[355]   *R (Al-Skeini and Others) v Secretary of State for the Home Department* [2007] UKHL 26, [2008] 1 AC 153.

[356]   *R (Al-Saadoon and Others) v Secretary of State for Defence* [2008] EWHC 3098 (Admin), [2008] All ER (D) 246 (Dec) and *R (Al-Saadoon and Others) v Secretary of State for Defence* [2009] EWCA Civ 7, [2010] 1 All ER 271. This case went to the European Court of Human Rights on the issue of breach of Art 6 of the ECHR (see *Al-Saadoon and another v United Kingdom* [2010] All ER (D) 37 (Mar)). See also *R (B) v Secretary of State for Foreign and Commonwealth Affairs* [2004] EWCA Civ 1344, [2005] QB 643 in which it was held that the Human Rights Act 1998 and Art 3 of the ECHR applied to the actions of diplomatic and consular officials but that the duty to provide diplomatic asylum could only arise under the ECHR where it was compatible with public international law. See also *Al-Adsani v United Kingdom* (2001) 34 EHRR 273.

[357]   See Art 15 ECHR and *Saadi v Italy* (2008) 24 BHRC 123, para 127.

[358]   See *Aksoy v Turkey* (1997) 23 EHRR 553, paras 98–99 relying on Art 12 of the UN Convention against Torture and Other Cruel, Inhuman or Degrading Treatment or Punishment.

[359]   *A v United Kingdom* (1999) 27 EHRR 611 concerning the failure by the State to prevent a child being caned by his father.

[360]   (2002) 35 EHRR 1, para 51.

[361]   Note that in *Pretty v United Kingdom* the European Court of Human Rights held that a requirement on the State to sanction actions intended to terminate life could not be derived from Art 3 of the Convention even where the person seeking to terminate their life faced the prospect of a distressing death ((2002) 35 EHRR 1, para 55).

effective deterrence, against serious breaches of personal integrity.[362] As noted by Baroness Hale in *Re E (A Child) (A) (Northern Ireland)*[363] the European Court of Human Rights has taken note of the vulnerability of children in its judgments on the obligations of the state to protect people from inhuman or degrading treatment with the landmark rulings in which the State has been found responsible for failing to protect victims from serious ill-treatment meted out by private individuals being cases concerning children. *A v United Kingdom*[364] concerned the failure by the State to prevent a child being caned by his father. The European Court of Human Rights held that 'Children and other vulnerable individuals, in particular, are entitled to State protection, in the form of effective deterrence, against such serious breaches of personal integrity'. In *Z v United Kingdom*[365] the UK Government accepted a finding by the European Commission that Art 3 of the ECHR had been violated by the State's failure to remove children from an abusive family situation of which the State was fully aware. In finding a similar violation in *E v United Kingdom*[366] the European Court of Human Rights made clear that in cases concerning the State's failure to remove children from abusive situations of which it is aware the test under Article 3 of the ECHR does not require it to be shown that 'but for' the failing or omission of the public authority ill-treatment would not have happened. A failure to take reasonably available measures which could have had a real prospect of altering the outcome or mitigating the harm is sufficient to engage the responsibility of the State under Art 3. The special vulnerability of children will be relevant to the scope of the positive obligation of the State to protect them from treatment which violates Art 3 of the ECHR.[367] States parties are under an obligation to protect children from domestic violence[368] and a failure to do so may constitute a breach of Art 3 of the ECHR.[369]

Obligation to Investigate Alleged Violations

15.146 The positive obligations arising under Art 3 of the ECHR will include an obligation to mount a prompt, impartial and effective official investigation based on sound evidence[370] and capable of leading to the identification and punishment of those responsible.[371] Failure to adhere to this duty will lead to a finding that there has been a

---

[362] *Opuz v Turkey* (2009) Application No 33401/02, para 159.
[363] [2008] UKHL 66, [2008] 3 WLR 1208, para 7.
[364] (1999) 27 EHRR 611.
[365] (2001) 34 EHRR 97, para 73. See also *DP and JC v United Kingdom* (2003) 36 EHRR.
[366] (2003) 36 EHRR 519, para 99.
[367] *Re E (A Child)(A)(Northern Ireland)* [2008] UKHL 66, [2008] 3 WLR 1208, para 9 per Baroness Hale citing *Mayeka v Belgium* (2008) 46 EHRR 23 at 53 ('... the obligation on high contracting parties under art 1 of the Convention to secure to everyone within their jurisdiction the rights and freedoms defined in the Convention, taken in conjunction with art 3, requires States to take measures designed to ensure that individuals within their jurisdiction are not subjected to torture or inhuman or degrading treatment, including such ill-treatment administered by private individuals ... Steps should be taken to enable effective protection to be provided, *particularly to children and other vulnerable members of society*, and should include reasonable measures to prevent ill-treatment of which the authorities have or ought to have knowledge ...'). See also *Gldani Congregation of Jehova's Witnesses v Georgia* (2008) 46 EHRR 613, para 96 ('This protection calls for reasonable and effective measures, including with regard to children and other vulnerable individuals, in order to prevent ill-treatment of which the authorities were or ought to have been aware').
[368] *ES and others v Slovakia* (2009), Application No 8227/04, para 40.
[369] *Opuz v Turkey* (2009), Application No 33401/02.
[370] *Yükshel v Turkey* (2005), 41 EHRR 316, para 29.
[371] *Assenov v Bulgaria* 28 EHRR 652, para 102, *Veznedaroglu v Turkey* (2001) 33 EHRR 1412, para 32, *Indelicato v Italy* (2002) 35 EHRR 1330, *Gldani Congregation of Jehova's Witnesses v Georgia* (2008) 46 EHRR 613, para 97 and *Krastanov v Bulgaria* (2005) 41 EHRR 1137, paras 57–58.

violation of Art 3 of the ECHR.[372] The duty to investigate arises only once the allegations of a breach of Art 3 have been made.[373]

ECHR, Art 3 – Ambit

(i)   ECHR, Art 3 – Relevant Treatment

Relevant Treatment – Minimum Level of Severity

15.147   Treatment must attain a minimum level of severity to fall within the ambit of Art 3 of the ECHR.[374] The test for whether particular treatment engages Art 3 of the ECHR is a relative one and is dependent on all the circumstances of the case including the duration of that treatment, the physical and mental effects of that treatment and, in some cases, the age, sex, state of health[375] and vulnerability of the victim of the treatment.[376] In assessing whether the relevant treatment falls within the ambit of Art 3 regard must be had to the fact that the ECHR is a 'living instrument which must be interpreted in the light of present-day conditions'.[377]

Relevant Treatment – Children

15.148   Van Bueren points out that the relative nature of the test for whether the minimum level of severity of treatment is reached for the purposes of Art 3 is beneficial to children as this relativist approach will include the age of the victim and, for example,

---

[372]   See *Assenov v Bulgaria* (1998) 28 EHRR 652 and *Veznedaroglu v Turkey* (2001) 33 EHRR 1412.

[373]   *Nasseri v Secretary of State for the Home Department* [2008] EWCA Civ 464, [2009] 1 All ER 116, para 16.

[374]   *Ireland v United Kingdom* (1980) 2 EHRR 25, para 162 and see *Costello-Roberts v United Kingdom* (1993) 19 EHRR 112, para 32 and *A v United Kingdom* (1999) 27 EHRR 611, para 21. See further *Kurt v Turkey* (1998) 27 EHRR 373 (anguish of mother over the disappearance of a child at the hands of the authorities amounted to treatment sufficient to engage and breach Art 3 of the ECHR on the basis that the mother had 'been left with the anguish of knowing that her son had been detained and that there is a complete absence of official information as to his subsequent fate ... over a prolonged period of time'). In this regard see also *Çakici v Turkey* (1999) 31 EHRR 133, para 98, *Cyprus v Turkey* (2002) 35 EHRR 731, para 157 and *Osmanoglu v Turkey* (2008) Application 48804/99 (unreported) ('The Court reiterates that the question whether a family member of a 'disappeared person' is a victim of treatment contrary to Article 3 will depend on the existence of special factors which gives the suffering of the applicant a dimension and character distinct from the emotional distress which may be regarded as inevitably caused to relatives of a victim of a serious human rights violation. Relevant elements will include the proximity of the family tie – in that context, a certain weight will attach to the parent-child bond –, the particular circumstances of the relationship, the extent to which the family member witnessed the events in question, the involvement of the family member in the attempts to obtain information about the disappeared person and the way in which the authorities responded to those enquiries. The Court further emphasises that the essence of such a violation does not so much lie in the fact of the 'disappearance' of the family member but rather concerns the authorities' reactions and attitudes to the situation when it is brought to their attention. It is especially in respect of the latter that a relative may claim directly to be a victim of the authorities' conduct').

[375]   See *Mouisel v France* (2004) 38 EHRR 735, paras 38 and 40 ('Although Article 3 of the Convention cannot be construed as laying down a general obligation to release detainees on health grounds, it nonetheless imposes an obligation on the State to protect the physical well-being of persons deprived of their liberty, for example by providing them with the requisite medical assistance. The Court has also emphasised the right of all prisoners to conditions of detention which are compatible with human dignity, so as to ensure that the manner and method of execution of the measures imposed do not subject them to distress or hardship of an intensity exceeding the unavoidable level of suffering inherent in detention; in addition, besides the health of prisoners, their well-being also has to be adequately secured, given the practical demands of imprisonment').

[376]   *Ireland v United Kingdom* (1980) 2 EHRR 25, para 162 and see *Price v United Kingdom* (2002) 34 EHRR 1285, para 30 ('... the Court considers that to detain a severely disabled person in conditions where she is dangerously cold, risks developing sores because her bed is too hard or unreachable, and is unable to go to the toilet or keep clean without the greatest of difficulty, constitutes degrading treatment contrary to Article 3 of the Convention').

[377]   See *Tyrer v United Kingdom* (1978) 2 EHRR 1, para 31.

developments in contemporary child discipline and punishment.[378] Baroness Hale in *Re E (A Child) (A) (Northern Ireland)*[379] held that the special vulnerability of children is relevant both as a factor in assessing whether the treatment to which they have been subject reaches the minimum level of severity needed to engage Art 3 and to the scope of the obligations of the State to protect children from such treatment.[380] Note that the victims own conduct is irrelevant to the question of whether the treatment falls within the ambit of Art 3, that article being absolute in its prohibition of treatment which amounts to torture or inhuman or degrading treatment or punishment.[381] Being threatened with torture may amount to treatment which violates Art 3 of the ECHR.[382]

Relevant Treatment and Standard and Burden of Proof

15.149 The standard of proof for establishing that the treatment complained of in fact occurred is that of 'beyond reasonable doubt' with the burden of proof falling on the applicant.[383] However, in circumstances where a person is taken into custody in good health and is found to have suffered injury upon being released the burden of proof falls on the State to demonstrate there is an acceptable explanation for those injuries.[384] Proof beyond reasonable doubt may follow from the coexistence of sufficiently strong, clear and concordant inferences or of similar unrebutted presumptions of fact.[385] Adverse inferences may be drawn by the court from procedural irregularities.[386] The absence of intention in relation to the treatment in issue will not prevent a finding that Art 3 of the ECHR has been violated.[387] For a breach of Art 3 of the ECHR to be established the victim of the torture, treatment or punishment must be aware that they are experiencing the same or at least to be in a state of physical or mental suffering.[388]

---

[378] Van Bueren, G *Child Rights in Europe* (2007) Council of Europe Publishing, p 168. See also *DG v Ireland* (2002) 35 EHRR 1153, para 97 and *Aydin v Turkey* (1998) 25 EHRR 251, para 84.

[379] [2008] UKHL 66, [2008] 3 WLR 1208, para 7.

[380] In respect of positive obligations arising under Art 3 of the ECHR see **15.144** below.

[381] *Ireland v United Kingdom* (1980) 2 EHRR 25, para 163 and *Lorsé v The Netherlands* (2003) 37 EHRR 105, para 58. See also *Abuki v A-G of Uganda* (1997) 3 BHRC 199 Constitutional Court of Uganda ('Let it be emphasised that an offender is a citizen with human dignity deserving to be protected').

[382] *Gafgen v Germany* (2008) Application 22978/05 (unreported) and see *Campbell and Cosans v United Kingdom* (1982) 4 EHRR 293, para 26 ('the Court is of the opinion that, provided it is sufficiently real and immediate, a mere threat of conduct prohibited by Article 3 (Art. 3) may itself be in conflict with that provision. Thus, to threaten an individual with torture might in some circumstances constitute at least 'inhuman treatment').

[383] *Ireland v United Kingdom* (1978) 2 EHRR 25, para 161.

[384] *Akdeniz v Turkey* (2001) Application No 23954/94 (unreported), para 85 ('Where an individual is taken into custody in good health but is found to be injured at the time of release, it is incumbent on the State to provide a plausible explanation of how those injuries were caused, failing which an issue arises under Article 3 of the Convention'). See also *Aksoy v Turkey* (1997) 23 EHRR 553, para 61, *Yavuz v Turkey* (2007) 45 EHRR 467, para 38 and *Nadrosov v Russia* (2008) Application No 9297/02, para 30 ('Where the events in issue lie wholly, or in large part, within the exclusive knowledge of the authorities, as in the case of persons within their control in custody, strong presumptions of fact will arise in respect of injuries occurring during such detention. Indeed, the burden of proof may be regarded as resting on the authorities to provide a satisfactory and convincing explanation').

[385] *Nadrosov v Russia* (2008) Application No 9297/02, para 30.

[386] See *Yavuz v Turkey* (2007) 45 EHRR 467, paras 40–41. But see also *Mentese v Turkey* (2007) 44 EHRR 147, paras 70–73.

[387] *Labita v Italy* (2000) Application No 26772/95 (unreported), para 120 ('In order for a punishment or treatment associated with it to be 'inhuman' or 'degrading', the suffering or humiliation involved must in any event go beyond that inevitable element of suffering or humiliation connected with a given form of legitimate treatment or punishment. The question whether the purpose of the treatment was to humiliate or debase the victim is a further factor to be taken into account, but the absence of any such purpose cannot conclusively rule out a finding of violation of Article 3').

[388] *NHS Trust A v M* [2001] Fam 348.

(ii) ECHR, Art 3 – 'Torture'

15.150 Under the ECHR torture has been defined as deliberate inhuman treatment causing very serious and cruel suffering.[389] It should be note that in determining whether the treatment in issue constitutes torture for the purposes of Art 3 of the ECHR certain acts which in the past did not amount to torture may be classified differently in the future having regard to the fact that 'the increasingly high standard being required in the area of the protection of human rights and fundamental liberties correspondingly and inevitably requires greater firmness in assessing breaches of the fundamental values of democratic societies'.[390] In *Aydin v Turkey*[391] the European Court of Human Rights held that the rape of and associated conduct[392] against a young girl aged 17 constituted torture, holding that:

> 'In order to determine whether any particular form of ill-treatment should be qualified as torture, regard must be had to the distinction drawn in Article 3 between this notion and that of inhuman treatment or degrading treatment. This distinction would appear to have been embodied in the Convention to allow the special stigma of 'torture' to attach only to deliberate inhuman treatment causing very serious and cruel suffering. While being held in detention the applicant was raped by a person whose identity has still to be determined. Rape of a detainee by an official of the State must be considered to be an especially grave and abhorrent form of ill-treatment given the ease with which the offender can exploit the vulnerability and weakened resistance of his victim. Furthermore, rape leaves deep psychological scars on the victim which do not respond to the passage of time as quickly as other forms of physical and mental violence. The applicant also experienced the acute physical pain of forced penetration, which must have left her feeling debased and violated both physically and emotionally. The applicant was also subjected to a series of particularly terrifying and humiliating experiences while in custody at the hands of the security forces at Derik gendarmerie headquarters having regard to her sex and youth and the circumstances under which she was held. She was detained over a period of three days during which she must have been bewildered and disoriented by being kept blindfolded, and in a constant state of physical pain and mental anguish brought on by the beatings administered to her during questioning and by the apprehension of what would happen to her next. She was also paraded naked in humiliating circumstances thus adding to her overall sense of vulnerability and on one occasion she was pummelled with high-pressure water while being spun around in a tyre. Against this background the Court is satisfied that the accumulation of acts of

---

[389]　*Ireland v United Kingdom* (1978) 2 EHRR 25, para 167. See also *Denmark v Greece (The Greek Case)* 12 YB 186 (1972), *Selmouni v France* (2000) 29 EHRR 403, para 96 and *Menesheva v Russia* (2007) 44 EHRR 1162, paras 57–59.

[390]　*Selmouni v France* (2000) 29 EHRR 403, para 101 noting again that the Convention is a 'living instrument which must be interpreted in the light of present-day conditions'. See also *Henaf v France* (2005) 40 EHRR 990, para 55 ('In this connection, the Court reiterates that, 'having regard to the fact that the Convention is a 'living instrument which must be interpreted in the light of present-day conditions', it has held: '… certain acts which were classified in the past as 'inhuman and degrading treatment' as opposed to 'torture' could be classified differently in future. It takes the view that the increasingly high standard being required in the area of the protection of human rights and fundamental liberties correspondingly and inevitably requires greater firmness in assessing breaches of the fundamental values of democratic societies'. As that statement applies to the possibility of a harsher classification under Article 3, it follows that certain acts previously falling outside the scope of Article 3 might in future attain the required level of severity').

[391]　(1998) 25 EHRR 251.

[392]　The applicant alleged that she was stripped of her clothes, put into a car tyre and spun round and round. She further stated that was beaten and sprayed with cold water from high-pressure jets. At a later stage she alleged that she was taken clothed but blindfolded to an interrogation room. With the door of the room locked, an individual in military clothing forcibly removed her clothes, laid her on her back and raped her. By the time he had finished she was in severe pain and covered in blood. She was ordered to get dressed and subsequently taken to another room. The applicant alleged that she was later brought back to the room where she had been raped. She was beaten for about an hour by several persons who warned her not to report on what they had done to her. The European Commission found the applicant's account to be consistent and credible, which finding the European Court of Human Rights accepted.

physical and mental violence inflicted on the applicant and the especially cruel act of rape to which she was subjected amounted to torture in breach of Article 3 of the Convention. Indeed the Court would have reached this conclusion on either of these grounds taken separately.'

(ii) ECHR, Art 3 – 'Inhuman or Degrading Treatment or Punishment'

15.151 In *Kalashnikov v Russia*[393] the European Court of Human Rights summarised its jurisprudence on the factors relevant to the question of whether treatment can be considered inhuman or degrading:

> 'The Court has considered treatment to be 'inhuman' because, *inter alia*, it was premeditated, was applied for hours at a stretch and caused either actual bodily injury or intense physical and mental suffering. It has deemed treatment to be 'degrading' because it was such as to arouse in the victims feeling of fear, anguish and inferiority capable of humiliating and debasing them ... In considering whether a particular form of treatment is 'degrading' within the meaning of Article 3, the Court will have regard to whether its object is to humiliate and debase the person concerned and whether, as far as the consequences are concerned, it adversely affected his or her personality in a manner incompatible with Article 3..However, the absence of any such purpose cannot conclusively rule out a finding of a violation of Article 3 ... The suffering and humiliation involved must in any event go beyond that inevitable element of suffering or humiliation connected with a given form of legitimate treatment or punishment.'

In *R (Limbuela) and others v Secretary of State for the Home Department*[394] Lord Bingham held as follows in respect of the meaning of inhuman or degrading for the purposes of Art 3 of the ECHR:

> 'Treatment is inhuman or degrading if, to a seriously detrimental extent, it denies the most basic needs of any human being. As in all Art 3 cases, the treatment, to be proscribed, must achieve a minimum standard of severity, and I would accept that in a context such as this, not involving the deliberate infliction of pain or suffering, the threshold is a high one. A general public duty to house the homeless or provide for the destitute cannot be spelled out of art 3. But I have no doubt that the threshold may be crossed if a late applicant with no means and no alternative sources of support, unable to support himself, is, by the deliberate action of the state, denied shelter, food or the most basic necessities of life. It is not necessary that treatment, to engage Art 3, should merit the description used, in an immigration context, by Shakespeare and others in *Sir Thomas More* when they referred to 'your mountainish inhumanity'.'

15.152 Note that Art 3 of the ECHR omits the word 'cruel' from the common formulation 'cruel, inhuman or degrading treatment or punishment'. Van Bueren notes that the omission of the word 'cruel' from Art 3 may have specific consequences for children as they suffer the effects of traumatic events in different ways to adults.[395] In this context is should be remembered that the ECHR must be read so as to give effect to the CRC.[396] Art 37(a) of the CRC provides that 'No child shall be subjected to torture or other *cruel*, inhuman or degrading treatment or punishment (emphasis added).[397]

15.153 A measure which is medically necessary by reference to established medical practice cannot in principle amount to inhuman or degrading treatment for the

---

[393] (2002) 36 EHRR 34, para 95.
[394] [2005] UKHL 66, [2006] 1 AC 396, para 7 per Lord Bingham.
[395] Van Bueren, G *Child Rights in Europe* (2007) Council of Europe Publishing, p 167.
[396] See **3.43–3.46** above.
[397] See **15.12** above.

purposes of Art 3 of the ECHR.[398] However, the European Court of Human Rights made clear in *Herczegfalvy v Austria*[399] that while it is for the medical authorities to decide, on the basis of the recognised rules of medical science, the therapeutic methods to be used, if necessary by force, to preserve the physical and mental health of patients who are entirely incapable of deciding for themselves and for whom they are therefore responsible, such patients nevertheless remain under the protection of Art 3 whose requirements permit of no derogation. Thus, forced feeding where there is no 'medical necessity' has been held to constitute a violation of Art 3 of the ECHR.[400] Medical necessity must be shown convincingly to exist.[401]

ECHR, Art 3 – Inhuman Treatment or Punishment

15.154 As noted, treatment will be considered inhuman for the purposes of Art 3 of the ECHR if it is premeditated, applied for hours at a stretch and causes actual bodily injury or intense physical and mental suffering.[402] In *Lorsé v Netherlands*[403] the European Court of Human Rights held that 'complete sensory isolation, coupled with total social isolation, can destroy the personality and constitutes a form of inhuman treatment which cannot be justified by the requirements of security or any other reason'. In *Campbell and Cosans v United Kingdom*[404] the Court held that:

> '... the Court is of the opinion that, provided it is sufficiently real and immediate, a mere threat of conduct prohibited by Article 3 may itself be in conflict with that provision. Thus, to threaten an individual with torture might in some circumstances constitute at least "inhuman treatment".'

ECHR, Art 3 – Degrading Treatment or Punishment

15.155 Treatment will be degrading if it arouses in the victim feelings of fear, anguish and inferiority capable of humiliating or debasing him or her and possibly breaking his or her physical or moral resistance.[405] In *Raninen v Finland*[406] the European Court of Human Rights held that:

> '... in considering whether a punishment or treatment is 'degrading' within the meaning of Article 3, the Court will have regard to whether its object is to humiliate and debase the person concerned and whether, as far as the consequences are concerned, it adversely affected his or her personality in a manner incompatible with Article 3. In this connection, the public nature of the punishment or treatment may be a relevant factor. At the same time,

---

[398] *Nevmerzhitsky v Ukraine* (2006) 43 EHRR 645, para 94 ('The Court reiterates that a measure which is of therapeutic necessity from the point of view of established principles of medicine cannot in principle be regarded as inhuman and degrading. The same can be said about force-feeding that is aimed at saving the life of a particular detainee who consciously refuses to take food. The Convention organs must nevertheless satisfy themselves that the medical necessity has been convincingly shown to exist. Furthermore, the Court must ascertain that the procedural guarantees for the decision to force-feed are complied with. Moreover, the manner in which the applicant is subjected to force-feeding during the hunger strike shall not trespass the threshold of a minimum level of severity envisaged by the Court's case law under Article 3 of the Convention').

[399] (1993) 15 EHRR 437, para 82.

[400] *Nevmerzhitsky v Ukraine* (2006) 43 EHRR 645, paras 96–106

[401] *Herczegfalvy v Austria* (1993) 15 EHRR 437.

[402] See *Kalashnikov v Russia* (2002) 36 EHRR 34, para 95 and *Becciev v Moldova* (2008) 45 EHRR 331, para 39.

[403] (2003) 37 EHRR 105, para 58.

[404] (1980) 3 EHRR 531.

[405] *Ireland v United Kingdom* (1978) 2 EHRR 25, para 167 and see the *East African Asians Cases* (1973) 3 EHRR 76 at 80.

[406] (1997) 26 EHRR 563, para 55.

it should be recalled, the absence of publicity will not necessarily prevent a given treatment from falling into that category: it may well suffice that the victim is humiliated in his or her own eyes, even if not in the eyes of others.'

15.156 Failure to provide medical assistance to a detainee may be considered degrading.[407] In *Akpinar v Turkey*[408] the European Court of Human Rights held that the mutilation of the body of a murdered relative prior to the return of that body amounted to degrading treatment.[409] In *Gongadze v Ukraine*[410] the European Court of Human Rights held that:

'... the attitude of the investigating authorities towards the applicant and her family [concerning the disappearance of her husband followed by a prolonged period of uncertainty prior to the identification of her husbands body in which conflicting information was given by the authorities] clearly caused her serious suffering which amounted to degrading treatment contrary to Article 3 of the Convention.'

15.157 Discrimination may amount to degrading treatment for the purposes of Art 3 of the ECHR.[411] Note however that discrimination against non-marital children has been held not to be degrading treatment for the purposes of Art 3 of the ECHR.[412] The decision to terminate a prosecution for assault on the grounds that it is not thought that the victim will make a credible witness may amount to a breach of the victims rights under Art 3 of the ECHR.[413]

15.158 As to whether a particular punishment is degrading for the purposes of Art 3 of the ECHR, a punishment which involves a degree of humiliation and debasement which attains a particular level and which is other than that usual element of humiliation almost invariably involved in punishment will be considered degrading.[414] The test for whether a punishment meets this criteria is a relative one and will depend on all the circumstances of the case including the nature and context of the punishment and the manner and method in which that punishment is executed.[415] The humiliation element does not need to constitute public humiliation for the punishment to fall within the degrees prohibited by Art 3 of the ECHR. Thus in *Tyrer v United Kingdom*[416] the 'birching' of a teenage boy in private by a stranger was held to be a degrading punishment notwithstanding the fact that the punishment was neither inflicted in public or by someone known to the victim.

---

[407] *Sarban v Moldova* (2005) Application No 3456/05 (unreported), para 90.
[408] (2007) Application No 56760/00 (unreported), paras 84–87.
[409] See also *Akkum v Turkey* (2006) 43 EHRR 526 (in which a father who was presented with the mutilated body of his son was held to be the victim of degrading treatment contrary to Art 3 of the ECHR).
[410] (2006) 43 EHRR, paras 184–186. See also *Kurt v Turkey* (1998) 27 EHRR 373, *Çakici v Turkey* (1999) 31 EHRR 133, para 98, *Cyprus v Turkey* (2002) 35 EHRR 731, para 157 and *Osmanoglu v Turkey* (2008) Application 48804/99 (unreported).
[411] *East African Asians Cases* (1973) 3 EHRR 76, *Cyprus v Turkey* (2002) 35 EHRR 30 and *Moldovan v Romania* (2007) 44 EHRR 302, paras 110–114. See also *Avsar v Turkey* (2003) 37 EHRR 1014, paras 418–420.
[412] See *Abdulaziz, Cabales and Balkandali v United Kingdom* (1985) 7 EHRR 471, para 91 and *Marckx v Belgium* (1979) 2 EHRR 330. See also *Smith and Grady v United Kingdom* (1999) 29 EHRR 493, paras 120–122 (discharge from the armed forces on the grounds of homosexuality not degrading treatment for the purposes of Art 3 of the ECHR)
[413] *R (on the application of B v Director of Public Prosecutions* [2009] EWHC 106 (Admin), para 70.
[414] *Kudla v Poland* (2002) 35 EHRR 11, paras 92–94.
[415] See for example *Chember v Russia* (2008) Application No 7188/03 (unreported), paras 47–57.
[416] (1978) 2 EHRR 1, para 30.

ECHR, Art 3 – Application

(i) Corporal Punishment

ECHR, Art 3 and Corporal Punishment

15.159   Van Bueren argues in the context of Art 3 of the ECHR that the term 'child physical punishment' should be used in place of 'corporal punishment' in order to divest of its legitimacy what would constitute an assault on an adult.[417] This section deals with corporal punishment in the context of the family home and in detention. The issue corporal punishment in school is dealt with in chapters 10 and 13 above.[418]

15.160   In *Tyrer v United Kingdom*[419] the European Court of Human Rights held that the 'birching' of a 15 year old boy to his bare posterior in private by a stranger as a result of which he was sore for about a week afterwards amounted to a punishment in which the element of humiliation attained the level inherent in the notion of 'degrading punishment' and constituted a violation of Art 3 of the ECHR. In *Y v UK*[420] the Commission held as follows:

> 'The Commission recalls that the Court held in the aforementioned *Tyrer* case for corporal punishment to be degrading, within the meaning of Article 3 of the Convention, the humiliation and debasement involved must attain a particular level of severity over and above the usual element of humiliation involved in any kind of punishment. The assessment of such matters is necessarily relative: it depends upon all the circumstances of the case and, in particular, on the nature and context of the punishment itself and the manner and method of its execution.'

15.161   In *A v United Kingdom*[421] the European Court of Human Rights held that punishment of a 9 year old boy by means of a physical assault with a garden cane on more than one occasion leading to a red linear bruise to the thigh and two linear bruises to the left calf reached the severity of treatment prohibited by Art 3 of the ECHR and constituted serious breaches of the child's personal integrity. Crucially, the Court held that the domestic defence of 'reasonable chastisement' did not provide adequate protection to the child against treatment contrary, or punishment contrary to Art 3 of the ECHR. In the circumstances the Court agreed with the European Commission and found a violation of Art 3 of the ECHR.[422] The United Kingdom Government expressly accepted that UK law failed to protect children from breaches of Art 3 rights under the ECHR and that it would require amendment.[423]

The Revised European Social Charter and Corporal Punishment

15.162   Whilst the European Commission and the European Court of Human Rights have not articulated a general prohibition on corporal punishment under Art 3 of the

---

[417]   Van Bueren, G *Child Rights in Europe* (2007) Council of Europe Publishing, p 169.
[418]   See **10.99** and **13.67** above.
[419]   (1978) 2 EHRR 1.
[420]   (1992) 17 EHRR 238, para 42.
[421]   (1998) 27 EHRR 611.
[422]   Note that in *A v United Kingdom* the European Commission had stressed that its finding that United Kingdom domestic law failed to provide adequate and effective protection against corporal punishment did not mean that Art 3 was to be interpreted as imposing an obligation on States to protect, through there criminal law, against any form of physical rebuke, however mild, by a parent of a child (27 EHRR 611 at 623–624).
[423]   See **15.208** below for the current state of the domestic law on corporal punishment.

ECHR, such punishment does not accord with the terms of the Revised European Social Charter. Article 17(1)(b) of the Revised European Social Charter provides that:

'With a view to ensuring the effective exercise of the right of children and young persons to grow up in an environment which encourages the full development of their personality and of their physical and mental capacities, the Parties undertake, either directly or in co-operation with public and private organisations, to take all appropriate and necessary measures designed ... 1(b) to protect children and young persons against negligence, violence or exploitation.'[424]

15.163 Article 17(1)(b) of the Charter has been held to require a prohibition in legislation against any form of violence against children, whether at school, in other institutions, in their home or elsewhere. It further requires that any other form of degrading punishment or treatment of children must be prohibited in legislation and combined with adequate sanctions in penal or civil law.[425] Within this context the European Committee of Social Rights has made clear that to comply with the Revised European Social Charter all States parties must ban corporal punishment in respect of children and act with due diligence to ensure that such violence is eliminated in practice.[426] To this end the Council of Europe has recommended a Europe-wide ban on the corporal punishment of children.[427] Such a ban on the physical punishment of children would not infringe parents' rights under Art 8 of the ECHR[428] In its recommendation the Parliamentary Assembly records that:

'The Assembly considers that any corporal punishment of children is in breach of their fundamental right to human dignity and physical integrity. The fact that such corporal punishment is still lawful in certain member states violates their equally fundamental right to the same legal protection as adults. Striking a human being is prohibited in European society and children are human beings. The social and legal acceptance of corporal punishment of children must be ended.'[429]

15.164 The European Committee on Social Rights received five collective complaints against Belgium,[430] Portugal,[431] Italy,[432] Ireland[433] and Greece[434] from the World Organisation against Torture complaining that each country had not effectively prohibited corporal punishment of children, nor had they prohibited other forms of degrading punishment or treatment of children and provided adequate sanctions in penal or civil law in accordance with the provisions of Art 17(1)(b) of the Revised European Social Charter. Save in respect of the complaints concerning Portugal and

---

[424] Note that the United Kingdom has not yet ratified the revised European Social Charter.

[425] See European Social Charter: European Committee of Social Rights Conclusions (2001), XV-2, Vol 1 General Introduction, p 26. See also *Eliminating corporal punishment: a human rights imperative for Europe's Children* (2005) Council of Europe Publishing.

[426] See European Social Charter: European Committee of Social Rights Conclusions (2001), XV-2, Vol 1 General Introduction, p 26.

[427] Recommendation 1666(2004) of the Parliamentary Assembly of the Council of Europe. See also CoE Resolution 1778 *Child Victims: stamping out all forms of violence, exploitation and abuse* (2007).

[428] *Seven Individuals v Sweden* (1982) Application No 8811/79 (unreported) (29 CDR 104).

[429] Note that the fact that the corporal punishment of children is supported by the majority of the population and therefore in accordance with democratic principles is not, by reason of the absolute prohibition on torture and inhuman or degrading treatment or punishment, a relevant consideration as once a punishment falls within Art 3 it is not open to states to accept public support of it (Van Bueren, G *Child Rights in Europe* (2007) Council of Europe Publishing, p 171).

[430] Complaint No 21/2003.

[431] Complaint No 20/2003.

[432] Complaint No 19/2003.

[433] Complaint No 18/2003.

[434] Complaint No 17/2003.

Italy the European Committee on Social Rights concluded in each case that there had been a violation of Art 17(1)(b) of the Charter, holding that the prohibition of all the forms of violence against children must have a legislative basis, must cover all forms of violence regardless of where it occurs or of the identity of the alleged perpetrator and must contain sanctions which are adequate, dissuasive and proportionate.[435]

(ii) Detention

15.165 Acts of violence and physical force against detainees will amount to a violation of Art 3 unless the violence was not gratuitous and was at the minimum possible level and made strictly necessary by the conduct of the person complaining of a breach.[436] The seriousness of the alleged offence or offences for which the person has been convicted plays no part in determining whether the treatment complained of is within the scope of Art 3 as the prohibition under the article is absolute.[437] The minimum level of severity of treatment triggering a violation of Art 3 of the ECHR in respect of a detained person is relative and depends on all the circumstances of the case, including in some cases the characteristics of the prisoner.[438] As to specific forms of treatment, handcuffing will not normally violate Art 3 of the ECHR[439] but shackling may if disproportionate.[440] The shaving of heads will constitute a violation of Art 3 of the ECHR.[441] Poor conditions of detention may likewise violate Art 3 of the Convention[442] and a lack of resources will not justify the breach.[443] Intrusive security measures such as strip searching may constitute degrading treatment[444] and may contravene Art 8 even if they do not contravene Art 3 of the ECHR.[445]

(iii) Immigration

Detention of Unaccompanied and Separated Children

15.166 The detention of children on the grounds of their immigration status can give rise to breaches of Art 3 of the ECHR prior to their removal taking place. In *Mayeka v*

---

[435] See Resolution ResChS (2005) 10 (Belgium) (finding an absence of an explicit ban on corporal punishment of children by parents and by other persons, including for educational purposes), Resolution ResCHS (2005) 9 (Ireland) (finding that a certain level of violence remains permitted within the home, including foster care, residential care and certain child minding settings, under the common law defence of 'reasonable chastisement') and Resolution ResCH S (2005) 12 (Greece) (finding an absence of a prohibition of all forms of violence against children, including for educational purposes, within the family home and no explicit prohibition on the use of corporal punishment in secondary schools).

[436] *Tomasi v France* (1992) 15 EHRR, para 113 and *Veznedaroğlu v Turkey* (2001) 33 EHRR 1412, para 29 ('In respect of a person deprived of his liberty, recourse to physical force which has not been made strictly necessary by his own conduct diminishes human dignity and is in principle an infringement of the right set forth in Article 3').

[437] *Jalloh v Germany* (2007) 44 EHRR 667 per the concurring opinion of Sir Nicholas Bratza.

[438] *Dougoz v Greece* (2002) 34 EHRR 1480, para 44 and *Keenan v United Kingdom* (2001) 33 EHRR 913, para 110.

[439] *Raninen v Finland* (1996) 21 EHRR 573, para 56 ('As regards the kind of treatment in question in the present case, the Court is of the view that handcuffing does not normally give rise to an issue under Article 3 of the Convention where the measure has been imposed in connection with lawful arrest or detention and does not entail use of force, or public exposure, exceeding what is reasonably considered necessary in the circumstances. In this regard, it is of importance for instance whether there is reason to believe that the person concerned would resist arrest or abscond, cause injury or damage or suppress evidence').

[440] *Henaf v France* (2005) 40 EHRR 990, paras 48–59 and see Weems v United States 217 US 349 (1920), US Sup Ct.

[441] *Yankov v Bulgaria* (2005) EHRR 854, paras 114–121.

[442] *Mathew v Netherlands* (2006) 43 EHRR 444, para 214 concerning a lack of protection from rain and snow and extreme temperatures.

[443] *Dankevich v Russia* (2004) 38 EHRR 542.

[444] *Lawńczuk v Poland* (2004) 38 EHRR 148, para 59.

[445] *Wainwright v United Kingdom* (2007) 44 EHRR 809, para 46.

Belgium[446] the European Court of Human Rights found that the detention of a Congolese child aged 5 violated Art 3 of the ECHR, the Court holding that:

'The second applicant's position was characterised by her very young age, the fact that she was an illegal immigrant in a foreign land and the fact that she was unaccompanied by her family from whom she had become separated so that she was effectively left to her own devices. She was thus in an extremely vulnerable situation. In view of the absolute nature of the protection afforded by Article 3 of the Convention, it is important to bear in mind that this is the decisive factor and it takes precedence over considerations relating to the second applicant's status as an illegal immigrant. She therefore indisputably came within the class of highly vulnerable members of society to whom the Belgian State owed a duty to take adequate measures to provide care and protection as part of its positive obligations under Article 3 of the Convention ... The Court is in no doubt that the second applicant's detention in the conditions described above caused her considerable distress. Nor could the authorities who ordered her detention have failed to be aware of the serious psychological effects it would have on her. In the Court's view, the second applicant's detention in such conditions demonstrated a lack of humanity to such a degree that it amounted to inhuman treatment ... There has therefore been a violation of Article 3 of the Convention.'

Deportation and ECHR, Art 3

15.167 A Contracting State which deports or extradites a person is liable for any action the 'direct consequence' of which is the exposure of that deported individual to ill-treatment proscribed by Art 3 of the ECHR.[447] In *Mamatkulov v Turkey*[448] the European Court of Human Rights reminded itself that:

'... it is the settled case-law of the Court that extradition by a Contracting State may give rise to an issue under Article 3, and hence engage the responsibility of that State under the Convention, where substantial grounds have been shown for believing that the person in question would, if extradited, face a real risk of being subjected to treatment contrary to Article 3 in the receiving country. The establishment of such responsibility inevitably involves an assessment of conditions in the requesting country against the standards of Article 3 of the Convention. Nonetheless, there is no question of adjudicating on or establishing the responsibility of the receiving country, whether under general international law, under the Convention or otherwise. In so far as any liability under the Convention is or may be incurred, it is liability incurred by the extraditing Contracting State by reason of its having taken action which has as a direct consequence the exposure of an individual to proscribed ill-treatment.'[449]

---

[446] (2008) 46 EHRR 23.
[447] *Mamatkulov v Turkey* (2003) 14 BHRC 149, para 66 and (2005) 41 EHRR 494 (Grand Chamber).
[448] 14 BHRC 149, para 66.
[449] See also *Soering v United Kingdom* (1989) 11 EHRR 439, para 88 ('That the abhorrence of torture has such implications is recognised in Article 3 of the United Nations Convention Against Torture and Other Cruel, Inhuman or Degrading Treatment or Punishment, which provides that 'no State Party shall ... extradite a person where there are substantial grounds for believing that he would be in danger of being subjected to torture'. The fact that a specialised treaty should spell out in detail a specific obligation attaching to the prohibition of torture does not mean that an essentially similar obligation is not already inherent in the general terms of Article 3 of the European Convention. It would hardly be compatible with the underlying values of the Convention, that 'common heritage of political traditions, ideals, freedom and the rule of law' to which the Preamble refers, were a Contracting State knowingly to surrender a fugitive to another State where there were substantial grounds for believing that he would be in danger of being subjected to torture, however heinous the crime allegedly committed. Extradition in such circumstances, while not explicitly referred to in the brief and general wording of Article 3, would plainly be contrary to the spirit and intendment of the Article, and in the Court's view this inherent obligation not to extradite also extends to cases in which the fugitive would be faced in the receiving State by a real risk of exposure to inhuman or degrading treatment or punishment proscribed by that Article 3').

15.168   The 'substantial grounds for believing' that there is a real risk that a person may be subjected to torture, or to inhuman or degrading treatment or punishment must arise as at the date of the court's consideration of the case.[450] The assessment of the risk, namely whether it can be said that there are 'substantial grounds for believing' is fact specific.[451] Once 'substantial grounds for believing' have been established on the available facts then no further balancing of rights is required even where the person in question has no right to remain under domestic law or poses a serious threat to public safety.[452] Note that the loss of any entitlement to benefit from medical, social or other forms of assistance provided by the expelling State will not normally be sufficient to give rise to a violation of Art 3 of the ECHR, even where the loss of such an entitlement may lead to a reduction in life expectancy.[453]

(iv)   Economic Harm

15.169   Withdrawal of benefits from those who are destitute and unable to work may amount to inhuman or degrading treatment for the purposes of Art 3 of the ECHR if it leads to the requisite degree of injury or suffering.[454]

---

[450]   *Chahal v United Kingdom* (1996) 23 EHRR, para 86 and *Ahmed v Austria* (1996) 24 EHRR 278, para 43. See also *Cruz Varas v Sweden* (1992) 14 EHRR 1, para 76 ('Since the nature of the Contracting States' responsibility under Article 3 (art. 3) in cases of this kind lies in the act of exposing an individual to the risk of ill-treatment, the existence of the risk must be assessed primarily with reference to those facts which were known or ought to have been known to the Contracting State at the time of the expulsion; the Court is not precluded, however, from having regard to information which comes to light subsequent to the expulsion. This may be of value in confirming or refuting the appreciation that has been made by the Contracting Party or the well-foundedness or otherwise of an applicant's fears') and *Vilvarajah v United Kingdom* (1992) 14 EHRR 248, para 108 ('The Court's examination of the existence of a risk of ill-treatment in breach of Article 3 at the relevant time must necessarily be a rigorous one in view of the absolute character of this provision and the fact that it enshrines one of the fundamental values of the democratic societies making up the Council of Europe').

[451]   *RB (Algeria) v Secretary of State for the Home Department* [2009] UKHL 10, [2009] 2 WLR 512.

[452]   *Saadi v Italy* (2008) 24 BHRC 123, paras 137–142 and *Chahal v United Kingdom* (1997) 23 EHRR 413, para 80 ('The prohibition provided by Article 3 against ill-treatment is equally absolute in expulsion cases. Thus, whenever substantial grounds have been shown for believing that an individual would face a real risk of being subjected to treatment contrary to Article 3 if removed to another State, the responsibility of the Contracting State to safeguard him or her against such treatment is engaged in the event of expulsion. In these circumstances, the activities of the individual in question, however undesirable or dangerous, cannot be a material consideration. The protection afforded by Article 3 is thus wider than that provided by Articles 32 and 33 of the United Nations 1951 Convention on the Status of Refugees'). Note that Art 33 of the UN Convention on the Status of Refugees provides that '1. No Contracting State shall expel or return ('refouler') a refugee in any manner whatsoever to the frontiers of territories where his life or freedom would be threatened on account of his race, religion, nationality, membership of a particular social group or political opinion. 2. The benefit of the present provision may not, however, be claimed by a refugee whom there are reasonable grounds for regarding as a danger to the security of the country in which he is, or who, having been convicted by a final judgment of a particularly serious crime, constitutes a danger to the community of that country.' Art 33 of the 1951 Convention was considered and applied by the House of Lords in *T v Secretary of State for the Home Department* [1996] AC 742, [1996] 2 All ER 865.

[453]   *N v United Kingdom* (2008) Application No 26565/05, para 42 ('Aliens who are subject to expulsion cannot in principle claim any entitlement to remain in the territory of a Contracting State in order to continue to benefit from medical, social or other forms of assistance and services provided by the expelling State. The fact that the applicant's circumstances, including his life expectancy, would be significantly reduced if he were to be removed from the Contracting State is not sufficient in itself to give rise to breach of Article 3. The decision to remove an alien who is suffering from a serious mental or physical illness to a country where the facilities for the treatment of that illness are inferior to those available in the Contracting State may raise an issue under Article 3, but only in a very exceptional case, where the humanitarian grounds against the removal are compelling'). For a case involving 'exceptional circumstances' see *D v United Kingdom* (1997) 24 EHRR 423.

[454]   *R (Limbuela) v Secretary of State for the Home Department* [2005] UKHL 66, [2006] 1 AC 396. But see also *R (Q) v Secretary of State for the Home Department* [2003] EWCA Civ 364, [2004] QB 36, paras 52–56.

ECHR, Article 4 – Slavery and Servitude

ECHR, Art 4

15.170 Article 4 of the ECHR provides as follows in respect of the prohibition on slavery and servitude:

> '1. No one shall be held in slavery or servitude.[455]

> 2. No one shall be required to perform forced or compulsory labour.

> 3. For the purpose of this article the term forced or compulsory labour shall not include:

> a)   any work required to be done in the ordinary course of detention imposed according to the provisions of Article 5 of this Convention or during conditional release from such detention;

> b)   any service of a military character or, in case of conscientious objectors in countries where they are recognised, service exacted instead of compulsory military service;

> c)   any service exacted in case of an emergency or calamity threatening the life or well-being of the community; any work or service which forms part of normal civic obligations.'

Art 4 of the ECHR constitutes an absolute prohibition on slavery and servitude from which no derogation is permitted pursuant to Art 15(2) of the ECHR, and a qualified prohibition on forced or compulsory labour.[456] The European Court of Human Rights has held that, together with Articles 2 and 3, Article 4 of the Convention enshrines one of the basic values of the democratic societies making up the Council of Europe.[457]

(i)   ECHR, Art 4 – Absolute Prohibition

15.171 The right enshrined in Art 4(1) of the ECHR not be held in slavery or servitude is an absolute right admitting of no exceptions.[458] Save for the narrowly construed and exhaustive list of exceptions contained in Art 4(3) of the ECHR the right enshrined in Art 4(2) of the ECHR that no one shall be required to perform forced or compulsory labour is likewise an absolute right admitting of no exceptions.[459]

(ii)   ECHR, Art 4 – Positive Obligations

15.172 In *Siliadin v France*[460] the European Court of Human Rights, having referred to the ILO Forced Labour Convention (No 29) 1930, the Supplementary Convention on the Abolition of Slavery, the Slave Trade, and Institutions and Practices Similar to Slavery and Art 19(1) and Art 32 of the CRC, held:

> 'In those circumstances, the Court considers that limiting compliance with Article 4 of the Convention only to direct action by the State authorities would be inconsistent with the international instruments specifically concerned with this issue and would amount to rendering it ineffective. Accordingly, it necessarily follows from this provision that States

---

[455]   Unlike Art 4 of the Universal Declaration of Human Rights and Art 8 of the ICCPR it makes not express reference to the slave trade.

[456]   Recommendation 1523 (2001) on Domestic Slavery.

[457]   *Siliadin v France* (2005) 20 BHRC 654, para 82.

[458]   *Siliadin v France* (2005) 20 BHRC 654, paras 90 and 112.

[459]   *Siliadin v France* (2005) 20 BHRC 654, paras 90 and 112.

[460]   (2005) 20 BHRC 654, para 89.

have positive obligations, in the same way as under Article 3 for example, to adopt criminal-law provisions which penalise the practices referred to in Article 4 and to apply them in practice'[461]

ECHR, Art 4(1) – Ambit

(i)   ECHR, Art 4(1) 'Slavery'

15.173   Article 4(1) of the ECHR provides that 'No one shall be held in slavery or servitude'. In considering the meaning of the word 'slavery' the European Court of Human Rights has pointed out that sight should not be lost of the fact that the ECHR is a 'living instrument' which must be interpreted in the light of present-day conditions, and that the increasingly high standard being required in the area of the protection of human rights and fundamental liberties correspondingly and inevitably requires greater firmness in assessing breaches of the fundamental values of democratic societies.[462] In *Siliadin v France*,[463] a case concerning a 15 year old girl forced to work in domestic servitude without respite and against her will, the Court adopted the definition of slavery contained in the Slavery Convention 1926 Art 1(1), namely 'the status or condition of a person over whom any or all of the powers attaching to the right of ownership are exercised'.

(ii)   ECHR, Art 4(1) 'Servitude'

15.174   A serf is obliged to work and live on the property of another with it being impossible for him or her to change his or her condition.[464] In *Van Droogenbroeck v Belgium*[465] the Commission indicated that a situation could only be regarded as 'servitude' if it involved a particularly serious form of denial of freedom. In *Siliadin v France*[466] the term 'servitude' in Art 4 of the ECHR was described as follows:

> '... that for Convention purposes 'servitude' means an obligation to provide one's services that is imposed by the use of coercion, and is to be linked with the concept of 'slavery' described above.'

ECHR, Art 4(2) – Ambit

15.175   Article 4(2) of the ECHR provides that 'No one shall be required to perform forced or compulsory labour'.

(i)   ECHR, Art 4(2) – 'Forced or Compulsory Labour'

15.176   In interpreting or the term 'forced or compulsory labour' for the purposes of Art 4(2) of the ECHR the European Court of Human Rights has had regard to the ILO Forced Labour Convention (No 29) as a starting point.[467] The term 'forced or compulsory labour' in Art 4(2) of the ECHR indicates physical or mental constraint and has been defined as work extracted from a person under threat of penalty for which he

---

[461]   See also para 112 ('... the Court considers that, in accordance with contemporary norms and trends in this field, the member States' positive obligations under Article 4 of the Convention must be seen as requiring the penalisation and effective prosecution of any act aimed at maintaining a person in such a situation').

[462]   *Siliadin v France* (2005) 20 BHRC 654, para 121.

[463]   (2005) 20 BHRC 654, para 89.

[464]   *Van Droogenbroeck v Belgium* B 44 (1980) Com Rep.

[465]   B 44 (1980) Com Rep, para 58.

[466]   (2005) 20 BHRC 654, para 124.

[467]   *Van der Mussele v Belgium* (1983) 6 EHRR 163, para 32.

or she has not voluntary offered him or herself.[468] In *Reitmayr v Austria*[469] the European Commission articulated the meaning of 'forced or compulsory labour' in Art 4(2) of the ECHR as follows:

> '... the concept of forced or compulsory labour within the meaning of Article 4 para 2 comprises two elements. These elements are first that the labour or service must be performed by the person concerned against his will and secondly that the obligation to perform this labour or service, must be either unjust or oppressive, or must itself constitute an avoidable hardship.'[470]

ECHR, Art 4(3) – Ambit

15.177   Article 4(3) of the ECHR provides the following exceptions to the prohibition on forced or compulsory labour contained in Art 4(2) of the ECHR:

> '3. For the purpose of this article the term forced or compulsory labour shall not include:
>
> a)   any work required to be done in the ordinary course of detention imposed according to the provisions of Article 5 of this Convention or during conditional release from such detention;
>
> b)   any service of a military character or, in case of conscientious objectors in countries where they are recognised, service exacted instead of compulsory military service;
>
> c)   any service exacted in case of an emergency or calamity threatening the life or well-being of the community; any work or service which forms part of normal civic obligations.'

15.178   Article 4(3) of the ECHR is not intended to limit the protection of the right guaranteed by Art 4(2) but to delimit that right. In *Schmidt v Germany*[471] the European Court of Human Rights held as follows in respect of the ambit of Art 4(3) of the ECHR:

> 'The Court reiterates that paragraph 3 of Article 4 is not intended to 'limit' the exercise of the right guaranteed by paragraph 2, but to 'delimit' the very content of that right, for it forms a whole with paragraph 2 and indicates what 'the term 'forced or compulsory labour' shall not include' (ce qui 'n'est pas considéré comme 'travail forcé ou obligatoire"). This being so, paragraph 3 serves as an aid to the interpretation of paragraph 2. The four subparagraphs of paragraph 3, notwithstanding their diversity, are grounded on the governing ideas of the general interest, social solidarity and what is normal in the ordinary course of affairs.'[472]

---

[468]   *Van der Mussele v Belgium* (1983) 6 EHRR 163, para 33 ('It remains to be ascertained whether there was 'forced or compulsory' labour. The first of these adjectives brings to mind the idea of physical or mental constraint, a factor that was certainly absent in the present case. As regards the second adjective, it cannot refer just to any form of legal compulsion or obligation. For example, work to be carried out in pursuance of a freely negotiated contract cannot be regarded as falling within the scope of Article 4 (art. 4) on the sole ground that one of the parties has undertaken with the other to do that work and will be subject to sanctions if he does not honour his promise. On this point, the minority of the Commission agreed with the majority. What there has to be is work 'exacted ... under the menace of any penalty' and also performed against the will of the person concerned, that is work for which he 'has not offered himself voluntarily') and *Siliadin v France* (2005) 20 BHRC 654, para 117.

[469]   (1995) 20 EHRR CD 89.

[470]   Note that a requirement that a lawyer represent a client for free pursuant to the requirements of his or her professional code will not constitute forced or compulsory labour (*Van der Mussele v Belgium* (1983) 6 EHRR 163 and see *X v Germany* 18 DR 216 (1979)).

[471]   (1994) 18 EHRR 513, para 22.

[472]   See also *Van der Mussele v Belgium* (1983) 6 EHRR 163, para 38.

The Revised European Social Charter[473]

Revised ESC Art 7

15.179 Part I of the Revised European Social Charter provides that children and young persons have the right to appropriate social, legal and economic protection.[474] To this end, Art 7 of the Revised Charter provides as follows:

'With a view to ensuring the effective exercise of the right of children and young persons to protection, the Parties undertake:

(1) to provide that the minimum age of admission to employment shall be 15 years, subject to exceptions for children employed in prescribed light work without harm to their health, morals or education;

(2) to provide that the minimum age of admission to employment shall be 18 years with respect to prescribed occupations regarded as dangerous or unhealthy;

(3) to provide that persons who are still subject to compulsory education shall not be employed in such work as would deprive them of the full benefit of their education;

(4) to provide that the working hours of persons under 18 years of age shall be limited in accordance with the needs of their development, and particularly with their need for vocational training;[475]

(5) to recognise the right of young workers and apprentices to a fair wage or other appropriate allowances;

(6) to provide that the time spent by young persons in vocational training during the normal working hours with the consent of the employer shall be treated as forming part of the working day;

(7) to provide that employed persons of under 18 years of age shall be entitled to a minimum of four weeks' annual holiday with pay;

(8) to provide that persons under 18 years of age shall not be employed in night work with the exception of certain occupations provided for by national laws or regulations;

(9) to provide that persons under 18 years of age employed in occupations prescribed by national laws or regulations shall be subject to regular medical control;

(10) to ensure special protection against physical and moral dangers to which children and young persons are exposed, and particularly against those resulting directly or indirectly from their work.'[476]

Council of Europe Convention on the Protection of Children against Sexual Exploitation and Sexual Abuse

15.180 The European Convention on the Protection of Children against Sexual Exploitation and Sexual Abuse[477] (CPCSESA) was signed by the United Kingdom on 5 May 2008 but has not yet been ratified by the United Kingdom. Further, as only two States Parties (Albania and Greece) have ratified the CPCSESA it has not yet come into force. According to the Explanatory Report on the Convention, its two main aims are to prevent and combat sexual exploitation and sexual abuse and to protect the rights of child victims.[478] Chapter II of the convention prescribes preventative measures and

---

[473] Note that the United Kingdom has not yet ratified the Revised European Social Charter.

[474] Revised European Social Charter Part I, para 17.

[475] See also the EU Directive 2003/88/EC Concerning Certain Aspects of the Organisation of Working Time.

[476] The Committee of Independent Experts has held that the term 'light work' does not automatically exclude domestic and agricultural work (Conclusions of the Committee of Independent Experts 1, p 42). See also CoE Recommendation 1336 – Combating Child Labour Exploitation as a Matter of Priority.

[477] (2007) CETS No 201. Signed by the United Kingdom on 5 May 2008 but not yet ratified.

[478] CPCSESA Explanatory Report, para 37. The preamble to the convention makes specific reference to Art 34 of the CRC and the Optional Protocol on the Sale of Children, Child Prostitution and Child Pornography,

Art 4 of the CPCSESA requires that 'Each Party shall take the necessary legislative or other measures to prevent all forms of sexual exploitation and sexual abuse of children and to protect children'. Chapter III of the CPCSESA makes provision for 'the co-ordination on a national or local level between the different agencies in charge of the protection from, the prevention of and the fight against sexual exploitation and sexual abuse of children'[479] and Chapter IV provides for the protection of child victims. Chapters VI and VII requires States Parties to take the necessary legislative measures to criminalise sexual abuse, child prostitution, child pornography and associated offences.[480]

The Child's Right to Freedom from Harmful Treatment under European Union Law

European Charter of Fundamental Rights

15.181 Article 4 of the European Charter of Fundamental Rights provides that 'No one shall be subjected to torture or to inhuman or degrading treatment or punishment'. Article 5 of the Charter provides that no one shall be held in slavery or servitude, be required to perform forced or compulsory labour and prohibits trafficking in human beings. Article 24 of the Charter provides that 'Children shall have the right to such protection and care as is necessary for their wellbeing'. In relation to economic exploitation, Art 32 of the European Charter of Fundamental Rights provides that:

> 'The employment of children is prohibited. The minimum age of admission to employment may not be lower than the minimum school-leaving age, without prejudice to such rules as may be more favourable to young people and except for limited derogations. Young people admitted to work must have working conditions appropriate to their age and be protected against economic exploitation and any work likely to harm their safety, health or physical, mental, moral or social development or to interfere with their education.'

15.182 In accordance with Art 52(3) of the European Charter,[481] the meaning and scope of the rights under Arts 4, 5, 24 and 32 of the European Charter are the same as the corresponding rights under the ECHR and its related protocols.

The Child's Right to Freedom from Harmful Treatment under Other Regional Instruments

American Convention on Human Rights

15.183 Article 19 of the American Convention on Human Rights provides that 'Every minor child has the right to the measures of protection required by his condition as a

---

the Protocol to Prevent, Suppress and Punish Trafficking in Persons, Especially Women and Children, supplementing the United Nations Convention against Transnational Organised Crime, as well as the International Labour Organisation Convention concerning the Prohibition and Immediate Action for the Elimination of the Worst Forms of Child Labour.

[479] CPCSESA, Art 10.

[480] See also CoE Recommendation 1307 – Sexual Exploitation: Zero Tolerance (2002) and CoE Recommendation – Child Prostitution (2007).

[481] Article 52(3) of the Charter provides that 'Insofar as this Charter contains rights which correspond to rights guaranteed by the Convention for the Protection of Human Rights and Fundamental Freedoms, the meaning and scope of those rights shall be the same as those laid down by the said Convention. This provision shall not prevent Union law providing more extensive protection.'

minor on the part of his family, society, and the state'.[482] Within this context, the American Convention stipulates that every person[483] has the right to have his or her physical, mental and moral integrity protected,[484] prohibits torture or cruel, inhuman or degrading treatment or punishment[485] and prohibits slavery, servitude and forced or compulsory labour.[486]

15.184 In its Advisory Opinion on the *Legal Status and Human Rights of the Child* the Inter-American Court of Human Rights opined that the States parties to the American Convention on Human Rights:[487]

> '... are under the obligation pursuant to Articles 19 (Rights of the Child) and 17 (Rights of the Family), in combination with Article 1(1) of this Convention to adopt all positive measures required to ensure protection of children against mistreatment, whether in their relations with public authorities, or in relations among individuals or with non-governmental entities ... the State has the duty to adopt positive measures to fully ensure effective exercise of the rights of the child.'

ACHR – Art 5

15.185 Article 5 of the American Convention on Human Rights provides as follows in respect of harmful treatment:

> '1. Every person has the right to have his physical, mental, and moral integrity respected.
>
> 2. No one shall be subjected to torture or to cruel, inhuman, or degrading punishment or treatment ...'

ACHR Art 5 – 'Torture'

15.186 Article 2 of the Inter-American Convention to Prevent and Punish Torture defines torture as follows:

> 'For the purposes of this Convention, torture shall be understood to be any act intentionally performed whereby physical or mental pain or suffering is inflicted on a person for purposes of criminal investigation, as a means of intimidation, as personal punishment, as a preventive measure, as a penalty, or for any other purpose. Torture shall also be understood to be the use of methods upon a person intended to obliterate the personality of the victim or to diminish his physical or mental capacities, even if they do not cause physical pain or mental anguish. The concept of torture shall not include physical or mental pain or suffering that is inherent in or solely the consequence of lawful measures, provided that they do not include the performance of the acts or use of the methods referred to in this article.'[488]

---

[482] See also Art 16 of the Protocol of San Salvador ('Every child, whatever his parentage, has the right to the protection that his status as a minor requires from his family, society and the State').

[483] Article 1(2) of the American Convention on Human Rights defines 'person' as meaning every human being.

[484] Article 5(1).

[485] Article 5(2).

[486] Article 6.

[487] Inter-American Court of Human Rights, Advisory Opinion OC-17/2002 of 28 August 2002, paras 87 and 91.

[488] Note that Art 5 of the Inter-American Convention to Prevent and Punish Torture provides that 'The existence of circumstances such as a state of war, threat of war, state of siege or of emergency, domestic disturbance or strife, suspension of constitutional guarantees, domestic political instability, or other public emergencies or disasters shall not be invoked or admitted as justification for the crime of torture. Neither the dangerous character of the detainee or prisoner, nor the lack of security of the prison establishment or penitentiary shall justify torture.'

15.187   In respect of the treatment of children, in *Jailton Neri Da Fonseca v Brazil*[489] the Inter-American Commission on Human Rights noted that:

'... in the case of children consideration must also be given to a more rigorous standard for the degree of suffering that could imply torture, taking into account, for instance, factors such as age, sex, the effect of the stress and fear experienced, the health of the victim, and his maturity.'

ACHR – Art 6

15.188   Article 6 of the American Convention on Human Rights provides as follows in respect of slavery, servitude and forced or compulsory labour:

'1. No one shall be subject to slavery or to involuntary servitude, which are prohibited in all their forms, as are the slave trade and traffic in women.

2. No one shall be required to perform forced or compulsory labor. This provision shall not be interpreted to mean that, in those countries in which the penalty established for certain crimes is deprivation of liberty at forced labor, the carrying out of such a sentence imposed by a competent court is prohibited. Forced labor shall not adversely affect the dignity or the physical or intellectual capacity of the prisoner.

3. For the purposes of this article, the following do not constitute forced or compulsory labor:

(a)   work or service normally required of a person imprisoned in execution of a sentence or formal decision passed by the competent judicial authority. Such work or service shall be carried out under the supervision and control of public authorities, and any persons performing such work or service shall not be placed at the disposal of any private party, company, or juridical person;

(b)   military service and, in countries in which conscientious objectors are recognised, national service that the law may provide for in lieu of military service;

(c)   service exacted in time of danger or calamity that threatens the existence or the well-being of the community; or

(d)   work or service that forms part of normal civic obligations.'

Ibero-American Convention on the Rights of Youth

15.189   Article 10 of the Ibero-American Convention on the Rights of Youth requires that States Parties shall adopt specific protection measures in favour of youth regarding their physical and mental integrity and security, as well as against torture and cruel, inhuman or degrading treatment. Article 11 of the Convention requires that States Parties shall take such measures as may be necessary to prevent from exploitation, abuse or sexual tourism or any other kind of violence or mistreatment of young people and shall promote the physical, psychological and economic recovery of victims. In respect of economic protection, Art 27 of the Convention stipulates that:

'1. Youth have the right to equal opportunities and treatment concerning integration, remuneration, promotion and working conditions, to the existence of programmes which promote a first employment, vocational qualification and to a special attention to youth who are temporarily unemployed.

---

[489]   IACHR, Report No 33/04, *Jailton Neri Da Fonseca (Brazil)*, Case 11.634 of March 11, 2004, para 64.

2. The States Parties recognise that working youth shall enjoy equal and working union rights as those recognised to all workers.

3. The States Parties recognise the right of youth to be protected against economic exploitation and any employment harmful to their health, education or physical or psychological development.

4. The work for youth with ages between 15 and 18 years shall be object of a special protection law according to the international working rules.

5. The States Parties shall adopt measures so that young minor women workers benefit from specific promotion additional measures which, in general, correspond to working legislation, Social Security and Social Assistance. In any case, they shall adopt in their favour special measures by developing Section 2, Article 10, of the International Covenant on Economic, Social and Cultural Rights. In the mentioned development, special attention shall be given to the application of Article 10, Covenant 102, of the International Labour Organisation.

6. The States Parties undertake to adopt the needed political and legislative measures to eradicate any kind of discrimination against young women in the working field.'[490]

The African Charter on the Rights and Welfare of the Child

15.190   The African Charter on the Rights and Welfare of the Child makes extensive provision for the protection of the child from harmful treatment and reflects the CRC in addressing the issues of torture and cruel, inhuman or degrading treatment or punishment, physical, mental and sexual abuse[491] and sexual exploitation,[492] sale, trafficking abduction,[493] narcotics and drug abuse,[494] economic exploitation and child labour[495] and involvement in armed conflict.[496] In addition, the Charter enshrines the right of the child to protection in respect of harmful social and cultural practices.[497] Art 13(1) of the Charter provides that every child who is mentally or physically disabled shall have the right to special measures of protection in keeping with his physical and moral needs and under conditions which ensure his or her dignity, promote his or her self-reliance and active participation in the community.

ACRWC – Art 16

15.191   Article 16 of the African Charter on the Rights and Welfare of the Child stipulates as follows in respect of the protection to be afforded to the child by States parties to the Charter against torture, cruel, inhuman or degrading treatment or punishment, physical or mental injury or abuse and neglect or maltreatment:

'1. States Parties to the present Charter shall take specific legislative, administrative, social and educational measures to protect the child from all forms of torture, inhuman or

---

[490]   See also Art 28(1).
[491]   Article 16.
[492]   Article 27.
[493]   Article 29.
[494]   Article 28.
[495]   Article 15.
[496]   Article 27.
[497]   Article 21.

degrading treatment and especially physical or mental injury or abuse, neglect or maltreatment including sexual abuse, while in the care of the child.[498]

2. Protective measures under this Article shall include effective procedures for the establishment of special monitoring units to provide necessary support for the child and for those who have the care of the child, as well as other forms of prevention and for identification, reporting referral investigation, treatment, and follow-up of instances of child abuse and neglect.'

ACRWC – Art 27

15.192   Article 27 of the Charter stipulates as follows in respect of the protection to be afforded by States parties to children in respect of sexual exploitation:

'1. States Parties to the present Charter shall undertake to protect the child from all forms of sexual exploitation and sexual abuse and shall in particular take measures to prevent:

(a)   the inducement, coercion or encouragement of a child to engage in any sexual activity;
(b)   the use of children in prostitution or other sexual practices;
(c)   the use of children in pornographic activities, performances and materials.'[499]

ACRWC – Art 29

15.193   Article 29 of the African Charter on the Rights and Welfare of the Child states as follows in respect of the protection to be afforded to children in respect sale, trafficking and abduction:

'States Parties to the present Charter shall take appropriate measures to prevent:

(a)   the abduction, the sale of, or traffick of children for any purpose or in any form, by any person including parents or legal guardians of the child;
(b)   the use of children in all forms of begging.'

ACRWC – Art 28

15.194   Article 28 of the African Charter on the Rights and Welfare of the Child states as follows in respect of the protection of children from narcotics and drug abuse:

'States Parties to the present Charter shall take all appropriate measures to protect the child from the use of narcotics and illicit use of psychotropic substances as defined in the relevant international treaties, and to prevent the use of children in the production and trafficking of such substances.'

ACRWC – Art 15

15.195   Article 15 of the African Charter on the Rights and Welfare of the Child provides as follows in respect of the prohibition on child labour:

---

[498]   See also Art 18(2)(a) of the African Youth Charter which provides that 'Ensure that youth who are detained or imprisoned or in rehabilitation centres are not subjected to torture, inhumane or degrading treatment or punishment.'

[499]   See also Art 23(l) of the African Youth Charter which requires States parties to 'Enact and enforce legislation that protect girls and young women from all forms of violence, genital mutilation, incest, rape, sexual abuse, sexual exploitation, trafficking, prostitution and pornography.' See further Art 23(m) of the African Youth Charter which stipulates that State parties 'Develop programmes of action that provide legal, physical and psychological support to girls and young women who have been subjected to violence and abuse such that they can fully re-integrate into social and economic life.'

'1. Every child shall be protected from all forms of economic exploitation and from performing any work that is likely to be hazardous or to interfere with the child's physical, mental, spiritual, moral, or social development.[500]

2. States Parties to the present Charter take all appropriate legislative and administrative measures to ensure the full implementation of this Article which covers both the formal and informal sectors of employment and having regard to the relevant provisions of the International Labour Organisation's instruments relating to children, States Parties shall in particular:

(a)   provide through legislation, minimum wages for admission to every employment;
(b)   provide for appropriate regulation of hours and conditions o employment;
(c)   provide for appropriate penalties or other sanctions to ensure the effective enforcement of this Article;
(d)   promote the dissemination of information on the hazards of child labour to all sectors of the community.'

ACRWC – Art 22

15.196   Article 22 Charter provides as follows in respect of the prohibition on the involvement of children in armed conflict:

'1. States Parties to this Charter shall undertake to respect and ensure respect for rules of international humanitarian law applicable in armed conflicts which affect the child.

2. States Parties to the present Charter shall take all necessary measures to ensure that no child shall take a direct part in hostilities and refrain in particular, from recruiting any child.[501]

3. States Parties to the present Charter shall, in accordance with their obligations under international humanitarian law, protect the civilian population in armed conflicts and shall take all feasible measures to ensure the protection and care[502] of children who are affected by armed conflicts. Such rules shall also apply to children in situations of internal armed conflicts, tension and strife.'[503]

ACRWC – Art 21

15.197   Article 21 of the African Charter on the Rights and Welfare of the Child states as follows in respect of the protection to be afforded to the child in respect of harmful social and cultural practices:

---

[500]   See also Art 23(i) of the African Youth Charter which requires States parties to 'Protect girls and young women from economic exploitation and from performing work that is hazardous, takes them away from education or that is harmful to their mental or physical health.'

[501]   Note that the level of protection provided to children by Art 22(2) of the African Charter on the Rights and Welfare of the Child is stronger than that provided under either the CRC or the Protocols to the Geneva Conventions.

[502]   See also Art 17(g) of the African Youth Charter ('States Parties shall ... Take appropriate measures to promote physical and psychological recovery and social reintegration of young victims of armed conflict and war by providing access to education and skills development such as vocational training to resume social and economic life').

[503]   See also Art 17(d) of the African Youth Charter ('States Parties shall ... Condemn armed conflict and prevent the participation, involvement, recruitment and sexual slavery of young people in armed conflict') and Art 17(e) ('States Parties shall ... Take all feasible measures to protect the civilian population, including youth, who are affected and displaced by armed conflict').

'1. States Parties to the present Charter shall take all appropriate measures[504] to eliminate harmful social and cultural practices affecting the welfare, dignity, normal growth and development of the child and in particular:

(a)   those customs and practices prejudicial to the health or life of the child; and
(b)   those customs and practices discriminatory to the child on the grounds of sex or other status.[505]

2. Child marriage and the betrothal of girls and boys shall be prohibited and effective action, including legislation, shall be taken to specify the minimum age of marriage to be 18 years and make registration of all marriages in an official registry compulsory.'[506]

African Charter on Human and Peoples' Rights

15.198   Article 5 of the African Charter on Human and Peoples' Rights provides as follows in respect of harmful treatment:

'Every individual shall have the right to the respect of the dignity inherent in a human being and to the recognition of his legal status. All forms of exploitation and degradation of man particularly slavery, slave trade, torture, cruel, inhuman or degrading punishment and treatment shall be prohibited.'[507]

Revised Arab Charter on Human Rights

15.199   Article 33(2) of the Revised Arab Charter on Human Rights requires that the State and society shall ensure the prohibition of all forms of violence against children and the protection and care of children.[508] Art 33(3) requires that State parties to the Charter take all necessary legislative, administrative and judicial measures to guarantee the protection, survival, development and well being of the child in an atmosphere of freedom and dignity.

Revised Arab Charter – Art 8

15.200   Article 8 of the Revised Arab Charter on Human Rights provides as follows in respect of the prohibition on torture and cruel, inhuman and degrading treatment or punishment:

---

[504]   See also Art 23(m) of the African Youth Charter which stipulates that State parties 'Develop programmes of action that provide legal, physical and psychological support to girls and young women who have been subjected to violence and abuse such that they can fully re-integrate into social and economic life.'

[505]   See also Art 23(l) of the African Youth Charter which requires States parties to 'Enact and enforce legislation that protect girls and young women from all forms of violence, genital mutilation, incest, rape, sexual abuse, sexual exploitation, trafficking, prostitution and pornography.'

[506]   See also Art 25 of the African Youth Charter ('State Parties shall take all appropriate steps to eliminate harmful social and cultural practices that affect the welfare and dignity of youth, in particular; a) Customs and practices that harm the health, life or dignity of the youth; b) Customs and practices discriminatory to youth on the basis of gender, age or other status.'

[507]   See *Curtis Francis Doebbler v Sudan*, Comm. No 236/2000 (2003) African Commission on Human and Peoples' Rights, para 42 ('There is no right for individuals, and particularly the government of a country to apply physical violence to individuals for offences. Such a right would be tantamount to sanctioning State sponsored torture under the Charter and contrary to the very nature of this human rights treaty').

[508]   Note that in relation to the protection of the child from participation in armed conflict Islamic law does not permit children under the age of 15 to participate in 'jihad' (see Elahi, M *The Rights of the Child under Islamic Law: Prohibition of the Child Soldier* (1988) 19 Columbia Human Rights Review 274).

'1. No one shall be subjected to physical or psychological torture or to cruel, degrading, humiliating or inhuman treatment.[509]

2. Each State party shall protect every individual subject to its jurisdiction from such practices and shall take effective measures to prevent them. The commission of, or participation in, such acts shall be regarded as crimes that are punishable by law and not subject to any statute of limitations. Each State party shall guarantee in its legal system redress for any victim of torture and the right to rehabilitation and compensation.'[510]

Revised Arab Charter – Art 10

15.201 Article 10 of the Revised Arab Charter on Human Rights prohibits all forms of slavery and trafficking in human beings as follows:

'1. All forms of slavery and trafficking in human beings are prohibited and are punishable by law. No one shall be held in slavery and servitude under any circumstances.

2. Forced labor, trafficking in human beings for the purposes of prostitution or sexual exploitation, the exploitation of the prostitution of others or any other form of exploitation or the exploitation of children in armed conflict are prohibited.'[511]

Revised Arab Charter Art 34(3)

15.202 Article 34(3) of the Revised Arab Charter on Human Rights provides as follows in respect of protecting children from economic exploitation and hazardous labour:

'3. The States parties recognise the right of the child to be protected from economic exploitation and from being forced to perform any work that is likely to be hazardous or to interfere with the child's education or to be harmful to the child's health or physical, mental, spiritual, moral or social development. To this end, and having regard to the relevant provisions of other international instruments, States parties shall in particular:

(a) Define a minimum age for admission to employment;
(b) Establish appropriate regulation of working hours and conditions;
(c) Establish appropriate penalties or other sanctions to ensure the effective endorsement of these provisions.'

---

[509] See also Art 9 of the Revised Arab Charter on Human Rights (' No one shall be subjected to medical or scientific experimentation or to the use of his organs without his free consent and full awareness of the consequences and provided that ethical, humanitarian and professional rules are followed and medical procedures are observed to ensure his personal safety pursuant to the relevant domestic laws in force in each State party. Trafficking in human organs is prohibited in all circumstances'). No derogation is permitted from Art 9 (see Art 4(2)).

[510] No derogation is permitted from Art 8 (see Art 4(2)).

[511] No derogation is permitted from Art 10 (see Art 4(2)).

Child's Right to Freedom from Harmful Treatment under Domestic Law

Domestic Law and Torture and Cruel, Inhuman or Degrading Treatment or Punishment

Domestic Law and Torture

15.203   In *A v Secretary of State for the Home Department (No 2)*[512] Lord Bingham of Cornhill noted that from its very earliest days the common law of England set its face firmly against the use of torture[513] and that, whilst torture continued to be used in the sixteenth and early seventeenth centuries, largely in the exercise of the Royal prerogative, no torture warrant has been issued in England since the Act of 1640 abolishing the Court of Star Chamber.[514] Lord Bingham concludes that Jardine's statement that 'As far as authority goes, therefore, the crimes of murder and robbery are not more distinctly forbidden by our criminal code than the application of the torture to witnesses or accused persons is condemned by the oracles of the Common law'[515] is aptly described as a constitutional principle. The English Bill of Rights of 1689 provides that 'cruell and unusuall punishments' should not be inflicted.[516]

15.204   Within this context the jus cogens nature of the international crime of torture has been recognised by the domestic courts[517] as has the fact that prohibition on torture is absolute.[518] The domestic courts have further reinforced the principle that, in respect of torture, there is a duty on States to do more than simply eschew the practice of torture.[519] This principle has been recognised as also encompassing the harmful treatment of children.[520] In *A v Secretary of State for the Home Department (No 2)*[521] the House of Lords affirmed the principle that evidence obtained by torture is inadmissible in judicial proceedings.[522]

---

[512]   [2005] UKHL 71, [2006] 2 AC 221, paras 11–13.

[513]   Lord Bingham noted that 'In rejecting the use of torture, whether applied to potential defendants or potential witnesses, the common law was moved by the cruelty of the practice as applied to those not convicted of crime, by the inherent unreliability of confessions or evidence so procured and by the belief that it degraded all those who lent themselves to the practice.'

[514]   Act of 16 Charles I, c 10. Commenting on this history in his seminal work *The Rule of Law*, Lord Bingham notes that 'It was early recognition that there are some practices so abhorrent as not to be tolerable, even when the safety of the state is said to be at risk, even where the price of restraint is that a guilty man may walk free. There are some things which even the supreme power in the state should not be allowed to do, ever.' (Bingham, T *The Rule of Law* (2010) Allen Lane, p 17).

[515]   Jardine, D *A Reading on the Use of Torture in the Criminal Law of England Previously to the Commonwealth* (1837) Baldwin & Craddock, p 13.

[516]   Bill of Rights, I.10.

[517]   *R v Bow Street Metropolitan Stipendiary Magistrate ex p Pinochet Ugarte (No 3)* [2000] 1 AC 147 HL.

[518]   *BA (Pakistan) v Secretary of State for the Home Department* [2009] EWCA Civ 1072, [2009] All ER (D) 308 (Nov) ('The prohibition under art 3 of the ECHR on torture, to take just one example, is absolute. Even a single incident of it may be sufficient to amount to persecution, unlike lesser harm, and there is ample authority to establish that a single incident may suffice').

[519]   *Kuwait Airways Corp v Iraqi Airways Co (No 3)* [2002] UKHL 19, [2002] 3 All ER 209, paras 12 and 117.

[520]   *Re E (A Child) (Northern Ireland)* [2008] UKHL 66, [2008] 3 WLR 1208, para 7 per Baroness Hale. See also *Van Eden v Minister of Safety and Security* (2003) (1) SA 389 Supreme Court of Appeal of South Africa.

[521]   [2005] UKHL 71, [2006] 2 AC 221, paras 11–13.

[522]   See the Police and Criminal Evidence Act 1984, s 78 ('In any proceedings the court may refuse to allow evidence on which the prosecution proposes to rely to be given if it appears to the court that, having regard to all the circumstances, including the circumstances in which the evidence was obtained, the admission of the evidence would have such an adverse effect on the fairness of the proceedings that the court ought not to admit it') giving effect to the intent of Art 15 of the UN Convention against Torture and Other Cruel, Inhuman or Degrading Treatment or Punishment ('Each State Party shall ensure that any statement which is established to have been made as a result of torture shall not be invoked as evidence in any proceedings, except against a person accused of torture as evidence that the statement was made').

15.205 In relation to the obligation not to 'refouler' persons who may be subject to torture or cruel, inhuman or degrading treatment or punishment, in *RB (Algeria) v Secretary of State for the Home Department*[523] the House of Lords held there is no need to demonstrate that assurances against inhuman treatment from States to which a person is liable to be returned must eliminate all risk of inhuman treatment before they can be relied on. The test is whether, after consideration of all the relevant circumstances of which assurances formed part, there were substantial grounds for believing that a deportee would be at real risk of inhuman treatment, if not there would be no basis for holding that deportation would violate Art 3 of the ECHR. Evaluation of the reliability of an assurance was a question of fact.[524]

Domestic Law and Cruel, Inhuman or Degrading Treatment or Punishment

15.206 In *A v Secretary of State for the Home Department (No 2)*[525] Lord Bingham noted that there remains a distinction between treatment which constitutes torture and that which constitutes cruel, inhuman or degrading treatment, acknowledging that the latter may come to constitute the former as present day conditions change:

'... I do not think the authorities on the Torture Convention justify the assimilation of these two kinds of abusive conduct. Special rules have always been thought to apply to torture, and for the present at least must continue to do so. It would, on the other hand, be wrong to regard as immutable the standard of what amounts to torture.'

15.207 In *R (Limbuela) and others v Secretary of State for the Home*[526] Lord Bingham considered the issue of what constitutes inhuman or degrading treatment, holding that:

'Treatment is inhuman or degrading if, to a seriously detrimental extent, it denies the most basic needs of any human being. As in all art 3 cases, the treatment, to be proscribed, must achieve a minimum standard of severity, and I would accept that in a context such as this, not involving the deliberate infliction of pain or suffering, the threshold is a high one. A general public duty to house the homeless or provide for the destitute cannot be spelled out of art 3. But I have no doubt that the threshold may be crossed if a late applicant with no means and no alternative sources of support, unable to support himself, is, by the deliberate action of the state, denied shelter, food or the most basic necessities of life. It is not necessary that treatment, to engage art 3, should merit the description used, in an immigration context, by Shakespeare and others in *Sir Thomas More* when they referred to 'your mountainish inhumanity.'

Domestic Law and Corporal Punishment at Home[527]

(i)   Current Domestic Legal Position

15.208 Historically at common law a person with parental responsibility for a child could lawfully physically chastise the child by the infliction of so called 'reasonable' corporal punishment. In *R v Hopley*[528] Lord Cockburn CJ reflected the common law position prior to the coming into force of the Human Rights Act 1998:

---

[523]   [2009] UKHL 10, [2009] 2 WLR 512.
[524]   See also see the Nationality, Immigration and Asylum Act 2002, s 84(1)(g). See further Lord Brown's dissenting judgment in *R (Wellington) (FC) v Secretary of State for the Home Department* [2008] UKHL 72, [2009] 2 WLR 48, paras 85–86 and *Saadi v Italy* (2008) 24 BHRC 123, paras 138–140.
[525]   [2005] UKHL 71, [2006] 2 AC 221, paras 11–13.
[526]   Department [2005] UKHL 66, [2006] 1 AC 396, para 7.
[527]   The domestic position in respect of corporal punishment in the context of education is dealt with at **10.124** and **13.146** above.
[528]   (1860) 2 F & F 202 at 206.

'By the law of England, a parent or a schoolmaster (who for this purpose represents the parent and has the parental authority delegated to him), may for the purpose of correcting what is evil in the child inflict moderate and reasonable corporal punishment, always, however, with this condition, that *it is* moderate and reasonable. If it be administered for the gratification of passion or of rage, or if it be immoderate and excessive in its nature or degree, or if it be protracted beyond the child's powers of endurance, or with an instrument unfitted for the purpose and calculated to produce danger to life or limb; in all such cases the punishment is excessive, the violence is unlawful, and if evil consequences to life or limb ensue, then the person inflicting it is answerable to the law, and if death ensues it will be manslaughter.'

15.209 The position at common law is now expressly limited by statute. The Children Act 2004, s 58, repealing the Children and Young Persons Act 1933, s 1(7), provides as follows in relation to corporal punishment:

'(1) In relation to any offence specified in subsection (2), battery of a child cannot be justified on the ground that it constituted reasonable punishment.

(2) The offences referred to in subsection (1) are –

(a)   an offence under section 18 or 20 of the Offences against the Person Act 1861 (c 100) (wounding and causing grievous bodily harm);

(b)   an offence under section 47 of that Act (assault occasioning actual bodily harm);

(c)   an offence under section 1 of the Children and Young Persons Act 1933 (c 12) (cruelty to persons under 16).

(3) Battery of a child causing actual bodily harm to the child cannot be justified in any civil proceedings on the ground that it constituted reasonable punishment.

(4) For the purposes of subsection (3) 'actual bodily harm' has the same meaning as it has for the purposes of section 47 of the Offences against the Person Act 1861.[529]

15.210 The effect of the Children Act 2004, s 58(3) is to leave open the defence of so called 'reasonably chastisement', now re-named as 'reasonable punishment', to a charge of common law assault against a person having care of the child.[530] The 2004 Act defines neither the nature nor the extent of what constitutes such 'reasonable punishment'. The most that can be said is that if chastisement goes beyond what is reasonable it is unlawful and renders the individual criminally liable for assault, or, depending on the gravity of the conduct, for more serious offences.[531] In *R v H (Assault of a Child: Reasonable Chastisement)*[532] the Court of Appeal held that in considering whether a given incident of chastisement constitutes 'reasonable punishment' regard must be had to the factors that are relevant for determining whether the treatment would violate the provisions of Art 3 of the ECHR. However, as the Court of Appeal itself noted in *R v H*, in its report in *A v United Kingdom*[533] the European Commission

---

[529]   See the *Review of Section 58 of the Children Act 2004* (Cm 7232, DCSF, 2007), following which the Government has decided to retain the law in its existing form in the absence of evidence that it is not working satisfactorily.

[530]   See the Explanatory Notes to the 2004 Act, para 236. See also *R v Woods* (1921) 85 JP 272 holding that it was unlawful for an elder brother to administer corporal punishment on his sibling where both were living with their father.

[531]   An unreasonable restraint of a child's movement can render a parent guilty of unlawful imprisonment (*R v Rahman* (1985) 81 Cr App Rep 349).

[532]   [2001] EWCA Crim 1024, [2002] 1 Cr App R 59.

[533]   (1998) 27 EHRR 611.

stated that it was not convinced that there is any true correlation between the Convention test of punishment which is inhuman or degrading and the domestic test of 'reasonable chastisement' as it then was.[534]

(ii) Criticism of the Domestic Law

Manifest Uncertainty

15.211 The first criticism that can be leveled at the current domestic law concerning corporal punishment in the context of the family home is that the law is manifestly unclear.[535] In the absence of a definition of 'reasonable punishment' there is no easily recognisable bright line between reasonable physical punishment and physical abuse. As Fortin points out, the state of confusion in this area of the domestic law is perhaps best illustrated in the DfES Review of Section 58 of the Children Act 2004[536] which produced the following statement of the law 'The current legal position is clear and appropriate, but can be difficult to understand. It is neither correct nor incorrect to say that 'smacking is legal'.[537] This leaves the position of the child in relation to physical assaults perpetrated against him or her, and accordingly the domestic ambit of the child's right to freedom from harmful treatment, manifestly uncertain with the attendant risk of subjective and arbitrary application. This position is arguably not compatible with the principle that the law must be intelligible, clear and predictable.[538]

Discriminatory Application

15.212 Fortin describes the law as representing a gross imbalance between parents' rights and children's rights.[539] The Children Act 2004, s 58(3) permits as lawful conduct against a child that would be unlawful if inflicted on an adult, permitting an assault on a child where no such assault would be permitted against an adult. It is arguable that, applying the principles of non-discrimination,[540] the difference between a child and an adult is insufficient to justify this difference in treatment having regard to the fact that children and adults are equal in their dignity as persons and their right to physical and psychological integrity.[541]

---

[534] 27 EHRR 611 at 623–624.

[535] See Buxton LJ in *R (Williamson) v Secretary of State for Education and Employment* [2002] EWCA Civ 1820, [2003] QB 1300 ('In the present state of English law, it is a defence to what would otherwise be a criminal assault by a parent on his child that the parent was inflicting 'reasonable chastisement' on the child. The limits of this parental right or liberty are obscure, as is the point at which such chastisement becomes unacceptable to the extent that a failure on the part of the state to use the criminal law to control the parent engages the state's responsibility under art 3 of the Convention').

[536] (2007) Cm 7232.

[537] Fortin, J *Children's Rights and the Developing Law* (2009) 3rd edn, Cambridge, p 330.

[538] See for example *Black-Clawson International Ltd v Papierwerke Waldhoff-Aschaffenburg AG* [1975 AC 591 at 638D per Lord Diplock ('The acceptance of the rule of law as a constitutional principle requires that a citizen, before committing himself to any course of action, should be able to know in advance what are the legal principles which flow from it') and *Sunday Times v United Kingdom* (1979) 2 EHRR 245, para 49 ('… the law must be adequately accessible: the citizen must be able to have an indication that is adequate in the circumstances of the legal rules applicable to a given case … a norm cannot be regarded as a 'law' unless it is formulated with sufficient precision to enable the citizen to regulate his conduct: he must be able – if need be with appropriate advice – to foresee, to a degree that is reasonable in the circumstances, the consequences which a given action may entail').

[539] Fortin, J *Children's Rights and the Developing Law* (2009) 3rd edn, Cambridge, p 330.

[540] See **4.71** above.

[541] Indeed, the relative vulnerability of children as a class compared to adults argues for equal treatment between children and adults in this context, the vulnerability of the class providing the rationale for equal treatment when it comes to physical assault (see *Pretty v United Kingdom* (2002) 35 EHRR 1, para 74).

15.213 The current domestic law on corporal punishment in the context of the family environment is also discriminatory as between different care settings. Whilst it might be tentatively argued that banning corporal punishment in schools is not inconsistent with permitting the practice at home given the differences between an educational and a home environment,[542] the argument becomes harder to make out where the distinction is between alternative 'home' environments. Whilst corporal punishment is permitted within the family home by parents and carers, corporal punishment is forbidden in all children's homes[543] and foster homes.[544] The effect of these provisions is that a child who has been removed from the family home has greater protection against corporal punishment than a child cared for by his or her parents. Again, it is difficult to see that there is a difference between these two classes of children sufficient to justify this divergence in treatment on such a fundamental issue, suggesting that the difference is discriminatory and therefore unlawful.

Incompatibility with International Treaty Obligations

15.214 The most powerful criticism of the current state of the domestic law on corporal punishment in the context of the family home is its incompatibility with the international and regional instruments which enshrine the rights of the child. Pursuant to the terms of the CRC, the Committee on the Rights of the Child considers that any form of corporal punishment of children, however light, is incompatible with the prohibition on torture or cruel, inhuman or degrading treatment or punishment contained in Art 37(a) of the CRC.[545] The best interests principle under Art 3 of the CRC cannot be used to justify 'reasonable' or 'moderate' corporal punishment at home, which punishment conflicts with the child's human dignity and right to physical integrity.[546] In *A v United Kingdom*[547] the Court held that domestic defence of 'reasonable chastisement' does not provide adequate protection to the child against treatment contrary or punishment contrary to Art 3 of the ECHR. The United Kingdom government expressly accepted that UK law failed to protect children from breaches of Art 3 rights under the ECHR and that it would require amendment.[548] Whilst the United Kingdom has not yet ratified the Revised European Social Charter, the decision of the European Committee on Social Rights that the common law defence of 'reasonable chastisement' in Ireland failed to meet the requirements of Art 17 of the Charter[549] would suggest that the domestic defence of 'reasonable punishment' would

---

[542] See *R (on the application of Williamson and others) v Secretary of State for Education and Employment and others* [2005] UKHL 15, [2005] 1 FCR 498, para 84 per Baroness Hale.

[543] Children's Homes Regulations 2001 SI 2001/3967, r 17(5)(a) and the Children's Homes (Wales) Regulations 2002, SI 2002/327, r 17(5)(a), which prohibit the use of any form of corporal punishment.

[544] Fostering Services Regulations 2002, SI 2002/57, r 28(5)(b), Sch 5, para 8 and the Fostering Services (Wales) Regulations 2003, SI 2003/237, Sch 5, point 8.

[545] See also CRC, Art 19. The Committee on the Rights of the Child has consistently interpreted Art 19, read with the CRC as a whole, as requiring the prohibition of corporal punishment in all settings (Newell, P and Hodgkin, R *Implementation Handbook for the Convention on the Rights of the Child* (2008) 3rd edn, UNICEF, p 249). In this context the Committee on the Rights of the Child has commented that the words 'all forms of physical and mental violence' in Art 19(1) of the CRC leave no room for any level of legalised violence against children in the form of corporal punishment (Committee on the Rights of the Child General Comment No 8 *The Right of the Child to Protection from Corporal Punishment and Other Cruel or Degrading Forms of Punishment* CRC/C/GC/8 p 6, para 18).

[546] Committee on the Rights of the Child General Comment No 8 *The Right of the Child to Protection from Corporal Punishment and Other Cruel or Degrading Forms of Punishment* CRC/C/GC/8 p 7, para 26.

[547] (1998) 27 EHRR 611.

[548] See **15.208** above for the current state of the domestic law on corporal punishment.

[549] See Resolution ResCHS (2005) 9 (Ireland).

likewise violate Art 17. Within the foregoing context, a whole range of international monitoring bodies have criticised the United Kingdom's position on domestic corporal punishment of children.[550]

15.215 A domestic ban on all forms of corporal punishment would be permissible. In the context of corporal punishment in educational settings, Baroness Hale observed in *R (on the application of Williamson and others) v Secretary of State for Education and Employment and others*[551] as follows:

> 'There can be no doubt that the ban on corporal punishment in schools pursues the legitimate aim of protecting the rights and freedoms of children. It has long been held that these are not limited to their rights under the European Convention. The appellants were anxious to stress that the corporal punishment in which they believe would not breach the child's rights under either art 3 or art 8. But it can still be legitimate for the state to prohibit it for the sake of the child. A child has the same right as anyone else not to be assaulted; the defence of lawful chastisement is an exception to that right. It has long been held in the context of art 8 that the rights and freedoms of the child include his interests. Even if it could be shown that a particular act of corporal punishment was in the interests of the individual child, it is clear that a universal or blanket ban may be justified to protect a vulnerable class: see *Pretty v UK* [2002] 2 FCR 97 at 135 (para 74) where a universal ban on assisting suicide could be justified for the protection of vulnerable people generally, even though Mrs Pretty herself was not vulnerable 'it is the vulnerability of the class which provides the rationale for the law in question'. Above all, the state is entitled to give children the protection they are given by an international instrument to which the United Kingdom is a party, the United Nations Convention on the Rights of the Child.'

Domestic Law and Corporal Punishment in Detention

15.216 In *R (Howard League for Penal Reform) v Secretary of State for the Home Department*[552] Munby J made clear that the CRC, the ECHR and the Charter of Fundamental Rights of the European Union are important sources of possible obligations both owed to and enforceable by children detained in young offender institutions. Munby J noted that in relation to the CRC that Art 3(1) and Art 37b are particularly relevant in the domestic context.[553] In this context, Munby J held that:

> 'In the first place, Arts 3 and 8 of the European Convention protect children in YOIs from those actions by members of the Prison Service which constitute inhuman or degrading treatment or punishment or which impact adversely and disproportionately on the child's physical or psychological integrity.

---

[550] See Committee on Economic, Social and Cultural Rights (2002) *Concluding Observations of the Committee on Economic, Social and Cultural Rights: United Kingdom of Great Britain and Northern Ireland – Dependent Territories* E/C12/1/Add 79, para 36 … Committee on the Elimination of Discrimination against Women (2008) *Concluding Observations of the Committee on the Elimination of Discrimination against Women: United Kingdom of Great Britain and Northern Ireland* CEDAW?c/GBR/CO/6, paras 33–34 as well as the Committee on the Rights of the Child (1995) *Concluding Observations of the Committee on the Rights of the Child: United Kingdom of Great Britain and Northern Ireland* CRC/C/15/Add 34, paras 16 and 31 and Committee on the Rights of the Child (2002) *Concluding Observations of the Committee on the Rights of the Child: United Kingdom of Great Britain and Northern Ireland* CRC/C/15/Add 188, paras 36–37 and the Committee on the Rights of the Child (2008) *Concluding Observations of the Committee on the Rights of the Child: United Kingdom of Great Britain and Northern Ireland* CRC/C/GBR/CO/4, paras 40 and 42(a).

[551] [2005] UKHL 15, [2005] 1 FCR 498, para 80.

[552] [2002] EWHC 2497, [2003] 1 FLR 484.

[553] Munby J concluded in relation to the CRC and the European Charter that 'both can, in my judgment, properly be consulted insofar as they proclaim, re-affirm or elucidate the content of those human rights that are generally recognised throughout the European family of nations, in particular the nature and scope of those fundamental rights that are guaranteed by the European Convention.' See **3.32–3.46** above.

[66] Secondly, however, Arts 3 and 8 of the European Convention, read in the light of Arts 3 and 37 of the UN Convention and Art 24 of the European Charter, impose on the Prison Service positive obligations to take reasonable and appropriate measures designed to ensure that:

(i)   children in YOIs are treated, both by members of the Prison Service and by fellow inmates, with humanity, with respect for their inherent dignity and personal integrity as human beings, and not in such a way as to humiliate or debase them;

(ii)   children in YOIs are not subjected to torture or to inhuman or degrading treatment or punishment by fellow inmates or to other behaviour by fellow inmates which impacts adversely and disproportionately on their physical or psychological integrity.

[67] Such measures must strike a fair balance between the competing interests of the particular child and the general interests of the community as a whole (including the other inmates of the YOI) but always having regard:

(i)   first, to the principle that the best interests of the child are at all times a primary consideration;

(ii)   secondly, to the inherent vulnerability of children in a YOI; and

(iii)   thirdly, to the need for the State – the Prison Service – to take effective deterrent steps to prevent, and to provide children in YOIs with effective protection from, ill-treatment (whether at the hands of Prison Service staff or of other inmates) of which the Prison Service has or ought to have knowledge.

[68] In short, human rights law imposes on the Prison Service enforceable obligations, that is, obligations enforceable by or on behalf of children in YOIs:

(i)   to have regard to the 'welfare' principle encapsulated in the UN Convention and the European Charter; and

(ii)   to take effective steps to protect children in YOIs from any ill-treatment, whether at the hands of Prison Service staff or of other inmates, of the type which engages either Arts 3 or 8 of the European Convention.

[69] In this connection it is to be borne in mind that, quite apart from any other remedies which there may be arising out of the State's – the Prison Service's – failure to meet its human rights obligations, ss 7 and 8 of the Human Rights Act 1998 enable a victim to bring a free-standing action in the High Court. In the case of a claimant who is a child, such a claim is appropriately brought in the Family Division: see *Re W and B; Re B (Care Plan)* at paras [71]-[76], *R (P) v Secretary of State for the Home Department and Another; R (Q) and Another v Secretary of State for the Home Department and Another* at paras [118], [120], and *C v Bury Metropolitan Borough Council* [2002] EWHC 1438 (Fam), [2002] 2 FLR 868 at paras [55]-[56].'

15.217   The domestic courts have continued to apply the principles set out in the CRC when dealing with the use of force against children in custody. In *R (Carol Pounder) v HM Coroner for the North and South Districts of Durham and Darlington*[554] Blake J held as follows:

'Moreover, it should have been clear to all properly self-directing public authorities that the limits on the use of force on children in custody was driven by the core principles set out in the United Nations Convention on the Rights of the Child, to which effect was designed to be given in United Kingdom law by the Children Act 1989, and which informs any detailed elaboration of human rights relating to children set out in the 1998 Act. Deliberate infliction of pain and force on children as young as 14 could only be justified by very compelling

---

[554]   [2009] EWHC 76 (Admin), [2009] 3 All ER 150, para 51.

reasons such as those contemplated by the STC rules, rather than generally to support staff orders. The authors of the Smallridge and Williamson report to the ministers were very much mistaken if they believed that the requirements of the United Nations Convention on the Rights of the Child were irrelevant to the limits of restraint that could be used in the United Kingdom'.

Domestic Law – Prevention of Abuse within the Family

15.218 The domestic legislative, administrative, social and educational measures to protect children from of physical or mental violence, injury or abuse, neglect or negligent treatment, maltreatment or exploitation, including sexual abuse, while in the care of parent(s), legal guardian(s) or any other person who has their care are extensive and a comprehensive account of them is beyond the scope of this work.[555] Reference should be made in particular to the Children Act 1989, the Children Act 2004, Working Together 2010,[556] the Framework for the Assessment of Children in Need and their Families[557] and the Children Act 1989 Guidance and Regulations Volume 1 *Court Orders*.[558] The position governing the removal of children from their families in circumstances where abuse has taken place or is suspected is dealt with in detail in chapter 8 above.[559]

15.219 Whilst commenting that the Children Act 1989 adopts an uneasy compromise between emphasising parents' rights to autonomy and privacy and fulfilling the child's right to protection, Fortin realistically acknowledges that no system which is required to balance these to ultimately insoluble positions will ever be perfect.[560] The domestic courts have been mindful of need for human rights to reinforce rather than undermine protection for children within the domestic context. In *Lawrence v Pembrokeshire County Council*[561] Auld LJ observed:

> 'Thus, in my view, the advent of Art 8 to our domestic law, bringing with it a discrete right to children and parents of respect for their family life, does not undermine or weaken as a matter of public policy the primacy of the need to protect children from abuse, or the risk of abuse, from, among others, their parents. Nor, when those interests are or may be in conflict, does Art 8 so enhance the status of family life as, in the balancing exercise involved, would require the development of the common law by the introduction of a duty of care to parents suspected of abusing their children, a duty precluded by that public policy.'[562]

Domestic Law – Prevention

15.220 One of the aims of the Children Act 1989 is to identify children in need and support families in order to ensure that their situations do not deteriorate to the point

---

[555] For a comprehensive account of the law and practice in this field reference should be made to Hershman, D and McFarlane, A *Children Law and Practice* Jordan Publishing.
[556] DOH (2010).
[557] DOH (2000).
[558] See also generally Lyon, C, Cobley, C, Petrie, S and Reid, C *Child Abuse* (2003) 3rd edn, Jordan Publishing.
[559] See **8.192–8.199** above.
[560] Fortin, J *Children's Rights and the Developing Law* (2009) 3rd edn, Cambridge, pp 553 and 555.
[561] [2007] EWCA Civ 446, [2007] 2 FLR 705, para 41.
[562] See also *Re L (Care: Threshold Criteria)* [2007] 1 FLR 2050 per Hedley J at para 50 ('... society must be willing to tolerate very diverse standards of parenting, including the eccentric, the barely adequate and the inconsistent. It follows too that children will inevitably have both very different experiences of parenting and very unequal consequences flowing from it. It means that some children will experience disadvantage and harm, while others flourish in atmospheres of loving security and emotional stability. These are the consequences of our fallible humanity and it is not the provenance of the state to spare children all the consequences of defective parenting. In any event, it simply could not be done').

where the child suffers abuse.[563] Part III of the Children Act 1989 sets out the general and specific duties imposed on local authorities in respect of the services which they must or may provide for children and their families. In providing these services, the local authority has a duty to consider whether any local education authority, local housing authority, health authority or other local authority can help in the provision of services and, if they can, to seek that help.[564] The scheme set out under Part III imposes:

(a) A general duty in respect of the welfare of children in need (including children with a disability) coupled with specific duties and powers aimed at facilitating the general duty of the local authority to provide a range and level of services to children in need.[565]

(b) Duties and powers in respect of children under five (whether they are in need or not).[566]

(c) Duties and powers in respect of other children (whether or not they are under five and whether or not they are in need).[567]

(d) Duties and powers in relation to the accommodation of children including children who are 'looked after' by the local authority.[568]

(e) Duties and powers in respect of children leaving care and formerly looked after by the Local Authority.[569]

Each of the duties prescribed under Part III is intended to enable local authorities to work with a family in a manner which seeks to promote the independent exercise of parental responsibility.

15.221 Specifically, the work of local authorities under Part III should be directed at avoiding the need for proceedings under Part IV of the 1989 Act.[570] Working in partnership with those holding parental responsibility and members of the wider family is the guiding principle in the effective discharge of the local authority's duties under Part III of the Act.[571] This requires local authorities to maximise the involvement of

---

[563] See Working Together to Safeguard Children (2010), para 1.6. For the non-exhaustive domestic definitions of abuse see Working Together to Safeguard Children (2010), paras 1.32–1.36.

[564] CA 1989, s 27. It should be noted that the Children Act 2004 and the Children Act 2004 (Children's Services) Regulations 2005, SI 2005/1972, now creates a framework whereby the provision by local government, national government and non-governmental organisations of 'children's services' is carried out co-operatively having regard to the need to safeguard and promote the welfare of children.

[565] CA 1989, s 17 and Sch 2. The specific duties to children in need include a duty to identify children in need (*R (Howard League for Penal Reform) v Secretary of State for the Home Department* [2002] EWHC 2497 (Admin), [2003] 1 FLR 484; *R (D) v Secretary of State for the Home Department* [2003] EWHC 155, [2003] 1 FLR 979), a duty to prevent abuse and neglect (CA 1989, Sch 2, para 4(1)), a duty to provide accommodation to a third party where it appears that a child is suffering or is likely to suffer ill-treatment at the hands of that person living at the same premises (CA 1989, Sch 2, para 5), a duty to promote the upbringing of children by their families by providing advice, guidance and counseling, occupational, social, cultural and recreational activities, home help, travel assistance and holiday provision (CA 1989, Sch 2, para 8), a duty to take steps to enable the child to live or have contact with his or her family home (CA 1989, Sch 2, para 10) and a duty to provide day care (CA 1989, s 18(1)).

[566] CA 1989, s 18(2). See also Education Act 1996, s 17.

[567] CA 1989, Sch 2, para 9.

[568] CA 1989, s 20(1).

[569] CA 1989, Sch 2, para 19A as inserted by the Children Leaving Care Act 2000, s 1.

[570] CA 1989, Sch 2, para 7(a)(i).

[571] The concept of partnership was introduced in the Guidance to the Act. See the Children Act 1989 Guidance

families at all stages of the planning and decision-making process such that the decision-making process in respect of those families is characterised by transparency and fairness.[572] This means that issues affecting a family's ability to participate in the decision-making process, for example a learning disability, should not be allowed to frustrate the principle of working in partnership[573] and that families should be provided with correct and complete information to facilitate that partnership.[574] It should be remembered however, that partnership cannot be permitted to compromise the duty to safeguard and promote the child's welfare. Authorities are required to facilitate the provision of Part III services by others, in particular voluntary organisations, and may make such arrangements as they see fit for others to provide such services (for example, day care or fostering services).[575] Further, a local authority may request the help of another authority, including an education authority, a housing authority, or a health authority or special health authority, Primary Care Trust or National Health Service Trust, to carry out duties under Part III. An authority so requested shall comply with the request if it is compatible with its own statutory or other duties and obligations and does not unduly prejudice the discharge of any of its functions.[576] A housing authority is not obliged to provide accommodation, but it does have a duty to ascertain whether it could provide a solution to the problems of homeless families so as to prevent children suffering from lack of accommodation.[577]

Domestic Law – Duty to Investigate Allegations of Abuse

15.222   Pursuant to s 47 of the Children Act 1989 where a local authority is informed that a child who lives or is found in its area is: (a) the subject of an emergency protection order; (b) is in police protection; (c) has contravened a ban imposed by a curfew notice under the Crime and Disorder Act 1998; (d) is the subject of an emergency protection order in favour of the local authority; (e) a child in respect of whom the local authority have reasonable cause to suspect is suffering or is likely to suffer significant harm; the local authority is under a *duty* to make, or cause to be made, such enquiries as it considers necessary to enable it to decide whether to take action to safeguard and promote the child's welfare.[578] The enquiries should be directed at establishing whether the local authority should apply for a child safety order,[579] whether in respect of a child who is subject to an emergency protection order[580] it would be in the child's best

---

and Regulations, Vol 2, Family Support, Day Care and Educational Provision for Young Children (1991) Department of Health, para 2.1 and Care of Children: Principles and Practice in Regulations and Guidance (1989) HMSO.

[572]   *Re L (Care: Assessment: Fair Trial)* [2002] EWHC 1379 (Fam), [2002] 2 FLR 730.

[573]   *Re G (Care: Challenge to Local Authority's Decision)* [2003] EWHC 551 (Fam), [2003] 2 FLR 42.

[574]   *Sahin v Germany* [2002] 1 FLR 119, [2002] Fam Law 94.

[575]   Section 17(5). See also the Children Act 1989 Guidance and Regulations, Vol 2, Family Support, Day Care and Educational Provision for Young Children (1991) Department of Health, para 2.11.

[576]   CA 1989, s 27.

[577]   *R v Northavon District Council, ex p Smith* [1994] 2 AC 402, HL.

[578]   CA 1989, s 47(1). Note that where a local authority believes that a child in its area is in need for the purposes of the Children Act 1989, that local authority *may* assess the child's needs for the purposes of s 17 of the Children Act 1989. See *Birmingham City Council v AG and A* [2009] EWHC 3720 (Fam), [2010] 2 FLR 580 for the consequences of the local authority not meeting its duties under CA 1989, s 47.

[579]   Crime and Disorder Act 1998, s 11. Section 11 provides for local authorities to apply for a child safety order, which is aimed at children under 10 years old and is designed to prevent them becoming involved in criminal or anti-social behaviour. See the Crime and Disorder Act Guidance Document: Child Safety Orders (June 2000) Home Office.

[580]   Pursuant to CA 1989, s 44.

interests for him or her to be accommodated by the local authority and whether, in respect of a child in police protection,[581] it would be in the child's best interests to apply for an emergency protection order.

15.223 The test for whether the duty to investigate under s 47 is triggered in relation to a child who may be suffering or at risk of suffering significant harm is whether there is 'reasonable cause to suspect' that this is the case. Suspicion is a standard that is 'quite low' and it is not necessary to establish facts on a balance of probabilities[582] but there must still be objectively reasonable grounds and not simply what the decision-maker thinks reasonable.[583] The fact that a child is 'looked after' by the local authority does not prevent a s 47 enquiry being carried out where the criteria for such an enquiry is met.[584] Where a local authority is conducting enquiries under s 47 in respect of a child who it appears to the local authority is ordinarily resident in the area of another local authority, the local authority making the enquiries is under a duty to consult the other local authority, which authority may undertake the enquiries in its place.[585] Enquiries pursuant to the Children Act 1989, s 47 generally do not constitute an infringement of the child's or the parents' rights under art 8 of the European Convention.[586]

15.224 Within 7 working days of receiving a referral the local authority should carry out a carefully planned initial assessment by a qualified social worker to establish (i) whether the child is in need, (ii) whether there is reasonable cause to suspect the child is suffering, or is likely to suffer, significant harm, (iii) whether any services are required and of what types and (iv) whether a further, more detailed core assessment should be undertaken using the Framework for the Assessment of Children in Need and their Families.[587] This initial assessment should be led by a qualified and experienced social worker who is supervised by a highly experienced and qualified social work manager.[588] Where concerns are revealed that justify further investigation under s 47 of the Children Act 1989 the local authority's s 47 enquiry should be carried out by means of undertaking a 'core assessment' utilising the Framework for the Assessment of Children in Need and their Families[589] in order to provide sound evidence on which to base the often difficult professional judgments about whether to intervene to safeguard a child and promote his welfare and, if so, how best to do so and with what intended outcomes.[590] The Guidance recommends that a Social Services Department has a maximum of 35 working days to complete this assessment.[591]

---

[581] Pursuant to CA 1989, s 46.

[582] *Re S (Sexual Abuse Allegations: Local Authority Response)* [2001] EWHC Admin 334, [2001] 2 FLR 776.

[583] *Gogay v Hertfordshire County Council* [2001] 1 FLR 280. See also the Family Law Act 1996, s 43 permitting a child under the age of 16 to apply for a non-molestation order or occupation order with the leave of the court where the child has sufficient understanding.

[584] *Gogay v Hertfordshire County Council* [2001] 1 FLR 280.

[585] CA 1989, s 47(12).

[586] *Gogay v Hertfordshire County Council* [2001] 1 FLR 280.

[587] Working Together to Safeguard Children (2010), para 5.38.

[588] Working Together to Safeguard Children (2010), para 5.41.

[589] DOH 2000.

[590] Working Together to Safeguard Children (2010), para 5.50. Once again, this enquiry should be lead by an experienced social work (Working Together to Safeguard Children (2010), para 5.62). The completion of the core assessment should include an analysis of the child's developmental needs and the parents' capacity to respond to those needs within the context of their family and environment. This analysis should include an understanding of the parents' capacity to ensure that the child is safe from harm. It should include consideration of the information gathered about the family's history and their present and past family functioning. The analysis of the child's needs and the capacity of the child's parents or caregivers to meet these needs within their family and environment should provide evidence on which to base judgments and decisions on how best to safeguard and promote the welfare of a child and where possible to support parents in achieving this aim. Decisions based on this analysis should consider what the child's future will be like if

15.225 If the local authority concludes as a result of its enquiries that it should take action to safeguard and promote the welfare of the child it is obligated to take that action in so far as it is within its power to do so and is reasonably practicable.[592] Where the agencies involved consider that a child may continue to, or be likely to, suffer significant harm, a Child Protection Case Conference should be convened.[593] Where, following enquiry into and assessment of the child's circumstances, emergency measures are required to safeguard that child's welfare, emergency protection provisions are provided for by the Act in the form of the emergency protection order[594] and police protection.[595] Where a local authority is being frustrated in its enquiry into and assessment of the child's circumstances, the Act provides a remedy in the form of a child assessment order where there is reasonable cause to suspect that he is or is likely to be suffering significant harm and an assessment of him is needed but cannot be carried out because his parents will not co-operate.[596] The Act also protects against the abduction of a child from the care of a local authority, from emergency protection and from police protection,[597] as well as making provision for the court ordered recovery of the child.[598] Where a child who is the subject of a care order requires additional protection, the court may grant injunctive relief ancillary to that care order. A court may also grant injunctive relief ancillary to making a care order if additional protection is required.[599] Where at the conclusion of its enquiries the local authority decides not to apply for an emergency protection order, a care order a child assessment order or a supervision order, it must consider whether it would be appropriate to review the case at a later date and, if so, set a date for that review.[600]

Domestic Law – Children's Views and Wishes

15.226 Pursuant to the Children Act 2004, ss 53 and 47 of the Children Act 1989 has been amended to make it a statutory obligation upon the local authority to ascertain the wishes and feelings of the child in relation to the action to be taken in respect of him and to give due consideration, having regard to his age and understanding, to such wishes and feelings.[601] When ascertaining the wishes and feelings of the child concerned care should be taken to communicate with the child in a way which facilitates the provision of accurate and complete information which is capable of constituting acceptable evidence should proceedings under s 31 of the Children Act 1989 be required.[602] Whilst the process of ascertaining the wishes and feelings of the child in respect of the course of action the local authority intends to pursue may not constitute

---

his or her met needs continue to be met, and if his or her unmet needs continue to be unmet. The key questions are, what is likely to happen if nothing changes in the child's current situation and what are the likely consequences for the child? (Working Together to Safeguard Children (2010), paras 5.120–5.121).

[591] The Assessment Framework, para 3.11.
[592] CA 1989, s 47(8).
[593] See Working Together to Safeguard Children (2010), para 5.81 et seq.
[594] CA 1989, s 44. Note that the domestic courts have emphasised the need to utilise emergency measures with great care and with scrupulous regard to the rights of the children and parents concerned. Such procedures should only be used where there is 'exceptional justification' and 'extraordinarily compelling reasons (see *X County Council v B (Emergency Protection Orders)* [2004] EWHC 2015 (Fam); [2005] 1 FLR 341; *Harringey LBC v C, E and another Intervening* [2004] EWHC 2580 (Fam), [2005] 2 FLR 47; *Re X (Emergency Protection Orders)* [2006] EWHC 510 (Fam), [2006] 2 FLR 701).
[595] CA 1989, s 46.
[596] CA 1989, s 43.
[597] CA 1989, s 49.
[598] CA 1989, s 50.
[599] *Re P (Care Orders: Injunctive Relief)* [2000] 2 FLR 385 and in the High Court and county court only.
[600] CA 1989, s 47(7).
[601] CA 1989, s 47(5A) as amended by the Children Act 2004, s 53. See Working Together to Safeguard Children (2010), paras 1.15–1.18.
[602] Working Together 2010.

a formal interview of the child, regard should be had to the applicable guidance regulating the interview of children.[603] If the child is unable to take part in an interview because of age or understanding, alternative means of understanding the child's wishes or feelings should be used, including observation where children are very young or where they have communication impairments.[604]

Domestic Law – Sale, Trafficking and Abduction

Prevention of Trafficking in Criminal Law

15.227 Section 57 of the Sexual Offences Act 2003 makes it a criminal offence to intentionally arrange or facilitate the arrival or entry into the United Kingdom of another person for the purposes of sexual exploitation[605] and s 59 renders it an offence to arrange or facilitate the departure from the United Kingdom for this purpose. Section 58 of the 2003 Act further makes it a criminal offence to arrange or facilitate travel within the United Kingdom of another person for the purposes of sexual exploitation. These provisions apply to acts done inside and outside of the United Kingdom.[606] In relation to exploitation otherwise than sexual exploitation, s 4 of the Asylum and Immigration (Treatment of Claimants etc) Act 2004 makes it a criminal offence for a person to arrange or facilitate the arrival or entry into the United Kingdom, travel within the United Kingdom or departure from the United Kingdom for the purposes of exploitation.[607] These provisions apply to acts done inside the United Kingdom and outside the United Kingdom if done by certain individuals defined by the Act.[608]

Prevention of Trafficking for Adoption

15.228 The Adoption and Children Act 2002, s 83 makes it a criminal offence for a person habitually resident in the British Islands to bring, or cause another to bring, a child who is habitually resident outside the British Islands into the United Kingdom for the purposes of adoption by a British resident save where the child is intended to be adopted under an order made pursuant to the Hague Convention on Protection of Children and Co-operation in respect of Inter-Country Adoption to which the United Kingdom is a party.[609] Under the Children and Adoption Act 2006, s 9(1) the Secretary of State may by order declare that the restrictions set out in Part II of the Child and

---

[603] Communicating with Children (2002) TSO: Department of Health (this provides guidance for interviewing children about adverse experiences and can be used as a basis for treatment) and Achieving Best Evidence in Criminal Proceedings: Guidance for Vulnerable or Intimidated Witnesses, including Children (2002) TSO (guidance published by the Department of Health, the Home Office and the Department for Education and Employment under s 7 of the Local Authority Social Services Act 1970). See also Dr David Jones Communicating with Vulnerable Children: A Guide for Practitioners (2003) Department of Health.

[604] Working Together 2010.

[605] Section 60 of the Sexual Offences Act 2003 defines the scope of acts prohibited.

[606] Sexual Offences Act 2003, s 60(2).

[607] Asylum and Immigration Act (Treatment of Claimants etc) Act 2004, s 4(4) defines exploitation as treatment that contravenes Art 4 of the ECHR, being encouraged, required or expected to do anything that would contravene the Human Organ Transplants Act 1989, Part I of the Human Tissue (Scotland) Act 2006 or the Human Tissue Act 2004, s 32 or 33, being subjected to force, threats or deception designed to induce him to provide services of any kind, to provide another person with benefits of any kind or to enable another person to acquire benefits of any kind or being requested or induced to undertake any activity, having been chosen as the subject of the request or inducement on the grounds that he is mentally or physically ill or disabled, he is young or he has a family relationship with a person and a person without the illness, disability, youth or family relationship would be likely to refuse the request or resist the inducement.

[608] The Asylum and Immigration Act (Treatment of Claimants etc) Act 2004, s 5(1)(b) and (2).

[609] See also the Adoptions with a Foreign Element Regulations 2005.

Adoption Act 2006 apply[610] to bringing a child into the United Kingdom from certain named States, known as 'restricted countries' where the Secretary of State has reason to believe that, because of practices taking place in a country or territory outside the British Islands in connection with the adoption of children, it would be contrary to public policy to further the bringing of children into the United Kingdom.[611]

15.229 A person who removes[612] a child who is a Commonwealth citizen or is habitually resident in the United Kingdom to a place outside the British Islands for the purposes of adoption will be guilty of a criminal offence unless a parental responsibility order has been made in respect of them pursuant to s 84 of the Adoption and Children Act 2002.[613] Section 92 of the Adoption and Children Act 2002 places restrictions on the persons who may arrange adoptions and s 95 makes the payment in consideration for the adoption or a child, the giving of consent to adoption, the removal from the United Kingdom of a child for the purposes of adoption and the preparation of an adoption report, the agreement or offer to make such a payment or the receipt of such a payment a criminal offence.[614]

Prevention of Abduction by Family Members

15.230 The domestic law also provides a comprehensive statutory framework in respect of children who are removed across international boundaries by one parent or relative. The Child Abduction and Custody Act 1985 incorporates into domestic law the Hague Convention on the Civil Aspects of International Child Abduction International Child Abduction and the European Convention on the Recognition and Enforcement of Decisions Concerning Custody of Children and on the Restoration of Custody of Children, the latter having been largely superseded by Brussels II Revised. Reference should be made to the seminal work '*International Movement of Children*'[615] for detailed discussion of the practice and procedure.

Prevention of Forced Marriages

15.231 Pursuant to s 63A(1) of the Family Law Act 1996 as amended by the Forced Marriage (Civil Protection) Act 2007, the court may make an order for the purposes of protecting a person from being forced[616] into a marriage or from any attempt to being forced into a marriage.[617] A forced marriage protection order may contain such prohibitions, restrictions or requirements and such other terms as the Court considers appropriate for the purposes of the order.[618] The terms of the forced marriage

---

[610] See Children and Adoption Act 2006, s 11(1).

[611] See also Children and Adoption Act 2006, s 11(2) and the Adoptions with Foreign Element Regulations (Special Restrictions on Adoption from Abroad) Regulations 2008.

[612] Pursuant to s 85(3) and 85(5) of the Adoption and Children Act 2002 removing a child for the purposes of the Act will include entering into an arrangement for the purposes of facilitating such a removal, initiating or taking part in negotiations of which the purpose is the conclusion of a removal or causing another person to take one or both of these steps (provided he knew or had reason to suspect the steps taken would contravene s 85(1)).

[613] Adoption and Children Act 2002, s 85(1) and (4).

[614] See also Adoption and Children Act 2002 for excepted payments.

[615] Lowe N, Everall M, and Nicholls, M (2004) Jordans Publishing.

[616] Pursuant to s 63A(6) 'force' includes to coerce by threats or other psychological means.

[617] Section 63A(4) defines a marriage as forced if person B forces person A to enter into a marriage with B or another person without A's free and full consent. Pursuant to s 63A(5) it does not matter whether B's conduct is directed against A, B or another person.

[618] Family Law Act 1996, s 63B(1).

protection order may relate to conduct outside England and Wales.[619] A court may make a forced marriage protection order of its own volition.[620]

Domestic Law – Economic Exploitation

15.232 The extensive domestic employment law concerning children is beyond the scope of this work. Reference should be made to Clarke, Hall & Morrison on Children and the DCSF *Guidance on the Employment of Children*.[621]

Domestic Law – Involvement in Armed Conflict

15.233 Whilst the United Kingdom has ratified the Optional Protocol to the Convention on the Rights of the Child on the Involvement of Children in Armed Conflict the minimum age for recruitment of children into the armed forces of the United Kingdom remains set at 16 years. Children under the age of 18 require the consent of those with parental responsibility. Children under the age of 18 are not permitted to take part in combat operations.

CONCLUSION

15.234 In his *World Report on Violence Against Children*[622] Pinheiro observes that no violence against children is justifiable and all violence against children is preventable. The CRC and the ECHR provide a comprehensive framework of rights which if given effect will go some way to protect children from the full gamut of harmful treatment to which they can be sadly subject. That the domestic courts have shown a willingness to apply not only the ECHR but also the CRC to this effect is encouraging, as is the willingness of domestic courts to mark their abhorrence of practices which exploit children and result in unimaginable suffering.[623]

15.235 There remain however areas of domestic law in which significant further progress needs to be made. In particular, the continuing legality of 'reasonable' physical punishment[624] and the recruitment into the United Kingdom armed forces of 16 year olds[625]requires further and careful consideration by the legislature in light of the

---

[619] Family Law Act 1996, s 63B(2)(a).

[620] Family Law Act 1996, s 63C(1)(b).

[621] (2009) Department of Children Schools and Families. See also Hobbs, S and McKechnie, J (eds) *Child Employment in Britain* (1997) Stationary Office Books.

[622] Pinheiro, P *World Report on Violence Against Children* (2006) United Nations.

[623] See for example *R v Maka Shaba* [2006] 2 Cr App R (S) 14 in which the Court of Appeal held that the sentence of 18 years imprisonment for trafficking a 15 year old Lithuanian girl and selling her into prostitution was an entirely appropriate sentence.

[624] See the Committee on the Rights of the Child *Concluding Observations of the Committee on the Rights of the Child: United Kingdom of Great Britain and Northern Ireland* on the United Kingdom's position on corporal punishment ('the Committee deeply regrets that the State party persists in retaining the defence of 'reasonable chastisement' and has taken no significant action towards prohibiting all corporal punishment of children in the family. The Committee is of the opinion that the Government's proposals to limit rather than to remove the 'reasonable chastisement' defence do not comply with the principles and provisions of the Convention and the aforementioned recommendations, particularly since they constitute a serious violation of the dignity of the child (CRC/C/15/Add.188)).

[625] See the Committee on the Rights of the Child *Concluding Observations of the Committee on the Rights of the Child: United Kingdom of Great Britain and Northern Ireland* on the United Kingdom's position in relation to the recruitment of children into the armed forces ('The Committee is deeply concerned that about one third of the annual intake of recruits into the armed forces are below the age of 18 years, that the armed

significant concerns expressed by the international monitoring bodies in respect of these practices. The case of *R (on the application of Mohamed) v Secretary of State for Foreign and Commonwealth Affairs*[626] demonstrates that torture should not be considered a remote issue simply because the United Kingdom has historically had a relatively impressive record concerning its prohibition and prevention.[627] In order to ensure that children are protected from the harmful treatment to which they are particularly vulnerable those charged with promoting and enforcing their rights must remain constantly vigilant to ensure that violations are promptly and effectively addressed using the full weight of the extensive provisions articulated in this chapter.

---

services target young people and that those recruited are required to serve for a minimum period of four years, increasing to six years in the case of very young recruits.' (UK CRC/C/15/Add.188, para 53)).

[626] [2010] EWCA Civ 65, [2010] 4 All ER 91.

[627] See also Report of the Special Rapporteur pursuant to Commission on Human Rights Resolution 1991/38 UN Doc E/CN.4/1992/17, para 262.

Chapter 16

THE CHILD'S RIGHT TO FAIR AND EQUAL TREATMENT UNDER THE LAW

'Lawyers, I suppose, were children once'

Harper Lee

INTRODUCTION

16.1　The preamble to the Universal Declaration of Human Rights states that 'it is essential, if man is not to be compelled to have recourse, as a last resort, to rebellion against tyranny and oppression, that human rights should be protected by the rule of law'. The right to fair and equal treatment under the law is a right which itself enshrines the fundamental principle of the rule of law.[1] It applies to criminal proceedings, civil proceedings and adjudicative procedures of a hybrid kind in which one or more of the parties may suffer a serious consequence if an adverse order is made.[2] The requirement of equality of treatment under the law means that the concept of fairness extends to both parties to a given dispute. In its Advisory Opinion entitled *The Right to Information on Consular Assistance within the Framework of the Guarantees of the Due Process of Law*[3] the Inter-American Court of Human Rights noted that 'the judicial process is a means to ensure, insofar as possible, an equitable resolution of a difference. The body of procedures, of diverse character and generally grouped under the heading of the due process, is all calculated to serve that end'.

16.2　In respect of children, the Human Rights Committee has noted that:

'Juveniles[4] are to enjoy at least the same guarantees and protection as are accorded to adults under article 14 [of the International Covenant of Civil and Political Rights].'[5]

In *Haly v Ohio*[6] Justice Douglas held in the US Supreme Court that 'Neither man nor child can be allowed to stand condemned by methods which flout constitutional requirements of due process of law'. In *Re Gault*[7] Justice Fortas said in the US Supreme Court that:

'Due process of law is the primary and indispensable foundation of individual freedom. It is the basic and essential term in the social compact which defines the rights of the individual

---

[1]　*Salabiaku v France* (1988) 13 EHRR 379, para 28. Lord Bingham describes the right to a fair trial as a 'cardinal requirement' of the rule of law (see Bingham, T *The Rule of Law* (2010) Allen Lane, p 90).

[2]　Bingham, T *The Rule of Law* (2010) Allen Lane, p 90.

[3]　Advisory Opinion OC-16/99 of October 1, 1999 Series A No 16, para 117.

[4]　See below at **16.5-16.6** for a discussion of the meaning of the word 'juvenile'.

[5]　Human Rights Committee General Comment No 13 *Article 14 (Administration of Justice)* HRI/GEN/1/Rev 8, p 177. Article 14 of the ICCPR provides *inter alia* that 'All persons shall be equal before the courts and tribunals.'

[6]　332 US 596 (1948).

[7]　387 US 1 (1967), US Supreme Court.

and delimits the powers which the state may exercise ... A boy is charged with misconduct. The boy is committed to an institution where he may be restrained of liberty for years. It is of no constitutional consequence and of limited practical meaning that the institution to which he is committed is called an Industrial School. The fact of the matter is that, however euphemistic the title, a "receiving home" or an "industrial school" for juveniles is an institution of confinement in which the child is incarcerated for a greater or lesser time. His world becomes "a building with whitewashed walls, regimented routine and institutional hours ..." Instead of mother and father and sisters and brothers and friends and classmates, his world is peopled by guards, custodians, state employees, and 'delinquents' confined with him for anything from waywardness to rape and homicide ... In view of this, it would be extraordinary if our Constitution did not require the procedural regularity and the exercise of care implied in the phrase "due process". In *Kent v United States* ... we stated that the Juvenile Court Judge's exercise of the power of the state as parens patriae was not unlimited ... we said that 'there is no place in our system of law for reaching a result of such tremendous consequences without ceremony without hearing, without effective assistance of counsel, without a statement of reasons.' We announced with respect to such waiver proceedings that while "We do not mean ... to indicate that the hearing to be held must conform with all of the requirements of a criminal trial or even of the usual administrative hearing; but we do hold that the hearing must measure up to the essentials of due process and fair treatment." We reiterate this view, here in connection with a juvenile court adjudication of 'delinquency,' as a requirement which is part of the Due Process Clause of the Fourteenth Amendment of our Constitution.'

16.3 However, as is made clear by Justice Fortas in *Re Gault* and as Van Bueren notes, for children respect for the basic principles of fairness and equality before the law does not imply that the administration of justice for children ought to be identical to adults, but merely that fairness demands that due process should be the principle on which hearings for children are based.[8] Furthermore, the application to children of the principle of fair and equal treatment under the law must take account of the child's need for special safeguards and care by reason of his or her physical and mental immaturity.[9] Thus, as Fortin has noted in respect of criminal proceedings, 'The law should undoubtedly protect children from the full rigours of the criminal justice system until they are old enough to take full responsibility for their actions'.[10] This protective principle applies equally to civil and hybrid proceedings, both of which may adversely affect the child. There is thus an important balance to be struck between giving effect to the child's cardinal right to fair and equal treatment under the law and recognising and facilitating the child's particular need for protection.[11]

16.4 The right to fair and equal treatment under the law is enshrined in the Universal Declaration of Human Rights.[12] Whilst the 1924 and 1959 Declarations on the Rights of the Child contained no provisions for the fair and equal treatment of the child under the law, the Universal Declaration of Human Rights, together with the ICCPR,[13] the CRC,[14] the regional human rights treaties and the 'Beijing Rules' provide a framework for applying the principles of due process to children.[15] This chapter considers the child's right to fair and equal treatment under the law as enshrined in the CRC, the ECHR and other key international and regional human rights instruments.

---

8   Van Bueren, G *The International Law on the Rights of the Child* (1998) Martinus Nijhoff, p 169.
9   See the CRC Preamble.
10   Fortin, J *Children's Rights and the Developing Law* (2009) 3rd edn, Cambridge, p 678.
11   See **16.9** below concerning the application of the best interests principle in this context.
12   See Universal Declaration of Human Rights, Arts 6, 7, 8, 10 and 11.
13   ICCPR, Art 14.
14   CRC, Art 40.
15   Van Bueren, G *The International Law on the Rights of the Child* (1998) Martinus Nijhoff, p 179.

Consideration is then given to specific issues concerning the application of the child's right to fair and equal treatment under the law in the domestic arena.

GENERAL PRINCIPLES

Application of the Child's Right to Fair and Equal Treatment under the Law to all Children

Application to all Children

16.5   The term 'juvenile justice' is closely associated with the right of children to fair and equal treatment under the law. It is however a term that presents a number of difficulties when considering that right. The word 'juvenile' as defined by the UN Standard Rules for the Administration of Juvenile Justice (the 'Beijing Rules') does not necessarily correspond to the concept of 'child'.[16] The 'Beijing Rules' define a juvenile as 'a child or young person who, under the respective legal systems, may be dealt with for an offence in a manner which is different from an adult'.[17] Thus under the 'Beijing Rules' it is the manner in which the child is dealt with by the criminal justice system rather than the child's age which determines whether or not the child is also considered a 'juvenile' for the purposes of rules facilitating the child's right to fair and equal treatment before the law. Van Bueren points out that this definition is circular, being no more than a statement that a person is a juvenile if he or she is treated as a juvenile, potentially eliminating some children from the protection conferred by 'juvenile' justice measures. As Van Bueren concludes, the net result is that whether a child gains the necessary protection is defined by the mode of trial rather than the fact of their age and vulnerability as a child.[18] The position outlined in this paragraph is now however mitigated to a certain extent.

16.6   The definition of 'juvenile' has effectively been amended in the United Nations Rules for the Protection of Children Deprived of their Liberty. Rule 18 of the UN Rules for the Protection of Children Deprived of their Liberty provides that 'A juvenile is every person under the age of 18'. This definition has been endorsed by the Human Rights Committee at least in so far as it relates to criminal justice.[19] Overarching this, Art 40 of the CRC applies the right of children to fair and equal treatment under the law to all children as defined in Art 1 of the CRC.[20] In its General Comment No 10 *Children's Rights in Juvenile Justice*[21] the Committee on the Rights of the Child makes clear that:

> 'The Committee wishes to remind States parties that they have recognised the right of every child alleged as, accused of, or recognised as having infringed the penal law to be treated in

---

[16]   Van Bueren, G *The International Law on the Rights of the Child* (1998) Martinus Nijhoff, p 171.

[17]   UN Standard Rules for the Administration of Juvenile Justice r 2(2).

[18]   Van Bueren, G *The International Law on the Rights of the Child* (1998) Martinus Nijhoff, p 171.

[19]   Human Rights Committee General Comment No 21 *Article 10 (Humane Treatment of Persons Deprived of their Liberty)* HRI/GEN/1/Rev 8, p 194, para 13.

[20]   Newell, P and Hodgkin, R Implementation Handbook for the Convention on the Rights of the Child (2008) 3rd edn, UNICEF, p 603. Article 1 of the CRC provides that 'For the purposes of the present Convention, a child means every human being below the age of eighteen years unless under the law applicable to the child, majority is attained earlier.' See also Human Rights Committee General Comment No 17 HRI/GEN/1/Rev.8, p 183 ('as individuals, children benefit from all of the civil rights enunciated in the Covenant').

[21]   CRC/C/GC/10, para 37.

accordance with the provisions of article 40 of CRC. This means that every person under the age of 18 years at the time of the alleged commission of an offence must be treated in accordance with the rules of juvenile justice.'

Application to all Proceedings

16.7   A further problem associated with the word 'juvenile' is that the use of the term 'juvenile justice' can act to emphasise the application of the right to fair and equal treatment under the law to criminal proceedings concerning children at the expense of recognising that this cardinal right applies to *all* proceedings concerning children. Article 10 of the Universal Declaration of Human Rights makes clear that the right of everyone to fair and equal treatment under the law applies in determination of 'rights and obligations' as well as in respect of any criminal charge. Article 14(1) of the ICCPR also makes clear that the principles of equality and fairness under the law apply to everyone in the determination of any criminal charge *or* rights and obligations. The UN Standard Minimum Rules on the Administration of Juvenile Justice require that States make an effort to extend the principles embodied in the rules to all juveniles who are dealt with in welfare and care proceedings.[22] Finally, the jurisprudence of the European Court of Human Rights makes clear that the cardinal elements of due process guaranteed within criminal proceedings are embodied in the notion of 'fair trial' generally.[23]

16.8   Thus, whilst the CRC omits to expressly confer on the child the right to fair and equal treatment under the law in determination of the child's civil rights and obligations, having regard to the foregoing international legal principles and the fact that, for children, the consequences of civil proceedings can be equally serious,[24] it is submitted that the child's right to fair and equal treatment before the law, as enshrined in Art 40 of the CRC, applies to civil and hybrid proceedings as well as criminal proceedings. Accordingly, whilst reference is commonly made in this chapter to 'juvenile justice' many of the principles discussed below in that context will apply, with necessary modifications, to civil and hybrid proceedings concerning children.

Best Interests and the Child's Right to Fair and Equal Treatment under the Law

16.9   The UN Standard Minimum Rules for the Administration of Juvenile Justice, which also provide for their extension to welfare and care proceedings concerning children, stipulate that 'Member States shall seek, in conformity with their respective general interests, to further the well-being of the juvenile and her or his family'.[25] Within the context of criminal justice systems, the Committee on the Rights of the Child has made clear that:[26]

'In all decisions taken within the context of the administration of juvenile justice, the best interests of the child should be a primary consideration. Children differ from adults in their physical and psychological development, and their emotional and educational needs. Such

---

[22]   UN Standard Minimum Rules on the Administration of Juvenile Justice r 3(2).

[23]   See for example *Albert and Le Compte v Belgium* (1983) 5 EHRR, para 30.

[24]   For example, care proceedings are civil in nature but can result in the permanent removal of the child from the care or his or her family.

[25]   UN Standard Minimum Rules for the Administration of Juvenile Justice, r 1(1). See also r 17(1)(d) ('The well-being of the juvenile shall be the guiding factor in the consideration of her or his case').

[26]   General Comment No 10 *Children's Rights in Juvenile Justice* CRC/C/GC/10 p 3 and p 5.

differences constitute the basis for the lesser culpability of children in conflict with the law. These and other differences are the reasons for a separate juvenile justice system and require a different treatment for children. The protection of the best interests of the child means, for instance, that the traditional objectives of criminal justice, such as repression/retribution, must give way to rehabilitation and restorative justice objectives in dealing with child offenders. This can be done in concert with attention to effective public safety.

16.10 The best interests principle applies from the inception of proceedings through to their conclusion. Article 14(4) of the ICCPR mandates that 'In the case of juvenile persons, the procedure[27] shall be such as will take account of their age and the desirability of promoting their rehabilitation'.[28] Rule 14(2) of the UN Standard Minimum Rules for the Administration of Juvenile Justice requires that 'The proceedings shall be conducive to the best interests of the juvenile'. In respect of the consequences of criminal proceedings for children, Art 40(4) of the CRC stipulates that a variety of dispositions, such as care, guidance and supervision orders, counselling, probation, foster care, education and vocational training programmes and other alternatives to institutional care shall be available to ensure that children are dealt with in a manner appropriate to their well-being and proportionate both to their circumstances and the offence.

16.11 The concepts of fairness and best interests are closely interrelated and may also lead to conflicting issues in the context of the child's right to fair and equal treatment under the law. For example, whilst as a cardinal element of the right to a fair trial and pursuant to Art 12 of the CRC the child has a right to participate in proceedings, there are a range of situations in which direct participation may not be considered in the child's best interests. In such situations, the application of the best interests principle requires the adaption of the proceedings so as to ensure both the best interests of the child and the right of the child, and all other involved parties, to fair and equal treatment under the law are safeguarded.

Participation and the Child's Right to Fair and Equal Treatment under the Law

16.12 Article 12 of the CRC enshrines the child's right to be heard in all matters affecting the child and in particular in any judicial and administrative proceedings affecting the child, either directly, or through a representative or an appropriate body, in a manner consistent with the procedural rules of national law.[29] Article 12(2) covers *all*

---

[27] The fact that this requirement is given its own paragraph within the context of Art 14 of the ICCPR rather than being incorporated into Art 14(3) concerning criminal charges, suggests that the word 'procedure' means procedure in the determination of any criminal charge or of his or her rights and obligations when read with Art 14(1).

[28] Note that the concept of 'rehabilitation' as set out in Art 14(4) of the ICCPR has been replaced by the concept of 'reintegration', the former concept being considered to hold unhelpful connotations of social control by the State and sole responsibility upon the individual, failing to reflect the multi-faceted causes of offending behaviour (Van Bueren, G *The International Law on the Rights of the Child* (1998) Martinus Nijhoff, p 173). The term reintegration is used in Art 39 of the CRC and Art 40(1) of the CRC and the 'Beijing Rules', r 80. Van Bueren submits that the term 'rehabilitation' in Art 14(4) of the ICCPR should be interpreted as 'the means by which the child can assume a constructive role in society' in order to avoid the creation of two different standards (Van Bueren, G *The International Law on the Rights of the Child* (1998) Martinus Nijhoff, p 173).

[29] See chapter 6 above.

judicial and administrative proceedings affecting the child.[30] In respect of judicial proceedings, it has been suggested that the term includes criminal prosecutions of parents, the outcome of which can affect children dramatically.[31] Note that the reference to national procedure qualifies only the method of participation and does not restrict the child's right to participate *per se*.[32] The term 'administrative proceedings' is a wide term in its application.[33] The rights under Art 12 apply equally to religious courts such as sharia courts.[34] Art 12 requires not only that children are heard but that their views are given appropriate weight. The Committee on the Rights of the Child has reminded States Parties that:[35]

'... the right of the child to be heard in judicial and administrative proceedings applies to all relevant settings without limitation, including children separated from their parents, custody and adoption cases, children in conflict with the law, children victims of physical violence, sexual abuse or other violent crimes, asylum seeking and refugee children and children who have been the victims of armed conflict and in emergencies.'

16.13 These principles should be adhered to throughout the course of the proceedings.[36] Within the context of juvenile justice, Art 40 of the CRC enshrines a series of rights designed to facilitate effective participation,[37] requiring that the child is informed promptly and directly of the charges against him or her,[38] that the child has access to legal and other appropriate assistance[39] and that the child is entitled to play a full part in the proceedings[40] with the assistance of an interpreter if required.[41] These rights are reflected in Art 6 of the ECHR.[42] The participation must be 'effective' participation and must be child sensitive. In this regard, reference should be made to the UN Standard Minimum Rules on the Administration of Juvenile Justice[43] and the UN

---

30   The words 'in all matters affecting the child' in Art 12(1) and the words 'any judicial and administrative proceedings' in Art 12(2) indicate that the child's right to be heard applies in criminal, civil and hybrid proceedings as well as administrative proceedings.

31   Newell, P and Hodgkin, R *Implementation Handbook for the Convention on the Rights of the Child* (2008) 3rd edn, UNICEF, p 156. Theoretically, this assertion could be taken further to encompass all court proceedings concerning parents and carers the outcome of which would impact adversely on the child, including proceedings for child maintenance and civil actions affecting the families' income.

32   Van Bueren, G *The International Law on the Rights of the Child* (1998) Martinus Nijhoff, p 181.

33   Van Bueren, G *The International Law on the Rights of the Child* (1998) Martinus Nijhoff, p 137. See also Fawcett, J *The Application of the European Convention on Human Rights* (1987) and **6.30** above.

34   Lebanon CRC/C/LBN/CO/3, paras 35–36.

35   Committee on the Rights of the Child, Report on the forty-third session, September 2006, Day of General Discussion, Recommendations, para 239. General Comment No 12 (2009) *The Right of the Child to Be Heard* (CRC/C/GC/12, paras 32)

36   See the Committee on the Rights of the Child General Comment No 10 *Children's Rights in Juvenile Justice* CRC/C/GC/10, pp 5–6 ('The right of the child to express his/her views freely in all matters affecting the child should be fully respected and implemented throughout every stage of the process of juvenile justice. The Committee notes that the voices of children involved in the juvenile justice system are increasingly becoming a powerful force for improvements and reform, and for the fulfillment of their rights').

37   See the Committee on the Rights of the Child General Comment No 10 *Children's Rights in Juvenile Justice* CRC/C/GC/10, para 46 ('A fair trial requires that the child alleged as or accused of having infringed the penal law be able to effectively participate in the trial, and therefore needs to comprehend the charges, and possible consequences and penalties, in order to direct the legal representative, to challenge witnesses, to provide an account of events, and to make appropriate decisions about evidence, testimony and the measure(s) to be imposed').

38   CRC, Art 40(2)(b)(ii).

39   CRC, Art 40(2)(b)(ii) and (iii).

40   CRC, Art 40(23)(b)(iv).

41   CRC, Art 40(2)(b)(vi).

42   See **16.72** below.

43   Rule 14(2) provides that 'The proceedings shall be conducive to the best interests of the juvenile and shall be conducted in an atmosphere of understanding, which shall allow the juvenile to participate therein and to express herself or himself freely.'

Economic and Social Council Resolution *Guidelines on Justice Involving Child Victims and Witnesses of Crime*[44] which defines 'child sensitive' in the context of the child's right to participate as an approach that 'balances the child's right to protection and that takes into account the child's individual needs and views'.[45] It must be remembered that the child has a right to silence[46] and that the child's right to participate does not equate to an obligation to express a view. The child must be able to choose whether or not he or she wants to exercise his or her right to be heard.[47]

Non-Discrimination and the Child's Right to Fair and Equal Treatment under the Law

Equality before the Law

16.14 In the US Supreme Court case of *Railway Express Agency Inc v New York*[48] Justice Jackson said 'Courts can take no better measure to assure that laws will be just than to require that laws be equal in operation'. The Universal Declaration of Human Rights Art 7 stipulates that 'All are equal before the law and are entitled without any discrimination to equal protection of the law'. Article 14(1) of the ICCPR provides that: 'All persons shall be equal before the courts and tribunals'. The CRC does not contain a provision expressly enshrining the child's equality before the law. However the CRC records in its Preamble a recognition of that the equal and inalienable rights of all members of the human family is the foundation of justice. Article 2(1) of the CRC requires that States Parties respect and ensure the rights set forth in the CRC concerning the child's treatment under the law to each child without discrimination of any kind, irrespective of the child's or his or her parent's or legal guardian's race, colour, sex, language, religion, political or other opinion, national, ethnic or social origin, property, disability, birth or other status. Further, Rule 2(1) of the UN Standard Minimum Rules for the Administration of Juvenile Justice provide that those rules 'shall be applied to juvenile offenders impartially, without distinction of any kind, for example as to race, colour, sex, language, religion, political or other opinions, national or social origin, property, birth or other status'. In its General Comment No 10 *Children's Rights in Juvenile Justice* the Committee on the Rights of the Child made clear that:

> 'States parties have to take all necessary measures to ensure that all children in conflict with the law are treated equally. Particular attention must be paid to de facto discrimination and disparities, which may be the result of a lack of a consistent policy and involve vulnerable groups of children, such as street children, children belonging to racial, ethnic, religious or linguistic minorities, indigenous children, girl children, children with disabilities and children who are repeatedly in conflict with the law (recidivists).'[49]

---

[44]   UNODC/UNICEF 2005/20 of 22 July 2005.
[45]   UNODC/UNICEF 2005/20 of 22 July 2005, para 9(d).
[46]   See Art 40(2)(b)(iv) and **16.50** below.
[47]   Newell, P and Hodgkin, R *Implementation Handbook for the Convention on the Rights of the Child* (2008) 3rd edn, UNICEF, pp 154 and 609.
[48]   336 US 106 (1949), US Supreme Court.
[49]   Committee on the Rights of the Child General Comment No 10 *Children's Rights in Juvenile Justice* CRC/C/GC/10 p 4, para 6. See also CRC, Art 23 ('States Parties recognise that a mentally or physically disabled child should enjoy a full and decent life, in conditions which ensure dignity, promote self-reliance and facilitate the child's active participation in the community), the Convention on the Rights of Persons with Disabilities Art 12(2) ('States Parties shall recognise that persons with disabilities enjoy legal capacity on an equal basis with others in all aspects of life') and the Committee on the Rights of the Child General Comment No 9 *The Rights of Children with Disabilities* CRC/C/GC/9 paras 73–74. See further the Committee on the Rights of the Child Report on the Thirty-Fourth Session September/October 2003 CRC/C/133, p 134 ("To the extent compatible with articles 37, 39 and 40 of the Convention and other

Status Offences

16.15 A 'status offence' is an offence which criminalises behaviour on the part of children which is not criminalised in respect of adults. The Committee on the Rights of the Child mandates the abolition of such 'status offences' in order to establish equal treatment under the law for children and adults.[50] Rule 56 of the UN Guidelines for the Prevention of Juvenile Delinquency (the 'Riyadh Guidelines') provide that:

'In order to prevent further stigmatisation, victimisation and criminalisation of young persons, legislation should be enacted to ensure that any conduct not considered an offence or not penalised if committed by an adult is not considered an offence and not penalised if committed by a young person.'

16.16 In respect of 'status offences' regard should be had to the views of the Inter-American Court of Human Rights in its Advisory Opinion on the Legal Status and Human Rights of the Child in which it observed that:[51]

'It is unacceptable to include in [the definition of criminal conduct] the situation of minors who have not incurred in conduct defined by law as a crime, but who are at risk or endangered, due to destitution, abandonment, extreme poverty or disease, and even less so those others who simply behave differently from how the majority does, those who differ from the generally accepted patterns of behavior, who are involved in conflicts regarding adaptation to the family, school, or social milieu, generally, or who alienate themselves from the customs and values of their society. The concept of crime committed by children or juvenile crime can only be applied to those who fall under the first aforementioned situation, that is, those who incur in conduct legally defined as a crime, not to those who are in the other situations.'

RIGHT TO FAIR AND EQUAL TREATMENT UNDER THE LAW

The Child's Right to Fair and Equal Treatment under the Law – CRC

CRC, Art 40

16.17 Article 40 of the CRC provides as follows in respect of the child's right to fair and equal treatment under the law in respect of children alleged as, accused of or recognised as having infringed the penal law:

'1. States Parties recognise the right of every child alleged as, accused of, or recognised as having infringed the penal law to be treated in a manner consistent with the promotion of the child's sense of dignity and worth, which reinforces the child's respect for the human rights and fundamental freedoms of others and which takes into account the child's age and the desirability of promoting the child's reintegration and the child's assuming a constructive role in society.

2. To this end, and having regard to the relevant provisions of international instruments, States Parties shall, in particular, ensure that:

United Nations standards and rules, the Committee suggests that States Parties respect the methods customarily practiced by indigenous peoples for dealing with criminal offences committed by children, when it is in the best interests of the child ...').

[50] Committee on the Rights of the Child General Comment No 10 *Children's Rights in Juvenile Justice* CRC/C/GC/10, p 4, para 8.

[51] Inter-American Court of Human Rights Advisory Opinion OC-17/2002, para 110.

(a)   No child shall be alleged as, be accused of, or recognised as having infringed the penal law by reason of acts or omissions that were not prohibited by national or international law at the time they were committed;

(b)   Every child alleged as or accused of having infringed the penal law has at least the following guarantees:

   (i)   To be presumed innocent until proven guilty according to law;

   (ii)   To be informed promptly and directly of the charges against him or her, and, if appropriate, through his or her parents or legal guardians, and to have legal or other appropriate assistance in the preparation and presentation of his or her defence;

   (iii) To have the matter determined without delay by a competent, independent and impartial authority or judicial body in a fair hearing according to law, in the presence of legal or other appropriate assistance and, unless it is considered not to be in the best interest of the child, in particular, taking into account his or her age or situation, his or her parents or legal guardians;

   (iv)   Not to be compelled to give testimony or to confess guilt; to examine or have examined adverse witnesses and to obtain the participation and examination of witnesses on his or her behalf under conditions of equality;

   (v)   If considered to have infringed the penal law, to have this decision and any measures imposed in consequence thereof reviewed by a higher competent, independent and impartial authority or judicial body according to law;

   (vi)   To have the free assistance of an interpreter if the child cannot understand or speak the language used;

   (vii) To have his or her privacy fully respected at all stages of the proceedings.

3. States Parties shall seek to promote the establishment of laws, procedures, authorities and institutions specifically applicable to children alleged as, accused of, or recognised as having infringed the penal law, and, in particular:

(a)   The establishment of a minimum age below which children shall be presumed not to have the capacity to infringe the penal law;

(b)   Whenever appropriate and desirable, measures for dealing with such children without resorting to judicial proceedings, providing that human rights and legal safeguards are fully respected.

4. A variety of dispositions, such as care, guidance and supervision orders; counseling; probation; foster care; education and vocational training programmes and other alternatives to institutional care shall be available to ensure that children are dealt with in a manner appropriate to their well-being and proportionate both to their circumstances and the offence.'

16.18 CRC, Art 40 enshrines the cardinal rights of all children alleged as, accused of or recognised as having infringed the penal law.[52] It is thus concerned with the criminal law and will apply from the point an allegation is levelled, through the investigation of that allegation, the arrest and charge or the child, pre-trial processes, trial and subsequent sentence. In its General Comment No 10 *Children's Rights in Juvenile Justice* the Committee on the Rights of the Child describes the cardinal elements of juvenile justice policy which should underpin the facilitation of the rights conferred by Art 40 of the CRC:[53]

'A comprehensive policy for juvenile justice must deal with the following core elements: the prevention of juvenile delinquency; interventions without resorting to judicial proceedings

---

[52]   Newell, P and Hodgkin, R Implementation Handbook for the Convention on the Rights of the Child (2008) 3rd edn, UNICEF, p 602.

[53]   Committee on the Rights of the Child General Comment No 10 *Children's Rights in Juvenile Justice* CRC/C/GC/10, para 15.

and interventions in the context of judicial proceedings; the minimum age of criminal responsibility and the upper age-limits for juvenile justice; the guarantees for a fair trial; and deprivation of liberty including pretrial detention and post-trial incarceration.'

16.19 As noted above, whilst the CRC, Art 40 omits to expressly confer on the child the right to fair and equal treatment under the law in determination of the child's civil rights and obligations, Art 10 of the Universal Declaration of Human Rights makes clear that the right of everyone to fair and equal treatment before the law applies in determination of 'rights and obligations' as well as in respect of any criminal charge. Article 14(1) of the ICCPR which makes clear that the principles of equality and fairness under the law apply to everyone in the determination or any criminal charge *or* rights and obligations. The UN Standard Minimum Rules on the Administration of Juvenile Justice require that States make an effort to extend the principles embodied in the rules to all juveniles who are dealt with in welfare and care proceedings.[54] The jurisprudence of the European Court of Human Rights makes clear that the cardinal elements of due process guaranteed within criminal proceedings are embodied in the notion of 'fair trial' generally.[55] Having regard to the foregoing international and regional legal principles and the fact that, for children, the consequences of civil proceedings can be equally serious,[56] it is submitted that the cardinal elements of the child's right to fair and equal treatment before the law, as enshrined in Art 40 of the CRC, apply to civil and hybrid proceedings as well as criminal proceedings.

CRC, Art 40 – Related Provisions

16.20 A number of related instruments provide detailed standards and guidance for the implementation of Art 40 of the CRC. In particular, regard must be had to the UN Guidelines on the Prevention of Juvenile Delinquency (the 'Riyadh Guidelines'), the UN Standard Minimum Rules for the Administration of Juvenile Justice (the 'Beijing Rules'), the UN Standard Minimum Standards for Non-Custodial Measures (the 'Tokyo Rules'), the UN Rules for the Protection of Juveniles Deprived of their Liberty and the Committee on the Rights of the Child General Comment No 10: *Children's Rights in Juvenile Justice*. Reference should also be made to the ESC Guidelines for Action on Children in the Criminal Justice System[57] and the ESC Guidelines on Justice in Matters involving Child Victims and Witnesses of Crime.[58] Rather than establishing rights the UN Standard Minimum Rules for the Administration of Juvenile Justice provide the detailed content of existing rights under the CRC.[59] Once again, it is important to note that these rules are not limited in their scope to criminal proceedings but, by r 3.2 extend to encompass children who are dealt with in welfare and care proceedings. Article 1(4) of the UN Standard Minimum Rules for the Administration of Juvenile Justice provides that:

> 'Juvenile Justice shall be conceived as an integral part of the national development process of each country, within a comprehensive framework of social justice for all juveniles, thus, at the same time contributing to the protection of the young and the maintenance of a peaceful order in society.'[60]

---

[54] UN Standard Minimum Rules on the Administration of Juvenile Justice, r 3(2).
[55] See for example *Albert and Le Compte v Belgium* (1983) 5 EHRR, para 30.
[56] For example, care proceedings are civil in nature but can result in the permanent removal of the child from the care or his or her family.
[57] ESC Resolution 1997/30.
[58] ESC Resolution 2005/20.
[59] Van Bueren, G *The International Law on the Rights of the Child* (1998) Martinus Nijhoff, p 170.
[60] See also the 'Guidelines for Action on Children in the Criminal Justice System' which aim to provide a

(i)   Preventative Measures

UN Guidelines on the Prevention of Juvenile Delinquency (the 'Riyadh Guidelines')

16.21 A fundamental aim of the provisions of Art 40 of the CRC is to minimise the necessity of intervention by the juvenile justice system to the greatest possible extent and in turn to minimise the potential harm inherent in such interventions.[61] In this context, the UN Guidelines on the Prevention of Juvenile Delinquency (the 'Riyadh Guidelines') recognise in Art 1(1) that 'The prevention of juvenile delinquency is an essential part of crime prevention in society'. The 'Riyadh Guidelines' articulate standards for the prevention of juvenile delinquency, including measures to protect vulnerable children and young people, with the emphasis placed on:

> '... preventative policies facilitating the successful socialisation and integration of all children and young persons, in particular through the family, the community, peer groups, schools, vocational training, the world of work, and voluntary organisations.'[62]

The Committee on the Rights of the Child has endorsed the 'Riyadh Guidelines' in the context of the children who may come into conflict with the law:[63]

> 'The Committee fully supports the Riyadh Guidelines and agrees that emphasis should be placed on prevention policies that facilitate the successful socialisation and integration of all children, in particular through the family, the community, peer groups, schools, vocational training and the world of work, as well as through voluntary organisations. This means, inter alia that prevention programmes should focus on support for particularly vulnerable families, the involvement of schools in teaching basic values (including information about the rights and responsibilities of children and parents under the law), and extending special care and attention to young persons at risk. In this regard, particular attention should also be given to children who drop out of school or otherwise do not complete their education. The use of peer group support and a strong involvement of parents are recommended. The States parties should also develop community-based services and programmes that respond to the special needs, problems, concerns and interests of children, in particular of children repeatedly in conflict with the law, and that provide appropriate counseling and guidance to their families.'

(ii)   Diversions

UN Standard Minimum Rules on the Administration of Juvenile Justice (the 'Beijing Rules')

16.22 The failure of preventative measures to stop a child becoming involved in activities which brings him or her into conflict with the law does not mean that the child must thereafter inevitably be exposed to the full force of the juvenile justice system. Rather, a fundamental principle of the juvenile justice system must be the 'diversion' where possible of children away from the more formal, and potentially more harmful, aspects of the juvenile justice system.[64] To this end Art 40(3)(b) of the CRC provides that:

---

framework for the implementation of those elements of the CRC concerned with children in the context of the administration of juvenile justice (Economic and Social Council resolution 1997/30 of 21 July 1997).

[61]   UN Standard Minimum Rules for the Administration of Juvenile Justice (the 'Beijing Rules') Commentary on r 1.

[62]   See Art 10.

[63]   Committee on the Rights of the Children General Comment No 10 *Children's Rights in Juvenile Justice* CRC/C/GC/10 p 7, para 18.

[64]   Van Bueren, G *Child Rights in Europe* (2007) Council of Europe Publishing, p 113.

'States Parties shall seek to promote the establishment of laws, procedures, authorities and institutions specifically applicable to children alleged as, accused of, or recognised as having infringed the penal law, and, in particular: (b) Whenever appropriate and desirable, measures for dealing with such children without resorting to judicial proceedings, providing that human rights and legal safeguards are fully respected.'

16.23 The UN Standard Minimum Rules on the Administration of Juvenile Justice further elaborate on the diversionary provisions of Art 40. In this regard Rule 11 provides as follows:

'(1) Consideration shall be given, wherever appropriate, to dealing with juvenile offenders without resorting to formal trial by the competent authority, referred to in rule 14(1) below.

(2) The police, the prosecution or other agencies dealing with juvenile cases shall be empowered to dispose of such cases, at their discretion, without recourse to formal hearings, in accordance with the criteria laid down for that purpose in the respective legal system and also in accordance with the principles contained in these Rules.

(3) Any diversion involving referral to appropriate community or other services shall require the consent of the juvenile, or her or his parents or guardian, provided that such decision to refer a case shall be subject to review by a competent authority, upon application.

(4) In order to facilitate the discretionary disposition of juvenile cases, efforts shall be made to provide for community programmes, such as temporary supervision and guidance, restitution, and compensation of victims.'

16.24 Within this context, the ESC Guidelines for Action on Children in the Criminal Justice System note that:

'Appropriate steps should be taken to make available throughout the State a broad range of alternative and educative measures at the pre-arrest, pre-trial, trial and post-trial stages, in order to prevent recidivism and promote the social rehabilitation of child offenders. Whenever appropriate, mechanisms for the informal resolution of disputes in cases involving a child offender should be utilised, including mediation and restorative justice practices, particularly processes involving victims. In the various measures to be adopted, the family should be involved, to the extent that it operates in favour of the good of the child offender. States should ensure that alternative measures comply with the Convention, the United Nations standards and norms in juvenile justice, as well as other existing standards and norms in crime prevention and criminal justice, such as the United Nations Standard Minimum Rules for Non-custodial Measures (The Tokyo Rules), with special regard to ensuring respect for due process rules in applying such measures and for the principle of minimum intervention.'[65]

16.25 In seeking to divert children who are in conflict with the criminal law from the more formal, and potentially more harmful, aspects of the juvenile justice system the

---

[65]   ESC Resolution 1997/30, para 15. See also Committee on the Rights of the Child General Comment No 10 *Children's Rights in Juvenile Justice* CRC/C/GC/10, para 24 ('Given the fact that the majority of child offenders commit only minor offences, a range of measures involving removal from criminal/juvenile justice processing and referral to alternative (social) services (ie diversion) should be a well-established practice that can and should be used in most cases') and para 25 ('In the opinion of the Committee, the obligation of States parties to promote measures for dealing with children in conflict with the law without resorting to judicial proceedings applies, but is certainly not limited to children who commit minor offences, such as shoplifting or other property offences with limited damage, and first-time child offenders').

following principles must be observed to ensure that the child's right to fair and equal treatment before the law are properly safeguarded:[66]

(a) The law must contain specific provisions indicating in which cases diversion is possible, and the powers of the police, prosecutors and/or other agencies to make decisions in this regard should be regulated and reviewed, in particular to protect the child from discrimination.

(b) Diversions should be used only when there is compelling evidence that the child committed the alleged offence.

(c) The child must be given the opportunity to seek legal or other appropriate assistance on the appropriateness and desirability of the diversion offered by the competent authorities, and on the possibility of review of the measure.

(d) Diversions should only be used where the child freely and voluntarily admits responsibility, and where no intimidation or pressure has been used to secure such an admission. Any admission made must not be used against the child in any subsequent legal proceeding.

(e) The child must freely and voluntarily give consent in writing to the diversion, a consent that should be based on adequate and specific information on the nature, content and duration of the measure, and on the consequences of a failure to cooperate, carry out and complete the measure. Consideration may also be given to requiring the consent of parents, in particular when the child is below the age of 16 years.

(f) The completion of the diversion by the child should result in a definite and final closure of the case.

(g) Although confidential records can be kept of diversion for administrative and review purposes, they should not be viewed as 'criminal records' and a child who has been previously diverted must not be seen as having a previous conviction. If any registration takes place of this event, access to that information should be given exclusively and for a limited period of time[67] to the competent authorities authorised to deal with children in conflict with the law.

CRC, Art 40(1) – Ambit

16.26 Article 40(1) of the CRC provides as follows concerning the proper treatment of a child who is alleged as, accused of or recognised has having infringed the penal law:

> 'States Parties recognise the right of every child alleged as, accused of, or recognised as having infringed the penal law to be treated in a manner consistent with the promotion of the child's sense of dignity and worth, which reinforces the child's respect for the human

---

[66] See Committee on the Rights of the Child General Comment No 10 *Children's Rights in Juvenile Justice* CRC/C/GC/10, para 27. See also the UN Standard Minimum Standards for Non-Custodial Measures (the 'Tokyo Rules') and the Economic and Social Council Resolution 2002/12 *Basic Principles for the Use of Restorative Justice Programmes in Criminal Matters*.

[67] The Committee on the Rights of the Child suggests a maximum of one year (Committee on the Rights of the Child General Comment No 10 *Children's Rights in Juvenile Justice* CRC/C/GC/10, para 27).

rights and fundamental freedoms of others and which takes into account the child's age and the desirability of promoting the child's reintegration and the child's assuming a constructive role in society.'[68]

16.27 Article 40(1) provides the overarching principles governing the child's right to fair and equal treatment under the law. In its General Comment No 10 *Children's Rights in Juvenile Justice* the Committee on the Rights of the Child explains that the concept of 'inherent right to dignity and worth', to which the preamble of CRC makes explicit reference, has to be respected and protected throughout the entire justice process, from the first contact with law enforcement agencies to the implementation of all measures for dealing with the child. The requirement to respect the child's dignity encompasses the requirement that all forms of violence in the treatment of children in conflict with the law must be prohibited and prevented. The necessity for treatment that reinforces respect for human rights and freedoms of others means that the treatment and education of children within the justice system shall be directed to the development of respect for human rights and freedoms. The obligation to take account of the child's age and the desirability of promoting his or her re-integration must again be applied, observed and respected throughout the entire process. These principles necessarily require that all professionals involved in the administration of juvenile justice be knowledgeable about child development, the dynamic and continuing growth of children, what is appropriate to their well-being, and the pervasive forms of violence against children.[69] The domestic courts have recognised the import of Art 40(1) of the CRC and the need to interpret the domestic criminal law in light of its provisions.[70]

16.28 There is an implicit acknowledgement in Art 40(1) of the CRC that whilst protecting the rights of children there is a balance to be struck between the rights of the child in conflict with the law and the rights of the wider community to public safety. The Committee has concluded that 'it is of the opinion that this aim is best served by a full respect for and implementation of the leading and overarching principles of juvenile justice as enshrined in CRC'.[71]

CRC, Art 40(2) – Ambit

16.29 Article 40(2) of the CRC stipulates as follows concerning the cardinal elements of fair and equal treatment under the law:

'2. To this end, and having regard to the relevant provisions of international instruments, States Parties shall, in particular, ensure that:

---

[68] See also Art 14(4) of the ICCPR.
[69] Committee on the Rights of the Child General Comment No 10 *Children's Rights in Juvenile Justice* CRC/C/GC/10, p 6, para 13.
[70] See *R v G and another* [2003] UKHL 50, [2003] 4 All ER 765, para 53 ('Ignoring the special position of children in the criminal justice system is not acceptable in a modern civil society. In 1990 the United Kingdom ratified the United Nations Convention on the Rights of the Child (New York, 20 November 1989; TS 44 (1992); Cm 1976) (the UN convention) which entered into force on 15 January 1992. Article 40(1) ... This provision imposes both procedural and substantive obligations on state parties to protect the special position of children in the criminal justice system. For example, it would plainly be contrary to Art 40(1) for a state to set the age of criminal responsibility of children at, say, 5 years. Similarly, it is contrary to art 40(1) to ignore in a crime punishable by life imprisonment, or detention during Her Majesty's pleasure, the age of a child in judging whether the mental element has been satisfied. It is true that the UN convention became binding on the United Kingdom after *R v Caldwell* was decided. But the House cannot ignore the norm created by the UN convention. This factor on its own justified a reappraisal of *R v Caldwell'*).
[71] Committee on the Rights of the Child General Comment No 10 *Children's Rights in Juvenile Justice* CRC/C/GC/10 p 7, para 14.

(a) No child shall be alleged as, be accused of, or recognised as having infringed the penal law by reason of acts or omissions that were not prohibited by national or international law at the time they were committed;

(b) Every child alleged as or accused of having infringed the penal law has at least the following guarantees:

(i) To be presumed innocent until proven guilty according to law;

(ii) To be informed promptly and directly of the charges against him or her, and, if appropriate, through his or her parents or legal guardians, and to have legal or other appropriate assistance in the preparation and presentation of his or her defence;

(iii) To have the matter determined without delay by a competent, independent and impartial authority or judicial body in a fair hearing according to law, in the presence of legal or other appropriate assistance and, unless it is considered not to be in the best interest of the child, in particular, taking into account his or her age or situation, his or her parents or legal guardians;

(iv) Not to be compelled to give testimony or to confess guilt; to examine or have examined adverse witnesses and to obtain the participation and examination of witnesses on his or her behalf under conditions of equality;

(v) If considered to have infringed the penal law, to have this decision and any measures imposed in consequence thereof reviewed by a higher competent, independent and impartial authority or judicial body according to law;

(vi) To have the free assistance of an interpreter if the child cannot understand or speak the language used;

(vii) To have his or her privacy fully respected at all stages of the proceedings.'

16.30 The provisions of Art 40(2) of the CRC must be read in the context of Art 40(1) and represent the *minimum* guarantees that must be available to children. The system of juvenile justice must have these basic procedural safeguards and they must be applicable at all stage of the proceedings.[72] These provisions represent the essential elements of a fair trial and are internationally recognised as such.[73] The implication of the words 'at least' in Art 40(2)(b) is that the protections included in the other international and regional human rights treaties are also applicable to children.[74] Many of the guarantees enshrined in Art 40(2) will plainly be relevant to welfare and care proceedings involving children, to which the UN Standard Minimum Rules on the Administration of Juvenile Justice should apply.[75] This will include in particular the right to have the matter determined without delay by a competent, independent and impartial authority or judicial body in a fair hearing according to law, in the presence of legal or other appropriate assistance and, unless it is considered not to be in the best interest of the child, in particular taking into account his or her age or situation, his or her parents or legal guardians.[76]

---

[72] See the UN Standard Minimum Rules for the Administration of Juvenile Justice, r 7(1) ('Basic procedural safeguards such as the presumption of innocence, the right to be notified of the charges, the right to remain silent, the right to counsel, the right to the presence of a parent or guardian, the right to confront and cross-examine witnesses and the right to appeal to a higher authority shall be guaranteed at all stages of proceedings').

[73] Newell, P and Hodgkin, R *Implementation Handbook for the Convention on the Rights of the Child* (2008) 3rd edn, UNICEF, p 613. Rule 14(1) of the UN Standard Minimum Rules on the Administration of Juvenile Justice provides that 'Where the case of a juvenile offender has not been diverted (under rule 11), she or he shall be dealt with by the competent authority (court, tribunal, board, council, etc.) according to the principles of a fair and just trial.'

[74] Van Bueren, G *The International Law on the Rights of the Child* (1998) Martinus Nijhoff, p 180.

[75] UN Standard Minimum Rules on the Administration of Juvenile Justice r 3(2). See the UN Standard Minimum Rules for the Administration of Juvenile Justice r 7(1) ('Basic procedural safeguards such as the presumption of innocence, the right to be notified of the charges, the right to remain silent, the right to counsel, the right to the presence of a parent or guardian, the right to confront and cross-examine witnesses and the right to appeal to a higher authority shall be guaranteed at all stages of proceedings').

[76] Article 40(2)(b)(iii).

16.31 Note that any steps taken to make the proceedings more informal in nature on the grounds that such steps are in the child's best interests must not be allowed to risk the absence of adherence to the minimum required international procedural safeguards.[77]

(i) CRC, Art 40(2)(a) – No Retrospective Legislation

16.32 Article 40(2)(a) of the CRC provides as follows in respect of the prohibition on retrospective legislation:

> 'No child shall be alleged as, be accused of, or recognised as having infringed the penal law by reason of acts or omissions that were not prohibited by national or international law at the time they were committed.'

16.33 This principle requiring the penal law not to be retrospective in nature is enshrined in Art 11(2) of the Universal Declaration of Human Rights which prohibits, unlike Art 40(2)(a) of the CRC,[78] retrospectivity in relation to both offences and any sentence passed in relation to an offence, stipulating that:

> 'No one shall be held guilty of any penal offence on account of any act or omission which did not constitute a penal offence, under national or international law, at the time when it was committed. Nor shall a heavier penalty be imposed than the one that was applicable at the time the penal offence was committed.'

Article 15(1) of the ICCPR, from which no derogation is permitted in accordance with Art 4(2) of the ICCPR, contains a similar prohibition prohibiting retrospective application in relation to both offences and any sentence passed in relation to an offence, although permitting the retrospective application of any general reduction on the penalty for an offence, stating that:

> 'No one shall be held guilty of any criminal offence on account of any act or omission which did not constitute a criminal offence, under national or international law, at the time when it was committed. Nor shall a heavier penalty be imposed than the one that was applicable at the time when the criminal offence was committed. If, subsequent to the commission of the offence, provision is made by law for the imposition of the lighter penalty, the offender shall benefit thereby.'

16.34 These provisions reflect the cardinal principle that to infringe the penal law the act in question must have been defined in the criminal law as an offence at the time the act was done.[79] Apparently importing a number of the provisions set out in the Universal Declaration of Human Rights Art 11(2) and the ICCPR Art 15(1) not expressed in the CRC concerning the non-retrospective nature of sentences, the

---

[77] See Pappas, A *Law and the Status of the Child* (1981) 13 Columbia Human Rights Review LII-LIII. See also Lehman, P *A Juvenile's Right to Counsel in a Delinquency Hearing* (1966) 17 Juvenile Court Judges Journal 53 p 54 ('Unfortunately, loose procedures, high-handed methods and crowded court calendars, either singly or in combination, all too often, have resulted in depriving some juveniles of fundamental rights that have resulted in a denial of due process').

[78] But see the Committee on the Rights of the Child General Comment No 10 *Children's Rights in Juvenile Justice* CRC/C/ GC/10, para 41 and **16.34** below.

[79] See *Black-Clawson International Ltd v Papierwerke Waldhoff-Aschaffenburg AG* [1975] AC 591 at 638D per Lord Diplock ('The acceptance of the rule of law as a constitutional principle requires that a citizen, before committing himself to any course of action, should be able to know in advance what are the legal principles which flow from it') and *Sunday Times v United Kingdom* (1979) 2 EHRR 245, para 49 ('... the law must be adequately accessible: the citizen must be able to have an indication that is adequate in the circumstances of the legal rules applicable to a given case ...a norm cannot be regarded as a 'law' unless it is formulated with

Committee on the Rights of the Child General Comment No 10 *Children's Rights in Juvenile Justice* makes clear that within the context of Children Art 40(2)(a):[80]

'... means that no child can be charged with or sentenced under the penal law for acts or omissions which at the time they were committed were not prohibited under national or international law ... No child shall be punished with a heavier penalty than the one applicable at the time of his/her infringement of the penal law. But if a change of law after the act provides for a lighter penalty, the child should benefit from this change.'

(ii) CRC, Art 40(2)(b) – Minimum Guarantees

CRC, Art 40(2)(b)(i) – Presumption of Innocence

16.35 CRC, Art 40(2)(b)(i) provides as follows concerning the presumption of innocence in respect of children:[81]

'2. To this end, and having regard to the relevant provisions of international instruments, States Parties shall, in particular, ensure that: (b) Every child alleged as or accused of having infringed the penal law has at least the following guarantees: (i) To be presumed innocent until proven guilty according to law...'

16.36 All children are presumed innocent until proven guilty according to law. The Committee on the Rights of the Child has observed that:[82]

'The presumption of innocence is fundamental to the protection of the human rights of children in conflict with the law. It means that the burden of proof of the charge(s) brought against the child is on the prosecution. The child alleged as or accused of having infringed the penal law has the benefit of doubt and is only guilty as charged if these charges have been proven beyond reasonable doubt. The child has the right to be treated in accordance with this presumption and it is the duty of all public authorities or others involved to refrain from prejudging the outcome of the trial. States parties should provide information about child development to ensure that this presumption of innocence is respected in practice. Due to the lack of understanding of the process, immaturity, fear or other reasons, the child may behave in a suspicious manner, but the authorities must not assume that the child is guilty without proof of guilt beyond any reasonable doubt.'

CRC, Art 40(2)(b)(ii) – Prompt Information on Charge and Legal Assistance

16.37 In relation to the child's minimum rights following arrest, the CRC, Art 40(2)(b)(ii) stipulates the right of the child:

'To be informed promptly and directly of the charges against him or her, and, if appropriate, through his or her parents or legal guardians, and to have legal or other appropriate assistance in the preparation and presentation of his or her defence.'[83]

---

sufficient precision to enable the citizen to regulate his conduct: he must be able – if need be with appropriate advice – to foresee, to a degree that is reasonable in the circumstances, the consequences which a given action may entail').

[80] Committee on the Rights of the Child General Comment No 10 *Children's Rights in Juvenile Justice* CRC/C/GC/10, para 41.

[81] See also the Universal Declaration of Human Rights, Art 11(1) ('Everyone charged with a penal offence has the right to be presumed innocent until proved guilty according to law in a public trial at which he has had all the guarantees necessary for his defence') and the ICCPR, Art 14(2) ('Everyone charged with a criminal offence shall have the right to be presumed innocent until proved guilty according to law').

[82] Committee on the Rights of the Child General Comment No 10 *Children's Rights in Juvenile Justice* CRC/C/GC/10, para 42.

[83] See also Art 14(3)(a) of the ICCPR ('In the determination of any criminal charge against him, everyone

CRC, Art 40(2)(b)(ii) – Prompt and Direct Information as to Charge

16.38 Direct Information as to Charge – The right of the child to be informed promptly and directly of the charges against him or her under CRC, Art 40(2)(b)(ii) is an unqualified right. The Committee on the Rights of the Child General Comment No 10 *Children's Rights in Juvenile Justice* provides that 'Prompt and direct means as soon as possible, and that is when the prosecutor or the judge initially takes procedural steps against the child'.[84] Providing a written document is not enough and an oral explanation may often be necessary.[85] Art 37(d) of the CRC provides that the child has the right to challenge the legality of any deprivation of liberty which right must imply a requirement that the child be informed promptly upon his or her arrest of the grounds for that arrest.[86] Note that when the authorities decide to deal with the matter without resort to judicial proceedings the child must nonetheless be informed of the charge(s) that may justify this approach.[87]

16.39 Information as to Charge provided through Parents or Legal Guardians – Article 40(2)(b)(ii) of the CRC includes the provision that the child may, if appropriate, be informed promptly of the charge through his or her parents or legal guardians. The provision of the information as to charge to parents or legal guardians should not be an alternative to communicating the information to the child.[88] In contrast to the unqualified right of the child to be informed promptly of the charge, the words 'if appropriate' qualify the right to the provision of that information through his or her parents or legal guardian. Hodgkin and Newell consider that the appropriateness or otherwise of informing a child of the charges against him or her through his or her parents pursuant to the provisions of Art 40(2)(b)(ii) of the CRC will be determined by reference to the child's best interests.[89] The evolving capacity of the child will also be relevant in determining the extent to which the child's parents should be involved in informing the child of the charges as will the views of the child. The Committee on the Rights of the Child encourages parental involvement, commenting that:[90]

> 'The Committee recommends that States parties explicitly provide by law for the maximum possible involvement of parents or legal guardians in the proceedings against the child. This involvement shall in general contribute to an effective response to the child's infringement of the penal law. To promote parental involvement, parents must be notified of the apprehension of their child as soon as possible.'

---

shall be entitled to the following minimum guarantees, in full equality: (a) To be informed promptly and in detail in a language which he understands of the nature and cause of the charge against him;').

[84] Committee on the Rights of the Child General Comment No 10 *Children's Rights in Juvenile Justice* CRC/C/GC/10, para 47.

[85] Committee on the Rights of the Child General Comment No 10 *Children's Rights in Juvenile Justice* CRC/C/GC/10, para 48.

[86] See Art 9(2) of the ICCPR ('Anyone who is arrested shall be informed, at the time of arrest, of the reasons for his arrest and shall be promptly informed of any charges against him').

[87] Committee on the Rights of the Child General Comment No 10 *Children's Rights in Juvenile Justice* CRC/C/GC/10, para 47.

[88] Committee on the Rights of the Child General Comment No 10 *Children's Rights in Juvenile Justice* CRC/C/GC/10, para 48.

[89] Newell, P and Hodgkin, R *Implementation Handbook for the Convention on the Rights of the Child* (2008) 3rd edn, UNICEF, p 614. See also Van Bueren, G *The International Law on the Rights of the Child* (1998) Martinus Nijhoff, p 177 and the 'Beijing Rules' r 15(2) ('The parents or the guardian shall be entitled to participate in the proceedings and may be required by the competent authority to attend them in the interest of the juvenile. They may, however, be denied participation by the competent authority if there are reasons to assume that such exclusion is necessary in the interest of the juvenile').

[90] Committee on the Rights of the Child General Comment No 10 *Children's Rights in Juvenile Justice* CRC/C/GC/10, para 54.

16.40 It should be noted that the UN Standard Minimum Rules on the Administration of Juvenile Justice place a somewhat higher duty on States Parties concerning the stage at which parents should be involved in the juvenile justice process. Whilst Art 40(2)(b)(ii) provides the option of the child being informed of the charge through his or her parents, r 10(1) of the UN Standard Minimum Rules on the Administration of Juvenile Justice obligates States parties as follows:

'Upon the apprehension of a juvenile, her or his parents or guardian shall be immediately notified of such apprehension, and, where such immediate notification is not possible, the parents or guardian[91] shall be notified within the shortest possible time thereafter.'

Having regard to the wording of Art 40(2)(b)(ii) of the CRC, there appears to be no corresponding duty under the Convention to inform a child's parents of his or her apprehension or interview, but only of his or her charge. Van Bueren records that this was not the intention of the States drafting the CRC but rather is a product of the use of the word 'charge' in the English language version of the Convention.[92] The Committee on the Rights of the Child has now made clear that there is a duty to notify the child's parents, and presumably his or her legal guardians, as soon as possible following the apprehension of the child.[93]

CRC, Art 40(2)(b)(ii) – Assistance in Preparation of Defence

16.41 As with the right to be informed promptly and directly of the charges against him or her, the child's right under Art 40(2)(b)(ii) to have legal or other appropriate assistance in the preparation and presentation of his or her defence is unqualified.[94] The assistance provided to the child should be free of charge. The assistance provided need not necessarily be legal assistance provided that the assistance made available is an appropriate.[95] Note however that given the specialist nature of the proceedings, both civil and criminal, involving children, the concept of 'appropriate assistance' is likely in most cases to encompass legal representation. The guarantee of legal assistance for children in the context of criminal proceedings is particularly important.[96] Rule 15(1) of the UN Standard Minimum Rules on the Administration of Juvenile Justice provides that 'Throughout the proceedings the juvenile shall have the right to be represented by a legal adviser or to apply for free legal aid where there is provision for such aid in the country'. The right to receive assistance with the preparation of his or her defence implies both the right to adequate time to prepare defence and the right to sufficient information through disclosure to enable this preparation to take place.[97] Communications between the child and the person providing him or her with assistance,

---

[91] Van Bueren suggests that the term 'guardians' is not limited to legal guardians but extends to those who have de facto responsibility for the child (Van Bueren, G *The International Law on the Rights of the Child* (1998) Martinus Nijhoff, p 177).

[92] Van Bueren, G *The International Law on the Rights of the Child* (1998) Martinus Nijhoff, p 177.

[93] Committee on the Rights of the Child General Comment No 10 *Children's Rights in Juvenile Justice* CRC/C/GC/10, para 54.

[94] See also Art 37(d) of the CRC ('Every child deprived of his or her liberty shall have the right to prompt access to legal and other appropriate assistance'). See further Art 14(3)(b) of the ICCPR ('In the determination of any criminal charge against him, everyone shall be entitled to the following minimum guarantees, in full equality: (b) To have adequate time and facilities for the preparation of his defence and to communicate with counsel of his own choosing').

[95] Committee on the Rights of the Child General Comment No 10 *Children's Rights in Juvenile Justice* CRC/C/GC/10, para 49.

[96] See Nigeria CRC/C/15/Add.257, para 81(b).

[97] Article 14(3)(b) of the ICCPR makes express provision in this regard by providing that 'In the determination of any criminal charge against him, everyone shall be entitled to the following minimum guarantees, in full equality: ... (b) To have adequate time and facilities for the preparation of his defence...'.

both in writing and orally, should take place under such conditions as ensure that the confidentiality of such communications is fully respected.[98]

CRC, Art 40(2)(b)(iii) – Prompt and Fair Hearing

16.42 CRC, Art 40(2)(b)(iii) sets out the cardinal elements of a fair hearing applied to children:

> 'To have the matter determined without delay by a competent, independent and impartial authority or judicial body in a fair hearing according to law, in the presence of legal or other appropriate assistance and, unless it is considered not to be in the best interest of the child, in particular, taking into account his or her age or situation, his or her parents or legal guardians.'[99]

CRC, Art 40(2)(b)(iii) – Determination without Delay

16.43 Whilst Art 14(3)(c) of the ICCPR provides a right to be tried without 'undue delay', Art 40(2)(b)(iii) provides in relation to children the right to have the matter determined without 'delay'. The removal of the word 'undue' from the terminology used in the CRC connotes an even greater need to avoid delay in relation to children in conflict with the law and in proceedings concerning children generally. The Committee on the Rights of the Child has made clear that the child's right to have the matter determined without delay is an essential element of the child's right to a fair hearing.[100]

16.44 In seeking to avoid delay it is important that the child's cardinal rights are not prejudiced in the effort to achieve a prompt determination. In this context, the period between the commencement of proceedings and their determination should only be as long as is necessary to ensure that the cardinal rights of the child, and of any other parties to the proceedings, are safeguarded.[101] In its General Comment No 10 *Children's Rights in Juvenile Justice* the Committee recognises that:[102]

> 'Internationally there is a consensus that for children in conflict with the law the time between the commission of the offence and the final response to this act should be as short as possible. The longer this period, the more likely it is that the response loses its desired positive, pedagogical impact, and the more the child will be stigmatised.'

CRC, Art 40(2)(b)(iii) – Presence of Legal or Other Appropriate Assistance

16.45 The words 'legal or other appropriate assistance' in Art 40(2)(b)(iii) indicate that the assistance provided need not necessarily be legal assistance provided that the

---

[98] Committee on the Rights of the Child General Comment No 10 *Children's Rights in Juvenile Justice* CRC/C/GC/10, para 50.

[99] See also the Universal Declaration of Human Rights Art 10 ('Everyone is entitled in full equality to a fair and public hearing by an independent and impartial tribunal, in the determination of his rights and obligations and of any criminal charge against him').

[100] See also Art 10(2)(b) of the ICCPR ('Accused juvenile persons shall be separated from adults and brought as speedily as possible for adjudication').

[101] See r 20 of the UN Standard Minimum Rules on the Administration of Juvenile Justice ('Each case shall from the outset be handled expeditiously, without any unnecessary delay').

[102] Committee on the Rights of the Child General Comment No 10 *Children's Rights in Juvenile Justice* CRC/C/GC/10, para 51. Note that the Committee on the Rights of the Child 'recommends that the States parties set and implement time limits for the period between the commission of the offence and the completion of the police investigation, the decision of the prosecutor (or other competent body) to bring charges against the child, and the final adjudication and decision by the court or other competent judicial body' (CRC/C/GC/10, para 52).

assistance made available is a 'appropriate'.[103] Note however that given the specialist nature of the proceedings, both civil and criminal, involving children, the 'appropriate assistance' is likely in most cases to encompass legal representation. The guarantee of legal assistance for children in the context of criminal proceedings is particularly important.[104] Art 14(3)(d) of the ICCPR guarantees to everybody 'legal assistance' in the determination of a criminal charge rather than the 'legal or other appropriate assistance' stipulated by Art 40(2)(b)(iii) of the CRC.[105]

16.46 Article 40(2)(b)(iii) of the CRC does not expressly articulate the right of the child to be present at the hearing. Whilst Art 14(3)(d) of the ICCPR requires the presence of the person charged,[106] on its face Art 40(2)(b)(iii) of the CRC appears only to mandate the presence of the child's representatives or parents rather than specifically the child him or herself. The Committee on the Rights of the Child has made clear that:[107]

> 'A fair trial requires that the child alleged as or accused of having infringed the penal law be able to effectively participate in the trial, and therefore needs to comprehend the charges, and possible consequences and penalties, in order to direct the legal representative, to challenge witnesses, to provide an account of events, and to make appropriate decisions about evidence, testimony and the measure(s) to be imposed.'

Within this context, and having regard to Arts 3, 5 and 12 of the CRC, it must be implicit in Art 40(2)(b)(iii) that the child has the right, subject to his or her best interests and capacity, to be present at any hearing which determines a criminal charge against the child and, having regard in particular to CRC, Art 12(2), where any right or obligation of the child is determined.[108]

CRC, Art 40(2)(b)(iii) – Presence of Parents or Legal Guardians

16.47 The child has the right to have the matter in question determined in the presence of his or her parents or legal guardians 'unless it is considered not to be in the best interest of the child, in particular, taking into account his or her age or situation.'. Hodgkin and Newell consider that the terms of Art 40(2)(b)(iii) imply that the child's parents or legal guardian can be required to be present during the hearing.[109] The words

---

[103] Committee on the Rights of the Child General Comment No 10 *Children's Rights in Juvenile Justice* CRC/C/GC/10, para 49.

[104] See Nigeria CRC/C/15/Add.257, para 81(b).

[105] See Art 14(3)(d) of the ICCPR ('In the determination of any criminal charge against him, everyone shall be entitled to the following minimum guarantees, in full equality: (d) To be tried in his presence, and to defend himself in person or through legal assistance of his own choosing; to be informed, if he does not have legal assistance, of this right; and to have legal assistance assigned to him, in any case where the interests of justice so require, and without payment by him in any such case if he does not have sufficient means to pay for it').

[106] See Art 14(3)(d) of the ICCPR ('In the determination of any criminal charge against him, everyone shall be entitled to the following minimum guarantees, in full equality: (d) To be tried in his presence, and to defend himself in person or through legal assistance of his own choosing ...').

[107] Committee on the Rights of the Child General Comment No 10 *Children's Rights in Juvenile Justice* CRC/C/GC/10, para 46.

[108] See also Art 13 of the UN Convention on the Rights of Persons with Disabilities ('1. States Parties shall ensure effective access to justice for persons with disabilities on an equal basis with others, including through the provision of procedural and age-appropriate accommodations, in order to facilitate their effective role as direct and indirect participants, including as witnesses, in all legal proceedings, including at investigative and other preliminary stages. 2. In order to help to ensure effective access to justice for persons with disabilities, States Parties shall promote appropriate training for those working in the field of administration of justice, including police and prison staff').

[109] Newell, P and Hodgkin, R *Implementation Handbook for the Convention on the Rights of the Child* (2008) 3rd edn, UNICEF, p 614.

'unless it is considered not to be in the best interests of the child' clearly indicate that it is acceptable to exclude the attendance of parents or legal guardians in certain cases.[110] The UN Standard Minimum Rules on the Administration of Juvenile Justice r 15(2) provide that:

> 'The parents or the guardian shall be entitled to participate in the proceedings and may be required by the competent authority to attend them in the interest of the juvenile. They may, however, be denied participation by the competent authority if there are reasons to assume that such exclusion is necessary in the interest of the juvenile.'[111]

CRC, Art 40(2)(b)(iii) – Competent, Independent and Impartial Authority or Judicial Body

16.48　The word 'authority' will encompass all bodies of a judicatory nature which have responsibility for juvenile justice.[112] For a further exploration of the meaning of the phrase 'independent and impartial authority or judicial body' reference should be made to the discussion of the jurisprudence of the European Court of Human Rights below.[113]

CRC, Art 40(2)(b)(iii) – Fair Hearing

16.49　Ensuring a fair hearing requires the diligent application of each of the cardinal aspects of due process contained in Art 40 of the CRC, applied within the context of the overarching aim set out in Art 40(1). Fairness will include taking into account all the circumstances of the case prior to final determination, including those aspects which mitigate the final disposition.[114]

CRC, Art 40(2)(b)(iv) – Protection Against Self Incrimination and Right to Call and Challenge Evidence

16.50　CRC, Art 40(2)(b)(iv) stipulates the essence of the child's right to silence as well as the child's right to challenge the evidence called against him or her and the child's right to call evidence in support of his or her case, stating that the child has the right:

> 'Not to be compelled to give testimony or to confess guilt; to examine or have examined adverse witnesses and to obtain the participation and examination of witnesses on his or her behalf under conditions of equality.'[115]

---

[110]　Note again however that 'The Committee recommends that States parties explicitly provide by law for the maximum possible involvement of parents or legal guardians in the proceedings against the child. This involvement shall in general contribute to an effective response to the child's infringement of the penal law' (Committee on the Rights of the Child General Comment No 10 *Children's Rights in Juvenile Justice* CRC/C/GC/10, para 54).

[111]　Rule 15(2) appears to apply a lower test than that of 'best interests' in determining whether or not the attendance of parents or guardians should be excluded. Where the issue arises, the 'best interests' test set out in Art 40(2)(b)(iii) is likely to be the appropriate test having regard to Art 3 of the CRC.

[112]　Van Bueren, G *The International Law on the Rights of the Child* (1998) Martinus Nijhoff, p 177

[113]　See **16.108–16.111**.

[114]　See UN Standard Minimum Rules for the Administration of Juvenile Justice, r 16 ('In all cases except those involving minor offences, before the competent authority renders a final disposition prior to sentencing, the background and circumstances in which the juvenile is living or the conditions under which the offence has been committed shall be properly investigated so as to facilitate judicious adjudication of the case by the competent authority').

[115]　See also Art 14(3)(g) of the ICCPR ('In the determination of any criminal charge against him, everyone shall be entitled to the following minimum guarantees, in full equality: (g) Not to be compelled to testify against himself or to confess guilt').

CRC, Art 40(2)(b)(iv) – No compulsion to Give Evidence or Confess Guilt

16.51 Self evidently the child's right not to be compelled to give testimony or confess guilt, in essence the child's right to silence, means that that torture, cruel, inhuman or degrading treatment in order to extract an admission or a confession constitutes a grave violation of the rights of the child and is wholly unacceptable. No such admission or confession can be admissible as evidence.[116] Note however that the term 'compelled' in Art 40(2)(b)(iv) should be interpreted in a broad manner and is not limited to physical force or other clear violations of human rights.[117] Art 40(2)(b)(iv) does not enshrine the child's right to silence in plain terms and nor does it articulate well the additional facets of the right to silence which operate upon apprehension and arrest, during the investigation and upon being charged. The UN Standard Minimum Rules on the Administration of Juvenile Justice however make clear that the child's right to silence applies at all stages of the proceedings.[118] In particular, the Committee on the Rights of the Child has commented that:[119]

> 'The court or other judicial body, when considering the voluntary nature and reliability of an admission or confession by a child, must take into account the age of the child, the length of custody and interrogation, and the presence of legal or other counsel, parent(s), or independent representatives of the child.'

CRC, Art 40(2)(b)(iv) – Examination of Witnesses under Conditions of Equality

16.52 This provision enshrines the right of the child to 'equality of arms' within the context of the administration of juvenile justice.[120] Pursuant to Art 40(2)(b)(iv) it is important that the lawyer or other representative informs the child of the possibility of examining witnesses and allows him or her to express his or her views in that regard. The views of the child in this regard should be given due weight in accordance with the age and maturity of the child.[121]

CRC, Art 40(2)(b)(v) – Right of Appeal

16.53 CRC, Art 40(2)(b)(v) enshrines the child's right of appeal in respect of any determination of the matter and any measures imposed in consequence of that

---

[116] See Committee on the Rights of the Child General Comment No 10 *Child's Rights in Juvenile Justice* CRC/C/ GC/10 p 16, para 56 and see the UN Convention against Torture and Other Cruel, Inhuman and Degrading Treatment or Punishment, Art 15.

[117] Committee on the Rights of the Child General Comment No 10 *Children's Rights in Juvenile Justice* CRC/C/GC/10, para 50.

[118] See UN Standard Minimum Rules on the Administration of Juvenile Justice, r 7 ('Basic procedural safeguards such as the presumption of innocence, the right to be notified of the charges, the right to remain silent, the right to counsel, the right to the presence of a parent or guardian, the right to confront and cross-examine witnesses and the right to appeal to a higher authority shall be guaranteed at all stages of proceedings').

[119] Committee on the Rights of the Child General Comment No 10 *Children's Rights in Juvenile Justice* CRC/C/GC/10, para 50.

[120] Committee on the Rights of the Child General Comment No 10 *Children's Rights in Juvenile Justice* CRC/C/GC/10, para 59. See also Art 14(3)(e) of the ICCPR ('In the determination of any criminal charge against him, everyone shall be entitled to the following minimum guarantees, in full equality: To examine, or have examined, the witnesses against him and to obtain the attendance and examination of witnesses on his behalf under the same conditions as witnesses against him').

[121] Committee on the Rights of the Child General Comment No 10 *Children's Rights in Juvenile Justice* CRC/C/GC/10, para 59.

determination. This right of the appeal is not limited to serious offences and should be available to every child.[122] CRC, Art 40(2)(b)(v) stipulates the right:

> 'If considered to have infringed the penal law, to have this decision and any measures imposed in consequence thereof reviewed by a higher competent, independent and impartial authority or judicial body according to law'.[123]

CRC, Art 40(2)(b)(vi) – Assistance of an Interpreter

16.54 CRC, Art 40(2)(b)(vi) provides as follows in respect of the child's right to an interpreter:[124]

> '(b)   Every child alleged as or accused of having infringed the penal law has at least the following guarantees ... (vi) To have the free assistance of an interpreter if the child cannot understand or speak the language used.'

16.55 As with the child's other cardinal procedural rights, the assistance of an interpreter should not be limited to the final determination of the matter but should be available at all stages of the proceedings.[125] The right to the services of an interpreter at all stages of the proceedings will extend to children who have difficulty communicating by reason of a disability.[126] Note that use of the term 'if' in the phrase 'if the child cannot understand or speak the language used' means that a child of foreign or ethnic origin who understands and speaks the official language of the State in question does not have to be provided with the free assistance of an interpreter.[127]

CRC, Art 40(2)(b)(vii) – Full Respect for Privacy

16.56 CRC, Art 40(2)(b)(vii) provides as follows in respect of the child's right to privacy in the context of the juvenile justice system:[128]

> '(b)   Every child alleged as or accused of having infringed the penal law has at least the following guarantees ... (vii) To have his or her privacy fully respected at all stages of the proceedings.'

Criminal Proceedings

16.57 Article 40(2)(b)(vii) of the CRC requires that a child accused of having infringed the penal law should 'have his or her privacy full respected at all stages of the

---

[122]   Committee on the Rights of the Child General Comment No 10 *Children's Rights in Juvenile Justice* CRC/C/GC/10, para 60.

[123]   See also Art 14(5) of the ICCPR ('Everyone convicted of a crime shall have the right to his conviction and sentence being reviewed by a higher tribunal according to law').

[124]   See also Art 14(3)(f) of the ICCPR ('In the determination of any criminal charge against him, everyone shall be entitled to the following minimum guarantees, in full equality: (f) To have the free assistance of an interpreter if he cannot understand or speak the language used in court').

[125]   Committee on the Rights of the Child General Comment No 10 *Children's Rights in Juvenile Justice* CRC/C/GC/10, para 62.

[126]   See Committee on the Rights of the Child General Comment No 9 *The Rights of Children with Disabilities* CRC/C/GC/9 p 9, para 32 ('Children should be provided with whatever form of communication they need to facilitate expressing their views'). See also the Committee on the Rights of the Child General Comment No 11 *Indigenous Children and their Rights under the Convention* CRC/C/GC/11, para 76 ('In the case of indigenous children, States parties should adopt measures to ensure that an interpreter is provided free of charge if required and that the child is guaranteed legal assistance, in a culturally sensitive manner').

[127]   Committee on the Rights of the Child General Comment No 10 *Children's Rights in Juvenile Justice* CRC/C/GC/10, para 62.

[128]   See also **9.11–9.13** above.

proceedings'. 'All stage of the proceedings' means from the point of initial contact with law enforcement agencies to the point of final determination by a competent authority.[129] This will include ensuring that communications between a child and his or her legal advisers take place in conditions of confidentiality.[130] The Committee on the Rights of the Child has made clear that the provisions of Art 16 of the CRC in respect of the child's right to privacy will also be applicable to juvenile justice. These provisions will not however extend to children who are indirectly involved in proceedings, for example as witnesses.[131] In its General Comment No 10 *Children's Rights in Juvenile Justice*:[132]

'The right of a child to have his/her privacy fully respected during all stages of the proceedings reflects the right to protection of privacy enshrined in article 16 of CRC. "All stages of the proceedings" includes from the initial contact with law enforcement (eg a request for information and identification) up until the final decision by a competent authority, or release from supervision, custody or deprivation of liberty. In this particular context, it is meant to avoid harm caused by undue publicity or by the process of labeling. No information shall be published that may lead to the identification of a child offender because of its effect of stigmatisation, and possible impact on his/her ability to have access to education, work, housing or to be safe. It means that a public authority should be very reluctant with press releases related to offences allegedly committed by children and limit them to very exceptional cases. They must take measures to guarantee that children are not identifiable via these press releases. Journalists who violate the right to privacy of a child in conflict with the law should be sanctioned with disciplinary and when necessary (eg in case of recidivism) with penal law sanctions.'

16.58 In addition to the provisions of Art 40(2)(b)(vii) and Art 16 of the CRC, Rule 8.1 of the UN Standard Minimum Rules for the Administration of Juvenile Justice (the 'Beijing Rules') requires that:

'The juveniles right to privacy shall be respected at all stages in order to avoid harm being caused to her or him by undue publicity or by the process of labeling ... In principle, no information that may lead to the identification of a juvenile offender shall be published.'[133]

16.59 Any exceptions to the principle that hearings in relation to children who are in conflict with law should be conducted in private should be very limited and clearly stated in the law.[134] Art 14(1) of the Covenant on Civil and Political Rights stipulates that:[135]

---

[129] Committee on the Rights of the Child General Comment No 10 *Children's Rights in Juvenile Justice* CRC/C/GC/10, para 64.

[130] Committee on the Rights of the Child General Comment No 10 *Children's Rights in Juvenile Justice* CRC/C/GC/10, para 50.

[131] See *Re S (A Child) (Identification: Restriction on Publication)* [2004] UKHL, [2004] 4 All ER 683, para 26.

[132] Committee on the Rights of the Child General Comment No 10 *Children's Rights in Juvenile Justice* CRC/C/GC/10, para 64.

[133] This will include records in respect of juvenile offenders ('Beijing Rules', r 21.1). Note that the Commentary to r 8 of the 'Beijing Rules' states that 'Rule 8 stresses the importance of the protection of the juvenile's right to privacy. Young persons are particularly susceptible to stigmatisation. Criminological research into labeling processes has provided evidence of the detrimental effects (of different kinds) resulting from the permanent identification of young persons as 'delinquent' or 'criminal'. Rule 8 stresses the importance of protecting the juvenile from the adverse effects that may result from the publication in the mass media of information about the case (for example the names of young offenders, alleged or convicted). The interest of the individual should be protected and upheld, at least in principle.'

[134] General Comment No 10 *Children's Rights in Juvenile Justice* CRC/C/GC/10, para 66.

[135] See the Committee on the Rights of the Child General Comment No 10 *Children's Rights in Juvenile Justice* CRC/C/GC/10, para 65.

'All persons shall be equal before the courts and tribunals. In the determination of any criminal charge against him, or of his rights and obligations in a suit at law, everyone shall be entitled to a fair and public hearing by a competent, independent and impartial tribunal established by law. The press and the public may be excluded from all or part of a trial for reasons of morals, public order (ordre public) or national security in a democratic society, or when the interest of the private lives of the parties so requires, or to the extent strictly necessary in the opinion of the court in special circumstances where publicity would prejudice the interests of justice; but any judgment rendered in a criminal case or in a suit at law shall be made public except where the interest of juvenile persons otherwise requires or the proceedings concern matrimonial disputes or the guardianship of children.'

The verdict and, if convicted, the sentence in respect of the child should be pronounced in public at a court session in such a way that the identity of the child is not revealed.[136]

Family Proceedings

16.60 Whilst there is no specific provision contained in the various international human rights instruments requiring family proceeding to be held in private, it is clearly established that those instruments support this proposition. Article 16 of the CRC, when read with Art 3 suggests that judicial proceedings under Art 9 of the CRC concerning the separation of children from their parents should be held in private.[137] The Committee on the Rights of the Child has stated that the principle articulated by Art 40(2)(b)(vii) that the child has a right in criminal proceedings to 'have his or her privacy full respected at all stages of the proceedings' should also apply to family proceedings and where children are the victims of violence, which latter category must include family proceedings concerning the alleged abuse of the child.[138] Art 14(1) of the Covenant on Civil and Political Rights contains a specific exception in respect of the publication of any judgment in proceedings concerning 'matrimonial disputes or the guardianship of children'. Finally, r 3(2) of the UN Standard Minimum Rules for the Administration of Juvenile Justice extends the scope of those Standard Minimum Rules to encompass care and welfare proceedings in respect of children, providing that '[e]fforts shall be made to extend the principles embodied in the Rules to all juveniles who are dealt with in welfare and care proceedings'. The UN Standard Minimum Rules for the Administration of Juvenile Justice themselves call for hearings to be conducted 'in an atmosphere of understanding'[139] and stress the need for privacy.[140]

---

[136] Committee on the Rights of the Child General Comment No 10 *Children's Rights in Juvenile Justice* CRC/C/GC/10, para 66.

[137] Newell, P and Hodgkin, R *Implementation Handbook for the Convention on the Rights of the Child* (2008) 3rd edn, UNICEF, p 128.

[138] Committee on the Rights of the Child *Report of the Eleventh Session* (1996) CRC/C/50/ Annex IX, p 80 and Newell, P and Hodgkin, R *Implementation Handbook for the Convention on the Rights of the Child* (2008) 3rd edn, UNICEF, p 203.

[139] UN Standard Minimum Rules for the Administration of Juvenile Justice r 14.2 ('The proceedings shall be conducive to the best interests of the juvenile and shall be conducted in an atmosphere of understanding, which shall allow the juvenile to participate therein and to express herself or himself freely').

[140] UN Standard Minimum Rules for the Administration of Juvenile Justice r 8 ('8(1) The juvenile's right to privacy shall be respected at all stages in order to avoid harm being caused to her or him by undue publicity or by the process of labeling. 8(2) In principle, no information that may lead to the identification of a juvenile offender shall be published').

CRC, Art 40(3) – Ambit

16.61 Article 40(3) of the CRC provides as follows in respect of the establishment of a minimum age of criminal responsibility and the desirability of dealing with a child alleged as, accused of or recognised as having infringed the penal law without resorting to judicial proceedings:

> 'States Parties shall seek to promote the establishment of laws, procedures, authorities and institutions specifically applicable to children alleged as, accused of, or recognised as having infringed the penal law, and, in particular:
>
> (a) The establishment of a minimum age below which children shall be presumed not to have the capacity to infringe the penal law;
>
> (b) Whenever appropriate and desirable, measures for dealing with such children without resorting to judicial proceedings, providing that human rights and legal safeguards are fully respected.'

The preliminary terms of Art 40(3) emphasise that States parties are under a duty to establish specific procedures and institutions applicable to children and attuned to their particular needs rather than simply adapting adult procedures to a best fit.[141] Within this context the Guidelines for Action on Children in the Criminal Justice System[142] suggest that 'States should establish juvenile courts with primary jurisdiction over juveniles who commit criminal acts and special procedures should be designed to take into account the specific needs of children'.

(i) Article 40(3)(a) – Minimum Age

16.62 As Van Bueren notes, the establishment of a minimum age is one of the foundation stones of a child rights based criminal justice system.[143] Art 40(3)(a) of the CRC provides that States Parties to the CRC shall in particular seek the 'establishment of a minimum age below which children shall be presumed not to have the capacity to infringe the penal law'. The Committee on the Rights of the Child defines the meaning of 'minimum age of criminal responsibility' as follows:

> 'Children who commit an offence at an age below that minimum cannot be held responsible in a penal law procedure. Even (very) young children do have the capacity to infringe the penal law but if they commit an offence when below MACR the irrefutable assumption is that they cannot be formally charged and held responsible in a penal law procedure. For these children special protective measures can be taken if necessary in their best interests; Children at or above the MACR at the time of the commission of an offence (or: infringement of the penal law) but younger than 18 years (see also paragraphs 35–38 below) can be formally charged and subject to penal law procedures. But these procedures, including the final outcome, must be in full compliance with the principles and provisions of CRC as elaborated in the present general comment.'

16.63 The appropriate age under Art 40(3)(a) should be set by reference to the UN Standard Minimum Rules for the Administration of Juvenile Justice r 4 which provides that 'the beginning of that age shall not be fixed at too low an age level, bearing in mind

---

[141] Van Bueren, G *The International Law on the Rights of the Child* (1998) Martinus Nijhoff, p 175.
[142] ESC Resolution 1997/30, para 14(d). Note that the Guidelines do allow for the adaption of 'regular' court procedures where necessary provided those adaption's are implemented in accordance with the principles set out in Arts 3, 37 and 40 of the CRC.
[143] Van Bueren, G *Child Rights in Europe* (2007) Council of Europe Publishing, p 168.

the facts of emotional, mental and intellectual maturity'.[144] The Committee on the Rights of the Child has made clear that 10 years is too low as a minimum age of criminal responsibility.[145] The Committee recommends that State parties should regard 12 as the absolute minimum age of criminal responsibility[146] and stipulates an ideal of between 14 and 16 years.[147] The Committee has however welcomed proposals to set the age at 18 years.[148] The Committee has further observed that:

> 'Alleging that the child is criminally responsible implies that he/she should be competent and able to effectively participate in the decisions regarding the most appropriate response to allegations of his/her infringement of the penal law.'[149]

16.64 Where there is no proof of age and it cannot be established that the child is at or above the minimum age of criminal responsibility the child shall not be held criminally responsible.[150] Exceptions to the minimum age of criminal responsibility in respect of serious offences should not be permitted.[151] Children should not be tried as adults.[152]

(ii) Article 40(3)(b) – Alternative Methods of Disposal

16.65 Article 40(3)(b) of the CRC provides that whenever appropriate and desirable, measures for dealing with children without resorting to judicial proceedings should be adopted, providing that human rights and legal safeguards are fully respected. These principles are dealt with above at **16.22–16.25.**

CRC, Art 40(4) – Ambit

16.66 Article 40(4) of the CRC makes provision for alternative dispositions in respect of children who have been found to have infringed the penal law, stating that:

---

[144] The commentary to r 4 of the UN Standard Minimum Rules for the Administration of Justice notes that 'The minimum age of criminal responsibility differs widely owing to history and culture. The modern approach would be to consider whether a child can live up to the moral and psychological components of criminal responsibility; that is, whether a child, by virtue of her or his individual discernment and understanding, can be held responsible for essentially antisocial behaviour. If the age of criminal responsibility is fixed too low or if there is no lower age limit at all, the notion of responsibility would become meaningless. In general, there is a close relationship between the notion of responsibility for delinquent or criminal behaviour and other social rights and responsibilities (such as marital status, civil majority, etc.). Efforts should therefore be made to agree on a reasonable lowest age limit that is applicable internationally.' See also Committee on the Rights of the Children General Comment No 10 *Children's Rights in Juvenile Justice* CRC/C/GC/10, paras 30–39.

[145] See United Kingdom CRC/C/15/Add.188, paras 59 and 62(a). See also Committee on the Rights of the Child, General Comment No 7 HRI/GEN/1/Rev 8, p 449, para 36(i)) ('Under no circumstances should young children (defined as under 8 years old; see paragraph 4) be included in legal definitions of minimum age of criminal responsibility. Young children who misbehave or violate laws require sympathetic help and understanding, with the goal of increasing their capacities for personal control, social empathy and conflict resolution').

[146] Committee on the Rights of the Child, General Comment No 10 *Children's Rights in Juvenile Justice* CRC/C/GC/10, para 32.

[147] Committee on the Rights of the Child General Comment No 10 *Children's Rights in Juvenile Justice* CRC/C/GC/10, para 33.

[148] See Nigeria CRC/C/15/Add.61, para 39.

[149] Committee on the Rights of the Child, General Comment No 10 *Children's Rights in Juvenile Justice* CRC/C/GC/10 p 14, para 45.

[150] Committee on the Rights of the Child, General Comment No 10 *Children's Rights in Juvenile Justice* CRC/C/GC/10, para 35.

[151] Committee on the Rights of the Child, General Comment No 10 *Children's Rights in Juvenile Justice* CRC/C/GC/10, para 34.

[152] United Kingdom CRC/C/15/Add.188, para 62(c).

'4. A variety of dispositions, such as care, guidance and supervision orders; counseling; probation; foster care; education and vocational training programmes and other alternatives to institutional care shall be available to ensure that children are dealt with in a manner appropriate to their well-being and proportionate both to their circumstances and the offence.'[153]

16.67 The UN Standard Minimum Rules for the Administration of Juvenile Justice r 17 sets out the detailed standards to be applied in relation to dispositions in respect of children who have been found to have infringed the penal law:

'17(1) The disposition of the competent authority shall be guided by the following principles:

(a) The reaction taken shall always be in proportion not only to the circumstances and the gravity of the offence but also to the circumstances and the needs of the juvenile as well as to the needs of the society;

(b) Restrictions on the personal liberty of the juvenile shall be imposed only after careful consideration and shall be limited to the possible minimum;

(c) Deprivation of personal liberty shall not be imposed unless the juvenile is adjudicated of a serious act involving violence against another person or of persistence in committing other serious offences and unless there is no other appropriate response;

(d) The well-being of the juvenile shall be the guiding factor in the consideration of her or his case.

17(2) Capital punishment shall not be imposed for any crime committed by juveniles.[154]

17(3) Juveniles shall not be subject to corporal punishment.

17(4) The competent authority shall have the power to discontinue the proceedings at any time.'[155]

16.68 Article 40(4) is dealt with in detail in chapter 14. The Committee on the Rights of the Child General Comment No 10 *Children's Rights in Juvenile Justice* makes clear that:

'The Committee wishes to emphasise that the reaction to an offence should always be in proportion not only to the circumstances and the gravity of the offence, but also to the age, lesser culpability, circumstances and needs of the child, as well as to the various and particularly long-term needs of the society. A strictly punitive approach is not in accordance with the leading principles for juvenile justice spelled out in article 40(1) of CRC.'[156]

---

[153] See also Art 37(a) of the CRC ('Neither capital punishment nor life imprisonment without possibility of release shall be imposed for offences committed by persons below eighteen years of age').

[154] See Art 37(a).

[155] Note that the Commentary to r 17 of the UN Standard Minimum Rules on the Administration of Juvenile Justice states that 'It is not the function of the Standard Minimum Rules for the Administration of Juvenile Justice to prescribe which approach is to be followed but rather to identify one that is most closely in consonance with internationally accepted principles. Therefore the essential elements as laid down in rule 17.1, in particular in subparagraphs (a) and (c), are mainly to be understood as practical guidelines that should ensure a common starting point; if heeded by the concerned authorities (see also rule 5), they could contribute considerably to ensuring that the fundamental rights of juvenile offenders are protected, especially the fundamental rights of personal development and education.'

[156] Committee on the Rights of the Child, General Comment No 10 *Children's Rights in Juvenile Justice* CRC/C/GC/10, para 71.

The Child's Right to Fair and Equal Treatment under the Law under other International Instruments

The Geneva Conventions

16.69 Articles 71–75 of the of the Geneva Convention relative to the Protection of Civilian Persons in Time of War (Geneva Convention IV) provide detailed provisions to ensure a fair trial is guaranteed by Occupying Powers. Those provisions enshrine the right of the accused to be informed promptly in writing in a language they can understand of the charges against them, the right to be brought to trial as rapidly as possible, the right to have the Protecting Power notified of all proceedings in respect of charges involving the death penalty or imprisonment of 2 years or more,[157] the right to present evidence necessary to their defence and to call witnesses, the right to be assisted by a qualified advocate or counsel of their choice who must be able to visit them freely and enjoy facilities necessary for the preparation of the defence, the right to be aided by an interpreter,[158] the right of appeal,[159] the right to have the Protecting Power attend the trial[160] and in the case of persons condemned to death the right of petition for pardon or reprieve.[161]

16.70 Article 5 of the Geneva Convention IV provides that the right to a fair trial prescribed by the Convention shall not be denied to protected persons suspected of or engaged in activities hostile to the State in the territory of a Party to the conflict or protected persons detained in occupied territory as spies or saboteurs or under definite suspicion of activity hostile to the security of an Occupying Power. Wilfully depriving a protected person of the right to a fair and regular trial will be considered a grave breach of the Convention.[162] Any person who has taken part in hostilities, who is not entitled to prisoner-of-war status and who does not benefit from more favourable treatment in accordance with the Geneva Convention IV nonetheless has the right at all times to a fair trial.[163]

16.71 Children should not be prosecuted for war crimes.[164] The Paris Principles make clear that children who are accused of crimes under international law allegedly committed while they were associated with armed forces or armed groups should be considered primarily as victims of offences against international law.[165] To this end the International Criminal Court has specifically excluded children under the age of 18 from its jurisdiction.[166]

---

[157] Geneva Convention IV, Art 71. See also Art 75(4)(a) of the Protocol Additional to the Geneva Conventions of 12 August 1949, and relating to the Protection of Victims of International Armed Conflicts (Protocol I) and Art 6 of the Protocol Additional to the Geneva Conventions of 12 August 1949, and Relating to the Protection of Victims of Non-International Armed Conflicts (Protocol II).

[158] Geneva Convention IV, Art 72.

[159] Geneva Convention IV, Art 73.

[160] Geneva Convention IV, Art 74.

[161] Geneva Convention IV, Art 75.

[162] Geneva Convention IV, Art 147. See also Art 85(4)(e) of the Protocol Additional to the Geneva Conventions of 12 August 1949, and relating to the Protection of Victims of International Armed Conflicts (Protocol I).

[163] Article 45(3) of the Protocol Additional to the Geneva Conventions of 12 August 1949, and relating to the Protection of Victims of International Armed Conflicts (Protocol I).

[164] Newell, P and Hodgkin, R *Implementation Handbook for the Convention on the Rights of the Child* (2008) 3rd edn, UNICEF, p 584 and see Rawanda CRC/C/15/Add.234, paras 70 and 71.

[165] *Paris Principles: Principles and Guidelines on Children Associated with Armed Forces or Armed Groups* (2007) UNICEF, para 3.6.

[166] Rome Statute of the International Criminal Court, Art 26 ('The Court shall have no jurisdiction over any person who was under the age of 18 at the time of the alleged commission of a crime').

The Child's Right to Fair and Equal Treatment under the Law – ECHR

ECHR, Art 6

16.72 Article 6 of the ECHR enshrines the right to fair and equal treatment before the law in the following terms:

'1. In the determination of his civil rights and obligations or of any criminal charge against him, everyone is entitled to a fair and public hearing within a reasonable time by an independent and impartial tribunal established by law. Judgment shall be pronounced publicly but the press and public may be excluded from all or part of the trial in the interests of morals, public order or national security in a democratic society, where the interests of juveniles or the protection of the private life of the parties so require, or to the extent strictly necessary in the opinion of the court in special circumstances where publicity would prejudice the interests of justice.

2. Everyone charged with a criminal offence shall be presumed innocent until proved guilty according to law.

3. Everyone charged with a criminal offence has the following minimum rights:

a)   to be informed promptly, in a language which he understands and in detail, of the nature and cause of the accusation against him;

b)   to have adequate time and facilities for the preparation of his defence;

c)   to defend himself in person or through legal assistance of his own choosing or, if he has not sufficient means to pay for legal assistance, to be given it free when the interests of justice so require;

d)   to examine or have examined witnesses against him and to obtain the attendance and examination of witnesses on his behalf under the same conditions as witnesses against him;

e)   to have the free assistance of an interpreter if he cannot understand or speak the language used in court.'

ECHR, Art 6 – Ambit

(i)   Object and Purpose

16.73 The object and purpose of Art 6 of the ECHR has been stated to be to 'enshrine the fundamental principle of the rule of law' by protecting the right to a fair trial and in particular the right to be presumed innocent.[167] By reason of their central importance within a democratic society, the rights enshrined in Art 6 of the ECHR as a whole must be given a broad and purposive interpretation.[168]

---

[167]   *Salabiaku v France* (1988) 13 EHRR 379, para 28. See also *Golder v United Kingdom* (1975) 1 EHRR 524, para 35 ('The principle whereby a civil claim must be capable of being submitted to a judge ranks as one of the universally 'recognised' fundamental principles of law; the same is true of the principle of international law which forbids the denial of justice. Article 6, para 1 must be read in the light of these principles').

[168]   *Delcourt v Belgium* (1970) 1 EHRR 355, para 25.

16.74 Article 6 of the ECHR applies to both criminal and civil proceedings, although State parties have a wider margin of appreciation in respect of the latter.[169] In *Albert and Le Compte v Belgium*[170] the European Court of Human Rights made clear that:

> 'For its part, the Court does not believe that the two aspects, civil and criminal, of Article 6 para 1 are necessarily mutually exclusive. Nonetheless, the Court does not consider it necessary to decide whether, in the specific circumstances, there was a "criminal charge". In point of fact, paragraph 1 of Article 6, violation of which was alleged by the two applicants, applies in civil matters as well as in the criminal sphere. Dr. Albert relied in addition on paragraph 2 and on sub-paragraphs (a), (b) and (d) of paragraph 3, but, in the opinion of the Court, the principles enshrined therein are, for the present purposes, already contained in the notion of a fair trial as embodied in paragraph 1; the Court will therefore take these principles into account in the context of paragraph 1.'

Article 6 will also govern administrative decisions where they are directly decisive of an individuals civil rights and obligations.[171]

(ii)   ECHR, Art 6 and Children

Criminal Proceedings

16.75 Van Bueren points out that Art 6, whilst applying to children, does not enshrine child-specific entitlements.[172] In *Nortier v Netherlands*[173] the question of whether Art 6 should be applied to juvenile criminal procedures in the same manner in which it was applied to adult criminal procedures was raised but not addressed save in the concurring judgments of Judge Walsh[174] and Judge Morenilla.[175] Van Bueren considers that a differential approach in the application of Art 6 of the ECHR as between adults and children is open to the court by interpreting Art 6 of the ECHR, as it must, in accordance with Art 40 of the CRC.[176] Such an approach must be one which affords to the child each of the fundamental rights enshrined in Art 6 applied in a manner which best takes account of the child's need for special care and assistance. In circumstances where children may be dealt with in more informal proceedings, the protected elements enshrined in Art 6 of the ECHR constituting a fair trial are essential.[177] In addition to

---

[169]   *Dombo Beheer v Netherlands* (1993) 18 EHRR 213, para 32 ('The requirements inherent in the concept of 'fair hearing' are not necessarily the same in cases concerning the determination of civil rights and obligations as they are in cases concerning the determination of a criminal charge. This is borne out by the absence of detailed provisions such as paragraphs 2 and 3 of Article 6 applying to cases of the former category. Thus, although these provisions have a certain relevance outside the strict confines of criminal law, the Contracting States have greater latitude when dealing with civil cases concerning civil rights and obligations than they have when dealing with criminal cases').

[170]   (1983) 5 EHRR, para 30.

[171]   *Albert and Le Compte v Belgium* (1983) 5 EHRR. See also *Mantovanelli v France* (1997) 24 EHRR 370 and *Re L (Care: Assessment Fair Trial)* [2002] EWHC 1379 (Fam), [2002] 2 FLR 730.

[172]   Van Bueren, G *Child Rights in Europe* (2007) Council of Europe Publishing, p 105.

[173]   (1993) 17 EHRR 273.

[174]   Judge Walsh stated that 'Juveniles facing criminal charges and trial are as fully entitled as adults to benefit from all the Convention requirements for a fair trial. Great care must always be taken to ensure that this entitlement is not diluted by considerations of rehabilitation or of reform. These are considerations which should be in addition to all the procedural protections available. Fair trial and proper proof of guilt are absolute conditions precedent.'

[175]   Judge Morenilla stated 'I think that minors are entitled to the same protection of their fundamental rights as adults but that the developing state of their personality – and consequently their limited social responsibility – should be taken into account in applying Article 6 (art. 6) of the Convention. In particular, the right of everyone charged with a criminal offence to be judged by an impartial tribunal should not be incompatible with the protective treatment of juvenile offenders.'

[176]   Van Bueren, G *Child Rights in Europe* (2007) Council of Europe Publishing, p 111.

[177]   Van Bueren, G *Child Rights in Europe* (2007) Council of Europe Publishing, p 112.

the requirement to interpret Art 6 of the ECHR in accordance with the CRC, the international rules governing the administration of juvenile justice, and specifically the UN Standard Minimum Rules for the Administration of Juvenile Justice (the 'Beijing Rules'), whilst not determinative, can act as subsidiary guidance on the parameters of a particular right in the application of Art 6 of the ECHR to children.[178]

Civil Proceedings

16.76 As noted above, the principles enshrined in Art 6(2) and 6(3) of the ECHR are also contained in the notion of a fair trial as embodied in Art 6(1), which is applicable to both criminal and civil proceedings. In civil proceedings concerning children, Art 6(1) of the ECHR has been engaged in cases concerning private family law disputes,[179] public law cases involving children in care where State action is determinative of the child or family's civil rights and obligations,[180] parental contact to children in care,[181] fostering[182] and adoption.[183]

(iii)   Need for a Dispute

16.77 Article 6 is engaged in relation to the determination of a criminal charge.[184] For Art 6 to be engaged in relation to civil rights and obligations there must be an actionable *domestic* claim as a matter of substantive law. In *H v Belgium*[185] the European Court of Human Rights made clear that:

'Article 6 paragraph 1 extends only to 'contestations' (disputes) over (civil) 'rights and obligations' which can be said, at least on arguable grounds, to be recognised under domestic law; it does not in itself guarantee any particular content for (civil) 'rights and obligations' in the substantive law of the Contracting States.'

Thus, Art 6(1) cannot be applied so as to create by way of interpretation a substantive right which has no legal basis in the domestic system of law.[186] It will however apply to disputes of a 'genuine and serious nature' concerning the actual existence of the right as well as to the scope or manner in which it is exercised.[187]

ECHR, Art 6(1) – Ambit

16.78 Article 6(1) of the ECHR provides as follows in respect of the right to a fair trial:

'In the determination of his civil rights and obligations or of any criminal charge against him, everyone is entitled to a fair and public hearing within a reasonable time by an independent and impartial tribunal established by law. Judgment shall be pronounced publicly but the press and public may be excluded from all or part of the trial in the interests of morals, public order or national security in a democratic society, where the interests of

---

[178]   Van Bueren, G *Child Rights in Europe* (2007) Council of Europe Publishing, p 112.

[179]   See for example *Airey v Ireland* (1979) 2 EHRR 305 and *Rasmussen v Denmark* (1984) 7 EHRR 371.

[180]   See for example *Olsson v Sweden* (No 1) (1988) 11 EHRR 259.

[181]   See for example *W v United Kingdom* (1987) 10 EHRR 29 and *Eriksson v Sweden* (1989) 12 EHRR 183.

[182]   See for example *Eriksson v Sweden* (1989) 12 EHRR 183.

[183]   See for example *Keegan v Ireland* (1994) 18 EHRR 342.

[184]   See **16.81** below in respect of determining whether a charge is 'criminal' for the purposes of Art 6 of the ECHR.

[185]   (1987) 10 EHRR 339, para 40.

[186]   See *R (Kehoe) v Secretary of State for Work and Pensions* [2005] UKHL 48, [2006] 1 AC 42, paras 38–41.

[187]   *Markovic v Italy* 44 EHRR 1045, para 93. See also *TP and KM v United Kingdom* (2001) 34 EHRR 42, para 94.

juveniles or the protection of the private life of the parties so require, or to the extent strictly necessary in the opinion of the court in special circumstances where publicity would prejudice the interests of justice.

(i)   Determination of Civil Rights and Obligations

16.79   To engage Art 6(1) of the ECHR the civil rights and obligations in question must be the object, or one of the objects, of the dispute and the result of proceedings must be directly decisive of such a right or obligation.[188] It is not necessary for both parties to the proceedings to be private persons.[189] Provided that civil rights and obligations are the object or one of the objects of the dispute and the proceedings are directly decisive of such a right or obligation Art 6 will apply to proceedings as between individuals as well as between individuals and the State[190] including those in a constitutional court.[191]

16.80   In determining whether the right or obligation at issue is a 'civil right or obligation' for the purposes of Art 6(1) it is the character of that right rather than the identity or nature of the parties which is key. In *Stran Greek Refineries and Stratis Andreadis v Greece*[192] the European Court of Human Rights made clear that:

> 'According to the Court's case-law, the concept of 'civil rights and obligations' is not to be interpreted solely by reference to the respondent State's domestic law. Article 6 para 1 applies irrespective of the status of the parties, of the nature of the legislation which governs the manner in which the dispute is to be determined and of the character of the authority which has jurisdiction in the matter; it is enough that the outcome of the proceedings should be decisive for private rights and obligations.'

The classification of a civil right in domestic law is not decisive.[193] The rights and obligations between private individuals are always civil rights and obligations for the purposes of Art 6 of the ECHR.[194] As between the individual and the State where State action is directly decisive of the individuals' rights and obligations those civil rights may attract the protection of Art 6 of the ECHR.

(ii)   Determination of a Criminal Charge

'Criminal'

16.81   Whether proceedings are 'criminal' for the purposes of Art 6(1) of the ECHR falls be determined by consideration of the classification of proceedings in domestic law, the nature of the offence and the severity of the penalty which may be imposed, which factors will be alternative and not cumulative.[195] The severity of the penalty will often be the decisive factor.[196] Anti-social behaviour orders do not constitute a criminal charge for the purposes of Art 6 of the ECHR.[197]

---

[188]   Lord Lester QC, Lord Pannick QC and Herberg, J *Human Rights Law and Practice* (2009) 3rd edn, LexisNexis, p 282.
[189]   *Ringeisen v Austria* (1971) 1 EHRR 455, para 94.
[190]   *Ringeisen v Austria* (1971) 1 EHRR 455, para 94.
[191]   *Süßmann v Germany* (1996) 25 EHRR 64, paras 39 and 41.
[192]   (1994) EHRR 293, para 39.
[193]   *Feldbrugge v Netherlands* (1986) 8 EHRR 425, para 29.
[194]   *Airey v Ireland* (1979) 2 EHRR 305.
[195]   *Engel v Netherlands* (1976) 1 EHRR 647, para 82 and *Lutz v Germany* (1998) 10 EHRR 182, para 55.
[196]   *Brown v United Kingdom* (1998) 28 EHRR CD 233 and *R (McCann) v Manchester Crown Court* [2002] UKHL 39, [2003] 1 AC 787, para 30.
[197]   *R (McCann) v Manchester Crown Court* [2002] UKHL 39, [2003] 1 AC 787, para 30 ('In *Engel v Netherlands (No 1)* (1976) 1 EHRR 647 at 678–679 (para 82), the European Court established three criteria for

'Charge'

16.82 A person will be the subject of a 'charge' for the purposes of Art 6(1) of the ECHR where that person is 'substantially affected' by the proceedings.[198] Thus whilst the point of charge will be relevant, a person may be considered to be under a 'charge' from the point of arrest.[199] Art 6 will not extend to the preliminary aspects of the criminal proceedings in respect of case management or procedure[200] or legal aid.[201]

(iii)   Access to the Court

16.83 Whilst Art 6(1) provides the right to a fair and public hearing it does not explicitly enshrine the right to access to the court. However, the European Court of Human Rights has made clear that the right of access to the court is inherent in Art 6(1) of the ECHR.[202]

Right of Access Not Absolute

16.84 The right to access to the Court under Art 6(1) is not an absolute right and States may regulate access according to the needs and resources of the community and of individuals within the margin of appreciation.[203] However, the measures regulating access to the court must not be such as to impair the very essence of the right under Art 6(1) of the ECHR, must pursue a legitimate aim and must comply with the principle of proportionality.[204] Any limitation must also be legally certain.[205] State immunity may limit the right of access to the court without impugning Art 6(1) of the ECHR even where the claim relates to torture.[206] The imposition of substantial court fees may amount to a disproportionate restriction on access to court.[207]

---

determining whether proceedings are 'criminal' within the meaning of the convention, namely (a) the domestic classification, (b) the nature of the offence, and (c) the severity of the potential penalty which the defendant risks incurring. The character and attributes of the proceedings for an anti-social behaviour order have been outlined. Domestically, they are properly classified as civil. That is, however, only a starting point. Turning to factor (b), the position is that the order under the first part of s 1 does not constitute a finding that an offence has been committed: contrast the community charge decision in *Benham v UK* (1996) 22 EHRR 293. It is right, however, to observe that the third factor is the most important. Here the position is that the order itself involves no penalty. The established criteria suggest that the proceedings were not in respect of a criminal charge').

[198] *Deweer v Belgium* (1980) 2 EHRR 439, para 46 ('The 'charge' could, for the purposes of Article 6 para 1, be defined as the official notification given to an individual by the competent authority of an allegation that he has committed a criminal offence. In several decisions and opinions the Commission has adopted a test that appears to be fairly closely related, namely whether 'the situation of the [suspect] has been substantially affected'').

[199] *X v United Kingdom* 14 DR 26 (1978).

[200] *X v United Kingdom* (1982) 5 EHRR 273.

[201] *Gutfreund v France* (2006) 42 EHRR 1076, paras 34–37 ('... the refusal of legal aid was not a decisive factor in the determination of the criminal charge against the applicant. Consequently, the criminal limb of Article 6(1) does not come into play').

[202] *Golder v United Kingdom* (1975) 1 EHRR 524.

[203] *Golder v United Kingdom* (1975) 1 EHRR 524, para 38.

[204] *Ashingdane v United Kingdom* (1985) 7 EHRR 528, para 57 ('Nonetheless, the limitations applied must not restrict or reduce the access left to the individual in such a way or to such an extent that the very essence of the right is impaired. Furthermore, a limitation will not be compatible with Article 6, para 1 if it does not pursue a legitimate aim and if there is not a reasonable relationship of proportionality between the means employed and the aim sought to be achieved') and *Stubbings v United Kingdom* (1996) 23 EHRR 213, para 48. See also *Golder v United Kingdom* 1 EHRR 524, para 39.

[205] *Société Levage Prestations v France* (1996) 24 EHRR 351.

[206] *Jones v Saudi Arabia, Mitchell and others v Al Dali and others* [2006] UKHL 26, [2007] 1 AC 270 and see *Al-Adsani v United Kingdom* (2001) 34 EHRR 273.

[207] *Jedamski and Jedamska v Poland* (2007) 45 EHRR 47. See also *MLB v SLJ* 516 US 102 (1996) US Supreme Court.

Access must be Effective Access

16.85 The right of access to court requires *effective* access.[208] In *Steel and Morris v United Kingdom*[209] the European Court of Human Rights stated 'The Court reiterates that the Convention is intended to guarantee practical and effective rights. This is particularly so of the right of access to a court in view of the prominent place held in a democratic society by the right to a fair trial'. Effective access is particularly important in respect of cases concerning the child's relationship with his or her parents.[210] The right to effective access to the court self evidently requires that the court should make a final decision one way or the other where it has jurisdiction.[211] Further, the right of effective access to the court will include the right to benefit from the success of any litigation and the results of any hearing must be effectively executed without unjustified and inordinate delay.[212] The right of effective access to the Court under Art 6(1) does not guarantee a right of appeal but where the national law provides a right of appeal Art 6 will apply to those appeal proceedings.[213]

Effective Access under ECHR, Art 6(1) and Legal Aid[214]

16.86 In *Airey v Ireland*[215] the European Court of Human Rights made clear that the right of access to court under Art 6(1) of the ECHR will not guarantee a party the right to free legal aid *per se* although the mere fact that such an interpretation of the Convention may extend its reach into the sphere of social and economic rights should not be a decisive factor against such an interpretation.[216] Thus in *P, C and S v United Kingdom*[217] the complexity of care proceedings meant that the parties right of access to the court required the provision of legal aid, the European Court of Human Rights observing with reference to *Airey v Ireland* that:

> 'Article 6(1) of the Convention embodies the right of access to a court for the determination of civil rights and obligations. Failure to provide an applicant with the assistance of a lawyer may breach this provision where such assistance is indispensable for effective access to court, either because legal representation is rendered compulsory as is the case in certain Contracting States for various types of litigation, or by reason of the complexity of the procedure or the type of case. Factors identified as relevant in *Airey* in determining whether the applicant would have been able to present her case properly and satisfactorily without the assistance of a lawyer included the complexity of the procedure, the necessity to address complicated points of law or to establish facts, involving expert evidence and the

---

208   *Airey v Ireland* (1979) 2 EHRR 305, para 26.
209   (2005) 41 EHRR 403.
210   See *MLB v SLJ* 516 US 102 (1996), US Supreme Court.
211   *Marini v Albania* (2007) Application No 3738/02 (unreported), para 120 ('The Court recalls that Article 6 of the Convention does not compel the Contracting States to set up courts of appeal or of cassation. Nevertheless, a State which does institute such courts is required to ensure that persons amenable to the law shall enjoy before these courts the fundamental guarantees contained in Article 6. These guarantees include the right to have a final determination on a matter submitted to a court including, in the applicant's case, a decision on the admissibility and/or merits of his constitutional complaint').
212   *Teteriny v Russia* (2005) Application No 11931/03 (unreported), para 41.
213   *Delcourt v Belgium* (1970) 1 EHRR 35.
214   See also **16.119** below.
215   (1979) 2 EHRR 305.
216   *Airey v Ireland* (1979) 2 EHRR 305, para 26 ('To hold that so far-reaching an obligation exists would, the Court agrees, sit ill with the fact that the Convention contains no provision on legal aid for those disputes, Article 6, para 3 (c) dealing only with criminal proceedings. However, despite the absence of a similar clause for civil litigation, Article 6, para 1 may sometimes compel the State to provide for the assistance of a lawyer when such assistance proves indispensable for an effective access to court either because legal representation is rendered compulsory, as is done by the domestic law of certain Contracting States for various types of litigation, or by reason of the complexity of the procedure or of the case').
217   (2002) 35 EHRR 1075.

examination of witnesses, and the fact that the subject matter of the marital dispute entailed an emotional involvement that was scarcely compatible with the degree of objectivity required by advocacy in court ... It may be noted that the right of access to a court is not absolute and may be subject to legitimate restrictions. Where an individual's access is limited either by operation of law or in fact, the restriction will not be incompatible with Article 6 where the limitation did not impair the very essence of the right and where it pursued a legitimate aim, and there was a reasonable relationship of proportionality between the means employed and the aim sought to be achieved. Thus, although the pursuit of proceedings as a litigant in person may on occasion not be an easy matter, the limited public funds available for civil actions renders a procedure of selection a necessary feature of the system of administration of justice, and the manner in which it functions in particular cases may be shown not to have been arbitrary or disproportionate, or to have impinged on the essence of the right of access to a court. It may be the case that other factors concerning the administration of justice (such as the necessity for expedition or the rights of others) also play a limiting role as regards the provision of assistance in a particular case, although such restriction would also have to satisfy the tests set out above. Secondly, the key principle governing the application of Article 6 is fairness. In cases where an applicant appears in court notwithstanding lack of assistance by a lawyer and manages to conduct his or her case in the teeth of all the difficulties, the question may nonetheless arise as to whether this procedure was fair. There is the importance of ensuring the appearance of the fair administration of justice and a party in civil proceedings must be able to participate effectively, *inter alia*, by being able to put forward the matters in support of his or her claims. Here, as in other aspects of Article 6, the seriousness of what is at stake for the applicant will be of relevance to assessing the adequacy and fairness of the procedures.'[218]

Right of Effective Access and Administrative Decisions

16.87 In relation to administrative decision making, the right of access to the court pursuant to Art 6(1) of the ECHR requires that States make available a process by which such decisions can be challenged before a judicial body with full jurisdiction providing the guarantees enshrined in Art 6(1) of the ECHR.[219] The right to effective access to the court implies a right to reasonable notice of administrative decisions which interfere with civil rights and obligations in order that a challenge may be mounted in court if necessary.[220] Note that the guarantees enshrined in Art 6(1) will encompass any administrative decisions taken prior to the commencement of proceedings, as well as the 'purely judicial' element of the proceedings, where such administrative decisions are determinative of the child's civil rights or obligations.[221]

Right of Effective Access and Limitation Periods

16.88 In *Stubbings v United Kingdom*[222] the European Court considered the claim that the limitation period attaching to actions in tort by virtue of the Limitation Act 1980 had impaired the right of effective access to the Court. The applicant, who had been the victim of sexual abuse as a child, contended that the very essence of her right of effective access to court had been impaired by the limitation period of 6 years from the age of majority applied in her case, as one of the effects of the sexual abuse she suffered was to prevent her from appreciating that it was the cause of her psychological problems

---

[218] See also *Steel and Morris v United Kingdom* (2005) 41 EHRR 403.

[219] *Albert and Le Compte v Belgium* (1983) 5 EHRR, para 29. For the meaning of 'full jurisdiction' see the opinion of Judge Bratza in *Bryan v United Kingdom* (1995) 21 EHRR 342. See also *W v United Kingdom* (1987) 10 EHRR 29, para 82 and *Re S (Minors) (Care Order: Implementation of Care Plan)* [2002] UKHL 10, [2002] 2 AC 291, para 79.

[220] *De La Pradelle v France* (1992) A 253–B, para 34.

[221] See *Mantovanelli v France* (1997) 24 EHRR 370 and *Re L (Care: Assessment Fair Trial)* [2002] EWHC 1379 (Fam), [2002] 2 FLR 730.

[222] (1996) 23 EHRR 213.

until after the expiry of the limitation period. The European Court of Human Rights, accepting that expert evidence showed that victims of child sexual abuse might commonly be unable to perceive the causal connection between the abuse and their psychological problems without medical assistance, rejected the applicant's claim on the basis that the very essence of the applicant's right of access to court had not been impaired, the limitation period allowing 6 years from the date of majority to institute proceedings and, if successful, criminal proceedings offering the possibility of a compensation order.[223] Van Bueren observes that 'The approach of the European Court of Human Rights [in *Stubbings v United Kingdom*] is, unfortunately, to cling to the traditional goals of statute of limitations without giving sufficient recognition to the distortions and complexities caused by the psychological trauma on children who have been sexually abused'.[224]

(iv) Right to a Fair Hearing

16.89 The right to a fair hearing applies to both criminal and civil proceedings. To establish whether a hearing has been fair the court will look at the proceedings as a whole[225] including whether any decision of appeal is capable of remedying unfairness which occurs at first instance[226] and the implementation of judicial decisions.[227] The right to a fair hearing is itself comprised of a number of cardinal rights, namely the right to a hearing in ones presence, equality of arms, access to evidence, the right to freedom from self incrimination and the right to a reasoned judgment.

Right to a Hearing in Ones Presence

16.90 The presence of the accused at a criminal trial is an essential requirement of fairness.[228] A procedure which determines civil rights without hearing the parties cannot comply with Art 6(1) of the ECHR.[229] In *Góç v Turkey*[230] the European Court of Human Rights reiterated once again that:

---

[223] (1996) 23 EHRR 213, paras 52–57. This was despite the Court expressly stating that 'There has been a developing awareness in recent years of the range of problems caused by child abuse and its psychological effects on victims, and it is possible that the rules on limitation of actions applying in member States of the Council of Europe may have to be amended to make special provision for this group of claimants in the near future' (Para 56).

[224] Van Bueren, G *Child Rights in Europe* (2007) Council of Europe Publishing, p 117. Note that in a dissenting judgment, Judge Foighel, finding a violation of Art 6(1) of the ECHR observed that 'The purpose of the rules of limitation, which is to strike a proportional balance between the prevention of stale claims and protecting the interests of the claimants, have no meaning when the victim is not aware that she even has a claim ... The margin of appreciation can never justify a State in depriving the individual altogether of the right in question.' Judge Macdonald, also dissenting and finding a violation of Art 6(1) held that 'Having regard to the nature of the injury involved and the fact that victims of childhood sexual abuse are frequently and for various periods of time unaware of the causal link between the damage suffered and the acts responsible, the imposition of a fixed statutory time-limit which expires 6 years after the date of the act or after the date on which the victim attains his or her majority (eighteen), regardless of the circumstances of an individual case and without the availability of a procedure to mitigate the consequences of the applicable period, is, in my view, disproportionate in that it unreasonably deprives the applicants of a right of access to court and thus lies beyond the margin of appreciation enjoyed by States in establishing time-limits for the introduction of proceedings.'

[225] *Barberá, Messegué and Jabardo v Spain* (1988) 11 EHRR 360, para 68 ('The Court must, however, determine – and in this it agrees with the Commission – whether the proceedings considered as a whole, including the way in which prosecution and defence evidence was taken, were fair as required by Article 6, para 1'). See also *Delcourt v Belgium* (1970) 1 EHRR 355, para 31 and *Borgers v Belgium* (1991) 15 EHRR 93, para 24.

[226] *Edwards v United Kingdom* (1993) 15 EHRR 417, paras 36–37 and *Rowe and Davis v United Kingdom* (2000) 30 EHRR 1, para 65.

[227] *Hornsby v Greece* (1997) 24 EHRR 250, paras 40–41 and *Ryabykh v Russian* (2005) 40 EHRR 615, para 51.

[228] *Ekbatani v Sweden* (1988) 13 EHRR 504, para 25 ('With regard to proceedings at first instance it flows from

'According to the Court's established case-law, in proceedings before a court of first and only instance the right to a 'public hearing' in the sense of Article 6(1) entails an entitlement to an 'oral hearing' unless there are exceptional circumstances that justify dispensing with such a hearing.'[231]

16.91 As Van Bueren notes, for children it is essential that they be dealt with in a manner which takes full account of their age, level of maturity and intellectual and emotional capacities, and that steps are taken to promote a child's ability to understand and participate.[232] In *V and T v United Kingdom*[233] the European Court of Human Rights observed as follows in relation to the application of Art 6(1) of the ECHR to children in criminal trials:[234]

'The Court notes that Article 6, read as a whole, guarantees the right of an accused to participate effectively in his criminal trial. It has not until the present time been called upon to consider how this Article 6(1) guarantee applies to criminal proceedings against children, and in particular whether procedures which are generally considered to safeguard the rights of adults on trial, such as publicity, should be abrogated in respect of children in order to promote their understanding and participation. The Court recalls its above findings that there is not at this stage any clear common standard amongst the member States of the Council of Europe as to the minimum age of criminal responsibility and that the attribution of criminal responsibility to the applicant does not in itself give rise to a breach of Article 3 of the Convention. Likewise, it cannot be said that the trial on criminal charges of a child, even one as young as eleven, as such violates the fair trial guarantee under Article 6(1). The Court does, however, agree with the Commission that it is essential that a child charged with an offence is dealt with in a manner which takes full account of his age, level of maturity and intellectual and emotional capacities, and that steps are taken to promote his ability to understand and participate in the proceedings. It follows that, in respect of a young child charged with a grave offence attracting high levels of media and public interest, it would be necessary to conduct the hearing in such a way as to reduce as far as possible his or her feelings of intimidation and inhibition ...'

16.92 Where the first stage of the proceedings is constituted by an oral hearing, the absence of an oral hearing at the appellate stage may not constitute a violation of Art 6(1) of the ECHR. In *Hoppe v Germany*[235] the European Court of Human Rights held that:

'The manner in which Article 6 of the Convention applies to proceedings before courts of appeal depends on the special features of the domestic proceedings viewed as a whole. Even

the notion of a fair trial that a person charged with a criminal offence should, as a general principle, be entitled to be present at the trial hearing'). See also *Raja v Van Hoogstraten* [2004] EWCA Civ 968, [2004] 4 All ER 793, para 94.

[229]   *Karakasis v Greece* (2003) 36 EHRR 507, para 26.

[230]   (2002) 35 EHRR 134, para 47.

[231]   As to waiver of the right to be present see *Poitrimol v France* (1993) 18 EHRR 130, para 31('a waiver must, if it is to be effective for Convention purposes, be established in an unequivocal manner and be attended by minimum safeguards commensurate to its importance').

[232]   Van Bueren, G *Child Rights in Europe* (2007) Council of Europe Publishing, p 107.

[233]   (1999) 30 EHRR 121, paras 85–91.

[234]   See now *Practice Direction (Crown Court: Young Defendants)* [2000] 1 WLR 659. See also *Uzunget v Turkey* (2010) Application No 21831/03, para 35 in which the European Court of Human Rights again emphasised that 'the Court considers that it is essential that a child charged with an offence is dealt with in a manner which takes full account of his age, level of maturity and intellectual and emotional capacities, and that steps are taken to promote his ability to understand and participate in the proceedings.'

[235]   (2002) 38 EHRR 285, para 63. See also *Ekbatani v Sweden* (1988) 13 EHRR 504, para 27 ('The manner of application of Article 6 to proceedings before courts of appeal does, however, depend on the special features of the proceedings involved; account must be taken of the entirety of the proceedings in the domestic legal order and of the role of the appellate court therein').

where the court of appeal has jurisdiction both over the facts and in law, Article 6 does not always require a right to a public hearing, irrespective of the nature of the issues to be decided. The publicity requirement is certainly one of the means whereby confidence in the courts is maintained. However, there are other considerations, including the right to a trial within a reasonable time and the related need for an expeditious handling of the courts' case-load, which must be taken into account in determining the necessity of public hearings in the proceedings subsequent to the trial at first-instance level. Provided a public hearing has been held at first instance, the absence of a hearing before a second or third instance may accordingly be justified by the special features of the proceedings at issue.'

Equality of Arms

16.93 A party to proceedings must have a reasonable opportunity of presenting his or her case in a manner which does not place him or her at a substantial disadvantage compared to his or her opponent. This involves striking a 'fair balance' between the parties, which principle will apply to both criminal proceedings and civil proceedings between individuals and between an individual and the state.[236] Equality of arms requires an adversarial process.[237] The principle of 'equality of arms' is particularly important in respect of children. For children accused of serious criminal offences, the principle that a party to proceedings must have a reasonable opportunity of presenting his or her case in a manner which does not place him or her at a substantial disadvantage compared to his or her opponent will require a specially adapted procedure which promotes the child's welfare, respects his or her privacy and enables him or her to understand and participate fully in the proceedings on an equal footing.[238] This principle will apply equally in proceedings concerning state intervention in the child's family.[239] A failure to provide children with representation in proceedings which are civil in nature may violate their rights under Art 6(1) of the ECHR.[240]

Equality of Arms and Administrative Decisions

16.94 In relation to administrative decisions, the principle of equality of arms will require that a party be informed of the detailed reasons for the decision to enable the applicant to mount a reasoned challenge to it.[241]

Access to Evidence

Equality of Arms and Access to Evidence

16.95 The principle of 'equality of arms' also requires that each party must be given the opportunity to have knowledge of and comment on the evidence adduced by the other party. In criminal proceedings this requires the prosecuting authorities to disclose material in their possession which may assist the defendant, including material which might undermine the witnesses relied on by the prosecution.[242] Note however that the duty of disclosure in criminal proceedings is not absolute.[243]

---

[236] *Dombo Beheer v Netherlands* (1993) 18 EHRR 213, para 33 (Nevertheless, certain principles concerning the notion of a 'fair hearing' in cases concerning civil rights and obligations emerge from the Court's case-law. Most significantly for the present case, it is clear that the requirement of 'equality of arms', in the sense of a 'fair balance' between the parties, applies in principle to such cases as well as to criminal cases').

[237] *McMichael v United Kingdom* (1995) 20 EHRR 205, paras 80 and 83

[238] *T and V v United Kingdom* (2000) 30 EHRR 121 and *SC v United Kingdom* (2005) 40 EHRR 226, para 27.

[239] *Buchberger v Austria* (2003) 37 EHRR 356, para 50.

[240] *S v Principal Reporter and the Lord Advocate* [2001] UKHRR 514.

[241] *Hentrich v France* (1994) 18 EHRR 440, para 56.

[242] *Jespers v Belgium* 27 DR 61 (1981).

[243] See *Rowe and Davis v United Kingdom* (1998) 25 EHRR CD 118 ('the entitlement to disclosure of relevant

16.96 The principle that each party must be given the opportunity to have knowledge of and comment on the evidence adduced by the other party will also apply in civil proceedings. This will include those where, by reason of them being concerned with the welfare of children, a less 'adversarial' approach is adopted. In *McMichael v United Kingdom*[244] the European Court of Human Rights held in relation to 'children's hearings' in Scotland that:

> 'The Court accepts that in this sensitive domain of family law there may be good reasons for opting for an adjudicatory body that does not have the composition or procedures of a court of law of the classic kind. Nevertheless, notwithstanding the special characteristics of the adjudication to be made, as a matter of general principle the right to a fair – adversarial – trial 'means the opportunity to have knowledge of and comment on the observations filed or evidence adduced by the other party'. In the context of the present case, the lack of disclosure of such vital documents as social reports is capable of affecting the ability of participating parents not only to influence the outcome of the children's hearing in question but also to assess their prospects of making an appeal to the Sheriff Court.'[245]

Freedom from Self Incrimination

16.97 Although not specifically mentioned in Art 6 of the ECHR, the right to silence and the right to freedom from self incrimination have been held by the European Court of Human Rights to be generally recognised international standards which lie at the heart of the notion of a fair procedure under Art 6, their rationale being based in the protection of the accused against improper compulsion by the authorities, thereby contributing to the avoidance of miscarriages of justice and to the fulfillment of the aims of Art 6 of the ECHR.[246] The right to freedom from self incrimination in particular presupposes that the prosecution in a criminal case seek to prove their case against the accused without resort to evidence obtained through methods of coercion or oppression in defiance of the will of the accused.[247] In order to determine whether the essence of the applicant's right to remain silent and his or her privilege against self-incrimination has been infringed, the Court will focus on the nature and degree of compulsion used to obtain the evidence, the existence of any relevant safeguards in the procedure, and the use to which any material so obtained was put.[248]

16.98 The right to silence is not absolute. For example, inferences may be drawn from silence.[249] In *O'Halloran and Francis v United Kingdom*[250] the European Court of Human Rights held that:

---

evidence is not an absolute right. In any criminal proceedings there may be competing interests, such as national security or the need to protect witnesses at risk of reprisals or keep secret police methods of investigation of crime, which must be weighed against the rights of the accused ... In some cases it may be necessary to withhold certain evidence from the defence so as to preserve the fundamental rights of another individual or to safeguard an important public interest. However, only such measures restricting the rights of the defence which are strictly necessary are permissible under Article 6(1) ... Moreover, in order to ensure that the accused receives a fair trial, any difficulties caused to the defence by a limitation on its rights must be sufficiently counterbalanced by the procedures followed by the judicial authorities').

[244] (1995) 20 EHRR 205, para 80. See also *McGinley and Egan v United Kingdom* (1998) 27 EHRR 1, para 86.

[245] Note that the requirement of 'equality of arms' may extend in the case of expert witnesses to the parties being properly involved in the process of securing the expert report including the examination of documents on which the report is to be based and interviewing witnesses on whom the expert will rely (see *Mantovanelli v France* (1997) 24 EHRR 370, para 33–36). See also *Bonisch v Austria* (1985) 9 EHRR 191, paras 32–34 and H v France (1989) 12 EHRR 74, paras 60–61.

[246] *Weh v Austria* (2005) 40 EHRR 37, para 39.

[247] *Weh v Austria* (2005) 40 EHRR 37, para 39 and see *Saunders v United Kingdom* (1996) 23 EHRR 313, para 68.

[248] *O'Halloran and Francis v United Kingdom* (2008) 46 EHRR 397, paras 55–57.

[249] *Condron v United Kingdom (No 2)* (2000) 31 EHRR 1, paras 56–57 ('... whether the drawing of adverse

'The applicants contended that the right to remain silent and the right not to incriminate oneself are absolute rights and that to apply any form of direct compulsion to require an accused person to make incriminatory statements against his will of itself destroys the very essence of that right. The Court is unable to accept this. It is true, as pointed out by the applicants, that in all the cases to date in which 'direct compulsion' was applied to require an actual or potential suspect to provide information which contributed, or might have contributed, to his conviction, the Court has found a violation of the applicant's privilege against self-incrimination. It does not, however, follow that any direct compulsion will automatically result in a violation.'

Right to a Reasoned Judgment

16.99 In *Ruiz Torrija v Spain*[251] the European Court of Human Rights made clear that the ambit of the right to a reasoned judgment is dependent on the circumstances of the case, holding that:

'Article 6 para 1 obliges the courts to give reasons for their judgments, but cannot be understood as requiring a detailed answer to every. The extent to which this duty to give reasons applies may vary according to the nature of the decision. It is moreover necessary to take into account, inter alia, the diversity of the submissions that a litigant may bring before the courts and the differences existing in the Contracting States with regard to statutory provisions, customary rules, legal opinion and the presentation and drafting of judgments. That is why the question whether a court has failed to fulfil the obligation to state reasons, deriving from Article 6 of the Convention, can only be determined in the light of the circumstances of the case.'

(v)   Right to a Public Hearing and Public Pronouncement of Judgment

Right to a Public Hearing

16.100   Pursuant to Art 6(1) of the EHCR everyone has the right to a public hearing save where the press and the public may be excluded from all or part of the hearing in the interests of morals, public order or national security in a democratic society, where the interests of juveniles or the protection of the private life of the parties require a private hearing or to the extent strictly necessary in the opinion of the court in special circumstances where publicity would prejudice the interests of justice. The presence of the press has been held to be of particular importance to facilitating the right to a public hearing.[252] Note that a person may waive his or her right to a public hearing. However,

---

inferences from an accused's silence infringes Article 6 is a matter to be determined in the light of all the circumstances of the case, having regard to the situations where inferences may be drawn, the weight attached to them by the national courts in their assessment of the evidence and the degree of compulsion inherent in the situation ... since the right to silence, like the privilege against self-incrimination, lay at the heart of the notion of a fair procedure under Article 6, particular caution was required before a domestic court could invoke an accused's silence against him ... it would be incompatible with the right to silence to base a conviction solely or mainly on the accused's silence or on a refusal to answer questions or to give evidence himself. Nevertheless ... it is obvious that the right cannot and should not prevent that the accused's silence, in situations which clearly call for an explanation from him, be taken into account in assessing the persuasiveness of the evidence adduced by the prosecution'). See also and *Beckles v United Kingdom* (2003) 36 EHRR 162, para 57.

[250]   (2008) 46 EHRR 397, para 53.

[251]   (1994) 19 EHRR 553, para 29. See also *Karakasis v Greece* (2003) 36 EHRR 507, para 27 and *Hirvisaari v Finland* (2004) 38 EHRR 139, para 30 ('The Court reiterates that, according to its established case-law reflecting a principle linked to the proper administration of justice, judgments of courts and tribunals should adequately state the reasons on which they are based').

[252]   *Pretto v Italy* (1983) 6 EHRR 182, para 21 ('The public character of proceedings before the judicial bodies referred to in Article 6(1) protects litigants against the administration of justice in secret with no public scrutiny; it is also one of the means whereby confidence in the courts, superior and inferior, can be

whilst neither the letter nor the spirit of this provision prevents a person from waiving of his or her own free will, either expressly or tacitly, the entitlement to have his or her case heard in public, any such waiver must be made in an unequivocal manner and must not run counter to any important public interest.[253]

Children and the Right to a Public Hearing[254]

16.101   The words 'in the interests of juveniles' in Art 6(1) appear to be a lower test than the best interests criterion, but ECHR must be interpreted in relation to children by reference to Art 3(1) of the CRC and this will necessarily import the customary international law status of best interests into consideration of the application of Art 6(1) of the ECHR.[255] Where the exclusion protects the child's right to privacy[256] and promotes the giving of full and frank evidence by the parties, including the child where a party, exclusion may be said to be in the child's best interests.[257]

16.102   In respect of criminal proceedings, in *V v United Kingdom*[258] the European Court of Human Rights said:

> '... in respect of a young child charged with a grave offence attracting high levels of media and public interest, it would be necessary to conduct the hearing in such a way as to reduce as far as possible his or her feelings of intimidation and inhibition ... where appropriate in view of the age and other characteristics of the child and the circumstances surrounding the criminal proceedings, this general interest [in the open administration of justice] could be satisfied by a modified procedure providing for selected attendance rights and judicious reporting'.

16.103   In *B and P v United Kingdom*[259] the Court considered the exceptions set out in Art 6(1) of the ECHR in the context of proceedings involving the family circumstances of children and held that:

> '... the requirement to hold a public hearing is subject to exceptions. This is apparent from the text of Article 6(1) itself, which contains the proviso that 'the press and public may be excluded from all or part of the trial ... where the interests of juveniles or the private life of the parties so require, or to the extent strictly necessary in the opinion of the court in special circumstances where publicity would prejudice the interests of justice'. Moreover, it is established in the Court's case-law that, even in a criminal-law context where there is a high expectation of publicity, it may on occasion be necessary under Article 6 to limit the open and public nature of proceedings in order, for example, to protect the safety or privacy of witnesses or to promote the free exchange of information and opinion in the pursuit of justice ... The proceedings which the present applicants wished to take place in public

---

maintained. By rendering the administration of justice visible, publicity contributes to the achievement of the aim of Article 6(1), namely a fair trial, the guarantee of which is one of the fundamental principles of any democratic society, within the meaning of the Convention') and *B and P v United Kingdom* (2002) 34 EHRR 529, para 36 ('The public character of proceedings protects litigants against the administration of justice in secret with no public scrutiny; it is also one of the means whereby confidence in the courts can be maintained. By rendering the administration of justice visible, publicity contributes to the achievement of the aim of Article 6(1), a fair hearing, the guarantee of which is one of the foundations of a democratic society').

[253] *Schuler-Zgraggen v Switzerland* (1993) 16 EHRR 405, para 58. See also *Zumtobel v Austria* (1993) 17 EHRR 116, para 34.

[254] See also **9.11–9.15** and **9.49–9.54** above.

[255] Van Bueren, G *Child Rights in Europe* (2007) Council of Europe Publishing, p 109.

[256] As widely defined by Art 8 of the ECHR (see **9.33** above).

[257] Van Bueren, G *Child Rights in Europe* (2007) Council of Europe Publishing, p 109.

[258] (2000) 30 EHRR 121, para 87.

[259] (2002) 34 EHRR 529.

concerned the residence of each man's son following the parents' divorce or separation. The Court considers that such proceedings are prime examples of cases where the exclusion of the press and public may be justified in order to protect the privacy of the child and parties and to avoid prejudicing the interests of justice. To enable the deciding judge to gain as full and accurate a picture as possible of the advantages and disadvantages of the various residence and contact options open to the child, it is essential that the parents and other witnesses feel able to express themselves candidly on highly personal issues without fear of public curiosity or comment ... while the Court agrees that Article 6(1) states a general rule that civil proceedings, *inter alia*, should take place in public, it does not find it inconsistent with this provision for a State to designate an entire class of case as an exception to the general rule where considered necessary in the interests of morals, public order or national security or where required by the interests of juveniles or the protection of the private life of the parties, although the need for such a measure must always be subject to the Court's control.'

Right to Public Pronouncement of Judgment

16.104 The right to the public pronouncement of judgment is not subject to the limitations in Art 6(1) governing the exclusion of the press and the public from the hearing.[260]

(vi) Right to a Hearing within a Reasonable Time

16.105 Article 6(1) of the ECHR mandates a hearing within a reasonable time. In calculating whether the period of time in issue is 'reasonable' for the purposes of Art 6(1) in both criminal and civil cases the length of proceedings must be assessed in the light of the circumstances of the case and particularly the complexity of the case and the conduct of the applicant[261] and of the relevant authorities.[262] It is not necessary to establish prejudice to rely on the right to a hearing within a reasonable time in civil proceedings.[263] The threshold for proving that the period in question is unreasonable for the purposes of Art 6(1) of the ECHR is a high one.[264] It is important to note that a

---

[260] *Campbell and Fell v United Kingdom* (1984) 7 EHRR 165, para 90. See also *Pretto v Italy* (1983) 6 EHRR 182, para 26

[261] *Fedorov v Russia* (2006) 43 EHRR 943, para 28. The State is not responsible for delay occasioned by the conduct of the applicant (see *König v Germany* (1978) 2 EHRR 170, paras 104–105 and *H v United Kingdom* (1987) 10 EHRR 95, paras 83–86). Note however that the existence of any possibility or right on the part of the applicant to take steps to expedite does not dispense the State from ensuring that the proceedings progressed reasonably quickly (see *McFarlane v Ireland* (2010) Application No 31333/06, para 152).

[262] *Vilho Eskelinen v Finland* (2007) 45 EHRR 43, paras 67–71 and see *McFarlane v Ireland* (2010) Application No 31333/06, para 140 ('The Court recalls its constant case law to the effect that the reasonableness of the length of proceedings must be assessed in the light of the circumstances of the case and with reference to the following criteria: the complexity of the case, the conduct of the applicant and of the relevant authorities and what was at stake for the applicant').

[263] *Porter v Magill* [2001] UKHL 67, [2002] 2 AC 357.

[264] *Dyer (Procurator Fiscal), Linlithgow v Watson and another; K v Lord Advocate* [2002] UKPC D1, [2002] 3 WLR 1488, para 52 ('In any case in which it is said that the reasonable time requirement (to which I will henceforward confine myself) has been or will be violated, the first step is to consider the period of time which has elapsed. Unless that period is one which, on its face and without more, gives grounds for real concern it is almost certainly unnecessary to go further, since the convention is directed not to departures from the ideal but to infringements of basic human rights. The threshold of proving a breach of the reasonable time requirement is a high one, not easily crossed. But if the period which has elapsed is one which, on its face and without more, gives ground for real concern, two consequences follow. First, it is necessary for the court to look into the detailed facts and circumstances of the particular case. The Strasbourg case law shows very clearly that the outcome is closely dependent on the facts of each case. Secondly, it is necessary for the contracting state to explain and justify any lapse of time which appears to be excessive'). See also *A-G's Reference (No 2 of 2001)* [2003] UKHL 68, [2004] 2 AC 72 (criminal cases should only be stayed as a result of a breach of the right to a hearing within a reasonable time where there can no longer be a fair hearing or it would be otherwise unfair to try the defendant).

balance is required between expedition and the proper administration of justice in accordance with the principles enshrined in Art 6 of the ECHR.[265] The State will be responsible for delays arising out of issues concerning the operation of the judicial system, for example where there is a long backlog of work.[266]

Period to be Taken into Account

16.106   The period of time to be considered runs, in civil cases, from the initiation of proceedings[267] although time may in certain cases begin to run prior to the issue of proceedings.[268] In criminal cases the time will run from charge[269] and will continue to run until the definitive determination of the proceedings, including any appeal.[270]

Children and the Right to a Hearing within a Reasonable Time

16.107   Particular diligence is required in respect of the time taken to conclude proceedings where issues of civil status and capacity are involved.[271] The European Court of Human Rights has acknowledged that it is essential that cases involving children are dealt with speedily.[272] The Art 6 right to a hearing within a reasonable time will apply to laws concerning education.[273] In proceedings in which the separation of children from their parents is being contemplated, 'exceptional diligence' is required in respect of ensuring proceedings are determined within a reasonable time. In *Johansen v Norway*[274] the European Court of Human Rights held that:[275]

> 'The Court observes that the proceedings leading to the deprivation of parental rights and access commenced before the Committee on 13 December 1989 and ended when the Supreme Court refused leave to appeal on 19 September 1991. They thus lasted altogether one year and nine months. The Court shares the applicant's and the Commission's opinion that, in view of what was at stake for the applicant and the irreversible and definitive character of the measures concerned, the competent national authorities were required by Article 6 para 1 to act with exceptional diligence in ensuring the progress of the proceedings. However, it does not find that they failed to discharge their obligations in this respect.'

---

[265]   See *Pafitis v Greece* (1999) 27 EHRR 566, para 97.
[266]   *Bucholz v Germany* (1981) 3 EHRR 597, para 51 and *Zimmerman and Steiner v Switzerland* (1983) 6 EHRR 17, paras 27–32.
[267]   *Guincho v Portugal* (1984) 7 EHRR 233, para 29.
[268]   *Golder v United Kingdom* (1975) 1 EHRR 524, para 32 and *König v Germany* (1978) 2 EHRR 170, para 98.
[269]   *Schaal v Luxembourg* (2005) 41 EHRR 1071, para 35 and see *McFarlane v Ireland* (2010) Application No 31333/06, para 143 ('The Court reiterates that in criminal matters, the "reasonable time" referred to in Article 6(1) begins to run as soon as a person is "charged". "Charge", for the purposes of Article 6(1), may be defined as "the official notification given to an individual by the competent authority of an allegation that he has committed a criminal offence", a definition that also corresponds to the test whether "the situation of the [suspect] has been substantially affected"').
[270]   *König v Germany* (1978) 2 EHRR 170, para 98.
[271]   *Mikulic v Croatia* (2002) 11 BHRC 689, para 44.
[272]   *Hokkanen v Finland* (1994) 19 EHRR 139, para 72.
[273]   See *Oršuš and Others v Croatia* (2010) Application No 15766/03 in which a period exceeding 4 years for the domestic courts to determine claims by a group of children concerning infringement of their right not to be discriminated against in the sphere of education, their right to education and their right not to be subjected to inhuman and degrading treatment was held to be excessive and in violation of Art 6(1).
[274]   (1996) 23 EHRR 33, para 88.
[275]   See also *H v United Kingdom* (1987) 10 EHRR 95, para 85 ('In the present case, the Court considers it right to place special emphasis on the importance of what was at stake for the applicant in the proceedings in question. Not only were they decisive for her future relations with her own child, but they had a particular quality of irreversibility, involving as they did what the High Court graphically described as the 'statutory guillotine' of adoption. In cases of this kind the authorities are under a duty to exercise exceptional diligence since, as the Commission rightly pointed out, there is always the danger that any procedural delay will result in the de facto determination of the issue submitted to the court before it has held its hearing. And, indeed, this was what happened here').

(vii)   Right to an Independent and Impartial Tribunal Established by Law

'Tribunal established by Law'

16.108   The definition of 'tribunal' for the purposes of Art 6(1) of the ECHR is a body which has the jurisdiction to examine all questions of fact and law relevant to the dispute before it.[276] It is characterised in the substantive sense of the term by its judicial function of determining matters within its competence on the basis of rules of law and after proceedings conducted in a prescribed manner.[277] In respect of the requirement that the tribunal be 'established by law' covers not only the legal basis for the very existence of a 'tribunal' but also the composition of the bench in each case.[278]

'Independent'

16.109   To establish whether a tribunal is independent for the purposes of Art 6(1) of the ECHR regard must be had to, amongst other factors, the manner of appointment of the members of the tribunal, to their term of office, to the existence of guarantees against outside pressure being exerted on the tribunal and to whether the tribunal body presents an appearance of independence.[279] The appearance of independence is an objective test bearing in mind the importance of justice not only being done but being seen to be done.[280] Independent means independent of the executive, the parties and of Parliament.[281]

'Impartial'

16.110   Impartial for the purpose of Art 6(1) of the ECHR equals an absence of prejudice or bias. In considering whether prejudice or bias is demonstrated, a distinction should be drawn between a subjective approach, that is endeavouring to ascertain the personal conviction of a given judge in a given case, and an objective approach, that is determining whether he or she offered guarantees sufficient to exclude any legitimate doubt in this respect.[282] In *Fey v Austria*[283] the European Court of Human Rights held that:

> 'Under the objective test, it must be determined whether, quite apart from the judge's personal conduct, there are ascertainable facts which may raise doubts as to his impartiality. In this respect even appearances may be of a certain importance. What is at stake is the confidence which the courts in a democratic society must inspire in the public and, above all, as far as criminal proceedings are concerned, in the accused. This implies that in deciding whether in a given case there is a legitimate reason to fear that a particular judge lacks

---

[276]   *Terra Woningen v Netherlands* (1996) 24 EHRR 456, para 52.
[277]   *Belilos v Switzerland* (1988) 10 EHRR 466, para 64.
[278]   *Posokhov v Russia* (2003) 39 EHRR 21.
[279]   *Bryan v United Kingdom* (1995) 21 EHRR 342, para 37.
[280]   *Campbell and Fell v United Kingdom* (1984) 7 EHRR 165, para 81.
[281]   *R (Haase) v Independent Adjudicator* [2008] EWCA Civ 1089, [2009] QB 550. In 1733 Charles Louis de Secondat, Baron de Montesquieu, observed that 'there is no liberty ... if the power of judging be not separated from the legislative and executive' (Montesquieu, Charles de Secondat, baron de, *L'Esprit des Lois*, vol I (c 1748). Alexander Hamilton later agreed: 'These considerations teach us to applaud the wisdom of those States who have committed the judicial power, in the last resort, not to a part of the legislature, but to distinct and independent bodies of men' (A. Hamilton, 'A further view of the judicial department in relation to its authority', *The Federalist*, No 81 (1788)). Section 3(6)(1) of the Constitutional Reform Act 2005 requires the Lord Chancellor to have regard to the need to defend the independence of the judiciary. Further, s 3(6)(1)(b) expressly recognises that, to uphold the continued independence of the judiciary, the Lord Chancellor must have regard to the need for the judiciary to have the support necessary to enable them to exercise their functions.
[282]   *Piersack v Belgium* (1982) 5 EHRR 169, para 30.
[283]   (1993) 16 EHRR 387, para 30,

impartiality, the standpoint of the accused is important but not decisive. What is determinant is whether this fear can be held to be objectively justified.'

Having regard to the European jurisprudence, the House of Lords has held that the proper test for bias is whether the relevant circumstances, as ascertained by the court, would lead a fair-minded and informed observer to conclude that there was a real possibility that the tribunal had been biased.[284]

16.111   In *Ferrantelli and Santangelo v Italy*[285] the Court made clear that whilst not decisive, the standpoint of the accused is important in determining whether there are ascertainable facts which may raise doubts as to the tribunal's impartiality. What however is ultimately important is not the subjective apprehensions of the suspect, however understandable, but whether, in the particular circumstances of the case, his or her fears can be held to be objectively justified.[286]

ECHR, Art 6(2) – Ambit

16.112   Article 6(2) of the ECHR provides as follows in respect of the right to be presumed innocent until proved guilty under the law:

'Everyone charged with a criminal offence shall be presumed innocent until proved guilty according to law.'

16.113   Article 6(2) of the ECHR guarantees the presumption of innocence in criminal proceedings, ensuring that the overall burden of proof remains on the prosecution. It should be noted that Art 6(2) does not prevent presumptions of law or fact provided that these are confined within reasonable limits.[287]

ECHR, Art 6(3) – Ambit

16.114   Article 6(3) of the ECHR provides the minimum guarantees of a fair trial in criminal proceedings. Those guarantees are the right to be informed promptly of an accusation, the right to adequate time and facilities to prepare a defence, the right to defend charges in person or through legal representation, the right to call and examine witnesses and the right to free insistence from an interpreter. Article 6(3) has been held by the European Court of Human Rights to enumerate the specific applications of the general principle stated in Art 6(1) of the ECHR, with the rights listed in Art 6(3) being non-exhaustive in scope. The Court specifically cautions that in applying Art 6(3) it must not be 'severed from its roots' in Art 6(1) of the ECHR.[288]

(i)   ECHR, Art 6(3)(a) – Right to be Informed Promptly of Accusation

16.115   The authorities must take positive steps to ensure that the accused has been informed of the accusation.[289] In order that the right of defence can be exercised in an effective manner, the defence must have at its disposal full, detailed information concerning the charges made, including the legal characterisation that the court might

---

[284]   *Porter v Magill* [2001] UKHL 67, [2002] 2 AC 357.
[285]   (1996) 23 EHRR 288, para 58.
[286]   *Nortier v Netherlands* (1993) Application No 13924/88 (unreported), para 43 (a case concerning the respect of the relevance of the perceptions of a 15-year-old boy).
[287]   *Salabiaku v France* (1988) 13 EHRR 379, para 28.
[288]   *Artico v Italy* (1980) 3 EHRR 1, para 32.
[289]   See *Brozicek v Italy* (1989) 12 EHRR 371, paras 38–42.

adopt in the matter. This information must either be given before the trial in the bill of indictment or at least in the course of the trial by other means such as formal or implicit extension of the charges.[290]

(ii)   ECHR, Art 6(3)(b) – Adequate Time and Facilities to Prepare a Defence

16.116   The right to be informed promptly of an accusation under Art 6(3)(a) is also an important element of the right under Art 6(3)(b) to adequate time to prepare a defence.[291] In determining the adequacy of the time allowed the court will take into account the complexity of the case.[292] The right under Art 6(3)(b) places a positive duty on the State to ensure its proper application in any given case.[293]

(iii)   ECHR, Art 6(3)(c) – Right to Defend in Person or through Legal Representation

The Right to defend in Person

16.117   The right to defend in person under ECHR, Art 6(3)(c) does not extend a right to be represented by a lay-person.[294]

The Right to Legal Representation

16.118   The appointment of counsel which runs counter to the expressed wishes of the defendant is incompatible with the notion of a fair trial under Art 6(1) of the ECHR if, having regard to the margin of appreciation accorded to State parties, such a course of action lacks relevant and sufficient justification.[295] The legal representation secured for the purposes of Art 6(3)(c) must be effective legal representation.[296] The accused must be able to communicate with his legal representatives without hindrance and in conditions of confidentiality. In *S v Switzerland*[297] the European Court of Human Rights stated:

> 'The Court notes that, unlike some national laws and unlike Article 8 para 2 (d) of the American Convention on Human Rights, the European Convention does not expressly guarantee the right of a person charged with a criminal offence to communicate with defence counsel without hindrance. That right is set forth, however, within the Council of Europe, in Article 93 of the Standard Minimum Rules for the Treatment of Prisoners[298] ... The Court considers that an accused's right to communicate with his advocate out of hearing of a third person is part of the basic requirements of a fair trial in a democratic society and follows

---

[290]   *IH and others v Austria* (2006) Application No 42780/98 (unreported), para 34.

[291]   *Sadak v Turkey* (2003) 36 EHRR 431, para 50.

[292]   *Albert and Le Compte v Belgium* (1982) 5 EHRR 533, para 41.

[293]   *Jespers v Belgium* 27 DR 61 (1981).

[294]   *Mayzit v Russia* (2005) Application No 63378/00 (unreported), para 70.

[295]   *Croissant v Germany* (1992) 16 EHRR 135, para 27.

[296]   *Artico v Italy* (1980) 3 EHRR 1, para 36 ('Admittedly, a State cannot be held responsible for every shortcoming on the part of a lawyer appointed for legal aid purposes but, in the particular circumstances, it was for the competent Italian authorities to take steps to ensure that the applicant enjoyed effectively the right to which they had recognised he was entitled').

[297]   (1991) 14 EHRR 670, para 48.

[298]   Article 93 of the Standard Minimum Rules for the Treatment of Prisoners states that 'An untried prisoner shall be entitled, as soon as he is imprisoned, to choose his legal representative, or shall be allowed to apply for free legal aid where such aid is available, and to receive visits from his legal adviser with a view to his defence and to prepare and hand to him, and to receive, confidential instructions. At his request he shall be given all necessary facilities for this purpose. In particular, he shall be given the free assistance of an interpreter for all essential contacts with the administration and for his defence. Interviews between the prisoner and his legal adviser may be within sight but not within hearing, either direct or indirect, of a police or institution official.'

from Article 6 para 3(c) of the Convention. If a lawyer were unable to confer with his client and receive confidential instructions from him without such surveillance, his assistance would lose much of its usefulness, whereas the Convention is intended to guarantee rights that are practical and effective.'

Legal Aid in Criminal Proceedings[299]

16.119   The provision of legal aid in criminal proceedings will be considered from the perspective of both Art 6(3)(c) and Art 6(1) of the ECHR.[300] Where the deprivation of liberty is at stake, in principle the interests of justice call for legal representation. The complexity of the applicable law in a given case will likewise be relevant. Taken together, these factors may compel the provision of legal aid in criminal proceedings having regard to the demands of Arts 6(1) and 6(3)(c) of the ECHR.[301] In *RD v Poland*[302] the European Court of Human Rights stated:

'The Court reiterates that the right of an accused to free legal assistance, laid down in Article 6(3)(c) of the Convention, is one of the elements inherent in the notion of fair trial. That provision attaches two conditions to this right. The first is lack of 'sufficient means to pay for legal assistance', the second is that 'the interests of justice' must require that such assistance be given free. While the manner in which Article 6 is to be applied to courts of appeal or of cassation depends on the special features of the proceedings in question, there can be no doubt that a State which does institute such courts is required to ensure that persons amenable to the law shall enjoy before them the fundamental guarantees of fair trial contained in that Article, including the right to free legal assistance. In discharging that obligation, the State must, moreover, display diligence so as to secure to those persons the genuine and effective enjoyment of the rights guaranteed under Article 6.'[303]

(iv)   ECHR, Art 6(3)(d) – Right to Call and Examine Witnesses

16.120   The right to call and examine witnesses under Art 6(3)(d) of the Convention has been described as a prima facie prohibition on the admission of hearsay evidence.[304] The national authorities have a considerable margin of appreciation in deciding whether or not to call a witness.[305] There may however be exceptional circumstances which could prompt the European Court of Human Rights to conclude that the failure to hear a person as a witness was incompatible with Article 6 of the ECHR.[306] The term 'witness' has an 'autonomous' meaning in the Convention system.[307] The right to call and examine witnesses pursuant to Art 6(3)(d) of the ECHR implies a right to have the information necessary to do so.[308]

---

[299]   See also **16.86** above.
[300]   *Benham v United Kingdom* (1996) 22 EHRR 293, para 52.
[301]   *Benham v United Kingdom* (1996) 22 EHRR 293, paras 61–64.
[302]   (2004) 39 EHRR 240, paras 43–44.
[303]   See also *Vaudelle v France* (2003) 37 EHRR 397 and *Beet v United Kingdom* (2005) 41 EHRR 441, para 38.
[304]   Lord Lester QC, Lord Pannick QC and Herberg, J *Human Rights Law and Practice* (2009) 3rd edn, LexisNexis, p 340. Note that the United Kingdom's domestic hearsay rules have been held as compatible with Art 6 of the ECHR (see *Trivedi v United Kingdom* [1997] EHRLR 520).
[305]   See *Doorson v Netherlands* (1996) 22 EHRR 330, para 67 ('The Court reiterates that the admissibility of evidence is primarily a matter for regulation by national law and as a general rule it is for the national courts to assess the evidence before them. The Court's task under the Convention is not to give a ruling as to whether statements of witnesses were properly admitted as evidence, but rather to ascertain whether the proceedings as a whole, including the way in which evidence was taken, were fair').
[306]   *Popov v Russia* (2006) Application No 26853/04 (unreported), paras 175–180.
[307]   *Lucà v Italy* (2003) 36 EHRR 46, para 41.
[308]   *Sadak v Turkey* (2003) 36 EHRR 431, para 65.

16.121   Article 6(1) taken together with Art 6(3) requires the Contracting States to take positive steps, in particular to enable the accused to examine or have examined witnesses against him. All the evidence must normally be produced at a public hearing, in the presence of the accused, with a view to adversarial argument.[309] There are exceptions to this principle however. As a general rule Arts 6(1) and 6(3)(d) cannot be interpreted as requiring in all cases that questions be put directly by the accused or his lawyer, whether by means of cross-examination or by any other means, but rather that the accused must be given an adequate and proper opportunity to challenge and question a witness against him, either when he makes his statements or at a later stage.[310] The statement of a witness does not always have to be made in court and in public if it is to be admitted as evidence. The opportunity to confront the witness need not necessarily be at the trial.[311] However, where a conviction is based solely or to a decisive degree on depositions that have been made by a person whom the accused has had no opportunity to examine or have examined, whether during the investigation or at the trial, the rights of the defence are restricted to an extent that is incompatible with the guarantees provided by Art 6 of the ECHR.[312]

Children and the Right to Call and Examine Witnesses

16.122   The fact that the relevant witness is a child will not relieve a State party from its obligations under Art 6(3)(d) of the ECHR although modifications to procedures are permitted to ensure the welfare of the child witness.[313] The impact of such modifications must not undermine the accused's right to a fair trial and must be counterbalanced by procedures to ensure this.[314] In *AS v Finland*[315] the European Court of Human Rights observed as follows in relation to the giving evidence by victims of sexual abuse:

> 'The Court would add that criminal proceedings concerning sexual offences are often perceived as an ordeal by the victim, in particular when the latter is unwillingly confronted with the defendant. These features are even more prominent in a case involving a minor. In

---

[309]   *AS v Finland* (2010) Application No 40156/07.

[310]   *Kostovski v Netherlands* (1989) 12 EHRR 434, paras 40–41. Note however that the right does not mean that in order to be used as evidence statements of witnesses should always be made at a public hearing in court provided the rights of the defence have been respected para 41. See also *AS v Finland* (2010) Application No 40156/07.

[311]   *Kostovski v Netherlands* (1989) 12 EHRR 434, para 41.

[312]   *PS v Germany* (2003) 36 EHRR 1139, para 24 concerning the giving of evidence by children who have made allegations of sexual abuse.

[313]   *Bocos-Cuesta v Netherlands* (2005) Application No 54789/00, para 71.

[314]   See *Doorson v Netherlands* (1996) 22 EHRR 330, para 72 ('The maintenance of the anonymity of the witnesses Y.15 and Y.16 presented the defence with difficulties which criminal proceedings should not normally involve. Nevertheless, no violation of Article 6, para 1 taken together with Article 6, para 3(d) of the Convention can be found if it is established that the handicaps under which the defence laboured were sufficiently counterbalanced by the procedures followed by the judicial authorities') and *Van Mechelen v Netherlands* (1997) 25 EHRR 647, para 54. In light of the European jurisprudence on this issue in *R v Camberwell Green Youth Court ex p D (a minor) (by his mother and litigation friend)* [2005] UKHL 4, [2005] 1 WLR 393, para 49 Baroness Hale held in relation to the special measures implemented to protect child witnesses pursuant to the Youth Justice and Criminal Evidence Act 1999, s 21(5) that 'All the evidence is produced at the trial in the presence of the accused, some of it in pre-recorded form and some of it by contemporaneous television transmission. The accused can see and hear it all. The accused has every opportunity to challenge and question the witnesses against him at the trial itself. The only thing missing is a face to face confrontation, but the appellants accept that the Convention does not guarantee a right to face to face confrontation. This case is completely different from the case of anonymous witnesses. Even then the Strasbourg Court has accepted that exceptions may be made, provided that sufficient steps are taken to counter-balance the handicaps under which the defence laboured and a conviction is not based solely or decisively on anonymous statements.' See also *R v A (No 2)* [2001] UKHL 25, [2002] 1 AC 45 and *R v Davis* [2008] UKHL 36, [2008] 1 AC 1128.

[315]   (2010) Application No 40156/07, paras 55–56.

the assessment of whether or not in such proceedings an accused received a fair trial, account must be taken of the right to respect for the private life of the alleged victim. Therefore, the Court accepts that in criminal proceedings concerning sexual abuse, certain measures may be taken for the purpose of protecting the victim, provided that such measures can be reconciled with an adequate and effective exercise of the rights of the defence. In securing the rights of the defence, the judicial authorities may be required to take measures which counterbalance the handicaps under which the defence labours ... In acknowledging the need to strike a balance between the rights of the defendant and those of the alleged child victim, the Court finds that the following minimum guarantees must be in place: the suspected person shall be informed of the hearing of the child, he or she shall be given an opportunity to observe that hearing, either as it is being conducted or later from an audiovisual recording, and to have questions put to the child, either directly or indirectly, in the course of the first hearing or on a later occasion.'

(v)   ECHR, Art 6(3)(e) – Right to Free Assistance of Interpreter.

16.123   The right to the free assistance from an interpreter is absolute.[316] The verification of the applicant's need for interpretation facilities is a matter for the judge to determine in consultation with the accused and, in the absence of apparent need, to reassure him or herself that the absence of an interpreter will not prejudice the accused's full involvement in a matter of crucial importance.[317] The right applies not only to oral statements made at the trial hearing but also to documentary material and the pre-trial proceedings. This means that an accused who cannot understand or speak the language used in court has the right to the free assistance of an interpreter for the translation or interpretation of all those documents or statements in the proceedings instituted against him which it is necessary for him to understand or to have rendered into the court's language in order to have the benefit of a fair trial.[318] Note however that Art 6(3)(e) does not compel a written translation of all items of written evidence or official documents in the procedure. The interpretation assistance provided should be such as to enable the defendant to have knowledge of the case against him and to defend himself, most importantly by being able to put before the court his version of the events.[319]

Age of Criminal Responsibility and the ECHR

16.124   Article 6 of the ECHR is silent as to the minimum age of criminal responsibility, primarily by reason of the lack of consistency across Europe on this fundamental issue. In *V v United Kingdom*[320] the European Court of Human Rights observed in relation to the imposition by the United Kingdom of an age of criminal responsibility of 10 years old that:

'In this connection, the Court observes that, at the present time there is not yet a commonly accepted minimum age for the imposition of criminal responsibility in Europe. While most of the Contracting States have adopted an age-limit which is higher than that in force in England and Wales, other States, such as Cyprus, Ireland, Liechtenstein and Switzerland, attribute criminal responsibility from a younger age. Moreover, no clear tendency can be ascertained from examination of the relevant international texts and instruments. Rule 4 of the Beijing Rules which, although not legally binding, might provide some indication of the existence of an international consensus, does not specify the age at which criminal responsibility should be fixed but merely invites States not to fix it too low, and Article 40(3)(a) of the UN Convention [on the Rights of the Child] requires States Parties to

---

[316]   *Luedicke, Belkacem and Koç v Germany* (1978) 2 EHRR 149, para 40.
[317]   *Cuscani v United Kingdom* (2002) 36 EHRR 11, paras 38–40.
[318]   *Hermi v Italy* (2008) 46 EHRR 1115, para 69.
[319]   *Hermi v Italy* (2008) 46 EHRR 1115, para 70.
[320]   (1999) 30 EHRR 121.

establish a minimum age below which children shall be presumed not to have the capacity to infringe the criminal law, but contains no provision as to what that age should be. The Court does not consider that there is at this stage any clear common standard amongst the member States of the Council of Europe as to the minimum age of criminal responsibility. Even if England and Wales is among the few European jurisdictions to retain a low age of criminal responsibility, the age of ten cannot be said to be so young as to differ disproportionately from the age-limit followed by other European States. The Court concludes that the attribution of criminal responsibility to the applicant does not in itself give rise to a breach of Article 3 of the Convention.'[321]

ECHR, Art 7

16.125   Article 7 of the ECHR provides as follows in relation to the requirement for non-retroactive penal laws:

'1. No one shall be held guilty of any criminal offence on account of any act or omission which did not constitute a criminal offence under national or international law at the time when it was committed. Nor shall a heavier penalty be imposed than the one that was applicable at the time the criminal offence was committed.

2 This article shall not prejudice the trial and punishment of any person for any act or omission which, at the time when it was committed, was criminal according to the general principles of law recognised by civilised nations.'[322]

16.126   Article 7 prohibits the retrospective application of the penal law and sentencing law.[323] Art 7 of the ECHR is not confined to prohibiting the retrospective application of the criminal law to the accused disadvantage but also embodies more generally the principle that only the law can define a crime and prescribe a penalty.[324] There can be no

---

[321]   See also *SC v United Kingdom* (2004) 40 EHRR 10, para 27 ('The Court observes, firstly, that the attribution of criminal responsibility to, or the trial on criminal charges of, an 11-year-old child does not in itself give rise to a breach of the Convention, as long as he or she is able to participate effectively in the trial'). Note however that in *V v United Kingdom* Judges Pastor Ridruejo, Ress, Makarczyk, Tulkens and Butkevych gave a joint partly dissenting judgment in which they held that 'As far as the age of criminal responsibility is concerned, we do not accept the conclusion of the Court that no clear tendency can be ascertained from the development amongst European States and from international instruments. Only four Contracting States out of forty-one are prepared to find criminal responsibility at an age as low as, or lower than, that applicable in England and Wales. We have no doubt that there is a general standard amongst the member States of the Council of Europe under which there is a system of relative criminal responsibility beginning at the age of thirteen or fourteen – with special court procedures for juveniles – and providing for full criminal responsibility at the age of eighteen or above. Where children aged from ten to about thirteen or fourteen have committed crimes, educational measures are imposed to try to integrate the young offender into society. Even if Rule 4 of the 'Beijing Rules' does not specify a minimum age of criminal responsibility, the very warning that the age should not be fixed too low indicates that criminal responsibility and maturity are related concepts. It is clearly the view of the vast majority of the Contracting States that this kind of maturity is not present in children below the age of thirteen or fourteen.' See also Gil-Robles, A *Report by Mr Alvaro Gil-Robles, Commissioner for Human Rights on his visit to the United Kingdom* (2005) Comm DH 6 Council of Europe, para 105.
[322]   The two paragraphs of Article 7 are interlinked and are to be interpreted in a concordant manner (*Kononov v Latvia* (2010) Application No 36376/04, para 186).
[323]   See *Waddington v Miah* [1974] 1 WLR 683 at 694 for consideration of Art 7 in a domestic context.
[324]   *Kokkinakis v Greece* (1993) 17 EHRR 397 at, para 52 ('The Court points out that Article 7, para 1 of the Convention is not confined to prohibiting the retrospective application of the criminal law to an accused's disadvantage. It also embodies, more generally, the principle that only the law can define a crime and prescribe a penalty (nullum crimen, nulla poena sine lege) and the principle that the criminal law must not be extensively construed to an accused's detriment, for instance by analogy; it follows from this that an offence must be clearly defined in law. This condition is satisfied where the individual can know from the wording of the relevant provision and, if need be, with the assistance of the courts' interpretation of it, what acts and omissions will make him liable'). The term 'law' in Art 7 of the ECHR was described in *Kononov v Latvia*

derogation from the prohibition on the retroactive application of penal laws.[325] Art 7 will only apply to criminal proceedings and not to extradition proceedings,[326] deportation,[327] internment[328] or generally to civil proceedings.[329] In *Kononov v Latvia*[330] the Grand Chamber described the guarantee enshrined in Art 7 of the ECHR as follows:

'The guarantee enshrined in Article 7, an essential element of the rule of law, occupies a prominent place in the Convention system of protection, as is underlined by the fact that no derogation from it is permissible under Article 15 in time of war or other public emergency. It should be construed and applied, as follows from its object and purpose, so as to provide effective safeguards against arbitrary prosecution, conviction and punishment. Accordingly, Article 7 is not confined to prohibiting the retrospective application of the criminal law to an accused's disadvantage: it also embodies, more generally, the principle that only the law can define a crime and prescribe a penalty (*nullum crimen, nulla poena sine lege*) and the principle that the criminal law must not be extensively construed to an accused's detriment, for instance by analogy. It follows that an offence must be clearly defined in law. This requirement is satisfied where the individual can know from the wording of the relevant provision – and, if need be, with the assistance of the courts' interpretation of it and with informed legal advice – what acts and omissions will make him criminally liable.'

16.127 The authorities on the application of Art 7 of the ECHR to children concentrate on sentencing. Notwithstanding the plain words of Art 7 that 'Nor shall a heavier penalty be imposed than the one that was applicable at the time the criminal offence was committed' both the European Court of Human Rights and the domestic course have held that there is no violation of Art 7 where a child is sentenced on the basis of the sentencing tariff applicable at the date of sentence as opposed to that applicable at the date of the commission of the offence. In *Taylor v United Kingdom*[331] the European Commission rejected a claim by a 15-year-old boy that his custodial sentence at the age of 15 for a crime he committed when aged 14, at which age a custodial sentence would not have been available, violated Art 7 of the ECHR. The Commission reached its decision on the basis that the child must have been aware that the proceedings against him may conclude after his 15th birthday and thus he would be liable to the custodial sentence applicable at that age. In the circumstances the Court held that the imposition of a custodial penalty on the applicant was prescribed by law in sufficiently clear and accessible terms and was applied to the applicant without any element of retrospectivity. In *R v Bowker*[332] the Court of Appeal applied these principles in upholding the heavier sentence of an offender who was under 18 at the time of the

---

(2010) Application No 36376/04, para 185 as follows: 'When speaking of "law", Article 7 alludes to the same concept as that to which the Convention refers elsewhere when using that term, a concept which comprises written and unwritten law and which implies qualitative requirements, notably those of accessibility and foreseeability. As regards foreseeability in particular, the Court recalls that however clearly drafted a legal provision may be in any system of law including criminal law, there is an inevitable element of judicial interpretation. There will always be a need for elucidation of doubtful points and for adaptation to changing circumstances. Indeed, in certain Convention States, the progressive development of the criminal law through judicial law-making is a well-entrenched and necessary part of legal tradition. Article 7 of the Convention cannot be read as outlawing the gradual clarification of the rules of criminal liability through judicial interpretation from case to case, provided that the resultant development is consistent with the essence of the offence and could reasonably be foreseen.'

[325] ECHR, Art 15(2).
[326] *X v Netherlands* 6 DR 184 (1976). See also *Soering v United Kingdom* (1989) 11 EHRR 439.
[327] *Moustaquim v Belgium* (1991) 13 EHRR 802, para 50.
[328] *Lawless v Ireland* (No 3) (1961) 1 EHRR 15.
[329] *X v Sweden* (1985) 9 EHRR 244.
[330] (2010) Application No 36376/04, para 185.
[331] (1999) Application No 48864/99 (unreported).
[332] (2008) 1 Cr App R (s) 72.

offence but over 18 at the time of sentence. Applying *Taylor v United Kingdom* and domestic authority,[333] the Court of Appeal held this did not violate Art 7 of the ECHR.

16.128 Whilst the Court in *R v Bowker* was keen to stress that the age of the child at the time of the commission of the offence would be relevant to judging the culpability of the child for the purpose of sentencing, the decisions in *Taylor v United Kingdom* and *R v Bowker* are hard to square with the plain wording of Art 7 of the ECHR. Article 7 provides that 'Nor shall a heavier penalty be imposed than the one that was applicable at the time the criminal offence was committed'. This must suggest that the applicable sentence is the one that could have been imposed by the sentencer on the child at the time the offence was committed and hence must take account of the age of the child at the time that the offence was committed where that factor is relevant to the sentence passed. This is the interpretation given to Art 7 by the Privy Council in *Flynn v HM Advocate*[334] and approved by the House of Lords in *R (on the application of Uttley) v Secretary of State for the Home Department*.[335] Whilst it may be argued that the penalties established by law for adults are still 'applicable' to the given offence at the time that offence is committed by a child, the undesirable results of the interpretation of Art 7 applied in *Taylor v United Kingdom* are best demonstrated in the context of crimes which still attract the death penalty for adults.[336] The interpretation of Art 7 in *Taylor v United Kingdom* opens up the possibility of a child committing a capital crime when under 18 but being liable to a sentence of death if sentenced for that crime after attaining the age of majority. Such a situation would plainly violate Art 37(a) of the CRC, the Committee on the Rights of the Child having made clear that under Art 37(a) that the death penalty may not be imposed for a crime committed by a person under 18 regardless of his/her age at the time of the trial or sentencing or of the execution of the sanction.[337] The execution as an adult of a person who committed a capital crime as a child would also violate an established norm of international customary law.[338]

ECHR Protocol No 7 Arts 2–4

16.129 Articles 2–4 of Protocol No 7 of the ECHR provide as follows in respect of the right to appeal in respect of a criminal conviction and sentence, the right to compensation for a miscarriage of justice and the right not to be tried or punished twice for the same crime:

ECHR, Art 2

---

[333] See *R v Ghafoor* [2002] All ER (D) 295 Jul; *R v Britton* [2007] 1 Cr App R (S) 121 and *R (on the application of Uttley) v Secretary of State for the Home Department* [2004] UKHL 38, [2004] 4 All ER 1.

[334] [2004] UKPC D1, [2004] SCCR 281 per Lord Carswell ('It seems to me difficult to escape the conclusion that the meaning of the provision is that the penalty which was 'applicable' at the time the criminal offence was committed is that which a sentencer could have imposed at that time, i e the maximum sentence then prescribed by law for the particular offence ... The object of the provision appears to have been to prevent a sentence being imposed which could not have been imposed at the time of the offence, because the maximum was then lower'). See also Baroness Hale, para 47 ('The question, as I believe all your lordships agree, is whether the penalty now legally applicable (and applied) to the offence is heavier than (or exceeds the limits of) the penalty which was legally applicable at the time it was committed').

[335] [2004] UKHL 38, [2004] 4 All ER 1, para 41 per Lord Roger. This case was cited to the Court of Appeal in *R v Bowker*.

[336] See **2.64** and **5.17** above.

[337] Committee on the Rights of the Child General Comment No 10 *Children's Rights in Juvenile Justice* CRC/C/GC/10 p 21, para 75. See also *The Michael Domingues Case*: Report on the Inter-American Commission on Human Rights, Report No 62/02, Merits, Case 12.285 (2002), para 84.

[338] *The Michael Domingues Case: Report on the Inter-American Commission on Human Rights*, Report No 62/02, Merits, Case 12.285 (2002), para 84.

'1. Everyone convicted of a criminal offence by a tribunal shall have the right to have his conviction or sentence reviewed by a higher tribunal. The exercise of this right, including the grounds on which it may be exercised, shall be governed by law.

2. This right may be subject to exceptions in regard to offences of a minor character,[339] as prescribed by law, or in cases in which the person concerned was tried in the first instance by the highest tribunal or was convicted following an appeal against acquittal.'[340]

ECHR, Art 3

'When a person has by a final decision been convicted of a criminal offence and when subsequently his conviction has been reversed, or he has been pardoned, on the ground that a new or newly discovered fact shows conclusively that there has been a miscarriage of justice, the person who has suffered punishment as a result of such conviction shall be compensated according to the law or the practice of the State concerned, unless it is proved that the non-disclosure of the unknown fact in time is wholly or partly attributable to him.'[341]

ECHR, Art 4

'1. No one shall be liable to be tried or punished again in criminal proceedings under the jurisdiction of the same State for an offence for which he has already been finally acquitted or convicted in accordance with the law and penal procedure of that State.

2. The provisions of the preceding paragraph shall not prevent the reopening of the case in accordance with the law and penal procedure of the State concerned, if there is evidence of new or newly discovered facts, or if there has been a fundamental defect in the previous proceedings, which could affect the outcome of the case.

3. No derogation from this Article shall be made under Article 15 of the Convention.'[342]

ECHR, Art 13

16.130 Article 13 of the ECHR provides as follows in respect to the right to an effective remedy before a national authority:

'Everyone whose rights and freedoms as set forth in this Convention are violated shall have an effective remedy before a national authority notwithstanding that the violation has been committed by persons acting in an official capacity.'

16.131 Pannick and others describe Art 13 as 'an autonomous principle of effective remedial protection that is subsidiary to the substantive rights protected by the Convention. It is the link between the Convention and the national legal systems, being the obligation on the international plane that requires states to provide domestic

---

[339] See Explanatory Memorandum to the Seventh Protocol CE Doc H(83)3, para 21.

[340] This provision have not yet been ratified by the United Kingdom and are not incorporated into the Human Rights Act 1998.

[341] The United Kingdom has not ratified this Art and it is not incorporated into the Human Rights Act 1998. Note however that Art 3 of Protocol No 7 of the ECHR follows the wording of Art 14(6) of the ICCPR which the United Kingdom has ratified. ICCPR, Art 14(6) is given effect in domestic law by s 133 of the Criminal Justice Act 1988 (see *R (Mullen) v Secretary of State for the Home Department* [2002] EWCA Civ 1882, [2003] QB 993). See also see Explanatory Memorandum to the Seventh Protocol CE Doc H(83)3, paras 22 and 23.

[342] See *X v Austria* 35 CD 151 (1970), *Nikitin v Russia* (2005) 41 EHRR 149 and *Zolotukhin v Russia* (2009) Application No 14939/03. See also *Connelly v DPP* [1964] AC 1254 HL

remedies to aggrieved citizens'.[343] Note that the Human Rights Act 1998 does not give effect to Art 13 in domestic law. However, the domestic courts have nonetheless continued to have regard to it.[344] In *Re S (Minors) (Care Order: Implementation of Care Plan); Re W (Minors) (Care Order: Adequacy of Care Plan)*[345] Lord Nicholls held that:

> 'However, I should elaborate a little further. In Convention terms, failure to provide an effective remedy for infringement of a right set out in the Convention is an infringement of Art 13. But Art 13 is not a Convention right as defined in s 1(1) of the Human Rights Act 1998. So legislation which fails to provide an effective remedy for infringement of Art 8 is not, for that reason, incompatible with a Convention right within the meaning of the Human Rights Act 1998. Where, then, does that leave the matter so far as English law is concerned? The domestic counterpart to Art 13 is ss 7 and 8 of the Human Rights Act 1998, read in conjunction with s 6. This domestic counterpart to Art 13 takes a different form from Art 13 itself. Unlike Art 13, which declares a right ("Everyone whose rights ... are violated shall have an effective remedy"), ss 7 and 8 of the Human Rights Act 1998 provide a remedy. Article 13 guarantees the availability at the national level of an effective remedy to enforce the substance of Convention rights. Sections 7 and 8 seek to provide that remedy in this country. The object of these sections is to provide in English law the very remedy Art 13 declares is the entitlement of everyone whose rights are violated.'

16.132 The effect of Art 13 is to require the provision of a domestic remedy allowing the competent national authority both to deal with the substance of the relevant Convention complaint and to grant appropriate relief.[346] The remedy need not be a judicial remedy[347] but a judicial remedy will usually satisfy Art 13 of the ECHR.[348] The concept of sufficiency requires that the remedial body is sufficiently independent of the national body which is challenged and the authority's powers are sufficiently strong to provide redress.[349] Art 13 requires that the applicant be permitted to put forward the substance of his or her Convention claim[350] and the remedy must be available in practice not just in theory.[351] The place of Article 13 in the scheme of human rights protection set up by the Convention would argue in favour of implied restrictions of Art 13 being

---

[343] Lord Lester QC, Lord Pannick QC and Herberg, J *Human Rights Law and Practice* (2009) 3rd edn, LexisNexis, p 565.

[344] *Brown v Stott* [2003] 1 AC 681 at 715D–715E per Lord Hope ('Article 13 of the convention provides that everyone whose rights and freedoms as set forth in the convention are violated shall have an effective remedy before a national authority. This article is not one of the convention rights to which effect is given by the Human Rights Act, but it has not been overlooked. The reason which was given for its omission from the articles set out in Sch 1 to that Act was that ss 7–9 of the Human Rights Act were intended to lay down an appropriate remedial structure for giving effect to the convention rights as defined by s 1(1) of that Act').

[345] [2002] UKHL 10, [2002] 2 AC 291, paras 60 and 61.

[346] Lord Lester QC, Lord Pannick QC and Herberg, J *Human Rights Law and Practice* (2009) 3rd edn, LexisNexis, p 565. See *DP and JC v United Kingdom*, para 134 ('The court reiterates that Art 13 of the Convention guarantees the availability at the national level of a remedy to enforce the substance of the Convention rights and freedoms in whatever form they might happen to be secured in the domestic legal order. The effect of Art 13 is thus to require the provision of a domestic remedy to deal with the substance of an 'arguable complaint' under the Convention and to grant appropriate relief, although Contracting States are afforded some discretion as to the manner in which they conform to their Convention obligations under this provision. The scope of the obligation under Art 13 varies depending on the nature of the applicant's complaint under the Convention. Nevertheless, the remedy required by Art 13 must be 'effective' in practice as well as in law').

[347] *Leander v Sweden* (1987) 9 EHRR 433, para 77 and *Chahal v United Kingdom* (1996) 23 EHRR 413, para 152.

[348] *The Greek Case* 12 YB 1 (1996) at 174.

[349] Lord Lester QC, Lord Pannick QC and Herberg, J *Human Rights Law and Practice* (2009) 3rd edn, LexisNexis, p 571.

[350] *Soering v United Kingdom* (1989) 11 EHRR 439, para 122 and *Vilvarajah v United Kingdom* (1991) 14 EHRR 248, paras 117–127

[351] *Airey v Ireland* (1979) 2 EHRR 305, *Aksoy v Turkey* (1996) 23 EHRR 553, para 95 and *Klass v Germany* (1978) 2 EHRR 213, para 64

kept to a minimum.[352] The more important the Convention right invoked the more effective must be the remedy.[353] A breach of Art 13 cannot amount to a freestanding violation separate from the violation of another right under the Convention. There can however be a breach of Art 13 absent any other breaches of Convention Rights.[354]

16.133 In *Silver v United Kingdom*[355] the European Court of Human Rights set out the following principles of application in relation to Art 13 of the ECHR:

(a) where an individual has an arguable claim to be the victim of a violation of the rights set forth in the ECHR, he should have a remedy before a national authority in order both to have his claim decided and, if appropriate, to obtain redress;

(b) the authority referred to in Art 13 may not necessarily be a judicial authority but, if it is not, its powers and the guarantees which it affords are relevant in determining whether the remedy before it is effective;

(c) although no single remedy may itself entirely satisfy the requirements of Art 13 the aggregate of remedies provided for under domestic law may do;

(d) neither Art 13 nor the ECHR in general lays down for the States parties any given manner for ensuring within their internal law the effective implementation of any of the provisions of the ECHR, for example, by incorporating the Convention into domestic law. The application of Art 13 in a given case will thus depend upon the manner in which the State party concerned has chosen to discharge its obligation under Art 1 directly to secure to anyone within its jurisdiction the rights and freedoms set out in section.[356]

The Child's Right to Fair and Equal Treatment under the Law under European Union Law

16.134 Article 47 of the European Charter on Fundamental Rights provides as follows in respect of the right to an effective remedy and to a fair trial:

'Everyone whose rights and freedoms guaranteed by the law of the Union are violated has the right to an effective remedy before a tribunal in compliance with the conditions laid down in this Article.

Everyone is entitled to a fair and public hearing within a reasonable time by an independent and impartial tribunal previously established by law. Everyone shall have the possibility of being advised, defended and represented.

---

[352] *Kudla v Poland* (2002) 35 EHRR 198, para 152.
[353] *Klass v Germany* (1978) 2 EHRR 214, para 55 and *Z v United Kingdom* (2002) 34 EHRR 97, para 109.
[354] *Bubbins v United Kingdom* (2005) 41 EHRR 458, paras 169–173.
[355] (1983) 5 EHRR 347, para 113.
[356] Note *Z and others v United Kingdom* (2001) 34 EHRR 97, para 109 ('Where alleged failure by the authorities to protect persons from the acts of others is concerned, Art 13 may not always require that the authorities undertake the responsibility for investigating the allegations. There should however be available to the victim or the victim's family a mechanism for establishing any liability of State officials or bodies for acts or omissions involving the breach of their rights under the Convention. Furthermore, in the case of a breach of Arts 2 and 3 of the Convention, which rank as the most fundamental provisions of the Convention, compensation for the non-pecuniary damage flowing from the breach should in principle be available as part of the range of redress'). See also *TP and KM v United Kingdom* (2001) 34 EHRR 42, para 109.

Legal aid shall be made available to those who lack sufficient resources in so far as such aid is necessary to ensure effective access to justice.'

16.135   Article 48 of the Charter provides that everyone who has been charged shall be presumed innocent until proved guilty according to law and that respect for the rights of the defence of anyone who has been charged shall be guaranteed. Article 49 of the Charter prohibits retrospective criminal and sentencing legislation[357] and provides that the severity of penalties must be proportionate to the criminal offence.[358] Art 50 of the European Charter provides that no one shall be liable to be tried or punished twice for the same offence within the European Union.

16.136   In accordance with Art 52(3) of the European Charter[359] the meaning and scope of the rights under the Charter set about above will be taken to be the same as that under the corresponding rights enshrined in the ECHR and its related protocols. As such, the interpretation and application of the relevant provisions of the ECHR will be applicable to the corresponding rights enshrined in the European Charter.

The Child's Right to Fair and Equal Treatment under the Law under other Regional Instruments

The American Convention on Human Rights[360]

16.137   Article 8 of the American Convention on Human Rights provides as follows in respect of the right to a fair trial:

'1. Every person has the right to a hearing, with due guarantees and within a reasonable time, by a competent, independent, and impartial tribunal, previously established by law, in the substantiation of any accusation of a criminal nature made against him or for the determination of his rights and obligations of a civil, labor, fiscal, or any other nature.

2. Every person accused of a criminal offense has the right to be presumed innocent so long as his guilt has not been proven according to law. During the proceedings, every person is entitled, with full equality, to the following minimum guarantees:

   a.   the right of the accused to be assisted without charge by a translator or interpreter, if he does not understand or does not speak the language of the tribunal or court;
   b.   prior notification in detail to the accused of the charges against him;

---

[357]   Article 49(2).
[358]   Article 49(3).
[359]   Article 52(3) of the Charter provides that 'Insofar as this Charter contains rights which correspond to rights guaranteed by the Convention for the Protection of Human Rights and Fundamental Freedoms, the meaning and scope of those rights shall be the same as those laid down by the said Convention. This provision shall not prevent Union law providing more extensive protection.'
[360]   See also Art 13 of the Ibero-American Convention on the Rights of Youth ('1.The States Parties recognise the right of youth to justice. This implies the right to report, audience, defence, fair and decent treatment, free justice, equal rights before law and all the guarantees of the corresponding procedure. 2. The States Parties shall take such measures as may be necessary to guarantee a legal procedure which takes into account the young condition, makes the exercise of this right real and includes all the guarantees of the corresponding procedure. 3. Youth charged with a criminal offence have the right to a decent treatment which stimulates their respect for human rights and takes account of their age and the need to promote their re-socialisation through alternative measures to the application of the penalty. 4. In all cases in which young minors are in conflict with the law, the rules of the corresponding procedure and effective legal guardianship shall be applied according to the rules and principles recognised under the International Law on Human Rights. 5. The States Parties shall take measures to ensure that the youth who are imprisoned have space and decent human conditions in the penal institution').

c. adequate time and means for the preparation of his defense;

d. the right of the accused to defend himself personally or to be assisted by legal counsel of his own choosing, and to communicate freely and privately with his counsel;

e. the inalienable right to be assisted by counsel provided by the state, paid or not as the domestic law provides, if the accused does not defend himself personally or engage his own counsel within the time period established by law;

f. the right of the defense to examine witnesses present in the court and to obtain the appearance, as witnesses, of experts or other persons who may throw light on the facts;

g. the right not to be compelled to be a witness against himself or to plead guilty; and

h. the right to appeal the judgment to a higher court.

3. A confession of guilt by the accused shall be valid only if it is made without coercion of any kind.

4. An accused person acquitted by a non-appealable judgment shall not be subjected to a new trial for the same cause.

5. Criminal proceedings shall be public, except insofar as may be necessary to protect the interests of justice.'[361]

16.138   The Advisory Opinion of the Inter-American Court of Human Rights on the Legal Status and Human Rights of the Child[362] provides extensive guidance on judicial and administrative proceedings concerning children within the context of the American Convention on Human Rights.

ACHR – Minimum Age of Criminal Responsibility

16.139   The Inter-American Court of Human Rights notes in its Advisory Opinion that the concept of the minimum age of criminal responsibility is a generic legal assessment, one that does not examine the specific conditions of the minors on a case by case basis, but rather excludes them completely from the sphere of criminal justice.[363] The Court does not in its Advisory Opinion proffer any view as to the appropriate age of criminal responsibility for the purposes of the American Convention on Human Rights. It should be noted however that the Advisory Opinion appears to suggest that children should be excluded from having to participate as defendants in criminal trials.[364]

---

[361] See also Art 25 of the ACHR which enshrines the right to judicial protection ('Everyone has the right to simple and prompt recourse, or any other effective recourse, to a competent court or tribunal for protection against acts that violate his fundamental rights recognised by the constitution or laws of the state concerned or by this Convention, even though such violation may have been committed by persons acting in the course of their official duties.'), Art 9 which enshrines the right to freedom from *ex post facto* laws ('No one shall be convicted of any act or omission that did not constitute a criminal offense, under the applicable law, at the time it was committed. A heavier penalty shall not be imposed than the one that was applicable at the time the criminal offense was committed. If subsequent to the commission of the offense the law provides for the imposition of a lighter punishment, the guilty person shall benefit therefrom') and Art 10 which stipulates the right to compensation for miscarriages of justice ('Every person has the right to be compensated in accordance with the law in the event he has been sentenced by a final judgment through a miscarriage of justice. See further Art 7(5) ('Any person detained shall be brought promptly before a judge or other officer authorised by law to exercise judicial power and shall be entitled to trial within a reasonable time …').

[362] Advisory Opinion OC-17/2002.

[363] Advisory Opinion OC-17/2002, para 105.

[364] Advisory Opinion OC-17/2002, para 131. The wording of this passage of the Opinion is difficult to interpret. It is unclear whether the Court meant that children should not be the subject of criminal proceedings or that children should not participate in such proceedings by way of attendance at court. The final sentence of para 131 ('Therefore, there should be no possibility of their rendering testimony that might correspond to the evidentiary category of an admission of guilt') tends to support the former interpretation.

16.140 Note also that the Inter-American Court also examined in its Advisory Opinion what may and what may not be considered 'criminal' behaviour by children, noting as follows:[365]

> 'It is unacceptable to include in [the definition of criminal conduct] the situation of minors who have not incurred in conduct defined by law as a crime, but who are at risk or endangered, due to destitution, abandonment, extreme poverty or disease, and even less so those others who simply behave differently from how the majority does, those who differ from the generally accepted patterns of behavior, who are involved in conflicts regarding adaptation to the family, school, or social milieu, generally, or who alienate themselves from the customs and values of their society. The concept of crime committed by children or juvenile crime can only be applied to those who fall under the first aforementioned situation, that is, those who incur in conduct legally defined as a crime, not to those who are in the other situations.'

ACHR – Prevention and Diversion

16.141 The Inter-American Court has also emphasised the need for alternative methods of dealing with children who are in conflict with the law having regard to the provision of Art 19 of the ACHR which provides that 'Every minor has the right to measures of protection required by his condition as a minor on the part of his family, society and the state'. In the context, the Court stated in its Advisory Opinion that:[366]

> 'International standards seek to exclude or reduce 'judicialisation' of social problems that affect children, which can and must be resolved, in many cases, through various types of measures, pursuant to Article 19 of the American Convention, but without altering or diminishing the rights of individual persons. In this regard, alternative means to solve controversies are fully admissible, insofar as they allow equitable decisions to be reached without detriment to individuals' rights. Therefore, it is necessary to regulate use of alternative means in an especially careful manner in those cases where the interests of minors are at stake.'

ACHR – Due Process and Children

16.142 The Inter-American Court notes in its Advisory Opinion that the principles and acts of legal due process are an irreducible and strict set.[367] The Court has made clear that the rules of due process apply not only to judicial proceedings but to any other proceedings conducted by the State.[368] The Court concludes in its Advisory Opinion that the child benefits equally from the fundamental principles of due process.[369] This will include the right to remain silent, the right to assistance from legal counsel, the right

---

[365] Advisory Opinion OC-17/2002, para 110. Note however that in dealing with issues that do not have the character of criminal acts the 'principles and provisions pertaining to due legal process must also be respected in such cases, both regarding minors and with respect to those who have rights in connection with them, derived from family statute, also taking into account the specific conditions of the children' (Advisory Opinion OC-17/2002 Chapter X, para 12).

[366] Advisory Opinion OC-17/2002, para 135. See also Advisory Opinion OC-17/2002, Chapter X, para 13 ('it is possible to resort to alternative paths to solve controversies regarding children, but it is necessary to regulate application of such alternative measures in an especially careful manner to ensure that they do not alter or diminish their rights').

[367] Advisory Opinion OC-17/2002, para 115.

[368] *Ivcher Bronstein Case*, February 6, 2001 Judgment Series C No 74, paras 102–104; *Baena Ricardo et al. Case*. February 2, 2001 Judgment Series C No 72, paras 124–126; *Constitutional Court Case*, January 31, 2001 Judgment Series C No 71, paras 69–71

[369] Advisory Opinion OC-17/2002 Chapter X, para 10 ('in judicial or administrative procedures where decisions are adopted on the rights of children, the principles and rules of due legal process must be respected. This includes rules regarding competent, independent, and impartial courts previously established by law, courts of review, presumption of innocence, the presence of both parties to an action, the right to a hearing and to

to make a statement before the authority legally empowered to receive it[370] and the right to be present in defence of his or her rights and interests.[371]

16.143   The Inter-American Court of Human Rights states that the rights and freedoms inherent in the human person, the guarantees applicable to them and the rule of law form a triad and that each component thereof defines itself, complements and depends on the others for its meaning.[372] Noting that these fundamental values include safeguarding children so as to ensure the exercise of their rights within the family, in society and with respect to the State, the Inter-American Court has stated that they must be reflected in regulation of judicial or administrative proceedings where decisions are reached regarding children's rights and, when appropriate, those of the persons under whose custody or guardianship they find themselves.[373] In this context, the Court notes that certain specific procedural measures must be adopted in respect of children because:[374]

> 'It is evident that a child participates in proceedings under different conditions from those of an adult. To argue otherwise would disregard reality and omit adoption of special measures for protection of children, to their grave detriment. Therefore, it is indispensable to recognise and respect differences in treatment which correspond to different situations among those participating in proceedings.'

16.144   Within this context, the Inter-American Court stipulates that children under 18 who are accused of conduct defined as crimes by penal law must be subject, for the case to be heard and appropriate measures to be taken, only to specific jurisdictional bodies different from those for adults.[375] The Court has further stated that decision makers must be especially careful when assessing the evidence of a child.[376]

ACHR – Child's Participation in Proceedings

16.145   In relation to the participation of children in judicial and administrative proceedings concerning them, the Inter-American Court notes that, by reason of the principle of evolving capacity, the degree of participation of a child in the proceedings must be reasonably adjusted, so as to attain effective protection of his or her best interests.[377] The aim, having regard to the child's specific conditions and his or her best interests, must be to seek as much access as possible by the child to examination of his or her own case.[378]

---

defense, taking into account the particularities derived from the specific situation of children and those that are reasonably projected, among other matters, on personal intervention in said proceedings and protective measures indispensable during such proceedings').

[370]   Advisory Opinion OC-17/2002, para 129.
[371]   Advisory Opinion OC-17/2002, para 132.
[372]   *Habeas Corpus in Emergency Situations* (Arts 27(2), 25(1) and 7(6), *American Convention on Human Rights* Advisory Opinion OC-8/87 of January 30, 1987 Series A No 8, para 26.
[373]   Advisory Opinion OC-17/2002, para 94.
[374]   Advisory Opinion OC-17/2002, para 96.
[375]   Advisory Opinion OC-17/2002, para 109. The Court concluded its Advisory Opinion on this issue by stating that 'children under 18 to whom criminal conduct is imputed must be subject to different courts than those for adults. Characteristics of State intervention in the case of minors who are offenders must be reflected in the composition and functioning of these courts, as well as in the nature of the measures they can adopt' (Advisory Opinion OC-17/2002 Chapter X, para 11).
[376]   Advisory Opinion OC-17/2002, para 130.
[377]   Advisory Opinion OC-17/2002, para 101.
[378]   Advisory Opinion OC-17/2002, para 102.

ACHR – Children and Public Proceedings

16.146 The Court has made clear that in respect of proceedings concerning children that it is appropriate to set certain limits to the broad principle of the public nature of the proceedings that applies to other cases.[379] It considers that the limits should take into account the best interests of the child, insofar as they protect him or her from opinions, judgments or stigmatisation that may have a substantial bearing on his or her future life.[380]

The African Charter on the Rights and Welfare on the Child[381]

16.147 Article 17(1) of the African Charter on the Rights and Welfare of the Child provides as follows in respect of children accused of having infringed the penal law:

> 'Every child accused or found guilty of having infringed penal law shall have the right to special treatment in a manner consistent with the child's sense of dignity and worth and which reinforces the child's respect for human rights and fundamental freedoms of others.'

Article 17(2)(c)(i) of the Charter requires that every child accused of having infringed the penal law shall be presumed innocent until duly recognised guilty. Pursuant to Art 17(2)(c)(ii) the child shall be shall be informed promptly in a language that he understands and in detail of the charge against him, and shall be entitled to the assistance of an interpreter if he or she cannot understand the language used and, pursuant to Art 17(2)(c)(iii) shall be afforded legal and other appropriate assistance in the preparation and presentation of his or her defence. The matter shall be determined as speedily as possible by an impartial tribunal pursuant to Art 17(2)(c)(iv) which article also enshrines a right of appeal upon conviction. Article 17(2)(d) of the African Charter requires that the press and public be prohibited from attending the trial of a child. Article 17(4) requires that 'There shall be a minimum age below which children shall be presumed not have the capacity to infringe the penal law'.

Revised Arab Charter on Human Rights

16.148 Article 13 of the Revised Arab Charter on Human Rights provides as follows in respect of the right to a fair trial:

> '1. Everyone has the right to a fair trial that affords adequate guarantees before a competent, independent and impartial court that has been constituted by law to hear any criminal charge against him or to decide on his rights or his obligations. Each State party shall guarantee to those without the requisite financial resources legal aid to enable them to defend their rights.

---

[379] Advisory Opinion OC-17/2002, para 134.

[380] Advisory Opinion OC-17/2002, para 134.

[381] See also Art 7 of the African Charter on Human and Peoples Rights ('1. Every individual shall have the right to have his cause heard. This comprises: (a) the right to an appeal to competent national organs against acts of violating his fundamental rights as recognised and guaranteed by conventions, laws, regulations and customs in force; (b) the right to be presumed innocent until proved guilty by a competent court or tribunal; (c) the right to defense, including the right to be defended by counsel of his choice; (d) the right to be tried within a reasonable time by an impartial court or tribunal. 2. No one may be condemned for an act or omission which did not constitute a legally punishable offence at the time it was committed. No penalty may be inflicted for an offence for which no provision was made at the time it was committed. Punishment is personal and can be imposed only on the offender').

2. Trials shall be public, except in exceptional cases that may be warranted by the interests of justice in a society that respects human freedoms and rights.'[382]

16.149 Article 16 of the Revised Arab Charter provides enshrines the detailed due process rights in relation to any person charged with a criminal offence, stating that:

'Everyone charged with a criminal offence shall be presumed innocent until proved guilty by a final judgment rendered according to law and, in the course of the investigation and trial, he shall enjoy the following minimum guarantees:

1. The right to be informed promptly, in detail and in a language which he understands, of the charges against him.

2. The right to have adequate time and facilities for the preparation of his defense and to be allowed to communicate with his family.

3. The right to be tried in his presence before an ordinary court and to defend himself in person or through a lawyer of his own choosing with whom he can communicate freely and confidentially.

4. The right to the free assistance of a lawyer who will defend him if he cannot defend himself or if the interests of justice so require, and the right to the free assistance of an interpreter if he cannot understand or does not speak the language used in court.

5. The right to examine or have his lawyer examine the prosecution witnesses and to on defense according to the conditions applied to the prosecution witnesses.

6. The right not to be compelled to testify against himself or to confess guilt.

7. The right, if convicted of the crime, to file an appeal in accordance with the law before a higher tribunal.

8. The right to respect for his security of person and his privacy in all circumstances.'

16.150 Within the context of the cardinal rights enshrined within Arts 13, 15, 16 and 19 of the Revised Arab Charter on Human Rights, Art 17 makes specific provision in respect of any child at risk of or charged with an offence as follows:

'Each State party shall ensure in particular to any child at risk or any delinquent charged with an offence the right to a special legal system for minors in all stages of investigation, trial and enforcement of sentence, as well as to special treatment that takes account of his age, protects his dignity, facilitates his rehabilitation and reintegration and enables him to play a constructive role in society.'

---

[382] See also Art 15 ('No crime and no penalty can be established without a prior provision of the law. In all circumstances, the law most favorable to the defendant shall be applied') and Art 19 ('1. No one may be tried twice for the same offence. Anyone against whom such proceedings are brought shall have the right to challenge their legality and to demand his release. 2. Anyone whose innocence is established by a final judgment shall be entitled to compensation for the damage suffered. 3. The aim of the penitentiary system shall be to reform prisoners and effect their social rehabilitation').

The Child's Right to Fair and Equal Treatment under the Law in Domestic Law

Domestic Law – Right to a Fair Trial

Magna Carta

16.151   Whilst it must be seen in its historical context,[383] Magna Carta demonstrates that as early as 1215 at least the gestation within the domestic sphere of the principle of due process was taking place. Chapters 39 and 40 of Magna Carta provide as follows:

> '39.   No free man shall be seized or imprisoned or stripped of his rights or possessions, or outlawed or exiled, or deprived of his standing in any other way, nor will we proceed with force against him, or send others to do so, except by lawful judgment of his equals or by the law of the land.

> 40.   To no one will we sell, to no one deny or delay right or justice.'

Constitutional Right of Access to the Court

16.152   Arguments concerning the right to fair and equal treatment before the law are now articulated in the domestic arena almost exclusively by reference to the Human Rights Act 1998, Sch 1 Art 6. However, within the domestic context it should be remembered that there is a constitutional right of unimpeded access to the Courts which can only be taken away by express enactment.[384] The unimpeded access to a solicitor is inseparable from the constitutional right of unimpeded access to the court.[385]

Domestic Separation of Powers

16.153   Section 3(6)(1) of the Constitutional Reform Act 2005 requires the Lord Chancellor to have regard to the need to defend the independence of the judiciary. Further, s 3(6)(1)(b) expressly recognises that, to uphold the continued independence of the judiciary, the Lord Chancellor must have regard to the need for the judiciary to have

---

[383]   Lord Bingham points out that it would be a travesty of history to regard the barons who confronted King John at Runnymede as altruistic liberals seeking to make the world a better place. Note however that as Lord Bingham makes clear, Magna Carta was not 'an instant response to the oppression and exactions of a tyrannous king' but had its roots in the oaths and writs of the Anglo-Saxon kings and the Charter of Henry I and was thus expressed the will of the people or at least the will of the articulate representatives of the people (see Bingham, T *The Rule of Law* (2010) Allen Lane, p 11–12).

[384]   *Raymond v Honey* [1983] 1 AC 1 and *R v Secretary of State for the Home Department ex p Leech (No 2)* [1994] QB 198 per Steyn LJ ('It is a principle of our law that every citizen has a right of unimpeded access to a court ... Even in our unwritten constitution it must rank as a constitutional right'). As to the requirements that need to be met by an express enactment removing a constitutional right see *R v Lord Chancellor ex p Witham* [1998] QB 575 per Laws J ('In the unwritten legal order of the British State, at a time when the common law continues to accord a legislative supremacy to Parliament, the notion of a constitutional right can in my judgment inhere only in this proposition, that the right in question cannot be abrogated by the state save by specific provision in an Act of Parliament, or by regulations whose vires in main legislation specifically confers the power to abrogate ... for my part, I find great difficulty in conceiving a form of words capable of making it plain beyond doubt to the statute's reader that the provision in question prevents him from going to court (for that is what would be required), save in a case where that is expressly stated. The class of cases where it could be done by necessary implication is, I venture to think, a class with no members.'). See also *R v Lord Chancellor ex p Lightfoot* [2000] QB 597.

[385]   *R v Secretary of State for the Home Department ex p Anderson* [1984] QB 778 ('It must, we consider, be inherent in the logic of the decision of the House of Lords in *Raymond v Honey* that an inmate's right of access to a solicitor for the purposes of obtaining advice and assistance with a view to instituting proceedings should be unimpeded, in the same way as his right to initiate proceedings by dispatching the necessary documents for that purpose by post is unimpeded').

the support necessary to enable them to exercise their functions. The principle that a person must have recourse to a court independent of state influence when their rights are threatened is thus now codified in domestic statute law.

Domestic Law – Preventative Measures and Diversions

16.154 The Crime and Disorder Act 1998 seeks to establish the principle that the aim of the domestic youth justice system is to prevent offending by children and young persons.[386] The Act places a duty on local authorities to ensure, in cooperation with the chief of police of police authority for their area, that youth justice services are available in their areas,[387] to establish youth offending teams[388] and formulate and implement a youth justice plan.[389] The Act further makes provision for the establishment of a Youth Justice Board to monitor the operation of the youth justice system and the provision of youth justice services.[390] Within the context of its aim to prevent offending by children and young persons, the Crime and Disorder Act 1998 introduced anti-social behaviour orders[391] in respect of children aged 10 or over prohibiting further anti-social behaviour on pain of criminal conviction,[392] parenting orders requiring a parent to comply with such matters specified in the order,[393] child safety orders in respect of children under 10 who have committed acts which would constitute an offence if they were over 10 years of age,[394] local child curfew schemes in respect of children under 16 years of age[395] and finally a system of reprimands and final warnings.[396] In addition to these provisions, local authorities are under a statutory duty to take reasonable steps designed to encourage children within their areas not to commit criminal offences and to reduce the need to bring criminal proceedings against such children.[397]

---

[386] Crime and Disorder Act 1998, s 37(1). See also the Anti-Social Behaviour Act 2003. For the historical context of the Crime and Disorder Act 1998 see *R (R) v Durham Constabulary* [2005] UKHL 21, [2005] 1 WLR 1184, paras 30–37.

[387] Crime and Disorder Act 1998, s 38.

[388] Crime and Disorder Act 1998, s 39.

[389] Crime and Disorder Act 1998, s 39.

[390] Crime and Disorder Act 1998, s 41.

[391] Crime and Disorder Act1998, s 1. Section 6 of the Act provides that 'The prohibitions that may be imposed by an anti-social behaviour order are those necessary for the purpose of protecting persons (whether relevant persons or persons elsewhere in England and Wales) from further anti-social acts by the defendant' and s 7 provides that 'An anti-social behaviour order shall have effect for a period (not less than 2 years) specified in the order or until further order.'

[392] Crime and Disorder Act 1998, s 1(10) ('If without reasonable excuse a person does anything which he is prohibited from doing by an anti-social behaviour order, he [is guilty of an offence and] liable (a) on summary conviction, to imprisonment for a term not exceeding 6 months or to a fine not exceeding the statutory maximum, or to both; or (b) on conviction on indictment, to imprisonment for a term not exceeding five years or to a fine, or to both').

[393] Crime and Disorder Act 1998, s 8.

[394] Crime and Disorder Act 1998, s 11. Section 11(3) prescribes the conditions for making a child safety order as '(a) that the child has committed an act which, if he had been aged 10 or over, would have constituted an offence; (b) that a child safety order is necessary for the purpose of preventing the commission by the child of such an act as is mentioned in paragraph (a) above; (c) ...; and (d) that the child has acted in a manner that caused or was likely to cause harassment, alarm or distress to one or more persons not of the same household as himself.' Section 13A of the Crime and Disorder Act 1998 provides for the making of parental compensation orders where the requirements of s 11(3)(a) or 11(3)(d) and it would be desirable to make an order in the interests of preventing a repetition of the behaviour in question.

[395] Crime and Disorder Act 1998, s 14.

[396] Crime and Disorder Act 1998, ss 65–66H.

[397] Children Act 1989, Sch 2, para 7. See also *R (Howard League for Penal Reform) v Secretary of State for the Home Department* [2002] EWHC 2497, [2003] 1 FLR 484, para 136 per Munby J ('... the law can, as it seems to me, be summarised in the following general propositions: (i) the 1989 Act does not confer or impose any functions, powers, duties, responsibilities or obligations on either the Prison Service (or any of its staff) or the Secretary of State for the Home Department; (ii) in that sense the Act does not apply as such either to

16.155 The language of the Crime and Disorder Act 1998 contrasts sharply with the language used in international law concerning the need for preventative and diversionary measures which move children and young people away from the youth justice system.[398] Within this context, the provisions of the Crime and Disorder Act 1998 have been the subject of sustained criticism.[399] Harmmarberg points out that the fact that anti-social behaviour proceedings are determined to be civil rather than criminal in nature means that the normal protections afforded by a higher standard of proof, strict rules of evidence and the procedural guarantees under Art 6(2) and 6(3) of the ECHR are unavailable.[400] Whilst commentators argue that the anti-social behaviour provisions are clearly in breach of the child's rights under the ECHR and should be analysed by reference to those rights,[401] the issue identified by Harmmarberg has been exacerbated by the apparent unwillingness of the courts to consider the Crime and Disorder Act 1998 and associated legislation within the framework of children's rights provided by the CRC and the ECHR.[402]

16.156 Whilst in *R (R) v Durham Constabulary*[403] the House of Lords determined that warnings given to young persons under the Crime and Disorder Act 1998, ss 65–66 do not involve the determination of a criminal charge for the purposes of Art 6(1) of the

---

the Prison Service or to YOIs; (iii) but the duties which a local authority would otherwise owe to a child either under s 17 or under s 47 of the Act do not cease to be owed merely because the child is currently detained in a YOI; (iv) in that sense the Act does apply to children in YOIs; (v) however, a local authority's functions, powers, duties and responsibilities under the Act, and specifically under ss 17 and 47 of the Act, take effect and operate subject to the necessary requirements of imprisonment'). See further Part III of the Crime and Disorder Act 1998 concerning the local provision of youth justice services including youth offending teams and the Youth Justice Board.

[398] See for example Art 10 of the UN Guidelines on the Prevention of Juvenile Delinquency ('... preventative policies facilitating the successful socialisation and integration of all children and young persons, in particular through the family, the community, peer groups, schools, vocational training, the world of work, and voluntary organisations'). See the comments of Baroness Hale in *R (R) v Durham Constabulary* [2005] UKHL 21, [2005] 1 WLR 1184, paras 26–29.

[399] See *UK Children's Commissioners' Report to the UN Committee on the Rights of the Child* (2008) 11 Million, p 33), domestic commentators (see Margo, J and Stevens, A *Make me a Criminal: Preventing Youth Crime* (2008) IPPR, pp 48–49), the European Commissioner for Human Rights (see Gil-Robles, A *Report by Mr Alvaro Gil-Robles, Commissioner for Human Rights on His Visit to the United Kingdom* (2005) CommDH 6 Council of Europe, paras 108–120 and 79–80 and Hammarberg, T *Memorandum by Thomas Hammarberg, Commissioner for Human Rights of the Council of Europe* (2008), paras 29–30) and by international human rights bodies (see Human Rights Committee *Concluding Observations of the Human Rights Committee: United Kingdom of Great Britain and Northern Ireland* (2008) CCPR/C/GBR/6, para 20 and the Committee on the Rights of the Child *Concluding Observations of the Committee on the Rights of the Child: United Kingdom of Great Britain and Northern Ireland* (2008) CRC/C/GBR/ CO/4, paras 34–35).

[400] Hammarberg, T *Memorandum by Thomas Hammarberg, Commissioner for Human Rights of the Council of Europe* (2008) CommDH Council of Europe, para 29. Hammarberg comments that this situation leaves the potential recipient of an anti-social behaviour order especially vulnerable to human rights violations.

[401] See Hollingsworth, K *R (W) v Commissioner of Police of the Metropolis and Another – Interpreting Child Curfews: A Question of Rights?* (2006) 18 Child and Family Law Quarterly 253 on the first instance decision in *R (on the application of W) v Commissioner of Police for the Metropolis and Richmond Upon Thames Borough Council (Secretary of State for the Home Department, Interested Party)* [2005] EWHC 1586 (Admin), [2005] 3 All ER 749 ('The case of *R (W)* provided the opportunity for the courts to make clear that children are 'persons' under the European Convention and, like adults, have rights worthy of protection. The outcome of the case is to be welcomed, but it would have been an even stronger decision if the reasoning had at least explicitly addressed the issue of the rights of children, and made clear that children's Convention rights can only be restricted in a justifiable and proportionate way').

[402] See *R (on the application of W) v Commissioner of Police for the Metropolis and Richmond Upon Thames Borough Council (Secretary of State for the Home Department, Interested Party)* [2005] EWHC 1586 (Admin), [2005] 3 All ER 749 (Divisional Court) and [2006] EWCA Civ 458, [2006] 3 All ER 458 (Court of Appeal) and *R (M) v Secretary of State for Constitutional Affairs and Lord Chancellor* [2004] EWCA Civ 312, [2004] 1 WLR 2298, para 39 (impossible to say that an interim anti-social behaviour order determined civil rights).

[403] [2005] UKHL 21, [2005] 1 WLR 1184.

ECHR,[404] Baroness Hale emphasised the applicability of the UN Standard Minimum Rules on the Administration of Juvenile Justice, the UN Guidelines on the Prevention of Juvenile Delinquency and the CRC, Arts 3(1), 37 and 40, both in their own right and as they affect the interpretation of the ECHR. Having reviewed the position under international law, her Ladyship stated:

'There can be no doubt, therefore, that constructive diversion policies and practices are thoroughly consistent with the fundamental principles of all these international instruments. However, diversion is not to be bought at the cost of basic fairness to the child. The child is a human being, not a mere object of social control. As Dame Elizabeth Butler-Sloss memorably put it in her report on *Child Abuse in Cleveland* (1987), "the child is a person and not an object of concern". Children will not be brought up to obey the law and respect the rights of others if they perceive that the system is treating them arbitrarily or unfairly. The fundamental issue in this appeal is whether it is fair to subject a child to a formal diversion process with mandatory legal consequences without first obtaining his informed consent.'

16.157 Whilst not finding a breach of the child's rights under the ECHR,[405] Baroness Hale noted that the lack of any requirement to obtain the consent of either the child or his parent to being dealt with by means of a warning under the 1998 Act appears inconsistent with the UN Standard Minimum Rules on the Administration of Juvenile Justice r 11(3) and potentially Art 40(3)(b) of the CRC. Within this context, Her Ladyship expressed significant reservations concerning the extent to which the warning scheme under the Crime and Disorder Act 1998 is consistent with the international law of children's rights:

'For these reasons, I have grave doubts about whether the statutory scheme is consistent with the child's rights under the international instruments dealing with children's rights. The rigidity of the scheme undermines the emphasis given to diverting children from the criminal justice system, propels them into it and on a higher rung of the ladder earlier than they would previously have arrived there, and thus seriously risks offending against the principle that intervention must be proportionate both to the circumstances of the offender and of the offence. There is also a risk that it is arbitrarily applied in the individual case. This particular case was not handled in the most sensible way. In particular, the failure to tell the child and his stepfather the full consequences of the warning, including the sex offender registration requirement, obviously upset them both and left them with a considerable sense of injustice. They are also concerned that the record on the PNC does not accurately reflect the admissions made. Any educational benefit to be gained from diversion is severely jeopardised if the offender feels unjustly treated. We are also told that no further steps were taken by the Youth Offending Team to work with the child in ways which might have helped him to see why his conduct was unacceptable and to engage with girls in a more sensible and ultimately more successful way.'

Domestic Law – Age of Criminal Responsibility

16.158 The domestic minimum age of criminal responsibility is set at 10 years old by the Children and Young Persons Act 1933, s 50 as amended by the Children and Young Persons Act 1963, s 16. The previous rebuttable presumption of *doli incapax*, holding

---

[404] [2005] UKHL 21, [2005] 1 WLR 1184, para 14 per Lord Bingham ('A process which can only culminate in measures of a preventative, curative, rehabilitative or welfare-promoting kind will not ordinarily be the determination of a criminal charge').

[405] [2005] UKHL 21, [2005] 1 WLR 1184, paras 44–49. Note that guidance has been issued requiring that the child and his or her parents, cares or other appropriate adult have access to information about the options available, including the final warning scheme and its consequences (*Final Warning Scheme: Guidance for the Police and Youth Offending Teams* (2002) Home Office, para 4.14).

that children under the age of 14 do not appreciate the wrongfulness of their actions unless proved to the contrary has been removed,[406] further reducing the protection afforded to young children and leaving the minimum age of criminal responsibility detached from any other reference point pertaining to the child's level of development.[407] The low domestic age of criminal responsibility has been repeatedly criticised by the Committee on the Rights of the Child.[408] Fortin pointedly draws a valid comparison between the criminal and civil justice systems 'Whilst the civil courts take great care to ensure that adolescents do not obtain legal capacity to reach decisions before being deemed sufficiently mature to comprehend their implications, the criminal law imposes criminal responsibility on juveniles at an extremely early age, presumably to protect society from their evident lawlessness'.[409]

Domestic Law – Best Interests and the Right to a Fair Trial

Criminal Proceedings

(i)   Child Defendants

16.159 Within the context of the low statutory minimum age of criminal responsibility, it has been left to the judges to ensure the efficacy of the available protection for young children who are subject to the criminal justice process. Every court dealing with a child or young person brought before it, either as an offender or otherwise, must have regard to the welfare of that child or young person.[410] In addition to any other duty to which they are subject, it is also the duty of all persons carrying out functions in relation to the youth justice system to have regard to the welfare of the child or young person.[411] This principle will thus encompass the police,[412] the Probation Service, social services, youth offending teams, the Crown Prosecution Service, defence lawyers, the Prison Service and the courts.[413] Pursuant to s 34A of the Children and Young Persons Act 1933 where a child or young person is charged with an offence or is for any other reason brought before the court, the court may in any case and shall in the case of a child under the age of 16 years require the child's parent or guardian, or where the child is in the care of the local authority the local authority, to attend court unless and to the extent that the court considers this unreasonable in the circumstances of the case. Section 37 of the Children and Young Persons Act 1933 gives the power to clear the court of all persons not being officers of the court, parties to the case or their legal

---

[406]   Crime and Disorder Act 1998, s 34.

[407]   The Government has argued that a low age of criminal responsibility benefits children by helping them 'develop a sense of personal responsibility for their behaviour' (HM Government *The Consolidated 3rd and 4th Periodic Report to the UN Committee on the Rights of the Child* (2007) p 160, para 54). It is unclear whether research into how many 10 year olds knew of or understood the concept of minimum age of criminal responsibility was undertaken prior to this conclusion being reached.

[408]   Committee on the Rights of the Child *Concluding Observations of the Committee on the Rights of the Child: Great Britain and Northern Ireland* 1995 CRC/C/15/Add.34, paras 17 and 36, *Concluding Observations of the Committee on the Rights of the Child: Great Britain and Northern Ireland* 2002 CRC/C/15 Add. 188, paras 59 and 62 and *Concluding Observations of the Committee on the Rights of the Child: Great Britain and Northern Ireland* 2008 CRC/C/GBR/CO/4, paras 77–78.

[409]   Fortin, J *Children's Rights and the Developing Law* (2009) 3rd edn, Cambridge, p 686.

[410]   Children and Young Persons Act 1933, s 44. See ss 45–48 of the Children and Young Persons Act 1933 for the constitution and powers of Youth Courts.

[411]   Crime and Disorder Act 1998, s 37(2).

[412]   Fortin notes that the PACE Codes of Practice based on the recognition that children in England and Wales should have at least as many due process rights as adults during the investigation by the police of alleged criminal offences (Fortin, J *Children's Rights and the Developing Law* (2009) 3rd edn, Cambridge, p 694). See PACE Codes A to H.

[413]   *No More Excuses – A New Approach to Tackling Youth Crime in England and Wales* Cm 3809 (1997) Home Office, para 2.5.

representatives, bona fide representatives of the press or persons otherwise directly connected with proceedings whilst the child gives evidence.

16.160　The domestic courts have acknowledged the vulnerable position of children in the criminal justice system by reference to the provisions of the CRC. In *R v G and another*[414] Lord Steyn recognised that in considering the element of recklessness in s 1 of the Criminal Damage Act 1971:

> 'Ignoring the special position of children in the criminal justice system is not acceptable in a modern civil society. In 1990 the United Kingdom ratified the United Nations Convention on the Rights of the Child (New York, 20 November 1989; TS 44 (1992); Cm 1976) (the UN convention) which entered into force on 15 January 1992. Article 40(1) ... This provision imposes both procedural and substantive obligations on state parties to protect the special position of children in the criminal justice system. For example, it would plainly be contrary to art 40(1) for a state to set the age of criminal responsibility of children at, say, five years. Similarly, it is contrary to art 40(1) to ignore in a crime punishable by life imprisonment, or detention during Her Majesty's pleasure, the age of a child in judging whether the mental element has been satisfied. It is true that the UN convention became binding on the United Kingdom after *R v Caldwell* was decided. But the House cannot ignore the norm created by the UN convention. This factor on its own justified a reappraisal of *R v Caldwell.*'[415]

16.161　Unlike child witness, the defendant who is a child must in most circumstances be present in court and is not eligible for the special measures directions under the Youth Justice and Criminal Evidence Act 1999 applicable to child witnesses.[416] Following the criticism of the domestic approach to the trial of children in *T v United Kingdom*[417] and *V v United Kingdom*[418] a Practice Direction entitled *Trial of Young Persons in the Crown Court*[419] was issued by the Lord Chief Justice. Paragraph 3 of the Practice Direction provides that:

> 'Some young defendants accused of committing serious crimes may be very young and very immature when standing trial and in the Crown Court. The purpose of such trial is to determine guilt (if that is in issue) and decide the appropriate sentence if the young defendant pleads guilty or is convicted. The trial process should not itself expose the young defendant to avoidable intimidation, humiliation or distress. All possible steps should be taken to assist the young defendant to understand and participate in the proceedings. The

---

[414]　[2003] UKHL 50, [2003] 4 All ER 765, para 53.

[415]　See also *R (on the application of P) v West London Youth Court* [2005] EWHC 2583 (Admin), [2006] 1 All ER 477, paras 9–11, *Director of Public Prosecutions v P (DPP v P)* [2007] EWHC 946 (Admin), [2007] 4 All ER 628, para 48 and 51–58, *R (W) v Thetford Youth Court, R (M) v Waltham Forest Youth Court* [2002] EWHC (Admin) 1252, [2003] 1 Cr App R (S) 67 per Sedley J, para 43 and *R (W) v Southampton Youth Court, R (K) v Wirral Borough Magistrates Court* [2002] EWHC 1640 (Admin), [2003] 1 Cr App R (S) 87 per Lord Woolf, para 16. See also Auld, R Lord Justice, *Review of the Criminal Courts of England and Wales* (2001) TSO, p 216.

[416]　See **16.163** below. Note however that pursuant to s 33A of the Youth Justice and Criminal Evidence Act 1999 the court may on the application of the accused give a direction that the accused provide evidence by a live link where the accused is under the age of 18 and his or her ability is compromised by his or her level of intellectual ability or social functioning and the use of a live link would enable him or her to participate more effectively in the proceedings (whether by improving the quality of his or her evidence or otherwise) or where it is in the interests of justice for the accused to give evidence through a live link. Pursuant to s 33B(2) the accused giving evidence by live link must be able to be seen by the tribunal, the other accused, the legal representatives acting in the proceedings and any interpreter or other person appointed to assist the accused.

[417]　[2000] Crim LR 187.

[418]　(1999) 30 EHRR 121.

[419]　16 February 2000

ordinary trial process should so far as necessary be adapted to meet those ends. Regard should be had to the welfare of the young defendant as required by section 44 of the Children and Young Persons Act 1933.'

16.162 Paragraphs 9–16 of the Practice Direction seek to ensure the child can effectively participate in the trial process. The measures stipulated by the Practice Direction include the provision of a court room in which all the participants are on the same or almost the same level, where the child can, if he or she wishes, be free to sit with members of his family or others in a like relationship and which permits easy, informal communication with his legal representatives. Further, the Practice Direction provides that the court should explain the course of proceedings to a young defendant in terms he or she can understand. The trial should be conducted according to a timetable which takes full account of a young defendant's inability to concentrate for long periods and robes and wigs should not be worn by the judge or advocates unless the young defendant asks that they should or the court for good reason orders that they should. Any person responsible for the security of a young defendant who is in custody should not be in uniform. There should be no recognisable Police presence in the court room unless there is a good reason. Finally, facilities for reporting the trial, subject to any direction given under s 39 of the 1933 Act or s 45 of the 1999 Act, must be provided but the court may restrict the number of those attending in the court room. The Practice Direction also stipulates that any other exercise of the courts discretion should be exercised in accordance with the principles in para 3 of the Practice Direction.

(ii) Child Witnesses

16.163 Children under 17 years of age[420] acting as witnesses in criminal proceedings[421] can take advantage of the provisions of Part II of the Youth Justice and Criminal Evidence Act 1999.[422] A number of special measures to assist children to give evidence in criminal cases are available,[423] including screens,[424] live television links,[425] using video-recordings as evidence-in-chief,[426] and cross-examination and re-examination,[427] the exclusion of specified persons from the court room during the giving of evidence,[428] providing aids to communication,[429] examining the witness through an approved intermediary[430] and the removal by advocates of their wigs and/or gowns.[431] Pursuant to s 35 of the Youth Justice and Criminal Evidence Act 1999 no person charged with an

---

[420] Youth Justice and Criminal Evidence Act 1999. Young people aged between 17 and 18 may be able to take advantage of the provisions of s 17 of the Act which allow special measures to be used where the quality of evidence given by the witness is likely to be diminished by reason of fear or distress on the part of the witness in connection with testifying in the proceedings.

[421] Note that under s 36 of the Children and Young Persons Act 1933, as amended by s 73(1) of the Access to Justice Act 1999, no child other than an infant is permitted to be present in court except when required as a witness.

[422] See also *Achieving Best Evidence in Criminal Proceedings: Guidance on Interviewing Victims and Witnesses, and Using Special Measures*(2007) Home Office.

[423] Recent research has shown that, although special measures have made the experience better for children giving evidence in the criminal courts, many still find it difficult and stressful (see Plotnikoff, J and Woolfson, R *Measuring up? Evaluating implementation of Government commitments to young witnesses in criminal proceedings* (2009) Nuffield Foundation and NSPCC).

[424] Youth Justice and Criminal Evidence Act 1999, s 23.

[425] Youth Justice and Criminal Evidence Act 1999, s 24.

[426] Youth Justice and Criminal Evidence Act 1999, s 27

[427] Youth Justice and Criminal Evidence Act 1999, s 28.

[428] Youth Justice and Criminal Evidence Act 1999, s 25.

[429] Youth Justice and Criminal Evidence Act 1999, s 30.

[430] Youth Justice and Criminal Evidence Act 1999, s 29. See also the Criminal Justice Act 2003, ss 114–118 which now allow for hearsay evidence to be given in criminal trials in a much wider set of circumstances than previously.

offence to which s 35 applies[432] may cross-examine in person a child[433] in connection with that offence or in connection with any other offence of whatever nature with which that person is charged in those proceedings. These provisions have been held by the House of Lords to be compliant with the requirements of Art 6 of the ECHR. In *R v Camberwell Green Youth Court ex p D (a minor)(by his mother and litigation friend)*[434] Baroness Hale held in relation to the special measures implemented to protect child witnesses pursuant to the Youth Justice and Criminal Evidence Act 1999, s 21(5) that:

> 'All the evidence is produced at the trial in the presence of the accused, some of it in pre-recorded form and some of it by contemporaneous television transmission. The accused can see and hear it all. The accused has every opportunity to challenge and question the witnesses against him at the trial itself. The only thing missing is a face to face confrontation, but the appellants accept that the Convention does not guarantee a right to face to face confrontation. This case is completely different from the case of anonymous witnesses. Even then the Strasbourg Court has accepted that exceptions may be made, provided that sufficient steps are taken to counter-balance the handicaps under which the defence laboured and a conviction is not based solely or decisively on anonymous statements.'

Domestic Law – Public Proceedings and Children

Criminal Proceedings

16.164   Domestic criminal proceedings are ordinarily open to the press and the public. Pursuant to the Children and Young Persons Act 1933, s 39 no newspaper report of the proceedings shall reveal the name, address or school, or include any particulars calculated to lead to the identification of any child or young person concerned in the proceedings, either as being the person by or against or in respect of whom the proceedings are taken, or as being a witness therein and no picture shall be published in any newspaper as being or including a picture of any child or young person so concerned in the proceedings save as permitted by direction of the court. Breach of these provisions constitutes a criminal offence.[435] Pursuant to s 49 of the Children and Young Person's Act 1933 within the context of the Youth Court and the magistrates court no matter relating to any child or young person concerned in proceedings as the accused or a witness[436] shall while he is under the age of 18 be included in any publication if it is likely to lead members of the public to identify him as someone concerned in the proceedings, namely his or her name, address, the identity of any school or other educational establishment, the identity of any place of work and any

---

[431]   Youth Justice and Criminal Evidence Act 1999, s 26. See ss 31–33 for the status of evidence given under special measures. See also the Criminal Evidence (Witness Anonymity) Act 2008.

[432]   Section 35 applies to offences under the Sexual Offences Act 1956, the Indecency with Children Act 1960, the Sexual Offences Act 1967, s 54 of the Criminal Law Act 1977, the Protection of Children Act 1978, offences of kidnapping, false imprisonment or offences under ss 1 or 2 of the Child Abduction Act 1984, any offence under s 1 of the Children and Young Persons Act 1933 and any offence which involves an assault on, or injury or threat of injury to any person. See ss 38–39 for the provisions concerning assistance to the accused in respect of cross-examination.

[433]   Pursuant to s 35(4) of the Act, 'child' means a person under the age of 17 where the offence is one under the Sexual Offences Act 1956, the Indecency with Children Act 1960, the Sexual Offences Act 1967, s 54 of the Criminal Law Act 1977 or the Protection of Children Act 1978 and a person under the age of 14 where the offence is one of kidnapping, false imprisonment or offences under ss 1 or 2 of the Child Abduction Act 1984, any offence under s 1 of the Children and Young Persons Act 1933 and any offence which involves an assault on, or injury or threat of injury to any person.

[434]   [2005] UKHL 4, [2005] 1 WLR 393, para 49.

[435]   See also s 44 of the Youth and Criminal Justice Act 1999.

[436]   Children and Young Persons Act 1933, s 49(4).

still or moving picture.[437] The term 'publication' includes any speech, writing, relevant programme or other communication in whatever form, which is addressed to the public at large or any section of the public (and for this purpose every relevant programme shall be taken to be so addressed), but does not include an indictment or other document prepared for use in particular legal proceedings.[438] The court may dispense with these provisions to any specified extent if satisfied it is in the interests of justice[439] to do so but must hear representations from the parties and take account of the same before doing so.[440] The court may also dispense with the provisions limiting publicity where it is appropriate to do so for the purpose of avoiding injustice to the child or young person or as respects a child or young person who is unlawfully at large and charged with a violent offence, a sexual offence or an offence attracting a maximum sentence of 14 years imprisonment,[441] it is necessary to dispense with those requirements for the purpose of apprehending him and bringing him before a court or returning him to the place in which he was in custody.[442] The efficacy of the provisions of the Children and Young Persons Act 1933 as to publicity have been the subject of particular criticism by the Committee on the Rights of the Child.[443]

Civil Proceedings

16.165 For the position in respect of publicity in the context of domestic family and civil proceedings concerning children and their families see chapter 9 on the child's right to a private life.[444]

Domestic Law – Administrative Procedures and Fair Trial

16.166 The domestic courts have recognised that Art 6(1) of the ECHR, and the procedural safeguards inherent in Art 8 of the ECHR,[445] will apply to the 'non-judicial' or administrative elements of procedures which precede litigation in court. In *Re L (Care: Assessment Fair Trial)*[446] Munby J, relying on *Mantovanelli v France*[447] held that Art 6 of the ECHR requires that a child should be entitled to participate effectively in the process by which the Local Authority identifies, assesses and approves prospective adopters for that child as:

> '... the fair trial guaranteed by Art 6 is not confined to the 'purely judicial' part of the proceedings. Unfairness at *any* stage of the litigation process may involve breaches not merely of Art 8 but also of Art 6. This is potentially very important bearing in mind that, as I explained in *Re B (Disclosure to Other Parties)* [2001] 2 FLR 1017, at [56], [64], [67], whereas rights under Art 8 are inherently qualified and can be – and often have to be – balanced against other rights, including other rights under Art 8, a parent's right to a fair trial under Art 6 is absolute. It cannot be qualified by reference to, or balanced against, the

---

[437] Children and Young Persons Act 1933, s 49(3A).
[438] Children and Young Persons Act 1933, s 49(3).
[439] Children and Young Persons Act 1933, s 49(4A).
[440] Children and Young Persons Act 1933, s 49(4B).
[441] Children and Young Persons Act 1933, s 49(6).
[442] Children and Young Persons Act 1933, s 49(5).
[443] Committee on the Rights of the Child *Concluding Observations: United Kingdom of Great Britain and Northern Ireland* CRC/C/15/Add.188, paras 60(d) and 62(d).
[444] See **9.11–9.15** and **9.49-9.54** above.
[445] See *R (P) v Secretary of State for the Home Department; R (Q) v Secretary of State for the Home Department* [2001] EWCA Civ 1151; [2001] 2 FLR 1122 and *CF v Secretary of State for the Home Department* [2004] EWHC 111 (Fam), [2004] 2 FLR 517.
[446] [2002] EWHC 1379 (Fam), [2002] 2 FLR 730.
[447] (1997) 24 EHRR 370.

child's or anyone else's rights under Art 8. The right to a fair trial under Art 6 cannot be compromised or watered down by reference to Art 8.'

Domestic Law – Legal Aid

16.167   The Rushcliffe Committee Report in May 1945 recognised that those members of society who cannot afford legal representation should be entitled to financial aid to ensure access to such representation.[448] The domestic provisions concerning legal aid are labyrinthine and reference should be made to the Legal Aid Handbook[449] for a detailed guide to the domestic civil and criminal legal aid scheme. The domestic legal aid system has been the subject of repeated reforms since 2005 and those reforms remain ongoing.[450] The importance of the provision of legal aid in ensuring access to justice for children is self evident. The extent to which this self evident proposition has been understood by successive governments remains unclear. In relation to care proceedings concerning children, Masson was forced to conclude that:[451]

'Overall, the [Legal Services] Commission appears to have lacked an adequate understanding of care proceedings to design a fair and workable system, which would allow it to control its expenditure whilst maintaining an economic incentive on solicitors to continue with this work.'

CONCLUSION

16.168   That a measured approach to children in conflict with the law is the most effective antidote to childhood offending was well recognised in the 1960s.[452] This approach did not however blossom and the United Kingdom has come under sustained criticism for the manner in which it treats children who are in conflict with the law.[453] Domestically there is a persistent tendency to view young offenders as bearing entire responsibility for their actions and deserving harsh punishment.[454] The arguably inaccurate public perspective on 'youth crime'[455] has in part been responsible for the 'general climate of intolerance and negative public attitudes towards young children, especially adolescents',[456] making it harder to implement a youth justice system which

---

[448]   *Report of the Committee on Legal Aid and Legal Advice in England and Wales* Cmd 6641 (1945). See also *Airey v Ireland* (1979) 2 EHRR 305.

[449]   Ling, V and Pugh, S (eds) (2011) Legal Action Group.

[450]   *Proposals for Reform of Legal Aid in England and Wales* (2010) Ministry of Justice Cm 7967.

[451]   Masson, *Controlling Costs and Maintaining Services – The Reform of Legal Aid Fees for Care Proceedings*, [2008] CFLQ 425. See also MacDonald, A *The Caustic Dichotomy – Political Vision and Resourcing in the Care System* [2009] CFLQ 30 and MacDonald, A *Legal Aid Reform – Beyond 'No More Money'* [2007] Fam Law 130.

[452]   Report of the Ingleby Committee HO (1960), para 106. See Fortin, J *Children's Rights and the Developing Law* (2009) 3rd edn, Cambridge, p 679.

[453]   Committee on the Rights of the Child *Concluding Observations of the Committee on the Rights of the Child: Great Britain and Northern Ireland* 1995 CRC/C/15/Add.34, paras 59 and 60 and *Concluding Observations of the Committee on the Rights of the Child: Great Britain and Northern Ireland* 2008 CRC/C/GBR/CO/4, paras 77–79.

[454]   see Gelsthorpe, L and Morris, A *Juvenile Justice 1945–1992* in Maguire, M Morgan, R and Reiner, R (eds) *The Oxford Handbook of Criminology* (1994) OUP, pp 971–973. See also Hamilton, C and Harvey, R *The Role of Public Opinion in the Implementation of International Juvenile Justice Standards* (2003) International Journal of Children's Rights 11 at 369.

[455]   See Fionda, J *New Labour, Old Hat: Youth Justice and the Crime and Disorder Act 1998* (2005) Criminal Law Review 36 p 83.

[456]   *Concluding Observations of the Committee on the Rights of the Child: Great Britain and Northern Ireland* 2008 CRC/C/GBR/CO/4, para 24.

reflects international norms which mandate a much higher domestic age of criminal responsibility coupled with a welfare based as opposed to punitive approach to diverting children from youth offending.

16.169   As with the domestic preference for imprisoning children,[457] there is an urgent need to appreciate that whilst the child may be responsible in the sense of having committed the offence in question he or she ought not to be liable only to a punitive response for the commission of the offence.[458] This proposition does not represent a contradiction if society is prepared to embrace a welfare driven response to offending by children rather than a response driven solely or primarily by the wish to satisfy a perceived public demand for punitive sanctions[459] and appreciate that any difference between a justice model and a welfare model of juvenile justice rests primarily in the manner the former is applied in order to achieve the latter. Once again, as Archard points out, 'A juvenile court can, for instance, both impose a penalty on a child *and* make provision for the child's needs to be addressed'.[460]

---

[457]   See **14.140** above.
[458]   Archard, D *Children – Rights and Childhood* (2004) 2nd edn, Routledge, p 133.
[459]   What Muncie has described as 'the ever-desperate measures to placate tabloid and mid-market newspaper law-and-order campaigns' (Muncie, J *Children's Rights and Youth Justice* in Franklin, B (ed) *The New Handbook of Children's Rights* (2002) Routledge 81, p 94).
[460]   Archard, D *Children – Rights and Childhood* (2004) 2nd edn, Routledge, p 133.

Chapter 17

CONCLUSION

'In the meantime I must uphold my ideals, for perhaps the time will come when I shall be able to carry them out'

Anne Frank
Born 12 June 1929
Died Bergen-Belsen 31 March 1945

17.1 Domestic jurisprudence,[1] and now statutory guidance[2] and secondary legislation,[3] evidences an increasing willingness to give the UN Convention on the Rights of the Child its proper status in domestic law as a binding international convention.[4] In *R (Axon) v Secretary of State for Health and the Family Planning Association*[5] Silber J, having reviewed the rights of children enshrined in the CRC felt compelled to observe that there has been a 'change in the landscape of family matters, in which the rights of children are becoming increasingly important.'

17.2 The need for the comprehensive and consistent application within the domestic jurisdiction of the rights enshrined in the CRC remains an urgent one. According to statistics compiled by the NSPCC at the dawn of the twenty-first century 1% of children experienced sexual abuse by a parent or carer and another 3% by another relative during childhood.[6] Eleven percent of children experienced sexual abuse by people known but unrelated to them. Five percent of children experienced sexual abuse by an adult stranger or someone they had just met.[7] Six percent of children experienced serious absence of care at home during childhood. Six percent of children experienced frequent and severe emotional maltreatment during childhood. Seven percent of children experience serious physical abuse at the hands of their parents or carers during childhood. Sixteen percent of children experienced serious maltreatment by parents, of whom one third experienced more than one type of maltreatment.[8] An NSPCC prevalence study in 2002 found that only a quarter of people who were sexually abused as children had told anyone at the time of the abuse; 31% per cent had still not told

---

1 See **3.32–3.36** above.
2 Statutory guidance of the UK Border Agency on making arrangements to safeguard and promote the welfare of children issued under s 55 of the Borders, Citizenship and Immigration Act 2009.
3 Children's Commissioner for Wales Appointment Regulations 2001, SI 2001/3121 and the Children's Trust Board (Children and Young People's Plan) (England) Regulations 2010, SI 2010/591, r 5(1).
4 See chapter 3 for a detailed discussion of the status of the CRC in domestic law.
5 [2006] EWHC 37 (Admin), [2006] 2 FLR 206, paras 76–80.
6 Cawson, P et al *Child Maltreatment in the UK: A Study of the Prevalence of Child Abuse and Neglect* (2000) NSPCC, pp 5 and 26.
7 Cawson, P et al *Child Maltreatment in the UK: A Study of the Prevalence of Child Abuse and Neglect* (2000) NSPCC.
8 Cawson, P et al *Child Maltreatment in the UK: A Study of the Prevalence of Child Abuse and Neglect* (2000) NSPCC. Cawson et al concluded that 'Every full double-decker school bus at the end of the day is likely to be taking home around 7 seriously unhappy children. Most of the lower deck would at some time during their childhood have been going home to serious worries. Approximately 10 children may be going home to a 'double-shift' of cleaning, laundry, shopping and preparing meals, and 2 or 3 will be in fear of violence between their parents while they were out, or of what might happen that evening' (Cawson et al, *Child Maltreatment in the UK: A Study of the Prevalence of Child Abuse and Neglect* (2000) NSPCC, p 93).

anyone by the time of their adulthood.[9] Later figures indicated in 2006 that one in five girls and one in ten boys are sexually abused before they reach the age of 16.[10] The latest figures from the NSPCC in 2011 indicate that almost one in five 11 to 17 year olds surveyed had been physically attacked by an adult, raped or sexually assaulted or severely neglected during their lives. One in four 18 to 24 year olds reported severe physical violence, sexual abuse or neglect during childhood.[11] Estimates suggest that disabled children are approximately three times more likely to be abused than other children.[12] Whilst there are no accurate figures of the *incidence* of child abuse, current figures suggest that nearly 40,000 children in England are at *risk* of such abuse.[13]

17.3   Infants under one are more at risk of being killed at the hands of another person than any other age group in England and Wales.[14] The second most at risk are persons between the ages of 16 and 29.[15] The Violence and Society Research Group at Cardiff University reported an unprecedented 100 per cent increase in the year 2007 to more than 8,000 in the number of children under 10 brought to Accident and Emergency departments with a history of violence-related injuries.[16] There is recent evidence that violence between children at school and in public places may be just as, or more frequent.[17]

17.4   Official figures show that 3.9 million children live in poverty in the UK.[18] Fuel poverty affects four million households, an increase of two million since 2004.[19] Estimates suggest that there are between 350,000 and 410,000 families with dependent children in England living in overcrowded conditions.[20] High rates of overcrowding persist amongst lone parent families.[21] Disabled children are at greater risk of living in

---

[9]   Cawson, P *Child maltreatment in the family: the experience of a national sample of children* (2002) NSPCC.

[10]   *'Don't Hide it' sex abuse campaign as rape reports to Child Line reach new high* (15 May 2006) NSPCC.

[11]   *Child Cruelty in the UK 2011 – An NSPCC Study into Childhood Abuse and Neglect over the Past 30 Years* (2011) NSPCC.

[12]   *It doesn't happen to disabled children: Child protection and disabled children* (2003) NSPCC. See also Sullivan, P and Knutson, J *Maltreatment and disabilities: a population based epidemiological study* (2000) Child Abuse and Neglect 24(10): 1257-73, Kennedy, M *The abuse of deaf children* (1989) Child Abuse Review 3(1), 3–7 and Westcott, H and Jones, D *The Abuse of Disabled Children* (1999) Journal of Child Psychology and Psychiatry 40(4), 497–506.

[13]   *Children Subject to Child Protection Plans – England 2006–2010* (2010) NSPCC citing Department for Education Children In Need in England 2009–10 Children in Need Census (Final) (2010) DfE Tables 16 and 17. The figure in Wales is 2,730 (Data Unit Wales (2009) Gwion: Data Unit Wales Dissemination Tool), for Scotland 2518 (Scottish Government (2010) Children's Social Work Statistics 2009/10 Tables 7 and 8) and Northern Ireland 2,488 (*Children Order Statistical Tables for Northern Ireland 2008/09* (2010) Northern Ireland, Department of Health, Social Services and Public Safety Tables 1.2 and 1.1).

[14]   *Homicides, Firearms Offences and Intimate Violence 2009/2010: Supplementary Volume Two to Crime in England and Wales 2009/2010*, (Home Office 2010), pp 11 and 19.

[15]   *Homicides, Firearms Offences and Intimate Violence 2009/2010: Supplementary Volume Two to Crime in England and Wales 2009/2010*, (Home Office 2010), pp 11 and 19.

[16]   V Sivarajasingam, S Moore, JP Shepherd, *Violence in England and Wales 2007– An Accident and Emergency Perspective* (2008) Violence and Society Research Group.

[17]   Tuthill D, Williams B, Shepherd JP. *Responses to children injured in violence* (2008) Arch Dis Child 93 (Suppl 1) A108.

[18]   Households Below Average Income 2008/2009 (2010) Department for Work and Pensions. This figure is calculated after housing costs are taken into account.

[19]   *The UK Fuel Poverty Strategy: 7th Annual Progress Report* (2009) Department for Energy and Climate Change, p 5.

[20]   *Tackling overcrowding in England: A discussion paper* (2006) Department for Communities and Local Government, p 4, para 1.2.

[21]   *Tackling overcrowding in England: A discussion paper* (2006) Department for Communities and Local Government, p 6, para 2.8.

poverty. A quarter of all children who live in poverty have a disabled parent and over half of families living with disabled children live in, or at the edge of, poverty.[22]

17.5 The mental health of children and young people in the UK has deteriorated over the last 30 years.[23] One in ten children aged 5-16 years have a clinically diagnosable mental health problem, including depression, anxiety or psychosis.[24] Nearly 80,000 children and young people suffer from severe depression.[25] It is estimated that 1 in 12 children and young people deliberately self-harm.[26] Rates of self harm among girls and young women aged 16 to 24 have increased dramatically since the year 2000.[27] Severely abused children are almost nine times more likely to attempt suicide and almost five times more likely to self harm than children not severely abused or neglected.[28]

17.6 Within the foregoing context, in its review of the Government's implementation of the CRC in 2008 the Children's Rights Alliance continued to highlight a broad range of areas in which the United Kingdom is in violation of the terms of the Convention in respect of general principles,[29] the definition of a child,[30] civil rights and freedoms,[31] family environment and alternative care,[32] basic health and welfare,[33] education, leisure and cultural activities[34] and special protection measures.[35] Many of these concerns are echoed by the United Kingdom Children's Commissioners.[36] The United Nations Committee on the Rights of the Child, whilst commending the United Kingdom for some progress has repeatedly made clear that it questions whether sufficient consideration is being given by the United Kingdom to the enjoyment of fundamental rights by children and in particular those belonging to the most vulnerable groups in society.[37]

17.7 It must be accepted that addressing these stubbornly persistent difficulties through the comprehensive and consistent application of the CRC does present some difficulties. There remain jurisprudential doubts about the true status of some of the

---

22 Preston G and Robinson M *Out of Reach: Benefits for Disabled Children* (2006) Child Poverty Action Group.

23 Bradshaw, J and Mayhew, E *The Wellbeing of Children in the UK* (2005) Save the Children.

24 Green, H, McGinnity, A, Meltzer, H, et al. *Mental health of children and young people in Great Britain 2004* (2005) Palgrave.

25 Office for National Statistics *Census 2001: national report for England and Wales (2004)* ONS.

26 *Truth hurts: Report of the national inquiry into self-harm among young people* (2006) Mental Health Foundation and Camelot Foundation and *Adult Psychiatric Morbidity in England 2007* (2009) The NHS Information Centre.

27 Colman, I, Murray, J, Abbott, R, Maughan, B, Kuh, D, Croudace, T and Jones, P *Outcomes of conduct problems in adolescence: forty-year follow-up of a national cohort* (2009) British Medical Journal 338.

28 *Child Cruelty in the UK 2011 – An NSPCC Study into Childhood Abuse and Neglect over the Past 30 Years* (2011) NSPCC.

29 CRAE *The State of Children's Rights in England* (2008), pp 1–5 and 7–13.

30 CRAE *The State of Children's Rights in England* (2008), p 6.

31 CRAE *The State of Children's Rights in England* (2008), pp 14–22.

32 CRAE *The State of Children's Rights in England* (2008), pp 23–24.

33 CRAE *The State of Children's Rights in England* (2008), pp 25–28.

34 CRAE *The State of Children's Rights in England* (2008), pp 30–33.

35 CRAE *The State of Children's Rights in England* (2008), pp 34–38.

36 *United Kingdom Children's Commissioners Report to the UN Committee on the Rights of the Child* (2008) 11 Million, NICCY, SCCYP and Children's Commissioner for Wales.

37 Committee on the Rights of the Child *Concluding Observations of the Committee on the Rights of the Child: United Kingdom of Great Britain and Northern Ireland* CRC/C/15/Add. 34, para 9, Committee on the Rights of the Child *Concluding Observations of the Committee on the Rights of the Child: United Kingdom of Great Britain and Northern Ireland* CRC/C/15/Add. 188, para 10 and Committee on the Rights of the Child *Concluding Observations of the Committee on the Rights of the Child: United Kingdom of Great Britain and Northern Ireland* CRC/C/GBR/CO/4, para 18.

rights listed in the CRC. Fortin argues that 'many of the rights listed are, in reality, no more than aspirations regarding what should happen if governments were to take children's needs seriously.'[38] That said, the declarative value of the CRC in relation to these more aspirational aspects must not be underestimated.[39] Eekelar argues persuasively that the symbolism of the CRC is as important as its practical efficacy.[40] However, most importantly, even accepting that *some* of the rights contained in the CRC may be more aspirational than current, it must be remembered that the CRC does enshrine a comprehensive set of rights for children that are plainly enforceable as such here and now.

17.8   Within this context, perhaps the greatest obstacle to the effective implementation of the CRC in the domestic jurisdiction is the fact that, whilst the Convention can be applied indirectly through the domestic rules on the status of binding international treaties and customary international law and through its influence on the interpretation of the ECHR,[41] there is at present no method of 'formal' enforcement of the provisions of the CRC available to individual children. Unlike the ECHR, the CRC is not the subject of a domestic statute giving its provisions formal status in domestic law. Further, the Convention lacks either a freestanding court in the mould of the European Court of Human Rights or the Inter-American Court of Human Rights or a Committee based complaints system similar to that complimenting the other United Nations human rights treaties.[42] Whilst it would appear increasingly likely that the Committee on the Rights of the Child will produce an Optional Protocol which establishes a complaints procedure under which children, as individuals or part of a group, can submit complaints directly to the Committee,[43] the absence of legislation giving the CRC the force of domestic law currently permits the legislature, the courts and administrative bodies to downplay the overall significance of the CRC.[44] The current reporting system employed by the Committee on the Rights of the Child does little to mitigate this difficulty.[45]

---

[38]   Fortin, J *Children's Rights and the Developing Law* (2009) 3rd edn, Cambridge, p 46.

[39]   Feinberg, J *Rights, Justice and the Bounds of Liberty* (1980) Princeton University Press, p 153 and Minow, M *Interpreting Rights: An Essay for Robert Cover* (1987) Yale Law Journal, p 1887.

[40]   Eekelar, J *The Importance of Thinking that Children have Rights* in Alston, P, Parker, S and Seymour, J (eds) *Children's Rights and the Law* (1992) Clarendon Press, p 234.

[41]   See chapter 3.

[42]   See **2.32 et seq.**

[43]   See the *Comments by the Committee on the Rights of the Child on the proposal for a draft optional protocol prepared by the Chairperson-Rapporteur of the Open-ended Working Group on an optional protocol to the Convention on the Rights of the Child to provide a communications procedure* (2010) A/HRC/WG.7/2/3. Note that the African Charter on the Rights and Welfare of the Child, which enshrines both first generation and second generation rights, provides a system of individual petition for all children (see Van Bueren *The International Law on the Rights of the Child* (1998) Martinus Nijhoff, p 411). The Committee on the Rights of the Child recommends that the Children's Commissioner be mandated to receive and investigate complaints from or on behalf of children concerning violations of their rights (Committee on the Rights of the Child *Concluding Observations in respect of the United Kingdom of Great Britain and Northern Ireland* (2008) CRC/G/GBR/C0/4, para 17). This provides a potential means of children accessing any complaints mechanism instigated by the Committee on the Rights of the Child.

[44]   For example, in the Government's response to the report of the House of Lords House of Commons Joint Committee on Human Rights Eleventh Report on the Use of Restraint in Secure Training Centres Ministers David Hanson and Beverly Hughes responded as follows to criticism by the JCHR of the Government's apparent lack of respect for the comments of the UN Committee on the Rights of the Child: 'The UN Committee is not a judicial body and its comments are not, and should not be seen as binding on signatory states' (*Government's Response to the Committees 11th Report* (2008) HL Paper 154/HC 979 p 6). Contrast this Ministerial view of the law with that expressed by the courts in *R (Williamson) v Secretary of State for Education* [2005] UKHL 15, [2005] 2 AC 246, [2005] 2 All ER 1 per Baroness Hale ('How can it not be a legitimate and proportionate limitation on the practice of parents' religious beliefs to heed such a recommendation from the bodies charged with monitoring our compliance with the obligations which we

17.9 A solution to these issues is to give the CRC the force of domestic law by embodying its terms within a domestic statute in a manner similar to that achieved in respect of the ECHR by the Human Rights Act 1998. The Committee on the Rights of the Child has urged the United Kingdom to take this step.⁴⁶ The House of Lords House of Commons Joint Committee on Human Rights considers that, within the context of the current discussion of a Bill of Rights for the United Kingdom, there is a strong case

---

have undertaken to respect the dignity of the individual and the rights of children?'); *R (on the application of C) v Secretary of State for Justice* [2008] EWCA Civ 882 per Lord Justice Buxton commenting specifically on the foregoing response of Ministers ('The [House of Lords and House of Commons Joint Committee on Human Rights] pointed out to the Secretary of State that General Comment 8 of the UN Committee states that deliberate infliction of pain is not permitted as a form of control of juveniles. The Secretary of State denied that he sanctions the use of 'violence' against children but, as the JCHR pointed out, that is exactly what PCC, at least in the form of distraction techniques, does provide for. Further, the Secretary of State appeared to suggest to the JCHR that he was bound only by the Convention, and not by the view of the UN Committee. The JCHR, at para 30, stated that it was very disappointed by the Secretary of State's apparent lack of respect for the views of the UN Committee. So am I. And in view of the observations of Baroness Hale of Richmond that must raise serious doubts as to the degree of understanding with which the Secretary of State approaches his obligations under art 3') and *R v (on the application of A) v Secretary of State for the Home Department* [2008] EWHC 2844 (Admin), [2008] All ER (D) 196 (Nov); *AL (Serbia) v Secretary of State for the Home Department* and *R (on the application of Rudi) v Secretary of State for the Home Department* [2008] UKHL 42, [2008] 4 All ER 1127, para 32 ('If anything, children who arrived here without a family required more protection than those who arrived with the support of their families. International law recognises that children who are separated from their families need special protection. The United Nations Convention on the Rights of the Child (New York, 20 November 1989; TS 44 (1998); Cm 1976) (UNCRC), art 2(2) prohibits discrimination on the basis of, among other things, the birth or other status of the child or his family; the UN Committee on the Rights of the Child has emphasised that this prohibits any discrimination on the basis of the status of the child being unaccompanied or separated (General Comment No 6, 2005); UNCRC, Art 22 requires appropriate protection and humanitarian assistance in the enjoyment of applicable rights for all asylum-seeking children, whether or not accompanied').

⁴⁵ The Parliamentary Joint Committee on Human Rights has observed that the reports provided by the United Kingdom to the Committee on the Rights of the Child contain 'little sense of how the information it provides relates to the principles of the Convention, or what the Government's strategic priorities for advancing children's rights are' (see the House of Lords House of Commons Joint Committee on Human Rights *The UN Convention on the Rights of the Child* Tenth Report of Session 2 (2003) HL Paper 117/HC81, para 10). Indeed some of the claims advanced by the Government have been truly remarkable. For example, in its second report the Government claimed that abolition of the *doli incapax* presumption in relation to children between the ages of 10 and 14 would promote children's rights on the basis that it will put 'all juveniles on the same footing as far as the courts are concerned, and will contribute to the *right* of children appearing there to develop responsibility for themselves' (see Department of Health *United Nations Convention on the Rights of the Child: Second Report to the UN Committee by the United Kingdom* (1999) The Stationary Office, para 10.30.1 and see HM Government *The Consolidated 3rd and 4th Periodic Report to the UN Committee on the Rights of the Child* (2007) DCSF, p 160, para 54).

⁴⁶ Committee on the Rights of the Child *Concluding Observations of the Committee on the Rights of the Child: United Kingdom of Great Britain and Northern Ireland* CRC/C/15/Add. 188, paras 8 and 9 ('While noting the entry into force of the Human Rights Act 1998, which incorporates the rights enshrined in the European Convention on Human Rights into domestic law, the Committee is concerned that the provisions and principles of the Convention on the Rights of the Child – which are much broader than those contained in the European Convention – have not yet been incorporated into domestic law, nor is there any formal process to ensure that new legislation fully complies with the Convention. and Committee on the Rights of the Child ... The Committee encourages the State party to incorporate into domestic law the rights, principles and provisions of the Convention in order to ensure that all legislation complies with the Convention and that the provisions and principles of the Convention are widely applied in legal and administrative proceedings') *Concluding Observations of the Committee on the Rights of the Child: United Kingdom of Great Britain and Northern Ireland* CRC/C/GBR/CO/4, para 11 ('The Committee recommends that the State party continue to take measures to bring its legislation into line with the Convention. To this aim, the State party could take the opportunity given in this regard by the development of a Bill of Rights in Northern Ireland and a British Bill of Rights, and incorporate into them the principles and provisions of the Convention, e g by having a special section in these bills devoted to child rights').

for any Bill of Rights to include detailed rights for children.[47] The opportunity presented by a Bill of Rights has also not been lost on the UN Committee on the Rights of the Child:[48]

> 'The Committee recommends that the State party continue to take measures to bring its legislation into line with the Convention. To this aim, the State party could take the opportunity given in this regard by the development of a Bill of Rights in Northern Ireland and a British Bill of Rights, and incorporate into them the principles and provisions of the Convention, e g by having a special section in these bills devoted to child rights.'

17.10 As Fortin notes there are powerful arguments for incorporating the terms of the CRC into domestic law.[49] Such a step is plainly suggested by Art 4 of the CRC[50] and would be the most effective way of ensuring the comprehensive domestic implementation of the rights of children enshrined in the Convention. For the time being however, ahead of such incorporation it is vital to remember that the CRC retains the status of a binding international convention in domestic law. The status of the CRC in the domestic sphere goes beyond a comprehensive set of standards against which ratifying states may measure the extent to which they fulfil children's rights.[51] Rather, as demonstrated in chapter 3, the domestic courts are bound to interpret domestic legislation, including the Human Rights Act 1998, and the common law in line with the provisions of the CRC. Likewise, domestic decision makers must have regard to the provisions of the CRC when exercising administrative discretion.[52] Thus, although not yet incorporated or transformed into domestic law, the CRC remains nonetheless a powerful tool for practitioners to advance the cause of children in the courts and administrative bodies of the United Kingdom. Alongside this the ECHR, which itself must be interpreted in accordance with the CRC, continues to protect and advance the rights of children within the domestic jurisdiction through the agency of the Human Rights Act 1998.

17.11 Children's rights apply to all children without limitation or qualification. They stand in the way of those who would seek to make swift, cheap and homogenised decisions concerning children without reference to children themselves or their interests. In particular, children's rights render the children who comprise the silent constituency evidenced in the grim statistics cited above visible and heard. The UNICEF report *Child Poverty in Perspective: an Overview of Child Well-being in Rich Countries* placed the United Kingdom near the bottom of twenty-one of the world's well-developed countries in each of the categories akin to those listed in *Every Child Matters*, namely being healthy, staying safe, enjoying and achieving, making a positive contribution and

---

47   House of Lords House of Commons Joint Committee on Human Rights *A Bill of Rights for the UK* Twenty Ninth Report of Session 2007–2008 HL Paper 165-I/HC150-I (2008) The Stationery Office, paras 139 and 145. The Children's Rights Alliance reports that Ministers indicated in 2008 that children would be at the heart of any new Bill of Rights (see CRAE *The State of Children's Rights in England* (2008) p.vii).

48   *Concluding Observations of the Committee on the Rights of the Child: United Kingdom of Great Britain and Northern Ireland* CRC/C/GBR/CO/4, para 11.

49   Fortin, J *Children's Rights and the Developing Law* (2009) 3rd edn, Cambridge, p 51.

50   Article 4 of the CRC provides that 'States Parties shall undertake all appropriate legislative, administrative, and other measures for the implementation of the rights recognised in the present Convention. With regard to economic, social and cultural rights, States Parties shall undertake such measures to the maximum extent of their available resources and, where needed, within the framework of international co-operation.'

51   Fortin, J *Children's Rights and the Developing Law* (2009) 3rd edn, Cambridge, p 45.

52   See **3.32–3.46** above. It must be remembered that this is how the ECHR gained currency in domestic law before it was given direct effect through the Human Rights Act 1998. See for example *Re KD (A Minor) (Ward: Termination of Access)* [1988] 1 All ER 577.

economic wellbeing.[53] As Rodham notes, ascribing rights to children will not immediately solve the diverse problems encompassed by this finding nor undermine the consensus that perpetuates some of those problems. Ascribing rights to children will, however, elicit from the legislature, from the judiciary and from administrative decision makers institutional support for the child's position and for the child's point of view.[54]

---

[53] UNICEF, *Child poverty in perspective: An overview of child well-being in rich countries*, Innocenti Report Card 7, (UNICEF Innocenti Research Centre, 2007).

[54] See Rodham, H *Children under the Law* (1973) Harvard Educational Review 43, pp 487–514 p 500.

Appendix 1

UN CONVENTION ON THE RIGHTS OF THE CHILD

Adopted and opened for signature, ratification and accession by General Assembly resolution 44/25 of 20 November 1989

Entry into force 2 September 1990, in accordance with article 49

Preamble

The States Parties to the present Convention,

Considering that, in accordance with the principles proclaimed in the Charter of the United Nations, recognition of the inherent dignity and of the equal and inalienable rights of all members of the human family is the foundation of freedom, justice and peace in the world,

Bearing in mind that the peoples of the United Nations have, in the Charter, reaffirmed their faith in fundamental human rights and in the dignity and worth of the human person, and have determined to promote social progress and better standards of life in larger freedom,

Recognizing that the United Nations has, in the Universal Declaration of Human Rights and in the International Covenants on Human Rights, proclaimed and agreed that everyone is entitled to all the rights and freedoms set forth therein, without distinction of any kind, such as race, colour, sex, language, religion, political or other opinion, national or social origin, property, birth or other status,

Recalling that, in the Universal Declaration of Human Rights, the United Nations has proclaimed that childhood is entitled to special care and assistance,

Convinced that the family, as the fundamental group of society and the natural environment for the growth and well-being of all its members and particularly children, should be afforded the necessary protection and assistance so that it can fully assume its responsibilities within the community,

Recognizing that the child, for the full and harmonious development of his or her personality, should grow up in a family environment, in an atmosphere of happiness, love and understanding,

Considering that the child should be fully prepared to live an individual life in society, and brought up in the spirit of the ideals proclaimed in the Charter of the United Nations, and in particular in the spirit of peace, dignity, tolerance, freedom, equality and solidarity,

Bearing in mind that the need to extend particular care to the child has been stated in the Geneva Declaration of the Rights of the Child of 1924 and in the Declaration of the Rights of the Child adopted by the General Assembly on 20 November 1959 and recognized in the Universal Declaration of Human Rights, in the International Covenant on Civil and Political Rights (in particular in articles 23 and 24), in the International Covenant on Economic, Social and Cultural Rights (in particular in article 10) and in the statutes and relevant instruments of specialized agencies and international organizations concerned with the welfare of children,

Bearing in mind that, as indicated in the Declaration of the Rights of the Child, 'the child, by reason of his physical and mental immaturity, needs special safeguards and care, including appropriate legal protection, before as well as after birth',

Recalling the provisions of the Declaration on Social and Legal Principles relating to the Protection and Welfare of Children, with Special Reference to Foster Placement and Adoption Nationally and Internationally; the United Nations Standard Minimum Rules for the Administration of Juvenile Justice (The Beijing Rules); and the Declaration on the Protection of Women and Children in Emergency and Armed Conflict, Recognizing that, in all countries in the world, there are children living in exceptionally difficult conditions, and that such children need special consideration,

Taking due account of the importance of the traditions and cultural values of each people for the protection and harmonious development of the child, Recognizing the importance of international co-operation for improving the living conditions of children in every country, in particular in the developing countries,

Have agreed as follows:

PART I

Article 1

For the purposes of the present Convention, a child means every human being below the age of eighteen years unless under the law applicable to the child, majority is attained earlier.

Article 2

1. States Parties shall respect and ensure the rights set forth in the present Convention to each child within their jurisdiction without discrimination of any kind, irrespective of the child's or his or her parent's or legal guardian's race, colour, sex, language, religion, political or other opinion, national, ethnic or social origin, property, disability, birth or other status.

2. States Parties shall take all appropriate measures to ensure that the child is protected against all forms of discrimination or punishment on the basis of the status, activities, expressed opinions, or beliefs of the child's parents, legal guardians, or family members.

Article 3

1. In all actions concerning children, whether undertaken by public or private social welfare institutions, courts of law, administrative authorities or legislative bodies, the best interests of the child shall be a primary consideration.

2. States Parties undertake to ensure the child such protection and care as is necessary for his or her well-being, taking into account the rights and duties of his or her parents, legal guardians, or other individuals legally responsible for him or her, and, to this end, shall take all appropriate legislative and administrative measures.

3. States Parties shall ensure that the institutions, services and facilities responsible for the care or protection of children shall conform with the standards established by competent authorities, particularly in the areas of safety, health, in the number and suitability of their staff, as well as competent supervision.

Article 4

States Parties shall undertake all appropriate legislative, administrative, and other measures for the implementation of the rights recognized in the present Convention. With regard to economic, social and cultural rights, States Parties shall undertake such measures to the maximum extent of their available resources and, where needed, within the framework of international co-operation.

Article 5

States Parties shall respect the responsibilities, rights and duties of parents or, where applicable, the members of the extended family or community as provided for by local custom, legal guardians or other persons legally responsible for the child, to provide, in a manner consistent with the evolving capacities of the child, appropriate direction and guidance in the exercise by the child of the rights recognized in the present Convention.

Article 6

1. States Parties recognize that every child has the inherent right to life.

2. States Parties shall ensure to the maximum extent possible the survival and development of the child.

Article 7

1. The child shall be registered immediately after birth and shall have the right from birth to a name, the right to acquire a nationality and. as far as possible, the right to know and be cared for by his or her parents.

2. States Parties shall ensure the implementation of these rights in accordance with their national law and their obligations under the relevant international instruments in this field, in particular where the child would otherwise be stateless.

Article 8

1. States Parties undertake to respect the right of the child to preserve his or her identity, including nationality, name and family relations as recognized by law without unlawful interference.

2. Where a child is illegally deprived of some or all of the elements of his or her identity, States Parties shall provide appropriate assistance and protection, with a view to re-establishing speedily his or her identity.

Article 9

1. States Parties shall ensure that a child shall not be separated from his or her parents against their will, except when competent authorities subject to judicial review determine, in accordance with applicable law and procedures, that such separation is necessary for the best interests of the child. Such determination may be necessary in a particular case such as one involving abuse or neglect of the child by the parents, or one where the parents are living separately and a decision must be made as to the child's place of residence.

2. In any proceedings pursuant to paragraph 1 of the present article, all interested parties shall be given an opportunity to participate in the proceedings and make their views known.

3. States Parties shall respect the right of the child who is separated from one or both parents to maintain personal relations and direct contact with both parents on a regular basis, except if it is contrary to the child's best interests.

4. Where such separation results from any action initiated by a State Party, such as the detention, imprisonment, exile, deportation or death (including death arising from any cause while the person is in the custody of the State) of one or both parents or of the child, that State Party shall, upon request, provide the parents, the child or, if appropriate, another member of the family with the essential information concerning the whereabouts of the absent member(s) of the family unless the provision of the information would be detrimental to the well-being of the child. States Parties shall further ensure that the submission of such a request shall of itself entail no adverse consequences for the person(s) concerned.

Article 10

1. In accordance with the obligation of States Parties under article 9, paragraph 1, applications by a child or his or her parents to enter or leave a State Party for the purpose of family reunification shall be dealt with by States Parties in a positive, humane and expeditious manner. States Parties shall further ensure that the submission of such a request shall entail no adverse consequences for the applicants and for the members of their family.

2. A child whose parents reside in different States shall have the right to maintain on a regular basis, save in exceptional circumstances personal relations and direct contacts with both parents. Towards that end and in accordance with the obligation of States Parties under article 9, paragraph 1, States Parties shall respect the right of the child and his or her parents to leave any country, including their own, and to enter their own country. The right to leave any country shall be subject only to such restrictions as are prescribed by law and which are necessary to protect the national security, public order (ordre public), public health or morals or the rights and freedoms of others and are consistent with the other rights recognized in the present Convention.

Article 11

1. States Parties shall take measures to combat the illicit transfer and non-return of children abroad.

2. To this end, States Parties shall promote the conclusion of bilateral or multilateral agreements or accession to existing agreements.

Article 12

1. States Parties shall assure to the child who is capable of forming his or her own views the right to express those views freely in all matters affecting the child, the views of the child being given due weight in accordance with the age and maturity of the child.

2. For this purpose, the child shall in particular be provided the opportunity to be heard in any judicial and administrative proceedings affecting the child, either directly, or through a representative or an appropriate body, in a manner consistent with the procedural rules of national law.

Article 13

1. The child shall have the right to freedom of expression; this right shall include freedom to seek, receive and impart information and ideas of all kinds, regardless of frontiers, either orally, in writing or in print, in the form of art, or through any other media of the child's choice.

2. The exercise of this right may be subject to certain restrictions, but these shall only be such as are provided by law and are necessary:

(a)   For respect of the rights or reputations of others; or
(b)   For the protection of national security or of public order (ordre public), or of public health or morals.

Article 14

1. States Parties shall respect the right of the child to freedom of thought, conscience and religion.

2. States Parties shall respect the rights and duties of the parents and, when applicable, legal guardians, to provide direction to the child in the exercise of his or her right in a manner consistent with the evolving capacities of the child.

3. Freedom to manifest one's religion or beliefs may be subject only to such limitations as are prescribed by law and are necessary to protect public safety, order, health or morals, or the fundamental rights and freedoms of others.

Article 15

1. States Parties recognize the rights of the child to freedom of association and to freedom of peaceful assembly.

2. No restrictions may be placed on the exercise of these rights other than those imposed in conformity with the law and which are necessary in a democratic society in the interests of national security or public safety, public order (ordre public), the protection of public health or morals or the protection of the rights and freedoms of others.

Article 16

1. No child shall be subjected to arbitrary or unlawful interference with his or her privacy, family, or correspondence, nor to unlawful attacks on his or her honour and reputation.

2. The child has the right to the protection of the law against such interference or attacks.

Article 17

States Parties recognize the important function performed by the mass media and shall ensure that the child has access to information and material from a diversity of national and international sources, especially those aimed at the promotion of his or her social, spiritual and moral well-being and physical and mental health.

To this end, States Parties shall:

(a)   Encourage the mass media to disseminate information and material of social and cultural benefit to the child and in accordance with the spirit of article 29;

(b)   Encourage international co-operation in the production, exchange and dissemination of such information and material from a diversity of cultural, national and international sources;

(c)   Encourage the production and dissemination of children's books;

(d)   Encourage the mass media to have particular regard to the linguistic needs of the child who belongs to a minority group or who is indigenous;

(e)   Encourage the development of appropriate guidelines for the protection of the child from information and material injurious to his or her well-being, bearing in mind the provisions of articles 13 and 18.

Article 18

1. States Parties shall use their best efforts to ensure recognition of the principle that both parents have common responsibilities for the upbringing and development of the child. Parents or, as the case may be, legal guardians, have the primary responsibility for the upbringing and development of the child. The best interests of the child will be their basic concern.

2. For the purpose of guaranteeing and promoting the rights set forth in the present Convention, States Parties shall render appropriate assistance to parents and legal guardians in the performance of their child-rearing responsibilities and shall ensure the development of institutions, facilities and services for the care of children.

3. States Parties shall take all appropriate measures to ensure that children of working parents have the right to benefit from child-care services and facilities for which they are eligible.

Article 19

1. States Parties shall take all appropriate legislative, administrative, social and educational measures to protect the child from all forms of physical or mental violence, injury or abuse, neglect or negligent treatment, maltreatment or exploitation, including sexual abuse, while in the care of parent(s), legal guardian(s) or any other person who has the care of the child.

2. Such protective measures should, as appropriate, include effective procedures for the establishment of social programmes to provide necessary support for the child and for those who have the care of the child, as well as for other forms of prevention and for identification, reporting, referral, investigation, treatment and follow-up of instances of child maltreatment described heretofore, and, as appropriate, for judicial involvement.

Article 20

1. A child temporarily or permanently deprived of his or her family environment, or in whose own best interests cannot be allowed to remain in that environment, shall be entitled to special protection and assistance provided by the State.

2. States Parties shall in accordance with their national laws ensure alternative care for such a child.

3. Such care could include, inter alia, foster placement, kafalah of Islamic law, adoption or if necessary placement in suitable institutions for the care of children. When considering solutions, due regard shall be paid to the desirability of continuity in a child's upbringing and to the child's ethnic, religious, cultural and linguistic background.

Article 21

States Parties that recognize and/or permit the system of adoption shall ensure that the best interests of the child shall be the paramount consideration and they shall:

(a) Ensure that the adoption of a child is authorized only by competent authorities who determine, in accordance with applicable law and procedures and on the basis of all pertinent and reliable information, that the adoption is permissible in view of the child's status concerning parents, relatives and legal guardians and that, if required, the persons concerned have given their informed consent to the adoption on the basis of such counselling as may be necessary;

(b) Recognize that inter-country adoption may be considered as an alternative means of child's care, if the child cannot be placed in a foster or an adoptive family or cannot in any suitable manner be cared for in the child's country of origin;

(c) Ensure that the child concerned by inter-country adoption enjoys safeguards and standards equivalent to those existing in the case of national adoption;

(d) Take all appropriate measures to ensure that, in inter-country adoption, the placement does not result in improper financial gain for those involved in it;

(e) Promote, where appropriate, the objectives of the present article by concluding bilateral or multilateral arrangements or agreements, and endeavour, within this framework, to ensure that the placement of the child in another country is carried out by competent authorities or organs.

Article 22

1. States Parties shall take appropriate measures to ensure that a child who is seeking refugee status or who is considered a refugee in accordance with applicable international or domestic law and procedures shall, whether unaccompanied or accompanied by his or her parents or by any other person, receive appropriate protection and humanitarian assistance in the enjoyment of applicable rights set forth in the present Convention and in other international human rights or humanitarian instruments to which the said States are Parties.

2. For this purpose, States Parties shall provide, as they consider appropriate, co-operation in any efforts by the United Nations and other competent intergovernmental organizations or non-governmental organizations co-operating with the United Nations to protect and assist such a child and to trace the parents or other members of the family of any refugee child in order to obtain information necessary for reunification with his or her family. In cases where no parents or other members of the family can be found, the child shall be accorded the same protection as any other child permanently or temporarily deprived of his or her family environment for any reason , as set forth in the present Convention.

Article 23

1. States Parties recognize that a mentally or physically disabled child should enjoy a full and decent life, in conditions which ensure dignity, promote self-reliance and facilitate the child's active participation in the community.

2. States Parties recognize the right of the disabled child to special care and shall encourage and ensure the extension, subject to available resources, to the eligible child

and those responsible for his or her care, of assistance for which application is made and which is appropriate to the child's condition and to the circumstances of the parents or others caring for the child.

3. Recognizing the special needs of a disabled child, assistance extended in accordance with paragraph 2 of the present article shall be provided free of charge, whenever possible, taking into account the financial resources of the parents or others caring for the child, and shall be designed to ensure that the disabled child has effective access to and receives education, training, health care services, rehabilitation services, preparation for employment and recreation opportunities in a manner conducive to the child's achieving the fullest possible social integration and individual development, including his or her cultural and spiritual development

4. States Parties shall promote, in the spirit of international cooperation, the exchange of appropriate information in the field of preventive health care and of medical, psychological and functional treatment of disabled children, including dissemination of and access to information concerning methods of rehabilitation, education and vocational services, with the aim of enabling States Parties to improve their capabilities and skills and to widen their experience in these areas. In this regard, particular account shall be taken of the needs of developing countries.

Article 24

1. States Parties recognize the right of the child to the enjoyment of the highest attainable standard of health and to facilities for the treatment of illness and rehabilitation of health. States Parties shall strive to ensure that no child is deprived of his or her right of access to such health care services.

2. States Parties shall pursue full implementation of this right and, in particular, shall take appropriate measures:

(a)   To diminish infant and child mortality;

(b)   To ensure the provision of necessary medical assistance and health care to all children with emphasis on the development of primary health care;

(c)   To combat disease and malnutrition, including within the framework of primary health care, through, inter alia, the application of readily available technology and through the provision of adequate nutritious foods and clean drinking-water, taking into consideration the dangers and risks of environmental pollution;

(d)   To ensure appropriate pre-natal and post-natal health care for mothers;

(e)   To ensure that all segments of society, in particular parents and children, are informed, have access to education and are supported in the use of basic knowledge of child health and nutrition, the advantages of breastfeeding, hygiene and environmental sanitation and the prevention of accidents;

(f)   To develop preventive health care, guidance for parents and family planning education and services.

3. States Parties shall take all effective and appropriate measures with a view to abolishing traditional practices prejudicial to the health of children.

4. States Parties undertake to promote and encourage international co-operation with a view to achieving progressively the full realization of the right recognized in the present article. In this regard, particular account shall be taken of the needs of developing countries.

Article 25

States Parties recognize the right of a child who has been placed by the competent authorities for the purposes of care, protection or treatment of his or her physical or mental health, to a periodic review of the treatment provided to the child and all other circumstances relevant to his or her placement.

Article 26

1. States Parties shall recognize for every child the right to benefit from social security, including social insurance, and shall take the necessary measures to achieve the full realization of this right in accordance with their national law.

2. The benefits should, where appropriate, be granted, taking into account the resources and the circumstances of the child and persons having responsibility for the maintenance of the child, as well as any other consideration relevant to an application for benefits made by or on behalf of the child.

Article 27

1. States Parties recognize the right of every child to a standard of living adequate for the child's physical, mental, spiritual, moral and social development.

2. The parent(s) or others responsible for the child have the primary responsibility to secure, within their abilities and financial capacities, the conditions of living necessary for the child's development.

3. States Parties, in accordance with national conditions and within their means, shall take appropriate measures to assist parents and others responsible for the child to implement this right and shall in case of need provide material assistance and support programmes, particularly with regard to nutrition, clothing and housing.

4. States Parties shall take all appropriate measures to secure the recovery of maintenance for the child from the parents or other persons having financial responsibility for the child, both within the State Party and from abroad. In particular, where the person having financial responsibility for the child lives in a State different from that of the child, States Parties shall promote the accession to international agreements or the conclusion of such agreements, as well as the making of other appropriate arrangements.

Article 28

1. States Parties recognize the right of the child to education, and with a view to achieving this right progressively and on the basis of equal opportunity, they shall, in particular:

(a) Make primary education compulsory and available free to all;
(b) Encourage the development of different forms of secondary education, including general and vocational education, make them available and accessible to every child, and take appropriate measures such as the introduction of free education and offering financial assistance in case of need;
(c) Make higher education accessible to all on the basis of capacity by every appropriate means;
(d) Make educational and vocational information and guidance available and accessible to all children;

(e)   Take measures to encourage regular attendance at schools and the reduction of drop-out rates.

2. States Parties shall take all appropriate measures to ensure that school discipline is administered in a manner consistent with the child's human dignity and in conformity with the present Convention.

3. States Parties shall promote and encourage international cooperation in matters relating to education, in particular with a view to contributing to the elimination of ignorance and illiteracy throughout the world and facilitating access to scientific and technical knowledge and modern teaching methods. In this regard, particular account shall be taken of the needs of developing countries.

Article 29

1. States Parties agree that the education of the child shall be directed to:

(a)   The development of the child's personality, talents and mental and physical abilities to their fullest potential;

(b)   The development of respect for human rights and fundamental freedoms, and for the principles enshrined in the Charter of the United Nations;

(c)   The development of respect for the child's parents, his or her own cultural identity, language and values, for the national values of the country in which the child is living, the country from which he or she may originate, and for civilizations different from his or her own;

(d)   The preparation of the child for responsible life in a free society, in the spirit of understanding, peace, tolerance, equality of sexes, and friendship among all peoples, ethnic, national and religious groups and persons of indigenous origin;

(e)   The development of respect for the natural environment.

2. No part of the present article or article 28 shall be construed so as to interfere with the liberty of individuals and bodies to establish and direct educational institutions, subject always to the observance of the principle set forth in paragraph 1 of the present article and to the requirements that the education given in such institutions shall conform to such minimum standards as may be laid down by the State.

Article 30

In those States in which ethnic, religious or linguistic minorities or persons of indigenous origin exist, a child belonging to such a minority or who is indigenous shall not be denied the right, in community with other members of his or her group, to enjoy his or her own culture, to profess and practise his or her own religion, or to use his or her own language.

Article 31

1. States Parties recognize the right of the child to rest and leisure, to engage in play and recreational activities appropriate to the age of the child and to participate freely in cultural life and the arts.

2. States Parties shall respect and promote the right of the child to participate fully in cultural and artistic life and shall encourage the provision of appropriate and equal opportunities for cultural, artistic, recreational and leisure activity.

Article 32

1. States Parties recognize the right of the child to be protected from economic exploitation and from performing any work that is likely to be hazardous or to interfere with the child's education, or to be harmful to the child's health or physical, mental, spiritual, moral or social development.

2. States Parties shall take legislative, administrative, social and educational measures to ensure the implementation of the present article. To this end, and having regard to the relevant provisions of other international instruments, States Parties shall in particular:

    (a)   Provide for a minimum age or minimum ages for admission to employment;

    (b)   Provide for appropriate regulation of the hours and conditions of employment;

    (c)   Provide for appropriate penalties or other sanctions to ensure the effective enforcement of the present article.

Article 33

States Parties shall take all appropriate measures, including legislative, administrative, social and educational measures, to protect children from the illicit use of narcotic drugs and psychotropic substances as defined in the relevant international treaties, and to prevent the use of children in the illicit production and trafficking of such substances.

Article 34

States Parties undertake to protect the child from all forms of sexual exploitation and sexual abuse. For these purposes, States Parties shall in particular take all appropriate national, bilateral and multilateral measures to prevent:

    (a)   The inducement or coercion of a child to engage in any unlawful sexual activity;

    (b)   The exploitative use of children in prostitution or other unlawful sexual practices;

    (c)   The exploitative use of children in pornographic performances and materials.

Article 35

States Parties shall take all appropriate national, bilateral and multilateral measures to prevent the abduction of, the sale of or traffic in children for any purpose or in any form.

Article 36

States Parties shall protect the child against all other forms of exploitation prejudicial to any aspects of the child's welfare.

Article 37

States Parties shall ensure that:

    (a)   No child shall be subjected to torture or other cruel, inhuman or degrading treatment or punishment. Neither capital punishment nor life imprisonment without possibility of release shall be imposed for offences committed by persons below eighteen years of age;

(b)   No child shall be deprived of his or her liberty unlawfully or arbitrarily. The arrest, detention or imprisonment of a child shall be in conformity with the law and shall be used only as a measure of last resort and for the shortest appropriate period of time;

(c)   Every child deprived of liberty shall be treated with humanity and respect for the inherent dignity of the human person, and in a manner which takes into account the needs of persons of his or her age. In particular, every child deprived of liberty shall be separated from adults unless it is considered in the child's best interest not to do so and shall have the right to maintain contact with his or her family through correspondence and visits, save in exceptional circumstances;

(d)   Every child deprived of his or her liberty shall have the right to prompt access to legal and other appropriate assistance, as well as the right to challenge the legality of the deprivation of his or her liberty before a court or other competent, independent and impartial authority, and to a prompt decision on any such action.

Article 38

1. States Parties undertake to respect and to ensure respect for rules of international humanitarian law applicable to them in armed conflicts which are relevant to the child.

2. States Parties shall take all feasible measures to ensure that persons who have not attained the age of fifteen years do not take a direct part in hostilities.

3. States Parties shall refrain from recruiting any person who has not attained the age of fifteen years into their armed forces. In recruiting among those persons who have attained the age of fifteen years but who have not attained the age of eighteen years, States Parties shall endeavour to give priority to those who are oldest.

4. In accordance with their obligations under international humanitarian law to protect the civilian population in armed conflicts, States Parties shall take all feasible measures to ensure protection and care of children who are affected by an armed conflict.

Article 39

States Parties shall take all appropriate measures to promote physical and psychological recovery and social reintegration of a child victim of: any form of neglect, exploitation, or abuse; torture or any other form of cruel, inhuman or degrading treatment or punishment; or armed conflicts. Such recovery and reintegration shall take place in an environment which fosters the health, self-respect and dignity of the child.

Article 40

1. States Parties recognize the right of every child alleged as, accused of, or recognized as having infringed the penal law to be treated in a manner consistent with the promotion of the child's sense of dignity and worth, which reinforces the child's respect for the human rights and fundamental freedoms of others and which takes into account the child's age and the desirability of promoting the child's reintegration and the child's assuming a constructive role in society.

2. To this end, and having regard to the relevant provisions of international instruments, States Parties shall, in particular, ensure that:

(a)   No child shall be alleged as, be accused of, or recognized as having infringed the penal law by reason of acts or omissions that were not prohibited by national or international law at the time they were committed;

(b)   Every child alleged as or accused of having infringed the penal law has at least the following guarantees:

    (i)   To be presumed innocent until proven guilty according to law;

    (ii)   To be informed promptly and directly of the charges against him or her, and, if appropriate, through his or her parents or legal guardians, and to have legal or other appropriate assistance in the preparation and presentation of his or her defence;

    (iii)   To have the matter determined without delay by a competent, independent and impartial authority or judicial body in a fair hearing according to law, in the presence of legal or other appropriate assistance and, unless it is considered not to be in the best interest of the child, in particular, taking into account his or her age or situation, his or her parents or legal guardians;

    (iv)   Not to be compelled to give testimony or to confess guilt; to examine or have examined adverse witnesses and to obtain the participation and examination of witnesses on his or her behalf under conditions of equality;

    (v)   If considered to have infringed the penal law, to have this decision and any measures imposed in consequence thereof reviewed by a higher competent, independent and impartial authority or judicial body according to law;

    (vi)   To have the free assistance of an interpreter if the child cannot understand or speak the language used;

    (vii)   To have his or her privacy fully respected at all stages of the proceedings.

3. States Parties shall seek to promote the establishment of laws, procedures, authorities and institutions specifically applicable to children alleged as, accused of, or recognized as having infringed the penal law, and, in particular:

(a)   The establishment of a minimum age below which children shall be presumed not to have the capacity to infringe the penal law;

(b)   Whenever appropriate and desirable, measures for dealing with such children without resorting to judicial proceedings, providing that human rights and legal safeguards are fully respected.

4. A variety of dispositions, such as care, guidance and supervision orders; counselling; probation; foster care; education and vocational training programmes and other alternatives to institutional care shall be available to ensure that children are dealt with in a manner appropriate to their well-being and proportionate both to their circumstances and the offence.

Article 41

Nothing in the present Convention shall affect any provisions which are more conducive to the realization of the rights of the child and which may be contained in:

(a)   The law of a State party; or

(b)   International law in force for that State.

PART II

Article 42

States Parties undertake to make the principles and provisions of the Convention widely known, by appropriate and active means, to adults and children alike.

Article 43

1. For the purpose of examining the progress made by States Parties in achieving the realization of the obligations undertaken in the present Convention, there shall be established a Committee on the Rights of the Child, which shall carry out the functions hereinafter provided.

2. The Committee shall consist of eighteen experts of high moral standing and recognized competence in the field covered by this Convention.[1] The members of the Committee shall be elected by States Parties from among their nationals and shall serve in their personal capacity, consideration being given to equitable geographical distribution, as well as to the principal legal systems.

3. The members of the Committee shall be elected by secret ballot from a list of persons nominated by States Parties. Each State Party may nominate one person from among its own nationals.

4. The initial election to the Committee shall be held no later than six months after the date of the entry into force of the present Convention and thereafter every second year. At least four months before the date of each election, the Secretary-General of the United Nations shall address a letter to States Parties inviting them to submit their nominations within two months. The Secretary-General shall subsequently prepare a list in alphabetical order of all persons thus nominated, indicating States Parties which have nominated them, and shall submit it to the States Parties to the present Convention.

5. The elections shall be held at meetings of States Parties convened by the Secretary-General at United Nations Headquarters. At those meetings, for which two thirds of States Parties shall constitute a quorum, the persons elected to the Committee shall be those who obtain the largest number of votes and an absolute majority of the votes of the representatives of States Parties present and voting.

6. The members of the Committee shall be elected for a term of four years. They shall be eligible for re-election if renominated. The term of five of the members elected at the first election shall expire at the end of two years; immediately after the first election, the names of these five members shall be chosen by lot by the Chairman of the meeting.

7. If a member of the Committee dies or resigns or declares that for any other cause he or she can no longer perform the duties of the Committee, the State Party which nominated the member shall appoint another expert from among its nationals to serve for the remainder of the term, subject to the approval of the Committee.

8. The Committee shall establish its own rules of procedure.

9. The Committee shall elect its officers for a period of two years.

10. The meetings of the Committee shall normally be held at United Nations Headquarters or at any other convenient place as determined by the Committee. The Committee shall normally meet annually. The duration of the meetings of the Committee shall be determined, and reviewed, if necessary, by a meeting of the States Parties to the present Convention, subject to the approval of the General Assembly.

11. The Secretary-General of the United Nations shall provide the necessary staff and facilities for the effective performance of the functions of the Committee under the present Convention.

12. With the approval of the General Assembly, the members of the Committee established under the present Convention shall receive emoluments from United Nations resources on such terms and conditions as the Assembly may decide.

1   The General Assembly, in its resolution 50/155 of 21 December 1995, approved the amendment to article 43, paragraph 2, of the Convention on the Rights of the Child, replacing the word "ten" with the word "eighteen". The amendment entered into force on 18 November 2002 when it had been accepted by a two-thirds majority of the States parties (128 out of 191).

Article 44

1. States Parties undertake to submit to the Committee, through the Secretary-General of the United Nations, reports on the measures they have adopted which give effect to the rights recognized herein and on the progress made on the enjoyment of those rights

  (a)   Within two years of the entry into force of the Convention for the State Party concerned;
  (b)   Thereafter every five years.

2. Reports made under the present article shall indicate factors and difficulties, if any, affecting the degree of fulfilment of the obligations under the present Convention. Reports shall also contain sufficient information to provide the Committee with a comprehensive understanding of the implementation of the Convention in the country concerned.

3. A State Party which has submitted a comprehensive initial report to the Committee need not, in its subsequent reports submitted in accordance with paragraph 1 (b) of the present article, repeat basic information previously provided.

4. The Committee may request from States Parties further information relevant to the implementation of the Convention.

5. he Committee shall submit to the General Assembly, through the Economic and Social Council, every two years, reports on its activities.

6. States Parties shall make their reports widely available to the public in their own countries.

Article 45

In order to foster the effective implementation of the Convention and to encourage international co-operation in the field covered by the Convention:

  (a)   The specialized agencies, the United Nations Children's Fund, and other United Nations organs shall be entitled to be represented at the consideration of the implementation of such provisions of the present Convention as fall within the scope of their mandate. The Committee may invite the specialized agencies, the United Nations Children's Fund and other competent bodies as it may consider appropriate to provide expert advice on the implementation of the Convention in areas falling within the scope of their respective mandates. The Committee may invite the specialized agencies, the United Nations Children's Fund, and other United Nations organs to submit reports on the implementation of the Convention in areas falling within the scope of their activities;

(b)   The Committee shall transmit, as it may consider appropriate, to the specialized agencies, the United Nations Children's Fund and other competent bodies, any reports from States Parties that contain a request, or indicate a need, for technical advice or assistance, along with the Committee's observations and suggestions, if any, on these requests or indications;

(c)   The Committee may recommend to the General Assembly to request the Secretary-General to undertake on its behalf studies on specific issues relating to the rights of the child;

(d)   The Committee may make suggestions and general recommendations based on information received pursuant to articles 44 and 45 of the present Convention. Such suggestions and general recommendations shall be transmitted to any State Party concerned and reported to the General Assembly, together with comments, if any, from States Parties.

PART III

Article 46

The present Convention shall be open for signature by all States.

Article 47

The present Convention is subject to ratification. Instruments of ratification shall be deposited with the Secretary-General of the United Nations.

Article 48

The present Convention shall remain open for accession by any State. The instruments of accession shall be deposited with the Secretary-General of the United Nations.

Article 49

1. The present Convention shall enter into force on the thirtieth day following the date of deposit with the Secretary-General of the United Nations of the twentieth instrument of ratification or accession.

2. For each State ratifying or acceding to the Convention after the deposit of the twentieth instrument of ratification or accession, the Convention shall enter into force on the thirtieth day after the deposit by such State of its instrument of ratification or accession.

Article 50

1. Any State Party may propose an amendment and file it with the Secretary-General of the United Nations. The Secretary-General shall thereupon communicate the proposed amendment to States Parties, with a request that they indicate whether they favour a conference of States Parties for the purpose of considering and voting upon the proposals. In the event that, within four months from the date of such communication, at least one third of the States Parties favour such a conference, the Secretary-General shall convene the conference under the auspices of the United Nations. Any amendment adopted by a majority of States Parties present and voting at the conference shall be submitted to the General Assembly for approval.

2. An amendment adopted in accordance with paragraph 1 of the present article shall enter into force when it has been approved by the General Assembly of the United Nations and accepted by a two-thirds majority of States Parties.

3. When an amendment enters into force, it shall be binding on those States Parties which have accepted it, other States Parties still being bound by the provisions of the present Convention and any earlier amendments which they have accepted.

Article 51

1. The Secretary-General of the United Nations shall receive and circulate to all States the text of reservations made by States at the time of ratification or accession.

2. A reservation incompatible with the object and purpose of the present Convention shall not be permitted.

3. Reservations may be withdrawn at any time by notification to that effect addressed to the Secretary-General of the United Nations, who shall then inform all States. Such notification shall take effect on the date on which it is received by the Secretary-General

Article 52

A State Party may denounce the present Convention by written notification to the Secretary-General of the United Nations. Denunciation becomes effective one year after the date of receipt of the notification by the Secretary-General.

Article 53

The Secretary-General of the United Nations is designated as the depositary of the present Convention.

Article 54

The original of the present Convention, of which the Arabic, Chinese, English, French, Russian and Spanish texts are equally authentic, shall be deposited with the Secretary-General of the United Nations. In witness thereof the undersigned plenipotentiaries, being duly authorized thereto by their respective Governments, have signed the present Convention.

Appendix 2

EUROPEAN CONVENTION FOR THE PROTECTION OF HUMAN RIGHTS AND FUNDAMENTAL FREEDOMS

Rome, 4.XI.1950

The governments signatory hereto, being members of the Council of Europe,

Considering the Universal Declaration of Human Rights proclaimed by the General Assembly of the United Nations on 10 December 1948;

Considering that this Declaration aims at securing the universal and effective recognition and observance of the Rights therein declared;

Considering that the aim of the Council of Europe is the achievement of greater unity between its members and that one of the methods by which that aim is to be pursued is the maintenance and further realisation of human rights and fundamental freedoms;

Reaffirming their profound belief in those fundamental freedoms which are the foundation of justice and peace in the world and are best maintained on the one hand by an effective political democracy and on the other by a common understanding and observance of the human rights upon which they depend;

Being resolved, as the governments of European countries which are likeminded and have a common heritage of political traditions, ideals, freedom and the rule of law, to take the first steps for the collective enforcement of certain of the rights stated in the Universal Declaration,

Have agreed as follows:

Article 1

Obligation to respect human rights

The High Contracting Parties shall secure to everyone within their jurisdiction the rights and freedoms defined in Section I of this Convention.

Section I — Rights and freedoms

Article 2

Right to life

1. Everyone's right to life shall be protected by law. No one shall be deprived of his life intentionally save in the execution of a sentence of a court following his conviction of a crime for which this penalty is provided by law.

2. Deprivation of life shall not be regarded as inflicted in contravention of this Article when it results from the use of force which is no more than absolutely necessary:

   (a)   in defence of any person from unlawful violence;

(b)   in order to effect a lawful arrest or to prevent the escape of a person lawfully detained;

(c)   in action lawfully taken for the purpose of quelling a riot or insurrection.

Article 3

Prohibition of torture

No one shall be subjected to torture or to inhuman or degrading treatment or punishment.

Article 4

Prohibition of slavery and forced labour

1.   No one shall be held in slavery or servitude.

2.   No one shall be required to perform forced or compulsory labour.

3.   For the purpose of this Article the term "forced or compulsory labour" shall not include:

(a)   any work required to be done in the ordinary course of detention imposed according to the provisions of Article 5 of this Convention or during conditional release from such detention;

(b)   any service of a military character or, in case of conscientious objectors in countries where they are recognised, service exacted instead of compulsory military service;

(c)   any service exacted in case of an emergency or calamity threatening the life or well-being of the community;

(d)   any work or service which forms part of normal civic obligations.

Article 5

Right to liberty and security

1.   Everyone has the right to liberty and security of person. No one shall be deprived of his liberty save in the following cases and in accordance with a procedure prescribed by law:

(a)   the lawful detention of a person after conviction by a competent court;

(b)   the lawful arrest or detention of a person for non-compliance with the lawful order of a court or in order to secure the fulfilment of any obligation prescribed by law;

(c)   the lawful arrest or detention of a person effected for the purpose of bringing him before the competent legal authority on reasonable suspicion of having committed an offence or when it is reasonably considered necessary to prevent his committing an offence or fleeing after having done so;

(d)   the detention of a minor by lawful order for the purpose of educational supervision or his lawful detention for the purpose of bringing him before the competent legal authority;

(e)   the lawful detention of persons for the prevention of the spreading of infectious diseases, of persons of unsound mind, alcoholics or drug addicts or vagrants;

(f)   the lawful arrest or detention of a person to prevent his effecting an unauthorised entry into the country or of a person against whom action is being taken with a view to deportation or extradition.

2. Everyone who is arrested shall be informed promptly, in a language which he understands, of the reasons for his arrest and of any charge against him.

3. Everyone arrested or detained in accordance with the provisions of paragraph 1(c) of this Article shall be brought promptly before a judge or other officer authorised by law to exercise judicial power and shall be entitled to trial within a reasonable time or to release pending trial. Release may be conditioned by guarantees to appear for trial.

4. Everyone who is deprived of his liberty by arrest or detention shall be entitled to take proceedings by which the lawfulness of his detention shall be decided speedily by a court and his release ordered if the detention is not lawful.

5. Everyone who has been the victim of arrest or detention in contravention of the provisions of this Article shall have an enforceable right to compensation.

Article 6

Right to a fair trial

1. In the determination of his civil rights and obligations or of any criminal charge against him, everyone is entitled to a fair and public hearing within a reasonable time by an independent and impartial tribunal established by law. Judgment shall be pronounced publicly but the press and public may be excluded from all or part of the trial in the interests of morals, public order or national security in a democratic society, where the interests of juveniles or the protection of the private life of the parties so require, or to the extent strictly necessary in the opinion of the court in special circumstances where publicity would prejudice the interests of justice.

2. Everyone charged with a criminal offence shall be presumed innocent until proved guilty according to law.

3. Everyone charged with a criminal offence has the following minimum rights:

    (a)   to be informed promptly, in a language which he understands and in detail, of the nature and cause of the accusation against him;

    (b)   to have adequate time and facilities for the preparation of his defence;

    (c)   to defend himself in person or through legal assistance of his own choosing or, if he has not sufficient means to pay for legal assistance, to be given it free when the interests of justice so require;

    (d)   to examine or have examined witnesses against him and to obtain the attendance and examination of witnesses on his behalf under the same conditions as witnesses against him;

    (e)   to have the free assistance of an interpreter if he cannot understand or speak the language used in court.

Article 7

No punishment without law

1. No one shall be held guilty of any criminal offence on account of any act or omission which did not constitute a criminal offence under national or international law at the time when it was committed. Nor shall a heavier penalty be imposed than the one that was applicable at the time the criminal offence was committed.

2. This Article shall not prejudice the trial and punishment of any person for any act or omission which, at the time when it was committed, was criminal according to the general principles of law recognised by civilised nations.

Article 8

Right to respect for private and family life

1. Everyone has the right to respect for his private and family life, his home and his correspondence.

2. There shall be no interference by a public authority with the exercise of this right except such as is in accordance with the law and is necessary in a democratic society in the interests of national security, public safety or the economic well-being of the country, for the prevention of disorder or crime, for the protection of health or morals, or for the protection of the rights and freedoms of others.

Article 9

Freedom of thought, conscience and religion

1. Everyone has the right to freedom of thought, conscience and religion; this right includes freedom to change his religion or belief and freedom, either alone or in community with others and in public or private, to manifest his religion or belief, in worship, teaching, practice and observance.

2. Freedom to manifest one's religion or beliefs shall be subject only to such limitations as are prescribed by law and are necessary in a democratic society in the interests of public safety, for the protection of public order, health or morals, or for the protection of the rights and freedoms of others.

Article 10

Freedom of expression

1. Everyone has the right to freedom of expression. This right shall include freedom to hold opinions and to receive and impart information and ideas without interference by public authority and regardless of frontiers. This Article shall not prevent States from requiring the licensing of broadcasting, television or cinema enterprises.

2. The exercise of these freedoms, since it carries with it duties and responsibilities, may be subject to such formalities, conditions, restrictions or penalties as are prescribed by law and are necessary in a democratic society, in the interests of national security, territorial integrity or public safety, for the prevention of disorder or crime, for the protection of health or morals, for the protection of the reputation or rights of others, for preventing the disclosure of information received in confidence, or for maintaining the authority and impartiality of the judiciary.

Article 11

Freedom of assembly and association

1. Everyone has the right to freedom of peaceful assembly and to freedom of association with others, including the right to form and to join trade unions for the protection of his interests.

2. No restrictions shall be placed on the exercise of these rights other than such as are prescribed by law and are necessary in a democratic society in the interests of national security or public safety, for the prevention of disorder or crime, for the protection of health or morals or for the protection of the rights and freedoms of others. This Article shall not prevent the imposition of lawful restrictions on the exercise of these rights by members of the armed forces, of the police or of the administration of the State.

Article 12

Right to marry

Men and women of marriageable age have the right to marry and to found a family, according to the national laws governing the exercise of this right.

Article 13

Right to an effective remedy

Everyone whose rights and freedoms as set forth in this Convention are violated shall have an effective remedy before a national authority notwithstanding that the violation has been committed by persons acting in an official capacity.

Article 14

Prohibition of discrimination

The enjoyment of the rights and freedoms set forth in this Convention shall be secured without discrimination on any ground such as sex, race, colour, language, religion, political or other opinion, national or social origin, association with a national minority, property, birth or other status.

Article 15

Derogation in time of emergency

1.   In time of war or other public emergency threatening the life of the nation any High Contracting Party may take measures derogating from its obligations under this Convention to the extent strictly required by the exigencies of the situation, provided that such measures are not inconsistent with its other obligations under international law.

2.   No derogation from Article 2, except in respect of deaths resulting from lawful acts of war, or from Articles 3, 4 § 1 and 7 shall be made under this provision.

3.   Any High Contracting Party availing itself of this right of derogation shall keep the Secretary General of the Council of Europe fully informed of the measures which it has taken and the reasons therefor. It shall also inform the Secretary General of the Council of Europe when such measures have ceased to operate and the provisions of the Convention are again being fully executed.

Article 16

Restrictions on political activity of aliens

Nothing in Articles 10, 11 and 14 shall be regarded as preventing the High Contracting Parties from imposing restrictions on the political activity of aliens.

Article 17

Prohibition of abuse of rights

Nothing in this Convention may be interpreted as implying for any State, group or person any right to engage in any activity or perform any act aimed at the destruction of any of the rights and freedoms set forth herein or at their limitation to a greater extent than is provided for in the Convention.

Article 18

Limitation on use of restrictions on rights

The restrictions permitted under this Convention to the said rights and freedoms shall not be applied for any purpose other than those for which they have been prescribed.

Section II — European Court of Human Rights

Article 19

Establishment of the Court

To ensure the observance of the engagements undertaken by the High Contracting Parties in the Convention and the Protocols thereto, there shall be set up a European Court of Human Rights, hereinafter referred to as "the Court". It shall function on a permanent basis.

Article 20

Number of judges

The Court shall consist of a number of judges equal to that of the High Contracting Parties.

Article 21

Criteria for office

1. The judges shall be of high moral character and must either possess the qualifications required for appointment to high judicial office or be jurisconsults of recognised competence.

2. The judges shall sit on the Court in their individual capacity.

3. During their term of office the judges shall not engage in any activity which is incompatible with their independence, impartiality or with the demands of a full-time office; all questions arising from the application of this paragraph shall be decided by the Court.

Article 22

Election of judges

The judges shall be elected by the Parliamentary Assembly with respect to each High Contracting Party by a majority of votes cast from a list of three candidates nominated by the High Contracting Party.

Article 23

Terms of office and dismissal

1. The judges shall be elected for a period of nine years. They may not be re-elected.

2. The terms of office of judges shall expire when they reach the age of 70.

3. The judges shall hold office until replaced. They shall, however, continue to deal with such cases as they already have under consideration.

4. No judge may be dismissed from office unless the other judges decide by a majority of two-thirds that that judge has ceased to fulfil the required conditions.

Article 24

Registry and rapporteurs

1. The Court shall have a Registry, the functions and organisation of which shall be laid down in the rules of the Court.

2. When sitting in a single-judge formation, the Court shall be assisted by rapporteurs who shall function under the authority of the President of the Court. They shall form part of the Court's Registry.

Article 25

Plenary Court

The plenary Court shall

- (a) elect its President and one or two Vice-Presidents for a period of three years; they may be re-elected;
- (b) set up Chambers, constituted for a fixed period of time;
- (c) elect the Presidents of the Chambers of the Court; they may be re-elected;
- (d) adopt the rules of the Court;
- (e) elect the Registrar and one or more Deputy Registrars;
- (f) make any request under Article 26 § 2.

Article 26

Single-judge formation, Committees, Chambers and Grand Chamber

1. To consider cases brought before it, the Court shall sit in a single-judge formation, in Committees of three judges, in Chambers of seven judges and in a Grand Chamber of seventeen judges. The Court's Chambers shall set up Committees for a fixed period of time.

2. At the request of the plenary Court, the Committee of Ministers may, by a unanimous decision and for a fixed period, reduce to five the number of judges of the Chambers.

3. When sitting as a single judge, a judge shall not examine any application against the High Contracting Party in respect of which that judge has been elected.

4. There shall sit as an *ex officio* member of the Chamber and the Grand Chamber the judge elected in respect of the High Contracting Party concerned. If there is none or if that judge is unable to sit, a person chosen by the President of the Court from a list submitted in advance by that Party shall sit in the capacity of judge.

5. The Grand Chamber shall also include the President of the Court, the Vice-Presidents, the Presidents of the Chambers and other judges chosen in accordance with the rules of the Court. When a case is referred to the Grand Chamber under Article 43, no judge from the Chamber which rendered the judgment shall sit in the Grand Chamber, with the exception of the President of the Chamber and the judge who sat in respect of the High Contracting Party concerned.

Article 27

Competence of single judges

1.   A single judge may declare inadmissible or strike out of the Court's list of cases an application submitted under Article 34, where such a decision can be taken without further examination.

2.   The decision shall be final.

3.   If the single judge does not declare an application inadmissible or strike it out, that judge shall forward it to a Committee or to a Chamber for further examination.

Article 28

Competence of Committees

1.   In respect of an application submitted under Article 34, a Committee may, by a unanimous vote,

   (a)   declare it inadmissible or strike it out of its list of cases, where such decision can be taken without further examination; or

   (b)   declare it admissible and render at the same time a judgment on the merits, if the underlying question in the case, concerning the interpretation or the application of the Convention or the Protocols thereto, is already the subject of well-established case-law of the Court.

2.   Decisions and judgments under paragraph 1 shall be final.

3.   If the judge elected in respect of the High Contracting Party concerned is not a member of the Committee, the Committee may at any stage of the proceedings invite that judge to take the place of one of the members of the Committee, having regard to all relevant factors, including whether that Party has contested the application of the procedure under paragraph 1(b).

Article 29

Decisions by Chambers on admissibility and merits

1.   If no decision is taken under Article 27 or 28, or no judgment rendered under Article 28, a Chamber shall decide on the admissibility and merits of individual applications submitted under Article 34. The decision on admissibility may be taken separately.

2.   A Chamber shall decide on the admissibility and merits of inter-State applications submitted under Article 33. The decision on admissibility shall be taken separately unless the Court, in exceptional cases, decides otherwise.

Article 30

Relinquishment of jurisdiction to the Grand Chamber

Where a case pending before a Chamber raises a serious question affecting the interpretation of the Convention or the Protocols thereto, or where the resolution of a question before the Chamber might have a result inconsistent with a judgment previously delivered by the Court, the Chamber may, at any time before it has rendered its judgment, relinquish jurisdiction in favour of the Grand Chamber, unless one of the parties to the case objects.

Article 31

Powers of the Grand Chamber

The Grand Chamber shall

(a) determine applications submitted either under Article 33 or Article 34 when a Chamber has relinquished jurisdiction under Article 30 or when the case has been referred to it under Article 43;

(b) decide on issues referred to the Court by the Committee of Ministers in accordance with Article 46 § 4; and

(c) consider requests for advisory opinions submitted under Article 47.

Article 32

Jurisdiction of the Court

1. The jurisdiction of the Court shall extend to all matters concerning the interpretation and application of the Convention and the Protocols thereto which are referred to it as provided in Articles 33, 34, 46 and 47.

2. In the event of dispute as to whether the Court has jurisdiction, the Court shall decide.

Article 33

Inter-State cases

Any High Contracting Party may refer to the Court any alleged breach of the provisions of the Convention and the Protocols thereto by another High Contracting Party.

Article 34

Individual applications

The Court may receive applications from any person, non-governmental organisation or group of individuals claiming to be the victim of a violation by one of the High Contracting Parties of the rights set forth in the Convention or the Protocols thereto. The High Contracting Parties undertake not to hinder in any way the effective exercise of this right.

Article 35

Admissibility criteria

1. The Court may only deal with the matter after all domestic remedies have been exhausted, according to the generally recognised rules of international law, and within a period of six months from the date on which the final decision was taken.

2. The Court shall not deal with any application submitted under Article 34 that

(a) is anonymous; or

(b) is substantially the same as a matter that has already been examined by the Court or has already been submitted to another procedure of international investigation or settlement and contains no relevant new information.

3. The Court shall declare inadmissible any individual application submitted under Article 34 if it considers that:

(a) the application is incompatible with the provisions of the Convention or the Protocols thereto, manifestly ill-founded, or an abuse of the right of individual application; or

(b) the applicant has not suffered a significant disadvantage, unless respect for human rights as defined in the Convention and the Protocols thereto requires an examination of the application on the merits and provided that no case may be rejected on this ground which has not been duly considered by a domestic tribunal.

4. The Court shall reject any application which it considers inadmissible under this Article. It may do so at any stage of the proceedings.

Article 36

Third party intervention

1. In all cases before a Chamber or the Grand Chamber, a High Contracting Party one of whose nationals is an applicant shall have the right to submit written comments and to take part in hearings.

2. The President of the Court may, in the interest of the proper administration of justice, invite any High Contracting Party which is not a party to the proceedings or any person concerned who is not the applicant to submit written comments or take part in hearings.

3. In all cases before a Chamber or the Grand Chamber, the Council of Europe Commissioner for Human Rights may submit written comments and take part in hearings.

Article 37

Striking out applications

1. The Court may at any stage of the proceedings decide to strike an application out of its list of cases where the circumstances lead to the conclusion that

(a) the applicant does not intend to pursue his application; or

(b) the matter has been resolved; or

(c) for any other reason established by the Court, it is no longer justified to continue the examination of the application.

However, the Court shall continue the examination of the application if respect for human rights as defined in the Convention and the Protocols thereto so requires.

2. The Court may decide to restore an application to its list of cases if it considers that the circumstances justify such a course.

Article 38

Examination of the case

The Court shall examine the case together with the representatives of the parties and, if need be, undertake an investigation, for the effective conduct of which the High Contracting Parties concerned shall furnish all necessary facilities.

Article 39

Friendly settlements

1.   At any stage of the proceedings, the Court may place itself at the disposal of the parties concerned with a view to securing a friendly settlement of the matter on the basis of respect for human rights as defined in the Convention and the Protocols thereto.

2.   Proceedings conducted under paragraph 1 shall be confidential.

3.   If a friendly settlement is effected, the Court shall strike the case out of its list by means of a decision which shall be confined to a brief statement of the facts and of the solution reached.

4.   This decision shall be transmitted to the Committee of Ministers, which shall supervise the execution of the terms of the friendly settlement as set out in the decision.

Article 40

Public hearings and access to documents

1.   Hearings shall be in public unless the Court in exceptional circumstances decides otherwise.

2.   Documents deposited with the Registrar shall be accessible to the public unless the President of the Court decides otherwise.

Article 41

Just satisfaction

If the Court finds that there has been a violation of the Convention or the Protocols thereto, and if the internal law of the High Contracting Party concerned allows only partial reparation to be made, the Court shall, if necessary, afford just satisfaction to the injured party.

Article 42

Judgments of Chambers

Judgments of Chambers shall become final in accordance with the provisions of Article 44 § 2.

Article 43

Referral to the Grand Chamber

1.   Within a period of three months from the date of the judgment of the Chamber, any party to the case may, in exceptional cases, request that the case be referred to the Grand Chamber.

2.   A panel of five judges of the Grand Chamber shall accept the request if the case raises a serious question affecting the interpretation or application of the Convention or the Protocols thereto, or a serious issue of general importance.

3.   If the panel accepts the request, the Grand Chamber shall decide the case by means of a judgment.

Article 44

Final judgments

1. The judgment of the Grand Chamber shall be final.

2. The judgment of a Chamber shall become final

    (a) when the parties declare that they will not request that the case be referred to the Grand Chamber; or

    (b) three months after the date of the judgment, if reference of the case to the Grand Chamber has not been requested; or

    (c) when the panel of the Grand Chamber rejects the request to refer under Article 43.

3. The final judgment shall be published.

Article 45

Reasons for judgments and decisions

1. Reasons shall be given for judgments as well as for decisions declaring applications admissible or inadmissible.

2. If a judgment does not represent, in whole or in part, the unanimous opinion of the judges, any judge shall be entitled to deliver a separate opinion.

Article 46

Binding force and execution of judgments

1. The High Contracting Parties undertake to abide by the final judgment of the Court in any case to which they are parties.

2. The final judgment of the Court shall be transmitted to the Committee of Ministers, which shall supervise its execution.

3. If the Committee of Ministers considers that the supervision of the execution of a final judgment is hindered by a problem of interpretation of the judgment, it may refer the matter to the Court for a ruling on the question of interpretation. A referral decision shall require a majority vote of two thirds of the representatives entitled to sit on the Committee.

4. If the Committee of Ministers considers that a High Contracting Party refuses to abide by a final judgment in a case to which it is a party, it may, after serving formal notice on that Party and by decision adopted by a majority vote of two-thirds of the representatives entitled to sit on the Committee, refer to the Court the question whether that Party has failed to fulfil its obligation under paragraph 1.

5. If the Court finds a violation of paragraph 1, it shall refer the case to the Committee of Ministers for consideration of the measures to be taken. If the Court finds no violation of paragraph 1, it shall refer the case to the Committee of Ministers, which shall close its examination of the case.

Article 47

Advisory opinions

1. The Court may, at the request of the Committee of Ministers, give advisory opinions on legal questions concerning the interpretation of the Convention and the Protocols thereto.

2. Such opinions shall not deal with any question relating to the content or scope of the rights or freedoms defined in Section I of the Convention and the Protocols thereto, or with any other question which the Court or the Committee of Ministers might have to consider in consequence of any such proceedings as could be instituted in accordance with the Convention.

3. Decisions of the Committee of Ministers to request an advisory opinion of the Court shall require a majority vote of the representatives entitled to sit on the Committee.

Article 48

Advisory jurisdiction of the Court

The Court shall decide whether a request for an advisory opinion submitted by the Committee of Ministers is within its competence as defined in Article 47.

Article 49

Reasons for advisory opinions

1. Reasons shall be given for advisory opinions of the Court.

2. If the advisory opinion does not represent, in whole or in part, the unanimous opinion of the judges, any judge shall be entitled to deliver a separate opinion.

3. Advisory opinions of the Court shall be communicated to the Committee of Ministers.

Article 50

Expenditure on the Court

The expenditure on the Court shall be borne by the Council of Europe.

Article 51

Privileges and immunities of judges

The judges shall be entitled, during the exercise of their functions, to the privileges and immunities provided for in Article 40 of the Statute of the Council of Europe and in the agreements made thereunder.

Section III — Miscellaneous provisions

Article 52

Inquiries by the Secretary General

On receipt of a request from the Secretary General of the Council of Europe any High Contracting Party shall furnish an explanation of the manner in which its internal law ensures the effective implementation of any of the provisions of the Convention.

Article 53

Safeguard for existing human rights

Nothing in this Convention shall be construed as limiting or derogating from any of the human rights and fundamental freedoms which may be ensured under the laws of any High Contracting Party or under any other agreement to which it is a party.

Article 54

Powers of the Committee of Ministers

Nothing in this Convention shall prejudice the powers conferred on the Committee of Ministers by the Statute of the Council of Europe.

Article 55

Exclusion of other means of dispute settlement

The High Contracting Parties agree that, except by special agreement, they will not avail themselves of treaties, conventions or declarations in force between them for the purpose of submitting, by way of petition, a dispute arising out of the interpretation or application of this Convention to a means of settlement other than those provided for in this Convention.

Article 56

Territorial application

1. Any State may at the time of its ratification or at any time thereafter declare by notification addressed to the Secretary General of the Council of Europe that the present Convention shall, subject to paragraph 4 of this Article, extend to all or any of the territories for whose international relations it is responsible.

2. The Convention shall extend to the territory or territories named in the notification as from the thirtieth day after the receipt of this notification by the Secretary General of the Council of Europe.

3. The provisions of this Convention shall be applied in such territories with due regard, however, to local requirements.

4. Any State which has made a declaration in accordance with paragraph 1 of this Article may at any time thereafter declare on behalf of one or more of the territories to which the declaration relates that it accepts the competence of the Court to receive applications from individuals, non-governmental organisations or groups of individuals as provided by Article 34 of the Convention.

Article 57

Reservations

1.   Any State may, when signing this Convention or when depositing its instrument of ratification, make a reservation in respect of any particular provision of the Convention to the extent that any law then in force in its territory is not in conformity with the provision. Reservations of a general character shall not be permitted under this Article.

2.   Any reservation made under this Article shall contain a brief statement of the law concerned.

Article 58

Denunciation

1.   A High Contracting Party may denounce the present Convention only after the expiry of five years from the date on which it became a party to it and after six months' notice contained in a notification addressed to the Secretary General of the Council of Europe, who shall inform the other High Contracting Parties.

2.   Such a denunciation shall not have the effect of releasing the High Contracting Party concerned from its obligations under this Convention in respect of any act which, being capable of constituting a violation of such obligations, may have been performed by it before the date at which the denunciation became effective.

3.   Any High Contracting Party which shall cease to be a member of the Council of Europe shall cease to be a party to this Convention under the same conditions.

4.   The Convention may be denounced in accordance with the provisions of the preceding paragraphs in respect of any territory to which it has been declared to extend under the terms of Article 56.

Article 59

Signature and ratification

1.   This Convention shall be open to the signature of the members of the Council of Europe. It shall be ratified. Ratifications shall be deposited with the Secretary General of the Council of Europe.

2.   The European Union may accede to this Convention.

3.   The present Convention shall come into force after the deposit of ten instruments of ratification.

4.   As regards any signatory ratifying subsequently, the Convention shall come into force at the date of the deposit of its instrument of ratification.

5.   The Secretary General of the Council of Europe shall notify all the members of the Council of Europe of the entry into force of the Convention, the names of the High Contracting Parties who have ratified it, and the deposit of all instruments of ratification which may be effected subsequently.

Done at Rome this 4th day of November 1950, in English and French, both texts being equally authentic, in a single copy which shall remain deposited in the archives of the Council of Europe. The Secretary General shall transmit certified copies to each of the signatories.

Protocol to the Convention for the Protection of Human Rights and Fundamental Freedoms

Paris, 20.III.1952

The governments signatory hereto, being members of the Council of Europe,

Being resolved to take steps to ensure the collective enforcement of certain rights and freedoms other than those already included in Section I of the Convention for the Protection of Human Rights and Fundamental Freedoms signed at Rome on 4 November 1950 (hereinafter referred to as "the Convention"),

Have agreed as follows:

Article 1

Protection of property

Every natural or legal person is entitled to the peaceful enjoyment of his possessions. No one shall be deprived of his possessions except in the public interest and subject to the conditions provided for by law and by the general principles of international law.

The preceding provisions shall not, however, in any way impair the right of a State to enforce such laws as it deems necessary to control the use of property in accordance with the general interest or to secure the payment of taxes or other contributions or penalties.

Article 2

Right to education

No person shall be denied the right to education. In the exercise of any functions which it assumes in relation to education and to teaching, the State shall respect the right of parents to ensure such education and teaching in conformity with their own religious and philosophical convictions.

Article 3

Right to free elections

The High Contracting Parties undertake to hold free elections at reasonable intervals by secret ballot, under conditions which will ensure the free expression of the opinion of the people in the choice of the legislature.

Article 4

Territorial application

Any High Contracting Party may at the time of signature or ratification or at any time thereafter communicate to the Secretary General of the Council of Europe a declaration stating the extent to which it undertakes that the provisions of the present Protocol shall apply to such of the territories for the international relations of which it is responsible as are named therein.

Any High Contracting Party which has communicated a declaration in virtue of the preceding paragraph may from time to time communicate a further declaration modifying the terms of any former declaration or terminating the application of the provisions of this Protocol in respect of any territory.

A declaration made in accordance with this Article shall be deemed to have been made in accordance with paragraph 1 of Article 56 of the Convention.

Article 5

Relationship to the Convention

As between the High Contracting Parties the provisions of Articles 1, 2, 3 and 4 of this Protocol shall be regarded as additional Articles to the Convention and all the provisions of the Convention shall apply accordingly.

Article 6

Signature and ratification

This Protocol shall be open for signature by the members of the Council of Europe, who are the signatories of the Convention; it shall be ratified at the same time as or after the ratification of the Convention. It shall enter into force after the deposit of ten instruments of ratification. As regards any signatory ratifying subsequently, the Protocol shall enter into force at the date of the deposit of its instrument of ratification.

The instruments of ratification shall be deposited with the Secretary General of the Council of Europe, who will notify all members of the names of those who have ratified.

Done at Paris on the 20th day of March 1952, in English and French, both texts being equally authentic, in a single copy which shall remain deposited in the archives of the Council of Europe. The Secretary General shall transmit certified copies to each of the signatory governments.

Protocol No. 4 to the Convention for the Protection of Human Rights and Fundamental Freedoms securing certain rights and freedoms other than those already included in the Convention and in the first Protocol thereto

Strasbourg, 16.IX.1963

The governments signatory hereto, being members of the Council of Europe,

Being resolved to take steps to ensure the collective enforcement of certain rights and freedoms other than those already included in Section I of the Convention for the Protection of Human Rights and Fundamental Freedoms signed at Rome on 4 November 1950 (hereinafter referred to as the "Convention") and in Articles 1 to 3 of the First Protocol to the Convention, signed at Paris on 20 March 1952,

Have agreed as follows:

Article 1

Prohibition of imprisonment for debt

No one shall be deprived of his liberty merely on the ground of inability to fulfil a contractual obligation.

Article 2

Freedom of movement

1.   Everyone lawfully within the territory of a State shall, within that territory, have the right to liberty of movement and freedom to choose his residence.

2.   Everyone shall be free to leave any country, including his own.

3.   No restrictions shall be placed on the exercise of these rights other than such as are in accordance with law and are necessary in a democratic society in the interests of national security or public safety, for the maintenance of ordre public, for the prevention of crime, for the protection of health or morals, or for the protection of the rights and freedoms of others.

4.   The rights set forth in paragraph 1 may also be subject, in particular areas, to restrictions imposed in accordance with law and justified by the public interest in a democratic society.

Article 3

Prohibition of expulsion of nationals

1.   No one shall be expelled, by means either of an individual or of a collective measure, from the territory of the State of which he is a national.

2.   No one shall be deprived of the right to enter the territory of the State of which he is a national.

Article 4

Prohibition of collective expulsion of aliens

Collective expulsion of aliens is prohibited.

Article 5

Territorial application

1.   Any High Contracting Party may, at the time of signature or ratification of this Protocol, or at any time thereafter, communicate to the Secretary General of the Council of Europe a declaration stating the extent to which it undertakes that the provisions of this Protocol shall apply to such of the territories for the international relations of which it is responsible as are named therein.

2.   Any High Contracting Party which has communicated a declaration in virtue of the preceding paragraph may, from time to time, communicate a further declaration modifying the terms of any former declaration or terminating the application of the provisions of this Protocol in respect of any territory.

3.   A declaration made in accordance with this Article shall be deemed to have been made in accordance with paragraph 1 of Article 56 of the Convention.

4.   The territory of any State to which this Protocol applies by virtue of ratification or acceptance by that State, and each territory to which this Protocol is applied by virtue of a declaration by that State under this Article, shall be treated as separate territories for the purpose of the references in Articles 2 and 3 to the territory of a State.

5.   Any State which has made a declaration in accordance with paragraph 1 or 2 of this Article may at any time thereafter declare on behalf of one or more of the territories to which the declaration relates that it accepts the competence of the Court to receive applications from individuals, non-governmental organisations or groups of individuals as provided in Article 34 of the Convention in respect of all or any of Articles 1 to 4 of this Protocol.

Article 6

Relationship to the Convention

As between the High Contracting Parties the provisions of Articles 1 to 5 of this Protocol shall be regarded as additional Articles to the Convention, and all the provisions of the Convention shall apply accordingly.

Article 7

Signature and ratification

1.   This Protocol shall be open for signature by the members of the Council of Europe who are the signatories of the Convention; it shall be ratified at the same time as or after the ratification of the Convention. It shall enter into force after the deposit of five instruments of ratification. As regards any signatory ratifying subsequently, the Protocol shall enter into force at the date of the deposit of its instrument of ratification.

2.   The instruments of ratification shall be deposited with the Secretary General of the Council of Europe, who will notify all members of the names of those who have ratified.

In witness whereof the undersigned, being duly authorised thereto, have signed this Protocol.

Done at Strasbourg, this 16th day of September 1963, in English and in French, both texts being equally authoritative, in a single copy which shall remain deposited in the archives of the Council of Europe. The Secretary General shall transmit certified copies to each of the signatory States.

Protocol No. 6 to the Convention for the Protection of Human Rights and Fundamental Freedoms concerning the abolition of the death penalty

Strasbourg, 28.IV.1983

The member States of the Council of Europe, signatory to this Protocol to the Convention for the Protection of Human Rights and Fundamental Freedoms, signed at Rome on 4 November 1950 (hereinafter referred to as "the Convention"),

Considering that the evolution that has occurred in several member States of the Council of Europe expresses a general tendency in favour of abolition of the death penalty;

Have agreed as follows:

Article 1

Abolition of the death penalty

The death penalty shall be abolished. No one shall be condemned to such penalty or executed.

Article 2

Death penalty in time of war

A State may make provision in its law for the death penalty in respect of acts committed in time of war or of imminent threat of war; such penalty shall be applied only in the instances laid down in the law and in accordance with its provisions. The State shall communicate to the Secretary General of the Council of Europe the relevant provisions of that law.

Article 3

Prohibition of derogations

No derogation from the provisions of this Protocol shall be made under Article 15 of the Convention.

Article 4

Prohibition of reservations

No reservation may be made under Article 57 of the Convention in respect of the provisions of this Protocol.

Article 5

Territorial application

1. Any State may at the time of signature or when depositing its instrument of ratification, acceptance or approval, specify the territory or territories to which this Protocol shall apply.

2. Any State may at any later date, by a declaration addressed to the Secretary General of the Council of Europe, extend the application of this Protocol to any other territory specified in the declaration. In respect of such territory the Protocol shall enter into force on the first day of the month following the date of receipt of such declaration by the Secretary General.

3. Any declaration made under the two preceding paragraphs may, in respect of any territory specified in such declaration, be withdrawn by a notification addressed to the Secretary General. The withdrawal shall become effective on the first day of the month following the date of receipt of such notification by the Secretary General.

Article 6

Relationship to the Convention

As between the States Parties the provisions of Articles 1 and 5 of this Protocol shall be regarded as additional Articles to the Convention and all the provisions of the Convention shall apply accordingly.

Article 7

Signature and ratification

The Protocol shall be open for signature by the member States of the Council of Europe, signatories to the Convention. It shall be subject to ratification, acceptance or approval. A member State of the Council of Europe may not ratify, accept or approve this Protocol unless it has, simultaneously or previously, ratified the Convention. Instruments of ratification, acceptance or approval shall be deposited with the Secretary General of the Council of Europe.

Article 8

Entry into force

1.   This Protocol shall enter into force on the first day of the month following the date on which five member States of the Council of Europe have expressed their consent to be bound by the Protocol in accordance with the provisions of Article 7.

2.   In respect of any member State which subsequently expresses its consent to be bound by it, the Protocol shall enter into force on the first day of the month following the date of the deposit of the instrument of ratification, acceptance or approval. Article 9

Depositary functions

The Secretary General of the Council of Europe shall notify the member States of the Council of:

(a)   any signature;
(b)   the deposit of any instrument of ratification, acceptance or approval;
(c)   any date of entry into force of this Protocol in accordance with Articles 5 and 8;
(d)   any other act, notification or communication relating to this Protocol.

In witness whereof the undersigned, being duly authorised thereto, have signed this Protocol.

Done at Strasbourg, this 28th day of April 1983, in English and in French, both texts being equally authentic, in a single copy which shall be deposited in the archives of the Council of Europe. The Secretary General of the Council of Europe shall transmit certified copies to each member State of the Council of Europe.

Protocol No. 7 to the Convention for the Protection of Human Rights and Fundamental Freedoms

Strasbourg, 22.XI.1984

The member States of the Council of Europe signatory hereto,

Being resolved to take further steps to ensure the collective enforcement of certain rights and freedoms by means of the Convention for the Protection of Human Rights and Fundamental Freedoms signed at Rome on 4 November 1950 (hereinafter referred to as "the Convention"),

Have agreed as follows:

Article 1

Procedural safeguards relating to expulsion of aliens

1.   An alien lawfully resident in the territory of a State shall not be expelled therefrom except in pursuance of a decision reached in accordance with law and shall be allowed:

(a)   to submit reasons against his expulsion,

(b)   to have his case reviewed, and

(c)   to be represented for these purposes before the competent authority or a person or persons designated by that authority.

2.   An alien may be expelled before the exercise of his rights under paragraph 1(a), (b) and (c) of this Article, when such expulsion is necessary in the interests of public order or is grounded on reasons of national security.

Article 2

Right of appeal in criminal matters

1.   Everyone convicted of a criminal offence by a tribunal shall have the right to have his conviction or sentence reviewed by a higher tribunal. The exercise of this right, including the grounds on which it may be exercised, shall be governed by law.

2.   This right may be subject to exceptions in regard to offences of a minor character, as prescribed by law, or in cases in which the person concerned was tried in the first instance by the highest tribunal or was convicted following an appeal against acquittal.

Article 3

Compensation for wrongful conviction

When a person has by a final decision been convicted of a criminal offence and when subsequently his conviction has been reversed, or he has been pardoned, on the ground that a new or newly discovered fact shows conclusively that there has been a miscarriage of justice, the person who has suffered punishment as a result of such conviction shall be compensated according to the law or the practice of the State concerned, unless it is proved that the non-disclosure of the unknown fact in time is wholly or partly attributable to him.

Article 4

Right not to be tried or punished twice

1.   No one shall be liable to be tried or punished again in criminal proceedings under the jurisdiction of the same State for an offence for which he has already been finally acquitted or convicted in accordance with the law and penal procedure of that State.

2.   The provisions of the preceding paragraph shall not prevent the reopening of the case in accordance with the law and penal procedure of the State concerned, if there is evidence of new or newly discovered facts, or if there has been a fundamental defect in the previous proceedings, which could affect the outcome of the case.

3.   No derogation from this Article shall be made under Article 15 of the Convention.

Article 5

Equality between spouses

Spouses shall enjoy equality of rights and responsibilities of a private law character between them, and in their relations with their children, as to marriage, during marriage and in the event of its dissolution. This Article shall not prevent States from taking such measures as are necessary in the interests of the children.

Article 6

Territorial application

1. Any State may at the time of signature or when depositing its instrument of ratification, acceptance or approval, specify the territory or territories to which the Protocol shall apply and state the extent to which it undertakes that the provisions of this Protocol shall apply to such territory or territories.

2. Any State may at any later date, by a declaration addressed to the Secretary General of the Council of Europe, extend the application of this Protocol to any other territory specified in the declaration. In respect of such territory the Protocol shall enter into force on the first day of the month following the expiration of a period of two months after the date of receipt by the Secretary General of such declaration.

3. Any declaration made under the two preceding paragraphs may, in respect of any territory specified in such declaration, be withdrawn or modified by a notification addressed to the Secretary General. The withdrawal or modification shall become effective on the first day of the month following the expiration of a period of two months after the date of receipt of such notification by the Secretary General.

4. A declaration made in accordance with this Article shall be deemed to have been made in accordance with paragraph 1 of Article 56 of the Convention.

5. The territory of any State to which this Protocol applies by virtue of ratification, acceptance or approval by that State, and each territory to which this Protocol is applied by virtue of a declaration by that State under this Article, may be treated as separate territories for the purpose of the reference in Article   1 to the territory of a State.

6. Any State which has made a declaration in accordance with paragraph 1 or 2 of this Article may at any time thereafter declare on behalf of one or more of the territories to which the declaration relates that it accepts the competence of the Court to receive applications from individuals, non-governmental organisations or groups of individuals as provided in Article 34 of the Convention in respect of Articles 1 to 5 of this Protocol.

Article 7

Relationship to the Convention

As between the States Parties, the provisions of Article 1 to 6 of this Protocol shall be regarded as additional Articles to the Convention, and all the provisions of the Convention shall apply accordingly.

Article 8

Signature and ratification

This Protocol shall be open for signature by member States of the Council of Europe which have signed the Convention. It is subject to ratification, acceptance or approval. A member State of the Council of Europe may not ratify, accept or approve this Protocol without previously or simultaneously ratifying the Convention. Instruments of ratification, acceptance or approval shall be deposited with the Secretary General of the Council of Europe.

Article 9

Entry into force

1.   This Protocol shall enter into force on the first day of the month following the expiration of a period of two months after the date on which seven member States of the Council of Europe have expressed their consent to be bound by the Protocol in accordance with the provisions of Article 8.

2.   In respect of any member State which subsequently expresses its consent to be bound by it, the Protocol shall enter into force on the first day of the month following the expiration of a period of two months after the date of the deposit of the instrument of ratification, acceptance or approval.

Article 10

Depositary functions

The Secretary General of the Council of Europe shall notify all the member States of the Council of Europe of:

   (a)   any signature;
   (b)   the deposit of any instrument of ratification, acceptance or approval;
   (c)   any date of entry into force of this Protocol in accordance with Articles 6 and 9;
   (d)   any other act, notification or declaration relating to this Protocol.

In witness whereof the undersigned, being duly authorised thereto, have signed this Protocol.

Done at Strasbourg, this 22nd day of November 1984, in English and French, both texts being equally authentic, in a single copy which shall be deposited in the archives of the Council of Europe. The Secretary General of the Council of Europe shall transmit certified copies to each member State of the Council of Europe.

Protocol No. 12 to the Convention for the Protection of Human Rights and Fundamental Freedoms

Rome, 4.XI.2000

The member States of the Council of Europe signatory hereto,

Having regard to the fundamental principle according to which all persons are equal before the law and are entitled to the equal protection of the law;

Being resolved to take further steps to promote the equality of all persons through the collective enforcement of a general prohibition of discrimination by means of the Convention for the Protection of Human Rights and Fundamental Freedoms signed at Rome on 4 November 1950 (hereinafter referred to as "the Convention");

Reaffirming that the principle of non-discrimination does not prevent States Parties from taking measures in order to promote full and effective equality, provided that there is an objective and reasonable justification for those measures,

Have agreed as follows:

Article 1

General prohibition of discrimination

1. The enjoyment of any right set forth by law shall be secured without discrimination on any ground such as sex, race, colour, language, religion, political or other opinion, national or social origin, association with a national minority, property, birth or other status.

2. No one shall be discriminated against by any public authority on any ground such as those mentioned in paragraph 1.

Article 2

Territorial application

1. Any State may, at the time of signature or when depositing its instrument of ratification, acceptance or approval, specify the territory or territories to which this Protocol shall apply.

2. Any State may at any later date, by a declaration addressed to the Secretary General of the Council of Europe, extend the application of this Protocol to any other territory specified in the declaration. In respect of such territory the Protocol shall enter into force on the first day of the month following the expiration of a period of three months after the date of receipt by the Secretary General of such declaration.

3. Any declaration made under the two preceding paragraphs may, in respect of any territory specified in such declaration, be withdrawn or modified by a notification addressed to the Secretary General of the Council of Europe. The withdrawal or modification shall become effective on the first day of the month following the expiration of a period of three months after the date of receipt of such notification by the Secretary General.

4. A declaration made in accordance with this Article shall be deemed to have been made in accordance with paragraph 1 of Article 56 of the Convention.

5. Any State which has made a declaration in accordance with paragraph 1 or 2 of this Article may at any time thereafter declare on behalf of one or more of the territories to which the declaration relates that it accepts the competence of the Court to receive applications from individuals, non-governmental organisations or groups of individuals as provided by Article 34 of the Convention in respect of Article 1 of this Protocol.

Article 3

Relationship to the Convention

As between the States Parties, the provisions of Articles 1 and 2 of this Protocol shall be regarded as additional Articles to the Convention, and all the provisions of the Convention shall apply accordingly.

Article 4

Signature and ratification

This Protocol shall be open for signature by member States of the Council of Europe which have signed the Convention. It is subject to ratification, acceptance or approval. A member State of the Council of Europe may not ratify, accept or approve this Protocol without previously or simultaneously ratifying the Convention. Instruments of ratification, acceptance or approval shall be deposited with the Secretary General of the Council of Europe.

Article 5

Entry into force

1. This Protocol shall enter into force on the first day of the month following the expiration of a period of three months after the date on which ten member States of the Council of Europe have expressed their consent to be bound by the Protocol in accordance with the provisions of Article 4.

2. In respect of any member State which subsequently expresses its consent to be bound by it, the Protocol shall enter into force on the first day of the month following the expiration of a period of three months after the date of the deposit of the instrument of ratification, acceptance or approval.

Article 6

Depositary functions

The Secretary General of the Council of Europe shall notify all the member States of the Council of Europe of:

(a)   any signature;
(b)   the deposit of any instrument of ratification, acceptance or approval;
(c)   any date of entry into force of this Protocol in accordance with Articles 2 and 5;
(d)   any other act, notification or communication relating to this Protocol.

In witness whereof the undersigned, being duly authorised thereto, have signed this Protocol.

Done at Rome, this 4th day of November 2000, in English and in French, both texts being equally authentic, in a single copy which shall be deposited in the archives of the Council of Europe. The Secretary General of the Council of Europe shall transmit certified copies to each member State of the Council of Europe.

Protocol No. 13 to the Convention for the Protection of Human Rights and Fundamental Freedoms concerning the abolition of the death penalty in all circumstances

Vilnius, 3.V.2002

The member States of the Council of Europe signatory hereto,

Convinced that everyone's right to life is a basic value in a democratic society and that the abolition of the death penalty is essential for the protection of this right and for the full recognition of the inherent dignity of all human beings;

Wishing to strengthen the protection of the right to life guaranteed by the Convention for the Protection of Human Rights and Fundamental Freedoms signed at Rome on 4 November 1950 (hereinafter referred to as "the Convention");

Noting that Protocol No. 6 to the Convention concerning the abolition of the death penalty, signed at Strasbourg on 28 April 1983, does not exclude the death penalty in respect of acts committed in time of war or of imminent threat of war;

Being resolved to take the final step in order to abolish the death penalty in all circumstances,

Have agreed as follows:

Article 1

Abolition of the death penalty

The death penalty shall be abolished. No one shall be condemned to such penalty or executed.

Article 2

Prohibitions of derogations

No derogation from the provisions of this Protocol shall be made under Article 15 of the Convention.

Article 3

Prohibitions of reservations

No reservation may be made under Article 57 of the Convention in respect of the provisions of this Protocol.

Article 4

Territorial application

1. Any State may, at the time of signature or when depositing its instrument of ratification, acceptance or approval, specify the territory or territories to which this Protocol shall apply.

2. Any State may at any later date, by a declaration addressed to the Secretary General of the Council of Europe, extend the application of this Protocol to any other territory specified in the declaration. In respect of such territory the Protocol shall enter into force on the first day of the month following the expiration of a period of three months after the date of receipt by the Secretary General of such declaration.

3. Any declaration made under the two preceding paragraphs may, in respect of any territory specified in such declaration, be withdrawn or modified by a notification addressed to the Secretary General. The withdrawal or modification shall become effective on the first day of the month following the expiration of a period of three months after the date of receipt of such notification by the Secretary General.

Article 5

Relationship to the Convention

As between the States Parties the provisions of Articles 1 to 4 of this Protocol shall be regarded as additional Articles to the Convention, and all the provisions of the Convention shall apply accordingly.

Article 6

Signature and ratification

This Protocol shall be open for signature by member States of the Council of Europe which have signed the Convention. It is subject to ratification, acceptance or approval. A member State of the Council of Europe may not ratify, accept or approve this Protocol without previously or simultaneously ratifying the Convention. Instruments of ratification, acceptance or approval shall be deposited with the Secretary General of the Council of Europe.

Article 7

Entry into force

1. This Protocol shall enter into force on the first day of the month following the expiration of a period of three months after the date on which ten member States of the Council of Europe have expressed their consent to be bound by the Protocol in accordance with the provisions of Article 6.

2. In respect of any member State which subsequently expresses its consent to be bound by it, the Protocol shall enter into force on the first day of the month following the expiration of a period of three months after the date of the deposit of the instrument of ratification, acceptance or approval.

Article 8

Depositary functions

The Secretary General of the Council of Europe shall notify all the member States of the Council of Europe of:

(a)   any signature;
(b)   the deposit of any instrument of ratification, acceptance or approval;
(c)   any date of entry into force of this Protocol in accordance with Articles 4 and 7;
(d)   any other act, notification or communication relating to this Protocol;

In witness whereof the undersigned, being duly authorised thereto, have signed this Protocol.

Done at Vilnius, this 3rd day of May 2002, in English and in French, both texts being equally authentic, in a single copy which shall be deposited in the archives of the Council of Europe. The Secretary General of the Council of Europe shall transmit certified copies to each member State of the Council of Europe

Appendix 3

HUMAN RIGHTS ACT 1998

Introduction

1   The Convention Rights

(1)   In this Act, 'the Convention rights' means the rights and fundamental freedoms set out in –

(a)   Articles 2 to 12 and 14 of the Convention, and
(b)   Articles 1 to 3 of the First Protocol, and
(c)   Article 1 of the Thirteenth Protocol,

as read with Articles 16 to 18 of the Convention.

(2)   Those Articles are to have effect for the purposes of this Act subject to any designated derogation or reservation (as to which see sections 14 and 15).

(3)   The Articles are set out in Schedule 1.

(4)   The Secretary of State may by order make such amendments to this Act as he considers appropriate to reflect the effect, in relation to the United Kingdom, of a protocol.

(5)   In subsection (4) 'protocol' means a protocol to the Convention –

(a)   which the United Kingdom has ratified; or
(b)   which the United Kingdom has signed with a view to ratification.

(6)   No amendment may be made by an order under subsection (4) so as to come into force before the protocol concerned is in force in relation to the United Kingdom.

Amendments: SI 2003/1887; SI 2004/1574.

2   Interpretation of Convention rights

(1)   A court or tribunal determining a question which has arisen under this Act in connection with a Convention right must take into account any –

(a)   judgment, decision, declaration or advisory opinion of the European Court of Human Rights,
(b)   opinion of the Commission given in a report adopted under Article 31 of the Convention,
(c)   decision of the Commission in connection with Article 26 or 27(2) of the Convention, or
(d)   decision of the Committee of Ministers taken under Article 46 of the Convention,

whenever made or given, so far as, in the opinion of the court or tribunal, it is relevant to the proceedings in which that question has arisen.

(2)   Evidence of any judgment, decision, declaration or opinion of which account may have to be taken under this section is to be given in proceedings before any court or tribunal in such manner as may be provided by rules.

(3)   In this section 'rules' means rules of court or, in the case of proceedings before a tribunal, rules made for the purposes of this section –

(a)   by the Lord Chancellor or the Secretary of State, in relation to any proceedings outside Scotland;

(b)   by the Secretary of State, in relation to proceedings in Scotland; or

(c)   by a Northern Ireland department, in relation to proceedings before a tribunal in Northern Ireland-

(i)   which deals with transferred matters; and

(ii)   for which no rules made under paragraph (a) are in force.

Amendments: SI 2003/1887; SI 2005/3429.

Legislation

3   Interpretation of legislation

(1)   So far as it is possible to do so, primary legislation and subordinate legislation must be read and given effect in a way which is compatible with the Convention rights.

(2)   This section –

(a)   applies to primary legislation and subordinate legislation whenever enacted;

(b)   does not affect the validity, continuing operation or enforcement of any incompatible primary legislation; and

(c)   does not affect the validity, continuing operation or enforcement of any incompatible subordinate legislation if (disregarding any possibility of revocation) primary legislation prevents removal of the incompatibility.

4   Declaration of incompatibility

(1)   Subsection (2) applies in any proceedings in which a court determines whether a provision of primary legislation is compatible with a Convention right.

(2)   If the court is satisfied that the provision is incompatible with a Convention right, it may make a declaration of that incompatibility.

(3)   Subsection (4) applies in any proceedings in which a court determines whether a provision of subordinate legislation, made in the exercise of a power conferred by primary legislation, is compatible with a Convention right.

(4)   If the court is satisfied –

(a)   that the provision is incompatible with a Convention right, and

(b)   that (disregarding any possibility of revocation) the primary legislation concerned prevents removal of the incompatibility,

it may make a declaration of that incompatibility.

(5)   In this section 'court' means –

(a)   the Supreme Court;

(b)   the Judicial Committee of the Privy Council;

(c)   the Court Martial Appeal Court;

(d) in Scotland, the High Court of Justiciary sitting otherwise than as a trial court or the Court of Session;

(e) in England and Wales or Northern Ireland, the High Court or the Court of Appeal.

(f) the Court of Protection, in any matter being dealt with by the President of the Family Division, the Vice-Chancellor or a puisne judge of the High Court.

(6) A declaration under this section ('a declaration of incompatibility') –

(a) does not affect the validity, continuing operation or enforcement of the provision in respect of which it is given; and

(b) is not binding on the parties to the proceedings in which it is made.

Amendments: Mental Capacity Act 2005, s 67(1), Sch 6, para 43; Constitutional Reform Act 2005, s 40(4), Sch 9, Pt 1, para 66(1), (2); Armed Forces Act 2006, s 378(1), Sch 16, para 156.

5 Right of Crown to intervene

(1) Where a court is considering whether to make a declaration of incompatibility, the Crown is entitled to notice in accordance with rules of court.

(2) In any case to which subsection (1) applies –

(a) a Minister of the Crown, or

(b) a member of the Scottish Executive,

(c) a Northern Ireland Minister,

(d) a Northern Ireland department,

is entitled, on an application made to the court in accordance with rules of court, to be joined as a party to the proceedings.

(3) An application under subsection (2) may be made at any time during the proceedings.

(4) A person who has been made a party to criminal proceedings (other than in Scotland) as the result of an application under subsection (2) may, with leave, appeal to the Supreme Court against any declaration of incompatibility made in the proceedings.

(5) In subsection (4) –

'criminal proceedings' includes all proceedings before the Court Martial Appeal Court; and

'leave' means leave granted by the court making the declaration of incompatibility or by the Supreme Court.

Amendments: Constitutional Reform Act 2005, s 40(4), Sch 9, Pt 1, para 66(1), (3); Armed Forces Act 2006, s 378(1), Sch 16, para 157.

Public authorities

6 Acts of public authorities

(1) It is unlawful for a public authority to act in a way which is incompatible with a Convention right.

(2) Subsection (1) does not apply to an act if –

(a) as the result of one or more provisions of primary legislation, the authority could not have acted differently; or

(b)   in the case of one or more provisions of, or made under, primary legislation which cannot be read or given effect in a way which is compatible with the Convention rights, the authority was acting so as to give effect to or enforce those provisions.

(3)   In this section, 'public authority' includes –

(a)   a court or tribunal, and
(b)   any person certain of whose functions are functions of a public nature,

but does not include either House of Parliament or a person exercising functions in connection with proceedings in Parliament.

(4)   . . .

(5)   In relation to a particular act, a person is not a public authority by virtue only of subsection (3)(b) if the nature of the act is private.

(6)   'An act' includes a failure to act but does not include a failure to –

(a)   introduce in, or lay before, Parliament a proposal for legislation; or
(b)   make any primary legislation or remedial order.

Amendments: Constitutional Reform Act 2005, ss 40(4), 146, Sch 9, Pt 1, para 66(1), (4), Sch 18, Pt 5.

7   Proceedings

(1)   A person who claims that a public authority has acted (or proposes to act) in a way which is made unlawful by section 6(1) may –

(a)   bring proceedings against the authority under this Act in the appropriate court or tribunal, or
(b)   rely on the Convention right or rights concerned in any legal proceedings,

but only if he is (or would be) a victim of the unlawful act.

(2)   In subsection (1)(a) 'appropriate court or tribunal' means such court or tribunal as may be determined in accordance with rules; and proceedings against an authority includes a counterclaim or similar proceeding.

(3)   If the proceedings are brought on an application for judicial review, the applicant is to be taken to have a sufficient interest in relation to the unlawful act only if he is, or would be, a victim of that act.

(4)   If the proceedings are made by way of a petition for judicial review in Scotland, the applicant shall be taken to have title and interest to sue in relation to the unlawful act only if he is, or would be, a victim of that act.

(5)   Proceedings under subsection (1)(a) must be brought before the end of –

(a)   the period of one year beginning with the date on which the act complained of took place; or
(b)   such longer period as the court or tribunal considers equitable having regard to all the circumstances,

but that is subject to any rule imposing a stricter time limit in relation to the procedure in question.

(6)   In subsection (1)(b) 'legal proceedings' includes –

(a)   proceedings brought by or at the instigation of a public authority; and

(b)   an appeal against the decision of a court or tribunal.

(7)   For the purposes of this section, a person is a victim of an unlawful act only if he would be a victim for the purposes of Article 34 of the Convention if proceedings were brought in the European Court of Human Rights in respect of that act.

(8)   Nothing in this Act creates a criminal offence.

(9)   In this section 'rules' means –

(a)   in relation to proceedings before a court or tribunal outside Scotland, rules made by the Lord Chancellor the Secretary of State for the purposes of this section or rules of court,

(b)   in relation to proceedings before a court or tribunal in Scotland, rules made by the Secretary of State for those purposes,

(c)   in relation to proceedings before a tribunal in Northern Ireland –
(i)   which deals with transferred matters; and
(ii)   for which no rules made under paragraph (a) are in force,
rules made by a Northern Ireland department for those purposes,

and includes provision made by order under section 1 of the Courts and Legal Services Act 1990.

(10)   In making rules regard must be had to section 9.

(11)   The Minister who has power to make rules in relation to a particular tribunal may, to the extent he considers it necessary to ensure that the tribunal can provide an appropriate remedy in relation to an act (or proposed act) of a public authority which is (or would be) unlawful as a result of section 6(1), by order add to –

(a)   the relief or remedies which the tribunal may grant; or
(b)   the grounds on which it may grant any of them.

(12)   An order made under subsection (11) may contain such incidental, supplemental, consequential or transitional provision as the Minister making it considers appropriate.

(13)   'The Minister' includes the Northern Ireland department concerned.

Amendments: SI 2003/1887; SI 2005/3429.

8   Judicial remedies

(1)   In relation to any act (or proposed act) of a public authority which the court finds is (or would be) unlawful, it may grant such relief or remedy, or make such order, within its jurisdiction as it considers just and appropriate.

(2)   But damages may be awarded only by a court which has power to award damages, or to order the payment of compensation, in civil proceedings.

(3)   No award of damages is to be made unless, taking account of all the circumstances of the case, including –

(a)   any other relief or remedy granted, or order made, in relation to the act in question (by that or any other court), and
(b)   the consequences of any decision (of that or any other court) in respect of that act,

the court is satisfied that the award is necessary to afford just satisfaction to the person in whose favour it is made.

(4)   In determining –

    (a)   whether to award damages, or

    (b)   the amount of an award,

the court must take into account the principles applied by the European Court of Human Rights in relation to the award of compensation under Article 41 of the Convention.

(5)   A public authority against which damages are awarded is to be treated –

    (a)   in Scotland, for the purposes of section 3 of the Law Reform (Miscellaneous Provisions) (Scotland) Act 1940 as if the award were made in an action of damages in which the authority has been found liable in respect of loss or damage to the person to whom the award is made;

    (b)   for the purposes of the Civil Liability (Contribution) Act 1978 as liable in respect of damage suffered by the person to whom the award is made.

(6)   In this section –

'court' includes a tribunal;
'damages' means damages for an unlawful act of a public authority; and
'unlawful' means unlawful under section 6(1).

9   Judicial acts

(1)   Proceedings under section 7(1)(a) in respect of a judicial act may be brought only –

    (a)   by exercising a right of appeal;

    (b)   on an application (in Scotland a petition) for judicial review; or

    (c)   in such other forum as may be prescribed by rules.

(2)   That does not affect any rule of law which prevents a court from being the subject of judicial review.

(3)   In proceedings under this Act in respect of a judicial act done in good faith, damages may not be awarded otherwise than to compensate a person to the extent required by Article 5(5) of the Convention.

(4)   An award of damages permitted by subsection (3) is to be made against the Crown; but no award may be made unless the appropriate person, if not a party to the proceedings, is joined.

(5)   In this section –

'appropriate person' means the Minister responsible for the court concerned, or a person or government department nominated by him;
'court' includes a tribunal;
'judge' includes a member of a tribunal, a justice of the peace (or, in Northern Ireland, a lay magistrate) and a clerk or other officer entitled to exercise the jurisdiction of a court;
'judicial act' means a judicial act of a court and includes an act done on the instructions, or on behalf, of a judge;
'rules' has the same meaning as in section 7(9).

Amendments: Justice (Northern Ireland) Act 2002, s 10(6), Sch 4, para 39.

Remedial action

10 Power to take remedial action

(1) This section applies if –

    (a)   a provision of legislation has been declared under section 4 to be incompatible with a Convention right and, if an appeal lies –

        (i)   all persons who may appeal have stated that they do not intend to do so;

        (ii)   the time for bringing an appeal has expired and no appeal has been brought within that time; or

        (iii)   an appeal brought within that time has been determined or abandoned; or

    (b)   it appears to a Minister of the Crown or Her Majesty in Council that, having regard to a finding of the European Court of Human Rights made after the coming into force of this section in proceedings against the United Kingdom, a provision of legislation is incompatible with an obligation of the United Kingdom arising from the Convention.

(2) If a Minister of the Crown considers that there are compelling reasons for proceeding under this section, he may by order make such amendments to the legislation as he considers necessary to remove the incompatibility.

(3) If, in the case of subordinate legislation, a Minister of the Crown considers –

    (a)   that it is necessary to amend the primary legislation under which the subordinate legislation in question was made, in order to enable the incompatibility to be removed, and

    (b)   that there are compelling reasons for proceeding under this section,

he may by order make such amendments to the primary legislation as he considers appropriate.

(4) This section also applies where the provision in question is in subordinate legislation and has been quashed, or declared invalid, by reason of incompatibility with a Convention right and the Minister proposes to proceed under paragraph 2(b) of Schedule 2.

(5) If the legislation is an Order in Council, the power conferred by subsection (2) or (3) is exercisable by Her Majesty in Council.

(6) In this section 'legislation' does not include a Measure of the Church Assembly or of the General Synod of the Church of England.

(7) Schedule 2 makes further provision about remedial orders.

Other rights and proceedings

11 Safeguard for existing human rights

A person's reliance on a Convention right does not restrict –

    (a)   any other right or freedom conferred on him by or under any law having effect in any part of the United Kingdom, or

    (b)   his right to make any claim or bring any proceedings which he could make or bring apart from sections 7 to 9.

12 Freedom of expression

(1)   This section applies if a court is considering whether to grant any relief which, if granted, might affect the exercise of the Convention right to freedom of expression.

(2)   If the person against whom the application for relief is made ('the respondent') is neither present nor represented, no such relief is to be granted unless the court is satisfied –

  (a)   that the applicant has taken all practicable steps to notify the respondent; or
  (b)   that there are compelling reasons why the respondent should not be notified.

(3)   No such relief is to be granted so as to restrain publication before trial unless the court is satisfied that the applicant is likely to establish that publication should not be allowed.

(4)   The court must have particular regard to the importance of the Convention right to freedom of expression and, where the proceedings relate to material which the respondent claims, or which appears to the court, to be journalistic, literary or artistic material (or to conduct connected with such material), to –

  (a)   the extent to which –
      (i)   the material has, or is about to, become available to the public; or
      (ii)   it is, or would be, in the public interest for the material to be published;
  (b)   any relevant privacy code.

(5)   In this section –

'court' includes a tribunal; and
'relief' includes any remedy or order (other than in criminal proceedings).

13 Freedom of thought, conscience and religion

(1)   If a court's determination of any question arising under this Act might affect the exercise by a religious organisation (itself or its members collectively) of the Convention right to freedom of thought, conscience and religion, it must have particular regard to the importance of that right.

(2)   In this section 'court' includes a tribunal.

Derogations and reservations

14 Derogations

(1)   In this Act, 'designated derogation' means –

any derogation by the United Kingdom from an Article of the Convention, or of any protocol to the Convention, which is designated for the purposes of this Act in an order made by the Secretary of State.

(2)   ...

(3)   If a designated derogation is amended or replaced it ceases to be a designated derogation.

(4)   But subsection (3) does not prevent the Secretary of State from exercising his power under subsection (1) to make a fresh designation order in respect of the Article concerned.

(5) The Secretary of State must by order make such amendments to Schedule 3 as he considers appropriate to reflect –

    (a)   any designation order; or

    (b)   the effect of subsection (3).

(6) A designation order may be made in anticipation of the making by the United Kingdom of a proposed derogation.

Amendments: SI 2001/1216; SI 2003/1887.

15 Reservations

(1) In this Act, 'designated reservation' means –

    (a)   the United Kingdom's reservation to Article 2 of the First Protocol to the Convention; and

    (b)   any other reservation by the United Kingdom to an Article of the Convention, or of any protocol to the Convention, which is designated for the purposes of this Act in an order made by the Secretary of State.

(2) The text of the reservation referred to in subsection (1)(a) is set out in Part II of Schedule 3.

(3) If a designated reservation is withdrawn wholly or in part it ceases to be a designated reservation.

(4) But subsection (3) does not prevent the Secretary of State from exercising his power under subsection (1)(b) to make a fresh designation order in respect of the Article concerned.

(5) The Secretary of State must by order make such amendments to this Act as he considers appropriate to reflect –

    (a)   any designation order; or

    (b)   the effect of subsection (3).

Amendments: SI 2003/1887.

16 Period for which designated derogations have effect

(1) If it has not already been withdrawn by the United Kingdom, a designated derogation ceases to have effect for the purposes of this Act –

at the end of the period of five years beginning with the date on which the order designating it was made.

(2) At any time before the period –

    (a)   fixed by subsection (1), or

    (b)   extended by an order under this subsection,

comes to an end, the Secretary of State may by order extend it by a further period of five years.

(3) An order under section 14(1)... ceases to have effect at the end of the period for consideration, unless a resolution has been passed by each House approving the order.

(4) Subsection (3) does not affect –

    (a)   anything done in reliance on the order; or

(b)   the power to make a fresh order under section 14(1)....

(5)   In subsection (3) 'period for consideration' means the period of forty days beginning with the day on which the order was made.

(6)   In calculating the period for consideration, no account is to be taken of any time during which –

(a)   Parliament is dissolved or prorogued; or
(b)   both Houses are adjourned for more than four days.

(7)   If a designated derogation is withdrawn by the United Kingdom, the Secretary of State must by order make such amendments to this Act as he considers are required to reflect that withdrawal.

Amendments: SI 2001/1216; SI 2003/1887.

17   Periodic review of designated reservations

(1)   The appropriate Minister must review the designated reservation referred to in section 15(1)(a) –

(a)   before the end of the period of five years beginning with the date on which section 1(2) came into force; and
(b)   if that designation is still in force, before the end of the period of five years beginning with the date on which the last report relating to it was laid under subsection (3).

(2)   The appropriate Minister must review each of the other designated reservations (if any) –

(a)   before the end of the period of five years beginning with the date on which the order designating the reservation first came into force; and
(b)   if the designation is still in force, before the end of the period of five years beginning with the date on which the last report relating to it was laid under subsection (3).

(3)   The Minister conducting a review under this section must prepare a report on the result of the review and lay a copy of it before each House of Parliament.

Judges of the European Court of Human Rights

18   Appointment to European Court of Human Rights

(1)   In this section 'judicial office' means the office of –

(a)   Lord Justice of Appeal, Justice of the High Court or Circuit judge, in England and Wales;
(b)   judge of the Court of Session or sheriff, in Scotland;
(c)   Lord Justice of Appeal, judge of the High Court or county court judge, in Northern Ireland.

(2)   The holder of a judicial office may become a judge of the European Court of Human Rights ('the Court') without being required to relinquish his office.

(3)   But he is not required to perform the duties of his judicial office while he is a judge of the Court.

(4)   In respect of any period during which he is a judge of the Court –

(a) a Lord Justice of Appeal or Justice of the High Court is not to count as a judge of the relevant court for the purposes of section 2(1) or 4(1) of the Senior Courts Act 1981 (maximum number of judges) nor as a judge of the Senior Courts for the purposes of section 12(1) to (6) of that Act (salaries etc);

(b) a judge of the Court of Session is not to count as a judge of that court for the purposes of section 1(1) of the Court of Session Act 1988 (maximum number of judges) or of section 9(1)(c) of the Administration of Justice Act 1973 ('the 1973 Act') (salaries etc);

(c) a Lord Justice of Appeal or a judge of the High Court in Northern Ireland is not to count as a judge of the relevant court for the purposes of section 2(1) or 3(1) of the Judicature (Northern Ireland) Act 1978 (maximum number of judges) nor as a judge of the Senior Courts of Northern Ireland for the purposes of section 9(1)(d) of the 1973 Act (salaries etc);

(d) a Circuit judge is not to count as such for the purposes of section 18 of the Courts Act 1971 (salaries etc);

(e) a sheriff is not to count as such for the purposes of section 14 of the Sheriff Courts (Scotland) Act 1907 (salaries etc);

(f) a county court judge of Northern Ireland is not to count as such for the purposes of section 106 of the County Courts Act (Northern Ireland) 1959 (salaries etc).

(5) If a sheriff principal is appointed a judge of the Court, section 11(1) of the Sheriff Courts (Scotland) Act 1971 (temporary appointment of sheriff principal) applies, while he holds that appointment, as if his office is vacant.

(6) Schedule 3 makes provision about judicial pensions in relation to the holder of a judicial office who serves as a judge of the Court.

(7) The Lord Chancellor or the Secretary of State may by order make such transitional provision (including, in particular, provision for a temporary increase in the maximum number of judges) as he considers appropriate in relation to any holder of a judicial office who has completed his service as a judge of the Court.

(7A) The following paragraphs apply to the making of an order under subsection (7) in relation to any holder of a judicial office listed in subsection (1)(a) –

(a) before deciding what transitional provision it is appropriate to make, the person making the order must consult the Lord Chief Justice of England and Wales;

(b) before making the order, that person must consult the Lord Chief Justice of England and Wales.

(7B) The following paragraphs apply to the making of an order under subsection (7) in relation to any holder of a judicial office listed in subsection (1)(c) –

(a) before deciding what transitional provision it is appropriate to make, the person making the order must consult the Lord Chief Justice of Northern Ireland;

(b) before making the order, that person must consult the Lord Chief Justice of Northern Ireland.

(7C) The Lord Chief Justice of England and Wales may nominate a judicial office holder (within the meaning of section 109(4) of the Constitutional Reform Act 2005) to exercise his functions under this section.

(7D) The Lord Chief Justice of Northern Ireland may nominate any of the following to exercise his functions under this section –

(a) the holder of one of the offices listed in Schedule 1 to the Justice (Northern Ireland) Act 2002;

(b) a Lord Justice of Appeal (as defined in section 88 of that Act).

Amendments: Constitutional Reform Act 2005, ss 15(1), 59(5), Sch 4, Pt 1, para 278, Sch 11, Pts 1-3, paras 1(2), 4(1), (3), 6(1), (3).

Parliamentary procedure

19 Statements of compatibility

(1) A Minister of the Crown in charge of a Bill in either House of Parliament must, before Second Reading of the Bill –

(a) make a statement to the effect that in his view the provisions of the Bill are compatible with the Convention rights ('a statement of compatibility'); or

(b) make a statement to the effect that although he is unable to make a statement of compatibility the government nevertheless wishes the House to proceed with the Bill.

(2) The statement must be in writing and be published in such manner as the Minister making it considers appropriate.

Supplemental

20 Orders etc under this Act

(1) Any power of a Minister of the Crown to make an order under this Act is exercisable by statutory instrument.

(2) The power of the Lord Chancellor or the Secretary of State to make rules (other than rules of court) under section 2(3) or 7(9) is exercisable by statutory instrument.

(3) Any statutory instrument made under section 14, 15 or 16(7) must be laid before Parliament.

(4) No order may be made by … the Lord Chancellor or the Secretary of State under section 1(4), 7(11) or 16(2) unless a draft of the order has been laid before, and approved by, each House of Parliament.

(5) Any statutory instrument made under section 18(7) or Schedule 4, or to which subsection (2) applies, shall be subject to annulment in pursuance of a resolution of either House of Parliament.

(6) The power of a Northern Ireland department to make –

(a) rules under section 2(3)(c) or 7(9)(c), or

(b) an order under section 7(11),

is exercisable by statutory rule for the purposes of the Statutory Rules (Northern Ireland) Order 1979.

(7) Any rules made under section 2(3)(c) or 7(9)(c) shall be subject to negative resolution; and section 41(6) of the Interpretation Act Northern Ireland) 1954 (meaning of 'subject to negative resolution') shall apply as if the power to make the rules were conferred by an Act of the Northern Ireland Assembly.

(8) No order may be made by a Northern Ireland department under section 7(11) unless a draft of the order has been laid before, and approved by, the Northern Ireland Assembly.

Amendments: SI 2003/1887, SI 2005/3429.

21 Interpretation, etc

(1) In this Act –

'amend' includes repeal and apply (with or without modifications);

'the appropriate Minister' means the Minister of the Crown having charge of the appropriate authorised government department (within the meaning of the Crown Proceedings Act 1947);

'the Commission' means the European Commission of Human Rights;

'the Convention' means the Convention for the Protection of Human Rights and Fundamental Freedoms, agreed by the Council of Europe at Rome on 4th November 1950 as it has effect for the time being in relation to the United Kingdom;

'declaration of incompatibility' means a declaration under section 4;

'Minister of the Crown' has the same meaning as in the Ministers of the Crown Act 1975;

'Northern Ireland Minister' includes the First Minister and the deputy First Minister in Northern Ireland;

'primary legislation' means any –

    (a)   public general Act;

    (b)   local and personal Act;

    (c)   private Act;

    (d)   Measure of the Church Assembly;

    (e)   Measure of the General Synod of the Church of England;

    (f)   Order in Council –

        (i)   made in exercise of Her Majesty's Royal Prerogative;

        (ii)   made under section 38(1)(a) of the Northern Ireland Constitution Act 1973 or the corresponding provision of the Northern Ireland Act 1998; or

        (iii)   amending an Act of a kind mentioned in paragraph (a), (b) or (c);

and includes an order or other instrument made under primary legislation (otherwise than by Welsh Ministers, the First Minister for Wales, the Counsel General to the Welsh Assembly Government, a member of the Scottish Executive, a Northern Ireland Minister or a Northern Ireland department) to the extent to which it operates to bring one or more provisions of that legislation into force or amends any primary legislation;

'the First Protocol' means the protocol to the Convention agreed at Paris on 20th March 1952;

'the Eleventh Protocol' means the protocol to the Convention (restructuring the control machinery established by the Convention) agreed at Strasbourg on 11th May 1994;

'the Thirteenth Protocol' means the protocol to the Convention (concerning the abolition of the death penalty in all circumstances) agreed at Vilnius on 3rd May 2002;

'remedial order' means an order under section 10;

'subordinate legislation' means any –

    (a)   Order in Council other than one –

        (i)   made in exercise of Her Majesty's Royal Prerogative;

        (ii)   made under section 38(1)(a) of the Northern Ireland Constitution Act 1973 or the corresponding provision of the Northern Ireland Act 1998; or

      (iii)   amending an Act of a kind mentioned in the definition of primary legislation;

(b)   Act of the Scottish Parliament;

(ba)   Measure of the National Assembly for Wales;

(bb)   Act of the National Assembly for Wales;

(c)   Act of the Parliament of Northern Ireland;

(d)   Measure of the Assembly established under section 1 of the Northern Ireland Assembly Act 1973;

(e)   Act of the Northern Ireland Assembly;

(f)   order, rules, regulations, scheme, warrant, byelaw or other instrument made under primary legislation (except to the extent to which it operates to bring one or more provisions of that legislation into force or amends any primary legislation);

(g)   order, rules, regulations, scheme, warrant, byelaw or other instrument made under legislation mentioned in paragraph (b), (c), (d) or (e) or made under an Order in Council applying only to Northern Ireland;

(h)   order, rules, regulations, scheme, warrant, byelaw or other instrument made by a member of the Scottish Executive, Welsh Ministers, the First Minister for Wales, the Counsel General to the Welsh Assembly Government, a Northern Ireland Minister or a Northern Ireland department in exercise of prerogative or

other executive functions of Her Majesty which are exercisable by such a person on behalf of Her Majesty;

'transferred matters' has the same meaning as in the Northern Ireland Act 1998; and 'tribunal' means any tribunal in which legal proceedings may be brought.

(2)   The references in paragraphs (b) and (c) of section 2(1) to Articles are to Articles of the Convention as they had effect immediately before the coming into force of the Eleventh Protocol.

(3)   The reference in paragraph (d) of section 2(1) to Article 46 includes a reference to Articles 32 and 54 of the Convention as they had effect immediately before the coming into force of the Eleventh Protocol.

(4)   The references in section 2(1) to a report or decision of the Commission or a decision of the Committee of Ministers include references to a report or decision made as provided by paragraphs 3, 4 and 6 of Article 5 of the Eleventh Protocol (transitional provisions).

(5)   . . .

Amendments: SI 2004/1574; Government of Wales Act 2006, s 160(1), Sch 10, para 56; Armed Forces Act 2006, s 378(2), Sch 17.

22   Short title, commencement, application and extent

(1)   This Act may be cited as the Human Rights Act 1998.

(2)   Sections 18, 20 and 21(5) and this section come into force on the passing of this Act.

(3)   The other provisions of this Act come into force on such day as the Secretary of State may by order appoint; and different days may be appointed for different purposes.

(4)   Paragraph (b) of subsection (1) of section 7 applies to proceedings brought by or at the instigation of a public authority whenever the act in question took place; but otherwise that subsection does not apply to an act committed before the coming into force of that section.

(5)   This Act binds the Crown.

(6)   This Act extends to Northern Ireland.

(7)   . . .

Amendments: Armed Forces Act 2006, s 378(2), Sch 17.

Schedules

Schedule 1
The Articles

PART I
THE CONVENTION — RIGHTS AND FREEDOMS

Article 2
Right to life

1   Everyone's right to life shall be protected by law. No one shall be deprived of his life intentionally save in the execution of a sentence of a court following his conviction of a crime for which this penalty is provided by law.

2   Deprivation of life shall not be regarded as inflicted in contravention of this Article when it results from the use of force which is no more than absolutely necessary –

(a)   in defence of any person from unlawful violence;
(b)   in order to effect a lawful arrest or to prevent the escape of a person lawfully detained;
(c)   in action lawfully taken for the purpose of quelling a riot or insurrection.

Article 3
Prohibition of torture

No one shall be subjected to torture or to inhuman or degrading treatment or punishment.

Article 4
Prohibition of slavery and forced labour

1   No one shall be held in slavery or servitude.

2   No one shall be required to perform forced or compulsory labour.

3   For the purpose of this Article the term 'forced or compulsory labour' shall not include –

(a)   any work required to be done in the ordinary course of detention imposed according to the provisions of Article 5 of this Convention or during conditional release from such detention;

(b)   any service of a military character or, in case of conscientious objectors in countries where they are recognised, service exacted instead of compulsory military service;

(c)   any service exacted in case of an emergency or calamity threatening the life or well-being of the community;

(d)   any work or service which forms part of normal civic obligations.

Article 5
Right to liberty and security

1   Everyone has the right to liberty and security of person. No one shall be deprived of his liberty save in the following cases and in accordance with a procedure prescribed by law –

(a)   the lawful detention of a person after conviction by a competent court;

(b)   the lawful arrest or detention of a person for non-compliance with the lawful order of a court or in order to secure the fulfilment of any obligation prescribed by law;

(c)   the lawful arrest or detention of a person effected for the purpose of bringing him before the competent legal authority on reasonable suspicion of having committed an offence or when it is reasonably considered necessary to prevent his committing an offence or fleeing after having done so;

(d)   the detention of a minor by lawful order for the purpose of educational supervision or his lawful detention for the purpose of bringing him before the competent legal authority;

(e)   the lawful detention of persons for the prevention of the spreading of infectious diseases, of persons of unsound mind, alcoholics or drug addicts or vagrants;

(f)   the lawful arrest or detention of a person to prevent his effecting an unauthorised entry into the country or of a person against whom action is being taken with a view to deportation or extradition.

2   Everyone who is arrested shall be informed promptly, in a language which he understands, of the reasons for his arrest and of any charge against him.

3   Everyone arrested or detained in accordance with the provisions of paragraph 1(c) of this Article shall be brought promptly before a judge or other officer authorised by law to exercise judicial power and shall be entitled to trial within a reasonable time or to release pending trial. Release may be conditioned by guarantees to appear for trial.

4   Everyone who is deprived of his liberty by arrest or detention shall be entitled to take proceedings by which the lawfulness of his detention shall be decided speedily by a court and his release ordered if the detention is not lawful.

5   Everyone who has been the victim of arrest or detention in contravention of the provisions of this Article shall have an enforceable right to compensation.

Article 6
Right to a fair trial

1   In the determination of his civil rights and obligations or of any criminal charge against him, everyone is entitled to a fair and public hearing within a reasonable time by an independent and impartial tribunal established by law. Judgment shall be pronounced publicly but the press and public may be excluded from all or part of the trial in the interest of morals, public order or national security in a democratic society, where the interests of juveniles or the protection of the private life of the parties so require, or to the extent strictly necessary in the opinion of the court in special circumstances where publicity would prejudice the interests of justice.

2 Everyone charged with a criminal offence shall be presumed innocent until proved guilty according to law.

3 Everyone charged with a criminal offence has the following minimum rights –

    (a)   to be informed promptly, in a language which he understands and in detail, of the nature and cause of the accusation against him;

    (b)   to have adequate time and facilities for the preparation of his defence;

    (c)   to defend himself in person or through legal assistance of his own choosing or, if he has not sufficient means to pay for legal assistance, to be given it free when the interests of justice so require;

    (d)   to examine or have examined witnesses against him and to obtain the attendance and examination of witnesses on his behalf under the same conditions as witnesses against him;

    (e)   to have the free assistance of an interpreter if he cannot understand or speak the language used in court.

Article 7
No punishment without law

1 No one shall be held guilty of any criminal offence on account of any act or omission which did not constitute a criminal offence under national or international law at the time when it was committed. Nor shall a heavier penalty be imposed than the one that was applicable at the time the criminal offence was committed.

2 This Article shall not prejudice the trial and punishment of any person for any act or omission which, at the time when it was committed, was criminal according to the general principles of law recognised by civilised nations.

Article 8
Right to respect for private and family life

1 Everyone has the right to respect for his private and family life, his home and his correspondence.

2 There shall be no interference by a public authority with the exercise of this right except such as is in accordance with the law and is necessary in a democratic society in the interests of national security, public safety or the economic well-being of the country, for the prevention of disorder or crime, for the protection of health or morals, or for the protection of the rights and freedoms of others.

Article 9
Freedom of thought, conscience and religion

1 Everyone has the right to freedom of thought, conscience and religion; this right includes freedom to change his religion or belief and freedom, either alone or in community with others and in public or private, to manifest his religion or belief, in worship, teaching, practice and observance.

2 Freedom to manifest one's religion or beliefs shall be subject only to such limitations as are prescribed by law and are necessary in a democratic society in the interests of public safety, for the protection of public order, health or morals, or for the protection of the rights and freedoms of others.

Article 10
Freedom of expression

1 Everyone has the right to freedom of expression. This right shall include freedom to hold opinions and to receive and impart information and ideas without interference by public authority and regardless of frontiers. This Article shall not prevent States from requiring the licensing of broadcasting, television or cinema enterprises.

2 The exercise of these freedoms, since it carries with it duties and responsibilities, may be subject to such formalities, conditions, restrictions or penalties as are prescribed by law and are necessary in a democratic society, in the interests of national security, territorial integrity or public safety, for the prevention of disorder or crime, for the protection of health or morals, for the protection of the reputation or rights of others, for preventing the disclosure of information received in confidence, or for maintaining the authority and impartiality of the judiciary.

Article 11
Freedom of assembly and association

1 Everyone has the right to freedom of peaceful assembly and to freedom of association with others, including the right to form and to join trade unions for the protection of his interests.

2 No restrictions shall be placed on the exercise of these rights other than such as are prescribed by law and are necessary in a democratic society in the interests of national security or public safety, for the prevention of disorder or crime, for the protection of health or morals or for the protection of the rights and freedoms of others. This Article shall not prevent the imposition of lawful restrictions on the exercise of these rights by members of the armed forces, of the police or of the administration of the State.

Article 12
Right to marry

Men and women of marriageable age have the right to marry and to found a family, according to the national laws governing the exercise of this right.

Article 14
Prohibition of discrimination

The enjoyment of the rights and freedoms set forth in this Convention shall be secured without discrimination on any ground such as sex, race, colour, language, religion, political or other opinion, national or social origin, association with a national minority, property, birth or other status.

Article 16
Restrictions on political activity of aliens

Nothing in Articles 10, 11 and 14 shall be regarded as preventing the High Contracting Parties from imposing restrictions on the political activity of aliens.

Article 17
Prohibition of abuse of rights

Nothing in this Convention may be interpreted as implying for any State, group or person any right to engage in any activity or perform any act aimed at the destruction of any of the rights and freedoms set forth herein or at their limitation to a greater extent than is provided for in the Convention.

Article 18
Limitation on use of restrictions on rights

The restrictions permitted under this Convention to the said rights and freedoms shall not be applied for any purpose other than those for which they have been prescribed.

PART II
THE FIRST PROTOCOL

Article 1
Protection of property

Every natural or legal person is entitled to the peaceful enjoyment of his possessions. No one shall be deprived of his possessions except in the public interest and subject to the conditions provided for by law and by the general principles of international law.

The preceding provisions shall not, however, in any way impair the right of a State to enforce such laws as it deems necessary to control the use of property in accordance with the general interest or to secure the payment of taxes or other contributions or penalties.

Article 2
Right to education

No person shall be denied the right to education. In the exercise of any functions which it assumes in relation to education and to teaching, the State shall respect the right of parents to ensure such education and teaching in conformity with their own religious and philosophical convictions.

Article 3
Right to free elections

The High Contracting Parties undertake to hold free elections at reasonable intervals by secret ballot, under conditions which will ensure the free expression of the opinion of the people in the choice of the legislature.

PART III
ARTICLE 1 OF THE THIRTEENTH PROTOCOL

Article 1
Abolition of the death penalty

The death penalty shall be abolished. No one shall be condemned to such penalty or executed.

Amendments: SI 2004/1574.

Schedule 2
Remedial Orders

Orders

1

(1)   A remedial order may –

(a)   contain such incidental, supplemental, consequential or transitional provision as the person making it considers appropriate;

(b)   be made so as to have effect from a date earlier than that on which it is made;

(c)   make provision for the delegation of specific functions;

(d)   make different provision for different cases.

(2)   The power conferred by sub-paragraph (1)(a) includes –

(a)   power to amend primary legislation (including primary legislation other than that which contains the incompatible provision); and

(b)   power to amend or revoke subordinate legislation (including subordinate legislation other than that which contains the incompatible provision).

(3)   A remedial order may be made so as to have the same extent as the legislation which it affects.

(4)   No person is to be guilty of an offence solely as a result of the retrospective effect of a remedial order.

Procedure

2

No remedial order may be made unless –

(a)   a draft of the order has been approved by a resolution of each House of Parliament made after the end of the period of 60 days beginning with the day on which the draft was laid; or

(b)   it is declared in the order that it appears to the person making it that, because of the urgency of the matter, it is necessary to make the order without a draft being so approved.

Orders laid in draft

3

(1)   No draft may be laid under paragraph 2(a) unless –

(a)   the person proposing to make the order has laid before Parliament a document which contains a draft of the proposed order and the required information; and

(b)   the period of 60 days, beginning with the day on which the document required by this sub-paragraph was laid, has ended.

(2)   If representations have been made during that period, the draft laid under paragraph 2(a) must be accompanied by a statement containing –

(a)   a summary of the representations; and

(b)   if, as a result of the representations, the proposed order has been changed, details of the changes.

Urgent cases

4

(1)   If a remedial order ('the original order') is made without being approved in draft, the person making it must lay it before Parliament, accompanied by the required information, after it is made.

(2)   If representations have been made during the period of 60 days beginning with the day on which the original order was made, the person making it must (after the end of that period) lay before Parliament a statement containing –

(a)   a summary of the representations; and
(b)   if, as a result of the representations, he considers it appropriate to make changes to the original order, details of the changes.

(3)   If sub-paragraph (2)(b) applies, the person making the statement must –

(a)   make a further remedial order replacing the original order; and
(b)   lay the replacement order before Parliament.

(4)   If, at the end of the period of 120 days beginning with the day on which the original order was made, a resolution has not been passed by each House approving the original or replacement order, the order ceases to have effect (but without that affecting anything previously done under either order or the power to make a fresh remedial order).

Definitions

5

In this Schedule –

'representations' means representations about a remedial order (or proposed remedial order) made to the person making (or proposing to make) it and includes any relevant Parliamentary report or resolution; and
'required information' means –
(a)   an explanation of the incompatibility which the order (or proposed order) seeks to remove, including particulars of the relevant declaration, finding or order; and
(b)   a statement of the reasons for proceeding under section 10 and for making an order in those terms.

Calculating periods

6

In calculating any period for the purposes of this Schedule, no account is to be taken of any time during which –

(a)   Parliament is dissolved or prorogued; or
(b)   both Houses are adjourned for more than four days.

INDEX

References are to paragraph numbers.